THE
PENN STATE
FOOTBALL ENCYCLOPEDIA

BY
LOU PRATO

with Ron Falk

Forewords by Fran Fisher and George Paterno

SPORTS PUBLISHING, INC.
CHAMPAIGN, IL
www.SportsPublishingInc.com

Interior design: Michelle Dressen, Erin Prescher, Lisa Peretz
Cover Illustration: Joe Buck
Dust Jacket design: Joe Buck
Editors: Ron Falk
        Jeff Keiser

ISBN: 1-57167-178-1

Front and back cover photos: Steve Manuel
Photos courtesey of Penn State Sports Information Department, Penn State archives, Steve Manuel, Wally Triplett, Greg Guise.

Printed in the United States of America by Quebecor Printing, Inc.

First, to the women of my life:
my mother, Florence, who sent me to Penn State in the first place
but who is no longer around to share in this accomplishment...

my wife, Carole, a Penn State football fan long before I was, whose
patience, understanding and devotion is the backbone of my life...

my daughters, Vicki and Lori, who have always appreciated their dad
and mom, and no longer wonder about their parents' passion for Penn State
football...

Second, to my son, Scott, who bleeds blue and white even though he didn't
follow in my footsteps to Happy Valley...

Third, to the late Jim Coogan and Ridge Riley, Penn State fans in the
tradition of General James Beaver and Andy Lytle, who helped turn a young,
idealistic undergraduate journalism student into a loyal alum...

Finally, to Nittany Lion Football fans everywhere.....We Are! Penn State!

"Lou Prato's unbridled enthusiasm for the subject, a life-long passion for a man who bleeds Blue and White, makes for some comprehensive, refreshing, and vivid storytelling and makes this a must-have for not only Penn State fans but also for all college football fans."

—Rich Eisen

"Lou Prato bleeds Penn State. His blood is Penn State Blue. All this shows in his book which contains everything you want to know about the Nittany Lions and even more. As one who relishes the history of college football, I recomend this book. As for me, I'm buying it as an early Christmas present for myself."

—Beano Cook

"No one knows Penn State Football like Lou Prato, and he has succeeded in bringing to life the fabulous history of this program in a book that will be a delight to not just Nittanly Lion fans but football fans everywhere."

—Bob Smizik

TABLE OF CONTENTS

ACKNOWLEDGMENTS

This book is a culmination of two years of work and a great number of people helped bring this project to fruition. It started when Sagamore Publishing decided to produce a book on Penn State football as part of the company's expansion of its college sports book ventures. Sagamore's only encyclopedia in its college book line was about Notre Dame football and company officials believed a similar project about Penn State might be as successful as *The Fighting Irish Football Encyclopedia*. Sagamore was looking for a journalist willing to spend full time working on *The Penn State Football Encyclopedia* because the original release date had been set for the fall of 1997. I was brought into the project at the suggestion of Budd Thalman, associate athletic director for communications of Penn State, and was contacted by Mike Pearson, director of acquisitions and development for Sagamore. Since that time, the company has split into two divisions and Sports Publishing Inc. has taken over the publication of the commercial line of sports books. Due to a series of events, my teaching load at Penn State became far more demanding and after a few months of working on *The Penn State Football Encyclopedia*, it became obvious that I would need more time to complete the book. We agreed to delay the publication date until the fall of 1998 and Sports Publishing was able to utilize the original fall of 1997 release time to publish George Paterno's book about his brother, *Joe: The Coach from Byzantine*.

So, I must first thank Budd Thalman and Mike Pearson for selecting me to author this project. They also gave me advice and counseling throughout the two years. Budd did even more by giving me full access to the Penn State athletic department's archives and media guides. This book could not have been completed without the use of that material for research and photographs. The writing itself consumed a majority of my waking hours and nearly all of my spare time and my wife, Carole, made far too many sacrifices during this period. There were no vacations and few hours away from the computer—except for my teaching duties, some personal business or an occasional trip to a State sports event. Carole also helped with the research and compilation of records that were not available through any other source and you will find her hard work in much of what you read in Section 4.

No one was more vital to this project than my associate editor, fraternity brother and long time friend, Ron Falk. Ron knows books. He retired a few years ago after a long career as a top executive with John Wiley, Inc., one of the largest publishers of college text books in the U.S. Ron also is a devout PSU football fan and early on he volunteered to read my copy from the viewpoint of both a consumer and an editor. Did the writing make sense? Was the content and story line interesting? Were there any mistakes in commission or omission? Did I use the proper word? Or was there a grammatical error or misspelling? He found much for me to rewrite and/or correct. Later, he helped me choose the photographs, write the captions, and place the photographs within the text. Truth be told, Ron did most of that and I reviewed his initial effort. Because of size considerations, our photograph options were limited but it was my decision to emphasize the content rather than the pictorial aspects of this encyclopedia, so do not blame Ron if you are unhappy with the photographs. Ron's production expertise also helped develop the final parameters of the book's format and size. Frankly, without Ron's efforts, the release of *The Penn State Football Encyclopedia* probably would have been delayed for another year because I couldn't have finished it on time without him.

Ron Falk   Lou Prato

Two other people were invaluable to this project from the beginning. Sagamore recommended a researcher to help me and I could not have found one as enthusiastic as Patti Kenney. Some of Patti's preliminary research into the first few years of State football helped set the tone for the entire book. I expect we will be working on another book project in the near future. Then there is Steve Manuel, the best still photographer I have ever known (outside of my late uncle Merle Agnello of the Johnstown *Tribune-Democrat*, who unfortunately was a misguided Pitt fan). Steve is a retired marine corps officer now teaching at Penn State who has worked several years as a free lancer for both PSU's *Football Letter* and the sports information office. His collage is on the cover and several of his original photographs are included inside. He has a sense for the moment and if you want a good example of this, check out the photo of

Joe Paterno and Fran Ganter during the 1994 Illinois game or the photo of Curtis Enis diving for a touchdown at the 1996 Kickoff Classic. Steve helped in many other ways. I know he will be disappointed in most of the photos in the book because they don't measure up to his standards or quality.

One of my prime sources of game information for *The Penn State Football Encyclopedia* was the *Football Letter* produced by the PSU alumni office. The late Ridge Riley originated the letter in 1938 and John Black took it over following Ridge's death after the 1975 season. John, a friend since our undergraduate days on campus, also read my first draft of the player profiles found in Section 3 and offered advice on other matters and I am grateful to him. I would like to believe that Ridge would have been pleased with this book, too. Ridge's own work, *Road to Number One*, published in 1977 by Doubleday is still the authoritative history on Penn State football and I drew considerable insight from it. I am also most appreciative of the encouragement I had from Ridge's daughter, Anne Riley, who not only shared her wisdom but also explained the pitfalls Ridge encountered while working on his book. In some of my personal research, I found myself reading the same original newspaper clippings, scrapbooks, minutes of athletic department meetings and other books that Ridge had scoured when he was researching his book. It was intriguing to note what he included or left out of his book and, like Ridge, I found myself wanting to put much, much more into this book than space allowed.

Several other people were helpful at different stages of this project. Jeff Nelson and his Penn State sports information staff never hesitated to provide information and photographs. Judy Fenush, Barry Jones, Jeff Keiser and Valerie Cingle were especially cooperative with me and the Sports Publishing folks. Sections 3 & 4 could not have been completed without them. Mike Poorman, editor of the Barash Group of publications, eagerly provided me with all the Penn State Football Annuals and other work produced under his supervision dating back to 1982. *The Daily Collegian*, the PSU student newspaper which was the journalistic baptism for many of us over the decades, allowed me free access to its files and I especially want to thank the professional staff. The Penn State Archives Section in the Patee Library also was helpful to Patti in her research and we thank the library personnel for their assistance. Although, the pressure of time did not allow me to personally interview many ex-players for this book, I gained considerable insight from former player and coach Jim O'Hora, Carl Stravinski and members of the undefeated 1947 team, particularly Ed Czekaj and Wally Triplett.

In addition to the Riley book, several other books were good sources of information for various periods of Penn State's football history. These included: *Paterno: By the Book* by Joe Paterno and Bernard Asbell, *Joe Paterno: Football My Way* by Merv Hyman and Gordon White; *Lion Country: Inside Penn State Football* by Frank Bilovsky; *The Nittany Lions* by Ken Rappoport; *Beast of the East* by Tim Panaccio; *The Hig* by Rich Donnell; *Welcome to the Big Ten* by Kip Richeal; *Nittany Lions Handbook* by Ron Bracken; *For the Glory* by Ken Denlinger; and *Lion Kings* by Scott Brown. I also want to thank my brother-in-law Dart Harpster for allowing me to review the dozens of football programs he saved since the early 1960s. That's where I found the first mention of Chet Smith's All-Time team and other tidbits which were incorporated throughout this book. And, of course, there was my late mother, Florence Davis, who didn't know a quick kick from a screen pass, but for years she would clip and send to me every article she saw about Penn State football and I have used many quotes from those articles in the season-by-season rundowns. Most of the photographs were provided by the sports information office and the University Photo Graphics division. The photo of John Cappelletti on page 293 was taken by Greg Guise of WUSA-TV in Washington and a tailgate buddy. Among those who gave me advice and encouragement along the way were Fran Fisher and George Paterno; my college pals Bill Jaffee and Vince Marino; Kay Kustanbauter of the Nittany Lion Club; and my longtime broadcast news friends at the Radio Television News Directors Association, especially Eric Swanson and Mark Thalhimer of the RTNDF staff, Bill Yeager, a Colorado fan, Edie Emery, a Tenneseee fan, Larry Scharff, a Northwestern fan, Loren Tobia, a (ugh) Nebraska fan, and Jack Hogan, who is a (ugh, ugh) Michigan State devotee. And certaintly, I need to acknowledge the help of others at Sagamore/Sports Publishing, including Peter Bannon, Susan McKinney, Lisa Peretz, Jeff Ellish and especially Erin Prescher, who didn't know what she was getting into when she was assigned to be the production guru of *The Penn State Football Encyclopedia*.

Last, but not least, there is my tailgating family and friends who listened as I related stories from my research and said they would be first in line to buy a copy of the book if I ever finished it— the Laskeys, the Harpsters, the Coopers, the Rearicks, the Keatings, my son Scott and his Ohio pals, the O'Connors, the Agnellos, the Campagninis, the Browell brothers, the Mark Thalmans, the Youngs, the Corsons, the Stulls, Charlie & the Murrays and all the rest of you who have joined us at the Great Prato Tailgate from time to time over the years—it's your turn.

INTRODUCTION

This book is for everyone who loves Penn State football and even for some who don't. Although the volume fits the basic dictionary definition of an encyclopedia, it may not be the type a reader is accustomed to perusing. I simply did not want to compile an encyclopedia made up solely of facts and figures or one that would inform but not entertain. My intent was to tell the history of Penn State football but in a manner that would be interesting and appealing.

The publisher gave me the guidelines: write a season-by-season synopsis and short profiles on 200 or so key players plus a compendium of all-time records and statistics. After discussing the project with State's Associate Athletic Director Budd Thalman, I decided to widen the scope. Rather than summarize a season in a drab chronological way, my approach was as a story teller and a participant. As I discuss in more detail in Section 2, I wanted to put each year in context of what it meant to players and fans of that season and that era and how one season evolved into the next. I wanted to see each year from the perspective of the players, the coaches, the fans and the sportswriters who were there. Whenever possible, I tried to relate one game to another and the effect and impact specific games had on the eventual results for the season. In the most significant or crucial games of the year, I attempted to encapsulate as a contemporary sportswriter might do it, keeping the outcome in suspense at times and summing up the highlights at other times.

To do all this, I needed to read newspapers and magazines of the period and books published later that gave me a retrospective panorama of the season. The reader will find that I quote this material widely with proper attribution. I literally read stories on every 1,056 football games State has played, sometimes examining a half dozen or so accounts of a particular game to ferret out the details that properly explained what happened. Of course, I saw many of these games in person so I was able to add personal insight throughout the last 45 years. I am only sorry I could not talk with more players and coaches to get their input, or to the sportswriters and broadcasters who covered the beat. The original format and deadline of the project made it impractical to seek such personal viewpoints but perhaps that can be the germination of a future companion book for this encyclopedia.

Some of the information and statistics here already will be out of date by the time it is all being read. That is the nuisance in publishing material that is constantly changing. Current players will break individual records and ex-players will change jobs or pass away. I apologize ahead for any mistakes or errors of commission or omission. I have tried to be as accurate as possible but I am sure I have missed some things, maybe misinterpreted data, failed to spot and correct typos or just simply had it wrong. I know in my research I found many mistakes in my sources, printed and human, so I am sure I have more than my share. I also am sorry I could not include more photographs. The size of the project grew incrementally in gargantuan proportions and eventually choices had to be made. I will leave to another time a visual chronicle of PSU football history.

To say this book was a labor of love is an understatement. Anyone who knows me, from my young journalism students to my old friends, can tell you that I am one of those Nittany Lion fanatics and so is my wife, Carole. Like many of the readers, we bleed blue and white. Our house, our van and all my former offices have been a testimonial to the Football Gods of Mount Nittany. We have followed the team from coast to coast and have made many long overnight drives from distant sites to return from games in time to go to work Monday mornings. When unable to attend a game in person we often have watched the drama on TV in hotel sports bars at 11 a.m. or listened to the radio broadcast over a telephone line a thousand miles away. We've made a lot of new friends that way—Penn State, friends, of course. Yes, we have a life, and so do our children and the rest of our family. But a tailgate at Beaver Stadium or Ohio Stadium or at a bowl game is often like a family reunion with sons, daughters, grandchildren, brothers, sisters, cousins, aunts, uncles, in-laws, high school classmates, neighborhood pals, students, new friends, old friends and college fraternity brothers all there to have fun and root for the Nittany Lions. Before my 90-year-old mother died in June of 1997 she had wanted to attend one more tailgate. We called her "The Tailgate Grandma."

Now, this may come as a shock, especially to my longtime acquaintances, but I was once a Notre Dame and Pitt fan. Growing up in Western Pennsylvania in the late 1940s and early 1950s, we huddled by our radios and cheered for Old Notre Dame, with our "local" superheroes and Heisman Trophy winners, Johnny Lujack of Connellsville and Leon Hart of Turtle Creek. And Pitt or Indiana State Teachers College (now Indiana University of Pennsylvania) was our hometown teams. It is difficult to believe I once rooted for Joe Schmidt and Bimbo Cecconi. But Penn State was that "other school," the "cow college up in the mountains." This personal reflection is not meant to bore the reader but to make a point about the vacuous image of Penn State football to a generation of kids who were growing up 80 to 150 miles away. Frankly, I have no memory of the great 1947 team and the 13-13 Cotton Bowl. I vaguely remember hearing about Tony Rados at the time. I do remember the Snowbowl of 1950. I broke my leg that week while sled riding and had to listen to the "Pitt game" the next Saturday with my leg in a cast. The only distinct recollection I have of Penn State at the time is "Pop" Hewitt. Pop was a businessman in my town of Indiana and already a grey-haired old man when I first heard of him. But in Indiana, even someone my age who was interested in sports knew that Pop had run back a punt 65-yards for the only touchdown to beat Army, 6-0, in 1899. Heck, Pop was as famous to us as our other hometown celebrity, movie actor Jimmy Stewart.

I didn't see my first Penn State game until 1955 when I was a naive, snot-nosed freshman wearing that little "dink" cap on my head to the season opener at New Beaver Field against Boston University. The field was across the street from the third floor room of my dormitory in McKee Hall and we could watch people buying tickets at the entrance no more than 50 yards away. A couple of freshmen football players lived down the hall and I spent a lot of time kibitzing with Steve Garban and Dick Dill. Steve became captain of the 1958 team and later was the university's chief financial officer and Joe Paterno's boss. Dick was slowed down by injuries but he made his mark in lacrosse and then went off to a business career in his hometown of Erie. I vaguely remember that the star of my first game was this sophomore fullback I never heard of named Joe Sabol. Joe later was the captain of the 1957 team and by that time my Theta Delta Chi fraternity brother. I recall 1955 was State's Centennial Year because all the billboards leading into town told you so. Frankly, I don't remember the Homecoming game three weeks later when Navy was at Beaver Field with a quarterback named George Welsh—who I had heard about— and buried State. But the first game I really remember was a month later when Syracuse came to town. The boys in McKee had to guard the Nittany Lion Shrine outside Beaver Field that Friday night to protect it from that nasty Syracuse crowd. The next afternoon, I sat in the bleachers as our great back Lenny Moore went toe-to-toe with Syracuse's great back, Jimmy Brown. God, what a performance by both those two. And, most importantly, State won, 21-20. I was hooked.

So, now it was more than 40 years later and I was asked if I wanted to write a book about Penn State football. Is the sky Blue? I had been there when State won its two National Championships on the field and I had been there when it lost them. I had been to the 1969 Orange Bowl with the unbeaten team of 1968 and to the 1995 Rose Bowl cheering for the Big 10 Champions of 1994. You name the bowl and I was probably there. Even while working in radio and television news in the midwest for nearly 14 years, when my job prevented me from seeing many games in person, I still followed the team, occasionally seeing a game in South Bend, Columbus, Lexington or Pittsburgh and once in a while in State College. If any fan knew about Penn State football it was me. I covered it for the *Daily Collegian*, the AP, *Pittsburgh Weekly Sports*, *Football News*, Channel 11 in Pittsburgh and occasionally wrote a story for the football program. I was there for Rip's last game and Joe's first game. I was there at a low point against Notre Dame in '84 and at a high point against Miami in '87. Did I know Penn State football? Not as much as I thought I did.

I didn't know about Charlie Atherton, the first college player ever to kick a field goal from a placement rather than drop kick. I didn't know about the near riot at Ohio State in 1912 or the visit by Gus Dorias and Knute Rockne of Notre Dame in 1913. I didn't know about the 1921 Mystery Team nor about the 1931 All-Time Losers. I had never heard of "Wrong-Way" Cyphers, who ran the wrong way with a blocked punt and cost the team a big upset. I did not know about Carl Forkum, a great running back from New Castle whose feats should be in the record books but are not. Nor did I recognize the name of Gus Michalske, a holy terror whether playing guard or fullback who was the first State player elected to the Pro Football Hall of Fame. I had all but forgotten that Engle's 1961 team with All-American Dave Robinson broke the color line at the Gator Bowl. But I didn't know that State had canceled a game at Miami in 1946 because the "Negro" players—Wally Triplett and Dennie Hoggard—were told by Miami officials to stay home. Perhaps I had once known that Triplett and Hoggard were the first Blacks to play in the Cotton Bowl, in 1948. But I sure didn't remember anything about Lenny Moore being the first Black to play in Fort Worth, TX, when State went there in 1954 to play TCU. I didn't know my friend Carl Stravinski was actually as good as he always told me he was and that his tackle on Dick Cassiano helped beat Pitt for the first time in 20 years in 1939. I didn't know that Joe Paterno didn't receive his first game ball until 1962 after beating California, 23-21, in a thriller at Berkeley. And I sure didn't know that my old broadcast pal Fran Fisher first came to the Penn State campus as a student in the 1940s and played saxophone in the Blue Band before leaving for personal reasons. Frankly, there was a lot I didn't know. For some reason, I had never read Ridge Riley's excellent book, *Road To Number One*. If I had, I wouldn't have been so ignorant about the past. Ridge's book remains the penultimate account of our rich tradition and goes into much greater detail in certain areas. I recommend it highly to any who have not read it. I have attempted to build on that work in the "Penn State Football Encyclopedia" without repeating or revealing too much of the information that makes Riley's book so appealing.

Except for my family, I am not sure how many people will read this book from cover-to-cover. There are snippets of information in every chapter that should delight the typical Penn State fan and some fans may be surprised at the recurring similarities in the 112 seasons between 1887 and 1997. You want bad weather like the 1996 Iowa or 1985 Notre Dame games? The first four times State played night games from 1940 to 1948 it rained, and the weather was so bad for the first meeting with Pitt in 1893 that the game was postponed for two days and everyone partied at the State fraternities. You want wild post-game celebrations like 1994 after the Michigan win in Ann Arbor or 1956 after the beating of Ohio State in Columbus? Check out what happened in 1911 after the big upset at Cornell and 1914 after the momentous tie with Harvard. Now, those were celebrations. Thought you saw everything in 1982 when State blocked its own punt and lost in the showdown at Alabama? Happened 50 years before in a loss at Colgate. Wondered how a team could be selected for a post season bowl game before the season even began, such as in 1992? That's how the Lions of 1922 wound up in the 1923 Rose Bowl.

The section on player profiles includes write-ups on many of the pioneers and every All-American and Hall of Fame inductee as well as tidbits about some virtually unknown modern day players who made an unusual contribution to the Nittany Lion football legacy. A special chapter of the book recounts Significant Dates in Penn State Football History. This list is extensive and reveals many heretofore unknown or long forgotten facts such as when the first game was televised and which U.S. President was the first to attend a State game. No jersey has ever been retired and, as best as I can determine, a listing of jersey numbers worn by State's biggest stars had never been compiled before. You'll find such a rundown in Chapter 18. Other chapters list the team physicians, trainers, equipment managers and student managers. The appendices includes the first compilation of a Year by Year summary of games against each opponent, giving not only the score and location but also the attendance. I have passed this material on to the PSU Sports Information office for inclusion in the 1998 Media Guide.

Nowadays, folks marvel at the way the dedicated State fans follow their team, traveling en masse to far away games via plane, vans, motor homes and chartered busses. But it has been that way almost from the beginning when townspeople and students would go by carriage, horseback and train to games in Lewisburg, Wilkes-Barre, Philadelphia, Ithaca, West Point and elsewhere. Two particular fans gained notoriety. Andy Lytle was a State College farmer who went to his first game in 1892 when he was 44 years old. Through those early years he became known as the team's "most loyal rooter" and he claimed he saw just about every game, home and away, until his death in January of 1928. They called him Penn State's "oldest freshman" and he was honored at the 1924 North Carolina State game in an elaborate ceremony that saw him carried by the freshman class from the president's box to the middle of the freshman section while the sophomore class formed his name in letters on the field. But the most important fan of all may have been General James Beaver, the former Civil War general, Pennsylvania governor and Board of Trustees president whose name has been memorialized in that 97,000-plus seat edifice in the shadows of Mount Nittany. Certainly, General Beaver's influence helped the growth of Penn State football in the early years. The general and his lady traveled regularly to see State play and was well known for the betting he did on the games, as was the practice of that era. So, the next time you are in Beaver Stadium, think about the "oldest freshman" and give a little pause of thanks to the general who, like us was—a FAN! GO LIONS!

Lou Prato
Happy Valley
September 1, 1998

FOREWORD

by
Fran Fisher

There had to be a few times during the research and even while composing this monumental work of prose that Lou Prato said to himself, or to his wife Carole, "What have I gotten myself into?" I'll tell you this, Lou Prato gets into anything he undertakes. That being the case, *The Penn State Football Encyclopedia* is a must for Penn Staters of every vintage.

Lou is a writer by trade — no — make that a journalist, because only a guy with ink in his blood to go along with the Penn State blue could build such a treatise! Oh yes, Lou is a Penn Stater. He has always been close to the Nittany Lions even when he was doing radio and TV in Pittsburgh, Chicago, Detroit or Dayton, or teaching journalism for Northwestern University's graduate program in Washington, D.C.

Even before he settled in State College, he was doing the rah-rah thing. You know, blue and white van, big PRATO/PSU flag for tailgating, second guessing radio announcers, basking in Nittany Lion victories, lamenting in defeats. That doesn't make him all bad, you know.

While he was putting this package together, we probably talked on the average of once a week. He would call to tell me how he uncovered some obscure football tidbit, found an unhearlded star, or discovered some long forgotten great game. He couldn't get over the fact that there was indeed outstanding football at Penn State B.J. before JoePa. He was always enthusiastic about doing this project. If he could write as fast as he talks, this book would have been completed long ago!

Do yourself a favor. Add this to your library. I know, I know, your book shelf is filled with Penn State-type "books." This baby is not a book, it's a masterpiece!

I say that not because Lou is a friend of mine (and I feel privileged for that) or that I feel reasonably certain I'll get a complimentary copy. I say it because I mean it.

No comp copy? I'll buy it. Gotta' have it! Who knows, George and I may still be doing the radio thing at the turn of the century.

Heaven help us all!

-- Fran Fisher, Penn State Broadcaster, 1966 to Present

FOREWORD
by
George Paterno

Lou Prato has managed to write a superb athletic tome on Penn State football. For all Penn Staters who consider themselves blue blood Nittany Lions, Lou's book is a must read. It will be a great edition for your library.

I only wish Lou had finished his enlightened production before I wrote my own. Without a doubt, it's the quintessential reference work on Penn State football.

Lou could be called the man for all seasons concerning his beloved Lions. Lou is not only a skilled writer but also a former radio and TV personality. Lou and his wife Carole tailgated with the best as this distinguished professor collected his information.

Lou's book gives all trivia fans an insight into the storied history of Nittany Lion football. I intend to purchase his book not only for professional reference but to win some arguments (tough to do with my big brother Joe). I only hope Lou has disclosed the true ages of JoePa and the George Burns of announcers, my dear friend and partner, Fran Fisher.

Lou and I are still young.

-- George Paterno, Penn State Broadcaster, 1975 to Present

Head Coach Joe Paterno joins his brother George (far left) and Fran Fisher (far right) in the broadcast booth each spring to help broadcast the annual Blue-White game over the Penn State radio network.

CHAPTER 1
THE ROAD TO NUMBER ONE
THE FIRST 715 WINS

Joe Paterno is so synonymous with Penn State football today that even among the 97,000-plus who pack Beaver Stadium six times each fall, there is little knowledge of what and who came before Paterno. The rousing touchdown runs of Lenny Moore in the '50s, Elwood Petchel in the '40s and Pepper Petrella in the '30s are fading memories for the aging fans of those eras. The exploits of Earl Hewitt, Hef Hershman and Glenn Killinger are all but forgotten except by some history buffs.

Of course, there was football before Paterno. Even the neophyte freshmen throwing the traditional marshmallows for the first time in the South end zone of Beaver Stadium realize that. What they and thousands of others who follow Penn State football don't know about is the almost supernatural legacy that binds Paterno and all Nittany Lion football fans with the once glorious past. Even before Joe Paterno was born on December 21, 1926, he was destined to coach Penn State football to it greatest fame. Sounds weird, right? But Paterno's Penn State roots can be traced directly back to George Atherton, the president of the school when George (Lucy) Linsz and Charlie Hildebrand organized the first team in 1887.

Follow this and see if you don't agree that Paterno was born to become the now legendary "Joe Pa." Atherton encouraged the expansion of football as an intercollegiate sport and was still president at Pennsylvania State College in 1900 when he hired Pop Golden to be the coach. As coach and later athletic director, Golden personally sought

Old Main as it is today but the front lawn is almost the same as it was in 1887 when State played its first home game there.

out and recruited a few players each year from the state's high schools and prep schools to play football for Penn State. Pop's predecessors had never used these tactics. Two of the players he recruited were the starting tackles on the 1910 and 1911 teams, Dick Harlow and Lloyd "Dad" Engle. As an assistant coach in 1913, Harlow persuaded Bob Higgins to attend Penn State instead of Princeton, once reportedly hiding Higgins from opposing coaches in a Pocono Mountain retreat. Then in 1915-16, Harlow was Higgins' head coach and they remained friends for life. Some 20 years later, Harlow would recruit Dad's nephew, Rip Engle, to play for him at Western Maryland. When Rip was offered the head coaching position at Penn State in 1950, he sought the advice of his uncle and his former coach, who had left State with bad feelings. Both men encouraged Rip to take the job. One of Rip's concerns was following the popular Higgins, who had retired as State's head coach in 1949 after a highly respected 18-year career. In a magnanimous gesture of respect for Higgins, Engle agreed to keep the current staff of assistants intact as long as he could bring one of his own. None of his assistants at Brown wanted to go with him. However, the graduating quarterback of his 1949 team said he would go along for one year before attending law school. Ergo, Joseph V. Paterno and the rest is now history. Sure, there were a lot of what ifs and maybes in that 63-year span that converged in the spring of 1950 to place Paterno on the Penn State campus. But there is an old quotation that says, "Each man has his destiny." Paterno's destiny was to coach the Penn State football team and to coach it to great distinction.

The link from 1998 back to 1887 is filled with similar eerie circumstances and situations which relate to the happenings of today. Take the contemporary complaints about the isolated location of State College and the difficulty for visiting teams and their fans to travel there. "A camping trip," Indiana University's famed basketball coach Bobby Knight says in one of the best known quotes about traveling to Penn State in this modern day. In 1953, the Texas Christian football team flew into Harrisburg believing the university was located there. The late great sportswriter Stanley Woodward wryly summed up the sentiments of his New York City colleagues a generation ago when he wrote that to reach State College, "you drive to Harrisburg, then swing through the trees." There is nothing new about the discontent. These were the laments of State opponents from the beginning. In the early years, no decent team wanted to make the long trek into State College and for decades the majority of games each season were played on the road. Dale R. Mason, a student and chronicler of the Athletic Department's history, wrote about the travel problem at the end of the 1907 season while filing stories for the *Pittsburgh Dispatch*. "As State must play all her hard games away from home, the brilliant record she has made against the athletic teams of larger colleges is wonderful, no matter from what angle it is reviewed," Mason wrote. "Too many hard games and the long, tiresome trips often play havoc with the varsity's condition."

The size of State's playing site and its grandstand seating capacity was a related consideration in avoiding State College in the early years, even for such neighborhood foes as Dickinson and the Carlisle Indians and games against those teams were played at neutral sites in Harrisburg and Wilkes-Barre to please and attract more fans. None of the major powers of that turn-of-the-century generation would visit Penn State. But State played on their grounds—Harvard, Yale, Princeton—usually to crowds three to five times larger than ones that would show up for games at home. Even as New Beaver Field expanded in the first 60 years of the century, most of the college football elite shied away from the Nittany Valley. In fact, in 47 games with Pennsylvania dating from 1890 to 1958, not one was played outside of Philadelphia. So, to fill the home schedule, State was forced to play weaker teams—Muhlenberg, Lebanon Valley, Susquehanna—and sportswriters of the times often cited the inferior schedule to denigrate the team's accomplishments. Sound familiar? The early pioneers of those Penn State teams would be amazed to see Beaver Stadium filled to capacity today, with the Lions now playing the likes of Michigan and Ohio State, when the stadium becomes the fifth most populous city in the state after Philadelphia, Pittsburgh, Erie and Allentown.

What is also uncanny is the strange bond between some of the foremost opponents of the Paterno era and the past. Notre Dame, for example. Notre Dame, gained almost overnight renown in 1913 *after* upsetting Army, 35-13, at West Point. That day Gus Dorias and Knute Rockne supposedly invented the forward pass—which, isn't true, of course, but that's another story. Just six days after playing that historic game at West Point, the Irish were in State College to play Penn State for the first time. State's defense contained the Notre Dame passing for the most part but the Irish won, 14-7, in an encounter that ended in a controversy over an offside call against State nullifying a Lion touchdown in the last minutes. That also was the team's first loss ever at New Beaver Field but this game, unlike the one a few days before which was seen by all the big name New York sportswriters, made hardly a blip in the college football world. One year later, Michigan State, then known as the Michigan Aggies, became the second intersectional opponent to visit Beaver Field. It would be six years before the third and fourth intersectional foe showed up in State College. The third would be North Carolina State and the fourth, a power from the Missouri Valley Conference named Nebraska. If the historical coupling to Notre Dame, Michigan State, North Carolina State and Nebraska are not enough, there also is the bizarre connection to Ohio State, which precedes all the rest.

To many Nittany Lion football fans of today, the most detested rival is Ohio State—at least since the demise of the traditional annual eastern series against Pitt and Syracuse and the end of the string of games with Notre Dame and Alabama. A few more trips to the snake pit in East Lansing at the end of the season could distort that perspective. Except for Michigan followers no one dislikes the Buckeyes and their fans more than the PSU constituency, particularly since entering the Big Ten in 1993. Of course, like the OSU-Michigan antagonism, this one's a natural. Not only do the two states share a common border but the rivalry is fed by a pursuit of many of the same high school players and an annual scholastic all-star game that pits the recruits of both schools against each other. State's devastating upset victories in Columbus under Engle and Paterno in 1956, 1963 and 1964 infuriated the Buckeye following who believed the Big Ten titan was invincible against any team from "the effete East." The thrashings of the Lion teams in Columbus in 1993 and 1996 and PSU's overwhelming victory in the 1994 championship season increased the animosity on both sides for a lot of reasons. And it all goes back to 1912. That was the year of the first game between the teams and it ended prematurely in a near riot in Columbus when the Ohio State team quit before the game was over because it was getting beaten up so badly in losing 37-0. So, you see, antipathy towards Ohio State didn't start with Paterno's time. It's been in the Nittany Lion football genes for 86 years.

Paterno's "Grand Experiment," the concept that good students who are good athletes can play big time football, also has connections to yesteryear. Most of the players of the late 1800s and early 1900s were students first, football players second. Two of State's stars of that era were Ed Yeckley and William "Mother" Dunn. Yeckley was supposed to go to Michigan or Dickinson but wound up at State where he was a running back and end. Dunn, a center and linebacker, was an exceptional student and class leader who became the school's first All-American. During their football years of 1902-1906, State had its greatest success up to that time, with a record of 34-14-1. Yeckley later owned a prosperous manufacturing business in Lorain, Ohio, while Dunn, a Youngstown, Ohio, native, became a surgeon and lived most of his life in Hawaii. "The boys came to school with a purpose and took their school work seriously—the faculty saw to that," Yeckley once said, as quoted in Ken Rappoport's Book *The Nittany Lions*. One of the stars who followed Yeckley and Dunn was Pete Mauthe, captain of the outstanding unbeaten team of 1912 that had only six points scored against it. Mauthe, the fullback and kicker, graduated in metallurgy and eventually became president and chairman of Youngstown Sheet & Tube Co. He and teammate Shorty Miller, quarterback and captain of the 1913 team and later a school administrator in Harrisburg, are both in the College Football Hall of Fame. Mauthe was also one the first football players to later join the school's Board of Trustees—a trend that continues today with ex-players like Jesse Arnelle, Ted Junker, Paul Suhey and Steve Garban now serving as trustees, as well as Ed Hintz, student manager of the 1958 team.

However, not all of the players during these early years were good students and the vague eligibility rules at the time led to abuses in the system. Although State athletes were required to have a five percent higher standing than the ordinary student to participate in their sports, there were ways around the rule. It was not unusual for a good player but marginal student to drift from school to school over the years and the practitioners of this custom became known as "tramp athletes." In helping to lead a campaign at the time to tighten eligibility, the student newspaper, *The Collegian*, pointed out alarming statistics which showed that of 89 football lettermen over a 17 year period, 30 failed to graduate and of those 30, 21 had won letters as freshmen.

In 1915, a new rule banned freshmen from varsity competition so the new students could devote their time to the classroom. Joe Paterno, with his well known aversion towards playing freshmen, would have been proud.

In the next few years, State attempted to recruit better students than the norm to play football and sometimes the coaches were quite successful. Higgins, in fact, was a prize catch because his prep school academic achievements were outstanding and several Ivy League schools wanted him. It was this unwavering commitment to education which led to the elimination of athletic scholarships and the de-emphasis of football in the late 1920s. While most of its chief opponents continued to operate with scholarships and other favorable trappings, State abided by a different set of rules. Just when the team was becoming a national power—with its first post-season bowl game in Pasadena, two outstanding undefeated teams and a string of six All-Americans from 1919 to 1923—school officials led by new president Ralph Hetzel changed everything. It would take more than 50 years and a coach named Paterno to restore the grandeur that had been lost by this reasonable but ultimately foolish and ingenuous move. During the interim, the Notre Dames and Pitts would reap the glory and the gridiron accomplishments of Hinkey Haines, Red Griffiths, Newsh Bentz and others would fade into oblivion.

Through the latter half of the Higgins years and on into Engle's tenure, State resurrected from the depths of the 1930s and became a regional force with an occasional foray into the national limelight. Higgins' 1940 team should have gone to a bowl game and the 1947 squad may have been the best two-way team of all time. Engle's teams of the 1950s rarely received the widespread recognition they deserved and even his bowl teams of the early 1960s were not completely appreciated for everything they accomplished. In fact, look how long it has taken Paterno's teams to gain esteem. And based on what happened in 1994 when Paterno's unbeaten Rose Bowl champions were denied a national title by the writers and coaches voting in the polls, there is still a lack of respect in some quarters for Penn State football. Perhaps, it comes with the territory—literally.

People who have never visited Penn State still are confused about its location. Some non-football fans continue to believe it is near Philadelphia, rather than 200 miles west, close to the virtual center of the state. The fact that the university has its own post office designation also adds to the uncertainty. In 1955, the Penn State campus became University Park, PA, surrounded by the borough of State College, PA. Yet, strangers frequently refer to the locale as College Park, which is where the University of Maryland is located, or College Station, the home of Texas A &M.

State College is far from any major city and Penn State has no media power base, especially now that it has abandoned its eastern roots for the Big Ten. The Lions may no longer have to fight the image problem that lasted for decades when they were often confused by outsiders with the Quakers of the University of Pennsylvania. But a bias appears to remain against State and Paterno that skews the reasoning of many in the college football world. *Sports Illustrated* took note of this 25 years ago when a reporter wrote in 1973 about the PSU schedule: "Texas grows fat on people like Rice, TCU and Baylor and it matters not. Notre Dame on Army, Navy and Pitt and it bothers no one. But let Penn State take on Ohio University and sirens go off." Substitute Nebraska for Texas and Temple for Ohio University and you have 1994 and 1997 revisited.

But things are changing. Instead of being asked about the location of "College Park", Penn State followers around the country are now asked, "What is a Nittany Lion?"

For the record, the mountain that overlooks Beaver Stadium is named Mt. Nittany after a folklore Indian princess, Nitta-Nee. Thus, mountain lions once found on Mt. Nittany were called Nittany Lions. The Nittany Lion has been the school mascot since H. D. "Joe" Mason, older brother of Dale mentioned above, led a campaign for the Lion in 1906 after seeing the Princeton Tiger mascot while playing baseball in Princeton. A student body vote made it official and Joe Paterno has made the Lion the symbol of college football excellence.

Beaver Stadium is a symbol, too. It exemplifies success, on and off the field. The people who flock there every fall to party outside and cheer inside are the same ones who give money—and lots of it—to build the new classroom buildings, fund the library expansion, create scholarships and endow the prestigious professorship. Because of the demand for tickets, the seating capacity of the Lions' home field will increase to 103,500 in the next three years and one should not be surprised if there is additional expansion in another decade. During an earlier enlargement in the late 1970s, the administration said that as many as 120,000 could eventually be seated in the outdoor arena. Naturally, not all future predictions have worked out but it is remarkable that the planning for Beaver Stadium began in 1938 when the area was farm land owned by the college. New Beaver Field located in the heart of the campus near the Nittany Lion Inn could seat about 12,000 at the time but even then the college hierarchy was anticipating a major growth in the student body. The farm site was designated for future athletic projects. Of course, it wasn't until after the 1959 season, that the steel structure of New Beaver Field was moved to its current site and rechristened Beaver Stadium. It also should be noted that when the new area was being designed in the late 1950s, the architectural plans included a special area with picnic tables adjacent to the stadium for fans to "bring their lunches" as was traditional in the Ivy League. However, it wasn't until the early 1970s that "tailgating" as we now know it began to take off. Winning under Paterno has made tailgating at Penn State as much of an event as the game itself.

And Paterno has won. No major college football coach has won more games at one college than Paterno. Entering the 1998 season, Paterno has 298. The coaches who have won more games did it at three or four different schools with Bear Bryant at 323, Amos Alonzo Stagg at 314 and Glenn "Pop" Warner at 313. Curiously, Bryant beat Penn State four times while at Alabama and Warner nine times while coaching at Cornell, Pitt and the Carlisle Indians but Stagg never coached against State. Paterno's victories give Penn State 715 in the past 112 years and only five colleges have won more: Michigan, Notre Dame, Alabama, Texas and Nebraska.

It took State a lot longer than the others to travel the Road to Number One. But the players who helped build the road—from Lucy Linsz and Charlie Hildebrand to the Collins brother of Cinnaminson, New Jersey, deserve the credit equally with Paterno, Engle, Higgins, et al. This book tells who they were and how they did it.

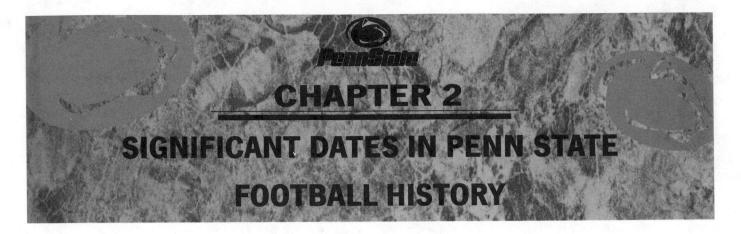

CHAPTER 2

SIGNIFICANT DATES IN PENN STATE FOOTBALL HISTORY

February 22, 1855 - Pennsylvania Governor James Pollock signs charter creating the Farmers' High School of Pennsylvania with location to be determined.

September, 1855 - Two-hundred acres of farm land outside the village of Centre Furnace in Centre County are chosen as location of Farmer's High School after review committee headed by Governor Pollock visits other proposed sites in Erie, Butler, Allegheny County and Perry County.

February 16, 1859 - Sixty-nine students show up for first day of classes at the new Farmer's High School of Pennsylvania.

1862 - Farmers High School of Pennsylvania is given a new name as the Agriculture College of Pennsylvania in anticipation of being given official recognition as a land grant college under the federal Morrill Act.

1874 - Name of college is officially changed to Pennsylvania State College. The town's post office takes the name, State College.

November 12, 1881 - Penn State College students organize team without administration support and play first football game against University of Lewisburg (renamed Bucknell University in 1896) in Lewisburg; State wins, 9-0 in cold, sleet-like drizzle.

September, 1887 - George "Lucy" Linsz arrives on campus as freshman and with help of fellow freshman Charles Hildebrand get approval by President George Atherton to organize first official football team for Penn State College.

Fall, 1887 - Pink and Black are picked as team colors.

November 12, 1887 - First official game is played against Bucknell at Lewisburg; State wins, 54-0.

November 19, 1887 - First home game is played with Old Main lawn used as the field; Captain and quarterback Lucy Linsz scores three second half touchdowns to lead 24-0 win over Bucknell.

Fall, 1888 - Team colors changed to Blue and White.
- Student Athletic Association is formed to help support athletics with three divisions including football, baseball and general.

November 11, 1889 - Penn State is handed worst all-time defeat, 106-0, by Lehigh at Bethlehem; State plays first half with only nine players; referee mercifully stops game with five minutes left.

March 18, 1890 - Blue and White are formally adopted as college colors at a meeting of the Athletic Association.

November 7, 1891 - Penn State plays biggest game since 1887 against Bucknell for lead in the Pennsylvania Intercollegiate Foot-Ball Association championship and loses mistake-prone game, 12-10.

January 9, 1892 - Penn State is awarded first championship of Pennsylvania Intercollegiate Foot-Ball Association after finishing with 4-1 league record, edging out "bitter rival" Bucknell at 3-1-1.

January, 1892	- George (The General) Hoskins is hired as first "official" head football coach and first director of physical training for athletic department.
Spring, 1892	- Football players participate in first spring practice as Hoskins stresses physical conditioning and teamwork.
November 6, 1893	- Beaver Field (later to be known as Old Beaver Field) is dedicated with General James Beaver and wife present, as Penn State plays first game ever against Pitt, then known as Western University of Pennsylvania, and wins easily, 32-0; funding of $15,000 from State Legislature helps construct field, including 500-seat grandstand.
October 13, 1894	- Charlie Atherton sets four all-time records that still stand in opening game 60-0 win against Gettysburg. Atherton kicks 10 of 10 extra points attempts to set the single game extra points record for accuracy, points and attempts, and also adds three touchdowns for most ever points in a single game by a senior (32).
November 10, 1894	- Bill Suter establishes a Penn State record that has never been broken for the longest touchdown run from scrimmage with a 90-yard dash around right end for the only State touchdown in a 6-6 tie with Navy in Annapolis.
November 24, 1894	- Charlie Atherton kicks first placement from scrimmage in history of college football; his 25-yard boot in 9-6 win against Oberlin is ignored by historians.
November 29, 1894	- State records first unbeaten season since the beginning of football in 1887 with a 14-0 win over Pittsburgh Athletic Club and a final 6-0-1 record.
Summer, 1896	- George Hoskins resigns as "head coach" to become coach at Pitt and Dr. Sam Newton is hired as replacement.
September, 1897	- "Henny" Scholl introduces the first helmet to Penn State football during fall practice; helmet is really a derby hat with the brim cut off and rags stuffed inside for padding; helmet gets little usage. - Athletic Association sets mandatory student fee of $2.00 to support athletic programs, including football.
October 30, 1897	- "Hidden Ball Trick" is used for first time in intercollegiate football by Cornell against Penn State in game at Ithaca; Cornell wins, 45-0.
Summer, 1898	- Dr. Sam Newton resigns as "head coach" to coach at Lafayette and Sam Boyle is hired as his replacement.
Fall, 1898	- School's loosely-organized drum and bugle corps expands to create full sized Cadet Band, which later changes name to the Blue Band.
December, 1898	- Junior guard "Brute" Randolph becomes first State player named to All-America team when selected by Walter Camp for 1898 Third Team.
Spring-Fall, 1899	- Sam Boyle of Penn is hired as "head coach" but leaves at end of season.
October 7, 1899	- Star quarterback Earl Hewitt runs back punt 65 yards for only touchdown, then makes game-saving tackle on State six-yard line late in game as State upsets Army, 6-0, in first meeting of the two teams at West Point; State will not beat Army again for 60 years.
Winter, 1900	- William (Pop) Golden hired as head coach and director of physical training for athletic department.
October, 1903	- Pop Golden chosen as school's first athletic director and gives up position as head coach of football team; Dan Reed of Cornell is hired as coach for last month of season and decides not to return in 1904.
October 24, 1903	- In first game at Pitt, Carl Forkum scores 39 points on 5 TDs and 9-of-10 PATs and Irish McIlveen scores two touchdowns—one on a 56-yard run—as State clobbers Pitt, 59-0, in what would be biggest margin of victory in the series for 65 years.
Winter, 1904	- Tom Fennell, Cornell star of 1890s, hired as first full-time head coach.
October 1, 1904	- Carl Forkum sets all-time kickoff return record with 115-yard runback for TD in 50-0 win over Allegheny but his feat is never listed in Penn State record books.

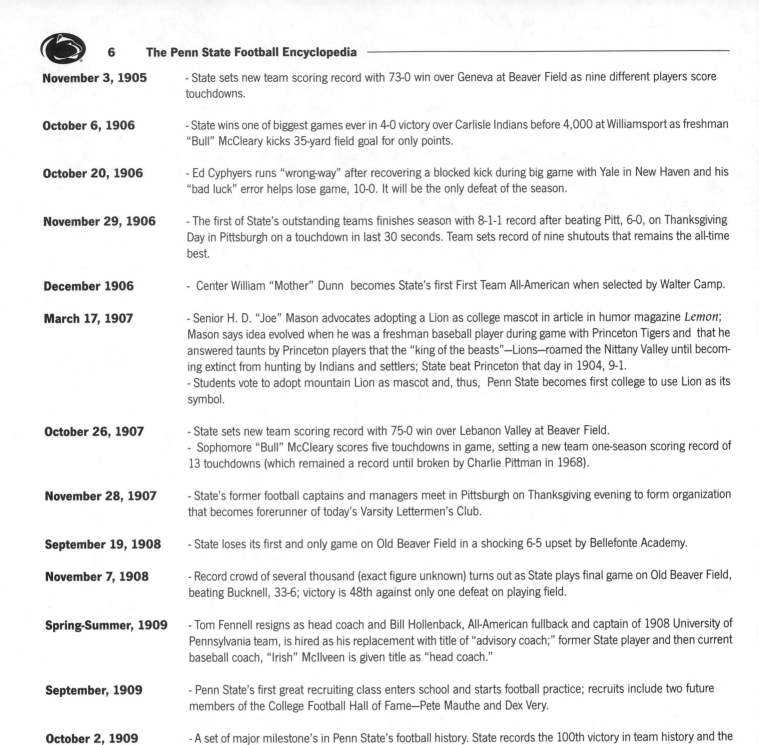

November 3, 1905 — State sets new team scoring record with 73-0 win over Geneva at Beaver Field as nine different players score touchdowns.

October 6, 1906 — State wins one of biggest games ever in 4-0 victory over Carlisle Indians before 4,000 at Williamsport as freshman "Bull" McCleary kicks 35-yard field goal for only points.

October 20, 1906 — Ed Cyphyers runs "wrong-way" after recovering a blocked kick during big game with Yale in New Haven and his "bad luck" error helps lose game, 10-0. It will be the only defeat of the season.

November 29, 1906 — The first of State's outstanding teams finishes season with 8-1-1 record after beating Pitt, 6-0, on Thanksgiving Day in Pittsburgh on a touchdown in last 30 seconds. Team sets record of nine shutouts that remains the all-time best.

December 1906 — Center William "Mother" Dunn becomes State's first First Team All-American when selected by Walter Camp.

March 17, 1907 — Senior H. D. "Joe" Mason advocates adopting a Lion as college mascot in article in humor magazine *Lemon*; Mason says idea evolved when he was a freshman baseball player during game with Princeton Tigers and that he answered taunts by Princeton players that the "king of the beasts"—Lions—roamed the Nittany Valley until becoming extinct from hunting by Indians and settlers; State beat Princeton that day in 1904, 9-1.
— Students vote to adopt mountain Lion as mascot and, thus, Penn State becomes first college to use Lion as its symbol.

October 26, 1907 — State sets new team scoring record with 75-0 win over Lebanon Valley at Beaver Field.
— Sophomore "Bull" McCleary scores five touchdowns in game, setting a new team one-season scoring record of 13 touchdowns (which remained a record until broken by Charlie Pittman in 1968).

November 28, 1907 — State's former football captains and managers meet in Pittsburgh on Thanksgiving evening to form organization that becomes forerunner of today's Varsity Lettermen's Club.

September 19, 1908 — State loses its first and only game on Old Beaver Field in a shocking 6-5 upset by Bellefonte Academy.

November 7, 1908 — Record crowd of several thousand (exact figure unknown) turns out as State plays final game on Old Beaver Field, beating Bucknell, 33-6; victory is 48th against only one defeat on playing field.

Spring-Summer, 1909 — Tom Fennell resigns as head coach and Bill Hollenback, All-American fullback and captain of 1908 University of Pennsylvania team, is hired as his replacement with title of "advisory coach;" former State player and then current baseball coach, "Irish" McIlveen is given title as "head coach."

September, 1909 — Penn State's first great recruiting class enters school and starts football practice; recruits include two future members of the College Football Hall of Fame—Pete Mauthe and Dex Very.

October 2, 1909 — A set of major milestone's in Penn State's football history. State records the 100th victory in team history and the first game is played on New Beaver Field; 500 watch as State beats Grove City, 31-0, with Captain Larry Vorhis, the quarterback, scoring the first touchdown and kicking a field goal.

October 9, 1909 — State gives up lead on two-point safety in last minute to allow Pop Warner's Carlisle Indians to gain 8-8 tie before 10,000 at the neutral site of Wilkes-Barre; a major brawl breaks out after game when State and Carlisle players fight over which team gets the "victory" ball.

October 23, 1909 — After 15 consecutive defeats since series began in 1890, State ties Penn 3-3 at Franklin Field. Lions go on to finish year at 5-0-2 for second undefeated season in history.

Summer, 1910 — Bill Hollenback resigns as coach to accept one-year position as head coach at Missouri; Hollenback's older brother, Jack, takes over "advisory coach" position at State; McIlveen continues as "head coach."

Summer, 1911 — Bill Hollenback returns from Missouri to again become coach, still with title "advisory coach;" former star running back and 1908 captain "Bull" McCleary named "head coach."

October 14, 1911	-State pulls off major upset over Cornell, 5-0, in Ithaca, touching off a riot back in State College that has been called the worst in history following a football game; students and towns people fight with fists, clubs and shovels throughout the streets and alleys of the borough; school officials apologized.
October 28, 1911	- State beats Pennsylvania for first time, 22-6, as Shorty Miller shocks crowd of 15,000 at Franklin Field by running back opening kickoff 95-yards for a touchdown.
December 12, 1911	- New eligibility rules are adopted by Athletic Association requiring athletes to finish education in four years and eliminating rules that allowed athletes to take less credit hours than the minimum requirements for freshmen.
Spring, 1912	- Pop Golden resigns as athletic director to enter private business.
Summer, 1912	- Bill Hollenback is formally given title "head coach."
October 12, 1912	- The largest crowd at New Beaver Field since its opening in 1909—4,000 fans—watch as State beats Washington & Jefferson, 30-0. - Pete Mauthe kicks three field goals to set record for most field goals a one game.
November 16, 1912	- Penn State "upsets" Ohio State at Columbus in first game between the two teams by official score of 37-0 but Buckeyes walk off field with nine minutes to play with claim of "unnecessary roughness" and score is officially recorded as a 1-0 forfeit.
November 28, 1912	- State's greatest team to date beats Pitt 38-0 on Thanksgiving Day at Forbes Field to finish with an 8-0 record, outscoring opponents 256-to-6 and ending a two-year run of 16-0-1. - Pete Mauthe sets record for longest field goal in a game with a 51-yard boot; kick remains record until broken by Chris Bahr in 1975; Mauthe scores total of 20 points with two touchdowns and five extra points. - Mauthe also sets individual season scoring record of 119 points that is not broken until 1971 with 11 TDs, 8 FGs & 29 PATs
February 5, 1913	- Rule is adopted by Athletic Association requiring athletes to "be in good standing for a four year collegiate course." This tightened eligibility requirements and eliminated the so-called "tramp athlete" who would be on a campus for only one year to play a specific sport while taking a few courses and then move on to another college.
Fall 1913	- A new fight song called "Victory" ("Fight, Fight, Fight, For the Blue and White") is introduced by its author, undergraduate Jimmy Leydon, and sung at all football games.
October 4, 1913	- Shorty Miller sets single game rushing record that lasts 68 years with 250 yards, including five touchdowns on runs of 23, 55, 47, 37 and 40 as State beats Carnegie Tech, 49-0, at Beaver Field in 1913 season opener.
November 8, 1913	- State loses first home game at New Beaver Field before record crowd of "several thousand" in its first ever major intersectional game and first game against Notre Dame; Fighting Irish win 14-7 in game that ends with controversial referee decision nullifying State touchdown; Knute Rockne catches a touchdown pass from Gus Dorias that helps end State's 20-game home unbeaten streak.
October 25, 1914	- State stops Harvard's 22-game winning streak with a 13-13 tie at Cambridge, as Harvard, considered the best team in the country, rallies on a trick-play touchdown in last minutes of game; celebration on campus two days later causes injuries and major damages to school buildings as bonfire explodes.
November 13, 1914	- A record crowd of 10,000, including governor John K. Tener, watch on Pennsylvania Day as State loses its second major intersectional game at Beaver Field in first game with Michigan State, 6-3.
December, 1914	- Bill Hollenback resigns as coach to enter private business in Philadelphia.
January 2, 1915	- Assistant Coach Dick Harlow becomes first former Penn State player to be named head coach of football team.
December 1, 1915	- Sophomore end Bob Higgins becomes first State underclassman to earn First Team All-American honors when picked by International News Service.

November 4, 1916 - State breaks nine-year old single game scoring record with 79-0 rout over Geneva at Beaver Field.

October 6, 1917 - Junior Harry Robb sets record that has never been broken for most touchdowns in one game with six in 80-0 rout of Gettysburg at Beaver Field as team again shatters single game scoring record.

October 13, 1917 - State breaks the one-week old team scoring record with a 99-0 win over St. Bonaventure at Beaver Field as nine players score touchdowns, including three by Harry Robb.

November 17, 1917 - Harry Robb ties "Bull" McCleary's one season record for touchdowns with 13 by scoring three TDs as State plays Maryland for first time in game at Beaver Field and wins, 57-0.

July, 1918 - Harlow asks out of his contract as head coach to enter military service; says he will return.

July 18, 1918 - Lt. Levi Lamb, a star lineman on the teams of 1912-14, is killed near Soissons, France, while leading his army platoon against German stronghold. He is one of two former players to die in World War I as 1912 teammate Red Bebout is killed on French battlefield on Sept. 29, 1918.

August 25, 1918 - Hugo Bezdek, manager of the Pittsburgh Pirates, is hired as head football coach and director of physical education with supervision over intercollegiate sports.

November 27, 1918 - State completes weirdest season in history because of World War I by losing 28-6 at Pitt and finishing with a 1-2-1 record.

Fall, 1919 - Dick Harlow returns to State to serve as assistant coach to Hugo Bezdek.

October 4, 1919 - A new tune, "The Nittany Lion," is introduced at the opening game against Gettysburg at Beaver Field. The first words, "Hail to the Lion, Loyal and True," written by Jimmy Leyden will become familiar to generations of State fans.

November 27, 1919 - End Bob Higgins takes flat pass near own goal line from Bill Hess on fake punt and officially runs 92 yards for touchdown for the longest pass play in State history (historians say it should have been recorded as 95 yards); surprise play helps State win, 20-0, and finish with best season since 1912 but State will not beat Pitt again for 20 years.

September 25, 1920 -New wood grandstands are added to Beaver Field's east side raising seating capacity to 5,500 but only 2,500 show up for opening season 27-7 victory over Muhlenberg.

October 9, 1920 - In first alumni "Home-Coming" day, a record standing-room crowd of 12,000 turns out to see Penn State beat Dartmouth, 14-7.

October 16, 1920 - In only the third major intersectional game at Beaver Field, and first since 1914, Penn State clobbers North Carolina State, 41-0.

October 23, 1920 - State sets all-time team scoring record with 109-7 win over Lebanon Valley at Beaver Field, coming back from a 7-0 first quarter deficit; Charlie Way scores three touchdowns in first quarter to lead the rout.

November 6, 1920 - State wins fourth major intersectional game at Beaver Field in first game against Nebraska, 20-0, on Pennsylvania Day, as Glenn Killinger and Charlie Way combine to lead victory as each scores a touchdown and Killinger passes for another.

September 24, 1921 - New Beaver Field constructs its first press box, located atop the West Stands; press box is used for first time in 53-0 season opening win over Lebanon Valley.

October 22, 1921 - State gives up touchdown in fourth quarter darkness at Cambridge as heavily-favored Harvard manages to come back for 21-21 tie in a game many sportswriters at the time called "one of the greatest football games ever."

October 29, 1921 — In first Penn State game played in New York City, State easily beats national power Georgia Tech, 28-7, at the Polo Grounds as Killinger runs back 85-yard kickoff for touchdown that breaks open game and helps make him a First Team All-American.

December 3, 1921 — State plays first game on West Coast, beating Washington 21-7, before 35,000 in Seattle to complete 8-0-2 season and 24th straight game without a defeat.

Spring, 1922 — Dick Harlow quits as assistant coach after final dispute with Hugo Bezdek and becomes head coach at Colgate.

September 23, 1922 — New Beaver Field seating capacity increased to 12,000 as 1922 season opens with 54-0 victory over St. Bonaventure.

October 27, 1922 — Ten surviving members of first official team in 1887 honored in New York City by Alumni Association for being "founders" of Penn State football.

October 28, 1922 — Nittany Lion Mascot makes first appearance ever on field dressed in African Lion uniform during Penn State's first game against Syracuse played at New York's Polo Grounds; Dick Hoffman, class of '23, dresses in uniform of maned African Lion that he had worn while appearing in Penn State Player's production of George Bernard Shaw's Androcles and the Lion. State and Syracuse battle to 0-0 tie before a crowd of 25,000.

November 3, 1922 — Navy uses a fake punt and fumble recovery to end State's 30-game unbeaten streak, 14-0, in a game played at Washington's American League Park before 35,000; dozens of congressional, government and foreign leaders and many of college football's leading coaches, players and sportswriters, were in attendance.

January 1, 1923 — Penn State plays in first post-season bowl game, the 1923 Rose Bowl at Pasadena, and loses to Southern California, 14-7, but receives $21,350 for participating in game; it is the first Rose Bowl played at its present site in Pasadena's Arroyo Secco section and the first ever appearance of USC.

September 29, 1923 — Additional wooden bleachers are constructed at New Beaver Field raising seating capacity to 13,500 but only 3,000 turn out to see State beat Lebanon Valley, 58-0 in season opener.

October 20, 1923 — New Beaver Field attendance record of 20,000 is set as State upsets unbeaten Navy 21-3 in Homecoming Game; "Light-Horse" Harry Wilson has his greatest game in rushing for 218 yards and scoring all three State touchdowns, with a 55-yard interception return, a 95-yard kickoff return and a 72-yard run off a fake reverse.

Spring 1924 — Bas Gray becomes first junior elected captain of Nittany Lion football team.

September 15, 1924 — Football team moves into new Varsity Hall, across the street from New Beaver Field; Varsity Hall includes dormitory rooms, training table and football locker room. (Building name is later changed to Irvin Hall after athletes leave building and still exists today as undergraduate residence hall.)

October 25, 1924 — State's 29-game winning streak at New Beaver Field comes to an end as Syracuse wins Homecoming game, 10-6; streak began after loss to Rutgers in World War I year of 1918.

November 7, 1925 — State surprises Notre Dame by tying Irish, 0-0, in driving rain and mud on Homecoming Day at New Beaver Field before a record-breaking crowd reported by several newspapers at 25,000 but official attendance is given at 20,000.

November 14, 1925 — State visits West Virginia for first time to participate in dedication ceremonies for West Virginia's new Mountaineer Stadium, and loses, 14-0.

November 26, 1925 — Annual Thanksgiving Day game with Pittsburgh is played for first time at new Pitt Stadium and State loses, 23-7.

January 14, 1926 — State administration appoints Alumni committee to study football policies in wake of allegations by Carnegie Foundation and others that State overemphasizes sport to the detriment of educational goals of higher education.

October 9, 1926 — State wins 200th football game by beating Marietta, 48-6, at New Beaver Field as Cy Lungren runs back kickoff 95 yards for touchdown to spark victory.

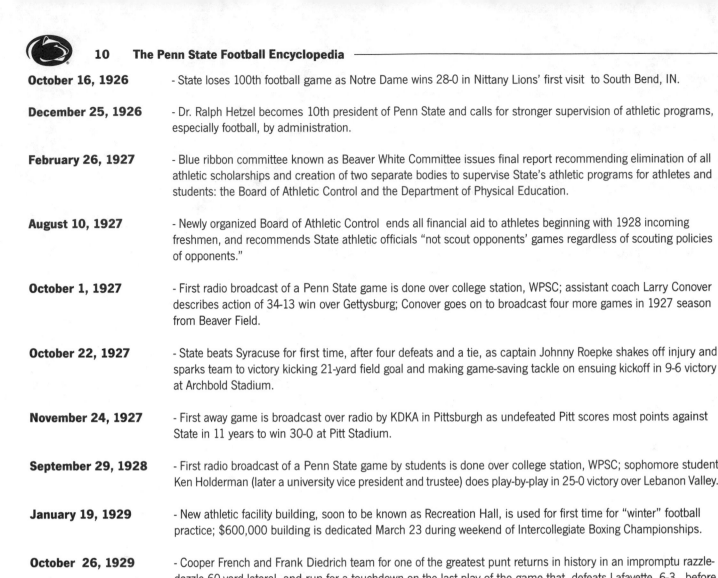

October 16, 1926 — State loses 100th football game as Notre Dame wins 28-0 in Nittany Lions' first visit to South Bend, IN.

December 25, 1926 — Dr. Ralph Hetzel becomes 10th president of Penn State and calls for stronger supervision of athletic programs, especially football, by administration.

February 26, 1927 — Blue ribbon committee known as Beaver White Committee issues final report recommending elimination of all athletic scholarships and creation of two separate bodies to supervise State's athletic programs for athletes and students: the Board of Athletic Control and the Department of Physical Education.

August 10, 1927 — Newly organized Board of Athletic Control ends all financial aid to athletes beginning with 1928 incoming freshmen, and recommends State athletic officials "not scout opponents' games regardless of scouting policies of opponents."

October 1, 1927 — First radio broadcast of a Penn State game is done over college station, WPSC; assistant coach Larry Conover describes action of 34-13 win over Gettysburg; Conover goes on to broadcast four more games in 1927 season from Beaver Field.

October 22, 1927 — State beats Syracuse for first time, after four defeats and a tie, as captain Johnny Roepke shakes off injury and sparks team to victory kicking 21-yard field goal and making game-saving tackle on ensuing kickoff in 9-6 victory at Archbold Stadium.

November 24, 1927 — First away game is broadcast over radio by KDKA in Pittsburgh as undefeated Pitt scores most points against State in 11 years to win 30-0 at Pitt Stadium.

September 29, 1928 — First radio broadcast of a Penn State game by students is done over college station, WPSC; sophomore student Ken Holderman (later a university vice president and trustee) does play-by-play in 25-0 victory over Lebanon Valley.

January 19, 1929 — New athletic facility building, soon to be known as Recreation Hall, is used for first time for "winter" football practice; $600,000 building is dedicated March 23 during weekend of Intercollegiate Boxing Championships.

October 26, 1929 — Cooper French and Frank Diedrich team for one of the greatest punt returns in history in an impromptu razzle-dazzle 60-yard lateral and run for a touchdown on the last play of the game that defeats Lafayette, 6-3, before a disbelieving but cheering Homecoming crowd of 10,000 at Beaver Field.

October 29, 1929 — Carnegie Foundation releases 383-page report on the Advancement of Teaching condemning Penn State and other colleges for dishonesty in overemphasizing football and other intercollegiate sports by giving athletic scholarships and urged a return to amateurism; Carnegie later issues addendum declaring State had changed policies two years previously but addendum is virtually ignored by public and press and State's educational image is damaged. (This same day the stock market crashed, precipitating a nationwide depression.)

January 20, 1930 — Hugo Bezdek is relieved of head coaching duties of football team and named first director of the new School of Physical Education.

March 27, 1930 — Former two-time All-American Bob Higgins is promoted from assistant coach to head coach of football team.

October 31, 1931 — Pitt coach Jock Sutherland rests his first team and plays scrubs for entire game as Panthers clobber Lions, 41-6, scoring most points since series began, then insults Beaver Field Homecoming crowd by working out his first team for 15 minutes after game; fans did not realize Sutherland had received Higgins' approval before game for the workout; this was Pitt's first visit to State since 1902 and the teams did not play again until 1935.

November 28, 1931 — State ends seven-game losing streak, which remains the school record, by beating Lehigh, 31-0, in post-season game for charity at Philadelphia's Franklin Field and ends season with the worst record in history, 2-8.

December, 1931 — State football team elects first married captain in history when senior quarterback Red Collins is picked by his teammates.

August, 1932   - Friends of Coach Higgins, including former player Ben "Casey" Jones of Pittsburgh and Jim Gilligan of Dunmore set up way to circumvent school policy and recruit good players by getting players jobs in fraternities, restaurants and other State College businesses; first class of those players entering as freshmen include Jim O'Hora, who later becomes a long-time coaching assistant to Rip Engle and Joe Paterno.

October 14, 1933   - State football hits bottom when Muhlenberg wins major upset, 3-0, at Beaver Field; team goes on to 3-3-1 record.

October 20, 1934   - State wins first regular season road game in five years and first away game in Higgins era with 31-0 win over Lehigh in Bethlehem, PA.

September 1, 1936   - State opens preseason practice with the first all-alumni coaching staff: Bob Higgins ('20), head coach; Joe Bedenk ('24), Earle Edwards ('31) and Al Michaels (Mikelonis) ('35), varsity assistants; and Marty McAndrews ('30), freshmen coach.

October 1, 1936   - Former coach Hugo Bezdek agrees to one year leave of absence with pay from position as director of Physical Education School, and resigns one year later.

October 6, 1936   - Four surviving members of 1881 "forgotten pioneers" team are officially recognized as playing in Penn State's first intercollegiate football game and given varsity "S" letters.

Fall 1937   - Dr. Carl P. Schott is hired as new director of Physical Education and is defacto Dean of Athletics.

October 2, 1937   - First game is filmed on request by coaches to help team during practice; State beats Gettysburg, 32-6, at Beaver Field but film shot by student camera operators turns out too dark and Higgins hires zoology instructor and part-time track coach Ray Conger to take charge of filming; Conger remains in position for 39 years.

November 13, 1937   - State clinches first winning season since 1929 and first in Higgins coaching regime by beating Maryland in last minute at Beaver Field, 21-14, but loses the next week to National Champion Pitt and finishes with 5-3 record.

September 26, 1938   - Ridge Riley writes and publishes first "Football Newsletter" in pre-season analysis of 1938 season.

October 1, 1938   - First Penn State radio network is set up and starts broadcasting with opening game against Maryland at Beaver Field; KDKA Pittsburgh originates broadcast with Bill Sutherland on play-by-play and Jack Barry doing color commentary as Penn State wins, 38-0.

October 29, 1938   - Two players each get 100 yards in one game for the first time as sophomore Chuck Peters (156 yards) and junior Steve Rollins (122 yards) help lead State to 33-6 win over Syracuse at Beaver Field.

November 20, 1938   - State loses 26-0 at Pitt to finish with 3-4-1 record that will be the last losing season for 49 years; despite this, team sets three NCAA defensive records including one for fewest yards passing allowed per game (13.1 yards average) that still stands.

November 25, 1939   - Future All-American Leon Gajecki leads State to first victory over Pitt in 20 years in 10-0 upset before record-tying crowd of 20,000 at Beaver Field and State finishes year with best record since 1921 at 5-1-2.

November 9, 1940   - Juniors Bill Smaltz and Lenny Krouse team for greatest passing day to date as Smaltz completes 14-of-21 passes (including 12 passes in succession that remained a record until 1994) for 193 yards and two touchdowns and Krouse catches 10 for 2 touchdowns and 155 yards (yardage is still the most in single game by a junior).

November 16, 1940   - Chuck Peters sets all-time kickoff return record with 101-yard touchdown return on opening kickoff in 25-0 win over NYU; it's his second touchdown runback of the season (96 yards against Temple opening second half) and sets season record for kickoff touchdown returns that is now shared by Curt Warner (1980).

November 23, 1940   - State loses first and only game of season and chance for post-season bowl game when upset by Pitt, 20-7, at Pitt Stadium.

September, 1941 — Dave Alston and his brother Harry of Midland, PA, become first black players on football team. (Dave becomes star of unbeaten freshman team and selection by some preseason magazines as college football's "sophomore of the year."

September, 1941 — State College Quarterback Club organizes and meets for the first time to sponsor luncheons on Wednesday with head football coach Higgins, players and other assistant coaches attending.

October 31, 1941 — State plays its first night game, at New York's Polo Grounds against New York University and wins 42-0 in heavy rain on sloppy field.

November 12, 1941 — Led by Dave and Harry Alston, Steve Suhey and Red Moore, freshmen team goes unbeaten for first time since 1916 with 5-0 record. Dave Alston scores 8 touchdowns, passes for 4 others and drop-kick's 6 extra points in one of the school's outstanding individual freshmen performances ever.

September 10, 1941 — Athletic Board authorizes freshmen to play on varsity for the duration of World War II.

August 15, 1942 — Freshman star Dave Alston, State's first black player, dies in Bellefonte Hospital after a tonsillectomy operation but death is traced to injuries suffered in spring practice scrimmage against Navy. (Brother Harry is so shaken he never returns to school.)

September 1, 1942 — First Radio Network is organized by KDKA dissolves because of World War II; major gasoline sponsor can't get enough gas to sell.

October 24, 1942 — Nittany Lion Statue created by famed sculptor Heinz Warneke near the entrance of Beaver Field is dedicated during halftime of 13-10 Homecoming win over Colgate; H. D. "Joe" Mason, class of 1907, who instigated the move for a Lion as mascot, is among the crowd of 11,510 on hand.

November 14, 1942 — In one of biggest upsets of the Higgins era, State shocks Penn, 13-7, before 50,000 at Franklin Field behind the punting of Joe Colone and the running and defensive play of Larry Joe who is carried off the field at the end of the game.

November 30, 1942 — State is ranked for the first time by the Associated Press at the end of the season, tying at number 19 with defending National Champion Minnesota and Holy Cross, as team dominated by sophomores and freshmen surprise nation with 6-1-1 record.

October 21, 1944 — Larry Cooney, 16, of Pittsburgh becomes the youngest player ever to start a State football game, when he opens at right halfback against Colgate in fourth game of season, when frosh were eligible because of World War II, and carries ball 5 times for 8 yards rushing.
— Johnny Chuckran of Lansford becomes only freshman ever to serve as captain for a season, and runs back punt 50 yards in last minute to spark 6-0 upset win over Colgate in Hamilton, NY.

October 28, 1944 — For first time in history, an all-freshmen starting lineup takes the field and loses thriller to West Virginia at Beaver Field, 28-27, in first defeat at home since 1938.

November 17, 1945 — Freshman Wally Triplett becomes first black to start a State game when he takes field at right halfback (or tailback position in single-wing formation) against Michigan State at East Lansing, MI.; Lions proceed to lose, 33-0, but Triplett is praised for his all around play.

Summer 1946 — Jim O'Hora, a center at State from 1933-1935, and Earl Bruce, high school coach from Brownsville, join Bob Higgins' coaching staff, O'Hora as assistant line coach and Bruce as freshmen coach based at California State Teachers College.

Summer 1946 — Casey Jones and other Pittsburgh area alumni raise $19,000 to buy on old fraternity house off campus to house football players; new assistant coach O'Hora agrees to be "counselor" of the new facility and he and his family move in; all freshmen players are assigned to the campus of California State Teachers College where they will train under the direction of Bruce.

November 9, 1946	- State cancels final game of season on November 29 at Miami when Miami University officials request that State not bring its two black players, Wally Triplett and Dennie Hoggard, on trip.
November 16, 1946	- This is the first known attendance at a Penn State game by a U.S. President as Harry Truman gives Navy pep talks before game and at halftime in Annapolis but State upsets heavily favored Middies, 12-7, as Elwood Petchel runs back a pass interception for one touchdown and scores another on a one-yard run.
October 18, 1947	- '47 team sets NCAA defensive record for fewest total yards Allowed in a single game by holding Syracuse to a minus 47 yards in 40-0 Homecoming victory at Beaver Field; record continues into 1998 season.
October 25, 1947	- In what was the key game of the 1947 season, State comes from behind to beat undefeated West Virginia, 21-14, before the largest Beaver Field crowd since the 1925 Notre Dame game (20,313) and stays on track for first postseason bowl game in 25 years.
November 15, 1947	- State wins 300th game with 20-7 conquest of Navy at Baltimore's Memorial Stadium as fullback Jeff Durkota runs 48 and 42 yards for touchdowns on identical inside reverse play.
November 22, 1947	- '47 team beats Pitt 29-0 to become first State squad in history to win all nine games of regular season and sets school record for giving up least amount of points (27) and shutouts (6); team also sets NCAA defensive records for fewest rushing yards allowed per game (17) and per rush (0.64); records still intact after 1997 season.
December 8, 1947	- State finishes in Top 10 for first time when ranked 4th in final Associated Press college football poll of 1947. - Lions also awarded Lambert Trophy as best team in the East for first time since trophy's inception in 1936.
January 1, 1948	- Tailback Wally Triplett and end Dennie Hoggard become first blacks to play in the Cotton Bowl game and Triplett scores a TD and plays outstanding defensive game as State and SMU battle to 13-13 tie.
October 23, 1948	- New Beaver Field attendance record of 24,579 is set during Homecoming as State ties Michigan State, 14-14, in a game marked by controversy over a clipping penalty that nullified a MSC 100-yard touchdown on an interception.
November 6, 1948	- State plays before largest crowd to date—71,180—and defeats Penn at Franklin Field, 13-0, sparked by a razzle-dazzle touchdown run-and-pass play of Fran Rogel-to-Chuck Drazenovich-to-Elwood Petchel-to-Rogel.
November 27, 1948	- A State team travels by airplane for first time to play Washington State at Tacoma and wins game, 7-0, to finish season at 7-1-1 and achieve 18th ranking in Associated Press college football poll.
March 12, 1949	- Bob Higgins announces his resignation as head coach of football team and long-time assistant coach Joe Bedenk is named as his successor.
Spring 1949	- Earle Edwards resigns from football coaching staff following spring practice and joins Michigan State as an assistant coach. Bedenk names former State lineman, Sever Toretti (1936-38), as line coach and ex-Pitt star Frank Patrick as defensive backfield coach.
May 1949	- Tuition scholarships for all sports re-established by Board of Trustees on recommendation from Athletic Board; 100 total scholarships are approved.
September 1949	- First class of scholarship players since 1927 enter State but are sent to California State Teachers College because of crowded housing conditions on main campus; among the freshmen are future starters Joe Yukica, Don Barney and Joe Gratson.
October 1, 1949	- State plays 500th game since 1887 and loses 42-7 to an Army team that would stay unbeaten and be rated #4 in country. - This is also the first known televising of a State football game as game is carried by WNBT-TV in New York City.
March 5, 1950	- Joe Bedenk resigns after one year as head football coach but remains on staff as an assistant coach.
March 31, 1950	- Athletic Board sets 30 scholarships exclusively for football to include tuition, room and board.

April 22, 1950 — Charles A. "Rip" Engle, head coach at Brown University, is named head football coach by acting college president James Milholland.

May 27, 1950 — Rip Engle names Joe Paterno, his senior quarterback at Brown, to coaching staff and assigns him to coach quarterbacks.

October 14, 1950 — State loses for the first time at night after four night game victories dating back to 1941, all played in rainy weather, as Syracuse wins, 27-7, on a clear night at Archbold Stadium.

October 28, 1950 — First Band Day is held at Beaver Field as part of Homecoming, with eight Centre County high school bands participating as State and Temple tie, 7-7, before 20,782.

December 2, 1950 — Major snow storm forces postponement of final game of season against Pitt at Pitt Stadium on November 25 and game is switched to Forbes Field one week later, where State wins 21-20 in what becomes known at "the Snowbowl."

December 1950 — Athletic Board adds 15 scholarships for football, bringing total to 45.

September 1, 1951 — Athletic Board and Eastern Intercollegiate Athletic Conference agree to make freshmen eligible for varsity because of Korean War. (Authorization only lasts one year before freshmen are banned again.)

October 21, 1951 — Another New Beaver Field attendance record—30,321—is set, again in a Homecoming game against unbeaten (and eventual #2) Michigan State, but this time Penn State loses, 32-21.

July, 1952 — Ernest (Ernie) McCoy, basketball coach at Michigan since 1948, takes over as Director of Athletics and Dean of Physical Education Department.

September 20, 1952 — Former player and coach Joe Bedenk watches first game since 1917 as spectator after stepping down as assistant coach; sees 20-13 win over Temple at Beaver Field.

September 27, 1952 — Junior Tony Rados surprises fans and makes national headlines by giving State its greatest passing day in 12 years, completing 17-of-30 passes for 179 yards and one TD (and 2 interceptions), and outdueling Purdue's All-American passing sensation, Dale Samuels, in leading State to a surprising 20-20 tie at Beaver Field.

November 13, 1952 — State goes over 100,000 in total one season home attendance for the first time in history (103,751 in 5 games) as 15,957 at Beaver Field watch Lions escape with 7-6 win over underdog Rutgers.

November 22, 1952 — State upsets Pitt, 17-0, to knock Panthers from Orange Bowl before 53,766 at Pitt Stadium; Lions defense, led by Jack Sherry's two interceptions, and Ted Kemmerer's punting throttles Pitt attack; Rados' passing sparks Lions offense.

October 17, 1953 — Mickey Bergstein, color man and engineer for State's radio network, makes spectacular debut as play-by-play announcer in game against Syracuse at Beaver Field, when he takes over fourth quarter for regular announcer Bob Prince, who has to leave to broadcast a Steelers-Eagle game in Philadelphia Saturday night; Bergstein describes how Lions score two touchdowns in fourth quarter in come-from-behind 20-14 win that ends with a full fledge brawl at Syracuse bench.

November 7, 1953 — Heavy snow blankets State College in 24-hour period, forcing major snow removal at Beaver Field for game against Fordham; kickoff delayed by two hours because of late arrival of State team, which was trapped in Clinton County hunting camp known as "Camp-Hate-To-Leave-It;" Lions go on to win 28-21 thriller before some 13,897 hearty fans.

November 13, 1953 — State officially becomes Pennsylvania State University and the next day the Lions play first game as PSU and come from behind a 14-6 second quarter deficit to wallop Rutgers 54-26 at New Brunswick.

December, 1953 — Levi Lamb Fund, named for former State star, is established at suggestion of athletic director Ernie McCoy, to assist in obtaining financial aid for athletes and athletic department.

March 1, 1954 - J. T. White, who played on Michigan's 1948 National Champion team as well as at Ohio State as a center, joins Rip Engle staff as an assistant coach.

September 25, 1954 - Underdog State stuns preseason Big Ten conference favorite Illinois 14-12 in opening game of season played at Champaign, shocking college football world and becoming overnight front-runner to win Lambert Trophy.

October 23, 1954 - Lenny Moore becomes first black to play college football in Fort Worth, Texas, but Lions make too many mistakes and lose to Texas Christian, 20-7.

October 30, 1954 - State plays first game on national television and beats Penn, 35-13, at Franklin Field, scoring most points in long time series against Quakers; Lenny Moore rushes for 140 yards and scores three touchdowns.

September 1, 1955 - State begins year long celebration of Centennial Year with Navy scheduled to visit Beaver Field for first time since 1923; establishes new dateline of "University Park" with opening of a campus post office.

September 29, 1955 - First game is televised from Beaver Field as CBS transmits season opener against Boston University to limited region in East; Lions win 35-0 and unknown fifth-string sophomore fullback Joe Sabol scores two touchdowns to lead victory.

November 5, 1955 - Syracuse's Jim Brown outgains Lenny Moore, 159 yards to 146, and scores all Syracuse points on three touch downs and two extra points, but State comes from behind 20-7 deficit on quarterbacking of Milt Plum to win thrilling 21-20 Band Day contest in one of greatest games ever at New Beaver Field as 30,321 and a CBS regional TV audience look on.

September 29, 1956 - First all-Penn State alumni broadcasting team works first game for the Lions football radio network as Mickey Bergstein ('43) moves from color commentary to play-by-play and Bob Wilson ('40) takes over color; State beats Pennsylvania, 34-0, at Franklin Field in Philadelphia.

October 20, 1956 - State stuns heavily-favored Ohio State in Columbus, winning 7-6 on Milt Plum's extra point kick before the largest crowd to see a Penn State football game up to that time, 82, 584.

October 19, 1957 - Pete Mauthe, captain of undefeated 1912 team, becomes first Penn State player inducted into the College Football Hall of Fame during halftime ceremonies of Homecoming game against Vanderbilt; Lions blow 13-point lead and are upset, 32-20.

October 26, 1957 - The third game of Engle era is televised by CBS on a regional basis from Syracuse as State beats Orangemen, 21-12, behind the surprise quarterbacking of sophomore Richie Lucas, who was forced to take over for the injured starter, Al Jacks.

December, 1957 - Outstanding freshman running back Robert "Red" Worrell, who was a potential varsity starter on 1958 team, is electrocuted at his family home in Denbo, PA, while helping his father erect a TV antenna; Athletic officials establish award in his name to honor the most improved player after spring practice; lineman Andy Stynchula wins first award in 1958.

September 27, 1958 - State ends longest running series with one of oldest opponents, Pennsylvania, with 43-0 victory at Franklin Field; series which began in 1890 was never played outside of Philadelphia and finished with State winning 18, losing 25 and tying 4.
- First ever two-point conversion is scored when Al Jacks passes to end John Bozick after State's second touchdown; later in game, Richie Lucas passes to Jim Schwab for second two-point conversion.

December 19, 1959 - Penn State plays in first ever Liberty Bowl and tackle Charlie Janerette becomes first black to play against Alabama as Lions beat Crimson Tide coached by Bear Bryant, 7-0, in Philadelphia's Municipal Stadium.

April, 1959 - Nittany Lion Club is organized by 15 alumni who want to arouse interest in Penn State athletic affairs through contributions to the Levi Lamb Fund; membership stipulated annual contribution to fund of at least $50 or at least $25 for graduates of less than 10 years; members will receive "special consideration" on game tickets and "preferred parking" at stadium.

November 7, 1959
- All-Time attendance record is set at New Beaver Field as 34,000 watch a memorable battle of unbeatens play with national rankings and bowl berths at stake; Syracuse edges Penn State 20-18 despite electrifying 100-yard kickoff return by sophomore Roger Kochman as Lions fail to make an extra point kick and two 2-point conversions.

November 14, 1959
- Penn State clobbers Holy Cross, 46-0, in last game played at New Beaver Field as 20,000 spectators watch final quarter in rain and heavy wind; Lions close out 229th game played on this site with record of 184-34-11.

September 17, 1960
- State plays first game in Beaver Stadium and a less than capacity crowd of 22,559 watch as Lions beat Boston University, 20-0, with senior halfback Eddie Caye scoring the first touchdown at 10:25 of the first quarter.

October 3, 1960
- What later becomes known as "Tailgating" is first suggested in front page column by "Centre Daily Times" Editor Jerry Weinstein after monumental traffic jams before and after Homecoming game against Illinois at Beaver Stadium on Saturday, October 1; Weinstein advocates adoption of Ivy League tradition of pregame "picnic lunches" and says State fans should add "picnic suppers" for after game while traffic disperses.

October 8, 1960
- "Hero" defensive back makes debut in 27-16 victory over Army at West Point; Senior Sam Sobczak is first player designated as "Hero."

September 29, 1961
- Athletic Department experiments with closed circuit television by televising first game ever against Miami from Orange Bowl Stadium to Rec Hall and Schwab Auditorium on Penn State campus but paid attendance is disappointing when less than 40 percent of the seating capacity is filled.

November 4, 1961
- Maryland beats State for only time in 37-game series, 21-17, at College Park behind passing combination of Dick Shiner and Gary Collins.

December 30, 1961
- End Dave Robinson becomes first black to play in Gator Bowl and makes the defensive "play-of-the-game" with a quarterback sack and fumble recovery that helps Lions beat Georgia Tech, 30-15.

Spring, 1962
- Penn State joins Pitt, Syracuse and West Virginia in agreeing to forbid "redshirting," a practice that withholds athletes from competition for a year so they can "mature."

October 13, 1962
- State becomes first team to play three service academies in one season, losing to Army at West Point on this date, 9-6, after beating Navy, 41-7, and Air Force, 20-6, earlier in season at Beaver Stadium.

October 27, 1962
- Assistant coach Joe Paterno is presented a game ball by team for the first time since he joined Rip Engle's staff in 1950, when Lions overcome sensational debut of sophomore quarterback Craig Morton and defeat California, 23-21, in Berkeley.

December 1962
- End Dave Robinson becomes first black player in State's football history to be named First Team All-American when selected by Associated Press, Football Writers and others.

Summer 1963
- State joins Syracuse, Pitt and West Virginia in Letter of Intent agreement for incoming freshmen football players, obligating recruit to a specific school for at least one year. National agreement being worked on would also include the following conferences: Big Ten, Southwest, Southeast, Atlantic Coast, Big Eight and Missouri Valley.

Summer 1964
- Joe Paterno is named associate coach and heir-apparent to succeed Rip Engle as head coach when Engle decides to retire.

November 7, 1964
- State, with 3-4 record, shocks unbeaten #2 Ohio State, 27-0, in what Associated Press calls the "college upset of the year" as Lions defense limits Buckeyes to 60 net yards while State's offense gets 341 total yards.

November 24, 1964
- In closed door meeting without coaches, players vote down opportunity to play post-season game in Gator Bowl after overcoming 0-3 start and ending 6-4 season with stunning shutout victories over Ohio State and Pitt and winning Lambert Trophy; this will be the last time players are given chance to vote on bowl games.

December 4, 1965	- Rip Engle coaches last game as State beats Maryland, 19-7, at Byrd Stadium, on game televised nationally by NBC, to finish season at 5-5 and wind up 16 years at State with 104-48-4 record and no losing seasons.
February 18, 1966	- Rip Engle officially announces his retirement as head coach, about one month from his 60th birthday on March 26.
February 19, 1966	- Associate Coach Joseph V. Paterno, 38, is named head football coach by University President Eric Walker and Dean of Athletic Department Ernest McCoy at annual salary of $20,000.
September 17, 1966	- Paterno wins first game, 15-7, in season opener against Maryland at Beaver Stadium as sophomore middle guard Mike Reid sets team record by scoring three safeties before less than capacity crowd of 40,911; team presents Paterno with game ball for only second time in his coaching career.
September 24, 1966	- Paterno suffers first loss as then #1 Michigan State led by All-Americans Bubba Smith and George Webster whip Lions, 42-8, before 65,763 at East Lansing.
October 15, 1966	- State loses at UCLA, 49-11, in what becomes worse loss ever for a Paterno team.
September 29, 1967	- In what becomes the "turning point" game of Paterno's career, he replaces several defensive veterans with untested sophomores, including future All-American Dennis Onkotz, and tackle Steve Smear and State beats Miami, 17-8, in Orange Bowl Stadium behind the running of Bobby Campbell and pass receiving of another future All-American, Ted Kwalick. - Among the 39,516 spectators are 150 members of Penn State's first Alumni Holiday Tour.
October 7, 1967	- New policy requires students to buy tickets (at $4 each) for home games at Beaver Stadium as University eliminates use of pre-paid activity fees for football; several thousand students among 46,007 watch State lose 17-15 to then #3 UCLA.
November 11, 1967	- A Paterno-coached team gains national recognition for the first time with a 13-8 upset over then #3 North Carolina State after a fourth down goal line stand in last minute preserves win at Beaver Stadium.
November/December	- Junior End Ted Kwalick becomes first First-Team All-American coached by Joe Paterno when named by Newspaper Enterprise Association and Football Coaches; also is first junior to win honor and first underclassman selected since Bob Higgins in 1915.
December 30, 1967	- Paterno gains nationwide attention in Gator Bowl by gambling for first down on own 15-yard line with a 17-0 third quarter lead and when gamble fails, Florida State rallies to tie 17-17. - Among the record crowd of 68,019 are 119 members of Penn States first Alumni Holiday Bowl Tour.
December 7, 1968	- The first Paterno team to have a regular season game televised nationally, beats Syracuse 30-12 at Beaver Stadium to become first PSU team to be unbeaten in regular season since 1947 and the first one to win 10 games.
January 1, 1969	- State beats Kansas 15-14 in thrilling Orange Bowl game after Jayhawks are penalized for having 12 men on the field; team finishes highest ever in final Associated Press poll after bowl games, #2 behind Ohio State which beats previous #1 USC and Heisman Trophy winner O.J. Simpson in Rose Bowl.
July 1, 1969	- Ed Czekaj, placekicker and end on the undefeated 1947 team, becomes Athletic Director succeeding Ernie McCoy, who retired.
September 27, 1969	- Some 2,000 seats and enlarged press box are added to Beaver Stadium as new record crowd of 51,402 turn out to see State beat Colorado, 27-3, with Paul Johnson returning kickoff 91-yards for touchdown, 15th longest in team history.
November 29, 1969	- State completes second straight unbeaten regular season with 21st straight win by beating North Carolina State in Raleigh 33-8, as part of second half of national television doubleheader on ABC following Army-Navy game; All-American Charlie Pittman scores two touchdowns to stretch his career touchdown record to 31, and break Pete Mauthe's 67-year-old career scoring record with 186 points.

December 31, 1969   - Earl Bruce, long time assistant coach, retires.

January 1, 1970   - State's defense led by Outland & Maxwell Trophy Winner Mike Reid sets new Orange Bowl record with seven intercepted passes as State beats Missouri, 10-3, for second consecutive 11-0 season, tying 30-game school unbeaten streak set by teams from 1919-to-1922, but again finishes #2 in AP (and UPI) poll to Texas, which beats first Notre Dame bowl team in 45 years in Cotton Bowl.

September 19, 1970   - Team sets new record for consecutive games won—23—and most unbeaten games in a row–31— with 55-7 pasting of Navy in opening season game at Beaver Stadium.
- Senior Mike Cooper of Harrisburg becomes first black to start at quarterback for PSU and throws for two touchdowns.
- New six-station Pennsylvania television network broadcasts first of five home games on a delayed basis at 11 p.m.; games are carried in Philadelphia, Altoona, Harrisburg, Scranton, Lancaster and York as Governor Ray Shafer helps do color commentary of games with Dick Scherr of WTAF (Philadelphia) and Dick Richards of WFBG (Altoona) handling play-by-play and other commentary.

September 26, 1970   - Colorado ends State's consecutive game winning and unbeaten streaks by beating Lions 41-13 in Boulder before an ABC national television audience.

September 18, 1971   - Albert Vitiello, a native of Naples, Italy, becomes first junior college transfer to play for PSU, the first placekicking specialist to be recruited and given a "grant in aid" and the first soccer style placekicker; makes debut by kicking eight extra points as State opens season with 56-3 victory over Navy in Annapolis.

November 20, 1971   - Lydell Mitchell establishes NCAA record for scoring and touchdowns and breaks Pete Mauthe's 59-year individual one-season scoring record with 174 points and Charlie Pittman's career touchdown record with 29 by scoring three TDs in 55-18 win over Pitt.

December 4, 1971   - In one of most signifcant losses of the Paterno era, Lions are upset by Tennesee, 31-11, in Knoxville, ruining unbeaten season and intensifying criticism about State's "overrated" football program.

December 1971   - Tackle Dave Joyner of State College becomes State's first pure offensive interior lineman to be named a First Team All-American when selected by six organizations, including UPI, American Football Coaches and Football Writers.

January 1, 1972   - State comes from behind in second half to stun Texas 30-6 in Cotton Bowl in a game Paterno said was one the Lions "had to win" more than any other in State history; victory helps quiet criticism of State football program and establishes Lions solidly as a legitimate national power.

Spring, 1972   - For first time in history, team elects four co-captains, choosing quarterback John Hufnagel and guard Carl Schaukowitch for offense and tackle Jim Heller and safety Greg Ducatte on defense.

September 23 1972   - Beaver Stadium seating capacity expands to 57,537 as 5,600 seats are added to east side and 3,570 to north end zone but just 50,547 turn out to watch State come from behind to beat four touchdown underdog Navy, 21-10, in opening season game.

September 30, 1972   - Majorettes debut with Blue Band as a corps of 12 coeds, led by junior Judy Shearer, parade before record crowd of 58,065 at Iowa game.

November 25, 1972   - Pitt announces it will no longer follow mutual agreement with State, Syracuse and West Virginia prohibiting "red-shirting" and a maximum of 25 football grants-in-aid per year.

December 31, 1972   - State plays in first Sugar Bowl ever held on New Year's Eve and lose 14-0 to second-ranked Oklahoma after star running back John Cappelletti is forced to miss game with virus; later Oklahoma is forced to forfeit game to PSU after NCAA penalties for using ineligible players.

September, 1973	- Defensive tackle Randy Crowder becomes first black elected captain when chosen as a defensive co-captain along with linebacker Ed O'Neil with tailback John Cappelletti and center Mark Markovich elected offensive co-captains.
September 22, 1973	- Dave Shukri and Brad Benson become first freshmen to play varsity football since 1951 when they enter game in second half of 39-0 rout of Navy at Annapolis.
September 19, 1973	- Women become members of marching Blue Band for first time in 60 years of existence as band entertains near record Homecoming crowd of 59,980 against Iowa in home season opener. The five coed pioneers include: Debbie Frisbee, flag carrier; Carol Gable, alto horn; Linda Hall, clarinet; Kit Murphie, alto horn; and, Susan Nowlin, drums.
December 13, 1973	- John Cappelletti becomes first State player to win Heisman Trophy as college football's outstanding player and accepts Heisman Trophy in emotional speech about his younger brother, stricken with leukemia, before Vice President Gerald Ford and 4,000 other dignitaries in New York.
January 1, 1974	- State's 1973 team beats LSU in Orange Bowl, 16-9, to become first Lion team to win 12 games without a loss but squad is snubbed in polls when voted #5 by AP and UPI; Paterno calls team "the best I've ever coached" and votes it #1 in the "Paterno Poll."
July 1, 1974	- State formally withdraws from Eastern Collegiate Athletic Conference in dispute over ECAC financial arrangements with 214 member schools; PSU athletic department balks at paying 1/5th of ECAC's total budget, plus 10 percent of all television and bowl revenues.
September 21, 1974	- In what is probably the biggest upset of a Paterno team ever, 24-point underdog Navy, coached by former Paterno assistant George Welsh, beats Lions, 7-6, in rain and wind at Beaver Stadium.
October 12, 1974	- Tight End Randy Sidler becomes first freshman to start since 1951 when two-year regular Dan Natale is sidelined by injury in Homecoming game against Wake Forest; Sidler catches two passes for 41 yards but another freshman, wingback Jimmy Cefalo, thrills crowd by scoring touchdowns on a 57-yard pass from Tom Shuman and a 39-yard run.
November 16, 1974	- State wins 500th game by beating Ohio University at Beaver Stadium, 35-16, despite 85 yards in penalties and four lost fumbles as Tom Donchez scores three touchdowns.
December 31, 1975	- State plays in first Sugar Bowl ever held at the New Orleans Superdome and loses to Alabama, 13-6.
January 6, 1976	- Ridge Riley, creator of the alumni "Football Letter," dies of heart attack in kitchen of coach Joe Paterno while interviewing Paterno for the final chapter of his soon-to-be-published book, "Road to Number One."
August, 1976	- John Black takes over the alumni "Football Letter" and writes first issue analyzing the team before fall practice.
September 18, 1976	- A record crowd of 62,503 and a regional TV audience watch as Ohio State visits Penn State for the first time in history and avenges four previous losses in five games at Columbus with 12-7 win.
November 6, 1976	- Joe Paterno wins 100th game as a head coach as Lions beat North Carolina State, 41-20, before 60,462 at Beaver Stadium.
July 1, 1977	- Assistant coaches Jim O'Hora and Frank Patrick retire; O'Hora after 31 years and Patrick after 24 years of coaching and three years as athletic academic counselor.
September 19, 1977	- The last record crowd before expansion of Beaver Stadium—a standing-room-only, 62,554— turns out in the second game of the season to see Penn State win second game by beating Houston, 31-4, as junior QB Chuck Fusina hits on 15-of-23 passes for 245 yards, one touchdown and no interceptions and All-American candidate Randy Sidler makes 11 tackles and causes one fumble to lead the victory.

October 15, 1977 - Paterno misses only game of his head coaching career when his 11-year-old son, David, is severely injured in a trampoline accident; Paterno spends day in a hospital in Danville, PA, as his team, coached by offensive coordinator Bob Phillips and defensive coordinator Jerry Sandusky, staves off fourth quarter comeback at Syracuse and wins, 31-24.

September 1, 1978 - Beaver Stadium completes addition of 16,000 seats after lifting steel pillars, closing the south end of the horseshoe, eliminating the track that had encircled the field, constructing 20-to-40 new rows of concrete stands and expanding press box.

September 11, 1978 - A new Beaver Stadium record crowd of 77,154 turns out to see Penn State beat Rutgers 26-10 in the opening home game of the season; Matt Bahr ties his brother's single game record of four field goals and Chuck Fusina hits Scott Fitzkee for a 53-yard touchdown pass in the first quarter to spark the victory.

November 6, 1978 - In a watershed battle of unbeaten teams before another record crowd of 78,019 and a national TV audience, #2 Penn State defeats #5 Maryland, 27-3, limiting the Terps to minus 32 yards rushing, intercepting five passes (3 by Pete Harris) and recording 10 QB sacks (3 by Larry Kubin) as Matt Bahr kicks two Field Goals and Chuck Fusina hits on a 63-yard TD pass to Tom Donovan.

November 13, 1978 - For the first time in 91 years of football, Penn State is voted #1 in the polls by the Associated Press and United Press International after beating North Carolina State, 19-10, thanks to another record four field goals by Matt Bahr.

November 30, 1978 - The Nittany Lion Statue near Recreation Hall is damaged for the first time since it was dedicated in 1942 when vandals smash off the right ear with a hammer.

January 1, 1979 - Number one ranked State plays for National Championship for first time ever and loses to #2 Alabama, 14-7, in Sugar Bowl when Mike Guman is stopped on fourth-and-inches at the goal line in fourth quarter in what was the biggest play of the game.

November 3, 1979 - Miami upsets State 26-10 at Beaver Stadium behind passing of suprise starting freshman quarterback Jim Kelly and the Hurricane's new coach Howard Schnellenberger tells reporters, "This day will do down in history of Miami football as the day we turned our football program around."

December 1, 1979 - The first State punt to be blocked in 10 years occurs when Ralph Giacomarro's punt is blocked by Pitt after 629 consecutive successful kicks in 29-14 loss to Panthers at Beaver Stadium.

March 1, 1980 - Joe Paterno becomes Athletic Director succeeding Ed Cezkaj but Paterno will remain as head football coach.

July 1, 1980 - J. T. White, the last assistant coach from the Rip Engle era except for Joe Paterno, retires after 26 years of coaching defensive ends.

September 6, 1980 - Beaver Stadium adds 7,000 seats, expanding seating capacity to 83,600, and also introduces new electronic scoreboard as record crowd of 78,926 watches State wallop Colgate 54-10.

October 10, 1981 - New Hall of Fame room and Indoor Sports Complex is dedicated at Homecoming festivities as #2 Lions win fourth straight by beating Boston College, 38-7, before a then record crowd of 84,473.

October 20, 1981 - State is voted #1 for only second time in history after beating Syracuse 41-16 in first appearance at Carrier Dome.
- Curt Warner breaks Shorty Miller's 69-year single game rushing record with 256 yards and a touchdown on 26 carries. (But with Warner sidelined by injury, Lions lose two weeks later at Miami, 17-14, and drop to #6 as Pitt moves up to #1.)

November 28, 1981 - State pulls off one of its finest come-from-behind victories, snapping back from a 14-0 first quarter deficit to rout then #1 Pitt, 42-14, and kill national title chances of Sugar Bowl-bound Panthers before national television audience and 60,260 at Pitt Stadium; victory sparked by interceptions of Dan Marino passes by Roger Jackson and Mark Robinson and the passing combination of Todd Blackledge to Kenny Jackson.

January 1, 1982 - State plays in first Fiesta Bowl ever held on New Years Day and beats USC, 26-10, holding Heisman Trophy winner Marcus Allen to 85-yards as Curt Warner gains 145 yards in 26 carries; State finishes #3 in AP and UPI ratings.

March 1, 1982 - Associate Athletic Director Jim Tarman succeeds Joe Paterno as Athletic Director as Paterno continues as head coach of football team..

September 11, 1982 - State achieves 100th victory at Beaver Stadium in a 39-31 shoot-out with Maryland as Todd Blackledge passes for 262 yards and four touchdowns and Boomer Esiason throws for 276 yards and two touchdowns before sellout crowd of 84,567.

September 25, 1982 - In one of the most thrilling games ever at Beaver Stadium, #8 State comes from behind with 65-yard drive in last 1:18 to beat #3 Nebraska as Todd Blackledge throws winning pass of 2-yards to reserve tight end Kirk Bowman with four seconds left on clock before record crowd of 85,304 and a national television audience.

November 26, 1982 - Curt Warner establishes career rushing record of 3,398 yards and Todd Blackledge sets career touchdown passing record of 41 as they lead 19-10 win over once-beaten Pitt at Beaver Stadium and take #2 ranking to Sugar Bowl; Warner gains 118 yardsand Blackledge throws 31-yard touchdown to Kenny Jackson in victory.

January 1, 1983 - State wins first National Championship by beating previously #1 Georgia, 27-23, in Sugar Bowl as Todd Blackledge passes 47 yards to Gregg Garrity for key fourth quarter touchdown and Curt Warner outduels Heisman Trophy winner Herschel Walker with 117 yards and two TDs.

August 29, 1983 - State plays in first ever Kickoff Classic at Giants Stadium in New Jersey Meadowlands and loses to Nebraska, 44-6, in worse loss since 1966 UCLA game.

September 9, 1983 - New sports logo is introduced featuring a sleek, Lion head.

October 8, 1983 - Unranked Penn State upsets #3 Alabama, 34-28, at Beaver Stadium on two last minute defensive plays that lead to one of the biggest controversies in PSU football history when back judge nullifies an end zone pass reception by Alabama, saying the receiver juggled the ball as he fell out of bounds. Despite videotape replays which indicate pass should have been complete, official review of game films show juggling occurred and validity of complaint is "inconclusive" but that Alabama should have been penalized for man-in-motion on play but was not.

October 22, 1983 - State bans media from locker room after 41-23 Homecoming win over West Virginia, and institutes new policy for interviewing coaches and players in separate room at adjoining Greenberg Indoor Sports complex; policy change is triggered after complaint by female reporter Sarahjane Freligh of Philadelphia Inquirer who was not allowed in State locker room after Alabama game two weeks earlier.

November 19, 1983 - In one of most bizarre finishes in PSU football history, Nick Gancitanto kicks 32-yard field goal to tie Pitt 24-24 after most of the 60,283 spectators and TV viewers in Pittsburgh and Johnstown thought game at Pitt Stadium had ended; clock showed no time left after a Lion running play had been stopped but officials said six seconds remained because of a penalty a few moments earlier; players had to be called back from the dressing room and the field cleared for the game to finish; it was only second tie game in Paterno's coaching career.

Spring 1983 - Running backs coach Fran Ganter is promoted to offensive coordinator to succeed Dick Anderson, who takes head coaching position at Rutgers.

September 8, 1984 - Former offensive coordinator Dick Anderson returns to Beaver Stadium as head coach of Rutgers and in first game of his career, his team loses to PSU 15-12.
- The "Hawaiian Wave" makes its first appearance in Beaver Stadium as 84,409 spectators help "wave" roll around stadium several times during the game.

Fall, 1984 - Permanent lights costing $575,000 are installed at Beaver Stadium after U.S. Supreme Court rules against NCAA's control of televised games and permits individual colleges to make their own arrangements.

September 14, 1985 — New home team locker room and media room open at Beaver Stadium along with additional permanent seats in North End Zone for handicaped and visiting band; four circular concrete ramps to help spectators are also part of renovation.

October 26, 1985 — State wins 600th game by beating West Virginia 27-0 before a sellout Homecoming crowd of 85,534 and ABC regional TV audience as John Shaffer throws two touchdown passes and defense limits Mountaineers to 268 yards with three interceptions, two fumble recoveries and four sacks.

November 6, 1985 — State is voted #1 for only fourth time in history when UPI coaches board select Lions after 16-12 come-from-behind fourth quarter win over Boston College but in AP poll Lions remain #2 behind Florida coached by former PSU quarterback Galen Hall.

November 13, 1985 — State moves to #1 in AP rankings after beating Cincinnati, 31-10, at Cincinnati's Riverfront Stadium while Florida loses to Georgia, 24-3.

January 1, 1986 — Oklahoma beats #1 Lions in Orange Bowl, 25-10, to win National Championship as two PSU interceptions and a fumble help Sooners to victory.

September 6, 1986 — State plays first night game at Beaver Stadium in season opener against Temple that helps launch celebration of first 100 years of Lions football; quarterback John Shaffer passes for three touchdowns and runs for another in 45-15 victory.

October 25, 1986 — Sixth-ranked Lions shock country with dominating 23-3 upset win over #2 Alabama in Tuscaloosa behind defense led by linebackers Shane Conlan and Trey Bauer and running of D. J. Dozier to hand Crimson Tide just its third loss in 25 years at Bryant-Denny Stadium; victory pushed State into #2 in polls and on track to play #1 Miami for national title.

January 2, 1987 — State wins second National Championship by upsetting previous #1 Miami, 14-10, in Fiesta Bowl behind defense led by All-American Shane Conlan with a four-down goal line stand in last minute of game; Lions fluster Heisman Trophy winner Vinny Testaverde with five sacks and five interceptions, including one by linebacker Pete Giftopoulos at goal line on last play of game.

September 5, 1987 — Paterno wins 200th game in 45-19 victory over Bowling Green in season opening game at Beaver Stadium and later tells media, "I may live to be 100, but I'll never be around for another 100 victories."

August 9, 1988 — State announces the end of traditional series with Syracuse at conclusion of current contract in 1990 season when Syracuse refuses to change home-and-home arrangement to allow six games at Penn State during new 10-year contract.

October 1, 1988 — Tony Sacca becomes first true freshman to start at quarterback in the Paterno and Engle eras and leads State to 45-9 win over Temple at Veterans Stadium in Philadelphia.

November 19, 1988 — State loses to Notre Dame, 21-3, in South Bend to finish with record of 5-6 and first losing season in 49 years.

June, 1989 — John Mitchell becomes first male baton twirler in Blue Band

December 19, 1989 — Representatives of Penn State and the Big Ten Conference announce an "invitation in principle" has been extended for State to join the Big Ten; invitation is made formal on January 4, 1990, in a 7-3 vote of the Council of 10 ruling body and Stae accepts; full integration of all sports, including football, is expected by 1995.

December 29, 1989 — In one of the zaniest games in State history, Lions beat BYU in Holiday Bowl shoot-out, 50-39, scoring 21 points in a wild fourth quarter that included two spectacular plays by defensive back Gary Brown; he scores PSU's first ever two-points off an opponent conversion attempt when he returns an interception 102 yards, then strips the ball from BYU quarterback Ty Detmer and runs 53 yards for another touchdown with 45 seconds remaining.

November 17, 1990 — State pulls off one of the biggest upsets in history as freshman Craig Fayak kicks 34-yard field goal with 58 seconds left to give the 18th ranked Lions 24-21 win over #1 Notre Dame after trailing at halftime, 21-7.

Spring, 1991 - Big Ten announces State football will be fully integrated into Big Ten for 1993 season. Iowa becomes first opponent on schedule fulfilling dates previously set with Notre Dame in 1993 and 1994; new Big Ten schedule expected to mark end of games with traditional rivals Pitt and West Virginia.

September 7, 1991 - 10,000 seats are added to Beaver Stadium with construction of a new upper deck in north end zone and new attendance record of 94,000 is set as State beats Cincinnati, 81-0, in home opener of 1991 season; score is the largest winning point differential in the Paterno era.

January 1, 1992 - In the most bizarre and exciting four minute span in history, the Lions come from behind a 17-7 third quarter deficit with 28 points in less than four minutes and go on to beat Tennessee, 42-17, in Fiesta Bowl.
- Crowd of 71,133 helps take State's total season attendance over one million for first time, with 1,017,843 in 13 games.

September 12, 1992 - A new policy is implemented banning smoking inside Beaver Stadium, starting with season opener against Temple.
- For just the second time in the Paterno era, a true freshman starts at quarterback as Wally Richardson leads Lions to 49-8 victory over Temple.

October 10, 1992 - In what is the biggest game at Beaver Stadium in years and a clash of unbeaten teams, #2 Miami beats #5 State with the help of an interception return for a touchdown, 17-14, and sends Lions into a tailspin for the season.

January 1, 1993 - State plays its worst bowl game ever and is embarassed by Stanford, 24-3, in Blockbuster Bowl at Florida's Joe Robbie Stadium.

September 5, 1993 - State ends 106 years of independence with 38-20 win over Minnesota in first game of Big Ten conference.
- Redshirt sophomore wideout Bobby Engram catches four touchdown passes of 29, 31, 20 and 31 yards from junior quarterback John Sacca to set new all-time touchdown receiving record; Minnesota quarterback Tim Schade also sets two individual records by a PSU opponent by completing 34-of-66 pass attempts.

September 18, 1993 - Paterno wins 250th game as State head coach and receives game ball from players as Lions shutout Iowa in Iowa City, 31-0, behind a defense that sets up three touchdowns with interceptions and sacks Hawkeye quarterback nine times for 89 yards in losses.

October 16, 1993 - State plays 1,000th game in history and loses at Beaver Stadium in first ever meeting with Michigan, 21-13, for initial defeat in Big Ten conference.

November 27, 1994 - Lions come from behind a 37-14 deficit late in the third quarter on the passing of Kerry Collins to Bobby Engram to beat Michigan State at East Lansing, 38-37, and clinch third place in first year of Big Ten conference play.

July 1, 1994 - Jim Tarman retires as Athletic Director and is succeeded by former football walk-on Tim Curley.

October 15, 1994 - Unbeaten State beats Michigan 31-24 in Ann Arbor before largest crowd ever to see Lions play, 106,832, and is voted #1 for first time since 1987 Fiesta Bowl victory over Miami in polls by both AP writers and broadcasters and USAToday/CNN coaches.

October 29, 1994 - Lions trounce Ohio State 63-14 but still lose #1 AP ranking to previously #3 Nebraska; two OSU beat writers vote State #2; Ohio native Ki-Jana Carter scores four touchdowns and runs for 137 yards and quarterback Kerry Collins passes for 265 yards and two touchdowns as defense limits Buckeyes to 214 net yards while intercepting three passes.

November 5, 1994 - Lions lose #1 USAToday/CNN ranking to Nebraska after two last minute touchdowns by Indiana make 35-29 victory in Bloomington look closer than it was.

November 12, 1994 - Lions clinch first Big Ten Championship by coming from behind a 21-0 first quarter deficit with one of the greatest clutch drives in history, a 96-yard, 15-play march into the rain and wind late in the fourth quarter to beat Illinois, 35-31, at Champaign in late afternoon game televised by ABC.
- Drive keyed by passes from Quarterback Kerry Collins to Bobby Engram and Kyle Brady and running of Ki-Jana Carter and Brian Milne, who scores winning touchdown on 2-yard plunge with 57 second left in game.

January 2, 1995 - State beats Oregon, 38-20, to win Rose Bowl but despite 12-0 season finishes #2 to Nebraska, which is named National Champion by AP and USAToday/CNN; New York Times computer rankings list State #1 with schedule rated 19th toughest by NCAA compared to Nebraska's 57th rating.

November 25, 1995 - Wide receiver Bobby Engram climaxes his career and his standing as one of the greatest clutch players in State history, scoring the winning touchdown with eight seconds left and no time outs on a 4-yard flanker screen pass from Wally Richardson, ducking under two Michigan State tacklers, to give the Lions a thrilling 24-20 win over Michigan State at East Lansing.

August 25, 1996 - State introduces a new logo with Lion head looking more fierce as State upsets Southern California, 24-7, before record Kickoff Classic crowd as redshirt sophomore tailback Curtis Enis comes within 15 yards of Curt Warner's single game rushing record with 241 yards and three touchdowns at Giants Stadium in the New Jersey Meadowlands.

September 28, 1996 - State becomes just sixth school in college football history to win 700 games by beating Wisconsin, 23-20, at Madison in last second thriller.

October 12, 1996 - Tackle John Blick of Saylorsburg becomes first true freshman to start in interior offensive line in Paterno era in Homecoming win over Purdue, 31-14.

April 26, 1997 - A record crowd of 60,000 show up to watch annual intrasquad scrimmage game at Beaver Stadium, beating the previous record of 40,000 set in the Blue-White game of 1996.

September 6, 1997 - For first time in history, Penn State is rated #1 in preseason rankings by AP media poll; USAToday/CNN coaches poll rate Lions #2 behind Washington.

September 20, 1997 - State scores 50 points in first half to tie record of unbeaten 1947 team in 57-21 romp at Louisville but lose #1 ranking in AP poll to Florida, which beats Tennessee, 33-20, while #3 Nebraska beats Washington.

October 11, 1997 - Lions come from behind to beat #7 Ohio State, 31-27, before record crowd of 97,282 at Beaver Stadium and go to #1 in both AP and USAToday/CNN polls for first time since October 23, 1994, as LSU upsets previous #1 Florida.

October 18, 1997 - State has to come from behind to beat 34-point underdog Minnesota, 16-15, and lose #1 ranking in both AP and USAToday/CNN polls to Nebraska, which beats Texas Tech, 29-0.

November 8, 1997 - A Paterno team suffers worst loss ever in Beaver Stadium before another record crowd of 97,498 as #4 Michigan wins first game in four years against Lions, 34-8.

December 23, 1993 - All-American tailback Curtis Enis becomes first State player in history to admit to knowingly violate NCAA rules after allowing a sports agent to buy him $1,100 worth of clothing at a shopping mall in Harrisburg in early December and is suspended from Citrus Bowl by Coach Paterno.

Fall 1998 - Joe Paterno wins 300th game.

April 1, 2000 - Joe Paterno retires as head football coach of Penn State. (Only fooling!!!)

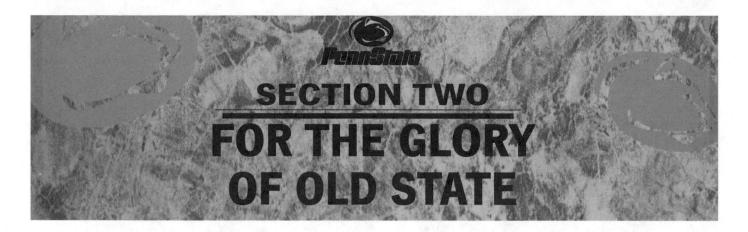

Joe Paterno likes to say that the outcome of a football game is determined by no more than five or six plays. Sometimes, it comes down to one play. A long touchdown pass. An interception. A penalty. A blocked punt. A sack. A tackle at the line of scrimmage. One play that changes the direction of the game. One play that determines the outcome. One play that makes heroes on one side and losers on the other. The turning point. The climactic instant. The defining moment that determines which team wins and which loses.

And so it is with a football season.

There, too, is that defining moment—the moment when the whole season hangs in the balance; that one point in time when the course of the season is determined; that turning point when the personality of the team solidifies and the essence of the season is set for the ages.

Often, that too, comes down to one play. One play in the thousands that occur throughout the season. Six months of hard work. Spring practice. Hot August two-a-days. Aches and pains. Cheers and boos. Through rain, sleet and snow and fourth quarter exhaustion. And it may well come down to one play.

Or maybe a couple of plays. A goal-line stand. A last-minute 90-yard drive with no time on the clock. A fumble recovery and a bomb on the next play for a touchdown. A winning season or a losing season. New Year's Day in Pasadena or in State College. The defining moment when the historic significance of the season is on the line.

Sometimes, the moment transcends the actual playing on the field. An injury in practice and the star running back is gone for the year. A fiery halftime speech by the coach and the team goes instantly from losing to winning. A controversial decision behind closed doors in the off-season and an entire team loses its desire to play.

It's the defining moment of the season although they may not realize it at the time. But, later, when everyone has time to reflect, they know. Sometimes, they disagree on the specific event, combining one moment in the season with another: a play in the regular season game and a bowl showdown; a player injury and the on-field result of his absence. However, it is still "the" moment or moments and they usually remember where they were when "the" moment occurred. On the field. In the stands. Watching on TV. Listening on the radio. Reading about it in the newspaper. Hearing about it from a friend.

They talk about it for years. At home. In the bars. On the sideline. In the press box. At the tailgates. If they sometimes forget about it, there's always someone around to remind them of it. If it happened before they were born or they were too young to care, there's always a book to read about it later. This book, perhaps.

I was there for some of "the" moments. I asked others what they remembered—former players, retired coaches, athletic department officials, broadcasters, writers and fans, in order to get an accurate rendition of each game and each season. For the early years and into the 1930s, there were books and newspaper articles that told of the significance of one play or a series of events. Sometimes, the information was sketchy and "the" moment was not easy to determine. But there was always something that one could point to and say, "Yes, this may have been it!"

One needs to note the research and observations for the early years. Newspapers were the prime source of game information. So was Ridge Riley's outstanding book, *The Road to Number One*. The author reviewed each season game-by-game in an attempt to get an overall perspective of what had occurred. This was especially crucial for the first few decades when there was little information about the games and the players, except from newspaper coverage, Riley's research and other source material in the Penn State Athletic Offices and the Pattee Library Archives. What I tried to do then was inject myself into that specific year, to think as the players, coaches and fans did at that time. Using this method, I wanted each season to come alive, to be as real today as it was then. Rather than a methodical, boring rundown of game-by-game minutiae, I wanted readers to get a true feeling and understanding for what that season was like a long, long time ago. In some instances, I have taken some liberties and made certain assumptions as to how a person (or persons) might have reacted to an event. In such instances, I have applied logic and basic rules of human nature in reporting the probable outcome. Whenever possible, I have tried to back up my observations with quotes, primarily from newspapers.

There also was a problem over the ever-changing football rules of the 1890s and 1900s. Football is played a lot differently today than it was at that time or even into the 1920s and 1930s. Rather than attempt to recite all the rule changes over the years, I chose to write about each season with today's game in mind. Where the rule change was crucial as to how a specific game or season was played, the information was included as part of the narrative. Thus, the reader may not need to know that in the early days, touchdowns counted four points and field goals scored five and "goals after" touchdowns were worth two points. Or that three downs were allowed to make a first down. Or that just about everyone on the team could carry the ball and that players could be "carried or pushed over the goal line" by their teammates. At one time quarterbacks were not permitted to run for touch-

Ridge Riley (R), author of the first history of Penn State football, The Road to Number One, *talks to Dex Very, captain of the unbeaten 1911 team and a member of the National Football Foundation College Football Hall of Fame, during a meeting in the 1960s. Riley also was creator of the Penn State Alumni Association "Football Letter" in 1938. Very never missed a game in his four-year career and was one of the first players in college football to be known as a pass receiver.*

downs and passing—backward, forward or sideward—was highly restricted. Kicking was different, too, and so was the way teams gained and kept possession by kicking. The field was longer than 100 yards at one time and it took three downs to make a first down five yards away. The time of games varied from 15- to 30-minute halves and sometimes teams played three or four games in a 10-day period.

As college football took its place in the culture of America, the rules were standardized. But even in the modern day, the game continues to be refined. Just two years ago, in 1996, the overtime rule for major college games was changed to provide for an overtime winner. For decades, participants played both offense and defense—and it was not unusual for many players to stay in the entire game. Some of Penn State's greatest players excelled on both offense and defense—and they kicked field goals and punted, too. Then, in the 1950s, along came two-platoon football, followed by unlimited substitution and, today, the age of the specialists: pass rushers, pulling guards, strong tackles, short tackles, field goal kickers, punters—you name it. In the beginning, players did not wear pads or helmets, and the equipment changed gradually over decades. Look at the average college player in uniform today and it is difficult to envision the game's forebears pounding each other so viciously without such protection—but they did. If the rules are different today, so are the sizes and physical abilities of the players. They evolved over the decades as coaching, conditioning, practice,

weight lifting, running, etc. became year-round activities. The variances in the rules, the physical makeup of the players and refinement in strategy and tactics go on and on, but what the reader should keep in mind is that the overall structure of the game has not changed fundamentally since its inception.

What I found most surprising in composing the season-by-season analysis in this manner was the number of similarities between Penn State football today and Penn State football over the generations. It was a little eerie to discover that kicking and defense often won games in the late 1800s and early 1900s, just as kicking and defense have won in the Paterno era, and that opponents have always been reluctant to play games at State because it was "too isolated." Home field was just as much an advantage then as now, and during one stretch from 1887 to 1908, State did not lose at home, winning 48 games and tying three, and most of the time holding the opposition scoreless. And weather—rain, cold, sleet, snow, mud—has always been a part of Penn State football. In fact, when you look at 112 seasons, the weather is as much a tradition as the blue and white uniforms, black shoes and the Nittany Lion mascot.

So, here is this writer's view of the defining moments of Penn State football. Season by season. From 1881 to 1997. One play. Several plays. No plays. One-hundred-and-twelve years of defining moments For the Glory of Old State.

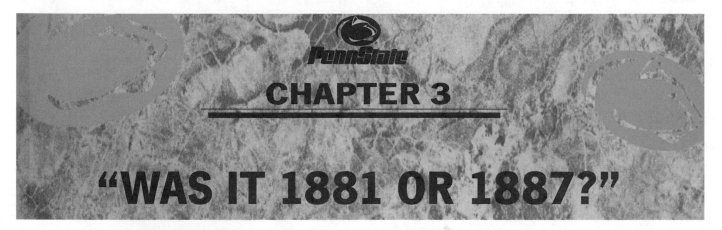

CHAPTER 3

"WAS IT 1881 OR 1887?"

1881-1891

Perhaps it was so long ago that it doesn't really matter which year Penn State began playing football. The young men who played one game in 1881 are long gone and even their living relatives may not be aware of what they did that dreary, cold and rainy November day at the University of Lewisburg.

You won't find a note of that game in the official Penn State athletic department record books. When the university celebrated its 100th anniversary of football with a series of events, the year was 1986, not 1981. The 1881 game doesn't count among the Lions' 705 all-time victories. Nor is the game recorded in the annals of Bucknell University, which was known as the University of Lewisburg until a name change in 1886.

The fact is, the single 1881 game was all but forgotten until 1922. On October 27 of 1922, ten surviving players and the manager from the 1887 team were re-united and honored by Penn State's New York (City) Alumni Club on the eve of a big football game at the Polo Grounds, the first-ever game with Syracuse. Each of the players were presented with a gold football charm—engraved with the words "1887, The First Penn State Team"—by then Coach Hugo Bezdek, whose own team that year would go on to play in the school's first post-season bowl game—the 1923 Rose Bowl. So much publicity was generated by the reunion and the scoreless tie with Syracuse the next day, that when the men from 1881 heard about it, they immediately complained in a flurry of letters to the school's alumni office.

Ivan P. McCreary, who graduated in 1882 and was the manager of the 1881 team, led the campaign for recognition. McCreary also should be cited as Penn State's first sports publicity director. He wrote that he not only managed the team and umpired the game but also sent out the initial word of the result via telegraph back to the campus: "We have met the enemy and they are ours, nine to nothing."

The 1881 team also took credit for originating the colors of uniforms, saying the "togs" were made by tailor Billy Hoover of Shingletown Gap. In 1922 and 1923, that claim angered the 1887 team as much as anything. The 1887 players retaliated with their own letters to the alumni office, arguing that the earlier game was either a "pickup game" or played under English rugby rules, not American football. McCreary countered by producing the actual rulebook used in the game, but even that did not dissuade many from believing it was more of a rugby match than a football game.

George Linsz (Lins), considered one of the two "fathers of Penn State football" and captain of the 1887 team, was particularly angered, and wrote: "It is quite certain that football was instrumental in putting Penn State on the map, but surely not through any team that played in one game in 1881 and then dropped completely out of existence."

The argument raged back and forth for three decades until every player who was alive in 1881 had died. The alumni office was caught in the middle. Except for what the players wrote, there was little proof to back them up. One has to remember, too, there were just 145 students enrolled at Penn State in 1881 and there was no local newspaper, student paper or college yearbook.

Over the years, evidence emerged that a game had actually been played! A newspaper in Bellefonte, *The Democratic Watchman*, noted in its November 25, 1881, issue that "a match game" had been played at Lewisburg "two weeks hence[sic]" and that Penn State had won. An editorial in the January, 1882, edition of the *University of Lewisburg Mirror* reported: "The first football match which has been played for some time on our campus came off near the close of last term, between the University team and the State College boys..." and went on to describe the game (see 1881 season review).

The late Alumni Secretary Ridge Riley, who helped research the situation in the 1930s as a student and later as the school's first official sports publicity director, detailed the controversy in the first chapter of his definitive book, *Road to Number One*. Riley believed the game had been played under an amalgam of rules that were part rugby and part American football—11 men to a side with kicking a major factor, and played at a line of scrimmage with no system of downs so that one team could keep the ball indefinitely unless fumbling or giving it up voluntarily by kicking.

Riley credited one of his predecessors, E. N. (Mike) Sullivan, the alumni secretary (1919-1929) at the height of the controversy, with officially recognizing the 1881 team as "the real pioneers . . . for playing Penn State's first intercollegiate contest, however informal, and for selecting the blue and white worn ever since by Lion teams except for one season..."

On October 6, 1936, the four surviving members of the 1881 team—Captain Robert Tait, Manager Ivan McCreary, Cummings C. Chesney and Umpire James G. White—were given gold footballs and varsity "S" letters to mark their achievement. Their teammates were honored posthumously: Marcus Baldwin, William Brunner, George Chadman, John Dale, Philip Foster, W. Ross Foster, Joseph Hollis, James McKee and Robert Whitmer.

None of their names are listed in the Penn State athletic department's official All-Time Letterman roster.

"The Real Pioneers"

If ever there was a perfect defining moment for the birth of Penn State football it was the weather in nearby Lewisburg on November 12, 1881.

Cold and drizzling rain!

Shades of 1996 and Iowa! Or 1985 and Notre Dame. Or any number of games played by Penn State at home—and sometimes away—in the next 116 years. Bad weather and Penn State football are synonymous and it is not surprising that it has been that way from this very beginning.

The field at the University of Lewisburg was muddy from all the rain, and by the time the game started the rain was almost like sleet.

Ivan McCreary had set up the game through a friend attending the University of Lewisburg (now Bucknell). He and some students had been playing the game among themselves on the lawn of Old Main. But, unlike what was happening at the time at such colleges as Columbia, Princeton, Yale and Rutgers, there was no faculty interest to help the students form an official university team or to give them some financial support. So McCreary and the others assembled their own team, with McCreary as manager. He mailed a challenge to the Lewisburg team manager and it was quickly accepted. The team made the 50-mile trek to Lewisburg on Friday via horse buggies and train.

There are no accounts of what actually happened during the game. But the final score of 9-0 suggests the team established another tradition that day that has become synonymous with Penn State football—DEFENSE!

Senior George Chadman apparently was the star, but what he did and which players scored the points will never be known. The best player on the field may have been tackle Marcus (Mike) Baldwin. He was one of six men that day who also played for the Penn State baseball team and he would become the school's first professional baseball player. Baldwin, who later became a medical doctor, dropped out of school after 1881 but returned to get a degree in 1887 after playing one year of professional baseball. He then went on to play six more years of baseball with National League teams in Chicago, New York and Pittsburgh and finished with a pitching record of 156-165 and a 3.36 ERA.

The only known write-up of the game appeared in the student newspaper, the *University of Lewisburg Mirror* of January, 1882, which reported in part:

"The State College team was well uniformed and disciplined, whereas our boys, although having considerable practice, were not up to all their dodges. It was apparent in this game that our team was a match for, if not superior to, their antagonists, in all but practice and knowledge of their arts."

The team celebrated the victory that evening with a dinner at the Myers Hotel in Old Fort and didn't get back to campus until just before midnight. As McCreary recalled later, the team was greeted by most of the students, "waiting our coming to give us an enthusiastic and appreciative team reception" and shouting a new college yell that had been written to mark the historic event. The team gave the game ball to the secretary of the alumni association, Professor William Buckhout,

who was also secretary of the faculty. But, as Ridge Riley later wrote in *The Road to Number One,* "neither the yell nor the football have survived the ages."

The game almost didn't either.

Season Record 1-0
Not Counted In Official Records

"Lucy's Football"

It was Lucy's football.

Every one who knew George Linsz called the outgoing freshman by his nickname, "Lucy." Later, he would drop the "z" from his paternal name and be known formally as George H. Lins.

Lucy not only owned the football; he had experience. He had played at Episcopal Academy of Philadelphia and they had used his football there, too. So the 18-year-old Linsz had his battered football with him when he arrived on the rural Penn State campus in September of 1887.

In those days, most of the 170 students enrolled at the college stayed in the big five-story Old Main building and "horsed around" on the lawn out front. When Lucy showed up one day with his football and suggested they play a pick-up game, a dozen or so students eagerly joined in. Before long, the pick-up games were a regular occurrence. One of the players was another freshman from Philadelphia, Charles C. Hildebrand, called "Charlie" by his classmates. Hildebrand, who already was 21 years old, also had played football back home.

Linsz and Hildebrand talked about the University of Pennsylvania football team they had seen play back in Philadelphia and wondered why Penn State College didn't have a team. They soon learned that organized football had been discouraged by the school's president, George Atherton, who had instituted a rigorous academic schedule after intense criticism years before about the way his predecessors had been running the school.

By this time, organized football was gaining a hold on many college campuses. Such schools as Harvard, Dartmouth, Lafayette, Navy, Michigan and Minnesota now had sanctioned football teams playing against each other. So, when Linsz, Hildebrand and others proposed a team for Penn State, President Atherton and the faculty agreed.

The students reorganized the one-year-old Penn State Athletic Association and eventually set up a Football Department to run the team. George Meek, an upperclassman and campus leader, didn't want to play any formal games but through his connections he obtained an official American Football rulebook for the team to use. The rules had been refined during the mid 1880s, and when the Penn State team began practicing that fall, the format for games no longer resembled rugby but was more like football as we know it—except for the scoring: five points for a field goal, four for a touchdown, two for a "goal-after-touchdown" and two for a safety. There were also two halves with an intermission but no quarters. The time of the halves would be anywhere from 10 to 20 minutes in length.

Linsz, of course, was the quarterback and apparently the best runner. Hildebrand liked to hit, so he was in the line at guard. A couple dozen students tried out, and soon the best players emerged: Linsz, Hildebrand, John Mitchell, James Rose, John Jackson, Watson Barclay, John Weller, Charles Kessler, James Mock, Harvey Mclean, Harry Leyden. They chose Linsz as captain—after all, it was still his ball and the only one the team had!

Down the road at Lewisburg, students at Bucknell heard about the Penn State team. Bucknell already had a team, dating officially back to 1883, and it issued a challenge to Penn State. The leaders of two teams probably didn't know it at the time but when they worked out a home-and-away agreement, they established a generally accepted scheduling precedent that lives to this day. There was one other stipulation: each team would pay its own expenses.

With the first game set for November 12 at Lewisburg, Linsz and his teammates felt they needed a coach and manager. They recruited two upperclass pre-law students, both class of '90, to help: Clarence G. Cleaver to coach and John F. Morris to manage. Unlike today, the coach was more of an advisor with little authority, who also pitched in to officiate the games. The manager handled the business affairs, which included working on the travel arrangements.

Of course, the team also needed uniforms. They went to the State College tailor who made their school military uniforms, Schaffer and Sons. They could only afford 12 pairs of Canton flannel pants, they said, knee length. They also ordered canvas jerseys with initials "PSC-FB" (Penn State College Football) on the front. When the proprietor asked about colors, the players huddled briefly.

Pink and black, they said! Pink and black?

Later, some of the players would deny they had chosen the embarrassing pink, claiming the "pink" color was really cerise, a moderate red. "We wanted something bright and attractive, Meek recalled, according to Ken Rappoport's book, *The Nittany Lions*, "but we could not use red or orange as these colors were already in use by other colleges. So we had a very deep pink—really cerise—which with black made a very pretty combination."

(Sure, and that's why the college yearbook, *LaVie*, had that pink and black cover that year. But never mind.)

They also needed a cheer, and their fellow students came up with a doozie:

Yah! Yah! (Pause) Yah! Yah! Yah!
Wish, Wack—Pink, Black!
P! S! C!

Now came another defining, prophetic and consequential moment in the history of Penn State football, one that would set the tone for all future away games and would forever characterize Penn State's fanatical followers over the next 100-plus years—12 fans decided to accompany the 12-man team on the road!

And it wasn't easy. First, it took everyone a half hour on stage coaches to get from Old Main to the train station in Lemont and then another few hours by train to reach Lewisburg, 60 miles away. But, like the fans of today, the rigors of the trip didn't deter the entourage (probably all students) from cheering loudly ('Wish, Wack—Pink, Black!') when the visitors took the field that Saturday in their garish uniforms—no pads, black stockings, tennis shoes and ski-caps with tassles on their heads.

The Bucknell players obviously tried to intimidate the Penn Staters on the first play from scrimmage. They went after the ski-cap tassels and apparently succeeded in ripping them off. That must have made Lucy and the boys mad. Penn State went on to win, 54-0—thus reaffirming the legacy started by the forgotten pioneers of 1881, that the foundation of Penn State's football tradition is DEFENSE! DEFENSE! DEFENSE!

As Ridge Riley wrote in *Road to Number One*: "Few other details of the game were recorded. According to one source, the 'two teams were well matched in size and strength' and 'neither side could gain anything by what is called rough playing.' All points, said Penn

The 1887 squad is widely recognized as the first Penn State football team. George Linsz (Lins) holds the ball in the photo because he truly owned the ball. The team was 2-0 that initial season one of the thirteen unbeaten teams in the school's history. The players are (left to right): Front Row: Watson Barclay, Harvey McClean, John Weller, Charles Kessler, Charlie Hildebrand, James Rose and Harry Leyden; Second Row: Advisory coach Clarence Cleaver, John Jackson, John Mitchell, James

The original Old Main was opened in 1863 and for decades was the center for all campus activities. It was five stories and included lodging rooms, the library, classrooms laboratories, a chapel and an infirmary. For six years from 1887 through 1892 the lawn in front of Old Main as used for home football games.

State's student newspaper, 'were made by the skillful playing of tricks.'"

One week later, on the morning of November 19, the first home game in history was played on the front lawn of Old Main. Once again, Penn State won another shutout, 24-0, behind a typical stout defense and opportunistic offense with Captain Lucy Linsz leading the way by scoring three second half touchdowns (for 12 points). John Jackson also scored a touchdown, John Mitchell kicked two "goals after" touchdowns and the State defense, led by the tackling of end Watson Barclay, forced Bucknell to take two safeties.

Penn State established another tradition that day that also continues to live on—home-field advantage! One must remember that the Penn State lads had been practicing regularly on the home field—running up and down the grassy hill that separates Old Main at the north from what is now College Avenue to the south.

Here's how *The Bellefonte Republican* of November 24 described what happened with that home-field advantage:

"The game began at 10 o'clock and the toss was won by Bucknell, who chose the south goal, thereby gaining an important advantage over the State College eleven who had to play up-hill with the wind against them. In almost ten minutes after the game began, after a good deal of running and returning—the ball all the time being in Bucknell's field—a touchdown was made by a good play of S. P. Jackson..."

Penn State played defense the rest of the half and the score at the intermission was 4-0 in State's favor.

"In the beginning of the second half," *The Bellefonte Republican* continued, "State College had the south goal and they then began to score. After a few moments of moving around the field, Linze [sic] made a touchdown for State College...Bucknell had to make a safety...adding two more to the State College score. After this two touchdowns were made by Linze [sic], goals being kicked by Mitchell. This was very near the close of the game..." Obviously, running down-hill with the football was easier!

The students probably celebrated the 24-0 victory into the night but there is no record of the type of rampages through campus and

town that would mark such momentous victories in future generations.

One more game had been scheduled for '87, a contest the following Tuesday with Dickinson College at Carlisle. But it was canceled when the Dickinson team refused to give State a $40 guarantee for expenses. Dickinson also rejected a $50 offer to play the game at Penn State.

And so, the first official Penn State season was over.

The '87 team would go down in history as the first of 13 unbeaten teams. But not before the occurrence of one more historic, defining moment—about those pink and black uniforms (Wish, Wack—Pink, Black!).

After several weeks of exposure to the sun, sweat and several washings, the uniforms faded and the pink—most thankfully—changed to plain white. At closer look, the black seemed more like a dark blue. So, by the 1888 season, blue and white were adopted as the official team colors.

The team yell also faded into history.

Eventually, so did Lucy Linsz and his semi-deflated football. But not before Linsz played in what would become the worst defeat in the history of Penn State football. Unfortunately, Linsz had given away or thrown away his football by then.

Season Record 2-0
Record to Date 2-0
Winning percentage 100%

"The First 'Bitter Rival'"

Bucknell's players and students were angry. Two losses. Two shutouts.

How dare those farmer yokels over in Centre Furnace think they are better at football than us!

Bucknell could hardly wait for a rematch in 1888. It was scheduled for October 27 in Lewisburg, and Captain Linsz and his Penn State team were guaranteed $20 for expenses. But there is no record of that game in either team's football history.

An argument erupted early in the game when Bucknell players complained about Penn State's snapback. They said it was against the rules. The referee was Penn State's advisory coach, George Cleaver. He said the snapback was legal, but he didn't have a rulebook with him. Neither did Bucknell. To stop the quarrel and get the game going again, Cleaver said he would rule in Bucknell's favor for the time being but would get an official ruling after the game from the proper authority. But the Bucknell players refused to accept that. So, the Penn State team walked off the field and left without asking for its $20 in expenses.

Whether that was a forfeit or not has never been resolved. Furthermore, the Penn State team complained that Bucknell had not paid for the players' expenses in the inaugural game of 1887 and, thus, was owed $62.50. But the controversy and bad blood continued for almost two years, for it was Thanksgiving Day of 1889 before football teams from the two schools would play each other again.

The dispute with Bucknell was the defining moment of the season and a bad omen. This wasn't the same team that had started it all the year before. Lucy Linsz had moved to end and Harry Leyden was now the quarterback with two newcomers, D. C. Reber and Phillip Foster at halfbacks, and Jim Mock back at fullback. Hildebrand was still at one guard and Harry McLean at center but the rest of the seven-man line and two substitutes were newcomers, too.

Four days after the Bucknell debacle, Penn State's 17-game, 44-year rivalry with Dickinson began. So did the first official losing season. The first game with Dickinson in Penn State was a 6-6 tie. In a return engagement at Dickinson on November 7, the Penn State team suffered its first loss ever, 16-0.

Lehigh closed out the disastrous season by handing State its initial defeat at home, 30-0. Lucy and the boys could not believe they could get whipped so badly on their own field, even against a team with more experience.

Wait until next year, they said. Unhappily, next year came too quickly.

Season Record 0-2-1
Record to Date 2-2-1
Winning percentage .500

"The Lehigh Licking"

Lehigh 106, Penn State 0!
Need any more be said?

It is still in the record books as the worst Penn State football defeat of all-time—November 11, 1889, at Bethlehem, PA—and was the defining moment of the season.

"We couldn't get at the son-of-a-bitch with the ball," rookie guard Charlie Aull, told the shocked students who greeted the disheartened team at the Lemont railroad station.

No wonder. For one thing, Penn State played the first half with just nine men, and when the half ended, Lehigh already had a 58-0 lead. However, there were a couple of other factors. Lehigh had more skilled players to begin with and the team was of better caliber. More significantly, under veteran coach J. S. Robeson, Lehigh had innovated and perfected the feared "wedge."

The "wedge" was an offensive formation in which all the players grouped together in a "V" and stormed down the field in one ferocious mass—elbowing, slugging and stomping on anyone in their way. It was a vicious formation that often led to serious injury and an occasional death and almost brought an end to college football until it was outlawed in the early 1900s.

Although battered and bruised, none of the Penn State players were hurt badly in the Lehigh game. They were thankful that Lehigh's coach, J. S. Robeson, agreed with the referee to stop the game with

five minutes left. They admitted later they should not have started play with just nine men but Lehigh had threatened to drop the $25 guarantee unless the game started on time. Not that it probably would have mattered. The players weren't in the best physical shape, anyhow, after tough games earlier against Swarthmore and Lafayette.

Lafayette was considered one of the best teams in the East, and the game was especially fatiguing and arduous. What's more, the game had been played just two days earlier in nearby Easton.

Aull and Charlie Hildebrand had missed the season-opening 20-6 win at home against lightly regarded Swarthmore because of injuries suffered while practicing on the Old Main lawn. Nor had Hildebrand's sprained ankle healed enough for him to play in the bruising 26-0 loss to Lafayette. Hildebrand still wasn't himself when he and two teammates finally arrived at Lehigh toward the end of the first half. (The three had gone to Philadelphia after the Lafayette game because Hildebrand's young sister had died.) Further, State's veteran center, Harry McLean was still limping from an injury that kept him on the sidelines for most of the Lafayette game.

After Lehigh, they had nearly two weeks to rest before taking on their chief rival, Bucknell, at home on Thanksgiving Day. The respite helped. So did the lower caliber of competition. State won, 12-0, in a game the student newspaper, *Free Lance*, said "to some extent redeemed its season."

That was apparently Lucy Linsz' last game. Lucy, who had given up his captaincy in '89 to veteran fullback Jim Mock, must have tired of the game. Perhaps he quit to concentrate on academics. Or maybe he had a career-ending injury. He didn't graduate until 1892, but his name does not appear on the team rosters of the '90 and '91 teams listed in the college yearbook, *LaVie*, nor is he in the team photos.

The "father of Penn State football" had been there for the historic victory in '87 and the equally historic loss in '89. It would be up to Lucy Linsz' football heirs to avenge that humiliating loss to Lehigh and it would take more than a decade to do it!

Season Record 2-2
Record to Date 4-4-1
Winning percentage .500

"Time to Rebuild"

By the time the first football practice began in the fall of 1890, everyone realized this would be a rebuilding year.

Just seven players returned from the 14-man 1889 squad, and three of those—center Gus Read, end Wellington Bohn and guard Charlie Aull—had been rookies. Halfback Phil Foster and end Charlie Hile had played in '88 and '89 and only Charlie Hildebrand and Harvey McLean had been on the original '87 team. Hildebrand and McLean would be the leaders.

Hildebrand, still a fierce hitter and tackler, would continue to anchor the line from his guard position and McLean, the center in '87, was now at halfback and would be the team's captain. Aull, the popular young guard from '89, moved to quarterback to take advantage of his running and leadership skills. It was a good nucleus, but the veterans knew they would need immediate help to win some games.

Nearly a dozen newcomers tried out in September on the Old Main lawn and most of them made the team. For the first time, State would use five men as key substitutions and three other rookies would play at least one game. One of the new players stood out above the rest—first, because of his name: Atherton. Young Charlie Atherton was the son of the college president, George Atherton. He also was one heckuva football player and would eventually be recognized as one of school's greatest stars of those early years.

In putting together the schedule that year, the State players wanted to show their fans that the Lehigh calamity of '89 had been an aberration. They believed they could hold their own with the best teams in the East and they wanted to prove it. They would even go on the road if necessary to show their mettle. So, back-to-back games were scheduled two days apart in mid-October against two of the best, the University of Pennsylvania in Philadelphia and Franklin & Marshall in Lancaster. But first, they would have to play their old nemesis, Bucknell.

After ending the '89 season with a conciliatory game with Bucknell, State had scheduled its opening game of 1890 at Lewisburg in a continued effort to improve relations with its nearest rival and erase the bitterness of the contentious '88 contest. But when the State team took the field in Lewisburg that October day, the Bucknell players complained that three of the visiting players were ineligible. There would be no game if they played, Bucknell warned. McLean and Hildebrand protested but the Bucknell players were insistent. So, McLean and his team walked off the field, went to the train station and returned to State College, cursing the Bucknell players and vowing to get even some day.

Then it was time to meet the challenge of Penn and Franklin & Marshall (F & M). They should have stayed home. On Oct. 11, State lost to Penn, 20-0, in a game that defined the season. It also would be the start of a 15-game losing streak against Penn that would last until a 3-3 tie in 1910. Two days later, the team was shut out again by F&M 10-0.

But the last two games were easier. In the only home game of the year, State walloped an outclassed Altoona Athletic Association squad, 68-0, on Nov. 15; then closed the season at Bellefonte Academy with another defensive win, 23-0.

The fourth season of Penn State football was history. What was to come next might surprise even the most ardent State fans—perhaps even now, more than 100 years later. For after just five years of playing this new game of football, Penn State would have its first championship team!

Season Record 2-2
Record to Date 6-6-1
Winning percentage .500

"The First Champions"

Everyone knew it would come down to the Bucknell game for the championship.

Bucknell, those #@$#%&^%#$&!!!!

Gutless. Crybabies. Fakers. No one had forgotten what happened in '88 and '90 in Lewisburg, and those new to Penn State football were quickly told of those "no game" fiascoes and of Bucknell's bad manners and arrogance.

Both teams had joined the new Pennsylvania Intercollegiate Football Association, which officially organized in Harrisburg on Sept. 26. State's manager, J. Frank Shields, was there to help form the league along with representatives of Bucknell, Dickinson, Franklin & Marshall, Haverford and Swarthmore. They had talked about including Lafayette and Lehigh but decided those schools were so much better they would dominate the league. So Lafayette and Lehigh were out, as was Pennsylvania, already a member of the esteemed "Big Four" conference that included four of the best teams in the country—Penn, Yale, Harvard and Princeton.

Manager Shields, who would later serve as president of Penn State's Board of Trustees from 1929-46, was so respected by his peers that the first thing they did was elect him president of the conference. Each team agreed to pay $10 for membership and another $2 for administrative traveling expenses. Then, the first dispute broke out. It was an issue that would live on in intercollegiate football into the next 100-plus years. Everyone wanted to play their league games at home!

And, in what would soon become an eternal lament by Penn State opponents of all eras, none of the other teams wanted to travel to the "isolated" hills of Centre County. Boondocks, they shouted. Backwoods and primitive. Didn't even have a train station, thank you. (A "camping trip?" Shades of Bobby Knight and his infamous rebuke a century later!)

So, Shields, ever the diplomat, agreed that Penn State would play all but one of its games on the road. But, he argued, the team would do so only if it received an equal share of the net receipts. That precipitated another heated exchange as to what was meant by "net receipts." Would that include the $5 each that would be paid to both the referee and umpire, chosen from neutral colleges, who would officiate the game? What about other expenses? Shields worked out a compromise and they moved on to the question of eligibility.

It was not uncommon in those days for teams to use players with questionable ties to the colleges. Sometimes, they would graduate, take money to play some "professional" ball and then return for a few more seasons at that school, or another. In one notable Penn State incident in 1890, Clarence Cleaver, the "advisor" coach of the '87 team, who was in law school at Dickinson, showed up as a spectator to watch the Lafayette game in Easton, and wound up playing the entire game for State.

After several hours of vehement discussions, the league representatives agreed to a vital rule that, in retrospect, may very well have been the birth of the "student athlete." The rule stated: "A man may play only six years, and no professionals are allowed; a player must be a bona fide member of the college community with at least fifteen hours of classroom work assigned." Think of that today—six years and no redshirt restrictions!

Penn State's first league game was set for Oct. 17 at Swarthmore. But Shields and the players came up with another resourceful idea that would become part of a legacy for Penn State's future schedule makers. They set up two non-league games before the league opener to get some experience as a team. The opponents were not patsies.

Playing Lafayette and Lehigh, they reasoned, would toughen them for the more intense league contests.

They were right, and in the process, they defined their season. When they beat Lafayette, 14-4, on Oct. 2 in Easton they realized how good they could be. Even the 24-2 loss to Lehigh the next day in Bethlehem didn't diminish their confidence. Charlie Aull, now the captain, told them they would only get better.

After the team's performance against Lafayette and Lehigh, State was seen as the favorite to win the first league title and the silk pennant that would go with it. Enthusiasm among students and faculty was at an all-time high. Baseball was still the most popular sport among the student body, but now everyone on campus was talking about the football team. This was State's best team ever and it was "loaded," said the *Bellefonte Democratic Watchman*.

The team was "in pink condition," and ready, the paper reported. "State College presents a stronger rush this fall than she has ever put before. [Gus] Read at center has never been in such fine form, while [Charlie] Hildebrand and [Henry] Dowler . . . [the] right and left guards are working with an enthusiasm that is bound to win. [Charlie] Hile and [C.R.] Cartwright, [who] as tackles, are doing great work and their sure grips and splendid blocking will be features of the seasons games. The ends [A.P.] Knittle and [Frank] Mattern, are both guarded by new men on the team, but they are showing up nicely in practice and good work is expected.''

But the best was the "Charlie" backfield: "Back of the line, [Charlie] Aull, [Charlie] Fay, [H.S.] Taylor and [Charlie] Atherton, a whole team in themselves, will represent the college," the paper said. "Aull at quarter is quick and cool headed while in Fay and Taylor, the half [sic], he has two fleet runners with just enough weight to make them sure tacklers. Atherton, the fullback has always played 'a pretty mean game' and is leading right off in practice."

Swarthmore was no match for this team. State won, 44-0, and, the *Democratic Watchman* reported Oct. 23 that, "The students are highly elated over the excellent showing the first team made and are now more certain than ever that the championship will come to the big Centre County institution."

Franklin & Marshall decided it didn't want to travel to "isolated" Penn State after all but agreed to play the Oct. 24 game on a neutral field in Gettysburg, then changed its mind again because the Gettysburg grandstand was not enclosed. So, State went to Lancaster, a little angrier than usual, and smashed F & M on its home field, 26-6. A third league game had been set at Haverford Nov. 4 but it was postponed until Dec. 5. So, three days after the F&M victory, the team tuned up with another non-league game against Gettysburg, winning 28-0.

It was now time for the big game with Bucknell in Lewisburg. Both teams were 2-0 in the league, but State was clearly favored, as the *Democratic Watchman* declared on the eve of the Nov. 7 game:

"...every evidence points to ending the season as champion. Two of the scheduled games have already been played and from comparisons drawn as to the relative strength of the other teams in the League, it is safe to say P.S.C. will be the sure winner. Tomorrow, the

The 1891 team won the first and only Pennsylvania Intercollegiate Foot-Ball Assoc. Championship with a 58-0 victory over Haverford before 60 spectators in Philadelphia. Captain Charlie Aull is in the front row, third from left, and so is Charlie Atherton on the far right.

eleven will play their strongest game against Bucknell and the outcome of the game will practically decide the championship as Bucknell is looked upon as the strongest team in the League outside of State College."

A couple of hundred noisy Penn State fans accompanied the team to Lewisburg, naturally, and a large Bucknell crowd greeted the visitors upon arrival at the train station. That's when the betting started. (Some things haven't changed in 100 years—except back then, the gambling was public, legal and wide open.) The betting was heavy, particularly in the two hotels where the team and fans were staying, according to the *Democratic Watchman*. At first, the bets were even money, but State fans were so confident in their team they began to give odds to attract Bucknell dollars.

The first sign that this might not be State's day came with the news that the sophomore star, Atherton, would not play, but the reason was never made clear. Big C.R. Cartwright would move to fullback and rookie Ed Haley would go in at tackle.

State fans of all generations could easily relate to the particulars of the game. A superior Penn State team (even without its star running back) would dominate play but waste opportunities, make too many mistakes—including several crucial fumbles—and finally lose when, late in the game, an attempted kick for two points after a touchdown would fail.

More than 1,000 people saw Bucknell win the toss and gain 15 yards on the first play, using the "wedge" formation. The home team got to within 25 yards of the State goal, when State's defense stiffened and Bucknell kicked (or punted). Aull ran the kick back to midfield and the offense quickly moved into Bucknell territory. The rest of the half was played on Bucknell's side but State's own errors cost it numerous chances to score. Twice the team lost the ball on fumbles and twice on decisions by the umpire. As time was winding down in the half, the visitors ran the ball to the Bucknell 10-yard line. Cartwright bulled his way over for the touchdown, kicked the two extra points, and State took a 6-0 lead into the half.

Later, the disappointed State fans—and all the disgruntled bettors—would accuse the team of being too overconfident—which also sounds all too familiar in this modern television age of second guessing. No doubt that the 6-0 lead had bolstered the confidence of Aull and his men. As badly as they played, they were winning and they were sure they would run up the points in the second half. But in the early moments of the second half, State fumbled deep in its own territory and Bucknell recovered. Bucknell couldn't move in three plays and kicked. The sure-handed Aull couldn't hold on, fumbled and Bucknell recovered close to the State goal line. A couple plays later, Bucknell tied the score with a TD and two extra points.

State banged through the Bucknell line several times and moved upfield. Then it happened again. State fumbled, Bucknell recovered, and with seven minutes to play Bucknell scored another touchdown and two points, to take a 12-6 lead.

"With defeat staring them in the face, the State College boys then gave the finest exhibition of football playing we have seen," wrote the *Democratic Watchman* reporter covering the game. "In three minutes they had secured a touch-down [sic] from the middle of the field and then Cartwright tried for a goal [after touchdown] but the angle was so great that he missed by two feet. A few scrimmages more and the game was done . . . The fact that only fifteen minutes of

the game were played in State's territory and that Bucknell was compelled to play almost an entire kicking game is evidence that had it not been for hard luck the score would have been decidedly different."

So, the dejected and humbled Penn State players and their angry, dispirited fans plodded back to State College, certain that they had just lost the championship to their bitterest rival. More than a century later, in 1982, another disheartened Penn State team would make a similar long and morose trip back from a big midseason loss at Alabama, equally convinced they had just blown the (national) championship! But for the 1891 team, there were two more games to play and despite what happened in Lewisburg, Aull and Hildebrand had to get their teammates back in the groove to salvage the season.

A game with Dickinson was scheduled for November 26—in Altoona because State was ostensibly the home team. As the team worked out on the Old Main lawn, its luck turned. Bucknell lost to F&M and tied with Dickinson. State was back in the championship race.

But State's game with Dickinson never occurred. The field where the game was to be played had inadvertently been cut into building lots. Manager Shields scrambled and came up with the Altoona Cricket Club Field as an alternative. Dickinson balked over expenses and demanded a guarantee of full expenses. Knowing he had a sellout crowd, Shields sent a telegram early in the week to the Dickinson manager but there was no acknowledged reply. The day before the scheduled game, Shields received a telegram from Dickinson which said, "Men scattered. Telegram came too late. Sorry."

State claimed a 2-0 forfeit, despite the protestations from Dickinson. Dickinson claimed the game contract was only verbal and that the exchange of telegrams was invalid because of the time element.

Now, Aull and his teammates knew they had the league championship in their sights. Bucknell's season was over with a record of 3-1-1. A sure victory over winless Haverford would give State a 4-1 record. Some 60 spectators, mostly Haverford fans, turned out in miserable weather in the Philadelphia area to watch State take an easy 58-0 win on Dec. 5.

On January 9, 1892, officials of the Pennsylvania Intercollegiate Football Association met in Harrisburg and awarded its first championship to Penn State. There was jubilation in State College.

"Never since the addition of football to the list of State College sports, five years ago, has the team been so ably captained and so carefully managed as during the fall just passed," commented the college yearbook, *LaVie*, "and as a result of this we have experienced the most brilliant and successful season in our history."

There would be many more brilliant and successful seasons to come.

Season Record 6-2
Record to Date 12-8-1
Winning percentage .595

CHAPTER 4

GEORGE, SAM AND POP

1892-1903

President George Atherton was proud of his school's championship football team and why not? His son, Charlie, was the star.

But there was more. Now, his football team was getting the respect of his contemporaries. The presidents at Bucknell, Lafayette and, yes, even Pennsylvania knew now that his little "school for farmers in the middle of nowhere" could match athletic skills with almost anyone.

Atherton had taken over Penn State College during that tenuous and tumultuous spring of 1881 and had spent the next several years reviving its academic standards and strengthening the faculty. Now, it was time to upgrade the athletic program.

So, in January of 1892, around the time the football team was being honored as Pennsylvania Intercollegiate Foot-Ball Association champions, Atherton hired George Hoskins. Hoskins would fill the newly created position as trainer of all athletic teams and help "coach" those teams as well as teach physical education to the student body.

Thus, did George W. (The General) Hoskins, a native of Vermont, become Penn State's first "official" football coach. But he was unlike any other official coach the school ever had, for George also played on three of State's football teams, even though he already had graduated from Swarthmore after taking a four-year course in physical training and anatomy.

George had little experience playing organized football. He was a good athlete, though, who excelled in rowing, wrestling, track and lacrosse. But once he started helping the football players get into condition, he began to enjoy the sport—especially the contact. He found his natural playing position at center.

Hoskins didn't have any real authority over the team. The Football Department still selected the players and manager. George's prime responsibility was to get the team into good physical shape and to keep them there. He was accommodating, diligent and extremely well liked by his fellow players. In 1896, Hoskins decided to take a similar job at the Western University of Pittsburgh (now commonly known as Pitt), and, in doing, so became the traitorous midwife of a rivalry that would become one of the most contentious in intercollegiate sports.

Hoskins had been so successful as a trainer-coach that when he departed after three winning and one tying seasons, President Atherton decided he needed a replacement who was not only similarly trained but also had additional medical skills.

So, in came Dr. Silvanus (Sam) Newton, a practicing gynecologist and a medical school graduate of the University of Pennsylvania, where he also helped coach the football team as a hobby. "Under his

direction, the important branch of training will be raised to its proper standard as a means of promoting the development of a complete physical manhood," Atherton wrote in the school's 1896 Annual Report.

Dr. Sam might have been a great trainer and a great doctor, but he was a lousy football coach at Penn State. In three years, his teams lost more games than they won and had two losing seasons. He left at the end of '98 in the wake of newspaper stories calling for his dismissal and moved on to Lafayette as head coach in 1899 (where he had better success). Sam Boyle, a star at Penn in 1897, succeeded him and Boyle, lasted one year—another losing one. President Atherton realized a more experienced trainer and "coach" was needed once again. So, he hired William Nelson (Pop) Golden, who had once been the athletic trainer at Purdue and also had been in charge of physical education at YMCA's in Syracuse, Johnstown and Williamsport. It was to be a propitious appointment.

Pop Golden did as much off the field to help the football team as he did on it, and in the process revitalized a football program that had only one winning season in the five years before he took over in 1900. It was costing about $3,000 a year for the student-run Athletic Association to administer football and its main revenue came from passing the hat at home games. They usually carried over a small debt from season to season. Within two years, Golden had them making money.

Golden's personality and enthusiasm were infectious and he seemed to care about people as individuals. He became a friend to all the students, not just the athletes, and he was popular with the faculty, too. Soon, the student body agreed to raise its small "athletic fee" to $4 a year and the faculty chipped in with "major" contributions. Before long, he had solicited alumni donations, too. He used some of the money to upgrade the equipment and uniforms, improve traveling accommodations and to establish a training table to feed the athletes.

By 1903, Golden's fund-raising efforts had enabled the college to start construction of the Track House, a multi-purpose building which became the home for football players and other athletes when it opened a year later. The facilities in the Track House included living and dining quarters, a club room, training rooms and locker rooms for home and visiting teams. Over the next 20 years, the Track House was a prime recruiting tool—much like Holuba Hall, the Greenberg complex and the other contemporary training facilities are today in the Paterno era.

Better players—bigger, stronger and faster—began to show up in State College. Golden and his managers continued to upgrade the schedule that President Atherton had encouraged since the hiring of Hoskins. Instead of just playing Gettysburg and Dickinson, State began playing the powers of the East on a regular basis. Virginia, Navy, Cornell, Princeton, Army, Yale and others were added in the late 1890s and by the end of the next decade, State was even playing and beating the powerful and famous Carlisle Indians.

Most of the big games were still being played on the road. Opposing teams simply didn't want to make the long and difficult trip into the barren mountains of Central Pennsylvania and they said so. Frequently and loudly. Even a new field with a grandstand in 1893 was not enough to attract prime teams. Hence, many games were scheduled on neutral grounds, such as in Williamsport and Harrisburg. The local fans would still follow, loading up train cars and traveling for hours to get to the site.

In the fall of 1903, the Athletic Association asked Pop to become its first Athletic Director and he agreed. The season was almost half over and State was 2-2, so Pop recruited former All-America guard Dan Reed from Cornell to take over for a couple of games. Reed won two out of three games but returned to his home in Buffalo before the biggest game of the season against Washington & Jefferson and Pop went looking for another coach. Only this time, Pop told President Atherton and the Athletic Association, "We'll find someone who can spend more time on campus!"

"Spring Practice"

Winter was over and the trees were starting to bloom. The birds were singing again and the warm spring days were luring the students out of their classrooms and onto the Old Main lawn.

A group of young men were tossing baseballs back and forth, getting ready for another PSC season. Suddenly, a football dropped into their midst. A football! What the heck is a football doing here?, someone shouted.

They looked across the lawn and were shocked. The football team was practicing. The football team? It was spring, not fall. Why the heck were the football players practicing now?

It was "The General's" idea. Hoskins said the players needed to be in better physical condition. Run, run, run. Hit, hit, hit. Gotta get ready to win another championship. The team in the best condition will win, he implored. Conditioning and teamwork. So, we'll run some plays, too. Practice. Practice. Practice.

And, thus, Penn State's spring practice was born.

It was the defining moment of the '92 season and certainly paid off in the fall. But there was no second league championship. The P.I.C.F.B.A. went out of business before September. But that didn't stop State. With captain and center Gus Read and quarterback Charlie Atherton leading the way, the '92 team held five teams scoreless and lost only once in six games. And no one was ashamed of the defeat. It was to powerful Penn, which had won 15 of 16 games in previous years, and it occurred in the season opener at Philadelphia, 20-0.

Only one game was played at home that year and it was on a new field. The Old Main lawn was no longer feasible for playing games. The campus was expanding and enrollment, now at about 250, was growing. Thanks in part to state government appropriations, several new buildings had been constructed. An Armory (that would be used often to help celebrate big football victories) was built right across the walk from the west side of Old Main and an Engineering Building was nearby.

A new field was carved out of a site a little bit to the east. (The area is now a parking lot between the Osmond and Frear labs, across the street from what is now a major Penn State landmark, the Hetzel Student Union Building.) Thanks to the fund-raising of President Atherton and the Board of Trustees under the presidency of General James Beaver, construction began on a new grandstand with an overhanging roof and three flag polls. But the grandstand would not be ready until the '93 season. That didn't help the hundreds of spectators on Nov. 12, when State played the "hated" team from Bucknell in the mud and snow. State won 18-0 in a rough, physical game that was stopped with four minutes to play after a Bucknell player had been seriously injured and carried off the field. The State players didn't want to hear anything more about '91!

Hoskins' team had roared back from the Penn loss in the season opener to beat Wyoming Seminary in Kingston, 44-0. Then it was off to Pittsburgh for a match on Nov. 5 with a non-college team, the Pittsburg (sic) Athletic Club (also known as the East End Gym), led by none other than Charlie Aull, the captain and quarterback of State's '91 champion team.

Hoskins, now starting at right tackle as well as coaching, was worried. Aull knew a lot about the State strategy and several of State's front-line players were hobbling. That's when Hoskins' conditioning program paid off. "The game was hotly contested from start to finish, but the superior training of the College boys was more than their doughty opponents could master," reported the *Bellefonte Democratic Watchman*. "Fifteen hundred people watched [halfbacks H.F.] Taylor [and Charlie] Fay, [and fullbacks S. E.] Morrow [and Sydney] Brown shoot through the [Pittsburgh] line and run around their ends until they had scored three touch-downs" and four extra points. Final score 16-0.

The Altoona Athletic Association was next in a game at Tyrone and State won, 56-0, but the victory is not listed in the official football records, only in the school yearbook, *LaVie*. Then came the avenging shutout victory over Bucknell. Lafayette, weakening as a football power, went down, 18-0, at Wilkes-Barre Nov. 23. Two days later, in a Thanksgiving Day game at Harrisburg's Island Park, Hoskins' team

George W. Hoskins, known as "The General," became State's first official football coach in 1892. His job description was apparently quite broad as he served as trainer, taught physical education and played on the team for three years as well.

closed the season with another satisfying win, 16-0, over the "quitters" from Dickinson. This time the Dickinson players showed up, but they walked off the field late in the game after disputing a touchdown by Hoskins—of all people—on a long run back of a fielded punt. State had been ahead, 10-0, when Dickinson's Ben Caswell failed to cover a punt. Hoskins grabbed the ball and went nearly the length of the field. Caswell, who would join the Carlisle Indians the next season, claimed he had hollered "down," thus ending the play according to the rules at the time. If he had, the referee didn't hear him and neither did the State players. The referee said the touchdown was good and the Dickinson players stormed off the field ending the game. Same old Dickinson!

Five wins, 108 points and only 20 points scored against them. The players, fans and students then tried to claim another championship, for as the college newspaper, *Free Lance*, stated, State had been unbeaten against "teams in our class." So began another legacy that would some day become as much a part of Penn State's football reputation as the winning tradition: lack of recognition for its winning teams.

The *Free Lance* bragged that "only five or seven teams in the country" could beat State, and the newspaper may have been right. However, just as would happen in later years—particularly in the Paterno era—there was no official championship for this team. The players celebrated their successful season in the snowy, remote hills and roads of Central Pennsylvania and eagerly awaited the next spring practice.

Season Record 5-1
Record to Date 17-9-1
Winning percentage .648

"Beaver Field, Pitt & Fisticuffs!"

The new 500-seat grandstand with its impressive overhanging blue and white roof and three flag poles was ready and the grassy football playing field was in fine shape.

President Atherton and the students had decided to name the facility after General James Beaver, the long-time head of the college Board of Trustees and former governor. They invited the ex-Civil War general and his wife over from their home in Bellefonte for the dedication ceremonies at the opening game of the season against Dickinson on Oct. 7.

Three new opponents were on the nine-game schedule for Hoskins' boys this year but only that amiable bunch from Western University of Pennsylvania (WUP) in Pittsburgh was willing to play in State College. Johns Hopkins and Rutgers wanted their games on their home grounds or neutral fields. As it turned out, both Johns Hopkins and Rutgers canceled.

So did Dickinson—apparently still upset by the brouhaha that ended the '92 game prematurely and by that controversial forfeit in '91.

Team managers quickly scheduled another new opponent—the University of Virginia—for the first game, but that game also had to be on the other team's field. So, instead of one game, a weekend trip to the Washington, D.C. area was planned for Oct. 13 and 14, with State playing the semi-pro Columbia Athletic Club on Friday and Virginia in Charlottesville the next day.

The 1892 team was the first to have spring practice and the first to play in Old Beaver Field, a site across the street from where the Hetzel Student Union Building now stands. The team had a 5-1 record. Star Henry Dowler in front row, second from left, and future star Bull McCaskey is in back row, fifth from left, with Charlie Atherton seventh from left.

A 500-seat grandstand was added to the new playing field in 1893 and named in honor of General James Beaver and dedicated on November 4 when State played a new opponent, Western University of Pennsylvania, known later as University of Pittsburgh. This scene is from a practice session in 1894.

Since the game with Penn in Philadelphia was already scheduled for Oct. 26, the dedication of Beaver Field would have to wait until the Nov. 4 home game with WUP.

The players knew the games in the South would be slugfests. They knew of Virginia's reputation as brawlers and they knew what happens anytime you play a semi-pro team. Captain Ed Haley and his veteran teammates never backed down from anyone and they were in excellent condition, again, thanks to Hoskins' training methods. They also knew that tough old Charlie Hildebrand, one of the original players from '87, would be playing too. Charlie had graduated the year before and was playing semi-pro ball in Pottstown when Hopkins asked him to come back and help coach. Knowing that Hildebrand could handle anything that the Columbia AC or Virginia players dished out, Hoskins asked Charlie to play that weekend at his old guard position. To get around any eligibility questions, Hoskins simply gave Hildebrand a new name: "Wolfe."

Because of heavy rain in Washington on Friday, the 13th, no less, the game with the Columbia AC was postponed until Monday. So, the team went on to Charlottesville to play Virginia first. It was not a pleasant experience. The townspeople were hostile from the time the State team got off the train and the abuse only got worse when the game started.

On the first play of the game, the Virginia captain belted Haley in the mouth and the State captain retaliated with a fist to his opponent's nose. Or maybe it was the other way around. No matter, it was a defining moment, and the two slugged it out until their faces were bloody. The officials didn't know what to do. They huddled. They didn't want to throw out the two team captains on the first play. No problem. They simply made a new rule on the spot. There would be no penalty on the "first offense." Play ball.

Slam. Bam. Wop. On every play, players traded punches. "First offense, no penalty," the officials shouted. Blood soaked through the jerseys of almost every player. From the sideline, the malevolent home crowd cursed at the State players and urged the Virginia players towards more mayhem.

Towards the end of the half, Virginia fumbled and State recovered. State's star player, halfback Charlie Atherton, smashed in for a touchdown, drop-kicked the two-point conversion and the visitors led 6-0 as the teams went into the intermission.

The Virginia coach, Johnny Poe, blew up. He had been a recent star at Princeton, so he put himself into the game. That inspired the Virginia players and when the second half started, the home team started to take charge. With 12 minutes left, Virginia moved to State's 30-yard line. Then it happened. Another of those defining moments.

Smack! Atherton hit a Virginia player in the nose, perhaps in retaliation, and was thrown out of the game as the crowd snarled with anger. Poe ranted, inflaming the crowd. He walked quickly towards Atherton heading to the State sideline and threw a punch. Atherton ducked, but he didn't see the spectator who dashed under the ropes and smashed him over the head. Atherton fell to the ground, out cold!

That's it, Haley yelled. Let's go. We're out of here! And he took his team off the field as the crowd booed and cursed. Not until the next day did they learn that the officials had given them the win, 6-0.

It was more of the same two days later in Washington. The Columbia AC team was a mixture of former college players and street-smart brawlers. The two teams slugged it out from the opening moment, only this time the officials let the home town players get away with more. Few penalties were called against the Columbia AC and the referee changed the rules as the game progressed. Charlie "Wolfe" scored after a Columbia fumble to help give State a 6-0 halftime lead. But the referee helped make that up in the second half.

They continued fighting throughout the second half and Columbia finally tied the score with three minutes left. As darkness fell, the game should have been over. But the ref kept the "official" time and insisted there was a lot of time left. Later, the State players insisted they must have played an extra half hour because the ref kept extending the time as Columbia drove down the field again. Play after play, State's defense beat back the home team but the ref wouldn't call the game. As time "wound down," additional players and spectators ran onto the field to help Columbia try to score. Finally, Haley could take it no longer. State stopped Columbia at the goal line but the ref shouted there were "five seconds to play." Haley waved his hands and shouted that that was enough and took his players off the field again. Columbia then scored what was supposedly the winning touchdown. To heck with that, the State players said. This wasn't a game. Just a practice. A bloody one, yes, but just practice. So the score doesn't count. And that is why the game is not listed in the official Penn State football records, although the college yearbook, "*LaVie,*" counts the game as a 6-0 State victory.

The *Bellefonte Democratic Watchman* of Oct. 20 was complimentary about State's opening two-game road trip without mentioning that the team had stalked off the field before the games had ended. "In as much as Johnny Poe, the great Princeton coach had been training [Virginia] this victory is looked upon as very satisfactory," the paper said, "...The game with the Columbia Athletic club on Monday was more of a slugging match than a foot-ball contest and resulted in a score of 12-6 in favor of Columbia after the umpire and three Subs [sic] had all been taken into the fight for the home club. They made two touchdowns in the last three minutes of play, which seems evidence that Capt. Haley did not even attempt to have his men hold up the robbers."

As expected, the team (with "Wolfe" no longer playing) was no match for Pennsylvania 10 days later, losing 18-6, but scoring on Penn for the first time in three games. The players rested up for their first game with WUP, which the *Democratic Watchman* called "the strongest team in the Western part of the state..."

Everyone anticipated a hard-fought game with WUP (which would be renamed the University of Pittsburgh in 1908). But a severe rainstorm on Saturday Nov. 4 forced postponement of the game until Monday. The visiting players were invited to spend the weekend at the campus fraternities, and according to reports, they must have had one heckuva a good time. Perhaps, as some sportswriters have suggested, this is where State's reputation as "a party school" started. Undoubtedly, it was the last time State's players and students partied happily with a team from Pitt.

Before the game started, there was an informal ceremony dedicating the field in honor of General Beaver. But few of the spectators paid any attention to it. Get on with it, they shouted, after some polite applause. They came to see some football.

The game was completely opposite of the slugfests earlier in the season. State got the ball at the start and immediately fumbled for a 5-yard loss. The two teams exchanged possession a couple of times before State's fullback, Chauncey Stuart, grabbed a WUP kick (punt) and ran it back nearly the length of a field for a touchdown. Just before the half ended, Captain Haley also got a touchdown and the home team led 12-0.

In the second half, State scored at will. Haley got another touchdown on a run, Jim Dunsmore recovered a fumble in the end zone, Charlie Atherton scored on a rush and booted three more "goals after" to make it 5-for-5 for the day, and State also picked up a safety to win easily, 32-0. "The superior training of the P.S.C. men was plainly evident...," reported the *Democratic Watchman* in its Nov. 10 coverage, hinting that some of WUP's best players may have missed the game. "State's interference and tackling was particularly fine and the visitors could have made a far better showing had they guarded their players while running with the ball."

The *Pittsburgh Times* was equally complimentary, saying WUP was "beaten in a clean manly game by a lot of hardy young Pennsylvanians."

The 1893 team enjoyed another fine 4-1. Coach George Hoskins is in the second row, far left, and captain Ed Haley in the same row holding the ball.

"We must compliment the players on the marked absence of slugging," reported State's student newspaper, *Free Lance*. "Both teams behaved like gentlemen...we want the Western boys to come again and come often."

They did. The series of games with Pitt would eventually be the longest and bitterest for Penn State and become one of the greatest rivalries in college football. But in '93 it was just another win for State.

Bucknell was next and when the team got to the field in Lewisburg November 11, some 2,000 belligerent Bucknell fans armed with fish-horns, pick-handles and baseball bats greeted the visitors. Must be remembering last year, the players figured. The Bucknell players must have been more intimidated than the crowd for they lost, 36-8

State went on to win the final game of the season against the Pittsburgh Athletic Club on Nov. 30, 12-0, and again tried to claim another championship. (Sound familiar, eh?) "In the East we scored against the University of Pennsylvania's best team," asserted the "*LaVie*." "In the South, we defeated the champions of the Southern League, the University of Virginia. In the West we defeated both the Pittsburg [sic] Athletic Club and the Western University of Pennsylvania. By the results of these games we claim first place in colleges of our class, for no college in the country, taking size into consideration, has a better record than ours."

Okay, so it was another mythical championship. But, just as in 1912 and 1921 and 1969 and 1973 and 1994 and many other years, the rest of the country ignored State's demand for a title. Perhaps there was a reason in 1893. For as "*LaVie*" had further noted: "It is much to be regretted that we were unable to meet the Princeton, U.S. Naval Academy, and Cornell teams."

So, if playing Princeton, Navy and Cornell would enhance the team's championship aspirations, then State's managers of that age would do just what Paterno would do decades later when his teams were similarly deprecated because of the quality of the opposition—upgrade the schedule. PSC would play Navy in '94, Cornell in '96, Princeton in '97 and all three in '98, but by then it would be too late to claim a championship.

Still, 1894 was just ahead and the "*LaVie*" figured it would be a good year: "With many of the old men back we have every right to expect that the coming seasons will be one of advancement. With hard, conscientious practice the team of 1894 should meet with nothing but success."

The team did. Especially on Beaver Field.

Season Record 4-1
Record to Date 21-10-1
Winning percentage .672

"Charlie Kicks Into History"

Hoskins had his veteran team running more in the spring and fall of 1894. This year's team was not as big or as strong as the '93 crew and Hoskins knew he would need speed and quickness to get through the challenging schedule he and the team manager George Spence had worked out.

The opener with Gettysburg looked like the easiest game ahead. After that came Lafayette, Penn, Princeton, Virginia, Navy, Bucknell, Washington & Jefferson (W&J) and the Pittsburg AC. Hoskins' boys were especially looking forward to the re-match with Virginia at Beaver Field and the road games with Penn, Princeton and Navy. Finally, they would get their chance to prove they could play football with anyone.

Hoskins believed this was his best backfield in three years, with two-year letterman "Bull" McCaskey returning at quarterback and standout runner and kicker Charlie Atherton, now at fullback, back for his final season. The newcomers at halfbacks, Fred Robison and W. A. (Bill) Suter, were speedsters who could run away from pursuing tacklers. The backfield would be playing behind an experienced line that had three players who had been starters for two years—Hoskins again at center, team Captain Ben (Big) Fisher at left guard, and J. L. Harris at left end—plus the Dunsmore boys, James A. and James G., who had been the first team tackles in '93.

The speed and experience showed as the team clobbered an outmanned Gettysburg, 60-0 on Oct. 13 at Beaver Field. Atherton, who scored three touchdowns, set four Penn State scoring records that day that have never been broken. He scored a total of 32 points, the most ever in one game for a senior. His three extra point records were even more spectacular. He was 10-for-10 in booting "goals after" touchdowns and, thus, established single-game records for number of extra points scored, extra point attempts and extra point accuracy. (What makes his records even more impressive today is the kicking rule of that era. The extra point kicks were rarely made from directly in front of the goal posts. Rather, the ball usually was placed in a straight line from the spot where the runner had crossed the goal line, forcing the kickers to boot often from severe angles.) Even that significant kicking feat was simply a harbinger of a more momentous kick Atherton would make later in the season.

Lafayette was expected to be a better test for State the following Saturday. Two weeks before, Lafayette had also creamed Gettysburg, 34-0, in a game stopped after a 30 minute half. But, as Joe Paterno was to say often many decades later, a team should improve the most between its first and second game. Hoskins' '94 team did—wiping out Lafayette, 72-0, before 400 people at Beaver Field as Atherton scored four touchdowns and kicked five "goals after" while Robison also had four touchdowns and Hoskins, himself, booted five "goals after."

"At no time during the game," the *Bellefonte Democratic Watchman* reported, "did the visitors give any evidence that they could play the game. Their wind was as poor as their judgment and they were completely dazed at the rapidly successive brilliant plays of their smaller antagonists."

Talk about your defining moments. When word of the Lafayette results got around the East, it caused a little panic on certain campuses. In the next few days, Penn, Princeton and Virginia canceled their scheduled games with State. The Penn State students and players hooted. Bullies!!! Cowards!!! "Is it possible that Penn was afraid of not running up the score? Or even being defeated by 'little State College?" the student newspaper, *Free Lance*, asked. When Princeton canceled one day before its scheduled game with a telegram saying the team was "in no condition to meet with such a strong team as State," the *Free Lance* crowed: "Such is the penalty for greatness."

Navy didn't back down. The Middies were 3-1, with only a close loss to Penn marring their record, when they hosted State in Annapolis Nov. 10. In the first quarter, Navy's rugged defense had State pinned back on its own 10-yard line. That's when left halfback Bill Suter made the run that put him into the all-time Penn State record books. He grabbed the ball, headed around the right end and didn't stop until he had a touchdown. Suter's epic run remains the longest touchdown run from scrimmage ever by a State player. Atherton booted the goal after and State took a 6-0 lead at the half.

During the intermission, Hoskins and the players continued to complain to the officials about a ruling the officials had made that had disallowed the use of a new State "trick play." The play would have permitted the players to use "handlebars" sewn on the seat of the pants of halfbacks Suter and Robison to lift the two men over the heads of the Navy players. There was nothing in the rules against it but the referee said it was illegal.

Navy came back in the second half with a TD but missed the extra points. However the Middies got two points on a safety and the game ended in a 6-6 tie. The State players said they could have won if the referee had not banned the "trick play." The reporter for the *Democratic Watchman* disagreed, saying they didn't win "because of the 'horse play' the boys indulged in the first half when they had the chance to win." Still, there was delight with the tie against a supposedly superior Navy team.

With the Princeton game canceled, State and its chief rival Bucknell agreed to move up the Thanksgiving Day game to Nov. 17 with the incentive that 75 percent of the gate receipts would go to the winner. Bucknell outweighed State by an average of 15 pounds per man but the betting was even when the game started on a neutral field in Williamsport with 1,500 looking on. The first half was scoreless. State tallied a TD and "goal after" within five minutes of the start of the

second half but Bucknell came back on a long drive with a touchdown and goal to tie. State controlled the ball the rest of the game. As time was running out, Robison scored the winning touchdown on a 10-yard run and Atherton kicked the "goal after." It was a narrow 12-6 victory that disappointed many of the State fans. The *Democratic Watchman* criticized the team for blowing too many opportunities in the first half and for repeated confusion in the play calling. But, the reporter also complained about Bucknell's stalling tactics that disrupted State's speed and "winning-fast" offensive formation "by...having a man feign injury after every scrimmage."

The next weekend, Hoskins took his team West for games with two new opponents, Washington & Jefferson on Nov. 23 in Washington, PA, and Oberlin the next day in Ohio. However, State was not at full strength. Robison, who already had 10 touchdowns, and a couple of other regulars missed the trip because of scholastic problems. That made the W&J game a lot closer and State escaped with a 6-0 win. And it nearly cost them the game with Oberlin, too.

Oberlin had been added to the schedule after one of the cancellations in October. It was a team with a good reputation and coached by one of football's early legends, John Heisman. (Yes, the same Heisman whose name is on the trophy now given annually to college football's outstanding player.) In the first half, Oberlin was all State could handle. Oberlin scored one TD and "goal after" and missed another because of a penalty and took a 6-0 lead at halftime. State roared back in the second half and before long Atherton had a touchdown. For once his leg failed him and he missed the two-point "goal after," keeping Oberlin in the lead, 6-4. Atherton was distressed but his teammates shouted encouragement. Hang in there, they yelled. He would soon have *his moment*.

There were about 10 minutes left in the game when Atherton's *moment* happened. Oberlin was on its own 10-yard line and had to punt into the wind. The ball went a measly 10 yards and halfback Charlie Thomas, subbing for Robison, made a "free catch" at the Oberlin 20-yard line. Atherton ran over to Hoskins. He had an idea. It was

The 1894 team went 6-0-1 and two of its players made history. Charlie Atherton (second row, second from right) kicked the first ever placekick field goal in college football history against Oberlin and Bill Suter (first row, fourth from left) set an all-time school record that still stands by running 90 yards from scrimmage for a TD against Navy.

something that had never been tried before—anywhere, as far as they knew. Charlie said he wanted to try and kick a field goal but instead of doing a dropkick as usual he wanted someone to hold the ball behind the line of scrimmage. Are you crazy? Someone hold the ball for a field goal? That's okay for a "goal after" touchdown. But a field goal? Nothing in the rules against it, someone said. Hoskins told Thomas to be the holder.

So, Thomas kneeled down on the 25-yard line, close to the sideline and Atherton lined up a few yards behind him. The State team lined up and the befuddled Oberlin players watched as Hoskins got set to center the ball back to Thomas. A trick play? The officials ordered play to resume. Hoskins centered. Thomas grabbed the ball, set it down and Atherton kicked the ball over the crossbar for five points and a 9-6 lead.

Hold on, Heisman and the Oberlin players screamed. Illegal. Illegal. They argued for a few minutes until a resolution was reached. Hoskins and Heisman accepted the decision by Referee Fred White of Oberlin to resume the game without counting the field goal. But they agreed to have a higher authority rule on the situation later. They finished the game without any more scoring. Oberlin claimed a 6-4 win and State a 9-6 victory. Weeks later, the ultimate decision was made by Walter Camp of Yale, who was considered the final arbiter in football rules since he had been one of the originators of the organized college games. Penn State wins, 9-6, he ruled.

Atherton had made history—but he didn't get the credit in his lifetime. Perhaps, it was because no one thought the kick was very significant at the time. Or, maybe once again, the isolation of State College kept people from talking about it. After all, it happened in Ohio and how many fans saw it? Newspapers virtually ignored his accomplishment and it wasn't until 1950 that Atherton's historic kick was first cited in a college football record book.

Atherton played his final game for Penn State on Thanksgiving Day against the Pittsburg (sic) AC and led State to a 14-0 victory. In his collegiate career, he had played in only six losing games and had been on the winning side 23 times. He was just 21 and would some day play one season of major league baseball and coach other State football teams before turning to a full time career in choir music. At the end of the 1894 season, Charlie and his teammates could claim to be the best team in Penn State's eight-year football history and the school's first truly unbeaten one. It would be another 15 seasons before State would field another unbeaten team and there were a few lean years just ahead.

Season Record 6-0-1
Record to Date 27-10-2
Winning percentage .718

"CHAUNCEY STRIKES BACK"

The General had been concerned about the Nov. 16th game against the Pittsburgh Athletic Club ever since he learned that several former State players were on the team, including Charlie Aull and Chauncey Stuart.

Aull had never played for Hoskins but The General knew Charlie and was well aware of his playing skills and his ability to lead a team. Around State College they were still talking about the first championship team in '91 when Charlie was the captain and quarterback.

Hoskins was even more worried about Chauncey Stuart. Chauncey had been a starting halfback on The General's '93 team, and it was Chauncey's long punt return for a touchdown in the opening minutes of the Pitt game that had sparked State to that big 32-0 win at Beaver Field. If Stuart has a big day against us, Hoskins had warned his team on the eve of the game, then we are in trouble.

On paper, State was a far superior team. That's what the sportswriters said and Hoskins believed it, too. After all, his team was mentally tough, galvanized by a solid schedule that had all but one game played on the road. But Hoskins was worried about his so-called "skill players," the backs and the ends. Except for "Bull" McCaskey, his quarterback and captain, and right end Jim McKibbin, they were all rookies. He might have felt better if Fred Robison was still at halfback, but the outstanding running back from '94 had left school after the well-earned 0-0 tie with favored Cornell in the second game of this season back in October. None of the first-year backs, Ed Brown and Charlie Thomas at halfbacks and Sam Walker at fullback, were in Robison's class.

Hoskins felt his rookie left end Joe Curtin was going to be a good one some day but right now he and McKibbin were both having problems stopping the opponents' runs around the flanks. The only part of the team Hoskins was pleased about was the middle of the front line, from tackle-to-tackle. That had been the heart and strength of the squad since the opening game win over Gettysburg at Beaver Field, 40-4.

Hoskins believed no team in State's class had a better pair of tackles than the Dunsmore's, James A. and James G., and that a third veteran, right guard Charlie Scott, was almost as good. He also was highly satisfied with his two rookies, W. W. "Bill" Murray at center and "Brute" Randolph at left guard. They were already playing like experienced lettermen, Hoskins told everyone, and they would only get better.

In fact, Hoskins believed the front line was so good that he was no longer upset that the opposing teams refused to let him play in the games. Gettysburg did in the opener on Sept. 25 and look what happened. The General also wanted to play in State's first ever game with powerful Cornell. Cornell said no, but let him be part of the officiating crew, and some of the partisan home team fans in Ithaca on Oct. 5 believed The General had been less than objective in carrying out his duties.

In the three weeks between the Cornell game and the annual big match with Bucknell at Williamsport, Hoskins decided not to play again. He almost regretted his decision in the first half against Bucknell when the team was sluggish and the score at the intermission was 0-0. But as the crowd of 4,000 looked on, State's superior size and strength overwhelmed the Lewisburg team in the second half for a 16-0 win.

No one expected State to beat Penn at Franklin Field on Nov. 9 for Pennsylvania was still one of the best teams in the country. In fact, most of the betting that day was on whether "the 'Agriculturists' from Centre County" would score any points. By halftime the score was 18-0 in Penn's favor. That's when General James Beaver of the Board of Trustees, one of State's biggest football fans who frequently followed the team on the road, went down on the field and told the

State players he would give new neckties to any of them who scored a TD. After the intermission Penn increased its lead to 29-0. But late in the game, J. A. Dunsmore recovered a Penn fumble at Penn's 25-yard line. Charlie Thomas ran 15 yards up the middle, Dunsmore picked up five more over right guard and then Thomas went the last five into the end zone for the touchdown—and a new necktie. The final score was 35-4 but sportswriters were impressed that State had scored. As the headline in the *Keystone Gazette* of Oct. 15, 1895, stated in part, "The Touchdown Made Fair and Square—Thomas was the Hero of the Hour and Highly Complimented."

The next opponent, the Pittsburgh AC, also had been impressed by State's showing against Penn and so had their fans. Few in the crowd of 2,000 at the P.A.C.'s East End Pittsburgh park that November Saturday afternoon gave the home team a chance. The expected win by State would guarantee a fifth straight winning season, no matter what happened in the remaining games against the tougher opposition of Washington & Jefferson and Western Reserve, another newcomer to the schedule. The only question anyone had was, how many points State would score?

Maybe Hoskins' men were looking ahead to its encounter with W & J two days away. Or, maybe as Hoskins feared, the old State lads—Aull and Stuart—brewed up some of their leftover blue and white magic. Hoskins would later remember this game as one of the worst in his coaching career at State. Chauncey Stuart set the tone eight minutes into the first half.

State was on a drive and had crossed midfield into Pittsburgh's territory when Ed Brown fumbled. Stuart grabbed the ball on a bounce and was in the clear before anyone on either team knew what happened. Walker took up the chase and finally tackled Stuart at the State 10-yard line. Before State's players could regroup, Pittsburgh's captain and left halfback, Tom Broderick, followed a block by Stuart on the first play and smashed over the center into the end zone. Stuart coolly drop-kicked the "goal after" and the P.A.C. had a stunning 6-0 lead.

The State players were furious and within a couple minutes after the kickoff they were within a few inches of the Pittsburgh goal line. But a fine goal line stand prevented a score. A frustrated Hoskins paced the sidelines, yelling and screaming. Pittsburgh couldn't move the ball and had to kick. McCaskey took the punt and ran it back 10 yards to the Pittsburgh 15-yard line. Two plays later J.A. "Jim" Dunsmore bulled through the P.A.C. line for 10 yards and the TD. The "goal after" would tie the score but the sure-footed McCaskey missed the kick. Hoskins couldn't believe it. What the hell was happening? He ranted at his players as they prepared for the kickoff.

Under the rules of that day, the team that scored a TD also received the next kickoff. Charlie Thomas took Stuart's kickoff and ran it back 20 yards to P.A.C.'s 29-yard line. Five plays later, J. A. Dunsmore scored his second TD on a 4-yard rush up the middle. Walker booted the "goal after" and Hoskins relaxed as State took its 10-6 lead into the intermission. "We have them now, boys" Hoskins probably shouted. "Let's take it to them in the second half."

Now that State had been aroused, the crowd sensed blood. As the writer covering the game for the *Pittsburgh Post* wrote later, "State was greatly surprised at the showing of the P.A.C. during the first half but was confident of rolling up a big score in the second half, as they thought their condition would stand better than P.A.C...."

Then, the writer added the now infamous punchline: "...but in this they were greatly fooled."

What happened in the second half will go down as one of the most surprising—and unnerving—endings in the history of State football. For most of the 30 minutes, the team struggled at midfield. As the game was winding down, Pittsburgh had possession at State's 50-yard line. Two running plays by Broderick and "Human Pile Driver" Weakly, picked up 25-yards and captain Broderick called time out. He huddled with his team, and, as the *Pittsburgh Post* writer later reported, Broderick knew "he must do something desperate..."

The State players dug in for what they felt was another run coming by Broderick or Weakly, the Pittsburgh substitute right half who had almost scored a breakaway TD a few minutes earlier. Charlie Aull called the signals. P.A.C.'s center, Reed, snapped the ball back to Aull, and before the State team realized it, Aull had tossed the ball back to Stuart, who had slyly maneuvered into a clear-sight position to attempt a dropkick field goal.

Hoskins and the State players could not believe what was happening. "Trick Play, Trick Play," someone hollered. "Field Goal, Field Goal," screamed another. But it was too late. "Stuart dropped the ball and catching it about six inches from the ground sent it sailing over the goal for five points, which won the game," the *Pittsburgh Post* reported. "Pandemonium broke loose. Stuart jumping and yelling...ran down the field with all his brother players at his heels. When they caught him....everyone tried to hug him at the same time..."

But the game wasn't over! State had one more chance. There was still time for State to get the ball back and it did. And for one moment, it looked as if State might pull out the victory: Sam Walker bolted through the line and was in the clear, heading for the Pittsburgh goal line, when he was brought down from behind by—you guessed it— Chauncey Stuart! State was still on the attack at the P.A.C. 15-yard line when time finally ran out. The *Pittsburgh Post* called it "The Greatest Victory P.A.C. Ever Achieved."

For Hoskins and State, it was the defining moment of the '95 season. The team never recovered from the devastating loss. Two days later, State was held to a 6-6 tie by W & J, another team it had been expected to beat, and Hoskins took out his frustration by starting a major all-out brawl late in the game when he slugged a W & J team member named B. E. Wilson. "No arrests were made," the *Keystone Gazette* reported, after "...the fight was quelled with some difficulty..." Ten days later, State finished the year with another tie, 8-8, against Western Reserve before "an immense crowd" in Cleveland.

So, for the first time since 1890, State did not have a winning season. Charlie Aull and Chauncey Stuart must have felt a little regret for what they did to their Alma Mater. But, then again, what happened that day in Pittsburgh, may have been providential.

Perhaps, it was then that The General made his decision to leave Penn State. Maybe his frustration with the loss and the ensuing near-riot he caused at W & J was the catalyst for his departure. Certainly, it must have had an influence on him when the Pitt job was offered. With The General at Pitt, a great rivalry began. So did the fist fights.

Season Record 2-2-3
Record to Date 29-12-5
Winning percentage .685

"TRAITOR HOSKINS!"

Hoskins was gone. The Western University of Pennsylvania—Pitt—had hired him away. More money and more prestige, he had said. Hogwash, said the few players who had returned for '96.

J. A. "Jim" Dunsmore, the captain, vowed to make Hoskins remember what he left behind when Hoskins brought Pitt to Beaver Field on Oct. 3. As State's starting right tackle for three years, Dunsmore had played alongside Hoskins in '93 and '94 and he liked The General. But there was just something wrong about the way George left.

Maybe, George realized the '96 team would be too green to be competitive with its schedule. After all, the last year under Hoskins had not been a rousing success and the only starters back were Dunsmore and sophomore center W. A. "Bill" Murray. Dunsmore especially missed Carlton "Brute" Randolph at left guard. "Brute" had lived up to his nickname as a freshman last year but he left school at the end of the spring and word had it he was now at Drexel. Still, Dunsmore was sure the new guy at left tackle, LeRoy "Henny" Scholl, would at least take up where "Brute" left off. Real tough guy, older than most of us. Brought that blackjack with him on the first day of practice and told the coach it was needed to survive the football games they played over in Williamsport. Uh, huh. "Henny" will do just right.

Dunsmore wasn't sure about the new coach, however. Dr. Sam was a nice guy, all right, but there was something missing. Seems okay as a trainer. And a doctor too. But Sam Newton doesn't seem to be all that sharp about the field techniques of this game. Yeah, he played at Penn from '91 to '93 and coached a bit at Penn, too, but that was just assisting. And that Trinity College job in North Carolina last year didn't really amount to a lot. Dunsmore wondered if he was worrying too much. Many of the other players and the fans seemed to have confidence in Dr. Sam. At least he'll start with three games at home, Dunsmore thought, and the opener with that pathetic Gettysburg should get him, and us, some valuable experience.

Newspaper observers felt the same. "...While it is expected the latter [State] will win," the *Bellefonte Democratic Watchman* reporter wrote on the eve of the opener, "the game...will give an opportunity of judging what strength the blue and white will develop on the grid-iron [sic] this fall...a new trainer, Dr. Newton...is on the ground and the men seem to have confidence that he will prove a valuable coach."

Gettysburg went down easily 40-0 on Sept. 26 and the State team was feeling confident when Western University of Pennsylvania rolled into town for the Oct. 3 game. Even the students were eager. Many of them remembered the festive atmosphere that surrounded the first Pitt game in '93 when everyone partied at the fraternities beforehand. But the ambience changed as soon as word got around that The General would be playing center for Pitt.

Many in the crowd booed when Hoskins took the field and it didn't take George long to antagonize the home town fans even more. There was one fight, then another and before the game finally ended Hoskins had instigated another of his all out brawls. State gave Hoskins the final comeuppance, though, by winning the game, 10-4, giving up the only Pitt TD on a blocked kick. Jim Dunsmore was in the middle of it all, and had one of his best ever games as the leading rusher and scoring both State TDs.

"...at more than one time during the game it looked as if State's colors would be black and blue instead of the gayer combination that designates her brawny athletes from those of other institutions," wrote the reporter for the *Democratic Watchman*, who said the score could have been much worse if not for Hoskins' antics. "...every scrimmage would evolve the hobbling 'General' with red face and hand raised in protest of some imaginary advantage that had been taken of him or his team."

The student newspaper, the *Free Lance*, berated Hoskins and his Pitt team's brutish style of play, hinting that college football might not survive people like The General. "Not only did trainer and captain Hoskins make it a disinteresting game," the *Free Lance* said, "but he gave such an exhibition of unmanly defiance of all fair rules which degrades the game as to make a lasting example for the 'antis' who hold up to public opinion." The newspaper then apologized to all past State opponents that might have lost because of ex-coach Hoskins' "unfair and unmanly tactics."

The two teams would not meet again until four years later but after the disruptive '96 slugfest, there was no doubt that the atmosphere had been set for all future Pitt-Penn State games. State also may have learned another lesson: that it is better to play Pitt at the end of a season rather than in the beginning. In what as the defining moment of the season, the '96 team was not the same after its physical combat with Pitt.

Dickinson made its first visit ever to State College the next week. The teams had not met since the '92 "walk out" at Harrisburg

The 1896 team lost its coach to the Western University of Pennsylvania before the season but managed to beat them on the playing field in a fierce battle marred by several brawls.

but this time the Dickinson players didn't back down. "The visitors proved more than a surprise to the home team by playing all around them in the first half," reported the *Democratic Watchman*, "and so successful were their rushes through State's line that the ball was once within two feet of her goal line." That's when a rookie substitute full-back named Lalon Hayes took charge. "...Hayes deserves nearly all the credit for having prevented the score...," the *Democratic Watchman* continued. "His punting was superb and he got into the plays with a daring and a purpose that ought to prove a 'line' to some others on the team."

State scored two TDs in the second half but missed both "goals after" and escaped with a listless, but hard-fought victory, 8-0. They wouldn't win another game the rest of the year. Two weeks later, Dr. Sam's team was overrun at Princeton, 39-0. "Though the blue and white didn't expect to do much with the Tigers and nine new men went to make up a discouragingly green team...there were optimists who could see State holding her opponents score below the twenties, while at least once Captain Dunsmore would be shoved over the other line with the ball," wrote the *Democratic Watchman*. "It didn't turn out that way, however, and...[State] rooters are not feeling as chirp as their wont..."

Then came Bucknell's revenge at Williamsport on Halloween day. Bucknell had lost four straight to State, but this year Bucknell was bigger and more experienced, and the heavy betting favorite. One newspaper reporter covering the game wrote that the Bucknell players looked much older—one was at least 35—and "there was a decided contrast when the lithe, vigorous State team came on the field." Dunsmore and his young players were a little intimidated and even before the game started they were telling fans they would lose.

"State's men looked like pigmies when lined up against the strapping wearers of the orange and blue," the *Democratic Watchman* reporter wrote. "They did not act like pigmies after the play had commenced, however, for they repeatedly broke up the Bucknell interference and tore holes through their line, with an ease that encourage those along the side lines to think she would even the long odds against her." Three quarters of the time they were playing in Bucknell's territory but, eventually, the brawn and experience overwhelmed State. Bucknell scored a TD on a 20-yard run in the first half to take a 6-0 lead, then came back with a couple of goal line stands and a line plunge for a TD late in the game to make the final score 10-0.

Dunsmore knew he would have to work hard to keep the players' spirits up for the last two games. Pennsylvania and the Carlisle Indians would be heavy favorites and both games would be on the road. It was a dismal November for Dunsmore and his teammates, and not just because they had to practice in the typical rain and cold of State College.

Penn beat State for the fifth time, 27-0, in Philadelphia on Nov. 14. Then, in State's first ever game with the powerful Carlisle Indians, State suffered its worst defeat since the Lehigh disaster in '89, losing to the Indians, 48-5, at Harrisburg. "The one feature of the game was Hayes' fine field goal from the 35-yard line," reported the *Democratic Watchman*.

Dunsmore would graduate that spring but he figured the worst was over for his teammates who would return in 1897. He didn't think it could get any worse than it was in '96. Neither did the reporters covering the team. "Next season, she [State] will appear on the grid-iron with all the benefit of this year's experience," the *Democratic*

Watchman noted on Nov. 11, "and having lost only three men by graduation there is every reason to believe that she will take her former position as leader in the class in which she is rated." They were wrong.

Season Record 3-4
Record to Date 32-16-5
Winning percentage .651

"The Hidden Ball Trick"

The schedule Doc Newton and Manager J. S. Albert had put together was daunting. Only two games were at Beaver Field: Gettysburg and Bloomsburg Normal, a new opponent. The '97 team once again would have to play on the home grounds of its toughest foes: Lafayette, Princeton, Penn, Navy and Cornell. Then, it would have to take on its biggest rivals on neutral fields—Bucknell at Williamsport and Dickinson at Sunbury on Thanksgiving Day. No wonder there was concern about the season.

Eight players had returned from '96 but three had been sub-stitutes and would remain so throughout '97. Joe Curtin, who sat out the '96 season, was back and would play quarterback and halfback and be the captain. But, again, there was no Charlie Atherton in the backfield, no one exceptional, except maybe Lalon Hayes, who had made a name for himself on defense and kicking after coming on in midseason. Atherton, in fact, was doing graduate work on the campus that fall and agreed to assist with the coaching. But Charlie must have been dismayed at the lack of running and scoring talent.

Up front it was a little better and the team's followers hoped the experienced linemen could overcome the weaknesses in the backfield. The only rookie was C.K. Cartwright at tackle. Murray was back for his third year at center and "Brute" Randolph had returned after his one season at Drexel to pair with tough "Henny" Scholl at the guards. John Clapper was back for his final season at the other tackle while Joe Ruble and Fred Heckel would be at the end positions again.

Scholl had returned to campus with another surprise for the players—a helmet. No one had seen a player wear a helmet on the football field before. But Scholl showed them his helmet when fall prac-tice opened in September. "Henny" had taken an old derby hat and cut off the brim. Then, he had stuffed the inside of the derby with some rags for padding. Protects the old noggin' from some of those fists, "Henny" told them. Some of the players liked Scholl's helmet so much that they got their own from the local shoemaker, who sewed leather protectors on the top of the hats and attached straps for the boys to tie under their chins. Some fans thought they all looked a little funny wearing the hats, or helmets, but it didn't help them play any better.

Doc and his boys also wondered how the new scoring change would affect the games. A touchdown would now be worth six points instead of four and the "goal after" would be reduced from two points to one and called "an extra point." Field goals would stay at five points and a safety at two points. With a questionable offense and running attack, most of the fans doubted if the scoring changes would make any difference this year.

Tackle James A. Dunmore, a four year starter and captain of the '96 team, played a major role in the win over Western U. of Pennsylvania that year–the start of a bitter rivalry.

Everyone knew the Gettysburg opener would be easy. State had played Gettysburg four times since 1891 and Gettysburg had yet to score, let alone win. It was no different this year, with State winning another shutout, 32-0, on Sept. 25. But as State fans feared, the next five games were pure agony. Dr. Sam's crew didn't score a point, losing in succession to: Lafayette, 24-0; Princeton, 34-0; Pennsylvania, 24-0; Navy, 4-0; and, finally, to "Pop" Warner's mighty Cornell team, 45-0.

When the battered team returned from Ithaca on Nov. 1, they grumbled about a "trick play" Cornell had used when the game was far out of reach. Bad sports, they complained. Dirty trick, someone said. What'd they do, the fans asked, what'd they do? They hid the ball and ran for a touchdown!

The score had been 39-0, the players recounted, and everyone was wet and cold from the icy rain that had fallen all afternoon. With a just a few minutes left and darkness imminent State kicked off following a Cornell TD. (The kickoff rule that gave the ball back to the scoring team had not changed.) Cornell's C.V.P. "Tar" Young grabbed the ball and was immediately surrounded by his teammates as the State players ran downfield to make the tackle. As the State players got closer to the mass of Cornell players, the Cornell men scattered in all directions, yelling and screaming. A couple of State players went after Young. Then, they realized he didn't have the ball. "Who has the ball?" The State players shouted, "Who has the ball?" They looked around quickly for the ball carrier. No one on the Cornell team had the ball. After a few hectic seconds, the confused and befuddled State players looked behind them. There in the end zone stood halfback Mike Whiting, waving the football. The referee threw up his hands. Touchdown, Cornell!!! What the hell happened? the State players wondered.

Here is how State's student newspaper, the *Free Lance*, described it: "...darkness fell on the gridiron long before the end of the game, and, aided by this cloak of gloom, Cornell was able to score a final touchdown in a most novel manner. When (C. A.) Mechesney kicked off, the Cornellians at once bunched together, and, while State was vainly searching for the ball, Whiting, with the pigskin neatly tucked beneath his sweater, was making tracks for our goal line, which he reached in safety, to the intense amusement of the cold, shivering spectators."

It would become known as "the hidden ball trick" and eventually would be outlawed because of "unsportsmanlike conduct." None of the players on either side realized they were making football history on that day, Oct. 30, 1897. For nearly 40 years, historians believed that Glenn "Pop" Warner first introduced the "hidden ball trick" in 1903 while coaching the Carlisle Indians against Harvard. Then in 1932, Warner admitted in a newspaper article he had innovated the trick in what he called "a practice game" in 1897.

"The most unusual play I remember," the coaching legend wrote, "was the ball-under-the-jersey play. It was first worked on Penn State by Cornell when I was coaching at Cornell in 1897."

After Warner's controversial admission, Whiting, the Cornell player who scored the touchdown, told about it in a letter to Cornell officials. Whiting said the team also used it in a couple of later games. "One day, Pop arranged to have a strong elastic placed in the bottom of my jersey," Whiting wrote. "He then got us out on the field to coach us in the new play. It would only be used on kickoffs." Whiting said Young was designated to receive the ball and run ahead to where the other Cornell payers had circled. "As he caught the ball, I placed myself directly ahead of him, with the other nine men in a circle ahead of me," Whiting wrote. "Tar would stuff the ball up my back, and, as soon as I realized it was well placed, I would yell and the whole team would yell and start to fan shape in all directions. I would go straight down the field; both my hands being free, it was obvious I did not have the ball...I would go between opponents close enough to almost touch them and they would stand open-eyed wondering where the ball was. Generally, we would go straight for a touchdown. Someone would follow and extract the ball from me after I was over the line and touch it down."

The "Hidden Ball Trick" became the defining moment for the season. The loss at Cornell meant another losing year, for now the team was 1-5 with just three games left. The players were depressed but they knew they had to do something to salvage the season and regain some pride. Unfortunately, they stumbled along the way.

In their annual grudge game with Bucknell at Williamsport, State pounded out a 27-4 win with some 400 fans from State College and Bellefonte in the crowd. "Miserable fumbling characterized the play of both teams," reported the *Bellefonte Democratic Watchman*. "...the superiority of the blue and white was so much in evidence as to justify the assertion that had both teams played the best game they were capable of, the score would have been about 40-0, instead of 27-4, in State's favor."

They shut out Bloomsburg 10-0 a week later at Beaver Field in a game that was so unexpectedly rough that the veteran center Murray was knocked out cold and missed much of the game. But the winning streak didn't last. In the final game with their other arch-rival, Dickinson, they were beaten 6-0 and they dejectedly walked off the field in Sunbury as the biggest losers in Penn State football history.

This was worse than the previous year. For the first time since State began playing football 10 years earlier, the team had been losers two years in a row. Figure in the 2-2-3 season of '95 and you had a team that was going downhill fast. Something had to be done.

Maybe what they really need, the newspapers were saying, is a new coach!

Season Record 3-6
Record to Date 35-22-5
Winning percentage .605

"The Coach Must Go"

Even before the season started, the new weekly newspaper in State College was calling for a new coach.

The *State College Times* didn't believe Dr. Sam Newton was spending enough time getting the team ready for its '98 schedule. Criticism was not new to Dr. Sam. The *Democratic Watchman* in nearby Bellefonte and the monthly student newspaper, *Free Lance*, hadn't been happy with Doc Newton either. They had chastised him in both '96 and '97 for concentrating on his medical practice in Philadelphia rather than being on campus training the football players. That's why the team was losing, they claimed, and the *Times* agreed.

Even another easy win over hapless Gettysburg in the season opener at Beaver Field, 47-0, didn't deter the *Times'* from carping. "Bright Outlook for State," blared the front page headline of the Sept. 29 edition. Then, even before detailing what happened in the game, the *Times'* reporter called for the re-hiring of The General: "The football season was opened on Saturday and from present indications, State will have the strongest aggregation of foot-ballists she has ever had. What is lacking now is a first class coach, and we know of no man in the country who would develop this team other than George W. Hoskins..."

Surprisingly, the *Times* backed down the following week, even though the team was creamed by Penn, 40-0, at Philadelphia's Franklin Field. But the *Democratic Watchman* was livid, saying "all State needs is the proper coaching to make the team one of the strongest in the country" and the *Free Lance* claimed "the trouble wasn't poor coaching, there just wasn't any coaching at all." But the *Times* was more optimistic.

"...The team will probably not be in such deplorable shape again this season as it was Saturday when it played against the strongest team in this year's schedule," said the *Times*. "Dr. Newton, the coach, has been getting good work from the men this week and with a little more ginger in the play back of the line, the team need not be afraid of the best of them." The reporter blamed the big score on the fact the State players were "scared half out of their boots" by playing such a good team before the largest crowd they'd ever seen. Some 4,000 spectators watched as Penn scored 34 points in the first half before the State players settled down. The *Times* reporter believed State was so much better than it had played in the first half that he said any rematch with Penn would end in a much closer result, and—like a modern day Beano Cook—he boldly predicted victory over a solid Lafayette team a week later. He was right on both counts.

The Lafayette game would prove to be a defining moment in Penn State football history but no one knew it on that Oct. 8 afternoon when State beat Lafayette for the first time ever, in Easton, 5-0. The students and townspeople of State College went wild. Some 500 fans celebrated on the streets until late Saturday night and 200 were on hand Monday, along with the newly-formed Cadet Band (forerunner of today's Blue Band), to greet the victorious team when it returned home. The *Times* reporter gloated, saying "if the game had been on neutral grounds...[State] would have beaten them from 10 to 20 points more" but hinted that it was probably the playing talent more than the coaching that made the difference. "Dr. Newton as a coach is all right," the

Times said. "Let the players train honestly and follow his directions and teachings" the reporter wrote, and they'd have a chance of beating Princeton down the road.

Princeton had been scheduled as part of a rigorous three game October road swing stretching from Annapolis to Pittsburgh that would have the team playing three times in eight days. The team and its fans were confident the three away games would show that State had one of the best teams in the country, just below the "Big Four" of Yale, Harvard, Princeton and Pennsylvania. Before that, however, there would be the second (and, as it turned out, final) home game. Susquehanna was the opponent for the first time. Like a lot of teams that would play on State's home turf in the future, Susquehanna got a good dose of Penn State's power and Beaver Field's lousy weather. About 400 spectators sat in a drizzling rain and fierce wind as junior fullback Dave Cure scored three touchdowns and kicked four extra points to lead State to a 45-6 win.

En route to Annapolis a few days later, Doc Newton took the team to Franklin Field to watch Penn practice and to pick up some pointers from his former boss, Coach George Woodruff. As the State players watched Penn punish its scrub team, Woodruff asked Doc if he wanted a scrimmage game. Soon, Penn's first team was banging away at the State players and in no time John Outland (yes, the same man whose name is on the trophy given nowadays to collegiate football's outstanding lineman) ran 40 yards for a touchdown. But the State players were not intimidated as they had been in the official game earlier that season. State took Penn's next kickoff and got to midfield. In a half dozen plays, State scored easily and Woodruff blew up. He challenged Doc Newton's team to repeat what it did and asked that the ball be placed on Penn's 25-yard line. "The visitors went through the big Quaker guards and scored another touchdown without any apparent difficulty," wrote the *State College Times* reporter who was watching. An angry Woodruff could not believe it and asked State to do it again. This time, State reached the 15-yard line where Cure took a pass and drop-kicked a field goal. Woodruff abruptly pulled his team off the field, gave them a stern lecture and sent them to the dressing room.

State and its followers treated the scrimmage against Penn almost like a game. The *Times* called it a 15-5 victory, although the game is not in the official State football records. Neither is the 10-10 tie in another "practice game" with Penn a few days later when the team stopped by again on the way to Pittsburgh. "The fact of the matter is that it was not generally known just how strong State was until after the practice games with Pennsylvania," wrote the unidentified *Times* reporter, who had long ago lost his objectivity, "and it is no wonder that it gave the Princeton coaches a chill when they learned what they would have to go against on Wednesday."

State lost to both Navy, 16-11, and Princeton, 5-0, but the State fans, like the *Times* reporter, considered the practice games against Penn more important. The Navy defeat was rationalized by the claim that most of the State regulars were held out of the game to get them rested for mighty Princeton and to prevent possible injury. Playing well against Princeton was more important than beating Navy, the reporter asserted. State came close as Cure missed a field goal by inches that could have tied the score against a Princeton team that would finish the year at 8-0-1. As for the loss, the reporter wrote, "The result was practically a victory for State, notwithstanding the score, for Princeton could not claim a victory from State by anything less than 40-0." In Pittsburgh Oct. 29, State lost to an all-star team of ex-collegians and semi-pros playing for the Duquesne Athletic Club, 18-15, but the *Times* reporter was convinced "that if State had a rest of a week, she would have no trouble in defeating" Duquesne. Uh huh!

The team was 3-4 at this point and staring at a third straight losing season, with big games coming up against its two main rivals, Bucknell and Dickinson, a final home game against Bloomsburg, and a major confrontation at Washington & Jefferson—the best team in Western Pennsylvania and Eastern Ohio. Splitting those games would not be good enough. They'd have to win at least three out of four to avoid what would be the most disappointing season in school history.

Some 2,500 watched in Williamsport Nov. 5 as State and Bucknell struggled through a fumbling first half. With about two minutes left in the half, veteran guard Henny Scholl got the ball and rambled 60 yards for a TD. State got another TD in the second half on a complete somersault over the goal line by Cure, who also kicked a couple of goals, and State won, 16-0. The Nov. 12 game with Bloomsburg was canceled because of the poor conditions of Beaver Field and the team traveled to Washington, PA, Nov. 19.

W&J was unbeaten with nine wins, including a 16-0 victory over a mutual opponent, Lafayette, and had not lost at home in five years. The headline of the Nov. 20 *Pittsburgh Post* succinctly told what happened: "Plunged in Gloom Was Washington." "The sturdy sons of the oldest college west of the Alleghenies have been conquered by a foreign foe on her home grounds...[and] the defeat is a bitter one," the Pittsburgh paper said. After a 6-6 tie in the first half of a bruising battle that went up and down the field, State came back after the intermission and won 11-6 with a tough defense and a touchdown by Scholl. "A Case of Swelled Heads Greatly Reduced," the *State College Times* crowed.

A winning season was assured. Now, all State had to do was beat it's other main rival, Dickinson, again on Thanksgiving Day in Williamsport, to have its best season in four years. After the '97 upset, Dickinson followers were sure they now had State's number and they bet heavily on their team. They were wrong. In "a blinding snow storm" State ran all over Dickinson with 20 points in the first half and another 12 in the second for an easy 34-0 win.

Three weeks later, the young *State College Times* did something for the first time that the hometown newspaper readers would see frequently over the next 100 years. It published a special "illustrated foot-ball edition" with a front page devoted entirely to the 1898 season, complete with photos, game summaries and biographical sketches on the players.

And, in what was the first of many examples of hometown hubris, the *Times* tried to claim a championship, displaying a large team photo at the top of the front page with a bold headline that stated, "State's Champion Foot-Ball Team." A smaller headline on the accompanying story noted, "This Years Team Surpasses any in the History of the College." The *Times* based its pronouncement on the fact State had beaten the best football teams in Pennsylvania, with the exception of "Big Four" power Penn, and had given both Princeton and Penn a scare—calling the 10-5 win over Penn in "practice" the team's llth game.

Of course, no one really went along with the championship claim. Although this was the first winning season since '94, most of the fans were disappointed. It had been a veteran team, led by the so-called "fabulous trio" of linemen— captain Bill Murray at center and guards Scholl and "Brute" Randolph. Randolph's play had been so impressive that his notoriety spread throughout the East and he was

named to Walter Camp's third team All-American squad—the first in what would become a long list of Penn State players to be honored as "All-America." Another player, fullback-placekicker-punter Dave Cure, led the country in kicking goals that year. And a 23-year-old freshman running back named Earl Hewitt, who had played football in prep school, had made a convincing debut with his running and backup punting.

The individual accolades aside, more had been expected of the '98 team. The talent was there, everyone said. Maybe if they had received better coaching. Dr. Sam had to go! Sam Newton did—on his own. Officials at Lafayette liked the way State had played in beating their team at Easton, 5-0. Unlike the disgruntled State fans, they thought Newton was clever and football smart. So they offered Newton more money to be their head coach in 1899. Dr. Sam accepted and State fans rejoiced. The fans figured State's losing days were over. They were wrong.

Season Record 6-4
Record to Date 41-26-5
Winning percentage .604

"BEAT ARMY!"

It had taken the team nearly a day and a half to get to picturesque West Point for Penn State's first game ever with Army. They had left State College at 6:20 Friday morning, stopped in New York City overnight and then made the trek up the Hudson to the Academy.

The players thought the place was as charming as everyone had said it was, almost like back home. But they had not come here to admire the autumn beauty. They had come here to play one of the best teams in the country, better, maybe, than any team outside the "Big Four" and certainly better than Navy.

State had been trying to schedule a game with Army for years, another of those efforts to gain respect for the school's improving football program. Army had always balked, deeming the State brand of football beneath them. Finally, manager Diller was able to make it happen. Maybe Coach Sam had something to do with it too. Sam Boyle had connections. He had been a three-year letterman on those powerful Pennsylvania teams and a Second Team All-American end in his last year, 1897. Now Sam was the coach. He had been recommended by the man he replaced, Doc Newton, an old friend from Penn. Everyone expected Sam Boyle to coach better than Doc Sam. "Boyle is one of the best coaches in the country," the *State College Times* reported on Sept. 14 as fall practice began, "and should be able to make State's team of 1899 a hummer."

With most of the starters from '98 returning this was expected to be a big year. Brute Randolph, now the captain, and Henny Scholl were back to anchor the line and star fullback and kicker Dave Cure was heading up a good crop of running backs. Center was a major question because of the graduation of last year's captain, Bill Murray, but a solid replacement was found among the freshmen, Ralph Cummings. Quarterback Fred Heckel also had departed but Randolph and Boyle simply moved last year's sensational freshman running back, Earl Hewitt, into the signal-calling position.

Now, with Cure, Hewitt, veteran Daniel "Push" Miller at right half and Billy Burns at the other halfback position, they felt the backfield was "loaded." They especially expected big things from Burns. He was the star of State's baseball team and playing football for the first time. But he was a speedster, perhaps the fastest man ever on the team

Eleven games were on the schedule with the most difficult on the road as usual—Army—Oct. 3—then, Princeton, Navy, Yale, Bucknell, Penn, Lafayette and the semi-pro Duquesne Athletic Club. Still, the *State College Times* beat reporter was highly optimistic, writing: "We are not at all afraid to predict something extraordinary...for State this year..."

For the first time in six years, Gettysburg was not the traditional opener. Gettysburg would follow a game with Mansfield Normal, and, although no one knew it at the time, this would be the only time State would ever play Mansfield.

State looked especially sharp in the smashing of Mansfield at Beaver Field Sept. 23, 38-0. "We were agreeably surprised to see so little fumbling on State's part so early in this season," wrote the *Times* reporter. The sports editor of the *Philadelphia Times* also was impressed: "State shows an offensive and defensive strength against Mansfield Normal School that augurs well for the success of the team later under efficient coaching and under Sam Boyle's tutelage they should have this...Even among the larger colleges few have stronger material than State. For her line and for her backfield she has lithe, active, heavy men. If they play fast football and play along well developed systematic lines, they should [give a good] game with even the Big Four." Upbeat words, indeed.

Gettysburg was walloped as usual, this time 38-0 as State scored 28 points in the first half, then brought in several substitutes. Two starting backs, Cure and Miller, sat out with minor injuries but they weren't missed. Burns led the scoring with two TDs and five extra points and even Randolph and Scholl had touchdowns. "Burns surprised everybody with his punting and excellent end-running," the State College reporter wrote. "Too much can not be said of the excellent all-around work of State. Everyman played for all that was in him...Cummings at center is filling old Bill Murray's post beyond the most sanguine expectations."

So, now it was time for Army. Everyone on State's team was healthy and eager when the Cadets kicked off at 3:40 p.m on the West Point parade and drill ground. Probably too eager. In a sequence of plays that would remind State fans a century later of their modern day heroes, the visitors bumbled through the opening minutes. The kickoff return man, Miller, was tackled deep in State's territory and State fumbled away the ball a few plays later. State's defense took charge, halting the first Army surge towards the end zone and State took over the ball. But they couldn't move far and soon the Cadets were on the march again, this time getting big gains up the middle. They reached State's 5-yard line but, again, State's traditional "bend-but-don't break" defense stiffened and got the ball back.

Then came what was the "*second*" most dramatic play of the game—and maybe of the season. Billy Burns took the ball close to the State goal line and "like a deer, sped downfield." In seconds he was in the clear and running yards ahead of the closest Army pursuers, who were slowly losing ground. It was a sure touchdown! Well, almost. With the goal posts just five yards away, Burns unexpectedly slipped and fell. His teammates ran up, picked him up and patted him on the back. Bad break, they said. We'll get the touchdown anyway.

Now, do Penn State fans really expect it to be that easy? On the next play, State fumbled all the way back to the 25-yard line and Army recovered. The State players and coaches were visibly frustrated, stomping their feet angrily into the ground and punching the air with their fists.

In the next few minutes, neither team could advance the ball and they exchanged punts. As time was running out in the first half, Army punted again. It now was time for a defining moment. Hewitt, the sophomore quarterback they called "the silent man," took the ball and dashed down the middle of the field, cut to the sidelines, avoiding tacklers, and went all the way. "I took the ball and with the assistance of 10 other fellows was able to run 65 yards for a score," Hewitt told this writer, then a young *Daily Collegian* reporter, 58 years later. "Army's captain [W. W. Smith] was the last man standing between me and the goal and when I saw [right end] Ed Wood knock him down it was clear sailing ahead." Burns kicked the extra point as State's sideline hooped it up and the half ended with State ahead 6-0.

That punt return won the game for State and would be remembered for decades to come. And although it was the defining moment of the game, it really wasn't the defining moment of the season. That came in the second half and, again, involved "the silent man" on a spectacular play. With 45 seconds left in the game, Army's left halfback Rockwell went back to punt deep in West Point territory. But it was a fake! Rockwell took off through the surprised State players and ran 60 yards before Hewitt tackled him from behind on the Army 6-yard line, saving the victory. Because of the rules in those days, it was State's ball and Cure punted out beyond midfield and the game was over. But Hewitt had already been carried off the field. He had severely injured his ankle on the game-saving tackle and was taken to the West Point hospital.

Hewitt's injury would be devastating to the team and would be a portent of things to come. He would not play the rest of the year and the season would never be the same. His replacement, Howard "Johnny" Johnson, had nowhere near Hewitt's signal calling-talent or quiet leadership and it showed. Furthermore, injuries to other players also would cripple the team and sap morale as the season wore on.

Hewitt wasn't with the team the following Monday, when a big crowd welcomed the players back with a large march through town and a ceremony on the steps of Old Main. He heard about the march as well as the Saturday night bonfires and the big celebration dance at the Armory. But he watched from the sidelines the next Friday—Friday the 13th, no less-when Washington & Jefferson visited Beaver Field with vengeance on its mind.

W & J was still fuming from its upset loss in '98 and intended to make State pay for that embarrassment. The brutal hitting started on the kickoff with elbows flying as the teams converged at midfield. The scrimmages were rough and the defenses seemed in control. Then Burns began showing his speed again, clipping off chunks of yards. Ten minutes into the half, Burns took a pass in Penn State territory and sped 68 yards until forced out of bounds at the W& J's 15-yard line.

"Burns was still lying on the ground when [W&J's halfback] Reed made a flying leap and landed on Burns' chest with both knees," wrote the *Times* reporter. "The State team as well as the spectators came to Burns' assistance and for a few minutes a general melee ensued." The referee threw Reed out of the game, then conferred with Randolph and the W&J captain. They all agreed to end the game. The referee declared it official, 0-0, even though it had only gone 10 minutes.

The players were tired and battered but had little time to recover. Mighty Princeton was just six days away. Burns was limping but would play. So would Dan Miller who also was hurt in the W&J fracas. Cure would not. He had been injured in the Army game but no one realized how serious the injury had been and now he would be out for nearly a month. Still, even with the injuries to their key offensive personnel, the other players were confident they could at least stay even with Princeton. They were wrong.

"The game was a complete triumph for Princeton...," the unidentified *Times* reporter wrote in an explicit analysis of the game won by Princeton, 12-0. "Had State been at her best and kept her nerve a better game might have been expected...Whether it was discouragement or from these changes [because of injuries] or stage fright of the big 'P', it is certain that State fell below the game she is reputed to be capable of...The line could not withstand the onslaught of the 'Tigers' and State's tackling was ineffective. Whether State has a strong attack could not be told from Wednesday's game as they seldom had the ball, and when they did get it, they lost it immediately on a fumble, generally by Johnson in putting the ball in play." (So you want honest reporting, you got honest reporting. In other words, they stunk out the joint and Hewitt's replacement at quarterback wasn't worth a tinkers damn!)

It got a little better four days later at Annapolis but not by much and State still lost, 6-0. "State seemed to lack snap throughout the game," the same intuitive *Times* reporter wrote, "whether it was because of their drubbing at Princeton or the absence of two of their stars, it is hard to say, but only once did they show their true form, when for forty yards they carried the ball by hard plunges through the Cadets' lines." Navy almost scored twice in the first half but lost both opportunities on offside penalties near the goal line. But in the second half, the Middies scored the only points they needed after a short drive following a poor State punt.

With State faltering, big rival Dickinson believed State was ripe for an upset at Beaver Field the next week. Dickinson already had come close to beating the Carlisle Indians and "everyone" knew the Indians were a much better team than State. Beat State, the Dickinson fans shouted as the teams kicked off. Not this year, you Dicks! Two first half fumbles inside Dickinson's 15-yard line thwarted two State scoring attempts until a 5-play, 38-yard drive got a TD, with Billy Burns going around right end for the score. They got the ball back a short time later on a fumble at the Dickinson 23, and Burns scored again, this time taking it over from the eight. Both times State missed the extra point and the half ended 10-0. Burns scored his third TD midway through the second half and State walked way with a decisive 15-0 victory.

So, they had bounced back. They were 4-2-1 at this point with their other major rival, Bucknell, up next at Williamsport. Beating the Bisons would be vital if they wanted to regain the momentum and salvage this injury-plagued season. Some 3,000 boisterous spectators were in their seats when Bucknell's Christy Mathewson (the same Christy Mathewson who later became a Hall of Fame major league baseball great) kicked off as a stiff, cold wind blew diagonally across the slippery field. Fans on both sides wondered if this football game would come down to another duel between Mathewson and Burns. The two men were star pitchers of their respective baseball teams and in June they had battled in a game still being talked about on both campuses. Burns had outpitched and out hit Matthewson and State had won, 4-3. Now, here it was on the gridiron, with Christy the fullback and kicker for Bucknell and Billy the best running back for State.

The ball was hard to handle because of the wetness, and fumbles hampered both teams as they wallowed through the muck. Both Mathewson and State's kicker Cure had difficulty on their punts and placements. Midway through the first half, a poor punt by Mathewson gave State the ball on Bucknell's 25-yard line. Four plays later, Burns took the ball and was sweeping around right end at the 20 with a clear field ahead when he slipped—again. That was the closest State would come to a TD, although Burns continued to pick up large gains, including runs of 24 and 20 yards near the end of the game. Bucknell scored the only points it needed shortly after Burn's slip with a short plunge for a TD. Mathewson missed the extra point but it didn't matter. Cure tried a placement field goal to avoid a shutout late in the second half but the wind carried the ball wide and the game ended with Bucknell winning, 5-0.

The Bucknell team and their fans marched nosily through the streets of Williamsport as the State players made the 5 and a half hour trip back to State College wondering realistically about their chances in the last four games. They didn't look good—and they weren't. The next week they played Yale for the first time and they were completely outclassed. Yale scored five of its seven touchdowns in the first half and coasted to a 42-0 win. Penn made it worse with a 47-0 triumph. A week later Penn State suffered its worst defeat since the record-breaking Lehigh disaster of 1889 in a 65-4 loss to the semi-pro Duquesne Athletic Club. Fortunately, the Thanksgiving Day finale with Lafayette was canceled.

What started out in September as a season full of potential and great expectations had turned sour. Army had been the turning point. The team was never the same after that. This was supposed to be Penn State's year and it wasn't. And next season there would be too much uncertainty. Hewitt would be back next year. So would Scholl, Miller and a few others. But Cure and "Brute" would be gone. So, would Burns, who would give up football to concentrate on baseball (and later become a dentist in Tacoma, WA)—a one-year wonder who may have been the most exciting State runner of his era.

Sam Boyle would not be back either. He had had enough with this team. Dickinson offered him its head coaching job and he took it. That would make it two in a row. They coach a losing team here one year and its off to a big rival the next. This has to end. Find a coach who can win, and find one who will like Penn State. President Atherton did. But State couldn't beat Army again for 60 years!

Season Record 4-6-1
Record to Date 45-32-6
Winning percentage .578

1900

"Fumble, Fumble, Fumble"

Henny Scholl knew the team was in trouble before pre-season practice started. So did Earl Hewitt. The new coach, Pop Golden, probably did too. Pop had been the director of physical education at the Williamsport YMCA when President Atherton hired him and previously held the same position at the Johnstown YMCA. So he was familiar with the Penn State team and many of its players. He couldn't have been surprised by Scholl and Hewitt's pessimism when the players reported to Beaver Field.

Scholl, now in his fifth year, was the captain. Hewitt, "the silent man," was back at quarterback and fully recovered from the ankle injury that sidelined him most of the season. Joe Ruble would be in his fourth season at left end and Tom Miller in his third year at right end. That tough sophomore Ralph Cummings returned at center and could be used in the backfield if needed. But that was it. The rest were rookies or seldom-used substitutes from '99. Percy Martin might make it in the backfield. He played enough behind Cure and Burns to earn a letter last year but he still lacked experience. But in looking over the dozen men who turned out in September for practice, Scholl and Hewitt realized their team had a serious problem—lack of talent.

Another severe travel schedule had been put together by the manager. The better quality teams that State needed to play to enhance its status and reputation continued to refuse to make the burdensome trip to State's campus. There would be only two games at Beaver Field this season and both were chalked up as easy wins— newcomer Susquehanna in the opener and traditional opponent Gettysburg in November. Of course, Pitt might be considered a "home" game since it was scheduled on a neutral field in nearby Bellefonte. The other eight games would be on the road, including those against Army, Princeton, Penn and Navy.

The defining moment of the season came on the first play of the first game against little Susquehanna on September 23. Even with an inexperienced starting lineup, State was a heavy favorite. State won the toss and elected to receive the kickoff. Hewitt was the return man and ran the ball back 15 yards. On the first play from scrimmage someone fumbled. State recovered but this was the omen. Fumbles, inexperience and ineptness was to be the trademark of the season. State beat Susquehanna by just 17-0, scoring all the points in the first half despite five fumbles. There were at least four more fumbles in the second half. "[State] should have scored at least twice in the second half," reported the *State College Times*, "but ugly fumbles by her runners prevented the score from being higher." Susquehanna's right tackle, Spotts, picked up one fumble on State's 20-yard line and almost scored a TD but was brought down from behind at the 3-yard line on a flying tackle by Hewitt, and the defense held. "Fumbleitis" even hit the normally sure-handed Scholl, who had at least four of the dropped balls to go along with his two TDs. One of the few runners who didn't fumble was Percy Martin who had several good runs over 10 yards, including a 25-yarder for State's first TD and a "brilliant run of 70 yards" that set up the final TD.

One week later against Pitt, fumbles again helped determine the winner—only this time it was the opponent doing the fumbling. The two teams had not met since "Traitor" Hoskins had caused all that mayhem in '96 so maybe the Pitt players were too tight. Perhaps it was the "gentle rain" and wet grounds. The rain certainly kept spectators away for a disappointing crowd of just 1,000 was in Bellefonte for the kickoff, including State's number one fan, General Beaver. They watched as a fumble on Pitt's third possession in the first half led to State's first TD by Cummings, and another fumble in the second half on the Pitt 10-yard line set up the final TD by Scholl in a 12-0 win. (Martin kicked both PATs.) Of course, State fumbled—at least three times, but Pitt couldn't take advantage. "Hewitt's leadership guided the team to success," reported the *Times*, but pointing out State's main weakness was the team's right guard, George Craft, because Pitt's "strongest plays...were through the right guard." Poor George. He may have been singled out but he wasn't the only weakness on the team—as the next nine games would show.

State played perhaps its best game of the season a week later at West Point in what turned out to be the last game with Army for 39 years. There were no fumbles by either team in the two 15-minute halves but neither team scored. Army came the closest. Late in the first half, the Cadets drove to within six inches of State's goal line but Scholl led his teammates on a staunch defensive stand that kept Army out of the end zone. Unfortunately Frank Yocum, the rookie starting right tackle, was severely hurt and never played another game. As the *Times* reported, "...Yocum had his cheek bone crushed in the game, and may be permanently disfigured."

The team went on from West Point to Princeton for its game with the Tigers four days later. It was no contest as Princeton won, 26-0, with the *Times* reporting: "As State is not in Princeton's class, the coach determined merely to play a defensive game and not allow the team to risk themselves to the utmost only to be beaten...we are expecting better results from such games as Dickinson and Bucknell, in which by all means, we ought to win." (We? Journalism has changed a bit in 98 years!)

But, Dickinson was 10 days away. First there was Penn, which had won five easy victories in a row over State by such scores as 47-0 and 40-0, and everyone knew what was going to happen this year, right? Not exactly. The final score was 17-5 and State fans considered it a moral victory. State's defense kept Penn out of the end zone, forcing the frustrated home team to settle for field goals. Meanwhile, State scored the only TD on Hewitt's quick kick—then known as a "quarterback kick"— from the Penn 30-yard line. In those days, such a punt was "a free ball" and allowed the kicking team to score such a touchdown. So, a little known substitute named Art Gill, who would not play enough that year to earn a letter, recovered Hewitt's kick in the end

Pop Golden is one of the most historic figures in Penn State athletics. He coached football from 1900-1903, turning State into a winning team, then became the school's first athletic director. Under his direction, football became a revenue producer and he led a fund raising effort that helped establish a training table for athletes and the construction of the Track House where athletes lived.

zone. What made the touchdown even more gratifying to State—and more galling to Penn—was that the "quarterback kick" had been invented by Penn's coach George Woodruff and was one of his favorite plays.

After their performance against Penn, Scholl, Hewitt and their teammates were convinced they could beat Dickinson in Carlisle three days later. They also wanted to show up Sam Boyle who they now blamed for the way last season fell apart. But they underestimated the mind of the man on the other sidelines. Coach Sam knew all the strengths and weaknesses of the team he left behind and he used his knowledge to smash State, 18-0. It was a demoralized bunch of players who plodded back to State College to prepare for the menacing semi-pro Duquesne Athletic Club the next week in Pittsburgh. Even the *Times* sportswriter covering the team noticed the depressing mood.

"We are passing through a crisis," he wrote the day before the Duquesne AC game. "We are in a slump. It can be seen on the faces of all and if it could not be, it could be felt. Now evidently what we need is a positive effort of courage, a putting of the shoulder to the wheel." He urged the players to push themselves harder in practice and he encouraged Pop Golden and his assistant coaches to work harder on getting the substitutes and "new material" better prepared to play. He said such "supreme effort" would be needed the next week when State played its big rival Bucknell. The players must have been looking ahead, too, for they were soundly defeated by the Duquesne AC, 29-0.

To fans of both teams, the State-Bucknell game was the only one that counted. The taunts started weeks beforehand, and as the day of the game drew closer, the atmosphere was spirited and intense. Both schools held rousing pep rallies to fire up their teams. "Everybody go to the game," urged the Bucknell newspaper, "you will regret it a thousand times if you do not. Don't let the 'farmers' cheer you down. Keep together...and 'whoop her up for Bucknell. If these directions are followed, victory is assured." No way countered the *Times*, which printed the Bucknell story. "Away we go to Williamsport to show Bucknell how to play football, and how to [cheer from] the sidelines," the Times wrote on the eve of the game. "A hot game? Well, you bet...Do you want to see State knock the bottom out of Bucknell? Go to Williamsport."

Bucknell's strategy was to keep State off balance by kicking the ball back immediately whenever play moved into Bucknell's territory. Someone must have scouted the State games and pointed out how State's offense sputtered and made mistakes. Like fumbling. Sure enough, two fumbles in the opening minutes of the first half gave Bucknell the ball on the State 45-yard-line. Two end runs of 15 and 30 yards and Bucknell had a touchdown. The PAT was good and Bucknell led, 6-0. As the first half was winding down, Bucknell punted from midfield and—you guessed it—State fumbled and Bucknell recovered at State's 5-yard line. Bingo. Another touchdown and PAT and the half ended, 12-0.

State's players were frustrated and it showed on their faces. They had dominated the action, moving the ball up field consistently. They had been held on downs just once and forced to kick just once, yet Bucknell was leading. Bucknell's strategy was paying off and their large crowd of fans were jubilant. They jeered at the State contingent, which couldn't believe what they were seeing—again. Fumble, fumble, fumble.

State took the second half kickoff and immediately powered its way quickly towards the Bucknell end zone. Bam, bam, bam and

State was at Bucknell's 3-yard line as the State fans roared from the sideline. Then it happened again. FUMBLE! Bucknell, which never fumbled in the entire game, recovered and the threat was over. Pop Golden, Scholl and Hewitt huddled on the sidelines. They called the team together and urged everyone to pull together. They were a better team and they were going to show it. Bam, bam, bam and they had a TD. Now it was 12-4.

With 11 minutes to play they had the ball back again at their own 60-yard line. (It was the 60-yard line because of the way the playing field was configured in that era.) Martin took the ball and dashed down the sidelines until he was forced out of bounds at the Bucknell 5-yard line. State players hurried downfield, lined up and veteran Joe Ruble stepped in bounds from the sideline and kicked the ball closer to the Bucknell goal line while officials were still determining the precise spot where Martin had stepped out. Bucknell players cried foul, claiming time had been called. However, it was a "trick play" allowed by the rules at the time. "Rule 22, Section A," the referee said and the Bucknell players and coaches protested angrily. Their fans joined in with boos. Play ball, the ref said. No way, the Bucknell players screamed and stomped off the field. Forfeit to Penn State, 6-0, said the ref.

"It was a dissatisfied crowd that left the grounds," the *Times* reported, "...[with] both sides claiming victory, neither side having completely earned it...[but Bucknell complained] just as she always does about something. And why...? Because she knew that if the game continued she would have been beaten." The prestigious *Williamsport Grit* agreed that State would have won the game because it was playing better: "Bucknell...could do little in battering against State' stonewall defense. State's strength was in its line plunging, which seldom failed to gain the required distance. In the second half, State clearly outclassed their opponents and were pressing to almost certain victory when the game broke up in a row."

That game caused such animosity that Bucknell refused to play the next year, and they did not play each other again until eight years later. By that time the intense rivalry that had marked these games since the beginning in 1881, or 1887—take your pick—was over. Other more competitive teams would replace "the Orange and Blue" as a big State rival, including Navy, the next opponent in 1900.

Navy clobbered State, 44-0, and once again fumbles tormented the team and its fans. "Annapolis played a fast, snappy game," wrote the *Times* reporter, "...But the trouble was State could not hold the ball at critical points. This happened eight distinct times, many of them being near the Cadets' goal line. Wash the butter off and put resin on your fingers next time, State." Sure!

Maybe it was the resin, or maybe just the quality of the opposition, but a week later, State fumbled just twice in blasting Gettysburg, 44-0, at Beaver Field. Gettysburg only had the ball twice in State territory as eight different players scored touchdowns and Martin kicked six goals after.

All that was left was a Thanksgiving Day clash with new opponent, Buffalo, in Buffalo. The game was played on a field described as "a veritable mud hole." It was a sloppy game and both teams fumbled but Buffalo dominated the game, playing its best game of the year, according to its captain, and won, 10-0.

The season was finally over. Considering all the newcomers in the lineup, the final record was not bad, equaling last year's team, which had better talent but maybe worse luck. We have to find some way to stop fumbling, Pop Golden said. Hewitt and Scholl agreed. Hewitt would be the captain and Scholl, my gosh, was going to come back for an unprecedented sixth year. Wash that butter off your fingers, boys!!!

**Season Record 4-6-1
Record to Date 49-38-7
Winning percentage .559**

"Henny's 6th Year"

Henny was back. It was that simple. The captain of last year's fumbling team had returned to play a sixth year. Six years, mind you. No one had ever played that many years for State—and never would ever again!

Captain Hewitt and Coach Golden welcomed him back with great enthusiasm. They sure needed him. This would be a very, very young team, more inexperienced than last year's squad. Seven newcomers would start against Susquehanna on Sept. 22, although Lynn Sweet the center wasn't exactly a rookie. Lynn had played for Bucknell last season and apparently liked the way State handled itself in last year's disputed game. So, eligibility rules being what they were—or weren't—in those days, Sweet migrated 60 miles east to play football for State—and presumably go to class, too!

There was another youngster working out in pre-season whom Hewitt had recruited from DuBois, but the kid would need a couple more weeks before he was ready to play. Hewitt had befriended Andy Smith after watching him play at DuBois High School. Now, Smith was Hewitt's roommate at Sigma Alpha Epsilon fraternity and Hewitt told everyone it would just be a matter of time before Andy became the biggest star in Penn State history. Sure, Earl, the older guys kidded.

Pop Golden was just happy to have Henny back. But no more fumbles this year, Pop undoubtedly said to his 6-foot tackle, okay? Certainly, Henny smiled back sheepishly. He was still angry at himself for the way he and "his" team fumbled away last season. He was determined to make it up this Fall.

Pop and the team managers had decided to make this season's schedule a little easier—nine games at tops, with the usual two or three home games. But they still had to play the toughest opponents on the road: Penn and Navy, naturally, with Yale—perhaps the best team in the country—back on the schedule after a year's absence and a game in November with another mighty semi-pro outfit, the Homestead Athletic Club. No one could ever accuse State of ducking strong opponents.

Susquehanna proved to be a tougher than expected opening foe at Beaver Field. Maybe that was because the old fumble bugaboo hit again. State won by just 17-0. But after another week of practice, the fumbling all but disappeared as State clobbered Pitt, 37-0, at Bellefonte. Scholl had two touchdowns in the first half and another in the second and Ed Whitworth also scored three times as the heavier State team "outclassed" the lighter Pitt squad. "There was little fumbling," reported the *State College Times*, "while the men played together like clockwork, the interference, with but one exception was splendid."

Now it was time for Pop to see what this young team was really made of with the meat of the schedule coming up. But State never stood a chance against Penn the next week and went down for the eighth straight year, 23-6.

They had two weeks to prepare for Yale and it was a game the players were looking forward to. Despite the Elis' deserved reputation as a football power, the State players were not intimidated. The first time State had played in New Haven two years ago, Yale had won easily, 42-0. Scholl remembered how disconcerted the team had been then, coming off the shocking loss to Bucknell the week before. They might be outmanned against Yale, Scholl assured everyone, but they wouldn't be outplayed. Hewitt had missed that '99 game because of his injury against Army but he was determined, now that he was the captain, to make it up this year. Hewitt also was pleased to have his young protégé, Smith, finally in the backfield with him. Smith was just too good to be a substitute. He could run and kick as well as anyone on the team, including Hewitt and Scholl.

Smith didn't help get a win at Yale. State still lost, this time 22-0, but, as is often the case, the score did not indicate how close the game actually was. Once again, fumbles spoiled any chance State had for an upset as State fumbled three times within the Yale 15-yard line. "State Holds Yale to 22 Points," blared the headline in the *New Haven Register*. "...no eleven has torn up the Yale line so persistently, and broken her interference," the *Register* reporter wrote. Hewitt was ecstatic. "We showed we weren't afraid of the 'Y' on the Yale sweaters," declared Hewitt to sportswriters after the game.

Hewitt had no doubts his team could beat Navy and it did, in an 11-6 upset at Annapolis on Oct. 26. The *Times* said Navy was "too over confident" and the *Baltimore American* agreed. "The Cadets (SIC) were perfectly confident of winning this game," the *American* reported, "but they were decidedly outplayed, and their touchdown was made on a fumble by a State player, while State made one touchdown straight, hard football, and go into position for her try at goal by steady punting down the field."

Fumbles were still nagging State but, at least now, it was able to overcome its bobbles and win a big game. Scholl and Smith led the way, doing most of the running and all the scoring. State scored on its second possession when Scholl made a 25-yard field goal on a difficult placement that is "seldom attempted, and requires greater quickness and accuracy." Navy recovered a State fumble late in the half near the goal line and scored a TD and PAT to take a 6-5 halftime lead. State snatched the second half kickoff and from its own 28-yard line drove methodically to Navy's 18-yard line before Smith fumbled. Navy recovered but Smith redeemed himself by blocking the Middies' punt on the next play and State had the ball back on the 5-yard line. Scholl crashed into the end zone immediately for a TD and Smith booted the PAT. On the last play of the game, Navy faked a kick and tried to run for a tying touchdown but Smith and Art Biesecker brought the runner down 10 yards behind the line of scrimmage and the game ended.

"Scholl again proved that he is one of the best players in the country," wrote the *Baltimore American*. "He made wonderful gains throughout, and was a bulwark of defense..." Yes, once again Henny Scholl had come through to lead State to victory. But it wouldn't be the last time.

Pop Golden didn't expect his charges to beat the Homestead AC. on Nov. 2 but he knew they wouldn't give in without a determined struggle. "State's line seemed like a stone wall," the *Pittsburgh Dispatch* reported, and that line held Homestead to a TD and a field goal in the first half. But in the second half, the home team simply wore down the overmatched State players and captured a 38-0 win.

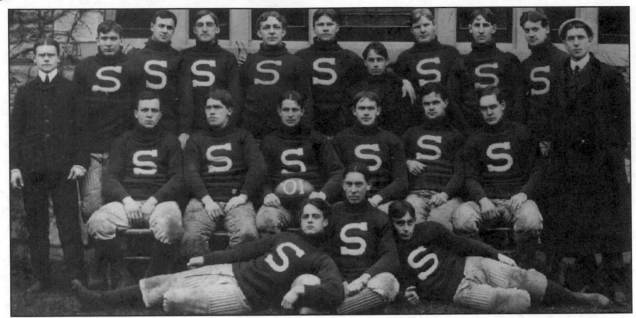

The 1901 Team put State back on the winning track as Henny Scholl returned for a sixth year, Andy Smith made his debut and legendary Earl Hewitt captained the team. Scholl and Smith are standing together in the back row, fifth and sixth from left with coach Pop Golden on the far right wearing the coat and hat. Hewitt is in the middle row holding the ball.

The team was now 3-3 and everyone was optimistic that they would attain the school's first winning season in three years. All they had to do was beat Lehigh at Williamsport and rival Dickinson at home. A possible ninth game with Gettysburg had been canceled.

Some 200 students and the Cadet Band accompanied the team on its trip to Williamsport early Saturday morning, Nov. 16. When they reached the field, they were surprised to find football players from Bucknell and dozens of Bucknell followers among the crowd. Bucknell's game with Susquehanna had been canceled, they were told, and Bucknell was there to give vocal support to Lehigh. To heck with you cheating farmers, the folks in Orange and Blue fans yelled!

The appearance of the Bucknell partisans probably brought a smile to Hewitt, Scholl and their teammates. So, we'll beat Lehigh and Bucknell, too, they thought. And as 1,500 jostling spectators watched, State proceeded to give both teams a lesson in how to play football. After trading possession twice after the kickoff, State took the ball and with Scholl and Smith alternating at "bucking the line" Scholl scored State's first touchdown. The PAT failed. Lehigh couldn't get a first down on the kickoff and as soon as State got the ball it was off to the end zone again and the rout was on. Scholl scored three more touchdowns in the second half and also kicked three PATs as State won easily, 38-0.

Another 1,500 spectators turned out in miserable, rainy weather at Beaver Field on Nov. 23 to see Scholl and Smith do it again. Smith's punting kept Dickinson out of scoring range all game and he kicked both PATs as Scholl scored touchdowns in each half to give State a 12-0 win over its number one rival.

The winning season was in the books and State would not have another losing year until 1913. A new star had been discovered. Andy Smith finished as the team's leading ground gainer and no one was happier than Hewitt, who was planning to return for a fifth year so he could be with his apprentice. Then there was old Henny Scholl. He had done it all. Without him, 1901 might have been another dismal year. He had defined the season the day he showed up back on cam-

pus in September, just as everyone knew he would.

So, now everyone looked ahead to '02. Young Smith would be "the man" for Pop Golden and Ralph Cummings, the new captain. They all figured the new season would depend as much on Smith's running and kicking ability as anything. And with two years remaining after that, Smith was all but certain to become one of Penn State's greatest football heroes, right? Perhaps he would even make Walter Camp's All-America team. And true to everyone's expectations, Smith did make Camp's All-America team, but by that time he wasn't playing for Penn State and Pop was no longer the coach.

Season Record 5-3
Record to Date 54-41-7
Winning percentage .564

"Andy Smith & The Other Kids"

Nobody expected State to come close against Yale. As the teams lined up for the kickoff in New Haven for the mid-October game, the overbearing and disdainful Eli supporters were giving 25 to 40 points to anyone foolish enough to back "the farmers."

Of course, Yale should win. The Elis were the best, the power of the "Big Four," usually winning by large margins, and, frequently keeping their opponents from scoring few, if any, points. Their fans knew the only reason they agreed to play the "farmers" from State College, Pennsylvania—wherever that is—is because they needed the practice. They had to stay sharp for the games with "real" football teams like Harvard and Princeton.

Still, the Yale players were not overconfident. They knew they were better but they also remembered last year when State had given them a good tussle. They remembered State's leaders, Earl Hewitt, the quarterback, and Henny Scholl, the tough inside runner, blocker and tackler, and that young kid, Andy Smith, who was a dandy runner, blocker and kicker.

And, yes, they knew about State's game against Pennsylvania two weeks before. Penn had won, 17-0, but not before a scare. State had taken the opening kickoff and marched right through Penn until fumbling away the ball on the 8-yard line. No one knows how that game might have turned out if State had gotten that first TD because State's offense played well all day. This was not the same team that played Penn two weeks ago or played Yale last year. Hewitt had left State after the Penn game to join Connie Mack's new pro football team in Philadelphia. Lynn Sweet, last year's center, was already with Mack. Scholl, who was no longer playing but had been helping Pop Golden coach this year, also was going pro. Ed Wood, too. A letterman in '99, Wood also was helping Golden coach and had devised some special plays and techniques to use against Yale. State would miss them all for their leadership.

Still, Yale had to admit State was a pretty good team in its class. State had won its other three games this season on shutouts and the Smith kid was looking pretty good again. What the Yale players didn't realize is that no one at State expected such a fine start for the season.

"The football outlook is certainly gloomy this year," the *State College Times* had reported on September 12, eight days before the season opener with Dickinson Seminary at Beaver Field. "Perhaps at no time in State's history has the situation been so discouraging to the coach and admirers...The fault for this is certainly not the coach...Golden has worked faithfully and earnestly to make the team of 1902 a winner, but it seems that nearly all his effort has been in vain." The problem, the reporter continued, was the lack of talent (Again?). "...after careful considering of all the available material ...State's team will be weak this year.," the writer said, bemoaning the fact that only Smith and three linemen would be back from the '01 squad. "Whitworth will not be in the line because of parental objections. Hewitt will not be able to get out because of his college work, and it is not certain that Cummings and Miles will be on the team for the same reason."

How the academic problems of Hewitt, who was playing his fifth season, Ralph Cummings, the elected captain, and Billy Miles, the veteran end, were rectified were never reported. Maybe Pop Golden did some wheeling and dealing with some of the faculty because all three were in the starting lineup on opening day, and Ed Whitworth's parents would relent later and he would be back in time for the Yale game.

What really changed the outlook—and early success—for State was the arrival of several skilled newcomers who would soon be rated among State's best players of that time. Three men in particular stood out, backs Carl Forkum and Henry "Irish" McIlveen and end Ed Yeckley. Another freshman, John Elder, would be Hewitt's back up at quarterback and take over when Hewitt left for the pros.

There was something else in State's favor—the home schedule. Never before had there been five games at Beaver Field, and the opponents were all teams State could easily defeat if everything went well. And it did.

Forkum was an immediate sensation. In the first half against Dickinson Seminary, a new opponent, Forkum scored two touchdowns in the first half, one on a 35-yard return of a punt, and teamed with

Smith, now at fullback, to run all over the visitors. Smith also had a touchdown and three PATs as State won, 27-0, in very hot weather. The *Times* reporter was impressed. "Forkum assured the side lines that he is to be one of State's ground gainers as well as a strong factor on the defensive," he wrote. "The general sentiment of the side lines was that State had some very excellent material and with the efficient corps of coaches, State's prospects for a good season is believed to be assured."

A week later against Pitt at Beaver Field, it was McIlveen's turn. Perhaps because of the muddy field conditions after an all night rain, Pop Golden started McIlveen in place of Forkum. On State's second possession of the game, after an exchange of fumbles, McIlveen dashed 35 yards for a TD, getting a key block from Hewitt. The next time State got the ball, McIlveen's 3-yard run for a touchdown climaxed a 50-yard drive in which he and Smith did most of the rushing. McIlveen just missed a third TD near the end of the half but he was tackled from behind at the 1-yard line after a 14-yard run. Forkum took over in the second half and scored a TD on a 10-yard run but wrenched his back on the play and left the game. Smith was Smith. He scored one TD, kicked two PATs and ran, tackled, blocked and kicked Pitt up one side of the field and down the other as State won, 27-0.

Forkum was back as the starter against Penn on October 4 and Yeckley made his debut at the starting left end. Forkum, Smith, and McIlveen ran well and guards Fred Dodge and Dan Junk opened big holes in the center of the line but Penn had too much manpower and won, 17-0.

Another new opponent, Villa Nova, visited Beaver Field next and State expected a close, defensive game. Villa Nova was supposed to be good but the weather was not. It rained before and during the game, keeping attendance down, and the field was extremely muddy. That didn't stop Forkum. He scored two TDs, set up two others with his running and kicked two PATs. Smith sat out for some unknown reason and another youngster, Britt Seely, scored the other TDs in the second half. Most of the game was played in Villa Nova territory as State won, 32-0.

Now the day was here. Yale at New Haven, October 18. In the opening minutes, Yale made it look easy, bashing through the State line for big yardage and scoring a quick touchdown. Just as we said it would, the Eli's supporters undoubtedly yelled. They probably felt the rout was on as they expected. But Golden and his captain, Cummings, must have said something to the team because from that point on State played as good of a game as it would play all year. The half ended 6-0. State almost got a TD in the second half on Smith's 35-yard run off a fake punt but Yale stopped it and then scored another TD late in the game to take away a tough 11-0 victory. Yale would go on to an 11-0-1 record and score 286 points while holding opponents to 22, so State's feat that day became even more impressive as the season progressed. "Penn State," wrote the great Walter Camp in Sunday's paper, "... met the hitherto unbroken stonewall lines of Yale, and not only held them to two scores, one in each half, but made things so particularly interesting that Yale was not only not in a position to make experiments by changing players, but was looking for the very best to put the game out of danger." So much for a practice game!

Back in State College, the students celebrated as if it had been a victory. They built a bonfire, marched around the campus and then held a "victory" dance at the Armory. When the team returned Monday morning, about 300 students led a parade from town to Old Main where nearly every player spoke. Pop Golden was smiling and not just because of the "moral victory." Yale had paid a $400 guarantee and the trip had cost $376.51 cents. State had made some money in the deal. Not bad, not bad.

Thus, we have the defining moment of the 1902 season. The young team, led by the kids, showed it could play on a football field with anyone, and make a financial profit at it, too. The rest of this season would be a cinch, and Pop Golden would show for the first time how football could be a profit-making sport. Despite the loss at Yale, the team would win more games than any in school history to that point. Pop would not only overhaul the finances of the football team but he would change the business structure of the entire athletic program—and get a promotion for doing it!

The following Saturday, Forkum, Smith and their teammates ran all over hapless Susquehanna, 55-0, at Beaver Field with Smith scoring five touchdowns. "Forkum and Smith carried the ball directly through the line for gains of from 5 to 25 yards [each time]," the *Times* reported. "Smith not only gained his usual amount of ground but showed up excellent in protecting and helping the end runs."

Navy claimed some of its best players were sidelined with injuries when State visited Annapolis on Nov. 1. Perhaps, it was true, or maybe it was simply a pre-game excuse in case this became the first Navy team in history to lose two-in-a-row to "the farmers." The first half was scoreless but played mainly in Navy territory. State blew the only scoring opportunity of the half when Navy blocked a field goal attempt. The defensive struggle continued into the second half. Then, with three minutes left, Navy fumbled Smith's punt and Yeckley recovered on Navy's 25-yard line. On the next play, Smith rambled around end for the touchdown and Forkum kicked the PAT. That's where it ended, 6-0, with the *Times* reporter again praising the play of Forkum and Smith: "At times, the Navy was at a loss especially in the beginning of the second half to stop State's hurdling and tandem play [of Forkum and Smith]. They seemed invincible as ground gainers."

Three games remained and all were winnable. But on the eve of the Nov. 8 game against Gettysburg at Beaver Field, there was another defining moment in the history of Penn State football, only this one wasn't good. Andy Smith quit the team!

Not only was he leaving the team, but he was leaving school—transferring to the University of Pennsylvania. Penn had offered Smith financial aid to go to school—and play football, of course. Smith said he loved Penn State and his teammates but he was having problems paying his bills. He had to work odd jobs just to cover his expenses. State could not help at all. The offer from Penn was too good to pass up.

Smith's teammates must have been stunned by his announcement. They played terribly the next day in the opening minutes against Gettysburg as the underweight visitors took the opening kickoff and drove nearly the length of the field until forced to punt at State's 25-yard line. That must have been the wake-up call. State immediately retaliated with a strong running attack that carried all the way to the Gettysburg 15-yard line before a fumble stopped the drive. But the defense got the ball back minutes later, forcing a punt, and this time State was not denied. On the first play following the punt, Ed Whitworth, starting in place of Smith, went around end and dashed 60 yards for the TD with Forkum, now playing at Smith's old fullback slot, running interference. A few minutes later, State got the ball back at Gettysburg's 25-yard line and two plays later McIlveen ran for a 20-yard TD. Before the half, State fumbled another touchdown away on the 1-yard line after another drive nearly the length of the field but scored moment

later with Forkum gong the final 10 yards. They piled it on in the second half with Whitworth scoring three more TDs and Forkum another on a dazzling 105-yard run to give State a 55-0 win—the most points scored since the 72-0 rout of Lafayette eight years earlier.

Smith apparently was a spectator at the game but he departed the next week to enroll at Penn. What no one realized at the time is that the young kid from DuBois would one day revolutionize college football on the West Coast. He played three years at fullback for Penn and was a Camp All-American in 1904. He stayed on at Penn as an assistant coach after his last season in 1905 and was the head coach from 1909 to 1913 when left for Purdue. In 1916 he became the head coach at the University of California at Berkeley and it was there that he became recognized as "the father of West Coast football." In the 10 years before his premature death in 1926, Smith's California "Wonder Teams" dominated football. Between 1920 and 1924 Cal was unbeaten with a 44-0-4 record and won one Rose Bowl and tied another.

State had two games left after Gettysburg. On Thanksgiving Day, State beat Dickinson in the "big game" at Carlisle, 23-0. Whitworth scored three touchdowns and Forkum got one touchdown on a 100-yard return of a kickoff and three PATs in leading the offense, and quarterback Elder played an outstanding defensive game. Jubilant State students paraded through the streets of Carlisle for a couple of hours, and when their train back to Lemont stopped for a short layover in Harrisburg, they marched to the governor's mansion for another impromptu celebration. Perhaps, it was an emotional letdown five days later which caused the football team to lose a close 6-5 game to the semi-pro Steelton YMCA. State probably a better team than Steelton but something just didn't jell.

The final record was 7-3, certainly a surprise from the preseason expectations. The team had scored the most points ever for State up to that time, 219, while holding opponents to just 34. Most of the kids would be back in '03 and so would Pop. They would miss Andy Smith but they had to move on. State football was on the rise and before the decade was finished the entire country would know how good Penn State's team could be—especially Andy Smith.

Season Record 7-3
Record to Date 61-44-7
Winning percentage .576

"Pop Gets the Weasels"

Washington & Jefferson wasn't on the original schedule. The Steelton YMCA was supposed to be the final opponent for the Thanksgiving Day game on Nov. 26. But Steelton had canceled a few weeks earlier and Pop Golden and his managers started hustling for an alternative.

Playing the last game of the season on Thanksgiving Day was now a tradition and for the last two years State's biggest rival Dickinson was the foe. But Thanksgiving wouldn't work out for Dickinson this year and the teams had scheduled their annual battle for Nov. 14 in Williamsport.

Why Steelton canceled was never fully explained. Player problems it was said. Geneva said the same thing about its Sept. 26 cancellation. Different excuse than West Virginia, which canceled its scheduled game of Nov. 7, supposedly because it couldn't find the right playing field. Uh, huh, and that was right after State had defeated Navy the week before. Maybe Steelton, Geneva and West Virginia were simply afraid of getting whipped—just as Pitt had been walloped in late October.

State had developed into a darn good football team under Pop Golden and was in a transitional stage of moving up in class. Many schools it once played with regularity were reluctant to play State now. Besides, there was still the problem of location. State still had to travel to meet the best competition, but Pop began to use the away games as part of his recruiting strategy, just as Joe Paterno would do decades later. So, Pop didn't mind scheduling games in Philadelphia, Pittsburgh, Harrisburg, Williamsport or Carlisle. Pittsburgh, in particular, was a fertile ground for players because so many alumni lived there and those alums touted PSC and steered the high school and prep school stars on to State.

Maybe that's how State wound up playing W&J before a then-record crowd of 7,000 at Exposition Park in Pittsburgh on Thanksgiving Day. Pop must have figured the Pittsburgh area alumni would be so happy to see their school play against a tough W&J team they would contribute heavily to his new "football fund." He already was planning to construct a building adjacent to Beaver Field that would be a housing, eating and training facility for the football players, and the more money he could generate from the alums, the quicker the project would be completed. Pop had moved all the players into the Armory that year for the first time and the Armory was a lot better than the small, cramped dormitory rooms. But wait until everyone saw the new Track House next year!

Pop also was back on the sidelines as the head coach again. When Pop had been named the school's first Athletic Director in October, he had hired Dan Reed to coach the team. But Reed had returned to Ithaca after the Dickinson game. In the short time he was in State College, Reed had done what Pop had wanted. The one-time Cornell guard, who had been a third-team All-American in '98 and had played against State in the famous "hidden ball trick" game of '97, coached just three games. But he had given the team a fresh, mid-season impetus. As the *State College Times* of Nov. 6 had noted, "[Reed's] system of coaching has been a revelation...The ex-Cornell guard is onto every trick of the game and knows how to teach 'em all too."

With Reed gone, Pop asked Charlie Aull, the captain of the '91 team, and a couple of other ex-players to help him get the team ready for W&J. They already knew that they had to beat W&J to have another winning season. They were 4-3 but coming off a disappointing 6-0 upset loss to big rival Dickinson 12 days before. Many of their followers didn't think they had much of a chance against a W&J team known for its "unsportsmanlike" behavior and intimidating rough-house play. Still, the State team had surprised many observers who had been alarmed when only seven players reported to the first day of practice on September 1.

However, by the time the team opened the season against Dickinson Seminary at Beaver Field on September 19, there was a good mix of veterans and newcomers who had come together as a team under the training of Pop and Lynn Sweet. Sweet, the center in '01 who had played for Connie Mack's professional team last year, was

helping Pop in the preseason. Sweet was particularly enthusiastic about a quiet, but aggressive and hard-hitting freshman from Youngstown, Ohio, named William Dunn.

Dunn was playing at Sweet's old center position. At 22, he was older than most of his teammates because he had worked several years in the steel mills to get enough money for his education. He was heavier and taller than his teammates, too, and his body looked like it was made of the steel he had forged back in Youngstown. Surprisingly, he had never played football in high school or the sandlots but on an impulse decided to try out for State's football team. He had read somewhere about "a flying tackle" and on his first day of practice he tried to make a "flying tackle" during a scrimmage. Bam! He hit the runner like a sledge-hammer. From that moment on, Dunn was the team's starting center. A few days later, Dunn was selected freshman class president, and as he was leading some fellow frosh across campus to challenge the sophomores in a school "rush," an upperclassman teased: "There goes Mother Dunn and all her baby chicks." The nickname caught on and William Dunn was no more. "Mother" Dunn would become one of the greatest players in Penn State football.

Pop felt optimistic with Dunn and another standout freshman, tackle Andy Moscrip, joining such veterans as ends Ed Yeckley and Art Biesicker and tackle Jim Arbuthnot in the line. He also had a veteran backfield of quarterback Fred ("Jack") Elder, halfbacks Irish McIlveen and Ed Whitworth and Fullback Carl Forkum. State opened with a 60-0 romp over Dickinson Seminary. Whitworth, now the captain (obviously with parental permission), scored the first touchdown of the season on a run around right end after a short punt early in the game. Forkum booted the PAT and scored the next touchdown himself. The score was 16-0 at the half and Pop substituted freely in the second half.

Geneva canceled at midweek, claiming injuries had decimated its team, so Pop scheduled an intrasquad game between the varsity and scrubs for that Saturday. Dunn and Moscript played with the scrubs and they beat the varsity 6-0 as several varsity players, including Forkum and Elder, went down with injuries. Next time, Pop, let the scrubs play Geneva!

Forkum missed the next game against Allegheny at Beaver Field on Oct. 3 but not Elder, who scored the first TD on a 45-yard run as State took the opening kickoff and made it look easy with a 7-play, 100-yard drive. Elder booted the PAT and about four minutes later McIlveen plunged over from the one on another quick 5-play, 65-yard drive. Elder booted the PAT and it was 12-0 just like that. Another thrashing was on! Not this time, fellows.

Maybe it was State's' overconfidence. Or maybe the power of prayer, since Allegheny was a theology school at the time. Allegheny's coach, Hachman gathered his players at the sideline and, as the *Times* reported, "ad-

Former Cornell All-American Dan Reed succeeded Golden as coach in the middle of the 1903 season. He left after three games belying the stability of the coaching staff that now exists.

dressed several urgent phrases to his men which sounded like passages of the scripture." Whether it was Providence or not, a penalty and fumble put State back in deep punt formation and when the punter Whitworth dropped the ball, Allegheny recovered at the State 5-yard line. Three plays later, Allegheny scored the first points given up by a State team at Beaver Field in 14 games, with a one-yard run around end for touchdown. The extra point was missed but it didn't matter. The Allegheny partisans went wild as the State players sulked. Near the end of the half, Whitworth scored again, Elder got the PAT and State went on to win, 24-5. "The varsity's play throughout was ragged and unaggressive with a few exceptions," the *Times* reporter wrote, adding that a major improvement would be needed to have any chance against Penn.

They didn't stand a chance against Penn anyway. With their former teammate, Andy Smith, leading the way, Penn scored the most points against State in five years in a 39-0 stomping. The next week Yale made up for its embarrassment the previous year by blasting State, 27-0, in an all-out slugging match, scoring three touchdowns in the second half to overcome a stiff State defense. But both defeats had been predictable. While still not in the class of the "Big Four," State was a solid team. "...our boys fought valiantly from start to finish," reported the *Times*, after the Yale game, "and according to Yale's own statement, gave her the hardest battle this season...Judging from present indications, for State's team play is showing steady improvement, and if 'grit' added to aggressive play is forthcoming in large enough quantities, there is no reason why we shouldn't win every remaining game on the schedule."

For the first time ever, the Pitt game was scheduled at Pittsburgh. State had won all five games since the series began in 1893 and was favored to make it six straight. Reed arrived from Ithaca in time to help prepare the players. "...Reed is an elegant coach," the *Times* reported, "and will probably benefit State's team immensely, as the men are already working together in pretty fair shape." It was quite a debut for Reed. As would eventually become customary in the future of this hostile series, Pitt's coaches and players whined before the game about the character and integrity of State's players. They were professionals, not college kids, Pitt complained. In describing the dispute later, the *Times* reporter put on paper what would become another attribute of Penn State football for the next 100 plus years. "Let it be said and right here," the *Times* said, "that's State's present status in athletics is as clean as possible, and 100 per cent cleaner than that of many of our prominent colleges."

Pitt's accusations must have made State angry as Forkum, McIlveen, Whitworth and the boys went out and pounded Pitt, 59-0, in what would be the biggest margin of victory for 65 years. Forkum set an all-time individual scoring record with 38 points on 5 TDs and 9-of-10 PATs and rushed for some 200 yards but neither of his achievements are noted in State's athletic record books. McIlveen had two TDs on runs of 41 and 56 yards. Back on campus, the students built a bonfire at Beaver Field to celebrate the win but that was only a prelude to their celebration the next weekend.

They burned down the old Beaver Field grandstand the next Saturday night after word reached State College that Navy had fallen for the third straight year, 17-0. It was a rough game with injuries to players on both teams but State dominated the game. Navy gained only two first downs and got as close as the State 10-yard line just once. Whitworth scored a TD in the first five minutes on a 50-yard run

around end and then kicked a 30-yard field goal before the half to give State an 11-0 lead. Forkum finished the scoring with a touchdown and two PATs. Another field goal and a couple of potential touchdowns were voided by some questionable officiating. The *Times* credited Reed's coaching for much of the victory, saying "...the team's improvement has been simply wonderful for the last two weeks...through the coaching of Reed, our linemen are learning to give the back field the necessary support and assistance on offense or defense."

Before the team could start preparing for West Virginia, the game was canceled and Reed and the players shifted their focus to the biggest rival, Dickinson. The game was set for November 14 at Williamsport and the two week wait enabled the injured players to recover. McIlveen was the most seriously hurt. He had torn the ligaments in his knee after a scrimmage with the scrubs and doctors said he might miss the rest of the season. Moscrip also was hurt as was guard L.R. White. But they were all in the starting lineup when Dickinson kicked off at 2 p.m. on a cold but windless day. Dickinson also had gotten a new coach at midseason and maybe that's why the game was a lot closer than anyone expected.

This may have been the best played game in the entire 16-game series with Dickinson that lasted until 1931. There was hard running and hard tackling on both sides as the teams went up and down the field in the first half without any scoring. At one point Forkum was carried off the field after a vicious tackle that *he* had made on Dickinson's halfback Rich but he returned minutes later. Dickinson fumbled on the first play after the second half kickoff and State recovered at the Dickinson 31-yard line. It took State eight hard-earned smashes into Dickinson's line to reach the 9-yard line from where, on third down, Whitworth tried what looked like an easy field goal. But it was blocked and Dickinson took over. Dickinson punted out of the hole and as the clocked ticked away the two teams hammered at each other again, neither one able to gain much ground before kicking the ball away.

With just a couple minutes left, State made a daring gamble. It was the type of decision that Bob Higgins, Rip Engle and Joe Paterno would be proud of. With the ball at its own 46-yard line and inches to go for a first down, Reed called for a run for the first down instead of a punt. Dunn centered the ball to State's best back, Forkum. Bam, up the middle! But, no! He didn't make it! Dickinson's ball.

What happened in the next few minutes is not unlike what happened many times in the ensuing 94 years of Penn State football. Five yards, first down Dickinson. No gain. Five yards, first down Dickinson. Yeckley, Moscrip, Arbuthnot, Forkum, McIlveen all tried to stop the Dickinson runner but Dickinson moved the ball relentlessly. And why not? It was the former State man, Brit Seely, a little known sub on PSC's '02 team, doing the brunt of the running for Dickinson. Seely for a first down. Seely for another first down. Seely for still another first down. In 14 hard-fought plays, Dickinson had the ball on State's 5-yard line. Less than a minute left. First down, no gain. On second down, Seely smashed his way to within inches of the State goal line. Forty seconds were left in the game. Everyone knew what was coming next and it did. Seely—bam, bam—TOUCHDOWN! Dickinson's fans went wild. The PAT was good. Dickinson kicked off and two plays later it was over. The "Dicks" had won 6-0 and fans from both sides swarmed onto the field to commend their players. Someone had to lose but what a game!!! Dickinson would not win again for another 28 years, and in less than four years, Pitt would replace Dickinson as

State's bitterest rival. This was the last hurrah for Dickinson and the significance of the game didn't last a week. "State's biggest game of this decade," as the *Times* put it in it's Nov. 27 edition, was set for Thanksgiving Day in Pittsburgh and "our defeat by Dickinson [while] hard to beat will be all forgiven if our boys beat W & J."

State had not played W&J since the scoreless '99 game which had ended prematurely after an on-field brawl involving players and spectators at Beaver Field. None of the current State players had been in that game but they had been hearing about it for years. Henny Scholl and Earl Hewitt told them all about the slugging, elbowing and, especially, the vicious out-of-bounds hit on Billy Burns that ignited the brawl. W&J believed it still was the toughest team in Pennsylvania, if not Ohio, West Virginia and other nearby states, and the team expected a vengeful victory over "the farmers" to prove it once and for all. State and its followers anticipated the roughest game of the year, even more violent than the one against Yale. "It is hoped that both sides will play clean football," wrote the *Times* reporter before the game. "W&J has made an enviable reputation for herself this season at home by unsportsmanlike methods but we hope the 'Red and Black' will brace up and do the right thing." The *Times* writer declared that State would play a "clean game" no matter what and picked State to win by 10 points.

There would be one major change in State's team. Reed had gone back to Cornell, perhaps abashed by the hard loss to Dickinson. Pop was back as the coach and in the 10 days of practice leading up to the game he had help from old Charlie Aull, the captain of the '91 team. Judging from the way the game turned out, Charlie must have taught Yeckley, Whitworth and the boys a few combat tricks from the old days.

Despite an intense cold and a periodic blinding snowstorm, the 7,000 fans hooped and hollered throughout the game. But it was all but over by halftime. State made few mistakes in the entire game

and manhandled the bigger W&J players. That the game was rough was undeniable and at least one W&J player was carried off the field with dislocated ribs and missing teeth. Pop's boys took the opening kickoff and in four quick rushes picked up 50 yards. Soon, Forkum ran across for the first touchdown and before the half ended he had another. During the half, State's brass Cadet Band "paraded with military precision around the gridiron...[and] the crowd simply went wild." The enthusiasm from State's fans carried into the second half and State pounded W&J unmercifully as Whitworth and Yeckley also scored touchdowns and State won easily, 22-0, in what was the defining moment of the season.

That night the team and its Pittsburgh area alumni celebrated with a big banquet that helped raise more money for Pop's futuristic endeavors in his Athletic Department. Folks talked about making this an annual Thanksgiving tradition in Pittsburgh, playing a game against W&J with a follow up banquet after the game. When the idea was broached to W&J, it decided to pass. The beating before the virtually hometown crowd apparently had been too humiliating for W&J. But, in the next few weeks, Pitt would pick up on the holiday game suggestion and the two teams would create one of the greatest and most competitive rivalries in football. But that would have to wait another year. And Pop would not be the coach then.

Officially, Pop wasn't the coach this year. Dan Reed is listed as the coach of record in Penn State's football history. But Reed was there for just three games and he lost the "big one" against Dickinson. This stalwart team was really Pop's and, if he had been coaching, maybe he wouldn't have lost to Dickinson. No matter, Pop and his players defined the moment. No one could out hustle State this year. Just ask the weasles. Both of 'em—W&J and Pitt!

**Season Record 5-3
Record to Date 66-47-7
Winning percentage .579**

CHAPTER 5

THE FIRST "FULL-TIME" COACH

1904-1908

Dan Reed told Pop Golden he thought his old Cornell team-mate, Tom Fennell might be interested in helping coach the State team in '04.

Tom's a lawyer up in Elmira, Dan probably said, but I think he misses football a little. Let's see if we can get him down here to talk to us, Pop may have replied, and show him our friendly little campus.

Fennell must have been impressed when he first visited the Penn State campus. He had heard all about the "farmers" down there in those mountains and he knew how difficult it was to get there. The picturesque countryside probably reminded him of Ithaca, and the enthusiasm and spirit of the students and faculty had to bring back warm memories of his undergraduate days at Cornell. He was probably a little surprised by the sparkling new Track House adjacent to Beaver Field and its little grandstand that Reed had told him about. Construction was almost complete. Full-time housing and training facilities for the football players and a training table too. Just like the big time. Wow!

And the players he met surely encouraged him. That Dunn lad, "Mother" they call him, looks solid as a rock. Yeckley, Moscrip, McIlveen and Forkum, the captain, they sure look like they can play, just as Dan said. Look a little bigger and faster than those fellows I played against in '97. Maybe not yet in the class of the "Big Four" but getting there, yes, getting there.

Pop told Fennell he wanted to hire him to coach the team full time in the fall. No other duties. President Atherton had agreed. Fennell said the offer was a good one but he still couldn't give up his law practice back in Elmira. Okay, Pop said, you be here whenever you can during the football season and when you're not here I'll do the coaching. They shook hands, and so began the five-year Fennell era at Penn State.

Fennell was never on campus for the entire season. He would be there for two-to-eight weeks each year. At other times, Pop Golden would run things on the practice field and during the games. The players weren't always happy about the arrangement but they came to accept it. They respected Pop so much that they simply followed his leadership. The team captain and some of the other veterans would run the practices when Pop couldn't be there and usually there were a couple of former players on campus to assist in the training and help out during the games. The players soon realized Fennell had a mind for football techniques, tactics and strategy. Fennell was so renown for his football knowledge that some of the new professional football teams would often seek him out for advice. In fact, one of the greatest pro teams of all time, the Canton Bulldogs, spent several days on the State campus in the middle of the 1906 season to get guidance and instruction from Fennell.

What football Pop didn't know, Fennell did. And like Pop, Fennell also knew how to relate to people, especially the temperamental athlete—encouraging them when they needed it and criticizing them constructively when they faltered. And, boy, could he talk. His halftime speeches became legendary.

Fennell's five-year tenure also was marked by change. Enrollment more than double from the time Fennell started in 1904 until he left after 1908, when the student body was about 2,000. It was a time of turmoil on campus. The student body was growing and wanted a bigger voice in self-government. In 1905 there were nearly 700 full time students and at one point during the year they staged a major protest, walking out of classes because of rules about cutting classes around holidays and vacations. (Little progress has been made on this issue in 100 years for in the 1997-98 academic year Penn State students were still complaining about having to be in class on days before holidays and vacations!) In July of 1906, the football team's major benefactor, President Atherton, died. A full time successor would not be found for two years and his death fractured the academic and administrative structure of the college. No one seemed to be in charge and this caused anxiety throughout every facet of the college, including the Athletic Department.

The rules of football were changing too. The rule makers were under pressure to lessen the brutality and open up the game. Passing started to come into vogue but everything seemed to change from one year to the next. Players were easily confused and it was up to the coaches, Golden and Fennell, to keep the team stabilized. Pop was the steady hand throughout. He was not only concerned about the team's play on the field but also the facilities.

Pop knew the college needed a new playing field. The team was outgrowing Beaver Field. Playing two or three games a year at home against the weaker teams was no longer practical. More revenue was needed to support the football team, which had grown to several dozen players and a scrub team as well as the varsity. At 50 cents a seat, little money could be produced in a site holding no more than 500-800 spectators. The team was playing away games before crowds of 5,000-to-8,000 in Philadelphia, Pittsburgh, Harrisburg and elsewhere. Pop envisioned a home field so big it could easily provide the type of financial guarantees that would attract even the most reluctant oppo-

The Track House opened in 1904 thanks to the fund raising efforts of Pop Golden. It was adjacent to Old Beaver Field and offered full-time housing and training facilities for the players and other athletes. For 20 years, the Track House was a prime recruiting tool as State built up its football program to compete with the major powers in the country.

nent to travel to "isolated" State College. Think of the type of players who would come here, too, he told anyone who would listen.

So, as Fennell helped develop the team on the field, Pop worked behind the scenes on everything else. Obviously, it worked. Tom Fennell would reluctantly quit coaching at the conclusion of the 1908 season to devote full time to the law. He would not have a losing season, finishing with a 37-17-1 record. He would produce the first of State's all-time great teams in 1906 and would create the environment for even further glory in the future.

Not bad for Penn State's first 'full-time' coach.

1904

"Injuries, Injuries & More Injuries"

Carl Forkum was having another brilliant day running and kicking. The Penn State captain already had one touchdown and two extra points against Washington & Jefferson and had just been tackled after another long run deep into W&J's territory. He was rising slowly to his feet when it happened! W&J's left end Hupp smashed into him from the blind slide with a savage hit that sent Forkum into the air. Hupp was going full speed and caught Forkum with a forearm from an angle at the side and a little low, and the shocked crowd at Pittsburgh's Exposition Park winced as Forkum fell hard onto the turf.

The State fans booed while the W&J partisans cheered and as Pop Golden and others ran from the sidelines towards Forkum's still body, players from both sides jostled each other and for a moment it looked like a major brawl would break out. It had been a rough game as expected and W&J had been playing dirty as usual. The four game officials had done little to restrain W&J, especially the umpire Art Poe of Princeton, who not only ignored the slugging by W&J players but also went out of his way to call penalties against State. Pop insisted that his players not retaliate and use dirty tactics themselves. He told his team to hit hard and to simply out play the SOBs, and that's precisely what they were doing when Forkum went down.

State was already ahead, 12-0, late in the second half and everyone knew the score would have been higher if not for some bad

calls by Poe at crucial times. The despicable hit on the popular State captain was almost more than the State players could take, but, reluctantly, they continued to heed Coach Golden's counsel about playing clean, and as a dazed and injured Forkum watched from the sideline in the last few minutes of an abbreviated 20-minute half, State insured the victory with an aggressive defense.

The win was the third in five games for State and the rest of the 10-game schedule favored State. But the illegal hit on Forkum would be the defining moment of the '04 season. It also brought about a temporary end to the games against W&J.

"There are few college teams on the gridiron today that play cleaner football than the eleven representing the White and Blue..." wrote the reporter for the State College *Times*, after the game. "The attempts of several W&J players to play "dirty ball" against State were so apparent that they cannot but reflect discredit upon the Washington institution. If this annual game cannot be decided by hard, clean, manly football, then it is time that the old rivals should cease playing."

They did. The W&J series was terminated and not resumed again until 1912. By that time, Pitt (still known then as the University of Western Pennsylvania) had surpassed W&J as a regional football power, and State's annual Thanksgiving Day game against Pitt in Pittsburgh had become one of the best traditional rivalries in college football, and every bit as rough as the old games with W&J.

Before his injury, Forkum had been playing the best football of his career. He had dedicated himself in pre-season practice and was enthusiastically leading the 50 varsity and scrub players around the campus on the strenuous one mile jogs which wound up the workouts each night. State captains were expected to take charge when the coaches weren't around but Forkum was into it even during the daily 3:30-6:30 p.m. sessions organized by Coaches Golden, Fennell and their assistants. He would lead the team up and down Beaver Field several times in the warm ups. When they broke into their three squads of linemen, ends and backs, he would occasionally wander from group to group shouting encouragement. He would hit the tackling dummies as hard as anyone during the first half hour of tackling drills and he was booming his punts so well during the half hour of kicking and running drills that even the press was taking notice. "Captain Forkum has improved to a great extent both in the length of his punts and the speed and accuracy with which he gets them away," the *Times* reporter had written. During the final 30 minutes of the day when the varsity scrimmaged the scrubs, Forkum would run as if he was playing Penn—the opening opponent of the '04 season.

This was not a team of great depth and Forkum and the coaches knew it. Of the 24 men at the training table in the new Track House, Forkum was the only returnee from last year's high scoring backfield, although Irish McIlveen might be back if he could overcome his personal problems in Pittsburgh. The candidates for the backfield were so thin that the new head coach, Tom Fennell, was planning to move Big Ed Yeckley from end to halfback to take advantage of his "ground gaining" talent, but the quarterback slot would have to be handled by a couple of untested seniors. Mother Dunn and Andy Moscrip were as good as anyone in the country up front but it would be a rebuilt line that would depend on a couple of newcomers, like Cal Moorehead at end and Charlie Smith at tackle, to make everything work. One bright spot was the kicking game where Forkum was taking full advantage of some new punting rules and Moscrip, of all people, looked like the best dropkicker ever seen on the State campus. Golden and Fennell knew the team could not afford many injuries or the 10-game schedule could turn into a disaster, and when Dunn, with a sore knee, and Yeckley, with a charley horse, missed most of practice in the week leading up to the opener with Penn, the coaches bemoaned their luck.

It had been 12 years since Penn had been the season opener and the newspapers were saying this was the best Penn team in years with the former State star, Andy Smith, leading the way as captain. So, when the students back in State College heard the halftime score of 0-0 they didn't believe it. They were even more doubtful when they learned the final at Franklin Field was just 6-0 in Penn's favor. One touchdown? Penn had never scored less than 17 points in the previous 12 games. When the students realized the score was correct, they paraded around State College with the Cadet Band leading the way, then started a large bonfire near "the ruins of the old Inn." On Monday, everyone learned that Penn had barely won, scoring the only points in the last minute of the game. The administration and faculty canceled the second period class to allow the students to welcome the team home in the traditional parade and ceremony, pulling the cart full of players through town and up to Old Main, where all the players spoke.

"Our team not only played Penn to a stand still but actually outplayed them in nearly every department," reported the *Times*. "Notwithstanding the final score...all the Philadelphia papers admitted that State played the better football and that Pennsy's only touchdown...was a very lucky one for the 'Red and Blue'." Forkum's punting had been a key to the close game as had the play calling and punt returns of the new senior quarterback Joe Saunders. The narrow loss would become even more significant as the season went on because Penn would finish the season unbeaten at 12-0 and former teammate Smith would be selected First Team All-America by Walter Camp.

There was one bad omen. While making a tackle on a Penn running back, Dunn reinjured the shoulder he had dislocated last year against Dickinson. He would sit out the home opener against Allegheny and see if he could be ready for the Yale game on October 8. Actually, everyone was looking one week beyond to the game at New Haven, including the local press. Scheduling such tough games at the start of the season was not wise, the *Times* reporter wrote, but it was equally imprudent to have more than five or six tough games a year. "...The necessity of easing up the football schedule is a very urgent one," he wrote, "to give the team breathing space" between "big" games. Maybe, but Forkum and his teammates would not have wanted any other arrangement than to play the best.

The enthusiasm from the close loss to Penn carried over in the week before the Allegheny game. As the coaches ran the team through practice at Beaver Field that week, the students turned out in droves to encourage the team with applause and a new cheer:

("Siss! Boom! Ah! Cuckoo!!! (Pause) The team! The team! The Team!!!)

Allegheny was too easy for "The Team!!!" Forkum had another great scoring day in a 50-0 romp on October 1. He had the first touchdown within a minute and eventually got five TDs, including one on a record 115-yard kickoff return, and kicked 2 PATs. Perhaps remembering last year's game when Allegheny surprised everybody by becoming the first opponent to score at Beaver Field in years, State held the visitors without a first down in a game cut short by 10 minutes at the request of the Allegheny coach.

Dunn was back for the Yale game but, as expected, State lost, 24-0. Yale simply wore down the undermanned State team. Be-

cause of State's defense, Yale did not score until more than midway through the first half but then tallied two TDs in each half for the win. "In all the newspaper accounts," wrote the *Times*, "State was given great credit for her plucky, scientific play, which made the Yale men work mightily for every point scored."

Fennell left the team after the Yale game to take care of his legal business in Elmira and would not return for a month. As the team practiced under Pop

Tom Fennell didn't completely give up his law practice in Elmira, N.Y. to become State's first "full-time" coach in 1904. With a little help from Pop Golden, he managed to do both for five years.

Golden's direction for its first ever game with West Virginia the following week at home, tackle Charlie Smith decided to skip classes and practice and take the day off. Pop was furious and threatened to suspend Smith. Pop must have put the fear of God into Smith for the big tackle went out the next Saturday and played like Forkum. He scored three TDs and gained 137 yards on 10 carries and was a demon on defense and punt coverage, stopping WVU's only serious scoring threat with a flying tackle to end a 70-yard punt runback. His frenzied performance forever earned him the name of "Rough House" Smith from the *Times* reporter, who also praised Forkum, who had one TD and 4 PATs and a sensational day of punting with one punt going 65 yards. The students were so happy about how the team played, they ran out onto the field and carried the players off on their shoulders to Pop's new Track House.

In the week before the W&J game, McIlveen returned to campus eager to play, but he needed time to get into shape and was not expected to be ready for at least three weeks. Forkum's injury against W&J accelerated McIlveen's workouts for it was apparent that Forkum's recovery would be slow and his return uncertain. When Westminster canceled its October 29 game at Beaver Field, Golden was able to schedule a pro team from nearby Jersey Shore to fill in but the pros were no match for State's varsity. Pop was able to rest his best players, including Yeckley, Dunn, Smith and Saunders. McIlveen came in as a substitute late in the game and the first time he carried the ball he ran for 50 yards much to the delight of the crowd. State won 30-0 as five different players scored TDs and Moscrip booted five PATs.

Dunn's shoulder injury was more serious than originally believed and he did not play the next week at Navy. Forkum tried but lasted only three minutes and went to the sidelines for the rest of the game. With a new end run formation developed by Pop, State outgained the Middies and McIlveen ran well while playing most of the second half. But without Forkum and Dunn the team was not sharp and fumbled frequently. Fumbles led to both Navy TDs and one of the two field goals as Navy beat State for the first time in four years, 22-9.

Pop and the players had no time to reflect on the Navy loss. The "biggest" game of the season was next—Dickinson at Williamsport November 12. Fennell returned that week to take charge again and he and Pop got the team properly motivated. Dunn was on the field but Forkum was back home when the teams kicked off promptly at 3 p.m. before a roaring crowd. State took the opening kick and methodically moved deep into Dickinson's territory before fumbling and was forced to punt. Moments later, they had the ball again and in 11 plays they marched 57 yards to the Dickinson 7-yard line when suddenly the injury jinx hit again. Moscrip was not getting up from the bottom of the pile and was writhing in pain. His day and his career was over. He had a broken collarbone. One play later, McIlveen, kicking in place of Moscrip, tried a field goal from a tough angle at the 15-yard line and missed by several yards. With new life, Dickinson's defense began to play better and although the entire half was played in Dickinson's territory, State never got close again. At one point, a Dickinson tackle named "Davy" Davis tried to injure State's quarterback Saunders by violently twisting Saunders' ankle after a tackle. A penalty was called and Saunders limped off the field and did not return until the second half.

During the halftime break, Pop Golden brought Bill Murray, the tough old center and captain of the '98 team, into the locker room to give a pep talk. Fennell and Pop spoke too. It must have been some oration. "State's team came dashing out of the field with renewed vigor and determination, spurred on by [the] spirited words...," the *Times* reported. Dickinson took the kickoff but could not get a first down and punted. McIlveen grabbed the punt and darted 35 yards to the Dickinson 33-yard line. Six plays later junior George McGee of Clearfield, playing fullback for the absent Forkum, bulled over from the 7-yard line for a touchdown. Saunders, still feeling the effects from his twisted ankle, missed the PAT. State got the ball back a few minutes later and with McGee gaining 43 yards on six carries, State moved 78 yards in 13 plays for the second TD with Yeckley, the captain in place of Forkum, going over from the two. Saunders was perfect this time and made the score 11-0 as the State fans went wild, throwing their hats onto the field and screaming and yelling at the top of their lungs. For all intent, the game was over—but not quite. During the second TD drive, Dickinson's Davis again tried to take Saunders out of the game with a sharp knee to the back as the quarterback lay on the ground. A few plays after the State kickoff, the referee watched (and smiled) but did nothing when McIlveen smashed into Davis with a hit so vicious Davis had to be carried off the field and he never returned. That one was for Forkie and Mossie, McIlveen yelled!

State had won "THE GAME" once again. However, it would be one of the '05 team's last days of glory. Geneva, a new opponent, was beaten easily, 44-0, at Beaver Field a week later as Yeckley scored three TDs and kicked 4 PATs and "Rough House" Smith also had a couple TDs. Even without Forkum and Moscrip, the State players had expected to beat Pitt on Thanksgiving Day at Exposition Park. After all, State had not only won all six previous games with Pitt but had scored 177 points to Pitt's four.

However, this was a vastly different Pitt team. It was unbeaten and unscored upon and had amassed 304 points. The State players obviously compared schedules and decided Pitt had not played anyone of any caliber, such as a Yale or Penn. They were wrong. State was outplayed almost from the opening kickoff. And when Yeckley, their leader, went out with an injury early in the game, the team lost its fighting spirit. As 8,500 watched, Pitt won "unexpectedly and decisively" 22-5 in what was described as a "catastrophe" but a "clean" game. Earl Hewitt, the veteran captain of the '01 team, wept openly on the State sideline. "If three of [Pitt's] stars had been out of the game,

the Gold and Blue would have been up against it just as badly as State was," reported the *Times*. Probably true. But as Paterno would say 80 years later, and probably coaches Fennell and Golden said then, injuries are part of the game.

No doubt the injury to Forkum was devastating. His leadership was as vital to the team as his playing ability. Without him, the team was never the same. The team's record could easily have been 8-2 but injuries to Forkum and others hurt them badly. History tells us that one man can make a difference in life and for the 1904 Penn State football team, one man did.

Season Record 6-4
Record to Date 72-51-7
Winning percentage .581

"The Yale(boys) & The Indians"

The Indians came first. Then Yale. They were as good as they come in college football, and Penn State had never beaten either team.

State had played the Carlisle Indians only once before, almost 10 years ago, and the Indians had clobbered that '96 team, 48-5. Since then, the Indians had gotten even better under the coaching of Glenn "Pop" Warner. And Yale? My God, in five games played since the first one in '99, State had been outscored 126 to Zero! Zero, mind you, Zero! Of course, all those games had been on the road. None of the big guys would visit Penn State. Never had. Too isolated, they said.

So, for State to prove it could play football with the best, the team had to travel constantly. Only the lower class or inferior teams agreed to play at Beaver Field—teams such as Lebanon Valley and California (PA) Normal, which would help State open this year's season. Even teams at State's level didn't want to play "in the mountains." That was why the annual games with the school's biggest rival, Dickinson, was always some other place. Navy, too. State beat them three times and tied once but this year's 10th game in the series would be at Annapolis again. At least they wouldn't have to play at Franklin Field this year. Penn was off the schedule for the first time in 10 years, but Gettysburg was back on for the first time in three years. That didn't mean Pop was easing back on the schedule though, just insuring that there weren't more "big" games than the team could handle.

As he juggled the schedule, Pop also decided to take advantage of the home field if possible. So, he set up seven home games. Westminster bowed out of the Sept. 23 date, but the six games were still the most that would ever be played in one season at Old Beaver Field. The State players knew they would be favored in every home game. All of the tough games would be on the road, starting with the Indians on Oct. 7 in Harrisburg. Everyone wondered if this team was up to the challenge.

This would be a young team, with some 20 freshmen making the 32-man roster. Five key players, including Forkum and Moscrip, had graduated but nine others were back, including the two team leaders, halfback-kicker Ed Yeckley and center "Mother" Dunn. Yeckley was the captain. Dunn, the fearless junior, had started every game in the last two years. Yeckley, wrote the reporter for the *State College Times* on the eve of the first game, is "a leader of unusual grit and aggressiveness; and the infusion of his spirit into the varsity team will mean an aggregation of nervy fighters" for State. The reporter raved about the "exceptionally husky squad" and the freshmen, which he said, are "by far the best looking lot of youngsters seen on Beaver Field for many years."

But there was an omen that would come back and haunt this team as the season progressed. Coach Tom Fennell was busy with his law work in Elmira and would not join the team until midseason. Pop Golden was doing the coaching with the assistance of the wily old tough guy from earlier years, Leroy "Henny" Scholl. Pop and Henny were good, no doubt about it. But, in retrospect, Fennell's style of coaching, with his emphasis on offensive techniques, might have made a difference in the outcome of a couple of games, including the first big one with the Indians.

As expected, State blew past Lebanon Valley in the September 16 opener, 23-0, in what the *Times* reporter said was a "listless game" in which "State's back-field [sic] was slow in getting off plays..." The sloppy offensive play carried over into the first half of the next game against California Normal. The 85 degrees temperature was "really far too hot for football, the *Times* reporter wrote, "...[and] State's team played miserable football [in the first half], getting their plays off aimlessly and fumbling outrageously..." The game was scoreless at the intermission but "Between halves State Coaches and Captain Yeckley gave the squad a spirited talking to, and the men looked determined when they came out for the second half...and urged on by the enthusiasm of 700 loyal students, the varsity jumped in and played some real football." Mother Dunn came through with his specialty in the first minute of the second half and blocked a California punt, leading to a quick TD, and State rolled on to a 29-0 victory. But the defining moment of the season had been set—State's defense would have to carry the team until the offense got going. It didn't help that the Carlisle Indians were next.

The festive atmosphere for the game on Oct. 7 was not unlike a typical Penn State game of today. The crowds began streaming into Harrisburg's Island Park an hour and a half before the 2:30 p.m. kickoff. The fans were noisy and enthusiastic with thousands of Indians' supporters cheering from the bleachers on the west side and an equal number of State fans yelling from across the field. The weather was perfect with "a glorious October Sun [sic]" pumping up the eventual crowd of 8,000. "...for half an hour preceding the game, the rival bands fought for supremacy, while the cheers and yells of the rivals echoed and re-echoed across the field," the *Times* reported. "Finally, the lusty squad of Carlisle braves, numbering over fifty, and resplendent in their flaunting 'gold and maroon' sweaters, dashed down the side lines amid an uproar. Then State's squad of 20 stockily build warriors trotted out led by Captain Yeckley and the State stands aroused enmassed, and welcomed them with a thunderous cheer."

Of course, State was a heavy underdog but as Joe Paterno would often say decades later, kicking and defense wins games. That's precisely what happened on this day as the game came down to Carlisle's tremendous punting, both teams' tough defense, and State's ineffective offense. The Indians' great quarterback, Mt. Pleasant, averaged 42 yards on nine punts, including two quick kicks, that kept State bottled up throughout the game. Carlisle had the edge in punt returns too. "Neither eleven showed good offensive power," the *Times* reporter wrote in his coverage of the game, "...although the Indians outclassed State in ground gaining ability." The Indians also showed better "speed and interference" while "on the defense State's men performed grandly, their all around tackling being especially fine."

Carlisle won, 11-0, but the scoring didn't come easy. The Indians tallied their first touchdown 15 minutes into the first half on a rugged 13-play, 50-yard drive but missed the extra point. The second touchdown and extra point came midway through the second half after an exchange of punts gave the Indians great field position on the State 24-yard line, but it took them 10 hard-fought plays to cross the goal.

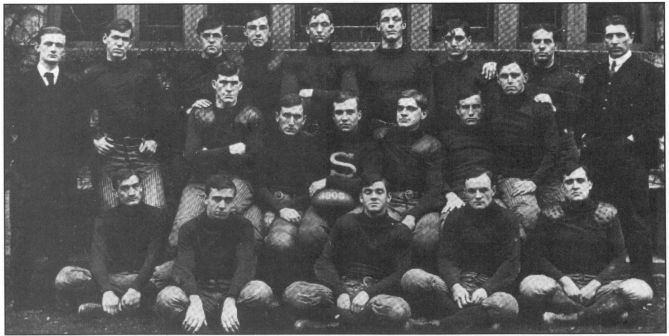

The young 1905 team won more games than any State team to date and gave the mighty Carlisle Indians and undefeated Yale all they could handle. The school's first First Team All-American, "Mother" Dunn is standing in the last row (fifth from left) and captain Ed Yeckley is in the middle row holding the ball.

State's offense never threatened and State played most of the game in its own territory or at midfield.

Yeckley, Dunn and their teammates were disappointed but not crushed. They knew they had a great defensive team. They just needed to keep trying to improve their offensive game before playing that Yale bunch. They didn't have much time. Yale was just two weeks away.

Gettysburg was next. In eight previous games, Gettysburg had not scored a point. State kept the scoreless streak intact at Beaver Field in a "hard fought and well played" 18-0 win that was marred by too many State fumbles and punts. The game at New Haven loomed directly ahead and everyone was uneasy. Until they saw Fennell at practice Monday. The head coach was back. By the end of the week, so was the offense.

Unbeaten Yale was in the midst of one of its greatest seasons. The Ivy Leaguers were always one of the best teams in the country and this year they would eventually win 10 games without a loss and would be scored upon only by Princeton. Perhaps the Yale players were too cocky. After all, they had never had much difficulty with the "farm boys" from the "cow college" before. But the Yale players were in trouble right from the opening kickoff when they were smashed into the ground by the vicious hits of Yeckley and his mates.

State's backfield of Yeckley, quarterback Cal Moorehead, halfback Sam Miller and fullback George McGee pounded away at the Yale defense, picking up two to seven yards at a crack. Most of the first half and much of the second was played in Yale's territory. Midway in the first half, State was trying to maintain possession on its 30-yard line when it ran a center-buck and fumbled. Yale's captain, Shevelin, picked up the fumble and rambled to about the 2-yard line before being tackled from behind. Halfback Veeder scored on the next play and kicked the extra point to give Yale a 6-0 lead. As the half wound down, State hammered away at the Yale line and twice got close enough to Yale's goal to attempt field goals but both kicks missed. The State team trotted into the dressing room believing they were the better team, despite the score.

The visitors didn't let up in the second half. They battered away at Yale's befuddled line but couldn't quite get into scoring territory. Both teams were playing great defense. Then, late in the half, Yale moved the ball across midfield, found a weakness on State's left side and backup quarterback Jones skirted around the end for 30 yards to State's 10-yard line. A couple plays later, Veeder went over again and then booted the extra point, and that's how it ended, 12-0. State had outgained Yale 203 yards to 110 but all to naught. Missed opportunities and a couple of mistakes. The story of many Penn State defeats, past and future.

Yeckley and his teammates were in no mood to celebrate because they felt they should have won. So did the Times reporter in his coverage of the game. He blamed bad officiating: "...had fair play been given by referee Hammand [the score] would have been without a doubt 6-0 in favor of State, while many believe had the game been played on Beaver Field, Yale would have been defeated by a score of 18-0...no man on State's team was outplayed by his opponent." The Eastern newspapers also lauded the State team for its outstanding play and almost overnight the team was seen as one of the best in the East.

Back on campus that Saturday night, most of the students gathered at Beaver Field and built a large bonfire to celebrate what they believed was a "moral victory." (Sounds familiar, doesn't it?) When the team returned home on Monday morning several hundreds students and townspeople met the players at the horse-taxi station in downtown State College. In the tradition of the day, the enthusiastic students unhitched the horses and with 200 students clinging to long ropes, they pulled the cart carrying the players around town and up the long hill to the front of Old Main for a spirited ceremony. The players were happy and pleased but felt a twinge of regret for what might have been. What if Coach Tom had been here all year?

With Fennel on the sidelines again, the team played almost flawlessly the next week in beating a respected Villanova squad, 29-0, at Beaver Field. It was over by the half as State scored 24 points with Yeckley getting one TD and booting all four extra points. "During the entire first half," wrote the Times reporter, "State's team played fast, smooth, aggressive football. There was never even the semblance of a fumble...Every man knew his place in every play so systematically that our team swept the full length of the field four time in succession against Villanova's fierce defense."

They wouldn't be so fortunate at Annapolis the following week. It was State's worst game of the season. They admittedly had underestimated the Middies and, maybe, overestimated what they had done against Yale and Villanova. "Although State's team failed to play its best game," the Times reporter wrote, "the fact is undisputed that the Navy outplayed our eleven at all points..." Injuries also took a toll as both of State's best players, Yeckley and Dunn, were hurt. Yeckley played most of the game with a "badly injured" arm that hurt his effectiveness. Dunn was knocked out of the game the first half but not until after he and Yeckley combined on a spectacular play that gave State it's only touchdown. Navy was attempting a field goal from State's 30-yard line when Dunn pulled off his specialty by breaking through and blocking the kick. Yeckley picked up the ball and rambled 80 yards for the score. Yeckley missed the extra point but it didn't matter. Navy came back with two TDs and an extra point to win, 11-5, before a crowd of 5,000.

Now, the team pointed to arch-rival Dickinson. First, there was a "tune up" with a thoroughly outclassed Geneva team at Beaver Field. Yeckley and Dunn were held out of the game to recover from their injuries. After taking a 29-0 halftime lead, Coach Fennel inserted substitutes the rest of the game. Nine different players had touchdowns as State broke the team scoring record set against Lafayette in 1894 with a 73-0 win.

Since the 1897 Thanksgiving Day game won by Dickinson, 6-0, in Sunbury, the annual contest with the college from Carlisle was the biggest game of the season for both teams. Forget Yale. Forget the Indians. Forget all the other victories at Beaver Field. If State couldn't beat Dickinson on November 18 at Williamsport, this season was ruined.

The largest crowd ever to see a football game in North Central Pennsylvania turned out to watch the game in cool but dry weather. Among the 8,000 spectators were some 700 rollicking State fans from State College and Bellefonte who had jammed 12 cars of a special train to follow their team. They weren't disappointed.

This may have been the most exciting—if not the best—game ever in the 17-game series played between 1888 and 1931. Although both teams moved the ball well, it was the defenses that had the crowd roaring. On its first possession, Dickinson's Captain "Davy" Davis, the "villain" of the '04 game, tried a fake punt from midfield but Yeckley stopped it with a tackle so vicious that the game was held up for several minutes for Davis to wake up and recover. State then moved 51 yards to the Dickinson 15-yard line where Dickinson held on downs. After a couple changes of possessions, Davis went back to punt again. This time, Dunn pulled off his specialty, blocking the punt, and State recovered at the Dickinson 40. Six plays later newcomer guard John Gotwals plowed through the line from 15 yards out and with several Dickinson players hanging on at the goal line, Gotwals "reached out and clasped the upright, pulling himself across the line with a magnificent effort." Yeckley kicked the extra point. Dickinson got another drive going and had the ball on State's 31-yard line when the half ended.

State's offense took control in the second half but couldn't quite overcome the determined Dickinson defense. One State drive was stopped on a great goal line stand at the Dickinson 2-yard line. Another time, Dunn picked up the ball on a fumbled punt at the Dickinson 6-yard line and crossed into the end zone but the play was nullified because of a State penalty. When the game ended without any more scoring, fans of both teams rushed onto the field to "carry off their varsity warriors upon their shoulders," as the *Times* reporter wrote.

One of the spectators watching was a halfback from Pitt named Rice. When asked by the *Times* reporter about the upcoming Thanksgiving Day game with State, Rice replied: "We will swamp State, simply swamp them." This may have been the first instance where the derogatory comments by an opponent in a newspaper was used to fire-up a State football team. The team was probably still seething at the remarks a week later and looking ahead to Pitt when it almost lost in an upset to West Virginia at Beaver Field. Playing in cold and mud, State lost the ball on several fumbles and got its only score in a last minute, 50-yard drive on the running of Yeckley, who gained 21 yards, scoring on an 8-yard TD and kicking the extra point.

Pitt had put together another solid team. The Pitt players were bigger, faster and more experienced than their State counterparts and they had never lost at Exposition Park. They were the obvious favorite on that Thanksgiving Day and their 2,000 fans jeered at State and its 400 partisans in the crowd. But State was looking for revenge from last year's upset. The Pitt cheering stopped early and State won, 6-0, with Irish McIlveen scoring the only TD in the last moments of the first half. The *Times* reporter wrote "No State eleven has ever fought 'more manfully, or fearlessly, for the honor of the 'Blue and White' and Captain Yeckley and his ten stalwart comrades will go down emblazoned in States proud gridiron history as men deserving of the highest praise and commendation."

That would be true. Yeckley was ending his career with one of the best individual performances a Penn State back would ever have. But, for the captain and his 1905 teammates, the season was over. They had won more games than any Penn State team ever. And they had played to the best of their ability. Could they have won more if Coach Tom had been around earlier to coach the offense? They would never know, but next year's team would find out. And it would have to play Yale and the Indians, too.

Season Record 8-3
Record to Date 80-54-7
Winning percentage .592

"'Mother' Dunn & 'Wrong Way' Cyphers"

Cy Cyphers could not believe his luck. The sophomore guard had scooped up the ball after Mother Dunn had blocked the Yale punt and he was running towards the goal line. Cy knew that his touchdown and an extra point would tie the score. And because of the way he and his teammates had been outplaying Yale throughout the first half, he knew they would win. Win, can you believe? Win over one of the greatest teams in the country.

The rain striking his face felt good. That rain had helped give Yale its 6-0 lead. Five minutes into the game, State mishandled the slippery ball and Yale's right tackle ran the fumbled punt 35 yards into the end zone. But now it was State's break. Dunn had done it again. He had smashed through and blocked All-America Howard Roome's punt at the 40-yard line and the ball had bounced high in the air. Cyphers had grabbed it and now he was pounding his way downfield over the soggy turf with nary a Yale player in sight.

His teammates were shouting him encouragement. Go, Cy, Go! Wait a minute. That's not what they were saying. What? No, Cy, No! Cy had to think quickly but he couldn't stop. He glanced around him and saw his teammates frantically waving their arms the other way. He stared for a moment at the Yale goal posts ahead of him, and in an instant it hit him. He was running the wrong way!!!

Oh, no, he thought. He slammed his feet into the ground, stopping abruptly, and turned to run back the other way. But it was too late. The whole Yale team was on top of him—or, at least it seemed that way. He was down. The ball was on the Penn State 20-yard line. There would be no touchdown. There would be no tie. Cy Cyphers, the sophomore from Stroudsburg playing his first season on the varsity, had just consummated one of the strangest plays in the history of Penn State football.

A few moments after Cyphers' embarrassing faux pas, Yale kicked a 25-yard field goal (worth four points) and State could not get close again. The players tried. They fumbled away another opportunity on the Yale 10-yard line and in the second half missed on four attempted field goals—two kicks were blocked, one was wide and the other from such a poor angle that it hit one of the goal posts. Hard luck, everyone said, including the cynical Eastern sportswriters covering the game. "The second half was full of Penn State's hard luck," wrote the reporter for the *Philadelphia North American*. "But the way State's big backs opened up Yale's rush time for material gains was sufficient to make Yale men admit the visitors deserved to score...it was a game of forward passes and punts. Yale was out-punted and out-passed but her team work and proverbial luck saved the day."

One of the spectators that October 20 was Yale's own renowned Walter Camp, the patriarch of modern day football. He and he alone selected the best teams in the country and the All-America teams. What he saw of Mother Dunn was good enough for him. At the end of the season, Camp made Dunn the first Penn State player ever named to a First-Team All-America team. "...it was he who led his team to such a remarkable record, a good deal of it depending on Dunn himself,"

Runner, punter and drop-kicker, Bull McCleary was also an exceptional defensive player. His 35-yard field goal were the only points in State's outstanding 1906 win over the powerful Carlisle Indians.

Camp wrote in *Collier's* magazine, " [Dunn is] absolutely reliable in his passing, secure in blocking, active in breaking through and in diagnosing plays..."

Yale had four players on that same Camp First-Team All-America as the '06 Eli squad went on to finish undefeated again, but tied with Princeton. Meanwhile, the 10 points Yale scored on State would be the only points Captain Dunn and his teammates would give up that season. Dunn's blocked punts, including the aberrant one against Yale and Cyphers' faux pas, would help define the season.

Cyphers' "wrong-way" run would be all but forgotten. Like the *Philadelphia North American*, most newspaper stories of the game ignored the Cyphers' goof or downplayed it. Twenty-two years later, Roy Riegels' would become famous for a similar "wrong-way" run in the Rose Bowl. Cyphers was fortunate to have played in an era when communications were primitive compared to today. Nowadays, Cyphers would be a household name and his humiliating run would have been seen by millions overnight on videotape. What he did remained virtually unknown until the late Ridge Riley uncovered the incident and wrote about it in his 1977 book, *The Road to Number One*.

Still, Cyphers' historic run and the subsequent loss to Yale had a significant affect on the outcome of the season. State had been unbeaten in five games before playing Yale and the players believed

they would have won if not for Cypher's mental error. They dedicated themselves to proving it in the five remaining games and they succeeded. This would be State's best season since football began in 1887 (or 1881, if you prefer). The team would finish 8-1-1 and set a record for shutouts—nine—that still stands. One of the victories was of historic proportions—a 4-0 win over the Carlisle Indians thanks to another Mother Dunn blocked kick. The tie was momentous, too, a shocking 0-0 deadlock at home with a hapless Gettysburg team.

Then, again, as in '05, there was the feeling of what might have been if Coach Fennell had joined the team earlier, particularly in how he might have handled the talented freshmen in the backfield. That, too, defined the season. For Fennell didn't show up until after the Yale game and by that time the damage had been done.

Perhaps, Fennell would have used the spectacular freshman quarterback Larry Vorhis sooner. Vorhis was an excellent passer—believed now to be one of the best in State history—and the rules had been changed that season to allow more passing. The passing rules were highly restrictive—for instance, an incomplete pass resulted in a 5-yard penalty and passes over 20 yards were prohibited. Still, just as it is today, pinpoint passing could help make the running attack more effective. Passing also was used effectively to set up field goals. In fact, it was primarily Vorhis' passing in the second half of the Yale game that led to the four failed field goal attempts.

No one really knew how good Vorhis and the other freshmen were when fall practice opened September 1. The best players returning were veterans on the line, like Dunn, three-year starter Bill Wray of Greensburg, and seniors John Gotwals and Bayard Kunkle. But Vorhis made an immediate impression with his dropkicks and veterans compared him favorably to Andy Moscrip of the '04 team. Another freshman, Walter "Bull" McCleary, was punting better than any returnee. Vorhis and McCleary also looked good running the ball. So did fellow freshmen Charles "Hef" Hershman and Bob Coulson. And the Maxwell kid, Larry, seemed to have great potential as an end and runner. The first two games gave Pop Golden and the former players assisting him—including last year's captain Ed Yeckley—the opportunity to fully evaluate the newcomers' talent.

Substitutes were used freely in the lopsided Beaver Field wins over Lebanon Valley, 24-0, and Allegheny, 26-0. State scored its first touchdown of the year within three minutes against Lebanon Valley on Sept. 22 as Coulson scored two touchdowns, including one on an 85-yard run, and Vorhis drop-kicked field goals from the 25- and 35-yard lines. A week later, Pop Golden unleashed Coulson, Maxwell, Hershman and McCleary as they ran all over Allegheny, with McCleary scoring two TDs and two extra points and Hershman getting his first TD. Vorhis had another field goal, this time booting one from a difficult angle at the 45-yard line.

The freshmen were good, very good, and they were eager to take on the intimidating Carlisle Indians next. The game at Williamsport was played "on a soft, slippery field in a driving rain" before a boisterous crowd of 4,000. Once again, the punting of the Indians' star player, Mt. Pleasant, was astounding as he hit on punts of 80, 55, 45, and 50-yards thrice to keep State away from scoring territory. However, late in the first half, Mt. Pleasant made a mistake. He couldn't avoid the rush of—guess who—Mother Dunn, who blocked the Indians' punt. Maxwell recovered and a few moment later McCleary went back to attempt a 35-yard field goal. His kick was a little low and an Indian defender reached up to try to block the ball. But the ball bounced off the Indian and went over the goal posts to give State a 4-0 lead.

And that's where it ended despite other State drives deep into Carlisle's domain. Another freak play had given State a victory that the reporter for the *State College Times* called "one of the most signal [sic] football victories ever" for Penn State. "...the final score does not indicate by any means the strength of the two teams," the reporter added, "...the Indians were exceedingly fortunate to escape at least two touchdowns." The State fans were so jubilant by this first win ever over the seemingly invincible Indians that they rushed onto the muddy field and carried the players off on their shoulders.

The players obviously had a let down seven days later when lightly regarded Gettysburg visited Beaver Field. State had won all 10 previous games with Gettysburg, mostly by large margins. And, talk about home field advantage! State had only lost one game ever at home (to Lehigh back in 1888 on the Old Main lawn) and had 42 victories with one tie. But on this bright sunny day, kicking, defense and Penn State mistakes had the visitors primed to pull off a major upset. Gettysburg's captain and star, Sieber, engaged in the finest punting duel anyone had ever seen at Beaver Field. Both Sieber and McCleary averaged over 40 yards a punt on some dozen kicks.

State's players seemed jittery and tense. The kick receivers bobbled the ball several times, later blaming the sun in their eyes, and penalties against State kept the home team off balance all afternoon. In the opening minutes of the second half, Gettysburg got two opportunities to score after State fumbles. Sieber's attempt at a 25-yard field goal was blocked but moments later Gettysburg had the ball back on a fumble. This time State's defense made a tremendous goal line stand to keep Gettysburg out of the end zone.

As time was winding down, State's junior pass-catching end Bobby Burns got the ball and "electrified the crowd by a beautiful 20 yard run" into the end zone, but the TD was wiped out by a holding penalty (And you thought holding penalties nullifying touchdowns were a modern thing, eh?) Vorhis then tried a dropkick field goal from the 30-yard line but the ball went out of bounds. Sieber immediately punted and Vorhis made a fair catch. Vorhis then held the ball as McCleary attempted a placekick field goal from about the 35-yard line. The kick was wide. Sieber punted out again but Gettysburg got the ball back a few moments later on a penalty.

"Then," as the *Times* reporter put it, "came the most spectacular play of the day. On a delayed pass, Sieber darted out through a broken field for a beautiful run of 60 yards before he was tackled [from behind] by Vorhis on State's 20-yard line. Gettysburg couldn't gain an inch in two downs, and Sieber dropped back for a try at a field goal. The pass from the center was low, and the Gettysburg captain was buried beneath an avalanche of State tacklers." That was about it. There was another exchange of punts and the game was over.

State had gained 192 yards and Gettysburg 96, with 60 of the visitor's yards coming on Sieber's great run. But the score was 0-0. It was the first time State had *NOT* scored at home in 24 games. And it was the last hurrah for Gettysburg. The team would never get that close to beating Penn State again. Gettysburg would lose 27 games before the series was finally canceled in 1937. But they had spoiled Penn State's home record, and, almost the season.

Perhaps the State players were so angry by almost losing to such an inferior Gettysburg team that they were more than just a little fired-up when they visited Yale. Or, maybe, it was the coming together of the all-freshmen backfield. They were the ones who ran through

Yale's vaunted line and impressed everyone watching. McCleary, Coulson and Hershman were full time starters by then. Vorhis usually replaced senior quarterback Hi Henry for the entire second half. Against Yale, Vorhis played most of the game after Henry and a Yale player were thrown out for "slugging." If Vorhis was good enough to almost beat Yale he was good enough to start. At least everyone thought.

Henry was back as the starting quarterback Nov. 3 at Annapolis, perhaps at the direction of Coach Fennell, who was now back in charge. Henry made the most of his reprieve with a key play on the drive that gave State the game's only touchdown in a 5-0 win. After an exchange of punts in the second half, Henry took off from midfield on a 30-yard run. Hershman then made several plunges to get the ball to the 2-yard line and McCleary went over left tackle for the score. It was the first win over Navy in three years but the Middies felt they would have won if both their captain and star quarterback had not missed the game.

The Bellefonte Academy went down 12-0 at Beaver Field on Nov. 3 and then it was time for the annual "biggest game of the year" with Dickinson. Some 8,000 spectators saw another punting duel in Williamsport with Dickinson's captain Davis getting the best of McCleary, accumulating 445 yards to the "Bull's" 285 yards. Dickinson stopped three Penn State drives at its own 15-, 10- and 5-yard lines before giving up the only TD in another 6-0 State win. The following Saturday State beat West Virginia at Beaver Field, 10-0, before traveling to Pittsburgh to close out the season on Thanksgiving Day.

State was the clear favorite but the game was still scoreless late in the second half when State got possession and drove deep into Pitt territory. With just a few seconds left in the game, a Pitt sub named William "Big Ban" Banbury was called for unsportsmanlike conduct for allegedly slugging a State blocker and Pitt was penalized half the distance to the goal. The Pitt players and coaches protested the call by head linesman Ed Young, claiming Banbury was a gentle man who would never punch anyone, and a fight almost broke out. But the game resumed and with just 30 seconds left, McCleary bolted over for the touchdown, kicked the extra point and State won, 6-0.

And so it was over. The best season ever for Penn State. The team won eight games by shutouts and had another in the 0-0 tie with Gettysburg. The nine shutouts would still be the school record 91 years later. In his final season, Mother Dunn not only made Camp's All-America team but he was a near unanimous choice on the All-State teams of both Pittsburgh newspapers. Dunn had closed out a glorious career and become State's first true football folk hero. Some wondered if the "fabulous frosh" could ever equal Dunn's stature with State fans: Vorhis, McCleary, Maxwell, Hershman and Coulson. They also wondered if what they had been hearing all season was true. Did Cy Cyphers really run the "wrong way" in New Haven?

Nah, the players must be joking, could never happen.

Dr. William T. "Mother" Dunn, State's first nationally known player and first team All-American in 1906, poses with a football at his home in Hawaii where he practiced medicine.

Season Record 8-1-1
Record to Date 88-55-8
Winning percentage .609

"Heff Goes Down"

Tom Fennell winced when he saw "Heff" Hershman go down underneath the pile late in the first half. It was as hard a tackle as he had seen on Cornell's Percy Field and he had seen many as a player, assistant coach and spectator. Now one of his best runners was out of the game but the team had not let Heff's loss upset them. State had driven downfield for a touchdown and now had a surprising 4-0 half-time lead over Coach Fennell's alma mater.

Fennell and the players could smell an upset. It had been 10 years since the two schools had last played a football game and, thankfully, no one on this team had seen that 45-0 loss. Nor had they been around for the first game in '95, when another underdog State squad had held Cornell to a 0-0 tie on this same field. Even before they kicked off on this sunny and pleasant October day, Fennell had sensed this team could win. They had been playing well so far this season, with three wins and only a tough 18-5 loss to the Carlisle Indians.

The "fabulous freshmen" backfield on last year's outstanding team and grown up and was playing even better this year, just as everyone had expected. No problem there with Hershman at fullback, Bull McCleary and Bob Coulson at the halves and Larry Vorhis at quarterback. The main worry had been in the line, particularly at center where freshmen Alex Gray of California Normal and Henry Weaver were battling to succeed—certainly not replace—the great Mother Dunn. Dunn was still on campus helping to coach the line and his work with Gray and Weaver was obvious. The two tackles also were new, senior Jessie Ritchey and sophomore R. M. "Dick" Smith. The three were developing well, the coaches believed, thanks to the help they were getting from the veteran guards, Cy Cyphers and Bayard Kunkle, and ends, Bobby Burns and Larry Maxwell. Fennell and Pop Golden marveled at the leadership of Burns, the senior captain and left end. He wasn't "Mother" but he was the steady hand with all these kids.

Once again, Pop Golden and some former players like Dunn and Irish McIlveen had guided the team through its preseason practices. The workouts had been strenuous, often lasting more than two hours, but a September headline in the *Pittsburgh Dispatch* indicated the heavy drills were paying off: "Penn State's Football Outlook Never Brighter." Fennell did not join the team until the Indians game in the third week of the season and some fans thought that may have been why the team had faltered there, but it really wasn't.

The schedule had been set up to help bring the newcomers along. The Altoona Athletic Association were pushovers and Pop had used the opening game at Altoona to "try-out" all the new material. The 27-0 score didn't indicate how superior State was over that collection of ex-college players. Neither did the 34-0 win over Geneva the next week at Beaver Field when five different players scored touchdowns as Bull and Heff ran all over the visitors and Vorhis impressed everyone with his play-calling, passing and kicking.

But Pop didn't think they were quite ready for the Indians and Fennell had he same feelings as soon as he saw the team. That was an experienced bunch of Indians Pop Warner was coaching and they were simply too much for the young State team. Still, State had kept the game at Williamsport close in the first half and at one time led 5-4 on an outstanding 70-yard touchdown run by McCleary. However, the Indians came back to take a 10-5 halftime lead, then used the punting of Mt. Pleasant and two more field goals by Hauser (who also had kicked two in the first half) to win, 18-5.

The team had learned from that defeat. Even without Fennell on the sidelines again the next week, State clobbered Grove City, 46-0, mainly on the passing of Vorhis to Burns and Maxwell. "It was a treat to watch Captain Bobby Burns and his fellow end, Maxwell, take the long passes from Larry Vorhis," reported one newspaper. "Again and again did this trusty pair of ends make twenty or thirty yards by catching passes with utmost accuracy and precision." The passing helped set up the running as McCleary scored three TDs and booted six extra points and Hershman tallied two TDs.

Fennell met the team when it arrived in Ithaca and first huddled with Pop Golden and the other coaches. Everyone knew Cornell was the test. This was a damn good Cornell team, Fennell said. Some folks said it was almost as good as teams on which Fennell had played. Maybe.

The first half had been a battle in the trenches and Fennell couldn't have been more pleased about the defense. Cornell had been on the attack most of the half and several times drove deep into State territory only to be turned back by State's aggressive defense. Just before halftime, Fennell's offense began a long march toward the Cornell goal line. That's when Heff went down on one of the first plays of the drive, injuring his left shoulder. But McCleary and Vorhis had picked up the slack and with time running out, State had reached Cornell's 14-yard line. As the large partisan crowd yelled as loud as they could to distract State's players, Vorhis calmly took the snap from Gray and dropkicked a field goal from the 20-yard line for a 4-point lead.

During the halftime intermission, Fennell delivered another of his inspirational speeches. "Play like Lions!" he may have implored. That's what the team was being called now, the Penn State Lions. It had been the suggestion of H. D. "Joe" Mason, editor of the off-beat campus publication, *The Lemon*. In an issue last March, Mason writing under another name, said the team needed a mascot and nickname and he suggested "The King of the Beasts,—The Lion!!!" The students had quickly picked up on the idea. "Go, Lions, Go," they undoubtedly shouted when watching the team practice or play on Beaver Field, but there were few cheering for the Lions when the second half resumed. Cornell's 2,000 fans noisily prodded their team to make a comeback. The halftime rest had not diminished the intensity of the combat and the play on the field continued to be savage and vicious. Cornell relentlessly pushed the attack and State just as resolutely fought back. Midway through the half, State made another tremendous goal line stand, stopping Cornell within five inches of the end zone and taking over the ball. But moments later, a poor kick went out of bounds at the State 5-yard line, and in three hard-fought plunges into the line Cornell scored a TD to take a 6-4 lead.

Cornell's delirious fans may have thought the game was over but they had underestimated Fennell's determined team. State got the ball and with Vorhis, McCleary and Coulson banging away, State reached the Cornell 35-yard line before the drive sputtered. Once again, Vorhis

Charles "Heff" Hershman was the starting FB and a defensive star from 1906-09 when State was holding 18 of 20 opponents scoreless during one stretch.

took the ball as the din of the hometown crowd increased and from 40 yards out he calmly dropkicked another field goal.

With seven minutes left, State led 8-6. As time was running out , the Big Red roared back and tried at least twice to kick field goals to win the game, once from the 42 and again from inside the 30. The State players were tired but they stopped every Cornell thrust. The game continued long after it should have been over because the time-keeper refused to call time. State's student newspaper, the *Collegian*, later accused Cornell of creating an impromptu "ten minute overtime" in an attempt to take the victory away from State. The game was finally called when State got the ball and began another long march towards the Cornell end zone. Losing 8-6 was better than losing 14-6, Cornell's biased timekeeper decided and blew the whistle.

"Penn State Team Wins Over Cornell in Hotley Contested Game...," said the headline in the *Ithaca News*. "Collegians Show Clearly That They Are Better Trained Than Their Ithaca Rivals." Penn State's "*LaVie*" called the game "the most memorable gridiron battle ever fought by a State team."

However, it was a costly victory. Hershman's injury would define the season. Heff would hardly play for the remainder of the season. The rest of the team was battered and bruised by the physical intensity of the Cornell game, and as the season wore on, they appeared to wear out.

Nothing appeared to be wrong at first. The next week the "Lions" set a new team scoring record with a 75-0 win over outclassed Lebanon Valley at Beaver Field as Burns scored twice on runs of 40 and 60 yards, Vorhis had one a 45-yard scamper and also kicked a 30-

yard field goal, and a sub back named Bill Barnett had 3 TDs. A week later, they walloped traditional foe Dickinson, 55-0, on a muddy field at Williamsport. Vorhis scored one TD and kicked field goals of 45 and 35 yards but the star was McCleary, who scored five TDs, and, in the process, set a new single-season record for touchdowns with 13. But he wouldn't get any more.

The victory over Dickinson marked the 20th shutout in 23 games for State, dating back to the 73-0 win over Geneva in 1905. Their record was now 5-1 and the fans were now talking about another season equal to '06.

Then, West Virginia canceled its Nov. 23 game at Beaver Field, which meant the last three games would be on the road. The first one was against Penn at Franklin Field on November 9, and even though the Quakers were favored, State believed it could win. That confidence must have been shattered when Fennell again stayed in Ithaca. State played its worst game of the season in losing, 28-0. State never threat-ened as Penn's All-American fullback, Bill Hollenback, scored three touchdowns, including one on a 55-yard run off a fake field goal, and set up another with a 25-yard punt return. "The Quakers simply ran away with the visitors and scored almost at will," one reporter wrote. Neither the reporter, nor State fans knew it then, but Hollenback's per-formance that day would change Penn State's football history. But that was a year or two down the road.

Fennell was back for the game the following week against Navy in Annapolis. State dominated the contest as the defense held the Middies to just three first downs and the offense went up and down the field. But Navy's defense also was tough in the clutch and stopped the Lions on the Middies' 3-, 7- and 10-yard lines. A Vorhis field goal midway through the first half had given State a 4-0 lead. The score should have been 6-0 at that juncture but the referee erred when he didn't grant a safety after Navy blocked a Vorhis field goal attempt. A Navy player picked up the ball near the goal line, then retreated into the end zone where he was tackled. Despite the protests of State's coaches and players, the referee ruled a touchback. So, as the clock wound down in the second half, it appeared as if Vorhis' field goal would win the game. But with less than a minute to play, State fumbled a Navy punt at midfield. End Bill Dauge, who was to become Navy's very first First-Team All-American, picked up the ball and ran 50 yards for a TD to give the Middies the shocking 6-4 victory.

If that wasn't enough to dishearten the team, the quirky loss to Pitt on Thanksgiving Day was. The game before 11,000 on a sunny day at Exposition Park was a battle between State's offense and Pitt's defense and time and again Pitt throttled State's many scoring chances. The teams had played evenly all afternoon and with about a minute left, it looked as if the game would end in a scoreless tie. Then, on a first down at State 40-yard line, Pitt quarterback Swenson threw a desperation pass to Quincy "Little Ban" Banbury, whose brother, Will, had been the goat in the State victory the previous year. Banbury took the pass on the 10-yard line but before he could cross the goal line he fumbled. FUMBLE! LIVE BALL! Players from both teams grappled for the ball and when the officials dug under the pile they found Pitt's substitute fullback, J.F. Campbell, with the ball at the bottom. There was time for a couple more plays by State following the kickoff but it was too late. Pitt won, 6-0.

"Deep Gloom Reigning at Penn State," noted one newspaper headline in summing up the season following the distressing back-to-back defeats to Navy and Pitt. So, what started as a season with potential and a great victory over Cornell ended in anguish and gloom. Some fans believed it would have been different if Fennell had been with the team more during the season. Fennell may have thought so, too, but he felt it would have been different if Heff had not been injured. The team's character was different without Hershman. Fennell and Pop Golden also knew the Cornell game had taken more out of the team than they had first realized.

They also lost the last two games but in such a demoralizing way that the depression caused by the defeats carried over into the next season. The players were bewildered and Fennell could see it in their eyes as they walked off the field in Pittsburgh. Before he left for Elmira, Fennell was asked by the Athletic Board to spend more time on campus in '08 and the board gave him another $1,500 to do so. It wasn't just the money that would bring him back earlier next year. He had to make those kids forget what happened this year. He'd have to work on their psyche before next season began or it could be another long season.

Season Record 6-4
Record to Date 94-59-8
Winning percentage .609

"The Blocked Kick "

Vic Ballou couldn't believe what just happened. One of Penn's charging linemen had just blocked his punt inside the State 10-yard line and the ball was rolling into the end zone with only Penn players chasing it.

Ballou ran towards the goal but it was too late. Penn's Fred Gaston had recovered it for a touchdown and Penn was now leading, 6-0, with less than five minutes left in the game. The angry Penn State freshman slammed his fist against his leg pads and cursed. As he walked towards the State bench, his teammates patted him on the back to console him. "Not your fault," someone yelled. "They were lucky," said another.

The blocked kick would define the season. Ballou's excellent punting and State's stout defense had stymied the heavily favored Penn team all afternoon. Until that moment no one had even come close to blocking one of the youngster's punts. State's attacking defense led by veteran guard Cy Cyphers had blocked four punts by Penn's All-American captain, "Big Bill" Hollenback, but the "lucky" Quakers had recovered all of them.

Another of Ballou's kicks in the first half had been bobbled by Keinath near the goal line and "Crazy Henny" Weaver had bulled past Keinath and his blocker to pick up the ball and roll into the end zone. But Referee Evans had disallowed the score on a technical ruling, despite the protestations of Coach Tom Fennell.

"Hang in there, guys, we'll get 'em," Captain "Bull" McCleary probably shouted as the teams lined up for the kickoff. McCleary knew there was plenty of time left in the game for State to come back. His teammates had been playing their hearts out, particularly on defense. Twice they had stopped almost sure Penn touchdowns with goal line stands at the one and two yard lines. Another Quaker drive had ended

abruptly at the State 20-yard line on a defensive thrust led by Cyphers, Weaver and center Alex Gray.

Now with time running out, the visiting Lions were moving the ball downfield on Penn. The home crowd at Franklin Field was yelling encouragement to their proud warriors. This was unbeaten Penn, number one team in the nation, many said. Never lost to the "farmers" and never will. Heff Hershman blasted over tackle for an apparent first down at the Penn 20-yard line, but wait—Evans has called another penalty. "Hurdling," Evans said to State's big fullback and walked off the penalty yardage. Hershman and his teammates screamed at the referee and Fennell shouted at him from the sidelines. "Homer!" "Baloney!" But Evans ordered play to resume. Penn stiffened and the game was over. State had played valiantly but it wasn't enough. A Philadelphia newspaper praised "the plucky eleven from Bellefonte" for its "determination" that held "Penn down so well that but for the blocked kick the game might have ended at 0-0." Penn would go on to win 11 of 12 games with the only blemish coming from a 6-6 tie against Pop Warner's Carlisle Indians with the great Jim Thorpe, and many sportswriters and coaches would rate the Quakers number one in the nation.

That was no solace to McCleary and his teammates on that early October day. They felt they had beaten—or, at the very least, tied—Penn, and that their achievement had been stripped from them by a duplicitous official. They'd have to forget it, Fennell told them as they went through practice for their next game, or the '08 season would be a disaster. The loss to Penn was the third in four games, and with Cornell, Navy, Pitt and old traditional foe Bucknell among the six games left, they'd have to snap out of their slump quickly. It had been eight years since State's last losing season and Fennell had not expected this to be another one when he opened preseason practice back in September.

Sure, he had told himself, he had some problems to overcome with the graduation of several starters and the unexpected absence of two star underclassmen who had left school, end Larry Maxwell (who left to get married) and halfback Bob "Buster" Coulson, who was now playing major league baseball with the Cincinnati National League team. But the rest of his "fabulous' backfield had returned—McCleary, Hershman and quarterback Larry Vorhis—and the rookie Ballou had fit in perfectly with that trio at Coulson's old right halfback slot. The veterans Cyphers, Weaver, Gray and Dick Smith were the nucleus of a rebuilt line, and Fennell was particularly impressed by his new right end, Tom Piollet, who had been a scrub at Cornell last year. The kid was tough on both offense and defense and could be a star. But McCleary had some doubts about the team's chances. "We have excellent backfield material but the line is lamentably weak," the captain told *Pittsburgh Press* reporter Dale R. Mason after the stunning upset in the opening game.

Fennell had been so sure his first team was solid that he had made one of the biggest mistakes of his coaching career in that opening game. The opponent was Bellefonte Academy, the nearby prep school. On paper the high school age youngsters were no match for the college boys, so Fennell started 10 substitutes with only center Alex Gray in there from the first team. Fennell figured he could get experience for his backups while resting the regulars for the tougher games ahead.

The youngsters from Bellefonte had other ideas. They held their own throughout the first half as State scored but one touchdown and missed the extra point. Despite the narrow 5-0 lead, Fennell kept his reserves in the game. Late in the second half, Bellefonte's right end, Dillon recovered a State fumble and ran 40 yards for a touchdown. Elsey kicked the extra point and Bellefonte led, 6-5. Fennell rushed in the first team but it was too late. The prepsters had the momentum and the confidence and won the game. It was the first (and would be the only) loss on Old Beaver Field. It also was a humbling experience for Fennell and his team, and perhaps an omen for the rest of the season.

The next week, the team took its ire out on Grove City, 31-0, as five different players scored touchdowns, including Vorhis, who also kicked 4 PATs. Then, it was off to Wilkes-Barre for the game with the Carlisle Indians. Pop Warner had a new star that year. His name was Jim Thorpe and everyone who saw him play said he might be the best player the Indians ever had. As a crowd of 10,000 looked on, State stopped Thorpe's running but they couldn't stop his kicking. Thorpe's first field goal from the 25-yard line gave the Indians the early lead but State came back before the half to take a 5-4 lead when Weaver picked up a blocked kick and ran 25 yards for a TD. But that was the only points State would get. Despite the rugged play of Cyphers, who was praised for his performance against Carlisle's toughest lineman, Afraid-of-a-Bear, the Indians overcame several lost fumbles and won, 12-5, as Thorpe booted additional field goals of 25 and 45 yards (and missed two others from the 40 and 50).

So, after the demoralizing loss at Penn, the team was 1-3 and Fennell worked hard the next week to get his team mentally prepared for the last six games. Geneva was expected to be an easy game and it was. But State paid a steep price for the 51-0 win at Beaver Field when McCleary went down early with a broken shoulderblade. The doctors told Fennell the "Bull" was done for the season but the obstinate Lion captain told them they were full of it.

With Cyphers again playing an outstanding game on both sides of the ball, State beat a tougher-than-expected West Virginia team at Beaver Field, 12-0. Ballou's runs of 60 and 35 yards behind the blocking of Cyphers set up both TDs. It was off to Cornell the next week where the Big Red was looking for revenge. The entire game was played in snow and heavy wind but weather was not really a factor. Once again a blocked punt led to State's demise. The recovered punt set up the first Cornell TD on a series of forward passes in the first half but Vorhis kicked a field goal late in the half to keep State in the game, 5-4. Midway through the second half State fumbled away a TD opportunity deep in Cornell territory. Cornell then marched all the way down field to the State 4-yard line. Two

"Dutch" Herman served as back-up QB behind early greats Vorhis and Miller playing effectively at every opportunity. He is best remembered in Penn State lore for his 50 years as assistant football coach, head basketball coach and

plays gained nothing but on third down, Cornell scored on another pass play to clinch the game, 10-4.

The Nov. 7 game with Bucknell was the last game ever played on Old Beaver Field. It also was the first game with State's original opponent since the infamous 1900 game at Williamsport when Bucknell walked off the field with the lead and State won by forfeit, 6-0. This time it was no match, as State won, 33-6, before what the *State College Times* called "..the Biggest Crowd Ever on Beaver Field." Just how many people actually saw the game is unknown because the newspaper only mentioned the "between 300 and 400" Bucknell rooters and wrote nothing about the number of State fans in attendance. The victory was the 48th in 49 games played on the old field. Hershman scored two TDs and Ballou had one but it was Vorhis who had everyone talking with his 50-yard run for a TD and his 35-yard field goal. Tough old Bull McCleary also started but left after the second TD because of a broken foot. This time he would be done for the season.

With McCleary out, Fennell tried to surprise Navy by switching Vorhis to left half and inserting old reliable "Dutch" Herman in at QB. The switch didn't work. Sportswriters thought the State team looked a little tired as State's offense sputtered. Navy scored the game's only TD in the first half on a 75-yard march and won a close 5-0 decision in what one newspaper described as one of "the hardest, cleanest football games" of the season.

And so, a losing or break even season came down to the annual Thanksgiving Day finale at Pitt. Some 9,000 fans showed up at Exposition Park, many of them waving banners extolling the new name of the Pittsburgh institution. It was no longer Western University of Pennsylvania. Forevermore, it would be known as the University of Pittsburgh. The name change meant nothing to Fennell's spirited troops. They had to win the game or go down in history as losers. Thanks in a large part to Pitt's mistakes and Vorhis' foot, they won.

Both offenses sputtered. State twice lost the ball on downs within Pitt's 10-yard line and Pitt fumbled away several opportunities. Vorhis kicked a 25-yard field goal to give State the halftime lead, 4-0, then booted two more field goals in the second half, from 30 and 25 yards, before Pitt mounted a long, 72-yard drive for the game's only touchdown. By winning, 12-6, State also won the Spalding Cup, a new trophy that was to go annually to the winner of this Thanksgiving Day game. (Somewhere, the Spalding Cup—a silver football once displayed at the Track House—was lost into history.)

After the game, Fennell told Pop Golden he would not be back in '09. He wanted to devote full time to his law practice, he said. Most everyone took him at his word, but some wondered whether he was just too frustrated by the ups and downs of the last two seasons. Fennell had been the best coach yet, everyone said, and he would have a veteran team returning next year, led by the newly-elected captain, Larry Vorhis. Too bad he doesn't want to stay around. We have a new field next season, and we could have one heckuva football team.

Season Record 5-5
Record to Date 99-64-8
Winning percentage .602

CHAPTER 6

THE BROTHERS HOLLENBACK

1909-1914

"Big Bill" Hollenback was just 23 years old and fresh out of Penn where he had been an All-America fullback and everyone told Pop Golden he would make one heckuva football coach. So, despite the fact that Hollenback would be younger than some of his players, he was hired to take over for Tom Fennell.

Hollenback was a football mastermind and a lot of people had expected him to get the coaching job at the University of Pennsylvania after captaining the 1908 team the previous fall. However, the vacant Penn job went to former Penn State star running back Andy Smith, who had been an assistant coach there for three years, and actually had helped coach Hollenback. So, "Big Bill" took the State offer, even though he had once contemplated a career in dentistry.

But there was one "catch." Although he would have total authority over the team for three months, his title would be simply "advisory coach." The Athletic Board believed it was vital that a measure of control be maintained by someone who was part of the Penn State system, so former four-year letterman Irish McIlveen, who was the baseball coach, was named "head coach" of the football team. McIlveen had not played football since 1905 and had spent part of the past four years trying to play major league baseball with the Pittsburgh Pirates and New York Yankees. He had finally finished up his mining degree in the spring and with his major league baseball aspirations faltering he eagerly accepted the football offer.

Irish might be the head coach but there was no question that Hollenback was in charge of the team. Hollenback was not unfamiliar with Penn State football or the State College area. As Penn's 6-3, 200 pound fullback, he had helped shut out Fennell's 1907 and 1908 teams and he had occasionally visited State College and Bellefonte because it was not far from his hometown of Phillipsburg. So, he was enthusiastic about taking charge of the 1909 team. He knew there was a good mix of veterans returning and a brand new playing field for home games. He also had been hearing whispers about some of the young talent State was trying to bring in and he figured that could make for an exciting couple of years, especially when playing his alma mater. That was one of his goals, he told Pop and the Athletic Board. He'd make Penn regret not giving him the head coaching job.

And he may have. By the time Hollenback gave up coaching State after the 1914 season and going into the coal brokerage business back in Philadelphia, he had stopped Penn's mastery of State. In fact, Hollenback never lost to his old team in three games. But he did more then beat Penn. Three of his State teams were unbeaten and one of them, the 8-0 1912 squad, is considered one of the greatest in school history. By the time he left, he had established a winning legacy that continues to this day.

His first team in 1909 was so successful that Missouri offered him more money to coach in Columbia for the 1910 season. Hollenback told Pop and the Athletic Board he needed the money but would return in 1911 if they hired his older brother Jack to replace him for the one year. Some folks thought that was strictly a ploy to get Jack the Penn State job full time, but Bill was so popular his request was granted and brother Jack was made "advisory coach" for 1910.

Coach "Big Bill" Hollenback was just 23 years old when he was hired in 1909 and was younger than some of his players. His off-field rules included "no swearing, no smoking and no chewing."

Jack Hollenback was one year older, had also been a star at Penn, but not an All-America, and had been the head coach at Franklin and Marshall in 1908 and 1909. He looked a lot like Bill but he didn't have his younger brother's coaching skills or personality. The players had little respect for him. Thus, when "Big Bill" asked for his old job after a 5-1-2 season at Missouri, the Athletic Board enthusiastically agreed. But he would still be "advisory coach." The Athletic Board decided someone within "the Penn State system" (and that meant only former players) was needed to be the "head coach." Thus, the "head coach" for 1911 would be one of Bill's 1909 stars, Bull McCleary.

Bill Hollenback's 1911 team was even better than his first one in 1909, and after the season he was finally named "head coach." The next year, he had the finest team of his tenure—and one of the all-time great teams in State history. But Pop was not around to share in the success. After 12 years of virtually running the athletic department, Pop had decided it was time to move on. He resigned in the spring of 1912 to go into the insurance business in Pittsburgh and there were many who believed it was Pop's absence that caused Hollenback to eventually leave State after the 1914 season.

For it was Pop Golden who had recruited many of the players who had made Hollenback so successful. Pete Mauthe, Shorty Miller, Dad Engle, Dick Harlow and the rest were all Pop's "boys." He had gone to their schools and to their homes to convince them to attend Penn State, and, thus, became Penn State's first "unofficial" recruiter. After Pop left, Hollenback may have felt that the quality of incoming players was diminishing, even though had more men to choose from as enrollment passed 3,000 in the 1912-13 academic year. Hollenback also was concerned about new eligibility rules instigated by the student newspaper *The Daily Collegian*, and implemented for the 1915 season by University President Edwin Sparks that made freshmen ineligible for varsity play and forced transfers to sit out a full year before they could play. Since most of State's football opponents were not adhering to similar rules, "Big Bill" told friends Penn State would be at a serious competitive disadvantage. Winning might be more difficult, he said.

He was wrong.

"Hoo Ray for Larry's Foot"

The football had left Larry Vorhis' foot and was headed directly towards the goal posts. State had just scored a touchdown on the Indians after two 15-yard runs by Dick Smith and Vorhis' extra point kick would tie the game at 6-6 three minutes into the second half.

Vorhis watched intently as the ball sailed into the air straight and true. Suddenly the ball seemed to die. Bong! The ball hit the crossbar and bounced back onto the field. The Lions' captain closed his eyes and shook his head. The crowd of 10,000 at the field in Wilkes-Barre groaned. Pop Warner and his Carlisle Indians team clapped and hollered. They still had the lead.

"Big Bill" Hollenback shouted encouragement from the Penn State sidelines as the two teams lined up for the kickoff. Behind the bench, the 30-piece Penn State band played a rousing, upbeat tune while head cheerleader George Ogilvie led the Penn State faithful in the cheer he had written special for this game. He had the words printed in song books and the cheerleaders handed out the books to the several hundred students who had paid $3.75 for the round-trip train ticket from Lemont: "*We've come to beat the Indians, Hoo Ray, Hoo Ray...*" they yelled. "*It seems a shame to take the game, But this is Penn State's day...*"

No one rooting for State could believe Vorhis had missed. It was a chip shot. Vorhis was one of the best kickers in the country and

had successfully drop-kicked many field goals from long distances at difficult angles. Yet he missed a chip shot! (Some things never change in Penn State football.) Minutes later, he got a chance to redeem himself. After a good drive from its own side of the field, State's offense sputtered inside the Indians' 15-yard line and Vorhis kicked a 20-yard field goal to give State its first lead, 8-6.

State appeared to be in command, now, as this second game of the season turned into a defensive struggle at midfield. But as the minutes ticked away, Carlisle drove into field goal range. The points for field goals had been changed this season from four points to three but that was still enough for an Indians' field goal to win. The Indians' Libby made the attempt. Wide right! The State crowd cheered as the football rolled into the end zone towards where Vorhis was standing.

Then came a moment Vorhis would regret for the rest of his career. Under the rules at the time, he had the option of picking up the ball and downing it for a touchback or running or kicking it out of the end zone. For reasons even he could not rationally explain later, Vorhis grabbed the ball and did nothing. The Indians' star left tackle, Wauseka, smashed into Vorhis and threw him to the ground. Safety, the referee yelled. Two points.

The crowd groaned again. Tie game, 8-8. Moments later that's where it ended. The disheartened State players trudged off the field. They knew they should have won. The Indians' whooped and hollered. A Carlisle player picked up the football and started to carry it off the field over his head. This was the trophy and the Indians' felt they earned it. A State player knocked the football to the ground and started to go after it. Wauseka jumped him. Someone in blue and white leaped onto Wauseka. Another Indian went to Wauseka's aid and the brawl was on! The players slugged it out as Hollenback and Pop Warner tried to get everyone off the field and back to the dressing rooms. Spectators began fighting in the stands, then poured onto the field to continue their battles. It took more than a dozen Pennsylvania State Troopers to restore order. When it was over someone asked what happened to the football. It was never found.

So, after two games in his first year as head coach, Hollenback was 1-0-1, with the really "big" game against his Penn teammates of last year coming up in two weeks. Hollenback still believed in his heart that he should have been coaching Penn this year, not Penn State. But the job had been given to another former All-America running back, Andy Smith, who had served a couple years as an assistant when his playing days were over. Hollenback would remind his State team how Smith had deserted Penn State a few years ago. That should help the incentive. State had not beaten Penn in 15 previous tries but Hollenback was convinced he could do it this year.

"Big Bill" had not been a bit surprised by the talent on this Penn State team. He had known all about Vorhis and the other veterans. He had played against some of them for three or four years: Hershman, McCleary, Weaver, Smith, Gray and Piloett. They were good, very good. The two new starting linemen, center Burley Watson and left guard Fred Johnson, both juniors, fit in well, and would get better with experience. He also liked one of the sophomore backup tackles, Dick Harlow. But Hollenback had been surprised—and was most impressed—by two freshmen whom he had promoted to the first team, "Pete" Mauthe at halfback and Dex Very at right end. Pop Golden said they had recruited a couple of good players and the Mauthe kid was just one fine all-around player who could run, tackle, pass and kick. Ed Yeckley, captain of the '05 team had helped find Mauthe in Dubois. Very showed up on campus on his own. Hollenback wondered how

The 1909 team was unbeaten and happy with a tie against Penn after fifteen straight losses. Coach Bill Hollenback was not pleased and vowed that this would be the last time State would leave Franklin Field without a victory.

everyone missed him, since he had played at Mercersburg Academy. Dex had speed, agility and intelligence and was one of the best tacklers Hollenback had ever seen. They could just as easily be playing for Penn or another of the Ivies. Already, Hollenback had let the two freshmen play the entire games against Grove City and the Indians and he intended to do that for most of the season.

"Big Bill" already felt comfortable with this squad. The preseason practices had gone well and the players had a good team spirit. Hollenback was a disciplinarian and he showed it on and off the field. "One of Hollenback's pet schemes is a most rigid discipline among the players and such a course will surely bring nothing but success to Old State's energetic eleven tucked away up here among the mountains," one newspaper reporter wrote. "...so firm has been his grip that the (football) candidates are rapidly rounding into form. Daily work at punting and tackling the dummy with long drills at some formations entirely new to 'Pop' Golden's boys have been brought the men into shape."

Hollenback had set new off-field rules and the players were following them with few complaints: no swearing, no smoking and no chewing. They seemed to enjoy playing with each other and they listened to what "advisory coach" Hollenback and "head coach" Irish McIlveen told them. That was why they looked so good in the season opener with Grove City on the new field. New Beaver Field on the western edge of the campus looked a lot better than that muddy old field over by the Track House. Hollenback was still mystified as to why there were no dressing rooms built at the new field but Pop said money had been tight, and besides, Pop said, they can warm up for the game as they walked the quarter mile from the Track House to New Beaver Field.

It really didn't matter. There would be just three home games and none of the opponents were toughies. Hollenback was sorry Cornell and Navy had been dropped. As Dale Mason had written in the *Pittsburgh Press* earlier, "Now that it has been found necessary, on account of long, tiresome trips, to pass up the games with such friendly rivals as Cornell and the Navy, the Nittany Mountain Lions will have no chance to show their prowess outside of the state of Pennsylvania." So be it, Hollenback must have thought. At least Penn was still on the schedule.

Hollenback was happy that Vorhis was his captain. The quarterback was a true leader who led by action, not just words. He had taken charge immediately in the Grove City opener by scoring the first touchdown, then later added another TD, three extra points and one of his patented field goals. McClearly also had two TDs. It was a relative easy 31-0 win and the home crowd did a little extra celebrating be-

cause it also was the schools' 100th victory since football began in 1887.

Hollenback would overlook Vorhis' last minute faux paus against the Indians. Everyone on the team had to forget it, Hollenback told them, and they did. A week later, they took out their frustrations on an outclassed Geneva club, as McCleary scored three TDs and Heff Hersham and Dad Engle got two apiece in a 46-0 win. With a little more practice in the next week, Hollenback was convinced they would be ready to defeat Penn.

Then came a defining moment off-field that undoubtedly affected the outcome of the Penn game. Hollenback was in downtown State College one afternoon before practice when he ran into his star left halfback, Hershman. Heff had a wad of tobacco in his cheek. "Big

Henny Weaver teamed with Dick Harlow at the tackle position on the undefeated 1909 team. He loved to hit and be hit.

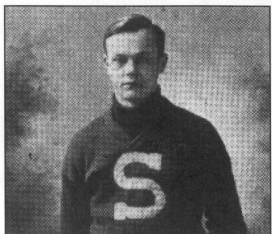

Captain Larry Vorhis of the unbeaten '09 team was one of the first QBs in the country to utilize passing when the rules were very restrictive.

Bill" didn't say anything at first but as they walked back towards Old Main, Hershman almost choked on his chew and had to spit it out. Hershman knew the rules. Break the rules and you sit.

So, for the Penn game, Hollenback shifted Vorhis to Hershman's position and moved dependable Dutch Herman in at starting quarterback. Dutch was a good quarterback but the switch seemed to take some of the rhythm out of the State attack. The first half turned into a punting duel between Penn's captain, Alex Thayer, and State's kicking tandem of Vorhis and Mauthe. State couldn't get a sustained attack going and the favored Quakers fumbled two scoring opportunities deep in State territory. The 12,000 mostly Penn fans could not believe their eyes. A scoreless tie at halftime? With the "farmers?"

Hollenback made one of the rousing halftime talks he would become known for. State quickly took the offensive in the second half and midway through the period moved into field goal range, but Vorhis missed a field goal. What happened next is not clear. Three sportswriters reported the next few minutes a little differently. The teams exchanged a couple of kicks before Penn got the ball at midfield, either by recovering a blocked punt or by a poor punt out-of-bounds by Mauthe. In any event, that put the Quakers into position for Thayer to kick a field goal from somewhere between the 35 and 22 yard markers to give Penn a 3-0 lead.

Minutes later, Alex Gray blocked a Penn punt that went out-of-bounds with Herman chasing it. A block must have sent Herman crashing to the ground, and as he lay there, Penn's captain Miller ran over and kicked him squarely in the head. That was too much for umpire Bill Edwards. He tossed Miller out of the game and marched off a 25-yard penalty. In went Hershman for the first time and after he gained a few yards on two rushes, Vorhis went back to try another field goal. This one was good—from somewhere between the 20 and 25 yard lines, and the score was tied.

But the game wasn't over yet. Penn got the ball back and as the clock wound down Thayer dropped back to attempt a game-winning field goal. Very saw that Thayer would have a sharp angle and shouted at McCleary to trade places in the line because he was bigger and had a better chance to block the kick. McCleary was skeptical of the rookie but switched positions. Sure enough, McCleary blocked the attempt and the game was over.

The players were jubilant and everyone on the State team seemed happy about the tie except Hollenback. "The State boys were inclined to be gay at the expense of the university (of Pennsylvania)," reported a newspaper (*Herald*). "They would have preferred to win, but they considered tieing [sic] the score after Pennsylvania had taken the lead almost equivalent to success, considering the fact that their opponents could not make a touchdown against them and were fairly fortunate to make a goal from the field."

But Hollenback was not pleased. "This is the last time Penn State will come to Franklin Field without a victory," he told reporters.

When the team returned home that Monday, they were greeted downtown by the entire 1,500 student body, which had been granted recess from classes by President Edward Sparks. "Big Bill" had to remind everyone that the season wasn't over yet.

Four games remained. But Lafayette canceled its scheduled contest at Altoona Oct. 30 and the team had two weeks to rest before playing original rival Bucknell. A familiar face was on the Bucknell sidelines in Lewisburg, "The General" himself, George Hoskins. But Hoskins' coaching did little good for Bucknell. State won by the highest score since teams started playing, 33-0, with McCleary scoring three TDs again and Hershman another in a 50-yard run. A week later McCleary had another three touchdown day and also kicked three extra points the Lions crushed West Virginia at Beaver Field, 40-0.

State was heavily favored in the annual season finale on Thanksgiving Day at Pittsburgh. The game was to be played on the new field built by the owner of the Pittsburgh Pirates, Barney Drefuss. He called it Forbes Field. The State players apparently didn't like how the field had been converted from baseball to football because they later complained about running up hill all day. Maybe it was the field. Maybe the long 10 day delay between games. Or maybe just overconfidence. But State struggled. Hershman's runs set up a 2-yard TD by McCleary in the second quarter but Mauthe missed the extra point. Later in the half, Vorhis also blew another chip shot field goal. But Pitt was simply awful all day. The Panthers got only two first downs, both in the second half, and picked up 76 yards rushing while State was grinding out 12 first downs and 241 yards. Still, it was a victory, 5-0—and the first unbeaten season since 1894.

"The city belongs to State College from five o'clock in the afternoon until the wee small hours of the morning," wrote one Pittsburgh sportswriter. "...Pitt was vanquished because the wearers of the gold and blue were outclassed....(State's) margin of supremacy was not evident throughout the game, but it was visible to the naked eye long enough to demonstrate its truth to Pittsburghers."

The team had scored 166 points and gave up just 11. "Big Bill" Hollenback had brought respectability—and more—back to the program. Pittsburgh area newspapers declared the Lions the champs of Western Pennsylvania and a *Philadelphia* paper said the team was in the top five of the East. Everyone hailed Hollenback as a coaching virtuoso. With Hollenback coaching up there again next year, some sportswriters said, State could probably do it again. Unfortunately, next year would be the wrong Hollenback.

Season Record 5-0-2
Record to Date 104-64-10
Winning percentage .612

"The Wrong Brother"

Jack Hollenback ran over to Pete Mauthe who was on the ground writhing in pain and clutching his ankle. The sophomore half-back had just gone down under a pile of players and Hollenback feared the worst.

It was only a routine scrimmage. Nothing out of the ordinary. Mauthe was carrying the ball through the line and was tackled. Happens every day in practice. Only this time it would be different.

The team had been practicing at Beaver Field for its third game of the year against the Sterling Athletic Club of Wilkinsburg. Despite the 2-0 season start, things had not been going well for Jack Hollenback. He had left his coaching job at Franklin & Marshall to take over the State team for his younger brother, Bill, who was now coaching at Missouri. "Big Bill" had told everyone he would be back after a year but some folks had become skeptical when Jack was hired as the coach. It's a ruse to get his brother this job, some people said. At this juncture in the season it didn't matter because Jack was in charge and Bill was a thousand miles away.

Everyone had expected another year like the last one. "State's Prospects in Football Bright," blared the headline in the *State College Times* on September 16, two weeks before the season opener at home against the Harrisburg Athletic Club. "There is plenty of good material on the ground...," the *Times* reporter wrote.

Much of the optimism was spawned by the return of all but one of the starting linemen: Very and Piolett at the ends, "Crazy" Henry Weaver at right tackle, Johnson and captain Alex Gray at the guards and Watson at center. The other starting tackle, Dick Smith, had left school over the summer but his replacement, junior Dick Harlow, had seen lots of playing time as a prime substitute in '09 and some assistant coaches felt he had more natural talent than Smith.

Jack Hollenback served as coach for the 1910 season when his younger brother, Bill, took a one year leave of absence.

No one had seemed overly concerned that the backfield would have to be completely revamped, with only Mauthe returning from last year's first team. As the pre-season practice progressed, two sophomores and a freshman emerged as starters: Dad Engle at left half, Fritz Barrett at fullback and newcomer Eugene Miller at quarterback.

Miller was the real surprise. Everyone called him "Shorty" and with reason. He was only 5-foot-5. He was stocky and weighed about 140 pounds. When he showed up for the first day of practice everyone laughed. They couldn't believe this "midget" (which is what they called him when they first saw him) was the whiz kid they heard about from Harrisburg Central High School. But the laughter stopped when they saw him run. He was fast, real fast. And he could spin, twist, cut and sidestep away from tackler after tackler. He also had a personality that matched his running style and his wisecracks kept the team loose.

Hollenback had figured the backfield would need a couple of games to jell into a synchronized unit but he had mixed feelings about the three easy games manager L. A. Cuthbert had lined up at Beaver Field to start the season. The Harrisburg Athletic Club was okay for the opener but he would have preferred a little tougher opposition before the big game with Penn at Franklin Field Oct. 22. Cuthburt had tried to schedule a game at Yale on Oct. 15 but Hollenback was just as glad that had not worked out. He would have enjoyed taking on Yale later in the season, if it could have been set up, but one game before playing his alma mater would have been too soon.

The game against Harrisburg turned out to be a disappointment because the visitors were so weak. The first team didn't play all that much and Hollenback had cleared his bench, using 24 players, so as not to run up the score. Barrett scored three TDs and Engle two and Mauthe had been 6-for-6 in extra points in the 58-0 win. But it had been interesting to see how the new passing and onside kick rules worked out. It felt a little strange playing four quarters instead of two halves but the short rest between quarters helped.

Hollenback worked some new wrinkles into his offense before the next game with Carnegie Tech but that game hadn't been much of a test, either. This was the first game with the "other" Pittsburgh school and there were some fans at Beaver Field who said it should be the last. The score was 61-0 and Tech never made a first down. The juniors, Engle and Barrett, again were the stars. Dad scored four TDs and Fritz had two, including one on a 100-yard kickoff return. Hollenback had been somewhat pleased with his new passing offense, with 9-of-12 completions and a TD by Piollet, but he realized Tech wasn't a true test.

Hollenback knew Sterling wouldn't be much better than Harrisburg or Tech. He figured State's second team would be tougher on the first team than anyone, so that was why he was putting the squad through such a rigorous scrimmage when Mauthe was hurt. It would be a costly scrimmage and would define the season. Mauthe's ankle was broken and he would be lost for the year. Once again, Hollenback would have to revamp his offense, using another untested freshman, A. M. Barron in his place.

State beat Sterling 45-0 with Miller, Piollett, Gray and Harlow leading the way but the team's play was ragged. "There was a lack of dash and concerted effort on the part of the state eleven," reported the *Times*, "and none of the three games thus far played have proved anything more than a variation in the practices, so that Pennsylvania will be the real opponent worthy of State's mettle..."

Rain fell throughout the first half of the game at Franklin Field and a sparse crowd made up most of students saw the game. The wet and muddy conditions caused all sorts of havoc in the State backfield. Twice in the first half, State fumbles led to Quaker touchdowns, one from inside the 5-yard line. The TDs gave Penn a 10-0 lead at the intermission but Hollenback gave a halftime talk that his brother would have appreciated and the State team dominated the Quakers throughout the second half. The Lions controlled the play in Penn's territory for 22 of the 25 minutes and the only time Penn threatened, State held on downs at the 3-yard line. But State blew a couple of scoring opportunities, including once when Engle was stopped on three successive plays inside the Penn 2-yard line. Another time, Miller went 95 yards on a thrilling punt return, only to have the play called back because he had supposedly stepped out of bounds back in State territory. So, the 10-0 Penn lead held up as the Quakers won the 16th game in the series dating back to 1890. "Big Bill" Hollenback's vow of 1909 would have to wait another year.

Despite the defeat, sportswriters praised the team's performance and another large crowd of fans greeted the team upon its return to State College. But the welcoming reception was not enough to boost the spirits of the downcast players. The following week's practices did not go well, no matter what was said by Hollenback, or the ex-players who were helping out as assistant coaches. As Joe Paterno would later say, if you practice well, you play well. That Saturdays' game against Villa Nova was a perfect example. In the first half, Villa Nova never got past its own 30-yard line but State couldn't punch in a score. The second half was equally frustrating. State missed three field goal attempts and lost another scoring chance at the Villa Nova 10-yard line. The game ended when a Villa Nova's quarterback, Skelton, avoided a safety by six inches after being tackled for a 10-yard loss at the goal line. The 0-0 score would go down as a tie but everyone on campus and elsewhere considered it a major "defeat."

The Villa Nova tie took a lot luster off the close loss to Penn and sportswriters criticized Hollenback's team as underachievers. Hollenback knew his team would never beat its other big rival, Pitt, unless he could get the players out of their stupor. Apparently, the advice the team got in practice the next week from ex-players like Henny Scholl and Fred Heckel must have helped. In its first ever meeting against St. Bonaventure at Beaver Field the following Saturday, State won, 34-0. Very and his substitute at left end, Al Wilson, both scored on onside kicks by Shorty Miller and Harlow also got a TD on a pass from Miller. A week later it was more of the same against the old traditional foe, Bucknell, at Beaver Field, winning this time, 45-3. Now they were ready for Pitt.

The 18,000 that showed up at Forbes Field on Thanksgiving day was the largest crowd to date to see a Penn State-Pitt game. The betting favored Pitt as the Panthers entered the game unbeaten and unscored upon in eight games. It turned out to be a rough game with State picking up some 200 yards in penalties and Pitt getting 100. Early in the first quarter, Pitt's Bill Hittner took a pass from quarterback Dave Richards, evaded several State defenders and went 42 yards before Barrett brought him down at the 8-yard line. Richards ran up the middle on the next play and just barely got the ball in the end zone. Pitt missed the extra point. In the second quarter State used a poor Pitt punt and a Watson-to-Miller pass to get to the Pitt 31-yard line as time was running out. But Miller's pass was intercepted to end the drive. State's only other serious threat came in the second half when Very ran

45 yards to the Pitt 2-yard line but State's sputtering offense could do nothing more against the attacking Pitt defense. Pitt got another TD in the fourth quarter on a 45-yard punt return and the final score was 11-0. No one knew it at the time, but State would not lose another game for the next two years.

The erratic season had finally come to an end. Many fans thought it might have been different if Mauthe had been able to play all year. No doubt, his absence seemed to take some spark out of the team, but most followers thought there was another spark missing. Yes, the alums complained, it would have been different if the other Hollenback brother had been coaching.

Season Record 5-2-1
Record to Date 109-66-11
Winning percentage .616

"'Big Bill' Returns With Vengeance"

Shorty Miller waited anxiously near the goal line for the kickoff from Penn's Captain Roy Mercer. The 15,000 people filling Franklin Field were screaming and cheering and the bands of both teams were playing louder and louder. Miller had never heard so much noise.

The little quarterback glanced over toward the bench and the grandstands where the 20-piece school band was blaring away as the hundreds of Penn State fans sitting behind the band waved their blue and white hats and banners. Among that crowd of more than a thousand for this fifth game of State's season were some 400-to-600 students, faculty and staff who had accompanied the team on the long 10-hour railroad trip from Lemont. They sure had gotten the team pumped up with their rousing cheers and songs throughout the journey.

As usual, Penn was favored, with the odds at 6-5. But everyone rooting for State knew this team would never be more ready. It had been one heckuva season up to now, going back to the first day of preseason practice when captain Dex Very led a "welcome back" cheer for coach "Big Bill" Hollenback. Yes, he could have stayed at Missouri but Hollenback said he had missed his friends and family in Pennsylvania, and, besides, hadn't he promised he would be back. The team had responded quickly to his return. Sportswriters observing the preseason workouts noticed how sharp and conditioned the team was—more precise on offense and more fundamentally sound in tackling and defensive techniques. This has the makings of a great team, everyone said.

Mauthe, the fullback, looked as good as ever and fully recovered from his ankle injury and quarterback Miller seemed faster than ever. The veteran and very dependable Dutch Herman also had returned as the backup quarterback after dropping out of school for a year. Hollenback, still the "advisory coach" and the official "head coach" Bull McCleary had a half dozen newcomers trying out for the halfback positions and they believed any two of them would adapt well to the State attack. Punk Berryman at right half looked like the best of them, even though he wasn't much taller than Shorty. The two transfers from Penn, Philip Barry and Francis Xavier King, were also quite talented,

The great, undefeated 1911 team set off a riot back in State College after word of its victory over Cornell hit town but its biggest accomplishment was the first-ever win over Penn. The players are (left to right): Punk Berryman, Fritz Barrett, Frank King, P.A. Barry, Dick Harlow, Pete Mauthe, Dad Engle, Captain Dex Very, Al Hansen, Al Goedecke, John Clark, Red Bebout, Al Wilson, Dutch Herman and Shorty Miller. Bebout was one of two State players killed in World War I.

but they were having some problems about their admission and they might not be eligible for the first two games. Hollenback believed his line was even stronger than the backfield, with the veterans Very and Wilson back at ends and Harlow and Engle at the tackles. Al Hansen, once in "Big Bill's" doghouse, and fiery "Red" Bebout at the guards and John Clark at center were new starters but they all had played a lot last year as substitutes.

"Big Bill" was also happy about the schedule manager F. W. Orr had arranged: nine games with four at Beaver Field, including the first two, but set up so that the team would not be away from home two weeks in succession. (Joe Paterno would have been impressed.) And the biggest game of the year—with his alma mater—would be right in the middle—game number five. Hollenback and the team were pointing for it. "Big Bill" said he would never lose to Penn again after the '09 tie and he was determined to keep his word.

State easily won the season opener at Beaver Field against Geneva. Junior sub Fritz Barrett started at fullback after Mauthe moved to left end for the injured Wilson and scored four touchdowns, including one on a 109-yard run. Miller and Berryman also scored two TDs apiece and Mauthe kicked two field goals and six extra points in the 57-0 win. The following week against Gettysburg, a crowd of 4,000 watched as the Nittany Lions scored two touchdowns in the first six minutes. Five different players scored TDs, including Mauthe, who also kicked a field goal and two extra points, as State won, 37-0.

In the practice week before the first road game, against Cornell, Hollenback drilled the team extra on kick and pass coverage and added "bucking" drills to the offense. He scrimmaged them hard, "from a half hour to an hour," the *Pittsburgh Post* reported, with the result that "the line has shown great improvement in strength and speed" and the offense showed "snappy open play formations." The intense practice paid off in Ithaca. Two of Cornell's stars were put out of the game in the first quarter with injuries and by halftime the Big Red captain also was sidelined. The only score came in the second quarter when Harlow blocked a punt at Cornell's 15-yard line and Engle picked the ball up at the 6-yard line and ran in for the touchdown. Mauthe missed the extra point. The State offense moved the ball well but Mauthe, who was having one of his worst kicking days, missed four field goal attempts. Late in the game, Herman took over for Miller at quarterback and led State on a drive for an apparent TD by Mauthe, but the referee disallowed it saying Hollenback had "coached from the sidelines."

When word of the great 5-0 victory reached the State campus, the students went "wild." This wasn't the first nor the last time State's students would celebrate a big win a little too enthusiastically but this one was probably the most destructive and unruly of all time. The students first celebrated around the traditional bonfire but when additional wood was needed to keep the bonfire going, they literally tore up the town, breaking up board walks, fences and anything else they could find throughout the village. Fights between students and townspeople broke out all over the area. The *State College Times* of Oct. 20, described one incident where "in a melee between residents of the west end, who were defending their property, and the mob, several of the latter [the students] received the contents of a shotgun while another had his face flattened by a blow from a shovel." The volunteer town deputies were overwhelmed until they attacked the student ringleaders and brought the riot to an end after several hours. School officials later apologized but the relationship between town-and-gown had suffered another major setback. (So, what's new?)

When Hollenback and the team returned from Ithaca, they, too, were disturbed by what had occurred. But they had to concentrate on the season, not the boorish behavior of their classmates. Villa Nova was not expected to be a tough opponent, but it was. Maybe the State team was looking ahead one week to its major confrontation with Penn but whatever the reason, the game was "one of the roughest battles ever witnessed on the home grounds," according to the "*LaVie.*" It was scoreless at halftime and Hollenback must have made another of his famous talks, for the Lions roared out and scored 18 points, including one TD on a 45-yard run by Miller, for an 18-0 win.

So, Miller now stood in Franklin Field awaiting Mercer's kickoff. He and his teammates had been surprised when Penn won the toss and decided to kick instead of receive. It would turn out to be a fatal mistake.

Miller grabbed the ball on the 5-yard line and started up the middle, directly towards "a swarm of Penn tacklers" who were closing in quickly. "Miller squirmed through the bunch," reported the *Philadelphia North American*, "dashing, sprinting, sidling, and once in a while coming to a dead stop to let an enemy overrun him." His teammates were "knocking everyone down," just as "Big Bill" and Bull had told them and Shorty cut to the sideline. Mercer came up near the 35-yard line to make the tackle and almost at that instant Very belted Mercer from the side and Shorty jumped right over both of them. In a second he was in the clear and he crossed the goal line amid the

Some action in the 1911 Penn game. State defeated the favored Quakers 22-6 for their first win in 17 tries. Here a Penn back (left) runs behind some good blocking.

cheers of the Penn State throng. It was only the second return of an opening kickoff in Franklin Field history and the Penn fans couldn't believe it.

"It was this play, startling in its suddenness, blasting in its effect on Penn's team that demoralized the Quakers at the start," reported the *Pittsburgh Post*. It was also the defining moment of the season. But Hollenback's boys had just begun.

State got the ball back a few moments later and drove nearly 70 yards on Miller's running and passing to the 25-yard line, when Shorty did it again. He broke through the line, spun and twisted and went into the end zone again. Everyone in the stadium was stunned The game was hardly five minutes old and already State led, 12-0 (with two PATs also by Mauthe).

Penn's coach Andy Smith must have said something inspirational to his players at that point because when State got the ball again a short time later, the Quakers stopped the Lions cold and forced Mauthe to punt out of the end zone. Now, it was Dex's turn. Mauthe's long and high spiral hit the ground near the sideline at State's 40-yard line and bounced into the air. Mercer must misjudged the ball because Very grabbed the ball without breaking stride and dashed 70 yards for State's third TD. Mauthe booted the extra point and within some eight minutes of the first quarter, State had an unthinkable 18-0 lead.

By the time the game was over, State had added two safeties after a blocked kick by Harlow and an errant Penn lateral, and Penn had scored a lone TD in the second quarter. "Pennsylvania was outplayed, outgeneraled and outspeeded by Hollenback's finished product of the new school of football," said the *Pittsburgh Post*.

Back in State College, the students celebrated the 22-6 victory in a calmer manner Saturday night, and when the team returned on Monday it received the traditional welcome home "wagon-pull" march through town and up to the Track House. Hollenback had coached a State team to its biggest victory of all time but he reminded the crowd that the season wasn't over yet.

As "Big Bill" spent the next week getting the team to calm down from its exhilaration, he was accused by Philadelphia papers of "stealing" two players from Pennsylvania that helped him win the big game. Those two sophomore halfbacks Barry and King might have helped Penn win, they said, if Hollenback hadn't stolen them and then "ignored the one year residence rule." Hollenback said he had done nothing wrong and reminded the critics of how Penn had "stolen" it's current coach, Andy Smith, from State back in 1902. The controversy soon died as State geared up for its final four games.

State had no trouble at home against St. Bonaventure as Hollenback rested the first team in the second half. Seven different players scored touchdowns with Barrett getting two. Colgate was a new foe on the schedule for the final home game and the visitors were somewhat of an unknown quantity. The team was "fast and snappy" and within the first four minutes of the game had kicked a field goal. Twice in the first half, State lost the ball on fumbles inside Colgate's 10-yard line and Hollenback wasn't pleased by the narrow 3-0 halftime lead. He told the team how he felt in an angry halftime talk. Four minutes after the second half kickoff, State scored on a pass from Miller to Very. Another Miller-to-Very pass later in the quarter brought another TD as State won 17-9. It was so dark when the game ended that the spectators who had automobiles had to ring the playing field to produce enough light to finish the game. Colgate got some solace by scoring the first touchdown ever by an opponent at New Beaver Field when a quick kick in the fourth quarter led to a 3-yard TD plunge by the visitor's captain and quarterback, Huntington.

Navy was unbeaten and twice tied but heavily favored in the Nov. 18 game at Annapolis. Hollenback thought his team could win if it played its best game. He was even more convinced they would win at the kickoff when Navy rested most of its starters because of its upcoming clash with its major rival Army. But State played perhaps its worst game of the year on the rain soaked, muddy field. Hollenback later complained that nothing seemed to go right. Both offenses fumbled and stumbled and kicking dominated the game. Once in the third period, Mauthe thought he had a field goal but the ball fell short of the cross bar. Another State drive ended with a fumble by Barrett at the goal line. Near the end of the game, Navy fumbled at its own 2-yard line and Herman fell on the ball instead of picking it up and running in for a touchdown, and Navy held on downs. The scoreless tie didn't matter much to Navy but Hollenback and his players were embarrassed.

The weather was sunny but chilly for the annual Thanksgiving Day game against Pitt and some 15,000 turned out for what was becoming a major "social event" for alumni of both schools. Once again kicking dominated the play. The only points came in the second quarter when Miller's short punt return set up a 32-yard field goal by Mauthe. Late in the third period, State drove 45 yards for a first down at the Pitt 3-yard line. King carried to the goal line but the referee ruled he did not cross, despite protestations from the players and coaches. State got the ball back moments later on the Pitt 37-yard line but Miller's pass was intercepted by Pitt's star, Hubie Wagner, who almost broke away for a long TD before being tackled from behind by Very. The final score was 3-0 but Pitt's coach Joe Thompson complained that he felt his team played a better game and should have won. McCleary told the *Pittsburgh Post* the score should have been 9-0 because "King clearly scored" and "we won because we outplayed them."

As usual after the Pitt-Penn State game, the Pittsburgh area alumni honored the team with a banquet at the Fort Pitt Hotel. This time, they also were celebrating the finest season in history, with the most victories ever and a team that gave up just 15 points while scoring 199 on opponents. That evening Mauthe was elected captain for 1912. "He's the best all around backfield man I have ever seen," said Hollenback.

"With a leader of such caliber for next year," wrote the *"LaVie,"* "may we not look forward to a season of gridiron achievements which shall equal, if not surpass, our extraordinary record for 1911?"

Season Record 8-0-1
Record to Date 117-66-12
Winning percentage .631

"Pete's Year"

There were nine minutes left in the game when it happened. Ohio State simply quit and walked off the field!

Ohio State had sought this first ever game with Penn State in part to show it deserved to join the prestigious Big Ten, then known as the Intercollegiate Conference of Faculty Representatives. The way OSC's athletic board figured, beating one of the best teams in the East would increase its prestige beyond the pedestrian Ohio Conference.

With few exceptions, Penn State had rarely traveled beyond the East to meet an opponent. For PSC officials, playing as far away as Columbus would be a way of proving it was one of the best teams in the country, not just the East. Penn State's president, Edwin Sparks, also encouraged the game. He was an Ohio State grad and figured the game could be the start of a nice friendly rivalry—which goes to prove, once again, how wrong college presidents can be when they get too deeply involved with the playing fields.

When Hollenback's team arrived in Columbus for the November 16 game, the players couldn't believe what they were hearing. In a disrespectful atmosphere that—amazingly—would set the tone for future games between the two schools in the Engle and Paterno eras, Ohio State's media and fans arrogantly predicted a rout. Two-to-three touchdowns and more, was the word around town.

Here we are unbeaten in six games against the likes of Cornell, Penn and Washington & Jefferson, the cocky Penn State players railed, with only six points scored on us all year, and these "Westerners" have the audacity to believe they can walk all over us. We'll see who will do the walking.

Before the team left the dressing room that afternoon, "Big Bill" showed them newspaper clippings from the local press belittling their exploits and questioning the quality of Eastern football. He reminded them of all the abuse "we farmers" have taken over the years and told them it was now payback time. He wouldn't have had to say a thing for Mauthe and his gang were so angry they were ready to kick OSC's butt into the Olgetangy River. And they did!

Unbeaten and untied, the outstanding 1912 team scored 285 points while yielding just 6. The "Farmers" scored a big win for Eastern football by destroying Ohio State 37-0 in a game where the badly out-classed Buckeyes simply left the field with nine minutes remaining in the game. The starting lineup was (left to right): backfield: Coach Bill Hollenback, Punk Berryman, Dan Welty, Pete Mauthe, Shorty Miller and manager Bill Kerr; front line: Dex Very, Levy Lamb, Al Hansen, John Clark, Red Bebout, Dad Engle and Al Wilson.

When the State players trotted out onto the field, many of the 3,500 spectators laughed. The visiting team looked quite small compared to beefy men in scarlet and gray and many of the fans pointed mockingly at the little squirt tossing the football to the big man they called Pete. The crowd stopped laughing after the first few plays. The fists and elbows started flying early and the blocking and tackling by the Penn Staters seemed overly vicious to the partisan Ohio fans.

Within the first couple of minutes, State moved into Ohio's territory and Mauthe calmly booted a 41-yard field goal that surprised the home fans. After the defense got the ball back, Shorty Miller took charge, and after a couple of good runs and a long pass to Al Wilson, Shorty rammed up the middle for a touchdown from five yards out. Mauthe's extra point was good and the visitors led, 10-0. Moments later, State had the ball again and this time Miller zipped past several would-be tacklers on a 30-yard run for another TD. Mauthe missed the point after and the first quarter came to a close with the Lions leading the stunned Buckeyes, 16-0.

Ohio State coach John Richards complained to the officials about the "unnecessary roughness" by the visitors but he was virtually ignored. They told him there was rough play all around. Throughout the second quarter, the players hammered away at each other and blood flowed on both sides. Someone smashed Wilson in the mouth from behind and knocked him out. When he came to he was missing several teeth, but he stayed in and finished the game. At one point, an Ohio player stomped on Red Bebout's face, "cutting the flesh badly," as the *Pittsburgh Post* reported. "The Pittsburgher's nose and one eye were considerably lacerated," the *Post* went on, "but no sooner had his

wounds been bandaged than he gamely resumed his place...and resumed play." Richards ran up and down the sidelines chastising the officials for not calling penalties against Penn State and the half ended with no additional scoring.

The irate Ohio crowd milled about the field and some even threatened the Penn State players, who had to rest under a tree because the dressing rooms were so far away. The second half was only moments old when Ohio's quarterback fumbled. Very grabbed the ball and ran 35 yards into the end zone. Just before the quarter ended, Miller picked up a muffed hand off from the center and dashed 40 yards for his third TD. Mauthe kicked both extra points and State had a 30-0 lead to start the final period. Another drive early in the fourth quarter brought the ball to the 1-yard line when one of Ohio's star lineman coming into the game challenged Miller to run the ball at him. As Shorty told the story later, he replied, "All right, cocky, here she comes," and gave the ball to Mauthe who barreled right through the Ohio challenger and into the end zone. Mauthe kicked the extra point and State now led 37-0.

James Lester "Pete" Mauthe captained the undefeated 1912 squad that outscored opponents 285 to 6. He was the fourth State player inducted into the National Football Foundation College Football Hall of Fame in 1957.

There were about nine minutes left when State kicked off. Very hit one of the Buckeye blockers so hard the Ohio player went flying at least 10 feet backwards. "That's enough," screamed coach Richards. "Illegal block. Illegal block. We're outta here." He signaled his players to follow him and they left the field and headed back to the dressing room as the disorderly crowd jeered and taunted the Penn State players.

Mauthe started to lead the State players to the dressing room, too, but he stopped when told by the referee that the rules required the team to remain on the field for at least five minutes to claim the forfeit. So, the players milled around as the crowd fomented, hurling verbal insults and debris at them. One spectator ran towards the team but got no further than assistant coach Dick Harlow, who decked him with a hard right fist. Police wielding nightsticks quickly surrounded the team as it stood around in the north end of the field. They watched as an Ohio fan further riled the crowd by lighting a fire to a blue and white bunting on the goal posts. The culprit escaped into the throng without being caught.

Finally, the five minutes were up, and the team went back to the dressing room, then headed back to their hotel. The sooner they could get out of this horsemanure town the better, they probably thought. An embarrassed delegation of Ohio State officials were at the train station the next day as the team departed, and they apologized to Hollenback, Mauthe and the Penn State officials. Apologies accepted. Now, let's get out of this bleep-bleep place and never come back. It would

College Football Hall of Fame members (from left) Shorty Miller, Pete Mauthe and Dex Very played together from 1909-1912.

The great 1912 backfield (l to r) Berryman, Mauthe, Miller and Welty.

be 44 years before a Penn State football team did—and, Ohio State would regret that, too!

The score of the game was officially recorded as 1-0 and a football used in the game is on display with that scored at the Penn State football Hall of Fame room. But it is a 37-0 win in the State record books. "The score could easily have been 60-0 or more," Hollenback said many years later.

That was probably the most satisfying win of the entire season for Mauthe and his teammates and it defined the season. They were 7-0 at that point and as they prepared the next two weeks for the traditional closer at Pitt on Thanksgiving Day, they could reflect on their record-breaking accomplishments. If they could not only beat Pitt but hold them scoreless, they could have the best record of all-time for State.

Pitt was fast becoming State's hottest rival. Penn was still the team everyone wanted to beat and Gettysburg was getting less and less competitive while Bucknell was no longer on the schedule. But playing Pitt on a major holiday in the last game of the year was taking on special significance and winning that game could now "make or break" each school's season, no matter what the overall record was.

Hollenback was not surprised his team was unbeaten going into the finale at Forbes Field. Almost all the starters from his outstanding 1911 team had returned in September. The two controversial expatriates from Penn—Barry and King—had dropped out of school but sophomore Dan Welty was a very capable replacement at left halfback. Besides, with Mauthe, Miller and Punk Berryman in the backfield, Hollenback figured Welty would do more blocking than running. Except for another sophomore, Levi Lamb at right tackle, all starting linemen were back: Dex Very and Wilson at ends, Dad Engle at left tackle, Bebout and Al Hansen at the guards and John Clark at center. Hollenback was happy he had shifted Lamb from the backfield to tackle. At 6-foot-4, 210-pounds, he was the biggest player on the field but Hollenback

thought he had a touch of laziness so "Big Bill" was constantly nagging at him during practice. This starting eleven was so good on defense as well as offense that Hollenback intended to let everyone play most of the season without substitution—and he did. Only 13 players won varsity letters that year.

Hollenback was now officially the "head coach" as the athletic board dropped the ersatz "advisory" title. Hollenback brought back last year's starting right tackle, Dick Harlow, to assist him as the line coach and the pair made a successful combination, with "Big Bill" plotting strategy and offense and Harlow concentrating on the line and helping out on game tactics. Some past State stars would drop by every couple of weeks to assist in the coaching and everyone was especially impressed by one-time captains Mother Dunn and Carl Forkum. One of the former players told Hollenback he thought the backfield was good but the line was weak. So, Hollenback called the line over, placed the ball on the 5-yard line and told the former player he had five chances to take the ball over the goal line. "After the third try, he was back on the 20-yard line...and decided he had enough," Engle later recalled. So much for a weak line.

Team manager Bill Kerr had worked up another schedule that always gave the team a couple of "breathers" before big games. The season opener at Beaver Field with Carnegie Tech also gave everyone a chance to play for the first time under the year's major changes in the rules: the field was shortened to 100 yards and now teams had four downs, instead of three, to make 10 yards for another first down; a touchdown was increased to six points. The new rules made little difference to Hollenback's team as Mauthe scored three TDs, Miller had two and Berryman one in an easy 41-0 win over Tech. Shorty had one of the longest runs of the year from scrimmage when he went 78-yards for a TD.

Hollenback closed practice most of the next week (See, Paterno wasn't the first coach to do it!) as the team prepared in secret

Tackle Lloyd "Dad" Engle was part of the great undefeated 1911 and 1912 squads and the uncle of future State coach Rip Engle.

for Washington & Jefferson. State had not played W&J since the nasty game of 1904 when Forkum had been intentionally injured. That was one of the reasons Forkum showed up that week to assist Hollenback and Harlow. W&J was no patsy. The Presidents had tied the Carlisle Indians led by Jim Thorpe, 0-0, and held powerful Cornell to a 3-0 win.

Some 4,000 fans, the largest crowd ever on New Beaver Field since it opened in 1909, turned out and saw three field goals by Mauthe give State a 9-0 halftime lead. State had a chance for a TD that half but fumbled on the W&J 1-yard line. What happened in the second half is best summed up by the headline in the *State College Times*, which reported: "W. And J. Was Crushed...The Westerners Were Completely Surprised at Penn State's Whirlwind Plays and Lost Their Nerve." Mauthe ran back the second half kickoff 95 yards to the 5-yard line and on third down Miller passed to Very for the first touchdown. Miller scored the next TD after picking up a fumble caused by Lamb's crunching tackle on the W&J quarterback. In the fourth quarter Miller hit Very again on a 50-yard passing play for another TD. Final score, 30-0.

The ease of the W&J win made State the slight favorite in its first road game the next week at Cornell. Perhaps they were a bit overconfident, but the players were not as sharp in the opening quarter.

Miller botched a punt return when he touched the ball and let it roll into the end zone where Cornell recovered for a touchdown. That woke up the Lions. Engle told his teammates he was never going to stand under his own goal post "like this again." A few minutes later, they got into position for Mauthe to kick a field goal, and they took the lead on the ensuing kickoff when Berryman ran it all the way back for a 75-yard TD. (Yes, the rules at the time still gave the scoring team the choice to receive the next kickoff.) In the second half, Hollenback stuck mainly to a rushing attack to grind out the yardage but used passes to score TDs as Miller hit Very, Mauthe and Wilson for touchdowns. The game ended at 29-6 and Cornell players complained that the visitors were "overly rough." Indeed!

Hollenback was so confident of beating Gettysburg at home the next week that he took Miller with him to Philadelphia and scouted Pennsylvania's game against Lafayette. With Harlow coaching on a muddy field in a heavy wind, the rest of the team struggled a bit but beat Gettysburg, 25-0. Only one forward pass was thrown all day as Very and Mauthe scored TDs and Mauthe kicked a field and two extra points.

For the first time since they began playing in 1890, Penn State was favored over Penn, which had lost three straight games. Old Andy Smith surprised Hollenback on the opening kickoff with an onside kick that Penn recovered. The Quakers moved to State's 10-yard line but State held on downs. That would be the closest Penn would get to scoring all day. Engle set up State's first TD with a blocked punt in the second quarter but scoring wasn't easy. Penn's defense made State earn the 6-points and Mauthe finally went over after three plunges from the 1-yard line. Penn, kicking off again to start the second half recovered another onside kick but went nowhere. Early in the fourth period Lamb recovered a fumbled punt at the Penn 12-yard line. Penn dug in and three plays picked up just six yards. On 4th-and-4, Miller tossed an arching pass to Very, who was covered in the end zone by two defenders. Very almost tripped trying to break away from the Penn players but leaped, stretched and fell to the ground clutching the ball.

The 1912 team is honored during the 1957 Homecoming game at New Beaver Field when Pete Mauthe was named to the National Football Foundation College Football Hall of Fame. Athletic Director Ernest McCoy (with the microphone) introduces (left to right): Pete Mauthe, former coach Bob Higgins, Dick Harlow, Shorty Miller, Dex Very, Dad Engle, Frank Keller, Punk Berryman, J.D. McVean, Ollie Vogel, Dan Welty, Bert Barron, Manager Bill Kerr, former coach Jack Hollenback, representing his brother Bill who was coach in 1912.

Mauthe's extra point made it 14-0. Late in the game Very caught another pass of 57-yards from Miller for an apparent TD but the play was called back because two officials erred by blowing the whistle to start the play. The final score was 14-0 and Very was acclaimed for his outstanding play on offense and defense.

The final home game against Villa Nova was simply a slaughter as State won, 71-0. Lamb had his greatest day ever on offense, scoring three TDs, one on a pass reception, while playing at both tackle and halfback. Very and Mauthe each had two TDs and Mauthe also had a field goal and a record 8 PATs as Hollenback substituted freely.

So, after the Ohio State "walkoff" it was down to Pitt. The team had two weeks of rest and practice to prepare for the Panthers and it showed. Pitt was 3-5 and on paper no match for powerful State. But Hollenback continually reminded the team of how last year's season was almost spoiled by the Panthers. Not this year, baby!!! In his last game for State, Mauthe played what sportswriters said was his greatest game. He ran, passed, tackled and kicked State to a 38-0 victory, accounting for 20 points. He led off the scoring in the first quarter when Miller surprised his teammates and shocked the crowd by calling for a field goal from midfield. His teammates looked at Miller as if he was crazy but Shorty called the signals, held the ball and Mauthe kicked into the history books with a 51-yard field goal that would be the team record for 63 years. Early in the second quarter, Mauthe gained 32 yards in a 45-yard drive and got the TD on a 5-yard run, then kicked the PAT. A few minutes later, after State had recovered a fumble at Pitt's 35-yard line, Mauthe again carried most of the way to score another touchdown on a 3-yard dive. His extra point made it 17-0 at halftime. He became a passer in the third quarter, hitting Very on successive passes of 30 and 32 yards for State's third TD. Berryman scored next on a 42-yard interception return and Miller added the coup de grace with a 16-yard scoot as Mauthe booted the PATs. State's defense stopped three Pitt scoring threats inside the 25-yard line in the second half, including an attempted 15-yard field goal by Pitt's All-American Hubie Wagner, and State's greatest season to date came to an end.

Hollenback and most of the players had only one regret. Pop Golden hadn't been around to share in the glory. Pop had resigned in the spring to go into the insurance business in Pittsburgh and they had seen him there after the Pitt game. The success of this year belonged to him, too, for he had recruited many of the players and had hired the coach.

The team had scored 285 points and given up only six, on a fluky fumble. Mauthe had scored 119 points, which would remain the State individual scoring record for 59 years. He had scored 11 TDs, eight field goals and 29 extra points and had rushed for 710 yards. His eight field goals that season was the official team record until 1970 and he was one of the few players in the early years to kick three field goals in one game. Total passing statistics were not kept but Mauthe and Miller certainly had outstanding numbers. Very is one of State's all-time receivers even though his statistics may not show it. He caught at least eight passes for 187 yards at a time when passing was extremely rare. He also scored at least 9 TDs and gained 234 yards on 17 end-around carries that season and was the team leader in kickoff returns with 12 for 240 yards. Those three, plus another lineman or two, should also be on State's All-Time All-Americans list, but only the Walter Camp team was recognized officially in that era. Newspapers in Philadelphia, Pittsburgh and New York cited several State players on their All-America teams and Very was probably the most honored because of his all-around offensive and defensive play, making the First Team All-American selections of two Pittsburgh papers, two Philadelphia papers and papers in Washington, Boston and New York but he could only make Camp's Second Team.

But neither the players nor the team received the national recognition they deserved. Camp and many other influential sportswriters of the day picked undefeated Harvard as not only the best team in the East but the best in the nation and Penn State usually was selected as number two. It's a legacy of disrespect, rejection and scorn that continues to this day.

Of course, as the old saying goes, "there is always next year." The team's unbeaten streak was now at 17 games. Unfortunately, it wouldn't last much longer. And neither would the victories over Pitt.

Season Record 8-0-0
Record to Date 125-66-12
Winning percentage .645

"'Shorty's' Year"

Bill Hollenback knew before preseason practice started that he could not duplicate the record of his last two teams. He had lost too many standout players by graduation.

But with Miller and Berryman returning in the backfield and Lamb, Bebout and Clark up front, he believed he had a good nucleus to build his squad. Once practice started in September, however, he and his assistant Harlow knew this would be a difficult season. There just wasn't enough talent around to make up for losses of Mauthe, Very, and company. Without Pop Golden helping Harlow recruit in the high schools and prep schools last year, the pickings were slim.

As an example of how thin the team was, Hollenback could point to his starting left guard, Ralph Sayre. Ralph was a senior who was playing interclass football two years ago and hardly played on the

QB of the great '11 and '12 teams and one of State's early, nationally-known stars, the 5'5", 140 lb. Eugene "Shorty" Miller set records that stood for decades.

scrub team in 1912. He was a hard working kid and Harlow was spending a lot of time with him, but he was an obvious weakness on the left side. The left tackle, sophomore Cecil McDowell, and left end, freshman George Morris, were pretty good but lacked experience. The right side was okay, now that Andy Barron was in at right end. Barron had lettered in 1910 as Mauthe's substitute running back but had left school for two years. Hollenback switched him to end because he was satisfied with his newcomers in the backfield, freshman Harold "Fats" (also known as Jeff) Clark at fullback, and junior "Yeggs" Tobin at right half. Tobin had been one of only two substitutes off last year's team to letter, and although he was no Mauthe, Hollenback felt Tobin was consistent and dependable.

Still, Shorty, Punk and three vets up front would have to carry this club until it could mature. Hollenback was thankful the schedule was made for a developing team such as this, with four very beatable teams to start and the toughest four games at the end. There was one new opponent and Hollenback was looking forward to that game. Notre Dame, the up-and-coming little Catholic team from the Midwest, had agreed to visit Beaver Field on November 7th. This would be the biggest intersectional game ever for Penn State. Like State, Notre Dame had been unbeaten the previous two seasons and had played at Pitt both years, getting a 0-0 tie in 1911 and winning 3-0 in 1912. Hollenback had been hearing a lot about Notre Dame's quarterback "Gus" Dorais and end Knute Rockne and he figured this would be a good match of two evolving big-time football programs. It ought to be a marquee match up between Shorty and Gus.

Hollenback was confident that Shorty would make this a winning team. And he wasn't disappointed in the opening season game at Beaver Field against Carnegie Tech. Miller had a running day that was not surpassed at Penn State for 68 years, when he set a single-game rushing record of 250 yards and scored five touchdowns on runs of 23, 55, 47, 37 and 40 yards. Miller's initial TD came in the first quarter when he and Berryman scored to give State a 14-0 lead. State was scoreless in the second quarter as Tech moved the ball around State's ends for three first downs but couldn't get near the goal. State broke open the game early in the third quarter. On the second play after the kickoff, Miller got his second TD, and he scored two more in the next six minutes to turn the game into an eventual 49-0 rout.

The following wek, Gettysburg came to Beaver Field with a familiar face coaching on the sidelines–last year's State captain, Pete Mauthe. Mauthe knew all of Hollenback's techniques and all of Shorty's tactics, so it was not surprising he held State to an unexpected low score, 16-0.

As the team practiced that week for its trip to Washington & Jefferson, something was happening off the field that would ultimately define the season. State's graduate manager Ray Smith went to New York City at the request of Harvard football administrators to discuss a possible game in Cambridge in two weeks. Harvard had suddenly found itself with an open date because Norwich had canceled after its captain had died from injuries in another game. Remembering the controversy over who was the champion last year, Harvard sought State as a make-up opponent. Obviously, State was eager for such a game to show its detractors that it was the equal of any team in the country. Harvard also dangled an extra incentive—future games. But, the Harvard officials had a caveat. Unsure about the State team's reputation as a "rough house gang," they told Smith that additional games would depend on "the conduct of its players."

There was a small snag but it was quickly overcome. State already had a game with Villa Nova scheduled for Oct. 25. Villa Nova had been humiliated 71-0 the year before and had never scored in five previous games against State, so it was more than willing to give up the date.

So, with the big game with Harvard looming over the horizon, State traveled to Washington, PA, to play W&J. State was favored by odds as much as 10-to-7, and when Miller won the coin toss, the State fans in the crowd of 7,000 were sure it would be their day. But the tempo of the game was set immediately after the kickoff. W&J's defense threw Miller for a big loss on the first play and after three more losses, State punted. W&J drove downfield relentlessly with a combination of running and passing and reached State's 7-yard line before settling for an 18-yard field goal by halfback Red Fleming. The rest of the half turned into a defensive battle, but early in the third quarter, Miller returned a punt to the W&J 42-yard line. The next few plays virtually decided the game. "Then, W&J simply tore State's offense to tatters," reported the *Pittsburgh Sunday Post*, " pushing the Center [sic] countians back until State was on its own 20-yard line. In other words, State on the offensive lost 40 yards..." State punted out but W&J was soon back at State's 22-yard line. Then came the play of the game. W&J's fullback Young faked a plunge into the line but stopped and flipped a pass to captain Goodwin who "picked the oval off his shoestrings," according to the Post, "and with Fleming bowling would-be tacklers out of his way, made the first touchdown of the game." Fleming booted the PAT and it was 10-0.

Another W&J field goal attempt in the fourth quarter was blocked by State's center, Big John Clark, but the Little Presidents got a final score with three minutes left in the game after Tobin was hit as he tried to pass and W&J recovered the ball on State's 22-yard line. On the next play, Goodwin faked a run around right end, hit a short pass on the left flank to Spiegel and the W&J halfback ran untouched for the touchdown. Fleming's PAT made the final score, 17-0. "W&J's victory was due to superior playing in every department," reported the *Post*. "Both on offense and defense...Man for man, State was outplayed, even the noted 'Shorty' Miller...[who] was harmless...[and] usually he was thrown for a loss when he carried the ball..." State was thoroughly whipped in a shocking upset. Perhaps the players were looking ahead or maybe they simply took the veteran W&J team too lightly. W&J had beaten State for the first time in history, bringing the 19-game unbeaten streak to a crashing end and handing Hollenback his first loss as State's head coach.

Observers eventually would look back at the next week as the turning point of the season. If Villa Nova and not Harvard had been the opponent, some believe the disconcerted State team may have been able to recover fully for the stretch run of the season. Others believe the powerful W&J eleven simply exposed State's dearth of talent and that what followed was inevitable.

Not even Hollenback expected State to beat Harvard. Harvard was "loaded" again with it's biggest stars—Charlie Brickley, Eddie Mahan and Tack Hardwick—leading the team through another unbeaten season. "Conditions were probably the worst that any team ever encountered," reported the "*LaVie*." "The mud was ankle deep while rain fell in torrents almost continually." The weather admittedly hampered the State attack, which was based on speed. Miller, in particular could not play his type of game." Captain Miller...was easily the star of the game and had the field been dry the visitors might have scored," reported the *Pittsburgh Sunday Post*. Harvard won, 29-0, but it was a closer game than the final score suggested. Brickley scored two TDs, one on a 35-yard run off a fake kick formation, and a 35-yard field goal and Mahan had 50-yard run around right end for another TD. "Shorty Miller lived up to his reputation, rain or shine," reported the *Boston Globe*, which added: "Penn State plays good, rough football with no 'pardon me's.'"

The next week at Franklin Field, in better weather, State again played better than the score indicated but still lost. Penn won, 17-0, scoring both TDs on deceptive plays as frequent penalties curtailed State's offense and defense. Early in the first quarter, Berryman was thrown out of the game for "roughing" and State was penalized a whopping 35 yards or "half the distance to her goal line." The Quakers' first TD came that quarter after a 35-yard pass and two runs got the ball to the State 7-yard line. From there, Penn's captain, Young, took a double pass that completely fooled State and went into the end zone for the score. In the second quarter, State's defenders went for a fake pass and Marshall rambled around right end for a TD. The second half was more even. Marshall dropkicked a 35-yard field goal in the third quarter and Penn's defense stopped State on the Quaker 4-yard line in the last minute to preserve the shutout.

The same day that State was losing to Penn, Notre Dame was making history a little further north at West Point. It was "THE GAME" that is credited with revolutionizing modern day football. Both teams were unbeaten but Army was heavily favored because Notre Dame's three easy victories had been over Ohio Northern, South Dakota and Alma. Notre Dame's new coach Jesse Harper shocked Army and the dumbfounded big city sportswriters covering the game by unveiling a high-powered passing attack that had never been seen before. Dorais hit on 14-of-17 pass attempts for 243 yards and two touchdowns as Notre Dame walloped Army 35-13. The Irish captain, Rockne, was Dorais' favorite target, catching passes and scoring one of the TDs on a 25-yard throw. Newspapers headlined the Dorais-to-Rockne passing combination, making them famous almost overnight. "The visitors showed a beautiful brand of wide-open game and had the Cadets completely baffled by their forward passing," reported the *Pittsburgh Sunday Post*.

Upon learning of Notre Dame's passing wizardry, Hollenback devised a game plan that would try to neutralize the Irish aerial offense while utilizing Miller's running and passing

One of State's early all-around athletes, Levi Lamb played several positions during the 1912-14 seasons. Killed during WW I, his memory is honored by the Athletic Dept. fund for financial contributions which is named for him.

strengths. Establishing a tradition for future Notre Dame games that would carry into the Paterno era, a record crowd turned out for the game, which was played on a Friday as part of the Pennsylvania Day festivities. "The game was one of the hardest fought and one of the most brilliantly played ever seen on a local gridiron," reported the *"LaVie."* "There were end runs, line smashes, shifts, fakes, short and long forward passes and quick kicks."

"With the exception of a few minutes in the middle of the game, the Blue and White forced the playing and had the ball almost continually in the visitors territory," reported the *Penn State Collegian*. Dame intercepted a pass to end that threat.

Notre Dame struck quickly late in the first half after getting the ball on a punt at about its own 22-yard line. On the first play, Dorais passed 40 yards to his other favorite receiver, Joe Pliska, then ran 35 yards on a quarterback keeper. On the next play, Rockne apparently fooled the State defense by feigning a limp, then caught a short pass from Dorais and went untouched into the end zone for the TD. Dorais kicked the PAT for a 7-0 halftime lead. Notre Dame took the second half kickoff and marched 75 yards behind the passing of Dorais and running of fullback Ray Eichenlaub who went over for the TD. Dorais again kicked the extra point. State couldn't move the ball and Notre Dame was soon back in scoring territory. This time, State held on downs.

What happened from that point on would become typical of many games these two teams would play in future decades. Hollenback probably said something on the sidelines, for State's offense went on a long march deep into Notre Dame territory before the Irish held on downs But moments later, State got the ball back at the Notre Dame 25-yard line on a fumble recovery by McDowell. Three rushes and State was on the 12 but Notre Dame intercepted another pass to halt the threat. After two fruitless runs and a 15-yard penalty for "illegal use of the hands," Notre Dame had to punt from behind its goal and Dorais' kick went out of bounds at the 33-yard line. A few plays later, Miller passed to Lamb in the end zone and then kicked the extra point, narrowing the score to 14-7. The teams exchanged possession several times until late in the game when State got the ball at its own 40-yard line. Miller carried, then Tobin, then Berryman, then Tobin. They drove determinedly towards the Notre Dame goal line with the trio of State backs running through Rockne, Dorais and their teammates. Soon, State had the ball on the Notre Dame 3-yard line with time running out. Miller called the play. He faked one way, then stuffed the ball into the stomach of "Yeggs" Tobin, who barreled over a block by Bebout and went into the end zone. The State fans went wild. But wait!!! Penalty, the referee signaled. Offside. (Boo! Hiss! Where'd you learn to referee, you bum!!) It was all but over. Notre Dame stopped a running play and pass attempt and won, 14-7. For the first time since New Beaver Field had opened, 20 games ago, the Lions had lost.

"The Westeners came east with a great reputation and fully lived up to it," reported the *Collegian*. "The whole (Penn State) team played by far the best football it has shown this season..." but it wasn't enough. State's record was now 2-4 and the only way to salvage the season was to win the last two games.

But a 10-0 loss the next week at favored Navy assured the first losing season in 13 years. Once again, it was State's inconsistent offense that let down. State's only serious threat on a rain soaked field ended with Navy stopping a drive on its own 5-yard line. Meanwhile, State's defense was outstanding, halting Navy four times on goal line stands, but the Middies were too powerful and scored a TD in the first quarter and field goal in the second period to win.

A win over Pitt on Thanksgiving Day would have given some solace to a dejected team. However, the way State lost this game made everything worse, and encapsulated the entire disappointing season. Despite Pitt's 5-2-1 record, the game was rated a toss-up. One of Pitt's defeats had been to a mutual opponent, W&J, 18-6. As usual for this late November outing, the field was wet and slippery, again, and a steady drizzle that fell throughout the game made the atmosphere gloomy.

Most of the action was at midfield as the teams battled between the 25-yard lines. All the scoring occurred in the second quarter. Fats Clark led a State drive from the 50, running through Pitt's line for 35 yards, including the final two over right tackle for a touchdown. Miller missed the extra point but no one thought much about it at the time. Pitt scored on the ensuing kickoff. After a 13-yard return and a five-yard run on the first play, Pitt's Guy Williamson broke through the State line, evaded Miller and Berryman, and rambled 67 yards for a TD. He then kicked the PAT and Pitt led, 7-6, at the intermission. The second half was all State's—except for the scoring. The Lions had several drives into Pitt territory but penalties kept stopping them. Pitt went nowhere, but when the game ended, the Panthers had won, 7-6. (No one knew it at the time, but the victory would mark the beginning of a long period of dominance by Pitt in this annual backyard clash.)

The year had not been kind to Shorty Miller. What started with a remarkable performance against Carnegie Tech ended eight games later in a frustrating day against the biggest rival, when nothing went right and his foot failed him. But Shorty took it all in stride and no one blamed him for the dismal season. And when he graduated the next spring, the popular Miller received one of the college's highest accolades by being named Honor Man on Class Day.

Meanwhile, his coach was determined not to have another losing season at State. Hollenback also knew he would need better players and he set out to try and duplicate Pop Golden's recruiting efforts. There was one kid in particular whom he wanted, a real "blue chipper" playing at a prep school in New Jersey. His name was Higgins and everyone in the country wanted him because he was the type who could turn around a program. And that's exactly what he eventually did at Penn State—in a way that Hollenback never would have imagined.

Season Record 2-6
Record to Date 127-72-12
Winning percentage .630

"The Bonfire Celebration"

The crowd of some 3,500 students and townspeople cheered, yelled and sang "The Victory Song" as the players encircled the gigantic pile of wood in the candlelight darkness. Student leaders had said they were going to celebrate the team's Saturday achievement at Harvard with the biggest bonfire ever and all day Monday they had been hauling in wood to the Armory's drill field.

The woodpile of telegraph poles, fences, boardwalks, wagons and boxes was now more than 50 feet high. At precisely 9 o'clock, Captain Yeggs Tobin was going to throw the torch into the mass of timber to climax the two days of revelry. Tobin deserved the honor, they all said. His leadership had helped inspire the team to play its best game of the year against Harvard. Sure, they had won the first four games before Harvard, but even the players agreed they had been sluggish and had not looked very good in those games.

Hollenback figured the Harvard game would make or break this team. From the day practice started in early September, he knew he'd have to do some rebuilding. "Big Bill" thought his biggest problem would be to find a successor to Shorty Miller at quarterback. He also was looking for a new fullback but he was counting on Tobin and Punk Berryman at the halfbacks to be the offensive leaders. However, Punk was having academic problems and was declared ineligible for the year. That now meant three-fourths of the backfield would be new. Even with Barron, Wood, McDowell and Lamb back in the line, neither Hollenback nor his line coach, Harlow, were satisfied with things, and before the first game with Westminster at Beaver Field he had shifted McDowell from tackle to right guard. He still wondered if Lamb would ever play up to his potential. The "big man" had improved a great deal last season and this year Hollenback intended to take advantage of Lamb's running, receiving and kicking skills. But sometimes Lamb seemed to loaf at practice and that constantly irritated the coach. At least his "blue chip" recruit, Bob Higgins, was looking good at left end, and so was the hot-shot sophomore, "Whitey" Thomas, at end and left halfback.

Westminster was supposed to be an easy opener at Beaver Field but the visitors shocked State in the first half by almost scoring three times. The game was still scoreless in the fourth quarter when State struck quickly on a 4-play 64-yard drive with the new junior quarterback Don "Jimmy" James going 20 yards around right end for the first touchdown and Lamb kicking the extra point. State got the ball back inside its own 30-yard line on a punt and four plays later, Higgins faked a punt and ran 58 yards to set up a short Lamb plunge for the TD, and a final score of 13-0.

Against Muhlenberg the next week, State was as hot as the weather, scoring seven minutes into the game on a sparkling 65-yard drive with Tobin getting the TD on a short run and Lamb kicking the PAT. After State recovered a fumble at the 50-yard line midway in the second quarter, Hollenback sent in his freshman quarterback from Pittsburgh, Stan Ewing. "Ewing immediately uncorked a dandy forward pass to Higgins," reported the *Pittsburgh Post*, "who ran 50 yards for a touchdown...but he stepped out of bounds on the 25-yard line." So, on the next play, Ewing passed to Lamb near the goal line and the big tackle stepped into the end zone for the TD. In the second half, State added a TD by sophomore fullback Harold "Fats" Clark, Lamb booted a 35-yard field goal and extra point, and the Lions defense kept the visitors mostly at midfield to take a 22-0 victory.

With Tobin sidelined with an injury seven days later, State struggled, again, but still beat Gettysburg, 13-0. Fats Clark and Tobin's substitute, George Dippe, scored TDs, and Gettysburg never seriously threatened until the last three minutes of the game, when it made four successive first downs before being stopped by State's defense deep in State territory. Tobin was back the next week when State played Ursinus for the first time and helped lead the 30-0 victory, scoring the first TD in the second period. Lamb was the star of the game with his running,

The 1914 tie against Harvard created the "spark" that resulted in a near-tragedy. At the victory celebration following the game, several key players were injured influencing the team's performance for the rest of the year. Captain Yeggs Tobin, who was hurt, is in the front row holding the football.

receiving and kicking, scoring two TDs, a field goal and three extra points.

Pete Mauthe, who had left Gettysburg at the end of the '13 season and gone to work for a steel company, took a week off from his job to help Hollenback and Harlow get the team ready for the big game at Harvard. Practically the entire student body of about 2,500 turned out at the Lemont Train Station Thursday at noon to give the team a send off with speeches, cheers and the singing of the alma mater. It was a gruelling trip but still some 150 students accompanied the team. The contingent did not reach Boston until well after Midnight but Hollenback put the team through a vigorous workout Friday afternoon at a country club on the outskirts of Boston.

Like State, Harvard was undefeated, but most sportswriters believed the game was a mismatch because Harvard was considered the best team in the country. However, five of the Crimson's best players were injured, including Brickely, Mahan and Hardwick, who had starred in last year's win over State. Even without these five standouts, Harvard was still a superior team and Harvard coach Percy Haughton knew it. Haughton was so confident he decided to turn the team over to one of his assistants and take his starting quarterback off on a scouting trip at the campus of one of his Ivy rivals. It was one of the biggest mistakes of his otherwise illustrious coaching career.

Within three minutes of the opening kickoff, State had hushed the crowd of 22,000 with an impressive drive that climaxed with Lamb's field goal from the 33-yard line. After the kickoff and a Harvard punt, State got the ball at midfield. On the first play, James passed to Higgins upfield but the freshman juggled the ball and as it fell towards the ground, Whitey Thomas snared it for a 27-yard gain. Tobin made five yards, then Fats Clark rambled 13 yards for a touchdown. Lamb kicked the extra point and State led by a shocking 10-0 margin at the end of the first quarter. State's defense held off Harvard's fired-up offense for most of the second quarter but as time was running out, Harvard's punter nailed one that backed State near its own goal line. State tried to kill time and get out of danger, but Clark fumbled at the 8-yard line and Harvard recovered. All-American halfback Fred Bradlee threw a touchdown pass to Jeff Coolidge on the next play. Bradlee missed the extra point and the half ended, 10-6.

"The terrific battle continued during the second half," the *"LaVie" reported*, "and the game was in State's favor. She would advance the ball, but only to be driven back by Bradlee's mighty punts." Early in the fourth quarter, Tobin intercepted a Bradlee pass in Harvard territory and a couple of plays later, Lamb kicked another field goal, this time from the 25-yard line. As time wound down, it appeared that State would pull off one of the greatest upsets in college football history. Harvard had won 22 straight games and had not lost at home since Jim Thorpe's Carlisle Indians did it in 1911. Then it happened! Another costly mistake. With about a minute left in the game Harvard punted. Lamb, of all people, fumbled the ball and Harvard recovered at the State 38-yard line.

Harvard then used a play it had been saving just for this extreme situation to take advantage of the aggressiveness of State's defensive ends. A little known substitute named Wes Wilcox entered the game. He was a track man who was a speedster. Harvard's fullback Hugs Francke faked a run into the line and as he was hit by Barron, he lateralled to Wilcox on the left flank and the track star sprinted all the way for a touchdown. Ted Withington kicked the extra point and Harvard escaped with a 13-13 tie. Whenever there was a tie game, the home team usually kept the "victory" ball. However, in a sign of respect for what Penn State had done, Harvard's captain, Wally Trumbull, gave the game ball to Tobin to take back to State College.

So, now, Tobin stood with the lighted torch in the darkness of the Armory grounds as State's students celebrated. Alongside him was the sophomore class president, George Sauerhoff. Tobin took a step toward the big woodpile and flung the torch. KERBOOM! KERBOOM! The two explosions and large ball of flames sent Tobin and Sauerhoff flying backwards to the ground. The ground shook and windows shattered at the Armory, the Carnegie Library and the Engineering Building. Plaster fell inside the President's house nearby and the memorial window in the Beta Theta Pi fraternity house was destroyed. People screamed and knocked each other down in the stampede that followed. Some were hit by burning wood and many were putting out the fires burning on their clothes. Tobin, Sauerhoff and several other students were rushed to the hospital in Bellefonte with serious burns of the face, throat and hands.

The cause of the explosion was five gallons of gasoline which had been used instead of the traditional kerosene to saturate the woodpile. A spark from Tobin's torch had ignited a leftover half filled barrel of gasoline and immediately caused the second explosion of the woodpile. Tobin suffered head and shoulder injuries and was so badly hurt he was not expected to play the rest of the season. The mood of the team suddenly changed. They were a little less enthusiastic on the practice field and they couldn't keep focused on Hollenback's drills. The explosion had changed everything.

Because of other injuries, Higgins and Thomas also missed the next game at Easton against Lafayette and Lamb did not play until the second half because of an injured ankle. But State still had enough to beat Lafayette, 17-0, scoring all the points in the second half, including three on a Lamb field goal.

With their captain still in the Bellefonte Hospital, State traveled to South Bethlehem for its first meeting with Lehigh since 1901. Several hundred State fans and the school band saw a ragged, uncharacteristic performance. "Fumbling was incessant, interference slow and ineffective, and tackling poor," the *"LaVie"* reported. Twice in the first half, Lehigh picked up State fumbles and went for touchdowns, including one on a 45-yard run. State got only four first downs to Lehigh's 20 and avoided a shut out in the last two minutes of the game on a pass from James to Clark, losing 20-7.

Even though this was just the first defeat of the season, there was a feeling of uneasiness among State followers. Some wondered if Hollenback was losing his touch. He would have to pull the team together quickly because the Michigan Agricultural College (now known as Michigan State) was next on the schedule. This would be the biggest game at Beaver Field since Notre Dame and the first ever with the Aggies, one of the best teams from the Midwest. Hollenback intended to win the game, no matter what.

Pennsylvania Governor John K. Tener was among the record crowd of 10,000 that showed up on Pennsylvania Day—a Friday, the 13th! Tobin, two days out of the hospital, was on the sideline in uniform but with bandages on his head and hands. A high wind stymied the offenses of both teams but in the second quarter a 50-yard run by Aggie fullback H. Miller set up a one yard TD by Captain George Julian. With State going nowhere in the second half, Hollenback made a fateful decision. He inserted the bandaged Tobin into the game. That must have inspired State, for in the third quarter, Tobin valiantly held the ball with his bandaged hands and Lamb placekicked a field goal to make it 6-3. With Tobin firing-up the offense, State attacked the Aggies goal line relentlessly late in the fourth quarter. Once, the Lions were six-inches from the goal but the MAC held on downs. A few minutes later,

they were back again at the Aggies 10-yard line and aTD seemed inevitable. But State fumbled, the visitors recovered and the game was over. The final score was 6-3 and Hollenback was criticized by fans and some sportswriters for using the injured Tobin.

Tobin was in the lineup again on Thanksgiving Day when 17,000 showed up for the annual battle with once-beaten Pitt. State was outplayed in the first half as Pitt gained 176 total yards to State's 55 yards but the game was scoreless at that point. Pitt took the kickoff to start the second half and drove into State territory, where Sandy Hastings booted a 34-yard field goal. On the next possession, Pitt pulled off a quick kick that Tobin fumbled in his bandaged hands at the State 35-yard line and Pitt recovered on the 23. "...It took 12 bucks by the Pitt backs to cover the distance in face of the desperate opposition of State," reported the *Pittsburgh Post*, and on fourth down-and-goal at the one-inch line, Pitt's Leo Collins scored. That appeared to seal State's doom. Late in the third quarter State faked a field goal and Lamb tried to pass for a TD but his pass was intercepted. Then in the fourth quarter, Lamb kicked a 30-yard field goal and Hastings got another one for Pitt from the 28-yard line, and Pitt won, 13-3.

That brought the once promising season to an unhappy close. Some fans continued to second guess Hollenback's coaching and particularly his use of Tobin in the last two games. That rankled "Big Bill" and he started to talk about quitting. Shortly after the end of the season, the Athletic Committee declared that new eligibility requirements would go into effect starting with the 1915 season. The new rules, which had been in the making for three years, eliminated freshman eligibility and implemented a one-year residency regulation for transfers from other schools. That was enough for Hollenback. Even though many other Eastern and Midwestern schools had similar rules, Hollenback didn't think State could win with the new restrictions. When he was offered a position in December with a Philadelphia coal company he resigned as coach.

So, State again went looking for a new coach. This time they wouldn't look too far. This time, they would pick one of their own.

Season Record 5-3-1
Record to Date 132-75-13
Winning percentage .630

CHAPTER 7

HARLOW'S HERE – FOR NOW

1915-1917

Dick Harlow was the natural replacement for "Big Bill" Hollenback and the Athletic Committee made its decision quickly. On January 2, 1915, only a few days after an informal interview, Harlow became the first Penn State player to be named head coach.

Harlow had been recruited by Pop Golden out of Philadelphia and had been one of the best linemen (at tackle) on the 1910 and 1911 teams. After getting his degree in forestry, he stayed on to get a master's degree and help coach, and soon he was Hollenback's top assistant and line coach. It was a good fit and in the next three years Harlow learned as much from "Big Bill" as Hollenback did from him.

With the new school rule that fall of 1915 prohibiting freshmen from playing on the varsity, Harlow asked that his one year contract include a full-time freshman coach and a varsity assistant. Okay, the committee said, but "in order receive the best ideas from other coaching systems," one of those positions must be filled by someone outside the Penn State system. That was quite a change from the philosophy under which Hollenback had been retained but Harlow was all for it. Inbreeding can be detrimental. He still needed to learn, too, and what better way than to bring in someone from one of the best teams in the country.

Oh, and one more thing, the committee added. We want one of the new assistants to be the head coach of another sport. It will make us more efficient that way. Sure, said the genial Harlow. So, he hired his one-time teammate Dutch Herman, the luckless backup quarterback to Larry Vorhis and Shorty Miller to coach the freshmen, and the Athletic Committee made Herman the school's first head basketball coach. For his "outside" assistant, Harlow picked Bud Whitney, the captain of last year's Dartmouth team, a Third-Team Camp All-American at fullback and a bronze medal winner in the 1912 Olympic Games.

With Harlow spearheading the recruiting efforts, State was soon attracting good young players, like "Red" Griffiths of Taylor, PA, and little Charlie Way of Downington. That remained true throughout his three-year regime as the freshman team went unbeaten every season and included noteworthy victories over Penn and Pitt.

Beating Penn and Pitt at any time had become an obsession for everyone connected with Penn State. And, eventually, it was Harlow's inability to stop Pitt's varsity powerhouse that had as much to do with ending his head coaching career at Penn State than anything else. Pitt was at the height of its power under the legendary Coach Glenn "Pop" Warner, and would claim two National Championships during Harlow's short tenure at State.

The beginning of Harlow's end actually came on the day the Athletic Committee renewed his contract for two-years on November 25, 1915. It was Thanksgiving Day and in Pittsburgh earlier that afternoon, undefeated Pitt had hammered Harlow's previously once-beaten team, 20-0. We're giving you a new contract, he was told, but beating Pitt was a priority, and he agreed.

One year later, Harlow took another once-beaten Penn State team into Pittsburgh on Thanksgiving Day to face another powerful undefeated Warner-coached Pitt team. This time Pitt won, 31-0, and Harlow was so disappointed he almost resigned on the spot. Some alumni were hoping he would for they felt his on-field coaching probably lost the game. (And you thought second-guessing the coach was a modern-day phenomenon, eh? Pop Warner later said the 1916 Pitt team was the best he ever coached, but no one associated with Penn State cared then—or, now, come to think of it!!)

Within two months of that defeat, the Athletic Committee quietly stripped Harlow of his on-field authority, by naming "Zen" Scott of Cleveland as the "Field Coach" and referring to Harlow as "Resident Coach." What that meant was Harlow would conduct the practices and Scott would devise the game plan and run the team during the game.

Harlow held his famous temper in check. He was angry but he also was hurt. Inside, he was heartbroken for this was still his team. He had recruited most of the players. He or Dutch had coached them from the beginning. And the players were loyal. When they heard about what happened, they wanted to go tell the Athletic Committee, President Sparks and anyone else connected with this stupid decision to stuff it. They weren't going to take orders from some "son of a gun" from Cleveland. Cleveland, mind you. Harlow convinced the players to forget about his personal dilemma and to think about playing football that fall.

But by the time the 1917 season started, the U.S. had entered World War I. Several college teams called off their seasons. There was a manpower shortage on every campus. Many of Harlow's players were gone. Almost all of State's regulars from 1916 had been called up by the armed forces, and Harlow went looking for men to play football. Olympic miler Larry Shields and basketball star Lloyd Wilson turned out. So did a bunch of eager youngsters whose only experience was on the sandlots. Penn canceled its game. So did Lafayette. The season was in a turmoil. Later, observers would say Harlow's classy attitude during this crucial period as the "Resident Coach" kept State football from incurring irreparable damage.

Dick Harlow as a player in 1912. He is best known as a coach at Penn State, Western Maryland, Colgate and Harvard.

"The Players' Coach"

Dick Harlow threw his fist into the air. His team had just recovered Pitt's fumble on the opening kickoff and it was first down-and-goal at the Pitt 6-yard line.

The unbeaten Panthers were favored in the annual Thanksgiving Day game but even the great sportswriters Walter Camp and Grantland Rice had given Harlow's once-beaten State team a good chance at winning.

Sure, it was the legendary Pop Warner coaching in his first season at Pitt against the rookie State coach. But State had surprised everyone all year. Only a loss to powerful Harvard had marred the record after eight games and even that game might have turned out differently if not for fumbles and penalties at crucial times. Not even the Athletic Committee members who had picked Harlow as Hollenback's replacement had expected this to be a successful year. Holdover player talent was thin, and without incoming freshmen and transfers who could play immediately, everyone figured Harlow would need time to develop a competitive team. Then, too, the players would have to adjust to a different style of coaching and that was expected to take a lot of time, too.

But, in what would become a pattern throughout Harlow's coaching career at State, everyone had underestimated him. Despite his well-known temper, he communicated easily with his players and they liked him. He believed in fundamental football and that started with coaching the basics in practice. His drills were organized and repetitive and he kept everything simple. Because of his playing and coaching background, defense was at the heart of his coaching concept. His offense was simple, with only a few plays utilized in each game, so that even his most inexperienced players could master them.

It was this simplicity that impressed a *Philadelphia Public Ledger* columnist known as "Touchdown" who praised Harlow and his coaching methods. "The 'new Penn State football system' [under Harlow] has made good this fall," the columnist wrote. "...Another theory that Coach Harlow has worked on this year is that a team with a few plays well-learned is superior to a team with a variety of plays that have not been perfected."

Harlow was not much for innovation. Line bucks and end runs formed the basis of his attack. But he believed passing was vital to winning. So, in the spring he devised a wooden target about the size of a man and had everyone in the backfield throwing at the target from every conceivable positions. Later, the *Public Ledger* columnist, "Touchdown," would rave about how the wooden target drills had vastly improved the "speed and accuracy" of State's passers. Harlow also had his centers utilize the spiral pass that his new assistant coach Bud Whitney of Dartmouth had advocated because the spiral increased accuracy in getting the ball to the backs and cut down on fumbling. At one point in the fall, Harlow also brought in Harvard's erstwhile All-American Charlie Brickley (who had turned down a full time assistant's job) to work with the kickers and Brickley's coaching is credited with improving the otherwise mediocre punting and dropkicking of Ewing and other kickers.

As for the Pitt game that year, well, another undefeated Pitt team stomped on the Harlow-Scott club, 28-6. State finished 5-4 but even before the end, some sportswriters were claiming the record would be worse but for the on-field coaching of Zen Scott. That had been enough for Harlow. On the eve of the Pitt game, he had challenged the Athletic Committee to either give him the authority or get rid of him. The committee rescinded the "dual authority" system, fired Scott, declared that only Penn Staters would be permitted on the coaching staff and gave Harlow a 12-month contract with the authority to pick his own assistants. Thanks, he said, but that's not enough. Three years and a raise and I'll take it. Granted. But if the war makes it necessary to cancel football, the contract is null and void, they said. So be it. They shook hands.

Harlow was vindicated. But he wasn't through. With the war still raging in July of 1918, Harlow asked for release from his contract to enter the military service. Duty calls, but I'll be back. The Athletic Committee was shocked. We can't guarantee the head coaching position when you return, the committee told him. Doesn't matter, Harlow said. I love this place. I'll be back.

Practice, simplicity, discipline and execution were the elements that turned the 1915 team into a winner from the opening game. Within days of being named coach that winter, Harlow had his players out practicing in the Armory. In May, he had them working out vigorously on Beaver Field. And in the month before the first game with Westminster, the starting team fell into place. The veterans were the keys.

Higgins at right end was probably the best player on the team. There were reports that the 23-year-old sophomore would transfer to Rutgers because his roommate had done so but Higgins denied everything, saying he was happy at State. One of the running and defensive stars of the unbeaten 1911-12 teams, Punk Berryman, also was back at left half after sitting out '14 because of academics. Starter Thomas and his sub Morris also had returned at right end, with both guards, McDowell and Miller, and captain Wood at center. Fats Clark was back at fullback but last year's starting quarterback, James, had dropped out of school. Harlow wasn't worried. He felt that Ewing, the little soph from Pittsburgh who had played last year but did not letter, was a better athlete who simply needed experience to become a fine quarterback. Harlow also was impressed by another sophomore, Stan "Zarney" Czarnecki, who eventually became the starter at right tackle. Czarnecki also had missed lettering as a frosh substitute but Harlow believed Zarney was a potential All-American. The two tackle positions and the right half slot were the trouble spots and except for Czarnecki, Harlow was not fully comfortable with any of the newcomers playing there.

Harlow had the team primed for Westminster for he was determined to avoid the letdown in last year's opener when Westminster had outplayed the home team most of the game. Ewing threw a touchdown pass to Higgins for the first score of the game and after State took a 19-0 lead, Harlow substituted freely to get more players experience. State won easily, 26-0, as the new right halfback, Chuck Yerger, scored two TDs.

One of the great historic figures in Penn State football is End Bob Higgins, seen here as a player in 1916. He was State's first two-time, First Team All-American and was inducted into the National Football Foundation College Football Hall of Fame in 1954.

State started out the next week against Lebanon Valley where it had left off, storming down field early in the first quarter on line plunges by Berryman, Clark and Yerger to score a TD. But the team was out of synch for the rest of the game, perhaps because of the wet and slippery field. Lebanon Valley was not about to be embarrassed as it was, 75-0, when the teams had last met in 1907. The visitors kept the Lions in check except for a 65-yard TD run by Ewing in the third quarter and State escaped with a 13-0 win.

The Lebanon Valley game had exposed a major weakness at the tackles. Before the first away game at Penn seven days later, Harlow made Czarnecki the starter at right tackle, shifted captain Wood from center to left tackle and inserted newcomer Heister Painter at center. Unbeaten Penn was the favorite at Franklin Field and played like it in the first half as it outgained State in rushing and, as the *"LaVie"* reported, "seemed to be excelling in every point of the game except in punting..." But the Quakers could score only a field goal by the intermission for a 3-0 lead. State changed tactics in the second half, resorting mostly to a running attack, and in the third quarter Berryman ran 40 yards behind the blocking of Czarnecki to score a TD after a drive that began deep in State's territory. After the kickoff and an exchange punts, Higgins broke loose just across the scrimmage line, caught the only successful State pass of the game from Ewing and ran for another 40-yard TD. The final score was 13-3. "When Harlow's men started to play real football, at the beginning of the second half, they swept the Penn players off their feet," wrote "Touchdown," in the *Public Ledger*. "...the quarterback used but seven plays. The fact that these plays secured a total of two touchdowns ought to vindicate Coach Harlow's plans."

The surprising win over Penn got the State fans all excited, particularly about Harlow's defense. This was a much better team than anyone expected and maybe a National Champion. But the next week Gettysburg brought the fans back to normal. The *"LaVie"* succinctly described what happened: "Seldom has a State team exhibited such a falling off in form as was shown in the game with the boys from the historic battlefield. There was no semblance of the mighty machine which had taken Penn's first scalp of the season. The playing was weak and slovenly...(and)...Both teams were weak on defense but gained almost at will in offensive play." Perhaps, it had seemed too easy at the start when Berryman and Clark scored TDs within the first five minutes. State eventually won, 27-12, but this was the first time in 13 games played since 1895 that Gettysburg had scored.

Harlow's players must have been humbled by their poor Gettysburg performance. In the first game ever against West Virginia Wesleyan, State won easily, 28-0, with Berryman's long runs setting up the first three TDs on line plunges by Clark. The game was typical of Harlow's coaching style. He never rolled up the score against an opponent and substituted freely whenever he felt he had enough points to win. By the fourth period of this game State led, 21-0. Harlow inserted an entire new eleven players, and one of them, a scrub named Bob Edgerton (who would not letter that year) scored a fourth touchdwon. The game also produced State's first field goal of the year when Ewing dropkicked a 25-yard three-pointer.

When the team left for Harvard on Thursday, hundreds of students were at the train station to see them off. The feeling of victory was in the air as the students rallied with rousing cheers and songs. The loss to heavily favored Harvard two days later at Boston's Soldiers Field would go down as one of the most frustrating defeats in Harlow's

State coaching career because the Lions out played the favored Crimson all day. Some 22,000 fans watched in almost perfect late October football weather as State gained 393 yards rushing and 19 first downs to Harvard's 239 yards and 11 first downs. But State's 100 yards in penalties (compared to Harvard's 67), a fumbled punt and a couple of questionable rulings by the officials was the difference in the game.

After Harvard's opening kickoff went into the end zone, Berryman shocked the crowd on the first play by running around right end for 30 yards. Two plays later, he went around right end again, this time for 15 yards. State picked up another first down before the drive stalled on the Harvard 20-yard line and on 4th-and-5 Ewing tried to drop-kick a field goal into the wind. The ball squirted off Ewing's foot and with the help of the wind bounced backwards, and Harvard took over at its own 29-yard line.

The two teams traded possession several times and as the second quarter started, Harvard fumbled a punt and Higgins recovered at the Crimson 40-yard line. On the first play, Ewing passed to Clark for 13 yards. Clark then ran up the middle for four yards. Now it was Berryman's turn. He followed his interference through the right side of the Harvard line and ran 23 yards into the end zone. But referee Billy Morice said someone was holding and the TD was nullified. Later, a newspaper columnist from Princeton wrote that the play "seemed to most of the spectators a perfectly legitimate play" and that "this score, if allowed, might have made all the difference in the outcome of the game." Two plays later, Harvard blocked a forward pass and, under the rules at the time, gained possession when it recovered the ball, ending State's second threat.

The outstanding punting by Harvard's three-time All-American fullback, Eddie Mahan, stymied State all day and midway through the second quarter he booted one deep into State territory. Ewing had to wait for the ball to bounce and when it did he accidentally kicked it into State's end zone. Harvard's right tackle Ken Parsons jumped on it and suddenly Harvard had a touchdown. Mahan kicked the extra point and Harvard led 7-0. Moments later State was on the march again and was inside Harvard's 13-yard line, when on fourth down Ewing passed to Higgins for an apparent first down, but the referee ruled that the ball had touched the ground, and Harvard took its 7-0 lead into the intermission.

After another exchange of punts early in the third period, Harvard got the ball at its own 44-yard line. With all four Harvard backs alternating on carrying the ball, the Crimson drove to the 6-yard line from where Mahan crashed up the middle to the goal line. Referee Morice signaled touchdown but State's players claimed Mahan was a foot short of the goal. Sorry, boys, touchdown Harvard! Mahan's PAT failed and Harvard led 13-0. State continued to hammer away and midway in the fourth quarter, marched 38 yards to Harvard's 10-yard line. But that threat died there when a third down pass attempt hit the ground, giving the ball to the Crimson (as mandated by the rules at the time). Near the end of the game Berryman almost got away for a TD when he ran 50 yards around right end. He carried three more times to reach the Harvard 11-yard line but that's where the game ended.

The Collegian called the loss "heartbreaking" but Harlow and his team didn't have time to brood about it. Lehigh would be at New Beaver Field the following Friday for the annual Pennsylvania Day football game and the visitors were reported to be better than the Michigan Aggies and Notre Dame teams that had defeated State at the last two Pennsylvania Day events. Again, State was the underdog as Lehigh outweighed State by almost 20 pounds to a man. "State played her

best and hardest football of the season," reported the "*LaVie.*" A crowd of 7,000 was on hand as Higgins scored the game's only TD on a 25-yard pass from Ewing in the first quarter. The play was notable because Higgins had to score twice. The first time the TD was called back because of a penalty but they used the identical play and Higgins did it again immediately after the penalty. Captain Clark was cited as the game's standout player with his blocking and tackling in the 7-0 win. "A line that held like a stone wall, a splendid forward pass defense, and fine secondary defense, said "*LaVie,*" "made it impossible for Lehigh to advance into State's territory beyond the 45-yard line more than once during the entire contest."

Lafayette was no match for State the following Saturday in Easton. Berryman scored twice, in the 33-3 win which featured Ewing's passing. State lost the shutout in the last seconds of play when a 70-yard pass reception set up a field goal.

Harlow knew his team would have to play its best and get some breaks in order to defeat Pitt in the annual Thanksgiving Day game. In hiring Pop Warner, Pitt had determined to become a national power. Warner's success with Cornell and the Carlisle Indians had already made him a legend, and after seven games his first Pitt team was undefeated. Harlow admired Warner and since becoming a head coach he had consulted with Warner about offensive strategy. He even adapted some of Warner's single-wing plays. But Harlow, ever the pugnacious fighter, was not intimidated by Warner.

The worst news for Harlow came in the days leading up to the big game. Berryman got sick and missed practice. He was still weak when the team left for Pittsburgh and Harlow knew his best back could not play a full game.

The crowd was slow arriving at Forbes Field that day and there were thousands of empty seats remaining when State kicked off. Eventually close to 30,000 would fill the stands, including a large delegation from Japan who were the guests of H. J. Heinz and the Pittsburgh Chamber of Commerce. Most of the Japanese were seeing their first ever football game and they must have been mystified by the sight of the hulking Americans banging each other around in the mud.

Harlow's desired break came early. Pitt's quarterback Meadows fumbled the kickoff, picked the ball up and threw it to the Panther captain and right halfback, G. M. Williamson, who also fumbled and State's three-year starting guard Cecil McDowell recovered at the 6-yard line. The Penn State fans in the left field bleachers went wild as the marching band erupted with a brassy tune. Everyone but the Japanese knew that a touchdown now could have a psychological effect on the entire game.

On the first play fullback Clark crashed up the middle but got only one yard. Then he tried right tackle and made just two. Next it was Berryman carrying between left tackle and guard but he was stopped after just one yard. Fourth down-and-goal at the 2. The ball went to Berryman again. He started around right end but there were too many Pitt players there and they tackled him for no gain. Now, it was the Pitt fans jumping up and down and cheering. Everyone but the Japanese knew the psychology had just been reversed on a great goal line stand.

"The magnificent display of strength may have had some result upon the final outcome of the game," wrote Florent Gibson in the *Pittsburgh Post*. "Certainly it was enough to daunt even the lion-hearted State men..."

Pitt punted out to about the 30-yard line and State was back in business. But again, the aggressive Pitt defense led by two-time All-American center Bob Peck stopped the Lions almost cold. A fourth down pass at the 27-yard line was incomplete and the Panthers took over again. The teams traded possession and just before the end of the quarter, Pitt got the ball on its own 30-yard line. If the opening goal line stand had set the tone for the defense, what happened next set the mode for the rest of the game. On the first play, Pitt's star left half, Andy Hastings, went off right tackle for 25 yards. A few plays later fullback George McLaren broke into the clear and was tackled from behind by Ewing after a 16-yard gain. State's defense stiffened and on fourth down, Hastings kicked a field goal from the 23-yard line.

State's captain and left tackle, Wood, and the starting left guard, Miller, apparently had been hurt during the drive but remained in the game because Harlow didn't have many substitutes to match Pitt's talented linemen. "Miller was kicked in the spine...and so badly injured that he could not charge...(while) Wood's knees became wobbly...," wrote the *Collegian* in reporting the impact of the injuries and Berryman's illness on the eventual outcome. "It is rather easy to see why Pitt's battle was made easier."

Pitt's battle was made easier because it had more depth and probably better players. As the rules of the time determined, Penn State kicked off following the field goal and Williamson ran the ball back 50 yards to State's 40-yard line. Pitt's runners bashed into State's hearty but sagging defense 12 times to reach the 2-yard line, where on fourth down, Hastings smashed over right tackle and crossed the goal by inches. Hastings then kicked the PAT, and for all practical purposes the game was over.

An intercepted pass midway through the third quarter set up another quick Pitt TD. The Panthers' second-team quarterback, Jimmy Dehart, picked off Ewing's pass at the Pitt 25-yard line and returned it 20 yards. On the first play, Williamson ran for 35 yards and on the next play Hastings barreled past Ewing and Berryman and swept into the end zone untouched. His PAT made it 17-0. With Pitt subs playing much of the fourth quarter, the Panthers drove from midfield to the State 7-yard line where Pitt's sub kicker booted a field goal to end the scoring.

"The (20-0) victory was clean cut and there's no doubt about which is the better team," wrote Florent Gibson. "But this is not belittling the Penn State team. Dick Harlow's eleven is a regular whale of a team. The visitors are a smoother-working combination than Pitt and...their attack would have overwhelmed almost any other team in the country..."

With its impressive victory, Pitt claimed the national title and received the support of most Eastern sportswriters, though some believed undefeated Cornell was more worthy because it had stopped Harvard's four year unbeaten streak, 10-0.

Despite the two losses, State had some solace when Higgins became only the second player in school history to be named a First Team All-American, when selected by the International News Service. Walter Camp, picking the other major All-America team at the time, tabbed Higgins for the Second Team and named Berryman to his Third Team.

On Thanksgiving evening, the Athletic Committee acknowledged the surprising success of Harlow in his first year by giving him a two year contract with a $300 a year raise. But, they told him, beating Pitt was still a priority. He agreed and said he could hardly wait for next year when they would get even.

Season Record 7-2
Record to Date 139-77-13
Winning percentage .635

"The Surprise at Penn"

As soon as Harlow got his first close look at the freshmen during spring practice, he knew he would have another good team that could challenge Pitt. With six starters and another half dozen lettermen returning from 1915, Harlow already had the experienced players who were familiar with his disciplined system. He would use the spring and fall practice sessions to work some of the talented sophomores into the lineup, and as the team gained game experience, he knew it would get better and better. By Thanksgiving Day, he figured, the team would be at its peak—and beating Pitt was the priority.

Harlow had to adjust his plans when practice started on Labor Day and only 25 players showed up. Two-year starting left end Whitey Thomas transferred to the University of Pennsylvania and Joe Gill, a letterman expected to start at right guard, was forbidden to play by his parents. Then, as classes started one week before the season opener against Susquehanna, starting center Heister Painter was declared ineligible because of academics. Those departures left five positions unsettled as the season began, because Harlow and his backfield coach, Bud Whitney, also were trying to find replacements at halfback for Berryman, now the head coach at Gettysburg, and Yerger.

The core of the team was built around four starters from 1915—All-American Higgins at right end, Ewing at quarterback, captain Clark at fullback and Czarnecki at right tackle. But as the season evolved, Harlow never used the same starting team in any two games and he constantly tinkered with the lineup—especially at left end, center and the running back positions. Six different players started at left end, including three-year veteran substitute George Morris, and sophomores Larry Conover and senior Ward Swain, both of whom also played center. Perhaps the most versatile player was sophomore Ben Jones, quarterback of the strong 1915 frosh team, who opened the season as the starting left halfback and later started two games at quarterback and two games at—yes—left end, including the Pitt game. Three other sophs were interchangeable at the halfbacks, Harry Robb, Harold "Bill" Hess and Carl Beck, and two more sophs became the primary starters at left tackle (Al Krushank) and right guard (Jim O'Donnell).

With all this maneuvering, one would think the team might be too unstabilized to perform well. But, not under Harlow's "small squad" coaching system, which the *Collegian* described this way: "In this manner, each man on the team will receive the maximum amount of individual instruction. Scrimmage will be held not oftener than twice a week and actual work on the field will be supplemented by numerous blackboard talks." Harlow also kept the "concept of team togetherness" by designating 18 players as "the varsity" and setting up a separate training table for them at the Track House.

For the first time since 1908, a 10-game schedule had been arranged, including the return of three teams that had been off the schedule for years: Susquehanna (1902), Bucknell (1910) and Geneva (1911). Seven of the games would be at home but the toughest three opponents—Penn, Lehigh and Pitt—would be on the road. The Athletic Committee was still having difficulty getting big name schools to travel to "the hills" of State College, and the lack of dressing room facilities at New Beaver Field didn't help. Both teams still had to dress at the Track House and walk to the playing field a quarter mile away.

Even though the quality of the opposition was suspect, neither Harlow nor the fans expected the team to do as well as it did in the first four games. Harlow substituted many players in beating Susquehanna, 27-0, as Jones scored two TDs, Hess got one and a little used sub quarterback named Thorpe (who would never letter) tallied another. Then State blasted Westminster, running up a 28-0 halftime lead and winning, 55-0. State had 20 first downs to the visitors' three and six different players scored TDs with Clark getting three, and guard-kicker Ben Cubbage booting six PATs. Clark scored two more TDs the next week against Bucknell and so did Beck as State pummeled its oldest rival, 55-7. One of Beck's TDs came on a 95-yard kickoff return. Cubbage booted five more PATs to run his three game total to 14. Bucknell's TD came late in the game when Laurence picked up a State fumble and ran 80 yards for the score.

West Virginia Wesleyan was more difficult than expected. The visitors played an outstanding defensive game even though their offense never got inside the State 30-yard line. Ewing got the first TD on a 15-yard scamper in the first quarter and starting left end Ed Ege grabbed a tipped pass from Ewing and ran 30 yards for another TD in the second quarter. State made it 21-0 at the half when Ewing completed two passes of about 15-to-20 yards to set up Clark's four-yard plunge and Cubbage kicked his third extra point. With State's starters still playing in the third period, Wesleyan held the home team scoreless. But when Harlow sent more than half a dozen subs into the game in the last quarter, the fresh troops wore out the visitors. State scored three more TDs, including one on a 95-yard kickoff return by Hess, to win, 39-0.

State was now leading the East in scoring with 171 points to just seven for its opponents. Even though the game against Pennsylvania was next, the fans were already talking about the "big showdown" with Pitt a month and a half away. Sure, they realized Penn would be tough and out to avenge last year's upset. But the Quakers were vulnerable. Didn't they just lose to Swarthmore? Swarthmore of all teams!!!

Perhaps, as the "*LaVie*" would later report, the State team was "overconfident" and Penn was "out to retrieve its reputation" after the Swarthmore loss. Or maybe it was the psychological boost the Quakers got by the return of their star fullback Howard Berry, who had been serving in the military on the Mexican border, and was playing in his first game of the season. Whatever the reason, Penn played a better game, particularly on offense, and Berry made the big plays. But the game was not a walkaway.

Penn led by just three points at the half on Berry's 35-yard field goal and the game might have been tied if Cubbage had hit on his 30-yard field goal attempt midway in the first quarter. Berry booted another field goal from the 40-yard line early in the third period and then sealed the victory in the same quarter with a 55-yard run for a touchdown off a short pass from quarterback Light. State blew a golden opportunity in the second half when an intercepted pass gave State the ball on the Penn 26-yard line. The Lions reached the 13 but an attempted first down pass by Ewing was grounded and (as the rules called for at the time), Penn took the ball on the 20-yard line. Penn added another field goal in the last quarter and won, 15-0.

The game had been rough and several players were carried off the field, including Berry late in the fourth quarter. Both teams accused the other of "dirty play." When Penn traveled to Pitt the next week, several players told *Post* sportswriter Harold Keck that Harlow was the instigator of it all. "For a time we did not begin to repay State

with its own tactics," a player was quoted as saying. "We hesitated to see just how far Harlow's men would go. They went the limit. They were egged on by Harlow himself, who from the side lines [sic], kept admonishing them to 'get' Berry." The players said Penn State would be "permanently dropped from Penn's schedule" and that also would mean "State will almost automatically forfeit its chances of being scheduled with Harvard, Yale, Princeton or any of the other large institutions in the East in the future."

For his part, Harlow was more critical of his own team, and uncharacteristically berated several players by name publicly and promised a shakeup. He was especially critical of Ewing's first down pass attempt at the 13-yard line and told the *Collegian* that State lost because of "a green backfield and lack of judgment at critical moments. We took second to Penn in brains and brawn. Our secondary defense played back too far in spite of all instructions, and allowed Penn's runners to come to them instead of meeting the ball carriers."

The Penn game would be the defining moment of the season. Harlow had succumbed to the pressure and had lost his cool in public. Although the team would go on to win more games, it would not be the efficient, well-drilled machine Harlow had tried to mold. It would be no match for Pitt. Penn also kept its promise—sort of. For a couple of years, State's Athletic Committee had been trying to get Penn officials to increase the compensation for playing at Franklin Field but Penn had declined. There was talk of not scheduling Penn unless the financial arrangements changed. Because of the war in Europe, most football schedules were in turmoil in 1917 and 1918 and there were many cancellations and shortened seasons. As a result, Penn and State would not play again until 1919 and by that time Harlow was no longer the head coach.

True to his words, Harlow "shookup" the starting lineup before the following week's game against Gettysburg. He benched Ewing for Jones at quarterback and switched Conover from end to center, where he had played as a frosh, sending Swain to the sidelines. There also was a change at both ends because of injuries. Cubbage went to right end to replace the ailing Higgins and Morris to left end for Ege, who was out for the season. Senior Ralph Parish, who had started his first game against Penn at right guard for O'Donnell, moved to Cubbage's guard position on the left. Captain Clark also would miss the game because he was with his senior chemistry class on its annual inspection tour of Pennsylvania industrial plants. So, with Jones at quarterback, Robb and Hess at the halfbacks and Beck at fullback, Harlow would start an all sophomore backfield. With all the changes, Harlow worked the team extra hard during the week. In one long, rough scrimmage against Dutch Herman's freshman offense, the first team defensive line looked pitiful as the frosh backs consistently got into the secondary. Harlow was furious and vowed to make more changes if needed.

It was a nervous and jumpy team that took the field against Gettysburg October 28th. Early in the first period, State had the ball deep in its own territory when Conover centered the ball over the head of Beck. The ball bounced into the end zone where Beck fell on it for a Gettysburg safety, and the State fans gasped. Gettysburg maintained its 2-0 lead well into the second quarter as State's attack sputtered. It was obvious to everyone that Jones was having difficulty running the reconstructed offense and Harlow was forced to bring in Ewing. That turned the game around. State scored 13 points in the second quarter, 14 in the third and 21 in the fourth for a 48-2 win. Ewing scored two TDs and five other players scored one, including guard O'Donnell, who

Coach Harlow constantly juggled the starting lineup and the sophomore-laden 1916 team won eight games. A 31-0 loss to Pitt, however, was a cause for great concern by the alumni. The starters seen here were (left to right) in the line: Bob Higgins, Stan Czarnecki, Jim O'Donnell, Larry Conover, Floyd Parish, Al Krushank and Ben Jones; backfield: Stan Ewing, Carl Beck, Bill Hess and Captain Harold "Fats" Clark. Hess and Higgins combined for the longest pass play in State history in 1919 Pitt game.

was the defensive star of the game. Robb made the most spectacular play of the day by running back a kickoff more than 80 yards before being tackled from behind on the 1-yard line. Conover made up for his early error by kicking six extra points and blocking and tackling all over the field.

Beaver Field was muddy and wet after several days of bad weather when Geneva came to town, but that didn't stop State. Eleven years earlier, the Lions had beaten Geneva, 73-0. This time the score was 79-0 in a game both the *Collegian* and *"LaVie"* dubbed "Water Polo." So many State scrubs got into the game that six of them were playing for the first time ever! State's domination was so overwhelming that Geneva had just six offensive plays and punted twice. State led by 20 points at the end of the first quarter and by 41 at the half. Eight different players scored TDs with Hess getting three. Jones scored two TDs and passed 35 yards to Cubbage for another and Robb ran 70 yards for one TD off a fake kick. Conover, still at center, even got a TD by recovering one of his own team's six fumbles in the end zone. Cubbage also had six PATs. Ewing, Clark and Higgins didn't get in for one play.

Ewing, Clark and Higgins were back in the starting lineup the next week at Lehigh. This was the team's best game of the year, but it was back-up kicker-halfback Bob Edgerton, in the game for less than a minute, who made the difference. Edgerton kicked State's first field goal of the season in the second quarter to give the Lions a 3-0 halftime lead in what was another penalty-filled, defensive struggle. State made it 10 0 on the first play of the fourth quarter when Ewing ran 15 yards through several would-be tacklers for the TD to climax a drive from midfield and Conover booted the extra point. Lehigh came right back with a brilliant passing attack. A 60-yard kickoff return had given Lehigh the ball at State's 36-yard line but the threat died on a grounded forward pass. After getting the ball back on a punt, a 40-yard pass from Brunner to McIsaacs put the ball on the State 8-yard line and Herrington passed to Hurley on the next play for the TD. The PAT made it 10-7 but State's defense held on for the win.

Despite cold, raw weather, the Beaver Field stands overflowed for the Pennsylvania Day contest against Lafayette. This was one of Lafayette's weakest teams, with a record of 2-4-1 entering the game, including shutout losses of Princeton and Penn. State won 40-0 with Hess getting two TDs and Robb and Ewing each getting one on long runs. State's pass defense was outstanding as Lafayette could complete just 4-of-22 pass attempts.

Even though State was the definite underdog to another unbeaten Warner powerhouse, Harlow actually felt his team could beat Pitt. He had nearly two weeks to prepare and he had everyone healthy. It didn't matter.

Warner would later say this was one of his all-time greatest teams. Pitt took control from the opening kickoff and moved to midfield from where Hastings startled the crowd of 29,000 by dropping back to attempt a 50-yard field goal. The kick was low and to the side. After a State punt and 10-yard penalty for interfering with the kick receiver, Pitt got the ball on the State 42-yard line. With the chants of "Let's Go Pitt" roaring from the student section, the Panthers drove relentlessly through the mud to the 6-yard line before being stopped, and on fourth down Hastings booted a 12 yard field goal. After an exchange of punts, Pitt had the ball again at its own 40-yard line. Five plays and a penalty later, Pitt was on State's 48-yard line. Hastings, the right halfback, got the ball, ran to his right and threw a pass to Pat Herron, who had gotten behind the State secondary at the 25 and Herron ran into the end zone for the TD. Hastings missed the PAT and Pitt led 9-0 going into the second quarter.

Pitt—and Hastings, who would be named a First Team All-American—put the game out of reach in the second quarter. Early in the period, State punted to Pitt's 25-yard line. On the first play, Hastings passed to McLaren behind the scrimmage line. McLaren passed back and Hastings ran around right end behind the blocking of DeHart and Morrow and dashed 75 yards for another TD. Again, the PAT failed. After another exchange of punts, Pitt got the ball on its own 39-yard line. Three plays later, Hastings passed to quarterback DeHart for a

28-yard TD. Pitt's band began playing "Hail, Hail The Gang's All Here" and it didn't matter that Hastings PAT attempt hit the goal post and failed. A few minutes later, Pitt was back again and Hastings kicked a 32-yard field goal for a 26-0 halftime lead.

The Pitt faithful rubbed it in at halftime with their taunting and singing and cheers for more touchdowns, but the scoring was almost over. Early in the third quarter, Hess intercepted a Hastings pass at the Pitt 44-yard line. Determined to salvage something out of the beating they were taking, the Lions marched down to the 18-yard line before losing the ball on downs. Pitt then added the *coup de grace* by going on its only sustained drive of the day with McLaren plunging over from the 1-yard line for the TD.

The 31-0 loss was the worst defeat by a State team since the 29-0 loss to Harvard in 1913 and the worst beating ever by Pitt. For the second year in a row the Lions had been shutout by the Panthers, who would again be acclaimed the consensus National Champion. Harlow was so devastated he almost resigned that night at the annual team banquet but was talked out of it by friends. "*LaVie*" called the game "a sad ending" and a "disappointment" that would be "deep and lasting" to "students and alumni all over the country." The alumni living in Pittsburgh were more than disappointed. They were angry and many wanted Harlow fired. They were particularly critical of his offensive strategy and tactics. Behind the scenes the more influential Western Pennsylvania alumni worked out a plan that would keep Harlow in overall charge of the team but take away his authority for developing the game plan and running the team during a game.

At another time, that might have caused Harlow to quit or fight openly for full control. But he was still a loyal graduate and did not want to do anything that would hurt "his" school.

World War I would change his mind.

Season Record 8-2
Record to Date 147-79-13
Winning percentage .642

"A War on Two Fronts"

What happened on the playing field in 1917 was overshadowed by events that occurred off it long before the season started.

As freezing, snowy weather engulfed State College in mid January, the United States was preparing to go to war. World War I was raging in Europe and by June the U.S. and many of the country's football players would be into it. But back at Penn State that January, Harlow was already in a personal war over his coaching position.

As historian Ridge Riley described in his book "*The Road to Number One,*" the Pittsburgh alumni who dominated the Athletic Committee pressured for a coaching change. Unable to get support for Harlow's outright firing, the Pittsburghers came up with a scheme to usurp his authority.

In an Athletic Committee meeting at the Duquesne Athletic Club in Pittsburgh on February 16, the committee interviewed and hired Xeonphen C. (Zen) Scott of Cleveland as the "field coach" with "full

responsibility for development of the 1917 team." Harlow, who attended the meeting with his captain-elect Higgins, was given a new title as "resident coach." The committee fully expected Harlow would resign and Scott to be the "head coach" by the fall. As the official minutes of the meeting stipulated, the committee reserved "the right after spring practice to ask Mr. Scott to assume full charge of the coaching of the team during the 1917 playing season." One month after spring practice, the committee said, Harlow would decide his responsibility.

One can imagine what went through Harlow's mind. Obviously, he was hurt and thought of quitting. Whatever made him accept the situation is not known. As Riley wrote, "His sensitive nature rebelled against the arrangement, but he tried to live with it, and his restraint probably kept the bottom from falling out of Penn State football during the first war year of 1917."

Harlow never had to make a choice after spring practice because spring practice was canceled because of the war. Unrestricted submarine warfare by the Germans had thrust the U.S. into the war that spring and college men all over the nation left the campuses for the military.

The annual preseason September practice session before the semester also was canceled and when Harlow, Scott and their assistants greeted the candidates on the first day of classes, they surely had no delusions about the season ahead. Only three regulars from 1916 had returned—Conover, Robb and Czarnecki—and no other lettermen. Clark and Morris had graduated but everyone else was in the armed services, even frosh coach Dutch Herman. Conover, who would eventually start every game at Higgins' right end position, was elected co-captain to supersede Higgins. Harlow could easily afford to move Conover from center because he had widely-heralded sophomore Red Griffiths up from the freshman team. Another sophomore, Frank Wolf, would be the starting quarterback in the opening game, and two other scrubs from '16, Al Pond and Red Gross, would join Robb in the backfield. The other starters also would be sophomores and, of those, only the left end Dick Rauch would ever make an impact after the war.

Schedule changes also were needed as Penn and Lafayette canceled their November games and two new opponents were added, Dartmouth and Maryland. Muhlenberg, which had been scheduled as the opening game in Allentown, also bowed out but city officials prevailed to have another game played there, and that's how State wound up opening the season against a team from the U.S. Army Ambulance Corps, which was based in Allentown.

The game was played Friday, September 29th, on behalf of the American Red Cross and the Ambulance team was actually an all-star college team that included three starters on State's 1916 team—Cubbage, Beck and O'Donnell. No one knew it at the time, but the game marked the debut of one of State's greatest players, Charlie Way. Way, then weighing about 125 pounds, had hardly played on the frosh team and he probably got his chance in 1917 only because of the dearth of talent. Although he didn't score against the Ambulance team, the *Pittsburgh Post* reported that Way, subbing for Robb at left halfback, "led the attack and his open field running thrilled the crowd." State won 10-0 as "The Blue and White team played a magnificent game, winning on superior defensive ability." State scored in the first quarter when Wolf dropkicked a 45-yard field goal and then sealed the game late in the third period, when Pond picked up a fumbled punt and ran for a TD, with Conover booting the PAT.

The home opener against Gettysburg was a historic game. Robb scored six touchdowns—a record that has never been equalled—as State blasted Gettysburg, 80-0. Wolf and Pond also had two TDs each and Conover kicked eight extra points. Gettysburg only gained one first down the entire game. The score broke the record for biggest margin of victory set the previous year against Geneva but it didn't last long. The next week, State battered St. Bonaventure, 99-0, with Robb scoring three TDs and Pond, Gross and a sub named A. McKelvey getting two apiece. Conover has seven PATs. St. Bonaventure was so inept it allowed two TDs to be scored when it failed to cover State kickoffs into its end zone and State players fell on the ball.

State could have used some of that offense the next week when it traveled to Washington, PA, to play Washington & Jefferson for the first time since 1913. That was the day W&J ended State's longest unbeaten streak at 19 games in a major upset. This time the game was rated even but, as the *Pittsburgh Post* reported, State was outclassed: "In the first half State was on the defensive all the time and in the entire game had only two first downs...It never had the ball nearer the Wash-Jeff goal than the 40-yard line." The only points were scored midway through the First Quarter when W&J got the ball on its own 40-yard line after a punt. Propelled by two long runs of 28 and 20 yards, W&J drove to the one yard line and fullback McCreight plunged into the end zone. The PAT made it 7-0 and that was it.

But something had happened during that drive that would impact Penn State football for the next several years. On the third play of the drive, Wolf was hurt making a tackle and was done for the day; nor would he play the next week either. His initial replacement was a reserve named R. S. Clarke who was ineffective. Early in the fourth quarter, Way came in as the quarterback and on the second play made the longest State run of the day for 12 yards. The youngster from Downingtown was about to become a starter and in the next game against West Virginia Wesleyan he became a star.

Coach Earl (Greasy) Neal had his Wesleyan team ready for State. Perhaps, Neal's scouts had seen how W&J had shut out the Lions and he may have deployed the same tactics. Wesleyan scored a TD in the first quarter and its defense made the 7-0 lead hold up until late in the fourth quarter. With his team backed up close to its own goal line, Neal ordered his punter to take a safety to avoid a blocked kick. Under the rules at the time, Wesleyan kept the ball, so it tried to run out the clock. But on fourth down, Wesleyan had to punt. Way picked up the ball as it bounced on wet Beaver Field and ran for a 45-yard touchdown and an 8-7 win.

Way was now the star of the team, even surpassing Robb as the fans' favorite player. But neither he nor Robb could win all the games on their own.

If the 1917 season was defined by World War I and the hiring of Zen Scott, then the next game at Dartmouth determined the fate of the team record that year. Even with the war on, Dartmouth was a stronger team on paper. State surprised the home crowd in Hanover by recovering an onside kick to start the game and moved into position to try a field goal. But Pond's attempt failed and Dartmouth got the ball on its own 35-yard line. An unusual backfield shift confused the State linemen and State was penalized four times for offside as Dartmouth drove downfield on a series of line bucks. The home team's left half-back, A. Holbrook, scored a TD on a 3-yard plunge and his brother C. Holbrook booted the extra point for a 7-0 lead. Midway in the second quarter, State got even and it was Charlie "all the Way." With the ball on

State's 40-yard line, Way ran around left end for 30 yards. On the next play he did it again for 25 yards. Conover was held for no gain on a trick play. Then, Way banged over center for the touchdown from the 5-yard line and Conover kicked the PAT to tie the game.

State controlled the game *almost* the rest of the way. As the *Pittsburgh Post* reported, "...although the visitors several times threatened Dartmouth's goal, they lacked the necessary punch to register a score." As time was winding down and a tie game appeared to be the conclusion, Conover misfired on his center snap and Way could not handle the errant pass. Dartmouth recovered the ball at State's 30-yard line. In five plays, Dartmouth moved inside the 20 and on fourth down with two minutes left, a sub named Phillips kicked a placement field goal from the 23-yard line to give Dartmouth the lead. State tried desperately to come back with a passing attack but one of Way's throws was intercepted and Dartmouth had the ball on State's 3-yard line when the game ended.

"The visitors outplayed the Dartmouth eleven, excepting at the start of the contest, and at its close," the *Post* reported. "State's speedy backfield, led by Way, repeatedly smashed through the Green line and got many substantial gains around ends...The work of Penn State's quarterback was the best seen here in recent years and he excelled in broken field running." Czarnecki had played an outstanding game as a blocker and tackler and partially because of his performance on this day he would be selected to Walter Camp's Second Team All-American squad at the end of the season.

What had become apparent since the W&J game, however, was that State's offense was not very effective. Stop Way and Robb and you stopped the offense. The friction between Harlow and Smith and the confusion over their lines of responsibility undoubtedly contributed to—if not directly caused—the problem. Whether Harlow or Smith was in charge of the offense is not known. But the fact also was that some of State's players weren't very good and they made too many mistakes.

The heart-breaking loss to Dartmouth had a psychological affect on the team's play the next week in the Pennsylvania Day game against Lehigh. State fumbled six times with two fumbles leading to Lehigh scores and another bobble stopping a State drive on the Lehigh 1-yard line. Early in the first period, Lehigh scored an 11-yard TD on a pass from fullback Vince Wysocki to the team's star, quarterback Herrington. The PAT was no good. In the second quarter, State stopped a short Lehigh drive on the 8-yard line and the visitors settled for a 15-yard field goal. State's only real offense came on fourth quarter punt returns by Way. Twice he took Herrington's punts at full speed and ran for 45 and 55 yards only to be stopped by the last man who had a chance—Herrington. But State could not take advantage of either return and the game ended in a 9-0 loss.

The game against Maryland, then known as Maryland State, was another mismatch on Beaver Field. It was only scheduled because Maryland's president at the time, Dr. Harry Patterson, was a graduate of Penn State's class of '86. (So, now modern day fans know why Maryland could beat State just once in their 37-game series—the Terps were jinxed from the beginning by an inside set-up!) Robb scored three TDs and Way scored two on runs of 75 and 55 yards with another 45 yard run setting up one of Gross' two TDs. State racked up 28 first downs while Maryland didn't make any and only gained a total of 24 yards.

For the third straight year, Pitt was unbeaten when the teams met before a less than capacity crowd of 20,000 on a dreary Thanksgiving Day at muddy Forbes Field. The Panthers were heavy favorites and they played like it from the opening kickoff. Starting at their own 22-yard line, the Panthers took just four minutes and 10 plays to get a touchdown with the big plays coming from runs of 14 and 18 yards by right half Easterday. Left half H. C. McCarter got the TD with a five yard plunge, carrying several State tacklers with him as he crossed the goal. The PAT was good and Pitt led, 7-0.

State kicked off again (under the rules) and McCarter's 18-yard run back off Conover's short kick to the 20, gave Pitt the ball at its own 38-yard line. Pitt moved quickly to State's 30-yard line before a costly holding penalty stifled the drive and forced a punt. A Panther player downfield interfered with Way's attempt to catch the ball and State got possession for the first time at its own 30-yard line. But State couldn't get a first down and punted. Pond got away a great punt that forced Pitt to take possession back at its own 22-yard line. The Panthers used most of the time remaining in the quarter to grind out another touchdown with a 32-yard run by Easterday sparking the drive. The TD came on a 32-yard double pass from star fullback George McLaren to Easterday to reserve halfback A. C. Gugler, who caught the ball on the 10 and slid into the end zone after being tackled at the 3. The extra point made it 14-0 and, again, State kicked off. The Pitt fans were euphoric for it looked like this was another blowout similar to last year.

However, as the second quarter began, Pitt's fourth down pass attempt failed at the State 48-yard line and the Lions got the ball again. When State's players lined-up on offense they were in a new formation no one had seen before. The linemen had spread out, leaving a yard or two of space between each man. Two backs lined up behind an end on one side with the other two backs behind the line but shifted in the direction of the other backs. The center stood at a slant so that he could toss the ball directly to any of the running backs. The Pitt defense was stunned and didn't know what to do. On the first play, Way—now called "Gang-Way" by Pittsburgh sportswriters—went around end for seven yards. In nine plays, State reached the Pitt 19-yard line before a fourth down failed. Pitt took over but was forced to punt and State got the ball back at its own 35-yard line. On the second play, Robb ran 35 yards out of the spread formation. This time, State made a couple changes with the formation, allowing the guards and tackles

to be eligible to carry the ball and Griffiths centered it to Czarnecki, who gained four yards. Now, the Pitt players were really confused. Six plays later, at the Pitt 20-yard line, State scored on one of the most razzle-dazzle plays in history, with Gross taking the center pass from Griffiths and tossing it to Robb. Robb then flipped the ball to Way, who threw it to Conover for the TD. Now it was the State fans' turn to cheer. "The Penn State followers began to sing after their shouting died out," reported Harry Keck in the *Pittsburgh Post*. "They were a joyous bunch." Conover's PAT attempt was wide and with four minutes left in the half, Pitt kicked off to State.

Down the field, the Lions went again, starting from their 16-yard line. Way ran for 15. Conover got 4. Way picked up 6. But the drive stalled at the Pitt 41 and a terrible punt gave Pitt the ball at its own 39. Now it was Pitt on the march in the closing minutes of the half. Easterday broke away for 19 yards and Way saved a TD with a tackle from behind. An Easterday to Gugler pass brought the ball to State's 7 and it looked like Pitt would score again. But a forward pass by McLaren failed behind the goal and as the rules dictated at the time, State took possession at the 20 and one play later the first half ended.

State's radical formation had everyone buzzing during the intermission. State took the second half kickoff and moved up field before punting. Easterday fumbled the punt and Conover recovered at the 26-yard line. A Way to Conover pass got the ball to the Pitt 8 and State's fans went wild again. But Way lost eight, then had a pass intercepted at the 8 and the Pitt fans cheered— but only for a moment. Easterday fumbled trying to go around right end and Griffiths recovered at the 20. Robb got four and Way two but that was the dying gasp of the State offense. Two pass attempts failed and Pitt took over. The next time State got the ball, it was stopped cold. Pop Warner used the halftime break to devise a defense against the spread formation and it worked.

With State's offense no longer effective, Pitt took charge again in the fourth quarter as Gougler and Easterday scored TDs and Gougler booted two PATS to give Pitt a 28-6 win. "Blue and White's Weird Attack Puzzles Panthers During Most of Contest," said the headline in the *Post*. Later, it was learned that Zen Scott had developed the unorthodox spread formation. Some sportswriters wondered why State had not waited until the second half to use it. Thus, they reasoned, Warner

The 1917 team was decimated through graduation and military service. Captain Larry Conover is on the far left at right end and Stan Czarnecki is the right guard and All-American Red Griffiths is at center. The backfield includes QB Charlie Way, second from left, and HB Harry Robb, far right.

would not have had the time to concoct a successful defensive strategy. Such criticism overlooked the fact that Pitt was threatening to turn the game into a rout early in the second period.

Whether it was Scott or Harlow's decision to use the spread formation in the first half is not known. The Scott-Harlow relationship already had become intolerable and had reached the breaking point on the night before the Pitt game, when the Athletic Committee gave Harlow back his coaching authority. The committee rescinded the "dual system of coaching," declined to renew Scott's contract and named Harlow head coach for 1918 with "instructions to select his own coaches" from former Penn State players.

Some sportswriters of the day credited Scott for whatever success State had in 1917 but no one knows for sure how Harlow's wartime team would have done without Scott's presence or the stress over who was in charge. The fact is, this was the worst State record since 1913 and as World War I continued into 1918, even more turmoil—and a worse record—was just ahead.

Season Record 5-4
Record to Date 152-83-13
Winning percentage .639

CHAPTER 8

IN & OUT OF THE BIG TIME WITH BEZDEK

1918-1929

Everyone was tired of getting beaten by Pitt. Five losses in a row was a little too much, especially for the alumni who lived in Pittsburgh. They wanted a "real" coach, someone with experience and a track record for winning; someone like that SOB Pitt hired, Pop Warner. We beat Warner and the Indians in '06, they said, and we can beat him and the Panthers this year or next if we get the right coach.

C.W. Heppenstall talked it over with his fellow alums. When the Pittsburgh industrialist quietly told some of the folks in the athletic administration what he and the others had in mind, they weren't so sure. The Athletic Advisory Committee was more concerned about finding someone to take over expansion of the physical education program. In the wake of World War I, the U.S. Army had issued a report on the poor physical fitness of young American men, and the report said colleges had an obligation to help fix the problem. We want someone to do more than coach football, Heppenstall was told. We want someone to get the entire student body involved in sports and exercise.

Heppenstall and his colleagues were convinced they had the man who could do both—someone who could take over the new Department of Physical Education and coach the football team to victory over Pitt: Hugo Bezdek, the manager of the Pittsburgh Pirates baseball team.

Bezdek had become manager of the slumping Pirates midway through the 1917 season and had revived the team. This year the Pirates were in the first division and a definite pennant

contender. But, as everyone knew, he had first gained prominence as a college football coach. He had coached unbeaten teams at Oregon and Arkansas and he had been a star fullback and coaching assistant under the master, Amos Alonzo Stagg, at the University of Chicago. In fact, Bezdek's teams had won the last two Rose Bowls. Two years ago, his Oregon squad beat Penn, 14-0, and last January, in the wartime Rose Bowl game, his Mare Island Marines defeated the Army's Camp Lewis team, 19-7. If anyone can match up with Pop Warner, it was Hugo.

But why in the world would he want to become director of physical education—and football coach—of some school in the sticks of Pennsylvania? And, doesn't he have a contract with the Pirates? Bezdek's Pirates' agreement ran into 1919 and he said he was happy running the National League team. But he missed the college atmosphere, just as his friends told him he would. Football was in his blood. Bezdek was not only a baseball mastermind, but also a football innovator. He already was known for originating and developing the screen pass and his spread formations and fullback/halfback spinner plays were being copied by his contemporaries.

Thus, in early September of 1918, Hugo Bezdek became the first "real" coach of Penn State's football team. However, that wasn't his primary job, said the Athletic Advisory Committee and the Board of Trustees. He would be the director of the new Department of Physical Education and an associate professor and, as such, would have overall authority over all of State's intercollegiate

Hugo Bezdek was hired as coach in 1918 while still under contract as manager of the Pittsburgh Pirates. He was an experienced football coach as well, and had a record of being a winner.

athletic programs. He'll coach football in the fall, yes, but he'll also do whatever it takes the rest of the year to improve the quality of State's athletic training.

What about the Pirates, someone asked. There will be a little overlap, came the official reply, but much of the major league season was in the summer when school was not in session. He'll finish out his Pirates contract in 1919 and then we'll see.

Bezdek moved quickly to salvage the abbreviated wartime 1918 season by getting the ban lifted on freshmen eligibility. By 1919 he had not only beaten Pitt and received a new three-year contract but also had outlined a master plan to the Board of Trustees that completely changed physical education and athletics on the campus. "Athletics for all," was his slogan. Much of what he advocated would not be fulfilled until after he stepped down as football coach. But he basically created State's intramural program and physical education curriculum while also upgrading the varsity sports program and facilities. He hired many of the non-football coaches who would someday be university legends—baseball's Joe Bedenk, wrestling's Charlie Speidel, boxing's Leo Houck, soccer's Bill Jeffrey and track's Chick Warner, among others. He expanded athletic facilities in golf, baseball and track and built a new housing facility for athletes (now called Irvin Hall) to go along with the Track House. His crowning achievement was Recreation Hall. The building was his idea and he nurtured the planning, fund raising, and construction right into the 1930s.

He also produced winning football teams that brought national recognition. Both the 1920 and 1921 teams were unbeaten and among the greatest in State history. His 1922 team played in the school's first bowl game, the '23 Rose Bowl. His teams were not hesitant about taking on the best from coast-to-coast, and he helped recruit and develop some of the school's all-time stars—Glenn Killinger, "Light Horse" Harry Wilson, Joe Bedenk, Gus Michalske and many others. Midway through the 1920 season he was given a new seven-year contract and when he asked that the Trustees also increase athletic scholarships from 38 to 48 that year they willingly agreed.

Early on, alumni called him the "miracle worker" and students and newspapermen loved him. When word got out during the 1922 season that the Philadelphia Phillies wanted to hire him as manager, the students marched around campus chanting and carrying signs that said, "Don't Hu-Go Bezdek." He turned down the Phillies and got a new 10-year Penn State contract in the process.

So, why isn't Bezdek as honored and revered in Penn State football and athletic history as his successors Bob Higgins, Rip Engle and Joe Paterno?

It wasn't just because he could never beat Pitt again after that 1919 win, although losing to Pitt seven straight years contributed heavily to his downfall. Bezdek was a complicated man and a forward-thinker with a genius for organization and innovation. But he also was power-hungry, egocentric and abrasive. His tactics were harsh on and off the field. Above all, he rarely gave credit to others and did not inspire loyalty.

When Dick Harlow returned from the military for the 1919 season, he was openly embraced by Bezdek as his number one assistant. However, they clashed constantly as Bezdek refused to acknowledge Harlow's expertise as a scout and line coach and was jealous of Harlow's rapport with the players. Their antagonistic relationship fi-

nally forced Harlow to leave, and when he took the head coaching job at Colgate in the spring of 1922, more than a half dozen players followed him. Bezdek may not have realized it at the time but that was the beginning of his end as head coach.

The '22 season was disappointing despite the Rose Bowl participation as the team finished the year with three straight losses, including a 14-0 defeat at Pitt. The next year, a 20-3 end-of-season loss to Pitt had the western Pennsylvania alumni grumbling. As the football team's record slipped over the next couple of years, other alumni groups began complaining, and not just about winning or losing but also about Bezdek's attitude, arrogance and dictatorial control. Some wanted Bezdek replaced as football coach. Other alumni wanted to take complete control of the athletic department. And one alumni faction joined with a group within the administration and called for the elimination of all financial aid to athletes. One by one Bezdek lost the support of his backers, especially the former players, like Ed Yeckley, the captain in '05, who had been recruiting players for him. He also was losing the respect of his players, who were rebelling under his brutal treatment.

The catalyst that ended the Bezdek era came in 1926 from outsiders unconnected with State's athletic program. The Carnegie Foundation for the Advancement of Teaching funded a nationwide study that examined the place of athletics on college campuses. (This was 1926, mind you, not 1996! *Déjà vu*.) The inception of the study in January prompted Penn State's alumni to conduct a similar evaluation of the State athletic program. Bezdek was furious at the way the internal assessment was being handled and he took out his displeasure on his team. A 26-4 loss to Pitt that gave State a final 5-4 record in 1926 didn't help.

In late February of 1927, two months after the installation of a new college president, Ralph Hetzel, the alumni committee delivered a report with several stunning recommendations. The committee advocated an end to all financial aid to athletes and the establishment of a Board of Athletic Control comprised of trustees, faculty, students and alumni to oversee the athletic department. The report also recommended that the Department/School of Physical Education and Athletics—Bezdek's domain—be split into two schools and that the director—Bezdek—not be permitted to coach in *any* sport.

Although the latter recommendations were delayed for a couple of years, the new Board of Athletic Control was in place by August. At its first meeting on August 10, 1927, the board not only eliminated all athletic scholarships, effective with the 1928-29 academic year, but also established a policy whereby Penn State "will not scout opponents' games regardless of the scouting policies of opponents." It was a shocking but honorable decision.

In retrospect, one can debate the merits, morality and rightfulness of what the board did that day. But one could also argue that the new policies—particularly the end of financial aid— set back Penn State's growing reputation as a football power by almost 50 years. Scholarships were not reinstituted until the Engle years and it took until the late 1970s for the Paterno-coached teams to be recognized among the nation's elite football programs.

President Hetzel was praised for what he had done to bring academic sanity back into athletics. His presidential colleagues at other schools, particularly those that were opponents on the playing fields, were quick with their acclaim. Of course, most other schools did not follow State's lead and with schedules that included such scholarship teams as Pitt, Syracuse, West Virginia and Bucknell, Bezdek could see the proverbial "writing on the wall."

Bezdek pushed them to his last winning records, 6-2-1 in 1927 and 6-3 in 1929. But he still could not beat Pitt, and after Pitt had back to back shutouts in '27 and '28, the Pittsburgh area alumni had had enough. They called for his head, with his original benefactor, C. W. Heppenstall, leading the way. He made it through the 1929 season— and another loss to Pitt—but in mid January of 1930, the Board of Trustees asked him to give up coaching and be the director of the new School of Physical Education and Athletics. It was a reward for a man who had done so much for Penn State's athletic program and especially football.

"Professor" Bezdek would stay on at State for another six years, improving the facilities and athletic programs beneficial to all students. But he would eventually lose the confidence of the administration, students, faculty and—of course—the alums. He accepted a one year leave of absence with pay on October 1, 1936 and one year later he left State completely.

The ultimate irony of the Bezdek coaching era is that President Hetzel and those who supported the de-emphasis of athletics never got the credit they deserved. When the Carnegie Foundation issued its final report on October 23, 1929, after visiting 130 schools in the U.S. and Canada, it called college officials who give athletic scholarships "the Fagins of American sport and American higher education." One of the "Fagins' school's cited was Penn State, despite the fact that financial aid to athletes had ended two years earlier.

Still, State was among the small minority of schools that endorsed the study, formally known as "Bulletin No. 23." Hetzel also persuaded the foundation to add a footnote mentioning how State had already "cleaned-up" its program with its new policies. But few outsiders paid any attention to the footnote and for years State was unfairly branded as an "out-of-control" athletic factory.

Bezdek did have a hand in choosing his successor. But he even botched that, telling the public he had reluctantly but voluntarily stepped down to give Bob Higgins "the benefit of good material" in his first year.

It was a crock and Bezdek knew it. He had been given no choice. If he had not stepped aside he might not have lasted another season. Nor would he have been permitted to stay on as athletic director. But in the end it would not matter. Higgins would become a Penn State legend and Bezdek would be almost a footnote. The Hig would also beat Pitt five times.

"The Weird Season of World War I"

In the long history of Penn State football, there has never been a season as chaotic and as weird as 1918.

A major coaching change, the deaths of two former star players killed in action on the battlefield and the subtle debut of a future

Hall of Fame player were part of the fabric of the shortened '18 season.

Most of the players from the 1917 squad had already left for military service when Harlow held a limited spring practice session. The students who turned out at Harlow's call had even less football talent than their predecessors. But there was one freshman who Harlow had personally invited to join the workouts.

Harlow had seen Glenn Killinger play basketball that winter and had asked if Killinger had played football before. In high school at Harrisburg Tech, Killinger replied, but he didn't think he was good enough to play at Penn State so he had not come out for the freshman team in the fall. Harlow saw a natural athlete in the rather skinny 5-10, 125-pound youngster and persuaded him to try out for the team in the spring. But Killinger didn't stay around long. He quit when baseball practice started.

As the war droned on in Europe that summer, word reached State that one of its former star players—and a Harlow teammate—had been killed near Soissons, France. Lt. Levi Lamb, class of 1915, died July 18 while leading his platoon against the Germans. It was about this time that Harlow decided that he, too, should join the military. The Athletic Committee graciously agreed to release Harlow from his three-year contract and immediately began looking for a coach.

On August 25, the committee hired Hugo Bezdek, a highly-respected former coach at Oregon and Arkansas, who was then managing baseball's Pittsburgh Pirates. Bezdek would be in charge of State's new physical education department and coach football as part of his duties. He also could continue managing the Pirates, at least until his contract expired after the 1919 National League season.

Bezdek looked at the roster of potential players and at the daunting eight-game schedule, which included Dartmouth, Cornell, Penn, W&J, Lehigh and Pitt. I need more players, he told the Athletic Committee. Let's make freshmen eligible. The committee agreed.

Before the players gathered at the start of classes, all games scheduled in September and October were canceled. Because of the war, the U.S. government had pressured the universities to emphasize intramurals instead of intercollegiate games and State's games with Penn and Dartmouth were eliminated. A flu epidemic later forced cancellation of the Cornell game and potential games with Bucknell and Carnegie Tech. Three games were set for November, including the traditional Thanksgiving Day finale against Pitt, and graduate manager Neil Fleming was pursuing another early November game as the team worked out in early October. That's when the Athletic Committee learned that another of its star players from the 1912 unbeaten team, infantry Lt. Red Bebout, had also been killed in action in France. The news further dampened the morale of the State athletic family as Bezdek and his assistant , Chuck Yerger, a running back on the '15 team, ran the football players through the daily practices.

In late October, Fleming came up with a fourth game to open the season. It was a navy team, Wissahickon Barracks, based at Cape May, NJ. The team was comprised of college players serving their military duty and included center Duke Osborn, who had enrolled at Penn State but had left for the Navy before playing any football.

An enthusiastic crowd of students turned out on Nov. 2 at Beaver Field to see what six weeks of practice would do for Bezdek's untried team of unknowns. Nary a letterman was in sight. Killinger, who had re-joined the team in September at the urging of his friend, Gene Farley, a substitute tackle, was the starter at right half. Ron "Buck"

Williams was the quarterback with Art Lundberg at left half and Frank Unger at fullback. Unger was elected the captain, replacing Robb, who was now playing for Columbia under the military's Student Army Training Corps (SATC) program (and would be picked to Walter Camp's Second Team All-American team at the end of the year).

Although outweighed by several pounds per man, State battled Wissahickon evenly throughout the first half, which was scoreless. State missed one opportunity when a field goal attempt at the visitor's 30-yard line was blocked. After an exchange of punts early in the third quarter, State started a drive from midfield. A nice end run by Williams got the ball to the Wissahickon 30-yard line again and an Unger to Williams pass moved State to the 10. On fourth down-and-two, half-back Al Knabb, subbing for Killinger, who had been injured, bolted over center for the touchdown. The PAT failed but the 6-0 lead continued to hold up into the fourth quarter as the teams exchanged possession several times without threatening. Then, with less than a minute left in the game, Wissahickon ran back a punt into State territory. Two plays later, with the ball at the State 30-yard line, right end George Uritis, a former star at Georgetown, took a short pass from Ruble and ran 30 yards for the tying score. But the attempt at the game-winning extra point was wide and the final score was 6-6.

State was a heavy underdog the next week in its first ever meeting with Rutgers led by All-American end Paul Robeson, who would later achieve fame as a major Black leader. (State's African American Center is named after Robeson.) Rutgers had piled up 147 points while winning four games without a loss. State was further hampered by the absence of starting backs Killinger and Unger, who were both hurt in the Wissahickon game. Killinger had three broken ribs after a collision with—of all people—the erstwhile State lineman, Osborn. Knabb replaced Killinger but Unger's sub at fullback was a freshman named Joe Lightner. The same day as the Wissahickon game, Lightner had started for the frosh team against Bellefonte Academy and had scored the only TD in a 7-0 win. The kid had never played high school football back in Harrisburg and now he was starting at halfback before 7,000 in the annual Pennsylvania Day Game at Beaver Field.

Bezdek knew it would take a lot of breaks and a lot of luck to beat the powerful visitors and he got his first break soon after the opening kickoff to Rutgers. On the first play from scrimmage at its own 20-yard line, Rutgers fumbled. State recovered and the partisan State crowd went crazy. Three bucks into the line picked up a few yards and on fourth down, tackle Red Henry booted a field goal from about the 20 for a 3-0 State lead. But from that point on it was all Rutgers. The visitors scored six points in the first quarter, 14 points in the second and six more in the fourth to win, 26-3. State got no closer than the 26-yard line late in the fourth quarter as Rutgers pushed the Lions up and down the field. "The determined fight during the second half by the boys held Rutgers to a single touchdown," reported the "LaVie," "and this was the pleasing factor to all who witnessed the fray."

Two days later, on November 11, the war in Europe officially came to an end. Armistice Day. The men would be returning home soon, but not in time to salvage the 1918 football season.

Killinger and Unger were back as starters the next week when State traveled to Bethlehem to play Lehigh. Lightner was back on the frosh team and would not earn a varsity letter. Lehigh was a slight favorite because of the home field but it seemed to be a far superior team in the first five minutes. Taking the opening kickoff, the home team drove the length of the field with the little left halfback, Savaris,

scoring the touchdown on a short plunge. Lehigh's kicker, Booth, missed the extra point but that didn't seem to matter to the cheering Lehigh fans. It soon would. Moments later, Lehigh star fullback Wysocki went back in punt formation inside his own 15-yard line. Red Henry burst through, blocked the kick, scooped up the ball and ran into the end zone for the TD. Killinger dropkicked the PAT and State led 7-6. That's how the game ended. The *Pittsburgh Post* thought Lehigh played a better game except "several times used poor generalship" but the "*LaVie*" disagreed, saying "The boys played a hard and consistent game all the time and only for a few decisive breaks against them and they would have scored at least two more touchdowns."

Even in this war-torn season, Bezdek knew his ragtag team was no match for Pitt. The war had not devastated the Pitt roster as much as it had State's. The Panthers had several veterans back, including the powerhouse backfield led by All-Americans McLaren and Tommy Davies. In easy victories over Penn, W&J and Georgia Tech, Pop Warner's crew had not been scored upon. Playing on a muddy field had become part of the tradition of this Thanksgiving Day game, but this year the Forbes Field turf was even sloppier than usual. That may have had something to do with the poor punt by McLaren that was partially blocked early in the first quarter and gave State the ball on Pitt's 19-yard line. Pitt dug in as State made a few yards at a time, once on fourth down-and-inches. With Pitt fans screaming, "Hold them, Pitt! Hold them, Pitt!" Killinger, Williams and Lundberg hit the line with Unger going over right guard for the final foot and a touchdown. State fans, of course, were delirious. They didn't mind that the PAT was missed.

"Pitt went stark fighting mad right then," wrote Harry Keck in the *Pittsburgh Post*. "Not angry, mind you, but mad. Mad over the presumption of those State hosts in scoring so soon, in scoring at all. And in just seven plays after the succeeding kickoff, Pitt crossed the Blue and White goal line for its first touchdown and...never again was State to lead." Pitt scored another TD in the second quarter and two in the third quarter to win, 28-6, with McLaren getting three of the TDs and Davies one.

Despite the decisive loss, fans and sportswriters were quick to praise Bezdek. "The prospects for next season are bright, as Coach Bezdek will have all but one man of this year's eleven on hand in the fall," wrote the "*LaVie.*" "Best of all is the news that no less than sixteen former stars are expected to return to college in the fall." Keck of the *Post* was even more impressed. "Bezdek has turned out a wonderful team," wrote Keck. "It is full of spirit and plays hard every minute it is on the field...Bezdek has made good at State...(and)...Given more material next fall... (he) will make a wide swath in Eastern circles."

No one could have been more prophetic. The tempestuous first golden age of Penn State football was about to begin.

Season Record 1-2-1
Record to Date 153-85-14
Winning percentage .635

"Victory for the Veterans"

The team leaders were angry and wanted a showdown with "Bez." They stormed around the Track House cursing his name and denouncing his competence. Two days had passed since losing the first game of the season at Dartmouth and the team's record was now 2-1.

It wasn't just the 19-13 defeat that bothered these half dozen or so players. They were certain it was Bezdek's coaching that lost the game. He keeps shifting players around, they complained. Some are out of position. Some of the best are on the bench. He works us hard during the week, they moaned, and then won't let us play our game on Saturday. And then all he does is complain about how poorly we play and how out of condition we are. Harlow's tried to tell him but he won't listen. So, we'll do it.

Higgins and Conover agreed to talk to Bezdek. Higgins, who had been elected captain before the first game, made it clear that Bez would not have many choices.

These were not your run-of-the-mill player mutineers. They were wise and mature veterans, not only of the football field but of the military and many, like Higgins, had seen real combat on the battlefields of Europe. Some had taken an instant dislike to Bezdek and his martinet ways and wondered why the likable Harlow had not been given his old job back.

Bezdek had not even been on campus when the 27-lettermen and a dozen of other prospects showed up for preseason practice on September 3. Bezdek was still managing the Pirates, so Harlow and Dutch Herman—signing back on as assistant coaches—ran the team through the daily workouts for almost four weeks. When he did show up a week before the opening game, Bezdek immediately tried to show them all who was boss with his intense conditioning drills and hard scrimmages, and he loudly criticized what Harlow and Herman had been doing. The grumbling over Bezdek's abrasive style was pervasive.

Despite his antagonistic attitude, Bezdek was impressed with all the talented players who had returned. He was especially pleased with his backs—Way, Killinger, Robb, Hess, Lightner, Williams and the two newcomers, Henry "Hinkey" Haines and George Snell. Up front he had Higgins, Conover, Cubbage, Rauch, Griffiths, Beck, Henry, Ege, Osborn, George Brown and sophomore Stan McCollum among others. Bezdek knew many starters from last year's team would be fortunate to get much, if any, playing time but he would try to play a lot of substitutes. Who would start where was Bezdek's prime dilemma and that's what irritated the players. Conover, for example, was placed at tackle, rather than his pre-war positions of end and center and Henry, a natural tackle, became a guard.

Fan enthusiasm was running high for the opening game at Beaver Field against Gettysburg on October 4th. The *Collegian* predicted an Eastern Championship. Alum Jimmy Leyden had composed another fight song to go along with the "Victory" tune ("Fight, Fight, Fight, For the Blue and White") he had introduced as an undergrad in 1913. This one he called "The Nittany Lion" ("Hail to the Lion, Loyal and True") and the fans at the Gettysburg game quickly picked up the words as Leyden sang them through a megaphone.

Bezdek's team did not get off to a good start. State sputtered in the first half as the heavily underdog Gettysburg team outgained the Lions and held them scoreless. Early in the third quarter, Higgins picked up a Gettysburg fumble and ran 30 yards for State's first touchdown. Way, held out in the first half, came into the game a few minutes later and his running got the team going. The Lions scored four more TDs and won, 33-0.

Henry "Hinkey" Haines started at HB for the 1919 and 1920 teams that lost only one game. He went on to play pro baseball for the Yankees and pro football for the first N.Y. Giant team.

Juggling the starting lineup the next week against Bucknell, Bezdek changed the entire left side of the line, benched Osborn at center in favor or Rauch and moved Robb back to right half in place of Haines, inserting Way in at quarterback. A steady drizzle at the start of the game turned into a downpour by halftime and kept the scoring down. Conover booted a 30-yard field goal with Robb holding to give State a 3-0 lead early in the first quarter. Midway in the second quarter, Way went around left end for 50 yards before being shoved out of bounds on the Bucknell 5-yard line. Bucknell held on the 2-yard line but a poor punt went out of bounds at the 12-yard line and on the first play from scrimmage, Way "slipped through tackle" for a touchdown. Conover missed the PAT. The rain turned Beaver Field into "a sea of mud" in the second half and Hess outdueled Bucknell's Bower in what became a punting match. Neither team could score in the half and the Lions took away a 9-0 win over their rivals from Lewisburg.

As the team prepared to travel to Hanover to play Dartmouth, Bezdek made more changes in his unsettled lineup. Dartmouth was unbeaten in three games but State was considered the favorite by sportswriters. A record Hanover crowd of 4,500 turned out at "Alumni Oval" for the game, which was part of Dartmouth's 150th anniversary celebration. Way got the game off to a rousing start when he returned the opening kickoff 85 yards for a touchdown and State led 6-0 after Hess' PAT attempt failed. Dartmouth was stunned but only momentarily. The home team took the next kickoff and with quarterback Jack Cannel and triple-threat left halfback Jim Robertson ripping holes in State's defense, Dartmouth drove the length of the field to go ahead, 7-6, with Robertson getting both the TD and PAT. A few minutes later, Dartmouth was deep in State territory again when Robertson fumbled. Way picked up the ball at the State 15-yard line and ran untouched another 85 yards for the touchdown. This time Hess's PAT was good and State led 13-7 as the first quarter neared an end. Dartmouth came back again in the second quarter after getting possession deep in State territory following a punt and Robertson scored the tying TD but missed the extra point. Midway through the third quarter, Dartmouth got the ball on its own 40-yard line and a couple of plays later, sub halfback Pat Holbrook dashed 43 yards for the TD and the eventual 19-13 win.

"The local team was decidedly superior of the Penn State eleven in every department," said the dispatch from Hanover in the *Pittsburgh Sunday Post*. "...the Green had possession of the ball at least twice as long as State did...In addition, the ball was in the State territory for practically three quarters of the total time." Still, the State students, who believed the team had played a fine game, gave the squad a spirited welcome home celebration, lining the campus all the way from downtown State College to the Track House. The students were unaware of the displeasure of the team leaders.

And so, Higgins and Conover, the 25-years-old "old men" of the team, confronted Bezdek. At the meeting, "Higgins claimed he could pick a team from the squad that could be the Dartmouth game starter," historian Ridge Riley wrote later. "Bezdek made some concessions, and the future looked a little brighter." This was the defining moment of the 1918 season for after this meeting, State was a different team. For one thing, Bezdek solidified his lineup. In the last four games, Bezdek stuck virtually with the same lineup with few substitutions except for injuries: Brown and Higgins at ends, Cubbage and Henry at tackles, Rauch and Osborn at the guards, Conover at center, Robb at quarterback with Way, Haines, Snell and Hess as the running backs. (Surprisingly, neither Killinger nor Lightner would play enough to earn a letter.)

Despite the players' concerns over Bezdek's coaching style, State's Athletic Committee and alumni had been quite happy with his accomplishments. In early October, even before the internal dispute with the players had been resolved, Bezdek had been rewarded with a three-year contract as both football coach and director of physical education. As part of the arrangement, Bezdek gave up managing the Pirates and agreed to spend 10 months a year on campus.

The Beaver Field contest against winless Ursinus on Oct. 25 was the last time many players on State's varsity got into a game. Bezdek used three complete teams as State won 48-7 with Way again running back the opening kickoff for a TD, this time going 95 yards, Robb getting two TDs and a little used halfback named Ullery scoring three. Ursinus, which had not scored in any previous game, got its only TD late in the game on 80-yard run off a recovered fumble.

The next game, against favored Penn at Franklin Field, would prove to be the pivotal game of the year. A few days before the game, Bezdek and Higgins called a mass open meeting for "all disgruntled" players, students and faculty. "The coach succeeded in ironing out the difficulties between the various members of the squad," wrote Walter Dunn in the *Philadelphia Public Ledger*, "and made it known to them that the success of the present season depended on the cooperation" among all of them.

Unbeaten Penn had scored 237 points to just seven by five opponents but some of State's players, including Higgins, Conover and Robb, remembered the accusations of "dirty play" that followed the last time the teams had met in 1916. Rain turned Franklin Field into mud before a crowd of 20,000 and a wet ball helped determine the outcome, but as the *Philadelphia Inquirer* and *Pittsburgh Post* later reported, "there was nothing flukey (sic) about State's great victory. The burley visitors did everything better" than Penn.

Outstanding RB Charlie Way did not earn a frosh numeral in 1917 when he weighed 115 pounds. He returned after WW I military duty to earn Second Team All-American honors in '19 and First Team honors in '20.

In the second quarter, Way made one of his rare mistakes when he fumbled a punt at State's 10-yard line and Penn recovered. But three plays later, Way made up for his error when he intercepted a pass thrown by quarterback Bert Bell (the man who would one day become commissioner of the National Football League) and Penn would never again get inside State's 25-yard line. Higgins, who would dominate the game with his great punting, booted one far down field out of danger. After neither team could move the ball, Higgins punted again from his own 26-yard line. This time Penn's receiver fumbled the punt and the ball bounced towards the Penn goal before Conover recovered at the 3-yard line. On fourth down, Robb plunged one yard for the touchdown and Cubbage booted the PAT. State scored again in the fourth quarter after a 12-yard Robb to Higgins pass set up a 25-yard field goal by Conover and won, 10-0. "State's grim determination," reported the *Philadelphia Inquirer*, "and fight—her alertness in taking advantage of ever Penn mistake—the superior kicking of Higgins, and her sureness in handling of the ball brought her the triumph..." Robert "Tiny" Maxwell, the sports editor for the *Philadelphia Public Ledger*, who refereed the game, would later cite it as the one that made State the best team in the East.

The same day that State beat Penn, its next opponent, Lehigh, lost its first game of the season after five wins. Pitt not only shut out the Engineers but scored the first points of the year against them in winning, 19-0. So, Lehigh was looking to regain respect when it invaded Beaver Field for the annual Pennsylvania Day game. A crowd of 6,000 saw State overwhelm the visitors in the final home game of the year, getting 17 first downs to Lehigh's three. State took the opening kickoff and marched to the Lehigh 20-yard line from where Conover placekicked a 30-yard field goal for an early 3-0 lead. Before the day was over,

Conover had kicked another field goal and Robb and Snell had scored touchdowns to lead a 20-7 victory. Lehigh's only score came late in the fourth quarter on the recovery of a blocked kick in the end zone.

State surprised Cornell with a well-executed passing attack the next week at Ithaca. With Higgins as the prime receiver, the Lions gained more than 100 yards in passes—a remarkable total at the time because of all the passing restrictions. A 25-yard pass from Robb to Higgins helped set up State's first score in the second period. Higgins' reception and a run by Robb got the ball to the Cornell 2-yard line. Cornell held but punted to its own 31-yard line. In two plays, State had a touchdown with Hess running for 15 yards and Robb for 16 and the TD. A few minutes later, State was on the Cornell 2-yard line after three pass receptions—two by Higgins— from midfield. Hess plunged over for the TD and State led 13-0 at the half. Midway through the third quarter, Higgins caught a Robb pass and ran 20 yards to the Cornell 5-yard line. Three plays later, with the Cornell line stacked up tight, Robb circled right end. Conover kicked the PAT and State went home with a 20-0 win.

For the first time in years, the annual Thanksgiving Day game against Pitt was rated a toss-up. Pop Warner's team had been beaten by Syracuse and tied by Penn but it still had not lost a home game since 1914 and many sportswriters predicted a seventh straight win over State. What happened in the first four minutes of the game was one of the greatest moments in the history of Penn State football.

In the 10 days of practice leading up to the big game, State's two punters, Higgins and Hess, had been working on a surprise pass play from punt formation. The play had been devised by Harlow who had scouted Pitt and noticed the Panthers almost always rushed nine or ten men when it had an opponent backed up near the enemy's own goal line. Harlow's plan was to have Hess in punt formation throw a short pass to the team's best receiver, Higgins. The problem was Hess was a lousy passer and as they practiced the trick play, Hess's passes continually failed to reach Higgins. As described by Riley in "*Road to Number One*," Hess, quickly losing confidence in himself, tried to get Harlow to use another passer. But Harlow said the play would work only if State's regular punters were used and since Higgins was such a great receiver, Hess had to be the passer. Surprisingly, Bezdek had not been told about the play and when he saw Hess and Higgins practicing he asked what they were doing. When told, he reportedly replied: "It sounds okay, but next time let me know what's going on around here."

Another record crowd estimated at 35,000-to-40,000 was at muddy Forbes Field on a foggy, wet day as Pitt kicked off to State. Way returned the kickoff to State's 28-yard line but two running plays went nowhere and Hess dropped back to punt on third down. Robb, at quarterback, called for a punt. Because of the mud, Hess had a problem getting the punt off and it was blocked. Pitt recovered at State's 23-yard line. In seven plays, Pitt was at 6-yard line with fourth down-and-one. At first, the Panthers lined up in field goal formation, but shifted to a running formation and lost two yards. State took over but instead of running a play, the Lions went immediately into punt formation, ostensibly to get itself out of a hole and improve field position. This time Robb called "the play."

Hess stood in the end zone and Higgins was on the right at the line of scrimmage. The Pitt linebacker, Herb Stein, cheated up towards his front line. Conover snapped the ball. Ten Pitt players rushed with only fullback Andy Hastings back to receive the punt. Hess drifted to his right as the Pitt linemen surged. No one was watching Higgins, who made a brush block and took several steps towards the 10-yard

line. Suddenly, Hess stopped and tossed the ball to Higgins. Bingo! Higgins caught it and with the other end, Brown, out front, he started downfield. Hastings dashed in but Brown nailed him and Higgins ran all the way for a touchdown. The State fans jumped up and down with joy as the Blue Band blared away the Victory song.

The play was officially listed as a 92-yard pass reception and it was still the team record 79 years later.

The play "took the heart out of Pitt, who appeared helpless from that stage on," wrote Dunn in the *Public Ledger*. "There have been few games in the last quarter century where the Blue and Gold was beaten in the first two minutes of play."

Another big play off a fake field goal helped set up State's second touchdown in the second quarter. Robb, the holder for Conover, took the ball from center and passed to Higgins who passed quickly to Way who ran 30 yards to get inside the Pitt 5-yard line. A couple plays later, Hess plunged over from the 1-yard line. State missed two more scoring chances in the second period when a holding penalty stopped one drive at the Pitt 3-yard line and a 45-yard field goal attempt by Conover fell short. So, State took a 13-0 lead into the intermission. Early in the third quarter, Way broke away on a 50-yard run for another touchdown, Cubbage kicked his second PAT and State won, 20-0. Pitt was thoroughly beaten, coming no closer to scoring than a futile 35-yard field goal attempt. State gained 238 yards on the ground to 110 for Pitt and added another 127 yards on passing. "Panthers Like Babies in Penn State's Hands," blared one headline.

State fans celebrated on the streets of Pittsburgh until the early hours of Friday morning. At the annual team and alumni dinner that night at a Pittsburgh hotel, Bezdek and his men were treated like conquering heroes. In the days that followed, most sportswriters would select State as the best team in the East over Syracuse, Colgate and undefeated Harvard, which had a weak schedule but went on to win the Rose Bowl. Higgins would be named a First Team All-American by Walter Camp, thus becoming the school's first two-time All American (selected by INS in 1915) and Way would be selected to the Third Team.

Bezdek, his new contract in hand, vowed that his 1920 team would be even better and would beat old nemesis Pitt again and again. He was half right.

Season Record 7-1
Record to Date 160-86-14
Winning percentage .642

"Gang-Way for Killinger & Nebraska"

Despite being on campus from the beginning of preseason practice on September 1, Bezdek was again having trouble picking a permanent starting lineup. The team had already defeated Muhlenberg and Gettysburg at the remodeled Beaver Field but it had not been impressive and powerful Dartmouth was about to visit for the first time to play in what was being called the "Alumni Home-Coming Day" game.

Although there was dissension, the players were not as rebellious as they had been last year. Maybe that was because they

A record crowd of 12,000 was in New Beaver Field for this first ever "Home-Coming" game, then known officially as Alumni Day, on October 9, 1920, as State beats Dartmouth, 14-7.

understood Bezdek's methods a little better, or, maybe it was because such strong team leaders as Higgins, Conover and Robb had graduated. Veterans like Rauch, Brown and others still chafed under Bezdek's harsh training and strict discipline. No one liked the tough mid-week scrimmages, especially the first one every Tuesday. "Bloody Tuesday" they called it and with reason. But many players appreciated Bezdek's football knowledge and tactical expertise and were willing to tolerate the coach's brutality and sarcasm to win.

With the exception of Robb, the entire corps of outstanding backs had returned from Bezdek's fine 1919 team. Bezdek was so confident in the returnees that he moved captain Bill Hess from full back to right guard to take advantage of his speed in leading interference. Eventually he would use Haines, Way and Lightner to share the halfback slots with Snell at fullback. For some reason, Bezdek was still uncertain about the ability of Killinger to be a winning quarterback and in the pre-season he tagged Buck Williams as his starter and had Killinger, who reported a tad late, battling for the second team with soph Pete Ruos.

The heart of his front line —Higgins, Conover, Cubbage, Henry and Osborn—had graduated. Rather than re-build, Bezdek simply had to re-tool because there was so much talent available among the non-letter substitutes of 1919 and incoming sophomores. Although there was considerable maneuvering in the first couple of games, Bezdek eventually would settle on a front line of Brown and soph Ross "Squeak" Hufford at ends, Rauch and either Beck or soph Dick Schuster at the tackles, Hess and Red Griffiths at guard and soph Newsh Bentz at center with juniors Ray Baer and Stan McCollum the prime backups at tackle and end, respectively.

The first game with heavy underdog Muhlenberg on September 25 was the earliest season opener in four years and the game was played under a blistering sun more fitting for baseball. Perhaps it was the heat that affected the players. But after Lightner scored the first touchdown early in the game, the team seemed to let up, and the final score of 27-7 was disappointing to the fans, many of whom sat in the new permanent stands erected on the east side of the field.

The weather was better for football the next week against weak Gettysburg but again State was sloppy. The Lions fumbled several times, stopping drives deep into Gettysburg territory, and the 13-0

victory was disappointing. However, Bezdek made a momentous decision after the game. He named Killinger, now packing a solid 166-pounds on his 5-10 frame, his starting quarterback in place of Williams. This was probably the defining moment of the season—if not, the next season, too.

Although many alumni had returned on their own each year for the big game on Pennsylvania Day, officials in Old Main had decided to make one game special for alumni this year. A series of parties, rallies and other events were planned around the Saturday afternoon football match with Dartmouth and by Thursday the alums began streaming into town by car, train and buggy. By Friday evening, the town and campus were jumping and the State marching band paraded around town. "The sidewalks were lined with people watching the hilarious mob invade the town," Alumni secretary Mike Sullivan later wrote for the *Alumni News* magazine. There was a big meeting inside Schwab auditorium Friday night and just before the game, some 4,000 people gathered on the Old Main lawn for a pep rally and march to Beaver Field.

With the new grandstands on the east side of Beaver Field raising the seating capacity to 5,500, a record standing-room-only crowd of 12,000 was on hand Oct. 9 to watch the "Home-Coming Day" game. Dartmouth was favored and scored first when captain Jim Robertson tossed a short pass to Holbrook after a drive from midfield. With the PAT the visitors led 7-0. But State retaliated after getting the ball on the Dartmouth 40-yard line following a punt. With passes from Killinger to Brown getting most of the yardage, State moved inside the 5-yard line and Snell plunged over for the TD. Rauch kicked the extra point and the score remained tied into the intermission.

The teams battled up and down the field throughout the second half and a tie seemed inevitable, particularly after Way left the game with an injury. But as time was running down, Killinger stepped in front of a

Squeak Hufford was a fine pass receiver and blocker on three of State's outstanding teams, including the 1921 "Mystery Team" and the 1922 Rose Bowl team.

Penn State beats Nebraska 20-0 in first meeting of the two teams at New Beaver Field in 1920. They would not play again until 1949.

Dartmouth receiver to intercept Robertson's pass at the State 46-yard line and he was not stopped until shoved out of bounds at the Dartmouth 2. On the next play, Lightner, subbing for Way, bulled over for the TD. Rauch booted his second PAT and the Lions left the field with a pleasing 14-7 victory. The *Alumni News* described the game as "a thrilling, gripping intense game" and the "*LaVie*" said there was great "satisfaction of winning from the only team that defeated the 1919 eleven." That night the players, students and alumni celebrated with a big party at the Armory and smaller parties at the fraternities. It was then, Sullivan wrote later, that he and others decided to make this "Home-coming Day" an annual event. More important for the moment was that Killinger was the talk of the campus. Another Penn State football star had been born.

Bezdek also received a personal reward. The Athletic Association tore up his three-year contract and gave him a seven-year pact for 12 months at a new salary of $10,000 with a separate verbal agreement that more athletic scholarships would be added to his Department of Physical Education.

Two new opponents were on State's schedule that year and the first one the Lions played was a patsy, North Carolina State. Bezdek substituted two full teams throughout the game and State won handily before 3,500 fans at Beaver Field, 41-0. Way led the rout with his running and scored two touchdowns.

The next week, Way scored three TDs in the first quarter as the 1920 team made history in destroying Lebanon Valley, 109-7. The score remains the biggest winning point differential in the State record book. What was even more unusual is that the outmanned visitors scored first. State fumbled near midfield on its first possession and Lebanon Valley's captain, Behman, picked up the ball and went 30 yards before being tackled near the 10-yard line. Two plays later, Behman fired a pass to his right end, Weushinski. Killinger tipped the ball at the 6-yard line but Weushinski grabbed it out of the air and scooted into the end zone. The PAT made it 7-0. But on the ensuing kickoff, State swiftly moved downfield in seven plays, with Way running the last 26 for State's first TD and the rout was on. Eight different players scored TDs while Beck and Lightner kicked the extra points as Bezdek went into his third team and scrubs before the game was over. "The one unfortunate result of the contest," reported the *State College Times*, "was the injury obtained by Killinger....who was taken out of the game in the

second quarter and who may be out for several weeks due to an injury to his shoulder."

No way, Killy. Despite his aching shoulder, the tough and resilient junior was back in the starting lineup the next week against Penn at Franklin Field and scored the first TD in the opening quarter after a 25-yard run by Way got the ball inside the Penn 5-yard line. Late in the second quarter, Penn drove to the 1-yard line before a fumble apparently ended the threat and State took a slim 7-0 lead into the intermission. In the State locker room, Bezdek told the team Way would not start the second half and that Hinkey Haines would take his place as the middle kickoff receiver. As historian Ridge Riley wrote, Haines later recalled "he felt something good was going to happen." It did. Haines took the Penn kickoff at the 15-yard line, sped up the middle, dashed to his right and then back to the middle as State blockers dumped the would-be Quaker tacklers and Hinkey went all the way for the score. The spectacular return unnerved the Penn players. State scored two more times that quarter, with Snell and Lightner getting the touchdowns, and won easily, 28-0.

State's Pennsylvania Day foe was another new opponent, Nebraska, a power in the Missouri Valley Conference. This was State's biggest intersectional game since the Michigan Aggies had visited—and won—in the 1914 Pennsylvania Day contest. Nebraska had only lost to Notre Dame, 16-7, in five games and had held its four victims scoreless. That included a 28-0 win over Rutgers just five days earlier in New Brunswick, NJ. "The Nebraska team was very heavy as well as fast," reported "*LaVie*," and outweighed State by an average of seven pounds per man. To get his team properly warmed up, Bezdek did a most unusual thing. A half hour before the team left its dressing room at the Track House for the walk to New Beaver Field, Bezdek sent the players through an intense and hard conditioning drill on the Old Beaver Field practice area. Bezdek also decided to rest "Gang-Way" and he started Lightner at right halfback instead.

"It was one of the fastest and most exciting games every witnessed on New Beaver Field," "*LaVie*" reported. Monte Munn, the 6-5, 202-pound guard, was Nebraska's best player and his brother, Wade, at the other guard, was another star, and they led the visitors on a long opening drive to the State 1-yard line. But a fourth down pass for a touchdown hit the goal post and State took over. After exchanging punts, State started a drive from near its 40-yard line and scored on a

Coach Bezdek and the unbeaten team of 1920 are superimposed on the back of an African Lion in this publicity photo of that era. Always the autocrat, Bezdek banned the Lion mascot from appearing at games in 1923.

35-yard pass from Killinger to Hufford. The 7-0 score remained through the halftime intermission and with Way still on the sidelines, State nursed the precarious lead into the fourth quarter. When State got possession of the ball at its own 47-yard line following a punt, Bezdek sent in Way. On the first play, Killinger called for Way to run directly at Monte Munn. Bentz snapped the ball to Way, who ran behind Griffith's block on Munn and dashed 53 yards for the touchdown that broke up the game. A few minutes later, Way broke loose for a 67-yard run to Nebraska's 15-yard line, from where Killinger sprinted the last yards for the TD, and State won 20-0. It would be 29 years before the two teams would play again but the rivalry that began that day would one day become the focal point of two National Championship controversies.

Lehigh was up next and State was heavily favored in the game at Bethlehem. Perhaps, Bezdek and the boys were looking ahead to the final game against hated Pitt. "The Lehigh team were (sic) especially pointed for this game and they fought fiercely throughout," "*LaVie*" reported, "...in a very loosely played game..." State outgained Lehigh 167 yards to 66 but Lehigh's defense stymied the Lions defense for most of the game. The first half was scoreless but in the third quarter, Lehigh drove from midfield and scored on a touchdown pass. With 10 minutes remaining in the game, State drove 80 yards with Way scoring a touchdown from the 5-yard line and Rauch booting the tying point. Lehigh had one last chance to pull off the major upset, when it tried a field goal in the waning moments. The kick missed the goal posts and as the ball bounced around the end zone, a Lehigh player could have fallen on it for a TD under the rules at the time. But a spectator came out, picked up the ball and handed it to the referee. Moments later, the game was over, and so was State's perfect season.

The unexpected 7-7 tie with Lehigh tarnished the luster of State's wins over Dartmouth, Penn and Nebraska and probably made the annual Thanksgiving Day finale against Pitt a toss-up. The Panthers also had a tie—7-7 with Syracuse—marring its otherwise unbeaten seven game record, which included wins over Georgia Tech, Penn and W&J. Once again, the mud of Forbes Field had an impact on the outcome. Both teams were hurt by the fumbles of their star players and the speedy runners on both sides had difficulty picking up yardage in the

slop. The final score of 0-0 was probably appropriate, although both teams missed great scoring opportunities near the opponent's goal line.

Pitt had the better of it in the first half and twice came close to scoring. The first time State stopped a fourth down running play at the 4-yard line and later Pitt's Davies missed a field goal by inches. At the start of the third quarter, Pitt blew another chance when a fourth down pass failed inside the 5-yard line. But then it was State's turn. The Lions reached the Pitt 10-yard line but Killinger was stopped four straight times trying to get over the goal line. In the fourth quarter, State got to the Pitt 15-yard line but on fourth-and-two at the 7, Way was thrown for a three yard loss.

The tie pleased no one and probably cost both teams the Eastern Championship. With one tie, a winner in this game would have challenged Harvard for the title. Harvard also was undefeated but also had a tie, with Princeton. Tying twice also eliminated State and Pitt from the mythical national title. Unbeaten Notre Dame claimed the National Championship but so did undefeated California, which clobbered another unbeaten team, Ohio State, in the Rose Bowl.

State received some consolation when two players were named First Team All-Americans and another made the Second Team. Walter Camp named Charlie "Gang-Way" to his All-American backfield, that also included the now-legendary George Gipp of Notre Dame. The International News Service placed Red Griffiths at guard on its First Team. Hinkey Haines made the Second Team as a halfback.

Despite the frustrating tie against Pitt, no one blamed Bezdek so much as they blamed the weather. The crusty Czechoslovakian had re-energized State's football fans. His teams now had a 14-game unbeaten streak going and everyone was looking forward to next year. Everyone but Bezdek. He was losing seven starters from this 1920 team and he didn't think his remaining eight lettermen or the incoming prospects from the freshman team could fill all the critical positions needed to extend that undefeated string in 1921. He was wrong.

Season Record 7-0-2
Record to Date 167-86-16
Winning percentage .651

1921

"The Mighty 'Mystery Team'"

Sportswriters from all the big Eastern city newspapers converged at Harvard's Soldiers Field to get a first hand look at this Penn State football team they called "the mystery team." It was another battle of unbeaten between the two teams that had been the best in the East for the last two years, but this game had a different context.

Penn State was not supposed to be very good this season, and despite four conclusive victories, all at Beaver Field, the Lions were still unknown and unappreciated. Harvard, with a veteran team that had trampled over five teams with ease, was once again the powerhouse of the East and had not lost a game in five years.

Even Bezdek and his staff had been surprised by the team's performance to this point. He had been unsure of the talent when preseason practice started and he had not really expected the veterans and newcomers to play together as well as they had been doing. Their self-discipline was remarkable. And the leadership of the seniors was obvious, especially Snell, the captain and fullback, quarterback Killinger and Lightner, the starting right halfback. The tough sophomore right guard Joe Bedenk was rapidly becoming a great interior lineman and with Bentz at center and Baer at left guard, Bezdek believed he now had one of the best middle lines in the country. The veteran ends, Hufford and McCollum, were solid but Bezdek had been most surprised by the continued development and improvement of his inexperienced tackles, Rags Madera (who would eventually win the Intercollegiate heavyweight wrestling championship) and Jay "Tiny" McMahon. Still, he could have used Shuster, a starter last year as a soph, who had transferred to Dayton. Pete Redinger was a fine complement to Lightner at halfback and the sophomore Harry Wilson—"Handsome Harry," they called him—was showing promise as a backup.

Bezdek also had been concerned that this team might not be able to handle the difficult schedule that had been arranged. Two good teams, Lehigh and Carnegie Tech would be at home, but the toughest games would be on the road, starting with Harvard on October 22 and ending with Pitt on Thanksgiving Day. For the first time, the school had succeeded in scheduling a game in New York City, partly to please alumni but also to enhance the team's reputation and recruiting endeavors. The opponent would be the team rated the best team in the South for several years, Georgia Tech. Navy also was back on the schedule for the first time since 1913 but this time the game was set for Philadelphia's Franklin Field. Even before the first game, the fans and some sportswriters began calling the team "the Nittany Nomads."

The sportswriters who covered the opening game against Lebanon Valley were pleased to find a press box now available on the west side of Beaver Field. The team looked a lot better than the visiting writers and fans expected, even without Killinger starting at quarterback because of an injury in a pre-season scrimmage. State only had a 7-0 lead at the end of the first quarter but when Killinger came into the game in the second quarter, he led State to two more TDs before the half. State scored three more TDs in the third quarter and 12 points in the fourth to win, 53-0.

State scored in the first two minutes of its game the next week against Gettysburg when McMahan blocked a punt and Hufford recovered at the visitor's 20-yard line. On the first play, halfback Ed "Eggs" Cornwall, subbing for the injured Lightner, ran off tackle for the touchdown and then kicked the PAT. Cornwall also had a field goal later and Snell, playing perhaps the best game of his career, also had a touchdown as State won easily, 24-0.

Snell had another great game against North Carolina State, including a 50-yard run in the second quarter for State's second touchdown. That game also got off to a sensational defensive start early in the first quarter when Bedenk crashed through to block a pass, picked the ball

Halfback Joe Lightner was a Second Team All-American in 1921 but was often overlooked because he played in the same backfield as First Team All-Americans Glenn Killinger and Light-Horse Harry Wilson.

out of the air before it hit the ground and ran in for the touchdown. Killinger brought the crowd to its feet at the start of the second half by returning the kickoff for a touchdown and scored on a 70-yard run from scrimmage as State won going away, 35-0.

With the three decisive and definitive shutouts, State was now attracting the attention of out-of-town sportswriters, who began to wonder in print about the "miracle" the great disciplinarian Bezdek was pulling off up in hills of Central Pennsylvania. It also was about this time that Bezdek scheduled an additional tough game at the end of the season—one that would take a State team as far West as it had ever been—the University of Washington. Now, instead of ending the season at Pitt on Thanksgiving Day, the team would play Washington in Seattle on Dec. 3. (Later, State officials would claim they rejected an invitation to play in the 1922 Rose Bowl because two West Coast trips in one year was impossible, but there is no record of the bowl bid in the official State or Rose Bowl records.)

On the eve of the second annual "Home-Coming Day" game against Lehigh, Bezdek got some bad news. Captain Snell was sick with an abscess in his throat and could not play. Little used Frank Hess was his replacement. The game started as the last three home games did with a great defensive play in the opening minute. Lehigh's receiver fumbled the kickoff and McCollum picked up the ball and ran into the end zone. Redinger's TD helped make it 14-0 in the second quarter. Just before halftime, State gave up the first points of the season when Lehigh used a series of forward passes to get a TD. The teams battled through a hard third quarter but State hung on to the slim 14-7 lead until the fourth quarter when Lightner and Killinger banged over to give State a 28-7 victory.

Before the players left for Cambridge to play Harvard, they stopped at the infirmary to see Snell, whose throat infection had worsened. What was said in the hospital room is not known but one can imagine the captain saying, "Win this one for me, you guys!" Or something like that.

Harvard was the favorite and Bezdek warned the team not to be intimidated or overconfident. They also were reminded of the classic 13-13 tie in 1914 when State had victory snatched away in the last minute. The crowd that watched the 3 o'clock kickoff was estimated at anywhere from 30,000-to-40,000 by the sportswriters covering the game but thousands were Harvard haters cheering for State. Later, some sportswriters would call this "one of the greatest games ever played."

Harvard took the opening kickoff with the wind to its back and disaster struck State immediately. Madera, the starting left tackle, suffered a broken thigh as Harvard returned the kickoff to its 37-yard line. Lee Hills, an unknown senior, replaced Madera, who was carried off the field, screaming at his teammates to "Fight 'em State." He never played football again. The Crimson drove relentlessly downfield almost at ease and scored to take a 7-0 lead. State kick ed off again and, as the *New York Tribune* reported, "once more the Crimson started downfield, sweeping the Pennsylvanians

Harry Wilson (arrow) goes 60 yards to the 4-yard line at Harvard's Soldiers Field in the 1921 21-21 tie game that many sportswriters said was one of the greatest games ever played.

before it." Suddenly, adversity struck State again. Hess injured his foot making a tackle and in went the third-team fullback, Al Knabb. But an offside penalty stopped the Harvard drive and State got the ball for the first time after a punt at its own 32-yard line. Wary of Harvard's reputation for taking advantage of fumbles, Bezdek had ordered Killinger to run the ball on the first play "because *you* won't lose it." He did. Harvard recovered Killinger's fumble on the 27-yard line. The Crimson drove to the 5 as the quarter ended but moments later with fourth-and-goal from the 2, Chapin bowled over for the second TD. At this point, wrote Boston writer Burt Whitman, State seemed to be suffering from "stage fright" and just about everyone expected a rout.

Killy ran back the kickoff to the State 30-yard line. Then it was Killinger, Lightner and Killinger and the ball was at the 50. But wait! Redinger was down. Bezdek raged on the sidelines. Not another injury. What next? Out went Redinger. In came one of the youngest players on the squad, 19-year-old Harry Edgar Wilson, all 166-pounds and 5-foot-8 inches of him. "That substitution appeared to work a turn in the contest," the *Tribune* reported later. Another star was about to emerge from the Pennsylvania mountains. Wilson got three yards and Killinger got 13. Killinger got eight, then five. Wilson carried three straight times and Killinger once and with the ball on the 1-yard line Lightner hit the middle and dragged tacklers into the end zone. Lightner made the PAT and it was 14-7. Harvard threatened again late in the half after recovering a midfield fumble by Knabb the first time he carried the ball. But the quarter ended on State's 27-yard line.

In the early moments of the second half, Killinger made two costly mistakes. His fumble on State's first possession gave Harvard the ball at midfield. But the Crimson couldn't move and punted. Instead of letting the ball bounce into the end zone, Killinger caught it on the 3-yard line and was tackled immediately. Under the normal strategy at the time, teams usually "punted out" but Killinger called for running plays and on third-and-one at the 12, Wilson broke loose for 21 yards. Two plays later, Wilson took what was described as a delayed pass and "twisting and turning" ran 60 yards before tackled at Harvard's 4-yard-line. On fourth down-and-inches, Lightner again smashed over the goal line for the TD. His extra point made it 14-14. Now, State was in control. Early in the fourth quarter, Wilson's 23-yard run and a Kill-

inger to Lightner pass set up another one-yard TD plunge by Lightner and with Lightner's PAT State led for the first time, 21-14.

After the kickoff, State forced Harvard to punt but the home team got the ball back moments later at the State 43-yard line when a 15-yard penalty for illegal use of the hands stopped a State drive and forced Killinger to punt from near his end zone. About six minutes were left in the game. "Darkness was falling fast," reported the *Pittsburgh Dispatch*. "...Here and there men scratched matches and these flared up like fire flies. The chalk marks which a few hours before had gleaned so bravely along the green turf, now no longer could be discerned. It was hard to tell which player had a crimson jersey and which wore the somber black of Penn State." In three running plays, Harvard moved the ball to the 34 and on fourth-and-one surprised State with a forward pass for a first down at the 27. With less than three minutes left and the field almost dark, Harvard had the ball on the 15-yard line. State's defense set in tight for another run. Harvard's quarterback Charlie Buell took the ball and feinted into the line, then dashed to his right and threw a pass to sub halfback Winthrop Churchill, who had gotten behind the State secondary, somehow saw the ball in the darkness, caught it and went into the end zone. Buell's PAT tied it but State wasn't done. Taking possession on the 10-yard line, State ran and passed downfield and with seconds left had a first down inside the Harvard 10. Three carries into the line got to the one. Rather than try a field goal that might not have been seen in the darkness, State attempted a pass on fourth down. It failed and the game was over.

"Penn State left the field with what is regarded as a moral victory," reported the *Dispatch*. "The Nittany Lions had trampled the Crimson...had outrushed it by a great margin (294 yards to 105 with 19 first downs to nine)...and had (State) left its fumbling in Center (sic) County it would have

Glenn Killinger, All-American HB in 1921, was selected to the College Football Hall of Fame 50 years later.

beaten Harvard by a couple of touchdowns." A Boston newspaper agreed, adding that "Penn State might have won had not Fullback Hess been hurt early." There also was some criticism of the referee for not calling the game because of darkness but the rules at time had been followed and State did not blame the tie on the officials.

The tie with Harvard boosted the prestige of Bezdek and his "mystery team." Sportswriters raved at Bezdek's ability to overcome injuries and rally a team from behind with superior on-field tactics. Most of the leading football writers and columnists were at New York's Polo Grounds the next Saturday, along with an estimated 25,000-to-30,000 fans, including the Mayor of Atlanta, to see if this feisty State team could upset another powerful favorite, Georgia Tech. With its brassy band blaring away, Tech made a "dramatic" entrance onto the playing field, running single file behind "two pretty girls" through the goal posts at both ends before going to the benches. State's players trotted on the field "unostentatious (sic)...and were kept in the background." It was an omen for the day.

State got the first break, recovering a Tech fumble after the opening kickoff but Tech's defense forced Lightner to try a field goal and his drop-kick from the 25-yard line was no good. After an exchange of punts, the Golden Tornado (as Tech was called then) got possession at midfield and using the so-called –Heisman shift," named after its former coach, Tech marched steadily downfield for a touchdown and extra point. The "two pretty girls" on the Tech bench led the cheering as the teams lined up for the kickoff. Bezdek would describe what happened next as one of the greatest plays of his coaching career. It was also the defining moment of the season. Killinger took the kickoff at about the 15-yard line, ran straight up field for a few yards, evading a couple tacklers, then, as Bezdek had told him to do, he cut to the right sideline at a 90-degree angle. The State blockers had formed a wall and Killinger ran down the open lane untouched and into the end zone for a touchdown. "Up out of the throats and hearts of the crowd...came a great roar," wrote Arthur Robinson in the *New York Tribune*. "The State thundered continuously...Now, the State attack broke loose."

Killinger's kickoff return demoralized the overconfident Tech team. Killinger's running in the second quarter set up a TD dash by Wilson and with Lightner's two PAT's State led, 14-7, at the half. State scored two more touchdowns in the second half on short runs by Killinger and Lightner, missed a fifth TD when a Killinger-to-Lightner pass was negated by a penalty and won easily, 28-7. "Golden Tornado Re-

duced to Mild Zephyr by the Brilliant Smashing and Wriggling of Killinger and His Husky Teammates," read one New York newspaper headline, and Walter Camp personally congratulated Killinger in the dressing room after the game. Even captain Snell got into the game late in the fourth quarter but it would be the last one he would play for his throat infection returned and sidelined him for the year.

The win over Georgia Tech broke the unbeaten record set from 1911-1913. State was now undefeated in 20 straight games and the players had become superstitious. Some of the players took the same route to and from practice and others wore the same neckties on road trips. Killinger got in and out of the same side of the bed everyday and Bentz always turned his practice pants inside out after every practice.

In the final home game of the season against Carnegie Tech on Friday November 5, State again trailed in the first quarter following a 55-yard TD off a triple pass. But the Lions stormed back before the Pennsylvania Day crowd of 6,000 with two drives the length of the field in the second and third quarters and won, 28-7, with Wilson scoring two TDs.

Giving up the early lead and then coming back was getting to be the pattern for this team. It happened again the following Friday against unbeaten Navy in what was billed as the battle for the "mythical Eastern Championship." Playing on a wet and somewhat muddy field, the Middies used a surprise onside kick on the opening kickoff to get the ball on State's 40-yard line and in seven plays had a touchdown and extra point. But after getting the ensuing kickoff on the 25-yard line, State drove methodically for a touchdown with Killinger going the final five yards dragging two Navy tacklers with him. However, Lightner missed the extra point and State still trailed. But not for long. With Wilson doing most of the running, State came back in the second quarter on a 58-yard march and Lightner scored the go-ahead TD. This time his PAT was good. State almost scored again that quarter but an apparent TD was nullified by an offside penalty.

Defenses took over in the second half, and when Navy's star halfback Steve Barchet mistakenly fielded a punt at his own 5-yard line late in the fourth quarter, it looked as if State had wrapped up the game. But Navy wasn't through. The Middies charged downfield as the minutes and seconds ticked away and the corps of Midshipmen chanted "Fight Like Hell." The capacity crowd of 25,000 watched as Navy reached State's 17-yard line. Then on a fourth down-and-3 play, Barchet hurled into the line and was stopped after gaining just a yard. State

Killinger (arrow) goes up the middle in the 1921 Georgia Tech game played at the Polo Grounds in New York City. Killinger's 85-yard kickoff return for a TD demoralized the favored Tech team and State won, 28-7.

Action from the 1921 Pitt game played in the mud at Forbes Field. Neither offense could hold onto the ball or keep their footing and the game ended in a scoreless tie.

took the ball and moments later the game was over. " State had the better team and deserved the victory," reported New York sportswriter Ray McCarthy. "...there is little doubt that had the field been dry State would have won by a larger margin."

The Pitt game 12 days later was the most disappointing of the season for State fans who believed State was the stronger team. Pitt had lost three games but the wily Pop Warner was still the coach. "History Repeats," reported "*LaVie*." It was *deja vu* on the muddy infield of Forbes Field. When Bezdek woke up in his hotel room at 5 a.m. on Thanksgiving Day he heard raindrops and opened the window. Not again, he thought. At breakfast that morning he told reporters, "I can tell you the score this afternoon. It's going to be nothing to nothing." It rained all day and the field was worse than anyone expected. Bezdek discarded most of the plays he had been saving for Pitt and used only the simplest formations with a couple of special plays. On the other side, Warner had devised a defense to stop some of State's special plays and it worked.

"It was a great day for the tacklers and no one else," wrote Cullen Cain for the *Philadelphia Public Ledger*. "No one could get started quickly in the mud, there were no long runs, few spectacular dashes and but little running back of punts...Penn State did not win because Killinger could not run in the mud." Fumbles were rampant. State had its best opportunity to score in the second period after recovering a Pitt fumble at the Panther 30-yard line. On the next play, State lost a fumble, then recovered another Pitt fumble at the 25. Three plunges into the line gained a couple of yards and on fourth down, a Killinger pass fell incomplete. Warner adjusted Pitt's offense during the intermission and after Lightner fumbled the second half kickoff, the Panthers marched 45-yards behind the running of Tommy Davies to reach the State 3-yard line. But State's defense threw Davies for a loss and on the second play Davies pass attempt was intercepted by Wilson. Pitt also got into State territory in the fourth quarter but another Davies pass was intercepted and the game ended as Bezdek had predicted, 0-0.

There was no traditional dinner for the team that night. The players returned to the hotel immediately after the game, picked up their bags and left for the West Coast on an 8:30 p.m. train after a rousing send off by several hundred State students at Union Station.

The 1921 "Mystery Team. (Left to right) Backs: Joe Lightner, RHB; Glenn Killinger, QB; Al Knabb, FB; Harry Wilson, LHB. Line: "Squeak" Hufford, RE; "Tiny" McMahon, RT; Joe Bedenk, RG; Newsh Bentz, C; Ray Baer, LG; Lee Hills, LT; Stan McCollum, LE. Not shown is Captain George Snell, the regular fullback, who missed much of the season with a throat infection.

They arrived on Monday morning and practiced in secret for most of the week for Bezdek was determined to win this game because of his previous West Coast coaching ties. The only difference between West Coast and Eastern football, Bezdek told *Seattle Star* columnist Leo Lassen upon the team's arrival, is the competition. "On the Coast, a team usually has one or two hard games, while in the East, every game is a tough one," Bezdek said. With another great crowd of 35,000 looking on, State gave Washington a lesson in Eastern football. Killinger dazzled the fans with his passes to McCollum. The big end set a school record that day by catching 11 of Killinger's 12 completions and scored a TD on one aerial in the second quarter. Knabb tallied State's first TD in the opening period and Redinger, subbing for Lightner, who had been injured in practice, got the third TD in the third quarter. Washington scored its only TD on an 86-yard march in the third period. Killinger booted three extra points and State won handily, 21-7. A prominent West Coast industrialist hosted a banquet for State after the game and the team left later that night for the week-long sight-seeing trip back to State College—no longer the "mystery team" but now unbeaten in 24 games.

Killinger, who had scored 10 TDs during the season, was a First Team selection on several All-American teams, including the most prestigious one chosen by Walter Camp. He also was a pick of 267 college football coaches in a poll by *Football World* magazine. Bedenk became the first State sophomore selected for any All-American team when Camp named him a Second Team guard. Lightner, McCollum and Baer also were placed on the Second Team by several sportswriters.

Bezdek spent the winter believing his team should have gone to the Rose Bowl and played unbeaten California, the host team now coached by former Penn State and Penn player, Andy Smith. W&J, also unbeaten with wins over Pitt, Syracuse and West Virginia, was the Rose Bowl's Eastern choice over two other undefeated teams, Lafayette and Cornell, and on January 1, 1922 battled Cal to a 0-0 deadlock.

Certainly, the 1921 "mystery team" or "Nittany Nomads" was one of the school's all-time best teams and maybe the greatest group of overachievers in State's 111 years of football. It also was the school's first big money maker, showing a $33,000 profit while all other intercollegiate sports had a deficit of $23,000 for the 1921-22 academic year. Part of the profit would be used to increase Beaver Field seating to 12,000. Bezdek was riding high as he prepared for the next season and in 1922 he would get his chance to take a Penn State team to the Rose Bowl. But it would be one year too late.

Season Record 8-0-2
Record to Date 175-86-18
Winning percentage .659

"The Rose Bowl"

Hugo Bezdek looked down the end of his bench as Navy prepared for the kickoff and saw Killinger, Snell, Haines, Lightner, Higgins and several more of his former star players. They had come to Washington on this Friday afternoon in early November to support their Alma Mater as it tried to extend the 31-game unbeaten streak that they helped create. Bezdek would have preferred to have some of his ex-players in uniform rather than in street clothes. There would be no doubts about winning then, he surmised.

But the team on the field of American League Park (later to be known as Griffith Stadium) was not as good as the last three State teams, and everyone knew it. The overall talent was not there. And, after six games, the squad was still developing. There was still too much disorder and once again Bezdek was continually changing the starting lineup.

Sure they were still unbeaten. It was up to 30 straight, now. But last Saturday's 0-0 tie with underdog Syracuse at New York's Polo Grounds had been distressing, and not just because of the poor way the team played. What had started out as a celebratory weekend honoring the old time players who had organized the school's first football team in 1887 had turned into a chastening experience. Not only did State not win the game as expected, but the whole country now knew what only Bezdek and a handful of other school officials had known for months—this team would play in the Rose Bowl on January 1, 1923!

The student newspaper, *The Collegian*, had broken the story the day before the Syracuse game. The invitation by the Pacific Coast Intercollegiate Conference, reported *The Collegian*, came as " a tribute to past achievements." In other words, the '22 team would be rewarded for what the teams of Killinger, Higgins and company had accomplished. What was still not public knowledge—and would not be generally known for months later—was the fact that the Rose Bowl invitation apparently had been given the *previous* spring and had been accepted privately in August by Bezdek and the Athletic Advisory Committee. (Modern day followers of State's football fortunes certainly can compare the irony of this situation in 1922 with what happened 70 years later to the 1992 team of the Paterno era, when a post-season appearance in the Blockbuster Bowl was guaranteed the previous spring.)

The tie with Syracuse had taken some luster off the Rose Bowl invitation, and Bezdek and those close to State knew a loss to Navy would be downright embarrassing. Bezdek knew Syracuse had achieved a tie by exploiting all the weaknesses that State fans had overlooked in the first five victories, all at Beaver Field.

Bezdek had realized since the previous November that he would have a relatively inexperienced team this season. That was one reason he had moved sophomore Mike Palm from third team halfback to quarterback midway through the '21 season and then promoted him to second team before the year was complete. But Palm never got into a game last year and since he had not played high school football, his only game experience was as a frosh running back, not quarterback. Bezdek was convinced Palm could be an outstanding quarterback because of his overall leadership and athletic skills. Palm had entered State as a standout in track and baseball. Bezdek, who was also the baseball coach, encouraged him to try out for football. He had speed and could run, and under Bezdek's guidance, Palm was developing into a decent passer and kicker. Still, as a junior, he would be one of the three newcomers in the backfield, with only "Handsome" Harry Wilson, the sensational sophomore of '21, returning from the great unbeaten team.

The line was only slightly better off with four starters back, including the superb right guard Bedenk, who had become the first sophomore in school history to be a Walter Camp All-American. The fun-loving center, Bentz, who was now the captain, also had returned along with Squeeks Hufford at end and Tiny McMahon at tackle. Bezdek was especially pleased at Tiny, who was playing with a neck brace after his severe neck injury while wrestling over the winter. But there was little depth in the line, with just three returnees from the second team—end Hap Frank, tackle Hal Logue and guard Bill Hamilton.

Bezdek had lost 15 varsity players from the '21 team and not all by graduation. Several potential starters had left with Dick Harlow when Harlow quit to take the head football coaching job at Colgate. It had been a bitter departure, coming after Harlow, who was also the boxing coach, clashed that spring with athletic director Bezdek over a boxing team matter. Bezdek was not sorry to see Harlow leave for the two had feuded ever since Harlow had returned from World War I. However, Bezdek would miss Harlow's expertise as a line coach and scout more than he would ever admit. And he would eventually blame Harlow for the failure that was to follow.

The exodus of Harlow and his loyal following, including another assistant coach and ex-player, Dick Rauch, may have been the defining moment of the season, for the play of the line was faulted throughout the last half of the schedule, when the team fell apart, starting with Syracuse. But another defining moment may have occurred on the last play of the second game of the season against William & Mary when Mike Palm sprained his ankle. The ankle bothered him the entire year, forced him to miss practices and leave games early and impeded his overall development at the team's most crucial position.

State breezed through its first five games, starting with a 54-0 win over St. Bonaventure on Sept. 23. Then came the easy wins over William & Mary, 27-7, Gettysburg, 20-0, Lebanon Valley, 32-6, and Middlebury, 33-0. Wilson had scored 55 points on nine touchdowns and an extra point to lead the nation in scoring at that point. But Bezdek shuffled his starting lineup for each game, particularly at the offensive skill positions in the backfield and at the ends. Injuries didn't help and State was hobbling when it met Syracuse. Bentz had a bad shoulder

and didn't start, while Palm and McMahon were still bothered by injuries. Even Bezdek was hurting on the sidelines, for he pulled a tendon while running with the players at the last practice in State College.

Syracuse, like William & Mary and Middlebury, was a first time opponent for State. Middlebury was only on the schedule because it was the Alma Mater of State's then President, John Thomas, and State would never play the Vermont college again. But the game with Syracuse would begin a long and often belligerent rivalry that would one day produce more animosity than the competition with Pitt.

The Syracuse game also marked the first appearance of the Lion mascot, when a senior named Dick Hoffman pranced around the Polo Grounds wearing a uniform of a maned African Lion that he had used while appearing in a Penn State Player's production of George Bernard Shaw's "Androcles and the Lion." The 500 State students and several thousand alumni in the crowd of 25,000 cheered and laughed as Hoffman mingled with the players and cheerleaders. With the 10 surviving members of the 1887 pioneer football team among the throng, the atmosphere was ripe for a notable game. And it was—for about two minutes.

State took the opening kickoff and moved from it's 37-yard line to Syracuse's 45-yard line before forced to punt. Palm booted to the Orange quarterback, Simmons, who fumbled and Bedenk dove on the ball at the Syracuse 5-yard line. The jubilant State fans sensed a sure TD. But with Wilson and Palm carrying the ball the Lions got only

H.N. "Newsh" Bentz was a three-year starter at center and captain of the 1922 team that played in the '23 Rose Bowl. Bentz later helped coach.

The Nittany Lion Mascot makes its first public debut at the Polo Grounds in New York City at the first game ever against Syracuse, which finished in a 0-0 tie.

two yards in four downs. Syracuse punted out and for the rest of the half the Orange held on as State continually pushed into Syracuse territory, with two drives ending inside the Syracuse 25-yard line. Twice, Palm attempted to dropkick field goals but neither were close to the goal posts. One Syracuse field goal attempt was blocked by Wilson and another Orange drive ended at State's 24-yard line.

Early in the third period, Palm was hurt and the referee refused to let him play any more in the game. That's when Syracuse took control and dominated the rest of the afternoon. The Orange tried and missed two field goal attempts inside the 35-yard line, twice lost the ball on fumbles deep in State territory, and twice lost the ball on downs, including once on a fake field goal late in the game that could have given the victory to Syracuse. Without Palm, State's offense did practically nothing. The tie was seen as a moral victory for Syracuse, which had already been thoroughly beaten by Pitt and tied by Brown.

"Today's contest was the first difficult test for the Bezdek disciples," wrote Chet Smith in the *Pittsburgh Gazette Times*, "and the crafty Hugo could not have been pleased with the way in which his line performed at times when Syracuse ripped it to shreds, especially at the tackles, and lunged through for big gains. The one bright spot...was the performance of Mike Palm who...did everything he could have been expected to do... [until injured.]"

The team had just three days to get ready for what many now saw as the "make or break" game of the season against Navy. Navy had been defeated the previous week by Penn, 13-7, but was still a strong team that had only lost five games in five years. The Middies came into the State game in healthy condition. Not State. Palm, Bentz, McMahan and Frank were still hurting and there were questions about who would start and how long they would play. "Bezdek Gloomy At Navy Prospects," said the headline in the *Harrisburg Patriot*. It got even gloomier when starting tackle Dick Shuster was declared ineligible after a complaint by Pitt officials. (Of course, it would be Pitt!!) Shuster had been a starter on the 1920 team but played at Dayton in 1921 when Charlie Way went there to coach. Shuster said he had been told his Dayton games would not prevent him from going back to State in 1922 but the Athletic Committee said he had violated the one-year residence rule and he was disqualified for the rest of the year.

President Warren Harding had planned to attend the game but canceled because of the illness to his wife. But dozens of congressmen, foreign dignitaries and other high government officials were in the crowd of 35,000. So were many of the nation's leading football coaches, who were able to attend because the game was on a Friday. Pitt's Pop Warner and Penn's John Heisman were there. So were Tad Jones of Yale, Curley Byrd of Maryland and Ken Scott of Alabama, and the coaches from Army, West Virginia, North Carolina and Carnegie Tech. Many players from other teams were there, too. And so were most of the best known sportswriters in the East, including

Myron "Mike" Palm was the QB and kicker for the 1922 team which played in State's first post season bowl game at the Rose Bowl in 1923.

the patriarch, Walter Camp, who sat on the Penn State bench beside Lightner.

The entire regiment of 2,400 Midshipmen were in the stands as were about 250 Penn State students, including 50 who had walked and hitchhiked from State College. But it was not a capacity crowd, perhaps because the game was on a working day. Both teams had wanted to play on Saturday but another game already had been scheduled for the ball park the next day. So, Navy kicked off.

Fumbles by both teams marred the entire game. Twice in the first quarter Palm attempted to dropkick field goals: the first one from the 35-yard line, following a Navy fumble, went wide and the second one from the 40-yard line, after a short punt, didn't have the distance. On the second play of the second quarter, Navy recovered Palm's fumble at the State 33-yard line. State's defense stiffened and Navy punted. The ball bounced on the 10-yard line and looked as if it was going into the end zone but it touched State's starting right halfback Harry Kratz. Palm picked up the ball in the end zone and got to the 5-yard line before being tackled. Navy held, Palm punted out of the end zone and the Middies got the ball on the State 41-yard line. That's when Navy's coach Bob Folwell surprised Bezdek, who had devised State's defensive plan to stop the Middies' running game. Navy came out passing. A 14-yard pass picked up one first down but after three downs and a penalty, it was fourth-and-15 at the 35-yard line and Navy's Pete McKee went back into punt formation. It was a fake! McKee hit D.C. native "Shaggy" Cullen with a 19-yard pass for a first down. Two plays later, McKee passed 16 yards to Taylor for the TD, and with the successful PAT, Navy led 7-0 going into the half.

Neither team made much headway early in the second half, but late in the third quarter, State found itself with the ball on its own 15-yard line after a booming 65-yard punt by Cullen. In what sportswriter Gordon McKay of the *Philadelphia Inquirer* later called "a bonehead...mental error," Palm tried to pass out of danger. Two passes were incomplete. His third pass was intercepted at State's 20-yard line. However, Navy could not pick up a first down and State took over on the 12. On the next play, Kratz rolled around left end but fumbled—again! Old reliable Cullen scooped up the ball and ran untouched into the end zone. Navy 14, State 0. State tried desperately to come back in the final period but Navy's defense and Cullen's punting kept the Lions from the goal. The undefeated streak was over.

In the final statistics, State had gained 213 yards and nine first downs compared to Navy's 100 yards and just four first downs. Palm hit on 16 of 27 passes but it was Navy's more conservative passing—and State errors—that lost the game. Many sportswriters said Bezdek was simply outcoached. But Bezdek would never admit that. In fact, he knew precisely who was to blame, as he told reporters at the Willard Hotel after the game.

"Navy has a great eleven," he said, "...however, I really feel Navy got all the breaks and with any luck...it should have been a 7-7 tie, at least. This team of mine is a good team...The line is great—one of the best I have ever had and the backfield is fair. If only Dick Harlow, my former assistant hadn't taken most of our backfield with him to Colgate when he left State this year, what a ripping, snorting team we would have had. He took our best men and scattered my plans to the four winds. No wonder we can't take the spoils in all the games this year."

So, whatever bad happened the rest of the season would be Harlow's fault! Uh, huh! But the season was far from over.

Harry Wilson runs for several yards in 10-0 win over Carnegie Tech before a record crowd of 17,000 at Beaver Field.

The following Monday, more than 2,000 students and the Marching Band turned out for football practice in a driving rain to cheer the team as it prepared for Carnegie Tech in the final game at home. That week Bezdek made a major change in his backfield, shifting his great two-year starting right end Hufford to right halfback and moving unknown sophomore scrub Barney Wentz in at fullback. Sophomore Ted Artelt would replace Hufford and another sophomore, Hank Lafferty, would backup Wentz. That would get more weight into the lineup, Bezdek said. It also would remove "fumbles" Kratz and the "midget" fullback (5-foot-5, 145-pound) Earl Singer from his wrath.

Walter Camp believed Bezdek's backfield problem was at quarterback. In a syndicated article printed in the *Philadelphia Evening Bulletin* two days before the Tech game, Camp suggested that Wilson be shifted to quarterback. "Palm seems to lack the punch necessary...[and his] forward passing is hardly up to the mark..."

Meanwhile, Bezdek, who had his State contract extended for 10 years in September with an increase in salary and bonuses, also confirmed he had been offered the manager's job with baseball's Philadelphia Phillies. He was considering the offer, he said, but he had a game to win on Saturday. Later in the week, Bezdek also was denying reports out of the West Coast that he would not take Penn State to Pasadena on January, 1. "We will be there with bells on and a good team," he emphatically told Chet Smith, to which Smith added, "How the false rumor found its way on the wire is a mystery to State athletic officials." (Sure!)

Another record Beaver Field crowd of 17,000 saw State play its best game of the year against Carnegie Tech in a 10-0 win. State's defense won the game, stopping two Tech drives inside the 10-yard line and another at the 20. Palm kept the offense moving, grinding out 18 first downs to seven. The Lions scored all their points in the second quarter. Wilson carried the ball most of the way on a 9-play, 40-yard drive and got the TD—his 12th of the season—on a 1-yard plunge. Palm booted the PAT. As the quarter neared an end, State marched from its own 20 to the Tech 20 where Palm kicked a 30-yard field goal, and that finished the scoring for the day.

Bezdek made only one change for the Penn game at Franklin Field, inserting Al McCoy at end for Artelt, who was injured against Tech. After watching Navy beat State, several Penn players boldly predicted victory. "I feel mighty sure we'll lick State," said captain "Poss" Miller. Penn's coach John Heisman predicted a "close and hard fought battle throughout" and he was right. Some 50,000 fans, including 10,000 State supporters, watched as the teams battled evenly through a scoreless first half.

Early in the third quarter, Penn intercepted a Palm pass at midfield and drove 42 yards for a touchdown. Miller scored the TD on what sportswriters described as a "trick formation." With the ball at the 12-yard line, McGraw, a left handed quarterback, rolled to his right behind three blockers, then stopped and threw across field to Miller, who caught the ball at the 5 and ran into the end zone. Tex Hamer, who had missed a 27-yard field goal in the first half, drop-kicked the PAT and Penn led, 7-0. State took the ensuing kickoff and with Wilson gaining 38 yards running and 15 yards passing, the team drove to Penn's 12-yard line. On fourth-and-6, Palm went into a drop-kick formation but instead of kicking passed to Wilson wide open on the right side of the goal line for six points. Palm dropped back to kick what was expected to be the tying point. But he missed—by inches! The next day's headline in the *Philadelphia Inquirer* told the story: "Quakers Trap Lion When Palm Misses Goal After Score." Wilson had been sensational, gaining 119 yards on 25 carries and 42 yards on four pass receptions. But Palm's missed kick meant a 7-6 loss.

It was nearly two weeks before the traditional Thanksgiving Day game at Pitt and Bezdek worked the team hard trying to get the players ready. But it wasn't enough to beat the favored Panthers before a crowd of 35,000 at Forbes Field. Playing conditions were not as bad as they had been the last two years but the first half still turned into another defensive battle with both teams stopping offensive thrusts deep in their own territory. Palm tried field goals from the 35 and 45 but both missed and the score was 0-0 at the intermission. On its first two possessions following the second half kickoff, Pitt drove deep into State territory only to be stopped, missing one opportunity on a 34-yard field goal attempt. Then Hoot Flanagan made the play of the game with a 44-yard punt return to State's 6-yard line. Two running plays failed but on third down Flanagan slid off right tackle and went into the end zone. The PAT was good and Pitt had a 7-0 lead. The rest of the game was played on State's side of the field and late in the final period, Pitt scored another touchdown on a 15-yard pass from Flanagan to John Anderson. The final score, 14-0.

The 6-3-1 record was the worst of Bezdek's regime, discounting the dysfunctional 1918 season that was disrupted by World War I. His brutal coaching style was still being questioned and, now, even his on field strategy was being criticized. It would have been easy to accept the Phillies' lucrative offer and leave State. But many alumni and most of the students didn't want him to go. A week before the Pitt game, the students had posted signs throughout the campus urging him to stay. "We Want You, Bez," read one sign. "Penn State and Bezdek Make A Wonderful Team," said another.

Before reassembling the team for Rose Bowl workouts, Bezdek made his announcement. "Bezdek Officially Turns Down Offer To Manage Phils," said the headline in one newspaper. Bezdek said the appeals by alumni and students were a major influence in his decision. "This means the sacrifice of several thousand dollars a year," Bezdek told reporters. "But ideals cost money and I find my ideals can best be worked out in college ranks."

Now, it was time to prepare for his personal return to the Rose Bowl. He had taken his Oregon team there in 1917 and the Mare Island Marines in 1918. They had won and he was convinced this team would too, despite its record.

THE 1923 ROSE BOWL GAME
Jan. 1, 1923
Southern Cal 14, Penn State 3

The trip to Pasadena was enjoyable for the players, who stopped at the Grand Canyon enroute, visited Hollywood while there, and toured Southern Texas and Chicago on the way back. But the Rose Bowl game against the University of Southern California was anti-climactic. It is noteworthy in Rose Bowl history for being the first game played in the then-new stadium at its present site in the city's Arroyo Secco section, and the first ever appearance of USC. It also should be known as "The Game of Losers." USC was asked to be the host team only after the three-time Pacific Coast Conference champion, California, rejected the invitation. Still, USC was the favorite after losing only to California, 12-0, in eight games.

As he had been doing all season, Bezdek was still fiddling with his starting team as the players went through intense practices on the West Coast. He told reporters he would shift the lineup a dozen times if necessary to find his best eleven. Unfortunately, his star guard, Bedenk, broke four ribs on the first day of work outs and would not play. Captain Bentz broke curfew or some other pregame training rule and would not get into the game until it was too late.

There also was bad blood between Bezdek and USC's coach Elmer "Gloomy Gus" Henderson, dating from Bezdek's days as coach at Oregon. The animus erupted into a shouting match and near fist fight on the field when the State team arrived late because of a major traffic jam following the Rose Bowl parade (Editor's Note: Nice to know some things haven't changed over the years!) and the game had to be delayed 45 minutes. Henderson accused Bezdek of deliberately holding up the game as a psychological ploy. But, as Ridge Riley wrote in *Road to Number One*, "Bez was innocent." The team did not have a police escort to get to the new stadium, and even after the taxis carrying the team plowed over lawns to get close, the players still had to walk a mile down the gorge to reach the stadium.

USC's opening kickoff bounced off the goal post (that made it a fair ball by the rules at the time) and put State in an immediate hole at its own 5-yard line. State punted out, then stopped USC on downs at the State 34-yard line. On the next exchange of punts, a USC player interfered with a fair catch by Palm and State got the ball on the USC 40-yard line. With Wilson again bearing the brunt of the running, State drove to the 12-yard line before faltering and Palm kicked a 20-yard field goal for a 3-0 lead.

But it was USC's game from that point on. For one thing, State made too many mistakes and the Trojans capitalized on the breaks. The hot weather also appeared to be too much for State and the players seemed to wilt as the afternoon wore on. "Their hard jaunt across the country and the week they spent in conditioning had a telling effect," wrote Mark Kelly of the Universal News Service. "Their attack

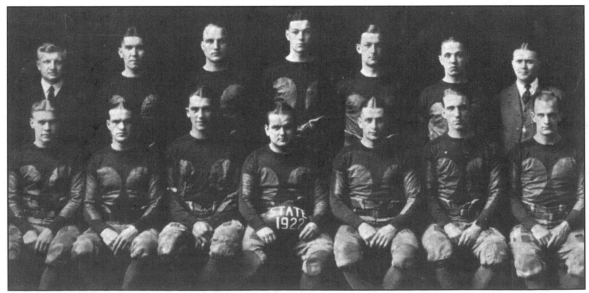

The 1922 Team that played in '23 Rose Bowl. (Left to Right) Back Row: Coach Bezdek, Les Logue, Bill Hamilton, Art Artelt, Freddy Flock, Barney Wentz, and Manager W. H. Parsons. Front Row: Harry Wilson, Squeak Hufford, Tiny McMahon, Newsh Bentz, Joe Bedenk, Hap Frank and Mike Palm.

lacked fire and dash. They were lethargic after the first 10 minutes..."

Henderson also had devised a defense to stop Harry Wilson and Bezdek's short pass offense, a scheme that was based on "inside" information from USC's freshman coach, Bill Hess, the same man who had been captain of State's unbeaten 1920 team! After State's drive for the field goal, USC's captain and on-field assistant coach, Leo Calland, went to the bench to confer with Hess, and from that point on USC's defense seemed to stymie State's offense. Wilson gained 55 yards on 20 carries, far below his average, and also caught one pass. Some sportswriters later criticized Bezdek's mundane offensive plan, which they claimed was more like the one he had used before the Navy game, with just a handful of running plays and little passing. That tactic seemed to play right into the Hess-Henderson defensive strategy.

As the first quarter was ending, Palm fumbled a punt at State's 27-yard line and the Trojans recovered at the 21. In five plays, USC was at the 1-yard line but Howard Kincaid then fumbled into the end zone and State recovered for a touchback. For the next several minutes the teams moved back and forth across the 50 with an exchange of punts and pass interceptions dominating the action. Then, late in the period the Trojans got another break when Palm's poor 12-yard punt went out of bounds at the State 30-yard line. With halfback Roy Baker running for 22 yards and passing four yards, USC reached the 1-yard line in five plays. On a double pass, Baker threw to fullback Gordon Campbell for the touchdown, John Hawkins kicked the extra point and USC led 7-3 at the half.

USC took control of the game in the second half. State took the kickoff but could not get a first down and Palm punted the ball out of bounds at USC's 44-yard line. Baker again led the charge downfield. He went around left end for 21 yards, up the middle for 15 yards and through left tackle for four. Then it was Campbell's turn as he ran over State's substitute center for five. With either Baker or Campbell carrying, USC moved to within inches of the end zone and Baker then plunged over for second TD. Hawkins booted the PAT and it was 14-3. Later in the period, Hawkins tried a field goal from inside the 30-yard line but it was no good. There would be no more points by either team. The rest of the game was played mostly in State's territory and only a standout effort by the Lions defense kept the Trojans from scoring more. By the time the game was over it was almost dark. Much of the fourth quarter had been played in twilight because of the late start of the game and the announced crowd of 43,000 had already dwindled when the players left the field.

But the game was not a total loss for State. A check of $21,349.64 was State's share of the Rose Bowl profits. That was some solace to athletic director Bezdek. But Coach Bezdek was not happy. He vowed that next year would be different.

Calvin "Hap" Frank played end in the 1923 Rose Bowl and went on to become a World War II hero as Commander of the 79th Infantry Division.

Season Record 6-4-1
Record to Date 181-90-19
Winning percentage .657

"The Birth of 'Light Horse' Harry"

From the moment Bezdek stormed off the field at Pasadena he was determined not to have a repeat of the curse 1922 season.

One of the first things he did was to prohibit any further appearances of the Nittany Lion mascot. "That thing's a jinx," he told reporters, recalling that last year's collapse started when the costumed student first showed up at the Polo Grounds for the Syracuse game, then cavorted around Annapolis, Philadelphia and Pittsburgh. He intended to make Syracuse, Navy, Penn and Pitt pay for what they did to spoil his return to the Rose Bowl and he didn't want any black cats or #$@%^& lions crossing his path.

Half of his starting team had graduated but from the beginning of practice on September 1, Bezdek felt he had the nucleus for a good team. He was particularly counting on some of the sophomores from Dutch Herman's fine freshman team to fill the places of his departed vets. His strategy was to concentrate on defense and build the offense around his senior backs, Wilson at left half and Palm at quarterback. The rest of the backfield was unsettled, just as it was last year, but as the rigorous preseason progressed, two more sophomores, Ray Johnston at right half and "Hobie" Light at fullback, moved ahead of everyone else, including the sometimes 1922 starters Wentz and Lafferty.

The line came together much easier. The ends were veterans, Frank and Artelt. Bedenk, the captain and a Third Team All-American in '22, had fully recovered from the broken ribs that kept him out of the Rose Bowl and Bezdek believed Bedenk's leadership would be especially helpful to the two talented sophomores, "Gus" Michalske at left guard and "Bas" Gray, the new center. They had great potential, Bezdek said. He also was pleased with his tackles, junior Jules Prevost, who had moved up from the second team to McMahon's old right tackle spot, and Dick Shuster, who was a starter again at the other tackle now that his eligibility was no longer a question.

Shuster also had used practice time to show off his placekicking and Bezdek intended to use the Philadelphia senior to handle kickoffs, extra points and field goals. Palm would continue to do some of the goal kicking, utilizing his drop kick technique, but after what happened in 1922 Bezdek wanted other options. Palm would still do the punting but Light, the State College kid, also was being groomed as the alternate punter. But there was little experienced depth elsewhere on offense and defense and Bezdek knew he could not afford many injuries.

Bezdek counted on the schedule— "Toughest...In East," headlined the *Scranton Times*— to give him time to develop some good backups. The first three games were against weaker opponents and all would be played at friendly Beaver Field. State would not get into the tough games until Navy came to town for the first time ever on October 29. That would be the test for this team and everyone knew it. The Middies had a veteran team returning and many of the eastern sportswriters were saying Navy had the best team in the country.

Bezdek got what he wanted in the opening game against Lebanon Valley. He used three complete teams as State won, 58-0, with Wilson scoring three touchdowns, Palm getting two and Shuster

"Light-Horse" Harry Wilson became a major star during the 1923 season and was eventually elected to the College Football Hall of Fame. Later he was a World War II hero as a pilot flying 45 combat missions.

booting six extra points and a 20-yard field goal.

The next week against North Carolina State, the coach surprised everyone by moving Wilson to fullback. On the second play of the game, Harry ran 80 yards for an apparent TD but both teams were offside and the play was nullified. That penalty must have boosted the visitors' morale because they played a surprisingly rugged defensive game the rest of the way. State led by just 6-0 at the half on a 20-yard run by Johnson in the first quarter. The Lions took the second half kickoff and marched 70 yards with Palm plunging 1-yard for the TD. Shuster, who had missed earlier, kicked the extra point. A few minutes later Palm dropkicked a 40-yard field goal and that's how the scoring ended, 16-0, although the second team was on NC State's 14-yard line when the game ended. Bezdek was frustrated. His team had 18 first downs to Wolfpack's four and Wilson had run up and down the field but couldn't get a TD.

Wilson was back at left half against Gettysburg with Wentz at fullback but again the team was sluggish against an inferior opponent. Palm dropkicked field goals of 47 and 22 yards to give State an early second quarter lead and Johnson's 20-yard dash and Shuster's PAT made it 13-0 at the half. But Gettysburg came out passing after the intermission and twice reached the State 12-yard line before the Lions' defense stiffened. Palm intercepted a pass in the fourth quarter to set up Wilson's one-yard TD around end and the final score was 20-0. "The Penn State line functioned fairly well on defense but failed to open up holes for the Nittany backs," reported one dispatch from State

College that circulated in several newspapers. "The team, as a whole, did not show the drive that was expected, and a big improvement must be made this week if the Navy is to be defeated next Saturday."

Practice did not go well that week. Johnson injured his shoulder and was ruled out of the game. Shuster also was hobbling and would not start nor handle kicks. Bezdek also contemplated some other roster shifts to shake up the squad. On Thursday, Bezdek told reporters his team would not win without an extraordinary effort. "I can't see that we have a chance," the coach said. "The team has not developed as it should and we will probably have several new men in the lineup. Of course, there is always the hope that a team will find itself in a big game and that is our only hope on Saturday." Bezdek was not being coy. This was practically the same starting Navy team that had defeated State last year and it was now unbeaten and heavily favored.

What happened at Beaver Field that October 20 before a record standing-room only Homecoming crowd of 20,000 ranks as one of the all-time great all-around one-man performances in State's football history and changed Harry Wilson's life—and name—forever. The game got off slowly as the teams battled back and forth at midfield but mostly on State's side of the 50-yard line. Midway through the first quarter, a Palm pass was intercepted by Navy's center Matthews at about the Navy 40-yard line and Matthews appeared to be in the clear and on the way to a touchdown when he was pulled down from behind at the State 38-yard line by Wilson. That tackle was an omen for the day. State's defense stopped that serious Navy threat without giving up another yard and as the game moved into the second quarter a series of punt exchanges found Navy with the ball on it's own 33-yard line.

Navy's sub quarterback Pete McKee [Some accounts of the game claim starting QB Shaggy Cullen was in the game, not McKee] threw a pass towards his left end Taylor who was wide open at about the 50-yard line. Suddenly, seemingly out of nowhere, Wilson dashed in, leaped up and intercepted the ball. He ran past the Middie players before they realized what had happened, "and with splendid interference from his teammates and a burst of speed" (as one reporter wrote) he was into the end zone. With Wilson holding the ball, Palm kicked the extra point from the placement rather than using his normal drop kick

Mike Palm attempts a field goal in the stunning 21-3 win over Navy.

Some 50,000 fans in New York's Yankee Stadium watched as Penn State and West Virginia fought to a 13-13 tie in the 1923 game.

technique. The surprised State fans were still cheering Wilson's spectacular interception when State lined up to receive the kickoff (as the rules still permitted in that era). Wilson was deep and he took the ball on the 5-yard line, dashed down the sideline past several Navy players, got a great block at midfield from Artelt on Middie fullback Steve Barchet and sped into the end zone without being touched. The partisan crowd was delirious as Palm added the extra point, with Wilson again holding.

The Navy players were shocked but they were not about to give up. Throughout the rest of the second quarter and on into the third quarter the Middies were constantly on the attack in State's territory, primarily using a ferocious passing offense. Gray stopped one drive with an interception and the defense led by Wilson, Gray and Bedenk batted down pass after pass. Once, the Middies were held on a fourth down inside the State 5-yard line. Two other threats were halted at the 20. Then late in the third quarter, State got the ball on its own 20-yard line. Two running plays gained eight yards. On third down, Wilson took the ball from Bas Gray, faked a reverse to Palm and burst up the middle, shook off two would-be tacklers and rambled 72 yards for another TD. Palm's PAT made it 21-0. There was more than a full quarter left but State's stout defense would only give up a meaningless 15-yard field goal late in the game. "Remarkable Runs by Wilson Brings Victory to Lions," hailed the *Pittsburgh Post*. "Nittanys Batter Down the Middies' Vicious Assaults." Navy had piled up 16 first downs and 285 yards to State's five first downs and 220 yards but it couldn't stop Wilson on offense or defense. In addition to his interception Wilson had 123 yards rushing on 16 carries and 137 yards on three kickoff returns. A syndicated sportswriter for the *New York Sun*, George Trevor, was so impressed by Wilson's one-man show that he gave him a new nickname. No longer was he "Handsome Harry". Now he was "Light Horse" Harry. The nickname didn't catch on right away at Penn State but by the next season, when Wilson was then starring for West Point, every football fan in the country knew him as "Light Horse" Harry Wilson.

Wilson's extraordinary performance against Navy was a defining moment of the 1923 season but there were at least two other "moments" that eventually affected the outcome of the season—injuries to Palm and Bedenk. Palm had suffered a hip injury in the Navy win, even though he played the entire game. Bezdek had no adequate backup. He tried three different players at quarterback while Palm recovered but no one could make up for Palm's absence. The team

missed his leadership, his running and passing, his defensive prowess and his placekicking.

That was obvious the next week when State played West Virginia at New York's Yankee Stadium. Playing an annual game in New York was now part of the athletic department's plan to gain notoriety as well as financial support. State had tried to arrange a game with Vanderbilt but that didn't work out and West Virginia had eagerly accepted. The Mountaineers had never played in New York before and they wanted to show that they were now the equal of State, a neighboring rival they had not played in 14 years and had never beaten in five games. Most of the top Eastern sportswriters believed WVC was better, but with both teams unbeaten and State coming off the big upset over Navy, the game was rated a toss up. Walter Camp, who usually sat on the bench of the team he favored, was on the West Virginia sideline.

Some 50,000 watched as two plays after the kickoff, West Virginia's star halfback Nick Narducci fumbled and State recovered on the 17-yard line. One play later, Wilson went up the middle for a 16-yard TD. Hobie Light kicked the extra point and State led 7-0 and many State fans figured a rout was on, but they were wrong. Neither team could get their offenses cranked up in the first half as fumbles, intercepted passes and punting dominated play. In the third quarter, State's sub quarterback Johnny Patton fumbled a punt and the Moutaineers' Tallman picked up the ball and raced to State's 25-yard line. Two plays later, Narducci caught a 17 yard pass from Guy Ekberg for a TD and Ekberg booted the tying point. As the quarter was coming to a close a few minutes later, West Virginia recovered a partially blocked punt at State's 38-yard line. At this point Bedenk was ordered out of the game by State's trainer because,

Guard Joe Bedenk was an All-American in 1921, 1922 and 1923 and later returned to State to coach football and baseball for more than 30 years.

The great Harry Wilson scored the only touchdown in State's 7-0 win over Georgia Tech at Beaver Field in 1923.

as a reporter wrote, "Bedenk's great playing had resulted in him being battered so that he was staggering around half unconscious..." He never returned and the team would miss him. With fourth-and-2 at the 20-yard line early in the fourth quarter, Ekberg threw a short pass to Pete Barnam who ran 18 yards for the go-ahead touchdown. But Provost, Gray and Michalske led a surge of the front line that blocked Ekberg's PAT attempt and WVC led, 13-7.

West Virginia's TD seemed to spark the State players. The Lions took the kickoff and moved to near the 50 before punting. The defense then forced WVC to punt the ball back and that's when Johnson, who didn't start because of his injury, made the big play. He took a punt at State's 32-yard line and ran it back 42 yards to WVC's 26. The Mountaineers defense dug in but with Wilson doing the brunt of the running, the Lions drove relentlessly towards the end zone. Twice on fourth-and-one, Wilson ran for the first down. Then on first-and-goal, Wilson bowled over for the tying score. State took a time out to settle down and Bezdek, not confident with Light as the placekicker, sent in the still-ailing Shuster to kick the point that would win the game. As everyone watched in almost a quiet murmur, Johnson held the ball as Shuster stepped forward and kicked. The crowd groaned. The kick was wide! Both teams had one more chance with the ball but couldn't mount a drive and the final score was a frustrating 13-13 tie.

The tie was a letdown for Bezdek and the players but they would have to forget it quickly because another unbeaten team was waiting for them in Syracuse. Bezdek was happy to have Johnson back as a starter to team with the rampaging Wilson but he was still worried about his quarterback. Now, he also had problems in his line, with Bedenk out with an injury and Shuster still not able to start. Wilson could not do it all on his own and it was obvious that State was not the same team without Palm and Bedenk.

Syracuse proved that beyond a doubt at Archbold Stadium when the Orange handed State its first loss of the season, 10-0. The sputtering State offense never got closer than the Syracuse 34-yard line and had just three first downs in the entire game. The defense played well after allowing Syracuse to score its only touchdown the first time it had the ball. Starting at its own 42-yard line after a punt, Syracuse utilized the line bucks of fullback John McBride, who carried the ball 14 times in 17 plays, to go the 58 yards for the touchdown, with McBride plunging over from the 1-yard line, then kicking the extra point. Midway in the second quarter, Syracuse surprised the defense with a quick kick that the usually sure-handed Wilson fumbled at State's 15-

yard line. Five plays later, McBride booted a 10-yard field goal and the scoring was over as defenses dominated the rest of the game.

Neither Palm nor Bedenk started the next week when Georgia Tech made its first visit to Beaver Field in a major intersectional clash, but both men entered the game in the fourth quarter to help preserve a State win, 7-0. Wilson got the only touchdown in the first quarter, gaining most of the yardage in a 72-yard drive, including the final 10 yards on a slick run around the left end. State recorded 16 first downs to Tech's four but once again it was the defensive units of both teams that set the tone of the game.

Palm and Bedenk were back at full strength for the Penn game and it showed. The largest crowd ever at Franklin Field up to that time, 56,000, saw Wilson go on another scoring binge. He scored all three TDs in what sportswriters called "an easy victory." "State's offense was super-mighty in its power, smooth and speedy in its execution," wrote one Pittsburgh reporter. "...Wilson could have been eliminated from the team...and the Blue and White would still have been triumphant." Perhaps. But Wilson was great, rushing for at least 162 yards on 32 carries and catching three passes for 42 yards. He scored his first TD as the climax of an 80-yard drive late in the second quarter by taking a swing pass from Johnson and sprinting 24 yards for the score. Early in the third period, he ran 48 yards for another touchdown. Then in the fourth quarter he intercepted a pass and ran 45 yards for the TD. Shuster kicked all three PATs and State won, 21-0. Wilson now had 13 TDs for the season, tying the school record held by Bull McCleary and Harry Robb.

Bezdek and the players were confident that Wilson would break the record and that they would beat arch rival Pitt on Thanksgiving Day. After all, they reasoned, all the injured players had healed, the offense had finally jelled and Pitt was not as good as any of the last five opponents. But everyone, including State's passionate followers, had once again overlooked the Pop Warner factor. This was Warner's last game as the Panthers coach for he had already announced that he was leaving for the coaching job at Stanford. His team had stormed back from a 0-4 start to win four straight, including a major upset over Washington & Jefferson and he had it primed for State. Warner figured that if he could stop Wilson, he could stop State, so he designed a defense that would do just that.

Another record crowd of 33,000 turned out in the usual rain and mud at Forbes Field for the holiday game. State scored in the first quarter on a 29-yard field goal by Shuster following a short punt. Then, at the start of the second quarter, Pitt surprised State's defense by going to the air and Karl Bohren hit Hoot Flanagan on 22-yard pass for the TD. A Pitt fumble on the next series gave State a break at Pitt's 26-yard line. But then came what was probably the play of the game. Flanagan intercepted a Johnson pass near the line of scrimmage and ran 74 yards for a Panther touchdown. With a 14-3 lead at the half, Pitt took the kickoff to start the third period and marched into field goal range, but a 24-yard field goal attempt failed and State got the ball on the 2-yard line. State couldn't move and Light dropped back in the end zone to punt. He apparently took too much time as right end Milo Gwosden broke through to block the kick and recover the ball for a touchdown. That was it, as Pitt upset State, 20-3. State didn't get a first down until late in the game against the Panther subs and netted just 69 yard rushing and none passing. "(Pitt) ran roughshod over their opponents, breaks for themselves, and took advantage of every opening left them by the visitors...," reported the *Pittsburgh Sun*. "Probably never in the annals of local football was a good team outclassed more decisively than Pitt outclassed State. The highly-touted Harry Wilson was stopped dead, just as admirers of the Warner system predicted that he would."

For the second year in a row, State's season had ended on a downer. Bezdek felt even worse about this one than he did last year. He might not admit it but he had been outcoached again by Warner. Sure, the West Virginia tie and Syracuse loss could be blamed on injuries. But not Pitt. Warner's team had been better prepared, and everyone knew it, especially the alumni from the Pittsburgh area. They were grumbling and that wasn't good. But Bezdek wasn't worried. Hadn't he beaten Navy? And the unbeaten Middies were in the Rose Bowl, right? And what about Georgia Tech and the once mighty Quakers?

Still, Bezdek had not beaten Pitt since 1919 and he knew what the game meant to State fans. Pitt was getting a new coach and that could change everything. But he was losing five of his best players: Wilson and Bedenk—the First Team All-Americans—plus Palm, Shuster and Frank. And he wasn't confident his returnees could do any better than this year's team. Bezdek needed some new players. And quickly.

Season Record 6-2-1
Record to Date 187-92-20
Winning percentage .659

"Quarterbacks Lost"

After three high-scoring victories to open the 1924 season, Bezdek was telling sportswriters this was "the heaviest and fastest" team he had ever coached. He even believed he had found the quarterback who might rekindle memories of Glenn Killinger. He would soon be proven wrong.

Bill Baker had quarterbacked the freshman team in 1922 but had been ineligible last season. Now, he was the field general in Bezdek's revamped backfield and the coach liked how the young man from Johnstown was handling the responsibility. Except for returning starter Hobie Light at fullback, the starting backfield was comprised of

The Varsity House located close to Beaver Field became the new living and dining quarters for the football players and other athletes. The building still remains and is now used as a dormitory and renamed Irvin Hall.

inexperienced sophomores. Baker's brother, Gene, and George Gier, were the halfbacks but together they could not come close to replacing "Light Horse" Harry, who had graduated and been recruited by West Point.

The heart of Bezdek's team was up front in the experienced line, anchored by junior center Bas Gray, who had been elected captain. Artelt was back at one end and sophomore Ken Weston at the other, Prevost and spot starter Ernie McCann at the tackles, and Michalske and Fred Flock, who had lettered in '22, at the guards. Prevost had developed into an excellent place kicker and already had 11 extra points and a field goal to his credit. Because of Michalske's speed, height, weight (6-foot, 196-pounds) and accurate passing ability, Bezdek had designed some offensive plays that utilized the junior in the backfield and Michalske had scored a touchdown against Gettysburg. No wonder his teammates had begun calling him "Iron Mike."

Preseason practice had been smoother than at any time in Bezdek's tenure. There were still complaints about the coach's tough and combative methods but the players now on the team had become used to Bezdek's techniques. They also realized he was the man chiefly responsible for their new living and dining quarters, Varsity Hall. The players had moved out of the old Track House and into Varsity Hall about two weeks before the first game with Lebanon Valley. It was bigger and better than the Track House and right across from New Beaver Field. But there was no locker room there. The players still had to dress at the Track House and make the long walks before and after games!

Lebanon Valley was an easy opener in the usual September heat. State gained an astounding 841 yards (622 in the official PSU records) rushing in overwhelming the visitors, 47-3. Light led the scoring with three touchdowns and Gier had two. Lebanon Valley avoided the shutout with a field goal in the closing minutes.

The next week against North Carolina State, Bill Baker ran back punts for 60 and 55 yard touchdowns to highlight a 51-6 romp. Baker also scored a third TD on a run as State gained 580 yards. Gray recovered two fumbles and intercepted a pass to lead a defense that held NC State to 50 yards.

Bezdek surprised everyone, including the 6,000 fans at Beaver Field, by starting his second team against Gettysburg and playing the backups the entire first half, which ended in a scoreless tie. When the regulars entered the game at the start of the third quarter, they took the kickoff and marched downfield with Michalske going off tackle

Jules Prevost was a Second Team All-American in 1924 as a tackle on one of the best lines in college football. He also was State's placekicker and won several games with his field goals.

for the TD. Minutes later, Gene Baker intercepted a pass and ran 60 yards to set up a 12-yard TD run by his brother. Then Prevost blocked a punt at the Gettysburg 30-yard line, scooped up the ball inside the 10 and rolled into the end zone. A 15-yard run around right end by Bill Baker finished the scoring in the fourth period and State won, 26-0.

The skilled performance of the team, particularly Bill Baker and his sophomore backs, against these obviously weak opponents may have lulled Bezdek and the team into thinking they were better than they actually were. They weren't overconfident when they departed on Thursday, October 16 for the 1,000 mile trip to Atlanta to play Georgia Tech. But they had not really faced adversity, and when they did for the first time they couldn't handle it. What happened against Tech defined the season.

As an estimated 30,000 looked on at Grant Field, Georgia Tech took the opening kickoff but couldn't move and punted. Bill Baker fumbled the ball at the State 40-yard lined but recovered. It was an omen. An off tackle run lost two yards, and then Baker made his second error. His pass was intercepted by Tech's quarterback Moore who ran to the 8-yard line before being pushed out of bounds by Light. With fourth-and-goal from the 3-yard line, fullback Doug Wycoff kicked a 3-yard field goal and State trailed for the first time in the season. Just before the quarter ended, Prevost tried to tie the game with a 45-yard field goal but he missed. After an exchange of punts early in the second quarter, State got the ball on about its own 40-yard line but was penalized 15 yards for holding. On third-and-10, Baker made another mistake. He had another pass intercepted. This time, the Golden Tornado's right tackle, Gardner, picked it off and ran it back more than 20 yards for a TD. Wycoff booted the PAT and it was 10-0. When Tech kicked off, Hank Lafferty, who had backed-up Palm in '23, had replaced Baker at quarterback. The first time he carried the ball, he gained 12 yards. But late in the second quarter, State failed to

make a first down at midfield on Lafferty's run around right end and, after an exchange of possession, State found itself in deep punt formation near its own goal line. Gray's snap went over Light's head and into the end zone where Light fell on the ball for a Tech Safety. That gave the home team a 12-0 half-time lead, yet Tech had still not made a first down.

State took the second half kickoff and couldn't move very far and punted. Tech couldn't move either and punted back. Bill Baker, back in at quarterback, waited for the ball on State's 15-yard line. You guessed it. He fumbled and Tech recovered on the 10. Three plays later, Wycoff kicked a field goal from the 17-yard line and Tech led, 15-0. The teams exchanged possession several times through the third and into the fourth quarters without either team making progress until State got the ball on its own 45-yard line after a punt. With Michalske carrying twice on big plays for 13 and 6 yards, State moved to the Tech 23-yard line. Iron Mike then bolted off tackle and dashed into the end zone. Prevost missed the PAT and it was 15-6. As time was winding down, State got the ball on Tech's 43-yard line and six plays later Gier went 10 yards over right tackle for the touchdown. Prevost's PAT made it 15-13. But it was too little, too late. Tech ran out the clock—and still had not recorded a first down!

Was it bad breaks or an incompetent quarterback that caused the defeat? Bezdek obviously believed the latter, for the following week Lafferty was the starting quarterback when State met Syracuse at Beaver Field in the third annual Homecoming game. Bezdek had two other fresh faces in his revised backfield, replacing Baker's brother at left half with another sophomore, Bud Bergman, and subbing junior Ed Buckley at fullback for Light.

The game was considered a toss-up and throughout most of the first quarter the game was even as the teams traded possession three times with State getting the only first down. Then, late in the quarter, State got the ball at its own 32-yard line after Syracuse's fourth punt of the day. Buckley went around end for five yards. What happened on the next play would further personify the 1924 season. Lafferty called "a double pass" play. Philadelphia sportswriter Stoney McLinn described what happened: "The ball was snapped to Bergman, who handed it to Lafferty as he swung across close to the scrimmage line. A groan arose from the State supporters when the ball slipped through Lafferty's hands and rolled behind him some 10 yards. Lafferty went after it and managed to touch the ball, but did not hold it.

State and Navy players scramble to recover one of several fumbles during 1924 game at Annapolis won by Lions, 6-0.

State's defense stops a run by Penn in the 1924 scoreless tie played in the rain, sleet and snow at Franklin Field. The outcome was a moral victory for the Lions.

Hanson, the energetic Syracuse end, who had hurried through, stooped, picked up the loose pigskin and raced 21 yards for a touchdown." Fullback John McBride kicked the extra point and Syracuse led 7-0.

State would be frustrated the rest of the day by its own mistakes and its missed opportunities. "Penn State completely outplayed Syracuse on the attack," McLinn wrote later. State would go on to rush for 179 yards to three for Syracuse and hold the visitors to one first down while getting seven. But the Lions passing attack was a disaster. They completed just one of seven and had two interceptions late in the game that stopped potential game-winning drives. In the second quarter, Prevost booted a field goal from a difficult angle at the 36-yard line to narrow the score to 7-3. Early in the second half, Prevost tried another field goal from the 48-yard line but it fell short. Syracuse then moved the ball upfield from where McBride connected on a field goal from the State 33-yard line. Prevost came back in the fourth quarter with another field goal from the 32-yard line to make the score, 10-6. A few minutes later, State blew a major opportunity when Jim Foley fumbled a low punt at the Syracuse 10-yard line. "The ball struck his knees and bounded away from him directly into the chest of (Bob) Hayes, State end," wrote McLinn. "Hayes made a desperate clutch for the oval, but it struck him so hard it bounded away too fast for him to grab it. Foley turned quickly, fell on the ball, which was a couple of feet behind him, and Syracuse was saved." It was the first defeat on Beaver Field since Rutgers won in the war-shortened 1918 season—29 games ago.

The team's spirit sagged noticeably after the frustrating loss to Syracuse. As the team worked out in preparation for its next game at Navy, a report from State College that appeared in a Philadelphia newspaper told of the poor mental attitude on the team. "It is to be hoped that the players have snapped out of their losing spirit and have imbibed some of the fighting qualities that are traditional at Penn State," the dispatch said. "Some of the worst offenders to date are players from whom the most was expected, and instead of setting a stirring example for the newer members of the team, these veterans have been falling down." No names were mentioned, of course.

The Navy game at Annapolis did not have the same significance as the three previous clashes between the two teams. Both

schools were having so-called "down" years and it showed on the field. Baker was back as the starting quarterback for State but the offense still had trouble scoring and holding on to the ball. In fact, neither team had much of an attack. Both teams fumbled several times and the first half was scoreless. Midway through the third quarter, Prevost recovered a fumbled punt at the Navy 20-yard line, and after a penalty prevented a first down, the big tackle booted a 30-yard field goal. In the fourth quarter, State got the ball at the Navy 48-yard line after a holding penalty. Bergman completed two passes for 27 yards but the drive bogged down and Prevost then booted another field goal from the 14-yard line. Final score: State 6, Navy 0.

Bezdek wasn't happy despite the win and he made several more changes in his starting lineup for the Pennsylvania Day game against Carnegie Tech. Lafferty was back at quarterback with Bill Helbig at right half and R. S. Watson, who was not even on the official roster, in at left half. Artelt and Michalske also were benched as Bezdek tried some psychology to rile up his team. It worked. Tech had won four games including a 6-0 victory over Pitt and had lost only to powerful Washington & Jefferson, 10-0. But State played its best game of the year before 15,000 at Beaver Field and showed real character after a frustrating start. After the opening kickoff, the Lions drove from their own 20-yard line to the Tech four before losing a fumble. But a short punt moments later gave State the ball near the Tech 40-yard line and the team marched to the goal, with Bergman scoring the TD on a short plunge. Prevost missed the PAT but it wouldn't matter this day. A Tech fumble on its own 22-yard line set up a 7-yard Lafferty TD run in the second period and in the third quarter Bill Baker got another TD and Prevost kicked a field goal to give State a 22-7. Tech's only score came late in the fourth quarter on a 60-yard interception return of a pass thrown by Bergman. "How Syracuse and Georgia Tech trounced the powerful Bezdekian outfit continues to remain a mystery to all who witnessed today's contest," wrote Harry Camins for the *Pittsburgh Gazette Times*.

Bezdek now felt he had the team turned around but he knew the next game would be the biggest challenge. Penn was unbeaten in eight games and one of the best teams in the country. It would be heavily favored at Franklin Field but maybe just ripe for an upset. "I would make myself appear like a fool if I said we would beat that strong Pennsylvania eleven," Bezdek told sportswriter Stoney McLinn. "...We can win in Philadelphia...But we lack the spark—perhaps the spark that a smart, snappy, skillful field general would provide. If that spark comes to life before we run onto Franklin Field, then there is hope."

Rain, sleet and snow turned the game into a defensive battle before some 52,000 fans, including Pennsylvania Governor Pinchot. Penn gained 149 yards to State's 140 yards but neither could mount any scoring drives. The biggest play of the game came in the third quarter when former starter Ted Artelt, subbing for Tom Wilson at right end, picked up a Penn fumble and dashed 60 yards for an apparent touchdown. But the referee nullified the TD, saying the whistle had blown the Penn running play dead before the fumble. State's players protested but to no avail. Penn tried five field goals and had two blocked. One from the 27-yard line in the fourth quarter just missed but the soggy ball went under the cross bar. Prevost tried two field goals for State but neither hit. The 0-0 final was seen as a moral victory for the Lions.

With some 10 days, as usual, to prepare for the big game against Pitt, Bezdek had scheduled another contest to keep his team on edge. So Marietta had agreed to visit Beaver Field on Nov. 22. State looked ragged and lacked punched and scored two of its four TDs by recovering fumbles and running for scores. Michalske and Artelt started at halfbacks and Iron Mike dashed 18 yards for another TD as State won, 28-0.

After defeating Carnegie Tech so decisively and holding mighty Penn scoreless, Bezdek, the team and State's loyal fans were convinced that Pitt would be no match. Pop Warner was gone and Jock Sutherland, a former star player, was now the Panther coach, and he was struggling. Pitt's 4-3-1 record (the tie was against Syracuse) was the worst in years and the Panthers had not looked good even in winning. State not only had not won since 1919 but had not scored since then either. To State's beleaguered fans, it was now payback time.

For once, the Forbes Field turf was dry on Thanksgiving Day as 33,000 showed up on a cloudy afternoon for the 2:10 kickoff. State won the toss and received the ball and drove to midfield before forced to punt. Pitt got the ball on its own 20-yard line and after a running play got two yards, a bad snap from center sent the ball way over the head of Pitt quarterback Jesse Brown. The ball went into the end zone but Brown beat several State linemen to the ball and got it just past the goal line before he was tackled. Pitt immediately punted out of danger, with Lafferty returning five yards to the Pitt 25. Three plays lost three yard and on fourth down, Prevost kicked a 36-yard field goal and the State fans cheered lustily. The rout was on!!!

The State fans were jolted back to reality following the ensuing kickoff. After trading punts, Pitt got the ball on its own 42-yard line. In several plays, the Panthers moved quickly inside State's 20 but the Lion defense held and Pitt's sub end, Milo Gwosden tried a field goal from 26-yard line but it missed. Pitt gained possession again at the start of the second quarter but was unable to move the ball at midfield and punted. Lafferty stood back on the 12 to make the run back. This would become the play of the game and the definitive, recurring statement about the entire season. Lafferty fumbled the kick! Pitt recovered at the 11. The Panthers couldn't get more than three yards and on fourth down Gwosden dropped back to try another field goal from the 16. Michalske crashed through and blocked the kick but Gwosden recovered at the 20-yard line, and under the rules at the time, it was still

Pitt's ball. Four runs later, Andy Gustafson banged over from the one for the Pitt touchdown. Gwosden missed the PAT but Pitt led 6-3 and took that lead into the intermission.

Whatever the two coaches said to their teams in the locker rooms has been lost in history. But it was Pitt which exploded in the second half and turned the game into a rout. After an exchange of punts to open the third quarter, Pitt got the ball on State's 48-yard line. Aided by a crucial pass interference penalty, Pitt went all the way in 11 plays with Gustafson plunging over for his second touchdown from five yards out. Again, Gwosden missed the extra point but Pitt was now in control. A few minutes later, Pitt intercepted a pass near midfield that set up a quick 38-yard drive for another touchdown and early in the fourth quarter another State fumble at its own 29-yard line resulted in a final TD and Pitt walked off with a humiliating 24-3 win. Some sportswriters blamed the loss directly on Bezdek.

"The downfall of State was pitiful," wrote Regis Welsh, Sporting Editor, of the *Pittsburgh Post*, accompanied by one headline that said: "Taking the Ego out of Hugo." "...they lacked the plays; lacked the ability to put them over...and when (things) went bad the whole team seemed to follow without murmur of protest. And the frantic actions of a beaten, bewildered coach on the bench, gave them little or not solace or confidence."

The Pittsburgh area alumni also were grumbling again. This game had been an embarrassment. Of course, Bezdek never blamed himself for what happened on Thanksgiving Day—or for the rest of the frustrating season. "I don't know what happens to my teams when they go to Pittsburgh," Bezdek told sportswriters. All he needed was a good quarterback, he said. And with next year's tough schedule that included intersectional games against Notre Dame, Michigan State and Georgia Tech, he had better find one who didn't fumble.

Season Record 6-3-1
Record to Date 193-95-21
Winning percentage .659

"Iron Mike & Notre Dame"

Bezdek had been thinking about switching Michalske to fullback full time ever since the end of the 1924 season. Now, as his struggling 2-0 team prepared for it's first true test of the young season against Georgia Tech, he figured it was almost time to make the move.

There was no doubt that taking Iron Mike out of the front line would weaken the Lions forward wall. Michalske was the best lineman on the team whether playing guard or tackle. But Bezdek was having more problems with his backfield than with his line and he needed some punch and leadership back there. "My men are too light," Bezdek told Allison Danzig of *The New York Times*. "They're a lot of ponies." The 206-pound Michalske would add the weight. He also was the best passer on the team and Bezdek believed he needed to get more passing into his lethargic attack.

The Lions had beaten Lebanon Valley in the season opener at Beaver Field, 14-0, and then defeated Franklin & Marshall, 13-0. But in both games they had been held score-less in the first half and the backfield was a mish-mash of sophomores and underachieving juniors and seniors. Soph Johnny Pincura had replaced fellow soph Cy Lungren at quarterback in the second half of the Lebanon Valley game and scored a touchdown to lead the victory. As the starter against F&M, Pincura ran for the TD that broke the 0-0 tie but his lack of experience showed as the team rolled up 16 first downs to F&M's 2 but still couldn't score much. Still, Pincura had emerged as the best quarterback and Bezdek was just as happy that the Baker brothers had left the team and that Lafferty had graduated.

Another soph, Harry Dangerfield, was the designated starter at right half but he missed the first two games because of an injury. Junior Bill Pritchard, Helbig, Light and a couple of others were battling for the other halfback spot and Bergman was now at fullback. Bezdek also was impressed with sophomore halfback John Roepke who had come out of nowhere in the preseason and was promoted from the scrubs to the varsity just in time to start against F&M for Dangerfield. Still, there wasn't a "game-breaker" among them. That's why Bezdek was contemplating the Michalske move. The front line also was unsettled but partially because of injuries to veterans Gray at center and John Filak at guard. Gray, elected captain again, had been replaced by sophomore Rog Mahoney and Bezdek had used veterans McCann, House, and Weston along with sophomores Hal Hastings, Barney Slamp and Tom Wilson in the line with Iron Mike. Bezdek was only sorry he could not use Prevost, who was a senior but ineligible because he had played 12 minutes against Pitt three years ago. Bezdek missed Prevost's blocking and tackling as well as his placekicking. He also was concerned about the team's punting and was not completely happy with Light, Gray and others who had been doing the punting.

Six weeks of spring practice, nearly a month of preseason workouts and the team still wasn't ready for what was the toughest schedule in Bezdek's eight-year tenure. Getting Michigan State and Notre Dame at home would be a break, although the defending National Champion Irish would be heavily favored. But the team also would have to win on the road in two new stadiums at West Virginia and Pitt and at unfriendly Syracuse. At least the Georgia Tech game was on neutral ground at New York's Yankee Stadium. But Bezdek knew his team would have to play better than it did in the first two games to beat Tech, which was a slight favorite. The team also would have to avoid the fumbles and other mistakes which cost them so dearly last year in Atlanta.

Bezdek decided to keep Iron Mike in the line since Tech outweighed State by at least 10 pounds per man. But it was the weather that caused State the biggest problem in New York. Gale force winds and "shivering cold" kept the crowd down to a mere 8,000 and eventually led to State's defeat on a bad break. Tech won the toss and started the first quarter with the wind to its back. However, the Golden Tor-

August "Gus" Michalske, guard and fullback from the early 1920s, was one of the best guards ever to play for State and the school's first player selected to the Pro Football Hall of Fame.

nados couldn't take advantage of the wind and neither could State for most of the second quarter. Neither team came close to scoring until the last 30 seconds of the half. Tech tried to punt from about its own 25-yard line and the wind was so stiff, the ball never made it past the 30. On the first play, the Associated Press reported, "Pincura flung a low, hard pass to Dangerfield from a fake cross buck formation and the latter shook off three tacklers to cross the goal line..." Bergman kicked the PAT "just as the whistle blew."

Taking advantage of the gale, Tech kicked deep to State and kept the Lions pinned inside the 5-yard line. Now, came the break of the game. Gray, in the game as a sub, went back to punt from his goal line. But, as the AP reported, "...the wind sailed the ball back to him" and a State player fell on the ball near the goal line. A couple of moments later Wycoff went over for the touchdown and the extra point tied the game. As the teams played through the third and fourth quarters, the game developed into a punting duel. Midway through the last period, State moved to within field goal range, but a 42-yard attempt by Weston fell short. Tech then proved it was the superior team with or without a gale by marching 80 yards on mostly "short, sharp dashes through the line" (the AP reported) and scored the go-ahead TD. The wind blew the extra point attempt wide but Tech left the field with a well-earned 13-7 victory.

Whether moving Michalske to fullback would have prevented the Tech defeat is questionable but Bezdek's offense had been ineffective. So, before the following week's game with Marietta at Beaver Field, Iron Mike was placed at fullback. Michalske scored State's first TD on a line plunge in the second quarter but State's offense continued "to be ragged," as one dispatch reported. State lost the ball five times on fumbles, most of them in scoring territory, and rolled up 458 yards and 23 first downs against the team coached by ex-Lion All-American Red Griffiths. State won 13-0 before a "Mother's Day" crowd of 3,500 but most of the fans, including the mothers, left the game wondering what was wrong with Bezdek's team.

Michigan State was just 2-2 when it visited Beaver Field on Pennsylvania Day and had been walloped by Michigan, 39-0. The field was what State's athletic department officials called "a veritable sea of mud," and a blocked kick eventually was the difference in the game. The Lions took the opening kickoff and marched down field and scored with Michalske going over on a 10-yard burst off tackle. Then in the second period, McCann blocked a punt and recovered the ball deep in MSC territory. Michalske again scored on a 10-yard run and the home team led, 13-0. MSC recovered a State fumble late in the third quarter and used a passing attack to get a TD but the Aggies would get no more. The final score was 13-6.

Syracuse was unbeaten and favored at Archbold Stadium but for the first time all season, Bezdek was not changing the starting lineup that had opened and won against Michigan State. He finally believed the team was beginning to play up to its potential and he was certain moving Iron Mike had been the catalyst. The teams battled evenly in the first half with both missing field goals from the 35-yard line, including one attempted by Michalske in the second quarter. Then came perhaps the most significant play of the season. With State moving upfield in the third quarter from about its own 35-yard line, Pritchard fumbled and Syracuse recovered. (Shades of 1924!) The Orange quickly moved to State's 2-yard line where it was second-and-one for a first down. But State's defense dug in, and it took all three downs for Syracuse to pick up a first down at the State one. Fullback Ray Barbutti scored after two plunges into the line, Syracuse kicked the PAT and that was it. Syracuse dominated the rest of the game, finishing with 136 yards and 10 first downs to States' 80 yards and four first downs and won, 7-0.

Bezdek now realized he had been too hopeful about Michalske's having a major positive affect on the inexperienced sophomores and particularly Pincura at quarterback. "If we only had a quarterback who would instinctively do the right thing..." Bezdek told Philadelphia sportswriter Stoney McLinn, "we'd have a much better record to show for our hard work on the gridiron." With the Homecoming game against Knute Rockne's powerhouse Notre Dame looming next, Bezdek was desperate and knew he had to make another change. Since the Marietta game he had been using Helbig at quarterback as well as right half and when the team resumed practice after the Syracuse loss, Bezdek promoted the Newark (NJ) senior to first team and moved Lungren up to the second team. He also demoted Dangerfield and inserted a little used junior fullback named George Greene in at right half.

The Notre Dame game had been virtually sold out since mid-September when Notre Dame had requested the last block of 400 tickets. "According to the South Bend institution," said a story in the September 23 edition of the *Altoona Tribune*, "no other away from home game has ever created the demand for tickets that the game with Penn State this fall is creating." With State's alumni also demanding tickets, State expected to break the Beaver Field attendance record. The game had been scheduled last December, even before Notre Dame had beaten Stanford 27-10 in the Rose Bowl and claimed the National Championship.

But this was not the same team. All eleven starters from the unbeaten '24 team had graduated, including the famed "Four Horsemen" backfield. Rockne's latest squad had been beaten badly by Army two weeks ago, 27-0, but was still 5-1 after knocking off Georgia Tech the previous Saturday in Atlanta, 13-0. This was Rockne's eighth season as coach of the Irish but he had been a player the only other time State and Notre Dame had met in 1913. Still, Notre Dame and its famed passing attack was expected to roll over Bezdek's floundering team. The rain started long before the 2:30 p.m. kickoff but a record crowd of 25,000 still turned out as the rain continued all day. The field was as muddy as it had ever been and the game turned into a defensive struggle where one small break could determine victory.

The first half was scoreless but in the third quarter Irish quarterback Red Edwards made a superb punt that the Irish downed at the State 1-yard line. Gray punted out immediately and Edwards returned it five yards to State's 25. Two running plays gave Notre Dame a first down at the State 12. On the next play, Edwards tried to pass and was nailed for a 17-yard loss by Weston and Filak. With fourth-and-long, Edwards tried another pass but the ball sailed over the head of the potential receiver and the State fans cheered lustily. Wait! The referee had blown his whistle and signaled penalty. Interference, he screamed, and gave the Irish a first down at the State 10-yard line. Three times the Irish backs slammed into the State line but could gain only one yard. On fourth down fullback Rex Enright tried a field goal from the 13 but missed.

A few minutes later State got its break when Gray recovered an Enright fumble at the Notre Dame 43-yard line. Michalske went around left end and rambled 23 yards, which was the longest run of the day by any player. But, now the Irish defense got tough, and State

could gain just five yards in three plays. Weston then tried a field goal from the 34 but he muffed the placement and the ball dribbled forward to the 30 where Notre Dame fell on the ball, and the Lions threat was over.

That was it. The final score was 0-0. "State Holds Irish to Scoreless Tie On Muddy Gridiron," said the headline in one Pittsburgh newspaper. Notre Dame made six first downs to three for State but the Irish lost two of four fumbles and the Lions lost two of three fumbles. Notre Dame's passing attack was stymied throughout with just two completions in seven attempts. "Perhaps there are some who will say that the rain and mud of new Beaver Field saved the day for the Nittany Lion," wrote one reporter. "But the greatest factor today was the old-time fighting spirit displayed by the 11 blue-clad warriors of Penn State...For once, the goddess of chance did not go back on Penn State and there was no unfortunate Lion fumble to pave the way to defeat."

Bezdek kept the same starting lineup for the game the following Saturday in Morgantown, although Helbig was hobbled by an injury during a midweek scrimmage. State had been invited the previous fall to dedicate West Virginia's new Mountaineer Stadium and the 50-man State Marching Band also was there among the largest crowd to ever see a football game in that state. The teams had played regularly at Beaver Field from 1904-1909 with State winning each game but they had tied 13-13 the last time the teams had met in 1923 at Yankee Stadium. This time West Virginia was favored.

State got its big break on the opening kickoff by recovering West Virginia's fumble at the Mountaineers 10-yard line. But State got only one yard in three plays and instead of trying a field goal punted out of bounds at the WVC 5-yard line. The Mountaineers punted immediately but ball only went two yards and out of bounds at the seven. Three running plays went nowhere and on fourth down Weston tried a field goal from the 17 but the attempt was blocked and WVC recovered at the 30. But WVC couldn't move either and punted to State's 34-yard line. State was on the attack again. With a 19-yard run by Michalske leading the way, State drove to the Mountaineer 14-yard line before losing the ball on downs. From that point on it was all West Virginia. In the second quarter, a blocked kick set up a 33-yard drive for a TD and a 7-0 lead. In the fourth quarter, the Mountaineers drove 69 yards after holding State on a fourth down play and scored another TD on a surprise lateral pass play from the 13-yard line. The final was 14-0 but it was Michalske who got the most praise after the game. "Michalske's play, both defensively and on the offense, was as strong an exhibition as has been seen this fall...," wrote Chester Smith, Sporting Editor of the *Pittsburgh Gazette-Times*.

Now it was three straight games without scoring and arch rival Pitt, with a strong 7-1-1 record—and another team with a new stadium—was up next on Thanksgiving Day. Helbig's injury forced him to the bench and Bezdek promoted Lungren, who had not started since the opening game. The coach also substituted Roepke for Pritchard at left half to get more speed into his lineup. Again, Bezdek had scheduled a "tune-up"—this time with an alumni team—on the Saturday before Thanksgiving to try out some techniques to use against the Panthers. But the alumni game was canceled when not enough ex-players could get away from their jobs.

Pitt was such a heavy favorite that the *Pittsburgh Post* reported "Penn State supporters are asking odds of three and four to one, and even they are loath to invest very heavily." Might as well enjoy and party, they all must have felt. On Thanksgiving eve, fans, students and alumni gathered at the Pittsburgh Chamber of Commerce auditorium for the "annual smoker." The team, which never attended these events before a game, also showed up, as did State's military band, varsity singing quartet, the Thespian Orchestra and Thespian entertainers. Good old Pop Golden, who helped develop the football program years before, was the master of ceremonies and KDKA, the first radio station in the country, broadcast the affair nationwide from 10:30-to-midnight.

State's team appeared to be more relaxed than usual when the Panthers kicked off in perfect November weather on a dry field before a crowd estimated at 45,000-to-50,000 at the new Pitt Stadium. On the first play from scrimmage, Michalske passed to Weston for 22 yards but a penalty stopped the momentum and the teams exchanged punts twice before State got the ball on it's own 27-yard line. Then it happened again! On the first play, Roepke couldn't handle Gray's poor snap and fumbled. Pitt tackle Andy Salata picked up the ball and ran 25-yards for a touchdown. Gustafson's PAT made it 7-0. Pitt got the ball again on the kickoff, and, starting from it's own 27-yard line drove quickly to State's 28-yard line from where Gustafson booted a 27-yard field goal. State took the kickoff next (as the rules mandated) and with a Michalske to Weston pass picking up 37 yards, State moved to Pitt's 29-yard line. On fourth down, Weston dropped back to attempt a field goal with Lungren holding. But it was a fake! Lungren passed to Roekpe who was wide open at the 10 and easily scored. Weston made the extra point. Early in the second quarter, Pitt marched 70 yards for another TD, this one by Gustafson, and Pitt led, 17-7. Just before the half, the worst thing that could happen to State did—Iron Mike was hurt trying to make a tackle and was helped off the field. He didn't return until late in the game and by that time it was too late. Early in the third quarter, Pitt sophomore Gibby Welch made the play-of-the-game with a spectacular 81-yard run that made the score 23-7. But the determined State team wasn't through. Near the end of the quarter the Lions drove 60-yards after Bergman's pass interception but Pitt's defense stopped State at the goal line on a fourth-and-inches play. (A photograph in the *Pittsburgh Gazette-Times* the next day appeared to show a touchdown but the referees ruled otherwise.) State was back at the start of the fourth quarter after a Pitt punt from behind the goal squirted out of bounds at the Pitt six. Two runs and a pass gained only one yard and on fourth-and-goal another Lungren pass attempt to Watson was batted down. Most of the last quarter was played in Pitt territory as the Panther defense continued to stop Lion offensive thrusts and Pitt won, 23-7.

It's doubtful that the outcome would have been different even if Iron Mike had played the second half and Bezdek probably knew it. "It was (our) best game of the season," Bezdek said afterwards, "...and the boys looked as good today as they did in 1919...We had a couple of bad breaks go against us...I am proud of our boys."

Sportswriters covering the game praised the performance of State. "A reincarnation of the powerful Penn State elevens which roam now only in the shifting shadows of memory, was outscored, but not outplayed, by the Pittsburgh Panthers...," wrote Chester Smith. But once again, the influential Pittsburgh area alumni were not pleased. They and other State supporters were wondering if Bezdek had lost his edge. His constant lineup changes were becoming the norm rather than the exception and some people were seriously questioning his judgment and his use of talent. Wasn't Iron Mike a good example? Some alumni also had joined prominent educators in wondering if State

and other colleges were emphasizing athletics too much, especially football. But as long as football made a profit and helped finance general physical education programs as well as athletic teams, there didn't appear to be any danger for Bezdek, (The football team made the only profit for the year and the $50,000 paid for heavy losses in track, baseball and basketball while also contributing $15,000 toward the funding of a new, but unbuilt, gymnasium.) The schedule, which had been set before this year's Pitt game, would be a little easier next year with five major games instead of six. This had been Bezdek's worst record yet. He didn't expect it would ever get worse. It did—but not right away.

Season Record 4-4-1
Record to Date 197-99-22
Winning percentage .654

"'Work Them Harder'"

After his record of the last four years, Bezdek had lost some of his esteem as a head coach. But he was still highly-respected nationally and many sportswriters believed it was only a matter of time when he would return State to the elite of college football.

"Victory does not come first with Bez," wrote Stoney McLinn for the *Philadelphia Public Ledger* one day in the Fall of 1926. "He is an idealist. He wants to have a part in graduating men from Penn State by developing the strength of body and sportsmanship that may be learned in intercollegiate games."

That philosophy seemed to fit in with the nationwide evaluation of college football now underway by the Carnegie Foundation for the Advancement of Teaching and a similar internal examination of State's football program by State officials and alumni. But Bezdek did not like the way the State appraisal was being handled and believed it was personally aimed at him.

However, many within the Penn State football family believed winning was important and Bezdek's ability to win was being questioned more and more. Much of the criticism was coming from former players and alumni who were helping to recruit players. The Pittsburgh area contingent had just about given up on Bezdek and few Western Pennsylvania scholastic players of any merit were now entering State. Philadelphia was now supplying many of State's players, thanks to the recruiting efforts of Charlie Hildebrand, who helped George Linz start football at State in 1887. Big Ed Yeckley, a star in early 1900's, was shipping in Blue Chip youngsters from Ohio and alumni in the New York and New Jersey area were also coming up with their share of gems.

As most of Bezdek's critics saw it, he simply didn't know how to utilize the good players he had. His frequent lineup changes were symptomatic of his ineptness, they thought. His idea of coaching was more physical than cerebral and the end result was a team that made a lot of mistakes and misjudgments on the field. "Work them harder," appeared to be his by-word when displeased and that certainly was true in the early part of the 1926 season.

Although he was openly pessimistic about 1926 because he had to rebuild his starting line, he had a good nucleus of veterans

The assistants on Hugo Bezdek's coaching staff in 1926 were all former players, (left to right): Newsh Bentz, Larry Conover, Bezdek, Dutch Herman and Bas Gray. The next year Conover would also broadcast the first State game on radio.

returning and some highly-touted sophomores when he opened practice Sept. 1. He also had the help of two former star linemen, Larry Conover and Newsh Bentz, who had become his top assistants on the varsity. But injuries in the pre-season plus ineligibility of a couple players hampered the team's progress. Still, Bezdek knew his first three opponents were not even close to being in State's class and that his first big game would be October 16 at Notre Dame. That was the one to point to.

When the team lined up against Susquehanna in the opener at Beaver Field Sept. 25, six of the seven starters in the line were newcomers with only Mahoney back at center. Weston, now the captain, was out indefinitely at one end as was sometimes starting end, Slamp. Filak, a two-year veteran at guard, would not be eligible until after several games. The backs were all veterans who had started some games in '25 with Lungren at quarterback, Roepke and Dangerfield at the halves and senior Greene at fullback. Roepke also was the placekicker and punter. The game was a mismatch as State ran up the third highest score of all time in an 82-0 victory, getting 34 points in the first quarter and 27 in the second. Greene scored five touchdowns and Roepke had two TDs and seven extra points. The only bad thing that happened was a injury to Dangerfield, who would miss several games.

Junior Bud Harrington took Dangerfield's spot at right half the next week against Lebanon Valley. Bezdek also made a change at right end but it had little impact on the outcome. Early in the first quarter Roepke intercepted a pass and dashed 60 yards for a TD but broke his cheekbone a few minutes later and would eventually miss several games. The offense was sluggish and State had just a 14-0 lead at the half. At the start of the third quarter, Bezdek sent in a new backfield, with Pincura at QB, sophomore Steve Hamas and junior Earl Hewitt, II, (son of the "silent man" of '99) at the halfbacks and Pritchard at fullback. Hamas scored on an 8-yard plunge near the end of the period and the Lions got two more TDs in the fourth quarter to win, 35-0.

But Bezdek was mad. "Work them, harder!" He ordered his team to stay on the field and practice. Despite the moaning and com-

plaints, they worked out for two hours. Ridge Riley described the incident in *Road to Number One*: "It was six-thirty before the players dragged themselves down to the Track House for a shower and back up the hill to Varsity Hall, where most of them fell into bed. Beginning Monday, they scrimmaged nearly every afternoon, sometimes under the lights with the 'ghost' ball."

Bezdek replaced the entire starting backfield for the game with Marietta, using Pincura, Pritchard and the two New Jersey soph halfbacks, Hamas and Allie Wolf. But it was former starter Lungren who made the play of the game with a 95-yard kickoff return for a touchdown in the second quarter, the first such runback in three years. Lungren had another TD, Pritchard had two and former starting fullback Greene also had two, including one on a 70-yard run, as Bezdek cleared his bench in a 48-6 win. The game was a milestone in State's football history for this was the 200th victory since the sport began on campus in 1887. Another milestone followed one week later when State visited South Bend for the first time.

Practice eased up only slightly for Notre Dame. The team did not scrimmage after Tuesday, practiced in the rain Wednesday and departed for South Bend Thursday afternoon. The Lions certainly were prepared for the rain that started Friday night and fell all through the game. But they weren't prepared for the unbeaten Irish. A headline in the *Pittsburgh Gazette-Times* succinctly described what happened: "Penn State Unable to Solve Notre Dame's Attack, Bows in 28-0 Defeat...Quick, Deceptive Plays of Rockne's Men Make Lions Appear Slow and Cumbersome—Superb Aerial Game Helps Irish Roll Up Big Score" This was the 100th loss in State's 39 years of football. Notre Dame was so dominant that it rolled up 461 yards from scrimmage to State's 64, and with penalties State's net loss was 39 yards. "They call 'em the Nittany Lions but these lions played like puppies," reported sportswriter James Cruisinberry, who said Rockne had so many substitutes in the game that he probably "started pulling out boys from the rooters section" of the grandstands. Later, it was disclosed that most of State's players had gotten sick on the Indiana water Friday night and spent much of the night and Saturday morning in the bathroom. Oh yes, Bezdek used a starting backfield of Lungren at QB, Greene at FB and Hamas and Harrington at the HBs.

Back in State College the following Monday, Bezdek continued his rigorous workouts. He also decided to install a new offense for the Homecoming game against Syracuse. The Orange also had lost for the first time the previous week, 27-21, to Army. The game was rated a toss-up and both teams had serious injuries. Weston, who played in his first game, was hurt again as was substitute end George Delp, Lungren and Greene. Roepke also was still on the sidelines. Okay, so who is in the starting backfield this week with the new offense? Pincura, Harrington, Dangerfield and Pritchard. As for the line, Filak was now at one tackle and the rest of the players had started most of the four games. The new offense was no better and maybe worse than the previous offense. Syracuse outplayed the Lions in a clash of defenses and won, 10-0. "The courageous defense (sic) play of Bezdek's line was all that kept the peppery York Staters from running up a high score," wrote Chilly Doyle for a Pittsburgh paper. Yet both scores were made after State mistakes. A fumble on a punt attempt in the second quarter helped set up the Orange touchdown. The Orange recovered the fumble but couldn't get past the 3-yard line. State tried to punt again but this one was short and the Orange drove 35 yards for the only TD of the game. Midway through the fourth quarter, Syracuse put a capper on the game with a 12-yard field goal after a pass interception at the 24. It was a disappointing loss and Bezdek prepared to "work them harder" on Monday. But the players had had enough.

At the Monday skull session before practice, Roepke, sophomore tackle Donn Greenshields, and Lungren led a delegation of players that confronted Bezdek. According to Ridge Riley, who disclosed the secret meeting years later, the players informed Bezdek "that practice would be omitted that day unless there were less scrimmaging, less time on the practice field and a return to the offense used prior to the Syracuse game. Bezdek capitulated, as he had before (in 1919) when the players (including his current assistant Conover) threatened revolt. A written schedule of practice sessions was set up, and all the players pledged to keep the uprising secret."

This was one of the defining moments of the season but it wouldn't be the last.

Either the players or some alumni must have talked about getting Dick Harlow back to coach. Later in the week, State officials had to deny a report that Harlow, now coaching at Western Maryland, would replace Bezdek as coach and athletic director. "Bezdek has a long contract and the report regarding Harlow is news to me," said Neil Flemming, graduate manager of athletics.

Practice was still tough that week by most standards but the players were a looser bunch. The next opponent, George Washington, was new to the schedule and State was favored at Beaver Field. Bezdek figured he would get some rest for his regulars so he started a patchwork lineup that included seven players who had seen little action, including Hewitt and Pete Houserman in the backfield with Pincura and Pritchard. State seemed to take command at the start and was driving for an apparent touchdown in the first quarter at the GW 30-yard line when there was a fumble in the backfield. GW's Harris picked up the ball and ran 70 yards for a touchdown. That was enough for Bezdek. He sent in the first team, including Lungren, Dangerfield and Greene. It was all over in the second quarter. Lungren scored twice on pass receptions of 25 and 15 yards from Dangerfield and Greene bucked over for another TD to give State a 20-6 halftime lead. Back in went the reserves and in the fourth quarter GW's quarterback Sapp intercepted a pass and ran 50 yards for a TD that made the final score of 20-12 look respectable.

Bezdek was satisfied and now prepared for the game he wanted to win almost as much as the Pitt contest set for Thanksgiving Day. Pennsylvania was back on the schedule after a one year absence and Bezdek still remembered the 0-0 tie that year and the Artelt TD run with a fumble that had been called back by a referee. Bezdek had known a lot of Penn scouts would be at the GW game, so he had intentionally stuck to his basic plays. He would show Penn a few surprises, he thought, as he worked his team out in secret during the week.

"The State team is at a turning point in the road," said the report in the *Philadelphia Public Ledger*. "A victory means a successful campaign but a defeat will add to the two disappointments already suffered..."

Penn was still reeling from a surprising 3-0 loss to Illinois that had stopped its winning streak at five but was still favored when the Lions invaded Franklin Field on November 6. Some 15,000 State fans, including celebrity musician Fred Waring, were among the 55,000-to-65,000 who watched as Roepke and Weston returned to the starting lineup for the first time in weeks. Hometown boy Lungren was at quarterback with Hamas at the other half and Greene back at fullback.

The game turned on three plays, one for both teams in the first quarter and the other for State in the second. Midway through the opening period, the Lions got the ball on their own 30-yard line after a punt. On the first play, Roepke passed to Lungren, who had an open field ahead of him. Lungren caught the ball and started running but slipped and was tackled after a 16-yard gain. State couldn't move further and had to punt. After the teams exchanged punts, Penn got the ball at State's 35-yard line. The Quakers got five yards in three plays and on fourth down, Penn's halfback Paul Scholl stood on his 40-yard line and dropkicked a perfect field goal for a 3-0 lead.

Following the kickoff the teams traded possession again until Mahoney intercepted a pass at State's 47-yard line. On third down, Roepke threw a pass which was caught for a 28-yard gain by Lungren after bouncing off another State player's fingers. That got the ball to the 24. Three plays later it was first-and-goal at the Penn six. Greene bucked for two yards, then two more. Then he bucked to the one. The players conferred in a makeshift huddle. Everyone expected Greene to run the ball again. That's what Lungren felt the Penn players thought, too. So, he called a play that would be a surprise. Roepke got the ball instead of Greene and stepped back a couple of yards, preparing to pass. Lungren was open on one side of the line and Delp on the other. Roepke hurried the pass, perhaps because of an onrushing lineman. There are two versions of what happened, sportswriters covering the game did not agree in what they later wrote. Either the ball sailed over the head of Delp or it fell short at the feet of Lungren. No matter. The pass failed and the threat was over. Later in the period, Roepke would also try placekicking a 40-yard field goal from an angle but the kick would barely miss the south goal post. Penn's Scholl also tried and missed two other field goals from the 35- and 48-yard lines but neither team really came close to scoring again. Penn won and many sportswriters blamed State's defeat on the play calling of Lungren, who was replaced by Pincura for much of the second half. Penn gained 213 yards and 11 first downs to State's 145 yards and five first downs but Scholl's kick was the difference—and another defining moment for the season.

With the disappointing loss, a winning season would depend on at least one victory in the last two games against Bucknell and Pitt. Bucknell, the first ever State opponent, was back on the schedule after a seven year absence. The Bisons did not play the caliber of teams as State did but included in its 3-3-1 record was a 13-0 win over George Washington. Bezdek could not afford to lose this game and he knew it. He made another shift in his backfield, partly out of necessity when Greene turned up lame after the Penn game. Bezdek placed Pritchard at fullback and moved Lungren to right half with Pincura at quarterback and Roepke at left half. He figured this gave him the most speed and offensive power since all of them could run, pass and kick. However, the offense was sluggish, perhaps because of the slippery field. Except for Roepke and Pritchard, the backs didn't do much. Bucknell got past midfield just twice, once to State's 30-yard line, as the Lions won, 9-0. Roepke's 35-yard run immediately following the recovery of a Bucknell fumble in the second quarter set up Pritchard's one-yard touchdown plunge and Roepke kicked a 34-yard field goal in the third period to complete the scoring. Roepke also missed field goal attempts of 45, 35 and 20 and Pritchard failed in field goal tries from the 40 and 45.

Bezdek gave the team Monday off, which certainly must have shocked everyone who thought Bez had no heart. But practice resumed Tuesday with the same intensity of old. Pitt was having a similar mediocre year, with a 3-2-2 record and an underperforming offense. Still, the Panthers were favored when 50,000 jammed Pitt Stadium on Thanksgiving Day. The game had been dedicated to the great college football pioneer and sportswriter, Walter Camp, who had died in 1925, and part of the proceeds was to be sent to the "Walter Camp Memorial Fund" at Yale.

The outcome of the game was probably determined by what happened in the opening moments. Pincura ran back the opening kickoff 29 yards to State's 39-yard line. On the first play, Roepke threw a short pass over the center to Delp, who broke through a gang of Pitt linemen who seemed to have him in their grasp and dashed all the way into the end zone. The State fans erupted with all the hoopla one might expect until they saw the referee's signal. He ruled that Delp's knee had touched at the 50. No touchdown. First Down. But with two more passes for first downs and a nifty run by Lungren on a triple pass, State quickly moved the ball to Pitt's 6-yard line, and Pitt took a time out. Pitt had scouted every game State played that season and they must have talked about State's surprising passing offense on the sideline. It didn't matter. State tried three running plays into the Pitt line and gained three yards. Roepke went back to attempt a field goal but it was a fake. He threw the ball to Delp, who was wide open at the goal line. Delp dropped the ball! Pitt took over and immediately punted, and State had the ball again on the Pitt 23. But State couldn't move further, tried another fake kick that failed and Pitt had the ball again.

The State threat ended but the Lions didn't give up. As sportswriters reported, the Lions gave it their all in the first half. That's also when Pitt's Gibby Welch made the play of the game. After Pitt had run back a State punt to the Pitt 45-yard line midway in the Second Quarter, Welch went around right end 55 yards for a touchdown, and with the PAT Pitt led, 7-0. Before the half ended, State was near the Pitt goal twice and scored once on a Roepke one-yard run for a TD, but Roepke's PAT attempt failed and it was 7-6 at the intermission.. "The Nittany Lions seemed to give everything they had in the first half...," wrote James Murray for the *Pittsburgh Post*, "...(and) the Panthers raced to victory in the second (half)..." State's passing attack kept Pitt on the defensive for most of the third quarter but neither team scored. In the fourth quarter, State's passing fell apart as the Panthers made three interceptions to set up 17 points. Early in the period, Pitt intercepted a Roepke aerial at midfield and drove downfield to kick an 18-yard field goal. The next two times State had the ball, Pitt intercepted passes in State territory and scored TDs, including one on a 35-yard run by Welch, and the Panthers won, 24-6.

Within a week after the Pitt defeat, newspapers reported that Bezdek might be leaving State for the head coaching job at Boston College, Rutgers or Northwestern. Another report had Bezdek finishing one more year before being replaced in 1928 by Lafayette's Herb Mc-Cracken, who ran a three-week course for coaches on the State campus during the summer. The rumors were not triggered simply by the usual complaints of the Pittsburgh alumni. Word also may have been filtering out about the negative results of the administration's evaluation of football. That was due to be released in early 1927.

Bezdek could easily blame the poor results of 1926 on injuries, which plagued his team all year. But the questions about his coaching competency were still there, no matter what some of his sportswriting friends said.

Season Record 5-4
Record to Date 202-103-22
Winning percentage .651

"Roping In Bezdek"

Bezdek could not believe it was happening again. The players were making demands once more. Ease the practices. Fewer scrimmages. Pass more during the games.

They had surrounded him in the dining hall of Varsity Hall after the unexpected loss to Bucknell in the third game. The entire varsity was there, challenging him, yelling and screaming at him to change—blaming him for wearing them out in practice and for a conservative offensive game plan that allowed Bucknell to win. Bucknell, of all teams! Hadn't beaten State since 1896, they shouted, and, you, Bez let it happen.

Okay, Bezdek said, you get one week. We'll cut back on the hard practice sessions this week and open up against Penn next Saturday. We win and the new routine stays. We lose and its back to my way, boys. Agreed? You got it Bez, they said.

Word of this latest players revolt remained a secret for nearly three weeks. Then Pittsburgh alumni, long disenchanted with Bezdek, leaked tidbits about the rebellion to some sportswriters. By that time, the team had not only beaten previously-undefeated Penn thoroughly, but also had upset another unbeaten powerhouse, Syracuse, and the anti-Bezdek faction was saying the players were running the team, not the head coach.

Certainly, with such a strong personality and large ego, Bezdek would never allow the players to take control. Compromise, sure. Particularly these days. But he was still in charge, no matter what anyone said. He certainly was under siege and it was more involved than just winning football games. Penn State had decided to de-emphasize athletics—all sports teams—not just football and the restrictions already were "tying his hands."

Three weeks before practice, the newly created Board of Athletic Control established an immediate policy not to "scout opponents' games regardless of the scouting policies of opponents." That wasn't the worst, as the board also eliminated all athletic scholarships, effective with the 1928-29 academic year. Bezdek knew that meant the end of big time football at State. If he wanted to continue coaching college football at the highest level, he would have to move on in a couple of years. Or, if State went through with a proposal to create a separate department of physical education, he could give up coaching altogether and perhaps stay on campus to run that new department.

The Board's edict had been another jolt in a year that had not gone well from the start. After dismissing the rumors at the end of last season about other coaching jobs, Bezdek suddenly developed an infection in his leg in February, on the eve of spring practice. The infection was so serious that he was forced not only to miss practice but to

The 1927 team managed a 6-2-1 record despite the school's decision to de-emphasize athletics. Captain Johnny Roepke, who was named to Grantland Rice's All-American team, is in the center of the first row holding the ball.

stay home for nearly six months and he had spent part of July and August in Atlantic City utilizing the salt water to help him recover.

Thus, Bezdek was not in a very good mood when 50 players reported for practice on September 1. Perhaps that is why he seemed to work them harder than in past years. He had a veteran team back and without any more incoming freshmen, he knew this year or next would probably be his last good team. Of course, if the frosh were anything like last year's crop, it might not matter. That team had been the worst freshman squad in history, not only losing all five games but getting just one touchdown all year, and that on a fumble recovery.

After a couple weeks of workouts, Bezdek could only see one sophomore breaking into a veteran starting lineup, Joe Miller at half-back. Captain Johnny Roepke would be the other half with Pincura at quarterback and Hamas at fullback. The ends would be Delp, Slamp or Al Lesko, with Greenshields and Joe Krall at the tackles, Red Darragh and Hal Hastings at the guards and Mahoney—one of the best defensive linemen in the East—at center. Of course, as the season wore on several sophs would eventually start primarily because of injuries, including interior linemen Marty McAndrew, Ralph "Dutch" Ricker, T. S. "Toots" Panaccion and Jack Martin. In fact, because of injuries, McAndrew, Ricker and Panaccion started in the opener against Lebanon Valley September 23 and, in the backfield, Wolff replaced the injured Miller.

Once again the schedule was a tough one that was front loaded with a couple of easier opponents. Lafayette was back for the first time in 11 years and New York University was on the schedule for the first time. Both had been unbeaten and among the best teams in the country in '26. State and Notre Dame also had agreed to play another game but a scheduling conflict forced the Irish to slate the game in 1928.

A fine passing attack helped State overcome a good defensive effort by a stubborn Lebanon Valley team in the Beaver Field opener. State hit on 11 of 16 passes for 233 yards and three touchdowns with Roepke scoring on a 35-yard screen pass in the first quarter for the first TD. But State led by just 7-0 at the half and needed a 13 point spurt in the final period to put the game away. That's when second team backs scored, Dangerfield on a 20-yard reception and Lungren on a 40-yard screen pass. There was another little quirk to this game

and the next one with Gettysburg. In both contests, State's players wore scarlet colored jerseys instead of their traditional blue and white because the Lebanon Valley and Gettysburg uniforms were too similar to State's normal colors.

Before that next game with Gettysburg, State also announced it would broadcast the rest of the team's home games and the Friday night pep rallies over the campus radio station, WPSC. Assistant coach Larry Conover would describe the game from a location "on top of the New Beaver Field stands."

The State fans listening to the Gettysburg game the next week heard Conover rave about Roepke. The Lion captain scored 28 points on four touchdowns and four extra points in the intense heat of a Dad's Day crowd of 4,000. Roepke also had kickoff returns of 25, 40 and 60 yards. State continued its aerial bombardment by completing 19 of 23 passes, including nine-for-nine in the first half when State took a 21-6 lead. State won, 34-13, with Gettysburg scoring both TDs after recovering State's fumbled punts.

With all that passing, one was unlikely to call the Bezdek attack conservative. But he had ordered the backs not to pass within State's own 40-yard line and the players believed that would make it easier for opponents to defend against. Bucknell's scouts must have spotted some flaw in both the offense and defense, for coach Carl Snavely's visitors stymied the Lions from the opening kickoff. Bucknell was a veteran club but its captain and leader, fullback Walter Diehl, had a slight leg fracture and did not start. Pincura also was out after aggravating an old arm injury and Bezdek gave Dangerfield the start at quarterback instead of Lungren. Bucknell scored in the opening moments by marching downfield after the kickoff. Its defense stopped one State drive in the second quarter on an intercepted pass, and another intercepted pass almost gave Bucknell a second TD. "When my boys found they had an attack that would score and a defense that could stop State, they played great football, " Snavely later told Stoney McLinn of the *Philadelphia Public Ledger*. But State took the second half kickoff and marched 65 yards to tie the score on Hamas' run and Roepke's PAT. That's when Snavely put Diehl back into the game to give his team a spark. He apparently did, for the Bisons seemed to become more aggressive on both offense and defense and in the fourth quarter, Bucknell quarterback Quinn ran around right end, reversed his field and dodging several tacklers in the secondary dashed 45 yards for a TD. The extra point failed but Bucknell's defense held on for the 13-7 victory.

A month later, a newspaper story out of Lewisburg had Bucknell players praising the State team for its sportsmanship in what was obviously a devastating defeat. According to Bucknell, the State players knew that with Diehl in the game, Bucknell's offense would be extremely better, and they could have forced Diehl out of the game by tackling his injured ankle. But, said Bucknell, State intentionally avoided hurting him. The first time Diehl was tackled, a State player reportedly said: "Don't worry, Wally, we'll be careful of your bad ankle." And apparently they were. The newspaper story concluded: "Whether or not Penn State's fine sportsmanship cost them a victory is hard to say, assert Bucknellians, but if it did the loss was not commensurable with the gift it made to American football."

Such sportsmanship was not unknown during this era. In fact, State's next opponent, Penn, had agreed not to scout any State games because of State's new athletic policy forbidding scouting. After the Bucknell loss, sportswriters gave little chance to the Lions against the 3-0 Quakers. Pincura was still sidelined with an injury, so Bezdek started Lungren at QB. Lungren decided to call his own plays and Bezdek must have gulped midway in the first quarter when the one-time Philadelphia schoolboy star startled the record crowd of 65,000 at Franklin Field with a daring play. A Roepke fumble had given Penn the ball at its own 40-yard line but the Quakers could not make a first down and downed a punt on the 1-yard line. On the first play, Roepke went deep into the end zone as if to punt. Instead, he hit Lungren on a short pass and the quarterback sped all the way to State's 32-yard line. That may have been the key play of the game, not only because it set the tone for the Lions offense that day but also because the Penn quarterback, John Shober, was injured and was sidelined the rest of the day. Shober's substitute Paul Murphy was responsible for most of the six Penn fumbles which disrupted the Quaker offense and set up State's touchdowns. In the second quarter, Penn also lost its starting left halfback, Scull, who had beaten State with his foot in '26.

But Shober and Scull might not have made a difference anyway, for it was State's uptempo passing attack that carried the day. Lungren's play calling had Roepke throwing passes from all over the field and the successful passing also opened up the running lanes for Roepke, Lungren, Wolff and Hamas. Neither team had a serious threat in the first half. But State took the opening second half kickoff and quickly went 80 yards, primarily on a 32-yard end run by Roepke and a 46-yard dash around the other end by Lungren. Hamas bulled one-yard into the end zone for the touchdown but Roepke missed the placement. Penn roared back into State territory but a fumble at the 30-yard line and a 15-yard penalty at the 3-yard line stopped potential scores.

As the third quarter was winding down, Murphy fumbled a punt at Penn's 43-yard line and Hamas recovered. Roepke passed to Lesko for 15 yards and when the fourth quarter started, State had the ball at the Penn 15. But the Quaker defense stiffened and Roepke tried a field goal from the 25-yard line. With the goal posts now 10 yards back from the goal line this year because of a rules change, the kick failed and Penn took over at the 20. On the next play Murphy fumbled again and Hamas recovered again at the 21. On first down Roepke passed to Lesko at the 10-yard line and the big end scooted into the end zone for a touchdown. Roepke booted the extra point and the 75-piece State Marching Band blasted away. The band was still playing when Mahoney kicked off. Murphy got the ball on the 10-yard line and ran upfield to about the 35 when he fumbled!!! Delp picked up the ball and ran to Penn's 20. Four plays later, Roepke bolted over from the two, kicked the extra point and State led, 20-0. The Lions almost scored again minutes later but lost the ball at the Penn 16 and the game ended.

"Nittany Team's Daring Use of Air From First Whistle Figures Largely in Victory," said the headline in one Philadelphia newspaper. State had completed 11 of 24 passes, mostly by Roepke, for 201 yards with just two interceptions. The Lions also had 169 yards rushing and 13 first downs.

As Bezdek had promised, the new practice routine was now set. He still worked them hard but the workouts were less intense and scrimmages were held to a minimum. "First-Stringers Left Off With Light Signal Drill After Defeat of Penn," said the article in Tuesday's *Philadelphia Inquirer*. The team left Thursday afternoon for Syracuse, which also was undefeated after upsetting Georgetown the previous Saturday.

State had never beaten Syracuse since the teams started playing in 1922, nor had the Lions scored a touchdown in the four losses and one tie. Roepke has been battered during the Penn game and Bezdek started the sophomore Miller in his place. Syracuse's star running back and captain, Ray Barbuti, also was out because of an injury in the Georgetown game. Syracuse intercepted two pass attempts by Wolff in the first quarter and the second interception led to a 17-yard touchdown run by Sammy Sebo. The PAT failed. Late in the half, Bezdek made his biggest on-field decision of the year. He inserted Roepke back into the lineup.

Despite Roepke's running and passing, Syracuse continued to hold a 6-0 lead until late in the third quarter. State then drove 66 yards for the tying score early in the final period, with the big play being a dazzling 20-yard fourth down pass off a fake field goal. Roepke, the kicker, took the snap, threw a short pass to Hamas who then lateralled to Delp. Delp ran down the sidelines and almost had the TD but stepped out of bounds at the 15-yard line. Lungren swept around end on a fake double pass for the final 9 yards and the TD. Roepke missed the PAT and the score was tied. State got the ball back minutes later when Lungren intercepted a pass to stop a Syracuse drive at the State 20-yard line and ran it back 16 yards. Using the clock, the Lions drove determinedly downfield, helped by a fourth down penalty for roughing the punter that gave State new life at midfield. In 17 plays, State moved to the 9-yard line, where on fourth-and-8, Roepke, with Lungren holding, booted a 21-yard field goal that cleared the uprights by several yards. But the game was far from over. As the 25,000 stunned fans looked on at Archbold Stadium, Syracuse's Jonah Goldman almost ran back the kickoff for a touchdown and was nearly in the clear at the 50 when he was tackled by—of course—Roepke. Relying solely on short passes as time was running out, Syracuse drove to State's 12-yard line where the game ended before the Orange could attempt a tying field goal.

State's upsets over Penn and Syracuse on the road had surprised the Eastern sportswriters who had given up on the team after the Bucknell loss. The writers were even more impressed after the Lions clobbered another strong once-beaten team, Lafayette, 40-6, in the annual Homecoming game at Beaver Field. Roepke scored four touchdowns, kicked three extra points and electrified the alumni with his passing, running and kicking. "Tonight, on the streets of State College, they are calling the captain an All American," wrote Stan Baumgartner for the *Philadelphia Inquirer*. "Roepke was a combination of a gazelle, a kangaroo, an intercollegiate broadjumper," "170 pounds of upholstered springs and padded T.N.T."

For the first time ever, State was playing three of its last four games at home. George Washington was next in the Pennsylvania Day game and, as he had done last year against GW, Bezdek again started the second team. This time he let them play the entire first half and the game was scoreless. The first team was inserted in the third quarter and, despite the regulars' listless play, it scored 13 points that period to win, 13-0. Roepke ran 21 yards for a touchdown and Hamas got the other on a 1-yard plunge following Lesko's blocked kick and recovery.

State was again the underdog in the final home game against New York University. The Chuck Meehan coached team was unbeaten and had lost just once in two years. It was the best game on Beaver Field in years with both teams at their peak and making few mistakes. One of NYU's errors early in the first quarter set up State's first touchdown. A bad snap by the center was recovered by Mahoney at NYU's 8-yard line and Roepke ran for a touchdown on the next play, then booted the PAT for the 7-0 lead. NYU tied the game in the second quarter. After being stopped once at State's 3-yard line, this visitors took advantage of a short punt and 19-yard run back to score on a 10-yard run. Ken Strong booted the PAT. Lungren ran back the ensuing kickoff 28 yards but was injured on the tackle and left the game, never to return. State quickly drove for a touchdown with Wolff going the last 20 yards. Roepke missed the extra point and State led at the half, 13-6.

Late in the third quarter, NYU marched 70 yards for a touchdown, with Strong going over from the one-inch line. But Strong then flubbed the extra point kick which could have put NYU ahead. As the teams battled in the fourth quarter, a tie looked inevitable. Then, NYU intercepted a Roepke pass at the State 28-yard line. A sub NYU back ran to the 10-yard line but the play was called back. NYU was penalized 15 yards for holding and the threat ended. With less than two minutes left in the game, State got the ball on its own 45-yard line and on the first play Roepke darted 47 yards. It was now first-and-goal at the 8-yard line. A victory was in sight. But three plays went nowhere and when Roepke tried a field goal, the hard charging NYU line raised up to block it. Moments later the game was over.

The 13-13 tie did not diminish Bezdek's team in the minds of the sportswriters and college football fans. Even though Pitt was unbeaten and apparently headed for the Rose Bowl, State was only a slight underdog for the annual Thanksgiving Day clash. If Roepke and his teammates played as well as they have against Penn, Syracuse and NYU, they could win, some said. Pitt, with only a scoreless tie with W&J marring its 7-0-1 record, was still awaiting an official invitation to play Pop Warner's Stanford team in the Rose Bowl. On the morning of the game, a Pittsburgh newspaper reported that the Rose Bowl invite depended upon beating State and hinted that State also was being considered. "'Contingent' Telegram Likely to Spur Both Teams to Spectacular," the newspaper headline said. "Unofficial Communication Reveals Panthers Must Win to Offset State's Startling Comeback."

What everyone apparently overlooked was Pitt's track record for scouting every State game. Without any scouting, Bezdek's team was at a distinct disadvantage. Nearly 60,000 people at Pitt Stadium and another few thousand listening to the game on KDKA radio were shocked by what happened. Pitt ran up the biggest score in 11 years with an easy 30-0 victory. Playing without the injured Lungren, State

never got past the Pitt 39-yard line. Roepke was stopped cold but the defense had made a game out of it and State had trailed by just 9-0 at the half. Pitt "demoralized" State, wrote *Pittsburgh Post-Gazette* sportswriter Jack Sell, as the Panthers "rode roughshod through the line, raced around the ends and passed over the head of the visitors, a smashing triumph which startled the entire country with its decisiveness."

A week later, Roepke was named to Grantland Rice's 35-man All-American team but Pitt's Gibby Welch beat him out for the First Team. Roepke also finished as the fourth highest scorer in the East with 89 points on 12 touchdowns (one less than the school record), 1 PAT and 14 Field Goals.

Of course, the way the team lost at Pittsburgh intensified the criticism of Bezdek, and not just from the Pittsburgh area alumni. All the plaudits and prestige that had come Bezdek's way with the post-Bucknell comeback had vanished in the aftermath of the thrashing by Pitt. He could recoup some of the respect with another good season in '28. But without any more scholarship players and a continuance of the no-scouting policy, Bezdek must have realized it would become even more difficult to win in the future—and it was.

Season Record 6-2-1
Record to Date 208-105-23
Winning percentage .653

"Score Less & Scoreless"

It is ironic that Penn State's most traditional opponent, Bucknell, would be so pivotal to the decline of Nittany Lion football and the end of State's first golden era.

The 1927 game, which triggered State's energizing comeback for the season, had been only the sixth with Bucknell since the bitter game of 1900 when the Bucknell players had stomped off the field before the game was over in protest of a referee's decision and State was awarded a forfeit. From that juncture, the two teams had gone in different directions in the college football world, with State becoming a nationally known power and Bucknell playing competitively at a lower level. The hiring of the well-regarded prep school coach, Carl Snavely, from the Bellefonte Academy had signaled a change in Bucknell's philosophy, and in 1929 Bucknell would be cited, along with State, by the Carnegie report as one of the many schools that overemphasized athletics.

Thus, when the 1928 game was played at Beaver Field on October 13, Bucknell was a much better team than most sportswriters and football fans realized. What happened in the closing seconds of that game not only defined the season but also epitomized why Bezdek's teams had fallen so far from the pinnacle of success in the early 20s.

With just seven lettermen returning from '27, Bezdek wanted to get an early start on training. So, shortly after his return from a Chicago hospital where he had been treated for a recurrence of his leg infection, he called for "winter practice." On February 15, all linemen candidates who were not playing other sports reported to the stock pavilion on the west side of campus for indoor training. The backs

During winter practice of 1928 the players practiced the "Charleston" dance to supposedly help their agility. Practices were normally held inside the Agriculture Department's Bull Ring (left of players). The building is now known as the Pavillion and stage plays are held in the old Bull Ring.

would not be required until the weather permitted workouts outside as part of the normal spring practice. Bezdek, who was still the baseball coach, also had invited his pitchers and catchers to participate in the pavilion drills. "...the men will be confined to the tanbark floor of the stock pavilion," said a story in the *Philadelphia Inquirer*. "The arena is large enough to permit line drill and individual instruction for small groups, but will not accommodate more than a few candidates at one time."

Another item appearing the newspapers that day which would eventually have a profound affect on Penn State football. The Lions' two-time All-American end, Bob Higgins, had resigned after three years as head coach of Washington University in St. Louis without giving a reason for his departure. A month later, Higgins joined Bezdek's coaching staff.

Bezdek had declared that "every position was open" in '28 but he was more concerned about his backfield than his line because fullback Hamas was the only full-time backfield starter returning. Hamas's New Jersey buddy, Wolff, also was back as was Miller, who had not lettered while playing mostly at halfback. The line was led by captain Donn Greenshields, who had been a starting tackle since the first game of his sophomore year. Panaccion, the other starting tackle from '26, also was back as were the guards, Ricker and Martin, and Delp at one end. McAndrews, who had not lettered, eventually would share center with another junior, Herb Eschbach, and junior Skip Stahley would be at another end. Bezdek did not have many experienced backups and was counting on the sophomores, his last class of scholarship players, to develop quickly, particularly in the backfield.

Despite the scarcity of talent and the continuing pressure from alumni, the 43-year old Bezdek was looking forward to this season. In December, he had become a naturalized U.S. citizen and he was now president-elect of the National Association of College Football Coaches. He told sportswriters he could at least break even and, with some luck, could be good. "Bez does not expect a world-beating eleven," opined Jesse Carver for the *Pittsburgh Sun-Telegraph*, "nor does he anticipate a season filled with disappointments." Bezdek certainly didn't expect to lose his captain for the season.

Greenshields reported a few days late for preseason practice because he was still suffering from the effects of a tonsillectomy. Then on September 15 he was rushed to State College Hospital with pneumonia. He was in the hospital for weeks and by mid-October he dropped out of school and returned to his home in Ohio. As a sophomore, Greenshields had been one of the leaders to confront Bezdek about his harsh practices. His illness and subsequent absence had a debilitating psychological affect on the team—an overall defining moment of the season.

There would be no player revolts this year. Bezdek was back to his old ways. "Work them harder." The players continued to complain but there was no consensus, no strong leader without Greenshields, and perhaps, because they were mostly inexperienced, Bezdek convinced them that they had to work hard to win.

The tough schedule was almost the same as last year with only NYU missing, replaced by Notre Dame in a game set for Franklin Field in Philadelphia on November 3. Syracuse would be the Homecoming foe and the Lafayette game would be played in Easton for the first time since 1915. Many State fans also had been pressing for the season-ending Pitt game to be switched every other year to Philadelphia, where they felt the environment would be less hostile than in Pittsburgh, but Pitt officials would not change the contract.

When the team opened the season against Lebanon Valley on September 29, sophomore Cal Shawley of State College was at Greenshields' old tackle slot with another soph, Frank "Yutz" Diedrich, at left half. Miller had been shifted back to start at quarterback and Wolff was the other halfback. Delp was the acting captain and place-kicker. Sportswriters noted that it was a fast but light team. It also was a running team. Bezdek didn't feel he had the material that could utilize a passing attack. He also had a major weakness in the kicking game for there didn't seem to be anyone around who could kick points or punt for distance consistently.

The Lions did very little passing in wiping out Lebanon Valley, 25-0, but the visitors gave them a harder game than expected. Wolff scored two TDs and Diedrich made the play of the day on a 51-yard TD run. Miller ran back a kickoff 70 yards to set up another score. Delp made just one of four extra point attempts and tried no field goals.

State was fortunate to get by Gettysburg the next week. "Although outplayed and outfought by a veteran Gettysburg eleven for most of the game," said a newspaper report of the game, "Penn State ground out a 12-0 victory here today." Gettysburg lost five fumbles and had one pass intercepted at the goal line. Diedrich got a touchdown on a one-yard run in the second quarter at the conclusion of a hard-earned 45-yard drive and State nursed the 6-0 lead well into the fourth quarter. The Lions, who were outgained, didn't seal the game until Stahley picked up a fumble and ran 32 yards for a TD.

Bezdek worked his team harder after the Gettysburg game, with a couple of long scrimmages and extra running and hitting drills. Delp was out because of an injury in the Gettysburg game, and Bezdek also replaced Miller at quarterback with sophomore Cooper French, younger brother of the one-time Rutgers and Army star, Walter, now playing center field with the Philadelphia Athletics. French had been the quarterback of the freshman team and was believed to be the best field general on the varsity but Bezdek did not have full confidence in him. He needed more experience in the "big games," Bezdek told sportswriters.

Bucknell was "a big game" but not even Bezdek believed the Bisons compared to Penn, Notre Dame or Pitt. But Bucknell had 10 veterans returning from the team that upset State in '28, and led by captain and fullback Ed Halicki the Bisons already had won three in a row. Bezdek warned his team of what happened last year and they came out before the crowd of 12,000 on Dad's Day fired up and ready to avenge the '27 debacle. Most of the first quarter was played in Bucknell territory but State couldn't quite sustain enough drives to score. Shortly before the end of the period, State lost the ball on downs at the Bucknell 23-yard line. Playing in spite of a broken nose, Halicki carried the ball on almost every play as Bucknell ran the ball right at the State defensive line, driving the 77-yards with the big fullback going over for the touchdown from four yards out. Halicki was a good kicker but the Lions roared through to block the extra point attempt. From that point on, State controlled the tempo of the game but the Lions' erratic offense couldn't quite overcome the Bison's stubborn defense.

Then, with time running out in the fourth quarter, State took the ball on its own 13-yard line after a punt. Miller had replaced French at quarterback earlier in the game and now he took charge. Miller slashed through tackle and around end on play after play, sometimes giving the ball to Hamas or sophomore sub George Collins just to keep the Bucknell defense guessing. Downfield they went with Miller gaining 55 yards until it was second-and-goal from the 1-yard line. The fans were screaming and everyone knew the tying touchdown was a sure thing. Only the extra point was in doubt. Collins got the ball and banged into the middle and from the grandstands a loud cheer went up. He was across. No! No!, shouted the referee. An inch or two short. The yelling got louder. Miller, Hamas, Collins or Wolff, who was going to get the ball on fourth down? It went to old dependable Hamas, and the rugged senior blasted forward and—Fumbled! Bucknell's left halfback Hambaucher leaped on the ball, and the threat was over. Bucknell punted out, and the Lions attempted several passes but never got close to the Bisons goal. Bucknell had possession at midfield when the game came to an end. The Lions had lost, 6-0, and they would never recover.

Except for a big 50-point scoring explosion against weak George Washington, State would score only six more points—one touchdown—in its last six games. Lebanon Valley, Gettysburg and Bucknell had exposed the ineptness and futility of Bezdek's offense. And when your most reliable running back can't make one inch without fumbling, you know your offense is ineffective and your team is destined to fail. Only an aggressive defense kept opponents from scoring more in almost every game.

With Penn sporting a 3-0 record and scoring 147 points to zero for its opponents, the Quakers were a three touchdown favorite the next week at Franklin Field. After last year's stunning upset, Penn was determined to win. No non-scouting agreement this year! Penn's scrub coach Pat Duncan had watched the Bucknell game and warned the Penn players that State was a much better team then they might believe. Sportswriters also cautioned against overconfidence, reminding readers that State always seemed to play a good game against Penn while doing just the opposite every year against Pittsburgh.

The largest crowd ever to see State play—65,000—turned out at Franklin Field and it would be 30 years before State would play

before more people. Seven minutes into the game, State's punting team interfered with a Penn return man at State's 45-yard line and the 15-yard penalty set up a two-yard touchdown run by Murphy, the goat of last year's game. In the second quarter, captain Scull intercepted a pass and dashed 70 yards for a second touchdown. Both of Scull's attempts to drop-kick the extra points failed but Penn was given the two points (as the rules then required) because State was offside both times. Although the Quakers were in scoring territory at least four more times during the game, State's defense beat them back and the final score was 14-0. "The Nittany Lions looked more like cubs than lions," wrote Ed Dooley for a Philadelphia newspaper. "They were young, overanxious and lacking in football experience. They tried hard but they were no match for their Philadelphia rivals."

The Homecoming game against Syracuse may have been the best one the team played all year but it still ended in deep frustration for the Lions. Syracuse had just been defeated by Nebraska but was still favored by two touchdowns. Wolff ran back the opening kickoff 45 yards and State marched down to the Syracuse 6-yard line before giving up the ball on downs. After an exchange of punts, Syracuse drove from midfield for a touchdown, with the Orange captain Harold Baysinger diving for the six points from two yards out on fourth down. Syracuse tried to fool the Lions by passing for the extra point but Baysinger overthrew his receiver. It was at this point that Bezdek inserted French in at quarterback for Miller and what happened during the rest of the game turned French into a star. Bezdek gave French the go ahead to pass and before the day was over State would gain 206 yards and 17 first downs on 15-of-26 completions. The Lion defense stopped Syracuse at nearly every turn and the Orange never seriously threatened again, going without any first downs in the second half. However, State's offense also was kept from the end zone until the fourth quarter.

Then, with French running, throwing and catching passes, the Lions rallied to tie the game early in the period, with French getting the TD on an 11-yard run after a 39-yard drive . The kick failed but the Lions were right back moments later, passing downfield to the Syracuse 2-yard line before Diedrich dropped a pass while crossing the goal line. After Syracuse punted out, State had one more chance and with French leading the way, the Lions had a first down at the Syracuse five. Delp appeared open for what would have been the game-winning touchdown but a Syracuse defender knocked down the ball and State's last threat died a short time later inside the 1-yard line. Once again, the offense couldn't quite do it.

The Notre Dame game the following week did not have the same buildup as the three previous games the teams had played. The Irish also were having a down year and had already lost to Wisconsin and Georgia Tech. Only 30,000 showed up at Franklin Field and they saw a boring game played with little passing from either team. State didn't complete a pass in 10 attempts and Notre Dame completed just 1-of-8 passes for 12 yards and had three interceptions. But the Irish overwhelmed the Lions on the ground, running up 286 yards and 18 first downs to the Lions 114 yards and just two first downs. Most of State's yardage came on some nifty runs by French but the Lions never got close to the Irish goal line. Notre Dame scored on the opening kickoff when it drove 72 yards, with third-string quarterback Charlie Corrido going over from the one for the TD and Jack Niemic booting the PAT. The only other Irish points came in the fourth quarter when left end Eddie Collins sacked Miller for a safety, and Notre Dame won, 9-0. This would be the last time State would play Notre Dame until the 1976 Gator Bowl.

In the final home game of the season, State scored 44 points in the first half and trounced George Washington, 50-0, as Hamas (who had been elected to replace Greenshields as captain), Diedrich and the third-team quarterback Johnny McCracken scored two TDs apiece. McCracken was the younger brother of Lafayette coach, Herb Mc-Cracken, who, despite his rejuvenation of the Lafayette program and a current 4-1-2 record, was fighting for his job when Lafayette hosted State the next Saturday afternoon. Bezdek had been so frustrated by his team's performance against Notre Dame that he held an open scrimmage at Thursday's practice. He picked two teams and had them scrimmage for the right to start against Lafayette. First team to score starts, he said. The tough scrimmage lasted two hours and, as was typical of the entire season neither team could score!

They couldn't score against Lafayette, either. Lafayette got its only points on a 50-yard march in the second quarter. Late in the fourth quarter, Johnny McCracken almost ran back a punt for a TD but was caught on the Lafayette 40-yard line, and a pass interception ended that threat. Then, with only seconds left in the game, and State with the ball on its own 20-yard line after a punt, Miller passed to Diedrich who ran to the 50-yard line. Time for one last play. Miller found Diedrich wide open at the goal line only to have the pass knocked down at the last moment on a lunge by Lafayette's captain, Paul Shellenberger. Lafayette won, 7-0, and, now, only a victory over Pitt stood between State and the first losing season since the shortened 1918 war year.

Beating Pitt had become an obsession for Bezdek and sportswriters had wondered why State always seemed to be "psyched out" when playing the Panthers. Bezdek didn't know either but was trying to find out. Since early fall he had been using the services of a Penn State psychology professor to help him learn more about understanding the mental peculiarities of his players and how to use these idiosyncrasies to motivate them. The professor was in the locker room and on the bench Thanksgiving Day when Pitt once again destroyed State. The Panthers were just 5-2-1 going into the game but they looked like national champs again in blasting State, 26-0, before a relatively small turnout of 33,000. State never seriously threatened to score until late in the fourth quarter and only got three first downs, all on passing. The game was probably over in the opening seconds when Tony Uansa ran back the kickoff 96 yards for a touchdown. He scored another in the third quarter on a 40-yard sprint, then added the proverbial "insult to injury" by intercepting a pass on the 15-yard line that ended State's lone scoring opportunity. The psychology professor later reported to Bezdek that 'defeat was due to the lack of preparation in executing finer details of the plays." No kidding!

This was the sixth straight year State had lost by nearly three touchdowns or more and Pittsburgh sportswriters were now questioning the worthiness of State as a holiday opponent. "Penn State is no longer the drawing card it once was," wrote columnist Ralph Davis, and, "...they never play their best brand of football here, according to their mentor." A *Pittsburgh Post-Gazette* writer suggested Carnegie Tech or some other "outstanding team" be played "instead of forever automatically handing it over to a team which year after year insists on making almost 'no contest.'"

How the mighty had fallen. Now, even his sportswriting friends were beginning to snip at Bezdek and emphasize his failings. But he

was not about to give up. He had at least one more year left in him, if not more. He would "work them harder" if he had to but he was going to go out a winner.

Season Record 3-5-1
Record to Date 211-110-24
Winning percentage .646

"The Great Punt Return"

The Homecoming crowd of 15,000 groaned as Lafayette's fullback Eddie Woodfin picked up a first down at the Lafayette 25-yard line with less than two minutes remaining in the game and State called its last time out. A 3-0 defeat was now inevitable, for Lafayette could simply run out the clock and hand Bezdek's team its second loss in a row. There were many alumni in the Beaver Field grandstands who were ready to lynch the Lions' beleaguered coach. "Fire the bum!" someone probably yelled.

With 15 lettermen returning, including triple-threat junior quarterback Cooper French, this was expected to be a team that could challenge for the Eastern championship. Now, the team would be 3-2 with its toughest four games ahead. This couldn't be happening, the fans must have thought. After more than a half dozen years, Bezdek had said he now had a quarterback with the potential of a Glenn Killinger. He also had a front line that most observers believed was State's overall best since at least '22 or '23, led by two of the best defensive ends in the country, juniors Earle Edwards and Myron "Mike" Kaplan. This could be a good team—maybe even a great one if things go right.

It had been a long winter after the dismal '28 season and some alumni groups had openly called for Bezdek's dismissal. One organized group in Youngstown, Ohio, spearheaded a campaign in mid-December to persuade the Athletic Board of Control to oust Bezdek before another season began. Even as the pressure from off campus was increasing, Bezdek was getting his players ready. Winter practice was earlier than ever because of the new athletic facility building that had opened near Beaver Field. Although the building (soon to be known as Recreation Hall) would not be dedicated officially until March 3, Bezdek began using the expansive gymnasium for football practice in mid January. No longer restricted to the confined space of the pavilion, he now had all the backs and linemen drilling at the same time, and he worked them harder than ever.

By the time preseason practice got underway on September 3, Bezdek already had a pretty good assessment of his players, including last year's freshmen. He never said so publicly but he knew there would be little help from this year's sophomores, the first of the non-scholarship players. In fact, only one soph, fullback George "Judy" Lasich, would become a regular. Cooper's long-time pal and roommate, Diedrich, would start at left halfback with junior letterman Tom Evans sharing the right half slot with non-letterman, Jack Livitzey, among others. In the line, Bezdek had Stahley backing up Edwards and Kaplan at end with McAndrews and Eschbach back to share the center position and Shawley, Panaccion, Ricker, Zorella, DuVall, Martin and non-letterman Jim Love at the guard and tackle positions. Bezdek felt so confident about the ability of his line that he shifted Jack Martin, who was the captain, to the backfield in the preseason and Martin stayed there, playing all four positions, until the Pitt game. However, A.G. "Red" DuVall, perhaps the best interior lineman of all, originally decided not to play but changed his mind in mid-October and returned to regain a starting position. With Higgins, Conover and now another ex-Lion All-American lineman, Joe Bedenk, on the coaching staff, it was not surprising that the line was the heart of the team.

"If we are fortunate enough to escape many injuries we will have a much better team than we had last season," Bezdek told sports-writers. "It will be faster, more experienced, and, I hope, more fortunate in getting its share of the breaks that always play a big part in football games." Practices continued to be hard and long but the players had one major break. A locker room with showers had been set aside for them in the new recreation building. No longer did they have to make the quarter mile trek up and down the hill to the "old" Track House for practice and games.

The schedule was front-loaded again with weaker opponents and two new foes, Niagara and Marshall, sandwiched around Lebanon Valley. The first major game would be against NYU on October 19 when State would visit New York City for the first time since '23. State's most traditional rivals—Penn, Bucknell and Pitt— would be played back-to-back at the end of the year. There also had been one change in the no-scouting policy. State officials would try to work out no-scouting agreements with each opponent but without such an arrangement, scouting would be permitted.

Niagara was beating up on smaller colleges in New York state but it was overpowered by State in the opener. Edwards scored a touchdown on a long pass from French in the first quarter and French's 48-yard run in the second quarter set up a line plunge for a TD by Diedrich, who kicked both PATs. State also got a safety in the last period in winning, 16-0. Niagara almost scored near the end when its quarterback intercepted a pass and ran 90 yards to State's 5-yard line but the visitors couldn't get into the end zone.

Looking for another quarterback to back up French, Bezdek used Martin as the signal caller for the entire game against Lebanon Valley and had French playing as a backup halfback. Diedrich ran back the opening kickoff 65 yards to set up a short TD run by Lasich but Lebanon Valley stayed in the game until Diedrich intercepted a pass near midfield in the second quarter. French entered the game at this point and Diedrich hit him on a short pass over the line and French ran the rest of the way for a touchdown. In the second half the Lions racked up 12 first downs to one for LV but could only score a safety and won, 15-0.

Diedrich was again the star in a penalty-filled game against Marshall, scoring all the points as State won, 26-7, before 8,000 on Dad's Day. In the first quarter, Diedrich recovered French's fumble into the end zone for one TD and minutes later ran for another on a 40-yard pass from French. He scored again on short runs in the third and fourth quarters and also kicked two extra points. Bezdek never subbed for Diedrich and French but deployed his captain, Martin, at left half.

On the same day that State beat Marshall, NYU had been upset by cross-town rival Fordham. Coach Chick Meehan shook up his team for State, moving his standout running guard, Dave Myers, to quarterback and replacing replacing the remainder of his backfield. Still, NYU was the betting favorite when more than 30,000 showed up at Yankee Stadium. This was probably the most disappointing game of

the season for the Lions because they outplayed NYU all afternoon but lost, 7-0. NYU's only score came in the opening quarter and was helped by two big 15-yard penalties. A holding penalty following a punt gave the Violets the ball on State's 29-yard line and moments later an unnecessary roughness penalty put the ball on State's 3-yard line, from where fullback Herman Lemark bolted over. Twice in the first half State was near the NYU 10-yard line thanks to a furious passing attack but NYU held both times, with Myers knocking down a short pass from French to Kaplan at the goal line that looked like a sure touchdown. It was more of the same after the intermission as the Lions passed and ran deep into NYU territory but were stopped three times near the 10 and twice at the 30. Once, Kaplan was wide open as he reached for a 40-yard pass thrown by French but the ball slipped off his fingertips. Meanwhile, State's defense led by Kaplan and Edwards was outstanding and NYU never seriously threatened again as State got 18 first downs to NYU's 10. "It might be said that the Violet was lucky to win...," wrote G. W. Daley for the *New York Herald-Tribune*. So much for the breaks Bezdek had yearned for.

The team sulked back to State with everyone wondering how it would rebound for the Homecoming game against Lafayette. At mid-week, everyone on campus was stunned when the long-awaited Carnegie report on college athletics lumped State among the dozens of colleges it criticized for "selling out" education for athletics, focusing on the recruiting and scholarships. The fact that State had disavowed scholarships two years before and was already de-emphasizing was not mentioned by the Carnegie task force, which criticized almost every State opponent, too. (The same day that the foundation report was released, the U.S. stock market crashed, precipitating a nationwide depression. There is no evidence to date that this was anything more than an incredible coincidence.)

Bezdek, who had played only 13 men against NYU, stuck with the same starting lineup for Lafayette, inserting Evans at right half. Lafayette also had suffered its first loss of the season the previous Saturday, 6-3, to Bucknell when a fumble on a fourth down punt late in the game gave the Bisons the chance to score the come-from-behind touchdown. After the game, coach McCracken, who had been given another one-year contract after almost losing his job last year, had criticized his quarterback, Tellier for waiting until the fourth down to punt and had warned him not to do it again. McCracken's advice would come back to haunt him.

Lafayette kicked off to State after the Lafayette band had delayed the start of the game by staying on the field too long. After the teams traded punts on the first possession, State took over the ball at its own 20-yard line. On the first play, Evans blasted over center and—fumbled! Lafayette recovered at the 26. Three plays later Lafayette had lost two yards. So, tackle Alan Cook booted a perfect field goal from the 36-yard line for a 3-0 lead. That was the extent of the excitement until midway through the fourth quarter as both teams stuck to the ground in a rather drab demonstration of offensive football. Lafayette was satisfied with nursing its narrow lead and a quick kick soon found State with the ball at its own 32-yard line. In seven plays, State was at the Lafayette 28 thanks largely to a 22-yard pass from Evans to Kaplan. Evans got another first down on an 11-yard run to the 15-yard line and the State Homecoming crowd cheered wildly. Lasich was stopped for no gain and Evans gained three but a lateral lost three and it was fourth down. Disdaining a field goal to tie, Diedrich threw a short pass to Kaplan who dashed across the goal for the apparent touchdown as the crowd screamed. But Lafayette protested that Diedrich had not been five yards deep (as the passing rules then required) when he threw the ball and the referee agreed. Lafayette's ball on the 15-yard line. State had one time out left and had to prevent Lafayette from getting a first down to have one last chance. Three running plays, first down Lafayette, time out State. Bezdek had not substituted the entire game and didn't do it now. It was all but over and some of the fans started heading home. (Something else that hasn't changed over the years, right?)

Woodfin went up the middle for a yard. Penalty, signaled the referee: 15 yards for unnecessary roughness against Lafayette. Woodfin carried for no gain. Woodfin again for two yards. The clock was ticking down and the small contingent of Lafayette fans were cheering. Suddenly, Woodfin dropped back to punt from the goal line. Everyone wondered what the heck was happening. Lafayette's quarterback, Tellier, had been told not to wait until fourth down to kick so there was Woodfin booting one high into the air almost at the same time as the timekeeper's air horn sounded ending the game.

French and Diedrich had rushed back in twin safety and Woodfin booted it 60 yards. The ball sailed lazily to French at the State 40 and Diedrich drifted towards the sideline. Three Lafayette linemen barreled in to make the game-ending tackle and just as French was about to be swarmed under, he turned and passed it back to Diedrich 15 yards away. It was an impromptu play the two had been practicing since their school boy days at Staunton Military Academy and had not been planned or sent in from the bench. Diedrich darted down the sideline, was almost trapped, reversed his field and was nearly in the clear. Only one Lafayette defender remained and he was wiped out by an unknown State player as Diedrich streaked by and into the end zone for a 6-3 victory.

"Fifteen thousand fans rolled on the gridiron like a tidal wave breaking over the sands of Florida," wrote Stan Baumgartner in the *Philadelphia Inquirer*. "Strong men wept and old men suddenly became strong under the emotional stimulus of the great victory. Hugo Bezdek hugged the water boy. Hats, coats, programs and even blankets were tossed into the air. For three minutes, fifteen thousand persons went stark mad. Thousands danced around the goal posts and it was almost impossible to keep them on the sidelines so that Diedrich could have his chance to kick the extra point...A moment later, the hysterical throng gathered about the Nittany eleven, hugging, kissing and patting them on the back. Diedrich was hoisted to the shoulders and borne triumphantly to the field house. French also was lifted high in the air and carried to the training house. Other members of the victorious cast were have dragged, pushed and half carried to town."

If ever one play defined the season this was it. The extemporaneous French-Diedrich punt return gave the team momentum as it traveled to Syracuse and Penn in the next two weeks. State was again the underdog at Archbold Stadium and almost gave away a touchdown early in the first quarter when French, following a punt to State's 7-yard line, fumbled a pass from center and fell on the ball in the end zone for a Syracuse safety. A few minutes later, he redeemed himself by calling a triple reverse pass play that took the Orange completely by surprise. The last man on the reverse, Diedrich, threw the ball from behind State's 40-yard line and hit Kaplan running on the fly at the 20-yard line for a 60-yard touchdown. Diedrich missed the PAT but State had a lead it never gave up. Although State seemed to be in control most of the game, Syracuse almost scored a touchdown in the third quarter after

intercepting a pass on State's 18-yard line and in the fourth quarter the Orange reached State's 10-yard line before giving up the ball. French intentionally took another safety towards the end of the game in order to place-kick the ball out of danger and State went on to win by the unusual score of 6-4.

Because the no-scouting policy had been modified, Bezdek had sent Bedenk to scout Penn. Bedenk's advice helped State intercept six passes and upset the once-beaten Quakers, 19-7, in a game that most sportswriters agreed was "the roughest played on Franklin Field in the last ten or twelve years." State was heavily penalized for unnecessary roughness and the crowd of 60,00 got so upset at the referee for not controlling the game that it showered the field with boos and cat calls through much of the second half. State had jumped off to a 13-0 lead with Lasich scoring on a 1-yard dive after a 59-yard drive in the first quarter and going over again in the second quarter after a pass interception by French. Diedrich had hit one of his two extra point attempts. Penn scored late in the second quarter with a 12-yard pass climaxing a 63-yard drive. The PAT made it 13-7. Penn dominated most of the second half and was driving for what could have been the winning points midway in the fourth quarter when French made the play of the game. On a third-and-9 at the State 28, French picked off a pass by Warren Gette at the 18-yard line and ran 82-yards for a touchdown, setting a new school record for the longest interception return. Diedrich missed the PAT but it was all over. "The Penn State dressing room was a scene of jollification after beating Penn, 19-7," reported the *Philadelphia Evening Bulletin*. "Coach Hugo Bezdek came into the quarters yelling: ' Bucknell,' meaning the Nittany Lions' next victim."

Victim? The sportswriter was a little premature because the next victim was State itself. Perhaps it was State's overconfidence or maybe the team was looking ahead at Pitt, which was unbeaten and on its way to the Eastern championship. But Bezdek and the team certainly underestimated the Bucknell team that had only lost to W&J, 14-6, and had a future College and Pro Football Hall of Famer at fullback, Clark Hinkle. "Hinkle Mighty As Bisons Run Through State," said the headline in the *Philadelphia Inquirer*. State was never really in the Beaver Field game. Hinkle figured in all the scoring as Bucknell erupted for 20 points in the second quarter, after almost scoring twice in the opening period, and overwhelmed State, 27-6, in what sportswriters called a major upset. Hinkle ran for touchdowns of four and one yards and threw touchdown passes of 30 and 12 yards in gaining 130 yards on the ground and passing for a phenomenal 140 yards. Hinkle also led the alert Bucknell defense with two of the six pass interceptions that helped set up two of the Bison touchdowns.

This may have been the most devastating loss of Bezdek's career for it virtually sealed his fate as coach of the Nittany Lions. With his track record against Pitt, he would need more than luck to upset what was another powerful Panthers team on Thanksgiving Day. Pitt was unbeaten with wins over Ohio State, Nebraska, W&J and Duke and had averaged 32 points a game while limiting opponents to a total of 32 points. The Rose Bowl invitation was all but official and no one expected Pitt to collapse with the incentive of a potential National Championship. "Only the greatest upset and form reversal of the year could prevent the Panthers from...downing the Lions tomorrow," wrote columnist James Long on the eve of the battle.

State did not go down easily, though, and for the first time since 1919 led at halftime, 7-6, thanks to a French-to-Stahley pass and Diedrich's kick. It was the first time all season that Pitt had been behind in a game. With a shivering crowd of less than 30,000 looking on, the Panthers drove 65-yards in the first quarter to score with fullback Tom Parkinson bowling over from the one but he missed the extra point kick. French returned the ensuing kickoff 47 yards and early in the second quarter French passed 24-yards to Stahley for the tying touchdown and Diedrich booted the go-ahead point. State's tough defense held Pitt in check for the rest of the half and for much of the third quarter but it tired under the relentless Pitt attack. Pitt drove 84 yards with Parkinson diving over for his second TD with four minutes left in the quarter and he scored a third time after another long drive in the final period. Pitt had 22 first downs to State's six and won 20-6. Pitt went on to the Rose Bowl and lost to USC. State went home and lost a coach.

In January, the college's board of trustees announced that Bezdek had voluntarily stepped down as coach after being promoted to be the first director of the new School of Physical Education and Athletics. In March, assistant Bob Higgins, the only experienced head coach on the Penn State staff, was elevated to the top job. The first "Golden Era" of Penn State football was officially over and it would be 40 years before the next "Golden Era" would occur. The "Great Depression" of Nittany Lion football was about to begin.

Season Record 6-3
Record to Date 217-113-24
Winning percentage .647

CHAPTER 9

THE ONE AND ONLY "HIG"

1930-1949

Bob Higgins already was a Penn State legend when he ascended to the head coaching job in 1930. At the time, he was probably the school's greatest all-around football player. He may not have been as famous as such running backs as Glenn Killinger, Charlie Way, "Light-Horse" Harry Wilson and Bull McCleary but in his playing days he was regarded by coaches and sportswriters alike as the best offensive and defensive end in the county, and an outstanding leader who was like a coach on the field.

Coaching was in his blood and he had become a head coach shortly after graduation in 1920 when hired by West Virginia Wesleyan. He was 4-1-1 in his initial year, including a tie with W&J, but took a leave of absence the following year to play professional football for the Canton Bulldogs. He returned in 1922 after Wesleyan had lost all seven games in '21 and posted an 8-2 record. His best year was in 1924 when Wesleyan was 9-2, including a victory over Southern Meth-

odist University in Dallas on New Year's Day of 1925 in a postseason game that was the predecessor to the Cotton Bowl. Ironically, a New Year's Day game against SMU in the official Cotton Bowl 23 years later would mark the high point of Higgins' coaching tenure at Penn State.

Higgins' success at West Virginia Wesleyan led to a three-year contract with Washington University in St. Louis, which was a member of the then potent Missouri Valley Intercollegiate Association and included such teams as Nebraska, Oklahoma and Missouri. After seasons of 2-5-1 and 1-7, his 1927 team went 5-2-2. But he decided to leave at the end of the year when the conference broke up and the other major schools reorganized another conference without Washington. When he contacted Bezdek to say he wanted to get back to his alma mater, Bezdek was eager to have him.

Despite the player revolt that he and Larry Conover led that turned around the 1919 season, Hig-

Former two-time All-American end Bob Higgins took over as head coach in 1930 and became a legend as he coached State for almost 20 years during a period of de-emphasis and the resurgent era of post World War II.

gins respected Bezdek's coaching skills. Higgins' easygoing, laid-back style was the opposite that of the snappish, militaristic nature of Bezdek. He may even have been a settling influence on Bezdek and a confidential liaison between the players. There was much less complaining about Bezdek and his practices after Higgins joined the staff.

After Bezdek had stepped down and Higgins promoted on March 27, 1930, there were reports that Higgins had been hired originally as an assistant to be Bezdek's replacement. But Higgins' biographer, Rich Donnell, found no evidence of that and says it was personal, not professional, reasons that took him back to State College. His wife wanted to be closer to her family in Clarksburg, WV, and they were looking for a nice place to raise their two children. So, as Donnell writes in his book "*The Hig*," they "packed up and headed for the only real home Higgins had ever known..."

Higgins certainly had no delusions of what he was getting into as head coach at State. He could see the school's purist policy taking effect and he certainly realized what it would mean to play without scholarships, especially without the "blue chip" players like himself. But there were many State followers who saw Higgins as a miracle man who would not only overcome the talent problem but would breathe fresh air into a program bogged down in recent years by Bezdek's harsh, autocratic methods.

The optimism barely lasted his first season when a team that many believed had championship potential went into a nose dive after the third game and finished with a 3-4-2 record. By the start of the 1932 campaign, many alumni were calling for another change as State's tailspin continued and the alleged inept coaching of Higgins was getting as much blame as the purity policies induced by President Hetzel and influential alumni. That's when certain friends of Higgins stepped in.

Two men, in particular, led the way to circumvent school policy and recruit good players—Ben "Casey" Jones of Pittsburgh and Jim Gilligan of Dunmore. Jones was a former teammate and close friend of Higgins on the 1916 team but an injury forced him to give up football after he returned from World War I and by the early 1930s he was a businessman in Western Pennsylvania. Gilligan, a 1912 graduate who did not play football, was a school principal in the heart of the hard coal region, Dunmore, PA. The scheme they developed was simple. Instead of free scholarships, the recruits would get jobs to pay for their own education. Fraternities, restaurants and other State College businesses eagerly cooperated and by the late 1930s there was an influx of young men from the coal mining and steel towns of Pennsylvania who might not have otherwise attended college.

The alumni also came up with other gimmicks to help the athletes. One book store provided books "on loan" to the athletes. To help raise funds, Jones conducted a statewide raffle of an automobile every year after the Pitt game. The money often would be used to pay fraternities for helping to support the players or to help subsidize the team training table. Sometimes, cash was given outright to players in the form of "necessary assistance." No one ever charged Jones or others with breaking NCAA rules but one can not believe the financial aid to the players was all proper, legal or ethical.

The jobs were real and the players did work. They went to classes and they played football and through the 1930s they got better and better, and by 1941 State was rated among the top teams in the country. Higgins brought the Nittany Lions back from the depths, survived a Depression and even another World War, and in 1947 he pro-

duced what may have been the greatest team in school history. The '47 team— with players who were older and matured by a war as their coach had been 30 years before—went unbeaten, was tied by SMU 13-13 in the Cotton Bowl and finished fourth in the nation. The next year, they lost only to Pitt—unfortunately, still the old bugaboo—and Higgins, concerned about his heart condition, decided to retire.

When he resigned after 19 years, he had won 97 games, lost 57 and tied 11. By staying one more year, he undoubtedly would have achieved what few college football coaches have ever accomplished—winning 100 games at one school. But today he is relatively unknown outside of the Penn State universe and it's probable that many Nittany Lion fans of the Paterno era don't even know his name. Yet, he is the man who directly links the early days of Pop Golden to Joe Paterno.

Higgins had expected the Board of Trustees would hire his hand-picked successor, Earle Edwards, an end on Higgins' first team in 1930, who had stayed on as a Higgins' assistant. But in another political maneuver reminiscent of the Harlow treatment decades earlier, the board selected another Higgins assistant and former great player, Joe Bedenk. Bedenk, who had been the head baseball coach since 1931, took the job only after the urging of friends, including World War II hero and ex-teammate, Hap Frank. But after one year he told everyone baseball was the sport he truly loved and he went back to be an assistant. This strange episode was perhaps the most significant turning point in Penn State football. For if Edwards had been hired instead of Bedenk, Joe Paterno might be practicing law in Brooklyn.

"The Debut Dud"

The hiring of Bob Higgins as head coach was a popular choice among Penn State fans and even within the sportswriting fraternity that admired Bezdek. As columnist James J. Long of the *Pittsburgh Sun-Telegraph* had written: "...there (isn't) any doubt that football on Mt. Nittany will improve with the direction of gridiron affairs in new hands...the general opinion (is) that a new coaching system and the new spirit that usually results from a coaching change after a long period of adversity...(was) needed, and an uplift is likely to follow..."

The consensus among fans and sportswriters alike was that Higgins was taking over a team with a lot of good players and that he would be able to get more out of them than Bezdek. With 10 lettermen returning, including the entire regular backfield and the two starting ends, Higgins' first team was expected to be one of the best in the East. And for a few weeks it was.

Diedrich was now the captain and he, French, Edwards and Kaplan were being touted as potential All-Americans. But Higgins and his assistants—Bedenk and Dutch Herman, who had turned over the freshman team to Conover—had to rebuild the entire middle of the line with just Shawley, DuVall and Zorella returning. The bench talent was thin, with not much to pick from in the non-scholarship junior or sophomore classes. Still, no one was really prepared for what happened.

Preseason practice may not have been a delight but it certainly was different. The squad went through the normal drills and scrimmages but the atmosphere was less intense and harsh. The spirit that pervaded gave no hint of the disaster that was to follow.

There had been one major change in the schedule. Penn had canceled it's November 18 scheduled game at Franklin Field, perhaps because of State's supposedly rough-house play in the '29 game. Graduate Manager Neil Fleming hustled for a replacement and found Iowa willing to host the Lions in Iowa City on that date. State had never played the Hawkeyes and had not been that far West since the '23 Rose Bowl. The Associated Press item reporting on the arrangement is memorable in the retrospective of 67 years later: "Fleming said other games with the Big Ten Conference may be arranged within the next few years." Right! Two other schedule changes were noteworthy. Colgate, considered a national title contender, would visit for Homecoming on Oct. 25, taking NYU's place on the slate, and, for the first time in 20 years, State would travel to Lewisburg for the Bucknell game. There was one remnant from 1929—the mutual agreement scouting policy would remain in effect indefinitely.

Higgins had a typical coach's debut in the season opener against Niagara. The team did not look good in the first half and the game was scoreless at the intermission. But with the "line smashing" of Diedrich and Lasich and the broken field running and passing of French, State erupted for 31 points and beat Niagara, 31-14. French scored three touchdowns and kicked one PAT and threw two TD passes to junior substitute end Bob Snyder. Niagara scored twice in the fourth quarter, including one on the recovery of a State fumble.

The Lions' offensive still looked a little sluggish in the opening minutes of the Lebanon Valley game and near the end of the first quarter, LV moved inside the Lions' five-yard line. But a LV fumble recovered by Laslich ended the threat and the visitors never came close again. Still, it was scoreless until the third quarter, when the Lions drove downfield twice for touchdowns by French and Lasich. French also threw a TD pass to Lasich and State won, 27-0.

One week later, Red Evans ran back the opening kickoff 98 yards for a TD to break Shorty Miller's 1911 record and State went on to rout Marshall, 65-0, on Dad's Day. Higgins used 37 players as Evans, French, Lasich and senior backup halfback Joe Miller scored two touchdowns apiece. Another reserve, Bill Martz, made the game's second most spectacular play late in the game, when a teammate swatting at a Marshall pass batted the ball inadvertently into Martz's hands and the big end ran 55 yards for State's final TD of the game.

After three games, Higgins' first team had the same record as Bezdek's last one, and the squad went to Easton heavily favored to defeat McCracken's inexperienced Lafayette team. Higgins had formulated a game plan based on running power plays to the strong-side of his single wing formation. Don't go to the weak side and keep the passing and reverses to the minimum, he told his quarterback, French, and his captain, Diedrich. "Penn State's offensive, heretofore unusually strong, seemed to lack that certain punch necessary to score when the ball was maneuvered into position," the anonymous writer for the official *"Penn State Athletic Records Scrapbook"* reported later. State got seven first downs to Lafayette's six but neither team scored in a 0-0 tie. Lafayette never got close to State's goal line but missed two field goals from about the 30-yard line. State thought it had a touchdown in the first half when Edwards caught a pass from French but the referee ruled Edwards was out of the end zone. In the fourth quarter, the Lions thought they had a safety after chasing a Lafayette fumble into the end zone and jumping on the Lafayette player who recovered the ball. But the referee also negated that score, saying the ball was dead when a State player touched it at Lafayette's 15-yard line, and the home team held there on downs.

This was probably the defining moment of the season because Higgins' team would not win another game and would only score a total of three touchdowns in the last five contests.

When the team began practicing for Colgate, the senior players led by Diedrich complained to Higgins about his conservative offense against Lafayette and Higgins agreed to "open up." Colgate never let him. Coach Andy Kerr's team had been stunned by Michigan State the previous weekend and his Maroons took it out on State, giving the Lions it's worst beating in 31 years, 40-0. Many in the Homecoming crowd of 8,000 must have regretted ever championing Higgins for the coaching job and surely yearned for the return of Bezdek. The closest State got to Colgate's goal line was in the fourth quarter when two passes helped reach Colgate's 25-yard line. But Colgate's All-American fullback Len Macaluso intercepted Diedrich's pass attempt on the next play and it was all over. Macaluso, who would become the nation's scoring leader that year with 144 points, got four touchdowns as he and Colgate's captain Les Hart and end Johnny Orsini ripped the State line to shreds. Kerr could not believe his team was that much better than State's and that week he wrote a letter to Higgins praising the Lions' on-field efforts. "As I told you on Saturday," Kerr wrote, as reported in Rich Donnell's book, *The Hig,* "things broke very well for us and we had a very fair share of good luck...I am convinced that no team on the rest of your schedule will beat you by anything like the one-sided defeat you suffered last Saturday."

Something else occurred in the Colgate loss that also helped define the season. French was injured and would miss the following game at Bucknell. Edwards also was hobbling and would not play again until Pitt on Thanksgiving Day. French's replacement was a senior with little game experience, Johnny Batdorf. Bucknell coach Carl Snavely had told sportswriters he points his team to the Penn State game every year. Win that one and we make our season, he said. And he did it again for the fourth straight year with a 19-7 victory. Without French, the State attack sputtered and Bucknell's defense had few serious problems. The Lion offense didn't cross the 50 until the fourth quarter and Bucknell intercepted a pass to halt that threat at its 40-yard line. Higgins had set the Lions defense to stop Hinkle after his one-man show of last year. "...The Lion gridmen succeed in crushing this line crasher on almost every occasion," reported the *"Penn State Athletic Records Scrapbook."* "In doing so, however, the Lions seemed to forget about Brumbaugh and Ross who swept the ends at will." Brumbaugh scored touchdowns twice in the first quarter, first at the end of a 50-yard march and then after a Hinkle pass interception. Hinkle bulled over for another TD in the second quarter following another drive and Bucknell might have scored more that period but State's defense came up with two fine goal line stands. The Lion defense continued to play well in the second half and held Bucknell scoreless. But State's offense also continued to struggle and the Lions didn't score until late in the game when Batdorf ran back a pass interception 45 yards to Bucknell's 10-yard line. Three downs could gain just one yard but on fourth down Diedrich hit Batdorf with a pass as the quarterback crossed the goal line. It was another case of too little too late.

French practiced with the second team the next week but he was the starter when State kicked off to Syracuse before more than 10,000 in the annual Pennsylvania Day game. The Orange had lost only to Pitt and with a big team that averaged 10 pounds more per man than State, the visitors were favored. But State took control from the beginning and played its best all-around game of the season. State outplayed Syracuse most of the day, gaining 226 yards, including 138 on passing, while the Orange had 131 yards on the ground and 45 passing. But neither team could score. State missed one opportunity in the opening period after starting a drive from its own 30-yard line and reaching the Syracuse eight, thanks to a backhanded pass reception by Evans. But Syracuse held and Diedrich missed a field goal from the 18-yard line. Syracuse threatened just once in the entire game, in the second quarter when a pass interference call on Diedrich gave Syracuse the ball at the State 15-yard line. However, Syracuse fumbled on the next play and Shawley recovered and French punted out of danger. A few minutes later, State reached the Syracuse 18-yard line on a pass following the recovery of another Orange fumble but Lasich fumbled the ball right back to Syracuse. State almost won in the fourth quarter after two passes from midfield put the ball at the 20 but on fourth down-and-goal at the four, Diedrich's attempt for a field goal missed and the Lions left Beaver Field with a 0-0 tie. Ironically, State's soccer team had the same offensive problems that day as the football team and despite playing in Syracuse's territory most of the game, the team also had a scoreless game.

If there was one game Higgins' team should have won this season and didn't it was at Iowa. The Hawkeyes were not very good, sporting a 2-4 record, and had been mauled so badly by Marquette the week before that several regulars did not start against State. Maybe the players were tired by the long 850 mile trip to Iowa City but mistakes cost State the game before an Iowa Homecoming crowd of 20,000. The first half was fairly even and scoreless and was marked by two record quick kicks of 79 and 70 yards by French that got State out of one jam and put Iowa in another. French is credited with a 90-yard punt in the official Penn State record books but newspaper accounts of the game and the *"Penn State Athletic Records Scrapbook"* make no mention of a kick that long. According to Bert McGrane, who covered the game for *Des Moines Register,* the 79-yard kick in the first quarter was the longest that day. "One Penn State punt was one of those things that must be seen to be appreciated," wrote McGrane. "With the ball on his own 18-yard line, French sent a might punt sailing far over the Iowa safetyman's head. The ball traveled seventy nine yards and was downed on Iowa's 1-yard line."

State lost its best scoring chance in the first quarter when a French pass was intercepted at the Iowa 10-yard line. The break of the game came late in the third quarter when Miller fumbled a punt as two Iowa ends barreled towards him and one of them, Rogge, recovered at the State 10-yard line. Three plays later Iowa scored from the 1-yard line but missed the extra point. Early in the fourth quarter, State found itself backed up to its own 10-yard line after a punt and 5-yard penalty. Iowa intercepted a pass attempt by reserve running back Hoguet and ran it back to the 9. On fourth down-and-goal from the 6, Randall Hickman crashed over for the TD and with the PAT, and Iowa led, 13-0. Another pass interception on the ensuing kickoff gave Iowa the ball at the State 19-yard line and five plays later Jack Warrington went around end for eight yards and another TD. Iowa won, 19-0. "Breaks Enable Iowa To Win In Last Half," said the headline in the *Des Moines Register.* The headline in the *Philadelphia Inquirer* said, "Iowa Awakens and Spills Penn State."

Even before State and Pitt kicked off at Pitt Stadium, everyone knew this would be the last time the teams would meet for the traditional Thanksgiving Day closer. Pitt had agreed to visit State in 1931 and that game had been set for Homecoming in October. After 27 years, the tradition was over—but not Pitt's dominance of the holiday affair. The smallest crowd in years—officially reported at 15,816—turned out in zero weather with snow still on the sidelines and saw one heckuva game. The opening period was a punting duel. But early in the second quarter, Pitt's sophomore halfback Warren Heller ran 30 yards for a touchdown just moments after State had made a goal line stand, and the 6-0 lead held up through halftime.

State came out throwing in the third quarter and French, playing his last game with his old buddy Diedrich, combined with him on a 63-yard pass play that put the ball on Pitt's four-yard line. Lasich bulled over from the three for the touchdown but a bad pass from center spoiled the extra point attempt. A few minutes later French intercepted a pass and ran it back to the 23-yard line but on fourth down Diedrich tried a field goal from Pitt's 25-yard line that was just wide to the left. The play of the game was next. Heller smashed over left tackle, found an open field ahead of him and raced 80-yards for the touchdown. The extra point made it 13-6 and State was never able to get back into the game. Midway in the fourth quarter, the Panthers drove 80 yards and scored on a four-yard pass. As the game was winding down, State got a consolation TD when Duvall blocked a punt at the Pitt 35-yard line. Edwards caught the ball in the air at the 40 and raced into the end zone. Another bad pass from center stopped the PAT attempt. State tried an onside kick but Pitt recovered and virtually ran out the clock, winning, 19-12. "At no time did the State men concede an inch to the Panther, who was forced to bring into play everything at his command...., wrote Harvey J. Boyle for the *Pittsburgh Post-Gazette.*

No one could explain completely why the season had deteriorated so badly. The Hig's debut had been a dud. Some outsiders claimed Bezdek had caused dissension because of his relationship with certain players and had constantly sniped at Higgins. Others blamed injuries and the lack of capable replacements that was the direct result of the purist policies. Another faction, the minority, felt it was simple—Higgins had been overrated as a coach.

There was another simple fact. Losing meant less money in the athletic department coffers. A $46,000 net profit from the 1929 season dropped to $29,300 in 1930. But if money had been critical to the success of Penn State football, there would have been no de-emphasis. So, what's a losing season or two? Higgins and the alumni would soon find out.

Season Record 3-4-2
Record to Date 220-117-26
Winning percentage .642

"The Losers"

This team is the biggest bunch of losers in Penn State's football history!

There is no way of getting around that fact. No team before or since has lost as many games—eight—and the seven defeats in a row that season is still the team record for consecutive losses.

Yet, difficult as this may be to believe, the '31 team also went to a postseason game and won a shutout by more than six touchdowns.

Perhaps the defining moment of the season came when Higgins looked at the roster of returnees and freshmen during the winter and realized he had to find more players. So, he turned to a football coaching class that was part the required curriculum in physical education and by mid-April had 140 men out for spring practice, the largest number of candidates in history. "The practice is more intramural in nature than required work for varsity candidates, and many of the men in uniform have never played in the game before," reported a revealing item in the *Towanda Daily Review Journal*. "Men now practicing were drawn largely from classes conducted during the winter by members of the coaching staff. The theoretical phases of the game, taught in those classes, is now being carried out in practice."

By the time the season started, a couple of those neophytes were battling for starting positions. The entire squad may have been epitomized by senior Ken Thomas of Plymouth, who was just 5-foot-5 and 130 pounds. As a sophomore, Thomas had been a scrub quarterback who didn't play in a game in '29 and had not gone out for football at all in '30 because of poor health. Now, he was the team's third-string quarterback.

Poor George Lasich, the captain, and one of only two regulars from last season. He had been the starting fullback for two years and now he was surrounded by a pack of klutzes. Surprisingly, the team did have some talent. Five other lettermen had returned but Tom Curry already had been beaten out at center by sophomore Stan Zawacki. Three other spot starters in the line also were back—Bill McMillen, Stan Stempeck and Chuck Gilliard—as was backup quarterback Snyder. George "Red" Collins also was there. Collins had started some games at halfback in '28 but had quit school to get married. He would be the starting left halfback to go with Lasich, Snyder and a non-letterman senior named Phil Moonves, who would have an up and down season, at right halfback. That was the extent of the experience in Higgins' lineup. A couple of other sophomores did not look too bad, particularly two ends, Harold Rosenberg and Tom Slusser. Last year's seniors also had been high on Slusser of Schenley High School in Pittsburgh, because they had given him "the tradition hat," a battered old felt headpiece passed on each year by senior players to the "outstanding athlete of the freshman class."

Actually, considering what he had to work with, Higgins' came up with a team that was hard working and never gave up, staying in many games until it tired in the last quarter. They certainly upheld the Nittany Lions' tradition on defense but were simply overmatched by just about all the teams on the schedule.

Three games defined the season, the Beaver Field opener against Waynesburg, the Homecoming encounter with Pitt six games later, and the season finale against Lehigh.

State had never played Waynesburg before and even during this time of no-scholarships, the Southwestern Pennsylvania school was considered a lightweight in football. It was coached by Frank Wolf, the quarterback on State's 1917 wartime team whose injury against W&J had been the big break for Charlie Way to get into the lineup and eventually become an All-American. Wolf had his team well-prepared for his return to Beaver Field. As the writer for the *"Penn State Athletic Records Scrapbook"* reported: "From the opening whistle the Yellow Jackets played as good a brand of football as has been seen here in many a year." Waynesburg scored the only touchdown of the game in the second quarter on a two-yard sprint around right end following a drive from midfield and walked away with a shocking, 7-0 victory. Writ-

ing about what happened, Ted Hoyt of the *Philadelphia Evening Ledger* asked the same question many State fans did : "And who ever heard of Waynesburg in football? Offhand, it's an even bet no local (Philadelphia) rooter knows whether Waynesburg is a school, a small college or a semipro eleven."

This was the first time State had lost the opening season game since the Bellefonte Academy upset in 1908. By the time the Nittany Lions met Pitt on October 31, they had lost three more games and had posted their only win of the "regular" season. The victory came in the second game of the year over Lebanon Valley, 19-0, and surprised the students who realized early that they were rooting for a very poor team. "...although the student body seemed to be of the opinion that the outcome was doubtful," the writer of the *"Penn State Athletic Records Scrapbook"* noted, "it was one we were expected to take easily...On the whole the game was not an exceptional one." At least the writer was honest. Lasich was the star and the writer wondered about "our fears for what will happen when Lasich is gone."

State traveled to Philadelphia the following week to play another first time opponent, Temple, at Owls Stadium. The highlight of the day for State fans was in the morning, several hours before kickoff, when the school's celebrated 75-piece marching Blue Band paraded through downtown Philadelphia and around City Hall. Actually, the team played an excellent defensive game against the favored Owls, who outweighed State by a remarkable 30 pounds per man and eventually wore out the Lions. And the outcome might have been different if not for a major error late in the second quarter.

A crowd of some 20,000 watched on a very hot day as the teams battled fairly evenly through much of the first half. Then, Curry recovered a Temple fumble at the Owl 40-yard line and despite a 15-yard penalty on the first play, two successive pass completions took State to the Temple 25. A pass interference call moved the ball another five yards and that's when Temple's center Henry Reese made the play of the game. Reese picked off Snyder's pass at the line of scrimmage and raced 80 yards untouched for a touchdown. State blocked the kick and the half ended moments later. Temple took the second half kickoff and marched 75 yards for another TD but missed the PAT. The rest of the game was played between the 30-yard lines until midway in the fourth quarter when Temple reached State's four-yard line and another TD seemed inevitable. But the Lions stopped Temple three times at the one-inch line and the Owls settled for a 12-0 win. "The State team deserves a word of praise," wrote Lud Wray, former coach at Penn, who covered the game for the *Philadelphia Record*, "for, led by Captain Lasich, they refused to quit and fought doggedly against a more experienced and far stronger opponent."

There appeared to be a natural letdown the next week when State played old-time rival Dickinson for the first time in 24 years. The game had been arranged last season by one-time Lions' star Red Griffiths who was coaching Dickinson at the time but he had resigned to return to graduate school and Joe McCormick was now at the helm. A Dad's Day crowd of 6,000 saw the favored Lions lose, 10-6, as Dickinson scored on a 55-yard pass in the second quarter and a 20-yard field goal in the third. Both teams were penalized for about 100 yards. State avoided a shutout late in the game on a 20-yard pass from little used QB Don Conn to Slusser. It was only the second win in 13 games for the visitors and the Dickinson students back in Carlisle celebrated the surprise win over "the big school" the entire weekend. "...Carlisle police officers used more than a dozen tear gas bombs to quell the demonstration...," the *Philadelphia Inquirer* reported, "...(and) a truce was called by the officers when five of the participants were locked in the local jail."

So, with demoralizing losses to Waynesburg, Temple and Dickinson, you might wonder what would happen next. Two days after the Dickinson embarrassment, State's president Hetzel announced that the football team would play a post-season game against Lehigh in Philadelphia on the Saturday of the Thanksgiving holiday weekend, November 28, to benefit the unemployed. This was the Depression and such a charity game seemed natural when proposed by Philadelphia city officials. Both teams had begun de-emphasizing football and other sports years before and both had big followings in the Philadelphia area. The University of Pennsylvania, which was just starting its own de-emphasis, donated Franklin Field as the site of the game and Penn State and Lehigh agreed to donate the proceeds to charity after taking off minimum expenses.

Whether it was the enticement of the post-season game or just the annual ritual of getting fired-up for Syracuse, but Higgins' misfits went out the next week and played what was their best game of the season against a vastly superior opponent. The 4-0 Orange was the third highest scoring team in the East with 176 points against 25 for its opponents and was heavily favored. "Hill Hopes to Run Up Score," said the headline in the *Syracuse Journal* preview story of the game, which went on to say that "an ordinary victory over Penn State will not add to Syracuse's prestige..." Another headline in the *Syracuse Post Standard* the next day told what happened: "Orange Lucky To Win Over Penn Staters."

Bedenk's scouting report may have made the difference. Except for the first quarter, when Syracuse scored a touchdown at the end of a 45-yard drive, the Nittany Lions outplayed the home team before a capacity crowd of 20,000 at Archbold Stadium. A dropped pass and Syracuse's aggressive goal line defense kept State from winning. Moonves took the opening kickoff of the second half and ran 91 yards before being tackled at the four-yard line but Syracuse held on downs. Late in the fourth quarter, State recovered a Syracuse fumble at the Orange 20-yard line and moments later Lasich threw a perfect pass to Moonves wide open at the goal line but Moonves dropped the ball. The Lions had one last chance a minute later when a poor punt and a 15-yard penalty gave them the ball near the 20. But a completed pass to the five-yard line brought the game to an end and Syracuse (which went on to a 7-1-1 record, losing only to Colgate) beat State for the first time in five years, 7-0.

With State no longer a holiday attraction in Pittsburgh, Pitt had agreed to visit Beaver Field for the first time since 1902. Only the most die hard of Nittany Lions fans could have believed the change of scenery would help State overcome the annual let down in Pittsburgh. Pitt was again contending for the National Championship and some players on its fourth team could have cracked State's starting lineup. Pitt's coach Jock Sutherland knew it, so he decided to rest his first team. He started the second team, played the third and fourth teams in the last three quarters and Pitt coasted to a 41-6 victory, scoring the most points ever against State since the series began in 1893. The game was over almost when it began. Moonves fumbled the opening kickoff, Pitt recovered at the 16-yard line and scored four plays later. Pitt's ensuing kickoff went over the end zone but on State's first play from the 20, Moonves fumbled again, Pitt recovered at the 24 and on the next play had another TD. Three minute had been played and it

was 13-0. By the end of the first quarter it was 27-0 and Pitt had a 41-0 lead in the third quarter before the thoroughly outclassed Lions scored on a 10-yard pass at the end of a 44-yard drive.

As the Homecoming crowd of about 10,000 drifted out of Beaver Field, they were stunned to see Pitt's first team take the field to work out. Some of the State fans booed and yelled names at Pitt's coach. It had been insulting enough that Sutherland had not started his first team, but sending the regulars out for a 15-minute workout on the home field of your traditional rival was an outrage. Many sportswriters who witnessed the incident criticized Sutherland "unmercifully" for his effrontery. The truth apparently did not reach the public until early December when it was confirmed in print that Sutherland had received Higgins' permission before the game to conduct the post-game workout. Sutherland wanted to keep his first eleven in shape for Pitt's next game with Carnegie Tech and he said he had waited until most fans had left the field before sending the players out. Of course, many State fans never did learn of the real circumstances and stewed about the "insult" for years.

Colgate was also heavily favored in the Pennsylvania Day game the following week but Andy Kerr started his first team, and scored a touchdown midway in the first quarter for a 6-0 lead. But a few minutes later, State took a surprising 7-6 lead after recovering a fumbled punt. Colgate marched 80 yards in the second quarter for another score but State's defense kept the Lions in the game until the fourth quarter when injuries forced Higgins to put most of his third and fourth string scrubs into the game and Colgate drove for TDs twice from midfield to win, 32-7.

The sixth straight loss that tied the record of the 1913 team came in Easton the next Saturday when unbeaten and unscored upon Lafayette used a passing offense and two intercepted passes to romp over State, 33-0. State never got closer to scoring than the 17-yard line early in the third period.

The record-setting seventh consecutive defeat occurred before a West Virginia Homecoming crowd in Morgantown but Higgins' weary troops didn't go down easily. WVC was favored and finished the game with overwhelming statistics, such as 16 first downs to five, as State's offense never threatened. But until the fourth quarter the Mountaineers could only manage one TD a 50-yard run in the opening period. Then, with a slim 6-0 lead early in the last quarter, WV's backup QB Bill Parriott replaced captain Doyle and passed the Mountaineers to two quick touchdowns and West Virginia won, 19-0.

Most of the sportswriters expected Lehigh to extend State's losing streak to eight in their post-season matchup the following Saturday at Franklin Field. Lehigh was almost as lousy as State with a 3-6 record but the Bears (as they were called then) had demonstrated a greater scoring punch and had lost to Lafayette by just six points. It had been 10 years since the schools had met on a football field and because of State's large following in the Philadelphia area and Lehigh's nearby location, city officials figured a huge crowd would be there for the charity event. Some pre-game newspaper accounts speculated about which "needy" organization would be selected to get the financial windfall.

The weather was chilly and damp and a meager 2,500 persons showed up. What they saw was a Penn State team that shocked everyone when the 31-0 score was reported around the East. State's attack led by Lasich was nearly flawless and its defense was insurmountable and the score might have been higher had Lehigh not made two fine goal line stands in the third quarter. State scored in the first five minutes, marching 40 yards after recovering a Lehigh fumble, with Snyder catching a 14-yard pass from Moonves for the TD. In the second quarter, another drive from midfield following a punt put the ball on the four-yard line from where Lasich faked a run and handed off to Moonves who bolted into the end zone. Moonves got his second TD with a 50 yard run in the third quarter and Lasich finished off the scoring in the final period with one TD on a six yard run and another on a 34-yard return of an intercepted pass. "No man could have shown to better advantage than did Lasich yesterday," wrote Stan Baumgartner in the *Philadelphia Inquirer*. "He did everything perfectly. Even the weakness of the opposition could not dim the brilliance of his sustained drive (on offense)...(or) his sturdy backing up the line on defense. These attributes would have won him recognition against any team in the country."

As for the big financial bonanza for the unemployed, the total receipts were $3,492.50 and expenses for State and Lehigh amounted to $2,348.92. That meant $1,143.52 for the jobless—which may not have been too bad considering the cost of living in 1931-32.

With the big victory, Higgins, reflecting on State's purity policies—and only partly kidding—claimed to be "the best amateur team in the East." In a speech he made after the season, and reported in Rich Donnell's book, *The Hig*, Higgins said: "The only other strictly amateur teams that I know were the University of Princeton (sic) and the University of Lehigh (sic). Lehigh defeated Princeton in the middle of the season by a rather large score and in our post season game with Lehigh we won with a score of 31-0, giving Penn State the championship of the three pioneers."

But the best summation of the 1931 season as well as a prediction of the one that would follow may have been best made by a 1922 State graduate from Emporia, KS, named Jim Benfer who wrote a letter to the *Philadelphia Ledger* which said: "I understand Bob Higgins has had to play half of the glee club this year, and if I follow your (columnist) correctly Penn [also in a de-emphasizing period] will be playing the cheerleaders next year. Why not get Penn State and Penn, real natural rivals, together?"

Penn wasn't on the 1932 schedule but based on what occurred, Higgins must have thought about using the glee club *and* the cheerleaders, at least to find a kicker.

Season Record 2-8
Record to Date 222-125-26
Winning percentage .630

"Oh, For A Placekicker"

When one looks back through 110 years of Penn State football and sees the 2-5 record of the 1932 team, it is easy to dismiss the squad as another batch of no-talent bums. Considering the schedule it played and the continued dependence on the general student body for players, this may have been the hard luck team of all time. With just a break or two, the team easily could have been 5-2. A dependable placekicker would have helped.

Harvard and Colgate were the only teams on the schedule that were of a far higher caliber and one wonders why Harvard was even there. Harvard was still a football power and the teams had not met on the field since the famous 21-21 tie of 1921. After the '32 game, they never played again. Colgate was fulfilling the end of a three-year contract and by time State played Colgate again in 1941 the teams were of equal quality. Syracuse and Temple were the only other teams on the schedule besides Harvard and Colgate which were still giving out scholarships to athletes and subsidizing their football players and both were fortunate to escape their '32 games against State with victories. One other superior team, Pitt, had been on the original '32 schedule for a Thanksgiving Day engagement in Pittsburgh. But when athletic director Bezdek insisted on a $20,000 guarantee instead of a percentage of the gate, Pitt canceled that game as well as the one in 1933 that had been scheduled for Pitt Stadium in early November. The cancellation meant that for the first time in five years, State would be playing just three games on the road. It also was the shortest schedule since the abbreviated one of four games in 1918 because of World War I.

Once again, it was the Nittany Lions' erratic offense which brought about their demise. A consistent kicker could have tied if not won a couple of games and the backfield lacked a player who could deliver a big play in the clutch. Red Collins, the first married man in history to be elected captain, was the team's best running back and one of several players who Higgins used as a kicker, but his supporting cast was thin. Before the season ended, Higgins would depend on several sophomores to help lead the team.

The defining moment of the season came late in the fourth quarter of the second game when Waynesburg pulled off another upset, winning 7-6, before another Dad's Day crowd of 4,000 at Beaver Field. The manner by which State lost would set the tempo for additional losses later in the year. For three periods the game was scoreless as the defenses of both teams held each other's offense in check. Then, with about three minutes left in the game, Lion sophomore Leo Skemp scampered 57 yards to set up a Bill Lohr's 13-yard touchdown run. Collins' PAT was wide, giving coach Frank Wolfe's team hope. The Lions appeared to clinch the game moments later when Lohr intercepted an errant Waynesburg pass that had bounced off two Waynesburg players and a State player before Lohr had grabbed it. But, according to the rules, it was an illegal pass because two Waynesburg players had touched it before the interception and required a mandatory loss of down penalty. "This penalty may not be declined," Rule seven, Section five, Item two stated. On the next play, Waynesburg halfback Rob Curry, who had 163 yards on 10 carries, ran 45-yards to the State one-inch line. Sub quarterback Adam Donnelly, who had just entered the game, plunged over for the tying touchdown, then kicked the extra point that gave Waynesburg the shocking victory. "Odd Play Marks Waynesburg's Victory over Penn State," said the headline in the *Pittsburgh Post-Gazette*. "Waynesburg, apparent loser, went on suddenly to victory," the reporter wrote. "The result of the game has created another uproar in little Waynesburg...It is almost certain that the townsfolk will gather up all the old furniture, fences and other combustibles which were overlooked one year ago and repeat the big bonfire..." It would also be the last bonfire after a Penn State game because the two teams would never play each other again.

One week before Waynesburg, State had beaten Lebanon Valley in the season opener, 27-0, scoring within the first six minutes, getting another touchdown minutes later on the return of a 25-yard pass interception by sophomore Lou Kreizman and a third by another sophomore, Harry Sigel, before the second quarter was over. In the first and third quarters Lebanon Valley advanced to State's five-yard line only to lose the ball on downs but the defense had some problems coping with the visitor's passing attack, particularly in the second half. Higgins took advantage of the new substitution rule which virtually created the two-platoon system of substituting full teams once during each quarter and used 32 players.

The first away game at Harvard caused so many injuries that not many observers believed the team would recover for the following week's Homecoming game against Syracuse. "Lions Put Up Great Battle Against Odds," was the headline in the *Pittsburgh Press*. "Nittany Eleven Wilts After Making Fine Early Stand." Harvard led by just 19-7 at the half thanks to a 64-yard run with a recovered fumble by tackle Irad Hardy. The Crimson broke it open when State's outmanned team tired in the second half and Harvard gave the Lions a physical beating in winning 46-13. Still, State's players took some solace knowing they scored the most points against the Harvard line in two years.

Syracuse was in a partial rebuilding year with nearly 30 sophomores on the varsity and a few key seniors on its first team. The Orange came into Beaver Field a slight favorite with a 2-2 record and in the first quarter looked as if it was going to finally win big against State. Syracuse had never been able to score more than 10 points in a game against the Lions since the series began 10 years before but by the end of the opening period it had a 12-0 lead. State's defense tightened up after that and the offense got a touchdown in the second quarter but missed the extra point. As had been the case in the Waynesburg defeat, the game came down to the fourth quarter. This time it was State's inability to score from the six-inch line that lost the game. Late in the quarter, three long runs put the ball on the Syracuse 14-yard line but the Orange held and punted out. Moments later, State was a half-foot away from the goal with a third down but the final whistle sounded before the Lions could get another play off and they lost, 12-6.

The game at Colgate the following Saturday was the lowest point of the season. Colgate, which would end the season unbeaten, untied and unscored upon, clobbered the Lions, 31-0, before its own Homecoming crowd. As Ridge Riley would write more than 50 years later, "What happened in the third quarter symbolized the nadir for Penn State football: The Lion punter kicked the ball right into the rear end of his halfback, who was therefore credited with blocking his own kick." That may have been a weird gaffe that typified the incompetence of the '32 team but to show again that history does repeat itself, a similar goof on a punt in a big game at Alabama in 1982 almost cost State a chance at it's first National Championship.

In the final home game of the season, State met Sewanee, the University of the South, for the first and only time in history. Junior Clyde "King" Cole, a wrestler who had been urged to come out for football this year and was now a starter at tackle, recovered two fumbles in the first half to set up two touchdowns that won the Pennsylvania Day game. Cole's first recovery came when Sewanee muffed the opening kickoff and Cole recovered at the Sewanee 30-yard line. Sigel went around end for the TD moments later. Cole also made his next recovery at Sewanee's 30-yard line and sophomore Merrill Morrison got that TD on a four-yard burst up the middle. As usual, State missed both extra point attempts. Sewanee, which eventually had a negative yardage of 37 yards, narrowed the score to 12-6 at the half before Collins

put the game out of reach late in the fourth quarter by intercepting a pass and running 42-yards for the TD. Again State missed the PAT but won, 18-6.

Some 15,000 were at Owls Stadium on November 12 expecting to see unbeaten Temple easily defeat the visitors from State College in State's final game of the season. Again, the Lions were outweighed by about 24 pounds per man but they stymied the heavier Owl backs throughout the game. State stunned the hometown crowd with a first quarter charge that had Temple holding on with two great goal line stands. State first drove 46 yards to Temple's one-yard line before losing the ball on downs but got the ball back at the one moments later when Slusser blocked a Temple punt. Again, Temple held and punted out as the period ended. On the first play of the second quarter, Lohr hit senior end Jerry Brewster on 33-yard pass for a touchdown. State lined up to kick the extra point but tried to pass for the point. Collins' throw to Slusser was batted down. Temple stormed back with two TDs to take a 13-6 lead but early in the fourth quarter State had a chance to tie it. Lohr's 21-yard pass to Collins bounced off a Temple back's hands into Collins' arms and he went into the end zone. This time, Collins tried to kick to tie the game but his boot was wide right. The *Philadelphia Inquirer's* report of the game pretty well summarized the entire season: "A raging, roaring Nittany Lion, snarling its defiance to the very last, bowed its head in defeat to a courageous but unwary Owl yesterday only because it lacked a leader who could convert either of the extra points after its two touchdowns."

The anonymous writer for "*The Penn State Athletic Records Scrapbook*" tried his best to rationalize the dismal finish. "The season as a whole was very successful, considering that most of the teams on the schedule had subsidized athletes, several of the schools being considered the leading eastern teams," he opined. Very successful? Hardly. The team, despite its effort and bad luck, was another of the big losers in State history, one of only nine teams to win just two games or less, and that included the first four pioneer teams (1887-through-1890) and the World War I team of 1918.

But help was on the way. The Hig's old alumni friends had figured out a way to get him some good high school football players and there were already several of those fine athletes on the freshmen team. Things were about to get better for Higgins.

Season Record 2-5
Record to Date 224-130-26
Winning percentage .624

"The Turning Point"

No one knew it at the time but this was the turning point season for Higgins and the beginning of Penn State's long climb back to football respectability. Regaining elite status as a perennial national power would not occur until nearly a half-century later under Joe Paterno. But in 1933, State football hit the bottom and began inching back up.

There were still two more losing seasons just ahead but the '33 team went from the outhouse to—well, not the penthouse but at least to the first floor. It was the last game of the year at Penn that defined the season but it was the second game, against little Muhlenberg, that State reached its nadir.

Higgins had 10 lettermen returning from the '32 team but he was again counting on several sophomores to fill key positions, including Frank "Red" O'Hora at quarterback and his distant cousin, Jim, at center. Both had been "recruited" by Dunmore High School principal Jim Gilligan, who helped them find jobs to pay for their education. They had been starters, along with two good looking running backs, Bill Cooper and Ron Knapp, on

Coach Bob Higgins (right) and Captain Tommy Slusser, an all-around offensive and defensive end, pose at the railroad station enroute to an away game in 1933.

what everyone said was the school's best freshman team in years, one that had a 2-2-1 record and lost to Pitt's subsidized freshman team by just 13-0. In Cooper, Higgins also had found the placekicker he desperately had needed in '32. Red O'Hora was the best punter on the varsity in years.

Slusser, now the captain, headed up the returning letterman, which also included running backs, Sigel, Morrison and Skemp, and the regular tackles, Cole and Dick Woolbert. End Hal Rosenberg, who had lettered in '31, also was back as were linemen Kreizman, Parker Berry, Wilson Anderson, and Tony Bedoski. Quarterback Al Mikelonis (Michaels) had not lettered but Higgins was planning to use him to spell O'Hora at QB. (Mikelonis later changed his last name to the Americanized version, Michaels, and became a long-time assistant coach to Higgins.)

Ever since State stopped playing with scholarship players, it had been curtailing and downgrading its schedule and the one set for this season was seen as "nearly perfect" for State's situation. Columbia, a newcomer, was the only team completely outside of State's class, and one of the rationalizations for scheduling Columbia was to obtain exposure in New York City. Syracuse and Penn also were still on a higher level than State for they had not de-emphasized athletics on the same scale as the Nittany Lions. Higgins and others within the athletic administration didn't want to completely emasculate the football program and so it continued to schedule some tougher teams.

Not for the opener, of course. The game with good old Lebanon Valley on October 7 was the latest State had started a season since 1918. The result was the same as it always would be with Lebanon Valley. State turned a 26-0 halftime lead into a 32-6 victory as Higgins used many substitutes after the intermission. Five different players scored touchdowns and Cooper had a pair of extra points.

State had not played Muhlenberg since 1920 and a Dad's Day crowd of 4,000 showed up expecting to see State repeat its thrashing of Lebanon Valley. But Muhlenberg's defense was exceptionally tough in its own territory, stopping several State drives on downs, including one at the 15-yard line. State gained 129 yards on the ground to 74 for

the visitors, but one Muhlenberg thrust reached State's two-yard line before being halted. Midway through the fourth quarter, Red Weiner kicked a 38-yard field goal to give the visitors a 3-0 lead. With time running out, State fans thought it had a come-from-behind victory when Mikelonis hit Slusser on a long pass but Slusser was out of the end zone when he made the catch. Muhlenberg's 3-0 upset stunned the East and many State fans figured a fourth straight losing season was now a certainty. "Penn State Falls Before Muhlenberg in Surprise," said the headline in the *Pittsburgh Press*, "State's Attack Appears Woefully Weak." That would be an understatement.

The night before the Homecoming game against Lehigh, students and alumni turned out enmasse for what the chronicler of the *"Penn State Athletic Records Scrapbook"* called "one of the largest and best pep rallys (sic) ever staged on the Penn State campus." Inspired by the rally, the writer added, "State's aggregation looked like an entirely different team from the week before." As a crowd of 8,000 looked on, Slusser caught touchdown passes from O'Hora in the first and second quarters and set up another TD in the second quarter with a fumble recovery as State walloped the visitors, 33-0.

The following week, the score was reversed as Columbia hammered State 33-0 at Baker Field in New York City. State held its own for most of the first half and trailed by just 13-0 after Columbia recovered a State fumble just before the intermission and turned it into a TD pass. But the Lions, outweighed by 15 pounds per man, tired in the second half and Columbia made it look easy with three more TDs, rolling up a total of 368 yards and 14 first downs to just 45 yards and three first downs for State. Considering that Lou Little's team went on to beat Stanford in the Rose Bowl, Higgins' "amateurs" certainly were not dishonored by this defeat.

No one could have predicted that the outcome of the game against heavily-favored Syracuse at Archbold Stadium would be similar to the one at Beaver Field in '32. The Orange had lost to Michigan State and Brown after starting the season with three wins and was fired up for State. But State was fired up, too, and after Syracuse had scored a touchdown in the first quarter on a series of line bucks and end runs to go ahead 6-0, the defenses took over and stopped each other's offense several times close to the goal lines. Early in the fourth quarter, Mikelonis' passing set up a TD run by Sigel that tied the score but once again State missed the PAT. Syracuse stormed back and made it 12-6 as time was winding down. State had one last chance and marched all the way to the Syracuse 12-yard line as time ran out just as it had the previous season.

For the first and only time State played Johns Hopkins, in a Pennsylvania Day game closing out the home schedule. The Nittany

Lions scored two touchdowns before the visitors could run one play. Johns Hopkins fumbled the opening kickoff and Cooper scored from the five-yard line after a short 30-yard drive. Because of the rules at the time, State was on the receiving end of the ensuing kickoff and Morrison ran it back 50 yards to the Blue Jay's 35-yard line. Sigel got the TD a short time later and Cooper's extra point made it 13-0 with just a few minutes gone in the game. After it was 20-0 early in the second quarter, Higgins sent in his reserves. And that was when junior Jim Boring, who would never play enough in his three-year career to earn a letter, made the play that is still in State's record books. He ran back a punt 100 yards for a touchdown, breaking Dex Very's record 70-yard punt return against Penn in 1911. State went on to win, 40-6, scoring the most points since beating Marshall in 1930.

Now, the difference between a winning and losing season would come down to the season finale against traditional rival Penn at Franklin Field. Penn had broken off relations after State's "roughhouse tactics" had helped beat the Quakers in 1929 but the bad blood had dissipated in the wake of purity policies at both schools. Still, Penn was playing and winning against a better class of opponents and it was favored to continue State's seasonal losing streak.

State was in control almost from the opening kickoff and continually drove deep into Penn territory during the first half only to be frustrated by the Quaker defense and lose the ball on downs. The Lions lost a major scoring opportunity midway in the second quarter when Sigel ran back a punt to Penn's 13-yard line but Cooper fumbled on the next play and Penn recovered. Then, with about a minute left in the half, Slusser made a sensational catch over his shoulders in the end zone on a 45-yard pass thrown by O'Hora. Cooper was out of the game, so O'Hora tried the extra point but it skidded to the right. State continued to dominate the third quarter but again was thwarted by Penn's defense. Midway through the fourth quarter, Penn tied the game on a 45-yard pass similar to the State TD as Don Kellett hit Johnny Pennypacker but Kellet also missed the PAT with a kick that was wide right. After forcing State to punt, Penn drove down to the State 20-yard line as the clock ticked away. Once again, the Lions defense came through, stopping the Quakers in four downs, and the game ended two plays later. "Another Centre County eleven, true to the glorious fighting traditions of the Nittany Lions, arose from the stygian [extremely dark] blackness of a mediocre season," wrote Stan Baumgartner in the *Philadelphia Inquirer*, "to shatter all pre-game prognostications and hold an acknowledgedly superior Penn machine to a 6-6 tie before 20,000 astonished and thrilled gridiron fans." Higgins told sportswriters he was "overjoyed with the results of the game." It was a moral victory and it brought an end to the losing seasons.

But winning was still four years away, and by then State's best and toughest player of the 1930s had graduated and was playing in the National Football League.

Season Record 3-3-1
Record to Date 227-133-27
Winning percentage .621

"Little Mike & Big Chuck"

No one in the crowd of 23,000 at Baker Field could believe what was happening. Here it was, early in the fourth quarter, and State was leading the great Columbia team, 7-0. Not even the few thousand Penn State rooters who were seeing it for their own eyes had given the Nittany Lions much of a chance against the defending Rose Bowl champions.

Sure, State had been unbeaten going into this game. Just like the old days, Higgins' team had won its first three games at Beaver Field and had looked impressive doing it, too. But this wasn't Gettysburg and Lehigh out there in the New York City October sunshine. This was Lou Little's juggernaut, one of the powers in college football. But, so far, it was Penn State that playing like the team seeking the National Championship.

Al Mikelonis, the senior quarterback who everyone called "Shorty," was playing the game of his life. He had engineered the surprisingly quick touchdown in the first quarter, place-kicked the extra point and, since then, had been keeping Columbia off balance with his punting. The punts had helped contain Columbia in its own territory for much of the game, allowing State's aggressive defense to take some chances as it continually smeared Columbia's speedy backs at the line of scrimmage. After three quarters, the highly-favored home team had been no closer to State's goal than the 23-yard line. Mikelonis' 24-yard pass to sophomore end Frank Smith following a Columbia punt to midfield had beaten the touted Columbia defense, setting up the State touchdown. On the next play, Bill Knapp had skirted right end for another 28 yards and then fullback Tommy Silvano had plunged through right tackle one yard for the touchdown. From that point on, Mikelonis' punting and State's tough defense had been dominating the game.

Mikelonis' performance had been a surprise to Columbia. Although he was a senior, he was a relative unknown. In fact, he probably would be nothing more than a little used substitute in this game if last year's starting quarterback, Red O'Hora, had not dropped out of school after spending most of the preseason sidelined with an ankle injury. That had given the 5-10, 158-pounder from DuBois his chance, starting with the opening season game against Lebanon Valley, and Mikelonis had taken full advantage of it. He had become good at calling plays and thinking under pressure and, despite his size, was a fine blocker.

Silvano also was a significant addition to State's backfield. He was another of Jim Gilligan's Dunmore boys—the same high school class as Red and Jim O'Hora—and originally had gone to Notre Dame but transferred to State in '33 and had sat out last season. He was now the starting fullback, replacing the veteran Bill Cooper, who had opened the season against Lebanon Valley. Higgins had been tinkering with his starting lineup ever since preseason practice started September 9. His backfield was pretty much set now with lettermen Knapp and Sigel sharing one halfback position and Morrison, now the captain, starting at the other half. Sigel also was used at fullback.

Up front it was a different story. Higgins had just six lettermen returning and the line was constantly changing. It was a mix of veterans, hot-shot sophomores and untested juniors and seniors. "Much

Depends on Work of Sophomore Material," the *Centre Daily Times* had heralded in a preseason analysis. Higgins had been optimistic about the season because of the sophomores, saying they were "strong sophomores, all with a great deal of potential ability and plenty of skill...We have only nine seniors on the entire squad this year, and with an incoming freshman group of more than average strength, we feel better about the football future of Penn State right now than at any time for a number of years."

Higgins and his line coach, Bedenk, were particularly impressed with a sophomore recruited by Gilligan—Chuck Cherundolo of Old Forge. Cherundolo was a throwback to another era. He loved to hit people and was a ferocious tackler. He was as good of a linebacker as Higgins had seen at State in years and he seemed to make everyone around him play better. Cherundolo already had displaced the veteran Jim O'Hora as the starting center for the Columbia game. Other sophs now starting included Smith at right end, Roy Schuyler at right tackle, Lou Barth at left guard. Veterans Kreizman at right guard and Weber at left tackle and junior Art Fry at left end rounded out the line. As the season progressed, Higgins would come to depend on several more sophomores and inexperienced reserves, including a senior end named Hugh Rodham, a big kid from the hard coal region who was out for the team for the first time. (Sixty years later Rodham would become better known as the father of First Lady Hillary Rodham Clinton.)

A large crowd at Beaver Field sometime in the 1930s or early 1940s. The field was located across the street from Recreation Hall and near the Nittany Lion Inn.

After scrimmaging Lock Haven and the freshman team in the preseason, word spread that this team could be the best in years. Higgins contributed to the high expectations when he penned an article for the *Beaver Field Pictorial*, saying "our team this year will be a decided improvement over those of recent years." Higgins' enthusiasm helped bring out a record opening day crowd of 5,422 that saw State beat Lebanon Valley, 13-0. Higgins substituted freely and limited his offense to a few plays. Silvano scored a touchdown in the opening quarter on a two-yard plunge to climax a 45-yard drive and Morrison got the second TD a short time later on an end run. LV once reached State's three-yard line but the Lion held on downs.

An even bigger crowd of 6,797 turned out the following week to see State crush Gettysburg, 32-6. It had been six years since Gettysburg was on the schedule but the result was the same as it had been in 26 of 27 previous games. (The teams tied 0-0 tie in 1901.) Silvano made the most spectacular play of the day when he intercepted a pass in the second quarter and ran it back 83 yards for State's second touchdown. Gettysburg scored on a long pass in the second half when Higgins again cleared his bench.

State won its first away game in five years at Bethlehem with a trouncing of Lehigh, ironically by the same score as its 1931 post-season clash, 31-0. State recovered three Lehigh fumbles and blocked

two kicks to set up five of the six TDs. Sigel scored three of the TDs as State turned a 14-0 first quarter lead into an easy win. There was one disquieting note. The Lions could convert just one of six extra point attempts. Last year's prime kicker, Cooper, was having a tough time breaking into the lineup and Mikelonis' PAT kicking was inconsistent.

The State players were not deceiving themselves when they traveled to New York City for the October 27 game against Columbia. They knew they'd have to play 60 minutes of near perfect football to beat Little's team. Forty-five minutes, yes; 60 minutes, no. They still had that 7-0 lead at the end of the third quarter, but the State players were obviously tiring, and as the fourth quarter started, Columbia's Rose Bowl standouts, Ed Brominski and Al Barabas, took charge. Starting at it's own 48-yard line, Columbia tied the score in seven plays with a lateral from Brominski-to-Barabas picking up 23 yards. Barabas carried three straight plays from State's 11-yard line, the final six for the touchdown, then kicked the extra point to make it 7-7. After the kickoff, Columbia's defense forced State to punt and Columbia took the ball on its own 44-yard line. On the first play, Brominski raced 36 yards before sophomore reserve end, Bob Morini, tackled him to save a touchdown. But five plays later, Brominski went three yards through a big hole over his left tackle for the go-ahead TD and Barabas booted another extra point. Columbia's defense stopped State and Columbia escaped with a 14-7 victory.

"Columbia's Rally Downs Penn State," said the headline in the *New York Times*. "Aerial Attack Saves Day." Daniel C. McCarthy, who covered the game, wrote: "It was expected that the Nittany Lions would make a close battle of it, but it never was thought that Coach Bob Higgins' pupils would come so close to toppling Columbia." Despite the loss, this was the defining moment of the season for it showed that Higgins' 1934 squad could stay on the same field against a superior opponent but simply didn't have enough manpower to dominate an entire game. It was a circumstance that would mark the team for the rest of the season.

There was an obvious let down the next week even though it was a Homecoming game and the opponent was Syracuse. All 12 previous games with the Orange had been close, even when Syracuse was highly-favored. This was Syracuse's best team in years and it was undefeated when it invaded Beaver Field November 4. State had about as many opportunities to score as the Orange but Syracuse's heavier line meant the difference in the game. Midway through the first quarter, Knapp intercepted a pass at midfield. State drove all the way to the Syracuse one-yard line before being held on downs. Syracuse punted out but on the first play State fumbled, Syracuse recovered and then drove 74 yards for a touchdown. State's defense kept the Lions in the game but Syracuse scored another TD in the third quarter, picked up two points on a blocked kick for a safety and gained 440 yards and 23 first downs rushing to win with the highest score since the series began in 1922, 16-0.

State's offensive problems continued against Penn before a shivering crowd of 35,000 at Franklin Field. The Lions blew two big scoring opportunities, reaching the Quaker 10-yard line in the first quarter and the 14-yard line in the fourth quarter. But each time, State lost the ball on downs. In the third period, Penn mounted its only threat of the game. An 18-yard punt return and a 26-yard run set up a fourth down 23-yard field goal by Penn quarterback Frank Murray and that won the game, 3-0. Philadelphia sportswriters were impressed by State's performance. "Balked by the ferocious and determined defense of Penn State's Nittany Lion against running plays and passes yesterday afternoon on Franklin Field," wrote Perry Lewis in the *Philadelphia Inquirer,* "the Quakers of Penn staked all on the accuracy of Frank Murray's right foot—and he did not fail them." Many State fans considered this a moral victory, but the fact was this was a game the Lions should have won but didn't.

The players had difficulty getting over their stumble against Penn because their laggard spirit carried over three quarters in the final home game against Lafayette. "The first half was one of the sloppiest seen on Beaver Field in recent years," opined the writer for the *"Penn State Athletic Records Scrapbook."* "The game was featured by the marvelous comeback by State when it looked as if they (sic) were to lose to an apparently weaker team." Lafayette had taken a 6-0 lead in the second quarter when halfback Charley Stabley returned a punt 64-yards for a touchdown. Early in the fourth quarter, State tallied its first TD of the game on a 52-yard pass from sub halfback Dick Mauer to Fry to tie the score. That brought the team out of its lethargy. Cooper scored two touchdowns, one set up by a Cherundolo interception, and threw a 37-yard pass to Morrison for a third TD as State won, 25-6.

The victory guaranteed that State would have another non-losing season and, perhaps with a little extra effort and luck against Bucknell, the first winning season in six years. But, alas, a winning year would have to wait. A strong wind that blew up and down the muddy field at Memorial Stadium in Lewisburg seemed to affect State more than Bucknell. Higgins had decided to start his second team and three times in the first quarter, the reserves were near the Bucknell goal line but only scored once. The first time the Lions were close, Bucknell held on at its six-inch line and punted out. On the third attempt, Knapp ran 26-yards for a TD off a fake field goal. State hit the PAT and the 7-0 lead held up until the second half when Bucknell took control. "Maddened by a sudden Lion score in the first quarter," read the dispatch of the game in the *Philadelphia Inquirer,* "the bellowing Bisons of Bucknell ripped the Penn State line to shreds in the last three quarters, scoring twice in the third period to gain their fifth consecutive victory, 13 to 7, in a series that began 34 years ago." Once again, State had been able to battle evenly with a better team for much of a game, only to wear out at the end. Bucknell would go on to beat Miami in the first Orange Bowl game on January 1, 1935 and State would go back home wondering when the bleeding would stop.

So, Higgins ended his fifth year with another break-even season. Sure, the players were getting better thanks to Gilligan, Casey Jones and some other alumni. The freshmen team had won four games and only lost to Pitt's more talented frosh by a narrow, 13-0, score. For the first time in years, some individuals were starting to get national recognition. Mikelonis had made honorable mention on several All-American teams and some sportswriters believed Cherundolo could

be the next one.

But the schedule also was getting tougher. Pitt would be back in '35 after a three-year absence and Dick Harlow had agreed to bring his fine Western Maryland team to Beaver Field for the first time on Columbus Day. Villanova, another Eastern power, had replaced Columbia and the traditional games with Syracuse, Penn and Bucknell also were set. If Higgins was not careful, next season could be another long one.

Season Record 4-4
Record to Date 231-137-27
Winning percentage .619

"Defense Is Not Enough"

When one looks back at all the Penn State teams Bob Higgins coached, this squad may have been the best one that didn't reach its full potential. In the typical Nittany Lion tradition of the "purity" era, it was a very good defensive team with a fair offense and an inconsistent kicking game. But it seemed to lack that nebulous and abstract ingredient that often takes a team over the top or even beyond its capabilities.

A controversial decision by a referee cost it an upset win over Syracuse and the listless play of the offense led to another defeat by Bucknell. Two games were decided by a safety and a quirky 2-0 score, one a victory and the other a defeat. But it was the 33-6 loss to Penn—when the defense faltered for the only time during the year—that defined the season. The final record could have just as easily been 7-1 or 6-2 with a little luck and a big play or two.

The defense kept State in every game, even against Penn until the fourth quarter. The defensive line, including the linebackers, was the best Higgins had up to then and three players stood out the entire year. Captain Bob "Iron Man" Weber was a three-year starter at left tackle and for the second year in a row led the team in playing time with several games of 60 minutes. Cherundolo was as good as any center/linebacker in the East and eventually would be given an honorable mention on several All-America teams. But many fans and sportswriters were convinced the best defensive player of all that year was a sophomore from Pittsburgh via Kiski Prep named John Economos. Economos had been chosen by his teammates on last year's freshmen team to be the honorary captain and he quickly became a leader on the varsity from his right guard position.

Higgins had more letterman returning this year than ever before in his tenure. The 13 returnees included quarterback Red O'Hora, who had returned to school after one year's absence, and senior Bill Cooper, the fullback and sometimes kicker, who had won a letter as a sophomore but had limited playing time in '34. Knapp, another three-year vet, and Silvano had also returned to the backfield. The best running back on the team was another sophomore, Wendell "Wendy" Wear, who was nicknamed "Rabbit" because of his speed and elusive running style. Wear had been offered scholarships by several major colleges but chose State and its "job for education" program because he wanted to be close to his home in nearby Huntingdon, PA. Wear was a lightweight at 5-9, 130 pounds but he was a triple-threat who was not only an excellent runner but also a good passer, pass receiver and punter. The rest of the returning lettermen were linemen: Barth, Fry, Harry Latorre, Jim O'Hora, Schuyler, Smith and Frank Wismer. There also was an interesting addition to the coaching staff. Mikelonis, the star QB of '34, was now a varsity backfield coach.

The team got off to a slow start in the opener against Lebanon Valley at a refurbished Beaver Field. All the wooden grandstands on the west side had been torn down over the previous three years and now most of the 5,800 fans were sitting on steel benches. They must have been shocked to see underdog Lebanon Valley hold the Lions scoreless through three quarters and then take a 6-0 lead early in the fourth quarter. Lebanon Valley's shocking TD brought the team out of its sluggishness and the Lions took the kickoff and went 60 yards on seven plays, thanks largely to a 44-yard pass from O'Hora to Smith. Cooper tied the score on a plunge at the goal line but his PAT attempt was wide. As time was winding down, the Lions marched 53 yards on the ground for the winning TD, with Cooper going over from the three-yard line with about a minute left. He missed the extra point again and State got away with a 12-6 win. It was the closest score against Lebanon Valley since the series began in 1905 and would remain the closest because the teams would never play each other again.

Former Lion Dick Harlow had recruited Higgins out of a New Jersey prep school and had been the Hig's head coach when he first made All-American as a sophomore. Harlow was now the successful coach at Western Maryland and despite his bitter departure from State in a clash with Bezdek a decade earlier, he readily agreed to bring his team to Beaver Field as a favor to Higgins. Western Maryland was favored but the visitors never got past State's 25-yard line and their only scoring attempt was a third quarter field goal that failed. State won 2-0 on a safety in the middle of the first quarter. The Lions had driven deep into WM territory but O'Hora's fourth down pass had been intercepted by WM at its own two-yard line. On the first play, Western Maryland tried a pass from the end zone but the ball was short of the receiver and a State player fell on it in the end zone for two-points (as the rule of the day required). Late in the fourth quarter, the Lions almost scored again after getting the ball on their own 32-yard line. With Wear running for 41 yards himself, the Lions drove all the way to Western Maryland's seven-yard line before the whistle ended the game.

The day before the Homecoming game against Lehigh, a front page editorial in the daily student newspaper, *The Collegian*, criticized President Hetzel's administration and Bezdek's Athletic Association for exploiting the football players. The editorial railed at the hypocrisy of not giving players financial aid while collecting a lot of money in gate receipts and for scheduling "professional" opponents that used subsidized players. Higgins and his team must have been encouraged by the editorial because they went out and shut out undefeated Lehigh 26-0 before more than 7,000 fans. The Lions scored twice in the first quarter and never allowed Lehigh inside the 15-yard line until late in the fourth quarter. Reserve back Frank "Fritz" Andrews made the play of the day by running back a punt 80 yards for a touchdown. Andrews also threw a 33-yard pass for another TD. The students were so elated by the overwhelming victory they set two victory bonfires in downtown State College and caused some $1,000 in damages. President Hetzel said the students were "silly." (This wouldn't be the first time a State president would make such a comment about his students.)

The financial dispute which had caused a break off with Pitt after the 1931 game had been resolved and State traveled to Pittsburgh to renew the old rivalry on October 26. The Panthers were still out of State's class and had just come off another outstanding season

where they had claimed the National Championship. They were so heavily favored that only 18,000 showed up at Pitt Stadium. State's defense was outstanding, led by the tackling of Economos, who made several touchdown-saving tackles and got a standing ovation from his hometown Pittsburgh crowd when Higgins pulled him out near the end of the game. The Lions "clutch" defense stopped at least 10 Pitt scoring opportunities, including three inside the five-yard line, as the Panthers piled up 329 yards to State's 72. Pitt didn't score until less than a minute remained in the third quarter when Frank Patrick booted an 11-yard field goal after a fumble recovery set up a short drive from midfield to State's four-yard line. The Panthers, who lost three fumbles to State's alert defense, finally got a touchdown in the fourth quarter and, again, it was Patrick who scored. Years later, after Patrick had joined the Penn State coaching staff in the Engle era, he would frequently tease his fellow coach, Jim O'Hora, about his big day against O'Hora's team. "Lions Stage Great Fight But Weaken," said the headline in the *Pittsburgh Press* of the 9-0 Pitt victory. "Sutherland Scythe Commits Many Errors, Meets Stubborn Defense."

Of all the games played this season, the one before 12,000 at Archbold Stadium November 2 ultimately would have the most historical significance. It would be the first of many games with Syracuse that would end in controversy over a referee's decision. Syracuse was unbeaten in four games and favored but the game was close all the way and the outcome was not decided until the final, controversial play. State surprised the Orange in the first quarter with a drive that led to a 20-yard field goal by Cooper from a difficult angle. From that point, the game developed into defensive see-saw with both teams marching up and down the field without scoring. At least five times the Syracuse offense led by fullback Vannie Albanese penetrated deep into State territory only to be stopped by the Lions' defense, twice at the four-yard line. On one drive, Albanese carried the ball 19 straight times over the middle and he finished the game with 70 of Syracuse's 115 rushing yards.

With its running offense thwarted for more than three quarters, Syracuse decided to go to the air late in the fourth quarter. There was a minute left when Albanese caught a pass in the flat at State's 17-yard line and rambled into the end zone for a touchdown. The PAT made it 7-3 and Syracuse kicked off. On the first play, O'Hora threw a high pass to midfield where reserve end Bob Morini stood surrounded by several Syracuse defenders. Morini leaped high to grab the pass but as he did a Syracuse defender slapped the ball. Miraculously, it fell into the hands of a substitute State running back, Art Yett, who clutched it into his chest and ran nearly 50 yards for what would have been the winning touchdown. Syracuse's coach, Vic Hanson, protested vigorously that the play was illegal, claiming that Morini had last touched the ball and that no Syracuse player had handled it. The referee ruled for Syracuse and the game ended 7-3 with State players shouting that they were robbed. Some newspaper photos the next day showed a Syracuse defender batting the ball out of Morini's hands but the visual proof didn't change the score.

Determined to prove they should have won the Syracuse game, the players prepared themselves mentally all week in practice for the Villanova contest at Beaver Field. State showed "the strongest offensive and the greatest form of the year to date," according to the writer of the "*Penn State Athletic Records Scrapbook*." The 27-13 victory was considered the first major upset for Higgins since he became the coach six years earlier. The Lions had a three touchdown lead early in the second quarter before Villanova tried to come back.

Cooper scored three of the TDs and gained 113 yards in leading the attack and his punting kept Villanova "in constant trouble" all day. Near the end of the game, his punt of 65 yards from the State goal line sailed over the head of the Villanova safety man and virtually iced the win for the Lions.

With a 4-2 record and winnable games left with Penn and Bucknell, State fans were confident this would be the first winning team in six years. No one cheering for State expected the Penn game to be as embarrassing as it was. Penn's scouts must have found all the flaws in State's defense as well as offense because the Quakers dominated the game from the opening kickoff. The writer for the *Athletic Records* summed up what occurred: "More than 40,000 spectators (at Franklin Field) watched the Red and Blue warriors crumple what was considered State's impregnable line, which had yielded only one touchdown via rushing previously in the season. The Quakers had a defense for every State attack and (its offense) found a loop-hole in every Lion defense." Still, the Lions trailed by just 7-6 at halftime and 14-6 at the end of three quarters.

Penn scored early in the first quarter on a crushing 62-yard drive that ended with a 33-yard TD run by Lew Elverson for a TD. Cherundolo's pass interception at Penn's 42-yard led to a State TD on a 12-yard pass from O'Hora to sophomore Walt Komic in the second quarter but the Lions missed the extra point kick. And that was the extent of State's offense. The defense hung on until the final period when Penn exploded with three TDs to send the Lions whimpering back to State College. The Quakers had netted 267 yards rushing, getting 172 yards in the second half and most of those came in the final period. Meanwhile, State's pathetic offense got just 12 yards on the ground and had 76 through the air on 5-of-19 passes but five other passes were intercepted by the Penn defense.

The Penn defeat seemed to take everything out of the players. This is when they needed that undefined trait that is characteristic of teams that overcome adversity. But this team had left its spirit in the dirt of Franklin Field. It should have come out against Bucknell determined to be Higgins' first winning team. Instead, State was "listless," according to the "*Penn State Athletic Records Scrapbook.*"

For the second year in a row, Bucknell was hosting the game in Lewisburg but State was a 2-1 favorite, said the *Philadelphia Inquirer,* "largely because the Lions easily trounced a strong Villanova team that had defeated Bucknell by four touchdowns." The Lions were in trouble almost from the start. A fumble gave Bucknell the ball at the State 40-yard line early in the first quarter and the Bisons drove to State's four-yard line before giving up the ball on downs. State couldn't get much ground and was forced to punt from behind the goal line. The usually reliable O'Hora fumbled the snap from center and, as the writer of the *Athletic Records Scrapbook* reported, "was tackled in his tracks by two Bucknell players" for a safety. For the rest of the game, Bucknell was on the defensive protecting its slim 2-0 lead and State's offense bumbled away several opportunities to score. "State kept hammering at the (Bucknell) line, gaining yardage almost every time," the scrapbook writer reported, "but individuals making mistakes at crucial moments, fumbling and bad passes (sic) kept the Lions from getting a score." With six minutes left in the fourth quarter, State's offense took over the ball at its own 20-yard line and came alive. With Wear and Silvano doing the bulk of the running, the Lions picked up six first downs and got within field goal range. Junior letterman Luther Barth was sent in on first down to try a field goal but the players realized the wind was too strong and Barth went back to the bench. Two

plays into the line yielded no gain. Then Wear tried to throw a pass to Smith. But Bucknell center Bob Pethick intercepted at the 10 and moments later the game ended.

The players trudged out of Bucknell's Memorial Stadium thinking about what might have been. They were neither winners nor losers but for the third straight season they had broken even. That may have been good enough in 1933 and 1934, they all thought, but not in 1935. Nor would another break even season be good enough for the players next year. Cherundolo, Economos, Wear and the other juniors and sophomores were determined to make the 1936 season a winner.

Season Record 4-4
Record to Date 235-141-27
Winning percentage .617

"'High School Harry' & The 'Babies'"

The words of the *Collegian* sportswriter were insulting and humiliating and the players were incensed. "Babies," Charles M. Wheeler Jr. called the team that had unexpectedly lost on Saturday to Lehigh, 7-6.

"Squabbling among themselves like babies, and playing listless and uninspired football," Wheeler had written, "Penn State's 1936 excuse [for a team] was thoroughly outplayed and beaten in Saturday's Lehigh game." Wheeler had gone on to accuse the team of letting down and he criticized the seniors for causing much of the problems. "What fight there was in the team was displayed by the players mixing it up with their teammates, rather than with the common foe," Wheeler wrote.

Many of the fans at Beaver Field on Oct. 17 for the third game of the season undoubtedly agreed with Wheeler. "There were practically no highlights from the State side of the picture whatsoever," penned the writer for the "*Penn State Athletics Record Scrapbook.*" The Lions had looked horrible against a far weaker opponent and now had a 1-2 record with the toughest part of the schedule ahead. Unless they got their act together and could pull off an upset or two, they surely were headed for the first losing football season in four years.

This was not something Captain Chuck Cherundolo had anticipated. Even though he was one of just nine senior lettermen, he had expected to lead the team to the first winning season ever for Coach Higgins. The heart of the team were the veterans, with Smith at one end, Danny DeMarino and Schulyer at the tackles, Barth and Economos at guards, Cherundolo at center, O'Hora at quarterback and Silvano at fullback. Two sophomores had broken into the starting lineup, big Alex Barantovich (one of Casey Jones's recruits out of Monogahela) at one end and John G. Patrick at halfback. Junior Sam Donato was the other halfback but Wear and a flashy sophomore named Harry Harrison out of West Philadelphia would see plenty of playing time at running back. And before too many games, sophomores Sever Toretti, another Monogahela kid, and Dean Hanley would become spot starters in the line and Joe Metro would start occasionally in the backfield.

A big win against Muhlenberg seemed to be a good sign for

this team. A record opening day crowd of 7,535—some sitting in the new steel grandstands on both sides of Beaver Field— saw State roll up its biggest score in six years with a 45-0 victory. The Lions scored in every period, exploding for three touchdowns in the third quarter after jumping off to a 21-0 halftime lead. Wear, Silvano and third-string half back Metro each scored two touchdowns as Higgins used 39 players.

But the team did not play well the next week in the Home-coming game against Villanova. The game had been rated even but Villanova was in control the entire afternoon, racking up 15 first downs to State's four. The 13-0 score made the game seem closer than it was and only the play of the Lions defense kept the score down. Villanova got a TD early in the first quarter on a long drive and made the 6-0 lead hold up until late in the third quarter when it recovered a State fumble at the Lions 15-yard line and scored a TD two plays later. "State played listless ball and did not deserve to win," reported the *Athletic Records* writer.

Whatever was bothering the team carried over the next week against Lehigh. Maybe part of the problem was the absence of Economos. Last year's sophomore star guard had been injured in the Muhlenberg game and sat out both the Villanova and Lehigh contests.

time later.

So, as the team practiced for the next game at Cornell, they seethed at the epithet in the *Collegian*. And, as Ridge Riley, then State's sports information director, later reported in his book, *Road to Number One*: "When the players' bus set out for Ithaca the following week, sportswriter Wheeler was missing. The angry seniors had ejected him." So much for freedom of the press!

Perhaps they would not admit it, but Wheeler's criticism may have helped the players change the course of the season. "Playing vastly improved football," reported the writer in the *"Penn State Athletic Records Scrapbook,"* "Penn State's Nittany Lions reversed their course of last week and made an interesting game at Ithaca against Cornell, almost coming home with the laurels by outplaying the Big Red in the second half." Something must have been said in the locker room at halftime. Heavily favored Cornell had a 13-0 lead by then as two long passes had set up a pair of touchdown runs and the Big Red had dominated both sides of the ball. But in the second half it was State's offense and defense that took control. Cornell could pick up just 11 yards and two first downs with both first downs coming in the closing minutes of the game, one on a penalty. Late in the third quarter

The coaching staff of 1936 poses in the positions each man played at Penn State. They are (left to right): Earle Edwards, Marty McAndrews, Joe Bedenk, Jim O'Hora, Bill Miller, Al Michaels and Bob Higgins. Edwards and Michaels later were head coaches at North Carolina State and O'Hora was a long time assistant for Higgins, Rip Engle and Joe Paterno.

The underdog Engineers deployed an eight man line with two linebackers and a lone defensive back and that completely stifled State's supposedly power running attack. When the Lions tried passing, the passers didn't throw very well, often passing the ball far over the heads of the wide open receivers. Neither team scored until Lehigh shocked the Lions late in the third quarter. Lehigh had a third down at midfield and went into punt formation. "State, apparently expecting a kick, was caught napping," said the dispatch in the *Philadelphia Inquirer*, "when...Wertz, substitute Lehigh secondary (sic), faded back and, with plenty of time, heaved a 50-yard pass. (Pat) Pazzetti was at the goal line ready to receive it and stepped across the goal line for the touchdown." Ayre's kick made it 7-0. State didn't score until getting a break with time running out in the fourth quarter when a Lehigh fumble gave the Lions the ball at the Lehigh 10-yard line. But a great defensive stand by Lehigh stopped the Lions at the three. Lehigh immediately punted out and State got the ball on the 25-yard line. O'Hora quickly passed to Harrison who caught the ball near the five and went into the end zone standing up. Barth set up to try the tying extra point that would have saved some embarrassment but the kick was wide and the game ended a short

State scored after Harrison's 29-yard punt return got the ball to Cornell's 29-yard line. Harrison picked up 10 yards on a reverse and several plays later O'Hora plunged over from the one-foot line, then faked a placekick and passed to Smith for the extra point. Trailing by 13-7, State "then charged into the shadows of the Red goal line three times in the last session," said a story in the *New York Times*, but Cornell held and won what was historically the 500th game State had played since starting football in 1887.

Revived by their second half performance against Cornell, the Lions battered Syracuse the following Halloween Saturday, 18-0, at Beaver Field. It was State's first victory over the Orange since 1929 and the most points scored by either team in the series—and there were no controversies. This was one of Syracuse's worst teams and it would lose seven straight games to finish 1-7 in Vic Hanson's last year as coach. But that should not take away from State's overpowering victory. The Lions rushed for 310 yards and 21 first downs to Syracuse's 78 yards and eight first downs and the Syracuse attack never penetrated past State's 33-yard line. State scored two touchdowns on drives of 72 and 65 yards with sophomore Bill Denise getting one TD on an 11-yard delayed reverse in the first quarter and another sophomore, Metro, going over from the one-yard line in the third. The third TD came in the fourth quarter on a 28-yard pass from O'Hora to Harrison at the goal line. The Lions almost had another TD in the closing seconds of the first half when Harrison ran 60 yards before behind hauled down from behind at the Syracuse six-yard line as the whistle blew. The fact that the team still had trouble kicking extra points was lost in the revelry of what some called "a major victory."

In spite of their new found spirit and offensive fire power, the Lions were decisive underdogs the following two weeks against their two traditional rivals, Pitt and Penn. Both Pitt and Penn were angling for the Rose Bowl and expected to use State as fodder to get there. The small crowd of 15,692 at Pitt Stadium was surprised when State went on the offensive in the first quarter and marched all the way to the Panther 30-yard line before losing the ball on a fumble. Pitt then drove 70 yards and scored on a 25-yard pass from Marshall Goldberg to Curly Stebbins. The Lions didn't let up and continued to surprise the Panthers throughout the first half as the teams traded possession several times before Pitt's passing attack helped the Panthers reach State's four-yard in the closing minute of the second quarter. Another Panthers TD seemed all but assured but four passes in a row were broken up by the Lions secondary and the team went to the locker room feeling pretty good about the 7-0 halftime deficit.

Pitt's coach Jock Sutherland must have realized during the intermission that he might not win if he didn't do something different in the second half. So, he pulled his regulars and started his second team when the Panthers kicked off to start the third quarter. The crowd was still muttering about Sutherland's unexpected move when Harrison took the kickoff at the two and with great blocking was about to break into the clear near midfield. Suddenly, he stumbled and went down and when the people in the stadium realized what had happened they began laughing. The elastic in the sophomore's pants had snapped and the falling pants had tripped him up (after a 49-yard gain). A few minutes later, Pitt began an 80-yard drive that gave it a 14-0 lead on Frank Patrick's one-yard TD run. But the Lions weren't phased. State moved quickly from its own 35 to the Pitt 13 on the running of Harrison and Wear with Wear's 33-yard dash setting up the first down at the 13. Then came a play that would make history and give Harrison a new name for all time. Harrison stayed at the State sidelines after Wear's run and when the rest of the team went into its huddle, Harrison laid flat on his stomach, unobserved by the Pitt players but noticed by Lions tackle Marino, who told Wear. Wear took the snap from Cherundolo and threw it immediately to Harrison in the flat and the sophomore ran into the end zone with nary a Pitt player within 25 yards of him. The howls of protest from the Pitt sideline and the Panther fans continued as Metro booted the PAT and State kicked off.

Whether the old "sleeper" play incensed the Pitt players, as Pitt fans and some sportswriters claim, or whether the Lions simply wore out when Sutherland put his first team back into the game in the fourth quarter, Pitt broke the game wide open in the final period. Pitt made it 20-7 on a 71-yard drive, then scored another TD on a short run and a third TD on the 44-yard return of a State fumble by Johnny Urban to win going away 34-7. "...For a fleeting few minutes," wrote Chester Smith, sports editor of the *Pittsburgh Press*, "a Penn State eleven that had come rolling down from Mt. Nittany with fire in its eyes and steel in its spines made a grand and gallant fight of it..." Other Pittsburgh sportswriters mocked State's performance the next day and specifi-

cally criticized Harrison's touchdown as a "high school play." But the State fans were proud of how their team played and when they heard later that the players were calling Harrison "High School Harry," they began referring to him that way, too. The nickname stuck the rest of his career.

"High School Harry" gave the 40,000 fans at Franklin Field another big thrill the following week when he ran back a Penn kickoff 94 yards for a touchdown late in the first half. Harrison's return—the fifth longest in Lion history—came as State trailed, 13-6. The Lions had taken a 6-0 lead with a march downfield in the first six minutes of the game but Penn had gone ahead 7-6 in the second quarter on a 50-yard run by Lew Elverson. With three minutes left in the half, Penn had scored on a 36-yard razzle-dazzle pass and lateral play, with Frank Murray going the last seven yards on the lateral, but State had blocked Murray's extra point attempt. Harrison then made his big play—keeping his pants on, of course—but Silvano missed the extra point and State trailed at the half, 13-12.

State could have won the game in the second half but the offense wasn't quite up to it. The Lions took the second half kickoff and marched to the Penn 25-yard line before turning over the ball. Moments later, Murray's surprise quick kick put State in a hole at its own six-yard line and when State couldn't move, its short punt set up a third Penn touchdown on a 27-yard run by Ed Warwick. State blocked the PAT attempt again, setting the stage for a fourth quarter drive that could have tied the game. State missed other scoring opportunities when Morini bobbled one pass in the third quarter and Barantovich dropped another one when he was wide open in the fourth. A tricky "Statue of Liberty" play could have got another TD but Wear juggled the ball with a clear field ahead of him and was smeared. Then in the final period, the Lions went all the way to the Penn 4-yard line before the Quakers held on downs with Wear stopped on a fourth down run through tackle that had the fans second guessing the play called by O'Hora. Penn won, 19-12, and later, when #3 Pitt (7-1-1) got the Rose Bowl bid over #10 Penn (7-1), the Philadelphia sportswriters blamed the snub on Penn's "poor showing against the subpar Lions."

The loss to Penn doomed State to its first losing season in four years but Cherundolo and the seniors were determined not to lose the last game of their careers. State had not beaten Bucknell in 10 years and the Lions were the underdog primarily because the Bisons, with a 4-3 record, had beaten common opponent Villanova. But this was not the same State team that lost earlier to Villanova (eventually 7-2-1). It was all Penn State from the opening kickoff when Patrick, who would never play another game, duplicated Harrison's return against Penn and went 94 yards untouched for a touchdown. Patrick scored the Lions other TD in the third quarter on a one-yard plunge that climaxed a 94-yard drive. State could have had three other TDs but fumbles ended drives at Bucknell's 24 and the goal line and another TD was nullified by an offside penalty. State's ground attack rolled up 359 yards to Bucknell's 84 and when the whistle ended the game at 14-0 the players carried Cherundolo off the field.

The season was probably best summed up after the Bucknell game by the writer of the *"Penn State Athletic Records Scrapbook."* "With three victories against five defeats, the season was far from a howling success," he wrote. "From the middle of the Cornell tilt, the Lions performed in sensational style, but it was those two and one-half games before that spelled disaster for the season...The year proves that the Lions can click when they want to and that no player, no matter how great, can get national recognition without a winning club."

Cherundolo would go on to become a big star in the National Football League. "High School Harry" would go on to be one of State's best running backs of his era. And Higgins would go on to have his first winning season—and only one more losing season. Bezdek was now gone and State football was rising from his ashes—thanks in part to a little known student sportswriter named Wheeler.

Season Record 3-5
Record to Date 238-146-27
Winning percentage .612

"Gambling For A Winning Season"

It's an old axiom that to win in football a team sometimes has to take chances. Games have been won and lost on a big risk. The difference between a winning and losing season often has been determined by a major gamble in a single game. So it was in 1937 that State's first winning season under Higgins and the school's first in nine years came down to two similar gambles late in the fourth quarter of games played two weeks apart.

The opponents were two teams whose sometimes contentious rivalry with State would last for more than 50 years—Syracuse and Maryland. And in both instances, the team that *lost* the gamble *lost* the game.

Despite the losing season of 1936, many sportswriters were optimistic about State in 1937. New York columnist George Trevor, analyzing "The East" in a preseason magazine, the *1937 Illustrated Football Annual*, wrote: Football has been on the upgrade in the mountain-cradled fastness of the Nittany Lion for several years, and in spite of heavy graduation losses, the trend should continued upwards...For once in his life, coach Bob Higgins can't complain that he isn't two deep at every position."

The Gilligan-Casey "jobs for education" scheme was picking up momentum and more good, tough, lean and mean kids from the coal mining and steel making regions of Pennsylvania were enrolling at Penn State to play football. Higgins had 11 lettermen back from his '36 squad and several fine sophomore prospects up from what was considered by sportswriter Trevor, "an unusually powerful freshman squad." A couple of those sophs, end Spike Alter and running back Lloyd Ickes, would play well in '37 and would eventually help lead State completely out of the football doldrums as seniors, but this season it was the veterans who would take charge: Economos and Donato (who were co-captains) plus Barantovich, DeMarino, Harrison, Wear, Hanley, Metro, Toretti, Carl Waugaman and Joe Adessa. Two juniors who had won minor letters also would be instrumental, running back Anthony ("Little Gee") Giannantonio and tackle Joe Peel.

Then there was Ben Pollock, the sophomore placekicker from little Hunlock Creek, PA. Higgins had not had a reliable extra point and field goal kicker since becoming head coach and State had lost several games over the years because of bad kicking. Pollock was a reserve guard, but after the season began, Higgins noticed Pollock kicking suc-

cessful placements in practice and designated him to boot PATs and field goals. Thus, Pollock become the first man in school history to be a placekicking specialist. He would go on to convert 12-of-13 PAT's during the year but would not earn a letter because he wouldn't get enough playing time then required under the stringent eligibility rules.

The opening game marked a distinct change in the philosophy of scheduling by Higgins. For more than three decades, State had opened the season at home against a weaker team. (Does this sound familiar?) This not only gave the coach the opportunity to give his entire varsity game experience under ideal conditions but almost always guaranteed a victory for the home crowd. But in a change, the first game this year would be at Ithaca against Cornell and for the next six years State would open with a tough opponent, usually at home.

State's old Bucknell nemesis, Carl Snavely, was now coaching at Cornell and he had weathered a 3-5 losing year with a starting lineup of mostly sophomores in '36 to rebuild the Big Red's program. Sportswriters expected Cornell to compete for Eastern supremacy in '37 and the Big Red were favored over the Lions on September 25. This was State's earliest opening game in 10 years and the late September heat that soared to an official 87 degrees bothered both teams. State surprised the home team with a passing attack in the opening minutes. With about seven minutes gone in the quarter, a 34-yard pass from Ickes, starting at left half, to his right end, Adessa, gave State the ball on the Cornell 15-yard line. On the next play, Harrison hit Ickes in the end zone for the touchdown. State missed the extra point (not Pollock) but the quick TD had awakened the Cornell team.

Cornell roared back on the strength of its own passing onslaught, driving 70, 85 and 52 yards to score three touchdowns by halftime and the Big Red held that 19-6 lead into the fourth quarter. What happened next was described by a reporter in the *Pittsburgh Press*: "Almost hopelessly outclassed for three periods, and trailing by two touchdowns midway in the final quarter, Penn State, with two perfectly executed plays, tied the score with less than five minutes to play." Cornell was methodically driving again for another TD when it fumbled and Toretti recovered at the State 30-yard line. After gaining one yard, State stunned the Cornell defense with a razzle-dazzle play. Wear took the snap, passed laterally to fullback Metro, who threw a short pass upfield to Adessa at the Lions' 40 and the big right end ran down the sideline with perfect blocking to score. State again missed the extra point to make it 19-12 but the Lions were back moments later after the aroused defense forced Cornell to punt. The ball went out of bounds at the State 35-yard line. On the first play, Wear "took the ball on a fake reverse, circled his own left end and was not stopped until he had traveled 64 yards and was forced out of bounds on the one-yard stripe." Metro plunged for the TD and Harrison tied the game with four minutes left when he kicked the extra point. Cornell then drove the length of the field with a diverse running and passing attack, and with a 20-yard pass the Big Red had reached the one-inch line for a first down and time running out. Two plays lost a yard and the small contingent of State fans went wild. On third down, Cornell was offside and penalized five yards. The Lions line led by Economos, Barantovich and Toretti dug in as the crowd screamed. Cornell fullback Dick Baker took the snap and sliced through a hole on the weak side for the winning touchdown. Cornell kicked the PAT and won, 26-19. "Penn State Loses Thriller to Cornell," headlined the *Pittsburgh Press*.

A last minute defeat like that could have affected the mental attitude of the team for the rest of the season but this squad had more character than some of Higgins' past teams. The next week, State overwhelmed Gettysburg, 32-6, in what would be the last game ever with its one-time big rival. This also is believed to be the first game Higgins had filmed in order to study what his team was doing on the field. State scored five times on drives of 73, 39,37,78 and 30 yards with Wear picking up two of the touchdowns. Gettysburg's lone score came on an 83-yard return of a pass interception.

Bucknell, the next opponent, had a new coach in Al Humphreys and a green team dominated by sophomores but the Bisons already had won their first two games when they visited Beaver Field for the annual Homecoming game. A steady downpour of rain kept the game close and more than 11,300 fans watched another thriller as State had to come from behind in the fourth quarter to win, 20-14. The Lions rushed for 225 yards and 10 first downs to Bucknell's 128 yards and six first downs and passed for additional yardage but fumbles and the slippery field kept State from blowing the game open.

Harrison's 20-yard touchdown run following a blocked punt by Barantovich gave State an early lead and it was 13-7 at the half as Pollock got his first PAT of the season after a Harrison punt return set up the second touchdown late in the second quarter. The teams slugged it out in the third quarter and Bucknell almost scored when a Bisons runner broke loose with three blockers out front and seemed headed for a sure touchdown until "High School Harry" brought him down from behind. But a Harrison fumble at State's 25-yard line midway in the fourth quarter enabled Bucknell to take the lead again. 14-13. After an exchange of punts, State got the ball on Bucknell's 45-yard line and with Wear running for nearly 40 yards on three plays, the Lions moved to the Bucknell four. As time was running out, Patrick scored on a reverse around left end. Pollock's boot made it 20-14 and the game soon ended. The writer for the "Penn State Athletic Records Scrapbook" reported that the score was no indication of the "severe drubbing" Bucknell took, "and many fans remarked that if the weather had been fair, the Lions would probably (have) run up a big score on the Bisons."

The weather was "ideal" the following week when Harrison gained 190 of State's total 285 yards running and passing in leading State to a 14-7 win over Lehigh before 10,000 at Beaver Field. State did not appear as sharp as in previous games and it showed against an inferior opponent as the Lions had to work for their scores. Harrison set up his own six-yard touchdown run early in the second quarter after catching a 28-yard pass from Ickes that moved the ball close to Lehigh's goal. Early in the third quarter, Barantovich made a spectacular catch on his back in the end zone of a 14-yard pass thrown by backup sophomore halfback Steve Rollins. Pollock kicked the extra point, his fifth in a row, and State led, 14-0. Lehigh scored midway through the fourth quarter after driving from midfield on a flurry of passes but State took control of the game after that and won it's third in a row.

The game against Syracuse the next week at Archbold Stadium was probably the most significant one for Higgins since he became the head coach. His mediocre teams had won a couple of upsets over the years and had come close to winning on occasion against superior opponents. The clash with Syracuse was different. Both teams were good and the victor would gain status. But Syracuse had been there before. State had not been in this situation since the Bezdek regime. Syracuse, under new coach Ossie Solem, was also 3-1 and had upset Cornell at Ithaca, 14-6, before being upset itself the previous week by Maryland, 13-0. That win over Cornell had made the Orange the slight favorites but State started out as if it was going to blow the home team out of its own stadium. "Penn State outrushed Syracuse in

the first half and, aided by several fumbles and a blocked kick, pushed over one score in the opening period and another in the second," wrote the reporter for the *Pittsburgh Press*. Barantovich recovered a fumble by Syracuse star Marty Glickman (who later became a well known as an Olympian and a sportscaster) at the Orange 32-yard line to set up the first touchdown on one-yard plunge by 200-pound sophomore Dick Skemp but Pollock's PAT attempt was wide. In the second quarter, DeMarino blocked a punt and Toretti recovered at the Syracuse 26. On the second play, Wear went around right end on a reverse for the TD and Pollock's kick made it 13-0 at the half.

The Lions may have let down a bit after the intermission. Syracuse certainly looked like a different team. The inspired Orange scored a touchdown early in the third quarter on the running and passing of young Wilmeth Sidat-Singh, then tied the score at 13-13 with five minutes left in the fourth quarter on another Sidat-Singh pass but missed the extra point that could have put them ahead. The Lions ran back the kickoff to their own 28-yard line and it was here that State decided to gamble with a pass on the first down. The aggressive Syracuse linemen overpowered the State front line and chased Wear almost to the State goal line. Wear spotted Alter downfield and launched a high spiral towards him. But Sidat-Singh, who would not letter that season, intercepted Wear's throw at the 25 and ran it back for a touchdown and the 19-13 victory. "The boys were rather disheartened after the game," reported the writer in the "Penn State Athletic Records Scrapbook," "and swore to get even next year..."

State fans, remembering how other Higgins teams had folded, feared another let down when the team traveled to Franklin Field for the Penn game. The Quakers were having a down year with a 2-3 record but they were still considered in a different class of football than the Lions and were a slight favorite. It was a sloppy game as State lost four fumbles and Penn dropped six. The largest crowd since 1929— 50,000—watched as State won for the first time since '29, 7-0. The TD came in the second quarter after Harrison's quick kick had forced Penn

End Alex Barantovich makes a spectacular catch for the winning touchdown on a pass from "Windy" Wear that gave State a 14-7 victory over Lehigh in 1937.

to punt from near its goal line and State got the ball on the 39-yard line. Wear passed to Harrison for a first down at the 17 and then Harrison returned the favor by throwing to Wear as he crossed the goal line. Pollock's PAT made it 7-0, and Penn could never catch up. The Quakers stopped another State threat in the third quarter with an end zone interception of a Metro pass. Barantovich clinched the game late in the fourth quarter when he crashed into the Penn punt receiver, forcing a fumble that he recovered, and State ran out the clock in Penn territory. "A light, fast Penn State team took advantage of every break today to squeeze out a 7-0 victory over Pennsylvania," said a *United Press* dispatch of the game, "State, averaging 15 pounds lighter than Penn, never was seriously threatened."

With a 4-2 record, a winning season would come down to beating either Maryland or Pitt. That didn't seem possible to many sportswriters. At this juncture, Maryland was 6-1, winning five straight after a 28-21 loss to Penn, and Pitt was 6-0-1 and contending for the National Championship again.

State had played Maryland just once before, winning 57-0 in 1917, but in 20 years the Terrapins had become a solid team in the South. Perhaps the jaunt into the mountains of Pennsylvania intimidated the visitors because State dominated the first half at Beaver Field, and in a repeat of the Syracuse game, had a two touchdown lead at the intermission, 14-0. Barantovich scored the first TD five minutes into the game on a 15-yard pass and Skemp's TD early in the second quarter and Pollock's two PATs gave State its points. But Maryland came out passing in the second half and by the end of the third quarter had tied the game 14-14. Maryland almost went ahead twice in the fourth quarter but was stopped on two outstanding individual defensive plays. The Terps' left end intercepted a pass at the State 27 and seemed to be in the clear but was stopped when Harrison made a shoestring tackle while sprawled on the ground. A few minutes later, Maryland drove inside the State 15 and set up for a field goal on third down. But it was a fake and the runner was stopped short of the first down on a nifty tackle by Giannantonio. On fourth down, Maryland's Pershing Mondorff tried to placekick a field goal from the four-yard line but the kick was low and wide.

With about three minutes to play in the fourth quarter, Maryland got the ball again but bogged down at its own 30-yard line with a fourth down and more than five yards to go. Now, it was Maryland which decided to gamble, believing it had found a weakness in State's suspect pass defense. So, instead of punting, the Terps passed. It was incomplete and State took over. Harrison made six yards on the first play, then Wear called for a reverse. He took the snap from center, started to his right and gave the ball to "High School Harry" going the other way. The play completely fooled the Maryland defenders and Harrison sprinted into the end zone. Pollock's PAT made it 21-14 and the more than 7,500 fans at Beaver Field cheered as the team walked off the field with the first winning season in eight years. "The same midget combination of Harry Harrison and Rabbit Wear that last week accounted for Penn's defeat functioned in Merrywell style in the last two minutes of play today as Penn State defeated a favored Maryland team...," said the game story in the *Pittsburgh Press*.

If State had beaten Pitt in the cold and snow at Pitt Stadium on November 20 it would have been one of the great upsets in college football history. Of course, Pitt won easily, 28-7, and after beating Duke the following week it was declared undisputed National Champion. Pitt scored two touchdowns in the first quarter and got another on Dick Cassiano's 79-yard run in the second quarter to take a com-

Sever "Tor" Toretti was a tackle on the teams of the late 1930s and later became a long time assistant coach under Joe Bedenk and Rip Engle and the first recruiting coordinator for Joe Paterno.

manding 21-0 lead at the half. State scored its only TD in the third quarter on a 27-yard pass from Wear to Alter and Pollock booted his 12th PAT.

In the grand overview of the Higgins era, the 13th straight loss to Pitt was not important to the '37 team. These Lions were winners. With just a slight more luck, this team could have been 7-1. But luck works both ways and gambling only pays off the winner. Still, this was a winning season and the outlook for next year was bright. Everyone figured winning was back for good at Penn State. Not quite.

Season Record 5-3
Record to Date 243-149-27
Winning percentage .612

"History's Scapegoats"

The most maligned team of all time in the history of Penn State football is this one. It was the last losing team for 50 years and as State re-emerged as an Eastern power under Higgins and Engle and then gained status among the football elite under Paterno, the public was constantly reminded that the 1938 team epitomized failure and defeat.

By the time the next losing team came along in 1988, an NCAA record had been set for 49 "Consecutive Non-Losing Seasons."

But as that record was being set year in and year out, the players of '38 had to suffer the ignominy of public embarrassment. When the survivors of the team would gather for reunions or tailgates in a State College hotel or at Beaver Field and Beaver Stadium, they'd wince when outsiders would frequently laugh and say, "Oh, yeah, the last losers."

When they tried to explain what they had done, how they had set four NCAA defensive pass records—including one that still stands—and how they had scored the biggest victory up to that time over hated Syracuse, no one would listen. Now that they are fading even more quickly into history, it's time to set the record straight. But for a startling 94-yard run on a mis-timed new defensive maneuver and a blocked kick—the defining moments of the season—we probably would be talking about a 51-year non-losing record and the 1936 team of "losers."

Higgins had 11 lettermen back from '37 but he had several positions to fill and sportswriters did not like the Lion's chances against what columnist George Trevor called, "a squad-shredding schedule." Trevor, analyzing "The East" for the *1938 Illustrated Football Annual*, wrote: "The Nittany Lions look for a stronger team than last year's...but they don't expect to do as well...In practically every major contest, Penn State will be outmatched by enemy manpower."

That tough schedule would start with Maryland at Beaver Field on October 1. In the same football magazine, sportswriter William F. Boand wrote that Maryland has "a fine shot at a perfect record. Veterans in abundance and many speedy sophs."

Higgins' starting lineup for Maryland were all upperclassman and included three men who had not lettered: Rollins at quarterback, Patrick at right half and Ted Nemeth at guard. Metro and Giannantonio were the other backs with Barantovich and Alter back at end, Captain Hanley and Bill Ellwood at the tackles, Joe Peel at the other guard and Toretti at center. Before the year was out, veterans Ickes and Harrison would start occasionally in the backfield and sophomore running back Chuck Peters would become a star. In the line, Higgins would move sophomore Leon Gejecki permanently to center and shift Toretti to tackle and guard. He also would utilize junior guard Grover Washabaugh, sophomore end Tom Vargo and "redshirt sophomore" tackle Carl Stravinski, who had sat out '37 with a broken leg, as spot starters. There was one major absence. Pollock, the fine placekicker, had dropped out of school, and another John Patrick, "John R.", would kick extra points and field goals.

Ridge Riley, writing the first of his now famous *"Football Letter"* series for the Penn State alumni on September 26, predicted that the sophomore reserves would make "the difference between a good team and a very good team," and reported that the team's biggest weaknesses would be pass offense and pass defense since "some of our shorter backs may be inept against a good passing team."

Beaver Field was set literally for "a banner year." The permanent seating capacity had been increased to 12,076 with all-steel seats and an electric scoreboard and timer had been constructed at one end of the field. Flags—representing the colors of all 1938 opponents and alumni classes holding reunions that year—had been mounted on both sides of the field. A new steel fence enclosed the football field as well as the nearby baseball diamond and football practice area. There also were changes inside the press box where a public address system had been set up for the first time and an area built for the new Penn State radio network team that would be broadcasting the games statewide and occasionally into Maryland, New York and New Jersey. And down on the field, the team was wearing new uniforms of light blue jerseys with silver pants and headgear (not exactly the blue and white with which we are now familiar).

Maryland turned out to be a patsy, just like in the old opening games. The Terps had already played Richmond and had been upset, 19-6. Less than four minutes into the game, Ickes ran off tackle on a routine spinner play and dashed past the confused Maryland defenders for a 69-yard touchdown. Patrick kicked the extra point. After an exchange of punts, State took possession on its own 15-yard line and in three quick plays had another TD. Harrison ran around end for 44 yards, sophomore sub fullback Craig White ran 39 yards on a reverse and Ickes dove over from the one for the TD and the rout was on. State marched 80 yards at the start of the third quarter, featuring the running and passing of Harrison and the running of Ickes, with Ickes scoring his third TD on another one-yard plunge. State gained 413 yards rushing and 59 yards on 4-of-6 passes to win in a breeze, 33-0.

Bucknell had a veteran team and two wins already when it visited Beaver Field for Homecoming. The game was considered a tossup but what happened in the first few minutes after the kickoff not only determined the outcome but also set the tone for the rest of the season. The Lions ran back the opening kickoff to the 27-yard line and without throwing a pass smashed through the Bucknell defense behind the running of Ickes and Rollins and picked up three first downs to reach the Bucknell six-yard line. But they couldn't move further and Bucknell took over on downs at the six.

As the defense lined up, Toretti got set to surprise Bucknell with a "loop," a new tactic Bedenk had taught the linemen but had never been used in a game. As Riley best described in his book, *The Road to Number One*, the "looping line" was originally devised by former coach Dick Harlow. "Defensive players changed positions just before the snap of the ball," Riley wrote, "slanting through the line at a confusing angle to mystify the opposing blockers...Higgins was skeptical about this 'looping'...Toretti, the defensive signal caller, was told to wait for the right spot, and now he thought he had it. Sure that the Bisons would use only straight off-tackle plays, Toretti looked over to the bench, got a nod from Higgins, and called for the line to loop toward the wingback. Bucknell ran a wide reverse the other way, and Frank "King" Funair went 94 yards down the left sideline for a touchdown." That ended the "looping" for the day. That also destroyed the team's frame of mind. The players continued to make mistakes at crucial times, fumbling away another opportunity at the Bucknell 24-yard line in the first quarter and throwing the ball helter-skelter. They completed just 1-of-14 passes and had two intercepted. In spite of gaining 218 yards on the ground, backs slipped when they had open holes. Once they recovered a blocked punt near Bucknell's goal and couldn't go in. Bucknell scored again late in the game following a pass interception and won, 14-0. "Bucknell Surprises Lion Gridders," said the headline in the *Daily Collegian*. "Something went wrong with everything we tried," Higgins told reporter Bill Engel. "Bucknell had a good team—better than we expected. They were set for this game."

Most of the 12,000 fans at Beaver Field probably didn't know it but there was a providential omen for the future that Homecoming Day. In the morning, State's freshmen beat the Pitt frosh, 13-12. Parity with the Panthers was not far away.

To their credit, the players did not sulk for the next week. At Bethlehem the following Saturday, the Lions took their wrath out on Lehigh and rolled up the largest score in eight years with a 59-6 victory. "High School Harry" had three touchdowns in the first quarter on runs of 29, 27 and three yards as Higgins used his entire 29-man traveling squad. Lehigh's score came on a spectacular freak play as State was going in for its apparent 10th touchdown when Lehigh's Steve Smoke picked up an errant lateral by Rollins and ran 102 yards untouched for the TD. (It remains a record for a fumble return by an opponent and is officially listed at 100 yards.)

Carl Snavely's veteran Cornell team, picked to be among the nation's best, had been upset by Syracuse, 19-17, that same day but the Big Red was still heavily-favored at Ithaca the next Saturday. Trying to take advantage of State's supposed weak pass defense, Cornell started passing the first time it had the ball. The Lions were ready, sacking the passer once, knocking down a couple of throws and intercepting one in the first quarter. After an exchange of punts, State got the ball on the Cornell 42-yard line and in three plays moved to the 33. Now came a gamble that was the turning point of the game. Instead of punting and putting Cornell in a hole, the Lions went for it and were held. (Gambling only pays off the winners, remember?) Once again, the mental state of the defense seemed to collapse. Cornell moved quickly down field, picking up four first downs, and scored. An interception a few minutes later set up another Cornell touchdown and for the rest of the afternoon, the Big Red used their rushing attack and their heavier line to dominate the game. The Lions scored with less than 30 seconds in the game on a pass of 55 yards from Peters that Harrison caught in stride on the two as he was covered by two defenders. Cornell won, 21-6, and now State faced the prospect of facing Cornell's only conqueror, Syracuse.

As the team practiced that week, the players knew they had been beaten by a better team. But they were upset that some sportswriters covering the Cornell game said they had been "hopelessly outclassed." That stung. The veterans also remembered what happened in '36 at Syracuse when they blew a two-touchdown lead and lost on a gambling last-minute pass that was intercepted. They had vowed then to "get even." They also knew a loss to Syracuse would ruin their season. Now, they had another incentive.

Syracuse, of course, was favored, thanks in part to Sidat-Singh, who was one of the best passers in the country. Sidat-Singh also was the man who made the game-winning interception against State last season. If State's pass defense was as bad as some sportswriters still believed, then State would be in for a long day. Higgins planned a special sequence of plays to surprise Syracuse the first time State had the ball. He shifted Harrison to wing back and installed Peters at tailback. He intended to have Harrison and Peters run off tackle a couple of plays, then give the ball to Harrison on a wide reverse, hopefully sucking in the right end and other Syracuse defenders concentrating on the middle.

Harrison ran the opening kickoff back to State's 18-yard line. On the first play, Harrison went off tackle for two yards. On the second play, Peters took a handoff from Metro on an inside reverse and ran off tackle. Suddenly, he was in the open. Bingo. Touchdown: 80 yards and a new State record for the longest run from scrimmage. After the kickoff, Syracuse moved to State's 26-yard line before losing the ball on downs and State then drove back down field before being stopped at the Syracuse six. In the second quarter, Toretti recovered a Syracuse fumble at the Orange 11-yard line. Two plays lost six yards but on third down, Peters started around left end on a sweep, stopped and threw a 16-yard pass to Alter all alone in the end zone. Both extra points were good. Two plays after the kickoff, Sidat-Singh, who was being harassed by State's pass rush, broke away for a 60-yard TD but the PAT attempt

failed. Just before the half, Sidat-Singh intercepted a State pass in the end zone to end another State threat and the Lions led at the intermission, 14-6.

State took the second half kickoff and drove all the way to the Syracuse 11-yard line before giving up the ball but the Lions got it back a few minutes later and Metro plunged over from the one for a TD. That, and State's defense, seemed to take the fight out of Syracuse. From that point, it was all State. Peters scored his second TD on a 14-yard run off tackle in the third quarter and Craig White ran 40 yards for another in the fourth. Syracuse got no closer than the State 30. The final was 33-6 and another star was born. Peters, the soph from Shamokin, had ran for 156 yards on 11 carries, hit on three-of-five passes and stopped one Syracuse drive with a pass interception. Rollins had 122 yards rushing. This was the first time on record that two State backs had gained 100 yards in the same game. It also was the biggest margin of victory ever in the State-Syracuse series. "Spectacular Upset Stuns Grid World," said the headline in the *Daily Collegian*.

Now, a victory over Lafayette in the Beaver Field finale would clinch at least a break even season. Lafayette was 3-2 after losing big to Brown and Penn but upsetting NYU by a point, and with Hooks Mylin now the coach, the Leopards were a dangerous opponent—and they showed why. This was probably the most disappointing game of the season for it was the one State should have won but didn't. Rain and a slippery field helped cause State's downfall but the team didn't play up to its potential, and, once again, a first quarter shock seemed to deflate the players' spirit. With about nine minutes left in the first quarter and neither team moving the ball well, Lafayette blocked White's punt at State's 20-yard line. Lafayette end Norbert Weldon picked up the ball on a bounce and ran in for a touchdown. Lafayette made the extra point and the 7-0 score held up for the rest of the game. State had the ball 17 times but couldn't get past the Lafayette 39-yard line. Lafayette had possession 16 times and except for the TD never made it past State's 44-yard line. State fumbled twice and lost one and completed two-of-eight passes for just 14 yards while Lafayette never fumbled or threw a pass. "It is difficult to explain the 'hot and cold' performances of Penn State's eleven this year," Riley reported in his "*Football Letter*." "It doesn't take a gridiron sage to note that the team doesn't have recuperating powers, that a first quarter shock takes the fire out of our players."

There were no first quarter shocks the next week when the team got "hot" again against favored Penn at Franklin Field. This was not one of Penn's best teams but even with a 3-3 record the Quakers were still considered far superior to State. The game turned into a defensive struggle, but unlike State's encounter with Lafayette, the offenses for both teams moved the ball, only to be stopped by the defensive units or a mistake. Three times State held for downs within its 25-yard line, once on the five. Penn stopped State three times with a pass interception or fumble recovery and held on downs on other occasions. State's pass defense was sensational, batting down at least 10 pass attempts and none of Penn's 12 throws was completed.

After a scoreless first half, both teams scored on breaks. Penn stopped State at its 30-yard line midway in the third quarter, and then drove to State's 15-yard line before losing the ball on downs. On the first play, Peters fumbled and Penn recovered at the 21. As the fourth quarter began, Penn had a fourth-and-goal at the one. Halfback Herb Rainwater hit the center of the line and seemed to be stopped short of the goal. But the referee signaled touchdown much to the disgust of the players (some of whom still believe, nearly 60 years

The 1938 team was 3-4-1 and the last losing team at State for 49 years until 1988 but it was an outstanding defensive unit and set four NCAA defensive passing records. The team included (by number) Front Row: Joe Peel (13) "High School Harry" Harrison (7) and Sever Toretti (22). Back Row: Leon Gajecki (26), Chuck Peters (5), Sid Alter (17), Grover Washbaugh (4), Steve Rollins (21) Lloyd Ickes (21) and Tom Vargo (27).

later, that the TD should not have counted). Captain Walt Shin kicked the extra point and the some 50,000 fans thought that would clinch it for Penn. But after an exchange of possessions, Ickes punted deep into Penn territory. The Quaker safety, Johnny Dutcher, tried to scoop up the ball and it brushed his leg and "bounced crazily toward the Penn goal." Players from both sides scrambled and touched the ball but Peters finally fell on it at the one-yard line. On the first play Ickes vaulted over right tackle for the TD. Patrick went back to placekick for the tie but the Penn front line stormed through and blocked the kick. The ball bounced back to the 20-yard line. Ickes picked up the ball, ran towards the corner, cut inside and as he was hit on the three-yard line he lunged over the goal with tacklers hanging on. Penn desperately tried passing to win the game but it was all over and State had a "moral victory," 7-7 tie.

State's large group of students stormed the field in an attempt to tear down the goal posts on the East side. But another throng of Penn students ran out of the South stands to meet them. In an instant the field turned into a fist-swinging melee. "It was a battle royal with everyone hitting," reported the *Philadelphia Inquirer*. "In less than it takes time to tell it, there were 10,000 people on the field, coats off, whaling one another. Alumni joined students in the battle which continued more than a half hour after the game...As the fight progressed, the first aggressors, their places taken by added volunteers, walked off the field of honor battered and, in some cases, bloody. Few of them escaped with their clothing intact..."

Later, Higgins told reporters: "All season we have been alternating, playing well one Saturday and poorly the next. This was our Saturday to play well and I think we did." And next Saturday?

The team knew it would have to beat Pitt to avoid a losing season and even today, now that they have had 60 years to reflect on that game, the Lions of '38 realize it would have taken a supreme effort and a lot of luck to beat the Panthers. This was still the Pitt team

of All-Americans "Mad Marshall" Goldberg and "Big Bill" Daddio and the "Dream Backfield" of Goldberg, Stebbins, Dick Cassiano and Johhny Chickerno, and although it would lose its next game against Duke and finish 8-2 and eighth in the country, it was an awesome unit. Three State fumbles set up touchdowns as Pitt won rather handily, 26-0, with Cassiano scoring three TDs and Jock Sutherland coaching his last game against the Lions. You're going to get yours some day, a few of the Lions muttered as they walked dejectedly off the Pitt Stadium grass.

Losers? Yes, the team of 1938 had a losing season. But did the players deserve to be tarnished for decades by that disparaging label? The 3-4-1 finish is in the record books. So is the NCAA team defensive record for fewest yards passing allowed per game (13.1 yards average). The team set three other defensive passing records that year that have since been broken: fewest yards per pass attempts (1.78 yards), fewest passes completed (10) and lowest percentage of passes completed (16.9 percent). Not too shoddy for a bunch of "losers."

Season Record 3-4-1
Record to Date 246-153-28
Winning percentage .609

1939

"Take That, Pitt!"

Leon Gajecki and his teammates stared gloomily at the ground, shaking their heads as the large crowd around them at Syracuse's Archbold Stadium roared in delight. It was precisely one minute and seven seconds into the game and already heavily-favored

Syracuse had a touchdown because of Gajecki's mental error, and no one felt worse than the junior center from the little coal mining town of Colver in Cambria County.

"That's okay, Caw-Jeck," a couple of his buddies shouted, "We'll get it back." This can't be happening again, some of the players thought as they trotted into position to take their second kickoff. Shades of last week at Cornell.

They had gone into Ithaca a decided underdog despite a 2-0 record but fully confident they could defeat unbeaten Cornell. And for the first five minutes they had held their own. Cornell had won the toss and instead of receiving the ball the Big Red chose to take the South goal because of the strong wind. Junior tailback Steve Rollins, starting at tailback in place of Peters, who was fumbling too much, ran the kickoff back to State's 41-yard line. Three conservative running plays into the line gained seven yards and Ickes punted. The runback was just two yards to Cornell's 31-yard line. But Cornell could gain just five yards and Hal McCullough got away a booming punt, thanks to the wind. Rollins caught the ball on State's 20-yard line and headed up field when disaster struck.

Cornell end Kirk Hershey plowed into Rollins at the 30 and the ball squirted up in the air. The speedy McCullough, already downfield, snatched the ball in flight and dashed untouched into the end zone. The Lions couldn't believe it. The Cornell punter had scored a touchdown on his own punt! The veterans began to think of last year on this same field when their failure on a fourth down gamble in the first quarter changed the momentum of the game and they never recovered. They were determined not to let that happen again. White took Cornell's kickoff at the eight-yard line and returned it to the State 42. Ickes banged up the middle for a yard. The ball went to Rollins who started through a nice hole at the left tackle when—BAM!—he was hit by Whit Baker and—BANG!—the ball shot out of his hands again. This time Cornell's Ken Brown snared it out of the air and ran 45 yards for the touchdown. Just like that, Cornell 13, Penn State 0. The Lions were dumbfounded and they literally sagged. "These (TDs) appeared to take the heart out of the visitors," wrote the Associated Press reporter covering the game. As the State players struggled in the first quarter to overcome their mental shock and physical inertia, they watched as two of their sensational sophomores were knocked out of the game with injuries. John "Pepper" Petrella, the 140-pound elusive and speedy runner everyone was comparing to Charlie Way and "Light-Horse" Harry Wilson, had his ribs kicked in and Bill Smaltz, the team's best passer in more than 10 years, twisted his ankle.

The rest of the game was no contest. Cornell ran and passed over, around and through the Lions, intercepted four passes while stopping State's attack at every point and gave a State team its worst defeat since 1899, 47-0. In a fine gesture of sportsmanship after the game, Cornell's coach, Carl Snavely, the one-time mentor at Bellefonte Academy, told the dejected State players in the locker room that they were a much better team than the score showed and that his team had all the breaks. It was Ridge Riley, in his *"Football Letter"* that week, who succinctly summed up the critical situation for the Lions. "What lies in the future for Penn State's 1939 football team is dependent upon how quickly the team can shake off the effects of not only a depressing psychological experience but also a serious physical beating." Riley, of course, remembered what happened in '38 and the 10 lettermen on this team did too.

Could this group bounce back and be the team sportswriters and its fans thought it could? "Despite a schedule that includes Pitt,

Army, Cornell, Syracuse and Pennsylvania," George Trevor had written in the preseason *1939 Illustrated Football Annual*, "the Nittany Lions are licking their chops as they anticipate their best season in a decade." And why not? Veterans Alter (the captain), Gajecki, Stravinski, Washabaugh and Vargo were in the line along with three fine junior linemen—Frank Platt, Wade Mori and Walt Kniaz—and two outstanding sophomores—Mike Garbinski and 300-pound Len Frketich, the biggest man in college football. In the backfield, Higgins had Peters, White, Patrick and Rollins and three standout sophs, Petrella, Smaltz and Len Krouse. What's more, the kicking game was the best in years. Ben Pollock, the great extra point kicker of '37, was back after his one-year absence and junior John R. Patrick was continuing to get better. Ickes was one of the best punters in the country and before too long into the season, Stravinski was booming the kickoffs into the end zone.

It had not been an easy season opener against underdog Bucknell. With the construction of new steel bleachers on the East side, the seating capacity of Beaver Field was now at 16,000. The press box on the West side also had been expanded to add a special section for President Hetzel and other college officials and guests and another area for visiting scouts. The biggest opening crowd in history, 11,143, saw State overcome its own mistakes and come from behind to beat Bucknell, 13-3. Peters made the first big error when he let a punt go through his fingers in the first quarter and Bucknell recovered at State's 20-yard line. Four plays later, the Bisons kicked a 30-yard field goal. Bucknell intercepted a pass at the goal line just before the half and took its narrow 3-0 lead into the locker room. The Lions finally went ahead in the third quarter on the passing of Smaltz, who threw one 29-yards to Rollins for the touchdown. Pollack booted the PAT and the fans breathed easier. But the Lions didn't clinch the game until 30 seconds were left when Petrella went 23 yards around left end after State had taken over the ball on downs. State had possession 20 times but lost the ball six times on fumbles, twice on interceptions and once had a kick blocked. Still, unlike last season, the Lions had surmounted their own problems and avenged the Bucknell debacle of '38.

A Homecoming crowd watched State clobber outmanned Lehigh the following week, 49-7. Five different players scored touchdowns as the Lions rolled up 563 total yards with Petrella's 68-yard TD run in the second quarter being the most thrilling play of the day. But the stars were really Ickes and Smaltz. Ickes scored the 48-yard run off a simple line buck in the first quarter, then caught TD passes of 25 and 16 yards from Smaltz, who was three-for-five for the day. Maybe the ease of the win made the team a little too confident for Cornell. "Underdog Nittany Gridders Point For Upset Win Over Cornell At Ithaca Tomorrow," said the headline in the October 20 *Centre Daily Times*.

The Cornell loss was debilitating but as the players practiced for Syracuse, they had vowed to turn things around. And now, here they stood, in the dreariness of Archbold Stadium, and they were suddenly in deep trouble again, behind 6-0 on Gajecki's mistake. They had downed the kickoff at the 21-yard line but there was confusion about the first play called and Gajecki had centered the ball over Rollins' head. Syracuse recovered at the State five-yard line and scored two plays later on a two-yard slant off tackle by quarterback Cliff Wilson. The kick had failed but Syracuse had the lead. Now, with the wind blowing the rain into their faces and their minds wondering if the heavens were against them, the Lions were set to receive the kickoff again. If ever there was a defining moment in a season, this was it.

Patrick ran the kickoff back to the State 41-yard line but an offside and holding penalty forced a punt. The teams changed posses sion again before Alter blocked a Syracuse punt and State recovered at midfield. Smaltz's passes to Krause picked up two first downs but the drive was stopped by another offside penalty and Smaltz punted out of bounds at the Syracuse 10-yard line. The defense went to work and Syracuse had to punt again. The kick was terrible and went out of bounds at the 19. A break. Higgins inserted Petrella. He got eight yards in two plays and Smaltz picked up the first down on a two-yard run up the middle. Petrella ran for four yards as the first quarter ended. When time resumed, Smaltz carried twice for three yards and it was now fourth-and-goal at the two. Petrella got the call. He swept wide to the right and the Syracuse defense, anticipating the play, bowled over the Lions blockers forcing Petrella back to the six where he appeared to be trapped by three Syracuse defenders. Suddenly he spurted through the would-be-tacklers and charged into the end zone. The PAT was no good but the Lions were back in the game.

It was a defensive game the rest of the way as the rain changed to snow and the 6-6 score was the final. Syracuse's offense had the better statistics, with 140 yards rushing and 11 first downs to 87 yards and six first downs for State. But it was a game of punting, 12 by State and 10 by Syracuse. Ickes was a defensive star, recovering a fumble to prevent one Syracuse score on a muffed punt by Petrella near the goal line and stopping another threat with an interception at the State seven. Gajecki also redeemed himself with a fourth down tackle at the eight-yard line that saved a touchdown. "Seldom, if ever, have football teams faced more trying (weather) conditions than those experienced yesterday," wrote Lawrence J. Skiddy, sports editor of a Syracuse newspaper, "and what started out as though it was going to be a whirlwind in the matter of producing action, soon settled down into a drab exhibition, each team playing ineffectively." Riley had another take for the *"Football Letter."* "...Under the circumstances," wrote Riley, "a tie game was strangely satisfying...and we believe it will give our players the incentive to carry them through the tough opposition ahead."

State was favored over Maryland the following week but the Terps had scouted well and stopped the Lions' passing attack in the first half. State tried 11 passes, completed just one for nine yards and had another intercepted in a scoreless half. So, Higgins switched to straight power running after the intermission and midway through the third quarter, the Lions scored two quick touchdowns. First, they stopped the Terps on downs at the State 47-yard line. On the second play, Rollins dashed around left end, cut diagonally across the field at the 30 and was forced out of bounds at the three. Ickes hit the line twice and scored the second time from the three. Smaltz missed the PAT. After Maryland failed to gain on the ensuing kickoff, State took the ball on the 47 again after a punt. Petrella, in for Rollins, ran the ball on five straight plays and scored on a spectacular play from the six when,

Leon Gajecki was State's 6th All-American and in 1939 made the tackle and recovered the fumble that led to the first victory over Pitt in 20 years, 10-0.

seemingly trapped off tackle, he ran across the field, then cut sharply left to the goal and his speed carried him in for the TD untouched. Pollock missed his first PAT of the season but State protected the 12-0 lead for the rest of the game with Maryland getting no closer than the 25-yard line.

The tie with Syracuse and win over Maryland did not impress the oddsmakers. The Lions were 4-1 underdogs for their annual clash against Penn at Franklin Field on Armistice Day. According to sportswriters, the Quakers' "vaunted passing attack" would be too much for the Lions. Actually, it was State's ball control running offense that was too much for Penn. State played its best game of the season with few mistakes, great play calling and a strong running with spot passing. The 10-0 score does not begin to indicate how superior State was. The Lions gained 230 yards and 12 first downs rushing compared to 84 yards and six first downs for the Quakers and Penn completed just two-of-11 passes for 13 yards and one first down. It was a typical game of ball control and in the third quarter, Penn had the ball for just eight plays.

The Lions scored their only touchdown early in the first quarter after an exchange of punts. They drove 73 yards in 11 plays and scored when Pepper Petrella, on one of his typical cut back runs, went around right end, then veered back off tackle and dashed 17 yards for the TD. Pollock booted the PAT. A Krouse interception in the second quarter set up another drive from the Lions 48-yard line. But that one bogged down at the Penn eight. So, Patrick came in and kicked State's first field goal in four years, a 15-yarder. Penn fumbled the kickoff and State had the ball on the Quaker 11-yard line as the half ended. State played a conservative second half, controlling the ball with its running offense and stopping Penn's passing cold. Penn never got past State's 44-yard line and when the game was over, most of the 50,000 fans could not believe it. These Lions were for real.

"The wildfire of football redemption roared down from the Nittany ridges yesterday," wrote Cy Peterman in the *Philadelphia Record*, "licked hungrily at Franklin Field, and flaming with the kickoff, raged unabated through four periods as Penn State burned down the banners of old Penn. In one of the greatest exhibitions of pure power and keen play, the Blue and White...went home with their 10th victory in the long series..."

The upset victory assured State of another winning season but this team now had its mind riveted on an even bigger goal—wins over Army and Pitt that would give this team the best State record in 18 years! The game at West Point was an anomaly on State's schedule. Though seemingly a natural rival because of its prime Eastern location up the Hudson River from New York City, Army had shunned State since the scoreless tie they had played at West Point in 1900. This contest on November 18 was a one-time-only affair and the teams would not play again for another 10 years.

More than one thousand State alumni and students made the trek to the picturesque Bear Mountain area, many of them frolicking the night before in Manhattan at the Hotel Pennsylvania where the world-famous Fred Waring's Orchestra and the Blue Band entertained at a festive alumni "smoker" gathering. Army authorities would not permit a radio broadcast out of Michie Stadium, and so for the first time that season, the Lion fans back in Pennsylvania would not know what happened until after the game.

Because of a leg injury, Stravinski could not kick off and his replacement's boot fell far short, giving the favored 3-3-1 Army team good field position at its 39-yard line on the return. But three plays later, a strong rush forced a hurried pass and Kniaz, playing for the injured Platt at tackle, intercepted and ran 45 yards untouched into the end zone. Pollock's PAT made it 7-0, stunning the corps of cadets. But Army came back in the first quarter, fumbling away one opportunity inside State's 10 but then returning a blocked punt 15 yards for the TD and a 7-7 tie as the quarter came to an end. The teams fought evenly without scoring in the second quarter but midway in the third period State got the ball on its own 45-yard line after a series of punts. Two plays later, Ickes fooled Army with a beautiful fake to White up the middle and ran 55 yards around left end for a touchdown. Pollock's kick made it 14-7. As the game went into the fourth quarter, Ickes and Krause came up with two big pass interceptions to shock Army, and the defense, led by Gajecki, took command. The game seemed nearly sewed up late in the fourth quarter when Army took possession at State's 44. On the first play, John Hatch passed to a wide open Don Heffner and the big end ran to the three before being tackled from behind by Ickes. Two plays later, Army scored and kicked the PAT and the game was all but over. In four plays, State couldn't move. Army was so happy to get out with a tie that when it got possession the Cadets took two delay of game penalties and lost 25 yards on the last play of the game. At long last, Ridge Riley wrote in his *"Football Letter,"* "we have a team that *cannot be counted out before the starting whistle."*

Now, it was back to State College and Pitt's first visit to Beaver Field since 1931. Jock Sutherland had quit as coach after last season when the Pitt administration announced it was going to de-emphasize football. This might not be a Pitt team as strong as the National Champs of '37 or the "Dream Backfield" team of '38 but it was still a potent aggregation and was favored. A standing room, overflow crowd of more than 20,000, the largest since the Notre Dame game of 1926, watched as a fired-up State team completely overpowered the Panthers and beat Pitt for the first time in 20 years, 10-0. In 1919, Higgins, then a two-time All-American end, had been the star of the victory. This time it was the "goat" at Syracuse, Gajecki, who played the entire 60 minutes and more than made up for his faux paus in Archbold Stadium earlier in the season with a sensational one-man defensive performance that had not been seen in years on the home field.

Midway through the first quarter, Cassiano broke loose on a 33-yard run that looked like a sure Pitt TD until Gajecki hauled him down from behind at the State 29-yard line. An interception by Smaltz quickly stopped the Pitt opportunity and the Lions then drove into field goal range. Patrick's 33-yard attempt was wide and Pitt took over at the 20. Then came the play of the season. Cassiano tried to go off tackle and was slammed so hard by Stravinski and Gajecki that the ball popped out and Gajecki recovered at the line of scrimmage. Peters ran off tackle for two yards and then White went around left end on a reverse

for 18 yards. Smaltz bulled over right tackle from one yard out for the TD and Pollock booted his 18th extra point in 19 attempts.

Pitt would never recover. The Panthers only threatened once more in the game, late in the fourth quarter, when they reached the 25-yard line. That was just moments before Patrick had booted a 24-yard field goal at the end of a 46-yard drive. State's defense led by Gajecki, Vargo and Alter held Pitt's high powered offense—which had scored in every other game—to 113 yards rushing and just 16 yards passing on two-for-10 pass attempts with two interceptions. Meanwhile, Peters was leading State's running game with 102 yards as the Lions piled up 17 first downs in gaining 205 yards on the ground and 61 through the air. The Pittsburgh Steelers were so impressed by Gajecki's performance against Pitt and other teams that season that they soon offered him a contract believing he was a senior.

Of course, the upset win touched off another wild celebration. "Virtually every man, woman and child in the overflow crowd of 20,000 fans was ready tonight to celebrate," wrote Claire M. Burcky in the *Pittsburgh Press*, "to tear the town wide open over an occurrence that when it comes no more often than once every 20 years must be observed fittingly, even fightingly." The students stormed on to the field, ripped down the goal posts and the typical party atmosphere carried them all over campus and into downtown State College. Town and school officials feared the worst but the students' over-eager celebration came to a halt when President Hetzel agreed to make Monday a school holiday.

"We realized we had a chance to win and we were up for the game," Higgins told sportswriters in the noisy dressing room. Higgins not only had a winning team, he had a very good team. And, everyone said, next year should be even better; maybe even a nationally-ranked team, by God. But the Panther was growling. She didn't like being mauled by the Lion from the mountain.

Season Record 5-1-2
Record to Date 251-154-30
Winning percentage .611

"Snow in The Seven Mountains"

This may have been one of the greatest teams that never was, at least before the Paterno era began.

Before the 1940 season, the Lion football team was rated among the best teams in the East, if not the country. One respected magazine rated the team as high as 13th in the preseason and the players lived up to that ranking throughout October and November as they won six games and tied one. As they prepared to play the down-trodden 2-4-1 Pitt Panthers in the final game of the year on November 23, a Rose Bowl bid was in the offing.

But they screwed it up!

In the modern day vernacular, some would say they "choked." To this day, the men still alive who were on the field that afternoon at Pitt Stadium aren't sure what happened. They remember losing the Pitt game but they are not sure how or why.

Perhaps the best explanation is that they simply didn't know how to handle success. This was a team dominated by seniors without a sophomore in the starting lineup. Some of them, like their captain and center Gajecki and their big left tackle and kickoff specialist Stravinski, were three-year starters. When those seniors and juniors arrived on campus, State was among the dregs of college football. They had to wait on tables or sweep the floors if they wanted to go to class and play football, too. It helped them develop a work ethic but it didn't teach them how to mentally handle affluence. Thus, when they neared the pinnacle that they never truly believed they would attain, it slipped away.

However, no Penn State football fan should ever forget the accomplishments of the 1940 team. It had the best record since the great unbeaten "Mystery Team" of 1921 and it helped set the stage that produced one of the greatest teams of all time, the 1948 Cotton Bowl squad.

In retrospect, this team probably did a lot better than it should have. Despite the game experience of most players, particularly in the front line, it had some weaknesses—first and foremost was a lack of reserve strength. The backups to Gajecki at center and three year vet Tom Vargo at right end were sophs, and although the left end, Lloyd Parsons, was a senior, he had not played enough in '39 to earn even a minor letter. Many of the other reserves were sophs, too, and as the season proceeded, the sophs did not develop very well. Only one, fullback Earl "Sparky" Brown, would letter and much of his playing time was contingent on an injury to State's key player, Bill Smaltz.

A preseason analysis of State in the *Street & Smith's 1940 Football Yearbook,* said if the Lions were to duplicate their success of '39, then "Bill Smaltz will hold the answer. Smaltz is the threat back replacing the departed Lloyd Ickes. As Smaltz goes, so goes the Lions." The words eventually proved to be prescient.

Smaltz, a junior, was both an excellent runner and passer. Petella, another junior, and the best running back on the team, shared the tailback position with the senior Peters, another gifted runner and the best defensive back and kick returner but who would be injured much of the year. J. R "Pat" Patrick was a fine blocker and signal caller at quarterback. Another three year veteran, White, was the starting wingback, with the exciting junior pass receiver, Krouse, as his backup. The fiber of the team was in the front line, which was nicknamed "The Seven Mountains," after the Allegheny Mountain range just east of State College. It was an outstanding defensive alignment, in particular, with Gajecki (who called defensive signals) at linebacker, Vargo and Parsons at the ends, Stravinski and Platt at the tackles (with veterans Kniaz and Frketich as backups) and Garbinski and Mori at guards. In the kicking corps, Pollock

Tackle Carl Stravinski was a three-year starter and one of the famous "Seven Mountain" linemen of the 1940 team. He also handled kickoffs in 1939 and '40 and is credited with his All-American teammate Leon Gajecki with making the big play that helped upset Pitt in '39.

had returned for extra points, Patrick for field goals and Stravinski for kickoffs. Punting was weaker without Ickes and none of the players who punted during the season matched him. In his pre-season analysis for the *"Football Letter,"* Riley predicted the team would be "a very good team, not a great team. It could be great if Lady Luck smiles." He was right—and Lady Luck didn't smile.

The team almost stumbled in the first game, against old rival Bucknell, before a record opening day home crowd of 12,091. State was heavily-favored and maybe overconfident. With Peters and Stravinski sidelined with injuries, the offense sputtered and Bucknell's fired up defense played well. Krouse scored the only touchdown of the game on a 25-yard TD pass from Smaltz after a 67-yard drive in the second quarter and Patrick booted the PAT. Patrick missed a 25-yard field goal in the fourth quarter but State got a safety when a Bucknell back standing in deep formation failed to catch the snap and the ball bounced out of the end zone for two points. State won, 9-0, with an overpowering statistical edge, including 238 total yards to Bucknell's 84. Petrella rushed for 96 yards on 24 carries but there were some offensive phases not up to par. The Lions completed just eight-of-22 passes with one interception and punts averaged just 34 yards. It was not a good sign.

During practice that week for West Virginia in the Homecoming game, Lady Luck gave her first nasty look at the Lions. Smaltz and his two backup fullbacks went down with injuries. Higgins desperately went to his fourth-string sophomore, Number 13, Sparky Brown. Under the circumstances, the nervous Brown played an exceptional game, making four first downs with his running and coming up with a crucial interception late in the fourth quarter that saved the game. In what was State's first game against West Virginia since it helped dedicate Mountaineer Stadium in 1931, the Lions overwhelmingly dominated the statistics yet trailed by three points in the fourth quarter. With Petrella running for 129 yards on 22 carries, State had 289 yards on the ground to a minus six for West Virginia and recovered two Mountaineer fumbles. But WVU's timely defensive plays, a big fourth down gamble and two long touchdown passes that fooled State's defensive backs kept the game tight.

State led 10-0 late in the second quarter on a 21-yard Patrick field goal and Petrella's three-yard TD but the complexion of the game changed with less than a minute left in the half when the Mountaineers scored a TD on 59-yard pass. Midway through the third period Smaltz entered the game and his first pass was intercepted and run back to State's 39-yard line. Three plays went nowhere and West Virginia's Charlie Seabright dropped back to the 45 in kick formation. But instead of punting, Seabright threw the ball high over the heads of three surprised State defenders to end Bob Mellace who caught the ball in full stride at the State 2-yard line. The extra point attempt was botched on a fumble but West Virginia suddenly had the lead, 13-10. Being snookered by an old-fashioned fake punt must have brought the Lions to their senses. Petrella returned the kickoff to State's 41-yard line and with Petrella doing the bulk of the running, the Lions moved swiftly down field at the start of the fourth quarter and Petrella circled right end from the 4 for the TD. Patrick's boot made it 17-13 but the Lions weren't out of danger until Gajecki and Brown intercepted Mountaineers passes. "Line Power And Petrella Stop W. Virginia," said the headline in the *Centre Daily Times*. Still, with a pass-happy Temple team looming two weeks away, sportswriters wondered if the Lions' apparent pass weakness would be fatal.

The Lions were obviously looking ahead to Temple when they traveled to Bethlehem to play Lehigh the following week. State led by just 7-0 at the half and even Peters' 96-yard touchdown run on the opening kickoff of the second half did not put much spark into the first team and the score was just 13-0 when Higgins put the second and third teams in during the fourth quarter. The reserves exploded over the tired Lehigh regulars and State won, 34-0.

Temple had been off the schedule since '32 but had won both previous games. The Owls were coming off a big upset over Michigan State in a game Higgins has personally scouted. With their 3-1 record and the home field, Temple was made a slight favorite over the Lions. "For the first time this season," reported Riley in his *"Football Letter"* after the game, "(State) looked like the team we had dreamed about during the summer months." The Lions played probably their best game of the season in winning, 18-0. Even though Temple completed 11-of-22 passes for 166 yards, State intercepted five and the Owls never seriously threatened the end zone. Meanwhile, State completed eight-of-nine passes for 75 yards and kept Temple's defense off balance because the Lions crunching ground game gained 292 yards with Krouse getting 89 yards on 12 carries and Petrella 86 yards on 17 carries. Petrella scored two touchdowns on runs of 35 and five yards and Peters went eight yards for another as the Lions scored in all but the third quarter. Patrick missed two PATs and Pollock another. That was the only bad note of the entire day but it had ominous implications for the rest of the season." Visions of their greatest year—their first undefeated season since 1921 and a bid to a bowl game—loomed in the eyes of thousands of loyal Penn State rooters yesterday...," wrote Stan Baumgartner in the *Philadelphia Inquirer*. "A mighty line, averaging more than 200 pounds to the man that was not only fast but football wise, paved the way for the easy victory."

A new opponent, South Carolina, visited Beaver Field the following week. The Gamecocks, with seven Pennsylvanians on their roster, had one of the best passing teams in the South but it wasn't one of that region's strongest teams and State was favored. The Lions put on another of their outstanding defensive games but something happened when these same players went on the offensive—they had a tough time scoring. State's pass defense was so good that Carolina passed only six times and four were intercepted—three by Peters, who set a one-game record that day that stood for 30 years. State's offense netted 308 yards but lost the ball three times on fumbles and had two 15-yard penalties that halted them deep in Carolina territory.

Still, the Lions won, 12-0, thanks to two big breaks. In the opening minutes Carolina tried to pass from its 23-yard line. White intercepted and run back to the eight set up a Peters touchdown. State

did not score again until midway in the third quarter after Vargo had recovered a fumble at the Carolina 33. It took nine plays to get the TD and when it finally came, it was scored by a sophomore end playing in his first varsity game and carrying the ball for the first time. Wilbur Van Lenten, who would not letter that year, went around right end on a third-and-goal at the five. Once more, Patrick's kick failed. "The boys play their heads off when it is necessary, but perform without any real spark against weaker opponents," Riley reported.

With five wins in a row since the opening game, State was off to its best start since the Rose Bowl year of 1922. That team's five-game winning steak was snapped by Syracuse in a 0-0 tie at New York's Polo Grounds in what was the first game ever between the two schools, and, ironically, this team's sixth game also would be against Syracuse, at Archbold Stadium. Syracuse was coming off a big loss to powerful Georgetown and wanted to redeem itself by knocking the Lions from the unbeaten ranks. State went into the game a slight favorite with the third best total offense in the nation and the second best defense against the rush. The score was tied at the half, 6-6, with Syracuse scoring on a second quarter 58-yard drive and the Lions striking back with 50 seconds left in the half when Krouse ran through two defenders to take a 14-yard TD pass from Smaltz. Pollock's PAT attempt was blocked.

Syracuse went ahead early in the third quarter on a spectacular 60-yard play. Sophomore fullback Sal "Toots" Mirabito took the snap, faked a line buck and handed off to quarterback Ed Rodiek, who took a step, lateralled to halfback Dick Banger on the right and Banger raced untouched past the bewildered State players for the touchdown. Mirabito's kick made it 13-6 over the stunned Lions. A fumble gave the Orangemen another opportunity but State stopped them at the 29. As the third quarter came to a close Petrella almost broke away for a TD but was tripped up at the Syracuse 17 on a shoestring tackle and moments later Petrella lost a fumble. There were about six minutes left in the game when State took the ball on its own 31-yard line after a punt. In three plays, the Lions were at the Syracuse 38 but a 15-yard penalty set them back. Then on first down, Smaltz faded back to pass. The Syracuse secondary anticipated a pass to Krouse, who already had caught eight passes from Smaltz during the game. As the Orange defenders converge on Krouse, Smaltz threw. Krouse leaped into the air between a couple of defenders at the three-yard line, reached out and caught the ball on his finger tips and bulled across the goal line carrying Syracuse tacklers with him. Syracuse Coach Ossie protested that Krouse was not over the goal but the referee said he was. Pollock came in, calmly kicked the extra point tying the game, 13-13, and that's how it ended.

Smaltz and Krouse had record setting days. Smaltz hit on 14-of-21 passes for 193 yards, the greatest passing day ever for a Nittany Lion up to that time, and his 12 straight completions remained the team record until broken by Kerry Collins in 1994. The nine receptions by Krouse that afternoon remained the record until broken by Jack Curry in 1965 and the 155 yards he gained is still the team record for most receiving yardage in a game by a junior. "Each time after scoring, the Orangemen went to sleep just long enough for Fullback Bill Smaltz to ship touchdown passes to the acrobatic Lenny Krouse," wrote Gerald Ashe in the *Syracuse Post Standard*. But Smaltz and Krouse probably would have given up all their records if the team would have won. "Hillmen Spatter State Record and Outplay Foes," said the biased *Post Standard* headline. The winning streak was over and so was the dream of an all-winning season. But the Lions were still unbeaten and only six teams in 53 years had ever gone undefeated before.

State easily beat NYU, 25-0, the next week at Beaver Field in snow flurries and a stiff wind. Peters, fully recovered from the shoulder injury that kept him out of games earlier in the season, got the Lions rocking by running the opening kickoff back 101 yards for a touchdown, setting a record that still remains after 58 years. Krouse caught a 47-yard pass from Brown for another touchdown, Smaltz scored twice and State had two others called back on penalties as Higgins cleared his bench in the fourth quarter. NYU got into State territory twice, once getting to the 48-yard line and then reaching the 47 on a long pass on the last play of the game.

In midweek, Higgins had a telephone call from Pasadena telling him the Lions were being seriously considered for the Rose Bowl. All they had to do was beat Pitt. The Lions were undefeated in 12 straight games over two years but some sportswriters favored Pitt, now in the middle of its own de-emphasis period.. "Some of the experts...questioned the caliber of opposition faced by the invaders," wrote Jack Sell in the *Pittsburgh Post-Gazette*, "and figured their six wins and one tie were no better than Pitt's two triumphs, three losses and one deadlock against sterner tests." Plus, Sell wrote, there was the "jinx angle in granting the Blue and Gold their narrow edge."

The largest crowd to watch a State-Pitt game in 12 years—30,083—was at Pitt Stadium for what Lions fans expected to be the victorious culmination to one of State's best seasons in history. Yes, a post-season bowl could extend the season. But this is what Lion fans had been waiting to see for two decades, beating the Panthers on their own field and avenging all those beatings by Warner and Sutherland. If there was a psychological edge, it may have belonged to Pitt. On the eve of the game, Pitt's new coach, Charlie Bowser, and his team had been booed at a planned pep rally at the Pitt dental school, apparently because the students were unhappy that Bower had replaced the popular Sutherland. They were still angry when they took the field the next day. The nervousness showed for both teams in the opening minute when each jumped offside before State could run a play from scrimmage after the kickoff. When the Lions got the first break in the first quarter, it looked like Lady Luck was smiling as Platt recovered a fumble by Ernie Bonelli at the Pitt 26-yard line. But three downs gained just one yard and Smaltz's fourth down throw into the end zone was batted down and Pitt took over. That may have been the most costly play of the game for State because Peters re-injured his ankle and didn't play the rest of the day. Lady Luck had stuck out her tongue. After an exchange of punts, Pitt got the ball at midfield and then came the play that seemed to take the heart out of the State players. With the ball at State's 49, fullback George Kracum ran around the short left-side end on a naked reverse and down the sidelines to the five. As Petrella tackled him, Kracum lateralled to one of his blockers, guard Ralph Fife, who scored the touchdown. Bonelli's PAT attempt was blocked by Parsons. The teams battled fairly evenly until late in the half, when State drove all the way from its 22-yard line to the Pitt 26 but on fourth down, Brown was tackled trying to pass and the Panthers took their slightly surprising 6-0 lead into the intermission.

After an exchange of possession to open the third quarter, Pitt got the ball on State's 48 and moments later on a fourth down play at the 18, Edgar Jones hit Bobby Thurborn on a pass in the center of the end zone. Fife's PAT made it 13-0 and the Lion fans groaned. The team was in trouble and the players knew it. On the first play of the

fourth quarter, Smaltz intercepted a pass at the State 30 and returned it 16 yards. Smaltz passed for nine and Petrella ran for 16 before fumbling but State recovered at the Pitt 28. Pitt was called for pass interference on Vargo and Smaltz connected on a six-yarder to Patrick. On second down from the 15, Smaltz passed to Krouse in the flat and the wingback sped into the end zone for his sixth TD of the year. Pollock's kick made it 13-7 and the Lions were fired up. Stravinski kicked off and State's defense held Pitt on downs at the Panther 33. The State fans roared. Another comeback, just like against West Virginia and Syracuse, they thought, only this time for a big victory.

But it never happened. Petrella, who would gain 71 yards from scrimmage and play an outstanding defensive game, fumbled the punt and Pitt recovered at the State 31. Lady Luck sneered at the Nittany Lions. Three running plays and Pitt had a first down. An offside penalty and another run and the Panthers had another first down, at the State nine. But the Lions dug in and held, taking over the ball at the 20 on Pitt's fourth down pass into the end zone. After an exchange of punts, State got the ball on its own 20 with four minutes left. Brown, in at fullback as Smaltz got a rest, passed on the first play. Kracum intercepted at the 35 and dashed into the end zone. If there was one defining moment of the season, this was it! The comeback victory, national ranking and bowl bid disintegrated on one play. Lady Luck delivered the death blow to the Nittany Lions. Fife's boot made it 20-7 and that's where the game ended.

"With the grimness of the Pitt Stadium," Riley wrote in his "*Football Letter*," "Penn State's visions of an undefeated season went up in the murky Pittsburgh sky and heavy Penn State hearts finished out a weekend (sic) in the Smokey (sic) City with forced gaiety and dreams of what might have been."

Lady Luck was chortling. "As Smaltz goes, so goes the Lions."

There was some consolation over the team's disappointment when Gajecki became the first First Team All-American since Bedenk in '24. But Gajecki and The Seven Mountains were now history. Higgins would have to rebuild his entire front line for 1941. The heart of his backfield would be back but unless he could find the right replacements for Gajecki and company, he knew it could be a return to those long seasons of the '30s. And more frustration at Syracuse and Pittsburgh.

Season Record 6-1-1
Record to Date 257-155-31
Winning percentage .615

"The Young Lions"

Bob Higgins paced the sidelines of Buffalo's Civic Stadium as his inexperienced team dug in at the one-foot line late in the fourth quarter to try and stop Colgate from clinching this season-opening game. State had not been given much of a chance against Andy Kerr's veteran Colgate team. Yet, until a couple of minutes ago, the young Nittany Lions, outweighed and outmanned, had played well and had held the Red Raiders scoreless. Then came the type of mistakes that green running backs often make.

First, third-string junior tailback, Ralph Ventresco, had made a "rookie" error in judgment. Ventresco was the team's only other able passer besides the triple-threat star, Bill Smaltz, and as the final period got underway, Ventresco's passing and running had helped take State quickly from its own 15-yard line to the 50. But on third-and-10, the junior had been rushed hard and trapped and foolishly flipped the ball towards a State player out in the flat. Colgate intercepted at the State 45-yard line. The Lions had held but moments later Smaltz was forced to punt from the end zone and Colgate had moved swiftly from the State 24 to score on Jo-Jo McCourt's five-yard end run for a 7-0 lead.

The team had re-grouped around Captain Krouse for the kick-off, and Krouse had reminded them of the kickoff that started the game. Running from the goal line, Petrella had been in the clear at the 50 when hauled down from behind at Colgate's 31-yard line by "Indian Bill" Geyer, said to be the fastest man in college football. But Colgate wasn't taking any more chances and had kicked the ball out of bounds. On the second play from the 20, State's third-team fullback, sophomore Charlie McFarland, had fumbled an attempted pass and Colgate had recovered at the 21.

A back-to-back jolt like that frequently destroys teams loaded with veterans. Ever since pre-season practice began, Higgins had wondered how his inexperienced squad would react to just such a circumstance. He never thought it would happen so early in the season. Now, as Higgins watched stonefaced, Colgate's heralded running backs of Geyer, McCourt and Mike Micka pounded through the young State line until it was second-down-and-goal just inches from the end zone. Just about everyone in the crowd of 23,467 was certain a touchdown was imminent. Bam, Micka up the middle, no gain. Third down. Bam, McCourt up the middle, two-yard loss. Fourth down. Bam, Geyer up the middle, one-yard loss. State's ball! The State players unpiled from the mass of arms and legs and jumped up cheering and patting each other. It was the season's defining moment. The game wasn't over but the spirited young Lions still believed they had a chance of winning, or at least tying.

But, alas, after an exchange of punts and three desperation passes by Smaltz, the dejected State players left the field in defeat but with their pride intact. "There is no one to disagree that the Lions established themselves as highly in defeat as the Red Raiders did in their 7-0 triumph," wrote Bill Kelley, sports editor of the *Buffalo Courier Express*. "Nice Try, Lions!" read a headline in the *Pittsburgh Press*. " Strangely enough," wrote Pat Nagelberg in *The Daily Collegian*, "it took a defeat in the first game to really convince the students (ourselves included) that Penn State has a football club this year." Unfortunately, the team would go on to lose two of their first three games and be given up as a "lost cause' by some fans and sportswriters. But by the time the season was over in the hot sunshine of South Carolina, that goal line stand against Colgate would be the defining moment of the year.

Higgins had figured it would take time for this team to mature. He was counting on his three senior backs—Krouse, Smaltz and Petrella—to provide the leadership to help bring the sophomore-dominated team along. He had lost his entire starting line of '40, including senior Mike Garbiniski, the two-year regular at guard who had been drafted into the Army. He knew he had a lot of raw talent up from the frosh team and some capable prospects in the handful of last year's reserves. But only two of the reserves had played enough to earn letters and Mike Kern was the only lineman. The other vet, "Sparky' Brown,

ultimately would miss the entire season because of a severe injury to both his ankles. As the team practiced for the October 6 opener against Colgate, Higgins and his coaches were especially pleased by the mental attitude of the team, particularly the youngsters. "...It is not the kind of squad that would normally set things on fire in top-notch (sic) college competition," Riley wrote in his preseason *Football Letter*. "But if the present spirit continues, if a few breaks come our way, you'll have lots of fun (following this team)."

Higgins had no problem picking his starting backfield. Smaltz was back at fullback, Krouse at wingback and Petrella at tailback. Smaltz would also handle the place-kicking for the first time and everyone was surprised at how accurate he had become. Smaltz also would kick off and he and Krouse would share the punting. Krouse was assigned to run the team on the field and do the play calling so that 215-pound junior quarterback Paul "Manny" Weaver could concentrate on blocking. In the line, Higgins would eventually go with a lineup of junior Van Lenten and soph John Potsklan at ends with soph Bob Davis as backup, junior Ken Schoonover and soph Bernie Brosky at tackles, sophs John Jaffurs and Ted Kratzke at guards with soph Jim Bonham, junior Bob Perugini and senior Red Yoho as spot starters. Senior Chuck Raysor started at center until he was injured early and then senior Bob Wear and soph Lou Palazzi took over. Once again, the offense would be pass oriented because of the Smaltz-Krouse combination. Petrella was the prime runner. Pass defense was seen as the prime weakness because of the inexperienced line, Petrella's small size and Smaltz' lack of speed.

Colgate only tossed eight passes against State, completing two for 19 yards and had two intercepted. But, in the Beaver Field opener the next week, underdog Bucknell came out throwing and startled the largest Homecoming crowd in 16 years—16,000—by capitalizing on fumbles by Petrella and Krouse to take a 13-0 lead in the first 10 minutes. Before the quarter was over Schoonover blocked a punt at the Bucknell 15-yard line and Van Lenten ran the ball to the one from where Petrella scored. Early in the second quarter, Van Lenten also blocked a punt—at the Bucknell 11—and this time Schooner recovered at the three. Petrella scored again, Smaltz kicked his second extra point and the Lions took the lead for good. Petrella got his third TD before the end of the half and his fourth in the third quarter as the Lions won, 27-13. Bucknell completed 11-of-20 passes for 150 yards with one interception but had a minus 24 yards on the ground on 33 carries. Not bad for an inexperienced line.

State didn't have much of a chance the next week against a superior Temple team in Philadelphia after Smaltz was knocked out of the game 10 minutes into the first quarter with a head injury. State's other passer, Ventresco, had not made the trip because of a knee injury and Temple was able to stack the line with virtually an eight-man front. When both starting guards, Jaffurs and Yoho and the first two centers went out with injuries, it was all over. Temple went 67 yards for a touchdown in the first quarter and scored another in the third quarter after a pass interception but the young Lions didn't go down easily. Despite losing the ball four times on interceptions and three times on fumbles, the defense stopped Temple nearly a dozen times near State's 20-yard line and in the fourth quarter held on downs at the seven. The final score was 14-0.

The Dad's Day contest with outclassed Lehigh on October 25 gave Higgins the chance for his team to recover from the tough Temple game but it also re-affirmed his concern about the squad's pass defense. Lehigh passed long, short, in the flat and down the middle and completed 16-of-34 passes for 206 yards. The Lions intercepted five but most of those were almost by accident rather than by any adroit tactical defensive maneuver. Still, the Lions won easily, 40-6, as Higgins played all of his reserves. The Smaltz-Krouse passing combination scored on TDs of 40 and 21 yards in the first quarter before leaving the game. Sophomore Fullback Jack Banbury scored three TDs and Smaltz was four-for-four in extra points.

The next Friday night, State played its first ever night game in the Polo Grounds of New York City against New York University. State was a slight favorite and the heavy rain that soaked the field kept the crowd down below 11,000. Miserable weather conditions almost always benefit the underdog and with a break or two, the weaker team can often pull off a magnificent upset. The game started out like a possible upset-in-the-making as the teams traded punts until State got the ball at the NYU 41 with about four minutes left in the first quarter. On third-and-three, Smaltz passed to Krouse in the clear at the 10 and the Lion captain went into the end zone. That seemed to wilt NYU. The Lions built a 21-0 lead by halftime and the reserves were in before the third quarter had gone halfway as State breezed to a 42-0 win.

State was now 3-2 but the biggest game of the season was just ahead. Against Cornell, Coach Ossie Solem had introduced a new formation he called the "reverse-center Y." It was unorthodox and had the center turning his back on the opposition and facing his own backfield. This enabled him to pass accurately to all his backs, especially the two flankers on both ends of the "Y." It also placed the center more in the backfield where he became a more deadly blocker for his runners. Against Cornell, the Syracuse center also took return passes from his backs and ran with the ball. But early in the game, the officials had declared the center's running illegal and also said his rear end was offside. Syracuse's offense sputtered and the team lost. But Solem made some refinements in the "reverse-center Y" and now it was the talk of the football world after victories over Holy Cross, NYU, Rutgers and Wisconsin.

But after State's assistant coach Earle Edwards had scouted Syracuse, Higgins and his staff devised a defense that was basically a seven-man line with a linebacker playing man-to-man on the center. Wherever the center went, the linebacker followed. But instead of hitting the center, the linebacker would go after the ball carrier. Meanwhile, the defensive ends played wide and crashed, the tackles stayed

home and bumped the offensive ends and the guards raced straight in. Higgins assigned Jaffurs as the linebacker trailer and when Jaffurs was injured in the game, Palazzi took his place and the two of them wound up making more solo tackles than had been seen in recent years on Beaver Field. Higgins also figured that controlling the ball on offense would make Syracuse work even harder for its yardage and if his new defensive strategy worked, the Orange game plan would be completely disrupted.

The defense worked to near perfection and the offense controlled the ball so well that Syracuse ran only 15 plays in the first half and by that time the score was 27-0. In another planned surprise, Higgins and Krouse decided to pass on the first play of the game if State got the ball. Since everyone knew Krouse was Smaltz's favorite target, they decided that Petrella would be the prime receiver but that Smaltz would have the option to go to Krouse if the wingback was open. Sure enough, Syracuse chose to kick off and State started on its own 35-yard line. Smaltz went back to pass, saw that Krouse was open and hit him for a 14-yard gain. With Petrella doing most of the running, the Lions went the rest of the way for a touchdown with "Pepper" going over from the three. The Orange did not know what hit them and they lost their poise. A fumble recovery by Ventresco at the State 20 early in the second quarter set up another touchdown by Petrella and minutes later the Syracuse punt receiver fumbled at his own 28 when hit by Van Lenten and the Lions stormed down the field for another TD. State got its fourth TD on the last play of the half when Smaltz passed 19 yards to Krouse in the end zone to climax another 51-yard drive. The final was 34-19. That's one for 1940! That was also the end of the "reverse-center Y" as Syracuse reverted to the single-wing to score two touchdowns late in the game. "An impressive Syracuse record and a heretofore baffling 'Y' formation failed to overcome tradition here today as Penn State's football team upset the Orange...," reported the *Pittsburgh Press*.

State fans now knew they had a good team. But having been deluded before by teams with fine records early on who subsequently lost their direction or their composure, the students and alumni were not completely convinced these Lions would be different. And it didn't help when State almost lost to a fired-up West Virginia team on Beaver Field. Once again, the win was defined by two goal line stands and the all-around play of Smaltz and Krouse, who played the entire 60 min-

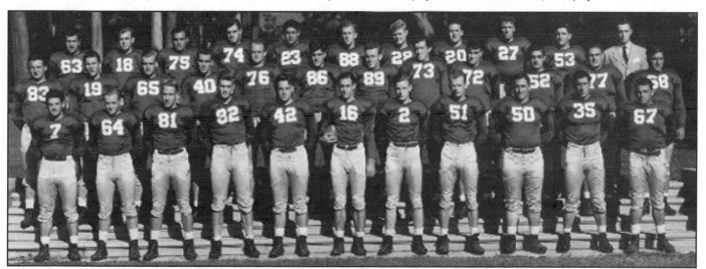

The young 1941 team brought big-time football back to State with a 7-2 season. The stars were (by number in front row): Pepper Petrella (7), Bill Smaltz (42) and Captain Lenny Krouse (16).

utes. The Lions scored the only touchdown of the game late in the second quarter on another great pass reception by Krouse at the end of a 65-yard march. On fourth down at the Mountaineers 28-yard line, Krouse ran down the middle with two defenders guarding him close, leaped up in the air at the one-yard line and came down with Smaltz' pass in the end zone. Smaltz extra point made it 7-0 at halftime. The second half was all defense as West Virginia halted one State drive at its 15-yard line and the Lions defense led by Jaffurs and Potsklan stopped the Mountaineers at State's 6- and 8-yard lines to preserve the victory.

Maybe the closeness of the West Virginia game was the consequence of a natural letdown after the avenging win over Syracuse. Or perhaps, the team was just looking ahead to Pitt. The senior leaders had been pointing to Pitt ever since the preseason. They owed the Panthers, not just for last year's humiliating upset but for the more than 20 years of frustrating defeats that Higgins and the Lion football family had endured at Pitt Stadium.

Pitt was hot. After being clobbered by Michigan and eventual National Champion Minnesota early in the season, the Panthers had revived and handed Fordham its only defeat of the year, 13-0. They also had upset Nebraska, 14-7. With another crowd of 30,000 watching in typical late November weather, the teams battled evenly for the first 10 minutes of the game. Then, an exchange of punts gave Pitt the ball at its own 43-yard line. Four plays later, Edgar "Special Delivery" Jones banged over left tackle on a weak-side reverse play and rambled 43-yards for a touchdown. The Lions fans were still groaning when Jones, the holder for the PAT, bobbled the pass from center, then picked up the ball and ran around right end for the extra point.

As the play continued in the second quarter, it appeared as if the Pittsburgh jinx was about to strike again. Pitt was playing a fine defensive game and State did not get a first down until Smaltz hit Krouse on an 18-yard pass during a short drive from midfield that Pitt stopped at its 17-yard line. But when State got the ball back at its 43-yard line moments later after a punt, the Lions quickly drove for a touchdown on the running of Petrella and a 30-yard pass from Smaltz to sophomore backup quarterback Aldo Cenci. Petrella went over left tackle from one yard out for the TD, Smaltz's PAT tied the game and State fans relaxed a bit. Pitt fumbled on its next possession and Van Lenten recovered at the 12. Petrella got 11 of the 12 yards on four plays and went over for the TD from the two. Smaltz's PAT made it 14-7 and the half ended a minute and a half later. The second half was all State. Pitt never crossed the 50-yard line. Meanwhile, the Lions drove 51 yards on its first possession with Petrella going 24 yards over left tackle for his third TD and Smaltz kicking the first field goal of his career (for 16 yards) later in the third quarter following a Jones fumble at the State 10. The final score of 31-7 was the most points scored by either team in this series since 1912 and the victory was State's first in Pittsburgh since the famous Higgins pass reception win of 1919. "In all the 41 games these teams have played," wrote Chester Smith, Sports Editor of the *Pittsburgh Press*, "it is questionable whether any was more decisively won, no matter what the margin of the score may have been..." and "...so far as State's supremacy was concerned, neither the 40 points scored against Pitt by Michigan nor the 39 by Minnesota represented a rout of any greater proportions than was unfolded in the green pit of the Stadium." Higgins told Eddie Beachler of the *Press*, "We waited a long time for this one. This is the best one of all to win." The celebration by State's alumni and students went on into Sunday afternoon.

The Lions had one more game left, 700 miles away from Pittsburgh and State College in Columbia, SC. South Carolina had not lost at home and had upset in-state neighbor Clemson and Higgins was concerned. The game played in 80 degree weather was close all the way despite a big statistical advantage for the Lions, who had 204 yards rushing, 146 passing and 19 first downs to South Carolina's 101 yards rushing 71 passing and five first downs. However, State blew three close-in scoring opportunities and got burned on a 62-yard bomb early in the second half. With head cheerleader Johnny Dague leading the cheers, a small contingent of State fans, comprised mostly of men from nearby Army and Navy bases, watched as the Lions scored on their first possession of the game, driving 65 yards with Petrella scoring from the one. Smaltz missed the PAT and the Gamecocks tied the game following the kickoff by going 64 yards on six plays. State took the ensuing kickoff and went on another 65-yard march, with a 43-yard pass from Smaltz to Krouse setting up Smaltz's one-yard TD and Smaltz booted the extra point just before the half ended. South Carolina made it 13-12 early in the third quarter on a 62-yard pass and the Lions got to the one-foot line later in the period but Krouse dropped a fourth down pass in the end zone. The Gamecocks almost took the lead midway in the fourth quarter on an interception but Krouse halted that threat with his own interception and a 13-yard runback to the State 43. From there, State drove for its final touchdown with Petrella getting the last five of his 110 yards off left tackle for the score. Smaltz missed the PAT again but the Lions defense stopped Carolina after the kickoff and the Lions were on the Gamecock's seven-yard line when the whistle sounded. The final score was 19-12 and Petrella got a new automobile. Petrella's mother, who had driven from Philadelphia to see her son play, had promised she would buy him a car if he had more touchdowns that season than his old high school rival, Andy Tomsic, now playing for Temple. His two touchdowns that day got him the new car keys.

The win over South Carolina prompted immediate speculation of a post-season bowl and the Lions were seriously considered by the Orange and Cotton Bowls but the bids never came. So, the young Lions of '41 finished with a surprising 7-2 record, in what may have been the best coaching job ever by Higgins and his staff. Krouse and Smaltz made the All-American team picked by the *New York Sun* and they, along with Petrella, played in post-season All Star games. This team had heart, spirit and determination and Higgins left South Carolina eager for the next season to begin. With the veterans returning and an outstanding group of players from the unbeaten freshman team, led by triple threat tailback Dave Alston—the school's first ever black player—there was reason to be optimistic about '42. Unfortunately, a World War was just a week away and before the next season began an off-field tragedy would shock the Penn State family and the college football world.

Season Record 7-2
Record to Date 264-157-31
Winning percentage .618

"Remember Pearl Harbor"

The defining moment of the 1942 season occurred on December 7, 1941 when the Japanese bombed Pearl Harbor. No matter what happened in the eight-game schedule that followed, Penn State football, like the rest of college sports, was changed by the nation's entrance into World War II.

By the time the '42 season started, 20 players had left the campus to serve in the armed forces, including six starters and several other lettermen off the '41 team along with nine members of the great undefeated freshman squad. That prompted the Athletic Board in September to make freshmen eligible for the varsity for the duration of the war and a couple of those frosh became immediate standouts.

Spring practice was a little more intense than usual under Higgins as he worked out his players without knowing who would still be around by October's opening game with Bucknell. With school remaining in session all summer, Higgins and his staff would hold periodic practices and sometimes would have enough players for full-scale scrimmages. This was not illegal and the same thing was happening on other campuses. Throughout these scrimmages, Higgins continued to be impressed by his sophomore tailback, Dave Alston. Alston and his brother, Harry, had been recruited by Casey Jones out of Midland High School and they were the first blacks ever on a State football team. Alston had been so exceptional as a freshman that one national magazine had featured him on its cover in July as "College Football's Sophomore of the Year." He had scored eight touchdowns, thrown for four other TDs, including three to his brother, and had drop-kicked more than a half dozen extra points. With his speed and agility, the 6-foot, 200-pounder also was an excellent defensive back. Harry had left school to work in the war industry but Higgins believed Dave could become one of the great players in State history.

In mid-August, Alston entered Bellefonte Hospital for a long-awaited but routine operation to remove his tonsils. He died there on August 15 of a blood clot following the surgery. Doctors said injuries Alston had suffered in a spring practice scrimmage at Navy apparently had been more severe than originally diagnosed. Late in that scrimmage, Alston had been swarmed over by Navy linemen while handing off the ball and had incurred a severe eye bruise. What no one knew was that he also had been hurt internally and those internal injuries had contributed to his death. Higgins and the team were in shock. "This is a terrible catastrophe that...leaves us all greatly shocked," Higgins told the *Centre Daily Times*. This was another defining moment for the team, especially for Altson's frosh teammates who were still on campus—Steve Suhey, Leo Nobile, John Wolsky, Jeff Durkota, Red Moore, Cliff St. Clair, Bucky Walters and others.

Higgins called off practice for the rest of the summer and didn't reassemble the team until September 8, the day before the fall semester began. Twenty-five players showed up and from that group, Higgins and the staff forged a starting lineup for Bucknell made up mostly of experienced reserves from '41. Four men who had started much of last season had returned—Van Lenten at end, Schoonover at tackle and Jaffurs and Perugini at guards. The rest of the line was filled with lettermen, senior Mike Kearns at tackle, junior Bob Davis at end, and Palazzi at center. Potsklan, the outstanding defensive end, had left for the service. So had the starting quarterback, Weaver, and Higgins promoted the 225-pound Cenci to the first team. Junior letterman Jack Banbury was now the fullback and Sparky Brown had returned after his one year absence because of injuries to be the tailback. The only sophomore in the lineup was St. Clair at wingback for the graduated Krouse. But the other sophs, Suhey, Nobile, etc., filled out the second team along with two freshmen, Larry Joe at tailback and Hal Pratt at

tackle. Another freshman, Joe Colone, would become the starting fullback by midseason and develop into one of the greatest punters of all time. A week before the Bucknell opener at Beaver Field, the squad elected Palazzi, another of the Dunmore boys, as captain.

Some schedules had been disrupted by the war, just like in World War I, but not State's. In fact, State and Pitt had scheduled a unique back-to-back doubleheader in Pittsburgh to end the season, with the games one week apart separated by Thanksgiving and the second game for the benefit of the Army Relief charity. But in early November, the second game was called off when the government ordered no more charity games after November 15 and the Pitt game was switched to Beaver Field. With State's opponents facing similar manpower problems, no one could predict what kind of season this would be. Higgins told friends he should be able to win half the games and beat Pitt. Still, some sportswriters believed State was among the best teams in the country. Chet Smith, sports editor of the *Pittsburgh Press*, picked the Lions as the best team in the East. Francis Wallace of *The Saturday Evening Post* went even further, tabbing State as the 16th best in the nation and predicting the Lions would play Mississippi State in the 1943 Orange Bowl.

Bucknell, with just three starters from 1941 returning, had already beaten Lebanon Valley when it made the 50-mile trek to Beaver Field on October 3. The smallest opening day crowd in four years, 10,303, saw Bucknell deploy its new T-formation offense and take a 7-0 lead in the first quarter on a 19-yard pass play. As the game moved into the second quarter, Higgins worked two freshmen into the game. Pratt, the tackle, became the first frosh to play in a varsity game since Higgins, himself, played at end in 1914. Joe was next and the high school sprint champ of Western Pennsylvania carried for eight yards on his first play—an omen for his and Penn State's future. A few minutes later, Joe ran 11 yards for a touchdown and Van Lenten's PAT tied the score. The Lions almost scored on its first possession of the second half but an intercepted pass thwarted a 70-yard drive at the Bucknell 12. Then late in the third quarter, Brown broke away over left tackle and with a key block by Moore on the Bucknell safety, Sparky ran 79 yards for the TD, the longest run from scrimmage in four years. Van Lenten booted the PAT and that's how the game ended, 14-7.

Van Lenten and St. Clair were left home with injuries when State traveled to Bethlehem the following week for the final game ever with Lehigh. The Lions went up and down the field in the first half but couldn't crack the Lehigh end zone until late in the second quarter. By that time, Lehigh had taken a 3-0 lead off a 28-yard field goal following a blocked punt. State moved ahead 6-3 before the half when Colone, on his first ever passing attempt, hit Durkota on a 34-yard pass that set up a one-yard touchdown plunge by Banbury. The PAT kick was blocked. Late in the third quarter, Joe brought the crowd to its feet with a 65-yard punt return for a TD. It was the longest punt run back in four years, and Cenci's kick made the score 13-3. The Lions added another touchdown after a roughing the kicker penalty set up a 37-yard drive and soph fullback Bob Weitzel got his 101st yard of the game with a one-yard plunge. The 19-3 score didn't begin to tell how much State dominated with 261 yards rushing, 96 passing an 18 first downs to Lehigh's 37 yards on the ground, 22 through the air and three first downs.

State could have used some of that offense at Ithaca when it battled to a 0-0 tie with a veteran Cornell team in the rain, wind and several inches of mud before a Homecoming crowd of 5,000 at

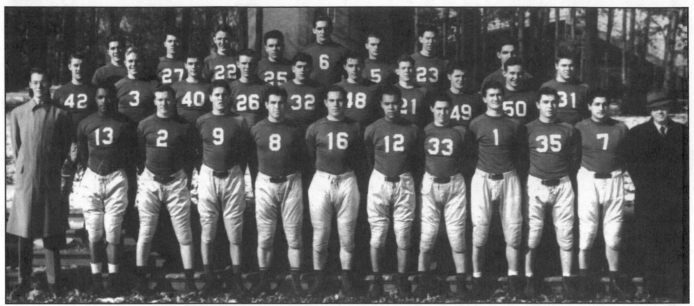

Penn State's first Black players, Dave and Harry Alston, were on the unbeaten 1940 freshman team. Both are in the front row with Dave wearing #13 and Harry, #12. Dave was expected to be a superstar but died before the 1941 season began and Harry left school. Also on the team were future stars of the great unbeaten team of 1947, including (by number in front row) Red Moore (2), Leo Nobile (8), Steve Suhey (16), George Durkota (1), John Wolosky (35) and (second row) Ray Ulinski (2).

Schoellkopf Field. This was perhaps he all-time "punting game" in State history. The Lions had net rushing yards of 39, fumbled seven times and didn't complete its only pass attempt while Cornell, which was favored, had 60 yards on the ground, 13 yards on two-of-three passes and five fumbles. The teams traded punts all day—27 by State and 24 by Cornell—and State discovered a new kicker. Brown did most of the punting early in the game, getting off a 54-yarder that was the longest by either team, but when Higgins inserted Colone, the freshman from Berwick got everyone's attention. "He kicked high, booming punts;" reported Ridge Riley in his *"Football Letter,"* "he kicked low, fast ones that went in a straight line down the edge of the field; he quick-kicked; he kicked out of bounds. His performance on a dry field would have been noteworthy." Colone averaged more than 40 yards on 14 punts and didn't have one blocked. (More than 50 years later, Colone still could not believe the number and variety of punts he made that day.) Cornell's lone scoring threat came early in the game after blocking one of Cenci's punts in the end zone. The ball bounced to the State 25-yard line but Cornell fumbled the ball away at the 10. State got as far as the Cornell 11 in the third quarter after recovering another fumble but Cornell held on downs. "Muddy Gridiron Stops Lion-Big Red Offenses," said the headline in *The Daily Collegian.* There was one ironic sidebar to the game. Because of wartime restrictions, the sportscaster doing the play-by-play on radio couldn't describe the miserable weather conditions in Ithaca, and State fans listening back home didn't learn until later how much the weather affected the outcome.

As Higgins prepared his team for the Homecoming game against favored Colgate, he decided that a surprise was needed to rattle the confidence of Coach Andy Kerr's squad and get the home crowd into the game. Kerr was known for his razzle-dazzle innovations and Higgins wanted something that would even flabbergast the master of surprise. He thought of "the play" while lying in bed Thursday night. The situation would have to be just right, he told his players as they practiced "the play" the next day.

With a combination alumni Homecoming and Dad's Day crowd of 11,510 looking on, Colgate jumped out to a 3-0 lead on a 22-yard field goal after recovering a State fumble midway through the first quarter. A pass interception gave Colgate another field goal opportunity as the second quarter began but this attempt was wide. The teams traded punts and fumbles around midfield and midway through the period Red Moore, starting his first game at right tackle, recovered a Colgate fumble at State's 47-yard line. Higgins knew it was time for "the play" and he signaled Cenci. Palazzi centered the ball to Colone who dropped back to the State 40. Walters, the left end, cut over the middle to Colgate's 40, came to a dead stop and turned to face Colone. Colone threw a perfect pass to Walters. The Colgate safety raced up to tackle Walters. But just as the safety was about to hit Walters from behind, the Lion end handed the ball off to St. Clair speeding down his left side and St. Clair ran into the end zone untouched. Van Lenten's PAT hit the upright and bounced back but State had taken the lead 6-3 on "the play" and that's how the first half ended.

Halftime ceremonies usually are not historic but this one was. The now famous Nittany Lion Statue created by famed sculptor Heinz Warneke, and then located near the entrances of New Beaver Field and the Nittany Lion Inn, was dedicated with Warneke and H. D. "Joe" Mason, class of 1907, who instigated the move for a Lion as mascot, among the participants.

The teams battled evenly when the third quarter got underway but midway through the period Higgins unleashed his second surprise. Into the game at tailback went a pint-sized walk-on freshman from Pittsburgh named Bobby Williams who had been playing on the junior varsity until the previous week. Two weeks earlier, Williams had completed 20-of-30 passes in a "JV" game and that performance earned him a promotion to the varsity when Higgins realized the 5-8, 165-pounder was the best passer on campus. Unfortunately, Williams' first pass was intercepted on Colgate's 32-yard line and that led directly to a touchdown that regained the lead for the visitors, 10-6. State got the ball on its 35-yard line following the kickoff and had a first down at the 46 as the fourth quarter started. Higgins, not deterred by the interception, sent the "little guy" back into the game. Two plays later, with second-and-13, Williams found St. Clair in the clear along the right sideline at the 20-yard line, hit him in stride and St. Clair scored his second touchdown. With Van Lenten's kick it was 13-10 and the defense kept Colgate in check the rest of the way. Higgins had made the alumni happy—and discovered a new star. "'Find a freshman—he'll do it' seems to be the battle cry of the Nittany Lion gridders," wrote Fred Clever in *The Daily Collegian*, "Latest yearling to come to the fore is Bobby Williams...Saturday, it was Williams who stole the show."

With a 3-0-1 record, the Lions were feeling pretty good about themselves when they went to Morgantown to play West Virginia on Halloween. A State team had not been to Morgantown since the dedication of Mountaineer Stadium in 1931 and this young Lions team obviously had little respect for the Mountaineers, even though a *Collegian* sportswriter predicted the Mountaineers were "overdue." Ridge Riley's lead in his "*Football Letter*" description of the game succinctly reported what happened. "Exactly 17 years ago, our Nittany Lions helped West Virginia dedicate its concrete stadium around Mountaineer Field," Riley wrote. "Saturday, it fell in on them." West Virginia got a touchdown quickly in the first quarter on a 41-yard drive following a punt and went on to score in every quarter for a convincing 24-0 win. "Everything went wrong," Higgins told the *Collegian*. The lone highlight for State was the punting of Colone who averaged 40 yards on nine kicks, but what Lions fans now wanted to know was whether this chastened team could bounce back after such a thorough beating.

Unbeaten Syracuse, with lettermen two deep at every position, was next and the Orange rushing defense was among the best in the nation, holding opponents to an average of about 50 yards per game. The Lions looked like a completely different team as they came from behind in the second half at Beaver Field to upset Syracuse, 18-13, and Colone's punting was even more astounding. Colone's nine punts, including quick kicks averaged 57 yards, and often came at critical times when a big play was needed. The Lions shredded Syracuse's defense for 282 yards with Brown getting 108 yards and two touchdowns on 13 carries and State's defense intercepted four of 14 Syracuse pass attempts to stop Orange drives. "Penn State played an entirely different species of football Saturday than we have seen all year," wrote Don Davis, sports editor of the *Collegian*. "For the first time this year we saw a well-poised team that knew where it was going."

Now, it was on to Franklin Field and the biggest game of the year against heavily-favored traditional rival, Penn. Penn officials had decided not to schedule any more games with State after this one and that irritated Higgins and the State fandom. The Hig was not much for locker room orations, but before the game he spoke quietly to his troops about the tradition: "This is the last time Lions will roar out of the dressing room and tear at their city cousins with every bit of strength they possess," he said. "This is the last game. Let's make them remember it. Let's make them remember us."

The Quakers remembered and so did the 50,000 fans who watched as Colone's punting, a staunch defense and an opportunistic offense led State to a convincing 13-7 victory. Penn, a veteran team, had the statistical edge but that was all, getting 272 yards rushing and 15 first downs from its ground-oriented attack while State had 131

Sparky Brown runs up the middle with blocks from Joe Colone, Aldo Cenci, Ken Schoonover and Jeff Durkota for a touchdown that helps State beat Penn, 13-7, at Franklin Field.

yards and six first downs ands didn't attempt one pass. Despite a stiff wind, Colone averaged 35 yards on 13 punts but several of the kicks were quick kicks or well-placed boots that backed Penn deep into its own territory. Three times in the first quarter, Colone's punts put the Quakers in trouble and midway through the period the defensive strategy paid off. Schoonover slammed through to block a Penn punt, picked up the ball at the Quaker 24-yard line and ran to the two before being tackled. Brown went over right tackle for the touchdown and Van Lenten's PAT made it 7-0. Penn stormed back in the second quarter and three times State's defense stopped Penn scoring drives—at the six, 12 and four yard lines. The Lions stopped another drive at the 10-yard line in the third quarter and almost had their own touchdown but a holding

Freshman tailback Larry Joe runs the second half kickoff back 90 yards for a touchdown that helps give State a 14-6 win over Pitt at Beaver Field.

penalty nullified Joe's 39-yard run. In the fourth quarter, the Lions put it away, recovering a Penn fumble at the Quaker 41 and scoring in four plays with Joe getting 34 of the yards, including the final nine. A penalty forced the Lions to try a pass for the extra point but it was no good. Penn scored with about two minutes left on a 58-yard drive but it was too late and the Lion's left Franklin Field with the sweetest victory of the season. Joe, who had played nearly the entire game after Brown went out with an injury and was as outstanding on defense as he was on offense, was carried off the field by a group of sailors in uniform as State students tore down the goal posts. "Today the Nittany Mountains ring and echo the praises of two guys named Joe," wrote Leo Riordan in the *Philadelphia Inquirer,* "State College is enjoying a story-book victory in an incredible season...This, the 11th victory in 39 meetings with their arch-rival Pennsylvania would go down in the books as possibly the sweetest of all. Certainly, it would have to be close to the most surprising."

The final game at Beaver Field on Nov 21 was anti-climactic. Higgins said he would beat Pittsburgh and he did but it wasn't pretty. Davis fumbled the opening kickoff at the 41-yard line but the Lions got the ball back three plays later on a Cenci interception. That's how it went throughout the scoreless first half as the Lions stumbled and the oft-beaten Panthers bumbled. Joe woke up the damp crowd of nearly 12,000 by taking the second half kickoff at the 10-yard line, running straight up the middle through the blocking alley and going for a touchdown. Van Letten's kick was good. Pitt came back and reached the State three before one drive was stopped but scored the next time it had the ball on a nine-yard pass. The PAT was blocked and a Pitt player picked up the ball near the goal line but Colone's tackle brought him down short, keeping the Lions in the lead. Pitt never threatened again and with three minutes to play, Williams tossed a six-yard pass to Cenci in the end zone for the big quarterback's first ever TD. The extra point made it 14-6 and for the first time since 1911-12, State had beaten Pitt twice in succession. This also was State's 16th straight home victory dating to 1939.

"The victory established State unquestionably as one of the better elevens in the East," wrote Chet Smith. "The record speaks for

itself, for this Nittany Lion squad, decimated by graduation and enlistment, has completed its season with six triumphs..." The Orange Bowl showed some interest but chose Boston College (8-1) and Alabama (7-3) instead.

In December, the Lions were ranked 19th in the country by the AP, tied with Minnesota and Holy Cross. That was quite an accomplishment, especially when one considers this team never scored more than 19 points a game and barely outscored opponents, 77 points to 64. Riley put it best in his final *"Football Letter"* of the season: "This is not the record of a great team, but it is the record of a courageous, resourceful group of young men who don't know what it means to quit trying."

The freshmen and sophomores had been magnificent. No one knew how many would return the next year. After all, there was a war to fight. But there was one man who had a strong premonition about the future once the war was over. "We're looking forward to that great season—not in the too distant future we firmly believe—when all of you who have had your college careers interrupted will return to the campus, "Riley wrote. "What a team we'll have THAT year." He was right. But that was a half a decade and many defeats away.

Season Record 6-1-1
Record to Date 270-158-32
Winning percentage .622

"The Army, Navy & Marines"

"Hupt, Hopt, Taaree, Fooh!" "Hupt, Hopt, Taaree, Fooh!"
The sounds of 2,500 Army, Navy and Marine recruits marching through campus was more prevalent in the fall of 1943 than the signal-calling cadence of Higgins' quarterback resounding off of Bea-

ver Field. There were many Penn State fans and faculty who believed the school should have given up football that year as some of its opponents, including Syracuse, had done.

But Higgins' experience during World War I gave him an insight that few on campus could comprehend. He had left State in 1917 and had seen heavy combat in Europe. He believed the game was a morale booster for students and others on the home front and remembered how he still tried to keep up with the Penn State game results while overseas in '17 and '18. He wasn't sure where he was going to get all his players but he was determined to put a competitive team on the field no matter what. And he did, but not without help from the Army, Navy and Marines.

Spring practice had been canceled and every member of his fine varsity team of '42 had left for the armed service. Every single one! A week before the start of fall classes, Higgins knew he would have one player back from Marty McAndrews' junior varsity and maybe two or three incoming freshmen who had been high school standouts. Then, the military came to the rescue, not only at State but at other schools which were fielding teams.

With so many American males volunteering for service, the military could not keep up with the training. So, the War Department used the campuses as a way-station for the recruits until they could be assimilated into the training programs. Anyone enrolled in the Advanced ROTC for officer training was allowed to return to his school until he graduated or was re-called but he had to pay his own tuition and expenses. The Navy and Marines had developed what was called the V-12 program and they were shipping recruits en masse to colleges throughout the nation to await openings. The Army frowned on football, believing its rigorous mass physical training was best for the would-be athletes. But the Navy felt football and physical activity was beneficial as long as the V-12 students could maintain their grades.

So, as the semester was about to start in mid August, three ROTC seniors showed up, all of them starters in '43—Brown, Cenci and Jaffurs. Then, a few days later, 600 men in the V-12 program arrived in State College and more than 60 went out for the football team. The V-12's had no choice of their destination since the Navy was paying but among the State contingent was Apprentice Seaman Red Moore and Marine recruit Bobby Williams. Dozens of other V-12's had played football at such schools at Pitt, Ohio State, Dayton and George Washington. They practiced when they could, an hour here and an hour there, and slowly the newcomers learned the Penn State system and began to actually care about winning for the Blue and White.

"The squad has produced an abundance of good material and the boys are shaping up favorably at this point, but we still have a long way to go," Higgins told the *Collegian* halfway through preseason practice. He added that rebuilding his line had been his biggest problem but he had some fine candidates among his V-12 contingent.

By the time Higgins opened the season on September 25 against Bucknell at Beaver Field, he had two full teams comprised mostly of V-12 Marines, the ROTC bunch and a couple of freshmen linemen. There were two significant uncertainties. A new V-12 ruling mandated that all Navy and Marines maintain their sports eligibility on a month-to-month basis. "...A single failure in any subject for any month would knock a student out of sports competition during the next month," reported the *Collegian*. In addition, neither Higgins nor the players knew when the men would be called back for training and, as the season progressed, several key players suddenly left. (Not many of

these V-12 surrogates returned to State after the War. But the starting end, a big kid out of Mount Pleasant, PA, by way of George Washington, would not only come back but would be a key player in one of State's most controversial games of all time, and, later, the top administrator of the Penn State Athletic Department. His name was Ed Czekaj.)

The starting backfield against Bucknell had only one unfamiliar name. Cenci, now called "Mt. Aldo" by his teammates because of his bulk (5'10", 230 pounds), was back at quarterback and Brown was again the fullback. Williams, the pint-sized star of the '43 Homecoming win over Syracuse, was at tailback. Jack Castignola, a Marine speedster from the University of Dayton, was the new wingback. Czekaj, Moore and Jaffurs (who would be named captain by Higgins) started on the right side of the line and four Marines took the other positions, Bill Powers, Dan Ross, Ted Hapanowicz and Bill Smyth. For the first time in years, State's proud Blue Band did not march upon the field before the 2 p.m. kickoff. Instead, a jeep circled the field draped with posters that said "Buy War Bonds." The team trotted out in all-white uniforms because new Blue and White attire had not arrived and the 7,000 fans, hundreds in military uniform, cheered lustily.

The referee signaled for the opening kickoff and Czekaj thundered towards the ball. He swung his foot lustily into the leather, aiming for the Bucknell end zone, 60 yards away. POOF! The ball traveled just 22 yards and wags in the press box wondered if Czekaj should be traded back to George Washington for a couple of 4-F civilians. This botched kickoff was a portent of the erratic season ahead, starting with this game. The first two passes Williams threw were intercepted. But early in the second quarter, Williams hit Castignola for a 39-yard touchdown to complete a 66-yard drive and Marine Private Dick Trumbull, formerly of Ohio State, kicked the extra point for a 7-0 lead. Using the new T-Formation, Bucknell spent almost the rest of the game trying to score and reached the State 12 twice and the 11 once but was thrown back on good defensive plays. The Lions offense sputtered, outgaining Bucknell 162 yards to 31, but was continually halted by penalties and had 107 yards total for the game. Midway through the fourth quarter, Brown ran back a punt 18 yards to Bucknell's 27. On the next play, Brown bolted off tackle, then reversed his field and ran to the six. Two plays later, Brown ran to his right and threw back towards a crowd and hit Castignola for the touchdown. As he headed towards the sidelines, Brown playfully stuck out his tongue at Higgins and the other coaches, silently reminding them they had razzed him about his lousy passing. Czekaj's PAT made it 14-0 and that was the final score.

Now came what was considered the toughest three games on the schedule—North Carolina, Colgate and Navy with only Colgate at home. The North Carolina game had been scheduled after Syracuse, Michigan State and Georgia dropped football for the year, West Virginia and Cornell also were added for later in the season.

The tiring trip and hot weather didn't help State against a well-stocked team that was almost like a Southern Conference All-Star team. The players had left Washington at midnight on the day of the game in four separate trains heading to Greensboro and then rode busses to Raleigh. The last group didn't reach Chapel Hill until two hours before the game and everyone was exhausted. Once the game started, the heat and the bigger and fresher Carolina players took their toll. A bad snap from center on a punt attempt in the first two minutes almost cost State a touchdown. However, Carolina didn't score until three minutes were left in the half when a punt return helped set up a short 35-yard drive. The TarHeels scored two more times in the second half with a steady ground game and some timely punt runbacks, then turned back a fourth period Lion drive at their own 11 and won, 19-0. "Except for this closing drive," wrote Chiles Coleman of the United Press, "the offense all belonged to (a Navy-bolstered) North Carolina."

The next week a Homecoming crowd of some 7,000 watched two bruised teams battle to a scoreless tie at Beaver Field. The Associated Press said State and Colgate lacked a " scoring punch after suffering physically from games a week ago." While State was getting a physical pounding at Chapel Hill, Colgate was being hammered by West Point. On this day, neither team could muster a consistent offensive and by the fourth quarter they both were tiring. A break could have determined the outcome but they both lost opportunities in scoring territory. The best chances either team had came in the second half but interceptions, penalties and fumbles frustrated the squads. State reached Colgate's six-yard line in the third quarter but gave up the ball after an offside penalty and a failed pass attempt. Colgate stopped another threat with a pass interception near the six. Early in the fourth quarter, Brown was in the clear at the Colgate 37 after taking a lateral from Williams but fumbled the ball away. Castignola stopped one Colgate drive in the final period with a pass interception at the 10. As the game was winding down, an interference penalty gave Colgate the ball on the State 14 but a field goal attempt from the 20 that could have won the game was partially blocked and went wide. The 0-0 final did not satisfy either coach but they agreed the score accurately reflected the game.

Unbeaten Navy was an overwhelming favorite over State the following week at Thompson Stadium in Annapolis. The Naval Academy, like its counterpart at West Point, had some of the best athletes in the country. Some observers believed Navy's third and fourth teams could have beaten most college teams that year and the Middies eventually finished third in the country in the AP ratings. With a nationwide CBS radio audience listening to Ted Husing's play-by-play, a hearty crowd of 10,000 that included the Navy's top brass of Admiral Ernest King and Secretary of the Navy Frank Knox braved the atrocious weather to watch what was nearly a historic upset. It was rainy and windy throughout the contest and when a squall with hail and gale force winds blew in off the Chesapeake River late in the first quarter, players could not see from one sideline to the other. That's when Navy got a big break, blocking its second punt with an aggressive rush that pressured State kickers all day. Taking the ball on the State 30-yard line, the Middies called the same play twice, a pass to a flanker in the flat. The State defender was caught napping both times and the play went for 19 yards the first time and for a 12-yard touchdown the second time. The PAT made it 7-0 and most of the rain-soaked fans figured a rout was on. It certainly appeared that way moments later when Navy drove quickly from State's 44 to the 15-yard line before the Lions' defense took the ball away on downs at the 16. In three plays the Lions lost 15 yards. Despite the wind and rain in his face, second team wingback Jim Graham got away a booming 60-yard punt and was hit as he went down. The roughing the kicker penalty gave State the ball on the 20 as the first quarter came to an end. State was forced to punt again moments later but from that point on the Lions' defense brought the Middies offense to a near standstill.

Using an overshifted seven-man line, the Lions continually stopped Navy's off-tackle power plays and end sweeps and an active defensive backfield neutralized the passing. On its first possession of the second half, Navy fumbled and State recovered at the home team's

36-yard line. On third down, Williams passed 28 yards to Castignola at the five. Then, Williams carried four straight times to get the TD. But Trumbull's extra point attempt was wide and State trailed, 7-6. Navy turned the ball over twice more that quarter on a pass interception and fumble but early in the fourth quarter another Navy rush on State's punter forced a short punt and Navy took over at the State 43. On second down Bill Barron skirted left end 39-yards for a touchdown and the extra point made it 14-6. That didn't stop State. With time expiring, the Lions recovered a fumble at the State 48 and then picked up a first down at the Navy 35. That's when Navy's pass defense stiffened, knocking down two Williams' pass attempts and finally intercepting a third down throw at the 15. "Navy Turns Back Stubborn Penn State," said the headline in the *Washington Post*. "...There was hardly a time on the field when I didn't think we had a good chance to come out ahead," Higgins told Riley after the game. "But we had enough to upset them, and frankly, I can't help feeling that we didn't take advantage of our opportunities."

Before the next game against Maryland at College Park, Brown was called up for officer training and never played for State again. Allan Richards, a Marine out of the University of Cincinnati, replaced Brown at fullback and scored the first touchdown in a 49-0 rout. The game was all but over in the first quarter as a fumble recovery by Czekaj and two pass interceptions by Williams quickly led to three TDs and a 20-0 first quarter lead and Higgins played substitutes practically the rest of the way. Williams scored three TDs with the Lions rushing for 212 yards and 13 first downs while the defense was limiting the Terps to a minus 18 yards rushing and 25 yards passing—a defensive performance that helped make State the seventh best defensive team in the country by the end of the weekend. But Sparky's departure had been the early warning signal. After the game, many of the Marine V-12 recruits were ordered to training, including Castignola, Graham, Powers, and Smith. In the following weeks, others would depart and Higgins would go week to week without knowing how to prepare his players for the upcoming opponent.

Before the West Virginia game at Beaver Field, the clairvoyant Higgins predicted a blocked kick by his team would be a big play in the outcome. The blocked kick set up State's second touchdown in the second quarter after the Lions had driven 53 yards for its first TD. Czekaj recovered the blocked kick at Lion 36 and after 20 yards in penalties against the Lions, Richards ran 49 yards off tackle for the TD. That seemed to take the fight out of the Mountaineers. Before the day was over the Lions scored three more touchdowns, including one by Williams, in a 32-7 win.

The team that Higgins put on the field the next week at Cornell was a mishmash of Marines and freshmen with Cenci, Jaffurs, Czekaj and Ross the only starters who had opened the season against Bucknell. Williams, Moore, Hapanowicz and others were history. In their place were such players as (Cass) Sisler, (Mike) Slobodnjak, (John) Misiewicz, (Frank) Veneroso and (Chuck) Klausing. Despite a transient lineup, the Lions played an outstanding defensive game but lost because of an ineffective offense. A blocked kick gave Cornell the ball on the State eight-yard line in the first two minutes of the game but the Lions held and punted out to the Lion 41-yard line. On first down Cornell scored on a pass but missed the extra point and the score remained 6-0 until late in the fourth quarter. State missed several scoring opportunities, reaching the Cornell 15, four and nine yard lines but couldn't get a TD. Desperately trying to score in the final period, Veneroso fumbled while trying to pass at the State nine-yard line; Cornell recovered and then scored a touchdown to put the game out of reach, 13-0.

With a 3-3-1 record, State fans wondered if this would be the first losing season in five years. Higgins simply wondered who his players would be. Veneroso was gone before the final home game against Temple and in his place at tailback was Bill Abromitis, of all people. Abromitis was a V-12 Marine who earlier in the year had been a star for the hated Pitt Panthers but had been called up and re-assigned to the State campus. His backup was Rowan "Tubby" Crawford, who just two weeks before had been the starting *goalie* on State's soccer team! Of course, Temple was not much better off. All but one of its starters was a freshman. And as if all the player shuffling wasn't enough, the game started with a makeshift set of officials because the original officials were delayed by a car accident in Altoona caused by the heavy snow that was falling and they did not arrive until the second quarter. So, when the game started, there was Doggie Alexander, owner of the popular State College beer joint, The Rathskeller, filling in as the field judge, and *Philadelphia Inquirer* sportswriter Stan Baumgartner, who was yanked out of the press box, substituting as the head linesman. Surprisingly, only one 15-yard penalty was called the entire game, against State, as the Lions won, 13-0. Temple never got past State's 34-yard line and the Lions scored on drives of 60 yards in the first quarter and 80 yards in the fourth quarter with "Goalie" Crawford's running setting up the first touchdown and his 44-yard dash around left end getting the second touchdown. Czekaj was one-for-two in extra points. "Without Crawford, the score would have been 0-0," wrote Baumgartner in his coverage of the game, who said the "goalie" swept "the ends with surprising speed and a baffling hip shift, made possible by the clever use of his sturdy legs."

The Pitt game was almost anti-climactic, again, but it was different than any other in the long State-Pitt series. Unlike State with its military contingent, Pitt was considered a "civilian" school and had virtually the same players all season. They weren't very good, however, despite now being coached by the master of the T-Formation, Clark Shaughnessy, and had a 3-4 record going into the game at Pitt Stadium on Nov. 20. State's defensive strategy, with the same 5-3-2-1 alignment that beat Bucknell's T-Formation, completely mystified Pitt. The Lions stopped the Panthers with a net minus 26 yards rushing and gave up only 97 yards passing on 18 attempts with 48 yards coming on the last play of the game. The Ex-Panther, Abromitis, scored the Lions first TD on a four-yard run in the first quarter and completed State's first pass before he left the game with an injury. In the second quarter, Czekaj faked a field goal from the Pitt 12 and the holder, Dick McCown ran for the TD. Czekaj's two PATs finished off the scoring. "...The outcome was hardly in doubt in the minds of the 20,000 spectators for more than a few minutes," wrote Chester Smith, sport editor of the *Pittsburgh Press*. "...Thrills were on a rationed basis...Abromitis...won the game against his former cronies almost before the late arrivals were seated." The 14-0 win made it the third straight victory for State over Pitt, the first time that had happened since 1900-03!

Of the 23 men who won letters in 1943, 16 were one-year wonders who never wore the Blue and White uniform again. Abromitis, the Pitt man, would only receive a minor letter from State but his old school would reward him with a full letter. By the following September, Abromitis and Ted Hapanowicz would be playing against State as recruits for the Naval Academy. Most of the other soldiers, sailors and

marines, would be gone before fall practice started for the 1944 season and by the fourth game of '44 only a few military stragglers would be left. In their place would be a squad of eager, pink-faced, 17-year-old freshmen, and even Higgins would be surprised by what they did.

Season Record 5-3-1
Record to Date 275-161-33
Winning percentage .622

"'Johnny Chuck' & The Freshmen"

Johnny Chuckran and the Colgate captain stood stiffly in the middle of the field, buffeted by the heavy wind and rain, as the referee prepared to toss the coin. Chuckran could not believe it. With the departure of all the Marines—including six starters—after last week's win over Bucknell, Higgins had named him captain.

A year ago, Chuckran had been playing for his high school back in Lansford. Today, October 21, 1944, he was captain and starting tailback of the Penn State football team and about to play favored Colgate on Colgate's home field in Hamilton, NY. Of course, most of his teammates were freshmen, too. That made this responsibility even more significant. Only four servicemen remained from the 30 or so who were on campus for the opening game against Muhlenberg four weeks ago. And one, Earl Bruhn, the starting quarterback, was only playing today because he was on furlough from the Marines and this would be his last game. Then, only the three sailors would be left: guards Bob Rutkowski and Carl Dimerling and second string tackle Bob Painter.

Another freshman, Elwood Petchel, had been the starter at tailback in State's first two games against Muhlenberg and Navy. Higgins had decided the peppy, 5-foot-8, 140-pound speedster—and the team's best passer—might be more effective as a spot player. He had moved the 168-pound Chuckran in as the starter last week against Bucknell and "Johnny Chuck" had run for 77 yards to lead the team to a 20-6 win. But six other starters from the Bucknell game were now gone for good, called up by the Marines. In the starting backfield with Chuckran and Bruhn today would be the youngest player on the team, Larry Cooney of Langley High in Pittsburgh who was just 16-years-old. Four weeks ago, Cooney had been the fourth string wingback but everyone else ahead of him had departed for active duty. Another frosh, Al Bellas of Kingston, was now the fullback, in place of Al Richards, the veteran Marine who had been the captain for the first three games. Five freshmen were also starting in the front line: Bob Hicks and Don Miltenberger at ends, Howard Caskey and Negley Norton at tackles and Bronco Kosanovich at center.

The Lions were 2-1 at this juncture, with the only loss to a mighty Naval Academy team, 55-14, at Annapolis. State had opened the season with an easy 58-13 victory over outmanned Muhlenberg at Beaver Field September 30. Petchel and Chuckran had made sensational debuts. A minute and a half into the game, Petchel ran back a punt 55-yards untouched for a touchdown, and scored another touchdown on a two-yard run in the second quarter. "I still remember that punt," Petchel recalled nearly six decades later. "It was the first time I ever got my hands on the ball." Chuckran, subbing for Petchel, threw touchdown passes of five and 22 yards and scored a TD on a 30-yard run as he led all rushers with 86 yards. Higgins used 40 players and threw only seven passes in rolling up 462 yards and 16 first downs.

But the following week, State discovered how it felt to be on the other end of a rout in losing to Navy. The Middies, fired-up because of an upset loss the week before to North Carolina Pre-Flight coached by former Lion All-American Glenn Killinger, racked up 340 yards on the ground and 252 in the air in lambasting the Lions. State had the ball for only 19 scrimmage plays as Navy used four teams and went on drives of 73 and 95 yards to score touchdowns and had another touchdown on a 74-yard run by Jim Pettit. Chuckran's 55 yard kickoff return after Navy's fifth touchdown late in the first half helped set up State's first touchdown by Richards but it was third-string end Al Auer, a V-12 Marine, who scored the other touchdown on the most spectacular play of the day. Navy was leading 42-7 and poised at State's 13-yard line when Ralph Ellsworth fumbled. Auer picked up the ball at the 20 and ran 80 yards for the touchdown—a feat that was the State record for longest run with a fumble recovery until broken in 1973. There was one other unusual and humorous play by a State player that went unnoticed by nearly everyone in Thompson Stadium except for Higgins and a few of his Lions. Navy's "Pistol Pete" Williams had broken into the clear running down the sidelines when Petchel dashed over from his safety position and jumped onto Williams' back. But the heavier Williams kept running as he carried the lightweight Petchel on his back for another 10 yards or so. As the duo passed close by the State bench Petchel spotted Higgins and in his best imitation of the Lone Ranger yelled, "Hi, ho, Silver!" Considering the black humor of a war time environment and the frivolity of college football in a world gone mad, this may have been the defining moment of the season.

The joke also may have been on Petchel for Chuckran was the starter the following week in the Homecoming game against Bucknell. However, it was Petchel's passing that gave State a 13-0 first half lead as he hit Hicks on a fourth-and-goal from the two-yard line and then found Marine Ed Meyer for a 22-yarder with 20 seconds left in the half. A crowd of 9,000 watched tensely as Bucknell came back to control most of the second half, getting a TD on a 75-yard drive in the third quarter but the Lions finally put the game out of reach on a Chuckran TD with three minutes left in the game. Still, the Lions almost got burned for another TD when Bucknell pulled the old "sleeper

Johnny Chuckran was the only freshman ever elected captain when chosen in the war year of 1944 and was a star that year. He also played in 1948 and 1949 and later returned as an assistant coach under Joe Paterno.

play" after the ensuing kickoff but the pass receiver was tackled on the State 30-yard line and the game ended in a 20-6 win.

So, now, here was Chuckran, the new captain, about to make the fateful call on the referee's coin toss. Everyone in the stadium knew the winner of the coin toss would undoubtedly choose the wind. Like a lot of bad weather games, this one could be won on the first break. Taking the wind is a psychological gambit that often puts the other team on the defensive the entire game. And when your team is the underdog, that can be the one tiny thread that sews up the victory. "Heads!" Chuckran yelled, and "heads" it was. State kicked off with a strong wind at its back and Colgate struggled the entire first quarter as the Lions defense and some good punting kept Colgate on the defensive in its own territory. As time was winding down in the quarter, it appeared as if Colgate would finally get to kick with the wind when the teams changed sides. Higgins had another ploy that was as much psychological as it was real. State stopped the clock three times with time outs and before the quarter was over Colgate had to punt into a strong gale. Then, when the Red Raiders defense stopped State's attack before the quarter was over, the Lions punter, Bruhn, was able to kick one 60 yards and Colgate was on the defensive again.

But with the wind to their backs in the second quarter, the Raiders moved quickly onto State's side of the field and stayed there. Using both the traditional single-wing and new T-Formation, sometimes from one play to the next, Andy Kerr's team pounded at State but the Lions' defense was up to the task, stopping Colgate on downs three times inside their 10-yard line, once on a fourth-and-goal at the one. The 0-0 tie at halftime was a good sign for State and a heavy downpour during the intermission turned the field into a quagmire, stymieing both teams in the second half. "...the footing was terrible," wrote Roscoe McGowen in *The New York Times*, "Everytime a player went down, water splashed as if the boys were playing water polo instead of football."

As time ticked away in the fourth quarter, a scoreless tie looked inevitable. But with wind now in State's favor, Petchel punted out of bounds on Colgate's four-yard line. The Red Raiders couldn't move and had to punt from their end zone. Petchel took the ball on the 35 and dashed back to Colgate's 13. After an offside penalty and two incomplete passes, the Lions lined up in a field goal formation. Colgate wasn't fooled by the fake and its front line smashed through and tackled the holder its own 30. Once again the Lions' defense was up to the challenge and sent Colgate reeling back. There was about one minute to play and Colgate had to punt again. Chuckran dropped back to the 50-yard line. The kick was low and short but bounced a couple of times. Instead of letting the ball roll as punt returners are taught to do around bouncing footballs, Chuckran picked up the football in a two-handed baseball motion at his own 47-yard line and dashed towards the right sideline. He got a great block from Cooney, then sprinted past two other Colgate defenders and went down the sideline with a blocker in front of him. The blocker, Dino Taccalozzi, screened out the last would-be tackler and Chuckran went into the end zone standing up. Joe Drazenovich, the freshman backup quarterback and placekicker, missed the extra point. Colgate still had a chance. But Higgins surprised Kerr and the Raiders by calling for a modified onside kick and Drazenovich recovered his own short kickoff at the Colgate 35-yard line and the game was over. For almost 30 seconds, the players muddled about the field as if they did not believe what had happened. Then they started cheering and ran over to Chuckran, picked him up and carried him off the field on their shoulders. It was the defining moment of the season. "Long Kick Return Halts Colgate, 6-0," said the headline in the *New York Times*. The freshmen of '44 were now in control of the season destiny.

The freshmen made history the next week when, for the first time in State's 67-year football history, the entire starting lineup was made up of frosh. They also played liked freshmen in a game at Beaver Field against West Virginia, which also had nine freshman starters. Ridge Riley's opening lines in his *"Football Letter"* summary of the game aptly describes what happened: "Those freshmen can take you up in the air, and then let you down; they can send shivers up your spine, and then drive you half crazy. On Saturday, they dropped a ball game which should have been won, but gave the home folks one of the most exciting, [and] the daffiest 60 minutes ever experienced on Beaver Field."

The Lions scored the first two times they had the ball, driving more than 70 yards for the first touchdown with Chuckran going over from the one, then scoring again moments later when Chuckran passed 34 yards to Hicks, and the Lions led, 13-0. Joe Drazenovich's missed extra point after the first TD seemed harmless. But a stunning 69-yard quick kick by West Virginia's star freshman Jimmy Walthall that went out of bounds on the Lions one-yard line led to the Mountaineers first touchdown early in the second quarter and then Walthall threw a 55-yard TD pass to give West Virginia a surprising 14-13 lead. Four plays later, Walthall intercepted Petchel's pass and returned it 33 yards to the one and the Mountaineers scored to go ahead, 21-13. Chuckran's 60-yard kickoff return helped take the Lions to the Mountaineers six-yard line as time was running in the half but Petchel's hurried pass fell incomplete and West Virginia had the lead at intermission. State scored on its first possession of the second half as Chuckran ran back a punt 12 yards, then darted 39-yards around end for the TD. Drazenovich's PAT made it 21-20. State was back at the West Virginia seven-yard line moments later but Chuckran's pass was intercepted in the end zone. Early in the fourth quarter, Chuckran fumbled a punt on the State 29 and West Virginia scored in four plays, extending its lead to 28-20. The Lions clawed back, driving 63 yards with Chuckran scoring his third TD of the day on a 24-yard run off tackle. With about four minutes to play, Cooney recovered a West Virginia fumble at the Mountaineer 34-yard line. Chuckran's running helped get the ball to the 18 but a second down pass by Petchel was picked off at the five-yard line and West Virginia ran out the clock for the 28-27 upset victory. Never before had a State team scored as many as 27 points and lost a game. The Lions had won the statistical battle, with 411 total yards and 19 first downs to

West Virginia's 207 yards and eight first downs, but three Mountaineers' interceptions made the difference. The greatest running day of Chuckran's career—157 yards and three TDs on 21 carries and 78 yards in kickoff returns—had gone for naught. "Little Johnny Chuckran tried to deliver the victory personally in the wild and woolly last period," said the *Pittsburgh Press*. "He fell short..." It was State's first loss at home since 1938, snapping a 23-game streak.

Before the game at Syracuse the following week, Drazenovich and Bellas were declared ineligible because of academics and Taccalozzi and Lang moved up as starters at QB and FB, respectively. Syracuse had resumed its football program after one year and with a team of young civilians hand-picked by Coach Ossie Solem, the Orange had beaten Lafayette and tied Temple and were given an even chance by some sportswriters to defeat the Lions. Some chance. State handed Syracuse its worst loss of the 22-game series, 41-0, as Chuckran and Petchel threw two touchdowns each and Chuckran also scored two TDs in an offensive attack that had 240 yards on the ground and 162 through the air. Syracuse netted just 65 yards rushing and 47 yards passing and never seriously threatened the State goal line.

On Wednesday, November 9, three days prior to the game at Philadelphia against Temple, the team sang "Happy Birthday" to Larry Cooney. He was now 17-years-old. Perhaps the ease of their victory over Syracuse had given Cooney and these very young Lions a false gauge of their talent but the underdog Owls brought them to their senses. The first half was all Temple as State ran just 16 plays, and only a crucial holding penalty kept the Owls from taking the lead. The Owls drove 80 yards in the second quarter for a first down at State's two-yard line but the holding penalty nullified Jimmy Wilson's two-yard TD run. With a first-and-goal at the 16, Temple fumbled and State's left guard, John Simon, recovered ending the big Temple threat. Still, it did not look good for State, particularly after Chuckran was carried off the field on a stretcher following the Temple drive. Then, with the game still scoreless in the opening minutes of the third quarter, Wilson intercepted a Petchel pass at the State 36-yard line and ran it back to the six. Three plays later, Temple had a TD. But Simon again came to the forefront and blocked Wilson's PAT attempt. That block would make the difference in the game as State took control from that point. Petchel ran five-yards for a touchdown that tied the game early in the fourth quarter following a drive from midfield after a punt. Harry Muckle, now the reserve fullback, dropped back to try the all-important extra point. This was only his second PAT attempt of the season and a strong cross-wind was blowing. Muckle's boot cleared the goal posts and State won its fifth game, 7-6, to clinch another winning season. The *Philadelphia Inquirer*'s Stan Baumgartner thought State was lucky. "Not given even an outside chance to win and figured to lose by at least two touchdowns," he wrote, "...(Temple) outplayed the up-Staters except for a few minutes in the third period."

Chuckran's bruised hip kept him out of the final home game against Maryland but the team didn't need him. Maryland had tied West Virginia earlier in the season and for a while, this game took on the same overtones as the clash with the Mountaineers. Lang ran 65 yards for a touchdown seven minutes into the first quarter but the Terps made it 7-6 early in the second quarter after blocking a quick kick by Petchel at the State four-yard line. The Lions scored twice before the half with Petchel running for TDs on short yardage at the end of 36- and 62-yard drives. A roughing the kicker penalty gave Maryland a break early in the third quarter and the Terps tallied on the second of two running plays from midfield to narrow the score to 21-13. But that's as close as Maryland got. Petchel ran back a punt 30 yards to set up a 39-yard drive that climaxed with his 12-yard pass for a TD. Then he hit Hicks on a six-yard pass for another touchdown following a 69-yard drive and Muckle's PAT's gave State 34 points. Maryland got a consolation TD after recovering a fumble at State's 14 but the game was never really as close as the 34-19 final score may have indicated.

To many State fans, a fourth straight victory over Pitt seemed all but certain. On paper, the Lions looked like the better team. The Panthers had a 3-5 record and had been badly beaten by Army, 69-7, and Notre Dame, 59-0. But Pitt had a full squad of players and Higgins had just 20, including Chuckran and Lang who were hurting and hardly played. Panthers coach Clark Shaughnessy started substituting early and even took more than a dozen five-yard penalties (under the rules at the time) to get fresh players into the game. In the end, Pitt simply wore out the Lions but it was a fairly even game most of the way. It also may have been little Elwood Petchel's finest game despite the outcome The Panthers dominated the first quarter and State the second but neither scored. State reached Pitt's five-yard line once but the Panthers held on downs while penalties kept Pitt from mustering any sustained drives. Then came the play of the game. Pitt's Bernie Sniscak, a high school teammate of Chuckran's in '43, took the opening kickoff of the second half and ran straight up field 93 yards for a touchdown. As the Lions were trying to come back late in the third quarter, a Petchel pass was intercepted at midfield and run back to the Lion 15-yard line. An offside penalty put the ball on the 10 and Pitt scored two plays later. Pitt almost scored again in the fourth quarter but a two-yard TD run was nullified by a penalty. State drove 53 yards late in the game but a 15-yard running pass from Petchel to Miltenberger, who made a circus catch between two Pitt defenders in the end zone, was called back by an offside penalty and that was it. The final score was 14-0. Because Chuckran could only play for a couple of minutes, Petchel had to go almost all the way at tailback and he took a physical beating. He carried the ball 29 of 46 running plays, threw 14 of State's 17 passes, punted all nine times for the team and was in on many tackles. On the last play of the game he intercepted a Pitt pass and tried to run for a TD but could hardly move. "He (Petchel) was a continual nuisance to the Panthers on sweeps and slants, together with handling all the kicking and nearly all the passing," wrote Chet Smith in the *Pittsburgh Press*. "If there was ever a Handy Andy on the gridiron, it was Master Elwood yesterday."

Ridge Riley summed up the season as only he could. "So let this final sentence in the last *"Football Letter"* of the 1944 season serve as a tribute to the kids who have kept the Nittany Lion football tradition strong; they are worthy of their fine heritage; they have made the future of Penn State football bright." He was right, but he was one year off.

Season Record 6-3
Record to Date 281-164-33
Winning percentage .622

"The War Hero & The Pitt Jinx"

This was another of those seasons that might have been but wasn't. And, once again, the denouement came down to 60 putrid minutes in Pittsburgh.

The Japanese surrender on August 14 that brought an end to World War II emitted a nationwide euphoria that carried on to the college football fields of 1945. The men would be coming back and the boys would be staying home.

Higgins had a stable team once again. It was made up predominantly of sophomores, a handful of V-12 refugees, some war veterans and a couple of super-talented freshmen. His two star freshmen running backs from '44, Chuckran and Petchel, would be in the Army by the September 29 opening game against Muhlenberg and would have to serve out their military duty before returning. But among their ex-teammates who were now civilians and would be sophomore starters were Simon at guard, Kosonovich at center, Miltenberger at end, Taccalozzi at quarterback, Cooney at wingback and Bellas at fullback. The four V-12 recruits still on the team— guards Rutkowski and Dimmerling, tackle John Nolan and end Bob Gernand—would start against Muhlenberg but only Rutkowski and Nolan, a transfer V-12 from Holy Cross, would become regulars. Gernand would be replaced at left end in the second game of the season by freshman Sam Tamburo of New Kensington, who would not relinquish the position until he graduated four years later. Marino Marichi, who lettered as a frosh in '43 but missed most of '44 because of a broken collar bone, would be the other tackle and the only true junior on the team. Another freshman, Chuck Drazenovich, younger brother of Joe (who was out of school) started out the season as a reserve center but by midseason he replaced Taccalozzi as the starting quarterback and would join Tamburo as a four year fixture in the Lions' starting lineup. Two old-time lettermen who were combat war veterans also returned after the season got underway and would eventually start some games: 27-year-old Mike Garbinski, one of the "Seven Mountains" of the '40 team, at right guard and 25-year-old Ralph Ventresco from the '41 team at fullback.

There were two notable freshmen additions in the backfield— unheralded Joe Tepsic and Wallace Triplett, III.

Tepsic was a genuine war hero. He had been in the first wave of Marines that landed at Guadalcanal in August of 1942 and had been severely wounded in the shoulder by a Japanese bayonet during hand-to-hand combat. "Jumping Joe" from the tiny town of Slovan, west of Pittsburgh, came out for the team on his own that September and wound up being the star running back from his tailback position. Triplett was State's third black player since the Alston brothers of the 1941 freshman team. Dennie Hoggard of Philadelphia had joined the team in 1942 but did not make the varsity and had been in the Army since 1943. Triplett, another Philadelphia area high schooler, thus became the first black to play on the varsity. Although he would play sparingly, this would be a learning year for the man who would eventually star on one of Penn State's greatest teams and help his school break down a momentous racial barrier.

Still, as the Lions prepared for Muhlenberg, Higgins was pessimistic. "There is a lot of work to do," he told the *Collegian*. "The boys just don't know their plays and until they do we can't do very much. They didn't look too good at all...as yet, we don't have a team."

Perhaps, that is why Higgins treated the opening game against Muhlenberg more like a scrimmage than a real game. Higgins' first team scored four touchdowns in the first 13 minutes and the second team tallied three more in the second quarter. The 47-0 halftime score only changed when the visitors got a TD on a flurry of passes late in the second half, which had been shortened to 24 minutes by mutual agreement. Tepsic, who also called signals, went 52 yards for a TD on the fourth play of the game and scored another six minutes later on a two-yard run after he recovered a fumble at the 21-yard line. Cooney intercepted a pass and ran it back 65 yards for the fourth TD of the first quarter and Tamburo recorded a safety in the second period when he tackled a befuddled Muhlenberg punt receiver at the goal line.

The largest Homecoming crowd since before the war, 9,619, was at Beaver Field the following week for the game against favored Colgate. The Lions drove 59-yards early in the first quarter on the running of Tepsic to take the lead with the ex-Marine getting the touchdown on a plunge over right tackle, but after the ensuing kickoff Colgate tied the game at 7-7 with a passing attack that covered 68 yards. Midway through the second quarter, second team end Ross Herron, a freshman, blocked a Colgate punt at about the visitor's 40-yard line. The ball bounced high in the air and came down on the 20. Reserve end Bob McCoy kicked the ball 10 yards further while trying to pick it up, then scooped it up and ran into the end zone for a 14-7 halftime lead. The Lions extended the lead three minutes into the second half, going 68 yards on the passing of Bellas, who hit Cooney with a six-yard pass for the TD. Colgate kept trying to come back, primarily with a passing attack that eventually had 226 yards on 14-of-26 attempts but three interceptions kept the Red Raiders away from the end zone. In the fourth quarter, a punt by Tubby Lang backed up Colgate near the goal line where a hard tackle caused a fumble that was recovered by Simon. Tepsic dove over right tackle, Taccalozzi kicked his third PAT of the game and the Lions won, 27-7. "Tepsic, With the Marines on Guadalcanal, Sparks Attack and Crosses Goal Twice," said the headline in the *New York Times*.

No one gave State a chance the following week in Annapolis against unbeaten and unscored upon Navy, the second ranked team in the nation and a four-touchdown favorite. The Academy was celebrating its 100th year anniversary at this game and the Lions were the cake and icing. As part of the pre-game festivities, 78 Navy dive bombers, many of them survivors of the Pacific Aircraft Carrier battles, flew over Thompson Stadium. That was no doubt an omen. All that military firepower must have brought back some bad memories to Tepsic because he was not himself the entire day and his first five minutes of the game was a near disaster. Thanks to a major penalty on the opening kickoff, State got the ball at the Navy 40-yard line. But on the second play Tepsic fumbled and Navy recovered. After an exchange of punts, State's Miltenberger recovered another Navy fumble at the Navy 26. But on the next play, Tepsic fumbled the ball away again. The Middies then drove to State's 34 before losing the ball on downs but when State was forced to punt from the end zone, Navy blocked the kick and the ball went out of the end zone for a safety. Navy ran back the free kick 42 yards to State's 29-yard line and in four plays had a touchdown and an 8-0 lead. The Middies made 14-0 by halftime after Triplett's errant pass into the flat was intercepted and run back 20 yards for a TD. Navy got another seven in the third quarter at the end of a sustained drive, then added the capper in the final period, when Tepsic's pass from the Lions 45 was intercepted and run back for a TD despite an official's

whistle that had stopped most State players from pursuing the interceptor. Navy had 204 yards rushing and 110 passing in the 28-0 win but its defense really won the game by limiting State to 51 yards rushing (Tepsic had just 16 net yards on 10 carries) and 72 yards passing while intercepting three passes, recovering three fumbles and blocking two punts. "The statistics proved nothing except that Navy was superior on the offense but far from the powerhouse it was supposed to be," reported the *Centre Daily Times*. "The Middies booted just as many opportunities as the Lions..." Al Costello of the *Washington Post* had a less biased view. "Penn State went down swinging," he wrote, "trying desperately to score right down to the finish. Even after Navy had locked the game in its duffle bag, the Lions fought...before the Tars braced and put on the brake." Navy would eventually finish 7-1-1 and third in the country, and, for a time, it appeared as if this would be the only defeat on the Lions' schedule.

Drazenovich was at quarterback the next week against Bucknell and Bellas took over signal-calling duties from Tepsic. Once again, the third and fourth quarters were shortened to 12 minutes as State turned a 33-0 halftime lead into a 46-7 win. For the first time in six years, two players gained over 100 yards with Cooney getting 144 on four carries and Tubby Lang, the backup fullback and punter, recording 118 on 14 carries. Cooney scored one TD on a 65-yard run and another on a pass from Tepsic. Lang also scored two TDs and passed for two others as State amassed 469 total yards.

After a week off, the Lions entertained hapless Syracuse, which had only a victory over West Virginia in four games. Tepsic was captain for the day and he played like one. He rushed for 135 yards on 15 carries and scored two touchdowns. His first TD on a 26-yard off tackle play in the second quarter gave State a 6-0 halftime lead and his second score came at the end of a 41-yard play in the third quarter when he took a lateral from Bellas at the 25-yard line and ran into the end zone. Triplett's first TD of his career on a 6-yard run in the fourth quarter made the final score 26-0. The game also marked the return of the combat veterans—Garbinski, Ventresco and tackle Ted Kratzke—and the end of Miltenberger, who became academically ineligible.

Now came the game that should have defined the season. Temple was unbeaten in six games and seemed headed for a post-season bowl game. It was State's final home game but the Owls were a slight favorite. Despite the threat of rain, four thousand spectators jammed the ticket office between 12:30 p.m. and the 2 p.m. kickoff. They became part of the largest crowd at Beaver Field since the '39 Pitt game (officially 13,135) and they watched as game captain Garbinski, starting his first game in five years, lost the toss and State kicked off. The Lions stopped Temple on it's first possession and were on the move themselves following a Temple punt, when they got into a jam on a juggled pass by Cooney that was intercepted and run back to State's 22-yard line. But on third down, Cooney came up with an interception himself on the five-yard line and ran it all the way back to Temple's 45. Bellas, Cooney and Tepsic carried to a first down at the 25. Then Tepsic went off tackle for four yards and as he was about to be tackled, he lateraled back to the center, Bronco Kosanovich, who rambled 21 yards for the first touchdown of his career. Taccalozzi's PAT made it 7-0. Before the quarter ended, State was back at the Temple eight-yard line again but penalties stopped the threat.

Early in the second quarter, Cooney returned a punt 35 yards to Temple's 47-yard line. Then Cooney caught a 21-yard pass from Bellas. Two plays later, Tepsic sped around the end and dashed 28 yards for State's second TD and Taccalozzi's kick made it 14-0. With two minutes left in the half, Simon broke through to block a Temple punt at the Owl's 26-yard line and Marichi picked up the ball at the 17 and ran into the end zone and State led 20-7 at halftime. It started raining in the third quarter and that helped State continue its domination in the second half. Two minutes before the end of the third quarter, Temple intercepted a Tepsic pass at it's own nine-yard line and on third down attempted a lateral that went wild and the ball rolled into the end zone. Kosanovich fell on it, giving the big lineman his second TD of the game and State won, 27-0. "Hard Charging Line Ends Owls' Dream Of Unbeaten Season," said the headline in the *Philadelphia Inquirer*. "Completely outclassed by a line that towered over every Temple man except...(one)...by two to three inches and outweighed every man at least 10 pounds," wrote the *Inquirer's* Baumgartner, "the Owls were soaked in a shower of touchdowns that matched the rain drops..." The Lion defense had held Temple's highly-touted rushing game to a minus 13 yards, recovered four fumbles and intercepted three passes and what they did that day should have defined the season.

Now, it was State players who were talking about a post-season bowl invitation. There were two away games left but neither Michigan State nor Pitt were thought to be in Penn State's class. The 4-2-1 Spartans had lost 40-0 to its chief rival, Michigan, and had beaten a pathetic Pitt team by just five points. But in scouting the Lions, the Spartans had spotted a weakness in State's pass defense. They also were able to take advantage of the absence of State's best player, Tepsic, who came down with a charley horse a day before the game in East Lansing and was held out by Higgins. "In a game which was almost a replica of State's upset victory over Temple last Saturday," reported the *Pittsburgh Press*, "Halfback Russ Reader of the Spartans passed the Lions dizzy in a spectacular one-man show." Using running plays to compliment its passing, Michigan State hit on 16-of-30 passes for 268 yards and scored three touchdowns without an interception and upset State with a 33-0 thrashing at Macklin Field. Michigan State's first two touchdowns were easy, scoring in the first and second quarters after recovering Lions fumbles at Penn State's 29- and 11-yard lines. The Lions never got closer than the Spartans' 22-yard line in the first quarter and were obviously missing Tepsic. "Tepsic's Absence Felt By Lions," said the headline in the *Pittsburgh Press*. Triplett started his first ever game and took a hard, physical beating as the Spartans keyed on him and he finished the game with a minus 18 yards on 10 carries. His performance earned him respect from his dejected teammates but that was about all.

What happened at Pitt Stadium on November 24 could not be explained any better than what had happened in 1940 or any other season when the Lions went into the Pitt game as the prohibitive favorite and left the loser. Some longtime observers of the State-Pitt games in the first 50 years of the century believed the Lions were jinxed, caught under the hypnotic spell of a some mysterious voodoo magic. That's okay if one believes in witchcraft. But since most people don't, the only way to rationalize this demoralizing defeat in 1945 is by simply saying that the Lions played badly and Pitt got the big play. State's passing was simply dreadful as the Lions completed just four-of-19 attempts for 64 yards and gave up two interceptions, including one at the Panther 11-yard line in the first quarter that could have been the turning point of the game. That frustrating interception came at the end of a drive from State's 36-yard line and followed the only score of the game. Pitt freshman, Jimmy Joe Robertson, tallied the lone TD midway in the opening period on a thrilling 84-yard punt return. Robinson

scooped up Ventresco's punt on the first bounce, ran to his right, then reversed his field and sped down the left sideline untouched for the touchdown.

Pitt played conservatively for three quarters, keeping the ball on the ground and attempting just three passes, none of which were completed. The game became a defensive struggle. After the first interception, State had come back all the way to the Pitt 18 before giving up the ball on downs. In the second quarter, the Panthers reached State's 13-yard line following a drive from its 44-yard line but the Lions held on fourth-down-and-two running play. Early in the fourth quarter, State took advantage of a partially blocked punt and had its own fourth down-and-two at the Pitt 14-yard line but Tepsic was thrown for a five-yard loss and that was the Lions' last gasp. The 7-0 victory gave Pitt a 3-5 record and marked the end of the Shaughnessy coaching regime. "The play of the lines was the dominant factor on each side," wrote Chet Smith. "Their inability to hook together a passing attack with the exemplary ball-carrying of Jungle Joe Tepsic, the Guadalcanal veteran, was a chronic weakness Penn State was unable to overcome from beginning to end."

"It was a bitterly disappointing end to a season that at times had brought high hopes...," wrote Ridge Riley in his *"Football Letter."* "Collectively our players got absolutely nowhere; individually they fought their hearts out." Riley went on to praise Tepsic, Simon, Rutkowski, Tamburo and others, then added, "We have witnessed few instances in the past where football players have put out so much and received so little in return."

Perhaps, the outcome of the season should not have been a surprise. Maybe, there was a leadership vacuum with so many freshmen and sophomores and the obvious differences between the fresh-faced kids and the battle-weary military men. After all, there was no election for a captain and this would be the first and only season since 1891 that the team would have no captain.

But, with the war over, some alumni were complaining again about State's inability to defeat its number one rival. Next year would be different they said. The men will all be back. We'll get even with Pitt and Michigan State. Uh, huh, and beat that new Southern team on the schedule, too. Look out, Miami, here we come!

Season Record 5-3
Record to Date 286-167-33
Winning percentage .622

"Black Clouds Over Miami"

The trip to Miami in late November was expected to be a fun way to close out the 1946 season. Even though Higgins and the schedule makers felt the game could be a tough one, they believed it would give Penn State the opportunity to show itself to a new and unfamiliar audience. A State team had never played farther south than Atlanta and that had been 22 years ago, a far different era than this post-World War II period of uncertainty. Some people in State's athletic family also saw the trip as a partial reward for the players who would be spending the previous eight weekends banging their heads in the rain and cold of the East. Trainer Leo Houck, who was also the boxing coach, had another reason. His two sons played for Miami.

But the Miami game was still far off when Higgins gathered his team for preseason practice at Beaver Field in September. The war had been over for more than a year but there was still much upheaval on college campuses. Many of the younger men fresh out of high school were still going off and serving their time in the military and the older ones who had done their duty were coming back to resume their education—the financial burden removed now that the government's GI Bill was paying the way. That gave the football players more time to concentrate on football, after their studies, of course.

There were so many veterans coming back to school that housing, classroom and athletic facility space became a problem. The 11,000 mostly men enrolled at State crowded the campus and that produced a special housing problem for football players. To resolve the housing dilemma, Casey Jones and some Pittsburgh area alumni raised $19,000 to buy an old fraternity house off campus. This became the late 40's version of the old Varsity House of the 20's and 30's minus a locker room. Jim O'Hora, Higgins' center from his mid-1930s teams, had just been hired as an assistant line coach, and he, too, needed a place to live. So, he agreed to be the "counselor" of the new facility and later moved his wife and new son into the residence. With all the veterans of the wartime teams returning, Higgins decided there wasn't enough room for any freshmen on the team. His top assistant, Earle Edwards, came up with the idea of "farming out" all frosh recruits to California State Teachers College, a few miles southeast of Pittsburgh. Then, in cooperation with California's athletic director, Earl Bruce was hired from nearby Brownsville High School to be the coach. Thus, Bruce, paid by State, was in the highly unusual situation of being a head coach and freshman coach at the same time. It was a natural fit since Bruce had sent several of his Brownsville players to State, including Johnny Potsklan, John Wolosky, John Simon and the Drazenovich brothers.

In fact Potsklan, a sophomore starter on the '41 team, was back in a Penn State uniform for the first time since then, having survived nearly three years in a German prison camp. Wolosky of '42 had also returned and, now, the Drazenovich brothers and Simon were in the service. With all the veterans back, Higgins had more talent available this season than he had had in years. Potsklan resumed his starting spot at right end and Bucky Walters of '42 pushed Tamburo out of the starting left end position. Steve Suhey of the great '41 freshman team relegated Rutkowski to second team right guard. Nolan at left guard and the 18-year-old Kosanovich at center kept their starting slots from '45 but two of Suhey's '41 frosh teammates were also now starting: left guard Leo Nobile and left tackle Red Moore, and Moore would be elected captain. Tamburo, Rutkowski and end Ed Czekaj ('44) would get their share of starts during the season and Czekaj would be the prime placekicker.

In the backfield, Cooney and Bellas were also in the service but Higgins didn't miss them. He was loaded and really didn't miss Tepsic, who left school to play major league baseball for the Brooklyn Dodgers. The starters were all vets, with Manny Weaver ('41) at quarterback, Bobby Williams ('42) at tailback, Bob Uiron ('42) and Jeff Durkota ('42) at wingback and Joe Colone ('42) at fullback and the prime punter. Also returning were a pair of crowd-pleasing running backs Larry Joe ('42) and Ellwood Petchel ('44) who Higgins planned to use as spot starters. This would also give him time to bring along the maturing Triplett, who didn't have the speed of other backs but was

one of the hardest to bring down and was better on defense than most of the others.

For the first time, State also had two black players on the varsity. Dennie Hoggard, the freshman from the '42 team had been in the Army for three years and was now a reserve end. Ironically, Triplett and Hoggard were both from metropolitan Philadelphia area but had not known of each other because of the age difference. They didn't realize it at the time but their presence on the varsity made them racial pioneers, and, before the '46 and '47 seasons were over, they would become the central figures in the State football team's historic assault against racial discrimination.

With so much versatility, Higgins had built his single-wing offense around the speed of his backs. He also felt he had a quick and tough defense that was capable of meeting the challenge of any formation: single-wing, T or the spread (or kick formation). He deployed a now popular 5-3-2-1 defense with a "looping" style that had the linemen shifting and "looping" instead of driving straight ahead. He was confident about his team but he warned fans about getting too optimistic. "You must remember that everyone will be stronger this year," he told the *Collegian*. "With everyone having star-studded teams, college football will be better this year than ever before."

The biggest opening day crowd in Beaver Field history, nearly 12,500, turned out in 77 degree weather on October 5, and watched Bucknell hold the Lions scoreless for about 27 1/2 minutes. Then, Tamburo caught a 30-yard touchdown pass from Petchel that ricocheted off a Bucknell player. With five seconds left in the half, reserve defensive end Fred Bell stole the ball from a Bucknell runner trying to run out the clock at the Bucknell 11-yard line and Petchel went around end with one second to play for the TD and a 14-0 lead. The second half belonged to Joe and he was in on only five plays. He went into the game for the first time on State's initial possession of the third quarter and scored on a seven-yard run. After Bucknell had scored a TD, Joe ran back the kickoff 39 yards, then went off tackle for 59 yards and his second TD. Petchel scored again on a 16-yard run and Joe was back with his third TD on a seven-yard run. Czekaj missed only one of seven PAT attempts in the 48-6 victory. Potsklan, who made it through the war with hardly a scratch, suffered what was thought to be a broken nose on the opening kickoff and sat out the rest of the game. But he was back the next week when the Lions visited Archbold Stadium for the first night game ever with Syracuse.

More than 25,000 tickets had been sold for the game but less than half of that number showed up after an eight-hour downpour. The night before the game, Higgins and Syracuse coach Biggie Munn had argued about State wearing white jerseys. Munn said State was wrong since the game ball would be white. Believing that they had each lost the argument, Higgins switched to blue jerseys and Munn had the game ball painted a neutral color. The sportswriters filled the press box with laughter over the high-jinks but the playing conditions were so miserable it wouldn't have mattered what State was wearing. Colone's great punting kept Syracuse contained much of the game deep in its own territory. He punted for distance and punted for position, sometimes quick kicking on second or third down and, as usual, he seem to boot 'em better with a wet ball than a dry ball. One kick went 68 yards and another went 71 yards (neither of which are in the Penn State official record books) and his kicks helped set up both State scores. In the second quarter, Colone's surprise quick kick led to a Syracuse fumble at its own 13-yard line and when the Orange defense held for three

Wally Triplett of Philadelphia was the first black to make the varsity and start a Penn State football game in 1945. He was a star running and defensive back for three years and had one of his finest games in the 1948 Cotton Bowl.

downs, Czekaj kicked the first field goal of his career from the 17-yard line. In the third quarter, Syracuse couldn't move after Colone's kick into the end zone and Williams ran back the Orange punt to the Syracuse 43-yard line. On the next play, Williams passed to Durkota down the middle for a touchdown. State almost scored again late in the game, getting to Syracuse's four-yard line but Syracuse stopped a fourth down running play and the game ended at 9-0. "Joe Colone's brilliant quick kicks and 'playing for breaks' were the keys to Coach Bob Higgins' mud strategy...in a driving rain at Syracuse," reported the *Collegian*.

The Homecoming game against Michigan State drew the largest alumni day crowd since Notre Dame in '25. The 17,149 watched nervously as the Spartans drove downfield 47 yards on their first possession before being stopped at State's 26-yard line. After an exchange of punts, State took the ball on its own 34 and started on a drive of its own. Joe almost had a touchdown on a 35-yard scamper but was brought down from behind by one of Michigan State's star freshmen, Lynn Chadnois, at the MSC 18-yard line. Then came two plays that would help define the season. The Spartans were ready for Joe's trademark quick, naked runs around end without interference and twice they hammered him for losses. The second time, Joe did not get up immediately, and when he did, he left the field in pain. His shoulder was separated.

Michigan State stopped the Lions drive but as the second quarter got underway, the Spartans fumbled and Petchel recovered at the MSC 20-yard line. On fourth down Triplett made a one-handed circus-like catch at the 15-yard line on a pass from Petchel and raced for a touchdown. Czekaj's kick made it 7-0. Late in the quarter, Penn State's sub fullback Bob Weitzel brought the crowd to its feet with a 48-

yard run to MSC's 22-yard line. He also was hurt on the tackle and left the game, never to return. It was getting rough out there. Williams ran for four yards, then passed to Triplett for nine. On the next play, the Spartans were called for interfering with Tamburo's pass reception in the end zone and the Lions got the ball on the one. Williams banged over for the TD, Czekaj booted the point and the home team took a 14-0 lead into the intermission, much to the delight of the old grads.

However, the Spartans made a change during the halftime that would determine the outcome of the game. Into the backfield went sophomore speedster George Guerre. Three minutes into the third quarter, Guerre bolted up the middle and ran 52 yards for a touchdown. The Spartans defense got the ball back for the offense a couple of minutes later and Michigan State went 75 yards for another TD with Guerre's 46-yard dash to the State two-yard line setting up the TD. Fortunately for State fans, the visitors missed both extra points and the Lions clung to a 14-12 lead into the fourth quarter. Not for long. After an exchange of punts, the Spartans drove from their 34-yard line and seemed to be stopped on the State 39 with fourth-and-21. But they crossed up the Lions with a fake pass as Horace Smith ran 25 yards for the first down and the Spartans scored the go-ahead TD two plays later. Trailing 19-14, the Lions roared back upfield to the MSC 17 before Frank "Muddy" Waters intercepted Williams' pass at the five. The Spartans took an intentional safety than came up with another pass interception at midfield as the game ended. Guerre, who would be named Michigan State's Most Valuable Player at the end of the season, had the best individual performance by an opposing player on New Beaver Field since its dedication. He rushed for 152 yards on 14 carries, completed three passes, recovered a key fumble, intercepted a crucial pass late in the game and quick kicked once for 53 yards. "Michigan State Springs Surprise," said the headline in the *Pittsburgh Press*.

This game was certainly one of the defining moments of the season. Not only did the Lions lose, but several first line players were injured and would miss future games, including Joe, Petchel, Moore and Suhey. The team would bounce back and win four straight but the after affects of blowing a two touchdown lead and getting a physical beating on the home field would take its toll.

The team was rather listless in the game against Colgate at Hamilton, NY, the next week. But Colgate wasn't very good either and State won, 6-2. The Lions held the Red Raiders to a minus 27 yards rushing and 61 yards passing while getting just 118 yards on the ground and 93 thorough the air. Colgate scored a safety in the first quarter when a miscommunications in the State backfield resulted in a center's pass going into the end zone and Petchel was tackled with the ball. State scored the winning TD in the second quarter after a short drive following a punt, with Colone hitting Triplett on a 19-yard pass play.

As the team practiced for the Fordham game, the *Collegian* reported on a rumor that Miami would pull out of its scheduled game with the Lions rather than play against the team's two blacks, Hoggard and Triplett. Triplett had known since the preseason that Miami had problems with "Negroes." Two years before, Miami had offered Triplett a scholarship sight unseen until the school's officials found out he was "a Negro." As he and others recalled, practices became more intense after the rumor was reported in the student newspaper. Some teammates seemed to be hitting and tackling Triplett and Hoggard extra hard.

But the rumor didn't affect the Lions play against Fordham. Higgins used four complete teams as State ran up the highest score since 1926 in beating the Rams, 68-0. Triplett carried four times and had touchdowns of 42 and 53 yards in his 98-yard rushing total. Williams and Petchel each scored one TD and passed for one as the Lions amassed 428 total yards to Fordham's 35. The game also gave Higgins the opportunity to rest his battered players and several did not even dress for the game.

As the team prepared for the next game against Temple, athletic department officials made a startling announcement that would have ramifications far beyond Beaver Field. Dr. Carl Schott, dean of the School of Physical Education and Athletics, disclosed publicly that University of Miami officials had strongly requested State not bring its two black players, Triplett and Hoggard, to Miami for the Nov. 29 game, saying "it would be difficult to carry out arrangements for the game."

"We recently advised Miami that two colored boys (sic) are regular members of the Penn State football squad," Schott announced, "and that it is the policy of the College to compete only under circumstances which will permit the playing of any or all members of its athletic team. The officials of the Miami school advised us that it would be difficult for them to carry out the arrangements for the game under these circumstances."

Game canceled. No moon over Miami. Not all the State players agreed privately with the decision. After all, this was 1946 and the undercurrent of racism still pervaded the nation's culture. But in a meeting with Higgins at midweek, the team had voted unanimously to support Hoggard and Triplett. The Penn State team had made a statement, one that has gotten lost in the passing of time. It also was a "moment of truth" for the State family and not the last one on the race issue.

So, the trip to Miami was off. Annapolis and Pittsburgh, here we come. But, first, there was Temple. Despite the Michigan State setback, the Lions had the third best defense in the country and Temple

found out why. The Lions won, 26-0, as Temple compiled just 11 yards rushing and 124 yards through the air on 13-of-28 passes, with two interceptions. The closest the Owls came to scoring was in the second quarter when they reached State's 10-yard line but Triplett picked off a pass at the one-yard line to end the threat. Williams ran for two TDs and Petchel passed for the other two as the Lions rushed for 226 yards (with Petchel getting 86) and completed 8-of-12 passes for 131 yards.

When the team arrived in Annapolis on Friday afternoon, there was a problem at the hotel. The players were getting the keys to their assigned rooms when it became apparent that Triplett and Hoggard were being neglected in the lobby. Inquires were made. Sorry, the hotel manager said, no more rooms. State officials decided it was too late to change hotels and the two black players were sent to another hotel. Later, both players would also remember the racial taunts by the Navy players during the game at Thompson Stadium the next day.

President Harry Truman gave the favored Navy team a pre-game pep talk and went back to the Middies locker room at halftime to do it again after State had taken a 12-0 lead. State just missed scoring in the first quarter when it drove 83 yards only to come up an inch short after Durkota dropped a third down pass from Williams in the end zone. But early in the second quarter, Petchel intercepted a pass at Navy's 20-yard line and ran over the goal line. The Lions then stopped Navy after the kickoff and drove 53 yards for another TD with Petchel scoring from the one. State missed other scoring chances during the half, once when Triplett was caught from behind at the 10 after a 40-yard run, and another on a fake field goal attempt.

Truman's halftime words must have had some effect because Navy recovered a State fumble early in the third quarter and went 66 yards for a TD, and with the PAT trailed by only five points. The Lions came back and seemed headed for another TD on a drive from their

The 1946 lettermen who voted not to play Miami because Miami would not allow State to bring its "Negro" players. They are (left to right): Front row: Kosanovich, Martella, Moore (Captain), Weaver, Rutkowski and Walters. Second Row: Tamburo, Triplett, Colone, Nobile, Suhey, Durkota, Kyle. Back Row: Williams, Potsklan, Czekaj, Petchel, Wolosky, Finley, Bell.

own 15 to the Navy eight but a Petchel pass was intercepted in the end zone. This seemed to fire up Navy and momentarily deflate the Lions. Navy drove all the way to State's eight-yard line before halted on a fourth down play. Navy kept State bottled up deep in its own territory for a couple of possessions but State soon regained control and almost scored again in the fourth quarter when Tamburo forced a fumble and recovered in the Navy end zone but the play was nullified by a mysterious five-yard penalty called by the referee. The final was a 12-7 upset, with no apologies to President Truman for spoiling his day. "...It was apparent in the first quarter that whomever had placed the Sailors in the favorite's role was guilty of a great miscalculation," wrote Morrie Siegel in the *Washington Post*. "The Nittany Lions showed one of the top teams to perform here in recent years and in tailback Elwood Petchel, one of the Nation's better backs...It was a rough, bruising battle with the Tars getting the worst if it."

Now, it was on to Pitt Stadium for the final game of the year. The biggest crowd since 1927—42,124—was there to see the Panthers do it again to the Lions, 14-7. Voodoo? A jinx? Or did Pitt just play better football? Certainly, the pre-game records were deceiving, with State at 6-1 and Pitt at 2-5-1 under new coach Wes Fesler. Yes, the Panthers had tied Temple 0-0 and lost big to four Big Nine opponents and Notre Dame. But it was a tough schedule and undoubtedly prepared Pitt well for its arch rival.

The Lions had a half dozen scoring opportunities and only cashed in on one while opportunistic Pitt made the most of what it had. State's failure near the Pitt goal seemed to inspire the Panthers offense and Pitt scored both TDs after defensive stands. Early in the second quarter, the Lions drove from their own 19 to Pitt's two-yard line before losing the ball on downs. Pitt punted out and then intercepted a Petchel pass at the Pitt 34-yard line. Pitt drove 66 yards for a TD, getting a big 37-yard gain on a pass from Carl DePasqua to Bimbo Cecconi, and scoring on a two-yard run by Bill Abraham. The extra point was good. As the first half wound down, State's backup center, Oggie Martella, recovered a fumble at the Panthers 33 but after getting a first down at the four, the Lions got no further than the one on three running plays and an incomplete pass as time ran out.

Midway through the third quarter, State reached the Pitt 22 before giving up the ball on downs. Behind the running of Cecconi and passing of DePasqua, Pitt marched into the fourth quarter and to the State 10-yard line where DePasqua passed to Leo Skladany for the TD. Now, it was 14-0 and the Lions were in deep trouble. After a fumble and a punt, State took the ball on its own 39-yard line went all the way for a touchdown with Wietzel getting the TD on a one-yard plunge and Czekaj kicking the PAT. But with less than five minutes to play, Pitt grabbed the kickoff and kept the ball until time ran out. Petchel had run for 117 yards on 20 carries without a loss but his performance went to naught. Joe was in for several plays but he was still hurting and it showed.

"It was a bitter dose to swallow in the Pitt Stadium Saturday afternoon," wrote Ridge Riley in the "*Football Letter*" "—all the more disappointing when the 'might have beens' are counted up on Monday morning." In the *Pittsburgh Press*, Chet Smith wrote: "Of all the football games Pitt and Penn State have played—46 since 1893—none has given the Panthers more satisfaction that their 14-7 victory over the Lions at the Stadium yesterday...State came to Pittsburgh super-charged and with every intention of making this their best campaign in more than 20 years...(but Pitt) throttled every Lion threat save one..."

So, once again it was Pitt who spoiled the season. The loss to Michigan State may have been a fluke, but not this one. Only 10 points separated the Lions from an unbeaten year but it might as well have been 50 or 100. As for Miami, it would be 1961 before a Penn State team would play there. But it would only be another year before Triplett, Hoggard and the rest of the returnees from the '46 team would make another statement and then the entire nation would know it.

Season Record 6-2
Record to Date 292-169-33
Winning percentage .624

"The Men of '47 & The 'Chocolate Bowl'"

Of all the teams in Penn State football history, the team of 1947 is arguably the greatest.

This conclusion may be heresy to those fans brought up in the 30-year glories of the Paterno era. The '47 team did not win a national title nor even its post-season bowl game. The 13-13 tie with Southern Methodist on New Year's Day 1948 in the Cotton Bowl scarred an otherwise unbeaten season. But this team needs to be celebrated for what it accomplished on and off the field in spite of itself.

No State team ever had the overall talent *AND* maturity of the 1947 squad. None! That's not even debatable. These weren't a bunch of 18 or 19 year old kids. These were mostly 24 and 25 year old men, the veterans of World War II who were at the prime of their football careers who should have been playing in the NFL. The handful of non-service veterans who made the team are among the school's all-time best—Triplett, Tamburo, Rogel. Some of the "old men" like Potsklan had started playing for Higgins as far back as '41 and '42. Four had been standouts on the great unbeaten freshman team of '41—Durkota, Suhey, Wolosky and Ray Ulinski. Many of the others were already State football stars—Petchel, Joe, Williams, Colone, Czekaj. Their exploits in these post-war years have been all but forgotten in the statistical blitz of modern day football. But their passing, running and defensive proficiency were every bit as intimidating in those waning days of single-wing power football. The 319 points scored was second in the country that year only to Michigan's Rose Bowl champions. They set a school rushing record of 2,713 yards that stood for 21 years and is still one of the best in Lion history. Only two other State teams—1994 and 1971—have a better average per carry. On defense, the team gave up just 27 points and had six shutouts—both of which are school records—and, after 50 years, the team still holds NCAA defensive records for fewest rushing yards allowed per game (17) and per rush (0.64) and fewest total yards allowed in a single game (minus 47 against Syracuse). The Cotton Bowl game that climaxed the season was the first postseason bowl appearance for a State team since the 1923 Rose Bowl. But unlike the '22 team, this team earned its right to play on New Year's Day. It would be 21 years and two coaches later before another State team would have the same honor. By then, the '48 Cotton Bowl would be a distant memory and so would the historical significance and controversy that surrounded the team's appearance in Dallas—a magnified and more disruptive version of the '46 Miami situation.

There was a different type of controversy at the beginning of the season when Higgins and his assistants were trying to put together a starting lineup before the first game against Washington State on September 20. Players who might be full time starters in any other year would have to share their positions as Higgins figured out a way to get the most out of all the talent he had. Thirty-three players would eventually letter in a year when playing both ways was still in vogue.

Although the starting lineup would be altered occasionally throughout the season, the regular lineup had Tamburo and Potsklan at the ends, Nolan and Norton at the tackles, Suhey and Joe Drazenovich at the guards and Wolosky at center. Hoggard, Hicks and Czekaj were the prime backups at end and Ulinski sometimes would sub for Drazenovich at linebacker on defense. Simon, Misiewicz, Bill Kyle and a half dozen sophomores from the outstanding freshman team that went 9-0 at California State also would see considerable action in the front line. In the backfield, Higgins had three or four men for each position. Chuck Drazenovich sometimes played the entire game at quarterback and linebacker but Ulinski and others substituted there, too, Williams, Joe and Petchel were the tailbacks with Durkota, Colone and Rogel the fullbacks. Triplett was the starting wingback and usually played most of the game. Sometimes Higgins would move the backs around to other positions and would insert Cooney, Bill Luther, Weitzel and a couple of sophomores into the lineup. There were two notable players missing. Chuckran, the frosh star of '44, was injured most of the year and hardly played. Starting guard Leo

Ed Czekaj is best known as Athletic Director from 1969–1980 but also was an end and placekicker on the unbeaten 1947 team and became famous for missing a point after touchdown kick that resulted in a 13-13 tie with SMU in the '48 Cotton Bowl.

Nobile, another of the fabulousfreshmen of '41, had jumped to the Washington Redskins, much to the dismay and anger of Higgins. The kicking was in excellent shape with Colone on punts and Czekaj on extra points and several players, including Triplett, handling kickoffs. Nolan and Potsklan were elected captains shortly after the season started.

In his first *"Football Letter"* of the season, Ridge Riley summed up the explosive and upbeat potential of the multi-talented backs of '47: "It is obvious that Bob Higgins' major problem from here is one of selection. With the possible exception of Drazenovich, the blocking back, it is difficult to imagine a Lion backfield player staying on the field for any length of time. Petchel, the smallest, can do more things well. He can pass and kick and run. He can hold his own defensively despite his 155 pounds. Larry Joe is the strongest and the fastest. He's so fast that he doesn't need to dodge. Bobby Williams, a good passer directs the team well. He's at his best when the boys need steadying down, or a particular careful selection of plays. Bill Luther, the tallest of the tailbacks, is potentially one of the very best. New this year, he's come a long way, is a brilliant passer and runner...The three fullbacks—Colone, Rogel and Weitzel—likewise have varying talents. Because of his kicking and defensive play it is difficult to keep Joe Colone out of the starting lineup. Yet, Rogel is the surest ground gainer, and Weitzel, the best when he gets in the open. Triplett, Cooney and Durkota are three experienced wingbacks—all good runners...Yes, the problem of selection will be very important and very difficult. But ain't it wonderful?"

Most of the teams on the schedule had either switched to the T-formation or were using a combination of the T and single-wing. Higgins was committed to the single-wing to the end but he often modified his 5-3-2-1 defense to utilize blitzing linebackers. It was an aggressive bunch on both offense and defense and the result of their determination and teamwork showed from the start.

With transcontinental trips becoming easier in the late 1940s because of air transportation, State had arranged a two-game home-and-away series with a new opponent, Washington State. The first game

The 1947 Penn State football team.

was originally set for Beaver Field but was shifted to Hershey Stadium after pressure from Pennsylvania politicians and Harrisburg area alumni and promoted as "The Chocolate Bowl." So on a damp and wet Saturday night in Hershey, the "Men of '47" played one of the biggest opening games in school history against a team considered a leading Rose Bowl contender. As some 15,000 watched, State fumbled away the ball at midfield on its first two possessions, then marched 64 yards in the second quarter to take a 7-0 lead when Petchel surprised the Huskies by throwing an 18-yard running pass to the blocking back, Drazenovich. Later in the quarter, Colone, who already had a 61-yard punt on a quick kick, booted another one 47-yards that went out of bounds at the visitor's four-yard line. An offside penalty against the Cougars put the ball back at the one and Washington State decided to punt. Nolan, Simon and Kyle smothered the punter and Kyle recovered the ball in the end zone. Czekaj's second kick made it 14-0. The Lions almost scored again before the half but Williams' pass was intercepted in the end zone.

The Lions drove 65 yards on their first possession of the second half with Triplett getting the 15-yard TD on a reverse around right end. An 85-yard march ended in Rogel's five-yard plunge for the TD on the first play of the fourth quarter and State went on to win, 27-6. The Lions had garnered 17 first downs on 279 yards rushing and 57 yards passing while the defense held Washington State's Double-T offense to 79 yards rushing and 90 passing. "..It didn't seem to make much difference who ran the ball against the Pacific Coast club," reported the *Centre Daily Times*, adding that the Lions strong defense "...keep the Cougars pretty well bottled up on the ground." It was an auspicious and prophetic beginning.

The team had two weeks off before Bucknell visited Beaver Field for the official home opener. Many in the crowd of 12,294 had not reached their seats when Joe literally bumped Triplett out of the way at the five-yard line, took the opening kickoff and ran it back 95 yards for a touchdown. A couple of moments later, four State players swarmed the Bucknell punter and Chuck Drazenovich recovered at the Bucknell 25. Triplett then ran 14 yards for the TD. Bucknell tried passing on its next possession and Nolan intercepted from his right tackle

position and ran 34 yards into the end zone. After five minutes the game was virtually over. Petchel and Hoggard teamed up on the game's most spectacular TD on a 42-yard pass just before the half and the final was 54-0. The defense set a school record that still stands (but is unrecognized in the official Athletic Records) by intercepting 10 passes in holding the Bisons to 37 yards passing and 18 yards rushing while the offense had 405 total yards.

The next week, "The Men of '47" scored the most points since the boys of '26 with a 75-0 rout over hapless Fordham before a relatively sparse crowd at New York's Polo Grounds. State ran up 40 points to take a 55-0 halftime lead and scored 10 of the 12 times it had the ball. Durkota, playing as backup wingback, was the star with four touchdowns and 95 yards on just three carries. He ran 69 yards on a reverse for one TD, scored twice on pass receptions of eight and 38 yards and returned an intercepted pass 27 yards for a fourth TD. Petchel carried the ball only once from scrimmage, making a spectacular 78-yard run for a TD, and Czekaj booted eight extra points to tie Pete Mauthe's 1912 record as the Lions moved up to #12 in the AP poll with the victory. The following Monday at a New York football luncheon, Higgins publicly apologized to Fordham for the big score. He had tried to hold down the score by agreeing to shorten the second half and altering the rules to keep the clock running but his team was simply too good.

One week later, the '47 team equaled the school record of the '40 team with its third consecutive shutout. This time, the victim was Syracuse as State overcame the heat and a scoreless first quarter to batter the Orange, 40-0, before a Homecoming crowd. Nine Syracuse backs carried the ball 28 times and lost 125 yards while gaining 18 yards for a net yards rushing of minus 107. Syracuse gained 58 yards passing on 6-of-21 attempts and two interceptions. The total net yards of minus 47 set a new NCAA game record that has never been broken. Rogel was State's offensive star, rushing for 72 yards and two touchdowns on 13 carries. Petchel hit Durkota on a 10-yard running pass for another TD and then scored himself on a seven-yard run. Czekaj booted four extra points to run his four-game total to 20-for-30. The Lions didn't seem to miss Potsklan, Wolosky and Joe who were out

Wally Triplett runs around left end behind the blocks of Joe Drazenovich (23) and Steve Suhey (62) against undefeated West Virginia as the largest Beaver Field crowd in 22 years watches. Lions won 21-14 with Triplett scoring winning TD on a 49-yard pass from Elwood Petchel.

with injuries, nor Colone who left the game early with a shoulder separation after kicking punts of 67 and 68 yards. But they would need all four players the next week for what was billed as the biggest game of the season.

Undefeated West Virginia, like State, had rolled up the points in winning four games. The Mountaineers featured a passing attack that was reputed as one of the best in the country and some sportswriters figured this was the type of offense that would give State the most trouble. For the fifth straight game, Potsklan and Nolan won the toss and chose to receive. The Lions took the opening kickoff and drove 64 yards in 10 plays to score behind the running of Rogel, Joe and Triplett with Rogel getting the TD and Czekaj booting the PAT. Triplett's ensuing kickoff bounced off a Mountaineer tackle and Triplett recovered on the 50. The largest State crowd since the 1925 Notre Dame game (20,313) roared as they smelled a rout. But on the first play Rogel banged off tackle for six yards and fumbled when he tried to lateral and West Virginia recovered. The Mountaineers tied the score with the help of two questionable interference calls on Rogel and Wolosky and the crowd jeered when fullback Pete Zinaich plunged for the TD. The quick TD pumped up the Mountaineer defense. They stopped the Lions at the 11-yard line on the kickoff, then partially blocked a punt to set up a 24-yard TD pass and a 14-7 lead as the first quarter came to a close.

For the first time this season, the team was facing adversity and the game was getting rough. "There were a lot of fist fights," Norton recalled 50 years later, "and the officials didn't call it like they do today." The players gathered around each other on the sidelines, exhorting one another to pick up the challenge. State fought for field position, driving inside the Mountaineer 25 yard line twice before tying the game, 14-14, on sophomore fullback Chuck Gorinski's one-yard TD and Czekaj's PAT. The Lions almost scored again just before intermission but missed a first down by inches at the West Virginia 12-yard line. State took control in the second half, losing another scoring opportunity at the WV 14-yard line early in the third quarter, then getting a TD when Petchel 18-yard punt return set up his 49-yard pass to Triplett. Czekaj's third PAT made it 21-14 and that's how the game ended. The Lions ran all over the visitors in the second half but missed two other scoring chances deep in WV territory.

The comeback victory was a good indication of what kind of team this would be and Higgins proved once again that best way to stop the opponent's offense is to not give up the ball. The Mountaineers vaunted passing game gained just 26 yards on two-of-six attempts and their eight backs netted another piddling 25 yards on the ground on 29 carries. The Lions' ball control attack netted 340 yards rushing on 69 plays with Rogel going over 100 yards for the first time in his career with 114 yards on 17 carries. "It was a game that caught the fancy of the crowd...(and) worked them into an hysterical pitch and finally left them limp," wrote Chester Smith for the *Pittsburgh Press*. "It was game too in which there were costly penalties and tempers flared frequently. But the errors that occurred were offset by magnificent line play on both sides and the hard running of an almost endless stream of Lion backs." So much for adversity.

The team recorded another shut out in the final home game of the season against Colgate, 46-0. The Lions led by just 13 points at intermission but scored three touchdowns within four minutes of the third quarter and turned the game into a romp. Durkota scored TDs on runs of 22 and 24 yards and Luther also got two TDs on runs of 40 and nine yards as the team rolled up 390 yards on the ground and 100

yards in the air. The defense held Colgate to a minus 16 yards rushing and 84 yards passing while intercepting four passes and recovering a fumble. This was the first time since 1920 that a State team had won its first six games and the Lions were now ranked anywhere from number five to number eight in the polls. With three games left, Bowl talk was in the air. Even though State would be playing Temple, Navy and Pitt away from home, none of the opponents were having good years. Higgins warned his team not to get overconfident or complacent.

Still, the Lions had difficulty getting primed for Temple. The Owls were 3-3 and had lost to Syracuse 28-12 and barely defeated Muhlenberg by one point. State was favored by as much as five touchdowns, partly because the Lions led the nation in points scored, total offense and total defense. "On paper, it doesn't look like much of a contest," wrote Stan Baumgartner in the *Philadelphia Inquirer* on game day. Still, some sportswriters gave the Owls a chance because of their tailback, Phil Slosberg, who was the leading rusher in the East and second in the nation and had gained over 100 yards in each game. But on November 8 in Philadelphia, Slosberg turned out to be less of a factor than the rain, wind and mud. Temple won the toss and took the wind. The decision appeared to have paid off when State bogged down on its first possession and Colone's middling quick kick gave Temple the ball on the Owl 41-yard line. Two runs lost two yards but on third-and-12, Temple used a special play it had been preparing for State. It was a version of the "hidden ball" play that Temple called the "Setting-Hen" and it nearly worked to perfection. Neither the State players on the field nor the 20,000 spectators realized what had happened until days later. State's movies of the game showed the quarterback had taken the ball from center and sat on it while the line and backs were carrying out their fakes. The left end, Joe Lee, simply drifted over, picked up the ball nonchalantly and dashed out of the pack. Luckily, Potsklan saw him running down the right sideline and saved a TD by hauling him down at the State 15-yard line. The Lion defense rose up and smashed the Temple offense back to the 29-yard line in four downs and took over the ball. But the play seemed to give Temple a psychological edge. Before the first quarter was over, Petchel, Suhey and Wolosky would leave the game with injuries. Wading through the muck in the first half, State controlled the ball but lost one scoring opportunity at the Owl 27 and another when a Williams pass was intercepted in the end zone.

In the State locker room at halftime, Higgins outlined his strategy. We kick off, he said, hold Temple, take the ball on a punt, and run, run, run it down their throats for a touchdown. Nothing fancy. No reverses. No passing. Up the middle, power football And that's precisely what happened. Williams ran back the punt 12 yards to the Temple 49-yard line. In 16 plays with just Williams and Rogel going up the middle, the Lions scored with Williams getting the final two yards for the touchdown. Twice they went for it on fourth down and often there was no hole but Williams and Rogel just slithered through. It was 'The Defining Moment" of the season—a brash and challenging display of raw power and man-against-man combat that exemplified the spirit and talent of the "Men of '47" and set the tone for the entire season. Czekaj kicked the extra point and the scoring was over for the day. State lost another scoring chance on a pass interception and Czekaj's missed a 15-yard field goal after another drive withered at the six. But it didn't matter. State had won the game, 7-0, rushing for 176 yards and 9 first downs. Slosberg was held to a minus 15 yards on 15 carries and Temple got just 30 yards and two first downs. "It would be difficult

The 1947 team poses for a photo with Joe Paterno (front row left) at its 40th reunion in 1987.

to say whether the condition of the field, Coach Higgins' desire to with-hold his secrets from the U.S. Naval Academy team, the upstaters' rival next week, or the Owls; stalwart defense held down the score," Baumgartner wrote after the game.

Based strictly on records, the game with Navy at Baltimore's old, wooden dilapidated Memorial Stadium seemed to be another mis-match. Navy had a woeful 1-5-1 record but the losses had been to some of the best teams in the country, including Notre Dame and Georgia Tech. The Middies and their supporters believed the Lions' unbeaten streak was the result of a "soft" schedule and some sports-writers agreed. This would be the real test, they said. Soon after the opening kickoff, the taunting started. "You're playing in the big time now," the Navy players yelled as they stopped State's opening drive and then moved downfield through the mud to the Lions' 30-yard line before punting out of bounds at the one. The insults angered the first team and they wanted to play the entire game. Suhey and Chuck Drazenovich did as Higgins used only 21 players. Late in the first quar-ter, Durkota brought the rain-soaked crowd of about 25,000 to its feet when he ran 48-yards for a TD behind a big block by Tamburo on Navy's defensive end on an inside reverse play and Czekaj's kick made it 7-0. Navy tied it early in the second quarter on a 46-yard first down pass but the Lions took the lead for good a few minutes later after Joe ran back the ensuing kickoff 59 yards to the Navy 13-yard line. From there, Williams carried seven straight times off tackle and powered his way into the end zone. A holding penalty on the PAT nullified Czekaj's kick and a pass for the extra point failed and State led, 13-7.

After an emotional halftime in the locker room where the play-ers vented their anger over Navy's taunting, the team came out and took control. "Navy came out in the second half with dry and clean jerseys on and that just made us angrier," recalled tackle Negley Norton five decades later. With three minutes gone in the third period, State called the same inside reverse that had scored earlier and this time Durkota went 42 yards, getting an initial block by Tamburo at the line of scrimmage and another one downfield by Suhey to earn the TD. In what became a mostly defen-sive game the rest of the way, the Lions reached Navy's seven- and 31-yard lines before drives stalled in the mud while the Middies only threat came in the last minute of the game when they reached the Lion 12 before three passes fell incomplete. Navy had gained more yards against this team than any other foe—120 rushing and 123 passing—but still lost,

20-7. The victory also was a milestone in State history—the 300th win since football began in 1887. "It's not very often we have a chance for an undefeated season," Higgins told Tom Lyon of the *Centre Daily Times* after the game. "You have to be good and you have to be lucky."

Lyon also wrote that, "Reports from Pittsburgh indicate that the Panthers...are calmly confident they will beat the Blue and White. They merely point to the records to prove it." But there was no jinx at Pitt Stadium this year. A crowd of 47,000 watched as State tallied in every quarter to win, 29-0. Five different players scored, including Czekaj, who kicked his first and only field goal of the season from the 21-yard line in the fourth quarter. Czekaj also kicked two extra points, giving him 32-of-46 for the year and a new State record. On one spectacular play in the third quarter, Rogel lateraled to Petchel as Rogel was being dragged down by tacklers at the 20-yard line and Petchel ran the rest of the way to complete a 40-yard TD. But the play of the game came in the last period with Pitt in a deep passing formation. Hoggard, subbing for Tamburo, rushed in, hit the Pitt quarterback Bobby Lee at the same time that Lee took the snap from the center, then snatched the ball out of the air and ran 25 yards for the final TD. The game had been an-other display of State's power offense and stingy defense as the Lions amassed 276 yards and 15 first downs rushing while holding Pitt to a minus 26 yards on the ground and 71 in the air. And when it was over, the Penn State fans at Pitt Stadium celebrated the first win over the Panthers in four years by tearing down the goal posts and carrying Higgins off the field. "We'll be glad to listen (to any Bowl invitations) if anyone invites us," Higgins told Carl Hughes of the *Pittsburgh Press* in the locker room. "However, we won't go if the Negro boys on our team (Triplett and Hoggard) can't play."

That probably meant no bowl, wrote Hughes, because the Orange and Sugar Bowls would never accept blacks and the Cotton Bowl was unlikely to do so. No team with black players had ever been invited to the Cotton Bowl and the city of Dallas was segregated. But SMU assistant coach Red McClean, who was at Pitt Stadium to scout the Panthers for the opening game of the 1948 season, told Hughes SMU would be eager to play State if the Mustangs win the Southwest Conference. "He intimated, however, that there was some opposition among Cotton Bowl officials," Hughes wrote, "but said enough pres-sure might be brought to bear to overcome it."

A few days later, State was awarded the Lambert Trophy for the first time as the best team in the East. The final AP poll released on

December 8 named the Lions the fourth best team in the country after Notre Dame (9-0), Michigan (9-0) and SMU (9-0-1). Texas, defeated by SMU, was fifth, and twice-beaten Alabama sixth. With Michigan committed to the Rose Bowl and Notre Dame declining post-season invitations, Cotton Bowl officials knew they could have the marquee game on New Year's Day by pairing hometown SMU, featuring the sophomore All-America Doak Walker, against Penn State. The Cotton Bowl hierarchy knew about the furor over the cancellation of State's '46 game at Miami and sought SMU's opinion. SMU's Coach Matty Bell endorsed the matchup, saying: "SMU has broken precedent before. We were the first school of the Southwest Conference to play against Negroes in another section. After all, we're supposed to live in a Democracy." So, with SMU's blessing, Cotton Bowl officials setup the game. That didn't please everyone and some intolerant zealots referred to the game derisively as, "The Chocolate Bowl."

THE 1948 COTTON BOWL GAME
Jan. 1, 1923
Penn State 13, Southern Methodist U. 13

When the players first heard about the Cotton Bowl invitation, they were exhilarated. Now, they would get a chance to show the nation how good they were. And they would have fun, too, they thought, as they talked about the parties, girls, swimming pools and festive hospitality that they knew were part of Bowl trips. Remember, these were mostly bachelors in their mid-20s who were salivating at the prospect of the holiday excursion. Practicing outside in the December cold and snow of State College soon brought the first dose of reality. Higgins had warned the players that the Bowl trip would be no vacation and he made the point quickly with his two-a-day practices. The situation worsened when the players learned that Dallas had no hotels that would allow Blacks and that they would have to stay at a busy Naval Air Station 14 miles from the city. That exacerbated their resentment when they arrived in Texas just before Christmas and many of them cursed Higgins for spoiling their ultimate dream.

Higgins shocked the players when he forced them to scrimmage on Christmas afternoon. "It was a little tough for a Christmas Day present," Higgins told the *Centre Daily Times*, "but the boys didn't seem to mind and they needed it badly." The players were actually seething and some of them rebelled Christmas Night when the team was taken into downtown Dallas for a dinner on the top floor of a skyscraper. They simply walked away from a bus returning them to the military base and hit the streets of Dallas. Spending the rest of the holiday week on the base was simply too much for many of the "Men of '47." They figured they had left the rigors and harshness of military life when they returned to the campus. This was like a prison, with guarded fences, bunk beds and chow lines and lousy food in the mess hall. Throughout the week, some of the players hopped the fence and snuck away to enjoy better food, a few beers and female companionship. "One of the places we hit was Jack Ruby's Carousel (night club)," recalled Jeff Durkota, who admitted 50 years later he was one of the carousers. "Our morale was bad and we just had to get out." Some of the players complained privately about Triplett and Hoggard, partly because the two men who brought on the situation were spending *their* nights partying in the Dallas black community where they were considered heroes. "Every day after practice, Dennie and I would get

picked up and taken to some social function," Triplett remembered. "It made strained relations between me and some of my teammates because I was thoroughly enjoying myself. The 'Hig' did not treat the players right."

Higgins and his assistants tried to cope with the dissension and they overlooked much of the players' off-field antics. Higgins later admitted "mistakes were made on both sides." When sportswriters found out about the forays into town they accused the players of "partying," insolence and disobedience and some suggested this team was not worthy of playing in such a high profile game. "The Lions' conduct preceding and during the Cotton Bowl game gave Penn State and the East a black eye...," wrote Tom Lyon of the *CDT*. "All of the Lions' gripes were petty."

Dallas' quirky winter weather didn't help either and on New Year's Day it was windy and near freezing. The pre-game hype had focused the on-field battle as a match between SMU's high-powered passing and running attack led by Walker and State's rushing and defensive prowess. Walker had finished third in the Heisman Trophy race and did everything for SMU—run, pass, catch passes, punt, intercept passes and kick extra points and field goals. During the regular season, his 653 yards and 11 touchdowns rushing and his 344 yards and two touchdowns in 30-of-52 pass attempts were among the best in the country. Stop Walker and you stop SMU.

Of the 43,000 shivering fans in the Cotton Bowl stadium on January 1, 1948, there were just 3,000 who got their tickets from Penn State. That was the full State ticket allotment and was 2,200 more than Bowl officials originally gave to State. With 20,000 requests, the Athletic Department needed a lottery in order for 1,500 students to attend the game. So, with a hostile crowd rooting for hometown SMU, the Mustangs won the toss and chose the take the wind. Joe almost broke away on the kickoff return but was cut down by a shoestring tackle at the Lions' 39-yard line. Two plays gained three yards and Colone's quick kick slithered out of bounds at SMU's 37-yard line. On second-and-four, Walker carried for the first time and Potsklan smashed through an SMU blocker and nailed Walker for a 12-yard loss. Walker punted to State's 47-yard line and the Lions went to work with Rogel pounding through the SMU line for most of the yardage until it was fourth-and-two at the SMU 18. Williams went off tackle and was stopped for no gain. It was SMU's turn again and as millions listened on network radio Walker showed why he was an All-American. SMU moved quickly to the 38-yard line on Walker's running, then Walker completed his first pass for 12 yards. On second-and-10 at SMU's 47, Walker faded back and threw more than 50 yards in the air to Paul Page who shook off Durkota at the 13 to make the catch and run into the end zone. Walker then kicked the PAT as the partisan Dallas crowd cheered and sang the SMU fight song. Higgins, who had blamed Durkota for the pregame player rebellion, removed Durkota from the game and he didn't play again. Minutes later, Walker recovered Rogel's fumble at the State 44-yard line and the first quarter came to an end.

For the next 12 minutes the game belonged to Walker and SMU and State looked listless on the field. Later, many of the players would say they simply were not in the right mental state because of all the hassle, disillusionment and inconvenience of the pre-game encampment at the military base. State stopped one SMU thrust at the 30-yard line, and after losing the ball on a blocked kick near midfield, the Lions needed a fumble recovery by Cooney to halt SMU at the eight-yard line. But shortly after the fumble, SMU scored on a short 38-yard drive with

Coach Higgins shouts encouragement to his team during the 1948 Cotton Bowl game in Dallas. This would be Higgins' finest team in his 19-year coaching career at State.

Walker getting the final three yards off tackle for a TD. Now came one of the crucial plays of the game. Walker stepped back to try the PAT but before the ball could be centered, Wolosky crashed into the SMU backfield. There was no penalty and the teams lined up again. Walker poised to make the kick and he may have been a little too concerned about Wolosky. The Lion center barreled in at the snap of the ball and Walker appeared to hurry his kick. It missed but no one in the press box seemed to think it was a big deal. State looked badly beaten already and many of the Texas sportswriters were speculating on how high the score would be.

But down on the field, the State players were fuming. They shouted and screamed at each other to get their heads out of their butts! Less than two minutes remained in the half when Cooney took the ensuing kickoff and ran it back to the State 35. In went Petchel. On the first play, Petchel passed to Hicks at the SMU 47. On the next play Petchel appeared trapped on another running pass play but somehow got away and sprinted 15 yards for a first down at the SMU 32. Next, he hit Triplett on short pass but Triplett was stopped immediately for just a one-yard gain. A five-yard penalty for delay of game put State back to the 36 as the clocked ticked down. Petchel tried a pass; incomplete. Petchel tried another pass, incomplete. Less than 30 seconds remained. Petchel took the snap, ran back and fired to Cooney running down the middle. Cooney took the pass in stride at the 10 and went into the end zone. Czekaj's kick was perfect but the half wasn't over. Triplett kicked off to Walker on the three and the Lions converged quickly on the SMU ace. Walker cut across the field and in a criss-cross maneuver handed off to Page who broke away from the mass of players and was almost in the clear when he was pushed out of bounds by Triplett at the 40 and the half ended.

In the locker room the State players continued hollering and screaming at each other. "We can beat these guys and we're not doing the job out there," Suhey yelled. "I know some of you are mad at The

Hig," one player shouted, "but let's win this for us." The angry Lions roared out of the dressing room. After the kickoff, State's defense forced SMU to punt from its 28-yard line and with Williams and Rogel doing the brunt of the running, the Lions drove from the SMU 44 to the one before SMU stopped a fourth down plunge by Rogel. The defense forced another punt that Petchel ran back 25 yards to the Mustang nine-yard line. In two plays Rogel got five yards, then it was Petchel's turn again. He ran to his right, saw Triplett racing towards the left corner of the end zone and threw a perfect pass to tie the game with 10 and a half minutes gone in the third quarter.

Now came one of the most controversial and significant plays in State football history. Williams held as Czekaj attempted the extra point that would put State ahead. The wind was hardly blowing and everything seemed to work perfectly—the snap, the hold and the kick. Czekaj booted the ball high, far above the goal posts. For a few seconds the referee made no signal. "Well, is it good or not?" Williams and Czekaj yelled at the referee. " Tell us." The referee hesitated, then shook his head. "No good," he said. "Wide right." To this day, the players on the field that afternoon are convinced the kick was good. "I knew damn well it was good," recalled Petchel. "I saw it go right inside the right goal post." Everyone knew but Czekaj. He never saw it. As Czekaj came off the Cotton Bowl turf, Higgins ran over and asked if the kick had been good. "I don't know coach, " Czekaj replied. "You always told me to keep my head down when I kicked and I did."

Neither the game nor the excitement was over. State's defense shut down Walker and the Mustangs for nearly the rest of the game as an SMU offense that had generated nearly 100 yards passing and 100 yards running in the first half got only 24 yards on three passes in the second half and just 15 yards on the ground. But the SMU defense saved the game and the Mustangs almost won it on a fake field goal. State lost the ball on a fumble at the SMU 43 and another time SMU held on downs at the 20. Twice the Mustangs intercepted Petchel passes to stop State drives inside their territory and the second time Walker ran the ball back to midfield to spark a last minute rally. On the first play following the interception, SMU picked up 15 yards on a pass, then had two long pass attempts batted down by State's defenders. On fourth down, Walker went back to attempt a field goal but the holder, Page, grabbed the ball, shook off a couple of State tacklers and ran all the way to the five before being hauled down. The SMU crowd went wild until they saw the penalty flag. Page had stepped out of bounds five yards back of the original line of scrimmage.

Now it was State's turn for some last minute heroics. On the first play, Petchel passed to Hicks who was in the clear on the SMU 37. But the ball was high and Hicks had to make a circus-like catch and fell to the ground. There was time for one more play. "48-Sweep Pass," Petchel shouted—a pass to Hoggard. Petchel ran to his right as Triplett and Hoggard sprinted into the end zone and got behind SMU's defenders, including Walker. "He was open," Petchel recalled years later, "and I threw it." Hoggard converged on the ball with Triplett nearby. An SMU back leaped and deflected it. The ball hit Hoggard squarely in the stomach. He tried to grab it and so did Triplett and Walker but it bounced harmlessly away. Hoggard walked off the field as disconsolate as anyone. If he or Triplett could have caught the ball, he remembered years later, it would have been a perfect ending to an otherwise less than happy experience in Dallas.

It was "one of the most thrilling Cotton Bowl games ever unreeled," wrote Jere R. Hayes, sports editor of the *Dallas Times Herald*. "We played a little better in the second half," a disappointed Higgins told the Associated Press. "But we'd gone too long without a game." Triplett was cited for his defensive play and had made three tackles that saved touchdowns. Drazenovich, Cooney, Nolan and Suhey also were praised for their defensive performance and Suhey and Petchel were named as Penn State's stars of the game. Rogel was the leading rusher with 97 yards on 27 carries, beating beat out Walker who had 57 yards on 15 carries.

Despite the tie, this group won more games in one season than any State team before them. They fell short of duplicating the all-winning season of the 1912 squad but they had set a new standard for Penn State football. Many of the records they set would live on long after some of the men themselves had passed away. Suhey would get a special honor—the school's first All-American since Gajecki in 1940, and he would leave behind a legacy that would continue deep into the Paterno era.

The tie in the Cotton Bowl did not dampen the enthusiasm of State's long-suffering fans. They knew many of the "Men of '47" would be back in '48. They talked of another unbeaten season, another high ranking and maybe another bowl game. They also talked of another payback at Pitt.

Season Record 9-0-1
Record to Date 301-169-34
Winning percentage .631

"Hi-Diddle-Diddle, Rogel-Up-the-Middle"

The several thousand Penn State fans shivering in the cold and dampness of Pitt Stadium could not believe it was happening again. Hundreds of them had seen it occur many times before in this Godforsaken concrete pit but they still were shocked and dumbfounded.

Pitt, a decided underdog in this annual late November game, was leading unbeaten State 7-0 on a fluke pass interception by a tackle—a sophomore tackle, mind you—and time was quickly running out in the fourth quarter. If the Lions were to salvage the game, the Bowl bid and the season, they needed to score quickly. Another Petchel pass had just been intercepted on Pitt's 5-yard line and now there were less than five minutes remaining. State needed a TD and extra point just to

tie, and everyone sitting in the stadium or listening to the game on radio knew a tie wouldn't be enough to get the Bowl invitation. One tie a season was enough and that already had occurred against the cry babies from Michigan State.

How could it have come down to this again? A jinx? Who knows? The fact was Pitt had spoiled many a State season over the past 40 years and every die-hard Nittany loyalist figured it would take decades to even the score. There was still time for a miracle but State's hope for another great season like '47 was fading fast.

Before the year began, some sportswriters had said this team was a contender for the national championship, right up there with Notre Dame, Michigan and North Carolina. And why not with many of the starters and a lot of the reserves back from the '48 Cotton Bowl team. Although not quite as deep at every position, this was another veteran team and some starters were in their fourth varsity season. Colone was the captain and starting fullback with Rogel and Joe in reserve. Triplett was at wingback with Cooney and Urion behind him. Luther started at tailback with Petchel and Chuckran backing him. Chuck Drazenovich was the quarterback and would again play most of every game with little or no relief. In the line, Higgins had Tamburo, Hicks, Hoggard and sophomore John Smidansky at ends; Norton, Finley and junior non-letterman Don Murray at tackles; Joe Drazenovich, Simon and junior letterwinner Paul Kelly at guards and juniors Chuck Beatty (a letterman) and Ray Hedderick at centers. Another Black player also was on the varsity, Chuck Murray, a reserve quarterback. Several other lettermen and sophomores filled in the second and third team positions. Colone and Triplett would again handle the punting and kickoffs. With Czekaj graduated, a senior named Carl Sturges of Washington, DC, a one-time halfback who had left the team two years earlier because of a leg injury, tried out as a kicking specialist in September and became the placekicker.

Another record opening-day crowd of 14,423 turned out in hot weather at Beaver Field October 2 to watch State shut out Bucknell for the second straight year. The spectators didn't know it at the time but they were seeing the last football game ever with State's first rival. Many of the fans were disappointed, despite a 35-0 score, for they felt the team didn't measure up to its preseason buildup. Triplett scored two TDs, one on a pass from Petchel, who also had a TD and Sturges booted all five PATs as Higgins used 40 players but the Lions had other drives stopped by a fumble, penalty and pass interception.

When the team arrived in Syracuse the following Thursday night for another Friday night game at Archbold Stadium, many of the players could not believe the weather forecast. Rain. Deja Vu. Two years earlier State had played through the rain in a Friday night game at Archbold and last season it had rained in Hershey for the Saturday night opener with Washington State. Add in the rain at the first night game ever, at NYU in 1940, and one had to wonder if the Lions somehow brought the lousy hometown weather of State College with them for these night games—after all, State had won every time. It would be no different this year, although the game (in the rain as promised) was much closer than the final score of 34-14.

The Lions vaulted to a 13-0 lead in the first 11 minutes, then withstood a sensational one-man passing and running performance by Syracuse sophomore Bernie Custis before putting the game out of reach in the fourth quarter. Triplett had his greatest running day ever, with 154 yards on eight carries, including a 48-yard TD off an inside reverse around right end. Custis went to work about the time the rain stopped

Bill Luther runs for several yards in 35-0 victory over Bucknell in the 1948 game that was the final one ever played between State and its first ever opponent.

in the second quarter and passed for 181 yards and two TDs and getting 26 of his team's net 36 yards on the ground. But State never trailed and with two fourth quarter touchdowns turned its 20-7 half-time lead into a 20-point victory margin. "As a runner, Wally combines speed, strength and intelligence," Riley wrote in his *"Football Letter."* "Above all he runs—or so it seems—with indomitable spirit. He gives you the impression that he is obsessed with an unconquerable desire to get to the goal line...He is the real Mr. Outside of Penn State football, complementing Francis Rogel..."

Triplett had another outstanding day the next week when he turned a tight 14-0 halftime lead over West Virginia into a 37-7 rout at Beaver Field. State led 7-0 on a first quarter touchdown pass from Petchel to Tamburo but West Virginia was holding its own until late in the second quarter, when Triplett dazzled the crowd with a 69-yard punt return for what appeared to be a touchdown. The TD was nullified because Triplett had stepped out of bounds at the West Virginia 42, but the runback set up the Lions second TD seven plays later on a two-yard run by Petchel. Early in the third quarter, Triplett raced around right end and went untouched 54 yards for the third TD. Then, Triplett took a Mountaineer punt at State's 15-yard line, faked a handoff to Luther and dashed down the left sideline 85 yards with Hoggard as his blocker for another TD. State finished the scoring in the fourth quarter with Petchel's 34-yard TD pass to sophomore wingback Owen Daughtery and a blocked kick by Simon for a safety. Triplett had 105 yards rushing on nine carries and his performance made the crowd of nearly 18,000 forget how much trouble the Mountaineers' passing attack had been: 15-of-23 passes for 124 yards.

Higgins blamed some of his pass defense problems on injuries that kept several players out of the lineup against both Syracuse and West Virginia. Against the Mountaineers, he was so short of guards that he moved the untested Murray from QB to guard toward the end of the game. With tough Michigan State coming to town for Homecoming, Higgins stressed pass defense during practice that week. And it paid off when the Lions intercepted four passes in the second half to stop Michigan State drives deep in State territory. But the Michigan State game, itself, ended in controversy, and complaints from the visitors about State's discourtesy and boorish behavior. Lions fans expected

that from Biggie Munn, the irascible former Syracuse coach who was now at the helm of the Spartans.

Although Michigan State was just 2-2, the losses had been to two of the nation's best, Michigan (13-7) and Notre Dame (26-7) and the Spartans had scored over 60 points in both victories (over Hawaii and Arizona). The largest crowd in Beaver Field history arrived early despite the threatening weather and hundreds of fans stood in line for hours to get the last 2,000 seats. By the time the Lions kicked off at 2:15 the standing-room-only throng of 24,479 people completely ringed the field and obliterated yard markers. Others sat in trees and step ladders outside the fence.

Both teams had tailored their defenses to stop the other team's best runners, and it worked. Triplett got only 20 yards while Rogel led all ball carriers with 83 yards. Lynn Chadnois, made 59 yards and George Guerre, the star of the '46 game, had just 16 but a young Spartan fullback named Frank "Muddy" Waters got 82 yards, mostly in the second half, when Munn tried to surprise the Lions with some different rushing plays. The first half was a defensive battle and fumbles led to each team's initial touchdowns. MSC took a 7-0 lead with five seconds left in the first quarter after recovering Rogel's fumble at the State 22-yard line. On fourth-and-goal from the five, Guerre took a pitchout to his left, faked a pass and went in for the score. Five minutes later, Guerre fumbled and Beatty recovered at the MSC 24. On the fifth play, Petchel passed 11 yards to Smidansky for the TD and Sturges tied it at 7-7. The Lions got the ball back late in the quarter following a punt and drove 74 yards for a first down at the Spartans' six-yard line with just 10 seconds left in the half. Then came the "play of the game" and one that many old-time Michigan State fans are still crying about. Petchel started to his right, saw Tamburo in the end zone and threw the ball. The pass was a little short. Guerre intercepted at the goal line and took off. He faked out three would-be State tacklers and went 100 yards for an apparent touchdown that stunned the partisan crowd. But back upfield, field judge Karl Bohren was waving his arms. He had spotted a clipping penalty at the MSC 20-yard line and nullified the TD. Michigan State officials would later claim their movies did not show a clip and their complaint about a "mystery" penalty gained credence when the field judge could not identify the number of the culprit. "I saw Penn

State's Number 78 (John Finley) get clipped," Bohren told the *Centre Daily Times* after the game. "I did not get the number of the Michigan State man who did it." Later, the *CDT's* sports editor Tom Lyon wrote: "Penn State's movies clearly show a clip. John Finley, Lion tackle, was cut down from behind by a lineman name Yocum, whose hometown is Windber, PA. It's a perfect clip and the official called it." The play and ensuing controversy certainly was one of the defining moments of the season.

Angered by the penalty, the Spartans kicked off the second half and trapped Luther at the six-yard line, then forced a punt. Three plays later, Gene Glick passed 47 yards to Ed Sobszak for a touchdown and a 14-7 lead. (State's game film showed Sobszak was way offside before the play but no penalty was called.) The Lions took the ensuing kickoff and marched 73 yards in 15 plays to tie the score on a bit of razzle-dazzle from an old Higgins playbook. With a first down at the MSC 20, Petchel hit Tamburo on a pass down the middle. Tamburo faked a lateral to Rogel, then handed the ball to guard John Simon, who ran in for the first and only TD of his career. Sturges kicked the tying PAT. Penn State was on the defensive most of the fourth quarter as interceptions by Cooney and Triplett and two by Rogel—one at the five-yard line—helped stop the Spartans inside the 33-yard line. The Lions lost one scoring opportunity at the MSC 25-yard line on a muffed pass play and almost gave away the game when a fourth down gamble at the Lions 32-yard line failed by inches, but Triplett's interception saved the Lions from embarrassment. Neither team was satisfied with the final 14-14 tie. "It was a tough game." Higgins told the *CDT*. Munn said, "It was a wonderful game." But after returning to East Lansing, Michigan State claimed it was treated rudely by Penn State and its fans. Among the gripes was one about the dressing room in Recreation Hall being too far from Beaver Field (although it was right across the street) and lacking privacy from the noisy, mocking Nittany Lions fans. MSC also complained that the State Blue Band never played the Spartans' Alma Mater. From such whining come great rivalries—even if they take 50 years to develop.

Higgins had to guard against a let down the following week against Colgate in Hamilton and he blew up when a starter with a minor shoulder bruise asked to sit out so he could be rested for Penn. The Hig played his starters for most of the first three quarters and five different players scored TDs as the Lions won easily, 32-13. Triplett had 71 yards, and an 11-yard TD, on nine carries and was outstanding on defense..

No game in the Higgins era had more pre-game pressure and hype than the one against Penn at Franklin Field on November 6. The old rivals had not played since '42 and no future games were scheduled. Even this game had been scheduled reluctantly by Penn officials who believed Philadelphia sportswriters were correct in labeling the State players as "unnecessarily rough" and the State fans as "crude and rowdy." What made this year's pre-game build-up even more fervent was that both teams were unbeaten and protecting non-losing streaks. State had not lost in 15 games and Penn had not been beaten in 14 contests, although State had two ties and Penn one tie in that span. Thousands of students cut classes on Friday and traveled to Philadelphia for the game. Many never got inside Franklin Field as the largest crowd ever to see a State or Penn game up to that time—71,180, including Governor James Duff—jammed the two-deck stadium on a sunny, cool day. The fans went wild when the mascots of both teams made their entrance on a tandem bicycle just before the kickoff. The State fans didn't learn until later that the Nittany Lion mascot had

planned to enter the field from a rope ladder dangling out of a helicopter but Penn officials had denied permission.

State played its finest game of the season on both offense and defense, holding the Quakers to a net rushing of 19 yards and net passing of 80 yards on 10-of-24 passes, in a 13-0 victory. But it wasn't easy. Rogel was the offensive star, scoring both touchdowns and running for 75 yards on 16 carries. Triplett, who played all but two minutes, and Chuck Drazenovich, who played all 60 minutes, led a tough defense that stopped Penn's only serious threat with one of the great goal line stands in school history. Rogel's first touchdown was a beauty and came in the second quarter on a drive that started at State's 11-yard line following a Quaker quick kick. The Lions had moved to Penn's 44-yard line when Rogel took the snap, spun and faked a pass to Petchel and bolted up the middle. Penn's mighty All-American Chuck Bednarik was just behind the line of scrimmage. Rogel lowered his shoulders, hit Bednarik, spun off to his left and ran all the way to the end zone. Sturges' PAT made it 7-0 at the half.

State's goal line stand came late in the third quarter. Following a punt runback, the Quakers moved from State's 45-yard line to the four for a first down. State called time out, then went into an eight-man line, with three guards—Kelly, Simon and Joe Drazenovich—in the middle. On first down, Finely nailed Penn's quarterback Bill Talarico for a four-yard loss. On second down, Triplett batted down a pass in the end zone. On third down, a pass was short of the receiver and Triplett almost intercepted. Riley vividly described what happened on the fourth down: "(Francis) Bagnell hit (Carmen) Falcone (with a diagonal pass) just a few yards from the goal line. Just as he was about to cross the goal line he was met by Triplett. The players hit the sod together with the ball resting under Falcone, just a few inches short of a touchdown." Colone, the hero of the last win over Penn in '42, punted out to the 30. On fourth down at the 25, Bagnell passed to end Lou Roberts wide open in the end zone but Triplett came "out of nowhere" and leaped to bat the ball away. Penn never threatened again. State scored again six minutes into the fourth quarter on two quick plays from the Lions' 35-yard line capped by a razzle-dazzle TD pass. On the first play, Petchel passed to Tamburo who ran all the way to Penn's 13-yard line before being hauled down from behind by Bednarik on a lunging tackle that caused an injury to Bednarik's hand and forced him out of the game. On the next play, Rogel took the snap from center, handed off to Drazenovich on a half spinner and faked a buck up the middle. Drazenovich pitched out to Petchel running to his left and Petchel threw it on the run to Rogel who was in the end zone. Penn's Henry Rossell tipped the ball and it hit Rogel on the shoulder but the big fullback lunged for the ball as it bounced away and caught it just before hitting the ground. Sturges missed the extra point and a few minutes later the game was over. "The Lions yesterday possessed too much speed for the Quakers,' wrote Art Morrow in the *Philadelphia Inquirer*, which featured a photograph of Rogel diving for the tipped pass. "Their linemen seem faster, most times, than Penn's backs...It was one of State's greatest victories." The rowdy State fans tore down the goal posts and celebrated in downtown Philadelphia. "While the band marched and countermarched on Broad St., hundreds of happy fans poured into the Bellevue(-Stratford Hotel) lobby and swamped elevator service in scenes reminiscent of the mid-summer political conventions," reported the *Inquirer*.

In the final home game of the season, the Lions smashed Temple 47-0 as seven different players scored touchdowns. Colone, who scored the first TD on a two-yard run, had the longest run of his

Elwood Petchel, a star on Coach Higgins' last teams, runs for several yards during a game at Beaver Field in 1948.

The Lions picked up a first down at the 35-yard line but Pitt stiffened and forced a fourth-and-14 play with less than a minute left. Petchel tried to hit Hoggard on a pass over the middle but Jimmy Joe Robinson intercepted and the Pitt fans jumped up and down in celebration. But wait. There was a flag. Offensive interference by Robinson. Penn State's ball, first down on the Pitt 20. Thirty seconds were left but State had no time outs. Petchel passed to Cooney at the 11. First down and 20 seconds left. The crowd was on its feet. Petchel passed to Smidansky at the two. First down and 12 seconds left. Time for one more play. The Stadium was rocking and the noise could be heard several blocks away. Beatty snapped the ball to Rogel who smashed into the right side of the

career, when he rambled 66 yards just before halftime to set up State's third TD by Chuckran. Temple had a net yards rushing of seven yards in suffering its worst defeat of the series with the Lions.

Now, it was on to Pittsburgh. The word was out that a win over Pitt and another over Washington State in the final game of the year and the team would be off to another bowl game. "We understood we were going back to the Cotton Bowl and resolve that tie with SMU," center Beatty remembered years later. Pitt was 5-3 and had lost big to SMU, Notre Dame and Ohio State. State players knew they should never take the Panthers lightly no matter what the record and the game was very physical. Perhaps the euphoria of the big victory over Penn was still on their minds but State's offense couldn't seem to get going. For more than three quarters, the offense sputtered, reaching Pitt territory several times but getting no closer than the 15-yard line. Meanwhile, the defense was holding Pitt in check and the Panthers got no further than State's 30-yard line on just three incursions into Lions territory. The nearly 50,000 fans at Pitt Stadium expected the Lions offense to explode at any moment and it did in the fourth quarter—but this time it blew itself up.

Three minutes into the final period, State took the ball on its own 20 following a punt into the end zone. On third-down-and-five, Petchel ran back to pass. Pitt guard Ralph Coleman crashed in and tipped the ball as it left Petchel's hand and it sailed into the hands of Nick Bolkovac, the sophomore tackle who also was Pitt's placekicker. Bolkovac had nothing but daylight in front of him and he ran 23 yards for the touchdown. His extra point made it 7-0 and the Lions knew they were in trouble. But there was still plenty of time left. They took the kickoff and marched down field. The interception had awakened the giant and the State fans were sure the tying TD was only a play or two away. Then it happened again. Petchel's pass was intercepted on the five-yard line. On fourth down, Pitt punted and State got the ball on the Panthers 48-yard line.

line and churned towards the goal line under a mass of humanity. Everyone held their breath for an instant. Then the referee's hands made the signal. No touchdown. Pitt wins. State fans groaned and thousands of Pitt fans charged across the field. "It was poetic justice," wrote Chet Smith in the *Pittsburgh Press*, "that the hands that finally pulled Rogel down were attached to Bolkovac." It was State's first loss since the Pitt game of '46. The jinx was back. Rogel had rushed for 116 yards on 31 carries but he couldn't get the most important two yards when it counted and his futile plunge was THE defining moment of the season.

Traveling to Tacoma, Washington, was the last thing the players wanted to do. Practice was dismal that week and on Wednesday night the team was forced to stay overnight in Pittsburgh again before flying out. Despite the rain, slippery field and 65 yards in penalties, State rushed for 217 yards—with Rogel getting 110 on 27 carries and setting a new season rushing record for fullbacks at 602 yards—and held Washington State's outstanding passing offense to 34 yards in a 7-0 victory. Cooney, starting in place of Triplett who had injured his wrist in a Friday practice and didn't play on offense, scored the only touchdown late in the first half on an 18-yard deep reverse. Sturges kicked his 25th of 32 extra point attempts to complete the scoring.

Despite the loss to Pitt, the Lions still finished 18th in the Associated Press poll and Tamburo became the school's 10th All-American. But it was the last hurrah for Higgins. He didn't know it then but he had coached his last game at Washington State. He would re-sign in March and let one of his long-time assistants pick up the football legacy. Or so he thought.

Season Record 7-1-1
Record to Date 308-170-35
Winning percentage .635

"Lost in the Shuffle"

Joe Bedenk had never expected to be the head football coach at Penn State. Although he had been one of State's finest football players in the early 1920s and a long-time assistant to Bob Higgins, Bedenk's true love was baseball. He had been the school's head baseball coach since 1931 and he was happy with his subordinate role in football as line coach and scout.

When the Hig decided to retire after the 1948 season for health reasons, Bedenk had no intention of applying for the job. But friends within the Athletic Department and ex-teammates had manipulated behind the scenes to get him the position and he reluctantly accepted. By early October he knew he had made a mistake and he told a few people confidentially that he would give up the post at the end of the year.

It wasn't the mixed success he had on the gridiron that season that drove Bedenk back to the diamond. He simply wasn't comfortable with the pressure of being the full time head coach. His tenure is noted more for a decision he made off the field than anything his team did on it. Before the season began, Bedenk hired two new assistant coaches, one to succeed him as line coach and the other to replace backfield coach Earle Edwards, who quit because he didn't get the head coaching job. Bedenk's hires would have ramifications on into the Paterno era. One of Bedenk's favorite former players, Sever Toretti, then a high school coach, came aboard as line coach. Frank Patrick, a star fullback at Pitt during the Panthers' heyday of the late '30s, was retained as defensive backfield coach. Both would become key assistants for both Rip Engle and Joe Paterno with Toretti distinguishing himself as Paterno's first recruiting guru. If he had stayed on, Bedenk also would have benefited from the first group of scholarship players since 1927. In May, the Board of Trustees re-instituted tuition scholarships for all sports. The initial football class was sent to California State Teachers College because of crowded housing conditions on the main campus. Among the freshmen were future starters Joe Yukica, Don Barney and Joe Gratson.

Edwards did not leave the team until spring practice was over. This was a most unusual spring practice because Bedenk had allowed most of his veterans to skip it. "Spring football practice is used to teach the fundamentals of the game to the boys," Bedenk told sportswriters, as quoted in Ken Rappoport's book, "The Nittany Lions." "If some of the more experienced letter-winners go out for other sports, the boys who need the practice will have a better chance to learn the things the seniors already know." And Bedenk had a lot of players who needed practice because he had less than a dozen lettermen returning for 1949.

From the start of preseason practice on August 28, Bedenk knew he would have a good first team but no depth. Most of the starters were veterans of the great unbeaten 1947 team and all but one were lettermen. The lone greenhorn was junior Owen "Doc" Dougherty, a flashy lefthanded passer out of Dunmore, who started at right halfback ahead of Orsini. In the backfield with Doc were Rogel at fullback, junior Vince O'Bara or Luther at left half and Chuck Drazenovich at quarterback. Up front, it was Hicks and Smidansky at ends, Norton and Don Murray at tackles, Joe Drazenovich and Kelly at guards and

Hedderick or Beatty at center. Hicks and Norton were co-captains and Joe Drazenovich and O'Bara handled the placekicking. With Colone graduated, the punting was turned over primarily to Dougherty and O'Bara. Bedenk retained Higgins' power-running single-wing attack but as the season progressed, he would begin dabbling in the popular T-formation with its more wide-open passing plays.

"Few will argue that State will have a good first team this season," wrote Tom Lyon, sports editor of the Centre Daily Times, a week before the September 24th season opener. "A couple of backs need seasoning, but on the whole the Lion starters are capable of holding their own with the first eleven of any club in the country."

The tempo of the season—and, thus, its defining moment—was set in the first two games against two of the best teams in the country, Villanova and Army. Villanova, with a 31-0 win over Texas A&M already, was the toughest opening season game since before the war. The Wildcats eventually would lose just one game and be rated #13 by the Associated Press. With student enrollment peaking on the main campus this year at 14,732, the crowd of 22,080 far surpassed any other opening day turnout at Beaver Field. They watched as State stumbled in the first half, tired in the second and lost, 27-6. The score was just 7-0 at the intermission, even though the Lions had not played well, but Villanova broke it open in the third quarter with one touchdown following a pass interception and another on a seven-play, 85 yard drive. The loss was the first at Beaver Field since the '46 Michigan State game and the first opening game defeat at home since the 7-0 shocker against Waynesburg in 1931.

Embarrassed by their performance, the players worked harder on pass defense and tackling at practice that week for what would be the school's 500th football game since 1887. They knew Army would be heavily favored in the game at West Point that following Saturday. But they were determined to regain the pride that had carried them through the last two outstanding seasons. The thousands of Penn State fans who traveled up the Hudson after a rousing Friday night party at the Commodore Hotel in New York city helped give Michie Stadium the biggest crowd in its 25-year history. The 27,000 in the stadium and thousands of others watching over WNBT-TV (sic) in New York looked on as the fired up Lions took charge of the first half. State's defense led by the Drazenovich brothers, Norton and Murray stuffed the Cadets' high-powered offense and Rogel's running helped State move the ball. Army almost scored on a 63-yard pass play early in the second quarter but the TD was nullified because both teams were offside. Midway through the quarter, State got the ball on its own 35-yard line following a punt. With the help of a roughing the kicker penalty, the Lions drove 65 yards in 14 plays to score on a six-yard pass from Dougherty to Luther. Drazenovich kicked the PAT and State took a surprising 7-0 lead into the locker room. The Lions fans smelled an upset and they cheered lustily when the team came onto the field to receive the second half kickoff.

Rogel returned the kickoff to the Lions' 21-yard line but State couldn't move further and Luther went back to punt. Now came what some sportswriters said was probably the play of the game. Luther shanked the punt out of bounds at the State 33 and Army quickly moved to the eight-yard line. That's when Luther redeemed himself. Army's All-American quarterback Arnold Galiffa fired a pass to his All-American end, Dan Foldberg, at the goal line but Luther ripped the ball out of Foldberg's hands and struggled to the two before being tackled. The Army defense forced State to punt again and a clipping penalty on the run back set the Cadets back to the Lions 41-yard line. But this time the Cadets would not be stopped. They marched for a TD behind the running and passing of Galiffa with the Army quarterback scoring after two rushes from the four. The PAT made it 7-7. After an exchange of punts, the Lions made another mistake. State's third string left half, Roy Shaginaw, fumbled. Army recovered at the State 32 and on the first play Galiffa threw a touchdown pass to Army's "other" All-American, fullback Gil Stephenson. O'Bara ran the kickoff back to the 17 and on the first play O'Bara tried to pass but was tackled for a 16-yard loss. As the fourth quarter began, State punted out of the end zone, and two plays later half back Jim Cain (no, he wasn't an All-American) dashed 38 yards for a TD and broke the spirit of the Lions. Two interceptions and a fumble set up three more Army TDs in the fourth quarter and the Cadets won, 42-7. "It was no fitting climax to as gallant a first half battle as any eleven has ever waged," wrote Riley in his *"Football Letter"*, "but no team without adequate shock troops could possibly absorb the might of Army's four full offensive and defensive alignments which poured back and forth into the fray as the ball changed sides." Michael Strauss of *The New York Times*, wrote that Bedenk "said he had a fine first team but that he was weak in reserves. Such proved to be the case as Army, loaded with material and using its famed platoons, battered away at the failing State players." Army would go on to a 9-0 record and number four AP rating. Bedenk would go back to State College and think about resigning. "Joe was upset about the game and didn't spare any feelings," assistant coach Jim O'Hora recalled. "I remember walking with him after the game and he said, 'For a nickel, I'd quit now.' From then on, he was uncertain about the season and whether he should be the coach."

A State team had not lost three games in a row since 1936 and the captains—Norton and Hicks— exhorted their teammates not to let down as the team practiced for its first game ever with Boston College. The Eagles had the East's leading passer in Ed Songin and one of the country's best linemen and kickers in Ernie Stautner. But even without linebacker Chuck Drazenovich, who was sidelined with an injury, State's passing defense was outstanding as Songin completed just six-of-21 passes for 95 yards and had three interceptions. The first interception by a virtually unknown sophomore tackle named Ed Hoover came two minutes into the game and was run back 22 yards for a touchdown. Meanwhile, State's passing accounted for three TDs and the Lions never trailed in winning, 32-14.

Drazenovich was still missing the following week when the Lions beat up on Nebraska, 22-7, before nearly 24,000 Homecoming fans. State's defense limited the Cornhuskers to 11 net yards rushing and 10 yards passing while the offense rushed for 265 yards and passed for 86 yards in picking up 16 first downs. Luther ran for one TD and passed to Smidansky for another. Charlie Murray, filling in for Drazenovich at QB and linebacker, was singled out for his fine play-calling and defensive tackling. But the joy of the victory was diminished by a first quarter ankle injury that sidelined Rogel, the team's clutch runner and leading rusher. That did not bode well for the next game, against Michigan State at East Lansing.

The Spartans were still upset about their trip to State College in '48 when they claimed State fans taunted them on and off the field. They got more incentive from their end coach, Earle Edwards, who told them he had been snubbed and embarrassed when passed over for the head coaching job—as if the Spartans needed any psychological inducements. They had won four games with only a 7-3 opening sea-

son loss to hated Michigan marring their record. They also had three bonafide All-Americans in halfback Lynn Chadnois and guards Ed Bagdon and Don Mason. Bagdon would go on to win the Outland Trophy as the nation's best lineman.

It was a game of mistakes and the Lions made most of them. In the opening minutes of the game, the usually reliable Smidansky dropped a pass from Dougherty when he was wide open and that was the defining moment of the game. Three times the Lions recovered Michigan State fumbles inside the Spartans 26-yard line but couldn't take advantage. The Lions also had five passes intercepted and lost a fumble. Chadnois scored the first TD on a 60-yard run in the second period and the last on a 56-yard runback of an interception with two minutes left in the game as the Spartans won, 24-0. Rogel did not play and Chuck Drazenovich saw only limited action.

Syracuse had a new coach named Floyd "Ben" Schwartzwalder and he had his team primed for his first visit to Beaver Field as the Orange took a 7-0 lead on a quick 80-yard drive on its first possession. State made it 7-6 before the end of the first quarter when Dougherty hit Smidansky on a 31-yard pass and the PAT kick failed. Syracuse extended its lead to 14-6 early in the second period on the passing of sub quarterback Bernie Custis, who had played so well against the Lions in '48. But with four minutes left in the half, Luther made the key play in the game, when he returned a punt 80 yards for a TD. Joe Drazenovich's kick was good this time and the Lions trailed by just 14-13 at the half. As the third quarter started, Rogel pleaded with Bedenk to get into the game, and the crowd of 18,758 roared when the senior fullback ran onto the field. Bedenk said later he inserted Rogel despite his better judgment. Moments later, with the ball at the State 48-yard line, Chuck Drazenovich took the snap, pitched out to Luther running right and Luther threw a short pass to Rogel who rambled to the Syracuse four-yard line before being tackled. Four plays later Rogel bulled over for the TD, O'Bara kicked the PAT and with State leading for the first time, 20-14, the Orange appeared to wilt. A 72-yard, 12-play drive led by O'Bara that straddled the third and fourth quarters gave the Lions another TD with O'Bara scoring on a 12-yard run and Dougherty wrapped it up with a 49-yard return of an interception off a Syracuse fake punt. The Lions won, 33-21, for their eighth straight win over their old rivals. "Fran Rogel is a bigger psychological factor in the Nittany offense than anyone realized," wrote the *CDT*'s Lyon. "His brief appearance in the game Saturday gave the Lions a tremendous lift..." Riley's *"Football Letter"* summed up the game the following Monday: "Better football has been played in the East this year, but few games have been more enjoyed by the paid customers...Excitement kept up to the very end."

The last three games were away, starting with State's first visit to Morgantown in seven years. Rogel was still not fully recovered from his ankle injury but that was difficult for West Virginia fans to believe after they watched what he did on Mountaineer Field that afternoon. He entered the game midway in the first quarter on State's second possession. The ball was at the 50-yard line. Rogel sandwiched six runs up the gut around a 30-yard Luther pass to sophomore Jack Storer and scored on a one-yard plunge. It was the first TD ever made by a State player in four games at Mountaineer Field. Rogel carried 25 times and was stopped only once, for a one-yard loss, finishing the day with 116 yards and two touchdowns as the Lions beat the Mountaineers, 34-14. "He's dynamite. He's dynamite," an assistant WVC coach, LeRoy Zimmerman kept yelling from his team's spotting booth in the Press

Box. "We can't stop him." Rogel wasn't the whole show. Luther and O'Bara also ran well, getting 68 and 64 yards, respectively, and a TD apiece, as State rushed for a net of 315 yards and passed for 113.

The Lions were now over the .500 mark for the first time this season and needed a win over Temple or Pitt to have their 11th straight winning record. Temple's new coach, Al Kawal, devised a 6-2-2-1 defense designed to stop Rogel. The defense not only failed to stop Rogel, who got 62 yards on 14 carries, but it also was vulnerable to passes and sweeps. Yet, it was a fumble on State's 17-yard line early in the first quarter that may have been the turning point of the game. After recovering the fumble, State drove 84 yards for a touchdown—getting 38 yards on a surprise Statue of Liberty pass play from Luther to Dougherty—with Luther later scoring the TD and Joe Drazenovich booting the PAT. By the end of the half it was 21-0 on another three-yard run by Luther and a spectacular 66-yard pass play from Dougherty to Hicks. Temple tried to get back in the second half but fumbled away another opportunity at State's seven-yard line and the Lions won, 28-7.

Although both teams had 5-3 records, Pitt was favored in the annual showdown at Pitt Stadium. The game may have turned when Rogel re-injured his ankle midway in the second period and was unable to play any more. Pitt had a narrow 6-0 lead at the time but Rogel was shredding the vaunted Panthers line with his line bucks, picking up 50 yards on 12 carries. With starting right tackle Don Murray also out with an injury and Chuck Drazenovich still hurting but playing, the Lions could not cope in the second half with Pitt's star backs, Bimbo Cecconi and Carl DePasqua. The duo had given Pitt its first touchdown when DePasqua ran off tackle for five yards, then lateraled to Cecconi who

ran another 30 yards for the TD. DePasqua's 67-yard pass early in the third quarter set up another Cecconi TD of eight yards and Cecconi put it out of reach in the fourth quarter on a 59-yard TD pass to Jimmy Joe Robinson. Cecconi, Pitt's captain, also intercepted three passes, including two in the final period— and a big one in the end zone when the score was still 13-0 and State was mounting a comeback. The final score was 19-0. "The Lions unquestionably suffered when their hard-to-stop fullback...Fran Rogel left the game...," reported Carl Hughes in the *Pittsburgh Press*. "Penn State missed first downs several times by small margins where Rogel undoubtedly would have made the difference."

For Rogel, the Drazenovich brothers, Norton, Hicks and the others who had reveled in the glory of the undefeated '47 team, this had been a disappointing and frustrating year. Still, they went out with a winning team and no one could ever take that away from them.

Bedenk did not resign until winter was nearly over. He may have had second thoughts as friends tried to make him reconsider his private decision at midseason. When the official announcement was made on March 4, 1950, the *Daily Collegian* began campaigning for "a big-time coach for a big-time college." What State fans got was both a "big-time" coach and a future "legend" but no one knew it at the time.

Season Record 5-4
Record to Date 313-174-35
Winning percentage .633

CHAPTER 10

RIP AND HIS PROTEGE

1950-1965

Charles A. "Rip" Engle had plenty of sensible reasons to reject Penn State's offer to be the new head football coach.

Engle already had turned down the chance to coach at Yale, Wisconsin and Pitt and those jobs seemed to have much more potential for immediate success than the one at Penn State. He also was familiar with the internal politics that had forced the bungled hiring of Joe Bedenk and resentful departure of Earle Edwards. It was not unlike the backstabbing circumstances that had embittered Engle's college coach at Western Maryland, Dick Harlow, when Harlow left State nearly 30 years ago.

That the factionalism continued was obvious by the stipulation from State officials that Engle retain all the current assistant coaches, including Bedenk. This was—and is— highly unusual because new coaches normally get to choose their own staffs. Engle wondered how he would get along with them, especially the three who were former State players, and particularly Bedenk.

And why leave Brown at this juncture? In six years since being promoted from an assistant to the head coach, he had turned the struggling football program around. The team had lost only to Princeton in '49 and was 7-2 the year before. Brown football was on the verge of cracking the "big-time" and he was the man responsible. He was also developing a reputation as an innovator with an offensive formation known as the Wing-T, where the quarterback was under center and one halfback out as a flanker, behind an end. He was just 42 years old and if his success continued as everyone expected, there would be many other coaching opportunities ahead. Besides, he and his family had fallen in love with Providence and the seacoast and it would be a culture shock to take them back into the mountains and farmlands of Central Pennsylvania.

Not that he was unfamiliar with the area or with Penn State. After all, he had grown up about 150 miles southeast in the small Somerset County town of Elk Lick (now known as Salisbury) and had coached high school football for 11 years in Waynesboro, another 150 miles south just across the Pennsylvania-Maryland border from Hagerstown. He had talked about Penn State football many times with his uncle, Lloyd "Dad" Engle, who had played alongside Harlow on the unbeaten 1911 team, and he had spent many hours also kibitzing with Harlow about the Nittany Lions.

Before he made his final decision, Engle talked it over with Harlow. Although still angered by what happened to him, Harlow encouraged Engle to accept the position, even with the requirement to keep the entire staff. Dad Engle said the same thing. It's a great opportunity and a challenge, they both told him. He felt so, too. He also figured he might be able to make State, with all its traditions and recent success, a national football power, again—if everything went right. He would have job security, too, since academic rank and tenure came with the offer.

So, Engle called the athletic director, Dr. Carl P. Schott, and accepted the job, with one caveat. He wanted to bring one of his assistants from Brown to help him. Agreed. But none of his assistants wanted to make the move. So, Engle asked his graduating quarterback, Joseph V. Paterno, if he would postpone law school for a year and help him get through the first season. The 23-year-old Paterno agreed and the rest is history.

Paterno became Engle's closest confidante. As State slowly regained prominence in college football in the 1950s, Paterno received almost as much credit as an assistant as Engle did as the head coach. Engle never left Penn State and Paterno never went to law school.

Still, Engle had "a lot of misgivings" when he took the job. "I had never met these coaches," he later told author Ken Rappoport. "They were all single-wing coaches. The whole staff that was here had been here long before me...and then Joe had never coached, although I knew he had great possibilities. It was a pretty precarious situation, and I just wondered how smart I was, really. But we worked real hard

Charles A. (Rip) Engle had some misgivings in 1950 when he accepted the coaching position at Penn State. Before the decade was over, he had the Nittany Lions on the verge of becoming a football power.

together, and it was the greatest thing that could have happened. I always say I owe so much to these coaches here."

Engle's chemistry and rapport with his assistants had a lot to do with the success that followed. In his 16-year tenure, there were only four changes on the staff. Bedenk left in 1952 and was not replaced until the ex-Michigan star, J.T. White, came aboard in 1954. Dan Radakovich, a fearless linebacker on the late 1950s' squads, was added as linebacker coach in 1960. Joe McMullen, who played for Engle at Brown, succeeded Sever Toretti when Toretti became an assistant athletic director and recruiter in 1963, and George Welsh, now the head coach at Virginia and a star at Navy in the early 1950s, also was added in 1963. The rest—Jim O'Hora, Frank Patrick and Earl Bruce—were still on the staff the day Engle retired.

Even before Engle's hiring, State's Board of Trustees had agreed to stablize the new athletic scholarship program for football. A month before the formal announcement of Engle's hiring, the Trustees established 30 football scholarships (later called grants-in-aid) with full tuition, room and board. Additional tuition aid for out of state applicants was added in May of 1950 and after the 1950 season, the number of full football scholarships was increased to 45. With the new financial wherewithal, Engle was able to attract the type of talent that would not only make his team a consistent winner but would help a football program develop and reach a new plateau—players like Lenny Moore, Rosey Grier, Milt Plum, Richie Lucas, Bob Mitinger and Dave Robinson.

By 1959, Engle's teams were flirting with the Top 10 and getting into bowl games. Ernest McCoy, who joined State as Director of Athletics and Dean of Physical Education in 1953, began upgrading the schedule at about this time. As they played into the early 1960s, Engle's teams were playing and beating teams from the Big Ten, Big Eight, Pac Eight, Southwest and Southeast conferences. But they had still not cracked the upper echelon of college football when Engle decided to retire after the 1965 season. He had become the first Penn State football coach to win 100 games and his record of 104-48-4 is surpassed at State by only one man.

Engle coached six All-Americans and his teams won three post-season bowl games and three Lambert Trophies in the 1960s as the best team in the East. In 1974, Engle was inducted as a coach into the National Football Foundation College Football Hall of Fame and he spent much of his retirement watching his protégé, Joe Paterno, fulfill their dreams of college football glory. When State won its first National Championship on January 1, 1983, the crowning moment belonged to Rip Engle almost as much as it did to Joe Paterno. Unfortunately, Charles A. Engle, ill with Alzheimer's disease, didn't know that when he died two months later, not far from the Beaver Field practice field where it all started.

"Can Anyone Here Pass?"

The four weeks of spring practice were almost over when acting president James Milholland announced on April 22 that Charles A. "Rip" Engle, the coach at Brown University, would become the next head football coach at Penn State.

Earl Bruce and the other assistant coaches wondered what would happen next. Though still based at California State Teachers College where he was overseeing State's freshmen, Bruce had been in charge of the varsity's spring practice on the State College campus. With just nine lettermen returning, there had been considerable work to do. Not knowing who the next coach would be simply compounded the problem. But Bruce, O'Hora, Toretti and Patrick had done their best to train the eager sophomores and juniors, stressing the fundamentals but also re-emphasizing the components of the single-wing. Now, they were getting a boss who utilized the intricate Wing-T formation instead of the single-wing and it was too late to do any indoctrination at spring practice. The preseason sessions were going to be pure hell.

Then came word that Engle would be there on the last day of spring drills for the practice scrimmage against Duquesne. The assistants were surprised by how quiet Engle was. His hair was prematurely white, which made him look older than his 44 years. But he seemed like a nice man. After the practice game, he asked Bruce if he could speak to the team. Sure, Bruce said, after all, it's your team now. The players were a little excited in meeting their new coach for the first time, and Rip gave a little pep talk about the future. At the end, he asked how many of them would come back for two more weeks to learn his Wing-T system. They all agreed enthusiastically and even some of the assistants were surprised. "We had to be taught the new formation first, then we had to teach the players," O'Hara recalled. "It wasn't easy."

And that's how the 1950 season began. Bruce quickly learned Engle's new formation and took it back to California for two weeks of training with the freshmen. Then, after classes were over at California, Bruce brought the frosh up to State College for two more weeks of training. This may have been the longest spring practice in the history of college football but it brought dividends when preseason drills began August 24.

Over the summer, another war had erupted. But this one was called a "police action" and it was in some place called Korea. Unlike the last two wars, this one would cause few disruptions on the Penn State campus, even less on the football field. It was, as everyone would later say, "the Forgotten War."

Certainly, the war was not Engle's problem. His biggest dilemma was to find a quarterback who could run the Wing-T offense. That meant someone who could call the plays, take the snaps from under center, handoff or pitch out to the other backs, run the ball and pass it—and do all this with equal proficiency, if possible. To help him find and develop his quarterback and teach everyone the Wing-T, Engle had hired the quarterback from his '49 Brown team, a Brooklyn kid named Joe Paterno who agreed to coach until he entered law school. Initially, sophomore Joe Gratson, who had been a single-wing blocking "quarterback" was trained by Bruce at California, and installed at quarterback. Gratson soon gave way to the 170-pound senior single-wing tailback, Vince O'Bara of Johnstown, despite Paterno's misgivings. When first asked by Engle to assess O'Bara, Paterno replied (according to *Football My Way*): "I'll tell you one thing, Vince O'Bara will never be a starting quarterback."

Finding a quarterback was just the beginning for Engle as he reconstructed the State team. All but two of the starters from '49 had graduated and only seven other lettermen had returned. Engle also was trying to figure out how to take advantage of the liberalized substitution rules which now enabled some schools to put separate teams on the field for offense and defense. Engle was not an advocate of this so-called "two-platoon" system because he believed it would lead to a disparity in college football between what he termed the "haves" and the "have nots." But he also realized he could not match the caliber of State's opposition with a traditional single "all-purpose" eleven. Further, he was realistic in recognizing that two-platoon football was the trend. So, he attempted to put together separate offensive and defensive units but many players still played both ways.

Engle's basic starting lineup in his 41-man traveling squad consisted of seven letterman, six of whom were seniors. Dougherty, now the captain, was at right half and pint-sized Tony Orsini at left half. Junior non-letterman Jim Pollard or sophomore Paul Anders was the fullback. The right side of the line was made up of veterans with Smidansky at end, Chuck Godlasky at tackle, junior Jim Barr at guard and Ken Bunn at center. On the left side it was all non-letter juniors with Art Betts at end, Hoover at tackle and Len Bartek at guard. Other players were substituted on defense, including former QB Gratson, who became one of the best linebackers, and another sophomore, Don Barney, at middle guard. Since he had started almost from scratch, Engle drilled the team intensely during the preseason and that included "practice games" with one-time opponents Duquesne, Bucknell, Colgate and Cornell.

No doubt all that practice helped get Engle and the team off to an impressive start against a Georgetown team that was dropping football after the season. But the 16,617 in the opening day crowd at Beaver Field must have thought they were seeing one of the worst coaching and quarterback debuts in history when Georgetown intercepted an O'Bara pass on the first play from scrimmage and scored after a 27-yard drive. However, the rest of the game belonged to State as the Lions won, 34-14 with five different players scoring TDs. "Only the restraining factor that the mighty Cadets are coming up, followed by Syracuse and Nebraska (all to be played on foreign fields) throws a shadow on the future of our relatively unseasoned gridiron forces, struggling to master an intricate system of modern football," wrote Riley in his "*Football Letter.*"

Riley's prudence was warranted. The next week at West Point, Army clobbered State 41-7 in what Riley termed "a rather cruel physical hammering...that took courage against the kind of vicious football the West Pointers are apparently taught." Army rolled up 345 yards rushing and 159 passing behind the running of Al Pollard, receiving of All-American Dan Foldberg and quarterbacking of Bob Blaik, the coach's son. The Cadets also had 148 yards in penalties, including six 15-yarders for "illegal use of the hands." O'Bara's passing was horrendous as State completed just four-of-17 passes for 34 yards with four interceptions. Still, some saw hope in the team's overall performance. "Penn State...had the look of a team which, with a less difficult assignment, might do very well for itself," wrote Al Laney in the *New York Herald-Tribune.* "It played intelligently and hard and was well drilled in the fundamentals of the game and in its own offense, but was hopelessly outclassed today." (Army would finish rated number two in the country by the AP but after the last poll would lose in what the *Pittsburgh Press* called "the upset of the year" to unranked Navy, 14-2),

Syracuse was not in Army's class either and had lost two of its first three games. Furthermore, the Orange had not beaten State in 11 years. But Syracuse Coach Ben Schwartzwalder had devised the consummate game plan when the teams met in a night game at

Archbold Stadium the following Saturday. Schwartzwalder figured Engle would concentrate on stopping Syracuse's fine passer, Bernie Custis, so he countered State's 5-3-3 defense with a power running attack. He also set up his own defense to stop State's running and force State's erratic quarterbacks to pass. His plan worked to near perfection as two Syracuse backs, Bill Haskins and Bob Young, rushed for a total of 225 yards and the Orange defense turned four pass interceptions into touchdowns for a 27-7 victory. Of course, some goofball fans blamed the defeat on the weather for this was the first time in five night games that State had lost and the victories had all been played in the rain. Actually, the Lions were keeping the game close, trailing by just 7-0, until a disastrous five minute stretch midway through the third quarter killed them. With about 7:45 left in the period, Syracuse sophomore Avatus Stone picked off an O'Bara's pass at the Orange 49 and on the first play Haskins ran around left end for a touchdown. After an exchange of possessions, State moved to the Syracuse 25-yard line when it happened again. This time Stone intercepted a pass by backup quarterback Dick Koerber and ran 85 yards for a TD. The PAT made it 20-0. Moments later, another Syracuse soph, Pete Lessard, intercepted an attempted pitchout by O'Bara at the State 36 and went in for the TD and it was all over.

More frustration followed the next week against Nebraska in Lincoln. On the eve of the game, the players were reminded of their crushing loss at West Point when they went to a movie and saw excerpts from the game on a newsreel. The next day, State's passing was abominable again and Nebraska's running attack behind sophomore halfback Bobby Reynolds was outstanding. The Cornhuskers grabbed a 6-0 lead on Reynolds' 19-yard touchdown early in the first quarter and held on to the lead tenuously into the fourth quarter as they stopped three State drives inside the 10-yard line. With 12 minutes left in the game, Reynolds went 26 yards for his second TD, capping a drive from midfield, and he got his third a short time later on a 43-yard dash. The future All-American would finish with 183 yards on 24 carries as Nebraska (which would be rated 17th in the country at seasons' end) rushed for a total of 375 yards in winning 19-0. "If Penn State's football team never meets a sophomore streak of lightning named Bobby Reynolds again it will be more than satisfied," wrote Ed Watson, sports editor of the *Centre Daily Times.* O'Bara and Koerber missed wide open receivers all afternoon, completing just five-of-21 passes with three interceptions, and even Engle was now wondering if his two quarterbacks would ever learn to throw the ball effectively.

Temple's passing was worse than State's but the Owls had beaten Syracuse, 7-6, and the Homecoming (and first Band Day) crowd of 20,782 didn't know what to expect when the team returned to Beaver Field for the first time in a month. The Lions scored in the first quarter on a 63-yard drive with Orsini getting the TD on a seven-yard run and O'Bara booting the extra point. Temple tied it at 7-7 just before the half after recovering an O'Bara fumble and going 60 yards for the TD. And that's how it ended as the Lions offense sputtered, fumbling away two more scoring opportunities and losing another on an interception. O'Bara completed four-of-14 passes, all in the first half, and had two interceptions. With a record of 1-3-1, State fans began looking ahead to 1951. The first losing season in 12 years seemed inevitable.

The Lions were on the road again the following Saturday, playing Boston College on the home field of the Boston Braves baseball team. A heavy rain fell all morning and by the time of the kickoff, the field was slippery and the infield was turning to mud. State found itself in deep trouble at the start when a clipping penalty moments after the kickoff backed the Lions to their own six-yard line. What happened in the game from that point on defined the season and turned the team from a loser into a winner. In three quick running plays, the Lions were up to their 28-yard line with a second-and-two. O'Bara faded back to pass, spotted Smidansky dashing down the right sideline and hit him in perfect stride at the BC 30, and the senior end raced untouched into the end zone. It was the best pass O'Bara had ever thrown. O'Bara's kick was wide but no one on State's side seemed too disturbed, even after the Eagles came back on the ensuing kickoff to take a 7-6 lead on a 75-yard drive. Twice in the second quarter, the Lions drove deep into BC territory but failed to score, once missing on an O'Bara field goal attempt from the 15. On State's first possession of the second half, the Lions drove 59 yards on 12 straight running plays to take the lead on Anders' 13-yard run, then recovered a BC fumble at the 18-yard line and Anders scored again on a three-yard bolt up the middle. Late in the fourth quarter, BC almost got a break on a nearly botched State punt. O'Bara was back to punt when the ball sailed over his head to the State 25-yard line, but he beat two BC players to the ball, picked it up and punted it all the way to the BC 20. Boston College scored late in the game to make it look close as State won, 20-13. O'Bara's final passing statistics were still bad— two-for-nine and one interception—but he had crossed the threshold with his 72-yard bomb and even Engle knew it.

O'Bara's passing continued to improve against West Virginia at Beaver Field. He connected on six-of-11 attempts for 95 yards to help State maintain ball control as the Lions recorded their first shutout in 17 games. "Defense Shines in 27-0 Tilt," said the headline in the *Centre Daily Times*. State scored once through the air but O'Bara wasn't the passer, Dougherty was. The Lions' captain threw one of his typical left handed reverse passes to Smidansky for a 20-yard touchdown in the second quarter. Otherwise, the Lions used their running attack to smother the Mountaineers, with sophomore Ted Shattuck getting two touchdowns and Orsini one as the Lions piled up 246 yards. "With Vince O'Bara gaining more poise in every contest," wrote Riley in the *"Football Letter,"* "our offense has shown definite signs of coming to life. There have been many times this year when Vince...might have been excused for adopting a defeatist attitude. He never did and his courage and developed skill have been an inspiration to all the squad."

That O'Bara and this team had character was never more apparent than in the final home game against Rutgers. The Lions got behind early when Rutgers drove 79 yards in the first quarter to take a 7-0 lead and State was still trailing by 14-12 after three quarters. O'Bara's 24-yard pass to Dougherty had given State its first TD midway in the second quarter and after Rutgers scored again near the end of the half, a 78-yard drive by State on the second half kickoff had narrowed the visitor's lead to two points. O'Bara had missed both extra point kicks but no one was blaming him. Referee John Coles had denied O'Bara use of the special kicking tee he had been utilizing all season and that had forced O'Bara to alter his kicking style. State took command in the fourth quarter and scored the winning touchdown on a drive from midfield following a punt. Orisini got the TD on a 10-yard pitchout from O'Bara and moments later State clinched the 18-14 win on a pass interception by senior George Jacob at the Lions 20-yard line. The State players mobbed Engle and O'Bara. The State quarterback had called a great game and, for the first time, had not thrown one interception while hitting on nine-of-18 passes for 160 yards.

Once again, a winning season came down to the traditional final game against Pittsburgh. Pitt was just 1-7 under new coach Len Casanova but State fans were always wary of the Pitt jinx. This would turn out to be one of the most memorable games in the long series between the two schools and not just because of the excitement on the field. Snow began falling before the team left by bus for Pittsburgh early Friday afternoon and by the time the players reached their hotel the snow was several inches deep and still coming down. Soon, the city was paralyzed, and as the snow continued Saturday morning, the State team and many of their fans were virtually marooned in hotels. "The city itself was deserted except for the hotels," wrote Watson of the *CDT*. "...There wasn't a car to be seen on the main drag and there weren't many more people." The game was postponed until Monday, and at one point Saturday night, Engle went outside, tumbled into a snow drift and lost his wallet. But as the snow continued, the game was postponed again. It wasn't until Monday, after a record 23 inches of snow had fallen, that the team could leave the hotel. They were picked up by Army trucks and taken to the train station for the trip back to State College, via Tyrone. Pitt Stadium was buried by the snow and there was talk of canceling the game entirely. But, with the cooperation of the Pirates baseball team and the Steelers, the game was switched to Forbes Field and set for the following Saturday. The Steelers were scheduled to play the Redskins on Sunday so it was agreed to remove the snow from the field in time for State and Pitt to meet the day before. But the upper deck of Forbes Field was not cleared and mounds of snow were piled all along the surface of the gridiron layout. A crowd estimated at 7,000—but cited officially in the record at 12,250—often could not see the playing surface because of snow drifts. The field, itself, was best described as "a morass" and the cleats of the players' shoe sank easily into the soft turf.

Bill Leonard, a sophomore walk-on from State College High School who was playing on the special defensive platoon, got the Lions off to a hot start by intercepting a pass into the flat by Pitt QB Bob Bestwick and running 65-yards in the slush and mud for a touchdown. O'Bara, using his special kicking tee again, made it 7-0. A few minutes later, a 35-yard punt return by Jacobs gave the Lions the ball at the Panthers 30 and they scored quickly behind the running of Orsini and Anders with Anders getting the TD on a five-yard run. O'Bara's PAT put State ahead, 14-0, at the end of the first quarter. Late in the second quarter, Chuck Wilson recovered a Pitt fumble at the Panther 21 and three plays later, Anders dashed up the middle 13 yards for another TD. O'Bara kicked the PAT and the small State crowd went into a frenzy. They could not believe this. It was too good to be true. And it was. With less than a minute to play in the half, a State sophomore lineman was called for unnecessary roughness, giving Pitt the ball at the State 24-yard line and Bestwick hit Chis Warriner for a touchdown pass. Tackle Nick Bolkovac, who had not missed an extra point all season, came in. He needed three attempts before he was successful. First, the snap was bad and the ball rolled up field but State was offside. Then Bolkovac's kick was wide but again a State player was offside. His third attempt was good and the half ended at 21-7. Was the jinx about to return?

A 93-yard, 23-play drive by Pitt ate up more than 10 minutes in the third quarter and Bolkovac's 13th straight extra point narrowed State's lead to 21-14, and State fans began to worry. The momentum was shifting. Early in the fourth quarter, it shifted further when Pitt's Bill Reynolds ran back O'Bara's punt 49 yards to the State 14-yard line. Now it was Pitt's fans who were screaming. After a penalty and another play, Bestwick passed 14-yards to Nick DeRosa who leaped high in the air to grab the ball in the end zone. On came Bolkovac to tie the game. Fans on both sides remembered how Bolkovac had personally ruined State's 1949 season with his quirky pass interception in State's only loss that year. Here he was again. Boom! The kick was good and the Pitt players began celebrating. But wait. Penalty—12 men on the field. Bolkovac had to do it again. This time the kick was slightly to the right of the goal post, and the State fans cheered loudly. Ten minutes were left to play but, as the *Pittsburgh Press* headline said the next day, "Penn State Staves Off Pitt Rally." The Lions reached the Pitt 18 before losing the ball on downs and in the last five minutes they intercepted two of Bestwick's passes with the second one by Leonard taking State to Pitt's 16-yard line as the clock wound down. State held on and won, 21-20, in what would become known in history as "The Snowbowl."

"The Ripper was carted off the field by a group of happy, mud-covered footballers," wrote the *CDT*'s Watson. "He was smiling as they reached the dressing rooms...The Lion locker room was a scene of joy and happiness...O'Bara could have gotten rich if he had charged a dollar for each kiss he was given."

The Engle era was now underway. He and his young assistant, Paterno, had transformed O'Bara from an ordinary running back into a capable quarterback. Where they would find their next quarterback was a matter of conjecture that winter. Let's get one who can pass, the fans were saying, and not throw interceptions! Sure, and make him the best passer in the East, if not all of America. Are you all dreaming?

Season Record 5-3-1
Record to Date 318-177-36
Winning percentage .633

"Coming From Behind"

The opening game of the season with Boston University was hours away and Engle still had not decided upon his starting quarterback. He had two choices, and both kids were sophomores. Tony Rados, the transfer from Notre Dame who sat out last year, appeared to have the most potential but he had missed more practice during the week because of a recurring injury. Bob Szajna, up from the freshman team, had been looking better in recent days, and there was not much separating them at this point, except for Szajna's unpronounceable last name (SHINE'-A).

Rados and Szajna had been battling since spring practice and after four weeks of preseason drills, they were about even. Rados was a smoother ball-handler and a better passer. Szajna's mechanics were good but until the past couple of weeks he had been having some trouble finding his receivers. He was coming on fast and had looked good in a scrimmage against Cornell. Engle and his quarterback coach, Paterno, had been encouraged by Szajna's development because the kid from Reading had played only one year of football in high school. He was a baseball player with major league potential, yet in his senior year he had led Reading's T-formation offense to a share of the state football championship with Rados' Steelton team. Engle and Paterno were pleased with the play-calling of both and that had been a pleasant

surprise since neither had ever played a varsity game. Engle had hoped that one of his incoming scholarship players could help out but Rados and Szajna were much further advanced.

Freshmen were eligible to play this year. One of the freshmen quarterbacks, Don Bailey, looked like he would make a great kick-off man but he still needed polish at the quarterback . Engle was very high on the other freshmen. "They have a good attitude," he told *The Daily Collegian* in mid September. "Some of the boys are going to be a big help to us in a couple of years." It didn't take a couple of years. Before the '51 season was over, four frosh were starting on the defensive line—Roosevelt Grier, Jesse Arnelle, Jim Garrity and Don Shank—and one, Buddy Rowell, at left halfback, and they would soon become household names to Nittany Lions fans.

Engle needed the freshmen because he had reluctantly decided to follow the college football trend and field separate teams on offense and defense. Some players would go both ways on occasion and at least one, wingback Bob Pollard, would start on both offense and defense and usually play 60 minutes. But Engle still opposed two-platoon football and was pleased that State's athletic department had asked the Eastern College Athletic Conference to re-examine the platoon system. Dean Schott also was pushing a plan to eliminate spring practice but Engle wasn't sure he fully agreed with that one. Make it shorter, maybe, but don't end it.

He needed spring practice this year just as he did last year. The five weeks of drills and practice scrimmages, especially the one against Navy, helped everyone, not just the 20 lettermen who were returning but also the reserves and kids up from the freshmen team. That was when he experimented with two platoons and realized he would need some freshmen who could play quickly in the fall. Engle believed there were some good athletes on this team but they were young. The co-captains, Art at offensive end and Len Shephard at linebacker, were among the handful of seniors. That also included Ed Hoover, whom some preseason magazines called one of the outstanding offensive tackles in the East.

After last season's surprising finish, State fans were enthused about the prospects. But Engle felt the schedule, which included first time opponents Boston University and Purdue and nationally-ranked Michigan State and Nebraska, was more difficult this year. "I honestly believe that this is the toughest schedule a Penn State team has ever faced," he told the *Collegian*. "All the teams that remain on the schedule have improved and all the new opponents are stronger than the ones we have dropped." Coaches are known to build up their opponents but this time sportswriters agreed. "...The experts say that Penn State will be lucky to win half of its games," wrote *Collegian* sports editor Ernie Moore. "And it might well turn out that way. It seems that practically all of the opponents have hit a peak year."

One such team was Boston University, which had 45 lettermen returning. Many sportswriters believed Buff Donelli's team could be one of the best in the country once quarterback Harry Agganis was discharged by the Marines. Agganis, a legitimate Heisman candidate, had been called up by the Marines because of the Korean War. He was discharged on a "dependency release" three days before BU's opener against William & Mary, and despite knowing only a few plays, he had almost salvaged a 34-25 defeat by passing for two touchdowns and running for another. Engle could only wonder what a quarterback like Agganis would do for his team. "He could play in the pro league next week," Engle told reporters.

Agganis, whom sportswriters had nicknamed "The Golden Greek," more than lived up to his billing in the season opener at Beaver Field on September 29. He played practically the entire game, including safety on defense, as he completed 10-of-14 passes for 219 yards and two TDs, kicked three extra points and passed for another and averaged 47 yards on three punts. But Agganis wasn't perfect. Twice on defense he was called for interference in situations that helped State score touchdowns, and the only pass interception he threw almost led to another State TD in the closing minutes of the game when the outcome was still in doubt. "I thought I had seen everything when I played against Nebraska's Bobby Reynolds last year," halfback-placekicker Bill Leonard told Ed Watson of the *Centre Daily Times*, "but this Agganis is better yet. He can do everything."

Despite the outstanding performance by Agganis, what the State players did against BU defined the entire '51 season and set the tempo for the other eight games. It started from the opening kickoff when the Lions took the ball at their 20-yard line with Szajna as Engle's choice at quarterback. Szajna didn't pass once as he led the team in 15 plays to the BU 7-yard line before losing the ball on a fumble. That's all Agganis needed and by the end of the first quarter, he had led BU on two long drives for a 14-0 lead. Both teams bogged down during the second quarter but with about 30 seconds left, BU fumbled at its own 40. Szajna threw a perfect pass to sophomore right end Joe Yukica, who leaped between Agganis and another defender to take the ball and step out of bounds at the BU four. Sophomore fullback Pete Shopa banged over for the TD and the veteran Leonard booted the extra point to make it 14-7 at the half.

Five minutes into the second half the game turned into a shootout and for 17 minutes of the third and fourth quarters the teams scored 55 points and the lead changed hands five times. BU's John Kastan—a Pennsylvanian who would score four TDs, gain 99 yards rushing and catch six passes for 155 yards—extended BU's lead to 21-7 with an eight-yard TD on the Terrier's second possession of the third quarter. However, State struck back quickly on a 10-play, 71-yard drive, with Szajna's passing and an interference called on Agganis, getting the ball to the five-yard line from where Shattuck scored. Leonard's PAT made it 21-14. BU fumbled the kickoff and Leonard recovered at the Terriers' 25. Three plays later, Shattuck went up the middle from the 20 for his second TD. This time Leonard's kick attempt was blocked because the Lions only had 10 men on the field and BU still led 21-20. The Lions got the ball back when Pollard's punt return put them at the BU 41 and four plays later first team fullback Paul Anders scored to give State the lead for the first time. Leonard's PAT made it 27-21. Back came Agganis and the Terriers. On the first play following the kickoff, Agganis found Kastan wide open and the 64-yard pass play plus Agganis' PAT put BU ahead again, 28-27. But not for long.

Agganis' second interference call gave the Lions the ball at the BU 41 and three plays later Shattuck rambled 32 yards for his third TD. Leonard missed the PAT but State was back in the lead, 33-28 two minutes into the fourth quarter. Back came Agganis again, leading an 85-yard drive with Kastan getting the last 27 yards on a run over right tackle. Reserve end Charlie Wilson blocked Agganis' kick and BU had the lead at 34-33, but Szajna and the young Lions were determined. They fought back after the kickoff and with Anders running 42 yards to set up the go ahead TD, the Lions went in front, 40-34, on Shopa's three-yard plunge and Leonard's kick. Agganis tried desperately to bring the Terriers back in the last seven minutes. Pollard stopped him once

with an interception and the Lions ate up the clock with a rushing game that drove deep into BU territory. Less than a minute was left when BU stopped State at the BU 16-yard line. Agganis completed two passes to Kastan and end Bob Capuano to reach the State 43. With time for one more play, BU tried to fool State's defense as Agganis pitched out to a freshman in for his only play of the game, Joe Terrasi. Terrasi ran to his right, stopped and flung a wobbly pass towards Capuano down the sideline. The ball hit Capuano at about the same time as two State defenders, bounced in the air and Capuano caught it on his knees at the nine-yard line—and the game was over. The 40-34 final was the highest score produced by two teams on Beaver Field since State's record 109-7 thrashing of Lebanon Valley in 1920. "They did everything but blow the top off Nittany Mountain this afternoon," wrote Ernie Roberts in the *Boston Globe*, "and some of the folks staggering out of Beaver Field thought that too might have happened in the confusion."

In the jubilant State dressing room, the school's new president, Milton Eisenhower told the players: "Congratulations, boys. It was the greatest game I've ever seen." Certainly, the 15,536 fans must have agreed. In the final statistics, BU had gained 269 yards through the air and 186 on the ground. State had 346 yards on the ground and for the first time since 1938, two players had rushed over 100 yards in a single game—Shattuck for 160 and Anders for 123. But the most valuable player for State was Szajna, who completed five-of-12 passes for 81 yards without an interception, and showed he could fake, hand off, call plays and keep his cool. Boston University would go on to win more games than the Lions that year and be ranked 16th in the country by the AP. But State, with Szajna at the QB controls much of the time, would play every opponent close and keep its poise under pressure, coming from behind in almost every game and winning a few along the way.

The next week against Villanova, State overcame a 6-0 first quarter deficit to take a 7-6 halftime edge but lost, 20-14, when a wide-open receiver dropped a long pass from Rados in the waning minutes. Villanova set up all three TDs off mistakes the Lions made on punts, recovering two bad snaps from center and partially blocking a kick. The contest was played in Allentown at the behest of State's Lehigh Valley alumni and among the spectators was a hotshot high school running back from Reading whom State was recruiting. His name was Lenny Moore. The game itself was marked by numerous "personal foul" penalties against Villanova and a near riot in front of the Villanova bench after Pollard was tackled and kneed by two Wildcat players late in the third quarter. The Wildcats lost 138 yards on penalties, causing Ridge Riley to note in his "*Football Letter*" that "It took self control and high moral courage to keep Saturday's game from developing into a bedlam of flying fists...State's players demonstrated qualities of character we like to think football teaches." Unfortunately, one of Villanova's questionable hits knocked Szajna out of the game. The injury caused Engle to start Rados the next week at Nebraska.

The Lions finally scored first in their game against the Cornhuskers, who were playing without their injured star halfback, Bobby Reynolds. With the wind swirling at 35 miles an hour, 39,000 watched as a poor punt by the Cornhuskers gave State the ball at the Nebraska 19-yard line early in the second quarter. On the first play, Szajna, recovered from his injury, passed to Betts in the open at the goal and State had a 6-0 halftime lead. After Nebraska went in front 7-6 in the third quarter, State drove 66 yards before Shattuck fumbled on the goal line and Nebraska recovered. State was right back minutes later, moving 81 yards to take a 9-7 lead on Leonard's 15-yard field goal. In the fourth period, State's Carl Pfirman blocked a Nebraska field goal attempt from the 20-yard line and State finally put the game out of reach with three minutes left when sophomore end Don Malinak forced a fumble at the Cornhusker three-yard line and Shopa got the TD for a 15-7 win. "Nebraskans take their football serious but they are very nice people," wrote Riley, "...nearly everybody on the Cornhusker side appeared to take the defeat with fine grace. Players from the two teams seem to fraternize nicely."

The largest Beaver Field crowd since the Michigan State game in 1948 turned out for another Homecoming clash against Michigan State's unbeaten powerhouse team of 1951. Among the 30,321 in attendance and honored that day were lettermen from the Lions teams of 1887 to 1901 and the 1926 team holding its 25-year reunion. The Spartans were now in the Big Ten but were still playing an independent football schedule until they could be integrated into the rest of the league. Biggie Munn had loaded his team with kids from Western Pennsylvania, including quarterback Tommy Yewcic of Conemaugh Township and were riding a 10-game winning streak. Michigan State jumped off to a 13-0 first quarter lead but the Lions narrowed it to 13-7 at the half behind the passing of Rados. Two minutes into the second half, Pollard took Yewcic's punt on the Lions 35-yard line and ran it back for a touchdown on a twisting and turning run that put the home team ahead, 14-13. But seven minutes later, the Spartans scored on their own 57-yard punt return to recapture the lead, 19-14, and made it 26-14 a few seconds before the end of the quarter on a 41-yard pass from Don McAuliffe to Al Dorow. That seemed to bolster Michigan State and the next time it gained possession, freshman Leroy Bolden ran 66 yards to seal what eventually was a 32-21 victory. "I think we're two years away from playing in the same league with Michigan State," Engle told sportswriters. It would be longer than that. Michigan State remained unbeaten and at 9-0 was rated number two by both the AP and UP. The next year, the Spartans would win their first National Championship.

After playing even with one of the best teams in the country for three quarters, the Lions had difficulty getting up for a West Virginia squad that had beaten Furman, Waynesburg and Geneva. And it almost cost them. On State's first running play after the opening kickoff, Shattuck fumbled a pitchout and the Mountaineers recovered at the State 47-yard line. They scored in nine plays, shocking the Band Day crowd. West Virginia's defense kept State bottled up until senior defensive guard Joe Shumock intercepted a pass and ran it back 15-yards to the Mountaineer 46. Six plays later Shattuck dove two yards for the TD but Leonard missed the PAT and the Mountaineers still led, 7-6. The teams traded possession in the third quarter with West Virginia fumbling away a scoring opportunity at the State 30 and the Lions having a 60-yard runback of a fumble by Malinak nullified by a quick whistle. With less than 10 minutes to play, State got a break when a Mountaineer player inadvertently touched a low punt, giving State the ball at the WVU 44. Rados, who started again, hit Yukica for 14 yards and Shattuck carried five straight plays, plunging for the TD from the one. Leonard's PAT made it 13-7 and the defense stymied West Virginia for the rest of the game. But the fans were not pleased and Engle heard about it all week. "We're going to have enough defeats to alibi without having to alibi victories," Engle snorted.

There were no alibis the next week when Purdue shut out the Lions 28-0 in a near snow blizzard at Purdue's Ross-Ade Stadium.

Some 400 State fans were among the 21,000 who sat in 20 degree temperatures and 30-mile winds and watched Purdue dominate the entire 60 minutes. Despite a 1-4 record, the Boilermakers were favored by 10 points and they had 21 by the half behind the leadership and passing of their crack junior quarterback, Dale Samuels. Rados was again the starter but neither he nor Szajna nor the rest of the team could muster up any sustained offensive. Still, the Lions played as if they could come from behind and win, and their determination was noted by Gordon Graham of the *Lafayette Journal and Courier* who wrote prophetically: "What a dreary outlook Penn State had as it returned to the field in a near blizzard to start the second half...they didn't have one chance in a 100...(yet) the Lions battled even harder and more effectively in the last half than they did in the first...we must remember that when we invade Penn State next year."

With a 3-3 record, the Lions needed to beat or tie a couple of their Eastern rivals to avoid their first losing season in 13 years. Szajna was back as the starting QB when the Lions closed out the home season against Syracuse on Nov. 10 and Engle shook-up the defensive platoon by starting four freshmen. For only the second game State scored first, going 91 yards in 10 plays on their second possession with Pollard getting the TD on a 13-yard run. But Syracuse tied it up with five minutes left in the half, following the interception of a Szajna pass. State took the lead back, 13-7, just before the intermission on the running of Shattuck, and then blew the game wide open in the second half, building up a 32-7 lead on the rushing of Anders, who ran for 87 yards and scored two TDs. "Lions Play 'Best Game' To Win Fourth," said the headline in the *Collegian* of the 32-13 victory.

State was a 14-point favorite the next week at Rutgers but had to rally from a 7-6 deficit in the second half for a 13-7 victory to clinch a winning season. The Lions lost the ball five times on fumbles and needed a near-record performance by Pollard to pull out the victory. Pollard ran for 243 yards, seven shy of Shorty Miller's 1912 record and scored both TDs on runs of 75 and 71 yards, with the 71-yarder midway in the third period putting State ahead to stay. For the second time in the season, two players ran for more than 100 yards with Anders getting 122 on 22 carries.

Pitt had lost seven of eight games, including a 53-26 defeat to Michigan State, but was favored because of its supposedly tougher schedule. Despite its record, some sportswriters said this was the Panthers' best team since the Jock Sutherland era of the 1930s. The game was scoreless until 30 seconds were left in the half, when Pitt freshman Henry Ford ran back a punt 30 yards to State's 32-yard line and Bestwick immediately hit Warriner on a TD pass for a 7-0 halftime lead. Of course, being behind had not bothered the Lions all year and they tied it up early in the fourth quarter on a 78-yard drive. Arnelle, playing on offense for one of the few occasions, caught four straight passes, starting with a 31-yard toss from Rados, who was hurt on the play. Szajna came in and passed three straight to Arnelle and the last one went nine-yards for the TD. Leonard's boot made it 7-7.

Pitt took the kick off and drove 71 yards to go ahead again, 13-7, on Paul Chess's 13-yard run. But the comeback team was not done. Pollard ran back the kickoff to the 34 and State quickly picked up a first down at its own 45. Szajna passed to Malinak for another first down at the Pitt 37 as the clock ticked down to two minutes. But on the next play, Pitt picked off its only interception of the day, coming down with Szajna's toss at the 28 and the team that came back all season could not do it one last time. Bestwick ran out the clock with three quarterback sneaks for the 13-7 victory. Sportswriters credited the win to the Panther line, led by a 203-pound junior guard named Joe Schmidt.

Arnelle also came in for accolades. "...After his performance against the Panthers, it looks like he will be a double duty man (on offense and defense) next year, wrote the *Collegian*'s Ernie Moore. "He and Bobby Szajna could team up as a nice passing combination." Moore was right about Arnelle but he had the wrong quarterback.

Season Record 5-4
Record to Date 323-181-36
Winning percentage .631

"Tony's Surprise"

Most of the 20,506 fans at Beaver Field for the game against Purdue on September 27 anticipated the appearance of the Boilermaker's passing wizard Dale Samuels. Sure, most of the crowd was rooting for the home team to stymie the All-American quarterback and pull off an upset. However, State's pass defense had almost lost the season opener against Temple the previous week and Samuels was the best passer in the country. In his sophomore and junior seasons he had averaged a touchdown on every nine pass completions, hitting on 155-of-331 attempts for 2,023 yards and 17 touchdowns. Engle had a couple of quarterbacks who were still having problems throwing the ball even in practice.

Engle and his quarterback coach, Paterno, were still not completely satisfied with Szajna and Rados. Szajna was fairly accurate with his short passes but he still threw a wobbly ball on the long ones. Rados sometimes showed flashes of brilliance but he had been inconsistent and was still plagued by a knee injury that had hampered him since spring practice. Bailey, the sophomore, was still developing as a quarterback but he had turned into a first-rate defensive back and was now a starter on the defensive platoon.

Rados had spent most of the preseason trying to recuperate from his injury. Szajna, steady as a play-caller and ball handler, was the logical starter for the opening game against Temple at Beaver Field but Rados, weak knee and all, had come off the bench to lead the Lions to a 20-13 come-from-behind victory. Rados completed just three of nine passes, but one was for State's first touchdown and the others set up the game-winning TD in the fourth quarter. "One of the most surprising elements of the Temple game was Rados' appearance in the lineup at all," wrote Jake Highton, sports editor of *The Daily Collegian*. "Even those closest to the team thought Coach Rip Engle was crazy when he shouted 'Rados' during the first period...(for) Rados had one contact scrimmage [before] the game." As the team prepared for Purdue, Highton and other sportswriters wondered who would start at quarterback.

Rados had not been the only surprise in the season opener. Scatback Dick Jones, a 5-foot-9, 165-pound junior playing at left half in place of the injured sophomore Buddy Rowell, had led all rushers with 56 yards on 16 carries and had scored the first TD on a 32-yard pass from Rados. Jones, who had been in Engle's doghouse as a sopho-

more because of his tendency to fumble, had been thrust into the limelight because of the loss of two of the Lions' leading runners of '51. Shattuck and Anders had dropped out of school over the winter and Engle had moved Pollard from left halfback to Anders' old fullback position, inserting Rowell and Jones as Pollard's replacement. As for the rest of the backfield, Leonard, still the prime placekicker, and sophomore Don Eyer, the punter, were the prime wingbacks but they also would be playing on the defensive platoon. Juniors Shopa and Matt Yanosich backed up Pollard at fullback while sophs Keith Vesling and Ron Younker also would see action at halfback.

Although he had 20 lettermen returning, including the three outstanding sophomores—Arnelle, Grier and Shank—and his co-captains, Gratson and Scheetz, Engle was concerned about his depth. He would field an offensive and defensive platoon but many players would have to go both ways. As Engle explained to the sportswriters the first team offensive line is the second and third team defense and the first team defensive line is the second and third team offensive line. That meant the fans would need to constantly refer to their programs to keep up to all the changes as Malinak, Garrity, Sherry, Yukica, Barney, Jim Dooley, Don Balthaser and others made their appearances. Engle regretted that he could no longer use freshmen. With the end of the Korean War, the Eastern Collegiate Athletic Conference had again banned freshmen. That meant frosh coach Earl Bruce, not Engle, would get to use that big running back they recruited from Reading. Engle also had the first change on his coaching staff as line coach Joe Bedenk resigned as an assistant to concentrate on baseball. He was not replaced.

Engle wasn't sure he had the manpower to get through the demanding schedule. For the first time since 1931, 10 games had been scheduled, and that included the preseason favorite for number one, Michigan State. Although he continued worrying about his manpower, Engle was pleased with the conditioning and spirit of his team. The "wonderful morale" and "good esprit de corps" he had talked

Roosevelt Grier, an outstanding interior lineman of the early 50s who became nationally known later in life, was a four-year starter who helped to turn the program around after the 20-year period of de-emphasis.

about in spring practice had carried over through the fall's preseason drills. They had looked a little shaky against Temple. But, as he told Riley the morning after that victory, "It's a young squad and our boys made the mistakes we thought they would—with a few extra—but they won the game by scoring twice in the last ten minutes. That took the kind of stuff we like."

The biggest mistakes had been on pass defense and the Owls had scored both of its TDs on passes in the third quarter. So, as the crowd drifted into sunny Beaver Field for the two o'clock kickoff against Purdue, they wondered what Engle had done in practice that week to shore up this glaring weakness. Perhaps, some said, it would be just like Rocky Marciano beating Jersey Joe Walcott for the heavyweight championship two days earlier—the young upstart Lions winning over the veteran, old pro Boilermakers.

Purdue, a front-runner in the Big Ten title chase since Michigan State was still playing its last independent schedule, was a one-to-three touchdown favorite but there was an omen that some sportswriters believed could benefit Penn State. This was the Boilermakers first game of the season and they had not won an opener since Stu Holcomb had become head coach five years before. Engle had decided to start Rados but Rados did little but hand off in the first quarter. Purdue got the opening kickoff, and as a nationwide audience listened over the Mutual radio network's "Game of the Week," the Boilermakers drove quickly downfield until fumbling away the ball at the Lions' 33-yard line. In came Rados. On the first play Rados handed off to Jones, who was trapped running to one side, reversed his field and reached Purdue's 47-yard line before being tackled—and fumbling. Out came Rados. The teams exchanged possession again before Purdue took the ball at midfield near the end of the first quarter and scored on a 14-yard pass from Samuels to Bernie Flowers to take a 7-0 lead.

Purdue's kickoff put the Lions in a hole at their own 14-yard line as the second quarter opened. In came Rados. What transpired in the next few minutes marked the beginning of a new epoch in State football—the quarterback as the star. Rados completed his first pass to Yukica for a big gain and State was on its way. With five pass completions by Rados eating up most of the yardage, the Lions reached the Purdue four-yard line from where Pollard banged off left tackle for the TD. Leonard missed the kick but Purdue was penalized for having 12-men on the field and Leonard's second attempt tied the score at 7-7. Early in the third quarter, a 52-yard punt return by Eyer set up a 17-yard TD pass from Rados to Yukica and State took a 13-7 lead. Purdue tied it up three minutes later as Samuels passed downfield to set up a six-yard TD run but the PAT attempt failed. Purdue went back into the lead two minutes later, 20-13, when Phil Klezek dashed 63 yards around left end for a TD and Samuels kicked the extra point. Back came Rados, passing the Lions upfield, but as the fourth quarter started, a Rados aerial into the Purdue end zone was intercepted. Purdue gave up the ball on a punt but Rados was again intercepted deep in Boilermaker territory. However, interceptions work both ways. Three plays later Eyer picked off a Samuels pass at the Purdue 31-yard line.

The next sequence of events certainly rank as among the most bizarre in Lions' football history. Rados hit on two passes to the Purdue 13 but the second completion was nullified and the Lions were penalized back to the Purdue 44 for pushing. No sweat. Rados found Arnelle open for a 20-yard gain and as the teams lined up, the referee signaled fourth down-and-three. Rados tried to pass for the first down but his pass attempt failed. State's defensive platoon ran onto the field

but Gratson, who often played both ways at tackle and linebacker, rushed over to the referee and argued that the Lions were entitled to another down because of the penalty. The officials conferred and agreed. Back came Rados and the offense. This time, the Lions surprised Purdue with a pitchout to Jones who picked up a first down at the 16-yard line. Seven plays later, Rados sneaked over from the two-yard line and Leonard booted the extra point that tied the score at 20-20. But Samuels wasn't done and neither were the Lions. Samuels passed Purdue to the Lion 33 before Eyer picked him off again at the 15 and ran back to the State 43. Now, as the clock ran down, it was State's turn to try for a win. But after Jones ran 16 yards to the Purdue 44, the Boilermakers stopped Rados twice attempting to pass, smothering him under on the last play of the game. Still, the unexpected tie was a moral victory and the State fans went wild as they ran onto the field to congratulate Rados and his teammates. "Probably not for some time will grid fans see a passing exhibition such as was witnessed on...Saturday," wrote Jim Peters, sports editor of the *Centre Daily Times*. "Half of it was expected...the show put on by Rados was not expected, yet it turned out to be the best performance of the day."

Rados had accomplished what many thought was impossible—he had outpassed the master, completing 17-of-30 passes for 179 yards and one TD with two interceptions, while Samuels hit on 14-of-27 for 131 yards and one TD and three interceptions. It was the best passing performance by a Nittany Lion since the days of Bill Smaltz more than a decade ago and it made Rados an overnight campus hero. It also established Engle's team as an instant contender for Eastern honors while Purdue would go on to be co-champ of Big Ten and finish 18th in AP ratings.

The following Saturday, Rados again led the team in a come-from-behind win over William & Mary. The Lions trailed 16-14 at the half but then went ahead, 35-16, in the fourth quarter before getting a 35-32 victory that boosted them to #20 in the AP rankings. Rados' passing was not as sharp as it had been the previous week but his ball handling and play-calling was superb and his brilliant fakes were the talk of the press box. Once again State's pass defense did well, limiting the visitors to 62 passing yards on three-of-12 attempts.

West Virginia was all pumped up to host the Lions in Morgantown and had been pointing to the State game since blowing a lead and losing last season's game. This was the game the Mountaineers and their fans wanted. The WVC players were so hyper that they blocked three State punts and at one point in the second quarter had a 14-7 lead. Coach "Pappy" Lewis apparently didn't believe Rados was for real because his Mountaineers used an 8-3 defense for most of the game. Rados mixed short passes with reverses and end-around plays and the Lions overcame a 14-14 halftime tie to win, 35-21. Rados completed 13-of-20 passes for 139 yards and a TD with just one interception. Arnelle caught six of Rados' passes until he left the game with a broken nose late in the fourth quarter. "The Lions continue to scare the daylights out of their rooters during the first half and then amaze them the second," the *Collegian*'s Highton wrote. Engle told the *Centre Daily Times* "the boys played better in the second half than any team I have ever coached."

A homecoming crowd of 28,551 was on hand at Beaver Field the following week for a clash with unbeaten Nebraska, the Big Seven Conference leader. It was a classic defensive struggle as the teams battled for more than three quarters before anyone scored. Nebraska stopped State three times inside the 10-yard line. Bailey nipped one

Cornhusker scoring threat with an end zone interception. Early in the final period, the Lions drove from midfield and scored on a three-yard pass from Rados to Arnelle that tied the school record for completions in one season (48). Leonard booted a 16-yard field goal a short time later and the Lions won, 10-0. After five games, Rados was now ranked among the best passers in the country with 603 yards and six TDs on 49-of-93 attempts. Unfortunately, he lost one of his prime targets, Yukica, who was injured and lost for the rest of the season.

State was unbeaten but the number one team in the country, Michigan State, was next and the Lions were a decided underdog as the teams kicked off before the third largest crowd in history (51,162) at East Lansing's Macklin Field. Michigan State had won 19 straight but Engle's spirited team was not intimidated. The punting of senior Ted Kemmerer—a State College kid who was not even on the team when the season started—kept the Spartans bottled up for most of the first half as the Lions took a 7-0 lead late in the first quarter on a Rados-to-Malinak pass following a fumble recovery. Midway in the second quarter, Michigan State tied it up on a 45-yard TD pass from Tommy Yewcic to Doug Bobo and with less than two minutes left in the half Yewcic hit Ellis Duckett on a 56-yard TD pass that put the Spartans ahead to stay. Yewcic hit for another TD pass of 61 yards in the third quarter and his sub, Willie Thrower of New Kensington, tossed one of 26 yards in the fourth quarter and Michigan State won, 34-7. "They beat us on passes," Riley wrote, "but our pass defense, on the whole, was good." So was the pass offense, with 14-of-25 passes for 138 yards and no interceptions. Despite the margin of defeat, the loss did not diminish State's status among the college elite. The Cotton Bowl now had the Lions high on its list for the New Year's Day game.

Still, the Lions were underdogs again when they met Penn at Franklin Field. The Quakers with their single-wing passing offense were unbeaten with four wins and two ties and had been scored on only by Columbia. Early in the first quarter, Penn intercepted a Rados pass at midfield and proceeded to take it in for a touchdown and a 7-0 lead. State tied it in the second after Grier forced a fumble with a hard tackle at the Penn 25-yard line, then recovered the ball at the five. Pollard went in from the three and Leonard kicked the PAT. Defenses dominated the rest of the way as Eyer, Sherry and Leonard intercepted five Quaker passes and Kemmerer's punting kept the Quakers in a hole. With less than five minutes remaining in the game, it appeared that a tie was inevitable. Then, Kemmerer boomed a 57-yard punt over the safety man's head to the Penn 20-yard line. On the first play, sophomore Sam Green deflected a pass that Scheetz intercepted and carried to the eight. Two plays later, Jones slanted between the tackle and guard for a five-yard TD. Leonard's PAT made it 14-7 and the 25,000 State fans among the 67,000 "cut loose with as loud a chorus imaginable—without competition," as the *Collegian* reported. Penn tried desperately to pass the Quakers back into the game but could complete just one. A sack ended the game, which was fitting since the Lions had nailed Quaker passers for 87 yards in losses, and the players carried Engle off the field and into the dressing room. "Defense Unit Stars," said the *Collegian* headline. It was "an outstanding defensive unit which repeatedly stopped Penn scoring threats at crucial points and which was directly responsible for both Nittany touchdowns," Highton wrote.

Ben Schwartzwalder must have been impressed, too. The Syracuse coach had personally scouted State's game against Penn because his team had a week off and he was ready for the Lions when they invaded Archbold Stadium on November 8. Engle said later that it had not been a good week of practice and he had felt what was coming. Perhaps, the election of Milton Eisenhower's brother, Dwight, as President of the United States that week was just one distraction. Perhaps, Rados and his teammates got a little complacent. The Lions were a slight favorite and Syracuse was just 4-2, including a 48-7 loss to Michigan State. The first two minutes and 18 seconds were all State's as the Lion defense stopped Syracuse in three plays after the kickoff, then watched as Bailey returned Syracuse's punt 77 yards for a touchdown. Leonard's 15th straight PAT made it 7-0. But from that point it was Syracuse's game. The Orange defense harassed Rados, Szajna and State's runners the rest of the afternoon and took away a 25-7 victory. State netted just 59 yards passing (on seven-of-24 attempts with three interceptions) and 48 yards rushing, while the Syracuse offense was grinding out 287 net yards on the ground and 169 through the air. Schwartzwalder told sportswriters it was the "best game since I have been coaching Syracuse," which meant 1949. Engle said his team seemed "helpless." Good-bye Cotton Bowl. The old adage about playing on Saturday the way you practice during the week proved true again.

The Lions were even worse against Rutgers in the final home game of the season. They couldn't seem to do anything right, giving up seven fumbles, dropping passes when wide open and stopping their own drives with motion and offside penalties. Rutgers, a heavy underdog, nursed a 6-0 lead for most of the game after recovering a fumble in the first quarter at the Lions 25-yard line and scoring on a 22-yard TD pass. The PAT attempt was wide and that would be the eventual difference. In the fourth quarter, Rutgers recovered another fumble at State's 19 but Eyer stopped a TD with a goal line interception and a runback to the 17. State then drove all the way for its only TD of the game, with Rados passing 18 yards to Simon for the six-pointer. Leonard's 16th straight kick gave State the lead, 7-6. Eyer's third interception of the game at the State five-yard line on the last play preserved the Lions frustrating victory. The game was a milestone in Beaver Field attendance. The 15,957 fans on hand helped boost State over the 100,000 season total for the first time in history (103,751).

No way could they beat the Panthers at Pitt Stadium, the sportswriters said. Pitt was 6-2 with victories over such top 20 teams as Notre Dame and Ohio State and had the Orange Bowl all but locked up. State was still shaky from its last two games and Rados had gone into a slump. He didn't even start against Rutgers after his dreadful performance against Syracuse (5-for-16 and a minus three yards) and there was talk that Engle and Paterno had lost confidence in him. The game attracted the largest crowd in the series since 1927—53,766—and Pitt was a 14-point favorite at the kickoff. But with Rados again at the controls, the Lions were a fired-up team and they smashed Pitt and its Orange Bowl hopes, 17-0. It was payback time for 1940 and 1948 when Pitt knocked the Lions out of post-season bowls. "I've waited four years for this," Gratson told the *Pittsburgh Press*' Carl Hughes. Kemmerer's 61-yard punt in the first quarter helped keep Pitt in trouble right from the start and his continued good punting and the Lions defense did the rest. A 20-yard runback of an interception by Sherry and passes from Rados to Garrity and Arnelle set up Rowell's three-yard touchdown run early in the second quarter and that was all the scoring really needed. The defense throttled every Panther offensive and State's offense controlled the tempo of the game. Early in the fourth quarter, Leonard kicked a 12-yard field goal and minutes later Sherry ran back another interception 25 yards to the Pitt 10 and Rados sneaked over for the TD. Leonard put a capper on the season by kicking his 18th straight extra point and his 19th in 21 attempts—and many State followers ruefully recalled the big one he missed which could have won the Purdue game and may have put the Lions in a bowl game. As the teams left the field, the dejected Pitt players were pelted with oranges taken from crates that had been brought to the stadium to "celebrate" a Panthers' win. "This is the greatest day we've ever had," Engle said after being carried off the field after the game. "We wanted to win this one and we never worked harder for any victory."

So, 14th-ranked Syracuse went to the Orange Bowl (and got clobbered by Alabama, 61-6) and the Lions went back to State College. Arnelle had broken the season pass receiving record with 33 catches and Rados had become a star. But the Lions could finish just 8th in the Lambert Trophy race despite big wins over teams that finished higher. Regardless of this lack of respect, Engle and his coaches were happy about '52 and optimistic about '53. And then the rules changed.

Season Record 7-2-1
Record to Date 330-183-37
Winning percentage .634

"Changing the Rules"

Rip Engle had never liked two-platoon football but he was even more disturbed by the constant rule changes that forced him to re-evaluate and overhaul his team each year.

"Give me a rule and let it stay," Engle told *The Daily Collegian* when asked about the new rule that eliminated two-platoon football and restricted substitution. In essence, the convoluted rule that would apply to the 1953 season stated that a man who played during a particular quarter and left the field could not re-enter the game until a subsequent quarter, except in the last four minutes of the second and fourth quarters when a player could return if he had already played that specific quarter. Get it?

What the rule meant was that everyone would have to play offense and defense and that kicking specialists would have to learn to block and tackle or sit on the bench. Fortunately, some of Engle's 16 returning lettermen were experienced two-way players—Grier, Arnelle, Malinak, Garrity, Eyer, Sherry, DeFalco, Rowell, Green, Schoderbek and Balthaser—but he was overstocked at offensive end and undermanned at the guard and linebacker positions. And he wasn't sure about his sophomores, such as halfback Lenny Moore, fullbacks Charlie Blockson and Billy Straub, quarterback Bobby Hoffman, end-turned-tackle Otto Kneidinger, center Frank Reich and guard Earl Shumaker. Rados, the co-captain along with Malinak, had not played any defense since high school, but he and Jones, Younger, Vesling, Wayne Wolfkeil and the other running backs would have to learn defense quickly if the team had any chance of matching the '52 record.

Engle began the re-tooling during spring practice but many of his players did not participate because of baseball and track commitments. Rados was held out the entire spring because he was still

recovering from an operation to repair his knee. With Szajna, Shopa, and other veterans not returning to school, Engle had many problems to overcome before the team's tough season opener September 26 at Wisconsin, a first time opponent and the defending Big Ten co-champ and Rose Bowl team. Teaching Rados to play defense and punt was exasperating. "He had that bad knee and he was so slow anyway that, when the ball was snapped, he would begin back-pedaling toward his own goal line," Paterno later recalled in the book, *"Football My Way,"* "He wasn't going to let anyone get behind him." Finding a new punter and placekicker were also major concerns. But there was one bright spot during all this turmoil—Lenny Moore. "He has a lot to learn," assistant coach Frank Patrick cautioned late that spring. "Nevertheless, don't take your eyes off him," wrote outgoing *Collegian* sports editor, Jake Highton. "He runs, blocks, and tackles well with authority."

A crowd of 49,000 in Wisconsin's Camp Randall Stadium gasped early in the second quarter of a scoreless game when Moore took a pitch out from Rados and dashed 64 yards around right end for an apparent touchdown. However, the TD was nullified by a back in motion penalty and the infraction seemed to demoralize the Lions. With junior All-American Alan (The Horse) Ameche leading the way by rushing for 109 yards and a TD, the Badgers pounded out a 20-0 win. "'The Horse' ran wild inside and outside the Penn State line...," wrote Sam Procopio, the new sports editor of the *Collegian*. "...Ameche did almost as much damage on the defense...he batted down two passes and was in on almost every tackle." Wisconsin picked up 21 first downs, getting 222 yards on the ground and 114 through the air (on 11-of-16 passes) while holding State to five first downs with just 50 yards rushing and 70 yards passing (on eight-of-18 attempts with two interceptions). "Did our boys just have an especially bad day?...," Ridge Riley wrote in his *"Football Letter."* "Our blocking was almost nil and unless it improves in the next few weeks, slightly built backs like Moore, (Buddy) Rowell and Jones are going to get killed." Moore had just 10 yards on 10 carries. It would be Moore's lowest one-game total of his career.

For the first time since 1892, a State team was starting the season with three road games. But, historically, the Lions had always played well against traditional rival Penn. So, it didn't matter that they were a six-point underdog when the teams kicked off in unusually sweltering, 80 degree weather before 51,000 at Franklin Field. In the pre-game hoopla, the Penn players were quoted as saying they wanted to win this game for their coach, George Munger, who had never beaten State and already had said he would quit at the end of the season. On State's second possession following a quick kick, the Lions drove 92-yards for a TD with Garrity scoring on a 29-yard pass from Rados, then kicking the PAT. But those were the last points State would get for the day. Penn tied it in the second quarter, then recovered Moore's fumble at the State 39 midway in the fourth period to set up a 26-yard TD pass that won the game, 13-7. "...Nothing rankles quite so much as a Penn defeat," Riley wrote. Despite the fumble, Moore was singled out for his play on offense and defense. "In Leonard Moore, it (Penn State) has a menace," wrote Leo Riordan of the *Philadelphia Inquirer*. "Moore is overdue and future opponents will get it."

The 0-2 start might have dazed a team with less character but these players were evolving mentally as they continued to develop under the new substitution rule. It all came together the following week at Boston University and Rados, Moore and Jones were the catalysts. Rados threw three TD passes, two to Jones, as State battered the Terriers, 35-13. Jones set a new record (later broken by Blair Thomas) by making the longest run from scrimmage without scoring. With State ahead 28-7 in the third quarter, DeFalco recovered a fumble at the Lion 14-yard line. Jones took a pitchout and started around the right end but was trapped, reversed his field and evaded several Terrier defenders as he darted down the left sideline. Running out of breath, he puffed into the end zone, but an official ruled he stepped out of bounds at the nine. The run was officially 77 yards. Moore scored his second TD of the game on the next play and Rip emptied his bench.

Syracuse, the spoiler of the '52 season, invaded Beaver Field for the home opener the following week and the Lions had made it clear they wanted revenge. The game turned into one of the all-time classics in the long series with Syracuse and further strained the bitterness that had been germinating between the teams for years. State's offense sputtered early with both Rados and Bailey at the controls and the Lions twice missed scoring opportunities deep in Syracuse territory. The underdog Orange drove 78-yards for a score in the first quarter and made the 7-0 lead hold up into the intermission. Syracuse increased it to 14-0 with five minutes left in the third quarter after stopping another State drive by recovering a fumble at the Syracuse 17 and then roaring downfield for a TD that appeared to give the Orange command of the game. But after the ensuing kickoff, the Lions got their first down and went 76 yards in five plays with Blockson running 45-yards off tackle for the TD and sophomore reserve tackle Jim Harding kicking the PAT. A few minutes later, Arnelle recovered a fumble at the State 45-yard line and with Blockson and Moore doing most the running the Lions reached the Syracuse 3 with a fourth-and-goal. Rados called time out and went to the sideline to discuss the play with Engle and Paterno. When time resumed, Rados faked to wingback Younker up the middle, then faked to Blockson up the middle and pitched out to Moore running all alone on the right and the sophomore speedster swept into the end zone behind the block of tackle Gene Danser. Garrity's kick tied the game with 10 minutes left.

Back came Syracuse, driving to State's 21 with a fourth-and-two before a desperation pass off a failed option play was intercepted by Schoderbek. But the Lions couldn't move very far and with two minutes left, Eyer punted and Syracuse took over at its own 29. The Orange tried three plays but gained only a few yards and with about a minute left, State called another time out, forcing Syracuse to punt. Engle, using the substitution rules, sent in four players who had been resting—Garrity and Arnelle at the ends and DeFalco and Danser at the tackles. Because Moore had been successful in returning punts in earlier games, Syracuse's punting team set up to stop a State return. Now came one of the defining moments of the season, one that was a consequence of the new substitution rule. Moore's ex-teammate at Reading High School Ed Albright, was the Syracuse punter. But Coach Schwartzwalder had been concerned about his punting since the preseason, calling it "a major headache." The center snapped the ball and 10 Lions surged at Albright. Albright's boot smashed into DeFalco's chest and Garrity scooped up the ball at the 23 and ran untouched into the end zone. The kick failed but the Lions now had a 20-14 lead. But Syracuse was not through. A short kickoff, a pass and a penalty gave the Orange the ball at the Lions' 40. The Syracuse QB faded back to pass and heaved the ball towards the end zone. Moore, the offensive star turned defender, intercepted at the 11 and ran back to the 36 before being shoved out of bounds in front of the Syracuse bench. And then all hell broke loose.

Lenny Moore never made First-Team All-American but is one of the Nittany Lions' greatest all-around offensive and defensive backs and one of just four Penn Staters in the Pro Football Hall of Fame.

"Something happened to Moore in the crowd and Arnelle went to protect him," recalls Mickey Bergstein, then the color man for State's radio network. "The next thing you know they were swinging all over the place." Jim Peters of the *Centre Daily Times* described what happened: "...an Orange player unnecessarily jumped on (Moore) and a free-for-all between both squads broke out. Players rushed from both benches, as well as coaches, and fans poured on the field from the stands. Fists were flying in all directions for several minutes before peace was restored and the game was allowed to end quietly." The Lions ran the last 10 seconds off the clock and walked off with their revenge. "Our boys never gave up," Engle told sportswriters.

Another new opponent, Texas Christian, was the Homecoming guest the next week. Apparently, TCU did not look at a map before the game was scheduled, because the visitors flew into Harrisburg, believing State College was close and not 90 miles away. The Horned Frogs were forced to take a bus Saturday morning to get to the game and perhaps that's why State was able to take a 14-0 lead early in the second quarter on a touchdown pass by Rados and a 41-yard TD run by Moore. By halftime it was tied, 14-14. TCU had the reputation of being a typical team out of the pass-happy Southwestern Conference, and, indeed, scored its first two TDs on passes. But it was Rados' passing and Moore's running that dazzled the crowd and sparked the victory. Early in the third quarter, Rados broke away from two tacklers and hit Garrity for a 26-yard TD that put State ahead 21-14 after Garrity's PAT. Before the quarter was over, a blocked punt at State's 36-yard line helped TCU tie the score but Rados led a 61-yard drive that climaxed with his two-yard run for a go-ahead TD. Harding's PAT attempt hit the crossbar but State's defense made the 27-21 lead hold up throughout a torrid fourth quarter of TCU passing. Rados finally sealed the win by making an interception—yes, slow, backpedaling Rados—in the last minute of play. Rados was the player of the game as he completed 13-of-19 passes for 164 yards but Moore also stood out as he rushed for over 100 yards for the first time in his career, gaining 127 yards on 16 carries.

Unbeaten and fifth-ranked West Virginia, with its best team in years led by quarterback Fred Wyatt and fullback Joe Marconi, was a six-point favorite to make the Lions its sixth victim in a Halloween Day encounter at Beaver Field. This probably was the pivotal game in the '53 season with a defining moment similar but little less dramatic than the one in the last minute of the Syracuse game. The Mountaineers were leading the nation in rushing and averaging 500 yards in total offense per game. But they got just 72 on the ground and 137 in the air as the Lions offense and defense outplayed Coach Pappy Lewis' team most of the game. Rados, the leading passer in the East, had one of his greatest games as he broke the single-game passing record he set against Purdue in '52 by passing for 239 yards and two touchdowns on 16-of-27 attempts. But it wasn't enough to give State a victory. Two controversial non-calls by the officials helped the Mountaineers.

With State leading 12-6 in the third quarter, the Lions appeared to have stopped West Virginia with a goal-line stand inside the five-yard line. However, the officials gave Wyatt a TD on a fourth down quarterback sneak even though the State players protested and movies later showed Wyatt's knee had touched before he crossed the goal line by inches. With the PAT, the Mountaineers led 13-12 late in the third quarter when the second—and more significant non-call—occurred. State went back to punt from its own 14-yard line. Most of the 24,670 fans—and Engle—thought they saw West Virginia's middle guard, Tommy Allman, jump offside before the ball was snapped. "Someone was across that line awful fast," Engle told sportswriters in the locker room, "and I will be plenty surprised if the movies don't show a West Virginia lineman offside." The movies did but it didn't matter. No penalty was called. Allman and sophomore tackle Bruce Bosley crashed through the Lions' defense. Allman blocked Eyer's punt and Bosley chased the ball into the end zone where he fell on it. The PAT made the score 20-12. Rados threw a 20-yard TD pass to Younker early in the fourth quarter but a fumble stopped another scoring opportunity a few minutes later and West Virginia won, 20-19. Two successful extra points might have given the Lions the win but Garrity's first attempt had been wide and Straub—the third backup kicker—had missed the second one. So much for the new substitution rule. "West Virginia Survives at Penn State," said the headline in the *Pittsburgh Press*. "Around 25,000 jittery fans watched the Lions out-fight and out-play the Mountaineers in every department but the final score and even that was in doubt until the gun ended the game," reported the *Centre Daily Times*. Eventually, West Virginia would finish 8-1 in regular season, be ranked 10th in the country, and lose to Georgia Tech in the Sugar Bowl (42-19). But the heartbreaking defeat was difficult for the Lions to accept and they pouted all week in practice.

So, on the eve of State's final home game of the season against Fordham, Engle decided to take the team out of town to loosen it up. "They need relaxation," Engle had said. "Football players can't relax in State College on Junior Prom weekend." It would be a fateful decision. They left that afternoon for a hunting camp deep in the woods about 30 miles from State College. The weather forecast in the *Collegian* for Friday and Saturday predicted "clear and cold." The snow began falling before they reached the camp and by 8 a.m. Saturday it was 13 inches deep at Beaver Field and more than 20 inches at the hunting camp. As Riley later described it humorously in his *"Football Letter"* and his book, the team was stranded for hours at "Camp Hate-to-Leave-It" until the caretaker located a rescue team. Eventually the players had to trudge a half hour through snow drifts to an awaiting

bus—with the coaches first making the trail, followed in order by the third, second and first teams. "Lenny Moore was expected to go last," recalled O'Hora. "We were all cold and wet by the time we reached that bus."

Back at Beaver Field, 200 students volunteers, including 98 members of the Blue Band, had shoveled the snow off the field and cleared the grandstands—just as a similar contingent of volunteers would do 42 years later when a surprise snow storm hit before a Michigan game. The State team arrived at the scheduled kickoff time of 1:30 and after a brief warm-up by both teams on the field, the game started at 2:15 before some 13,897 stalwart fans. Neither team seemed to be bothered by a fine snow that continued throughout the game and made the field slippery. But Rados, the third best passer in the country, had lost his concentration after the shattering experience at "Camp Hate-to-Leave-It" and had one of his worst passing days. Fortunately, Moore, Blockson and Younker picked up the slack on the ground. Moore, who would gain 108 yards on 11 carries, scored State's first touchdown early in the second quarter on a 58-yard run and picked up another TD in the third quarter. But the game was tied three times and the score was 21-21 midway in the fourth quarter when an interception by Rados gave State the ball at midfield. Two plays later, Younker, who set up Moore's second TD by recovering a fumbled punt, slanted off left end and ran 35 yards for a touchdown and State won, 28-21. The college's meteorology department apologized, saying that the staff should have "trusted its instincts rather than its instruments" in its weather prediction.

The next game was a milestone of sorts. Thanks to Milton Eisenhower's lobbying, Penn State officially became a "University" the day before the game against Rutgers at New Brunswick. What that did to help the team win football games was absolutely nothing but for anyone who is superstitious it should be noted that the date was Friday, the 13th, 1953! The Lions were heavy favorites, again, as they had been in the three previous games against Rutgers. But, with eight minutes left in the second quarter, Rutgers, winners of just two of six games, had a 14-6 lead and Engle and his coaches were steamed. They let the players know it along the sidelines and that had an instant reaction. Penn State scored three TDs before the intermission and won, 54-26, in what was the highest score produced by an Engle-coached State team in four years. Eight different players scored TDs. Rados was again a little shaky in his passing and Hoffman and Bailey spent a lot of time at QB with the sophomore Hoffman scoring one TD and passing to Garrity for another.

Rados was back in passing form for the traditional season's finale against Pitt. The Panthers were favored by six points despite a 2-5-1 record. For long-time State followers who sat through many humiliating losses to Pitt over the years, this game was a delight to watch. The Lions thoroughly dominated the Panthers and the 17-0 score (ironically the same as '52) was deceiving. Only the outstanding defensive play of Pitt's safetyman Henry Ford kept the game from being a rout as he intercepted three of Rados' passes in the end zone. Pitt's defense kept the Panthers in the game in the first half, stopping State's first two drives at the Pitt 22 and 19, then holding the Lions to a 15-yard field goal by Garrity after they had marched 75-yards early in the second quarter. But State scored a touchdown the next time it got the ball. Moore returned a punt to the Lions 21-yard line, then two plays later Moore went up the middle on a draw play, cut to the left and ran untouched into the end zone as the State fans in the crowd of 39,642 romped with joy. The 79-yard run was State's longest from scrimmage since Chuck Peters' record 80 yards in 1938. A 63-yard drive on the second half kickoff put the game out of reach as Rowell scored the TD from less than a yard out and Garrity's PAT made it 17-0. Pitt surprised State with a "spread formation" for much of the second half but it didn't amount to much. Pitt, held to 59 yards rushing and 60 yards passing, finally reached Penn State's 6-yard line at the end of the game as Engle played all his reserves. "The Lions allowed their hosts few enjoyable moments and not until the last play of the game did Pitt even get within sight of the enemy end zone," wrote Carl Hughes for the *Pittsburgh Press.* "I knew the boys wouldn't let me down," Engle told the *Collegian,* "but I did not think we'd win so decisively."

In his final game, Rados completed 13-of-25 passes for 160 yards, giving him 1,026 yards (on 81-for-171 attempts) for the year and a new State yardage record that lasted for 10 years before broken by Pete Liske in 1963. But Rados was now history. State fans looking ahead to 1954 were now talking about Moore, the elusive speedster whom sportswriters had nicknamed *"The Reading Express."* The 120 yards he gained against Pitt was the third time he had gone over 100 yards in a game and broke the school record 100-yard plus record held by three players. He had rushed for 601 yards, the most since Rogel in '48, and his 5.6 per yard average was the best in more than a decade. The best was yet to come.

Season Record 6-3
Record to Date 336-186-37
Winning percentage .634

"Here Comes Lenny"

Joe Paterno didn't think much of senior Don Bailey's quarterbacking skills and he urged Rip Engle to start the sophomore Paterno had recruited personally from Westville, New Jersey. Paterno believed Milt Plum could be a star while Bailey was barely adequate. "I didn't want to use him (Bailey)," Paterno recalled in his book, *"Football My Way."* "You never knew what he was going to do."

Bailey was a good defensive halfback, a fine punter and a decent runner but he was not much of a passer. Paterno also was wary of his play-calling and ball handling. "He had the smallest hands you ever saw for a quarterback," Paterno recalled. " He was a tough runner but the only trouble was we would be running an option play to the left and he'd come out of the backfield running to the right."

But Plum was having problems throwing in the preseason. He also seemed to lack confidence in himself. The third quarterback was a hustling 5-foot-9, 165-pound junior named Bobby Hoffman. Hoffman and Bailey had shared the back-up slot behind Rados in '53 but neither one had distinguished himself in that role. As State's tough season opener at Illinois approached on September 29, Engle still did not have a starting quarterback. And it was until minutes before the kickoff that he finally selected Hoffman.

Without a passer as proficient as Rados, Engle realized as early as spring practice that his '54 team would depend more on running than passing. Because of this, he added the quarterback option to the playbook. That would give his elusive junior left halfback, Lenny Moore, additional running schemes. The All-American candidate was among 17 returning lettermen, including most of the starting eleven. With all the veterans returning, the sportswriters figured State could have another good year but the perennially pessimistic Engle wasn't so sure. "...About 80 percent of the teams in the nation have that many (letter)men returning," Engle told the *Daily Collegian.*

Arnelle and Grier were back for their fourth year as starters and other regulars returning from '53 included Garrity and Balthaser, the co-captains, plus Kneidinger and Shumaker. However, before the first game, Balthaser would injure his leg and junior Frank Reich would play most of the year as the regular center. The spunky Younker would start at right half and Blockson at fullback but Younker would be pressed later by sophomore Billy Kane and Blockson would miss much of the season because of injuries. In fact, injuries hampered the Lions throughout the year, particularly at fullback where Engle would be forced to start a fourth string sophomore named Jim Lockerman late in the year. Two sophomore linemen, Sam Valentine and Dick DeLuca, also would get starting nods at some point and Valentine would share placekicking with Garrity. An almost forgotten man would be Rowell, a three-year letterman who had the misfortune of playing behind Moore at left half. In an effort to beef up his defense, Engle also added a new assistant coach to his staff in the spring, the first change since Bedenk had quit before the '52 season. J.T. White, a starter on Michigan's unbeaten 1948 Rose Bowl champion, was brought on to coach defensive ends. That proved to be a fortuitous hire for the defense—with Garrity, Arnelle and Sherry at the ends—became the team's backbone from the opening game.

For the second straight year, Engle was faced with opening the season on the foreign field of a heavily-favored Big Ten opponent. This time, assistant athletic director Ike Gilbert had scheduled another first ever foe, Illinois. The Illini had shared the 1953 conference title with Michigan State and was a preseason favorite to win it all this year. They had three of the most highly-touted and fastest backs in the country in J.C. Caroline, Mickey Bates and sophomore Abe Woodson. The All-American Caroline was the nation's rushing leader in '53 and already had broken all the Illinois records of the "immortal" Red Grange and the Big Ten rushing record, too. Bates was the Big Ten scoring champion and Woodson held several conference hurdling marks. The Illini were favored by six-to-14 points but Paul Poorman, sports editor of the *Centre Daily Times,* had a hunch the Lions would win in a close game, "which will make us a genius if they do...," he wrote. "But Penn State has the stuff and a top-notch performance...could bring home a winner."

The Lions won the toss, elected to receive and as an ABC radio network audience listened, Bill Straub ran the kickoff back to the State 42-yard line. Moore carried twice for a first down at the Illinois 45. A pass and run gained nothing and on third down disaster struck. Illinois quarterback Em Lindbeck intercepted Hoffman's deep pass and returned it 19 yards to the State 41-yard line. Four plays later, Illinois had a touchdown on a 28-yard screen pass from Lindbeck to Woodson. Caroline's kick for the extra point failed but the record opening day crowd of 54,090 cheered and hollered. The rout they all expected had begun.

Engle had seen enough of Hoffman. In came Bailey. It was one of the defining moments of the season but no one knew it at the time. Bailey couldn't move the team and he had to punt. He got off a beauty that went out of bounds at the Illini 16-yard line. State's defense forced Illinois to punt the ball back and Moore returned it 21 yards to the Illini 37-yard line. Three plays later disaster struck again when Bailey's pass was intercepted inside the Illinois 20. The partisan fans at Memorial Stadium whooped it up. But their cheers turned to groans moment later when Moore's tackle on Bates caused a fumble that Arnelle recovered at the Illini 28-yard line. Two plays later, Bailey passed to Arnelle running full stride at the goal line for a 24-yard touchdown. Garrity's PAT put the Lions ahead, 7-6, and, one could sense the confidence rising along the PSU sidelines. Now, the State defense took over and, with Grier and Shumaker leading the charge, the tackling was hard and sometimes vicious. Moore's shoestring tackle on Caroline in the clear saved one touchdown and with less than a minute left in the half, the Lions got the ball on its own 26-yard line following a punt. On the first play, Bailey kept the ball on an option around the left end and ran 50 yards before forced out of bounds by Woodson at the Illini 24. Younker got six yards and on second down, Bailey started around left end again, faked to Moore and ran downfield. He was hit at the eight but turned and lateraled back to Moore, who blasted past three defenders and dashed into the end zone. The center pass was wide but Bailey got the ball down and Garrity's kick made it 14-6 as the half ended.

Illinois took the second half kickoff and marched 77 yards for a touchdown, with Woodson scoring on a 17-yard run. But fullback Bob Wiman's extra point attempt hit the cross bar and bounced back, and State still had the lead, 14-12. Illinois thundered back moments after the ensuing kickoff by recovering a Lions fumble at the Illini 46. A few minutes later, it was fourth-and-six at the PSU 16-yard line. Caroline took the pitchout and started around right end but was nailed for a loss at the 20 by Garrity and Reich. It was the crucial defensive play of the game for the Illini never seriously threatened after that. Moore (who ran for 137 yards on 18 carries) intercepted an Illini pass at the State 48 with four minutes left in the game and when time ran out, the Lions were on the Illini five-yard line. "A determined Penn State football team methodically cut down an illustrious opponent Saturday afternoon and emerged with a victory that will probably rank with the greatest Nittany Lion wins in modern times," the *CDT*'s Poorman wrote. "We stopped Illinois by playing alert football," Riley reported in his *"Football Letter,"* "—every player on the field under the intelligent leadership of Coach Engle, gave every once of energy he possessed for the full sixty minutes."

The stunning upset caused ripples throughout the football world and made State an instant contender for the Lambert Trophy. But the loss thoroughly demolished the Illini, which lost seven more games and was winless in the Big Ten. Engle had found the quarterback to run the option plays that enhanced the running of Lenny Moore. However, he was not satisfied with Bailey's passing and he sent the team through three hard practices that week, concentrating on the passing attack.

The next game was against State's old nemesis, Syracuse, at Archbold Stadium. After the way the '53 game had ended, the Lions expected some hostility from the crowd of 18,000 but a 24-hour rain that lasted almost to kickoff kept the antagonism in check. State got itself into a critical jam on the second play of the game when a pitchout from Bailey to Moore went awry and Syracuse recovered the fumble at the Lions 18-yard line. But a great defensive stand stopped Syracuse on a fourth down at the 14. Another fumble moments later gave Syra-cuse a second opportunity at the State 35-yard line. Again, the Lions defense throttled the Syracuse attack, forcing the Orange back to the 43 where they punted on fourth down. The two defensive efforts set the tempo for the rest of the game and in the next few minutes the offense scored the only points needed to win in a 76-yard, all-running drive that climaxed with Moore's 22-yard touchdown. Garrity's PAT attempt was blocked but Syracuse never really got back into the game. Early in the second half, Younker ran back a punt 50 yards to the Syracuse 18-yard line and six plays later he bolted into the end zone for a TD. Garrity's kick made it 13-0. Syracuse had one last gasp in a 72-yard drive that ended on a fourth down play at the Lion 17-yard line with four minutes to play. The defense had limited Syracuse to 75 yards rushing and 22 passing while the offense ground out 207 yards rushing with Moore just missing another 100-yard game at 93 yards. "I now have confidence in this team and even more important, I think our players have confidence in themselves," a happy Engle said after the game. "I believe we have a good chance in every game." He was still concerned about the team's passing, however. "We have yet to hit our real stride," he told Poorman. "One of these days, we'll begin to connect on our passes."

It had been 61 years since a State team had played Virginia, the opponent for the home opener on October 9. The Cavaliers should have waited a few more years. Despite a 2-0 record, Virginia was no match for the Nittany Lions as State won easily 34-7. Moore rushed for 120 yards and two touchdowns but Younker had the most spectacular TD of the day when he ran 80 yards in the second quarter to tie the school record set by Chuck Peters in 1938. The victory moved the Lions into the AP Top 10 for the first time in years, tying with Navy for the number nine spot.

If there was one game the Lions wanted to win in '54—outside of Pitt, of course—it was West Virginia. They remembered what happened last year when a couple of blown calls by the officials helped the Mountaineers eke out a win that led to a Top 10 ranking and the Sugar Bowl. West Virginia was unbeaten once again, ranked #14 and with another veteran team led by Wyant at quarterback and All-American Bruce Bosley and Sam Huff in the line. Toretti, who scouted the Mountaineers said they were a "good sized squad with surprising speed, a strong ground game and plenty of defensive savvy." Another record-breaking, standing room crowd of 32,384—largest since the 1948 Michigan State game—turned out for the Homecoming game played on a wet field in the aftermath of Hurricane Hazel. West Virginia dominated the first quarter and took a 6-0 lead. But the Lions, who were favored by six points, went ahead, 7-6, early in the second quarter on a 46-yard drive, following Moore's 19-yard punt return, with Bailey passing 24-yards to Younker for the TD. Minutes later, State started on a 76-yard drive for another score, with Moore scampering 41-yards on one play and taking an option pass from Bailey for the eight-yard TD. Garrity's PAT made it 14-6 and the fans were pretty happy at halftime when they watched onfield ceremonies formally induct coaches Higgins and Bezdek (posthumously) into the National Football Foundation Hall of Fame.

West Virginia's defense kept the Lions from crossing midfield throughout the second half and with 11 minutes left in the game, the Mountaineers drove 68 yards to narrow the gap to 14-12. They stopped the Lions on the next series and took over at midfield following a punt. Three plays later, Dick Nicholson took an option pass from Wyant and ran 40 yards for the TD, then kicked the PAT that thrust WVU into the lead, 19-14. State tried desperately to come back—first on a pass from

Bailey to Garrity, who was almost in the clear when he slipped, then on a pass from Plum to Sherry, who tried to lateral to Garrity inside the Mountaineer 35 but they fumbled the ball and West Virginia recovered with less than a minute left. Moore had another great day running with 139 yards but the Lions lost five fumbles and 85 yards on penalties to help seal the defeat. "What a difference one touchdown can make," Engle told Riley the next day. "I don't think anyone touched Jim Garrity. It was just one of those things. He cut fast and slipped." But Poorman blamed the defeat on the players. "Fumbles, plays that didn't work, seeming errors of judgment (were the cause)...," he wrote. "The Lions seemed unsure of their own proven abilities. Their poise—class, if you will—was missing..."

The Lions made more mistakes against Texas Christian the next week when Moore made history by becoming the first black to play a college football game in Fort Worth. Moore rushed for 109 yards on 19 carries and scored a TD on a 29-yard pass from Hoffman in the fourth quarter. But the Lions lost the ball four times on fumbles and interceptions, dropped at least a half dozen passes and had a punt blocked for a touchdown. Despite winning the statistical battle, with 316 yards in total offense and 20 first downs to 211 yards and 10 first downs for TCU, the Lions lost 20-7. "It was the most frustrating game I've ever coached," Engle said in the dressing room.

The following Saturday, it was the team which made history. For the first time ever, a State football game was televised nationally. The site was Franklin Field and 33,145 were there in person as an estimated 40 million watched on television. They saw quite a performance from Moore, who rushed for 143 yards and scored three touchdowns on a slippery turf in a 35-13 victory over an underdog but hustling Penn team. Moore's first TD near the end of the half broke up a surprising 7-7 tie as he bulled over tacklers on a nine-yard trap play up the middle. On the second running play of the third quarter, Moore took a pitchout from Bailey, dashed inside Penn's left end and sped 60 yards, tip-toeing down the sideline, for the TD. Then, with the score 28-13 midway in the final quarter, and Penn battling back, Moore clinched the win by intercepting a pass and running it back 53-yards for his third TD. "Spindle-legged Lenny Moore, a hot rod in football togs, ran wild on Franklin Field yesterday..." reported Herb Good in the *Philadelphia Inquirer*. "Moore, extremely fast and very elusive proved...why is rated with State's all-time greats."

A week later, Moore broke the season rushing record set by Shorty Miller in 1912 with 127 yards on nine carries, giving him 843

yards for the year, as the Lions pummeled Holy Cross, 39-7. Moore scored touchdowns on runs of 33 and 16 yards and Younker ran 35 yards for one TD and 46 for another as State rushed for 405 yards. Moore's senior backup, Rowell, also had his best rushing day ever with 79 yards on 11 carries as Engle removed Moore after his second TD three minutes into the second half. "This game belonged to the lithe...Lenny Moore, the most exciting performer in Penn State football for more than a quarter of a century," wrote Riley in his *Football Letter*. "Someone overheard a few of our players discussing what makes Lenny run: 'I guess,' said Jesse Arnelle, 'It's because Lenny just doesn't like to be tackled.'"

Moore was at it again against Rutgers in the final home game of the season. This time he rushed for his most yards ever in a single game, 171 on 12 carries, stretching his record of 100-plus yards to 10 games over two seasons. But the Lions struggled in the first half as they usually did when playing Rutgers. Trailing, 7-6 early in the second quarter, State went 80 yards behind the running and receiving of Moore to take the lead they never relinquished. In that drive, Moore gained 36 yards on a pitchout and seven yards on a reception

The great Lenny Moore became the first Lion running back to gain over 1,000 yards when he finished second in the nation in rushing in 1954. Here he is in this reverse photo running for yardage in a game at Beaver Field.

before slicing off right tackle from the three for the TD. His 54-yard touchdown dash off a pitchout in the fourth quarter capped the Lions 37-14 victory and tied the school record for touchdowns in one season—13. Moore now had 1,014 yards for the year and was just 11 yards behind the country's rushing leader, Art Luppino of Arizona. With one game left, against arch rival Pitt, Moore seemed a cinch to break the TD record he now shared with Bull McCleary, Harry Robb and Harry Wilson, and maybe even surpass Luppino's rushing mark.

But, Engle had decided to use Moore as a decoy when Pitt set up a 6-3-2 defense—that was virtually an eight-man line—to stop the option. By the time Engle gave the go ahead to give Moore the ball, it was too late on a slippery field and he gained just 68 yards and had no TDs on 16 carries. Pitt was 4-4 and coming off another big upset, this time over Nebraska, and many sportswriters picked the Panthers to do it again against State. But the Lions defense was too much for Pitt. Early in the second quarter, the second team took the ball on PSU's 45 following a punt and drove to a score behind the running of Rowell and Kane with Hoffman hitting Sherry on a 19-yard pass for the TD. The kick was wide but it wouldn't matter. With Moore playing a spectacular game on defense—intercepting two passes and recovering a fumble that stopped three Pitt drives—the Lions' defense kept Pitt in check and the offense scored again in the third quarter after Moore's fumble recovery at the State 44. It was appropriate that Bailey—the underrated quarterback from a Pittsburgh high school who had been so vital to Moore's success—scored the final TD on a three-yard sneak up the middle. Garrity's kick made it 13-0 and that's how it ended.

"Seniors 47: Pitt 0," the seniors scribbled on the blackboard in the winners' locker room, reflecting the third straight shutout over the Panthers. Engle apologized to Moore for not giving him the ball earlier in the game. "Maybe your yardage wasn't as high, but you never played a better game," Engle told him after the game.

"Used for part of the game as a decoy," wrote Chet Smith in the *Pittsburgh Press*, "State's great halfback Lenny Moore still played a vital role in the victory and was rewarded...(with) a new University record for offense over one season...(totalling) 1082 yards in nine game to break the mark of 1031 set by Shorty Miller in 1912..Moore also was worth his weight in gold defensively, turning in a pair of pass interceptions that helped no little in taking the heat off his team."

It would be more than a decade before Pittman, Mitchell and others would break the rushing records Moore set that season. He would get a few more records the next year but, surprisingly, would never be more than a second team All-American. Still, because of him, an Engle team was ranked in the Top 20 at the end of the season for the first time—16th by UP and 20th by AP. Engle would miss the seniors in 1955 and two of them, Arnelle and Sherry, would help lead the PSU basketball team to State's only appearance ever in Final Four before they graduated that spring. But with Moore returning for State's Centennial Year of 1955, the football fans were looking forward to next year. Then they looked at the schedule.

Season Record 7-2
Record to Date 343-188-37
Winning percentage .636

"The Centennial Season"

The half was winding down at Beaver Field and a frustrated Rip Engle still could not believe the score. Syracuse was winning 13-0 and Engle's Lions had been completely shut down. Sure, Syracuse had been the favorite but all week Engle had felt this would be the breakthrough game for his team.

After six games, State was just 3-3 and getting little respect. The defeats against Army, Navy and West Virginia—all top 20 teams—had been decisive and the relatively easy wins against Boston University, Virginia and Penn had been expected. Syracuse was ranked 18th in the country and number two in the East behind Navy after beating Army and thrashing undefeated Holy Cross while the unranked Lions were down to number eight in the Lambert listing of Eastern teams. Still, Engle believed his squad had done the best it could under the circumstances and was ready for an upset.

This was not how "The Centennial Season" was supposed to go. With enrollment at an all-time high of 13,400, State was celebrating its 100th year as a college and the school's athletic officials had begun planning for this season a few years earlier. At one time, Ike

Gilbert had tried to set up a football schedule with all nine games played at home but that didn't work out. Still, Navy had visited for the first time since 1923 and Pitt was set for its first Beaver Field appearance since 1942. The hierarchy of the university had hoped State could field a team that would be one of the best ever but that was not to be.

Engle had realized from spring practice that this would be a difficult season. Lenny Moore, his star halfback, had been placed on academic probation over the winter and had dropped out of school. Fortunately, Moore had been reinstated after summer school and was back on the team in the fall. But Moore was among just 11 lettermen returning and that included just five linemen and three fullbacks. Engle had no veterans at end, only one at tackle and his only letterman at quarterback was backup Bobby Hoffman. Engle told *Daily Collegian* sports editor Roy Williams in the spring that he "lacked depth in several spots and the speed of his line and backfield was another problem." His problems compounded during the preseason workouts when injuries decimated his fullback position.

When the team opened "The Centennial Season" against Boston University at Beaver Field on September 24, Engle was still manipulating his starting lineup. He didn't have the manpower to field two teams of equal ability but the new substitution rule that allowed players to re-enter a game once during each quarter gave him some flexibility. His basic starting lineup would have co-captain Reich at center with junior Dan Radakovich subbing often as a linebacker on defense; Shumaker, DeLuca or Valentine at guards; Calderone and co-captain Kneidinger at tackles; with numerous players at the ends, including four highly-touted sophomores: Les Walters, Paul North, Jim Caldwell and Jack Farls. Moore and Kane were the halfbacks and Straub the fullback. Hoffman shared the quarterback slot with Plum during the early games but Engle and his coaches were not satisfied with either one through the first few weeks of the season. Their passing was spotty and neither could run the option well. That meant opponents could try to cripple the Lions offense by concentrating on stopping Moore.

Boston University tried that tactic but didn't succeed very well as the Lions won, 35-0, on a soggy, rain-soaked field. This was the first game ever televised from Beaver Field and carried on a limited regional telecast by CBS. BU had been a late addition to the schedule, replacing Fordham, which had given up football the previous December, but the Terriers had been expected to give PSU a tough battle. An unknown 5-foot-11 187-pound sophomore fullback from Shamokin named Joe Sabol came off the bench to spark the victory. Sabol had started the year on the fifth string but injuries to Straub, Blockson and fellow sophomore Babe Caprara thrust Sabol into the limelight. Sabol carried the ball five times for 52 yards, scored two touchdowns, including one on a 34-yard run, and set up another TD on an 18-yard pass reception. With the BU defense primed to stop Moore—who got just 68 yards on 12 carries—Sabol's running and Hoffman's passing was quite effective. "Moore Overshadowed by Unknown Sophomore," said one newspaper headline. "Sabol came out of nowhere and looked like a sophomore All-American," Williams wrote in the *Collegian*. "Sabol, Hoffman, Moore and Kane ran and passed BU dizzy."

Neither Sabol nor any one else could overcome Army's gang-tackling of Moore the following week at West Point and the Lions lost, 35-6. Moore played 56 minutes, gained 75 yards on 16 carries, intercepted one pass and made several touchdown-saving tackles as the favored Cadets led by quarterback Don Hollender mauled the outmanned Lions. "Moore, a truly great player, lost no stature in this game," Riley wrote in the *"Football Letter."* "He played a superb defensive game...returned three kickoffs for 60 yards...and...made practically all his yardage through the tough Army forwards where it was worth your life to stick in your head...He was a marked man on every play, took a severe physical beating and came back time and time again for more."

Engle replaced Hoffman with Plum as the starting quarterback the following week for State's game against Virginia in what was billed as the "Tobacco Festival" bowl game played at the Richmond City Stadium. But it was Hoffman who was at the controls after Virginia took a 7-0 lead early in the second quarter and led the Lions to a come-from-behind 26-7 victory in a steady rain. Moore gained 92 yards on 16 carries and the Lions recovered two fumbles deep in Virginia territory to help set up two TDs. The game was tougher than the Lions had expected, perhaps because it was sandwiched between Army and Navy.

Navy had 17 vets back from the so-called "Team Named Desire" that had beaten Mississippi in the '55 Sugar Bowl and the Middies were unbeaten and unscored upon in three games with the best total defense in the country. The returnees included quarterback George Welsh, who would one day become an assistant coach at State in the Paterno era, and fellow All-American Ron Beagle at end. A heavy rain fell for 24 hours before the kickoff but that didn't stop a sellout Homecoming crowd of 32,209 from turning out to root for an upset. They were already buzzing about the daring bunch of PSU Sigma Chi fraternity brothers who had kidnapped the Navy mascot, Billy XIV, the previous week.

"Nobody, but nobody will cross the Navy goal line," a Middie player had declared in writing on the bulletin board after beating Pitt. He was wrong. Navy scored on a drive following the kickoff to take a 6-0 lead but the Lions came right back. Welsh stopped State's first scoring threat with a pass interception at the Navy 12-yard line but the Lions then went 45 yards following Navy's punt to go ahead 7-6 at the end of the first quarter on a nine-yard inside reverse by Kane and Valentine's PAT. But State would not score again until late in the game as Navy's defense zeroed in on stopping Moore and Welsh carved up the State defense with his passing. Navy won 34-14, holding Moore to his lowest rushing yardage in more than two years—37 yards on 18 carries. Welsh broke Tony Rados' three-year-old Beaver Field passing record by hitting on 15 of 20 passes for 285 yards and two TDs and scoring another TD on a quarterback sneak. "Oh, That Welsh—" said the headline in the *Centre Daily Times*. "Penn State played one quarter of fine football Saturday afternoon, won it 7-6, then succumbed to the brilliant passing of Navy's George Welsh...," wrote sports editor Paul Poorman.

State was a 14-point underdog the following week in Morgantown against another unbeaten team, eighth-ranked West Virginia. The faces of the opponents were familiar with Wyant, Bosley, Huff and Marconi back for their fourth season. State was outweighed 20 pounds per man and the Mountaineers had many more men with a bench full of young and talented reserves. But the Lions were not intimidated and they drove 64 yards primarily on the ground early in the second quarter to lead 7-0 with Hoffman scoring the TD on a sneak and Plum booting the extra point. Wyant's second interception of the half stopped another Lions threat at the Mountaineers 25-yard line and State took its narrow margin into the third quarter. Then, WVU drove 93 yards midway through the quarter to tie the score. Only the punting of

State's reserve quarterback Jim Hochberg kept the game from getting out of hand. The home team went into the lead on a 50-yard drive early in the fourth quarter and scored its final TD with less than two minutes left in the game following a Lions fumble. "W.VA Manpower Whips Lions, 21-7," said the headline in the *Collegian*. "In the final 21 minutes," wrote sports editor Williams, "the effect of Coach Art Lewis' merry-go-round substitution techniques was felt as he replaced a solid first string with equally powerful and well-rested gridders."

Penn had refused to move its 1955 game to Beaver Field and so, for the 44th time since the series began in 1890, the Lions traveled to Philadelphia for the October 29th encounter at Franklin Field. De-emphasis had emasculated Penn football and the Quakers had lost 14 straight games over the last two years. The Lions were a 26-point favorite but seemed to relax after taking a 13-0 lead in the first quarter and the game had little excitement after that because Penn never seriously threatened. Late in the final period, State's second team drove 65 yards, mostly on the passing of Plum, and scored with less than 30 seconds left on a nine-yard pass from Plum to little used senior end Leo Kwalik, causing Penn's coach Steve Sebo to complain that Engle was "rubbing it in" and rolling up the score to 20-0. (Wonder what Steve Sebo of 1951 would think of Steve Spurrier of 1998?)

Sebo's grumbling aside, Engle had seen something in Plum's quarterbacking during that last two-minute drive that he had not seen before. The junior appeared more confident about himself, more in control of the situation, relying on his instincts and his natural ability to carry him. Maybe he was ready to become the big-time quarterback Engle and Paterno had always thought he could be.

It didn't seem that way during the first half against Syracuse. Another sellout Band Day crowd of 30,321 and a CBS regional television audience watched as Plum fumbled on State's first possession and Syracuse recovered at the Lions 29-yard line. Syracuse scored in five plays with Jim Brown, the future Hall-of-Fame halfback, carrying four times and getting the touchdown on a fourth-and-two. Brown kicked the extra point and the Orange led 7-0. Neither Plum nor Hoffman could get the Lions offense moving despite some solid running by Moore and midway through the second quarter, Syracuse drove 68-yards in 12 plays on the running and pass receiving of Brown to score another touchdown. A 15-yard pass from Albright to Brown just outside the 10-yard line set up another clutch fourth down play for the TD when Albright passed five-yards to Brown in the corner of the end zone. Brown went back to kick the extra point but this time, soph end Farls, who was making his first start because of injuries, threw off a Syracuse defender and blocked the kick. But the Lions' offense still couldn't move and Syracuse took the ball again as time was running out in the half. Engle was exasperated as he looked at the scoreboard and saw the score. Syracuse had not won on Beaver Field since 1934, losing nine straight to the State on the Lions' home turf, but that streak was now in serious jeopardy.

Then came the break of the game. With the clock under a minute, Albright called a pass play from the Syracuse 32-yard line. His pass seemed to be on target to Brown at the sideline, but at the last second young Sabol—the star of the BU game who was now the third team fullback and spot substitute at linebacker—leaped in front of Brown to intercept the pass. Sabol rambled toward the goal line, evading tacklers at least four times before being hauled down from behind at the 10. Plum started off the field, expecting Hoffman to take over the offense, but Engle waved him back on. With 15 seconds left on the clock, Plum passed to Kane running at the two-yard line and Kane stepped into the end zone. Plum's PAT made it 13-7 and the partisan crowd went wild as the half ended. But the home fans' glee didn't last too long into the third quarter.

Brown took the second half kickoff three yards into end zone and was almost in the clear when Moore's ankle tackle brought him down at the Syracuse 47. But Moore's heroics only postponed the inevitable. Six plays later, Brown went around right end from the six for the TD. His extra point made it 20-7 with 11 minutes still remaining in the third quarter and the crowd fell into a near silence. But the fans perked up again when Plum ran back Syracuse's short kick to the State 41-yard line. With Moore, Kane, Sabol and Plum doing the running and Plum passing 20-yards to Kane on one play, the Lions drove for a score with Moore going up the middle from two yards out for the TD. Plum's PAT was good and the Lions were back within six midway through the third quarter. For the rest of the game, the two teams hammered away at each other, trying to take advantage of breaks by recovering fumbles and intercepting passes. Early in the fourth quarter, Brown intercepted a Plum pass at the Orange 41, then moments later ran 42 yards before Plum saved a TD with the tackle at the State 13. Syracuse looked like it would score but Plum again stopped a TD when he intercepted Albright in the end zone with six minutes left in the game. The Lions took over on their own 20 and the defining moment of the season was about to begin.

Milt Plum (22) about to break up a pass. Best remembered as a passer, quarterback Plum was an outstanding defender, leading team in interceptions in '55 and '56. He also punted and handled placekicking duties for the Lions.

Now it was Moore, Straub, Plum and the offensive line's turn. With Moore making runs of 22, 14, five and four yards and Straub banging out 14 yards for a first down, Plum guided the Lions to the Syracuse one-yard line, then took the ball over on a sneak to tie the game. Plum stepped back to try the go-ahead extra point. Kane took the snap and set the ball as Syracuse defenders crashed in. Plum hurried and the kick was low—but it cleared the cross bar by inches and the crowd erupted. The Syracuse players could not believe it. Three plays after the kickoff, Syracuse fumbled and Valentine recovered at the Orange 46. Down the field went Plum and the Lions, all the way to the Syracuse two when the game ended. One point was enough this time and the Lions won, 21-20.

Jim Brown had run for 159 yards on 20 carries, caught two passes, scored three TDs and two extra points, returned three kickoffs for 95 yards and intercepted one pass in one of the greatest individual performances ever on New Beaver Field. Moore also had been outstanding with his best offensive day of the season, 146 yards and a TD on 22 carries. "...He came up with an old time performance when it was needed most," wrote Carl Hughes in the *Pittsburgh Press.* "In Coach Rip Engle's jubilant words, 'Lenny never in his life was greater.'" But the biggest star of the day was Plum, who played all but 10 min-

utes, and it was Engle who again summed up Plum's day when he told the *Collegian*'s Williams, "If, as I believe, Plum found himself against Syracuse, our quarterback troubles are ended."

The next week the Lions clinched State's 17th consecutive winning season with a 34-13 win at Rutgers. Moore had the last of his great running days, rushing for 179 yards and three touchdowns on nine carries, including an 80-yard sprint for the Lions first TD. Plum also had his best rushing day of the season before his home state New Jersey crowd, sprinting for 87 yards on 11 carries, scoring one TD and booting three extra points.

It would have been satisfying to have capped "The Centennial Season" with a victory over Pitt at Beaver Field. But Pitt's new coach, John Michelosen, had revitalized the Panthers and they were again among the best teams in the nation. Their 6-3 record was deceiving and one week earlier they had knocked off unbeaten West Virginia 26-7. That victory made Pitt the leading candidate for the Sugar and Gator Bowls. They were big and tough with such standouts as Joe Walton and John Paluck. Still, the Lions were only a touchdown underdog and some sportswriters believed Moore's speed, Plum's quarterbacking and an attacking defense would give State a good chance. A snow that fell overnight and continued throughout the game in freezing weather literally put a damper on State's offense and defense. "The agility required by this (5-3-3 looping) defense needs sure footing and there wasn't much footing at all," Riley wrote in his *"Football Letter."*

"Pittsburgh just ran over us. In their first drive and until they were stymied by a fumble, no one in the Pitt backfield made less than six yards in a try. It was sort of frightening."

But as the 29,361 bundled up fans watched through the snow flakes, State didn't back down. Twice when the game was scoreless the Lions drove into Pitt territory only to be stopped when Plum's passes were intercepted. The second interception by Bobby Grier inside the Panther 35-yard line was returned to the State 32 and led to Pitt's first TD on a fourth-and-one with six minutes left in the half. Pitt carried the 7-0 lead into the second half and then drove 77 yards at the end of the third quarter to up the lead to 14-0. The Lions tried to score but the Panthers' defense was too good and they ganged-up on Moore, holding him to 10 yards on 13 carries. Quarterback Corny Salvaterra's 62-yard run off an option around right end in the fourth quarter made it 20-0 and that's how it ended. "Neither a driving snowstorm nor a charging Penn State team could keep Pitt from posting its best football record since the era of the late Jock Sutherland," wrote Hughes in the *Pittsburgh Press.* Pitt went on to a #11 rating and a Sugar Bowl game against Georgia Tech. Penn State went into its second century and Lenny Moore went on to be one of the all-time greats in professional football.

It would be years before State would again have a running back with the all-around talent of Moore. But now Engle had a big-time quarterback, one who could win games in the clutch against the odds. And in 1956, Milt Plum would beat the biggest odds of all with the help of his defense and some tips from an Oklahoman named Wiliknson.

Season Record 5-4
Record to Date 348-192-37
Winning percentage .635

"The Somersault in Columbus"

Assistant coach Tor Toretti stood before the 600 cheering students at the Thursday night pep rally outside Recreation Hall and flatly predicted an upset victory over Ohio State in Columbus on Saturday. The Lions were a two-to-three touchdown underdog against the undefeated, fifth-ranked Buckeyes and many sportswriters figured the game would be a runaway.

Toretti wasn't just trying to pump up the spirits of the students with patronizing mishmash. He had scouted the Buckeyes and he really believed what he was saying. "You will be proud to be here when you join the thousands who will be here Sunday morning (welcoming our victorious team home)," he confidently told the crowd in a voice choking with emotion. He said the game would be between schools where "football means everything" and one where "it is part of an education."

The schools had not met on the football field since the infamous encounter in 1912 at Columbus when the beleaguered Ohio State team quit before the end of the game because of the physical and mental beating it was taking. The bitterness from that game lasted for decades and many old time OSU alumni wondered why this one was ever scheduled. Pete Mauthe, one of the Penn State's stars of the 1912 game, had something to do with it. Mauthe was now the president of the Youngstown (Ohio) Sheet & Tube Co. and a member of Penn State's Board of Trustees. Mauthe's Ohio connections, especially his friendship with Columbus-based businessman John Galbreath, owner of the Pittsburgh Pirates and an OSU grad, helped bring the game about.

This year's pregame circumstances were eerily similar to that skirmish 44 years ago. Ohio State was again a heavy favorite and Columbus sportswriters and fans were disparaging the quality of an Eastern football team. "Buckeyes In For Easy Time," read one newspaper headline. "They are an intruder on the Big Ten schedule," said the *Columbus Dispatch*. "Ohio State practices Wisconsin plays," wrote another Columbus sportswriter. "The attitude of the people here in Columbus," wrote Fran Fanucci, sports editor of *The Daily Collegian*, "was that the Lions were a breather; everyone, including the team, was looking toward Wisconsin."

In truth, the Lions looked like easy pickings to Ohio State, a perennial Top 20 team and the defending National Champion. Although the Lions were 2-1, both victories had been over Eastern patsies, Penn and Holy Cross, and even Engle knew he lacked the manpower to compete with the Buckeye legions. Since spring practice, Engle believed he would have a solid first team but would be thin in reserves. He was especially worried about the tackle position where Calderone was the

only returning letterman. Senior Walt Mazur, the biggest man on the team at 6-foot, 230-pounds would be the other tackle. Engle had the most experience at end with five lettermen back: Farls, Walters, North, Jim Caldwell and Doug Mechling. The rest of the first line had Valentine, the captain, and DeLuca at the guards and Radakovich at center. Plum and Kane were the prime backs. "Plum doesn't have any faults," Paterno said in mid September. "He's the best all around quarterback on the team since we've been here." Senior Ray Alberigi was installed at Moore's old left half position and junior Babe Caprara, who was hurt much of '55, at fullback. Engle was so confident about Caprara and his sophomore backup, Maurice Schleicher, that he moved his surprise fullback star of last season, Sabol, to a second team guard slot. Engle also had high hopes for an elusive sophomore running back named Bruce Gilmore, who had followed Lenny Moore as a high school star in Reading. Engle lacked a breakaway runner like Moore but he believed he had more team speed. He also altered some of his offensive and defensive schemes after he, Paterno and O'Hora had driven to Oklahoma in the summer to see what they could learn from Bud Wilkinson, coach of what was then the nation's premier football program. Wilkinson's advice also helped Engle reorganize his practice session, making them more flexible for the players. The players responded by working hard in practices. They had the best spirit and more desire than any team he had coached and Rip had a prophetic hunch. "He (Engle) believes that this team will surprise somebody," wrote Ridge Riley in his preseason analysis for alumni, "some favorite opponent, and will upset one of our rivals when they are least expecting it."

Engle wasn't thinking of Penn. The Quakers had lost 18 games in a row and the Lions made it 19 with an easy 34-0 win at Philadelphia, amassing 414 total yards and 20 first downs to Penn's 99 yards and two first downs. In the process, Engle deployed a Split-T formation, rather than the Wing-T, which he helped develop, because his personnel was better suited for that orthodox formation.

As usual, the Lions traveled to West Point as a 13-point underdog against a seventh-ranked Army team. With the corps of cadets screaming non-stop over amplified speakers from the opening kickoff, Army appeared to be on the verge of a rout in the first quarter with two touchdown drives from midfield and a 14-0 lead. However, the Lions settled down and stopped the Cadets from any more scoring, with Plum twice making touchdown-saving tackles. Sabol's pass interception at the Army 35-yard line late in the third quarter set up a State touchdown on a two-yard burst by Schleicher and Caprara's PAT made it 14-7. The Lions almost tied it a few minutes later when Gilmore, broke away on a long run from PSU's six-yard line but was forced out of bounds at the Army 40 by the last man who had any chance, safetyman and quarterback Bob Kyasky. The final was 14-7 and Fanucci wrote in the *Collegian*: "Oh! If the Nittany Lions could only play those first 11 minutes...over again...If Engle's crew stood out in any phase of the game it was in its highly competitive spirit. For not in the past four years has a Penn State team displayed a never-say-die spirit as this team."

A Homecoming crowd and regional CBS TV audience watched the following week as the Lions demolished a 1-1 Holy Cross team, 43-0. Engle's second unit led by the passing of sophomore quarterback Al Jacks scored three first half TDs as Engle cleared his bench. State was so dominant that it never had to punt and only once did the defense led by "Bad Rad" Radakovich allow the Crusaders to venture past the 50-yard line. But Army's shocking 48-14 loss to Michigan the same day took much of the luster off State's spirited performance against the Cadets and undoubtedly contributed to the disparaging remarks about Eastern football that emanated from Columbus throughout the next week. "We are looking forward to the game," Ohio State's All-American guard Jim Parker told a sportswriter on the eve of the game, "because we want to show an Eastern team what Big Ten football looks like."

The night before the game, Engle got the players in the proper mood by taking them to see a Jack Palance war movie called "Attack." As they dressed in the locker room the next day, they listened as Engle read the denigrating remarks of Parker and others in the Columbus newspapers. They were slightly awed when they walked out into the horseshoe of the stadium and looked up at what was then the largest crowd to see a Penn State football game—82,584 hostiles screaming for their heads. Then, as a regional TV audience watched, Ohio State kicked off into a 12-mile wind and the Lions shocked the throng by driving all the way to the OSU 20 before a Plum pass was intercepted at the 10-yard line. Ohio State couldn't move, punted, and the Lions did it again—this time going 51 yards before another Plum pass was intercepted. That would be the

Rip Engle poses at Beaver Field with his first First-Team All-American and team captain in 1956, guard Sam Valentine.

Buckeye's last interception. The Lions had set the tone for the rest of the afternoon. OSU's offense, which had been averaging 333 yards per game behind the running of Galen Cisco and John Roseboro, came to a virtual halt as the Lions defense led by Valentine and Radakovich and Plum's punting—one for 56 yards that went out of bounds on the one-yard-line and another for 72-yards that rolled out on the three—completely stymied the Buckeyes. In the second quarter, OSU recovered a fumble at the Lions 45 but State held for downs at the 18 and the Buckeyes' second-team field goal kicker, sophomore Frank Kremblas, missed a 25-yard field goal attempt, and the half ended, 0-0.

The Lions took the second half kickoff and did it again, marching from its own 28 to the OSU 13 before another fumble stopped the drive. Now, the Buckeyes finally made their move, driving to State's 25-yard line, and they seemed to have a TD when sophomore Don Clark broke into the clear only to be tackled from behind at the five by Gilmore. Three plays and two yards later, OSU quarterback Frank Elwood tried to pass into the end zone but Gilmore was there again to intercept. Midway in the fourth quarter, Plum's 72-yard punt help lead to the Lions' TD when OSU had to punt to State at midfield. With Gilmore, Kane and Plum doing the running, the Lions went 45 yards for the games first score. A 12-yard Plum-to-Kane pass took the ball to the one-foot line and on third down Gilmore bolted over. Plum kicked the PAT and the Lions led 7-0 with about 3 and a half minutes left in the game. When OSU got the ball at the 20 following the kickoff, Coach Woody Hayes did the unthinkable. He resorted to trickery and gave the go ahead for halfback Roseboro to pass on the option play. Roseboro completed the only two passes of the game in hitting end Leo Brown for 33 and 42 yards on successive plays that reached the Lion three-

yard line from where Clark went off tackle for the TD. Less than two minutes remained when Kremblas was sent in to try for the tying point. His substitution resulted in a five-yard penalty for having 12-men on the field and when he finally tried the kick, it was wide and the home-town crowd fell silent as the State players jumped up and down. "You could have heard a pin drop," Ticket Manager Ed Czekaj said to the *Centre Daily Times.*. "That was the most surprised crowd you ever saw." In what may have been the defining moment in the defining game of the season, Kane did a somersault in the end zone as Farls ran by Kremblas, patted him on the back and said, "That's the way to kick Frank." The Lions recovered the onside kick, ran out the clock and carried Engle and defensive line coach O'Hora off on their shoulders.

"Lions Overthrow Ohio State, 7-6," said the headline in the *CDT*. "I've never had a bigger victory," Engle told sports editor Jim Snyder. "What tickled me was that it came against a Western team. This will team then a little more respect for Eastern football."

Back in State College, students had rushed from the dormitories and fraternities to celebrate, as reported by Ed Dubbs in a *Collegian* extra edition published the next day: "The students went wild. Toilet paper hung from trees on the Mall. Cars, all vintages, all marked went down the Mall. The Alma Mater sang loud—but still with reverence. Even towns-people were joining in. Cheers ran wild. Chorus-line and snake-line dancing was the thing. Noise was the result." Eric Walker, who had succeeded Milton Eisenhower as president of the university three weeks earlier, was in Columbus but his wife watched the revelry from their campus home near the Mall and was relieved that it never turned violent. A proud and cheering crowd of more than 2,000 greeted the victorious team at Rec Hall Sunday morning, just as Toretti had predicted. Toretti also was credited with part of the victory for while scouting the Buckeyes he had discovered that OSU's QB Elwood tipped off the plays by where he looked coming out of the huddle and with his "audibles" at the line. So, the Lions knew where the ball carrier was going. That might not have mattered if State's offense had bogged down. "I thought all along they would have a fine defense," said OSU coach Woody Hayes. "But their offense was stronger than we expected."

State was a six-point favorite at home against West Virginia the following week but most of the nation's sportswriters predicted an upset sensing a State letdown. The Lions led 16-0 and stopped two Mountaineer drives near the end zone before winning 16-6 as Kane ran for 129 yards and a TD on 20 carries. WVU coach Pappy Lewis praised State as a "team that makes its own breaks, then hurts you with them." The victory moved the Lions up to #11 (UP) or #12 (AP) in the polls and the post-season bowls were expressing interest.

The Ohio State game may have defined the season but the November 3 clash against Syracuse at Archbold Stadium was the pivotal game of the year and defined a rivalry. It ended in a controversy that reverberated long into the Paterno era. Syracuse was also 4-1, flirting with the Top 10 and a bowl bid, and the game was rated a toss-up. The Orange, using its heavier line and backfield to control the ball, and running off a total of 90 plays to State's 53, won, 13-9, but it was a game the Lions could have had. The Lions lost three fumbles and had three pass interceptions but still had a 9-6 lead in the fourth quarter until a sack on Jacks gave Syracuse the ball at the PSU 24-yard line and the Orange scored eight plays later. With 1:49 left in the game, Syracuse was about to punt on a fourth-and-15 from its own 35-yard line when Engle sent in his starter Plum to relieve Jacks. Syracuse coach Ben Schwartzwalder protested that the substitution was illegal. Engle and his players argued vociferously that Plum was eligible but the officials agreed with Syracuse and marked off a 15-yard penalty. However, the game wasn't over, and it ended in a fury. Syracuse lost a fumble. Jacks threw an interception. Syracuse lost another fumble. Jacks had a desperation pass partially blocked on the last play of the game and that was it. Engle was furious at the officials but he couldn't prove anything until the game film was developed. "Films Prove Plum's Eligibility," said the page one headline in the *Collegian* the following Tuesday. "Subject to intense criticism by many newspapers and fans for pulling a 'blunder' which cost the Lions a possible victory," Fanucci wrote, "Engle was proven correct by game movies which showed clearly that quarterback Milt Plum...was a legal substitution when Engle sent him into the game..." No one will ever know whether State could have come back to win the game with Plum at quarterback. But Lions fans pointed to the fact that Plum had driven the team 61 yards with less than two minutes left in the first half and then kicked a 19-yard field goal that had given State the 9-6 lead. Plum's last minute heroics two weeks later against North Carolina State made a come-from-behind scenario even more credible. The frustrating defeat not only knocked the Lions out of the Top 20 but, correspondingly, propelled the Orange to an eventual number eight ranking and a Cotton Bowl game against TCU.

The Lions took out their frustration against Boston University the next week at Beaver Field, winning 40-7 to guarantee the 17th straight non-losing season. Gilmore had 110 of State's 314 rushing yards and scored the first TD on a 33-yard slant off right tackle in the first period. Walters caught two passes for TDs, including one for 72 yards in the fourth quarter that was State's longest TD reception since Bob Higgins' 92-yard catch against Pitt in 1919.

The matchup against North Carolina State in the final home game of the season was intriguing because the Lions' one-time star end and assistant coach, Earle Edwards, was now the head coach at NC State. Edwards, who had been passed over for the Penn State job because of some backroom politics when Higgins retired in 1949, had two other former Lion stars as his assistants—Al Michaels of '35 and Bill Smaltz of '42. He also had 27 Pennsylvania recruits on his team including seven starters. But with just a 3-5 record in his first year, Edwards' Wolfpack were a 20-point underdog to the Lions. It was a cold day with light snow but the weather didn't bother the crowd of 22,864 nor the visitors with all those Pennsylvanians on the squad. NC State with its multiple offense was the aggressor and the Lions seemed listless for most of the game. Twice in the first half, the defense stopped Wolfpack drives near the goal, once at the seven and then at the three. Penn State got no closer than the NC State 17 and both teams missed a field goal. As time was winding down in the fourth quarter, a scoreless tie seemed inevitable. Then came the explosion.

There were seven and a half minutes on the clock when NC State's star, Dick Hunter of Leechburg, quick kicked on third down from his own 25-yard line and the ball went out of bounds at the PSU 43. Plum passed to Kane for 22 yards on second down and seven plays later Kane vaulted over the goal line from two yards out for the first score of the game. Plum's PAT made it 7-0 with 3:15 on the clock and the cheering State fans were certain the Lions defense would end it in four more plays. But Plum's kickoff only reached the 30-yard line and the runback took the ball to the 44. With the help of two fine passes, a holding penalty and two offside penalties inside the 10, the Wolfpack reached the one-yard line. However, an unusual pushing penalty on NC State's halfback moved the ball back to the 16. Three plays later, on third-and-one from the six, Bill Franklin passed over the middle to Bob Pepe, who made a spectacular catch in the end zone while surrounded by several defenders. Hunter tied the game with minute and a half left.

This time, NC State's kickoff was short and Kane returned it 12 yards to the Lion 37. On the first play, Plum pitched out to Alberigi who swept around right end for 19 yards. Students began pouring out of their seats and ringing the south end of the field. Plum passed twice to Walters for a first down at the Wolfpack 21 with 45 seconds left and only one time out remaining. An offside penalty put the ball back to the 26. Then, Plum hit Kane twice on the same sideline pass pattern to stop the clock, first at the 16 and then at the nine. Twenty-five seconds remained and the crowd was screaming. Plum decided to try one more pass before calling time out and getting the kicking tee. He spotted Walters on the three covered by three defenders but threw the ball perfectly. Walters leaped and nabbed the ball over his shoulders and barreled into the end zone carrying three NC State tacklers with him. There were 15 seconds remaining when Plum made it 14-7. The flat kickoff was a formality after a 15-yard penalty had been walked off against NC State for unnecessary roughness and the exhilarated students ran out onto the field to carry several of the players off on their shoulders. "We've been talking about the great courage and spirit of our players all season," wrote Riley in the *"Football Letter."* "It was evident now...Milt Plum supplied the expert direction. Never have we seen a more skillful use of available time. As the seconds ticked away, Milt proved his All-American stature...One mistake anywhere would have been fatal."

Despite the thrilling victory, the Lions were seven-point underdogs against Pitt in the season finale. Both the Orange and Cotton bowls were courting the Panthers, who had beaten Army and Syracuse, and 51,308 turned out at Pitt Stadium in 25 degree weather for the annual battle. At first, it appeared as if Pitt would blow the Lions right out of the stadium as the Panthers marched all the way to the goal line on the opening kickoff before a fourth down tackle by Valentine, Kane and Caprara at the one-foot line ended the threat. Late in the first quarter, State started a drive from its own 40 yard line and three minutes into the second quarter Kane went off right tackle from four yards out for the TD. Plum's PAT made it 7-0 but Pitt stormed back after the kickoff, driving 75 yards to tie the score on an 18-yard pass from Corny Salvaterra to Bob Rosborough and Amby Bagamery's PAT. Both teams threatened again over the next two and a half quarters but neither could score. Plum had a chance to win it late in the game but his field goal attempt from the 13-yard line missed by a few feet to the right. "I thought he would make it," Engle said after the game. "He could probably kick nine out of ten like that any time."

Despite the tie, Pitt got a Gator Bowl bid and a #12 ranking.

The Lions had to settle for an All-American as Valentine became State's first, First Team All-American since Sam Tamburo in 1948. "He's a great defensive performer and an outstanding leader and the best linebacker I've coached," said Engle upon hearing the news.

"There have been Penn State teams with better overall records than the one compiled by our current eleven," wrote Riley, "but it is doubtful if any team in our history ever got more mileage out of its potential." It would be different a year later.

Season Record 6-2-1
Record to Date 354-194-38
Winning percentage .637

"Close, But No Cigar"

Rip Engle looked uneasily at his untested sophomore quarterback Richie Lucas as captain Joe Sabol led the team out of the decrepit visitor's locker room at Archbold Stadium for the second half against Syracuse.

In four games, Lucas had done a capable, if unspectacular, job as quarterback of State's sophomore-laden second unit. Now, with starter Al Jacks out indefinitely with a dislocated shoulder, Lucas would have to take over the first team in the middle of the biggest game of the season—a game they had to win to turn the season around. Lucas, who had started the preseason as the number three quarterback, had great potential but even Engle's quarterback coach, Paterno, believed the kid from Glassport in suburban Pittsburgh needed seasoning. And here he was, about to replace the second best passer in the East and one of the nation's leaders in total offense.

Sure, the Lions were beating the undefeated and favored Orangemen, 13-12, but they had blown a 13-0 second quarter lead and, again, it was the pass defense that was responsible. Six of the last seven touchdowns scored against State had been by the air and Engle wasn't sure the defensive adjustments they just made in the locker room could stop the Syracuse aerial attack. That meant Lucas, who was accurate on short passes but not a great long passer, might be forced to throw long to win the game. It was not a comforting thought.

Engle had been worried that something like this would happen. It was the way the season was going. He had known since spring practice that this would be a young team with a major weakness at tackle and guard and limited speed in the backfield. Jacks, technically a "redshirt" junior, had been a fine successor to Plum and because he was such an outstanding passer, the offense had been getting more pass catching out of the ends. Five of the 18 returning lettermen were ends—including seniors Walters, Farls and North— and their experience on defense as well as offense was valuable. Center was solid, too, with junior veterans Chuck Ruslavage and Steve Garban. Sabol was a fine leader and a standout at left guard. Veteran Richie McMullen had started the season opener against Penn at the other guard but now was out with fractured ribs and his replacements were untested underclassmen with junior Willard "Bull" Smith and sophs Bud Kolhass, a converted center, and Sam Stellatella getting the most playing time at that position. Tackle had been weak from the start with only veteran Bill

Wehmer returning. Junior Joe Bohart was at the other tackle but Engle had three sophomores behind them who had great potential: Charlie Janerette, Tom Mulraney and Andy Stynchula—perhaps the best of all, who had been switched from right end at the start of preseason practice. Underclassmen also dominated the backfield with Caprara, the only senior, returning to start at fullback. McConyi was back as the regular right half but last year's sophomore standout, Gilmore, was bothered by a preseason knee injury (which would eventually sideline him for the year) and Army veteran, Dave Kasperian, who had been an unheralded walk-on sub from last year, was starting at left half. Lucas had beaten out junior "redshirt" Bob Scrabis for the backup quarterback slot and a couple of sophomores, Pat Botula and Eddie Caye, also were seeing a lot of action at running back along with the veteran Schleicher at fullback and non-letterman Army veteran Bucky Paolone at halfback.

Despite the relative inexperience of the team, some sportswriters had projected the Lions as a possible bowl team. "*Look*" magazine picked them #10 in the nation and second in the East behind Navy. Francis Wallace of "*Playboy*" had them 14th in the country and Jesse Abramson, writing in the *New York Herald-Tribune*, said they were "the choice here for Eastern champion," after Pitt. Beano Cook, then the sports publicity director at Pitt—but even then making errant predictions he would later become famous for as a radio and TV college football analyst—said State would go to the Cotton Bowl. Engle, always the pessimist anyway, knew his players would have to jell as a team—as the '56 squad did—if it was to be as good as the sportswriters expected.

The season opening win over Penn at Franklin Field, 19-14, did little to give Engle optimism. Although they were overwhelming favorites, the Lions struggled. They never trailed and for most of the game they had a two touchdown lead. However, the Quakers made it look close with a determined effort that gave them one touchdown on a 47-yard run just before the half and another in the last four minutes of the game that led their fans to claim a "moral victory."

Army visited Beaver Field for the first time in an eight-game series that started in 1899 when State won for the only time. Army's Coach, Earl "Red" Blaik, had convinced the college football world that

this was a rebuilding year at West Point and most of the partisan crowd of 31,979 believed State would win. The fans were even more confident after the Lions took the opening kickoff and marched 57 yards for a 6-0 lead on Kasperian's two-yard TD run. Minutes later, Army recovered a fumble at State's 48-yard line and scored in 12 plays with sophomore Bob Anderson getting the TD on a crucial fourth-and-five run

Tackle Andy Stynchula was one of the premier linemen of the mid-Engle era and went on to play several years for the Washington Redskins.

off left tackle to make it 6-6. State regained the lead early in the second quarter after forcing Army to kick from deep in its own territory and getting the ball at the Army 38. Jacks virtually passed the rest of the way for the TD, hitting Walters all alone in the end zone for the TD on an 18-yarder. Caprara's PAT made it 13-6. As the half was winding down, Army started a drive downfield. On one particular play in front of the PSU sideline, fullback Harry Walters and two of his blockers were hit by three State tacklers and the entire gang went careening out of bounds and into a crowd at the Lion bench. When the group unpiled, an old man in street clothes was on the bottom. He literally jumped up and could be seen by most of the crowd shaking his fist at the Army players and shouting something. A couple of minutes later he was identified as Earl "Pop" Hewitt, now 78, and the star of the 1899 victory over Army when he ran back a punt 65-yards for State's only touchdown. "You couldn't get me in 1899," he had shouted at Walters and company, "and you can't get me now." Pop must have put the curse on Army for the drive died and the Lions took their 13-6 lead into intermission.

But if there was a hex, it was gone by the time State kicked off to open the second half. Army spent the next 15 minutes driving the ball right down State's throat, scoring three times on marches of 71, 66 and 40 yards. Led by a relatively unknown junior named Pete Dawkins, the visitors finished the game with 303 yards rushing while holding State to 78 yards on the ground. Army's rushing defense was so good in the second half that the Lions had only 10 running plays and tried to get back into the game in the fourth quarter on Jacks' arm. When the game was over, Jacks had tied Tony Rados' single game record for completed passes (set in '52 against Purdue) by completing 17 of 32 attempts for 166 yards. However, Army had the 27-13 victory and would go on to lose only two games and finish 18th in the country. Joseph M. Sheehan, covering for *The New York Times* praised Army's "devastating attack power" but also Jack's performance. "This clever junior quarterback bedeviled Army's secondary early and late in the game with his bullseye passing," Sheehan wrote. Engle told the *Centre Daily Times* "Our kids were real disappointed that we didn't win. But, as I told them, our season began today—it didn't end."

The "kids" didn't do much better the following Saturday at home against a three-touchdown underdog William & Mary team that had won only two games in three years. Lucas engineered his first career touchdown drive, taking the alternate unit 81-yards for a 7-0 lead, but W&M stormed back to go ahead 13-7 at the end of the third quarter. As the teams traded sides, Paterno turned to fellow assistant Earl Bruce on the sideline and said, "Now, we'll find out if we have a football team." Kasperian led the comeback, running for 35 yards in a 56-yard march that put the Lions ahead 14-13 on Caprara's TD plunge and PAT. Kasperian sparked another drive late in the game to clinch the game, 21-13. "At least we know we have a football team," Paterno told Vince Carocci, sports editor of the *Daily Collegian*. "Now, we need to find out just how good we are."

The Lions did not have a good week leading up to the Homecoming game against a new opponent, Vanderbilt. A flu epidemic that hit campus kept many players away from practice. Then on Thursday, Engle's father died. The elder Engle had sat on the bench at the William & Mary game and was given the game ball by Sabol. Coach Engle was on the sideline Saturday afternoon but some players were not because of the flu. The Lions had a 20-7 lead midway through the second quarter, then fell apart as Vanderbilt, a six-point underdog, scored on TD passes of 11, 78 and 39 yards for a 32-20 upset win. State had 23 first downs to the Vanderbilt's 19 but lost three fumbles and had two passes intercepted as the Commodores took full advantages of State's shaky pass defense. Engle blamed the flu and mistakes on pass defense for the loss. "Our mistakes are coming at particularly wrong spots and are hurting us," he told sportswriters.

With three of the last four games away from Beaver Field, the pressure was intensifying for this erratic '57 squad and everyone knew it. "Syracuse Victory Called Necessary In Winning Year," said the front page headline in the *Collegian* on the day of the game. "The outcome could determine to a great extent the future of the Lion squad for the remainder of the year," wrote Carocci. Syracuse was 3-0-1 and a six-point favorite on its home field. "We don't like to play on that field," Engle admitted.

State took a 6-0 lead with just over a minute gone in the first quarter when a bad snap from center on a Syracuse punt attempt gave the Lions the ball at the Syracuse one-yard line and Caprara plunged over. A 51-yard pass from Jacks to Walters made it 13-0 a minute into the second quarter. But as a regional CBS TV audience looked on, Syracuse struck back in the quarter with drives of 65 and 46 yards that led to TD passes of 25 and 10 yards. The Orange missed both extra points and the Nittany Lions clung to a 13-12 lead. State almost scored another TD before the half on a pass from Lucas to Paolone but the officials ruled Paolone had been stopped at the one-inch line as the clock ran out. Paolone and his teammates protested vigorously but the ruling stood and another "Syracuse controversy" seemed to be in the making. "There were many who thought the State halfback had reached paydirt," wrote Michael Strauss in *The New York Times*. A few days later Engle told the *CDT,* "Even in the movies it's difficult to see how much forward progress he made and where his knee touched the ground."

But Paolone's near miss was all but forgotten in the aftermath of the second half. It was State's much maligned pass defense that set up the winning touchdown, then stopped Syracuse's passing comeback. Early in the third quarter, Syracuse quarterback Chuck Zimmerman was sacked at the Orange one-yard line by Walters after losing 11 yards while trying to pass. That set up a short punt which Kasperian returned four yards to the 27. What came on the next play was not only the defining moment of the season but perhaps the defining moment of a career. "Those who saw it are still talking about (it)...," Riley wrote in his *"Football Letter."* Lucas faked to Caprara, then appeared to hand off to Kasperian. The fake to Kasperian was so good it fooled just about all 35,000 spectators as well as sportscaster Lindsey Nelson and his CBS TV crew as the cameras followed Kasperian, who was tackled after an apparent five-yard gain. Lucas had kept the ball on an option right, then stopped and passed to Walters, who had streaked by Zimmerman, the safetyman. Walters caught the ball in stride at the five and crossed into the end zone. With Lucas holding, Caprara made it 20-12 and that was the final score. Syracuse ate up a lot of time with a stodgy ground attack and State's pass defense throttled Zimmerman the rest of the game. The Orange's only serious threat late in the fourth quarter was stopped when Sabol chased Zimmerman for a 20-yard loss on one pass play and moments later Walters tackled another receiver two yards short of a crucial first down near the State 15-yard line. For his all-around play, Walters was named "Lineman of the Week" by the Associated Press. "Don't expect miracles of Richie Lucas," Carocci wrote in the *Collegian*. "...The sophomore quarterback handled himself with the poise and ability of a veteran...(But) now that he finds himself in the first string drivers seat...this is quite a task for a soph in first varsity season." Paterno also was concerned, saying "You just can't lose a boy like Jacks without getting hurt."

The Lions didn't miss Jacks a bit the next week as Lucas led the team to a 27-6 win over a 4-1-1 West Virginia team at Beaver Field. Lucas hit on eight of 14 passes for 102 yards and two touchdowns and ran for 48 yards on seven carries as the Lions exploded for three second half TDs after leading by just 7-6 at the intermission. "Unquestionably our team performance against the Mountaineers was at its season peak," wrote Riley in the *Football Letter.* "...Engle was 'delighted with the manner in which Lucas 'took charge'...Richie rarely lost his poise under pressure and at times exhibited the kind of imaginative quarterbacking you would expect from a seasoned veteran."

There was a slight letdown at Milwaukee's County Stadium the following week when the Lions met Marquette for the first time ever. Marquette was in the throes of the nation's longest losing streak at 17 and few could blame the Lions for looking ahead to Holy Cross and Pitt. The smallest crowd to see State play since 1944—4,719—watched the Lions take a 20-0 lead in the first minute of the third quarter and win, 20-7, in a dull ground battle. Lucas and Scrabis combined for seven pass completions on 13 attempts for 132 yards but only to keep Marquette off balance as 10 State ball carriers rushed for 185 yards. "How do you get ready for a team like that," Engle said after the game. "...It was natural for our kids to get slightly complacent." The win assured State of its 19th straight winning season.

A high scoring game was expected when the Lions visited Holy Cross for the first time because Tom Greene, the Crusader quarterback, was the nation's total offensive leader and the top-rated passer. Holy Cross had upset Syracuse the week before on the running and passing of Greene. In the end, this game belonged to Kasperian who was playing before several hundred of his relatives and friends in his hometown of Worcester. The improving Lions pass defense broke up Greene's first seven passes and at halftime, Holy Cross led by the odd score of 2-0, after getting a second quarter safety when the center's snap sailed over Lucas' head on a punt from the State 12-yard line. On the first play after the second half kickoff, Greene dazzled the home fans with a pass that was caught by 6-foot-2 Charlie Pacunas over the head of the 5-foot-9 Kasperian at the Lions 35-yard line and Pacunas ran into the end zone for an 8-0 Crusader lead. But on the kickoff, Kasperian redeemed himself by running the ball back 67 yards to the Holy Cross 23. Two plays later, Lucas faked to Caprara and passed to Walters for a 16-yard TD. Caprara's PAT made it 8-7. Holy Cross return men fumbled the next kickoff and Ruslavage recovered at the Crusader 17. Four plays later, Lucas walked over from the one when his handoff never reached the intended ball carrier, and Caprara's kick made it 14-8. Two other Lion scoring threats were halted by penalties inside Crusader territory and a third one was stopped on downs at the Holy Cross 20 with seven minutes left in the game. That's when the excitement really began. Greene hit on a spectacular 56-yard pass and Holy Cross soon had a first-and-goal at the 8. Two running plays gained three yards and a third down pass was batted away by Walters. On fourth down, Greene rolled out right as if to pass and dashed toward the end zone but he was met by Wehmer and Walters and he got no further than the one-inch line. Two minutes were left in the game as Lucas tried to run out the clock. With 12 second remaining, Lucas went into punt formation, then simply walked out of the end zone with the ball for another

Holy Cross safety. Holy Cross had one more play after the free kick and Greene tried to throw a long one but Kasperian reached up and intercepted, ending the game and giving the Lions a 14-10 win. More than 200 members of the Armenian Club of Worcester swarmed onto the field, lifted Kasperian on their shoulders and carried him off the field.

After a two week layoff, it was on to Pitt and a possible bid to the Gator Bowl. Pitt, the preseason Eastern favorite, was just 3-5 after being upset by Syracuse (24-21) and West Virginia (7-6) but the Panthers were still a six-point favorite. Jacks was ready to play again but Lucas started and when three first half drives sputtered, Lucas kept Pitt contained with excellent punts that died on the 2-, 6- and 10-yard lines. Midway in the second quarter, State took the ball on the PSU 42 after a short Pitt punt and Engle sent in Jacks with the alternate unit. Jacks connected to Schleicher on a 43-yard pass and five plays later, on fourth-and-goal from the three, Caye took a handoff and circled left on an option. He was hit by two Pitt tacklers at the five but spun around, saw senior end Ron Markiewicz on his far right and threw the ball. Markiewicz leaped and caught the ball as he fell into the end zone. Caprara's PAT made it 7-0 with less than four minutes in the half. Pitt drove all the way to the State 13 before the Lion defense held as the half ended. Although he had been punting well, Lucas did not look sharp at quarterback, so Engle put Jacks in with the first team. A penalty on a fair catch punt gave State the ball at Pitt's 36-yard line late in the third quarter and six plays later Jacks passed to North for a nine-yard TD. Caprara's kick was wide and the Lions took its 13-0 lead into the fourth quarter. The State fans in the crowd of 44,710 at Pitt Stadium were shocked at what happened next. Led by quarterback Bill Kaliden, Pitt drove nearly the length of the field and scored on Fred Riddle's one-yard plunge with Ivan Tonsic's PAT making it 13-7. Moments later, Pitt forced State to punt and the Panthers soon had the ball at the State 45. Kaliden immediately hit his best receiver, Dick Scherer, in the open and the score was now tied. Tonsic was not eligible to re-enter the game, so Coach John Michelosen put in a third-string guard named Norton Seaman. His kick was good but the Panthers were penalized for a five-man backfield and he had to do it again from the seven. The second kick was good, too, and the Panthers took the lead they never relinquished. "I don't know when I've felt worse about losing one," Engle told sportswriters. "They were just too big and strong...they just wore you out."

About 10 days later, the Lions were invited to the relatively unknown Cigar Bowl that was scheduled in late December for a 15,000 seat stadium in Tampa. State officials expressed some interest when told TCU or Mississippi State would be the opponent. But when both of those schools declined, so did the Lions. "When we go to a bowl," a State spokesman told the *Collegian,* "we want to go to a bowl that will do some good for the prestige of the University." It would be two years before that would happen. Until then, Engle would have to endure another year of frustration and it would start almost from the opening kickoff.

Season Record 6-3
Record to Date 360-197-38
Winning percentage .637

"The Kickoff"

Penn State's opening game against Nebraska in 1958 looked like a breather, one that would get the veteran team ready for its more rigorous Eastern schedule. Once again Navy and Army, in that order, were being picked by sportswriters as the "teams to beat" in the battle for the Lambert Trophy with Penn State, tagged as "the sleeping giant" and Pitt and Syracuse rated on the next level.

The Lions were a two-touchdown favorite over Nebraska, which was then the doormat of Big Eight Conference. In Coach Bill Jennings first year in 1957, the Cornhuskers had their worst record ever, 1-9, and with 27 newcomers on its 42-man roster little improvement was expected in 1958.

Engle wasn't sure how good his team was. His veteran quarterbacks were the heart of it and neither he nor Paterno were worried about them. "What can be said about our quarterbacks that hasn't been said before," Paterno told the *Collegian* three days before the opener. "They're great. In fact, our only problem is who will start against Nebraska." Both Jacks, a who already had been drafted by the Los Angeles Rams, and Lucas, last year's sophomore flash, could run the first team and "redshirt" Scrabis (who would later play for the New York Titans/Jets) was a solid backup. Sophomore Dick Hoak of Jeannette, who quarterbacked the impressive, unbeaten freshman team, was so good on defense that Engle knew Hoak would force his way into the lineup.

Elsewhere, Engle was worried and uncomfortable. He fretted about team speed and the graduation of his five top ends. He was so uncertain about his team that in the preseason he shifted several '57 starters to different positions in an attempt to find the right mix. Tackle Wehmer, the best defensive tackler on the team, and center Ruslavage were moved to guards to get junior Stynchula and captain Garban into the first team lineup. Starting right halfback Moconyi (the third leading receiver in '57) and his backup Botula both moved to fullback and the 230-pound Schleicher shifted from fullback to end to get more punch in both the running and passing attacks. Engle had several lettermen returning, including Kasperian, Gilmore, Paolone and Caye in the backfield and Bohart, Kohlhass, Jannerette, Mulraney and Smith in the line. He would go with two non-lettermen as his starting ends, juniors John Bozik and Norm Neff but he was high on several sophomores, including Stew Barber, Dave Alexander and Henry Opperman. Four more sophs also figured to get plenty of playing time: Billy Popp at guard, Wayne Berfield at center, Jim Kerr at halfback and Don Jonas, a running back and placekicker.

The coach also was concerned that the first three games were on the road, especially the one at West Point on October 4 against a veteran Army team. Engle hoped the experience the Lions would get at Nebraska and Penn would have them primed for the Army and the Cadets' explosive running backs, junior All-American Bob Anderson and senior Captain Pete Dawkins. But after analyzing the Lions, some sportswriters, such as the *Centre Daily Times* sports editor, Ron Field, said the team "would be in trouble" if it gets more than a touchdown behind "because they don't have the explosive type of team that can overcome a big lead."

As preseason practice moved on, Engle had even more reason to worry. Injuries sidelined so many players in the 10 days before the Nebraska kickoff that the coach had to ease back on the hard contact drills. By the time the Lions took the field before 30,000 partisan Cornhusker fans at Lincoln Memorial Stadium on September 20, the team had lost starting backs Caye (for the season with a knee injury) and Moconyi and at least half dozen other key players off the first three units. Engle, always reluctant to use sophomores, had no choice. He inserted four sophs into the lineups of his first two teams—Sam Sobczak, who started the preseason on the sixth team, at fullback and Barber at end with Hoak and Jonas at halfbacks.

The Lions were in trouble within minutes of the opening kickoff when they were stunned by a 65-yard quick kick by highly-touted sophomore Pat Fischer that pinned them back on their own 14-yard line. Nebraska's surprising punt set the tone for the rest of the first half. The Lions' traditional Wing-T offense moved the ball but could never get a solid drive going. Two more booming punts by Fischer died on State's 11- and 2-yard lines. The half ended with the game scoreless and Engle and the players trotted uneasily into the locker room.

It was more of the same after the intermission. Another Nebraska punt, this one for 58 yards, rolled out of bounds at the PSU three-yard line early in the third quarter. As they had done in the first half, the Lions again punched out of the hole but couldn't sustain their attack. Punt. Minutes later, Nebraska lined up for a field goal. But it was a fake. The holder, Fischer, threw a pass that went incomplete and the Lions took over on their 29-yard line. With Lucas at quarterback, the Lions began to grind through Nebraska's beleaguered defense. Kasperian showed why he was All-East and the team's leading rusher the year before. He and Botula (who would gain 122 yards for the game, the most for a State fullback in eight years) led the 71-yard charge down field. Early in the fourth quarter, Kasperian picked up the last of his 43 yards in the drive with a one-yard bolt over left guard for a touchdown. Jonas booted the extra point and the State's small contingent of players and fans was exuberant. Finally, the Nittany Lions were in charge as everyone, including the Cornhuskers, had expected them to be.

And then it happened! The defining moment of the 1958 season. There was no live television and only black and white films and still photos would record the next moment for history. Stellatella kicked off. Fischer was back to receive. The Fischer family of Omaha was part of Cornhusker football history. Three brothers had preceded Pat at Lincoln and everyone was saying the kid brother was the best of them all. Fischer took the kick on the eight-yard line and ran down the left sideline. No one touched him and he sped 92 yards for a touchdown. Nebraska Captain Dick McCashland kicked the extra point to make the score 7-7. The Penn Staters were shocked and demoralized as they lined up for the Nebraska kickoff. Fischer, who would later be an All-Pro for the Washington Redskins, changed the direction of the game and, ultimately, the course of the season.

The Lions were spiritually down but not yet beaten, and they didn't give in easily. After the kickoff, they moved from their own 30-yard line to the Nebraska 49 before the usually sure-handed Kasperian fumbled and the Cornhuskers recovered. A surprise run around end picked up 30 yards for Nebraska and a 26-yard pass moved the Cornhuskers deep into Penn State territory. Then, it was fourth-and-goal at the one. Nebraska fullback Carroll Zaruba plunged over for the TD and McCashland kicked his second extra point to make it 14-7.

Still, the Lions didn't fade. There were seven minutes left to play when Paolone ran the kickoff back 36 yards to the Nebraska 49-yard line. In a few plays the Lions were at the Cornhusker nine-yard line and a score seemed imminent. But two running plays went nowhere and two pass attempts by Jacks were batted down. State got one more chance with 30 seconds remaining at the Nebraska 29-yard line but two plays gained three yards and it was over. Penn State's offense had dominated the game, recording 334 yards and 20 first downs on 83 plays while Nebraska had 181 yards and nine first downs on 49 plays. But the offense could never get completely on track. Nebraska had pulled off the stunning upset. The Cornhusker's coach, Jennings, admitted after the game that his team "had the psychological edge as do all underdog teams" and had been lucky Penn State dropped a couple of long, wide-open passes that would have been sure touchdowns. "In a nutshell," wrote Field, in the *CDT*, "spirit whipped experience, speed conquered power, determination swallowed up sluggishness in spots, great punting won over a passing game far off its stride..." But Engle, who in 28-years of coaching had never seen a kickoff returned for a touchdown against his team, summed up the game best: "That kick-off broke our morale."

The Lions next game was historic for it marked the end to State's longest rivalry. Pennsylvania and Penn State began meeting in 1890 and never once in the 47 games played did the Quakers ever travel to Beaver Field. Penn held the advantage, winning 25 games and tying four but it had not won since 1953 and it wouldn't win this final game either. Although favored by just over a touchdown, the Lions wanted to show the Nebraska loss had been a fluke and they had no problem shutting out the Quakers 43-0. "Instead of (Penn's) 82nd football season being ushered in with a rip-snorting battle as everyone had a reason to expect," wrote Herb Good in the *Philadelphia Inquirer*, "it turned out to be a nightmare and little more than a practice romp for Penn State ..." Again, Botula led all rushers with 72 yards on 15 carries but suffered a bad elbow sprain late in the first half on a blindside block while running downfield on a kickoff. It would prove to be a devastating loss, for Botula would not return until after the Syracuse game. The Penn game was historic for another reason. A new rule change for 1958 brought about the option for a two-point conversion following a touchdown. Engle didn't like it, saying before the season "it will bring a new era of second guessing." There was no second guessing when he used "it" three times against Penn, with Jacks throwing twice and Lucas once for the two points.

The Lions were a two-touchdown underdog the following week against sixth-ranked Army at Michie Stadium. The outcome was worse. Before the game everyone was talking about Coach Earl Blaik's radically new formation, with an end standing 15-18 yards away from his nearest teammate and never entering the huddle. This was the now-famous "lonesome end" with speedy junior Bill Carpenter (a Pennsylvania native who was later a Vietnam war hero) in the spotlight. It wasn't just the "lonesome end" who beat the Lions that day. Carpenter caught three passes for 119 yards, including a 55-yard touchdown. Dawkins and Anderson, whom Blaik had called "the best pair of half-backs in my 17 years at the Point" did the rest. Dawkins (who would win the 1958 Heisman Trophy) rushed for 73 yards and scored the first Army touchdown 3 and a half minutes into the game. He scored the Cadets' fourth TD on a dazzling, tackle-breaking 72-yard run after a short pass from quarterback Joe Caldwell. Anderson picked up 71 yards and a TD on 13 carries. The Lions never quit but it was all over by halftime and the 26-0 score didn't change after the intermission. Penn State limped back to State College for its home opener and Homecoming game against Marquette while Army moved up to number three in

Steve Garban was captain of the 1958 team and later, as senior vice president of financial affairs at Penn State and in charge of Athletic Department, he was influential in State's entrance into the Big Ten Conference and the expansion of Beaver Stadium.

the polls and soon would be number one. "After Saturday's game, Penn State became a football team without a country," Field wrote in the *CDT*. "Apparently too tough for teams like Penn, the Lions proved they don't have the personnel to travel with the big ones."

There were just 22,000 (11,000 less than capacity) on hand at Beaver Field as the Lions overwhelmed a weak Marquette team, 40-8. Primarily because of injuries, six sophomores started the game, including Sobczak and Kerr in the backfield, Opperman and Dave Truitt at the ends and Hoak in the defensive backfield. Kerr, one of the few Ohio (St. Clairsville) high school players Engle had recruited, was outstanding on defense in his debut, recovering a fumble and intercepting two passes, including one he ran back 44 yards for a touchdown. But it was a neglected senior who was the star. Halfback Bruce Gilmore, who had been a sophomore sensation himself in '56 but injured most of '57, racked-up 142 yards and two touchdowns on 19 carries. Lucas, also starting at QB for the first time this year, set a new team record for the longest touchdown run by a T-formation quarterback by scampering 49-yards in a passing situation. Marquette netted just 62 yards running and passing. "We thought they would be much tougher," Engle told the *Collegian* after the game. "But they weren't a good football team...Lucas ran and faked well and his passing was better than usual. The starting job is his as long as he keeps up his present work."

Engle altered his lineup again for the game at Boston University. By this time, only Garban and Stynchula had started every game. BU was coming off a surprising 36-30 upset over West Virginia and a tough 28-14 loss to Navy but the Terriers were no match for Lucas and the Lions defense. In a game televised regionally by NBC, State flattened BU 34-0 with Lucas running for 57 yards and two TDs, passing for 83 yards and intercepting a pass. But the game is remembered for one of those historic moments. With the score 13-0 early in the second period, Wayne Berfield, a sophomore center/linebacker inserted into the lineup when Garban went out with a concussion, intercepted a pass on the Lions' two-yard-line. Berfield shook off one tackler, leaped over another and raced 98 yards for a touchdown. It was the longest interception return in history and remained a record as the 1998 season began. The team also set another record that stood for 12 years with a total of six interceptions. "That line played a great game," said Red Grange, the Illinois football legend who covered the game for television. Engle told Ridge Riley, "For the first time we put offense and defense together...Now, I'm pretty sure we have a football team."

But State's next opponent was its old nemesis, Syracuse, and the Orange also had a good team and led the nation in scoring when they came to town as a six-point underdog on a rainy October 25. The Orangemen were led by quarterback Chuck Zimmerman, third in the nation on TD passes and that week's cover boy for *Sports Illustrated*. Engle's personal rivalry with Syracuse coach Ben Schwartzwalder was intensifying and Schwartzwalder was still smoldering from his team's 20-12 upset loss in Archbold Stadium in 1957. Syracuse had lost five of the last seven games against State and had lost 10 straight on Beaver Field dating to 1934. The Orangemen also were missing star lineman Ron Luciano (later a flamboyant major league baseball umpire) because of an injury. But there was an omen: Syracuse had walloped Nebraska 38-0 the previous weekend.

Syracuse took advantage of breaks and State errors and won 14-6 in a victory that helped propel them into the Orange Bowl and a top 10 final ranking. But to this day, most of the 27,000 partisan Lion fans who were at Beaver Field believe Schwartzwalder's team had help from the officials, specifically the referee—one Robert W. VanLengen, a graduate of the Syracuse law school who also lived in Syracuse. State was penalized seven times for 55 yards, mostly for controversial interpretations of "illegal procedure" or "illegal shifts" called by VanLengen at crucial times. Syracuse, however, did not have one penalty until there was less than a minute left in the game. Engle said to Riley "its inconceivable to me that a team like this could go for 59 minutes without a penalty of any kind." Somehow, as the game films would show, the officials missed a blatant out of bounds block on Kasperian and a number of holding and motion infractions by Syracuse while calling key penalties on the Lions. Perhaps, the defining moment—and the most demoralizing penalty—came late in the fourth quarter when sophomore flanker Jonas made an acrobatic 39-yard catch on a pass from Jacks to set up a potential tying touchdown only to have the play nullified by a motion call against Jonas. Films showed there was no motion. An angry Engle said in the locker room it was "the worst refereeing I've seen in 28 years" and he later complained in writing to the Eastern Collegiate Athletic Conference which assigned officials for the independent Eastern teams.

Even with the penalties, the Lions might have won if not for their own mistakes. The first time the Lions had the ball they drove 72 yards before fumbling on the Syracuse eight-yard line. In the second quarter, Lucas threw a perfect pass to a wide open receiver in the corner of the Syracuse end zone on a fourth down play from the 11-yard line but the end dropped the ball. "We're not alibing because of the penalties," Engle told the *Collegian*. "Even with all the penalties

we still should have beaten Syracuse." The defeat was a milestone in State's football history for it was the 200th loss since football began officially in 1887.

No one was worried about the next opponent, Furman. But with tough games also remaining against West Virginia, Holy Cross and Pitt there was apprehension about a potential losing season, especially with the star-crossed Gilmore now out for the season with another knee injury sustained in practice after the Syracuse loss. Furman went down 36-0 on Band Day as the Lions unleashed a high-powered passing offense for the first time. Lucas, now established as quarterback of the first unit, completed eight of 15 passes for 131 yards and one TD and also passed twice for two-point conversions. Schleicher finally lived up to Engle's expectations, catching five of Lucas's throws for 87 yards

But the next week in Morgantown, the Lions once again struggled, outplaying the Mountaineers before a screaming, hostile Homecoming crowd of 26,000 but allowing their own mistakes to hurt them. State lost six of seven fumbles, including two inside the West Virginia five-yard line, and had 85 yards in penalties. One holding call at the line of scrimmage negated an electrifying 80-yard touchdown by Hoak who grabbed a two-yard flat pass from Lucas and cruised into the end zone. State had to settle for a frustrating 14-14 tie. "We've never been a fumbling team," Engle moaned after the game. "We haven't given up. These kids deserve a break."

With a 4-3-1 record, the first losing season since 1938 was now a real possibility. But, in the final home game of the season, the Lions walloped a solid, once-beaten Holy Cross team that had bowl aspirations after upsetting Syracuse, 14-13. Only 18,000 showed up to see State win 32-0 with a combined rushing and passing offense that amassed 412 yards and a defense that allowed the Crusaders across the 50-yard line only once.

Pitt had tied Army 14-14, lost to Syracuse 16-13, beaten West Virginia 15-8 and clearly was the favorite. But there was another omen. Nebraska had upset the Panthers the previous week. Gator Bowl officials virtually guaranteed Pitt would be chosen with a victory and hinted that State could get the bid with an upset. For the first time in years, the game was played on Thanksgiving Day. It had been shifted to the old traditional holiday as a way to kick off the year-long 200th anniversary celebration for the city of Pittsburgh.

A crowd of 39,000 watched in 20-degree temperatures as Pitt took a 14-0 halftime lead with the only State threat in the first half ending in frustration as time ran out on the two-yard line. But on Pitt's first possession in the second half, sophomore punter Mike Ditka bobbled the snap and was tackled at the 25-yard line. Five plays later Botula went in for the TD but the two-point conversion failed. On Pitt's first play after the kickoff, Riddle fumbled and Stynchula recovered on the Pitt 32. On the fifth play, a halfback option pass from Hoak to Norm Neff got an eight-yard TD, but again the two-point conversion failed. Pitt made it 21-12 moments later on a 48-yard TD run by Chuck Rienhold. But State recovered Rienhold's fumbled a punt on the Panther 36 and Jacks passed two yards to Neff for the TD early in the fourth quarter. A third two-point conversion attempt failed. Midway through the final quarter, Kerr ran back a punt 43 yards to the Pitt 28. After a pass gained 10, what came next was another of those great game "moments." Hoak took a pitchout to the right, saw that he was trapped, reversed his field and evaded tacklers until stopped at the nine. Jonas barreled in for the TD and kicked the extra point to give the Lions the lead for the first time, 25-21. The PSU defense held the rest of the way and the goal posts came down a minute before the gun sounded as State students streamed onto the field to celebrate the gutsy comeback and one of the all-time upset victories over its traditional opponent.

But the Gator Bowl wasn't interested. "Gator Bowl Snub Upsets State," said the headline in the *Pittsburgh Press*. "Why? Why? Tell me why?" an irate Engle snapped at the *Press'* Roy McHugh. "This is the best team I've ever coached and they're wrong when they say we didn't play anybody." So, the Lions season was over. It was left to Garban, an All-East choice that year, to best sum up the season a couple weeks earlier after the frustrating tie with West Virginia. "We sure have been a hard luck team," he told the *Collegian*. The Lions would get luckier in '59 but not with its tormentor from Syracuse.

Season Record 6-3-1
Record to Date 366-200-39
Winning percentage .637

"The First Liberty Bowl"

Philadelphia? A bowl game in Philadelphia? In December? You gotta be kidding?

The players could not believe it. We deserve better, they said, as they practiced for the final game of the season against Pitt. We're 8-1, we came within two points of beating the nation's number one team and what's our reward? We have to play in some new bowl game in Philadelphia. Some reward. We should be going to Florida for New Years, not to Philadelphia in the middle of December.

For months behind closed doors, the bigwigs in Philadelphia led by one time Villanova athletic director Bud Dudley, who had conceived the new post-season game, had been pressuring Penn State officials to be the host team. It would be good for the state, they said, and, thus, good for the state university. Politicians who controlled the state budget that helped fund the university talked ambiguously about the long-term financial benefits that could accrue. Philadelphia area sportswriters claimed the bowl would enhance Eastern football, and, of course, the "City of Brotherly Love." Two weeks into the season, State's athletic director, Ernie McCoy, was brazenly added to the Liberty Bowl's executive council. Lost in all the back hall maneuvering were the feelings of the players. Over the years, the Lion players had watched enviously as their high school teammates and others had played in the Orange, Sugar, Cotton and Gator Bowls. Now, it was their turn.

This was Engle's best team in his 10 years at State with a representative schedule that would eventually include five teams in the AP Top 20. It also was a veteran team with 15 of 22 starters from the first two teams returning. It had a genuine superstar in quarterback Richie Lucas, whose daring play-calling and spontaneous running had inspired Jim Tarman's sports information office to nickname him "Riverboat Richie" before the opening game against Missouri to help hype his Heisman Trophy chances. And it had a handful of talented sophomores—including two future All-Americans, Roger Kochman of Wilkinsburg and Bob Mitinger of Greensburg—who would make a difference before the season ended.

Joining Lucas in the starting backfield was Botula, the captain and fullback, with Hoak, Kerr or junior Dick Pae at the halfbacks. Neff and Opperman were at the ends, Mulraney and Janerette or Stynchula at the tackles and Kohlhass and Korbini or Popp at the guards. When injuries in preseason sidelined the first two centers, sophomore Jay Huffman was promoted from the third string and he started every game. In the second unit, Engle had such stalwarts as Sobczak at fullback, Stellatella, the placekicker, at guard, Stew Barber at tackle and sophomores Mitinger at end and Galen Hall of nearby Williamsburg at quarterback. "The key to our 1959 season can be found in one man, Richie Lucas," wrote Ridge Riley in his preseason "*Football Letter*." "...He is the best running quarterback we've had in many years...but...he must pass better than he has so far." Inexperienced linebackers and the lack of a break-away runner were the team's main weakness, Riley added, in predicting a 7-3 season.

This year's season opener was no breather. Missouri, a first time opponent, was expected to challenge Oklahoma for the Big Eight title and go to the Orange Bowl. A nightmarish plane ride to Columbia did nothing to help the Lions prepare for the game and the 83 degree weather at kickoff was totally unexpected. But Lucas' passing was the real surprise of the day. He completed 10 of 11 passes for 154 yards and a touchdown in leading State to a 19-8 win. Missouri didn't score until late in the game as Lucas also led the Lions' ball-control offense with 48 yards rushing on eight carries. "If he isn't the best quarterback in the country," wrote Bob Boerg in the *St. Louis Post Dispatch*, "he'll sure do until a better one comes along." The victory over Missouri moved the Lions into the AP Top 20 at #18.

The next week, another first time opponent, Virginia Military Institute, helped the Lions open its final season at New Beaver Field. The steel structure in the heart of the campus was scheduled to be dismantled at the end of the season and re-assembled and enlarged on a remote farm field at the far Western edge of university property. This would be the only time State would ever play VMI and the Lions obviously took their opponent too lightly after Missouri because they struggled before winning, 21-0. They didn't score until 1:25 remained in the half and recorded the final TD with less than three minutes left in the game. Lucas threw two touchdown passes to Neff, including one for 33 yards, as he hit on eight-of-11 passes for 120 yards. So much for the doubts about Lucas's passing. "The chief difference between the two teams," wrote Riley in his "*Football Letter*," is "our replacement team was too good."

The following Saturday, the Lions scored the most points they ever would for an Engle coached team in beating Colgate, 58-20. Stellatella kicked State's first field goal in three years with a 32-yard boot in the second quarter as six different players scored touchdowns with Botula getting two. Hoak made the most spectacular play of the game on a non-scoring 87-yard kickoff return to open the second half. Despite the lopsided score, the pass defense was severely criticized for giving up 284 yards on 13-of-34 completions. "Our secondary men are just too small to break up some of those pass plays," Engle lamented to *Collegian* sports editor Sandy Padwe.

In preparing for fourth-ranked Army at West Point, Engle resorted to some psychology suggested by an alum named Hal Hein. Hein, a psychology major, had compiled a recording of West Point songs, cheers and crowd noise and had sent the material to Engle with the recommendation that the recording be played during practice sessions to prepare the 16th-ranked Lions for the intimidating atmosphere they would encounter at Michie Stadium. Engle took the advice and when the Lions lined up for the opening kickoff in a game rated about even they were oblivious to the noise all around them. Midway in the first quarter, the Lions got the ball at midfield following a punt and drove for a touchdown with Lucas scoring on a fourth down run from the two. Army kicked a 22-yard field goal in the second quarter but the Lions went 68 yards after the kickoff to get its own field goal on Stellatella's boot from the 10. With about two minutes left in the half, the Lions reached Army's 36 before losing a fumble but got

The starting backfield on the 1959 team that may have been the best of the Engle era, and went to State's first bowl in 12 years: Left to right, HB Jim Kerr, Captain and FB Pat Botula, HB Dick Hoak and QB Richie Lucas.

the ball back moments later when Huffman intercepted a pass. An interference penalty gave the Lions the ball at the Army four-yard line and with 10 seconds remaining, Lucas ran a quarterback sneak for the TD. Stellatella's kick made it 17-3 at the half. In previous games with Army, the Cadets' superior manpower had overcome the Lions in the second half. But not this time. Army made it 17-11 in the third quarter after intercepting a Lucas pass on the State 15-yard line but the Lions defense kept the Cadets away from the goal line the rest of the game. Lucas stopped Army's final threat on a gambling interception at the Lions 16-yard line with two minutes remaining when he anticipated a throw over the middle and left his receiver uncovered to pick off the ball. For his overall performance, Lucas was named "Back of the Week" by *Sports Illustrated*. It was the first victory over Army since 1899 and it was no fluke. The Lions dominated the statistics, making 21 first downs to 12 and getting 185 yards rushing to Army's 70. The frustrated Cadets also were penalized 12 times for 138 yards, including a five-yard offside penalty late in the second quarter that erased a 90-yard TD off an interception. "The team wanted to win this one," Botula told the *Collegian's* Bill Jaffee as the players gave the game ball to Engle.

Back in State College, the momentous win touched off another celebration by students. "Horns and screams rose to a howling crescendo...," Jim Moran reported in the *Collegian*. "A motorcade of student-filled cars moved down the mall...and met (another) motorcade preceding in both directions along College Avenue...(The) Old Main lawn became a race course as several cars were driven around flag polls...Rolls of toilet tissue hung from tree branches...and other rolls streamed...from passing cars." The dean of student affairs called the revelry "orderly and in good spirit."

Engle warned his team not to underrate Boston University but it was difficult not to have a let down following the historic win over Army. BU had won just one of three games but the Terriers played the Lions even for most of the first half. The Lions never trailed but the visitors kept the PSU Homecoming crowd on edge until the fourth quarter, when a 73-yard drive put the game out of reach and gave State a

21-12 win. Lucas scored two TDs on short runs and was a leading tackler on defense.

By this time, it was becoming apparent that State's November 7 game against Syracuse at Beaver Field would be the game of the year. Syracuse was also unbeaten and crunching opponents at a furious pace, averaging more than 36 points and leading the nation in both offensive and defensive team statistics. But the Lions knew they could not overlook their next two opponents, Illinois and West Virginia.

The city of Cleveland had convinced Penn State and Illinois administrators it would give their schools great exposure and a financial windfall to play their scheduled game at Municipal Stadium as part of Cleveland's "Seaway Year" celebration. But only 15,045 fans turned out in the 80,000-seat stadium to watch the game and one Cleveland announcer who had graduated from Ohio State blamed Penn State, saying: "Penn State plays strictly minor league football. People in Cleveland are used to the big time." (And, you still wonder why true Penn State fans dislike Ohio State so much, eh?) Illinois was the best defensive team in the Big Ten and still contending for the conference title and a Rose Bowl berth. The Illini intercepted four of Lucas' passes but couldn't stop his running as he gained 71 of State's 179 rushing yards and scored a TD in leading a 20-9 victory. State "went right to work from the opening whistle," wrote Doug McDonald, sports editor of the *Centre Daily Times*, "and proved that an Eastern power could lick a supposedly-stronger Big Ten club..."

West Virginia, coming off a 44-0 loss to Syracuse, made the final score in the rain at Mountaineer Field look respectable, 28-10. But with State's defense playing its best game of the season, the Mountaineers had trailed by 20-0 at the half and 28-3 late in the fourth quarter before recovering a fumble at the State 15-yard line. The game saw the advent of a new running star when Engle promoted sophomore Roger Kochman from third team to the alternate unit. Starting with the Army game, Kochman had seen spot duty at defense halfback and receiver. But on this day he became the first State back in more than a year to run for over 100 yards, with 111 yards on eight carries, including a 52-yard sprint for a TD in the first quarter. "...He can run," Riley wrote in his "*Football Letter*." The entire country would learn how well he could run the following week.

Not surprisingly, the largest crowd ever to see a game at New Beaver Field—34,000—was there for the clash of the unbeatens. Syracuse was ranked third and favored by a touchdown over the seventh-rated Lions. More than the Eastern Championship was at stake. Many sportswriters believed the winner also could win the National Championship. Early in the first quarter, Popp stripped the ball from Syracuse's sophomore quarterback Dave Sarette and Lucas recovered at the Orange 45-yard line. Six plays later the Lions were at the 17 with a fourth down. Lucas faked to Botula and handed off to Kochman, who was in for Hoak. Kochman bolted between guard and tackle, got a good block from Kerr on the Orange All-American end, Fred Mautino, and ran into the end zone, dragging Syracuse backs Ernie Davis and Gil Schwedes with him. The partisan crowd went berserk and no one seemed too upset when Stellatella's kick was wide. It was only the second PAT miss of the year for Stellatella but it would be one of the defining moments of the season. As the game moved into the second quarter, Syracuse's alternate unit appeared to take control. Hoak's interception in the end zone stopped one drive but the Orange got the ball back on a short punt to the PSU 43-yard line and scored six plays later on a six-yard run by Schwedes off a pitchout. Bob Yates' PAT made it 7-6 and that was the score at the half.

Syracuse drove 56 yards in the third period to go ahead 14-6, scoring on the first pass of the season thrown to the fullback, a fourth down 10-yard aerial from Sarette to Art Baker. Early in the fourth quarter, the Orange seemed to clinch the game by driving 41 yards in nine plays with the sophomore Davis getting the TD from the one. Yates missed the PAT and Syracuse led 20-6. What came next was another of the defining moments of the season. Kochman took Yates kickoff with one foot on the goal line and sped upfield. Getting key blocks from Kerr and Kohlhass, Kochman ran it back all the way, breaking two tackles and pulling away from Davis at the 20. Sportswriters later described the kickoff return as "electrifying." (To this day, it ranks as the second longest kickoff return in Lions history, second only to Chuck Peters' 101-yard return against NYU in 1940.) State went for two as the crowd went berserk again, but Lucas' hurried pass to Hoak was short. There was 11:20 left in the game. The teams traded punts and State's defense forced Syracuse to punt again, this time from its own nine-yard line. In a Herculean effort, Stynchula crashed through three Syracuse blockers and hit the ball with his right hand. As the ball bounced crazily to the left, Syracuse's Mautino stooped to pick it up and was blasted by Sobczak. The ball continued bouncing to the one-yard line and Mitinger fell on it. Sobczak scored on the next play. Now, two points would tie. Lucas called the same play that gave the Lions their first TD. He faked a roll out left and handed off to Kochman but Syracuse had jammed the inside and Kochman was stopped short of the goal. Now, there was 4:15 to play. Too much time for an onside kick. Engle turned it over to his defense. But Syracuse's offense was simply too overpowering. The Orange ground out four first downs and ran out the clock and State fans saluted both teams with a lengthy standing ovation. "Two points," Engle said to Roy McHugh of the *Pittsburgh Press* as he stuck two fingers into the air. "They kicked the points and we didn't." Coach Schwartzwalder told sportswriters State was "the greatest team I've ever come up against." Riley's perspective in the *"Football Letter"* was poignant: "Encounters between Penn State and Syracuse have ended in bitterness with almost comic regularity. This one ended in mutual respect. Coach Rip Engle went to the Syracuse dressing room to congratulate Coach Ben Schwartzwalder and the Orange players. His remarks were applauded by the tired and happy warriors. In this atmosphere of friendship and good will let the great rivalry continue. It's much more fun that way."

Syracuse jumped to number one with the victory (combined with a defeat by LSU). But despite the heartbreaking loss, the Lions did not let up the next week against Holy Cross in the final game ever at New Beaver Field. Holy Cross had lost just once, to Syracuse, but the

Lions turned the game into a rout, winning 46-0, despite not having Kochman who went out with a bruised knee on the first offensive play. Lucas set a new total offense record for the season at 1,184 yards by passing for 176 yards and one TD and running for 40 yards and another TD. The game ended appropriately in rain and a heavy wind with the students fruitlessly trying to tear down the steel goal posts anchored in concrete and the Blue Band marching off playing "Auld Lang Syne." "Penn State is as good and perhaps a better team than Syracuse and I don't see how it lost to anyone," said Holy Cross coach Eddie Anderson after the game. "Richie Lucas is simply terrific, the best back I've seen in years."

So, as the Lions practiced for Pitt with their glittering record and Heisman Trophy candidate, they seemed to be a great attraction to the post-season bowls. But the options were not as clear as many fans believed. The Rose Bowl was locked up by conference tie-ups. The Cotton Bowl had already grabbed Syracuse and the Sugar Bowl had avoided Eastern teams since inviting Pitt in a controversial racial uproar in 1956. Since Oklahoma could not go back to the Orange Bowl under the Big Eight's non-repeat clause, Missouri appeared headed there and Orange Bowl officials said they were uncertain about a potential rematch. The Gator and the new Bluebonnet Bowl were possibilities. The new Liberty Bowl was a lock.

Late Monday night, McCoy confirmed that the Lions had been invited to host the Liberty Bowl but he said no decision would be made until after the Pitt game. On Friday, the *Collegian*'s Padwe broke an exclusive that the "players had voted unanimously" at a secret meeting Wednesday night to accept the Liberty Bowl bid. The *Collegian* also quoted university president Walker as saying he prefers the Liberty

Quarterbacks Richie Lucas and John Unitas of the Baltimore Colts compare Maxwell Club awards in 1959 when Lucas was named the Outstanding Collegiate Player and Unitas the Outstanding Professional Player. Lucas just missed winning the Heisman Trophy won by LSU's Billy Cannon.

Bowl because "we have a special obligation to a bowl in Pennsylvania." A week later, some disgruntled players revealed they had been given the opportunity to vote only on the Liberty Bowl and no other bowl.

Distracted and perturbed by the closed door shenanigans about the Liberty Bowl, the team was not mentally prepared for the game with its biggest rival. In the past, each school often had spoiled the other's season and this year would be no different. Pitt was 5-4 and had lost to Syracuse (35-0) and West Virginia and some of its fans wanted Coach John Michelosen fired. But the Pitt players knew they could salvage the season by upsetting State, and they admittedly "were really up for

This is Beaver Stadium as it was being reconstructed between the 1959 and 1960 seasons as the steel structure that was New Beaver Field was taken apart and moved to the present field site on the north edge of campus.

the game," as fullback Jim Cunningham said later. The Lions, playing again without Kochman, were never in the game after a goal line stand early in the first quarter. The Panthers caught Lucas in the end zone for a safety, then drove 40 yards after the free kick for a TD and extra point and 9-0 lead. It was 16-0 at the half after a 32-yard TD run by Bob Clemens. The clincher came on the first play after the second half kickoff . Fred Cox, the third member of Pitt's "3-C's" who were starting together for the first time, dashed around right end for 86 yards for the third TD and a 22-7 victory. Cox and Clemens ran for over 100 yards each while the Lions total rushing came to 107 yards, with Sobczak's 27 yards being the best of any State back. "It was evident from the second play of the game which team was hitting harder, charging faster and had more desire," wrote John Black in the *Collegian*.

The Liberty Bowl still beckoned but in a December 1st editorial, the *Collegian* blasted Walker and McCoy for embarrassing the team and not properly rewarding the players for their fine season "Penn State has become the laughing stock of the football world," the editorial charged, "and for no reason at all if it hadn't been for the political and administration pressure." The editorial claimed State officials rejected interest from the Houston's Bluebonnet and Jacksonville's Gator bowls and thereby denied the players a choice.

However, in the next few days, the Liberty Bowl took on a different aspect. This would give the team a chance to redeem itself, everyone said. Depends on the opponent, and the bowl's organizers were having problems getting a second team. Georgia and Georgia Tech turned them down. So did TCU. They got invitations from better bowls, they said. Then, Bear Bryant came to the rescue, saying he would be happy to take his once-beaten Alabama team up North. Alabama was ranked 10th by the AP but with two ties in 10 games it trailed LSU, Mississippi and Georgia in the Southeastern Conference standings. Still, the Bear said his team rated among Alabama's all time best and he believed the Liberty Bowl would give him an opportunity to impress the influential Eastern media. The selection did not please the Philadelphia branch of the NAACP, which blasted the Liberty Bowl for picking Alabama because the school "doesn't admit Negroes."

THE 1959 LIBERTY BOWL GAME
Dec. 19, 1959
Penn State 7, Alabama 0

Alabama had not been to a bowl since 1953 when Bryant was still coaching at Kentucky. The Bear had taken three of his Kentucky teams to bowls but the last time was the 1952 Cotton Bowl. Engle had never coached a team in a post-season bowl. He asked Georgia Tech coach, Bobby Dodd, for some advice. "Keep 'em busy and interested," Dodd replied, "and put in some new plays." While watching Alabama game films, Engle and the coaches noted a flaw in the Tide's kick rush. So, four days before the December 19th game, they had the team practice a new fake field goal and screen pass play.

Both teams devised game plans that anticipated adverse weather conditions, with State concentrating on a ball control running game and Alabama utilizing quick kicks and a hard-hitting defense that was ranked fourth in the country. The temperature was 42 degrees but a 20-mile wind that virtually shut down the passing on both sides made it seem colder for the small crowd of 36,211 spectators at the 100,000-seat Municipal Stadium (later renamed JFK Stadium). Both teams lost the ball four times on fumbles and Alabama recovered another three of its own fumbles. On its first possession, Alabama reached the State 27-yard line but that would be the closest the Tide would be all afternoon. A quick kick put State in trouble at the PSU 3. With Lucas doing most of the running, the Lions drove 89 yards only to lose the ball on Kochman's fumble at the Alabama nine-yard line as the first quarter drew to a close. Early in the second quarter, disaster appeared to strike the Lions when Lucas left the game with a badly bruised hip. He would not return, yet, he would lead all rushers with 55 yards on nine carries. A few minutes later, Huffman recovered Pat Trammell's fumble at the Alabama 28-yard line and with Hall now directing the offense, the Lions soon had a first down at the five. But the Tide defense stiffened and on fourth-and-goal at the one, Hall's pass to Mitinger in the end zone was batted down by an Alabama defender in a collision of players. A short punt into the wind gave the Lions the ball on the Alabama 19 and when this drive bogged down at the five with two and a half minutes left, Stellatella tried a field goal from the 12 that was blocked. Again, Alabama couldn't move and had to punt into the wind and, again, the punt was short. State took over at the Alabama 22 with time running out in the half and no time-outs left and Engle signaled for the fake field goal play. A pass to Botula picked up four. Then, without a huddle, the Lions quickly lined up for a field goal. When some State players shouted, "Where's the kicking tee?" Alabama figured this could be a fake. But two fakes?

Hall, the holder, grabbed the ball and rolled to his right as the Alabama defense surged towards him. Neff ran down field for the pass and the Alabama safety man ran over to cover him. But it was a fake pass. Instead, Hall whirled and threw to Kochman who was waiting for the screen pass behind four blockers on the left sideline. Kochman took the ball and as Barber, Opperman, Wilson and Botula took out the Tide defenders, Kochman ran towards the end zone, getting a final block from Neff who wiped out two tacklers at the five, and went in for the touchdown as time ran out on the clock. Stellatella booted the PAT and the Lions took the 7-0 lead into the intermission. The second half was anti-climactic as neither team could muster a sustained offense until the fourth quarter when State drove 52 yards to the Alabama 10-yard line before letting time run out.

"I think we were very fortunate we weren't beaten by four or five touchdowns," Bryant told Frank Dolson of the *Philadelphia Inquirer*. "Penn State out-hit us, outsmarted us, out-blocked us, out-tackled us and out-coached us." The Lions had impressed the Southern press and the national television audience with its offense and defense, finishing with 269 yards rushing and 46 passing while holding Alabama to 111 yards on he ground and 27 through the air. Harry Mehre of the *Atlanta Journal* wrote that "the Nittany Lions could play anyone from any section of the country and do very well, thank you." Leave it to syndicated columnist Red Smith of the *New York Herald-Tribune* to sum up the game: "...One point has been proved. It is possible to play college football at this season in these climes, give the show away on television and still peddle $175,000 worth of tickets. People do the damndest things."

The disappointing turnout at Municipal Stadium reduced the financial payout to $98,000 to each team. Nor did the victory change the Lions' standing in the final polls which were released before the bowl games. State rated 12th and Syracuse won the National Championship. Lucas became State's first back to be named All-American since Light-Horse Harry Wilson in 1923. He also won the Maxwell Award as college football's outstanding player and finished second in the Heisman to LSU's Billy Cannon. Hall would be a more than adequate replacement in 1960 as the team moved into a new home field and Hall would take the players back to the Liberty Bowl again—whether they liked it or not.

Season Record 9-2
Record to Date 375-202-39
Winning percentage .640

"Roger's Knee & Galen's Shoe"

Dick Hoak had not played a game at quarterback since he was a freshman but when Engle and Paterno asked the senior running back to switch back to quarterback at the start of spring practice he willingly agreed. Whatever's best for the team, he said.

Hoak had been one of the team's leading rushers in his sophomore and junior years and as the starting left halfback last season he had been the leading pass receiver with 14 receptions for 167 yards.

Now, he would be throwing the ball instead of catching it and even the coaches realized he would need time to refine his passing techniques. He was a better dropback passer than Hall but Hall could throw better on rollouts. They both could run, not as well as Lucas, of course, but both were difficult to bring down.

Shifting Hoak to the alternate unit quarterback was a way to take advantage of his versatility on offense and defense and to get more use out of the other running backs. Everyone was back from '59 except Lucas and Botula. That included senior lettermen Kerr, Sobczak, Caye and Pae along with last year's explosive sophomore, Kochman. Don Jonas, the kid from Scranton who was one of the other young stars of the '58 team, also had returned after a stint in the Army but would miss the first two games. Reserve junior Al Gursky and a couple of sophomore fullbacks, Buddy Torris (Hoak's cousin) and Dave Hayes, also were in the mix. Engle was planning a more wide open offense, running from a multiple T-formation with everything from unbalanced lines to slots and double slots. That was another reason for moving Hoak because Engle and Paterno did not think their sophomore quarterback, Pete Liske of Plainfield, N.J., was good enough for this upbeat offense. To make it all work Engle needed good ends and he had a set of skillful veterans in, Opperman (the captain from Connellsville who was recovering from a knee operation), Mitinger, Bozik and Alexander who were all good blockers and tacklers as well as receivers. The lines of both units would be a mix of experience and youngsters with veterans like tackle Barber, guard Popp and center Huffman sharing time with such sophomores as Charlie Siemenski and Gerry Farkas at tackles and Joe Blasenstein and Dave Robinson at guards. Juniors Jim Smith, Dick Wilson and Bill Saul along with senior Berfield also would see action in the line. But the key to the offense would be Kochman, bigger and at least as fast as Engle's last superstar running back, Lenny Moore. With Kochman as the prime running back, State was picked at #20 in the AP preseason poll. Tim Cohane of *Look Magazine* predicted the Lions would finish 7-2 and meet Air Force in the Liberty Bowl. "This year," wrote Ridge Riley in his preseason *"Football Letter,"* two weeks before the season opener, "Roger Kochman could easily lift us from a good team to a great one." (How prophetic Riley would be once again.)

The defining moment of the season may have occurred that summer when Kochman injured his knee playing baseball. He was believed to be okay before preseason practice started September 1 but he went down on the first day and an operation three days before the opening game sidelined him for the season. "This isn't likely to be a spectacular team (without him)," Engle said. "You get a running back like Kochman maybe once in 10 years...our squad this year will be a good one—capable and hard-working and reliable—but we won't razzle-dazzle anyone." (Rip could be prophetic, too.) Kochman wasn't the only injury in the preseason. There were so many players hurt that veteran trainer Chuck Medlar said it was "one of the worst years for preseason injuries" he had seen.

The first game against Boston University on September 17th was the earliest opening date since 1905 and it was fitting that a team from that era—1909—was on hand to help dedicate the new all-steel Beaver Stadium. The 1909 team had been the first State squad to go unbeaten (5-0-2) and also the first one to play in New Beaver Field, a mile away. Coach Bill Hollenback and several of his players, including stars Pete Mauthe and Dex Very, watched as this latest team kept it simple and overpowered BU, 20-0, in the rain. The crowd of 22,559 was disappointing since the expanded seating capacity was up to 46,000 but thousands of students and faculty were not there because classes didn't start until the following Monday. Caye, plagued much of his career by injuries, scored the first touchdown on the new home field at 10:45 of the first quarter after running back a pass interception 10 yards and diving one-yard for the TD. One sportswriter described the game as "desultory." The Lions threw just nine passes but ran the ball 72 times for 326 yards. "With the press box full of scouts from Missouri, State's next opponent, there is a strong possibility that Engle wanted to keep some of his pet plays under wraps," wrote Sandy Padwe in the *Collegian*.

The Lions had two weeks to prepare for its Homecoming game against Dan Devine's Missouri team led by All-American end Danny LaRose and speedy running back Mel West. By that time State had fallen out of the Top 20 despite the BU victory and 2-0 Missouri had jumped in at #19. The two-week respite enabled Engle to get Mitinger and some other injured players back into the lineup and Mitinger sparked a defense that held Missou's fine running attack to 185 yards, mostly in the first half when the Tigers took a 14-0 lead. The Lions scored on a 73-yard drive in the third quarter with Hall passing to Opperman for the TD and two-point conversion. But Missouri blocked a punt a short time later that led to a 36-yard TD drive and the Tigers won, 21-8, helped by three intercepted passes and two recovered fumbles. "Fumbles, interceptions and Dan LaRose...haunted (State)...," wrote Doug McDonald of the *Centre Daily Times*. "LaRose crashed through and upset many Lion ball carriers in their own backfield with all the force of a midwestern cyclone in season." Engle told sportswriters his team was "outplayed" but also "made too many mistakes." (Missouri would go on to lose only once, rank number five by AP and defeat Navy in the Orange Bowl.)

The record Homecoming crowd of 33,613 was more upset at the monstrous traffic jam that occurred before and after the game than by the defeat and their post-game ire targeted the local, state and campus traffic cops rather than the student athletes. (Some things never change!) "...the traffic pileup before and after the game had police sweating, drivers cursing and pedestrians jumping for their lives...," said the front page story in the *CDT*. "The blockage seem concentrated on the campus before the game and in town after the game...There were some reporters of traffic using lawns and private driveways to get around the jams... 'Think what it would have been if we'd won,' said one weary policeman." In an accompanying front page column, Jerry Weinstein, the editor of the *CDT*, suggested fans could avoid future traffic jams by adopting the Ivy League tradition taking "picnic lunches to be eaten before the opening kickoffs." He also suggested "a picnic supper. Then after the game people could take their time eating. When desert rolls around a good bit of the crowd should be dispersed and the traffic jam ended." (And now we know who created State's now famous six-hour "Tailgating.")

Now, the Lions had to take to the road for what everyone realized was the toughest part of their schedule—Army, Syracuse and Illinois. "...They'll all be undefeated when we meet them," Engle predicted, and they almost were.

Engle tried to use psychology again to get his team prepared for another visit to intimidating Michie Stadium. The sounds of the Army fight song, "On Brave Old Army Team," and loud cheers from the corps of West Point cadets again blared over the loud speakers at practice all week. Since Michie had opened in 1924, only Notre Dame had

been able to win back-to-back games there and Engle and the coaches believed this was a game the Lions had to win to have a good season. Engle unveiled a new defensive wrinkle that would become synonymous with Penn State defenses for decades. He deployed the fullback as a roving combination linebacker and defensive back, giving the man the freedom and flexibility to roam the secondary depending on what the offense does when the play begins. It was designed to be especially effective against long passes. The defensive position was named "Hero" because, if the defender guessed right, he could make big plays that could decide the outcome of a game. Sobczak was designated the first "Hero" and his backup, Torris, became one against Army.

Part of the Army mystique at Michie was to stimulate the screaming corps of cadets into a frenzy that would unnerve the opponent and nothing did this better than when Army scored first. On its second possession, Army, 3-0 and favored by six points, methodically drove 70 yards in 13 plays to take a 7-0 lead and the cadets in the stands were nearly uncontrollable. But many of the Lions had been here before and they shrugged it off. Midway through the second quarter, Hall recovered a fumble at the Army 42. Hall's 12-yard pass to Opperman and his 16-yard bootleg helped set up Kerr's one-yard TD and Opperman's PAT tied the game. At halftime, the entire corps of cadets streamed onto the field for a spontaneous pep rally to inspire their team. Only the Superintendent, Major General William Westmoreland, was missing. That pep rally may have helped Army regain the lead, 13-7, early in the third quarter but the Lions stormed back on the kickoff. They drove 64 yards in eight plays, with Hall passing 25 yards to Kerr for the TD and Opperman's kick putting State ahead again, 14-13. Back came Army, driving to State's three-yard line early in the fourth quarter before settling for a 10-yard field goal by quarterback Tom Blanda. A few minutes later, Kerr ran back an Army punt 18 yards to the Cadets' 32-yard line. Opperman made a first down with a spectacular reception at the Army 20 and three plays later Kerr blasted over right tackle from the 11 for his third TD. The Lions tried for two points but the attempt failed and they led 20-16 with five minutes left. Army tried to come back but a Blanda pass was intercepted at the Army 37 by "Hero" Torris, who ran to the 18. Three plays later Hayes went up the middle for the clinching TD. Opperman's PAT made it 27-16 and the corps of cadets went silent as the game ended and Sobczak and Saul carried Engle off the field. The players gave the game ball to assistant coach Toretti, who had scouted the Cadets in all three wins. "The way we came from behind was indicative of our kids' spirit," Toretti told the *CDT*'s McDonald.

The game with unbeaten and fifth-rated Syracuse at Archbold Stadium was typical of this intense rivalry with another controversial ending that helped define the season. The score was 7-7 in the third quarter with the Lions on the move at the Syracuse 38-yard line when Hall made perhaps his biggest mistake of the year. Under a fierce rush on a bootleg, he forced a third-down pass into heavy coverage. Syracuse's Mark Weber intercepted at the 40 and ran untouched down the sidelines for a touchdown. The seemingly demoralized Lions gave up another TD minutes later on a 66-yard drive and the Orangemen led 21-7 going into the final period, when State struck back. A great Syracuse goal line stand stopped one PSU drive at the one-foot line early in the quarter but when Syracuse had to punt, a 23-yard runback by Jonas—who started a left half and would be the game's outstanding player—got the Lions back to the 20. Five plays later Hall threw a three-yard pass to Pae for the TD, then ran a bootleg for the two-point conversion that made the score 21-15 with seven minutes remaining. Syracuse tried to control the ball for the rest of the game but had to punt from midfield and with 2 and a half minutes left State got the ball at its own 11-yard line with no time-outs. Two pass plays went nowhere. Then, Jonas took a pitchout from Hall, started to run right, stopped and heaved the ball 50 yards to Mitinger, who made a leaping catch as he tumbled at the Syracuse 40. There was 1:12 remaining. Two more sideline passes and the Lions were at the 12. Hall then tried to hit Caye on the sideline at the three. One official ruled complete but Referee Francis Brennan ran up and overruled, saying Caye was out of bounds. Thirty seconds remained and it was second down. Hall ran the option pass right and reached the Syracuse four-yard line for a first down but in the tackle he lost his shoe. The clock was running. Hall asked Referee Brennan for time to put his shoe back on. Brennan shook his head and said, "play ball." Quarterbacking with one shoe, Hall tried to pass to Caye in the end zone but the ball was deflected. With the clock officially stopped, Opperman asked Brennan to give Hall time to put on his shoe. Brennan said no and Hall hopped up to center for the fourth down. Not being too mobile with just one shoe, Hall disdained the option and tried to pass to Mitinger in the end zone but Baker batted the ball away and the game was over. "I might have hit it (the pass) if I hadn't been off-balance," Hall told the AP after the game. Under NCAA rules, the referee can call time for an equipment change if he believes such equipment will endanger other players. State fans believed the referee's overly strict interpretation of the rules took away the Lions' golden opportunity to win what *New York Times* writer Howard Tuckner called a "Herculean" Syracuse effort "over a relentless Penn State football team."

Illinois, ranked fourth earlier in the season, was coming off its first loss of the season when it hosted the disheartened Lions the following week at Champaign. The Lions were flat but it was the wind which gave the Illini the 10-8 victory. Illinois won the toss and took advantage of a 20-mile wind in the first quarter to score its only points on the passing of John Easterbrook and receiving of Ed O'Bradovich as poor State punts set up a touchdown and field goal. Both Hall and Hoak had problems throwing in the wind but State receivers also dropped six passes. The Lions launched a fourth quarter comeback by marching 74-yards in the last four minutes but an onside kick failed with less than two minutes left and the Illini ran out the clock. With three losses in its last four games and a 2-3 record, State appeared to be sliding quickly towards college football oblivion. But Engle and the coaches had more confidence in this hard working squad. "I honestly believe our boys are playing up to their full potential and what more can a coach ask for than that," Engle told sportswriters.

The Lions were a heavy favorite over thrice-beaten West Virginia in the annual Band Day game on October 29. This was the day Hoak came into his own as a quarterback, passing for two touchdowns and scoring another as the Lions won easily, 34-13. One of the TD passes was a 17-yarder off a bootleg to Torris. Hoak's alternate unit scored four of the five State TDs and the defense held the Mountaineers scoreless until late in the fourth quarter. Unfortunately, the Lions also lost alternate unit end Bozik for the season when he broke a leg in the first quarter.

Maryland was back on the schedule for the first time since 1944 and this game was the beginning of a new series with one of State's natural rivals. Perhaps it was symbolic, then, that the game was played at Beaver Stadium in a cold drizzle, for rain and bad weather would haunt Maryland on many of its future visits to University Park. The smallest home crowd of the season showed up as more than 10,000

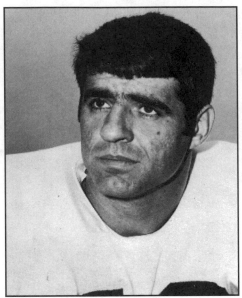

Dick Hoak, one of the most versatile and clutch players of the Engle era, was a fine two-way player as a QB, HB and DB and led the team in punt returns and kick returns in '58 and receiving in '59. He went on to play and coach for the Pittsburgh Steelers and earned four Super Bowl rings.

of the 30,126 who had bought tickets stayed away. The Lions scored on a long opening drive, going 91-yards in 17 plays with Kerr getting the TD on an eight-yard run, and they never trailed, winning 28-9. Jonas emerged as the player of the game by returning a punt 65 yards for one touchdown, setting up another with a recovered fumble and stopping a Maryland drive with an interception.

Five days after the election of John F. Kennedy to be the nation's President, State pasted Holy Cross at Worcester, 33-8, to give the Lions another winning season. Five different players scored TDs and Hoak was voted the outstanding back of the game as he completed six-of-seven passes for 164 yards and a touchdown and led all rushers with 54 yards on seven carries. "I don't know how Syracuse ever beat you," Crusader Coach Eddie Anderson told Engle. Before the game Engle made a seemingly minor personnel move that would impact the future direction of his football teams. Because of injuries to Bozik and Alexander at end, Engle switched his reserve sophomore guard Dave Robinson to the alternate left end spot behind Opperman, and he was one of the defensive stars against Holy Cross.

Something Engle said in the Holy Cross dressing room accelerated the usual pregame hostility before the Pitt game. Reminded that the Gator Bowl was interested in Pitt while no bowl seemed to want State, the usually cool Engle exploded: "They've been talking about bowls over there and what have they got to shout about. Four wins and three ties. That's not much to shout about." His remarks angered the Panthers, particularly after the Gator Bowl said it was no longer interested because Pitt had played so badly in a 7-7 tie against Army that same Holy Cross Saturday. The *Pittsburgh Press'* Roy McHugh reported on Monday that the Gator Bowl now had State on its list but no Gator representative showed up at Pitt Stadium on November 19. Bud Dudley, the mastermind of the Liberty Bowl, did, flying up from Miami after watching the Miami-Syracuse game Friday night.

Four days before the game, Pitt rewarded Coach Michelosen with a new contract and captain Mike "The Hammer" Ditka told sportswriters, "every senior on the team wants to win this one." The Panthers

(4-2-3) were favored and when Kerr fumbled the opening kickoff at the 14-yard line and Pitt kicked a 25-yard field goal, it looked like the odds-makers were right. But those were the last points until the fourth quarter as the teams slugged it out in their typical backyard fashion. The Panthers' offense dominated well into the third quarter by playing possession football but the Lions defense held its own and Hoak and Jonas intercepted passes to stop two scoring threats. The momentum changed with Jonas' interception at the PSU 6-yard line on a fake field goal play late in the third quarter. In four plays, State was at the Pitt 30. Michelosen belatedly tried to substitute his starting quarterback, Ed Shrockman, into the defensive backfield but in the confusion over Pitt having 12 men on the field, and before a penalty could be called, Hall ran a play and passed to a wide open Kerr at the goal line for a touchdown. The PAT attempt was wide but State led for the first time, 6-3, with 12 minutes left. State's defense held Pitt on downs near midfield and Kerr all but took the life out of the Panthers with a brilliant 41-yard punt return to the Panther 42-yard line—and an extra 15 yards for a "piling on" penalty that moved the ball to the 27. It took seven plays to score but on fourth-and-goal from the three, Hoak ran a bootleg to the right, spotted Mitinger racing to the right corner and threw a perfect pass. Hayes ran a draw off tackle for the two-point conversion. The Lions almost scored again minutes later after a short punt but a 26-yard TD pass from Hall to Kerr was nullified by an illegal receiver penalty and the Lions won, 14-3.

In the depressing Pitt dressing room, Michelosen singled out Kerr as "a great money player" and Hoak as "dangerous with the ball." Ditka, who had hardly played after a shoulder injury in the second quarter, told Les Biederman of the *Pittsburgh Press* that he never felt worse in losing a game, "I would have preferred beating State than any other team on our schedule. Boy, they'll gloat for a long time but give them credit." And they were gloating. "Instead of Nittany Lions the Penn State football squad resembled Indians on the warpath as they jumped, danced and ran their way into the dressing room yesterday," reported the *Press'* Bob Drum. "The young men with paint-blackened faces stormed around in various forms of undress congratulating each other—and anyone else near on the 14-3 win..."

On Monday, the Liberty Bowl made its offer and the players voted "unanimously" that night to return to Philadelphia. This time, the players were eager to accept. As Padwe wrote in the *Collegian*, "Penn State helped Bud Dudley when things didn't look bright for him (last year). The time has come to return the favor back." The players didn't need warm weather to show the country what kind of a football team they were. They were steaming because the Lambert Trophy had been awarded to "co-champions" Yale and Navy and they had finished third by one point.

THE 1960 LIBERTY BOWL GAME
Dec. 17, 1960
Penn State 41, Oregon 12
Leftwich Memorial Trophy: Dick Hoak

Initially, Baylor, Rice and Texas were being sought as opponents for the December 17 contest. But Dudley's bowl promoters, trying to sell the Liberty Bowl as the "East Coast Rose Bowl," came up with the team that had lost by just one point to Rose Bowl bound Washington, 7-6. Oregon had a 7-2-1 record, losing also to Michigan (21-0) and tying Oregon State (14-14). One of its wins was over West Virginia, 20-6. The Ducks'

coach, Len Casanova, had a direct tie to Engle's first season at State for he was the head mentor at Pitt in the famous "Snowbowl" game at Forbes Field. There was a minor controversy in early December when Dudley sought to cut expenses by hiring an Eastern officiating crew. Oregon officials balked at first but relented after Ernie McCoy proposed that an all Pac Eight crew be on the field in Eugene in 1963 when the two teams met for the first time in the regular season.

Dudley had hoped to double the attendance of the first Liberty Bowl in 1959 but a major 14-inch snow storm the week before and freezing cold and a swirling 25-mile wind on game day kept the Municipal Stadium crowd down to 16,624, including Pennsylvania's governor, David Lawrence. They and a national television audience saw Hoak play perhaps his best game ever along with a defense that virtually shut down Oregon's speedy razzle-dazzle offense led by quarterback Dave Grosz, who already had been drafted by the Philadelphia Eagles. But the first quarter belonged to Oregon. Backed up to their two-yard line on their second possession, the Ducks rammed it down the Lions throat, driving 98-yards on 12 plays for a 6-0 lead on Grosz' one-yard TD. But the Lions exploded for 21 points in the second quarter as Hoak led two scoring drives and Hall the other. One of TDs was set up by Jonas' 23-yard punt return and another by a Kerr's fumble recovery on the ensuing kickoff. However, Oregon wasn't done. The Ducks scored on their opening possession of the third quarter and with the Lions lead shrinking, 21-12, Paterno tried to rally the seniors from the sideline, yelling, "Come on boys, this is it. You'll never play college ball again." That's when Hall took the Lions on a 95-yard TD drive that broke the game open early in the fourth quarter. Hoak ran for his second TD of the game and passed 33-yards to Pae for the final score that gave State the 41-12 victory and won a salmon dinner for Governor Lawrence from his counterpart in Oregon. Hoak led State rushers with 61 yards on nine carries, hit on three of five passes for 66 yards, intercepted two passes himself to set up two TDs and was named the game's Most Valuable Player. "I guess that was about as good a day as I've ever had," Hoak said in the locker room. Opperman finished his career as a captain should by being named the Most Valuable Lineman as he caught four passes for 66 yards. But it was Hoak and Opperman's performance on State's tight defense and ball control that gave State the edge as the Lions ran off 91 plays to Oregon's 57 and picked up 27 first downs to 17. "We beat a very good football team today," Engle said after the game. "I figured we'd win but the score was more one-sided than we had a right to expect...That drive in the fourth quarter broke their backs." Casanova told Frank Dolson of the *Philadelphia Inquirer* that "we made more mistakes in this game, I think, than we did the rest of the season...I was really disappointed in our defense. We haven't had that many points scored on us in...maybe 10 years." Red Smith, the syndicated columnist for the *New York Herald Tribune*, wrote that "The only thing lacking was an opponent worthy of Penn State, whose inalienable right to top eastern ranking was established today beyond cavil. Nobody watching the flashy Dick Hoak and his boisterous accomplices could conscientiously place them behind Yale or Navy in this region."

So, once again, the Lions' bowl win gave them the prestige they had been seeking since the mid '50s. The financial payoff of $55,000 wasn't up to last year but that didn't matter as much as the victory. Despite the snub by the Lambert Trophy committee, State finished 16th in the country in the final poll before the bowl games. Hoak would be drafted by his hometown Pittsburgh Steelers and go on to a great professional career as a clutch running back. Hall, Kochman, Mitinger and Robinson would return for another year and this time the boys would get their bowl game in the sun—but it wouldn't be what they expected.

Season Record 7-3
Record to Date 382-205-39
Winning percentage .641

"Galen's Day & Robby's Play"

Injuries to indispensable players before or during a season is sometimes the defining moment of that year and in 1961 the loss of starting quarterback Galen Hall for 2 and a half games early in the season made a significant difference.

Injuries also sidelined two other important players for several games—junior end Dave Robinson and senior halfback-placekicker Don Jonas—and their absences had a major impact. But when they went down, some one was there to pick up the challenge. The shoulder injury that knocked out Hall in the second game of the season at Miami rattled the players and forced Engle to rely on two inexperienced sophomores for leadership. At a stubby 5-foot-9, 190-pounds, Hall was not a great passer or runner but he was a thinking man's quarterback. It was an era when quarterbacks called their own plays, and Engle said Hall was "like a coach on the field." Before Hall returned, the Lions were upset twice and their preseason selection as the "team to beat in the East" had soured.

Even though he felt this team would be better than '60, Engle had not been happy with the preseason praise by sportswriters. Most preseason magazines had the Lions among the nation's Top 10 and a *Newsweek* poll of 125 coaches selected them #5. What Murray Olderman of the *Newspaper Enterprise Association* and president of the Football Writers of America wrote was typical: "Rip Engle is trying to hide what he's got at Penn State—a genuine powerhouse."

"There's no reason for it...," Engle said, "(Not) with that schedule." Two first time major intersectional opponents were on the schedule—Miami and California—and for the first time the Lions would play both Army and Navy in the same year. Maryland was already considered a post-season bowl candidate while traditional rivals Syracuse and Pitt were still part of the Eastern elite. With 15 lettermen returning, mostly in the line, and several rugged sophomores, Engle expected his team to be physical but lacking in overall team speed. "I look for us to be hard hitting, tough, rugged and physically strong," he said. "We should block and tackle hard."

His first unit had two of the best defensive ends in the country in Robinson and Mitinger, and the rest of the veteran starting line also was sound, with Sieminski and Smith (the captain) at tackles, Blasentstein and Bob Hart at guards and Huffman at center. The alternate unit line would develop into a solid group with veterans like Saul, Wilson and Farkas, non-letter upperclassmen such as Joe Galardi, Ron Tietjens and Jim Schwab and sophomores who would soon become familiar names to State fans—ends Dick Anderson and Ralph Baker, guard Harrison "Hatch" Rosdahl and tackle Terry Monaghan. Nor was Engle worried about his first team backfield with Kochman—fully recovered from the knee injury that sidelined him all of 1960—and Jonas at

halfbacks and Hayes at fullback. Gursky and Torris also had returned as running backs and Engle liked what he saw in hustling sophomore Harold "Junior" Powell from nearby Lewistown. Engle's dilemma was in choosing a backup quarterback and by the end of preseason, soph Don Caum, the high school All-American from Harrisburg, had beaten out "redshirt" soph Pete Liske and another highly recruited soph from Corning, N.Y., Gary Wydman. However, Liske was designated as the punter and "wild card" substitution for Hall on defense and Wydman was shifted to halfback to take advantage of his speed and pass catching ability since the Engle pass offense relied more on running backs as receivers than the ends.

A virus struck the team in the week leading up to the September 23 opener against Navy at Beaver Stadium, sidelining nine players, and the hot, sticky 90 degree weather appeared to bother the Lions more than the Middies. State was favored but the score was close for three periods and after the game Navy players, including end Greg Mather, told the *Daily Collegian* that State's linemen were "out of shape" and gave "no second effort." That angered the Lion players, particularly since they had dominated the game offensively with 328 yards on the ground, 59 yards on 3-of-10 passes and 23 first downs in running off 85 plays to Navy's 64 plays and 13 first downs. After getting 50 yards rushing on a 60-yard TD drive after the opening kickoff, the Middies gained only 42 yards on the ground for the rest of the game and a total of 120 yards through the air on 10-of-29 pass attempts and four interceptions. But the Lions did have to come from behind first half deficits of 7-0 and 10-7 before scoring 13 points after the intermission and winning 20-10. Jonas, who had not kicked field goals since high school in 1957 and rarely practiced them either, booted field goals of 31 and 25 yards and rushed for 68 yards on 17 carries including a 6-yard TD to lead the victory and Caum darted 19 yards on a rollout for the clinching TD with 6:10 left in the game. The downside was that Robinson dislocated his shoulder while throwing a block on the second half kickoff and would miss the next 5 1/2 games. "You just can't lose one of the best ends in the East and not be hurt," assistant coach J.T. White told the *Collegian*.

It was hot and sticky again the following Friday night in the Orange Bowl stadium when State played its first night game in 11 years against Miami (1-1). The game was televised on closed circuit back to two sites on the Penn State campus but less than 40 percent of the available seats were filled. The eighth-ranked Lions stumbled in the first quarter, giving up the ball on a fumble and interception and blowing a 50-yard pass completion from Hall to Kochman on a holding penalty. That gave Miami the impetus to take charge in the second quarter and score a touchdown on a 7-yard pass by the Hurricane's outstanding sophomore quarterback George Mira. Mira was playing with rib and wrist injuries and the Miami crowd of 46,687 didn't like the way State's linemen were harassing and tackling him, especially Mitinger. One section of fans led by the Miami cheerleaders chanted "Get That Killer" and "Savage! Savage!" When Mitinger slammed Mira down for an 8-yard loss on the last play of the half, the fans booed lustily as the Lions left the field, trailing 7-0.

Engle expected Hall to take the team downfield after the second half kickoff but Hall bruised his shoulder on the first play and Engle sent Caum in to run the first unit. It was three plays and out. Mira also was now on the sidelines and senior Bobby Weaver then led the Hurricanes on an 81-yard drive in 11 plays to take what became an insurmountable 14-0 lead. State's offense continued to flounder and

Miami extended its lead to 25-0 lead with 1:21 left in game when State finally scored. Liske guided the first unit 71 yards in 5 plays for the TD on a 6-yard pass to reserve Frank Sincek with 10 seconds remaining. Liske then passed to Sincek for two points and a 25-8 final score.

Much of the post-game analysis centered around Mitinger's vicious hits on Mira. "Mitinger...rocked Mira on several occasions," reported Doug McDonald in the *Centre Daily Times*. "And just about every time he did, Mira lay prone on the warm Orange Bowl turf. Soon, the Miami fans started booing Mitinger for his supposedly rough tactics. But it was not warranted. 'He better learn to take it,' Mitinger said on the flight home. 'He's going to get hit a lot harder before he's through.'" *Miami Herald* sportswriter Ray Crawford lambasted Mitinger, calling him a "killer." But Tommy Devine of the *Miami News* said the crowd was "idiotic...They seemed to have the attitude that George should be accorded the same deferential treatment as a Sacred Cow...it is ridiculous to label Penn State's tactics as 'dirty.'" Miami's coach Andy Gustafson, the old Pitt player, agreed with Devine. The Lions and their fans got some solace the following week when Navy went down to the Orange Bowl and whipped Miami. Meanwhile, State dropped out of the Top 10 and got a new quarterback.

Pete Liske made his first start the next Friday night in Boston when State played Boston University for the last time. Liske led the team to a 32-0 victory, scoring one TD and setting up another with an interception as he hit on 7-of-12 passes for 98 yards and ran for 38 yards. Hayes scored twice in leading rushers with 90 yards and Caum threw a 50-yard TD pass to Powell as the Lions amassed more than 400 total yards. "I like to play defense but I'd be crazy if I said I didn't like to play offense," Liske told the *CDT*'s McDonald.

The first capacity crowd at Beaver Stadium—45,306, including 1,200 West Point cadets and their commander, General William Westmoreland—saw the Lions play their worst game of the season on October 14 in losing to underdog Army, 10-6. The light rain and gloomy skies were appropriate for the way State's offense sputtered. Between them, Liske and Caum could complete just five passes in 18 attempts for 66 yards and Army's gang-tackling defense stuffed most of State's runners at the line of scrimmage except for Kochman who gained 55 yards on 12 carries. Army, with seven starters from Pennsylvania, led 10-0 before the Lions scored with six minutes remaining in the fourth quarter on Liske's 17-yard TD pass to Jonas. That seemed spur the players but a last minute drive that started at the State 33-yard line was stopped at the Army 36 as time ran out.

Hall was ready to go the next Saturday and it was just in time, for 3-1 Syracuse was visiting Beaver Stadium and the Lions had not beaten the Orangemen since 1957. This time it was Ben Schwartzwalder who had to play without his starting quarterback, Dave Sarette, and four other regulars who were injured. Whether Sarette would have made a difference is a matter of conjecture, but Hall certainly did. He had the best State passing statistics since Richie Lucas against Missouri in 1959 as a regional TV audience, a Gator Bowl scout and 44,674 others looked on. Hall completed 10-of-12 passes for 169 yards, including touchdown tosses of 48 yards to Kochman and 13 yards to Anderson, to lead State to a 14-0 upset over the favored Orange. Kochman became the first Lion player in two years to run for more than 100 yards as he gained 105 yards on 14 carries. The State defense led by linebacker Saul was at its best, stopping the only real Syracuse scoring opportunity with a great goal line stand inside the 5-yard line in the first quarter after the Orangemen had recovered a fumble

First-Team All–American end Bob Mitinger is about to collar an opposing runner. Marv Levy, then coaching at California, called him "the best college football player in the U.S." in 1961.

at midfield. It was one of the defining moments of the season. Ernie Davis, who would win the Heisman Trophy in December, carried the ball twice in the first three downs but could gain no more than a yard each time as Saul, Liske and Torris wrapped him up. Syracuse gave it to Davis again on fourth-and-1 and he was met by Saul, with help from Gursky and Galardi, and went down inches short of the end zone. Then in the third quarter, Saul forced a fumble that Baker recovered at the Orange 15 and two plays later Anderson scored State's second TD. The score could have been higher as the Lions missed two field goals and two TDs 'by a hair," including one on the last play of the first half that could have created another typical "Syracuse controversy" if the Orangmen had won. As game films showed, the officials botched an interference call in the end zone on a pass to Wydman and when the hobbled Jonas could not get on the field quick enough to boot a field goal, Hayes was stopped inches short of the goal on a run from the 3-yard line. Engle was so upset, he chased after the officials at the intermission, then mistakenly entered the Syracuse locker room before realizing where he was. It was Rip's 100 victory in his coaching career and the players carried him off the field. "The team almost to a man agreed that (Joe) Paterno's pre-game talk which concerned Engle going for this 100th coaching win was a big factor in boosting team morale...," wrote Jim Karl, sports editor of the *Collegian*. "I can't help thinking of all the kids who made this possible," Engle told Riley. But the turning point victory came with a cost. Jonas injured his shoulder and had attempted both field goals with his arm in a sling. He would continue to be the team's placekicker but would never again carry the ball for the Lions.

Hall and Kochman would have another outstanding performance before a Homecoming crowd against a 1-2-1 California team. The Lions overcame two fumbles and a 10-3 deficit in the first quarter to win, 33-16, as Hall tossed a 36-yard TD pass to Kochman and a 51-yarder to Junior Powell in the second quarter, then scored the final TD himself on a sneak in the fourth quarter. Kochman ran for 107 yards on 21 carries and the Lion defense held Marv Levy's Bears to 93 yards on the ground and 137 in the air. Levy called Mitinger "the best college football player in the United States."

Another last minute judgment call by an official spoiled State's dramatic come back the following week against 4-2 Maryland. Gator Bowl scout George Olson was among the 34,000 in Byrd Stadium who watched as the underdog Terps, with 19 Pennsylvanians on the squad, took a 21-6 first half lead on the excellent passing of sophomore Dick Shiner of Lebanon. Shiner completed 11-of-16 passes for nearly 150 yards and three touchdowns, including a 7-yard toss to Gary Collins of Williamstown with 1:15 left in the half. Collins caught 6 of Shiner's tosses as the Terps twice drove 69 yards for TDs and set up another with a sack on Hall at PSU's 35-yard line. But Engle and his coaches made some defensive passing adjustments during the intermission and the Lions virtually shut down the Terp attack when Maryland coach Tommy Nugent kept Shiner on the sideline most of the second half because of a leg injury.

State's offense took over after the intermission, driving to the MD 25 before losing the ball on downs but minutes later going 65 yards for a TD on a 1-yard pass from Hall to Gursky. An attempt for two points failed but with nine minutes left in the fourth quarter Jonas kicked a 27-yard field goal when a Lion drive bogged down at the Terp 10, narrowing Maryland's lead to 21-15. The Terps controlled the ball for the next five minutes, driving to State's 25 yard line before Schwab, starting in Robinson's old position, intercepted a Shiner pass that bounced off the chest of a Terp receiver. After a fumble that put the Lions back to its own 12-yard line, Hall passed to Schwab for a first down at State's 37. On the next play, Hall found Powell in the open past midfield and the sophomore dashed to Maryland's 19 before being tackled. Hall then rolled out for 9 yards and Kochman ran off right tackle for a first down at the Terp 5. "Defense, Defense," screamed the home crowd and the Maryland defense responded. Kochman got only a yard. A Maryland blitz broke up a pass attempt to Mitinger and caught Hall for a 5-yard loss on a rollout. Third-and-goal at the 9 with less than two minutes remaining. Hall rolled right and passed to Powell in the end zone. The ball bounced out of Powell's hands but he dove for it and seemed to have caught it before hitting the ground but the closest official ruled no catch. Powell jumped up and down in protest but to no avail. On fourth down, Hall underthrew Powell near the one and Maryland took over. Moments later, the Terps took an intentional safety.

Collins punted 52 yards on the free kick and the Maryland defense stopped State's three last-ditch plays at midfield. State won the battle of statistics but Maryland won the game, 21-17. No one realized it at the time but the game would be historic, for the two teams would play 29 more times and Maryland would never win again!

Game films could not determine if Powell had "trapped" or caught the end zone pass. Powell told sportswriters the official who called the play probably was in a poor position but that he was in control of the ball "from the moment I caught it." Engle didn't blame that play for the loss. "We are making fundamental mistakes," he told McDonald of the *CDT*. "There were 50 different ways to win that game...and we didn't come up with one of them." In his *"Football Letter,"* Riley wrote: "It was a bitter experience for our players to lose a game they might have won. Artistically, it would seem the season has passed us by." However, there were three encouraging signs. Hall's passing was back in stride (10-of-23 for 162 yards and 1 TD), Kochman was running as well as ever (16 carries for 99 yards and 1 TD) and Robinson was back in the lineup ("He came out of the game in good shape," trainer Chuck Medlar said.)

Engle was worried about a let down the following week against 4-4 West Virginia before a Mountaineer Homecoming crowd. Kochman scored on a 66-yard TD pass from Hall in the first quarter and ran for another TD in the second quarter and the Lions let the defense do the rest in a 20-6 win. With Hayes out with an injury, Torris did most of the running at fullback and had led all rushers with 108 yards and a TD on 21 carries. The attack-minded Lions defense with Mitinger at left end, Robinson at right end and Saul at linebacker stopped the Mountaineers twice inside the 10-yard line, including a late fourth quarter thrust when WVU was trying to rally.

The Lions clinched another winning season in a 34-14 Band Day win over Holy Cross on November 18. PSU went into the game ranked 7th in the nation in total offense and the running of Kochman and Torris helped the Lions gain 487 yards. Kochman rushed for 133 yards and three TDs on 26 carries and Torris got 145 yards and three TDs on 22 carries as they became the first Lion tandem to go over 100 yards in a single game since Lenny Moore and Billy Kane in 1954. Holy Cross didn't go down easily, coming back in the third quarter from a 21-0 halftime deficit to narrow State's lead to seven points. But an interception by Gursky late in the third quarter and a short punt that led to Torris' second TD early in the fourth wrapped up the game for the Lions.

The 1961 team had an 8-3 record but ended the season with an outstanding and turning point upset over Georgia Tech in the Gator Bowl.

Prior to the Holy Cross game, the relatively new bowls—Liberty, Bluebonnet and Gotham—had indicated an interest in State but on the eve of its traditional closer with Pitt, the Gator Bowl also came back into the picture, after its initial choice, Maryland, had been upset by Virginia. State was a 6-point favorite over the 3-6 Panthers and the game at Pitt Stadium was close in the first half. Pitt led 14-13 on the running and passing of Paul Martha as the second quarter was winding down when Mitinger's tackle caused a fumble that Gursky recovered at the Pitt 23. Calling a play before Pitt could get the right defense on the field, Hall hit Gursky all alone in the middle of the end zone and the Lions took a 19-14 lead into the intermission. That appeared to stun the Panthers for it was 40-14 before Pitt would score again in the fourth quarter as State won by the highest score since 1903, 47-26. Hall played the best game of his career, setting a new single game record for passing yardage, completing 11-of-14 passes for 256 yards and two touchdowns and scoring two TDs himself. After the game, Pitt's sports information director Beano Cook and other Pitt officials complained about State "rolling up the score." The claim was ludicrous to State fans who reminded the whining Pitt followers that the Lions threw just two passes in the final quarter and that Pitt scored its final TD on a 6-yard pass from Jim Traficant with one second left in the game. In the victorious dressing room, Paterno told Bob Drum of the *Pittsburgh Press* the season might have been even better if Hall had not been hurt. "Who knows what would have happened if Hall had played in the second-half at Miami (and against Army)?" Paterno said. Speaking for all his teammates, Captain Smith said, "The Maryland game was the turning point of the season for us. We were determined to prove we were a good team...We reached our peak and have momentum now and we're ready to play in any bowl game to prove it."

There was no controversy over the bowl invitation. Two days later, the team turned down a bid from New York City's fledging Gotham Bowl and voted to play the school's first bowl game ever in the Deep South—the Gator Bowl at Jacksonville on December 30. That's when the controversies began.

THE 1961 GATOR BOWL GAME
Dec. 30, 1961
Penn State 30, Georgia Tech 15
Burkhalter Award: Galen Hall

Many Southern sportswriters, particularly from Atlanta, were surprised by the choice of 17th-rated State as the opponent for 13th-ranked Georgia Tech and they were equally dismayed when the oddsmakers made the Engineers just a three-point favorite. Tech was 7-3 and fourth in the tough Southeastern Conference and had allowed only 4.4 points per game, registering four shutouts against a schedule that included three top five teams: Alabama (the National Champ), LSU and Mississippi.

The contrast in the pregame preparations was startling. Tech coach Bobby Dodd, who had won 9 of 10 bowl games in 16 years at Tech, gave his players a couple of weeks off following its final game, let the team go home for Christmas and then had just two brief workouts in Jacksonville. Meanwhile, two weeks before the game, Engle took the Lions to an Army post at Fort Eustis, Va., and worked the team hard for a week, then reassembled the squad in out-of-the-way St. Augustine after Christmas for several more days of closed practice sessions. It was not the pleasant experience the players had expected at a "major bowl game." Staying at a military barracks was not unlike the bleak

experience of the '48 Cotton Bowl team and for the same reasons. Jacksonville was still a segregated city and Dave Robinson would become the first black to play in a Gator Bowl game. In fact, when an airport restaurant would not serve the team because of Robinson, all the players walked out. Robinson never got mad but he got even during the game when he distinguished himself and made one of the most memorable plays in college football history.

"...The haughty Southerners ruled the town Friday night," wrote *Collegian* Editor John Black in describing the eve of the game. "As they blustered from party to party, they condescended to infer to the infidel Yankees (in town) that Penn State didn't play quite the same brand of ball as the Southeastern Conference teams." The Tech players were as cocky as their fans who made up most of the Gator Bowl record crowd of 50,000. And after a little more than a quarter had been played, it looked like Tech had reason for its confidence as Tech led 9-0 on a safety and a 68-yard touchdown run by sophomore Joe Auer that was another Gator Bowl record. Remembering Dodd's previous advice about inserting new plays, Engle had added a couple of pass plays off a fake draw to Kochman. For the rest of the second quarter, Hall used those new plays in spot passes to Robinson and Anderson to help drive the Lions for two touchdowns. State went 78 yards in 10 plays to score on a diving over-the-shoulder catch by Gursky, then traveled 87 yards in seven plays with time running out in the quar-

Rip Engle called Galen Hall "a coach on the field." Hall quarterbacked the Lions to a Liberty Bowl victory in 1960 and was MVP in the turn around 1961 Gator Bowl win over Georgia Tech.

ter before Hall hit Kochman in the corner of the end zone with a 27-yard pass. Jonas' two PAT's gave State a surprising 14-9 lead a the half.

Robinson stunned Tech and the national TV audience midway in the third quarter with what *Philadelphia Daily News* sportswriter Larry Merchant later called "possibly the play of the Century." Tech was driving from its own 43-yard line when quarterback Stan Gann faded back to pass. Robinson literally leaped over two blockers, grabbed Gann around the neck and slammed him to the turf, causing a fumble which Robinson then recovered on the Tech 35-yard line. As he had done against Pitt, Hall quickly called a play. He faked to Kochman, circled right and found Powell all alone near the 15-yard line and Powell did a victory jig into the end zone, and State led 20-9 after the PAT failed. Early in the fourth quarter, Tech made it 20-15 after Auer overcame a muffed pitchout and ran 25 yards with impromptu blocking for the TD. A few minutes later with a fourth-and-6 at its own 12-yard line, Tech gambled on a faked punt but the pass failed and Jonas kicked a 23-yard field goal to make it 23-15 with four minutes left. On the first play after the kickoff, Schwab intercepted Gann's pass at the 20 and ran to the 11. Four running plays later Torris smashed over the goal for the TD and the Lions won, 30-15. Hall was named the game's outstanding player as he completed 12-of-22 passes for 175 yards and

three TDs and in congratulating him immediately after the game, Dodd said: "you are one of the greatest players a Tech team has had the privilege of playing against in my 17 years of coaching." Sportswriters not only praised Hall but also credited States' aggressive defense and the punting of Liske for the surprising win.

The decisive Gator Bowl victory over what was then one of the nation's perennial bowl teams helped State gain additional prestige within the college football world. The Lions still would need a game on New Year's Day before they could think about being part of the football elite. But this was a start. Thanks in a large part to Hall, the Lions achieved the sportswriters' preseason expectations and for just the second time won the Lambert Trophy as the best team in the East. Engle also had another All-American in Mitinger and by the next pre-season the sportswriters were saying that more two potential All-Americans—Robinson and Kochman—could put the Lions into the final Top 10 for the first time since '47. They did.

Rip Engle with his 1962 stars, left to right: All-American end Dave Robinson, All-East tackle Chuck Sieminski, and All-American halfback Roger Kochman.

Season Record 8-3
Record to Date 390-208-39
Winning percentage .643

"The Season That 'Could Have Been'"

After his more than 20 years as a player and coach at Penn State, Dick Anderson still believes the pass he dropped in the Army end zone in 1962 may have cost the Lions a shot at the National Championship. State was 3-0 and ranked 3rd in the country by AP and UP but lost 9-6 and didn't lose again in the regular season to finish 9-1. Anderson's botched reception was just one mistake in the critical upset loss at Michie Stadium that mid-October day and it helped define a season that "could have been" one of State's greatest. But what really gave '62 its final destiny was the post-season bowl fiasco that resulted in an embarrassing loss of prestige for State in a repeat appearance at the Gator Bowl.

From the start of preseason, State was touted by sportswriters as one of the nation's best and was picked #5 by the AP. Again, Engle was dismayed. He knew he would have a good first unit that could play offense and defense but he was undecided about a starting quarterback and he was unsure about the capability of his alternate unit. Before the opening game against Navy at Beaver Stadium September 22, Liske won the quarterback job. Caum and Wydman were bothered by injuries for part of the preseason and Wydman's knee injury would be so severe he would miss the entire year. Sophomore Ron Coates, a fine passer who also was in the running at QB, became the prime placekicker. The starting backs were big and fast and all were two-year veterans: Kochman and Gursky at the halves and Hayes at fullback with Torris, Powell, junior Ed Stuckrath of Baltimore and sophomores Frank Hershey and Bud Yost in reserve. Anderson and Robinson were the ends, Sieminski and Farkas the tackles, Blasenstein and Rosdahl the guards and Galardi, the captain, was moved from guard to center. Monaghan, Baker, Tietjens, Bernie Sabol (brother of Engle's 1957 captain) and

non-letterman Jim Williams were among the backups in the line along with two fine sophomores, Glenn Ressler of little Dornsife and Billy Bowes. "We have three returning players of potential All-American caliber in Robinson, Kochman and Sieminski," Engle told sportswriters. "We should have a strong first unit, adequate size...Line depth, especially at end, center and guard, is our chief concern because we proved by our recent success with alternating units that it takes 25 to 30 good players to succeed on our level of competition." Engle also would have to do without fifth year, "redshirt" seniors. In the spring, State had joined Pitt, Syracuse and West Virginia in a ban of "redshirting" except for injuries. Although he was for the agreement, he was unhappy the Lions' other Eastern rivals, including Army and Navy, were not included.

The first five games were crucial and they included all three service academies, marking the first time any school would play Army, Navy and Air Force in one season. Engle worried about playing the academies so early because he knew their players would be in top physical shape. The first of a two-game series with Rice would be played in the heat and humidity of Houston and perennial nemesis Syracuse would be the Homecoming foe October 20.

State was given the slight edge over Navy and Middies coach Wayne Hardin predicted his defense would slow down State's quick offense. It didn't. In the first quarter, a record opening day crowd of 42,653 watched as Liske threw a 55-yard TD pass to Powell and Kochman ran 8-yards for another. Two minutes into the second quarter, Gursky returned an intercepted pass 77-yards for a TD and the rout was on. The Lions won easily, 41-7, as the Lions gained 234 yards passing on 16-of-24 completions by Liske and Coates and Powell caught seven passes. The 5-foot-9, 160-pound scatback also scored State's final TD on a 48-yard interception in the fourth quarter. Engle, who had been concerned about his pass defense, said it was "our best opener ever." Sieminski had played so well he was picked as Lineman of the Week by *Sports Illustrated*. A Washington sportswriter wrote: "Penn State, billed as the number one football team in the East, played like it was the number one team in the nation."

The first ever game with Air Force was not as easy. For nearly three quarters, a crowd of 45,200 sat glumly as the underdog Falcons outfought the Lions, who were playing without Gursky and Galardi. State held a slim 7-6 lead late in the third period when an Air Force quick kick backed State to its own 10-yard line. With Liske and Caum shuttling at quarterback, the Lions drove 90 yards in 16 plays for a TD with Liske passing to Kochman on a fourth-and-goal at the 3 for the TD. Powell's PAT made it 14-6. Air Force battled back behind the quarterbacking of Terry Isaacson and reached State's 21 before two great defensive plays by Robinson stymied the Falcons and State took over on downs at the 19. Liske then took the team 81-yards in 9 plays for the clinching TD,with Kochman making a diving catch in the end zone on a 15-yard pass from Liske and the Lions won, 20-6.

The oppressive heat and humidity almost wiped out the fourth-ranked Lions at underdog Rice the next Saturday night as Gursky, Kochman and Baker were hobbled by injuries. To keep cool throughout the game, State's players continually dropped crushed ice down their blue jerseys. The Lions trailed at the half, 7-6, after a short punt led to Rice's 7-points and a bad snap from center bungled State's PAT in the first quarter. It could have been worse. The Owls drove to the PSU 5 before the Lions held with about 1:30 left in the first half and Rice missed a 17-yard field goal. Moments later, Rice intercepted a Liske pass but Liske redeemed himself with a touchdown-saving tackle at the 3-yard line on a 15-yard screen pass on the last play of the half. A surprise tactic by Engle at the start of the third quarter helped turn them in for a series, then utilized three units the rest of the game. Engle started his inexperienced third unit, kept them in for a series, then utilized three unites the rest of the game. With the first unit and Kochman out on the field, Liske drove the team 68-yards in 10 plays for the go-ahead score at 10:04 of the third quarter. A fourth-down, 21-yard pass to Powell that went to Rice's 6-yard line set up a 3-yard TD by Hayes; a screen pass for 2-points failed and the Lions led 12-7.

State's defense led by Robinson and Sieminski stopped Rice on a drive to the Lions 23-yard line and a short time later, Chuck Raisig, the nation's leading punter, put Rice on its own 1-inch line with a 58-yard boot. Minutes later, a Caum interception gave the Lions a chance for a 27-yard field goal but Rice blocked it. The Lions finally scored the clincher in the fourth quarter after Liske returned an interception 42 yards to the Rice 17 and two plays later Hayes bounced off left tackle and ran around right end for a 16-yard touchdown and State had a tiring 18-7 victory. "...The third unit meant the difference...," wrote Doug McDonald, sports editor of the *Centre Daily Times*. "'Those guys saved us,' guard Joe Blasenstein said.'"

Now, it was on to noisy Michie Stadium and 2-1 Army for the third-rated Lions. State was a six point favorite and that worried Engle. "I know of few teams that respond to an underdog role the way Army does," Engle told John Morris of the *Daily Collegian*. Coach Paul Dietzel, who had won the national title with LSU in '58 with his special defensive unit he called the "Chinese Bandits," was the new coach at West Point and he brought his "Chinese Bandits" tactics with him. As a regional CBS television audience looked on, Dietzel ran his three units in and out of the game, used plays without a huddle, deployed a 9-man line, kicked on third down and even tried to surprise State with a heretofore unused "spread formation" in the opening series. Still playing without Gursky, the Lions offense had problems in the first half and the score was tied, 3-3, when Army kicked off in the third quarter. Starting from the State 33-yard line, Liske drove the team for a first down at the Army 8. Kochman was stopped for no gain and Liske overthrew Powell. On third down, Liske spotted Anderson wide open in the end zone. "I wasn't the primary receiver but the ball bounced right

of my chest," Anderson said, recalling his defining moment 35 years later. On fourth down Coates attempted a field goal but one of the "Bandits" blocked it. After the PSU defense forced Army to punt, Coates and Liske combined to the take the Lions on another drive of 58-yards to the Army 12. On first down, Bowes made a spectacular catch in the end zone but the touchdown was called back by an offside penalty. Four plays later Coates' 24-yard field goal put the Lions ahead 6-3 as the third quarter came to a close. After the kickoff, the defense stopped Army at midfield and the Cadets punted out of bounds at State's 14-yard line. Three plays later, Powell fumbled at the 18 and Army's Tom Kerns recovered. On fourth-and-goal at the 7, Army's Dick Peterson scored on a pass over the middle from QB Cammy Lewis. The conversion failed but Army now led, 9-6. After the kickoff, State drove to the Army 38 but was held on a fourth down run and State never seriously threatened again. The game closed with a brawl when Army enticed Rosdhal to jump offside and players on both sides started swinging as hundreds of bellicose Cadets rushed on to the field before the final plays could be run. "The defeat was a heavy blow to Engle's fine team," wrote Allison Danzig in *The New York Times*, "but it lost to an Army eleven worthy of West Point's best traditions."

The defeat did not demoralize the Lions, who fell #14, and they showed their character in the next two weeks when they beat Syracuse and California by a total of three points. The record Homecoming crowd of 48,356 saw the favored Lions use a fumble recovery and interception to take a 14-0 first quarter lead over Syracuse (1-2) on two Kochman touchdowns. But the Orangemen battled back behind sophomore quarterback Walt Mahle and tight end John Mackey for two touchdowns and trailed going into the fourth quarter by just 14-13 after missing a third quarter extra point on a holding penalty. The Syracuse momentum helped carry them to a go-ahead touchdown on an 86-yard drive early in the final stanza but a two-point run for the conversion was stopped on a tackle by Liske. Then Coach Ben Schwartzwalder made a gambling decision that backfired. He ordered an onside kick but the

Dave Robinson, a First-Team All-American in 1962 and later a star with the Green Bay Packers, is the latest Penn State player elected to the National Football Foundation College Football Hall of Fame. Engle called him the greatest lineman he ever coached.

kick went too far. Robinson scooped up the ball and ran five yards to State's 42. That rejuvenated the Lions. With Liske passing once to Kochman for 37 yards and three times to Robinson—the last a fourth down throw to the Army 1-yard line—State drove downfield and took the lead on Hayes' plunge. Liske stumbled trying to pass for the two-points and with less than five minutes remaining. the Lions led, 20-19. Syracuse was out of time outs, but the Orange moved the ball upfield and Tom Mingo went back to attempt a game winning field goal from the 34-yard line. But Rosdahl smashed through and blocked the kick. Robinson recovered and the game was over.

The Lions had another close call at California in State's first West Coast game since 1948. In the first quarter, the Lions looked like they would run the 1-and-4 Bears off the field but they couldn't score as they gained nearly 150 yards but lost 70 yards on penalties, including three holding infractions and an offensive interference call. An 80-yard touchdown drive and Coates' 27-yard field goal put State ahead 10-0 midway in the second quarter when Bears Coach Marv Levy inserted a sophomore into his first varsity game. *The Saturday Evening Post* had labeled young Craig Morton as the probably the best soph in college football and he looked like it that day in Berkeley. Morton immediately took Cal 73-yards in six plays for a touchdown and the half ended at 10-6. Kochman's one-yard plunge and Coates' PAT made it 17-6 at the end of a 77-yard drive early in the third quarter, but Morton quickly passed the Bears back, going 75-yards in nine plays and a two-point pass narrowed the score to 17-14. The Lions scored again on the ensuing kickoff, going 75 yards on the running of Kochman and Hayes and the passing of Liske, with a 10-yard pass to Gursky getting the touchdown at the start of the fourth quarter. The kick failed and State led, 23-14. Back came Morton with a 73-yard, 10-play drive and PAT that made it 23-21 with eight minutes remaining. State gave up the ball with four minutes left and it was the defense which saved the game. With third-and-four at the State 33, Morton had to scramble to avoid Robinson and was hit by Rosdahl. The ball popped into the air and Robinson recovered. But the Lions had to give up the ball again with 1:14 left and Liske punted into the end zone. Morton completed two passes to stop the clock, then just missed a bomb to a wide open receiver before Liske intercepted another long pass to end it all. In the locker room, the team gave Paterno the game ball, the first and only time he was given a game ball as an assistant coach. The

Lions had survived one of the greatest passing exhibitions by an opposing quarterback as Morton completed 20 of 30 attempts for 273 yards and three touchdowns. Liske also had his best game as a starter, hitting on 13-of-16 passes (eight to Gursky) for 132 yards. "For the second Saturday in a row, the excellent quarterbacking of Pete Liske [14 for 17 and 150 yards] has been overshadowed by a sophomore," wrote McDonald in the *CDT*. "...Craig Morton captured most of the headlines...in a losing effort."

Despite a heavy snowfall that started two hours before game time and continued most the game, 41,834 turned out when Maryland and the nation's leading passer, Dick Shiner, visited Beaver Stadium on November 3. However, Shiner had the worst game of his career as State's defense led by Robinson, Rosdahl, Baker, Sieminski and Caum held Shiner to 5 completions on 13 attempts (for 33 yards) and Liske ran the Lions to a 23-7 victory. Caum picked off two of Shiner's three interceptions to set up fourth quarter touchdowns when the score was still close. His 35-yard return on the first play of the fourth quarter led immediately to Liske's 13-yard touchdown run that gave the Lions a 16-7 lead and Caum sealed the game a moment later with a 13-yard pickoff that led to Kochman's clinching touchdown. Robinson harassed Shiner all afternoon and set what is

All-American Roger Kochman gets a block from Al Gursky in the 23-7 win over Maryland in 1962 as an early November snowstorm hit Beaver Stadium.

probably a school record by recovering three fumbles. Liske ran for 76 yards to lead all rushers and scored on touchdowns of 11 and 13 yards on quarterback keeper plays that offensive backfield coach Paterno designed just for Maryland.

The Lions closed out the home season by breaking a 40-year team record for first downs in a 34-6 win over West Virginia. The score was just 7-0 at the half but State erupted with three fourth quarter touchdowns as the offense gained 337 yards on the ground and 193 in the air for a total of 38 first downs. Liske passed for three touchdowns and Powell caught two of them. It was more of the same the next week at Worcester when State exploded with three touchdowns in the second quarter and turned a 7-6 first quarter lead into a 48-20 romp over Holy Cross. The offense gained 357 yards on the ground and 130 through the air as seven different players scored touchdowns. The win moved the Lions back into #9 in the AP ratings.

State was now a leading candidate for another bowl trip. As the team practiced for the traditional final at Pitt Stadium, the Gator Bowl said it wanted the Lions back in Jacksonville. The Cotton and Orange bowls also mentioned State as an outside possibility and the Liberty and Gotham bowls said State and Pitt were being considered. Pitt was just 5-4 but a 24-6 win over Syracuse and a 7-6 upset over Army had put the Panthers back into bowl contention and the race for the Lambert Trophy. State was favored by eight points and Engle reminded the team about previous games in this rivalry when the upset winner kept the loser from going to a bowl game. In a psychological move, Pitt coach John Michelosen started his alternate unit led by sophomore quarterback Fred Mazurek and on Pitt's first possession, Marzurek led the Panthers to State's 5-yard line before Robinson and Baker stopped two runs with hard tackles and Pitt fumbled away the ball on third down in what may have been the turning point of the game. State's offense had problems moving against Pitt's tough defensive line and it wasn't until the Panthers' starting quarterback, Jim Traficant, fumbled on Pitt's 30-yard line late in the second quarter that the Lions got their first score. Traficant's bobble led to a 26-yard field goal by Coates and it was just 3-0 at the half. Pitt's first unit took the second half kickoff and drove from its 33-yard line to the State 30 before Gursky intercepted Traficant in the end zone. Pitt never came close again. From that point, Liske drove the Lions downfield and at the State 44 he tossed a pass to Kochman at the Pitt 40 and Kochman romped untouched for a touchdown. The PAT made it 10-0. On the last play of the third quarter, Powell made his fifth interception of the season, running back 47 yards to set up an 18-yard TD pass to Gursky that Pitt protested. Pitt's Eddie Clark seemed to have an interception on the play but Gursky yanked the ball out of Clark's hands. Pitt claimed Gursky had been out of the playing field and that Liske had crossed the scrimmage line but the referee disagreed. State went on to win, 16-0, as Liske broke three team records for one season, including the most TD passes (12), total offense (1,302) and most yards passing (1,047). For his performance he was named the game's outstanding player and became the first recipient of the James H. Coogan Memorial Award, named after State's one-time sports information director who had died that April.

It became apparent in the locker room after the game that the Lions would be ignored by the January 1st bowls and the best they could get would be a Gator Bowl encore. State kept the locker room closed for a half hour after the game and Engle admitted they were discussing a bowl bid but had reached no decision. "The Lions may be miffed about being shunned by the other major bowls and wanted time to cool off before making a decision," wrote Bob Drum in the *Pittsburgh Press*. In that era, State's players voted on whether or not to accept bowl invitations and in the dingy visitor's enclave at Pitt Stadium, most of the seniors were adamant about rejecting the Gator invitation. They believed they had earned a New Year's Day game and they resented the snub. They also were not looking forward to another hard-working and extended stay at dreary Fort Eustis and St. Augustine over the holidays, nor the continued racial ostracism of the South. But on Monday following the Pitt win, the team voted to go to the Gator Bowl December 29 with the stipulation that "Christmas must be spent at home." The players' sour attitude towards the bowl wasn't helped when a 6-4 Florida team was selected as their opponent and soon the newspapers were hinting at the team's lack of enthusiasm for the game. "I'm hoping that our players don't underrate Florida," Engle told the *Centre Daily Times*. "In a one-game effort such as this, there's no telling how high a team can get up mentally against you...Florida has a lot to gain by beating us."

Even before they started practicing for the game, the Lions learned they had won the Lambert Trophy, again, and finished 9th in

the final AP poll. But they were the odd team out as all the teams ahead of them were playing on New Year' Day: #1 USC vs #2 Wisconsin in the Rose Bowl; #3 Mississippi vs #6 Arkansas in the Sugar Bowl; #4 Texas vs #7 LSU in the Cotton Bowl; and, #5 Alabama vs #8 Oklahoma in the Orange Bowl. They also learned that for the first time since 1923, two State players were selected First Team All-Americans, Robinson and Kochman.

THE 1962 GATOR BOWL GAME
Dec. 29, 1962
Florida 17, Penn State 7
Miller Award: Dave Robinson

Because the racial and travel circumstances would not allow Engle to take the team too far South until after Christmas, the squad practiced for more than a week at the Naval Academy in Annapolis where the lousy weather forced them into the field house much of the time. The best experience out of the entire period was a side trip to the White House where they gave President John F. Kennedy a Nittany Lion statuette. Kennedy told the team he had a kinship with them because he had played halfback at Harvard for former Lion player and coach, Dick Harlow, who also had coached Engle at Western Maryland. They reassembled in Harrisburg on Christmas night and had a disconcerting travel experience before reaching St. Augustine. The plane to Jacksonville couldn't leave Harrisburg because of a snow storm so the team took a bus to Greater Pittsburgh Airport, arriving at a Pittsburgh motel at about midnight. Then, when their airplane tried to land at Jacksonville on instruments because of low cloud ceiling, the pilot almost crashed into a hanger before getting the plane airborne again. The plane went on to Orlando and the players boarded another bus to St. Augustine. Once practice started in St. Augustine, several of the key seniors, including Robinson, Kochman and Sieminski, were being badgered by the professional football teams. "We had so many guys eligible for the pros that nobody had his mind on the game," Kochman told writer Ken Rappoport years later. Meanwhile, the Southern newspapers continued to spread the word that State was denigrating its opponent. "...The word is out," wrote one writer, "that Penn State's Nittany Lions, angry at having been over-looked by other bowl committees, are regarding their December 29 Gator Bowl date with the Florida Gators as 'just another stop along the road' and haven't been practicing regularly." Another writer said the Gators were "unrated and unwanted." Engle had a hunch of what was coming. "They're as fine a team as we've faced in our last three bowl games," he told McDonald of the *CDT*. "We're concerned with our timing reaction and conditioning. I just don't think we're near the team we were in November."

"There is no tougher opponent than a team comprised of southern boys whose pride had been injured," wrote Riley in his *"Football Letter."* "The Gators came on the field with Confederate flags newly painted on their helmets and fire in their eyes...(they were) angry young men." In its previous six games, the Lions had lost a total of three fumbles but on this day, they gave up three fumbles and the first one by Kochman in the opening period led to a 3-0 Florida lead when a reserve tackle named Bob Lyle kicked his and Florida's *first* field goal of the season from the 33-yard line. In the second quarter, Caum fumbled a punt at State's 24-yard line and Florida's supposedly run-oriented offense led by sophomores Tom Shannon and Larry Dupree *passed* its way to a touchdown and a 10-0 lead. With six minutes left before intermission, State drove 76 yards and made the score 10-7 on

Liske's fourth-down, one-yard run and Coates' PAT with 36 seconds remaining. "On other similar occasions this season we have fought back in the third and fourth periods to overcome the opposition with drive and determination," wrote Riley. "But the third quarter found our team again listless and the Gators full of beans." Late in the third quarter, Florida intercepted a Liske pass at midfield and on the first play of the last period, Florida scored another TD on a 19-yard pass and that was the ball game as State ran just four plays in the fourth quarter. The Lions' ball-control offense had withered, as they had the ball for just 19 minutes and could run off but 58 plays, including 6 punts.

"They were hungrier than we were," Engle told sportswriters. "They also had more incentive." Florida coach Ray Graves said, "The only way we knew we could beat State was to come up with a strong pre-game practice program...They were willing to sacrifice and it paid off." Robinson was voted State's outstanding player as he, Kochman and Sieminski signed pro contracts right after the game. "I always attributed the loss in the 1962 Gator Bowl to the fact that nobody cared about winning it," Kochman said years later, in summing up what was, ultimately, the defining moment of the season.

"We are...firmly convinced," wrote Riley in his *"Football Letter,"* "that no team should play in any Bowl unless the players are completely in favor of the venture and willing to make all the necessary sacrifices, if not for their own benefit, then for the benefit of the University, and the sport which has made their education possible."

The players would turn down another bowl opportunity two years later and it would be five more years before State would play in a post-season bowl game again. By then, the team would have a new coach and it would be his choice, not the players. There would be no National Championship for two decades. But there would be a couple of big surprises in 1963 and a shock.

Season Record 9-2
Record to Date 399-210-39
Winning percentage .646

"The 'Z-Back'"

Engle and his coaches looked at their material following spring practice and knew they would have to make some changes. There was a shortage of veteran running backs and experienced linemen.

All the top rushers from '62 were graduating, except for Liske at quarterback. Of the returning lettermen, Powell was more a pass receiver than a running halfback and Stuckrath, battling for a starting position at fullback, had been used more on defense in the "Hero" position. Caum also was starting on defense but running third at quarterback behind Coates. Yost was a defensive specialist, too. The rest of the backs were an amalgam of mostly non-letter juniors like halfback Gary Klingensmith of Uniontown and fullback Tom Urbanik of Donora or unproven sophomores—Bob Riggle, Dave McNaugton and Dick Gingrich, another quarterback. Up front, the veterans Rosdahl, Ressler, Sabol, Anderson, Bowes, Monaghan, and Baker, the captain, were superb. But Engle's line coaches Jim O'Hora and J. T. White would need

to find help from a batch of reserves and sophomores or there would be a lot of linemen on the field for a long time playing both ways. Their dilemma was further complicated by the confusing new substitution rules which restricted some individual as well as team deployment. Still, with young linemen like Jerry Sandusky, Joe Bellas, Gary Eberle, John Diebert and Ellery Setiz coming up, Engle was more concerned about the early development of his backfield than his line. State's upgraded schedule put together a few years back by athletic director McCoy also was part of Engle's quandry. His first three games were against high-quality intersectional opponents—Oregon, UCLA and Rice—and he needed a good offense to match up. He also knew he would need more than defense for the rest of the schedule, which included another game at Columbus with mighty Ohio State. So, he and Paterno spent the summer secretly creating the Swing-T formation and the "Z-Back" to capitalize on the passing ability of Liske and Coates and to get the most of the inexperienced linemen.

Over the summer, Engle mailed a batch of information about the Swing-T to all players and told them to keep the data secret. He wanted to surprise Oregon when the Lions opened the season at Portland September 21. Sportswriters covering the team's preseason workouts also were sworn to secrecy and no mention of the Swing-T was made by the press until after the Saturday night game at Multnomah Stadium. The Swing-T centers around a position called the Z-Back, which is actually a split end position in the line. The player sets himself a few yards from the nearest lineman and "swings" from one side to the other. When on the right, the line is unbalanced and the right end is ineligible as a receiver. When on the left, the line is balanced and the left end is ineligible. In either position, other linemen and backs have blocking assignments and pass patterns designed to confuse the opposition. "Our coaches believed it was a psychological time for something new with which to harass our opponents, provide stimulus to veteran players, and at the same time be a relatively easy adjustment for the many sophomores, not yet inured to the old system," wrote Riley in his *"Football Letter."* And with the former quarterbacks Caum and Gingrich designated as the "Z-Back" it worked—for a while.

The Z-Back did not make his debut against two-point favorite Oregon until the second possession. The Lions won the toss and received but on the first play from the traditional Wing-T formation, Klingensmith, who is totally deaf, went in motion and was into the Ducks' secondary before the ball was snapped. When asked by State's sports information director Jim Tarman after the game what made him jump offside, Klingensmith said through an interpreter, "Well, everyone is always asking you about that deaf player, so I decided it was time to let them know who he was." After the penalty, the Lions lost yardage and had to punt. But the defense held and State got the ball back on its own 20 and out trotted Caum on the right end, wearing a number (80) not on the depth chart. In the press box, Tarman began distributing a news release about the Z-Back to the puzzled sportswriters. Liske hit Caum immediately on a hook pattern for 8-yards. Now, the surprised Oregon defense spread out to cover the new formation and with Caum mostly a decoy, the Lions drove downfield on the power running of Urbanik, Klingensmith and Yost to a 4th-and-1 at the 8-yard line. Instead of kicking a field goal, Liske used a special Swing-T play that had Powell as a receiver following behind Caum who would block the only defender. The pass play worked perfectly and with Coates' PAT the Lions led 7-0. State's defense held Oregon's explosive running attack in check until late in the third quarter, when Quarterback Bob

Berry marched the Ducks 80 yards in 7 plays to tie, 7-7, with All-American Mel Renfro getting the TD from the one. But the Lions came back with a 63-yard drive that gave them the lead on a 32-yard field goal by Coates on the first play of the fourth quarter. After the kickoff, Oregon reached State's 25-yard line with a third-and-2 before Rosdahl tackled Renfro behind the scrimmage line. Oregon set up for a long field goal but the State defense figured it would be a fake and Yost tackled Renfro for a loss on a pitchout from the holder.

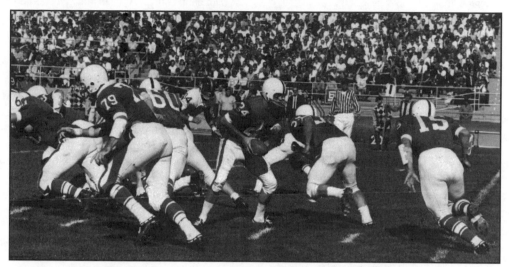

QB Pete Liske, seen here handing off at the start of a play at Beaver Stadium, led the team in total offense in 1962 and 1963, and was also a fine defensive back.

The Lions moved into the Top 10 at #9 the following week after beating Rice at Beaver Stadium, 28-7. The defense led by Stuckrath and Caum held Rice to 30 yards rushing and intercepted three Walter McReynolds' passes as the Owls tried to pass their way to victory. Stuckrath was in Rice's backfield half of the day with his blitzes and Caum intercepted two aerials, including one in the third quarter that set up a touchdown that put the Lions ahead, 14-7, early in the third quarter. Stuckrath also scored a TD on a one-yard dive and Urbanik ran 17 yards for another as the duo led the rushing with more than 60 yards each.

State took over and moved to the Oregon 41 where on third-and-11, Liske called another special Swing-T play. Up to this time, Caum and Gingrich had caught three passes apiece, mostly on third down short hook patterns. Now came the surprise. Oregon's defender bit on the hook pattern and Caum caught Liske's perfect pass in stride at the 10-yard line and out ran Renfro into the end zone. Coates' boot made it 17-0 and it was all over. State had just won its 400th game in history. "Oregon was caught flat-footed," wrote Doug McDonald of the *Centre Daily Times*. "According to reports, the Ducks were prepared for a tight line and a passing attack from a tight line... 'We had to adjust to it,' (Oregon coach Len) Casanova said. 'Maybe we should have had those press releases a little sooner.'"

The Swing-T worked again as State beat UCLA, 17-14, in the home opener before 36,327 a week later. Liske broke the single-game completion record held by Tony Rados and Al Jacks with 19 of 27 passes for 176 yards and a touchdown and Powell tied the 1940 game record of Lenny Krouse by catching 9 passes. But the outcome of the game depended on a 32-yard field goal under pressure by Coates. Powell's 52-yard reception and elusive dash down the sideline with a minute and a half left in the second quarter helped give the Lions a 14-7 halftime lead. Midway through the third quarter, quarterback Larry Zeno and halfback Mel Profit led a 74-yard UCLA drive following a Lions fumble that tied the game. State almost scored after the kickoff, reaching the UCLA 13 before giving the ball up on downs. Then with six minutes left in the game, Coates had to kick the ball twice for the the winning points. His first boot from the 18 was nullified when State had too many men on the field, so he dropped back and kicked from 22. Caum, who had been mostly a decoy on offense, came up with his second interception of the game to halt a UCLA comeback at the Lions' 37-yard line and State almost scored again as the game neared an end but a fourth-and-goal pass to Powell from the 2 was overthrown. "That field goal by Coates will always be one of the top pays of my coaching experience," Engle told the *CDT*'s McDonald. "He's a tremendous kicker—the best one we've ever had."

In the last two seasons, an underdog Army team had become the worst nightmare for State fans and another record standing room only crowd of 49,389 could not believe it when it happened again. Despite the demise of his defensive specialists—the "Chinese Bandits"—because of the new substitution rules, Paul Dietzel's 2-1 Army team brought the Swing-T to a virtual halt. The Lions, favored by two TDs, gained just 37 yards rushing and 99 yards passing—and 69 of the passing yards came on a Liske to Powell touchdown bomb with 30 seconds left in the half. Army got all the points it needed on a 32-yard field goal by Dick Heydt in the first period and a fourth-and-2 touchdown pass from Carl Stichweh to Sam Champi that culminated an 85-yard drive early in the second quarter. Army totally dominated the second half. Engle replaced Liske with Coates but the Cadets still kept the Lion offense from crossing their own 40-yard line. State had to stop Army twice with goal line stands in the second half but still had a chance to win when Ressler forced and recovered a fumble at the Cadets 31-yard line in the last minute. However, two running plays and two passes were futile and Army won, 10-7. "We just got licked and by a big strong football team," Engle said after the game. Dietzel told sportswriters, "Our players really love to play against Penn State...The only thing that could have been better is if Navy had been on the other side and you can quote me on that."

Engle knew the Lions would have to improve on defense to stop fullback Jim Nance and the best rushing attack in the nation at Syracuse the following Saturday. He also did some tinkering with the Swing-T. And on an unusually hot 85-degree day in Archbold Stadium, it all might have worked if not for two defensive lapses and several dropped passes by State's receivers. Late in the second quarter, Syracuse's Billy Hunter scampered around left end with some devastating blocking and ran 53 yards for a touchdown and a 6-0 lead. The Lions drove quickly to the Orange 5 as time was running out in the half but Syracuse's pass defense halted four attempts by Liske, including a fourth down throw that Caum dropped when he was wide open in the end zone. On the first play of the second half, Mike Koski went around left end for 58 yards to the PSU 7 and four plays later Syracuse booted a field goal from the 14 and that was the final, 9-0. Midway in the final quarter, the Lions almost avoided a shut out but Anderson muffed a 40-yard throw at the goal. It was the first time PSU had been scoreless since 1958 and Syracuse's first whitewash of State since 1934. The Lions defense had held the powerful Syracuse rushing attack to 233 yards but as Joseph Sheehan pointed out in the *New York Times*, "Trying too hard, perhaps, to redeem their defeat a week ago by Army, the Nittany Lions just couldn't get any cohesion into their attack in scoring territory."

That was it for the Swing-T. It was back to the Multiple-T for the Band Day game against West Virginia on an Indian Summer afternoon at Beaver Stadium and the Lions broke open a 6-6 tie in the third quarter to win, 20-9. A dazzling Liske to Powell lateral that went for 35 yards set up State's go ahead touchdown and a 5-yard Liske to Anderson TD pass sealed the game in the fourth quarter. State's offense racked up 268 yards rushing and 102 yards passing while holding WVU to 59 yards on the ground and 100 in the air. "We weren't surprised State didn't use the Z-Back because it had sort of worn off the past few weeks," said Mountaineer Coach Gene Corum. "(State) buried the Swing-T formation today and it was West Virginia's funeral," wrote one sportswriter. "...the Z-back is dead like the sea," wrote another. "Not so," Engle told Riley. "We hope the Swing-T will continue to be an important part of our offense. It was effective against the first three opponents and it will be again...It's a formation we'll still have and will still use

Ralph Baker was captain of the 1963 team and one of the early graduates of "Linebacker U" who later played on the NFL's famous 1969 New York Jets team.

at the right time." But in writing about the last four games, Riley never mentioned the Swing-T nor the Z-Back again!

After six games in near perfect football weather, the winds changed—literally. Of course it would, because the next game was against Maryland in Byrd Stadium. It rained for nearly 24 hours before the game and a cold 30-mile wind greeted the teams and the 35,500 Terp Homecoming fans. Injuries were now affecting Engle's game plan. State was seriously hampered at tackle on his first two units with Rosdahl and Eberle out for the season and Monaghan also sidelined. Powell also was among the missing because of an ankle sprain. As expected, Maryland took the wind, kicked off and scored with less than two minutes in the first quarter on Shiner's 5-yard rollout. But when State got the wind in the second quarter, Frank Hershey put Maryland in a hole with a punt out of bounds at the Terp 1-yard line. Maryland muffed a handoff in the end zone and Bowes, Stuckrath, Sabol and Gingrich nailed the ball carrier for a safety. Maryland's punt barely went 30 yards and Stuckrath ran it back the the Terp 20. Five plays later, Liske

rolled out and passed 14-yards to a wide open Anderson for the TD, despite 12 men on the field for the Terps. Liske hit Bowes on the two-point conversion and State led, 10-7. Maryland flubbed a field goal in the third period but had moved into State territory midway in the fourth before losing a fumble that Liske recovered at the 34-yard line. Maryland knew what was coming next but couldn't stop it. On the first play, Liske rolled out and hit a wide open Klingensmith at the Maryland 25 and Klingensmith outran two pursuing tacklers for a 66-yard touchdown. "We call it a disaster play," Maryland Coach Tommy Nugent told thre *CDT*'s McDonald. "It's right in our scouting report. It was a perfect bomb." Coates' PAT made it 17-7. As time was running out, Maryland got the ball on an exchange of fumbles and scored on a 22-yard deflected pass. The two-point conversion made it 17-15 with 1:30 left but Maryland's onside kick failed and the Lions ran out the clock. "We were able to take advantae of the win and played it smart," Engle told Ira Miller of the *Daily Collegian*.

As expected, the Lions were again a heavy underdog against Ohio State at Columbus. The Buckeyes were one of the favorites to win the Big Ten and would eventually finish with a 4-1-1 conference record and a tie with Michigan State behind champion Illinois. The *Columbus Citizen-Journal* called the game with Penn State "Non-League Nonsense." The Buckeyes were loaded as usual with such future All-Pros as Matt Snell and Paul Warfield leading a crushing ground game. The Lions' injury problem at tackle had continued as Bellas also was sidelined and Buchan and Diebert were playing with leg problems. Not since State had visited Columbus in 1956 had a PSU team played before such a huge crowd as 83,519 showed up for the televised game. On the first play from scrimmage, Liske almost hit a wide open Klingensmith on a bomb and although the pass was overthrown it set the tone for the day for State's offense. A Lions' fourth-and-inches gamble that failed at State's 45-yard line with five minutes left in the first half helped give OSU a 7-0 lead as the Buckeyes then drove the distance for a 5-yard TD by Warfield. State tied it on its first possession of the third quarter, driving 61 yards and scoring on an 18-yard pass from Liske to Bowes. Throughout the game, State's defense came through in the clutch and three times OSU went for a first down on fourth down and short yardage and three times State's defenders led by Ressler, Baker and Sabol stopped them. The second time, in the third quarter, they halted sophomore Tom Barrington at the 50 and Liske faked and passed State downfield to set up Coates' 23 yard field goal. As time was running out, State stopped Snell on a fourth down at the OSU 44 and then almost scored another TD but Liske's pass was intercepted in the end zone. It didn't matter. The Lions had pulled off another upset, 10-7, with a well rounded offense that gained 155 yards rushing (on 46 attempts) and 171 yards passing (on 14-of-24 passes). "Our offense beat us," Coach Woody Hayes told Roy McHugh of the *Pittsburgh Press*.

In the final game ever with Holy Cross, the Lions scored 28 points in the second and third periods and coasted to a 28-14 win at Beaver Stadium. Caum scored one TD on a 9-yard run off a fake field goal and picked up another when he combined with Coates on a 60-yard pass. Sophomore reserve McNaughton also had two TDs and led all rushers with 46 yards on 14 carries.

Pitt had its best team in more than a decade and had lost only to Roger Staubach's unbeaten second-ranked Navy squad, 21-14, at Annapolis. The Panthers were rated fifth and had the third best offense in the country. The oddsmakers made Pitt an eight point favorite for the

November 23 game and the Orange, Sugar, Cotton and Gator Bowls had all expressed a strong interest in the Panthers. The Lions also were mentioned by the Cotton and Gator bowls but no one in State's official family believed they would get a bowl bid even with a win over Pitt.

But as State was traveling to Pittsburgh the day before the scheduled game, the nation was shocked by the assassination of President Kennedy in Dallas. All the college games were postponed for a week. When the two teams finally met before a Pitt Stadium crowd of 51,477 on December 7, only the Cotton and Gator Bowls had spots still open and Navy was a shoe-in for a Cotton Bowl encounter with #1 Texas. Those long-time State and Pitt fans who saw this one believe it was one of the best-played games ever in the traditional series. But another strict rule interpretation by a familiar referee may have cost PSU the opportunity to win the game.

State dominated the first quarter and took a 7-0 lead on Klingensmith's fourth down, 9-yard TD run and Coates' PAT. Pitt's All-American Paul Martha ran 1-yard for a TD early in the second quarter but Fred Mazurek's flare pass to Martha for two points was stopped by Stuckrath. It would be a play that would influence both sides for the rest of the game. With about five minutes left in the half, State recovered a Pitt fumble at the Panther 36 and seven plays later, Sandusky twisted around in the end zone to catch a 9-yard pass thrown behind him by Liske. With Coates' kick the Lions led 14-6. But Pitt rebounded with a 10-play, 80 yard drive with Rick Leeson going over from the one on fourth down. Mazurek again tried to pass for two but Ressler broke up the play and it was 14-12 at the half.

State recovered another Pitt fumble at the Panther 30 early in the third period but when an offensive interference penalty moved the Lions back from the Pitt 11 to the 26 the referee—one Francis Brennan—signaled fourth down to Liske but failed to make his notification clear to the State sideline. Liske completed a pass to the 12 but Pitt took over on downs. "Had I known it was fourth down, I would have had Coates try a field goal," Engle told sportswriters after the game, blaming Brennan's subtle movements on the field for confusing the coaches and many of the fans. Brennan, of course, was the same referee who refused to allow Galen Hall time to put his shoe back on in the waning moments of the 1960 Syracuse game. A short time later, Pitt went ahead 15-14 on Leeson's 25-yard field goal. But State thundered right back on a 78-yard drive in eight plays with Caum making a leaping catch of a Liske pass at the back of the end zone for a 9-yard TD. Then came a decision Engle said he would always regret. Coates went in for the apparent kick but it was supposed to be a fake and a two-point conversion try. "We had a play off the fake kick but I didn't act in time and couldn't get my players into the game," Engle told Les Biederman of the *Pittsburgh Press.* Coates' kick made it 21-15 as the game moved into the fourth quarter. But Pitt retaliated with a 77-yard drive in 11 plays as Mazurek scored on a 17-yard rollout. Leeson's PAT made it 22-21 with 12 minutes left. Late in the game, State almost had a TD when Liske tried to hit Caum in the clear with a bomb but Pitt's safety Glenn Lehner broke it up with an intentional interference call that gave PSU the ball on Pitt's 43. State got to the Panther 20 with 70 seconds remaining and on fourth down Coates tried a field goal against the wind from the 27. The kick was barely wide left and Pitt ran out the clock for the victory.

"Pitt makes a field goal by inches and we miss one by inches and that's all the difference there was in the two football teams," Engle told this writer for the Associated Press. Pitt coach John Michelosen

said it "was a tremendous football game. I can't remember a game with Penn State that has been so close." Pitt moved up to #4 in the ratings and State finished 16th but Navy got the Cotton Bowl berth and unranked teams, Air Force and North Carolina, went to the Gator Bowl. The only solace for Pitt was the Panthers had beaten their prime rival for the first time in four years.

The innovative Swing-T and the Z-Back had helped to make the '63 season a successful one despite it's short life. Now, as Engle, Paterno and the coaches looked ahead to 1964, they wondered who their quarterback would be. "I'm much more worried over who will quarterback against us," Engle told Riley. The junior Heisman Trophy winner, Roger Staubach, would be the first one and he would start the Lions off to their worst opening three games in history.

Season Record 7-3
Record to Date 406-213-39
Winning percentage .647

"Paul Bunyan and His Ox"

Jim Tarman could not believe what Joe Paterno had just said. They were sitting in the cocktail lounge of the Columbus hotel on the eve of Penn State's game against unbeaten and #2 Ohio State and the Lions sports information director had just asked if the team was going to be humiliated the next day.

It was an honest question. The season was almost over and the Lions were still trying to recover from the most horrendous start in team history while the Buckeyes were once again one of the elite teams in the country. Sure, the '56 and '63 Penn State teams had pulled off great upsets at Ohio Stadium. But this November 7 game appeared to be the biggest mismatch in the series. The Lions already had gone down as the first State team in history to lose its first three games and the squad was 1-4 before beating weaklings West Virginia and Maryland in the last two weeks. Ohio State, with six relatively easy wins that limited opponents to a total of 39 points, was leading the Big Ten and battling it out in the polls with Ara Parseghian's rejuvenated Notre Dame, which, coincidentally, was playing at Pitt this same weekend.

So, with assistant coach Jim O'Hora listening, Tarman had said he knew the Lions couldn't possibly win but worried about being humiliated. "We're going to shut out Woody (Hayes)," Paterno replied matter-of-factly. "How do you figure that?" a flabbergasted Tarman responded. "We've put in some changes that will neutralize some of the things they do best on offense and we've scrapped our regular offense," Paterno said, according to a description of the incident in his book, *Football My Way.* If Tarman had told sportswriters of Paterno's prediction before the game, he would have been laughed right out of the press box.

Sure, the Lions had improved since bumbling their way through successive losses to Navy, UCLA and Oregon at the start of the season, when they had given up 64 points by fumbling 16 times and throwing four interceptions. But even after winning three of its last four games, State did not appear ready to take on the likes of Ohio State, a team of powerful runners and defensive opportunists who had turned 19 fumble recoveries and interceptions into 10 touchdowns.

No one had expected this to be a great season, not with such inexperience at quarterback, halfback, defensive end and guard. Gary Wydman, a fifth-year senior who had lettered as a defensive back in '61 but missed the last two seasons because of a knee injury and mononucleosis, had beaten out Gingrich, the former Z-back, and sophomore transfer Jack White of Wilkinsburg for the starting quarterback. He was a good rollout runner and a decent passer but he needed time to master the State offense. Stuckrath was back at fullback but would be used more on defense as the season progressed because of the resurgence of Urbanik,

Workhorse FB Tom Urbanik was the "Ox" for Glenn Ressler's "Paul Bunyon" and had one of his finest games in the great 1964 upset over then #2 Ohio State, 27-0.

who had struggled in '63 and started this preseason as the number three fullback. The halfbacks were mostly non-lettering juniors or sophomores with potential but none of them stood out in the first month or so. Engle had 10 lettermen back in the line but another mercurial change in the substitution rules restricting the number and timing of substitutions limited the coach's options. Is this ever going to stop? Engle complained. He wanted to use three units, one each for offense and defense and another one that would go both ways. But he didn't have enough manpower so he intended to use one unit on offense 80 percent of the time and another on defense 80 percent. Some players still would go both ways, including Ressler, the man everyone considered the best athlete on the team, who was back at center and defensive guard. Ressler was the type of player who could dominate a game up front and in the preseason Ridge Riley nicknamed him "Paul Bunyan" after the legendary lumberjack of the storybooks. With so many question marks, sportswriters, like those at *Street & Smith* magazine, picked State as the "sleeper" in the East behind two State opponents, Navy and Syracuse. "We feel obliged to pursue a policy of *cautious* optimism," Riley wrote.

There was one other notable change that had occurred even before the players had arrived on campus. Engle promoted Paterno to Associate Coach, making official what had been evolving over the years. The 37-year-old offensive guru was now the number two man in charge and heir-apparent as Engle began to contemplate retirement.

Because of changes in the University's four term system, most of the 19,000 students had not returned to campus when the Lions opened the season September 19 against Navy and Roger Staubach. Many of the students watching the regional televised game in their homes must have been shocked to see State's defense completely halt Staubach, as the Heisman winner of 1963 ran 12 times for a minus-14 yards and totaled just 43 yards passing on 5-of-13 passes. But Wydman and the offense was ineffectual. Urbanik's fumble at the Navy 13 set up a touchdown in the first quarter and Navy ran back a 58-yard interception of a Wydman pass in the third quarter to take a 14-0 lead it never gave up. Urbanik's 43-yard run helped spark a drive on the ensuing kickoff that narrowed the gap to 14-8 on a 12-yard sweep by sophomore Tim Montgomery of Kane and a 2-point pass completion from

Wydman to converted end Bill Huber. But a nearly 70-yard drive in the fourth quarter that could have given the Lions the win fizzled when Huber dropped a pass at the goal line on a daring fourth-and-2 from the 17. With two minutes left, Navy intercepted another Wydman pass deep in State territory and scored on a 5-yard run to make the final score 21-8. "It was the blocking—or lack of it—which caused the Lions to lose their first season opener in seven years," reported this writer for *Pittsburgh Weekly Sports*. "...to give Wydman a chance, Engle might be forced to use some of his excellent defensive linemen on the offensive platoon..."

The offensive mistakes continued the following Saturday night in the Los Angeles Coliseum against UCLA and this time the defense, without Sandusky and Deibert who were injured, also withered. A 52-yard pass from Larry Zeno to Kurt Altenberg set up UCLA's first TD the first time it had the ball and a 40-yard run by Cornell Champion gave the Bruins a 14-0 lead early in the third quarter. Before the quarter was over, a UCLA fumble at its own 12-yard line on a punt led to a State touchdown on a fourth down, 4-yard halfback pass from Montgomery to junior Don Kunit and the Lions tied it on a 73-yard drive, with Stuckrath, subbing on offense for the injured Urbanik, getting the final four yards. UCLA went ahead, 21-14, early in the fourth quarter on a 16-yard Zeno-to-Altenberg pass that capped a 43-yard drive following a punt. State rallied late in the game with a drive from its own 43 to the UCLA 13-yard line but fumbled its last opportunity with just over a minute to play. "It was a tragic ending to a valiant effort," wrote Riley, who added, "One of these weeks when the gears mesh, this team is going to capitalize on somebody else's mistakes. To put it crudely, our boys are going to bust loose."

Because of injuries, Wydman was joined by three new starters in the backfield against unbeaten Oregon on Band Day: Stuckrath, Kunit and senior reserve Dirk Nye. With 44,803 watching, State fumbled three times in the first quarter but recovered all of them. Both teams recovered fumbles that led to touchdowns in the first half and State had a 7-6 lead going into the third quarter. The Lions blew it early in the third quarter as Oregon quarterback Bob Berry capitalized on back-to-back State fumbles deep in Ducks' territory to score 13 points and take charge. The Lions lost a total of six fumbles for the day and Wydman had two more passes intercepted near the end of the game when he tried to rally the team from a 22-14 deficit. For the first time since football started at State in 1887, a team had lost its first three games and the unhappy Lions fans and sportswriters were calling for Engle to replace the erratic and shaky Wydman at QB. Engle told *Pittsburgh Weekly Sports* he was "never more frustrated in my life" and felt his line and the news substitution rules were the problem. But privately, even Engle and some of his assistants wondered if a change at quarterback should be made. Paterno defended Wydman vigorously behind the scenes. "If we drop Wydman now," Paterno said, according to *"Football My Way,"* "we'll just be going backwards." With the Michie Stadium whammy looming next and Syracuse after that, it appeared that this group of fumblers might go through the worst season since the all-time losers of 1931.

And a fumble did cost State a touchdown at Army (2-1) but not the game. With some 6,000 State fans in the record Michie Stadium crowd of 32,268 and Paul Dietzel's "Chinese Bandits" back in action because of the revised substitution rules, the teams fought through a scoreless first half. However, the Lions got a 25-yard runback from Nye on the second half kickoff and marched 62-yards for touchdown.

Wydman's 36-yard pass to Huber was the big play in the drive and on third-and-goal at the 2, injury prone junior Bob Riggle, playing for the first time, took a pitchout, got a block from Joe Bellas and outran Army fullback Don Parcells to the corner of the goal for the TD. The kick for the PAT was wide and State led, 6-0. Minutes later the offense was banging near Army's goal again after linebacker Bob Kane, a senior non-letterman who was now a starter, intercepted Rollie Stichweh's pass at the State 43-yard line. But State's only fumble of the day ended the threat as the third quarter drew to a close. With 10 minutes left in the game, Army took the ball on its own 20 following a punt and relentlessly moved up field. As the corps of cadets screamed, "The fourth quarter is ours, the fourth quarter is ours," Army ate up the clock, passed only when necessary, made two first downs by inches and soon had a second-and-goal at the two with 3:15 remaining. O'Hora's defensive troops dug in with seven-man front line of Stuckrath, Bowes, Bellas, Ressler, three-year veteran John Simko, sophomore John Runnells and Huber; Kane and Gingrich were the linebackers and Hershey and sophomore Mike Irwin manned the corners. Kane dropped tailback Mark Hamilton for no gain. Third down and Stichweh tried a pass to Sam Champi and Huber batted it down. Fourth down. Surprisingly, Stichweh attempted another pass to Champi and it was overthrown as Huber blitzed and took Stichweh's legs out from under him. The Lions took over and tried to run out the clock but Army used its last time outs and on fourth down with 45 seconds left, punter Hershey scrambled around the end zone for 11 seconds before taking a safety. Army ran back Hershey's 53-yard free kick to midfield but an interception by Runnells finished the game and ended State's three-game victory drought, 6-2. "This has to be one of our greatest wins," Engle told Ira Miller of the *Centre Daily Times*. "That goal line stand was one of those things you hope you get but never know if you will." Dietzel said, "They knew exactly what they came up here to do and they went out and did it. They outhit us, outcharged us and outplayed us."

The Lions lost again the following week to 7th-ranked Syracuse but not in

All-American Glenn Ressler fights off a double-teaming effort by Pitt to block him in 1964 game. This great two-way player was one of the few linemen to win the Maxwell Award as the Outstanding Collegiate Player.

the same way they dropped the first three games. This game before a packed Homecoming crowd of 45,998 went down to the final minute and at the half State led 14-7 after setting up two second quarter touchdowns with interceptions. But State could not stop Jim Nance, who rushed for 107 yards on 23 carries, nor Floyd Little. The sophomore Little returned a punt 71-yards for a first quarter TD and Nance carried the ball six of 12 plays in a third quarter drive of 65-yards that tied the score, then did the bulk of the running late in the fourth quarter when Syracuse pulled out the 21-14 win. Syracuse's winning TD was set up with about three minutes left when Orange linebacker Roger Smith outfought Riggle for a pass from Wydman and returned it 36 yards to State's 22-yard line. With 37 seconds remaining on a third-and-goal at the 3, quarterback Walt Mahle faked to Nance and scampered around

the right end for the winning TD. "That kid made a great play (on the interception). That wasn't Wydman's fault," Paterno told this writer for *Pittsburgh Weekly Sports*. Wydman knew the fans were still blaming him for the loss. "I can read the papers...and it hurts," he told *PWS*. "But the coaches have stuck with me...and I'm thankful for that." Syracuse Coach Ben Schwartzwalder told sportswriters, "They are the best team we've played this season...It wouldn't surprise me a bit if they won the rest of their games."

When Riggle fumbled at the West Virginia 4-yard line following a long drive on the opening kickoff at Mountaineer Field the next Saturday, it appeared as if State's blundering disease had returned. But another outstanding goal line stand at the 1-yard line early in the second quarter was the turning point. Moments later, Riggle ran 86-yards for a touchdown—the longest TD run from scrimmage since 1894—and the Lions went on to win, 37-8, with Paterno and O'Hora coaching the team in Engle's absence. Rip missed his first ever game because of the unexpected death of his younger brother. Paterno told the *Centre Daily Times* the big play of the game was the goal line stand and WVU coach Gene Corum agreed, saying "The tide turned on that goal line stand." Riggle, who continued to play with a torn ligament in his knee that was heavily bandaged, became the first Lion back in three years to rush for over 100 yards as he gained 172 yards and scored two TDs on 13 carries.

One week later at Beaver Stadium, it was Urbanik with the big rushing day, getting 109 yards and two TDs on 29 carries, in a 17-9 victory over 2-4 Maryland. After seven games, Urbanik, behind the blocking of Ressler, first team center Bob Andronici and others, was the team's leading rusher with 317 yards and 5 TDs on 79 carries and some sportswriters began referring to the Ressler-Urbanik tandem as "Paul Bunyan and His Ox." But the sportswriters also figured Ohio State would have no difficulties reining-in "the Ox" the next week in Columbus. No one in his or her right mind would have predicted what happened on November 7 in Columbus— except Paterno!!! Certainly not the *Chicago Sun-Times* writer whose quote, "The Buckeyes have a breather in Penn State this week," had been posted all week in the Lions' University Park dressing room.

On the first play after the kickoff, Ohio State tried to surprise State with a pass from quarterback Don Unverferth. But Paterno had predicted that would happeand, too, and Irwin almost intercepted. The Buckeyes punted on third down and after another exchange of punts, the Lions took the ball on their own 35 and shocked the 84,279 fans by driving for a touchdown. A 35-yard pass from Wydman to Kunit set up a third down, one-yard burst up the middle by Urbanik—who fumbled into the end zone! But Nye dove for the ball and recovered for the 6-points. Sophomore Gary Sanger's kick made it 7-0 and the Lions were on their way to one of the greatest upsets in college football history. A few minutes later, State drove to the OSU 13 but missed a 20-yard field goal at the start of the second quarter. But they were back on another 65-yard drive, with Wydman scoring on an 18-yard rollout and the Lions led at halftime, 14-0. At this juncture, OSU had a minus-14 yards rushing, no yards passing and no first downs on just 16 plays. "It'll be a helluva story if the Buckeyes win," an Ohio writer told *Collegian* sports editor John Lott in the press box. No way. Gingrich's interception of a Unverferth pass at midfield led to Kunit's 2-yard run in the third quarter and in the fourth quarter State's third team went 63-yards for Kunit's second TD. The Buckeyes with its star rusher Tom Barrington didn't get a first down until late in the third quarter and couldn't even avoid a shutout against State's reserves when their only drive of the game ended with an interception at the one and the Lions won, 27-0. Wydman had completed 12-of-22 passes for 147 yards and Urbanik had rushed for 74 of State's 194 yards on the ground and the team had not one fumble or interception. State's defense led by Ressler, Sandusky, Diebert, Yost, Stuckrath, Gingrich, Irwin and Kane held OSU to a total of 60 net yards and five first downs while recovering two fumbles and making three interceptions. "The performance of the Lions was unbelievably good and they, in turn, made the Bucks look unbelievably bad," wrote Lester J. Biederman of the *Pittsburgh Press*. "That was the soundest trouncing we've ever gotten," Woody Hayes whispered to sportswriters in the locker room...How could a team like that lose four games?" Engle praised his center and middle guard: "If Ressler doesn't get Lineman of the Year or the Heisman Trophy, there's something wrong in Denmark," he told sportswriters.

Paterno and assistant Frank Patrick, who had scouted the Buckeyes, had seen it all coming while watching game films of Ohio State. More than 30 years later O'Hora still remembered that the position of the hands and feet of the OSU backs gave away the play. "Actually, Woody had gotten into a pattern with his offense," Paterno said in *"Football My Way."* "...We felt we could tell which side they were going to run without any chance for error. We changed our defense to put Ressler directly on the head of the Ohio State center...We always knew where the play was going before the ball was snapped and our kids were always there."

Of course, the students went crazy again back in State College. Student government president Ben Novak (a university Trustee 30 years later) led a march of 5,000 screaming, confetti-throwing celebrants from the student union building down College Avenue to Old Main to President Walker's home, where coeds were tossed into the swimming pool along with a Volkswagen. Then the mob attacked a Pittsburgh bound bus, yelling "We Want Pitt, We Want Pitt. "

But Pitt—which had almost upset Notre Dame, losing 17-15 on a missed chip shot field goal in the last seconds—would have to wait. The following Saturday night, the Lions played Houston in the 84 degree heat and 95 percent humidity of Rice Stadium. Some fans expected a let down. However, State marched 73-yards with the opening kickoff, set up another TD on a Yost interception and clinched the 24-7 victory with Joe Vargo's 78-yard punt return for a TD in the fourth quarter. Urbanik rushed for 122 yards and a touchdown on 19 carries, Wydman threw his first TD pass of the year and Gingrich, who hadn't place-kicked since high school, booted three extra points and a field goal.

For the first time since the Centennial Year of 1955, the Lions hosted Pitt at home and it was freezing and windy, with temperatures at 25 degrees and a wind chill near zero. But a record standing-room crowd of 50,144 turned out to watch the Lions thoroughly dominate

their main rival. Pitt had crushed Army 24-8 and despite a 3-4-2 record was expected to give State a good game. But it was all over by halftime. State capitalized on a good runback from Kunit on the opening kickoff and went 56 yards for the first TD on a 1-yard plunge by Urbanik—who would have another great day in running for 107 yards on 20 carries and would just miss Fran Rogel's season rushing record for fullbacks. Then, after the defense stopped Pitt's only serious threat a few minutes later on Stuckrath's interception, Wydman led the offense on drives of 69-yards and 59-yards for two second quarter TDs and cruised to victory. "State Annihilates Pitt, 28-0," said the headline in the *Pittsburgh Press*. "[This was] a great climax to the most gratifying season I've ever had," Engle said in the locker room. "I'm just amazed when I think of the way this team picked itself off the floor and came through in the last five weeks. It's as fine a football team right now as I have ever had."

By Monday, the Lions had won the Lambert Trophy as best team in the East, even though 7-3 Syracuse would go to the Sugar Bowl (and lose to LSU). And now, the Gator Bowl came courting, talking about matching the Lions against an 8-1-1 Florida State team. The Liberty and Sun Bowls also expressed interest. As was policy, Engle let the team vote and the athletic department officials figured this would be a shoo-in. "But Ressler and the seniors were against it," recalled O'Hora. In a closed meeting without the coaches Tuesday night at the Nittany Lion Inn, the players surprised everyone by rejecting the bowl bid. "(The players) decided to quit while they were...at the top," wrote Lott in the *Collegian*. "The three bowls...offered little incentive to a team that had just knocked off such outfits as Ohio State and Pitt. To get themselves 'up' for a big game, players needed a challenge, especially if they are to practice a whole month for it. Why risk losing everything for a game against a team inferior to those on the regular schedule?" Years later, Ressler told Frank Bilovsky in the book, *"Lion Country,"* the seniors remembered the bad experience of '62 when they had reluctantly gone to the Gator Bowl against Florida: "The training facilities were poor...There was the travel, the hassle. The seniors remembered it...Needless to say, the university fathers-to-be were a little upset at us and that was the last time the players were given that option."

Ressler became Engle's sixth All-American and was named College Player of the Year by the Maxwell Club. Paul Bunyan and His Ox would be history before the next season. And after one more year, so would Rip Engle.

Season Record 6-4
Record to Date 412-217-39
Winning percentage .646

"The Day The Clock Stood Still"

Rip Engle first started to think about when he would retire after the 1962 season. He was then 57 years old and he figured he would quit at age 60. "Once you reach 55, you have to work longer and harder to get the job done," Engle told his assistant coaches. Although he was in good health, he was concerned that his health would deteriorate as the pressures increased to keep winning, going to bowl games and competing for national honors. So, he knew going into the '65 season that this would be his last, even though he wouldn't make the official announcement until after it was finished. If ever there was a year that confirmed Engle's foresight and apprehension, this was it!

Little did he know his team would lose one game when it was already over, drop another in the very last second, lose a third on some unfair but legal shenanigans with a two-way radio and blow another because the defense couldn't tackle one man. And that didn't count the fact that the Lions would open against the eventual National Champion and play both teams that went to the Rose Bowl.

Because of the 1964 team's strong finish, many sportswriters figured State would take up where it left off as the team to beat in the East. *Look* magazine predicted the Lions would be #7 in the nation and go to the Orange Bowl. *Street & Smith* rated the team #9 and *Sports Illustrated* ranked PSU #11. Engle wasn't just being his pessimistic self when he complained about the predictions. "We have to start fresh and we're right back where we were last September," he told Riley. He was right, starting with an inexperienced quarterback and another change in the substitution rules. Jack White had backed up Wydman in '64 but had not even played enough to earn a letter. White, a transfer from Florida, was a quick runner on the option but his passing was still a question. Gingrich had shifted permanently to defense and was the starting safety, so that left a pair of sophomores to compete with White, Tom Sherman and Mel Frye. Engle was pleased that the rulemakers finally came to their senses and installed free substitution. But now he had to find enough quality players to man separate offensive and defensive platoons in order to compete on the same level as his opponents.

After quarterback, his biggest concern was on the line. He wanted to avoid the early debacle with the offense in '64 so he concentrated first on the offensive line. In the spring, he had shifted Sandusky back to offense to pair at end with Huber, giving him a veteran front wall anchored at center by Andronici, the captain. The halfbacks also were lettermen with Nye, Kunit and Irwin (transferred from defense) and so he was able to move sophomore halfback Jack Curry, a one-time high school quarterback at Danville, to end to bolster the offense. It would prove to be a critical maneuver. McNaughton, another non-letter senior, was the starting fullback but everyone was counting on sophomore Roger Grimes, a highly-recruited 6-foot 210-pound speedster out of Cornwall who was being compared to Lenny Moore and Roger Kochman. "Grimes has power, speed and wonderful balance," Paterno told Doug McDonald of the *Centre Daily Times*. "He still need a lot of polish." Engle figured an effective offense would give O'Hora and the other defensive coaches time to develop their mixture of lettermen, inexperienced reserves and well-regarded sophomores. Fans would soon become familiar with the names of these out-of-state sophomore imports: Rich Buzin of Youngstown, OH, Mike McBath of Woodbury, NJ, and Jim Litterelle of Mineola, NY.

The original opponent for the September season opener was Maryland. But because Maryland also was expected to be one of the regional powers, NBC asked that the game be moved to December 4 so that it could be televised nationally. That meant for the first time since 1948, the regular season would not end with the traditional battle against Pitt. It also resulted in a one week delay before the scheduled game against Michigan State, a team with 22 lettermen coming off a 4-

5 season but which sportswriters said was on the same level in '65 as the Lions. What the experts didn't acknowledge or didn't realize was that coach Duffy Daugherty had put together a powerhouse with such players as Gene Washington, Bubba Smith, George Webster, Clint Jones, Bob Apisa and a barefoot Hawaiian kicker named Dick Kenny—all of whom would become All-Americans. With an opening season win over UCLA, State's next opponent, the Spartans cruised into Beaver Stadium and wiped out the Lions, 23-0. Jones ran outside, Apisa ran inside, Webster creamed the runners, Bubba blitzed the quarterback and Kenny booted three field goals and an extra point as the Spartans shocked the 46,121 fans with their might. "We're a good medium sized team and Saturday we ran into a good big team and that was the difference," Engle said after the game. Michigan State would split the National Championship and be voted #1 by UP but #2 by AP after losing the Rose Bowl in a rematch with UCLA.

UCLA, under new coach Tommy Prothro, had a week off to recover from its loss to the Spartans when the Bruins invaded Beaver Stadium for the annual Band Day game. A crunching tackle by Runnells and Riggle on the opening kickoff that forced a UCLA fumble at the Bruins' 16-yard line appeared to be a good omen. The Lions couldn't score but after keeping UCLA trapped in its own territory, State gained possession on the Bruins' 47 following a punt. Five plays later, Grimes slanted off tackle from the 2 for the TD. Sherman, who had caught a 29-yard pass from White during the drive while playing at split end for the injured Curry, kicked the PAT and the Lions led 7-0. But a short kickoff gave UCLA the ball at midfield and the Bruins' sophomore quarterback, Gary Beban, quickly drove the visitors to a score, going in for the TD himself on a 16-yard option and the score was tied. Before the first quarter was over, State had another opportunity at the PSU 43. But McNaughton, who had been running well, fumbled at the 6, ending the threat. That seemed to be all UCLA needed. In the second quarter, another State fumble led to Larry Zimmerman's 31-yard field goal and UCLA then marched 61-yards for another Beban touchdown on a 6-yard rollout and a 17-7 halftime lead. Less than five minutes into the third quarter, Mel Farr ran 58 yards for another TD and UCLA had a commanding 24-7 lead. In the fourth quarter, State marched 92 yards before losing the ball on downs but came back to score twice, including a 4-yard TD run by White with nine seconds left but it was too late, UCLA won 24-22.

It wasn't until the next morning that sportswriters learned that UCLA assistant coach Pepper Rodgers had been calling the plays and directing Beban on what to do over a two-way radio from the press box. Beban wore a transistorized receiver in his helmet. When Rodgers saw how the defense lined up, he would give Beban an audible to overcome that defense and even tell him when to run when his receivers were covered—as Beban did on his first touchdown. State found out about it when a university traffic supervisor named Ed Sarson stumbled upon Rodgers' chatter over a walkie-talkie radio. Sarson alerted the State bench of the situation late in the third quarter but the coaches did not believe there was anything they could do. Technically, what UCLA did violated Rule 9, Section 2, Article 2, Part D of the rule book which stated, "There shall be no direct communication from the sideline with players on the field." The punishment for what was officially listed as a "prohibited act" was a 5-yard penalty. Still, it was unethical, at best, and gave UCLA an unfair advantage. When confronted, Prothro denied ordering or even knowing about the high-tech high-jinks. "Beban called most of the plays and had a fine day," Prothro had told Al Wolf of

A longtime PSU tradition is for students to pass the Lion mascot up the grandstand seats to the top. Here, the cadets of Army get into the act during a game at Beaver Stadium in the 1960s.

the *Los Angeles Times*. "The only way to counter a situation like that would be to have one of our men wired for sound on the field," Engle said to the State College Quarterback club the following Wednesday at the Nittany Lion Inn. "But football's getting out of hand when you have to rely on those tactics."

The controversy over the radio transmissions overshadowed the grim report that Grimes would be sidelined for weeks by a twisted knee suffered while catching a pass in the third quarter. A month later he would also contact mononucleosis and miss the rest of the season. Even without the highly-regarded soph, the Lions overcame their own mistakes at Boston College the next week to make Engle the first coach ever to win 100 games at State. Sherman kicked a 24-yard field goal in the first quarter and after being stymied by four pass interceptions and a lost fumble, the Lions scored two touchdowns in the fourth quarter and won, 17-0. The players carried Engle off the field.

Curry was back for Engle's final visit to Syracuse's Archbold Stadium and he had a career day, catching 10 passes to break the single game record shared by Lenny Krouse and Junior Powell. But neither he nor McNaughton—who ran for 138 yards and 2 TDs on 27 carries—were enough to overcome Syracuse's elusive junior, Floyd Little. The 2-2 Orangemen drove 73-yards for a TD early in the second quarter, and after State fumbled moments later, Little took a pitchout and went 25-yards to give Syracuse a 14-0 halftime lead. Taking the second half kickoff, the Lions reached the Syracuse 20 before losing the ball and that's when Little broke a Syracuse record by running back Wayne Corbett's punt 91-yards for a TD. But State did not fold. The Lions scored minutes later after recovering a fumble at the Orange 29 and McNaughton pounded over from the 4 with White rolling out for the 2-point conversion. The defense held Syracuse into the fourth quarter and the Lions mounted a 73-yard drive with McNaughton back-flipping into the end zone from one-yard out for the TD and Sherman making it 21-15 with his kick. Less then seven minutes remained when the Lions kicked off and on the first play from scrimmage, Little virtually sealed the victory by running 69-yards off tackle for his third TD. State came back and drove 68-yards for a TD on a pass from White to Huber with 1:11 to play. Sherman hurried his kick because of the Syracuse rush

and after an onside kick failed the Orange ran out the clock and won, 28-21. State had netted 391 total yards and 25 first downs to Syracuse's 194 yards and 8 first downs but Little's 258 yards on runs, kick returns and pass receptions had won the day. "Fumbles, penalties, interceptions and a ghost named Floyd Little haunted Penn State all afternoon," wrote Russ Franke in the *Pittsburgh Press*. "We got licked by a guy we couldn't catch," Engle told sportswriters. "This is the toughest luck football team I've ever coached."

So State was 1-3 and seemingly heading for another potential disaster with high scoring West Virginia (4-1) coming into Beaver Stadium for the Homecoming game. The Mountaineers had blasted Pitt 63-48 but had been averaging 45 points a game before being shocked by Virginia 41-0 the previous week. Apparently, the Mountaineers defense was worse than their offense for the Lions amassed 423 yards in a 44-6 victory. Sherman, who was doing triple duty as the backup QB, a split end and the prime placekicker, set a modern day record by kicking for 14 points. His three field goals of 21, 29 and 28 yards also tied the record set a half century earlier by Larry Vorhis ('09) and Pete Mauthe ('12). Irwin, a junior from Altoona, had his best day ever with three touchdowns on a 23-yard TD run, a 24-yard pass from White and a 74 yard punt return.

The game at California (3-3) the following Saturday was the one that defined the season and it all came down to sloppy officiating and a question of how much time was left on the clock. An end zone fumble recovery following a botched State handoff gave Cal a 7-0 lead in the second quarter but the Lions, favored by 7, immediately tied the game on a 72-yard drive with McNaughton getting the TD on a one-yard dive. A good return on the second half kickoff gave the Bears the ball at their own 43-yard line and they drove the rest of the way in 12 plays for a 14-7 lead. Late in the third quarter, the Lions found themselves in trouble at their own 2-yard line after a punt, but with White passing to Curry in clutch situations, they drove to the Cal 3 with a third-and-goal as the fourth period began. A loss on another mix-up in the backfield and a delay of game penalty forced State to settle for a field goal and Sherman's boot from the 21 made it 14-10 with 12 and a half minutes left. The teams traded possessions as the defenses took control but with 3:22

Rip Engle poses with his coaching staff in 1965: (Left to right) Earl Bruce, Joe Paterno, Joe McMullen, Dan Radakovich, J.T. White, Frank Patrick, George Welsh and Jim O'Hora.

remaining, the Lions took the ball on their 19 after a punt. Behind White's passing and McNaughton's running, State reached the Cal 37 and called time out, but 9 seconds ran off because the referee would not stop the clock until he was given the official signal from captain Andronici at 1:32 . On the next play, White overcame a ferocious blitz and hit Curry who made a spectacular catch at the 13, and with 53 seconds left, State called its last time out. Cal blitzed again and seemed to have White trapped but he jumped and threw to Curry who was barely inside the goal at the corner flag. Curry leaped. Touchdown!!! State's bench was in bedlam as Sherman's kick made it 17-14 with 42 seconds remaining.

Cal ran back the short kickoff to its own 37 and with State in a "prevent defense," the Bears picked up a first down at State's 43 with 10 seconds left and called time out. They had one more remaining. State rushed on the next play and Cal's second team QB Jim Hunt scrambled to find a receiver. The clock flashed two seconds as he was nailed for a 3-yard loss by Buzin. Everyone looked at the clock. It showed one second left. "How the referee was able to stop the play with his whistle, how the California *captain* was able to request a time out and get the clock stopped in that remaining two seconds, we'll never know," Riley wrote in the *"Football Letter."* Cal Coach Ray Willsey sent in the play he called "our last Chance Play"— a Hail Mary to a lone receiver, Jerry Bradley. Hunt heaved from midfield. State's three defenders surrounded the 5-foot-10, 155-pound Bradley and they all leaped for the ball. John Sladki had it, Seitz did too, but the ball miraculously bounced out of their hands and into Bradley's as he lunged into the end zone. "A mighty roar went up as most of the crowd of 38,000 flooded the playing field, completely obscuring all players from view," Riley wrote. The final score was 21-17 as Cal kicked a meaningless PAT minutes later after a few State players were herded back from the locker room. Game films would show Bradley had "pushed off" Sladki and Engle told sportwriters "the back judge should have called it (a penalty)." White

had his best passing day of the season with 17-of-26 completions for 227 yards. Curry set a record in single game receiving yardage with 148 yards on 10 catches. And McNaughton had another fine day running, getting 116 yards on 23 carries, as the Lions completely dominated the statistics again. But a mysteriously stopped clock had allowed Cal time to get the victory. "You won't see another ending like that one in 100 years," O'Hora told sportwriters in the depressed State locker room.

No one expected the Lions to lose to Kent State, which was on the schedule only because of a cancellation of a contract by Holy Cross two years ago. The Mid American conference team was not on the same level as State but it did have the nation's seventh leading rusher in 6-foot-1, 225-pound "Willie" (Bill) Asbury. Asbury ran for 97 yards on 26 carries but he was overshadowed by McNaughton who ran for 112 yards and a TD in 22 carries as State coasted to a 21-0 victory. Ironically, 30 years later, Bill Asbury would be a high Penn State administration official and sometimes master-of-ceremonies at the weekly meetings of the State College Quarterback Club.

McNaughton broke Fran Rogel's season rushing record for a fullback the following week when he ran for 81 yards on 18 carries against a "tenacious" Navy team that had held eight strong opponents (including Syracuse and Notre Dame) to an average 84 yards rushing per game. Navy's new coach, Bill Elias, had nicknamed his squad the "Team Called Tenacity" and the 4-3-1 Middies took the Lions down to the last play before losing 14-6 at Beaver Stadium. State gained 208 yards on the ground and 141 in the air and had a 14-0 lead in the fourth quarter when Sherman missed a 26-yard field goal. That seemed to spark Navy, for the Middies went 78-yards before fumbling at the 2, then stopped the Lions on downs at their 18 with two minutes left and drove for a TD with less than 30 seconds remaining. A two-point pass for the conversion was broken up by Seitz but the Middies' kicker, Rob Hester, recovered his own onside kick at the State 48. Gingrich batted down Navy's first pass attempt and the Middies completed one for 14-yards but couldn't get another play off and State evened its record at 4-4. "The final score indicates a close, hard fought contest," wrote Alex Ward, sports editor of the *Daily Collegian*. "Hard fought it was. Close it wasn't...the Middies were outweighed, outplayed and completely dismayed until those last few minutes."

Now, the Lions would have to win their last two games, or win one and tie one, to keep their 27-year victory streak alive. That didn't seem improbable against 2-7 Pitt and 4-5 Maryland. But the Panthers came out of their Pitt Stadium locker room on November 20 fired up by the belief they could save Coach John Michelosen's job. Pitt Chancellor Edward Litchfield had been critical of Michelosen even after his 9-1 record in '63 and in '64 he was just 3-5-2. Pitt's senior quarterback, Kenny Lucas, also was filled with emotion. Lucas had wanted to follow his All-American brother Richie to State but had not been offered a scholarship by Engle. Pitt's groundskeeper also got into the act by placing a large "No Visitors" sign behind the Pitt end zone. All that Pitt emotion may have caused State to give away four fumbles in the first half and help the Panthers take what seemed like an insurmountable 20-0 lead.

Andronici, McNaughton and their fellow seniors steamed in the State locker room at the intermission and when the second half started the Lions were the ones who were fired up. After the defense forced Pitt to punt from near its end zone, the Lions drove 48-yards and scored from the 2 when White salvaged a muffed handoff to McNaughton and ran the ball into the end zone. But Pitt came right back and used seven minutes to drive 70-yards and stretch its lead to 27-7 with two minutes left in the third quarter. Now, State took charge. The Lions took the ensuing kickoff and went 59 yards for one TD, then Riggle intercepted a Lucas pass at State's 32 and the Lions drove for another as Kunit scored both times and Sherman's extra points made it 27-21. State's defense held Pitt on downs at midfield and with about three minutes remaining, PSU gained possession on its own 12-yard line. With White passing to different receivers and McNaughton and Kunit running up yardage, State reached the Pitt 6 and then tied the game on a pass from White to Kunit. Sherman had only missed one PAT all season but his kick was wide and it appeared the two rivals would have to settle for their first deadlock in nine years. But Eric Crabtree broke through State's kickoff containment and reached the Pitt 40. There were 55 seconds

left and it was deja' vu for the anguished State fans. Using his timeouts and the sidelines wisely, Lucas fired four successive passes from a shotgun formation, three to Bob Longo. Then on an 8-yard bootleg Lucas took the ball to the one-yard line and called time out with three seconds left. Michelosen sent in junior Frank Clark, the namesake son of a Pennsylvania congressman who dressed only for home games and was not listed on the Pitt roster as a placekicking specialist but had already booted an extra point. Supposedly, the 5-foot-6 Clark had a bad back, but his boot from the 18-yard line was perfect. Pitt kicked off with one second left and Riggle zig-zagged up field for almost 10 seconds trying to break away but he was tackled at midfield and the game was over. "Unknown Sub's Kick Beats Lions in Photo," said the headline in the *Pittsburgh Press*. "Our kids showed a terrific amount of guts coming back the way they did," Engle told the *Collegian*. "Our last scoring drive was great but so was Pitt's."

Two weeks later in a cold 20-mile wind at Maryland's Byrd Stadium, three State backs set a new team record by becoming the first trio in school history to rush for over 100 yards in a game as State prevented a losing season by beating the Terps, 19-7. Sophomore Bill Rettig (105), Irwin (105) and McNaughton (103) did the running but most of Irwin's yardage came when he picked up Rettig's forward fumble at State's 14-yard line and officially ran 65-yards for a touchdown and another team record. A nationwide TV audience missed the play because of a commercial time out. The TV audience almost missed the kickoff, too, because NBC frequently cut away from the game for the launch of the Gemini-7 space capsule.

The frustrating, heart-stopping season was now over and Engle quietly made plans to announce his retirement. All in all, it had been a good 16-year run and he had made State a sustaining power in the East again and an occasional national contender. He was leaving the program in good shape, even with the freshmen who would play next season. He was sure the fans would soon be talking about some of them: Mike Reid, Ted Kwalik, and Bobby Campbell. It was now time for the Kid from Brooklyn to take charge.

Season Record 5-5
Record to Date 417-222-39
Winning percentage .644

CHAPTER 11

THE GRAND EXPERIMENT

1966-1979

It would have been a shock if someone else other than Joe Paterno had been named to succeed Rip Engle as Penn State's football coach in February of 1966.

A year earlier, Paterno had turned down an offer to be the coach at Yale after being assured by athletic director Ernie McCoy that, "barring unforeseen circumstances," he would be Engle's successor when Rip decided to quit. Of course, State had a history of "unforeseen circumstances" when picking a head coach. The old-timers on campus still remembered the "circumstances" that caused the bitter departures of Dick Harlow and Earle Edwards.

But McCoy and university president Eric Walker moved swiftly after Pittsburgh sportscaster Tom Bender, the play-by-play man on State's football radio network, broke the story of Engle's planned retirement. Engle had planned to make a formal announcement on Friday, February 18. But Bender gave the initial word on KDKA-TV's 11 o'clock newscast the night before. At a news conference Saturday morning, February 19, 1966, Joseph V. Paterno, 39, formerly of Brooklyn, N.Y, was named the 14th coach in the 79-year history of Penn State football.

"I've said this before and I meant it," Paterno told sportswriters that day, "this is the finest program in the country and I feel extremely fortunate in getting the job. Rip has built the program up extremely well and all I have to do is keep it going." Engle said, "They couldn't have picked a better man anywhere in the country."

The staff would have only a minor change. Jim O'Hora, Earl Bruce, Frank Patrick, J. T. White, Dan Radakovich, Joe McMullen and

A man of great vision, Joseph V. Paterno took over the head coaching position in 1965.

George Welsh would be retained. These were Paterno's friends as well as his cohorts. "...There are five or six other coaches here that are just as qualified as I am," Paterno told sportswriters. "That will give you an idea of how strong our staff is." Bob Phillips, who had sent several players to State as coach at Montour High School in suburban Pittsburgh, would replace Paterno on the staff. No one knew it at the time, but two of Phillips' former high school players—freshman Ted Kwalick and incoming freshman Chuck Burkhart—would help lead Paterno's teams into the big time.

Even before he became the head coach, Paterno had talked about recruiting more football players who also were exceptional students. He wanted to go far beyond the athlete majoring in physical education and attract the athletes who wanted to become doctors, lawyers and engineers. Engle was supportive of the philosophy and had brought in some players who were outstanding in the classroom. Joe Bellas, John Runnells and Bill Lenkaitis from the '65 team were good examples. Bellas, a starter at offensive tackle for two years and All-East in '65, became State's first player to make the First Team Academic All-American with a 3.5 grade average in accounting. Runnells, a pre-law major with a near perfect 4.0 average, was an Academic All-American as a junior linebacker in '65 and would do it again in '66. Lenkaitis, a sophomore center in '65, was a pre-dental major who would eventually graduate with a 3.37 average, play pro football for 15 years and become a practicing dentist.

But Paterno wanted to go even further than Engle, both on and off the field. He not only wanted to bring in more scholar-athletes but he wanted them to play so well that they would make the Nittany Lions football team a perennial contender for the National Championship. "What's needed," he told Ridge Riley for the *"Football Letter"* in the summer of 1967 before his second season, "is about 40 good football players, fifteen excellent ones and four or five great ones. They must all have pride and enthusiasm. Among the superstars, there should be a breakaway runner, a great kicker, a versatile quarterback and so on...Sure, there are only a dozen or so schools in the country which will come up with these standards year after year. Penn State can do it if everyone gets behind us. Eventually we should have this kind of team. It's more than just 'should.' We *must* because we've already committed ourselves to the kind of schedule demanding it."

Paterno also wanted to do this without breaking the rules, no under-the-table deals, no cheating and no false promises. He called this "The Grand Experiment," and when he first started talking publicly about what he intended to do, his coaching elders thought he was either crazy, brash or just plain full of it. Many of them laughed when the outspoken hot-shot barely made it through his first season. Even after his team went unbeaten in 31 straight games and won two Orange Bowls in the next four years, they still didn't believe he was doing it the way he claimed.

"It sounds corny, I know...," Paterno told Bill Conlin of the *Philadelphia Daily News* midway through the 1967 season. "Everybody assumes if you have a great football team there have been some sacrifices made in the area of standards. People tell me it can't be done without sacrificing standards, they tell me I'm day dreaming..."

He wasn't day dreaming. Throughout the rest of the '60's and '70's, Paterno's team of scholar-athletes became a national power against some of the toughest opposition. He had three unbeaten teams, three others that lost only once in a season and 11 that finished in the AP or UPI Top 10 from 1967 through 1979. His teams played and won post-season bowl games with regularity and twice he was named "Coach of the Year" by the American Football Coaches Association. He nearly doubled the number of State's First Team All-Americans, producing 28 during this stretch, and his players won all the major trophies in collegiate football: Heisman, Outland, Lombardi. His teams became a major pipeline for professional football and some went on to the Pro Football Hall of Fame. At the same time, dozens of his players graduated with academic honors. Eight were chosen as First Team Academic All-Americans, seven won NCAA post-graduate scholarships and five were honored as "scholar-athletes" with $18,000 academic fellowships by the National Football Foundation and College Football Hall of Fame. Year in and year out, the graduation rate of Paterno's football players usually surpassed the percentage of all students in the university and, as Paterno had wanted, they were becoming lawyers, doctors, bankers, businessmen and engineers.

Paterno, himself, had become a well-known and popular sports figure. His success on the field attracted the professional teams and the Pittsburgh Steelers, Green Bay Packers, New York Jets, New York Giants and New England Patriots made serious attempts to hire him. He actually accepted the Patriots' lucrative $1.4 million offer after the 1972 season and then changed his mind overnight. The on-going success of his "Grand Experiment" was spreading his fame beyond the stadium walls and the campus environs, and in the late '70's there was talk in Pennsylvania about Paterno running for governor. People who had little interest in football knew about the big-nosed coach with the dark horn-rimmed glasses and white socks prancing the sidelines

Joe Bellas was a good offensive tackle in the mid-60s and the first of State's Academic All-Americans. He was also the first State athlete to win a prestigious NCAA Post Graduate Scholarship.

as he watched his players in those non-descript white uniforms and black shoes. An educated man who quoted Greek philosophers and listened to opera music was winning football games with "real" students. No athletic dormitories. No special privileges. No skipping class, even if it means taking a test on the Saturday morning before a game. Maintain a better than 2.0 average or you don't play. Many of the players didn't like it. Some of them even thought Paterno was too sanctimonious at times and some questioned his sincerity about education when he pushed them hard to win games. But they won and they graduated and the entire country knew about it.

But what Paterno wanted the most for himself, his assistants, his players and his adopted University and their fans eluded him—a National Championship. His unbeaten teams of 1968 and 1969 finished second in the ratings but were squeezed out of a national title by disbelieving writers, jealous coaches and the politics of a United States President. An upset loss in the final game of the regular season knocked the 1971 squad out of contention, although that team redeemed itself with a monumental victory over Texas in the Cotton Bowl. The overachieving undefeated team of 1973 led by Heisman winner John Cappelletti simply had too many power-laden competitors the same year and a four-point midseason defeat in 1977 to an opponent on probation ruined that campaign. Then, on November 8, 1978, Paterno's team was named #1 for the first time in the history of Penn State football. The Lions were still #1 and 11-0 when they played Alabama on New Year's Day of 1979 in the Sugar Bowl but they were #4 and 11-1 when the game was over. That was the day "The Grand Experiment" began to crumble.

By the end of the 1979 season, trouble had entangled Paterno's football paradise. Three players, including an All-American, were thrown off the team for poor academics. Two were arrested for drunkeness, another for drunk driving, a fourth for starting a brawl at a dormitory party and a fifth for a first-degree burglary. A couple of team leaders defied him openly on the practice field and to try to regain their confidence, Paterno eased up on his discipline. Then after the unexpected

8-and-4 season in 1979 came the *Sports Illustrated* story examining Paterno's situation entitled, "There Are a Lot of People Who Think I'm a Phony and Now They Think They Have the Proof."

What started in the last decade as "The Grand Experiment" was ending in this decade as "The Grand Debacle."

"A Year of Confusion"

Quarterback Jack White did not have a good spring practice and neither did Joe Paterno, although the rookie coach didn't realize it at the time. Paterno worked the players hard and long during the spring and the approach backfired. The resentment that built up carried over into the fall when the strenuous practice sessions continued as Paterno tried to push the players beyond their capabilities. "I must have driven those kids to reach too far beyond their grasp," Paterno wrote years later in his book, *"Paterno: By The Book."* "...They had played well under Rip Engle who had formed them and played well for me as Rip's assistant. Now they were unhappy with their overeager new coach."

White was symbolic of Paterno's mistaken approach. The senior quarterback had set several team passing records in '65 and so had his favorite receiver, split end Jack Curry. Many sportswriters figured the return of White and Curry, along with highly-regarded sophomore receivers Ted Kwalick of McKees Rocks, Bobby Campbell of Apalachin, NY, and Leon Angevine would give State a good passing attack. But despite his record-setting performance, White was considered little more than an average passer but a strong runner. To best utilize the talents of White and the other running backs, Paterno installed an I-Formation offense during spring practice.

White was bothered throughout the spring workouts by a leg muscle problem. He also missed time taking exams for dental school and his concentration was further distracted by his marriage in late March. His backup, Tom Sherman, didn't look sharp in the spring either. But that was more understandable. The versatile Sherman had hardly played at quarterback in '65 but had been impressive as a defensive halfback and placekicker and even spent some time relieving Curry at split end. Paterno designated Sherman as a defensive starter in '66 and figured the Rimersburg junior might have to play both ways. A 6-foot, 205-pound "do everything" sophomore named Frank Spaziani had been impressive in the spring and by the time preseason practice started, Spaziani was listed as the #2 quarterback and possible backup at tailback.

But quarterback wasn't Paterno's only concern as he prepared to open his head coaching career against the same team that Engle had ended his—Maryland. With just 14 lettermen back, Paterno was worried about his inexperience, particularly on offense. Grimes, the junior tailback who had the potential of being a game-breaker, reinjured his knee in the winter while working out and underwent an operation just before spring practice. He was still trying to get himself up to speed in early September and Paterno was looking at a couple of sophomores to possibly step in. Sophomores Angevine and Campbell also were being counted on at wingback but Paterno planned to use Irwin as both a wingback and defensive back if necessary. Both of the two

junior fullbacks, Rettig and Dan Lucyk, also were struggling. The interior line was being virtually rebuilt with junior center Bill Lenkaitis the lone regular from last season. Paterno told the media he would have to depend on his defense to carry the team until the offense could mesh.

The defense lacked depth but the first team was strong, especially at linebacker and the interior line. Two-year starter Runnels and Litterelle returned at linebacker with newcomer Jim McCormick. Rowe and McBath also were back at the tackles but Paterno and O'Hora believed the best lineman of all might be sophomore middle guard Mike Reid from nearby Altoona, who majored in music and was a classical pianist. "If Reid doesn't turn out to be a great football player, then I don't know football," Paterno told the State College Quarterback Club before the Maryland opener. Non-lettermen and sophomores would be needed to help out at defensive end as well as in the secondary, particularly with Tim Montgomery coming off a year's absence because of knee surgery and Irwin out much of the preseason with an injury.

In another move that bothered the players, Paterno broke tradition and decided to appoint game captains and elect an honorary captain at the end of the season. He initially irritated the sportswriters and sportscasters when he closed his first practice, but he won the media over with his frank appraisal of his players' talent. Paterno's candor was refreshing, they said. And when he gave sportswriters covering the team an honest assessment of the schedule, they agreed. "Outside of a fluke or a lot of luck," he told Ira Miller of the *Associated Press*, "I don't see how we can handle at least four teams on our schedule," naming Michigan State, UCLA, Georgia Tech and Syracuse. Even though he said he was "worried about Maryland" because "they have a veteran team," his comments didn't go over very well with the Terps when printed in the *Washington Post* and the players felt insulted when they invaded Beaver Stadium September 17.

The 40,911 fans who showed up on a warm and sunny Band Day were less than the 46,284 seating capacity. Few of State's 21,000 students were in the crowd because classes still had not started. Maryland also had a new coach but Lou Saban was not a rookie. He had spent the last six years as head coach of the Boston Patriots and Buffalo Bills in the American Football League. State was favored but Paterno had predicted a close, low-scoring game with lots of mistakes and that's what it was. It was also a game that made Reid a star—and in a most unusual way. The tempo was set in the early minutes when two penalties cost the Lions a 50-yard touchdown and a 21-yard gain on passes from White to Curry. Then when Maryland gained possession, an interference penalty on a third-and-12 put the Terps on the State 15-yard line and Ernie Torgain scored on the next play as Maryland took a 7-0 lead. But early in the second quarter, State's defense forced a Maryland punt from the end zone and Reid broke through to block it for a safety. "There's a sophomore for you," Paterno joked after the game. "If he'd blocked it with his hands, we'd had a touchdown." State scored the touchdown minutes later on a 60-yard drive with White running in from 2-yards out. The 2-point conversion failed but State never trailed again.

Bob Capretto's interception set up Sherman's 23-yard field goal that made it 11-7 at the half and Reid was credited with another safety on the second play of the fourth quarter when he and defensive ends Bill Morgan and Bob Vukmer tackled Terp quarterback Al Pastrana in the end zone. Maryland almost scored midway through the final period when State lost a fumble at the Maryland 46 and the Terps drove to the PSU 8 for a first down before the defense led by Reid, Runnells and

Litterelle stopped them on a fourth down at the one. Then, with about 30 seconds left, Reid was awarded his third safety when Maryland's second string quarterback threw the ball out of the end zone rather than be sacked by the sophomore. The final score was 15-7 with White passing for 110 yards on 9-of-17 passes and leading all rushers with 85 yards. "Our defense was great and that goal line stand was terrific," Paterno told Doug McDonald of the **Centre Daily Times**. For only the second time in his 16-year coaching career at State, Paterno was given the game ball by the team. Saban ran off the field without shaking hands with Paterno but he telephoned the next week and apologized, saying, "You really stunk. We just stunk a lot more." As Paterno related the conversation in his book, **"Football My Way,"** he said Saban's analysis was "damn near the truth"

So, Paterno had the first victory as Penn State's head coach and no one realized then how historic it would be. His first defeat would be memorable, too, and it came the next week at East Lansing against the nation's number one team, Michigan State. This was the outstanding Spartan team that would play the momentous and controversial 10-10 tie at midseason with Notre Dame and go undefeated but finish second behind the Irish in the final national rankings. The veteran Spartans were a 21-point favorite and they hammered the Lions, 42-8, losing a shutout with 3 and a half minutes left in the game when Duffy Daugherty refused to reinsert his first team defense despite the exhortations of the 65,763 hometown fans. That MSU defense had already done its damage with All-American Bubba Smith's blindside tackle of White on the third play of the second quarter that knocked the Lions QB out of the game with a bleeding kidney. "It was a legal tackle," Paterno said later, "but one of the hardest tackles I've ever seen." Spaziani had finished the game in place of White as the Lions were held to 79 yards rushing and 88 yards passing while the Spartans rolled up 230 yards on the ground and 149 through the air. "A game like that will help us for the future," Paterno told sportswriters." We came of 'age' today."

White was back in the starting lineup against Army at Michie Stadium in what turned out to be the crucial game of Paterno's first season. Army (2-0) also had a first year coach in Tom Cahill and an inexperienced team similar to State's. The game was rated a toss up and a sellout crowd of 31,000 was expected but the cold rain that began on Friday night and continued through Saturday kept the actual attendance down to 18,000. The sloppy conditions seemed to affect the Lions more than the Cadets. State gave up four fumbles and three interceptions and the first interception by Henry Uberecken was run back 40 yards to the 1-foot line resulting in a third down touchdown in the second quarter. With Army ahead 6-0, the Lions blew scoring opportunities on two interceptions by Runnells in Army territory. The first time the Cadets held for downs at the 9-yard line and the second time White fumbled a handoff at the 2-yard line. Army quarterback Steve

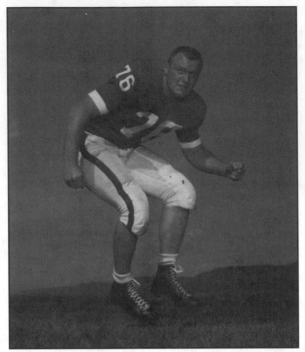
DT Dave Rowe was one of the transitional stars who bridged the Engle and Paterno years in 1965-66 and then went on to a career in pro football and sports broadcasting.

Lindell booted a 27-yard field goal with about a minute left in the half and the Cadets used the punting of Nick Kurilko to help get a safety less than four minutes from the end of the game and won, 11-0. The game energized Army for the Cadets went on to a 9-2 record and Cahill was voted "Coach of the Year." "So far, football in '66 hasn't been much fun," wrote Riley. Some impatient fans thought it was time to get rid of the new coach.

What followed in the week after the Army defeat was the defining moment of the season. Heeding the advice of some of his critics, including athletic director McCoy, Paterno decided to abandon the I-formation and return to the power-running Wing-T for the Boston College game. Out went White at quarterback and in came Sherman. "White wasn't the kind of man to have at quarterback in the different type of offense where you had to throw back across the field, pitch back and do other things," Paterno recalled in **"Football My Way."** In addition to installing Sherman at quarterback, Paterno also replaced Grimes at tailback with Irwin. After three games, Grimes was the Lions' leading rusher with 147 yards on 53 carries but he still had not regained his old form. The move of Sherman and Irwin to offensive starters also gave veteran John Sladi and junior Bob Capretto starting positions in the defensive secondary.

A disappointing and apathetic crowd of 30,924 were at Beaver Stadium October 8 when Sherman made his debut. The first quarter did not go well. On the third play from scrimmage Sherman threw a 39-yard touchdown to Irwin but the touchdown was nullified by a backfield in motion penalty. Late in the period, Sherman's fumbled handoff near midfield led to a TD and an 8-0 BC lead. State blew an opportunity early in the second quarter when Frank Pringle recovered a fumble at the BC 17 and State moved to the 3 before Sherman's attempted field goal from the 10 went wide. A few minutes later, State gained possession near the 50-yard line on Litterelle's interception and Sherman quickly passed to Kwalick for a 49-yard touchdown, then tied the game on a bootleg around left end. But BC used up the next 5 1/2 minutes to drive downfield for a touchdown and a 15-8 halftime lead. In the locker room, Paterno made what was his first emotional halftime speech. He told the players they were at a crossroads for the season and in the next 30 minutes they would "find out if we have any men on this team."

With Sherman's play-calling and passing providing the spark, the Lions went 74 yards on 10 plays after the second half to take the lead. 16-15. Sherman threw five passes in the drive with the last one for 17-yards to Kwalick getting the touchdown, then he passed to Spaziani for the 2-point conversion. Sherman led a 7-play, 67-yard drive that gave State another touchdown on Rettig's 2-yard run early in the fourth quarter and Lucyk ran 44 yards for the clinching touchdown with four minutes left as State won, 30-21. Sherman had been spectacular, completing 13-of-26 passes for 220 yards and two touchdowns with just one interception. Kwalick also had made an impression with his six receptions for 126 yards and two touchdowns, but the Lions lost Angevine for the season with a broken foot. "Tom Sherman gave us the spark I had hoped he would," Paterno told the *CDT*'s McDonald, adding that "we must come up with a running attack (because) teams like UCLA and Georgia Tech aren't going to let us pass all the time."

The euphoria over the revitalized passing offense didn't last long. The next Saturday night at the Los Angeles Coliseum, 4th-ranked UCLA turned a 21-11 halftime lead into a 49-11 nightmare for the Lions. Once again, coach Prothro resorted to a legal but unfair gimmick to obtain his victory by having his assistant coaches monitor the closed circuit TV replays in the press box to help make immediate onfield adjustments. The PAC 8 conference had banned the practice but Prothro used it in outside games. But what really rankled Paterno and the out-manned State team was UCLA's successful onside kick with 38 seconds left in the game when the Bruins already led 42-11. "We felt like naked jerks 2,500 miles from home, and I the exposed head jerk," Paterno recalled years later in *"Paterno: By The Book."* Paterno vowed to get even one day.

Paterno took it easy on another rookie coach, Jim Carlen, the following week in Morgantown. The Lions had a 28-0 halftime lead and beat West Virginia 38-6 as they rushed for 276 yards and passed for another 219 yards while limiting the Mountaineers to 139 net yards. Sherman had another great day, hitting six different receivers for 15 completions and 182 yards in 27 attempts while scoring one touchdown, kicking three field goals (tying the team record again), throwing for one 2-point conversion and booting two other extra points. The new first team offensive backfield of Sherman, Irwin, Lucyk and Campbell was coming together and so was the offensive line with Lenkaitis and Dave Bradley at the tackles, Bryan Hondru and Jim Kollar at guards and John Kulka at center. Paterno also changed his mind about captains. Prior to the game Irwin and Runnells had been elected co-captains for the rest of the season.

More than 2,000 cheering students surprised Paterno and the team by turning out for a pep rally in Pollock Circle on the night before the Homecoming game against California. "It was great and it helped us a lot," Paterno told Riley later. Paterno and the veterans who remembered last year's controversial ending at Berkeley and the defeat after time had expired were concerned about the Cal passing game. But a 20-mile an hour wind and gusts up to 30 on a dull gray and cold afternoon kept both passing offenses in check. Sherman still completed 7-of-18 passes for 103 yards but he used the running of Lucyk and Campbell to get the victory, stretching a narrow 12-7 halftime lead into a 33-15 win. Lucyk rushed for 132 yards on 23 carries and Campbell picked up 84 yards on 15 carries as State recorded 320 yards on the ground to just 39 for Cal. Sherman made the record books that day, scoring more points in a game than anyone since Johnny Roepke in 1927 with 25 points on four touchdowns and one extra point.

No game was more frustrating to Paterno in his first year than the final home game of the season against Syracuse. The Orange had won five straight after early season defeats to Baylor and UCLA (31-12) and they were favored to beat the Lions for the fourth straight year. Naturally, there was another controversy. This one occurred the day *before*. The game was set for a regional telecast and coach Schwartzwalder requested the use of TV replays in the press box, ala UCLA. When Paterno and McCoy refused, Schwartzwalder and his assistants boycotted the traditional Friday night press party and the piqued

Syracuse coach never again attended a Penn State press function. "All we wanted to use was a lousy little bit of electricity," Schwartzwalder told a Syracuse newspaper, which called State "bush" for its decision. Schwartzwalder got even in the game. Despite two lost fumbles and an interception in the first half, the Lions led 10-6 at the half on drives of 72 and 76 yards with a Sherman-to-Kwalick 26-yard pass getting the touchdown and Sherman booting a 29-yard field goal after Campbell had been tackled from behind on a 57-yard run. The trick play that helped give Syracuse the 12-10 victory came with 25 seconds left in the third quarter and State *knew it was coming!* With fourth-and-4 at the State 43, Syracuse went into punt formation. "They're going to pass, Timmy," Paterno yelled to halfback Montgomery, covering one of the potential Syracuse receivers, end Dick Towne. "Yeah, I know Coach," Montgomery shouted back, according to a description of the incident in *"Football My Way."* But Montgomery slipped and Towne caught a pass for a first down at the 30. Eight power-running plays later, Larry Csonka bulled over from the one. The kick failed and with 10:41 left in the game there was still time for State to come back. But the Orange defense stopped the Lions and Syracuse controlled the clock for nearly eight minutes, almost scoring again but losing a fourth-and-goal fumble at the State one-yard line as darkness began to envelop Beaver Stadium. Conska and the Syracuse captain, Floyd Little had been the difference. They carried the ball on 49 of 54 running plays with Conska getting 131 yards and Little 110 yards.

For the third time that season, State met an undefeated and Top 10 team when it traveled to Atlanta for the November 12 encounter with #5 Georgia Tech. The Lion offense also chose that day to play its worst game. Tech turned a 14-0 first quarter lead into a 21-0 victory despite a great performance by the defense led by Runnells, Reid and Montgomery. The Lions only first downs in the first half came on penalties and Sherman didn't complete his first pass until 11 minutes remained in the game. Tech went on to lose to Georgia but play in the Orange Bowl. State, with a 4-5 record, went to Pittsburgh to try and prevent the first losing season in 28 years.

Pitt was having even a worse year under its first year coach, Dave Hart, but it could get some respect back with an upset over State. The Panthers were 1-8 and the Pittsburgh newspapers reminded everyone that no Pitt team had *ever* lost nine games before. Disturbed by the way his offense played against both Syracuse and Georgia Tech, Paterno told his team before the game that "We will run every play just as if we were behind." With Campbell scoring two touchdowns and Kwalick and Curry each catching a touchdown pass from Sherman, the score was 33-0 before Pitt scored on a blocked a punt midway through the third quarter. By that time, most of the 30,467 chilled spectators had left to go home and watch the Michigan State-Notre Dame game on TV. With the score 41-12 in the fourth quarter, Wayne Corbett faked a punt from the PSU 25-yard line and passed to Curry for 32 yards. A few plays later, White threw a TD pass and that prompted Pitt fans and some Pittsburgh sportswriters to accuse Paterno of "running up the score." Pitt scored two TDs in the fourth quarter against a bunch of third stringers who had rarely played all year making the 48-24 final seem closer than it was. The Lion offense netted a total of 546 yards while the defense intercepted five passes, recovered two fumbles and blocked a kick as State scored the highest total of points against Pitt since the series began in 1893. State also set what was believed to be a team record in penalties as overzealous officials penalized the Lions 12 times for 142 1/2 yards. Campbell won the Coogan Award as the game's outstanding player by running for 138 yards, including TDs of 41 and 16 yards, and scoring another TD on a 9-yard pass. "Something about a victory over Pittsburgh adds zest to the long winter months," Riley concluded.

Paterno didn't blame anyone but himself for his mediocre start. "We just shouldn't have stuck with that I formation so long," Paterno recalled in *"Football My Way."* "I think if we had had Sherman in there from the start of the season we might have been a 6-4 team, or better." He also blamed himself for mishandling his staff, not listening to them when he should have and trusting his own instincts at other times. That had a desultory effect on the players. "We lost boys in that 1966 season by moving them up and down too much," he recalled. "We were confused and there was doubt in the players' minds that we were doing the right things. We didn't make it work right."

Paterno vowed to make it work right in 1967. And he did. But not before utilizing his brilliant offensive mind to devise a revolutionary defensive strategy and making it all come together with a bunch of gung-ho sophomores on a hot and humid night in Miami.

Season Record 5-5
Record to Date 422-227-39
Winning percentage .642

"The Year the Legend Began"

It is easy to look back decades later and pinpoint 1967 as the beginning of the Joe Paterno legend. The previous season had been an admitted flop. Paterno knew he had to do things differently or his career as a head coach could end quickly. The decisions he would make during the year—some daring, some calculated and some lucky—would set the course of his actions for decades. But no one knew that at the time.

In evaluating his players during spring practice, Paterno realized the defense would be his major problem. He wasn't satisfied with the 5-3-3 defensive schemes the '66 team used nor was he satisfied with the overall quality of the defensive players returning. "I had to find a way of playing a great defense without great defensive athletes," he wrote years later in *"Paterno: By The Book."* "I needed something that might take three years for other coaches to figure out—truly a new system." So, that summer, Paterno virtually locked himself in the den of his home and spent months developing a new defensive formation. What he came up with was an attacking and mobile 4-4-3 defense that had a lot of variations that no one had used before. To this day, Paterno has not received the credit he deserves for conceiving the revolutionary defense.

As Paterno and his assistants installed the new defense during preseason practice, they found it necessary to shift some players to take advantage of their specific skills. Co-captain Litterelle went from the eliminated middle guard position to end. Spaziani, a backup quarterback and punter for two years, went from offense also to defensive end, and Angevine moved from wingback to defensive halfback. Paterno also worried that his best defensive player, Mike Reid who was

now at left linebacker, might miss the entire season. Paterno had said Reid was the best sophomore lineman he had seen at State and that "included Roosevelt Grier and Dave Robinson." But the junior had torn a knee ligament during the quarterfinals of the NCAA wrestling championships that winter and the knee was not responding. Paterno also was coming to the realization that some of his untested sophomore defenders were better athletes than his experienced juniors and seniors. As the September 23 season opener at Navy approached, Paterno continued to complain to sportswriters about "our lack of team speed and quickness up front, especially on defense."

Paterno didn't have the same concern about his offense because all his starters would be veterans except for senior left guard Dan Coccoli who was being pressed by sophomore Tom Jackson. Co-captain Lenkaitis at center anchored a formidable line that included two of the best receivers in the country, tight end Kwalick and split end Curry. Buzin, who would just miss being a First-Team All-American, was at one tackle and Kukla and Bradley filled in the rest of the line. Sherman was back at quarterback, although Paterno worried about his inconsistent passing, and last year's leading rusher, Campbell, was now the tailback. Lucyk started at fullback but was being pressed by sophomore Don Abbey of South Hadley, MA, who would share placekicking with Sherman. Grimes was switched to wingback but in the preseason he didn't seem to have the spark he had originally shown as a sophomore and before the season was too far along he would be a backup to sophomore Paul Johnson of Cazenovia, NY.

The '67 schedule left no room for Paterno to experiment or dawdle. Sportswriters picked the Lions and their first opponent, Navy, to challenge for Eastern supremacy. The next two foes, Miami and UCLA, were preseason picks for the Top 10. *Playboy* magazine had even tapped the Hurricanes as #1 with State as #12. ABC Sports thought so highly of the game at Navy-Marine Corps Memorial Stadium that it planned to have its prime team of Chris Schenkel and Bud Wilkinson broadcast the regional televised game. But when Schenkel and Wilkinson arrived at the press box, they were told ABC technicians had gone out on strike and they left.

Anticipating a possible strike, Director Chuck Howard had taken over play-by-play and had recruited the sports information directors of each team—Jim Tarman of State and Budd Thalman of Navy—to do the color. During the halftime intermission, the press box transmission cables were cut and after being off the air for about 15 minutes, the trio resumed the broadcast with a single microphone from a restricted view behind the Navy

Bill Lenkaitis, co-captain and center of the 1967 team that turned around Joe Paterno's coaching career, went on to attend dental school during his 15-year NFL career.

bench. "We'd like to tell you what's going on but we can't see a thing," Thalman told the audience.

Paterno had predicted a "high scoring game" that could be "decided by less than a touchdown." The score was just 10-3 at halftime with Navy in the lead, when the Lions offense took charge. On State's first possession of the second half, it moved to the Navy 6 before disdaining a sure field goal and missing on a fourth down pass. Minutes later, a 64-yard, 10 play drive put PSU ahead, 11-10, on Campbell's 7-yard run and Curry's run for the extra points off a fake kick. Late in the third quarter, Montgomery's second interception of the day set up Abbey's second field goal of 26-yards. But the Middies regained the lead, 17-14, with 8:22 remaining by driving 72-yards and scoring on QB John Cartwright's one-yard TD pass to his favorite receiver, Rob Taylor. Navy's defense stopped the Lions after the next kickoff but State forced a punt and took over at its own 19 with 4:20 left in the game. Hitting on key passes to Campbell, Kwalick and Curry, Sherman moved the Lions steadily downfield and on fourth-and-2 from the 20 he hit Campbell behind a defender for a TD. Again, State faked the PAT and Campbell went in to give the Lions a 22-17 lead with 1:44 left as the Blue Band, cheerleaders and other PSU rooters celebrated. Navy returned Abbey's kickoff to its 22-yard line and in six plays and 47 seconds, Cartwright shattered the Lions defense as the Middies scored on a 16-yard pass to Taylor that regained the lead. But the PAT failed and the Lions still had a chance. Campbell returned the kickoff to midfield and Paterno told Sherman to try and set-up a game winning field goal. But Sherman missed a couple of wide open receivers and on fourth down he was sacked by Navy's All-American end, Bill Dow, and Navy won, 23-22. In his *"Football Letter,"* Riley called the defense "porous" and wrote, "Normally a team that amasses nearly 400 yards in rushing and passing, to say nothing of 162 yards in kickoff returns and more than a hundred through interceptions, had enough to win...It could be a long season."

Paterno thought so, too. "After the game I felt, for the first time, concerned about my future as a coach," he recalled in *"Football My Way,"* and, initially, he wondered about his new defensive formation. "I knew I needed a drastic change—but what change?" he wrote in *"Paterno: By The Book."* "On the long, downcast bus ride home that night from Annapolis, the crazy thought entered my mind of dumping almost the whole crew and starting from scratch with fresh kids." He wasn't helped by the game injuries to Reid, who would be lost for the season, to sophomore starting defensive tackle John Ebersole and to senior defensive halfback Capretto. Before the team left State College Thursday afternoon for its Friday night game at Miami, Paterno knew what he was going to do but he didn't tell the players.

Aware that the heat and humidity at the Orange Bowl could shock and overwhelm his team of Northerners, Paterno had used some psychology in planning the trip to Miami. He didn't want the players to know about the heat until they walked out onto the Orange Bowl field. So, the team traveled in air-condition comfort all the way, bussing to Pittsburgh and staying overnight at a motel near the airport instead of flying down to Miami the night before the game as was custom. Upon arrival in Miami, they were assigned rooms at the Miami Airport hotel and told to stay off their feet and rest up for several hours before the game. "We can't afford to be tired tonight," he told them.

Miami had dropped out of the Top 10 after being upset by Northwestern, 12-7, but the Hurricanes were still an 11-point favorite with a

lineup that included 6-foot-7 defensive end Ted Hendricks, who had made All-American as a sophomore in '66. Paterno started virtually the same senior-laden defense that he had against Navy, except sophomore Steve Smear of Johnstown was at tackle for the injured Ebersole. On the first play he sent in sophomore Jim Kates of Plainfield, NJ, at linebacker. A few plays later, another sophomore entered the game. Before the end of the first quarter, Kates had been joined at linebacker by Dennis Onkotz of North Hampton; Pete Johnson of North Plainfield, NJ, at "Hero;" former walk-on Neal Smith of Port Trevorton at halfback; and Wally Cirafesei of South Plainfield, NJ at another halfback. What Paterno did that night is now part of the legend and is deemed by many to be the defining moment of his coaching career, not just the defining moment of the season. But the significance of his action was not as apparent at the time.

The temperature was 78 degrees on the Orange Bowl field and with Hurricane Edith approaching the Florida coast, it drizzled sporadically throughout the game as 39,516 looked on. Using his hustling sophomores and junior Spaziani with such seniors as Litterelle, McBath, Montgomery and Pringle, Paterno's attacking defense swarmed all over Miami's backs and receivers. The first half was virtually a punting duel between Campbell and Miami's Hank Collins until a scintillating 50-yard zig-zag run by Campbell with about four minutes left. The run set up a 15-yard TD pass from Sherman to Kwalick at the end of an 8-play, 90-yard drive and State led 6-0 at the intermission. In the third quarter, Sherman's passing to Kwalick set up a 7-yard TD pass from Sherman to Abbey and a two-point pass from Sherman to Curry. Abbey's 28-yard field goal made it 17-0 in the fourth quarter and with five minutes left the defense stopped the Hurricanes on four downs inside the PSU 8-yard line to seal the victory. Miami scored with less than 30 seconds left after recovering the ball when Campbell botched a punt near the State 30-yard line, making the final 17-8. Campbell's running (72 yards on 9 carries), Sherman's passing (15-for-25 for 187 yards and two TDs) and the receiving of Kwalick (9 receptions for 88 Yards) and Curry (4 catches for 85 yards) was credited by many for the victory but the young, aggressive defense also was noticed. The six sophomores led by Kates made a total of 26 unassisted tackles, assisted on nine others and had three interceptions. "Teen-Agers Ambush Miami," said the headline in the *Centre Daily Times*. "That Campbell really killed us with his run," Miami coach Charlie Tate told Paul Levine, sports editor of the *Collegian*. "It was the key play...Their defense was stronger than I expected." Paterno told Levine, "The defense played a great game. All the sophomores did well." Still, in reflecting on the game years later in *"Football, My Way,"* Paterno said, "I felt he (Campbell) and Kwalick turned our season around in that game."

Back on the PSU campus, the students had celebrated as they often do after emotional upset victories. They paraded up and down College Avenue and the Mall chanting, "We Want the Bruins! We Want UCLA!" But Paterno wasn't celebrating. After the game, he had caught a couple of seniors from the defensive team trying to sneak a beer at an out-of-the-way airport bar. He threw one player off the team and suspended the other for two weeks. On Monday evening the players held a stormy meeting and asked Paterno to change his mind. He refused and challenged the team to "live by the rules" or leave. They stayed and resumed practice the next day for UCLA with no further doubts about who was in charge. "The morale and support of the entire squad hung in the air," Paterno recalled later in *"Paterno: By The*

Book." "If I backed off, the message was clear as a bell: I'm afraid of you guys." It was, to say the least, another defining moment in his still embryonic coaching career.

Undefeated UCLA with Beban back at quarterback was now #3 in the nation and averaging 37 points in three games. A sportswriter for the *Los Angeles Times* predicted UCLA would "wash its hands" with Penn State. Not quite. Coach Prothro

Versatile and selfless, Pete Johnson made significant contributions at the Hero position as a sophomore, LB as a junior and TE in his senior year during the unbeaten streak of the late '60s.

ran for 120 yards on 18 carries and booted six extra points in what would be the greatest offensive day of his career. Led by Smear and Onkotz, who had 16 tackles between them, the Lion defense recovered two fumbles and intercepted three passes, scoring 28 points in the first quarter and had a 43-8 halftime lead before the reserve defense gave up 20 points in the fourth quarter. *Boston Globe* sportswriter Ernie Roberts accused Paterno of "pouring it on" by keeping his

didn't use any electronic trickery this time but Beban, who would go on to win the Heisman Trophy, used the referee to constantly silence the loud Beaver Stadium crowd of 46,007 and move his offense. However, two big mistakes, not Beban's antics, cost the Lions the upset. State scored on its first possession, moving 79 yards in 10 plays with Campbell running for 49 of those yards, including a 3-yard TD, and the defense helped PSU take that 7-0 lead into the intermission. Zenon Andrusyshyn's 47-yard field goal made it 7-3 in the third quarter and with six minutes left in the quarter UCLA made the play of the game. With an 8-to-10 man rush, the Bruins blocked Campbell's punt at the State 25-yard line. The ball bounded back into the end zone where UCLA tackle Hal Griffith pounced on it and the Bruins led 10-7. "That blocked punt was the turning point," Paterno told sportswriters later. "Without it I have a feeling this would have turned out differently. Midway through the fourth quarter Sherman fumbled at the PSU 29 and eight hard-earned plays later, Beban rolled out from the 3 for the TD. The PAT gave UCLA a 17-7 lead. A few fist fights broke out along the line of scrimmage as the clock wound down and a player from each side was thrown out of the game. With about three minutes left, the Lions drove 40 yards after a punt and scored on a 2-yard run by reserve tailback Tom Cherry, subbing for Campbell who had been injured on a tackle. Sherman ran for the extra points and with 1:08 remaining State tried an onside kick. UCLA recovered and ran out the clock to escape with a 17-15 win. The State fans were on their feet cheering as Paterno and the team left the field. After the game Paterno said "this was one of the best games our team has played in a long time" but it was big plays like the blocked punt that separates good teams from great ones. "I don't think I've had to face a tougher pass rush," Beban told the *Los Angeles Times* after being thrown for 45 yards in losses by the defense.

Worse than the defeat was the loss of Campbell for the season. He was well on his way to possible All-American honors and was leading the nation in punting but the torn ligaments in his left knee required surgery. That gave sophomore Charlie Pittman of Baltimore the opportunity to start the next week against Boston College at Chestnut Hill. But it was the defense and another sophomore, Abbey, playing before a homestate crowd, who helped lead the Lions to an easy 50-28 victory. Alternating with Lucyk at fullback, Abbey scored three touchdowns,

first team in the game in the third quarter but Paterno said, "honestly, there was just too much time left to use what I have for a second team...(and) you saw the way they ran through our subs when we did use them."

The following Saturday, it was Pittman and the defense who made the difference in a 21-14 Homecoming win over once-beaten West Virginia. The Lions were clinging to a 14-7 lead at halftime when Pittman returned the second half kickoff for an 83-yard touchdown, the first such runback since Roger Kochman's historic return against Syracuse in 1959. "Without (that kick return) we probably wouldn't have won the ball game," Paterno told the *Collegian*'s Levine after the game. Pittman also gained 137 yards on 24 carries and caught two passes for 45 yards to delight the 44,460 fans. The Mountaineers scored midway in the fourth quarter on a 26-yard pass but State's defense, with seven sophomores now in the starting lineup, held WVU inside its own 33-yard line for the rest of the game.

State had not beaten Syracuse (4-1) in five years and had not won at Archbold Stadium since 1957. Paterno and his staff didn't believe the Lions could "slug it out" with a potent Syracuse offense led by All-American fullback Csonka and quarterback Rick Cassata. Paterno wanted to hold Csonka to 100 yards and beat the Orange with a "big play." Csonka ran for 112 yards and two touchdowns on 32 carries and Syracuse won the statistics with 363 total yards and 24 first downs to State's 283 yards and 14 first downs. But the young Lions won the tight game on a couple of big plays and never trailed after taking a 7-0 lead early in the first quarter on Pittman's 3-yard TD. Syracuse used up 7 and a half minutes of the quarter, primarily on Csonka's running, to tie the game, but State retaliated in 15 seconds with a "big play"—a 60-yard "bomb" from Sherman to Kwalick to go ahead 13-7. It was 22-14 at the half and midway through the fourth quarter Syracuse made it 22-20. That's when State's defense clinched the game, with McBath recovering a fumble to halt one Syracuse threat and Onkontz making the final "big play" by picking off a Cassata pass and running 47 yards for a touchdown as the Lions won, 29-20.

State scored the first time it had the ball at College Park and went on to destroy winless Maryland, 38-3, for its fourth straight win. Pittman scored three touchdowns on runs of 2, 15 and 6 yards and rushed for 127 yards on 15 carries. The most spectacular play came on an 80-yard pass from Sherman to sophomore Paul Johnson, who started at wingback in place of Grimes,

The Lions were now 5-2 and leading in the Lambert Trophy race but they had hardly made a dent in the Top 20. That would all change after the November 11 game against North Carolina State at Beaver Stadium. NC State was on the verge of its first unbeaten season since 1910 with eight wins and was #3 in both AP & UPI polls with a major bowl bid a certainty if it could win its last two games against PSU and Clemson. Unlike the Lions, the Wolfpack were a veteran team with 17 seniors starting on their offensive and defensive units. Earle Edwards, the Penn Stater passed over for the Lions coaching job in 1949, was still NC State's head coach and ex-Lions Bill Smaltz and Al Michaels were still his assistants—just as they had been in 1956 when the two teams had last played. Paterno's game plan again focused on his opportunistic defense, a big play from the offense and a break or two with no mistakes. Even though the pollsters had not noticed the Lions, the oddsmakers did because they made the Lions a surprising two-point favorite.

A standing-room only crowd of 46,497 and scouts from the Orange, Sugar and Liberty Bowls turned out on a sunny but windy day and when NC State won the coin toss it chose to take the wind. That would be the first break. Pittman ran the kickoff out of the end zone to the PSU 41 yard line. To deter double coverage of his best receiver—Kwalick—Paterno surprised the Wolfpack defense by placing Kwalick and Curry on the same side of the line, with Kwalick in the slot. That confused NC State and the Lions quickly moved the ball to NC State's 18-yard line on Sherman's passes to Abbey and Curry and two short runs by Pittman. The Wolfpack had not given up a first quarter score all

Two-time All-American LB Dennis Onkotz epitomized Paterno's "Grand Experiment" of scholar athletes. He was a team leader in tackles, interceptions and punt returns. He graduated with a 3.5 average in Biophysics and was inducted into the National Football Foundation College Football Hall of Fame in 1995.

year but Kwalick broke open in the end zone and made a spectacular catch when Sherman overthrew him. Sherman's PAT made it 7-0 with just 3 and a half minutes gone in the game. Three minutes later, Onkotz intercepted Jim Donnan's pass at the PSU 33 and with a block from Litterelle, dashed 67-yards for another touchdown. Sherman's kick failed but the 13-0 lead shocked everyone, especially the Wolfpack defense. The Lions had three more opportunities to score in the first half but NC State's defense stopped one with an end zone interception and another with a fourth down play at the 5 and Sherman missed a 33-yard field goal.

The second half was mostly a battle of defenses as NC State shut down the Lions offense. State had the ball eight times and could only move past the PSU 37. Meanwhile, the Wolfpack offense was able to get field goals of 12 and 26 yards from Gerald Warren, the nation's leading placekicker, to make the score 13-6. Another threat was stopped when Montgomery literally took the ball away from an NC State receiver in the end zone early in the fourth quarter. But with 4:47 left in the game, the Wolfpack took over at their 32 following a punt and drove for a first down just inside the PSU 10 with 1:41 remaining. Tailback Tony Barchuk, who already had gained 92 yards in the game, carried for one, then fullback Bobby Hall for six. After a time out, Hall made two and with 40 seconds left, NC State called another time out with a fourth-and-goal at the one. Paterno figured NC State would fake inside to the fullback then go outside. But all week, the Lions had practiced against the fake and a run *inside* by the Wolfpack's best runner, Barchuk. Along the Lion sidelines, assistant coach O'Hora and safety Montgomery, who called the defensive signals, argued for an inside defense and Paterno gave the okay. On the other side, Edwards, thought about calling a pitchout, then reluctantly agreed to the play his quarterback wanted. The center snapped the ball and another part of the Paterno legend was born. Donnan faked to the fullback, then handed off to Barchuk *inside*. McBath submarined at the hole to grab a leg, Kates smashed into Barchuk low, Onkotz hit him high and the three of Lions slammed the tailback backwards onto the turf as the stadium crowd went crazy. However, the game wasn't over. The Wolfpack used its last three time outs to stop the clock and the Lions' punter, Tom Cherry, took an intentional safety. Two seconds remained after the free kick but Onkotz ended it with a tackle on Barchuk at the 39 and the Lions won, 13-8. The crowd inundated the field and tried to take down the concrete-imbedded goal posts as the players carried Paterno off the field. "The (interception) by Onkotz was the big one," Paterno told Doug McDonald of the *Centre Daily Times*. "At the same time you have give the whole defensive unit credit for that goal line stand." Later, Paterno would call the fourth down stop "one of the greatest plays in Penn State history," and fully credit Montgomery for the decision, saying "I sure as hell would have screwed it up." Onkotz was chosen as the AP "Lineman of the Week" and when it was revealed that he had taken a test at an 8 o'clock German class earlier that morning, some people couldn't believe it. "The Grand Experiment" was for real.

Now, the Gator Bowl focused on the Lions, and the bowl's executive vice president, George Olson, was at Beaver Stadium the following Saturday when State beat Ohio University 35-14. The game was a surprisingly tight 7-6 for nearly a half until Capretto scored a touchdown on a 50-yard pass interception and Onkotz returned a punt 56 yards for another TD. On Monday evening, the Lions accepted an invitation to play in the Gator Bowl December 30 against the winner of

Two-time All-American Ted Kwalick caught this pass for a touchdown to help upset then #3 North Carolina State, 13-8, in the pivotal 1967 game that first put Paterno's program into the national spotlight. Kwalick, a fine blocker as well as an excellent receiver, was inducted into the National Football Foundation College Hall of Fame in 1989.

the Florida-Florida State game. "This team deserves the honor," Paterno told the *CDT*. "It's a fitting reward for the outstanding job it has done this year. But the most important thing right now is Saturday's game with Pitt." Five days later, the Lions wound up the season with a relatively easy 42-6 win over Pitt at Beaver Stadium. Sherman threw four TD passes to set a new record for TDs passes in one game that was not broken until 1991. That gave him 13 touchdown passes for the season, breaking Pete Liske's five-year record, and Sherman held that one for 10 years. Curry caught 7 passes to extend several of his career and seasonal records and Abbey scored two touchdowns and kicked six extra points to give him 88 points for the year and the most since Pete Mauthe's 119 in 1912. The margin of victory also was the biggest over Pitt since Mauthe's team won, 38-0. Buzin achieved an offensive lineman's dream by scoring a TD on an end zone fumble recovery and his teammates presented him with the game ball in the locker room. Florida State also won that day. The Gator Bowl was ahead and it was there that the Paterno legend gained momentum.

THE 1967 GATOR BOWL GAME
Dec. 30, 1967
Penn State 17, Florida State 17
Burkhalter Award: Tom Sherman

Paterno wanted no repeat of the previous fiascoes when Engle's '61 & '62 teams prepared for the Gator Bowl. This time Paterno convinced Dean McCoy and President Walker to make the trip a reward for everyone, from players and coaches to the managers, cheerleaders and Blue Band. Instead of cold Fort Eustis (VA) and Annapolis and isolated St. Augustine, the team trained in the warm sunshine of bustling Daytona Beach for nine days, then went to Jacksonville three

days before the game. Behind closed practices, Paterno made a couple of drastic changes to counter Florida State's high-powered passing offense led by quarterback Kim Hammond and receiver Ron Sellers. To get more speed and quickness on defense and better man-to-man coverage, he changed several defensive alignments, including moving linebacker Kates to middle guard, halfback Neal Smith to "Hero" and halfback Cirafesi to safety with Capretto and Montgomery. He confided to PSU beat writers that he might use a 3-6-2 and 5-5-1 defense as well as the 4-4-4. On offense, he switched Kwalick to wingback so that Kwalick could line up again on the same side as Curry, inserted sophomore Gary Williams at tight end and added a "Y" formation to the backfield. "We put in new stuff to keep the boys from going flat, to give them a new challenge," Paterno told Riley. He also changed his kickers after Abbey twisted a knee in practice and Campbell, still recovering from his knee injury, returned to do the punting.

Florida State also had started the season slowly, with a tie and two defeats, including a 20-10 loss to NC State, then had won seven straight. Despite the similar records, the Seminoles were favored by several points when a new record Gator Bowl crowd of 68,019 turned out on a sunny 60-degree day and millions watched on television. But Paterno had the Lions primed. Montgomery made two great defensive plays at the goal line in the first quarter to stop FSU drives, forcing a receiver to drop a sure touchdown with a jarring tackle and running back an intercepted pass for 42 yards. Later in the quarter, State reached the Seminole 6-yard line on the running of Pittman but had to settle for a 27-yard field goal by Sherman. The Lions went ahead 10-0 in the second quarter following a diving interception at midfield by Smith. State appeared to be stopped when a fourth down field goal attempt failed but an offside penalty gave the Lions new life and Sherman threw a 10-yard pass to Curry, who made a leaping catch in the end zone. Late in the half Pittman—who would gain 127 yards on 21 carries to lead all rushers—ran 35 yards on a draw play to help set up a 12-yard TD pass from Sherman to Kwalick and the Lions took a surprising 17-0 lead into the intermission.

In the locker room, Paterno told the players to "play as if we're behind and have to make good on every down." It was a bold—and sometimes intemperate—philosophy that was about to become part of the Paterno legend. Florida State bolted out of the dressing room and within minutes of the second half kickoff, the Seminoles had a first down at the Lion 3-yard line. But another outstanding goal line stand stopped FSU and after a fourth down mix-up in the Seminole backfield, PSU took over at the 5. Pittman ran three times and appeared to make a first down at the 15 but a measurement showed the Lions about 6 inches short. The players wanted to go for it and up in the press box, Tarman said, "Joe's going to go for it." As Riley later described in his book, *The Road to Number One,* McCoy and Walker were aghast, with Walker exclaiming, "He'd better not!" and McCoy saying, "He'd never!" Down on the field, Paterno remembered his half time talk and gave the go ahead. It was another defining moment of Paterno's career. As thousands of disbelieving Penn State fans watched on TV, Sherman tried a sneak behind Lenkaitis, and, after the game Sherman told Riley, "...I looked down and the ball was more than a foot past the line. Someone caught the seat of my pants and pulled me back...the official came in...and spotted the ball where I ended up after they finished pulling me back. We made that first down." As it turned out, it was probably the worst football gamble in State history. Two plays later, Hammond passed to Sellers for a touchdown and when Pittman fumbled the kickoff at the 23, FSU needed just three plays to get another TD and just like that the score was 17-14. State's offense sputtered the rest of the game but Campbell's punting—including one for 68 yards—kept FSU at bay until late in the game when the Seminoles drove 46-yards to a first down at the Lion 14 with less than a minute remaining. A run picked up six yards but then Onkotz broke up one pass and Capretto another and with 15 seconds left, Seminole coach Bill Peterson decided to go for the tie because "our boys had made a tremendous comeback." Grant Guthrie's 25-yard kick was successful and the game ended at 17-17.

Many sportswriters and fans criticized Paterno for blowing the game with his foolish gamble. But others praised the young coach for his daring go-for-the-win philosophy, particularly in contrast to Peterson's play-it-safe denouncement. "I blew it," Paterno said outside the locker room, then reflected on it later, and told Sandy Padwe of the *Philadelphia Inquirer*, "If I had ordered a punt on that play instead of a run, I wouldn't have had the courage to be the football coach a want to be. I took a chance. I know it turned the game around but I took it." Later, Paterno said, "I may be rationalizing, but in the long run that fourth down call may be the best thing I ever did for Penn State football."

So, Paterno had his first winning team and his ever first ranking in the Top 10 (#10 by the AP). He also had his first All-American as Ted Kwalick became the first underclassman since Bob Higgins in 1915 to gain such status. But when he flew home from Jacksonville on New Year's Eve Day, Joe Paterno was more than just a football coach. Neither he nor anyone else realized it, but he was on his way to becoming a legend. It had started in the Orange Bowl some three months earlier and in 366 days it would grow even further in the same Orange Bowl—thanks to a piano playing tackle from Altoona, a resourceful, underrated quarterback from McKees Rocks and a 12th man from Kansas.

Season Record 8-2-1
Record to Date 430-229-40
Winning percentage .644

1968

"Chuck & 'The Rover Boys'"

Whenever Penn State football fans reminisce about the great 1968 season, they first think of quarterback Chuck Burkhart's daring last minute plays in the Orange Bowl and the 12th man penalty that gave unbeaten State the thrilling 15-14 victory. That was undoubtedly the ultimate defining moment of the season, and another personification of the Paterno legend.

Yet, that moment must be shared with at least one other in the regular season in a sequential overview. For if the first one had not occurred, the '68 squad would have never played in the 1969 Orange Bowl nor been noted today among State's all-time greatest teams. It is prophetic as to how Paterno's teams would play over the next 30 years, that the second moment was the handiwork of special teams and the logic of a "big play" that wins games.

Paterno knew he had a good team with an outstanding defense returning for '68 but as he told the State College Quarterback Club in his preseason analysis, he wouldn't have a great team "until the of-

fense became more cohesive." Burkhart, his inexperienced junior quarterback, had not played enough in '67 to letter and sportswriters were questioning Burkhart's ability. But the 6-foot, 185-pound bespectacled Burkhart, who wore contact lenses on the field, had never lost a game as a starter at McKees Rocks. And now his high school coach Bob Phillips was on Paterno's staff and his scholastic teammate was State's exceptional tight end, All-American Ted Kwalick. Paterno was convinced the rest of his starting backfield was as good as any in the country with the explosive Pittman and Campbell at halfbacks and Abbey at fullback. Of course, Paterno was counting on Campbell's and Abbey's injured knees to hold up. (Their knees did but other parts of their bodies did not.) Paterno hoped veteran Angevine or sophomore Greg Edmonds could fill some of the void at split end left by Curry, who graduated with all the team's major receiving records, but he was more concerned about his offensive interior line and his depth. There wasn't much experience after Bradley and Kukla (one of the tri-captains) at the tackles and before the season went too far, Paterno would be starting sophomores Warren Koegel of Seaford, NY, at center and Charlie Zapiec of Philadelphia at guard along with junior Jackson at the other guard and Dave Rakiecki in reserve.

Paterno's veteran defense was the team's strength. It will be the "smallest defense I can remember," he told Jim O'Brien, editor of *Pittsburgh Weekly Sports*, before the September 21 opener against Navy, but it will be "quick, tough and alert." With Reid fully recovered from *his* knee injury, Paterno had moved him back to defensive tackle to pair with Smear—who had been picked as the most improved player in spring practice—with Ebersole as the prime backup. Reid and Smear also were defensive captains, the first time juniors had that role since Bas Gray in 1924. Spaziani returned at one defensive end and Lincoln Lippincott, III, a non-lettering senior who had bounced around from offensive end to defensive halfback, was the other end. Kates and Onkotz were the inside linebackers with Pete Johnson and sophomore Gary Hull sharing time at one outside linebacker position. The other outside linebacker would be a 6-foot-2, 205-pound sophomore named Jack Ham who had been given the last scholarship two years ago on the recommendation of Smear, his high school teammate at Johnstown's Bishop McCourt. Paul Johnson was back on defense at one halfback and sophomore Mike Smith was the other with Neal Smith switched to safety. It was a mobile and opportunistic defense befitting Paterno's innovative 4-4-3 alignment and would soon earn the nickname, "The Rover Boys."

Sportswriters who evaluated the team saw great potential and most predicted another Top 10 finish. The Dunkel computer ratings went the furthest with a #2 ranking while the AP and *Look* magazine picked a 10th place finish, with *Look* also forecasting a victory over Florida in the Orange Bowl. "We've talked about (the high rankings)," Paterno told Ron Kolb, sports editor of the *Daily Collegian*. "We feel it's a better challenge and it will make the season much more exciting." The schedule was similar to '67 except that the traditional mid-October game against Syracuse was switched to December 7 so that ABC could televise it nationally (and provide each team with an extra $185,000 in revenue). That caused the November 2 game against Army to be designated as Homecoming and 49,653 would be there to witness a defining moment.

The 49,273 who turned out on a warm afternoon at Beaver Stadium for the Navy game was the largest up to that time for a home opener. They shook their heads when they saw Burkhart overthrow

Don Abbey, another scholar-athlete of Paterno's "Grand Experiment," was State's fullback on the unbeaten 1968 and 1969 teams, who also handled kickoffs and place kicking.

tempt at the PSU 10-yard line set up a 22-yard field goal for K-State in the first quarter but the Lions went ahead 7-3 in the second period on a 17-play, 74-yard drive with Campbell scoring from the three. The Wildcats ran back the kickoff to their own 41-yard line and two plays later sophomore substitute quarterback Lynn Dickey threw a short pass to junior speedster Mark Herron and Herron ran the rest of the 56-yards for the TD and K-State led at the half, 9-7. The Lions appeared to be in deep trouble on the second half kickoff when they couldn't get the return past their own 9-yard line. But on the first play Campbell burst off tackle for 56-yards and five plays later a 5-yard TD by Pittman regained the lead for good, 13-9. However, Campbell's run had been costly. The hard-luck senior had suffered a shoulder separation and doctors said he would be out for at least a month. Still, Campbell had played long enough to gain 112 yards on 18 carries and when Pittman finished the game with 106 yards on 25 carries, they became just the sixth PSU duo in history to run for more than 100 yards in a game. A minute after Pittman's TD, Ham intercepted Dickey at the Lion 41 and Cherry, in at fullback for Abbey, scored from the 2. Burkhart threw his first TD pass of the year early in the fourth quarter to Angevine for 25 yards and the Lions won, 25-9. The defense had held the Wildcats to 28 yards rushing and 138 yards passing while sacking Dickey for about 25 yards in losses and intercepting two passes. "When I heard (Campbell) might be out for a year, he and I sat down and cried like babies," Paterno told Paul Levine of the *Daily Collegian*. "I'll be back and sooner than you think," Campbell said.

State moved up another notch in the polls behind #1 Purdue and #2 USC but the Lions still had to come from behind again the following week before a rowdy throng in Morgantown before beating West Virginia, 31-20. A brawl erupted on the field before the game when West Virginia students, egged on by thousands of cheering, hostile Mountaineer fans, attacked a PSU group, including cheerleaders, participating in some pre-game festivities. State scored first on an opening drive of 73 yards with Kwalick getting the 1-yard TD on an end-

Kwalick in the end zone early in the first quarter and some shouted for Paterno to make a change. Nor were they comfortable when they saw Abbey limp off the second time he carried the ball. But the defense forced a fumble minutes later and that set up a 20-yard field goal by sophomore Bob Garthwaite. Two minutes into the second quarter, Pittman ran for a 57-yard touchdown and three minutes later Pete Johnson intercepted a pass at the Navy 28 and ran for another TD. Before the day was over, Pittman would rush for 162 yards on 18 carries and the defense would pick off five Navy passes and recover four fumbles to spark a 31-6 win. "The defense won the game for us," Paterno told sportswriters. The final TD was scored by the special teams in an unusual festive atmosphere on the opening play of the fourth quarter. Because classes had not yet begun, there was no halftime ceremony because the Blue Band was not ready to perform. Between the third and fourth quarters, the fans stood on their feet and sang the Alma Mater. They were still singing the last stanza when Paul Johnson took a Navy punt and ran 52-yards into the end zone. For PSU loyalists, that was an omen. After the game, the cheerleaders found a small bamboo horseshoe lying in the end zone grass and for the rest of the season the little horseshoe was taken to every game, draped over the goal posts for home games and placed near the team bench on away games. "We figured...it had to be our good luck omen for the season," said cheerleader Gary Cotler.

The win over Navy jumped State to #4 in both the AP and UPI polls. But the bad news was that Abbey would be sidelined indefinitely with a sprained left knee and ankle. The news worsened the next week when the Lions had to come from behind twice against underdog Kansas State at Beaver Stadium. A bad snap from center on a punt at-

Steve Smear was co-captain of the great undefeated teams of 1968 and 1969 and, along with Mike Reid, part of one of the greatest defensive tackle tandems in college football history.

around. But sophomore Mike Sherwood threw TD passes of 27 and 67 yards to Austin Patrick before the first quarter was over for a 14-7 lead. An interception by Onkotz in the second quarter set up the tying TD on 21-yard pass from Burkhart to sophomore Charlie Wilson, subbing for Campbell, and a 78-yard drive early in the third quarter made it 21-14. Onkotz clinched the game when he intercepted an attempted screen pass at the WVU 9-yard line midway in the fourth quarter and ran for a TD. After the game Mountaineer coach Jim Carlen said he had designed his offensive game plan to avoid Onkotz, "but everywhere we went, he was there." Carlen also had pointed his defense to stop Pittman but he gained 127 yards and a TD on 25 carries. "With Charlie Pittman carrying an abundance of his team's striking power on his dancing, spindly legs, and Denny Onkotz again leading the fierce defensive charge of the 'Rover Boys,' our Lions justified their high national ranking in Mountaineer Stadium Saturday," wrote Riley in the *"Football Letter."*

Paterno agreed to take the "Lucky Horseshoe" to Los Angeles for the UCLA game the next week because the cheerleaders couldn't make the trip. Neither did Paterno's two starting defensive ends, Spaziani and Lippincott, who were hurt. But Abbey was there, although he was still hurting and would see only limited action. UCLA had been upset at the Coliseum by Syracuse, 20-7, and LA sportswriters said there was no way another "Eastern team" could beat Prothro twice in a row on UCLA's home field. The AP picked the Bruins by two points. They all had underestimated the "Rover Boys" and the resourcefulness of Burkhart. The defensive play of the game came in the second quarter with the game scoreless and the Bruins punting from their 35-yard line. With a regional TV audience watching as Keith Jackson and Bud Wilkinson described the play, Reid, Smear, Ebersole, Kates and Ham barreled across the line. Ham hit the ball solidly with his arm and it ricocheted off the punter's chest. Kates accidentally kicked the ball, then picked it up and ran 36 yards for a touchdown accompanied by Reid. Garthwaite's PAT made it 7-0 and State never trailed, although UCLA kept it close into the second half. A missed extra point by Andrusyshyn after UCLA had scored in the second quarter made it 7-6 at the half and the Bruins were driving early in the third quarter when Pete Johnson made a diving interception at the PSU 24-yard line. On second down, Burkhart rolled left as his primary receiver, Kwalick, crossed over the middle. The big tight end was being

double-teamed, so Burkhart glanced at his fullback, Cherry, who had flared out on the right. Cherry was wide open. He took Burkhart's pass and roared down the sideline, picked up a downfield block on two defenders from Kwalick and went 76-yards for a TD. UCLA never recovered. The Lions iced the game in the fourth quarter when a 23-yard punt return by Onkotz set up a 10-yard TD sprint by Pittman, and they won, 21-6, carrying Paterno (and probably the "Lucky Horseshoe") off the field. "The unbeaten Nittany Lions were anything but Paper Lions," wrote Jeff Prugh in the *Los Angeles Times*. "They were every bit as good as advertised—tough, quick and precision-built." After losing because of a blocked punt to then #2 UCLA in '67, Paterno and the team reveled in the way this year's victory was achieved. "A revenge blocked punt started the festivities that were to continue from Anaheim to Pittsburgh to State College," wrote the *Collegian*'s Kolb. Back in State College, more than 2,000 students paraded up and down College Avenue, rocking busses and cars. Then they marched to President Walker's campus home near the Mall, where the usually reserved president greeted them with a big smile and yelled "We're Number One!" As many as 3,000 students and the Blue Band met the team at 5 a.m. Sunday when the team busses rolled up to Rec Hall, repeating Walker's refrain: "We're Number One! We're Number One!"

But the Lions didn't move to Number One. USC with Heisman Trophy front-runner O. J. Simpson did and Ohio State leaped over PSU to #2 after dumping the previous #1, Purdue, 18-0. With the Syracuse game moved to December, State had a week off before its next game at Boston College. On Monday night, October 21, Paterno's wife, Sue, gave birth to their second son, Joseph Vincent Paterno, Jr.(who 30 years later would be better known as "Jay" and an assistant on his dad's coaching staff). Tuesday morning, the idle Lions slipped to #4 in both AP & UPI as surprising Kansas, which had not even been ranked in the preseason Top 20, jumped ahead. It was the type of shifting in the polls that would haunt Paterno's teams for the next three decades and frustrate four of his unbeaten teams.

Boston College had a Nittany Lion flavor because its new head coach was Joe Yukica, a star end on Engle's early teams, and two of Yukica's assistants also had played end for Engle—Bill Bowes, captain in '64, and his teammate, Jerry Sandusky, one of the defensive stars of the '64 upset over Ohio State. The pass-oriented Eagles had lost to Tulane during State's

The first of Paterno's major running backs, Bobby Campbell (23) gets blocking help from Dave Bradley (73) and Tom Jackson (63) in the big win over Army in 1968. Campbell's two clutch plays in the final minutes of the 1969 Orange Bowl will enshrine him forever in the history of Penn State football.

All-American tailback Charlie Pittman starts one of his patented sweeps in 1968 behind a phalanx of blockers led by FB Don Abbey (36), Charlie Zapiec (60) and John Kulka (78).

idle week and despite a 3-1 record were an 11-point underdog. But with scouts from the Orange and Sugar Bowls looking on, Yukica surprised Paterno by switching quarterbacks and going to a running offense, and for more than 20 minutes the game was scoreless as State's offense also struggled with Burkhart missing 9 of his first 10 passes. Then with less than 5 minutes left in the half, Garthwaite kicked a 22-yard field goal at the end of a 73-yard drive. In the next four minutes, State scored two touchdowns, one on a 31-yard pass to Kwalick and another on an 11-yard run by Cherry that Paul Johnson had set up with an interception. State went on to win 29-0 as the defense intercepted three more passes in the second half, recovered a fumble and Ham blocked another punt. Richie Lucas, who had quit pro football and joined the Athletic Department, returned the "Lucky Horseshoe" to the cheerleaders the next day.

Since migrating from Brown to State in 1950, Paterno had seen the Lions lose nine times to Army, win just three and never win at home. On the eve of the game at Beaver Stadium, Paterno told an enthusiastic pep rally at Rec Hall, "I'm fed up to here with Army." So were a group of radical students who demonstrated outside of President Walker's home that night and the next day. But those students cared little about football. They were protesting against the escalating Vietnam War and Walker's house guest, General William Westmoreland, the superintendent at West Point. State troopers had to help get Westmoreland and Walker to the stadium Saturday morning where 1,200 Cadets joined the Homecoming crowd. To the delight of the home fans, Campbell was back in the starting lineup, and he had an outstanding return—rushing for 104 yards and two touchdowns on 17 carries. But it was special teams, two key Army mistakes and maybe the "Lucky Horseshoe" that helped give State the 28-24 victory.

The Lions scored on the opening drive with Campbell taking a reverse handoff from Pittman for the 9-yard TD. When the defense forced a punt at the Army 29-yard line after the ensuing kickoff, the Army snap sailed over punter Charlie Jarvis' head into the end zone. Jarvis fell on the ball and the safety gave State a 9-0 lead. But Army marched 87 yards before the end of the second quarter and it was 9-7

at the half. PSU's defense stopped Army on the second half kickoff and the offense made it 16-7 on a drive from midfield, with Pittman getting the TD on a 5-yard sweep around the left end. The defense continued to stymie Army's attack but four minutes into the fourth quarter the Cadets kicked a 30-yard field goal. Then came another Army blunder. A State drive from the PSU 24 stalled at the Army 21 and Garthwaite tried a field goal into the wind. The ball never made it but as it stopped dead near the goal line, an Army player touched it with his leg and Kulka recovered. Three plays later, Campbell burst two yards over tackle for the touchdown and State led 22-10 after the two-point conversion failed. But Army stormed back quickly after the kickoff, with a 60-yard pass from Steve Lindell to Gary Steele that set up a Jarvis 1-yard TD and with the PAT Army trailed by just 6 with 2 and a half minutes left. Then came the play of the game and the defining moment of the regular season.

Army tried an onside kick and it was a good one. Zapiec tried to fall on the ball but it rolled towards Bradley who seemed to have it as several Army defenders leaped on top of him. Suddenly, the ball squirted beneath the pile. Kwalick, standing alone a couple feet away, swooped down, grabbed the ball and ran all alone into the end zone for a 53-yard TD. The PAT failed but State had control. But Army still wasn't done as Lindell passed Army 60 yards in six plays for another 7 points. The crowd was edgy as Army set for another onside kick. This time Zapiec grabbed the ball tightly and the game was over. "We made some mistakes but that onside kick was a unique mistake," Army's Coach Tom Cahill told sportswriters. "We worked on that play in practice," Paterno joked in the locker room. The victory was the 13th in a row over two seasons and no PSU team in history had ever done that.

As the Lions prepared for dangerous Miami (5-2) the next week, they moved back to #3 in the polls on the heels of a Kansas loss to Oklahoma. And while they read about Richard Nixon's Presidential election victory over Hubert Humphrey, they also learned they were high on the list of the Orange and Cotton Bowl committees. Neil Amdur of the *New York Times* reported the Lions would get the Orange Bowl bid if they beat the Hurricanes. Georgia was the probable opponent. For 30

High school teammates Ted Kwalick (82) and Chuck Burkhart continued their careers at Penn State. Kwalick was a two-time All-American at TE and Burkhart was an outstanding leader who quarterbacked the great unbeaten teams of 1968 and 1969.

minutes that looked improbable to the standing-room only crowd of 50,132, including scouts from the Orange, Cotton, Sugar and Gator Bowls at Beaver Stadium. Miami stunned State with a 78-yard touchdown pass in the first quarter from David Olivo to Ray Bellamy, then just missed a field goal in the second quarter as the Hurricane defense, led by ends Ted Hendricks and Tony Cline stuffed PSU's offense, and Miami took a 7-0 halftime lead. When Cline was forced to the sidelines with a knee injury in the third quarter, the Miami defense began to wither. State's defense also picked up the tempo and after Spaziani recovered an Olivo fumble at the Miami 30, State scored in six plays with Pittman getting the TD. But a 2-point pass attempt failed and minutes later the Lions drove 57-yards in 10 plays to take a 12-7 lead on Pittman's second TD. On the first play of the fourth quarter, Olivo fumbled again, Ham recovered at Miami's 16 and four plays later Garthwaite kicked a 21-yard field goal. With less than four minutes remaining, Ham set a team record that still stands by blocking his third punt of the season. Lippincott recovered at the Miami 5 and Pittman, now limping with a sore ankle, carried four straight plays for the touchdown, and State won 22-7. "That second half was a fine a half of football I've ever seen a Penn State team play," Paterno told Doug McDonald of the *Centre Daily Times*. "Both offensively and defensively. We knew we couldn't dilly dally around. We had to go after people."

Despite a 21-inch snowfall that sent practice into disarray the next week, the Lions had no problem with Maryland at College Park. Five minutes into the game, Smear intercepted an attempted screen pass at the Terp 40 and ran for a touchdown and the 57-13 rout was on. Burkhart completed 12 of 17 passes for 121 yards, Pittman scored two TDs, and the defense had two interceptions, two fumble recoveries and another blocked kick to hand the Terps their worst defeat since State's 1917 victory the first time the schools played. In this era of the late 1960s, bowl pairings were set up in mid November before teams completed their seasons. On Monday afternoon, with two games remaining, the Lions accepted an invitation to play in the Orange Bowl against Kansas, the highest scoring team in the nation. "This is something you think about when you're a little kid," a happy Reid told the *Collegian*.

The following Saturday at Pitt Stadium, the Lions rolled up the highest point total in the history of the traditional series by battering the Panthers 65-9. The score could have been worse but Paterno took out his first team early in the third quarter, ordered no more passing and inserted every substitute he had, including two scrubs who paid their own way to Pittsburgh. Pittman scored three touchdowns, tying the school record for a season of 13 held by four others, including Lenny Moore, and Campbell rushed for 104 yards as the Lions amassed 618 yards in total offense. "In a complete mismatch, sympathy was the only thing Penn State gave Pitt yesterday," wrote Russ Franke in the *Pittsburgh Press*. As a national TV audience watched a week later, the '68 team became the first in school history to win 10 games in a season with a 30-12 win over Syracuse in 25 degree weather at Beaver Stadium. Pittman set a new season TD record with a 27-yard run in the first quarter and Campbell came within 12 yards of breaking Shorty Miller's one-game rushing record by running for 239 yards and two touchdowns on 24 carries. One of his TDs came on a second quarter 87-yard run that was the longest from scrimmage in 76 years. Campbell's most memorable run for himself that day came late in the fourth quarter when he ran a draw for an 18-yard TD right over a former high school antagonist and then tried to throw the football out of the north grandstands in celebration. As he trotted back to the bench, Paterno angrily greeted him on the field at the hash mark and told him he would have to pay for the football. "(Joe) wasn't real happy, " Campbell recalled years later to Neil Rudel for *Blue-White Illustrated*. "I didn't do it to be anti-whatever. I did it in the excitement of the game." Still, Paterno benched him for the rest of the game. So, with the regular season at an end, the offense, so maligned earlier in the season, broke the single season total offense mark of the 1961 team (4,025 yards) and the rushing record held by the 1947 squad (2,739 yards). The team also had two more All-Americans as both Onkotz and Kwalick were consensus First Team choices.

THE 1969 ORANGE BOWL
Jan. 1, 1969
Penn State 15, Kansas 14

The atmosphere in Miami in the week leading up to the Orange Bowl game New Year's Night was fresh, relaxing and full of the holiday spirit. Both teams worked hard in practice but the players and coaches reveled in the official events the Orange Bowl committee held in their honor. In their off times, the State players lolled around the pool and lobby at the Ivanhoe Hotel in Miami Beach and talked easily with alumni and fans who dropped by. Frequently, Mike Reid would entertain with some impromptu piano playing.

Playing in a such a glamour game was a new experience for both the State and Kansas teams. The Jayhawks had not been to any bowl game since their 1947 team (8-0-2 and ranked 12th) played and lost to Georgia Tech in this same Orange Bowl, 20-14. Of course, the last State team to play on New Year's also was its '47 squad, which tied SMU in the Cotton Bowl. One the attractions of this year's game was the two young coaches, Paterno and Kansas' Pepper Rodgers. In his second year at Kansas, Rodgers had surprised everyone with a team picked to finish third in the Big Eight. Now, the Jayhawks were 6th in the nation with a high octane offense featuring quarterback Bobby Douglass and running backs Donnie Shanklin and John Riggins and a hard-hitting defense with two of the best defensive ends in the country,

All-American John Zook and Vernon Vanoy. Rodgers had earned notoriety as an outstanding quarterback at Georgia Tech but State fans remembered him as the UCLA assistant in 1965 who was using a controversial electronic device from the Beaver Stadium press box to give plays to quarterback Gary Beban on the playing field. Rodgers was as talkative and as witty as Paterno and at their public events, they wowed the crowd with their remarks and impromptu comedy routine. That helped excite the local populace, who seemed to be looking ahead to the January 12th Super Bowl between the powerful Baltimore Colts and the 17-point underdog New York Jets and their cocky quarterback, Joe Namath.

Bob Holuba was one of Paterno's first scholar-athletes who was a two-year starter at guard on the great unbeaten teams of '68 and '69 and graduated with a 3.65 average in Business Administration. State's indoor practice field is named after his family.

Because the teams were similar, both Paterno and Rodgers predicted a wild, high-scoring game. Most sportswriters agreed and believed Kansas had the edge because of their quarterback, a big and mobile left-hander who could run and throw. Although Burkhart had thrown just seven interceptions, he also had tossed just six TD passes. He wasn't much of a runner and he was still criticized for being erratic. "Sure, he'll make some mistakes," Paterno said when queried about his QB, "but then he'll come up with the big play. All he does is win." With Burkhart in control, the Lion offense had just 14 turnovers all season and had scored more points than any State team since 1916, averaging 21 points per game. Some sportswriters said State's defense would make or break the game. The Rover Boys defense had set up or scored 145 of State 339 points.

Because Ohio State, now #1, was playing #2 USC in the Rose Bowl three hours earlier on New Years Day, the outcome in the Orange Bowl was not expected to have any bearing on the National Championship. Despite its record, State was still being criticized for its "Eastern" schedule, especially by sportswriters in the midwest, southeast and southwest. Even with a potential tie in the Rose Bowl, PSU was given only an outside chance to go to #1. Still, when hundreds of giddy fans gathered for a Noon time pep rally inside the Deauville Hotel, they chanted "We're Number One" and "Numero Uno" when Paterno and the players appeared. At a special prayer service just before the game, Dallas Cowboys coach Tom Landry spoke to the players and told them, "Don't give up, whatever may happen."

In spite of what the two coaches had predicted, the game turned into a defensive battle almost from the start. Kansas intercepted two Burkhart passes and recovered an Abbey fumble in the first quarter and after the second interception at the PSU 45-yard, Kansas ran eight straight running plays and scored on Mike Reeves' 2-yard plunge and Bill Bell's PAT. The Lions tied it in the second quarter after getting the ball at the their own 47 after a punt and on the sixth play of the drive

Pittman ran up the middle from the 13-yard line and Garthwaite made it 7-7. State's defense halted KU at PSU 35 later in the quarter and twice the Lions had scoring opportunities but Cherry fumbled at the Jayhawk 7 and Garthwaite missed a 21-yard field goal with four seconds remaining in the half.

In the third quarter, the Lions drove from their 33-yard line for a first down at the KU 5. Cherry carried three straight times to within a half yard but on fourth down Pittman was thrown for a 2-yard loss and State never got close again—until the end. Kansas drove all the way into State territory but a 33-yard field goal was short and wide as the period came to a close. On the opening series of the fourth quarter, KU's defense forced State to punt from the PSU 13-yard line. Now came what seemed to be the play of the game. Shanklin took the punt at the KU 47 and was not tackled until Pittman stopped him at the PSU 7. Riggins picked up 6 yards on the first play and a touchdown on the next one. Bell's PAT gave KU the 14-7 lead and the momentum. The KU defense forced the Lions into another punt and the Jayhawks moved from their 28 for a fourth-and-1 at the PSU 5 with 10 minutes still to play. Disdaining a "sure" field goal, Rodgers sent Riggins off tackle and he was stopped for no gain by Paul and Pete Johnson. But Kansas kept the Lions bottled up for the next eight minutes. When State was forced to punt with two minutes left and KU took possession at its 38 yard-line, the Kansas fans in the crowd of 77,719 began celebrating. "There was no way Penn State could win...," Roy McHugh of the *Pittsburgh Press* wrote later. "The last two minutes were pure unadulterated insanity."

State had all three time outs left and used them well. Douglass tried a keeper around the end but was stopped for no gain by Lippincott. Then on two successive plays Douglass was nailed for losses by Reid and with fourth-and-23, Kansas had to punt. State rushed 10 men and Neal Smith partially blocked the ball and it bounced and wobbled out of bounds at the 50. There was 1:16 left on the clock as Paterno conferred with Burkhart and Campbell on the sidelines. Paterno knew Kansas would defend against short passes, so he told Campbell to run deep and he told Burkhart to throw it over his head but not worry about a completion, just avoid an interception. That way, Paterno said, Kansas will have to defend deep and we'll come back with Kwalick over the middle. But as they returned to the huddle, Campbell told Burkhart, "Throw to the left goal post and I'll be there." Burkhart nodded and said the ball would be too. Up in the press box, came the announcement that Shanklin had been selected the game's "Most Valuable Player" and many sportswriters headed for the elevator and the dressing rooms. Burkhart dropped back and just as he was being whacked by two lineman he arched the ball towards Campbell, who split between two KU defenders, snared the pass on the 20 and reached the KU 3 before being tackled. The crowd roared as Kukla raced up to the referee and called State's last time out.

Burkhart and Paterno discussed a three-play sequence without any huddles, with Cherry carrying the first two times and Paterno sending in the third play. The TV camera cut to a shot of Reid on the bench, his hands clasped and ostensibly saying a prayer. When time resumed Kansas stopped Cherry twice for no gain and as the clock ticked down, Paterno sent in Edmonds with the play, a handoff to Pittman for a "scissors" slant over the left tackle with Campbell as a pass decoy out on the left flank. The KU defense figured Pittman would get the ball and the linebackers squeezed in towards the line. Burkhart realized the play wouldn't work but there was no time for an audible. Instead of giving Pittman the handoff, Burkhart faked, kept the ball and ran around a surprised Campbell at the left end. "I thought we had fumbled," said Pittman later. "Then I was tackled; then I saw Chuck score." It was the first touchdown of Burkhart's career. "I said I'd save my first touchdown for a time when it counted," he later told John Crittenden, sports editor of the *Miami News*.

The State fans cheered and Paterno, true to his go-for-the-win philosophy, sent in a 2-point option pass play that had Kwalick running near the goal, Campbell going deep into the end zone and Burkhart rolling out to either run or pass. But Kansas had the play defensed perfectly and when Burkhart tried to hit Campbell, two KU defenders knocked the ball away. The Kansas players and fans started to celebrate as their fans began pouring out of their seats. But the umpire Foster Grose was waving a red flag. Penalty. "Illegal procedure," signaled the referee but neither the fans nor the sportswriters in the press box learned until after the game that the penalty was for 12 men on the field. Actually, as the game film showed and the Kansas coaches later admitted, 12 men had been on the field for four plays, including Burkhart's touchdown. In the confusion after the sensational pass to Campbell, Linebacker Rick Abernathy had stayed on the field. Now with a second chance, Paterno sent in a play for Campbell to take a pitchout right but when the referees had to hold up the game because of the noise, Paterno changed the play to a Campbell sweep left. With Zapiec taking out Zook and Kwalick and Cherry blocking the linebackers, Campbell ran around left and dove into the end zone. Now it was the State players and fans who went crazy. Eight seconds were left and in the bedlam State kicked off. KU had one play left and Douglass threw the ball wildly trying to hit a receiver and it fell harmlessly to the ground. The final score was 15-14 and State became the first Eastern team to win the Orange Bowl since Duquesne in 1937. "This was a crazy to end all crazies," wrote Edwin Pope, sports editor of the *Miami Herald*. "...Folks will be examining their brains about this one for a long time."

"This Orange Bowl game put us on the map," Paterno would say later. The team finished with the best record since football began at State in 1887 and the highest place ever in the polls—#2. Paterno was hot and within the next month he would turn down a job offer from the Pittsburgh Steelers and be named "Coach of the Year" by his coaching colleagues. Everyone wondered if he, Chuck and "The Rover Boys" could do it again in 1969. He could and they would, even without the "Lucky Horseshoe." But then a football coach turned sportscaster and a conniving President of the United States spoiled it all.

Season Record 11-0
Record to Date 441-229-40
Winning percentage .649

"Say It Ain't So, Mr. President"

No year in the Paterno era had so much glory and so much controversy as 1969. What could have been the greatest year of all time in Penn State football history turned into an agitating political squabble that entangled the White House with the gridiron and had ramifications that still continue to haunt and frustrate Nittany Lion teams and their loyal fans. But for an ill-advised decision that seemed rational at the time, State might have won its first National Championship on the field in '69, not 13 years later. And instead of being known for having one of the outstanding defensive teams in the history of college football—as it should—the Lions of '69 are maligned by critics as overrated bullies who "ducked" a showdown with the nation's number one team.

No one will ever know if State could have beaten #1 Texas that season. Despite another 11-0 year and an unbeaten streak of 28 games, the Lions were demeaned for being a team from the "weak" East. It took years for Paterno's teams to overcome the disdain outsiders had for Eastern football, and even as his squads routinely beat the best teams from all the major conferences, the respect came grudg-

State's all-time career interception leader, Neal Smith, picks off one of two interceptions against Colorado as George Landis prepares to throw a block. The former walk-on became a First-Team All-American.

ingly. Yet, all of the criticism could have been moot if not for a fateful mid-November vote by the players of '69 to return to the Orange Bowl instead of going to the Cotton Bowl.

After the thrilling Orange Bowl victory over Kansas and his rejection of an offer to be head coach of the Pittsburgh Steelers, Paterno received a new contract with a modest raise to $30,000. He also sought and received academic tenure as a "full professor" because, he said, he considered himself an "educator" first and a coach second. It was the coach, not the educator, who was upset throughout spring practice by the lack of enthusiasm by his veteran defensive players. "Defensively, we could be outstanding if we avoid injuries," he said that summer, "(and) if we recapture that incentive and intensity that was lacking in spring practice." Paterno need not have worried. The defense, third in the nation in '68, was ready to go by the season opener at Navy. Although he was initially worried about his replacements at defensive end, everything fell into place with the shift of Ebersole from tackle and Hull from linebacker. Reid and Smear were, as most sportswriters acknowledged, "two of the best defensive tackles in the country." Onkotz, Kates and Ham returned at linebacker as did Paul Johnson and Neal Smith in the backfield. When junior thirdstringer George Landis developed so well in preseason at defensive half, Paterno switched halfback Mike Smith to the "Hero" slot. That also enabled Paterno to shift Pete Johnson from linebacker to tight end to succeed two-time All-American Kwalick.

On offense, Paterno was most concerned about "the smallest overall offensive line since I've been here." That interior line averaged 6-2, 220-pounds and Paterno wondered if his tackles were big

Eight members of State's great defensive unit of '69 surround Colorado's star quarterback, Bob Anderson. In the photo are: Jim Kates (55), Steve Smear (76), Neal Smith (26), Dennis Onkotz (35), Gary Hull (80), George Landis (31), John Ebersole (89) and Jack Ham (33). Mike Reid, Paul Johnson and Mike Smith were keeping Colorado's other 10 players pre-occupied.

enough. Jackson, the offensive tri-captain with Reid and Smear, moved from guard to left tackle and junior letterman Vic Surma became the starter at right tackle. Bob Holuba moved into Jackson's old guard spot to pair with Zapiec and center Koegel. Edmonds, who was voted the most improved player in spring practice, was again the split end. Three starters returned to the backfield with Burkhart, Pittman—a preseason All-American—and Abbey, who also kicked off. Junior letterman Gary Duel took over at wingback. Paterno was pleased with his corps of reserve running backs that included junior lettermen Joe Ramich and Fran Ganter and a pair of hot-shot sophomores from New Jersey, Lydell Mitchell of Salem and Franco Harris of Mt. Holly. Junior Mike Cooper continued as Burkhart's backup but a 6-4 220-pound sophomore named Bob Parsons of Wind Gap also was impressive in the preseason. By the time the season began, Parsons was the punter and another sophomore, Mike Reitz, had won the placekicking position from Garthwaite.

Because of PSU's awesome defense, many sportswriters picked the Lions for another Top 10 finish, and some, like Tom Siler of *Parade* Magazine had them #2 behind the defending national champ, Ohio State. *Sports Illustrated* tabbed State third behind OSU and Texas. Still, many forecasters griped about State's schedule and several writers called it "the softest of the major teams" since none of the Lions' 10 foes were in the preseason Top 20. The writers and many PSU fans also continued to belittle Burkhart despite his Orange Bowl heroics and winning record and the criticism went on throughout the season. "I think it bothered me at the time because of getting picked at for what you thought was a pretty decent job," Burkhart later told author Frank Bilovsky, a one-time PSU beat writer, for his book, *"Lion Country: Inside Penn State Football."*

The opener at Navy-Marine Corps Stadium in Annapolis on September 21 is noted for what happened before the game rather than

during it. The Maryland State Police escort was an hour late getting to the motel in Bowie where the team stayed and they all were caught in a major traffic jam. Blocked by the corps of middies crossing the College Creek bridge and marching into the stadium, the players finally had to walk through a mostly-jeering crowd to get to their dressing room only minutes before the scheduled kickoff. By the time they warmed up at the end of the first quarter, the heavily-favored Lions were leading 14-0 on the running of Pittman, who scored both touchdowns, one on a 58-yard run. By the time Pittman left early in the third quarter when Paterno put in the reserves, he had recorded his best rushing day ever with 177 yards on 19 carries—and he did it as his idol, Lenny Moore, watched from the State sidelines. Mitchell also scored the first of what would eventually be PSU's career touchdown record on a 39-yard run with only one shoe in the third quarter, and his soph running mate, Harris, recorded his first TD on a 6-yard run a minute later. Navy's new coach Rick Forzano thanked Paterno for taking it easy as the Lions won 45-22 and Paterno complained about the terrible conditions of the field, calling it "a cow pasture." The victory, without anything spectacular from the defense, jumped the Lions ahead of #3 Arkansas and #4 Texas in the AP poll, behind Ohio State, which had not played yet.

State was favored by 14-to-17 points in its first game ever with Colorado at expanded Beaver Stadium on Band Day. With 2,000 additional seats and an enlarged press box, a new record crowd of 51,402 watched and winced when Pittman went out early with a severe ankle sprain. Led by scrambling Bob Anderson, the best rushing quarterback in the nation for two years, the veteran Buffalo offense was hot in the first quarter but two interceptions by Neal Smith and another by Landis stopped any scoring threats. Then in the second quarter, a 65-yard punt by Parsons helped give the Lions field position from where Abbey scored on a 40-yard run. A few minutes later Reitz booted a 22-yard field goal and before the half was over, Harris scored on a 5-yard

Mike Reid was one of the finest defensive tackles in college football history, winning both the Maxwell Award and the Outland Trophy in 1969. He is in the College Football Hall of Fame and is now a well-known country songwriter and singer who has won Grammy Awards for his music.

sweep around left end and PSU led, 17-0. Moments after a 27-yard field goal put Colorado on the board midway through the third quarter, Paul Johnson returned a kickoff 91 yards for a touchdown and the Lions won, 27-3, as the defense held Anderson to 5 net yards rushing and sacked him for losses of 25 yards. "If we hadn't been a great defensive team," Paterno told Don McKee, sport editor of *The Daily Collegian*, "they might have bounced us right out of the stadium." One of those defenders getting the most notice was Reid who was named Lineman of the Week by *Sports Illustrated* after earning the same honor from the AP in the Navy game.

As rumors spread on campus that Dr. John Oswald of Cal-Berkley would succeed Eric Walker as university president, Paterno cautioned the State College Quarterback Club about under estimating the next opponent, Kansas State, now ranked 19th by UPI after two surprising wins. "They're anxious to knock off a top ranked school," Paterno said. A jeering, hostile crowd dressed in purple screamed insults at the Lions when they took the field on a windy, 84 degree day in Manhattan. "They want blood, not victory," a visiting PSU fan said to the *Collegian*'s McKee. It was the largest home crowd in the history of K-State, 37,000, and they cheered loudly as junior Lynn Dickey drove the Jayhawks inside the Lion 25-yard line five times in the first half—once to the 10-yard line—before State's defense took the ball away on two fumbles, two interceptions and a fourth down tackle by Smear. Then as the half was winding down, Mitchell, replacing the injured Pittman, ran 58 yards off tackle and Reitz kicked the PAT to give the Lions a 7-0 lead. With Parson's punting continuing to give K-State poor field position, the Lions stretched the lead to 17-0 in the third quarter. An Onkotz punt return led to Reitz' 33-yard field goal and Burkhart hit on five straight passes in a 9-play, 60-yard march that culminated in a 6-yard TD by Harris.

All-American LB Charlie Zapiec, who was one of Paterno's best players in the era of the two-way player, commiserates with an injured cheerleader.

Midway in the fourth quarter, K-State scored as Dickey avoided a heavy pass rush to guide the Jayhawks 50 yards in 7 plays with Mack Herron getting the touchdown on a 3-yard run. A pass for the 2-point conversion failed and the Lions controlled the ball for almost the rest of the game as Paterno put in the reserves with about seven minutes remaining. The crowd was filing out of the stadium when the Jayhawks got the ball with less than 30 seconds left at their own 37-yard line. In one instant, K-State had a TD as Dickey arched the ball some 56 yards in the air and a wide open receiver, Mike Creed, gathered it in and sped into the end zone. "We figured the No. 2 unit could hold them," Paterno told Doug McDonald of the *Centre Daily Times* after the game. Dickey passed for the 2-point conversion and the home crowd went wild. A tie and even an upset win was not inconceivable. But Surma recovered the onside kick and the Lions won, 17-14, as Mitchell rushed

for 123 yards on 19 carries to lead the sputtering offense. "Are you really Number Two?" some K-State fans taunted as the team left the field. Not after the polls came out as the Lions dropped to #5.

West Virginia had lost 10 straight to State but Coach Jim Carlen believed this was the Mountaineers year. WVU was ranked 17th with a 4-0 record and had the best offense in the country, two of the leading rushers in Bob Gresham and James Braxton, and the second best defense against the rush. With tickets selling for triple their face value of $6, another record crowd of 52,713 Homecoming fans saw State's defense give up 71 yards rushing in the first quarter but just 66 for the rest of the game and hand WVU its first shut out in 40 games, 20-0. The Mountaineer passing wasn't much better with 77 yards on 7-of-19 completions as the Lions picked off four passes, including two by Neal Smith, who broke Junior Powell's career record of 13. Meanwhile, State's offense, with Pittman and Duel back, gained 201 yards rushing and 186 yards passing. Still the game was scoreless until a surprising 66-yard pass from Burkhart to Mitchell set up a 2-yard TD by Harris midway in the second quarter and the defense took over from there. "They were ready for us," Carlen told sportswriters. "The Penn State defense is fantastic," adding, "how can you get ready for a Reid and Smear until you actually play a Reid and Smear?"

The campus was in an uproar the following Wednesday as students and faculty joined in the nationwide War Moratorium day protesting against U.S. involvement in Vietnam. Some 5,000 people jammed the Hetzel Student Union Building, but the team was hard at work practicing for its game at Syracuse. Perhaps no game in the eventual 68-game series with Syracuse had more meaning to Penn State than this one, including the 20-18 loss in 1959, although another one 17 years later was eerily similar. Certainly, this one had more post-game controversy than the other two. And what happened during and after the game defined the season. Both Paterno and Schwartzwalder expected a defensive struggle but unranked Syracuse (3-1) took advantage of three great punt returns by sophomore Greg Allen in the first half to take a shocking 14-0 halftime lead before 42,491 and scouts from the Orange and Sugar Bowls. And the score could have been worse. Allen's initial return of 61 yards helped put the Lions in a hole from the start but Landis blocked a field goal attempt by George Januszkiewicz. However, the Orange scored midway through the first quarter after a 32-yard return of a Burkhart interception set up a 25-yard drive. With Parsons consistently overkicking the punt coverage, Allen ran back another punt 65-yards to the PSU 8 late in the quarter and quarterback Randy Zur scored on a keeper with Januszkiewicz booting his second PAT. Landis blocked another Syracuse field goal attempt later in the second quarter and those two blocks had a psychological affect on Schwartzwalder that helped change the momentum of the game. When Allen ran back another punt 26 yards to the State 29-yard line as time was winding down in the second quarter, it appeared that Syracuse was on the verge of clinching the game. Syracuse moved to the 3-yard line with a fourth-and-less than two when Schwartzwalder made a decision that was similar to one Kansas' Pepper Rodgers had made in the '69 Orange Bowl. Instead of another field goal attempt, he sent Allen on a sweep around left end and Allen fell down as he was about to be tackled. "We couldn't afford to give them the big play," Schwartzwalder told sportswriters after the game. "The big play was when we didn't score that third touchdown." Paterno agreed, saying "If they score, it's all over. That was the turning point."

But it wouldn't start turning around for more than a quarter. Paterno talked quietly to the players during the intermission." I never saw a Penn State football team so bewildered," he said after the game. "I don't know whether we can win," he told his players, as recounted in the book, *"Football My Way.,"* "But I tell you what, I know you have the kind of pride that you're going out there and you're going to give it all you have. I know you won't quit and that's all I want you to prove to the world in the second half." When Landis recovered a fumble by Al Newton at the Syracuse 12 in the third quarter, it looked like the break State needed. Paterno pulled Burkhart for Cooper to try and get some spark but on fourth-and-3 at the 5, the Orange stopped Cooper's scamper a yard short and Syracuse took over. It continued to look bleak until the fourth quarter, when Allen fumbled and Ham recovered at the Syracuse 32. Burkhart went back into the game and moments later, with a fourth-and-6 at the 15, Burkhart tried to hit Pittman with a pass near the left corner. Pittman and linebacker Richard Kokosky went down in a tangle as the pass fell incomplete. But shades of Kansas once again. An official called pass interference on Syracuse and on the next play Mitchell scored. Now came another eerie similarity to the Kansas game. On the 2-point conversion attempt, Burkhart completed a pass in the flat to Harris, starting for the injured Abbey, but the fullback was stopped at the one by safety Tom Meyers. But wait! A holding penalty gave the Lions another chance and this time, as the Syracuse fans in decrepit Archbold Stadium booed, Harris ran around left end and it was now 14-8. Syracuse bobbled the kickoff and barely recovered at their own 14. State's fired up defense forced a punt and it was short, rolling out of bounds at the 39. On the second play, Burkhart faked to Pittman off tackle, handed off to Harris on a counter and Harris ran behind Holuba's block for a touchdown. Reitz kicked the point that put the Lions ahead with seven minutes still remaining and neither team could score again as Neal Smith intercepted again and the Lions rolled to the Orange 12-yard line as the clock expired. "A great football team beat a good football team on a bad day," wrote Phil Musick in the *Pittsburgh Press*, "and everyone agreed—as a character builder—Joe Paterno has few peers."

But on Monday Schwartzwalder stood before the weekly luncheon of the New York City football writers and railed against the officiating and blaming the defeat particularly on "three officials from the state of Pennsylvania where they earn a living." "If it were three or five calls there would be no reason to complain," Schwartzwalder said, according to Gordon White of the *New York Times*. "This is a case of 25 or more bad calls and it was seemingly unending." Schwartzwalder claimed the Syracuse game films did not show the fourth quarter inter-

John Ebersole (83) was an outstanding defensive lineman during State's record 31 game unbeaten streak in the late '60s.

ference or holding calls and he singled out "Number 63," Tom Jackson, saying, as reported by the AP, "their offensive left tackle was tackling and holding our defensive right tackle on practically every play. They continually and flagrantly held and tackled our boys while two of the three holding penalties against us were as legal as I've ever seen." It was true that three of the officials assigned to the game by the ECAC in May lived in the Philadelphia area but none had any ties to Penn State, and the man who made the interference call was from Massachusetts, the home of Al Newton and other Syracuse players. Ed Myer, the referee from Haddonfield, N.J., and a Temple graduate told the *New York Times*, he heard "nothing from any player during the game" except on the interference call, adding "I was late getting off the field after the game and even then heard no complaints." Paterno was livid, particularly when he pointed out that the State left tackle, Jackson, "Number 63," was used to shuttle in plays and had been in the game just 40 percent of the time. "Ben Schwartzwalder owes Tom Jackson an apology," Paterno said, "and if we don't get one I'm going to report him to the Ethics Committee of the American Football Coaches Association." Jackson told the *Daily Collegian*, "I know I wasn't holding because we aren't coached that way. It's pretty ironic because they are coached that way." The ECAC investigated and commissioner Asa Bushnell declared, "There was no evidence of any laxity in officiating."

On Tuesday, the Lions dropped to #8 in the AP poll as Missouri moved into #5 and Kansas State went to #18. The next week, Missouri lost to Colorado, 31-24, and slipped to #14 while the Lions easily beat Ohio University at Beaver Stadium, 42-3, and jumped back to #5, behind OSU, Texas, Tennessee and Arkansas. Kansas State beat Oklahoma for the Big 8 lead was now #12 with Colorado #18. A Cotton Bowl scout had watched the lopsided OU victory as Neal Smith returned a 70-yard interception for one TD and Mike Smith had another on the pickup of a blocked punt by Landis. "We like Penn State," the scout said. He may have but the sportswriters and sportscasters didn't. They continued harping on the Lions "weak" schedule. Despite the comparisons that showed State opponents with a record of 20-14-1, after six games, compared to Ohio State (8-33-1), Texas (16-24) and Arkansas (9-30), the writers and sportscasters snickered. "The talk now," wrote McKee in the *Collegian*, "is that the Lions were lucky to get Kansas State early in the season and couldn't win a rematch." ABC Sportscaster Howard Cosell told his radio and television listeners that Kansas State had been defeated "only by Penn State in a game perhaps they shouldn't have lost." Dan Jenkins of **Sports Illustrated,** an old Texan who believed in Southwest Conference football, wrote that the National Championship should be played between Ohio State's first and second teams. Even in the voting for the Lambert Trophy, some Eastern writers were favoring unbeaten Dartmouth from the Ivy League.

The next week, the Cotton Bowl scout was joined by scouts from several bowls, including the Orange and Sugar, as the Lions overcame stubborn Boston College before a regional CBS-TV audience at Beaver Stadium. Yukica's '68 assistant, Sandusky, was now on Paterno's staff and had scouted BC. But his tips didn't help in the first half as the Eagles came from behind a four point deficit to take a 13-10 halftime lead, which they stretched to 16-10 early in the third quarter. But shortly after Neal Smith's eighth interception of the year, Harris scored on a 19-yard run and the Lions tallied another 21 points in the fourth quarter for a 38-10

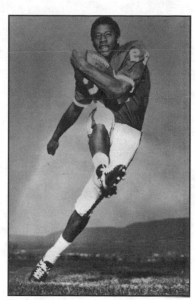

Charlie Pittman was the first Paterno running back to become an All-American in 1969. He was an Academic All-American, too, a distinction also achieved by his son, Tony, a defensive back on the great team of 1994.

win. For only the second time in history, three runners each went over 100 yards in a single game as Harris (136 yards and 3 TDs on 22 carries), Mitchell (120 yards on 13 carries) and Pittman (106 yards on 24 carries) helped State amass 398 yards on the ground. However, Paterno was criticized for allowing reserve QB Cooper to throw the ball late in the game, just as he had in the Ohio University encounter. A sportswriter asked if he was trying to impress the bowl scouts with his offensive fire power. Paterno said he may have been wrong. "'(Mike) was kind of frustrated,'" Paterno told Musick of the **Pittsburgh Press.** "'He asked me, 'Can I throw?' I said, "Do what you want, Mike.'""

State was off the next week but on the eve of the Lions game against woeful Maryland on November 15, the **New York Times** reported that the Cotton and Orange Bowls had State as their top choice. This was bowl weekend when the bowls could officially issue invitations. Often the bowl matches would backfire because teams would get upset and the pairings would lose their appeal. It was a tricky situation and it was about to entrap the Lions. Gordon White of the **Times** reported that a Cotton Bowl representative would stay over in State College to personally offer PSU officials an invitation at noon Monday. But White also reported that Paterno and Tennessee coach Doug Dickey had talked about meeting in the Orange Bowl if both teams stayed unbeaten. "It might be a safe assumption that Tennessee and Penn Stare are pretty much a package deal for here," and Orange Bowl official told White.

On a day when hundreds of thousands of peace marchers demonstrated in Washington at the Lincoln Memorial, some 46,106 turned out at Beaver Stadium in the cold, wind and snow to watch the

Lions demolish Maryland 48-0. Reid scored the first TD when Hull forced a quarterback fumble and Reid picked it up and went 25 yards for the first and only TD of his career. Paul Johnson's 56-yard punt return accounted for another TD and Mitchell dashed 71-yards for a third. Pittman had three TDs to break Lenny Moore's career record of 25. After the game, the team held a closed door meeting to discuss their bowl options but they didn't vote until Sunday night.

The Cotton, Orange and Sugar had all made offers. In his book, "**Football My Way**," Paterno says he talked privately with some of the Black players—Pittman, Mitchell and Harris—about their choice since "this was at the peak of the new civil rights awareness" and "they didn't want to go to Dallas" but would go if their teammates did. In discussing the alternatives, most of the veteran players did not believe they would accomplish anything by playing either Texas or Arkansas in the Cotton Bowl. Since they didn't have a shot at #1 Ohio State, why not return to Miami and have some fun again, they reasoned. Everyone in the country said there was no way OSU was going to lose to twice-beaten Michigan the next week, so a National Championship was not possible.

Texas and Arkansas were scheduled to meet December 4 and Paterno admitted Texas coach Darrell Royal asked him to "hold out for the Cotton Bowl." When the players voted on Sunday night, they "overwhelmingly" chose the Orange Bowl even though they didn't know who the opponent would be. Tennessee had been beaten that weekend and the **Miami Herald** had speculated that the other team might be Notre Dame, which had just changed its policy on post-season games and would be going to its first bowl game since the 1925 Rose Bowl. On Monday, November 17, the Orange Bowl announced a game between Penn State and Missouri, the Big Eight Conference champ, and the Cotton Bowl said Notre Dame would play the Texas-Arkansas winner.

Penn State was chastised immediately, even by many of their own, disappointed fans. "A victory over Texas or Arkansas would have been undeniable proof that Penn State wasn't indulging in hollow boasting when it said that the Lions could play on the same field as any other team...," wrote McKee in the **Collegian** on November 19. "No one anywhere else in the country will believe it. The public's feeling now is that State is scared of Texas or Arkansas..." Defending the decision in the **"Football Letter,"** Riley called the **Collegian** reporters "pipsqueaks."

The criticism intensified the following week after Michigan upset Ohio State at Ann Arbor, 24-12, and the Lions were sluggish in beating Pitt, 27-7. A 71-yard punt return by Onkotz with two minutes left in the third quarter and the score tied, 7-7, set up a 4-yard Pittman TD that was the turning point of the game at Pitt Stadium. Pittman scored again in the fourth quarter as he (104 yards) and Harris (107 yards) became the seventh duo in PSU history to get over 100 yards in a game. "I wish we were playing Texas," Harris said after the game. The Lions still had to play North Carolina State in what was the second game of a nationally televised doubleheader that followed the traditional Army-Navy game on ABC. Even before the game at Raleigh, four players were named All-Americans—Reid, Onkotz, Pittman and Neal Smith—the most ever in one year for the Nittany Lions. Reid also had been honored with the Outland Trophy as the country's best interior lineman and finished fifth in the Heisman Trophy balloting, highest for any lineman that year. Later he would win the Maxwell Club trophy as

The great 11-0 team from 1969 did not win the National Championship in part due to politics played by President Richard Nixon .

the outstanding player in college football. The Lion defense led by Reid, Onkotz and Smith held NC State to 50 net yards while recovering two fumbles and intercepting three passes—one by Smith for a PSU one season record of 10— to give the Lions their 21st straight win, 33-8. Pittman scored two more TDs—one on Burkhart's first TD pass of the year—stretching his career TD record to 31, and in the process breaking Pete Mauthe's 67-year-old career scoring record with 186 points.

But some luster was taken off the Lions' national televised performance by ABC. Throughout the game, ABC sportscasters promoted the following Saturday's Texas-Arkansas game "for the National Championship." When Paterno was interviewed during the telecast he said a championship should be won on the playing field and for the first time he pushed publicly for a playoff. After the game, several players complained about the criticism of their bowl choice. Kates said some players had received letters saying the team was second rate, and "It bothers the hell out of me." Smear told the *Collegian's* McKee: "A lot of us have really been disappointed in the reaction to our decision. We've done a tough job for three years and it hurts when people question our guts."

But the biggest insult was yet to come. One of the ABC sportscasters hyping the Texas-Arkansas game was Bud Wilkinson, the former Oklahoma coach who also was an advisor on physical fitness to the President of the United States, Richard Nixon. Nixon thought of himself as the "nation's number one sports fan." Wilkinson convinced Nixon it would be a political asset to attend the game in Austin as a climax to the 100th anniversary of college football and to present a National Championship Presidential "trophy" to the winner in the locker room. After Texas had won 15-14 on a daring 2-point conversion, Nixon delivered his championship plaque to Coach Royal in a noisy Longhorn dressing room and a photograph of the presentation was printed in the nation's newspapers the next day. Pennsylvania politicians had been quick to react, especially Republican Governor Ray Shafer, a diehard fan who had attended most home and away PSU games. During the network presentation, Nixon said he intended to honor Penn State with a plaque for having the longest winning streak in college football. Paterno exploded and issued a statement rejecting the award, saying "it would seem to me to be a waste of his very valuable time to present Penn State with a plaque for something it already indisputably owns..." The following Tuesday in New York City , while accepting a gold medal for his contributions to college football, President Nixon told his audience "I think Penn State is among those who should be considered for the Number one spot," and he thought about suggesting a possible playoff game after the bowl games but decided to skip it because "I was in deep enough already." When Paterno accepted the Lambert Trophy at a luncheon in New York the following day, he graciously read

a telegram from the President which said, "I join with football fans all across the nation in acknowledging the great achievement represented by the award you received today."

THE 1970 ORANGE BOWL
Jan. 1, 1970
Penn State 10, Missouri 3
Most Valuable Back: Chuck Burkhart
Most Valuable Lineman: Mike Reid

With the controversy about Number One still simmering, Paterno prepared his team for its New Year's Night game against Missouri. In adhering to his philosophy that bowl games "should be a reward and fun," Paterno persuaded university president Walker, new athletic director Ed Czekaj, and retiring athletic department dean McCoy to allow the team to be home for the Christmas holidays by making two trips to Florida. It was an expensive deal but a special reward to the seniors who had not been home for Christmas for three years. So, the Lions spent more than a week before Christmas in Fort Lauderdale before breaking off practice December 23 and reassembling in Miami December 26. Everything went smoothly except for an early evening altercation Burkhart—of all players—had in Fort Lauderdale with a young man from New York city who picked a fight with the Lion QB outside a local hamburger spot. Both Burkhart and his assailant were arrested and to restrain the publicity, Burkhart forfeited his bail and left town. One sportswriter critical of Burkhart's passing wrote that the quarterback had thrown a punch and missed by 10 yards. "Show them your boxing stance, Chuck," Paterno later joked at an Orange Bowl news conference.

In Miami, Paterno closed his practices again and, as was now customary for bowl games, added something new. Missouri coach Devine later said he knew Paterno was not going to change his defense and he guessed State might pass more—and he was right. Paterno and his assistants didn't believe the Lions could run inside on the underrated Missouri defense so he opened up the passing. Paterno also tinkered with the defense, which had allowed just 87 points in 10 games. He shifted from a man-to-man pass defense to a zone and worked on the techniques and formations that would stop Missouri's high scoring offensive. The Tigers offense had averaged 450 yards and 36 points per game in its nine wins and one loss. Their best running back, Joe Moore, had rushed for more than 1,300 yards and receiver Mel Gray had caught 26 passes for 705 yards. Quarterback Terry McMillan was an excellent passer and a good runner. Kansas State Coach Vince Gibson, who was in Miami for the game, told sportswriters it should be a close game. "Missouri can hurt you on the big play," he said. "Penn

State is better defensively but Missouri has the edge on offense." The pregame news conferences and luncheon appearances with Paterno and Devine were not as lively as the ones the year before with loquacious Pepper Rodgers but the atmosphere was never uptight. After being given an Orange Bowl sports jacket at the annual Orange Bowl Kickoff Luncheon, Paterno joked that he was thinking of sending his coat "up to the White House." Paterno also said, "I feel the team that wins (the Orange Bowl) has earned the right to be considered for Number One in the nation." Devine told the gathering, "I'd rather lose to a champion any day than some rinky-dink team."

At a spirited pep rally on New Year's morning in the ballroom of a Miami Beach hotel, Paterno introduced and joked with the new university president, John Oswald. In his best Italian, Oswald said, "I Giovanni Oswaldo, wish you, Giuseppe Paterno, and your team the greatest luck tonight. I know you will win. Numero Uno!" The fans went wild. Then, as Riley reported in his *"Football Letter,"* Governor Shafer told the players, "You don't have to prove you're Number One to the newspapers, the fans, or even to the President. Just go out there and win this game for yourselves."

As if the insults by the sportswriters were not enough, the oddsmakers also added to the indignity by making the sixth-ranked Tigers a two-point favorite. The first time State had the ball, Burkhart came out in a shotgun formation and threw a pass. "That surprised me," Devine later told Dick Wade of the *Kansas City Star*. Burkhart would go on to throw more passes against Missouri than he had against any opponent during the regular season and hit on 11 of 26 for 18 yards and the game's only touchdown. He would have one meaningless interception and after running Paterno's conservative game plan to conclusion he would be named the game's Most Valuable Back. But in the end, the crowd of 77,282 and the TV audience knew this game belonged—as it should have—to the Penn State defense. Midway through the first quarter, Burkhart's passing and the running of Pittman and Harris took State on a drive from the PSU 20 to the Missou 16 before the Tiger defense stiffened and the Lions settled for a 29-yard field goal by Reitz with 3:44 left in the quarter. Moore fumbled the kickoff when belted by Reid and Mike Smith recovered at the Missou 28. Burkhart struck immediately for a touchdown, passing to Mitchell on the left sideline at the 24. Mitchell eluded one defender, picked up a block and dashed into the end zone. Reitz' boot made it 10-0. Now, the Lions "bend-but-don't-break" defense took over and the next four times the Tigers had possession, they were stopped on interceptions inside State territory by Hull, Landis and Onkotz and a fumble recovery by Ebersole. The Ebersole play was spectacular as Missouri had moved from State's 43 to the 10 when, on third down, Ebersole caught Gray in the backfield on a flanker reverse, stripped the ball away and recovered the fumble at the Lion 22. Midway in the second quarter the Tigers went on a long drive from their own 8-yard line to the State 7. But after Reid tackled Moore for a 10-yard loss and a pass into the end zone failed, Missouri kicked a field goal from the 23 and the half ended, 10-3.

The second half was one of missed opportunities for State's offense and almost cost the game. Neal Smith intercepted another McMillan pass on Missouri's second possession of the third quarter and picked off another one later in the half but both times the Lions gave up the ball. Midway through the third quarter, Onkotz intercepted inside the Missouri 30-yard line but on third-and-2 at the 21 Burkhart's pass to Pete Johnson was incomplete. Then, near the end of the third

quarter, State took possession on its own 27 and with Burkhart throwing a 56-yard bomb to Pete Johnson, the Lions moved for a first down at the Missouri 7. A pair of offside penalties and a sack momentarily stopped the Lions but a screen pass to Mitchell and a run by Pittman up the middle put the ball at the one with a fourth down. Remembering Rogers' decision a year ago and Schwartzwalder's call in October, Paterno sent in Reitz to try a chip-shot field goal from about the 10. The snap and hold (by Ramich) were good but Reitz kicked the ball off the side of his foot and it was low and wide. "A field goal wins it," Paterno, told the *Press*'s Musick later.

Missouri, which could not get past the State 46 in the third quarter, finally caught a break early in the fourth when a partially blocked punt put the ball on the PSU 20. But penalties for offside and offensive pass interference plus State's ferocious pass rush pushed the Tigers back to the 36 and a field goal attempt from the 42 was short. The teams battled at midfield for nearly the rest of the game but as a heavy rain fell in the closing minutes, Missouri, with reserve QB Chuck Roper in for McMillan, moved from its own 42-yard line for a first down at the State 14 with 1:42 remaining. As the crowd roared and Paterno thought about the defense he might need against a 2-point conversion, State's defense thwarted Roper's first two pass attempts and third down Roper tried to hit Gray in the end zone. But Landis, who had shut down Gray all night despite a sore knee, made the final big play of the game by intercepting the ball at the 2 and reaching the State 42 before being tackled. Burkhart ran out the clock and the Lions were now unbeaten in 30 straight games, tying the school record set from 1920-1922. The State defense also had set an Orange Bowl record for interceptions with seven and with Reid—named the outstanding defensive player of the game—and Smear leading the way on the pass rush the Lions had held Missouri to 6 completions in 28 attempts. Missouri netted 175 yards rushing but Moore had just 36 yards on 15 carries. Pittman led the Lions with 90 yards rushing. Burkhart had lost 79 yards trying to pass and the Lions net rushing was just 60 yards.

In the dressing room, the happy players threw everyone into the showers, including Governor Shafer and some sportswriters. "A couple more games and we'll get the Big 8 title," Burkhart crowed. "It was a miracle," shouted Landis about his game-ending interception. "Penn State's Joe Paterno described it best," wrote Joe McGuff of the *Kansas City Star*, "when he said: 'You won't see college teams play better defense. It was a great defensive effort.'" After viewing the films, Devine agreed, saying State had "the best defensive team I've seen in college football." Devine told the *Star* shortly after the game that his Tigers made too many mistakes, but added "That's an awfully good team we played...This easily may be the best team in the country...If I voted, I might make it a two-way tie for first but I sure wouldn't put Penn State No. 2."

Earlier in the day Texas had come from behind late in the fourth quarter at the Cotton Bowl to beat Joe Theismann and Notre Dame, 21-17, and clinched the National Championship " I don't know if we're No. 1," Paterno said in the Lions locker room, "But I'm up to my ears in the polls. We have as much right as anybody else to be No. 1. I can't sit back and let Richard Nixon or anyone else say someone else is No. 1. I've got to stick up for my kids." In the final AP poll, Texas received 910 points with 36 first place votes and to State's 822 points and 7 for first place. Notre Dame was fifth behind USC and Ohio State and Missouri was sixth.

Paterno knew it was nearly impossible to have another unbeaten season in 1970. He was losing most of his defense and his winning quarterback. But he believed he had the players with the poise and pride to continue building on this new winning tradition. What he didn't realize in that winter was that it would take another quarterback from McKees Rocks to keep it going.

Season Record 11-0
Record to Date 452-229-40
Winning percentage .655

"The First Quarterback Controversy"

The streak had come to an end on September 26 in the sunshine and beauty of the Rocky Mountains as Colorado had blasted the Lions 41-13 on national television. It had been rocky for Paterno and his team ever since, and now cursed Syracuse had just embarrassed State on its home field before a disappointed and perturbed Homecoming crowd. After five games, the Lions were 2-3 and some disgruntled fans, spoiled already by three years of success, were questioning the coach's decisions and strategy. Paterno bristled as he ran off the Beaver Stadium field, trying not to think about more of those venomous and sometimes racist phone calls to his home and office.

Some of the fan complaints were typical of the type all coaches get when they are losing and few of the grumblers gave their names. But the worst were the mostly anonymous telephone calls and unsigned letters that denounced Paterno for choosing a young black man to be his quarterback. Mike Cooper, the senior from Harrisburg who had backed up Burkhart for two years, had earned the starting position after beating out junior Parsons and sophomore John Hufnagel in the preseason. Because this was a time of racial unrest on the nation's campuses, many outsiders figured Paterno started Cooper only because of his race. State did not have many blacks on the team, although the star running backs, Mitchell and Harris, also were black. But at many colleges, black players were revolting against their white coaches. Syracuse was in special turmoil and nine players, most of them starters including the team's two leading rushers, quit the team and were expelled from school before the beginning of the season.

Cooper was a good passer and ball handler and a decent runner. Paterno says he also was smart and enthusiastic. In the spring,

Paterno's first "Quarterback Controversy" in 1970 involved (left to right) Bob Parsons, John Hufnagel and Mike Cooper.

Paterno had decided to open up his offense and do more passing. He also planned to have the quarterback call his own plays. During practice, Parsons, bigger and stronger and a better runner than Cooper, appeared to be a great passer with a quick release, but when he went into game type situations, he was mediocre and erratic. Hufnagel never entered the mix, basically because of his inexperience but he was a good runner and Paterno began working him out at defensive halfback. Of course, Paterno realized a black quarterback would be controversial and he could have avoided the issue by alternating Cooper and Parsons. But he knew that would not have been fair to Cooper nor true to himself—a liberal on racial issues and a one-quarterback coach on the field. "I could tell I was bound to lose," he recalled later in his book, *"Paterno: By the Book,"* "If I picked Cooper, it was because he was black. If I picked Parsons, it was because Cooper was black."

Paterno believed Cooper was better suited to operate the new offensive formation, which had the left halfback moving far outside to a flanker slot. He figured his team would have to score more this year because his new defense would be drastically different because of the departure of so many starters. He had to rebuild the entire front line since he had shifted Hull back to the "Hero" linebacker position. Three sophomores would break into the front four, with Bruce Bannon of Rockaway, NJ at left end, Jim Heller of Pottsville at right tackle and Doug Allen of Corning, NY, sharing left tackle with junior Frank Ahrenhold. Senior Steve Prue would be at right end. Ham, the co-captain, was back at outside linebacker and Paterno moved his starting All-East offensive guard, Zapiec, to an inside linebacker to pair with non-lettering junior Gary Gray. But Zapiec would not play after the first game because of an appendectomy and another sophomore, John Skorupan of Beaver, would get promoted. Mike Smith went back to his old halfback spot, alongside Landis, with senior Terry Stump at safety. "(But) don't let anyone think we're going to play patsy defense," Paterno told Riley for the *"Football Letter"* during the preseason.

With veterans Mitchell and Ramich returning at right half and Harris and Ganter at fullback, Paterno needed a sure-handed pass catcher at flanker and he believed he had found one in sophomore speedster Gary Hayman of Newark, Del. But Hayman broke his ankle about 10 days before the season opener against Navy and veteran Deuel became the starter again. Four starters were back in the offensive line with co-captain Koegel at center and Holuba, Surma and Edmonds, the split end, on the right side. They were joined by juniors Bob Knechtel and Dave Joyner (of State College) and senior Jim McCord at tight end. Parsons would punt again, while Reitz would share placekicking with offensive lineman John Hull. Paterno also had two changes in his coaching staff. Earl Bruce retired after more than 20 years at State, and Johnny Chuckran, the Lions' star running back during World War II (see 1944), replaced him. Dan Radakovich left and Sandusky moved up to coach linebackers.

The sportswriters and coaches who voted in the polls evaluated Paterno's team and gave it another Top 10 ranking in the pre-season, with both the AP & UPI voting the Lions at #7. "Penn State lost 11 starters, including two first team All-Americans from the magnificent defensive unit," said the AP, "but coach Joe Paterno always comes up roses."

State was favored over Navy, which had already beaten Colgate, but Middies coach Forzano tried to use a little psychology by reminding his players that it was another Navy team in 1922 that had stopped the 30-game school un-beaten record that this PSU squad was trying to break. It didn't matter. Cooper made Paterno's quarterback decision look good on a balmy Saturday afternoon at Beaver Stadium as he led the Lions to a 55-7 pasting of Navy and a new record. After misfiring with an interception near the end zone in the first quarter, Cooper threw touchdown passes of 21 and 27 yards to Edmonds and ran one-yard for another TD as State built up a 35-0 early third quarter lead and Paterno cleared the bench. Mitchell ran for 144 yards on 19 carries, including a 53-yard TD run, and Smith ran back a punt 50 yards for another TD as Parsons and Hufnagel both saw action at QB in the second half. "I've just been waiting for my chance and when it came everything just naturally fell into place," Cooper told Dan Donovan, sports editor of the *Daily Collegian*. The revised defense also was complimented as the Lions moved up to #4 in the AP rankings. The game was the first of five home games to be televised on a delayed basis at 11 p.m. to six Pennsylvania stations in the central

All-American LB Jack Ham, seen here chasing the Syracuse QB, is the only Penn State player to be in both the College and Professional Football Halls of Fame. In 1990 he was honored by the University as a Distinguished Alumnus.

went back to pass, saw Edmonds and Mitchell wide open in the same vicinity and threw. For some reason, the ball sailed on him and went right to Colorado defensive back Pat Murphy at about the 40-yard line. In five plays, the Buffaloes had a touchdown on a one-yard dive by junior college transfer John Tarver but the first quarter nightmare was just beginning for Cooper and the Lions. A few minutes later, a fumbled handoff near midfield led to a 35-yard field goal by Dave Haney and before the quarter was over Cooper was intercepted again at the PSU 41 and Haney came in to boot a 48-yard field goal to make the score, 13-0.

In the second quarter, Colorado made its first mistake, losing a fumble at its 17. Three plays later Harris ran in from the 6 on a fake pitchout and Reitz's PAT narrowed the score to 13-7. But the Buffaloes got the next break when Stump was called for interference at the Colorado 45, nullifying an interception by Ham—who would have an outstanding day with 15 unassisted tackles and two fumble recoveries. The home team moved for a first down at the PSU 4 and after State's defense grudgingly gave up three yards on three downs, Colorado scored another TD and with the PAT led 20-7. But State wasn't through. The Lions drove from the Colorado 42 to the 12 with 30 seconds remaining in the half before two Cooper passes into the end zone failed and Reitz missed a field goal from the 20. Another junior college transfer named Cliff Branch, who had tied the world record in the 60-yard sprint over the winter, virtually clinched the game for the Buffaloes when he returned the second half kickoff 97 yards for a touchdown. State drove 71 yards after the kick-off to reach the Colorado 2 but on fourth down Cooper was tackled on

and eastern part of the state with the team's number one fan, Governor Shafer, helping with the commentary.

The ease and manner of the victory over what was really a bad football team—Navy beat an equally hapless Army squad and finished 2-9—gave the Lions a false sense of confidence when they traveled to Boulder the following week. But Colorado, now #18 after a victory over Indiana, had been pointing to State since the summer to salvage some respect for the Big 8, which had now lost five straight games in two years to State. Even before the players had gone to bed the night before, State had a bad omen. Zapiec was taken to a Denver hospital with appendicitis and by 2 a.m. he was in the operating room. The second omen—and one that set the mood for the next few weeks—came on the first play from scrimmage after the Lions won the toss and elected to receive. As a howling crowd of 42,850 at Folsom Stadium and a national ABC-TV audience watched dumbfounded, Cooper

a keeper. A few minutes later, State fumbled at its own 41 and the Buffaloes went in for another TD. In the final quarter, Landis recovered a Colorado fumble at the Buffaloes 45 and Parsons, now at quarter-back, passed the Lions downfield for a TD on a 2-yard pass to Edmonds. Colorado scored again and ran off the field celebrating a solid 41-13 victory. "I didn't do a very good job today," Paterno told sportswriters. "We were outcoached all around." State has never played Colorado again.

"In our locker room, we heard something that for some of our kids was a strange and shocking experience; the roar of celebration from the other team's room," Paterno wrote in *"Paterno: By The Book."* "I hated the feeling, too... 'Listen to them,' I said in a little locker-room speech I still remember. "Let them have their glory. We've had our share.'" Then Paterno did something few coaches would ever do in a similar situation. He went over to the Colorado dressing room and congratulated Eddie Crowder and his players. They couldn't believe it. "How can that man smile after what has happened to him," a player said to Gordon White of the *New York Times*. When the defeated Lions arrived back in State College at 3:30 a.m. Sunday, they were shocked by the 2,000 or so cheering students and townspeople who had been waiting for an hour in the rain in front of Rec Hall. After the crowd shouted, "You're Number One With Us," Paterno told them, "I've been at Penn State for 20 years and I have never been prouder of a team than I am at this moment and I have never been prouder of the student body than I am at this moment."

The telephone calls to Paterno's home started the next day and his wife, Sue, answered them because Joe was with his assistants getting ready for the next game at Wisconsin. "People called me all day, telling me how to run the team," she recalled years later in *"Football, My Way."* "They didn't give their names, of course, but I recognized some fair-weather fans. They charged Joe with misguiding the team..." Over the next few weeks, the calls got more abusive and racist as the team continued to skid and Cooper, who was getting his share of bigoted telephone calls and hate mail, floundered.

Cooper threw three interceptions at Wisconsin (0-1-1) and two of them led to 10 points but he wasn't the only one who had problems as the #16 Lions lost two straight for the first time in four years, 29-16, and dropped out of the Top 20. Parsons, playing most of the second half, also had an interception and Mitchell and Harris had fumbles that set up Wisconsin scores but it was the Lions erratic pass defense that lost the game as junior Neil Graff threw a 68-yard TD in the first quarter and TD passes of 27 and 52 yards in the fourth quarter when the Badgers broke a 16-all deadlock to win. Unbelievably, the Lion defense had sacked Graff and his substitute 16 times for 111 yards and had held 5-foot-6 sophomore Rufus "Roadrunner" Ferguson and his fellow rushers to a minus 22 yards in rushing but still lost. After the game, Paterno told sportswriters the Lions and coaches lost their poise. "The Penn State football, unlike many advertised products, is not getting better with age," wrote Doug McDonald in the *Centre Daily Times*.

Rumors of a shake-up in the backfield followed the team all the way to kickoff at Boston College. During practice that week, Cooper and Parsons told the *Collegian* they didn't know who would start at quarterback and Paterno refused to talk about it. "We're going to see how people react to different situations," Paterno said. "I've made no decisions about personnel." One decision he had made was to call the plays again, which he had done at Wisconsin. BC was 3-0 and some Boston writers seemed to be as confident as Yukica's players that this was the Eagles' year to be the best team in the East. But the State defense took control by intercepting seven passes and won, 28-3, after breaking it open in the third quarter when Gray blocked a punt at the Eagle 47 and Ham ran it in from the 42 for the first TD of his high school or college career. "That really was the ball game," wrote Jerry Nason in the *Boston Globe*, "and you spell it D-E-F-E-N-S-E." Cooper started but Paterno used more players on offense, interchanging Cooper and Parsons throughout the game and utilizing Hufnagel for more than mop-up duties. Ramich, a virtual unknown who had never carried the ball more than five times in a game or gained more than 10 yards, led all rushers with 60 yards on 14 carries while splitting tailback time with Mitchell, who had 40 yards before suffering an ankle injury.

The end of Mike Cooper's career as the Nittany Lions quarterback came when State returned to Beaver Stadium for the first time

Coach Paterno and his 1970 co-captains, Warren Koegel (center) and All-American Jack Ham, pose with the Lambert Trophy before the season. Dartmouth won the trophy in '70 and Paterno touched off a controversy by suggesting a post season charity game against Dartmouth.

in a month to play old rival Syracuse in the annual Homecoming rite. The Orange had beaten Maryland the previous week to stop a three-game losing slide and were a 7-point underdog after losing their starting quarterback, Randy Zur. Mitchell also was out for PSU and Ramich made his first ever start. Cooper started again but the offense sputtered in the first quarter as Syracuse took a 3-0 lead and Paterno inserted Parsons. Parsons threw three interceptions in the second quarter and one led to a 50-yard drive and a 7-yard touchdown by sophomore fullback Marty Januszkiewicz. With less than a minute remaining in the half, Tom Myers' punt return set up a 1-yard plunge by Januszkiewicz and Syracuse led at the half 17-0. Although Cooper returned in the third quarter and moved the offense, he overthrew one receiver in the end zone and another probable TD was dropped in the end zone by Edmonds. Three times the Lions were inside the Syracuse 10 in the second half but couldn't capitalize. Nor could State take advantage of the five fumbles the Orange gave up in the game. In the end, it was the inept Lion offense, including missed field goals by Reitz, and Syracuse's running attack, particularly in the first half, that provided the edge. The Orange recorded just one first down in the second half but with Januszkiewicz gaining a total of 159 yards on 36 carries, the visitors pounded out a 24-7 victory. "We stunk," Edmonds told the *Collegian's* Donovan, who wrote that the offense "needs a leader, be he a quarterback or running back or lineman and a leader could be the difference between winning and losing."

During practice that week for Army at West Point, Paterno made a change at quarterback and found his leader. It wasn't difficult. He was satisfied with the progress of his defense, so he decided to simplify his offense. He switched back to power running and the quarterback option with a more controlled passing attack. He moved the flanker back into the old wingback slot and began utilizing two tight ends. He also replaced his placekicker. "We had to get back to being a precise team again," he recalled in *"Football My Way."* "We just went back to doing nothing more than we could handle." Paterno believed the best quarterback to handle the revised offense was Hufnagel, the 19-year-old kid from the same Montour High School as Burkhart, who also had never lost a scholastic game he started.

Army had lost five straight after an opening season win over Holy Cross but the conquerors included three of the best teams in the country—Nebraska, Tennessee and Notre Dame. The Cadets were surprised by the Lions' revised running offense, which used about a half dozen plays featuring the option sweep and the wingback reverse. To help steady his sophomore quarterback in the hostile Michie Stadium atmosphere and the added pressure of regional television, Paterno started a senior backfield of Ramich, Ganter and Duel. "I really thought I had beaten out Franco at the time," Ganter recalled three decades later. "It makes me laugh to think about it now." The defining play in this defining moment of the season came about two minutes into the game as Hufnagel was leading the Lions on an opening drive from the PSU 27-yard line off the Double Wing formation. On the 10th play at the Army 32, Hufnagel ran an option left, kept the ball himself and ran into the end zone. John Hull's PAT made it 7-0 and the Lions were off to a 38-14 victory. "In that four-minute drive, Hufnagel prove his worth," wrote Gordon White in the *New York Times*. "He didn't appear at all bothered by the noisy and chanting cadets...Hufnagel may be the find of the midseason in college football this year." Hufnagel ran five more times for 66 yards and another TD and led State on touchdown marches of 69 and 77 yards and another drive that resulted in a Hull field goal. State's defense intercepted three passes and recovered two fumbles while only Lion turnover was a fumbled punt return. Hufnagel's center, Koegel, got the game ball but the sophomore captured the headlines. "Hufnagel is a take-charge player...," Riley wrote in the "*Football Letter*," "His presence seemed to give a lift to the team, igniting the spark that's been missing so far."

West Virginia, with the nation's sixth best rushing offense, a defense that held four opponents under 10 points and a 5-2 record under new coach Bobby Bowden, figured to be a better test for Hufnagel. However, State's punt teams made it easy for Hufnagel by setting up two touchdowns in the first six minutes on Mike Smith's 75-yard punt return and Gary Hull's blocked kick and Prue's recovery. Hufnagel scored one TD on an 8-yard option, threw a 42-yard TD to Edmonds and let the other backs and the defense do the rest in a 38-14 victory. The offense netted 452 yards running and passing and the defense held WVU to 30 yards net rushing while intercepting three passes and recovering a fumble.

Hufnagel never lost his poise in the final three games as Paterno continued to start his senior running backs, Ramich and Ganter, before sending in his reserve "shock" tandem of Mitchell and Harris. Mitchell scored two touchdowns and ran for 87 yards on 10 carries and Duel scored two more as the Lions easily defeated oft-beaten Maryland (1-7), 34-0 at College Park. The following week, the Lions moved back into the Top 20 as Mitchell scored three TDs and rushed for 112 yards on 18 carries while Harris had 133 yards and one TD on 19 carries in a 32-22 win over an inspired Ohio University team at Beaver Stadium. Hufnagel's running and passing were steady in both games, totaling 71 rushing yards on 14 option runs and hitting on 12-of-26 passes for 149 yards with just one interception. In the OU game, Mike Smith set a one-game interception record that is still the school record with four, including a 28-yard return for State's first TD.

Before the Pitt game, the Peach and Liberty bowls had expressed interest in the Lions with the Liberty Bowl, playing off the Cotton Bowl controversy of '69, talking about a match-up between the Lions and the loser of the Texas-Arkansas game. Pitt had its best team since the once-beaten squad of 1963 but Carl DePasqua's Panthers were no match for Hufnagel and the Lions in the final game of the year at Beaver Stadium on November 21. Ramich scored in the first 23 seconds after Landis recovered a fumble on Pitt's first scrimmage play and it was over by halftime when the score was 35-9. The final was 35-14 as Mitchell rushed for 111 yards on 14 carries and Harris scored three touchdowns while rushing for 91 yards. Hufnagel completed his longest pass of the year of 55 yards to set up one TD but for the first time all season he had minus yardage (9 yards) on eight carries.

Representatives of the Peach Bowl waited outside the Penn State locker room to offer an invitation to their game in Atlanta December 30 but inside the players voted to reject any bowl bid. "We finished 7-3 and we're willing to live through history with that record," Jack Ham told the *Collegian's* Donovan. "We're tired, really tired." Paterno surprised sportswriters by trying to promote a charity game in New York's Shea Stadium two weeks later against unbeaten Dartmouth, the Ivy League champion and winner of the Lambert Trophy. "It would be a great thing for eastern football," Paterno said, as Roy McHugh of the *Pittsburgh Press* reported. Paterno said he wanted the game to benefit the families of football players and coaches from Marshall and Wichita who were killed in plane crashes. Some sportswriters accused Paterno of "grandstanding" because he knew of the Ivy League's long time policy against post-season games. "I think Penn State is just trying to salvage the Lambert Trophy," Dartmouth's athletic director, Seaver Peters, told the *New York Times*. Dartmouth coach Bob Blackman, who would take the coaching job at Illinois a few weeks later, belittled Paterno and Syracuse officials also joined in by reminding everyone that the Orange buried the haughty Lions. Paterno later claimed his proposal was "kind of tongue-in-cheek" but few writers believed him.

Paterno and his players stayed home for Christmas and New Years. The last month blitz had given State a #18 ranking by AP and #19 by UPI. Ham was named to just about every All-American team and moved on to the Pittsburgh Steelers and, eventually, the Pro Football Hall of Fame. Mike Cooper went back to Harrisburg, a bitter but proud young man who felt he was never given a fair chance. Years later, Paterno would agree that maybe Cooper was right. But the fact remained that young Hufnagel was a natural leader and in 1971, he would lead the Lions to the turning point game they should have played two years earlier—a Cotton Bowl match with Texas.

Season Record 7-3
Record to Date 459-232-40
Winning percentage .655

"Deep in the Heart of Texas"

If there is one game in the Paterno era that any of his 31 teams "had" to win, it was the 1972 Cotton Bowl game against Texas. This was the game that finally gave Paterno's Nittany Lions the respect and prestige they had sought since the '69 Orange Bowl victory over

Kansas. The 300 plus victories and five undefeated seasons and two National Championships that went before or came later were the fruition of what happened in Dallas on January 1, 1972.

Now, after three decades, one can point to other "must win" games that have been crucial to State's rise to the pinnacle of college football and the expansion of the Paterno legend. But if the Lions had lost this one, it would have set the program back for years and, perhaps, caused Paterno to accept one of those lucrative early offers from professional football and leave Penn State.

Offensive tackle Dave Joyner, now a well-known orthopedic surgeon, was the first Paterno offensive lineman selected All-American in 1971. In 1997, he won the NCAA Silver Anniversary Award honoring former athletes who have distinguished themselves in their professions.

Yet the consequential game and its definitive result might never have occurred, if not for another unusual series of events that involved Texas Christian, Notre Dame and a demoralizing season ending loss at Tennessee.

Paterno knew he had a good team after what was the best spring practice since he became the head coach. And although he wouldn't admit it, he also had a favorable schedule that included only two teams in the preseason Top 20—Syracuse and Tennessee—and several mediocre Eastern rivals. For the first time since 1962, the Lions would be playing the three military academies and one of those games against the Air Force at Beaver Stadium would help define the regular season. Most sportswriters evaluating it all also tabbed the Lions as a Top 20 team, with the AP ranking the Lions #16, Syracuse #19 and Tennessee #7. Texas was #3 behind defending National Champ Nebraska and Notre Dame.

Paterno had used the spring to rebuild an offensive line that could stimulate an attack structured around the running of Mitchell and Harris, whom Paterno called "the two best backs I've had at Penn State." Joyner, the co-captain at right tackle, and Knechtel at right guard were the only starters back from '70. Senior center Mike Botts won the Worrell Award as the most improved player during spring practice and junior lettermen Carl Schaukowitch at guard and Craig Lyle at tackle became the other starters with junior Bob Rickenbach being the prime reserve at both left tackle and tight end. Junior John Skarzynski took over the split end position and halfway through spring practice Paterno surprised sportswriters by switching Parsons from quarterback to starting tight end. That made a highly-recruited sophomore from Havertown, Steve Joachim, the backup quarterback to Hufnagel. "He's one of the best sophomore quarterbacks we've had here," Paterno said. Senior Glen Cole moved into the wingback slot. Paterno also was high on sophomore linemen Charlie Getty, Mark Markovich and Phil LaPorta and two running backs who had been outstanding on the freshman team, a 6-foot-1, 205-pound tailback from Upper Darby named John Cappelletti and a 6-foot-2, 202-pound fullback from Bethlehem named Tom Donchez.

However, in the preseason, Paterno moved Cappelletti to defensive halfback because of his concern over the Lions secondary. Cappelletti, who would run back punts and kickoffs, and another sophomore, Ed O'Neil of Warren, would be the principal reserves in a secondary that included juniors Greg and Steve Davis and sophomore Buddy Ellis. Paterno believed his linebacking crew was the strength of the defense with Skorupan and Gray returning as well as Zapiec, the other co-captain, ready to play again after his "medical redshirt" year. Allen, switched from defensive tackle, was ticketed for the other linebacker slot until a preseason head injury put him out for the season. So that spot was filled by Tom Hull, Gary Hager and others, including a non-lettering senior named Paul Pasqualoni, who 30 years later would become the head coach at Syracuse. Junior Jim Laslavic, who had lettered at linebacker, joined Bannon at defensive end with Ahrehold and Heller at tackle and sophomore Randy Crowder of Farrell in reserve. Parsons was still the punter but because Paterno had been unhappy with the placekicking the last two years, he went out and recruited his first kicking specialist and his first junior college player, Al Vitiello. Vitiello was a native of Naples, Italy, who moved to the U.S. six years earlier and had set junior college placekicking records at Nassau (NY) Community College, including a 60-yard field goal.

"We will have to rely on speed and quickness to offset the weight advantage we'll give most of our opponents," Paterno said. "We have a young squad that should get better as the season progresses." He was almost right.

The Lions clobbered Navy in near-80 degree heat at Annapolis, 56-3, as Mitchell scored five touchdowns—one less than Harry Robb's 1917 record—and Vitiello kicked eight extra points, one shy of Pete Mauthe's 1912 record. One of Mitchell's TDs came on a 37-yard pass from Hufnagel, who was 7-for-7 for 133 yards on the day, including another 7-yard pass to Parsons. Joachim also threw an 86-yard bomb to sophomore speedster Jim Scott as Paterno used his second and third teams for most of the second half. "The tendency is to label this Lion team as a 'hungry one' and that's in direct opposition to last year's squad..." *Collegian* sports editor Terry Nau wrote after the game.

State traveled to Iowa City the next week for the first game against Iowa since 1930. The Hawkeyes under first year coach Frank Lauterbauer, a one time Pitt assistant, had been beaten badly in its first two games by Ohio State and Oregon State but Iowa had a record of rarely losing home openers. The Hawkeyes lost this one, 44-14, as Mitchell ran for a near record 211 yards and one touchdown and Harris rushed for 145 yards and four touchdowns before a regional TV audience in the rain at Niles Kinnick Stadium. It was the second time the duo had rushed for over 100 yards in a game and just the ninth time in PSU history. Zapiec, playing just his third game as a linebacker, was named the Defensive Player of the Game. The Lions moved up from #13 in the rankings to #9 in AP and #7 in UPI. "I'm not sure how good or bad we are because we haven't been in a game yet," Paterno told sportswriters. "We haven't had to come from behind in a game..."

Paterno got his wish the next Saturday in State's Beaver Stadium opener against Air Force. Despite their 2-0 record, the Falcons were a two-to-three touchdown underdog but possessed a strong running attack led by their all time leading rusher, Brian Bream. But they crossed-up State by passing and almost pulled off an upset. Midway in the first quarter the Falcons missed a field goal after Zapiec led a goal line stand inside the PSU 8-yard line. State then drove 80 yards for a touchdown with Donchez scoring from the one early in the second

First-Team All-American Lydell Mitchell breaks away on one of his TD runs as tight end Jim McCord (86) throws a block. Mitchell led the country in scoring while setting three NCAA records in 1971 and is still the Lion career leader in touchdowns with 38.

quarter. Air Force came back with a 67-yard drive that tied the score, 7-7 at the half. Hufnagel, who had a 100 degree temperature the previous night, was struggling and Paterno thought about inserting Joachim at the start of the third quarter. But he said later he had never seen Hufnagel in a game when "we were behind and I wanted to find out what he could do." He did put in his two sophomore defensive backs, Cappelletti and O'Neil, and O'Neil intercepted Rich Haynie's first pass of the second half as it was tipped by Bannon and returned the ball 34 yards to the AF 11-yard line. On fourth-and-goal at the 2, Hufnagel, faked to Donchez and Harris, then pitched out to Mitchell, who ran in for the TD. But Vitiello hooked the PAT attempt and the Lions led, 13-7. Zapiec stopped the Falcon's next drive with an interception at the State 9 but Harris fumbled moments later and Air Force recovered at the PSU 22. What came next was almost the play of the game. On third-and-one, Haynie was trapped by the Lion rush and tried to throw the ball out of the end zone. He was hit as he threw and the ball wobbled into the end zone where Paul Bassa leaped between Zapiec and Ducatte and grabbed the ball for a TD. Craig Barry's kick put the Falcons ahead, 14-13.

The partisan crowd of 50,459 tensed when Mitchell fumbled at the Lion 32 after the kickoff, but Barry missed a 41-yard field goal. Four times through the rest of the third quarter and into the fourth, the Falcon defense stopped the Lions and forced punts. Then, with about eight minutes left and rain coming down, the Lions took over at the PSU 34-yard line. With runs by Mitchell and Donchez, the Lions moved to the AF 41. What came next can only be described as luck. Hufnagel handed off to Harris but after Harris broke into the secondary he fumbled. Miraculously, the ball bounced into the arms of Hufnagel, who was out blocking, and the quarterback ran nine yards to the Falcon 14. "We didn't see that (play) in the films," Falcon coach Ben Martin told sportswriters after the game. On the sideline, Vitiello, still brooding over his missed PAT, was hoping for a touchdown, "so I wouldn't have to go back into the game. I knew I'd had to make a field goal or lose the game for us," he told Glenn Sheely of the *Collegian*. Three running plays reached the 5 and Paterno summoned Vitiello, who had hit only 5 of 7 previous field goal attempts. But this time, the snap from Botts and the hold by Hufnagel were good and so was the 22-yard kick with 4:07 remaining. Haynie tried to pass the Falcons to victory but Cappelletti and Ducatte intercepted for the fifth and sixth time and the Lions escaped, 16-14. "Our young men met their supreme challenge in the last seven minutes and will be a better team because of it," Riley wrote in the *"Football Letter."*

The Lions slipped to #12 in the ratings but bounced back to #9 the next week after shutting out Army, 42-0, at Beaver Stadium. However, the Lions didn't score until Ahrenhold recovered an Army fumble at the Cadet 32 with 36 seconds left in the half. On third-and-2 at the 14, Hufnagel threw a TD pass to Skarzynski and Vitiello's PAT made it 7-0. Skorupan partially blocked a punt early in the third quarter and three plays later Mitchell ran off tackle for 40-yards for the TD and a 14-0 lead. Then, Paterno surprised everyone by putting in Joachim to run the first time offense. "We decided to give Steve a chance with the first team under some pressure," Paterno told Riley later. By the time Joachim gave way to a reserve, he had thrown a 62-yard TD pass to Parsons, an 11-yard TD pass to Mitchell and guided another 42-yard drive and the Lions led 35-0. Mitchell scored another TD on the ground, rushing for 161 of the Lions' total 271 yards, as Harris saw limited action because of injured ribs.

Franco Harris blasts through the line in one of his patented runs. He and Mitchell formed a formidable backfield combination from '69–'71. He was inducted into the Pro Football Hall of Fame in 1990.

After being embarrassed by Syracuse in '70, Paterno was determined not to let it happen again this year. Paterno studied films of every game Syracuse played since that win over the Lions and before leaving the hotel for Archbold Stadium Saturday morning, Paterno used a little psychology by showing his team the film of last year's game "We were better prepared for this game than any other I can remember," Zapiec told the **Collegian** later. Syracuse was 2-1-1 after an upset loss to Northwestern and Schwartzwalder figured his team would regain its Eastern status before a noisy Homecoming crowd by beating the Lions again with its ground game. But with a new defensive formation that clogged the middle, State held the Orange to 110 yards rushing and won 31-0. Bannon was named AP Defensive Lineman of the Week after making a dozen tackles and blocking a punt that Gray picked up and ran 21 yards for a touchdown. Hufnagel scored two touchdowns on quarterback sneaks as Syracuse keyed on Mitchell and Harris still nursed his ribs. Vitiello hit his longest field goal of the season of 43-yards and ran his extra point total to 24. It was the first back to back shutouts by a State team since 1948 and moved the Lions up two places in the polls.

What happened the following week would presage New Year's Day but nobody realized it at the time. For the first time, a Paterno team would be up against the multi-faceted Wishbone offense that had helped make Texas the National Champion in '69. TCU's new coach, Jim Pittman, had switched to the run-oriented Wishbone, despite having a quarterback named Steve Judy who had broken all of the school passing records held by the fabled Davy O'Brien and Sammy Baugh. TCU was 2-1-1 and most of State's Homecoming crowd of 51,893 and scouts from the Orange, Cotton and Sugar Bowls looked for a close game. The 66-14 final was a shocker as the Lions limited the wishbone to 129 yards while the offense broke an all-time total offense record with 633 yards, 485 on the ground. "We defensed the Wishbone pretty well," defensive tackle Heller told Doug McDonald of the **Centre Daily Times**. Once again, Mitchell and Harris both went over 100 yards, with Mitchell getting 177 yards and four touchdowns (tying Pittman's seasonal record of 14) and Harris had 104 yards and one TD. Vitiello set a new record with 9 extra points and O'Neil scored the first TD of his career with a 54-yard punt return. TCU completed just 5 passes for 53 yards as the defense intercepted three of the 15 attempts. It was State's biggest point production since the 75-0 Fordham game of 1947. "They have a tremendous football team," Pittman told the **CDT**'s McDonald. "We got our tails whipped." Unfortunately, one week later, Pittman, 46, would collapse and die on the sideline during TCU's game at Baylor.

West Virginia was 6-1 and ranked in the Top 20, and their fans were all psyched up for State's visit to Mountaineer Stadium the following Saturday afternoon. The Mountaineers had not beaten State since 1955 but coach Bowden had convinced everyone that this was their year. The rowdy students, most of them dressed in hillbilly costumes for the WVU Homecoming crowd, booed and cursed the PSU players constantly but it was the aggressive Mountaineer defense that kept the game close into the third quarter. The Lions had scored with 30 seconds left in the first half after an 88-yard drive and WVU had tied it at 7-7 by scoring the first rushing TD of the year against the Lions after a 70-yard march opening the third quarter. The controversial turning point of the game came after the ensuing kickoff when the Mountaineer defense forced State to punt. John Billetz bobbled Parsons' punt at midfield and as the ball bounced towards the PSU sideline,

Dave Joyner (70) shakes the hand of Lydell Mitchell (23) after a touchdown during a 1971 game. These were two of Paterno's greatest stars who helped forge his career and both players made All-American in 1971.

State's Cole and Rickenbach dove for it. As they tumbled out of bounds, Cole seemed to have the ball first, then Rickenbach. The referee ruled Cole had possession before going out of bounds and gave the Lions the ball at the WVU 45 as the crowd shrieked and booed. West Virginia sportswriters were certain the Mountaineers "were robbed" but game films were inconclusive. Paterno said he "wasn't sure" the Lions had recovered but "I don't know what would have happened if we didn't." The fumble recovery seemed to take some of the spirit out of the Mountaineers and transfer it to the Lions. State drove for a touchdown, with Hufnagel passing to Harris from the 7-yard line and Vitiello's PAT made it 14-7 with less than five minutes remaining in the third quarter. Before the period was over, State drove 61-yards for another TD as Mitchell banged over from the one to set a new season record. Ellis' interception and 29-yard runback of a Bernie Galiffa pass in the fourth quarter set up a second Mitchell TD from the 2 and the Lions went on to win, 35-7, in a score Paterno said was "deceiving."

Harris missed the next game against Maryland (2-6) with a hamstring pull but he wasn't needed as Mitchell ran for 209 yards and five touchdowns (on 24 carries) and the Lions hammered the Terps, 63-27, at Beaver Stadium. Mitchell set three more school records with his performance, surpassing Lenny Moore's career and single season rushing yardage and snapping Pete Mauthe's one season point record of 119 set in 1912. With scouts from the Orange, Sugar, Cotton and Gator bowls looking on in Beaver Stadium the following week against North Carolina State, Mitchell scored four touchdowns to break the all-time college one season touchdown record set by Arizona's Art Luppino in 1954. The game was much closer than the 35-3 final score indicated as first year coach Al Michaels, the one time Lion quarterback in the Higgins era, had his team primed, despite a 2-7 record. The Wolfpack recovered four Lion fumbles and intercepted a Hufnagel pass and trailed by just 7-3 late in the third quarter when they drove for a first down at the PSU 11-yard line. But the defense forced a fourth-and-7 field goal attempt at the 8-yard line. A strong Lions rush led by Bannon and Laslavic caused the kick to go wide and that seemed to take the heart out of NC State as the Lions went on to break open the game with 28 fourth quarter points. Still, the Lions dropped from #5 to #6 in the rankings as they prepared to play Pitt and bowl rumors began to swirl.

Saturday, November 20 was bowl selection day and for the first time invitations would be allowed at 6 p.m. rather than the following Monday. According to speculation, #1 Nebraska and #2 Oklahoma were headed for a Thanksgiving Day showdown with the winner playing #4 Alabama in the Orange Bowl and the loser going to the Sugar Bowl against #5 Auburn. The Cotton Bowl wanted to match State or Georgia against the Southwest Conference winner, either #12 Texas or Arkansas, although both had already lost two games. However, the Gator Bowl thought it might have a "dream game" with Penn State against #7 Notre Dame at 8-1 and behind the scenes State seemed interested. "Except for money, there's little to be gained by playing in the Cotton Bowl," wrote Ron Bracken of the *Centre Daily Times*. "Certainly, there will be no prestige in turning a two-time loser into a three-time loser...A battle between to independent giants such as State and Notre Dame would guarantee the Gator Bowl an enormous television market and enough prestige to put it on a level with the Orange, Rose, Sugar and Cotton Bowls." But when Ara Parseghian said later in the week that Notre Dame would not play in any bowl that year, it looked like the Cotton Bowl was the best available. "Okay, its two years late," wrote Nau of the *Daily Collegian*., "but that kind of rivalry would stir emotions among players, coaches and fans." The Lions took care of business at Pitt Stadium, scoring 35 points in the first half and blasting the 2-and-7 Panthers, 55-18, as Mitchell scored three touchdowns and ran for 181 yards. In the locker room, Wilbur Evans and Field Scovell of the Cotton Bowl issued their formal invitation, the players voted and university administrators accepted. "We haven't even put Tennessee into the contingency," said Bob Scannell, who now ran the Athletic Department as Dean of the Physical Education School. "I'm sure Joe will take care of that."

Joe didn't, or, rather, his team didn't. Even before the game on national television between #5 PSU and twice-beaten #12 Tennessee, many sportswriters were again questioning the caliber of the State team and mocking "the soft schedule." On the morning of the game, the *Chattanooga Times* headline said, "Penn State: Powerhouse or Imposter—We Find Out This Afternoon." Tennessee, a 32-15 victim against Alabama and 10-9 loser to Auburn, would be the Lions' true test, everyone said, including the PSU supporters. It was a test, all right, and the Lions not only flunked but embarrassed themselves in the process. Hufnagel and the Lions special teams had a horrible day as the Volunteers alert defense and kicking game kept State's offense struggling all day. The tone was set in the first quarter with the Lions driving from their own 7-yard line to a second down at the UT 23-yard line. Hufnagel rolled out right on an option but as he was about to pitch the ball, his arm was hit and the ball flopped into the arms of cornerback Conrad Graham who ran unmolested down the sideline in front of the PSU bench and went 76 yards for a touchdown. Shortly after Vitiello's 27-yard field goal made it 7-3 early in the second quarter, Tennessee blew one score with a fumble into the end zone, then intercepted a Hufnagel pass at the Lion 30 to set up Bill Rudder's one-yard TD. On the kickoff, sophomore Chuck Herd mistakenly signaled for a fair catch at the PSU 5-yard line and after barely avoiding a safety, the Lions punted to UT star Bobby Majors, who returned the kick 44 yards for

another TD. Defensive lineman Jackie Walker picked off another Hufnagel pass midway in the fourth quarter and ran 43 yards for a fourth TD before Mitchell scored State's only TD of the game on a 14-yard pass from Hufnagel and the Lions lost, 31-11. Hufnagel had completed a school record of 19 passes in 29 attempts for 220 yards but had lost his first game since junior high school. "If you play lousy you're gonna lose," Mitchell told the *CDT*'s Bracken, "and we played lousy." Paterno said, "this isn't the end of the world" but it almost was. The Lions dropped out of the Top 10 and the naysayers crowed for weeks, predicting another embarrassment against Texas in the Cotton Bowl. Bill Conlin of the *Philadelphia Daily News* called State the "Paper Lions."

THE 1972 COTTON BOWL
Jan. 1, 1972
Penn State 30, Texas 6
Outstanding Offensive Player: Lydell Mitchell
Outstanding Defensive Player: Bruce Bannon

Getting his team ready for Texas was not easy for Paterno. A new NCAA rule for post-season games now prohibited a team to return home for Christmas if it had started practice in the south beforehand. So, even without a field house, Paterno decided to practice in the freezing cold and snow of University Park. When the team arrived in Dallas on December 26, they were still unsettled and the boisterous confidence of Texas fans didn't help. "Kick The Hell Out of Penn State," said one sign near the team's headquarters at the Fairmont Hotel. The first couple of workouts in Dallas did not go well and the team seemed listless and uninspired. "I'm really pessimistic...," Paterno told the *CDT's* Bracken four days before the game, "because I don't feel comfortable about what we plan to do...Some people may think I'm just playing a game but I'm not. I don't know if we can get good enough quick enough." When the popular Harris showed up late for practice, Paterno reprimanded him in front of the entire team. The next day Harris was three minutes late and Paterno publicly demoted him to the second team. It was a disciplinary action that seemed to anger some of the players rather than stimulate them. "Looking back, I think I handled that wrong," Paterno would write later. And as Paterno dejectedly talked more pessimistically during public appearances about his team's chances against Texas, the players just shook their heads. They didn't care for his psychology and some of them got mad at him

Defensive end Jim Laslavic makes one of his 10 first half tackles against Texas in the 1972 Cotton Bowl that the Lions won, 30-6, in what was then the biggest game of the Paterno era.

for implying they were not working hard and couldn't handle the Texas Wishbone. "I don't believe any one can stop the Wishbone," Paterno had said. "Of course, we'd like to contain it but we haven't had much luck even at that in practice." When Paterno continued that refrain at a news conference and said, "It will take a miracle for us to win," Texas coach Darrell Royal replied, "I think Joe's peeing on my leg."

Texas was favored by six points when the Longhorns kicked off on a rainy, 50-degree afternoon before an announced crowd of 72,000, including former President Lyndon Johnson, who flashed his "Hook 'Em Horns" sign to the fans and the cameras. The Lions drove to the Texas 37 on their first possession before an "illegal receiver downfield penalty" forced a punt. Starting from their own 14, the Longhorns ate up yardage with their Wishbone as quarterback Eddie Philips and halfback Jim Bertelsen ran inside and outside until reaching the PSU 30 where Phillips was trapped for losses on two plays and Texas punted to State's 2-yard line. State's offense couldn't get untracked and Parsons' uncharacteristic 28-yard punt gave the ball back to Texas at the State 35. A few plays later, State stopped the Longhorns on third down at the 19 and Steve Valek came in and kicked a 29-yard field goal with about 1:15 left in the first quarter. State's defense was now getting into the rhythm and early in the second quarter, Skorupan and Hull forced a fumble that Zapiec recovered at the UT 20. The Lions drove to the 5 before a third down play lost a yard and Vitiello booted a 21-yard field goal to tie. The defenses took over from this point and as the second quarter wound down, a halftime tie seemed inevitable. Then with less than a half minute remaining and State in possession at the Texas 32, Glen Gaspard made a one-handed interception of a Hufnagel pass at the 17 and returned it to the Longhorn 40. Phillips completed his only two passes of the half in the last 19 seconds to set up a 40-yard field goal by Valek on the last play that set a new Cotton Bowl record. The cocky Texas fans cheered lustily as their team headed into the locker room with the 6-3 lead for the Longhorns now had momentum on their side and "everyone" knew they'd break the game wide open in the second half.

In the PSU dressing room, the players and coaches made no fiery speeches. The Texas Wishbone had controlled the ball for 17 minutes and picked up nearly 200 yards. But as the half progressed, the Lions had throttled the Wishbone, just as they had learned to do in the TCU game, and they now felt certain they were going to win the game with their defense *and* offense. "We expected to stop the Wishbone and Joe Paterno expected to stop the Wishbone," Gray told sportswriters after the game. On the Longhorns first series, Phillips fumbled the handoff at midfield and after Laslavic had accidentally kicked the ball 10 yards downfield Zapiec recovered at the Texas 41. Mitchell ran up the middle for 20 yards and one play later Hufnagel found his secondary receiver Parsons wide open near the goal line and the Lions had a first down and goal at the one. Mitchell banged over for the TD, Vitiello kicked the PAT and State had a 10-6 lead that seemed to stun the Longhorn players and their fans. The Lions defense forced Texas to punt after the kickoff and on the first play from the PSU 35, Hufnagel found Skarzynski in the clear, 15 yards behind the Longhorn safetyman, and hit him for a 65-yard TD and a 17-6 lead with about 6 1/2 minutes into the third quarter. "I was so far open...," Skarzynski said later, "My grandmother could have made the play." It was the play of the game and the end for Texas. Vitiello kicked a 37-yard field goal later in the quarter and a 22-yard field goal seven minutes into the fourth period, setting a Cotton Bowl record with three. The Lions controlled the ball

for nearly 13 minutes in the final quarter, and scored another TD on a time consuming 64-yard drive with Hufnagel going the final 4 yards on a fourth down keeper and the Lions won, 30-6.

The Lions whooped it up in the locker room, tossing Governor Shapp into the showers with Paterno, as the contingent of PSU students outside chanted, "We Broke The Wishbone!" When they reached the Fairmont Hotel more than an hour later, the players were greeted by a howling mob of Lion fans celebrating the momentous victory. Mitchell, who had gained 146 yards on 27 carries was named the game's top offensive player and Bannon was the defensive player. Zapiec was given the game ball. Hufnagel passed for 137 yards on 7-of-12 completions and Harris, playing much of the second half, rushed for 47 yards on 11 carries. The Wishbone had netted 159 yards rushing and 83 yards passing as Texas was held without a TD for the first time in 80 games while the Lions had gained 239 yards on the ground and 137 through the air. "Penn State...stormed through, over and around the Longhorns for a resounding 30-6 victory," wrote Sam Blair in **The Dallas Morning News**. "When it was over, not a soul was making jokes about the so-called Eastern style football, which the Lions supposedly play...Rarely, if ever, has a good Royal team, supposedly operating under normal strength, been subjected to such a licking." Blackie Sherrod of **The Dallas Times-Herald**, wrote, "The vaunted Wishbone T offense...was most ineffective. This was due partly to poor execution on the part of the Steer offensive unit...and partly to a rather savage Penn State defense."

The Lions finished #5 in the final AP poll and set school scoring (454 points), rushing (3,347 yards) and total offense (4,995 yards) records that were not broken until 1994. Mitchell and Vitiello also set several team records and Mitchell also established three NCAA records for TDs (28), rushing TDs (26) and most points per season (174). Mitchell, Joyner and Zapiec were chosen to All-American teams with Joyner becoming the first pure offensive interior lineman in State history to be so chosen.

"The Cotton Bowl game is one of the greatest victories in Penn State history," Paterno said years later. "I don't think we've ever had a game that we had to win more than this one. There was so much that had been done that was ready to go down the drain if Texas had beaten us." The Lions finally won the respect they had sought for years but 1972 would have a more exasperating ending and State would nearly lose its coach as well.

Season Record 11-1
Record to Date 470-233-40
Winning percentage .659

"Don't Go Pro Joe"

The defining moment of the 1972 season occurred during spring practice when Paterno switched John Cappelletti from defensive halfback to tailback but even Paterno did not recognize the ultimate consequences of the move. Years later, he would point to "the historic moment" in the third quarter of the season opener at Tennes-

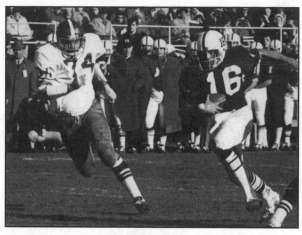

1972 All-American QB John Hufnagel was one of the best running quarterbacks of the Paterno era who also was a fine passer. State lost just three games during the 2 1/2 years that he started.

see when Cappelletti "launched Penn State's most famous career of power running" but it actually began in late April.

Mitchell had been so durable that his backups at tailback in '71 had hardly carried the ball. Cappelletti had played tailback on the freshman team when he and Donchez were the stars. Donchez had been fourth in rushing as a sophomore even though he was used more as a blocker and had started in the Cotton Bowl game when Paterno benched Harris. Paterno figured Cappelletti and Donchez would be the best replacements for his graduated running stars. But during the spring, Donchez injured his knee and Cappelletti hurt his ankle and both missed the Blue-White game, which turned into an aerial circus. Thus, Paterno really didn't know how good of a running back Cappelletti would be until he saw him in a few games. Even then, it would be another year before Cappelletti's true ability would be fully appreciated by everyone, including the coaches. As for Donchez, he continued to work out with the team all fall after a knee operation but he would miss the entire season, and no one really stepped up to do everything he had been expected to do. So the running burden fell on Cappelletti, who was bigger than Mitchell and matched his speed. What Paterno really wanted was more passing from Hufnagel and to do that, Paterno reasoned, he needed another strong running attack to keep the opposing defenses off balance.

Paterno believed Hufnagel was underrated as a passer, and even before preseason practice started, Paterno called Hufnagel "the best college quarterback in the county today, bar none." Many sportswriters agreed and he was the cover boy of two preseason magazines, *Street and Smith* and *Kick-Off.* His backup would be sophomore Tom Shuman of Pottstown, who played so well in the spring that he was named the #2 quarterback, causing Joachim to quit and transfer to Temple. Skarzynski returned at flanker but he was soon surpassed by a corps of wide receivers that included Scott, Herd, and junior Gary Hayman, who had returned to school after missing a year with personal problems. Sophomore Dan Natale of Glassport would break into the lineup as the starting tight end and the dependable Rickenbach would be utilized as a second tight end and a reserve tackle. Non-letter junior Bob Nagle who was a good blocker eventually became the starting fullback. The interior line was all veterans, except for brainy sophomore Jack Baiorunos of Quincy, MA, at center. Getty and LaPorta were

the tackles with Lyle in reserve while Schaukowitch, offensive co-captain with Hufnagel, and Markovich were the guards.

Paterno believed the defense was his strength and in the preseason he said it had the potential to match the great unit of '69. "They still have to prove they can make the big play and play with the reckless abandon that the '69 gang had," he told sportswriters. In the front line Paterno had Bannon and sophomore Dave Graf at the ends and Crowder and Heller at the tackles with sophomore Mike Hartenstine of Bethlehem in reserve. Skorupan returned at outside linebacker and senior Larry Ludwig, voted the most improved player in spring practice, manned the other outside LB position. For his inside linebackers, Paterno moved Laslavic back from defensive end and O'Neil over from halfback. Allen, fully recovered from his head injury, and Hull were prime backups. Ducatte, defensive co-captain with Heller, was back at safety with another '71 regular, Ellis, at halfback with junior Jack Koniszewski and Davis sharing the other slot. Vitiello was back to placekick with sophomore tight end John Reihner handling kickoffs and a sophomore reserve fullback named Brian Masella beat out Koniszewski for the punting job.

If Paterno had so desired, he could have brought up one of his outstanding freshmen, such as end Greg Buttle and guard Tom Rafferty, to fill in because the NCAA had lifted its ban on freshman eligibility. But the coach always believed freshmen should concentrate on the classroom while adjusting to college life and it would be another year before Paterno would give in to reality and utilize a freshman named Duane Taylor against Syracuse due to injuries to four tailbacks, including Cappelletti.

The '72 schedule wasn't criticized as much because three of the toughest foes were being played away from Beaver Stadium and all were preseason Top 20 teams: Tennessee, Illinois and West Virginia. Still, the Lions were rated #4 in the preseason by the AP and *Kick-Off*

Second-Team All-American OT Charlie Getty was one of the leaders of the underrated offensive lines that allowed Cappelletti to run for 1,117 yards in 1972.

Magazine and ranked in the Top 10 by most other sportswriters. Paterno wasn't happy about opening the season in Knoxville against Tennessee and not because the Lions had been disgraced there last December. In the original two-year contract, Tennessee had balked at traveling to State College in December, so the game had been scheduled for December 9 in Memphis—a so-called "neutral" site. But when State administrators realized that December 9 fell in the middle of exams, they had to break the contract. Since there were no lights at Beaver Stadium, State felt obligated to offer Tennessee the option of playing a day game at Beaver Stadium on the afternoon of September 16 or a night game in Knoxville that same evening. Tennessee wasn't daft or gracious, especially knowing the Lions would be out to revenge last year's embarrassment. The Volunteers also knew they would have another advantage—game experience. They would open their own season a week earlier against Georgia Tech on national television, and Paterno would be in Atlanta to see it as part of a new ABC game segment called, "Coaches' Corner." No one ever beats Tennessee in Knoxville," wrote Tennessee sportswriter Tom Siler in a bit of hyperbole. "There is no way, NO way a Northern team can win in Neyland Stadium," wrote another Southern writer.

Neyland Stadium is one of the most intimidating venues in college football with Orange everywhere inside the stadium and around Knoxville. This was the first night game in the history of Neyland and the largest crowd to watch a sports event in the state turned out in the humid 75 degree heat— 71,647—and all but a couple thousand where hollering and screaming for their Vols to kick butt again. Paterno had tried to play down the revenge factor and the players apparently bought into it. "The worst thing you can say," Bannon told the media in the preseason, "is that one of your games is going to make the whole season." Tennessee had beaten Georgia Tech and the players' one game experience showed in the first half when the Vols took intercepted two passes and recovered a pair of fumbles. About two minutes into the game, Eddie Brown's diving sideline interception at the UT 40 set up a 41-yard touchdown run up the middle by tailback Haskel Stanback. After the Lions lost one opportunity with a fumble at the Vol 25, Hufnagel's fumble at the PSU 30 led to fullback Steve Chancey's 3-yard touchdown and a 14-0 lead with four minutes left in the first quarter. Tennessee set up its third touchdown after a 20-yard punt runback as Chancey ran 22 yards for the score for a convincing 21-0 halftime lead.

During the intermission, Paterno quietly told the team it had to attack to win and three minutes into the third quarter, Hufnagel threw a 69-yard bomb to Scott. Minutes later, Allen hit Chancey so hard he fumbled and then left the game never to return. Graf recovered at the UT 22 and it was at this moment that Cappelletti showed Paterno the type of running that would ultimately win him the Heisman Trophy. Cappy carried six straight times and bulled his way to the one-yard line from where Nagle scored, and with Vitiello's second PAT it was 21-14. But Tennessee's sophomore quarterback Condredge Holloway led the Vols back on an 80-yard drive that carried into the fourth quarter with Stanback going 2-yards around left end with less than 9 minutes left in the game and a 28-14 lead. At one point in the third quarter, Paterno replaced Hufnagel with Shuman for a series, saying later he wanted Hufnagel ready for the fourth quarter. Hufnagel was ready and he took just three minutes to narrow the lead again, marching the team 79 yards on his passing and the running of Cappelletti and Nagle and climaxing with a 14-yard touchdown pass to Natale. A minute later,

Stanback fumbled and Ludwig recovered at the Vol 34. But the Tennessee defense gave up just two yards in four plays and took the ball back. The Lions had one last shot following a punt to State's 18-yard line with a minute left but Hufnagel's passing could get the team only as far as the UT 26 when time ran out. "This was a big game for us but losing it doesn't mean the end of our season," Paterno told Glenn Sheely, sports editor of the *Daily Collegian* after the 28-21 defeat. "...Our kids came back from what could have been a disaster game. They showed their poise."

First-Team All-American John Skorupan, who is part of the great linebacking legacy at Penn State, had one of his finest games in home opener win over Navy and was named "Lineman of the Week" by the AP.

Poise and determination would be the trademarks of this team and they would need both on many occasions before the year ended, starting with the home opener against Navy. Beaver Stadium had been expanded again over the summer with more than 9,200 seats added but classes had not yet begun and a "disappointing" crowd of 50,547 showed up for the game between the 11th ranked Lions and the four-touchdown underdog Middies. State's offense was ragged again in the first half as two fumbles, an interception and several dropped passes helped give Navy a surprising 3-0 halftime lead on a 38-yard field goal. A 90-yard drive at the start of the third quarter put the Lions ahead on a 2-yard TD by Cappelletti but Ike Owens ran back the kickoff 59 yards to set up another TD and a 10-7 Navy lead. Now it was Cappelletti's turn and he returned the Navy kickoff 40 yards. Hufnagel drove the Lions the rest of the way and Cappy scored again, on a one-yard dive up the middle after passes to Scott and Natale and some nifty running by Hayman, who was subbing occasionally at tailback because of some problems Cappelletti was having with his leg. State was now in control at 14-10 but the Lions didn't seal the win until Skorupan made an interception in the flat with about 1:20 left the game and ran for a 32-yard TD for a 21-10 final score. The interception had capped one of Skorupan's finest performances as he made 15 unassisted tackles and assisted on two others and was named the AP Lineman of the Week. "That number 81 was super," Navy coach Forzano told sportswriters. But the Lions dropped to #13 in the polls with Tennessee at #4 and West Virginia now at #20. Paterno complained that the polls were taking "a lot of fun out of Saturdays" because home fans were expecting big victory margins all the time, and "you can't go into a game any more and just win. You have to win big."

More fans were watching, too. All the games, home and away, were being videotaped and replayed over a three-state network of cable systems at 11 p.m. Saturday and 7 p.m. Tuesday with Dick Richards of WRTA in Altoona doing the play-by-play. They might have liked what they saw *before* the following week's game against Iowa when a corps of 12 majorettes made their debut with the Blue Band. But neither they nor the record-breaking crowd of 58,065 at Beaver Stadium were too happy about the narrow, but exciting last minute 14-10 victory over a weak Iowa team. Two fumbles and a missed field goal stopped Lion scoring opportunities in the first half and there was a loud chorus of boos as the team left the field at halftime trailing 3-0 on a 44-yard field goal by Harry Kokolus. State lost another fumble and missed two more field goals in the third quarter but Hayman's 32-yard punt return in the fourth period helped spark a 63-yard drive that ended with Cappelletti bolting 7-yards off right tackle for the touchdown with two linebackers on his back to give the Lions a 7-3 lead. However, Iowa marched 61-yards to go ahead 10-7 with just three minutes left, scoring on a 36-yard pass from Frank Sunderman to Brian Rollins that had Ducatte and Stilley miscommunicating on the coverage. Now came another defining moment in the season.

Iowa kicked off into the end zone. A 15-yard screen pass to Hayman and an 8-yard pass to Natale moved the Lions upfield but it was fourth-and-two at the PSU 43 when Hufnagel and Cappelletti combined for what may have been the play of the year. It was an option play and Hufnagel thought he saw an opening for the first down but decided to pitch back almost blindly to Cappelletti, who was still hampered by his leg injury. Cappy grabbed the ball and with the help of an open field block by Schaukowitch, rambled 32 yards to the Iowa 25. Hayman came in at tailback and gained 13 yards, then Cappelletti carried three times to reach the 2-yard line but a motion penalty set State back to the 10 with 49 seconds left. It was now third-and-eight and Hufnagel dropped back looking for Natale on a crossing pattern in the end zone but couldn't find him because he had been bumped by the Iowa linebackers and slipped. Hufnagel scrambled and then saw Natale heading for the corner of the end zone and he hit him perfectly. Vitiello kicked the PAT with 36 seconds left and the Lions won, 14-10. "That was shaving it awfully

close," wrote Riley in his *"Football Letter."* The offensive come back overshadowed what Paterno called "the best game by the defense." Crowder had been sensational again, making 12 tackles, 7 unassisted, giving him 23 tackles in the last two games. On one play he hit the Iowa fullback so hard he caused a fumble and then recovered the ball. "(Crowder) brought back some (Mike) Reid memories when he'd suddenly appear in the Hawkeyes' backfield," Riley reported.

The game at Illinois had the same eerie start as the others when the Illini picked off a Hufnagel pass on the second play of the game deep in Lion territory and scored two minutes later for a 7-0 lead. But before the first quarter was over, the Lions had stormed back to go ahead 21-10 and had a 35-10 lead in the fourth quarter when Paterno cleared the bench. The final score was 35-17 over an Illinois team coached by former Dartmouth mentor Bob Blackman—that obviously wasn't as good as sportswriters had expected. Cappelletti rushed for over 100 yards for the first time, getting 124 yards on 21 carries, including a 53-yard TD. The offense still gave up the ball four times on fumbles and twice on interceptions but Illinois was stymied by State's attacking defense. The Lions finally put it all together the following week at Michie Stadium with the second straight shutout over Army, 45-0. The defense limited the Cadets to just 93 yards net rushing and passing and intercepted three passes while the offense rolled up 395 yards. A 64-yard run off an option that helped set up one of two Cappelletti TDs helped Hufnagel lead all rushers with 71 yards. He also passed for two TDs while hitting on 12-of-18 passes for 152 yards and for the first time that season did not throw an interception. The Lions also shut out Syracuse for the second straight year, 17-0, before a standing-room-only record Homecoming crowd of 60,465. This was the 50th meeting between the two Eastern rivals and it was a typical physical affair dominated by defense and a running game. Two of Syracuse's best backs were out with injuries but whether they would have made a difference against the Lions swarming defense will never be known. Cappelletti gained 162 of State's net 188 rushing yards and scored the clinching TD in the fourth quarter after PSU had nursed a 7-0 second quarter lead through three periods. Vitiello continued to miss field goals, so Paterno turned to Reihner who booted one from the 32 early in the fourth quarter. Schwartzwalder, who was rumored to be on his way out as coach of the Orange, was uncharacteristically good-natured after the game and when asked by a Syracuse writer if he had any problems with the officiating as he did in '71 he said, "I have no complaints." Paterno told Ron Bracken of the *Centre Daily Times*, "our defense is just getting better and better...The only thing is that they're not making the big play yet."

West Virginia and its rabid followers had spent a year fuming about what they called "a highly controversial official's decision" that was the turning point of the '71 loss to State. In the preseason, coach Bowden said beating State would be his team's number one priority. "The percentages have got to run out on Penn State this year no matter what the circumstances," he said. For the second year in a row the game was in the inimical environs of Morgantown and the screaming overflow crowd of 37,000 at Mountain-

The great John Cappelletti, who would win the Heisman Trophy in 1973, makes a big gain against West Virginia, in his first year as a running back in 1972, after starting on defense in '71.

eer Stadium booed the Lion players at every opportunity, even when they were in street clothes 90 minutes before kickoff. Asked about the hostility the next week at the Quarterback Club, starting guard Markovich said all the booing "was inspirational...Why they even gave us a 10-minute standing boo when we came on the field." Chris Schenkel, Bud Wilkinson and the ABC-TV cameras were there to show it all to a regional audience, too. The opening moments kindled the explosive, emotional atmosphere even further when the Mountaineers' speedy Kerry Marbury took State's opening kickoff one yard deep in the end zone and ran it all the way back for a TD—only the second time in PSU football history a Cappelletti scored three TDs and his backup, sopho-more Walt Addie, had what would

Defensive end Bruce Bannon was another of Paterno's "Grand Experiment" great scholar athletes and a First-Team All-American in 1972 while maintaining a 3.91 academic average in Geology.

be the best game of his career, leading all rushers with 117 yards and a TD. NC State had won six straight under new coach Lou Holtz and at 6-2-1 and #23 in the ratings, the Wolfpack was given a good chance for an upset. Hufnagel ran for two TDs and passed for another as the Lions built up a 30-8 lead into the fourth quarter before the reserves took over. The final score, 37-22, allowed Holtz to save some face.

The bowl invitations were set for the following Saturday at 6 p.m. and during that week State received "serious feelers" from all the major bowls. The Orange Bowl mentioned a possible match-up of the Lions against #2 Alabama or #5 Nebraska and the Cotton Bowl suggested a possible rematch with #7 Texas. The Gator Bowl said it definitely wanted State because of its "Eastern television audience" and the Sugar Bowl included LSU, Oklahoma and Notre Dame as possible opponents for the Lions. Sportswriters speculated that Alabama's Bear Bryant would determine the pairings by picking the foe he believed his team could beat. Once the Bear "picked his bowl," they wrote, all the other bowl games would fall into place.

The word was out by kickoff at Boston College that the Sugar Bowl would invite State to play Oklahoma if the Lions beat BC. The State players may have lost some concentration by all the bowl rumors. A young 3-5 BC team battled from a 12-point halftime deficit and was driving for a go ahead TD at the PSU 20 late in the third quarter when the Eagle quarterback Gary Marangi was trapped for a 22 yard loss. A couple moments later in the fourth quarter Hufnagel threw a 77-yard bomb to Scott, then ran 57 yards on an option for another score and the Lions won, 45-26. The Sugar Bowl invitation was accepted that evening. A small crowd of 38,600 turned out at Beaver Stadium on Thanksgiving Saturday to watch State build a 42-0 third quarter lead over Pitt and win easily, 49-27. Hufnagel threw touchdown passes of 31, 21 and 41 yards and wound up his last regular season holding 16 school passing records. A few days before the game, Pitt had announced it was unilaterally withdrawing from the agreement with State, WVU and Syracuse that limited scholarships to 25 per year

and banned redshirting. Two days after the game, the Panthers (1-10) fired coach Carl DePasuqa.

THE 1972 SUGAR BOWL
Dec. 31, 1972
Oklamoma 14, Penn State 0

By the time both teams gathered in New Orleans, Oklahoma was #2 behind USC but was fretting about playing a #5 State team and missing out on the national title if #3 Ohio State upset the Trojans in the Rose Bowl. With Heisman Trophy runner-up Greg Pruitt in the backfield and All-American Lucious Selmon spearheading the line, the powerful Sooners coach by Chuck Fairbanks were established an early 13-point favorite. Of course, the Lions had a couple of All-Americans, too, in Hufnagel, Bannon and Skorupan but the oddsmakers figured Oklahoma's veer Wishbone attack and 5-2 defense was more than the Lions could overcome with their Power I and Wing T offense. As usual Paterno closed his practices while he secretly installed a "three wideout" formation of Heard, Scott and junior Frank Bland as receivers. Paterno expected this formation to spread out the Sooner defense and provide Cappelletti opportunities to gain big yardage inside on runs off the fake draw and to give Hufnagel more passing targets.

Paterno also was distracted from his normal pre-Bowl preparations and public appearances by the owner of the New England Patriots, Billy Sullivan, who was openly pursuing Paterno to be the general manager and coach of his club. Sullivan showed up at several Sugar Bowl events including a big party for both teams at the famous restaurant Antione's where he joked with Paterno and the crowd about the Patriots' job. Paterno told everyone he would not discuss the situation with Sullivan until the game was over but privately he told friends he was seriously interested in the Patriots' proposition. State fans in New Orleans for the game, took up the chant, "Don't Go Pro, Joe," whenever they saw Paterno and several signs with the same message were scattered throughout Tulane Stadium Sunday night at game time.

This was the first time in 49 years that an SEC team was not in the Sugar Bowl and the first time the game was being played on New Year's Eve, instead of New Year's Day. The less than capacity crowd of 80,123 did not learn until the starting lineups were introduced that Cappelletti would not play because of a virus infection that sent him to bed with a 102-degree temperature. His backup, Addie, had not practiced all week because of a badly bruised foot—which he would further aggravate in the first half of the game. Without having to worry about a running game (the Lions netted just 49 yards), Oklahoma's defense concentrated on Hufnagel and he was chased, harassed and hammered all night. He was thrown for 25 yards in losses and although he completed 12 of 31 passes for 147 yards with just one interception, his receivers were frequently double teamed or they dropped the ball at crucial times. State lost four fumbles but the Lion defense and Masella's punting kept the game close and State recovered five Sooner fumbles—three deep in PSU territory, including one by Ducatte on his tackle near the goal line that saved a touchdown. Midway in the second quarter, the Sooners drove from their 23 to the Lion 27 in 10 plays; then, quarterback Dave Robertson passed to freshman Tinker Owens—brother of the Sooners 1969 Heisman Trophy winner, Steve—who made an over-the-shoulder catch between two Lion defenders for the touchdown. Owens, whose receiving coach at OU was former PSU quarterback Galen Hall, would make a controversial catch for OU's second TD in the fourth quarter and be voted the game's MVP. That second reception came after the Lions fumbled a punt on their own 18-yard line. Robertson then passed to Owens who dove for the ball as he crossed the goal line and the official immediately signaled touchdown. Ducatte protested that Owens had made the catch on a bounce and the TV replays proved Ducatte right but the TD stood and the Lions lost, 14-0.

"Lions Offer No Excuses," said the headline in the *New Orleans State-Item*. "We just didn't have enough offense," Paterno told Ron Brocato. He compared the Sooners to Michigan State's 1966 juggernaut. "You can't keep kicking the football and expect to beat a team like Oklahoma." The coach "had a built-in (excuse) in John Cappelletti,...kayoed by a 102-degree temperature..." wrote Bob Rosler, sports editor of the *New Orleans Time-Picayune*, "...however, he wasn't looking for a crutch..." But some sportswriters were not as kind and demeaned State's heroic, underdog effort. One of the most severe critics was Dan Jenkins of *Sports Illustrated*, who obviously could not overcome his innate bias against Eastern teams and his partiality towards Southwestern football. "For some reason, Penn State has the knack of bringing out the worst in good teams," Jenkins wrote. "Maybe its because the Nittany Lions do not command enough respect, being from the East and all. Whatever the reason, Joe Paterno's bowl opposition seems to show up looking as if they had food poisoning and Oklahoma was no different....(Also) against the Sooners quickness and size, Penn State's celebrated quarterback, John Hufnagel, was not quite the operator he was against all the Armys and Marylands who made him an All-American." A few weeks later, Oklahoma was discovered using two ineligible freshmen players. The NCAA placed the Sooners on probation and made them forfeit their games, including the Sugar Bowl. Paterno and State's athletic officials refused to accept the win and the game continues to be listed as a defeat in PSU's records.

After the Sugar Bowl was over, Paterno spent the next several days talking with Sullivan about the Patriots and discussing the offer with his wife. As he later described in *"Paterno: By the Book,"* the following Thursday night he actually accepted the nearly $1.4 million offer that, he says, "could have made me financially secure for life." But he changed his mind, and surprised everyone with his decision at a 9 a.m. news conference on Saturday, January 6. "My decision virtually eliminates pro football from my career," he told reporters. "I think this is a decision I made with the idea that I'll stay here for the rest of my life." Of course, as they say, the rest is history—starting with a surprise Heisman Trophy winner and his kid brother, Joey.

Season Record 10-2
Record to Date 480-235-40
Winning percentage .662

"'Something for Joey and His Big Brother'"

No one predicted before the season that John Cappelletti would win the Heisman Trophy as the outstanding player in college football. Sure, there were a few sportswriters who mentioned the big tailback

as a possible All-American, including the AP college football writer. But even State's own sports information office wasn't promoting Cappelletti as a possible Heisman candidate as it did the year before with Hufnagel.

The 1973 Sugar Bowl proved how vital Cappelletti was to the Lion offense. He had been the third back in State history to run for more than 1,000 yards in a season and Paterno knew he could do it again if he could avoid serious injury. Paterno realized Cappelletti could make the difference between a good team and, perhaps, an exceptional one but the Lions would need a passing quarterback to go with him.

As Hufnagel's backup, Shuman had done little but mop-up and had never been tested under pressure. He did not have a good spring, either, and in both public scrimmages he had not thrown well and had a total of five interceptions. "I don't know how I'll react to the big game," Shuman admitted in the preseason to Ray McCallister of the *Daily Collegian*. "I can't play unless I'm psyched and I can't get psyched for practice." The rest of the offense was pretty well set with 9 of 11 starters returning, including the speedy wide receivers, Hayman and Scott, and the pass-catching tight end, Natale, whom people were starting to compare to Ted Kwalick. Nagle was back at fullback and so was Donchez, who had recovered from his knee injury but was bothered in the spring by a pulled hamstring. Markovich, offensive co-captain with Cappelletti, was up front with Baiorunos, LaPorta, Getty and non-lettering junior John Nessel at right guard. Paterno also planned to use sophomore Woody Petchel, son of the '48 Cotton Bowl star, at tailback and he was high on another soph, Rafferty, at tackle.

Crowder and O'Neil, the defensive co-captains, were the keys to the defense and when Crowder missed spring practice because of a knee operation, Paterno shifted Graf from end to tackle. But Crowder was fully recovered by the opening game at Stanford and Graf went back to end to pair with junior non-letterman Greg Murphy and Crowder teamed with Hartenstine at tackle. O'Neil manned one inside linebacker slot with Hull and veteran Chris Devlin and Allen took the outside LB spots. Ellis was back at one halfback position and Koniszewski and Mitchell would share the other. Junior Jim Bradley of Johnstown turned out to be a fine successor to Ducatte at safety. Masella returned as the punter and Paterno recruited Chris Bahr, captain of the soccer team, to do his placekicking. That would be an unusual arrangement for Bahr would continue playing soccer and would miss at least one game because his priority was playing soccer. When Bahr wasn't around, reserve tight end and sometimes kickoff man John Reihner would boot extra points and field goals.

Paterno was on a personal high and his team reflected his buoyant attitude. Since rejecting the coaching offer from the Patriots, Paterno had been invited by the senior class to be the commencement speaker that June and friends, alumni and others honored him with a state-proclaimed "Joe Paterno Day" and a banquet in Harrisburg. "I have a good feeling about this squad," Paterno told sportswriters in September. "They appear to like each other." However, there had been a couple of changes on his coaching staff. Offensive backfield coach George Welsh, believed by some sportswriters to be the man who would eventually succeed Paterno, left to become the head coach at his alma mater, Navy—which, ironically, would play State in the second game of the season. Former players Dick Anderson and Fran Ganter joined the staff.

Most sportswriters felt the Lion schedule would be more challenging than in recent years. *Kick-Off* magazine reported a "tougher-than-usual schedule that features early games at Stanford and Air Force." West Virginia, Maryland and North Carolina State were potential bowl contenders and everyone expected a resurgence from Pitt after its new coach, Johnny Majors, had recruited dozens of new junior college players and freshmen. However, *Sports Illustrated* continued to criticize State's schedule, reporting, "Given its schedule—oh so easy with the Marylands and Navys—10-1 is the worst it can be," and predicted the Lions would be number three in the country behind Texas and Southern Cal. *Street & Smith* magazine forecast a #11 ranking with AP picking State at #7 and UPI at #10. This also would be the last season the Lions would be part of the Eastern Collegiate Athletic Conference, which provided officials for home games. Before the season started, State announced it was withdrawing from the ECAC as of July, 1974, because of unhappiness with the organization's financial arrangements with member schools.

Stanford was a new opponent and the opening season game at Palo Alto on September 15 was part of a four-year series that had the Cardinals visiting Beaver Stadium the next three years for large monetary guarantees. It was PSU's first visit to the West Coast since 1968 and more than 3,000 Lion fans were there. Stanford was led by quarterback Mike Boryla, the fourth best passer in the nation in '72, and six seniors who had started and beaten Michigan in the '72 Rose Bowl. Former NFL defensive star Jack Christiansen was in his second year as coach and a few days before the game he boldly claimed the 6 and a half-point underdog Stanford would win "because hard work and enthusiasm will make the difference." As a nationwide ABC television audience watched, the "hard work and enthusiasm" of the Lion players was evident—particularly on defense—as they constantly blitzed Boryla, sacking him seven times for 40 yards in losses, and held Cardinal runners to a minus eight net yards in winning 20-6. Stanford barely avoided a shut out, scoring on a TD pass against the Lion reserves with less than two minutes remaining in the game. Neither Cappelletti nor Shuman looked especially sharp at the start but they both improved as

John Cappelletti captured the nation's heart with his acceptance speech when he won the Heisman Trophy in 1973. Here, he poses with Coach Paterno in New York the day after winning college football's most prestigious individual award.

the game went on. Cappelletti lost the ball twice on fumbles, gained just 76 yards on 26 carries but scored a 2-yard TD on a dramatic change-of-direction run up the middle with three tacklers hanging on his back. Shuman completed 11-of-18 passes, including a 14-yard TD to Hayman and also a 2-point conversion pass to Natale, and was named offensive player of the game by ABC. But the game belonged to the defense as Bradley returned an interception 51-yards and set up Hayman's TD with a fumble recovery just before the half. O'Neil led all tacklers with 10 and sportswriters were especially ebullient about the front four of Graf, Hartenstein, Crowder and Murphy and the blitzing linebackers. "Rarely used last season, the blitz was one of the tools with which Paterno said he shaped the defensive strategy...," wrote Bill Heufelder for the *Pittsburgh Press*, "...(and) the defense eased the pressure."

Navy was overmatched on both offense and defense in the heat at Annapolis the following Saturday and was shut out, 39-0. The 6th-ranked Lions controlled the ball for 43 minutes, as Cappelletti ran for 104 yards and a 10-yard TD in the second quarter. Shuman was excellent with 9-of-12 completions for 178 yards, including a 17-yard TD to Hayman and a 23-yard TD to Herd, and he scored himself on a 2-yard run that gave the Lions a 27-0 halftime lead. Bahr kicked four extra points and a 22-yard field goal, then flew back to State College after the game to play soccer against a college team from Great Britain. O'Neil missed the game because of a broken bone in his hand but soph Greg Buttle of Linwood, NJ, replaced him and called defensive signals like a veteran. The defense limited the Middies to 12 yards rushing and 76 passing, and for the first time since 1951 two freshmen played a varsity game as Dave Skurki and Brad Benson come on in the second half when Paterno used all 62 players on the traveling squad. An impressed Welsh told sportswriters the State team was as good as any he had seen, adding, "They were a lot better than I thought they would be."

A near record Homecoming crowd of 59,980 turned out in the rain for the Beaver Stadium opener against winless Iowa. The game

One of the most underrated of PSU's famed linebackers, Doug Allen, blocks a punt for a safety as the Lions defeat Stanford in opening game of their unbeaten 1973 season.

was all but over in the first quarter when the Lions scored 21 points and then coasted to a 27-8 win, with the PSU reserves allowing the Hawkeyes their only points with 1:36 left in the game. Cappelletti rushed for 88 yards on 22 carries and scored the first TD on a 10-yard run three minutes into the contest. Before the opening period was over, Shuman threw touchdowns of 9-yards to Herd and 32-yards to Bland. The defense, led by Hartenstine, who had 12 tackles and three sacks, hammered Iowa's quarterbacks for minus 87 yards and held Hawkeye runners to a net seven yards rushing. "We'll see how good we are when we get involved in a game where one mistake can cost you the whole thing," Paterno said, repeating one of the lines he would often use over his career in similar situations. The following Tuesday, the Lions dropped a notch in the ratings, giving credence to a mea culpa by ***Sports Illustrated*** which had reported two weeks earlier, "Texas grows fat on people like Rice, TCU and Baylor and it matters not. Notre Dame dines on Army, Navy and Pitt and it bothers no one. But let Penn State take on Ohio University and sirens go off."

The first noteworthy mention of Cappelletti as "the Heisman Trophy candidate" was by the ABC announcers handling the regional televised game at the Air Force Academy on October 6. Many sportswriters believed this was a game the Lions would lose primarily because the players would have difficulty playing in the high altitude. The writers also reminded everyone about PSU's last visit to this Rocky Mountain area when Colorado smashed the Lions 31-game unbeaten streak in 1970, 41-13. The Falcons were 2-0 and scored the initial points against State's first defense with a 44-yard field goal in the first quarter. But the Lions took the lead on an 85-yard drive in the second quarter with the touchdown coming after Shuman faked to Cappelletti and passed 38-yards to Hayman. Reihner kicked the PAT because Bahr stayed home to help State's soccer team beat West Virginia. Less than a minute later, Bradley recovered a fumble at the Air Force 26-yard line and on the third play Cappelletti bounced off a couple of tacklers and went into the end zone from the one-yard line. Cappelletti scored another TD in the third quarter, running eight yards at the end of an 80-yard drive, and as the Lions nursed their 19-3 lead past the midway

point of the fourth quarter, the defense got caught in a blitz and the Falcons scored suddenly on a 45-yard pass from Rich Haynie to Bill Berry. But Hager knocked the onside kick out of bounds and State won, 19-9. Without one of his 34 carries going more than 16 yards, Cappelletti had run for 187 yards and Falcon coach Ben Martin was amazed, calling him an All-American. "The altitude didn't affect him at all," Martin told the ***Collegian's*** McCallister. "He could have played another hour and a half and been just as effective." Cappelletti agreed that the altitude didn't bother him but said "the dry air did." Uh, huh. The defense, with O'Neil back in the lineup, held Air Force to 69 yards rushing but had just two sacks as Haynie avoided the Lion blitz attack with his rollouts. State has never played the Air Force again.

As the Lions prepared to entertain Army at Beaver Stadium, Spiro Agnew resigned as Vice President and the New York Mets won the National League pennant over Cincinnati. Neither event had any bearing on State's 54-3 beating of the Cadets as scouts from the Cotton and Orange Bowls looked on. Cappelletti had the longest run of his career of 60 yards and another run of 27 yards to help amass 151 yards on 17 carries but fullbacks Donchez and Nagle led the touchdown parade with two apiece. Shuman burned Army on a 66-yard bomb to Scott and the defense had four sacks while limiting Army to 78 yards passing and 54 yards rushing. "This is the best Penn State team we've seen," Army coach Tom Cahill said, as reported by Gordon White in the ***New York Times***. "(And) Cappelletti is the best we've seen."

The following week's game against old rival Syracuse at Archbold Stadium was a little melancholy because State's old antagonist, Ben Schwartzwalder, was closing out his distinguished coaching career in '73 and he had a lousy team. The Orange were 0-5 and for the first time that anyone could remember in this bitter series, the Lions—now up to #5 in the rankings—were 5 and a half touchdown favorites. Because of a slight shoulder injury that Paterno kept secret, Cappelletti was in for the game's first three plays as a decoy, then sat out the rest of the game as the Lions pounded Syracuse, 49-6, with several bowl scouts watching. Not only was Cappelletti out but so was his replacement, Addie, and their backup, Petchel, was sidelined for the season with a knee injury in the second quarter. Sophomore Rusty Boyle and freshman Duane Taylor took over at tailback and both scored touchdowns. Taylor also made the PSU record books with a fumble in the second quarter. The Lions were backed up to their own 8-yard line and leading 22-6 when Taylor broke away to the 20-yard where he fumbled. Natale, running interference, picked up the loose ball on a high bounce and ran down

First-Team All-American LB Ed O'Neil moves in for a tackle during a 1973 game.

the right sideline for a combined 92-yard TD run that is still the longest ever in Lion history (although it was tied by Blair Thomas in 1986). Bahr also made the record books after flying into Syracuse just before the kickoff because of a Friday night soccer game in State College where his two goals helped beat Maryland, 5-1. In the first quarter, Bahr came within a yard of beating Pete Mauthe's record 51-yard field goal set in 1912 and then he added two more field goals of 22 and 33 yards to tie four other players for the school's single game record. "Penn State's defense was superb again," wrote White

A first-Team All-American in 1973, co-captain Randy Crowder was named college football's Defensive Player- of- the-Year by the Washington Touchdown Club.

in the *New York Times*, "with four pass interceptions. Three of them led directly to scores (as did) two Syracuse fumbles..."

Cappelletti's four touchdowns and 130 yards against one-time Top 20 team West Virginia (now 3-3) the next Saturday in Beaver Stadium re-energized the Heisman talk. Actor Jack Palance, who watched the game with Pennsylvania Governor Shapp and ex-governor Ray Shafer, told a local TV reporter that Cappelletti ran with "quiet power." Cappy's first TD was typical of his jarring style—a 10-yard burst off right tackle that broke two tackles at the line of scrimmage and two more near the goal line. "That's one of the greatest runs you'll ever see," said Paterno "We knock people down at the line and Cappy comes through and knocks them down again," Markovich told sportswriters. Cappelletti also scored on two 2-yard runs and another of 5 yards, Shuman threw a 76-yard bomb to Herd and Buttle scored on a 25-yard interception as the Lions rolled up the highest score in the 40-year series history with the Mountaineers, 62-14. "I don't know whether I've been around a better football player than Cappelletti," Paterno said. "He's got speed, poise and he's a tremendous competitor."

The next week, State's sports information office noted the accelerated interest in Cappy. "It's obvious that Cappelletti is a 'hot item' in that everyone wants to write about him right now, everyone wants to talk to him and everyone wants information on him," Sport Information Director John Morris said to the *Collegian's* McCallister. Cappelletti told McCallister, "It's nice to hear all the talk about the Maxwell Trophy and the Heisman Trophy but we have some team goals that come first." One of those goals was to continue winning, move up in the ratings and get a bowl bid that could help win the National Championship. But the sportswriters were still not awed by the Lions, dropping them down to #6 in the AP rankings despite the WVU slaughter and leapfrogging previously #8 Notre Dame in at #5 after the Irish had stopped then #6 USC's 23-game unbeaten streak. An Orange Bowl scout who watched the WVU game had indicated a possible match with #2 Alabama was in the works for Penn State but he admitted that the Notre Dame upset probably changed things. *The New York Times* said the Lions may be headed to the Sugar Bowl and another report had the Cotton Bowl interested in the Lions as one of four teams for the visiting berth against the SWC champ.

What happened the next two weeks against Maryland and North Carolina State defined the season and catapulted Cappelletti to the front of the Heisman race. Jerry Claiborne had revitalized Maryland football and despite losses to West Virginia and NC State, his 5-2 team was the best Terp squad in more than a decade. The Lions and Terps were among the nation's leaders in defense against the rush, total defense and scoring but one wouldn't have known that by the final score. As a slew of bowl scouts watched, State took a 12-0 lead in less than two minutes of the first quarter at Byrd Stadium when Hayman ran back the opening kickoff a near-record 98 yards and Nagle scored following Buttle's fumble recovery at the Maryland 18 on the ensuing kickoff. A few minutes later, the Terps stripped the ball from Cappelletti and scored on a 34-yard halfback pass, then made it 12-10 near the end of the first quarter on Steve Mike-Mayer's 21-yard field goal. Another halfback pass of 11-yards to tight end Randy White following Bob Smith's 47-yard punt return gave Maryland a 16-12 lead early in the second quarter but the Lions regained the lead on a 17-yard pass in the flat from Shuman to Natale and stretched it to 22-16 with three minutes left in the half on Bahr's 39-yard field goal. But with just 22 second remaining, Smith broke free on an 83-yard punt return and Mike-Mayer's extra point tied the game as the half ended with the partisan crowd of 44,135 in bedlam.

Cappelletti and the State defense took control in the second half. Early in the third quarter Bradley's interception at the Terp 31 set up a 30-yard TD pass from Shuman to Scott. Minutes later, Murphy recovered a fumble at the Maryland 17 and Cappelletti carried three straight times to the 3 yard line from where Shuman passed to Natale for the score. Bahr kicked both extra points, then kicked field goals of 25 and 29 yards. Maryland's last chance at another TD in the closing minutes was stopped on an interception by Ellis in the end zone as the Lions won, 42-22. Cappelletti rushed for over 200 yards for the first time (202) and had 37 of the team's 66 carries, breaking the PSU single game record for carries. "So impressive was his performance," wrote Ron Bracken in the *Centre Daily Times*, "that even a partisan Maryland writer stood and applauded when the senior tailback left the field for the final time."

On the eve of the NC State game at Beaver Stadium, the AP reported that Orange Bowl had all but tied up

A young coach named Lou Holtz of North Carolina State and Joe Paterno shake hands after one of their games in the 1970s. The two were destined to meet many more times in later years.

#6 State against #7 LSU after Bear Bryant had said he wanted Alabama to play Notre Dame in the Sugar Bowl. Notre Dame would not commit until after its game the next day against #20 Pitt and Sugar Bowl sources said State would be Alabama's likely opponent if the Irish said no. Meanwhile, the Liberty Bowl was interested in NC State, which was leading the ACC with a 6-2 record and had one of the best offenses in the country. The game turned into another wild shoot-out in the freezing cold and snow before 59,424 and scouts from the Orange and Liberty bowls. The Lions fumbled away two first quarter opportunities, then allowed Lou Holtz' Wolfpack to become the first team of the season to score on the ground against them with a 50-yard drive early in the second quarter. By halftime, NC State had a 14-9 lead, after scoring another TD on the ground following a 53-yard kickoff return, with the Lions getting a 13-yard Bahr field goal and a 34-yard TD run by Cappelletti at the end of an 8-play, 78-yard drive.

At the start of the second half, Shuman led the Lions on another 78-yard drive in nine plays, with a 40-yard pass to Hayman into the wind setting up a 20-yard pitchout to Cappelletti for the TD. A two-point conversion pass attempt failed but State made it 22-14 on a dazzling 83-yard punt return by Hayman and Bahr's PAT. Before the quarter ended, NC State tied the game after a 70-yard drive and two-point conversion. The Lions went ahead again in the fourth quarter after another punt return by Hayman for 27 yards and Cappelletti's running led to a 10-yard TD by Nagle. But moments later, fullback Charlie Young's 69-yard TD run and another Ron Sewell PAT tied the score again at 29. The Lions regained the lead two minutes and six plays later as Cappelletti carried four times in a 60-yard drive and scored on a 27-yard run. But Bahr missed the PAT and the 35-29 score with about 8 and a half minutes left kept everyone in their seats. NC State almost blew the ensuing kickoff when the return man slipped at the one-yard line but the Wolfpack moved upfield to their own 40 before being forced to punt after trying to draw the Lions offside. NC State had one last gasp and sophomore quarterback Dave Buckey led the Wolfpack to the PSU 40 before giving up the ball on downs with two seconds left. "I thought we'd have an advantage because our players are accustomed to the cold and winds in this valley in November," Paterno told Riley for the *"Football Letter,"* but they seemed to adjust better than we did." But NC State still couldn't stop Cappelletti, who had his best running day ever with 231 yards and three TDs and an all-time record of 41 carries.

The next week at Beaver Stadium, Cappelletti set three records that have never been equaled when he rushed for 204 yards and scored four touchdowns in a playing span of 30 minutes as the Lions beat Ohio University 49-10 and accepted an invitation to the Orange Bowl. Cappelletti's third rushing day of 200 yards or more was a new school mark for consecutive games, most in one season and most in a career. The bowl invitation to play LSU was a formality since all the bowls had actually worked out ironclad agreements with their "committed team" before the Saturday 6 p.m. time sanctioned by the NCAA. Four bowl-bound teams had lost earlier in the day and LSU would lose to both Alabama and Tulane before playing State on New Year's Day—a factor that took more luster off the game and, thus, diminished the Lions' ultimate accomplishments. State also had one game left, against a fired-up Pitt rival, and to win that one required a second half comeback spearheaded by Cappelletti, of course.

For the first time in 71 years the Lions were playing Pitt twice in a row at home. Majors had Pitt (6-3-1) ready for an upset, just like the "old days" of this series when the underdog often spoiled the other team's bowl chances. State's offense seemed listless in the first half and a poor punt helped Pitt get a touchdown on a 14-yard run by freshman star Tony Dorsett, one of the nation's leading rushers who had gained 209 yards against #3 Notre Dame. Freshman Carson Long's field goals of 31 and 51 yards helped give Pitt a surprising 13-3 halftime lead. But the cocky Long had riled the State players at the end of the half after booting his 51-yarder in the closing seconds when he defiantly shook his fist at the State bench as the Panther players raced onto the field to congratulate him. "They acted like the game was over," Devlin later told Bob Smizik of the *Pittsburgh Press,* who quoted Dorsett after the game as saying, "When (State) came out in the second half, they were really psyched up."

The angry Lions took control after kicking off to the Panthers and forcing a punt from the 10-yard line to gain field position. State then drove from midfield with Shuman's 15-yard screen pass to Cappelletti giving PSU a first down at the Pitt 2. The Panthers stopped Cappelletti for no gain but an offside penalty against Pitt placed the ball at the one. Cappelletti tried again, twice, and the aroused Panthers sent him back to the 6. On third down, Shuman rolled out and under pressure threw the ball in the direction of tackle Getty. At the same time, an official called interference against Pitt in the end zone. Majors protested vehemently that Shuman should be called for intentional grounding, despite the rule which states it is not intentional grounding "If any player occupies the area into which a pass is thrown." With the ball back on the Pitt one, Cappelletti and Donchez were held for no gain before Shuman faked to Cappelletti and Nagle banged up the middle for the TD. Shuman's 2-point pass to Hayman made it 13-11. After the game, Majors said the non-call on Shuman's pass was the turning point, and Panther players claimed they were cheated. Of course, off-setting penalties at that crucial juncture would still have given Shuman another chance for a TD or a field goal.

The Lions took the lead on the third play of the fourth quarter after another drive from midfield with Cappelletti going over from the 5. A minute later Hull intercepted a Bill Daniels pass and ran 28 yards for another TD and it was all over for Pitt. Herd set a new record for career TD passes when he caught his 10th on a 32-yard throw from Shuman and Bahr also set a record with his 11th field goal of the season (covering 45 yards) and the Lions won, 35-13. Cappelletti, who won the Coogan Award as the game's outstanding player, finished with 161 yards on 37 carries, which gave him 1,522 yards for the season and 2,639 for his career—second only to Lydell Mitchell. "(Cappelletti's) the kind of guy who makes you undefeated," Paterno told sportswriters. Meanwhile, the State defense had held the Panthers to 93 net yards with Dorsett getting just 77 on 20 carries.

When the First Team All-American squads were announced, Cappelletti made most of them. Crowder and O'Neil also were selected to several and Crowder also was chosen Defensive Player-of-the-Year by the Washington Pigskin Club. Natale, Markovich and Getty were second-team choices. Never before had a State team had so many first and second team All-Americans in one year. But the biggest awards went to Cappelletti as he was an overwhelming choice for both the Heisman and (the lesser known) Maxwell awards. Cappelletti's emotional, heartfelt acceptance speech at the Heisman dinner on December 13 has become part of the Heisman and Penn State football legend. After thanking his father and mother, his high school and college coaches and his teammates, he focused on his 11-year-old brother,

Joey, who was stricken with leukemia and was in the audience at the New York Hilton Hotel that night. John was not sure of what he was going to say as he discarded his notes. "If I can dedicate this trophy to (Joey) tonight and give him a couple days of happiness, this is worth everything," Cappelletti said through tears as vice president Gerald Ford, Archbishop Fulton Sheen and hundreds of other dignitaries listened in reverent silence. "I think a lot of people think that I go through a lot on Saturdays and during the week...Only for me...it's only in the Fall. For Joseph, it is all year round and it is a battle that is unending with him and he puts up with much more than I'll ever put up with and I think that this trophy is more his than mine because he has been a great inspiration to me." The standing ovation lasted for minutes and there were few dry eyes in the crowded room that night. Joey died on April 6, 1976, and a year later a television movie, "Something For Joey" immortalized John and his kid brother and the most famous Heisman speech of all time.

THE 1974 ORANGE BOWL
Jan. 1, 1974
Penn State 16, Louisiana State U. 9
Most Valuable Back: Tom Shuman
Most Valuable Lineman: Randy Crowder

Even before the players arrived in Miami the day after Christmas they knew their chances for winning the National Championship were practically nil. For weeks, sportswriters and ABC had been promoting the Sugar Bowl game between undefeated and untied #1 Alabama and #3 Notre Dame as the one for the national title. State, #6 in the rankings at the end of the regular season, was the only other team with a spotless record. All the others ahead of the Lions had a tie. Oklahoma, now coached by Barry Switzer after Fairbanks had taken the Patriot job Paterno had rejected, was #2 but on probation and

Underrated QB Tom Shuman led the Lions to 22 wins in 24 starts in the 1973-74 seasons. He saved some of his best performances for the Orange and Cotton Bowl victories over LSU and Baylor.

banned from a bowl. No. 4 Ohio State was playing #7 USC in the Rose Bowl and #5 Michigan was through for the season. LSU's season-ending defeats to Alabama, 21-7, and Tulane, 14-0, had dropped the Tigers to #13 and taken much of the glamour off the New Year's Night Orange Bowl. Furthermore, in their pre-bowl analyses many of the country's leading sportswriters continued to demean State's schedule, despite three opponents who were in bowl games.

Many players watched the Sugar Bowl in their rooms of the Ivanhoe Hotel on New Year's Eve, so they knew long before kickoff that Notre Dame had upset Alabama in a thrilling 24-

Now an orthopedic surgeon and team doctor for the Pittsburgh Steelers, Jim Bradley made the tackle that turned around the Orange Bowl game against LSU in 1974. His brother Tom was captain of the 1978 special teams unit known as "The Scrap Pack" and is now an assistant coach and prime recruiter at PSU.

23 victory. Perhaps, that is why the defense looked sluggish in the opening minutes of the Orange Bowl game. A less than capacity crowd of 60,477 showed up just as the rain stopped and watched LSU run the opening kickoff to midfield, then drive 51 yards in nine plays behind the running of Brad Davis to score a touchdown and extra point three minutes later. That TD seemed to wake up the Lions. Despite a close score, the rest of the way, the Tigers only had two more serious scoring opportunities, getting the rest of its points when State botched a punt near the end zone early in the third quarter and gave up a safety. In fact, the game could have turned into a rout if the officials had not blown two calls in the first half on big plays that should have been touchdowns—as the television replays proved.

After the LSU TD, Bahr kicked a 44-yard field goal that set an Orange Bowl record and with the score 7-3 at the end of the first quarter, LSU drove into range for a long field goal. Graf blocked the kick and the ball bounced back upfield before Murphy recovered at the LSU 35. On the first play, Shuman hit Herd deep in the end zone but an official ruled Herd was out of bounds. The TV replay showed the senior did have one foot in the end zone when he caught the pass. Cappelletti then went around left end for a first down at the 25 but State was penalized to midfield and then had to punt. But the defense held the Tigers and they returned the punt. Hayman, the nation's leading punt returner, caught the ball near the PSU 30, slipped almost to his knees on the soaked Poly-Turf but gained his balance and was in the clear at the LSU 25 for an apparent TD when the officials stopped him, claiming his knee had touched. Again, the TV replay showed otherwise. Two plays later, with the LSU defense concentrating on stopping Cappelletti inside, Shuman found Herd in the clear at the LSU 35. The pass was a little high but Herd, running full speed, reached up, took the ball on the finger tips of his left hand and sped into the end zone for a 72-yard TD.

Bahr's PAT gave State a 10-7 lead. Minutes later Hayman returned a punt 25 yards to the LSU 26 and with 2:19 left in the half, Cappelletti vaulted over from the 2. Bahr's kick hit the left upright and State led 16-7.

With about 1:30 left in the half, State had LSU backed up to its 19 on a fourth-and-one and called a time out. The move almost backfired as the Lions were penalized on the punt and LSU quickly moved to a first down at the State 9 when LSU called its final time out. McClendon told his quarterback, Mike Miley, to try a pass to Davis but to throw out of bounds if Davis was covered and they'd go for a field goal. Miley hit Davis at the 5-yard line but Bradley hit him immediately and time ran out. The second half turned into a defensive battle with both Paterno and McClendon playing a conservative game that tried to get the other team to make a mistake. The 16-9 final drew some yawns from some of the sportswriters but Paterno and the team were happy. LSU had won the statistics but had never been in control. The Tigers held Cappelletti to the lowest yardage of his career—50 yards on 26 carries—and to their credit, neither the players nor Paterno used the excuse that they could have. Cappelletti had sprained his ankle in practice but the injury had been kept secret. "No, it didn't bother me," Cappelletti told Heufelder of the *Pittsburgh Press*. "Their defense just played well. Their linebackers were plugging the holes." Co-captain Markovich agreed, saying "The holes weren't there. We just had trouble blocking their defenses."

The victory had made this team the first in PSU history to win 12 games and in the locker room, Paterno said "This was the best team I've ever coached." He was asked about the number one ranking and replied, "We have as much right to claim the top place as anyone else. We're undefeated. Our players accomplished every goal they set for themselves and they have a right to think they are as good as anybody. I have my own poll—the Paterno poll. The vote was unanimous—Penn State is Number One!" But the AP and UPI polls snubbed the Lions by voting them #5. It would not be the last time Paterno would need the "Paterno Poll" to make one of his State teams Number One. And, eventually, he'd get his crack at Alabama, Notre Dame and Nebraska. But next year it would be an old friend and a new antagonist who would do him in, not a bunch of biased sportswriters and jealous coaches.

Season Record 12-0
Record to Date 492-235-40
Winning percentage .668

"The Christians and The Lions"

Joe Paterno didn't try to fool himself when he looked at his team as it went through preseason drills in early September. He had lost 13 starters from the undefeated squad of '73 and 10 of them had been drafted into the NFL. For the first time in his nine years as head coach, he did not have an outstanding running back. Nor did he have any wide receivers with the speed of his graduated trio—unless he counted freshman Jimmy Cefalo of Pittston and he didn't.

Although all his opponents were using freshmen, Paterno still insisted—stubbornly, some friends told him—that their playing time

be limited so they could concentrate on their academics. Before the season was over, Cefalo—who had been recruited by more than 100 colleges—would not only be starting but also would become one of the stars of the Cotton Bowl.

At least he had his quarterback back. "If I didn't have Shuman, I'd be down on my knees," he told sportswriters. If Shuman got hurt he would have a major problem because the backup was untried sophomore John Andress. Neither quarterback had looked that good in the annual spring Blue-White game, which took on a defensive character and ended in a 7-6 score. But with the September 14 opening game against Stanford on national television fast approaching, Shuman was getting his old rhythm back.

Paterno had been upset that many of the players were out of shape when they reported back after the summer. "This is the slowest team here since 1966," he told Rick Starr of the *Daily Collegian*. "A lot of people think we'll keep on winning because we've won before, but we're not going to make a yard on what we did last year." Still, he told Riley for the *"Football Letter,"* "It's going to be a fun season because it will be a challenge to all of us..." The preseason certainly became a challenge to sportswriters covering the PSU beat because Paterno closed many practices for the first time as he and his coaches overhauled the offense.

The coaches adapted the attack to fit the skills of their players so they restructured it around fullback Donchez, a running wingback and a short passing game that featured tight end Natale and all the running backs. Because of all the inexperience, particularly on offense, Paterno continued moving players around during the season. Addie, Petchel and Boyle would split the tailback assignment and Taylor would back up at fullback with senior letterman Jim Eaise at wingback and later at split end, along with senior Jerry Jeram. Co-captain Baiorunos was the center again and Nessel moved to left tackle and would be the starter most of the year until sophomore Brad Benson of Altoona took over late in the season. Senior letterman Jeff Bleamer had won the Worrell Award as the most improved player in the spring and would start at right tackle with last year's backup Rafferty at left guard and sophomore George Reihner (John's brother) alternating at right guard with junior Mark Thomas.

The defense was in better shape with three of the front line returning—Graf, Hartenstine and Murphy—along with co-captain Bradley at defensive halfback. Junior letterman John Quinn took Crowder's old tackle position and juniors Tom Odell and Jeff Hite shared the other halfback slot with Mike Johnson and Tom Giotto splitting time at safety.

Devlin returned at outside linebacker along with

Scholar athlete center Jack Baiorunos was a Third-Team All-American in 1974 and winner of a National Football Foundation and College Football Hall of Fame fellowship and a NCAA postgraduate scholarship in 1975.

last season's prime inside reserve, Buttle. Junior letterman Jim Rosecrans won the other inside spot and senior veterans Joe Jackson and Buddy Tenser shared the other outside position. A sophomore walk-on from State College named Tim Curley was listed as a reserve halfback, and some 20 years later he would become Paterno's boss as PSU's athletic director. There was another change on defense but this was in the coaching staff as Frank Patrick, who had been an assistant since the Higgins era, retired as defensive backs coach and was replaced by Ducatte, co-captain of the '72 team. "Our defense is going to have to carry us in that (first) game," Paterno said. His defense also included the kicking game, which had everyone returning: punter Masella, kickoff man Reihner and Bahr, who would again play soccer and placekick. Bahr and Reihner also would have to be sharper on field goals and extra points because of a new rule that stated successful kicks "must go between the two uprights" and not just over one.

Despite the inexperience and obvious problems on offense, the Lions were still picked among the Top 20 teams. But again there were jibes about the schedule, even though Maryland and North Carolina State were tabbed as the leaders of the ACC and were also in the Top 20 along with Pitt and Stanford. The AP rated State at #8 with the *Sporting News* picking the Lions at #4 and *Playboy* at #12. "The relatively easy schedule is a big aid towards another fine record," reported the Syracuse-based magazine, *Game Plan*, which placed the Lions #16, then rated Pitt, Stanford and Maryland ahead of them.

Over the summer, the university had formally withdrawn from the Eastern Collegiate Athletic Conference in a dispute over funding and so the athletic department worked out an arrangement with the Big Ten to provide officials for home games. Perhaps, it was not surprising then—as Lion fans have discovered three decades later—that Stanford coach Jack Christiansen said "the officiating stunk today" after State won a 24-20 thriller in the sun-drenched opener at Beaver Stadium. The Goodyear Blimp was in the air, Notre Dame coach Ara Parseghian was in the booth with Keith Jackson and Jim Lampley was on the sidelines when it all happened.

Christiansen was complaining specifically about two fourth quarter penalties for clipping and interference. The clip nullified a Stanford touchdown with the score tied 17-all with about six minutes left in the game and the Cardinals eventually had to settle for an 18-yard field goal that put them ahead, 20-17. The interference call came three minutes later against Stanford at its goal line as the Lions were driving 80-yards for what became the winning touchdown. The interference on a 13-yard pass from Shuman to reserve split end Dick Barvinchak set up a one-yard dive off tackle by Petchel and Bahr's PAT finished the scoring. Television replays appeared to support the officials. Of course, Christiansen didn't complain about the back-to-back penalties against the Lions for roughing-the-kicker and piling on that gave Stanford breaks deep in State territory in the second quarter when the Lions were leading 14-0.

Paterno had surprised the highly-touted Stanford defense led by All-American ends Roger Stillwell and Pat Donovan by using the wingback, Eaise, on "end-around" plays and that had helped set up TDs on a 6-yard pass from Shuman to Donchez and a 1-yard run by Addie. But after the two second quarter penalties against the Lions allowed Stanford good field position, sophomore Quarterback Mike Cordova's passing gave the Cardinals one TD and led to a 29-yard field goal by Mike Langford on the last play of the first half. Bahr, who had scored a goal in a soccer game at nearby Jeffrey Field Friday night,

booted a 22-yard field goal in the third quarter but after he missed another field goal from the 27 early in the fourth quarter, Cordova drove Stanford 80-yards to tie the game and set-up the whirlwind finish. With less than two minutes remaining, Cordova had one more chance to win the game but his 60-yard pass was intercepted by Giotto and the Lions ran out the clock. Cordova's 301 yards passing in 51 attempts set new Beaver Stadium records and his 32 completions tied another. Donchez rushed for over 100 yards

A typical second half comeback characteristic of a Paterno team seemed to be developing when State took the third quarter kickoff and drove inside the Navy 10-yard line. But the Middie defense held again and Bahr missed another field goal from the 19. Later in the quarter, the Lions reached the Navy 12 and early in the fourth quarter they were at the Navy 9 but lost the ball on fumbles by Donchez. Midway in the final quarter, the Lions finally scored, going 58 yards in 7 plays with Shuman passing to Jeram on a third-and-goal at the 5 for the TD with about 4:40 remaining. Paterno said after the game there was no doubt about going for two points but Shuman's pass to Eaise was batted down by Ed Jeter. State had one last chance when the defense forced Navy to punt and Eaise returned the kick 17 yards to the Navy 38. Paterno worked for field position and with 46 seconds left State had a fourth-and-9 at the 26 when Bahr went into to try and win. It was certainly within his range but the 43-yard boot veered right and just missed. Navy ran out the clock and won, 7-6. "I don't know how the hell we won it," a delighted but exhausted Welsh told sportswriters. "It seemed like they were going up and down the field." He was right. The Lions had 378 net yards and 21 first downs to the Middies' 172 net yards and 8 first downs. But losing five of seven fumbles and missing field goals cost them the game. It was no consolation to Donchez that he had his best ever running day with 166 yards on 35 carries for three of the fumbles were his. When Paterno was asked if the weather affected the game, he replied "it seemed to me it was raining over there (on the Navy side), too," adding, "if you're going to lose it, it might as well be to a member of the family."

The Lions dropped all the way to #19 in the AP poll as Pitt moved up to #7 and NC State to #13. The AP also picked Iowa, an upset winner over UCLA, 21-10, to beat the Lions by six points at Iowa City the following Saturday. It rained throughout the game again but it was nowhere near the type of downpour of the previous week in State College. The Lions won the toss and chose to kickoff with the wind and the decision kept Iowa in a hole all day. The Hawkeyes never reached Lion territory until late in the game as the defense led by Murphy and

Double-teaming First-Team All-American Mike Hartenstein made little difference as he led the underrated unbeaten 1973 team with 104 tackles. Hartenstein went on to be a star with the Chicago Bears.

Hartenstine held Iowa to 66 yards rushing and 43 yards passing in a 27-0 win. "That No. 79 (Hartenstine) should be All-World," Iowa's new coach Bob Cummins said. The PSU offense didn't make any mistakes either. Injuries to Addie and Petchel forced Paterno to use reserve tailbacks and third stringer Rusty Boyle led all rushers with 77 yards while fourth stringer Dave Stutts, a sophomore, scored two TDs. Bahr flew in from Pittsburgh but because he had been injured in a soccer game Friday night, Reihner did all the kicking and booted field goals of 30 and 19 yards and three extra points. "That guy is their second string kicker?" an Iowa newspaperman said after two of Reihner's kickoffs sailed into the end zone against the wind. The Lions moved back up to #15 and got set to travel to West Point to meet 1-and-2 Army, which also had a new coach named Homer Smith who had introduced the Wishbone offense to the Cadets.

The Wishbone gave State's defense some problems in the first quarter but it was more fumbling by Donchez that led to a surprising 14-0 Army lead that had the 41,221 at sunny Michie Stadium thinking about another upset. On the first play after the opening kickoff, Donchez muffed a handoff from Shuman and Army recovered at the 12-yard line. Three running plays later, Army had a TD and led 7-0. A short time later, Donchez fumbled again at the PSU 41. Army recovered at the 38 and using all running plays advanced into the end zone, with quarterback Scott Gillogly scoring on a fourth-and-goal at the one and plebe Mike Castelli booting his second extra point. Late in the quarter, another fumble by Duane Taylor at the Lion 39 almost gave Army the ball again but freshman tight end Randy Sidler, subbing for Natale who had been injured, recovered. The Lions went on to complete a 75-yard drive and get a TD on Donchez' 2-yard plunge as the second quarter started. Paterno surprised everyone by going for 2-points and wingback Cefalo scored on an "end around" Army's right side. The defense was now in control and just before the end of the half, it forced a short punt to the Army 38. With less than a minute remaining, Shuman hit Sidler for a TD on a third down pass from the 18-yard line and Reihner kicked the go-ahead extra point. The defense kept Army from penetrating past the 50 in the second half and the Lions added another TD in the final quarter on a 16-play, 83-yard drive with Taylor running 19 yards for the TD. A bad snap ruined the PAT attempt but the Lions won, 21-14. "Unless Penn State cuts down on mistakes and manages to mix an air attack with it inside ground moves," wrote Gordon White in the *New York Times*, "Coach Joe Paterno's team might lose again this season."

The only game ever with Wake Forest was a treat for 56,500 Homecoming fans as Paterno used 80 players in a 55-0 romp. Six different players scored TDs but it was two by Cefalo that had the fans and sportswrit-

ers buzzing. In the first quarter, Cefalo caught a 57-yard bomb from Shuman for State's second TD, then ran 39-yards on an end around in the third quarter to give the Lions a commanding 34-0 lead. Shuman hit on 12-of-14 passes for 183 yards and two TDs as the offense netted 536 yards rushing and passing. The game also was noteworthy when Sidler became the first frosh to start a varsity game in 23 years because Natale remained sidelined with an injury. The next week, Shuman led another comeback over Syracuse at Beaver Stadium after the Orange had stunned State and a standing-room-only crowd of 59,100 on the first play of the game by throwing a 77-yard pass for a touchdown. Rookie coach Frank Maloney's team took a 14-3 lead midway in the second quarter before Shuman directed an 80-yard drive and scored on a 2-yard run that narrowed the score to 14-10 at the intermission. The Lions took the lead 17-10 seven minutes into the third quarter as Shuman again marched the team 80 yards and scored on a 9-yard run. In the fourth quarter, Shuman threw a 10-yard pass to Taylor and the Lions won, 30-14. Shuman hit on 13-of-20 passes for 167 yards while Donchez picked up 120 of the Lions' 354 net yards rushing. Although pleased with his offense, Paterno complained after the game about his inconsistent defense, saying the Lions "have to be more reckless."

The crowd in Morgantown the following Saturday seemed less frenzied than in past appearances by State and there were several thousand empty seats despite the perfect weather. State was now #10 in the AP and a 10-point favorite over the Mountaineers who had lost four games but three by four points or less. As an Orange Bowl scout watched, the tone of the game was set on West Virginia's opening possession when punter Bernie Kirchner fumbled the snap and Hartenstine recovered at the 35. Three plays later Shuman fired a 30-yard pass to Jeram and with Reihner's PAT the Lions took a lead they never relinquished. With the score at 14-6 in the third quarter, State scored the clinching TD on a bizarre play when WVU blocked a Reihner field goal attempt from the 17-yard line. Mountaineer defender Jack Eastwood tried to pick up the ball but it bounded off his hands into the end zone where Eastwood fell on it with his legs. He didn't realize it was still a free ball and State's junior guard Ron Coder jumped on the ball and an official signaled touchdown. WVU scored again but the Lions won, 21-12. Bowden was disappointed with his team but said the official made the right call. "We make a great play and smell like a rose and then came out in the end smelling bad," he told sportswriters.

A regional ABC TV audience and a Beaver Stadium crowd of 60,125 including several bowl scouts would see something even more unusual the next week when #10 State clashed with #15 Maryland (5-2). On Maryland's second posses-

The Lion mascot does his traditional pushups following a Penn State score in front of the student section with help from the cheerleaders.

sion, quarterback Bob Avellini had moved the Terps to the Lion 19 when he tried to pass to speedster Lou Carter in the flat. Hite, subbing for the injured Bradley, stepped in front of Carter and ran 79-yards for a touchdown. A 34-yard TD pass from Avellini to Walter White had tied the game at 7-7 with 8:28 left in the half but State took the lead again 14-7 on a 7-yard pass to Barvinchak after an 80-yard drive. Then Hite struck again. Ricky Jennings was running back Reihner's kickoff from the 8-yard line and had reached the 21 when he turned to lateral to a trailing Carter. Hite, sensing a lateral because of what State's coaches had talked about in practice that week, speared the lateral with one hand and was across the goal line before many watching knew what happened. That made it 21-7 but on the first play after the kickoff, Avellini hit White on a 66-yard bomb and the half ended 21-14. The teams parried in the second half but could score only field goals in the fourth quarter as Masella's punting (9 punts averaging 47 yards) and State's harassing defense (6 sacks for 58 yards) kept Avellini's potent passing attack (302 total yards) off balance. The Terps came close, however. With 2:47 left, Maryland had a third-and-2 at the PSU 11 but sophomore linebacker Kurt Allerman stopped the Terps' runner for a one-yard loss and Avellini overthrew on fourth down when he was rushed hard. Maryland regained the ball with 27 seconds left but Avellini had three incompletions before his final pass was intercepted by Rosecrans and the Lions won, 24-17. In the locker room Avellini told Paul Attner of the *Washington Post* he was "shocked" that State's defense seemed to know Maryland's plays. "It was like they were hearing the plays in the huddle," he said. "I don't know who was tipping it off but they knew what was going on."

On Monday, athletic director Czekaj received a telephone call from the Cotton Bowl inquiring about the Lions' interest in playing the SWC champion. Official bowl invitations were not allowed until the next Saturday but once again all the bowls were scrambling to get firm commitments from contending teams. "It was revealed by a team spokesmen that Penn State players have already agreed to accept the anticipated Cotton Bowl invitation," wrote Starr of the *Collegian*, adding that the opponent probably would be Texas A & M or Texas or possibly Baylor, which still had an outside chance at the SWC title. State was now #7 in the polls and Texas A &M was #5. Czekaj told Starr he had not heard from any other bowls.

To say that Holtz had his North Carolina State team primed for an upset in Raleigh on November 9 would be an understatement. The Wolfpack had won seven games but blamed fumbles on its losses to North Carolina and Maryland away from home. In addition, Holtz was 13-0-1 at Carter Stadium. The Lions looked flat in the first half but NC State was sharp and drove 80 yards in 14 plays for a 6-0 lead in the second quarter. On the opening kickoff of the second half, the Wolfpack moved 73 yards to score again and this time the touchdown came on a play the Lions had seen before—against Navy—and again helped define the season. Wolfpack fullback Stan Fritts took a pitchout from Dave Buckey at the PSU 22 and passed to tight end Pat Horvance at the 5, and Horvance scored with Buttle and Johnson hanging on his back. That momentarily fired up the Lions. They took the kickoff and drove for a first down at the Wolfpack 6. But the Wolfpack stopped State on a goal line stand, halting a third down end around by Barvinchak for a 9-yard loss and hurrying Shuman into a fourth down incompletion. Then, with three minutes remaining in the game, the Lions went 80 yards in 10 plays to score with Shuman passing 13 yards to Eaise for the TD with 43 seconds left. Reihner made it 12-7 and Bahr tried an onside kick. The boot failed and NC State celebrated its upset victory, the first

ever in 11 games with the Lions. In the festive Wolfpack dressing room, the team presented the game ball to the former Lion player and assistant coach, Al Michaels, now NC State's defensive coordinator. Over in the quiet and grim PSU dressing room, three nattily dressed Cotton Bowl executives made their way to Paterno, offered condolences, then extended the invitation for New Year's Day. "We wanted Penn State before this game and we want you now," Field Scovell told the players. "We know today has been a big disappointment to Coach Paterno and to you players—more than it is to us. This makes the fifth straight year a team we've invited to the Cotton Bowl lost before it got to Dallas, so we're not embarrassed." Neither was Paterno, on the surface, at least." I wouldn't let one loss bother us," he said. "I'm looking forward to (the bowl)." Then he launched into another promotion for a post-season college football playoff "by 1980." (Dream on, Joe!) Riley had his own take on the game. "...Penn State should take measures to abolish the fullback pass," he wrote. "This play scored the winning points for Navy and N.C. State." Before the day was over, the Cotton Bowl folks had two more shocks—SMU had upset conference leading Texas A&M and Baylor had clobbered second place Texas.

A less than happy State team closed out the home season the next week with a 35-16 win over Ohio University, despite injuries to several players, 85 yards in penalties and four more lost fumbles. Donchez scored three TDs as the Lions built up a 35-0 lead before the reserves took over. Two facts made the game notable. It was the 500th victory in PSU football history and the first start ever for Cefalo, who ran for 36 yards on seven carries.

Ten days later, a national TV audience watched on Thanksgiving Night as State played Pitt at chilly Three Rivers Stadium in a game that hyped Pitt's sophomore Dorsett—who again had gained more than 1,000 yards—as a "Lion killer." Some wrote that State should have been playing in the "Turkey Bowl." The Lions players were so emotional in the dressing room before the game that when Donchez threw his helmet against a locker at the end of a passionate oratory the helmet bounced and hit Buttle between the eyes, knocking him cold. He came to just before kickoff and played the entire game with a bloody head gash, and continued to call the defensive signals. "Everything seemed to be in slow motion for the first quarter," Buttle told reporters later. Maybe that is one reason why Pitt was able to take a 7-6 halftime lead in the 25-degree, windy weather. A fumbled punt at the PSU 30 led to the Panthers TD. Bahr kicked a near record 50-yard field goal in the first quarter and a 20-yarder in the second quarter as State's defense played without three starting linebackers, who were injured. But that crippled defense led by Hartenstine, who had been named a First Team All-American and was ABC's defensive player of the game, gave up just three points in the second half and held Dorsett to 64 net yards. Meanwhile, the offense scored 25 points and the Lions won 31-10. Bahr kicked two more field goals to set a school single game record and Shuman hit Eaise on touchdown passes of 23 and 35 yards, giving Shuman the career record for TD passes at 28. It was Paterno's ninth straight victory over Pitt and the 100th game of his coaching career.

THE 1975 COTTON BOWL
Jan. 1, 1975
Penn State 41, Baylor 20
Outstanding Offensive Player: Tom Shuman

When Baylor surprised everyone by winning its first Southwest Conference championship in 50 years, the Cotton Bowl game took on a different flavor and piqued the interest of college football fans. There was no National Championship game. Oklahoma, #1 in the AP, was still on probation and ineligible for a bowl. Alabama, #2, was playing #9 Notre Dame in the Orange Bowl and #3 Ohio State was meeting #5 USC in the Rose Bowl. They were intriguing match-ups but so was the Cotton Bowl, which set the Christians against the Lions, as many sportswriters noted.

Second-Team All-American Dan Natale was one of the stars of the 1975 Cotton Bowl win over Baylor. The big TE had over 1,000 yards receiving during his career but may have been the best blocking TE in PSU history, until Kyle Brady came along in the 90s.

Baylor was a Cinderella team. The Bears had not had a winning team in 11 years and after a 2-9 record in '73 they were a pre-season pick for the Southwest Conference cellar in '74. Now, they were 8-3, 6-1 in the SWC and winners of five straight. Moreover, as the largest Baptist college in the world, Baylor had God on its side—at least that's what the sportswriters wrote, particularly after evangelist Billy Graham flew into Dallas to cheer for the Bears. In addition, Baylor's third-year coach, Grant Teaff was a lay minister and he preached a rousing sermon from a Dallas pulpit three days before the game. When Teaff and Paterno got together at one of the pregame Cotton Bowl luncheons they joked about the religious fervor of the game. "I'm glad to see Joe doesn't have any rosary beads," Teaff cracked. "Yes, but I'll put my mother and her rosary beads up against all that religion," Paterno replied and the crowd loved it.

There also was a David & Goliath touch to the affair and not just because the football teams had vastly different genealogies. Baylor's full time enrollment was 8,100 compared to the 30,200 on PSU's main campus. This size differential was easily seen at the Cotton Bowl parade when spectators watched the 175-piece State Blue Band march past followed by the 40-piece Golden Wave band of Baylor. But unlike the '72 Cotton Bowl when the Dallas citizenry mocked State's schedule and its Eastern roots, the ambiance this time was pleasant and admiring. There was no criticism about a soft schedule or any talk about the luck of Paterno and his Lions. More than 5,000 tickets were sold to State fans and they partied throughout Dallas as if they were long lost friends of the hosts.

Seventh-ranked State was a 4-point favorite but on the eve of the game, Baylor received a little spiritual boost when Teaff was named Coach of the Year by the Football Writers Association of America. A light rain fell in 44 degree weather before the game and Billy Graham visited both dressing rooms, offering a prayer to all the players, before taking his seat with all the Baylor followers wearing buttons that said, "I Believe." State blew a couple of scoring opportunities in the first half and Baylor drove 85 yards after a Donchez fumble in the first quarter to score with the help of a third down offside penalty against the Lions at the PSU 9-yard line. In the press box, the excited Texas writers had to

be reminded by the press box announcer that "We know its been 50 years, but no cheering." Bahr's 25-yard field goal a minute before the half made the score 7-3 at the intermission. The Lions took the second half kickoff and with Shuman passing twice to Natale for 62 yards and Donchez running the other 18 yards on 6 plays, including one-yard for the TD, State took a 10-7 lead. Midway in the quarter, Shuman hit Donchez on a sparkling 64-yard screen pass but the TD was nullified when the Lions were hit with an interference penalty and further penalized for unsportsmanlike conduct against Shuman after the Lion quarterback picked up the flag. The Lions were forced to punt from their 11-yard line and four plays later, with the help of a 15-yard penalty for piling on, Baylor regained the lead, 14-7, on a 35-yard pass tipped high in the air by Lion defender Mike Johnson that fell miraculously into the arms of split end Ricky Thompson. "They'd better look up," a Texas writer cracked in the press box, "They're getting help from somewhere."

But the help didn't last long. Two plays after the kickoff, Shuman switched from a running play to a pass a the line of scrimmage when he saw man-to-man coverage at the Baylor 49 and threw over onrushing linemen to a wide open Cefalo at the 20, and the Lions led 17-14 with 3:35 left in the third quarter. That took the momentum away from Baylor and was the beginning of the end for the Bears. After forcing a punt, State drove 68 yards for a TD early in the fourth quarter, with Cefalo circling right end 3-yards for the TD, then State went 70 yards for a 33-yard field goal by Bahr. One play later, Johnson returned an interception 15 yards to the Baylor 18 and on the sixth play Shuman ran in from the 2-yard line. Reihner's PAT made it 34-14 with a little more than three minutes remaining but the most spectacular play was still to come. Baylor drove 70 yards in the last three minutes against Lion reserves to score on an 11-yard pass but when the Bears tried an onside kick, Joe Jackson scooped up the ball and ran 50 yards for State's final TD and a 41-20 victory. The next day, the Lions had to share the headlines in Dallas with one that read, "Watergate Jurors Convict Nixon Aides in Coverup Scandal" and detailed guilty verdicts against H. R. Haldeman, John Mitchell and John Erlichman. "What was an uneventful yet close 39th Cotton Bowl for three quarters turned into a one-team show in the final period," wrote Bob Galt in the *Dallas Times Herald*. "Penn State allowed the neophyte Bears to dream on peacefully for almost three quarters before setting off the alarm clock," reported Mike Jones in the *Dallas Morning News*. "It rang like Big Ben. And so, the Rude Awakening." Paterno, more subdued than usual after a bowl game, told sportswriters "This team has played to more potential than any other team we've had." The game had been quite a finish for Shuman, who passed for over 200 yards for the first time in his career (226 on 10-of-20 attempts) and was named the Offensive Player of the Game.

For the seventh time in eight years, the team finished in the Top 10, selected #7 by both AP & UPI. But now Paterno had to get ready for next season with more questions about his backfield and another new, untested quarterback. Once again, he would surprise everyone by turning out a team that would play up to its potential. He would also run into the plague of his entire career—a friendly, soft talking man with a deep Southern drawl and a trademark houndstooth, porkpie hat whom friend and foe alike called, "The Bear."

Season Record 10-2
Record to Date 502-237-40
Winning percentage .670

"The Bahr & 'The Bear'"

Chris Bahr flexed his right leg on the sideline trying not to let the noise from the nearly 60,000 Beaver Stadium faithful impede his concentration. In a few moments he would have to go in and kick the winning field goal, just as he had done against Maryland the week before. Only this time he would get just one chance for there were less than 30 seconds left in the game. And if he missed? No, he couldn't miss. The New Year's bowl game was at stake.

After eight games, the Nittany Lions had lost only a close game to Ohio State, now the #1 team in the country, and Bahr's foot had been essential to the victories. He was not just the Lion placekicker but the punter and kickoff man, too. With his soccer eligibility used up, Bahr was now playing football full time this fall and his value was obvious. "He's worth at least a touchdown a game," sportswriters had written. He was leading the team in scoring and already had set a new school record by kicking 18 field goals in one season. The three he booted for 55 yards against Temple, Ohio State and Syracuse had wiped out the 63-year record of Pete Mauthe for State's longest. His punting was averaging 38 yards and the kicks were so good that returns were being kept to about 5 yards a runback. The kickoffs usually were into the end zone and less than 30 had been returned for about an 18-yard average. One kickoff against West Virginia had even gone through the uprights 70 yards away.

But now, Bahr was facing the biggest kick of the season. This was a game the Lions had to win or forget about the Sugar Bowl. At least that was the pregame speculation. Beat North Carolina State and they would play #5 Alabama in New Orleans, the newspapers had reported. Yes, they had another game left against Pitt, two weeks away. But the bowl invitations would be going out next Saturday and they were off that day. A win against the Wolfpack was a virtual guarantee of the Sugar Bowl, said the reports. And they had been expected to win, too. Unlike last year, this game was at home and NC State was not as strong. But the Lions had blown a 14-point lead and NC State was now winning 15-14. With less than two minutes left and no time outs the Lions had driven from their own 9-yard line into field goal range and now it would all depend on Bahr.

From the beginning of preseason practice, Paterno knew Bahr's kicking would be critical to his team's success. He was one of the few seniors on a young and relatively inexperienced squad and he was a natural leader. Certainly, no one on the team was in better physical shape. Because of an allowance within NCAA rules, Bahr already was a professional soccer player and had been the Rookie of the Year in the North American Soccer League that summer while playing for the Philadelphia Atoms. His competitive spirit rubbed off on everyone and Paterno knew that would help his young team.

Once again, Paterno had a quarterback with limited playing time, and before the opening game, injuries would alter his offensive scheme and his phi-

losophy about utilizing freshmen. Andress, who was a good runner but needed work on his passing, beat out another junior, John Carroll, for the starting quarterback position, and when injuries continued to plague Carroll, freshman Chuck Fusina of McKees Rocks emerged as the backup. Injuries also caused shuffling at tailback and flanker, with Hutton going out for the year and Boyle and Cefalo missing some early games. Petchel started at tailback with junior Rich Mauti dividing time between flanker and tailback and freshman Tom Donovan getting a start at flanker after Cefalo was sidelined with a broken thumb and sprained ankle. Junior Larry Suhey, son of State's '47 All-American and grandson of former coach Higgins was at fullback with Taylor. As the season progressed sophomore Steve Geise also was utilized as a running back and flanker. Paterno said he had a "good solid offensive line" anchored by co-captain Tom Rafferty and Thomas at the guards, with Benson and Reihner at the tackles and juniors Ron Argenta and Shukri playing at center when projected starter Rick Knechtel was injured. Senior Dick Barvinchak, a converted quarterback, started at split end and sophomore Mickey Shuler and junior Stutts were the tight ends. "We're not going to overpower too many people," Paterno said, "and it will be hard to replace Donchez but they have an excellent attitude."

Despite having to rebuild the defense and move some players around, Paterno and his coaches came up with a lineup that gave them "much more experience here than usual." The secondary was composed of veterans Johnson and Giotto at halfbacks and Odell at safety with sophomore Gary Petercuskie also at halfback or safety and Hite playing halfback and linebacker. Veterans Buttle, a co-captain, and Rosecrans were also at linebacker along with sophomore Ron Hostettler, senior Rich Kriston and Sidler, who was moved from tight end. Quinn, another co-captain, was the only returnee up front but Paterno switched Ron Coder from offensive guard to defensive tackle and inserted senior Dennis Zmudzin and junior Ron Crosby at the defensive ends. Allerman played both defensive end and linebacker.

"We've got awfully good potential," Paterno told sportswriters. The writers agreed for many picked the Lions to be among the Top

There is a long tradition of sons following fathers and brothers following brothers to play at Penn State. Here two close friends from the great 1947 team were reunited in 1975 when their sons played. From left, All-American guard Steve Suhey; his son Larry, a FB; Woody Petchel, a HB; and his father, Elwood, a star back on the '47 team.

10 teams. Some reporters believed this was State's most difficult schedule in years, especially with the addition of Ohio State and Kentucky and the continued improvement of Pitt and Maryland. All the games would be seen on television, too, although most on a delayed basis. The athletic department had set up a Penn State Football TV Network to televise the games over five stations in Pennsylvania, Ohio and West Virginia with former CBS announcer Ray Scott doing the play-by-play and one-time Green Bay Packer Max McGee handling commentary. Another six stations would carry a condensed one hour highlights show. The back-to-back games at Ohio State and Iowa were set to be televised live on closed-circuit back to University Park and the Pitt game at Three Rivers Stadium on November 22 would be the second game of an ABC doubleheader that also featured Michigan against Ohio State.

The Buckeyes had not been on PSU's original schedule but had approached the Lions over the winter about a game in Columbus on September 20. Navy, planning to end its series with State after 1976, agreed to give up that date and released State from its contract. So, the Buckeyes got their game in Columbus and agreed to visit University Park in place of the Middies in '76. The opening game also was moved up a week to September 6, when Temple and the city of Philadelphia asked State to switch the November 16th game against the Owls from Beaver Stadium to Franklin Field to help launch Philadelphia's Bicentennial celebration. The Lions had not played Temple since 1952 and when the game was first scheduled a few years back even Paterno had felt it would be a mismatch. But under coach Wayne Hardin the Owls had become competitive and in 1974 quarterback Steve Jaochim, the transfer quarterback from PSU, had led them to an 8-2 record and runner-up to State in the Lambert Trophy race. Jaochim was gone but Temple still had plenty of veterans returning, including preseason All-American middle guard Joe Klecko. Still, the Owls were a three-touchdown underdog when State kicked off before 57,112 on a warm Saturday night in Philly.

On the first play from scrimmage at the Temple 24-yard line, Hardin called a delayed draw designed to test State's 4-4-3 defense and gain three or four yards. Some test. Bob Harris went up the middle and shocked partisans from both sides when he ran 76-yards for a touchdown. There were more "big plays" to follow. Late in the first quarter with the score 10-3, Mauti took a Temple kickoff on the goal line, bolted straight up the middle, found an opening at the PSU 25-yard line and went 100 yards for a touchdown, the longest return since Roger Kochman's dramatic runback against Syracuse in 1959. A 2-point conversion attempt failed and the Owls held the lead until Bahr startled the crowd again near the end of the half with his record 55-yard field goal. "It was a lot of luck," Bahr said later, "(because) I only had about a half-yard over the bar." That was probably the defining moment of the season for it set the tone for everything else that followed throughout the year. Another field goal by Temple's Don Bitterlich regained the lead before the intermission and although the lead changed again in the third and fourth quarters the Owls appeared to be on the way to a 23-18 victory with less than five minutes left in the game. That's when Petchel hauled in a punt at the State 31-yard line, shook off three Owl tacklers and evaded two more before being tackled 66 yards later at the Temple 3-yard line. Taylor scored the go ahead TD and Shuler made a leaping catch of an Andress pass for the 2-point conversion and a 26-23 PSU lead. Temple quickly moved upfield but was forced to punt after a sack by Sidler. However, penalties and a fumble set the Lions back to their own 13-yard line and on fourth down

with 15 seconds left Andress ran out of the end zone for an intentional safety. Bahr's free kick went 51 yards and with seven seconds left Temple had one last gasp from its own 41-yard line but two passes gained just two yards and the game was over. "Penn State was beaten everywhere but on three plays," wrote Gordon Blain in the *Daily Collegian*. "A win's a win, right?" Rafferty told Ron Bracken of the *Centre Daily Times*.

Paterno's well-known philosophy about the improvement a team makes from its first game to its second was evident the following Saturday when the Lions beat Stanford, 34-14, before a record, standing-room-only crowd of 61,325

Greg Buttle, 1975 First-Team All-American LB, holds all of State's major tackle records and made 343 tackles during his three year career.

in windy but warm Beaver Stadium. State never trailed although Stanford punter Mike Michel helped keep the game close in the first half with punts to State's 1- and 2-yard lines. Although Cardinal quarterback Mike Cordova completed 21 of 44 passes for 244 yards, State's defense intercepted four passes and batted down several others to limit Stanford to two first half touchdowns. Meanwhile, the Lions were pounding away on the ground, rushing for 321 yards to Stanford's 75. Paterno surprised Stanford and the home fans by starting a freshman at tailback who was not on the depth charts and Tom Donovan became the first frosh in modern times to run for over 100 yards with 113 yards on 10 carries including a 61-yard TD run in the second period. Andress threw just 6 passes, completing 3 for 43 yards. Bahr kicked field goals of 39 and 33 yards, giving him 21 for his career and breaking the record set by Larry Vorhis from 1906-09. "Penn State played 50 to 75 percent better this week than the week before," Stanford coach Jack Christiansen told Doug McDonald of the *Centre Daily Times*.

The game at Columbus now had national title implications for Stanford had been a preseason pick as a Pac 8 Rose Bowl contender. Still, #3 Ohio State was a 14-to-17 point favorite over the Lions, who had moved up to #7 in the AP poll. The oddsmakers looked good when OSU marched 80 yards after the opening kickoff to take a 7-0 lead four minutes into the game. But the Lions were not blown off the field and by the start of the fourth quarter, they trailed by only a point, 10-9, as Bahr kicked field goals of 55, 31 and 25 yards and just missed another into a 15-mile wind from 57-yards out. The key play of the game occurred early in the fourth quarter when the Lions had the Buckeyes backed up to their 15-yard line on a third-and-15 play and State was penalized for interference on an attempted sideline pass from Cornelius Greene to Lenny Willis. It was a legitimate call and seemed to energize the home team and the crowd of 88,093—second largest in Ohio Stadium history. As 2,300 frustrated PSU fans watched on closed circuit back in Rec Hall, the Buckeyes used up more than seven minutes of the clock and drove for a touchdown behind the running of fullback Pete Johnson and a third down clutch pass reception of

23 yards by Heisman Trophy winner Archie Griffin. With less than five minutes remaining, the Lions took the kickoff and quickly moved into Buckeye territory but lost a fumble and OSU ran out the clock for the 17-9 victory. "That's as close a game as you'll see," Woody Hayes told sportswriters, and he had special praise for Bahr and Buttle, who made 16 tackles. "This isn't a great team," Paterno said, "but they're good and gonna get better."

They actually looked worse in the first quarter of the game against Iowa. Rosecrans jumped offside three times in the first two minutes and when the Lions finally gained possession after stopping an Iowa drive, they fumbled it away on their first play from scrimmage. Midway through the period, Nick Quartaro put Iowa ahead 3-0 with a 50-yard field goal into the wind that set a Kinnick Stadium record. State snapped out of its stupor early in the second quarter on a spectacular 75-yard pass from Andress to Barvinchak, who was hauled down at the Iowa 3-yard line. Taylor scored the TD, Bahr booted the PAT and the Lions never trailed again. State made it 14-3 at halftime after Mauti's 18-yard punt return set up an 8-play, 46 yard drive and Bahr's 45-yard field goal in the third quarter stretched the lead to 17-3. But Iowa narrowed the margin on a 58-yard drive early in the fourth quarter before Andress threw another bomb, this time to Rich Mauti for a 70-yard TD. The Lions went on to win 30-10, and for the first time since 1956 held an opponent without a pass completion (on 12 attempts). Paterno was especially pleased with Andress' passing. In the last two games against quality opponents, Andress had completed 19-of-31 attempts for 331 yards and a TD without throwing an interception. Another Paterno quarterback prodigy appeared to be in the making.

A Homecoming crowd of 60,225 turned out on a perfect autumn afternoon the following Saturday to see the "new" quarterback in action against Kentucky. They were pleased when Andress led the Lions on an 80-yard touchdown drive in the second quarter, completing passes of 15, 13 and 28 yards to Barvinchak, with Suhey getting the TD on a one-yard dive. After an Odell interception stopped Kentucky near the goal line, the Lions drove downfield and Bahr kicked a 29-yard field goal with eight seconds left in the half to give the Lions a 10-0 lead. After the intermission, Andress seemed to fall apart, as he threw three interceptions and completed just one of seven pass attempts. He wasn't told until after the game that his father had suffered a heart attack in the stands but perhaps he had a psychic premonition and it affected his performance. The defense saved the game, stopping Kentucky's unfamiliar Veer offense at the Lion 24 and 32 yard lines in the third quarter, giving up just a 36-yard field goal on another drive and making a fine goal line stand with time running out in the game when the Wildcats drove for a first down at the PSU 14-yard line. Ron Coder's sack on a third-and-eight was the big play at the end and after a fourth down pass fell incomplete, the Lions ran out the last 58 seconds to win, 10-3. "We were flat and we lost our poise a little...in the second half," Paterno told Jeff Young of the *Daily Collegian.* Sonny Collins had gained 140 yards against the Lions, more than the 128 Griffin had three weeks earlier, but Paterno was more upset at his offense, even though he defended the offense publicly on his midweek TV Quarterbacks' show that was seen throughout the state.

That week in practice, Paterno worked the team harder than he had since preseason. West Virginia was unbeaten and ranked #10, just behind State, in the AP poll. The Moutaineers (4-0) had been averaging 411 yards per game and was fourth in the nation in scoring, including a 50-7 whomping of Temple in mid-September. Bowden be-

lieved this was the best WVU team in his coaching tenure and he was especially high on his sophomore quarterback Dan Kendra. Mountaineer fans were convinced this was the year their losing to State would end. But with time to prepare for another Veer offense, Paterno and his defensive coordinator O'Hora came out of the game looking like geniuses. The Lions won easily at Beaver Stadium, 39-0, limiting the Mountaineers to 49 yards on the ground and 145 through the air while rushing for 376 yards and passing for 63. Four different players scored TDs and Bahr had three field goals, including a 52-yarder in the first quarter for the team's first points. Woody Petchel, subbing when starter Mauti pulled a hamstring, had 120 yards, including an 8-yard TD. Andress completed just 5-of-11 short passes for 59 yards and Cefalo, making his first start of the year, caught two for 30 yards.

But the offense sputtered again at decrepit Archbold Stadium before a sparse, but hostile Syracuse Homecoming crowd. The Lion players, sitting on the Syracuse side of the field for the first time, had to dodge oranges and other flying objects before and during the game but the 28,153 spectators were pretty much silenced by the ineptness of their own team's offense, whose only score came after recovering an Andress fumble at the PSU 20 in the third quarter. Bahr's field goals of 55 and 37 yards in the first quarter gave the Lions a 6-0 lead into second half. He missed another from 56 yards at the start of the third quarter, then came back moments later to try one from the 47. But with Syracuse basically rushing 11 men with no defenders deep, Paterno ordered a fake. Barvinchak, the holder, took the snap, rolled out right on an option to run or pass and threw to Stutts all alone at the goal line. Although the 2-point conversion failed, the 12 points were all that was needed to win but after Crosby recovered a fumble at the Orange 11 in the fourth quarter the Lions added an insurance TD on an Andress to Stutts pass and won, 19-7. Despite the touchdown throw, Andress missed several open receivers and hit on just 7-of-18 passes for 94 yards while eight Lion backs could gain just 173 yards on the ground. "They (the receivers) were open," Andress told the *Collegian,* "I just missed them...We just made too many mental mistakes, all on offense."

Despite losing five of seven fumbles against Army, the #9 Lions had no problems winning 31-0 at Beaver Stadium the following week, with Petchel getting 140 yards and two TDs and Andress hitting on 6-of -8 passes for 116 yards. That set up another showdown game, this time against #14 Maryland, which had been beaten only by Tennessee in its season opener. With scouts from the Cotton, Sugar and Gator bowls among the record Byrd Stadium crowd of 58,973, the game came down to field goals and fumbles. Maryland fumbles on its first two possessions led to 37 and 44 yard field goals by Bahr and before the first quarter was over the Lions drove 69 yards for a 12-0 lead on Petchel's 36-yard sweep around left end. But the Terps came back with 10 points in the second quarter on Mike Sochko's 26-yard field goal and a 68-yard TD drive. Bahr missed a 37-yard field goal just before the half and early in the third quarter Maryland took the lead when Sochko booted a 31-yard FG after Jim Brechbiel had stolen the ball from Suhey. Bahr had a rare miss later in the period when his 38-yard kick into a tricky wind was wide but midway through the fourth quarter he booted a 40-yarder to regain the lead at 15-13. With about 4 and a half minutes left, Maryland took the ball on its own 19 and without any time outs left, moved to a third-and-8 at the PSU 24-yard line with less than 30 seconds remaining. Sochko ran in to try to win the game on a 42-yard kick with the wind. Without time to concentrate,

Sochko said he was rattled and the kick was wide. "I just felt hurried," Sochko told sportswriters. "I hit it hard but it was two or three yards off to the right." Terp coach Jerry Claiborne told Mark Asher of the *Washington Post*, "We had plenty of time to kick the ball."

As the Lions practiced for NC State, sportswriters speculated on the bowl pairings. Once again the word was that Alabama's Bear Bryant would influence the invitations. Alabama had lost eight straight bowl game and Bryant reportedly wanted to play a team he felt confident of defeating. That team apparently was Penn State, sources said, and that meant a game in the Sugar Bowl, which was being played for the first time in the new New Orleans Superdome on New Years Eve. Of course, the Lions would still have to beat 13-point underdog NC State or Notre Dame, then 7-2, might be the choice. Lion fans remembered the upset in Raleigh in '74 and so did Paterno, who reminded his players to ignore NC State's 6-3 record. Holtz stirred up a little controversy during the week when he accused PSU of having "their own officials and many of their previous opponents have questioned their integrity." Even though Holtz apologized after the game, saying "I used very bad judgment," his remarks were resented for years.

It was an unusually warm November day with temperatures nearing 68 degrees and the crowd of 59,536 included two honored guests, author James Michener and Heinz Warneke, sculptor of the Nittany Line Shrine. They all had a good feeling when State took a 14-0 lead in the second quarter after recovering a fumble at the Wolfpack 26 in the opening period and driving 70-yards early in the second quarter. But with a minute left in the first half, NC State drove 65 yards on the passing of quarterback Dave Buckey to score a TD and trail by 14-6. NC State narrowed the score to 14-12 on its opening possession of the third quarter, going 76 yards with Buckey hitting his twin-brother, Don, on a 42-yard pass that helped set up freshman Ted Brown's six points. The Wolfpack made just one first down after that but the Lion offense struggled. Bahr missed a couple of field goal attempts in the period, one from 57 yards out, and the Wolfpack grabbed the lead on sophomore Jay Sherrill's 24-yard field goal early in the fourth quarter. Bahr missed another attempt midway in the quarter and when NC State stopped the Lions deep in their territory after a 78-yard quick kick, it looked like the game was over. But the defense regained the ball at the PSU 20 with 1:43 remaining and no time-outs left (shades of Maryland), and Andress drove State upfield on passes to Barvinchak and Cefalo as Bahr loosened up on the sidelines. The Lions reached the NC State 29 with 13 seconds left and in came Bahr to attempt the game winner from the 36. But it was simply not Bahr's day. The kick was short and to the right and the final score was 15-14. But no one in the Penn State locker room blamed

Chris Bahr, who played collegiate and then professional soccer while kicking for the Lions, set several field goal records when he made All-American in 1975 and still holds school mark for longest FG at 55 yards.

Bahr for the defeat. "I wouldn't trade him for anyone else," Odell told Bracken of the *CDT*. Paterno said, "Chris Bahr's kicking did not lose that game for us...There were a lot of reasons why we lost." Andress admitted the team may have been thinking too much of the bowl game. "The only thing that was in the back of our minds was maybe a bowl game," he told sportswriters. "We all figure that's it for the bowl game, now."

Even with its two defeats, all the bowls were still interested in the Lions but they now seemed headed for one of the second tier bowls—the Gator, Sun or Fiesta. Ironically, it was State's oldest rival Pitt which put the Lions back into the Sugar Bowl. While State was idle on "bowl selection day," Paterno personally scouted the Panthers against Notre Dame at Pitt Stadium and he watched as Tony Dorsett led Pitt to a 34-20 upset with 303 yards rushing and another 71 yards on pass receptions. Bear Bryant had asked the Orange Bowl committee to hold up its invitation until after the Oklahoma-Nebraska game on November 22 but when the committee declined, he elected to go to the Sugar Bowl and said he wanted State as his opponent and not the Big Eight runner-up. On Monday, November 17, the Sugar Bowl made it official and invited the Lions to New Orleans.

Now, the November 22 clash with Pitt now took on special significance for both teams, with the Lions needing to prove they were worthy of the Sugar Bowl invitation and the Panthers wanting to embarrass State and all the New Year's bowl committees. As had been true all season, this final game on the schedule came down to defense, Bahr, the kicking game and some alert coaches. Pitt scored a TD in the second quarter after recovering a fumble at midfield but Odell blocked Carson Long's extra point. While scouting Pitt, assistant coaches Gregg Ducatte and J.T. White had noticed a quirk in the Pitt center's snapback and Odell had been trained to leap over the center at the right instant to get into the Panther backfield. After the kick had been blocked, Long realized what had happened and he became noticeably nervous on a subsequent missed field goal attempt from the 35-yard line. Pitt's defense kept the Lions and Bahr away from any scoring opportunity until midway in the fourth quarter when Paterno inserted Fusina to try and get some offensive spark. The decision worked because the freshman drove the Lions 69 yards with Guise scoring the TD from 28 yards out. Now, it was Bahr's turn. He had not missed in 34 straight PAT attempts. Ironically, Odell was the snapper and this time the snap was a little low. Barvinchak managed to jerk the ball into place and the Lions led 7-6. But Long and the Panthers weren't done. With less than seven minutes remaining, Long missed a 41-yard field goal attempt. Minutes later, Fusina fumbled at the PSU 29 and with 1:37 left in the game, Long had a chip shot from the PSU 13. Again, he missed. The Lions couldn't get a first down and with three seconds remaining, Long had one last chance at State's 35-yard line. He missed again and State fans watching on TV throughout the nation celebrated. Pitt won the statistics but State's bend-but-don't-break defense had held Dorsett to 128 yards and Bahr's punting had kept Pitt's exceptional punt returner Gordon Jones from breaking a big play. "No true followers of the Nittany Lions need such extraneous things as crazy bowl situations or the Eastern Championship...to sharpen their ardor for the holiday season...," wrote Ridge Riley in his *"Football Letter."* "A victory over Pitt suffices..."

THE 1975 SUGAR BOWL
Dec. 31, 1975
Alabama 13, Penn State 6

Weeks before the game, the #8 Lions were being disparaged as "unworthy" of playing #4 Alabama in the Sugar Bowl and the blame was placed on the The Bear. Bryant was accused of ducking #3 Oklahoma in the Orange Bowl and picking a patsy to break his bowl losing streak. Some sportswriters predicted a blow-out against an "Eastern pretender." Even some PSU beat reporters thought it was a mismatch. "Face the facts," wrote one for a Northeastern Pennsylvania daily, "John Andress is not a good quarterback. He can't move the offense. If you can't score points, you can't win ball games. John Andress and the Nittany Lions have not been scoring points and that's why Penn State is going to lose to Alabama."

When the Tide (10-1) was established as a 13-point favorite, even the Alabama players started believing what they were reading, as they later admitted after the game. The Lion players figured they had nothing to lose but they practiced to win. The Alabamans, led by their star quarterback Richard Todd, figured it was "party time" on Bourbon Street. Four days before the game, 23 Alabama players, including Todd and wide receiver Ozzie Newsome, broke the midnight curfew by up to 1 and a half hours. Two days later nearly a half dozen players were caught out of their rooms after hours and Bryant benched his starting split end and a linebacker.

The mood in the sold out and noisy Superdome before the 6:30 p.m. kickoff on New Year's Eve was festive with chants of "Let's Go Penn State! Let's Go!" competing with "Roll Tide!" When the small contingent of Lion fans inadvertently continued chanting through the pregame invocation, the Alabama cheering section retaliated with "Go to Hell Penn State, Go to Hell!" The crowd of 75,212 also noticed that Bryant was not wearing his trademark houndstooth, porkpie hat and sportswriters in the press box were informed that the Bear "thought it was impolite to wear a hat inside." True to form, the Lions' first scoring attempt was a field goal by Bahr, who had the crowd murmuring when he tried one of 62-yards five minutes into the game. Alabama was primarily a running team that utilized a Wishbone offense to roll up 302 yards rushing per game but Paterno had warned his team of Todd's ability to pass (84 yards per game) and pass he did. On Alabama's third play of the game, Todd completed one for 54 yards to Joe Dale Harris and after State's defense held at the PSU 3-yard line, Danny Ridgeway booted a 25-yard field goal to give Alabama a 3-0 lead. But the rest of the half belonged to the defensive teams. State's best scoring chance came late in the second quarter when the Lions reached the Alabama 37 but Mark Prudhomme's leaping interception at the 6-yard line ended the threat. That interception probably changed the complexion of the game for State might have been able to take a 7-3 lead into the intermission. Alabama made it no closer than the Lion 44 during the rest of the half even with Todd throwing six more passes. However, the Lions were now playing without Odell, who had left the game with a torn rib cartilage after tackling Newsome on the last play of the first quarter. His absence would prove crucial after the intermission.

After the State defense twice held Alabama for downs in the opening minutes of the second half, Andress drove the Lions from their own 31-yard line to the Tide 25 from where Bahr kicked a 42-yard field goal to tie the game. But four plays after the kickoff, Todd made the play of the game on a third-and-two at the Alabama 34. Seeing that he had called a play that would not work, Todd called time out and conferred with Bryant. The Bear called for a "slant-take-off-pass" to Newsome. It was the perfect call. Todd faked a pass down the middle,

then threw to Newsome who got behind freshman safety Bill Crummy, subbing for the injured Odell, and was at the State 10-yard line before being tackled. Buttle forced Todd to fumble on the next play but Todd recovered his own fumble for a 3-yard loss. Then Todd pitched out to Mike Stock who swept around left end for the touchdown. The PAT was good and for all practical purposes the game was over. Early in the fourth quarter, Bahr kicked a 37-yard field goal at the end of an 80-yard drive but Alabama came back on the next possession and went 62-yards in 14 plays for a 28-yard field goal by Ridgeway that made the score 13-6. The Lions had one last gasp in the final three minutes, but a fourth-and-inches play at the PSU 39 just missed and Alabama ran out the clock. Paterno ran on to the field and congratulated Bryant as he was being carried on the shoulders by his players, then the Lion coach shook hands with as many Tide players as he could find, including Todd. The 'Bama QB had the best passing day of his four-year career, hitting on 10-of-12 passes for 210 yards despite a cut finger on his throwing hand, and was the overwhelming choice for Most Valuable Player of the Game. Coder, with 14 tackles, and Buttle, with 13, were cited as State's standouts, along with Allerman and Crosby. "We beat a helluva football team tonight," Bryant told sportswriters in the Tide locker room. "Anybody who doesn't think that is an idiot. I'm glad we don't have to play them every week." Bob Roseler of *The New Orleans Times–Picayune* may have put it best when he wrote, "Penn State, downgraded by some critics...proved they had come south to give their best shot. It was a good effort but not quite good enough."

So, Paterno and the Lions returned home with their pride still intact but with their worst record in five years. Three more players were named All-Americans—Bahr, Buttle and Rafferty—but they would not be back in 1976. Twenty-eight other veterans would return. Yet, before the season was too far along, it would be an inexperienced sophomore and Paterno's change-of-heart about playing freshmen that would determine the destiny of his next team.

Season Record 9-3
Record to Date 511-240-40
Winning percentage .671

"The Freshmen Cometh"

Joe Paterno had no intention of playing so many freshmen before the season started but now he felt he had no choice. For the first time since he became the Nittany Lions head coach, his team had lost three in a row and he knew he had to do something to turn the season around.

"Kentucky just beat our ears off," Paterno had told sportswriters after State had lost 22-6 in its first game away from Beaver Stadium. But even the 15-12 win over Stanford in the season opener had been shaky. The Lion had their chances against Ohio State but the #1 Buckeyes had been too good and didn't make one mistake. Iowa simply had been a letdown and no one was mentally sharp, including the coaches. Sure, he could blame some of his problems on injuries if he wanted an excuse. But Paterno knew better. Injuries were part of the game. This team didn't have spark, didn't have cohesion. Unless he did something quickly he would have the first losing season of his career.

And now his senior quarterback, the offensive co-captain he had depended upon to help lead this young team, probably was out for the season. Sure, the fans had been critical of Andress but Paterno thought he had been playing well, if a little inconsistently. Besides, Fusina, his sophomore backup, still needed work. "Fusina probably has as much potential at quarterback as anyone we've had in all the years I've been here," Paterno had said in the preseason. But, Fusina also was inconsistent. Fusina had played the entire Kentucky game after Andress had injured his shoulder

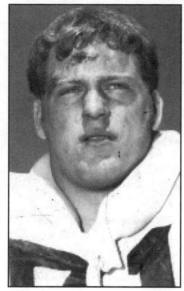

Brad Benson was a three-year offensive starter and co-captain and OT in 1976 but became better known after an all-pro career with the New York Giants.

on the second play from scrimmage. He had thrown for 151 yards and completed the Lions first touchdown pass of the year. But his 15-for-28 completions were diminished by two interceptions, one that stopped a PSU drive at the Kentucky 33 and the other that led to Kentucky's first TD in the first quarter. Still, Paterno was not blaming Fusina for the Kentucky loss as much as he was his defense, which had allowed the Wildcats to control the ball for 35 minutes and run off 83 plays to State's 58. By the time the score was 22-0 midway in the third quarter, Paterno had inserted some of his freshmen into the defensive lineup and at one point there were seven on the field at the same time. He still could count on veterans such as Crosby and Bill Banks at defensive end, Tony Petruccio at tackle, Sidler, Hostetler and Allerman at linebacker, Petercuskie at safety and a couple of others. But he needed some new blood, like that big kid Bruce Clark from New Castle and that free spirit Matt Millen from Hokendauqua. They had played for the first time against Kentucky and had looked good with Clark leading the team with eight unassisted tackles.

Despite the erratic performance of his offense, Paterno was generally pleased with his offensive line. Reihner was more comfortable now that he was back at tackle after being switched last spring to the defensive line. With Benson at the other tackle, Argenta, Shukri and sophomore Paul Renaud at the guards, sophomore Keith Dorney at center and Shuler at tight end, Paterno had a good set of blockers and pass protectors. Donovan and Mauti were skillful split ends and Cefalo and sophomore Scott Fitzkee were fine flankers, with Fitzkee doubling as a punter and a capable successor to Chris Bahr. No problem with the receivers if the quarterbacks could get the ball to them more often. Fullback and tailback were the problems areas and injuries had been playing havoc back there. Paterno had not had the same backs for any game. Larry Suhey, the projected starter at fullback, went out before the first game with a twisted knee and his younger brother, Matt, the freshman who started against Stanford and looked sensational, was hurt against Iowa. Stutts was moved from tight end to fullback and sophomore Bob Torrey and freshman Tony Alguero were also there. Geise, sophomore Rich Milot and freshman Ken Thrower

had played tailback but Paterno still wasn't completely comfortable with his lineup. He also was not satisfied with his placekicking, with Chris Bahr's younger brother Matt and fellow freshman Herb Menhardt both dividing their time between soccer and football.

Before the season, Paterno had thought his team would be among the Top 20 in the country and he had developed a more wide open offense around various formations, including the I, Wing-T and Double-Wing, that used a man in motion and widely split receivers. Many sportswriters believed the Lions would be better than Top 20 and the AP ranked State #10 in its preseason poll, just ahead of Notre Dame and Maryland, and one place behind Pitt. Playing five of the first six games at home appeared to be a distinct advantage, although Paterno believed his first two against Stanford and Ohio State would be among his toughest.

Both Stanford and OSU attracted record crowds, with 61,645 watching on a partially sunny day as the Lions capitalized on Stanford mistakes to take a 15-0 first quarter lead, then relied on the defense for a 15-12 victory. A fumbled punt by Stanford after State's first possession set up a 44-yard pass from Andress to Cefalo that led to a 2-yard touchdown run by Geise in the first 3 and a half minutes. Stanford fumbled the ensuing kickoff and four plays later Bahr kicked a 33-yard field goal. On the next possession, Cardinal quarterback Mike Cordova fumbled at midfield and eight plays later Matt Suhey went six yards for the TD. Field goals of 52 and 27 yards by Mike Mickel put Stanford on the boards by halftime. Cordova threw a 48-yard bomb near the end of the third quarter to give the Cardinals their final points but the Lions needed an end zone interception by sophomore Bill Crummy, another interception by linebacker Joe Diange and a 15-yard sack by Banks near the end of the game to secure the victory. Suhey rushed for 119 yards on 23 carries but Andress completed just 4-of-18 passes and had one interception. "Our defense deserves great credit," Paterno told John Black for the *"Football Letter."* "They didn't miss any assignments and didn't give up anything either."

The following week, the biggest home crowd of the season— 62,503—was on hand on a drizzling late afternoon day to witness Ohio State's first ever visit to Happy Valley. Paterno was so hyper that after his pregame introduction on regional television, he ran across the field and leaped into a mob of his fist-waving players who were jumping up and down in front of the Lion bench. But enthusiasm alone doesn't win games. Three times in the first half, the Lions were deep in OSU territory but couldn't score. In the first quarter they were stopped on a fourth-and-inches at the 25, even though TV replays showed Geise made the sticks. Then after a penalty had given them good field position in the second quarter, Andress' pass to Shuler on a second-and-goal from the 6 was intercepted by Ray Griffin. From there, OSU drove 82 yards for a touchdown with Jeff Logan going 48 yards for the TD and a 6-0 lead. PSU retaliated with its own drive following the kickoff but on a second-and-goal at the 4, Geise fumbled a pitchout and the Buckeyes recovered. After the game Geise admitted his right arm had been numbed on the previous play and he couldn't grip the ball. OSU dominated most of the second half with defense and Woody Hayes' classic "three downs and a cloud of dust" ball control strategy. The Buckeyes extended their lead to 12-0 on a 35-yard, 6-play drive five minutes into the fourth quarter after the Lions were forced to punt out of the end zone. The Lions then drove 87 yards with both Andress and Fusina shuttling in at quarterback and Suhey scored the TD on a one-yard dive. Bahr's PAT made it 12-7. PSU had one more chance with time running out but an Andress pass interception ended the threat and OSU ran out the clock. Hayes ducked the traditional handshake with his fellow coach and told reporters, "It had nothing to do with him (Paterno). I just wanted to get out of there." The first downs had been even and Andress had thrown more passes than ever before, completing 16-of-29 but his two interceptions had been costly. "Ohio State played a great game on offense," Paterno told Barbara Parmer of the *Daily Collegian*. "They didn't

Rich Mauti was on a team with so many stars he never achieved the recognition he should have as a TB and WR and is best known for his exciting kick returns in the mid-70s.

fumble and they didn't give up the interception. We had the chances and we blew them."

The weather was perfect the next Saturday with 65 degree temperatures and sunny skies. But the Lions, down to #11 in the polls, were lethargic all afternoon and Iowa didn't need to do much to win. Another short punt out of the end zone following an interception led to an Iowa TD in the first quarter and Nick Quartaro's PAT gave the Hawkeyes a 7-0 lead they carried into the fourth quarter. Neil Hutton, now playing at defensive halfback, blocked a Quartaro field goal attempt in the third quarter, then in the fourth quarter stripped the ball from the Iowa fullback and recovered the fumble at the Iowa 30. Fusina led an 8-play drive with Suhey getting the TD on a one-yard plunge with 10 minutes left in the game. But Fusina's pass for the 2-point conversion fell incomplete when Milot was tackled before he could reach the ball but no penalty was called. As Iowa tried to run out the clock with two minutes remaining, Petercuskie forced a fumble on a blitz and Hostetler recovered at the Iowa 26. With Fusina at the controls, the Lions moved for a first-and-goal at the Hawkeye 7. Fusina rolled out for two yards, threw out of bounds to stop the clock on second down, then lost three yards on a boot leg. With 51 seconds remaining, Paterno sent in Menhardt to attempt a winning field goal from a hard angle on the right hash mark and Iowa called time out to try and fluster the freshman. The center snap was low, the holder had difficulty getting the ball down and Menhardt shanked the ball wide left. Asked later why he had not put in Bahr, Paterno said Bahr had not been kicking well and already had missed a field goal attempt. "You play a hunch and sometimes it doesn't work out," Paterno told sportswriters. "We weren't ready for them mentally. They came ready to play."

As the Lions tried to regroup for their trip to Kentucky, University President John Oswald and the Board of Trustees announced plans to increase Beaver Stadium's seating capacity by another 16,000 before the 1978 season. The move had been expected after an 11,000 increase in season ticket demand and the sell out of all home games by early June. Kentucky's three-year old Commonwealth Stadium also was sold out with a record 57,733 for its October 2 meeting with the Lions, and before that game a building adjacent to the stadium was

dedicated in honor of Oswald, who had once been president at Kentucky. Once the game started, a neutral observer would not have blamed Oswald for cheering a bit for his old school because State was never in the game. Coach Fran Curci's Wildcats nursed a 7-0 first quarter lead into the second half but in a two-minute span midway through the third quarter they scored a touchdown and a field goal after recovering back-to-back fumbles inside the PSU 25-yard line, and the game was virtually over. Curci, a Pittsburgh native who had played against the Lions as a Miami quarterback, said the victory was the most important win of his career and one of the most important in Kentucky history. "I'm going to take a good hard look at everything," Paterno told Black after the game. "I'm not going to panic but I can't tell you what I'm going to do right now because I just don't know."

By Monday afternoon he knew, and it was the defining moment of the season. Practice that week for Army was the toughest it had been since the preseason. "I've been soft on the squad the last couple of weeks," Paterno told the *Collegian*. "We've got to start getting tough again, both mentally and physically." Said Fusina, "There was a lot of hitting in practice." Paterno shook up his lineup with seven new starters who were either freshmen or sophomores and he eventually played 15 freshmen against the 3-1 Army team. There were some 25,000 no shows at rainy, soggy Beaver Stadium when State kicked off with three freshmen starting on the defensive unit—Clark and Millen at inside linebackers and Paul Matasavage at defensive tackle. On the second play of the game, Millen intercepted an Army pass at the Cadet 21-yard line and returned it 13 yards but Fusina, who was also making his first start in place of the injured Andress, fumbled away a fourth-and-goal scoring opportunity at the 3-yard line. Frosh Alguero had started at fullback when the Lions went on offense but before the first quarter was over two other freshmen would make impressive debuts. When a 58-yard drive bogged down 10 minutes into the game, Paterno sent in frosh quarterback Tony Capozzoli to kick a field goal and his 40-yard boot was successful. Although Geise started at tailback, Paterno was quick to substitute frosh Mike Guman of Bethlehem, who had been a backup at safety since the season began. With a minute left in the first quarter, Guman took a screen pass from Fusina and ran 25-yards for a touchdown, Capozzoli kicked the first of four PATs, and State went on to win easily, 38-16. Guman scored three more touchdowns on runs of 3, 15 and 1 yards as he rushed for 107 yards in 25 attempts. Geise had 110 yards on 16 carries, marking the first time since 1971 that two Lion backs had rushed for over 100 yards in a single game. Fusina connected on 6-of-11 passes, including another TD of 31 yards to Donovan that had given State a 31-0 halftime lead. Meanwhile, the defense held Army to minus 9 yards rushing and intercepted three passes. "Making the most extensive in-season realignment of players in his 11 years at the helm, Paterno came up with a young and enthusiastic combination that trounced Army...and ended the Nittany Lions' three-game losing streak," wrote Gordon White of the *New York Times*. "...(Future) opponents had better beware..."

The following Saturday, Guman scored two touchdowns on runs of 3 and 1 yards, Geise scored on a 27-yard run and Capozzoli kicked field goals of 25 and 34 yards as the Lions capitalized on Syracuse mistakes to beat the Orange 27-3 before a Homecoming crowd of 61,474. Paterno used 10 different running backs to roll up 250 yards rushing, including the Suhey brothers who were coming off injuries. "I'll continue alternating our running backs because...I don't have to worry about anyone getting tired," Paterno told sportswriters. "We in-

tend to play a lot of people from here on in (on both offense and defense) and give everybody a chance to develop." A week later, Paterno
switched to a passing attack to wallop West Virginia, 33-0, at
Morgantown. The Mountaineers went into the game with the best pass
defense in the nation, giving up just 59 yards per game. But Fusina
had the third best passing performance in PSU history up to that time,
completing 15 of 24 passes for 261 yards and two touchdowns with
only one interception. Ten different receivers caught his tosses, with
Shuler getting three, including a 16-yard touchdown. Bahr, kicking for
the slightly injured Capozzoli, booted field goals of 30 and 4 yards and
three PATs. The Lion defense limited the Mountaineers to 75 yards
rushing and shut down WVU's passing with two interceptions on Kendra,
who was benched in the third quarter after completing just 7 of 17
passes. "We were outclassed, outplayed, outexecuted and outcoached
today," West Virginia rookie coach, Frank Cignetti told sportswriters. "I
think Joe's got them back where he wants them."

Not quite. Paterno did not think his team had played two
good halves in any game and, worse, didn't seem to have the killer
instinct. Temple proved he was right. The Owls were a two-touchdown
underdog at Veteran's Stadium and included in their 2-4 record was a
47-0 loss to West Virginia and defeats against Syracuse and Pitt. A 60-
yard bomb from Fusina to Fitzkee on the third play of the game gave
the Lions a false sense of superiority. Before the first quarter was over,
the score was 14-14. Led by junior quarterback Terry Gregory who was
getting his first start, Temple drove 86-yards in 14 plays for a TD on a 9-
yard pass to Mike Hober. Moments later the Owls intercepted a Fusina
pass to set up a 48-yard TD pass from Gregory to Ken Williams before
the Lions scored again on a 13-play, 76-yard drive. The Lions regained
the lead early in the second quarter on a 78-yard drive that culminated
with a 27-yard TD run by Matt Suhey. Temple narrowed the score to 21-
17 by halftime with a 40-yard field goal but the Owls missed two other
scoring chances when Hutton recovered a fumble at the PSU 13 and
then intercepted a pass at the Lions 5-yard line. A 26-yard field goal by
Capozzoli in the third period and a 23-yard TD pass from Fusina to
Donovan that climaxed an 80-yard drive seemed to give the Lions an
insurmountable 31-17 lead five minutes into the fourth quarter. But,
with the help of a fourth down penalty against PSU for illegal procedure
on a punt, Temple drove 72 yards to narrow the score to 31-24 on a 34-
yard TD pass from Gregory to Williams.

With about two minutes remaining and no time outs left, the
Owls took the ball on their own 20 following a punt and with some pinpoint passing, a couple of draw plays and two pass interference penalties, they had a first-and-goal at the PSU 5 with 44 seconds left. State's
defense dug in and twice stopped Temple runners for no gain. There
didn't seem to be any time for Temple to run another play but suddenly
the officials stopped the clock when a spectator dashed into the end
zone as the crowd screamed and an injured Temple player limped off
the field. When the clock started after the confusion, Gregory threw a
dump-off pass for the TD to a wide open Hober, who had subbed for
the injured player and had not gone into the huddle. It was Gregory's
fourth touchdown pass of the game, tying the all-time PSU record for
TD passes by an opponent. Time had expired when Temple lined up for
the 2-point conversion attempt. Gregory rolled right as the left side of
the Lion line surged and just as he was about to be tackled by Rick
Donaldson, he threw a pass—over the head Williams, and the Lions
escaped with a 31-30 victory. "It's the kind of game we needed," Paterno told Bill Lyon of the *Philadelphia Inquirer*, "tough, a lot of pressure. It develops your poise and confidence."

Despite the narrow win, the Lions' 5-3 record attracted scouts
from the Fiesta and Sun Bowls to Beaver Stadium November 6 for the
final home game of the season against North Carolina State, which
was 3-5-1 under its rookie coach Bo Rein. What they and 60,462 others saw was State's best performance of the season in windy, 42 degree weather, as the Lions gave Paterno his 100th coaching victory, 41-
20, and clinched State's 38 straight non-losing season. The offense
totaled 530 yards as Geise and Guman again ran for over 100 yards
with Geise getting 145, including a 64-yard TD, and Guman rushing for
102, including a 46-yard TD. Fusina passed for 131 yards and a 29-
yard TD to Cefalo while Capozzoli booted field goals of 34 and 28
yards and four PATs. The aggressive Lion defense forced six turnovers
to set up four of State's scores, including two off fumble recoveries by
Petruccio and Millen midway in the first quarter that gave the Lions
momentum for the rest of the day. "We seemed inspired," Paterno
said. When asked about bowl possibilities, Paterno said he might not
want his team to play in a bowl because "they might not be ready."
Besides, he added, he was only "concerned with the Orange Bowl"
where his team was playing Miami the following Saturday night.

Paterno thought the only way his team could beat Miami was
by passing and he was right. Fusina, getting better each week, completed 17 of 26 passes for 212 yards, including a 16-yard TD to Guman
and a 3-yard strike to Shuler as the Lions won their sixth in a row, 21-7.
Because of NCAA rules the game could be televised to one "hometown
station" and TV viewers who could pick up Channel 11 in Pittsburgh
watched as Capozzoli kicked field goals of 28 and 23 yards in the first
quarter to give the Lions a 6-0 lead and from that point it was a battle
of the defenses. State could not score a TD until late in the third quarter at the end of a 9-play, 70-yard drive and Miami didn't score until
there were less than five minutes remaining in the game. The Lion

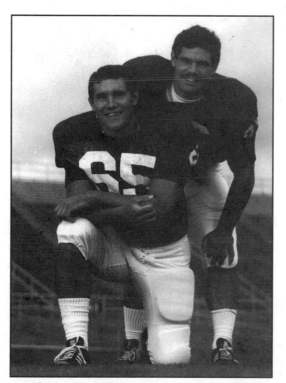

*LB Paul Suhey (kneeling) poses with his younger brother Matt.
Paul was defensive captain and Matt one of the star running
backs of the '78 team that lost to Alabama in the National
Championship Sugar Bowl game. Their older brother Larry was
a fullback for Paterno but injuries curtailed his career.*

defense, with four freshman starters, intercepted two passes and recovered two fumbles to stop Hurricane drives. "We played a little stronger on defense," Paterno told sportswriters.

The Lions had nearly two weeks to get ready for Pitt, now the #1 team in the nation. The game originally had been scheduled for Beaver Stadium on November 20, but Paterno and PSU officials had agreed to move it to Three Rivers Stadium on the Friday night after Thanksgiving, November 26, when ABC offered $250,000 and a national television audience. In the interim the bowl invitations were issued and the Lions seemed headed for either the Peach, Liberty or Sun Bowl until Notre Dame intervened. Notre Dame was asked to play in the Gator Bowl with Nebraska as the possible opponent but the Irish insisted on Penn State. "Our decision was based on enthusiasm of the Notre Dame team for this game plus the opportunity it gives us to meet Penn State...," admitted the Rev. Edumund P. Joyce of Notre Dame. Meanwhile, Pitt headed to the Sugar Bowl and a game against #5 Georgia.

For one rainy half, the Lions battled the favored Panthers evenly, holding eventual Heisman Trophy winner Tony Dorsett to a mere 51 yards on 16 carries and taking a 7-7 deadlock into the intermission, thanks in part to a 21-yard TD pass from Fusina to Torrey. But in the second half, Pitt shifted into an unbalanced line and began running Dorsett from the fullback position in an I-formation and the State defenders could not cope. Dorsett and the Panthers took control of the game and late in the third quarter, Dorsett scored on a 40-yard run to break the game open. Dorsett rushed for 224 yards on 38 carries, while the Panther defense was limiting Lion runners to 106 yards and intercepting three Fusina passes. Pitt beat State for the first time in 10 years, 24-7, and coach Johnny Majors said, it was "the most memorable moment of my life, so far." (It couldn't have been that memorable because two weeks later Majors resigned to become the head coach at his alma mater, Tennessee.) "We wanted to beat Penn State more than anything," said Dorsett. The PSU coaches had not expected to see Dorsett at fullback nor were they ready for the unbalanced line. "I didn't think they could run up the gut against us like that," Paterno told sportswriters. "They are a great football team." A week later it was revealed that Paterno, three assistant coaches—O'Hora, Chuckran and White—and Fusina had been receiving death threats for five weeks from someone in Pittsburgh who claimed to be "a disgruntled father." The FBI investigated but no one was ever arrested.

THE 1976 GATOR BOWL
Dec. 27, 1976
Notre Dame 20, Penn State 9
Outstanding Penn State Player: Jimmy Cefalo

Even many long time fans of both schools did not realize Penn State and Notre Dame had a football legacy going back more than a half century. But the schools had taken different paths since their last meeting in 1928, with the Irish becoming a football legend and Lions just now regaining the national prominence they had held before de-emphasizing the sport. They were natural competitors and already had agreed to renew their rivalry in the regular season starting in 1981. "In the days before the (Gator Bowl) game," wrote Black in the *"Football Letter,"* "Penn State and Notre Dame officials sounded like a mutual admiration society, continually expressing how delighted they were to be playing a team with the tradition and class of the other."

This also could have been called the "Gator Brothers Bowl" for among the brothers on both teams were the three Penn State Suheys—Larry, Paul and Matt—and the Notre Dame Browners—Ross and Jim.

Another of the outstanding graduates of "Linebacker U," Kurt Allerman was co-captain of the 1976 squad and a First-Team All-American who led the team in tackles.

The two teams were similar in that they were both young with great potential and both had lost to Pitt. But the Irish, now coached by Dan Devine, were a different team since losing to the Panthers 31-10 in the season opener. They were #12 in the AP poll with other losses to Georgia Tech, 23-14, in an upset and to #3 USC, 17-14, in a game with a controversy about officiating. Of course, State also was a different team since its defeat against Kentucky, which now ranked 18th in the polls and was playing in the Peach Bowl. But with a defense that included junior Ross Browner—winner of the Outland Trophy as the nation's best interior lineman—and an offense boasting All-American tight end Ken MacAfee, another junior, and runners Vagas Ferguson and Al Hunter, the Irish were established as a 7-4 betting favorite.

Most of the 67,827 spectators in the Jacksonville stadium on that chilly and blustery Monday night appeared to be rooting for Notre Dame. And it was true that the game had not generated that much enthusiasm among PSU fans, spoiled by the team's string of appearances in the Sugar, Cotton and Orange Bowls. State sold just 7,000 of its allotted 11,000 tickets but a strong contingent of alumni from Florida helped beef up the crowd of Blue and White rooters. The game can be summed up in halves. Notre Dame won the first half, winning the statistics and taking a 20-3 lead. The Lions captured the stats in the second half and scored six points while shutting out the Irish. Ergo, Notre Dame won, 20-9. The Irish did not have a turnover while the Lions had two passes intercepted, a lost fumble and a half dozen crucial penalties. State actually scored first on a 26-yard field goal by Capozzoli midway through the first quarter but a 65-yard kickoff return by Terry Eurick set up a 10-play 35-yard drive and a one-yard TD by Hunter that put ND in the lead to stay. Perhaps, the key play of the game came a few minutes into the second quarter after State's defense held for downs at the 2-yard line. Three plays later, Guman took a short pass from Fusina but fumbled when hit by linebacker Steve Heimkreiter and Jim Browner recovered at the PSU 23. Notre Dame settled for a 23-yard field goal by Dan Reeve but Hunter scored another one-yard TD six minutes later after a short Fitzkee punt gave the Irish field position at the PSU 49-yard line. Another short Fitzkee punt of only 22 yards gave Notre Dame the ball at the Lion 47 with 20 seconds left and two plays and an interference penalty later, Reeve kicked a 23-yard field goal as time ran out in the half. End of Notre Dame scoring. Twice in the second half, the Lions drove some 70 yards only to have their scoring chance thwarted by goal line interceptions. State did get a TD in the final period after Clark blocked a Notre Dame punt at the 30-yard line and sophomore linebacker Paul Suhey recovered at the 8. Two plays later Fusina hit Matt Suhey on a flare pass for an 8-yard TD. But it was too late. Cefalo, who caught 5 passes for 60 yards, was named Penn State's Outstanding Player and Allerman, who had won All-American honors, was cited on defense for his game-leading 16 tackles. "I had hoped that we had reached the stage where we could play a good football team and beat them," Paterno told sportswriters after the game. "But we made a lot of mistakes. I was disappointed."

Sportswriters who saw the game predicted that both teams would be vying for the national title in 1977 and they favored Notre Dame to win it all. They were right. The Lions would rebound and get close once more to the mythical championship Paterno so desperately wanted. But once again, it would be Kentucky and politics in the post season bowls that would help do them in.

Season Record 7-5
Record to Date 518-245-40
Winning percentage .670

"Missing Out on New Year's Day"

Of all the outstanding Paterno teams that didn't win the National Championship, the young squad of 1977 is probably the most overlooked. That may be because most of the stars that season also were on the unforgettable 1978 team that played for the national title in the Sugar Bowl—Fusina, Fitzkee, Guman, Clark, Millen, Dorney and Matt Suhey to name a few. But for a second half breakdown against Kentucky in the fourth game of the season, this is the team that might have given Paterno his first champion.

In the end, even though the team won 11 of 12 games, it didn't even get the opportunity to show how good it was on New Year's Day. The desire to play Pitt on national television for a payday and the usual post-season bowl politics forced the Nittany Lions off the January 1 calendar. Instead, they met a 13-point underdog on Christmas Day and their 12-point victory did little to impress the pollsters.

But at the beginning, in spring practice and the first few days of preseason workouts, Paterno was not sure how good this team would be. He had 31 lettermen returning, including nine starters on defense and his placekickers Bahr and Capozzoli and punter Fitzkee. The offensive line was his first priority with Dorney the only starter back from '76. Injuries had sidelined several offensive and defensive players in the spring and none of his tailbacks had looked impressive. Even though Fusina had dazzled everyone at the Blue-White game with his passing—21-of-30 completions for 263 yards and four touchdowns—Paterno felt Fusina was still a little careless and needed more discipline. Actually, the whole team needed discipline, Paterno said. "We have to learn how to win again," he told sportswriters as preseason practices got underway. "We have to develop discipline, mental toughness, poise— the ability to play 60 minutes in a tough game and eliminate erratic and careless play..."

Paterno knew he had talent on defense but he wondered how all the veterans would be affected by the retirement of longtime

associate coach and defensive coordinator Jim O'Hora and the switch from the traditional 4-4-3 defense to the new 5-3-3. Sandusky was now in charge of the defense and he would have to make it all work. Before the earliest opener ever— on September 2 against Rutgers in the new Giants Stadium in the New Jersey Meadowlands— Sandusky had his unit. Clark and Millen were shifted to tackles with Petruccio and Matasavage backing them. Sidler was switched to middle guard with Banks, Joe Diange

Unheralded Rich Milot typified the type of PSU player who has helped make State one of the elite football programs in the last 30 year. He played everything from RB to LB and is part of the tradition of "Linebacker U." He went on to a long NFL career playing in two Super Bowls on the Washington Redskins with teammate Larry Kubin.

and junior Joe Lally at ends. The linebackers included Hostetler, back after a knee operation, and his brother Ron, Paul Suhey, Donaldson and DePaso. Hutton and Petercuskie returned to the secondary but Crummy injured his knee and was lost for the season. Milot moved over from offense to replace him. Later, sophomore Pete Harris, Franco's younger brother, and junior Joe Diminick also would see a lot of action, and after the Kentucky game, Guman would shift from tailback to defense to shore up the shaky pass defense.

Paterno and offensive coordinator Bob Phillips could afford to move Guman by then because the starters at tailback—Geise—and fullback—Matt Suhey—had avoided serious injuries and reserves Ed Guthrie, Duane Taylor, Torrey, Alguero and freshman Booker Moore had developed well. Paterno did not plan to alternate his running backs, anyway, as he did last season. He also expected to pass more because of Fusina and his three top receivers. Cefalo was back at flanker and also would return punts for the first time with Fitzkee at split end and Shuler at tight end. Unfortunately, the projected wide receiver backup, Donovan, was lost for the year with an ankle injury. Junior Chuck Correal anchored the new offensive line at center with Dorney shifted to tackle to pair with sophomore Irv Pankey of Aberdeen and juniors John Dunn and Eric Cunningham at guards with Renaud and senior Tony Williott also in the mix. As the season progressed, the special teams led by junior backup defensive back Tom Bradley—and including freshmen Larry Kubin of Union, NJ, and Lance Mehl of Bellaire, OH—became a factor in giving the offense field position and were nicknamed "The Scrap Pack." Eventually, Bradley became captain of the special teams but only game day captains were named on offense and defense during the season and permanent captains were elected at the end.

Paterno was not pleased when sportswriters once again picked the Lions among the Top 20 teams, with *Sports Illustrated* rating them #10. "We're overrated," he said. "We've lost our last two games against Pitt and Notre Dame. We haven't beaten a really good football team in a long time. We have to stop talking about potential and wait until we beat somebody before we can say how good we are." State was #1 in one ranking but it wasn't the football team but the PSU cheerleaders, who had been chosen best in the country by the International Cheerleading Foundation. Only one game was scheduled to be televised, Maryland, in an ABC regional on September 24, and Lion fans who could not get to Beaver Stadium would have to be satisfied with a one-hour highlights show featuring Ray Scott and Joe's

One of State's best Tight Ends, Second-Team All-American Mickey Shuler led all receivers in 1976 and 1977 seasons and went on to have an outstanding pro career with the New York Jets.

younger brother George because the delayed broadcast network that had started with such fanfare in '74 had collapsed.

A crowd of 64,790, many of them Lion fans, showed up at the Meadowlands on a hot Friday night before Labor Day to help inaugurate the 1977 college football season. State had not played Rutgers since 1955 and this game marked the start of a new series that would last for two decades but would never be competitive. At the time, Rutgers owned the nation's longest winning streak of 18 games and under coach Frank Burns had posted a 33-10-1 record over four years. But the 45-7 result would typify the next two decades. The Lions rolled up 504 total yards with Suhey getting 100 yards and two TDs and Guman also scoring two touchdowns. Paterno used his reserves for most of the second half, including some 18 freshmen, and Burns thanked Paterno after the game. "He could have run up the score a lot more," Burns told sportswriters.

State had two weeks to get ready for its home opener against the defending Southwest Conference and Cotton Bowl champion Houston Cougars. By that time, both teams had jumped into the AP Top 10 with Houston #9 after beating UCLA on national TV and PSU #10. Despite threatening showers in the morning and a heavy downpour in the first half, a record standing-room-only crowd of 62,554 watched as State rolled up another 521 total yards while the defense was limiting Houston's potent Veer offense to 138 yards on the ground and 154 in the air in a 31-14 victory. Fusina passed for 245 yards, including a 29-yard TD to Fitzkee, on 15 completions in 23 attempts and didn't throw an interception. Four of his passes were to Shuler who gained 100 yards for the second game in a row, matching the record of Jack Curry set a decade earlier. Bahr kicked field goals of 28, 38 and 25 yards and three extra points to lead all scorers. "This game did a lot for our young people," Paterno told Black of the *"Football Letter."* "We have a balanced attack now between running and passing and we have depth at the skill positions...(but) we must get more consistent." The AP and UPI pollsters also took notice and jumped the Lions up to #5.

It rained again the following week when State broke open a 3-3 halftime tie with Maryland and won, 27-9, as scouts from the Or-

ange and Sugar Bowls watched. A 58-yard touchdown bomb from Fusina to a wide open Cefalo six minutes into the third quarter broke the stalemate after Paterno had challenged the team in the locker room at intermission to "find out something about themselves." In the fourth quarter, Cefalo caught a 7-yard TD pass from backup QB Capozzoli and with his 6 receptions for 107 yards and three flanker reverses for 30 yards, he was named Outstanding Player by the PSU football TV network. ABC TV's announcers, Chris Schenkel and Frank Broyles, selected Fusina as their offensive MVP after the junior had hit on 19-of-29 passes for 286 yards, including a 20-yard TD to Guman, and again had no interceptions. Sidler was named the outstanding defensive player of the week by *Sports Illustrated* for making 11 tackles, including two sacks, blocking a Maryland field goal attempt and deflecting at least two passes. "We can be as good as our attitude makes us," Cefalo told Ken Denlinger of the *Washington Post*. He was almost right.

The Lions moved up another notch in the polls, just behind Oklahoma, USC and Michigan and they were favored by more than a TD over a 2-1 Kentucky team that was now on probation for recruiting violations. Once again, rain drenched the tailgaters at Beaver Stadium but they were in a good mood by halftime when the sun came out with the Lions out front, 20-14. Cefalo had thrilled the crowd of 61,000 with a 75-yard punt return for a touchdown in the second quarter and had caught two long passes in the opening quarter to set up a 20-yard Bahr field goal. Bahr kicked another field goal of 24 yards and Fusina had hit Guman for a 29-yard TD at the end of a 6-play, 60-yard drive to give State its lead. But the Lions had missed a TD in the opening minutes when an illegal procedure penalty at the Kentucky one-yard line forced State to settle for a field goal. And despite passing for 195 yards on 12 of 20 attempts in the first half, Fusina had thrown his first two interceptions of the season and they had kept the Wildcats in the game. In the first quarter Dallas Owens had picked off Fusina's overthrown pass in the flat and made an easy 23-yard TD. Moments later in the second quarter, Mike Siganos' interception at the State 27-yard line set up the other Kentucky TD. During the intermission, Kentucky's coach Curci came up with an offensive strategy to pass on first down and a defensive scheme that had his linebackers dropping back deeper and jamming the Lion receivers while the defensive line applied a more aggressive pass rush—and it worked. The Wildcats' quarterback, Derrick Ramsey, who was better known as a runner than a passer, completed five first down passes in the third quarter that seemed to baffle the Lion defense. Another first down attempt resulted in 30-yard interference penalty. The strategy en-

Flanker Jim Cefalo, who was one of the best receivers and kick returners of the 70s and later became known as a sportscaster, is helped off the field by assistant trainer Eddie Sulkowski (left) and head trainer Chuck Medlar after an injury.

abled Kentucky to control the ball for the rest of the game, keeping it for about 10 minutes in each of the last two quarters. Meanwhile, Kentucky's defense led by end Art Still harassed State's receivers, sacked Fusina twice in the second half and caused another interception as well as a half dozen incompletions. "I was trying to force the ball too much," Fusina admitted later. And when the Lions tried to run the ball, the visitors were there to stop PSU's runners, as State totaled just 24 yards on 14 carries in the last two quarters and fumbled away its only penetration into Kentucky territory. The Wildcats won the game in the third quarter with a 30-yard field goal and a 44-yard TD drive that was helped by an offside penalty against the Lions. "It was one of those games where the underdogs pull it off," Curci told sportswriters after the 24-20 upset. Paterno said the difference were "the big mistakes" State made. "We gave away two touchdowns...," he said. "We had them early, but let them off the hook." The pivotal loss dropped the Lions to #10 in the AP poll, one place ahead of Notre Dame and Kentucky moved up to #16, just behind Pitt.

Although there were seven games to go, the manner in which the Lions were defeated would define the rest of the season. They lost some of their zip and enthusiasm but they were too good to disintegrate. "We all had dreams of an undefeated season and then we lost it and it took a while to figure out that we still could have a heckuva season," Dorney told the *Daily Collegian*'s Jerry Lucci a month later. The team floundered the next week against 31-point underdog Utah State (1-3) on another rainy and cold afternoon at Beaver Stadium. Eric Hipple's 50-yard touchdown bomb following a PSU fumble two minutes into the game provided the visitors with a 7-6 margin they carried into the fourth quarter. Utah State never seriously threatened again after the big play and had only 100 yards for the rest of the game. But State's offense strained as Geise ran for 108 yards and Suhey for 105 and Fusina had just 6-of-12 passes for 99 yards. Bahr missed four field goals in the first three quarters and after the game Paterno revealed that the junior had pulled a groin muscle while playing soccer at West Point Friday night and had not arrived home until 1:30 a.m. Bahr finally hit on a 22-yard field goal 2 and a half minutes into the fourth quarter, giving the Lions a 9-7 lead. The score was set up after a tackle by Clark on tailback Tony Gipson forced a fumble that Diange recovered at the Utes' 25-yard line. On Utah State's first play from scrimmage following the kickoff, Clark hit Hipple as he tried to pass and Sidler grabbed the errant ball at the Utes' 17-yard line. Four plays later, Moore ran two yards for the TD and the Lions won, 16-7. "They just didn't seem to have it together," a Utah State defensive back told sportswriters. The next week "they" had to play without their coach.

Paterno missed the only game of his head coaching career when the Lions played at Syracuse on October 15. His son David, then 11, suffered a fractured skull in a trampoline accident at school Friday afternoon and Paterno spent Saturday at a hospital in Danville while Phillips and Sandusky ran the team. The capacity crowd of 27,029 in Archbold Stadium observed a moment of silence for Paterno's son, then watched as State took a 31-10 lead late into the third quarter. But a questionable call by an official gave 17-point underdog Syracuse new life and almost cost State a victory. The Lion defense had the Orange in a third-and-18 situation at the Syracuse 16-yard line when Syracuse quarterback Bill Hurley passed to tight end Dave Farneski at midfield. Farneski was hit by Hutton and Petercuskie as he caught the ball and fumbled with Millen recovering. But the official ruled that Farneski's knee had touched the ground before the fumble. "It was a bad call,"

Phillips said later. Two more questionable calls for defensive holding and interference helped keep the Orangemen drive alive and they scored on a 30-yard pass as the fourth quarter began. State's offense couldn't muster any momentum and Syracuse scored another TD with five minutes remaining on a 7-play, 57-yard drive to narrow the margin to 31-24. With time running out the Orange got the ball back again and Hurley—who set a single game Syracuse passing record that day—nearly passed them to victory. His 40-yard pass completion to the PSU 6-yard line was nullified by a holding penalty and with 10 seconds left a fourth down pass was dropped near the 5-yard line by the game's leading receiver, Bruce Smeal. "Without Joe the organization was just not the same," Dorney told the *Collegian*.

Paterno had a difficult time concentrating on 4-and-2 West Virginia while his son lay in a coma for four days. But by the next Saturday young David was taken off the serious list and the Lions went out and hammered the Mountaineers, 49-28, on the first sunny game day of the year. As scouts from the Orange, Sugar, Cotton and Tangerine Bowls watched, State scored 21 points in the first five minutes, with Millen picking up a punt blocked by Sidler to give the Lions their first touchdown at 1:38 of the opening period. Fusina threw a 41-yard TD pass to Shuler after WVU punted again and moments later Geise went 7-yards for a TD after Donaldson had recovered a fumble at the Mountaineer 17. Just before the half Cefalo ran back a punt 57 yards for a TD and a 42-7 lead. In the third quarter, WVU's safety Tom Pridemore set a Beaver Stadium record that still stands by intercepting Capozzoli's pass in the end zone and running 100 yards for a TD.

The win did little to help the Lions in what turned out to be a critical week of voting by the pollsters. Notre Dame's 49-19 win over USC vaulted the Irish from #11 to #5 in the AP while State inched up one slot to #9, just behind Arkansas. Texas became #1 and the nation's only major unbeaten team after Michigan's upset loss to Minnesota with Alabama, Ohio State and Oklahoma next in line. All the poll shuffling would have negative repercussions for the Lions when the bowl invitations were given four weeks later. So would the change of date for the Pitt game which also was announced that week. The game originally had been scheduled on the day the bowl bids were issued, November 19. But the game was moved one week to November 26 so that it could be televised by ABC as the first part of a national doubleheader that included the Army-Navy game. Pitt, rated #13, also figured in the bowl picture. Even though it was still premature to develop pairings because too much could change before the 19th, the bowls were not happy with the date change. As the behind the scenes maneuvering evolved, some sportswriters in Pittsburgh suggested that the bowls wait for the outcome of the State-Pitt game before completing their selections. The Cotton and Sugar Bowls had State and Pitt among their four or five top contenders with Texas and Alabama having the inside track as their "host' teams. The Orange Bowl leaned towards PSU to play Oklahoma and reportedly was not too keen about Pitt because it was still upset the Panthers had gone to the Sugar Bowl last year when they were #1. "I can't see any major bowls waiting" the Cotton Bowl's Wilbur Evans told sportswriters. When State clobbered a good Miami team 49-7 at Beaver Stadium the following Saturday, the talk of an Orange Bowl match against Oklahoma intensified. "This was our best effort of the year," Paterno said after the Lions rolled up 461 yards against a Hurricane team that had been the fifth best in total defense before the game. Fusina threw a 56-yard screen pass to Guthrie and a 72-yard bomb to Fitzkee as 72 players saw action.

The next week, Fusina and the Lions showed how good they really were in the clutch by overcoming a determined North Carolina State (6-3) team with a thrilling, last minute 83-yard drive in the heat and humidity at Raleigh. PSU was a 9 and a half point favorite and within the first three minutes drove 80 yards in 8 plays for a 7-0 lead, capped by a 36-yard TD pass to Cefalo. But the Lions did not score again until late in the third quarter after a 76-yard drive as the Wolfpack controlled the ball most of the game with six time-consuming marches behind the running of tailback Ted Brown. Brown would set a record still unbroken by gaining the most yards ever by one back against a State team, 251 yards on 37 carries. PSU's defense stopped three scoring opportunities deep in Lion territory and forced NC State to settle for a field goal on another. But with 2:35 left in the game, the Wolfpack led 17-14 and had the Lions backed up to the PSU 17-yard line after a punt. Fusina, changing most of the plays at the line of scrimmage and throwing the ball out of bounds at least three times to stop the clock, quickly led the Lions downfield. He passed to Cefalo for 24 yards, then to Shuler for 9 and Cefalo again for 11. With the Wolfpack expecting another pass, Fusina fooled them with a draw to Suhey that gained 16 yards. Short passes to Shuler and Cefalo gained 10 more yards, and with a first down at the NC State 11-yard line, Fusina improvised a play by telling Fitzkee to change his running lane and run a flag pattern. Fitzkee faked out the NC State defender and caught Fusina's perfect pass for a touchdown with 58 seconds left on the clock. Bahr's PAT made it 21-17 and the defense stopped NC State's frantic effort to win as Millen sacked the Wolfpack quarterback for a 12-yard loss, then made an interception that ended the game. "We have to be able to make that kind of drive, in the clutch, away from home, against a good team with so much on the line, to get the confidence that we can win against anyone at any time," Paterno said in the locker room. With his 22-of-36 passes for 315 yards for the day, Fusina was now State's second all-time best passer in career and one season yardage behind John Hufnagel. The following Saturday, Fusina broke Hugnagel's season record by throwing for 249 yards and three touchdowns on 12-of-22 attempts as State manhandled Temple for the first time in three years, easily beating the Owls, 44-7, amid snow squalls at Beaver Stadium.

Before and after the Temple game, the maneuvering for the bowl slots continued. The Cotton Bowl appeared to want a match between Texas and Notre Dame and the Sugar Bowl, with Bear Bryant again pulling the strings, wanted the Big Ten runner-up against Alabama. The Orange Bowl still favored a Penn State-Oklahoma matchup with the Gator Bowl seeking Pitt as one of its teams. But some sportswriters, prodded by Pitt officials who told anyone who would listen that the Panthers would beat State and embarrass the Orange Bowl, proposed that the winner of the Pitt-Penn State game get the Orange Bowl berth with the loser going to the Gator Bowl. Paterno didn't like the idea and publicly said so. He was criticized for his stand by some sportswriters and before the bowl invitations went out November 19, Paterno changed his mind and agreed to the so-called playoff. But by then, the Orange Bowl also changed its mind after heavy pressure from Oklahoma's head coach, Barry Switzer and the governor of Arkansas. "I told the Orange Bowl officials that I wanted the highest-ranked team they could get," Switzer said to the AP. "I wanted to win the national title. I didn't think playing Penn State would give us that chance." Meanwhile, the governor of Arkansas promised the Razorbacks—coached by Lou Holtz—would bring at least 35,000 fans to Miami the help that

Chuck Fusina looks for a receiver downfield. He is one of the McKees Rocks QBs including Burkhart and Hufnagel who were so important to Coach Paterno's success in his first 15 years.

city's tourist business. So, when the bowl pairings were made November 19th, Switzer's alma mater, Arkansas, ranked one spot higher than PSU by the AP, was chosen for the Orange Bowl. The Gator Bowl tabbed Pitt and the Lions were fortunate to work out an agreement with the seven-year old Fiesta Bowl, which was still trying to gain respect in the post-season circus. "The developments saw Penn State wind up with a lesser bowl than Pitt despite a higher national ranking and a better record," wrote Russ Franke in the *Pittsburgh Press*. "It is now Penn State that will be the offended party in...a game that already had enough built-in emotion..."

All the backroom maneuvering cost Penn State nearly a million dollars since the Fiesta Bowl guarantee was about $250,000, which was $100,000 less than the Gator Bowl. Paterno blamed Herschel Nissenson, college football writer for the Associated Press, for part of the Orange Bowl snub, telling him, "a lot of people like you are enamored of other parts of the country." But some sportswriters could not believe what had happened and criticized the way the bowls chose its teams. "The Orange Bowl people really pulled a rock by letting Barry Switzer talk them into taking Arkansas instead of Penn State," wrote Dick Young of the *New York Daily News*. "Arkansas-Oklahoma has about as much national TV appeals as the gubernatorial election of Utah."

The game against Pitt, beaten only by Notre Dame but tied once, turned out to be a close one that was not decided until the last play. With 56,500 in Pitt Stadium looking on in freezing weather with a wind chill of minus 7-degrees, the Lions led most of the way in a tight defensive battle. Three Bahr field goals of 34, 31 and 20 yards and a 52-yard punt return by Guman on a reverse handoff from Cefalo late in the second quarter had given State a 15-7 lead with less than a minute left in the game. Then, in dramatic fashion, Pitt's Matt Cavanaugh—who had been sacked five times and intercepted thrice by a Lion defense led by Ron Hostetler—took the Panthers 52 yards on four plays, throwing a 17-yard pass to Gordon Jones with 12 seconds remaining. Tailback Elliot Walker banged into the left side of line for the 2-point conversion attempt that would tie the game but he was stopped short of the goal line by Millen, Diange and Donaldson to preserve State's 15-13 victory. "I've been coming to Pitt Stadium for 28 years and this win could be the sweetest one," Paterno told sportswriters in the locker room. It also was revealed that Fusina—the offensive player of the game—again had received threats on his life before the game and that his mother also had been threatened, but no one was ever arrested.

THE 1977 FIESTA BOWL
Dec. 25, 1977
Penn State 42, Arizona State 30
Outstanding Defensive Player: Matt Millen

State's opponent in the Fiesta Bowl, Arizona State, also had been struggling for national recognition in the last decade and this bowl in the Sun Devils home stadium at Tempe had been created partially to help boost the fortunes of ASU. The Sun Devils had played in four of the six Fiesta Bowl games and won each time over quality teams such as Nebraska and Pitt. Despite unbeaten seasons in 1970 and 1975 and two years with just one loss ('71 & ''73), the Sun Devils' highest finish in the rankings was #2 in '75 when it was the only major college team with an undefeated record. Their coach was Frank Kush, who grew up 50 miles from State College in Windber and had played against Rip Engle's team as a Michigan State All-American. He not only looked at this encounter with PSU as another way to earn more respect for his football program but also as a personal challenge. ASU was 9-2 and rated #12 by UPI and #15 by AP but its losses had been to unranked Missouri and Colorado State. This also had been the Sun Devils last season in the lightly-regarded Western Athletic Conference, which they had won seven times since 1969, and Kush knew a victory over the Lions would get his team off to a good start in the more prestigious and expanded Pac Ten next season.

The Lions were a nine-point favorite and admittedly did not have their heart completely into playing on Christmas afternoon when they really wanted to be in Miami on New Year's night. They also found it difficult to get into the Christmas spirit. "...It's hard to get in the Christmas spirit when it's sand blowing in your eyes instead of snow and the outdoor lights are draped around cactus plants instead of evergreens," wrote Ron Bracken in the *Centre Daily Times*. "It might have been Christmas Day but it wasn't Christmas," said Ron Hostetler. "This was just another game day for us," Geise said. Kush hoped to surprise Paterno with a new formation that eliminated the tight end. In addition, he started a little used freshman at halfback in place of his leading ground gainer. But PSU took a 14-0 lead at the end of the first quarter, thanks to a fumble recovery by DePaso that set up a 3-yard TD pass from Fusina to Torrey and a blocked punt by Banks that Lally scooped up at the 21-yard line and ran in for a touchdown. ASU Quarterback Dennis Sproul, who was still hurting from a back injury suffered in the regular season, led an 86-yard drive that put the Sun Devils back into the game on an 11-yard TD pass early in the second quarter. Late in the quarter a 67-yard punt return by Cefalo enabled Bahr to kick a 23-yard field goal but with the help of a questionable roughing the kicker penalty, ASU narrowed the score to 17-14 at the half as Sproul threw a 13-yard TD pass with 22 seconds left.

Paterno's halftime talk helped spur the Lions into a 31-14 lead early in the fourth quarter on two good drives sparked by the running of Geise, Suhey and Torrey. But, as Bracken wrote, "the fourth quarter was an absolute track meet as the two teams ripped up and down the field..." ASU stormed back on Sproul's passing and closed the gap to 34-28 before a 54-yard run by Torrey set up Suhey's second one-yard TD plunge of the day with three minutes left that seemed to clinch the game. However, the Sun Devils were not done. They were driving for another apparent TD with the clock winding down when Diminick intercepted Sproul at the PSU 5-yard line. The Lions then took a two-point safety off a punt formation to win, 42-30. Relying mostly on a rushing game to control the ball, the Lions had 351 total yards but just 83 on Fusina's passing as Geise had 111 yards and Torrey had 107. State's suspect pass defense was hit for 336 yards as Sproul completed 23 of 47 for 336 yards and three TDs but three interceptions helped slow the ASU attack, which could muster just 90 yards on the ground. "Right now, I'd say we're capable of beating anyone in the country," Paterno said in the locker room. Millen was cited as the game's outstanding defensive player for his 18 tackles and constant harassment of Sproul and after the game he told Bill Heufelder of the *Pittsburgh Press*, "As soon as that last second ticked off, I was thinking about next year."

So were most of the Penn State players and a lot of their fans. This was a young team that finished #5 in the final AP ratings and #4 in UPI with only 11 seniors among the first 44 players, including Sidler who had been named an All-American. The squad's other All-American, Dorney, would be back in '78 and so would most of the starting offense. "I don't think we'll settle for second place next year," Fusina told Heufelder. "...There hasn't been a National Championship here and we want it so bad."

"Unless they get politicized right out of contention for a major bowl bid (next season)," wrote Neil Rudel for the *Collegian*, "they will have the chance at what was pulled out from under their noses this year. Roads to National Championships are paved with seasons like this one." Sure enough. But on this road one had to watch out for Woody & The Bear.

Keith Dorney was another of Paterno's scholar athletes who was a two-time First-Team All-American in 1977-78 as an offensive lineman and had an outstanding NFL career with the Detroit Lions.

Season Record 11-1
Record to Date 529-246-40
Winning percentage .674

"'We're Number One!'"

In the 110 years of Penn State football, no season had a more frustrating and disappointing ending than this one. For the first time in history, the Lions became the Number One team in the nation, then lost it all at the Sugar Bowl on New Year's night.

If ever there was a defining moment for a season it was the instant tailback Mike Guman was stopped on fourth-and-inches at the Alabama goal line in the fourth quarter of that National Championship game. The play itself did not lose the game nor cost State the national title. There were other factors that night that also contributed to the devastating 14-7 defeat. But *that* play, more than any other, epitomized the anguish of a coach who betrayed his own judgment under pressure, and the futility of a team and a football program that had reached the crest of the ultimate goal only to be denied and rejected by a greater force.

The players who were in the New Orleans Superdome that night still can not believe they lost. They remember the Guman play and at least a half dozen others which could have changed the outcome: the Fitzkee pass reception that ended on the one-yard line instead of the end zone two plays before the Guman dive; the 61-yard Alabama punt return against the Lions' outstanding special teams unit that set up the winning TD; the controversial second quarter touchdown catch by an Alabama receiver who dropped the ball but was given the TD by an official despite what a TV replay showed; the obvious interference that wasn't called on a pass to tight end Brad Scovill at the Alabama goal line late in the game; and, the 12 men on the field penalty that negated a fourth quarter PSU scoring opportunity following a shanked punt at the Alabama 20-yard line; etc.

This team deserved a better fate and so did its quarterback, Fusina, who lost the Heisman Trophy to Oklahoma's Billy Simms by just 87 votes, the closest vote in 14 years, and actually had more first place votes. Fusina, who won the Maxwell Trophy as college football's Player-of-the-Year, was one of six First-Team All-Americans, the most ever in one year for State, and that included Clark who won the Lombardi Award as the nation's outstanding lineman/linebacker. The other All-Americans were Dorney (for the second time), Matt Bahr, Millen and Pete Harris. Also starting on the team were such standouts as Fitzkee, Matt Suhey, Correal, Pankey, Mehl and Milot—all of whom would later play in the NFL. This certainly was one of the greatest teams in Lion history and some may argue the best of all time in spite of the heartbreaking Sugar Bowl loss.

Everyone in the country, including Paterno and his staff, knew it was going to be a very good team. There were 40 lettermen returning and many, like Fusina, Clark, et al, were three year starters. A consensus of more than a dozen preseason football publications rated the Lions as #3, including AP, UPI. *Football News* and *Sporting News*. *Sports Illustrated* and *Playboy* tabbed them as #2 and *Argosy College Football* made them #1. Ironically, Alabama was a near unanimous choice of #1 by all the major publications except *Sports Illustrated*, which chose Arkansas. Oklahoma was the consensus #2 with Arkansas #4, followed by defending National Champion Notre Dame and Ohio State at #6. That meant the Lions would have an early test to determine how good they really were since the third game of the sea-

son was against the Buckeyes in Columbus. Three other opponents were rated in the Top 20: Pitt, Kentucky and Maryland

State had another early opener set for the Labor Day weekend, Friday night, September 1 against Temple at Philadelphia's Veterans Stadium. Then it was Rutgers in the home opener in the expanded Beaver Stadium. Some 16,000 seats had been added to help accommodate the Lions growing legion of fans, including 45,000 season ticket holders. The track had been eliminated and 20 rows of concrete stands were added at the base. The south end of the horseshoe was closed and 40 rows of concrete seats were built, turning the stadium into a bowl for the first time. That pushed the new seating capacity to 78,000 but still did not meet the demand of the 32,000 students, who complained throughout the year about their 20,000 ticket allotment.

Even before the preseason started, Paterno told sportswriters, "we should have an explosive team—an exciting team to watch." He said Fusina, who already owned most school passing records, was "without question the best quarterback we have ever had at Penn State." Paterno's running backs included veterans Suhey, Torrey and Moore. Guman, who Paterno called "one of the finest all around athletes" ever at PSU, was moved back from defense to tailback and Milot was switched permanently to outside linebacker. The interior line consisted of Dorney, Correal, Cunningham and a couple of sophomores, John Wojtowicz and Jim Brown. Pankey was moved from tackle to tight end but played tackle when injuries hit the team with sophomore walk-on Brad Scovill backing up at tight end. Fitzkee was back at split end (and still the punter) and Tom Donovan, recovered from his injuries, was the flanker, along with senior Bob Bassett. The prime concern on defense was the secondary but by the end of August Paterno was happy with the combination of Harris at safety and Diminick and senior Mike Gilsenan at halfbacks with sophomore Karl McCoy in reserve. "We put them under a lot of pressure and they've improved a lot," Paterno said. Clark, Millen and Lally returned to the defensive line with Kubin and senior letterman Fred Ragucci battling it out for the other defensive end slot and Petruccio taking over at middle guard, backed by sophomores Greg Jones and Frank Case. Donaldson, Paul Suhey and Mehl started at linebacker with Milot taking over when Donaldson was hurt in

Center Chuck Correal, another fine scholar athlete, was co-captain of the 1978 team. He received the National Football Foundation's College Football Hall of Fame fellowship and a NCAA Postgraduate Scholarship.

midseason. Tom "Scrap Iron" Bradley and many of his "Scrap Pack" buddies from the punting and kicking teams also were back as was placekicker Matt Bahr, who had played pro soccer that summer for the Tulsa Roughnecks. Fusina and Paul Suhey were elected co-captains and Bradley continued as the unofficial captain of the "Scrap Pack." Yes, this definitely was a team of National Championship caliber. But it didn't look like one against Temple.

The Lions were favored by three-to-four touchdowns but once again Wayne Hardin has his Owls well prepared for an upset. For nearly three quarters, Temple held State's touted "explosive offense" scoreless with a defensive strategy based on punting on third down. Because Paterno and Sandusky were concerned about Temple faking a punt on third down and passing, the Lions did not drop back a return man and seven times Temple's Casey Murphy punted over the defenders' heads and deep into State territory. One PSU drive started at its own 3-yard line and another at the 5 as Temple's fired-up defense kept the Lions offense from crossing midfield until midway in the third quarter. The Lions finally scored on a 5-play, 57-yard drive near the end of the third quarter with Moore getting the TD on a 26-yard run and Bahr adding the placement. But the Owls tied it five minutes later with their own 54-yard drive on a 21-yard TD pass reception by Zack Dixon. With six minutes left in the game, Temple seemed to get a break when it intercepted a Fusina pass and returned the ball to the State 30. But on first down Kubin sacked the quarterback for a 13-yard loss and on the next play Clark forced a fumble at that Mehl recovered at the PSU 48. With time winding down, the Lions drove down field in 11 plays solely on the running of Moore and Suhey and with just 15 seconds remaining Bahr kicked a 23-yard field goal for a 10-7 Lion win. "We were sloppy and imprecise," Paterno told sportswriters. Still, in an indication of what was to follow, State's defense held Temple to a measly 15 yards rushing on 34 carries while giving up 111 yards passing.

The following week it was more of the same in the home opener before a record crowd of 77,154 as the defense held Rutgers to 72 yards rushing (on 28 carries) and 117 yards passing, with two interceptions, and the offense sputtered again. Bahr tied a school record set by his brother Chris against Pitt in '74 by kicking four field goals (of 32, 37, 28 and 27 yards) and Fitzkee caught a 53-yard TD pass from Fusina to give the Lions a 26-10 victory, with the Rutgers TD coming against the reserves in the last two minutes of the game. Paterno was not pleased in the locker room and when the media began asking questions he did not like he threw them out after 15 minutes, prompting such comments as this one from Eric Yoder of the *Daily Collegian*: "He was rude, overbearing, obnoxious. He answered legitimate questions curtly if he answered them at all." Paterno did admit he was mystified by the inconsistency of his offense, saying "as individuals they play well but there's no cohesion." Seven days later he would acknowledge he held back two thirds of his passing offense until the Ohio State game. That's when he also told sportswriters he and his staff began planning for the Buckeyes in the summer.

Because this was OSU's opening game, the #5 Lions had the advantage of playing two games but the #6 Buckeyes had the benefit of scouting PSU and surprising Paterno with different offensive and defensive tactics as well as playing at home. True to past form, some Ohio writers were picking the Buckeyes by as much as 17 points, even though they were just a 3-to-6 point favorite by the oddsmakers. Much of the pregame analysis centered around OSU's highly-publicized 18-year-old freshman quarterback, Art Schlichter, and whether he would start over the veteran Rod Gerald, who had taken the Buckeyes to a 9-3 record and a Sugar Bowl game in '77. Paterno knew Schlichter well because he had recruited the Bloomingsburg, Ohio, native, who never lost a high school game. It rained most of the morning and the field was slick when OSU kicked off before a crowd of 88,202 and a regional television audience. The Buckeye defense stopped the Lions on their first possession and Hayes sent in his offense—with Schlichter at quarterback and Gerald at split end. On the first play Schlichter surprised the home fans by completing a pass. No one in the press box could

recall the last time OSU threw on the first play of the season—at least since Woody began coaching. Schlichter completed two more passes as the Buckeyes moved upfield into Lion territory. On Schlichter's fourth passing attempt, Harris stepped in front of the intended receiver at the 21 and returned the interception to the OSU 46-yard line. It was a portent of things to come. The Lions drove for a 30-yard field goal by Bahr and a 3-0 lead. Before the half was over, the Lions in-

Pete Harris was a First-Team All-American in 1978 when he led the country with ten interceptions.

tercepted another Schlichter pass and recovered fumbles by Schlichter and Gerald but could not capitalize on the OSU turnovers. In the locker room Paterno calmly told his troops they were not going to sit on a three-point lead. "We're going to play this baby like we were behind, like we are desperate," he said. On State's second possession of the third quarter, Fusina guided the Lions on a six-minute, run-oriented 13-play, 80-yard drive for a 10-0 lead with Suhey getting the TD on a 3-yard run. From there, the Lion defense led by Clark and Kubin took over, harassing Schlichter and the OSU offense by intercepting three more passes—another by Harris—and recovering another fumble. In the fourth quarter, Bahr kicked three more field goals to tie his single game record and the Lions shut out the Buckeyes for the second time in 14 years, 19-0. "Overall, the Lions, while less than spectacular, were capable of making folks forget the two previous weeks...," wrote Bill Heufelder of the *Pittsburgh Press*. "The defense was so strong that there wasn't any time in the game that we thought Ohio State could hurt us," Paterno told sportswriters. The defense held Buckeye runners to 89 yards and the 247 yards OSU earned by passing was meaningless since it never scored. Suhey, who had almost gone to Ohio State, had 96 of the Lions' 139 yards on the ground. It would be the last time Hayes coached against PSU for he would be fired in a few months after losing his temper and slugging a Clemson player at the Gator Bowl. Back in State College, the students celebrated all over the downtown streets and campus, throwing toilet paper, water balloons and eggs and tying up traffic on the major arteries, and some 5,000 fans greeted the team when it arrived home.

With its solid thrashing of OSU the Lions were now the credible national contender the preseason oracles had expected. But the offense was still struggling and continued to do so in the first half against Southern Methodist the following Saturday at Beaver Stadium. What happened in the second half was the defining moment of the regular season. Although favored by 17 points, State trailed at halftime, 14-12, with Bahr getting the only PSU points on another record four field goals and the defense giving up both Mustang touchdowns after long drives of 72 and 67 yards. When David Hill returned an interception 40 yards for a touchdown three minutes into the third quarter, the Lions appeared to be in deep trouble. However, the shock of being behind by nine points seemed to motivate the offense. After the kickoff, Fusina drove the Lions 69 yards in 9 plays, capped by a 16-yard TD to Fitzkee, to narrow the score to 21-19. Minutes later, the Lions took over the ball on the PSU 27-yard line following a punt and in three plays moved 9 yards. With a fourth-and-one Paterno surprised the crowd of 77,404 by gambling for the first down. "We didn't have control of the game and we couldn't kick it and guarantee we could keep them in a hole," Paterno told the *Collegian*. The second guessing would have been terrible if they had not made it and then lost the game. But Moore ran off the right side for the first down and Fusina took the Lions the rest of the way with Suhey banging over for the TD on a 3-yard plunge and Bahr kicking the PAT to take the lead, 26-21, with two minutes left in third quarter. There was no more scoring, as the Lion defense controlled the rest of the game, putting on a furious pass rush that negated SMU QB Mike Ford's 60 percent completion average. When it was over, SMU had a minus five yards rushing and 289 yards passing as the defense sacked Ford five times and intercepted two passes. Meanwhile, the Lions had 422 total yards and Fusina had a good passing day, hitting on 13-of-24 attempts for 129 yards. "We knew we were up against a tough team," Fusina told Black for the *"Football Letter,"* "but there was no time when we didn't think we could win it." Still, Paterno was upset at the failure to score touchdowns in the red zone. "We may need more variety in our goal line play selection," he told Black. "...We ought to be better inside the 10." That same day, USC upset #1 Alabama in Birmingham but the Lions stayed at #5 in the ratings and Alabama dropped to #7.

One week later, the Lions were much better inside the 10-yard line, scoring six of their nine touchdowns from nine yards or less in routing outmanned Texas Christian, 58-0. Moore had three TDs and Fusina threw TD passes of 9 and 53 yards as State rolled up the highest victory margin since the unbeaten '47 team walloped Fordham, 75-0. Again, the defense was superb, limiting TCU rushers to 55 yards on 37 carries, intercepting three passes and recovering a fumble. That performance helped make the defense the best in the country against the rush and they fortified their ranking the following Saturday night in a revenge game against Kentucky (1-1-1) at Lexington. The defense held Kentucky to 27 yards rushing on 33 carries and 115 yards passing while making two interceptions and recovering two fumbles and shut out the Wildcats, 30-0, as four bowl scouts looked on. Fusina threw for 211 yards, including a 15-yard TD pass to Fitzkee and a 57-yard bomb to Donovan that set up Bahr's record-setting eighth consecutive field goal (of 33 yards) in the second quarter. The defeat was the worst ever for Kentucky at five-year-old Commonwealth Stadium and its first loss at home in two years. "We were disappointed in the way we've played here and in Tennessee," Paterno told sportswriters, who had pointed out that State had been 2-5 against Southeastern Conference teams "and we wanted to gain some respect." Kentucky coach Curci said: "I hope this answers their question (about respect)." The win moved the Lions into a tie with Arkansas for #3 in the AP poll. One week later, without even playing, State replaced USC as the #2 team and was now on track to meet #1 Oklahoma in the Orange Bowl.

Syracuse, 1-5 and playing without its star quarterback Hurley, who was out for the year with cracked ribs, was no match for State in the Homecoming game. Fusina threw four TD passes, two of them to Fitzkee for 21 and 11 yards, and accumulated 293 yards on 15-of-27 passes in leading the Lions to a 45-15 victory. Millen even scored a TD by recovering a punt in the end zone that had been blocked by Micky Urquhart. No one expected the heavily favored Lions to have any problem with the 1-6 Mountaineers at West Virginia on October 28 in State's

last game ever played at old Mountaineer Field. But the early 14-0 score in WVU's favor must have been a shocker when it was sent around the nation. The Mountaineers had taken the opening kickoff and driven 78 yards for a touchdown, then intercepted a Fusina pass a minute later to set up a 28-yard TD drive for the second score. But Bradley's "Scrap Pack" had helped tie it up by the end of the first quarter, when Lally's blocked punt led to a Suhey one-yard TD and Guman ran back a punt 85 yards for another TD. Harris returned an interception 28-yards to set up Fusina's one-yard sneak midway into the second quarter that gave the Lions the lead for the first time and they went on to win, 49-21.

Matt Bahr was a First-Team All-American in 1978 when he broke his brother's NCAA field goal percentage record by hitting 22 of 27 attempts for an 81.5% average.

What came next was the biggest game in University Park since the epic 1959 "battle of unbeatens" against Syracuse. This was another "battle of unbeatens" only this time the foe was #5 Maryland, which had won 12 straight games but had lost 14 in a row to Penn State since 1961. "I've waited a long time to be where we are tonight," Paterno told a cheering pep rally of 8,500 at Rec Hall the night before the game. "We're No. 1!" the fans screamed back. The game was on national TV and was hyped as a defensive battle, with the favored Lions still the best against the rush and the Terps' defense ranked fourth overall. Maryland also had a vaunted running game led by Steve Atkins, the Terps' all-time rushing leader, who had been averaging more than 119 yards per game. With five bowl scouts and a new record crowd of 78,019 watching in crisp but perfect early November weather, the Lion defense and offense blistered the Terps' from every direction and won, 27-3. On defense, State drilled the Maryland rushers for a minus 32 yards on 43 carries, sacked two Terp quarterbacks five times—three by Kubin—and intercepted five passes, with Harris picking off three and McCoy two. Fusina passed for 234 yards, including a 63-yard TD bomb to Donovan who was the alternate receiver on the play, Bahr kicked field goals of 33 and 32 yards and seven running backs gained 210 yards on 51 rushes. Fans celebrating the victory threw oranges all over Beaver Stadium and the adjoining parking lots. "The defense looked like the old '69 group," Paterno said. "...The wide-awake Penn State football team is casting a lengthening shadow as it arrives on the threshold of what could be its first national championship...," wrote John Underwood in a *Sports Illustrated* story of the game that featured Fusina on the cover. "Don't get cocky," Paterno told his team in the locker room, Underwood reported. "We're not there yet."

Nine days later, two days after beating North Carolina State, 19-10 at Beaver Stadium, the Lions reached the pinnacle when they were ranked #1 for the first time in history, following #4 Nebraska's upset of Oklahoma. But if Paterno wanted to rewarn his team about overconfidence, this was the game he could cite. "The Lions looked

Who is that man beside Chuck Fusina at the AP All-American Awards program? Fusina won the Maxwell Award and was runner-up to Billy Sims for the Heisman in 1978.

very flat in the first half and were particularly sloppy on offense," wrote Black for his *"Football Letter."* "They frittered away good field position with costly penalties, wasted four scoring opportunities and came away with only three points..." They actually were behind at the half, 7-3, after 17-point underdog NC State (7-2) turned an intercepted pass into a 28-yard drive for a TD with 8 seconds left. In the third quarter, Bahr kicked three more field goals to break his brother's season record of 18 and career record of 35 but the Lions were still holding on to a narrow 12-10 lead with about 4 and a half minutes to play when Suhey returned a punt 43-yards for a TD to clinch the victory. "Penn State deserves top ranking," NC State linebacker Bill Cowher told Doug McDonald of the *Centre Daily Times*. Cowher, who led the Wolfpack with nine tackles and nine assists, said, "Penn State doesn't have a weakness...(They) just keep coming after you." NC State eventually would finish 18th in the country with a 9-3 record after beating Pitt in the Tangerine Bowl. Fifteen years later Cowher was coaching the Pittsburgh Steelers.

Now that the Lions were atop of the polls, and the only unbeaten major college team in the country, they could go to the bowl of their choice and even pick the team they wanted to play. But it was not an easy decision for a team still trying to overcome an anti-Eastern bias and yearning to win its first National Championship. The quality of the bowl opponent was important to Paterno and the players but once again the bowl pairings would have to be made before all the games had been played. They knew they would have to beat Pitt no matter what but that game was two weeks off and the bowl invitations were due the following Saturday evening. As usual all the bowls were manipulating behind the scenes and so were some coaches.

With Nebraska at #2 that week, the Orange Bowl seemed to be the logical choice for State but the Associated Press reported that Paterno might snub the Miami game because of how the Orange Bowl committee spurned State in '77. Eighth-ranked Georgia seemed headed for the SEC title and the Sugar Bowl and #6 Houston for the SWC championship and the Cotton Bowl. Paterno talked about the possibil-

ity of all three bowls and the desire of the Lions to play "the highest ranked team." He also admitted to the AP that Bear Bryant had called him about meeting #3 Alabama in the Gator Bowl. Naturally, everything changed the afternoon of November 18 when Missouri upset Nebraska, 35-31, and Georgia and Auburn tied, 22-22. Now, Alabama—which had lost only to USC and beaten Nebraska—could win the Sugar Bowl berth if it beat Auburn Dec. 2. No matter what State did, it would be a gamble but this time the odds would be in State's favor. So, at 6 p.m., Paterno and President Oswald sat in the Rec Hall football lounge and formally accepted an offer from the Sugar Bowl to play either Georgia or Alabama on New Year's night. "As I told Joe, I hoped the road to number one ends in the Superdome," Jim Flowers of the Sugar Bowl said to Ron Bracken of the *Centre Daily Times*. "Hopefully, this will give us a chance to settle the National Championship on the field."

Pitt and its cocky young coach, Jackie Sherrill, would have liked nothing better than to knock State off its #1 pedestal and out of the national title race. And the Panthers came very close in what was a classic defensive matchup before a national TV audience on the Friday after Thanksgiving at Beaver Stadium. Even before the game started, a controversy erupted over the cleats being worn by the Pitt team and when Paterno asked officials for an inspection of the cleats 90 minutes before the game, Sherrill accused the PSU coach of "unethical" behavior. The Panthers, 8-2 and going to the Tangerine Bowl, were a two-touchdown underdog but they didn't play like it. A fumble recovery by Donaldson at the Pitt 15-yard line had helped give the Lions a 7-0 lead midway through the first quarter but by the end of the third quarter the Panthers had taken a 10-7 lead. In the fourth quarter, the Lions took the ball on the Pitt 42 following a punt and as darkness began to envelop the field, they were faced with a fourth down just inside the Panther 5-yard line with about five minutes left in the game. Confused by assistants as to how far it was for a first down, Paterno had Fusina call a time out, then sent him to determine the exact yardage needed for a first down. A field goal might have seemed like a "safe" play for if the game ended in a tie, the #1 ranking would probably have been retained since no other team was undefeated. "I wanted to go for it," Paterno said after the game. If it was more than two yards, Paterno was going to have Bahr try to tie the game with a field goal, then rely on his aggressive defense to get the ball back so that another field goal could win it. When Fusina returned to the sideline, he held his hands about two feet apart. Actually, the Lions were two full yards away from the first down. "I lied a little," Fusina later told reporters. The Pitt de-

Running back Mike Guman, shown here going for some tough yardage, was a fine running back but is probably better known as one of the runners stopped by Alabama in its great goal line stand that cost State the national title in the 1979 Sugar Bowl.

fense was fired up and earlier had stopped State on back-to-back third and fourth down tries with one yard to go. Paterno said to go for the first down and they discussed the play. "He really had his mind made up," Fusina said. Fusina figured it would be a rollout after a fake to the fullback. But Paterno called a "40 pitch." Fusina sent two receivers wide to the right to stretch the Panther defense, then pitched out left to Guman. Guman cut inside between the blocks of Dorney and Pankey, got two more blocks by Cunningham and Suhey on the defensive backs and ran into the end zone standing up. Bahr's PAT made it 14-10 and the crowd of 77,465 went wild. A minute later Milot intercepted Rick Trocano's pass at the 33-yard line and on third down Bahr kicked a 38-yard field goal that set a new NCAA record for most field goals in a season at 22. With less than two minutes remaining, Mehl made the Lions fourth interception of the afternoon at the 40 and the Lions won 17-10. The winning TD was "nothing fancy" Paterno told sportswriters in the locker room. "Guman could go wide or cut back. When the crack opened up inside, he cut through it. We run it all the time."

A few days later Alabama beat Auburn, 34-16.

THE 1979 SUGAR BOWL
Jan. 1, 1979
Alabama 14, Penn State 7

After 20 years of reflecting on why State lost the National Championship to Alabama on New Year's night, one can not help but return to an obscure newspaper headline in the sports page of the *Louisville Courier-Journal* two days after the game. "Paterno shows class, shoulders blame for loss to Tide," the headline said. The accompanying story like many of the post mortems of the game told how Paterno frankly admitted he was outcoached. He didn't blame any of his players for losing their poise, as some did. Nor did he fault his assistants for some questionable strategy or complain about not getting a break or a crucial call by the officials. Reacting immediately to the most excruciating defeat of his entire career, he blamed no one but himself. And he was right, even though he would wonder about it later.

It had been seven years since the #1 team faced the #2 team in a bowl game and the last time that happened, at the 1972 Orange Bowl, Bear Bryant's Alabama team also was #2 and was embarrassed by Nebraska, 38-6. For Bryant, the '79 Sugar Bowl was a crusade. For Paterno, it was the fulfillment of a dream—to settle the National Championship on the field and not in the polls. The Lions could have easily chosen to play in the Orange or Cotton Bowls and probably backed into the national title. But that wasn't the Paterno way then, or now.

That Alabama, the consensus preseason #1, was now playing the reigning #1 for the championship seemed as if it had been scripted in Hollywood. But for that 24-14 loss to USC, the positions may have been reversed. Alabama, with a powerful wishbone running attack sparked by Tony Nathan and Major Ogilvie and a good but underrated defense led by All-American linebacker Barry Krauss, end E. J. Junior and tackle Marty Lyons, had captured its seventh SEC title in eight years. The Tide had won 10 of 11 games, including a 20-3 victory over Nebraska, which was playing Oklahoma in a rematch at the Orange Bowl. State, on the other hand, had the nation's longest winning streak of 19 games and a balanced offense with the number one defense in the country, the nation's leading kicker and coached by the Chevrolet Coach-of-the-Year. The betting line favored Alabama by one point.

In the two or three days leading up to the game, the sounds of "Roll Tide Roll" seemed to drown out the yells for "We Are...Penn State" that reverberated throughout Bourbon Street and the French Quarter. The Alabamans in their bright Crimson outnumbered the PSU fans in their traditional Blue and White by three or four fold. Inside the Superdome near game time, the noise from both sides was deafening and the signs demeaning. One banner on the Penn State side read: "Around the bowl, Down the hole, Roll Tide Roll." Across the way, in the middle of all the red, was a sign that said, "Remember Gettysburg." "The affair was somewhat unusual at the beginning because there seemed to be more tension in the air than enthusiasm," wrote Wes Jackson for the *New Orleans Times-Picayune*. A record Sugar Bowl crowd of 76,824 was stomping and screaming in the 72 degree temperature while outside the Dome rain was pouring down on a windy 58-degree early evening.

Everything seemed to go wrong for the Lions right from the first offensive play when Guman's 8-yard run was nullified by a holding penalty that pushed State back to its own 7-yard line. The Lions could never get out of the hole in the first half as Alabama surprised State with a stunting, blitzing defense that pressured Fusina while controlling the line of scrimmage to stop the run. "We were not ready for them..."Paterno said after the game. "My play-calling wasn't sharp and I didn't adjust to what they were doing on defense." Bryant said it was probably "the greatest pass rush" his team ever had. Although the Lions adjusted in the second half, Fusina was sacked five times for nearly 70 yards. Once in the first half he beat the blitz and completed a 32-yard pass to Guman only to have the play called back on an illegal motion penalty. And that's how the entire evening went, with Alabama's defense stymieing PSU's offense and penalties at crucial times thwarting several State opportunities.

During the first 25 minutes of the game, Alabama's offense also found gaps in the Lion defense and moved for several first downs on the running of Nathan and Ogilvie and spot passing by quarterback Jeff Rutledge. But State kept the Tide away from the end zone and late in the second quarter, the Lions came up with a big play when Milot picked off a Rutledge pass at the PSU 8-yard line and ran 55 yards

One of the clutch players of his time, Scott Fitzkee pulls down a pass against Pitt. This exciting WR and punter had one of his biggest games in the classic 1979 Sugar Bowl battle against Alabama for the national title.

Matt Millen, seen here returning an intercepted pass, teamed with Bruce Clark for three years to give State one of the best defensive tackle combinations ever and was an All-American and a Lombardi Award finalist in 1978. He is even better known today as a TV sportscaster.

down the sideline to the Alabama 37. However, a 15-yard sack ended the threat and forced a punt into the end zone with just 1:11 remaining. It was here that Paterno made another questionable decision by calling two time outs to stop the clock, figuring his defense could get the ball back for a field goal attempt. But Nathan ran 30 yards for a first down on a play called by Bryant and suddenly the Tide was on a "roll." The number one defense in the country was flustered and with just eight seconds left in the half, Rutledge passed to Bruce Bolton over the middle at the goal line. Bolton had to dive for the ball and it seemed to slip from his grasp as he rolled on the ground. Newspaper photographs and videotape confirmed the ball had bounced on the ground and landed in Bolton's arms after he rolled over. But the official ruled a touchdown and no one argued at the time. That gave Alabama a 7-0 lead but the worst was yet to come. "When we went out in the second half, the enthusiasm didn't seem to be there," a PSU player said after the game. "I just had a bad feeling going out."

The teams continued to parry in the third quarter until Harris intercepted a Rutledge pass at the Alabama 48. For the first time the Lion offense came alive and in five plays, the game was tied, with Fitzkee getting the TD on a 17-yard catch that he made just over the head of a defender while tip-toeing inside the end line. State's defense then forced a punt but so did the Tide and that's when the Lions made another big mistake. Fitzkee boomed his punt 50 yards but it was too far for the coverage. The "Scrap Pack," which had not allowed any opponent to return a punt more than 10 yards all season, was caught flat footed and a second string return man named Lou Inker went 62 yards to the PSU 11 before being tackled. On third down, Rutledge

barely escaped a tackle by Millen as he pitched out to Ogilvie for an 8-yard TD and a 14-7 lead. State continued to fight back and was on a drive in the fourth quarter when another Fusina pass was intercepted in the end zone by Alabama safety Don McNeal. But a moment later, Millen forced Rutledge to fumble on a pitchout and Lally recovered at the Alabama 19 with about seven minutes to play.

What followed was a sequence of plays and events that live forever in the annals of both teams. Suhey bolted up the middle for a first down at the Tide 8-yard line. Guman dove for two yards. Fusina then hit Fitzkee near the flag at the right side of the end zone for what looked like a TD but as he turned to cross the goal McNeal sprinted up and knocked him out of bounds inside the one-yard line. With two feet to go, Suhey dove into the Alabama line but was stopped short by about six inches. State called time out and Fusina went to the sidelines to confer with Paterno. "...I wanted...Fusina to fake a run and throw a little pop pass to the tight end...," Paterno recalled in his book, *"Football My Way."* "A couple of my soundest coaches insisted I play the percentages—just crash through the couple of feet for the touchdown...That moment was one of the few in my life when I backed off from a strong instinct and let myself worry about what people might say if a decision was wrong." Over on the Alabama side, they also were discussing the play. "We expected them to dive over or run off tackle like they did against Pittsburgh" Bryant told sportswriters later. But Lyons told Mike Bolton of the *Birmingham News*, "We never dreamed they would come back with the same play. We were sort of expecting a pass. Krauss told *Times-Picayune* writer Jimmy Smith, "I had a hunch." The atmosphere in the Dome was electrifying as Fusina handed off to Guman who dove at the left tackle with the option to go through a hole or dive over the pile. Alabama's defense surged and as Guman leaped to go over the pile he was hit by Krauss and they all went down. Krauss was in a daze and did not get up. But the official signaled Alabama's ball and the Tide linemen jumped up and down in celebration as the Lion offense walked dejectedly off the field. Krauss would be selected the MVP of the game and later a hallowed photograph of that play would be turned into a lithograph and become one of Alabama's most treasured memorabilia.

But the Lions weren't done. Two minutes later they forced Alabama to punt and Woody Umphrey shanked it out of bounds at the Tide 20. The State crowd cheered and the Alabama fans groaned until they saw the red flag. In an ironic twist that could be traced back to State's 15-14 victory over Kansas in the '69 Orange Bowl, the Lions were penalized for having 12 men on the field. The coaches knew it and had yelled to get the offender out. "The kid just didn't come out," Paterno said later. Asked who it was, Paterno said, "It doesn't make any difference. It wasn't his fault any way." Still, the Lions had one more chance and Fusina thought he had a TD when he threw a long pass down the middle to Scovill as the clock was running out. Scovill was tripped up as the defender came in and they tangled legs but there was no penalty and the incident was hardly mentioned in either locker room after the game. Like their coach, the State players didn't blame anyone for the loss but themselves. They had been outplayed and they knew it. "It seemed like the world fell in on us but...we looked around after the game and decided we gave it everything we had," said Suhey. "We didn't underestimate them," said Fusina. "It was sad, the way things worked out...for the most beloved, respected coach in college football," wrote Billy Reed in the *Courier-Journal*. "My biggest disappointment is for our seniors," Paterno said in the locker room after the game. "They worked hard, and it is unfortunate they lost without playing their best game...They accomplished a lot." Bryant told sportswriters "It was one of the greatest victories we've ever had. I think we could have beaten any team in America today." Yet, when it was over, he had to share the national title with USC, which was tabbed #1 by the UPI coaches board while Alabama was selected by AP and the Football Writers of America.

State finished fourth in both major polls and Paterno went home to brood. "It got to me," he later wrote in *"Football: By the Book."* "It hammered at my ego. When I stood toe to toe with Bear Bryant, he outcoached me." Paterno also began to second guess himself and as he thought more about what had occurred he lost his perspective. "Much as I blamed myself, I couldn't tolerate all that self-blame," he wrote. "I let my anger turn against the staff and against the team, even though the decision was purely mine...I still think my distraction and demoralization helped lead to some of the things that went wrong in the terrible season that followed, 1979."

Season Record 11-1
Record to Date 540-247-40
Winning percentage .677

"Troubled Times in Happy Valley"

No year was more star-crossed and unpleasant for Joe Paterno than this one. In the next two decades, he would have other discouraging seasons but 1979 would be the most depressing and much of what occurred was beyond his control. Later, he would admit he made some mistakes and miscalculations, particularly early in the year when he was still distracted by self-pity over the humbling Sugar Bowl loss. But he could not be held accountable for the irresponsibility of several players, who embarrassed themselves, their families and the football program with their academic failures and their run-ins with the law. Nor could he do anything about the injuries that pecked at the team all year and finally sent the two best players to the sidelines permanently just as the squad was regaining its winning mode. Injuries are part of the game. Bad judgment off the field is not. Taken altogether, the contretemps melded to define the season.

The serious problems started with the opening of preseason practice in August. In the spring, Paterno had tried to develop a new quarterback and offensive line to replace Fusina, Dorney and company but from the first day of fall practice, his critical problem was the secondary. Safety Pete Harris, who led the nation in interceptions in '78, and starting corner Karl McCoy had left school for academic reasons along with Frank Case, who was considered a possible starter in the defensive line. Junior Grover Edwards, set to start in Harris' place, also was sidelined from injuries suffered in a July auto accident and before practice was too far along, the other projected corner, junior Tom Wise, also went down with an injury. Paterno's dilemma worsened when two prime reserve defensive backs, junior Brian Kistler and sophomore Bill Meade, quit the team as Paterno shuffled players. Before the first game

against Rutgers on September 15, Paterno moved sophomore Joel Coles from tailback to starting safety, and switched sophomore Giuseppe Harris, Pete and Franco's younger brother, from linebacker to pair with converted quarterback John Walsh at the corner positions. Later he would juggle the lineup with Wise and Urquhart, who also played linebacker, and move Coles back to tailback.

With Clark, Millen and Kubin returning, Paterno figured junior lettermen Gene Gladys at the other defensive end and Jones at the nose guard with sophomore Leo Wisniewski in reserve would make the defensive line the strength of the team. Veterans Mehl, a co-captain, Donaldson and junior Steve Griffiths were the linebackers with Urquhart and Matt Bradley, Tom's younger brother, in reserve. "I don't know if any team has better people at those positions," Paterno said in mid September. But Millen was no longer a co-captain. Midway through preseason practice, Paterno had taken away the captaincy after Millen dropped out of a required one mile running drill one afternoon, saying simply that he couldn't do it. Two days later he ran the drill and apologized but the damage had been done. "...the morale and concentration of the team was severely shaken," Paterno later wrote in his book, *"Football: By the Book."* Millen admitted it afterwards, too, saying "I wasn't a real leader like I should have been out on the field...I think it set the tone for the team and, psychologically, it hurt the team."

Paterno had absolutely no experience at quarterback. Fusina's back up Capozzoli had seldom played in '77 and '78 and he left school before the preseason because of personal problems. The designated starter since the spring was junior Dayle Tate, who missed one season with a broken hand and was out nearly all of '78 after suffering a broken collar bone in the Rutgers opener. Behind Tate were five untested freshmen and sophomores and the best of them, redshirt frosh Frank Rocco, was still nursing an ankle injury from a pickup basketball game before spring practice. True freshmen Jeff Hostetler of Holsopple, whose brothers had played on defense the last couple of years, and Todd Blackledge of Canton, OH, looked like great prospects but Paterno would not think about turning over this team to an inexperienced rookie. But he had a different opinion about his freshman tailback, Curt Warner of Wyoming, WV, who was the backup to starter Moore with sophomore Leo McClelland right behind. The indestructible Suhey was back at fullback with sophomore Mike Meade in reserve. Because of the need for wide receivers, Guman was moved to flanker and Donovan, fully recovered from injuries, was installed at split end. Later, when both were hurting, Paterno would go to a two tight end offense, featuring Scovill and sophomore Vyto Kab or freshman Mike McCluskey. Pankey, the offensive co-captain, was shifted back to left guard with sophomores Sean Farrell of Westhampton Beach, NY and Mike Munchak of Scranton, battling at the other guard. Junior Bill Dugan, winner of the Worrell Award as the most improved offensive player in spring practice, started at one tackle and junior Pete Kugler, who moved from defense, was the other tackle after Brown broke his leg, with Ron LaPointe and others as backup. The centers were Bob Jagers and two-year veteran Jim Romano. Menhardt, back on the team after giving up his last year of soccer eligibility, succeeded Bahr on field goals with junior Brian Franco on kickoffs and freshman Ralph Giacomarro on punts.

Because they did not know or understand the depth of State's problems, sportswriters again picked the Lions for a Top 10 finish and both AP and UPI selected the team #5. There were four changes on the schedule from '78, including #8 Nebraska and first time foe, Texas

A&M, tagged #14 by AP and #20 by UPI. Miami and Army also were back on the schedule along with the traditional Eastern opponents like Pitt, which was selected #17 in the preseason AP. Six of the teams had been to bowls last season and four had finished in the final Top 20. Based on the records of '78, the NCAA rated the Lions schedule as the fourth toughest in the country for '79.

The preseason turmoil was completely forgotten in the satisfying 45-10 victory over Rutgers on opening day at Beaver Stadium. After a shaky 3-3 tie in the first quarter, the Lions exploded as Paterno introduced his newest superstar—Warner—to the crowd of 77,309. Warner scored three touchdowns, including one on a 62-yard pass from Tate with three seconds left in the second quarter that gave State a 27-3 lead. His other two TDs came on runs of 7 and 18 yards as he rushed for 100 yards on 12 carries and also returned four kickoffs for 109 yards. The Lion defense held Rutgers to eight yards rushing on 30 carries and sacked the quarterback eight times, with Clark's blindside tackle in the end zone resulting in a fourth quarter safety. PSU also had another safety when the Rutgers center snapped the ball out of the end zone and Menhardt picked up where Bahr left off with field goals of 21 and 41 yards. Rutgers' only TD came on a 72-yard bomb in the third quarter over the head of a sophomore defensive back who was in for his first play. Paterno said "it was a good beginning. We tried to be as precise as we could...without getting too fancy."

While the Lions practiced for their game against Texas A&M Paterno found himself with another disciplinary problem. Dugan and reserve tackle Bob Hladun were arrested by University police for drinking openly while sitting on a campus bench. Paterno suspended both players indefinitely and told *Sports Illustrated* later "we lost our concentration during the week." Texas A&M had not lived up to expectations and had lost close games to BYU and Baylor so coach Tom Wilson had benched his starting quarterback Mike Mosley in favor of Gary Kubiak. On the Aggies first play from scrimmage after the kickoff, Millen smashed into Kubiak and knocked him out of the game. On the third play, Mosley bobbled the ball as he was being hit by Clark and Millen recovered the fumble at the Aggie 24-yard line. Five plays later Moore sliced off left tackle for a 3-yard TD and Menhardt's PAT made it 7-0. The Beaver Stadium crowd of 77,576 sat back to enjoy the rest of the warm but overcast afternoon. Thirty seconds later they groaned when the Aggie's all-time rusher Curtis Dickey dashed around PSU's left side and went 69-yards untouched for a TD and a 7-7 tie. A&M had found a weakness and with their speed and quickness they exploited it the rest of the afternoon, with Dickey skirting the ends and Mosley evading sacks and sprinting for big gains. Meanwhile, the Aggie defense stuffed State's inside running game and smothered the passing. Tate was erratic, completing just 13 of 30 passes, including an 8-yard TD to Suhey midway in the fourth quarter, and throwing one interception. By the final period, the crowd was booing. Warner could muster just 65 yards on 14 carries but Dickey pierced State's defense for 184 of his team's 259 yards rushing and scored two more TDs on runs of 11 and 21 yards as A&M won, 27-14. "This is the greatest win in A&M history," Wilson said after the game. Paterno told sportswriters his team was terrible. "We were not ready for a dog fight," he said. "We didn't tackle well and we didn't block well."

As Paterno tried to re-energize the team for its battle at Lincoln, he lamented the lack of leadership. "We've got to be able to withstand some adversity," he told Tom Verducci of the *Daily Collegian*. "Somebody has to come through when we're in trouble." To prepare the Lions for the thunderous environment at Nebraska's Memorial Stadium, Paterno used an old tactic from games at West Point by setting up speakers on the practice field to simulate the Cornhuskers 76,000 screaming fans. The loss to A&M had dropped State all the way down to #18 and Nebraska was now #6 with two victories and favored to make it number three before a national TV audience. The Lions took it to the Cornhuskers on the opening kickoff, marching 82 yards on 9 plays with Tate throwing 19 yards to Scovill for the TD and a 7-0 lead. A few minutes later, Wise intercepted Tim Hager's pass and ran 30 yards for another TD and suddenly State was ahead, 14-0. Now came the adversity. "When you jump out to an unexpected lead," Nebraska coach Tom Osborne said after the game, "sometimes you relax a little bit and all of a sudden, boom, here comes the other team." It was boom, all right. Nebraska scored four touchdowns in the second quarter, getting a pair within a minute on a 72-yard bomb and a 16-yard reverse following a fumble recovery at the PSU 15-yard line on a bad pitchout by Tate. The Cornhuskers' 42-17 stomping was the worst for Paterno since the 41-13 loss to Colorado in 1970 that ended State's all-time unbeaten streak. Nebraska dominated every phase of the game, rushing for 298 yards and four TDs and shredding State's pass defense by completing 15-of-23 passes for 232 yards. State had just 60 yards rushing on 35 carries and 123 yards passing. "I didn't envision losing by 25 points to Nebraska...," Paterno told sportswriters.

This was the fourth Paterno team to lose two of its first three games and, just as he had made changes in '67 and '76, he knew he had to do something to turn the squad around. Both Texas A&M and Nebraska had been able to neutralize State's All-American tackles Clark and Millen by double teaming both. Jones, the middle guard, was being trapped too much as were the linebackers. Paterno and his assistants believed they could stifle the opponents' offensive schemes with one move and so they switched Clark to nose guard and moved Jones to tackle. Clark didn't like it but agreed if it would help the team. "It's the worst position on the team," Clark told the *Collegian's* Jon Saraceno. "Everybody just beats on you and I just don't like getting beat on. I like to do the beating."

Maryland did not know about the switch until the defense took the field after the opening kickoff in College Park. The Terps, 3-1 after a narrow 14-7 defeat to Kentucky the previous week, were convinced this was the year they would end their 16-game losing streak against the Lions. The new defensive lineup surprised them but they didn't see it until they were already seven points down. The Terps stopped State's offense in three plays after the kickoff but their punt returner Mike Lewis dropped the ball when hit by Edwards and Bradley recovered at the Maryland 14-yard line. Suhey blasted up the middle on the next play and with just 1:46 elapsed State led, 7-0. Then the modified defense took over and it was "lights out" for Maryland. The Terps crossed the 50-yard line just two times and it wasn't until late in the fourth quarter that they scored their only TD on a 55-yard drive. State's defense sacked Maryland quarterbacks seven times, intercepted three passes and recovered four fumbles to set up three TDs in a 27-7 whipping. Charlie Wysocki, the nation's third leading ground gainer who had been averaging nearly 135 yards per game, picked up just 51 on 19 carries as the Terps netted 35 yards rushing and 118 passing on 7-of-28 attempts. The Lions offense had 318 yards but Paterno said it still needed to be "more consistent." "If the Terrapins were a professional franchise," wrote Black for the *"Football Letter,"* "one would swear they were owned by a Penn State alumnus."

The revitalized defense did it again the following week in a 24-3 Homecoming win over Army only this time the running attack cranked it up, too. The defense had six sacks, three interceptions and a fumble recovery in holding the Cadets to 76 yards rushing on 46 carries and 120 meaningless pass yards. An interception by Mehl led to a 17-yard TD by Suhey and a fumble recovery by Kubin after a tackle by Clark produced a 24-yard field goal that gave the Lions a 17-0 lead over Lou Saban's team. Suhey, who was featured on the cover of the game program as part of a salute to the Higgins-Suhey family, ran for 225 yards on 23 carries, including a 61-yard TD on a third-and-one situation in the fourth quarter that iced the game. The 225 yards still ranks as the eighth best of all time in the PSU record books. With Warner on the sideline with a pulled hamstring and ankle injury, Moore had more carries and in 24 rushes he gained 103 yards, marking the 16th time two State runners had gained over 100 yards in the same game. The downside of the day was the passing of Tate, who threw three interceptions, was sacked three times and missed open receivers in the end zone as he completed 6-of-14 passes for a measly 51 yards. "Suhey's effort was the big difference," Saban told sportswriters after the game.

Before the Lions played Syracuse at Giants Stadium in the New Jersey Meadowlands the following Saturday, the Pirates beat the Orioles to win the World Series, four games to three, and reserve tailback McClelland quit the team to transfer elsewhere because he was not getting enough playing time. He wasn't missed as the Lions hammered the Orange 35-7 behind another strong defensive performance and the surprise first-rate passing of Tate. Syracuse (4-2) used an eight-man front to force PSU to pass and Tate did, hitting on 14-of-18 passes for 199 yards, including two TD passes to Scovill of 10 and 2 yards and a 17-yard TD to Donovan. The Lion defense limited the country's 7th ranked offense to 250 yards, negating Joe Morris' running and virtually shutting down Syracuse's outstanding passing combination of Bill Hurley-to-Art Monk. "Dayle Tate proved today that he could take command of this football team," Paterno told sportswriters. "I believe I can be the team leader now," Tate said.

Tate had another fine game against West Virginia (4-3) but it was Moore's running that thrilled the 77,923 at Beaver Stadium. Tate was 11-for-17 for 128 yards and a 23-yard TD and Moore ran for 166 yards, scoring TDs of 52, 7 and one yards, as the Lions spotted WVU 6 points in the first quarter, then thundered back to win 31-6. Suhey, who led the blocking for many of Moore's runs, also had 124 yards on 20 carries. Because of ankle and back injuries, Clark and Millen did not start but came in during WVU's initial 86-yard TD drive in the first quarter to provide a spark, then saw limited action the rest of the way as the defense recovered two fumbles deep in Mountaineer territory to

Bruce Clark, the first junior in the country to win the Lombardi Award and a two-time All-American, puts one of his big hits on a Maryland runner.

set up TDs. The victory moved the Lions back into the AP Top 20 at #19 and Paterno said the Lions were "ready to make our stretch run" He also praised Moore after the game, saying "He's getting a little better each week. He's been developing better judgment all along."

Unfortunately, Moore's better judgment did not include overcelebrating and shortly after midnight Saturday, the junior from Flint, MI, was arrested for driving while intoxicated. By Monday afternoon, Paterno had his second disciplinary problem when freshman tailback Dave Paffenroth was arrested for starting a fight that morning with a student he had scuffled with at a Saturday night dormitory party. Both players were suspended for the upcoming Miami game and late in the week—Halloween week, no less— Paterno received more bad news when Millen was sent to the Hershey Medical Center for tests and also would miss the game.

On paper, the Hurricanes were no match for the Lions. Their 3-4 record included a loss to little Florida A&M and to Syracuse and their offense was struggling despite the passing of sophomore quarterback Mike Rodrique, who already was Miami's 9th best passer in history. But Miami's new coach Howard Schnellenberger had a little surprise for State and after a disruptive week of practice, the Lions were caught off guard. Redshirt freshman quarterback Jim Kelly, who Paterno had once tried to recruit as a linebacker, didn't know he was going to start until about 10 minutes before the game. On the first play from scrimmage, Kelly hit halfback Chris Hobbs on a 57-yard pass and Miami was "off and passing." A goal line stand forced Miami to settle for a 26-yard field goal but on the ensuing kickoff, the Lion return team ignored a little blooper kicked to the right side and the Hurricanes recovered at the 28-yard line. Three plays later, Kelly threw an 8-yard TD to Jim Joiner. State drove 76 yards for a TD late in the first quarter but by halftime Miami was leading 20-7 after intercepting a Tate pass in the end zone and marching 80 yards to score on Kelly's 25-yard pass to Pat Walker. State's offense stumbled in the third quarter, controlling the ball for an astounding 13 minutes but it could not score as another long drive ended with an interception at the goal line. That was the end for State. Kelly threw another TD pass of 17 yards in the fourth quarter and many of the 75,332 fans booed as the game wound down with Miami winning, 26-10. "Linebacker" Kelly had hit on 18-of-30 passes for 280 yards and three TDs without an interception while quarterback Tate had completed 11-of-20 with three interceptions. "This day will do down in history of Miami football as the day we turned our football program around," Schnellenberger said in the jubilant Miami locker room. "They made the big plays and we didn't," Paterno said. Miami assistant Mike Archer, who played high school football for State College, told Doug McDonald of the *Centre Daily Times* that he thought the Lions underrated the Hurricanes. "I don't think they took us seriously," Archer said. "All week the Miami papers were saying how Penn State was going to put it to us...I think our kids got all fired up."

The Lions not only lost the game—and, thus, ruined their chances of a major bowl invitation—but they also lost Clark for the rest of the season, after he tore ligaments in his right knee while chasing a pitchout in the fourth quarter. Before the team traveled to North Carolina State the next Saturday, Gladys, Donovan and Donaldson joined Clark and Millen on the injured list with several other players hobbling. Warner and Moore were back in the lineup and Dugan was starting again at offensive tackle with Kugler, Wisniewski, sophomore Rich D'Amico and walk-on senior Ron Walchack in the defensive front line with Kubin and Jones and several other changes on both sides of the ball.. "The guys will rally around and hustle a little bit harder...," Paterno told the *Collegian's* Saraceno, "Some other guys will have to rise up (and show leadership) and I think they will." Even Paterno could not have envisioned how "the guys rallied" at NC State.

For nearly four quarters, the Lions' patched-up defense held the underdog Wolfpack's high-powered offense in check but the Lion offense also sputtered. Menhardt kicked field goals of 38 and 37 yards in the first and third quarters and PSU held a 6-0 lead until 1:18 was left in the game when NC State went ahead, 7-6, after a six minute, 72-yard, 14-play drive. The Lions moved to their own 41 following the kickoff but on third-and-10 Tate was sacked for a 14-yard loss and State called time out with 34 seconds left as the partisan NC State fans in Carter Stadium crowd of 47,200 went wild. What happened in the next few moments now ranks as one of the all-time great endings in PSU history. When time resumed, Tate faded back as four receivers streaked down field. He scrambled to avoid a hard rush and saw sophomore split end Terry Rakowsky—his backup at QB until the Army game—near the side-

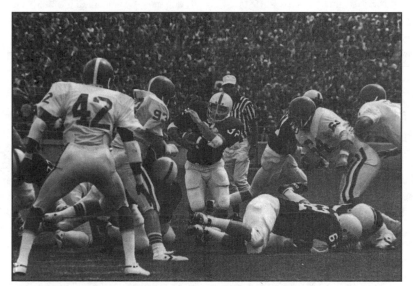

FB Matt Suhey goes up the middle in a 1979 Beaver Stadium game. Suhey led the team in rushing for three seasons but, unfortunately, also is known for being stopped by Alabama at the goal line in the famous 1979 Sugar Bowl.

line at the NC State 37-yard line. Tate threw and Rakowsky leaped between two defenders and as the ball was tipped he grabbed it for the first catch of his career and stepped out of bounds for a 36-yard gain. The crowd could not believe it but there was more to come. Tate tried a sideline pass again. Incomplete. Time for one more play, possibly two. Another pass. Incomplete. And everyone looked at the clock. There was one second left. In came Menhardt. What? A 54-yard field goal? Only Chris Bahr had ever kicked one farther for PSU. Later, Menhardt said the longest one he had ever booted was for 47 yards in high school. His regular holder was Donovan, who had not made the trip, so Guman was holding. Sophomore walk-on Bill Rishell snapped the ball and Guman placed the ball perfectly on the left hashmark. Menhardt knew it was long enough but was it too far right? The ball grazed the inside of the right goal post and sailed through and the entire Lion bench poured

onto the field as Menhardt was pummeled by delirious teammates. "Herbie," Paterno told him later, "In all the years I've been coaching, 30 years, that's the greatest football play I've ever seen." Paterno also told sportswriters it was one of PSU's greatest wins, saying, "This victory meant more to me because of the team—because these guys showed they could come back from adversity. This has to give us some momentum and confidence."

Although none of the New Year's Day bowls were interested in the Lions, several others were, including the Hall of Fame in Birmingham, AL, and the new Garden State Bowl being played at Giants Stadium. "The Garden State Bowl would like Saturday's Temple-Penn State winner as its host but Penn State might not look on it as a true bowl trip," Herschel Nissenson of the AP wrote with a touch of sarcasm. "Could Joe Paterno, Eastern football's biggest booster, turn down a bowl designed to feature an Eastern team?"

When the bowl invitations were handed out at 6 p.m. the following Saturday, it was Temple that gained the Garden State bid but it was State that won the game thanks to a reserve quarterback. The Lions were leading the 8-and-1 Owls late in the first quarter on a 30-yard Menhardt field goal when Tate injured the thumb on his throwing hand and was replaced by Rocco. The backup QB had thrown a total of three incomplete passes and run twice for four yards in previous games. One of his first passes was a 17-yarder to Scovill that set up another Menhardt field goal but by halftime Temple led 7-6 on a 64-yard sprint draw by Kevin Duckett. However, the second half belonged to Rocco and the defense as Rocco ran and passed the Lions to a 22-7 victory. Rocco had a total of 16 carries for 60 yards and hit on 4-of-9 passes for 54 yards in leading scoring drives of 56, 85, 33 and 71 yards as the Lions controlled the ball for more than 42 minutes in the game. Several of his runs and passes were on key third down plays, including an 11-yard TD pass to Suhey on a third-and-goal situation in the third quarter. State's defense had three interceptions and a half dozen sacks as the Lions gave up just six first downs in holding the Owls to 134 net yards. "(The Lions) won this game in the way they're accustomed to, with a brutalizing defense and an offense that is no more fancy than plain brown slacks...," wrote Bill Lyon in the *Philadelphia Inquirer*. After the game the Lions accepted an invitation to play Tulane in the Liberty Bowl in Memphis, December 22. The Liberty Bowl had been courting Pitt but the Panthers, 9-1, accepted a Fiesta Bowl bid instead. "Very frankly, we're happy the way things worked out," Liberty Bowl chairman Jim Kinney told the *CDT*.

When practice resumed Monday, Paterno had a minor quarterback controversy. Once again the Pitt game had been delayed a week to accommodate national television and that would give Tate time to recover from his injury. Paterno admitted Rocco's performance against Temple gave him a dilemma about whom to start against the Panthers. Then, at midweek, Rocco developed severe headaches and was sent to Hershey to be examined for possible brain damage. Doctors diagnosed his problem as severe migraine headaches but Rocco also began having back problems which were related to his migraines and couldn't practice. So, Tate started when Pitt invaded Beaver Stadium December 1 with the nation's fourth best defense led by two-time All-American Hugh Green. The Panthers also had a rookie quarterback named Dan Marino, who had taken over at midseason when veteran Rick Trocano pulled a hamstring. In five games Marino had already passed for more than 1,000 yards, and as 76,968 watched on a blustery day, the future NFL superstar led Pitt to a 29-14 win over State and its injury-riddled defense, which now included Mehl who was in for just one play. A 65-yard TD run by Suhey midway through the first quarter had put the Lions ahead 7-0 and a stunning 95-yard kickoff return by Warner in the second quarter had given State another 14-10 lead. But with tailback Randy McMillan scoring TDs on runs of 9 and 6 yards, Pitt went ahead 23-14 at the half, then shut down State the rest of the way. Early in the third quarter, Paterno inserted Hostetler for Tate but the freshman could not revive the struggling Lion offense, which had just 95 yards passing and 142 on the ground. The swarming Pitt defense also partially blocked a Giacomarro punt, ending a PSU streak of 629 consecutive successful punts dating back to 1968. Marino hit on 17-of-32 passes for 279 yards including a 50-yard screen pass to McMillan for Pitt's final TD late in the fourth quarter. McMillan ran for 114 yards on 26 carries and caught another 43-yard screen pass from Marino and was voted the outstanding player of the game. It was Pitt's first win ever at Beaver Stadium and Pitt coach Sherrill told sportswriters it was "the biggest day of my football life." This also marked the first time since 1931 that State had lost its final three games at home and Paterno said the Lions "were obviously outclassed."

THE 1979 LIBERTY BOWL
Dec. 22, 1979
Penn State 9, Tulane 6

There was little enthusiasm among the PSU fans to travel to Memphis for the Saturday afternoon Liberty Bowl game three days before Christmas. A week before, travel agencies in State College still had vacancies on a 100-seat airplane and a 52-seat bus that had been chartered. The University returned 1,800 of its 5,000 ticket allotment and those tickets were quickly sold by Tulane, which had more than 8,500 followers among the 41,036 that actually attended the game. "Memphis Is No Miami," said the headline in the *Centre Daily Times* after the team arrived five days before the game. "...Nobody on the Penn State team could mistake Memphis for Miami," wrote Dennis Gildea. "Or New Orleans or Dallas." Sportswriters speculated about the team's attitude, noting how it had been embarrassed on national TV by Nebraska and Pitt. "I think we owe something to the seniors to go out there and finish the season right," Kugler told the *Collegian's* Verducci. Of course, not all players cared about the seniors. When two reserves showed up late for the first team meeting in Memphis, Paterno sent them home. Then, reserve tight end Bill LeBlanc was arrested on first-degree burglary charges after wandering into a private house and being shot at. Later he would plead guilty to malicious mischief but it was another in the string of troubling incidents that shadowed the team all year.

Paterno once said Lance Mehl was "as good an inside linebacker" as any who ever played at State. He was a Second-Team All-American and led the team in tackles in 1978-79.

Tulane had not been to a bowl since losing to Houston in the '73 Bluebonnet Bowl. Now coached by Larry Smith, the Green Wave had a better record at 9-2 but one of their losses had been to West Virginia and State was a three-point favorite at kickoff. The heavy rains that fell throughout the game didn't dampen the spirit of the less than capacity crowd, which included comedian Danny Thomas and the reigning Miss America. But the rain and ineffective offenses helped turn the game into a field goal kicking contest. With Tate hurting from a shoulder injury he had received just before being pulled from the Pitt game, Paterno started Rocco, who had overcome his migraine problem. The first three times the Lions had the ball, they gave it up—twice on fumbles by Suhey and once on an interception. Injuries also took an early toll as Kugler and Wisniewski left the game in the first quarter and little used subs Steve Stupar and Hladun took over on defense. Sticking mainly to the ground, the Lions were able to turn 68 and 63 yard drives in the second quarter into two Menhardt field goals of 33 and 27 yards and State kept that lead until Tulane tied it with its own two field goals in the fourth quarter.

After Tulane's second field goal with only 2 and a half minutes left in the game, Coles ran the kickoff back to the PSU 23-yard line and a 6-6 tie seemed probable. But in a minute and a half, the Lions reached the 50-yard line with a third-and-two situation. From the press box, assistant coach Phillips called the surprise play the team had been practicing since the Pitt game. It was a halfback option pass. Phillips had called the play in the first half but it had not worked because Coles was tackled before showing he was going to pass. Now, Tulane defender Terry Daffin thought it was going to be a pitchout from Rocco to Coles and he ignored Donovan who dashed past Daffin and was wide open when Coles hit him on a 39-yard pass to the Tulane 11. Two conservative running plays moved the ball to the 3-yard line and Paterno called time out. In went Menhardt and Tulane called another time out. "If you don't love a situation like that, you're not a kicker," Menhardt told sportswriters later. The kick was perfect and the Lions won, 9-6. "We wanted to win this one to end it right for the seniors and to start our comeback," Paterno said in the locker room.

Paterno was right. It was the start of the Lions comeback. The best for Paterno and Penn State fans was still ahead. There would never be another schizophrenic year like 1979. In 1980, Paterno would have most of the building blocks for his first National Championship team, starting with a young quarterback with a penchant for throwing interceptions.

Season Record 8-4
Record to Date 548-251-40
Winning percentage .677

CHAPTER 12

THE NATIONAL CHAMPIONS

1980-1986

When the decade of the 1980s began, Joe Paterno was filled with self doubt. The culture had changed and so had students now entering college. He wasn't sure he really understood the kids he was now recruiting and coaching and he wondered if his old style of discipline was making them rebel. He had tried to ease up in 1979 and his relaxed approach had backfired.

His critics, and especially his coaching enemies, were gloating. They said he was too pious and self righteous and too quick to condemn others for doing what the system allowed. He bends the rules just like us, some of his colleagues claimed, and now it was all coming home to show what a hypocrite he is. They had smirked when he talked about "The Grand Experiment" and using students who are athletes to win big time football games, not athletes who may be dubious students. He had proven it could be done but times were changing and more borderline students were filling college football rosters, including his own.

Even before the '79 season had concluded, Paterno began discussing it all with his players. And the conversations continued into the spring after he had succeeded Ed Czekaj as athletic director. The players told him he had lost touch. We don't mind discipline, they said, but we need your help and counsel when we have problems. You're too busy being Mr. Athletic Director and Mr. Public Speaker. He vowed to change and he did. That didn't mean he lowered his standards. He adjusted to the times but not his own rules. Players still had to get the grades and obey the laws. "Don't do anything that will embarrass yourself, the team or the university," he continued to preach.

The players understood, maybe not at first, but eventually. Free-spirit Matt Millen may have summed it up best in November of '79 when he realized his sometimes tendentious four-year career in Paterno's "penal colony" was about to end. "You can play big time football and do it the right way—Joe's way—whether (you think) it's right or wrong," he told Jon Saraceno, sports editor of the *Daily Collegian*. "You chose to come here and be under him and those are the rules...I think Joe practices what he preaches. He's really sincere in what he says..." Another former star, Lydell Mitchell, told *Sports Illustrated*, "I enjoyed playing for him much more after I was through playing for him."

As he tried to get closer to his players, Paterno stepped back from many of the sportswriters who had once been his leading cheerleaders. Sportswriters were changing, too, and he could no longer trust them with the team's innermost secrets as he once did. Closed practices were now the norm. He became more snappish in answering questions. Candid, off-the-record conversations at press functions became a thing of the past. It was now more of a business than a working friendship and Paterno could not believe some of the things that were now being written about him and his football program.

Joe Paterno gets a victory ride of his life from his players after defeating Georgia, 27-23, in the 1983 Sugar Bowl for Penn State's first national championship.

With renewed fervor, Paterno plunged into the 1980 season and before it was over the Lions were back in the Top 10. He and his players were in synch again and not a season too soon. If you want to be the best, you have to play the best was the Paterno philosophy. So, a few years earlier, State began revising its schedules for the 1980s, scheduling perennial powers like Nebraska, Alabama and Notre Dame on a regular basis. It would all pay off in 1982 with a National Championship victory at the Sugar Bowl and a second national title four years later at the Fiesta Bowl. In between, there were a couple of precarious seasons. But he weathered them through, made the changes he deemed necessary and emerged with more respect than ever. In both championship years he was named Coach of the Year by his peers and in December of 1986 he became the first and only college football coach ever honored as *Sports Illustrated's* prestigious "Sportsman of the Year."

During this glory period, he and his loyal assistants continued to turn out scholars and athletes. Four players were honored as "scholar-athletes" by the National Football Foundation and College Football Hall of Fame and awarded $18,000 post-graduate fellowships, four were recipients of the NCAA's post-graduate $5,000 scholarship award and six were named Academic All-Americans, including two-time winners Harry and Lance Hamilton. Eleven players were selected to First-Team All-American teams and 54 were drafted by the National Football League, including eight selected as number one choices. "The Grand Experiment" was still alive and well in Happy Valley.

Perhaps 1986 was the grandest season of all. Paterno and the team began the year by celebrating Penn State's 100 years of college football with three black-tie dinners across the state that summer and fireworks at the Beaver Stadium season opener on September 6. The year ended on the night of January 2, 1987, in Tempe, AZ, with a 14-10 upset victory over previous #1 Miami and a second National Championship.

After the 1981 season, Paterno relinquished the athletic director's position. He realized it was too difficult to be both the coach of a premier football team and the head of an ever expanding intercollegiate men's and women's sports program. As athletic director he had tried to convince his contemporaries in the East to form an all-sports conference that could rival the Big Ten and the SEC. But the effort had failed when a couple of key participants at Syracuse, Boston College and Pitt rejected the idea over fear that Paterno and Penn State would dominate the league on and off the field like an Eastern version of Bear Bryant—or worse. Years later, the rebuff would have after affects on Paterno and Penn State as the Lions veered away from their traditional Eastern roots and joined the Big Ten.

It also was during this era that Paterno became more vocal about the future of Penn State as an educational entity and the welfare of the general student body. His efforts were not always appreciated, particularly by student and faculty factions who believed Paterno and football had too much power over the university. But Paterno wanted football to be more than a producer of revenue that would support all the other sports and intramural programs. He also wanted football to be the catalyst for a major fund raising effort that would help the university become one of the leading academic institutions in the country, on the same level as the Ivy League schools from whence he came. When invited to his first Board of Trustees meeting after winning the National Championship in 1982, Paterno went public with his ideal. "It bothers me to see Penn State football number one and then, a few

weeks later, to pick up a newspaper and find a report that many of our academic departments and disciplines are not rated up there with the leading institutions of the country," he told the Trustees, as he wrote in *"Paterno: By The Book."* He went on to challenge the Trustees to help raise the money that would begin the process. Paterno was aided and abetted by the arrival of a new president, Bryce Jordan, and within months a five-year capital campaign was started to raise $200 Million. Paterno talked other friends, associates and business acquaintances to contribute and he gave some of his own money—$120,000—to seed a special Library Endowment. Within three years the goal of the major fund had been raised to $300 Million. And it succeeded beyond even Paterno's imagination.

At the end of 1986, Paterno began to think about retirement. He had just turned 59 years old and he began hinting at getting out at 65. Of course, no one believed him. He had been State's head coach longer than any other man. Twenty-one years had gone by since he succeeded his mentor Rip Engle. He had won 199 games, lost just 43, tied 2 and never had a losing season. His teams had played in 18 bowl games and won 13. He was at the pinnacle of his career so why not get out and do something else. Five more years? Hogwash!

"Oh, No, Not Another Interception"

Todd Blackledge ran out of the tunnel at Missouri's Faurot Field and tried to block the hostile crowd of 75,000-plus out of his mind. Sure he was nervous. This was his first start at quarterback for the Nittany Lions and that's heady stuff for any freshman, even a "redshirt" freshman who already had played in three games. Paterno had given him a hefty responsibility. The Lions had just lost to Nebraska at home on national television and another defeat at this juncture to a quality opponent would be most damaging for such a young team. It was up to Blackledge to change the momentum.

Of course, he wouldn't be doing it alone. But everyone knew the quarterback was the key and that is why Paterno had just switched starters. Hostetler was now the backup, at least on this Saturday afternoon. That could change again next Saturday if Blackledge had a bad game and both he and Hostetler knew it. It was not beyond reasoning to say that their long term careers at Penn State could depend on this game.

Hostetler had started the first three games after winning the three-way battle with Blackledge and Rocco that began in the spring when Tate was sidelined with a broken jaw. Tate had decided to graduate and because of Rocco's experience he seemed to have the inside track when preseason practice began. Hostetler had been the most impressive quarterback in the Blue-White game but Blackledge, who had been "redshirted" in '79 because of a broken hand, was not far behind. Paterno felt all three young men had similar abilities, although Blackledge was the classic "dropback" QB who had rarely run in high school, while the other two were decent runners and passers. Paterno had waited until the eve of the season opener against Colgate to select a starter.

The chaos of '79 was history and Paterno was pleased with the attitude and leadership of this squad. "I don't know if we've ever had a better preseason," he told sportswriters. He had 36 lettermen returning but many were sophomores and juniors who were still learning. He also had a couple of true freshmen whom he would use despite his continued opposition to freshmen eligibility. One of those frosh was wide receiver Kenny Jackson of Toms River, NJ, whom Pitt coach Sherrill called "the most sought after athlete in the country." Paterno knew he had a weakness at wide receiver and so he moved Wise, Urquhart and sophomore walk-on Gregg Garrity from the defensive secondary to wide receiver and later used Rakowsky and freshman Kevin Baugh there with Jackson. The running backs were all veterans with Warner and Coles at tailback and Moore shifted to fullback with Meade in reserve. Freshman Jonathan Williams of Somerville, NJ, also would see action in the backfield and would run back kickoffs and punts along with Warner and Jackson. It was a veteran offensive line, too, with all the tight ends back—Scovill, Kab and McCloskey. Co-captain Jagers was at center, Farrell and Wojtowicz at guards and Dugan at tackle along with newcomers Dave Laube and Pete Speros. Munchak injured his knee and would sit out the season and another veteran, Romano, also would take a redshirt year, giving an opportunity in the offensive line to such youngsters as Mark Battaglia and Bill Contz.

Despite the loss of Clark and Millen, the defense was considered a major strong point with nine starters returning from the Liberty Bowl team, along with former All-American Pete Harris, who had overcome his academic problems. Harris, his brother Giuseppe and Edwards gave Paterno a fine starting secondary with Walsh and sophomore lettermen Dan Biondi and Dan Rocco in reserve. But before too long Paul Lankford broke into the lineup. Lankford was a world class hurdler who had stayed out of football for two years trying for the Olympics but returned to the team in the preseason after the U.S. boycott of the Olympics. The linebackers included returning starters Matt Bradley and Griffiths with lettermen Chet Parlavecchio in the middle and Walker Lee Ashley and Ed Pryts also involved. Up front, Kubin and Gladys were back at the ends with D'Amico, Case and Paffenroth in reserve, co-captain Jones was in the middle backed by Jeff Bergstrom and Kugler, Case, Wisniewski and Hladun split the tackles. All the kickers had also returned: Menhardt, Giacomarro and Franco.

"I think we have a good, solid squad with some young people who may not be quite as good now as they are going to be...," Paterno told Mike Poorman of the *Daily*

Pete Kugler was a starter on the offensive line in 1979, then switched to defense and played nose tackle for two years. He went on to play in three Super Bowls with the 49ers.

Collegian two days before the opener. To stress his flexibility, Paterno listed 17 players on what he called the first team offense, including three quarterbacks, four wide receivers and four running backs. In their preseason predictions, sportswriters generally rated the Lions in the middle of the second 10. The AP had State at #18, Pitt at #3 and Nebraska at #8. There was one noteworthy change on Paterno's coaching staff. J. T. White, the last of the holdovers from the Engle era, retired after 26 years of coaching the defensive ends and was replaced by Tom Bradley, the feisty leader of the '77-'78 special teams known as the "Scrap Pack." The Lions also would now play before larger home crowds. Beaver Stadium continued to expand. This time another 7,000 seats and an electronic scoreboard were added, bringing seating capacity up to 83,600 with 75,000 in season tickets.

With classes not yet in session, a less than capacity record crowd of 78,926 turned out on a warm, late summer day to watch what was no more than a dressed up scrimmage game against Colgate. The game had been moved up a week to September 6 when Duke backed out of a previously scheduled contest. The new Lion mascot, Roy Scott, did 317 pushups in front of the student section as the Lions clobbered the Red Raiders, 54-10, amassing 562 total yards. Warner scored touchdowns on runs of 58 and 11 yards and an 89-yard kickoff return in rushing for 149 yards on 10 carries. Hostetler threw an 11-yard TD pass to Wise, Menhardt kicked three field goals and Baugh scored on an 80-yard run in what is still the longest run from scrimmage ever by a freshman. Another freshman had an embarrassing debut when Jackson fumbled away a punt on the PSU 9-yard line the first time he touched the ball. Hostetler was 4-for-12 for 47 yards and Blackledge 6-for-11 for 70 yards while Rocco had two incompletions as Paterno used 89 players, including 25 freshmen.

Texas A&M was a better test for the young team two weeks later in the heat and humidity of College Station. The night game was televised live back to KDKA in Pittsburgh and seen on a delayed basis over cable via ESPN. The temperature was 83 degrees at the kickoff with the humidity at over 80 percent. A&M was still reeling from a 42-0 shellacking a week earlier by Georgia, which would go on to win the national title. The Lions took the opening kickoff and drove 80 yards in 11 plays for a 2-yard TD by Moore and A&M had made it 7-3 at the end of the first quarter with a 58-yard punt return that set up a 27-yard field goal. State put the game away with an 18-point barrage in the second quarter sparked by the special teams. Jackson's 31-yard punt return set up a 35-yard Menhardt field goal, then Ashley blocked a punt out of the end zone for a safety. Jackson's 23-yard return of the ensuing free kick led to a 2-yard TD by Meade and Giuseppe Harris partially blocked another punt to set up Hostetler's 5-yard bootleg. The second half was scoreless until A&M tallied on a 32-yard pass late in the fourth quarter as the Lions won, 25-9. Hostetler was 3-for-9 for 41 yards and Blackledge 6-for-8 for 78 yards. In the locker room, the players talked about Nebraska.

The #3 Cornhuskers had 35 fifth-year seniors and led the nation in total offense behind the running of tailback Jarvis Redwine who averaged 166 yards per game. The night before the game several thousand PSU fans turned out at a boisterous pep rally in Rec Hall and another several hundred attended a special concert at Eisenhower Auditorium by 80-year-old alumnus Fred Waring, who was marking his 65th year in show business. Before the kickoff, the record crowd of 84,585 honored two All-Americans who had led State to a 20-0 win over Nebraska in the teams' first meeting in 1920—Glenn Killinger and

Charlie Way. But all the pregame fanfare couldn't help the #11 Lions avoid a 21-7 loss. Hostetler fumbled twice in the first quarter and his second bobble at the PSU 30-yard line led to a 7-0 Nebraska lead. By the second quarter Blackledge was in. Midway through the period Blackledge had a pass intercepted near midfield and returned by Sammy Simms and in three plays the score was 14-0 on Redwine's 3-yard dive. But after the kickoff, Blackledge led the Lions on a 74-yard drive in 8 plays, hitting Jackson on a 40-yard pass that set up Warner's 3-yard TD and narrowed the score to 14-7. State was driving again late in the half when another Blackledge interception ended the threat. After Nebraska made it 21-7 six minutes into the third quarter on a 74-yard drive, the Lions had to go to the air and made too many mistakes. Blackledge gave up another interception and a fumble and Jackson fumbled at the Cornhusker 11 to end the Lions final scoring opportunity in the fourth quarter as Nebraska used State mistakes and ball control to win. The two Lion quarterbacks were sacked nine times by the blitzing Cornhuskers for a total of 89 yards in losses as Blackledge completed 6-of-17 pass attempts for 111 yards and Hostetler was 1-for-4 for 12 yards before being pulled. Jackson set a freshman record (since tied) with four receptions that day and the 93 yards he gained is still the record for a frosh. "Both quarterbacks contributed to their own difficulties...," wrote Ron Bracken in the *Centre Daily Times*. "...It's a matter of inexperience...and when it's not going well at any times, it's back to the drawing board."

As Paterno and his offensive assistants Phillips and Ganter contemplated the change at starting quarterback, the defense received some bad news. Kubin, the team's all-time sack leader with 30 and a preseason All-American, tore his right knee in practice and was out for the year, ending his career. That didn't make it any easier getting the younger players ready for Missouri, which was 3-0 and now #9 in both polls. So, at 3:30 p.m., Eastern time on October 6, Blackledge made his first start for the Lions as ESPN cameras recorded the moment for delayed broadcast. He had an erratic first half, throwing a 24-yard TD pass to Scovill for State's initial touchdown in the first quarter and showing surprising running ability by scampering for several gains, including a one-yard TD in the second quarter that had helped give State a temporary 16-7 lead. But he threw two interceptions and that helped Missouri take a 29-21 halftime lead on TD passes of 31 and 53 yards by Big 8 star quarterback Phil Bradley. "We came in at halftime and felt we had the better football team," Paterno said later. "We just made too many mistakes in the first half." The errors continued on State's first two possessions of the third quarter when Warner lost a fumble and Blackledge had another pass intercepted. But moments after the

Larry Kubin, who would have been an All-American but for injuries, set the all-time Lion record for most sacks in a career (30) and season (15 in '79) while playing defensive end from 1977-80.

Blackledge interception, Lankford picked off a Bradley pass and returned it 33 yards to the Missouri 23. Five plays later, Menhardt kicked a 27-yard field goal. Then Lankford did it again, intercepting another pass, and setting up another Menhardt field goal from 34-yards out that gave State the 22-21 lead. With the Lion defense bottling up Bradley and shutting down the Missouri runners, State's offense took command of the game. Midway in the fourth quarter, Blackledge led the Lions on an 86-yard drive that sealed the game. It started and ended with two plays that would personify the Blackledge style for the rest of his career. With a third-and-10 at the PSU 14-yard line, Blackledge switched plays when he recognized a blitz coming and on a rollout right he passed 27-yards to a wide open Jackson at the sideline. Six plays later, the Lions had a third-and-four at the Missouri 43 when Blackledge rolled left on an option. The Missouri linebacker went for Warner but Blackledge kept the ball and out ran Tiger safety Eric Wright into the end zone. Mendhardt's PAT made it 29-21 with about six minutes left and the Lions had the victory. "You can attribute this win to the character of this team," Blackledge told Bracken of the *CDT*. "We're winners and we're believers."

Of course, it was Blackledge who was the winner and Paterno and the players who became the believers. Blackledge was making freshmen type mistakes but despite his inconsistent passing and his interceptions, he seemed to have the confidence of his teammates. The crux of the Lions offense was running and controlled passing and Paterno figured a better attack would give him more time to help Blackledge overcome his passing faults. The next two games against Maryland and Syracuse showed he was right. The Lions ran the ball 58 times, threw just 10 passes and relied as usual on their opportunistic defense to beat the Terps, 24-10, at Byrd Stadium. Trailing by 10-3 in the third quarter, the Lions took the lead on a 55-yard TD run by Moore and a 5-yard TD pass from Blackledge to Jackson that was set up by a Williams punt return. Early in the fourth quarter, Parlavecchio intercepted a Mike Tice pass and returned it 37 yards and moments later on a third-and-goal from the 6, Williams threw a TD pass to Meade off a halfback option that clinched the win. Blackledge completed 5-of-8 passes for 63 yards and had one interception while State's backs gained 293 yards, led by Warner's 100 and Moore's 98. The defense gave up 162 yards passing and 178 rushing but had three interceptions, five sacks and a fumble recovery to hand Maryland its third defeat. "The key was stopping the turnovers," Blackledge told sportswriters.

The running of Warner and Moore and the aggressive and alert State defense made the difference again against Syracuse after Blackledge gave up a touchdown on an 11-yard interception return in the second half and then fumbled away a scoring opportunity at the Orange 13. The 12th-ranked Lions were leading 10-0 at the half but on the second play of the third quarter, Blackledge was chased out of the pocket and when he tried to force a pass to avoid a sack, linebacker Mike Zunick picked it off and ran for a TD. "I felt it was my fault," Paterno said later," because I really jumped on him (in the first half) when he did take a sack, instead of passing." The interception fired up the Orange and the 84,000 in the rain-drenched Homecoming crowd at Beaver Stadium watched apprehensively when Syracuse drove downfield a few minutes later for a third-and-6 at the PSU 28. Syracuse called a screen pass but Parlavecchio and Kugler beat the blocking and smeared Orange QB Dave Warner for a 14 yard loss, taking Syracuse out of field goal range and changing the complexion of the game. It was one of seven sacks by the State defense, which also had an interception and fumble recovery (both by Giuseppe Harris) and stopped Syracuse four times inside the Lion 30-yard line. After that Parlavecchio sack, State went 80 yards in mostly running plays and Moore sprinted 40 yards for a TD. A few minutes later, Blackledge threw a 13-yard TD pass to Jackson following a Jackson punt return of 22 yards and the Lions won, 24-7. Moore had 100 yards on 11 carries, Warner had 76 yards and two TDs rushing and 57 yards on four pass receptions and Blackledge completed 8-of-13 passes for 108 yards with one interceptions. "Moore's move to fullback is one of the best things we've ever done," Paterno told sportswriters.

The Lions traveled to Morgantown the following week to play their first game in West Virginia's new $22 million Mountaineer Stadium against 4-3 WVU and their new coach, Don Nehlen. A steady rain and cold wind that increased as the game progressed kept the normally obstreperous Mountaineer crowd from getting out of hand and the stadium was half empty by halftime with the Lions leading, 10-0. Blackledge was shaken up early in the first quarter and Hostetler had led a 14-play, 66-yard drive for State's TD, with Menhardt kicking his school record 44th straight PAT. But the Lions almost let the game get away from them early in the third quarter. WVU returned the second half kickoff 41 yards and two plays later Robert Alexander broke away for what looked like a sure TD only to be forced out of bounds by Lankford inside the one-yard line. On the next play, Kugler stripped the ball from Alexander and Pete Harris recovered near the goal line. The Mountaineers forced a punt and Giacomarro's kick was blocked out of the end zone for a safety. Giacomarro's booming free kick went all the way to WVU's 17-yard line but Steve Newberry streaked down the left sideline for 78 yards before Rocco caught him at the 5. A 15-yard penalty delayed WVU momentarily but Oliver Luck hit Billy Evans on a post pattern for a 23-yard TD and only an incomplete pass on the 2-point conversion attempt kept the game from being tied. But seconds later, Warner brought WVU's momentum to a halt when he returned the kickoff 88 yards for a TD, tying Chuck Peters' 40-year record for two such TD kickoff returns in one season. Late in the quarter, Blackledge was hurt again and Hostetler led a time consuming drive of nearly eight minutes that gave State a 20-8 lead on Menhardt's 29-yard field goal. Midway in the final quarter, Hostetler fumbled at the Lion 38 and the Mountaineers scored to make it 20-15, then recovered an onside kick with 3:45 remaining and the few thousand WVU fans who were still in the stadium came alive. But six plays later, Giuseppe Harris intercepted Luck's long pass and State ran out the clock for the victory. "We stayed a little close to the vest because of the weather conditions," Paterno told Bob Black of the **Pittsburgh Press**. "We were playing well defensively so there was no sense in getting foolish."

With scouts from the Sugar, Fiesta, Gator and Garden State bowls looking on the following week at Beaver Stadium, the Lions ripped a good Miami team with a 4-2 record that included an upset over 5th-ranked Florida State. Blackledge had his best day passing with 10-of-24 completions for 130 yards and a 25-yard TD to Kab in the 27-12 victory but he also threw an interception and missed two probable TDs with overthrown passes to wide open receivers. Warner ran for 146 yards and Jackson scored a 25-yard TD on a halfback option pass from Coles. State's defense recovered three fumbles, held Miami to 48 yards rushing and intercepted Jim Kelly twice and sacked him three times but the special teams gave up a TD in the fourth quarter on a 53-yard punt return, the first against State since 1973. "Overall, it was the best balanced football game we have played," Paterno told sportswriters. "We're getting better and better..." Even Blackledge—maybe.

Five days after the election of Ronald Reagan as president of the United States, Blackledge's in-and-out play turned a near blow-out against North Carolina State into a close, 21-13, win before 83,847 home fans and four bowl scouts. After setting up State's first touchdown with a 32-yard pass to Baugh and passing 39-yards to Jackson for the second TD for a 14-0 lead, Blackledge fumbled at the NC State one-yard line late in the first quarter and that gave the Wolfpack new life. NC State went 70 yards for a TD early in the second quarter, then as the Lions were driving minutes later safety Louie Meadows picked off a Blackledge pass at the goal line and returned the ball 77 yards before Blackledge caught him. NC State had to settle for a 34-yard field goal before the half and another Wolfpack field goal five minutes into the third quarter made it 14-13. Blackledge then showed his mettle by leading a 79-yard, 8-play drive that concluded with a 10-yard TD toss to Scovill and Menhardt's PAT ended the scoring for the day. But the game was not over until Pete Harris threw halfback Wayne McClean for a 2-yard loss on a fourth-and-one at the PSU 4 in the final quarter. Coles had his best day ever with 151 yards on 12 carries and State's "bend-but-don't-break" defense twice stopped the Wolfpack inside the 5-yard line. "That game is an example of why coaches get nervous about every game," Paterno said in the locker room. "We let them off the hook. We encouraged them and then we were in for a tough game. I thought Todd did well overall. He made some mistakes that almost killed us but you have to expect that because he's still a young kid."

Because of the U.S. boycott of the 1980 Olympics, Paterno invited world-class hurdler Paul Lankford to re-join the football team where he soon became a star in the defensive secondary.

Despite their surprising 8-1 record, the Lions were having a difficult time attracting interest for a New Year's Day bowl game. Only the Sugar Bowl was seriously interested, having watched State in its last three games, but Notre Dame, with just a tie marring its record, had the inside track. Pitt, loser only to Florida State in its season opener, was in the same predicament. But by the time of their showdown on national television the day after Thanksgiving, the bowl pairings would be wrapped up because the invitations were due at 6 p.m. on November 15. State played Temple in Veteran's Stadium that day and the Lions won easily, 50-7, after spotting the Owls to a 7-0 lead in the first quarter. Blackledge looked brilliant on State's second scrimmage play when he hit a wide-open Jackson for a 51-yard pass to the Temple 2-yard line. But Blackledge then fumbled twice, recovering the ball the first time but turning it over to the Owls on the next play. When he threw an interception into the end zone minutes later, Paterno replaced him with Hostetler. Hostetler completed 7-of-10 passes for 111 yards and scored two touchdowns on option runs of one and two yards. Rocco also scored on a 25-yard option and in the locker room Paterno said, "My problem is that all three are good young quarterbacks. I go to bed at night worrying about being fair to them and my nights are restless." A few hours later, Paterno accepted an invitation to meet Ohio State in the Fiesta Bowl the day after Christmas. "Obviously, we would have liked to go to a New Year's Day bowl and play in a game that might figure in the National Championship," Paterno told a news conference. "But short of that, we wanted the Fiesta Bowl."

Pitt had accepted a Gator Bowl bid to play South Carolina and Sherrill made no secret of his unhappiness that his #4 Panthers were not getting a shot at a higher-ranked team. Sherrill thought his squad could have won the national title and they played like it against then #5 State on November 28. Pitt had the nation's leading defense, led again by Hugh Green and Ricky Jackson, and twice the Panthers stopped the Lions on crucial fourth-and-one plays in the fourth quarter at the Pitt 15 and 36-yard lines. Still, the Lion defense had kept State in the game, holding Panther rushers to 91 yards and allowing Pitt QB Trocano to complete just 8-of-22 passes while intercepting three. A "freshman" type mistake by Blackledge cost the Lions a chance to pull off the upset in the waning moments of the game. With a crowd of 82,459 watching in a chilling drizzle and sometimes snow flurries, Pitt took a 14-3 lead early in the third quarter after recovering a Warner fumble at the Lions 6-yard line. But State still had a chance for victory late in the fourth quarter as State's defense kept the Panthers powerful offense inside its own 43-yard line throughout most of the second half. Blackledge had completed 13-of-32 passes for 152 yards, including a 13-yard third quarter TD pass to Jackson, when he made his biggest mistake of the year. With two minutes remaining in the game, the Lions gained possession on the State 27 and Blackledge moved the Lions to a first down at the Pitt 34 with less than a minute to play. But in trying to stop the clock, Blackledge miscalculated his throw out of bounds and safety Carlton Williamson intercepted to end the threat and the game. It was the first time since 1949 that Pitt had beaten State two years straight. "We failed to take advantage of some good field position," Paterno said in the locker room. " (Pitt) made the big plays when they had to...Right up until the end it was anyone's game."

THE 1980 FIESTA BOWL
Dec. 26, 1980
Penn State 31, Ohio State 19
Outstanding Offensive Player: Curt Warner
Outstanding Defensive Player: Frank Case
Sportsmanship Award: Frank Case

The tension and stress that pervaded the atmosphere for the last two bowl games was missing as the team prepared for its December 26 game against Ohio State. While the Lions practiced in University Park, the seniors told the younger players about the fun they had at the '77 Fiesta Bowl and Paterno encouraged the relaxed mood. He reminded them to concentrate on winning the game and to practice that way but to enjoy themselves—within his rules, of course. And they did. It was a week in Arizona of country club style living and temperatures in the high 80s with gourmet meals, swimming pools and horse back riding—and sweat on the practice field. The players were determined to rebound from their disappointing loss to Pitt and they practiced with vigor and effort. Paterno might not have shown it outwardly but he wanted to win this game as much as any bowl game he had coached. His teams had won only one of six games on national televi-

Todd Blackledge became the starting QB early in 1980 and before graduating became PSU's most prolific passer in history. He led the Lions to their first national championship in 1982 and was elected to Phi Beta Kappa.

sion in the last two years and that was starting to bother him because he brought it up to his players in Arizona. More importantly, he believed winning the Fiesta Bowl would be vindication for they way he ran his football program and overcame the disciplinary problems of 1979. He also believed an impressive victory over Ohio State by this young team would set the stage for another run at the national title in 1981.

Unlike Penn State, this had been a disappointing year for OSU and its second year coach, Earl Bruce. The Buckeyes had been the consensus preseason favorite for National Champion but an early 17-0 upset by UCLA had destroyed their title chances and a 9-3 loss to Michigan ruined their Rose Bowl aspirations. Still, the OSU seniors had never won a bowl game and as Bruce told Spike Lukens of the *Centre Daily Times*, "a lot of them played in the 1978 game (won by the Lions, 19-0), so that may be in our favor." Buckeye defensive back Ray Ellis said that '78 loss had been "hard for us to take. We'd kind of like to get a little revenge for that one." OSU was now ranked #11 with PSU at #10 but the Buckeyes were still a one-point favorite for the Friday afternoon, encounter. The Fiesta Bowl promoters believed this was the most prestigious match-up in the bowl's 10-year history and was equal in fan appeal to the New Years' Day pairings. They were right.

A record crowd of 68,738 and a large television audience watched as the Lions kicked off in 75 degree sunshine and stopped the Buckeyes on its first series. The OSU quarterback was junior All-American Art Schlichter who had made his debut as a true freshman against the Lions in '78 and had started in every game for the Bucks since then. But Schlichter's first three pass attempts gained just six yards, OSU punted and the Lions took over at their own 36-yard line. On the first play, Warner dashed off the left side of the line behind a block by Farrell and ran 64 yards for a touchdown that set a Fiesta Bowl record. Menhardt's kick made it 7-0 and Lion fans viewing the NBC telecast around the country screamed with joy. But their ecstasy was short lived. Within two minutes the score was 7-6 as OSU went 83-yards in six plays with Schlichter passing 23-yards to Doug Donley for the touchdown. Vlade Janakievski missed his first extra point after 45 straight kicks and the Lions kept the one point lead into the second quarter. That's when Schlichter made up for all his previous frustration against PSU. He led the Buckeyes on drives of 84 and 77 yards, passing for touchdowns of 33 yards to Gary Williams and 19 yards to Donley, as OSU sprinted to a 12-point lead before Menhardt's 38-yard field goal with eight seconds left in the half made the score 19-10. By this time Schlichter had completed 15-of 22 passes for 244 yards and figured to do more of the same in the second half. "We were very confident," Schlichter told Bob Baptist of the *Columbus Dispatch*. "We thought we had their number." In the PSU locker room, Sandusky and the defensive coaches made some adjustments on the pass coverage and Paterno told the players, "You guys got 30 minutes left. You'd better go play."

And play they did. In the type of a second half comeback that has become a trademark of Paterno's bowl teams, the Lions took the game away from the Buckeyes right from the kickoff. They marched 75 yards in 10 plays with Blackledge running 3 yards for the TD and Menhardt kicking the PAT. Then the defense stopped Schlichter and his mates cold. OSU didn't gain a yard in the third quarter as Schlichter went 0-for-4. Just before the end of the third quarter, Williams returned a punt 17 yards to the OSU 37 and five plays later he ran 4 yards for a TD and State led 24-19. In the fourth quarter, the Buckeyes gained just 15 yards on the ground and 57 in the air, mostly on desperation passes in the closing seconds after a 37-yard TD run by Moore. That run climaxed an 85-yard drive late in the game and made the final score 31-19. The Lions set a team bowl record with 351 yards rushing and Warner also had an individual record with 155 yards in 18 carries to beat Lydell Mitchell's record set in the '72 Cotton Bowl. Blackledge completed just 8-of-22 passes but had 117 yards and didn't throw an interception. "I have more respect for this team than any I've coached," Paterno told the Fiesta Bowl crowd over the public address system when he accepted the winning trophy. "This team came a long way this year." Frank Case, the game's Outstanding Defensive Player, said "Beating a team like Ohio State on national TV helps restore our reputation." Perhaps Bracken of the *CDT* put it best when he wrote, "There have been other 10-2 seasons at Penn State but neither of them brought the satisfaction of the newly-finished campaign."

The Lions returned to University Park with their pride back and the #8 ranking by both AP and UPI. Farrell and Dugan were named First Team All-Americans and before the next season began, Farrell would be elected co-captain of a team that would again become #1 in the nation in midseason. But this time, being #1 would only last two weeks. Then, another pass interception against the new #1 team would rejuvenate and memorialize the 1981 season for all time.

Season Record 10-2
Record to Date 558-253-40
Winning percentage .679

"The End Zone Interception"

Chet Parlavecchio and Leo Wisniewski walked around the defensive huddle uttering words of encouragement and guidance to their teammates. The Lion co-captains didn't have to say much. Everyone on the field knew the team was in trouble. The first quarter had just come to an end and Pitt was within a few yards of putting the Lions 21 points behind.

It was bad enough that the Panthers were now the #1 team in the nation, just as the Lions had been only a month ago. But at this moment they were humiliating the Penn State players on national television. Parlavecchio had publicly ridiculed Pitt's schedule with the quote "Who have they played, Thiel?" and Panther coach Sherrill had retorted by saying the fiery PSU linebacker didn't have the class to play for Pitt. Later, the two would almost get into a fist fight in front of the Pitt bench but now, Parlavecchio and his teammates had to stop Dan Marino. Marino had looked like an all-pro, missing only one of 10 pass attempts in the quarter and throwing touchdowns of 28 and 9 yards to Dwight Collins to give Pitt its 14-0 lead. State's defense already had given up 121 yards through the air and in the last minute of the quarter, it had allowed Marino to march quickly downfield again. And State's offense had been no help. Pitt's defense—best in the country in total defense and against the rush—had held the impotent State attack to a minus one yard in the quarter and Blackledge, still hurting from a tackle on the game's second play, had completed just one of three passes for five yards.

To the 60,260 in Pitt Stadium and the millions watching over ABC-TV, a rout by the Panthers was imminent. That sure would make the Sugar Bowl happy with a National Championship game looming between Pitt and #3 Georgia on New Year's Night. But it would be downright embarrassing for the Fiesta Bowl, which used its switch to New Year's Day to set up an intriguing game between Penn State and Southern Cal. One of the best of the East versus one of the best of the West. Paterno versus John Robinson. Curt Warner versus Marcus Allen. A blow out by Pitt would send the Fiesta committee reaching for the aspirin bottle and NBC-TV might want a rebate for televising the dud. What started out last spring as a run at the national title had come down to this.

Until Halloween, everything had worked out as Paterno and the players had expected it would if they played up to their potential and had a little bit of luck. It was still a young team but one with experience on both offense and defense. The starting backfield was practically intact from '80 with Blackledge, Warner and wide receiver Jackson returning and Coles moving from tailback to join Meade at fullback. Hostetler had transferred to West Virginia and Rocco was now the backup quarterback with Williams behind Warner and Garrity playing both flanker and split end, along with Baugh and Rakowsky. The offensive line may have been the best in the country and

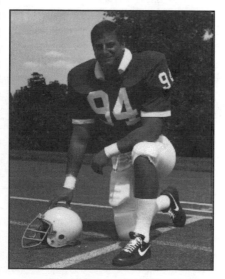

An exceptional leader, LB Chet Parlavecchio was Second-Team All-American at LB and captain of the 1981 team. He led the team in tackles that year as well as in 1980.

was also loaded with veterans led by Farrell, the co-captain at one guard, and Munchuk, back after his injury, at the other guard. Romano, also returning after taking a "redshirt" year, was now the center with Battaglia and sophomore Dick Magginis in reserve. The tackles included starters Contz and Speros, backed by Laube and Jim Brown, finally recovered from the broken leg that sidelined him for nearly two years. Kab and McCloskey were again the tight ends with sophomore Ron Heller of Farmingdale, NY, also in the rotation.

Mike Munchak teamed with Sean Farrell to give Penn State the finest guards in the country in 1980-81. Both went on to outstanding careers in the NFL.

Paterno and his new offensive coordinator, Anderson, had devised a balanced attack which continued to stress a traditional running game that would open up a myriad of passing opportunities. "I think our offense has a chance to be excellent," Paterno told sportswriters.

Through the spring and preseason practices, Paterno and the staff concentrated on developing the defense, which returned six players from the unit that started against Ohio State in the Fiesta Bowl. He and defensive coordinator Sandusky were mostly concerned with the front line and they decided to alter the 4-4-3 defensive scheme to fit the personnel. They put the defensive ends in a standup position where they virtually became outside linebackers. Ashley was at one end and D'Amico was switched from nose guard to the other end. The tackles included Wisniewski, Paffenroth, Opfar, Joe Hines and sophomores Greg Gattuso and Kirk Bowman with one tackle usually playing over the center. Parlavecchio, Pryts and Bradley were the starting linebackers again along with two-time letterman Ken Kelley with sophomores Harry Hamilton of Wilkes-Barre, Scott Radecic of Pittsburgh and Steve Sefter and Villanova transfer Al Harris in reserve. Lankford and Giuseppe Harris returned to the defensive backfield but Harris was pressed by Kenny Jackson's brother Roger, who had taken a "redshirt" year after transferring in 1980 from a junior college. Another sophomore, Mark Robinson, would beat out Biondi and sophomore Mike Suter at safety. Giacomarro, who already held State's one season and career punting records, returned and Franco took over as the placekicker. "If our down people get good in a hurry, we could be a good defensive team," Paterno told sportswriters. " The key to any great football team is depth. We have to be at least two deep in every position."

Paterno knew he would need depth to take on a beefed-up schedule that included four preseason Top 10 teams—Notre Dame, Alabama, Nebraska and Pitt—as well as up and coming Miami, Syracuse and West Virginia. This would be State's first regular season game ever with Alabama and first against Notre Dame since 1926. The NCAA rated the schedule as the second toughest in the country behind Florida State and associate athletic director Jim Tarman admitted the schedule was "an overreaction" to the years when undefeated PSU teams were criticized for supposedly playing weak teams. The final three games

against Alabama and Notre Dame at home and Pittsburgh in Pitt Stadium were seen by most sportswriters as the most challenging part of the schedule. But in the preseason, Paterno told Sharon Fink of the *Daily Collegian* that he was just as worried about Nebraska in Lincoln and Miami in the Orange Bowl. "We play (Miami) down in Florida in October, in the day time," he said. "And I think that will be a very difficult challenge for us..." Most sportswriters believed the Lions were at least equal to the task and they were rated sixth or seventh in most major preseason forecasts, including AP, UPI and *Sports Illustrated*. Michigan was the consensus choice for #1 with Oklahoma, Notre Dame and Alabama seen as the prime challengers.

SMU and Missouri were on the original schedule when it was first announced but SMU asked out of the contract and the Missouri game was canceled by mutual agreement. Thus, the Lions opened with Cincinnati at home on September 12, then had a week off before traveling to Nebraska. State hammered Cincinnati and its new coach, Mike Gottfried, 52-0, with Warner scoring three first half touchdowns and getting 122 yards on 17 carries before leaving the game three minutes into the third quarter. The Bearcats never crossed their own 45-yard line as Paterno used 69 players. Michigan, Alabama and Nebraska were upset that day and by the Nebraska game State was #3 in the AP behind Southern Cal and Oklahoma. Ironically, USC and Oklahoma were playing the same afternoon as State met Nebraska and ABC TV decided to pass on the game in Lincoln for various reasons but ESPN was there for a delayed telecast. Despite their 10-7 loss to Iowa, the Cornhuskers were a 4 and a half point favorite over the Lions but the game was closer than that. The lead changed hands six times and was tied once and in the end Franco and Warner made the difference. Franco set a school record that still stands (but has been tied) by kicking five field goals of 29, 48, 39, 20 and 32 yards. Two kicks followed fumble recoveries in the first half when the Lions took a 17-10 lead thanks in part to a 33-yard TD pass from Blackledge to Jackson near the end of the half that climaxed an 82-yard drive. Franco's record setting kick was for State's final points, when the Lions came from a 24-20 deficit at the start of the fourth quarter to score a TD on a 61-yard drive, then went 65 yards for Franco's 32-yarder with five minutes remaining and made the final score, 30-24. Warner didn't get a touchdown but he ran for a near record 238 yards on 28 carries, marking the seventh time he was over 100 yards in a game. After the game, Franco publicly thanked walk-on snapper Bill Rishell of Georgia and holder Rakowsky. "Without them doing their job," he told sportswriters, "I'd never get a chance to do mine."

Before the next game against Temple, the Lions had moved up to #2 behind USC, which had defeated Oklahoma. Paterno also denied a report by CBS sportscaster Brent Musberger that he would retire as coach if State won a national title and would be succeeded by former assistant George Welsh of Navy. "I might get out of this athletic directorship job sooner than four or five years, but not coaching," he said on his weekly "TV Quarterback Show."

The Lions stayed at #2 a week later after getting another shutout, 30-0, over Temple at Beaver Stadium. Warner had his fourth straight game of over 100 yards with 117 in 22 carries, including touchdowns of 3 and 19 yards. Paterno also utilized his passing more, as Blackledge completed 9-of-15 passes for 123 yards, including a 5-yard TD to Jackson in the third quarter, before Rocco replaced him. State's defense kept Temple on its own side of the field for most of the game and the closest the Owls came to scoring was a missed 21-yard field goal in the second half. After the game, Temple coach Hardin singled out the Lion offensive line. "They have the best five-man offensive line that I've seen," Hardin said. "Then when they add their two tight ends, they have the best seven-man offensive line I've ever seen." But there was a downside when Coles was carried off the field on a stretcher after severely breaking his ankle. He would be lost for the rest of the season.

The Lions were impressive again the following Saturday in beating Boston College, 38-7, before a Homecoming crowd of 84,473. For the first time since 1979, two backs went over 100 yards in

Ralph Giacomarro may be the best punter in State history and still holds several punting records including best punting average for a season in '81. Only had 5 of 230 punt attempts blocked in his four-year career and he was instrumental in winning the '82 national championship.

a game as Warner had 105 yards and Meade 107 yards with Warner scoring two TDs and Meade getting one. Blackledge hit on 8-of-17 passes for 182 yards, including a 39-yard bomb to Jackson late in the second quarter that capped a 72-yard drive. While the offense was rolling up 483 total yards, the defense limited BC to 231, with most of the visitors' yardage coming in the fourth quarter when second team quarterback freshman Doug Flutie led BC to its only TD against State's reserves. The Lion defense intercepted four passes, recovered four fumbles and had four sacks as Paterno again cleared his bench. Later that day, Arizona upset USC, 13-10, and the Homecoming crowd partying into the night expected State to automatically move to #1. But when the polls came out the following Tuesday, Texas had hopped over State after beating Oklahoma 34-14. Paterno did not complain, saying :"I don't care about the polls, I really don't" but Lion fans wondered if the old bias against Eastern football had returned. One week later they had their answer.

Syracuse had a new stadium, a 50,037-seat indoor arena called the Carrier Dome, which had been built on the same site as old, decrepit Archbold Stadium, site of many knock-down battles with Penn State. The Orange also had a new coach, Dick McPherson, and even though Syracuse was 1-3-1, and had not beaten State in 10 years, McPherson had his players believing they could win this year. Even Syracuse's all-time leading rusher, Joe Morris, thought so. Dreamers. It was a record-breaking day for Warner and Giacomarro, a brilliant passing day for Blackledge and an outstanding defensive show by the Lions as they won, 41-16. Warner broke Shorty Miller's single game rushing record set in 1912 with 256 yards on 26 carries, including a 69-yard TD, and with his two pass receptions for 20 yards and three kickoff returns for 65 yards, he also set a team all-purpose yardage record of 341 yards. Both are still the records going into the 1998 season. It was Warner's sixth consecutive 100-yard game and tied the team record then held jointly by Lydell Mitchell and John Cappelletti. Giacomarro's average of 54.8 yards on four punts that day, including one for 64 yards, also remains the team single game record. Blackledge threw TD passes of seven and 12 yards and hit on 10 straight passes

for 121 yards before missing his first and only attempt at the start of the fourth quarter. He also scored the Lions' initial touchdown with a 5-yard scamper three minutes into the game. Meanwhile, the Lion defense held Morris to 67 yards on 18 carries, intercepted three passes and sacked Orange quarterback Dave Warner eight times for 49 yards in losses. "(Warner) may be the best running back we've ever had at Penn State," Paterno told sportswriters, "but he'll have plenty of chances to prove that."

The following Tuesday proved how unpredictable life can be. At practice that afternoon, Warner pulled a hamstring and the injury would be one of the defining moments of the season. That same evening came word from the wire services that the Lions had been named #1 in the wake of Texas' 42-11 loss to Lou Holtz' Arkansas team. State had 36 and a half first place votes in the AP poll compared to 26 and a half to second place Pitt. So much for the Eastern bias. "We're No. 1—At last," said the front page headline in the *Daily Collegian*. But the veteran Lion players had no illusions. "Our freshman year going into the Sugar Bowl, I thought it meant a lot being No. 1," Wisniewski told Tom Verducci of the *Collegian*. "But I learned that unless you're No. 1 when the season's over, it doesn't mean a thing."

Parlavecchio joined Warner on the sidelines when the Lions set a new Beaver Stadium attendance record of 85,012 against West Virginia on October 24. The Mountaineers were 5-1 and ranked #20 with just a 17-0 loss to Pitt marring their record. With Oliver Luck throwing passes all over the field, WVU kept the game close for nearly three quarters as scouts from the Orange, Sugar, Cotton, Tangerine, Sun and Garden State bowls watched. Leading by just 10-7 midway through the third quarter, Blackledge led the Lions on a 10-play, 72-yard drive that climaxed with Jackson catching a tipped pass for an 11-yard TD. Early in the fourth quarter, Jackson dashed 44-yards on a flanker reverse to set up Meade's one yard TD and the Lions went on to win, 30-7. Luck had blistered State's defense for 226 yards on 24-of-39 passes and his 54-yard bomb in the second quarter was the Mountaineers lone TD. But the defense had sacked Luck three times, intercepted a pass and held WVU's rushing to 38 yards on 29 carries as the Lion offense totaled 469 yards against what had been the country's fourth best total defense. Williams and Meade took up the slack from Warner's absence with Williams gaining 140 yards on 27 carries, including a TD, and Meade getting 97 yards on 18 carries while Blackledge hit on 9-of-15 passes for 118 yards. "They're big and strong and they keep coming at you," WVU coach Nehlen said in the locker room.

The game Paterno feared most since the

Co-captain Leo Wisniewski, seen here attacking the Temple QB, was Defensive Player-of-the-Game in the 1982 Fiesta Bowl victory over USC nailing Heisman winner Marcus Allen for three big losses. His brother Steve followed him and was a mainstay on the '86 national championship team.

preseason turned out to be the team's downfall. But for penalties that nullified touchdowns, Miami might have been undefeated. The 5-2 Hurricanes had lost 14-0 to Texas and 14-10 to Mississippi State and they were fired up to play the #1 team in their first nationally televised game in 13 years. As John Black later wrote for the *"Football Letter,"* "It was a perfect example of Murphy's Law—if anything can possibly go wrong, it will." The Lions made too many mistakes, including a rash of illegal procedure penalties, two lost fumbles, four missed field goals and two interceptions, and still almost rallied from a 17-0 fourth quarter deficit. The *Miami Herald* called the 17-14 victory the Hurricanes "Biggest Victory Ever." With Warner still hobbled by his hamstring and forced to leave the game in the second quarter, the Lion "bread-and-butter" rushing offense couldn't cope with Miami's stunting defensive line and gained just 69 yards on 38 carries. Franco, who had missed just one field goal all year, tried one 47-yarder into wind gusts of 15 to 20 miles an hour and another from 23 yards during a torrential downpour but had no luck. The turning point of the game came midway in the second quarter with Miami holding a narrow 6-0 lead on two first quarter field goals. Lankford intercepted a pass at the PSU 8-yard line and ran 63-yards before being caught from behind when he had to slow down to avoid his own blockers. Four plays later, State was on the Miami one-yard line but Warner was dumped for a four yard loss and Franco missed a 22-yard field goal from a sharp angle at the left hashmark. On Miami's first play, Art Brodsky caught a pass from Jim Kelly and when Lankford slipped trying to make the tackle, Brodsky went 80 yards for the touchdown and a 14-0 halftime lead. Just before the half, the Lions had a first-and-goal at the Miami 6 after recovering a fumble by the Hurricane punter but time ran out when Blackledge was tackled as he rolled out and tried to run when he couldn't find a receiver open. State changed its defensive scheme at halftime and limited Kelly to 50 yards in passing in the second half and continued to shut down the Miami running game. But a fumble recovery at the PSU 9-yard line led to another field goal early in the fourth quarter as a heavy rain storm inundated the Orange Bowl stadium and many in the announced crowd of 32,117 began leaving.

Just when it appeared as if the game was over, Blackledge took the Lions downfield 80 yards in nine plays and hit McCloskey for a 13-yard TD. His pass for two points failed but moments later Lankford recovered a fumble at the Miami 26-yard line and on the second play Blackledge passed 26 yards to Williams for the TD and his two-point completion to Jackson made it 17-14 with eight minutes remaining. Even Schnellenberger admitted later he thought the Lions were going to pull out the victory. With about three minutes left, the Lions were driving again after a 36-yard pass from Blackledge to Williams put the ball on the Miami 25. But on the next play, Williams fumbled a soft pitchout and the threat ended. "It's our bread and butter play," Paterno said later. "That's the safest play we've got." State had one last shot with 41 seconds remaining but Blackledge threw another interception and the game was over. Blackledge had set three new records by passing 358 yards on 26-of-41 attempts and his total yardage and 255 yards in the second half remain team records to this day. "They showed a great deal of determination and character and championship form by coming back and almost catching us," said Schnellenberger, while sipping champagne in the locker room. "This has to be the biggest win in our history. It was like playing poker with all of Penn State's money." Blackledge told reporters the team would rebound. "We still plan on having a great season," he said. The teams would not play again until

the showdown game of '86 in the Fiesta Bowl on January 2, 1987. But a week after this game, the NCAA placed Miami on two years' probation for 66 recruiting violations between 1976 and 1980. The ban included the loss of 10 scholarships and no bowl games.

As one might expect for a team that just lost its #1 ranking and was looking two weeks ahead to Alabama, the Lions were nearly upset by North Carolina State in Raleigh. As usual when playing PSU, NC State was at an emotional high despite its 4-4 record. The Wolfpack controlled the ball for nearly 37 minutes and won most of the statistics but the now #6 Nittany Lions were saved by the big plays of their special punt teams. With Warner still out, Lion rushers gained just 95 yards on 35 carries and Blackledge picked up only 52 yards on 8-of-19 completions with two interceptions. But a 56-yard punt return by Baugh, who was just getting over a season-long injury, set up a 7-yard Blackledge TD to Garrity that gave State a 7-6 half time lead. Then, with NC State back in front 9-7 midway in the third quarter, the Lions faked a punt from their own 49-yard line and the blocker, Kelley, threw a pass to Hamilton, who dashed 51 yards for a TD that put the Lions ahead for good. In the fourth quarter, Giuseppe Harris blocked the third punt of his career and it went out of the end zone from 33 yards away for a safety. A few minutes later, Biondi blocked another NC State punt at the Wolfpack 4 and Meade scored from the one with Franco's kick making it 22-9. NC State scored on an 80-yard drive with about 45 seconds left but missed the PAT and the game ended at 22-15.

The Alabama game had even more emotion with both teams still striving to get back into the national title race and secure a New Year's Day bowl slot. But #6 Alabama had an added incentive. With a 7-1-1 record, Bear Bryant was on the verge of breaking Alonzo Stagg's all-time record for coaching victories. One more win for Bryant would tie Stagg at 314 and this regionally televised game gave Bryant and his players the opportunity to do it with at least half the nation watching. Another record Beaver Stadium crowd of 85,133 saw the Bear surprise Paterno, again, with another passing attack and an aggressive defense that stymied the #5 Lions for at least the first half. That was all Alabama needed to take a 24-3 halftime lead on a 17-point blitz in the second quarter that capitalized on a fumble recovery at the PSU 19-yard line and an interception that led to a 3-yard TD pass eight seconds before the intermission. "We played over our heads in the first half," Bryant admitted later. The Tide had averaged just 98 yards on 10 passes in its previous games but against the Lions they completed 7-of-13 passes for 190 yards and two TDs, including a 37-yard bomb from Walter Lewis to Jesse Bendross in the first quarter. "They had us well scouted and seemed to know what we were going to do," Parlavecchio told sportswriters after the game. Even though State fought back with two touchdowns in the fourth quarter, the Tide probably clinched the game early in the third quarter with a goal line stand that reminded everyone of the '79 Sugar Bowl. This time the Lions had seven attempts stopped from inside the 4-yard line following the second half kickoff. After failing to get a TD in the first two downs, a pass interference penalty gave the Lions a new opportunity at the one-yard line but three runs into the line and a fourth down sweep by Warner to the outside went nowhere and Bryant told sportswriters later, "That was as good a goal line defense as we've ever had. Lyons and Krauss must be jealous." The final score was 31-16 and the Alabama players carried the Bear off the field. "Paterno, who will be second guessed for years over the play calling on the goal line series, was ready for the line of questioning..." wrote Ron Bracken in the *Centre Daily Times*. "...

'The game was lost in the first half when we weren't precise in doing some things. When you get down around the goal line you do what you think will work for you...'." Paterno also told sportswriters, "if you can't play any better than that, you have to blame the coach." Many Lion fans did as State slipped to #13 and prepared to try and salvage its faltering season against unranked Notre Dame. "The Penn State program is at a crossroads now," wrote Bracken, noting that the Lions had now lost seven of their last nine games on television and had looked bad in doing so, "and another loss to a nationally-respected team could just about completely undo the reputation Paterno has built for the school over his career."

In the week before the Notre Dame game, Paterno maneuvered behind the scenes for a lucrative bowl invitation. When the Sugar Bowl moved its game to New Year's Night against the Orange Bowl, the Fiesta Bowl switched to New Year's Day as competition for the Cotton Bowl and increased its payoff from $450,000 to $650,000 per team. The Fiesta officials believed that State had helped raise the prestige of its game, starting with the Christmas Day contest of 1977. So, they were eager to work out a deal with the Lions—if State could beat the Irish. After the Alabama defeat, State's options were limited. Notre Dame also had been #1 in September but after a defeat by Michigan the Irish had tottered to a 5-3 record and they needed a win to get any kind of bowl bid for their new coach, Gerry Faust. State scored within the first minute after Hamilton's 50-yard kickoff return set up a 39-yard run by Williams and his 4-yard TD, but Notre Dame tied it less than two minutes later. Fumble recoveries helped each team score touchdowns before the half and State led 17-14 when Notre Dame kicked off in the third quarter. Two minutes later, the Irish took the lead, 21-17, on Blair Kiel's second TD pass after All-American linebacker Bob Crable intercepted a Blackledge pass into heavy coverage and returned it 27 yards to the Lion 5-yard line. Now, Notre Dame had the momentum and as 84,175 watched nervously, the Irish twice moved into scoring territory. Pryts, Parlavecchio and Robinson stopped Greg Bell on a fourth-and-goal at the one, then on the next series, Gattuso intercepted Kiel at the PSU 18-yard line. That seemed to fire up the offense and Blackledge led the Lions on an 82-yard drive in nine plays with Blackledge diving over from the one-yard line for the game winning TD with about four minutes left. State's defense then stopped the Irish and the Lions won, 24-21. "It was a great game for both sides," a dejected Faust told sportswriters. "It was good to come from behind in the closing minutes with the pressure on," said Paterno. Two hours later the Lions accepted a Fiesta Bowl invitation to play USC, runner-up to Washington in the PAC Ten conference.

Now, the Lions felt that could truly redeem themselves by dumping arch-rival Pitt. The Panthers had stayed #1 since State's Miami debacle but some of the Lions players were skeptical of Pitt's schedule and said so publicly. One newspaper clipping in the Pitt dressing room quoted Parlavecchio as saying: "Our schedule was like going through a hurricane and Pitt's was like going through a Bermuda shower." Another newspaper story had Paterno saying: "I would rather have a tough schedule and lose a couple of games than have a patsy schedule and be rated No. 1." The words intensified the already bitter relationship between Paterno and Sherrill and the Panther coach was sure the quotes would incense his team and help give him a nice present on his 38th birthday.

So, now it was the end of the first quarter on Saturday, November 28, in Pitt Stadium. Many in the crowd of 60,260 must have

been thinking that Parlavecchio and Paterno would have to eat their words. Even Sue Paterno must have wondered about taking off the button she was wearing that said, " Parlavecchio, the Italian Enforcer." Play resumed. The Lion defense went into its deep zone coverage with a three man rush. As expected, Marino faded back for another pass into the end zone. He was looking for Collins again. "I just kind of threw it up there and thought Dwight could get under it," Marino said later. Roger Jackson leaped in front of Collins and grabbed the interception. It was the defining

Sean Farrell was another of State's two-time First-Team All-Americans, teaming with Mike Munchak to give the Lions as fine a pair of guards that ever played the college game.

moment of the season and from that instant the game belonged to the Lions. Suddenly, State's offense came alive and with Blackledge hitting on several passes, the Lions went 80 yards in three minutes for a touchdown. Back came Marino to give Pitt another opportunity. This time he drilled a pass to Julius Dawkins crossing in front of the goal line. The ball and Roger Jackson were there at the same time and Jackson's hit jarred the ball into the air where Robinson snagged it for another interception. The Lions had to punt but moments later Marino fumbled at the Pitt 46 and Gattuso recovered. Again the Lions were kept from the end zone but with about five minutes left in the half, State took possession on its own 20 following a Pitt punt. Four plays later from the PSU 39, Kenny Jackson sped past Pitt's All-American safety, Tom Flynn, caught a perfect pass from Blackledge and reached the Panther 8-yard line before being tackled by Flynn at the Panther 8-yard line. On the next play, Blackledge ran in for a TD and Franco tied the game with his second PAT. The Lion defense forced a punt but Kenny Jackson fumbled at the PSU 41 and Marino had another chance, reaching the Lion 22 before a personal foul penalty and another fumble recovery by Gattuso ended the threat.

The game was virtually over six minutes into the second half. On the fourth play of the third quarter, Roger Jackson belted Pitt fullback Bill Beach after a 13-yard gain and forced another fumble that Parlavecchio recovered at the State 44-yard line. Three plays later from the Pitt 42, Blackledge hit Kenny Jackson tip-toeing along the side line at the 10-yard line and Jackson cut across the middle leaving Flynn and others in his wake for another TD. Three minutes later following a punt, Blackledge and Jackson combined for a 45-yard bomb that gave State a 28-14 lead and Franco's field goals of 39 and 38 yards made it 34-14 four minutes into the fourth quarter. Farrell, already named to three All-American teams and a leading candidate for the Lombardi and Outland trophies, achieved a lineman's dream by recovering Warner's fumble in the end zone for State's next TD. "You know, I wanted to spike the ball," Farrell said later. Then, with about six minutes left, Robinson put the final punctuation on the shocking turnaround when he picked off another Marino pass at the Lions 9-yard line and ran 91 yards for the TD and a 48-14 final. "I didn't think anyone could score that many points on us," Pitt's All-American linebacker, Sal Sunseri, told sportswriters. "We had our pride on the line today," said Wisniewski. Parlavecchio, added, "We went out to win against the No. 1 team in the country and prove we were a better team than a lot of people were giving us credit for being. We're on the verge of a really great season."

THE 1982 FIESTA BOWL
Jan. 1, 1982
Penn State 26, Southern Cal 10
Outstanding Offensive Player: Curt Warner
Outstanding Defensive Player: Leo Wisniewski

The Penn State players were enthusiastic about returning to Phoenix and playing on New Year's Day against Southern Cal and their Heisman Trophy winner, Marcus Allen. USC was the most famous bowl team in the country at the time, with a record 25 bowl appearances, mostly in the Rose Bowl. In fact, the only time the two schools had played before was the 1923 Rose Bowl, which was USC's very first Rose Bowl and State's only one.

But the Trojans had missed out on the Rose Bowl this season and were not happy about it. They had been upset by Arizona at home early in the season, then eliminated from the PAC-10 title race by Rose Bowl bound Washington. Their 9-2 record was identical to State's and they were similarly ranked by the polls, with PSU at #7 and USC at #8. After all the shakeup in the polls, Clemson was the lone unbeaten team and ranked #1 but was an underdog to #4 Nebraska (9-2) in the Orange Bowl. Even if Clemson lost, both State and USC had no chance to win the national title because there were four other bowl teams that had lost just one game and they were playing each other—#3 Georgia vs #10 Pitt in the Sugar Bowl and #3 Alabama vs. #6 Texas in the Cotton Bowl. Still, Paterno said before the Fiesta Bowl that he felt the winner had as much right as any other team to be acclaimed the National Champion. Upon arriving in Phoenix, Robinson agreed.

State worked out at its new indoor sports complex before Christmas, then regrouped and flew to Phoenix on December 26. After the first day of workouts, Paterno closed his practices. USC coach John Robinson took the opposite approach and let anyone into the Southern Cal practices, including the Trojan marching band. The day before the game, the band interrupted USC's practice with a mini-concert that had the players dancing with the cheerleaders in a festive party atmosphere.

Penn State had sold its entire ticket allotment of 11,675 tickets but on game day, most of the record crowd of 71,053 were rooting for USC, which had been designated as the "home team." Parking signs outside Sun Devil Stadium were indicative of the atmosphere inside. "USC, left. All others, right," the signs said. Some sportswriters billed the game as a match between "Tailback Tech" and "Linebacker U," and they were partially right. Allen was another in the long line of outstanding USC All-American tailbacks and this season he had averaged nearly 213 yards per game rushing as well as being a key pass receiver. But Sandusky and Paterno had designed a special defense featuring linebackers that they expected would neutralize Allen. Meanwhile, Anderson had his offense completely healthy for the first time all

season, with Warner, Jackson and Blackledge and the offensive line at their peak. Warner, in particular, was expected to have a good game and he was now a bonafide First Team All-American—the first Lion running back to be honored since Cappelletti in 1973.

The tone of the game was set in the first 15 seconds. On the first play from scrimmage, Opar crashed into the USC backfield and stripped the ball from Allen with Roger Jackson recovering in mid air and running three yards to the USC 17-yard line. On the next play, Blackledge surprised everyone by passing but he overthrew Kab in the end zone. Then, Warner took a delayed handoff and darted off tackle for the touchdown and with Franco's PAT State led, 7-0. Now, the Lion defense took control and continually stopped the Trojans. Franco missed a 36-yard field goal attempt and then with about three minutes left in the quarter, the Lions made a mistake in their own territory. USC's Keith Browner blitzed and hit Blackledge just as he was throwing. All-American Chip Banks picked the errant ball out of the air and dashed 20 yards for a TD and suddenly the score was tied. Early in the second quarter, the Lions gained possession at their 31 following a punt and five plays later Blackledge hit Garrity on a 52-yard bomb that put the Lions back into the lead. Franco kicked a 21-yard field goal later in the quarter after Wisniewski recovered another Allen fumble at the USC 20-yard line. But State missed three other scoring opportunities in the quarter, including one just before halftime when the Trojans stopped Blackledge on a short run at the 2.

With a 17-7 lead, State took the second half kickoff and jammed it right down USC's throat, marching 80 yards in nine plays as Blackledge threw three passes to different receivers for long gains before Warner took a quick pitch from the 21 and scored his second TD. USC had a field goal a few minutes later but the Lions clinched the game on the last play of the third quarter when Paffenroth blocked a punt that went out of the end zone 19 yards away for a safety. The fourth quarter was all defense and was so predictable that even before the final gun, NBC-TV left the game to start its Rose Bowl coverage. The final score was 26-10 and when Robinson congratulated Paterno at midfield, he said, "Sorry we couldn't give you a better game, Joe." Later, Robinson told sportswriters he and his team were confused by the Lion defense. "I've looked at them 10-12 years and have no idea what the hell they are doing," he said. The defense had held Allen to 85 yards in 30 carries, his worst day of the season, and USC rushers netted just 60 yards as the defense came up with 11 tackles behind the line of scrimmage, including a half dozen sacks. The Lions also had three pass interceptions while the offense was running and passing for 393 yards, with Warner outplaying Allen with 145 yards and two TDs on 26 carries. "Penn State pounds USC in Fiesta Bowl," said the headline in the *Arizona Republic*. "The final difference could have been much larger," wrote the reporter for the *Phoenix Gazette*.

"We feel we could probably beat any team in the country right now," Paterno said after the game. "That doesn't mean we will be voted the best team in the country." They weren't. Clemson beat Nebraska in the Orange Bowl and was voted #1 with Texas second and Penn State third. Lion opponents had a cumulative record of 82-37-2 for a winning percentage of .686 compared to .483 for Clemson foes and six of State's 12 opponents finished in the Top 20. But Clemson had finished unbeaten. Leave it to Parlavecchio to sum up the sentiments of his team. "Clemson wouldn't finish the season undefeated against our schedule," he said. "Any body who knows football should recognize that we are the best team in the country..." But, alas, it was not to be. Paterno was chosen "Bobby Dodd Coach of the Year" but his team fell short of the National Championship once again. Parlavecchio, Wisniewski, Farrell and their graduating teammates would miss it all by just one year.

Season Record 10-2
Record to Date 568-255-40
Winning percentage .681

"We Are!–Number One! (Finally)"

No one honestly predicted this would be the team that would give Penn State its first National Championship. There were far too many questions before the season began and another imposing schedule. Most importantly, the '82 Lions would not have been in position to win the national title without the one, vital component that had evaded most of its predecessors—luck.

Not that it was just lucky on the field. Sure, Paterno and his players had some of that. But every team has some sort of luck during a 60 minute game and a four month season. Good luck and bad luck. A juggled pass that winds up as an interception, perhaps. Or a referee's instant decision on a "bang-bang" play that nullifies or produces a last minute touchdown that wins the game. Sometimes you win, sometimes you lose. No, the type of good luck the '82 team had was totally out of its control. It's the luck that flows capriciously back and forth across the college football landscape every year, thrusting one team after another into the national title race until only two teams are actually left to have a true National Championship playoff in a bowl game. Paterno's teams of '68, '69 and '73 did not have this luck despite their unbeaten seasons. Neither did the undefeated 1994 team 12 years later nor a couple of Paterno's other once-beaten squads. But the '78, '82, '85 and '86 teams all had that particular kind of luck. And on the night of January 1, 1983, the team played its best game of the year and brought the National Championship back to Happy Valley for the first time.

In a season with at least a half dozen defining moments, none were more consequential than what happened at Legion Field in Birmingham, AL, on the afternoon of October 9—first during the game and then in the locker room after the game. Both incidents have been recounted many times in the media over the years, including by Paterno in his tome *"Paterno: By The Book."* With the #3 unbeaten Lions trailing #4 unbeaten Alabama 27-21 with less than five minutes remaining in the game, substitute blocker Mike Suter backed into punter Ralph Giacomarro and unintentionally blocked the punt with his elbow. Alabama recovered at the Lion 12-yard line, scored a touchdown two plays later and won the game, 42-21. In the locker room, the players were disconsolate and depressed as any one would be after losing a big game in such a manner. Then senior Joel Coles, now a backup running back whose career had been ravaged by an assortment of injuries, did something that will live forever in the annals of Nittany Lion football. As Paterno described in his book, Coles "just let his inner voice take possession of him, and he got up on a bench and let it out with a yell: 'Listen, you guys, we've still got six games to prove that

we're a good football team!' You could just see a dark cloud of discouragement explode and disintegrate. The kids began to cheer for themselves." They not only began cheering for themselves, they went on to win the rest of their games and, with the right type of luck, played themselves right into a National Championship.

But no one knew that in the spring when some 20,000 fans and a statewide television audience watched the annual Blue-White game and saw sophomore tailback Skeeter Nichols and two sophomore quarterbacks, Doug Strang and Dan Longren, steal the show. And no one knew that in the preseason, either, when *Sports Illustrated* picked the Lions to finish #9 and its principal rival Pitt, under new coach Foge Fazio, to be #1. With the loss of 11 starters, including two first round NFL draft choices and most of the offensive line, said *SI*, "Penn State will be pressed to equal last season's 10-2 record." The sportswriters who picked in the AP poll agreed because they tabbed the Lions at #8 in the preseason with Pitt at #1 and State opponents Alabama at #3, Nebraska at #4 and Notre Dame at #20. What no one counted on was Paterno—again concentrating on football after giving up the athletic directorship—to overhaul his offense and infuse his defense with some new blood.

Paterno and his staff had decided before preseason practices began in mid-August to build his offense in the spring around a "big play" attack that would combine passing with the speed and quickness of his running backs. With Blackledge, he had the quarterback who could throw and with Jackson, Garrity, Baugh and McCloskey he had the receivers. Warner, Williams and Coles also were fine receivers and without a prototype fullback, he devised a split-back offense that would use the speedy Warner and Williams at the same time with Nichols, sophomore Tony Mumford and senior Tom Barr in reserve. Later, walk-on Rocky Washington, who played minor league baseball in the Cincinnati farm system, would add depth at flanker, even though he hadn't played football since the midget league in Beaver Falls. Bowman shifted from defense and added depth at tight end. Up front, Paterno would move Speros to guard to team with Maginnis and Heller to tackle to pair with returning starter Contz with Battaglia at center. The second unit had junior Nick Haden at center, sophomores Stan Short and Jerome Wilson at tackles and veteran Lauge and senior Lou Bartek at guards. Paterno said he wasn't "entirely comfortable" with a "big play" attack. "We're going to have to put up with interceptions and we're going to have to put up with turnovers," he told Ron Gardner of the *Daily Collegian*. "We absolutely have to have a different kind of offensive concept."

On defense, Paterno and Sandusky shifted some personnel between the front line and linebacker as they worked with various defensive schemes. The basic defensive front had Gattuso, Opfar and Hines at the tackles with freshman Todd Moules of Wilkes-Barre in reserve and Ashley at one defensive end with Al Harris, Kelley, Sefter and sophomore Mike Garrett in the mix at the other end. Harris and Kelly also played linebacker, along with Radecic, Paffenroth, Putz, redshirt sophomore Carmen Masciantonio and freshman Michael Zordich of Youngstown, OH. Hamilton was the "Hero" back again with Suter in reserve. The starting secondary was all veterans with Roger Jackson, Robinson and Biondi with Mark Fruehan and Chris Sydnor as prime backups. Giacomarro was back for his fourth year as punter and the place kicking was shared by sophomore Nick Gancitano and freshman Massimo Manca, a native of Italy who played high school football in Reno, NV. Ashley, Kelley and Speros were the co-captains and senior

Stuart McMunn captained the special teams. Paterno admitted the defense would not be overpowering but would be quick and opportunistic. "We have the skill people but we're just not going to be able to dominate people physically as we have done," he told sportswriters. "I thinks this will prove to be a very smart team, an alert team that will be able to handle many things."

Paterno's new offense stunned the opening day crowd of about 80,000 at Beaver Stadium on an un-

Walker Lee Ashley, First-Team All-American DE, led the 1982 national championship team in sacks with five.

usually cool Labor Day weekend. The game against Temple was televised live to Pittsburgh and Philadelphia and carried later on a delayed basis by ESPN. On the first play of the game, Blackledge threw a 9-yard swing pass to Williams, then just missed Garrity on a 55-yard bomb that fell off Garrity's fingertips. Four plays later he threw a screen pass to Warner and the tailback went 40 yards for a TD. Before the first quarter was over Blackledge tossed two more TD passes, 31 yards to Baugh and 16 yards to Williams, and he added a 4-yard TD to Williams in the fourth quarter as the Lions won, 31-14. Blackledge completed 14-of-25 attempts for 203 yards with just one interception and his four TDs tied the record held jointly by Tom Sherman and Chuck Fusina. "I think I've really matured as a quarterback," Blackledge told sportswriters. "We have a great combination of receivers, maybe the four best as a unit in the country." However, the emphasis on passing changed the team's traditional running style and Warner gained just 49 yards on 13 carries as the Lions rushed for just 100 yards. The game did nothing to help Warner's Heisman Trophy hopes and sportswriters appeared to dwell on that fact in their post game reports, citing Warner's downcast mood in the locker room. "...No injury-free triumph has been more disappointing to Curt Warner...who broke down and wept in the locker room when it was over," wrote Ron Reid in the *Philadelphia Inquirer*. "Warner was the forgotten man in the debut of the 'new look' Nittany Lions...." Warner told sportswriters he "didn't like to be the guinea pig. I expected to see the ball more."

The air was filled with even more passes the following week when Blackledge dueled with Maryland's junior quarterback Boomer Esiason in one of the wildest games ever at Beaver Stadium. Blackledge threw for another four touchdowns and 262 yards while Esiason fired two TD bombs and had 276 yards as the two combined for 67 pass attempts and kept the crowd of 84,597 on its feet throughout the hot and hazy afternoon. The Lions led at the half 20-10 on an 11-yard TD pass to Warner, a 22-yard TD pass to Jackson and Manca field goals of 20 and 29 yards. But two minutes into the third quarter Blackledge threw an interception and on the next play Esiason hit Russell Davis on a 50-yard bomb. Eight minutes later, Manca booted a 21-yard field goal at the end of a time consuming 70-yard drive but Esiason came back with another 60-yard bomb to a wide open Davis to give Maryland the lead 24-23 with about two minutes left in the quarter. That's when

Paterno inserted his young second team offensive line and in a little over a minute State went 78 yards in five plays—with Williams gaining 33 on one run—to take back the lead, 29-24, on a 23-yard pass to Garrity. With the second team offensive line still in the game, the Lions marched 60 yards in five plays for a TD early in the fourth quarter, helped by a 15-yard penalty against Maryland's new coach Bobby Ross on the Terp punt that started the drive. Ross thought State had 12 men on the punt return team and he ran onto the field complaining to the officials. The referee penalized Maryland instead and a few moments later Jackson scored on a 10-yard TD pass from Blackledge and Manca kicked his third PAT for a 36-24 lead. Maryland narrowed the scored to five points again, 36-31, on an 80-yard, 14-play drive midway through the quarter but State's defense stopped the Terps the rest of the way, and near the end of the game, Manca tied the school record with his fourth field goal and the Lions won, 39-31. Paterno credited his reserve offensive line with winning the game. "We decided we might as well stick the 'green' kids in and let them go," he told sportswriters, referring to the color of jerseys the second team wore during practice. "They played without making mistakes and without jumping offsides." Paterno was not so pleased with his defense. "Esiason was good," he said, "but our tackling was sloppy and I'm being charitable..." Maryland's new coach Bobby Ross said the Lions "kept their poise" and simply had "too much depth." Warner suffered a hip pointer in the third quarter and had jut 45 yards on 15 carries but said he now understood the offensive game plan. "Some games you have to run and some games you have to pass," he said in the locker room.

Both Blackledge and Jackson had set new team records in the Maryland game. Blackledge became the first player to throw four TD passes in more than one game and Jackson's two TD catches gave him 13 for the all-time career high. They added to their records the next Saturday when Blackledge again threw four TD passes, including a 7-yard toss to Jackson, in a 49-14 defeat of Rutgers at Beaver Stadium. Blackledge's other TDs were to Warner for 22 yards, Garrity for 8 yards and McCloskey for 8 yards as he again threw for over 200 yards, with 213 on 15-of-24 attempts. "He's played three great games for us and he's a strong leader out on the field," Paterno told sportswriters. The Lions also scored on the ground for the first time in the season, with Williams going in from the one in the second quarter and Nichols running 15 yards for the final TD late in the fourth quarter. Both rushing TDs had been set up by punt returns but the most spectacular return was by Robinson who went 92 yards down the right sideline for a TD in the first quarter. It was the longest return for a TD since Wally Triplett's 85 yard runback in 1948 and still ranks as the second longest in PSU history.

Despite the three victories, the Lions were still #8 in the polls as they prepared for their biggest game of the year against Nebraska. Since the season began, Pitt had dropped to #3 in the AP rankings even though it was still unbeaten and Washington and Nebraska had jumped ahead with Alabama down one notch to #4. Because of a new NCAA television contract, both ABC and CBS were now showing games head-to-head, and after State's win over Rutgers and Nebraska's 68-0 rout of New Mexico State, CBS decided to nationally televise the State-Nebraska game starting at 3:45 p.m. Eastern time. With a player strike about to begin in the NFL, CBS needed a competitive major college game to assuage its football viewers. Portable lights were brought by an Iowa company but some of State's season ticket holders were not happy with the late start, the latest since the 1976 Ohio State game. In

The 1982 team was the first to win Penn State a National Championship after beating Georgia, 27-23, in the Sugar Bowl on January 1, 1983.

its thrashing of New Mexico State, the Cornhuskers had set new NCAA records for total offense (883 yards), rushing (677 yards) and first downs (43). Nebraska also had beaten Iowa, 45-7, with a backfield that included I-back Mike Rozier, fullback Roger Craig and quarterback Turner Gill and oddsmakers made the visitors a slight favorite. Paterno, still concerned about his defense, said the Lions needed a high-scoring game. "If it's low scoring from our end," he told sportswriters at his weekly news conference, "we won't be in it." On PSU's "TV Quarterbacks" Show, Paterno said the fans should "bring candles to light to St. Jude," the patron saint of lost causes.

As every devout PSU fan now knows, the game was one of the most thrilling ever played at Beaver Stadium with an electrifying come-back ending that had two controversial pass receptions. What John Black wrote in the ***"Football Letter"*** at the time is still true "Anything anyone writes or says about this game is an understatement," Black penned. "You'll never see a more exciting college football game." The pregame atmosphere was unlike any other previously in Happy Valley, surpassing the exhilarating aura of the '78 showdown with Maryland and the '59 " battle of unbeatens" against Syracuse. Another record crowd of 85,304 watched State take a 14-0 lead early in the second quarter on drives of 83 and 71 yards. A 43-yard pass to Warner set up the first TD with Bowman catching the first pass of his career for a 14-yard TD. Warner's running sparked the second drive as he went 31 yards on one play, 15 on another, then scored on a 2-yard scamper. The Lions missed several other scoring opportunities when Manca failed on field goal attempts of 50, 47 and 14 yards and Blackledge had two TD passes nullified by man-in-motion penalties. That kept Nebraska in the game at halftime, 14-7, as Gill drove the Cornhuskers a quick 80 yards in the last minute of the second quarter, completing four of seven passes with a 30-yard strike to Irving Fryar for the TD.

After Nebraska botched a 35-yard field goal attempt following the second half kickoff, State stretched its lead to 14 points again on another 83-yard drive with Jackson getting the TD on an 18-yard pass from Blackledge. But with Warner now out of the game because of muscle cramps, the offense seemed to sag a bit just as Nebraska, still upset by State's 6-point win at Lincoln the year before, regained its

emotional verve. The Cornhuskers drove 80 yards in 15 plays to score on Gill's 2-yard pass to Rozier with 3 and a half minutes left in the third quarter, then recovered a Nichols fumble at the PSU 36 and kicked a 37-yard field goal two minutes into the fourth quarter to trail by just 21-17. Midway through the final period, the Lions moved into scoring territory but a Blackledge pass into the end zone was intercepted. Now, the Cornhuskers had momentum and they drove methodically downfield 80 yards, eating up the clock and taking the lead, 24-21, with 1:18 left in the game on Gill's one-yard run and Kevin Seibel's PAT. The Nebraska kickoff went into the end zone but a 15-yard personal foul on defensive end Dave Ridder gave the Lions the ball at their own 35-yard line with no time outs. "I thought we could do it," Blackledge told sportswriters later. "There was no panic." Indeed, it was another defining moment for the season.

Two 16-yard passes to Nichols and Jackson moved the ball quickly up field to the Nebraska 33-yard line with 52 seconds left. A draw by Williams lost a year and passes to Garrity and Nichols were incomplete. It was now fourth-and-11 with 32 seconds remaining. Paterno thought about kicking a field goal to tie but he wasn't confident Manca or Gancitano could make it. So, Blackledge scrambled and found Jackson down the middle on a curl pattern for a first down at the 23, then made 6 yards running out of bounds on another scramble. Now there were just 13 seconds left. With a second-and-4 at the 17, Blackledge threw to McCloskey tip-toeing at the 2-yard line and stepping out of bounds. The Nebraska defenders protested, saying McCloskey was already out of bounds when he caught the ball and video replays later showed the Cornhuskers were right. "The decisions of officials, wrong or right, are among the breaks of the game," Paterno wrote of the incident in his book. (Nearly 16 years later, in a speech in Boys Town, Nebraska, McCloskey admitted publicly to Cornhusker fans that he was out of bounds.) Nine seconds were left and many in the crowd had now left their seats and were ringing the field. The stadium was thumping. Time for one or two more plays. It was a full house backfield and both tight ends sprinted into the end zone. McCloskey was covered so Blackledge threw a low pass to Bowman cutting across the middle of the end zone. Teammates had nicknamed Bowman "Stonehands" after he dropped an easy pass against Rutgers the week before. But this time, the converted lineman dove and scooped up the ball just before it hit the grass. He stood up waving the football at the referee and the Nittany Lion mascot tackled him. Nebraska defenders again protested frantically but the referee had signaled a touchdown and video replays would show he was right. "I caught the ball about six inches above the ground," Bowman said later. Delirious PSU fans poured onto the field. In the bedlam, Manca missed the PAT and State was penalized five yards on the kickoff for delay of game. But Rozier was tackled quickly on the kickoff and the game was over. The fans rushed onto the field again and this time the goal posts came down at the South end of the field where the winning TD had just been made. The celebration went on for hours as students paraded the goal posts through downtown State College and then to the steps of Old Main and spectators tailgated in the dark parking lots. "This one will take its place right up there in Penn State football history...," wrote Ron Bracken of the *Centre Daily Times*. "It had to be one of the finest wins we've had," Paterno told sportswriters. "I was delighted for our kids that they were able to comeback and make that drive at the end." *Sports Illustrated* called it, "The Miracle of Mount Nittany."

The victory shot the Lions to #3 in the ratings and placed Blackledge on the cover of *Sports Illustrated* under the headline: "Prodigious Penn State, Todd Blackledge Throws Nebraska For A Loop." State had a week off to prepare for its next big game against Alabama and the first away game of the season. Paterno welcomed the time off to give his injured players, especially Warner, more time to recuperate and also to add a few new plays. In the interim, some sportswriters and fans speculated about the reputed curse of *Sports Illustrated*. "The *SI* Cover Jinx--Will Blackledge and the Lions be Next?" said the headline in the *Collegian*. Greg Loder's story outlined seven examples where an athlete appeared on the cover and then lost or failed, including baseball's Pete Rose and horse racing's Spectacular Bid. Of course, Paterno ridiculed the notion of any jinx but after what happened in the regionally televised game at Alabama, many State followers weren't as certain. Even before the bizarre blocked punt in the fourth quarter, the Lions looked uncharacteristically ragged in the 80 degree heat. On the first series of the game a bad snap from center caused Giacomarro's first punt to be blocked inside the 20-yard line and that set up a 4-yard run by quarterback Walter Lewis that gave Alabama a 7-0 lead. State had stormed back two minutes later with Blackledge throwing a 69-yard bomb to Warner but then Lion mistakes helped give the Tide two TDs in the second quarter and a 21-7 halftime lead. State's normally sure-handed receivers were having difficulty holding on to the ball when hit by the Tide defenders but midway through the third quarter, the Lions scored on a 10-play drive from midfield with Williams going in from five yards out on a reverse handoff from Warner. After an Alabama field goal, the Lions drove 75 yards in 10 plays for a 13-yard TD pass from Blackledge to Baugh to narrow the score to 24-21 early in the fourth quarter. But after forcing the Tide to punt, Blackledge threw his third interception of the day near the PSU 37-yard line and Alabama kicked a field goal for a 27-21 lead. Just before the ill-fated punt blocked by Suter, an outstanding defensive play by Alabama end Russ Woods, who brushed off a block by McCluskey and stopped Warner for a 3-yard loss on a third-and-one play from the Alabama 45. It may have been the play of the game. Moments later, Suter backed into Giacomarro's kick, the Tide scored, and when Blackledge tried to pass the Lions back into the game on the ensuing kickoff, Eddie Lowe intercepted on the first play at the PSU 31 and ran in for a touchdown that

clinched the game. "It certainly wasn't one of (Blackledge's) better days," Paterno said. "(But) the kicking game is what lost the game for us. You just don't believe those things can happen to you as much as you practice punting." Warner gained 40 yards on 12 carries and later, Paterno would say he should have given Warner more opportunities to run. The victory was the 320th of Bear Bryant's career and he told sportswriters, "We're either real lucky or a lot better than most people thought we were." They were lucky. Alabama would win only three more

Two-time Academic All-American DB Harry Hamilton (17) and exciting WR and kick returner Kevin Baugh (11) were an integral part of the first national champions in 1982.

games, including a 21-15 win over Illinois in the Liberty Bowl. The 69-year-old Bryant would retire after that game and would be dead within six months, taking his incredible mastery over Paterno with him to the grave.

The Lions fell to #8 in the polls on the same day that the stock market broke through the "magic" 1,000 point level. "I never thought we'd go unbeaten," Paterno said, but now he had to revitalize his team, and with the help of Coles' impassioned locker room plea he did. But it wasn't easy. At first Paterno contemplated several changes. "Right now, I'm not very happy with the team," he said. "We have some players who think they're playing well but they're not." So, in the week before the Homecoming game against Syracuse, he juggled the defensive front a bit and moved Kelley to outside linebacker and the blocking back position on punts. He also refocused on his running game and with the backs gaining the most yardage of the season up to then—225 yards—the Lions whipped 1-4 Syracuse, 28-7, without throwing a touchdown pass. The lousy weather with rain, snow and winds up to 25 miles per hour had forced the Lions to limit the passing but Blackledge had still hit on 10-of-15 passes for 120 yards and scored two TDs by running. Warner led the rushers with 148 yards and TDs of 4 and 34 yards in 25 carries and the defense intercepted five passes, recovered two fumbles and had seven sacks as 84,762 looked on, including the University's newly-announced president, Bryce Jordan. Some Syracuse players were not impressed. "There's no way they should be ranked that high," said defensive tackle Mike Charles. "We basically shut them down..." Paterno agreed the offense was "a little sloppy with the ball" and that the "defense sputtered a little bit" but he was pleased with the rejuvenated running game, saying he needed a more "balanced offense" to keep opponents guessing. The win didn't impress the pollsters, either, as State slipped to #9 before its game with West Virginia.

The West Virginia Homecoming game at Morgantown was intriguing because Hostetler was now the WVU quarterback and had led the Mountaineers to a #13 ranking with a 5-1 record, including a shocking opening season upset at Oklahoma. He had passed for 1,305 yards and 7 TDs with just three interceptions and Paterno admitted his one-time starting quarterback has "more confidence in himself...and

Tailback Curt Warner was a two time First-Team All-American in 1981-82 and is the PSU career leader in rushing yardage and TDs. He helped lead State to its first national championship as a senior.

has a better feel for throwing..." Despite being hobbled by assorted ailments, including bruised ribs, a sprained right ankle and "turf toe," Hostetler passed for 267 yards on 20-of-40 passes and led the Mountaineers on five long drives but came up empty as State's "bend-but-don't break" defense intercepted him three times and shut out WVU for a 24-0 victory. A first quarter fumble by Hostetler at the WVU 23-yard line led to a 31-yard field goal by Gancitano in the first quarter and a 4-yard TD by Williams off a reverse made it 10-0 at the half. An 85-yard interception return by Radecic early in the fourth quarter clinched the game and Jackson's 9-yard run off a flanker reverse with three minutes left capped the scoring. Eight State backs gained 225 yards on 49 carries as Blackledge reined in his passing again with 11-of-21 completions for 118 yards but threw key blocks on both rushing TDs. "The defense played very well," Paterno said, and "the running backs were outstanding."

Boston College was another up and coming team and had posted a 5-1-1 record, including a tie with defending National Champion Clemson. That had propelled Jack Bicknell's team to #20 in the UPI rankings and BC followers were convinced the Eagles could upset the Lions with a pass-happy offense led by sophomore Doug Flutie. State had tried to get the game moved to Schaefer Stadium in Foxboro which had nearly double the capacity of the Eagles' Chestnut Hill playing field but BC declined because it was Parents Weekend. So, a record crowd of 33,205, including House Speaker Tip O'Neill, squeezed into Alumni Stadium on an Indian summer afternoon and watched Flutie set school records for passing and total offense. His 520 yards passing on 26-of-44 completions and 507 yards of total offense also is a PSU

individual record by an opponent. But the Lions won rather easily, 52-17, as Warner ran for 183 yards and three TDs to become State's all-time leading rusher and Blackledge threw three TD passes—two to Jackson for 59 and 29 yards— to set a new career TD record of 33. The Lion defense recovered four fumbles, picked off two Flutie passes and had five sacks as 68 players saw action. Bicknell called the game "a nightmare," adding "In real life, Penn State is more of a threat than in their game films." Michael Madden of the *Boston Globe* wrote that the Lions were "a cold, lethal football team."

North Carolina State, with a 5-3 record, believed it had a good chance against the now #7 Lions, too, and with a history of many close games in the 19-year series, some sportswriters felt an upset was possible. As Black wrote in the *"Football Letter,"* "It was the kind of game writers like to describe by saying the turning point came when the band played the national anthem." With scouts from the Sugar and Cotton Bowls among the 84,837 Beaver Stadium spectators, State won 54-0 as the defense set up four touchdowns with two interceptions and two fumble recoveries and the offense gained 491 total yards. One of the interceptions was returned for a 32-yard TD by Radecic, tying the PSU record of two TD interceptions in one season held by Dennis Onkotz and Jeff Hite. Warner and Williams scored two TDs each with Warner breaking the 100 yard barrier for the 15th time in his career (106 yards on 19 carries) to tie Lydell Mitchell's record. "Two shutouts in the last three game speaks very well of our defense," Paterno said in the locker room. "This was the best (overall) game we've played." That same day, State's next opponent, Notre Dame, knocked Pitt from #1 with a 31-16 victory at Pitt Stadium and Georgia moved to the top of the polls, followed by the nation's only other undefeated-untied teams, SMU and Arizona State. Nebraska was now #4 and State #5. Pitt fell to #8 and Notre Dame was at #13. The bowl invitations would not come out for another two weeks but the race for the national title was still wide open with three weeks left in the regular season and the Lions were still in it. "We have a three-game playoff now for the National Championship," Paterno said. "We have to handle our own affairs and not worry about anyone else."

State had played in South Bend only once before and that was in 1928 when Joe Paterno was one-year old. So when the Lions arrived Friday night Paterno was surprised by the questions of two TV reporters, who asked him how it felt bringing his team into such a traditional football setting for a big game. "I wondered to myself, 'Who the hell do the Notre Dame fans think they are?'" he wrote in *"Paterno: By the Book."* Years later, Kenny Jackson remembered the situation. "A lot of us were enamored by Notre Dame," he recalled. "We had been hearing about it for years. Touchdown Jesus, the Golden Dome and all that. Joe sensed it and the night before the game and he talked to us

All-American safety Mark Robinson was credited with nine tackles and two interceptions in the 1983 Sugar Bowl National Championship game.

about Penn State's tradition, our plain uniforms and things like that. He said he didn't think Notre Dame could beat us because we were something special and we would go out the next day and show everyone."

Fresh from its upset over #1 Pitt, Notre Dame had a 6-1-1 record that included a 16-13 loss to Arizona and a 13-13 tie against Oregon, but the oddsmakers had established State as a six-point favorite. Scouts from the Sugar, Cotton, Orange, Fiesta and Gator Bowls were on hand when the Lions kicked off in subfreezing, blustery weather before an ABC regional television audience shortly after 3:45 p.m. Eastern time. The Irish stormed down the field, eating up nearly eight minutes of the clock and in 15 plays they had marched 76 yards for a 7-0 lead on an 8-yard pass from sophomore Ken Karcher to Chris Smith. Karcher was subbing for starting quarterback Blair Kiel who left the game midway through the drive after aggravating a shoulder injury and he never returned. It took the Lions about 12 minutes to tie with Blackledge completing three passes to Jackson in a 59-yard, 8-play drive and diving in for the TD from one yard out. Two Irish fumbles deep in their own territory led to field goals of 42 and 29 yards by Gancitano and with less than two minutes left in the half, the Lions led, 13-7. Then freshman Alvin Pinkett stunned the Lions and the 59,075 spectators by running back the kickoff 93 yards for a touchdown and with Mike Johnston's PAT Notre Dame suddenly had the lead, 14-13, as the half ended. "The mistake I made was deciding to kick off to Pinkett...because I know how good he is," admitted Paterno later. The Irish momentum seemed to carry into the third quarter as the teams slugged it out but no one came close to scoring. Then, as the fourth quarter began, the Lions took over on their own 20-yard line. Warner gained four yards and on second down Blackledge passed to Jackson for 28 yards to the Irish 48. Blackledge called a running play but when he noticed no one covering Warner in the slot of the double wing formation, he switched the play in an audible. Warner dashed past the Irish safety and was wide open when Blackledge connected and went all the way for the TD. A pass for two points failed but when Manca booted the ball away from Pinkett on the kickoff, Pat Ballage inadvertently touched his knee at the one-yard line. On the next play, Ashley barreled over two blockers and tackled Pinkett for a safety and the Lions led 21-14. With about five minutes remaining, Warner ran 44 yards to set up Gancitano's 27-yard field goal and the Lions won, 24-14. Warner finished with 143 yards on 25 carries and Blackledge had 189 passing yards on 11-of-27 attempts and Notre Dame fans wondered if the game would have been different if Kiel had played. "Kiel would have helped," wrote Bill Moor, in the *South Bend Tribune*, "but probably not enough...Penn State was the better team on Saturday." Paterno said, "We're playing about as well as any football team we've ever had at Penn State."

When the polls came out the following Tuesday, State had leaped into #3 as Arizona State had lost. Now the bowls made their moves. Official invitations would go out on Saturday, November 20, but the Lions would not be playing that day. They didn't meet Pitt until the Friday after Thanksgiving at Beaver Stadium. Everything pointed to the Sugar Bowl because Georgia was #1 and had only a game left with Georgia Tech on November 27. That meant SMU would remain #2 even if it defeated Arkansas on November 20. So, in keeping with Paterno's philosophy of playing "the highest ranked team," the players voted to accept a Sugar Bowl invitation if it came. It did and so did that quirk of luck when SMU was tied by Arkansas, 17-17. Now all the Lions had to do was beat Pitt and root for Georgia against Georgia Tech and they would have their shot at the National Championship.

Once again, the traditional game with Pitt would help clarify the national title race. Pitt had accepted a bid to play SMU in the Cotton Bowl so the Panthers still had an outside chance at #1. The winner of this game would still be a contender. The loser—an also ran, no matter what happened on New Year's Day. The tenor leading up to the nationally televised game had none of the bitter feelings of the previous year. Sherrill had left for a lucrative job at Texas A&M and had taken much of the animosity with him. Fazio had been the defensive genius behind the Panthers under Sherrill and he again had an outstanding defense that was second in the nation, giving up just 87 yards per game. In the end, the game came down to defense and it was the Lion defense that prevailed—with an outstanding goal line stand in the fourth quarter as another record crowd of 85,522 looked on in 20 degree, windy weather. The first half belonged to Pitt as the Panthers took a 7-3 lead and thwarted three State scoring chances by intercepting a pass in the end zone and recovering two fumbles. Sugar Bowl representative paced nervously in Beaver Stadium during the intermission. But with a gusty, swirling 30-mile-an hour wind at their backs in the third quarter, the Lions kept Pitt deep in Panther territory and forced three short punts of 21, 32 and 34 yards. One punt set up a 43-yard drive that led to State's only touchdown of the day on a 31-yard pass from Blackledge to Jackson. Then, later in the quarter, a high snap forced the Pitt punter to run for a first down but he was short at the Panther 30-yard line and a few plays later, Gancitano booted a 31-yard field goal that gave State a 13-7 lead. Gancitano kicked a 19-yard field goal one play into the fourth quarter after a 58-yard PSU drive stalled at the Pitt 2 and the Lions led 16-7. Now, Pitt had the wind and midway through the quarter the Panthers drove 76 yards to State's one-yard line. After four plays, including an interference call, Pitt was still at the one and Fazio decided to go for the field goal, setting himself up for second guessing after the game. "I question myself about whether we should have gone for the touchdown...," Fazio said later. The field goal made it 16-10. Shortly thereafter a low 51-yard punt by Giacomarro into the wind helped get the Lions out of trouble and Pitt took what would be its last shot with a field goal attempt on a fourth-and-five at the PSU 30 but was short. Gancitano's record tying fourth field goal with a minute left made the final score, 19-10. Blackledge's TD pass was the 41st of his career and is still the school record. Warner ran for 118 yards to run his four-year total to 3,398 yards and that, too, remains the career rushing record. "What has impressed me about this squad is how many times it did what it had to do under pressure," Paterno said in the locker room.

But the Lions still needed some of that special type of luck. The next day Georgia beat Georgia Tech, 38-18, and it was back to the Sugar Bowl for another National Championship game. Only this time, the return to Happy Valley would be different.

THE 1983 SUGAR BOWL
Jan. 1, 1983
Penn State 27, Georgia 23
Outstanding Player: Todd Blackledge

"How 'Bout Them Dawgs?" came the Georgia cheer echoing down Bourbon Street and the French Quarter."Woof-Woof-Woff." But the yells didn't have the same sting and were nowhere near as aggravating as the "Roll Tide" hoots that State fans had heard on their last visit to the Sugar Bowl. They may have been outnumbered but the Lion followers in New Orleans this time were not outdone by Bulldog fans and screams of "We Are—Penn State!" could be heard throughout the downtown and especially in and around the team's headquarters at the Hilton Hotel. The manager of the hotel was a PSU graduate and the lobby seemed like one gigantic tailgate for hours on end. Blue and White signs proclaiming "Lions #1...No Bull" were plastered on billboards and buses and "Love Ya Lions" placards hung in windows of many New Orleans shops and bars. One "watering hole" on Bourbon Street catering to PSU fans renamed itself "Fritzel's Lion's Den," hanging a giant State football helmet on its second floor balcony and playing recordings day and night of "Hail to the Lions" and "Fight on State." A pep rally outside the Superdome around 4 o'clock on New Years Eve attracted thousands of fans, who were given large blue or white foam hands with the index finger pointed in the air and a #1 printed on it. Most of the souvenir hands were toted into the Dome the next evening and thrust high into the air continuously by the exuberant State followers.

Following the usual routine for a New Year's Day game, the team arrived in New Orleans the day after Christmas. Once again, Paterno closed practices. He also tried to keep the players away from their ardent fans who crowded the lobby of the Hilton Hotel for hours each day to socialize and catch glimpses of the team coming and going on buses. This was Paterno's chance to redeem himself and the Lions for what happened at the '79 Sugar Bowl and he didn't want any major distractions to deter the ultimate goal. Still, some players were able to cruise Bourbon Street early in the week as Paterno kept his word to let them have some fun.

Sportswriters saw this game as a match-up between State's explosive offense and the Georgia's running game and pass defense. For the first time, a State team had gained more yards passing (2,369) than rushing (2,283) but it was a balanced attack with an attacking defense and boasted four All-Americans in Warner, Jackson, Ashley and Robinson and a Phi Beta Kappa quarterback in Blackledge. But Georgia had junior Herschel Walker, who had just won the Heisman Trophy and already owned 10 NCAA and 15 SEC records. The Bulldogs also led the nation in interceptions with 31, had the two leading pass interceptors in All-American Terry Hoage (12) and Jeff Sanchez (9) and had given up just seven TD passes all season. What Georgia didn't have was a passer. Quarterback John Lastinger completed less than 50 percent of his passes but he was a leader who made the clutch plays "that allows us to win," according to coach Vince Dooley. The Bulldogs also had been here before. For the third

Second-Team and Academic All-American LB Scott Radecic led the team with 14 tackles in the 1982 championship game. After an NFL career, he is now a consulting engineer and involved with the expansion of Beaver Stadium into the 21st Century.

straight year, Georgia was playing in the Sugar Bowl and in '80 had beaten Notre Dame to win the national title. Paterno had lost all three Sugar Bowl games and had admitted that the Superdome is "a tough place to coach." To get his players ready for the noise of the Superdome, he had used some of the 10 days of practice in State College to work indoors with speakers blaring loud crowd noises. "It would give you a headache when you walked out of practice," said Garrity. Despite Herschel Walker, the oddsmakers had made the Lions a three-to-four point favorite. Bill Conlin of the *Philadelphia Daily News* picked the Lions by 27-24, saying: "Balance of Blackledge, Warner offsets brilliant effort by H. Walker. Fans will talk about this one for years."

Walk-on WR Greg Garrity made the unforgettable, diving, fourth quarter catch in the 1983 Sugar Bowl victory over Georgia. His father also played for State and was a fine receiver in the early 1950s.

The weather was rainy, foggy and dreary outside the Dome that night when the Lions won the toss and chose to receive. Dooley had figured Paterno would first test his "bruised" defensive line by running the ball up the gut. But Paterno's strategy was to use the speed and dexterity of his receivers and to throw long. After Warner made four yards up the middle on the first play, Blackledge passed to McCloskey for 33 yards, then to Garrity for 27 yards. With two more passes and two runs, the Lions went 78 yards and Warner then ran two yards around left end for the touchdown. Gancitano kicked the PAT and the Lions led, 7-0. But Georgia came right back. With Walker carrying six times for 40 yards, including runs of 12 and 11 yards, the Bulldogs marched 70 yards in 15 plays before halted by State's defense and forced into a 27-yard field goal by Kevin Butler. For nearly the rest of the half, the game belonged to State. Sandusky's constantly shifting defensive scheme concentrated on stopping Walker with three waves of tacklers that stripped away the blockers and gang tackled him high and low. He would gain 49 yards in the first quarter but only 107 on 28 carries for the entire game. With the help of three punt returns by Baugh, including one of 66 yards, the Lions built up a 20-3 lead late in the second quarter on field goals of 38 and 45 yards by Gancitano and a 9-yard Warner TD that climaxed a 5-play, 65-yard drive. With just 39 seconds left in the half, Walker ran back the kickoff 23 yards and Georgia went into its "two-minute" drill. Lastinger passed four times to reach the PSU 10-yard line, including the fourth one for 26-yards that had split end Kevin Harris catching the ball for 16-yards and lateralling to Walker who ran for 10 more. Then, with just five seconds remaining in the half, 6-foot-5 Herman Archie out jumped 5-foot-9 Biondi on a Lastinger floater to the left corner of the end zone and with Butler's PAT Georgia was back in the game, 20-10.

With their confidence restored by Lastinger's passing and the momentum still in their favor, the Bulldogs took the second half kickoff and marched 69-yards for a TD. Twice State appeared to have Georgia stopped on third-and-long situations, only to have Lastinger get the first downs on clutch tosses to Harris for 11 and 24 yards. Walker scored the TD on a one-yard dive and Butler's kick made it 20-17. Now, the Lion offense broke down. After a few plays, Warner left the game with leg cramps and Blackledge was sacked twice. Throughout the third quarter, Warner made some good runs but had to leave the field several times because of cramps. Blackledge was sacked again and missed seeing open receivers several times. "I lost my poise," he would tell sportswriters later. "I wasn't picking up the blitzes and throwing the ball when I should have." But State's defense was halting Walker and Lastinger, with Robinson stopping two threats with pass interceptions, and just before the teams changed sides at the end of the third quarter, the Lions took the ball on their own 19-yard line. Warner gained 11 yards up the middle and during the time out, Paterno and Blackledge discussed a pass play Blackledge wanted to call. Now, 90 seconds into the period, the Lions were at the Georgia 47 with a first down. Paterno sent in that play— "643." Blackledge faked to Warner up the middle as four receivers sped downfield. Blackledge saw Garrity—the team's "other receiver" all season long—getting a step on freshman cornerback Tony Flack down the left side. "I threw the ball as far as I could," Blackledge said later. It was a perfect pass to Garrity who made a diving catch in the end zone for a touchdown. "I think that was the most important play of the game," Dooley said later. Gancitano's PAT gave State the 27-17 lead and for the next several minutes, the Lion defense took control. A sack by Ashley with about five minutes remaining forced the Bulldogs to punt from their own 25 and it was here that Baugh made a mistake, trying to run with the ball instead of signaling for a fair catch or letting the ball bounce and, uncharacteristically, he fumbled. Georgia recovered State's only turnover of the evening and in six plays the Bulldogs had a TD on a 9-yard pass to Clarence Kay. The Lion defense stopped Walker short on the 2-point conversion but now, with 4:54 left, the Bulldogs would need more than a field goal to tie or win. Later, Dooley would second guess himself for not trying an onside kick because his defense would never get the ball back. They almost did with about two minutes left, and the Lions with a third-and-3 at the State 32. Georgia called time out and Blackledge went to the sideline to discuss the play. Paterno said a run was the safe play but Blackledge wanted to throw a pass. "Throw it," Paterno said. The 6-yard square out to Garrity for the first down caught the Bulldogs completely by surprise. Years later, when talking about the game, Paterno would tell his listeners that it was this play that best epitomized Blackledge and he team that season.

As the seconds ticked off the clock with the scoreboard showing a 27-23 score, it was obvious to the players and their fans in the record Superdome crowd of 78,184 that the Lions were about to reach college football's Holy Grail. "We're Number One, We're Number One" they started chanting. And when the game was finally over they stood and cheered for nearly 15 minutes as the players hoisted Paterno on their shoulders and carried him into the center of the field with his right arm outstretched and his index finger pointing to the top of the Dome. It is an indelible image captured by photographers and flashed to newspapers around the country that remains the symbolic icon of that historical moment. "This is the best football team "I've ever had," a jubilant Paterno told sportswriters. Dooley said, "Penn State is the best-balanced football team that I've seen since I've been coaching." Meanwhile, in the locker room, Blackledge broke out the cigars for himself and his teammates.

"No. 1 At Last!" said the headline on the cover of *Sports Illustrated*, featuring Garrity celebrating after his touchdown. "There is nothing phony about college football's newest champion," wrote Peter Finney, sports editor of the *New Orleans Times- Picayune.* With his 228 yards on 13-of-23 passes and the TD toss to Garrity, Blackledge was named the Most Valuable Player of the game. Warner, despite his cramps, had outdueled the Heisman Trophy winner for the second year in a row, this time gaining 117 yards and two TDs on 18 carries and 23 yards on two pass receptions. Radecic, an Academic All-American like Blackledge, had led the Lion defense with 14 tackles and his fellow Academic All-American, Hamilton, had 10 tackles. Paterno's Grand Experiment had finally paid the biggest dividend of all.

A crowd of nearly 8,000, including Governor Dick Thornburg, met the team upon its arrival at the Harrisburg airport the next morning. Then, as the team busses made the 100 mile trip back to State College through the small towns in the Central Pennsylvania mountains, thousands of well-wishers were on the road along the way to cheer, wave and honk their horns into the night as their new heroes passed by. "...I learned as never before how much this team and its success are an expression of so many people," Paterno would later write in his book. "I never saw such love between people who didn't know each other." When the team reached State College they were greeted by a large crowd in the parking lot of a shopping mall, then another rally at the indoor sports complex. A few days later, they were honored with parade through downtown State College and thousands turned out despite a heavy snow storm.

It was a heady few days for Paterno and Penn State fans. The euphoria carried over for months as Lion football fans continued to celebrate their first taste of the ultimate glory. Then in late August the new season began. And it all came crashing down.

Season Record 11-1
Record to Date 579-256-40
Winning percentage .685

"'You Either Get Better or You Get Worse'"

Joe Paterno has a favorite saying that he tells his players every year: "You either get better or you get worse, but you don't stay the same."

Never was that philosophy more true for Paterno's teams than it was between the end of the 1982 championship season and the beginning of 1983. Not even Paterno was prepared for what occurred.

"I don't think repeating (as National Champion) is out of sight," he told sportswriters in the preseason. "But you've got to be good and you've got to be lucky. Whether the drop-off offensively that we are going to have...for a while can be made up with the plusses of the defense or the field goal kicking in the early part of the season, we'll just have to wait and see." He didn't have long to wait.

In the inaugural Kickoff Classic game created by the NCAA as a benefit for the National Football Foundation to match the two best teams from the previous year, Nebraska humiliated the Lions before a Monday night national television audience, 44-6. It wasn't just his offense that failed but his veteran defense, too. And before he pulled his team together, the Lions lost two more games for the worst start since 1964. Then on the eve of the biggest game of the season he had to publicly chastise some of his best players for bragging about how good they thought they were.

When it started off so badly, some of the more superstitious fans blamed everything from the new Lion logo to the new play-by-play broadcaster on the Penn State radio network. In the end, the season would turn on an ironic fourth quarter goal line stand and a controversial last minute pass play by Alabama. The Lions would pull off two major upsets and get a bowl bid by getting a tie on the last play of the regular season. And when it was over, they would wind up with the worst record in four years and still spend Christmas in Hawaii.

Prior to the August 29th Kickoff Classic at Giants Stadium in the New Jersey Meadowlands, Nebraska had been anointed as the favorite to succeed State as National Champions. The Lions were picked at #4 in the AP preseason poll behind Oklahoma and Texas with three opponents also among the Top 20 selections: Notre Dame at #6, Alabama at #13 and Iowa at #16. Paterno was starting out with a new quarterback again and a new tailback since Blackledge had given up his last season of eligibility to turn professional and both he and Warner had been #1 draft choices by the NFL. Williams was moved back to tailback with Mumford succeeding him at fullback. Jackson, who already owned 22 State receiving records, returned at flanker and Baugh moved up to start at split end but Paterno needed someone to get the ball to the them. Neither Lonergan nor Strang had played much while backing up Blackledge but both juniors had impressed the record crowd of 31,000 that turned out for the annual spring Blue-White game. Paterno didn't decide on starting Strang until two days before the Nebraska opener and even then he was ambivalent. He said he hoped his defense could hold the Cornhuskers to three touchdowns because he wasn't sure his offense was "good enough to win a high scoring game."

Nebraska's veteran players led by Gill, Rozier and Fryar were still miffed at their last second loss to the Lions at Beaver Stadium in '82 and they had spent the winter blaming the judgment call on the sideline pass to McCluskey for costing them the national title. They took their revenge on a hot August night by rolling up 500 total yards on touchdown drives of 78, 86, 66, 40 and 88 yards and returning a pass 27 yards for another TD in a 44-6 romp. "I think the thing just snowballed," Nebraska coach Osborne said after the game. The Lions barely avoided their first shutout in a decade when Lonergan threw a 35-yard TD pass to redshirt freshman Sid Lewis with 20 seconds left in the game. Strang had started but both quarterbacks played and neither had looked good, completing just 13-of-39 passes for 227 yards and one interception. "I don't think our defense played badly," Paterno said. "I just think our offense couldn't get anything going."

It didn't get better when the Lions opened their regular schedule two weeks later against Cincinnati at Beaver Stadium. Keeping with Paterno's philosophy, it got worse. In one of the biggest upsets in the Paterno era, upstart Cincinnati beat the Lions, 14-3, on a hot, sweltering day. The Lion offense was awful again as the Bearcats controlled the clock for nearly 38 minutes and the overworked defense was listless in the second half. Even the kicking game fell apart as two fumbles by Baugh within 2 and a half minutes early in the second quarter led to all of Cincinnati's points. The Bearcats went 38 yards in five plays for their first TD after Baugh fumbled a punt, then when Baugh dropped the ensuing kickoff return at the PSU 38-yard line, another five plays brought the second TD and a classic "insurmountable" 14-0 lead. Pa-

terno even used true freshman quarterback John Shaffer of Moeller High School in Cincinnati to try to spark the offense but it didn't help. The three quarterbacks completed just 7-of-25 passes for 112 yards and had three interceptions while the Bearcats pro style offense of coach Warren Brown completed 25-of-36 passes for 261 yards and didn't have one intercepted. "Nobody played well at any position," Paterno said in the locker room. "There was no second effort, no enthusiasm, confidence or leadership." He was wrong. Punter George Reynolds had a 44.4 yard average in 8 punts.

The next day the players held a private team meeting without the coaches. "When you lose a couple of games," you start to feel a little animosity on the squad," Robinson later told *Sports Illustrated*. "Everybody had to get things off his chest." Robinson and the other team captains—Jackson, Radecic and Heller—took the player complaints to Paterno. One of their biggest gripes was the shuttling of three quarterbacks. Paterno agreed, telling *USA Today*, "I thought we could do a little experimenting and still beat Cincinnati. Obviously, I underestimated them. That was my mistake as coach." He named Strang the number one quarterback but before the game against #12 Iowa, Lonergan was sidelined with severe headaches and Shaffer moved up to number two.

For the most part, Paterno was satisfied with his rebuilt first team offensive line. He had two starters from the championship team, Heller at right tackle and Maginnis at left guard. Haden was at center and Short teamed with Heller. Moules, who lettered as a defensive lineman in '82 and played there in the opener against Nebraska, was now the short guard. Paterno made one other key offensive change before Iowa, starting sophomore Dean Dimidio at tight end in place of Bowman. That move paid off three minutes into the first quarter when Dimidio caught a 9-yard TD pass from Strang to cap a 33-yard drive set up by Gattuso's partially blocked punt. Strang threw two more touchdown passes to Jackson for seven yards and Baugh for 18 yards but Iowa came from a 21-14 halftime deficit on the quarterbacking of Chuck Long to hand the Lions their third straight defeat, 42-34. Paterno also discovered a new running back in true freshman D. J. Dozier of Virginia Beach, VA, who entered the game in the second half when Williams strained a knee. Dozier gained 102 yards on 8 carries, including a 57-yard run that set up Baugh's TD early in the third quarter and gave the Lions a momentary 28-21 lead. But Dozier also fumbled twice and both bobbles led to Iowa scores. With Strang going all the way at quarterback, the offense gained 492 yards but the defense couldn't stop Long or the Iowa runners as Long set a Beaver Stadium record by completing 16-of-30 passes without an interception for 345 yards and two TDs while Hawkeye rushers led by Owen Gill gained 242 yards on 53 carries. Paterno said he was pleased with the offense but very disappointed in the defense. "It was the poorest tackling by any team that I've ever been associated with," he told sportswriters.

So before the Temple game, Paterno made some changes in the first team defense. He was pretty well set in the line with Sefter, junior John Walter and redshirt freshman Bob White of Freeport as the primary ends and Gattuso, Hines and senior Scott Carraher at the tackles. Radecic and Masciantonio were the inside linebackers with returning starter Harry Hamilton at the "hero" position. Now, Paterno moved Zordich from outside linebacker to the wideside corner back and shifted All-American safety Robinson to the short side corner spot. Sophomore Rogers Alexander took over at outside linebacker and "redshirt" freshman Darrell Giles went to safety. Syndor and Fuehan were now in backup roles and as the season continued other youngsters would get heavy playing time behind the defensive line, including Hamilton's brother, Lance, two redshirt freshmen, Shane Conlan of Frewsburg, NY, and Don Graham of Pittsburgh and true freshman Tim Johnson of Sarasota, FL.

The defensive changes helped make the difference as the Lions stopped the bleeding with a 23-18 win over Temple (1-1) at Veteran's Stadium. On Temple's second possession of the game, Alexander sacked veteran quarterback Tim Riordan, sending him to the sidelines for the rest of the afternoon. That enabled

Ron Heller was one of the best offensive linemen of the Paterno era, a key member of the 1982 national championship team and co-captain of the '83 squad who later had an outstanding pro career.

State to build up a 23-3 lead early in the fourth quarter on two TD passes by Strang for 23 and 21 yards, three Gancitano field goals, a 31-yard punt return by Robinson and the running of Dozier and Mumford. But Strang also missed the second half with an injury and Shaffer's second pass interception nearly led to a dramatic comeback by Temple in the last six minutes. Freshman quarterback Lee Saltz threw a 44-yard TD following the interception, then hit a 52-yard bomb with 2:34 left. State recovered an onside kick but gave up the ball on downs and clinched the game with a sack on the last play. Dozier gained 107 yards on 27 carries and Mumford had 85 yards in 11 carries as Lions stuck to a basic running game most of the second half with Shaffer throwing just 7 passes and completing two. "This was a win for Penn State and that's all it was," wrote Bill Lyon in the *Philadelphia Inquirer*. "It was hardly decisive and hardly encouraging." Paterno was "glad to get one" but said, "we still have a long way to go."

Returning to Giants Stadium in the Meadowlands the next Saturday, the Lions made it two straight with a 36-25 win over a fired-up Rutgers team. State led by just 20-19 at the half but seemed to have control of the second half with a 29-19 lead midway through the fourth quarter when Rutgers quarterback Rusty Hochberg threw a 76-yard pass that trimmed the score to 29-25. Hochberg, whose father Jim was PSU's trainer, was injured on the play and would be sidelined the rest of the season after setting a school passing record with 367 yards. Dozier, who set a new freshman single game rushing record with 196 yards on 27 carries, sealed State's victory minutes later on a 50-yard TD that capped an 8-play, 89-yard drive. Strang threw for two TDs in hitting on 11-of-26 passes for 173 yards and Paterno said he was "pleased" with the way Strang was maturing. "Obviously, we've got to straighten out a couple of things (on defense)," Paterno told sportswriters.

Now, the resurgent Lions faced their biggest test—undefeated and third-ranked Alabama in a late afternoon national televised game at Beaver Stadium. Former Alabama All-American Ray Perkins had quit as head coach of the NFL's New York Giants to take over the Crimson Tide for the late Bear Bryant. Perkins had thrown out Bryant's wish-

bone offense and installed a multiple wide-open passing attack and the Tide had been averaging 37 points in four games. Three days before the game, Paterno, still upset by the poor play of the defense he had counted upon, lashed out at some his players during his weekly news conference. "Too many players talk about how good they are," he said. "I think some of my players are shooting their mouths off too much. That's been part of the problem with this football team from the beginning." Paterno's angry words singed a few ears. With a record crowd of 85,614 looking on in sunny, warm weather, the Lions forced six turnovers and turned two fumbles and two interceptions into points to take a shocking 34-7 lead into the fourth quarter. Strang had thrown three TD passes, including an 80-yard bomb to Dimidio for State's first TD that had tied the score in the first period at 7-7. But as the fourth quarter began, Alabama was in the middle of an 87-yard drive that made the score 34-14 less than a minute later. On their next possession, the Tide drove 69-yards for another TD and with less than six minutes remaining, Alabama narrowed the score to 34-28 with another drive of 78 yards. State appeared on the ropes but the Lion offense perked up and moved downfield towards a clinching TD. Then, it fell apart as Strang misfired on two pass attempts and a wide-open Dimidio dropped another one. Gancitano tried a 43-yard field goal but Stan Gay broke through to block it. Now, Alabama had the ball at its own 49-yard line with three minutes remaining.

Four pass completions by Walter Lewis and a run by tailback Kerry Goode gave Alabama a first down at the State 6-yard line with 28 seconds left. The crowd was on its feet and knew Lewis was going to pass because Alabama had just one time out remaining. Lewis already had completed 24-of-32 attempts, including 13-of-14 in the fourth quarter, but his first two passes were incomplete. On third down, Lewis had to scramble and was tackled by Alexander at the four. Now, there were eight seconds left. Harry Hamilton blitzed and forced Lewis to throw a high pass to his secondary receiver, tight end Preston Gothard. Gothard had to jump for the ball. He juggled it as he came down and field judge Jack O'Rourke ruled Gothard didn't have possession when he hit the end line with the upper part of his body. The State fans went wild until they saw the flag. Sefter was offside and 'Bama had one last chance at the one-yard line. Perkins sent in the play for his two-tight end formation. Sandusky flashed his defensive signal to Gattuso, who shifted into the gap. In what was an ironic reversal of the '79 Sugar Bowl, Perkins called the play ("Toss 28") Sandusky and Gattuso were expecting, a pitchout to Goode which had gained yardage on all afternoon. Goode swept right, cut back when his path was blocked by Sefter and was hit first by Fruehan and then by Gattuso. No gain. Game over. And the fans swarmed onto the field. "I played sweep all the way," Gattuso told Mike Poorman of the *Lebanon Daily News*. "If they had run up the middle, I would have been the goat."

The controversy started in the locker room when Alabama players claimed Gothard's last second catch was a touchdown. "Our players said he had it," Perkins said. CBS-TV replays seemed to support the Tide. Sportswriters emphasized that the reception was made in the same South end zone as the disputed catches by McCluskey and Bowman that beat Nebraska in '82. "Lions Upset 'Bama Behind End Zone Curse," said the headline in the *Daily Collegian*. But the next week TV cameramen from Johnstown and Wilkes-Barre showed film from different angles that proved Gothard was out of bounds. "It showed the kid did not have control," Paterno said after viewing the film. A few days later, the *New York Times* reported that a review of 16-millimeter films by the Collegiate Independent Football Officiating Association showed Gothard had bobbled the ball "but that the film was 'inconclusive' on whether (he) had regained possession before rolling out of the end zone." However, Art Hyland, supervisor of officials, revealed that a motion penalty should have been called on Alabama's other tight end, Thornton Chandler. Chandler may have drawn Sefter offside. Hyland said either off-setting penalties should have been called or Alabama penalized for encroachment and given the ball at the 9-yard line for one last play. Therefore, a Gothard TD shouldn't have counted anyway. Still, some in the media claimed the Lions got away with another "hometown" decision. ABC-TV sports commentator Beano Cook produced a diagram on a national telecast a week later that humorously showed a weird South end zone with part of the end line cut out where Gothard "caught" the pass and an extra piece added on the left sideline at the 2-yard line where McCloskey had "caught" his pass against Nebraska. *USA Today* and *Sports Illustrated* soon printed their own versions of the drawing and to this day Alabama fans complain about "that crazy end zone."

The defensive heroics against Alabama and ensuing controversy were among the defining moments of the season. Almost overshadowed in the aftermath was the fine passing performance of Strang and the running of Dozier. Strang hit on 13-of-21 passes for 241 yards while Dozier broke Matt Suhey's freshman rushing record by gaining 163 yards on 17 carries to run his total to 619 yards. But in the process the Lions lost Robinson for the season because of a fractured ankle. The media also lost their access to the Penn State locker room. Sarajane Freleigh of the *Philadelphia Inquirer* complained that she was not allowed admission to the locker room after the game and a few days later State adopted a new policy that closed the dressing room and set up an interview area in an adjoining classroom. However, there were still no plans to build a locker room at the stadium as players and reporters continued to use busses after the game to reach the facility near

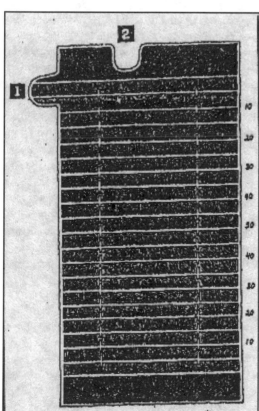

This is the whimsical diagram of a redsigned South end zone at Beaver Stadium created by ABC-TV's Beano Cook and published in Sports Illustrated after two controversial decisions by game officials helped State beat Nebraska in 1982 (1) and Alabama in 1983 (2).

Tailback D.J. Dozier was a four-year starter and the backfield star of the second national championship team in 1986 when he made First-Team All-American. As a freshman he ran for more than 100 yards in five games.

the Greenberg indoor sports complex.

State came out flat against Syracuse (3-3) in the Carrier Dome the next week and trailed by two field goals, 6-0, late in the third quarter. The Orange might have had more points but lost fumbles in the first half that stopped drives at the Lion 11 and 46-yard lines. When Syracuse lost another fumble on a punt return late in the third quarter, the Lions took the lead on a 6-play, 36-yard drive with Strang running one-yard for the TD. A Gattuso interception four plays later gave State the ball at the Syracuse 25 and Dozier scored form the one-yard line. A 21-yard Gancitano field goal at the end of a 72-yard drive in the closing minutes gave the Lions a 17-6 victory and a winning record for the first time in the season. "The players kept their poise and learned a good lesson," said Paterno.

West Virginia was certain it was about to end its long 27-year winless drought against the Lions in State's Homecoming game on October 22. The Mountaineers were 6-0 and ranked #4 with one of the best quarterbacks in the country in erstwhile Lion, Jeff Hostetler, who had thrown for 1,126 yards in completing 56 percent of his passes. Another record crowd of 86,309, including PSU astronaut Guion Bluford and scouts from six bowls watched in 50 degree weather as WVU took the kickoff and quickly moved upfield until White's hit on a pass receiver caused a fumble that Syndor recovered at the Mountaineer 44. Strang immediately completed passes to Baugh and Dimidio and six plays later Strang ran one-yard for the TD, Gancitano booted the PAT and the Lions never trailed. The game was tight until late in the third quarter when a 57-yard punt return for a TD by Baugh gave the Lions a 31-17 lead and WVU could only score two field goals after that as State pulled off another upset, 41-23. Strang had outplayed Hostetler, passing for touchdowns of 8, 16 and 46 yards in a 16-for-26, 220-yard afternoon. Dozier sat out most of the game and Williams ran for 106 yards on 24 carries and caught an 8-yard TD pass. Hostetler hit on 18-of-30 for a season high 273 yards but was sacked twice for a loss of 10 yards and had one interception. "We did particularly well against one of the great athletes in the country, Jeff Hostetler," Paterno told sportswriters.

The Lions didn't fare as well the following week against another of the country's outstanding quarterbacks as Doug Flutie led #19 Boston College to its first ever win over State after 11 defeats. In a late afternoon regional televised game from Sullivan Stadium in Foxboro, Flutie threw for 380 yards and two touchdowns in completing 24-of-43 pass attempts, including a 67-yard TD that tailback Troy Stradford scored after picking off a pass tipped by a Lion defensive back. Still, the Lions fought back after BC had jumped to a 21-0 lead early in the second quarter and were within a TD until Flutie engineered a 59-yard drive for a 40-yard field goal in the fourth quarter that made the final score, 27-17. Paterno blamed the loss primarily on State's offensive line, which failed to cope with a steady BC blitz. The Eagles sacked Strang four times for 30 yards in losses and forced him to throw several incompletions while holding State runners to 164 yards on 40 carries. "BC deserved to win," Paterno said. "They wanted the game more than we did."

The next opponent would not have been on the schedule if Tennessee had not reneged on a commitment to play at Beaver Stadium. So Brown, Paterno's Ivy League alma mater, agreed to the November 5 date. "As one Brown player said," wrote Black for the *"Football Letter,"* Penn State had almost as many no-shows Saturday as Brown's average home attendance." Another Brown player said, "what shocked us when we arrived was all those campers (tailgating)...we've never seen anything like that." The atmosphere surrounding the game on a snowy day was loose and casual and seemed almost like a lark to both the estimated 75,000 fans and the players. State had a 38-7 lead early in the fourth quarter when Brown came up with two TDs against the Lion reserves and the final score was 38-21. The Brown players surrounded Paterno to shake his hand after the game. "This feels like a win," said Brown fullback Steve Heffernan.

While State was beating overmatched Brown, Notre Dame was losing to Pitt, 21-16, and seeing its bowl hopes fade. The 6-4 Irish needed a victory as much as the Lions if they wanted to snag a possible Fiesta Bowl invitation. The game played in subfreezing weather was tied twice in the first half and the lead change hands six times in the second half before State pulled out a thrilling 34-30 victory with a 50-yard drive in the last minute. Notre Dame had gone ahead 30-27 midway through the fourth quarter on a 77-yard drive that climaxed with Pinkett's one-yard touchdown for his fourth TD of the game, tying a PSU record for TDs by an opposing player in one game. State charged back but when Dozier fumbled the only turnover of the game at the Irish 12-yard line with 2:55 left, it looked like a Notre Dame win. But the defense stopped the Irish, with Alexander making the biggest play of the game by blitzing past his blocker and smashing Pinkett for a 4-yard loss on a third-and-one situation at the ND 21. Kiel then shanked a punt 33 yards and the Lions had the ball at the 50 with 53 seconds remaining. Williams gained five on a draw play and Strang threw a 36-yard pass to Dimidio off the same formation that put the Lions at the 9-yard line. Two plays gained just one yard and with the clock ticking, Strang rolled right looking to pass to Jackson or Baugh but both were covered so he dashed towards the end zone, got a block by Williams and scored the winning TD with just 19 seconds left. "Doug did the job when it had to be done," Paterno told Ron Bracken of the *Centre Daily Times*.

Before the final game at Pitt Stadium on November 19, several minor bowls approached State. Representatives of the one-year old Aloha Bowl expressed the strongest interest, saying it would like to match the Lions with either UCLA or Washington—"Whoever's not in the Rose Bowl"—for its December 26 game in Honolulu. "We've gone to a minor bowl in the past when Joe has had a young team," athletic director Tarman told the *Pittsburgh Press*. "Whether he and the squad want to go this year, I don't know." Pitt, with an 8-2 record, already had the Fiesta Bowl bid sewed up and would play the loser of the Big Ten championship game, either Michigan or Ohio State.

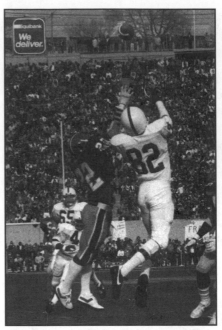

All-American Kenny Jackson outleaps a Pitt defender for a reception in the 24-24 1983 game at Pitt Stadium. Jackson had two TD catches in this game best remembered for its bizarre ending and one of only three ties in Paterno's coaching career.

Of all the games with Pitt over the decades, this one had the most bizarre ending. Games had been won or lost on the last play before but none had been tied when the game was over. Actually, there were six seconds left when Gancitano booted a 32-yard field goal that made the final score 24-24 but most of the players, the 60,283 spectators and TV viewers watching in Pittsburgh and Johnstown were convinced the game had ended a few minutes earlier. In fact, hundreds of Pitt fans had run onto the field in celebration of a 24-21 victory and some Pitt players had already headed for the dressing room when the officials signaled that time remained. The confusion occurred because of what happened three plays earlier, with 19 seconds left, and State at the Pitt 40-yard line. Before the snap of the ball, a State lineman had jumped offside and six seconds had run off the scoreboard clock. The Lions were penalized five yards but the officials were told the scoreboard clock could not be turned backwards, so the officials informed both coaches, Paterno and Fazio, but nobody else.

Pitt was on the verge of victory after coming from a 21-10 deficit early in the third quarter to score two touchdowns on passes from John Congemi to split end Bill Wallace. The second TD of 23 yards came at the end of a 74-yard drive with 1:15 left in the game. Strang had already thrown TD passes of 24 and 57 yards to Jackson, so a last minute rally was conceivable and after the kickoff he had led State from its own 31 to the Pitt 40 in four plays. Following the offside penalty, Strang passed to Dozier, who caught the ball off his shoetops after it had been tipped by one of Pitt's six defensive backs and he stepped out of bounds at the 19-yard line. Now, Paterno tried to fool Pitt with a reverse to Dozier but he was tackled after a 4-yard gain and immediately called time out. But the scoreboard clock showed: "00:00" and Pitt fans believed they had won.

When the officials were finally able to clear the field, Paterno sent out his field goal team but he had called a fake. State lined up in what Paterno called the "muddle huddle" formation, with eight players lined up on one hash mark and the snapper, holder and kicker on the other hash mark. It's designed to confuse the opponents and utilize a quick snap with the snapper, Mike Sullivan centering the ball to the holder, Strang, who would run into the end zone. But Pitt called timeout before the formation was set. When time resumed, Pitt safety Tom Flynn saw the "muddle huddle" and sent three players over to cover it. Now, Gancitano had to kick and he was successful. "I'm not overjoyed with the tie," Paterno told Dan Donovan of the *Pittsburgh Press*.

"That's the first time in my career, I went for the tie." Pitt players and coaches were upset, believing the victory had been taken away from them. "They say a tie is like kissing your sister," Fazio told sportswriters. "But I sure as hell don't want to kiss Joe after that one." Gattuso may have defined the entire season when he told Donovan, "You just don't know how to accept it. In a way it's disappointing...This game typifies our season. We were always falling a little short."

It was the first tie for Paterno since the 17-17 deadlock with Florida State in the 1967 Gator Bowl and this tie helped bring the Lions an invitation to the Aloha Bowl. "So we'll give (the players) a couple of days off so they can think about all those Aloha girls and beaches and then we'll go to work and have a good time," Paterno told sportswriters. "These guys deserve it."

THE 1983 ALOHA BOWL
Dec. 26, 1983
Penn State 13, Washington 10
Outstanding Player: George Reynolds

The enticement of Christmas in Hawaii already had made the Aloha Bowl a success after just one year. In its inaugural game, the bowl had pitted #9 Washington, runner-up to UCLA for the Pac-10 title and the Rose Bowl, against #16 Maryland. Washington had expected to get back into the Rose Bowl this season but had been upset by Washington State, 17-6, on the final Saturday of conference play while UCLA was defeating USC. So, Washington (8-3) returned to the Aloha to play Penn State.

Before flying to Honolulu on December 21, Paterno had worked the team hard but not necessarily preparing them for the Huskies. The Lions didn't dwell on watching films of Washington. The practices were geared to fundamentals and improving the skills of the younger players who would be returning next year. Jackson, Heller and other seniors were almost like assistant coaches during the workouts. But the workouts were strenuous. "It's not a rest period at all," Jackson told the *Collegian*. Paterno and Sandusky also made some changes in the defensive alignment, experimenting with different formations that varied around the traditional 4-3-3 or the 3-4-4. The team of 116 players flew out of Harrisburg with an alumni charter group and were given the traditional Hawaii welcome by hula dancers in grass skirts. That set the mood for everyone and Paterno eased the training rules. There was only one hard practice the entire time and no practice on a rainy Christmas day, one day before the game. Players had plenty of free time. After practice, they hit the beach at Waikiki. After dinner, they hit the bars. "It was definitely a vacation," Conlan told the *Collegian* later.

But it was a working vacation and Paterno and his staff had prepared the team well. Washington's offensive strength—passing—was State's defensive weakness and the Huskies were a big favorite. Washington had one of the nation's best passers in Steve Pelluer, the Offensive Player of the Year in the Pac-10. Pelluer had a completion ratio of 67 percent in throwing for 2,212 yards and 11 touchdowns as Washington averaged 400 yards and 25 points per game. But on this sunny day of 81 degree temperatures and high humidity (on a cold night back East), Pelluer couldn't cope with a revamped PSU pass defense. Pelluer's best pass was a 37-yarder in the last minute of the first half that set up a 36-yard field goal and gave Washington a 10-3 halftime lead. He completed just 19-of-40 passes for 153 yards for the day and Huskie runners didn't do much better, gaining 126 yards on 33 carries.

Washington's only TD came on a 57-yard punt return six minutes into the second quarter. The second half belonged to State. The Lion defense and George Reynolds' punting helped keep the Huskies under control and in the fourth quarter, the Lions scored twice on drives from midfield. Gancitano's 49-yard field goal narrowed the score to 10-6 early in the period. Then Strang went to work. On passes to Williams and Baugh and a 12-yard scramble, Strang led the Lions on a 51-yard scoring drive that climaxed with Dozier's 2-yard run off right tackle for the winning TD with three minutes left

Kenny Jackson was the first Penn State WR to be named First-Team All-American in 1982 and he repeated again in 1983. Jackson set 27 school records some of which still stand and has been an assistant PSU coach since '93.

Gancitano's PAT made it 13-10 and that's how it finished. State's offense gained just 118 yards through the air and 95 on the ground but had once again came through in the clutch. Masciantonio and Radecic had led the defense with 14 tackles apiece and each had a deflected pass but the Outstanding Defensive Player Award went to Reynolds, who had a 46.8-yard average in eight punts, including one for 62 yards into the wind and another downed at the Washington 6-yard line. "It hasn't been a great year for us defensively," Sandusky told sportswriters, "so we kind of deserved this one today."

During the game, Paterno had used many true and "redshirt" freshmen on both offense and defense—Johnson, Graham, White, Conlan, Tim Manoa, Chris Conlin, Dan Morgan and Brian Silverling, to name a few. He was already thinking of '84 even before '83 had ended. "You either get better or worse," right? Paterno expected his team to get better in '84. It didn't.

Season Record 8-4-1
Record to Date 587-260-41
Winning percentage .684

"'A Bunch of Babies'"

"We had a bunch of babies playing out there today," an angry Joe Paterno railed over the Penn State radio network as he stormed off the Beaver Stadium playing field after seeing himself and his team embarrassed by Pitt, 31-11, in the final game of the season.

Lion fans were aghast. They had never heard Paterno denounce his team so brutally in public before. Over 19 years, the Lion head coach had occasionally teed off on his players but never with such venom as this. And he didn't cool off when he reached the media room minutes later to talk to sportswriters. "We stunk," he said. "We don't have any men and that's not taking anything away from Pitt. They manhandled us and just humiliated us...We've got some kids who don't understand what tough football is all about."

As he thought about it more, he also blamed himself, saying "There's something not right and that's where I have to look at this whole thing." But Paterno's tirade had already triggered a reaction among his players. Some were offended by his attack on their manhood. Some simply passed it off as a temporary aberration by their often emotional coach . Others agreed that something was wrong but they weren't sure what. "There's not a quitter on this team," co-captain Nick Haden told sportswriters. "But we should have been more emotional than we were."

It wasn't just the way his players lost to a 2-7 Pitt team by itself that had elicited Paterno's diatribe. One week earlier there had been a similar result on the field at South Bend when a 5-4 Notre Dame team had drubbed the Lions 44-7. What had appeared to be another successful season with two major upsets and a 15th straight bowl appearance suddenly had been whisked away. The 6-5 record was the worst since Paterno's first year and it is not a season he likes to remember even today. "Please don't press me to name names or give details," he wrote in his book, *"Paterno: By The Book."* "We disbanded for a not-too-merry Christmas..." Paterno's outburst was the defining moment of the season because no matter what happened in the previous three months, the ultimate outcome was determined on that afternoon, two days after Thanksgiving.

But the signs had been there all along. It started as far back as spring practice when the annual Blue-White game had to be shortened by seven minutes because of thunder storms which had sent the 23,000 spectators and the players scurrying for cover. Near the start of preseason practice, Paterno had told the media, "Right now, this is the lousiest football team we ever had. They better go at it...it's a tough schedule." The schedule included eight teams that had played in bowl games in '83, including the first ever regular season game with Texas, which had just missed winning the national title. Paterno had 31 lettermen returning including more than a half dozen starters on both offense and defense but it was a young team and Paterno said it needed leadership.

Paterno was counting on Strang, one of the co-captains, to provide some of that leadership at quarterback. Strang had been second in the country in '83 with 19 touchdowns and had just seven interceptions but Paterno was concerned about his inconsistency and the lack of proven wide receivers. "I hope there will be a couple of guys come in here and be big league wideouts," he said. Eventually, redshirt freshman Herb Bellamy, sophomore Eric Hamilton and senior Rocky Washington, out all of '83 with a knee injury, would be the team's best wideouts but none would match the departed two-time All-American Jackson nor last year's team receiving leader Baugh. Strang and his two backups, Shaffer and redshirt freshman Matt Knizner, also would pass more to the backs, including starting tailback Dozier and the two sophomore fullbacks, Steve Smith and Manoa, who was shifted from defensive end. The offensive line would include Dimidio at tight end, Haden at center, co-captain Short pairing at tackle with Conlin and senior Steve Woofter and underclassmen Mark Sickler and Mitch Frerotte at guards. There was one other change on offense. Anderson had taken the head coaching job at Rutgers and running backs coach Ganter had been promoted to offensive coordinator.

Paterno and Sandusky liked the potential of the young defense and they had worked since the spring to improve the pass rush. The starters were mostly veterans although some had switched positions. The heart of the defense were the linebackers with Masciantonio, Conlan and Graham starting and Alexander and newcomers Trey Bauer, Chris Collins and Bob Ontko in reserve. Zordich was switched to the "Hero" slot with Syndor and Lance Hamilton at the corners and Giles at safety. White teamed with junior Don Ginnetti at end with Moules, back from offensive guard, paired with sophomore Mike Russo at tackle. Among others who would see action on defense were Morgan, Tim Johnson (after recovering from an injury at midseason) and freshman Peter Curkendall of Elmira, NY, in the line and freshmen Duffy Cobbs, a walk-on from Alexandria, VA, and Ray Isom of Harrisburg in the backfield. Gancitano was back again to do the placekicking along with Manca, who sat out '83 as a redshirt, and walk-on sophomore John Bruno of Upper St. Clair was the punter. Major rule changes affected the defense and placekickers. Pass interference was now a standard 15-yard penalty and kickoffs out of the end zone would give the receiving team the ball on the 30-yard line instead of the 20.

Paterno had been pleased with the team's progress in preseason workouts. "I think this team has the potential to be really good," he told sportswriters as the season opener with Rutgers approached. "We are going to have some difficulties until we gain experience." Once again the schedule was among the most difficult in the country with four opponents picked in the preseason AP Top 10: Pitt #3, Texas #6, Notre Dame #8 and Alabama #9. The Lions were selected at #11 with Iowa at #12 and Boston College at #19. Paterno was also wary of Maryland and West Virginia, two teams that had not beaten State in years. For the first time, most of the games would be televised live either by the networks or through special arrangements made by Total Communications System (TCS) which had handled State's delayed TV broadcasts for 11 years. The new TV set up resulted from a decision by the U.S. Supreme Court which ruled against the NCAA's control of TV games and freed schools to make their own deals. As a result, permanent lights were installed at Beaver Stadium in early fall.

It was a bit ironic that the September 8 opener was with Rutgers since Anderson was making his head coaching debut and he knew the Lions well. Several of his assistants also were former PSU players, including All-American linebacker Ed O'Neil and former captains Otto Kneidinger and Warren Koegel. The 84,409 seemed less interested in the Rutgers coaches than they were in doing the "Hawaiian Wave" for the first time in Beaver Stadium. On Rutgers first possession after the kickoff, Anderson gambled with a fourth-and-

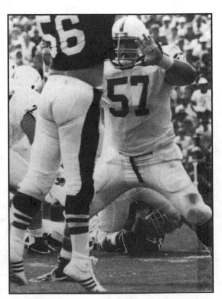

Three-year starter Chris Conlin was First-Team All-American OT in 1986. His brothers Keith and Kevin followed him to Penn State.

one at the PSU 45. Moules stopped the run for a no gain and four plays later Dozier dashed 43 yards for a TD and the Lions seemed on their way to a big victory before a short-sleeves crowd of 84,409. A 20-yard Gancitano field goal made it 10-0 at the end of the first quarter but by halftime Rusty Hochberg had led the Scarlet Knights to a 10-10 tie. The second half turned into a defensive battle as the Lions gave up just four rushing yards and caused Hochberg to misfire on 9-of-14 pass attempts. The Rutgers defense stopped the Lions on a fourth-and-2 at the PSU 4 late in the third quarter, but moments later Morgan sacked Hochberg in the end zone for a safety. Gancitano added a 36-yard field goal in the fourth quarter and State's punter Bruno took an intentional safety with seven seconds left in the game to make the final score, 15-12. Paterno's earlier concern about his passing had been valid. Strang completed just 7-of-20 attempts for a paltry 50 yards and two interceptions. "Dick Anderson knew exactly what we were going to do," Strang told Greg Loder of the **Daily Collegian**. Anderson seemed to agree in his post-game remarks. "I thought Penn State played the game the way I thought they would," he said. "But we lost the game and I'm not happy."

The Lions were a six-point underdog at #5 Iowa the following week but an aggressive hard-hitting defense led by Conlan, second-team safety Isom and Cobbs sparked the Lions to an exciting 20-17 upset. A Strang interception had given Iowa a 3-0 first quarter lead when Conlan blitzed, stripped the ball from All-Big Ten QB Chuck Long and recovered at the Iowa 4. State's offense had to settle for a Gancitano 21-yard field goal but five minutes later Conlan hit Owen Gill as he was about to catch a pass from Long and Ontko made a diving interception at the 50. Again, State had to settle for a field goal. But late in the half the Lion offense, which was playing without an injured Dozier, finally broke out of its slumber and went on a 13-play, 82-yard drive capped by Strang's 24-yard TD pass to Bellamy with 47 seconds remaining. But the kickoff team then fell asleep. Ronnie Harmon returned the kick 50 yards and with four seconds left from the 15-yard line Harmon fooled the defense, which was expecting a pass, and ran a sprint draw for a TD. Suddenly the halftime score was 13-10. Another Strang interception thwarted a Lion scoring opportunity after the second half kick-off but early in the fourth quarter Strang scored from the one after a 61-yard drive. Iowa came back after the kickoff with a 12-play, 80-yard march for a TD that made the score 20-17 with 10 minutes left but the Lion defense took control the rest of the way. First Cobbs forced a fumble on a punt return that allowed the offense to run more time off the clock. But Iowa was on the march again late in the quarter and had a fourth-and-one at the PSU 29 with less than two minutes remaining. Harmon took a pitchout left but was met by a swarm of tacklers including Isom, Cobbs, Zordich and Syndor. State ran out the clock and won. Isom led the team with nine tackles and his hard hits on Iowa receivers caused several incompletions, leading him to be named the Defensive Player of the Game. "...This Penn State defense played the game in much the same manner as many of its more storied predecessors," wrote Ron Bracken in the **Centre Daily Times**. "It flew to the football, punished ball-carriers, mugged receivers... the defense played well but could have done better." Paterno said "We still made a lot of mistakes and we still have a lot of work to do to be a good football team."

The victory moved the Lions up to #9 in the polls and they went up to #5 after walloping undermanned William & Mary, 56-18, the following week at sunny Beaver Stadium. Paterno used 75 players and seven scored touchdowns, including two apiece by backups Knizner and sophomore tailback Dave Clark, who ran 80 yards in the second

quarter for one of his. State's clash with #2 Texas at Giants Stadium in the Meadowlands now had national championship implications, even so early in the season. Ten thousand noisy Texans and many more cheering PSU fans were among the 76,883 spectators and an ESPN audience who watched the Lions kick off shortly after noon and stop the Longhorns first drive with an interception by Syndor at the PSU 15-yard line. On State's first offensive play, Strang had Bellamy wide open behind the Texas secondary but the ball skidded of Bellamy's finger-tips. The failed pass would be an omen, for Strang would complete just 9-of-26 passes as he overthrew and underthrew and receivers dropped balls all afternoon. On their next possession, the Longhorns caught State in a blitz and fullback Terry Orr ran up the middle for a 51-yard touchdown. But Isom's interception at the Texas 22 set up a 35-yard Gancitano field goal that made the score 7-3 at the end of the first quarter. The outcome of the game was actually determined in the next 15 minutes. On Texas' first possession of the second quarter, the Lions blitzed again on a third-and-9 at the Texas 16 and Todd Dodge threw a perfect pass to tight end William Harris who went all the way for a TD. State forced two fumbles later in the quarter but couldn't capitalize and Texas led 14-3 at the half. Lion fumbles in the second half put the game on ice for Texas. A fumbled punt by freshman Kevin Woods at the PSU 11 led to another Texas TD in the third quarter, Dozier's fumble stopped a State drive at the Texas 35 a few minutes later, then Strang's fumble at the PSU 14 set up the Longhorns' final score and they won, 28-3. Paterno felt his defense had played well, intercepting two passes and recovering two fumbles, but he also praised the Texas defense, which held Lion rushers to 82 net yards on 40 attempts and had more than a half dozen sacks on State's three quarterbacks. "Maybe we have too much (offense)," Paterno said after the game. "We've got to get back to some basic things we can do well and execute." That same afternoon, Syracuse upset #1 Nebraska, 17-9, in the Carrier Dome and Texas went atop the polls as the Lions slipped to #11.

The following week, Strang pulled himself together against Maryland (2-2) but the Lions blew a 25-11 lead early in the fourth quarter and almost lost to the Terps on the last play of the game. When Strang threw an interception at the PSU 29-yard line on his first pass early in the first quarter and Jess Atkinson kicked a 31-yard field goal, a smattering of boos were heard among the 84,486 at Beaver Stadium. But later in the quarter, Strang hit Washington on a 30-yard TD, scored another TD himself in the second quarter on a one-yard run, then listened to the cheers after a 27-yard TD pass to Mumford following a Syndor interception had given the Lions the 25-11 lead a minute into the final period. But five minutes later, the Terps junior quarterback Stan Gelbaugh—playing only because starter Frank Reich had been sidelined with an injury—caught the Lion secondary by surprise with a 45-yard TD pass, narrowing the score to 25-18. With Dozier injured again, the Lion offense sputtered with conservative play-calling by Paterno and State failed to pick up a first down the rest of the game. That continued to give the Maryland offense life and after taking over at their own 43 following a punt, the Terps drove for a TD on Alvin Blount's 18-yard fullback draw with less than two minutes left. With the score now 25-24, Gelbaugh tried to pass for the 2-point conversion that could win the game but he failed to see a wide open receiver over the middle and overthrew Greg Hill in the corner of the end zone. Steve Smith recovered the onside kick at the PSU 46 and the game seemed over with 1:52 remaining. But State's offense couldn't pick up a first down and Maryland used its last three timeouts to force a fourth down punt. Bruno shanked it to the Terp 46-yard line. Now Gelbaugh was hot. He completed three of five short passes and with eight seconds remaining he crossed up the defense which was protecting the sidelines and hit Sean Sullivan slanting across the middle. Sullivan bobbed the ball but pulled it in for a 20-yard gain and a first down at the PSU 35. Maryland coach Ross had told Gelbaugh earlier that if such a situation occurred, to line up the team quickly and throw the ball out of bounds to stop the clock so they could get Atkinson into the game. But someone on the

Lance Hamilton followed his brother to State as DB and, like his brother, was also a two-time Academic All-American in '84 and '85.

Maryland sideline had yelled for a field goal and the Maryland players scrambled in and out of the formation. Back up QB Dan Henning, who holds for snaps, ran under center and threw the ball out of bounds. But Maryland was penalized for illegal motion and before Maryland could line up again the game was over. Ross did not know who screwed up his plan, but he took the blame, telling the media, "When that happens, the ultimate person responsible is myself." Paterno blamed himself for making the game close. "We sat on some things," he told sportswriters. "When we got into the fourth quarter, I thought we had it."

Alabama had lost 7 of 11 games since its defeat at Beaver Stadium in '83 and Perkins was under heavy pressure. His team was 1-4 and had looked terrible, giving up 17 turnovers and drawing many penalties. But Perkins fired up his players for Penn State with a pep talk from Joe Namath, who was the quarterback and a Perkins teammate on Alabama's 1964 National Champions. He also moved the original game site from Birmingham to Bryant-Denny Stadium in Tuscaloosa to jack up everyone's emotions. With temperatures reaching into the high 80s on a humid afternoon, the Lions seemed listless from the start and they wilted as the game went on. It was another battle of inept offenses and strong defenses. The Lions were in Alabama territory just twice and their only scoring opportunity went awry when a 42-yard Gancitano field goal attempt bounced off the left upright in the first half. When Gancitano complained to the referee that the upright was bent inward, he said the Lion kicker should have protested before the kickoff. (Of course, it was the Alabama version of "the end zone curse.") Less than two minutes into the fourth quarter, the Tide's Van Tiffin broke a school record with a 53-yard field goal, then hit another one from 23 yards six minutes later and Alabama won, 6-0, as the players carried Perkins off the field. Strang had been ineffective with 6-of-18 passes and one interception when he left the game with a shoulder injury in the fourth quarter after being hit by Jon Hand. Shaffer was no better and threw an interception and was sacked once in completing 2-of-4 short passes. "Both defenses played well," Paterno told sportswriters. "Our offense was very spotty...It was a classic shutout." It was the first time the Lions had been scoreless in 190 regular season games, dating to 1966. "You get shut out when you punt eight times, have receivers drop passes, run for just 159 yards and never

get inside Alabama's 20-yard line," wrote Jim Carlson for the **Centre Daily Times**.

Strang's injury was bad enough for Shaffer to start against Syracuse (3-3) in the Homecoming game the next week. Dozier also was healthy and Paterno simplified the offense. With a sellout crowd that included all-time defensive great Mike Reid, who was honored at halftime, the Lions were crisp in the first half and turned a 21-0 halftime lead into a 21-3 victory. Shaffer hit on 10-of-23 passes for 140 yards and Dozier had his best day since '83, running for 159 yards on 22 carries, including a 58-yard TD in the first quarter. State's defense held the Orange to 130 yards passing and 68 on the ground while intercepting four passes, two by Zordich. "We're turning the defense around to be an intimidating Penn State defense," Zordich told the media after the game.

As the Lions prepared for #14 West Virginia, **USA Today** published a list of the "Toughest schedules of the last five years" based on opponents' won-lost records from 1980-84 and State topped the list with a record 40-11-1, followed by Florida State and Temple. Boston college, Pitt and Syracuse also were in the top 10 with Notre Dame, Maryland, Alabama and West Virginia in the second 10. "You get better playing good people," Paterno was quoted as saying.

The best way to describe what happened the following Saturday evening in Morgantown is to refer to Black's lead in the **"Football Letter."** "All hell broke loose in Almost Heaven Saturday night," he wrote. For the first time since 1954, West Virginia beat State as an ESPN audience watched and some 64,879 victory-starved Mountaineer crazies went wild. Ten bowl scouts were on hand for what was the first night game ever in Mountaineer Stadium and most of them were there to see WVU, which was 6-1 and had just upset undefeated Boston College. State did not go down easily. The game was tied 7-7 at the half but shortly after kicking a 49-yard field goal at the start of the fourth quarter, the Mountaineers recovered a fumble by Shaffer at the PSU 39-yard line and scored three plays later for a 17-7 lead. Shaffer engineered an 83-yard drive after the kickoff to make it 17-14 and seemed to be bringing the Lions back on a winning drive when Larry Holley intercepted at the WVU 18-yard line with 35 seconds remaining. As the Mountaineer fans poured onto the field and began tearing down the goal posts, Paterno sent his team to the dressing room and sprinted across the field to congratulate WVU coach Nehlen. "The fans waited a long time for this," Paterno told the media in an equipment truck where he went to avoid the crowd outside the dressing room. "It's tough to bridle that kind of enthusiasm...Let (the fans) enjoy it." Then, he went to the WVU locker room to personally congratulate the Mountaineer players and coaches.

State was the underdog again November 3 when Heisman Trophy front runner Doug Flutie led #9 Boston College into Beaver Stadium. Flutie didn't disappoint the ABC regional television audience nor the 10

LB Carmen Masciantonio was an Academic All-American with a 3.54 average in Chemical Engineering and a winner of the National Football Foundation and College Football Hall of Fame Scholarship in 1984.

bowl scouts with his performance as he passed for 447 yards and one touchdown on 29-of-53 completions. Nor did Flutie disappoint State's largest home crowd of the season, 85,690, because the Lions won, 37-30, and never trailed after taking a 10-7 lead four minutes into the second quarter. Shaffer started again but suffered a mild concussion in the first quarter and Strang engineered the Lion upset behind a revitalized running game and an alert defense. Strang's running, not his passing, was the key to the game as he scrambled 11 times in picking up 52 yards, usually at crucial times. His 6-yard run for a first down with 1:34 left with BC rallying clinched the victory. Smith had his finest rushing day ever with 126 yards and two touchdowns on 23 carries and Dozier ran for 143 yards on 21 carries including a 39-yard TD that put State ahead, 37-23 midway in the fourth quarter. The defense intercepted two Flutie passes, turning one by Johnson into a 24-yard Gancitano field goal in the first quarter, recovered three fumbles, had a couple of sacks and forced receivers to drop passes with several jarring tackles. "I thought the defense did a super job," Paterno said. "There were a couple of throws I just couldn't believe Flutie made." Ian Thomsen in the *Boston Globe* summed it up with this lead: "It was all you ever read about. Control the ball with the running game. Avoid the key turnovers that stop drives. Stay healthy. Bend, don't break."

Now the Lions had two weeks to prepare for Notre Dame and on the Saturday they were idle, Rutgers shocked the East with a 23-19 upset over West Virginia. Meanwhile, the bowl talk began. The Fiesta and Gator Bowls expressed a strong interest in State as did the Holiday, Liberty and the new Freedom Bowl set for Anaheim, CA, on December 26. Perhaps the players were deceived by Notre Dame's 5-4 record but at his weekly meeting with the media three days before the game, Paterno had said, "At this stage, with their momentum and their injuries healed, Notre Dame will be the toughest team we've played all year." Of course, few fans believed him so maybe the players didn't either. The Irish broke a 7-7 first quarter tie with 24 points in the second quarter and cruised to its 44-7 win. Notre Dame ripped State's defense for 276 yards on the ground as Pinkett scored four TDs again, including one on a 66-yard run in the second quarter and Steve Beuerlein passed for 267 yards on 20-of-29 passes. "The score is not indicative of how they dominated us," Paterno told the media. While Paterno was talking, he had to stop because of all the noise from the celebrating Irish fans outside the media interview room. "I hope that's the Notre Dame band and not the Penn State alumni," he said.

At his midweek news conference before the Pitt game, Paterno said, "I hope we have enough people who have enough pride that they will rebound after a licking such as that." He was wrong again. A 92-yard drive in the first quarter gave the Panthers a 7-3 lead and before halftime they had driven 65 and 75 yards for two more TDs and had kicked a 39-yard field goal after an interception at the PSU 29 yards line to make the score 24-3. Another 65-yard drive late in the fourth quarter ended the Lions misery as Pitt controlled the ball for almost 36 minutes while netting 420 yards. Paterno's tirade followed but the fans were also upset. "After the game," wrote Ron Leonard in the *Daily Collegian*, "(the players) were forced to hear people underneath Beaver Stadium's south end zone calling the Lions 'chickens' as they made their way to the busses outside the stadium."

Despite the 6-5 record, three bowls still wanted State and one was particularly intriguing. BYU was now the #1 team in the nation but as the Western Athletic Conference champ it was committed to the Holiday Bowl, being played in Provo, UT. State was asked to be BYU's opponent and declined and Michigan eventually went and lost. The Freedom Bowl still wanted to match the Lions against Iowa and the new Cherry Bowl was seeking a pairing with Michigan State. But State declined again, saying it had already beaten Iowa and was not interested in the other bowl because of exams.

So, Paterno once again turned inward. As he had done after '66, '76, '79 and '83, he said "it is time to regroup, reevaluate and consider new approaches. We're down but we're not going to stay down. I'm determined we shall go on to greater things." He wasn't wrong this time.

Season Record 6-5
Record to Date 593-265-41
Winning percentage .682

"The Cardiac Kids"

The temperature was already 96 degrees with the humidity at 74 percent and the opening game of the season had just started. Mike Zordich could not believe how hot he was as he waited for Maryland's second play from scrimmage in sweltering Byrd Stadium. This was Maryland's year, everyone was saying. Picked #1 by *Sport Magazine*, #5 by *Sports Illustrated*, #7 by the AP and a definite contender for the national title with a veteran team led by quarterback Stan Gelbaugh.

Well, State was a veteran team, too. Nineteen of the first 22 players back on defense and 15 of the top 22 back on offense, right? But no one could forget how shameful last season had ended, least of all the media and the Lion fans. Maybe a Top 20 team, maybe not, they said. They have some talent, the sportswriters wrote, but where are their heads? Maybe Paterno has lost his touch, some speculated. Those critical letters Paterno had read to the team in the spring made that point, too. But no one outside the team and its coaches really knew.

Paterno had first talked to them in the winter. He had made it clear to everyone that things were going to be different in '85. Everyone would have to prove themselves again. "I was too soft on you," he had told them. He outlined his plan for a harsh schedule of weight-training off season, winter conditioning and punishing spring and fall practices ahead. "If you don't want to do it, fine," he said, as Malcolm Moran later reported in the *New York Times*. You're out. "But if you say you want to be part of this Penn State football team this year, this is the kind of commitment we're going to make..." Only two players quit and now Zordich and his fellow co-captains Alexander and Moules and the rest of their teammates were about to find out if all the sacrifice and hard work would pay off as Paterno had promised.

Defense would again be the quintessence of this team but Paterno, Sandusky and the new defensive backfield coach, Ron Dickerson, tinkered a bit with the 4-4-3 defense and they needed to be sure they had the right players in the right positions, so they reevaluated all the personnel. The backups would be just as vital to the team's success as the starters and many of them would play as much if not more than others as the season progressed. The new alignment was more like a 4-1-4-2 set up with a defensive tackle over the center and an outside linebacker actually playing at left defensive end. The hero position was now a strong safety playing on the back line across from the free safety. Zordich and sophomore Barry Buchman were the "heroes" with a set of linebackers that included Alexander, Conlan, Graham, Bauer, Ontko, junior Chris Collins and sophomore Pete Giftopoulos of Hamilton, Ontario. Graham or sometimes Conlan usually would line up at the left defensive end slot with White on the right and Curkendall, sophomore Greg Johns and Mike Uhlar in reserve. The tackles were Russo (over center), Tim Johnson, Ginnetti, Matt Johnson and sophomore Aoatoa Polamalu. Isom, Cobbs and Lance Hamilton were in the secondary again with sophomores Marques Henderson and Dwayne Downing and freshman Eddie Johnson among the reserves.

The offense was more difficult to reconstruct. Dozier had missed spring practice because of arthroscopic knee surgery and no one knew what effect this would have on him until the season started. His backups, Clark and sophomore Kevin Woods, were good but not in Dozier's class. At least Smith and Manoa gave the Lions versatility at fullback. As for quarterback, Shaffer and Knizner battled through the spring and preseason until Paterno named Shaffer the starter for Maryland. Dimidio returned at tight end with Siverling and senior Bob Williams in reserve. Bellamy was academically ineligible at wide receiver but there was new blood in freshman Michael Timpson of Hialeah, FL, and junior college transfer Mike Alexander. They were challenging Eric Hamilton, Giles (who switched over from defense), sophomore Ray Roundtree of Aiken, SC and sophomore walk-on Jim Coates, who also ran back punts and kickoffs along with Timpson and freshman Blair Thomas of Philadelphia. In the rebuilt offensive line, seniors Rob Smith and Keith Radecic (Scott's brother) shared the center slot with Sickler and Conlin starting at tackle backed by Morgan and junior Stan Clayton. Moules was at long guard and Frerotte at short guard with freshman Steve Wisniewski of Spring, TX, and redshirt junior Rich Kuzy in reserve. Bruno was again the punter and Manca took over all the placekicking for the graduated Gancitano. Sophomore Greg Truitt was the designated snapper with Knizner the holder. A few days before the opener with Maryland, Paterno was still concerned with his offense. "I'm still concerned about getting overpowered across the front on pass protection," he told Mike Poorman of *Blue-White Illustrated*. "(And) I still wonder whether we can have a big-league system passing game...we have not caught the ball consistently."

Maryland had not lost since its one-point defeat at Beaver Stadium and had a seven-game winning streak that included a Sun Bowl victory over Tennessee. The Terps also had lost 20 straight to the Lions and many sportswriters saw this as "the day of atonement." The game had been hyped for weeks and more than 400 media credentials were issued by Maryland, the most since 1957 when the just-coronated Queen of England attended a game against North Carolina. But the Queen didn't have to sit

Because of his versatility, Todd Moules switched back and forth from offense to defense every year he played. He was a third-Team All-American as an offensive guard in 1985 while serving as co-captain.

through such heat. Even before the 1:30 kickoff several tailgaters were treated for heat exhaustion and before the day was over more than 350 persons visited the first aid station. Two fire hydrants near the stadium were turned on in the afternoon so spectators could seek relief and throughout the second half the public address announcer kept advising the fans to seek assistance if they weren't feeling well. On the sidelines, the players had electric cooling fans and liquid to help them get relief as temperatures reached 105 degrees but during the game several of them threw up, including Bauer near the 50-yard line. Eventually, Paterno would use 61 players, substituting throughout the game to give everyone some rest. So as the sweltering sellout crowd of 50,750 and a syndicated national television audience watched, State won the toss and surprisingly elected to kick off. Let's go with our strength, Paterno had reasoned. Sandusky warned his defense that it had to prevent Maryland from jumping off to an early lead because the potent Terp offense could "grind out and keep the ball."

Maryland ran the kickoff up past the 25 and there was nothing unusual about the conservative first down running play intended to feel out the defense and settle all the players down. But on second down, Gelbaugh took a quick drop and tried to hit his wide receiver Azizuddin Abur-Ra'oof on a quick screen pass into the right flat. From his roving "hero" slot, Zordich sensed what has happening even before Gelbaugh released the ball, and he leaped in front of Abur-Ra'oof to intercept the pass, losing his right shoe in the process, and ran unmolested into the end zone. Everyone in the stadium was shocked. Manca booted the PAT as the 5,000 PSU fans cheered noisily. There were still 59 minutes and 10 seconds left in the game and 659 minutes in the season but the stunning interception by Zordich not only set the tone for the day but would define the season. Before the year was over, the Lions would again be the #1 team in the country and play for the National Championship in the 1986 Orange Bowl. They would go undefeated in the regular season and win most of their 11 games with alert and critical defensive plays, many in the fourth quarter. If any PSU team deserved the now overused sports nickname of "The Cardiac Kids," this was the bunch. And it started that hot afternoon in College Park.

Later in the first quarter, the Terps launched a drive and seemed to be headed for the tying score. But Giftopoulos picked off another Gelbaugh pass at the Lion 47 and eight plays later Manca booted a 28-yard field goal. On the last play of the quarter, State had the ball at the 20 following a punt when Shaffer avoided a rushing lineman and hit Timpson with a perfect 50-yard bomb down the left sideline. Three minutes later, reserve tight end Williams caught the first pass of his career for a 2-yard TD and State led 17-0. Bobby Ross chewed out his team on the sideline. "We were hanging our heads...I got after them," he later told Michael Wilbon of the *Washington Post*. The Terps drove 66 yards for a 22-yard field goal with five minutes left in the half, then got the break that put them back into the game. Thomas fumbled the ensuing kickoff at the State 32-yard line and with fullback Rick Badanjek getting most of the yardage including an 8-yard TD, Maryland closed to 17-10 at halftime. Early in the third quarter, Shaffer threw his second interception of the day at the State 28-yard line and five plays later Badanjek had a 5-yard TD. Then the Terps faked the PAT kick as holder Henning passed to tight end Chris Knight for two points and suddenly Maryland was in the lead for the first time, 18-17. But not for long as the Lions took back the lead 90 seconds later, 20-18, on a 45-yard field goal by Manca. Now, few people watch-

In perhaps the biggest play of the 1985 season against then #1 Marylan in the season opener, All-American Michael Zordich intercepts a pass on the second play of the game and runs in for a TD that helps spark a 20-18 upset that puts Lions on track towards the national title game in the Orange Bowl.

ing the game expected the scoring to end there. Twice in the fourth quarter, Maryland's Ramon Paredes missed field goal attempts from 34 and 51 yards and the Terps had one last chance to win when State couldn't convert a first down with 1:24 left and had to punt. The Terps were 76 yards away but Gelbaugh struck quickly when Abur-Ra'oof caught a pass tipped by Alexander for a 39-yard gain to the PSU 37 with a minute remaining. Ten more yards and a field goal could win it. Two passes were incomplete, one dropped at the 10. Then on third down and 39 seconds left, Gelbaugh passed to tailback Alvin Blount at the 30 and as Blount ran upfield to about the 24-yard line, Lance Hamilton stripped away the ball and recovered the fumble. The game was over. Maryland had controlled the ball for 36 minutes and run off 83 plays for a net 342 yards to State's 59 plays and 249 yards but the Lion defense had won it. "We felt we needed this game to re-establish ourselves as a defense," Zordich told sportswriters, "and we went out and did it." The victory shot the Lions from #18 to #11 in the AP poll and to #9 in the UPI rankings and commentator Beano Cook of ABC Sports made a prediction everyone ridiculed. He said State would play for the National Championship in the Orange Bowl against Oklahoma, the AP and consensus preseason #1.

A week later State's special kicking teams now coached by "Scrap Iron" Tom Bradley of the late '70s squads made the difference in the fourth quarter of the Beaver Stadium opener against Temple before 84,651. State's offense sputtered after giving the Lions a 24-10 halftime lead and Temple turned a Shaffer fumble at midfield into a 29-yard TD by Paul Palmer late in the third quarter to make it a 7-point game. Midway into the final period Dwayne Downing tore the ball away from the Temple punt receiver and Henderson recovered at the Owl 26. Manca, who minutes earlier had shanked a 30-yard field goal attempt after the recovery of another fumbled Owl punt, hit on this one from 43 yards and State led, 27-17. But Temple made it even closer three minutes later with a 72-yard drive behind the running of Palmer. Palmer, who gained 206 yards for the day, rushed for 68 yards in this march, including a 10-yard TD. A pass for two points made it 27-25 with about four minutes left and Owl coach Bruce Arians figured his defense could get the ball back. But Thomas ran the kickoff back 58 yards and the Lions were on the Owl 6-yard line when time ran out. In the media room near the new Beaver Stadium dressing rooms under-

neath the South End Zone seating area, Paterno said the team "missed too many scoring chances that could have blown the game open...We were lucky." Part of the second half offensive problems may have been caused by the loss of Dozier. He had gained 81 yards on 13 carries before going out early in the third quarter with a pulled hamstring and his running (along with Smith's 96 yards) had helped generate 265 yards in rushing against Temple compared to just 67 yards in the Maryland game.

Dozier's injury would keep him out of the next two games against East Carolina and Rutgers and without him in the lineup the Nittany offense was different. But it would be the defense, again, that would spur the victories, which were ironically by the identical 17-0 score. East Carolina also was unbeaten at 2-0 and a dangerous team with a reputation for upsets over major powers. The Pirates were on the schedule because Minnesota had backed out of a tentative two-game contract and ECU was willing to fill in for a lucrative Beaver Stadium pay day. Dozier wasn't the only Lion who missed the game. White, Russo and Frerotte also were sidelined and a half dozen other starters were ailing and saw limited action. The Lions were now #9 in the AP poll but they were in constant jeopardy again in the second half after taking a 14-3 lead at the intermission. East Carolina drove 64 yards for a touchdown midway through the third quarter and minutes later started on an 82-yard drive for what appeared to be the go ahead score. But a jarring tackle by Conlan on Tony Baker at the PSU 9-yard line caused a fumble that Ginnetti recovered to end the threat. On the Pirates' next possession, Graham belted option quarterback Ron Jones, forcing another fumble that Graham recovered. State made it 17-10 with less than four minutes left in the game on a 38-yard Manca field goal after a 7-play, 40-yard drive but the Pirates continued the pressure. Starting on their own 19 with less than four minutes left, they marched methodically downfield to the PSU 34 in 16 plays, picking up extra yardage on two pass interference and two offside penalties. Jones had one final play to try and tie or win the game but his last pass was overthrown and the Lions had the victory. "There's got to be an easier way to make a living," Paterno said in the media room. Then he praised his team, saying: "I think this club has a lot of things about it that's going to make it tough to beat it. There are a lot of kids on this team that, if you were going to war, you'd want to have right next to you."

Two long runs helped the #9 Lions beat Rutgers before 54,360 in Giants Stadium at the New Jersey Meadowlands the day after Hurricane Gloria hit the East Coast. But it was the kicking team and "bend-but-don't-break" defense that again had to preserve the win. Clark finally broke out of Dozier's shadow when he went up the middle for 76 yards to set up a 4-yard TD by Kevin Woods that gave the Lions a 7-0 lead early in the second quarter. But after stopping one scoring threat in the first quarter with a Cobbs interception, the Lion defense needed a goal line stand near the end of the half to keep Rutgers out of the end zone after a 75-yard drive and the Scarlet Knights settled for a 22-yard field goal. That's where it stood until a 24-yard punt return by Timpson to the Rutgers 40 late in the third quarter. State let the time run out in the quarter to get the wind and two plays later Manca kicked a 53-yard field goal, the longest of his career. The defense continued to shut down the Knights and with about five minutes left in the game, State took the ball at its own 24. Knizner was now the quarterback and after picking up a first down on a rollout for four yards, he gave the ball to Smith, who blasted off tackle, found an opening and ran 63 yards for a touchdown. Coach Anderson's familiarity with State's prevent defense enabled his team to go 77 yards in two minutes to make the score 17-10 but the Lions recovered the onside kick and the game was over. "I'm glad we got out of here with a win," Paterno told the media. "We haven't really improved since the week before Maryland."

The Lions were now 4-0—an "ugly 4-0," some said—and their close victories over three lightly regarded opponents spawned a legion of doubters. They need a better offense, some sportswriters wrote and many fans agreed. Alabama would be the test, everyone said. The Lions had two weeks to prepare for the Tide's visit to Beaver Stadium and by then they had moved up to #8 in the AP poll (#6 in UPI) and unbeaten Alabama was #10. The kickoff was set for late afternoon to accommodate ABC's national television audience and advertisers must have been happy for the game went down to the last minute but this time it was both the Lion defense and offense that won it—with help from some daring play calling by Paterno. Although there were no turnovers in the game and each offense kept the ball about half the time, State's defense held Alabama rushers to 90 yards on 34 carries, far under the Tide's 250 yard average. Alabama quarterback Mike Shula passed for 211 yards and two touchdowns but he was sacked five times and a third of his yardage came in the last minute against the Lion's "prevent" defense. Meanwhile, the Tide's equally aggressive defense led by All-American linebacker Cornelius Bennett was keeping State out of the end zone and three Manca field goals of 38, 44 and 50 yards had given State a 9-7 lead late in the third quarter. When Alabama's defense stopped the Lion offense again on three downs inside the 5-yard line to force another field goal as the fourth quarter started, it seemed obvious to the partisan crowd of 85,444 and the scouts from all the New Year's Day bowls that State's defense would have to win it. With the help of controversial penalties for roughing the passer on Alexander and a personal foul on Zordich (that replays showed did not happen), the Tide reached the Lion 17. On third-and-13, Cobbs sacked Shula, forcing Alabama to settle for a 45-yard field goal by Van Tiffin to make the score 12-10.

Now the offense had the ball again with about nine minutes remaining. On a second-and-8 from the PSU 22 following the kickoff, Paterno called for a reverse by Timpson. Before the play was over, the flanker had dashed 29 yards down the sideline and two Alabama players and the field judge had been injured by the devastating blocking. "I was going to call it on the first down but lost my guts," Paterno admitted later. "...I called it and held my breath. He made me look good." Dozier and Smith picked up first downs at the Alabama 22 but two plays later, Shaffer had the wind knocked out of him after gaining six yards to the Alabama 11. It was now third-and-one and Paterno could either call a time out or send in Knizner without warming up. Paterno gave Knizner the play— "Boot 157" —and sent him in. Perkins yelled for his defense to be alert for a bad snap and set the formation to anticipate a run up the middle by Smith. Knizner faked to Smith as Dozier led the blocking, then put the ball on his hip and bootlegged to the right with the option to run or pass. He spotted Siverling open at the 2-yard line and the tight end caught the pass and bowled over the Alabama cornerback into the end zone. "It was a gutsy call," Perkins said after the game. Alabama had one last gasp near the end and scored after a 74-yard drive in seven plays with 10 seconds left, to make the score 19-17. The Tide almost had a last shot when they recovered the onside kick but the recovery was nullified by an offside penalty and Coates hauled down the second kick to end the game. Bob

Smizik of the *Pittsburgh Press* said the victory proved "the Lions were worthy of their No. 5 ranking. And maybe a lot more. Penn State has achieved this status with an offense that is adequate and can become good, and a defenses that is good and can become great." Nick Horvath, sport editor of the *Harrisburg Patriot-News*, had a different take. "The heat generated by 1984's nightmare has exited," he wrote. "...Let the record show that Penn State has finally bagged a football prize of substance, done in a style that reminded of yesteryear. Heaven."

It was back to "winning ugly" again the following week against Syracuse (2-3) at the Carrier Dome. Bradley's special kicking teams had helped give the fourth-ranked Lions a 14-0 lead as Coates returned the opening kickoff 78 yards to set up Smith's 5-yard TD and Timpson ran back a punt 48 yards to spark a 4-play, 26-yard drive with five minutes left in the half. But Syracuse kicked a 41-yard field goal as the second quarter ended and midway through the third period quarterback Don McPherson evaded a blitz and scrambled for a 26-yard TD at the end of an 80-yard drive. The Orange narrowed the score to 14-13 on another Don McAulay field goal before the end of the period but Ontko's fumble recovery at the Syracuse 34 led to Manca's 44-yard field goal a minute into the final quarter. Syracuse roared back 82 yards after the ensuing kickoff to take the lead for the first time, 20-17, as McPherson avoided another blitz and threw a 45-yard TD pass to Mike Siano. Shaffer brought the Lions upfield to the Syracuse 44 before crossing the scrimmage line on a third down pass and State had to punt with about six minutes left in the game. In moments, McPherson had moved the Orange near midfield and the sellout Homecoming crowd of 50,021 sensed the first victory over PSU in 15 years. But suddenly fullback Roland Grimes fumbled when hit by White and Graham recovered at the Syracuse 42. So unlikely was the fumble, wrote Matt Herb in the *Daily Collegian*, that "it would not have been difficult to imagine the hand of God poking through the Carrier Dome ceiling and sneaking up behind Grimes to knock the ball free..." Dozier ran for 13 yards and almost before the Orange defense and their All-American tackle Tim Green knew it, the Lions were at the 8-yard line with a third-and-3 with less than two minutes left in the game. Syracuse set for a run or a possible pass off the option. Paterno and Ganter crossed them up having Shaffer throw his first pass of the day to Smith, who dashed into the flat, snagged the ball and went into the end zone. Manca's PAT made it 24-20 and the Lions kicked off. McPherson tried to give Syracuse one more chance but his long pass was intercepted by Cobbs and the Lions won. "They go to the bank with these games and the rest of us are standing in the bread lines," Syracuse Coach Dick MacPherson told sportswriters.

The win coupled with Miami's 27-14 upset over Oklahoma moved State up to #2 in the UPI rankings behind Iowa and #3 in the AP behind Iowa and Florida, which was on probation and not rated by UPI, and, ironically, was coached by former Lion quarterback Galen Hall. The next Saturday the offense pulled it altogether for the first time all year and smashed West Virginia (4-1-1) before a sellout Homecoming crowd of 85,534 and an ABC regional TV audience on a perfect autumn afternoon, 27-0. Shaffer threw TD passes of 51 and 15 yards to Roundtree and Dozier gained 125 yards, including a 14-yard TD, on 17 carries as the offense netted 349 yards. Meanwhile, the defense allowed the Mountaineers across the 50 just three times, limiting them to 268 yards with three interceptions, two fumble recoveries and four sacks. "We thought we owed West Virginia one from last year the way they treated us down there after they won," Isom told the media. It was the 600th victory in Penn State's history, a milestone only Michigan, Notre Dame, Texas and Alabama had achieved at the time. "There have been a lot of outstanding football players go through here, for me to be the quarterback of the team that won number 600 is exciting," Shaffer said.

Ray Roundtree was one of the best receivers of the 1980s but his career was cut short by injuries. He was a key performer on both the 1985 and 1986 teams that played for the national championship.

But it was back to "normal" the next week at Beaver Stadium with another fourth quarter thriller won by the defense, the kicking game and another bold gamble by Paterno. Boston College was 3-6 and on a three game losing skid against Army, West Virginia and Cincinnati but the Eagles had a spirited defense led by nose guard Mike Ruth and linebacker Bill Romanowski. The Lion offense struggled again from the start. Despite good field position in the entire first quarter, State could muster only a 35-yard Manca field goal on four possessions. Early in the second quarter, BC drove nearly the length of the field for a first-and-goal at the one-yard line. But fullback Ken Bell fumbled when hit by Conlan as he tried to leap over the middle of State's line and White recovered. On the next play, however, Shaffer was sacked in the end zone for a safety. By halftime, BC had kicked another field goal to lead by the unusual score of 5-3 and State's offense had hardly moved.

Early in the third quarter, Shaffer fumbled when he was sacked again and on the first play Bell ran 54 yards for a touchdown that gave the Eagles a 12-3 lead. Late in the third quarter the Lions finally mounted a drive from their own 26 after a punt but they reached their own 46 with a fourth-and-one and Paterno sent in the punting team. Then he changed his mind, called time out and summoned everyone to the sidelines. He went into conference with Ganter, Shaffer and offensive line coach Nick Gasparato. Gasparato said the offensive line wanted "Sweep 49" with Dozier running left to the short side. That was the call and with BC's defense expecting a run up the middle or a quarterback sneak, Dozier took the handoff from Shaffer and cutting inside behind the blocks of Smith, Manoa and Sickler he found a hole and ran 42 yards to the BC 11. A 10-yard pass to Hamilton led to Shaffer's sneak for the TD and Manca's kick narrowed the score to 12-10. A few minutes later, an outstanding 71-yard punt by Bruno put the Eagles back on their 20-yard line. The defense rushed hard, flushing quarterback Shawn Halloran out of the pocket and as he tried to pass Tim Johnson tipped the ball right into the hands of nose tackle Russo, who caught it and ran 21-yards for a touchdown. A two-point pass for the conversion failed but the Lions now had the lead, 16-12, with 14 minutes still left

in the game. Now, it was up to the defense again and they needed an all-out effort because BC continued its offensive assault. BC missed a 31-yard field goal at one point, then lost the ball when Alexander and Zordich forced another fumble. As time was winding down, Cobbs blitzed and sacked Halloran for a 22 yard loss and on fourth-and-32 from the BC 13, Halloran threw a pass that Alexander intercepted and State ran out the clock. "I don't know whether a defense could play much better than ours today," Paterno told Black for the *"Football Letter."* Speaking for the defense, White said, "You win a few close games and you establish the attitude that regardless of the situation you can get out of it...We win, get a positive attitude and things go our way."

Things obviously went their way that afternoon because Iowa lost to Ohio State and the Lions went to #1 in the UPI poll. "This is a team that always uses its head. And its heart," wrote Jack McCallum in a *Sports Illustrated* cover story that asked: "Who's No. 1 Now? Florida (7-0-1) Or Penn State (8-0)." There was no question after the following Saturday when the Lions wiped out Cincinnati, 31-10, at Riverfront Stadium and Florida lost to Georgia, 24-3. Interceptions by Hamilton, Isom and Zordich and a fumble recovery by Russo set up all four touchdowns and Dozier ran for 112 yards, including a 2-yard TD, to pace the offense, which rolled up 269 yards running. State was now #1 in both major polls with Nebraska #2 and Ohio State #3. But Paterno's philosophy about being #1 was the same as it had been since he first became the head coach. "Nobody's anything until the season's over," he said at his midweek news conference.

Now, the bowl speculation started in earnest. But with two weeks before the invitations could officially go out, it was really too early for anyone to get serious about the Lions' destination. For starters, State still had to play Notre Dame and Pitt and both were dangerous opponents who could salvage their mediocre seasons with an upset over the Lions. However, the bowls already were maneuvering to lock up their teams before the official bids went out. Bowl executives said the pairings would be made after next week. If State beat Notre Dame, it would be in the proverbial driver's seat, they said, and could select the bowl it wanted. "The Lions' destiny is in their own hands," wrote Phil Grosz for *Blue-White Illustrated*. Among the possibilities for State, Grosz speculated, were these: the Air Force was still unbeaten and could be a possible PSU foe in the Fiesta Bowl; three once beaten teams still had a chance to win the Big 8 conference and the Orange Bowl bid—Nebraska, Oklahoma and Oklahoma State—and once-beaten Arkansas was the front-runner to be the Southwest Conference host team in the Cotton Bowl. "... only luck will determine if there's a New Year's Day match-up that will decide the National Championship," Grosz concluded.

Although there were still doubts in some quarters about the caliber of the PSU team, there should have been no qualms about the team's desire to beat Notre Dame and Pitt and finish undefeated. "In the back of our minds, we know that Notre Dame and Pitt put us to shame last year," Frerotte told Poorman of *Blue-White Illustrated*, "We have something to prove to them." Two days before the Notre Dame game, Paterno told his squad, "that a day hasn't gone by where I haven't thought about this game and the one coming up." Neither Notre Dame (5-3) nor Pitt (5-4-1) was having a good year and the job of both coaches, Faust and Fazio, was in jeopardy. Still, State was only a one-point favorite for the late afternoon ABC regional TV game on November 16. Despite a heavy rain that started Friday night and continued without letup for the next 24 hours, an estimated Beaver Stadium crowd of 84,000 and scouts from eight bowls watched the Lions annihilate Notre Dame, 36-6, as Manca set a new school record with five field goals. Fittingly, Manca's boots of 32, 27, 50, 26 and 35 yards were all set up by the defense and the kicking teams as the defense intercepted three passes and recovered two fumbles and the special teams blocked a punt and returned another into scoring territory.

QB John Shaffer, an Academic All-American, lost only one game as a high school and college starter and as co-captain led the '86 team to the national championship.

That same day Air Force and Arkansas were beaten and although State officials wouldn't' confirm it publicly, the Orange Bowl was looming ahead. A week later, as ESPN's viewers and a sellout crowd watched at Pitt Stadium on a cold Saturday night, the Lions walloped Pitt, 31-0, and accepted a bid to play Oklahoma in the Orange Bowl New Year's Night. The defense intercepted three passes and recovered two fumbles, including one by Giftopoulos in the end zone as Manoa scored TDs on runs of 60 and 3-yards in what turned out to be Fazio's last game. Faust quit a week later after Miami coach Jimmy Johnson ran up the score on Notre Dame, 58-7, in an attempt to impress pollsters and horn in on the national title race.

The Hurricanes jumped over Oklahoma and Iowa into #2 in the AP poll. The only defeat for the #3 Sooners had been early in the season to Miami, which had then lost only to Florida. Miami was headed to the Sugar Bowl to play #8 Tennessee and Johnson figured a victory there combined with an Oklahoma win over State in the Orange Bowl would give his Hurricanes a good shot at the National Championship. Johnson's politicking was aided by some Miami sportswriters, who appeared to go out of their way to deride Penn State's worthiness as #1. "Penn State is viewed as a fraud," wrote Bob Rubin of the *Miami Herald*, "Nittany Paper Lions."

THE 1986 ORANGE BOWL
Jan. 1, 1986
Oklahoma 25, Penn State 10

The plush Fountainbleau Hotel in Miami Beach usually served as the headquarters for the Big 8 champion but Paterno insisted his #1 Lions should also stay there. So, with players and fans of both teams wandering the lobbies and bantering at the pool side bar and restaurants, the friendly pregame atmosphere was somewhat disconcerting. Penn State fans drew icy stares from Oklahoma's All-American sophomore linebacker Brian Bosworth but the overall mood was more like a convention or a family reunion than a hostile battleground. Some sportswriters tried to get a feud going between Paterno and Sooner Coach Barry Switzer over a flippant remark Paterno had made about Switzer years before at an off the record session with reporters. But both coaches said Paterno had apologized soon after the statement became public

and they insisted they were now friends. The only mild controversy came when Oklahoma's covered wagon mascot, the Sooner Schooner, was banned from the field on game night because of an incident the previous year when the Schooner galloped onto the field at the wrong time and cost Oklahoma a 15-yard penalty.

As usual, Paterno closed his practices and later said he may have worked the team harder in preparing for this game than in any other of his post-season appearances. He also kept his players away from many of the Orange Bowl functions. Switzer was the opposite. He had brought his team to Miami a week before Christmas and told them to have a good time because he intended to do likewise. Later, when some sportswriters claimed the Lions were too tight and that's why they lost, Conlan said the players felt Paterno "had the right approach. It was just the wrong result."

By game time, Oklahoma was favored by 6 1/2 points, primarily because of its defense and triple option wishbone running attack led by freshman quarterback Jamelle Holieway. The defense, which had held opponents to 90 yards rushing per game and 104 yards passing, featured nose guard Tony Casillas, the Lombardi award winner as the nation's outstanding lineman, and Bosworth, who won the Butkus award as best linebacker. Holieway had taken over in the fourth game of the season when starting QB Troy Aikman broke his leg and Switzer switched his offense from passing to running. Holieway now led Sooner rushers with 861 yards on 61 carries and had thrown just 58 passes, completing 24 with 5 TDs. State's defense led by All-Americans Conlan and Zordich would hold Holieway to one-yard rushing and he would complete just 3-of-6 passes but one would be the game breaker.

If the State offense had played the entire game as it did the first seven minutes, the Lions probably would have won the national title that night. After the defense stopped Oklahoma on the opening kickoff, Shaffer took the Lions 62-yards on a 10-play drive that featured two first down passes to Eric Hamilton and a couple of nifty runs by the backs, with Manoa scoring from the one. Manca's PAT gave State the 7-0 lead. Tim Lashar's 26-yard field goal made it 7-3 at the start of the second quarter but a few minutes later Oklahoma made the play of the game. The Sooners were facing a third-and-24 at their own 29-yard line following a sack by Matt Johnson. Sandusky sent in a fifth defensive back and then called a safety blitz for only the third time all year. Holieway beat Isom's blitz and hit his wide open tight end Keith Jackson who went the rest of the way for the TD. The Lions never recovered but only because the offense faltered. Twice in the quarter Shaffer overthrew or underthrew into double or triple coverage and the Sooners intercepted. Both interceptions led to Lashar field goals. As Oklahoma was trying to run out the clock before the half, White stripped the ball from Holieway and Conlan recov-

Linebacker Shane Conlan made All-American in '85 and his decision to return as a "fifth-year senior" in 1986 was one of the reasons the Lions went on to win the national title in 1986.

ered at the OU 11-yard line with 9 seconds left. Manca booted a 27-yard field goal and Oklahoma led at the half, 16-10.

The game was virtually over after State's 70-yard drive that opened the third quarter. Shaffer had moved State to a first down at the OU 20-yard line when he again underthrew into double coverage, not seeing the tight end who was wide open. Sonny Brown picked off his second interception at the one-yard line and the Lion threat was over. Later in the quarter, Timpson fumbled a punt on a handoff from Coates and Oklahoma used that turnover for another Lashar field goal. The Lion offense continued to stumble throughout the early part of the fourth quarter and with less than seven minutes remaining, Paterno replaced Shaffer with Knizner. Knizner hit on four passes to move State to the OU 9-yard line before Manca attempted a 26-yard field goal that was wide with 2:46 remaining. About a minute later, fullback Lydell Carr bolted over right guard and went 61 yards for a TD that made the final score, 25-10.

In the locker room, Shaffer took the blame for the defeat. "I can't believe that one person could do so much to cause a team to lose," Shaffer told Leo Suarez of the *Miami News*. "I didn't throw the ball well...It hurt because I could see my teammates on defense playing their hearts out and all I could do was run three plays and get off the field..." But none of his teammates nor his coach would condemn Shaffer, who lost as a starter for the first time since 7th grade after 55 games. "We here at Penn State try to win and lose with class," said Alexander. "We have nothing to be ashamed of...We gave it all we had and it wasn't enough." Paterno told reporters that the "the turnovers killed us...(we) were just beaten by a better team tonight."

When the final polls were released the next day, Oklahoma was a unanimous #1 with Michigan #2, State at #3 and Tennessee at #4 after clobbering Miami 35-7. "Losing a national championship game is never easy," wrote Neil Rudel in the *Altoona Mirror*, "especially when the opponent was beatable—but Penn State accomplished far more than anybody expected this year and the future looks bright. The Road to No. 1 is paved with seasons like this one and considering the wealth of talent returning it will not be surprising if Penn State negotiates that road in 1986."

Season Record 11-1
Record to Date 604-266-41
Winning percentage .686

"A Century of Excellence"

No matter how many National Champions or undefeated teams Penn State ever has, no year will compare to 1986. It was one of a kind that will never be duplicated—for how many times can a school celebrate its 100th year of football by winning the national title.

Some sportswriters called it a "Storybook" season that seemed to be scripted in Hollywood. It started with a tribute to "A Century of Excellence" on the football field and ended with the most momentous goal line stand in Nittany Lion history. In between, there was everything from elegant black tie dinners in three cities to a ceremonious fireworks display over Beaver Stadium. During the regular season, some games would be virtual blowouts and others would be fourth quarter thrillers. But on January 2, 1987, the Lions of '86 would beat Miami 14-10 in the Fiesta Bowl and give State its second National Championship.

That the Lions were again playing for the national title was not the surprise it had been in '85. Everyone knew Paterno was going to have one of his most experienced teams, with the return of 19 of the top 22 offensive players and 18 of the best defensive players. He excused a dozen of his "fifth-year seniors" such as Conlan and Smith from most of spring practice while he and his assistants concentrated on offensive and defensive refinements and position changes. His main concern through the spring and preseason practice sessions was the development of a better passing game but unlike a lot of the fans Paterno blamed the system rather than the quarterback for '85's shortcomings in passing.

"I have been very, very uptight about the criticism John Shaffer has received," Paterno told sportswriters during the spring. "We may have asked him to do too many things." So, Paterno dumped the passing offense he had been using since Todd Blackledge was the quarterback and went to a controlled-type of attack with more short passes thrown to the backs and tight end. Still, throughout the spring and preseason, Paterno declined to name Shaffer the starting quarterback and ostensibly gave Knizner a crack at winning the job. "We've got two kids who are both capable of taking this football team and winning games with it," Paterno told sportswriters. "That's a great situation for a coach."

But many fans had already made up their minds. Knizner seemed to be "The People's Choice," as the cover story in *Penn State Football Preview* magazine proclaimed. "Of course," wrote the author, Gordie Jones of the *Lancaster Intelligencer Journal*, "the No. 2 quarterback tends to be the most popular person in town." And in a preseason poll by the *Harrisburg Patriot-News*, Knizner was the clear winner, 355-73. Naturally, Paterno said he "didn't care what the fans think" but he didn't chose his starter until two days before the opening game against Temple on September 6.

The rest of the offense appeared to be sound. Dozier, who needed just 983 yards to surpass Curt Warner as the Lions all-time rusher, was being touted as a Heisman Trophy candidate. However, sportswriters cautioned that Dozier would have to avoid the injuries which had plagued him since his sensational freshman season. Clark was his prime backup at tailback with Thomas in reserve. The tandem of Smith and Manoa at fullback may have been the best ever in the Paterno era. Although Timpson was redshirted, the wide receivers included Roundtree, Alexander, Coates and Eric Hamilton, whom Paterno believed was under utilized in '85. Silverling, who was one of the best blockers on the team, started at tight end with sophomore Bob Mrosko and Paul Pomfret behind him. The offensive line were all veterans with Radecic at center backed by Truitt; Morgan, Wisniewski, Kuzy and sophomore Ed Monaghan at guards; and, Conlin, Sickler, Clayton and Frerotte at the tackles.

Defense again was the backbone of the team and the linebacking corps was one of the best in the nation with Conlan, Bauer, Giftopoulos and Graham starting and Mike Beckish, junior Kurt Bernier and sophomore Keith Karpinski the prime back-ups. Up front, Russo was back at nose tackle with Tim Johnson, White or Curkendall at the ends and Matt Johnson, Polamalu and freshman Rich Schonewolf also seeing action. The secondary was led by Isom at safety with Cobbs and sophomore Eddie Johnson at the corners and Henderson, Downing and Gary Wilkerson in reserve. The kicking game was another major strength with the kickers Bruno and Manca back again as well as the returners Thomas, Timpson and Coates. For the first time in years, Paterno decided to pick game captains, then elect permanent captains at the end of the season. "We've got so many leaders," Paterno told *Sports Illustrated*, "I didn't think it would be fair (to elect captains)."

Sports Illustrated was quite high on the Lions and picked them at #2 behind defending champion Oklahoma, saying: "This year the football team is celebrating its 100th anniversary with a season-long salute to 'A Century of Excellence.' The 1986 Lions should live up to that billing." The AP tabbed State at #6, right behind Alabama, which was #8 in the *SI* selections. Barring a major upset in State's first six games, most sportswriters looked towards the October 25 showdown against Alabama at Tuscaloosa as the one that would "make or break" State's season. They were right. But not everything went as smoothly as the first game.

It's doubtful that any opening game was planned more thoroughly than the one against Temple. Paterno, athletic director Jim Tarman and others in the PSU football hierarchy wanted to make it something special and they did. Scheduling the kickoff for 7 p.m. made this the first night game ever at Beaver Stadium. Three hours before the game, Paterno and Temple coach Bruce Arians made a highly-unusual joint appearance with their captains at a pep rally for both teams at nearby Jeffrey Field. Then, minutes before the kickoff, two parachutists from the Green Beret unit at Fort Bragg, NC, delivered the game ball and ceremonial coin for the coin toss to the referees at midfield. In July, the "Century of Excellence" celebration had honored the undefeated teams of 1968-1969, 1973 and 1982 with formal dinners in Pittsburgh, Philadelphia and Hershey. So, during halftime ceremonies, 87,732 watched as players representing lettermen from each era of State football were recognized on the field, including All-Americans Charlie Way, Leon Gejecki, Lenny Moore, Bob Mitinger and Dave Joyner. And as the halftime ceremonies concluded, the darkened skies over the stadium were lighted up by a 10-minute fireworks show.

By that time, the Lions were leading, 24-0, and they went on to an easy 45-15 win behind the quarterbacking of Shaffer, who was celebrating his own 22nd birthday. Shaffer threw touchdown passes for the first time in his career, hitting on passes of 10, 14 and 12 yards, and scored another TD on a 5-yard rollout as he completed 12-of-18 passes for 194 yards without an interception. Seven of his completions were to Dozier or Smith on screen or swing passes and Dozier led all receivers with four receptions for 73 yards and scored a TD on a 9-yard run. The offense also churned out 259 yards on the ground while the defense held Temple star running back Palmer to 96 yards on 29 carriers, and scored the most spectacular TD when

Defensive lineman Tim Johnson became a First-Team All-American selection in 1986 when he was one of the stars of the national championship team and one of the team's truly clutch players.

Karpinski returned an interception 64 yards in the fourth quarter. "I really needed this game," Shaffer told sportswriters. Paterno used 67 players and inserted his second offensive and defensive units into the game in the first quarter to get them better game experience. In the media room he said the team was "way ahead of where we were this time last year because we're so much better offensively."

But something was missing from the offense two weeks later when the now #5 Lions met Boston College in a Saturday night ESPN game at Sullivan Stadium in Foxboro. State never trailed after a fumble recovery on the opening kickoff led to an 8-yard TD by Smith less than two minutes into the game. However, the offense sputtered most of the evening as Shaffer connected on just 7-of-21 pass attempts for 95 yards and threw one interception while Knizner also threw a pair of interceptions while going 0-for-6. Without the short passing, the Lion rushing game couldn't get the big play and Manca also missed three field goals. Fortunately, BC's offense was worse, giving up five interceptions and two fumbles and even a safety on a bad snap from center. The Eagles also lost 142 yards on 15 penalties. An end zone interception by Conlan stopped one BC threat when State's lead was 19-7 late in the third quarter and Isom's 30-yard runback of another interception in the fourth quarter set up a 35-yard TD drive that clinched the 26-14 victory. "We needed a tough game like this," Paterno told sportswriters. "It tells us more about ourselves than the Temple game."

Despite the win, the Lions slipped to #7 in the AP rankings but a week later they were back at #5 after clobbering East Carolina 42-17 at soggy Beaver Stadium. Another Isom interception on the second play of the game set up the Lions initial TD and the score was 35-0 by halftime. Shaffer was back in stride, throwing TD passes of 8 yards to Roundtree and 7 yards to Hamilton as he connected on 11-of-16 passes for 160 yards and no interceptions. Dozier led the rushers with 71 yards and a TD on 12 carries but it was Thomas who thrilled the crowd with 67 yards and two TDs on nine carries and a 44-yard kickoff return. "We got a chance to play a lot of kids that will pay off later," Paterno said in the media room. "We have hopes Thomas can be a really good back for us." The coach would soon find out how good Thomas could be. In a more notable game that same day, #2 Miami beat #1 Oklahoma and moved to the top of all the major polls.

Rutgers was touted as State's most formidable Eastern opponent in three years. With victories over Boston College, Cincinnati and Syracuse and a tie with Kentucky, Dick Anderson's team came into Beaver Stadium all fired up. A crowd of about 84,000 including baseball Hall of Famer Joe DiMaggio watched in the rain as the Lions doused the Scarlet Knights fire with a 31-6 victory. Shaffer had another good day, throwing for 154 yards, including a 7-yard TD to Hamilton while completing 13-of-23 passes with one interception. Eleven backs gained 287 yards on the ground with Roundtree's so called "end aroundtree" TD romp of 34 yards in the third quarter being the longest and best run of the afternoon. The aggressive defense held Rutgers to 45 yards on the ground and set up one TD with a fumble recovery. But Paterno was upset at the nine penalties, mostly on defense, that cost his team 102 yards. After the game he said he was "very, very concerned in our (lack of) poise...I've never had a team draw as many foolish penalties...You can't be aggressive and not have penalties, but some are nonsense, just plain stupid." Still, Paterno added, "it was by far our best effort of the year."

Now came the game that defined the season—and the opponent wasn't Alabama but mediocre 3-2 Cincinnati. The weather was nearly perfect for a mid October afternoon at Beaver Stadium but the

A great defense helped this 1986 team give Penn State its second National Championship with a last minute defensive stand against Miami in the 1987 Fiesta Bowl.

Lions were not. Coates fumbled the first two Cincinnati punts and the Bearcats recovered the second one in the end zone for a 7-0 lead five minutes into the second quarter. But before the half was over, State took a 14-7 lead on two touchdown drives from midfield and narrowly missed another score when the clock ran out too late to try a field goal with the Lions at the Cincy 5-yard line. However, with Danny McCoin directing the Bearcats ball-control, short-passing attack, Cincinnati surged into a 17-14 lead two minutes into the fourth quarter. Thomas' 34-yard kickoff return and his 20-yard run off a draw helped Shaffer take State to a third-and-2 at the Bearcat 24-yard line but Shaffer was sacked for a 14-yard loss and the Lions had to punt. Trying to use up time on the clock, McCoin moved Cincy slowly from its 4-yard line to the PSU 49 before Curkendall stopped Reggie Taylor on a third-and-one play, forcing the Bearcats to punt. With 5:57 left in the game, the Lions gained possession at their own 25-yard line. An incomplete pass and a run for no gain had the sellout crowd of 84,812 shifting nervously in their seats. It was now possible for Cincinnati to get the ball back and run out the clock. Shaffer called a pass play that sent two wide receivers, the tight end and the tailback into the Bearcat secondary. He threw to Thomas who leaped at the Cincy 43 and caught the ball for a 32-yard gain. On first down, Thomas gained five yards on a draw. On second down he took a pitchout towards the right and with blocks from Conlin and Morgan dashed 27 yards to the Cincy 11-yard line. Smith gained five up the middle, then Clark blasted into the end zone with three would-be tacklers hanging on for the go-ahead TD with 3:07 left in the game. McCoin tried to rally the Bearcats but he was sacked twice for a minus 20 yards and Conlan blocked a punt for a safety to make the final score, 23-17. "We didn't play really well but we played tough when we had to," Paterno told sportswriters. "Playing tough when they had to would be the ultimate defining characteristic of this team.

The pollsters didn't think much of the victory for they dropped State back to #6 behind Miami, Alabama, Nebraska, Michigan and Oklahoma. However, as the Lions prepared for their Homecoming game with 1-and-4 Syracuse, *USA Today* reported that ABC-TV was trying to get the Citrus Bowl interested in matching Miami against State on New Year's Day. "...Wouldn't it be nice...?," Citrus Bowl scout John Day told Dave Ailes of the *Greensburg Tribune-Review* in the Press Box

during the Syracuse game. But Day admitted that NBC also was looking into a potential Fiesta Bowl game between the two teams. With all the other major bowls tied up with conference deals, the Citrus, Fiesta and Gator Bowls were the only ones capable of handling such a game between the two independents. But they would have to come up with additional money to make it attractive to both teams. Of course, much would depend on both Miami and State continuing unbeaten as well as the financial arrangements. "Penn State would want to play Miami but Miami might want to go somewhere else," Manny Garcia of the Citrus Bowl told Mark Ashenfelter of the *Daily Collegian*. A 42-3 win over outclassed Syracuse continued the Citrus Bowl speculation for another week. For the first time all season, a Lion runner gained over 100 yards and in the process of doing so Thomas broke the school record for the longest run from scrimmage set by Bill Suter in 1894. Late in third quarter, the sophomore dashed 92 yards before being knocked out of bounds at the Syracuse one-yard line. He carried just two more times and had a total of 132 yards as the Lions piled up 434 yards on the ground. Five different players scored touchdowns and the defense set up two of the scores with an interception by Cobbs and a blocked punt by Matt Johnson. "That might be as well as we've played defense all year," Paterno said.

Most of the nation's sports media figured the #6 Lions would get their comeuppance in Tuscaloosa against the #2 Crimson Tide. Alabama had beaten Ohio State, Florida, Notre Dame and Tennessee and the continued bias against Eastern football was obvious in some of the pregame analysis. "After disposing of a bum a week since the start of the football season," wrote Bill Lumpkin in the *Birmingham Post-Herald*, "Penn State returns to the big time today." Coach Ray Perkins' team had averaged 33 points and 412 yards per game and possessed the country's longest unbeaten streak at 12-0-1. Furthermore, Alabama had lost just 12 games in Bryant-Denny Stadium since it was built in 1929 and only two in the last 25 years. So, it was not surprising the Tide was a 6 1/2 point favorite and that angered the Lion players and Paterno. When the team arrived in Tuscaloosa on a rainy Friday afternoon, Paterno was asked by a couple of sportswriters if the rain and a wet field would help State because of Alabama's speed. "Naw, I don't want it to rain because I don't want them to have any excuses when we beat them," he confidently told the shocked sportswriters. In his pregame speech to his players, Paterno compared the schedules of the two teams and pointed out that only two of Alabama's opponents had records over .500 and that the Tide also had played patsies such as Vanderbilt and Memphis State. "We've got something to prove and they've got something to prove," he said. The Lions not only beat the Tide, they destroyed them as a national television audience and scouts from nine bowls watched and the 23-3 score did not begin to tell what happened. "The surprise...was not that Penn State beat Alabama," wrote Douglas Looney in *Sports Illustrated*, "...the surprise was in the scope and sweep of the devastating 23-3 victory...The Crimson Tide played very well. The Crimson Tied also had no chance." Alabama scored its only points seven minutes into the first quarter for a 3-0 lead on a 40-yard field goal by Van Tiffin after a 41-yard drive and never came within 30 yards of the PSU goal line again. The defense led by Bauer, Conlan and Graham set up a touchdown and two field goals as they intercepted two passes, forced five fumbles, recovering three, and sacked Tide QB Mike Shula five times for 32 yards in losses while holding Alabama back Bobby Humphrey and his running mates to a total of 44 yards on 33 carries. The biggest play of the came shortly after the fourth quarter started and the Lions ahead 17-3. Two minutes into the quarter Bennett tackled Thomas from behind forcing a fumble the Tide recovered at the Lions 39-yard line. Three plays gained nine yards and on fourth-and-one, Humphrey tried to dive over the middle and was hit so hard by Bauer that he fumbled. Curkendall recovered and the Lions drove for a 30-yard Manca field goal that put the game out of reach. Later Bauer recovered a fumble that led to Manca's 42-yard field goal and the 23-3 final score. For his defensive effort, which included nine tackles and a pass deflection, Bauer was ABC's pick as the State's Player of the Game. But the offense also was sharp, rolling up 210 yards on the ground and 168 through the air as Shaffer played one of his finest games, completing 13-of-17 passes without an interception. The blocking was so good that neither Dozier nor Thomas was hardly touched when they ran 16 yards and 3 yards, respectively, for second quarter touchdowns that climaxed drives of 65 and 77 yards. "They're the best team we've played since I've been here," Perkins told sportswriters. Paterno said, "it will take an awfully good team to beat us as well as we are playing now." Perhaps Bob Smizik of the *Pittsburgh Press* summed the game up best when he wrote: "In the glowing aftermath of victories over Florida and Tennessee, Alabama coach Ray

Place kicker Massimo Manca, the only player to be on both national championship teams, still holds a number of PSU placekicking records, including field goals in consecutive games.

Perkins modestly announced that his team had 'touched greatness.' You bet the Tide touched greatness," Smizik wrote. "It touched great-

ness all afternoon...The greatness on this afternoon belonged to Penn State."

With Nebraska losing to Colorado that same day, the Lions jumped into #2 in both polls, then headed to Morgantown for a Saturday night encounter against 2-5 West Virginia televised by ESPN. Sportswriters believed this game would give them a chance to compare State with Miami since the Hurricanes had battered the Mountaineers before a WVU Homecoming crowd two weeks earlier, 58-14. The Lions took the opening kickoff and drove 91 yards in eight plays for a TD on a 23-yard pass from Shaffer to Dozier. But from that point it became a defensive game with Manca kicking field goals of 42, 37, 22 and 27 yards to give the Lions a 19-0 victory. The defense held the Mountaineers to 8 yards rushing on 27 carries and 126 yards passing while intercepting two passes, recovering a fumble and allowing WVU past the 50 yard line just three times. Although the offense controlled the ball for more than 37 minutes and Shaffer had a good day passing (11-for-20 for 171 yards), they blew several scoring opportunities and Paterno wasn't happy. "It shows we still have a lot of work to do," he told sportswriters. As for comparing State to Miami, wrote Black in the *"Football Letter,"* "the consensus of the Mountaineer gridders was that Penn State is as good as anyone defensively but Miami is more explosive offensively."

In retrospect, what happened the following week against Maryland (4-4) at rainy Beaver Stadium may have presaged what eventually occurred in the Fiesta Bowl. The "explosive" passing of Terp QB Don Henning pushed State's highly-praised defense to the breaking point and probably made it better prepared later in the confrontation with Miami. Henning threw for 302 yards and two TDs on 23-of-40 completions but his three interceptions and a hard rush by the Lions' defensive ends salvaged the 17-15 victory that went down to the last play of the game. Once again, the Lions missed several scoring opportunities in the first half when they controlled the ball for nearly 20 minutes and held the Terps to 84 yards in total offense. One first quarter drive ended when Shaffer was intercepted on the one-yard line and another fizzled at the 16 when Dozier was sacked for a 10-yard loss on a third down option pass and Manca missed a 43-yard field goal. In the second quarter the Lions finally scored after a 15-play, 84-yard drive. Three Dozier runs covered 38 of those yards, including the final nine, and Dozier would eventually post his only 100-yard game of the season with 111 yards on 25 carries. Even though State held a shaky 7-0 halftime lead, few if any of the 85,651 partisan fans could have envisioned the second half Maryland aerial fireworks. The Terps took the second half kickoff and nearly drove for a TD but were stopped at the Lion 2-yard line when White tipped a pass that Bauer intercepted. After a State punt, the Terps were back again at the PSU 2 but on a fourth-and-goal settled for an 18-yard field goal that made the score 7-3. The Lion offense continued to founder and early in the fourth quarter Henning marched the Terps back to the Lion 7-yard line when he called an audible and tried to pass to Alvin Blount in the flat. As Henning went down under a heavy rush led by White, Curkendall stepped in front of Blount and intercepted the pass. He was finally caught at the Terps 9-yard line by guard John Rugg after running 82 yards for what is still a record for the longest interception in school history without scoring a touchdown. Dozier took care of the TD on the next play and with Manca's PAT the Lions seemed to have a comfortable 14-3 lead with about eight minutes left in the game.

Back came Henning on a 73-yard, 10-play drive that took up just three minutes. Henderson dropped an interception that was a sure TD that could have ended the game but on fourth-and-7 at the PSU 16, Henning picked on Wilkerson, who had just replaced an injured Johnson, and hit Vernon Joines in the corner of the end zone for the TD. Brent Lowery tried to run for the 2-point conversion but was stopped by Bauer and State still led 14-9. Now, it was up to the Lion offense and Shaffer used up almost four minutes on a 53-yard drive that culminated in a 36-yard field goal with 1:04 left in the game. But in 47 seconds, Henning took the Terps 76 yards and on another fourth down, and seven, at the PSU 27-yard line, he hit John Bonato, who leaped between Henderson and Johnson for the TD in the end zone. Two points would tie the game and knock the Lions out of the national title race. Sandusky signaled the defense. Karpinski, in for Conlan who had sprained his knee, rushed Henning, forcing him to throw earlier than he wanted to and Cobbs dove over the intended receiver James Milling to knock the ball down at the 1-yard line—preserving the 17-15 victory. "The ending was a surprise," wrote Ronnie Christ in the **Harrisburg Patriot-News**. "Perhaps it shouldn't have been. Penn State has now beaten Maryland by five points the last three times they've met." When Paterno entered the media room, he said "You probably have to win one that maybe you don't deserve if you're going to go unbeaten...We've got to get the killer instinct and until we do we'll find ourselves in some tough games."

The narrow victory didn't help the Lions in the polls as they dropped to #3 behind Michigan but the speculation about a championship game between State and Miami continued. Herschel Nissenson of the AP reported that the Fiesta, Citrus and Gator Bowls were still trying to put together proposals and he quoted a Fiesta Bowl official as saying State would rather not play in Orlando or Jacksonville but on a neutral field outside of Florida. Nissenson wrote that Miami Athletic Director Sam Jankovich told him the Hurricanes would prefer to play in the hometown Orange Bowl but would meet State elsewhere if the Lions remained unbeaten. He did not rule out the Citrus or Gator bowls. "Jankovich hinted that he might be easier to deal with if the Lions agreed to some regular season games with Miami (in the future)," wrote Nissenson. "Those are the kind of people I think this football team deserves to play," Jankovich told Nissenson, "and we surely would hope that Joe Paterno would consider that."

Notre Dame was 4-4 under new coach Lou Holtz but State fans remembered how Holtz had coached North Carolina State to a pair of upsets over Paterno a decade earlier and he almost did it again with the Irish in a nationally televised thriller at South Bend. In the end, the game came down to a magnificent goal line stand that presaged the last minute heroics in the Fiesta Bowl and was another defining moment in this "Century of Ex-

Duffy Cobbs, a fine defensive back on both the ' 85 and ' 86 teams, made the key play in the 1986 Maryland game that preserved the unbeaten season leading up to the national championship.

cellence" season. Vice president George Bush was among the 59,075 spectators who watched State's defense stop the fired-up Irish three times deep in Lion territory in the first half to help give State a 10-6 lead. A sack by Graham and White forced a fumble by Irish QB Steve Beuerlein that Giftopoulos recovered at the 18-yard line and led to a 78-yard drive for a touchdown in the first quarter. Then in the second quarter, the Irish drove 84 and 54 yards but had to settle for field goals of 20 and 38 yards by John Carney. With about a minute left in the half, Conlan forced another fumble on another sack of Beuerlein. Curkendall recovered at the Irish 23-yard line and Manca's 19-yard field goal made it a four point halftime margin. But Notre Dame grabbed the lead, 13-10, on a quick 6-play, 92-yard drive early in the third quarter with Tim Brown scoring the TD on a 14-yard pass from Beuerlein. Shaffer led the Lions back, throwing a 37-yard TD pass to Roundtree to cap an 82-yard drive with two minutes left in the third quarter and scoring on a one-yard run after a 56-yard march early in the fourth quarter. The Irish narrowed the score to 24-19 midway through the quarter, scoring a TD on an 8-yard pass from Beuerlein to Brown at the end of a 64-yard drive but missing the two points on a gimmick pass attempt from Brown to Beuerlein. After the teams traded punts, the Irish gained possession on their own 15-yard line with 2:29 left. Now, it was up to State's defense again. But Beuerlein was having a career day (311 yards passing on 24-of-39 completions) and in a minute and a half he had the Irish pounding at the State 6-yard line with a first-and-goal.

On first down, Beuerlein pitched to Brown going left and Isom dashed in and hit him for a 3-yard loss. Then White sacked Beuerlein for a 9-yard loss. "He saved us," Conlan later told sportswriters. "I think they were surprised we got it." On third down, Beuerlein tried to hit tight end Joel Williams cutting across the end zone but just as he touched the ball he was blasted by Wilkerson and the ball fell incomplete. Fourth down and with his receivers covered, Beuerlein flipped the ball to tailback Mark Green at the 13 but he slipped and was immediately tackled. The Lions ran out the last 39 seconds on the clock. "...Penn State, a team that knows better than all others how to look dull but play sharp, squeezed out a 24-19 victory and let out a sigh of relief," wrote Bill Bilinski for the **South Bend Tribune**. "It was a great effort by both squads," Paterno told sportswriters. "We played as well as we could and they played as well as they could. Fortunately, we had more points."

Michigan's upset loss to Minnesota thrust the Lions back to #2 and Miami's athletic director Jankovich and coach Jimmy Johnson told the media the Hurricanes would play State in the Fiesta Bowl on the evening of January 2, providing State beats Pitt the following Saturday. "Jankovich said he discussed the situation with Penn State," reported the **Daily Collegian's** Joey

LB Don Graham was part of the "sack gang" of the great 1985-86 teams. Three of his sacks came in the ' 86 win over Notre Dame.

Holleman, "but (said) the Hurricane decision to play outside of Florida was in no way tied into a decision to schedule the Nittany Lions during the regular season in the future." The announcement touched off a flurry of complaints from several coaches, including two Big Ten mentors. "National championship? No way," said Iowa's Hayden Fry. " Strictly a bowl concoction, a TV deal," snapped Michigan's Bo Schembechler.

Hawaiian Tim Manoa shared FB duties with Steve Smith during the 1986 championship season giving the Lions the finest one-two combination in the country. Both went on to have fine pro careers.

After two weeks of "down-to-the-wire" scares, the Lions made it look easy in a 34-14 win over Pitt on an unusually warm late November afternoon at Beaver Stadium. Thomas scored a pair of touchdowns, including one on a stunning 91-yard kickoff return that gave State a 10-7 lead in the first quarter and demoralized the Panthers. Knizner combined with Hamilton for the longest TD pass of the year on an 82-yard bomb in the third quarter but he also gave up an 82-yard interception return for a TD in the fourth quarter that made the final score look closer than the game really was. The game was marred by five fist fights and several late hits and four cases of offsetting penalties for unsportsmanlike conduct, and late in the game Paterno ran across the field to help break up a scuffle in front of the Pitt bench. The Panthers new coach Mike Gottfried took it personally and told his team in the locker room, "I'm never going to forget what their coach did to me on that sideline and how their fans embarrassed us." Paterno blamed the officials for letting the game get out of hand and said, "I've never been in a football game with Pitt when we had so much of this kind of stuff." Later, Pittsburgh police reported receiving an anonymous telephone call about a bomb planted in Paterno's State College home but none was found.

But all the on field combat faded in the revelry of the PSU coaches and players in the locker room. "I've never had a bunch of seniors who have been more committed and made more personal sacrifices and worked harder," Paterno said. "When you go out saying that you played on two undefeated teams, there is not much more to say," Isom told sportswriters. Dozier, who finished 172 yards short of the 983 he needed to surpass Warner, said "the key this year is we've been together for four years. We work well together." Shaffer told how the team had pitched in $800 to fly Manoa's parents in from Hawaii to see the Pitt game. "I just love the guys for doing what they did," Manoa said. Conlan said "the last two years have been hell, bustin' our butts in practice, but we knew that's what it would take to win." Bauer probably summed it up best. "This year we have a lot of guys who know how to win," he said. "We're still that big, slow team with no talent wearing the black shoes but playing again for the National Championship."

The bowl invitations officially went out at 6 p.m. that day but the championship game between State and Miami still had a loose end. Bruce Skinner, the director of the Fiesta Bowl, said nothing would be official until after Miami played East Carolina the following Thursday night. Should Miami lose, Skinner said, State would have the option of going to the Orange Bowl and play Oklahoma again. But five days later Miami beat East Carolina 36-10 and the "Duel in the Desert" was set.

THE 1987 FIESTA BOWL
Jan. 2, 1987
Penn State 14, Miami (Fla.) 10
Most Valuable Offensive Player: D.J. Dozier
Most Valuable Defensive Player: Shane Conlan

With a corporate sponsorship from the Sunkist Citrus Growers enabling the Fiesta Bowl to pay each team $2.4 million and NBC anxious to air the game in prime time without competition from other bowls, the pregame atmosphere and hype was unlike any other in college football history. It was almost like a Super Bowl. Certainly, there had been other bowl games for the National Championship matching #1 against #2. But this was the first time such a game was being played *after* New Year's Day and *outside* one of the traditional and more glamorous bowls—Orange, Sugar, Cotton and Rose. In fact, this title game would instantly thrust the Fiesta Bowl into the New Year's Day elite and ultimately lead to the so-called "bowl coalition" and its successor the "bowl alliance" which now orchestrates the postseason bowl pairings. Because Penn State had helped get the Fiesta Bowl better established in its embryonic days by playing here three times—including the first New Year's Day game in 1982—the Lions were sort of adopted as the "hometown" team.

Of course, Miami made it easy for State to be the fans' favorite by their pregame antics and behavior. It started the moment the Hurricanes arrived in Phoenix on a chartered jet at 7:47 p.m. on Saturday, December 27. A dozen players, including quarterback Vinny Testaverde, who had just won the Heisman Trophy, stepped off the plane in camouflage fatigues, caps, combat boots and sunglasses. "That was a great idea," Miami coach Jimmy Johnson told Jon Masson of the *Phoenix Gazette*. "I wish I had thought of it." All-American tackle Jerome Brown and running back Alonzo Highsmith had been the instigators as sophomore wide receiver Michael Irvin explained to Masson: "Jerome said, 'Get your gold, get your fatigues, we're going to war.'" The combat fatigues may have been seen inside the Miami camp as a joke or psychological inspiration but it all backfired when the Hurricanes continued talking about war and wearing the fatigues in public appearances.

It came to a head the next night when both teams were entertained at the Rawhide western theme park. After a steak dinner, the players were expected to put on a little entertainment. When it was Miami's turn, three players including Brown got up on the stage and stripped down to the fatigues they had been wearing under their clothes. Then Brown grabbed the microphone, looked at all his teammates and said, "Did the Japanese have dinner at Pearl Harbor before they bombed it? Let's go." And he stunned the crowd by leading the entire team out of the room to the team bus. In the momentarily silence, Lion punter John Bruno jumped up on the stage, cracked a joke about Miami players having to "go film Rambo III," then returned with a line that has become part of the Penn State football legend. "Excuse me," said Bruno, "but didn't the Japanese lose?" and the crowd of some 1,000 roared with laughter. "After the major-league tacky stunt," wrote Gail Tabor in the *Arizona Republic*, "a member of the Miami coaching staff explained it away as, 'That's the way they feel. They're here on a mission.'... "If there's any justice in the world," Tabor wrote, "the Miami Hurricanes will leave here Saturday with a championship. For rudeness, not football."

Miami's boorish behavior clashed with the quiet, good-natured demeanor of the PSU players and their no-nonsense coach, who had just been honored by *Sports Illustrated* as the magazine's "Sportsman of the Year." During a joint appearance with Jimmy Johnson, the Miami coach referred to Paterno as "St. Joe" and without missing a beat Paterno responded by saying "I left my halo at home" for this game. Both teams were loaded with stars. Four of the Lions had been chosen All-Americans with Conlan being selected for the second year in a row and Dozier, Tim Johnson and Conlin picked on various teams. Despite the flamboyant pranks and braggadocio, Miami was a very good football team and the 6 1/2 points that it was favored by did not seem out of line. The Hurricanes explosive offense had averaged 38 points a game and Testaverde had thrown for 26 touchdowns and just nine interceptions in completing 63.4 percent of his passes. He had excellent receivers in Irvin, who had caught 53 passes for 11 TDs, Brett Perriman, who had 34 receptions and four TDs and Brian Blades. Highsmith and Melvin Bratton were also good runners and receivers. The defense led by Brown, linebacker George Mira Jr., and All-American safety Bennie Blades had held opponents to less than 13 points a game. "They're the best balanced team we've seen in many years," Paterno told sportswriters. "We can't trade touchdowns. If it's that kind of game, we're out of our league. The more it gets into the 20s the worse our chances are." So, behind closed practices, the Lion defense worked on a radical new technique designed by Sandusky and Dickerson to fool and confuse Testaverde and disguise pass coverage. Rather than blitz, the defense would dropped eight players into the passing zones and give Conlan the flexibility to roam a bit.

Meanwhile, the Hurricane attempt at intimidation continued right up to game time. A full page advertisement in the *Phoenix Gazette* on the day of the game that was sponsored by the *Miami Herald* boldly proclaimed a "HURRICANE WARNING!" "Hurricane Vinny is now approaching Southern Arizona," the ad read. "At 8 p.m., EST, the center of the hurricane was near the 50-yard line...Hurricane Vinny is moving rapidly toward the Penn State end zone at 10-33 yards per play and is expected to cross the goal line repeatedly throughout the game." The Miami players were back wearing combat fatigues when they made their entrance into the stadium on January 2 and they started taunting the State players as soon as they saw them in street clothes getting off the bus by shouting epithets. They ran through the Lions formation during pregame calisthenics and during the warm-ups zeroed in on State's defensive backs, whom they had criticized as being too small and too slow. Isom later recalled Irvin saying, "You Isom? We're gonna get you tonight."

Obeying Paterno's orders, the Lion players did not talk back, although the always feisty Bauer zipped a ball past the helmet of one Miami player and made sure he knew who had thrown it. However, the linebackers and defensive backs already had decided that the way to answer the taunts was by hitting the pass receivers hard whenever Testaverde threw the ball their way. Soon after the kickoff, the hitting started. On Miami's second possession, Irvin reached for a pass and was belted so hard he dropped the ball. A few moments later in the same series, Irvin caught a 23-yard pass and as he turned to run at the

Second-Team All-American safety Ray Isom will always be remembered for the punishing tackles put on Miami's highly touted trio of receivers in the 1987 Fiesta Bowl.

Miami 45-yard line he was blasted by Isom, fumbled the ball and Cobbs recovered. The tone for the game was now set. The Miami receivers would drop a total of seven perfect passes and it was clear they were hesitating in running some of their routes. "Our little, slow guys back there just rocked 'em, and soon they didn't want to catch the ball," said Conlan after the game. "Later on, we were helping their receivers up after we hit them and patting them on their butts," said Cobbs, who would have 12 tackles. "Receivers *hate* that."

The first quarter was scoreless as the teams traded punts but five minutes into the second quarter, Brown sacked Shaffer, forcing a fumble that Miami recovered at the Lion 23-yard line. Two runs by Highsmith for 16 yards and a Testaverde pass to tight end Charles Henry put the ball on the one and Bratton dived over for the TD. Greg Cox booted the PAT for the 7-0 lead. But State tied the score after the ensuing kickoff with the only sustained drive of the evening, going 74 yards in 13 plays. Three times the Lions converted on third down plays, once on a 24-yard pass from Shaffer to Hamilton at the PSU 37. Manoa ran 19 yards on another big play, then caught a 12-yard swing pass that set up Shaffer's 4-yard rollout right for the TD with 1:14 left in the quarter. Manca's kick made it 7-7 at the half.

During the intermission, Conlan tried to nurse his left knee. It was the same knee he had hurt in the Maryland game and he had reinjured it in the first quarter, forcing him out of the game a few times. In the third quarter he injured his right ankle but not before stopping one Miami drive with an interception and running eight yards before the knee gave out. Shaffer also threw an interception in the third quarter and was clubbed in the aftermath by Hurricane linebacker Randy Shannon who took off his helmet and hit Shaffer over the head with it. Dozier tried to get the officials to call a penalty but they said they didn't see it. "It was very unnecessary," Dozier said later. Both teams missed field goal attempts during the period as the defenses dominated play, trading interceptions with State losing a fumble, and the score was still 7-7 as the final period began. Thus far, Sandusky's defensive plan had worked to near perfection with Bruno's punting keeping the Hurricanes from getting good field position and Testaverde showing his frustration on the sideline. One minute into the third quarter, Manca missed another field goal from 49-yards out. When the Hurricanes took over the ball they moved back into field goal range, getting a 20-yard run from Highsmith and two Testaverde pass completions for 19 yards that helped set up Mark Seelig's 38-yard field goal with 11:49 left in the game. Now, Miami seemed to take control. The Miami defense stopped the

Lions and the Hurricanes were on the move again.

But with about 8:35 remaining, Conlan made perhaps the biggest play of his career. Testaverde never saw him. Conlan intercepted the ball at the Miami 44-yard line and bad knee and ankle aside he ran all the way to the Hurricane 5 before being tackled. Shaffer almost blew it by fumbling the next snap but Smith recovered at the 6 and on second down Dozier

While best remembered for his interception against Miami in the final seconds of the 1987 Fiesta Bowl, Canadian LB Pete Giftopoulous was a solid contributor to the success of the 1985 and 1986 teams that played for the national title.

went up the middle for the TD. Manca kicked the PAT and the Lions led, 14-10 with 8:13 on the clock. That was more than enough time for Testaverde to bring the Hurricanes back. But after the kickoff Bauer stripped Alfredo Roberts of the ball after a pass reception and Russo recovered at the Miami 49-yard line. However, the Lion offense couldn't move and had to punt. The defense held again and after Miami's punt, State had the ball at its own 43-yard line with 4:56 remaining. tackle Maurice Maddox. Time out with 25 seconds left. Third down and Testaverde missed halfback Warren Williams. eighteen seconds left. After months of hard practices, winning games and a lot of talk, the entire season for both teams had come down to one play. "Somebody's got to make a play," Conlan yelled. Testaverde went back, looked for Perriman in the left corner of the end zone and threw. "The middle linebacker dropped back and went right to the throw just like he knew what I was going to do exactly," Testaverde said later. Giftopoulos swept in at the goal line, grabbed the ball and ran to the 10-yard line before falling to his knees with the ball firmly clutched the ball to his bosom. Nine seconds showed on the clock but it was over. They had just won the National Championship! The Lions and their fans celebrated on the field for nearly a half hour and when it was over the Blue Band led a march of delirious supporters out of the stadium and down the main street of Tempe.

With his two clutch interceptions and eight tackles, Conlan was named the Outstanding Defensive Player of the Game but in the locker room he made sure it was shared with the rest of his defensive teammates. "Everybody on our defense had a big play one way or another," he told sportswriters. Miami had run off 93 plays to State's 59 and had a total offense of 445 yards and 22 first downs to State's 162 yards and eight first downs. But Testaverde had been sacked five times and thrown five interceptions in hitting on 26-of-50 passes for 285 yards. Highsmith gained 119 of Miami's 160 rushing yards but Dozier's 99 yards on 20 carries made him the Outstanding Offensive Player of the Game. "It doesn't mean as much to me as being No. 1," Dozier said. Shaffer, who had lost only one game since 7th grade, was asked if he felt vindicated after being so maligned by the fans. "If I

could spell the word, maybe I could feel it," he joked. Not to be forgotten was the punting of Bruno, who averaged 43.4 yards on nine kicks and once backed Miami inside its own 10-yard line. "I can't put into words how happy I am for these kids," Paterno told sportswriters. "They worked hard, believed in themselves and had the poise to withstand the pressure." Unlike their pregame boorishness, the Hurricanes were gracious in defeat as Johnson and Brown both made appearances in the State locker room. "Penn State is a deserving National Champion," Johnson said. "We won the battle but lost the war," said Brown. "We gave our all...we just got beat. Penn State is a helluva team. They did what they had to do. They deserved to win."

"Class Beat's Crass," said the headline in the *Phoenix Gazette* over a story by Joe Gilmartin. "...It's nice to see nice guys finish first," wrote Gilmartin. "Maybe if it happens often enough, it will start a trend." Joe Henderson of the *Tampa Tribune* wrote, "The bad boys were bad and the good guys were good..." and Robbie Andreu of the *Fort Lauderdale News & Sun Sentinel* wrote, "They arrived in battle fatigues, boastful and confident of winning the war for the National Championship. In the end, they left in confused retreat." In the *Philadelphia Inquirer*, Bill Lyon wrote, "It was the kind of game Penn State almost always wins. Keep it close; make it come down to making the big play at the end. We have watched this same scenario unfold over and over." And Ed Pope, writing in the *Miami Herald*, said, "Penn State still deserves to be No. 1 simply because it did what it had to when it had to."

A two-time First-Team All-American, the great LB Shane Conlan was selected Most Valuable Defensive Player in the 1986 National Championship game.

The championship was a popular one with the public and the game made an impression on the nation. The game had been seen by a record 21.9 million households watching on NBC, breaking the previous record for a college football telecast set by USC and Ohio State in the 1980 Rose Bowl. To this day, millions of football fans not associated with Penn State remember the pregame controversy and the whirlwind finish and Paterno still hears about it from strangers when he travels. When the team returned to Pennsylvania, two days later, they were greeted by thousands in Harrisburg, including Governor Dick Thornburgh. There was another motorcade up to State College similar to the victory celebration of '82 with well-wishers cheering as fire engines and ambulances escorted the PSU contingent through the small towns in the hills and valleys of Central Pennsylvania. The following Saturday, 30,000 more turned out for an hour and a half parade down College Avenue that was televised live by several area stations and 10,000 stayed for the rally that followed on the Old Main lawn honoring the team.

"For the first time, undefeated and No. 1," said one headline in the *Philadelphia Inquirer*. The "Century of Excellence" had come to an end but another was about to begin. Paterno had his second National Championship and he wanted more. No, he told sportswriters, he was not going to retire. Maybe in five or six years but not now. He had more challenges ahead. The coach was right about that—several seasons of challenges.

Season Record 12-0
Record to Date 616-266-41
Winning percentage .690

1987-1997

One of the newest and most popular cheers emerging from the National Championship years was one that went like this:

Cheerleaders: "We say 'JoePa' ... You Say, 'Terno"
Cheerleaders: "JoePa"
Crowd: "'Terno"
Cheerleaders: "JoePa"
Crowd: "'Terno"
Everyone: "Yeahhhhhhhh!!!!"

Paterno's 5-foot-10 image on life-size cardboard cut outs, known as "Stand-Up Joes," were now selling by the thousands in and around Happy Valley. His face with an overexaggeration of that prominent nose was turned into coffee cups and book ends, plastered all over golf balls and coke bottles and imprinted on everything from hand towels to serving trays. He had become a commodity and a cult figure. Songs were written about him. An ice cream at the University's world-renown creamery was named after him, "Peachy Paterno." His words helped sell credit cards, telephone yellow pages and pizza. Much of the money he made on the merchandise went to the fund he had set up to expand the Penn State library. In the next decade he would become a wealthy man from endorsements and investments but always he would be giving back to help his adopted school.

But after the ecstasy of the '86 championship, things didn't go so well on the football field. It went to hell in 1988 when State had its first losing season in 49 years and lost six games in a row on national television. Just before a midseason game against perennial State whipping-boy West Virginia, a letter in the Centre Daily Times suggested someone kidnap Paterno on game day. He was told by sports-

"JoePa"

writers and fans that his offense was too predictable and out of style with the go-go late '80s. "These are dismal days in Happy Valley...," wrote a columnist for the Boston Globe, "...Joe Paterno now seeming a tad old and set in his ways..." Many said he and his staff had grown stale and had lost their recruiting touch. Some critics believed he was spending too much time on his outside activities and a high profile appearance at the '88 Republican convention seconding the nomination of George Bush for President was seen as being symbolic of what was wrong. He later told Sports Illustrated that he had considered retiring after that disastrous '88 season.

What he did was not to quit but to back off on his outside activities and concentrate on football, re-energizing himself, his coaches and his young players. By the end of 1989, the Lions appeared to be on the way back. And Paterno gained more motivation when the Big Ten shocked the college athletic community by inviting Penn State to join. This traditionally Eastern school was pulling up its roots and moving to the midwest. Although many Lion fans didn't like it and blamed Paterno, he and other University officials were convinced the change was in the best athletic and academic interests of State. The Big Ten's maneuver was the catalyst for other conference shakeups that soon found two other major independents, Miami and Florida State, hooking up with league affiliations. The SEC and the Big 8 were overhauled and the Southwest Conference went out of business. A month before his '91 team finished 11-2 and third in the ratings, Paterno was honored by being the first active coach to receive the "Distinguished American" award from the National Football Foundation College Football Hall of Fame. He also helped to bring in more money to build a new indoor basketball arena and convocation center planned for a site adjacent to Beaver Stadium. And he began to seriously talk publicly about retiring in five more years, December 1996, when he would be 70 years old.

However, even as his team was winning again, some of the criticism about his coaching continued, particularly when the team failed to win some big games against the likes of Alabama, Miami and Notre Dame. Then in 1992, as he and the players waited to begin Big Ten play the following year, the major post season bowls made an agreement before the season that virtually eliminated the Lions from a chance at a National Championship game on New Year's Day. Additional off field personnel problems didn't help and the season turned into another embarrassment when the team seemed to quit in three or four games that were televised nationally.

"Pasadena, Here We Come!" heralded one 1993 preseason football magazine catering to Penn State fans. But many in the Big Ten resented the interloper and the entire conference and its followers, including the media, seemed to take special pleasure when the Lions lost two midseason games to the league's elite team, Michigan and Ohio State. A year later, Paterno and his latest participants of "The Grand Experiment" took their revenge and went unbeaten, won the Big Ten title and the Rose Bowl only to see another National Championship denied them by the personal politics of college football.

As Paterno and his team headed towards the last years of the 20th Century, he was determined to get that national title again—and maybe again and again. His recruiting techniques which been criticized when the decade started had brought more blue chip athletes to Happy Valley. They were signing on as their fathers and uncles had once done to play for this legend in the mountains of Pennsylvania. Five more years, just five more years.

"'Out of Whack'"

The best way to describe and define the 1987 season is to use a phrase that frequently pops up in Paterno's lexicon. Everything was "out of whack." According to the "American Heritage Dictionary," it means, "improperly ordered or balanced; not functioning correctly." That certainly would characterize what happened in the year following the second National Championship.

Although the Lions lost 24 letterman and 15 starters, including the heart of the defense and offense, there was still enough talent returning to believe this team could still compete for another national title. Certainly, the sportswriters who covered State thought so. "... it is not crazy to think that the Lions could be 9-0 heading into (the end of the season games with) Pitt and Notre Dame next year," wrote Neil Rudel of the Altoona Mirror. Ronnie Christ of the Harrisburg Patriot News agreed. "I'm not about to predict that Penn State is going to win it all again," he wrote in Penn State Football Preview magazine. "Let's just say I won't be tremendously surprised if it does happen." The national press was a little more cautious. Sports Illustrated picked the Lions #7 and the AP had them #11 in the initial preseason poll.

Paterno was optimistic but realistic. "Obviously, we're going into this season understanding that things can't possibly go as well as they did last year," he said on the annual media day as preseason practice began in mid-August. He was right. His problems had started in the spring with serious injuries to Giftopoulos and Roundtree and continued on the eve of the preseason when co-captain Bauer showed up on crutches after straining a tendon in his foot while jogging. Injuries, particularly on defense, would hamper the team all season and Paterno would never be able to start the same lineup in any game. Giftopoulos was in and out and Roundtree didn't play the last part of the season. Of course, injuries are part football and every team has them. But these injuries, and others to such defensive veterans as Matt Johnson, Karpinski and Polamalu before the opening game, were the first sign of a season that would be "out of whack."

Paterno knew he had a lot of spots to fill in both the defensive and offensive units and he had used the spring to "teach the kids how to play." "I don't think we've ever had as many areas to start from scratch as we have with this group," he said at the end of spring practice. He was particularly concerned about his kicking game with the need for a new punter and placekicker. Inexperienced fifth-year senior Chris Clauss eventually would beat out two walk-ons, including basketball letterman Christian Appleman, and do well. Two other walk-ons, senior Eric Etze and sophomore Ray Tarasi, would share the placekicking and neither would distinguish himself. However, other parts of his rebuilding also would be "out of whack" as the season progressed.

This was Knizner's team from the start and a lot of fans expected the Lion co-captain would finally get his chance to show he was a better quarterback than Shaffer. "I think Matt has a chance to be as good a quarterback as there is in the East and maybe one of the best in the country," Paterno told sportswriters. Paterno was also high on his wideouts—Roundtree, Timpson, Coates and Mike Alexander—and he said "I think we'll have to have a good passing year if we're going to be a good team." But running was still the foundation of the Paterno offense and except for Thomas, the backfield was inexperienced. Even Thomas had never started a game. Still, he was a proven factor and vital to the attack. "I think we have to give him the ball 30 times a game for us to win," Paterno said before the preseason. To get depth behind Thomas, Paterno moved junior John Greene from safety to tailback in the spring and Greene shared the Worrell award with offensive tackle Tim Freeman as the most improved offensive player. The fullbacks also were new with redshirt sophomore Sean Redman and redshirt freshman Sean Barkowski battling for the starting position. Paterno and offensive coordinator Ganter also expected some help from three true freshmen running backs: Leroy Thompson of Knoxville, TN, Gary Brown of Williamsport and Sam Gash of Hendersonville, NC. Paterno was more confident about his offensive line, saying "The offensive line has a chance to be a good one." The tight ends would be Pomfret and Mrosko with Clayton, Sickler and Freeman at the tackles, Wisniewski, Kuzy and Monaghan at the guards with senior letterman Mike Wolf and sophomore Roger Duffy of Canton, OH, at center. A change on the offensive coaching staff also marked a milestone for Paterno as the first assistant he ever hired, Bob Phillips, retired but continued to help out as a volunteer.

With Bauer and Giftopoulos returning at inside linebackers and Polamalu at nose tackle backed by Matt Johnson, the middle of the defense was expected to be a major strength. Curkendall, Schonewolf and sophomore Dave Szott of Clifton, NJ, were set at the defensive tackles but the outside linebacker slots were more unsettled with veterans Karpinski and Bernier, junior Quintus McDonald, redshirt sophomores Scott Gob and Dave Jakob and true freshman Andre Powell all

Stan Clayton, OT and a starter on the 1986 National Championship team and again in 1987, went on to a professional football career with three different NFL teams.

figured in the mix. Much was expected from McDonald, who was one of the nation's most recruited athletes in '85 out of Montclair, NJ, when he was the USA Today Defensive Player of the Year. McDonald had struggled as a backup in his first two years but now he seemed ready to live up to his potential after winning the O'Hora award as the most improved defensive player in spring practice. The secondary was anchored by cornerback Eddie Johnson, whom Paterno said was "the best cornerback we've ever had." Wilkerson and Downing battled for the other corner with redshirt junior Kevin Woods and freshmen Hernon Henderson and Willie Thomas in reserve. Co-captain Marques Henderson was moved to free safety with sophomore Andre Collins of Cinnaminson, NJ, backing him up and sophomores Brian Chizmar and Sherrod Rainge took over at the "Hero" position. "It's difficult to assess...what we're capable of," defensive coordinator Sandusky told Ron Bracken of the Centre Daily Times before the season. "It will be a learning experience from the beginning...We have the potential to be solid..."

The schedule was another indication that this was a season "out of whack." Two home games had been changed from the original schedule. When North Carolina State asked for more money to visit Beaver Stadium, PSU officials said "no" and the contract was canceled. Arizona State was sought as a replacement but only wanted to play in Tempe, and that is how Bowling Green of the Mid-American Conference became a first time opponent and the season opening game on September 5. The other change involved the shift of the Alabama game from October 24 to the second game of the season on the night of September 12 so that it could be televised nationally in prime time by CBS. "If I knew the defensive guys were that hurt I wouldn't have scheduled Alabama so early in the season," Paterno told sportswriters as the Bowling Green game approached.

The 45-19 victory over Bowling Green was historic for it was the 200th win in Paterno's career. Bowling Green actually led, 7-3, at the end of the first quarter but the Lions exploded for four touchdowns in the second quarter, including one on a 63-yard punt return by

Roundtree and another on a 67-yard screen pass from Knizner to Thomas. McDonald also scored a TD in the third quarter when Curkendall sacked the Bowling Green quarterback in the end zone and McDonald recovered the fumble. Paterno was honored for his landmark victory in a post-game ceremony on the field and later told reporters, "I may live to be 100 but I'll never be around for another 100 victories." He also said his team made too many mistakes. "We have a lot of loose ends obviously...We're certainly not ready to bring on a good team yet..."

Alabama may not have been that good but under new coach Bill Curry it was much better than State on both sides of the ball the following Saturday night in the rain at Beaver Stadium. The game belonged to Tide halfback Bobby Humphrey who had the fourth best rushing day ever against the Lions with 220 yards on 36 carries to spark a 24-13 victory. Seven minutes into the game, Humphrey brushed off several Lion would-be tacklers and ran 73 yards for a touchdown. Early in the second quarter, he surprised the PSU defense by throwing a 57-yard pass off a pitchout to set up Alabama's second TD and a 17-0 lead. But the tone of the game may have been set three minutes before Humphrey's TD run in the first quarter when Alabama linebacker Derrick Thomas sacked Knizner and literally knocked him silly. Knizner had hit on three of his first four passes but after the Thomas hit Knizner wandered around the Alabama backfield looking for his huddle until the Lions called time out. He convinced Paterno and the doctors that he was okay but the next three times he tried to pass he was sacked. "For a while, I didn't know where I was," Knizner admitted later. "I thought I was all right but I was still woozy and my vision was blurry." Paterno inserted redshirt freshman Tom Bill at quarterback in the second quarter and late in the period Bill completed 5-of-7 passes in a 76-yard drive that climaxed with a 21-yard TD pass to Roundtree. Knizner was back in the third quarter but Alabama's offense took charge of the second half and controlled the ball for nearly 20 minutes. The Tide scored another TD early in the fourth quarter on a 58-yard drive and just as Paterno was about to take Knizner out of the game with nine minutes left, he combined with Roundtree on a 60-yard bomb. But that was State's last gasp as Alabama dominated the rest of the way. "Alabama just played a better game than we did," Paterno told the media, but he said he was pleased with Knizner's performance and the TD to Roundtree. "He had a lot of pressure on him," Paterno said. "He was out of whack."

Of course, the team was "out of whack," too, and Paterno knew it. Many of the players were dispirited because they had never played in a game that the Lions had lost in the regular season. Paterno wasn't pleased with everything either and several of his defensive players were still nursing injuries. Before the next game against Cincinnati, he moved some players on the defense, including the shift of Marques Henderson back to Hero and Rainge to free safety. But his most significant maneuver was to switch Greene from backup tailback to starting fullback to get more blocking for Thomas. Thomas ran for 154 yards and a touchdown on 22 carries and Greene gained 124 yards and had two TDs as the #20 Lions romped over Cincinnati, 41-0, on another rainy Saturday. The offense piled up 559 yards while the defense was limiting the Bearcats pro-style attack to 117 passing yards and a minus three rushing yards with four sacks and a fumble recovery. "They just stuffed us," said Cincy coach Dave Currey. "I think this shows that Penn State's better than people think."

Thomas did even better the following Saturday night against Boston College at Sullivan Stadium in Foxboro when he gained 164 yards on 30 carries, including a 17-yard TD, and caught a 40-yard pass for another TD. But as an ESPN television audience watched, the now #15 Lions almost blew a 17-0 lead early in the second quarter as BC quarterback Mike Power got hot. Power hit Darren Flutie with first half scoring passes of 18 and 41 yards and set up a 26-yard field goal with a 39-yard pass that tied the game five minutes into the second half. "He looked like (Doug) Flutie, (Dan) Marino and everyone else rolled into one," Paterno told sportswriters later. "But I didn't want what he was doing to get us out of whack." So, the defense, playing without Bauer, intensified its blitzing. The Lions sacked Power a total of 10 times for 78 yards in losses, including five big sacks that stopped BC cold on its last six possessions. Early in the fourth quarter, a 5-yard running into the punter penalty on a fourth down at the BC 35-yard line allowed the Lions to take a 20-17 lead on Etze's 46-yard field goal. Then, after an exchange of interceptions, Timpson ran back a punt 26 yards to the BC 47-yard line. With Thomas, Greene and Timpson running, the Lions quickly drove for the clinching score with Greene pounding in for the TD from 4-yards out. Etze's PAT made it 27-17 and that's how it finished. BC's All-American linebacker Bill Romanowski said Thomas is so strong that "You have to wrap him up and then gang-tackle him...it also helps that they have one of the toughest offensive lines I've ever faced." Paterno said, "it was really a good (defensive) effort, especially since we didn't have Bauer in there."

Even with Bauer and Karpinski sidelined by injuries, the Lions seemed back on track the next two weeks as Thomas continued his exceptional running against Temple and Rutgers. Knizner also broke out of his lethargy, perhaps responding to some of the boos directed his way. Temple was off to its best start since 1979 with a 4-1 record that included a 24-21 upset over Pitt but the Owls were no threat after a 3-3 tie in the first quarter. Knizner directed touchdown drives of 80 and 87 yards in the second quarter and a 95-yard march at the start of the third quarter as the Lions whipped the Owls, 27-13, on another soggy day. Thomas scored both second quarter TDs on runs of 3 and 45 yards and before he left in the middle of the fourth quarter he had rushed for 167 yards on 24 carries, caught three passes for 51 yards and returned three kickoffs for 41 yards. Knizner had the first 200 yard passing day of his career, hitting on 15-of-27 passes for 200 yards, including a 21-yard TD pass to Coates and a 41-yarder to Timpson that set up Thomas' first TD. Temple's only TD came against PSU reserves late in the fourth quarter as the Lion defense throttled the Owls star halfback Todd McNair who gained just 88 yards on 34 carries. The Lions played even better before a Homecoming crowd of 85,376 a week later when Rutgers brought its 4-1 record into Beaver Stadium on the first sunny day of the season. The first half was close as touchdown runs of 9 and 3 yards by Thomas helped give the Lions a 14-7 lead. Knizner then led State on drives of 81 and 61 yards to take a 28-7 lead early in the fourth quarter, passing 39-yards to Roundtree for one TD, and State went on to win, 35-21. Knizner had what would be the best day of his career, completing 16-of-26 passes for 215 yards with just one interception, while Thomas rushed for 116 yards on 20 carries and Roundtree caught four passes for 107 yards. The passing of Scott Erney kept Rutgers in the game as he hit on 32-of-55 passes for 346 yards but the Lion defense led by Chizmar picked off two passes, sacked Erney three times for 33 yards in losses and held Rutgers runners to 10 yards on 23 carries. "We played well until we got a little sloppy in the end," Paterno said in the media room. "This club may be 5-1," wrote Mark Ashenfelter of the Daily Collegian, "but nobody's really sure just how good the Lions can be."

The test would be at Syracuse on October 17 in the Carrier Dome and CBS-TV's cameras would show a regional TV audience how "out of whack" this Penn State season was going to be. The Lions were now #10 in the AP poll and unbeaten Syracuse was #13 and off to its best start since the 1960 team went 7-2. The Orange had not beaten State in 16 years and it was not a good omen when the Nittany Lion shrine was painted orange Thursday night and Rainge and Wilkerson were left home because of injuries when the team left for Syracuse the next morning. Then, when Giftopoulous and Eddie Johnson showed up in the pregame warm-ups wearing street clothes, even the most fervent PSU fan realized something was "out of whack." Just before the kickoff the public address announcer got carried away and told the 50,011 screaming partisans that this was the most important game ever for Syracuse. It was virtually over in 10 seconds. On the first play after the kickoff, Rob Moore raced past Downing and Chizmar, who slipped as he was changing directions, and caught an 80-yard bomb from Don McPherson and the crowd went wild. By halftime the score was 27-0 and it was an embarrassing 41-0 midway in the third quarter when freshman Gary Brown sped 80 yards for a Lion TD. In the fourth quarter, Schonewolf blocked a punt and ran 18-yards for a TD and Bill threw a 59-yard TD to Roundtree as Syracuse won, 48-21, scoring the most points ever against State since the series began in 1922. Thomas was held to 42 yards on 14 carries and Knizner had just 4-of-13 competitions for 24 yards and one interception. "All the trappings were in place for this kind of exorcism...and (Syracuse) made the defending National Champions grovel," wrote Ray Parrillo in the Philadelphia Inquirer. "(Coach) Dick (MacPherson) took it easy on us," Paterno said after going into the Syracuse locker room to congratulate the winners. "It could have been a lot worse than it was."

What happened at Syracuse was a shock but the Lions had two weeks to recover before playing 4-and-3 West Virginia at Beaver Stadium on a warm Halloween afternoon in what was the turning point of the season. Except for the absence of Roundtree, who was hurt in practice, everything seemed back to normal when the Lions went 68-yards in the first five minutes of the game to take a 7-0 lead on Greene's one-yard run and Tarasi's PAT. But then, things just seemed to go "out of whack." With State still leading 10-7 late in the third quarter, the Mountaineers intercepted a Knizner pass at the Lion 29-yard line and took a 14-10 lead six plays later on a 6-yard TD pass from redshirt freshman Major Harris to tight end Keith Winn. Five minutes into the fourth quarter, the Mountaineers stretched their lead to 21-10 after a quick 71-yard drive with Harris running 21 yards on one play and throwing a 30-yard pass to former QB John Talley for the touchdown. The WVU players celebrated on the sidelines as if the game was over and that angered the Lions. Thompson took the kickoff and ran 35 yards to the PSU 42-yard line in what both Paterno and WVU's Nehlen would call "the play of the game." No longer the "People's Choice," Knizner was booed when he came onto the field. But a 13-yard pass to Timpson and a 20-yard pass to Alexander picked up first downs. Thomas, who would gain 181 yards for the afternoon, went 16-yards on a draw to put the ball at the one-yard line, then banged over the middle for the touchdown. Knizner hit Thomas with a swing pass for the 2-point conversion and the Lions trailed 21-18 with eight minutes remaining. A moment later Harris scrambled and completed a pass that would have given WVU the ball at the State 6-yard line but the play was nullified by a penalty for an illegal receiver downfield. That forced a punt and the Lions took over at their own 38-yard line. Thomas carried four times for 21 yards and Knizner passed 14 yards to Alexander and soon State

Aggressive LB Trey Bauer was a starter in the 1986 and 1987 championship games and a Third-Team All-American as a senior.

was at the WVU 19-yard line. Brown then swept left, cut back inside and dashed into the end zone standing up. Tarasi's PAT made it 25-21 and the defense stopped Harris and WVU the rest of the way for the victory. "When you're down by 11 points with nine minutes to go, you'd better decide you're going to be a team right then and there," Matt Johnson told sportswriters. "We're going to have to fight like dogs every game of the season," Paterno said.

Maryland tried some psychology to break its long losing streak against the Lions. First it shifted the game to Baltimore's Memorial Stadium, then came out on the field with different uniforms, wearing black shirts for the first time since 1946. All that seemed to fire up the 4-and-4 Terps and their hungry fans and they dominated the first half, controlling the ball for 11 minutes of the first quarter and twice driving inside the PSU 10-yard line before the intermission. But both times Maryland had to settle for 27-yard field goals and when Downing intercepted sophomore Neil O'Donnell's pass and returned it 38-yards for a touchdown with 4:23 left in the half, the frustrated Terps were stunned. State stretched its halftime lead to 14-6 on an 81-yard drive at the start of the third quarter with Pomfret scoring on a 5-yard pass from Knizner. Another Maryland drive to the State 4 in the third quarter ended in more frustration for the Terps when O'Donnell was sacked by Chizmar on a third-and-goal and Dan Plocki missed a 25-yard field goal. Early in the fourth quarter, Maryland again had to settle for a Plocki field goal after a 71-yard drive. State appeared to seal the game a few minutes later when Knizner switched plays after sensing an all-out blitz and

pitched out to Thomas who ran 58-yards for a touchdown. But with Henning now at quarterback, Maryland drove 59 yards for a TD to make the score 21-15 with five minutes remaining. A botched punt by Clauss enabled the Terps to get the ball on its own 42-yard line with 2:22 left. But on the first play, Karpinski and Schonewolf broke through and as Henning tried to get rid of the ball he threw directly to Giftopoulos, playing for the first time in three games. The interception virtually ended the game. "(Penn State) can be beat," said Maryland's new coach Joe Krivak, who had turned down Paterno's offer to be State's offensive coordinator only a few months earlier. "But you have to beat them. They don't beat themselves."

Krivak was wrong. The next week, State helped beat themselves as an ESPN audience watched Pitt win 10-0 on a cold night at Pitt Stadium. It was another night when everything was "out of whack" as the Panthers blocked two Tarasi field goal attempts from inside the 30-yard line—one with five minutes left in the game—and Pomfret dropped a sure 44-yard TD pass when he was wide open at the Pitt 10-yard line. Jeff Van Horne's 44-yard field goal four minutes into the first quarter was all the Panthers really needed and Van Horne missed three other chip shot field goal attempts that could have extended the lead. The Panthers stacked eight men on the line, shutting down State's running game and daring Knizner to throw. His throws were often way off target and he hit on just 7-of-28 attempts for 126 yards with two interceptions, including one in the last 20 seconds that Billy Owens returned for a 69-yard TD. Later, Paterno admitted the Lions should have passed earlier in the game. "I did a lousy job," he said. "I got my offensive coaches all screwed up. Our defense played well enough for us to win."

Despite the loss, the unranked Lions were still an attractive bowl team and in the week before the final game against #7 Notre Dame, the Citrus Bowl talked about pairing State against Atlantic Coast Conference champion Clemson. With only a 30-22 loss to Pitt, Notre Dame still had an outside chance for the national title and was trying to persuade Orange Bowl officials to wait until after the Irish's final game against Miami two weeks later before selecting an opponent to play #1 Oklahoma. A national television audience watched in the comfort of their homes as the teams kicked off on an icy field before 84,000 in snow flurry weather with 30 mile an hour winds and a wind chill temperature at 18 degrees. What they saw was a solid, evenly played game that came down once again to the last seconds of play. Part of Paterno's game plan was to try an avoid punting to Tim Brown whose punt returns for touchdowns in earlier games had made him the front-runner for the Heisman Trophy. So on the Lions first possession, they punted on third down before Brown could get into the game. Defensive back Brandy Wells fumbled and Chizmar recovered at the Irish 19-yard line. In two plays, State scored with Thomas going over the left side for nine yards and Greene then getting the TD and the Lions led 7-0 midway through the first quarter. But the Irish tied it in 20 seconds on a quick three-play drive following the kickoff, with quarterback Tony Rice scampering 32 yards for the TD. That set the tempo for the game and after the Lions had taken a 14-7 lead at halftime on a one-yard Thomas TD, Notre Dame tied it on a Rice run of 11 yards at 6:44 of the third quarter. The game was so even that when it was finally over both teams had a total of 312 yards running and passing, although the Lions ran off nine more plays. After the second Irish TD, the Lions drove 77 yards but Etze missed a 28-yard field goal. Then, in the fourth quarter another time consuming, 15-play drive into the wind gave State the lead again, 21-14, on Greene's 3-yard TD. By the time Notre Dame took possession on its 38-yard line with about four minutes remaining, the shivering crowd and the CBS announcers were raving about Thomas, who had rushed for his best day ever with 214 yards on 35 carries. But the game wasn't over and Rice methodically moved the Irish for a TD on 12 plays, with fullback Anthony Johnson getting the one-yard TD with 30 seconds left. On the sideline, the Notre Dame players told Holtz they wanted to go for the win. Sandusky called the defense. Rice rolled out right on an option and Karpinski was waiting. Rice turned inside and was smashed down short of the goal line by Curkendall. "I knew I had him by the ankle..." Curkendall said later, "Then eight or nine guys jumped on top of me." Mike DeCourcy of the Pittsburgh Press wrote, "It was a moment that will always be frozen in the history of Penn State football." Paterno told sportswriters, "For the first time these kids finally felt the National Championship cross was off their backs."

After the game, the Lions accepted an invitation to meet Clemson at noon on New Year's Day in the Citrus Bowl. Notre Dame settled for the Cotton Bowl. "I promised some people we weren't going to go to Florida with a 7-4 football team," Paterno said.

THE 1988 CITRUS BOWL
Jan. 1, 1988
Clemson 35, Penn State 10

For all intents and purposes, State's fate in the Citrus Bowl was determined on December 9 in State College when Thomas injured his right knee during a private running drill in the Lions' new indoor field house, Holuba Hall. But that wasn't the only indication that this post-season endeavor was simply "out of whack." Paterno decided to take the team to Orlando two days earlier than usual for a New Year's Day game. But the chartered flight on December 24 was nearly two hours late and the team had to sit around the barren Harrisburg Airport all that time. Still, Paterno was able to keep his sense of humor. When presented with the "key to the city" upon arrival at the Orlando airport, Paterno cracked, "I want to remind all the players that this key also doesn't open the jail." In keeping with his philosophy, he wanted the players to have a good time in this tourist mecca where Disney World, Sea World and the downtown Church Street entertainment complex were just some of the distractions. He also wanted them to know the real reason they were there.

As usual Paterno closed his practices but he told sportswriters he wasn't happy with how they were going. He blamed part of the problem on the heat of Central Florida, which surprised him. At first, Paterno said he hoped Thomas would play but by the time he reached Florida he knew Thomas had suffered a torn cruciate ligament. Thomas was with the team but he eventually underwent surgery on January 11. Losing Thomas was like losing three-quarters of the offense for the junior was the team's leading rusher with 1,414 yards and 11 touchdowns on 268 carries and leading pass receiver with 23 catches for 300 yards and two TDs. With Roundtree also still sidelined and Knizner's passing erratic in recent games, the Lions were in a hole even before the kickoff.

Clemson coach Danny Ford looked at the game as redemption for a season that "could have been." Although the #14 Tigers had won the ACC title, they believed they could have been playing for the National Championship as they had in '81. A midseason upset to North

Carolina State, 30-28, and a surprise 20-7 loss to arch rival South Carolina in the last game of the season had ended their title aspirations. A win over Paterno and the defending National Champions, Ford said, would restore pride. To insure his team was ready, he took it to Daytona Beach two weeks before the game and put the players through intense, hard hitting two-a-day workouts. He also revamped his passing attack which had been criticized during the season for being inconsistent.

Although both schools were allocated 11,000 tickets, most of the record crowd of 53,142 seemed to be wearing Orange colors and cheering for Clemson. Tiger officials said they had such a demand they could have sold 30,000 more tickets and thousands of their fans had scooped up tickets sold through newspaper advertisements and ticket agencies. The weather was perfect when the Lions kicked off in 75 degree temperatures with Giftopoulos also out with an injury and freshmen tailbacks Thompson and Brown subbing for Thomas. The Lions were "out of whack" from the kickoff as sophomore Wesley McFadden returned the boot 42 yards. Clemson surprised State with a pass on the first play as quarterback Rodney Williams hit Keith Jennings for a 24-yard gain. Williams would go on to have his best passing day of the year, completing 15-of-24 passes for 214 yards, and be named the offensive MVP. Seven plays later fullback Tracy Johnson went 7-yards for the TD and with David Tredwell's PAT the Tigers led 7-0. On their second possession, the Lions drove to a third-and-goal at the 3-yard line but Brown botched a handoff on a reverse to Greene and Clemson recovered the fumble ending the threat. However, State scored the next time it had the ball as Timpson returned a punt 36 yards to the Clemson 44 and three plays later Knizner found Alexander open on the right sideline for a 38-yard TD. Etze's PAT tied it but Clemson came right back with an 8-play 76-yard drive to take a 14-7 lead at halftime. At that point, State's offense had gained just 20 yards rushing on 19 plays and even loyal PSU fans sensed the Clemson defense led by All-American Michael Dean Perry was about to prove why it was the fifth best defense in the nation and the second best against the rush.

The Lions made it look good at the start of the second half when Thompson's 32-yard kickoff return set up a 76-yard drive that carried to the 11-yard line. But State had to settle for a 27-yard Etze field goal and Clemson took the ensuing kickoff and went 70 yards for the TD that virtually clinched the game. State had one last fling, driving 71 yards following the Clemson TD before Knizner an threw an interception in the end zone that Dorian Mariable returned 46 yards. Clemson added another TD early in the fourth quarter, then with time running out in the fourth quarter, Donnell Woolford picked off another Knizner pass in the end zone, setting up an 80-yard drive that made the final score, 35-10. It was State's worst loss in a bowl game and Paterno told the media, "Clemson kicked our ears in. Obviously, Danny and his staff did a much better job preparing than we did. Clemson played a great game." Jerry Greene of the Orlando Sentinel wrote, "Clemson was not supposed to pass because nobody thought Williams could. Wrong...the Lions (also) had to throw the ball some...Without superior running back Blair Thomas, they didn't run effectively. Unfortunately...they didn't pass effectively either. Come to think of it, they didn't play defense effectively either." Paterno said he was especially sorry for his seniors. "They did a lot for Penn State and for college football in general," he told sportswriters.

Not everything was "out of whack" that season. Wisniewski became the 14th offensive lineman in PSU history to be named a First-

Team All-American. He would be back in '88 to help lead the team. So would Thomas and Roundtree. At least that's what Paterno believed when he left Orlando. He was wrong. Paterno didn't know it on January 2, 1988, but the year ahead was about to make history. And for all the wrong reasons.

Season Record 8-4
Record to Date 624-270-41
Winning percentage .689

"The Hellfires"

In his book published after the 1988 season, Paterno called this year, "The Hellfires of '88." That certainly is a succinct description of what became the school's first losing season in 49 years.

It wasn't just a season "out of whack," it was a season out of control. And unlike what happened during the turmoil of 1979, there was not much Paterno could do about it. Certainly, he made some mistakes and a few bad coaching decisions. But a good portion of the collapse was the result of outside forces. With a few moves here or there, Paterno may have avoided a 5-6 season. However, its unlikely it would have improved that much—perhaps 7-4 at the very best. Maybe not as much hell, but still hell for Paterno and the inhabitants of the Lion football kingdom.

The defining moments of the season came in the second half of the game against Rutgers at Beaver Stadium when the Lions were 2-0 and seemingly headed for another winning year. But the seeds of what occurred that day had been planted months before. It started with the slow healing of Thomas' knee injury and the medical decision to keep him off the playing field for another year. Then, the NCAA ruled against giving Roundtree another year of eligibility because of his injury. As a freshman in 1984, Roundtree had been in 38 plays in two early games before being cut down by a groin injury. But in the seventh game against Syracuse, he was in for just two plays and that was enough for him to be ineligible by a strict interpretation of the rule. So, even before spring practice was over, Paterno had lost his best two offensive weapons. He also lost their leadership and that was significant because this was his most inexperienced team.

"More players faced their first year of college football—either as redshirts or 'true' freshmen—than on any team in my coaching career," he wrote in "Paterno: By the Book." But even the upperclassmen were young and the final three-deep depth chart had more freshmen and sophomores (30) than seniors (27). "On this year's depth chart," Paterno wrote, "the potential leaders, those who lift the others to a vision of winning, had not yet stepped out to stake their claim."

Nowhere were the Lions more inexperienced than at quarterback. Redshirt sophomore Bill was tabbed as the #1 quarterback after spring practice but he had thrown just 36 passes as a backup to Knizner in '87. His backups, senior Lance Lonergan and redshirt freshman Doug Sieg, had even less experience. Paterno had recruited two outstanding quarterbacks, including Tony Sacca of Delran, NJ, who was rated by most recruiting services as the best scholastic QB in the coun-

try. But both he and Matt Nardolillo of Randolph, NJ, were slated to be "redshirted." However, by the time the season started at Virginia, Sieg was out for the year with a herniated disc and Sacca was practicing as the third QB.

With Thomas out, Paterno made a decision that even he wondered about later. Instead of designating a starting tailback, he used a three-man rotation of youngsters—Brown, Thompson and Redman. Some sportswriters said this indicated Paterno was

Paterno called Roger Duffy the "best center to ever play for Penn State." He won a NCAA Post Graduate Scholarship in 1990 and went on to an NFL career.

unwilling to make decisions. "If Paterno couldn't choose a starting tailback," Matt Dorney of the York Daily Record would later write for "Penn State Football Preview" magazine, "how could one expect him to use one for a key fourth-down call against Pittsburgh?" Fullback was set with co-captain Greene and sophomore Gash as Barkowski had transferred to Syracuse. "We've got a different backfield," Paterno told Adam Gusdorft of the Daily Collegian. "I think those five guys are going to have to carry the load in some combination." Paterno received one break when his best wide receiver, Timpson, didn't qualify for the U.S. Olympic team as a sprinter and was ready for the first game. The other prime receivers were inexperienced redshirt freshmen with strong credentials, David Daniels of Sarasota, FL, and Terry Smith of Monroeville. Paterno said both would have to "step up" if the team was going to have a good passing attack. Jakob was switched from linebacker to tight end and became the starter with juniors Todd Young and John Wolfe in reserve. Co-captain Wisniewski and center Duffy were the only starters back on the offensive line but veteran Monaghan became the other starter at guard with sophomore Sean Love and senior Bob Vernaglia as backups. The tackles were Freeman, junior Eric Jonassen, senior Jeff Brubaker and sophomore Matt McCartin, who had transferred from SMU. "We have a big job ahead of us," Paterno said during the preseason.

The defense was also inexperienced as Paterno lost 12 lettermen, including six starters from '87. That included defensive backs Wilkerson and Woods, who had left school with academic problems. Co-captain Eddie Johnson was back and moved to strong safety with Chizmar returning to the Hero slot. The cornerbacks included Willie Thomas, Rainge and redshirt freshman Darren Perry of Cheapeake, VA. Andre Collins was moved to inside linebacker where he won the O'Hora award for most improved player during the spring, and paired with Gob with Powell and redshirt freshman Mark D'Onofrio of North Bergen, NJ, while Karpinski, McDonald, juniors Neil Hamilton and Geoff

Japachen and redshirt freshman Keith Goganious were on the outside. Karpinski, the fourth co-captain, later would move to strong safety as Paterno juggled the secondary and utilized true freshmen Chris Cisar and Mark Graham there too. The starting nose tackle was Szott with true freshman Eric Renkey of Pittsburgh as his backup. In a surprise move, Paterno turned senior Mrosko from a tight end into a defensive tackle and he started there, teaming with Schonewolf, with sophomores Frank Giannetti and Jim Deter in reserve. Redshirt freshman Doug Helkowski was the punter with Tarasi doing most of the placekicking. "The word is that while the new (defensive) crew may lack experience," wrote Ron Christ of the Harrisburg Patriot-News, "it's going to be tougher, quicker and much more physical."

Christ and most of the PSU beat writers figured the Lions would be no worse than '87 and probably better. "All those opposing coaches out there are licking their chops at the prospect of catching Penn State in a down cycle had better beware," he wrote for the "Penn State Football Preview" magazine. "A wounded Lion is the most dangerous kind." Neil Rudel of the Altoona Mirror picked the Lions to be 8-3 "with a good coaching job." The AP preseason poll had State at #20 with opponents Notre Dame at #13, Alabama at #14 and West Virginia at #16.

Even before the Lions were out of the preseason, Paterno had two controversies on his hands. In early August, athletic director Tarman announced that State would no longer play Syracuse after the end of the current contract in 1990. Instead of an equal number of games home and away as had been customary in the series, the Lions had wanted six games at Beaver Stadium over the next 10 years. Tarman said such an arrangement was needed to help finance PSU's 27 other sports teams. Syracuse cried foul and blamed Paterno and State for being selfish. It was a little more complicated than that. Partly, it could be traced to Syracuse's bolt into the Big East basketball conference several years earlier without helping Penn State gain entrance and then dropping the Lions from its basketball schedule in 1982. There also was the demise of Paterno's plan for an all-sports Eastern conference when he was athletic director and Syracuse's role as a leader in that rejection. The second controversy was purely political and involved Paterno leaving preseason practice for a few days in late August to second the nomination of George Bush for President at the Republican convention in New Orleans. Many Pennsylvania Democratic officials were furious and some fans were, too. Paterno never backed away from the dispute but after the season admitted it had been a distraction from his coaching duties.

The opening game in Charlottesville had the most ballyhoo of any season opener since '83 when State's defending National Champions faced Nebraska in the inaugural Kickoff Classic. In six years as head coach at Virginia, George Welsh had transformed a dormant program into a winner and in '87 had finished second in the ACC to Clemson, conquerors of State in the Citrus Bowl. That '87 season also put Virginia into only its second bowl game ever and it had been impressive in knocking off BYU. This year's team was expected to be UVA's best in history and, like Penn State the previous year, this was Virginia's Centennial season. There also was the "family" angle since Welsh had coached under Paterno for nine years and was once considered the heir apparent to succeed Paterno. Three members of Welsh's coaching staff had Lion ties, including defensive coordinator Frank Spaziani, who was co-captain of State's undefeated '68 team, and receivers coach Tom Sherman, the quarterback of Paterno's first bowl

team in 1967. The rivalry was intensified in the recruiting of players and Virginia was now pursuing some of the same scholastic athletes as State. In fact, some recruiting guru's believed the winner of this game would give that team the inside track to a highly-sought Virginia high school running back named Terry Kirby.

Paterno knew this was going to be a crucial game even before spring practice started. Over the summer, he had written to his players reminding them of what was ahead. "This is the biggest game Virginia has ever played," he wrote. "They changed the date of their William and Mary game to September 3 (the week before we play them) so as to give their new QB a chance to get some game experience...They have superb speed on defense and I do mean superb speed. One of their wideouts will be a #1 draft choice...They will be waiting to get us and they will be ready. So will we."

Winning under Welsh had enabled the Cavaliers to expand and improve Scott Stadium and a new artificial turf and additional seats added for '88 brought the seating capacity up to 45,000. With so many PSU alumni living in the Virginia-DC-Maryland area, the demand for tickets rivaled a post-season bowl game and 5,000 State fans were among the sellout crowd that jammed Scott on a warm Saturday night for the game. The atmosphere reminded older State fans of games at New Beaver Field in the 1950s with Virginia students wearing coat and ties and party dresses and socializing on the hill behind one end zone. Their stadium party was over by the end of the first quarter.

After State stopped Virginia at the PSU 27 following the opening kickoff, Bill led a well-executed 61-yard march in 6-plays, passing 18-yards to Jakob to help set up Gash's 1-yard TD. Virginia fumbled the ensuing kickoff and Perry recovered at the 7-yard line. Brown's 5-yard run and Tarasi's PAT made it 14-0 with less than five minutes gone in the quarter. UVA didn't fumble the next kickoff but as quarterback Shawn Moore tried to move his team upfield, he threw a pass that was intercepted by Johnson and returned to the UVA 35-yard line. Eight plays later, Bill hit Timpson on a 5-yard pass for a TD and the Lions led 21-0. Virginia finally scored with about five minutes remaining in the half after recovering a Thompson fumble at PSU's 35-yard line but State came back with an 82-yard drive and Brown ran 19-yards that gave the Lions a 28-7 halftime lead. Brown scored another TD in the third quarter on a 19-yard pass from Bill and the final score was a surprising 42-14. "The big kids came to town tonight; and the Virginia Cavaliers couldn't do anything but cower and look for somewhere to hide," wrote Mark Maske for the Washington Post. "Did we have some kind of miracle team here?" Paterno would later write in "Paterno: By the Book." "If they were this good on opening night, how good might they get by the end of October?" Bill had looked especially sharp, completing 15-of-22 passes for 179 yards and two TDs without an interception. Brown and Jacob each caught three passes and 11 backs helped gain 237 yards rushing on 50 carries. "(Tommy Bill) was very accurate and very poised," Paterno said in the locker room. "(The backs) blocked well, they ran hard and we got what we hoped to get out of them." But Paterno also had to do something during the game that he had hoped not to do. When second team QB Lonergan stubbed his thumb against a helmet in the fourth quarter, Paterno put in Sacca "for game experience." Sacca completed his only pass for 15 yards. Four years, 400 passes and 5,854 yards later, Sacca would own the all-time career record for completions and yardage.

Of course, no one knew it but the Lions had just played their best game of the season. The Beaver Stadium opener against Boston

Paterno once called Eddie Johnson the best cornerback he ever coached. Johnson was at safety when he led all tacklers in the Fiesta Bowl title game against Miami in 1987, and was a Third-Team All-American in 1988.

College the following Saturday would be far less precise and much more mistake prone but State would pull off a typical last minute victory on a rainy day. A 30-yard Tarasi field goal gave the Lions a 3-0 lead after the opening kickoff but BC had a 10-3 lead nine seconds into the second quarter after a TD pass by Mark Kamphaus and a 43-yard field goal by Brian Lowe. State came back to tie at 10-10 when Chizmar's interception set up a 43-yard TD run by Brown on a draw play and by halftime the Lions led 17-13 after a 50-yard TD drive and Lowe's second field goal for BC. Tarasi's 22-yard field goal made it 20-13 six minutes into the third quarter and the Lions were driving for another TD early in the fourth quarter when three costly penalties thwarted them, including a holding penalty that nullified an 18-yard TD pass from Bill to Daniels. Tarasi's 43-yard field goal attempt was wide and a few minutes later BC drove 72 yards with the help of two more penalties, including a personal foul for 15-yards, to tie the score, 20-20, on another Kamphaus TD pass of 19 yards and Lowe's PAT. The Lions almost botched a punt that could have put the Eagles in scoring possession but as the clock was winding down under two minutes, the game seemed headed towards a tie as BC went into punt formation at its own 31-yard line. On the State sideline, specials teams coach Bradley asked Paterno for permission to block the punt. "OK, go after him," Paterno said, "But you'd better not rough the kicker." No one blocked Johnson in the rush and he hit the ball squarely. The ball went out of bounds at the BC 27 and two running plays picked up six yards. In came Tarasi and with his roommate Joe Markiewicz subbing for the regular holder Lonergan, Tarasi booted the ball through the uprights with 43 seconds remaining and the Lions won, 23-20. "Lions Kick Their Way Out of Trouble," said the headline in the Centre Daily Times. "A win like this keeps you humble and thankful," Paterno told the media. "We made enough mistakes to lose three games." He was particularly upset by the eight penalties for losses of 98 yards and the four sacks, which he blamed on the inexperience of his young backs for not picking up the BC blitz. But he was happy with Bill, who hit on 10-of-22 passes for 170 yards with just one interception. "I'm not going to get carried away with two wins," Paterno said. Good thing because the season was about to go into the hellhole.

Rutgers was coming off a major upset over Michigan State and Anderson and his Penn State bred coaching staff devised a game plan that would emphasize more running against the Lions' three-man front. But it was the Scarlet Knight defense that set up the TD that gave Rutgers a 7-0 lead less than four minutes into the game and then stifled several Lion first half scoring opportunities. The Lions stopped Rutgers after the opening kickoff but the offense lost 14 yards in three downs and had to punt. Eric Young returned Helkowski's kick 10 yards to the PSU 38 and on the first play Young beat linebacker Gob dashing down the middle and took an over-the-head pass from Scott Erney all the way into the end zone. On their next possession, the Lions drove into Rutgers territory but a hard rush caused Bill to throw an interception at the Rutgers 32. The next State march reached the Rutgers 11 before the Lions had to settle for a 28-yard Tarasi field goal. State's frustration continued when the Rutgers defense stopped State at the Scarlet Knight 13-yard line in the second quarter and Tarasi missed a 29-yard field goal attempt. But with 23 seconds left in the half, Daniels outleaped a Rutgers defensive back at the goal line and took a 38-yard pass from Bill that gave the Lions a 10-7 halftime lead. Thompson made a "freshman" type mistake on the second half kickoff when he picked up the Rutgers kick along the sideline at the PSU 2-yard line and tried to run across the field where he was tackled at the 9. The Scarlet Knight defense stopped State on a third-and-one at the 18-yard line and a 15-yard face mask penalty against the Lions on the punt runback put the ball at the PSU 37. Another 15-yard penalty on a late hit after an 11-yard gain by Young on a reverse took the ball to the 11-yard line and Mike Botti scored the TD on the next play to give Rutgers the lead, 14-10. Two possessions later, the Knights were on the move again after taking over at their own 30-yard line. On the fourth play of the series, Botti broke through the line and ran 57-yards for a touchdown that stunned the 85,531 in soggy Beaver Stadium and gave Rutgers a 21-10 lead. Late in the third quarter, Bill went down for the fifth time on a sack and didn't get up. It would be a defining moment of the season for Bill would leave the game with an apparent twisted knee injury that was more serious than anyone realized and would be lost for the season.

With Lonergan's thumb still ailing, Paterno had to insert freshman Sacca and the youngster led the Lions back. Early in the fourth quarter, Sacca drove the Lions 70 yards in 9 plays, hitting on a 17-yard pass to Smith and bootlegging for 18-yards to help set up 4-yard TD run by Brown. A 2-point pass for the conversion failed but now the Lions trailed by just four points with nine minutes remaining. The next few minutes were a battle of defenses but with 3:05 showing on the clock, the Lions took the ball at their own 10-yard line following a punt. It looked desperate for State with an untested rookie at the controls in a pressurized situation but suddenly Sacca had the Lions on the move again. A pass to Timpson gained 29 yards and a 20-yard screen pass to Brown picked up 20 yards. Then on a fourth-and-11 at the Rutgers 43, Sacca passed to Timpson on a slant-in pattern to the Rutgers 29-yard line. Four plays later, Sacca came through again on a fourth down-and-11 clutch play, scrambling to avoid tacklers and hitting Brown with a swing pass in the right flat. Brown ran all the way to the 3-yard line before being forced out of bounds and the crowd was on its feet with 53 seconds remaining. Yes, they thought, another Penn State legend was being born. Ganter sent in the plays. Thompson gained a yard off right tackle, then Brown was stopped for no gain trying to plunge through the left side. On third down, Sacca faked a handoff and rolled right on a play called "21 Shoot" with the option to pass or run and he passed to a wide open Jacob in the end zone. The ball was a little high but Jacob leaped—and it went right through his finger tips. "I feel I should

WR Michael Timpson missed the 1986 championship year when he tried out for the Olympics but led the team in receiving in 1988 and was the leading punt returner for three seasons.

have caught it," the tight end said later. Now, just like the '87 Fiesta Bowl, it was down to the last play. Sacca rolled right again and saw Timpson dashing near the corner. He fired, but the pass was a little high and wide of Timpson's outstretched fingertips and fell harmlessly to the ground. Another defining moment, indeed, for State had almost always won games such as this. Many fans believed it was the Lions birthright to win these last second games in dramatic fashion. But not this time. The hellfires of '88 were about to be fueled.

Rutgers had won for the first time in 17 games dating back to 1918. "They certainly deserve all the credit," Paterno said in the media room. "We played tough, determined football," said Anderson, who was hugged by Sue Paterno in the media room. "There probably aren't two teams anywhere intertwined like these two teams," Anderson said. Keeping with his ban against freshmen speaking to the media, Paterno refused to let Sacca say anything in the locker room. Fans who saw him later that night relaxing with a girl friend at a local pizzeria could only wonder what was on the mind of this 18-year-old who was suddenly the key to Penn State's football fortunes. At his midweek news conference, Paterno said, "I never dreamed that I'd be going into the fourth game with the situation we have...that we would have to think about who would be starting at quarterback."

When Sacca started against Temple the following Saturday night at Veterans Stadium in Philadelphia, he became the first true freshman to start at quarterback in the Paterno and Engle eras. Paterno and offensive coordinator Fran Ganter knew they would have to keep the offense simple for the young man only a few months out of high school. They shouldn't have been so worried about Temple. The Lions won easily, 45-9, before a sellout crowd of 66,592 mostly Nittany Lion fans as Sacca threw TD passes of 60 yards to Timpson and 4

yards to Jacob. Collins blocked a punt that Willie Thomas scooped up for a 19-yard TD in the second quarter and Brown raced 57-yards after a fumble recovery by Renkey that completed the scoring in the fourth quarter. Bowing to requests, Paterno let Sacca meet with the media. "I was nervous at the beginning but I relaxed after our first touchdown," he said.

Sacca was more harassed in the Homecoming game against Cincinnati the following Saturday. " (Cincinnati) made up their mind they were going to make us throw and see what the freshman could do, " Paterno told sportswriters. Sacca completed just 11 of 33 passes for 178 yards but two were for touchdowns of 17 and 15 yards in the second quarter when the Lions scored 28 points to break open the game. The final score was 35-9 as Timpson returned a punt 64 yards for a TD and Thomas scored again on a 19-yard interception return. Paterno bemoaned the fact that Sacca ran too much when he didn't' have to and didn't concentrate on his receivers but added, "(Tony) learned a lot today."

So, now the Lions were 4-1 and anxious to play Syracuse at Beaver Stadium and avenge '87's embarrassing loss in the Carrier Dome. "We're going to practice so it doesn't happen again," Brown told sportswriters. "No one is going to embarrass us two years in a row," said Chizmar. Oh no? Syracuse coach MacPherson wanted to prove last year "was no fluke" and he did as the Orange won, 24-10, before an ESPN nighttime audience and a crowd of 85,916 that included former Astronaut Frank Borman. Although outplayed in the first half, the Lions led at the intermission, 7-6, on a sudden 4-play, 70-yard drive in the last two minutes of the second quarter with Sacca's 42-yard pass to Brown setting up a 1-yard TD by Gash. The turning point came shortly after the second half kickoff. Thompson bobbled the kickoff but made it up to the 17-yard line. Sacca was sacked for a 10-yard loss on the first play and Brown fumbled the ball away at the 12 on the second play. Three plays later Syracuse had a TD on a 6-yard pass from Todd Philcox to Deval Glover, who actually came down beyond the end line as the TV replays showed. A 2-point pass made the score 14-7. On the next series, the Lions drove all the way to the Syracuse 4-yard line with a fourth-and-2 but settled for a 21-yard field goal by Tarasi. The rest of the game was one of frustration for the Lions as the Syracuse defense and the passing of Wilcox dominated the action while the State offense was sluggish and seemed disorganized. A 31-yard TD pass midway through the fourth quarter capped the Orange scoring and the Syracuse players and their coach gloated in the locker room. "...Now they have to gear it back up and get back at us," MacPherson said. "It was beautiful." Sacca hit on 15-of-27 passes for 215 yards but threw an interception, was sacked five times and penalized once for intentional grounding. "Sacca did well for a kid," said Paterno "This is the first really emotional really big game our young players have been in. I tell them you can't keep playing like freshmen."

Most of them played better than freshmen the next week at Legion Field in Birmingham but still lost to Alabama, 8-3, before another national TV audience. A 68-yard bomb from Sacca to Timpson in the second quarter that could have changed the complexion of the game was nullified by a questionable holding penalty and after a 3-3 halftime tie, Alabama altered its defense by turning All-American linebacker Derrick Thomas loose. "Once he starts flying around, all kinds of things happen," said Tide coach Bill Curry. Thomas sacked Sacca three times, including once for a safety in the fourth quarter, as the Alabama defense never allowed State past midfield in the second half, held Sacca to one pass completion in 12 attempts and gave up just five net yards rushing over the last 30 minutes. Still, Sacca almost had a chance to win the game in the last minute when he completed a long pass to Daniels. But Daniels was ruled out of bounds and Sacca threw an interception on the next play. "We played a better game than we have all year," Paterno said, "but we just couldn't make a play."

They couldn't make a lot of plays the following Saturday night in Morgantown when undefeated and sixth-ranked West Virginia turned an embarrassing 41-8 halftime lead into a 51-30 victory before another national television audience. The Mountaineers led by QB Major Harris netted 322 yards on the ground and 241 through the air in scoring the most points ever against a Paterno-coached team and took advantage of two interceptions, a fumble and many missed tackles to win for just the second time since 1955. Once again, the game ended prematurely when the overexuberant Mountaineer fans poured onto the field with 49 seconds left after a 16-yard sack on Lonergan, throwing a smoke bomb in the process and forcing Paterno to take the team into the dressing room. "It was a stupid end to a football game," said Paterno, who was cursed and shoved by several obnoxious West Virginia fans. Mountaineer coach Nehlen said "it was a shame" and WVU President Neil Bucklew later apologized to Penn State and the nation, telling the Associated Press, it was "an unfortunate conclusion to one of the most tremendous and exciting victories in WVU sports history."

When a Nittany Lion team is spiraling downward it can always count on Maryland for help. The game at Beaver Stadium on November 5 was played in a torrential downpour with wind gusts of up to 55 miles an hour and some fog that made seeing the other sideline difficult. "Those were unbelievable conditions," said Maryland coach Krivak. "It was like old times. The only things missing were the leather headgears without face masks." Lonergan was healthy again and he replaced Sacca as the starter. An estimated crowd of 78,000 watched State take a 10-3 lead in the first half on a 27-yard field goal by redshirt freshman Henry Adkins and a scintillating 79-yard TD run by Greene on a screen pass from Lonergan. But many in the crowd departed before Maryland tied the game on a 59-yard march during the day's heaviest downpour midway through the third quarter and even less were around for the usual thrilling fourth quarter finish. With less than five minutes left in the game, Lonergan led the Lions on a quick 5-play drive, hitting Daniels wide open on a 45-yard pass to the 18-yard line that set up two Brown runs of 8 and 10 yards for the TD. Adkins kick made it 17-10 with 2:18 remaining. Back came the Terps as Neil O'Donnell, still ailing from a bruised wrist on an earlier hit by Collins, took them to the PSU 14-yard line after a 31 yard pass to Vernon Jones with less than 60 seconds left. Then Rainge stepped up and batted down two O'Donnell tosses into the end zone and O'Donnell overthrew Jones in the end zone as time expired and the sun came out to punctuate State's 17-10 victory. "So it goes for the Terrapins. Year after year," wrote Ken Denlinger for the Washington Post. "An ordinary Penn State team plays well—and also gets lucky. Once more, Lucy pulls the football away from Charlie Brown." Paterno told the media: "It was a real good win for us...It was something we needed at this stage." It also was the last time they would win in '88.

Pitt's defense was rated #1 against the rush and #4 overall and they proved why to 85,701 spectators and an ESPN audience at Beaver Stadium on an unusually warm November afternoon, limiting Lonergan and the Lions to 114 yards in the air and 106 on the ground in a 14-7 victory. Freshman Curvin Richards led Pitt's offensive with

159 yards rushing on 31 carries, including a 6-yard TD that capped an 80-yard drive for the Panthers' only TD in the second quarter. A safety and field goal gave RH its other points and Gash scored for the Lions. With about nine minutes left in the game, the Lions had a fourth-and-2 at Pitt's 22-yard line. The players wanted to go for it but Paterno ordered a field goal. Since Tarasi had missed one field goal and had another blocked, Paterno used Adkins—who missed from 39 yards. And that was the game as Pitt's defense shut State down the rest of the way. "It wasn't a good call on my part," Paterno told the media later. "It's not a call you win football games with."

The loss that made this the losingest PSU team in 49 years came in South Bend against the team that would eventually win the National Championship. Once again, a national TV audience watched as the Lion offense sputtered and the defense was simply overpowered as Notre Dame controlled the ball for nearly 40 minutes in pounding out a 21-3 victory. State's only points were on a 52-yard field goal by Etze in the second quarter and the Lions never made it past the Irish 17-yard line. Lonergan completed just 3-of-16 passes—all in the first five minutes of the game—and had one interception as Notre Dame limited State to 179 net yards while getting 502. After the game, Paterno said his Lions were "a better team than the record shows. We knew what our problems were but we just weren't able to solve them."

The "Hellfires of '88" were finally over. Paterno swore it would be better next season. Forty-two of the players on his two-deep lineup would be back and so would Blair Thomas. Tom Bill would be healed and ready to take charge. It would be payback time again for the wounded "Beast of the East." Not quite.

Season Record 5-6
Record to Date 629-276-41
Winning percentage .687

"Washed UP & Over the Hill"

One game into the '89 season, Sports Illustrated suggested Paterno may be washed up and over the hill. The Lions had been upset by Virginia at Beaver Stadium, 14-6, and had been erratic on offense and defense. In a three-page article entitled, "A Very Sorry State," Austin Murphy wrote, "Either (Paterno's) not attracting to State College the same caliber of talent he once did, or he's squandering that talent...With each loss, the murmurs around State College grow louder: The Lions are playing in a time warp; Paterno has failed to change with the times. That's certainly true."

It wasn't one sportswriter's opinion either for others in the media and many fans were questioning Paterno's competence, wondering why his team had slid into mediocrity. Some writers who followed the team more closely also thought his coaching style may be out of touch. "Memo to Paterno: It's Time to Make Some Changes," said the headline over another article in "Penn State Football Preview" magazine. But the author, Ronnie Christ of the Harrisburg Patriot-News, also had written that Paterno is "a realist. His pride has been hurt. He'll do whatever it takes to return Penn State to contender status."

Paterno believed he had changed for '89. He and his staff worked closer over the winter and spring reevaluating the talent and analyzing the offensive and defensive strategy. You utilize the best players to fit the situation, he always said, and he was doing that again in '89. What made the opening game defeat against Virginia so "shocking, surprising and embarrassing" —as senior defensive tackle Rich Schonewolf had told sportswriters—was that Paterno, his staff and the players had worked hard in spring and preseason practices to prevent such a debacle. Except for the absence of a couple of key linemen sidelined by injuries, the players who started on that hot September 9 afternoon were the ones Paterno believed would lead the Lions back from those "Hellfires of '88." After all, they were mostly veterans and they had talent. He was counting specifically on tailback Blair Thomas and quarterback Bill to rekindle an offense that had faltered often last year.

Paterno intended to turn Thomas loose but knew the offensive captain would need better blocking from the other backs and the offensive line than the Lions had provided last year. Paterno felt so confident in Thomas' durability that he moved Thompson and Brown to fullback in the spring, then shifted Brown—last year's leading rusher—to the defensive secondary in the preseason when injuries weakened the team there. Thompson would share fullback with sophomore John Gerak and become the starter after the second game. Sophomore Gerry Collins, younger brother of Andre who had transferred from Colorado State, became the prime backup to Thomas after a starring in the Blue-White spring game with true freshman Richie Anderson of Sandy Springs, MD, in reserve. With Timpson turning professional despite another season of eligibility, Smith and Daniels became the starting wide receivers but by midseason McDuffie was also in the mix. Jakob again was the tight end backed by senior Todd Young. Duffy, who had started in every game in '88, was back at center. To beef up the interior line, Paterno moved Szott from defense to the short guard position, although he missed the Virginia game because of injury. The other guards were Monaghan, Love and redshirt senior Mike Flanagan. The tackles were Freeman and McMartin backed by sophomore Paul Siever and senior Pat Duffy. With Bill at QB, Paterno figured Sacca would be in a better position to learn and mature as well as improve on his 37 percent pass completion rate. Paterno avoided a crisis when he learned Sacca was thinking of quitting during the preseason because he was not getting enough practice time with the first team and the two QBs began sharing the snaps. Bill appeared to be fully recovered from his dislocated knee injury but Paterno was more worried about an off-field problem. Twice in the off season, Bill had been picked up for underage drinking and Paterno tried to help him while also issuing a warning. "There is no way he's going to run this football team if he doesn't handle himself in a way that the kids can look up to him," Paterno told Mike Poorman of "Penn State Football Preview" magazine.

Sandusky and Paterno wanted to make the defense more aggressive than it was in '88 and they had seven starters returning. Linebacking would again be the soul of the defense as Chizmar moved from Hero to inside linebacker to team with fellow co-captain Collins. D'Onofrio was at one outside position with Japchen starting most games at the other slot until giving way in the eighth game of the season to true freshman Reggie Givens of Sussex Central, VA. Goganious, Gob, sophomore Ivory Gethers and true freshman Eric Ravotti were among the others in the mix. Up front, junior Jim Deter was the nose tackle, although he missed the first two games and was replaced by senior

Jorge Oquendo and backed by redshirt sophomore Todd Burger. The other tackles were Giannetti and Schonewolf with sophomore Tony Matesic and Sean Moffitt in reserve. Perry became the Hero with Rainge and junior Mike Baggett at strong safety. The cornerbacks were Willie Thomas and Henderson with sophomore Leonard Humphries and true freshman Tisen Thomas in reserve. Paterno was confident about his punter, Helkowski, but he needed better placekicking from Tarasi and Adkins. He also wondered how the elimination of kicking tees would affect the placekickers' accuracy. Anderson and redshirt freshman Bobby Samuels were the designated kickoff return men with McDuffie and Blair Thomas running back punts.

Most of the nation's sports media expected the Lions to make a comeback from '88 and picked them in the second half of the Top 20. The AP had State at #11 in the preseason poll, with Syracuse a #13, Alabama at #16, West Virginia at #17 and Pitt at #20. "I really don't know where we are," Paterno said at his last news conference before the opener. "This squad has worked very hard...and at times it has looked good."

Perhaps the loss to Virginia should not have been that surprising considering the fact that George Welsh's Cavaliers already had played a game and Paterno's young team was still edgy after winning just one of its last six games '88. Virginia's trouncing by defending National Champion Notre Dame in the Kickoff Classic, 36-13, was a little deceiving because Virginia had played well in the second half after the veteran Irish team had taken a 33-0 lead. What the Cavaliers proved was one of the Paterno tenets about a team usually improving the most between its first and second games. Virginia turned Bill's only interception of the day into a 59-yard touchdown drive midway through the first quarter with Shawn Moore throwing a 24-yard TD alley-oop pass on a third-and-12 to freshman Herman Moore, who outleaped Baggett in a corner of the end zone. Early in the second quarter, the quarterback struck again at the end of a 64-yard drive with an 11-yard TD pass to Moore, giving the Cavaliers a 14-0 lead at the half. The Lions seemed to be making a comeback on the first series of the third quarter after taking the ball at their 46-yard line but an apparent 43-yard TD run by Thomas was called back when it was ruled he stepped out of bounds at the 31 and State had to settle for a 36-yard Tarasi field goal. Late in the quarter, three Bill passes helped the Lions on a 62-yard march that again wound up with a field goal instead of a TD. A D'Onofrio sack gave State another opportunity deep in Virginia territory in the fourth quarter but the Cavaliers forced a punt and Virginia then used almost seven minutes in a drive that ended with a missed field goal. The Lions had one last chance when they moved to the Virginia 32 with less than a minute left and no time outs but the Cavalier defense ended the threat at the 26 by forcing two incomplete passes as the clock expired. Because of the 83 degree heat and humidity, Paterno substituted frequently, particularly with his running backs, and Thomas carried just 13 times for a game high of 86 yards. "That was far too few for Thomas to make a significant contribution to the offense," wrote SI's Murphy. "We're not good enough right now to beat Virginia the way they played today," Paterno told sportswriters. It was State's first opening game loss played at home in 24 years and dropped the Lions out of the AP ratings. Virginia would lose just one more game in the regular season and play Illinois in the Citrus Bowl.

But just as the convincing win over Virginia in '88 had not been a harbinger of the season to come, this disappointing loss was not an omen for '89, despite the Sports Illustrated derision. However, what followed did not recapture the lost glory, either. Paterno showed he could change when the first play against Temple the next week at Beaver Stadium was a 75-yard bomb from Bill to Daniels that is still tied as the seventh longest TD pass in Lion history. State went on to clobber helpless Temple in the rain, 42-3, as Bill hit on 6-of-10 passes for 192 yards and another TD of 38 yards to Daniels, who was celebrating his 20th birthday. Thomas had the first of what would be nine games over 100 yards that season with 138 yards and two touchdowns on 21 carries and Andre Collins set up two scores by blocking one punt and tackling the punter near the goal line after a bad snap. Before Boston College came to town on September 23, Sacca was again the starting quarterback and Bill was suspended after being arrested for public intoxication Monday morning.

Sacca looked shaky for most of the water soaked afternoon. The remnants of Hurricane Hugo turned Beaver Stadium in a windy, cold and rainy amphitheater and by halftime many of the estimated 80,000 fans who showed up had left with Boston College holding a 3-0 lead on Brian Lowe's 28-yard field goal. One apparent Lion TD by Willie Thomas on an interception in the first quarter was nullified by a questionable roughing the passer penalty and it was the defense keeping State in the game. Sacca completed just three of his first 14 passes and the situation did not look good when the Lions took over the ball at their own 7-yard line midway through the final period. But Thomas and Thompson ran for first downs, Sacca connected on a 33-yard pass to Smith, Thomas went 16 yards on a draw and the Lions suddenly had a first down at the BC 17. But Thompson fumbled and the Eagles recovered. However, the State defense forced a punt four downs later and Lowe, who had been punting well, must have felt the pressure for he shanked it out of bounds at the BC 35. With 3:49 remaining, Thomas carried for a first down but a few moments later State faced a fourth-and-8 at the 21. Paterno called a time out and prepared to send in Tarasi for a field goal. "Aw, nuts, let's go for it," he told Ganter, as later described in Ken Denlinger's book, "For The Glory." "We're never going to be any good if we're going to start hoping they're going to make a mistake." It was the type of bold decision that SI said was passé in Paterno's Happy Valley realm and one of the defining moments of the season. Paterno and Ganter called for a "gimmick" fake screen pass to Thomas with a throw to the tight end over the middle. But after the fake, Sacca found Jakob covered so he instinctively took off around left end and made a first down and more to the BC 8. Two plays later Thomas bolted over from 4-yards for a TD but the officials ruled BC had called time out and nullified the score. When time resumed, Thomas ran it twice to the one-yard line. Now, with 44 seconds remaining and most of the fans and the BC defense expecting another run by Thomas, Paterno sent in the "21 Shoot" play which failed against Rutgers in '88. Sacca faked to Thomas inside, and bootlegged to the right and seeing no one but sophomore guard Greg Huntington in front of him ran into the end zone with his arms raised in a "V for Victory" sign. Rainge intercepted a long desperation pass at the State 11-yard line three plays later and the Lions won, 7-3, and gave the game ball to their missing teammate, Tom Bill. "This was a victory that really belonged to the Lion defense," wrote Black in the "Football Letter." Led by Chizmar and Collins, who had 33 tackles between them, the Lions held BC's sophisticated offense to 278 net yards and intercepted three passes. "It's the kind of game we like to win, with a fourth quarter drive," Paterno said in the media room. "I do think we're going to be a pretty good football team eventually."

The Lions came from behind again the following Saturday night against 1-2 Texas in Austin and it was Collins and the defense that came up with the big play. A 33-yard TD pass from Sacca to Daniels set up by a 31-yard run by Thomas capped an 80-yard drive that gave the Lions a 7-0 lead six minutes into the game. But as a Central Pennsylvania TV audience watched over Altoona's Channel 10, Texas took a 12-9 lead into the last nine minutes of the fourth quarter and the Longhorn fans chanted, "Eastern football...Eastern football." Then a sack by D'Onofrio forced Texas into a punt from its own 17-yard line and Paterno gave Bradley the go ahead for the special team's play the Lions had practiced all week. In the game films, Bradley had noticed that punter Bobby Lillejdahl stood closer to the line of scrimmage when backed up near the Longhorn goal line and took longer strides in kicking the ball away. Bradley adjusted State blocking angles and switched the rushing lanes of Collins and Deter. On the snap, Deter took the center's block and Collins rushed in and blocked Lillejdahl's kick. Humphries scooped up the ball and was in the Texas end zone before most of the 75,232 fans realized a kick had been blocked. Texas had three more possessions but couldn't get past the State 48-yard line and the Lions won, 16-12. "Joe always tells us that the special teams will win two or three games a year," Collins told sportswriters in the locker room. Paterno said, "we blew away too many chances on offense...(but) the win should give our guys a lot of confidence."

Collins tied Jack Ham's one-season and career records for blocked kicks the next Saturday afternoon at sunny Giants Stadium in the Meadowlands as the Lion defense shutdown Rutgers, 17-0. With a crowd of 52,688 that may have had more Blue and White fans than the home team, Collins blocked his third punt of the season and fourth of his career. The defense limited Rutgers to 59 yards rushing and held the Scarlet well below their game passing yardage with three sacks, a pass interception and a fumble recovery. Sacca had his best passing day of the season, hitting on 10-of-20 attempts for 120 yards, including a 23-yard TD to Smith that gave the Lions all the points they needed in the first quarter. "Our defense played very well," Paterno said. "But the offense has to knock the ball in after the defense makes the big play...Next week (at Syracuse) will be a real indication of how much we have improved."

The Lions were a 3 1/2 point underdog going into the Carrier Dome and once again the 2-2 Syracuse team and their fans were making noise about the new "Beast of the East." With lightning crackling outside and ESPN's cameras recording the scene inside, the Lions broke open a 10-6 halftime lead with a 17-point third quarter spurt that demoralized the Orange and gave State a convincing 34-12 victory. As nine bowl scouts watched, the defense set up two scores on turnovers, intercepting three passes and recovering a fumble, but it was McDuffie's 84-yard punt return for a TD late in the third quarter that silenced the crowd of 49,678 and sealed the win. Earlier in the third quarter, McDuffie had set up a Tarasi field goal on a 45-yard reverse and then a 7-yard TD pass from Sacca to Jakob with a 25-yard reception. He also ran back three other punts, caught another pass and was named player of the game. Thomas with 115 yards, including a 38-yard TD, on 17 carries and Gerry Collins with 104 yards on 19 rushes became the first Lion tandem in two years to go over 100 yards each in the same game. "Lions Delivered from Orange Taunts," said the headline over a column by Ron Bracken in the Centre Daily Times. "(Syracuse) liked to open their mouths the last two years," D'Onofrio told sportswriters, "they thought all of a sudden they have this great program, but we

Andre Collins, the first of the Collins brothers to attend State, was a First-Team All-American LB in 1989 and a Butkus Award finalist after leading the team in tackles for two seasons.

showed them today we're not down." "Ah, sweet deliverance," wrote Bracken. State moved back into the ratings for the first time since the preseason at #23 and went back to State College to await the invasion of unbeaten and sixth-ranked Alabama. It would be the defining game of the regular season.

In the two weeks before playing Alabama, the Lions moved up to #14 in the AP ratings and the bowl talk started. Scouts from 10 bowls including all the New Year's Day ones except the Rose were in Beaver Stadium along with 85,975 fans and CBS-TV cameras October 28 on what was a perfect autumn day for football. The game was tied 3-3 at the half but State took a 13-10 lead into the fourth quarter on a 19-yard TD pass from Sacca to McDuffie and another Tarasi field goal. Both teams had missed chances for more points, with State's defense stopping the Tide at the one-yard line as time ran out in the first half and the Alabama defense forcing field goals when the Lions twice penetrated inside the 10-yard line. State's "bend but don't break" defense finally broke early in the third quarter as quarterback Gary Hollingsworth mixed short passes with the running of tailback Siran Stacy and marched the Tide 76-yards in eight plays to give Alabama the lead for the first time on Stacy's 12-yard TD and Phillip Doyle's PAT. However, the Lions closed to within one point after the kickoff with a 46-yard drive that culminated in Tarasi's longest field goal of his career from 46-yards out. Alabama was on the move again with less than six minutes remaining in the game when Schonewolf intercepted a short pass at the PSU 27-yard line. On the first play, Sacca passed to Jakob for 15 yards. Now, Paterno did what he said he would do at the beginning of the season. He turned the ball over to Thomas.

Thomas to the right. Thomas to the left. Thomas up the middle. Ten straight times, Thomas carried the ball as the minutes ticked away. With the ball at the Alabama 4-yard line and less than 30 seconds remaining, Thomas bolted up the middle on his 35th carry of the day and appeared to cross the goal line under a swarm of tacklers. But the officials said he was down six inches from the goal line. He had run 160 yards for the afternoon and after all that he was six inches short. Thirteen seconds remained and State was out of time outs. "There wasn't any other option," Paterno told sportswriters later. "There wasn't anything to do but kick it." In came Tarasi for a "chip shot" from the 18-yard line. The snap from Mark Lawn was a little high and holder Markiewicz had to reach for it. Markiewicz put the ball on the ground and Tarasi kicked. But 6-foot-7 Thomas Rayam stretched his right arm and knocked the ball awry before it could get airborne. "Blocked kick foils State, 17-16," said the headline in the Philadelphia Inquirer. It was probably the most significant blocked field goal of the Paterno era. A victory on this day would have silenced all the critics and put the Lions back into the elite of college football. It would be another 13 months before that would finally happen and then it would be another field goal on a hallowed playing field in South Bend that would be the catalyst. "It wasn't lost on one play," Paterno said after the game. Maybe not but it was the one play everyone would remember for years.

Some sportswriters believed the heartbreaking defeat might shatter the confidence of this young team and send it spiraling to another losing season. Certainly, the Homecoming game against 13th-ranked West Virginia (6-1-1) would be a fair test. The score was again 3-3 at halftime when Ted Kwalick of the '67-'68 teams was honored for his induction into the College Football Hall of Fame. The defense had been responsible for the deadlock, stopping the Mountaineers three times near the PSU goal line as WVU used up nearly 19 minutes of the clock and outgained the Lions, 158 yards to 45. A fumble recovery by Rainge had led to State's points and Sacca had thrown seven incomplete passes. With another ESPN audience and more bowl scouts looking on in the late afternoon, the State defense took complete control in the second half. Another fumble recovery on the kickoff led to another Tarasi field goal and before the 30 minutes had elapsed, the defense set up two more field goals and a 31-yard TD pass from Sacca to Jakob with two more fumble recoveries and an interception and the Lions won, 19-9. State recovered five fumbles, intercepted one pass, batted down eight others and had three sacks in frustrating the Mountaineer's Heisman hopeful, Major Harris. "Penn State did a great job of stripping the ball," WVU's coach Nehlen said. "Penn State has a great defense. It's definitely something special." Of course, the offense was far less than special with Thomas getting 150 of PSU's net 262 yards and Sacca continuing to show his immaturity, hitting on just 2-of-13 passes, and virtually requiring Paterno to limit the offensive game plan.

The Lions were now back to #13 in the polls and in line for a possible New Year's Day game at the Citrus, Fiesta or Hall of Fame Bowls or one of the other late December games. "There may be some sort of package worked out with the Pitt-Penn State winner," the Gator Bowl's George Olson told Bracken of the CDT, with the victor going to one bowl and the loser another.

Maryland made up for nearly three decades of frustration on November 11 in Baltimore's Memorial Stadium by knocking State out of a New Year's Day bowl game and the Terps didn't even have to win to do it. With the Lions leading 13-10 after a 24-yard Tarasi field goal with five minutes remaining in the game, Neil O'Donnell led a 57-yard drive

First-Team All-American Blair Thomas gained over 1300 yards in 1987 and 1989. His 8.4 yards per carry in 1986 was the best seasonal rushing average ever.

to a fourth-and-5 at the PSU 9-yard line and Dan DeArmas kicked a 26-yard field goal with 55 seconds left that tied the game, 13-13. "I wasn't going to let this one get away," said coach Krivak as his players celebrated in the Terp dressing room. "Our players are tired of losing to Penn State." But the Lions only had themselves to blame. "For some reason we came out flat," Thomas told sportswriters. "It was dead on the sidelines and dead on the field. We didn't support each other and we didn't execute as we should have." State squandered scoring opportunities all day against the 3-6 Terps and twice had to settle for field goals, including the fourth period boot when Szott jumped offside on a third-and-goal at the Maryland 2-yard line. On State's first possession following a 20-yard punt return by McDuffie, the Lions moved 37 yards to a fourth-and-goal at the Terp one when Sacca slipped on a bootleg right with no one in front of him and Maryland took over at the 4. After a blocked punt had helped give Maryland a 7-0 lead with three minutes left in the second quarter, Paterno replaced Sacca with Bill. The reinstated QB played the rest of the game, leading State to a field goal two seconds before the intermission and taking the Lions 80 yards for a TD late in the third quarter. But he couldn't rally the Lions after the Terps' tying field goal as he was penalized for crossing the scrimmage line on one completion to Daniels and underthrew on another attempt. "It's a loss, a sickening loss," said Chizmar.

Nine bowl scouts had watched the Maryland tie and most agreed that even an upset the following week over #1 Notre Dame could not put the Lions back into the New Year's Day picture. Then two days before the Notre Dame game, the Knight-Ridder newspaper service reported that State would play the champion of the Western Athletic Conference in the Holiday Bowl December 29 in San Diego. A State spokesman would not comment but a source told Knight-Ridder "It's a done deal." Of course, official invitations could not go out until 6 p.m. November 25.

Sacca was back as the starter when the Irish rolled into Beaver Stadium for another national televised game. A half-inch snow fell before the game and snow squalls continued intermittently in the freezing afternoon as the Irish simply overpowered the Lions in winning, 34-23. With Tony Rice running for a season high 141 yards and Ricky Watters getting 128 yards, Notre Dame rushed for 425 yards and that is still a Beaver Stadium record by an opponent. Notre Dame passed just 10 times and gained 47 yards. "We made crucial mistakes and let them get big gainers," Collins told sportswriters. While State's defense faltered for the first time all season, the offense was at its best and

twice held leads in the first half. Thomas ran for 133 yards and scored two TDs while Sacca and Bill both led 79-yard touchdown drives. "Overall we played a pretty good football game," Paterno said in the media room. "I told (my players) we just got beaten by a better football team today."

After the loss to Notre Dame, Paterno felt his team needed a lift before closing out the season against Pitt (7-2) in another national televised game at Pitt Stadium. At the team meeting the night before the game, Paterno reminded the players of what they had accomplished so far in '89. They had come a long way, he told, them but they "still had a ways to go" and could lose to Pitt if they "didn't wake up." "Look in the mirror" and "dig down deep" he told them. Collins said later that Paterno's speech set the tone. Paterno had the Lions fired up and they took a 10-0 lead in the first quarter. Sacca led a 75-yard drive on the first possession, throwing a 19-yard TD pass to Daniels. Moments later Rainge stripped the ball from Curvin Richards and Givens recovered the fumble in midair, setting up a 19-yard field goal by Tarasi. Pitt tied it in the second quarter on the passing and running of quarterback Alex Van Pelt. But Paterno inserted Bill with less than two minutes left in the half and Bill led a "two-minute" offense downfield for Tarasi to boot a 37-yard field goal on the last play of the quarter to make it 13-10 at the intermission. The second half was a battle of defense and field position and with about four minutes remaining in the game Van Pelt connected on a 54-yard bomb that gave Pitt the ball inside the Lion 20. But after a 14-yard TD was called back for holding, Panther coach Gottfried went for the tie and Ed Frazier booted a 40-yard field goal with 2:23 remaining. But the Lions wanted a win. "Dig down deep," they shouted at each other. With Bill at quarterback, the Lions drove into Pitt territory, with Bill throwing one third-and-10 pass of 17 yards to Daniels and another on a 29-yard screen pass to Thompson that put the ball at the Pitt 14-yard line with 1:05 left. Paterno kept the clock running and so did Pitt, which had two time outs left. Thomas bolted up the middle for nine yards, then Thompson ran for two to put the ball right in front of the goal posts. The Lions called time out to get the field goal team on the field and Pitt then called another time out to try and psyche Tarasi, Markiewicz and Lawn. Everyone on the team remembered what had happened in a similar situation against Alabama. "We've waited five weeks for a chance to redeem ourselves," Lawn said later. The snap, hold and kick were perfect and Tarasi's 20-yard field goal was good. But the game ended in a full scale brawl in front of the Pitt bench after Rainge intercepted a desperation pass at the PSU 3 and ran to the 39 before being tackled at the Pitt sideline. When Rainge was pummeled by several Pitt players, the Lion players raced across the field and it took several minutes to restore order. "We looked like two jerks on national television," Scott Gob's brother Craig, a Pitt linebacker, told the Pittsburgh Press. "It took away from a great game."

Tarasi's kick gave State the 16-13 win, and, ironically, allowed the senior from Pittsburgh to break Matt Bahr's school record for field goal accuracy with an 82.6 percentage on 19-of-23 kicks. The kick and State's 7-3-1 record also gave the Lions the Lambert Trophy as Eastern champion for the first time in three years. Going to the Holiday Bowl was a fine reward but winning the Lambert Trophy was a major accomplishment for this team, Paterno told sportswriters after the game because "We've been fighting to get away from that business about us being a bunch of has-beens and the bad things that have been said about our program." (Take that Sports Illustrated!) Thomas had gained 131 yards, going over 100 for the 16th time in his career and his 1,134 yards for the year put him just behind Curt Warner in all-time PSU rushing records with 3,301 yards. Collins had the most tackles in any one game of his career with 16 and his total of 130 in the season remains the third best in the State record books. Within two weeks both were named First Team All-Americans.

Four days after the team resumed practice on December 15 for the Holiday Bowl, Paterno, Tarman and outgoing University president Bryce Jordan shocked State fans and much of the college sports world with the announcement that the school would leave its Eastern roots and join the Big Ten in the early 1990s. The Holiday Bowl game would be the prelude to a new and explosive sports age in Happy Valley and the second half fireworks in San Diego would set the tone.

THE 1989 HOLIDAY BOWL
Dec. 29, 1989
Penn State 50, Brigham Young 39
Player- of-the-Game: Blair Thomas & Ty Detmer

No one who saw this game in person or on ESPN December 29 will ever forget it. As BYU Coach LaVell Edwards said later, it was "as screwy a game as I've ever been associated with." Certainly, it ranks as the wackiest of the Paterno era. In his "Football Letter," John Black described It as "spectacular, sensational, phenomenal and even faaaaaaaantastic!"

This was State's first trip for a West Coast game since the '73 team played at Stanford. The team arrived on the afternoon of December 22 and after a welcoming ceremony at Lindberg Field Paterno took the team to San Diego State University for a workout. The media was allowed in for the first hour but after that all practices were closed. However, Paterno already had worked the team hard in State College. He followed a different routine than the one prior to the Citrus Bowl two years earlier. "When we went down to Orlando...," he told John Severance of the Centre Daily Times, "we were not ready to go. This year I ran them really hard before we came here. We got a lot accomplished." Still, Paterno was not on a crusade and he wanted the players to have fun. They did, not only around the swimming pool of their resort hotel on Mission Bay Drive but also in the team events at Sea World and aboard the aircraft carrier Independence. But some of the freshmen and sophomores who had never been away from home on Christmas weren't too happy and a few complained to Ronnie Christ of the Patriot-News after eating a Chinese dinner on Christmas Day. That irritated Paterno who could not believe some of his younger players were still that immature.

This was expected to be a battle between the Lions' run-oriented defensive opportunists and the high-scoring passing attack of BYU, which once again won the WAC. In the regular season, State had converted 18 interceptions and 11 fumbles into four touchdowns and eight field goals while holding opponents to under 12 points a game. Only twice, against Virginia and Notre Dame, did the defense let opponents cash in on the 17 turnovers by the Lion offense. With sophomore Ty Detmer at quarterback, BYU had passed for more yards—4,732—in one year than the Lions had totaled in the last three years. Detmer had thrown 45 touchdowns over two years and the Cougars had five receivers with more than 30 receptions, including tight end Chris Smith who had 60 catches for 1,090 yards and five TDs and wideout Jeff Frandsen, who had nine TDs and averaged 18.6 yards per catch. BYU also had the nation's top interior lineman in 6-foot-5, 290-pound Mohammed

Elewonibi, who had won the Outland Trophy. His nickname was Mount Mohammed but before the game was over Gary Brown would plant his flag on the mountain's summit.

What no one expected was a shootout. Nor did anyone expect Sacca to suddenly turn into a sharp passer. But that is what happened. Detmer would set several new Holiday Bowl records by passing for 576 yards and two TDs on 42-of-59 attempts but one interception would set up a State TD and another would result in a thrilling first ever runback of a two-point conversion attempt. Sacca hit on 10-of-20 passes for 206 yards and two TDs and Thomas had the second best running day of his career with 186 yards and a TD on 35 carries. Yet, in the end, the game would be won by the State defense in the last minute of play.

The game that would last four hours and 17 minutes started slowly with both sides kicking field goals for a 3-3 first quarter tie. State moved ahead 9-3 early in the second quarter as Sacca completed three passes in an 8-play 62-yard drive with Smith scoring the TD on a 24-yard toss. But by halftime, BYU was back in the lead 13-12 as the Lions could muster only a 36-yard field goal from Tarasi the rest of the quarter. That all changed almost from the second half kickoff which McDuffie ran back 46 yards to set up the longest field goal of Tarasi's career—51 yards and a Holiday Bowl record. The score was now 15-13 and the Lions never trailed again but the next 27 1/2 minutes would be among the most exciting in PSU history. State would score six more times and BYU four times as the teams cruised up and down the field of Jack Murphy Stadium. The first time State went into punt formation with about four minutes left in the third quarter, Terry Smith went into the game ostensibly as the punter but then threw a 9-yard pass to Tisen Thomas that kept a 66-yard drive going. Thompson's 14-yard run and the PAT made the score 29-20 but Detmer threw a 12-yard TD pass two minutes later and the Lions led by just 29-27 at the end of the third quarter. State pushed its lead to 35-27 less than three minutes into the final period after a 73-yard drive with Sacca hitting Thomas on passes of 29 and 17 yards and Thomas getting the TD on a 7-yard run.

Unselfish Gary Brown, the leading ground gainer as a sophomore, became an excellent defensive back in 1989 before returning to running back again as a senior.

Then came the most spectacular TD reception of the evening—and it wasn't by BYU. Rainge stopped a BYU drive with an interception at the PSU 13-yard line and ran the ball back to the Lion 40. Two plays later, Sacca heaved the ball to Daniels racing down the sideline. Daniels leaped high at the goal line and reached over the defensive back. The ball bounced off Daniels' hands as he was hit and as he went down the ball hit his face mask, then his hands again and finally landed on his chest as he hit the ground on his back, and he skidded into the end zone firmly clutching the ball. ESPN announcer Tim Brando called it "the catch of the decade."

The Lions now led 41-27 with less than nine minutes remaining but back came BYU with Detmer leading a 68-yard drive in 30 seconds for one TD and driving the Cougars 90 yards for another. The score was 41-39 with 2:58 left when BYU lined up for a 2-point conversion that would tie the game. Detmer tried to pass to his tight end but Collins leaped in front of the intended receiver two yards deep in the end zone and ran down the sidelines in full stride, pushing Detmer aside as the QB tried to make the tackle and going all the way to the other end zone. It was the first time since adoption of a new rule two years earlier that a conversion attempt had been run back for two points in a major college game. However, Detmer wasn't through. State stopped the kickoff return at BYU 12-yard line but with 45 seconds remaining the Cougars were at the PSU 38 and poised to take the 4-point victory away from the Lions. Sandusky signaled in a blitz. Brown rushed in from strong safety, pushed past Elewonibi, took the ball from Detmer as he prepared to pass and ran 53 yards for a touchdown that gave State the 50-39 win. "I beat the Outland Trophy winner," shouted Brown in the locker room. "I can't even pronounce his name but I beat him." "There's something about the wacky WAC that awakens sleeping offenses," wrote Ray Parillo in the Philadelphia Inquirer, "and State's offense never blinked." Paterno said he told "the young kids we owed this game to the seniors." He also told them "maybe we can play for all the marbles next year."

The Lions finished 15th in the AP rankings and 14th in UPI. Joe Paterno and Penn State were back. Then the 1990 season began and they had to start all over again.

Season Record 8-3
Record to Date 637-279-42
Winning percentage .687

"Cheer, Cheer for Old Notre Dame"

In the euphoria over Penn State's upcoming entry into the Big Ten and the '89 team's exciting Holiday Bowl victory over BYU, Paterno told anyone who would listen that he now planned to coach until he was 70. He was 63 and entering his "Silver Season" as head coach of the Lions but he had the indomitable spirit of a person half his age.

"As long as I'm healthy and still enthusiastic about coaching," I'll stay until I'm 70," he told the media. And why not? He had another world to conquer—the Big Ten and the Rose Bowl. If the foot-

ball team could not be integrated into the Big Ten schedule until 1995 as initially planned, then he would have to stay around until he turned 68 to have even one shot at climbing this new Mount Everest.

In the meantime, there was another National Championship to attain. And, he believed, with the right breaks, this was the team that could do it. Of course, it fit his mantra about the four-year cycle. As he wrote in "Paterno: By the Book," every one of his players who had "played out his football eligibility" had either "played an undefeated, untied season, or played in a bowl game for the National Championship, or played on a team that won the National Championship." This team would have to do it or the 25-year cycle would be broken. They were young, even younger than the snakebitten squad of '88. But there was talent underneath those drab Blue and White uniforms. They would have to mature quickly, avoid serious injury and get the right break, but the potential was there. Unfortunately, it didn't happen the way Paterno had hoped. But before the season was over, this team would pull off one of the school's greatest upsets of all time in the shadow of the Golden Dome.

No one had more potential than Sacca. When Bill left school over the winter to get rehabilitation for his drinking problem, Sacca was ordained the starting quarterback. Yet through spring and preseason practice he and Paterno clashed. Part of it was personality and part of it was coaching technique. But Paterno believed Sacca was not taking the game and his learning process seriously and was squandering away genuine talent by behaving immaturely. One day during spring practice Paterno became so frustrated with Sacca's attitude that he yelled, "Sacca, you're the biggest quarterback flop in Penn State history!" Sacca wasn't fond of Paterno's bullying and sarcastic style and felt he was being blamed unfairly for offensive problems beyond his control. "He has to crank it up one more notch," Paterno told Tom Luicci of the Newark Star-Ledger. "I think I'm ready...," Sacca said. "I think they're ready to center the offense around me and let me do a little more of what I do best." Despite his mediocre two-year 39 percent completion rate, Sacca rationalized by saying the Lions threw too many downfield passes on second-and-long and not enough high percentage passes. Paterno told Ken Denlinger of the Washington Post that Sacca needs a "better touch" and "he's got to read (defenses) a little better."

So, as Paterno and his staff prepared for the season opener against Texas on September 8 at Beaver Stadium, they remolded the offense to get Sacca more involved. Thompson was shifted back to tailback but he, too, was expected to "crank it up a notch" to fulfill the promise he had shown as a highly recruited running back out of Knoxville, TN. Brown took spring practice off to concentrate on his academics, and then was given his choice to stay on defense or return to the offense. He decided to join Collins as Thompson's backup rather than be a probable alternate at safety. Gash, fully recovered from the leg injury that sidelined him all of '89, started at fullback with sophomore Brian O'Neal in reserve. Anderson and Gerak were "redshirted." The starting wide receivers, Daniels and Smith, were back but McDuffie would get hurt in the Texas game and take a medical redshirt and youngsters Chip LaBarca and Rich Rosa would be the prime substitutes. Junior letterman Al Golden moved up to start at tight end and redshirt junior Rick Sayles shifted from linebacker to be the backup. In the line, the only starter returning was McMartin, who was elected offensive co-captain with Thompson. The rest of the front six had limited experience even though most were seniors with Rob Luedke at center, Pat Duffy (Roger's twin brother) at short tackle and Dave

Brzenchek and junior Huntington at the guards. Siever and redshirt sophomores Todd Rucci and Mike Malinoski were in reserve.

As usual, defense would be the strength of the team. D'Onofrio was moved from outside linebacker to inside and shared one side with redshirt junior Brett Wright while Goganious took over the other inside slot with junior Andre Powell in reserve. Givens and his fellow sophomore Rich McKenzie started on the outside and Baggett, shifted from the secondary, Ravotti and Gethers were the backups. Burger and Deter shared the nose tackle spot with Giannetti and redshirt freshman Lou Benfatti of Green Pond, NJ, at the outside tackles and junior Mark Flythe, redshirt freshman Tyoka Jackson of Forestville, MD, and Matesic in reserve. Perry was back at Hero with Willie Thomas, the defensive captain, at safety, and Humphries and senior Greg Fusetti at the corners. Henderson, junior Mark Graham, redshirt freshman Lee Rubin, true freshman Derek Bochna of Greensboro, PA, and redshirt sophomore Chris Cisar also would see action in the secondary as would redshirt freshman Shelly Hammonds of Barnwell, SC, who would move to tailback later because of injuries and make a dazzling debut on national television. Helkowski returned to punt and after Adkins stumbled in the opening game 18-year-old first semester freshman Craig Fayak of Belle Vernon became the placekicker. Lawn was the kick snapper for two games before getting in Paterno's doghouse and was replaced by sophomore Bob Ceh, who was a student manager when the season began. Walk-on Bill Spoor was the holder with Brown, Smith and Tisen Thomas returning kickoffs and punts.

Paterno may have thought his team was of National Championship caliber but most sportswriters did not. The AP preseason poll ranked the Lions #21 with traditional foes Pitt at #18 and West Virginia at #25. This may have been the toughest schedule of the Paterno era with three of its toughest games—#9 USC, #12 Alabama and #2 Notre Dame—on the road. "The sophomores and juniors aren't seasoned enough to handle a schedule that includes six bowl teams from last season," wrote Steve Halvonik of the Pittsburgh Post-Gazette for the Penn State Football Preview magazine. "Call me a nay soothsayer, but (State's) chance of playing for the 1990 National Championship is about as good as Jackie Sherill's chance of being coach of the year."

By the third game of the season, any thoughts of playing for the national title were over and now the Lions were fighting for their reputation again. With a play or two they could have beaten both Texas and Southern Cal. But they came up short because of a break down by the kicking teams and misfires on what could have been game-winning big plays. And in neither game did the running attack do anything to distinguish itself. It was obvious that if something didn't change, the defense would be carrying the offense once again. The game against unranked Texas had been moved up three weeks by mutual agreement and was expected to get the Lions better prepared for their West Coast visit the following week. A record opening day crowd of 85,973 watched in sunny Beaver Stadium as Brown took the opening kickoff and ran 95 yards before being pulled down from behind at the Texas 3-yard line. Thompson went up the middle three plays later for the TD and Adkins booted the PAT. But that would be the highlight of the day for State fans. Later in the quarter, Adkins had a 41-yard field goal attempt blocked and in the fourth quarter he missed one from 31-yards that could have narrowed the Texas lead to one point. Meanwhile, Texas' Michael Pollak kicked three field goals and the Longhorns scored its only touchdown in the same manner as State—by running back the second half kickoff 88 yards to set up a 6-yard TD and 2-point pass conversion. Still, Sacca

almost brought the Lions back from a 17-7 third quarter deficit, leading State on three long drives but getting just one score when Brown ran 5-yards for a TD to cap an 8-play, 81-yard drive early in the fourth period. Another march ended with Adkins' missed field goal. With 1:06 left in the game and no time outs, Sacca took the Lions from the PSU 24 to the Texas 20 on three pass completions and the help of an interference penalty. But on the last play of the game he failed to see a wide open Brown in the corner of the end zone and tried to hit a well covered Golden on a "Hail Mary" heave that fell incomplete. "We didn't play with a lot of poise or precision," Paterno said of the 17-13 loss. "We dropped passes, jumped offsides and were very sloppy in the first half offensively." Ronnie Christ of the Harrisburg Patriot-News blamed the offensive line for the loss, writing, "Unless Joe Paterno comes up with a quick fix, the Nittany Lions are going to have to circle the wagons when they head west." Texas went on to lose just one game in the regular season and win the SWC championship.

USC had beaten Syracuse in the Kickoff Classic and that had helped propel the Trojans to #6 in the country and made them a 13-point favorite over State in a nationally televised game at the Los Angeles Coliseum September 15. The bad sign came early when State's opening drive of 59 yards ended with a missed field goal of 39 yards by Fayak. After USC took a 7-0 lead late in the first quarter on a time consuming 16-play 78-yard drive, Sacca responded by leading a 73-yard march that climaxed with his 8-yard TD pass to Golden. Fayak's PAT tied it at 7-7. But the offense began to sputter and by the end of the third quarter USC's redshirt sophomore QB sensation, Todd Marinovich, had passed the Trojans into a 19-7 lead. The fourth quarter was nearly similar to the Texas game except this time it was the Lion defense that missed the chance to pull out the victory. On one drive the Lions had a first down at the USC 9-yard line after a Brown run of 32 yards and Brown almost scored on the next play but was ruled out of bounds at the one. USC's goal line defense then stopped two runs up the middle.

Hard-hitting LB Mark D'Onofrio set the record for causing the most fumbles in a season in 1990 and was one of the most combative players on the field.

Trying to outsmart USC on fourth down, Paterno called for a pass to the tight end but a blitz chased Sacca back to the 20-yard line before he threw an incompletion. However, State's defense forced a punt and Tisen Thomas's 11-yard run back set up a short 31-yard drive capped by Thompson's 2-yard TD. With Fayak's boot, State trailed by just five with five minutes remaining. Now came what may have been the key play of the game. State had USC deep in its own territory following the kickoff and when Marinovich tried to throw a flat pass and he threw it perfectly to Goganious who had no one in front of him at the USC 25-yard line. But Goganious dropped the ball and USC went on to win, 19-14. "It hit my hands and I just dropped it," Goganious told Jerry Crowe of the Los Angeles Times. Sacca had passed for 243 yards for the second week in a row but had still been inconsistent in hitting on 16-of-34 attempts while giving up two interceptions and two sacks.

"This team is frustrated and angry," Giannetti told Black for the "Football Letter," "and we're looking for someone to take it out on." They took it out on 2-and-0 Rutgers the following week at Beaver Field, rolling up all their points in the first half in a 28-0 victory. State had 374 net yards while limiting Rutgers to 148 as Thompson scored four touchdowns on short runs and Sacca set up two of the TDs with long passes, including one of 36 yards to Thompson before State's final score. After State's fencing team was honored at halftime for winning its first National Championship, the Lion reserves took over and just about everyone played, including Bill and Nardolillo at QB and fifth string tailback Brian Kurlej. However, Paterno was still frustrated by his kicking team. "We had another field goal blocked and we darn near had another punt blocked," he said in the media room. The public scolding would intensify the efforts of special teams coach Tom Bradley in practice and pay off big time seven games later.

However, the special teams had another punt blocked against Temple and the Owls scored a touchdown on the return. But it was Temple's only TD of the day as the Lions routed the Owls, 48-10, in 80 degree weather at Beaver Stadium. With a sellout Homecoming crowd of 85,874 looking on, Brown ran back the opening kickoff 82 yards to set up the first touchdown by Gash and Sacca threw a 33-yard TD to Smith and a 26-yard TD to Daniels to help give State a 31-7 halftime lead. Thompson rushed for 125 yards and Brown for 105 as Fayak booted two field goals—one for 45 yards—and the defense intercepted four passes in the easy win.

The final game of the series with traditional rival Syracuse did not end in a controversy nor a fist fight as many oldtimers on both sides might have expected—and even hoped. It was a well played football game despite a wet field soaked by three days of heavy rain from Hurricane Lilli. After all the flak the special teams had been taking, it was the kickoff team that came up with a key play of the game and the field goal team that provided the margin of victory in State's 27-21 win. An interception by Thomas on Syracuse's first possession set up a 16-yard TD scramble by Sacca that gave the Lions a 7-0 lead. With a national CBS-TV audience and a Beaver Stadium crowd of 86,002 looking on, State went ahead 14-6 after a 77-yard drive capped by Gash's 2-yard TD. On the ensuing kickoff Powell smashed the return man so hard he fumbled and Fusetti recovered at the 23-yard line. Fayak then kicked a 22-yard field goal but Syracuse stormed back on an 80-yard drive before the intermission to narrow State's lead to 17-14. Sandusky gave his defense a chewing out at halftime and Syracuse didn't score again until two minutes were left in the game. "The intensity in the second half was much higher," Deter said after the game. Sacca and

Daniels hooked up for a 36-yard TD pass four minutes into the fourth quarter and Fayak kicked a 42-yard field goal a few minutes later to finish off State's scoring. When it was all over, the bands of both teams met on the field at the end for a short concert that featured the twirlers—sisters Lori Branley of PSU and Lisa Branley of SU. Paterno had little to say about the end of the Syracuse series after 68 years but Orange coach MacPherson wasn't bashful. "I'm so damn mad," he told sportswriters. "I didn't want them to get out of here with a win."

The 40-21 winning score at Boston College the following week was deceiving to anyone who did not watch the game on CBS-TV or was not in Chestnut Hill to see it. Both teams were 3-2 and at halftime the score was tied 14-14 on the passing of the two quarterbacks. Sacca threw 6-yards to Smith for one touchdown and set up Gash's 2-yard TD with 26-yarder to Smith while BC quarterback Glenn Foley took advantage of a roughing the kicker penalty on the Lions and an interception to pass for two TDs as the teams went to the locker rooms. When they came out, a new State star emerged. Thompson had not even dressed for the game because of a toe injury and in the second quarter Brown went out with his own dislocated toe. In came Hammonds, who had started the year as third-string safety but moved to tailback when Collins and Kurlej were hurt. He had carried the ball four times against Temple for 26 yards and in his first five rushes on this day, he gained a total of 17 yards. On the third play of the second half, Hammonds took the handoff from Sacca and ran 65-yards down the right sideline for a TD. Two Fayak field goals made the score 27-14 as the fourth quarter began but two minutes later Foley hit Mark Chmura with a 13-yard TD pass to close the gap to 27-21. It was a defensive struggle for most of the fourth quarter and with three minutes left Humphries intercepted Foley at the PSU 37-yard line. Two plays later Hammonds burst through right tackle, cut back and ran 48-yards for another TD. A few moments later, D'Onofrio stripped Foley of the ball on a sack, Jackson recovered at the BC 2 and Gash went in for the TD to seal the game. The Lion defense had held BC runners to a minus 4 yards on 22 carries and also had two interceptions and three sacks but Hammonds had stolen the headlines. His 208 yards rushing on 24 carries is still the State record for a freshman back but he was a reluctant runner. "I really don't like playing running back," he told sportswriters after the game. "I'd rather play defense." Paterno said he wasn't sure "where (Hammonds) will end up" but said, "obviously, he's got a lot of ability."

State's last game in its 10-year series with Alabama took on special meaning for a variety of reasons. Despite winning six of the previous nine games, the Tide declined to negotiate a new contract and this last game at Bryant-Denny Stadium in Tuscaloosa was designated for Homecoming. It was Homecoming, all right, a "homecoming" for Penn State's new president, Joab Thomas, who previously had been president at Alabama but had been forced out partly in a quarrel about the non-Alabaman football coach he had hired. Now, Thomas and coach Bill Curry were both gone and former Bear Bryant disciple Gene Stallings was the coach. Thomas had unexpectedly showed up at State's practice in midweek and the usually soft-spoken academic had urged the players to "kick some butt." After three losses to open the season, Alabama had won three straight including an upset over #3 Tennessee the previous week. The Alabama followers still had difficulty respecting any Eastern team, even one coached by Paterno, and they didn't think this State team was very good. One Birmingham sportswriter compared the Lions to Slippery Rock. Still, the atmosphere in Tuscaloosa was like a bowl game only this time there were less than

6,000 State fans in the crowd of 70,123, most of whom were scream-ing "Rolllll TIDE!!!" when the teams kicked off before an ESPN audi-ence on Saturday evening.

The game lived up to its billing as a battle of defenses as Alabama entered with the nation's 6th best total defense and the Lions at 13th. The Tide also had the country's leading placekicker in Phillip Doyle who had kicked 16 of 18 field goal attempts. But this night be-longed to the State defense and the Lions young kicker, Fayak. Perry's interception of quarterback Gary Hollingsworth's first pass set up a 34-yard field goal by Fayak early in the first quarter and the 3-0 lead car-ried into the third quarter. Sacca was having problems moving the Lion offense and when he threw an interception on State's third possession of the second half, Paterno inserted Bill. Late in the third quarter, a 19-yard run by Bill helped put Fayak into position to kick his longest field goal of 50 yards. Early in the fourth quarter, Perry picked off another pass at midfield and six plays later Fayak booted a 34-yard field goal and the Lions won, 9-0. State's defense had come up with five inter-ceptions, a fumble recovery and four sacks while holding Alabama to 135 yards passing (on 19-of-47 attempts) and just 6 yards rushing on 33 carries. The only time the Tide was close to scoring Doyle missed a 43-yard field goal attempt. "This was a classic Joe Paterno win, fea-turing defense, kicking and offense. Mostly defense," wrote Ron Bracken in the Centre Daily Times. President Thomas celebrated in the dress-ing room with the State players. "It's about time we get the respect we deserve," D'Onofrio told the media. "Our defense played a strong game," Paterno said, and the offense "played well at times against an awfully good Alabama defense." Stallings said "their defense whipped us at the line of scrimmage."

Paterno was not about to start another quarterback contro-versy. As the team practiced for its visit to West Virginia, Paterno told Sacca he was still the starter but that he was getting careless. Sacca admitted later that he was angered by Paterno's remarks and it af-fected how he played against the Mountaineers. With scouts from the Fiesta, Cotton, Citrus, Gator, Hall of Fame and new Blockbuster bowls watching, State took a 7-0 lead on the second play of the game when Perry intercepted a Greg Jones pass and went 30 yards for a touch-down. But it had been too easy. Sacca couldn't move the offense in the first four possessions and noticing that Sacca didn't seem to be into the game, Paterno replaced him again with Bill. An interception by Bochna on a passed tipped by Jackson set up a 43-yard drive and a 9-yard TD pass from Bill to Smith gave State a 14-6 lead at halftime. But West Virginia went 90 yards after the second half kickoff to narrow the score to 14-12. That was as close as the Mountaineers would get. With Brown still out with an injury and Thompson bothered by his sore toe, Collins, Gash and Hammonds took over the running. Late in the third quarter Bill directed a 12-play, 80-yard drive, passing to Smith for 25-yards on one play and scoring himself from the 5-yard line when forced to run because a screen pass wouldn't work. The defense then forced WVU to punt from deep in its own territory and Collins capped a 40-yard drive with a 19-yard TD run. The Lions missed another TD when Perry was stripped of the ball at the WVU 3-yard line after running back another intercepted pass 48 yards but Fayak kicked a 37-yard field goal and State won, 31-19. "We were terrible offensively in the first half...(and) we were sloppy defensively," Paterno said. "We've got a lot of work ahead."

As the Lions worked a little harder in practice that week be-fore hosting Maryland, the post season bowls began to line up their

teams. Paterno wanted a New Year's Day game and the Sugar, Citrus, Fiesta and Hall of Fame seemed the most interested. Much specula-tion centered around a possible match-up against Virginia in the Fiesta Bowl but there were potential political problems because voters in Ari-zona had rejected a holiday in honor of Martin Luther King. Tarman told the AP, "that would be a concern."

Every game with Maryland in the last 10 years had been close and the one at Beaver Stadium in 40 degree weather on Novem-ber 10 was no different. Almost unbelievably, the game started the same way as it did in West Virginia with Humphries intercepting Scott Zolak on the sixth play and running 74-yards for a touchdown. But by halftime, the score was tied, 10-10, as the Lions fumbled away one scoring chance at the Terp 23-yard line and lost another opportunity after a long interception return by Perry was nullified by a roughing the passer penalty on McKenzie. Sacca had started again and even though he was ineffective in the first half, completing just 1-of-5 passes, Pa-terno did not replace him. Many in the estimated crowd of 83,000 expected to see Bill start the third quarter but after the Lions took the ball on the 20 following the kickoff, out trotted Sacca. What happened next surprised Sacca as well as the fans. Paterno and Ganter ordered a long pass on first down. It was complete for 40 yards to Daniels and the crowd was on its feet. A fourth-and-four pass to Gash picked up 9 yards but Maryland stiffened at the PSU 19-yard line and soon the Lions faced a fourth-and-21 at the Terp 30. With a stiff wind making a field goal attempt difficult, Paterno called for an intermediate pass to Smith that would at least give the Lion defense good field position if

Sam Gash was a team player, an excellent blocker, powerful runner and fine pass receiver who started every game at FB during the 1990 and 1991 seasons.

they couldn't pick up the first down. But Sacca saw that his secondary receiver Daniels had beaten the corner back and he threw it. Daniels dove in the back of the end zone and caught the pass for a touchdown and now State had momentum. Minutes later Sacca passed the team on another long drive to a first down at the Maryland 3 but five running plays into the line gained only two yards and the Terps took over. But not for long. The defense forced a punt from the end zone and after

Smith's punt run back of 11 yards, the Lions scored with Thompson going in from 10 yards to climax his finest day of running—gaining 132 yards on 26 carries—and the Lions won, 24-10. "This team is getting better each week," Paterno told the media. For the first time in weeks, he also had something good to say about his still maturing quarterback. "...He came through in the third quarter," Paterno said. "I think that shows he's got something in him we haven't seen before."

By the next day, the Lions were all but set to play Florida State in the new Blockbuster Bowl in Fort Lauderdale, December 28. The Blockbuster wanted a Florida team to be the host and Florida State agreed. State wouldn't confirm the pairing but an FSU official confirmed Florida State's participation. Blockbuster executive Bruce Keller had told the CDT's Bracken that State could lose all of its remaining games and still get the bowl invitation. However, there was a rumor State still had a chance at the Sugar Bowl.

Not many fans believed the 18th-ranked Lions could beat #1 Notre Dame in South Bend the next Saturday. Certainly not Sugar Bowl officials who had declined State's request to wait until after this game before selecting its teams. Later, the Sugar Bowl would try to get State to renege on a commitment to the Blockbuster Bowl but, win or lose, the newest post-season bowl wanted the Lions and PSU officials had unofficially accepted earlier in the week. A cloud of bitterness also enveloped the game because of Notre Dame's new television deal giving NBC exclusive rights to televising Irish home games starting in 1991. Paterno had been outspoken about what Penn State and other members of the College Football Association believed was deception in Notre Dame's breakaway from the CFA TV contract. His quip at a winter sports banquet that "Notre Dame has gone from an academic institution to a banking institution" had incensed some Notre Dame officials. Paterno also was angered that Notre Dame had wanted to end its current football contract with the Lions even before State's announcement about the Big Ten. So, he had some extra incentive when his team took the field in the late afternoon of November 17. After it was over, Paterno told sportswriters he had been confident his team could win but he "wasn't sure the squad had that confidence." The Irish were loaded with All-Americans and future All-Pros and they played like it in the first half as an ESPN audience and 59,075 fans watched. With the running of Ricky Watters, Tony Brooks and Rodney Culver, the passing of sophomore quarterback Rick Mirer, receiving of Raghib Ismail and a tenacious defense led by cornerback Todd Lyght, Notre Dame scored three touchdowns on drives of 63, 59 and 92 yards to take a convincing 21-7 lead at halftime. Already, the Irish had gained 151 yards on the ground and Mirer had completed 7-of-12 passes for 140 yards. Meanwhile, the Lions' only score had come with five minutes left in the first quarter on a 32-yard TD pass from Sacca to Smith that climaxed a 68-yard drive. In the locker room, Paterno told the team to quit giving Notre Dame so "much respect." He said to go out and "be more aggressive...take a chance and see if (you) can make something happen."

Nothing happened right away. State had one break when Ismail could not play the second half because of a thigh injury but the Lions were now playing with renewed spirit and its doubtful Ismail could have made a difference in the outcome. The teams traded possessions mostly around midfield although State missed one scoring opportunity when Fayak missed a 39-yard field goal. Then, late in the third quarter D'Onofrio intercepted Mirer at the Notre Dame 49 and ran down the left sideline to the 11 before being tackled from behind. It was the big break the Lions had needed. On third-and-10, Sacca heaved a pass to Sayles in the left corner of the end zone and he juggled it four times while trying to stay in bounds and finally clutched it for a touchdown. Fayak's PAT made it 21-14. Midway through the fourth quarter, the Lions took over at their own 42 following a punt. Sacca immediately threw a 24-yard pass to Smith, then two plays later hit Thompson on a 20-yard screen pass to the Irish 14. Sacca rolled right and threw back to Golden at the 3 and Golden barreled into the end zone with three tacklers on his back. Fayak's PAT tied the game and the Irish fans were stunned. There was 7:15 left in the game, time for Notre Dame to put on one of its legendary finishes. Not this time Leprechauns. With about two minutes remaining, a Helkowski punt backed up the Irish at their own 7-yard line. On first down, Burger almost sacked Mirer for a safety. The Irish could see their #1 ranking fading. Second down, one yard. Third-and-9 and Mirer overthrew his receiver cutting across the middle. Perry picked it off at midfield and ran to the Notre Dame 19. With 58 seconds left, Paterno decided to turn the game over to his freshman kicker. "Before that kick I told my holder that this was just like kicking in my backyard," Fayak said later. "I have a goal post there and I've made this kick a million times." Two running plays moved the ball into position and with four seconds left, Ceh snapped, Spoor held, the line blocked and Fayak calmly kicked a 34-yard field goal to give the Lions the 24-21 victory. "Penn State Boots No. 1 Notre Dame," said the full front page headline in The National Sports Daily. "If they play Penn State football for 1,000 years," wrote the CDT's Bracken, "men will look back and say: 'This was their finest hour.'" Notre Dame had never crossed midfield in the second half and Sacca had played the best game of his young career, hitting on 20-of-34 passes for 277 yards, three touchdowns, no interceptions and just one sack. "Tony grew up today," Paterno said. Holtz congratulated State, saying "they won the battle up front in the second half." Paterno told the media, "this team is much better than it has been given credit for all along...They've been in every game and made things happen." Back in State College, some 1,200 students tore down the goal posts in darkened Beaver Stadium and marched to Paterno's home before parading around campus and downtown.

The Pitt game at cold Beaver Stadium on November 24 was hardly anti-climactic. The underdog had often won this traditional series and the 3-6 Panthers now coached by Paul Hackett almost did it again. The Lions, now #11 in the AP poll, allowed a 10-0 lead in the second quarter to get away from them and with about 10 minutes left in the game State led 16-10 after Fayak's third field goal of the day. With another late afternoon CBS-TV audience watching, Pitt returned the kickoff to its own 33-yard line then moved to a second down at the 37. Now came what was almost the play of the game and it was one from Hackett's "bag of tricks." Sophomore quarterback Alex Van Pelt threw a cross-field lateral to wide receiver Darnell Dickerson, the former quarterback, who had dropped back from the line. Another wide receiver, Olanda Truitt, had dashed behind State's secondary and was wide open at the PSU 25. Dickerson threw a perfect pass to Truitt and Scott Kaplan's PAT put Pitt into the lead for the first time, 17-16. But it was the rejuvenated special teams which helped regain the lead on the kickoff. Tisen Thomas took the ball on a bounce over his head at the State 6-yard line, broke two tackles up the middle then ran down the right sideline before being tackled at the Pitt 35. Brown ran 11 yards on one play and three plays later Daniels took a screen pass in the left flat from Sacca and dashed 16-yards into the end zone. A two-point pass for the conversion failed but State led, 22-17. Van Pelt, who would pass for 246 yards on 22-of-44 attempts, had two more chances to get the victory but Humphries and Bochna ended each threat with an interception and the Lions celebrated their ninth straight victory. Sacca had another fine day, passing for 187 yards with 16-of-32 completions and thrilling the crowd by scrambling for a total of 113 yards on runs of 55 and 50 yards. For his performance, Sacca won the Coogan Award as the game's outstanding player. And after the game, State formally accepted a bid to the inaugural Blockbuster Bowl.

THE 1990 BLOCKBUSTER BOWL
Dec. 28, 1990
Florida State 24, Penn State 17

What made this new bowl game so special was that both teams still had a legitimate outside shot at the National Championship. No major college team had finished the regular season undefeated and untied and before the post season games began at least 10 teams believed they could win the title if things broke their way. The sole unbeaten team was surprising Georgia Tech but with a 10-0-1 record it was still number #2 to Colorado and relegated to playing #19 Nebraska in the Citrus Bowl. Colorado at 10-1-1 was playing #5 Notre Dame (9-2) in the Orange Bowl and #3 Texas (10-1) was meeting #4 Miami (9-2) in the Cotton Bowl with #8 Washington (9-2) against #17 Iowa in the Rose Bowl. The Sugar Bowl had blown it with #10 Tennessee (9-2-2) against unranked Virginia and most of the media rated the Blockbuster clash between #6 Florida State and #7 Penn State as the third best game of the post season. It certainly didn't pay as much as the other major bowls but once the Blockbuster Video corporation bought into what was originally titled the Sunshine Bowl, the payout increased to $1.6 million per team. The syndicated Raycom Sports Network had originated the idea for the bowl and had brought the owners of Joe Robbie Stadium—the Robbie family, who also owned the NFL Miami Dolphins—into the deal, then worked out an agreement for the bowl to become part of Fort Lauderdale's Winterfest celebration. For that reason, the Friday night game was being televised by Raycom and not one of the major networks, but Raycom had put together a group of some 150 stations in 90 percent of the country to carry the game. Ironically, one of the game's announcers would be Dave Rowe, an outstanding defensive tackle on Paterno's first team in '66.

The match-up also was emboldened by the two opposing coaches. FSU's coach Bobby Bowden had turned the Seminoles into a football power since going to Tallahassee from West Virginia in the late 1970s and he was all hepped up about this game with his erstwhile nemesis but now long time friend, Joe Paterno. With college football's two winningest coaches—who were both quick with the quip—the game was easy to market on television and in South Florida. In fact, there was such a demand for the 74,500 tickets from FSU alumni that it sold out quickly and days before the game scalpers were asking up to $250 for tickets originally priced at $18-$32. Once again there was a contrast in pregame preparations as Paterno continued his custom of closed practices while also limiting player interviews to a small group of individuals for 15 minutes each day. Everything was loose and informal at FSU with practices open and players always available. Paterno seemed a little more uptight about this game and canceled the team's participation in a bowl week cruise. Still, the atmosphere around the team headquarters at the Pier 66 Resort was typical for a Florida bowl game and was marred only when Paterno's son Jay and a female companion

were robbed at gunpoint while sitting on the beach. The thieves were arrested and the valuables recovered.

The game itself was expected to be a battle between Bowden's free-wheeling offense and Paterno's aggressive defense. What it came down to was too many mistakes by the Lions. The omen was in State's first series after FSU had taken a 3-0 lead thanks in part to a pass interference penalty. Daniels dropped a pass. Brown fumbled but recovered. And Sacca threw behind his open receiver. The Seminoles rushed Helkowski on the ensuing punt, partially blocking it. All-American corner back Terrell Buckley picked it up on the FSU 46, ran back to his own 30, then brushed away several would-be tacklers and dashed all the way to the State 15. Four plays later Amp Lee ran in from the one and FSU led 10-0. The Lions blew one scoring chance when Daniels, uncharacteristically, dropped another pass when he was wide open. But on State's third possession, Sacca hit Daniels on a 56-yard bomb and the Lions trailed, 10-7. However, in the second quarter, the special teams faltered and Fayak's 22-yard field goal attempt was blocked. Then, after a drive to the FSU 5, Sacca was intercepted following a holding penalty. That was what FSU needed and just before the half the Seminoles marched 70 yards in seven plays for a TD and a 17-7 lead. A Humphries interception helped set up a 67 yard drive that resulted in a 32-yard field goal by Fayak midway through the third quarter but then FSU's Casey Weldon led a 58-yard drive and scored on a 5-yard run that hiked the Seminole lead to 24-10 going into the fourth quarter. Trying to light a spark in his offense, Paterno replaced Sacca with Bill with 7:32 left and the senior struck quickly, going 62-yards in three plays with a 37-yard TD pass to Smith and Fayak's PAT making the score 24-17 with 6:27 remaining. The Lions had two more shots but FSU's defense forced a punt at midfield and then after State had reached the Seminole 31-yard line with three minutes remaining, an interception at the one-yard line virtually ended the game. "Nittany Lions Couldn't Edit Out Their Mistakes," said the headline in the Fort Lauderdale Sun-Sentinel. "We had a lot of opportunities but we just didn't do it," Paterno told sportswriters such as Elaine Sung of the Miami Herald. Paterno also touted Florida State for #1, saying "they're the best team I've seen this year." But when it was all over, Colorado shared the title with Georgia Tech and the Lions finished 10th in the UPI and 11th in the AP ratings.

So, the "Silver Season" was tarnished at the end but Paterno was optimistic with 50 of 60 players from his depth chart returning. "After the game I felt the same way I felt after the (1985) Orange Bowl," Paterno later told Black for the "Football Letter." Okay, then 1991 really would be the year for another run at the National Championship, right? And it was—until it all went "South" in Miami.

Season Record 9-3
Record to Date 646-282-42
Winning percentage .688

"'They Never Quit'"

Joe Paterno led his Nittany Lions out into the heat of the Orange Bowl convinced that they could upset Miami on this sunny October afternoon and stay in contention for the National Championship. If they lost, it would be all over because they had already dropped one game. No team had ever won the national title with two defeats since the wire services started ranking teams after the post-season bowls in 1968.

One loss can be overcome as State had learned in '82 and Colorado had found out last year. But unless something inconceivable occurred, two defeats would probably make the Lions an also ran once again. Southern Cal had helped see to that with another victory in the Los Angeles Coliseum a month before. Now, at 5-1, the #9 Lions could regain momentum by beating the #2 unbeaten Hurricanes, especially by doing it on their home field where Miami had not lost in 40 straight games. But to do it, Paterno had told his players, they would have to play a heckuva lot better than they had in the last two games. "We don't seem to be getting any better," he had told the media for the second week in a row after the Lions struggled to beat Temple the previous Saturday night. A week earlier they had barely survived against winless Boston College after blowing a 28-7 lead in the fourth quarter. They were making too many mistakes and careless errors. And, as he had feared as far back as spring practice, the offensive line was still his weakest link.

Despite the return of some 35 veterans, including 15 starters, only Huntington was a regular in the '90 offensive line and he was shifted from short guard to center in the spring. Seiver, who had started a couple games near the end of the season when Huntington was hurt, moved to long guard but the other linemen were inexperienced. Rucci won the Worrell Awards as most improved offensive player in the spring and became the long tackle. Burger was moved from defense to the short tackle spot and last years' backup center, Mac Gallagher, moved to short guard. At least that's how the season opened. But Rucci hurt his knee against Boston College and was now out for the season. Seiver was now at long tackle, Gallagher at long guard and John Gerak, who played fullback two years before and took a redshirt in '90, was now the starter at short guard. Derick Pickett also had started two games at short tackle and before the season was over Malinoski, redshirt freshman Bucky Greeley and E. J. Sandusky, the assistant coach's son, also would get starts on the offensive line. "Working with new people in new positions presents certain problems," Huntington had told sportswriters after Temple. "You must learn to play together as a unit." Tight end was solid with co-captain Golden and Sayles back but before too long redshirt freshman Kyle Brady of New Cumberland and junior walk-on Troy Drayton of Steelton would take over the position.

After the offensive line, Paterno also had been most concerned in the spring about his tailback position and after six games he still was. Collins and Anderson, who was redshirted in '90, had been splitting the starting slot with Hammonds in reserve. None of the trio had done anything exceptional and in three of the first six games, the fullback, Gash, had been the leading rusher. There was no worry about the passing with Sacca having two outstanding wide receivers to throw to in Smith and McDuffie. Daniels had turned pro against Paterno's advice but true freshman Bobby Engram of Camden, SC, and LaBarca were more than able reserves. Nardolillo and redshirt freshman Kerry Collins of West Lawn were the substitute quarterbacks but this was Sacca's team all the way. He had brushed off his erratic performance in the Blockbuster Bowl and finally had become the quarterback Paterno knew he could be. Going into the Miami game, he was ninth in the nation in passing efficiency and had thrown for 12 touchdowns and 1,322 yards with just three interceptions. And after three years of bickering and a somewhat contentious spring Sacca and Paterno were no

longer "The Odd Couple." They had adjusted to each other's foibles and although they would never be pals there was at least mutual respect now. In fact, Paterno had changed the offense to take advantage of Sacca's passing capabilities.

Until the offensive line and running game developed, Paterno had counted on the defense and kicking teams to give the Lions the winning edge. Some sportswriters compared the four starting linebackers to all the best ones of the past. A headline in a *Penn State Football Preview* magazine story entitled "Fab Four" by Rich Scarcella of the *Reading Eagle-Times*, wondered whether "D'Onofrio, McKenzie, Givens and Goganious may be the finest quartet to play for Linebacker U. at the same time." Behind them were Powell, Wright, Ivory Gethers, Ryan Grube and freshman Brian Gelzheiser. Ravotti moved from linebacker to left tackle with Benfatti on the right and Deter over the center with Jackson, Flythe and Rudy Glocker, shifted from tight end, in reserve. Darren Perry was back at Hero with Humphries and Bochna at the corners. Baggett started at safety but a neck injury in the third game of the season ended his career and Rubin developed quickly into a first class performer. Graham, Cisar and Frank Yeboah-Kodie were the primary reserves in the secondary. Paterno felt his kicking would also be a strength with Helkowski back for his fourth year as the punter with Fayak again placekicking and snapper Ceh and holder Spoor also returning. A change in the field goal kicking rules narrowed the distance between the goal posts to match what had already occurred in the NFL but that was not expected to hamper Fayak. McDuffie was the prime return man on punts and also ran back kickoffs with Anderson, Smith, Hammonds and Engram also returning kicks. There also was a major change on the coaching staff when defensive backfield coach Ron Dickerson left for Clemson

Florida State was the choice of most sportswriters in the preseason polls but the Lions were usually in the Top 10 along with several opponents. In the AP rankings, State was #7, sandwiched by #6 Notre Dame and #8 Georgia Tech. Miami was #3 with USC at #16 and BYU at #20. "With the most demanding schedule a Paterno team has ever played," wrote Ron Christ of the *Harrisburg Patriot-News* in *Penn State Football Preview* magazine, "the Lions could lose a game and still wind up as National Champion." This also was the next to the last year that the Lions would play an independent schedule. Their integration into the Big Ten had been accelerated and was now set for 1993.

The first game against the defending UPI National Champion Georgia Tech was not on the original schedule but was set up for the Kickoff Classic to open the college football season on August 28. Paterno originally declined the invitation to play in the game at Giants Stadium in the New Jersey Meadowlands but then let his players decide. Sacca admitted later that he argued against it but the co-captains—D'Onofrio, Gash, Goganious, Golden, Perry and Smith—were all for it. "Georgia Tech made us an offer we couldn't refuse," D'Onofrio told Christ of the *Patriot-News*. Based on the '90 season and the running that highlighted the spring Blue-White game, no one expected the Lions to come out throwing. But behind his usual closed practices in the preseason, Paterno had developed a more wide-open passing offense for Sacca to operate and it exploded on a warm Wednesday night as a record Kickoff Classic crowd of 77,409 and a national TV audience looked on. The game started slowly and was just 13-3 at the half after Sacca had thrown TD passes of 4 and 8 yards to Smith following drives of 46 and 85 yards. But in the third quarter, Sacca threw two more TD passes to McDuffie, including one incredible catch for 39 yards late in the third quarter that was reminiscent of Daniel's

LB Keith Goganious closes in on a Georgia Tech receiver in the 1991 Kickoff Classic. He was co-captain of the team that year.

spectacular TD reception in the '89 Holiday Bowl. The ball seemed to be knocked away after McDuffie outleaped defender Curly Day at the goal line but as McDuffie landed on his stomach, he rolled over, stuck out his left hand and snared the ball before it hit the ground. When Anderson turned a screen pass into a 52-yard TD less than a minute into the fourth quarter, that made the score 34-3 and Tech only made it look closer with three TDs against State's reserves for a final score of 34-22. It might have been worse but Fayak missed a pair of field goals in the third quarter. "Georgia Tech,...was reeducated by a physical, more-ready-to-play Penn State," wrote Steve Hummer in the *Atlanta Constitution*. Sacca's five TD passes are still a school record as he hit on 13-of-25 attempts for 206 yards without an interception. "Tony did a fine job out there tonight with a tough football because it was really humid and the ball got wet," Paterno said. Gash led Lion rushers with 80 of the net 159 yards and the defense set up three second half TDs by forcing three fumbles and intercepting a pass. "They're a great football team," Tech Coach Bobby Ross told the media. "Their speed and their depth are the most significant things you can see..."

Tech didn't complain that its two best runners were out for disciplinary reasons and several other starters went down early in the game. The Lions appeared to be in midseason form but the ease of the victory was deceptive. So was the 81-0 romp over Cincinnati 10 days later in the home opener at expanded Beaver Stadium. A new cantilevered second deck over the north end zone stands had increased seating capacity by 10,000 seats and a record crowd of 94,000 was there to watch State win by the largest point margin since 1926. The score was 40-0 by halftime and State threw just two passes in the second half as Paterno used everyone on the bench but the punter. Gash, Brady and Hammonds scored two TDs each as did true freshman J. T. Morris, the only one of four notable scholastic running backs Paterno had recruited who was not being "redshirted." Morris thrilled the crowd with TD runs of 53 and 57 yards to become the first freshman since D. J. Dozier in 1983 to run for over 100 yards (145 on 13 carries). Sacca's younger brother John, the fifth quarterback in the game, had the longest touchdown run of the day when he avoided a sack and scrambled 75 yards for the Lions final TD. Perhaps the hardest worker of all was Nittany Lion mascot Tim Curan who did a record 543 pushups in the traditional accounting of State's cumulative score. Paterno was so concerned about the limited amount of playing time his team had that he held an unusual Sunday workout without pads. "We may be deluding ourselves about what it will take to beat Southern Cal," Paterno told sportswriters at mid week. He was right.

Neither the Lion coaches nor the players were prepared for what happened in the LA Coliseum on prime time television the following Saturday night. USC was angry after being upset by lightly regarded Memphis State on Labor Day, 24-10, and coach Larry Smith had two weeks to get his team fired up and ready for the now #5 Lions. State could not handle the Trojan's all-out blitz nor overcome its own mistakes and carelessness and the Lions had none of the spark they showed against Georgia Tech. The Lions fumbled seven times and twice the Trojans recovered to set up short TD drives of 20 and 14 yards. State also had 90 yards in penalties and two 15-yard personal foul penalties on the defense helped keep USC TD drives alive. The offensive line and backs simply couldn't cope with the blitz, even after halftime adjustments, and Sacca was sacked five times and had to scramble and rush his passes at other times. He threw two interceptions and hit on just 18-of-40 passes, although one was a 13-yard TD pass in the second quarter that tied the score at 7-7. State was still in the game midway through the fourth quarter, trailing 14-10, and almost took the lead on a play eerily similar to one the year before. This time D'Onofrio dropped what looked like a sure TD on an interception at the USC 30. Then, a few minutes later, McDuffie and Smith fumbled a reverse handoff on a punt, backing the Lions to their own 6-yard line. Two plays later, Gash fumbled, USC recovered at the 14 and after six straight running plays the Trojans led 21-10 and held on to win. "Trojans bounce back from humiliation at hands of Memphis State to dominate Nittany Lions, 21-10," said the subheadline in the *Los Angeles Times*. "Nothing mystical or magical happened here tonight," Paterno told sportswriters, "Southern Cal just played good, tough football" and deserved to win, adding, "We kicked the ball around and didn't look very good."

As ill prepared as the Lions were for USC, they were more than ready to redeem themselves in another nationally televised night game against Brigham Young (0-2) the following Saturday at Beaver Stadium. In their last meeting at the '89 Holiday Bowl, the teams had battled to a 50-39 shootout and a similar high scoring game was expected, especially with both starting quarterbacks from '89 still on the scene. Detmer had won the Heisman Trophy in 1990 and was already the NCAA's all-time passing leader with a career completion record of 62.8 percent and an average of 305 yards and 2 1/2 touchdowns per game. But Paterno and his assistants designed a game plan that would be based on ball control and keeping Detmer off the field. They weren't even sure Sacca would play because of a dislocated finger he had suffered against USC. He hadn't taken any snaps in practice but no one knew that until after the game. The now #12 Lions led by just 10-7 at the half after missing two other scoring opportunities but State turned a BYU fumble on the second half kickoff into a TD, then scored another TD after recovering a fumbled punt and went on to smother the Cougars, 33-7. In the second half BYU had just 30 net yards and Detmer completed just 3-of-16 passes for 47 yards. State controlled the ball for 42 minutes and ran off twice as many plays as BYU, rushing for a net 292 yards to zero for the visitors. Sacca completed 12-of-24 passes for 187 yards and a 12-yard touchdown to Smith while the Lion defense held Detmer to 8-of-25 pass attempts for 158 yards while sacking him six times and intercepting him once. "Our defense played a strong, strong game," Paterno said in the media room. "In the second half our offensive line really took off and played like they're capable of playing."

But in the next two weeks, the team would regress and barely escape with victories over inferior opposition. The pattern would be the same against both Boston College and Temple with careless mistakes, missed opportunities, inopportune penalties and an erratic running game. In the September 28 game against Boston College at Beaver Stadium, the Lions were losing 7-6 at halftime despite pushing the Eagles all over the field while amassing 209 net yards. A blocked PAT attempt and two missed field goals by Fayak kept BC in the game. The Lions seemed to take charge early in the fourth quarter, 28-7, as interceptions by Givens and Perry set up two touchdowns and Perry returned another one 45 yards for a TD. But after the ensuing kickoff, BC quarterback Foley led the Eagles on a 7-play, 77-yard drive and a 20-yard TD to Chmura. Then BC forced a punt and Chmura's freshman substitute Pete Mitchell caught a 46-yard bomb behind Rubin on a fourth down pass to narrow the score to 28-21 with 5 1/2 minutes left in the game. Helkowski's shanked punt gave BC possession again at the BC 33-yard line with 2:54 left and despite a sack by Givens, Foley hit on five passes to move the Eagles for a first down at the State 17. Jackson sacked Foley for a big loss but the play was nullified by a personal foul penalty away from the ball. As time ran down, Foley threw two passes into the end zone, including one to a wide open receiver, but both fell incomplete and the Lions won. "We're not a very smart football team," Paterno told sportswriters. Sacca had the best passing day of his career with 16-of-22 completions for 292 yards and a 42-yard TD pass to Smith but Lion rushers had just 78 net yards on 38 carries and 56 yards came on a TD run by third string tailback Hammonds in the third quarter. Although State intercepted Foley five times and sacked him five times he almost beat State's so-called "prevent defense" with 277 yards on 17-of-34 attempts. "This was our second wake-up call," Smith told the media. "One should have been enough."

They had another one the next Saturday night against Temple at Veterans Stadium in Philadelphia when they let a 10-0 lead in the second quarter get away from them because of major penalties and shoddy play on both sides of the line. Trailing by just 10-7 at halftime, the 1-3 Owls dominated most of the second half and fumbled away scoring opportunities at State's 19 and 28 yard lines and missed a

A co-captain of the 1991 team, WR Terry Smith ranks among the top in number of PSU receiving records.

field goal from the Lion 18. D'Onofrio, who was playing with a painful shoulder he injured before the BYU game, recovered both fumbles and his second one with five minutes left seemed to give the Lions some spark. Sacca drove them 73-yards in 8 plays, passing twice to Smith including a 22-yard TD pass with two minutes remaining. On Temple's first play from scrimmage after the kickoff, Perry intercepted and ran 41 yards into the end zone, making the 24-7 final seem more decisive than it actually was. "We keep shooting ourselves in the foot," D'Onofrio said after the Lions had been penalized 10 times for 95 yards for the second week in a row. "If we play like this against Miami, we'll get killed."

So, why after they had looked so miserable in the last two weeks, did Paterno feel these players could knock off Miami? He reasoned it was the level of competition and the last chance for the 14 fifth-year seniors to stay in the national title race. Miami was a nine point favorite but some of the Hurricane players arrogantly predicted a blow out. "I think we'll beat them by 21 points because our offense is jut so explosive," offensive tackle Anthony Hamlet told the *Miami Herald*. Paterno's plan was to control the ball to keep State's defense off the field and to avoid giving up the big play. He believed he could match speed with speed and stymie the Hurricanes' pass rush with a new shovel pass play developed in practice that week. Although the game was supposed to be on national television, not many people saw it because much of the contest was preempted most of that Saturday afternoon by live ABC news coverage of the controversial hearings on Clarence Thomas' nomination to the U.S. Supreme Court and the emotional sexual harassment charges leveled by Anita Hill. A sellout crowd of 75,723 sat in the searing 90 degree heat and humidity and saw the two teams trade two field goals in the first half. A 15-yard TD pass from Sacca to Smith in the first quarter was nullified by an ineligible receiver penalty and the 6-6 score held up until midway in the third quarter. On the first series of the half, the Lions lost a scoring opportunity after Ravotti's sack of quarterback Gino Toretta at midfeld. The Hurricanes forced a punt and then did precisely what Paterno wanted to avoid. They hit on the big play. On first down at the Miami 20 Toretta found wide receiver Horace Copeland wide open behind Humphries and hit him on an 80-yard TD bomb. A few minutes later, Helkowski punted again from near midfield. Kevin Williams caught the punt on the Miami 9-yard line, found the lane and ran 91 yards for a school record touchdown and a 20-6 lead. "I thought my run would break them," Williams later told sportswriters.

Two 15-yard penalties on Miami, one for celebrating and another for a personal foul on the kickoff, put the ball at the Lion 43 and nine plays later Sacca threw a 2-yard TD to Smith on fourth down, narrowing the lead to 20-13. But Miami came back after the kickoff with another 42-yard bomb from Torretta to Thomas to go up by 26-13 on the first play of the fourth quarter. However, the Lions wouldn't go easily. Sacca led a 78-yard drive in 10 plays, passing to Smith for a 9-yard TD and Fayak's PAT made it 26-20 with 9 1/2 minutes remaining. The teams traded possessions until the Lions took over with 2:36 left at their own 26. Sacca, hit hard all day by the Hurricanes and sacked eight times, was exhausted. But he found McDuffie twice for 15 yard gains to move to Miami's 44 -yard line. A running play was stopped for no gain and two passes fell incomplete. On fourth down Sacca scrambled and could have picked up a first down if he had run for it. "I was so tired," he said later, "I wasn't seeing clearly." He lofted a desperation pass towards Drayton near the goal line. Williams intercepted at the one, stepped back into the end zone then came out and was tackled. State fans watching thought it was a safety and that the Lions would receive a free kick with 1:04 remaining. But the Big Ten officiating crew gave the ball to Miami at the one and the Hurricanes ran out the clock for the 26-20 victory. "Sweet victory emerged from a pile of crumpled bodies Saturday afternoon and staggered off the field exhausted," wrote Ken Rodriguez in the *Miami Herald*. "Our kids hung tough away from home," Paterno told the media. "We played a good game but got beaten by a really good team in a fine football game." Miami coach Dennis Erickson said it "was a great win for us" and praised State, saying "They never quit..." It was the defining characteristic of this team and led to the ultimate defining moment on New Year's Day.

Without a National Championship to play for, Paterno knew he had to do something to keep the team motivated. After all, there was a New Year's Day bowl game still attainable and the best season record since 1986. He made some changes on both offense and defense, removing Huntington, Siever, Gallagher and Golden as starters and moving up Sandusky, Malinoski, Greeley and Brady. D'Onofrio was done for the season because of his dislocated shoulder and Wright replaced him. Deter missed Miami and was still out and Jackson was now at nose tackle with Glocker at left tackle and Ravotti backing up at both defensive tackle and linebacker. Paterno also needed some leadership. "Paterno was taking a high stakes gamble...," Ken Denlinger would later write in his book, *"For The Glory."* "What if this latest bold move failed?"

It looked like failure for more than a quarter against Rutgers in the Homecoming game the following Saturday. With a 5-1 record including an upset of Michigan State and a win over Boston College, Rutgers was no pushover and led 14-7 midway through the second quarter. That's when McDuffie ran back a punt 55 yards for a touchdown to tie, then just before the half caught a 55-yard pass from Sacca to set up a 1-yard TD run by Collins that gave the Lions a 21-14 lead at the intermission. Both teams kicked field goals in the third quarter, then the Lions put it away with a Sacca 20-yard run that capped a 69-yard drive early in the fourth quarter. Graham's 12-yard interception return on the last play of the game made the final 37-17. McDuffie caught another pass and Smith had six for 75 yards giving them a total of 77 for the season—breaking the two player record set by Jack Curry and Ted Kwalick in 1967—and Smith moved ahead of Curry's individual record with his 43rd reception in the third quarter. Sacca had his fourth straight 200 yard passing day and was the leading rusher with 41 yards on six carries.

A week later, scouts from 10 bowls and a late afternoon ESPN audience watched the #8 Lions destroy a 5-2 West Virginia team in Indian Summer weather at Beaver Stadium, turning a 24-6 halftime lead into a 51-6 rout. "It was so one-sided," wrote Mike DeCourcy in the *Pittsburgh Press*, "(that) a large segment of the students included in the record crowd of 96,445 knew it was safe to leave at halftime." Sacca threw for three touchdowns, including two to McDuffie for 30 and 37 yards, and Anderson became the first back this season to run for 100 yards with a TD run of 26 yards among his 15 carries. Morris also had another TD on a 66-yard scamper in the fourth quarter and Fayak kicked field goals of 42, 31 and 19 yards as well as five extra points. The defense intercepted three passes, recovered two fumbles and had six sacks as it held the Mountaineers to a net 131 yards while the offense accumulated 529 yards. One pass Sacca didn't throw was by Kerry Collins in the fourth quarter when he completed the first pass

of his career to Drayton for a 27-yard gain. After the game, Paterno and the players said it had been a tough week of practice. "We went all out in practice," Anderson said. "There was a new cohesiveness among the whole offense."

The Lions had a week off before playing Maryland in Baltimore and Huntington, Seiver and Gallagher regained their starting positions on the offensive line. In that two week period, the bowl talk intensified and the Sugar, Citrus and Fiesta bowls appeared to be the most interested in the Lions. Scouts from those bowls plus four others were in Memorial Stadium on November 9th. Although the official invitations would not go out until November 17th, the bowls intended to line up their teams ahead of time as usual. This would be the last game at Memorial Stadium as the venerable old park was slated for demolition and the Baltimore Colts all-time great quarterback Johnny Unitas was on hand for the coin toss. "The Terrapins came out dressed in black shirts and black pants on a grey day..." wrote John Black for *"The Football Letter,"* "But they were appropriately attired for their own funeral." The Lions won 47-7 as Sacca moved past Chuck Fusina as PSU's career leader in passing yardage and completions by hitting on 13-of-18 passes for 198 yards and a 3-yard TD to Brady. For the first time all year, State had a balanced attack with 214 yards rushing and 266 yards passing with Anderson scoring two TDs in his 96 yards. McDuffie and Morris again thrilled the State fans in the crowd of 57,416 as McDuffie returned a punt 60 yards for a TD and Morris combined with Collins on a 64-yard screen pass for the Lions' final TD. "Tony has been a great player this year," Paterno raved in the locker room. "He's matured and has had a very positive effect on our football team."

That same day, Tennessee rallied from a 31-7 deficit to upset then #5 Notre Dame, 35-34, in South Bend and some sportswriters initially speculated this would lessen the Irish chances of going to the Sugar Bowl. Now, they wrote, the winner of the State-Notre Dame game the following week would play SEC champion Florida in New Orleans. But Sugar Bowl executives had already decided before the Tennessee game that they wanted the Irish, and so by Monday the Fiesta Bowl had arranged a New Year's Day match up between State and Tennessee. Despite its loss to Tennessee and another defeat earlier in the season to Michigan, #12 Notre Dame was a slight favorite over the #7 Lions and part of the reason was psychological. This was a veteran Notre Dame team, with 44 lettermen, including 12 starters, back from '90, and some in the media figured the Irish had the revenge factor on their side after losing their #1 ranking last year on that last play field goal by Fayak. On paper the teams seemed evenly matched and both were averaging 36.5 points per game with State giving up just 13.4 points and Notre Dame 18.4. A new record crowd of 96,672 turned out at Beaver Stadium on an unusually warm and sunny mid November day and they could not believe what they saw.

The ABC regional TV audience was still watching Miami beat #1 Florida State when the Irish kicked off at 3:30 and did not see the Lions methodically march 73 yards in 11 plays for a 3-yard touchdown by Anderson. But the TV audience was there when the Lions gained possession again at their own 27-yard line following a punt. And they must have been flabbergasted when Anderson broke free on a 57-yard run to set up Sacca's 8-yard TD pass to McDuffie. But there was more to come. The Lion defense forced the Irish to punt from about their 10-yard line and this time State went 53-yards on 10 plays with Anderson going over from the 4 to make the score a stunning 21-0 at the end of the first quarter. State had controlled the ball for nearly 12 minutes and

Darren Perry was one of the premier defensive backs for the Lions. He was a co-captain and All-American in 1991 as well as a finalist for the Jim Thorpe Award.

had gained almost 200 yards. Notre Dame tried to come back in the second quarter, getting a 2-yard TD by Jerome Bettis after a 65-yard drive. But another long drive to the State 2-yard line ended in four downs of frustration as State's outstanding goal line defense stopped the Irish from going any further. The Lions kicked off to start the second half and three minutes later had their fourth touchdown. Benfatti intercepted Rick Mirer at the Irish 37-yard line and on the next play McDuffie took a reverse handoff from Gash, got a savage block from Sacca and ran 37-yards for a touchdown. Early in the fourth quarter, a 45-yard TD pass from Sacca to McDuffie climaxed an 11-play, 91-yard drive that sealed the game and gave the Lions a 35-13 victory. "I knew going in that Penn State was probably the best team we played," Irish coach Holtz told the media, "and I feel the same way coming out." Paterno said the Lions "came out ready to play...Tonight we were a very fine football team." The next day, State officially accepted the Fiesta Bowl invitation.

Reviving an old tradition that dated to another era, State played Pitt on Thanksgiving day at Pitt Stadium. The teams had not met on Thanksgiving since 1974 and 52,519 spectators and another national TV audience watched as State took a 14-0 lead in the first quarter, then had to hold off a passing assault by Alex Van Pelt. The Lions never were behind but Pitt (6-4) rallied from a 23-7 halftime deficit to trail by just 26-20 with 11 minutes remaining. State's defense, which already had intercepted Van Pelt three times, needed two more in the fourth quarter to stop the Panthers. The final interception by Perry and his 12-yard runback set up a 29-yard TD run by Anderson that clinched the victory, 32-20. Van Pelt's 64 passing attempts set an individual record for a PSU opponent (since broken) as he completed 27 for 324 yards. Sacca was 11-for-27 and 162 yards—giving him a career record of 5,869 yards—and his 28-yard TD pass to Frayton in the first quarter tied Todd Blackledge's career TD record of 41. Anderson had the best running day of his career with 167 yards and two TDs on 27 carries and won the Coogan Award as the game's MVP. But the kicking game also was superb with Fayak kicking field goals of 25, 47, 24 and 48 yards and Helkowski averaging 44.2 yards on 9 punts in his final regular season game. The next week Paterno accepted the Lambert Trophy again as the best team in the East and Perry became the Lions first First-Team All-American in two years.

THE 1992 FIESTA BOWL
Jan. 1, 1992
Penn State 42, Tennessee 17
Most Valuable Offensive Player: O.J. McDuffie
Most Valuable Defensive Player: Reggie Givens

So much of State's football history in the Paterno era is linked to the Fiesta Bowl and the thrilling victory over Miami for the National Championship in the 1987 game could never be equaled. But no four minute span in 111 years and 1,056 games ever had such a bizarre and exciting turnaround as this New Year's Day game against Tennessee.

The teams had played just twice before and Tennessee had won both times in Knoxville, spoiling State's unbeaten season in the last game of 1971 and doing it again in the first game of 1972. The coach of the Volunteers was Johnny Majors who had resurrected Pitt football in the late '70s to challenge Paterno for Eastern supremacy. Since returning to his alma mater in 1977, Majors had revived the Volunteer program and Tennessee had won its last six bowl games. Like State, this year's Tennessee team had overcome two early season losses and its come from behind upset over Notre Dame had boosted the Volunteers into the Top 10. They were led by quarterback Andy Kelly, who had set several school passing records, and All-American wide receiver Carl Pickens. To beat them, Paterno had told some sportswriters, his defense and kicking teams, would have to help keep Tennessee from having field position and then the Lions would have to come up with some big plays. Tennessee, a four-point underdog, indicated it would try to beat the Lions with an all-out blitz as USC had done.

Although he continued to encourage his players to enjoy these post-season trips, Paterno had some internal problems which made some members of the team a little uneasy. He left three players home because they didn't measure up to his academic requirements, and in the days leading up to the game, a reserve lineman was sent home for breaking curfew and another starter was benched for drinking. Two players, including a second starter, were caught with girls in their rooms and others barely avoided detection for some rule violations. Perhaps, all that behind the scene high jinks was the reason the team played so poorly for almost three quarters.

State had the first break of the game when Tennessee fumbled the opening kickoff and freshman Geff Kerwin recovered at the Volunteer 11-yard line. Three plays later Sacca hit Gash on a 10-yard pass and the sixth-ranked Lions led 7-0. But the next 30-to-40 minutes were all Tennessees as the song "Rocky Top" bellowed throughout the stadium. A 62-yard drive following State's TD tied the game and a 24-yard field goal by John Becksvoort made it 10-7 at the half. But the Volunteers missed at least three other scoring opportunities, once on a 37-yard field goal attempt and another time when stopped on fourth-and-2 at the PSU 17. By the time the teams went to the locker room for intermission, Tennessee had netted 324 yards and 17 first downs to State's 59 yards and 5 first downs. Kelly was 16-of-26 for 204 yards while Sacca had hit on just 5-of-12 attempts for 49 yards and he had been sacked four times. Of course, Sacca was missing one of his favorite receivers, the record-breaking Smith, who was out with an injury, but the Lion quarterback was looking worse than he had all season. "I told our players at halftime to just keep hustling and something good would happen," Paterno said later. But, the second half didn't start any

QB Tony Sacca led Penn State to an 11-2 season and a #3 ranking in 1991. Sacca had a stormy relationship with Joe Paterno after becoming the first true freshman to start at QB in more than 50 years and he holds several career passing records.

better. State took the kickoff and it was three plays and a punt. Tennessee took over at its 32-yard line and six plays later, Kelly hit split end Cory Fleming on a 44-yard TD pass and Becksvoort's PAT made it 17-7. The Lions seemed to get another break a few minutes later when they forced another punt and the punter tried to run with the ball because of State's pressure and was tackled at the Tennessee 42. But it was another three plays and a punt. However, Tennessee also was forced to punt a couple of minutes later and none of the 71,133 fans in Tempe or the millions watching on national television could have predicted what was about to occur. This would be the defining four minutes of the season. *"They never quit..."*

McDuffie took the kick on the State 26, broke through the coverage and didn't stop until he reached the Tennessee 35-yard line. Three plays gained nothing but a Tennessee lineman jumped offside on third down and Paterno sent in another play. Sacca had thrown eight straight incomplete passes but this time he hit McDuffie at the 20 and McDuffie reached the 8-yard line before being tackled. On third-and-goal from the 3, State flooded the left side with three receivers and Sacca passed into the middle of the end zone to LaBarca for the sophomore's first TD. Fayak's PAT made the score 17-14 with 2:56 left in the third quarter. State kicked off and on the second play, Jackson beat his blocker, smashed into Kelly, stripped the ball and recovered at the UT 13. On the first play, Sacca rolled right and threw back across the field to Brady, who was wide open at the 10 and the Lions suddenly led, 21-17. Neither the Tennessee nor the State fans could believe it. But the barrage wasn't over. The Volunteers tried to regroup after the kickoff but on the second play from the UT 24, Givens intercepted Kelly at the 34 and ran to the 26. A pass to Drayton gained 18 yards to the 8, Anderson went up the middle for five, McDuffie picked up two on another pass and Anderson bolted over for the TD. With Fayak's PAT the score was now 28-17 less than a minute into the fourth quarter. Another kickoff. This time on the first play at the Tennessee 29, Bochna

and Givens blitzed from opposite ends. Bochna hit Kelly from the blind side. The ball popped into the air, Givens grabbed it and ran 23 yards for another touchdown. "It felt like a sack of money landed in my hands," Givens told sportswriters later. Fayak's kicked the PAT. In less than four minutes, the Lions had scored 28 points but there was more to come three minutes later after Tennessee finally ran three plays before punting. The Lions took over at the UT 48 and on third down Sacca and McDuffie combined for a 37-yard TD pass. There were still 10 minutes left in the game but it was virtually over and the Lions won, 42-17. "Penn State's dramatic turnaround...was one of those moments when everyone will remember what he/she was doing at the time it happened," wrote Black in *"The Football Letter."* "If you were sitting watching at home and you went to the bathroom, you probably missed the whole game," Sacca told Shelly Anderson of the *Pittsburgh Post-Gazette.* "This team responds to adversity," said McDuffie who received the offensive MVP trophy and dedicated it to the seniors. "We stuck together and came out with a big W."

The victory catapulted State into #3 in the AP, UPI and *USA Today*/CNN ratings behind the unbeaten co-National Champions Miami and Washington. The Lions were on the move upward again. Even with a new young quarterback, Paterno believed his next team could take another crack at the national title before entering the Big Ten in '93. Then, State was sabotaged by a new alliance among the Orange, Sugar, Cotton and Fiesta Bowls. A family picnic and another loss to Miami made the year even worse.

Season Record 11-2
Record to Date 657-284–42
Winning Percentage .690

"They Didn't Care"

This is a season longtime Penn State football fans would rather just forget. Perhaps Paterno, his coaches and the players that season would too. Like some of the years past, 1992 had its share of injuries, disciplinary problems and bad luck. But what made this season so dislikable is that the team squandered away its talent and in the end was a major embarrassment to itself and its loyal followers.

That doesn't mean there was any individual or group of players to blame, although there was a definite lack of leadership by the seniors and immaturity elsewhere. Nor were the coaches completely at fault, even though they failed to motivate and inspire the team at crucial junctures. But a football team is a unit and, strange as it may seem to outsiders, each team develops a personality and characteristics. Sometimes the absence or inclusion of one player can alter the chemistry of the team and subtle changes in team personality may happen often in the course of a season because of injuries and other misfortunes. It's what occurs over the entire year that forever sets the team's place in history. For 1992, it was a season that started with high expectations and ended in indifference.

The major post season bowls were the catalyst for it all. During the winter, the Cotton, Fiesta, Orange and Sugar Bowls came up with a plan to try and match the #1 and #2 teams in the AP writers' and *USA Today*/CNN coaches' polls for a National Championship game on New Year's Day. Included in the scheme were the Southeastern, Big 8, Southwest, Big East and Atlantic Coast conferences and Notre Dame. The Rose Bowl and the conferences affiliated with the Pasadena game—the Big Ten and Pac-10—declined to join what was being called "The Coalition." Because State was giving up its independence in 1993 to become part of the Big Ten, the bowls haughtily excluded the Lions from the new Coalition. Oh, State could have a long shot chance at one of the four Coalition bowls like any other of the remaining independents, the organizers admitted, but because of commitments to the conferences that was unlikely unless State finished unbeaten. So, finding themselves outside the Coalition's championship umbrella and its multi-million dollar payoffs, State officials went searching for an alternative.

The Blockbuster Bowl also was upset at being left out of the Coalition. On May 20, State and Blockbuster officials announced that the Lions would be the host team of the January 1 game at Joe Robbie Stadium and that CBS would televise it starting at 1:30 p.m. All State had to do was win the six games required by the NCAA for post season play. Opponent to be named later, of course. The unprecedented deal was ridiculed by many in the media and State's assistant coaches weren't exactly thrilled either. "It's an awkward situation," Tom Bradley told Kip Richeal for his book, *"Welcome To The Big Ten."* "It's tough from a coaching standpoint...the players come into the season knowing exactly what they're playing for. Their goal is still the National Championship...(but) if you lose one game, you have to redefine your goals." The scenario almost guaranteed a major letdown if the Lions lost one game and after the season was over many State fans wondered if the financial gain from the Blockbuster Bowl had been worth it all.

Neither the coaches nor the players knew about the Blockbuster Bowl when they went through spring practice and everyone came away optimistic about the fall. Paterno's prime objective that spring was to find a quarterback to succeed Tony Sacca. Nardolillo had passed up his fifth year figuring he had no chance to beat out the three underclassmen competing for the job. He was right. Kerry Collins had an outstanding spring and was most impressive during the rainy Blue and White game when he threw for 406 yards and four touchdowns while completing 24-of-41 passes. Collins also was a natural leader and Paterno designated him the starter, telling the media "Kerry has a strong personality and it shows in the way he runs the football team. He has an awful lot of poise." That move convinced redshirt freshman Danny White—son of Paterno's first quarterback in 1966—to transfer in June to Arizona. Redshirt sophomore John Sacca almost left for William & Mary, but Paterno talked him into staying, saying he would get his chance. Paterno also asked Nardolillo to return in the fall to back up Collins and Sacca.

The internal trouble that would eventually change the dynamics of this team had actually begun the previous winter when Gelzheiser was suspended from school after being charged with a questionable credit card fraud. Then Samuels complained that Paterno had taken away his scholarship even though he was no longer in school because of poor academics. Then, in mid-July there was a major incident when McDuffie, Sayles and Graham were involved in an early morning scuffle outside of a downtown State College bar and arrested for disorderly conduct. Around the same time, a highly-touted incoming freshman cornerback named Brian Miller was arrested for supposedly being part

of a drug ring in his hometown. Although charges against Miller were later dropped, all these incidents were not only disruptive but also a blot on the clean image of Paterno's program and the coach was testy when asked about this at Media Day on the opening of fall practice in early August. But it was something Paterno didn't talk about on Media Day that would be the defining moment of the season.

Reporters attending the team's first open scrimmage a few days later were surprised to see Collins in street clothes on the sideline. During his meeting with the media after the scrimmage, Paterno revealed that Collins had injured the index finger of his throwing hand during a volleyball game at a family reunion. The injury had occurred a few days before the preseason and State had kept it secret, Paterno said, because "there was the possibility he could have been out for the whole year. We were not sure until this morning." Collins would need surgery and just when he would be ready to play would depend on the healing process. PSU beat reporters were angry at not being told about Collins injury earlier and this further aggravated the tense atmosphere in Happy Valley. "(Why) cloak the injury before preseason practice ever got underway?" asked Ron Bracken in the *Centre Daily Times*. "That's just another brick in the wall between the media and the Penn State football program." John Sacca was now the starting quarterback and placekicker Craig Fayak would also work out there. Paterno did not want to use his incoming blue chip freshman, Wally Richardson of Sumter, SC, but Richardson would be around just in case.

The next tremor came 10 days before the season opener at Cincinnati. At 2 a.m. August 26, police arrested Engram and Sayles inside an apartment and charged them with burglary. They had gone to the apartment believing it was Anderson's but it wasn't. Once inside they were tempted to take some of the contents and that's when the police found them. Engram had been set to start at spilt end with Sayles as his backup. And now both were in jail. Their teammates were dumbfounded but the pair admitted their guilt. They were sentenced, placed on probation and thrown off the team. The black cloud over Happy Valley was growing bigger and there was more to come. As the September 5 opener drew closer, Sacca hurt his back and had to miss valuable practice time. Nardolillo suffered a shoulder injury that was even worse and would not be ready for Cincinnati. Richardson was now taking snaps with the #1 and #2 teams. The potential and optimism that had evolved in the spring was quickly disappearing.

Guard John Gerak was offensive co-captain of the 1992 team and another of Paterno's players who changed positions numerous times for the good of the team.

With the strong-armed Collins at quarterback and a corps of wide receivers that included McDuffie, Engram, Sayles, Tisen Thomas and LaBarca, Paterno had expected to have another wide-open passing attack. Sacca did not have Collins' arm but had a better "touch" than his older brother. McDuffie would still be the flanker and co-captain after being placed on a year's probation for his summer incident and also would return punts and kickoffs. "He's going to be one of the real exciting players in the country," Paterno told Lenn Robbins of the *Morristown Daily Record* and any other reporter who would listen. Paterno even mentioned McDuffie as a Heisman Trophy candidate, and in its preseason football issue, *Sports Illustrated* promoted McDuffie as the best "all-around player" in college football. Thomas—recovered from a severe knee injury—would now start at split end. Paterno also had two of the best tight ends in the country in Drayton and Brady, although Brady would be hampered all season by a severe virus and never reach his potential. The running game was expected to be much stronger than '91 with Anderson returning at tailback and backed by the three exceptional redshirt freshmen: Ki-Jana Carter of Columbus, OH, Mike Archie of Sharon and Stephen Pitts of Atlantic Highlands, NJ. "If he stays healthy and works at it," Paterno said, "I think Richie Anderson will be one of the best backs in the country in 1992." O'Neal, a redshirt in '91, and sophomore J. T. Morris gave the offense additional speed at fullback. Paterno also was more pleased about his offensive line than he had been most of '91. They were all experienced. Rucci still had problems with his knee and so Pickett started at long tackle early in the season until Rucci was fully ready while Huntington moved from center to short tackle and Sandusky took over center, backed by Greeley. Co-captain Gerak and Malinoski were the guards with redshirt freshmen Jeff Hartings of St. Henry, OH, Marco Rivera of Elmont, NY, and Keith Conlin of Glenside and senior Mike Heller also in the front line mix.

Richie Anderson dives in for a touchdown in a game at Beaver Stadium. Anderson led the team in rushing in 1991 and 1992.

Unlike the past couple of seasons, the defense had to be rebuilt and Paterno warned that the defense would "not be great in the early going." Givens and Wright were the co-captains with Givens and McKenzie back at outside linebacker and Wright joining sophomore Phil Yeboah-Kodie on the inside. Ravotti decided to take a redshirt so Gelzheiser, Gethers and sophomores Terry Killens, Willie Smith, Eric Clair and Jon Witman were in reserve. Benfatti and Jackson were back at the tackles with redshirt sophomore Vin Stewart moving from offense to nose tackle. Burger shifted back from offense to be on the defensive line along with sophomores Todd Atkins, David Thomas and Andre Johnson. Rubin was back at safety with Cisar backing him and Graham was at left corner. Hammonds finally had his wish and started at the Hero spot but he and Bochna traded positions after the first game and Hammonds was at the right corner the rest of the season. The main reserves in the secondary were either redshirt freshmen like

Cliff Dingle, Brian King and Josh Kroell or redshirt sophomores Tony Pittman (son of Paterno's star running back in '68-'69) and Marlon Forbes. Fayak was back to placekick and Ceh to snap with LaBarca as the holder. Redshirt juniors Jamie Dreese and V. J. Muscillo would share the punting with Muscillo also backing up Fayak.

Without knowing the extent of the team's preseason problems, most sportswriters picked State for a Top 10 finish with a consensus ranking at about #7 or #8. *Sports Illustrated* ranked the Lions at #2 behind Miami while both the AP and the *USAToday*/CNN poll had them #8. Practically everyone believed that the key game would be against Miami at Beaver Stadium on October 10. Most preseason polls selected the Hurricanes as the team to beat with Notre Dame at #3 behind Washington. "There's not much doubt that Joe Paterno and Co. will be 5-0," wrote Mike Poorman for the *Penn State Football Annual* magazine. "And even if the 'Canes aren't undefeated...they will provide Penn State's biggest test of 1992." Except for BYU and Notre Dame on the road no one else was expected to seriously challenge the Lions. However, the traditional games with Boston College, West Virginia and Pitt figured to be emotional since they would be the final ones before State cut its Eastern roots and entered the Big Ten.

The lightning and thunder storm that sent tailgaters scurrying outside Cincinnati's remodeled Nippert Stadium in the late afternoon of September 5 was a prelude to the imaginary thunderbolt that struck the Lions inside a short time later. It was bad enough that the underdog Bearcats ran back the opening kickoff 69 yards to set up a TD six plays later. A McDuffie punt return of 18 yards and his 46-yard run on a reverse helped the Lions tie the game before the quarter was over on O'Neal's 7-yard TD and Fayak's PAT. The misfortune came midway in the second quarter when Sacca went out with a collarbone injury. For the second time in four years, Paterno was forced to play a talented freshman he wanted to redshirt. Paterno and Ganter stripped State's offense to the bare essentials and midway in the third quarter Richardson drove the team 65 yards for a TD after Stewart had blocked a Cincinnati field goal attempt. Fayak's 44-yard field goal extended State's lead to 17-7 going into the fourth quarter but another foul-up by the special teams allowed Cincinnati back into the game when the Bearcats blocked Dresse's punt to set up an 8-yard TD pass. Richardson and Anderson led another time consuming drive of 64 yards with O'Neal getting his second TD on a 1-yard dive with less than six minutes left in the game. But Cincinnati made it close by marching 71 yards on 10 plays to score with eight seconds remaining. A pass for the two-point conversion pass failed and the Lions recovered the onside kick to escape with a 24-20 win. The ultra conservative offense generated 243 yards rushing and Richardson passed for 35 yards on 5-of-10 short completions but Paterno was pleased. "We were careful with (Richardson)," Paterno told the media. "We played pretty well in the second half except for the blocked kick."

Richardson started the next week in the home opener against Temple and looked like a veteran in a 49-8 victory. Of course, the Owls were terrible and that made it easier for Richardson to throw for 164 yards, including a 15-yard touchdown to Archie, on 10-of-19 passes. McDuffie caught 6 passes for 115 yards and Anderson ran for 103 yards and two TDs. About the only complaints some of the 94,892 spectators had was the new policy that prohibited smoking inside Beaver Stadium. Sacca was back for Eastern Michigan but it wouldn't have mattered if McDuffie had started at quarterback. EMU had been added to the schedule in the spring when Virginia Tech canceled its contract and the Mid-American Conference school was far over its head. State scored four touchdowns in the first quarter, including one on Hammond's 32-yard interception return, and romped to a 52-7 win. McDuffie caught two of Sacca's 10-of-17 completions for TDs of 17 and 38 yards and Anderson and Carter both scored two TDs while the defense forced five turnovers and had five sacks as the Lions moved up from #10 to #7 in the rankings.

As the Lions prepared for Maryland's new run and shoot offense that week, they had a surprise visitor at practice. President George Bush, in State College for a campaign stop, visited with the team after Paterno had introduced Bush at the Republican rally earlier in the day. But the Lions didn't need a presidential pep talk to beat Maryland. The Terps were not much better than Temple and Eastern Michigan despite accumulating 518 net yards. The Lions won 49-13 before a crowd of 94,578 including members of the 1982 National Championship team which was honored at halftime. Anderson scored on runs of 6, 25 and 22 yards and had another TD on a 26-yard pass from Sacca, who threw for 195 yards, including a 29-yard TD to McDuffie.

Rutgers at 3-1 was a little tougher the next Saturday night at Giants Stadium in the balmy New Jersey Meadowlands. The Scarlet Knights used an eight man line to stop the Lions' running attack and State gained just 142 yards on the ground. Anderson had only 16 yards on 12 carries before leaving with a sore knee in the third quarter. But Sacca beat Rutgers with his passing, becoming just the third PSU quarterback to throw for more than 300 yards. He hit on 21-of-37 attempts for 303 yards with TD passes of 10 and 20 yards to McDuffie and a 10-yard TD to Brady. The Lions built a 31-10 lead early in the fourth quarter and then held off the passing of Rutgers' reserve QB Bryan Fortay to win, 38-24. "I think we're a pretty good football team," Paterno told sportswriters, "but we'll find out next week." McDuffie, who caught 8 passes for 129 yards, said, "We've been looking forward to the Miami game since last year."

The unfamiliar rock music that blared over the loudspeakers in Beaver Stadium for an hour before the nationally televised noon kickoff pumped up the home crowd as Paterno had expected. But the main tune, "Taking Care of Business," also made the Hurricane players feel more at home, as they said later, and they weren't intimidated by the raucous crowd noise before or during the game. Some of the Hurricanes even tried to incite the record crowd of 95,704 by taunting the students in the South end zone, disrupting the Blue Band when it marched onto the field and refusing to shake hands with the PSU captains during the coin toss. But a game is won on the field and not in any antagonistic pre-game antics and it was the team with the better kicking , an opportunistic "bend-but-don't-break" defense and a quarterback who didn't make any mistakes that was the victor.

The pattern of the game was set on the first series when the #5 Lions marched to the Miami 38-yard line before having a field goal attempt by Fayak blocked. The #2 Hurricanes then went 51 yards for a touchdown on a 9-yard run by Donnell Bennett. McDuffie returned the kickoff 29 yards and Sacca moved the Lions to the Miami 12-yard line before Fayak's second field goal attempt sailed wide from the 20. After the game, Paterno would reveal that Fayak had been having severe back spasms that left him almost unable to practice. Later, the problem would be diagnosed as fractured vertabraes and he would miss the rest of the season. The teams traded possession until midway through the second quarter when Gino Toretta, who would go on to win the Heisman Trophy, methodically drove Miami 79 yards on 14 plays and a 26-yard field goal that made the score 10-0 at halftime. Despite the missed field goals and some inopportune penalties that had hampered the State offense, the Lions stormed back on the second half kickoff, going 72 yards primarily on the running of Anderson who scored the TD on a 10-yard run. As the third quarter continued, State's defense kept Miami's potent offense under control, and with about a minute left in the period, McDuffie's punt return of 18 yards gave the Lions the ball at the PSU 36-yard line. What happened next was another defining moment of the season.

Ganter called for a screen pass to Anderson to the right sideline. Miami linebacker Jesse Armstead blitzed past Anderson and was on top of Sacca so fast Sacca had little time to react. Instead of taking a sack he threw the ball as he was hit and the ball fluttered into the air. Defensive end Darren Krein was all alone in the flat at the 28-yard line. In 148 previous passing attempts by PSU's quarterbacks, not one interception had been thrown. But Krein had an easy run into the end zone. "Ninety-six thousand people have never been quieter," wrote Austin Murphy for *Sports Illustrated*, and with the PAT Miami led 17-7. Back came the Lions into Miami territory. Fayak missed a 36-yard field goal but an encroachment penalty kept the drive alive and State moved to a fourth-and-one at the Miami 5. Paterno called for a pitchout to Anderson swinging wide on the short side towards the Lion bench. But All-American linebacker Michael Barrow charged in and hit Anderson for a 2-yard loss. Another missed opportunity. The next time the Lions had the ball, they scored as McDuffie caught a 14-yard TD pass from Sacca at the end of a 54-yard drive. There were six minutes left. But that was State's last real shot. Neither team could mount another sustained offensive and Miami won, 17-14. "Canes Feeling Like No. 1 Again," said the headline in the *Miami Herald*. Despite outgaining the Hurricanes by 370 yards to 218 and controlling the ball for almost seven minutes longer, the Lions had faltered and it would take them nearly 14 months to recover. "We played our hearts out but came up short," McDuffie told sportswriters. Wright said, "This was an emotional letdown. We had high expectations for this season." Many of the fifth year seniors could not believe they had lost and they now felt their chance for a National Championship, and thus their season, was over. "There's nothing really to play for," Gerak told Ken Denlinger of the *Washington Post* for his book, *"For The Glory."* "Whether we're 6 and 5 or 10 and 1 doesn't matter. We go to the same place." The Blockbuster Bowl.

The shock and disbelief continued throughout practice the next week and neither the players nor the coaches truly focused on Boston College. The 20th-ranked Eagles were unbeaten at 4-0-1 and had two weeks to get ready for the now #9 Lions. A five minute period at the end of each half determined the outcome of the game and that 10 minutes characterized the changing fortunes of the '92 team. Bos-

TE Troy Drayton was a walk-on who became a Third-Team All-American his senior year.

ton College drove 72 yards on the opening kickoff for a 7-0 lead but State came back to go ahead 10-7 and with about five minutes left in the half, the Lion defense forced the Eagles into a fourth-and-11 punt near midfield. State went for the block but missed and Killens slammed into the punter for a roughing penalty. As the Homecoming crowd and another regional TV audience watched, Glenn Foley, who had missed seven straight passes, found Ivan Boyd wide open behind Dingle and BC had a 48-yard TD. The next four minutes were even worse and reminded PSU fans of the Lions blitzkrieg against Tennessee in the Fiesta Bowl a few months earlier. It was three downs and out for State and with 2:31 remaining, Foley passed the Eagles 79 yards in 7 plays, hitting tight end Mitchell with a 16-yard TD pass with 57 seconds left in the half. Again, State couldn't move as BC used its time outs and with 32 seconds remaining, the Eagles took the ball on their 33-yard line. Instead of playing it safe, BC moved quickly downfield again with Foley throwing a 29-yard TD pass to Mitchell with one second remaining. State fans were stunned and many left the stadium not to return.

BC increased its lead to 35-10 on another Foley TD pass midway in the third quarter before a 46 yard reverse by McDuffie appeared to finally fire up the Lions. They moved 72 yards for a TD in the third quarter and scored again midway in the fourth quarter when Sacca led them on an 80-yard drive in 13 plays. Now, State had the momentum and with three minutes left, the Lions had the ball again at their own 10-yard line and trailed 32-24. Sacca scrambled for seven yards but hurt his shoulder and left the game. In came Collins without a warm up for his first appearance of the year. He passed 24 yards to Justin Williams, then 41 yards to McDuffie and four plays later Anderson went around right end for a 2-yard TD. Collins hit McDuffie for more points and now the Lions were just three points behind. Muscillo, in for the injured Fayak, booted the onside kick high and Brady recovered at the BC 46 with 1:39 left. Plenty of time. The fans still remaining sensed a new Lion legend being born. McDuffie dashed to the left sideline and seemed open. But the BC safety had anticipated the Collins pass to State's best receiver and when Collins' heave was slightly overthrown, Joe Karma intercepted at the 17 and BC won, 35-32. "What made this victory sweeter," wrote Michael Vega in the *Boston Globe*, "was that it was the first for BC on the happy sod of Happy Valley where so many Eagles have dared, only to come up short." Foley said, "I couldn't think of a more perfect sendoff (to the Big Ten)." McDuffie's 212 yards in receptions that day is still the PSU team record and his 11 catches was the record until broken by Freddie Scott two years later.

"Boston College just beat us up," Paterno said, "but we lost a game we should not have lost."

With Sacca still hurt, Collins started the next week at Morgantown and he showed the 66,663 fans and a late afternoon regional TV audience why Paterno had been so high on him. He threw for 249 yards, including touchdowns of nine yards to Williams and 67 yards to Drayton while completing 15-of-30 passes, several on crucial third downs, without an interception or a sack. But with four defensive starters out with injuries, plus some fumbles and penalties at the wrong times, the now #14 Lions were tied with the 5-1 Mountaineers with just 5:40 left in the game. Then, Collins took charge at State's 11-yard line following a punt. Twice on third down plays Collins passed for first downs, including a 40-yard toss to Williams to the WVU 40-yard line. Five plays later, O'Neal broke up the middle for 21 yards to the 3-yard line and Anderson went around left end for the TD. Moments later, Yeboah-Kodie intercepted Jake Kelchner's pass at the WVU 23-yard line and ran into the end zone to make the score 40-26. "We needed to face some adversity and win," Paterno said in the locker room. "I made some mistakes but I just kept trying," said Collins.

In midweek, Collins moved permanently into the starting QB position after Sacca hurt his knee in practice. The injury would keep Sacca out until the Blockbuster Bowl but having the starting job didn't appear to bolster Collins' confidence. He looked shaky in the first half against BYU but just how hard his teammates tried was questionable. The only good that came out of the Lions visit to Provo was their Sunday morning side trip to Salt Lake City to see the Mormon Tabernacle Choir. In picturesque Cougar Stadium the previous afternoon, State was horrible. BYU (4-4) surprised the Lions with an unusually strong running attack and built up a 30-3 lead in the third quarter before giving up two fourth quarter TDs on the passing of Collins and beating State, 30-17. Collins' 54 passing attempts that day is still a PSU record and the 317 yards he accumulated on 28 completions is still fifth-best in team history. "Obviously, some players left their season in the locker room after the disheartening loss to Miami crushed their national title dreams...," wrote Black in the *"Football Letter."* "At the moment, the Penn State team seems to be wandering in the wilderness waiting for someone to climb Mt. Sinai and bring down the commandments,"

With two weeks off before traveling to South Bend, the players had plenty of time to ruminate about their disintegrating season. They realized everyone was questioning the team's character but so what? Fans were fickle. The players knew what they thought about themselves and they knew they were better than Miami, BC and BYU. They figured they would prove it by beating heavily favored Notre Dame on its home grounds, just as the '90 team had done. "We worked on toughness," McDuffie would tell sportswriters later. "We put our hearts into this one," said Rubin. Sometimes having heart is not enough and on this freezing day the Lions would come up short—several times. Two inches of snow blanketed the field as the teams battled to a 6-6 half-time deadlock. Notre Dame's points had come on Craig Hentrich field goals, including a 31-yarder with just 9 seconds left in the second quarter. The Lions could have been ahead after scoring a TD on a 72-yard drive late in the first quarter but Muscillo's PAT attempt had been blocked by safety Bobby Taylor. Another Hentrich field goal gave the once-beaten Irish the lead in the third quarter. Then, early in the fourth quarter, Collins, who was not having a good day, led the Lions on a 63-yard drive that gave them a first down at the Notre Dame one-yard line. But an Irish goal line stand stopped State on two runs and a pass and

Before he graduated in 1992, First-Team All-American O.J. McDuffie broke or tied 15 receiving, kick return and all purpose records.

the Lions had to settle for a 22-yard Muscillo field goal that tied the game. A few minutes later, Givens and Rubin forced tight end Irv Smith to fumble and Gelzheiser, starting at inside linebacker, recovered at the Notre Dame 44. Anderson ran for 13 yards and Collins hit McDuffie for 15 to the 13-yard line. On the sixth play of the drive, O'Neal went up the middle for the TD and Muscillo's PAT made it 16-9 with 4:25 left in the game. Now, it was up to the defense.

Notre Dame returned the kickoff to the ND 36-yard line and suddenly Rick Mirer had the Irish on the move. With a 21-yard screen pass to Bettis and a 15-yard scramble, Mirer drove the Irish for a first down at State's 9-yard line with a little more than a minute left in the game. Two running plays by Brooks gained six yards sandwiched around a pass incompletion and now it was fourth-and-goal at the 3 with about 30 seconds. Mirer dropped back looking for his tight end but saw Bettis open over the middle on a delay pattern and hit him perfectly. Sandusky set the Lions defense for the 2-point conversion attempt. Mirer faded back, looking to the left, then scrambling right and with Clair charging in he spotted Brooks in the right corner of the end zone. Mirer threw just before he was tackled. Brooks bobbled the ball but made a diving catch and the partisan Irish crowd cheered. There were still 20 seconds remaining and when Notre Dame screwed up the kickoff, the Lions got the ball at midfield. But there would be no miracle comeback this time in the shadow of "Touchdown Jesus." Collins tried three wild passes and Notre Dame won, 17-16. "This loss was tougher than the Miami loss," McDuffie told sportswriters, "because we thought we had this one, but it slipped away." Ray Parrillo of the *Philadelphia Inquirer* wrote, "...the Nittany Lions had answered the critics who suggested they had played without gumption since the Oct. 10 loss to Miami...(but) they didn't quite have enough to stop another Irish miracle."

Some fans now wondered which team would show up for the final game in the long series with Pitt—the one that played at Notre Dame or the one at BYU. Future games with Pitt were scheduled for the

1997 and 1998 seasons but they were set for the beginning of the year. Everyone knew the old rivalry, with the late November games and a bowl invitation often at stake, would never be the same. So, the question was whether this team would have the motivation and pride of its predecessors. It did. With an estimated 91,000 watching in the cold and rain of Beaver Stadium and another few million on ESPN, the Lions romped to a 57-13 victory over a Pitt team that really wasn't very good. McDuffie, who already had been named to two All-American teams, set several seasonal and career records that afternoon as he caught eight passes for 112 yards, including a 6-yard TD pass from Collins. Most of his records were broken or tied later by Engram but on this day he was hailed as State's all-time receiver. "He's as good an all-around player as I've ever been around," Paterno told sportswriters. O'Neal had his finest day ever with four TD runs while rushing for 105 yards on 14 carries and Anderson's 64-yard TD run in the second quarter helped him become the second leading scorer in the nation with 10 touchdowns as he led all rushers with 129 yards. Archie ran back a punt 62 yards for another TD and Rubin scored an unusual two points on the 82-yard return of a blocked extra point. "A win against Pitt was sentimentally of greater importance than wins against team like Notre Dame, or maybe even Miami...," wrote Jill Rosen for the *Centre Daily Times*. "There was no way we were going to lose this game," Gerak said in the locker room. "It meant too much to the older guys."

THE 1993 BLOCKBUSTER BOWL
Jan. 1, 1993
Stanford 24, Penn State 3

The less said about this bowl game, the better. Whatever pride the Lions had after beating Pitt didn't carry over into the first day of the new year. Some sportswriters who were in Joe Robbie Stadium refer to this game as "The Lackluster Bowl." To many of State fans in the disappointing crowd of 45,554, it was the low point of the Paterno era—worse than the humiliating end of season losses to Notre Dame and Pitt in 1984 and more embarrassing than the clobbering by Nebraska in 1983's first Kickoff Classic.

This team had the talent to be a National Champion. Even with just one loss to Miami, it still might have finished #2 and—with the right luck during the season—still would have had a shot at the national title on New Year's Day. But by the time the players arrived in Fort Lauderdale after Christmas, they didn't care. For many of them, they just wanted to party and get the game over with. "Sobriety, according to several players, wasn't high on the team's list of priorities," wrote Scott Brown in his book, *"Lion Kings."* "In fact, according to Jeff Hartings, the eve of the game was about the only night they didn't go out in full force." Any one around the players for even a short time noticed their lack of enthusiasm. Nowhere was it more obvious than at the traditional pregame pep rally at the Pier 66 Hotel where some players openly mocked Paterno, shaking their heads and smirking as he tried to rouse the crowd in the hotel's courtyard with some inspirational words.

Despite the Lions' "lackluster" record, the promoters of the bowl figured they had a natural seller in matching State against Stanford, the Pac 10 conference co-champion coached by Bill Walsh. Walsh had coached Stanford before achieving fame with the San Francisco 49ers in the 1980s and had come out of retirement this season to help revive the Stanford program. In his previous tenure, Walsh had won two post

season bowl games and this was the Cardinals first New Year's Day bowl since 1972. Along the way, Walsh had picked up the nickname "the Genius" for his coaching ability. Paterno had been winning for so long that he was usually referred to as "the legendary Joe Paterno." So, the newspapers and CBS willingly acquiesced to hyping the game as: "The Genius versus The Legend." In their public appearances the coaches tried to play down the hyperbole. "I didn't know which one I was," Paterno joked. They tried to talk about their players but the focus really never left Walsh and Paterno.

The highlight of game day for PSU fans was the tailgate party and pep rally underneath a tent outside the stadium two hours before the kickoff. With Walsh scripting all the plays, Stanford took the opening kickoff and drove 71 yards for a touchdown on the passing of Steve Stenstrom. The Lions came back on a 66-yard march with Collins throwing passes of 21 and 26 yards to McDuffie to set up Muscillo's 33-yard field goal. Interceptions by Rubin and Forbes stopped two more Stanford drives and the Lions reached the Cardinal 26 and 29 before giving up the ball on fourth down. State appeared listless on both offense and defense and towards the end of the half Stanford went ahead 14-3 on another 65-yard drive. Whatever Paterno and his coaches said to the players at halftime must have gone in one ear and out the other. In the second half, State crossed midfield just three times and got no closer than the Stanford 31-yard line. The Cardinals controlled the ball for nearly 20 minutes and scored 10 more points in the third quarter on a field goal and a 40-yard touchdown pass from Stenstrom to All-American tailback Glyn Milburn to win, 24-3. "I think the whole (State) team quit," Stanford cornerback Darrien Gordon told sportswriters. "I never thought a team with so much tradition would quit."

In the Lion locker room, Paterno said little to his players except to tell the seniors he was sorry the season ended "on a note like this." He told the media, his team didn't play well against Stanford and that the passing game fell apart. "We didn't do anything when we had the ball," Paterno said to Steve Wyche of the *Miami Herald*. "We weren't ready to play a big league football game," he told Robes Patton of the *Fort Lauderdale Sun-Sentinel*. Some players agreed. "We started the game poorly and I don't think we did a good job of keeping focused," said Gerak. Collins had hit on just 12-of-30 passes for 145 yards and one interception but that wasn't the worst of it. He had reinjured the index finger of his right hand on the helmet of a Stanford player and the swollen finger did not look good.

The next morning Paterno met with the media and he obviously had not had much sleep. "The whole program has to recommit itself," he said. "Football is a tough game. It's tough physically and mentally. It's really tough at this level and we are not that tough anymore. We have to go back to square one. Tomorrow, I am going to start changing things around."

The words were strong and Paterno did change things. But he couldn't fix all his problems at once, particularly the big one that continued to fester at quarterback. Nor were his new foes in the Big Ten about to lay out the welcome mat.

Season Record 7-5
Record to Date 664-289-42
Winning percentage .688

"'Welcome to the Big Ten, Joe!'"

If there is one singular positive trait about Joe Paterno, it is his ability to be introspective. He has faults like anyone else and he can be obstinate and irrational on and off the football field. But his continued willingness to look deeply inward and to readjust and adapt to the changing environment has been the backbone to his three decades of success. It first happened during the 1967 season and at other significant junctures in his career. And because he did it again at the end of 1992, Penn State's rightful place in the Big Ten is now established.

But it took another year for that to be proven. This season was the start of it all and there were disappointments and frustrations along the way. It was not until the very end that everything came together. And when it did, everyone had to admit that Paterno had done it again.

The embarrassment at the Blockbuster Bowl was but a few hours old when Paterno began the self-evaluation. "I think I let some of the kids get away from me in the latter part of the season," Paterno told Kip Richeal for his book, *"Welcome To The Big Ten."* "I overestimated some of the leadership on the squad and I wasn't as close to the situation as I should have been. It was not a solid Penn State football team, and that's what became frustrating. I blame myself for that."

He started that winter by talking to the players, first individually and then in groups. He wanted to clear the air, to hear what they had to say and hear their problems. He made them feel free to criticize and they did. He also conferred with his staff. What he discovered was a major communications gap. "We just weren't on the same page with (the players)," assistant coach Tom Bradley told Richeal. To help close the gap, Paterno created the "Breakfast Club." Elected representatives of each class would have breakfast with Paterno twice a month during the off season and weekly in season to discuss problems, not just football problems but personal and classroom situations as well. Paterno was now 66 years old but he was learning how to think like, understand and work with a new and different generation.

The enthusiasm and openness Paterno generated carried over into spring practice. He was looking for some leadership. "Talent will take you so far," he told the media, " but if you want to really be an outstanding football team, there have got to be a couple of people who know how to make some plays in the clutch, who know how to practice, know what it takes to win." He told the players it was going to be tough because the Big Ten was tough. And the spring was intense but the players had the right attitude. "You could see a change in the whole program," Kerry Collins told Richeal. "It was a different atmosphere," Brian Gelzheiser said. After spring practice was over, Paterno was happy. "We had a solid spring and got some work done," he told Mike Poorman for the *Penn State Football Annual* magazine. "The kids were kind of back in the groove."

However, not everything had gone well. Collins' index finger required additional surgery and he missed spring practice. So did O'Neal with back surgery. Anderson had decided to turn professional instead of return to compete at tailback and junior-to-be J. T. Morris had quit school in a pique over his playing time at fullback in '92. Sacca and Richardson both had good spring sessions but Paterno declined to name a starter until Collins had a chance to compete in the preseason.

Witman was moved from linebacker to fullback and Paterno also was counting on the fall return of redshirt sophomore Brian Milne, who had stayed out of football in '92 to concentrate on track. Losing Anderson opened the way for the three hotshot redshirt sophomores—Archie, Carter and Pitts—and Paterno and his offensive coaches came out of the spring thinking about playing all three without naming a permanent starter.

The uncertainty in the backfield cleared up during preseason practice that August. Collins was rusty and Paterno still wanted to redshirt Richardson if possible. Four days before the season and Big Ten opener against Minnesota, Paterno named Sacca the starting quarterback. O'Neal had recovered fully and was at fullback. Tailback was not so easy to resolve. The three tailbacks all had different styles and strengths—and nicknames. Archie, the most versatile, was "Cutback" because of his cutback ability. Carter was "Flash" because of his speed to get through a hole and into the open. Pitts was "Slash" because he could ramble and slash through the line. After the last practice before Minnesota, Ganter and Paterno told the trio that Pitts would start because they thought he had the best practices but that all three would split the time unless "somebody gets hot." Engram was back, humbled by his experience, and set to start in McDuffie's old flanker spot. Paterno had hoped Tisen Thomas would be the flanker after his performance during the spring but a severe injury to his other knee during the preseason ended his career. LaBarca got the initial call at split end with three other wide receivers in reserve: Justin Williams, redshirt junior Phil Collins of the notable Cinnaminson, NJ, Collins family and redshirt freshman Freddie Scott of Detroit, MI. Brady was the tight end with redshirt frosh Keith Olsommer backing him up after Grube was injured in preseason. Malinoski was the only fulltime starter back from '92's offensive line but Paterno was high on a trio of redshirt sophomores. Conlin was hurt in the spring so Hartings started at guard opposite Malinoski and Rivera teamed with veteran Pickett at the tackles. Greeley was at center, backed by Barry Tielsch with another redshirt sophomore, Andre Johnson of Southampton, NY, shifted from defense to be in reserve.

First Team All-American Lou Benfatti; (55) was a four-year starter in the early 1990s and a Lombardi semi-finalist as a senior.

With nine regulars returning, the defense was again expected to be the strength of the team. Tackles Benfatti and Jackson, who missed part of '92 because of an injury, were considered two of the best in the country with senior Jeff Perry, a redshirt in '92, Thomas and Mazyck in reserve. Clair moved from linebacker to share nose tackle with Stewart. Rubin was back at free safety and Bochna at Hero. The corners included Hammonds, Pittman, Forbes, Miller and Mark Tate with Dingle, Kroell and King also seeing action in the secondary. Unlike many seasons past, the linebacking crew was relatively new. Geltzheiser was at one inside post and senior Brian Monaghan beat out Yeboah-Kodie for the other slot with Willie Smith also in reserve. Ravotti returned from his redshirt year and started at outside linebacker along with Navy transfer Rob Holmberg with Atkins, Kerwin and Killens as backup. Fayak had recovered from his back injury and was back to kick field goals and extra points with true freshman Brett Conway of Lilburn, GA, handling the kickoffs. Muscillo returned to punt and LaBarca to be the holder with walk-on Brad Pantall doing the snapping. As was becoming practice, game captains were named weekly with an election to pick official captains at the end of the season. There also was a major change on the coaching staff as Jim Caldwell left to become the head coach at Wake Forest and one-time star Kenny Jackson returned to coach the wide receivers. Jackson would have an immediate impact with his first pupil, Engram.

Paterno knew playing in a conference would be a radical experience for everyone—the coaches, the players and the fans. In the past, the prime goal was the National Championship. That was still the main objective, he told the team, but now there would be the conference title and the Rose Bowl invitation that went with it. "I think we can get a licking, maybe get a couple of lickings and yet there's still a lot to play for and still be in it," Paterno told Poorman for *Penn State Football Annual*. But, for the first time in years he faced an unfamiliar schedule. Four conference teams were first time PSU opponents: Minnesota, Michigan, Indiana and Northwestern. The last time his team had played any of State's other league foes was in 1984 at Iowa. Except for the Hawkeyes' Hayden Fry, Paterno had not coached against any of the Big Ten coaches and he didn't know the style of their teams. Paterno called it "a challenge." So, he assigned each of his assistants to analyze one Big Ten team: dissect the game film, study the other coach's tendencies and devise a game plan. "I have had to do a lot of homework to get a feel for the different coaches in the conference," Paterno told sportswriters.

Paterno believed it was easier for his Big Ten contemporaries to focus on State because it would be like playing a non-conference foe for the first time. But his rival coaches weren't buying anything Paterno said. Many were still angry about the way State was brought into the league without their input. And since the 1993 schedule was announced, some of them railed about the special treatment that allowed State to have a week off before playing the league's other two heavyweights, Michigan and Ohio State, in October. To Paterno, the criticism was additional evidence that no one in the Big Ten wanted to see this erstwhile Eastern behemoth come in the first year and go to the Rose Bowl. "Every school in this conference, every one of 'em wants to see you fall flat on your face," he told the players, as described in *"Welcome To The Big Ten."*

Because of what happened in '92, many sportswriters and sportscasters were a little wary about State's maiden Big Ten season. Most of the preseason magazines had the Lions finishing in the latter

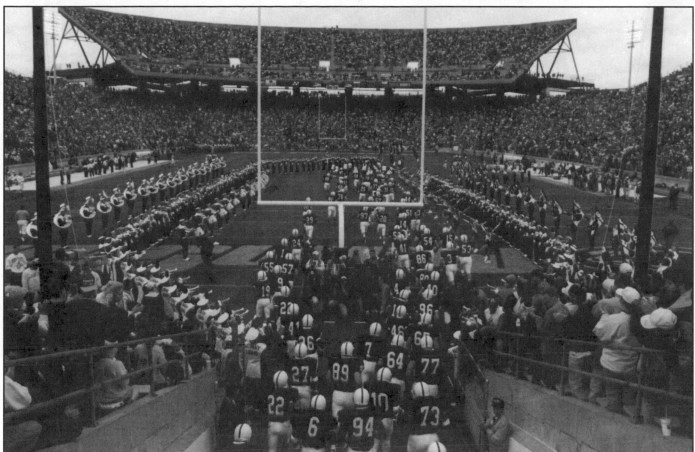

The Penn State Blue Band welcoming the Lions onto the field at Beaver Stadium before a game is a PSU tradition. The Blue Band's precision marching and outstanding music has been entertaining State fans for generations.

partof time the Top 20 but competing for the Big Ten title. The *USA*/CNN poll of coaches picked State #14 with conference favorite Michigan at #3 behind Florida State and Alabama and Ohio State at #17. *Sports Illustrated* had the Lions at #16 with Michigan at #2, Wisconsin at #22 and OSU at #30 and the AP tabbed State at #16 with Michigan #3, and OSU #17.

Twenty-four hours before the Labor Day weekend kickoff, a gunman barricaded himself in a construction site near Beaver Stadium and virtually shut down State College for more than eight hours. Thousands of visitors coming in for the game were told to stay in their hotel rooms or their motor homes and that included the visiting Minnesota team, which was staying at a hotel four miles away. The incident ended when a police swat team found the gunman's body but everyone who was in town when it happened was still talking about it the next day. "Next time I come here I'll have to bring a six-gun," cracked Minnesota coach Jim Wacker.

The Lions ended 106 years of independence on September 5, 1993, with an explosive 38-20 win over the perennial conference doormat. Before a sun-drenched crowd of 95,387 that included Big Ten Commissioner Jim Delany and Minnesota's governor, Engram broke State's all-time touchdown record for receivers by catching four TD passes of 29, 31, 20 and 31 yards from Sacca. "I wasn't aware that the record was only two," the redshirt sophomore told the media afterwards. "I thought it was probably four or five with all the great receivers we've had here." Actually, Engram had scored on State's first offensive play in the Big Ten, taking a 29-yard screen pass moments after Bochna's interception less than two minutes into the game. Gophers

quarterback Tim Schade, a nephew of coach Wacker, also set two State records for an individual opponent by attempting 66 passes and completing 34. Three of his completions were for touchdowns but State's defense intercepted four others. Engram caught four other passes for a total of 165 yards and Sacca hit on 18-of-32 passes for 274 yards. Lion runners accumulated 230 yards with Carter getting 120 on 15 carries and Pitts 89 on 18 carries. "You want to start out right and I feel pretty good about it," Paterno said in the media room. Despite the defeat, Wacker was enthusiastic about State being part of the Big Ten. "This is the greatest atmosphere that I've ever seen for college football," he said. With no other games scheduled in the Big Ten that day, Penn State took the conference lead for the first time in history.

Now that the inaugural game in the Big Ten was out of the way, the Lions zeroed in on their next opponent. For the upperclassmen who were around in '90 and '91, beating USC was as big a priority as winning the first conference game. Benfatti, Bochna and others still believed State was a better team in those two defeats at the Coliseum and now it was payback time. It didn't matter that USC had a new coach since then. John Robinson, who had coached the Trojans against Paterno in the 1982 Fiesta Bowl, had returned after a few years with the Los Angeles Rams. The crowd of 95,992 included State's Heisman Trophy winner, John Cappelletti, who was honored at halftime, and 86-year-old USC alum Giles Pellerin, who was the only person in the stadium who had seen State and USC play for the first time in the 1923 Rose Bowl. State dominated the game for 3 1/2 quarters and led 21-7 at the half with USC scoring its lone touchdown on a quarterback sneak by Rob Johnson after cornerback Jason Sehorn had intercepted and returned a Sacca pass 30 yards to the PSU 1-yard line in the second quarter. Although Sacca was not sharp, completing just 6-of-17 pass attempts for 65 yards in the entire game, he engineered touchdown drives of 41, 80 and 71 yards with key passes and the running of the tailback trio and O'Neal. Archie and Carter would both run for over 100 yards. When USC lost a fumble at the State 10-yard line following a drive after the second half kickoff, the Lions marched all the way on the ground to the Southern Cal 3-yard line and with a first-and-goal was on the verge of putting the game out of reach. But three runs up the gut by O'Neal gained just two yards and Paterno sent in Fayak for an 18-yard field goal attempt. Fayak, who had missed three out of four attempts against Minnesota, was wide right and USC still had life.

Then, with about seven minutes left in the game, USC suddenly came alive after taking the ball at the Trojan 46-yard line following a punt. On a third-and-18 following a 15-yard penalty, Johnson found

Defensive lineman Tyoka Jackson was the best QB sacker of the '90s. He ranks second all-time in total career sacks.

Johnny Morton open for 20-yard gain to the PSU 30, then hit Ken Grace on a middle screen and Grace ran for a touchdown. The PAT made it 21-14 with 4:11 left. State tried to run out the clock but the offense stalled and Muscillo's short punt gave USC the ball at the Trojan 30 with less than three minutes remaining. Down the field came the Trojans, with Johnson hitting on 8-of-9 passes, including one on a third-and-17, and another of 20 yards to Morton, who made a tip-toeing sideline catch at the 2-yard line. With 37 seconds left, Johnson found slotback Johnny McWilliams on a cut back in the end zone and now USC trailed by just a point. State called a time out to discuss the defense for the 2-point conversion. USC went for the same play but Jackson pressured Johnson out of the pocket and this time McWilliams trapped the ball after it hit the ground. Kroell recovered the onside kick and the Lions escaped with a 21-20 victory. "Lions Win, Holding Breath," said the headline in the *Harrisburg Patriot-News*. "It's nice to finally win one of these by stopping a two-pointer," Bochna told sportswriters. Paterno said "it was an ideal game for this squad...our kids learned how to play under pressure...We haven't won those kind of games recently."

What happened the following week in the cornfields of Iowa was one of the defining moments of the season and changed the course of Nittany Lion football. Outside of Columbus and Ann Arbor, Iowa City may be the toughest venue for a visiting team in the Big Ten. The intimidation starts in the visitors' dressing room, which is painted pink, and continues with the hostility of the hometown fans during the pre-game warm-ups. But if a team can survive Morgantown, it can endure in Niles Kinnick Stadium. An early morning rain that soaked the playing field couldn't stop an aggressive and opportunistic State defense and a staunch running and clutch passing game. Both teams were 2-0 but the #12 Lions turned three interceptions into 17 points and sacked Iowa quarterback Paul Burmeister nine times for 89 yards in losses to shut out the Hawkeyes for the first time at home in 15 years, 31-0. It was the 250th win in Paterno's coaching career and the players gave him the game ball in the locker room. Iowa crossed midfield just three times in the first half and not once in the second half after a 54-yard return by Hammonds of the second half kickoff set up a 36-yard drive that gave the Lions an insurmountable 17-0 lead. "In the second half, the roof caved in," said Coach Fry. "If Saturday's game is any indication," wrote Ed Sherman in the *Chicago Tribune*, "book Penn State for a trip to Pasadena right now." Carter, now starting at tailback, went over 100 yards for the third straight game. His 19 carries gave him 144 of State's net 244 yards compared to just 32 yards on 41 carries by the entire Hawkeye team. But it was the passing by State's quarterbacks that caused the biggest postgame ruckus.

Sacca started and had trouble moving the team early in the first quarter. A Hammonds interception set up State's third offensive series from the Lion 32-yard line and Sacca completed his only pass in seven attempts—a 22-yarder to Brady—that helped get the drive started. But the march bogged down at the Iowa 10-yard line. Twice Sacca missed wide open receivers in the end zone and the Lions settled for a 20-yard field goal by Fayak. Early in the second quarter, Paterno replaced Sacca with Collins and Sacca didn't play again until the game was out of reach with about nine minutes left. On the surface, Collins didn't appear to pass much better, hitting on just 6-of-16 attempts for 57 yards, but one completion was in a fourth down situation and two others on third downs that helped sustain three touchdown drives. After the game, ABC-TV's Dick Vermeil told the regional television audience, State's "passing game right now sucks, and they're going to have to get it going if they're going to be successful." Paterno admitted the passing game needed work and when asked why he had removed Sacca, he said he had planned all along to play Collins, who had not been in the first two games. "Kerry was getting away from it a little bit...," Paterno told sportswriters, and "I just felt it was time for a change." But Sacca was angry and told the media, he didn't see himself "as a backup" this late in his career. "If I'm gong to exit the football game in the first quarter, then I don't see myself as a quarterback here much longer," Sacca said.

Paterno tried to muffle this new controversy during his weekly news conference the following Tuesday, absolving Sacca for any intemperate remarks, and saying he wasn't sure who would start against Rutgers. But Sacca was now wearing the second team green jersey in practice and he began talking openly about transferring. Whereas Collins had kept his mouth shut and had practiced in a business-like manner when relegated to backup duty, Sacca was now openly defiant and pouting. Paterno told a closed meeting of the players not to allow the discord to be a distraction. Fortunately, the now #9 Lions had two non-conference games with familiar opponents before resuming Big Ten play in what everyone believed would be the "game of the year" against Michigan.

The game against Rutgers the following Saturday night convinced State fans that Paterno had made the right choice in starting Collins. To accommodate ESPN, the game was moved from Saturday afternoon and the heavy rain that came late in the day and continued during the evening turned the newly-resodded grass field into what ESPN commentator Beano Cook called "a cow pasture." Rutgers (2-0) came out with an eight-man line daring Collins to throw and he did—all night. He completed seven of his first eight passes to help give the Lions a 10-0 lead early in the second quarter and before he gave way to Sacca late in the fourth quarter, he had thrown four touchdown passes while completing 18-of-25 attempts for 222 yards with just one meaningless interception late in the game. Brady caught two TD passes of 15 and one yards and Engram and Archie had the other TDs on tosses of 20 and 4 yards, respectively. The Lion runners netted 206 yards, including a 28-yard bootleg by Collins that helped set up the first TD late in the opening quarter. The defense turned one of two interceptions and a blocked punt by Killens into touchdowns and Rutgers didn't score until 49 seconds were left. "There is good chemistry on this team," Paterno said in the media room. "I am having more fun coaching than I have in a long time."

Maryland had hoped to get some inspiration from the only Terp team to defeat Penn State when the schools closed out the 37-game series at Byrd Stadium the following Saturday night. The 1961 Maryland players must have been embarrassed at the halftime ceremonies honoring them on this mild fall evening for by then the 1993 Terps trailed, 46-7. "Too bad (the '61 team) wasn't suited up," wrote Black in his *"Football Letter."* "They probably could have given the

Nittany Lions a better game." The final score of 70-7 was the biggest Terp loss since 1913 and it could have been even worse. Collins passed for just 128 yards on 9-of-19 completions and touchdowns of 10 and 16 yards to Engram. State's runners gained 526 yards with Carter getting 159, including TD runs of 63, 36 and 4 yards, and Archie picking up 120 yards and a one-yard TD. Meanwhile, the defense intercepted four passes, had five sacks, two recovered fumbles and a blocked kick while limiting the Terps run-and-shoot offense to 21 yards rushing and 170 yards passing. "We are playing more consistently than last year and we are more focused," Paterno told sportswriters.

Paterno now had two weeks to get his team ready for Michigan and what happened in the next 14 days would reverberate throughout Happy Valley for more than a year. On Monday, Sacca met with Paterno and three other coaches and told them he was leaving the team. They wished him luck. But Sacca's departure was kept quiet for days as rumors circulated until Sacca's father revealed the information and Paterno confirmed it during his statewide call-in radio show Thursday evening. In retrospect, Sacca's abrupt exit was disruptive to the team but there were many players happy to see the malcontent leave. Collins was quickly becoming their leader. On Saturday, while the Lions were idle, Michigan State upset Michigan, 17-7, to hand the Wolverines their first Big Ten loss in three years. Earlier in the year, Notre Dame had upset Michigan 27-23 and now the Wolverines—winner of the last five conference titles—were 3-2 and their character was being questioned. Another defeat and it would be uphill in the Big Ten. And looming ahead was this upstart Eastern team talking about a Rose Bowl, Michigan's Rose Bowl! "That 11th team," as State was being called disdainfully by the Michigan coaches and players.

Although the Michigan State loss took a little luster off the game, the frenzied atmosphere in State College was similar to that of a national title bowl game. This was the game that would make up for all

The Penn State Cheerleaders go through one of their gymnastic-type routines in front of the student sections at Beaver Stadium during an early October game.

the heartaches of the last couple of years, the fans said, and show the arrogant Big Ten that the Lions were a force to be reckoned with. Ironically, this also would be the 1,000th game in PSU history and that added even more significance to the event. Paterno didn't need loud rock music to get this record crowd of 96,719 into the right spirit. But, it may have been an omen when early in the game the Big Ten referees blunted the noise by threatening to penalize State unless the crowd quieted down while Michigan was calling plays. Wasn't a loud crowd supposed to be a home field advantage? Welcome to the Big Ten, Penn State.

Unfortunately, the decisive elements on this sunny afternoon were similar to the ones that doomed the Lions against Miami in '91 and '92—missed opportunities, big plays and mental breakdowns at the worst time. A 40-yard Fayak field goal and a 37-yard touchdown pass from Collins to Engram had given the favored #7 Lions a 10-0 lead with 5 1/2 minutes left in the first half when the first big mistake occurred. State was punting from the end zone on a fourth down at the 5-yard line and Michigan coach Gary Moeller went for the block. But Muscillo got the punt away. Derrick Alexander caught the ball on the run, broke through the first wave of Lion tacklers, cut to the left and ran untouched into the end zone. The next error came after the teams traded possessions in the third quarter. Michigan drove from its own 20 for a third-and-five at the PSU 23. The Lions thought they had thwarted the Wolverines when Renkey sacked UM quarterback Todd Collins forcing a fumble that Benfatti picked up and ran to the Michigan 30. But as the crowd booed, the referee's ruled an incomplete pass and kicker Peter Elezovic went in to try a field goal from the 40-yard line. The Lions rushed and the kick was wide left and the State fans were cheering again. Until they saw the yellow flag, then the boos resumed. Hammonds was ruled offside and Michigan now had a first down. Three plays later, Collins hit Mercury Hayes for a 16-yard touchdown and Elezovic's PAT put the Wolverines ahead for the first time, 14-10. "It was a very big point in the game for us when we got that first down after the field goal," Moeller said later.

But an even bigger point was just ahead. Taking the ensuing kickoff, the Lions marched determinedly from their own 20 for a first down at the Michigan one-yard line on the passing of Collins, the running of Archie and two interference calls against the Wolverines' Ty Law. Then came a sequence of plays that was reminiscent of State's futile goal line surge in the National Championship Sugar Bowl game of 1979. Twice Collins tried a quarterback sneak only to be stopped by nose guard Tony Henderson. On third down, Paterno sent Carter up the middle but as Carter tried to hurdle the line he was met at the line of scrimmage. The fourth quarter was over and Collins went to the sidelines to discuss the next play. Some of the players wanted to call a sweep by Carter and the offensive linemen could not believe it when Collins returned with another Carter run up the middle. "It's my decision and my call," Paterno told the media afterwards, "You got to guess down there." The Michigan defensive coordinator guessed it would be a rollout right but when Carter bulled ahead the defensive line stunted and the Wolverine linebackers were there to smash Carter and his blockers to the ground and Michigan took over. "It was the right play," Paterno said. "We just didn't execute well." A few minutes later, the Lions were on the move again, driving from the PSU 40 for a third-and-goal at the Michigan 8. Collins tried to hit Engram on a curl back into the end zone but the pass fell incomplete when a Michigan defender knocked Engram to the ground. Engram appealed for an interference

call but didn't get it and Fayak made it a one-point game with a 25-yard field goal. Then came the play that broke the spirits of the Lions. Michigan's Tyrone Wheatley rambled 47 yards around the left corner to the PSU 6-yard line and on third down Collins threw a 5-yard TD pass to fullback Che Foster and the game was all but over. In the afterglow of the 21-13 win, the Wolverines and some Michigan newspapers gloated. "You have to pay your dues," Wheatley told Bob Wojnowski of the *Detroit News* and others. "We just had to show them we've been here a while." Said center Marc Milia, "We wanted to welcome Penn State to the Big Ten..."

Despite the demoralizing defeat, the players told anyone who asked that they were determined not to repeat what happened in '92. "We have to come out and win the rest of our games," said Carter. "We still have a chance (at the Big Ten championship)." The Lions had another week off before traveling to Columbus and during that time, Ohio State knocked off Michigan State and moved into #3 in the polls behind Florida State and Notre Dame. Everyone realized that a win over the Buckeyes would not only put the Lions back to the forefront of the Rose Bowl race but also regain lost prestige from the Michigan game. But, as one of the many signs in Columbus, said: "No More Cupcakes, Joe. Welcome To The Big Ten!" An unusually late October swirling snow storm turned the Ohio Stadium field into a sea of mud and the Lions wallowed in it all night. They were physically manhandled on both sides of the line and as the ABC TV audience watched, the Buckeyes led by All-American Dan "Big Daddy" Wilkerson harassed Collins and his receivers all evening, and won, 24-6. State's only points came on two first quarter field goals as Collins completed just 13-of-39 passes for 122 yards and had four interceptions. Playing before a hometown crowd, Carter had 123 yards on 24 carries but he and Fayak were it for the offense. Meanwhile, sophomore quarterback Bobby Hoying and wide receiver Joey Galloway had keyed a relentless Buckeye attack that accumulated 156 yards in the air and 224 on the ground. And as the game wore on through the mud and snow the Buckeye players mocked the Lions and their effete Eastern football roots, talking trash on the field while their obnoxious fans screamed obscenities from the stands. "There's no excuses," Paterno admitted to sportswriters. "They just kicked our butts." Up in the press box, OSU's president Gordon Gee, who watched Paterno beat West Virginia several times during his presidential tenure in Morgantown, walked around the sportswriters shouting scornfully, "John Cooper outcoached Joe Paterno! And I want you to print that!" But down in the locker room, behind closed doors, Paterno was angrily chastising his dejected players. "I'm mad 'cause I know we're better than both those teams we lost to...," he screamed, according to a description in Richeal's book, *"Welcome To The Big Ten."* "I'm not going to let last year happen all over again...You have to decide whether you want to take some pride in yourselves." Then Paterno abruptly walked out. Welcome to the Big Ten, Joe! The Lions of 1993 had four weeks to prove themselves.

Greeley had another reason for the two losses. On the Thursday before the season opener against Minnesota, Greeley and Malinoski had gone to the State College VFW for the $3.93 luncheon special. They also began enticing others in the offensive line to join them each Thursday for the VFW's cheesesteak, fries and Coke combination. But Greeley and Malinoski had both missed the Thursday before the Michigan and Ohio State games. Greeley, who was one of the most superstitious players on the team, vowed that neither he nor the rest of the line would forego another Thursday during the season no matter what the circumstances. Greeley's "Lunch Bunch" was about to make PSU football history.

Indiana was off to its best start in six years and at 7-1 was now ranked #13 with State dropping to #16 and sixth in the Big Ten standings. The Homecoming game at Beaver Stadium was expected to be a low-scoring defensive battle since the Hoosiers were leading the conference in total defense, pass defense and sacks. It turned into a wild passing shootout with State twice blowing 14-point leads, once at the end of the first quarter and again at the end of the third quarter. The Lions were leading 31-17 one minute into the final period and seemed about to put the game away when Muscillo's punt backed the Hoosiers to their own one-yard line. But on the first play IU quarterback John Paci found flanker Thomas Lewis open on the Indiana 37-yard line and Lewis took the pass in stride and ran for a 99-yard touchdown that set a record for the longest pass play against the Lions. Lewis would catch a total of 12 for 285 yards which is a record in yardage for the Big Ten, IU and a PSU opponent. A few minutes after Lewis' record catch, Paci drove the Hoosiers 80 yards to tie the game at 31-all with about eight minutes left. A short kickoff helped the Lions get possession at the PSU 42 and five plays later Collins hit Engram cutting over the middle for a 45-yard TD and Fayak's PAT made it 38-31. With less than two minutes in the game, Paci drove Indiana to the PSU 37-yard line but his pass towards the end zone was picked off by Pittman at the 7 and the Lions ran out the clock. It was Paci's only interception of the day but Collins didn't have any as he completed 18-of-29 attempts for 215 yards and another 10-yard TD pass to Engram. Carter also had another good running day to help the Lions maintain some ball control, going 138 yards in 23 carries before leaving the game with a hip pointer injury. "Kerry needed a game like this," Paterno said in the media room.

What Collins didn't need was a game like the one he had the following week at rainy Beaver Stadium against Illinois. The Illini had rebounded from three non conference defeats to post a 5-1 Big Ten record, including a win over fading Michigan, and still had a long shot chance at the Rose Bowl. With a late afternoon ABC TV audience watching, Carter left the game in the first quarter after pulling a hamstring muscle and Archie came in to take the Lions to a 28-0 lead midway through the second quarter. Archie scored two of the TDs on runs of 15 and 9 yards and would have had the other but he fumbled into the end zone after a 22-yard run and LaBarca recovered for the touchdown. For the day, Archie totaled 134 yards on 30 carries. Paterno went conservative in the second half, perhaps because his quarterback was having such a miserable afternoon, and the defense sacked Illini quarterback Johnny Johnson five times and intercepted him once in the last quarter and a half to preserve a 28-14 victory. Collins was just 5-for-18 for 49 yards and three interceptions and he was booed throughout the day as the estimated crowd of 90,000 dwindled to some 30,000 by the end of the game. "I'd be lying if I said I let (the booing) bounce off me," Collins told sportswriters. "...Sometimes I let it get to me more than I should." Paterno defended his inconsistent quarterback, saying "He'll be fine, and in all fairness, he's not played a lot of football."

Ohio State's victory over Indiana that same day eliminated the Lions from the conference championship and now OSU and surprising Wisconsin had the only chance for the Rose Bowl. However, the Lions could go to the Citrus or Holiday Bowls if they could beat Northwestern and Michigan State. Because of the Coalition, the Citrus, Holi-

day and Hall of Fame bowls had tied-in with the Big Ten to take the second, third and fourth place teams, respectively. There were a couple of specific exceptions, which made it possible for the Lions to wind up in Orlando even if they finished third.

Collins bounced back the following Saturday before a sparse crowd at Evanston's Dyche Stadium by completing 19-of-30 passes for 278 yards, including a 15-yard TD to Engram, as the Lions beat outmanned Northwestern, 43-21. Carter didn't even make the trip and Archie would have the best day ever in his four-year career by running for 173 yards on 27 carries and touchdown runs of 5 and 23 yards. Fayak kicked two field goals of 42 yards and another for 31 yards, then played quarterback for part of the fourth quarter as Paterno tried to maintain the redshirt status of Richardson and true freshman Mike McQueary of State College. Engram had 8 catches for 132 yards and Archie four receptions for 41 yards while the defense picked off two passes and had five sacks in holding Northwestern's all-time leading passer, Len Williams, in check except for one big 74-yard bomb in the second quarter. The Lion fans in the stands who were monitoring other games on their transistor radios were happy with the victory and even happier when they heard that Michigan had upset Ohio State.

Now, the final game of the season at Michigan State took on greater meaning. The Spartans had another game left against Wisconsin in Hawaii the following Saturday and by whipping both the Lions and Badgers, MSU could be the Big Ten representative at the Citrus Bowl. That scenario could also send the Lions plunging all the way down to fifth and a consolation trip to the Liberty Bowl. Michigan State was actually Penn State's second-oldest Big Ten rival although neither were in the conference, of course, when the team's first met in 1914. The last time they had played was in Paterno's first year as head coach and the unbeaten Spartans with a half dozen future All-Pros in their lineup had clobbered State 42-8 at East Lansing in a game that still ranks as the third worst defeat in Paterno's career. When PSU was invited into the Big Ten in 1989, MSU coach George Perles was one of the few conference athletic leaders who was enthusiastic. Looking for a season-ending game that could rival the great Michigan-Ohio State series, Perles had urged conference officials to schedule MSU against PSU and they agreed. Trying to pump up the rivalry, the two schools came up with "The Land Grant Trophy," symbolizing the founding of both institutions in February of 1855 as "two pioneer land-grant schools." Naturally, some traditional PSU fans scoffed at the trophy and the manufactured rivalry, longing for a resumption of the year-end series with Pitt and—for those who could still remember—the battle for "Old Ironsides," which went to the winner of the State-Pitt-West Virginia games.

A freezing rain and wet snow that fell on Friday night froze the astroturf of Spartan Stadium that Thanksgiving weekend. By the time the sun came out and helped melt the ice, the #24 Spartans had a 37-17 lead late in the third quarter. Their fans were celebrating in the stands, taunting the small contingent of Lion followers about the "patty-cake Eastern football" and the players were whooping it up and talking trash down on the field. Welcome to the Big Ten! A national TV audience had watched the #12 Lions self-destruct in the first quarter, fumbling away a potential TD at the 15-yard line and missing a 47-yard field goal after a drive had been halted by a blundering offside penalty. With an offensive line that outweighed the Lion defensive front by an average of 45 pounds per man, the Spartans roared to a 23-10 lead with 1:03 left in the half. But Collins had engineered a 6-play, 65-yard drive with a two minute drill on passes to Phil Collins, LaBarca and a 16-yard

TD to Scott with five seconds remaining. Fayak's PAT made it 23-17 and the Lions thought they would have the momentum in the third quarter. But with MSU's Jim Miller hitting on key passes and Duane Goulbourne and freshman Steve Holman running over the best rushing defense in the Big Ten, the Spartans scored two more touchdowns in the third quarter, including the last one on an embarrassing 3-yard pass to tackle-eligible Bob Denton. Then, with less than two minutes left in the third quarter, Miller threw his only interception of the day. Bochna picked it off at the Lion 42-yard line. What happened in the next five minutes would be another defining moment of the season, and although no one realized it at the time, this was another turning point of the Paterno era. Another championship team was about to be born.

On second down, Collins broke his string of seven incompletions, then on another pass found Scott for 18 yards. Engram, who had been out most of the game after being kneed in the back early, gave Collins the play he had suggested to Paterno on the sideline. Collins faded back, Engram streaked down the right sideline and caught the pass in stride for a 40-yard TD. Fayak hit the PAT and Conway kicked off. Two plays later Goulbourne fumbled and Gelzheiser recovered at the MSU 40. The Spartans forced a punt but as Muscillo took the bad snap and got the punt away he was blasted by MSU's Juan Hammonds and a roughing penalty gave the Lions new life. On second down Collins passed 20 yards to Brady at the 3-yard line and on the next play O'Neal followed the blocking of Witman and Milne over right tackle for the touchdown. Fayak booted the PAT and with just two minutes gone in the fourth quarter, State suddenly trailed by just six points. Now, the PAT kick by Bill Stoyanovich that bounced off the left upright after MSU's first TD in the first quarter was coming back to haunt the Spartans. Conway's kickoff into the end zone gave MSU the ball at the 20 and on second-and-10, Gelzheiser blitzed and sacked Miller for a 9-yard loss. A third down pass was incomplete and MSU punted to State's 48. On the first play, Engram streaked down the right sideline again and was wide open at the 7 to haul in Collins' pass for a 52-yard TD. Fayak's kick gave the Lions the lead for the first time with more than 11 minutes left in the game. "The Spartans, so comfortable for so long behind that huge front line and stunting defense, suddenly were groggy," wrote Marino Parascenzo for the *Pittsburgh Post-Gazette*. The Lion defense was now in charge, sacking Miller three more times and keeping the Spartans from even getting close enough for a field goal and the Lions ran out the clock for the victory. "This was the best comeback that I can remember in a long time," Paterno told sportswriters. Engram's two TDs gave him 13 for the season and a new State record that still stands. But the main star was Collins, who hit on 23-of-42 passes for 352 yards and three TDs, third all-time in PSU history. "Give Kerry credit," Paterno said. "...He hit some clutch throws for us." Collins told sportswriters the Lions used the "two-minute drill a lot more than two minutes. It has never, ever gone as smooth as it did today, even as much as we practice it." Paterno finally had the leader he thought he had in the spring of 1992.

On Monday, the Lions were invited to play in the Citrus Bowl on January 1. Ohio State had been there the previous year and a Big Ten rule prohibited the Buckeyes from returning. So, even if Wisconsin tied MSU and finished second to OSU, the rules permitted Citrus officials to invite another team. A week later, Wisconsin beat Michigan State to tie for the conference championship and get the Rose Bowl berth. Penn State, the interloper, was in the Big Ten's second best bowl. Welcome to the Big Ten, Joe. Thank you!

THE 1994 CITRUS BOWL
Jan. 1, 1994
Penn State 31, Tennessee 13
Most Valuable Offensive Player: Bobby Engram
Most Valuable Defensive Player: Lee Rubin

As soon as the pairing of State and Tennessee was announced, the aspersions and bad mouthing began. Fifth-ranked Tennessee was 9-1-1 and would have been playing in the Sugar Bowl against unbeaten West Virginia but for an early season loss to Florida, 41-34. With a potent offense averaging 43 points per game behind quarterback Heath Shuler and running back Charlie Garner, the Volunteers were established an early 9-to-10 point favorite. "It surprises me it's not more," Paterno told the media in praising Tennessee as "playing the best football in the country (right now)." But many sportswriters suggested that the Lions were not a worthy opponent and even some Tennessee players complained about it when the teams were together at Citrus Bowl events. One *Orlando Sentinel* writer predicted a 48-14 Tennessee blowout. Much of the pregame publicity focused around whether Shuler, runner-up for the Heisman trophy, would turn professional and which NFL team would draft such an outstanding "franchise" quarterback. Mentioning Collins in the same breath was not even an afterthought and Collins told writers later it bothered him. "It was Heath Shuler this and Heath Shuler that and they were going to beat us by a few touchdowns," Collins said. "I'd be lying if I said it didn't get a little personal. Nobody was giving me or Penn State any respect."

But this was not the same team that had lost to Michigan and Ohio State. Nor were these the same players who sleep-walked through the embarrassment at the '93 Blockbuster Bowl. When Paterno asked, they agreed to go to Florida four days earlier than required and spend a grueling four days in Melbourne with two-a-day practices in pads. The hard work continued after the Lions moved to Orlando on December 23 while the Volunteers were breezing through lighter workouts. Paterno also tried not to let the Disney World atmosphere of Orlando distract the team. He wanted to win this one and so did his players.

Orange seemed to be everywhere on New Year's Day in the Citrus Bowl, which had been expanded by 20,000 seats since State's first visit here in 1988. A record crowd of 72,456 turned out on a warm, overcast day and most of them appeared to be singing Tennessee's adopted school anthem, "Rocky Top." Tennessee fans figured this would be the day their team avenged the stunning 42-17 loss to State in the '92 Fiesta Bowl and they were stomping and screaming when Shuler and the boys came out sizzling. In less than six minutes the Volunteers led 10-0 on a 46-yard field goal by John Becksvort and Shuler's 19-yard TD pass to Cory Fleming. Welcome to the SEC, Joe! State started its second possession from the PSU 30-yard line following Tennessee's TD and on second down from the 36 Collins hit Engram on a wide receiver screen pass over the middle. Woosh! With a wicked block by Pickett, Engram dashed down the left sideline 36 yards to UT's 29-yard line. "That play helped set a tone," Engram said later. "They saw we had some speed after all, and you could just see it in their eyes they weren't sure they could stop us." Carter came on the field for the first time since his knee injury against Illinois and with his running and Collins passes to Archie and Engram, the Lions scored in seven plays with Carter banging over from the 3. Fayak kicked the PAT. Tennessee took the challenge and Shuler quickly marched the Volun-

Place kicker from 1990–1993, Craig Fayak is the all–time leading scorer for PSU. Another scholar athlete, Fayak was awarded a NCAA Post Graduate Scholarship in 1994.

four times and intimidating the Volunteer receivers into dropping passes while holding the UT rushers to just 135 yards. Late in the third quarter, another punt return of 16 yards by Engram set up a 49-yard drive with Engram getting the last 28 yards on passes, including a 15-yard TD he caught just inside the left corner of the goal line before stepping out of the end zone and the Lions won 31-13. For his performance, Engram was named the offensive MVP and Rubin, with the big interception and five tackles, was the MVP on defense. "Lions Teach Vols Lesson," said the headline in the *Orlando Sentinel*. "The nerdy-looking guy with the Coke-bottle glasses and white socks humbled the high-tech wizardry of the Tennessee Volunteers," wrote *Sentinel* writer George Diaz. "I never said we were a great team," Paterno told the media, "but that's a lot of points (to be an underdog). I'm sure that rankled some of the kids." Welcome to the Big Ten, Tennessee!

So, Paterno won an even bigger "big one" than he did at Michigan State. The victory tied him with the late Bear Bryant for most bowl victories at 15 and moved State back into #7 in the final polls. The demons of '92 had been exorcised and the challenges of '93 had been met. A new phase of the Paterno legend had begun and it was about to reach another pinnacle. Welcome to Happy Valley, Big Ten!

Season Record 10-2
Record to Date 674-291-42
Winning percentage .690

1994

"The Drive"

Kerry Collins looked once more through the rain, wind and artificial light at the Illinois scoreboard and knew what he had to do. "Illinois 31, Penn State 28"

In six minutes and seven seconds, the Lion quarterback would have to take this struggling team 96 yards for a touchdown or the unbeaten season, the chance for the National Championship everyone longed for and possibly the Big Ten title and the Rose Bowl and would be lost. With two games still left against Northwestern and Michigan State, they could lose tonight and still win the Big Ten and go to Pasadena. But that would stigmatize the accomplishment and give State's detractors another reason to rationalize their dismissive attitude in the national polls.

None of the players could believe you could lose the number one ranking after destroying one of your biggest rivals, 63-14. But that's precisely what happened two weeks earlier after the Homecoming game against Ohio State, when the AP voters—including two from Ohio who had predicted an upset—moved #3 Nebraska ahead of the Lions. "To beat a (good) team 63-14 and drop," Collins told Scott Brown for the book, *The Lion Kings,* "what else can you do?" Then a week later, when the defense of mostly reserves gave up two touchdowns in the last five minutes to Indiana, a 35-29 win looked much closer than it was and the *USA Today*/CNN coaches' poll followed suit. One coach even dropped State to #6. "That's a joke," Brady had told Brown. "Maybe it was just a coach we whupped up on one too many times."

But it was no joking matter. The pollsters were being biased and unpredictable as usual. The Lions had become #1 in mid October after beating then #5 Michigan in a showdown at Ann Arbor. That same

teers to the State 28-yard line. Then on a pass attempt, Jackson batted the ball into the air and Rubin grabbed it with a shoestring catch at the State 13-yard line. There was 1:26 left in the first period and, nobody knew it, but Tennessee would not get much closer to the goal line again. After an exchange of possession, Engram returned a punt 14-yards to State's 42-yard line. On the first play, he caught a 16-yard pass from Collins, then brushed off a would-be tackler and ran 35 yards on a reverse to the UT 7-yard line. Three downs reached the one and Fayak came on to kick a 19-yard field goal that tied the game at 4:38 of the second quarter. Minutes later, State was on the move again but Collins was intercepted at the UT 2-yard line and Tennessee drove to the PSU 32. With 1:08 remaining in the half, Becksvoort gave Tennessee the lead again with a Citrus bowl record 50-yard field goal. It was now time for Collins' to run the two-minute drill. Starting at the State 35-yard line, Archie gained 12 on a draw, Engram picked up 18 on a pass and O'Neal caught two passes out of the backfield and with 10 seconds left in the half the Lions had a second-and-10 at the UT 14. Paterno, Ganter and Collins conferred on the sideline during a time out. Some State fans screamed for a field goal but Fayak stayed on the bench. Tennessee set its defense for the expected pass into the end zone. Paterno crossed them up. Carter ran left on a counter draw, broke a tackle at the line of scrimmage and with blocks by Pickett and Engram dashed into the end zone. Fayak made it 17-13 at halftime.

In the dressing room, Paterno asked for no quarter. "Who do they think they are, telling us they need a better opponent," Paterno yelled, as described in Scott Brown's book, *"Lion Kings."* "I'm tired of this Orange team! I'm tired of this Orange Stadium! I'm tired of seeing Orange! Let's go out there and kick the Orange out of them!" And that's just what they did. State took the second half kickoff and drove 60-yards in 11 plays with Collins tossing an across the field TD pass of 7-yards to a wide open Brady at the goal that was similar to the one Tony Sacca threw to Brady in the '92 Fiesta Bowl. The defense took over and controlled Tennessee the rest of the game, sacking Shuler day, Auburn had upset then #1 Florida and Penn State, at #3 in both major polls, jumped over Nebraska, #2 in both the AP and the *USA Today*/CNN rankings. But two weeks later, when then #3 Nebraska beat #2 Colorado, 24-7, on the same day the Lions clobbered Ohio State, the writers and broadcasters who vote in the AP poll shifted their allegiance. When the coaches did it, too, it was obvious an anti-Penn State bias was at work. As the trend continued through the rest of the season, some voters, such as ESPN's Beano Cook, said it was because "Nebraska accomplished more" and that "a lot of coaches voted for (Nebraska's Tom) Osborne and against Paterno." None of the writers or coaches admitted any bias publicly, of course. Nor did the people who ran the four Coalition bowls—Orange, Sugar, Cotton and Fiesta—as they maneuvered behind the scene to keep State out of #1 so that they could present a "National Championship Game" on New Year's Day.

But none of that mattered now as Collins trotted back to the huddle after discussing strategy with Paterno and Ganter on the sidelines during the TV time out. As Lion fans watched the nationally televised game over ABC, they thought about the last time a State quarterback faced such a similar consequential and pressurized situation. They had to go back to '82 when Todd Blackledge led the last minute drive to beat—ironically—Nebraska. But that game had been early in the season at home and no one knew then that the '82 team would lose a game and still win the national title. This time there would be no chance at the National Championship unless the Lions won, particularly after what had happened in the first quarter when they were suddenly behind by three touchdowns.

It had not been a good trip from the time the team arrived in Champaign Friday and discovered their hotel was right in the middle of noisy fraternity row. Then, Saturday morning, the power went out in the hotel and the players had to hike up 15 flights of stairs to get taped for the game in the trainers' hotel facility and then walk back down for an abnormal pregame meal of pizza and hoagies while their regular nourishment sat uncooked in the kitchen. Paterno was unnerved by the chaotic break from the usual routine and so were some of the players. Still, no one expected what happened in the first 15 minutes of the game.

The game was expected to match State's explosive offense, number one in the country in total offense (533.5 yards) and number two in scoring (48.3 points), against a defense that ranked second against scoring (11.3 points) and fourth in total defense (253.6 yards). With three bonafide All-American linebackers in Dana Howard, Simeon Rice and Kevin Hardy, the #25 Illini had a 4-2 Big Ten record and an outside shot at the Big Ten title. State was a 12-point favorite but Coach Lou Tepper predicted earlier in the week that his team would win if the offense, quarterbacked by the veteran Jimmy Johnson, could score 29 points. The Illini had almost that many in the first quarter. With a frenzied crowd of 72,364 rocking Memorial Stadium, Illinois kicked off. On the third play, Carter fumbled at the PSU 24-yard line. Rice recovered and five straight running plays by fullback Ty Douthard gave Illinois a 7-0 lead 3 1/2 minutes into the game. The teams traded punts and on State's third possession, Collins threw just his sixth interception of the year into the hands of Tyrone Washington, who made a 5-yard return to the State 23. Douthard banged his way to the one-yard line in four plays, then Johnson rolled out and passed to tight end Ken Dilger for the touchdown and a 14-0 lead with just 6:21 elapsed in the quarter. A few minutes later, Brett Larson's punt backed the Lions to their 3-yard

One of the classic moments in PSU history. Joe Paterno and offensive coordinator Fran Ganter discuss strategy as the scoreboard shows Illinois leading PSU 21-0 with 10:06 remaining in the first quarter of their 1994 game in Champaign. A thrilling 96-yard drive late in the fourth quarter gave State the victory, 35-31, and clinched the Lions' first Big 10 championship.

line. The Illini defense stopped State's supposedly high-powered offense again, forcing a punt that gave Illinois the ball at the PSU 40. Johnson passed 22 yards to Dilger and three plays later fired a 12-yard TD pass to Shane Fisher with 10:06 remaining in the quarter and the Illini fans whooped it up. When the quarter was finally over, the team that had outscored its previous eight opponents 113-0 in the first quarter was way, way behind. Up in the press box, many sportswriters like Gene Wojciechowski of the *Los Angeles Times* and Ivan Maisel of *Newsday* were nodding their heads, saying "We told you so." Number one, indeed!

The small faction of State fans sitting mostly in the South end zone away from all the Illinois devastation couldn't believe it either. This was not the team they had been watching since the televised opener from the Minneapolis Metrodome the night of September 3 when the Lions bombed Minnesota, 56-3. Nor the one that had blitzed through five Big Ten and three outside opponents with the greatest offense Paterno had ever put on the field. Collins and Carter were already being pushed for the Heisman and Engram, Brady and maybe a lineman or two such as Jeff Hartings were almost certain All-Americans. This was a veteran and confident offense that was at least two deep at every position with Richardson backing up Collins at QB, Archie, Pitts and redshirt freshman Ambrose Fletcher behind Carter at tailback and Witman, Milne and redshirt freshman Jason Sload at fullback. Engram and Scott were the wide receivers with Phil Collins, Williams, sophomore Chris Campbell and redshirt freshman Joe Jurevicius of Chardon, OH, in reserve. Brady, who almost turned pro, was again the tight end with either Olsommer or true freshman Bob Stephenson coming in on the two tight end formations. Except for Malinoski, Greeley and his superstitious "Lunch Bunch" were back. Hartings and Rivera returned to start at guard with veterans Conlin and Johnson moving up to the first team tackles. Tielsch was the backup center with redshirt sophomores Peter Marczyk, Bill Anderson, Jason Henderson and Dale Harvey, junior Wayne Holmes and redshirt freshman Brad Jones the main subs at guard and tackle. The placekicker Conway also was part of the crushing offense with his accurate field goals and PATs and he was equally valuable on defense with his end zone kickoffs that were helping to give the Lions good field position.

Field position was critical to State's success because the defense was not as strong as usual for a Paterno team. In fact, it was the occasional breakdowns in the defense that many voters cited for denigrating the Lions in the polls. Sandusky had to replace eight starters and revise some of his techniques because of the inexperience and the lighter weight of some linemen. Perry and Atkins moved up to start at the two defensive end positions. Mazyck, fully recovered from a horrendous drive-by shooting near his South Carolina home in 1991, was at left tackle. Stewart started the season at right tackle but both he and Clair were bothered by injuries and redshirt sophomore Brian Noble of Virginia Beach, VA, became the starter after Ohio State with Thomas, redshirt freshman Chris Snyder, true freshman Brad Scioli of Bridgeport and sophomore Boris Oden also seeing playing time on the front line. Gelzheiser returned at inside linebacker with Smith and Yeboah-

Kodie taking over the outside. Killens, redshirt sophomore Gerald Filardi, true freshman Aaron Collins (the last of the Collins brothers), Cory Carlson, and Amhad Collins (no relation) were among the linebacker subs. Pittman and Miller were the starting corners with Forbes, Tate and redshirt sophomore Chuck Penzenik in reserve. Holes took over at Hero until sidelined with a knee injury against Ohio State and Aaron Collins' older brother, Jason, became the starter. With projected starter Kroell ending his career with a preseason concussion, Dingle and redshirt sophomore Kim Herring of Solon, OH, shared the free safety with Dingle also playing at Hero and King, Forbes and redshirt freshman Shino Prater also at safety. Injuries over the season would stretch the defense further. Punting also was weaker with Jurevicius starting out as the main punter but giving way later to walk-on sophomore Darrell Kania. Pantall returned as the snapper and Phil Collins was the holder. Archie and Engram returned punts with Archie, Fletcher and Carter handling kickoff returns.

Paterno knew he had the ingredients for a mighty offense even before spring practice started. But he wouldn't let the players or the media know it. "When things go fairly well for you one year, you have a tendency to get a little bit lax," he told Matt Herb of *Blue White Illustrated*, "and then the first thing you know, you're back in trouble again." Paterno continued to push the team in practice throughout the preseason and whenever he had a chance, he needled the offense to keep them from getting overconfident. "What's this great offense I keep hearing about?" he would yell whenever the offense made a mistake

All-American teammates Ki-Jana Carter, Kerry Collins and Kyle Brady were among the first ten selections in the NFL players draft following the 1994 season.

on the practice field. Obviously, the pollsters had some doubts about the Lions' ability because they rated State #9 in both the AP and *USAToday*/CNN preseason rankings with Michigan again the Big Ten favorite at #5. Defending Rose Bowl champ Wisconsin was at #10 in the AP with Ohio State at #20 and State's second opponent, Southern Cal, at #17. Nebraska was #4. *Football News* didn't even put the Lions in the Top 20. *USA Today's* sports analyst Danny Sheridan rated the Cornhuskers as a 5-1 favorite to win the National Championship with State at 75-1. Later, he told the *Penn State Football Annual* magazine that he didn't believe the Lions could go undefeated with its schedule. "If they did," he said, "I thought they'd lose the Rose Bowl." Most of the beat reporters who covered State also figured the Lions would lose at least one game in the regular season with Mike Poorman, editor of the *Football Annual*, being one of the few predicting a perfect 11-0. "Maybe, just maybe, 11-0," wrote Ron Christ of the *Harrisburg Patriot-News*. "Penn State has the ability to go 12-0 in 1994 and win the National Championship," wrote Don McKee of the *Philadelphia Inquirer*, "but the Lions have neither the wit nor the grit to carry it off."

What many fans thought was probably an aberration on Labor Day weekend in Minneapolis proved to be a harbinger of the season ahead. With Fran Fisher returning after a 12-year absence to describe the action on the Penn State radio network, the Lions took a 7-0 lead on a crisp 14-play, 77-yard drive in the opening minutes behind the running of Carter and passing of Collins, then watched as Minnesota returned the kickoff to the PSU 21. But the Lion defense, playing without their injured leader Gelzheiser, recovered a fumbled snap by Minnesota quarterback Scott Eckers on a third-and-one at the PSU 12-yard line. On second down, Carter darted through the right side of the line and ran 80 yards untouched for State's longest TD run since 1987. On the Gophers next possession, Dingle and Killens smashed into a receiver so hard the ball flew into the air and Dingle grabbed it as he fell on his back at the State 41. That was just about the end for Minnesota. Early in the second quarter, a 26-yard TD pass from Collins to Scott climaxed an 85-yard drive and on State's next possession following a punt, Carter went 62 yards on the first play and State led 28-0 on Conway's fourth PAT. Before Carter left the game midway in the third quarter, he had become just the 12th State player to run for 200 yards with 210 yards and two TDs on 20 carries. Collins completed 19-of-23 passes to six different receivers for 260 yards and three touchdowns and broke Bill Smaltz' 54-year record by throwing 14 consecutive passes in one stretch. The attack was unbelievably balanced with 345 yards rushing and 344 passing. "Let's not get carried away with this one," Paterno told the media. "You jump on somebody and they get out of whack. We have a long way to go."

It took just one more week for State fans to realize this offense was going to be something special. Southern Cal had beaten #23 Washington, 24-7, and earned a three-page spread in *Sports Illustrated* and a #13 ranking. Johnson, the quarterback who almost beat the Lions in '93, was being touted for the Heisman and offensive tackle Tony Boselli for the Lombardi and Outland trophies as the outstanding interior lineman. It was a perfect sunny and warm day for football with a 3:30 kickoff for national television. The sellout crowd of 96,463 had hardly settled into their seats when the Lions took the ball at the PSU 20-yard line after the opening kickoff. On the first play, Collins passed to Scott for 17 yards. Two plays later, Carter bolted up the middle for 13 yards. With Engram getting double coverage, Scott

was open again for another 14-yard completion to the USC 32. Then Carter went around left end behind a phalanx of blockers and streaked into the end zone. One minute and 15 seconds had elapsed and the Lions led 7-0. Less than a minute later, it was 14-0. On third-and-one near the USC 45, Johnson fumbled the snap and Gelzheiser recovered. Collins went for the TD on the first play as Scott outleaped USC cornerback John Herpin near the goal line and tip toed into the end zone. When USC took possession again, an 18-yard penalty and a sack on Johnson forced the Trojans to punt from the end zone. Engram almost had a TD on the runback but a penalty put the ball back at the Lion 43. On the first play, Brady buried the defensive end and Carter barreled around the corner for 19 yards. Two plays later, Brady went 20 yards on a pass from Collins to the USC 20. On the ninth play of the drive, Witman bulled 7-yards for the TD and with 7:09 still left in the first quarter, the Lions were ahead, 21-0. This was not a mirage. By the time the 1959 Liberty Bowl team was honored at halftime, State led by the shocking score of 35-0. "We got a little sloppy and lost our concentration in the second half," Paterno told the media after the game. Sure, and State won easily 38-14 as the offense accumulated 286 yards on the ground and 248 in the air. USC's first TD came early in the third quarter when Quincy Harrison intercepted a Collins pass and went 68 yards and the other came against the defensive reserves midway through the fourth quarter. Carter had 119 yards on 17 carries and Collins hit on 18-of-33 attempts for two TDs, with Scott catching 6 passes for 133 yards. "That Penn State football team overwhelmed us," USC coach Robinson told Terry Hess of the *Centre Daily Times*. "They got us back on our heels and could do just about anything (they) wanted." Paterno said, "I don't know how we could have been much better in the first half."

No one was comparing State's next opponent, Iowa, to USC but the Hawkeyes were 2-0 with eight starters back on offense. That offense never crossed the 50-yard line until after the score was 42-0—one minute into the second quarter. The #5 Lions scored 35 points in the first quarter to tie a one quarter scoring record set by the unbeaten 1968 team against Pitt and many members of the '68 team were in rainy Beaver Stadium on September 17 to see it as the great '68 and '69 teams were honored at halftime. The final score was 61-21 and the millions who watched on ESPN knew it could have been worse. State passed just 13 times and only the first TD came through the air, on a 10-yard pass to Archie. Eleven backs helped accumulate 309 yards on the ground with Archie getting two more touchdowns on runs of 35 and 4 yards and Carter scoring two TDs on runs of 41 and four yards. "The polls insist there are better college football teams than Penn State," wrote Jere Longman in the *New York Times*, "but no contender has proved more ruthlessly efficient or ravenously business-like in its dismantling of early-season opponents...There has been no such thing as a turning point in a Penn State game this season unless you count the coin toss." But the players were not being fooled by the ease of their victories. Unlike some past seasons, this group was listening to Paterno and remembering what happened in '93 against Michigan. "We're not a great team," Greeley told Randy Johnson of the *CDT*, "we haven't had any adversity."

They finally had a "taste" of adversity the following week against Rutgers in another Beaver Stadium game televised at noon by ESPN. This time Rutgers stopped the Lions on their first possession but with a fumble recovery by Killens and a pass interception by Miller, the Lions took a 19-0 lead 10 minutes into the first quarter on a pair of Carter TD runs for 22 and 12 yards and 3-yard dive by Witman. However, Rutgers made a game out of it for a while, going 80 yards for its first TD before the opening period was over, then closing to within six points late in the second quarter after Carter had scored again on a 16-yard run that capped a 65-yard drive. There was 1:07 left in the half when Collins went into his "two-minute" drill and took the Lions 80 yards in 8 plays, primarily on passes of 13 and 33 yards to Engram, a 10-yard pass to Brady and a 14-yard dash by Carter that set up Witman's 5-yard TD with five seconds remaining. Conway's PAT made it 33-20 going into the third quarter and that's when the Lions put the game away with the help of another big defensive play. Rutgers was still fired up after the second half kickoff and drove to State's 12-yard line for a field goal attempt. But Mazyck crashed through and blocked the kick with Pittman recovering the ball at the 18. Collins went for it all on the next play, hitting Scott in full stride cutting across the middle on a post pattern, and the 82-yard TD tied the record for the third longest pass in State history. Rutgers couldn't move after the kickoff and Engram's punt return and a 15-yard roughing penalty set up a 6-play 54-yard drive that sealed the game. The Lions scored their final TD four seconds into the fourth quarter on a 15-yard TD pass from Collins to Engram and won, 55-27. "Engram Breaks Out of 'Slump' for Penn State," said the headline in the *Greensburg Tribune-Review*. Engram, getting man-to-man coverage for the first time, was just 12 yards shy of O.J. McDuffie's record for yardage in one game with 200 yards on eight receptions and Scott caught three pass for 108 yards, becoming just the third pair of Lion receivers to go over 100 yards in a single game. Collins completed an amazing 14-of-16 attempts—Engram dropped one at the one-yard line—for 328 yards, which is still the fourth-highest passing yardage in team history. "Kerry Collins is playing as well as any quarterback has played for us," Paterno told the media, adding, "There was some adversity...it indicates there is some poise and character and leadership there." Still, Paterno had to be concerned about his defense, which gave up 513 yards, including a 46-yard second quarter TD pass from Ray Lucas to Reggie Funderburk. It was a sign of more adversity ahead.

The Lions could not be faulted for looking past Temple to the big game with Michigan on October 15. It was the type of situation players are constantly warned about. The Owls were a 45-point underdog and although they had won games over Army and Akron, they were coming off a 1-9 season and they couldn't match State's talent. But their coach, Ron Dickerson, had been State's defensive secondary coach from 1985-1990 and he knew the Lions well. Dickerson figured that the shortest path to an upset victory was to keep State's offense off the field. And that's precisely what Temple did in the first quarter of the late Saturday afternoon contest at Philadelphia's Franklin Field. As 38,410 predominantly State spectators watched in a pouring rain, Temple took the opening kickoff and drove 63 yards before settling for a 27-yard field goal by Rich Matson, then stopped State's offense on a three-and-out and drove 49 yards for a 25-yard field goal. With four minutes still left in the first quarter, Temple held a stunning 6-0 lead and had controlled the ball for nearly 10 minutes. The State defense was on the run and Temple players said later they could sense an upset. When State took possession again, Collins drove State 77 yards on 11 plays for a 12-yard TD pass to Brady one minute into the second quarter and a 7-6 lead. A few minutes later, a Temple punt backed State to its own 9-yard line. Collins found Engram streaking down the sideline for a 63-yard pass, then hit Scott for a 26-yard TD. Before the half was over the Lions had two more touchdowns on lightning strike drives, including a

First-Team All-American TE Kyle Brady, an outstanding blocker as well as receiver, came into his own during the 1993 and 1994 seasons.

3-play, 62-yard blitz in the last minute that ended with a 21-yard TD pass to Scott and a 27-12 halftime lead. However, one play before the Scott TD, Carter left the game with a dislocated thumb and was rushed to a nearby hospital. Temple booted another field goal to open the second half, then State scored three more quick TDs before the third quarter was over—one on a razzle-dazzle halfback pass of 51 yards from Archie to Scott and another after Clair picked up a Temple fumble and ran 17 yards to the one-yard line. The final score was 48-21. Although Temple held the ball for nearly 38 minutes and ran off 27 more plays, the Owls netted 385 yards compared to the Lions' 596. Once again Engram and Scott went over 100 yards in receptions with Engram catching four for 136 yards and Scott getting four for 115 yards as Collins completed 12-of-19 passes for 286 yards, three TDs and only one interception. Filling in for Carter, Archie gained 142 yards on 24 carries. "We were very sloppy on defense," Paterno told the media, including Black for the *"Football Letter."* "We had a lot of foolish penalties and did not give a very good effort...We can't play like that the rest of the season and win."

The week off before the Michigan game gave Paterno, the doctors and Carter a chance to assess his thumb injury. Surgery was needed but Carter was determined to play, no matter what. Meanwhile, the media speculated about the significance of the game in Ann Arbor and players on both teams were aware of what was at stake. Michigan would have been unbeaten but for a winning 65-yard "Hail Mary" pass on the last play of the game by Colorado's Kordell Stewart to Michael Westbrook. That had occurred at home in the so-called "Big House" and the Wolverine players made it clear they were not going to lose in the "Big House" again. The Lions had never forgotten what happened at *their* own big house a year before when they couldn't make 12 inches in four downs, nor stop a punt return that could have prevented everything that followed; and then they had to listen to Michigan players brag about teaching them some respect. In fact, the Wolverines continued to call them "the 11th team" as if they were still outsiders not good enough to play in their hallowed "Big House." There also were the skeptics among the media and the fans who wondered if Paterno and his players could really win "the big one." The come-from-behind victory over Tennessee in the Citrus Bowl was ancient history for these doubters. Their short memories were more vivid in recalling the last two seasons when the Lions were 5-0 at this same juncture and lost momentous games they should have won to Miami and Michigan.

For most outsiders, the game was rated a toss-up because the teams were so similar in makeup—with a pair of quarterbacks named Collins who already had passed for more than 1,000 yards apiece this season, two Heisman candidate running backs in Carter and Wheatley, a couple of potential All-American receivers in Engram and Scott and Mercury Hayes and Amani Toomer, fine placekickers in Conway and Remy Hamilton and, perhaps most importantly, a suspect defense. Only Purdue and Northwestern had given up more points in the Big Ten than Michigan. But some oddsmakers gave Michigan a one-point edge because of the home field advantage and a supposedly tougher schedule. "5-0 But Is Penn State Really That Good?" blared the headline in the *Detroit Free Press* a few days before the game.

The third largest crowd in football history and the most to ever see a Penn State team, 106,832, turned out on a perfect sunny autumn afternoon for the 3:30 kickoff televised nationally by ABC. It was a classic duel between two of the elite and most respected football powers in the country with a stereotypical "down to the last minute" ending. It appeared to be another State runaway at first with the Lions taking a 16-0 lead with a little over five minutes left in the first half. With Collins passing to all his prime receivers and Carter running with a splint and heavy bandages protecting his injured thumb, the Lions went 73 yards for a 24-yard Conway field goal and 80 yards for a 3-yard TD pass from Collins to Olsommer in the first quarter. Jason Collins, starting for the injured Holes, stripped the ball from Wheatley's backup, Tshimanga Biakabutuka, early in the second quarter, leading to a 28-yard field goal and a few minutes later a shanked Michigan punt and a 23-yard pass to Brady helped set up Conway's 29-yard field goal for the 16-0 score. A defensive mental error seconds before the intermission helped Michigan turn the game around. On a third-and-17 from midfield, Todd Collins fell five yards short on a scramble but Gelzheiser was penalized 15 yards for spearing. Collins threw a 20-yard pass to Hayes and Hamilton booted a 33-yard field goal on the final play of the half.

Capitalizing on the momentum at the end of the half, Michigan ran back the second half kickoff to its own 32-yard line. On the second play, the Lions blitzed and Wheatley found a seam and ran 67 yards for a touchdown. A few moments later, Michigan had the ball again on the UM 49 after a 17-yard shanked punt by Jurevicius. Collins hit Toomer for 30 yards and on the next play Wheatley took a pitchout and went 21 yards for another TD. Hamilton kicked the PAT and the Big House exploded as the Wolverines led for the first time, 17-16, with just 4:19 gone in the third quarter. When Michigan stopped the ensuing kickoff return by Fletcher at the Lion 14-yard line, the Wolverine fans screamed for more. But Engram picked up 29 yards on a reverse and the Lion offense was on the way again. Carter ran 13 yards on a draw, Brady caught a 14-yard pass and on the 10th play of the drive, Collins fooled Michigan by throwing to the fullback on a swing pass and Witman caught it for a 9-yard TD. Collins hit Scott for the 2-point conversion and State led again, 24-17. The teams traded possessions before Michigan went 59-yards on 7 plays early in the fourth quarter to tie the game

once more. For the next several minutes the defenses took over as the teams battled for field position. With 4:45 left in the game, State got the ball at the PSU 45-yard line. On the first play, Engram leaped to take a high pass from Collins for a first down at the Wolverine 41. Then with blocks by Rivera and Johnson, Carter raced up the middle on a draw all the way to the Michigan 15. But two plays lost a yard. On third down, Archie went in motion and with the Michigan secondary on man-to-man coverage, Engram was alone in the end zone to catch the 16-yard toss from Collins. Less than two minutes had elapsed since the start of the drive and Conway's PAT now made the score 31-24. But Michigan wasn't through. After the kickoff, Wheatley took a pitchout and ran 30 yards for a first down at the Wolverine 49. On first down, Toomer broke into the clear down the right sideline but the ball was slightly overthrown and bounced off his finger tips at the 20. Biakabutuka gained nine. On third down, Smith and Yeboah-Kodie tackled Biakabutuka for a 2-yard loss. Then with a three wide receivers set, Collins was rushed and Miller intercepted his pass near the Michigan sideline. The Lions ran out the clock and won their biggest game since the 1987 National Championship victory over Miami.

"The New Big Boys of the Big Ten," read the headline in the *Chicago Sun-Times*. "Critics of Nittany Lions Living in a Dream World," said the headline in the *Washington Post*. "We had two winners Saturday in Michigan Stadium," wrote Joe Falls for the *Detroit News*, " Penn State and the United States of America...viewers from coast to coast saw a truly great football game...Penn State simply was better, early and late and made the big plays..." Bob Verdi of the *Chicago Tribune* wrote, "Penn State didn't just win here Saturday, it staged a hostile takeover of this alleged chamber of horrors called, 'the Big House.'" Kerry Collins had completed 20-of-32 passes for 231 yards and three TDs without an interception and Carter outrushed Wheatley by running for 165 yards on 26 carries, "Michigan has dominated the Big Ten for so long," Carter told sportswriters, "we had to gain respect...this was the biggest game of my life." Paterno said his team beat "a great team...If the game goes another quarter, who knows who's gonna win it?" Michigan coach Moeller knew. "We know we got beat today by a better football team," he said.

On Monday, the Lions zoomed to the top of all the major polls. "Penn State: The New No. 1," said the cover of *Sports Illustrated*, which featured a photo of Scott running past a Michigan linebacker after catching a pass. But, ominously, only 19 voters in the AP polls named State #1 while 25 still had #3 Nebraska at the top of their ballot. As had been his custom for nearly 30 years, Paterno downplayed the polls and he had several of his players repeating his mantra. "All we have to do is keep playing hard," Engram told sportswriters. "The polls and the No. 1 ranking will take care of itself." With another idle week again before Ohio State, Paterno also cautioned his team about complacency. He reminded the players that OSU was the last team to beat them. But this group of Lions was not about to forget the humiliation in Columbus and the rude behavior by the Buckeyes' boorish fans. Collins & company wanted this game as much as they wanted to beat Michigan.

Normally, Homecoming games are reserved for the lightweights when an easy victory sends the alumni home happy for another year. Although State had been upset by Boston College in that Homecoming debacle of '92, this was supposed to be the toughest Homecoming opponent since Jeff Hostelter had brought fourth-ranked West Virginia to Beaver Stadium in 1983. The #14 Buckeyes (6-2) had

Heisman runner-up and Maxwell Award finalist as a junior, Ki-Jana Carter might have been the best PSU running back ever had he returned for his final year. Here he is headed for one of his four TDs in the 63-14 Homecoming blow-out of Ohio State in 1994.

lost to Washington, 25-16, and Illinois, 24-10, but were still dangerous with an offense that featured tailback Eddie George, who averaged 130 yards per game, wide receiver Joey Galloway and quarterback Bobby Hoying, who set a school record with five TD passes against Purdue the previous week. The weather was perfect and the crowd of 97,079 that set a new stadium record wasn't prepared for what happened after the first quarter. The Lions scored on their first possession, going 73-yards on 8-plays with Carter running 20 yards for the TD. But OSU kept the ball for much of the opening period, missing a 40-yard field goal but chalking up some good yardage on a couple of possessions while the Buckeye defense kept State's offense from breaking out. Even when Collins led a methodical 13-play march of 96 yards for a TD four minutes into the second quarter, there was no sign of what the regional TV audience was about to see. But as the State defense began to throttle the Buckeye attack, the Lion offense exploded. State scored three more touchdowns before the half on a pair of 15-yard passes to Engram and Archie and a 36-yard run by Carter to take a shocking 35-0 lead. On the Lions first play of the second half, Carter fumbled at the Lion 32 and the Buckeyes recovered. Five plays later Hoying passed 14 yards for a TD. Ohio State wouldn't get another until there were just four minutes left in the game. With Miller setting up another TD with his second interception and Mazyck returning an interception 10 yards for a TD, the Lions scored four more TDs to win, 63-14. It was Ohio State's worst defeat since 1946. "I don't feel like we tried to run up the score on them," Rivera told Randy Johnson of the *CDT*. "Because if we did, then they would have been in trouble." The Lions accumulated 572 net yards with Collins hitting on 19-of-23 passes for 265 yards and two TDs, Carter gaining 137 yards on 19 carries and four TDs and Engram catching six passes for 102 yards and a TD. The defense limited the Buckeyes to 214 net yards while intercepting three passes. "They put on a clinic," OSU coach Cooper told Marc Katz of the *Dayton Daily News*. "Ohio State's players decided Thursday to wear black socks for the game," Katz wrote. "They should have added black arm bands." ABC's Dick Vermeil said, "This is the best offensive team I've seen since I've been doing college broadcasting." "If ever a team approached perfection, this one certainly did," wrote Christ for the *Pa-*

triot-News. "It was just one of those days," Paterno said.

But it wasn't enough to keep 33 voters in the AP poll from voting Nebraska number one while 28 had the Lions at the top of their ballots and the Cornhuskers took over the AP rankings by six points—1,520 to 1,514. In the *USAToday*/CNN coaches poll, the Lions still held on to #1 by a narrow two points, 1,520 to 1,518, with 32 first place votes to 30 for Nebraska. "I won't lobby," Nebraska coach Tom Osborne told *USA Today*. "I don't see Tom Osborne arguing," Paterno said, "and I don't see any reason I should." The debate had only just begun.

In looking back at 1994, a myth has developed that the close score at Indiana on November 5 cost this team the National Championship. Hogwash. Politics by the media, the coaches and the bowl Coalition kept the Lions from at least sharing the title with Nebraska. State could have beaten Indiana by 50 points and it wouldn't have made a difference on January 3, 1995. For various reasons, most of the AP voters already had made their decision before the Indiana game was even played and the 35-29 final score simply gave the coaches the excuse they were looking for that would help Osborne get the championship he had never won.

What has been lost in all the furor over the Indiana game was that a team coming off an emotional high after two big, grudge match victories over its prime conference rivals played far below its level and still could have won by five touchdowns but for two crucial fourth quarter penalties and a last play Hail Mary pass. Any State follower who was among the crowd of 47,754 in Bloomington that overcast day or watched on ESPN knows this. The Lions offense did not play well for much of the game and the thin State defense was missing three starters. Still, State led 17-7 at the half on TD drives of 96 and 66 yards and a 30-yard field goal by Conway. Another Conway field goal of 38 yards made it 20-7 after three quarters and 90 seconds into the final period the Lions capped a 74 yard drive with a one-yard Archie TD and a 2-point conversion to go ahead 28-7. A few minutes later came the first questionable penalty which changed the final score. Archie had taken a punt return 89 yards for a TD only to have the run nullified by an illegal use of the hands infraction. Because of that penalty and a poor punt, Indiana had just 34 yards to go for its second TD. Still, one play after the Indiana TD, Carter became the only State player ever to run for an 80-yard TD twice in a season and the Lions led, 35-14, with 6:09 left in the game. Chris Dittoe, IU's backup quarterback who had come on in the second quarter and passed for both Indiana TDs, moved the Hoosiers into State territory. But he fumbled the ball when sacked from behind by Forbes at the Lion 25-yard line and Gelzheiser scooped it up and ran 75 yards to the end zone. But wait. An official threw a flag, claiming Forbes had inadvertently touched Dittoe's face mask, and IU retained the ball. Four plays later, Dittoe passed five yards to Eddie Baety for a touchdown with 1:49 remaining. Using its time outs, Indiana got the ball back and moved from its own 20 to the PSU 40 for one last play. Dittoe heaved the ball into the end zone and Dorian Wilkerson was there after Dingle and Pittman had both deflected it to grab the TD. A two-point pass made the final scored 35-29 and the Hoosier players and what was left of their fans celebrated as if they had won. Carter had run for 192 yards and Collins had thrown for 213 but Collins also threw two interceptions and the defense gave up 315 yards through the air. No one in the PSU locker room was happy. "You've got to win a game when you don't play well," Paterno told the media.

"Maybe we'll get everybody's feet on the ground again." Collins told Malcolm Moran of the *New York Times*, "...We weren't there today. Next time we'll know better." But as Moran ominously added, "When the polls and rankings are revised on Sunday, the Lions could discover that next time might be too late."

State lost 12 first place votes in the coaches poll and six more in the media voting and now Nebraska was #1 in both with a 27 point lead in the *USAToday*/CNN poll and an 18 point lead in the AP. "Evidently, style points count, too," wrote Verdi in the *Tribune*. "I was somewhat surprised by the swing in the coaches' vote," Osborne told the AP. "It must be how they perceived the games yesterday." Paterno declined comment. But the Lions were slipping and it was becoming obvious that even an eventual victory in the Rose Bowl might not help their chances. The Pac 10 race was in disarray and thrice-beaten Oregon loomed as the Big Ten's opponent. Nebraska was headed for the Orange Bowl against a team most likely to have lost just once. Paterno tried to be optimistic when asked about this at his weekly news conference. "I wouldn't say getting pigeon-holed into the Rose Bowl is the worst thing that could happen to you," he replied, refusing again to talk about the polls.

At approximately 4:15 p.m. Central Time on November 12, 1994, the Rose Bowl was just a blurred image in the far secluded corners of Paterno's mind. The Lions were losing 21-0 after one quarter to fired up Illinois and the hometown crowd was eating it up. Paterno had talked about his players needing adversity to prove how good they really were and now they had it up to their kiesters. And it seemed to get worse before it got better. A pooch punt by Brett Larson off a fake field goal had backed the Lions to their own one-yard line in the early moments of the second quarter and the Illini fans were screaming for their stalwart defense to cause a fumble or get a safety. But Witman gained five and Carter eased the pressure with a 14-yard run. A moment later Collins, who had thrown eight incomplete passes in a row,

Kerry Collins, winner of the Maxwell and Davy O'Brien awards, set numerous passing records while quarterbacking the great 1994 offensive unit. Following graduation, he endowed a scholarship for quarterbacks attending PSU.

hooked up with Brady for a 38-yard pass to the Illini 41. Brady caught two more passes and on the 11th play of the drive Milne blasted up the middle from one-yard for the TD. The defense held and the Lions got the ball back at the Illini 38 after a 13-yard punt partially blocked by Yeboah-Kodie. Collins went for it all on the first play, faking to Engram on a reverse and finding Scott wide open in the end zone. This was more like it. Conway's PAT made it 21-14 with 3:35 left in the half. But Johnson quickly found holes in State's secondary and with passes of 24, 27 and 4 yards to tight end Ken Dilger, he moved the Illini for a 5-yard TD by Douthard as the second quarter drew to a close.

The State locker room was relatively calm during the intermission as Paterno concentrated on inspiring his defense to toughen up. They did, stopping Illinois after the second half kickoff and forcing a punt to the State 41-yard line. A 22-yard pass to Engram and an 18-yard run by Carter helped get the ball to the Illini 7 and on second down Carter went four yards for the TD. Conway's PAT made it a 7-point game again but back came the Illini, consuming nearly seven

minutes of the clock on a 14-play, 71-yard drive that faltered at the PSU 9. Chris Richardson's 27-yard field goal made it 31-21 with about five minutes left in the third quarter. The Lions were on the move again and Collins found Archie wide open for a 27-yard pass to the Illini 13 but three plays later Conway came in to try a 33-yard field goal that was wide right. The rain started to fall in the fourth quarter when the Lions took possession on their own 45. On a fourth-and-two at the Illini 41, Collins hit Engram for 17 yards and five plays later Milne bolted up the middle for a 5-yard TD. Conway's kick narrowed it to three points with eight minutes left. The defense held again at the Illiniois 29 but this time Larsen boomed the punt 67 yards over Archie's head and the Illini kick team downed the ball at the PSU 4-yard line. Now came a TV time out with 6:07 left as the rain increased and the wind picked up.

"Ninety-six yards, fellas," Collins said as he stepped into the huddle. "Let's go. Let's do it." Collins knew he could not afford one mistake. Carter picked up one yard, then Milne gained six on a safety valve pass to the right. Brady caught a short pass on the left and rambled to the 18 for a first down. Collins hit Engram on a quick drop which Engram turned into an 11-yard gain and a face mask penalty added 15 more yards. First down at the PSU 44 with 4:25 left. A dump off pass to Carter over the middle gained five. Then Carter went around left end for five. Milne dove up the middle for three and Brady caught one crossing the middle to the left for six. The Illini fans were screaming as the Lions headed into the rain towards their small legion of fans who were on their feet with 3:10 remaining. Illinois blitzed and as Carter swung left he was tackled at the line of scrimmage. Out came the chains for a measurement. First down just inside the Illini 35. Now, Scott was open for a 16-yard shot over the middle to the 19. Carter was stopped for no gain and Collins called time out with 1:43 on the clock. The Lions had two time outs remaining. When time resumed, Collins found Engram over the middle for nine yards. On third-and-one, Milne went up the middle on a fullback trap for seven yards with Hartings, Ostrowski and Conlin leading the way. Now the Lions were just two yards away and Illinois called time out to set the defense. "Should Penn State pull this out," Brent Musburger told his TV audience, "they've got to consider moving them back to No. 1." In went another tight end, Olsommer, and another fullback, Sload. On first-and-goal Hartings pulled, Sload led the way into the hole being made by Rivera, Johnson and Olsommer and Milne took Collins' handoff and followed. Touchdown! And the Lion bench exploded. It wasn't over. There were 57 seconds remaining and on half dozen pass attempts against the prevent defense Johnson took the Illini all the way the State 31-yard line before his desperation shot into the end zone with two seconds left was intercepted by Herring. "It was a great comeback," Paterno said. "We never quit, we never lost faith," said Collins. "We have watched (Penn State) rise from the grave," wrote Bruce Keidan in the *Pittsburgh Post-Gazette*.

The Lions now had the Rose Bowl berth, no matter what happened in the last two games or the polls. But the players weren't celebrating. They still wanted the National Championship. That same evening, Nebraska needed two fourth quarter TDs to beat a very weak Iowa State team, 28-12, that had been hammered earlier by Iowa. But neither Nebraska's nor State's poll numbers budged the following Monday.

The next week, the much maligned defense led the way as Northwestern's Gary Barnett tried to use ball control to keep the State offense off the field. He did. State's offense was around for less than 19 minutes but pass interceptions by Herring and Scioli and a fumble recovery by Forbes set up three first half TDs and Herring ran 80 yards for a TD with another fumble recovery midway in the first quarter to help give State a 45-17 victory. The offense scored four times in drives of two minutes or less with Carter getting TDs on runs of 5, 23 and 1 yards in piling up 107 yards on 12 carries. Collins threw for 161 yards, including a 50-yard TD to Engram. The next Saturday, the Lion offense returned in force at Beaver Stadium to turn a 24-17 halftime lead over Michigan State into a 59-31 rout in what was George Perles' last game as the Spartan coach. Carter had his best rushing day ever, with 227 yards and five touchdowns on 27 carries to total 1,539 yards for the season, which was just 28 yards short of Lydell Mitchell's 1971 record. Collins completed 16-of-24 attempts for 289 yards, including a 56-yard TD to Scott, and set PSU season records for yardage (2,679) and completions (176) while also being the nation's leader in passing efficiency. For the third time, Scott and Engram each had over 100 yards in receptions with Scott catching six for 145 yards and Engram pulling in eight for 169, giving Engram a new season record in yardage with 1,029 yards. "It's a great football team," Paterno said in the media room. "Its hard for me to believe anybody can beat us." Unfortunately, the pollsters would.

THE 1995 ROSE BOWL
Jan. 2, 1995
Penn State 38, Oregon 20
Co-Most Valuable Players: Ki-Jana Carter & Danny O'Neil

By the time the Rose Bowl game started on January 2, the national title race was virtually over and State's players knew it. Nebraska had beaten #3 Miami in the Orange Bowl the night before, 24-17, and most of the media reports on that game said the Cornhuskers had all but clinched the National Championship. It wouldn't change even if State beat Oregon by 85 points, wrote Randy Hill in the *Pasadena Star-News*: "Hell, even that type of clouting would not enable the Snittany Lions to con pollsters into abandoning the party line that insists Nebraska should be known as the No. 1 team in America." In a team meeting after the Orange Bowl at State's hotel headquarters 40 miles away from Pasadena, Paterno tried to tell the players they still had a chance. But deep in their hearts, they knew otherwise. Earlier that day they had marveled at the 15,000 cheering fans who turned out for a pep rally near the Westin Plaza Hotel in Costa Mesa. The fans would enjoy the Rose Bowl parade the next morning and many would be tailgating before the game in the warmth and sunshine pouring down over the San Gabriel mountains. The Lions were a 17-point favorite and Paterno cautioned against a let down. "It would be a shame if you let anything that happened tonight affect your season," he had told them at the meeting, according to *"The Lion Kings."*

Paterno was right. In the regular season, the team had set two NCAA records for total offense at 520.2 yards per game and scoring offense with 47.8 points a game. The Lions also broke several school records, including points (526), total offense (5,722 yards) and passing yardage (2,962). Already, five players—Collins, Carter, Engram, Brady and Hartings—had made First-Team All-American, the most for State since 1978. Although Collins and Carter had seemed to cancel each other out for the Heisman, Collins won the Maxwell Award as "the outstanding college player" and also the Davy O'Brien Award as the nation's best quarterback. Engram was given the first Biletnikoff Award as the country's leading receiver. Of course, none of this mattered to Oregon, which had not been to the Rose Bowl in 27 years. Coach Rich Brooks' team had been an underdog all season and had gone 6-1 in the Pac 10 after losing two non-conference games at the start of the season to Hawaii and Utah. The Ducks had a defense that compared to Illinois but with more speed and had given up just 13.3 points a game. They also had a pair of quarterbacks in Danny O'Neil and Tony Graziani who had thrown for 1,756 yards and 20 TDs. Furthermore, the oft-criticized Lion defense had several key players still out with injuries and Sandusky was forced to start fourth string redshirt sophomore Chuck Penzenik at a new position, free safety.

State's offense seemed to be in typical form after the defense had stopped Oregon following the opening kickoff. On State's first play from scrimmage, Carter burst over right tackle and went 83 yards for a touchdown. The rout appeared to be on. But it took Oregon

1994 Penn State Football team.

just 45 seconds to go 80 yards in four plays to tie the score and the rest of the first half was a battle. Four times, the high-passing Oregon attack moved deep into PSU territory with chances to score. One drive was stopped by Penzenik's interception at the 9. Two others ended in missed field goals. And a long, last minute march just before the half ended at the 5 as the clock ran out. Meanwhile, State

As some 15,000 fans watched at the Rose Bowl pep rally near the team's hotel, the Lion mascot does a few traditional pushups with the cheerleaders encouraging. Paterno and the team are in the background.

much-maligned State pass defense also had come through with big plays to stop O'Neil, who broke five 32-year old Rose Bowl records with 41-of-61 passes for 456 yards. "Lions No. 1 in Pasadena," said the headline in the *Pasadena Star-News.* "We proved to everyone in the country we're certainly worthy to be National Champion as much as anyone else," Paterno told the media after his

had taken a 14-7 lead with 1:26 left in the half on a quick 7-play, 73-yard drive that was highlighted by a 44-yard pass from Collins to freshman Jurevicius. Engram also caught passes of 18 and 12 yards to help set up Milne's one-yard TD. The Lion fans among the throng of 102,247 expected the State offense to break it open in the third quarter. Instead, Collins threw his only interception of the afternoon. Oregon linebacker Reggie Jordan ran it back 38 yards to the PSU 17 and Oregon tied the score two plays later with five minutes left in the period. But freshman tailback Ambrose Fletcher made what may have been the play of the game by returning the kickoff 72 yards to the Oregon 21. Carter ran for four, then for 17 and the touchdown and Conway's PAT put the Lions back into the lead. Moments later, Penzenik made the defensive play of the game. He intercepted his second pass at the State 43 and didn't stop running until he was at the Oregon 13. Three plays later Carter scored from the 3 and the Lions were on their way to the Rose Bowl victory. With nine minutes left in the fourth quarter,

players had given him the game ball.

But it was not to be. "Undefeated. Untied. Unappreciated," said the front of a popular T-shirt sold in Happy Valley. Paterno had his fifth unbeaten team and became the only coach ever to win the traditional New Year's Rose, Orange, Sugar and Cotton Bowl games. He also was now the winningest coach in bowl history. But Nebraska won the national title by an overwhelming margin. Only one media voter split his ballot in the AP poll with Nebraska getting 51 1/2 first place votes and 1,539 1/2 total to State's 10 1/2 and 1,497 1/2. The coaches gave the Cornhuskers 54 first place votes and 1,542 points to State's 8 and 1,496 points. Only the *New York Times* and the Sagarin computer ratings made the Lions #1. Despite playing what the NCAA said was the 17th toughest schedule, the laurels went to Nebraska with the 57th hardest schedule.

Maybe, as Black wrote in his *"Football Letter"* the championship was determined by one play at Ann Arbor—a month before the

Conway kicked a 43-yard field goal and a few minutes later Witman scored from the nine after Oregon gambled and lost on a fourth down at its own 13-yard line. "Nittany Lions Finally Put Away Oregon, 38-20, to Complete 12-0 Season," said a subhead in the *Los Angeles Times.* Although the Lion offense netted 430 yards, the

Penn State fans whoop it up at the 1995 Rose Bowl won by Penn State over Oregon.

Lions' visited there. That was the day of Colorado's Hail Mary upset. "If Colorado had not upset Michigan on that improbable play," wrote Black, "the Wolverines would have been ranked #1 when Penn State went into Ann Arbor on October 15. Consequently, when the Lions moved into the top spot themselves after defeating Michigan, their hold on #1 would have been unbreakable, rather than tenuous." Perhaps, but that doesn't factor in the innate bias by the voters.

But 1994 was now part of the legacy. A new season started on January 4, 1995. The fans wanted to know if the Lions could do it again. They found out it takes more than winning in the clutch to win a championship.

Season Record 12-0
Record to Date 686-291-42
Winning percentage .694

"Mr. Clutch & The Big Snow"

Joe Paterno trotted across the field at Giants Stadium for the traditional handshake with his opposing coach when all hell broke loose. As a Saturday night ESPN audience watched and heard, Paterno and Rutgers coach Doug Graber exchanged words, then both muttered barnyard obscenities as Paterno lost his temper and had to be pulled back by his assistants.

Graber was upset at a 12-yard touchdown pass thrown by State's backup quarterback in the last minute of the game with State already ahead by 18 points. When it happened, Graber had ripped off his headset and hurled it to the ground. He believed Paterno was trying to roll up the score to impress the pollsters. Teams such as Nebraska and Miami were notorious for rubbing it in against weaker foes but Paterno often vowed he would never do it and in 30 years he never had. In fact, only a few days before the Rutgers game, Paterno had been widely quoted for again saying he would not embarrass opponents in this manner, even if it costs his team the National Championship. Some media folks had already said that compassionate philosophy may have cost his '94 squad the title because of what happened at Indiana.

As Paterno approached Graber trying to explain what happened on the pass, the Rutgers coach said calmly, "I really didn't think you'd pull that, Joe, I really didn't." "That's Bull——!" Paterno said angrily, turning abruptly to walk away. "Bull——!" Graber snapped as he headed towards the dressing room. The next thing the audience saw was Paterno chasing after Graber and one of the Rutgers' aides as State's assistant coach Bill Kenny tried to restrain him. In the chaos, someone shouted "F— You!" but who said the "F" word was not known. Up in the TV booth, play-by-play announcer Ron Franklin commented about the angry exchange. Color commentator Mike Gotfried, who had several run-ins with Paterno when coaching at Pitt a few years earlier said, " When you throw like that at the end you can expect that from the other side."

In the next 48 hours, that peppery confrontation was a bonanza for the sports media across the nation. ESPN played the one minute segment over and over and many radio sports talk shows and newspaper columns were critical of Paterno and what seemed to be a blatant example of hypocrisy. At his weekly news conference that following Tuesday, Paterno publicly apologized to Graber and for using an obscenity. He also was sorry for losing his cool and his poise. He ex-

plained that he wanted little-used redshirt sophomore Mike McQueary to throw a short pass just to test his arm. The pass was to go eight yards to the freshman tight end, Cuncho Brown. The plan then was to run out the clock. But when McQueary saw flanker Chris Campbell wide open heading towards the end zone, the young quarterback couldn't resist.   "I did not want to run up the score against Rutgers," Paterno said. "Our team, former players and coaches know how I feel about embarrassing anybody." What Paterno didn't say and what never really came out publicly was something else that was said to him by an unidentified Rutgers aide as Paterno stomped away from Graber. And it was this intemperate remark that infuriated Paterno and had him chasing after Graber. The man virtually accused Paterno of betting on the game and running up the score to beat the point spread. Still, there had been no excuse for Paterno's temper tantrum and he knew it. But this was the defining moment of the season for its after effects would last for at least two weeks and in that period, the fate of the 1995 season would be determined.

The 59-34 victory over Rutgers on September 23 gave the Lions a 3-0 record and was State's 20th straight victory dating back to the Ohio State game of 1993. Even with a new quarterback, tailback and tight end succeeding the three first round NFL draft choices from '94—Collins, Carter and Brady—the Lions had enough talent returning to make them the preseason favorite to defend their Big Ten title. The media also believed they had another chance at the national title, particularly with a schedule that had three lightly-regarded non-conference foes and the most critical league games against Wisconsin, Ohio State and Michigan at home. Except for the fact that the University's new president, Graham Spanier, had come directly from Nebraska, the controversy over the polls in 1994 was pushed into the background. The preseason AP poll had State ranked at #4 behind Florida State, Nebraska and Texas A&M with Ohio State #10, Michigan #12, Wisconsin #22 and Illinois #24. "This well could be another 12-0 season," wrote Neil Rudel of the *Altoona Mirror*, and several other PSU beat writers predicting for the *Penn State Football Annual* magazine agreed. But not Steve Halvonik of the *Pittsburgh Post-Gazette* who wrote, "History tells us the Lions will go 9-3. This is a rebuilding year." *USA Today* analyst Danny Sheridan also had his doubts, making the Lions a 75-1 shot to win the national crown and saying, "two undefeated seasons are too much to expect."

But even before the season began, some of the other Big Ten coaches were grumbling about this upstart "11th team" that had taken over their domain. "Papa Joe's got a great schedule," OSU coach Cooper complained to the *Columbus Dispatch*. "I'm not very happy." What especially rankled Cooper was that he had to take his team to Happy Valley two years in a row. He and other coaches believed State was given extra breaks on the scheduling. They were particularly upset at the off weeks State gets before big games—this year it would be before Michigan, again. They also complained because the Lions had not played Wisconsin when the Badgers won the Big Ten in '93 nor would State have to meet contending Illinois this season. "There's no question, they have the best of scheduling," Michigan's new coach Lloyd Carr told the AP. Some coaches even hinted at a Paterno power play on scheduling but Big Ten assistant commissioner Mark Rudner denied that, saying "The scheduling is done randomly. We try to be as fair as possible."

The reason for so much optimism about 1995 was the return of 42 lettermen with seven regulars and five other sometime starters from the record-breaking offense. That included the two flashy wideouts, Engram and Scott, and the offensive line, except for Greeley, that gave up just four sacks in '94. Tielsch was now the center of the "Lunch Bunch" flanked by Rivera and Hartings at guards and Conlin and Rivera at tackles with Olsommer at tight end. All three fullbacks were back—Witman, Milne and Sload—as well as the prime tailbacks behind Carter: Archie, Pitts and Fletcher. The offense had depth in these positions, too, with such returnees as Marczyk, Henderson, Anderson and Jones and redshirt sophomore Phil Ostrowski in the line, Stephenson at tight end and Jurevicius, Campbell and redshirt freshman Joe Nastasi at the wideouts. Engram, Archie, Fletcher and Pitts gave the offense experienced kick returners as well. But all this fire power would put the pressure on Wally Richardson to take over at quarterback where Collins left off. Richardson had enough game experience in '94 to throw 45 passes but he was still green in running a team full time. And, except for some pressure in his baptism as a freshman against Cincinnati in 1992, Richardson had never been in a game when he had to bring the team from behind in the fourth quarter to win. Paterno wasn't worried. "I've never had any questions about Wally's leadership," Paterno told the media. He also believed Richardson had a better arm and more mobility than Collins. "Wally is a big time quarterback," Paterno said. "He's got to get some experience."

Paterno was much more concerned about his defense. It had been too susceptible to a passing attack in '94, giving up 232 yards per game. He and Sandusky wanted the defense to be quicker and more aggressive. The lineup that they put on the field in the opener against Texas Tech September 9 had six new starters, including several redshirt sophomores. Killens and Scioli were at the ends with Atkins and Noble at the tackles, Aaron Collins and Jim Nelson were the outside linebackers with Filardi on the inside. Herring was back at free safety, fully recovered from the chop block injury that had ended his season against Northwestern, with Miller and Tate at the corners. Jason Collins started at Hero but would be lost for the season with an injury in the Rutgers game and Holes and Penzenik would share the position. Clair, true freshman Anthony Cleary, redshirt sophomores Clint Seace and Chris Snyder would be among the reserves in the line with Cory Carlson, Shino Prater, Shawn Lee and Brad Johnson also subbing on defense. A prized recruit named Floyd Wedderburn, who was 6-foot-7, 320 pounds, also was slated for defensive tackle but took a redshirt when he injured a knee severely in the preseason. Another highly-recruited freshman, Brandon Short of McKeesport, would break a bone in his foot against Tech and he, too, would take a medical redshirt. On paper, the kicking was strong, with placekicker Conway and punter Kania back as well as snapper Pantall with McQueary and Nastasi sharing the holding. But, as with Richardson, there was still a question of how Conway would kick under pressure when the game was on the line in the closing seconds and his foot would win it or lose it. No one expected that test to come in the first game.

Texas Tech was a decided underdog in the regionally televised opener at Beaver Stadium. The Red Raiders had finished 6-6 in '94 and had been demolished by USC, 55-14, in the '95 Cotton Bowl representing the Southwest Conference. But Coach Spike Dykes had devised a gambling defense with continued blitzes and stunts to stop State's running game and put the pressure on the Lions' new quarterback and it worked—for a while. It didn't help that Paterno was missing two of his tailbacks. Pitts was out with a stress fracture of his foot and Fletcher was embroiled in legal problems back home. Paterno moved

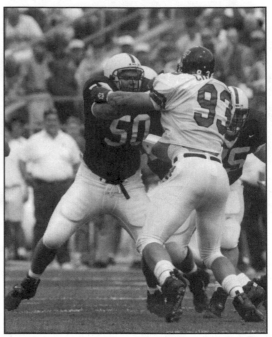

Two-time First-Team All-American offensive guard Jeff Hartings was also selected twice to the Academic All-American team and was a 1995 semi-finalist for the Lombardi Award.

redshirt freshman Chris Eberly from defense to tailback but Archie went the whole way at tailback. Yet it was mistakes by three of State's best offensive players that allowed Tech to take a shocking 20-7 lead in the first half. A Tech punt on its opening series had put the Lions in a hole near their own goal line and when State tried a tricky end reverse, Archie and Scott collided. The ball went into the end zone and was recovered by Tech for a 7-0 lead less than five minutes into the game. State tied it after the ensuing kickoff as Richardson led a 62-yard drive, hitting Scott on two key passes for 15 and 17 yards, with Witman getting the TD on a 2-yard plunge. But the game swiftly turned into a battle of defenses and an exchange of punts. That's when the usually sure-handed Engram dropped two punts in the second quarter that led to Tech TD drives of 20 and 40 yards.

The defensive parry continued into the third quarter and it was the Lion defense that put State back into the game with five minutes left in the period. Jason Collins stripped the ball from tailback Brian Hanspard and Killens recovered at the Tech 3-yard line. Witman scored on the next play. When the Lions took the ball back, Richardson found the groove again. With the help of three passes to Engram, including one for 24-yards on a third-and-22 situation, Richardson led an 8-play, 54-yard drive that climaxed with a 3-yard, fourth down TD pass to Olsommer. Conway's PAT gave State the lead, 21-20, 53 seconds into the final period. But Tech came back minutes later to go ahead again on a 42-yard field goal. There was 6:39 left in the game when State gained possession at the 20-yard line following the kickoff. The pressure was now on Richardson. Passing three times to Engram for good yardage, twice on third-and-long, Richardson methodically drove State for a first down at the Tech 11 as the clock wound down. Three running plays put the ball in position for a game winning field goal and now came the test for Conway. Paterno may have had confidence in Conway but the 96,034 fans were uneasy for he had already missed two field goal attempts and this 39-yarder was not a sure thing. There was no miss this time and with four seconds showing on the clock, the ball went through the uprights and State escaped with a 24-23 win. "You don't figure he's going to miss three in a row," Paterno said in the media room.

Before the Temple game, Paterno had another tailback. True freshman Curtis Enis of Union City, OH, who had spent a year at Kiski Prep before enrolling at State, was moved from backup linebacker and was an instant success. With just three days of practice at tailback, Enis ran for 132 yards on 14 carries, including touchdowns of 24, 1 and 6 yards as the Lions overwhelmed hapless Temple, 66-14. When Enis repeated his performance the following Saturday against Rutgers in the New Jersey Meadowlands, it was apparent that State's newest running star was being born. But Enis' 145 yards on 15 carries was all but forgotten in the aftermath of the testy Paterno-Graber incident and the unexpected high scoring shoot-out of the game. Although State never trailed, Rutgers rallied twice from 17 point deficits, primarily on the pass receiving of Marco Battaglia, who caught 13 passes for 184 yards and three touchdowns. He was matched by Engram, who caught eight passes for 158 yards and touchdowns of 47, 27 and 16 yards. Engram also had a TD on a 58-yard run after picking up Witman's fumble early in the first quarter. But the key play of the game was an interception by Herring one minute into the fourth quarter with State leading 38-27 and Rutgers gaining momentum. Herring, whose first interception led to Engram's TD run, stepped in front of Battaglia at the Rutgers 21-yard line and ran the ball in for the TD. A few minutes later, Engram caught his 18-yard TD at the end of an 80- yard drive to clinch the victory. Then came the ill-advised McQueary pass and the controversial postgame eruption.

The Lions were a two-touchdown favorite in their Big Ten opener against Wisconsin the following Saturday in an early evening game televised by ESPN. But Badger coach Barry Alvarez had his team well prepared and State looked out of sync all game. Later, those close to Paterno said he had been distracted by all the furor over the Graber episode. "The fiery taskmaster seemed to be in a fog," his brother George wrote in the book, *"Joe Paterno: The Coach From Byzantium."* "Some people who witnessed practice noticed his dismay and maybe the players did also." Perhaps, everyone also was looking one week ahead to Ohio State. But the offense dropped passes, gave up sacks, and could gain just 83 yards on the ground and lost, 17-9. Richardson completed a record 33 (of 48) passes for 259 yards without an interception but could only get one TD as Wisconsin staved off State drives at the Badger 22, 31, 24 and 37 yard lines. Late in the first half, Paterno even missed an opportunity for a field goal when he thought it was third down and a fourth down pass fell incomplete. Trailing by 17-3 with less than 10 minutes remaining, State scored on a 16-play 80 yard drive but a two-point conversion attempt off a fake kick failed. Then, with 3:31 left, Richardson tried to rally the team, moving to a first down at the Wisconsin 40. But a fourth-and-7 pass fell incomplete and the Badgers ran out the clock to end the Lions 20-game winning streak. "Wisconsin Plays Flawless Football in Breaking Streak," said the headline in the *Centre Daily Times.* "Penn State was a confused team tonight," wrote Michael Giarrusso for the AP. "Wisconsin took away all the big plays and kept good field position," Paterno said. "We couldn't make anything happen for ourselves."

The #12 Lions played like a different team against #5 Ohio State the following Saturday at Beaver Stadium and maybe they were just beaten by a better squad in the 28-25 defeat. But the way the nationally televised game was lost at the end had many fans wondering

if some distractions had carried over from the previous week. State had taken a 10-0 lead in the first quarter only to see Ohio State go ahead 21-10 in the third period after two 80-yard drives and another for 98, principally on the passing of Bobby Hoying to Rickey Dudley and Terry Glenn. But Richardson took the Lions 86 yards midway in the third quarter and then 84 yards early in the fourth quarter to give State a 25-21 lead. When Miller intercepted Hoying at the State 34 with 9:26 remaining, the Lions seemed to have momentum. But two running plays and a rushed pass gained just five yards and the Lions had to punt. A few minutes later, Miller stripped the ball from Glenn at the State 10 and the Lions took over with five minutes remaining. A couple of first downs and they might have been able to run out the clock. But the offense could gain just six yards as an offside penalty and some conservative play calling forced the Lions to punt. The Buckeyes took possession at their own 42 with 3:10 remaining. In 6 plays, the Buckeys scored with Dudley's 32-yard pass reception from Hoying setting up a 6-yard TD by Eddie George, who would go on to win the Heisman Trophy. The Lions had one last chance but a fourth down desperation pass from midfield by Richardson to a wide open Engram at the OSU 10 fell short and the fans gave State a standing ovation for effort. "There was a time when Penn State could take the ball and a four-point lead and drain the last few minutes off the clock like so much dishwater," wrote David Jones for the *Harrisburg Patriot-News.* "But yesterday was not the time..." Engram told Ed Morales of the *CDT.* "There was some confusion late in the game, and it was frustrating. We were not as sure about things as we should have been." Ergo, Rutgers? This was first time since 1992 that State had lost two games in a row and the players were in shock. "We did not expect to be 0-2 (in the conference) at this juncture," Herring said. The loss dumped the Lions into last place in the Big Ten and suddenly the league was turned around. Northwestern had upset Michigan that same day and the surprising Wildcats were now leading the conference. But there was one major bright light for Penn State in all the gloom. Enis had again shown his prowess, running for 146 yards on 25 carries to lead all ball carriers, including George, who had 105 yards on 24 carries.

In a 1995 game against Wisconsin, Freddie Scott had 13 receptions for 110 yards setting a record for most receptions in a game. He teamed with Engram to give the Lions a formidable pair of wide receivers.

What happened in the next two weeks at Purdue and Iowa not only set the tone for the rest of the season but also marked the final manifestation of Bobby Engram as perhaps the greatest clutch player in Penn State football. Both games were away and both had similar endings. Once again, mistakes by three of State's best players put the team in jeopardy. Fumbled punts by Archie and Engram plus a fumble and pass interception thrown by Richardson had set up two Purdue TDs and two field goals and helped give the Boilermakers a 23-16 lead five minutes into the fourth quarter. State's scoring to that point had come from three Conway field goals of 35, 33 and 33 yards and a 48-yard bomb from Richardson to Engram in the second quarter. With a Homecoming crowd and ESPN audience watching, the Lions drove 59-yards for another Conway kicked field goal of 25 yards to narrow the score to 23-16 with 7:39 left. The defense forced a punt and the Lions took over at their own 20-yard line with 4:11 remaining. On first down, Paterno ordered another bomb and Richardson hit his roommate Engram for 49 yards. Two plays later, Engram caught another Richardson pass for 14 yards and stepped out of bounds at the Purdue 16. On the next play, Engram started downfield taking two Purdue defenders with him but Richardson threw a screen pass to Archie instead and with blocks from Marczyk and Hartings, Archie dashed into the end zone with 2 1/2 minutes remaining. Conway's PAT made it 26-23 and that's how it finished after the defense sacked the Purdue quarterback twice and forced two incomplete passes. "We made enough mistakes today to lose five games," Paterno told sportswriters. "But we played with determination and character." Engram had his finest receiving day ever with 9 catches for 203 yards. "Penn State All-American Lives Up to Star Billing," said the headline in the *Lafayette Journal and Courier*.

Engram outdid himself the following week before a regional ABC-TV audience and an antagonistic Iowa crowd of 70,367 at Niles Kinnick Stadium. The game also marked the come back of Pitts, who subbed at tailback for the first time in the season and wound up as the leading ball carrier with 134 yards on 12 carries and 150 more yards on six kickoff returns. Two of his kickoff returns went for 43 yards and both set up field goals by Conway, including one with a little more than 11 minutes left in the game that tied the score at 27-all. Iowa was

unbeaten and had the best rushing attack in the Big Ten. But the Hawkeyes had used a passing attack and aggressive defense to keep pace with State throughout most of the game. After Conway's 26-yard field goal, Iowa resumed its passing mode but two sacks by Atkins forced the Hawkeyes to punt from their own end zone. Killens partially blocked the punt and Engram's return took the ball to the Iowa 25. Witman carried three straight times to the 13, then Richardson threw to Engram who made a diving catch in the far left corner of the end zone for the TD. It was the 26th TD catch of his career, breaking the record held by his position coach, Kenny Jackson. But Engram wasn't through. A few minutes later, Herring's interception at the State 39 set up a Richardson to Engram 43-yard TD pass that gave the Lions the 41-27 victory. "Little Bobby Engram is just unbelievable," said Iowa coach Hayden Fry. "He's a great clutch player," Paterno told sportswriters. Perhaps John Black put it best for *"The Football Letter:"* "The formula is simple for Penn State in 1995. When the game is on the line, go to Bobby Engram."

Engram's heroics weren't needed the following week when State trampled over Indiana, 45-21, in the annual Beaver Stadium Homecoming game. The Lions turned three interceptions, a fumble recovery and a blocked punt into scores and led 38-0 before IU scored in the fourth quarter. Aaron Collins had an 80-yard interception return for one TD and Killens had one for 25 yards after the runback of the kick he blocked. Killens, who was named Defensive Player of the Week by *Sports Illustrated*, also had four sacks, which gave him 11 for the season and just four shy of Larry Kubin's one season record set in 1979. The Lions were now 6-2 and the players figured they were now ready for the football world's Cinderella team, Northwestern. The Wildcats already had upset Notre Dame, Michigan and Wisconsin and would have been undefeated if they had not blown a lead and been upset themselves by Miami of Ohio in the second week of the season. Still, the oddsmakers were not convinced and made the Lions a 5-to-7 point favorite at Dyche Stadium. After Northwestern won, 21-10, Paterno told the media, "People just can't believe Northwestern's that good. But they are that good...They play football the way I like to see kids do it." Still, if State's offense had been more consistent and if Engram had not been hampered by a severely injured left hand, the Lions might have won. Behind by just 14-7 at the half, the Lions twice drove inside the Northwestern 10 in the third quarter and had to settle for one field goal. Conway missed another field goal on a referee's decision early in the fourth quarter after State blew a first-and-goal with a holding penalty. TV replays showed the field goal attempt was good but Northwestern turned the official's ruling into an 80-yard drive for the winning TD that was helped by a questionable pass interference penalty on a third-and-5 at the Wildcat 25. "We had a chance in the third quarter but they hung in there and hung in there and then they did what they had to do," Paterno said. "...The Lions have gone nine weeks and still haven't beaten a really good team," wrote Mark Brennan of *Blue White Illustrated*. "...Limping into the final two games of the season wasn't what the players had in mind when it began. If they let up now, things could get really ugly."

In the two weeks before the Michigan game, the players had time to ruminate about what might have been and what still could be. "People are upset, they're mad," Richardson told Bob Biertempfel of the *Greensburg Tribune-Review*. "It's been showing in practice." The players also could talk about the continued lack of respect emanating from the Michigan camp. "This year we have to go back and treat

The great Bobby Engram, First-Team All-American and winner of the first Bilentnikoff Award in 1994 as a junior, holds many major receiving records at Penn State. Here, he makes a reception in the Michigan State game of 1994.

(Penn State) like the stepchild they are," Wolverine linebacker Pierre Cooper told *Sports Illustrated* even before the season began. "...Why exactly did we let these rubes in (the Big Ten)?" wrote a columnist for the *Detroit News*. On State's idle Saturday, Michigan beat Purdue, 5-0, running its overall record to 8-2 and conference mark to 4-2. That now made the winner of the State-Michigan game the likely Big Ten representative for the New Year's Day Outback Bowl in Tampa. On Monday, #19 State was made a 4 1/2 point favorite over #12 Michigan. On Tuesday night, the snow started falling. By Wednesday night, 17 1/2 inches of snow had buried State College and Beaver Stadium.

The unexpected snowfall shocked an area that normally receives about 2.7 inches of snow in the entire month of November. Some 18,000 homes and businesses lost power and many of the electrical disruptions continued into Friday. Initially, State officials contemplated postponing or moving the football game to Ann Arbor. Then, with some old-timers remembering the famous "Snow" game of 1953 when New Beaver Field had to be shoveled out for the game against Fordham, an emergency plan was put into effect to remove the snow from Beaver Stadium and the adjacent paved parking lots. Some 300 volunteers, including 81 low-security inmates from four area prisons, were paid $5 an hour to clear the stadium field, seats and walkways. Because two-thirds of the normal 25,000 stadium parking spaces were on grass fields that would not be cleared of snow, shuttle lots were set up at malls and businesses for people going to the game. "Like long lines of banished citizens marching across Siberia to the Gulag Archipelago, hardy fans trudged through the deep snow covering unplowed areas around the stadium to arrive in time for the early kickoff, set at 12:08 to accommodate a telecast (by ABC) to 80 percent of the nation," wrote Black for the *"Football Letter."* Of course, not all the snow could be taken out of Beaver Stadium and the estimated 80,000 fans who showed up on November 18 in the near freezing weather still had to sit with their feet surrounded by piles of snow. Despite all this, the field was in good condition because it had been covered by a tarp. However, weather conditions were expected to favor Michigan, which was number one in the nation against the rush, holding teams to an average of 73 rushing yards per game. Paterno also had expressed concern earlier in the week about his own team's ground game and particularly the need for his tailbacks to be more consistent.

There was no scoring until the second quarter but by halftime State led, 13-7, on Conway field goals of 49 and 51 yards and a 13-yard TD pass from Richardson to Archie that capped an 83-yard drive. The Lions missed another scoring chance when Witman fumbled at the UM 9 after a pass reception and Michigan than drove 91-yards for its only TD of the half. State blew another TD in the third quarter after a 29-yard Remy Hamilton field goal narrowed State's lead to three points. The Lions marched 72 yards to the Wolverine one-yard line but Enis fumbled into the end zone and Michigan recovered. However, State scored on its next possession, going 57 yards in 10 plays with Engram leaping in front of State's student section to catch the 12-yard TD pass from Richardson. A hail of snowballs from the students almost caused a 15-yard penalty but the Lions now led, 20-10. However, with sophomore QB Brian Griese passing to Toomer, Hayes and Biakabutuka, Michigan went 73 yards following the kickoff with Biakabutuka scoring on an 18-yard pass and Hamilton's PAT making the score 20-17 with 7:48 left in the game. Now, it was anybody's game and after an exchange of punts, State took possession at its own 34-yard line with 4:08 remaining. On the first play, Pitts, who had been

in most of the second half at tailback, suddenly broke away for 58 yards to Michigan's 8-yard line. Three plays gained just six yards and Conway came in to kick another field goal. But Paterno had given Ganter the go ahead for the fake field goal play the Lions had practiced. Nastasi, the holder, had the option to run depending on the way the Michigan defense was lined up. "I saw they had three guys outside tackle," Nastasi said later, "and I called the audible at the line of scrimmage." Nastasi took the snap from Keith Conlin and dashed over right tackle for the touchdown and the Lions won, 27-17. "It was a great call," Michigan coach Lloyd Carr said later. "It never entered Lloyd Carr's mind that Michigan's defense would be the weak link," wrote Angelique Chengelis for the *Detroit News*. "'I did not expect Penn State to run the football the way they did,' said Carr..." The Lions had rushed for more yards than any UM opponent (245) with Pitts getting 164 on 17 carries. "You dream of having days like this," Pitts told sportswriters.

When the Big Ten coaches were complaining about State's off week before the Michigan game, no one mentioned Michigan State's two weeks to prepare for Penn State's visit over Thanksgiving weekend. And the Spartans were ready, throwing up a defense designed to smother State's rushing and pressure Richardson on passes. The Lions seemed to be on the defensive all day, starting in the first quarter when Miller stopped MSU with an interception in the end zone. PSU then drove 80 yards to take a 3-0 lead on a Conway field goal but by halftime the Spartans were ahead 10-7. Twice in the second half, the Lions tied the game but couldn't seem to regain the lead and with 5:13 left in the game, MSU led 20-17 after a 28-yard field goal by Chris Gardner. Then, when Richardson was sacked and State had to punt with 2:19 remaining, the Spartan fans began to celebrate. But utilizing their time outs and getting big defensive plays from Atkins and Miller, the Lions forced MSU to punt and with 1:45 left, PSU had the ball on its own 27-yard line and no time outs. Certainly, the Lion fans watching the early evening game at Spartan Stadium or on national TV did not have much confidence in Richardson at this point. The junior QB had hit on just 13-of-30 passes, thrown two interceptions and been sacked three times. But in a march downfield reminiscent of "The Drive" at Illinois in '94, Richardson took the Lions on a thrilling two-minute drill. He started with two passes to Milne for a first down. Then, throwing 10 more consecutive passes without a handoff, Richardson took the Lions to a first down at the MSU 4-yard line with 34 seconds left. He had completed 9-of-12 passes, throwing to five different receivers, and spiked the ball to stop the clock on one incompletion. The Spartans called time out to align their defense. On first down, Richardson passed to Archie but the tailback was tackled for no gain. The team hustled to the line and Richardson spiked the ball again and went to the sideline. Paterno told him to run the same play but to throw the flanker screen over the middle to Engram. There were 13 seconds left. The pass was perfect. Engram grabbed the ball just inside the 5-yard line, ducked under the attempted tackle by two MSU defenders at the 3 and dived over the goal line. Conway's PAT made the final 24-20. "If there's a better clutch player in the country than Engram, I want to see him," wrote Ronnie Christ for the *Harrisburg Patriot-News*. "I wanted the ball in my hands to see what I could do," Engram said, adding, "I think (Wally) grew up a little, just like Kerry (Collins) did two years ago here." Paterno praised Engram and Richardson but also his entire team. "We're a good football team...Outside of Wisconsin, we played hard and well (all season)."

THE 1996 OUTBACK BOWL
Jan. 1, 1996
Penn State 43, Auburn 14
Most Valuable Player: Bobby Engram

Season Record 9-3
Record to Date 695-294-42
Winning percentage .694

"Back Home Again, In Indiana"

Unlike the last two bowl trips which had added pressures on the players, this game was more for personal player, coach and conference pride than anything else. It matched the third place teams of the Big Ten and SEC and had no bearing on the Top 10 national rankings. In fact, the biggest news of all was the name of the bowl. A corporate contract with a steak house chain had changed the name of the 10-year-old bowl from the Hall of Fame to Outback. Still, the opposing coaches made the game an intriguing matchup. Auburn's Terry Bowden was the son of Florida State's Bobby Bowden and 30 years younger than Paterno. The *St. Petersburg Times* touted the match up as "The King and the Cub" while the *Tampa Tribune* used the headline, "Old Dog, New Tricks" to describe the two coaches. The teams had the same record at 8-3 with one of Auburn's losses being a 49-38 loss to Florida, which was playing Nebraska for the national title the next day. Most of the pregame analysis focused on a battle between State's defense and Auburn's high scoring offense. The Tigers had averaged almost 39 points per game behind the running of Stephen Davis and passing of Patrick Nix and sportscasters such as ESPN's Lee Corso figured that was enough for Auburn to overpower and run right over the Lions. They also figured Auburn had an extra incentive since this was the school's first bowl game in five years. A near sellout crowd of 65,000 was expected but then the rains came.

Heavy rain and thunderstorms hit Tampa Stadium just as the tailgaters were piling out of their cars, vans and campers and at least 15,000 paying customers stayed home when the teams kicked off at 11 a.m. before the ESPN cameras. It was apparent that the soggy conditions could affect the game and as the first half was drawing to a close, the Lions led by just 9-7 on three Conway field goals. Then, with 19 seconds before the half, Herring picked off a Nix pass at midfield. On the first play, Richardson passed to Jurevicius for 43 yards, then hit Archie for an 8-yard TD and with Conway's PAT, State took a 16-7 lead into the intermission. It was all over in the third quarter as the Lions exploded in the mud and two-inch rain fall for four touchdowns with Richardson throwing TD passes of 9 and 20 yards to Engram and another 4-yard TD to Pitts. One TD came after the recovery of a Davis fumble at the Auburn 25 and a second was set up by another Herring interception at the Auburn 34. The final score was 43-14 as Richardson set an Outback Bowl record with his four TD passes on 13-of-24 attempts for 217 yards with one interception but no sacks. Engram won the game's MVP award with his four catches for 113 yards and two TDs and Milne had a career high rushing day with 82 yards on 12 carries. "Penn State handled the elements much better than we did," Bowden told sportswriters, including Roger Mills of the *St. Petersburg Times*. "You don't let weather bother you," Paterno said. "It's there and there's nothing you can do about it." Paterno also lauded his graduating wideout. "Very few athletes have been the deciding factor in more Penn State football games than Bobby Engram," Paterno told Marino Parascenzo of the *Pittsburgh Post-Gazette*.

But Engram's Nittany Lion career was over. Richardson's was not. Paterno expected the quarterback to be even better in 1996. Maybe even take the Lions back to another New Year's Bowl game. Maybe even to Pasadena. But Paterno would miss Engram more than he knew.

The players trudged listlessly into the visitors' locker room at Indiana's Memorial Stadium for the halftime break and the sullen look on their faces told it all. They were a beaten team. And not just for this game. The whole season was etched into their countenance. The humiliating loss to Ohio State. The blundering defeat to Iowa. And now this thrashing by the worst team in the league. Their eyes mirrored their glum mood and Paterno knew he had to do something.

Indiana, winless in the Big Ten and 2-and-6 overall, was ahead 20-10 and it could have been worse. The Hoosiers had bulldozed through the defense for 211 yards on the ground and they had made the offense look so bad that Paterno had pulled his starting quarterback in the second quarter. "It's hard to remember a Penn State team that was punished the way this one was, especially in the first half," Ronnie Christ of the *Harrisburg Patriot-News* would write later. Coming on the heels of an unexpected and lethargic 21-20 loss to Iowa the week before, this first half fiasco was pushing the Lions to the precipice of a woeful season. Sure, State was 6-2. But if this game is lost, then the remaining three games against the conference elite would almost certainly push the Lions over the edge. A season that had looked so promising after the upset over Southern Cal in the Kickoff Classic was about to go into the garbage heap.

No one knew what type of team this would be when preseason practice started in early August. It figured to be a transition year on offense where eight starters had to be replaced, including all of the offensive line except for Tielsch at center. Richardson was back at quarterback and Olsommer at tight end but Paterno had to find a pair of new running backs and wide receivers. Although he never started in '95, Enis wound up as the leading rusher and he was the obvious choice at tailback. But, curiously, Paterno didn't name him the starter until just before the kickoff of the first game. To get depth at tailback, Eberly was shifted back from defense again and two red shirt freshmen, Chafie Fields of Philadelphia and Cordell Mitchell of Syracuse, NY, were in reserve along with West Virginia transfer Jeff Nixon of State College. Sload became the fullback and to give him relief, Paterno moved redshirt freshman Aaron Harris of Exton from tailback and switched Cleary from defensive tackle. Paterno had hoped Scott would stay around for his final year of eligibility but the fifth year senior decided to turn professional. That thrust Jurevicius into the prime receiving role at split end with Campbell and Nastasi battling for the flanker slot and Titcus Pettigrew in reserve. Stephenson and redshirt sophomore Concho Brown gave depth at tight end. The offensive line would be a problem all season because of inexperience and injuries. Promising junior Brad Jones started at short guard against USC but an injury in the game ended his career and Kevin Conlin took over for five games. Ostrowski started at long guard but moved to short guard after the Ohio State game when Paterno shuffled the lineup to get true freshman John Blick into the lineup at long tackle. Marczyk, the long tackle, went to long guard with Henderson and Anderson at the short tackle. Among the other reserves on the offensive line were underclassmen Ryan Fagan, Gabe Tincher, Eric Cole and Chance Bright. True freshman Kenny Watson of Harrisburg became the prime kick returner with Campbell and Herring running back punts. Paterno expected Richardson to be the glue that would fuse the offense into an attacking force. Despite some inconsistency in '95, the Academic All-American had shown his mettle in leading the team to several comeback victories. "I think Wally has an opportunity to be outstanding but he's got to have help (from his wideouts)," Paterno told Matt Herb of *Blue White Illustrated*.

Defense had none of the inexperience problems that the offense had with eight starters and nine other lettermen returning. But another regular, left tackle Scioli, tore up his right knee in the spring

David Macklin, and Derek Fox in the secondary. Paterno was concerned that his defense might not have size but felt that speed and quickness would overcome any deficiencies in bulk. "We will be tough but I don't know if we will be dominating," he told sportswriters. Even with Kania and Conway back to handle the kicking with Pantall as the long snapper and Nastasi as the holder, Paterno felt his special teams would have to play better. "We are going to have to have some great specialty teams if we are going to survive early," he said. He added a former winning high school coach from Maryland and Virginia, Larry Johnson, to his staff to take over the special teams with Bradley moving to the secondary.

Despite all the inexperience on offense, State was picked by the two major polls to battle Ohio State for the Big Ten title. *USAToday/*

Curtis Enis dives for one of his three touchdowns in the 1996 Kickoff Classic victory over USC at Giants Stadium in New Jersey. Enis gained a near-record 241 yards in the game.

and was forced to miss the entire season on a medical redshirt. Junior Matt Fornadel replaced him with Noble back at the other tackle. Short, fully recovered from his foot injury, moved into Killens' right end slot, the so-called X-position which required a rush on the passer. Junior Chris Snyder was at the other end. Aaron Collins, Filardi and Nelson returned at the linebackers with Tate and Miller at the corners and Herring at free safety. With an injury ending Holes career, Lee took over at Hero backed by Penzenik, who also would be injured and miss the season. When Miller was hurt later in the Iowa game, Prater finished up the season at the left corner. Others who would see action on defense included many youngsters from his last two highly-rated recruiting classes with Wedderburn, Seace, redshirt sophomore Mike Buzin, true freshmen Courtney Brown of Alvin, SC, and Eric Sturdifen and redshirt freshman David Fleischhauer in the line; redshirt freshman Maurice Daniels and true freshmen Aaron Gatten and Mack Morrison at linebacker; and redshirt freshman Askari Adams and true freshmen

CNN ranked the Lions 8th with OSU at #10 and Michigan at #11 while the AP had them at #11, with OSU at #9 and Michigan at #14. Northwestern and Iowa also were in the Top 25 with State's Kickoff Classic foe, USC, #6 in *USAToday/*CNN and #7 in the AP. Most of the beat writers covering the Lions figured they would finish with a record anywhere from 10-2 to 8-4. "I think it will be a pretty good year...although they will struggle in some areas," wrote Neil Rudel of the *Altoona Mirror* in picking a 10-2 season. "I don't think they can rebuild the offensive line and come up with the game-breaking receiver they need to win on the road," stated Dick Weiss of the *New York Daily News* with his 9-3 selection. Phil Grosz of *Blue White Illustrated* also chose a 9-3 finish but warned, "...this team could stumble to a 7-5 mark."

The Kickoff Classic against USC at Giants Stadium on August 25 was expected to be an excellent test for State because the three non-conference opponents after that were considered pushovers— at least by the media and fans. Southern Cal was coming off another

Pac-10 championship and a big victory over Northwestern in the Rose Bowl. Coach John Robinson had 29 players back from his two-deep Rose Bowl roster but he had similar problems on the offensive line as Paterno and his defense was supposedly the strong point of his team. A record sellout crowd of 77,716 and an ABC-TV audience watched on a warm Sunday afternoon in the New Jersey Meadowlands as Enis and his teammates ripped the USC defense for 462 net yards in a 24-7 victory. Enis came within 15 yards of Curt Warner's single game rushing record with 241 yards and three touchdowns on 27 carries and immediately had the media buzzing about the Heisman Trophy. "So impressive was Curtis Enis yesterday that, if he does not touch the ball the rest of the season, he still might get some Heisman Trophy votes," wrote David Waldstein in the *New York Post*. Meanwhile, the Lion defense was destroying the Heisman candidacy of USC quarterback Brad Otton who had a miserable day, overthrowing wide open receivers and misguiding the Trojan offense into one jam after another. The absence of USC's best runner, Delon Washington, didn't help but State's aggressive defense held the Trojans to 282 yards in total offense while recovering a fumble that set up State's first points on a 28-yard Conway field goal. USC didn't score until it recovered a fumble in the end zone by Fields with 30 seconds left in the game. Enis scored his first TD on a 24-yard run late in the first half and his third on a 4-yard dive in the fourth quarter. In between, he ran 57 yards early in the fourth quarter set up a 9-yard TD that capped a 93-yard drive and clinched the win. "We couldn't tackle him and that was the deciding factor in the game," Robinson told sportswriters. "When he came off tackle on that long run by our bench...I was the closest person to him, and I sure as hell wasn't gong to tackle him."

Lost in all the excitement about Enis was the performance of State's two quarterbacks. Richardson had looked a little shaky at the start and he threw two interceptions that stopped drives in the first half. "It was a case of everybody being a little nervous," Richardson said after the game. When he aggravated a groin muscle scrambling late in the third quarter, McQueary came on and engineered the two fourth quarter drives of 93 and 42 yards that put the game away. Now, Paterno saw that he had two quarterbacks he could count on.

The Lions had two weeks before the Beaver Stadium opener against Louisville and he warned his players not to get too impressed by their victory. "Southern Cal did not have a good day and didn't play particularly well," Paterno said at a midweek news conference. "I hope we are mature enough...around here that we don't all of a sudden think that we are the greatest thing that ever happened since jelly or something." The remnants of Hurricane Fran swept across Happy Valley on the eve of the Louisville game and it was still raining the next day when the now #7 Lions beat the Cardinals by another 24-7 score. "We didn't play very well on offense," Paterno told sportswriters, although Enis had another fine day, running for 104 yards and a TD on 23 carries. But Richardson hit on just 11-of-33 passes for 118 yards and threw two interceptions. Perhaps the presence of the defensive-minded 1986 National Championship team, which was honored at halftime, turned this into a victory by the defense. This defensive team held Louisville to 50 yards rushing on 31 carries, intercepted three passes and recovered a fumble that led to a first quarter TD that gave the Lions a 14-0 lead. In the second quarter, the special teams came through as Sturdifen blocked a punt which Prater scooped up at the 4-yard line and carried into the end zone. "We have a lot of work to do," Paterno said.

If the next two foes weren't pushovers they were the next thing to it. The first game ever with Northern Illinois ended in a 49-0

rout at Beaver Stadium as Jurevicius and Fields each scored two TDs and Richardson and McQueary both threw TD passes. Enis sat on the bench recovering from a week-long strep throat illness but the nine other running backs gained 310 yards while the two QBs passed for 190 yards on 10-of-15 completions. Before the next game with Temple at Giants Stadium, the Penn State campus was rocked by the sniper killing of a student near the student union building. Then, the team had another emotional letdown when Sandusky's father died and he left for a few days. "We talked all week about how fragile life is," Paterno told the media. In walloping Temple 41-0, State recorded the first back-to-back shutouts since 1978. With Penn State ticket manager Bud Meredith selling some 23,000 tickets, the crowd of 24,847 was the smallest to see the Lions play since the 1976 game at Miami. Six different players scored with Harris getting the first two TDs on runs of 14 and 7 yards and Conway kicking a pair of field goals. After the game Paterno was asked how good his team really was after playing such inferior teams. "I don't have the slightest idea," he said. He didn't really find out the next week either in the Big Ten opener at Wisconsin but he thought he did.

The two easy victories thrust the Lions into #3 in the polls behind Florida and Florida State and they looked the part when they took a 17-3 lead early in the second quarter over unbeaten Wisconsin (3-0) before the third largest crowd in the history of Camp Randall Stadium. But after an out of bounds kickoff by Conway five minutes into the period gave Wisconsin possession at its own 35, Badger coach Alvarez inserted his 260-pound freshman tailback Ron Dayne. As a regional ABC-TV audience watched, Dayne bulled his way for 53 of the next 65 yards, including a 6-yard TD, and Wisconsin was back in the game. With just 33 seconds left in the half, Richardson moved the Lions 49 yards in six plays so that Conway could boot a 28-yard field goal as time ran out and stretch State's lead to 20-10. The Lions had a chance to put the game away in the next 20 minutes but botched a fake field goal attempt at the Wisconsin 14 in the third quarter and failed to make a fourth-and-one at the Badger 30 with 11:34 left in the game. Nastasi had signaled for the fake field goal but the offensive linemen did not hear him because of the crowd noise. On the fourth down play, Enis was stopped for no gain. Later Paterno took the blame for both ill-fated plays as well as other poor play calling, saying, "I sure didn't help the situation...(The fake field goal) was not a good call...(But) We should be able to make a yard and a half (on fourth down)."

After stopping Enis' fourth down run, Wisconsin drove 70 yards in 10 plays for a TD with Dayne barreling into the end zone from 12 yards out carrying two Lion defenders with him. Minutes later, after an exchange of punts backed up the Lions to their own 10-yard line, a pass intended for Brown was batted in the air and intercepted by Wisconsin at the 13-yard line. On fourth down John Hall kicked a 24-yard field goal and with 3:22 remaining the score was tied, 20-20. Now, it was time for Richardson to do what he had done so often under pressure in '95. On the first play after the kickoff, Enis ran 14 yards to the PSU 34. Then, Jurevicius faked a post pattern and streaked down the sideline to grab Richardson's wobbly pass at the Wisconsin 26 before stumbling out of bounds. Three Enis carries and a face mask penalty later the Lions were at the Badger 7 and Conway booted a 23-yard field goal to put State back into the lead with 1:23 left. But the game was far from over even when Wisconsin took the ball at its own 7 following the kickoff. With a couple of key passes, Badger QB Mike Samuel moved his team to the State 40 and with 6 seconds left, Hall tried a 57-yard field goal that would have thrown the game into overtime. The kick was long enough but went wide left by just five feet and the Lions won. It was the 700th victory in PSU history and few had been closer. "Escape From Camp Randall," said the headline in the *Harrisburg Patriot-News*. "This was the kind of game the Nittany Lions needed to prove they could perform under pressure and you can't get much more pressure than yesterday," wrote Lori Shontz in the *Pittsburgh Post-Gazette*. "I didn't do a very good job for our kids today," Paterno told the media. "They won in spite of me."

On the same day of the State thriller over Wisconsin, Ohio State belted Notre Dame 29-16 in South Bend and jumped ahead of the Lions into #3 in both polls. "We're either a little ahead of schedule or a little overrated—one or the other," Paterno told his weekly news conference the following Tuesday. The oddsmakers figured they were overrated for the Buckeyes were made 10 1/2 point favorites for the late afternoon game televised by ABC from Ohio Stadium the following Saturday. "Showdown in the Horseshoe," said the headline in the *Centre Daily Times*. Some showdown. State was blown away and it was 38-0 before the Lions finally tallied midway through the fourth quarter. OSU rushed for 350 yards on the ground and passed for another 215 while limiting the PSU offense to 211 net yards in handing a Paterno team the worst defeat, 38-7, since the 44-7 loss to Notre Dame in 1984. It was a flat out total team defeat and neither Paterno nor his players had any excuses. "There was no excuse. They came right at us and kept going," said Short. "We just got a good whipping every which way," Paterno told sportswriters. "At least now we know how good Lions are," said the *CDT* headline over a column by Ed Morales. "A game as crushing as Saturday's can sometimes cause a ripple effect, giving a team pause in the weeks to come," Morales wrote. "'I would hope that wouldn't happen to us,' Paterno said. 'I would think we're mature enough to avoid something like that.'"

Some players may have been mature but others were not. Before the Lions Homecoming game against Purdue, two of the team's key players had earned Paterno's ire. Jurevicius, now leading the team in receiving, was suspended by Paterno for cutting a class. That might not have seemed like a serious infraction to outsiders nor to the 40,000 other PSU students. But Jurevicius' grades had been so poor in the spring that he had to attend summer school to gain reinstatement. Paterno's "Grand Experiment" has always meant going to class even for those who never make the Dean's List. "I told him the first time he cut a class he'd be suspended for a game and the second time he would be out for two games and the next time he would be out for the season," Paterno told Ron Bracken of the *Centre Daily Times*. "He's got to learn that he's here to get an education first." Some of the players weren't happy with Jurevicius either, particularly after the tough midweek practices. "Guys have to realize that they can hurt the team by not being there," Richardson said. Jurevicius said later he learned his lesson. "I came here and I had an idea stuff like this would happen," he said. "I think this will help me grow." Kania, the punter, had angered Paterno by injuring his ankle while attempting to kick a field goal after Thursday's practice. "It was a stupid thing to do on the Thursday before a big football game," Paterno said. "It didn't light me up." Redshirt freshman Pat Pidgeon became the new punter.

The Ohio State debacle appeared to be forgotten in the first half against mediocre Purdue (2-3). The now #10 Lions were ahead by 24-0 at the intermission as Richardson hit on 10-of-15 passes to set up TD runs of 9 and 3 yards by Enis and a 23-yard Conway field goal in drives of 50, 74 and 76 yards. With about a minute left in the half

Defensive back Kim Herring was a three-year starter and a First-Team All-American in 1996 when he led the Big Ten in interceptions.

Campbell gave the ESPN audience and the alumni crowd of 96,653 a thrill by running back a punt 59 yards for a TD, the first PSU TD return since 1992. But after the break, State looked like a different team. Although the outcome was never in serious doubt, the offense was erratic and could muster just one more TD, again by Enis on a 2-yard run that capped a 67-yard drive early in the fourth quarter. Purdue scored twice on passes midway through the third and fourth quarters and the final score was 31-14. Paterno was not happy. "We're gonna struggle if we don't get better because right now we're not very good." After viewing videotapes of the game, Paterno changed his mind slightly. "Overall, I think we played a pretty good game offensively," but he still wanted the offense to be more consistent. Many of the fans and some in the media were blaming Richardson, who was last in the Big Ten passing statistics. "Yes, the players around him are new. But Richardson's erratic play hasn't helped," said the subheadline over a column by Neil Rudel of the *Altoona Mirror*, "...beneath the surface lurks the suspicion that despite his 15-4 record as a starter, Richardson is mired in quicksand," wrote Rudel.

By the middle of the second half against Iowa, Richardson was being booed by the Beaver Stadium faithful. There were at least 16,000 no shows for the game televised by ESPN as freezing rain, wet snow and blustery winds pelted State College for more than 24 hours. By halftime more than a third of the estimated 80,000 who were there for the kickoff departed and did not return. The Lions were leading 20-14 at the time and Iowa, unbeaten in the Big Ten, was lucky to still be in the game. An 83-yard punt return by the Hawkeyes' All-American Tim Dwight gave Iowa its first TD midway in the first quarter. Then early in the second quarter, Iowa recovered Richardson's fumbled snap at the PSU 45-yard line. The defense seemed to have the Hawkeyes controlled, particularly after a holding penalty but on second-and-34, quarterback Matt Sherman found Dwight open streaking down the sideline and Dwight reached the State 4-yard line before being tackled. Two plays later Iowa's Tavian Banks had the TD. Still, the Lions had domi-

QB Wally Richardson was a master at the two-minute drill. The two-time Academic All-American consistently led the 1995 and 1996 State teams back from late-game deficits.

nated the half, with Harris running 49 yards for one TD, Richardson passing 12 yards to Enis for another and Conway kicking field goals of 24 and 37 yards. But after the intermission, the Lions went into their usual second half stupor. State could cross midfield just once and that was on its initial possession. With Iowa firing in on an all-out blitz, Richardson was sacked four times for 31 yards in losses and could complete just 5-of-16 passes for 45 yards, while the Hawkeyes also jammed the running lanes. An offense that totaled 247 yards in the first half had just 76 in the second. Iowa didn't do much better and was into State territory only three times in the second half but once was enough. Less than two minutes into the fourth quarter, Richardson fumbled after being sacked on a safety blitz and Iowa recovered at the PSU 33. On the first play, Coach Fry went to a trick play and freshman halfback Rob Thein threw an option pass to Demo Odems for 25 yards. Banks scored from the 8 and with Zack Bromert's PAT Iowa took a 21-20 lead. The Lions could not get past their own 38-yard line on three more possessions and a 152-yard rushing day by Harris had been wasted as Iowa won. Most of the post-game media analysis blamed the loss on three factors: the offensive line, Richardson's inept passing and a receiving corps that wasn't measuring up to expectations. "On an afternoon where the Penn State defense was exceptional, it was the offense, long thought to be suspect, that undid this team," wrote Bob Smizik in the *Pittsburgh Post-Gazette*, and Richardson was feeling the pressure. "When the offense doesn't do well, I feel bad...like its my fault," he told sportswriters. "We're gonna have to re-evaluate a lot of things because we didn't get things done today," Paterno said.

State was now sixth in the Big Ten and 17th in the polls but Indiana, 0-4 in the conference, appeared to be the perfect opponent for a rejuvenation. The last time the Lions visited Bloomington in 1994, they were #1 in the *USAToday*/CNN coaches poll but two last minute TDs by the Hoosiers had made the Lions' 35-29 victory seem closer

than it was and many fans believe that game cost State the national title. So that was another motivating component during the week and Paterno told his radio-call in show listeners this team was as ready to play as any team he had coached. Wrong. With Indiana leading 10-3 five minutes into the second quarter and State's offense going nowhere, Paterno yanked Richardson and inserted McQueary as State gained possession at the PSU 33-yard line. McQueary's first two passes were dropped by Jurevicius and Cuncho Brown. Then after a 5-yard penalty for a false start, McQueary found a wide open Jurevicius dashing down the right sideline and hit him for a 57-yard TD. But an 80-yard drive and a 28-yard field goal on the last play of the half had propelled the Hoosiers back in front, 20-10, as the dispirited Lions filed into their dressing room. What happened next would be the defining moment of the season.

Paterno's exact words to his team in that closed locker room have never been made public. But from what the players said later, it was an angry, X-rated tirade that questioned their toughness and challenged their manhood. "I wouldn't want to go down a back alley with any of you guys because I'd be the only one fighting," he reportedly shouted at them. After the game Paterno told the media, "We had a little prayer meeting...We challenged the kids at halftime to make some plays." McQueary stayed in at quarterback and with Enis hurting from a shoulder injury he aggravated in the first half, Eberly, who had just 28 carries in eight games, went in at tailback. Watson started the turnaround with a 52-yard kickoff return and 6-plays later Conway kicked a 44-yard field goal. The defense stopped the Hoosiers and State's next possession ended when McQueary's pass was intercepted at the IU 2-yard line. Then as the third quarter was drawing to a close, McQueary started a drive with a 41-yard pass to Jurevicius to the Indiana 10. Eberly gained 7 off tackle then took a fade pass from McQueary into the end zone. Conway's PAT tied it at 20-20. State got the ball back moments later at the Lion 33 and six plays later on a third-and-8, McQueary hit Jurevicius with a 27-yard pass to the IU 12. A face mask tacked on five more and Fields bolted up the middle for the go ahead TD. Conway's kick with 13:26 left in the game made it 27-20 and it was all over for Indiana. Eberly, who would run for 110 yards, scored another TD on a 4-yard run, Harris had one on a 10-yard dash following a fumble recovery by King, and Filardi scored another on a 24-yard interception before IU tallied in the last minute and the Lions won, 48-26. "Pep Rally (:) Paterno's blistering halftime tirade coupled with some key substitutions spurs PSU to win over Indiana," said the headline in *Blue White Illustrated*.

Even before the team left Bloomington, Paterno had a quarterback controversy. He told his post-game news conference he didn't know who the starter would be for the Northwestern game. "We'll practice them both this week...," he said. "Wally's too good to all of a sudden drop him...but we'll have to see." Richardson told the media, "I don't know exactly how to deal with it...I felt I should have been able to stay out there and play." McQueary said, "Wally is still the leader and...I'm the No. 2 guy." At his weekly Tuesday meeting with reporters, Paterno said Richardson was his quarterback but that didn't stop the fans and media from arguing about it—until the following Saturday evening.

Tenth-ranked Northwestern (7-1) was leading the Big Ten with a 5-0 record and had won 13 straight league games since losing to the Lions at Beaver Stadium in '94. With just Purdue and Iowa remaining on the Wildcat schedule and no game with Ohio State, a win over State

Coach Paterno leads the 1996 team onto the field prior to the Northwestern game.

meant a possible repeat trip to the Rose Bowl. ABC-TV was on hand to televise the late afternoon clash and 96,596 screaming State fans turned out in the chilly wind and light snow to see if the Lions could be a spoiler. State came out sizzling behind a revitalized quarterback, an angry running back and a fired-up defense. A snappy 6-play, 80-yard drive midway through the first quarter gave the Lions a 7-0 lead on a 39-yard run by Enis and on the ensuing kickoff Herring's tackle forced a fumble that Cleary recovered at the Northwestern 19. Six plays later Harris dove over for the TD and the Lions never looked back. In the second quarter, PSU scored on three straight possessions as Richardson threw a 63-yard TD pass to Jurevicius and Conway kicked field goals of 46 and 39 yards that were set up by a Herring interception and a fumble caused by Collins and recovered by Fornadel. Richardson added a 7-yard TD pass to Nastasi in the third quarter and the Lions won convincingly, 34-9. Richardson had his best game since the Wisconsin victory, hitting on 11-of-22 passes for 201 yards with just one interception. Enis ran for 167 yards on 21 carries and later told sportswriters he was mad because of last season's defeat in Evanston. "Their fans were yelling stuff at us after the game," he said. "I took it personal." Meanwhile, the Lion defense was hammering Wildcat quarterback Steve Schnur, the Big Ten total offense leader, and containing running back Darnell Autry. Schnur was sacked seven times for 54 yards in losses, intercepted three times and gained most of his 278 yards on 49 pass attempts when the game was already lost. Autry had 107 yards on 23 carries but never got near the end zone. Much of the post game commentary centered around Richardson, whose selection as a Hall of Fame scholar-athlete by the National Football Foundation was announced at halftime. "I expected Wally to play well," Paterno said. "He took the heat and didn't gripe. He didn't point fingers. He's a team player." Richardson told sportswriters, "We were on a mission today...I wasn't playing to the best of my ability before...I came through. I just tried to prove I can still do that."

It had been nearly 30 years since a team had beaten Michigan three years in a row and rarely did anyone do it twice in 'The Big House." But two weeks later, the Lions went into Ann Arbor and in a classic game of "smash-mouth" football, they took away a 29-17 victory before 105,898 and a national television audience. The game was fairly even in the first half as State led 13-10. But two minutes into the third quarter Richardson was hit on a Michigan blitz just as he tried to throw a swing pass behind the line of scrimmage to Harris and Michigan recovered the "fumbled lateral" at the PSU 30. Two plays later, Chris Howard ran 27-yards and the Wolverines had a 17-13 lead. Midway through the period, Herring's interception at midfield led to Conway's third field goal of the game to cut Michigan's lead to a point with 10:13 left in the quarter. State's defense forced a punt from the UM 18 four plays after the ensuing kickoff and Macklin then made the play of the game. He sprinted in from the left and blocked the punt. Ahmad Collins scooped up the ball at the 3 and went into the end zone. "We were trying to get (a block) because we knew it was there," assistant coach Johnson said after the game. A 2-point pass for the conversion failed but the Lions now led 22-17 with 3:45 left in the quarter. The Lion defense took charge from there as Paterno played it safe with a conservative ball control offense. After the kickoff, Scott Dreisbach drove the Wolverines to the PSU 20 before throwing a pass that Herring tipped and Lee intercepted at the 10-yard line with 12:44 remaining in the game. When Michigan got the ball back, a drive inside the State 40 ended when Nelson forced Dreisbach to fumble on a scramble and Filardi recovered at the 33 with 5:56 left. A minute later, the Wolverines had the ball again at their own 22 after a Lion punt and on the first play Herring again intercepted Dreisbach at the UM 38. Enis ran for a TD on the first down to seal the victory. But there was 4:42 still remaining and sub quarterback Brian Griese tried to rally the Wolverines but his pass to Tai Street in the end zone was literally taken away by Tate with 3:56 left and State ran out the clock. "...What Penn State did defensively here Saturday is what it has done for 30 years," wrote Bracken for the *CDT*. "—It frustrated an offense to the point where it couldn't leave the huddle without making a mistake. It's the way Ham and Reid did it in the 1960s...It is the way Joe Paterno-coached teams have won the vast majority of their games." Paterno told the media, "Beating Michigan, no matter where it is, is great."

Beating Michigan also thrust the Lions into the new Bowl Alliance, which had replaced the Coalition as a new way to try and get a matchup for the National Championship. The Big Ten/Pac-10 champions were still committed to the Rose Bowl, which continued to stay out of the postseason formula put together by the other bowls. But under the new Alliance plan, a Big Ten or Pac 10 team finishing in the Top 10 was eligible for one of the at-large slots in the other major New Year's Day bowls not hosting the national title game. That meant a possible Orange or Fiesta Bowl invitation for the now #7 Lions if they could beat Michigan State in the final game of the season November 23. At the very least, State would probably go to the Citrus Bowl.

Except for Michigan State fans, the 96,263 in Beaver Stadium and the regional television audience were not disappointed the following Saturday. Michigan State was 5-2 in the conference and also playing for a bowl game. The lead changed hands four times and was tied twice as the outcome went down to the final minutes when the Spartans missed their field goal and the Lions made theirs. And just as it was in '95, Richardson was the man who made it happen. After a 14-13 halftime score, Michigan State had gone ahead for the first time midway through the third quarter on a 34-yard TD by Duane Goulbourne

Brett Conway kicked 119 consecutive extra points and holds several PSU kicking records. He was a semi-finalist in both 1995 and 1996 for the Lou Groza Award.

but State regained the lead three minutes later on an 84 yard drive sparked by Enis running for 67 yards and Harris getting the 1-yard TD. Richardson's two-point pass to Jurevicius made it 22-19. Less than two minutes into the fourth quarter, the Spartans tied it on a 19-yard field goal by Chris Gardner after State had thwarted a MSU TD with a goal line stand. The Lions answered with a 69-yard drive that regained the lead 29-22 on a 4-yard TD by Enis and Conway's PAT but the Spartans retaliated with an 84-yard drive to tie it again with 9:02 left. With six minutes remaining the Lions took possession on their own 20 and on the first play Richardson was blindsided and fumbled. MSU recovered at the State 14. Three plays lost two yards and Gardner came in to attempt a 33-yard field goal. It was wide left. There was 4:27 remaining when Richardson entered the huddle and told his teammates, "This is it guys. This is why you all came here." Down the field they went with Enis and Cleary running and Richardson tossing a 27-yard pass to Jurevicius on third-and-7 and a 5-yard pass to Olsommer on third-and-three to the MSU 27. The Spartans took their last time out with 51 seconds and the Lions moved the ball to the 16-yard line, then played for position at the 13. With 16 seconds remaining, State called time out and Conway went in to kick the field goal. The kick was perfect and the Lions won, 32-29. "A kicker can't ask for any more than to have the last game come down to a field goal in the last seconds," Conway told the media. "That's something you prepare for your whole life."

In the next week, the media speculated about a possible Fiesta Bowl game between State and Notre Dame. The Fiesta had the third and fifth picks in the Alliance and made it known that such a game was possible, provided the Irish beat USC in their last game. Notre Dame lost and fell out of the Top 10. Texas surprised Nebraska with a gambling fourth down play that helped win the Big 12 title game and on Alliance Bowl selection day, December 8, State and Texas were picked to meet in the Fiesta Bowl on New Year's night.

THE 1997 FIESTA BOWL
Jan. 1, 1997
Penn State 38, Texas 15
Offensive Player-of-the-Game: Curtis Enis
Defensive Player-of-the-Game: Brandon Noble

Two days after the Lions arrived in Arizona on December 19th, they helped Joe Paterno celebrate his 70th birthday. When asked if he was any closer to retirement, Paterno replied "Right now, I'm having too much fun." His players were having fun, too, even with the two-a-day practices. This was the bowl they had all heard about, the one that State helped push into the big time when it first played here on Christmas Day of 1977, the site of the second national title ten years later and the bowl they had never lost in five appearances. And once again, the Lions were the underdogs. Despite an 8-4 record and 20th ranking, Texas' closing season victories over Texas A&M, 51-15, and Nebraska, 37-27, convinced oddsmakers the Longhorns were at least 1 1/2 points better than #7 State. They were led by a scrambling quarterback, James Brown, who completed 57 percent of his passes for 2,468 yards and 17 TDs and was the team's fifth-best rusher who had been sacked just 16 times. His favorite receiver was trash talker Mike Adams, a high school teammate of State's Shino Prater, who was the godfather of Adams' son. For days before the game, Adams and his mouthy teammate cornerback, Bryant Westbrook, told anyone who would listen what they were going to do to Prater, Richardson and the other Lions. As usual, the State players kept quiet. Their major complaint was about the Fiesta Bowl patch they would have to wear on their jerseys during the game. State had never worn such patches in other bowl games and this one was a garish tribute to the bowl's corporate sponsor, Tostitos. Herring called the patches, "cheesy" but the team was contractually-bound to wear them.

The patches were all forgotten by the second play of the game when Tate intercepted Brown's pass and returned 12 yards to the Texas 26-yard line. With thousands of fans watching on TV back in icy Happy Valley, Richardson passed four yards to Enis for the TD four plays later and the Lions led 7-0. The rest of the first half was a defensive struggle as the Lion offense sputtered and Texas twice drove some 65 yards to State's 11-yard line only to settle for a pair of field goals. If not for a controversial end zone interference penalty on Tate against Adams in the last seconds left in the half, the Lions might have had the halftime lead. But the penalty enabled Texas to cap a 69-yard drive with a 7-yard TD. A 2-point pass for the conversion failed but the Longhorns led 12-7 and seemed to have momentum. They had gained 242 yards to State's 95 in controlling the ball twice as long as the Lions and they appeared to be just one big play from breaking the game open. It was State's Watson who made the big play, exploding for 81 yards on the second half kickoff. Five plays later Harris went five yards off right end with a block from Enis for the TD and Richardson's 2-point pass to Enis made it 15-12. A few minutes later a 33-yard pass to Westbrook off a fake punt on a fourth-and-one at the Texas 34 enabled the Longhorns to move in for a 48-yard field goal to tie the game with 6:50 left in the third quarter. But the Lions launched an 8-play, 65-yard drive on the ensuing kickoff with Enis running four times for 40 yards, including the 2-yard TD that gave State the lead again, 22-15. With a minute left in the quarter, State took possession at the PSU 13 following a punt and here's where another of the young Lions helped clinch the game. Richardson rolled out and handed off to Eberly, who gave the ball to

Fields running left from the flanker slot and Fields broke loose for 84 yards before being tackled at the 3. Two plays later, Cleary bulled over and State led, 28-15 as the third quarter ended. In the fourth quarter Conway kicked a 23-yard field goal and Enis scored a 12-yard TD and the Lions won, 38-14, as the players drenched Paterno in water and Gatorade on the sideline.

The victory was especially significant for the 16 seniors who had compiled a 42-7 record and four bowl victories in four years. "This lunchbucket gang wanted to bow out a winner and jump start their young teammates of the future," wrote Christ of the *Patriot-News*. "They delivered on both counts." Some sportswriters also lauded Richardson for for what he had done to bring the Lions back from the edge and earn a final #7 rating. "Showered with boos early in the season, Richardson never received nor took credit for the (season's) second-half turn around," wrote Geoff Mosher for the *"Daily Collegian."* "(Now) he's the quarterback of the Outback Bowl and Fiesta Bowl champion Lion football teams."

"Let's win this game as the first step to even better things," Paterno had repeatedly told his team in Arizona. But the "better things" would have to wait at least another year, for the coach always says, "you either get better or you get worse." In 1997, it got better then much worse.

Season Record 11-2
Record to Date 706-296-42
Winning percentage .696

1997

"Say It Ain't So, Curtis & Joe"

Maybe State was jinxed from the beginning of the season. After all, there was Joe Jurevicius' photo on the cover of *Sports Illustrated's* college football preview issue over the headline "Penn State is No. 1." The JINXED cover of *SI*! Then, there was the #1 preseason ranking by the Associated Press. Since the AP's preseason poll started in 1950, only eight teams had gone on to win the National Championship and four of those teams were named Oklahoma. It should have been a bad omen that two of the last three teams to do it were Oklahoma in 1985 and Alabama in 1978 and all Penn State football fans remember what happened in those years! And if that was not enough, who ever heard of opening the season against Pitt? That was the one-time bitter backyard rivalry game that was supposed to end every season, not start it. Who did these Panthers from the inferior Big East think they were? Michigan State?

Now, is it any wonder that the 1997 season turned out the way it did? Lofty expectations, a Heisman Trophy candidate and another early run at the national title at the beginning. And an embarrassing defeat, a tough bowl loss and a mini-scandal at the end. "Whether we are as good as some people think we are or not we will find out," Paterno said on the first day of preseason practice. The day after the 21-6 loss to Florida in the Citrus Bowl Paterno told the media, "I'm never going to be satisfied with 9-3. That's not my nature. We want to be right there at the top...We probably came out as well as we could considering everything that happened to us."

Surely the record crowd of 60,000 that showed up on April 26 for the annual Blue-White game could not envision how the season eventually would be remembered. But there was an early sign in Beaver Stadium that day that most folks have forgotten. Despite having to break in a new quarterback, Paterno kept his leading receiver out of spring practice because Jurevicius had become what Paterno called "loosey-goosey" with his academics. So, when Paterno threw Jurevicius off the team prior to the Citrus Bowl for ignoring his classroom responsibilities, no one should have been surprised. When you play for Joe Paterno, you go to class. Period. And when you play for Joe Paterno, you don't consort with sports agents while you're still on the team. For 12 games, Curtis Enis was the darling of the fans, giving 100 percent and humbly thanking his teammates at every opportunity as he became the third leading rusher in Lion history and an All-American. Then, sadly, he blew it on a $325 suit and a clumsy cover-up story that he will have to live with for the rest of his life. In the end, Jurevicius and Enis had let their teammates down before the most important game of the season. Long after the 9-3 record is but a fading memory and the crushing losses to Michigan and Michigan State are nearly forgotten, 1997 will be remembered as the season of Curtis and Joe—for all the good that they did this year and for what they could have done but didn't. Say it ain't so, Curtis & Joe!

That does not mean Enis and Jurevicius are to blame for the 9-3 record. Even with one or both in the lineup, the Lions still might have lost to Florida. Perhaps, as the underclassmen who return in '98 have hinted, there was an overall lack of leadership by the seniors on the 1997 team. Perhaps. But there also were on field malfunctions, particularly by the veteran defense that was supposed to be the soul, if not the heart, of the team. In the post season analysis, many of the beat reporters covering the Lions were critical of the defensive strategy as well as the small size of the downfront linemen, the speed limitations of the linebackers and the height and speed of the secondary. "...Lack of size is part of the problem (but)..the common thread among (the dominating defenses in college football 1997) is that they use an attacking style," wrote Phil Grosz in *Blue White Illustrated*. "They've got to get with the defense of the '90s," wrote Ronnie Christ in the *Harrisburg Patriot-News*. The small size of the offensive line also was criticized and in looking ahead to 1998, the writers covering the Citrus Bowl made special note of two big true freshmen who saw a lot of playing time against Florida at tackle, 6-foot-7, 330-pound Kareem McKenzie and 6-foot-5, 305-pound Jordan Caruso. Of course, sportswriters are notorious second-guessers of coaches, even of 70-year-old legends. Only Paterno and his assistants know and understand what really happened with the defensive breakdowns in 1997.

Certainly, a fifth-year senior quarterback with limited experience didn't make it easier. But McQueary, the popular hometown favorite known fondly as "Big Red," probably played as well as he could have over the 12-game stretch. Another year's experience and who knows. It was an ineffective offense as well as an inept defense that led to the 34-8 defeat to Michigan in the pivotal game of the year and to the 48-14 loss to Michigan State. But it wasn't all the fault of the quarterback as many ill-informed State fans presume. Perhaps the defining moment of the season came in the Homecoming game against weak Minnesota when fullback Aaron Harris, one of the heroes of the Ohio State game a week earlier, went down with a knee injury in the second quarter and didn't play the rest of the season. Without Harris to balance the running of Enis and the receiving of the wideouts, the offense didn't seem the same, and Minnesota's defense was the first to exploit that weakness. Even though the Minnesota game was eventually won by the Lion defense, the heavily underdog Gophers probably uncovered a major flaw in the defense with the runs up the middle by tailback Thomas Hamner, who gained 154 yards on 32 carries despite a rather impotent Minnesota passing attack. Later, in the embarrassing losses to Michigan and Michigan State, the defense was simply manhandled and over matched, particularly in the running game.

Still, when preseason practice began there was every reason to be optimistic, with 42 lettermen returning, including 13 starters. McQueary was the "rookie" in the new starting backfield that had Enis and Harris at the running backs and Jurevicius and Nastasi at the wideouts. With Sload's career also finished by an injury, when Harris was hurt Cleary moved up to start at fullback while Fields and Pettigrew subbed as receivers. Blick and Ostrowski were back in the offensive line joined by Cole, Fagan and Conlin, who moved back to center where he also was the snapper on field goals and extra points. Wedderburn was switched from defense to short tackle and eventually replaced Fagan in the latter part of the season. Others who would see time on the offensive line included Rich Stankewicz, Gabe Tincher and Josh Mitchell. Cuncho Brown was at tight end, backed by Scioli, who moved over from defense after sitting out '96 recovering from his injury. On defense, Snyder returned at one end and Fornadel at left tackle. Fleischhauer moved up to the other tackle and Courtney Brown became the pass rushing left end as Short was shifted to his natural position at middle linebacker. Aaron Collins and Nelson were back to start for their third straight year as the outside linebackers and, along with Short, would be initial candidates for the Butkus Award as the nation's outstanding linebacker. Later, Daniels would start three games at the inside when Short was hurt in midseason with Morrison and true freshman LaVar Arrington of Pittsburgh and Gatten in reserve. Jason Collins, who had not played since breaking his leg in the Rutgers game of '95, received a sixth year of eligibility from the NCAA for medical reasons and took over at Hero with Lee moving to free safety. Prater and King started at the cornerbacks but by the Northwestern game Macklin took over at right corner. Fox, Adams, Ahmad Collins, Buzin, Seace, Amani Bell, Justin Kurpekis, Joe Sabolevski, Marc Kielmeyer and true freshman Greg Ransom were among the defensive reserves. Pidgeon did the punting and sophomore walk-on Travis Forney of nearby Lock Haven beat out highly regard freshman recruit Casey Hannon to succeed Conway as the placekicker. Eberly became the prime kick and punt returner along with Watson. It was a young team with just 13 seniors and 18 veterans who were redshirt or true sophomores. "The kids have worked hard," Paterno told the media a few days before the opening game with Pitt, "...but now they've got to be able to go out there and get skillful with what they're doing...I really don't know how good we are because we're so tired." But he was confident about his quarterback from State College. "Anytime we've asked him to do anything, he's done it well."

In tabbing State at #1, *Sports Illustrated* said, "Paterno has a lot of the pieces necessary to become the ninth coach to win at least three national championships." If the Lions weren't picked #1 in the preseason, they usually were #2 behind either Washington, Colorado, Tennessee or one of the Florida teams. That's where the *USAToday/CNN* coaches' poll and *Sporting News* had them. The AP placed OSU at #9 with Michigan at #14, Wisconsin at #24 and Michigan State at #25. Most of the PSU beat writers figured they would lose at least one game, two at the most, and Mark Brennan's comments for *BWI* were prophetic: "Look for PSU to crack under pressure in one game, per-

haps Michigan or Michigan State." Of the 14 contributors to the *Penn State Football Annual* making predictions, only freelance sportswriter Steve Halvonik went as low as 9-3, saying, "something tells me it's going to be a chilly autumn without a proven QB. PSU will be only a shadow of its former self."

The facile and flashy performance of the team in the first four games may have lulled everyone into a false sense of satisfaction, even though no one overrated the quality of the opposition. The warm, sunny weather for the September 6 opener at Beaver Stadium was perfect and a record crowd of 97,115 showed up for the first game with Pitt since State entered the Big Ten in 1993. The Panthers' new coach, Walt Harris, had been the offensive coordinator at Ohio State the last four years and he figured an 8-man defensive line was the way to stop Enis and Harris and put the pressure on the Lions' new quarterback. So, "Big Red" showed him. He broke Todd Blackledge's 16-year school record for yardage with 366 yards and two touchdowns on 21-of-36 passes without an interception. McQueary also snapped John Hufnagel's total offense record set in 1972 by adding four yards rushing for a total of 370 yards. He threw touchdown passes of 14 yards to Jurevicius and 32-yards to Nastasi as the Lions built up a 34-3 lead at the end of three quarters and won, 34-17. Enis was still able to gain 85 yards and two TDs on 20 carries but "Big Red" was the story of the game. "Red Dawn," screamed the headline across the sports page of the hometown paper, the *Centre Daily Times*. "You guys probably didn't think that I had that much of an arm," McQueary kidded the media after the game.

The next Saturday, it was more of the same against Temple, which was finally going off State's schedule after this game. A fumble by Concho Brown on the first play from scrimmage enabled Temple to score within 43 seconds on a quick 2-play strike from the Lion 48-yard line and the game was still 7-7 at the end of the first quarter. Then, Fields ran 43-yards for a TD on a reverse at 8:27 of the second quarter and the rout was on. Fields scored from the 47 on another reverse and McQueary threw TD passes of 25 yards to Nastasi and 35 yards to Jurevicius as the Lions won, 52-10. McQueary was 10-for-19 and 158 yards without an interception and Enis had just 81 yards rushing on 16 carries but Paterno said it was Temple's concentration on Enis that made the reverses work. Enis told reporters, "the most important thing is that we are winning and getting better...I can't control a defense keying on our running game...But I can control how hard I go out there and play..."

The first away game at Louisville had a similar start as the Temple game when the Cardinals' Sean Redman startled the national TV audience by throwing a 65-yard TV pass on the third play from scrimmage. Then, as a crowd of 39,826 including former heavyweight boxing champ Muhammad Ali looked on in the 80-degree heat of Cardinals Stadium, the Lions scored 50 points in the first half and won, 57-21. It was the first time since 1947 that a State team had rolled up that many points in the first half. McQueary and Jurevicius combined for three touchdown passes of 57, 8 and 67 yards as "Big Red" hit on 10-of-18 attempts for 219 yards without an interception. Enis carried just 14 times but had TDs of 29, 4 and 10 yards and Aaron Collins returned an interception 57 yards for another TD. "Don't read too much into (these victories)," wrote Neil Rudel of the *Altoona Mirror*. "...This nonconference schedule has proved almost nothing."

What it did prove is that the AP pollsters didn't think much of the three victories. Florida's 33-20 victory over Tennessee that followed the Louisville game on national TV moved the previously #3 Gators ahead of the Lions in the September 22 voting with Nebraska up to #3 following the Cornhuskers upset over then #2 Washington. "...Everyone knows that polls are a popularity contest at this stage," Paterno said in a Big Ten coaches' teleconference that Tuesday. "There will come a time, I would hope, when there will be legitimate reasons for picking one team over another...it's a guessing game right now."

Two weeks later, State opened it Big Ten schedule with another easy victory over winless Illinois at Champaign, 41-6. McQueary connected on TD passes of 57 and 20 yards to Jurevicius and a 60-yarder to Fields in rolling up 266 yards on 13-of-21 completions. He also threw his first interception of the year. Enis went over 100 yards for the first time in the season, with 108 yards an TDs of 11 and 4 yards on 14 carries. "The fun and games are over for Joe Paterno and his Penn State football team," wrote Ron Christ in the *Patriot-News*. "It's time for Ohio State to come to Beaver Stadium. It's time for Penn State to prove it deserves its No. 2 ranking in the national polls."

The October 11th clash with Ohio State at Beaver Stadium was the "biggest game" in Happy Valley since the 1992 confrontation with Miami. Certainly, there had been significant games in State College since then, including the first ever game with Michigan in '93 and the pasting of OSU in '94 but this one was another of those turning point type of encounters. Tickets were being sold for up to $350 and on game day five men were arrested for selling some 3,000 counterfeit tickets which led to dozens of squabbles inside the stadium when people showed up for the same seats. State was a 6 1/2 point favorite over the #7 Buckeyes and another record crowd of 97,282 was on hand in perfect weather for the late afternoon game televised by ABC. Except for Alabama, no team had beaten a Paterno squad three years in a row and the '96 thrashing at Ohio Stadium still rankled the Lion veterans, especially Enis. In the pre-game hype, some media mavens condensed

Hometown favorite Mike McQueary was the first quarterback from State College High School to start for Joe Paterno, waiting four years for his chance and helping lead the Lions to a 9-3 record.

the game into a battle between the team's two central impact players— Enis and OSU's sophomore All-American linebacker, Andy Katzenmoyer. Of course, it wasn't that simple. But Enis, the Ohio native who passed up the Buckeyes when they botched his recruiting, had taken this game as a personal challenge after receiving hate mail following his lackluster performance in the '96 loss at Columbus.

The Lions jumped off to a 10-0 lead in the first seven minutes on an opening drive of 81 yards keyed by the passing of McQueary and the running of Enis and Harris, then got a 23-yard Forney field goal after Lee recovered a Pepe Pearson fumble at the Buckeye 16-yard line on OSU's second play. The Bucks made it 10-3 by the end of the first quarter but with the Lion defense stuffing the Buckeye running game, coach Cooper inserted his passing quarterback Joe Germaine in the second quarter and Germaine immediately led a 70-yard drive to tie the score on a 35-yard TD pass to Dee Miller. But with Enis running for gains of 13 and 12 yards and McQueary passing 21 yards to Jurevicius, the Lions retaliated with a 7-play, 72-yard march and a 6-yard TD on a pass to Nastasi to regain the lead with 10 minutes left in the half. Now, OSU seemed to grab the momentum as McQueary misfired on his passes. One Buckeye drive of 72-yards resulted in another field goal and the Bucks just missed a third field goal after another 72-yard drive as the half ended. State still had the lead, 17-13, but not for long. The third quarter was nearly all OSU's. With the Lion passing attack still stuttering and the offense not moving, the Buckeyes scored two TDs on drives of 50 and 80 yards as Germaine picked apart the Lion defense with his passing. Pearson's 8-yard TD pass reception and the PAT put the Buckeyes ahead 27-17 with 1:42 left in the third quarter and the huge crowd was getting edgy. "I said to myself we'd find out what kind of team we are right now," Paterno told the media later.

Following the kickoff into the end zone, Enis ran for nine yards, then for seven. McQueary finally found a receiver and hit Jurevicius for 13 yards to the State 49-yard line. On the next play, Harris took the handoff, slashed left, zigzagged his way downfield, bouncing off three would-be tacklers and sprinted into the end zone. Forney's PAT made it a 3-point game with the crowd on its feet, screaming "Defense, Defense." Sacks by Short and Snyder and a pass reception that missed a first down by a yard forced OSU to punt and the Lions took over at their 14-yard line early in the fourth quarter. On the third play, Enis went off tackle for 25 yards and the Lions were on their way. McQueary hit Brown for 10 yards, then Jurevicius for 8 and in seven plays State was at the OSU 26. Enis blasted through a hole over right tackle, got a block by Scioli on Katzenmoyer and no one was about to stop him. Forney's PAT made it 31-27 with 10:31 still left. Back came the Buckeyes but Germaine was intercepted by Lee at the State 15. Ohio State had one more shot with about three minutes left and possession at its 39-yard line. Macklin broke up a deep pass. A blitz forced Germaine to overthrow a receiver, then Short tipped a pass that fell incomplete. On fourth down, Lee batted down a pass intended for Ken-Yon Rambo and the Lions took over with 2:24. Behind Enis' running, the Lions moved swiftly to the OSU 5-yard line but Paterno ordered McQueary to "take a knee" instead of trying to score again. The bend-but-don't-break pass defense which had given up 456 yards had saved the 31-27 victory. "Nittany Lions say their emotional win for Ohio State proves... 'We're for real,'" said the front page headline over Ron Bracken's report in the *Centre Daily Times*. Enis, who had his best rushing day since the '96 Kickoff Classic, gaining 211 yards on 23 carries, cried in the dressing room. "My heart bleeds blue and white and it always will," he told reporters. "I've never been so happy in my life, to play Ohio State and come out with a win," said Jurevicius, another Ohio native. "I think we're pretty good, obviously, but we've got a long way to go," Paterno said.

A few hours later, LSU upset Florida, 28-21, and on Monday, the Lions moved to the top of both the AP and *USAToday*/CNN polls. OSU dropped into a virtual tie with Michigan State at either #11 or #12, but coming up fast was Michigan at #5. "Penn State appears to have its fate in its own hands in its run to finish No. 1," wrote Ray Parrillo in the *Philadelphia Inquirer*. "Penn State's credentials would be hard to question if it swept through a remaining schedule that includes two currently undefeated teams—Michigan and Michigan State..." But first there was Minnesota, and Paterno told his weekly news conference the team needed "maturity, leadership and common sense" to put OSU in the past and concentrate on the Gophers. "Hopefully, they understand the need to be ready or they'll get licked."

Maybe the young Lions couldn't be faulted for looking ahead four weeks to the invasion of Michigan. Minnesota certainly didn't look like it posed a threat with a 0-2 conference record, 2-4 overall, and an underdog by 34 points. State's offense was sluggish from the start and McQueary's only pass completion in five attempts in the first half turned into a misfortune when Harris was tackled hard in the second quarter after running 10 yards on a screen pass and ripped his knee apart. McQueary also was stunned on a hard hit while scrambling in the first quarter and it seemed to affect him the entire game. The offensive line was ragged and the Minnesota running game was picking up yardage by the chunks. Still, State's defense was able to keep the Gophers out of the end zone but as the Homecoming crowd and ESPN audience watched, Minnesota used field goals of 52, 23 and 32 yards by Adam Bailey to take a surprising 9-3 halftime lead. After the undefeated team of 1947 was honored during the intermission, the third quarter didn't start much better. State's drive on the second half kickoff ended at the UM 30-yard line after a sack forced a punt and later in the period Bailey kicked a 50-yard field goal to stretch Minnesota's lead. The Gophers almost had another field goal late in the quarter after recovering an Enis fumble at the PSU 43 but Courtney Brown, who was playing with a bandaged left hand, broke through to block it. However on the next play, Cleary bobbled a flare pass and Minnesota intercepted. Seven plays later Bailey booted a 33-yard field goal for a 15-3 lead less than a minute into the fourth quarter. That seemed to wake up the offense. With McQueary hitting twice for first down passes, the Lions marched from the PSU 25 and, with the help of a questionable third down interference penalty on a pass to Enis, moved to a first-and-goal at the six. Enis banged over on the next play and Forney's boot made it 15-10 with 9:02 left in the game. Less than a minute later, Macklin intercepted and State had the ball at the Minnesota 34 with the home crowd smelling a come-back victory. A 20-yard scramble by McQueary helped reach the Minnesota 6 but McQueary's fourth down pass into the end zone fell off Scioli's finger tips. With less than six minutes remaining and the Lions out of time outs, Minnesota had a chance to run out the clock. Tailback Thomas Hamner, who had been running through the Lions all day, picked up eight yards on two plays but before the third down, Minnesota inexplicably called its last time out. Then, instead of a safe handoff play, first year coach Glen Mason called for a pitchout. Hamner fumbled it and Snyder recovered at the UM 10-yard line. Enis barreled around right end on the next play for the TD at the 3:59 mark and the crowd roared. A 2-point pass for the conversion

failed. The Lion defense stopped Minnesota's last possession inside the UM 10 with Brown smashing through two blockers to make a third down sack, and McQueary kneeled down to run out the clock and escape with the 16-15 victory. "This time there was no back-patting, no helmet-raising," wrote Kimberly Jones in the *Centre Daily Times*. "Whatever celebrating the top-ranked Nittany Lions did...on Saturday was subdued." "We got outcoached and outplayed," Paterno said. "Sometimes championship teams get lucky," Nelson told reporters.

But the narrow win gave the pollsters another excuse to discredit the Lions as Nebraska beat Texas Tech, 29-0, and leaped over State in both the AP and *USAToday*/CNN rankings. Two weeks later, State slipped to #3 in the coaches ratings and lost ground in the media voting after beating Northwestern, 30-27, in Evanston. This time, the Lions only had themselves to blame after blowing a 17-point lead over the 3-and-6 Wildcats with four minutes left in the game. State led 21-7 at the half and could have been ahead by four TDs. However, the kicking team gave up a 41-yard pass off a fake punt midway in the second quarter and that allowed Northwestern to score a TD. Then with time winding down in the half, the Lions moved to a first down at the Wildcat 9. But McQueary tripped over a guard and a holding penalty forced a 45-yard field goal attempt which bounced off a goal post. Still, the Lions held a 30-13 lead with 3:33 remaining in the game when Mitchell fumbled after a 14-yard run and Northwestern recovered at its own 41-yard line. Back into the game went the first team defense. Three plays later, quarterback Tim Hughes hit freshman tailback Brian Marshall over the middle and Marshall ran 45 yards for the TD. State tried to run out the clock but Northwestern stopped two running plays, calling time out each time, then sacked McQueary for an 11-yard loss. Pidgeon punted out of the end zone to the State 44 and with 1:47 left, Northwestern went the distance on 9 plays, with Musso catching passes of 15 and 11 yards before scoring the TD on a 9-yard pass. The PAT made it 30-27 with 28 seconds remaining. Pettigrew recovered the onside kick and State won but Northwestern had almost spoiled Enis' big day of 153 yards on 27 carries. "We played dumb...(and) we lost our poise a little bit at the end," said Paterno. "If they continue to play as they did yesterday," wrote Bruce Keidan in the *Pittsburgh Post Gazette*," they won't beat Michigan. They won't come close."

So, even if the fans did not want to believe it, the signs were there for what would happen two weeks later. State's offense was stumbling at crucial times and the defense was bumbling with a minus four in turnover ratio, recovering just three fumbles in seven games and intercepting just 8 passes for 76 yards. Fourth-ranked Michigan, led by All-American switch hitting cornerback/wide receiver, Charles Woodson, was among the top five defenses in almost every category and had not allowed a touchdown in the second half. "Michigan is riding high on a defense that takes no prisoners," wrote Christ of the *Patriot-News*. "Penn State is still riding high on a defense that allows its prisoners out on bail." This game was even bigger than the Ohio State game a month before. Bracken of the *CDT*, who had covered almost all of the Paterno era, wrote that it might even be the biggest game ever in Beaver Stadium, comparing it to the momentous '82 Nebraska game and the '80 Pitt game when both teams were 9-1 and ranked in the Top 5. "It's definitely the first time two ranked, unbeaten teams have collided in the steel structure this late in the season," he wrote.

Once again a record crowd of 97,498, some paying $500 a ticket, turned out for the late afternoon nationally televised contest. Four days before the game, Paterno told reporters he didn't "know

Aaron Collins was the last of the five Collins brothers. He was a starting LB for 36 consecutive games and co-captain of the 1997 team. He was the most recent Lion selected as a Hall of Fame scholar-athlete and to earn a NCAA Post Graduate Scholarship.

whether we're ready for this game or not." They weren't. The emotion was probably on Michigan's side from the beginning. After all, the Lions had beaten them three straight, including two in "the Big House," and the Wolverines may have had more pride on the line. State was favored by 3 but Michigan defensive end Glen Steele set the tone of the game on State's first play. Paterno wanted McQueary to fake a reverse to Fields, then throw a pass downfield. But Steele brushed past his blocker and sacked McQueary before he knew what hit him. The Lions punted and the second defining play of the game came on Michigan's possession when Griese threw an incompletion on a third-and-15 at the State 47 but was roughed up by Short. The 15-yard penalty enabled Michigan to score a 29-yard field goal and State's defense never seemed to recover. "Maybe we'll get the message about dumb penalties," Paterno said after the game. If there was any doubt about the type of day it was going to be for the Lions, it was settled in a two-play sequence early in the second quarter. On a second-and-7 at the Michigan 23, Griese, who was not known for his running, embarrassed the State defenders by scrambling for a 40-yard gain down the right sideline in front of the Wolverine bench. On the next play, Woodson blew past the State secondary and hauled in a 37-yard TD pass. The final score of 34-8 made this the worst home loss ever for Paterno. "And now we know," wrote Diane Pucin of the *Philadelphia Inquirer.* "The Penn State team that beat Ohio State, that was a fake. The Penn State team that should have lost to Minnesota and almost lost to Northwestern, that's the real team....Now we know." But comments like that didn't give enough credit to Michigan. "It's hard to remember when a Michigan team played this well," wrote long-time Wolverine follower Joe Falls for the *Detroit News.* "They were almost faultless in everything they did. Can you remember them playing so beautifully?" Leave it to an offensive lineman to sum up the realities of the game. "They kicked the crap out of us," Ostrowski told the media.

Even Paterno was not sure his demoralized team could bounce back. "We've got to find out if we're good enough to win a football game," Paterno said at his Tuesday news conference. "We may lose the next three football games." That afternoon at practice, the players said later, was "Bloody Tuesday." The Lions had fallen to #6 in the polls, behind #5 Ohio State, and now had to face red-hot

Purdue, which was 7-2 and #19 in country after coming from behind an 11-point deficit in the last two minutes to beat Michigan State, 22-21. The Boilermaker program had been resurrected by the run-and-shoot passing offense of new coach Joe Tiller and the ineffectiveness of State's pass defense against Northwestern and Michigan seemed to make another blowout loss possible. Purdue quarterback Billy Dicken threw 60 passes and completed 33 for 347 yards and two touchdowns in West Lafayette but the Lions picked off two interceptions in the fourth quarter to set up touchdowns in a 42-17 victory. The game was close in the first half with State leading by just 14-10 at the intermission. But a 72-yard drive capped by a 4-yard TD run by Enis stretched the lead with five minutes left in the third quarter, then McQueary threw a 67-yard bomb to Enis four minutes later to go up 28-9. Midway through the fourth quarter Jason Collins returned an interception 53 yards to set up a 30-yard run by Enis for a TD and Daniels finished the scoring with the runback of a 27-yard interception with about three minutes left in the game. Enis had his sixth straight rushing game over 100 yards with 186 yards on a personal record of 37 carries. He also had a third TD on a 14-yard run and caught three passes for 83 yards. McQueary also had his best day in a weeks, completing 16-of-24 passes for 253 yards and two TDs without an interception. The following week, Enis and McQueary followed up with an equally impressive performance in a 35-10 win over #24 Wisconsin in the Beaver Stadium finale. Enis ran for 138 yards on 17 carries, including a 78-yard TD around right end on State's first offensive play of the second half and another TD for 13 yards in the second quarter. McQueary threw TD passes of 20 and 42 yards to Jurevicius and one of 28-yards to Nastasi as he completed 16 of his 19 passes for 269 yards without an interception. Jurevicius' 42-yard reception was a crowd-pleasing Hail Mary on the last play of the half which gave State a 21-3 lead and broke open the game. "Obviously, it was a great way to go out in our last day in this Stadium," McQueary told sportswriters. Paterno said he "was really pleased with the defense," which had controlled the Badgers and their elephant sized offensive line and running backs, holding Ron Dayne and the others to 171 yards on 55 carries.

With Ohio State getting beaten by Michigan, the resurging Lions jumped back to #4 in both polls and now had another shot at an Alliance Bowl on New Year's Day. Michigan was now #1 and playing in the Rose Bowl with #2 Nebraska and #3 Tennessee all but set for the Alliance's so-called championship game in the Orange Bowl. The Sugar Bowl, with the third and fifth picks this year, wanted to match State against #5 Florida State, which had been knocked from the unbeaten ranks that same weekend by Florida, 32-29. "It all depends on what happens next week at Michigan State," the Sugar Bowl's Jim Flower told the media.

What happened at Michigan State, as we now know, was another beating even more painful than the one rendered by the Wolverines. This time, the Lions encountered a team that had lost *four straight* to Penn State, twice in the last minute and once blowing a 20-point lead. "I made a statement (after last year's game) that it didn't matter if we went 1-10 the next season as long as that one win was against Penn State," MSU's fifth-year senior linebacker Ike Reese told the *Detroit Free Press* a few days before the game. The Spartans' 3-4 conference record (6-4 overall) was deceiving for they had outplayed Purdue and Northwestern only to lose by quirks in the waning moments. Not only that, but a trip to Hawaii for the Aloha Bowl was in the wings if they beat the Lions. The determined look on the MSU players

State's assistant coaches have a combined service of more than 160 years at Penn State. They are (left to right): Front Row – Tom Bradley, Fran Ganter, Head Coach Joe Paterno, Jerry Sandusky, Joe Sarra, Josh Kroell (graduate assistant); Back row – Dick Anderson, Kenny Jackson, Jay Paterno, Larry Johnson, Bill Kenney, John Thomas (strength coach), Dave Opfar (graduate assistant).

as they made their traditional group march in stony silence from the athletic center to Spartan Stadium to put their uniforms on was the first clue of what was ahead. The MSU players said later they knew from watching videotapes that they could run on the Lions and run they did. Utilizing a two tight end, one-back set, the Spartans crunched the Lions as tailbacks Sedrick Irvin and Marc Renaud took turns going up the middle and around the ends until they became the second pair of backs in NCAA Division 1-A history to run for over 200 yards in a single game, with Irvin getting 238 yards on 28 carries and Renaud picking up 203 on 21 attempts. However, the Spartans led by just 14-7 at the half, after missing a couple of other scoring chances and allowing Enis to break away for a 54-yard TD run with just 1:43 left before intermission. When PSU opened the third quarter by marching 75-yards in 7 plays for a 14-yard TD pass from McQueary to Jurevicius, it looked like the Lions were about to make another of those patented second half comebacks against the Spartans. But MSU snapped back with an 8-play, 74-yard drive and a 19-yard Irvin TD, then sacked McQueary on the Lions next series to force a fumble at the PSU 17 and scored five plays later on an 8-yard pass to Irvin. The last 15 minutes were pure misery and Penn State's players looked like they just wanted to get out of Spartan Stadium as soon as they could. "They took it to us," McQueary said. The 49-14 beating was the worst lost for State since the Notre Dame game of 1984 and the first time in eight years a Lion team had lost the last game of the regular season. "We've walked off the field after we've kicked somebody's ears in," Paterno said. "Now, someone's done it to us." The headline in the *Michigan State Journal* the next morning told it all, "Redemption." "(This) may have been the greatest single performance in MSU's 101 seasons," wrote Jack Ebling. So, now it was the Lions turn to redeem themselves as they dropped to #12 and headed for the Citrus Bowl and a game with #6 Florida.

On Friday, December 19, Harrisburg TV station WHTM reported that sports agent Jeff Nalley had bought Enis a suit at a Harrisburg area mall in early December for Enis to wear on an ESPN awards show. No one could believe it and initially Enis and the agent both denied the story. The controversy swirled for five days until Enis joined the team in Melbourne, Florida, on December 23 and admitted to Paterno what he had done. Nalley had not only bought him a suit but other clothing worth a total of $1,100. Two days before, Paterno had announced that Jurevicius was no longer with the team because of academic reasons. Jurevicius had cut one too many classes and he knew what the penalty would be. Now, Paterno sent Enis home. For the first time in Paterno's 48 years as an assistant and coach at Penn State, a player had violated a major NCAA ruling and smeared the university's clean football image. Say it ain't so, Curtis & Joe.

THE 1998 CITRUS BOWL
Jan. 1, 1997
Florida 21, Penn State 6

The specter of Enis and Jurevicius permeated the Citrus Bowl even as the focus shifted to the game and the coaching styles of the two coaches. Florida's Steve Spurrier was the brash, innovative loud mouth product of a younger generation who relished running up the score on his opponents with his flashy, high scoring offense. Paterno was the sophisticated elder statesman from another era where you ran the ball more than you passed and respected your opponent on and off the field. The wiseacre from the South versus the legend from Brooklyn. But they had a lot in common as strong family men and grandfathers. There was even a personal family tie because the great uncle of Spurrier's wife was none other than Paterno's coach and his

Penn State patron saint, Rip Engle. To the surprise of a lot of sportswriters, Spurrier was a different person around Paterno and he was being genuine, too. In their pregame appearances, Spurrier consistently called Paterno, "Coach Joe." Paterno would smile and say, "I kind of like that. There's a certain respect." Then he would lavish praise on his younger cohort. They became so cozy with each other that Spurrier instigated a quirky side bet on the game, whereby he would wear Paterno's trademark glasses on the field after the game if State won or, if Florida won, "Coach Joe" would wear Spurrier's familiar sun visor. Paterno agreed.

The State players tried to put Enis, Jurevicius and Michigan State behind them as they practiced for the game. "This bowl game is a chance to redeem ourselves," Short said. But it would be uphill and everyone knew it. The Gators had finished second in the SEC with their 9-2 record but with a break or two they might have been playing Nebraska in the Orange Bowl. This was almost like another home game for them with Gainesville only a couple of hundred miles north of Orlando and Florida alumni swirling around like flies. The oddsmakers figured it could be another blowout and made the Gators a 13-point favorite.

That the Lions actually had a chance to win the game is a credit to the players and the coaching staff. But, in fact, Florida was simply too good and the 21-6 final score could have been much worse. Discarding the pass for most of the game, the Gators did what most of State's Big Ten foes did all season and ran the ball. Fred Taylor rushed for a career high 234 of Florida's 254 yards on 43 carries while the Gator defense stuffed State's running and passing game. The Lions gained just 47 yards on 29 rushes and McQueary picked up just 92 yards on 10-of-32 passes with three interceptions. One of his interceptions set up a 35-yard TD pass that gave Florida a 14-0 lead in the first quarter and another from the one-yard line into the end zone ended a State drive in the second quarter. That goal line interception with 54 seconds left in the half came minutes after Florida had stopped Eberly on a fourth-and-goal at the one on State's previous series. An earlier interception return by Lee helped give State a third first down opportunity at the Florida 7 but a sack pushed the Lions back and Forney kicked a 42-yard field goal that made the score 14-3 at the half. State took the second half kickoff and drove to the Florida 13 before settling for another Forney field goal of 30 yards and for all practical purposes the game was really over. The Lions never seriously threatened again. "It was a run-the-ball, run-the-clock-out kind've game," Spurrier said later. The Gators went 75 yards for a TD early in the fourth quarter and Paterno briefly wore Spurrier's visor off the field after the game. "You're never happy getting licked," Paterno said "It was a good effort. We played hard but we didn't play well. Losing is for the birds."

"So, it's a time for reassessment by Coach Paterno and his staff...," concluded John Black for the *"Football Letter."* Reassessment? Every year has been a reassessment for Penn State football going back the beginning. Which quarterback are we going to use Rip? Speed or more size on the line, Hig? Should he be a back or a lineman, Bez? What do you think Pop? Hail to the Lions!

Season Record 9-3
Record to Date 715-299-42
Winning percentage .697

CHAPTER 14

THE TRADITION CONTINUES

1998 & Beyond

The best known of Joe Paterno's favorite quotes is the line from a Robert Browning poem that has been used so often whenever anyone writes about Paterno that it has become a cliché. Still, the mystical phrase that has inspired and galvanized Paterno all his life succinctly defines the man and the future of Penn State football:

"Ah, but a man's reach should exceed his grasp, or what's a heaven for."

Thousands of Penn State fans and others in the college football community believe what Paterno is now reaching for is Bear Bryant's all-time winning record for victories by a major college coach. Bryant had 323 victories over a 38-year career at four different universities and early in the 1998 season Paterno will get victory number 300. He wants the record, goes the popular wisdom, because he couldn't beat the Bear on the field. Bryant won all four of their confrontations and none was more heartbreaking than the loss to Alabama in the 1979 Sugar Bowl game for the National Championship. Even today, Paterno will admit that was his "toughest" defeat. But he says he doesn't think about the record and is not interested in it. A great number of people don't believe him when he says that. Yet, it doesn't really matter. For if Paterno reaches, grasps and surpasses Bryant, that will not end it. As long as he is healthy and is excited about each season and each player he coaches, as long as he can motivate and influence others and help young men become better citizens and as long as he can still contribute to the well-being and growth of his adopted university, Joe Paterno will be Penn State's football coach. And nobody will have to tell Joe Paterno when he is over the hill. He'll know it.

His health is not an issue. He looks and acts younger than his 71 years. Paterno walks when he could ride and he runs when he could walk. Anyone who has seen him hustle around the Lion practice field or doing his daily exercises knows this man is in better shape than many half his age. He's also having too much fun being the head football coach off the field as well as on it. The Library wing named after him is now under construction and will be dedicated soon, a concrete tribute to his massive fund raising efforts and personal financial contributions. His personal donation of nearly $500,000 helped seed the library endowment fund that now has a value of $3.4 million. He continues to lead funding campaigns for other University projects, and in January of 1998, he and his wife Sue donated $3.5 million to Penn State, almost all of it for educational purposes, including endowed scholarships named after their parents and another named after Joe's high

school Latin teacher. He also has given a half million dollars for the construction of an All-Sports Hall of Fame building between Beaver Stadium and the Bryce Jordan Center. Paterno knows that getting more money for that sports entity as well as the assorted educational projects planned by Penn State are easier when the football team is winning.

Paterno also wants to be there when the latest expansion of Beaver Stadium is completed in 2001. A seating capacity raised to 103,500 with luxury suites, new high-tech scoreboards with instant replay capability and bigger and better locker rooms, restrooms and concession stands. Why shouldn't he be the first coach to run onto the field with his team in those familiar drab blue and white uniforms on the day the biggest crowd in State history shows up to help dedicate the new additions? After all, Beaver Stadium is truly the "House that Joe Built," a modest steel-structured edifice seating 46,284 when he became the head coach in 1966. Just look at it now.

This 1998 look of Beaver Stadium will soon change again. The seating capacity of 46,284 in 1960 has increased to more than 97,000 today and by 2001 will seat 103,500 with luxury boxes.

Of course, Paterno will not be the State coach forever and for years there has been speculation about his successor. Twenty-five years ago it was supposed to be his offensive assistant, George Welsh, who went to Navy in '73 and is now the Paterno of the University of Virginia. Then, in the early 1980s, the word was that another assistant, Dick Anderson, was the heir apparent. Anderson left for Rutgers in '84 but returned in '90 and now seems to be behind offensive coordinator Fran Ganter and defensive coordinator Jerry Sandusky in the media's pecking order. At the end of the great 1994 season, Ganter was offered the head coaching job at Michigan State and turned it down. In December of 1996, Sandusky applied for the Maryland position but it went to someone else. If that was a signal of Ganter's status as the inside candidate, as some in the media have theorized, then this is the best kept secret in Happy Valley. But nobody really knows whether Paterno's successor will come from within or from the outside. Perhaps by the time he does retire, there will be another aspirant from the loyal coaching staff—maybe Kenny Jackson or Tom Bradley or some one who is not yet on the staff. If the job stays in the Penn State family, it might go to one of the dozens of former players now a head coach elsewhere—a Galen Hall or a Bill Bowes type—or one of the younger kids still an assistant somewhere.

Most of the sport media covering State football agree that Paterno will hand pick his successor. He already has

Penn State and football fans across the nation hope that Joe Paterno's decision to coach for "a few more years" will go on and on. Honored by Sports Illustrated in 1986 as Sportsman of the Year, he is everything that is right about college football.

said he would like to do what Rip Engle did for him in 1964 when Engle promoted Paterno to Associate Head Coach. But the history of Penn State football suggests the ultimate selection process may not happen the way he truly wants it. In fact, as earlier chapters of this book indicate, internal, backroom politics has interceded in the natural process. Dick Harlow and Earle Edwards had to find their coaching fame elsewhere and Paterno, himself, would not have been here if the wisdom of Bob Higgins had been followed.

Whomever succeeds Paterno will have a legacy to live up to and that won't be easy. Under Paterno's leadership, Penn State has become one of the nation's football powers, restoring the glory that was there some 75 to 80 years ago. Finishing in the Top 10 every year and going to a bowl game is expected now. Winning a Big Ten title and going to the Rose Bowl has become a desire almost on par with going after another national title. But winning on the field will not be enough. "JoePa" also has been instrumental in the academic growth of the school and it is now recognized as one of the premier public universities in the country. The fact that State receives more applicants for admission than almost any other university is not a coincidence. The reputation of the football team has enticed non-athletes to look at the academic program and what they find is a school with a high caliber of curriculums and faculty. Superior athletics and superior academics are feeding upon one another in Happy Valley. State only recruits high school players with the potential to graduate and many players choose Penn State because of its academics. But even Paterno acknowledges that it will be a challenge to continue in that vein. "Our institution right now has gotten so tough academically, that we're going to have academic problems," he told reporters after the end of the 1997 season. "We're gonna have some academic problems unless kids go to class and un-

derstand they have to do things…They're there to get an education and that'll always be a problem (for some players)."

Paterno's "Grand Experiment" is no longer an experiment but a living testimonial that superior athletics and superior academics can be a successful mix. State's graduation rates for all athletes is extraordinary but especially for football with its stereotype image of the "dumb" player. Year in and year out, the graduation rates of Paterno's players have been among the top five in the country and often number one. In figures released by the NCAA in 1997 for athletes entering in the freshman class of 1990-91, PSU football players graduated at a rate of 71% compared to the average 52% of football players at other schools and a 58% for all students. A year earlier, the rate was 87% for Lion footballers, compared to 54% for the national average. A *Time* magazine study in 1994 comparing graduation rates of football programs in the AP Top 25 named State the clear winner with a 92% rate to second place UCLA's 85%. Paterno also proved that good students make good professional players, too. In the past 30 years, the NFL has been loaded with PSU graduates. And after they've left the pros, they have gone on to fine careers as lawyers, doctors and businessmen. More importantly, the hundreds of players who don't make the pros have received a diploma and they, too, have become leaders in their communities. That was all part of "The Grand Experiment." The high number of Paterno players who have been named Hall of Fame Scholar Athletes by the National Football Foundation and Academic All-Americans or whom have received the prestigious NCAA Postgraduate scholarships is further evidence that academics is a priority for the Nittany Lions. And it will be a priority for the next coach, too.

Certainly, 1998 and 1999 is not the time for Joe Paterno to retire. Nor is the beginning of the next millennium. The young talent who make up the core of the Nittany Lion football team could help Paterno win another National Championship. Of course, many still have to prove themselves. But the veterans like Brad Scioli, Aaron Harris, David Macklin, and Brandon Short will show the way for the LaVar Arringtons, Rashard Caseys and Ron Grahams. With the continuing flow of those blue chip student-athletes, maybe Paterno will get a couple more titles before he finally retires. At least, we know the reach will be there, if not the grasp. And he starts out with circumstances in '98 that are all too familiar to those who have followed Penn State football in the Paterno era. A quarterback controversy. Questions about the defensive strategy and the offensive play calling. Too many distracting outside activities. "Deja' Vu all over again," as Yogi Berra once said.

"Ah, but a man's reach should exceed his grasp, or what's a heaven for."

As the first words of the Penn State Alma Mater says, "For the Glory…"

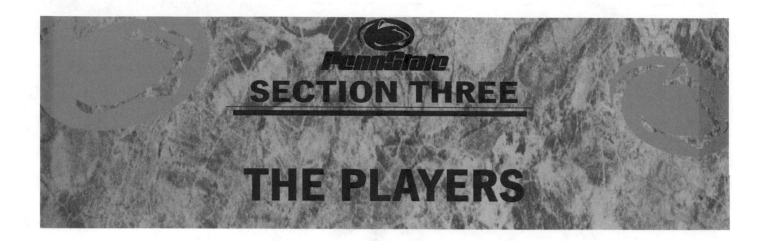

From (Don) Abbey to (Rod) Zur they're known as Penn State's football letterman. More than 1,100 of them since 1887.

Some of them are familiar names, recognized not only by Penn State alumni and fans but also by the nation's millions of football followers. John Cappelletti. Lenny Moore. Rosey Grier. Jack Ham. Kerry Collins.

There are others who were stars when they played but are now all but forgotten. Most are deceased and many of those who saw them play are gone, too. The memories of what they did at Beaver Field have faded into history and the library archives. Henny Scholl. Mother Dunn. Earl Hewitt. Red Griffiths. Bas Gray.

And there are the dozens who played in virtual obscurity. Many of them linemen, little known outside their circle of friends and class-mates. Guido Schiazza. Mike Slobodnjak. Mahlon Heist. James Wood-ward. Maybe they played just one season. Maybe more. But, they, too, are part of the 111 year tradition.

Penn State's Football Letterman's Club keeps track of all the lettermen. Executive Secretary Michelene (Mike) Franzetta and her staff update the roster continuously. A list of the players and their whereabouts are printed annually in the football media guide published by the Sports Information Office. That alphabetical listing is reprinted in Chapter 16 of this book.

Of course, some players have had more impact on the Penn State football program than others. This is not meant to demean the contributions of anyone. But, over the years, certain players have stood out from their teammates. Sometimes, it has been a full career of exploits. Sometimes, it has been for just a year. Sometimes, it has been because of one particular play. But these players did something that was different and they made an impression on the fans. Pete Mauthe with his running, punting and place kicking for the great teams from 1909-to-1912 that lost only twice in four years. Leon Gajecki with his bone-crushing tackling that made him a starter for three years in the late 1930s and one of State's first All-Americans. Mike Reid and Steve Smear with their pulverizing defensive wizardry that was the back-bone of the unbeaten 1968 and 1969 teams. Greg Garrity with his leaping pass reception for the winning touchdown that gave Penn State it's first National Championship in the 1983 Sugar Bowl. Ki-Jana Carter

with his three years of scintillating running, climaxed by that record 83-yard run in the 1995 Rose Bowl that guaranteed Joe Paterno his fifth unbeaten team.

Chapter 15 focuses on 401 of the men who played for Penn State. Most of them made a difference. A few are anomalies who are noted here for a historic purpose or an ironic circumstance. This list is woefully incomplete. That is especially true of offensive linemen who almost always labor in anonymity. The backs, ends and linebackers get the glory but it has always been that way. Many, many outstanding football players are not on this list. This is not Joe Paterno's list nor is it Bob Higgins' list. This is the author's list and the most difficult part of writing this project was deciding who to exclude. While carefully weighed, my decisions are extremely arbitrary and subjective and many of the players I have selected are probably not the same that many readers would select. Perhaps, this list will be longer in the author's next book. Or the next revision of this one. So, let the arguments begin.

Some of the best players—and certainly among the toughest—may have been those long forgotten early pioneers of the late 1880s and early 1900s who played when football games were more like bloody street brawls. They didn't wear pads or helmets; the rules were few; and, the referees frequently cheated openly for the home team. At least some of those players are remembered here.

The old-timers and hundreds of players who followed into the 1960s played for 60 minutes, offense and defense. Many were punters and place kickers, too. Ironmen, we now call them. Then came the expansion of substitution and two platoons. Unlimited substitution and the specialists we have today for offense, defense, kicking, runbacks, etc. didn't come into vogue until the last part of the 20th Century. Were the 60 minutes players of the bygone era better than the weight-lifting behemoths of today? Who really knows? But in the time that they played for Penn State, they were some of the school's best.

It is especially unfortunate that among those missing from this chapter are many of the players of the late 1950s and the 1960's who were classmates or friends of a certain young sports reporter. They, perhaps more than others, helped make this section and this book possible.

CHAPTER 15

THE LIONS

ABBEY, DON. 1967-68-69. FB & PK, 6'3", 241 lbs.; South Hadley, MA. A fine FB and "scholar athlete" on the back-to-back unbeaten and unappreciated teams of '68 & '69 who also was a very good kickoff and field goal man. Hampered by injuries, particularly in '68 after missing spring practice because of knee injury, then getting knee and ankle injury in the opening game against Navy that curtailed his playing time rest of year. Led team in scoring as soph with 88 points (on nine TDs, 3-of-14 FGs and 23-of-26 PATs and one two-point conversion), good for 12th in all-time record for career season points. Had his finest individual game early in soph year before hometown crowd in Boston, when he led team to 50-28 win over Boston College by gaining 119 yards and three TDs on 18 carries and averaging 55 yards on eight kickoffs; it would be the only 100-yards plus game of his career but he was a steady performer and great blocker throughout his career. Made great debut as placekicker against Navy in '67 opener with field goals of 42 and 26 yards and kickoffs to the goal line. Designated starter for all of '68 and '69 (except when he missed games because of injuries) but became more known for his blocking in senior year with the emergence of a sensational soph FB named Franco Harris. Seventh choice of Dallas Cowboys in '70 but didn't play pro ball. An honors major in pre-med who changed career choice and is now a prosperous managing partner in a real estate conglomerate in Southern California and living in Bradbury, CA.

ALEXANDER, ROGERS. 1982-83-84-85. LB, 6'2 ½", 215 lbs.; Riverdale, MD. One of the all-time big hitters but surprisingly never made anything higher than Honorable Mention All-American. Co-captain and defensive leader of the surprise '85 team that went unbeaten and played Oklahoma for the National Championship in the '86 Orange Bowl. Made one of the biggest plays of '85 season in tight early season game with East Carolina at Beaver Stadium, when he recovered fumble that led to first TD in eventual 17-10 win. Three weeks later he was leading tackler (12) in key fourth QT 24-20 come-from-behind win at Syracuse. Led team in tackles that year with 102 on 54 solo and 48 assists, which is 13th best for one season in records. Also 15th in career tackles with 137 solos, 89 assists for 226 total. A key

backup on the first National Championship team as a frosh and caused a fumble in the '83 Sugar Bowl title game with Georgia. In soph year he was the sack leader with six. Played in '86 Hula Bowl. Drafted fourth by New York Jets in '86 and played one year with Jets and another with New England before leaving pro ball. Now a security officer in State College.

ALLEN, DOUG. 1970-72-73. DE & LB, 6'2", 220 lbs.; Corning, NY. One of the least known fine linebackers of his era because he played at the same time as All-American's John Skorupan and Ed O'Neil, but an excellent outside man. A starting LB on the unbeaten team of '73 which may have been the most ignored of all Paterno squads after beating LSU, 16-9, in '74 Orange Bowl to become 1st State team ever to go 12-0 but finished only fifth in both AP & UPI polls. Got off to a great start as senior in nationally-televised opening game at Stanford when he and Greg Murphy partially blocked an end zone punt for a safety and the first score in an eventual 20-6 win. Played one of his best games in 49-6 win over Syracuse in '73 with tackles all over field and a 28-yard interception return to the Syracuse 11-yard line in second QT that set up PSU's second TD. Was a backup DE as soph but played as much as the starters. Switched to Inside Left LB in '71 and was set to start alongside Charlie Zapiec, Gary Gray and Skorupan but a head injury in opener against Navy sidelined him for season and doctors feared he might never play football again. But came back to be the prime backup at OLB in '72 and then started in '73. Known as a jarring tackler who caused a lot of fumbles, as he did in opening game against Tennessee in '72. Those who were there said he played one of his best games in losing cause at '72 Sugar Bowl. Number two choice of Buffalo Bills in '74 and played two years before career ended. Has become well known as the assistant executive director of the National Football League Players Association and lives in Alexandria, VA.

ALLERMAN, KURT. 1974-75-76. LB, 6'3", 220 lbs.; Kinnelon, NJ. Another of the outstanding graduates of "Linebacker U." A First-Team All-American in senior year, when he led team with 87 tackles in regular season, including 57 solo and 30 assists. Co-captain of the comeback '76 team that lost three of first four games but won six straight before loss to national champ Pitt and went to Gator Bowl against Notre Dame—where he played one of his best games with 11 solo tackles and five assists. Started off year as he ended it with an outstanding opening-season performance against Stanford: led team in tackles with five solos and four assists and recovered a fumble at Stanford 48-yard line in second QT that led to winning TD in 15-12 victory. Played one of his best games in losing cause, when named Defensive Player-of-the-Game with seven solo tackles and eight assists in 12-7 defeat by Ohio State. A backup ILB as soph but began starting games in junior year and couldn't be kept out of lineup. In junior year had one of his best games in 21-12 win over West Virginia with several tackles and a big interception. Finished career as 12th all-time best in tackles with 145 solos and 90 assists for 235 total. Played in '77 Senior Bowl. Third choice of St. Louis Cardinals in '76 and had fine pro career with Cardinals twice ('77-'79 & '83-'85), Green Bay ('80-'82) and Detroit ('85) before retiring. Now a wholesale lighting distributor in Hudson, OH.

ALSTON, DAVE. 1941. TB & Drop-kick PK, 6'1", 198 lbs.; Midland, PA. State's first Black football player, along with his brother Harry. One of the few "blue chip" athletes recruited in the pre-World War II de-emphasis period. No one will ever know his true potential because he died before playing a varsity game. A triple threat on offense and an outstanding tackler and pass defender. Built like Lydell Mitchell and was a similar runner with speed, strength and the ability to be elusive and shake off tacklers. He could throw bullet passes 50-to-60 yards. One of the last of the great dropkickers. Led talented '41 freshmen team to first unbeaten season in 25 years with 5-0 record; team scored 133 points to opponents' 26 and Alston scored eight TDs, passed for four others (including three to his brother) and kicked six PATs. In July of '42 he was selected by some preseason football magazines as college football's "Sophomore of the Year" for the '42 season. Had won 12 letters at Midland High School where he was captain of the football and basketball teams, valedictorian and president of his class. Majored in pre-med. Suffered internal injuries in spring practice scrimmage against Navy in '42 but severity of injuries were not discovered until a routine tonsillectomy operation in August and he died on August 15th in Bellefonte Hospital of complications following the tonsillectomy surgery. Ironically, his jersey number as a frosh was 13.

ALTER, SIDNEY ("SPIKE"). 1937-38-39. E, 6'0", 170 lbs.; Pittsburgh, PA. Captain of the '39 team that brought respectability back to State's program during the disastrous de-emphasis period; team had best record in 18 years, finishing 5-1-2, and setting the stage for the best years of the Higgins era. One of the team's leading pass receivers in junior and senior years. Also a fine defensive player, known for his aggressive style of play. Was one of reasons the '38 team set several NCAA pass defense records, including one for fewest yards passing allowed per game (13.1 average) that still stands. Played one of his best defensive games against Syracuse in '39, when his blocked punt at midfield led to the State TD that gave team a 6-6 tie over the favored Orange. Deceased.

ANDERSON, DICK. 1961-62-63. E, 6'4", 215 lbs.; East Patterson, NJ. A long-time assistant coach under Paterno, and even old time fans forget he was a fine pass receiver, defensive end and blocker in the Engle "bowl" era. Had excellent hands and deceptive speed. A starter for two years and led '63 team in receiving with 21 catches for 229 yards and two TDs and a 10.9 yards per catch average. Had one of his finest games in 28-14 win over Holy Cross in '63,

when he caught three passes, made a spectacular one-handed interception, recovered a fumble and partially blocked a kick. Starter on two Gator Bowl teams and caught three passes for 40 yards in '61 game. Also a star outfielder on baseball team. Varsity debut delayed one year by a kidney injury that kept him out of the '60 season. Made the first TD of career on a 13-yard pass over the middle from Galen Hall, taking two defenders across the goal line with him in a third QT score that sealed a 14-0 win over Syracuse in '61. Played in '63 Blue-Gray game. Drafted number 17 by Cleveland in '63 and played briefly but turned to coaching in '65. Coached at Lafayette and Penn before joining Paterno's staff in '73 as offensive line coach and developed five First-Team All-Americans; was offensive coordinator when he left in '84 for head coaching job at Rutgers. Coached six teams against State and was at helm when Rutgers beat State for first time since 1918, 21-16, at Beaver Stadium in pivotal '88 game that eventually led to PSU's first losing season in 49 years. Returned to Paterno's staff in '90 and is credited with developing QBs Kerry Collins and Wally Richardson. Now is quarterback coach and in charge of team's passing game. Lives in State College.

ANDERSON, RICHIE. 1991-92. TB, 6'2", 210 lbs.; Sandy Spring, MD. Never reached his full potential and left for the pros after his "redshirt" junior season after being a UPI Honorable Mention All-American. Had the speed and the size but sometimes seemed to be holding back. Bothered by off-and-on injuries as a true frosh and sat out '90 as "redshirt," then led the team in rushing in '91 & '92, and is 14th in career rushing with 1,756 yards and 29 TDs on 363 carries and a 4.84 yards average. Had a sensational debut as starter in '91 Kickoff Classic win over Georgia Tech, 34-22, but it was more as a pass receiver; caught four passes for 93 yards, including a 52-yard TD run off a screen pass from Tony Sacca. Had total of eight games rushing over 100 yards. Two of his best games were in back-to-back '91 wins over Notre Dame, 35-13, and Pitt, 32-20, that sent State to the '92 Fiesta Bowl; against Irish on regional TV he scored two TDs and set up two more on runs of 57 and 16 yards, as he rushed for 136 yards on 26 carries and caught three passes for 17 yards; the next week in a nationally televised Thanksgiving Day game at Pittsburgh he was Offensive-Player-of-the-Game with 167 yards rushing (his best yardage ever) on 27 carries and scored two TDs, one on a 28-yard run midway in the fourth quarter that clinched the victory. Leading rusher in 42-17 win over Tennessee in '92 Fiesta Bowl with 57 yards and one TD. Never gained 1,000 yards in a season but is 12th in career scoring with 188 points on 31 TDs and a two-point PAT; his season-leading 116 points in junior year is fifth most of all-time. His four TDs in 49-13 blowout of Maryland in '92 is tied for 7th in all-time single game scoring. A fine return man on kickoffs, he led team in junior year with nine returns for 222 yards and a 24.7 yards return average. Sixth choice of New York Jets in 1993 and still playing for Jets as sometimes starter.

ARCHIE, MIKE. 1992-93-94-95. TB, WR & KR, 5'8", 206 lbs.; Sharon, PA. A blue chip back who had the ill fortune of being at State at the same time as classmates Ki-Jana Carter and Stephen Pitts but developed into a fine "change-up" back. No running back ever caught as many passes and scored as many TDs on receptions as he did, and his 70 career receptions for 535 yards and seven TDs is 10th best of all receivers. Excellent pass receiver and kick returner. Fulfilled this role brilliantly on unbeaten '94 offensive powerhouse team that won '95

Rose Bowl. Led team that year in punt returns (11 for 126 yards and 11.5 yards average) and kickoff returns (11 for 240 yards and a 21.8 yards average). Played one of his finest games in 61-21 rout of Iowa, when he scored the first two TDs on a 10-yard pass and 35-yard run and added another TD in second QT on four-yard run. Sixth in career punt returns with a 14.0 yards average per runback on 24 returns for 337 yards and one TD. The TD came as a frosh, when he returned one 62 yards against Pitt. Led team in returns in junior year with 11 for 126 yards and an 11.5 yards per return average. Should have been the prime TB in '95 after Carter left, but hampered by muscle spasms and other injuries all season after fine opening season game against Texas Tech, when he was leading rusher with 76 yards on 17 carries; shared TB position rest of year with classmate Stephen Pitts and frosh Curtis Enis but still managed 512 yards rushing and one TD on 97 carries (second to Enis) and caught 21 passes for 141 yards and two TDs. Had one of best years rushing as a "redshirt" sophomore in '93, when he gained over 100 yards in four games with his best day being 173 yards and two TDs (in 27 carries) in 43-21 win at Northwestern. Played in '96 Japan Bowl . Seventh choice of Houston in '96 and still playing for the Oilers.

ARNELLE, JESSE. 1951-52-53-54. E, 6'5", 228 lbs.; New Rochelle, NY. One of PSU's best known three-sport athletes who was a First-Team All-American basketball player, and a starter on the baseball team but never made more than Honorable Mention All-American in football despite his outstanding performances on offense and defense. Also now recognized as one of the most prominent Penn State alumni, who is very active in Penn State affairs as a long time member and former president of the Board of Trustees. A leader in opening up the diversity of the campus in the '70s and '80s to improve the cultural atmosphere for Black students and not just Black athletes. Part of State's great recruiting class in '51, including his linemate Rosey Grier, that rejuvenated football after a 20-year de-emphasis period. He and Grier were an intimidating one-two defensive force starting in their freshmen years and they continued to get better and more daunting every season. Known for his crisp blocking, solid tackling and sure-handed pass catching. Played a position that was close to what is now a Tight End and was used more for blocking than receiving. Played one of his finest games as a senior in the opening game 14-12 upset over defending Big 10 co-champ Illinois; recovered a fumble caused by a Lenny Moore tackle midway in first QT and three plays later caught a 24-yard pass from Don Bailey for first TD; also was all over field on defense, smothering the Illini's highly-touted ball carriers, J.C. Caroline, Abe Woodson and Mickey Bates, for losses or very short gains and sacking the QB. Set the individual pass reception record that lasted 13 years, when he caught 33 passes for 291 yards and two TDs as a soph and led team in receiving. Often used as a decoy in junior and senior years as he, Jim Garrity and Jack Sherry gave State one of the best receiving corps of the Engle era. Made great impression in very first game as frosh before Homecoming crowd against Michigan State, when he came in as defensive end and tackled two MSU backs for 29 yards in losses on successive plays. Started next week against West Virginia and became regular on defensive platoon from that point. Was in three games on offense as frosh and had greatest game against Pitt, when he caught four straight passes, including nine-yard TD pass, in leading downfield fourth QT drive that tied Panthers in game State eventually lost, 13-7. Co-captain of '54-'55 basketball team that is the only PSU team to go

to Final Four. All-University President as undergraduate. Honored with the Distinguished American award from the National Football Foundation's College Football Hall of Fame in '92. Drafted number one by Fort Wayne Pistons in National Basketball Association but decided to play one year with Harlem Globetrotters before going to law school. Graduate of Dickinson Law School and for years was an attorney with international clients, and based in San Francisco, CA. Now semi-retired and chairman of a law firm in North Carolina.

ASHLEY, WALKER LEE. 1979-80-81-82. DE, 6'0", 235 lbs.; Jersey City, NJ. Known for his blistering sacks on QBs and hard tackling and a First-Team All-American in '82. Should have made more All-American teams that year, but there were so many stars on that first National Championship team (Warner, Jackson, Robinson, Blackledge, etc.) that he was by-passed for many post-season accolades. Was a big year for him, though, as he led team for second straight year with QB sacks (five). Recorded 52 tackles in regular season, when he also recovered three fumbles and caused two more. One of the stars of '83 Sugar Bowl win over Georgia 27-23, when he and fellow-All-American, safety Mark Robinson, were designated to stop Heisman Trophy winner Herschel Walker from getting around the corner, where he could use his speed—and they did; Walker got only 103 yards and one TD on 28 carries and Ashley was credited with seven tackles and a big QB sack. 13th in career sacks with 14. Won Jim O'Hora Award in '81 for most improvement by a defensive player in spring practice. Played in '83 East-West Shrine game. Third choice of Minnesota in '83 and played for Vikings from '83-'88 and again in '90 with two years at Kansas City in '88-'89 before retiring. Now living in suburban Minneapolis and working in environmental products marketing.

ATHERTON, CHARLES (CHARLIE). 1890-91-92-93-94. RB & PK, Ht & Wt Unknown; State College, PA. The running star of State's early teams. Second five-time letterman and son of then college president, George Atherton. Ignored by football historians but was first man to kick a FG placement from line of scrimmage in successful 25-yard attempt against Oberlin on Nov. 24, 1894—three years before John Minds of Penn and Clarence Herschberger of Chicago, who are credited with being among first in 1897. The kick was made after a free catch by halfback Charles Thomas who then held ball for Atherton to kick from a difficult angle. The referee, Fred White of Oberlin, ruled the kick was illegal. Oberlin claimed a 6-4 victory and Penn State claimed a 9-6 win. Walter Camp, who was the football authority at the time ruled in favor of State but some historians continue to ignore the Camp ruling. Atherton also set four State single game scoring records that still stand in opening game of 1894 season against Gettysburg on October 13—most points by a senior (32) and number of extra points, extra points attempts and extra points accuracy (by kicking 10-for-10 in 60-0 victory); his 10 extra points and three TDs that day also places him second in the all-time single game individual scoring record. Returned for graduate work and helped coach in '97. Played with Washington Senators professional baseball team in '99. A chemist by training, became a choir director and music teacher in later life. Died Dec. 19, 1934.

AULL, CHARLIE. 1889-90-91. G, E & FB, 5' 7", 125 lbs.; Pittsburgh, PA. Another of the stars of the early State teams. Captain & FB of the first championship team in 1891 when the 6-2 squad won the

Pennsylvania Intercollegiate Football Association title. Played in same backfield with Charlie Atherton in 1890 and 1891 and did a lot of blocking for Atherton. One of the most popular players on the team during his era and was always quick with a remark. As a sophomore G he also was on team that had worst all-time loss, 106-0 to Lehigh on the road, and when asked what happened upon his return to SC is reported to have uttered the immortal words, "We couldn't get the son-of-a-bitch with the ball." Deceased.

BAER, RAY. 1920-21. G, 6'0", 196 lbs.; Toledo, OH. Two-year starter on the back-to-back unbeaten teams of '20 & '21 that were State's best until the great '47 team. Sportswriters raved about the middle of State's line with "Newsh" Bentz at C, Baer at LG and All-American Joe Bedenk at RG. They were credited with helping make All-Americans out of Glenn Killinger and "Light Horse" Harry Wilson. Because of his size, he also played tackle in a few games, but fit into Bezdek's offense better as a guard and that's where he spent most of his time. In senior year, he was First-Team on the prestigious All-East team picked by the **New York Herald**, and Second-Team on "Tiny" Maxwell's equally celebrated All-East squad. Also stayed on after graduation to help coach for next couple of years. Deceased.

BAHR, CHRIS. 1973-74-75. PK & P, 5'9 ½", 160 lbs.; State College, PA. The best long yardage placekicker in PSU history with twice as many FGs of 50 yards or more (six) than any other kicker. First-Team All-American in senior year. In first two years he was kicking for Paterno he played varsity soccer and was captain of the '74 soccer team; in summer of '75 he was rookie of year of professional North American Soccer League with Philadelphia team. Also owns PSU record for the longest FG at 55 yards, which he first set in opening game of '75 season against Temple, breaking Pete Mauthe's 63-year record of a 51-yard FG, then, amazingly, did it two more times that year with boots against Ohio State and Syracuse; also had 52-yarder in '75 against West Virginia and kicks of 50 yards against Syracuse in '73 and Pitt in '74. His kick at Syracuse in '73 occurred in a most unusual of circumstances: he had played soccer in State College Friday night, scoring two goals in a 5-1 victory over Maryland, then caught an airplane to Syracuse in time for the 1:30 p.m. kickoff, and 15 minutes later, at about 1:45, kicked the longest FG since Mauthe's in 1912 as State went on to clobber Syracuse, 49-6. Made one of his most significant kicks in fourth QT that beat Pitt, 7-6, in '75, when holder Dick Barvinchak was able to overcome a low, off target snap. In '75 Beaver Stadium game against WVU he booted one kickoff 70 yards through the goal posts. Had four FGs in that '74 Pitt game, which also was the record (and tied four times by younger brother Matt in '78) until Brian Franco broke it with five at Nebraska in '81. First in most career attempts and tied for fourth with Brett Conway in most FGs for one season with 18 in '75 and sixth in career FGs with 35 on 63 attempts (for a 55.6% average). Set NCAA record on FG percentage for one season that was later broken by brother Matt. A soccer All-American in '72 before turning to football, he was a little erratic in '73 year, when he would miss "chip shot" PATs while kicking long FGs in same game; hit on only 32-of-42

PATs in '73 but was 19-for-20 in '75, when he also nailed 18-of-33 FGs and led scoring with 73 points. Kicked FGs in three Bowl games with a 42-yarder in 16-9 win over LSU in '74 Orange Bowl, two for 25 & 33 yards in 41-20 win over Baylor in '75 Cotton Bowl and 42 and 37 yard FGs for all PSU points in 13-6 loss to Alabama in '75 Sugar Bowl. Most people forget he also was the punter in senior season and his average of 38.6 yards per kick on 56 punts (for 2,163 yards) is seventh best career record of all time. His 48.5 yards average on four punts in '75 Sugar Bowl loss to Alabama is fourth in single game punting averages. Played in '76 Senior Bowl. Number two choice of Cincinnati in '76 and played with Bengals from '76-'79, then joined Raiders where he had his greatest All-Pro success from '80-'88, kicking in two Super Bowls, before spending one year at San Diego and then retiring in '90. He returned to the State College area, where he is a financial planner and lives in Boalsburg.

BAHR, MATT. 1976-77-78. PK, 5'10", 164 lbs.; State College, PA. Followed brother as a First-Team All-American in '78. More accurate and prolific than brother Chris. Owns record for most FGs in one season ('78) with 22 on 27 attempts for an 81.5% accuracy record that year—which was NCAA record for several years, too—and also hit on 31-of-31 extra points to set team accuracy record PATs (since tied by Massimo Manca and Brett Conway) and nailed 39-of-41 PATs the year before. Still holds NCAA record for kicking more field goals in more games. Four times in '78 he kicked four FGs in games against Rutgers, Ohio State, NC State and SMU, with his four against SMU being the most ever in one half. The four at distances of 33, 32, 37 and 30 yards in 19-10 win over NC State were crucial to victory that made Lions number one for first time in history. Also played soccer in '76 & '77 while kicking for Paterno and made All-American there, too. Has just one FG of 50 yards (Syracuse '78) but is fourth in career FGs with 39 (on 61 attempts for a 63.9% average). Led team in scoring in '77 & '78 with 97 points in senior year on 22 FGs and 31 PATs being his best. Ninth in career scoring (and fourth best among place-kickers) with 191 points on 39 FGs and 74 PATs. May have made his most critical kick in '78 opening season game against Temple when his 23-yard boot at end of 52-yard drive with 10 seconds left in fourth QT, won game and put Lions on track to be number one for first time in history. Only kicked two FGs in bowl games, both in 42-30 win over Arizona State in Christmas Day '77 Fiesta Bowl, when he hit from 23 and 32 yards and also had three PATs. Also played pro soccer in summer of '78 for Tulsa of the North American Soccer League. Played in '79 Hula Bowl. Sixth pick of Pittsburgh in '79 and kicked for Steelers two years, including for the '80 Super Bowl Champions, then moved on to San Francisco ('81), Cleveland ('81-'89), New York Giants ('90-'92 and another Super Bowl winner), and New England from '93 until his retirement in '97. Now a design engineer who makes his home in Pittsburgh.

BAILEY, DON. 1952-53-54. QB, P & PR, 6'1", 178 lbs.; Pittsburgh, PA. Backup to Tony Rados for most of career and very underrated. Was second team at beginning of senior year but came in as sub early in first QT of game against defending Big 10 champs Illinois at Champaign and engineered 14-12 upset; threw a 22-yard pass to Jesse Arnelle for first TD, ran 50-yards on an option to set up second TD—which was scored on another option when he first faked to Lenny Moore, then lateraled at the 12-yard line to Moore who ran the rest of the way for an 18-yard TD—and punted five times to keep star-studded Illini off balance. Started the rest of the season and helped lead team to best record in six years at 7-2. Had never run option before but Engle added it to PSU attack in '54 and Bailey adjusted beautifully because he was such a good runner. Put up more than adequate passing numbers with 393 yards and five TDs on 33-of-80 pass attempts with just two interceptions. Also led team in punting that year with 26 kicks for 898 yards and a 34.5 yard average. As soph, he started as a halfback on the defensive platoon and was the prime punt returner, leading '52 team in punt returns with 16 for 213 yards and a 13.3 average; his first return of season in opening game against Temple set up Lions' initial TD in 20-13 win and his 77-yard return for a TD at Syracuse later in season was his only TD return in 25-7 upset loss. Was #2 QB in junior year when rules eliminated two-platoon football. Outstanding Player in '55 East-West Shrine Game. Now a manufacturer's representative and lives in Berwyn, PA.

BAIORUNOS, JACK. 1972-73-74. C, 6'3", 225 lbs.; Quincy, MA. A fine college center who held down the starting position for two and a half years on teams that won 32 games and lost only four and was as steady as any C in the Paterno era. Third Team All-American in '74 and co-captain of team that lost in upsets to Navy and North Carolina State and defeated Southwest Conference champ Baylor in '75 Cotton Bowl to finish seventh in country. All-East in '73 & '74. Winner of a prestigious National Football Foundation and College Football Hall of Fame fellowship in '74 and an NCAA postgraduate scholarship in '75. Graduated with a 3.45 academic average in pre dentistry and is now a dentist in Ellicott City, MD.

BAKER, RALPH. 1961-62-63. TE, C & LB, 6'3", 215 lbs.; Lewistown, PA. One of the early graduates of "Linebacker U." Captain of '63 team that had 7-3 record and ranked in top 20 but missed bowl opportunity mainly through unfortunate circumstances when the assassination of President Kennedy postponed Pitt game by one week; team lost to Pitt 22-21. Began varsity career as a TE in '61 but moved to C and won Red Worrell Award in '62 as most improved player in spring practice. As spot player in soph year, his recovered fumble on Syracuse 15-yard line in third QT of '61 game led to (Galen) Hall-to-(Dick) Anderson TD pass that sealed victory, 14-0. Played on second unit behind Capt. Joe Galardi in junior year. Never one to give up, he played some of his best games in losses & two standout—the 17-7 loss to Florida in '62 Gator Bowl and the 9-0 defeat at Syracuse in '63 when he was voted the Outstanding Defensive Player. Played perhaps his greatest game in the 10-7 upset of Ohio State at Columbus in '63, when he led team with 12 solo tackles and 14 assists. Played in '63 East-West Shrine game & '64 Hula Bowl. Picked third by NFL Pittsburgh and sixth by AFL New York Jets and signed with Jets where he had a stellar 11 year career and was a mainstay on the '69 team that upset Baltimore to win Super Bowl III. Works in the New York City metropolitan area as an account representative and lives in Greenlawn, NY.

BANNON, BRUCE. 1970-71-72. DE & LB, 6'3", 224 lbs.; Rockaway, NJ. One of the school's great scholar-athletes with a 3.91 academic average in geological sciences and a consensus First-Team All-American in senior year, when picked by UPI, Football Coaches, Football Writers and Walter Camp among others. Started preseason as a backup DE as soph in '70 and was starter by opener against Navy

and never went back to bench in next two and a half years. His 223 tackles on 126 solos and 97 assists is the 15th best overall. Played perhaps his finest game in the "breakthrough" 30-6 win over Texas in '72 Cotton Bowl, when he was named the game's Outstanding Defensive Player, as he and defensive teammates held Longhorn offense without a TD for first time in 80 games. He was quick and quick-thinking. One play in the '71 win over Syracuse (31-0) epitomized his style of play; he blocked a punt deep in Syracuse territory, then knocked down the closest would-be tackler, as teammate Gary Gray scooped up the ball and ran for a TD. Played one of his best all-around games in '72's 28-19 win at West Virginia when he was named the Defensive Player-of-the-Game; with State leading 25-19 late in the third QT, he led a four-down goal line stand that kept WVU out of EZ and was turning point of the game. All-East in '71 & 72. Named Outstanding Collegiate Defensive Player by Washington Pigskin Club in '72. Academic All-American in '72, when he also was awarded a National Football Foundation and College Football Hall of Fame graduate school fellowships for outstanding "scholar-athletes." Also winner of NCAA postgraduate scholarship in '73. Played in '73 Hula Bowl. Fifth choice of New York Jets in '73 and wound up playing two years with Miami before quitting pro ball. Now a businessman living in North Hollywood, CA.

BARANTOVICH, ALEX. 1936-37-38. E, 6'1", 180 lbs.; Monongahela, PA. A three-year starter and one of the best players on teams that were struggling through the terrible period of de emphasis in the mid-'30s. Known for his aggressive defensive play and great blocking, which was the prime responsibility for the RE in the single wing attack. Scored one of his few TDs on a great 34-yard pass reception while lying flat on his back in 21-14 win over Maryland in '37, when series with Maryland resumed after 20 years. Part of the outstanding defensive team of '38 that set several NCAA pass defense records, including one for fewest yards passing allowed per game (13.1 average) which still stands. Played one of his best games in 33-6 upset of Syracuse in '37 when he recovered a fumble to set up first TD. But his finest games may have been against powerful Penn: in 7-0 upset in '37 he clinched game late in fourth QT when he crashed into the Penn punt receiver, forcing a fumble that he recovered, and State ran out the clock in Penn territory; in '38 he was cited by sportswriters for his performance in 7-7 tie with Quakers. Retired and living in Brownsville, PA.

BARBER, STEW. 1958-59-60. E & T, 6'3", 225 lbs.; Bradford, PA. A devastating blocker with good hands and decent speed who was used at both E & T. Might have been a prototype of the Tight End as a soph if more passes had been thrown his way. Moved to T in junior year and was regular on alternate unit, then became starter on defense with first unit as senior. Long-time line coach Jim O'Hora said Barber probably improved more through the years than any lineman he ever coached and by the time he was a senior was one of the best of the era between '46 and '75. Didn't get many headlines but was a solid, dependable blocker and a good tackler. Was involved in one of the great deceptive plays in history on the last play of the half in '59 Liberty Bowl, when Galen Hall threw a screen pass to Roger Kochman off a fake FG attempt and Barber and others led the phalanx of blockers into the EZ for the only score of the game, an 18-yard TD, in a 7-0 victory over Alabama. His fumble recovery in '59 Illinois game led to winning TD in 20-9 victory. Had one of his best games in 27-16 upset over Army in '60 with his blocking that helped open holes for the running of Jim Kerr and his hard-hitting tackling. Played in '60 Blue-Gray game. Chosen number three by NFL Dallas Cowboys and number five by AFL Buffalo Bills, signed with Bills and was one of their starting offensive tackles through the '69 season before he joined the Bills front office for a few years. Now a division vice president who lives in West Chester, PA.

BARNEY, DON. 1950-51-52. G, 6'0", 184 lbs.; Erie, PA. Three-year defensive starter at nose guard for Engle's first teams. Was in first scholarship class in 22 years following the debilitating de-emphasis period of the 1930s and 1940s and spent frosh year at California State Teachers College in '49 because of crowded conditions on main campus. Called "a watchcharm guard" by some sportswriters for his aggressive play. Frequently used to contain blocking at line of scrimmage so teammates could zero in on ball carrier. As a soph, his interception against West Virginia set up a TD in the second quarter that broke game open in State's 27-0 victory. Spent most of his professional career as a sales executive with Hallmark Cards. Now retired and living in Doylestown and season ticketholder for State football and basketball games.

BAUER, TREY. 1984-85-86-87. LB, 6'1", 215 lbs.; Paramus, NJ. One of the most aggressive LBs of the Paterno era. Third-Team All-American in '87. A starter on the back-to-back teams that played for national title and won it in '86. Played mean and nasty on the field and had a fiery temperament that often got him into trouble with Paterno. Once when State was playing on national TV, Paterno got so angry at an on-field indiscretion by Bauer the coach pulled him immediately from the game, and when Bauer got to the sideline Paterno grabbed him by the neck of his jersey and shook him angrily as the camera zoomed in for a close up. Never hesitated to speak his mind, which also got him into frequent collisions with Paterno. Seventh in career tackles with 256, one less than Andre Collins, but he had more solo tackles than Collins, 176, and 80 assists. Played one of his finest games in junior year in pivotal midseason contest in '86 against then number two Alabama; named by ABC as Player-of-the-Game, when he led team with nine tackles, recovered one fumble, caused another and deflected at least one pass, as State upset Tide, 23-3, and moved further towards the eventual National Championship game in '87 Fiesta Bowl. As soph in opening game of '85, he made one of the key plays in march towards number one ranking and the national title game by recovering a fumble with 38 seconds left against preseason number one Maryland to prevent an attempt at a game-winning FG, as State upset Terps, 20-18. The next year against the Terps he intercepted a pass at the PSU two-yard line that halted a drive that could have turned the eventual 17-15 win into a major upset and spoiled the '86 team's drive for the championship. Played in '88 Senior Bowl. Returned to State to receive his MBA. An accounts manager for an investment firm on Wall Street and lives in Paramus, NJ.

BAUGH, KEVIN. 1980-81-82-83. KR & WR, 5'9", 176 lbs.; Deer Park, NY. One of the best known kick returners in the Paterno era, because it was his specialty, but he did it all during his four years. Has record for most KO returns and yardage in a season (26 for 503 yards in '83) and in a career (62 runbacks for 1,216 yards). The only player to lead team in punt returns for four years. Also led in KO returns in '82

& '83. His returns were significant in winning the '82 National Championship, when he had 29 punt returns for 315 yards and 18 KO returns for 404 yards. Had one of his most dazzling punt runbacks in 52-17 win over Boston College that year with a 38-yard return that saw him cutting, spinning, faking and twisting his way to the BC 29-yard line to set up a TD. His best overall season was as senior, when he also led team in receptions (36 for 547 yards and 5 TDs) and all-purpose running with 670 yards in returns and seven yards in rushing to go with the 547 yards in receiving. The 547 yards is 17th best for one season. Had great back-to-back receiving games in '83 in wins over Rutgers, Alabama and Syracuse, when he led all receivers in each game, with best performance in 36-25 win over Rutgers as he scored two TDs on catches of six and 31 yards and set up a FG on another reception for 34 yards. He made a spectacular debut as a frosh in opening game against Colgate, when he had one of the longest runs from scrimmage in history with an 80-yard TD in 54-10 victory. Played one of his finest games against Boston College in '83, when he caught eight passes for 103 yards, setting up two TDs, returned two punts for 12 yards and a kickoff for 19 yards, as he was selected State's Player-of-the-Game. Leading receiver in '80 Fiesta Bowl win over Ohio State, 31-19, with three receptions for 53 yards. Played in '84 Senior Bowl. Eighth choice of Houston Oilers in '84 but didn't play pro ball. Has been living and working in New Jersey.

BEBOUT, JAMES ("RED"). 1911-12-13. G & T, 6'0", 180 lbs.; Pittsburgh, PA. One of the best interior linemen of his era. Tough infighter who wasn't afraid to use his fists if challenged by an opponent. Vicious tackler. Lettered as frosh, then was three-year starter and one of the stars at tackle of State's first great unbeaten team, the 1912 squad. Part of a great interior line that also included fellow tackle "Dad" Engle and guards Levi Lamb and Al Hansen that helped open the holes for Pete Mauthe and Shorty Miller to become All-Americans. Played perhaps his best game in the controversial, 37-0 win over Ohio State at Columbus in '12 and his blood-splattered uniform that day showed the intensity of his performance. Had another fine game in 14-7 loss to Notre Dame in '13, when he was so feared the Notre Dame players frequently shouted throughout the game to "Get Red; Get Red." Named All-East in '12. Became an officer in World War I and was one of two stars of the great '12 team to be killed in action. Died on Sept. 29, 1918 in France.

BEDENK, JOE. 1921-22-23. G, 5'11", 183 lbs.; Mansfield, PA. Considered one of the all-time great linemen at Penn State and teamed with sophomore Gus Michalske (and future Football Hall of Famer) in senior year to form one of the greatest guard combinations in collegiate football. Became State's second soph named All-American when picked for Second-Team by Walter Camp in '21. Then became first interior lineman named First-Team All-American since "Mother" Dunn as senior, after being Third-Team as a junior. Known as a great blocker for fellow All-American's Glen Killinger and "Light Horse" Harry Wilson. Killinger said Bedenk was the best "running" blocker he ever saw, who did more blocking for him than anyone on the team. Picked on the All-Time Penn State team in 1950s and again in 1967 by **Pittsburgh Press** sports editor Chet Smith, who covered Nittany Lion football for more than a half century. Scheduled to be starter on first bowl team ever, the '22 Rose Bowl squad, but broke three ribs in practice in California and missed the game. Captain of '23 team that had 6-2-1 record. Made a great interception that Walter Camp later cited in promoting forward pass in the historic 13-13 tie with West Virginia in New York's Yankee Stadium in '23, but injury that knocked him out of the game was considered a main reason why State didn't win game. After graduation he was a graduate assistant for Bezdek, then went to Rice as a full time assistant ('24) to the legendary coach, John Heisman, for whom the "Heisman Trophy" is named. Also coached at Florida before returning to assist Bezdek full time in '29. Then assisted Higgins ('30-'48), where he earned nationwide reputation as a line coach and for his ability in scouting opponents. Took over as head coach in '49 when Higgins retired but decided he didn't want to be a head coach and assisted Engle for two years ('50-'52) before concentrating on baseball. Was head baseball coach for three decades from '31 until his retirement in '63 and his once-beaten '57 team was runner-up to NCAA champion in '57 College World Series. Lived in State College until his death on May 2, 1978.

BELLAS, JOE. 1964-65. OT, 6'2", 230 lbs.; Colver, PA. One of the best offensive lineman of the '60s for Engle and the first of State's First-Team Academic All-Americans in '65. Also was first PSU athlete ever to win a prestigious NCAA post graduate scholarship ('66) for academics. He had a 3.5-plus average in accounting and was as fine a "scholar-athlete" as there was in the Engle era. Started for two years and was the "iron man" of the '64 team, when he had more playing time than any player. All-East in senior year. Played one of his finest games in shocking 27-0 upset of Ohio State in '64 as team racked up 221 yards rushing on what was then one of the country's best defenses.. Played in '66 Hula Bowl. Deceased.

BENFATTI, LOU. 1990-91-92-93. DE & DT, 6'3", 270 lbs.; Green Pond, NJ. One of the few players in the Paterno era who started in every game from his frosh season through senior season (49 total). First-Team All-American in senior year and Second-Team '92. Semifinalist in '93 for Lombardi Award as outstanding lineman/linebacker in nation when he had 64 tackles—six for losses—five sacks, an interception, three pass breakups, four forced fumbles and one fumble recovery. Finished career with 109 solo tackles and 70 assists, with 25 tackles for losses, 10 sacks and two interceptions. Seemed to always play his best against Notre Dame: as frosh he led team with nine tackles, including four solos, in "nailbiting" 24-21 win over then number one Irish, and in '91 his interception stopped a potential go-ahead TD for Notre Dame and set up an O.J. McDuffie TD in 35-13 win. Co-Capt of '93 team that finished third in first season as member of Big 10 and beat Tennessee 31-13 in '94 Citrus Bowl. Played one of best games of year in come-from-behind 38-37 win over Michigan State that put State into Citrus Bowl, when he had 8 tackles and caused a fumble. Won Hall Award in '93 as "outstanding senior player." Played in East-West Shrine game and Senior Bowl in '94. Picked third by New York Jets in '94 and still playing with the Jets. Lives in Oak Ridge, NJ.

BENSON, BRAD. 1974-75-76. OT, 6'3 ½", 262 lbs.; Altoona, PA. One of the fine offensive linemen who was overlooked by many because of such linemates as Tom Rafferty and Jeff Bleamer. Became better known as pro with New York Giants. A two-year starter at LT and co-captain of '76 team, when he made All-East and Honorable Mention on several All-American teams. Made an impression as frosh in several games but didn't play enough to win letter. Made his first start

as a soph against Ohio University in mid-November of '74 and was a regular from that point on. Along with Keith Dorney and George Rehiner, he was cited for his fine blocking in 38-16 win over Army that helped turn around '76 season and led to Gator Bowl finish with Notre Dame. Also praised for his pass protection in 33-0 victory over West Virginia in '76. Played in Hula and Japan Bowls in '77. Eighth choice of New England in '77 but moved on to New York Giants where he had an All-Pro career from '78-'86. Now living in Flemington, NJ.

BENTZ, H. N. 'NEWSH'. 1920-21-22. C, 5'7", 190 lbs.; Ebensburg, PA. A three-year starter at center on the back-to-back unbeaten teams of '20 and '21 and the '22 team that played in State's first bowl game, the '23 Rose Bowl. Often overlooked because he was 'sandwiched' between two All-American guards, Joe Bedenk and 'Red' Griffiths. Sportswriters of his day credit him as well as the others with the blocking that helped Glenn Killinger, "Light Horse" Harry Wilson, Charlie Way and Joe Lightner become national stars. Played one of his finest games as soph in big 28-7 win over Penn with blocking and tackling that had sportswriters "buzzing" in the press box. Had the physique that made his nickname apropos and no one ever called him by his long-forgotten first name. Had an outgoing personality on and off the field and wasn't afraid to take on the toughest man of the opposing team. Playing with blood flowing from cuts and bruises never bothered him. Captain of '22 team that went to Rose Bowl despite losing last two games to Penn and Pitt. Got all caught up in the pre-game hoopla as team visited Hollywood Studios and he and Bedenk had pictures taken with Mary Pickford and husband Douglas Fairbanks Sr.; then violated a training rule and didn't start against USC, but came in as substitute in a loss that he always said was one of the biggest disappointments in his otherwise standout career. Served as assistant coach in '26 and almost died of typhoid in '27 but went on to successful coaching and business career. Deceased.

BERRYMAN, BOB ("PUNK"). 1911-12-13-15. HB & FB, 5'11", 175 lbs.; Philadelphia, PA. One of the best running backs of his era but overshadowed by All-American's Pete Mauthe and Shorty Miller. Started as a frosh at HB and later at FB in place of injured Mauthe on the '11 team that went unbeaten. Continued as starting HB the next year on the great '12 team. Was academically ineligible in '14 but returned in '15, and with Mauthe and Miller gone he was the star running back and became a Third-Team All-American on head coach Dick Harlow's first team. Had perhaps his finest games against Penn and Harvard in '15: scored TD on 45-yard run in 13-3 win over Penn, and against Harvard, he had 177 yards rushing as State outplayed the favored Crimson, but lost on two key fumbles and a controversial holding penalty that cost them the game, 13-0. Made one of the key plays in the '12 season when, with State trailing 6-3 to underdog Cornell, he returned a KO 75-yards for a TD to break the game wide open as State won, 29-6. Was one of stars in classic first game ever with Notre Dame in '13 but Lions lost, 14-7, as Knute Rockne and Gus Dorias led Irish victory. Later coached professional football with Frankford Yellowjackets, then became a civil engineer in Cincinnati. Deceased.

BLACKLEDGE, TODD. 1980-81-82. QB, 6'4", 222 lbs.; North Canton, OH. The most prolific TD passer in State history and QB of the first National Championship team, but, surprisingly, never was higher than Honorable Mention All-American, although he was an Academic

All-American in '82. Won Davey O'Brien Award as the nation's best QB in '82, beating out such players as Dan Marino. Was sixth in balloting for Heisman Trophy that year and then outplayed Herschel Walker in '83 Sugar Bowl, where he was named Outstanding Player in 27-24 win over Georgia that gave team national title. Gave up last year of eligibility in senior year to enter pros and was number one choice of Kansas City in '83. He was one of Paterno's great scholar-athletes who graduated with a 3.80 GPA and Phi Beta Kappa key. In '97, he became the second Penn State player to be inducted into the GTE/CoSIDA Academic Hall of Fame. Holds passing records for career TDs with 41 (tied with Tony Sacca) and most TDs in one season ('82) with 22. But also threw a lot of interceptions and holds record for most interceptions in a career with 41, and twice (in '81 and '82) he was one short of Vince O'Bara's record of 15 interceptions in one season. Tied with Richie Lucas and Bob Parsons for most interceptions in one game, when he had four in demoralizing 42-21 loss at Alabama in mid-'82 that temporarily set back National Championship aspirations. Until '97 he held record for most passing yards in one game, with 358 yards—225 in the second half— on 26-for-41 passes (and two TDs & two interceptions) in devastating 17-14 loss at Miami that knocked State from number one rankings in mid-season of '81. Only QB to have four TDs in more than one game, and he did it three times, all in '82 (against Temple, Maryland and Rutgers). Battled fellow "redshirt" frosh Jeff Hostetler for starting QB position in spring and fall of '80 and had first start in fourth game against Missouri and never gave it up, although debut in 29-21 defensive win over Missouri wasn't great, with only 9-of-19 completions (for 92 yards) and three interceptions with one TD. But went on to set record that still stands for season passing yardage by a frosh (1,037) and also soph passing yardage record with 1,557 yards; and caused Hostetler to transfer to West Virginia. Total offense leader three years in a row. Fourth in career passing with 4,812 yards on 341 completions in 657 attempts and one-season passing yardage with 2,218 yards on 161-of-292 passes in '82. Passed for over 200 yards in nine games (fourth best of all time), including his final game in '83 Sugar Bowl, when he was 13-for-23 for 228 yards and one TD; the TD was a never-to-be-forgotten beauty of 47 yards into the EZ to a leaping Greg Garrity in the fourth QT that provided the victory margin. And no one will ever forget the last second two-yard TD pass to backup TE Kirk Bowman inches from the EZ turf that climaxed a desperate come-from-behind two-minute, 65-yard drive that upset then number two Nebraska, 27-24, in '82 and put the team on course for the eventual National Championship game; had another of his great one-game passing days against Nebraska, too, hitting on 23-of-39 passes for 295 yards, three TDs and just one interception, and that performance put him on the cover of **Sports Illustrated**. Also led team to '80 Fiesta Bowl win over Ohio State, 31-19, although he hit on just 8-of-22 passes for 117 yards but scored a TD on a three-yard run. Pro career never reached the heights of his collegiate years, even though he played five years for Chiefs and two years with Pittsburgh before retiring. Now a highly-successful sports broadcaster and has been living in his hometown of North Canton, OH.

BLASENTINE, JOE. 1960-61-62. LG, 5'11", 200 lbs.; West Philadelphia, PA. A tough little guard who was as intense as any lineman during the Engle era. Engle said he was a "blood-and-thunder" tackler. A favorite of the fans because of his take-charge attitude and "hard-nose" approach to every game. Teammates often said they were glad he was on their team. The only soph to start in '60 when the team overcame poor opening to season to win last five games in a row, including the Liberty Bowl over Oregon. Played one of his greatest all-around games in 35-15 win over Georgia Tech in '61 Gator Bowl; Line coach Jim O'Hora noted Blasentine hit one opponent so hard, "It was one of the finest tackles I've ever seen." Now an elementary school teacher in Cinnaminson, NJ.

BLEAMER, JEFF. 1973-74. OL, 6'4", 250 lbs.; Allentown, PA. Played behind three-year starter Charlie Getty in junior year but finally got chance as senior. Won Red Worrell Award in '74 as most improved player in spring practice and started in fall at RT. A fine pass protector. Along with Tom Rafferty, John Nessel and Jack Baiorunos he opened holes for the '74 team that finished 10th in country after going 8-2 and beating Baylor, 41-20, in '75 Cotton Bowl. Eighth pick of Philadelphia in '75 and played two years with Eagles, one year with the New York Jets and another year with the New York Giants before leaving pro ball in '79. Now an assistant football coach at East Tennessee State in Johnson City, TN.

BLOCKSON, CHARLIE. 1953-54-55. FB, 6'1", 210 lbs.; Norristown, PA. An all-purpose back who was a two-year starter at FB but was sidelined much of his junior and senior years by injuries. Fullbacks did more blocking than anything during this period of the Engle era and his blocking skills fit his name. Good at pounding the line and a first class linebacker in the era of one platoon football. Was a backup as soph when he made one of the most crucial and longest runs of year in fourth game of season against Syracuse; State was losing 14-0 late in third QT when Blockson ran off tackle for 45-yard TD that sparked eventual 20-14 comeback victory. Also had one of his best offensive days in famous "snow game" against Fordham in '53 when he was second to Lenny Moore in rushing with 42 yards on 10 carries, including a three-yard TD; also had a 20-yard pass reception that set up TD in 28-21 win. Teammates said he was a nice man who let his actions speak for him on the field. Now a well-known scholar and historian of Afro-American culture and a school district advisor; lives in Gwynedd, PA.

BOCHNA, DEREK. 1990-91-92-93. CB & SS, 5'11", 195 lbs.; Greensboro, PA. One of the best DB's of the 90's who gave Paterno consistency as a three-year starter at LCB. Had 12 interceptions during career, good for a fourth place tie with Junior Powell and Brian Miller in all-time records. As true frosh, broke into the lineup as backup CB and wound up as starter in '90 Blockbuster Bowl. Led team in pass deflections that year with 18, had two interceptions and was number three in tackles with 56. Became full-time starting CB in opening game as soph and stayed there until senior year, then moved to strong safety. Coaches considered Bochna a heady player who seldom made an error. Always seemed to play well before the "hometown" crowd at Pitt. Made one of the "clutch" interceptions of his career in final regular season game against Pitt in '90 with a pick off in last minute off of Darren Perry's deflection, preserving 22-17 win over Panthers and putting team into Blockbuster Bowl. The next year he intercepted two passes and broke up another in 32-20 victory over Pitt. One of his outstanding plays came in '91 Fiesta Bowl with a blind-side sack of Tennessee QB Andy Kelly, forcing fumble that teammate Reggie Givens snatched out of the air and ran 23 yards for a TD that virtually clinched the come-from-behind 42-17 win; also had eight solo tackles and two assists in game. As SS in '93 he missed first three games because of injury but came back and made immediate impact against Rutgers and Maryland with fumble recovery and interception that helped win both games. The final interception of his career was one of his biggest ever: with Michigan State leading 37-17 late in third QT at East Lansing and driving for another TD, Bochna made a diving interception at the State 42-yard line; three plays later State scored on a 40-yard pass from Collins to Engram and went on to win the game, 38-37, and get the Citrus Bowl bid. All-East in '92. A fine baseball player who was an outfielder for the '92 & '93 teams. Now an assistant football coach at Washington & Jefferson and living in hometown of Greensboro, PA.

BOTULA, PAT. 1957-58-59. HB & FB, 6'1", 195 lbs.; Pittsburgh, PA. One of the smartest runners in the Engle era who didn't have the natural speed of his contemporaries but was quick and determined in his running style. Solid defensive player who wasn't apprehensive about taking on a blocker or runner. Started out as third unit left halfback as soph but moved to second unit because of injuries and was one of leading ground gainers. Moved to FB in junior year and became starter in opening game against Nebraska, where he rushed for over 100 yards (122) for the only time in his career. The next week he was leading rusher again with 71 yards in 43-0 win over Penn but was injured in game and missed four games before coming back and being the leading rusher (66 yards on 13 carries) in 14-14 tie with West Virginia. Finished season as number two rusher behind Dave Kasperian. Was first back in six years to be elected Captain in '59, when team played in first bowl game of Engle era and finished 11th in country with 9-2 record. Rushed for 204 yards on 58 carries in senior year in the option offense led by QB Richie Lucas, and was leading ground gainer (with 43 yards) in the classic 20-18 loss to eventual National Champion Syracuse in the late season "clash of the unbeatens." Also led all rushers in final game of career at '59 Liberty Bowl win over Alabama with 44 yards on 12 carries, but actually made one of the biggest plays of his career as an "offensive lineman" in that game: with seconds left in the 1st half of scoreless game, Botula was in the line blocking for attempted FG at 18-yard line when QB-holder Galen Hall faked and passed to Roger Kochman on screen pass with Botula and others leading the charge into EZ for the only TD of the game in eventual 7-0 win in Coach Bear Bryant's first bowl game with the Crimson Tide. Now an investment broker in Pittsburgh, PA.

BOWMAN, KIRK. 1980-81-82-83. DE & TE, 6'1½", 246 lbs.; Mechanicsburg, PA. Teammates jokingly called him "Stonehands" because of his problems in catching passes but this converted defensive end made one of the most memorable receptions in history that led to first National Championship in '82. It happened in fourth game of season against Nebraska at Beaver Stadium, when with four seconds left and State trailing, 24-21, he made a near impossible diving catch close to the ground near the back of the EZ to scoop up a poorly thrown Todd Blackledge pass from the two-yard line to give State a 27-24 victory and thrust the team into contention for the national title; Nebraska players claimed he didn't catch the ball but to this day Bowman insists he had it six-inches off the ground; inserted into the game as the second TE in a basic running formation, he also had the first TD of the game on a 14-yard pass from Blackledge, and they were the first two passes he ever caught. What makes his feat even more miraculous in retrospect is that he never had another pass reception that season, nor ever scored

another TD and only had six more catches (for 60 yards) in his final year, when he started just two games. He was a good backup DE in his first two seasons and then was moved to OG in Spring practice of '82 but was moved to TE in the fall when Ron Heller was shifted to OT. A nice guy well liked by teammates who probably will be remembered long after many First-Team All-Americans are forgotten. Now in business in Colleyville, TX.

BRADLEY, DAVE. 1966-67-68. G & T, 6'4", 240 lbs.; Burham, PA. One of the forgotten fine offensive linemen of the early Paterno era. Started first three games at T as sophomore, then switched to G in '67 and back to T in '68 and was full-time starter both years. Along with fellow T John Kulka, he was singled out by offensive line coach Joe McMullen at end of great unbeaten '68 season as the reason Campbell, Pittman and the other running backs could do so well. Pittman said he wouldn't have led team in rushing that year without the great blocking off tackle by Bradley. Few remember that it was Bradley who originally almost recovered the late onside kick that Ted Kwalick ran back for a TD to beat Army, 28-24, in one of the biggest plays of the '68 season. Was biggest man on '68 team. Known as "the chief" because he had played football at Chief Logan High School near State College. Played in '69 Senior Bowl. Drafted number two by Green Bay and played with Packers ('69-'71) and St. Louis ('72). An accounting major at PSU who is now a steel corporate manager in Lewistown, PA.

BRADLEY, JIM. 1973-74. DB, 6'1", 186 lbs.; Johnstown, PA. One of the fine, opportunistic DBs who made things happen on the unbeaten '73 team that Paterno once called his "best team ever." Made perhaps the tackle of the year in 16-9 Orange Bowl victory over LSU that LSU coach Charlie McClendon thought was the turning point in game: on last play of half, Bradley surprised LSU when he stopped a wide open receiver at the five-yard line to prevent a TD that could have changed momentum of game. Hardly played as a reserve in his soph year, but when he got his chance he became a two-year starter and a terrific and aggressive tackler and pass defender. Had an outstanding season in '73: led team with four interceptions and three recoveries of opponent fumbles, beginning with a spectacular debut as a starter in nationally-televised opening season game against Stanford in '73, when he had a 51-yard interception return and recovered a fumble on the Stanford 10-yard line with two minutes left in the half to set up the Shuman-to-Hayman TD pass that broke open the game and led to 20-6 victory. Three games later his recovered fumble late in the first half at the Air Force 26 led to a quick TD that again broke open a tight game in a 19-9 victory. Against Syracuse his interception set up another TD in 49-6 blowout, and another interception two weeks later at the start of the second half against Maryland set up a TD that broke open a 22-22 tie and sparked the Lions to a 42-22 win in one of the crucial games of the season. Co-Captain of veteran defensive unit of '74 team that lost only two of 11 regular season games by a total of six points and beat Baylor, 41-20, in '75 Cotton Bowl. Missed two games that year with injury but still had an interception and two fumble recoveries. His performance set stage for his brothers Tom (see below) and Matt (three year LB starter, '79-'81) to follow in his footsteps. Now an orthopedic surgeon in Pittsburgh.

BRADLEY, TOM. 1977-78. DB, 5'9", 167 lbs.; Johnstown, PA. Perhaps the epitome of the Penn State player who was determined to make it despite lacking the natural ability and talent of most teammates. Better known now as a long time assistant coach in Paterno era, and recruiter of many players from Western Pennsylvania, but as a player he made the most of his skills. As hard-working and determined as any player in the Paterno era. Coaches say he had enthusiasm and tenacity and was smart. Originally a walk-on but later earned scholarship. Backup at DB back in both '77 & '78 but was leader of the special teams. Made initial impression on regional TV in third game of '77 season when he tackled punt receiver inside five-yard line to help give Lions good field position in eventual 27-9 victory. Teammates called him "Scrap Iron" because he was scrappy and not afraid to take on all blockers during KOs, FGs and punts. Was captain of the '78 special teams which became known as "The Scrap Pack." "The Scrap Pack" helped the '78 team become the first ever number one team in State history and during season, the "Pack" held opposing teams to less and 20 yards per kickoff and a total of 87 yards on punt returns. Unfortunately, a 62-yard punt return by Alabama in '79 Sugar Bowl which set up the game winning TD for the Tide is the one Bradley regretfully remembers the most. Joined Paterno's staff as a graduate assistant and has been full-time since '80 with various coaching responsibilities including linebackers, wide receivers, defensive ends, special teams and now defensive backs. Lives in State College.

BRADY, KYLE. 1991-92-93-94. TE, 6'6", 260 lbs.; New Cumberland, PA. May have been the best TE ever as a combination blocker/receiver and gained more recognition for his blocking ability than his pass catching. First-Team All-American in senior year, when he helped lead unbeaten '94 team to Big Ten title and '95 Rose Bowl championship. One of his most critical blocks came with less than a minute remaining in the Illinois game when FB Brian Milne crashed nine-yards over a big hole opened by Brady and tackles Jeff Hartings and Keith Conlin for the TD that climaxed the historic 96-yard drive that gave State the dramatic come-from-behind victory and the Rose Bowl berth. TV commentators praised his blocking all season as the team racked up 530.2 yards average and 47.8 points per game. One of the most highly-recruited players in the nation in high school but didn't fully develop until his junior and senior years, when he was named All-Big Ten both years. Saved best for last, when he caught 27 passes for 365 yards and two TDs and an average of 13.5 yards per reception in '94. Had one of his best all-around days in "big" game victory over Michigan, 31-24, that vaulted team into number one as he led all receivers with six receptions for 63 yards and had the crucial first Down catches on four scoring drives. His 76 career receptions is second only to Ted Kwalick among PSU TEs. Holds record for most TD receptions by a frosh in one game with two in 81-0 blowout of Cincinnati in '91; tied with Kenny Jackson and Terry Smith for most receptions in one game by a frosh with four in 35-13 loss to Notre Dame in '91. Made two of his best receptions on similar plays in comparable situations against Tennessee in the '92 Fiesta Bowl and '94 Citrus Bowl: in both games State came back from early large deficits to win games in second Half with Brady's third QT TDs helping to swing the momentum; in Fiesta Bowl he was wide open in EZ for Tony Sacca's "across-the-field" pass for a 13-yard TD that gave Lions first lead, 21-17, in eventual 42-17 win; two years later at Citrus Bowl, he was wide open again for an "across-the-field" pass from Kerry Collins for a seven-yard TD five minutes into the third QT that gave State an insurmountable 24-13 lead in eventual 31-13 victory. Won Red Worrell Award in '93 as most improved

offensive player in spring practice. Top choice of New York Jets in '95 (and 9th NFL pick overall). Still playing with the Jets and makes his off season home in New Cumberland, PA.

BROWN, GARY. 1987-88-89-90. RB, DB & KR , 5'11", 208 lbs.; Williamsport, PA. No one in the Paterno era better epitomizes the player who makes individual sacrifices for the betterment of the team than Brown. A highly recruited running back, he was the leading ground gainer in soph year as Tailback in '88 (689 yards and six TDs on 136 carries for a 5.1 yards average), when Blair Thomas was sidelined by season-long injury, then switched to DB as Hero when Thomas returned in '89 and was a sensation. Started in five games and finished 11th in tackles with 21 solos and 13 assists. Best remembered for his spectacular defensive performance in '89 Holiday Bowl against BYU, when he literally ran over Outland Trophy winner Mohammed Elewonibi, stripped the ball from Heisman Trophy winner Ty Detmer and ran 53 yards for a TD with 45 seconds remaining to clinch victory, 50-39. Was one of the best kickoff returners and still has record for the best KO return average in one season (43 yards on eight returns) in senior year. Tenth in career KO returns worth a 24.2 yards average on 38 runbacks for 920 yards. His 95-yard return against Texas in '90 is the longest without a TD in records; also set record in game yardage (201) and average (40.2 yards on five returns) that day. Holds records for most KO returns in a game with seven in '88 against West Virginia. Is 21st best in career rushing with 1,321 yards and 11 TDs on 260 carries for a 5.08 yards average. His 80-yard TD run as a frosh at Carrier Dome against Syracuse is tied with six others for seventh longest run in team history. Had best day rushing in '90 win against Temple with 105 yards and one TD on 16 carries. Played in '91 Senior Bowl. Eighth pick by Houston in '91 and was a starter there for nearly five years. Sat out '96 season but came back to NFL in '97 to be leading rusher for San Diego Chargers. Signed with New York Giants for '98.

BROWN, EARL ("SPARKY"). 1940, 42-43. TB & FB, 5'9", 165 lbs.; Cazenovia, NY. Another of the forgotten running backs of the Higgins era who was one of the stars of the war-torn '42 team that surprised the nation with a 6-1-1 record and was ranked 19th by AP. He had two games rushing over 100 yards that year, getting 125 yards on 18 carries and one TD in 14-7 opening season win over Bucknell and got 108 yards and two TDs on 13 carries in come-from-behind 18-13 victory over Syracuse, but neither games are listed in PSU record book. His 79-yard TD run against Bucknell was longest run from scrimmage in four years and still is one of State's all-time best. Only soph to letter in '40 as backup FB to Smaltz on team that had school's best record in 19 years; was only non-Pennsylvanian on squad. Wearing number 13 jersey in '40, had one of best games in 17-13 Homecoming win over West Virginia, when he came in from fourth string because of injuries to other FBs and made four crucial first downs and big interception in fourth QT. Sat out '41 because of severe injuries to ankles during winter but came back to be one of the running stars of '42. Was starting FB in early games of '43 while back in school under Advanced ROTC program waiting for call-up to Officer Candidate School and in opening game threw a 39-yard TD pass, then impishly stuck out his tongue at Higgins and the coaches because they had said he was a lousy passer; left after fourth game of season when team almost upset unbeaten Navy, 14-6, and never returned after war; carried four times for eight yards in last game. Also a fine pass receiver and defensive back. Retired and living in his hometown of Cazenovia, NY.

BRUNO, JOHN. 1984-85-86. P, 6'2", 187 lbs.; Upper St. Clair, PA. Will never be forgotten for what he did on and off the field at the '87 Fiesta Bowl that gave State its second National Championship, but, unfortunately, he died in April of '92 after the skin cancer few knew about when he was playing came back after remission. During a pre-game steak fry at Fiesta Bowl, the Miami team dressed in Army fatigues and walked out en masse proclaiming they wouldn't sit down for dinner with State players because "the Japanese [didn't] go and have dinner with Pearl Harbor before they bombed them..."; Bruno quickly grabbed the microphone and said: "...but didn't the Japanese lose that war?"; the incident gained such notoriety it is still remembered as one of the all-time great "put downs" in college football hype. He then went out on Jan. 2 and booted nine punts (for a 43.4 average) that kept Miami in a hole all night and helped State's "bend but don't break" defense throttle then number one Miami and win the game, 14-10. Three of his kicks were downed on the Miami two, nine and 11-yard lines and, despite running 93 plays and gaining 445, yards the Hurricanes heretofore high-powered offense scored just 10 points. One of the most likable players on the team with a great sense of humor. Many forget he was a walk-on sophomore in '82 who earned his way onto the team. Still holds record for most punts and most yardage in one season, when he kicked 79 for 3,273 yards in his soph year. Had one of his best punting days that year that helped Lions beat Maryland 25-24 when he averaged nearly 43 yards on eight kicks. In '85 his 46-yard average on nine punts, including one for 71 yards, was cited as a major factor in the Lions 16-12 victory over Boston College. Only had one blocked in 205 career attempts. Three-year punting average of 41.7 yards (on 204 punts for 8,508 yards) is fourth highest in career records. Also third, sixth and ninth in season averages with his best year being in '85, when he averaged 42.9 yards (60 punts for 2,575 yards)—including best punt ever, 71 yards against Boston College, fourth longest in school records. A cancerous mole discovered in summer of '85 was removed by surgery but came back in December of '91 and he died five months later at age 27. An award in his honor is now given annually to the outstanding member of the special teams. Drafted fifth by St. Louis in '87 and played one year with Pittsburgh. Deceased.

BURKHART, CHUCK. 1968-69. QB, 6'0", 190 lbs.; McKees Rocks, PA. The QB who could do nothing well but win. The leader of the great back-to-back unbeaten, uncrowned and unappreciated teams of '68 and '69 that set the tone for the Paterno era. His name is hardly in the State record books, yet he was one of the best clutch QBs of all time. Always played his greatest when the situation was desperate. Not much of a runner but will always be known for his dramatic spur-of-the-moment run for a TD in the last seconds that beat Kansas 15-14 in the momentous "12-man" '69 Orange Bowl; with third-and-Goal at the Kansas three-yard line, he was supposed to hand off to Charlie Pittman on State's patented scissors play but he kept the ball himself and went around left end all alone for the TD; only moments before he had thrown a dramatic 48-yard pass (as he went down under a mass of tacklers) to Bobby Campbell that put State at the Kansas three-yard line, from where Burkhart got the TD; then handed off to Campbell for the two-point conversion after the 12th man penalty. Showed his character and poise again in the '69 game at Syracuse, when he was benched in

second Half after a horrendous performance, yet came back in fourth QT to lead team from desperate 14-0 deficit to thrilling 15-14 win. In his last game in PS uniform, the '70 Orange Bowl, he was the Most Valuable Back as he completed 11-of-26 passes for 187 yards and the game's only TD on a 28-yard first QT throw to Lydell Mitchell in the 10-3 victory. Starter in both '68 & '69, when he led team in passing with his best stats in junior year when he was 87-for-177 and 1,170 yards and six TDs. The first of the McKees Rocks QB trio of Burkhart, John Hufnagel and Chuck Fusina who were so integral to the success of Paterno in his first 15 years. His 76-yard TD pass to little known Tom Cherry in '68 UCLA game is sixth longest pass play of all-time (although tied with two others). Played in 1970 Senior Bowl. Now president of a company in Dallas, TX.

BUTTLE, GREG. 1973-74-75. LB, 6'2 ½", 220 lbs.; Linwood, NJ. Penn State's "Mr. Tackle" who holds all the major tackle records and a consensus First-Team All-American in senior year, when picked by AP, UPI, Walter Camp, Football Writers and others. His three-year career total tackles of 343 (on 185 solos and 158 assists) is nearly 30 more than runner-up Brian Gelzheiser (who played four years) and his totals in '74 (165) and '75 (140) are 1-2 for most tackles in one season with the 86 solos and 79 assists in '74 being the best marks in solos & assists for one season. Also tied Jeff Hite for most interceptions in '74 season (three) and had two in 21-12 win over West Virginia. Had one of greatest tackling games against WVU the next year with 24 in 39-0 victory. In final regular season game of his career, he was named Defensive Player-of-the-Game as State beat Pitt 7-6 to clinch '75 Sugar Bowl bid. Picked off three opponent passes again in '75, one less than team leader. A TE in high school, he had great lateral speed, which enabled him to plug up seemingly open holes quickly. Had a fine soph year as a backup to All-American Ed O'Neil and made first ever start in second game of '73 season against Navy when O'Neil was injured and called defensive signals in 39-0 win; later in year was involved in one of the quickest scores of Paterno years when he recovered a fumble on the opening kickoff against Maryland at the MD 18-yard line and State scored TD in eventual 42-22 win. He also scored a TD one game earlier against West Virginia on a 25-yard interception return. Co-Captain and inside right LB of '75 team that was 9-3 and finished 10th in country; had 13 tackles in tough '76 Sugar Bowl loss to Alabama. The "object" in one of the most bizarre moments in State FB history prior to '74 Thanksgiving Night game at Pitt: in players-only locker room meeting before kickoff, FB Tom Donchez closed a fiery, inspirational speech by throwing his helmet against a locker where the helmet bounced off and hit Buttle between the eyes, knocking him out cold; a groggy, patched-up Buttle barely made kickoff; remembers practically nothing about first half and needed six-stitches over eye at halftime but played outstanding game in 31-10 win. Played in Hula and Japan Bowls in '76. Number three pick of New York Jets in '76 and had a fine nine-year career before retiring. Now a sports marketing representative and lives in East Meadow, NY.

BUZIN, RICH. 1965-66-67. DT & OT, 6'4", 243 lbs.; Youngstown, OH. Second-Team All-American and All-East in '67 and one of best seniors for Paterno in the year he turned around his coaching career. Academic All-American in '67 as an accounting major. One of the hardest working players on the team. Became a starter in midseason of soph year at OG and then played both OT and DT as junior and senior. Excellent at pass protection and was cited for his great work in '67 win over Syracuse, 29-20. Received the game ball from his teammates for his all-around performance in 42-6 pasting of Pitt to end '67 regular season; scored a rare TD for an offensive lineman when he recovered a State fumble in the EZ. Played in '68 Hula Bowl. Second choice of New York Giants in '68 and played with Giants ('68-'70), Los Angeles Rams ('71) and Chicago ('72) before quitting pro ball. His son Mike is starter at defensive line on the '98 team. Now an executive vice president of a company in Westlake, OH.

CALDERONE, JACK. 1955-56. T, 6'0", 219 lbs.; Chester, PA. Another of those unsung interior linemen but one of the best tackles of the Engle era. After playing behind Rosie Grier and co-captain Otto Kneidinger as a soph, he became a two-year starter at T and the only letterman at T in senior year. Engle and Toretti said he was a solid player on both offense and defense who rarely got headlines but always did his job. Still was one of the smallest tackles on the team. Didn't get as much credit as many of his teammates but was instrumental in helping Lions pull off one of the major upsets in team history, 7-6, over then number five Ohio State in Columbus in '56. Played in North-South game after senior season. Now a real estate broker in Glen Mills, PA.

CAMPBELL, BOBBY. 1966-67-68. TB, P & KR, 6'0", 190 lbs.; Apalachin, NY. The first standout running back of the Paterno era. Probably would have been an All-American but knee injury sidelined him for seven games in '67 and dislocated shoulder for almost four games in '68. Teamed with Charlie Pittman as the running stars on the first unbeaten team in 21 years in '68 and one of the heroes of the historic come-back 15-14 win over Kansas in the '69 Orange Bowl; made two of the greatest clutch plays in last minute of his career in that Orange Bowl game: with State trailing, 14-7, he first combined with QB Chuck Burkhart on a 48-yard pass reception that put State at the Kansas third-yard line, from where Burkhart got TD moments later; then after State got a second chance for a two-point PAT attempt because of 12 defenders on the field, Campbell scored the crucial two-points on a sweep around left end with 15 seconds left. Was game's leading rusher with 101 yards on 18 carries and also caught two passes for 55 yards. One of his most consequential runs was as junior in '67 in pivotal early season game in same Orange Bowl Stadium at Miami that was turning point of Paterno's embryonic coaching career; made a scintillating 50-yard run off a scissors play late in second QT to highlight 90-yard drive for TD and eventual 17-8 win on sophomore-laden team. However, he was injured the following week against UCLA and was sidelined for rest of season. In perhaps the best game of his career, he set a record that still stands for best rushing in one game by a senior (and fifth best of all-time), when he amassed 239 yards and two TDs on 24 attempts in his final regular season game, a 30-12 victory over Syracuse on Dec. 7 '68; his 87-yard run for TD in that game is still the fourth longest run for TD of all time; also caught three passes for another 20 yards. A deceptive and elusive runner who could fool tacklers and shake them loose in a quick stop-go maneuver. Did much of the punting as junior

and senior and was a boomer, with a 45.1 average in 12 punts in '67 when he led team (and led nation until sidelined with knee injury). His 52.4 yards average for five punts against Miami in '68 victory is second best single game punting average of all time. He was first soph since Lenny Moore in '53 to lead team in rushing with 482 yards and five TDs on 79 carries (for a 6.1 yard per carry) and in KO returns with five for 179 yards and a 35.8 average. Eighteenth in career rushing with 1,480 yards and 14 TDs on 242 carries for a 6.12 yards average. Had total of six games rushing more than 100 yards, including his first as a soph in 48-24 win over Pitt, when he compiled 137 yards and two TDs on 14 carries and won Coogan Award as "outstanding Player-of-the-Game. Played in '69 Senior Bowl. Fourth choice of Pittsburgh in '69 but never had his heart set on playing in NFL and quit after one year. Coached high school football for years in Syracuse, and is now head coach and teacher in Frederick, MD.

CAPPELLETTI, JOHN. 1971-72-73, TB, 6'1", 225 lbs.; Upper Darby, PA. The school's only Heisman Trophy winner as "outstanding intercollegiate football player" in '73. No one who saw it "live" or on TV will ever forget his from-the-heart emotional acceptance speech honoring his dying younger brother, Joey. Also won Maxwell Trophy that year as "outstanding player" and selected "Player-of-the-Year" by ABC-TV, UPI, the Walter Camp Foundation and Washington Touchdown Club. A consensus First-Team All-American, when picked by AP, UPI, Football Coaches, Football Writers, Walter Camp and others. Inducted in '93 into National Football Foundation College Football Hall of Fame and is one of 15 Penn State players in the Hall. A throwback to the days of the "two-way" star. Was faster runner than most people realized but relied on power and quickness. Led team in rushing as junior and senior with his Heisman year being his greatest, when he rushed for 1,522 yards and 17 TDs on 286 carries and a 5.3 yards average, numbers that still rank him third in one-season ground gaining, behind Lydell Mitchell and Ki-Jana Carter (see below). Eighth in career rushing with 2,639 yards and 29 TDs on 519 attempts (for a 5.1 yards average)—which is even more amazing, since he is the only player in the top 10 to accumulate all his numbers in just two years and not three or four. The reason? A shock when one looks back in retrospect, because Paterno played him at defensive back in frosh and soph years. And he was a good one, starting on the '71 team that hammered Texas in '72 Cotton Bowl in the "breakthrough" game of the Paterno era. Also an outstanding punt returner as soph and led team with 28 returns for 274 yards. His three consecutive 200-yard rushing games in '73 against Maryland, North Carolina State and Ohio U is a season and career PSU record, and, at the time, set an NCAA record that has since been broken; had a total of 13 games over 100-yards rushing, with his best being 220 yards and three TDs on 41 carries (a team record) in 35-29 win over NC State at Beaver Stadium in '73. That game also showed what he could do when the pressure was on, for with the score tied, 29-29, late in fourth QT, he carried four times in a 60-yard drive, including the final 27 yards for a TD that gave State the victory. Also all-purpose yards leader in '72 & '73 with additional yards as pass receiver and kick returner. His absence from '73 Sugar Bowl (played on New Years Eve of '72) because of illness probably cost team the game in 14-0 loss to Oklahoma, and put a blemish on a great 10-2 season and eighth ranking by UPI. But he came back next season as co-captain to lead '73 team to Paterno's third unbeaten season, including a 16-9 win over LSU in '74 Orange Bowl. But, again, team was unappreciated by pollsters who rated it fifth; he had an off night in Orange Bowl but did score one of the two TDs. His four TDs in 62-14 win over West Virginia in '73 and another four TDs in 49-10 victory over Ohio U three games later ties him with eight other players for third most TDs in one game. Played in Hula and Senior Bowls in '74. Number one choice of Los Angeles Rams in '74 and had All-Pro career with Rams ('74-'79) and San Diego ('80-'83) before retiring. Now involved in real estate acquisition & management in Southern California and lives in Laguna Niguel, CA.

CAPRARA, BABE. 1955-56-57. FB & PK, 5'10", 181 lbs.; Turtle Creek, PA. Probably the best FB to play for Engle during the time when FBs were mainly used as blockers or spot runners who helped disrupt defensive schemes concentrating on HBs. A two-year starter at FB who also was the prime PK in senior year. Was so good on frosh team he was set to be the starter on second unit in soph year but injuries held him back early in season, giving soph teammate Joe Sabol his big break. However, by '56 he was the full-time starter and Sabol was moved to G. Also a fine defensive LB. His blocking was credited with being a subtle part of the thrilling, last minute 14-7 win over North Carolina State in '56. Played probably his best game in 21-13 win over William & Mary in '57, when he was team's leading rusher for only time in career with 72 yards on 12 carries, scored one TD and booted two extra points as State won in fourth QT. Kicked the two PATs that helped upset Syracuse, 20-12, at Archbold Stadium later in year & was the workhorse back in 14-10 win over Holy Cross with 57 yards on 15 carries and two PATs, but ended career on downer when he missed a crucial extra point in 14-13 loss to Pitt in last game of '57 season. Played in '58 East-West Shrine Game. Later played semi-pro ball in Grand Rapids where he settled down and is now athletic director of Grand Rapids Junior College and lives in Rockford, MI.

CARTER, KI-JANA. 1992-93-94. TB, 5'10", 212 lbs.; Westerville, OH. Might have become the greatest State running back of all time but left at end of "redshirt" junior year for the NFL. Only the third PSU player to be runner-up to the Heisman Trophy when, he was also a consensus First-Team All-American in '94, selected by AP, UPI, Football Writers, Football Coaches and Walter Camp among others. Lost Maxwell Award as "outstanding collegiate player of year" to backfield teammate, QB Kerry Collins. He will never be forgotten as the running star of the offensive powerhouse team of '94 that went unbeaten and won first Big Ten championship, beat Oregon in '95 Rose Bowl and was snubbed by pollsters who relegated team to second in rankings. His 83-yard TD run on the first play from scrimmage in the Rose Bowl will go down as one of the most dramatic plays in State history, and he was the Co-Most Valuable Player of the game with 156 yards and three TDs on 21 carries. His '94 season was about as impressive as any running back could have with his 1,539 yards rushing, 23 TDs and 138 points being second only to Lydell Mitchell in the State career records; he is the only player to run more than once for 80 yards or more for a TD with 80-yard TD runs against Minnesota and Indiana in '94 and the 83-yard Rose Bowl run (which is the sixth longest run of all-time). He led Big Ten that year in rushing, scoring and all-purpose yards (1,743) and his scoring average of 10.8 points per game was second in nation, while his game rushing average of 139.9 yards was fourth best in country. Rushed for more than 100 yards in nine games, setting a team

record for one season and had a total of 17 100-yard rushing games in his career. Exploded on opening day of '94 at Minneapolis' Metrodome with a performance that was a preview of what was to come: scored State's first TD of season on two-yard run at end of 77-yard drive, which included his 18-yard run; then moments later, after a Minnesota fumble, he dashed 80 yards for a TD; scored third TD early in second QT on 62-yard run, and finished game with 210 yards on 20 carries in just two and a half quarters of play. He had his best rushing and scoring game ever in what became the final game of his regular season career with a sensational day against Michigan State, scoring five TDs and amassing 227 yards on 27 carries. The five TDs ties him for second with two others in PSU's single game records, and he also had four TDs in one of the most gratifying State wins of all time, a 63-14 pasting of Ohio State before a Homecoming crowd at Beaver Stadium. Sixth in career rushing with 2,829 yards and 34 TDs on 395 carries and a 7.2 yards average. Recruited as a potential FB and became backup TB in "redshirt" frosh year, when he was third leading rusher with 264 yards and four TDs on 42 carries. Actually began soph year behind fellow "redshirt" Stephen Pitts, but after sterling performances against Minnesota (leading ground gainer with 120 yards and one TD) and USC (104 yards on 21 carries), he was starting TB; and was leading rusher for next six games, gaining more than 1,000 yards for the season in ninth game, against Illinois; but pulled hamstring in that game and didn't play again until '94 Citrus Bowl, when he was one of stars of 31-13 come-from-behind win over Tennessee, leading all rushers with 93 yards and two TDs on 19 carries. Then came his momentous '94 season. First choice of entire '95 NFL draft by Cincinnati and still playing with Bengals.

CAUM, DON. 1961-62-63. QB, Z-B, 5'11", 172 lbs.; Harrisburg, PA The original Z-Back who became a standout in his senior year as receiver and runner after being a backup QB for two years. Engle created Z-Back as keystone of new Swing-T formation, where one player known as Z-Back (or a flanker) played at an open end position on either side of the line. The formation forced defenses to spread out and opened up more running and passing opportunities. It was developed in secret in preseason of '63 and unveiled against a surprised—and favored—Oregon in season-opening night game at Eugene. Caum was not listed in three-deep lineup throughout preseason and some fans thought he had left school. On State's first offensive play, QB Pete Liske threw a quick hook-pass to Caum for eight yards to start an 80-yard drive that ended in a TD when Liske passed eight yards to Junior Powell, who got a block from Caum for score. Late in fourth QT, Caum caught a perfect pass in stride from Liske as two defenders closed in to score a 41-yard TD that sealed 17-7 win & Z-Back was born. He was also an excellent defensive safety, and in the next game against UCLA he had two interceptions in 17-14 win. Ended his career with back-to-back outstanding games against Holy Cross and Pitt. In last game at Beaver Stadium against Holy Cross he scored first TD as holder on fake FG, running in from nine-yard line, then caught a 60-yard bomb for another TD in 28-14 victory. It was a fine ending to an otherwise frustrating career for a fiery competitor who was a highly sought QB out of Central Dauphin HS, but had misfortune of coming along at same time as Galen Hall and Pete Liske. Still, he was backup QB in soph and junior years and said he always gave his best. Had one of his best defensive games as junior when his two fourth quarter interceptions set up TDs that helped give State a 23-7 win over Maryland.

Played in '63 Blue-Gray game. Now a senior vice president & chief marketing officer in Topeka, KS.

CEFALO, JIM. 1974-75-76-77. FL & KR, 6'0", 185 lbs.; Pittston, PA. One of the most crowd-pleasing offensive players of the Paterno years and a great "clutch" player even though his name is hardly in State record books anymore, and he was never more than an Honorable Mention All-America. Became one of the all-time great punt returners in senior year, when Paterno put him in return slot for first time; ran back two for TDs, setting a one-season record later tied by O.J. McDuffie. His 13.7 average return on 18 runbacks (for 247 yards) is seventh best in career records and his 75-yard return for a TD against Kentucky in only team loss of '71 season, 21-20, is tied for the ninth longest return ever. Other TD return was a 57-yarder against West Virginia. Also helped Mike Guman score on a 52-yard return that helped beat Pitt, 15-13, by handing off to Guman on a reverse after catching the punt. Started out frosh year as fifth string flanker in preseason practice and by first game was the prime backup and running back kickoffs; led team with nine KO returns for 159 yards and a 17.7 yards average. Caught his first "bomb" ever on a 57-yard pass from Tom Shuman against Wake Forest in fifth game of '74 season and by next-to-last game against Ohio University he had his first career start. Had a sensational Cotton Bowl game as frosh against Baylor that gave him notoriety for rest of career; he nabbed three passes for 102 yards, including a 49-yard TD catch and scored another TD on a three-yard run over right tackle. Started for next three years, although injuries kept him on the sidelines for much of '75. Was a steady and often spectacular receiver and sometimes runner, especially on "end around" plays. Named Outstanding Penn State Player in 20-9 loss to Notre Dame in '76 Gator Bowl, as he caught five passes for 60 yards. Had one of his finest games in senior year against Maryland, when he scored on 58-yard and seven-yard pass plays, caught six passes for 107 yards total and was the leading rusher with 30 yards on three plays in regionally televised 27-9 win; was Outstanding Player-of-the-Game and won similar honors later in season against Kentucky and Temple. Made three of his "clutch" catches in the last minute 83-yard drive that gave State a come-from-behind 21-17 win over North Carolina State and helped send school to Fiesta Bowl. Closed out career with 1,058 yards and seven TDs on 56 receptions for 10th place in all-time career receiving yardage, and was team's leading receiver in his final game, the 42-30 Fiesta Bowl win over Arizona State on Christmas Day, with three crucial receptions for 39 yards, and also ran back punt 67 yards to set up a FG. Played in '78 Hula and Japan Bowls. Third choice of Miami in '78 and had fine seven-year career with Dolphins, including playing in the '83 & '85 Super Bowls. A journalism major who had several articles published in the **New York Times** while still in college, and is now a nationally-known sports broadcaster. Currently, the lead sports anchor at WPLG-TV in Miami, and makes his home in North Miami Beach, FL.

CENCI, ALDO. 1941-42-43. QB & P, 5'10", 235 lbs.; Scranton, PA. A bruising blocking back (QB) and standout middle linebacker for the war era Higgins' teams that had good winning records. His nickname was "Mt. Aldo" because he was so big and tough. But also had the speed to return kickoffs. Played two of his finest games at end of '42 season: in 13-7 win over Penn at Franklin Field, his blocking and defensive work earned him a Philadelphia Maxwell Club Award as Player-of-the-Game; the next week, he intercepted one pass, made several key

tackles and scored the first TD of his State career with a six-yard pass reception that sealed the 14-6 win over Pitt. Joined service in '43 but was back on campus in time for '43 season as part of the Army's ROTC program which sent officer trainees back to college until they could be processed through training. Starting QB and punter on the makeshift '43 team that was 5-3-1, and one of the few starters for the entire season. Cited by sportswriters for playing fine defensive game in closing out career with 14-0 win over Pitt. Retired plant superintendent in Bridgeport, CN.

CHERUNDOLO, CHUCK. 1934-35-36. C & LB, 6'1", 199 lbs.; Old Forge, PA. May have been the best player for State during the destructive years of de-emphasis in the '30s. Certainly, he was one of the toughest of all time but never got the respect he deserved because of State's overall mediocrity during the period. Picked on the All-Time Penn State team in 1950s and again in 1967 by **Pittsburgh Press** sports editor Chet Smith, who covered Nittany Lion football for more than a half century. Named to several All-American teams as honorable mention. He was a ferocious tackler who wasn't afraid of anyone at anytime. He played the game as if nothing else mattered. Probably made as many tackles as anyone in history but no one was counting for the records in his era. Never played on a team with a winning season and was captain of the soph-laden '36 team that was 3-5 but had first victory over Syracuse in seven years, 18-0, and first over Bucknell in 10 years, 14-0; in rousing the sophomore-dominated line in front of him would shout for them to "just take somebody out—anybody—I'll make the tackle" and he would, no matter how many blockers were running interference for the ball carrier. Had a great pro career with Cleveland ('37-'39), Philadelphia ('40) and Pittsburgh ('41-'42 & '45-'48). Lives in Des Plaines, IL.

CHIZMAR, BRIAN. 1986-87-88-89. DB & ILB, 6'1", 205 lbs.; Swissvale, PA. One of the most determined players of the Paterno era who always gave 100% on the field. With LB Andre Collins, he formed one of the best tackling combos in school history from '86-through-'89. Made an immediate impression on fans as frosh as a "gung-ho" hard-hitting member of the kicking team on National Championship team of '86. Had six solo tackles that year, which started him on the road to becoming one of the all-time tackling leaders. Became the starting strong safety in opening game of '87 season and never relinquished the position until senior year, when he was switched to inside linebacker. Led team in interceptions in '87 with three. Had one of his best games that year in 21-20 win over Notre Dame with a fumble recovery off a botched punt return that led to one TD and an interception in the EZ that stopped a ND scoring drive; also had six tackles in the game. In 7-3 '89 win over Boston College, he had best tackling performance in four years with 18 tackles on eight solos and 10 assists. His 241 career tackles on 161 solos and 80 assists is 10th best of all-time and his 110 tackles on 56 solos and 54 assists in senior season is tied with Collins for 10th best in one-season. Also led team in tackles as soph with 57 solos and 12 assists for a 69 total. Played in '90 Japan Bowl. Is an acute care specialist in Pittsburgh.

CHUCKRAN, JOHN. 1944, 1948-49. LHB, 5'11", 180 lbs.; Lansford, PA. A nice guy and fine football player whose best years were spent off the football field because of World War II. The only frosh ever chosen Captain during war year of '44 when PSU and most other teams (except Army & Navy) were decimated. Still, '44 team was 6-3, and Chuckran was a star from the opening game against Muhlenberg, when he scored one TD on a 30-yard run and passed for two other TDs in 58-13 win. In his first ever start against Bucknell, he was leading rusher with 77 yards (on 15 carries) and scored game-clinching TD with three minutes left in 20-6 victory. Made one of his biggest "clutch" plays as frosh in fourth game of season by running back a 50-yard punt for a TD with 30 seconds left in the mud and rain at Colgate to give State a 6-0 win, and was carried off the field. Played perhaps his finest game in 28-27 loss to West Virginia, when he had the only 100-yard rushing day of his career, scoring three TDs and gaining 157 yards on 21 carries, including a 39-yard TD, passing for 69 yards, and another TD, and returning kickoffs for 78 yards. Played little in last three games of year because of injury but did play in '44 Blue-Gray game when the game was one of only two all-star contests and underclassmen were eligible. Left for armed service in '45, and when he returned in '47 he was one of many tailbacks on the team. Injuries kept him on sideline most of '47 but in '48 he couldn't beat out Elwood Petchel, with whom he shared the '44 starting LHB position, nor young Bill Luther in '48, but was a solid and dependable backup the rest of his career. Considered a speedy and intelligent runner. Was head coach at Allegheny College for 12 years before getting a Ph.D. in Education at PSU in '69, then joining Paterno's staff as freshman coach in '70 and later becoming offensive line coach. Left to be Athletic Director at Rhode Island for several years before his retirement. Deceased.

CLARK, BRUCE. 1976-77-78-79. LB & DT, 6'2 ½", 255 lbs.; New Castle, PA. The first junior in the country to win the Lombardi Award as the nation's Outstanding Lineman/Linebacker in '78. State's fourth two-time First-Team All-American and a consensus AA in both '78 and '79, when selected by Football Writers, Football Coaches, UPI, Football News and others. But senior year ended at midseason when sidelined with a knee ligament injury that required surgery. Teamed with Matt Millen for three years as one of the best defensive tackle combinations in college football and Paterno said they were even better than the Reid-Smear combo of '68-'69. They had mutual respect for each other and nicknamed themselves, "Salt & Pepper." At start of '79 season, Paterno said Clark was so good "he has to be careful that he doesn't seriously hurt people." But without him late in '79, the team suffered a disappointing season. Best year was as junior on team that lost only to Alabama for National Championship in '79 Sugar Bowl. During season he had 51 tackles, 21 for losses, four QB sacks and recovered three fumbles (including one on TCU's nine-yard line that led immediately to the first TD in a 58-0 rout). In Sugar Bowl loss he had eight solo tackles and four assists with two tackles for losses. Had a tremendous debut, breaking into the starting lineup along with Millen as a frosh linebackers against Army after Paterno shook-up the team following a 1-3 start; his block of a Notre Dame punt in the Gator Bowl that year set up State's only TD from the eight-yard line in a 20-9 defeat. Moved to DT in soph year with Millen and they dominated scrimmage in most games as team posted 11-1 record and Fiesta Bowl victory over Arizona State. Played one of his best games in '78 19-0 win at Ohio State when he was named Defensive Player-of-the-Game. Used at MG most of senior year so that opponents could not double team he and Millen; he wasn't happy with move but it didn't affect his play: against Maryland he was in the backfield so quickly he grabbed the QB and the HB together and forced a big fumble in 27-7 win. Sixth

in career sacks with 19, which is all the more impressive when one realizes he also played alongside the school's all-time sack leader, Larry Kubin, for three years. He and Millen led team in sacks as sophs with six, then Kubin took over. First choice of Green Bay in '80 but played two years with Toronto Argonauts in Canadian League in '80 & '81 before joining New Orleans where he had a good career with Saints ('83-'88) and Kansas City ('89) before playing in the World League. Now an assistant football coach for the Orlando team in indoor football league and lives in Orlando, FL.

CLAYTON, STAN. 1985-86-87. OT, 6'3", 265 lbs.; Cherry Hill, NJ. Two-year starter at Short Tackle and played alongside All-American G Steve Wisniewski both years, including the '86 National Championship year. They were the main cogs in opening the running lanes for D. J. Dozier to lead unbeaten season that year. Played one of his best games in the '87 Fiesta Bowl in neutralizing Miami's All-American Jerome Brown. He was the quiet type and let his blocking on field do the talking. Was backup OT in beginning of "redshirt" frosh year of '85 but by midseason was starting on team that became number one and played Oklahoma for national title in '86 Orange Bowl. May not have lived up to his full potential but decided to give up last season of eligibility to turn pro. Played in '88 Senior Bowl. Number 10 choice of Atlanta in '88 and played with Falcons ('88-'89), New England ('90-'91) and Pittsburgh ('92) before leaving pro ball to be a financial consultant. Quit that to coach football, and is now an assistant at Alabama State University.

COBBS, DUFFY. 1983-84-85-86. DB, 5'11", 175 lbs.; Alexandria, VA. One of the fine defensive backs of the '80s, who made one of the most significant plays ever in '86 game against Maryland; he batted down an attempt for a two-point conversion on the last play of the game to save a 17-15 win and preserve unbeaten season that kept team on course for eventual National Championship. Had another great "clutch" play in '85 at Syracuse with an interception in the last two minutes that helped seal a great come-from-behind win, 24-20, and maintain that undefeated season. Was a starting cornerback on the '85 & '86 teams that played for national title and won it all in '86, 14-10 game over Miami in '87 Fiesta Bowl. Along with S Ray Isom, CB Eddie Johnson and others, he was part of the hard-hitting secondary that made devastating tackles on Miami's highly-touted wide receivers Michael Irvin, Brian Blades and Brett Perriman (all of whom became big pro stars) in the '87 Fiesta. He was the biggest of State's underrated "pony secondary," and in that game, he had 12 tackles, deflected two passes and recovered an early fumble by Irvin after a hit by Isom. Had three interceptions in championship year to lead team. Played as a Split End in his frosh season and moved to defensive back as soph where he became a three-year starter. Now a marketing representative in Alexandria, VA.

CODER, RON. 1974-75. OG & DT, 6'4", 232 lbs.; State College, PA. A star for only one year but a player who finally got a break when he was asked to switch from offense to defense in '75. All he did then is lead the team in sacks (five), passes batted down and stopping runners for losses as he made 93 tackles. Was a big reason why team was 9-3 and 10th in country. Made the key play of game in last minute to help defeat Kentucky, 10-3: Kentucky was driving for tying or winning score but on third-and-five at PSU nine-yard line, Coder sacked

Wildcat QB and then pressured fourth down pass attempt that failed. Final game was one of his best in '75 Sugar Bowl loss to Alabama, 13-6, when he led both teams in 14 tackles. Was a walk-on who played high school football at a military base in Japan, and moved to State College with family. Began career at OG and was a fine one, but couldn't break into the starting lineup (or even letter in soph year) because he was behind such talent as Tom Rafferty, Charlie Getty, John Nessel and Mark Markovich but he was a solid backup in junior year. Even had an offensive lineman's dream come true when he scored a TD under bizarre circumstances in 21-12 win over West Virginia in '74: An attempted FG by State in third QT was blocked and ball rolled into EZ; a WVU player on his back tried to grab the ball with his legs but it was knocked away by State's SE Jerry Jeram and Coder fell on it for the TD. Penn State was in his genes for his father Ron was a soccer star for the Lions in '49 & '50 and his brother Craig lettered in '77 & '78 at LB. Drafted number four by Seattle in '76 and played with Sea Hawks ('76-'79) and St. Louis Cardinals ('80-'81). Also played in USFL from '82-'85, primarily with Philadelphia Stars. Now an independent contractor in Roswell, GA.

COLES, JOEL. 1979-80-82. TB, FB & DB, 6'0", 212 lbs.; Pittsburgh, PA. The epitome of the "team player" who is credited by Paterno with turning around the '82 National Championship season after the devastating 42-21 midyear loss to Alabama. He was then a backup FB and a "fifth year" senior whose career had been meandering but in the locker room after the Alabama defeat, he was the man of the hour. As Paterno recalled in his book, **"Paterno: By the Book,"** the mood in the dressing room was somber and depressing with the players hanging their heads when Coles jumped up on a bench and yelled out: "Listen you guys, we've still got six games to prove that we're a good football team." Paterno wrote: "You could just see a dark cloud of discouragement explode and disintegrate. The kids began to cheer for themselves." Without Coles "seizing of leadership," Paterno says, the Lions probably would not have won the national title that year. By then, he was backing up Jon Williams at FB and did not carry the ball that much as Williams and Curt Warner led the running attack. Played as frosh on '78 team that nearly won National Championship, running back kicks, but didn't letter. Started as third-string TB in '79 and played offense and defense; cited as DB in 22-7 win over Maryland for jarring hits on Terp pass receivers; then as sub TB in Liberty Bowl against Tulane he set up game winning FG with a 32-yard halfback pass to Tom Donovan and a two-yard run in last minute. The next year he was a backup to Warner; against Miami he threw a 25-yard TD pass to Kenny Jackson in third QT to break open a tight game as Lions won, 27-12; then one week later had the finest day of his career when he rushed for 151 yards on 12 carries in 21-13 win over NC State and was named TV Player-of-the-Game; scored first TD of career following week against Temple and finished season with 406 yards rushing. Shifted to FB in '81 and was backing up his roommate Mike Meade when he broke his ankle in third game of season against Temple (after rushing for 40 yards on five carries and catching one pass for 12 yards) and missed rest of season. Continued as backup FB to Williams in '82 and carried ball five-to-10 times per game and caught passes too. Never complained about his subordinate role to the stars and remained an inspirational leader as an "unofficial" captain of the great '82 team. Played in East-West Shrine game in '83. Signed as free agent with USFL and played with Pittsburgh until '85. Now a supervisor for a data center in suburban Pittsburgh.

COLLINS, AARON. 1994-95-96-97. LB, 6'0", 234 lbs.; Cinnaminson, NJ. The last of the five Collins brothers to play for Paterno (See below) and started 36 consecutive games. Also the latest of Paterno players to be selected for a National Football Foundation Hall of Fame scholar-athlete fellowship and earn an NCAA Postgraduate scholarship. Was a quiet but spiritual leader of '97 team and was elected co-captain at end of season. Was on original candidate list during season for Butkus Award given to nation's outstanding linebacker. In senior year he had 62 tackles and his 227 career tackles places him number 14 in school history. Played one of his best games in 57-21 in over Louisville in '97 when he was named Big 10 Defensive Player-of-the-Week with five tackles, including a sack, and returned an interception 57-yards for a TD in second QT that broke open tight game. Also played a good game in losing to eventual National Champion Michigan with eight solo tackles. Perhaps his best game in junior year was 23-20 win over Wisconsin which helped team reach Fiesta Bowl, when he 13 tackles, including three sacks for a minus 18 yards. Finished career with five interceptions and two were for TDs. Named outstanding collegiate player from South Jersey as senior (following in footsteps of brother Andre) and was two-time second-team Big 10. Also Academic All-Big 10 for four years. Also played in '98 Senior Bowl. Signed as free agent by St. Louis Rams in '98. Lives in hometown of Cinnaminson, NJ.

COLLINS, ANDRE. 1986-87-88-89. LB & S, 6'1", 197 lbs.; Cinnaminson, NJ. First-Team All-American as senior and one of five finalist for Butkus Award as the country's best linebacker. That year he tied Jack Ham's 21-year record of three blocked kicks in one season and also tied with Ham for most blocked kicks in a career (four). One of the all-time great tacklers whose 130 tackles in '89 on 68 solos and 62 assists is second only to Greg Buttle's '74 and '75 marks for most tackles in one season. Sixth in career tackles with 257 total (147 solos and 110 assists). Also led team in tackles in junior year with 63 solos and 47 assists; that year he was the leading tackler in nine of the 11 games. Was a standout on kicking team as a frosh on '86 National Championship team, when he made five solo tackles. Stayed on kicking team in '87 when he also was a backup at free and strong safety. Switched to ILB in spring of '88 and became a star. Showed what he could do right from opening game of '88 when he had 12 tackles, including two QB sacks and caused a strategic fumble in 42-14 victory at Virginia. As defensive co-captain in senior year he was an outstanding leader as well as performer. Made the "clutch" play of his career in fourth game of year at Texas: With State trailing 12-9 midway through the fourth QT in a tough defensive struggle, he blocked a Texas punt at the Texas 17-yard line and soph Leonard Humphries took the ball in for the TD that won the game, 16-12. Had one of best games in last one of regular season, when he made a career high of 16 tackles and two deflected passes in 16-13 win over Pitt. In four other games he had 15 tackles. Scored two-points on one of the most unusual plays ever—and perhaps his greatest—in his last game, against Brigham Young in '89 Holiday Bowl, when he intercepted Heisman Trophy winner Ty Detmer's pass attempt for a two-point conversion that would have tied the game with 2:48 in the fourth QT and raced 102-yards into the EZ for a rare defensive two-point conversion that cinched an eventual 50-39 win. Four brothers have followed him to Penn State: Gerry ('89-'91), Phillip ('93-'94), Jason ('94) and Aaron (see above). Played in '90 Senior and Japan Bowls. Second choice of Washington in '90 and played five years with Redskins and two years with Cincinnati before signing with Bears for '98. Now lives in Arlington, VA.

COLLINS, KERRY. 1992-93-94 QB, 6'5", 235 lbs.; West Lawn, PA. No PSU QB ever had one season as he did in '94 when he did everything but win the Heisman Trophy. Won Maxwell Award as "the outstanding player in collegiate football," Davey O'Brien Award as nation's Outstanding QB, ABC-TV Player-of-the-Year and UPI Back-of-the-Year. Consensus First-Team All-American when picked by AP, UPI, Football Coaches, Walter Camp and others. Fourth in Heisman balloting when teammate Ki-Jana Carter finished second. His entire career was epitomized by the come-from-behind 96-yard drive late in fourth QT before a hostile crowd at Illinois in '94 that won Big 10 title and preserved unbeaten streak: trailing by as much as 21 points at one point, Collins rallied the team for two 90-yard plus drives, and in final six minutes he coolly completed seven-of-seven passes into a cold, stiff wind to take team all the way downfield 96 yards for thrilling 35-31 victory. Set several school records for one season including passing yardage (2,679 yards), completions (176), yards per attempt passing (10.15 yards), total offense (2,660 yards) and passing efficiency—172.86, which is just four points shy of the NCAA record. Also holds record for most consecutive games with a TD pass in both one season (11) and over two seasons (14), completion percentage in both one season (66.7%) and career (56.3%) and the lowest interception percentage for a season with 1.46%. Leader and co-captain of the blistering "TD-a-minute" attack for unbeaten team that led nation in total offense (520.2 yards-per-game) and scoring (47.8 points-per-game), broke 14 school records and won Big 10 title and '95 Rose Bowl, but was relegated to number two in ratings by fatuous pollsters. No one has more games passing over 300 yards (four) or 200 yards (16) with his all-time best being the final game of '93 that turned his career around, when he led team to come-from-behind 38-37 win at Michigan State, amassing 352 yards and three TDs on 23-of-42 attempts and just one interception. Followed MSU game with another outstanding performance in come-from-behind 31-13 win over Tennessee in '94 Citrus Bowl, when he hit on 15-of-24 passes for 162 yards and two TDs. He is third in career passing behind Tony Sacca and Chuck Fusina, both of whom started in more games over more seasons, with 5,304 yards and 39 TDs (second to Sacca and Todd Blackledge who are tied with 41) on 370 of 657 attempts. His career passing efficiency rating of 137.33 is third of all-time and his one season TD pass percentage of 7.95% is second only to Tom Shuman. Tied with six others behind Sacca with four TD passes in one game against Rutgers in' 94 and his 82-yard TD bomb to Freddie Scott that day is fourth longest pass play of all-time. Might have had even greater career if not for a freak accident during a family picnic prior to his soph season, when he broke the index finger on his throwing hand during a volleyball game and the injury kept him sidelined much of '92. He was still on bench as backup QB in early part of '93, when Paterno gave him the big break in sub role at Iowa, and he led team to 31-0 win. He was starter rest of season but was inconsistent until dramatic "turn-around" game at MSU. Made sensational debut in '92 season, playing for first time in second half of seventh game of year against Boston College and led tremendous fourth QT come-from-behind TD spurt before Homecoming crowd that fell short in last 30 seconds of eventual 35-32 defeat; two weeks later at Brigham Young he set record for most pass attempts (54) in 30-17 defeat, but could not beat out John Sacca. Didn't complain when he began '93 season as backup to Sacca again but when Sacca faltered in third game of '93 season against Iowa he took over. Struggled through season until second half of final game at MSU when he finally found

his true potential. Played in '95 Senior Bowl. Donated $250,000 to university to endow a scholarship for QB recruits as a way of showing personal appreciation for how PSU football helped him. First choice of new Carolina Panthers in '95 and has been the Panthers starting QB since mid-season of '95. Lives in Charlotte, NC.

COLONE, JOE. 1942-46-47-48. FB & P, 5'11", 200 lbs.; Berwick. Probably the greatest State punter of all time and another of the forgotten stars of the World War II and post war era who sacrificed football for duty to his country. Was a great punter from the beginning of frosh year in '42 who easily booted punts of 50-60 yards, including quick-kicks. Made his punting debut against Cornell and had one of his best punting days with 14 kicks. Also an outstanding defensive player on teams that posted an overall record of 28 wins, four losses and three ties. Began as backup FB in '42 when frosh were declared eligible because of the war and was so good at running, tackling and punting that he was a starter for last three games of season, but he spent the next three years in the armed services. The first time he entered a game, against Lehigh in '42, he completed a 34-yard pass to fellow frosh Jeff Durkota that set up TD in come-from-behind 14-3 victory. His punting and running helped lead State to one of its biggest upsets, 13-7, over traditional rival Penn later in the season; despite a stiff wind, he averaged 35 yards on 13 punts but several of the kicks were quick-kicks or well-placed boots that backed Penn deep into its own territory. Didn't play again until after the war, in '46, and was an instant star, particularly on defense and punting. Might have been an All-American on defense if he didn't have to play both ways. A good offensive FB but he couldn't match the running skills of Larry Joe and Fran Rogel so his defensive prowess and superb punting ability kept him the starting lineup most of the time. One of the best punters in the nation in the post World War II period. His sharp punting and quick-kicks helped beat many teams and could kick for distance or accuracy; his quick-kicks often would go 60-70 yards and he was even better with a wet ball. In '47 he averaged 40 yards on 28 punts for first unbeaten team in 26 years. His punting is credited with keeping SMU off balance and helping to tie the '48 Cotton Bowl. Started at FB most of '46 and in beginning of '47 until a separated shoulder in fourth game of '47 against Syracuse limited him on offense but he continued to kick. His punting helped beat Navy, 20-7, in key game near end of season when a 66-yard quick-kick set up a 46 yard TD by Jeff Durkota. The zenith of his career came in '48, when he was captain of a team that was 7-1-1 and finished 18th in country. He had another fine year punting but also was a solid runner and sometimes passer who started at FB in last five games of season as team lost only to Pitt in last game of season, 7-0, and tied Michigan State 14-14. Coached football briefly at Berwick. Retired high school teacher and lives in Berwick, PA.

CONLAN, SHANE. 1983-84-85-86. LB. 6'3", 225 lbs.; Frewsburg, NY. The outstanding linebacker of the '80s and one of State's greatest of all-time. One of 11 Two-Time First-Team All-Americans (in '85 & '86) and a consensus AA in '86 when chosen by AP, UPI, Football Writer, Football Coaches, Walter Camp and others. Selected Most Valuable Defensive Player in '87 Fiesta Bowl that brought State its second National Championship; he had eight tackles and intercepted two passes, including one he returned for 38 yards to five-yard line in fourth QT that set up winning TD by D. J. Dozier, and he did all that despite being hobbled by a left knee injury in first QT and a right ankle injury in third QT. A three-year starter and part of the "Sack Gang" of the '85 and '86 team that played for the National Championship both years and won it in '86. Along with Don Graham and Bob White, the trio had more sacks on opposing quarterbacks than any three defensive teammates before or since the years. Ninth on the career sack list with 16, three behind his teammates. Has more solo tackles than any State player ever with 186 and his additional 88 shared tackles gives him a 274 total that is tied for fourth best in the career tackles. His best year was '85 when he had 91 tackles (57 solo and 34 shared) but did not lead team that year; led team in '86 with 79 tackles (63 solo and 16 shared). In junior year he caused more fumbles than anyone on team and recovered a couple big ones. Played one of his finest games that season in 27-0 win at West Virginia when he led team with 14 tackles, caused a fumble that led to a 31-yard FG and deflected one pass. One week later against Boston College his tackle at the goal line forced another fumble on a first-and-Goal that preserved 16-12 victory. Had another fine game against BC the next year when his 11 tackles, a sack and end zone interception, helped spark State to a 26-14 win. Played one of his outstanding games as "fifth year senior" in pivotal midseason game in '86 against then number two Alabama that kept State on course for the National Championship in what he called "the biggest game of my life." Conlan led defense that sacked Tide QB Mike Shula five times, intercepted two passes, forced five fumbles, recovering three, and shut down flanker Al Bell. So good that he broke into the starting lineup as a "redshirt" frosh and was Defensive Player-of-the-Game in final game of '83 regular season against Pitt, when his two QB sacks caused fumbles deep in Pitt territory that led to quick TDs and eventual 24-24 tie that put State into Aloha Bowl. Played in '87 Japan Bowl. First choice of Buffalo in '87 and was the NFL's Defensive Rookie-of-the-Year. Played six years with Bills on three Super Bowl teams before winding up his career with two years for the Rams. Now working with Northwest Mutual and living in Sewickley , PA.

CONLIN, CHRIS ("BUCKY"). 1984-85-86. OT. 6'4", 280 lbs.; Glenside, PA. First-Team All-American in senior year when team won National Championship and nominated for Outland Trophy as nation's best interior lineman, despite missing three games with injuries. Won starting long tackle position as soph in '84 and was the starter for rest of career. A solid blocker who helped open holes for D.J. Dozier and the FB tandem of Tim Manoa and Steve Smith on the '85 & '86 teams that played for national title in consecutive years. Missed last part of '85 regular season after being injured in Cincinnati game but came back to play in '86 Orange Bowl loss to Oklahoma. Cited for his blocking in pivotal '86 Alabama game, when State won the "showdown" over favored Crimson Tide, 23-3, to put them into the front of the championship race. Brothers Keith (see below) and Kevin ('96) followed him to State. Played in '87 Hula Bowl. Fifth pick of Miami in '87 and played two years with Dolphins and three years with Indianapolis before leaving pro ball. Assistant coach in the Arena Football League and lives in East Rutherford, NJ.

CONLIN, KEITH. 1992-93-94-95. OL, 6'7", 300 lbs.; Glenside, PA. The long tackle in the great offensive line on one of the best offensive teams in college football history that won '94 Big 10 title and also '95 Rose Bowl but was unappreciated by pollsters. He was big but very athletic with more speed than the usual big man. The tallest of that

'94-'95 line who was so quick he was a reserve guard in '92 & '93. Got his chance at tackle in '94 and was a two-year starter on line that gave up only three sacks in '94. One of his most critical blocks came with less than a minute remaining in the '94 Illinois game, when FB Brian Milne crashed two-yards over a big hole opened by Conlin, TE Kyle Brady and T Jeff Hartings for the TD that climaxed the historic 96-yard drive that gave State the dramatic come-from-behind victory and the Rose Bowl berth. All-Big 10 in '95. A leader with a great sense of humor who may not have received the credit he was due because of the presence of teammate Jeff Hartings. The younger brother of Chris (see above). Played in '96 Senior Bowl. Sixth choice of Indianapolis in '96 and still playing in NFL. Lives in Glenside, PA.

CONOVER, LARRY. 1916-17-19. C, E, T & PK; 5'10", 185 lbs.; Hometown unknown. One of the best known players of his era and perhaps one of the least known among modern day State fans. An outstanding leader who was primarily a C but also played E and T and was team's main placekicker in '17 & '19. Also was first person to broadcast a State game over radio in '27 when he was an assistant coach for Bezdek. Started at C as soph in '16 and then shifted to LE in '17 to replace All-American end Bob Higgins who left for service in World War, then was named Co-Captain of '17 team to supersede Higgins. Was in armed service in '18 but moved back to C & teamed with Higgins in '19 for 7-1 record that was school's best in seven years, after he and Higgins had led revolt of players against Bezdek. Had one of his finest games in big 10-0 win over Penn in '19, when he recovered fumbled punt on three-yard line that set up State TD and kicked 25-yard FG that clinched game. Later kicked two FGs in 20-7 victory over Lehigh. Played one of his best games as a soph against Gettysburg, blocking and tackling all over the field and kicking six extra points. Had two of his finest days as a placekicker in back-to-back record shutouts of Gettysburg and St. Bonaventure in '17 when he booted eight and seven PATs, respectively. Scored more than 50 points in his career. Returned in '26 to assist Bezdek and during '27 season he broadcasted five home games at Beaver Field over campus radio station. Deceased.

CONTZ, BILL. 1980-81-82. DT & OT, 6'6", 252 lbs.; Belle Vernon, PA. Another of the outstanding offensive linemen who was overshadowed by some of his linemates such as Sean Farrell and Mike Munchak. A two-year starter at OT on two of the best teams in PSU history, including the first National Championship squad '82. Along with Pete Speros, Ron Heller, Dick Maginnis and Mark Battaglia, he was credited with helping make Curt Warner an All-American in '82. Started out on defense, then shifted to offense as soph where he backed up All-American tackle Bill Dugan. But got first start at other tackle in '81 Fiesta Bowl victory over Ohio State. Never missed a start in next two seasons. Played one of his best games in the classic 27-24 come-from-behind win over Nebraska in '82 and another in the 24-14 victory at Notre Dame near end of season. Played in East-West Shrine game in '83. Number five choice of Cleveland and was a starter for Browns ('83-'86) and New Orleans ('86-'88) before leaving pro football. Now a client systems administrator in Cranberry Twp., PA.

CONWAY, BRETT. 1993-94-95-96. PK; 6'2", 190 lbs.; Liburn, GA. Did everything but make All-American. Known to fans as the "kid from Georgia" who never missed a crucial extra point or FG attempt in his four-year career. Also noted for his booming kickoffs which usually went into the EZ and kept run backs to a minimum. Holds record for most extra points in a career (143), season (62 in '94), consecutive extra points (119), and FG accuracy (10-for-12 for 83.3% in '94). His kicking as soph in '94 helped the great offensive team that was unbeaten in Big 10 and Rose Bowl champ. Never missed an extra point in '95 season and didn't miss one in '96 until last game of season at Fiesta Bowl. Second to Craig Fayak in school career scoring and FGs with 276 extra points and 46 FGs in 62 attempts and his 18 FGs on 24 attempts in '96 is tied with Chris Bar for fourth best in one season. Never really had to kick under pressure until first game of junior year, when he booted 39-yard FG with four seconds left in season opener to beat Texas Tech, 24-23. Made his most important kick under pressure in final regular season game of career with a 30-yard FG with 12 seconds left that beat Michigan State, 32-29, and put State into Fiesta Bowl and an eventual number seven season ranking. First Team All-Big Ten in '96 when led team in scoring with 93 points; also led team in scoring in '95 with 83 points. Semi-finalist both years for Lou Groza Award as Placekicker-of-the-Year. Kicked longest FGs of career to help win '95 Beaver Stadium snow game with Michigan 27-17 with first half boots of 51- and 49-yards. Had career high four FGs in come-from-behind 26-23 win at Purdue in '95. Tied school and Outback Bowl record in '95 with FGs of 19, 22 and 38 yards. Missed first Extra point in two and a half years in '97 Fiesta Bowl win over Texas when he hit on three-of-four PATs and one FG. Played in 1997 Senior Bowl. Third choice of Green Bay in '97 draft. Traded to New York Jets in '98 and now playing for Jets.

COONEY, LARRY. 1944-45-47-48. RHB & PR, 5'11", 180 lbs., Pittsburgh, PA. Probably the youngest player ever to start a State game in the modern era. He was a 16-year old frosh when he started at RH (wingback) on October 21, 1944, against Colgate in fourth game of season, when frosh were eligible because of World War II. In historical 13-13 tie with SMU at '48 Cotton Bowl, he scored the second TD in last moments of first Half on 36-yard pass from Elwood Petchel and was praised by sportswriters for his outstanding play at defensive halfback. After breaking into '44 starting lineup, he started every game at RHB, or wingback position, rest of year; had already moved up from fourth-string, and played well all season. Threw the key block that sprung fellow frosh and captain Johnny Chuckran on his famous 50-yard punt return in last 30 seconds to beat Colgate, 6-0. Led team in rushing in big 41-0 win over Syracuse with 57 yards on five carries. In first game of '45 season, he returned an interception 65 yards to help beat Muhlenburg, 47-7, and was again the regular RHB. Made one of his best runs in 46-7 win over Bucknell with 65-yard scamper on a reverse play, which was his specialty. Left for Armed Services in '46 but came back in '47 and was a fine defensive back for next two years and spot duty at HB backing up Wally Triplett and Jeff Durkota on offense. Deceased.

COOPER, MIKE. 1968-69-70. QB 6'1", 188 lbs.; Harrisburg, PA. The first Black to start at QB but was replaced in sixth game of '70 season against Army by soph John Hufnagel and never got job back. Paterno has often said he regrets not giving Cooper more time to develop, and the aftermath of the Paterno-Cooper situation reverberated through the program for several years. Most people forget he was the backup to Chuck Burkhart as QB of the great back-to-back unbeaten

team of '68 & '69 that put Paterno and State into the upper echelon of college football. Although he saw plenty of playing time as Paterno substituted freely in many games, Cooper was frustrated by the restrictions on passing late in the game. Was a good ball handler and a fine passer with "quick feet." Had one of his best games in the '70 opening season win over Navy, 55-7, when he hit on 6-of-10 passes and two TDs and scored a TD himself. Unfortunately, had miserable game next week at Colorado when Buffaloes ended the school record 31-game unbeaten streak; he had two interceptions and missed several wide open receivers in seven-for-16 day and that was beginning of his end. After two more losses in next three games, when he threw three interceptions and just one TD while completing 14-of-27 passes, he was benched when Paterno changed his offense from passing to running, and he was in mop-up role rest of his career he threw just eight more passes, completing four and one for a TD. Later became a high school teacher and civil rights leader in his hometown of Harrisburg, PA, where he still lives.

CORREAL, CHUCK. 1977-78. C, 6'4", 244 lbs.; Uniontown, PA. One of the fine "scholar-athletes" of the Paterno era and co-captain of the great '78 team that lost the National Championship to Alabama in the '79 Sugar Bowl. As soph he backed up fellow soph Keith Dorney at C but didn't play enough to letter. When Dorney was switched to OT at start of junior year, he became starting C and stayed there for two years. May have been overshadowed in offensive line of '78 by Dorney but was a consistently good blocker and ball handler. An outstanding student who was a recipient of the prestigious National Football Foundation's College Football Hall of Fame "scholar-athlete" fellowship and NCAA Postgraduate scholarship in '78-'79. Played in '78 East-West Shrine Game and '79 Senior Bowl. Eighth pick of Philadelphia in '79 and played with Atlanta ('79-'80) and Cleveland ('81), then moved to USFL for several years and played for Pittsburgh. Now an investment broker and lives in Bethel Park, PA.

CROSBY, RON. 1974-75-76. LB & DE, 6'3", 215 lbs.; Glassport, PA. Another of the fine defensive players in the first decade of the Paterno era. Was a backup linebacker as soph and shifted to DE in spring of '75 and was starter for next two years. Was quick and a hard-hitting tackler. Almost had his first start in final game of '74 against Pitt when Buttle was hurt in pre-game locker room incident (see Buttle) but had to wait another year then became regular at LDE. Played one of his best games in 19-7 win over Syracuse in '75, including several tackles at key moments deep inside PSU territory and a fumble recovery that led to clinching fourth QT TD. Also cited for his defensive play against Alabama in '76 Sugar Bowl. Co-Captain of '76 team that relied on defense to carry it most of season and came from a 1-3 start to win six straight and earn invitation to Gator Bowl before losing to National Champion Pitt. Played one of his finest games that year in 21-17 win at Miami which clinched bowl bid, when he had five solo tackles and one assist, including a sack. Also had good game when Paterno shook up team against Army and Crosby had to lead front line which included new freshmen starters, Matt Millen and Bruce Clark; State won 38-16 and Crosby again had five solo tackles and one assist. Played in '77 Hula Bowl. Drafted fifth by Detroit in '77 and played for New Orleans ('78), Lions ('79) and Jets ('80-'82), then played in USFL, including time with the Pittsburgh franchise. Now a distributor account manager in Venetia, PA.

CROWDER, RANDY. 1971-72-73. DT, 6'2", 240 lbs.; Farrell, PA. One of the best defensive linemen of the Paterno era and the school's first Black Captain in history. A First-Team All-American in senior year when he also was named Defensive Player-of-the-Year by Washington Touchdown Club. Co-Captain of unbeaten and unappreciated '73 team that helped John Cappelletti win the Heisman Trophy and was the first State team ever to win 12 games. Selected Most Valuable Lineman in 16-9 win over LSU in '74 Orange Bowl, when the defense held LSU to a first QT TD. He was aggressive and quick, and Paterno often compared him to Mike Reid. Almost didn't play senior season when he injured knee in gym during winter and stayed out of spring practice but was in starting lineup for opening game at Stanford and was one of defensive stars in 20-6 win. A backup as soph who saw plenty of action on the '71 team that beat Texas in "breakthrough" '72 Cotton Bowl game. Then became two-year starter at RT. Had 95 tackles in '72. Played one of his two of best games early in '72, making 12 tackles in victory over Navy, then following it up the next week in 14-10 win over Iowa, getting into Hawkeye backfield all afternoon, causing a fumble and making the recovery. Against West Virginia that year he intercepted a pass and ran it back 10 yards to the WVU 12-yard line to set up State's first TD in eventual 28-19 win. Played in '74 Hula Bowl. 6th pick of Miami in '74 and had All-Pro career in three years with Dolphins and five years with Tampa Bay. Later coached two years at State but is now a mortgage broker in Tampa, FL.

CURE, DAVE. 1896-97-98-99. FB, P & PK; Jacquin, PA. Historians believe he was Penn State's first professional football player, joining the Canton Bulldogs after graduation. Started out as a HB in freshman year but moved to FB because of his line-plunging ability. Also developed a somersault technique at the goal and used it several times to score TDs. During his four years he was State's prime punter and dropkicker of field goals. Had probably his best season in junior year, when he led the nation in field goals and best scoring day in 45-6 win over Susquehanna at Old Beaver Field with three TDs and four FGs. Deceased.

CURKENDALL, PETE. 1985-86-87. DT & DE, 6'3", 262 lbs.; Elmira, NY. Third-Team All-American in '87 but may have been even more important to team in his soph and junior years, when he was defensive starter on back-to-back teams that played for national title. Made one of the crucial plays in the '86 championship season in late season game against Maryland; intercepted Bob White's tipped pass on the PSU one-yard line midway in the fourth QT with State leading by just 7-3 and ran it back 82-yards to set up a nine-yard D. J. Dozier TD that broke open the tight game and led to eventual 17-15 win; the runback is the longest return of an interception without scoring in school history and tied for fourth longest of all-time. The next week against Notre Dame he had another outstanding day with four tackles, one sack and a fumble recovery that set up a FG in 24-19 victory. Led team in sacks in senior year with nine. Played best game of year in his final one in State uniform, again against Notre Dame: led team with 10 tackles, including a sack, and saved 21-20 victory in last 30 seconds, when ND's QB Tony Rice tried to run for a two-point conversion after a TD but was stopped at the line by Curkendall. Had another fine game that year in 27-17 win over Boston College with three sacks. Also played well in losing effort against Alabama with eight tackles and a pass deflection in 24-13 defeat. Played in '88 East-West Shrine game. Re-

cipient in '96 of first State College Quarterback Club's Caring Award for adopting a child suffering from aids. Eleventh pick of Buffalo in '88 but didn't play in NFL. Now a social worker living in Liverpool, NY.

CURRY, JACK. 1965-66-67. SE, 6'0", 175 lbs.; Danville, PA. One of the forgotten receivers of the Paterno era who held most receiving records until O.J. McDuffie came along more than 20 years later. A three-year starter and one of the foremost transition players from the Engle era to Paterno. Had good hands and good speed but some opposing coaches said he was "too frail to play football." Third in career receiving behind Bobby Engram and McDuffie with 117 receptions for 1,837 yards and five TDs and a 15.7 yard average. Still holds record for most receptions in one game by a soph—10—and did it twice, against Syracuse and California; that is still good enough for third in record for most receptions ever in a game behind Freddie Scott and McDuffie. Also had nine catches as senior against Ohio U, which also is among top 10 in game receptions. Had three games with over 100 yards in receptions with the 148 yards and one TD on 10 catches at Cal in '65 being his best; the 148 yards still is in school record book as 13th most yards in one game. Made two of his greatest receptions in that game in last minute drive that won game, first taking a 24-yard pass from QB Jack White on a leaping ballet-like reach for a first down on the Cal 13 and then snaring White's scrambling throw just inches inside the EZ in the deep corner for the winning TD. Fifth in career reception yardage with 1,837 yards. Led team in receiving all three years he played with his 681 yards and two TDs on 41 receptions as senior being tops (and ninth on list for reception yardage in one season). Is an insurance and real estate broker in Danville, PA.

CYPHERS, ELLIS (CY). 1906-07-08. G & T, 5'9", 184 lbs.; Stroudsburg, PA. Tough blocker and tackler and one of the best defensive players of his time. But known to his teammates as "Wrong Way" after committing major blunder as soph guard in what was one of State's major games of the era with Yale: in a hard rain storm at New Haven, Cyphers picked up a punt blocked by All-American "Mother" Dunn at midfield and despite a clear field to Yale goal line for tying score, he ran towards the wrong goal before realizing what happened and was tackled inside the State 20; Yale kicked 25-yard-field goal moments later to win 10-0. They were the only points scored on the '06 squad, which was the best ever State team up to the time with an 8-1-1 record and set record of nine shutouts that still stands. May have played greatest game in '08 in another defeat, a 6-0 loss to unbeaten Pennsylvania, then number one team in the nation, when he blocked four punts by Penn Captain Bill Hollenback, who began coaching at State the next year. Deceased.

CZARNECKI, STAN ("ZARNEY"). 1915-16-17. G & T 6-1 199; Erie, PA. Second-Team All-American in senior year when selected by the number one All-American selector, Walter Camp. Probably the finest interior lineman of the Dick Harlow coaching era. Became a starter in third game of soph year against powerful Penn and was praised for his blocking that helped open holes for "Punk" Berryman in 13-3 win. Then became a three-year starter for Harlow on winning teams that were 20-8 and only lost two games in '15 & '16. Everyone, including sportswriters, called him by his nickname, "Zarney." Also a fine heavyweight wrestler for State. Deceased.

CZEKAJ, ED. 1943, 1946-47. E & PK, 6'2", 200 lbs.; Mt. Pleasant, PA. Best known in State's football history as the man who missed the controversial extra point in the '47 Cotton Bowl game that allowed favored Southern Methodist University to tie, 13-13. Always keeps sense of humor about missed kick, and reminds people that the great future Heisman Trophy winner Doak Walker also missed the extra point kick that could have won it for SMU. After the game Higgins asked him if the kick was good and Czekaj replied, "I don't know, Coach. You always told me to keep my head down." For the record, the referee said the kick was wide right, although many of State players on the field swear the high kick was good and that officials blew it. Set a season record for extra points that lasted for 22 years when he kicked 32-of-46 that senior year. Also tied Pete Mauthe's record for most extra points in one game with eight in 75-0 win over Fordham and held record until broken by Al Vitello in '71 against TCU. Started his career at George Washington University and transferred to State in '43 during World War II as part of the historic V-12 program that sent servicemen who were athletes back to college until they could be integrated into the armed forces. Was starting LE on '43 team, when he also did the placekicking and kickoffs. Returned after war to be the team's main kicker. In opening game of '46, he made six-of-seven extra points as State beat Bucknell 48-6. In second game of that season he attempted his first FG ever and it was good for 17-yards in 9-0 win over Syracuse. That started him on his way to being one of the best kickers in the country. Started occasionally at RE or LE throughout '46 & '47 and was known as an effective blocker and solid defensive end. Came back to State in '53 to work in Athletic Department and held several positions, including Athletic Director from '69 to his retirement in '80. Still a familiar sight at the major sports events in State College.

DANIELS, DAVID. 1988-89-90. SE, 6'1", 191 lbs.; Sarasota, FL. A first class receiver who may not have received the recognition he deserved because he played during one of the shaky periods of the Paterno era. Still is 11th in career receptions and ninth in career yardage with 69 for 1,222 yards, a 17.7 yards per catch average, and nine TDs. Led team in receiving as junior and senior with his best year being '90, when he caught 31 passes for 538 yards and four TDs (18th best for one season yardage). Played perhaps his finest game in his last one, the '90 Blockbuster Bowl against Florida State, when he recorded his most yardage ever in one game with 154 yards on seven receptions, including a 56-yard pass play from Tony Sacca for State's first TD. Had his most sensational reception the previous year in the '89 Holiday Bowl with a leaping, tumbling, juggling, fingertip catch over the back of a Brigham Young defender and into the EZ on a 52-yard bomb thrown by Sacca in the fourth QT of the pass-happy 50-39 win. Earlier that year, combined with Tom Bill for one of team's longest TD pass plays, a 75-yard bomb that helped beat Temple, 42-3. His nine receptions (for 119 yards and one TD) that year in 16-13 win over Pitt is tied with five others for fourth most receptions in one game; he was named State's Offensive Player-of-the-Game for his performance on that November '90 day. Started in '88 as "redshirt" frosh and was a regular the rest of career. Was known not just for his receiving but was an outstanding downfield blocker. Number three choice of Seattle in '91

and played two years before giving up pro ball. Lives in his hometown of Sarasota, FL.

DELUCA, DICK. 1954-55-56. G, 5'10", 188 lbs.; Monaca, PA. One of the best interior linemen in the early Engle era. Overshadowed by his All-American teammate, Sam Valentine, but is credited with being one of major factors in helping Lenny Moore become a star with the holes he helped open in the interior line. On defense he often had the unsung role of being the man who tied up opposing blockers so the State linebackers could make the tackles. Broke into starting lineup at LG midway through soph year and stayed there as starter in junior and senior seasons. Was on field more than any other lineman in senior year with 359 out of a possible 540 minutes, third best on team behind backs Milt Plum and Billy Kane. Cited for his all around play in the famous 7-6 upset of Ohio State in '56. Still teaching high school in Rochester, PA.

DIEDRICH, FRANK "YUTZ". 1928-29-30. RB & PK, 5'10", 175 lbs.; Woodburn, NJ. One of the stars in the last scholarship class before the disastrous de-emphasis period of the 1930s. Was a three-year starter at LHB and captain of Higgins' first team in '30, which had a disappointing 3-4-2 record. Recipient as soph of "the tradition hat"— a battered old felt headpiece—given by senior players to the "outstanding athlete of the freshman class." Was one of leading scorers in nation in '28 with 12 TDs but missed tying school record when Pitt shut out team, 26-0. Was a speedy runner, a fine pass receiver and passer and excellent defensive player. Combined with his roommate and one-time prep school teammate, QB Cooper French, for one of the most spectacular TD plays in history in '29 Homecoming game against Lafayette: Lafayette was ahead 3-0 with less than 30 seconds left in game and a third down on own 14-yard line and, surprisingly, decided to punt; Diedrich & French scurried back in double safety; French took the punt at 40-yard line, started to run to draw in all the Lafayette defenders, then threw the ball back across the field to Diedrich who ran 60 yards for winning TD as time expired; both were carried off the field by the jubilant fans. Also won three letters on baseball team as a center fielder. Selected as school's "most valuable athlete" for 1930-31 academic year. Retired and living in Sun City, AZ.

D'ONOFRIO, MARK. 1988-89-90-91. DL & LB, 6-2 233; North Bergen, NJ. A defensive tiger who tackled hard and loved to brush by blockers and nail the QB. Holds record for causing most fumbles in one season, when he forced five as junior. One of the career sack leaders with 15, which ties him for 10th with 11 of them as a soph. Next year led team in tackles with 71, including 45 solos. Made perhaps the biggest "clutch" play of his career as junior against number one Notre Dame: with ND leading, 21-7, late in third QT and driving for another apparent score, he intercepted a Rick Mirer pass and ran it down sidelines to ND 11-yard line, setting up a TD that gave State new life in game that PSU eventually won in major upset, 24-21; he also had seven tackles in game, including two QB sacks. Played one of his best games in the final game of the long time series with Syracuse in '90, when he was named State's Outstanding Player-of-the-Game with a team-leading eight tackles and a QB sack in 27-21 victory at Beaver Stadium. Starting ILB in senior season but missed last five games and '92 Fiesta Bowl with shoulder injury (suffered in BYU game) that needed surgery; yet still was third that year in tackles with 33 solos (two sacks) and 21 assists for 54 total, only six behind leader Lee Rubin and tied with Rubin for recovered fumbles with three. Had one of his outstanding games in '91 season opener against Georgia Tech in Kickoff Classic, when he had 10 tackles in leading defense in 34-22 victory; for that performance he was later named to the Kickoff Classic All-Decade team. Second choice of Green Bay Packers in '92 and played with Packers for two years before injuries shortened his pro career. Lives in Teaneck, NJ.

DONCHEZ, TOM. 1971, 1973-74. FB, 6'2", 216 lbs.; Bethlehem, PA. Came into his own in senior year, finally becoming full-time starter at FB. One of few Paterno FBs to lead team in rushing, scoring and pass receiving (in '74) and first to do so in rushing in nine years; had 880 yards and 7 TDs on 195 carries (for a 4.5 yards average) and caught 17 passes (tying with SE Jerry Jeram) for 176 yards and one TD and a total of 48 points. Was leading State rusher in six regular season games and '75 Cotton Bowl, and four times had over 100 yards, with best being 166 yards on 35 carries in the rain and mud at Beaver Stadium in upset loss to Navy, 7-6. But he had three fumbles in that game and another three in come-from-behind 21-14 win over underdog Army but finally got his act together. In his final PSU game in '75 Cotton Bowl win over Baylor, 41-20, he had 116 yards and a TD on 25 carries and had another TD off a screen pass nullified by a penalty; also leading receiver in the game with four receptions for 50 yards. Started a few games as soph, when Paterno benched senior Franco Harris, including the "breakthrough" '72 Cotton Bowl game against Teaxs, and had 29 yards on eight carries and caught a pass, in that 30-6 win. Set to be starting FB in '72 but missed entire year because of a knee injury. Nineteenth in career rushing with 1,422 yards and 11 TDs on 296 carries. The protagonist in one of the most bizarre moments in State FB history prior to '74 Thanksgiving Night game at Pitt; in players-only locker room meeting before kickoff, he closed a fiery, inspirational speech by throwing his helmet against a locker, but the helmet bounced off the locker and hit starting LB and defensive signal caller Greg Buttle between the eyes and knocked him out cold; a groggy, patched-up Buttle barely made kickoff; State won 31-10 with Donchez leading all rushers with 87 yards on 23 carries and Buttle playing outstanding game. Chosen number four by Buffalo in '75 draft and wound up playing two years with Chicago Bears before quitting pro ball. Graduated as a finance major and is now a business manager in Bethlehem, PA.

DOOLEY, JIM. 1951-52. C, 6'1", 205 lbs.; Williamsport, PA. The starting C on two of Engle's early teams and a Second-Team All-American and All-East as a senior. Praised for his excellent blocking in the two-platoon era but sometimes played defense at LB and was a good tackler. Didn't make too many mistakes. Also a good leader and a spirited hustler. His line coach, Toretti, said he was "the best offensive center in the country" in '52. Helped make it easy for Tony Rados to become best QB in East on '52 surprise team that upset Penn and Pitt and tied Big 10 co-champ Purdue while shooting to a 7-2-1 record. Was part of the first class to receive scholarships in '49 after more than two decades of de-emphasis. Never played under Bob Higgins but wound up marrying his youngest daughter and is an uncle to the Suhey brothers. Played in '52 Blue-Gray game and '53 Senior Bowl. Works in insurance sales and lives in Allentown, PA.

DORNEY, KEITH. 1975-76-77-78. OT, C & TE, 6'5", 257 lbs.; Allentown, PA. One of the great offensive linemen and a two-time First-Team All-American in '77 & '78. He was a consensus AA as senior, when picked by AP, UPI, Football Writers, NEA, Walter Camp and others. Finished 10th in balloting for Lombardi Award in '78—won by teammate Bruce Clark—as the nation's outstanding lineman/linebacker Another of Paterno's fine "scholar-athletes" who also was an Academic All-American in '78. A backup TE in frosh year, then became starting C as soph in '76. Along with Brad Benson and George Rehiner, he was cited for his fine blocking in 38-16 win over Army that helped turn around '76 season and led to Gator Bowl finish with Notre Dame. Switched to RT in junior season and became a star. He may have been the best OT of the '70s. One sportswriter said he was the type of player who "just knocked everyone down." A leader on the unbeaten '78 team that lost the National Championship to Alabama in the '79 Sugar Bowl. Played in East-West Shrine game and Senior Bowl in '79. Number one choice of Detroit in '79 and had a great 10-year All-Pro career with Lions until retirement in '88. Now works in time management products and lives in Sebastopol, CA.

DOUGHERTY, OWEN ("DOC"). 1949-50. HB, 5'9", 187 lbs.; Dunmore, PA. A transition player between Joe Bedenk and the Rip Engle era. Started at RHB for both and was known for his spectacular left handed passing, particularly off a reverse which often fooled opponents. Captain of Engle's first team in '50 that had 5-3-1 record. Led team in KO returns in '49 with eight for 132 yards and a 16.5 yards average. A nice person with a great sense of humor who knew how to "turn it on" on the field. One of the many frosh of '47 who were "farmed out" to Earl Bruce at California State Teacher's College because there was no room for the frosh at State with the return of the World War II veterans. Led team in passing in junior year, when State was still playing the Single-Wing and was among leading rushers in most games. His 57 yards on nine carries that led all rushers was the key to a big 22-7 win over Nebraska in '49. Also a fine defensive HB with the speed and quickness to nail runners and break up passes. His 49-yard return of an interception against Syracuse in '49 broke open a tight game and helped give State a 33-21 win. Hooked up with end Bob Hicks on a spectacular 66-yard pass play that helped beat Temple, 28-7. Easily made transition to Engle's Wing-T and was starting RH where he became more of a blocker for the LHB, FB and QB in the restructured offense. For years he was an assistant football coach, head baseball coach, athletic director and physical education professor at Indiana University of Pennsylvania. Deceased.

DOWLER, HENRY. 1889-90-91-92-93. G, 5'11", 178 lbs.; Burnside, PA. One of the State's football pioneers and one of its star linemen. One of few in his era who played more than four years; he lettered five years. May have been as "hard-nosed" as any State lineman of his time. Known to be tough and aggressive. Rules permitted linemen to run with ball in his years and he often carried it almost like a FB. A member of the first "championship" team which won the first Pennsylvania Intercollegiate Football Association title in 1891. Later came back to help coach. Deceased.

DOZIER, D. J.. 1983-84-85-86. TB, 6'1", 210 lbs.; Virginia Beach, VA. First-Team All-American in senior year when he was backfield star on team that won second National Championship. Eighth in balloting for Heisman Trophy that year. Led team that year in rushing and receiving with 811 yards and 10 TDs on 171 carries and 26 receptions for 287 yards and two TDs. Scored the game-winning TD in fourth QT of 14-10 win over Miami for national title at '87 Fiesta Bowl with a six-yard run; also led team that night in rushing (99 yards on 20 carries) and receiving (2-for-21 yards) and was named Most Valuable Offensive Player-of-the-game. Played one of his best games in '86 in 17-15 win over Maryland, scoring two TDs on nine-yard runs and setting up Massimo Manca's winning FG with a 15-yard run late in fourth QT, as he led all rushers with 111 yards on 25 carries and caught four passes for 18 yards. Was a star from the opening game of frosh year, when he succeeded Curt Warner at TB and had four straight games rushing over 100 yards, and eventually became the first back to lead in rushing four straight seasons. Because of later exploits, most fans forget how he helped turn around a losing season in '83 season after team had lost three straight at start of year and had narrow wins over Temple and Rutgers; in nationally televised upset over then number three Alabama at Beaver Stadium, he was State's Player-of-the-Game with 163 yards on 17 carries and one TD in 34-28 win. Had most yardage as frosh with 1,002 yards and seven TDs on 174 carries for a 5.8 yards average, which is still 13th best of all-time. Fourth in career rushing with 3,227 yards and 25 TDs on 624 carries for a 5.2 yards average. Rushed for over 100 yards in 11 games, with the 196 yards and two TDs (on 27 carries) in 36-25 win over Rutgers at the Meadowlands in frosh year being his all-time best. Good pass receiver, too; held record for more receptions in one season by a running back (26 in '86) until broken in '96 by Curtis Enis. Made one of his biggest "clutch runs" in '85 against Boston College, when with State trailing 12-3 late in third QT, he dashed 42 yards to the BC 11 to set up a TD that put State in position to eventually win 16-12. Played in '87 East-West Shrine game. Number one choice of Minnesota in '87 and played four years with Vikings and one with Detroit before turning full time to pro baseball for a few years. Always very religious, he is now out of athletics and a minister in Altamonte Springs, FL.

DRAYTON, TROY. 1991-92. WR & TE, 6'3", 220 lbs.; Steelton, PA. A walk-on who became a Third-Team All-American in senior year. A player who truly was still developing and getting better even as he graduated. Started out in junior year as fourth string WR and wound up as starting TE in '92 Fiesta Bowl against Tennessee, where he played key role in come-from-behind 42-17 victory, catching three passes for 35 yards and making key blocks to help the running of Richie Anderson and Sam Gash. Involved in one of the most bizarre and spectacular plays of the era when he took a behind-the-back shovel pass from Tony Sacca for 11 yards in 26-20 loss in the heat in Miami; he had four receptions that day, his best day of the year. Set record for one season receptions by a TE in '92 with 36 (for 488 yards and a TD). The TD was against West Virginia, when he caught 67-yard pass from Kerry Collins in second QT that put Lions into lead in eventual 40-26 victory. Also was PSU's Player-of-the-Game against BYU when he caught eight passes for 85 yards. Second choice of Los Angeles Rams in '93 and played three years with Rams before joining Miami in '96 and still playing for Dolphins.

DRAZENOVICH, CHUCK. 1945, 1947-48-49. QB & LB, 6'1", 215 lbs.; Brownsville, PA. The Iron Man of the late '40s. One of the toughest and most durable State players ever who played more than three-fourths of every game from his soph year on. Wasn't afraid of anyone and proved that as he also won the NCAA Heavyweight Boxing Championship and was named Outstanding Boxer by the Intercollegiate Boxing Association in 1950. Picked on the All-Time Penn State team in 1950s and again in 1967 by **Pittsburgh Press** sports editor Chet Smith, who covered Nittany Lion football for more than a half century. Primarily a blocking back and play caller and sometimes pass receiver in the Single-Wing offense and a LB on defense. Was truly the hardest hitter on the team, and everyone compared him to Penn's more famous All-American Chuck Bednarik. Gained national recognition in '48 Cotton Bowl as leader of the quick-hitting defensive team that stymied SMU's future Heisman Trophy winner, Doak Walker, in 13-13 tie. Was one of the reasons the undefeated '47 team set several NCAA defensive team records, including three that are still the record: fewest yards allowed rushing per game (17.0 yards on a total of 150 yards in nine games), fewest yards per rush in a season (0.64 yards on 240 carries) and fewest total yards allowed in a game (minus 47 yards in 40-0 Homecoming win over Syracuse). Got first start of career as frosh QB in '45 against Bucknell in fourth game of season, led team to 46-7 win and started rest of the season. After frosh season, he played in '46 East-West Shrine game at QB. Then left for armed service in '46. Returned in '47 and took over starting QB spot again in opening game and started there for next three years. Missed three games with injuries in '48 season. Had many key plays in games over the years and none was bigger than the fumble recovery that sealed late season 20-7 win over Navy and helped preserve unbeaten streak in '47. Also involved in one of the great razzle-dazzle pass plays of all-time that helped beat Penn, 13-0, in '48 that snapped Quakers 14-game winning streak: with nine minutes left in fourth QT and first-and-10 at Penn 13-yard line, he took handoff from FB Fran Rogel and pitched out to HB Elwood Petchel who then passed to Rogel in the EZ who juggled the ball, then made a desperation lunge as he hit the turf with the ball in his grasp for the TD. Scored one of the few TDs of his career when he tallied the season's first TD on an 18-yard pass from Petchel in '47 opening 27-6 win over Washington State. Played MLB on defense alongside his older brother Joe (see below) for three years. Became one of the best-known NFL defensive stars of the '50s and was an All-Pro linebacker with Washington Redskins until retiring in 1960. Deceased.

DRAZENOVICH, JOE. 1947-48-49. G, K & QB, 5'11", 200 lbs.; Brownsville, PA. A tough two-way lineman who was major part of the great undefeated '47 team that set several NCAA defensive records and allowed opponents only 26 points in regular season. May not be as well known as his younger brother Chuck (see above) because he never played pro football. But was just as tough and hard-nosed. Got chance to play in '44 when frosh were eligible because of World War II and was moved from G to QB because of his blocking ability. Started only one game, against West Virginia at midseason, before academic problems made him ineligible, and didn't letter. When he returned in '47, he was an immediate starter at LG and never missed a start for next three years except for injuries. Was a LB on defense and played alongside his brother Chuck for three years. Sometimes used as PK and P and scored his first point with PAT in 55-14 loss to powerful Navy in '44. Was a consistently fine blocker and hard-driving tackler, though often overshadowed by the ferocity and durability of his brother. Played one of the best games of his career in 22-7 win over Nebraska in '49, when credited with more than a half-dozen tackles and fumble recovery that led to winning TD in 22-7 victory. Son Andy ('78) was on special teams of the great '78 team. Retired and living in Wexford, PA.

DUCATTE, GREGG. 1969-71-72. LB & S, 6'1", 215 lbs.; Plattsburgh, NY. One of the best defensive backs of the early Paterno era and the first PSU player to play in the Orange, Sugar and Cotton Bowls. Co-Captain of the '72 team that was 10-2 and finished 10th in country after battling Oklahoma in Sugar Bowl. Had one of his greatest games in that game, making 10 tackles, including one that forced a fumble at the goal line and saved a touchdown; Sooner coach Chuck Fairbanks praised Ducatte for his performance, saying he never saw a safety play any better against the run. Also had another great game in the '71 "Breakthrough" Cotton Bowl game with 11 tackles and a fumble recovery. Made key interception in closing minutes of game against Air Force in '71 to preserve 16-14 victory that kept team unbeaten. Was a reserve linebacker as soph in '69 and played in '70 Orange Bowl. Missed '70 season because of back injury. Started in both junior and senior years and called defensive signals in the secondary. Married during his playing days and had his first child just before crucial game of '72 season against West Virginia. All-East in '71 & '72. Played in '73 Senior Bowl. Returned in '74 to coach defensive backs for a few years. Now an investment counselor in St. Petersburg, FL.

DUFFY, ROGER. 1987-88-89. C, 6'3", 274 lbs.; Canton, OH. Paterno called him "the best center ever to play for Penn State" on eve of his final game in a PSU uniform prior to the '89 Holiday Bowl. "Mother" Dunn, Chuck Cherundolo, Leon Gajecki and other two-way centers aside, he was a great three-year starter and never missed a start in 31 straight games when he graduated. One of the best blocking centers ever at State. Probably was the most consistent lineman in his three years but played in anonymity most of career. "The band never plays for a lineman," he once said. Centers rarely get noticed unless they make a big mistake and Duffy made few. Dressed but didn't play much on '86 Championship team. Got first start as soph in third game of season against Cincinnati because of injury to senior Mike Wolfe and two games later took over as full-time starter for rest of season, as Wolfe was sidelined, and he never came out of lineup until he graduated. Winner in '90 of an NCAA postgraduate scholarship that honors "scholar-athletes." Brother Pat ('90) followed him as an OT. Played in '90 Japan Bowl. Number eight pick of New York Jets in '90 and played with Jets until '98 when signed with Steelers. Lives in Long Beach, NY.

DUGAN, BILL. 1979-80. OT, 6'4", 278 lbs.; Hornell, NY. Another of the least known of State's All-American's, selected in senior year by Kodak Football Coaches. Largest offensive lineman on the team during his era and known as a punishing blocker. Succeeded another All-American, Keith Dorney, at left tackle in '79 after winning Worrell Award for being most improved player in Spring practice. But early in season he was suspended for a disciplinary problem and spent much of the season on the bench until injuries forced Paterno to use him again. Came into his own as a senior. Played one of best games in 24-10 win over Maryland in '80 while opening holes on short side of Terp line for Curt Warner & Booker Moore, including a 55-yard TD run by Moore that started State on the way to victory. Had another good game in 14-9 win over Pitt at end of season and later in 31-9 Fiesta Bowl win over Ohio State. By end of career, Paterno said Dugan "has

played as well as any player we have had in that position." An administration of justice major. Played in '81 East-West Shrine game. Drafted third by Seattle in '81 and played two years with Seahawks and one year with Minnesota. Now owns a plumbing & heating repair company in hometown of Hornell, NY.

DUNN, WILLIAM. T. ("Mother"). 1903-04-05-06. C; 6'1", 190 lbs.; Youngstown, OH. State's first nationally known player and first First-Team All-American; picked in '06 personally by Walter Camp who saw him play in 11-0 loss to Yale at New Haven—the only points scored on State all that season; in the game he made one of his trademark blocked kicks that should have been a State TD but the man who recovered for PSU ran the wrong way (see "Wrong-Way" Cyphers). Also blocked kick that led to only points via FG in historic first win over Carlisle Indians, 4-0. Camp later wrote in **Collier's** magazine: "Dunn of Penn State was the best center of the season, and it was he who led his team to such a remarkable record (8-1-1), a good deal of it depending on Dunn himself. He...is absolutely reliable in his passing, secure in blocking, active in breaking through and in diagnosing plays...He persistently broke through and blocked kicks. Able to run the 100 in 11 seconds, he was down under his own side's kicks with the ends. Beyond all and giving him added worth was his earnestness of purpose and character." Later, in typical modesty, Dunn credited fellow student Joe Mason, who was a campus news correspondent, with helping achieve his fame. Blocking kicks was Dunn's specialty and newspaper summaries of games in his era document that he blocked more kicks than any State player in history but no records were kept then so his blocks are not official. Also known for his great flying tackles and hard hitting. Centers didn't move around much in his era but he loved action and when opposing runners began avoiding him, he began to roam all over the field to tackle the ball carrier, and thus became known as one of college football's "roving centers." Sinewy, rangy and solid. Older than most when he entered college because he had to work in the steel mills in Youngstown to earn enough money to pay his way through school and was 29 years old when he became an All-American. Because of his maturity, he was the leader of his frosh class, and that was how he got his nickname: in often-told story, he was leading fellow frosh across campus one day in '03 when an upperclassman joked, "There goes Mother Dunn leading his chickens." Known as "Mother" Dunn ever since. Had great personal qualities and integrity and never swore, smoked or drank. Considered becoming a missionary after graduation while coaching for a year at Harrisburg Academy and went to University of Pennsylvania Medical School intent on becoming a doctor in China. Interned in Hawaii and never returned to mainland except for three years in San Diego, and spent most of his life as a physician and surgeon in Maui, Hawaii. Died in Maui on Nov. 17, 1962 at age 81.

DURKOTA, JEFF (GEORGE). 1942-46-47. FB & RHB, 6'2", 205 lbs.; Colver, PA. Another of the outstanding running backs of the World War II era who returned after the war to become a star on Higgins' best teams. Led the unbeaten '47 Cotton Bowl team in scoring with 10 TDs. Originally, part of the outstanding '41 frosh team that had best record in 25 years, 5-0, and was backup RHB as soph but then spent next three years in service. Came back in '46 when State was loaded with running backs but he couldn't be kept out of lineup. Got first start at RHB (or wingback in Single-Wing) in second game of '46 against Syracuse because of an injury and stayed on first team rest of year. Started games at both FB and RHB in senior year, when team was unbeaten, sharing playing time with Wally Triplett, Fran Rogel and Joe Colone, and was named Second Team AP All-East. In 75-0 rout of Fordham, he showed his all-around ability by scoring four TDs on runs, receptions and interceptions: he gained over 100 yards for the only time in his career with 102 yards (on three carries), including a 69-yard TD, caught passes of eight and 38 yards for two more TDs and ran back an interception 27 yards for his fourth TD. One of his finest games was in 20-7 win over mighty Navy late in '47 that was the catalyst to Cotton Bowl bid; he scored the first two TDs on reverses with runs of 48 and 42 yards to shock Navy and put game out of reach. Got on Higgins' bad side during preparations for Cotton Bowl and didn't play much in his final game. Played pro football with Los Angles Rams and Los Angles Dons before retiring. Longtime owner of an automobile dealership in Leola, PA.

DUVALL, A. G. ("RED"). 1928-29-30. T & G, 6'1", 190 lbs.; Monessen, PA. Probably the best all-around interior lineman on the teams at the beginning of the de-emphasis period that setback State football for decades. He was in the last batch of scholarship players and was a two and a half-year starter on teams that had two losing seasons. Intended not to play in junior year and did not report to team until early October but started late in season. In final game of career against Pitt, he blocked a punt that Earle Edwards picked up and ran in for a 40-yard TD but State lost 19-12. Deceased.

EBERSOLE, JOHN. 1967-68-69. DT, DE & LB, 6'4", 236 lbs.; Altoona, PA. An outstanding defensive lineman during State's record 31-game unbeaten streak between '67 & '70 who also is part of the "Linebacker U" tradition. May have been overshadowed by the reputation of DT's Mike Reid and Steve Smear, but he was a good compliment to that duo on the defensive line. Started out as the second team DT as soph in '67 but was injured in opening game of season against Navy. By end of year he was not only back but starting, and in 42-6 win over Pitt, he recovered a fumble on the Pitt 23 that set up one TD. Continued as backup at DT & DE on the great unbeaten team of '68 and found home as starter at DE (and sometimes also playing at LB) in '69, when team continued unbeaten streak and won '70 Orange Bowl in defensive struggle with Missouri, 10-3. Had affinity for playing good games against Maryland. Blocked a punt in 57-13 rout in '68 and recovered a fumble in 48-0 win in '69. Also won game ball for his courageous performance with an injured shoulder in a tough 17-14 win over Kansas State in '69. Fourth choice of New York Jets in '70 and had good career as a linebacker with Jets through '77 season before leaving pro ball. For years he has been a Blair County Commissioner and lives in Altoona, PA

ECONOMOS (EVANS), JOHN. 1935-36-37. G, 5'10", 170 lbs.; Pittsburgh, PA. May have been the best G of the mid and late 30's. A three-year starter at RG and co-captain in '37 of State's first winning team in nine years. Polished his football skills at Kiski Prep. Was outstanding as soph and might have had All-American honors if the team

had a better record (4-4). Played one of his best games when State beat Syracuse for first time in six years in '35, 18-0. His defensive play against Pitt in '35 is credited with keeping the score from getting out of hand despite 9-0 loss; he made several TD-saving tackles and got a standing ovation from the Pitt Stadium crowd. Was on several magazines' All-American checklist for '37 season when he was co-captain on 5-3 team. Tough and rugged despite his size. Stayed on after graduation to help Higgins coach the frosh. Deceased.

EDMONDS, GREG. 1968-69-70. SE, 6'3", 192 lbs.; Charleston, WV. Often overlooked when mentioning the outstanding receivers of the Paterno era but he was the first big pass catcher for Paterno. Played on the unbeaten teams of '68 & '69 which help thrust PSU Paterno into the big time of college football. Caught passes in both '69 & '70 Orange Bowl games which helped offense at critical times. Still 13th in career receptions with 66 (for 860 yards and six TDs). At one time the six TDs was the all-time record for one season. The record breaker was a 42-yard throw from John Hufnagel that helped beat WVU 42-8 in '70. Led team in receiving in junior and senior years with his 38 receptions (for 506 yards and the six TDs) in '70 being his best and still the 10th best in the one season record books. Was a backup as soph but used by Paterno to shuttle in plays and caught eight passes for 108 yards. Won Worrell award as the most improved player in spring practice in '69. All-East in '70. Number 16 choice of Minnesota in '71 but didn't play in NFL. Now a dessert manufacturer, Northfield, OH.

EDWARDS, EARLE. 1928-29-30. E, 5'11", 172 lbs.; Greensburg, PA. A man who bled Blue and White, even when he later faced PSU as the head coach at North Carolina State. Also was State's first football historian. He was in the last class of scholarship players before the 20-year de-emphasis period that set back State's football prominence for several decades. A three-year starting E and a solid player despite the dwindling cast of talent around him. Played one of his best games at the very end of his career against Pitt in '30, scooping up a punt blocked by Red Duvall and streaking 40 yards for a TD, but Pitt won, 19-12. His junior team was the last winning one for seven years, the worst losing streak in PSU history. But he also helped end the losing and regain some respectability as an assistant coach under Bob Higgins from '36-'48. Was a great scout of opposing teams and is credited with being the mastermind behind many game plans because of the weaknesses he would discover while watching opponents play. Higgins had hand-picked Edwards as his successor at the end of '48 but the Athletic Board which did the hiring passed him over for fellow alum and assistant coach Joe Bedenk. He resigned to become an assistant at Michigan State ('49-'53) and then went on to be a highly-respected head coach at North Carolina State from '54-'70. He coached three games against his alma mater in '56, '67 and '69 and lost all three, but the first two were "classic nail-biters" that weren't decided until the last minute of play; also recruited many Pennsylvania high school players who might have gone to PSU. After Ridge Riley, he was probably the leading historian of State football. His unpublished master's thesis in '39 traced the early days of State football as the title indicates "A History of A College Program of Football, An Historical Analysis of Intercollegiate Football at the Pennsylvania State College." After retirement, he lived in Raleigh, NC, until his death on February. 26, 1997, at age 88.

ENGLE, LLOYD ("DAD"). 1910-11-12. T, 5'11", 182 lbs.; California, PA. Another of State's "legends" with a historical football link to the Paterno era. He was the uncle of head coach 'Rip' Engle, who played at Western Maryland for Dick Harlow— "Dad's" linemate on State's unbeaten but once tied 1911 squad. Part of an outstanding interior line that also included fellow tackle "Red" Bebout and guards Levi Lamb and Al Hansen that had back-to-back unbeaten seasons in '11 & '12; they helped open the holes for Pete Mauthe and Shorty Miller to become All-Americans. Named All-East in senior season, when he played on one of the greatest teams in State history. Made one of the most significant TDs of '11 when he picked up a second QT punt blocked by Harlow at the Cornell 15-yard line and ran it into the EZ for the only points in a 5-0 win. In '12, he is reported to have fired up the team after Cornell scored a TD in third game by declaring no team would score on State again that season—and none did! Blocked punt deep in Penn territory in '12 that led to first TD and eventual 14-0 win. Played some HB in soph year after Mauthe was sidelined with broken ankle in opening game but was a starter at tackle in junior and senior season. Had long time career with the university as agricultural extension representative in Greene County. Deceased.

ENGRAM, BOBBY. 1991-93-94-95. WR & PR, 5'10", 187 lbs.; Camden, SC. May have been the greatest "clutch" receiver of all time in collegiate football. Holder of most State pass receiving records. A First-Team All-American and winner of the first Biletnikoff Award given to the nation's "outstanding pass receiver" as a junior. Underestimated by All-American selectors as senior, when he was even more valuable and crucial to State's offense, but picked to Second-Team and also a finalist in Biletnikoff Award. Made Third-Team All-American in soph year of '93. A protégé of assistant coach and former PSU All-American Kenny Jackson. He is the first and only State player to gain more than 1,000 yards on pass receptions in a season, and he did it twice— with 1,029 yards and seven TDs on 52 catches in '94 and 1,084 yards and 11 TDs on 63 receptions in '95 and only one to lead team in receiving for three years. Also career leader in receptions, reception yardage and TDs by receiving with 167 catches for 3,026 yards (an 18.1 yards average) and 31 TDs. His four TDs on receptions in 38-20 opening season win over Minnesota in soph year is the one-game record and so is his one-season total of 13 that year. Has twice as many games (16) with over 100 yards in receiving than runner-up O. J. McDuffie and is tied with McDuffie for most receptions in one season with 63. About only major records he doesn't hold is the number of receptions and yardage in one game; he had nine for 203 yards against Purdue in '95, but team-mate Freddie Scott set record that year with 13 catches against Wisconsin, and McDuffie had 212 yards on 11 catches in '92 Boston College game. Still, Engram has five of the best seven single games in reception yardage. Was also an excellent punt returner and led team in runbacks as soph and senior with best year in '93, when he had 33 returns and 402 yards for a 12.2 yards per return. The great (Kerry) Collins-to-Engram passing combination was a major reason why the '94 State team was one of the outstanding offensive teams of all-time, unbeaten and '95 Rose Bowl champs. Made one of his all-time "clutch" receptions with less than three minutes remaining in 24-24 tie with Michigan in '94, when he caught a 16-yard pass from Collins for the winning TD in game that propelled State to number one in the polls. But without Collins in '95, Engram prevented many defeats with his fourth quarter catches for TDs, often beating double and triple cover-

age. It happened in back-to-back games at Purdue and Iowa and again in the final game of the regular season at Michigan State, when a national TV audience watched as he took a pass in a crowd from Wally Richardson on the five-yard line with eight seconds left and no time outs and squirmed past two defenders for the winning TD, 24-20. Followed up with four receptions and two TDs and 113 yards in '96 Outback Bowl victory over Auburn to win MVP Award. Also Offensive MVP as sophomore in 31-13 Citrus Bowl win over Tennessee with seven receptions for 107 yards and a 15-yard TD and got another 35 yards on an end-around. Lettered as a "true" frosh in '91 but personal behavior problems caused Paterno to suspend him for a year. He came back a contrite and more mature individual and became in instant star in opening game of '93 and first game ever in Big 10 against Minnesota: he scored a 29-yard TD on the first play from scrimmage, added three more TDs on receptions of 31, 20 and 31 yards and was Big 10 Player-of-the-Week. Went on to be a Three-time First-Team All-Big 10 and winner of Hall Award in '95 as "outstanding senior player." Played in '96 Senior Bowl. Second choice of Chicago Bears in '96 and now a wide receiver and kick returner for the Bears.

ENIS, CURTIS. 1995-96-97. TB, 6'1", 231 lbs.; Union City, OH. One of the all-time great backs in PSU history whose career was tarnished at end when he accepted gifts from a sports agent in violation of NCAA rules, and thus became first player in Paterno era to be suspended for such a reason. Was the 12th Lion running back to be a First-Team All-American when selected in '97 by AP, Football Writers and Walter Camp. Also one of three finalists for Doak Walker Award as nation's outstanding running back. Selected Big 10 Offensive Player-of-the-Year after being named Player-of-the-Week three times in last six games as he rushed for over 100 yards in eight consecutive games, breaking school record held by Blair Thomas. His best game was 211 yards (and a TD on 23 carries) in crucial 31-27 win over Ohio State. Finished season with 1,363 yards and 19 TDs on 228 carries, which is the fifth best one season in school history. That made him just the fifth PSU player to rush for more than 1,000 yards in two seasons, finishing '96 with 1,210 yards and 13 TDs on 224 carries for a 5.4 yards average—the seventh highest one-season rushing yardage in school history, and the most ever by a soph, breaking Ki-Jana Carter's record set in '93. His three-year totals of 3,256 yards (and 36 TDs on 565 carries) is third in career record behind Curt Warner and Thomas. Also fourth in career scoring with 230 points and second in career rushing TDs to Lydell Mitchell with 36. His longest run for a TD was 78-yards that sparked Lions to 35-10 win over Wisconsin in '97. Also a fine pass receiver and in '96 broke D. J. Dozier's 10-year record for most receptions in one season by a running back with 32 catches (for 291 yards and one TD). Wound up career with 57 receptions for 416 yards and two TDs, including a 67-yard TD that broke up a tight game with Purdue in '97 and led to 42-17 victory. That was one of his finest games as he scored four TDs, rushed for 186 yards, caught three passes for 87 yards and had a career high 269 all-purpose yards. Big enough to be linebacker, which is where he played as a true frosh in the opening game of the '95 season against Texas Tech (and made two tackles). Switched to TB for second game against Temple because of injuries to other running backs, he entered game in second half and was an immediate hit; ran for a game high 132 yards on 14 carries, for a 9.4 yards average, and scored three TDs, including his first on a 24-yard run. Went on to rush for over 100 yards in next three games (including

146 yards against then number five Ohio State in losing effort) to become first frosh back to do so four straight times since D. J. Dozier in '83. Selected Big 10 Freshman-of-the-Year by media. Was sensational in nationally televised Kickoff Classic that opened '96 season when he exploded for 241 yards and three TDs (on 27 carries) in 24-7 win over Southern California and had everyone talking about him as a Heisman Trophy candidate; he was the unanimous selection as the game's Most Valuable Player. But injuries kept his production down for several games. However, he still made First-Team All-Big 10, as he came back to help lead victories over Purdue, Northwestern, Michigan State and '97 Fiesta Bowl opponent Texas—led running attack in 38-15 win over Texas with 95 yards and two TDs on 16 carries. Played one of his finest all-around games in 31-14 Homecoming victory over Purdue in '96, scoring three TDs and gaining 83 yard on the ground while catching a career high seven passes for 94 yards. Spent one year after high school at Kiski prep, and with his original class graduating in '98. Suspension cost him opportunity to play final game in Citrus Bowl, he turned pro and his presence was missed as Lion offense sputtered and lost to Florida. Number one draft choice of the Chicago Bears in '98 and now playing with the Bears.

EYER, DON. 1951-52-53. E, HB & P, 6'1", 189 lbs.; Chambersburg, PA. An excellent defensive back and fine pass receiver on Engle's early teams. His 11 career interceptions (for 143 yards) was the record for 10 years, and he is still fifth on all-time list. Had eight interceptions (for 67 yards) in junior year to tie with teammate Jack Sherry for team lead and a one season record that stood for 17 years until broken by Neal Smith in '69; still third in one-season interceptions. He didn't have any interceptions in senior year but led team in punting in '53 with 10 punts (for 330 Yards). Played one of his best defensive games in '52 in surprising 20-20 tie with Purdue that got the attention of the college football world and gave the Engle era its first prominence; his tackle from behind at PSU 17-yard line stopped an almost sure TD on Purdue's opening drive; then in last minute of game he intercepted All-American Dale Samuel's pass at the State 15-yard line and ran it back 28 yards to end a final Purdue scoring threat. In next to last game of season, against Rutgers, he made two interceptions late in the fourth QT—one on the goal line and another at the five—that stopped potential TD drives in 7-6 win. Also played offensive wingback in several games because of injuries and was among team's leading rushers in those games. Spent many years teaching at Chambersburg High School until retirement, and continues to live in Chambersburg, PA.

FARRELL, SEAN. 1979-80-81. OG, 6'3", 266 lbs.; Westhampton Beach, NY. One of State's best offensive lineman of all time and one of only 11 two-time First-Team All-Americans; picked by Football News in '80 and was consensus All-American in '81, when selected by AP, UPI, Sporting News and others. Finalist as senior for both Lombardi and Outland Awards given to outstanding linemen/linebackers. He was first three-year starter at offensive guard in 20 years and at end of career Paterno said "if there's a better guard in the

country (than Farrell), he's Superman." Along with fellow G Mike Munchak, helped open the holes that made Curt Warner a star from his frosh year. When Warner broke Shorty Miller's 69-year record for rushing in one game with 256 yards in 26 carries in 41-16 win over Syracuse in '81, it was Munchak, Farrell and center Jim Romano who were credited with providing the essential blocking. After playing against Farrell & Munchak in '81, a Nebraska LB said "I've never seen anyone tougher than those two and I hope I never do again." Co-captain of '81 team that was third in country after a 10-2 season, including a momentous 48-14 comeback win over then number one Pitt and 26-10 win over USC in '82 Fiesta Bowl. Had a lineman's dream come true, when he recovered a Warner fumble in EZ of '81 Pitt game for only TD of career. Winner of Hall Award in '81 given to State's "outstanding senior player." Played in East-West Shrine game and Japan Bowl in '82. Number one choice of Tampa Bay in '82 and had an All-Pro career with Bucs ('82-'86), New England ('87-'89) and Denver ('90-'91) before retiring. Now lives in Tampa, FL.

FAYAK, CRAIG. 1990-91-92-93. PK, 6'1", 190 lbs.; Belle Vernon, PA. The all-time scoring leader with 282 points on 132 PATs and 50 FGs, and another of Paterno's fine "scholar-athletes." As cool under pressure as any PSU kicker ever. Will always be remembered for his "clutch" 34-yard FG with four seconds left at South Bend as a frosh late in the '90 season that knocked off then number one and unbeaten Notre Dame, 24-21. Also holds record for most career FGs and attempts (80) and most points in one season by a frosh (74 in '90); his record points for a soph (93 in '91 and eighth in all-time for one season) was broken by Curtis Enis in '96; led team in scoring both years and as senior had 79 pts. Seventh in career FGs for one season with 15 in '90. Among eight players with four FGs in a game (one behind record); his four in 32-20 win over Pitt in '91 went for 48, 47, 25 and 24 yards. His 50-yarder that helped beat Alabama 9-0 in '90 is tied for sixth longest with three other kickers; also kicked two 34-yard FGs that day for all the points in final game of long regular season series with Crimson Tide. Kicked in three bowl games and best was the 19-yard FG and four PATs that helped beat Tennessee in '94 Citrus Bowl, 31-13. Hampered by a leg injury in junior and senior years and injury eventually kept him out of pro football. Winner in '94 of an NCAA post-graduate scholarship that honors "scholar athletes." Now working for Andersen consulting and living in Bryn Mawr, PA.

FITZKEE, SCOTT. 1976-77-78. WR & P, 6'0", 183 lbs.; Red Lion, PA. One of the most exciting players of the late '70s. Ninth in career reception yardage with 1,263 yards and 11 TDs on 65 receptions and 12th best for one season with 530 yards and six TDs on 37 catches (and 17 yards per reception average) in '78. Made one of the biggest "clutch" receptions of his career as junior in great comeback win at North Carolina State when he caught winning TD at end of 83-yard drive in last two and a half minutes by snatching an 11-yard throw from Chuck Fusina as he crossed towards the back corner of the EZ. His 72-yard catch on a pass from Fusina in 49-7 win over Miami in '77 is tied with three others for being eighth longest in records. Played one of his best games in the classic National Championship game against Ala-bama in the '79 Sugar Bowl: had a leaping 17-yard reception of Fusina pass for a TD in the third QT that virtually tied the game at 7-7; then almost scored another TD on a second down, seven-yard throw from Fusina but was shoved out of bounds at the one-yard line, setting up the historic two-play Alabama goal line stand that eventually won the game—and the national title—14-7; he had total of three receptions for 38 yards in the game; also punted 10 times for a 38.7 yards average. Was team's main punter for three years with his '77 average of 38.6 yards per punt on 44 kicks (for 1,699 yards) being his best. Career average of 36.43 yards is not among top 10 but his total yardage is fourth on all-time list, and he never had a punt blocked. His 64-yarder against Maryland in '77 is tied for 10th longest in records. Played in '79 Hula and Japan Bowls. Number five choice of Philadelphia in '79 and played two years with Eagles and two years with San Diego before going into the new United States Also holds record for most career FGs and attempts (80) and most points in one season by a frosh (74 in '90); his record points for a soph (93 in '91 and eighth in all-time for one season) was broken by Curtis Enis in '96; led team in scoring both years and as senior had 79 pts. Seventh in career FGs for one season with 15 in '90. Among eight players with four FGs in a game (one behind record); his four in 32-20 win over Pitt in '91 went for 48, 47, 25 and 24 yards. His 50-yarder that helped beat Alabama 9-0 in '90 is tied for sixth longest with three other kickers; also kicked two 34-yard FGs that day for all the points in final game of long regular season series with Crimson Tide. Kicked in three bowl games and best was the 19-yard FG and four PATs that helped beat Tennessee in '94 Citrus Bowl, 31-13. Hampered by a leg injury in junior and senior years and injury eventually kept him out of pro football. Winner in '94 of an NCAA postgraduate scholarship that honors "scholar athletes." Now working for Andersen consulting and living in Bryn Mawr, PA.

FORKUM, CARL. 1902-03-04. HB, FB & K, 6'0", 180 lbs.; New Castle, PA. One of the greatest State running backs of all time and also one of the most neglected in State's official records. He should hold the record for most points ever scored in a game and longest kickoff return for a TD, but neither of these deeds—nor the five TDs he scored against Pitt in '03 and Allegheny in '04—are in the record book because few records were kept in his era. In the '03 Pitt game, won by State 59-0, he also booted 9-of-10 extra points for a total of 38 points, two better than Harry Robb's "official" record against Gettysburg in '17. In the '04 Allegheny game, he had a 115-yard kickoff return (the playing field was 110-yards then)—which is better than Chuck Peters' 101-yard return in '40—scored five TDs and kicked two extra points in 50-0 win. He rushed for some 200 yards against Pitt in '03 but that isn't in the football record books either. He also scored on another KO return for over 100 yards at least once, and several times in his career he scored three TDs in a game. A fine FG kicker and a great punter known for his high kicks for long distance which would enable his tacklers to get downfield quickly. Also known as a tough tackler, who was not afraid of taking on several blockers and this caused him several injuries over three years. Made sensational debut in very first game by scoring two TDs and gaining big chunks of yardage to lead State to 27-0 win over Dickinson Seminary in '02 season opener. Combined with Irish McIlveen, Andy Smith, Ed Whitworth and Ed Yeckley in '02 for one of the most potent running attacks in the country. Scored two TDs in '03 22-0 victory over Washington & Jefferson, which was State's biggest victory in the first 15 years of football and was played before the largest crowd ever to see State up to that time—7,000 at Pittsburgh's Exposition Park. Captain of '04 team and leading scorer in first four games, but career ended prematurely, when he was intentionally injured by W&J player in midseason and played only three minutes in

team's last five games. Was first athlete to win four letters in a single year ('04): football, basketball, track and baseball. After graduation, returned occasionally in next decade to help coach for a few weeks at a time. Deceased.

FRANK, CALVIN (HAP). 1922-23. E, 6'0", 168 lbs.; Harrisburg PA. Another war hero who commanded the 79th Infantry Division in World War II. Shared starting end position on '22 team and regular in '23. Started first game as soph against Navy on great '21 "mystery team" and his blocking was instrumental in 13-7 upset; but didn't play enough that year to letter. The '22 team played in first bowl game, losing to USC in '23 Rose Bowl. His blocking is credited with helping make "Light Horse" Harry Wilson an All-American on '23 squad. Known for his rugged blocking and tackling style. Without much boxing experience he agreed to fight for coach Leo Houck's team and won intercollegiate light-heavyweight championship (175-pounds) in '24. Also captained '24 lacrosse team. After graduation, coached football at Dickinson and Gettysburg, then went into insurance business in hometown, later becoming a city councilman. Was active in Army Reserves and became a major general prior to World War II. Remained active in university affairs, serving on Athletic Board. Played major role in selection of his teammate, Joe Bedenk, as successor to coach Bob Higgins in '49. Deceased.

FRENCH, COOP. 1928-29-30. QB & RB, 5'8 ½", 163 lbs.; Moorestown, NJ. One of the truly forgotten stars, who had the misfortune of entering State when the college was under pressure for "overemphasizing football" and Coach Bezdek was being criticized for his "inhuman" style of coaching. Was in the last class of scholarship players before the drastic de-emphasis of football in the '30s and '40s that crippled PSU football for decades. Holds official record for longest punt with a 90-yard kick in 19-0 loss at Iowa in senior year but according to newspaper reports of the game, the kick was only 79-yards; also kicked a 70-yarder on that day—both on quick-kicks which went over the safety man's head—and that kick was the second longest punt until 1976. Also is still in records with fifth longest interception return, an 82-yard run for TD in 19-7 win at Penn in junior year. First showed star presence in '28 Homecoming game against Syracuse, when he came off bench to lead a comeback with his passing and running and scored first TD of his career in fourth QT 11-yard run that was State's only score in a 6-6 tie. Combined with his roommate and one-time prep school teammate, Frank Diedrich, for one of the most spectacular TD plays in history in '29 Homecoming game against Lafayette: Lafayette was ahead 3-0 with less than 30 seconds left in game and a third down on own 14-yard line and, surprisingly, decided to punt; French & Diedrich scurried back in double safety; French took the punt at 40-yard line, started to run to draw in all the Lafayette defenders, then threw the ball back across the field to Diedrich who ran for winning TD as time expired; both were carried off the field by the jubilant fans. Deceased.

FUSINA, CHUCK. 1976-77-78. QB, 6'1", 196 lbs.; McKees Rocks, PA. Some partisans believe he is the best PSU QB of all time. Won Maxwell Award in '78 as "outstanding player in collegiate football" and runner-up to Billy Sims for Heisman Trophy; also consensus All-American when selected by AP, UPI, Football Coaches and Football Writers, among others. Paterno once said Fusina was "without question the best QB we had had in my 29 years at Penn State. He is an excellent , a fine leader and a completely unselfish player." Co-captain of the first State team ever to become number one in the country in '78 but lost the National Championship to Alabama, 14-7, in the frustrating '79 Sugar Bowl; he hit on 15-for-30 passes and the only PSU TD but was stymied by the great 'Bama defense, which intercepted four passes. Previous year he was 9-for-23 for 83 yards and one TD in 42-30 Fiesta Bowl victory over Arizona State that set the enthusiastic tone for the future amicable relationship with that bowl. Played one of his outstanding games in the "classic" '78 November clash of the unbeatens against Maryland at Beaver Stadium, when he hit on 15-of-29 passes for 234 yards, including a 63-yard TD pass to Tom Donovan that gave State a 27-3 win on regional TV and made him Offensive Player-of-the-Game, and put him on the cover of *Sports Illustrated*. But his biggest "clutch" moment may have been against North Carolina State in '77 in what some called "a miracle march;" with about 2:30 left in game and State trailing, 17-14, he marched team 83 yards with six straight completions and tossed the game winning TD from 11 yards out to Scott Fitzkee as he cut across the EZ towards the back corner. Was State's record career passer for a decade, until topped by Tony Sacca, but still number two with 5,382 yards and 37 TDs (fourth best) on 371-for-665 attempts and 32 interceptions. Made an initial impression as frosh in last game of '75 season against Pitt when he relieved starter John Andress in fourth QT with State trailing 6-0 and quarterbacked team 69 yards for TD; Chris Bahr then kicked PAT that gave PSU 7-6 win and salvage prestige for season and Gator Bowl appearance against Notre Dame. His big chance came as a soph, when Andress suffered a severe shoulder injury on the second play of the fourth game of the season against Kentucky; Lions lost that day for a 1-3 record but Fusina helped turn around that season starting the next week against Army and he started the next 31 games, winning 27 and losing just four on teams that finished fourth in the country in '77 and '78. Led team in passing and total offense for three years. Fifth in career passing efficiency (132.48), third in career yards per attempt with 8.09 yards and 10th in career TD pass percentage with a 5.56 average. Tied with five others behind Sacca with most TDs in a game, when he passed for four in '78's 45-15 Homecoming win over Syracuse. Until Kerry Collins came along, he had the record for most 200-yard passing games with 11, and his 315 yards and two TDs on 22-of-36 attempts in the 21-17 victory at North Carolina State in '77 is sixth best of all-time. Also tied for eighth longest pass for a TD, when he and Scott Fitzkee combined for a 72-yarder that helped beat Miami, 49-7, in '77. Winner of first Hall Award in '78 given to State's "outstanding senior player." One of the McKees Rocks QB trio of Burkhart, Hufnagel and Fusina, who were so integral to the success of Paterno in his first 15 years. Played in Hula and Japan Bowls in '79. Fifth choice of Tampa Bay in '79 and played with Bucs from '79-'82 before joining Philadelphia Stars in new United States Football League and led team to championship during three years he played there, then played one year with Green Bay in '86 before retiring. Now a medical sales representative in Pittsburgh.

GAJECKI, LEON. 1938-39-40. C, 6'0", 225 lbs.; Colver, PA. One of the best centers of all time. Penn State's sixth All-American ('40) and only one from '23-to-'47. Captain of '40 team that had best Penn State record in 19 years, 6-1-1, and leader (he also called the defensive signals) of the highly-regarded front line known as "the Seven Mountains." Two-way player known for his hard hitting and tenacious blocking. One national football magazine called him "indestructible" and a sportswriter who followed the team cited his outstanding tackling and blocking as one of the key elements in producing the fine '39 & '40 seasons that rejuvenated State football. Started second game of '38 season as 180-pound soph against Bucknell, forcing the veteran Sever Toretti to switch to G, and never gave up starting position until graduation 23 games later. Part of tough '38 defensive team that set three NCAA pass-defense records despite having a losing season; the record for fewest yards passing allowed per game (13.1 average) still stands after 68 years. Played one of his finest games in 7-7 tie with powerful Penn in '38, making "three-fourths" of State's tackles before injuring a shoulder. His best game may have been in the 10-0 victory over Pitt in '39, the first win over State's bitterest rival in 20 years after 14 straight losses. Coach Higgins called him "the best man on the field" that day; he played the entire 60 minutes and helped make tackle and recovered fumble on Pitt 22-yard line that led to the Lions' only TD. Recruited during an era when State de-emphasized football and had to work during college to pay for his education. Played in '41 East-West Shrine game. Drafted by Pittsburgh Steelers but went into Army. After service in World War II he played pro ball with the Jersey City Giants of the American Professional Football League. Settled in Pitman, NJ, working for Humble Oil & Refinery Co. Helped recruit from New Jersey high schools such future Penn State stars as Milt Plum, Dave Robinson, Lydell Mitchell and Franco Harris. Now retired but still a fixture at Penn State home games where he tailgates regularly with the Lions' broadcaster Fran Fisher, friends and teammates from '38-'40.

GANCITANO, NICK. 1982-83-84. PK, 5'7", 164 lbs.; Coral Springs, FL. Very accurate kicker and great under pressure. As soph, he helped win first National Championship. He kicked FGs of 38 and 45 yards and three extra points that made the difference in the 27-23 win over Georgia Tech for the national title in the '83 Sugar Bowl. Still holds record for career FG accuracy, hitting on 38-of-49 FGs for a 77.6 average. Eleventh in all-time career scoring with 190 points on the 38 FGs and 76 extra points, and tied for 12th in one-season scoring with 85 points on 17 FGs and 34 PATs in '83. Led team in scoring in both '83 and '84. Fifth in career FGs and sixth in one-season total. Always kicked his best against arch rival Pitt. Tied with 11 other players who have kicked four FGs in a game behind co-leaders Brian Franco and Massimo Manca with five; his four were in big 19-10 win over Pittsburgh in '82 that sent team into National Championship game against number one Georgia in Sugar Bowl. Also made one of his outstanding kicks under pressure in final game of '83 season against Pitt, when six seconds was added to the clock after Pitt thought the game had ended in a 24-21 victory and everyone had to be recalled back to the Pitt Stadium field; Gancitano calmly booted a 32-yard FG that saved the year and put State into the Aloha Bowl. Now living in Coconut Creek, FL.

GANTER, FRAN. 1968-69-70. HB, 5'11", 200 lbs.; Bethel Park, PA. Now better known as Paterno's Offensive Coordinator for past decade but he was a three-year letterman at running back on Paterno's great teams in the early years. Unfortunately, he came along at the same time as Charlie Pittman, Lydell Mitchell and Franco Harris and was mostly a reserve. Played HB on the unbeaten '68 team and FB on the undefeated '69 and hard-luck '70 squad. In pre-season practice of '69 he was set to be backup to starter Don Abbey, but Harris soon moved ahead and became a star. Won Red Worrell Award as most improved player in spring practice of '70, and went on to have his best year in Fall, when he was team's fifth best rusher with 203 yards and three TDs on 59 carries. When Paterno shook up his struggling team and reconstructed his offense at midseason, he inserted Ganter as starter for last five games, partially to keep his hot-shot runners, Mitchell and Harris, fresh and motivated. Ganter, believing he had beaten out Harris, scored all of his TDs in this period. It was an early example of what would become a Paterno era trait—rewarding a less talented but hard working and loyal player who has "paid his dues." Had one of his best games ever as soph in 69-9 rout of Pitt in '68, when he carried 11 times for 51 yards and a TD. After graduating in '71 he served as a graduate assistant while completing Master's Degree. Few remember what he did to help beat Texas in the "breakthrough" '72 Cotton Bowl game: as the '71 team prepared in Dallas for the game, Ganter appeared in uniform at a Thursday practice to run the Texas Wishbone offense against the State defense; he did, but the practice was so rugged he watched the game on New Year's Day with his leg in a cast. Became full-time assistant coach in charge of frosh team in '72. Also has been in charge of running backs almost from the beginning, and he has been instrumental in the development of such TB's as Curt Warner, D. J. Dozier, Blair Thomas and Ki-Jana Carter. Became offensive coordinator in '84 when Dick Anderson left for Rutgers. Credited with developing the great "sudden strike" offense of '94 that set 14 school records and led nation in total offense (520.2 yards per game) and scoring (with 47.8 points). Lives in State College.

GARBAN, STEVE. 1956-57-58. C, 6'0", 195 lbs.; Grindstone, PA. A solid and consistent player on both offense and defense and an outstanding team leader. Soft-spoken off the field but knew how to motivate on it. Captain of "snake-bitten" '58 team that was 6-3-1 but missed out on bowl bid despite last game upset of Pitt that knocked Panthers out of major bowl game. That was one of his finest games— and his last—in 25-21 win at Pitt Stadium; he was a hard-charging defensive firestorm, making tackles all over field from his LB position and recovering a fumbled punt at the Pitt 36-yard line to set up State's final TD in fourth QT; his play was epitomized by a crucial solo tackle on a kickoff earlier in the game that pinned the Panthers on their 12-yard line and set up the Lions second TD moments later because of a mishandled punt snap by Mike Ditka. First went to work for U.S. Steel after graduation but returned to PSU in early '60s for an administrative position in the Athletic Department and later became senior vice president of financial affairs for Penn State until his retirement in '95. Lives in State College.

GARBINSKI, MIKE. 1939-40, 45. G, 6'0", 195 lbs.; Johnstown, PA. One of the original "Seven Mountains, " the great seven-man line of the '40 team, which had the best State record in 19 years and was one of the top teams in the country with a 6-1-1 record. Was strong and rough-hewn. A tough running guard noted for his blocking on inside plays. Played on teams that lost only five games in his career. Garbinski was only soph to make starting lineup in '39 and went on to start every game at LG in both soph and junior years before leaving for armed services. After four years in World War II, he came back at age 27, and

although his skills had deteriorated, he was a fine backup and spot starter who terrorized opposing backs for the comeback '45 team that surprised everyone with a 5-3 record. Retired and living in his hometown of Johnstown, PA.

GARRITY, GREGG. 1980-81-82. WR, 5'10", 170 lbs.; Bradford Woods, PA. Who can ever forget his diving fourth quarter catch of a 47-yard pass from Todd Blackledge in the EZ against Georgia in the '83 Sugar Bowl that gave State the eventual 27-23 victory and the school's first National Championship, and landed him on the cover of *Sports Illustrated*? Was leading receiver in that game with 116 yards from four receptions. Also went over 100-yards in the disheartening 17-14 loss to Miami that knocked State from number one in polls in '81 with 104 yards on six receptions, setting up the first TD with two fine catches of 16 and 21 yards. Overshadowed during his receiving career by All-American Kenny Jackson but one of the schools best "clutch" receivers. Led team in receptions as a junior on the 10-and-2 '81 team with 23 catches for 415 yards (18.0 yards per reception) and one TD. Ranks 14th in career reception yardage with 952 on 58 catches and four TDs. A backup WR as soph but got start in opening season game against Cincinnati in junior year. Played one of his finest games in '82 Fiesta Bowl when his 52-yard TD on a pass from Blackledge broke up a 7-7 tie in the second QT and led to a 26-10 victory. Two of his best games came in championship year against Maryland and Nebraska: scored a TD on a 23-yard pass and set up two more TDs with crucial catches as he led all receivers with four receptions for 73 yards in 39-31 shoot-out with Maryland; then in the historic 27-24 come-from-behind win over Nebraska, he had five receptions (some of the acrobatic variety) for 75 yards that kept drives alive. Son of Jim (see below) and was planning to attend Clarion but father talked him into being a "walk-on" at Penn State. Drafted fifth by Pittsburgh in '83 and played one year with Steelers but came into his own as a receiver with Philadelphia ('84-'89) before leaving the game and is now owns a construction company in his hometown of Bradford Woods, PA.

GARRITY, JIM. 1952-53-54. E & PK, 6'1", 177 lbs.; Monaca, PA. One of the country's leading pass receivers in the early '50s. Co-captain of '54 team that was 7-2 and upset Illinois 14-12 in the season opener, knocked Pitt from a probable Orange Bowl in a 13-0 win at Pittsburgh in the last game of the season and finished ranked 16th by UPI and 20th by AP. In Illinois game, he kicked two PATs that was the difference in victory and made game-clinching tackle with junior Frank Reich late in the fourth quarter: Illinois was at State's 16-yard line on fourth-and-six, when he and Reich tackled All-American J.C. Caroline for a four-yard loss that ended the last threat; the game set the tone for the rest of the successful season. His 30 pass receptions in '53 junior year not only led team but was one of the best in nation. Also team scoring leader that year with 48 points on four TDs, 17 extra points and one FG. Part of State's great recruiting class in '51 that rejuvenated football after a 20-year de-emphasis period. Started at LE on defensive platoon as soph but also played offense. Outstanding defensive player who was able to adjust to the elimination of two-platoon football after his soph year and play both ways with equal intensity. One of biggest defensive plays in his career came against Syracuse in '53, when he picked up a blocked kick by Dante DeFalco with a minute left in the game and ran 23 yards for a TD that broke a tie and gave State the 20-14 win. Father of Greg (see above). Was planning to attend Clarion but father talked him into being a "walk-on" at Penn State. Played in '55 East-West Shrine game and was one of stars along with teammate and QB Don Bailey. Also played in '55 Senior Bowl. Now semi-retired and living in Bradford Woods, PA.

GASH, SAM. 1988-90-91. FB, 5'11", 225 lbs.; Hendersonville, NC. An outstanding team player who is the prototype of a Paterno fullback: an excellent blocker, a good runner and a solid pass receiver. Second team FB as frosh and scored two TDs and selected State's Player-of-Game in loss to West Virginia, and started in last game of year against Notre Dame. Sat out '89 season after being injured in pre-season. Came back and won Red Worrell Award in '90 as most improved player in spring practice. Started in opening game of '90 against Texas and started every game at FB for next two years. Played one of his best games in the final game of the long series with Syracuse, when he scored one TD and set up two others with his running and pass receiving, as he led all rushers with 78 yards on nine carries and caught three passes for 33 yards. As usual for PSU FBs Gash didn't score much but picked up key yardage and was main blocker on many plays. Rushed for 391 yards and three TDs on 87 carries in senior year to finish second behind Richie Anderson. Had one of the finest days of his career in '91 opening season 34-22 win over Georgia Tech at Kick-off Classic, when he led all rushers with 89 yards on 12 carries. His best TD day was in 81-0 rout of Cincinnati, when he scored first two TDs of day on smashes of four and two yards. Closed out career with a different type of TD, taking a 10-yard pass from Tony Sacca in for the first score against Tennessee in '92 Fiesta Bowl victory. Number eight choice of New England Patriots in '92 and was starting fullback for Patriots until '98 when he joined the Buffalo Bills.

GATTUSO, GREG. 1981-82-83. DT, 6'3", 262 lbs.; Pittsburgh, PA. One of the defensive stars on the first National Championship Team of '82. Seemed to have a knack of forcing and recovering fumbles. Had two of his finest games as a soph: first against Notre Dame, when his late fourth QT interception at the PSU 18-yard line with ND leading, 21-17, sparked an 82-yard drive for the winning TD; then followed up the next week in great come-from-behind 48-14 upset over then number one Pitt, as he recovered two fumbles to stop Panther scoring threats. Helped turn around a losing season in '83 season after team had lost three straight at start of year and had narrow wins over Temple and Rutgers; in nationally televised upset over then number three Alabama at Beaver Stadium, he and sub DB Mark Fruehan stopped 'Bama TB Kerry Goode at goal line on fourth-and-Goal from PSU two with one second left to preserve 34-28 win; earlier in game he had forced two fumbles, including one at PSU goal line in second QT that saved TD. Had another of his best games in the memorable 27-24 win over Nebraska at Beaver Stadium when sportswriters said he outplayed the Cornhuskers' All-American center, Dave Rimington. Played in '84 East-West Shrine game. Went into football coaching following graduation and is now the head coach at Duquesne University.

GEISE, STEVE. 1975-76-77. RB, 6'1½", 207 lbs.; Lock Haven, PA. May not be as well known as other running backs of his era because he played during the major rebuilding years of '75 and '76. Co-captain of the 11-1 '77 team that lost only to Kentucky in 24-20 upset at Beaver Field but was dropped by the Orange Bowl at the last minute by "political maneuvering" from the Southwest Conference; team wound

up making its first ever appearance at the Fiesta Bowl on Christmas Day of '77, where he had one of his greatest games, running for 111 yards and an 18-yard TD on 26 carries, catching two passes for 10 yards, and scoring a two-point conversion in 42-30 victory over Arizona State. Three other times he gained over 100 yards in his career, including his biggest yardage day ever, against North Carolina State in '76, when he rushed for 145 yards and one TD on 12 carries in 41-20 win. Also had 110 yards in 16 carries against Army that junior year and combined with frosh Mike Guman, who had 107 yards, for first dual 100 yards by two State running backs in five years. Made one his most important TDs as soph in fourth QT of final game of regular season against Pitt: Lions were trailing 6-0 when he and frosh QB Chuck Fusina entered game and went on 69-yard drive with Geise scoring TD on 28-yard run; Chris Bahr's PAT gave State the 7-6 victory that helped regain prestige before Gator Bowl. Ranks 20th in career rushing with 1,362 yards and 11 TDs on 313 carries. Drafted sixth by Cincinnati in '78 but never made NFL a career and went to medical school instead. Now a practicing doctor in hometown of Lock Haven, PA.

GELZHEISER, BRIAN. 1991-92-93-94. LB, 6'1", 235 lbs.; Pittsburgh, PA. Leader of the often maligned defense on the unbeaten '94 team that won the '95 Rose Bowl; the defense that year was not up to the quality of outstanding defensive teams in the past but not this senior; his hard tackling stopped many potential long runs. Led the team in tackles as senior (126 tackles on 51 solos and 75 shared) and junior (113 on 57 solos and 56 shared) and is second in career tackles behind Greg Buttle with 315 (157 solos and 158 shared). His '94 and '93 statistics places him fifth and eighth on the all-time list for tackles in one season. Recruited as a LB or DB after playing QB in high school and was fourth string early in '91, when season-ending injury to Mark D'Onofrio and injuries to two backups forced Paterno to use him in middle of season against Rutgers. Started one game that year and had 32 tackles. Was backup most of soph year at OLB until injuries got him a start at ILB against Notre Dame and he was outstanding in last minute 17-15 loss, making 15 tackles (the highest for any State defender that season) and recovering a fumble. Started at ILB for next two years. Took up in opening game of '93 against Minnesota where he left off in '92 with a game high 10 tackles in 38-20 win. Usually had most tackles in each '93 game, hitting the double digit figures with 17 in 28-14 win over Illinois being his best. Played in '95 Senior Bowl. 6th choice of Indianapolis in '95 but no longer in NFL. Working and living in Pittsburgh.

GERAK, JOHN. 1989, 1991-92. G, TE & FB, 6'5", 278 lbs.; Struthers, OH. One of the players who typifies the philosophy of "positioning" that has marked the Paterno coaching era. Recruited as a FB & DE and played FB as true frosh, when he didn't letter, but had 108 yards and one TD on nine carries. Switched to shortside G in spring practice of '91 and became a standout in '91 & '92. Was the starting FB in opening game of soph year but after three games was replaced by Leroy Thompson; had decent year finishing fifth in rushing with 108 yards on 31 carries. Took "redshirt" year in '90 to make transformation to G and got first start there in fifth game of '91 season and was regular for next one and a half years. Became a solid blocker with good speed for pulling outside. Offensive co-captain of '92 team that didn't play up to potential and had disappointing 7-5 season. Played in '93 Senior Bowl. Drafted third by Minnesota in '93 and was starting offensive lineman for two years, then a backup and played with St. Louis Rams in '97. Lives in Youngstown, OH, in off season.

GETTY, CHARLIE. 1971-72-73. OT, 6'4", 260 lbs.; Pompton Lakes, NJ. Second-Team All-American in '73 and one of the leaders of probably the most underrated offensive line in the Paterno era that included Mark Markovich, John Nessel and Jack Baiorunos. This was the line that allowed John Cappelletti to run for 1,522 yards and 17 TDs and become State's only Heisman Trophy winner; also line that helped '73 team become first to win 12 games. Played behind All-American Dave Joyner as soph and was listed as backup after spring practice of '72 but was in starting lineup at RT as season opened and stayed there for two years. Paterno believed he was one of the best OT's in the country by the time he graduated. Wrestled as heavyweight in winter sports and won Eastern Collegiate championship after spurning $1,500 offer to play in Senior Bowl. Number two pick of Kansas City in '74 and had All-Pro career with Chiefs from '74-'82 and one year with Green Bay ('83). Now a teacher and coach in Blue Springs, MO.

GIACOMARRO, RALPH. 1979-80-81-82. P, 6'2", 190 lbs.; Upper Saddle Brook, NJ. Arguably the best punter in State history and holder of several punting records. Started punting in frosh year and led team all four years, and still holds down first, second and eighth slot in records for best punting average in a season: 43.6 yards on 55 punts in '81, 43.3 yards on 42 punts in '80 and 41.1 on 47 punts in 1982. Also holds first, fourth, fifth and sixth for best average in a game, with his '81 kicking in a 41-16 win at Syracuse being his best, averaging 54.8 yards on four punts. Had only five punts blocked in 230 attempts. Second in career punting yardage (41.8 average on 225 punts for 9,402 yards) to teammate George Reynolds, who was regular punter only one year and had just three kicks in '81 & '82 while sitting on bench behind Giacomarro. Among six players with most punts in a game (12) but no one has done it since he did it as a frosh against Pitt in '79. Perhaps his most important punting ever was the seven (for a 42.6-yard average) that helped the defense hold down Georgia in '83 Sugar bowl victory that gave State its first National Championship. But in midseason game against Alabama he figured in one of the most unusual plays in PSU history that almost cost the Lions a chance at the national title when his blocker, Mike Suter, backed into one of his punts; the mistake set up an Alabama TD that broke the game open a gave the Tide a 42-21 win. Played in '83 Senior Bowl. Tenth choice of Atlanta in '83 and played two seasons. Now an engineer living in Norcross, GA.

GIANNANTONIO, ANTHONY JOSEPH ("GEE"). 1936-37-38. HB, 5'10", 173 lbs.; South Philadelphia, PA. Another member of the "pint-sized" backfield who helped Higgins get through the era of de-emphasis. Usually played the blocking back position, or LHB, and was an excellent blocker and outstanding defensive player. Played one of his finest games in the thrilling 21-14 come-from-behind win over Maryland in '37, when he helped lead three goal line stands in the second half—including making a brilliant fourth down open field tackle for a loss—that stopped Terp drives and enabled State to set-up game-winning TD in final minutes. In '38 he was part of the great defense that set three NCAA pass-defense records despite a losing season; the record for fewest yards passing allowed per game (13.1 average) still stands after 68 years. Retired after a career as an industrial engineer. Now lives in Jamestown, NY, and is a regular attendee of home games at

Beaver Stadium where he tailgates with family and classmates from the '36-'38 teams.

GIFTOPOULOUS, PETE. 1985-86-87. LB. 6'2", 243 lbs.; Hamilton, Ontario. Will always be remembered for his fourth-down interception of Vinny Testaverde's pass at the PSU one-yard line with 15 seconds left that clinched a 14-10 Fiesta Bowl victory over then number one Miami and the '86 National Championship; also had another interception in second QT that halted a Miami threat. A starter on the outstanding "bend but don't break" defense that played for the national title in successive years in '85 and '86. Overshadowed during much of playing career by fellow linebackers Shane Conlan, Don Graham and Trey Bauer but had reputation among teammates as a hard working LB who never gave up. Played one of his finest games in 24-19 win over Notre Dame enroute to '86 title, when he was named TV Defensive Player-of-the-Game with 11 tackles, including a sack, a pass interception and a fumble recovery that set up State's first TD. Along with rest of his defensive teammates he had another great game in pivotal midseason game in '86 against then number two Alabama; had seven tackles and deflected at least one pass. Made one of his best "clutch" plays as a soph backup LB in first game of '85 season against pre-season number one Maryland, when his interception at the PSU five-yard line stopped a MD drive and his 25-yard runback led to a PSU FG that was the eventual game-winning margin, 20-18. Played in '88 Hula Bowl. As a native Canadian, he decided to play professionally in the Canadian Football League and recently retired. Now living and working in Connellsville, PA.

GILMORE, BRUCE. 1956-57-58. HB, 5'11", 180 lbs.; Reading, PA. The hard-luck running back of the late '50s. Touted as the successor to Lenny Moore when recruited out of the same hometown, he lived up to his high school and frosh team reputation in his first varsity year, '56, when he led the team in rushing yards-per-carry with a 5.6 average on 406 yards in 72 attempts. But a knee injury sidelined him for most of '57 and the last half of his senior season. Played a pivotal role in one of the momentous upsets in history, the 7-6 win over three-TD favorite Ohio State in Columbus in '56; his TD-saving tackle and EZ interception late in the third QT stopped an almost sure OSU TD and then he helped lead scoring drive and tallied State's only TD with dive from the one-foot line late in the game. Had his first 100-yard game in 40-7 win over Boston University, when he ran for 113 yards and two TDs on 13 carries. A nice, quiet man and a very good student who played "heads-up" football on defense and was known for his quickness when running the ball. Had best running day ever as a senior in 40-8 win over Marquette, when he rushed for 145 yards and 2 TDs on 19 carries, but his career ended two weeks later when he reinjured his knee in practice. That also ended what could have been a promising pro career. Now a commercial officer in Delran, NJ.

GINGRICH, DICK. 1963-64-65. QB, S, PK & Z-Back, 5'11", 183 lbs.; Burnham, PA. One of the fine defensive backs in the last years of the Engle era. Recruited as a QB because he was a fine left-handed passer and began preseason of '63 as third team QB but was switched to the new Z-back slot in preseason of '63 to back up Don Caum and caught six passes for 65 yards, but saw most of action at defensive HB and defense became his niche. Started at S in '64 and tied Frank Hershey and Mike Irwin for team lead in interceptions that year with three. Suddenly became the emergency PK in next-to-last game at Houston when regular kicker Gerry Sanker hurt foot in home accident: Gingrich had been holder for Sanker and had not kicked since HS; also kicked with left foot, and with starting QB Gary Wydman as holder, he kicked five-of-six PATs in 27-7 win over Houston and 28-0 victory over Pitt and booted the only FG of his career from a difficult angle at the 12-yard line against Houston. Had more interceptions as senior than anyone in previous nine years with seven for 66 yards; picked off two in 17-0 win over Holy Cross and got his last in the final game of the season, when his interception at Maryland 20 set up first TD in 19-7 victory. Those seven tie him with three others for third best in records. Made All-East as senior. Considered an excellent tackler who made up for his lack of speed by being smart, strong and durable. Now an attorney in Lewistown, PA.

GIVENS, REGGIE. 1989-90-91-92. LB, 6'0", 218 lbs.; Sussex, VA. One of the few "true" frosh to start for a Paterno-coached team. Will always be remembered for his dramatic "bang-bang" interception and fumble recovery early in the fourth QT of the '92 Fiesta Bowl against Tennessee that broke the game wide open: State had just taken the lead for the first time in the game, 21-17, when Givens intercepted a pass at the Tennessee 10-yard line and returned it eight yards, setting up a two-yard TD by Richie Anderson; on the first play after the KO, Derek Bochna hit the Vol QB so hard the football popped into the air from where Givens grabbed it and rambled 23 yards for a TD that virtually clinched the come-from-behind 42-17 win; he also had five tackles, including one on a fourth down fake punt, and his overall performance brought him the Defensive Player-of-the-Game award. Although not among career leaders, he had some 185 tackles and eight sacks in his career and many of them came at key moments. Became regular at OLB in eighth game of '89 season against West Virginia and started almost every game for the rest of career. Played at OLB position known as "Sam," which is half safety, half linebacker and requires speed as well as strength. Showed his poise and ability in big '89 Holiday Bowl win over BYU, when he had six unassisted tackles, including a sack of Helsman Trophy winner Ty Detmer and broke up at least one pass. Defensive co-captain of '92 team that never played up to its potential in the "purgatory" season before joining the Big 10. Played in '93 Senior and Japan Bowls. Eighth draft choice of Dallas in '93 and now with San Francisco '49ers. Lives in Emporia, VA.

GOGANIOUS, KEITH. 1988-89-90-91. LB, 6'3", 234 lbs.; Virginia Beach, VA. Another of the "Linebacker U" graduates who came into his own as a junior and senior on teams that were 9-3 and 11-2. Co-captain of '91 team that surprised everyone by finishing third in country and won one of the biggest come-from-behind bowl games of all time, a 42-17 win over Tennessee in the' 92 Fiesta Bowl. Goganious played perhaps his finest game in that victory; he was all over field from his inside linebacker position, stopping Tennessee backs and receivers and had the most tackles of his career with 15 and all but one unassisted; also had a QB sack in the game. Had 55 tackles in senior year, with 31 solos, when he started every game at ILB. A backup LB in frosh and soph years but won Jim O'Hora Award in '90 as most improved defensive player in spring practice and became full-time starter in junior year. Averaged eight tackles per game in '90 and led team in tackles in four games, including '91 Blockbuster Bowl, when he had eight. Had one of best games in 9-0 defensive win over Alabama in

junior year, with team-leading 10 tackles, including two for big losses. Played in '92 Hula and Senior Bowls. Third pick of Buffalo in '92 and played three years there and one year with Jacksonville team. Lives in hometown of Virginia Beach in off-season.

GRAF, DAVE. 1972-73-74. DE, 6'3", 205 lbs.; Dunkirk, NY. May be one of the most forgotten and best of the outstanding defensive linemen in the Paterno era. A starter at DE for three years, including what may be the most underrated defensive line of the Paterno era on the undefeated '73 team that was the first ever to win 12 games and beat LSU in '74 Orange Bowl. Blocked an LSU field goal in second QT of that game when LSU could have taken command of contest. Had a fine sophomore debut in opening game at Tennessee in '72 when he recovered a fumble that led to a TD but Lions lost, 28-21, for only defeat in regular season. May have made played one of finest games in season ending 35-13 win over Pitt that gave Lions unbeaten '73 season; assigned to be one of prime people to stop the Panther's sensational running back, Tony Dorsett, and helped hold Dorsett to 77 yards. Had a steady senior season with 16 solo tackles and 26 assists and recovered one fumble. Drafted number 17 by the Cleveland Browns in '75 and played with the Browns ('75-'79) and Redskins ('81-'82). Now an assistant vice president and financial consultant in Pompano Beach, FL.

GRAHAM, DON. 1983-84-85-86. LB, 6'2", 238 lbs.; Pittsburgh. Part of the "sack gang" of the '85 and '86 teams that twice played for the National Championship and won it in '86 with the famous 14-10 victory over Miami in the Fiesta Bowl. Along with Shane Conlan and Bob White, the trio had more sacks on opposing quarterbacks than any three defensive teammates before or since the years they played, '83-'86. Always seemed to play his best in the biggest games, such as the pivotal midseason game in '86 against then number two Alabama, when he had five tackles, including two big QB sacks for losses totaling 26 yards in dominant 23-3 win. Had one of his biggest games in late season win at South Bend in '86, when he sacked QB Steve Beuerlein three times for 17 yards in losses to lead a defensive charge that helped beat Notre Dame, 24-19, and preserve unbeaten season and march toward national title. In '85 his fumble recovery at midfield late in fourth QT at Syracuse with State trailing, 20-17, led to game-winning TD and preserved unbeaten season and eventual National Championship game in '86 Orange Bowl. Led team in sacks in both '85 (seven) and '86 (nine). Tied for seventh with teammate White on the career sack list with 18. Played in '87 East-West Shrine game. Fourth round choice of Atlanta in '87 but played with Tampa Bay ('87) and Buffalo ('88) before leaving pro football. Now living in Columbia, SC.

GRATSON, JOE. 1950-51-52. C, LB & T, 6'0", 210 lbs., Liesenring, PA. One of the toughest linemen of the early Engle era who could play offense and defense. Tough, smart and quick. Co-captain of Engle's surprise team of '52 that upset Penn and Pitt, knocking Panthers out of Orange Bowl, and had moral "victory" 20-20 tie with eventual Big 10 co-champion Purdue. Made one of smartest moves in Purdue game when referees had turned over ball to Purdue after a supposed fourth down play had failed; Gratson convinced officials they had given State only three downs and with another down, State scored TD and PAT that tied game. Started at offensive LT in '52 season of two-platoon football but often played defense at LB. One of frosh in post-World

War II era who played on the '49 frosh team under Earl Bruce at California State Teachers College. When Engle became coach in spring of '50, Gratson was playing QB and was so impressive he was set as the varsity's starting QB when fall practice opened in September but Engle shifted him to center and he played mostly on defense as LB. Started in '51 on defensive platoon at LB and was one of the team's leading tacklers. Deceased.

GRAY, BAS. 1923-24-25. C & P, 6'0", 185 lbs., Pittsburgh. The only two-time Captain in school history other than the father of PSU football, George Linsz. Part of the solid "ironman" center duo of the early '20s, when he succeeded the pugnacious "Newsh" Bentz at C as soph and, like Bentz, started for three years. Anchored some of the best lines of the Bezdek era, which also featured such players as All-American's Joe Bedenk, 'Gus' Michalske and Jules Prevost. The '24 line on hard-luck team that was 6-3-1 was considered one of the fastest and strongest lines of the Bezdek era. Had played on Kiski Prep team and was considered one of the best recruits ever when he entered State. Never played in a losing season but finished career in a 'downer" when '25 team lost three of last four games at Syracuse, West Virginia and Pitt. Still, he had well-deserved reputation for always playing at his best. Had what sportswriters said was perhaps his finest game defensively, when State pulled off one of the outstanding "upsets" in 0-0 tie with powerful Notre Dame in the mud at old Beaver Field in last home game of '25. Also a fine punter who did the kicking in both junior and senior years. Deceased.

GRAY, GARY. 1969-70-71. LB, 6'0", 208 lbs.; Levittown, PA. Not as nationally well known as other linebackers of his generation, because his teammates included such stars as Dennis Onkotz, Jack Ham, John Skorupan and Charlie Zapiec. A true Paterno "scholar-athlete" who had a 3.33 average in electrical engineering. One of only three players to lead team in both tackles and interceptions in same year; he did it in '71 with 115 tackles (60 solos and 55 assists) and five interceptions (for 11 yards); '71 total is sixth on all-time list. Also led team in tackles as a junior with 96 (50 solo and 46 shared). Backed up Jim Kates & Onkotz in soph year and got the first start of career at ILB as junior in '70, when Zapiec went out for year with emergency appendectomy before Colorado game. Two weeks later made crucial block of a punt that Ham ran in for a TD in third QT of tight game with Boston College in 28-3 victory that helped turn '70 season around after two straight losses following record 31-game undefeated streak. Starter and one of the leaders of the great defensive team of '71 that lost only one game in 12 and held Texas to two FGs in big "breakthrough" win, 30-6, at the '72 Cotton Bowl; led team in tackles in that game with nine solo tackles and five assists. Played two of best games in come-from-behind 16-14 win over Air Force and 31-0 win over Syracuse, scoring only TD of his career, when he picked up a blocked kick by Bruce Bannon, got a great block from Bannon and ran 21 yards for TD. Was All-East that year. Recipient in '96 of State College Quarterback Club's Alumni Achievement Award. Now vice president of an investment banking firm in the State College area and lives in Lamont.

GREELEY, BUCKY. 1991-92-93-94. C, 6'3", 277 lbs.; Wilkes-Barre, PA. Co-captain and the inspirational leader of the great offensive line on the unbeaten '94 Rose Bowl champions; offense was one of the most explosive in the history of college football in both running

and passing and never scored less than 31 points in a game. As a senior he won Maginnis award given to the offensive lineman who "exemplified the spirit, dedication and commitment" displayed by the late Dick Maginnis of the '82 National Championship team. Credited by sportswriters with being one of prime reasons Kerry Collins became a star in '94 because he could always depend on Greeley and they never had problems with the center snap. Also part of the blocking group that opened the holes for Ki-jana Carter to become one of the premier runners in the country. Although a C all his career, he actually got his first start in "redshirt" frosh year of '91 in the "long" G position because of injuries and played nine games there. Played behind E. J. Sandusky in soph year but became starter in '93 and was the regular until his graduation. An excellent team player with a great sense of humor. Signed as a free agent with the Carolina Panthers and still on the Panthers' roster.

GRIER, ROSEVELT (ROSEY). 1951-52-53-54. T, 6'4", 245 lbs.; Linden, NJ. One of State's great interior linemen but, surprisingly, never made any All-American team because State was considered one of the weaker teams in the East in the early '50s. Became a household name in football with an illustrious pro career and eventually became prominent in entertainment, politics and social work. Received the university's Distinguished Alumnus Award in '74. Part of State's great recruiting class in '51 that rejuvenated football after a 20-year de-emphasis period. Along with classmate Jesse Arnelle at end, he made immediate impact as a defensive tackle in his frosh year and started all four years. Known as a nice man, with a whimsical temperament, who "speaks softly and carries a big stick." Could hit as hard as anyone whether he was blocking or tackling. Took it easy in practice despite prodding by Engle and other coaches but was a terror on game day. Had one of his finest defensive games in State's 14-12 opening season upset at Illinois in '54 which shocked the football world; he was in the Illini backfield all day stopping their runners for losses and blocking pass attempts and was the talk of the Press Box. In his soph year, his fumble recovery inside the six-yard line against favored Penn was one of the biggest plays of the season for it led immediately to a TD and an eventual 14-7 upset win that guaranteed a winning season. Also lettered in track, serving as captain in senior year and was star in weight events. Drafted by New York Giants in '55 and was a starter on the defensive line during the Giants heyday. Played with Giants from '55-'62 (except '57 when he was in the Army and was named first team tackle on All-Service team) and then went to the Los Angeles Rams where he was part of the Rams' legendary "Fearsome Foursome" defensive line from '63 until his retirement after the '66 season. Selected All-Pro several times and considered one of the Giants' all-time stars. Is a big, gentle man noted for doing needle work. Involved in Democratic politics even while playing professional ball and was at the side of Sen. Robert Kennedy, when Kennedy was assassinated in Los Angeles in '68 while running for U.S. president. Later became an singer and entertainer. Now a minister and social worker in Los Angeles area.

GRIFFITHS, PERCY ("RED"). 1917-18-19-20. G & C, 5'8", 196 lbs.; Taylor, PA. Third State player *ever* named First-Team All-American when selected to a guard position in senior year by International News Service. One of leaders on the '19 & '20 teams that started an unbeaten streak that did not end until '22 and won State the unofficial Eastern Championship in '19. Star lineman on the undefeated but twice-tied '20 team that still holds the State record for most points ever in 109-7 win over Lebanon Valley. Persistent blocker and sharp tackler who was ahead of his time as an indefatigable "trash talker" who constantly bantered with opponents on the field. Against Cornell in '19 he so unnerved the Cornell punt receiver with his talking that the opponent let the ball fall into the hands of State's All-American Charlie Way, who ran it in for a TD in a 20-0 victory. Played one of his best all-around games in 28-7 win over powerful Penn in '20, as he and center Newsh Bentz opened holes for Glenn Killinger, Charlie Way and 'Hinkey' Haines and made big tackles on Penn backs. Started as a frosh center under Dick Harlow and became an outstanding lineman during the Bezdek regime but really didn't play guard until early in '20 season. Came back in fifth year to play lacrosse. Went into coaching after graduation in '21 and coached football, basketball at Marietta (Ohio) and was head coach at Dickinson before he turned to business and politics. Mayor of Marietta in '38-'39, then elected to U. S. Congress, representing Ohio's 15th District. Retired in '52 and lived in Clearwater, FL, until his death in '83 at age 91.

GUMAN, MIKE. 1976-77-78-79. RB, 6'2 $\frac{1}{2}$", 210 lbs.; Bethlehem, PA. Will always be remembered for a gutsy, but losing performance against Alabama in the National Championship game at the '79 Sugar Bowl. On fourth-and-goal, less than a yard away from the EZ, he was stopped on a dive play by Alabama's All-American LB Barry Krauss at the end of a classic Alabama goal line stand that eventually cost State the game and the National Championship in the '79 Sugar Bowl; the play was forever immortalized on the cover of *Sports Illustrated*. Academic All-American in senior year and one of the team's 17 players in last 30 years who have won an NCAA Post-Graduate scholarships. Shared running spotlight throughout career with classmate Matt Suhey. Leading scorer as frosh with eight TDs for 48 points thanks to a sensational four TD day in 38-16 win over Army (tying him with 11 other players for fourth in all-time single game scoring but still the best ever in one game by a frosh). Had big chance as frosh when Paterno shook up team after 1-3 start and switched Guman from safety to TB and he was a star by scoring four TDs and running for 107 yards on 25 carries in a 38-16 victory. Twice in frosh year had games over 100 yards rushing (against Army and 102 against North Carolina State) but never did it again because of the way he was used in State's powerful offensive attack of the latter '70s. Ran back punts throughout his career and was team leader in senior year with 14 returns for 102 yards. His 85-yard return against West Virginia in '78 is tied for third longest in team records. Scored on one of the outstanding punt plays in Paterno era on a 52-yard return against Pitt in '77, taking a handoff from Jimmy Cefalo on a reverse in 15-13 victory. Offensive player of the game in the nationally televised 17-10 win over Pitt in '78 that preserved State's number one ranking: he scored both TDs on runs of three and four yards, gained 43 yards on 15 carries and caught three passes for 22 yards. Also involved in one of the most breath-taking victories of all time, when he was substitute holder of Herb Mendhardt's near record 54-yard FG on the last play of the game that beat North Carolina State, 9-7, in '79. Twenty-fifth in career rushing with 1,130 yards and 12 TDs on 276 carries. Also won annual Ridge Riley Award which honors a senior for "sportsmanship, scholarship, leadership and friendship" and provides post-graduate scholarship and the State College QB Club's "unsung hero" award. Played in '79 East-West Shrine game and '80 Japan Bowl. Sixth choice of the Los Angeles Rams in '80 and went on to a solid

career with the Rams from '80 to '88. Now a regional vice president and investment manager in Allentown, PA.

HAINES, HENRY L. ("HINKEY"). 1919-20. HB, 5'8", 170 lbs.; Red Lion, PA. One of State's all-time all-around athletes in football, baseball and basketball. Starting HB on team that lost only once in two seasons and was unbeaten in '20 when he was named to Second- and Third-Team All-American squads. Despite his stocky build he was a breakaway threat who was well known nationally in his era, but few modern day PSU football fans have ever heard of him. Probably never received the credit he deserved because he played in the same backfield with Glenn Killinger and Charlie Way. Played some of his best games against big rivals Penn and Pitt. In '19 he played an incredible game on defense and intercepted three passes as State beat Penn, 10-0, and then as senior against powerful Penn, he replaced (First Team All-American) Way at start of second half as prime kickoff return man with a tight 7-0 lead and proceeded to take KO 85 yards untouched for TD that broke open game, prompting one sportswriter to praise him for being fast enough to "run 100 yards in 10 seconds and....[strong enough] to throw a grizzly bear." Never played football in HS but became a star with the tutoring of Coach Bezdek and his assistant Harlow. Unlike many of his teammates, "Hinkey" was not intimidated by Bezdek and consistently spoke up to him, gaining the respect of the entire team. Also had great season as Captain, CF and "clean-up" batter of '21 baseball team that won 20 straight games before first loss and had a 31-game winning streak over two years. Upon graduation he became "athletic" coach at Lebanon Valley College (where he had played briefly on junior varsity before entering State) but left there to play professional baseball with the New York Yankees. Was utility outfielder in the '23 World Series. Then played pro football with Philadelphia Quakers, Frankford Yellowjackets and became the star QB of first New York Football Giants teams in NFL and led Giants to NFL title in '27, retiring in '28. Once held the record for catching a football thrown the longest distance (324 feet) when Giant owner Tim Mara set up a publicity stunt to have a ball thrown by teammate Lynn Bomar to Haines from the 20th floor of New York's American Radiator Corp. Building in midtown Manhattan. Was a well-known college and NFL official from '33-'53. Became district chief of Philadelphia's IRS and office of Small Business Administration before retiring in '68. Deceased.

HALL, GALEN ("BUTCH"). 1959-60-61. QB, 5'9", 190 lbs.; Williamsburg, PA. Rip Engle called him "a coach on the field" because he had such a football mind. Selected to the All-Time Penn State team in 1967 by *Pittsburgh Press* sports editor Chet Smith, who covered Nittany Lion football for more than a half century. Starter in junior and senior years on teams that won Liberty Bowl, 41-12, over Oregon in '60, and Gator Bowl, 30-15, over Georgia Tech in '61. Selected Most Valuable Player in '61 Gator Bowl as he passed for three TDs, connecting on 12 of 22 passes for 175 yards, prompting Tech coach Bobby Dodd to say that Hall was one of "the greatest football players to play against Georgia Tech since I've been here." Also played crucial role as soph in winning the '59 Liberty Bowl, State's first bowl appearance in 12 years; subbed for injured starter Richie Lucas in second QT; with time running out in half and second-and-six from the 18-yard line, he was holding ball for an apparent FG attempt by Sam Stellatella when he faked it and threw screen pass to Roger Kochman who ran for a TD as time expired for only score in 7-0 victory. Made an immediate impression as soph in running the team's "alternate unit" with his poise and derring-do. Injured in second game of senior season and team lost two games but came back to lead team to five wins and Gator Bowl victory. Not a great passer but a good one who teamed with Roger Kochman in '61 on several long TD passes. A fine ball handler and excellent on-field general who looked more like a fullback in uniform. Had only one game passing over 200 yards but it was a beauty as he broke Tony Rados' eight-year record with 11 of 14 completions for 256 yards in 47-26 win at Pitt in '61 that gave team Gator Bowl bid; probably was the finest game he ever played. Fourth in career TD passing efficiency with 6.76% and eighth in career passing efficiency at 121.83. Sportswriters called him "bald, runty and squatty" but he knew how to win football games. "You try to evaluate Hall as a pro quarterback or for All-American and he doesn't stand a chance," Paterno said at the end of Hall's PSU career. "Yet he's invaluable to a college football team." Played in U.S. Bowl College All-Star game held in Washington, DC after '61 season. Signed with Washington as free agent in '62 and played with Redskins and New York Jets ('63) before starting coaching career in '64 as an assistant at West Virginia. Offensive coordinator for many years at Oklahoma and was head coach at Florida from '84-'89. Now coaching minor league pro football in Orlando and also in the NFL-supported NFL Europe.

HAM, JACK. 1968-69-70. LB, 6'3", 212 lbs.; Johnstown, PA. Arguably the greatest all-time graduate of "Linebacker U" and the only Penn State player to be in both College and Professional Football Hall of Fames. One of only 15 Penn State players in the National Football Foundation College Football Hall of Fame, inducted in '90. One of four Penn Staters in the Pro Football Hall of Fame, inducted in '88 after a brilliant career with the Pittsburgh Steelers (1971-82). Honored by University as Distinguished Alumnus in '90. All-American in '70, when he was senior Co-Captain and had 92 tackles and four intercepted passes. So quick and instinctive, he could roam the field in almost an instant, sacking the QB on one play, defending on a potential receiver the next and fighting off would-be-blockers to tackle the runner on the third. Made a sensational soph debut in '68 as a punt blocker and hard tackler. Played on the unbeaten Orange Bowl teams of '68 and '69 and only played in three losing games in entire college career. Teamed with Dennis Onkotz in '68 & '69 for one of best one-two linebacker combinations ever in college football. Shares record with Andre Collins for most punts blocked during a season (three in '68) and career (four). In fourth game of '68 season at UCLA, his crucial blocked punt was picked up by fellow LB Jim Kates and run back 36 yards for first TD in eventual 21-6 win; three games later his blocked punt deep in Miami territory led to one TD and he recovered a fumble at the Miami 32 that led to another in the keys to 22-7 come-from-behind win that propelled State to its first unbeaten record in 21 years and an eventual Orange Bowl victory. May have played one of his best games in the 41-13 loss at Colorado in '70 that ended the record 31-game unbeaten streak, when he led team with 15 unassisted tackles and two fumble recoveries. Had 143 solo tackles and 98 co-tackles in career (ninth on all-time list). Unheralded in high school at Bishop McCort as a second team offensive pulling guard, playing with future State teammate Steve Smear,

but went to prep school and when spotted by assistant coach George Welsh he was given the last scholarship in May of '66. By spring practice in frosh year he was playing on first team defense with Onkotz, Smear and Mike Reid. Played in '71 East-West Shrine Game and Hula Bowl. Drafted 2nd in '71 by Steelers and made immediate impact. Was unanimous choice for the All-NFL "Team of the Decade" for '70s and All-Pro for nine consecutive seasons. '75 NFL Defensive Player-of-the-Year. Played with PSU teammate Franco Harris in all four Steelers Super Bowl victories in '75, '76, '79 & '80. Intercepted 32 passes in NFL career. Now a successful businessman in Sewickley, PA, and a network radio sportscaster for college and professional football games.

HAMAS, STEVE. 1926-27-28. FB, 6'1", 190 lbs.; Wallington, NJ. One of the best players in the last part of the Bezdek era when State started de-emphasizing and eliminating scholarships. Not an outstanding runner but known for his hard line plunging when team was close to goal line. Also a bruiser on defense who was an outstanding tackler. Was a great fighter on the boxing team despite not competing most of winter because he also played varsity basketball. Won Intercollegiate Heavyweight Boxing Championship as a sophomore and senior and later became one of the leading heavyweight contenders in the country. Fought and beat Max Schmelling. Was a spot starter as sophomore but became regular fullback on the '27 team that was 6-2-1 and was talk of football world until final game. Captain of the '28 team that won just three games and eventually led to Bezdek's ouster as coach. Won a record nine varsity letters during time when frosh were not eligible for varsity and was first athlete to win letters in five different sports. Also lettered in lacrosse and track, where he was a weight tosser. Was selected "most valuable athlete" for 1928-29 academic year. Deceased.

HAMILTON, HARRY. 1980-81-82-83. S & Hero, 5'11½", 191 lbs.; Wilkes-Barre, PA. One of Paterno's great "scholar-athletes." Academic All-American in both junior and senior years and one of the team's 17 players in last 30 years who have won NCAA Post-Graduate Scholarships. Named Third-Team All-American as senior, when he was team's leading tackler with 53 solo and 47 shared for a total of 100, which still is among the top 15 for one season in State records. A starter at the "Hero" position on the National Championship team of '82. Played one of his finest games in 39-31 win over Maryland, when he led team with 12 tackles and had an interception that set up a FG. Perhaps his best defensive effort of the year was in the frustrating 42-21 loss to Alabama that temporarily de-railed the team's national title trek, when he again led team in tackles with 11, including one sack for a 13-yard loss. In Sugar Bowl win for over Georgia Tech for championship, he was second only to Scott Radecic in tackles with 10, including one sack. What may have been his finest game came as senior, when he helped turn around a losing season in '83 after team had lost three straight at start of year and had narrow wins over Temple and Rutgers; in nationally televised upset over then number three Alabama at Beaver Stadium, he led team with 11 tackles, recovered a fumble (to set up one TD) and caused another fumble in 34-28 win. Brother of Lance (see below). Played in '84 Hula Bowl. Drafted 7th by New York Jets in '84 and played three years with Jets and four years with Tampa Bay before retiring. Now working in Odenton, MD.

HAMILTON, LANCE. 1983-84-85. DB, 5'11", 185 lbs.; Wilkes-Barre, PA. Not as well known as his brother Harry (see above) but another outstanding "scholar-athlete." An Academic All-American in junior and senior years and winner of the National Football Foundation and College Football Hall of Fame graduate school fellowships. A hard-hitter, who always seemed to play his best against Maryland. Made one of the great "clutch" plays of the '85 season in the opening game against preseason number one Maryland: with 38 seconds left and State winning, 20-18, Maryland was driving for a FG attempt; MD's Al Bount caught a pass at the PSU 24-yard line and turned to head up field, when he was blasted by Hamilton, who stripped him of the ball; teammate Trey Bauer recovered the fumble and sealed the upset that put State on the road to the national title game against Oklahoma in the '86 Orange Bowl. Also played outstanding game in midseason clash of unbeatens when he led team with nine tackles in 19-17 win over Alabama. Played behind All-American Mark Robinson as soph and became starter in junior year. Was among team's leading tacklers in each game of '84 and played perhaps his best in 25-24 win over Maryland when he led all tacklers with nine. Winner of '85 Ridge Riley Award given to the senior for "sportsmanship, scholarship, leadership and friendship." Played in East-West Shrine game in '86. Now a law clerk in Tampa, FL.

HARLOW, DICK. 1910-11. T, 5'11½", 220 lbs.; Philadelphia, PA. One of the "Legends" with direct links to today's Paterno era. He and "Dad" Engle were the starting tackles in '10 & '11 and he later coached "Dad's" nephew and future State head coach "Rip" Engle at Western Maryland. May be better known for his coaching than his playing and was inducted into the National Football Foundation College Football Hall of Fame as a coach in '54. Was State's head coach from '15-'17, compiling 20-8 record, then went into World War I. Returned in '19 to be an assistant coach under Hugo Bezdek, until he left for the head coaching job at Colgate at end of '21 season after a dispute with Bezdek. Achieved his greatest fame as coach at Harvard ('35-'42 & '45-'47); named Coach-of-the-Year in '36 and Ivy League coach of the year in '37; also head coach at Colgate ('22-'25) and Western Maryland ('26-'34). He and Bezdek are both credited with perfecting the screen pass as coaches. Also was a great recruiter and fine game scout who made emotional halftime speeches as a head coach. Known for his fiery temper and sensitivity, which often got him in trouble as a player and a coach. A two-year starter at G and known at the time for blocking kicks. In third game of '11 season at Cornell, his blocked punt in second QT was picked up by "Dad" Engle and run into the EZ for the only points in a 5-0 win. He did it again two weeks later at Penn but neither he nor Engle could recover the ball and gained only a safety in a 22-6 victory. In the season final at Pitt he blocked another punt at the Pitt six-yard line late in the fourth QT, but the team was denied a TD on a controversial goal line decision by the referee as State won 3-0. The three blocked kicks that season should tie him with Jack Ham and Andre Collins for most blocked kicks in one year but Harlow's name is not in record books. Also played baseball and competed in track for State. Stayed on after graduation to be the line coach under Bill Hollenbeck, until named head coach when Hollenback departed in '15. Started boxing as a varsity sport at State in '19 and was head coach of State's boxing team for years. Died on Feb. 20, 1962 at age of 73.

HARRIS, FRANCO. 1969-70-71. FB, 6'2", 220 lbs.; Mt. Holly, NJ. Overshadowed during college career by teammate Lydell Mitchell but became a bigger star as a pro. Never made All-American but now

one of four Penn Staters in the Pro Football Hall of Fame; inducted in '90 after a sensational career with the Pittsburgh Steelers ('72-'83). Teamed with Mitchell in leading Lions to 30-6 "breakthrough" win over Texas in '72 Cotton Bowl, when he gained 47 yards on 11 carries, even though he was in Paterno's "doghouse" at the time for being late to team meetings; Paterno had demoted him to third string but put him back into game in 2nd half when Lions came from behind a 6-3 deficit to win. Leading scorer in junior season with 48 points on eight TDs and 13th among career rushing leaders with 2,002 yards on 380 carries for 24 TDs. Had five games with over 100 yards rushing with 145 yards and four TDs on 28 carries in 44-14 win at Iowa in '71 being his best. Three times he teamed with Mitchell for a "double" 100-yard game and in '69 against Boston College he, Mitchell and Charlie Pittman became just the second trio to get more than 100 yards each in a game. Started soph preseason as third team FB behind starter Don Abbey and Fran Ganter in Paterno's Power-I offense, but in opening season win over Navy, 45-22, he was third leading rusher behind Pittman and Mitchell with 36 yards and a TD on eight carries and soon was seeing as much playing time as Abbey's sub. Starting FB at Syracuse in fifth and pivotal game of '69 unbeaten season, when Abbey was out with injuries, and the opportunity made him a star: was leading rusher with 57 yards on eight carries and scored vital points in fourth QT when team was trailing; ran for two-point conversion to pull State within six and tied game (after a punt blocked by Jack Ham) on a 37-yard TD jaunt, as PSU pulled off a great 15-14 come-from-behind win. Was leading ground gainer in five of next six games and had three 100-yard games, as team completed second straight unbeaten season. In 10-3 win over Missouri in '70 Orange Bowl he carried 17 times for 46 yards and his 16-yard run up the middle on a trap play was the key to a 68-yard drive that gave State the only TD in the first QT in what was one of the toughest defensive struggles in State history. In next two years he and Mitchell were usually the top rushers in every game with the '70 Pitt game (when he gained 133 yards and one TD on 19 carries) and the '71 Iowa game being his best, as well as the '72 Cotton Bowl. Played in '72 Senior Bowl. Number one choice of Steelers and 13th choice overall in '72 draft, played in nine pro bowls and is in the top 10 of all-time leading NFL rushers with 12,120 yards on 2,949 carries and 91 TDs. Rushed for over 1,000 yards in eight seasons and had 47 games rushing 100 yards or more. Became well known for being the receiver on the now legendary "Immaculate reception" pass play against Oakland which put the Steelers into the AFC championship game in '72. Played with PSU teammate Jack Ham in all four Steelers Super Bowl victories in '75, '76, '79 & '80 and was Most Valuable Player of Super Bowl IX. Honored by University as Distinguished Alumnus in '82. Now a business executive with headquarters in Pittsburgh with emphasis on minority participation (one business partner includes former teammate Mitchell) and a frequent visitor to State's home sporting events.

HARRIS, PETE. 1977-78-80. S, 6'1", 200 lbs.; Mt. Holly, NJ. Not as well known as his brother Franco (see above) but he was a First-Team All-American in '78 junior season, when he led country with 10 interceptions (for 155 return yards); also that year had 28 tackles and recovered two fumbles on disappointed but great team that lost National Championship to Alabama in '79 Sugar Bowl. Paterno said he was "a great college safetyman who has great range and great instincts." Tied with Neal Smith for most interceptions in one season

(10) and tied for second (with Darren Perry) behind Smith in career interceptions (15). Had one of his biggest games ever in '78 in the nationally-televised late season "clash of the unbeatens" between then number two State and number five Maryland; with his trademark three interceptions for 38 yards, including one for 27 yards that helped State thump Maryland, 27-3, before a record Beaver Stadium crowd (78,019) and propel the Lions to number one for the first time ever in 91 years. Was an oft-used backup S in soph year until a broken ankle in NC State game sidelined him. Came back as starter in '78 and became a star. His first interception of season against Rutgers in second game of year set up a 53-yard Fusina-to-Fitzkee TD pass that got team off on a 26-10 romp and set tone for Harris's interception barrage the rest of the year. Sat out '79 season because of academic difficulties but came back to be starter again in '80. Had another fine season on 10-2 team; with one of best games being the 29-21 win at Missouri, when he had seven tackles and batted down three passes; had interceptions in key '80 wins over West Virginia, Miami and Pitt. Played in '82 Japan Bowl. Works in his hometown of Mt. Holly, NJ.

HARRISON, HARRY ("HIGH SCHOOL"). 1936-37-38. HB & QB, 5'9", 154 lbs.; West Philadelphia, PA. Perhaps the best of the "pint-sized" backs of his era, when Higgins struggled through the de-emphasis period. A three-year starter who certainly had one of the best nicknames in the history of State football, which he earned during '36 Pitt game, when he initiated a play the newspapers called "a high school play." It actually was a "sleeper" play that came with Pitt leading, 14-0, and State at Pitt's 11-yard line: Harrison lay flat on his stomach near the sideline, unnoticed by any Pitt player, and no one was within 25 yards of him when "Windy" Wear threw a pass for a TD—but it was the only State TD of game in 34-7 loss. Also in that game he was involved in one of the most hilarious incidents in State football history, when he took the kickoff at the opening of the second Half and with great blocking broke into the clear only to have the elastic snap in his pants and fall below his waste to trip him up. Always seemed to play his best against Penn: in '36 he ran back one kickoff 95 yards in 19-12 loss; in '37 threw a 17-yard pass to Wear for the only TD of the game just moments after catching a 21-yard pass from Wear to set up the scoring play; in '38 his spectacular running, including one dash of 45 yards when he was seemingly trapped, set up State's TD in 7-7 tie. Had another of his best games in '37 against Maryland, when he scored the winning TD with less than a minute left, going around left end and outrunning the Terp defensive halfbacks in 21-14 victory. In '38, he got team off and running to a 59-6 win over Lehigh with three TDs in first QT. Turned into a great pass receiver that year as soph Chuck Peters also became a running and passing star. Deceased.

HARTENSTINE, MIKE. 1972-73-74. DT, 6'4", 240 lbs.; Bethlehem, PA. An outstanding DT who was a near unanimous First-Team All-America in '74, including selection by AP, UPI, American Football Coaches and Football Writers. Led team in tackles as a junior on unbeaten '73 team that, beat LSU in Orange Bowl but finished only fifth in country; had 57 solos and 47 assists for 104 total tackles, which is 11th on all-time one season list. Despite being "double teamed" as senior, he still had 108 tackles—second to Greg Buttle who set all-time one season tackle record—and also recovered two fumbles and blocked a punt, against arch-rival Pitt. Backed up Randy Crowder as

soph, then started first game in '73 opener at Stanford and played alongside him at DT in '73 on a defensive line that was considered the best since the '68-'69 Reid-Smear group. Two plays in that opening 20-6 win over Stanford typified Hartenstein's never-give-up style of play: Stanford QB Mike Boryla twice went down seemingly untouched as he was dropping back to pass as Hartenstein, buried under a pile of blockers, reached up to grab him by the ankle both times; named Defensive Player-of-the-Game for that performance before national TV audience. Against Iowa he had an unbelievable four sacks as State won 27-8. Started off '74 as he ended '73 with a great game against Stanford that earned him Defensive Player-of-the-Game; repeated honor in final game of season against Pitt and then was named the nation's Defensive Player-of-the-Year by Chevrolet. Continued his performance in 41-20 victory over Baylor in Cotton Bowl when he was voted State's Defensive Player-of-the-Game. One of the least vocal members of the defensive team but a great inspirational leader. Drafted second by Chicago in '75 and spent 12 years with Bears and one with Minnesota before retiring in '88; played in '86 Super Bowl. Majored in food service and housing administration and is now a businessman in Chicago.

HARTINGS, JEFF. 1992-93-94-95. OG, 6'3", 284 lbs.; St. Henry, OH. Another of Paterno's great "scholar-athletes." One of only 11 two-time First-Team All-Americans; selected by Walter Camp and AP in '94 and Camp, UPI and Football Writers in '95. Three-time All-Big 10. Semi-finalist for Lombardi Award as "outstanding lineman or linebacker of the year" as a senior. Twice chosen to the Academic All-American team and winner in '95 of a National Football Foundation and College Football Hall of Fame graduate fellowship for "scholar-athletes." Leader of the great offensive line in '94 that helped the unbeaten Rose Bowl championship team top the nation in scoring and total offense and give up only five sacks. Known for his hard work and determination that combined with speed, agility, strength and endurance to make him one of the best who ever played offensive line in the Paterno era. Originally wanted to play for Notre Dame but Irish did not offer scholarship. After a "redshirt" season he became a backup as frosh and played in every game. But really came into his own at "long" G in '93 and started 10 of the 12 games, including the Fiesta Bowl victory over Tennessee. In '93 game at Maryland, he was one of the leaders as the team gained the most rushing yards in one game ever under Paterno with 626 yards in a 70-7 rout. The great 35-31 comeback win over Illinois in '94 that gave team Big Ten championship would not have occurred without Hartings and his linemates stopping the Illini's nation-leading sack defense without a sack. One of his most critical blocks in that game came with less than a minute to play when FB Brian Milne ran two-yards over a big hole opened by Hartings, TE Kyle Brady and T Keith Conlin for the TD that climaxed the historic 96-yard drive that put State ahead for the first time in the game. Co-winner along with teammate Andre Johnson and two others for first Frank Patrick Memorial Award in '95 honoring juniors for "Total Commitment" to academics, community service and year-around preparations. Maintained a B+ grade average in marketing. Number one pick of Detroit in '96 and now a starting tackle with Lions.

HAYMAN, GARY. 1972-73. WR, TB & KR, 6'2", 200 lbs.; Newark, DE. Another of the forgotten wide receivers whose outstanding performances in the run-oriented first decade of the Paterno era has been eclipsed by the upbeat pass offenses of the last 20 years. May be best remembered as a kick returner, since he led both the '72 and '73 teams in kickoff and punt returns and was leading punt return man in country as senior with 19.2 yards average. Is fourth in career KO returns with a 26.9 yards average on 18 returns and one TD—a 93-yard runback against Maryland in '73 that is fifth best return in history. 10th in career punt returns with a 12.8 yards average and two TDs on 56 returns; got his first TD in '72 win over Pitt on a 59-yard jaunt and picked up his second TD on an 83-yard return in '73's narrow 35-29 victory over North Carolina State in key game of that undefeated season, when team became first in history to win 12 games. Also had 77-yard return for TD in '74 Orange Bowl called back because of a penalty, but then returned one 35 yards to the LSU 26-yard line, setting up a John Cappelletti TD that clinched the 16-9 victory. As a receiver, he wasn't even on pre-season depth chart in '72 because he had left school the year before with personal problems but became a spot starter at WR and backed up at TB; in '72 21-10 win over Navy he led team in rushing with 87 yards on 16 carries and had another 47 yards on 10 carries the following week in 14-10 win over Iowa when he also had three receptions for 37 yards. Also was forced to play TB in '72 Sugar Bowl when Cappelletti became ill but couldn't help team avoid 14-0 loss to Oklahoma. Then led unbeaten '73 team in receptions with 30 for 525 yards and three TDs. Had two of his finest games against the academies in '73 with five catches for 123 yards and a TD in 39-0 win over Navy and six receptions for 122 yards and one TD in 19-9 victory over Air Force. Played in '74 Senior Bowl. Fifth choice of Buffalo in '74 and played two years. Now an attorney in New Castle, DE.

HELLER, JIM. 1970-71-72. DT, 6'3", 240 lbs.; Pottsville, PA. A three-year starter at DT who is probably one of the most underrated defensive linemen of the Paterno era. He was overshadowed by some of his better known linemates such as Randy Crowder and Bruce Bannon. But he was a strong and agile player and outstanding team man. He is 10th in career tackles with 237 on 133 solos and 104 assists but never led in any one year. His best was his junior year in '71 with 91 tackles, including 58 solos. Part of the great defense that throttled Texas in '72 "breakthrough" Cotton Bowl game, limiting high-powered Longhorn offense to two FGs and total 242 yards in 30-6 victory. Began '70 preseason as third string right DT but was starter by opening season game against Navy and stayed there rest of career. Led the front four in tackles that year with 71. Defensive co-captain of the '72 team that finished eighth in country and played Oklahoma in '73 Sugar Bowl. Seemed to play especially well against Navy and cited by sportswriters each year for his "ferocious" performance in Navy games. Had one of his finest games in 35-17 win over Illinois in '72, making several tackles at line of scrimmage and recovering a fumble that set up a TD. During Heller's playing days Paterno said he was "an extremely dedicated football player and leader who is one of the finest defensive tackles in the East." No relation to Ron Heller (see below). Now a highway maintenance foreman in Lewisberry, PA.

HELLER, RON. 1981-82-83. TE & OT, 6'6", 256 lbs.; Farmingdale, NY. One of the outstanding blockers of the Paterno era and a key member of offensive line on first National Championship team in '82. Surprisingly, never made an All-American team. Perhaps the reason is he was a TE as frosh and soph and didn't move to OT until preseason of '82. In '81 was third team TE better known for his blocking than receiving. So, Paterno moved him to LT and shifted Pete Speros to LG and the Heller-Speros-(Mike) Maginnis-(Bill) Contz-(Mark) Battaglia line became one of the best at blocking and pass protection of the Paterno era. The '82 & '83 teams were the best passing PSU squads in history until the 1990s. Switched from the short tackle to the long tackle position in '83 when he was Co-Captain of team that lost first three games but salvaged season and beat Washington in Aloha Bowl. (Younger brother Mike played OG in '91-92.) Played in '84 Senior Bowl. Drafted in fourth round by Tampa Bay in '85 and had great career with Bucs ('84-'87), Philadelphia ('88-'92) and Miami ('93-'95). Now a manufacturer's representative and living in Absarokee, MT.

HERD, CHUCK. 1971-72-73. WR & TB, 6'0", 201 lbs.; New York, NY. Still another of the outstanding but nearly forgotten pass receivers of the early Paterno era whose career overlapped Gary Hayman (see above). He will always be remembered for his spectacular one-handed, finger-tip catch in '73 Orange Bowl, grabbing the ball with his left hand at full speed at the LSU 35-yard line and out running defenders for the rest of a 72-yard TD in the second QT that stunned LSU and virtually locked up the game; it is still the sixth longest TD pass play in State history; what made the reception even more remarkable is that one play before he had taken another Tom Shuman bomb for an apparent TD but was ruled out-of-bounds in the EZ (TV replays showed he was in bounds). It was the climax of an unsteady but determined career that started somewhat ignominiously in soph year when he signaled for a fair catch on a kickoff reception inside the five-yard line in a season-ending 31-11 loss to Tennessee that knocked team from ranks of unbeaten. Scored 10 TDs in career, which was the record for wide receivers at one time, and are still more TDs than many of State's better known receivers have had in their time. He was a spot WR as soph but moved to TB in junior year and was backup to eventual Heisman Trophy winner John Cappelletti for first part of year, and moved to WR in fourth game against Illinois and caught his first TD pass on a 37-yard throw from John Hufnagel in 35-17 rout. Had one of his best games in 49-27 win over Pitt in '72, when he led all receivers with four receptions for 91 yards, including a 41-yard TD in third QT. In senior year he was the backup at flanker to classmate Jimmy Scott but wound up as starter in some games and then came his memorable reception in the Orange Bowl. Now working for the university in State College as a conference coordinator in the Continuing Education program.

HERMAN, BURKE M. ("DUTCH"). 1911. QB, 5'8", 160 lbs.; Wilkes-Barre, PA. One of Penn State's most loyal players and coaches who had the misfortune of being on team at the same time as the best two QBs of the first 25 years, Larry Vorhis and Shorty Miller. As a result, the greatest contribution of "Dutch" came after graduation, as he spent 50 years deeply involved in State athletics and academics. Involved in one of the most historic decisions in PSU football as part of the Athletic Board that hired Rip Engle (and, thus, Paterno) in '50. Reserve QB for '07, '08, '09 season and dropped out for a year only to return for the outstanding 8-0-1 '11 season. Started his first game in '08 against Navy when Vorhis was moved to HB and played a fine game in 5-0 loss. Also at the helm most of the way in the 3-3 tie with Penn in '09 when team was unbeaten. Played perhaps his finest game in 0-0 tie with Navy in '11, when he not only subbed for Miller at QB but also played in the line on defense and recovered a fumble deep in Navy territory that almost led to winning TD. Was a four-letter winner in basketball and eventually school's head basketball coach from '16 to '32 (except for duty in WW I). Coached in high school after graduation then became State's first full-time frosh coach under Harlow in '15 and stayed there under Bezdek. Higgins made him backfield coach in '30, but he quit coaching two years later to teach in the Department of History. As frosh coach, he is credited for discovering the talents of future All-American Charlie Way. Retired from PSU in '56. Deceased.

HERRING, KIM. 1993-94-95-96. FS, 6'0", 196 lbs.; Solon, OH. Another in the long line of great defensive backs in the Paterno era. First-Team Sporting News All-America in '96 and Second-Team AP. All-Big 10 on both media and coaches team in '96. Led Big 10 in interceptions in '96 with seven, which ties him with three others for third on State's all-time list for one season, and tied for Big 10 interception lead in '95 with six, counting two in '96 Outback Bowl win over Auburn. His 13 career interceptions (State records do not include Bowl games) is third best in school history. Known as a hard-hitter with the sixth sense of knowing where the ball was. Three-year starter at FS but played TB as frosh and lettered, playing in every game and gaining 46 yards on 11 carries. Moved to defense in spring of '94 and was a starter as a "true" soph on the unbeaten and unappreciated '94 powerhouse but missed the Rose Bowl because of severe knee injury in second QT of Northwestern game; just before injury he was having one of his best defensive days, going 80 yards for a TD with a fumble recovery on Northwestern's first possession and then intercepting a pass and returning it 21 yards to set up another State TD on Northwestern's second possession. A week earlier he sealed the great come-from-behind win over Illinois and Rose Bowl bid with an interception in the EZ on last play of the game. Picked up in '95 where he left off; two interceptions in the nationally-televised Rutgers game at the Meadowlands was key to the victory, and he was Outback Bowl Defensive Player-of-the-Game with two interceptions and a fumble recovery that led to 21 points in 43-14 victory. His senior leadership in '96, particularly after fellow DB Brian Miller was sidelined late in season, was big reason team surprised just about everyone with 11-2 season and '97 Fiesta Bowl win over Texas. Played two of his finest games of '96 in 29-17 win at Michigan when he led team with 10 tackles and batted down one pass attempt and in thrilling 32-29 win over Michigan State, when he had eight tackles and batted away four pass attempts. Played in '97 Hula Bowl. Number three draft choice of Baltimore in '97 and now playing with Ravens in NFL.

HERSHMAN, CHARLES ("HEFF"). 1906-07-08-09. FB, 6'0", 195 lbs.; New York City. Picked to All-Time Penn State team on 40th anniversary of State football in '27 by *New York Sun* sportswriter George Trevor, who wrote that Hershman was "a line-breaking fool when aroused." As good defensively as he was offensively and during his career State shutout 18 of 21 opponents in streak from '05 to '07. Starting FB and part of the "all frosh" backfield on what was the best ever State team at that time—the 8-1-1 '06 team. That team lost only to powerful Yale, 10-0, which scored only points on State that season, and had nine shutouts that is still a State team record. Perhaps his finest game was in 5-0 win over Navy in '06, when he carried ball on short bucks almost the entire length of the field to set up the only

points. Not exactly your puritan, he was known to chew tobacco, which was forbidden when Bill Hollenback took over as head coach in '09; benched before Penn game because of tobacco habits and his absence probably cost team win in 3-3 tie. In final game of career against Pitt at the new Forbes Field, his running on a mushy field in second QT led to only TD for 5-0 win that clinched first unbeaten record (5-0-2) in 15 years. Never made All-American but was picked on many regional "All" teams during his playing days. Deceased.

HESS, HAROLD ('BILL'). 1916, 1919-20. FB, G & P, 5'11", 178 lbs.; Indiana, PA. A starter first at FB in '19, then at G in '20 (when he was also Captain) on the back-to-back unbeaten teams that helped boost State into the nation's elite football powers. Overshadowed by All-Americans Charlie Way, Glenn Killinger, Bob Higgins and 'Red' Griffiths, but when switched to G in senior year he was outstanding in opening up holes for Way, Killinger, 'Hinkey' Haines and Joe Lightner. As a punter he was involved in one of the most daring Lion plays ever in first four minutes of final game of season against Pitt: without informing coach Bezdek, QB Harry Robb had Hess fake a punt from near State's goal line and pass to E Higgins all alone in the flat, whereby Higgins took the 15-yard pass and went rest of way for shocking TD and eventual 20-0 win and unofficial Eastern Championship; it was the only pass Hess ever threw, and the TD is still listed as the longest pass play in State history at 92-yards, but historians say it should have been recorded as 95 yards. Played one of his finest games at G in '20 in big 28-7 win against Penn. Upon graduation he went into coaching and played major role in State's loss in '23 Rose Bowl to USC, 14-3; as USC frosh coach in '22 he used State's offense, and, after the SC varsity practiced against it constantly they were easily able to fluster State's offense in the Jan. 1 game. Deceased.

HEWITT, SR, EARL. 1898-99-1900-02. HB, 5'9", 160 lbs.; Pennfield, PA. Best known for 65-yard run back of a punt for the only score that enabled State to beat Army for the first time in 1899; it would also be the last time until 1959. Called "the silent man" by his teammates. A standout runner starting in his frosh year but moved to QB as soph and stayed there as the starter for the rest of his career. Older than most fellow students but no one knew his true age at the time he played; actually was 26 years old in frosh year. An extremely accurate punter who was also adept at quick-kicks, one of which in '00 gave State its only points against Penn during a five-year stretch. Captain of '01 team that had 5-3 record. Left team after four games in '02 to play quarterback on Connie Mack's Philadelphia Athletics professional football team along with such former State teammates as "Henny" Scholl, "Brute" Randolph and Lynn Sweet. Also tried professional baseball. Helped coach '09 team. His son, Earl Junior also played for State in '27. Went into coal and real estate business and later served 16 years in Pennsylvania legislature. Rarely missed a home or away football game with Army and was usually found near the State bench. In a famous incident in '57 while he was sitting on bench he was hit by a half dozen players in a sideline pile up; he got up, shook his fist at the Army players and yelled, "You couldn't get me in 1899 and you can't get me now." He died in '72.

HIGGINS, BOB ("THE HIG"). 1914-15-16, 1919. E & Head Coach, 5'10", 181 lbs.; Corning, NY. The legend who is a vital element in the tradition that ties the past to the present Paterno era. May be better known today as a long time head coach but he also is one of State's greatest players. State's second *ever* First-Team All-American & the school's first two-time pick—selected by INS in '15 and Walter Camp in '19—and first sophomore; also named to Second-Team in '16. One of only 15 State players in the National Football Foundation College Football Hall of Fame, inducted in '54. Chosen on the All-Time Penn State team in 1950s and again in 1967 by *Pittsburgh Press* sports editor Chet Smith, who covered Nittany Lion football for more than a half century. Also one of only five players to earn five letters. Head coach for 19 years ('30-'49) during an uneasy period when State de-emphasized football and the best players were in World War II; still compiled a 91-57-10 record and had one of greatest teams in '47 that was unbeaten and tied SMU in '48 Cotton Bowl. His teams in the late '30s and throughout the '40s were better than most modern day State fans may realize. He also was a man of principle who led the charge to integrate the Cotton Bowl. One of his daughters married his '47 All-American G, Steve Suhey; and his three grandsons (Paul, Matt and Larry Suhey) played for Paterno in the '70s. As a player, his 92-yard TD on a short 15-yard pass from Harold Hess (see above) off a fake punt early first QT of 20-0 win over Pitt in '19 game gave State unofficial Eastern Championship and is still the longest State pass play ever, although historians say it should have been recorded as a 95-yard TD; and his 75-yard run for a TD that day is still among the top 15 longest runs in school history. One of the most highly recruited prep players of his era, who almost went to Princeton but was enticed to State by then assistant coach Dick Harlow. He was a great defensive player as well as an offensive threat and started as a frosh in '14. Captain-elect in '17 but left for service in World War I with the American Expeditionary Force, where he saw heavy combat in the trenches as a infantry lieu-tenant. When war ended, he was transferred to another army unit to play football and was one of the stars on the 89th Division team that won the A.E.F. championship, and further enhanced his national repu-tation as a great football player. When he returned to State for the '19 season, he was already well-regarded by sportswriters, opponents, and fans. He proceeded to prove he was worthy of their respect as captain of '19 team. That team lost only to Dartmouth and won seven, scoring 173 points to 33 for the opponents, and was named best team in the East (which was almost like being selected National Champion in those days). Hig helped save the season in mid-year when the team's only punter, Hess, sprained his ankle before Penn game, so he volunteered to punt even though he had never punted in a game before; had sev-eral kicks of 50 yards or more to keep Quakers bottled up, and then Penn's returner fumbled one, which led to State's only TD in 10-0 win. Also lettered in baseball, boxing and wrestling. As coach he had record of 97-57-1. His '47 team was first unbeaten and untied team in the regular season in 35 years but tied Southern Methodist in the Cotton Bowl, 13-13; his '39, '40, '42 and '48 teams only lost one game. Spent two years in pro football with the Canton Bulldogs. Also coached at West Virginia Wesleyan and Washington University in St. Louis be-fore becoming an assistant at State in '28. Lived in retirement in State College until his death on June 6, 1969.

HILDEBRAND, CHARLES (CHARLIE). 1887-88-89-90-91-93. G, 5'8", 180 lbs.; Philadelphia, PA. Helped George (Lucy) Linsz orga-nize first Penn State team in 1887 and, thus, considered "co-father of Penn State football." Became Penn State's first five-time letterman and even played a couple games in 1893 when he returned after 1892

graduation and one season of semi-pro football in Pottstown to play under the name of 'Wolfe.' Assisted in coaching 1893 and 1898 teams. Played on teams that won total of 16 games while losing nine and tying one. Older than most teammates. Known for his hard hitting. Played entire first official Penn State game, a 54-0 win over Bucknell at Lewisburg, Nov. 12, 1887. Hobbled by sprained ankle most of four-game season in 1889. Missed most of first half but played all of sec-ond half in Penn State's worst all-time loss, 106-0, to Lehigh at Bethlehem on Nov. 11, 1889. As businessman in Philadelphia, helped recruit Penn State players for 50 years. Started Philadelphia's alumni club. Attended all Penn State football games in Philadelphia after 1900 and many on campus, including nearly all Homecoming games, until his death on Feb. 24, 1950, at age 84.

HITE, JEFF. 1973-74-75. DB & LB, 6'0", 190 lbs.; Pittsburgh, PA. May exemplify the type of player who is not a star but a solid and consistent performer who is the foundation of State football teams. A sometimes starter on defense at DB and LB throughout his three-year career who, on one spectacular day, placed himself for all-time into the State record books with an unusual record—most interceptions run back for TDs in a single game—two. It all occurred before a near-record crowd and regional TV audience on Nov. 4, 1974 against Maryland: Late in first QT, he picked off a pass in the flat by MD's highly-touted QB Bob Avellini and streaked 79-yards down the sidelines for State's first TD; then in second QT, after State had tied the score at 14-14 and had kicked off to Maryland, he intercepted a Maryland lateral *on the kick-off* and dashed 21 yards for the TD that won the game, 24-17. For that he was named ABC's Player-of-the-Game. Had another interception that year to tie Greg Buttle for team lead with three for season. Captain of the special teams in '75 when the team was 9-3 and finished 10th in country. Now a brewing superintendent in Crown Point, IN.

HOAK, DICK. 1958-59-60. HB, QB & KR 5'11", 185 lbs.; Jeannette, PA. One of the most underrated players ever at State. A gutsy player who was one of the best in the "clutch" in team history. An outstanding defensive back with a sixth sense for knowing where the ball was. Perhaps his best game was his final one in the '60 Liberty Bowl victory over Oregon, 41-12, when he was named the Most Valuable Player-of-the-Game; as QB of second unit, he scored two TDs on runs of six and 11 yards, passed 33 yards to Dick Pae for another TD, and racked up 61 yards on nine carries, hit on three of five passes for 67 yards and intercepted a pass, running it back 15 yards to set up the Pae TD. Started out as a QB in frosh and soph years but began starting occasionally at HB as soph. Played HB as junior, then was QB of alternate unit as senior. Not really fast but a very deceptive runner. He was not a very talkative man and let his actions on the field speak for him. One long-forgotten play in Pitt Stadium as a soph best cap-tures the type of player he was; with State trailing late in the fourth QT and the ball on Pitt's 17, Hoak got the handoff and started around right end and was seemingly trapped for a large loss, when he reversed himself, shook off a couple of tacklers and went around the left end to the eight-yard line, setting up the winning TD and knocking arch-rival Pitt out of a certain bowl bid. Led team in punt returns in soph (nine returns for 135 yards) and junior years (six returns for 94 yards) and his career 15.3 yards average is fifth best of all-time and his 15.7 average in '59 is seventh best for one season. Also as junior led team in receiving with 14 receptions for 167 yards and kickoff returns with six runbacks for 215 yards and an outstanding 35.8 yards average. Played in Tucson's Copper Bowl All-Star game in '60. Although just a seventh round choice of Pittsburgh in '61, he had a solid 10-year career with the Steelers as the team's prime running back, and since his retirement after the '70 season he has been an assistant Steelers coach and wears four Super Bowl rings. Lives in Greensburg, PA.

HOGGARD, DENNIE. 1947-48. E, 6'0", 200 lbs.; Philadelphia, PA. Best remembered as one of first Black players in PSU history who, along with Wally Triplett, integrated the Cotton Bowl in '47. As frosh in '42 he was only Black player on team after the unexpected death of potential superstar Dave Alston and the departure from school of Alston's brother, Harry. Left school to enter Army in '43 and was on the European battlefields for three years. Returned on GI Bill in '46 and found a young Black freshman from Philadelphia on the team, Triplett, and they became almost like brothers. Even though both were reserves in '46, State canceled a scheduled game at Miami when told the Black players would not be allowed to play because of segregation rules. The next year, the Cotton Bowl broke the color line by allowing Hoggard and Triplett to play in the game on Jan. 1 '48. Hoggard might have been the hero of the Cotton Bowl if not for a quirk of fate involving Triplett: on the last play of the SMU game, with the score tied 13-13, QB Elwood Petchel fired a pass towards Hoggard in the EZ; a defender tipped the ball just enough for it to fall through the diving Hoggard's finger tips. Hoggard was a backup E to All-American Sam Tamburo in both '47 & '48, but played a lot on defense; scored one of his few TDs on an exceptional defensive play in fourth QT against Pitt in '47, when he beat the center's direct snap to the tailback at the Pitt 30-yard line, grabbed the ball out of the air and rambled into the EZ untouched in a 29-0 victory. After graduation, he first worked in city government in Philadelphia, then opened a jewelry business in West Philadelphia, which he ran for more than 25 years before his death.

HOLUBA, BOB. 1968-69-70. LG, 6'3", 238 lbs.; Closter, NJ. Another of Paterno's first "scholar-athletes" who made the Deans' List five straight terms and graduated with a 3.65 (out of a 4.0) average in Business Administration. A two-year starter at LG and mainstay as a backup soph and starting junior on the great back-to-back unbeaten and unappreciated teams of '68 & '69 that won two Orange Bowls and finished number two in the country. Helped open big holes for Pittman, Campbell, Abbey, Harris and Mitchell. "He's a top-notch guard and one of our best football players," Paterno said at the time. Winner in '71 of an NCAA postgraduate scholarship that honors "student athletes." Played in '70 Blue-Gray game. State's modern indoor practice facility, Holuba Hall, is named after his father, Stan, a former Nittany Lion boxer, and other members of the family who donated major funds to help construct the building. Now the president of a company in HoHoKus, NJ.

HOSTETLER, RON. 1975-76-77. LB, 6'2", 191 lbs.; Holsopple, PA. One of the many solid linebackers of the Paterno era who never made All-American but was a consistent performer. Played the "Hero" position and was good at playing against the pass as well as the run. Co-captain of '77 team that was fourth in country with 11-1 record and went to Fiesta Bowl for first time, recording a victory over Arizona State on Christmas Day. Made impact as a backup soph LB with his pass coverage and tackling ability. Cited in 10-3 win over Kentucky in '75 for

his pass defending in last minute that helped preserve victory. A two-year starter at OLB in junior and senior years, but missed last two games of junior season with knee injury. Had one of his best games that year in losing cause against Ohio State with five solo tackles, two assists and big QB sack. Called defensive signals in senior year on team that featured Bruce Clark and Matt Millen. Played one of his finest games in 21-17 win over North Carolina State in '77 with three solo tackles and nine assists. Brothers Doug ('76-'78) and Jeff ('80) both lettered but Jeff transferred to West Virginia after losing QB competition to Todd Blackledge and became a star, though he couldn't lead WVU to victory over State in '83. Eleventh choice of Los Angeles Rams in '78 but didn't play pro FB. Now a teacher in Hershey, PA.

HUFFMAN, JAY. 1959-60-61. C, 5'11", 206 lbs.; Clairton, PA. One of the toughest and most durable centers of the Engle era, who anchored the line for all three of Engle's bowl-winning teams. Played one of his best games as soph in 7-0 win over Alabama in first Liberty Bowl, when he was selected the game's Most Valuable Player because of his aggressive performance in blocking and tackling; also recovered a fumble that could have put game away early. Began soph year as third team center but got start in opening game of season against Missouri, when injuries sidelined two players ahead of him, and he never sat on the bench again. Made one of the biggest plays of his career as soph in State's first win over Army in 60 years, when he intercepted a pass with less than two minutes in the first half, leading to the TD that put game out of reach in eventual 17-11 win. Two years later against Army he played one of his finest defensive games in 10-7 loss. Some fans will always remember him for his bruising tackle in the final game of his career against Oregon in '61 Liberty Bowl, when he hit the Oregon FB so hard at the goal line the ball went bouncing back to the 10-yard line where State recovered in an eventual 41-12 victory. Was very active on campus and served as vice president of the Penn State student body as senior. Played with Quantico Marines after graduation but didn't go into pro football. Now owns a cleaning service in Guilford, CT.

HUFFORD, ROSS A. ("SQUEAK"). 1920-21-22. E, 5'11", 175 lbs.; Hillsboro, WV. Three-year starter at RE on the great back-to-back unbeaten teams of '20 & '21 and the '22 team that went to State's first post-season bowl game, the '23 Rose Bowl team. Best known for his blocking that helped Glenn Killinger and "Light Horse Harry" Wilson become All-Americans. Also cited for his rugged defensive play. A fine pass receiver, when necessary, but his teammate Stan McCollum was the prime passing target on the '20-'21 teams. He and McCollum formed the best end combination in the East in '21 and both were selected on several first or second Team All-East squads that year. First recipient of "the tradition hat"—a battered old felt headpiece— given by senior players to the "outstanding athlete of the freshman class." Played one of his best games as soph in State's first ever game with Nebraska, catching a 35-yard pass from Glenn Killinger for the first TD in 20-0 win at Beaver Field. Moved to RHB in final game of career against Pitt in '22 as Coach Hugo Bezdek attempted to catch Pitt off guard but it didn't help as State lost, 14-0, then went on to lose Rose Bowl. Returned in '27 as assistant coach, then went into high school coaching and was long-time coach and teacher at Lewistown (PA) High School. Deceased.

HUFNAGEL, JOHN. 1970-71-72. QB, 6'1", 194 lbs. ; McKees Rocks, PA. Some fans believe he may have been the best all-around QB of the Paterno era; he could run as well as pass and think. All-American in his senior year, when he led State to a 10-1 regular season record and a Sugar Bowl bid; finished sixth in Heisman Trophy vote that year. Began career as a second string safety and third string QB and became starter in sixth game of '70 season against Army as soph after Paterno benched two other QBs ahead of him following early losses to Colorado, Wisconsin and Syracuse; as starting QB, he lost just three games and won 26 over next two and a half years. QB of the 11-1 '71 team and led team to the "breakthrough" 30-6 win over Texas in '72 Cotton Bowl; he hit seven-for-13 passes for 137 yards and one TD and rushed for 14 yards and another TD; his 65-yard pass to Scott Skarzynski in the third QT with State ahead 10-6 stunned Texas and broke open the game; he ran four yards for the final TD in the fourth QT. Played one of his finest games in '71 against Iowa, when twice in the fourth QT he led team from deficit to go-ahead TDs, and in last three minutes took Lions 80 yards with his ball-handling, precision passing and leadership to score the winning TD on 10-yard pass in corner to TE Dan Natale with 36 seconds left for 14-10 victory. Perhaps State's most efficient passer of all-time with a three-year career passing efficiency rating of 140.83; his 151.84 efficiency rating in '71 is topped only by Kerry Collins for one-season and the 148.04 rating he got in '72 also is fourth best of all time. Also second in career yards per attempt (8.69 yards), seventh in career TD passing percentage with a 6.37 per-pass average, seventh in career passing yardage with 3,545 yards on 225 completions in 408 attempts for 26 TDs and 17 interceptions, and sixth in one season with 2,039 yards on 115-for-216 passes for 15 TDs and eight interceptions. Best passing day was in 46-16 win over Maryland at Beaver Stadium Field in '72 when he hit on 14-of-30 passes for 290 yards and one TD and one interception. Had five other games with over 200 yards passing. He was a good running QB who used the option play well and scored several TDs; one of best days was in 31-0 win over Syracuse in '71, when he had two TDs and was second leading rusher with 70 yards on 13 carries. Actually was leading rusher in '72 45-0 win over Army with 71 yards on eight carries, including a 64-yard sprint on the option that set up one of two Cappelletti TDs that day. One of the McKees Rocks QB trio of Burkhart, Hufnagel and Fusina who were so integral to the success of Paterno in his first 15 years. Played in '73 Hula Bowl. Drafted 14th by Denver but after two years with Broncos he decided to play with Saskatchewan in the Canadian Football League and became a star in a 12-year career. Now coach and general manager of the New Jersey team in the Arena Football League, and as well was coach and general manager of Calgary in CFL.

HULL, GARY. 1968-69-70. LB & DE, 6'3", 207 lbs.; Greenville, PA. May be the most forgotten starter on the great defensive team of '69. Played at right DE and was known for his pass rush but was overshadowed by left DE John Ebersole and such superstar teammates as Mike Reid and Dennis Onkotz. Was LB as soph and became starter in midseason. Had outstanding game as soph in nationally televised 30-12 win over Syracuse at end of season with four unassisted tackles and four assists. One of only three juniors to start on defense with seven three-year lettermen seniors. Steady and dependable but it was his linemates who made the spectacular plays in '68 & '69. Moved back to outside LB in senior season and continued to start and play fine football. Now a high school teacher and coach in Jamestown, PA.

ICKES, LLOYD. 1937-38-39. FB & QB, 5'10", 178 lbs.; Altoona, PA. One of the team leaders of the late '30s credited with helping to bring respectability back to State's football program after several non-winning seasons. Had his finest year as senior when he called the plays and signals; was fine runner, receiver and defender for team that posted best record in 18 years, losing just one game, tying two and winning five. Usually played 60 minutes and one sportswriter praised him for "his inspiring will to win, his versatility...(and)...his rugged re-sourcefulness." Was a good play caller and an excellent punter, the finest at State of his era, who often kicked for 50-to-60 yards. Played one of his best offensive games early in senior season in 49-7 win over Lehigh before Homecoming crowd: scoring three TDs in first Half, including one on a 49-yard run up the middle and two on pass receptions of 25 and 16 yards, and gained 91 yards on 11 carries. Was outstanding on defense in 6-6 tie with Syracuse, stopping two Syracuse drives near goal line, once with an interception at State's seven-yard line and again with a fumble recovery at the third-yard line. Made perhaps the best run of his career with a 55-yard dash for a TD off a fake reverse that enabled State to tie Army 14-14. As junior, scored three TDs in opening season game against Maryland, including 69-yard run off tackle. Also made crucial extra point in 7-7 tie with Penn in '38 when Penn blocked State's extra point try after TD late in game: Ickes picked up ball on 20-yard line and ran into end zone, carrying tacklers with him. Began career as an E but converted to a back and spent most of career as FB, starting most of junior season, when he was one of the defensive backfield stars on team that set three NCAA pass defense records, including the record for fewest yards passing allowed per game (13.1 average) that still stands. Deceased.

ISOM, RAY. 1984-85-86. FS & PR, 5-9 187; Harrisburg, PA. One of the hardest hitters ever to play in a State secondary. Second-Team All-American in senior year. He will never be forgotten for the devastating hits on Miami's highly touted wide receivers Michael Irvin, Brian Blades and Brett Perriman (all of whom became big pro stars) in the '87 Fiesta Bowl victory over then #1 Miami, 14-10, that gave State its Second National Championship. He sent an early message to Irvin and set the tempo early in the game when he hit Irvin so hard that the Miami receiver fumbled the ball and State recovered. Despite his small stature he was tough and fast and never afraid to take on receivers who were bigger and taller, such as the Miami trio. Tied for 6th in career interceptions with five players, including the great two-way players of the '50s—Lenny Moore and Milt Plum—with 10 pick offs for 121 yards. His best interception year was '85, when he led team with four for 39 yards; interceptions against Cincinnati and Notre Dame late in season set up TDs, as State cruised to #1 ranking. First interception in second game of '86 season led to clinching TD in 26-14 win over Boston College and his next one deep in East Carolina territory in first QT set up first TD in 42-17 win, but his biggest one that year was in pivotal midseason game in '86 against then #2 Alabama, when he stopped a 'Bama drive in an all-out defensive team win, 23-3; also made 6 tackles and knocked down another pass in that game. In soph year he began as a punt returner (ran back 15 for 67 yards) and backup DB, but by fourth game of season against Texas at the Meadowlands he was a starter and led team in tackles that season with 55 solos and 27 assists for 82 total. Moved to FS in junior year and started on both teams that played for National Title. Played in '87 Japan Bowl. Signed as free agent by Tampa Bay and played in '87 and '88 before injuries cut short his pro career. Now a claims adjuster in Harrisburg, PA.

JACKS, AL. 1956-57-58. QB, 6-0 185; Pittsburgh, PA. A better than average QB and defensive back with a good football mind, who had the bad luck of being at State at the same time as Milt Plum and Richie Lucas; thus, he has never received the recognition of other QBs on the Engle-Paterno teams of the '50s and '60s. A prototype dropback QB who usually ran only when forced. Paterno said he was the "best passing quarterback" of the '50s and '60s who had wonderful poise, never got rattled and was always thinking. He also was a nice person who shared with his backups, including Lucas and fellow "redshirt" Bob Scrabis. However, his name is but a footnote in today's State record books. His best year was '57, when he led team in passing despite missing three games late in the season with a shoulder separation; completed 53 of 103 passes for 673 yards and five TDs with just three intercepted. One of his finest games was in a losing cause to powerful Army, 27-13, at Beaver Field in '57, when he set what was then the State record for completed passes in one game with 17, hitting seven different receivers in 32 attempts and picking up 153 yards and one TD. As a senior shared starting position with Lucas, and in final game of career he helped rally team from a 14-0 deficit to a 25-21 upset victory at Pitt Stadium that knocked Pitt out of a post-season bowl game; he completed 10-of-17 passes, including one for a TD and helped keep the Panthers off balance with his punting. Drafted 10th by Los Angeles Rams at end of his junior "redshirt" year but decided not to play pro football and went into coaching instead. Head coach for several years at Clarion University and still on the faculty there.

JACKSON, KENNY. 1980-81-82-83. WR, 5-11 171; South River, NJ. One of the all-time great pass receivers and a two-time First-Team All-American. State's first wide receiver to be named First-Team All-American, selected as a junior on school's first National Championship team, when he caught 41 passes for 697 yards and seven TDs, which still ties for 8th in all-time one season receptions; then repeated as All-American in senior year. Probably his best single performance was the five receptions for 158 yards and two TDs in team's outstanding come-from-behind 48-14 victory over then #1 Pitt in last regular season game of '81; had a 52-yard reception that set up tying TD late in second QT & then scored on two quick passes from Todd Blackledge of 42- and 45- yards within six minutes of the third QT to break the game wide open. His seven TDs in '82 included two (on passes of 22 and 10 yards) in 39-31 win over Maryland, one (on an 18 yarder) in key 27-24 win over Nebraska and two (on passes of 59 and 28 yards) in 52-17 rout of Boston College. Obviously missed his favorite QB Blackledge in senior season but closed out career with another outstanding game against Pitt, scoring two TDs on passes of 24 & 57 yards and catching

two others for a total of 108 yards in 24-24 tie that sent team to Aloha Bowl. Set 27 school records before he graduated and still holds records for career yards per reception (18.4), most TDs in one season by a junior (7) and frosh (5) and most receptions and yardage by a frosh in a season (21 for 386 yards) and in a game (when he caught 13 for 93 yards in 21-0 loss to Nebraska). Fourth in all-time career receptions with 109 catches and second only to his protégé Bobby Engram in yardage (2006) and TDs (25). Seventh in all-time reception yardage for one game (158 yards) and 10th in season (697 yards). Six times had games with over 100 yards in pass receptions. Starter on teams that had a four-year record of 39-9-1 and went to two Fiesta Bowls, Sugar Bowl and Aloha Bowl. Co-captain his senior year when won Hall Award as the Outstanding Senior Player. Played in '84 Hula and Japan Bowls. First State receiver ever taken in first round of NFL draft and fourth player overall, when chosen by Philadelphia in '84; had best year as rookie with 40 pass receptions for 692 yards; gave up pro ball in early '88 to run his own restaurant business in New Jersey but returned to play '88, '90 and part of '91 with Eagles and '89 with Houston. Sold business and is now in sixth year as wide receiver coach for State and is credited with developing Bobby Engram (who broke many of Jackson's individual school records), Joe Jurevicius and other receivers.

JACKSON, ROGER. 1981-82. DB, 6-1 186 South River, NJ. Sometimes overlooked because he was in the same defensive backfield as All-American Mark Robinson and Olympic aspirant Paul Lankford and was older brother of superstar receiver Kenny Jackson (see above). Made one of the most memorable interceptions in State history against then #1 Pitt in final regular season game of '81; Pitt had 14-0 lead early in second QT on two Dan Marino TD passes and was driving for apparent third TD to take complete control of the game, when Jackson intercepted in the EZ; State went on to drive 80 yards for TD, turning game completely around and scored 48 unanswered points, as State upset Pitt, 48-14, in one of greatest games of bitter series; Jackson also caused another interception and a fumble with his hard tackles and knocked down three passes, and was named the Player-of-the-Game. In following game at '81 Fiesta Bowl, he had another outstanding defensive game, forcing a fumble late in the first QT on USC 17 that set up State's first TD by Curt Warner on next play and knocked down several passes in 26-10 win. Followed up with another fine year the following season as starting cornerback on first National Championship team that beat Georgia in Sugar Bowl. His blocked punt early in first QT of second game of '82 season against Maryland led to State's first TD and an eventual 39-31 win that gave momentum to championship season. Now living near his hometown of South River, NJ.

JACKSON, TOM. 1967-68-69. OG & OT, 6-3 228; Scotch Plains, NJ. Another of the "team" players of the early Paterno era who made the most of his talent in the most unglamorous of positions, offensive tackle. The only sophomore to start on offense (at LG) on Paterno's turnaround '67 team who then started at G on the great unbeaten team of '68 that beat Kansas 15-14 in '69 Orange Bowl. Willingly agreed to move to LT in '69 when he was the offensive captain (with defensive co-captains Reid and Smear), and team went on to repeat undefeated season and win Orange Bowl. Was one of the reasons Pittman, Mitchell and Harris were able to gain the yardage that helped make them stars. Became the object of major controversy after pivotal come-from-behind Syracuse game at Archbold Stadium in '69 when Orange coach

Ben Schwartzwalder complained to NY City media that Jackson "was tackling and holding our right tackle on probably every play." Jackson, who had been used by Paterno to shuttle in plays and was only the field about 55 percent of the time, denied the accusation, saying "we aren't coached that way...but Syracuse is...;" Paterno demanded an apology and threatened to report Schwartzwalder to the NCAA coaches' ethics committee. Not as big as some of the other OT's in Paterno era but a solid blocker and pass protector who was a leader off field as well as on it. Was in coaching for a time and coached at the University of Connecticut. Now a human resources manager in Bradenton, FL.

JACKSON, TYOKA. 1990-91-92-93. DT & DE, 6'2", 265 lbs.; Forestville, MD. The best QB sacker of the '90's. His four-year total of 24 ½ sacks places him second of all-time to Larry Kubin, who has 30. Best years were the nine and a half sacks in '91 and eight in '93. He made up what he lacked in size with his quickness and his natural instincts. Made one of his finest plays in the come-from-behind 42-17 win over Tennessee in '92 Fiesta Bowl; with State trailing, 17-14, Jackson sacked Vol QB Andy Kelly, forcing a fumble which he recovered at Tennessee 13-yard line; on the next play Tony Sacca passed to Kyle Brady for the TD that gave State the lead, 21-17, that it never relinquished. Even as backup DT as frosh he gained reputation for sacks with four. Became starter in "redshirt" soph year and played at both DT and NT, where he had 11 tackles behind scrimmage and nine and a half sacks. Played one of his best games in 28-21 win over Boston College when he twice sacked BC QB Glen Foley at key times and had six other tackles. Starter for most of junior year, although missed several games near end of season when sidelined with ankle injury. Had another fine year as senior, starting with season-opening 38-20 win over Minnesota, when his recovery of a fumble in second QT led to TD. Also cited by sportswriters the next week in 21-20 win over Southern Cal when he had six tackles, including two sacks and harrassed USC QB Rob Johnson all day. His six tackles, including two sacks for 15 yards in losses, then helped Lions to 31-0 win over Iowa. Had one of best days against Illinois when he recorded two big sacks for 18 yards in losses, eight tackles and caused two fumbles in 28-14 win. Played in '94 Senior Bowl. Signed as free agent by Miami in '94 and now on roster of Tampa Bay Buccaneers.

JAFFURS, JOHN. 1941-42-43. G, 5'10", 190 lbs.; Wilkinsburg, PA. Second-Team All-American in '43 and one of the toughest two-way players of his era. Started at G as a soph in '41 and was also a regular in '42 but left for the service at the end of season. Fortunately, returned in the fall of '43 as part of the Army's ROTC program that sent officer candidates who were athletes back to college until they could be integrated into the armed forces. Captain of '43 team that had 5-3-1 record, including a narrow 14-6 loss to powerful Navy and a big 14-0 win over Pitt, when Jaffurs, playing middle LB, had "a field day," as defense held Pitt to minus 26 yards rushing and 97 yards passing. He was short, husky and tough. Never played on a losing team and State was 18-4-1 when he was a starter. Was the leading player in one of the most historic—but long forgotten— milestones in college football in '41, when Syracuse developed the so-called "Y" formation whereby the center turned his back to the defense and would begin play by picking up ball and immediately throw shovel passes to ends or backs, almost like a QB of today; it was called the "reverse center" formation, and, after Syracuse had used it to dominate foes and post a 4-1 record, the for-

mation was thwarted by State in mid-season '41 game by having Jaffurs virtually tackle the Syracuse center on every play; Jaffurs and his backup, Lou Palazzi, made just about every tackle until Syracuse switched back to the Single-Wing; State won, 34-19, and by the '42 season the "Y" formation had been banned. The next year, he was again the defensive star of the 18-13 win over Syracuse with two fourth QT interceptions that stopped Orange scoring drives. Jaffurs closed out career by playing in East-West Shrine game in '44, then played one year with Washington Redskins in '46. Deceased

JANERRETTE, CHARLIE. 1957-58-59. T, 6'3", 234 lbs.; Germantown, PA. One of the fine two-way interior linemen on Engle's late '50s teams and a Second-Team All-American in senior year. First Black to play against Alabama when he started in '59 Liberty Bowl game in Philadelphia. Paired with fellow soph Andy Stynchula on second unit of '57 team but developed slower than anticipated and didn't really reach his full potential until senior year when he shared LT position with Stynchula and started most games. Began soph year playing on second Unit and was occasional starter in junior year. His blocked punt early in second QT of Pitt game in '58 was credited with being the psychological boost that led team to 25-21 win and dropped Pitt out of a New Year's Day Bowl. Had one of best games in '59 opening season win over Missouri, when he was cited for his defensive prowess. Had a great year and was a defensive standout in several games, including the 7-0 win over Alabama in first Liberty Bowl. Fifth round draft choice of AFL Los Angeles Chargers in '60 but signed with NFL LA Rams. Spent five years in pros with Rams ('60), New York Giants ('60-61), New York Jets ('63) and Denver Broncos ('64-65). Deceased.

JOE, LARRY. 1942, 1946-47-48. RB & KR, 5'9", 185 lbs.; Derry Township, PA. Perhaps State's greatest kickoff returner but also one of the best runners of Higgins' excellent post-World War II teams. Still holds record for career KO return average with 29.6 yards on 16 returns for 473 yards and one TD. Best year was as a junior in '47, when he averaged 32.6 yards on nine returns for 293 yards thanks to a 95-yard return for a TD on the opening kickoff in a 54-0 win over Bucknell; the 32.6 average was the school one season record for 33 years and is still third best of all-time. Led team in returns in both '47 & '48. Made a sensational debut as frosh when, in second game of season he ran back a punt 65 yards for a TD that clinched 19-3 win over Lehigh. Was running star of the freshmen-dominated '42 team that had 6-1-1 record; played one of best games of his career that year in 13-7 win over Penn, when he scored winning TD in fourth QT on nine-yard run and led rushers with 46 tough yards. Left for service in World War II and expected to take up where he left off in '46 and almost did, for he had perhaps the greatest five-play day of any runner in PSU history in opening game against Bucknell: scored three TDs on runs of 58, seven and three yards, ran back a KO another 39 yards and gained 112 total yards on four carries in 48-6 win; two games later he suffered a shoulder separation in 19-16 loss to Michigan State and missed the rest of the season. Came back in '47 and was one of the starters at tailback on unbeaten '48 Cotton Bowl team, except when hobbled by injuries. Got off to great start as leading rusher in first two games with 68 yards on nine carries in 27-6 win over Washington State and 43 yards and one TD on six carries—and the opening kickoff TD—in 54-0 win over Bucknell. Had the speed and quickness to get around the ends and scored many TDs that way. But because of his age he was slowing down and was moved to FB for most of '48 where he carried the ball less but was still an effective line smasher. Can trace his roots to Paterno because his real name was Lorenzo Giuseppe and in Italian that means "Larry Joe." Played in '46 Blue-Gray game, at the time the only post-season All-Star game, which also allowed underclassman to participate. Played one year for Buffalo Bills of All-American Conference in '49. Deceased.

JOHNSON, ANDRE. 1993-94-95. OT, 6'5", 299 lbs.; Southhampton, NY. Three year starter who played on the talented offensive line of the unbeaten' 95 Rose Bowl Champions that was one of the best offensive teams in college football history with an average 520.2 yards and 47.8 points per game; line gave up only three sacks all season. Known as the "short tackle" who was a key pass protector. Was the least known of the great offensive line of '94 until he was matched up with Illinois All-American Siemon Rice late in the season at Champaign; Rice, who led the Big 10 in sacks, was completely dominated by Johnson and didn't make a tackle in State's thrilling come-from-behind 35-31 win. Co-winner along with teammate Jeff Hartings and two others for first Frank Patrick Memorial Award in '95 honoring juniors for "Total Commitment" to academics, community service and year-around preparations. Recruited originally as a defensive lineman and played there in four games as a "redshirt" frosh in '92, before a knee injury knocked him out for the season. Switched to the offense in the spring of '92, he was slow at first in making the transition but progressed so well in the '93 season that he started the last three games, including the 31-13 come-from-behind win over favored Tennessee in the '94 Citrus Bowl. Played in '96 Senior Bowl. First round choice of Washington in '96 and played with the Miami Dophins in '97.

JOHNSON, EDDIE. 1985-86-87-88. CB & S, 5'10", 164 lbs.; Lindenwold, NJ. Paterno once called him "the best cornerback I ever coached," but it was at free safety in '88 that he made Third-Team All-American. A three-year starter who will never be forgotten for the devastating tackles he, Ray Isom, Duffy Cobbs and other DBs made on Miami's highly touted wide receivers such as Michael Irvin in the '87 Fiesta Bowl victory over then number one Miami, 14-10, that gave State its second National Championship. Johnson led all tacklers in the title game with 13 and also deflected two Vinny Testaverde passes. Co-Captain in senior year when he made AA despite playing on team that had State's first losing season in 49 years. Was backup on '85 team that played for national title against Oklahoma in '86 Orange Bowl, and then moved into starting LCB slot in '86. Played one of best games in '86 in close 23-17 win over Cincinnati, when he had four tackles, a fumble recovery and deflected two passes. Missed part of '87 with an injury but came back in '88 to be one of the few standouts in a disappointing year. Led team to 17-10 win over Maryland in the rain at Beaver Stadium Field with team-leading 10 tackles, a pass deflection and three punt returns for 15 yards. Shared Ridge Riley Award honoring a senior for "sportsmanship, scholarship, leadership and friendship" with John Greene. Played in '89 East-West Shrine Game and '89 Senior Bowl. Never played pro ball. Now living in Sparks, MD.

JOHNSON, PAUL. 1967-68-69. DB, SE & KR, 6'0", 186 lbs.; Cazenovia, NY. A two-year starter at RHB on the great defensive teams of '68 & '69. Paterno once called him "a great team man and one of the most unselfish players I ever coached." Recruited by the all-time

football hero of Cazenovia, NY, State All-American Steve Suhey, and began career as SE and wide receiver. Wound up starting some games in '67 at wing back and caught 80-yard TD pass that helped beat Maryland, 38-3, then willingly switched to DB on eve of '67 Gator Bowl game in one of many tactical player maneuvers Paterno made in effort to surprise bowl opponent Florida State. Unfortunately, he didn't get to play in that game, but came back in next two years to be one of the stars of the back-to-back Orange Bowls. In '68 Orange Bowl win over Kansas, he teamed with DB Pete Johnson (no relation) in fourth QT for one of the crucial tackles of the game: KU was leading, 14-7, with fourth-and-one at PSU 5-yard line but instead of going for a FG that might have put game out of reach, KU sent star running back John Riggins into the line where he was stopped for no gain by the Johnsons; State took over and eventually won game, 15-14, on the famous "12th man" penalty. In '69, he was cited for his devastating tackling and outstanding pass coverage, which helped State throttle Missouri's high-flying passing offense in 10-3 win. Played perhaps his finest defensive game in 17-14 win at Kansas State in '69, when he intercepted a pass, recovered a fumble and stopped an almost sure KS TD by overpowering a blocker and making an open field tackle on a runner who had broken into the clear. Also ran back kickoffs and punts. Led team in KO returns in '69 with 12 for 316 yards, including a 91-yard TD in 27-3 win over Colorado in 2nd game of season. Made one of the most exciting punt returns of the early Paterno years in opening season game against Navy in '68, when on first play of fourth QT, he literally took the ball away from teammate Dennis Onkotz (one of State's all time punt returners) and ran 52 yards for a TD in 31-6 victory. Finished year with eight returns for 84 yards. Number eight choice of Washington in '70 but didn't play in NFL. Now owns a lumber company in his hometown of Cazenovia, NY.

JOHNSON, PETE. 1967-68-69. Hero, LB & TE, 6'2", 215 lbs.; North Planfield, NJ. One of the most versatile players of Paterno's great teams during the record unbeaten streak of '67-'69. Willingly changed positions all three years and because of that he doesn't receive the credit he deserves. Played in "Hero" position as soph and took over starting slot early in season where he had 18 unassisted tackles and 11 assists. Shifted to outside left LB in '68 and shared position with Gary Hull; had 38 tackles, 20 assists and three interceptions. His 28-yard interception in opening game of '68 against Navy helped spark 31-6 win and put Lions on road to first ever Orange Bowl game. With graduation of two-time All-American TE Ted Kwalick, Pete moved to TE as senior and started ever game except when injured. Known for his speed and hard hitting. Now president of a commodity company in New Vernon NJ.

JOHNSON, TIM. 1983-84-85-86. DT & DE, 6'2½", 256 lbs.; Sarasota, FL. First Team All-American in senior year, when he was one of the stars on the '86 National Championship team that beat Miami, 10-7, in the '87 Fiesta Bowl. Made one of the great "clutch" plays in that game, as Miami was driving towards State goal in last minute: on second-and-Goal from the six-yard line with 30 seconds left, he sacked Miami's Heisman Trophy winner Vinny Testaverde for a seven-yard loss, and two plays later Pete Giftopoulos' interception at one-yard line ended the game. The play was similar to one he made two games earlier on Notre Dame QB Steve Beuerlein in 24-19 win. Also made Third Team All-American as a junior. Led team in tackles in '86 with 33 and also had five sacks. Played one of his best games as senior in pivotal midseason game against then number two Alabama; named by TCI television network as Co-Player-of -the-Game, when he had nine tackles, including two QB sacks, as State solidly beat the Tide, 23-3, and moved up from number six in rankings. Was backup at both DT & DE as frosh and mostly DE as soph but emerged in junior year after sharing the Jim O'Hora Award given to the most improved player in spring practice with Chris Collins. Started at DT next two years. Had one of best games in '85 in tough come-from-behind 24-20 win over Syracuse at Carrier Dome, when he had nine tackles, including two QB sacks and caused a fumble. Two games later, he made another of his patented "clutch" plays against Boston College to preserve undefeated season: with State trailing 12-10 in fourth QT, he batted a pass attempt by BC QB Shawn Halloran that teammate Mike Russo intercepted and ran in for TD that won game, 16-12. Closed out his regular season career with great game against Pitt, making eight tackles with one sack. Played in '87 Japan Bowl. Sixth round choice of Pittsburgh in '87 draft; played with Steelers ('87-'89), Washington ('90-'95) and Cincinnati ('96) but is no longer in the NFL. Lives in Ashburn, VA.

JONAS, DON. 1958, 60-61. HB, KR & PK, 5'11", 195 lbs.; Scranton, PA. May have been the most underrated running back of the Engle era who had an erratic career due to personal and injury problems. Along with Dick Hoak and Jim Kerr, he was a star on the unbeaten frosh team of '57 but had in-and-out soph year as backup. Still, made one of the biggest TDs of year in final season game against Pitt, scoring on eight-yard run around left end for TD that gave State come-from-behind 25-21 win and knocked Panthers out of Gator Bowl bid. Left team soon after and went into U.S. Army, but returned after beginning of preseason practice in '60; missed first game, but by fourth game of year against Syracuse he was starting at LHB and running back kickoffs and punts; named "outstanding player" in controversial 21-15 loss to Orange, scoring TD on 45-yard run, rushing for 77 yards and making key pass receptions. Went on to lead team in punt returns and pass interceptions that year and was fourth leading rusher on team with 238 yards; also caught six passes for 87 yards. Played one of his best games when series with Maryland resumed that season after 17-year lapse: made one of the year's most thrilling plays, when he picked up a Terp punt on a high bounce and dashed 65-yards down the left sideline for the TD; also recovered a fumble that helped maintain State's initial 91-yard scoring drive and intercepted a pass in EZ to stop a potential Maryland TD in 28-9 victory. Scored State's first TD in '60 Liberty Bowl win over Oregon, 41-21, when he gained 40 yards on 13 carries. Switched back to RHB in '61 because of Roger Kochman's return and was the star of 20-0 opening season win over Navy, when he scored first 13 points on a TD and FGs of 31 and 25 yards and was leading rusher with 68 yards on 17 carries; what made the performance even more startling is that the FGs were the first he attempted since high school and he kicked the first while wearing the wrong—and awkward—helmet of lineman Jim Smith. Finished year by making six-of-nine FGs, 17-of-22 PATs and handled most of the kickoffs. But a dislocated collarbone in mid-season of '61 limited him to FGs and PAT in last part of season and he ended his career with a PAT in '61 Gator Bowl. An all-around athlete who also was the starting catcher on baseball team. Played in U.S. Bowl College All-Star game held in Washington, DC after '61 season. Number 13 draft choice of Philadelphia in '61 and played one year with Eagles, then played and coached minor

league football before becoming first coach at Central Florida University. Now a sales director in Winter Springs, FL.

JONES, BEN C. ("CASEY"). 1916. QB, HB & LE, 5'10", 165 lbs.; Pittsburgh. One of the most instrumental persons in the history of Penn State football whose playing career was cut short by World War I and an injury. He simply loved State football and especially his one-time college roommate Bob Higgins. Came to State from Bellefonte Academy in '15 and was a versatile sophomore starter on Dick Harlow's '16 team that was 8-2; opened season at starting left half and scored two TDs in 27-0 win over Susquehanna, then started at QB and led team to victories against Gettysburg and Geneva when Harlow benched his regular QB, and finished up last two games of season starting at left end. Also lettered in track and lacrosse that year, then left to join Captain Eddie Rickenbacker's famous 9th Aero Pursuit Squadron in France and saw combat as flyer in Europe. Returned to State in '19 but injury forced him to give up football. Went to work in Pittsburgh for the West Penn Power Co. and became one of the biggest fund raisers and recruiters of football talent over next four decades. Most of State's stars from Western Pennsylvania were Casey Jones' recruits. Among the outstanding players he brought to State were Dave and Harry Alston, the school's first Black football players, and such talents as Sever Toretti, Chuck & Joe Drazenovich and Fran Rogel. He also was responsible for inducing Earl Bruce to leave his job as head coach at Brownsville H.S. to become frosh coach at State in '46, from where Bruce became the linchpin between the Higgins and Engle eras on into Paterno regime. During the late 20's he and other influential alumni lost confidence in the coaching and administration of Bezdek and he helped engineer Bezdek's replacement by Higgins. When State eliminated scholarships and de-emphasized in the 1930s, he worked behind-the-scene to entice players to State with jobs and other financial assistance; he and others always maintained he broke no NCAA rules but he circumvented official school policy until a new grants-in-aid system was established in late 1940s. Continually raised money to help the school's athletic program and especially football. Served on State's Board of Trustees from '51-'69 and also 14 terms on Executive Board of Alumni council. After retiring from West Penn Power he lived in Punta Gorda, FL, until his death.

JOYNER, DAVE. 1969-70-71. OT, 6'0", 235 lbs.; State College, PA. The university's first pure offensive lineman to be chosen All-American and one of Paterno's first great "scholar-athletes." A near unanimous First-Team All-American as senior when selected by UPI, Walter Camp, American Football Coaches and Football Writers among others. An academic All-American in senior year and also won a prestigious National Football Foundation and College Football Hall of Fame fellowship. Inducted into the GTE/CoSIDA Academic Hall of Fame in '91 and winner of the NCAA Silver Anniversary Award in '97 honoring former student-athletes who have distinguished themselves in their professions. At the time, Paterno said "Joyner may be the best tackle we've had at Penn State." A swift and devastating blocker, who also could transform into a great pass protector on the next play. Credits All-American G Steve Suhey with making him a good offensive lineman by voluntarily working with him while still in high school in State College. A backup on the great unbeaten team of '69; moved into the starting RT slot in '70 and stayed there rest of career. Co-captain of powerful '71 team that lost only last game of regular season in upset to Tennessee and went on to beat Texas 30-6 in "breakthrough" Cotton Bowl game, thanks in part to Joyner's inspirational leadership: at halftime of game with State behind 6-3, Joyner approached Paterno and said, "Don't worry coach, we got them where we wanted them," and then led the team out to prove it, making the lead block as Lydell Mitchell scored State's first TD early in third QT to take a lead it never relinquished. Co-captain of PSU wrestling team in senior year and was a two-time Eastern heavyweight wrestler and runner-up in the NCAAs. Winner of an NCAA Post-Graduate Scholarship in '72 and played in '72 Hula Bowl. His wife, Carolyn, was a State cheerleader. Son Matt was a reserve DB on '96 & '97 teams. Graduate of Penn State's Hershey Medical School and served as a team physician at the '92 Winter Olympics. Now an orthopedic surgeon in Hummelstown, PA., and owner of University Orthopedics and Sports Medicine Center in State College.

JUREVICIUS, JOE. 1994-95-96-97. WR, 6'5", 223 lbs.; Chardon, OH. Another in the line of outstanding wide receivers of the Paterno era but career ended prematurely when Paterno wouldn't let him play in '98 Citrus Bowl for academic reasons. Teamed with QB Mike McQueary in '97 for one of the best passing combinations in the Big 10 when he was a semi-finalist for the Biletnikoff Award as the nation's "outstanding receiver." Perhaps his finest day was in 57-21 win over Louisville, when he caught four passes, three of them for TDs, and racked up 150 yards and was named the Big 10 Offensive Player-of-the-Week. Also had two TDs and 101 yards on four receptions in 35-10 win over Wisconsin. Only Bobby Engram had more games catching passes for over 100 yards in his career as Jurevicius recorded nine in four years. His best was in the come-from-behind 48-26 win over Indiana in '96, when he caught four passes for 156 yards including a 57-yard TD. Finished career as number four in all-time receiving yardage (1,894), number six in receptions (94) and tied with Terry Smith for number four in TD receptions (15). His 10 TDs as senior made him number three behind Engram for the best in one season. Also, the 869 yards he made as a junior and 817 yards as senior are sixth and eighth in the one-season records. One of the most sought after high school players in the country in '92, and the tallest State receiver of the Paterno era. Combined good speed, agility and great hands with size that made it tough to defend against him. Waited in background until Engram left, but as "redshirt" frosh in '95 Rose Bowl, he exploded into the spotlight with a streak down the sidelines for a 53-yard reception in the second QT that set up State's second TD in the 38-20 win over Oregon. Although playing behind Engram in '95 he had the longest pass reception of the season and his first TD ever on a 55-yard catch in 45-21 win over Indiana. Had a fine start in '96 at Kickoff Classic, when he caught four passes for 63 yards, including a 35-yard throw from sub QB Mike McQueary for the final TD in 24-7 win over Southern Cal. Two games later he caught TD passes of 19 and 51 yards and another pass for 34 yards in 49-0 win over Northern Illinois; then had best receiving day of his career up to then against Wisconsin with five receptions for 135 yards. But tailed off and was benched by Paterno for scholastic reasons. That must have motivated him, for he came alive in the last four games to help carry team to 11-2 record and Fiesta Bowl win. Played in '97 Hula Bowl and was one of stars as he caught four passes for 102 yards and also threw a TD pass. Drafted number two by New York Giants in '98 draft and playing in the NFL.

KANE, BILLY. 1954-55-56. HB & KR, 5'10", 180 lbs. ; Munhall, PA. A durable and steady all-around player at running back, pass receiver and defensive back who never received the publicity he deserved because of the brilliance of teammates Lenny Moore and Milt Plum. Also tough on defense; he tackled hard and was quick at stopping end runs. After Moore's departure, he became the team's leading rusher in '56 with 544 yards and seven TDs on 105 attempts for 5.0 yards per carry and leading scorer with 42 points. As a soph, he and Moore became only the fourth duo in State history up to that time to both run over 100 yards game in 35-13 rout of Penn at Franklin Field as Moore got 143 yards (and three TDs) and Kane 133 (and one TD). Also had 130 yards and a TD in 16-6 win over West Virginia in '56. Leading receiver in '55 (nine catches for 184 yards and two TDs) and '56 (16 receptions for 232 yards) and his 20.4 yards per catch average in '55 is still one of the all-time best. The primary kick returner as a junior and senior, he led team in KO returns both years and punt returns in '56. Also led in all-purpose running in '56 with 1,085 yards from 530 rushing, 232 receiving and 333 on kick returns. His hard running and pass receiving and excellent defensive work in the secondary helped State pull off one of its biggest upsets, 7-6, over three-TD favorite Ohio State in Columbus in '56; he was leading rusher (47 yards on 13 carries) and receiver in the game and stopped one OSU drive deep into State territory with an interception late in first half. Later in season his crucial sideline pass receptions in the last minute against North Carolina State set up winning TD in thrilling 14-7 win at Beaver Field. His brother Bob was a fine linebacker on the Engle's last team of '64 & '65. Played in North-South All-Star game after senior year. Lives in his hometown of Munhall, PA.

KASPERIAN, DAVE. 1957-58. HB & KR, 5'8", 177 lbs.; Worcester, MA. Leading rusher and punishing defensive back in '57 and '58 in Engle's ground-oriented Wing-T offense. Nicknamed "the old man" after coming out for team as an unknown 25-year-old walk-on soph following a stint in paratroopers. Rushed for 469 yards on 122 carries and eight TDs as a junior in '57 and made All-East and Honorable Mention All-American. Had 381 yards on 98 carries and seven TDs in '58, when he also tied as leading pass receiver with nine receptions for 107 yards and two TDs. Led in all-purpose yards and scoring in '57 and '58. Also a good punt and kickoff returner and led team in '57 and '58 for a total of eight returns for 281 yards. Led '57 team with two pass interceptions and six punt returns for 62 yards. Holy Cross Coach Eddie Anderson called him "a man who has a blow torch for a heart" after his finest game, an exciting 14-10 win over the Crusaders before hometown Worcester crowd in '57; he was carried off the field on shoulders of dozens of friends and relatives after gaining 97 rushing, 28 yards pass receiving , 66 yards on one kickoff , 33 yards on two punts and making a daring interception on the last play of the game to preserve the Lions' victory. Played in '58 Blue-Gray game. Now retired after operating a business in Worcester for years.

KATES, JIM. 1967-68-69. LB & MG, 6'2", 230 lbs.; Plainfield, NJ. One of the all-time "clutch" defensive players but often overlooked because of the reputation of his defensive teammates, such as Mike

Reid, Jack Ham and Denny Onkotz. Crucial member of the back-to-back unbeaten and unappreciated teams of '68 and '69. Paterno called him the "most underrated and unpraised football player for his ability in the country." One of the "sophomore subs" who Paterno started playing as regulars early in '67 season that helped turn around his coaching career. Became a starter in third game of soph season at LB, when John Kollar was lost for season, and couldn't get him out of the lineup until he graduated. Made one of the biggest plays of his career in '67, when he, Onkotz and Mike McBath combined to stop North Carolina State's Tony Barchuk at the goal line on a fourth-and-one near the end of the game to preserve a 13-8 upset over then number three NC State that made the college football world first take notice of a Paterno team. Switched to MG for '67 Gator Bowl as part of a scheme to surprise opponent Florida State, and it worked as Kates and others kept Gator offense confused all day in a 17-17 tie. Had highest coaches rating of any lineman in '67. Played mostly inside linebacker but occasionally played MG in State defense. Made one of the key plays of '68 season at UCLA, when he scooped up a blocked punt by Ham and dashed 36 yards for first TD that gave State impetus for 21-6 win. Led LB's in tackles that year with 50 unassisted and 29 assisted. Had another crucial "big play" in senior year, when his recovery of a fumble in the fourth quarter with State trailing, 14-0, at Syracuse sparked a dramatic 15-point rally that won the game and kept unbeaten streak alive enroute to second straight Orange Bowl win. Played in '70 Hula Bowl with teammate Onkotz. Twelfth choice of Washington Redskins in '70 but didn't play in NFL. A marketing major, he is now a supervisor in corporate security and living in Middletown, CT.

KEMMERER, TED ("THE FOOT"). 1952. P, 5'10", 205 lbs.; State College, PA. Became the punter in '52 in one of the most unusual situations in team history since he was not on roster when season started and had not played at all until senior year. Led team in punting that year with 52 punts for 1,904 yards and a 36.7 average. His punting was credited with paving way for upset victories over Penn and Pitt; against Penn, a 52-yarder over head of safety man helped set up winning TD late in fourth QT in 14-7 victory. His first punt against Pitt went for 61 yards in first QT and rest of kicks helped keep Panthers bottled up all day in 17-0 win that knocked Pitt out of Orange Bowl. Surprisingly, he didn't become main punter until knee injury cut short Don Eyer's punting in sixth game of season against Nebraska. Played football at State College High School where father was coach but couldn't make varsity as frosh at Penn State and didn't play football again until asked by Engle to try out as a punter in late September of '52 after season had already started. Helped team achieve surprising 7-2-1 record and earned nickname from teammates as "The Foot." Now a season ticket holder and member of Quarterback and Tailback clubs and a frequent attendee at many Lion sports events. Retired after career as teacher and realtor and lives in Pine Grove Mills, PA.

KERR, JIM. 1958-59-60. HB & Kick Returner, 5'11", 182 lbs.; St. Clairsville, OH. One of the great "clutch" players of all time. A speedy running back who was even better as a defensive back. Probably would have been an All-American DB in a later era of specialization. May have changed the complexion of the '59 season when he scored a 52-yard TD on a short pass from Richie Lucas to break open tight game in the third QT with Missouri and get team off to an eventual great year. Played one of his finest games in State's historic 17-11 win over Army in '59—

State's first victory over the Cadets in 60 years—by topping all rushers with 82 yards on nine carries and leading team in tackles. Repeated his performance in '60 when State became only second team to beat Army in consecutive years at home since Michie Stadium opened in '24 by scoring three TDs and leading all rushers with 64 yards on 15 carries in 27-16 win. Made a crucial block in one of the most memorable State plays in history when soph Roger Kochman ran back KO for TD in classic '59 game with Syracuse, when he smashed the first player downfield (a charging Art Baker) to give Kochman the opening for his spectacular 100-yard KO return. Led '58 team in interceptions as soph with five, returning them for 122 yards and one TD. Had one of his best games at West Virginia in '58, when he scored on a 13-yard sprint, picked up 38 yards on eight carries and halted a WVU drive with an interception on the PSU 13 in a 14-14 tie that started State's 26-game unbeaten streak against the Mountaineers. The next year his interception and 25-yard run for the first TD sparked State to 28-10 win over WVU. In senior year of '60 he was leading rusher (389 yards on 93 carries) and scorer (52 points on eight TDs and two two-point conversions). Also KO return leader in '60 with eight for 158 yards. A fine pass receiver, who was team leader in all-purpose yards in '59 (710 yards on 320 yards rushing, 122 receiving and 268 on kick returns) and '60 (799 yards total on 389 rushing, 163 receiving and 247 on kick returns). Played in '60 East-West Shrine game and '61 Hula Bowl. Drafted seventh by NFL Washington and 19th by AFL New York Jets in '61 and played two years as a DB with the Redskins before an injury curtailed his career. Now a computer sales representative in Mount Pleasant, SC.

KILLENS, TERRY. 1992-93-94-95. LB & DE, 6'1", 223 lbs.; Cincinnati, OH. Didn't reach his full potential until his final season, when he found his natural position at left DE. Was small for a DE, but his quickness and speed enabled him to play off blockers and get to the QB or running backs. Tied with Mark D'Onofrio for 10th in career QB sacks with 15 and had most in '95 senior season, when he led team with 11 and Big Ten with 13, counting two in '96 Outback Bowl win over Auburn. Also had 62 tackles that year, most for a defensive lineman. Started with a "bang" in narrow season opening win over Texas Tech, when he had seven tackles, including one sack, broke up two passes and recovered a fumble at the Tech three-yard line, leading to a quick TD in third QT that turned game around in come-from-behind 24-23 win; for that performance he was named ABC-TV's Player-of-the-Game. Played perhaps his best game in 45-21 win over Indiana in '95, when he scored on his own blocked punt in third QT, picking up the football and rambling 25 yards into EZ; also made six solo tackles, one unassisted, forced a fumble and had a career high of four sacks (for 27 yards in losses), as Big 10 and *Sports Illustrated* named him Defensive-Player-of-the-Week. Played as a "true" frosh in '92 and was in every game either on special teams or as a backup LB; made fine impression with 13 solo tackles. Foot surgery prior to spring practice of '93 season seemed to bother him all year but he came back to start in '94 season opener at OLB against Minnesota and had great game, recovering a fumble on the third play of the game that led to State's first TD in 56-3 rout; had a season high eight tackles that day including a sack. But he struggled rest of year in backup role. Switched to DE in spring and had outstanding senior year. Third choice of Houston in '96 and still playing in with the Oilers.

KILLINGER, GLENN. 1918, 1920-21. QB & HB, 5'10", 166 lbs.; Harrisburg, PA. One of State's greatest all-around athletes, who was a Walter Camp All-American HB in '21, when the honor was almost like winning today's Heisman Trophy. One of 14 State players and three coaches named to the National Football Foundation's College Football Hall of Fame, inducted in '71. Quarterbacked the back-to-back unbeaten teams in '20 (7-0-2) and '21 (8-0-2), which may have been State's best teams ever until the Paterno era. An outstanding team leader who was an excellent passer and "juke" runner, who could dart away from would-be tacklers as well as smash into the line like a FB; also a good blocker and fine defensive player and dropkick specialist. Full of self-confidence with an outgoing personality. Had one of the most unusual career routes to stardom. Too small to play football in high school and not good enough to make State's team as a frosh but became a nine-letterman, who also played basketball and baseball. Came out for team in '18 when Bezdek sought candidates because there were so few men on campus due to World War I, and in his first game (against the Army Ambulance Corps based at Allentown) he broke three ribs but played rest of season with little fanfare. As soph was third stringer who played only occasionally and missed earning letter by being one quarter short of the letter-winning requirements. But by start of junior year he was the starting QB and had one of his finest performances in the key game of the season, a 14-7 homecoming win over Dartmouth, when he hit on two passes to set up one TD and returned an intercepted pass 52 yards to the Dartmouth two-yard line to set up the other TD. QB in the all-time biggest victory margin, 109-7, over Lebanon Valley in '20. In State's first ever meeting with Nebraska, he passed 35 yards for the first TD and ran 15 yards for the final TD in 20-0 win at Beaver Field late in year. Because of a preseason injury he didn't start the first game of senior season against Lebanon Valley but came on to lead team to 8-0-2 record with great games against North Carolina State, Georgia Tech and Navy. He scored 10 TDs, including a 70-yard TD run against NC State in 35-0 win. His most momentous play of the season was against Tech at New York's Polo Grounds and it probably was turning point of the entire season; after Tech had taken a 7-0 lead early in the first QT, Killinger took the ensuing KO and ran it back 85 yards for a TD that turned around the game and led to a 28-7 win; his leadership and quarterbacking that day probably made him All-American because Walter Camp was there and later congratulated him in the dressing room. In picking him AA, Camp wrote, in part, "he has the most peculiar elusiveness of any back on the field this year." Played 3B on '21 baseball team that won 20 straight games before first loss and had a 31-game winning streak over two years (still a school record) and usually batted in number two spot. State basketball teams had 37-5 record in his three years on team, and he was captain in '21. Played professional football for old New York Giants. Returned as assistant football coach to Bezdek and head baseball coach in '23 and '24. Was head coach at Dickinson, Rensselaer and Moravian before joining West Chester State (PA) in '34 where, over the years, he was head coach of football (146-31-6 record) and baseball, athletic director and dean of men. As coach of the North Carolina Preflight team during World War II, he is credited with changing future pro football hall-of-famer Otto Graham from HB to QB. He died on July 25, 1988, in Stanton, DE, as he was nearing his 90th birthday.

KLINGENSMITH, GARY. 1963-64. HB, 5'11", 190 lbs.; Uniontown, PA. Can hardly find his name in the Penn State record books but was one of the most inspirational players of all time because his hearing was impaired. Played sparingly as soph but had a fine debut in opening season game of '63 as starting HB; on first play of game he went in motion before snap of ball and was past the Oregon secondary anticipating a reception, when play was called back by his offside penalty; he then went on to be game's leading rusher with 85 yards on 12 carries. It was an omen for the season, as he led 7-3 team in rushing with 450 yards and three TDs on 102 carries for a 4.4 yards average; also led team in punt returns with 10 runbacks for 245 yards and a 24.5 yards average and all-purpose yards with 871 on 450 rushing, 173 receiving and 248 on kick returns. Had one of his best games that year in 10-7 upset win over Ohio State at Columbus, when he was leading rusher with 80 yards on 11 carries and picked up additional yardage on receptions and kick returns. Carried ball less in senior year, when Engle used FB & QB more in option running attack, but still had fine year with good runs and receptions in key situations. After graduation went into coaching and has had long career as a teacher and high school football coach at Juniata High School and lives in Mifflintown, PA.

KNEIDINGER, OTTO. 1953-54-55. T, 6'3", 205 lbs.; Bellwood, PA. One of the best interior linemen on Engle's early teams, he started at either LT or RT in junior and senior years and was co-captain in '55. Was especially fine defensive tackle who pursued well and was quick. Assistant Coach Jim O'Hora said Kneidinger was "the best tackle I worked with" in his first 10 years as line coach. "He's a coach's ball player, and he not only takes care of his own side but helps on the other side," O'Hora said. As junior he was "the other tackle" in the tandem with the great Rosey Grier and received less publicity. He played one of his finest games in first half of 36-13 win against Penn as junior but was injured and missed most of second half and next two games. Was solid throughout his senior year, and his leadership was instrumental in keeping team stable despite erratic year. Played in East-West Shrine game in December of '55 along with teammates Lenny Moore and fellow co-captain Frank Reich. Went into coaching, and at one time was on Rutgers staff under another alum and current State assistant, Dick Anderson. Also was an assistant football coach at the University of Delaware, but now retired and living in Altoona, PA.

KNIZNER, MATT. 1985-86-87. QB, 6'3", 197 lbs.; Youngwood, PA. A QB who probably never had the chance to prove how good he may have been. The "people's choice" for QB in the '85 & '86 seasons, when State twice played for the National Championship and won it in '86 with John Shaffer as the starter. Was better passer than Shaffer but it was defense, more than offense, that was the heart of the '85 & '86 teams Fans felt Knizner was the better QB, but Paterno stuck with Shaffer as starter, inserting Knizner in key situations and he almost always came through. In the '85 "showdown" game with Alabama at Beaver Stadium, Knizner came in after Shaffer had wind knocked out of him midway in fourth QT with score tied and ball on Alabama 11-yard line; without any warm-ups he immediately took snap, rolled right as if to run and fired a perfect pass to Brian Siverling for TD that actually won game, 19-17. He almost saved the '85 national title game against Oklahoma in '86 Orange Bowl when he entered with less than seven minutes left in fourth QT and the score 19-10, but even his 8-for-11 passes for 90 yards was not good enough in 25-10 loss. Didn't play as much in '86 as Shaffer's passing improved but got chance to be full-time starter as senior. Team talent was not same in '87 and Knizner was never able to fulfill his potential, as he led team in passing with 113-of-223 passes for 1,478 yards and 7 TD but his 12 interceptions that year are the most for any PSU QB in the last decade. Had one of best games in 21-16 win at Maryland, completing 13-of-21 passes for 143 yards and a TD. Won Hall Foundation Award in '87 as Outstanding Senior Player. Now an insurance executive in Greensburg, PA.

KOCHMAN, ROGER. 1959-61-62. HB & KR, 6'1", 200 lbs.; Wilkinsburg, PA. One of the most exciting runners of the Engle era and a First-Team All-American in '62, when he led team for the second year in row in rushing, scoring, kickoff returns and all-purpose yards. Was a great pass receiver as well as a runner. Picked on the All-Time Penn State team in 1967 by *Pittsburgh Press* sports editor Chet Smith, who covered Nittany Lion football for more than a half century. Made a sensational impact as a soph against Syracuse at Beaver Field in one of the biggest and most memorable games of the Rip Engle era, when both teams were unbeaten late in the season and vying for the national title; he scored State's first TD on a 16-yard run and then made an electrifying 100-yard kickoff return in the second half that brought State back from a 20-6 deficit and almost won the game; a botched kick for an extra point and two failures on two-point conversions cost State the game, and Syracuse eventually won the '59 National Championship. Kochman went on that year to score the dramatic winning TD in a 7-0 win over Alabama in the first Liberty Bowl: with time running down on the clock and no time outs left, State set up for a FG at the Alabama 18-yard line, but it was a fake as QB Galen Hall, the holder, threw a screen pass to Kochman at the three-yard line and Kochman launched into the end zone for the TD with one second left on the clock. Surprisingly, his '59 KO return is not a State record because of a quirk in the rules at the time but still ranks second of All-Time; also sixth on career kickoff returns with a 25.7-yard return average on 23 returns and 591 yards. Missed entire '60 season because of a preseason knee injury that required an operation three days before the opener but returned to have his finest years for State. Had to change his running style from speed to slashing, and in '61 he rushed for 666 yards and six TDs on 129 carries (5.2 yard average per carry) and scored three more TDs (and gained 226 yards) on pass receptions. In '62 he had another 652 yards and four TDs on 120 carries (5.4 average) in rushing while getting four more TDs (254 yards) on pass receptions. Ranks 17th in career rushing with 1,485 and 12 TDs on 264 carries. Rushed for more than 100 yards in four games with the 133 yards and three TDs he got in the 34-14 win over Holy Cross in '61 being his best. Had one of finest all-around games in '61 33-16 Homecoming win over California, when he ran for 109 yards, scored a TD on a 36-yard pass reception and ran back three KOs for 59 yards. He could turn a short pass into a great TD run as he did on a short pass from Galen Hall that went for a 66-yard TD in '61 West Virginia game. Along with Hall and linebacker Dave Robinson, he led State to 30-15 win over Georgia Tech in the "historic" integrated '61 Gator Bowl by rushing for 76 yards on 13 carries and scoring on a 27-yard pass in the second QT that put State ahead for the rest of the game. Also State's leading ground gainer in '62 Gator Bowl against Florida with 51 yards on six carries, but he still believes that 17-7 loss was the biggest disappointment of his collegiate career. Played in '63 Hula Bowl and College All-Star game. Drafted in '62 before his "medical redshirt" senior year by the NFL St. Louis Cardinals (#4) and the AFL Buffalo Bills (#15) and played HB less than

one year with Bills before severely injuring his leg in a game against Houston in late October of '62; injury on tackle severed an artery and the leg was nearly amputated; wore brace for years and still suffers great pain. Returned to State for his Masters Degree and then settled into a long career with the Bell Telephone Co. Now director of telephone security for Bell Atlantic in the Philadelphia area and living in Upper Darby, PA.

KOEGEL, WARREN. 1968-69-70. C, 6'4", 240 lbs.; Glascow, NY. Another in the long line of fine centers at State and so good he started as a soph. The starting C on the first of Joe Paterno's great teams, the unbeaten back-to-back squads of '68 and '69 that won two Orange Bowls and were snubbed by the pollsters, finishing number two each year. Usually always ranked among best blockers by coaches' internal ratings. He is credited with helping Chuck Burkhart become a fine QB as the two rarely bumbled a snap in both '68 & '69 seasons. Then as co-captain in '70 he had to keep the offense steady as Paterno alternated quarterbacks until putting sophomore John Hufnagel in charge and Koegel was again credited with helping make Hufnagel a success. That team lost two of the first three games before Hufnagel but came back to finish 7-3 and be rated 18th in country. Played two of his best games in '68 against West Virginia and Miami and sportswriters said he rarely had a bad day as a junior and senior. Played in East-West Shrine game and Hula Bowl in '71. Third choice of Oakland in '71 and played one year with Raiders, then with St. Louis Cardinals ('73) and New York Jets ('74) before retiring. Later was an assistant coach at Rutgers under then coach Dick Anderson. Currently assistant football coach at the University of Connecticut and lives in South Windsor, CT.

KOHLAAS, EARL ("BUD"). 1957-58-59. G, 6'0", 220 lbs.; Mechanicsburg, PA. One of the fine, tough two-way guards of the late '50s. Started out as third team C in soph season and was switched immediately to G and moved up to second unit. Basically a two-year starter at LG in junior and senior years although he alternated with Chuck Ruslavage in '58. Sportswriters said he was built like a truck and blocked like one, too. Made perhaps his foremost block in the "showdown of unbeatens" late in '59 season, when State battled Syracuse at Beaver Stadium in a game with national title implications; after Syracuse scored early in fourth QT to take a 20-6 lead, State soph Roger Kochman (see above) took the ensuing kickoff on goal line and Kohlhass wiped out the kicker Bob Yates to spring Kochman for what became a dazzling TD return that is one of the all-time great plays in PSU history (although State eventually lost and Syracuse became National Champion). Sportswriters said that was the best game of his career although he also was praised for his performance in his final game, the 7-0 win over Alabama in the '59 Liberty Bowl. Played in '59 Blue-Gray game. 20th choice of NFL Washington Redskins and late round pick by AFL Oakland Raiders in '60 but never played in NFL. Manages a tire store in his hometown of Mechanicsburg, PA.

KROUSE, LENNY. 1939-40-41. Wingback & P, 6'0", 180 lbs.; Rochester, PA. An outstanding pass receiver in an era when running and not passing was the prime thrust of Penn State's Single-Wing running offense. Also an outstanding defensive back, particularly on pass defense. Picked on the All-Time Penn State team in 1950s and again in 1967 by *Pittsburgh Press* sports editor Chet Smith, who covered Nittany

Lion football for more than a half century. Despite the team emphasis on running and defense, he and Bill Smaltz formed one of the finest passing combinations of that time. Leading receiver in the East and third best in country in both junior and senior years. For 25 years he held the record for most receptions and yardage in a game, when he caught eight for two TDs and 155 yards in '40 13-13 tie at Syracuse; that reception mark still ties him with five players for sixth best of all time. Made one of his outstanding catches in that game: with four minutes left and State trailing, 13-6, he leaped into the air between a couple of defenders to take a 57-yard throw from Smaltz on his finger tips at the three- yard line and bull his way over the goal for the TD; PAT tied score in what would be an outstanding 6-1-1 season. Captain of '41 team that lost two of its first three games then roared back to win six straight, including a big 31-7 win over arch rival Pitt. Also shared punting that year with Smaltz. Had another fine game in his final performance, when he caught eight passes from Smaltz including a 42-yarder to set up a TD as State beat South Carolina 19-12 win to complete a 7-2 season. Still holds the record for most receiving yards by a junior in a single game, when he gained 155 yards (and scored two TDs on 10 receptions). A excellent blocker. In the Single-Wing offense, the wingback was a key to the off-tackle power play and Krouse was one of the best in the country but didn't get the notoriety he deserved. Made several key interceptions in '40 while playing behind the school's famous "Seven Mountains" front line on team that only lost once and had best record in 19 years. Was president of his senior class and excellent student in mechanical engineering. Played in '42 East-West Shrine game. President of an elevator company in Springfield, PA.

KUBIN, LARRY. 1977-78-79-80. DE & LB, 6'1", 228 lbs.; Union, NJ. Penn State's "Mr. Sackman." Lost his chance for All-American in senior year, when he injured a knee in practice following the fourth game of the season and missed the rest of the '80 season. That makes his sack numbers even more amazing, as he is the school leader in sacking the quarterback for both career (30) and one season (15 in '79); also holds season record for most tackles for losses with 23 in junior year of '79; also led team in sacks as soph. Played as much as the starters as a soph on the great '78 team that played for (and, regretfully, lost) the National Championship against Alabama in the '79 Sugar Bowl. Had one of his biggest games ever that year in the nationally-televised late season "clash of the unbeatens" between then number two State and number five Maryland; was Defensive Player-of-the-Game with his trademark three sacks for 34 yards in losses and six unassisted and two assisted tackles that helped State thump Maryland 27-3 before a record Beaver Stadium crowd (78,019) and propel the Lions to number one for the first time ever in 91 years. Was a third-team backup DE at start of frosh season but got first start at Miami in eighth game of season and led all tacklers with six unassisted grabs, including two sacks, in 49-7 win. Started at DE in first game of soph year at Temple alongside Bruce Clark and had sack in third QT that helped stop Temple's momentum and led to 10-7 victory but didn't start again until West Virginia; then stayed there rest of year and had seven tackles in disappointing '79 Sugar Bowl loss of national title to Alabama. Made All-East that season. Started as junior on a line that also featured All-Americans and Lombardi Award candidates Clark (who won the Lombardi) and Matt Millen. At the time, Paterno said "Kubin is a great athlete but he probably won't get the attention he deserves because he is playing on the same line as Clark and Millen." Had

probably his best game of year in last play 9-7 win over North Carolina State with nine tackles and one sack; then had seven tackles and three sacks for 18 yards in losses as State beat Tulane, 9-6, in Liberty Bowl. Then came his unfortunate injury after Missouri game in '80. Sixth choice of Washington in '81 and played in '83 and '84 Super Bowls along with PSU teammate Rich Milot before leaving pro football in '85 because of his recurring knee injury. Working in Union, NJ.

KUGLER, PETE. 1979-80. DT, OT, Nose Tackle & DE, 6'4", 253 lbs.; Cherry Hill, NJ. One of the fine nose tackles who was still developing when he anchored State's defensive line in '79 and '80. Played behind standout DT Bruce Clark and Matt Millen as soph but usually played in "mop-up" role; as such, he had fine performance in pivotal '78 game against Maryland (see Kubin above) with three sacks totaling 20 yards in losses. Switched to OT as junior and started eight games before volunteering to switch back to DT before North Carolina State game after injuries to Clark and Millen, then played one of his best games with nine tackles and two sacks (for losses of seven yards) in the last second 9-7 win; almost repeated performance in final regular season game against Pitt with nine tackles. As NT in senior year his job was to clog the line to give teammates opportunity to make tackles and he did his job well, usually averaging 3-5 tackles a game. Had one of his best games in his finale, the 31-19 win over Ohio State in '81 Fiesta Bowl with three tackles, two sacks and a pass batted down. Played in Hula and Japan Bowls in '81. Drafted sixth by San Francisco in '81 and had excellent career with 49ers in '81-'82 and '86-'90, going to the Super Bowl in '82, '89 and '90. Also played for San Antonio in USFL ('83-'85). Majored in finance and is now working in San Francisco.

KULKA, JOHN. 1966-67-68. T & C, 6'4", 225 lbs.; Ludlow, PA. Another of the good offensive linemen of the early Paterno teams who started for two years at T after lettering as a reserve C & T as a sophomore. Along with fellow T Dave Bradley, he was singled out by offensive line coach Joe McMullen at end of great unbeaten '68 season as the reason Campbell, Pittman and the other running backs could do so well. Pittman said he wouldn't have led team in rushing that year without the great trap blocking by Kulka. Made perhaps the play of his career in the 28-24 win over Army by recovering the ball at the Army one-yard line after it was accidentally touched by a cadet when a PSU field goal attempt fell short; with new life, the Lions scored a TD and helped propel them into the Orange Bowl and the historic 15-14 win over Kansas. Brother George was a back up defensive lineman in '68 & '69. Drafted number seven by Miami in '69 but didn't play pro ball. Now a construction vice president in State College.

KWALICK, TED. 1966-67-68. TE, 6'4", 230 lbs.; McKees Rocks, PA. Probably State's greatest TE. The second two-time First-Team All-American and the first since Bob Higgins in '19; a near unanimous All-American as a senior, when selected by AP, UPI, Football Coaches, Football Writers, NEA, The Sporting News, Football News, Central Press Association, ABC-TV and the New York Daily News. Also first junior ever named First-Team All-American in '67. Finished fourth to O.J. Simpson in '68 Heisman Trophy race. One of 14 State players and three coaches in the National Football Foundation College Football Hall of Fame, inducted in '89. A fine blocker and an excellent receiver who made many clutch catches and blocks for his one-time high school teammate, QB

Chuck Burkhart, on the great unbeaten team of '68 that won the Orange Bowl over Kansas, 15-14; he was State's leading receiver in the game, which was his last for State, with six receptions for 74 yards. Was one of key players on the two-point conversion that won game after Kansas was penalized for having 12 men on the field; his block on one of the linebackers helped spring Bobby Campbell into the end zone on a sweep left and win the game. He holds the career record for most receptions, yardage and TDs by a TE and is eighth in career receptions with 86 catches for 1,520 yards and 10 TDs and a 15.6-yard per reception average. As a sophomore starting in just his second game he caught nine passes for 89 yards and one TD in a 17-8 victory over Miami that Joe Paterno says was the "turning point" game of his coaching career; Kwalick's statistics that day ties him with five other players for fourth most receptions in a single game. In senior year he led team in receptions with 31 catches for 403 yards and two TDs and an average of 13.0 yards a reception. His 563 yards on 33 receptions for four TDs in '67 is 16th best in one-season pass receiving yardage. He had four games with more than 100 yards, the most for any TE, and his 128 yards and one TD on three receptions against Boston College in his junior year was his best. The most memorable play of his career was not a pass reception or a block but a recovery of an onside kick by Army before a Homecoming crowd at Beaver Stadium on Nov. 2, '68; a 60-yard pass play with two and a half minutes left in the game had just pulled Army to within five points of State's tottering 22-17 lead, when Army tried an onside kick; three Army players and a State man fell on the ball at midfield but the ball suddenly popped out of the pile where Kwalick grabbed it and ran for a TD that clinched the game, and preserved State's first unbeaten season in 21 years. Played in the Senior Bowl, Coaches All-America game and College All-Star game in '69. Number four choice of San Francisco in '69 and played for 49ers ('69-'74) and Oakland ('75-'78) and was on Raiders' Super Bowl Championship team of '77. Played in three Pro Bowls and averaged 15.3 yards per catch before retiring. President of a sportswear company in Santa Ana, CA.

LALLY, JOE. 1976-77-78. LB, DE, 6'2", 233 lbs.; Upper Saddle River, NJ. May be one of the most overlooked defensive ends of the Paterno era because he started for two years on a line that included All-Americans Bruce Clark and Matt Millen and State's All-Time sack leader, Larry Kubin. Made what was perhaps the biggest play of his career in the National Championship game against Alabama in '79 Sugar Bowl, when he recovered a fumble at the Alabama 19-yard line in the fourth quarter that led to the now-famous 4th-and-inches goal line stand by Alabama that probably cost State the national title. Earlier in the year, his blocked punt helped spark the Lions to a 49-21 win over West Virginia. Had another big play in 42-30 Fiesta Bowl win over Arizona State in '77 when he picked up a blocked punt and ran 21 yards for a TD that game Lions a 14-0 first quarter lead. Sixth in tackles in '78 with 42 including five sacks and fifth in '77 with 46 tackles and four sacks. In '77 led defense in stopping opponent runners behind the line of scrimmage with six tackles for 24 yards in losses. Also was one of the best in deflecting passes near the line of scrimmage. Played one of

his best games in '78 in when he had six unassisted tackles in 49-21 victory. Had two of best games in '77 against Utah State when he had 10 tackles in come-from-behind 16-7 victory and 44-7 win over Temple when he led all tacklers with seven and also batted down a pass. Winner of the first Jim O'Hora award in '76 for "exemplary conduct, loyalty, interest, attitude and improvement" by a defensive player in spring practice. Showed his potential as soph in '76 when he was a back up that year at both ILB and DE. Now in financial printing sales and lives in Bryn Mawr, PA.

LAMB, LEVI. 1912-13-14. HB, G, C, E & PK, 6'4", 210 lbs.; California, PA. One of Penn State's first all-around athletes. He was killed in World War I and his memory is honored by the Athletic Department's fund for financial contributions, which is named after him. Picked on the All-Time Penn State team in 1950s and again in 1967 by *Pittsburgh Press* sports editor Chet Smith, who covered Nittany Lion football for more than a half century. One of the star linemen at G of the first great unbeaten team of '12; part of an outstanding interior line including fellow guard Al Hansen and tackles "Dad" Engle and "Red" Bebout that helped open holes for Pete Mauthe and Shorty Miller to become all stars. He was really one of the true "tramp athletes" of his time, having played two years at California Normal (now California University of Pennsylvania) and three years at Grove City before coming to State. Didn't letter in first year of '11 because Coach Bill Hollenback was loaded with running backs and thought Lamb was a show off; also believed he was not durable enough to take continued pounding by tacklers after a preseason practice field incident, when starting tackles Dick Harlow and Engle hit him so hard on a run that he was practically knocked out as his head gear went tumbling and he fumbled the ball. So, Hollenback (who goaded Lamb throughout his career) switched him to the line where he became quite good and was a starter at G by the time soph season began. In big late season game against Penn, his recovery of a fumbled punt at the Penn 12-yard line early in fourth QT broke up tight game and gave State a 14-0 victory. Despite his size, he could run the 100 in 10 seconds and was an outstanding open field runner. Sometimes played at End in '13 and he scored the only TD on a pass reception in the first game ever against Notre Dame (which also was the first defeat at New Beaver Field after 18 wins as Notre Dame won, 14-7). Also was placekicker in junior and senior seasons. His 33-yard FG early in '14 game at Harvard helped State tie, 13-13, in what was seen as a major upset. Lettered four years in track and wrestling; finished first more than 30 times while competing in dashes, hurdles and field events and lost only two wrestling matches in 21 bouts. Became an Army lieutenant after graduating and was killed in France in World War I while leading his platoon in battle on July 18, 1918.

LANDIS, GEORGE. 1968-69-70. DB, 5'11", 186 lbs.; Linwood, NJ. One of the overlooked defensive stars of the unbeaten '69 team that helped produce the longest winning streak in school history. Was an offensive back until switched to DB in Fall of '68 and didn't become full time starter until mid-'69 after being number two defensive RHB on undefeated '68 team. Was outstanding in two key games in '69 that kept streak alive and made team number two in country: In midseason he blocked two Syracuse FGs and recovered a fumble to help State overcome 14-0 Syracuse lead in fourth QT for thrilling 15-14 victory at Archbold Stadium; In '70 Orange Bowl win over Missouri, 10-3, he intercepted two passes, including one at the State three-yard line with

56 seconds to play to save victory and, despite playing with a knee injury during the game, he shut down Missou's great receiver Mel Gray, who didn't catch a pass. Now lives in Schwenksville, PA.

LANKFORD, PAUL. 1980-81. DB, 6'1", 173 lbs.; Farmingdale, NY. A world-class hurdler who didn't come out for football until junior year because of concentration on preparing for '80 Olympics. But U.S. boycott of Olympics caused Paterno to invite him to join the team in fall of '80; declined at first but won starter role, and despite ankle injury in third game of season against Nebraska, he came back the next week to intercept two passes, setting up Herb Menhardt FGs of 27 and 34 yards that beat Missouri, 29-21; had two more interceptions that year to lead team (with four). Always seemed to play his best against Miami (and maybe that's why Dolphins later drafted him). Perhaps his best game of '80 was in 27-12 win over Miami at Beaver Stadium when he had one interception, knocked down two other pass attempts and made six tackles. Played one of his finest games in 38-7 Homecoming win over Boston College, intercepting one pass and covering receivers so well the pass-happy BC QBs could complete just nine of 35 passes and only one completion in first three quarters. Had another fine but frustrating game at Miami in '81 with a 63-yard return of an interception, a fumble recovery, two batted down passes and four tackles but also gave up a TD when he slipped as he was making a tackle in disappointing 17-14 loss. So good at pass coverage from his corner position that he often was assigned to the opponent's best receiver and forced opposing QBs to throw away from him. Had an outstanding senior season in helping team rank number three in country and stop USC and Heisman Trophy winner Marcus Allen in '82 Fiesta Bowl. Played in '82 Senior Bowl. Third choice of Miami in '82 and starred with Dolphins defense through '91 season. Played in '83 and '85 Super Bowls. Now a sales manager living in Jacksonville, FL.

LASLAVIC, JIM. 1970-71-72. LB & DE, 6'2", 230 lbs.; Etna, PA. Another graduate of "Linebacker U" and fine defensive player, who was willing to play whatever position Paterno desired, but found his niche at Inside LB in senior year on the surprise team that won 10 straight after opening loss and played Oklahoma in Sugar Bowl. Third on team in tackles that year with 105. Played one of his best games of the year in 46-16 win over Maryland with nearly a dozen tackles and an interception. A backup LB as soph he switched to DE in junior year and became starter. Was one of stars in the 30-6 win over Texas in the "breakthrough" Cotton Bowl game of '72, making 10 tackles in first half when Longhorns got their only points on two FGs and finished game with 12 tackles, finishing second to Bruce Bannon as Outstanding Defensive Player-of-the-Game. Was number two choice of Detroit in '73 and played for Lions until '78, when he was traded to San Diego where he played through '82 season before retiring. Started sportscasting while still playing pro football and is now a full-time broadcaster living in Coronado, CA.

LENKAITIS, BILL. 1965-66-67. C, OT, OG, 6'2", 245 lbs.; Youngstown, OH. One of the transition players from the Engle to Paterno era and never received the credit he was due while in college, but became well known as an All-Pro lineman in a 15-year NFL career. Involved in perhaps the most momentous and controversial play of the Paterno era in '67 Gator Bowl against Florida State: with State leading by a surprising 17-0 score early in second half and a fourth-and-inches at

about the PSU 15-yard line, Paterno called for a daring QB sneak by Tom Sherman over Lenkaitis; to this day both Sherman and Lenkaitis swear Sherman was a foot past the scrimmage line when Sherman was pulled back under the pile by FSU players, and the official misplaced the ball; FS was given ball and scored two plays later, eventually holding on for 17-17 tie; but Paterno's gamble captured the imagination of the sportswriters and made him an overnight coaching sensation. Lenkaitis was co-captain and starting center of that '67 team that turned around Paterno's coaching career, when it won last seven games of season and became Paterno's first bowl team. As versatile an offensive lineman as there was with excellent strength, size and speed and a great pass protector. Began career on defense as MG for frosh team in '64 but was switched by Engle to C in pre-season of soph year and by midseason was a starter at OT. Began junior year under Paterno as starter at OT and was set to play DE if needed but was back at C by third game and stayed there for rest of career. Made All-East as senior. Played in '68 Hula Bowl. Second pick of San Diego in '68 draft and played with Chargers from '68-'70 before joining New England where he had a long career as a guard and center, and retired after the '81 season. Went to dental school while playing pro ball and is now a full time dentist living in Canton, MA.

Leonard, Bill ("The Toe"). 1950-51-52. HB & PK, 6'1", 190 lbs.; State College, PA. One of the few players from State College High School to become a Penn State regular. Became a part-time starter in his soph year and turned into a fine defensive back and placekicker. Known for his tough style of play and his speed and quickness. One of the biggest plays of his career came as a soph against heavily favored Pitt in a game postponed one week by the famous Thanksgiving Snow of '50 and played at Forbes Field; with just six minutes gone in the game, he intercepted a pass by Bobby Bestwick and raced down the sidelines 65 yards for State's first touchdown; also intercepted pass with two minutes left in game and ran it back 28 yards to Pitt 16 to take pressure off defense as State won, 21-20. His three interceptions (and 94 yards) in '50 tied him with Chan Johnson for team leadership. A backup HB in junior and senior years but the main PK in '52 as he hit on three FGs and 21-of-23 PATs (including 18 in a row) to lead the team in scoring with 27 points and earn nickname from his teammates of "The Toe." Kicked his first FG (for 15 yards) in a "clutch" situation in fourth QT at Nebraska in '51 that gave State a 9-7 lead and then made key interception late in game at PSU 37-yard line that helped preserve 15-7 win. In final game of career, he kicked a 12-yard FG & two PATs in surprising 17-0 win over arch rival Pitt; it was his 18th PAT in a row and 19th in 21 attempts that year. Played in '52 Blue-Gray Game. Turned to coaching after graduation and was head coach at State College High for many years and a realtor in State College. Deceased.

LIGHTNER, JOE. 1920-21. HB & PK, 5'11", 175 lbs.; Harrisburg, PA. One of the outstanding running stars of his era but often overlooked because he played in the backfield at the same time as First-Team All-American's Glenn Killinger, Charlie Way and "Lighthorse Harry" Wilson. A two-year starter at RH and the PK on the back-to-back unbeaten teams that were probably State's best until the Higgins' '48 Cotton Bowl team. Second-Team All-American in '21 along with teammates guard Joe Bedenk and end Stan McCollum on team that was last unbeaten one (8-0-2) for 26 years. He was more like the modern day FB than a HB. Didn't have the speed of his better known teammates but was great at picking up short yardage in crucial situations and was a fine blocker for his fellow running backs. He was known for his "fake double pass" in which he faked once or twice to other runners and then either ran up the middle himself or passed the ball. Never played football in high school and went practically unnoticed on scrub team for two years before head coach Bezdek and his assistant Harlow turned him into a star. In the big 14-7 win at Dartmouth in '20 he scored the winning TD while subbing for Way. One of his best games was in the classic 21-21 tie at powerful Harvard in midseason of '21, when he scored all the points with three TDs , including one on a 60-yard run, and kicked all the extra points. Missed first extra point of year in late season game against Navy in drizzling rain at Franklin Field but came back to score winning TD and PAT in narrow 13-7 win. Played LF on baseball team that won 20 straight games before first loss and had a 31-game winning streak over two years (that is still PSU record) and was a fine number five batter. Deceased.

LINSZ, GEORGE ("LUCY"). 1887-88-89. QB & E, 5'6", 152 lbs.; Philadelphia, PA. Considered "the father of Penn State football." He owned the football and, as an 18-year-old frosh, he and Charles (Charlie) Hildebrand organized the first official Penn State football team in 1887. Called "Lucy" by his teammates. Captain of '87 and '88 team and QB in '87. Smallest member of the team. Led team to 54-0 win over Bucknell in State's first official game at Lewisburg on Nov. 12, 1887. Scored three TDs (worth four points then) in State's first home victory, 24-0, over Bucknell on lawn in front of Old Main, Nov. 19, 1887. Also played in worst football defeat of all-time, 106-0, against Lehigh, Nov. 13. 1889, in Bethlehem. Graduated in 1892 and later formally changed name to George Lins. Lived most of his life in Philadelphia area. Deceased.

LISKE, PETE. 1961-62-63. QB & P, 6'2", 190 lbs.; Plainfield, NJ. Another in the long list of fine quarterbacks produced by Paterno when he was an assistant under Engle. Selected on the All-Time Penn State team in 1967 by *Pittsburgh Press* sports editor Chet Smith, who covered Nittany Lion football for more than a half century. Compared to Milt Plum as an all-around passer, ball handler, runner and defensive back. Very smart and "cool" under pressure. Two-year starter as junior and senior and led teams to 8-2 and 7-3 records: '62 team rated ninth by both AP & UPI and went to Gator Bowl; '63 team rated 10th by AP but missed bowl bid, when Pitt game was postponed one week because of assassination of President Kennedy. Many of the passing records he set have since been broken but he still owns the record for percentage of passes completed in one game with 91.7% in 17-7 opening season win at Oregon in '63. His career interception percentage of 2.82% was the record for 30 years until broken by John Sacca in '93 and his 2.47% interception percentage in '62 is sixth best for one season. Sixth in career passing efficiency with 127.71 and fifth in career TD pass efficiency with 6.76 TDs. Eighth in career TD passes with 24 and fourth in one season TD pass percentage at 7.41%. Until John Hufnagel came along a decade later, Liske was all-time passing leader with 1,037 yards and 12 TDs on 91-of-162 attempts and only four interceptions in '62 and 1,117 yards and 10 TDs on 87 of 161 attempts and five interceptions in '63. Also total offense leader in '62 & '63. Got his first start as soph in third game of season after injury to Galen Hall week before and led team to 32-0 win over BU. Usually subbed for Hall at defense on first unit and ran second unit as QB; also was best

punter that year, leading team with 24 punts for 880 yards for an average of 36.7 per punt and no blocked kicks. Was an outstanding defensive back. Sportswriters and coaches cited him for his outstanding defensive play in '61 Gator Bowl win over Georgia Tech, when he intercepted one pass and batted down another; his punting during game also credited with helping in 31-15 victory. Played one of his finest all-around "clutch" games as junior in Homecoming game against Syracuse in '62 when his tackle halted a two-point conversion attempt as Syracuse took 19-14 lead and then he passed and ran team to winning TD in 21-19 win. Perhaps his best game ever was the 17-7 opening season win over Oregon in '63, when he completed 11-of-12 passes for 113 yards and two TDs of eight and 41 yards; he followed up the next week by completing a record 19 passes on 27 attempts for 176 yards, including a sensational 52-yard TD by Junior Powell in 17-14 win over UCLA. Also had good game in 10-7 "upset" over Ohio State at Columbus in '63, when his play calling and faking befuddled the Buckeyes as he passed for one TD and set up the winning FG with other passes and made several key tackles on defense. Was All-East that year. Played in '63 East-West Shrine game and '64 Hula Bowl. Drafted as "redshirt" during senior year by NFL Philadelphia Eagles (10th) and AFL New York Titans (15th); spent 12 years in pro football as either a QB or DB with the Jets ('64), Calgary ('65-'67) of the Canadian Football League— where he was the CFL's Most Valuable Player in '67— Denver ('69-'70) and Philadelphia Eagles ('71-'72) before turning to coaching and athletic administration. Now the Athletic Director at the University of Toledo and lives in Holland, OH.

LUCAS, RICHIE. 1957-58-59. QB & P, 6'1", 185 lbs.; Glassport, PA. One of the most exciting players in State history and a triple-threat on both offense and defense. Won the Maxwell Award as "the outstanding player in collegiate football" in '59 and finished second to LSU's Billy Cannon for the Heisman Trophy. He could run, pass and kick as well as he could tackle and intercept passes. He called his own plays on offense and had a sixth sense for knowing where the ball was on defense. A consensus All-American as a senior, when chosen by UPI, Football Coaches, Football Writers, The Sporting News, NEA, Central Press Association, Hearst Syndicate and others. One of 14 State players and three coaches selected for the National Football Foundation College Football Hall of Fame, inducted in '86. Chosen on the All-Time Penn State team in 1967 by *Pittsburgh Press* sports editor Chet Smith, who covered Nittany Lion football for more than a half century. The only QB in the last 50 years to lead the team in rushing, when he scrambled for 325 yards and six TDs on 99 rushes and a 3.3 per carry average in '59. Engle called Lucas "the modern version of the old triple threat player. He runs, passes, punts blocks, holds the ball on extra point attempts and is an excellent defensive player both against running and passing....he's the complete man, the player who does it all." Paterno says Lucas was the best running quarterback State ever had during his time on campus. Paterno called him "a tremendous leader, a clever faker and a very, very fine ball handler." The media gave him the nickname "Riverboat Richie" because he was daring and not afraid to take chances. He made things happen. He was also tough and worked in the steel mills during the summers. Led team to its first bowl game in 12 years in '59 with a 9-2 record and 11th ranking by AP; was leading rusher (54 yards on nine carries) and passer (one-for-four and 23 yards) in 7-0 win over Alabama in first Liberty Bowl, although he missed more than half the game with an injury. His performance in the '59 season opener at Missouri was a preview of the spectacular All-American year ahead; he hit on 10-of-11 passes for 154 yards and a 52-yard TD and was game's leading rusher with 48 yards on eight carries in 19-8 victory. Four weeks later he led team to first win over Army in 60 years with his passing and running, scoring both TDs in 17-11 victory at West Point. Played one of his finest games in a losing cause that year in the great battle of unbeatens at Beaver Stadium between 7-0 State and 6-0 Syracuse and was particularly outstanding on defense as Syracuse won 20-18 and went on to win National Championship. A HB in high school who Engle and Paterno spotted while watching film of an opposing team's QB and were impressed by the running and defensive prowess of Lucas. He was switched to QB in his frosh year and improved in his passing from year to year. Became a starter as a soph in sixth game of year when Al Jacks, then the leading passer in the East, was sidelined for season with shoulder injury and had great debut with first unit, hitting on 8-of-14 passes for two TDs and 102 yards and running for 48 yards on seven carries in leading 27-6 win over West Virginia; led '57 team to two victories with his spectacular running and passing; finished second in total offense that year with 492 yards, gaining 426 passing, including four TDs, and 66 running. Replaced Jacks as starter midway through junior season and never gave position back, leading team in passing and total offense with 483 yards passing on 36 of 80 attempts and three TDs and another 218 yards and six TDs on rushing. Repeated in senior year with total offense of 1,238 yards and 10 TDs, completing 58 of 117 passes for 913 yards and five TDs. Led defensive team in interceptions as senior with five for 114 yards. Punted for three years and was punting leader in soph and junior years (with 21 punts for 750 yards and a 35.7 average in '57 and 29 punts for 1,083 yards and a 37.3 average in '58); also punted 20 times for a 34.0 per punt average in senior year and never had a punt attempt blocked. Still holds one passing record (tied by Bob Parsons and Todd Blackledge) and it is a dubious one—most interceptions in one game, with four thrown in '59 in 20-9 win over Illinois at Cleveland's Municipal Stadium. Played in '60 Hula Bowl. Number one choice of NFL Washington Redskins and AFL Buffalo Bills in '60 and played two years mostly as a defensive back before an injury ended his professional career. He returned to Penn State to work in the Continuing Education Department, then joined the athletic administration in '63, and became an assistant athletic director in '66. Most recently had been made responsible for all male sports teams except football and basketball. Retired in the spring of '98 and lives in State College.

MADERA, RAGS. 1921. T, 6'3", 197 lbs.; Pittsburgh. One of the outstanding interior linemen of the early era who was picked on the All-Time Penn State team in 1950s and again in 1967 by *Pittsburgh Press* sports editor Chet Smith, who covered Nittany Lion football for more than a half century. He was considered one of the toughest linemen of his era even though his career was shortened by a near crippling injury. A sophomore star of the great unbeaten teams of '21. He suffered a broken thigh on the kickoff in the crucial Harvard game at midseason of '21 and was carried off the field, screaming at his team-

mates to "Fight 'em State;" schools tied 21-21 in what sportswriters have called "one of the greatest games ever played" as team went on to 8-0-2 record. But Madera never played football again and sportswriters of that era say he would have been an All-American and perhaps one of State's all-time greats. Despite football injury, he was still able to box and became one of the best collegiate boxers of his generation and was a heavyweight champ for coach Leo Houck. Captain of boxing team in senior year when he won the Intercollegiate Boxing Association unlimited championship and was selected an alternate member of the 1924 Olympic Team. Only lost one bout in three years. Deceased.

MAGINNIS, DICK. 1981-82-83. OG, 6'3", 250 lbs.; State College, PA. Well-liked member of State's first National Championship team who died unexpectedly of cancer in '89. His '82 teammates established an award in his memory in '89 that is presented to the outstanding offensive lineman "who exemplifies the spirit, dedication and commitment" which Maginnis always displayed on the playing field. Very good college G. Began career as a DT but moved to offense, and as soph he was prime backup to two of the best offensive guards who ever played at State, Mike Munchak and Sean Farrell. Teamed with co-captain and RG Pete Speros at LG in championship year, although he missed some games because of a pinched nerve in neck. Played one of his finest games in 24-0 win over West Virginia in '82 when his blocking was cited as a key offensive factor in the game. Starter for most of senior season but missed last four games and Aloha Bowl because of another injury. Deceased.

MAHONEY, ROGER. 1925-26-27. C & K, 6'1", 196 lbs.; Philadelphia, PA. One of the best centers in the East during the latter part of the Bezdek era and an all-around athlete. Started as soph after injury to captain Bas Gray. Was two-year starter as junior and senior and usually played the entire 60 minutes without substitution. Known for his outstanding play on defense. Good speed. A fine tackler. Also handled kickoffs for two years and was so good that his boots usually gave Lions good field position. His snaps in the Single-Wing formation were so precise that he was rarely responsible for any fumbles during his career. Had one of his best games in 9-0 win over Bucknell in '26 when sportswriters noted his blocking and tackling and all around performance. Played another of his finest games in a 13-13 tie with NYU in '27 that was considered a moral victory and upset by State; recovered a fumble in game that led to State's first touchdown. Also lettered in boxing, lacrosse, track and wrestling and was a fine heavyweight boxer for two years under Leo Houck. Deceased.

MALINAK, DON. 1951-52-53. E, 6'1", 190 lbs.; Steelton, PA. As fine a defensive end as State had in Engle's early years but also played both ways in an era of two-platoon football and was a "possession" receiver. Co-captain of '53 team that lost first two games, then came back to win six of next seven. Started first game late in soph season against Purdue and became regular in junior and senior season. Led team in receiving as soph with 14 receptions for 138 yards and two TDs but was used more as spot receiver and blocker in '52 & '53, as Jesse Arnelle, Jim Garrity and Jack Sherry shared most of the pass-catching. Played probably his finest all-around game in the last game of his career when he led all receivers with six catches for 38 yards and was cited for his defensive performance in helping State upset and shut out rival Pitt for second year in row, 17-0. Also played an excellent defensive game against Pitt the year before. Had one of his best defensive days in '52 West Virginia game, including an interception in early moments of contest that set up first TD and eventual 35-21 win. Played in '54 Senior Bowl. Retired and living in Lock Haven, PA.

MANCA, MASSIMO. 1982, 1985-86. PK, 5'10", 192 lbs.; Reno, NV. Has the distinction of being the only state player to be on both National Championship teams. As frosh in '82 he handled kickoffs entire season and also was the main FG and PAT kicker in first four games (five FGs & 19 PATs) while soph Nick Gancitano recovered from a strained muscle in his thigh. Then was the prime kicker on '86 championship team (14 FGs & 37 PATs) and kicked two PATs in 14-10 victory over Miami at '87 Fiesta Bowl. Holds record for kicking FGs in most consecutive games (13 in the '85 and '86 seasons), most points in one game (18 against Notre Dame in '85) and most attempts (six against West Virginia in '86). His five FGs—one for 50 yards—in 36-6 win over Notre Dame in '85 ties with Brian Franco as most FGs ever in one game. Also kicked four FGs three times: as a frosh in 39-31 win over Maryland, in '85 in 19-17 win over Alabama and again in '86 game against West Virginia, which may have been his finest day ever when he booted FGs of 42, 37, 22 and 27 yards and a PAT in 19-0 win on Mountaineer Field. Made perhaps his most important FGs against Maryland; his 46-yarder with five minutes left in the '85 game gave the Lions a 20-18 victory and his 36-yard boot in the '86 contest provided the margin in 17-15 victory. Third in all-time FGs for a career (40 on 59 attempts) behind Craig Fayak and Brett Conway and second for season (21 of 26 in '85) behind Matt Bahr. Also third in longest FGs with 53-yard boot against Notre Dame in '85 and had two others of 50 yards. Fifth in all-time scoring with 206 points on 40 FGs and 86 PATs and 10th in one-season scoring with 91 points on 21 FGs and 28 PATs in '85. Never missed an extra point in either '85 or '86, hitting on 65 straight. Born and raised in Italy and learned to play football in high school after his family moved to Reno, when his father became a teacher at the University of Nevada. Used '83 as "redshirt" season and returned in soph year to handle KOs again and back up Gancitano before taking over in '85 & '86. Signed as free agent and played one year in NFL with Cincinnati. Now a sales representative in Easthampton, NJ.

MANOA, TIM. 1983-84-85-86. DE & FB, 6'0 ½", 227 lbs.; Pittsburgh, PA. Among the top 30 all-time career ground gainers with 1,098 yards and five TDs on 223 carries. Teamed with Steve Smith in senior year for a great one-two FB combination that helped unbeaten State win its second National Championship in '87 Fiesta Bowl; he rushed for 36 yards on eight carries and caught one pass for 12 yards in that game. Scored only State TD in national title game with Oklahoma the previous year in '86 Orange Bowl. He was the Player-of-the-Game in '85 31-0 victory over Pitt that climaxed an unbeaten regular season; he gained 91 yards on seven carries and scored two TDs, including one on a 60-yard draw play in the first QT that was the longest run of his career. Began career as DE and saw a lot of playing time as a prime backup in '83. Switched to FB in spring of '84 and from soph year on he and Smith were the team's FBs with Smith usually starting but Manoa playing equally. Had more speed than Smith and had more runs for big yardage. Had one of best running days in '85, when he was named Player-of-the-Game in 17-10 win over E. Carolina, as he was leading rusher with 73 yards on nine carries including a 27-yarder

to the EC 10-yard line in the first QT that set up State's initial TD. In '86 championship year he was usually the number two rusher behind D. J. Dozier, and had one of his finest running days in the opening season win over Temple with 89 yards on six carries and a 51-yard run that set up a TD in 46-15 rout. In 42-3 win over Syracuse he gained 96 yards (on 12 carries) and scored TDs on runs of 11 and three yards, and in big 23-3 win over Alabama it was his pass receiving (two catches for 31 yards) and running (43 yards on 11 carries) that helped carry the day. Played in '87 Hula and Senior Bowls. Third round choice of Cleveland in '87 and had solid pro career with Browns ('87-'90) and Indianapolis ('91) before leaving pro ball. Now a sports agent working out of Cleveland, OH.

MARKOVICH, MARK. 1971-72-73. OT & OG, 6'5", 241 lbs.; Latrobe, PA. Another fine "scholar-athlete" who was a Second-Team All-American in '73. Academic All-American in '73 and winner of a prestigious National Football Foundation and College Football Hall of Fame fellowship in '73 and an NCAA postgraduate scholarship in '74. One of the outstanding offensive linemen in Paterno's early years who played a big part in opening holes for his roommate and '73 Heisman Trophy winner, John Cappelletti. Made one of the classic statements about Cappelletti after Cappy had run for four TDs and 130 yards in 62-14 win over West Virginia when he told sportswriters, "We knock people down at the line and Cappy comes through and knocks them down again." Co-Captain (along with All-Americans Cappelletti, Randy Crowder and Ed O'Neil) of perhaps the most neglected State team in history—the powerhouse unbeaten '73 squad that defeated LSU in Orange Bowl, 16-9, but only finished fifth in AP & UPI polls. Also centered on placekicks. Played primarily as backup OT and sometimes starter in soph year but switched to OG and started as junior and senior. Played in '74 Senior Bowl. Number two pick of San Diego in '74 and played two years with Chargers and four years with Detroit Lions. Attended graduate school at San Diego State while playing for Chargers and is now the president of a company and living in Peoria, IL.

MASCIANTONIO, CARMEN. 1982-83-84. LB, 6'2", 224 lbs.; Jeannette, PA. Epitomizes the true "scholar-athlete of the Paterno era, for he never had the special ability to make pro football a long career. Graduated with a 3.54 in Chemical Engineering and was an Academic All-American in '84. Winner of prestigious National Football Foundation and College Football Hall of Fame fellowship in '84. A good college football player who gave his all, despite being a starter in one of Paterno's "down" periods. A backup on the '82 National Championship team but missed the last part of the season with an injury. Came back to start at ILB in '83 and on hard luck '84 team, when he was Captain of the defense. Had a fine game in PSU's first regular season win over Alabama, 34-28, in '83, including a tipped pass that frosh Shane Conlan intercepted to set up a TD. Played one of his finest games in '84 Aloha Bowl win over Washington, 13-10, when he led team with 14 tackles (tying Scott Radecic) and a deflected pass. Honored in '84 with the Ridge Riley Award given to a senior for "sportsmanship, scholarship, leadership and friendship." Now a district sales manager in Center Valley, PA.

MASELLA, BRIAN. 1972-73-74. P & TE, 6'1", 212 lbs., Bordentown, NJ. One of the best punters in school history who was at his best under pressure. In '74, Paterno said Masella and placekicker

Chris Bahr were the "best kicking" team in PSU's history. Also was backup TE but came along at the same time as one of Paterno's best, Dan Natale. Still ranks 11th in career punting with 38-yard average on 159 punts and never had one blocked. Had his finest year in '74 when kicking game was vital for team to get field position because of run oriented offense; had 56 boots for 2,201 yards, averaging 39.3 per kick. Consistently kicked high to allow good coverage and in '74 opponents averaged just 2.7 yards per return. That helped team post 10-2 record and win over Baylor in Cotton Bowl. His punting also was major factor in helping '73 team become first in school history to win 12 games, including Orange Bowl, but was snubbed by pollsters. Had one of his finest games in '73 Sugar Bowl when PSU offense was crippled by illness to John Cappelletti and Masella's punting (10 punts averaging 42.9 yards) helped in maintaining good defensive field position. Also in soph year was a third string FB and gained 38 yards on seven carries before being switched to TE in spring practice of '73. Also lettered in baseball and swimming. Now a teacher and special assistant in Fairview, NJ.

MAUTHE, JAMES LESTER (PETE). 1909-10-11-12. HB, FB, PK & P, 6'0", 165 lbs. Turkey City, PA. One of the first all-around offensive and defensive backs who helped bring State a national reputation. Captain of the first great State team, the unbeaten and untied '12 squad, which outscored opponents 285-to-6. Selected by Walter Camp as Third-Team All-American in '13, when any recognition by Camp was considered an outstanding achievement. Became first State player ever inducted into the National Football Foundation College Football Hall of Fame in '57. Picked on the All-Time Penn State team in 1950s and again in 1967 by *Pittsburgh Press* sports editor Chet Smith, who covered Nittany Lion football for more than a half century. Many of the records he set held up for six decades. Remarkably, he never played in a losing game in his career (but missed much of '10 season). Part of State's first great recruiting class entering in '09 that included Dex Very— another future member of the Hall of Fame. Combined with Very to be State's first great passing-receiving combination in an era when passing was restricted and everyone in the backfield passed. Most effective as a long passer. In senior year he scored 119 points (and 11 TDs) in eight-game season, which is still fourth most points in all-time seasonal scoring records behind Lydell Mitchell, Ki-Jana Carter and Curtis Enis. Also had 710 yards rushing that year. Kicked 51-yard FG in 38-0 win over Pitt in '12 for a record that was not broken until '75 by Chris Bahr. His eight FGs in '12 was school record for 58 years, and he is still one of only a handful of players to kick three FGs in a game. He did it in 30-0 win over Washington & Jefferson. Known as a tough man mentally and physically and a hard hitter on defense who saved many touchdowns with his tackling. Also known as a great blocker while running interference for teammates such as Shorty Miller (see below). Good punter but occasionally inconsistent. Was a starter from the opening game of his frosh season (on team that was only second one to go unbeaten) and immediately caught fancy of fans and sportswriters. Broke ankle in second game of soph season against Carnegie Tech and missed rest of the year. Came back to start at FB in junior and senior years and never lost another game. Had one of his best games as junior in 3-0 win over Pitt, when he kicked a 35-yard FG for only points and was cited for his running and tackling. That was the prelude to his senior year. Even though banged up part of the year, he had several fine games. In last home game of career, he scored 23 points

on two TDs, a 46-yard FG and eight PATs in 71-0 rout of Villanova. Played one of his finest games in the great (and controversial) 37-0 win over Ohio State in Columbus that was the first meeting ever between the two teams; his 41-yard FG early in game ignited the victory and he later scored two TDs and kicked four extra points before OSU stalked off field before game had officially ended. Then climaxed career with a passing, kicking, running and tackling demonstration that helped demolish Pitt, 37-0, scoring all of State's 17 first Half points and throwing a 60-yard "bomb" that set up another TD. Graduated in metallurgy and eventually became president and chairman of Youngstown Sheet & Tube Co. Served on Penn State's Board of Trustees until his death in '67 at 76.

MAUTI, RICH. 1975-76. TB, WR & KR, 6'0", 180 lbs.; East Meadow Ridge, NY. Played on teams that were not filled with many stars and were overachievers, and, thus, he didn't get as much recognition as others who played his position. Transferred from Nassau Community College but was held back by a severe knee injury in '73 that was so bad doctors did not think he would play again. Came back in '74 after being injured in preseason practice and saw limited playing time, but made sensational debut in 10th game of season against Ohio University by running opening KO back 68 yards to set up a 26-yard TD drive in 35-16 romp. Played at TB & WR in '75 and became team's prime kick returner and led in kickoff and punt returns. On his first KO return in the opening game of the '75 season against Temple, he took the ball on the goal line and went all the way untouched for a TD; it was the only kicking TD return of his career, but the run ties him with Roger Kochman for State's second longest return. He had seven other returns that year for another 124 yards and the next year he had 13 returns for 217 yards (and a 16.7 yards average). Also led in punt returns as a senior with 17 for 208 yards and a 12.2 yards average. Had one of his best games as a receiver in 30-10 win at Iowa in '75 and scored a 70-yard TD with a picture-perfect reception that he took in full stride on his fingertips just behind the Iowa defensive back; the TD thrown on a pass from QB John Andress still ranks among the longest ever in State records. Also had fine running game in 34-14 win over Stanford in '75, when he scored two TDs and had 58 yards rushing on 16 carries from TB position. Was an All-American in lacrosse in '74. Signed as a free agent by New Orleans and had a fine seven-year career with the Saints and one year with Washington before retiring. Now working as a marketing manager in Mandeville, LA.

MCBATH, MIKE. 1965-66-67. DT, 6'4", 240 lbs.; Woodbury, NJ. One of the fine defensive linemen in the transition years between Engle and Paterno. Was a three-year starter at DT and occasionally filled in at OT. Began career as standout OL on frosh team but Paterno said he was needed more on defense. Was tough and aggressive with good speed, and overcame a serious asthma condition that occasionally forced him to the sidelines. An excellent pass rusher. Teammates said he was "happy-go-lucky" and good natured and they nicknamed him "Pig Pen." Teamed with DT Dave Rowe for a outstanding one-two defensive line combination on Paterno's first team but because of the 5-5 record they were both overlooked in post-season honors. Played a major leadership and inspirational role in '67 when Paterno shook up the team in second game at Miami and replaced seniors with such sophs as Steve Smear and Jim Kates; McBath was credited with helping to solidify the young defense that helped turn around the season and Paterno's career. Never has been given credit for one of the outstanding plays in PSU history when he submarined and stuffed line to help Kates and Denny Onkotz stop North Carolina State's Tony Barchuk at the goal line on a fourth-and-one near the end of the game to preserve a 13-8 upset over then number three NC State in '67 that made the college football world first take notice of a Paterno team. Had started in every game since sophomore year (28) when freak knee injury coming off field after the NC State game sidelined him for last two games of '67. Made 42 tackles and 31 assists in senior year and made second Team All-East. Played in '68 Senior bowl; drafted 5th by Buffalo Bills in '68 and had fine career at DE until retiring after '72 season. Now a vice-president and stockbroker of investment company in Orlando, FL, and owner of an Arena Football League team.

MCCASKEY, WALTER ("BULL"). 1892-93-94-95. QB & HB, 5'6", 125 lbs.; Lancaster, PA.. One of the little known stars of the early teams. Overshadowed by such standouts as kicking great Charlie Atherton and Charlie Hildebrand (one of the "fathers" of State football) and played on three teams ('92-'94) that only lost two games and tied once while winning 15. Captain his senior year when team went 2-2-3 but held three of the toughest teams in the country to ties—Cornell, 0-0, Washington & Jefferson, 6-6, and Western Reserve, 8-8. QB of '94 team that opened the season with back-to-back shutouts, 60-0 over Gettysburg and 72-0 over Lafayette, the highest scores recorded by a State team until 1905. Attended West Point after graduating from State. Returned to State in 1930s as a Colonel and commandant of the Department of Military Science and Tactics. Deceased.

MCCLEARY, E. H. ("BULL"). 1906-07-08-09. HB, PK & P, 5'10 ½", 195 lbs.; Charleroi, PA. Picked to All-Time Penn State team on 40th anniversary of State football in '27 by *New York Sun* sportswriter George Trevor, who wrote that McCleary "was a demon on straight smashes or thrusts off tackle. A lethal straight arm, combined with a fadeaway pivot , made it almost impossible for a single tackler to stop him. He packed a tremendous drive that carried him ahead, even when thrown off his feet. An exceptional defensive man...could drop-kick accurately, and lead interference." Credited with 13 TDs in '07 10-game season, which was the record for decades, and tied by "Light Horse" Harry Wilson, Lenny Moore and Harry Robb, before broken by Charlie Pittman in '68. In rookie season of '06, his 35-yard FG placement in a driving rainstorm were the only points in State's first victory ever over the powerful Carlisle Indians, 4-0. In his senior year, his clutch play in two games preserved the school's first unbeaten season in 15 years (5-0-2): in midseason game against Penn, he blocked a last minute FG attempt to maintain 3-3 tie; and, in final game of year on Thanksgiving Day at new Forbes Field in Pittsburgh, he scored the only TD and then blocked a Pitt FG in the closing minutes to preserve a 5-0 win. Captain in junior year of '08 team that had 5-5 record but beat Pitt, 12-6. Member of the great "all freshman" backfield in '06 on team that had best record in history up to that time, 8-1-1. Stayed around area after graduation to help coach the '10 team and then was given official title as "head coach" by administration in '11 when Bill Hollenback returned as "advisory coach," but it was strictly because of "campus politics." Although '11 team produced the best record ever up to then with eight wins and a scoreless tie with Navy, Hollenback was the "hands-on" coach and credited for the great season. The next year Hollenback officially replaced McCleary. Deceased.

MCCLOSKEY, MIKE. 1979-80-81-82. TE, 6'5", 240 lbs.; Philadelphia, PA. May not be as well known as other TEs but had a significant role in his senior year on National Championship team of '82. Those who saw it at Beaver Stadium or on national TV will never forget his dramatic "controversial" catch "in bounds" at the two-yard line in the waning moments that helped beat Nebraska, 27-24, and keep State unbeaten and in the championship hunt. It was the reception of his career and came near the end of a 65-yard drive in the last 78 seconds with State trailing, 24-21: with less than 12 seconds remaining at the Nebraska 15-yard line, Todd Blackledge threw to McCloskey dashing down the left sideline; he grabbed the ball at the two going out of bounds and although the officials ruled he was in bounds when he caught the pass, TV replays showed he did not get a foot inside the line in time; it didn't matter, State scored on the next play on near impossible reception by his backup TE Kirk Bowman to win the game. He had 17 other receptions that year and one TD but none ever matched "the catch" against Nebraska. In the national title win over Georgia in Sugar Bowl, he caught three passes for 53 yards, including a 33-yard reception that helped set up the first TD and a 13-yarder that set up a FG. Like a lot of TEs in the Paterno era he was a fine blocker and his blocking is credited with helping Curt Warner become an All-American. Broke into lineup as frosh in the "tight end-wingback set" when Paterno used three TEs to beef up the running attack. A backup for his first three years, who started a couple of games as junior because of injury, but got his chance as senior and made the most of it. Played in Japan Bowl in '83; fourth round choice of Houston in '83 and played three years with Oilers and one year with Philadelphia before retiring. Presently a marketing vice president in Lower Gwynedd, PA.

MCCOLLUM, STAN. 1920-21. E, 5'11", 170 lbs.; Hometown unknown. One of the great receivers in school history but hardly known because he was surrounded by so many stars and passing was secondary to running in that era. Starting LE on two of the greatest teams in school history that had last back-to-back undefeated seasons until Paterno's '68-'69 teams. Second-Team All-American in '21, along with teammates guard Joe Bedenk and back Joe Lightner on team that was last unbeaten one (8-0-2) for 26 years. Two of his best games were the 21-21 tie at Harvard and 28-7 win over Georgia Tech at New York's Polo Grounds in '21, when he excited crowd by catching several passes on the "reverse throw" from All-American Glen Killinger. His greatest game was probably his last, when State played its first game ever on the West Coast, against Washington on Dec. 3, 1921: as 35,000 looked on, he caught 11 of State's 12 completed passes, including one for a TD from Glen Killinger in 21-7 win that clinched second straight unbeaten season. The 11 receptions that day was the unknown school record for single game receptions for 70 years. Selected to several All-East First Teams in '21. Tall and well built with "matinee idol" looks. Also was occasional starter at forward on basketball team. Deceased.

MCDUFFIE, OTIS JAMES ("O.J.") 1989, 1991-92. WR & KR, 5'11", 185 lbs.; Warrensville Heights, OH. A consensus All-American as a senior, when selected First-Team by AP, UPI, American Football Coaches, Football News, Walter Camp and others. Candidate for Heisman Trophy in '92 and had picture on cover of *Sports Illustrated*. A great receiver and kick return man. By the time he graduated, he had broken or tied 15 receiving, kick return or all-purpose records. Ran back more punts than any player and is leader in career returns (84), career yardage (1,059) and career TDs (three). Perhaps his most important punt return ever came in the '92 Fiesta Bowl against Tennessee: State was being badly outplayed and losing 17-7 with five minutes left in third QT, when O.J. ran back a punt 39 yards to the Tennessee 35-yard line that changed the momentum of the game; he then caught a 28-yard pass from Tony Sacca, setting up a three-yard Chip LaBarca TD reception that started State off on a romp of 35 unanswered points in the dramatic come-from-behind 42-17 win; he caught a total of four passes for 78 yards and a 37-yard TD and had 149 all-purpose yards, as he was selected the game's Most Valuable Offensive Player. One of his most memorable receptions was in the '91 Kickoff Classic against Georgia Tech when he made an acrobatic catch in the EZ for a 39-yard TD that helped spark a 34-22 victory. Still holds record for receiving yardage in one game with 212 yards (on 11 receptions for one TD) against Boston College in '92; also had 43 yards rushing and 24 in kick returns for 280 yard total that places him sixth on all-purpose yardage in a single game. Also has record for one season all-purpose yardage with 1,831 yards with 977 on receptions, 721 on kickoff and punt returns and 133 on rushing. Tied with Bobby Engram in receptions for one season (63 for 977 yards and nine TDs in '92). Second to Engram in career receptions (125) and one season yardage (977 in '92) and third to Engram and Kenny Jackson in career yardage (1,988). Had seven games in which he gained over 100 yards on pass receptions, including 111 against Stanford in '93 Blockbuster Bowl. Among top 10 in season and career punt return averages. One of his best all-around games was in 35-13 win over Notre Dame in '91, when he scored three TDs, including one on a spectacular 37-yard run off a flanker reverse, caught four passes for 2 TDs and picked up 20 yards on punt returns to be named ABC-TV's Most Valuable Player. Led team in punt returns in '89, '91 and '92; best year was as junior in '91, when he returned 33 punts for 358 yards and two TDs on returns of 55 yards against Rutgers and 60 yards against Maryland (tying him with Jimmy Cefalo for most punt return TDs in one season). His 84-yard return for a TD in 34-12 win at Syracuse in '89 is fifth best in history. Also led team in kickoff returns in senior year with 14 for 323 yards. He would have accumulated even more yardage and receptions, punt and kickoff returns if not for a knee sprain injury in the opening season game against Texas in '90 that sidelined him for the rest of the year. Co-captain in '92 and winner of Hall Award as outstanding senior player. Played in '93 Japan Bowl. First choice of Miami Dolphins in '93 NFL draft (25th player selected overall) and still playing wide receiver and punt returner for Dolphins.

MCILVEEN, HENRY ("IRISH"). 1902-03-04-05. HB, 6'0", 182 lbs.; Belfast, Ireland and Pittsburgh. Picked to All-Time Penn State team on 40th anniversary of State football in '27 by *New York Sun* sportswriter George Trevor, who called McIlveen a "crackerjack" runner. One of State's best all-around athletes of his generation. Had a "take no prisoners" attitude on both offense and defense and wasn't afraid to "mix it up" with opposing players. Combined with Carl Forkum, Andy Smith, Ed Whitworth and Ed Yeckley in '02 for one of the most potent running attacks in the country. Had one of his greatest games against Pitt in '02, scoring three TDs in 27-0 shutout. Played in shadow of Forkum most of career. Personal problems kept him at home in Pittsburgh most of '04 and '05, but in '04 he led running attack in last four games and set up winning TD in second half against big rival Dickinson with 35-yard punt return; also in that game he avenged an intentional

injury to QB Joe Saunders by retaliating in open field in front of referee and hit "culprit" so hard it knocked Dickinson player out of game, as State fans cheered wildly and referee smiled. Scored the only TD in 6-0 win over Pitt in '05, when he smashed over the goal with just six seconds left in first Half. Also a good left-handed pitcher for the baseball team and had short period in major leagues with Pittsburgh Pirates in '06 and New York Yankees in '06 and '08. Graduated with degree in mining in '08. Deceased.

MCMAHAN, JAY ("TINY"). 1921-22. RT, 6'7", 210 lbs.; Youngstown, Ohio. One of the star lineman of the great undefeated team of '21 and the '23 Rose Bowl team. Tallest man on State teams of that era, but his body was firm and muscular. Got his nickname from legendary newspaperman Damon Runyon, when McMahan was assigned as Runyon's escort while on campus to cover a State game. Was a backup T on the 7-0-2 '20 team and then the starting RT for next two years. Often had run-ins with Coach Bezdek in '21, who goaded McMahan because Bezdek didn't think Tiny could take punishment. Had one of his best games in the historic 21-21 tie at Harvard in '21, when credited with the lead blocks on Joe Lightner's three TDs. His blocked punt in second half of Gettysburg game set up a quick 20-yard TD and turned a 0-0 tie into a 24-0 win. Earned complete respect of Bezdek after recovering from potential career-ending neck injury while wrestling in winter of '22: injury was believed to be a broken neck, but a Youngstown doctor known as "Bonesetter" Reese helped repair the damage, and McMahan played entire senior year with a neck brace. In '22 Homecoming game against Middlebury, he scored the only TD of his career when he blocked a punt: teammate Joe Bedenk picked up the ball and ran 15 yards before fumbling; McMahan scooped up the ball and rambled rest of way for TD in 33-0 victory. Also was the star heavyweight wrestler in '21 and a track letterman. Was recruited by West Point at same time as his All-American teammate, "Light Horse" Harry Wilson, but turned down offer to attend academy after State graduation. Helped coach the '23 team, then went to work as laborer for National Tube, run by State's great Pete Mauthe, and eventually became an executive with the Steel Co. of Canada, and an internationally known expert on blast furnaces. Received the University's Distinguished Alumnus Award in 1975. Deceased.

MCQUEARY, MIKE ("BIG RED"). 1996-97. QB, 6'4", 222 lbs.; State College, PA. May have never reached his full potential because he waited patiently for four years before getting his chance to play as a regular in '97. Led team to a 9-3 record but season ended in a downer when State was clobbered by Michigan State, 49-14, in last regular season game and then lost to Florida in Citrus Bowl when team played without two critical offensive stars, Curtis Enis and Joe Jurevicius. Jurevicius was McQueary's favorite target since both entered PSU as frosh and they had one of the best passing combinations in the Big Ten in '97. With Jurevicius' doing much of the receiving, McQueary passed for 2,211 yards and 17 TDs, which is fifth best in State history for one season yardage and sixth best for touchdowns. He also set a new record for game yardage and total offense when he had 366 yards passing (and two TDs) and 370 total yards in opening season 34-12 win over Pitt and was named Big Ten Offensive Player-of-the-Week. He threw for three TDs in victories over Louisville, Illinois and Wisconsin and combined with Jurevicius for a 67-yard bomb against Louisville that was the longest TD throw of his career. One of his finest games was his last at Beaver Stadium when he completed 16-of-19 passes for 269 yards and three TDs in 35-10 win over Wisconsin win and was again named Big Ten Offensive Player-of-the-Week. May have played his best game ever in '96 when he came off bench in second half against Indiana with the Lions trailing by 10 points; he sparked a 48-26 win with what was then a career high of 9-of-19 pass completions for 184 yards and two TDs, including a 57-yard bomb to Jurevicius that was the turning point of the game. Easily recognized by his shocking red hair, he was the first State College HS player to start at QB for Paterno. However, he had to wait behind Kerry Collins and Wally Richards and saw only limited time in field. Although he didn't letter in '95, his first career TD pass against Rutgers that season was one of the most controversial of the Paterno era; the 42-yard toss to Chis Campbell in the closing minutes gave State a 59-34 lead and Paterno was challenged on the field after the game by Rutgers' coaches who accused him of "running up the score;" McQueary said Campbell was a secondary receiver but was so wide open he had to throw the ball. But the criticism so affected Paterno that he was distracted in preparing team for Wisconsin the next week and the Lions were upset. McQueary won Hall Award as "outstanding senior" in '97 and was elected Co-Captain at end of season but many PSU fans were sorry he didn't have one more year to show what he could really do. Signed as a free agent with the Oakland Raiders in '98.

MEHL, LANCE. 1977-78-79. LB 6'3 ½", 236 lbs.; Bellaire, OH. Another of the graduates of "Linebacker U." Paterno said Mehl was "as good an inside linebacker" as ever played at State. Named Second-Team All-American in senior year. He was overshadowed most of career by his more renown teammates Bruce Clark and Matt Millen but his laid back personality helped steady the defensive team. Led the team in tackles in both '78 (96 tackles with 46 solos and 50 shared) and '79 (99 with 68 solos and 31 shared). One of the best games he played was in '78 nationally televised 17-10 win over Pitt that preserved unbeaten season and sent team to '79 Sugar Bowl as number one team in country, when he was selected Outstanding Defensive Player-of-the-Game with six solo tackles, five assists, a deflected pass and a return of a pass interception for 55 yards. Played DE as frosh and didn't letter but moved to LB as soph and started in junior and senior years. Co-captain of '79 team which beat Tulane, 9-6, in defensive Liberty Bowl game; he had a great game in leading all tacklers with eight, including two sacks for 10 yards in losses. Led tacklers in most games that season and twice, against Texas A & M and Nebraska, he had 15 tackles. Played in '80 Hula Bowl; third draft choice of New York Jets in '80 and was a star linebacker with Jets until his retirement after the '87 season. Working in St. Clairsville, OH.

MENHARDT, HERB. 1978-79-80. PK, 6'0", 170 lbs.; Flourtown, PA. Another in the long-line of excellent place kickers. Made one of the greatest pressure kicks in State history in '78 with a 54-yard FG on the last play of the game that climaxed an 83-yard drive in 1:37 to give State a 9-7 win over North Carolina State. The FG is still the second longest on record, after Chris Bahr's three 55-yard FGs in '75. Later that year in '79 Liberty Bowl, his three FGs of 33, 27 and 20 yards were all the points needed in 9-6 victory over Tulane. Led team in scoring in '79 (70 points) & '80 (71 points) and never missed a PAT in 54 attempts, which is still the career record for accuracy. Also had 29

FGs in career. Seventh in career FGs and tied for seventh for most FGs in one season with 15 in '80. Was put on spot by Paterno in frosh year of '76 when inserted into game instead of Matt Bahr to attempt game-winning 20-yard field goal against Iowa; Menhardt shanked kick and Lions lost, 7-6. But that taught him a lesson and he later studied "performance enhancement and stress management" to help on the field. Played soccer in '76 & '77 and made Olympic tryouts in '79. Was second kicker behind Matt Bahr on '78 team that just missed national title but was prime kicker in junior and senior year. In '80 Fiesta Bowl he kicked a 38-yard FG and 4 PATs in 31-19 pasting of Ohio State. Played in '81 Senior Bowl. Lives in Flourtown, PA.

MICHAELS (MIKELONIS), AL. 1933-34. QB & P, 5'10", 158 lbs.; DuBois, PA. Better known to older Penn State fans as one of the best assistant coaches of his generation, but he was a two-year letterman in the early years of the Higgins era. Unfortunately, he played in the harmful de-emphasis period and on teams that had records of 2-5, 3-3-1 and 4-4. In '33, shared QB with Red O'Hora, then became the starter in senior year when O'Hora left school. Was a fine punter who did most of kicking in his years. Played one of his best games in near upset of Rose Bowl champion Columbia in '34, with his punting and passing, including a 24-yard pass that set up a TD and his extra point kick in 14-7 loss. Also led team to unexpected 6-6 tie with Penn in last game of '33 that prevented losing season. Became a graduate assistant in '35, then a full time assistant in '36. Considered a good scout of opposing teams and was credited with the 17-0 upset of Pitt in '52 that was one of the most satisfying victories of the Engle era. Stayed on with Higgins, Bedenk and Engle until '56, when he joined another ex-State man, Earle Edwards, at North Carolina State and coached against his alma mater in some great down-to-the-wire games. Was head coach of Wolfpack for one year, then became defensive coordinator under Lou Holtz. When NC State upset the Lions' Cotton-Bowl bound '75 team, 15-14, he was given the game ball. Deceased.

MICHALSKE, AUGUST ("GUS" or "Iron Mike"). 1923-24-25. G & FB, 6'0", 206 lbs.; Cleveland, OH. First PSU player ever selected to the Pro Football Hall of Fame ('64). Considered one of the all-time great guards at State. Picked on the All-Time Penn State team in 1950s and again in 1967 by *Pittsburgh Press* sports editor Chet Smith, who covered Nittany Lion football for more than a half century. Emerged as a star lineman as a soph, when teamed with senior captain Joe Bedenk to form one of the greatest guard combinations in collegiate football and helped make "Light Horse" Harry Wilson an All-American. Outstanding as lead guard on running plays. Hard tackler known for his "blitzing" techniques on defense. Nicknamed "Iron Mike" by his teammates. In junior year, he and linemates "Bas" Gray and Jules Prevost were better known nationally than any of the long-forgotten backs. He was so big and fast that he often moved to the backfield to run or pass and scored several touchdowns in junior and senior year. Switched full time to FB midway through senior season by coach Bezdek and was a crunching runner and accurate long-distance passer. Had his finest game at FB against Michigan State, when he scored both touchdowns in 13-6 victory. Played with New York Yankees pro teams in AFL ('26) and NFL ('27-'28) but had his best pro years at Green Bay ('29-'35, '37), where he was a member of three NFL championship teams ('29-'31) and was named All-NFL six times. After pro football, he coached football at Lafayette, St. Norbert, Iowa State, Baylor, Texas, Texas A&M and the Baltimore Colts before opening up a business in Tyler,TX, then retired to DePere, WI. Died in '83.

MILLEN, MATT. 1976-77-78-79. DL & LB, 6'1½", 255 lbs.; Hokendauqua, PA. One of the best defensive linemen ever at State. All-American and finalist in junior year for Lombardi Award as best lineman or linebacker in the country won by teammate Bruce Clark; made 54 tackles that year with nine sacks, blocking one punt and recovering two fumbles. Teamed with Clark for three years as one of the best defensive tackle combinations in college football and Paterno said they were even better than the Reid-Smear combo of '68-'69. They had mutual respect for each other and nicknamed themselves, "Salt & Pepper." Millen told sportswriters the only difference between he and Clark "is that I go crazy sometimes. Bruce keeps his cool." Often was in Paterno's "doghouse" because of his brash, head-strong, free-spirit attitude and they argued a lot on and off the field. Paterno never did like Millen's rowdy style of celebrating each good play he made with a leaping war dance. When Millen refused to complete two half-mile runs in the preseason of '79, Paterno stripped him of his captaincy and threw him off the team temporarily. Missed most of senior year because of ankle injury suffered at midseason and the team finished with a disappointing 8-4 record. Third in career sacks with 22; tied with Clark for most sacks in '77 season (six); and, tied with Bill Crummy for most interceptions in '76 season (three). In soph year he was named Outstanding Defensive Player-of-the-Game in '77 Fiesta Bowl, when he had 18 tackles as the defense held Arizona State to 90 yards rushing in a 42-30 Christmas Day victory. Had one of his most spectacular plays against West Virginia in '77, when he picked up a punt blocked by Randy Sidler two minutes into the game and scored his first TD in 49-28 win. Had a tremendous debut, breaking into the starting lineup along with Clark as a frosh linebackers against Army after Paterno shook-up the team following a 1-3 start; intercepted a pass on the second play of the game and returned it 13 yards to the Army eight-yard line and made 14 tackles to lead team. Moved to DT in soph year and teamed with Clark. Second round draft choice of Oakland in '80 and went on to great pro career with Raiders ('80-'88). San Francisco ('89-'90) and Washington ('91-'92); played in four Super Bowls (Raiders in '81 & '84, 49ers in '90 and Redskins in '92). Married former PSU gymnast Patty Spisak. Turned to sports broadcasting after the NFL and is now one of the leading pro football analysts in network television. Lives in Whitehall, PA.

MILLER, BRIAN. 1993-94-95-96. CB, 5'9", 186 lbs.; Donora, PA. Overcame serious personal behavior problems that threatened to halt his State career before it began to become a two-time All-Big 10. Started as a soph on the unbeaten Rose Bowl Champions and led team in interceptions (four). Perhaps the biggest play of his career was the diving interception at State's 23-yard line with less than 1:30 to play that stopped a Michigan drive and guaranteed 31-24 victory over Wolverines in '94 game that elevated team to number one in country. Led team in interceptions in '94 (four) and in '95 (five) when he was second in Big 10 in interceptions. Twice had two interceptions in a game, against Michigan State in '95 and Ohio State in '94. Tied with two others for fifth in career interceptions with 12. Very aggressive and a hard hitter who came through in the clutch. Senior year cut short after eight games by injury in mid-season but still had fine year with

three interceptions, 30 tackles and 10 deflected passes. Finished career with 115 solo tackles and 39 assists. Played in every game as a "redshirt" frosh and became starter the next year. Played in '97 Senior Bowl. Signed as free agent in NFL in '97 had been playing for the Tennessee Oilers.

MILLER, EUGENE ("SHORTY"). 1910-11-12-13. QB & KR, 5'5", 140 lbs.; Harrisburg, PA. One of State's early nationally known stars who set records that stood for decades. QB of the great '11 & '12 teams that were unbeaten. Named Third Team All-American in '12 by Walter Camp. One of only 14 Penn State players and three coaches in the National Football Foundation College Football Hall of Fame, inducted in '74. Picked on the All-Time Penn State team in 1950s and again in 1967 by *Pittsburgh Press* sports editor Chet Smith, who covered Nittany Lion football for more than a half century. His nickname was appropriate because he was so small but he was fast, stocky and tough and could shed tacklers with spinning, twisting and sidestepping; newspapers referred to him as the "Meteoric Midget." When he first showed up for practice as a frosh he looked too small to play but wound up as the starting QB for the next four years. His stunning 95-yard return of the opening kickoff for a TD against Penn in '11 is tied for fourth best KO return of all-time and he had a 32-yard TD run in the same game that led to first ever victory over then-powerful Penn, 22-6, at Franklin Field. Played one of finest games in 41-0 season-opening win over Carnegie Tech in '12, when he scored five TDs for 30 points which is still tied for the third best single game scoring record; his 250 rushing yards that day was the team record for 69 years, until broken by Curt Warner, and is still second on all-time single game list; yardage included a 78-yard TD that remains one of the top 10 longest runs in school history. In the controversial first game ever with "favored" Ohio State at Columbus in '12, he scored State's first two TDs early in first QT on runs of five and 30 yards and added a 40-yard TD later and another before frustrated OSU walked off field with six minutes left in game, as State won, 37-0. Missed only one game in career because of minor injury, and Coach Hollenback took him on scouting trip of Penn game that day; what he learned helped him run for 96 yards and pass to Dex Very for a six-yard TD in leading team to 14-0 win. His 1,397 all-purpose yards in '12 (801 rushing and 596 on kick returns) is 12th best in history. Was a great kick returner and averaged 17 yards on 35 punt returns for 396 yards in '13, which is still fourth on all-time punt return seasonal average list. Captain of '13 football and baseball teams. After graduation played professional football for the Massillon Tigers ('16, '17 & '19). Spent most of his life as a teacher, coach and administrator in the Harrisburg school system and was also highly respected as an official in college and professional football before his death on Sept. 20, 1966.

MILNE, BRIAN. 1993-94-95. FB, 6'3", 253 lbs.; Waterford, PA. An inspirational player who overcame cancer in high school to become a prototypical Paterno-type FB. A workhorse on the unbeaten '94 team who teamed at FB with normal starter Jon Witman to give that great offensive team a fine "full-house backfield" in short yardage situations. Played one of his finest games in the "clutch" in comeback win over Illinois that year, blocking for Ki-Jana Carter on runs and Kerry Collins in passing situations; scored three TDs; was especially effective in the outstanding 96-yard drive late in the fourth QT with State trailing, 31-28, and carried the ball the last nine yards, including the final two-yards over the middle for the TD that won the game; for that performance he was named State's Outstanding Player-of-the-Game. Had his best rushing day in his last game in PSU uniform, when he gained 82 yards on 12 carries in '96 Outback Bowl win over Auburn. Was third leading rusher on the '95 Rose Bowl team with 267 yards on 56 carries and his eight TDs on the ground was second only to Ki-Jana Carter. He also had 15 receptions for 78 yards that year, most of them in key situations. Also a world class discus and shot-put competitor who holds State record in discus and won NCAA discus title in '93. Is planning to tryout for Olympics in 2000. Played in '96 Hula Bowl. Drafted fourth by Indianapolis Colts in '96 but moved on to Cincinnati where he has become a starting FB and one of the best blockers on the team.

MILOT, RICH. 1977-78. LB, CB & RB, 6'3½", 214 lbs.; Coraopolis, PA. A late-blooming graduate of "Linebacker U." Position changes and injuries held him back for most of career. Made one of the biggest plays in final regular season game in '78 against Pitt with an interception late in fourth QT that led to Matt Bahr FG that sealed 17-10 come-from-behind win and sent number one Lions into National Championship game at '79 Sugar Bowl. Began career in '75 as a TB and, in eighth game of year against Army, he entered game in fourth QT as part of an all-frosh backfield featuring Chuck Fusina at QB. Moved to CB in '76 but still didn't letter. Finally switched to OLB in '77, where he became a starter senior year. Had one of biggest games in '78's 30-0 win over Kentucky, when he had five tackles, an interception and was awarded game ball. Seventh round choice of Washington in '79 and played with Redskins, until he retired after the '87 season; played with PSU teammate Larry Kubin in '83 and '84 Super Bowl; also played in '88 Super Bowl. Businessman in Haymaker, VA.

MITCHELL, LYDELL. 1969-70-71. HB, 6'0", 198 lbs.; Salem, NJ. One of the all-time great State runners who certainly was the best back on Paterno's early teams. A three-year starter and First-Team All-American in senior year when he also finished fifth in Heisman Trophy competition. He was so outstanding in '71 that in eight of 11 regular season games he went over 100 yards rushing and scored at least one TD in every game but one. Country's leading scorer that year with 174 points on 29 touchdowns, still the State one season records. At the time he set three NCAA records for TDs, TDs by rushing and most points per season and the 174 points is still fourth best in NCAA history. Only State player to score five TDs or more in two games, against Navy and Maryland in '71. Also holds the record for most TDs in a career (41) and consecutive games (seven), and three major State running records: most rushing yards in a season (1,567 yards on 254 carries in '71), most TDs in a season (26 in '71) and most TDs in a career (38). Fifth in career rushing yardage with 2,934 yards on 501 carries and among top 15 in single game rushing with 211 yards on 29 carries and two TDs against Iowa and 209 yards on 24 carries and five TDs against Maryland, both in '71. Won Red Worrell Award in spring practice of '71 as most improved player and went on to prove it in the fall. In senior year he had over 100 yards in eight of 11 regular season games, and his total of 15 games of more than 100 yards rushing is still third in records. His longest run of 71 yards for TD against Maryland as a soph is still among the team's all-time best. Led team in both total offense and ground gaining as junior and senior (rushing 751 yards on 134 carries as a junior) and his career total offense of 2,934 yards is 13th of all time. Also one of school's top 10 kickoff returners

and is seventh on all-time career return averages with 24.6 yards on 19 returns, team leader in '70 with 16 returns for 410 yards. Teamed with Franco Harris in leading Lions to 30-6 "breakthrough" win over Texas in '72 Cotton Bowl, when he gained 146 yards on 21 carries and scored first TD in second half that broke open the game; named Outstanding Offensive Player-of-the-Game. In 10-3 '70 Orange Bowl victory over Missouri, he scored only TD on a 28-yard pass reception and was leading pass receiver with five receptions for 81 yards. Three times in career he teamed with Harris for a "double" 100 yard game and in '69 against Boston College Mitchell, Harris and Charlie Pittman became just the second trio to get more than 100 yards each in a game. Played in '72 Hula Bowl. Drafted second by Baltimore in '72 and went on to great career with Colts ('72-'77), San Diego ('78-'79) and Los Angeles ('80). Now a public relations consultant and in business with teammate Harris, running a minority-owned meat packaging company out of Baltimore.

MITINGER, BOB. 1959-60-61. E, 6'2", 215 lbs.; Greensburg, PA. One of the great defensive linemen and a fine pass receiver and blocker in era of two-way players. First-Team All-American in senior year, when he became the 13th State player ever chosen to first team and only the third end in first 74 years of football. Selected on the All-Time Penn State team in 1967 by *Pittsburgh Press* sports editor Chet Smith, who covered Nittany Lion football for more than a half century. Basically a tight end on offense but in Rip Engle's Wing-T more passes were thrown to the backs and split ends. Made a big impression as soph when inserted to play with first team in the "game-of-the-year" against eventual National Champion Syracuse in battle of unbeatens at Beaver Field; recovered Andy Stynchula's critical blocked punt in fourth QT that gave State chance to tie game; he covered ball on one-yard line, Sam Sobczak scored the TD, but the two-point conversion failed and Syracuse went on to win, 20-18. Had one of his finest defensive games in 25-8 loss to Miami in Orange Bowl Stadium in '61, when he harassed and tackled Miami's popular QB George Mira so often the partisan Miami fans booed him all day; he belted Mira so hard that Mira left game at least three times; one Miami sportswriter referred to Mitinger that day as "a killer" who tackled ferociously" but another Miami writer said Mitinger's play was fair, legal and "brilliant." One long forgotten play in the '61 Syracuse game at Beaver Stadium best exemplifies Mitinger's style of play; in second QT with Syracuse threatening to score Mitinger literally threw off two blockers and nailed the great Ernie Davis for no gain as State went on to win, 14-0, holding Davis to 35 yards. Seemed to get even better defensively as '61 season progressed as he had outstanding games against Maryland, West Virginia, Pitt and Georgia Tech in Gator Bowl, usually fighting off two or three blockers to make tackles. Showed what type of receiver he was when he scored one of the few TDs of his career in 14-3 win over Pitt in '60; on a fourth-and-Goal situation at the Pitt three-yard line late in fourth QT of a close game, he made a fingertip catch in the right corner of the EZ on a pass from Dick Hoak for the final TD in a 14-3 win that put team into '60 Liberty Bowl. Became starting RE in junior year and never gave up position. One sportswriter wrote that he "blocks and tackles with the best and gives you the big defensive play when you need it most." In senior year he and Dave Robinson were the best pair of defensive ends in the country; after State beat California, Bears' coach Marv Levy called Mitinger "the best college football player in the United States." Played in '62 Hula Bowl. third draft choice of NFL

Washington and fifth round choice of AFL San Diego in '62 and signed with Chargers. Starting left LB for Chargers from '62 until mid-'66 when he was called up by Army to serve as an MP (and volunteer football coach) at West Point. Returned to Chargers for '68 but left pro football after that season. Went to law school while playing for the Chargers and is now an attorney in State College, PA.

MONTGOMERY, TIM. 1966-67. S & HB, 5'10", 185 lbs.; Kane, PA. An outstanding defensive back on Paterno's first two teams, who overcame a serious knee injury that almost destroyed his career to become a Second-Team All-American in '67 season. Also named "Defensive Back of the Year" in the Eastern College Athletic Conference that year and AP All-East. He was so good as a running back on the frosh team of '63 that he started at RHB in the '64 season opener against Navy and scored the team's only TD on a 12-yard run in 21-8 loss; the following week, he threw a four-yard TD pass and a two-point conversion off option plays for State's first points against powerful UCLA and then suffered a knee injury in fourth QT that sidelined him most of season, and he didn't even letter. Recurrence of injury kept him out in '65 (after a short trial at QB) but came back as DB in '66 and started at safety for two years. Despite his small size, he was tough and quick and had what Paterno called "football sense." Played one of his best games in '67 win over Syracuse, 29-20, with a goal line interception that stopped one scoring drive and an EZ tackle that caused a Syracuse receiver to drop the ball on a two-point conversion attempt that could have changed eventual outcome. Also credited by Paterno for helping change his mind on defensive strategy that stopped fourth down run by then number three North Carolina State and gave Lions 13-8 win and Paterno his first national attention by the media and bowl scouts. Had a great career finale in 17-17 tie with Florida State at '67 Gator Bowl with another goal line interception and several tackles that caused the pass happy Seminoles (38-of-55 passes) to drop potential completions. Played in '68 Senior Bowl. Now head coach and teacher in Williamsport, PA.

MOORE, BOOKER. 1977-78-79-80. RB & KR, 5'11", 205 lbs.; Flint, MI. A speedster who was sometimes overshadowed by Matt Suhey, Mike Guman and Curt Warner. Eleventh in career rushing with 2,072 yards and 20 TDs on 448 attempts for a 4.6 per carry average. As soph he started in same backfield as junior Matt Suhey on unbeaten '78 team that was number one at end of regular season but lost the national title game to Alabama, 14-7, in the '79 Sugar Bowl. Twice in following season ('79) he and Suhey had "double" 100 games, first against Army (103 yards and a TD on 24 carries) and then two weeks later against West Virginia when he had his best rushing day ever with 166 yards and three TDs on 18 carries in 31-6 win; also rushed for 100 twice in senior year. Played backup TB and ran back KOs as frosh and led team with six returns for 155 yards and a 25.8 return average. Made first start as soph against Texas Christian at midseason of '78 and scored team's first TD (nine yards) and third TD (one yard) in 58-0 rout. Won Hall Award in '80 as outstanding senior player. Scored final TD against Ohio State in '80 Fiesta Bowl on a 37-yard run and gained 76 yards on 10 carries in 31-19 win. Played in East-West Shrine game and Japan Bowl in '81. First choice of Buffalo Bills in '81 and played with Bills from '83-'85 but pro career cut short by injuries. Works in Flint, MI.

MOORE, LENNY. 1953-54-55. HB & KR, 6'0", 185 lbs.; Reading, PA. One of greatest running backs in State history but never made First-Team All-American; Second-Team choice in junior and senior years. Picked on the All-Time Penn State team in 1950s and again in 1967 by *Pittsburgh Press* sports editor Chet Smith, who covered Nittany Lion football for more than a half century. Nicknamed the "Reading Rambler" or the "Reading Comet." His high-stepping running style was a trademark that carried over into an illustrious pro career with the Baltimore Colts during their heyday. One of all-time all-purpose offensive leaders with his running, pass receiving and kick returns. First State player to ever gain over 1,000 yards in a season when he had 1,082 in junior year and was second leading ground gainer in nation. Also played great defense which most people forget, and is tied with four players at sixth in career pass interceptions with 10 (for 136 yards and one TD). Led team in interceptions as junior (three for 40 yards) and senior (six for 96 yards and a TD); senior mark still among 10 best ever in one season. Played one of finest defensive games against Pitt in '54 with two interceptions and fumble recovery credited with sparking 13-0 victory. Led State every year he played in all-purpose yards and in rushing: 601 yards on 108 carries and seven TDs in '53, 1082 yards on 136 carries for 10 TDs (averaging eight yards per carry) in '54 and 697 yards on 138 carries for fifth TDs in '55. Ninth in all-time rushing for one season ('54) and ninth on all-time career rushing with 2,380 yards on 519 carries and 29 TDs. Second only to Ki-Jana Carter on career average-per-carry with 6.2 yards. Had two of the longest TD runs in State history, going 80 yards in 34-13 win over Rutgers in '55 and 79 yards in 17-0 win over Pitt in '53. Leading scorer in '54 with 78 points for 13 TDs and '55 with 30 points for five TDs. The 13 TDs tied him with "Bull" McCleary, "Light Horse" Harry Wilson and Harry Robb for the single season record that was not broken until '68 by Charlie Pittman. Showed his all-around skills in opening game of junior season, when State upset Big 10 co-champion Illinois at Champaign, 14-10, when he gained 124 yards and one TD, ran back punts and was a tackling whiz on defense, while intercepting a pass to stop one Illini drive and setting up first TD by Jesse Arnelle in first QT, when his tackle on UI soph sensation Mickey Bates caused a fumble. Played one of his finest all-around games in the classic head-on duel with the great Jim Brown at Beaver Stadium in '55; gained 146 yards and a TD on 22 carries in the 21-20 come-from-behind win. Had 12 games rushing over 100 yards with 179 yards and three TDs against Rutgers in '55 being his best. Also great kick return man, fourth in all-time career punt return average (15.8 yards and one TD on 24 returns), ninth in all-time career kickoff return average (24.3 yards on 23 returns) and third in season punt return average (17.5 and 1 TD on 13 returns in '53). Played in East-West Shrine game in December of '55 along with teammates Frank Reich and Otto Kneidinger. One of four Penn Staters in the Pro Football Hall of Fame, inducted in '75 after a brilliant career with the Colts ('56-'67). Selected to Hall of Fame's All-Pro team of the 1950's. Running star of the Colts championship teams in late '50's and set NFL record by scoring at least one TD in 18 straight games; fourth in all-time NFL career touchdowns with 113. Selected All-Pro five-times and played in seven Pro Bowls. NFL's '64 "Comeback Player-of-the-Year," when he scored 20 TDs on more than 1,000 yards rushing and receiving. For years he complained about the poor isolated atmosphere for Blacks on the PSU campus but has mellowed in recent years in seeing changes during the Paterno era. Near retirement as a program specialist in suburban Baltimore.

MOORE, HAROLD ("RED"). 1942-43-46. G & T, 5'11", 205 lbs.; Rochester, PA. One of the finest linemen of the "war years" who helped resurrect State football following World War II, when he was Co-Captain of the '46 team that lost only to Michigan State and Pitt in close games. Picked on the All-Time Penn State team in 1950s and again in 1967 by *Pittsburgh Press* sports editor Chet Smith, who covered Nittany Lion football for more than a half century. Part of the great '41 frosh team including Steve Suhey, Dave and Harry Alston and Jeff Durkota that had best record in 25 years, 5-0, but was sidetracked by the war and other tragedies. As soph he was a backup G until midseason, when he started in Homecoming game against Colgate and helped team to 13-10 win and eventual 6-6-1 record. Scheduled for officer training in fall of '43 but military was overloaded at time and allowed Moore and other college football players to return to their campuses under the historic V-12 program until training schedule could start. Thus, he was a starter at LT on the '43 team that was 5-3-1 although he missed last couple games, when called up by Navy for training. Came back in '46 to be the starting LT and roomed with his best friend, Suhey. Team set tone for '47 undefeated Cotton Bowl season with six wins and tough losses to MSU, 19-16, and Pitt, 14-7. But Moore graduated and missed the big season. Played with Pittsburgh Steelers from '47-'49 and was All-Pro as rookie. Retired and living in Meadville, PA.

MOSCRIP, ANDY ("MOSSIE"). 1903-04. T & PK, height and weight unknown; Towanda, PA. Picked to All-Time Penn State team on 40th anniversary of State football in 1927 by New York Sun sportswriter George Trevor, who described Moscrip as a player "with an exceedingly wide range who could nail 'em out in the flanks." Called "Mossie" by his teammates. Solid blocker and a vicious tackler who flattened opponents on both offense and defense. Formed one of State's best front lines of the early era that included "Mother" Dunn and Ed Yeckley. Didn't start kicking until asked to try out in final season and did so well he was considered the best State dropkicker in history until Vorhis showed up in '06. College career ended abruptly, when he broke his collarbone in late season game against Dickinson in '04 and his absence from final game of the year against Pitt was considered a major reason for 22-5 loss. Deceased.

MOULES, TODD. 1982-83-84-85. DT & OG, 6'1", 262 lbs.; Wilkes-Barre, PA. A throwback to the days of the two-way player, he switched back and forth from defense to offense every year he played because he was so versatile. Third-Team All-American in '85 and Co-Captain on the hustling team which was number one in country, until losing to Oklahoma in '86 Orange Bowl. Began career as a DT as a frosh and played behind Greg Gattuso on the '82 National Championship team. Was in same backup role in opening game of '83 season but was switched to OG in second game against Cincinnati and became an immediate starter. Played one of his best games that year in 17-6 win over Syracuse with blocking and alertly recovered a State fumble on the one-yard line that preserved 38-yard drive and led to team's first TD. By the start of '84 he was back on the defense and started all season at DT. But he was moved back to OG for '85 and found his niche. Given credit for helping to make D. J. Dozier a star running back because of his fine blocking. Played two of the best games of his career that year in the 19-17 win over Alabama and 24-20 win over Syracuse that propelled State into national title hunt. Played in '86 Japan Bowl. Now in the commercial lending business in Cleveland, OH.

MUNCHAK, MIKE. 1979-80-81. G, 6'3", 257 lbs.; Scranton, PA. One of the excellent offensive linemen of the early '80s, who became an outstanding pro player. Named Third-Team All-American in '81. Often overlooked because of play of fellow G Sean Farrell, but teamed with Farrell and others to help make Curt Warner a running star from his frosh year. When Warner broke Shorty Miller's 69-year record for rushing in one game with 256 yards in 26 carries in 41-16 win over Syracuse in '81, it was Munchak, Farrell and center Jim Romano who were credited with providing the essential blocking. After playing against Farrell & Munchak in '81 a Nebraska LB said "I've never seen anyone tougher than those two and I hope I never do again." Played one of his finest games in his last in '82 Fiesta Bowl win over USC 26-10 when his crunching blocks were crucial in both TD runs (of 17 and 21 yards) by Curt Warner; helped Warner outplay USC's Heisman Trophy winner Marcus Allen. Broke into starting lineup as soph in '79 and teamed with Farrell to give State "two of the finest guards in the country," according to Paterno. Could pull and sweep the corners as well as anyone. Also great at pass protection. Missed '80 season with knee injury and redshirted. Decided to turn pro after junior year of '81. Number one draft choice of Houston in '82 and had an outstanding pro career with Houston from '83-'93. Now an assistant coach with the Oilers and lives in Brentwood, TX.

MURPHY, GREG. 1973-74. DE, 6'3", 230 lbs.; Brooklyn, NY. A fine DE on the forsaken unbeaten '73 team which was relegated to fifth in polls despite convincing win over LSU in '74 Orange Bowl, where Murphy had played well and recovered big fumble. He also was good enough to make Second-Team All-American in '74, when team beat Baylor in '75 Cotton Bowl. Made 80 tackles that year. Had one of best games in 27-0 win over Iowa, when he and Mike Harstenstine were given main credit for holding Hawkeyes to net rushing of 66 yards and net passing of 43. Was known for his great strength and quickness. After playing behind All-American Bruce Bannon in '72, he emerged out of '73 spring and fall practice as the regular for '73. Won Red Worrell Award in spring practice of '73 as most improved player. In his first ever start in nationally-televised opening game at Stanford, he scored two points when he and Doug Allen combined to block a Stanford punt from the EZ in fourth QT for safety in 20-6 win. Played LB as freshman and was a prime backup DE as soph but didn't play enough to letter. Twelfth choice of Pittsburgh in '75 but didn't play in NFL. Now in construction management and living in Brooklyn Heights, NY.

MURRAY, W. A. (BILL). 1895-96-97-98. C, 6-0 178; Williamsport, PA. Captain of 1898 team that had 6-4 record with big wins over Bucknell and Washington & Jefferson. Normally quiet man except on the football field. Four-year starter at center and part of the "famous trio" line of 1897 & 1898 teams that included Henny Scholl and "Brute" Randolph. One of few linemen who didn't run the ball as rules permitted in his era. Solid blocker and tackler; his halftime talk to the team in '04 against Dickinson in what was then State's "big game of the year' is credited with helping to arouse the team to an 11-0 victory. Deceased.

NATALE, DAN. 1972-73-74. TE, 6'3", 220 lbs.; Glassport, PA. Perhaps the most overlooked of the good PSU tight ends because of such First-Team All-Americans as Ted Kwalick and Kyle Brady. But he's the 12th best in career receptions and career yardage with 67 catches for 1,038 yards and eight TDs and a 15.5 yards per reception average. Second-Team All-American in junior year, when team was unbeaten and beat LSU, 16-9, in '74 Orange Bowl. Was considered an outstanding blocker, but also ran well after catching passes. Missed two and a half games in senior year because of injuries. Best statistical year was as soph, when he led team with 30 catches for 460 yards and five TDs. The five TDs ties him with Bob Parsons for most in one season by a TE. Made probably his most important TD of career in '72 Iowa game at Beaver Stadium; with State trailing 10-7 with 49 seconds left and facing a third-and-Goal at the Iowa eight-yard line after a 72-yard drive, QB John Hufnagel hustled a pass to Natale, who had slipped and then ran to the corner of the EZ to grab the throw for the winning TD, 14-10. Holds one of the most unusual records in combining with Duane Taylor on the longest run for a TD with a fumble recovery: it happened against Syracuse in '73, when Taylor, a frosh running back, was carrying the ball from the PSU eight-yard line on a third-and-10 when he neared the 20-line and fumbled, but Natale, who was running interference, picked up the ball and dashed down the sidelines 78 yards for a TD and a combined 92-yard run in a 49-6 win at Archbold Stadium. A very good blocker, who often sacrificed his pass catching potential to stay on the line and help block for Heisman Trophy winner John Cappelletti in '73 and Tom Donchez in '74. His 42-yard reception of a Tom Shuman pass in the opening minutes of the second half in '75 Cotton Bowl was considered the key play that turned a 7-3 deficit into an eventual 41-20 win over Baylor and a final number 10 ranking in the polls. Ninth round pick of San Francisco in '75 but didn't play pro in NFL. Owns and operates a sporting goods store in North Huntingdon, PA.

NESSEL, JOHN. 1973-74. OG & OT, 6'5½", 258 lbs.; Georgetown, CT. Perhaps one of the least known of State's All-Americans and the first offensive lineman of the Paterno era to be so honored. Chosen by Walter Camp in '74, when team went 10-2, beat Baylor, 41-20, in Cotton Bowl and was rated seventh in country. He was a starter for first nine games at left tackle but was then beaten out by soph Brad Benson who became an NFL great with the New York Giants. Shared time with Benson in '75 Cotton Bowl win over Baylor. Began career as a OG and started there as junior on the unbeaten '73 team (12-0) that brought John Cappelletti the Heisman Trophy and finished fifth in country. Number four choice of Atlanta in '75 draft but decided not to play pro ball. Now a technology education instructor in Ridgefield, CT and lives in Wilton, CT.

NOBILE, LEO. 1942, 46. G, 5'10", 210 lbs.; Ambridge, PA. Another of the WWII veterans whose career was interrupted by the war but he is considered one of the best interior linemen of that era. A standout on the unbeaten freshman team of '41 which had the best record in 25 years; he shared placekicking on that team with the star, Dave Elston. Was a close friend of teammate Steve Suhey and they started out as sophs in '42 on the second team but soon were playing almost as much as the regulars. He left for the service after the season and didn't return until '46. Then he started at LG with Suhey at RG. Was one of the toughest players on the field and never missed a game that year because of injuries. Surprised everyone by leaving school in '47 to play for the Washington Redskins and then moved on to the Steelers in '48 & '49. Retired after a career in recreation and living in Coraopolis, PA.

NOBLE, BRANDON. 1994-95-96. NG, 6'2", 270 lbs.; Virginia Beach, VA. One of the most underrated players of the 1990s. Named Outstanding Senior Player in '96 by State College Quarterback Club. Paterno called him "the best nose guard in the country" for his play and leadership on the seventh-ranked '96 team that beat Texas in Fiesta Bowl, 38-14. Had 72 tackles in senior year, including seven and a half sacks for losses of 54 yards and another 10 tackles for losses of 58 yards. Played perhaps his best game of year in key 34-9 win that stopped Northwestern's 13-game winning streak with seven tackles and three sacks and a pass breakup. Player-of-the-Game in '95 nationally televised come-from-behind, 24-20, win over Michigan State, when he made 10 tackles and had key interception. Good quickness and strength and very aggressive. Broken leg in '93 and mononucleosis in early '94 held him back, but he began to make an impact in the midseason of '94 in helping unbeaten Rose Bowl Champions. Started every game as junior and senior and finished career with 147 tackles, including 69 solos, and 13 ½ sacks. Played in '97 Senior Bowl. Signed as a free agent with the San Francisco 49ers of the NFL and also playing in the NFL Europe League.

NOLAN, JOHN. 1945-46-47. T, 6'3", 228 lbs.; Glen Falls, NY. One of the best interior linemen of the post World War II era and Co-Captain of the undefeated '47 Cotton Bowl team that was the best between '21 and '68. Picked on the All-Time Penn State team in 1950s and again in 1967 by *Pittsburgh Press* sports editor Chet Smith, who covered Nittany Lion football for more than a half century. Those who saw State tie SMU 13-13 in that bowl say Nolan was outstanding on defense. Part of Navy V-12 program at Holy Cross in World War II and then at Penn State and decided to stay on at State when discharged at end of war. He was an instant starter at RT as a soph and never missed starting another game in the next three years, even when hurt. In '45 he was cited for his outstanding defensive play in 26-0 win over Syracuse & in 7-0 loss at Pitt, when he played entire 60 minutes. He was an outstanding blocker and he made one of the most significant blocks of his career in '47 on Jeff Durkota's 46-yard TD run against Navy that provided spark in 20-7 win that made State the prime contender for Cotton Bowl bid. Teammate Wally Triplett, State's first Black player, credited Nolan for helping to lead team to vote against playing Miami in '46 when Miami asked State not to bring its Black players. Played pro ball with three teams in All-American Conference, the Boston Yanks ('48), the New York Bulldogs ('49) and the New York Yankees ('50). In 1971, he became the equipment manager for the PSU football team and remained in that position until his retirement after the 1978 season. Lived in retirement in Glenn Falls, NY, until his death in 1996.

NORTON, NEGLEY. 1944-47-48-49. T, 6'1", 225 lbs.; Albany, NY. Another of the outstanding linemen on the teams of the late 1940's. A four-year regular at tackle, starting as frosh on the wartime team of '44, and finishing as Co-Captain of '49 team. Was in Pacific Theater in

WWII. Returned to start at RT as soph on the great undefeated '47 team that finished fourth in country and set NCAA defensive records that still stand. Was a fine blocker and exceptional defensive tackle. Played one of his best games in 20-7 victory over Navy late in '47 season. Missed some games in '48 because of injuries but came back and had finest year in '49 in Joe Bedenk's only year as head coach. Played two of his best games in losing causes, against Villanova in season opener and against Pitt in final game of his career. Has had a successful business career since graduation and is now a sales representative for a Chicago company. Lives in Slingerland, NY.

O'BARA, VINCE. 1949-50. HB, QB & K, 5'11", 170 lbs.; Johnstown, PA. Rip Engle's first QB and Joe Paterno's first protégé. Had been a running back in the last year of the Single-Wing under Higgins, but Engle turned him into a Wing-T QB for one year with Paterno's tutoring. Not a natural passer and still holds the record for most intercepted passes in a season (15). But he was smart and worked hard, got better as the '50 season progressed and became a good enough QB to lead the team to a 5-3-1 season. He also did the punting and placekicking that year and showed great poise. His quick thinking on a botched punt attempt late in the fourth QT in crucial game at Boston College avoided a possible devastating defeat in midseason since team was 1-3-1 at that time; on fourth-and-nine at the BC 49-yard line O'Bara was back to punt when the ball sailed over his head to the State 25-yard line, but he beat two BC players to the ball, picked it up and ran five yards where he punted it all the way to the BC 20, and State held on to a 20-13 win. Earlier in the BC game he threw the biggest pass of his career, a 72-yard bomb to John Smidansky that is credited with being the play that turned the season around. Played his best game in a 16-9 win over West Virginia, when he gained 54 yards on three carries (including a 43-yard QB sneak), hit on 6-of-11 passes for 100 yards and booted three PATs. But his most important game was his last, when he kicked all three crucial extra points as State upset arch-rival Pitt, 21-20, in a game played at Forbes Field after a one-week postponement because of the famous so-called Thanksgiving Snow of '50. Led team in scoring (31 points on five TDs and one extra point), passing (640 yards and three TDs on 38-of-103 passes) total offense (692 yards on 140 plays) and punting (a 32.1 yards average and 1,638 yards on 51 punts). Played in '50 Blue-Gray game, when Engle was the head coach. Retired as a school district administrator and now lives in Sinking Spring, PA.

O'DELL, TOM. 1974-75. DB, 5'10", 180 lbs.; Summit, NJ. Made one of the biggest plays of the Paterno era when he blocked an extra point kick by Pitt's Carson Long that gave State a 7-6 victory in '75 and helped regain prestige for the Lions. Long was one of the nation's best placekickers and had a string of 60 straight PAT kicks when O'Dell blocked the kick in the first half as a national TV audience watched. The block so unnerved Long that he blew a chip shot field goal attempt from the 13 yard line with time running out that preserved State's victory and assured the Lions of a 9-2 regular season record. The blocked kick had been designed by assistant coaches J. T. White and Greg Ducatte, who had scouted Pitt and noted how the Panther center lifted

his shoulders an instant before snapping the ball. Odell was trained to take advantage of this mistake and he leaped over the center and blocked Long's kick perfectly with his chest. That was the climax to a fine season by Odell, who didn't come into his own until his senior year when he was the starting safety. Led team in interceptions that season with four. Unfortunately, he was injured in the first QT of the Sugar Bowl game against Alabama and his absence figured into Alabama passing to victory. Didn't play much until '74 when he got his first break in midseason as a replacement for starter Jeff Hite at DB in Syracuse game and O'Dell never came out of starting lineup. Lives in Madison, NJ.

O'HORA, JIM. 1933-34-35. C, 5'10", 166 lbs.; Dunmore, PA. Better known as the long time assistant football coach under Bob Higgins, Rip Engle and Joe Paterno. He was the mastermind of the State defenses in the Engle and early Paterno eras, and is the person credited with putting together the great '68-'69 defensive teams that many believe were the best ever in college football. He also was the architect of the classic "defensive" defeat of Ohio State in '64, 27-0. Played C on three Higgins teams and was occasional starter and backup to Chuck Cherundolo. Undersized for his position but a hard-working, determined player, who didn't back away from confrontations with bigger opponents. He is one of the few PSU players who never had a winning *or* losing season in his three years on the team; each team finished with a .500 record: '33 (3-3-1), '34 (4-4) and '35 (4-4). Played during the misguided period of football de-emphasis, when there were no scholarships or financial aid for State players, but most opposing teams didn't abide by similar restrictions. As a result, many players of this era, like O'Hora, were recruited from working class homes in the coal and steel regions and guided to State, where they were assisted in getting jobs to help pay for their room, board and tuition. O'Hora worked at campus fraternities during his years playing football. Coached in high school and was Navy officer in World War II before joining Higgins' staff as an assistant in '46. Remained on staff through Bedenk, Engle and Paterno eras. Also well known by State football aficionados for opening his home to the bachelor Paterno for a couple of years, when Paterno first came to State from Brown. For years he was the interior line coach and defensive coordinator and was named "assistant head coach' by Paterno in '74. When he retired in '77, an award was created in his honor that now is presented annually after spring practice to a defensive player for "exemplary conduct, loyalty, interest, attitude and improvement." Still living in State College and not as mobile because of some health problems but still active in meetings of the State College Quarterback and Tailback Clubs and a spectator at Beaver Stadium.

O'NEIL, ED. 1971-72-73. LB & DB, 6'3", 225 lbs.; Warren, PA. Another of the outstanding graduates of "Linebacker U." A First-Team All-American in senior year, when picked by Walter Camp, The Sporting News and Time magazine. Typical of the type of player converted from one position to another who becomes a star. Recruited as a QB and S, he began as a defensive back in soph season and was a first team starter in secondary with another soph, John Cappelletti. Played one of his best games at DB in third game of season against Air Force and made first interception of career, which he ran back 34 yards, deep into AF territory to set up State's first TD in eventual 16-14 win. Moved to LB in junior year and started at inside slot. Played another of his finest games in 28-19 win over West Virginia in '72; with State leading, 25-19, late in third QT he and teammates Bruce Bannon and John

Skorupan led a four-down goal line stand that kept WVU out of EZ and was turning point of the game, with O'Neil making two big tackles. He was quick and had great instincts. Led team in tackles in '72 with 72 solos and 54 assists for 126 total. Had another big game in '73 season-opening win over Stanford, 20-6, when he led team with 10 tackles as defense shut down Cardinal rushing game with minus eight yards. Scored one of few TDs in career with a 66-yard return of an interception against Ohio University in next to last game of regular season. Closed out career with another solid game in the '74 Orange Bowl win over LSU. Tied for fourth (with Brian Gelzheiser) in tackles for one season with 72 solos and 54 assists for a 126 total. Played in '74 Senior Bowl. Only the second State LB to be drafted number one (Dave Robinson was the first and Shane Conlan the most recent), when picked by Detroit in '74 and played with Lions until '80, then with New England and Green Bay for rest of '80 before quitting pro football. Coached for a time at Rutgers when PSU's Dick Anderson was head coach, and now coaching high school football in Amherst, NY.

ONKOTZ, DENNIS. 1967-68-69. LB & PR, 6'2", 210 lbs. North Hampton, PA. One of the greatest "scholar athletes" Paterno ever had, graduating with a 3.5 average as a biophysics major, and the second linebacker to gain All-American honors. He did as much as anyone to help give State the name of "Linebacker U." One of only 11 players to be a two-time First-Team All-American and a consensus All-American both years, when named by AP, UPI, Football Writers and others and a Second-Team All-American and All-East in his sensational soph year. Also one of only 14 State players and three coaches in the National Football Foundation College Football Hall of Fame, inducted in '95. Was an Academic All-American in '69. An outstanding star among many on the back-to-back unbeaten teams of '68 and '69 that was shunned by the pollsters despite the record, which included two Orange Bowl victories. Teamed with fellow Hall-of-Famer Jack Ham at LB to form one of the best one-two collegiate linebacking combinations of all-time. No linebacker ever was as good as he was at interceptions, tackles—and *returning punts*! He was the type of "scholar-athlete" who set the tone for Paterno's teams. He gained notoriety for doing the "unthinkable" by going to class Saturday morning before home games. His run back of three interceptions for TDs is still the team record (although Darren Perry tied it in his four-year career). He is tied (with Perry and two others) for the one season record on TD interceptions with two in his sophomore year ('67), when he also set a record that still stands for season interception return yardage (179 yards on six interceptions). Tied for fifth (with Don Eyer) for career interceptions with 11 (for 275 yards and the 3 TDs) but his 25 yards per interception return average is the best of all-time. What makes his interception records even more phenomenal is that he played all three years with PSU's career interception leader, Neal Smith. He and Smith intercepted two apiece in the 10-3 Orange Bowl win over Missouri in '69. He is third in the career tackles with a total of 287 on 165 solos and 122 assists and the 118 (74 solos and 44 assists) he had as a soph in '67 is sixth for one season. Played one of his outstanding games in '67 in 13-8 upset over then number three NC State that startled the college football world. Ran back an interception 33 yards for a TD in first QT to give State a 13-0 lead and then made one of his all-time most critical tackles when he, Jim Kates and Mike McBath stopped North Carolina State's Tony Barchuk at the goal line on a fourth-and-one near the end of the game to preserve a victory. Led the team in tackles every year he played.

Running backs, wide receivers or defensive backs usually return punts, but Onkotz ran back more punts than any player in State history except Gary Hayman. His 13.2 yards average per runback on 47 returns for 619 yards and two TDs place him eighth in career punt returns, which is based on averages. He led team in punt returns every year he played with his best year in '69, when he averaged 13.5 yards on 24 returns for 325 yards and one TD. His 71-yard return that helped beat Pitt, 22-7, in '69 is the 14th longest on record but the second longest that didn't result in a TD; he was voted Outstanding Player-of-the-Game that day with an interception late in the first half that set up a go-ahead TD, eight tackles and another spectacular punt return for 38 yards that set up another TD. Played in '70 Hula Bowl with teammate Jim Kates. Third choice of the New York Jets in '70 and played one year with the Jets before a severely broken leg ended his pro aspirations. Returned to the State College area and is now a successful financial planner who lives in Boalsburg, PA.

OPPERMAN, HENRY. 1959-60. E & K, 6'2", 205 lbs.; Connellsville, PA. A good all-around receiver and defensive end, who also was fine kicker. Captain of the comeback '60 team that overcame a 2-3 start to win five straight games, including the Liberty Bowl over Oregon, 41-12. He was named Most Valuable Lineman in that bowl game; played with both first & second units that day, leading State receivers with four catches for 49 yards, kicking four PATs, making more than a half dozen tackles and providing key blocks in a 420-yard offensive onslaught. He helped rally the '60 team after it had lost to Missouri, Syracuse and Illinois in close games that were not settled until late in fourth QT. Led all receivers in yardage as junior with 212 yards on 11 receptions and then tied HB Jim Kerr with most receptions in senior year with 13 for 131 yards and one TD. Known for his crisp blocking and determined tackling. Most forget he was a good kicker who did most of the booting for FGs, PATs and KOs. A knee injury almost wrecked his career in '58, but he came back to be one of the best all-around players on Engle's first two bowl teams. A great leader with a steady persona, who Engle depended on to motivate his team, particularly after the horrendous start in his senior season. Now the vice president of a brokerage office in Uniontown. Lives in Connellsville and is a long-time football season ticket holder who rarely misses a home game.

OSBORN, ROBERT (DUKE). 1919. C & G, 6'9", 170 lbs.; Hometown unknown. One of the toughest interior linemen of his era. Picked on the All-Time Penn State team in 1950s and again in 1967 by *Pittsburgh Press* sports editor Chet Smith, who covered Nittany Lion football for more than a half century. Only played one year on varsity before leaving school to play pro football. Enrolled at State as frosh but left for Navy and in shortened season of '18, he was the center for the Wissahickon Barracks team of Cape May, NJ, when it played State in opening season game at Beaver Field. He made an impact that day, colliding with State's Glenn Killinger at such a force that Killinger was sidelined with three broken ribs. Rejoined State in '19 and started at center but was benched by Bezdek before critical Dartmouth game and when State lost, team captain Bob Higgins led player revolt that forced Bezdek to reshuffle lineup and Osborn became starting right guard. Team didn't lose again, finishing with 7-1 record. Played pro football with the Canton Bulldogs ('21-'23), Cleveland ('24) and Pottsville ('25-'28). Deceased.

OSTROWSKI, PHIL. 1996-97. G, 6'4", 280 lbs.; Wilkes-Barre, PA. May be one of State's most underrated offensive linemen because he was surrounded by inexperienced linemates, who often struggled. Ostrowski is credited with helping to mold line that helped Curtis Enis become an All-American. Elected one of team's offensive co-captains at end of season and was named First-Team All-Big 10 by both coaches and media. Co-winner of Richard Maginnis Memorial award presented to team's outstanding offensive lineman. Originally recruited to play defensive end but switched to G in '94 to give depth to Big 10 champion team. Was prime backup in '95 and got first start against Ohio State but sprained ankle on 11th play and never fully recovered for rest of season. Started '96 in short guard position and switched to long guard in midseason. Had one of his finest games in come from behind 38-15 Fiesta Bowl victory over Texas, when Lions rushed for 292 yards in big second half explosion. Number five choice of '49ers in '98 draft and lives off-season in hometown of Wilkes-Barre.

PALAZZI, LOU. 1941-42. C & LB, 6'0", 190 lbs.; Dunmore, PA. Best known as a college and professional referee and spent many years officiating in the National Football League. Teammates said he was as tough as anyone on the team. Broke into starting lineup in fourth game of junior season as injuries sidelined first two centers and became regular C in '42 before graduating and going into Army. Elected captain a week before '42 season and became leader of the war time team dominated by freshmen and sophs that surprised country with 6-1-1 record and tied for 19th in AP ratings. A fine defensive linebacker who put on 20 pounds just before '41 season to give him more strength against his blockers. Part of a senior class that never lost a home game at Beaver Field. Was one of the key players in one of the most historic—but long forgotten— milestones in college football in '41 when Syracuse developed a new so-called "Y" formation whereby the center turned his back to the defense and would begin play by picking up ball and immediately throw shovel passes to ends or backs, almost like a QB of today; it was called the "reverse center" formation and after Syracuse had used it to dominate foes and post a 4-1 record, the formation was thwarted by State in mid-season '41 game by having the PSU center virtually tackle Syracuse center on every play; starter John Jaffurs and Palazzi, made just about every tackle until Syracuse switched back to the Single-Wing; State won by the biggest score in 20 years, 34-19, and by the '42 season the "Y" formation had been banned. Made game-saving tackle against South Carolina in final game of '41 season that helped beat Carolina, 19-12, and give team a surprising, 7-2 record; State was leading by just 13-12 in fourth QT when SC defender intercepted a State pass and ran 33 yards before being tackled from behind by Palazzi in State territory. After service in WWII he played with the NFL New York Giants in '46 and '47 before turning to officiating. Now semi-retired but working as a landscape architect and living in Santa Fe, NM.

PALM, MYRON ("MIKE"). 1922-23. QB, PK & P, 5'11", 165 lbs.; Carlisle, PA. Starting QB as junior of the '22 team that played in State's first bowl game, the '23 Rose Bowl. But he never fully reached his potential, primarily because of injuries. In Rose Bowl, his 20-yard dropkick FG gave State a 3-0 lead 10 minutes into the game, but the team tired and lost 14-3; it was one of Palm's worst passing and running games, he threw three interceptions and gained only one yard on three-of-nine passes and gained just 25 yards on 16 rushing attempts; also caught two passes for five yards and his 12 punts are still the team record for bowl games (tying with Bob Parsons), but much of his difficulties that day were caused by the captain of State's '20 team, Harold "Bill" Hess, who was a USC assistant and knew the intricacies of the PSU offense and, thus, helped with the USC defensive strategy. Palm was a fine leader. Not a natural passer but developed into a good one. Had speed and became a good dropkicker. Hampered much of his senior year by injuries and played little in last couple of games, missing key games, when team lost twice, and tied West Virginia, 13-13, in historic Yankee Stadium meeting. Did not play high school football and actually went to State because of his ability in track and was encouraged to go out for football because of his athletic skills. Originally was a HB but Bezdek moved him to QB in middle of soph year but he never played in a varsity game until the '22 opener against St. Bonaventure. Played one of his best games in surprise 10-0 win over Carnegie Tech when he drop-kicked a FG and a PAT after a "Light Horse" Harry Wilson TD in a 10-0 win; but was blamed for 7-6 loss to Penn despite hitting on 8-of-13 passes for 99 yards, when he missed extra point after Wilson TD. Ran the 100- and 200-yard dashes and threw the hammer and javelin on track team and played CF on baseball team. Went into coaching after graduation and was an assistant football coach with the New York Giants for one year, then an assistant at West Virginia, Harvard and Georgetown before becoming a restaurant owner in Washington, DC. For some 30 years, until his death in '74, he operated Mike Palm's Restaurant on Independence Avenue on Capitol Hill, which was a well-known hangout for Congressmen and their staffs. Deceased.

PANKEY, IRV. 1977-78-79 TE & OG/OT, 6'5", 251 lbs.; Aberdeen, PA. One of the best blockers of the '70s and Second-Team All-American at G in senior year, when he also was co-captain. Started at LT as soph but had speed and good hands so Paterno moved him to TE as junior, then back to LG as senior. He was a fine TE on the '78 team, which was undefeated in the regular season but lost the National Championship in the disappointing '79 Sugar Bowl to Alabama, 14-7 (where he caught one pass for five yards). Only caught nine passes for 94 yards in career and never more than one in a game except for his sensational day in the nationally-televised late season "clash of the unbeatens" between then number two State and number five Maryland; he had four receptions for 35 yards that helped State thump Maryland, 27-3, before a record Beaver Stadium crowd (78,019) and propel the Lions to number one for the first time ever in 91 years. Played in '79 East-West Shrine game and '80 Japan Bowl. Second choice of Los Angeles Rams in '80 and was one of the team's All-Pro linemen for 10 years, then played with Indianapolis for two years, before retiring after the '92 season. Spent '96 as a graduate assistant coach at State and is now living in Ithaca, NY.

PARLAVECCHIO, CHET. 1979-80-81. LB, 6'2", 227 lbs.; West Orange, NJ. Followed in the tradition of Lance Mehl and Greg Buttle as part of the 1980s class at "Linebacker U." A Second-Team All-American in '81. Led team in tackles in junior and senior years, with 72 (on

42 solos on 30 assists) in '80 and 70 (on 42 solos and 28 assists) in '81. An exceptional leader. Defensive coach Sandusky said Parlavecchio "doesn't know anything except an all-out effort." Co-captain of the '81 10-2 team that beat USC, 26-10, in first Fiesta Bowl played on January 1; led the stinging defense that held USC's Heisman Trophy winner Marcus Allen without a TD and to 85 yards rushing with 13 tackles and a recovered fumble. Backed up Mehl as soph and became regular in junior and senior seasons. Played one of his best games as junior in 24-10 win over Maryland, when he led team in tackles with nine and ran back an intercepted pass 37 yards in the fourth QT that led to a game-sealing TD. Made one of the great "clutch" tackles in '81 when he and S Matt Robinson stopped Notre Dame's Greg Bell on fourth-and-one at PSU four-yard line to stop potential game-clinching TD in fourth QT, as State roared back minutes later after Greg Gattuso interception to win, 24-21, and get Fiesta Bowl bid. Played in East-West Shrine game and Japan Bowl in '82. Drafted sixth by Green Bay in '82 and played for Packers one year, then St. Louis Cardinals for one year before quitting pro ball. Now a teacher and head football coach in Little Falls, NJ.

PARSONS, BOB. 1969-70-71. TE, P & QB, 6'4", 228 lbs.; Wind Gap, PA. Although he made All-East in his only year playing TE as a senior, he may be remembered more as a punter because he led team in punting all three years he played, including '69 when his 40.6 yards average on 58 punts (for 2,353 yards) as a soph helped State finish a second straight unbeaten season and number two in the ratings. His punting that year is still the team's 11th best for one season and included 12 punts for a 42.6 yards average against Missouri in the 1970 Orange Bowl that helped State win a defensive struggle, 10-3, and preserve a 30-game undefeated streak. (The 12 punts is still a team record for bowl games, tying with Mike Palm of '23 Rose Bowl.) He was the third team QB as soph and started junior year as backup QB to Mike Cooper but moved to TE in spring of senior year; Paterno said he had "great speed for his size, naturally soft hands" and was a very good blocker. Became leading receiver on '71 team that lost only last game of regular season in upset to Tennessee and went on to beat Texas, 30-6, in "breakthrough" Cotton Bowl game; he was the leading receiver in the game with three catches for 48 yards, including crucial 20-yard pass to one-yard line near start of third quarter that set up go ahead TD; also had a 36-yard punting average on five punts during game. His five TDs in '71 ties him with Dan Natale for most in one season by a TE; caught 30 passes for 489 yards and a 15.6 yards average that year. Had his biggest yardage day in 66-14 Homecoming win over TCU in '71, when he picked up 110 yards on five receptions. Punted all three years he played. Sixth in career punting with a 38.9 yards average on 153 punts (for 5,948 yards); only had one blocked (in '69). Shares record with 11 other players for most punts in a game, but the 12 he had in '70 Orange Bowl is the record for a soph. Always punted great against Colorado and his 69-yard kick in '70 is sixth longest in record, while the 65-yarder the previous year is the 13th all-time best. As QB in '70 he tied Richie Lucas with dubious record that still stands (and later tied by Todd Blackledge) for most interceptions in one game, when he tossed four in 24-7 Homecoming loss to Syracuse. Fifth choice of Chicago in '72 and had a fine 11-year career with the Bears and was the team's prime punter for most of that time. Now a businessman in Chicago and living in Lake Zurich, IL.

PATRICK, JOHN R. 1939-40. QB & PK, 6'0", 180 lbs.; Central City, PA. One of the unsung stars of the '39 & '40 teams which brought respectability back to State football after the "purity period" of the early '30s. Called the plays and directed the on-field tactics for those winning teams. QB was primarily a blocking back in Higgins' Single-Wing and Patrick helped open holes for outstanding runners such as "Pepper" Petrella and Chuck Peters. Also developed into fine field goal kicker and kicked State's first FG in four years with a 15-yard boot that helped beat Penn, 10-0, in '39; also kicked 24-yard FG against Pitt in '39 that gave State first victory over Pitt in 20 years, 10-0. Was two-year starter on teams that had combined 10-2-3 record. Played guard for Pittsburgh Steelers in '41 and in '45 & '46 after WWII service. Retired and living in Johnstown, PA.

PERRY, DARREN. 1989-90-91. H & DB, 5'10", 190 lbs.; Chesapeake, VA. Perhaps the premier defensive back for Paterno in the 1990s. All-American in senior year and finalist for the Jim Thorpe Award as college football's outstanding defensive back. Tied for second in career interceptions (with Pete Harris) behind Neal Smith with 15, scoring three TDs and gaining 299 yards for a 19.9 yards average; the three TDs ties him with two-time All-American Dennis Onkotz for the career record. Two of the TDs were in back-to-back games against Boston College and Temple in '91. Had one of finest games against BC in '91, when he intercepted three passes, including one he returned 56 yards for a TD, in helping thwart a BC rally and give PSU a 28-21 victory. The next week he had a 41-yard return for a TD late in fourth QT to seal 24-7 win over Temple. Tied with three others for third in one-season interceptions with seven (for 125 yards and one TD in returns and a 17.9 yards average) set as a junior in '90. Co-captain of '91 team that was 11-2 and came from behind in a wild second half to beat Tennessee, 42-17, in '92 Fiesta Bowl; he had eight tackles in game. Also led team in senior year interceptions with six (for two TDs and 122 yards and a 20.3 yards average). Had one interception as frosh in '88 but didn't play enough to letter, yet gave indication of what was to come, when he had that interception and fumble recovery in big game with Alabama. In '89 shared Hero position with converted RB Gary Brown and started six games, making 20 solo tackles and 17 assists. Played in Japan Bowl in '92. Unsung eighth round choice of Pittsburgh in '92 who developed into a starter and All-Pro and is still starting for the Steelers.

PETCHEL, ELWOOD. 1944, 1946-47-48. HB & KR, 5'8", 145 lbs.; Easton. One of State's first stars in the resurgence of football after World War II. What is even more amazing about his four-year performance is that he usually was the smallest player on the field and he was usually not the starter. But he was a true triple-threat, who could do everything well—run, pass, kick and play defense. One of the most popular players among his teammates with a sense of humor that kept the team and coaches loose. Led team to the school's first unbeaten season in 26 years in '47 and the now famous 13-13 tie with SMU in the Cotton Bowl. A Third-Team All-American in his senior year of '48, when he led team with what was then phenomenal passing statistics of 628 yards and nine TDs on 48-of-100 passes, punt returns with a 10.3 yards average and 144 yards on 14 returns and interceptions (four for 15 yards). He had even better statistics in his soph year after returning from World War II, when he led the team in passing, rushing, total offense, all-purpose, scoring and interceptions. Still holds the record for career TD pass percentage with 9.14% and is 12th in all-time passing efficiency with 117.32. Was one of the stars of the all-freshmen starting team of '44 and made remarkable debut a minute and a half into season opening game against Muhlenberg with a 55-yard punt return for a touchdown. Played one of the outstanding games of his career as a frosh in losing cause against Pitt, as he took a physical beating for nearly 60 minutes; carried the ball 29 of 46 running plays, threw 14 of State's 17 passes, punted all nine times for the team, was in on many tackles and on last play of the game intercepted a Pitt pass and tried to run for a TD but could hardly move. In his first game back from World War II in '46, he was spectacular: running for 97 yards and three TDs on 14 carries, throwing a 30-yard pass for another TD, catching two passes for 19 yards and returning a punt 29 yards in State's 48-6 opening season win over Bucknell. That year he led team in rushing with 373 yards and seven TDs on 71 carries and hit on 16-of-37 passes for 287 yards and two TDs. Had his only 100-yard plus running game in '46, rushing for 115 yards on 20 carries in 14-7 loss to Pitt. Led the team three years in passing and in '46 as the defensive leader in interceptions with four. His 78-yard run for a TD in 75-0 pounding of Fordham in junior year is among longest TD runs in history. Also a great punt returner. Set the record for punt returns in one game (seven) against West Virginia in '47 that is now shared by three other players. Played perhaps his best game as a junior in the '48 Cotton Bowl; with the team losing 13-0 in the first half to an SMU team led by the great Doak Walker, he sparked a rally with two minutes left in first half and threw a 38-yard pass to Larry Cooney for a TD just before the intermission and 13-7 deficit; came back in third QT on a six-yard TD pass to Wally Triplett to tie the game, but the referees said the State kicker missed the extra point; on the last play of the game he threw a pass for the potential winning TD from the SMU 45 into the EZ that was deflected and bounced off the chest of Denny Hoggard and 13-13 was the final. Played in first Hula Bowl in '49. One of the few married players of his era. His son Woody was a solid running back for State in '74 and '75 who was hampered by injuries but led '75 team in rushing. Coached his son during his time as head coach at Pen Argyl High School. Retired and living in Wind Gap, PA.

PETERS, CHUCK. 1938-39-40. HB, WB & KR, 6'0", 180 lbs.; Shamokin, PA. May have been the best kickoff returner of all-time but official seasonal records only go back to 1940, his senior year, when he led team with five returns for 261 yards and two TDs and a 52.2 yards average. That average was the NCAA record for decades. One of his returns in '40 is the official PSU record of 101 yards for a TD against NYU: it was a spectacular runback on the opening KO, when he actually fumbled the ball one-yard behind goal, then picked it up and dashed down sidelines, getting great blocking and eluding the safety man at the 30. He had another TD of 96 yards against Lehigh earlier in the year, and his two TDs is still a one season record that he held alone for 40 years, until tied by Curt Warner in '80. Also a great runner and outstanding defensive back. Until Roger Kochman came along 20 years later, he held record for most games with over 100 yards rushing (three), although Fran Rogel tied it in late '40s. His 156 yards rushing (and two TDs on 11 carries) in 33-6 win over Syracuse as a soph in '38 was remarkable considering he played in the era of Single-Wing power football. That included an 80-yard TD run that is still among the seventh

longest runs from scrimmage (and tied with six others). He had two other games running over 100 yards—102 yards on 20 carries in '39 10-0 upset over Pitt and 105 yards and one TD on 17 carries in 34-0 win over Lehigh in '40. He played both the tailback and wingback positions and had a galloping stride but could cut well and was deceptive with a natural instinct to pick his holes and utilize the stiff arm when needed. A fine tackler and pass defender, who intercepted many passes during his career. His three interceptions in 12-0 win over South Carolina in '40, was the record until broken by Mike Smith in '70. State coaches called him "the best pass defender in the country." Made an impressive debut in '38 season and was starting at midseason. Played one of the best games of his career as soph in that surprising 33-6 win over Syracuse: He scored one TD on an 80-yard run on the second play of the game, ran 14-yards off right tackle for another, threw a TD pass off a "dead" run and intercepted a pass to stop one Orange drive. Teamed with "Pepper" Petrella (see below) as the running stars of the '39 and '40 teams that lost just twice, tied three times and won 11 to start State's NCAA record of 49 consecutive undefeated seasons. Hampered much of his senior year because of a preseason shoulder injury but came back at midseason with his great record interceptions against South Carolina and kickoff return against NYU. Deceased.

PETRELLA, JOHN ("PEPPER"). 1939-40-41. HB, 5'8", 140 lbs.; Downingtown, PA. The speedster of his era. Teamed with Chuck Peters (see above) as the running stars of the '39 and '40 teams that lost just twice, tied three times and won 11 to start State's NCAA record of 49 consecutive undefeated seasons. Very difficult to tackle because of his running style, his stocky legs were constantly churning. In soph and junior years often didn't enter game until second quarter. Was also a fine defensive safety despite his size. Leading rusher as junior (488 yards on 105 carries for 4.65 yards per carry) and senior (482 yards on 135 carries and 3.57 yards per carry) and his 12 TDs as senior was one short of then team seasonal record. Had great soph debut. Scored the TD in a comeback 6-6 tie with Syracuse at midseason that was the turning point of the '39 season (5-1-2). Two weeks later his 17-yard run for TD in the first QT was the key to a major 10-0 upset over Penn and in the final game of the year he, Peters and Bill Smaltz were the offensive standouts of first win over Pitt in 21 years, 10-0. His best game as a junior came before a Homecoming crowd at Beaver Field when he ran for 119 yards and two TDs (on 21 carries) in a 17-13 come-from-behind win over West Virginia: did most of running in final drive, starting with 41-yard kickoff return and carried six times for 36 yards including four yard around shortside right end for winning TD. May have played his finest game ever in his last as a senior: scored two TDs in first half and led rushers with 63 yards to help demolish Syracuse, 34-19; and against Pitt scored three TDs and was the leading ground gainer with 90 yards on 24 carries in a 31-7 rout, then followed that a week later with 110 yards and two TDs (on 23 carries) in 19-12 win over South Carolina that gave the team a surprising 7-2 record. Chosen for North-South All-Star game in '41. Deceased.

PITTMAN, CHARLIE. 1967-68-69. TB, 6'1", 190 lbs.; Baltimore, MD. The first superstar running back of the Paterno era. First-Team All-American as a senior & Academic All-American, too. As soph he and junior Bobby Campbell were the first of Paterno's great running duos in the '68 season. He had first start as a wingback in the Paterno's historical "turnaround game" against Miami in '67 but became fulltime starter at TB in fourth game of year after knee injury against UCLA sidelined Campbell for season; in next game, he led team to 21-14 win over West Virginia, scoring a spectacular "turning point" 83-yard TD on the second half kickoff—State's first TD off a KO since '59—and ran for 136 yards on 24 carries, caught two passes for 45 yards, and threw a key block for another TD. Perhaps the most underrated of Paterno's great running backs because his exploits and records have been surpassed by Curt Warner, John Cappelletti, Ki-Jana Carter and others. He is still 10th in career yardage with 2,236 yards and 30 TDs on 454 carries. He led team in rushing and all purpose yards all three years he played, led scoring as a junior and senior and kickoff returns as a junior and was the prime running back of the back-to-back unbeaten teams of '68 and '69 that won two Orange Bowls but were relegated to second place in the national polls. In 15-14 win over Kansas in '69 Orange Bowl he was second to Campbell in rushing with 58 yards on 14 carries, scoring the first TD on a 13-yard run in second QT and had 12 yards on two pass receptions. In the next Orange Bowl he was the leading ground gainer in the 10-3 win over Missouri with 83 yards on 21 carries and 10 more yards on two pass receptions. Came to State because he idolized Lenny Moore when Moore was starring for Baltimore Colts and wore Moore's Colt number, 24. In '69, Moore watched Pittman play and said, "Pittman is the best in the country...I can see natural talent." A fast runner known for his quick starts. Best statistical year was as junior in '68, when he rushed for 950 yards and 14 TDs (then a record) on 186 carries (for a 5.1 yards average) and had another 296 yards on pass receptions and 116 yards on kickoff returns—all this despite a recurring ankle injury that hobbled him but didn't keep him out of a game. In All-American year he gained 706 yards and 10 TDs on 149 carries and had another 127 yards on 10 pass receptions and 86 yards on three KO returns. Had 10 games rushing over 100 yards with the first one against West Virginia in '67 also setting the record that still stands for all-purpose yards by a soph with a total of 265 yards, 137 yards and one TD rushing (24 carries) 45 yards on pass receptions and 83 yards on kickoff returns. His best rushing yardage came in the opening game of '69 season against Navy, when he ran for 177 yards and two TDs on 16 carries in a 45-22 victory. Third behind Warner and Larry Joe in career kickoff returns with a 28.4 yards average and 483 returns and one TD (as a soph) on 17 returns. His sophomore average return of 28.7 yards places him seventh in the one-season records. Played in '70 Senior Bowl. Drafted third by St. Louis Cardinals in '70 and played for Cards one year and Baltimore in '71 before injuries forced him to give up pro ball. His son Tony played defensive back three years, '92-'94, and was a starter and Academic All-American on the unbeaten '94 team that also was neglected by the pollsters and finished second. Charlie became a newspaper executive after graduation and for years worked and lived in Charlotte, NC. Now publisher of the *Decatur News-Herald*.

PITTS, STEPHEN. 1992-93-94-95. TB, 5'11", 190 lbs.; Atlantic Highlands, NJ. Perhaps the ultimate team player of Paterno's 1990s squads. Might have been a starter elsewhere if not for the presence of two other blue chip TB's, Ki-Jana Carter and Mike Archie. One of the most unselfish players of the Paterno era. Waited patiently and worked hard for his turn in senior year only to be sidelined for half of season by a stress fracture in right foot. Came back slowly as KO returner but provided running spark in last four games that helped salvage season.

Broke out in seventh game of '95 against Iowa: he returned six KOs for 150 yards (including one for 43 yards that set up Brett Conway's 52-yard FG), then substituted at TB in second QT and proceeded to make several key runs in rally that brought 41-27 victory; finished game as leading rusher with 134 yards on 12 carries; for that performance he was named State's Outstanding Player-of-the-Game. Earned the same Player-of-the-Game honors again against Michigan in "snowbowl" three weeks later, when he also was selected Big 10 Offensive Player-of-the-Week with a career high 164 yards on 17 carries, including a 58-yard run in the final minutes that set up Joe Nastasi's TD off a fake FG that won game, 27-17. Closed out career with another fine game in '96 Outback Bowl win over Auburn, 43-14, when he again led all rushers with 118 yards on 15 carries and scored TD on four-yard pass from Wally Richardson. Started only two games in his career, as "redshirt" soph in opening games of '93 against Minnesota and USC, but by third game he had been eclipsed by Carter and Archie and was relegated to backup and kick returns for next two years. Led team in KO returns in '95 with the most runbacks (17) and yardage (364) since '88. Despite his ill-fortune, he is still one of only 30 players to rush for more than 1,000 yards in career with a total 1,156 yards on 215 attempts and five TDs. Number six choice of San Francisco in '96 draft and still playing in NFL.

PLATT, FRANK. 1939-40. T, 6'3", 190 lbs.; Folsom, PA. One of the original "Seven Mountains," the great seven-man line of the '40 team, which had the best State record in 19 years and was one of the top teams in the country with a 6-1-1 record. Began '38 as a guard but didn't play enough to letter. Moved to LT before junior year and became a two-year starter on the teams that helped turn around State's football program during the disastrous de-emphasis period prior to World War II. Was more laid back than some of his teammates but was a solid tackler and good blocker. Played one of his best games in 10-0 upset over Pitt in '39 that was State's first against Pitt in 20 years. Had another of his finest games against NYU in '40. Retired and living in Alexandria, VA.

PLUM, MILT. 1955-56. QB, PK & P; 6'2", 190 lbs.; Westville, NJ. One of finest State QBs under pressure and a throwback to another era as a triple-threat player—passer, defender and kicker—when QBs called their own plays. Played outstanding defense as an open field tackler and is tied with four players at sixth in career pass interceptions with 10. Led team in interceptions in senior year with seven (sixth best in one season) and tied Sam Valentine in junior year (two). Played one of his outstanding all-around games in of come-from-behind 21-20 win over Syracuse at Beaver Field in '55; in fourth QT he saved one TD by tackling the great Jim Brown from behind after a 42-yard run, stopped another with a last-minute interception in the end zone and then drove the team 80 yards and passed to Billy Kane for a one-yard TD that tied the game with 15 seconds left, then won the game by kicking the extra point; and played 50 minutes on a day he became a star. In '56 his punting—one for 73 yards that went out of bounds on the three-yard line and one for 56 yards that died on the OSU one— helped pull off one of State's biggest upsets, 7-6, over Ohio State in Columbus; his PAT after State's only TD actually won the game; the 73-yard punt is third longest in school history. His coolness, fortitude and skills under pressure was typified by his last game at Beaver Field against North Carolina State: with score 0-0 midway in fourth QT, he drove team 43 yards for 7-0 lead with 3:15 to play; NC State roared back with tying TD at 1:30 left; starting from own 37-yard line, Plum called a successful running play for 19 yards, then hit on four straight sideline passes and then a final nine-yard aerial to Les Walters at the three with 15 seconds left and Walters went into the EZ with three defenders hanging on for the TD and the 14-7 victory. Career punting average of 38 yards on 47 punts is 10th on all-time list. Led team in punting in '56 with 33 punts for 1,297 yards and a 39.3 yards average and played most minutes on team that year with 374 of a possible 540 minutes. Most of the passing records he set in the mid-'50s have been broken but he is still eighth in season passing efficiency with 136.47 in '56, when he completed 40 of 75 passes for 675 yards and six TDs and seven interceptions. Played in East-West Shrine game and Senior Bowl in '57. Drafted by Cleveland in '57 and had fine career with Browns ('57-'61), Detroit ('62-'67), Los Angeles Rams ('68) and New York Giants ('69) before retiring. Now a sporting goods business representative out of Raleigh, NC.

POLLARD, BOB. 1950-51-52. HB & PR, 6'1", 185 lbs.; Berwyn, PA. One of the truly forgotten standout backs who was an offensive and defensive star on Engle's first teams. He is the only player in history to score more than one TD in a game on runs from scrimmage over 70 yards (Rutgers, '51). During an era of two-platoon football, he played many games for the full 60 minutes. A backup in his soph year, he started at RH or Wingback in Engle's Wing-T and became a star. Second leading ground gainer that year with 425 yards on 57 carries for a fine 7.5 yards average per attempt and his outstanding performance against Rutgers in the next to the last game of '51 is still third in the single game rushing records; he gained 243 yards (on 14 carries), scored both two TDs on runs of 75 and 71 yards and had another 35 yards on kick returns in a 13-7 win at Rutgers. Also led team in interceptions (six for 43 yards return) and punt returns in '51 and his 16.0 yards average return on 14 punts (for 224 yards) and one TD on a 65-yard return against Michigan State before a Homecoming crowd is sixth best on record for one season. In senior year he was the rushing and all-purpose yards leader on 7-2-1 team with 341 yards (in 110 carries) and two TDs on the ground, 84 in receptions and 164 on kick returns. Had one of his best games in senior year in 14-7 win over Penn with 94 yards on 18 carries and the TD that won the game. One of few lettermen whose whereabouts are unknown.

POLLOCK, BEN. 1939-40. PK & T, 5'10", 205 lbs.; Hunlock Creek, PA. The first man to specialize at placekicking at State. Began soph year in '37 as a backup G but Higgins noticed how good he was kicking placements, so he was designated to boot extra points and FGs. Converted 12-of-13 PAT's that year but didn't play enough to earn a major letter under the eligibility rules at the time. State's kicking had been a major problem in previous season and cost Higgins' teams several games and possible winning seasons but with Pollock kicking the '37 team had first winning season in eight years. Left school for a year. Returned in '39 and had grown to the size of a tackle. Became the prime PK as junior and senior, and made 29 of 33 extra points over three years. Was backup at T but was mainly used in reserve behind second team. Had a long career in secondary education and retired as a school superintendent. Lived in Benton, PA until his death in '98.

POPP, BILL. 1958-59-60. G, 5'11", 205 lbs.; Steelton, PA. One of the best interior linemen on Engle's best teams. His name was perfect for the type of player he was, a good blocker and a solid hitter. Considered as "rugged" a guard as any in the Engle era. Was steady and consistent and could always be counted upon in crucial situations. Broke into starting lineup in last half of soph year and remained there rest of career. Was only letterman G returning in '60 and made the most out if it when he was picked All-East. Had one of his best games against Syracuse in the historic '59 battle of unbeatens when he set up State's first TD by stripping the ball from Syracuse QB in first quarter. Also recognized for his all around play in 34-13 win over West Virginia in '60. Played another of his finest games in one of his last in '60 in helping Lions beat Pitt 14-3; cited by sportswriters for his tackling and led a third period defensive charge when he threw Pitt QB Ed Sharockman for a big loss that forced Panthers to try a fake field goal and ended their last chance at scoring. Starter on the Liberty Bowl teams that won back-to-back games against Alabama and Oregon in '59 & '60. Played in Tucson's Copper Bowl All-Star game in '60. Recently retired as head track coach at Albright College and living in Reading.

POTSKLAN, JOHN. 1941-46-47. E, 5'11", 183 lbs.; Brownsville, PA. No player symbolizes the World War II era better than Potsklan. Like Potsklan, many of his generation sacrificed football and a possible pro football career for duty to their country and didn't let the war deter their love for the game. One of the outstanding defensive players of his generation. He was a standout defensive lineman and starting RE from the opening game of '41 season as a soph and was noted for his hard tackling and for rushing kickers; blocked two punts during season. Went into the Army in '42 and didn't play football for five years as he saw heavy combat and survived a German prison camp. Returned in '46 and became an even bigger star on the post-war teams, eventually becoming Co-Captain of undefeated '47 Cotton Bowl team, which still holds three NCAA defensive records, including fewest yards allowed rushing per game (17.0 yards on a total of 150 yards in nine games) and fewest yards per rush (0.64 yards on 240 carries). Sportswriters said he was one of the defensive Players-of-the-Game in the 13-13 tie with SMU in '48 Cotton Bowl. As soph, played one of his best games in a stunning 34-19 win over Syracuse that virtually ended the Orange's use of its previously powerful Reverse Y Formation. When he returned after the war he was a two-year starter at RE. Made one of biggest plays of career against heavy underdog Temple near end of '47 that salvaged unbeaten season: Temple surprised State with a version of the "hidden ball trick" and Potsklan tackled the runner from behind on the PSU 15-yard line after a 46-yard run to prevent a TD in eventual 7-0 win. Then in game next week against powerful Navy he and QB Chuck Drazenovich were cited for their defensive prowess in 20-7 win that was the impetus to the Cotton Bowl bid. Later became a well-known small college coach at Albright. Deceased.

POWELL, HAROLD ("JUNIOR"). 1961-62-63. FL, DB & PR, 5'9", 162 lbs.; Lewistown, PA. One of the most popular players with the fans because he always showed his spirit and exuberance on the field. A fine two-way player on offense and defense. The leading receiver on Engle's last bowl team and for a short time held the career receiving record until Jack Curry broke it in '66. He caught more passes in '62 than any State receiver since Jesse Arnelle a decade earlier and scored more TDs on receptions than anyone since Les Walters in '57—had 32 receptions for 303 yards and three TDs. His nine receptions against UCLA in thrilling 17-14 win in Beaver Field opener in '63 is still fourth in the single game records for receptions (he shares with five other players) and at the time broke Lenny Krouse's 23-year record; made one of the most exciting plays of the Engle era in that game just before halftime, when he took a sideline pass from QB Pete Liske between three defenders and instead of stepping out of bounds to stop clock he dashed down sidelines for 52-yard TD and 14-7 lead. In '62 Gator Bowl loss to Florida, 17-7, he led all receivers with four receptions for 40 yards. In the '61 Gator Bowl win over Georgia Tech, 30-15, he was wide open for a 35-yard TD pass from Galen Hall that broke open a tight 14-9 game in the third QT. Played one of his finest games in a losing cause against Maryland in '61, when the Terps won the only game in the 37-year series, 21-17; he caught three passes for 74 yards and picked up another 24 yards rushing; late in the game he caught what he is sure to this day was the winning TD on a diving nab of a Galen Hall pass from the nine-yard line but the officials ruled incomplete. Also a fine defensive back who led the team in interceptions in both '61 (three) & '62 (five) and tied with Don Caum in '63 (four). Tied for fourth in career interceptions with 12 for 211 yards and one TD. Had most yardage on interceptions in '62 with 140 yards and one TD, and his 47-yard zig-zag return against Pitt helped achieve a 10-0 victory and an 8-1 regular season. Led team in punt returns as junior and senior with his 18 returns (for 222 yards) being the most runbacks since Bill Luther in '49. Has been a practicing attorney in Mifflintown, PA, for years.

PREVOST, JULES. 1923-24. T & PK, 6'2", 198 lbs.; Radnor, PA. One of the great linemen of the era. A Second-Team All-American in senior year. Starting T and PK in '23 and '24 on teams that had 6-2-1 and 6-3-1 records, respectively but couldn't beat two main rivals, Syracuse and Pitt. In his first year as starter in '23, he and guards Joe Bedenk and Gus Michalske and center Bas Gray were part of one of the most underrated lines in the country. Took over PK in '24 after the graduation of QB Mike Palm and was considered one of best PKs in country; kicked eight FGs and some 12 PATs during the year, including two second half FGs of 30 and 15 yards for only points that beat Navy 6-0. Scored only points with two FGs in hard luck 10-6 loss to Syracuse before Homecoming crowd in '24 and 30-yard FG for only points in 24-3 loss to Pitt. A good blocker but earned his reputation for his fierce tackling. Was difficult for opponents to block and made frequent tackles behind the line of scrimmage. The number three on his uniform was one of the best known to fans of his era. One of his finest games was against West Virginia in the classic 13-13 tie at New York's Yankee Stadium in '23; was a "bearcat on both offense and defense" said the Pittsburgh Press; also picked up a partially blocked kick to stop a WVU opportunity. Deceased.

PRITCHARD, BILL. 1925-26. HB, 5'11", 175 lbs.; Buffalo, NY. One of the team's prime running back in his junior and senior years but he was not surrounded by many other quality players. Became well-known later as a professional football official. The teams he was on broke even in '25 (4-4-1) and was 5-4 in '26. But he was one of the stars in the scoreless tie with Notre Dame in the Beaver Field mud on Nov. 7, '25 when his running kept State on the move consistently

despite the horrendous playing conditions. Played in first East-West Shrine game in '27 along with teammates Gary Green (B) and Ken Weston (E). After graduation he played pro football with Providence Steamrollers in '27 and New York Yankees football team in '28. He then coached high school football for six years and was the head coach at the University of Buffalo for a period. He spent 35 years as a teacher and administrator in the Buffalo public school system. During this time he officiated in the old All-American Conference and then the NFL. Deceased.

RADAKOVICH, DAN ("BAD RAD"). 1954-55-56. C & LB, 6'2", 184 lbs.; Kennywood, PA. One of the most intense players of the Engle era. Nicknamed " Bad Rad," he was tough and mean. As rugged a LB as any who played for Engle. Stayed on as graduate assistant for three years and then spent 10 years as full time assistant for Engle and Paterno. Paterno credits Radakovich for being the father of "Linebacker U" for Rad was in charge of linebackers ('60-'69) during the development of such early graduates of "Linebacker U" as Ralph Baker, Bill Saul and Dennis Onkotz. An outstanding blocker but even better tackler. Hard and aggressive with a "take-no-prisoners" approach to the game and loved to play defense and hit people. When he hit, the runner knew it. Admittedly sometimes stubborn as a youngster but as he matured, he became an outstanding player and defensive football coach. Had one of his finest games as a junior backup to Captain Frank Reich in the 21-20 come-from-behind victory over Syracuse in '55. Those who saw him play, say his best game was the great 7-6 upset over Ohio State in Columbus, when he and other members of the first unit hammered the heavily favored Buckeye backs all afternoon, allowing the only TD with less than two minutes in the game and holding the vaunted Buckeye ground game to 188 yards, half its normal game output. Blocked punt in opening minutes of Holy Cross game in senior year that both coaches said was the key play in State's eventual 43-0 rout. His cousin Dave was reserve lineman and linebacker on the great '68 & '69 teams when Bad Rad coached linebackers. Played in '55 Blue-Gray game. Didn't play pro football but coached at State in the last six years of the Engle era and then with Paterno before leaving after '69 season to coach elsewhere, and has been an assistant with several college and pro teams, including the Pittsburgh Steelers during their heyday of the 1970's. Currently assistant head coach under former Pitt All-American Joe Walton at Robert Morris College in suburban Pittsburgh.

RADECIC, SCOTT. 1980-81-82-83. LB, 6'3", 238 lbs.; Pittsburgh, PA. One of the most durable graduates of "Linebacker U" and one of the best in the clutch. Second-Team All-American in junior year, when he was one of the leaders of the defense that helped give State its first National Championship. Also an Academic All-American. He and DB Mark Robinson led team with four interceptions that year and he had two TDs, including one on a spectacular 85-yard TD return early in fourth QT against West Virginia that broke open a tight 10-0 game and sparked the team to a 24-0 win (also had 10 tackles that day to lead team and was named TV Defensive Player-of-the-Game). Leading tackler in '82 championship season with 48 solos and 23 assists for a 71 total; and had one of his best days in 24-14 win over Notre Dame at South Bend, when he had 11 tackles and deflected two passes. Played one of his finest games in 19-10 win over Pitt that put team into National Championship game, when he had seven tackles, including one on third down goal line stand in fourth QT that forced Pitt to kick FG and eventually gave PSU the victory. Was outstanding in 27-23 win over Georgia for national title in '83 Sugar Bowl, when he led team with 14 tackles, caused one fumble and harassed Heisman Trophy winner Herschel Walker all evening. Co-Captain of '83 team that came back from a horrendous 0-3 start to eventually achieve an 8-4-1 record and a 13-10 win over Washington in the Aloha Bowl. Played two of his best games at the end of his career in Aloha Bowl and last regular season game against Pitt, when he had a whopping 21 tackles, including three sacks and recovered two fumbles deep in Pitt territory that led directly to TDs in 24-24 tie that put State into Aloha Bowl; was named TV Defensive Player-of-the-Game. Then was defensive star with 14 tackles and a deflected pass in the Aloha Bowl. Won Ridge Riley Award in '83 given to senior player for "sportsmanship, scholarship, leadership and friendship." Brother Keith played on '85 & '86 teams. Played in Japan Bowl in '84. Drafted second by Kansas City in '84 and had solid pro career with Chiefs ('84-'86), Buffalo ('87-'89) and Indianapolis ('90-'96). Works as an engineer, and is now the project engineer for the latest expansion of Beaver Stadium to 103,500 seating capacity by 2001. Makes his home in Mission Hills, KS.

RADOS, TONY. 1951-52-53. QB & P, 6'1", 187 lbs.; Steelton, PA. The first quarterback who became a star under Paterno's tutelage as an assistant in the Engle era. Never made All-American but was All-East and an astute team leader. Fine passer and very good ball handler. Got off to slow start as soph, when hobbled by a preseason injury and was beaten out for the starting position by another soph hardly anyone ever remembers, Bob Zajna; eventually started several games in soph year, but became the regular in '52 and '53 and led team in passing and total offense. Still bothered by a severe knee injury in '52 which cut down on his productivity but had operation during winter that helped make him a big star in '53. Had to be taught how to play defensive back in '53 when rules changed ending two-platoon football, and performed admirably. Also became one of team's punters as senior and could kick high and place kicks well. Best statistical passing year was '53, when he was the leading passer in the East, hitting on 81-of-171 passes for 1,025 yards, eight TDs and 12 interceptions. For more than 25 years his 425 passing attempts was the career record, and he is still 12th in all-time career passing yardage with 2,437 yards on 199 completions for 18 TDs and 25 interceptions. Played one of his finest games in a 20-19 loss to West Virginia in '53, when he passed for 251 yards and two TDs (on 16-of-27 attempts) but the Mountaineers won the game on a controversial blocked kick by All-American Bruce Bosley. Was still bothered by injuries in preseason of junior year but burst into the national spotlight and became a star in the second game of the season by leading State to a stunning 20-20 tie with Purdue at Beaver Field; he outdueled Purdue's All-American QB Dale Samuels, completing 17 of 29 passes for 197 yards and a TD in what was then the best single passing performance by a Lion QB in a decade. Had another fine game against Pitt that year, hitting on 11-of-21 passes for 105 yards and scoring the final TD on a one-yard sneak in leading State to a 17-0 upset win at Pitt Stadium that knocked the Panthers out of the

Orange Bowl. Next year he led team to win over Pitt by identical score, completing 13-of-28 passes for 161 yards, and a 6-3 record. Played in '53 Blue-Gray game. Deceased.

RAFFERTY, TOM. 1973-74-75. OL, 6'4", 232 lbs.; Fayetteville, NY. Another of the excellent offensive linemen who became better known in his All-Pro career with Dallas. First-Team All-American by Football Writers and The Football News in '75, when he was just State's third offensive lineman to become an All-American. One of the few "blue chip" seniors and co-captain of the solid, overachievers of '75 that won nine and lost two in the regular season and played Alabama in the first New Year's Eve Sugar Bowl at Superdome on Dec. 31. A pulling guard who was quick and fast enough to get to the corners and throw shattering blocks to spring the backs for long gainers. Early in his junior year Paterno said he was one of two best offensive guards in country, and he proved that throughout season. Back up in '73 and became starter in '74 and started ever game on team that was 10-2 and beat Baylor, 41-20, in '75 Cotton Bowl. Played in Hula and Japan Bowls in '76. Fourth choice of Dallas Cowboys in '76 and had an All-Pro career for 14 years including starting in two Super Bowls. Retired at the end of the '89 season. Now lives in Southlake, TX.

RAMICH, JOEL. 1968-69-70. HB & TB, 5'10", 185 lbs.: Elmira, NY. One of the early examples of Paterno's "pay your dues" philosophy that has guided player personnel decisions throughout his era. No back has ever worked harder in practice. Primarily a backup on the back-to-back undefeated teams of '68 & '69, when he played behind Charlie Pittman and Lydell Mitchell. Carried ball less than 50 times in those two years and gained just over 200 yards, but always gave 100 percent in practice and on field. Began '70 as Mitchell's understudy, but was ready in fourth game of season against Boston College when Mitchell suffered ankle sprain in second QT; he came in and led all rushers with 60 yards on 14 carries, including a TD in 28-3 win. The next week he again led the rushing with 96 yards on 23 carries in 24-7 loss to Syracuse. When Paterno shook up his struggling team before the Army game, he designated Ramich the starter and Ramich was the first Team TB for last five games, as Paterno also wanted to keep his hot-shot runners, Mitchell and Franco Harris, fresh. The tactic worked as State won last five games to finish with a 7-3 record, 18th ranking in country. Ramich closed out his career on a high when he rambled 26 yards for the first TD in a 35-15 pasting of arch rival Pitt. Now a vice president of administration for a company in Mountain Lakes, NJ.

RANDOLPH, CARLTON ("Brute"). 1895-97-98-99. LG, 6'1", 199 lbs.; Lewisberry, PA. First Penn State player to be selected to an All-America team when Walter Camp named him to Third-Team in 1898. A good runner noted for brute strength, thus his nickname. One reporter wrote that "Brute" could "hit like a sledgehammer." Captain of 1899 team. Older than most teammates and took year off in 1896 to play for Drexel and Camden Athletic Club. Part of State's so-called "famous trio" of '97 & '98 teams that included Henny Scholl and W. A. "Bill" Murray. After graduation played pro football on Connie Mack's Philadelphia Athletics football team in 1902 along with such former State teammates as Scholl, Earl Hewitt and Lynn Sweet. Deceased

RAVOTTI, ERIC. 1989-90-91-93. DT & OLB, 6'3", 247 lbs.; Freeport, PA. A hard-working defensive player who played on the line and or at linebacker at various times in his four years. Decided not to play in '92 season to concentrate on academics, but came back in '93 to become a full time starter for the first time in career, at OLB. Was usually among the top tacklers in each game, while also covering receivers and sacking the QB. As a "true" frosh he played on the special teams, then started four games at OLB in soph year and six games at DT in junior year. Played one of his best games as junior against Miami, when he had four tackles behind the line of scrimmage and a QB sack. As senior, his best game may have been in 21-20 win over Southern Cal, when he had four tackles and a QB sack and was among defenders who kept USC's potent passing attack from winning game. Had two more sacks against Iowa the following week. Played another fine game in the team's 38-37 come-from-behind win at Michigan State that brought Citrus Bowl invitation when he had three tackles for losses of 20 yards and five other tackles and batted down a couple passes. Wound up with 14 $\frac{1}{2}$ sacks in career, which is 12th best in statistics since '75. Sixth choice of Pittsburgh in '94 and is now one of the prime backup LBs and played in '96 Super Bowl.

REICH, FRANK. 1953-54-55. C, 6'2", 201 lbs.; Steelton, PA. Another in the fine tradition of State centers dating from the days of George Hoskins and "Mother Dunn." Called the defensive signals and was considered by coaches to be "football smart." Overshadowed most of his career by Rosey Grier, Jesse Arnelle and Sam Valentine but a tough hard-working C and LB. Started in junior year after senior Co-Captain Don Balthaser injured knee before opening game. Had one of his best games as a junior when he played entire 60 minutes in State's 14-12 opening game upset of Big 10 co-champ Illinois at Champaign; along with Jim Garrity, he made game-clinching tackle late in fourth quarter when Illini threatened at PSU 16-yard line on fourth-and-six and they threw Illinois' All-American J.C. Caroline for a four-yard loss. Co-Captain of snake-bitten '55 team that was 5-4 and couldn't seem to catch a break in a year State celebrated it's 100th year of existence. But he had a fine opening game against Boston University with a goal line interception that broke the game open: State was leading 14-0 early in third QT when Reich picked off pass at the goal and ran it down sidelines for 78 yards to set up State's third TD in eventual 35-0 win. Played in East-West Shrine game in '55 with teammate Lenny Moore. Also known as the father of pro QB Frank Reich Jr. who played against State while at Maryland. Teaches high school in Lebanon, PA.

REID, MIKE. 1966, 1968-69. MG & DT, 6'3", 235 lbs.; Altoona, PA. One of the greatest defensive tackles in college football. The only State player ever to win the Outland Trophy as the Outstanding Interior Lineman of '69. Also that year he won the Maxwell Award as the "outstanding player in collegiate football" (one of the few lineman to ever win the award) and finished fifth in the Heisman Trophy balloting. One of 14 State players and three coaches selected for the National Football Foundation College Football Hall of Fame, inducted in '87. Winner of the NCAA Silver Anniversary Award in '95 honoring former student-athletes who have distinguished themselves in their professions. He was a unanimous First-Team All-American in '69 and was selected to the Second-Team in '68. Formed with Steve Smear one of the outstanding defensive tackle combinations in State history. They were Co-Captains for two years of the great back-to-back unbeaten teams of '68 & '69, but both years the teams were downgraded by the pollsters and finished number two in the country. A true student-athlete who ma-

jored in music and acted in several campus theater productions. Made an outstanding debut in his first game as a soph MG against Maryland in the '66 season opener, when he set an unbelievable record of three safeties in one game in a 15-7 win, blocking two punts and tackling a runner in the EZ; and that performance earned him Lineman of the Week honors by *Sports Illustrated* and the AP. Re-injured knee in the first game of the '67 season against Navy kept him out for an entire year and required a major operation, but it was a fortuitous injury for it enabled him to play in '69 when he won the Maxwell and Outland Awards. That year he had 87 tackles and returned a fumble 25-yards for his first career TD (against his old patsy, Maryland). Was Most Valuable Lineman in 10-3 win over Missouri in '70 Orange Bowl; one of his most spectacular plays came with Missouri poised for a TD late in the fourth quarter at State's seven when he broke through and nabbed the running back for a 10-yard loss, forcing Missouri to kick a FG, which was ultimately its only score. Another of the most memorable moments in his career were the two sacks on Kansas QB Bobby Douglass in the last two minutes of the '69 Orange Bowl that put the Lions in position to win the game; one newspaper wrote that "Mike Reid was on Quarterback Douglass so fast it looked as if he'd been passed back by the Jayhawk center;" and the national television audience that watched the game will never forget the picture of him apparently praying on the sidelines (he has maintained he was just wiping the sweat off his head) as State went for a two-point conversion that won the game over Kansas, 15-14. Without experience he decided to threw the shot put in track and broke the State record in his first meet. Also wrestled and won Eastern Intercollegiate Heavyweight title as soph and was nearing NCAA finals when he lost to eventual champ and injured the knee that sidelined him for '67 football season. First choice (and seventh overall) of Cincinnati in '70 and an instant star and All-Pro. But quit pro ball at the height of his career in '75 to work full time on his music career. Honored by University as Distinguished Alumnus in '87. Very well known country song writer and singer who has won Grammy Awards for his music. He now makes his home in Nashville, TN.

REIHNER, GEORGE. 1974-75-76. OG & OT, 6'5", 250 lbs.; Washington, PA. Often overlooked because he played alongside such future All-Pros as Tom Rafferty, Brad Benson and Keith Dorney. Started out in soph year as the seventh guard on the depth chart and by year end he was starting at OT, playing on same team with older brother John— the '75 Cotton Bowl winners. Started as junior on offensive line that included Rafferty and Benson; team finished 10th in country with 9-3 record and played first New Year's Eve Sugar Bowl at Superdome in '75. Was often used in soph and junior years to carry-in plays from coaching staff to QB. In senior year he was switched to DT in spring and preseason but moved back to offense before opening game with Stanford, and formed a solid tackle combination with fellow Co-Captain Benson on team that lost three of first four games but roared back with six straight wins before losing to eventual National Champ Pitt and to Notre Dame in the Gator Bowl. Along with Dorney and Benson, he was cited for his fine blocking in 38-16 win over Army that helped turn around that season and he made All-East that year. Played in '77 Senior Bowl. Second choice of Houston in '77 and had fine six-year career with Oilers before retiring. Now an attorney in Scranton, PA.

REITZ, MIKE. 1969. PK, OG & FB, 5'11", 208 lbs.; Reading, PA. Only lettered in soph season and was bitter about not playing so he transferred to Maryland in '71, but without his kicking, the school record 31-game unbeaten streak and the 11-0 finish in '69 might never have happened. Was a backup OG who became the PAT & FG kicker and went on to break Ed Czekaj's 22-year record by booting 33-of-37 extra points. Also kicked seven FGs in regular season and a 29-yard one that helped beat Missouri, 10-3, in '70 Orange Bowl. His 33-yard FG and two PATs was the difference in early season 17-14 victory over Kansas State. Made the biggest kick of his career in waning minutes of midseason game against Syracuse: after State had rallied from a 14-0 fourth QT deficit to tie the game, he booted the PAT that won the game, 15-14, and kept the team on track towards another unbeaten season. In '70 he didn't play enough to letter but shared kicking with John Hull, making 13-of-15 PATs and one FG. Also played FB that year behind Franco Harris and Fran Ganter and had 103 yards and one TD on 28 carries. First played guard behind Bob Holuba, then fullback and frustrated by his situation left PSU angry and didn't feel he had been given a fair chance at beating out Harris at FB. Played against Lions in '72 as MD fullback, and carried five times for 35 yards, in 46-16 State win. Now a national accounts manager in Harrisburg, PA.

RESSLER, GLENN. 1962-63-64. OG, C & MG, 6'2", 230 lbs.; Dornsife, PA. One of the few linemen in country to win the Maxwell Award as the "outstanding player in collegiate football" in '64. A consensus First-Team All-American in '64 when selected by Football Writers, U.S. Coaches, NEA, Sporting News, Time, Football News, and others. Chosen on the All-Time Penn State team in 1967 by *Pittsburgh Press* sports editor Chet Smith, who covered Nittany Lion football for more than a half century. He was credited with being the primary force behind the dramatic turnaround of the '64 team, which came back from a terrible 1-4 start to win last five games and capture Lambert Trophy as best team in the East and finish 14th in country. Because he was the prime blocker for FB Tom Urbanik, who sparked comeback by running for 100 yards in three games and nearly 75 in another during five-game winning streak, sportswriters dubbed the duo "Paul Bunyan and his Ox." Rip Engle called him "the best interior lineman I ever coached." Played both ways as junior and senior and was an outstanding blocker and even better on the defensive line. Best known by State fans for his exceptional defensive play in the big back-to-back upsets over Ohio State at Columbus in '63 (10-7) and '64 (27-0). In '63, he was credited with 14 tackles and four assists and went head-to-head with the Buckeye's best running backs, Matt Snell and Tom Barrington, three times on fourth-and-short situations and three times he stopped Snell and Barrington. One year later, when State started the season at 1-4 and was a three-TD underdog against the then number two Buckeyes, Ressler dominated the line of scrimmage on both sides of the ball, as State stunned OSU, 27-0, holding the Buckeyes to 30 yards rushing and 30 yards passing, and he was given the game ball by his teammates. A quiet farm boy who majored in agriculture; started on the fifth team in the spring of his soph year and wound up as a second team OG in the '62 season, then became the star lineman of the '63 & '64 seasons. Played in East-West Shrine game and Hula Bowl in '65. Drafted number three by both the NFL Baltimore Colts and the AFL Denver Broncos and had an All-Pro 10-year career with the Colts before retiring. Played in Super Bowls III and V (when the Colts became the champs). For a long time he has owned a restaurant chain based in Camp Hill, PA, and also runs a construction company involved in insurance restoration in the Harrisburg area.

REYNOLDS, GEORGE. 1981-83. P, 6'0", 194 lbs.; Walnut Creek, CA. The career punting leader just ahead of Ralph Giacomarro based on average per punt, but he really only punted one year, '83, after waiting for Giacomarro to graduate. He had his finest moment in his final game in a Lion uniform when chosen the Defensive Player-of-the-Game in the '83 Aloha Bowl victory over Washington, 13-10; his punts put the Huskies in bad field position all afternoon; he had eight punts for a 46.8 yards average, including a 62-yarder into the wind and a 40-yarder late in the fourth QT that was downed on the Washington six-yard line and set up the Lions' winning TD. Punted once as a soph and three times as a junior but had more kicks than any senior in history (68). He was a boomer with a 43.0 yards average on 72 punts (for 3,096 yards) and only had one blocked. His '83 season average of 42.6 yards is the fourth best behind Giacomarro's '81 and '80 seasons and the late John Bruno's '85 season. Probably would have been a three-year punter on any other team, except had the misfortune of coming along at the same time as Giacomarro. Ninth choice of the Los Angeles Rams in '84 but never played an entire season of pro ball. Lives in Freemont, CA.

RICHARDSON, WALLY. 1992-94-95-96. QB, 6'4", 222 lbs.; Sumter, SC. One of the most intelligent starting QBs ever but one who never was fully accepted by the fans, probably because he followed in the path of All-American Kerry Collins. State's first successful Black QB and as unselfish a QB as ever stepped on the field in a PSU uniform. A two time GTE Academic All-American. No one was better in the two-minute drill when the team was trailing. He showed that in his first game as the regular starter in '95, when he brought the team back from a 23-21 deficit with 10 straight pass completions to set up a last second Brett Conway FG that beat Texas Tech, 24-23. Three more times in '95 he led late fourth QT come-from-behind wins. Perhaps his finest games under pressure were against Michigan State in both '95 and '96, when he passed the team downfield in the last moments for victories that assured berths in the Outback and Fiesta Bowls. Perhaps his all-time best was against MSU in '95, when State trailed, 20-17, with 1:45 remaining and the ball on its own 27-yard line with no time outs; he completed 11-of-15 passes, with two incompletions being spikes to stop the clock, and with eight seconds left hit Bobby Engram from the four-yard line for the winning TD. Made an impressive debut as a true freshman in '92, when injuries forced Paterno to insert him in the second QT of the opening game at Cincinnati; the score was tied 7-7 and he led three scoring drives, hitting on five-of-10 passes, for a 24-20 win. Started next week at Temple and led team to another victory, 49-8, with 10-of-19 passes for 165 yards and one TD and scored another TD himself. He rarely played the rest of the year, although he did appear in the Blockbuster Bowl, and "redshirted" the next year. Had an outstanding Outback Bowl in '95, when, despite a constant rain and muddy field, he completed 13-of-24 passes for 217 yards and four TDs in 43-14 pasting of Auburn. A preseason groin injury and a less-than-stellar receiving corps hampered him during his senior year, but he never complained; had several shaky games but lived up to all expectations in last three games of season by leading team to wins over Michigan, Northwestern and MSU. With 4:27 remaining against MSU and the scored tied, 29-29, he cooly took the team 80 yards for a 30-yard Brett Conway field goal that won the game, 32-29, and put State into the Bowl Alliance '97 Fiesta Bowl. In 38-15 thumping of Texas he was the ultimate leader, with 12-of-20 pass completions for 95 yards and one TD that made State number seven in the country. Finished career as fifth best passer of all-time with 4,519 yards and 27 TDs (fifth best) on 378-of-692 attempts and holds record for most completions in one season (193) and one game (33 against Wisconsin) set in '95. Surpassed John Sacca with lowest career interception percentage (2.02) but had more interceptions in senior year (eight) than his previous three-year total of six; the 14 total over four years is still the lowest number of interceptions among State's 11 top career passers, except for Tom Shuman (12) and Tom Sherman (also 14). His '95 season is sixth best for one-season yardage and TDs, when he hit on 193-of-335 passes for 2,198 yards , 18 TDs and just six interceptions. Had nine games with more than 200 yards passing with the 281 yards and two TDs in come-from-behind 26-23 win over in '95 and the 281 yards against MSU in final regular season game of career being his best. Headed for law school and a possible career on Wall Street after a stop in the NFL. Number seven choice of Baltimore in '97 draft and now playing with Ravens and the NFL Europe League.

RIVERA, MARCO. 1992-93-94-95. T, 6'5", 282 lbs.; Elmont, NY. Never made All-American but probably should have. A three-year starter who was part of the great offensive line in '94 that helped the unbeaten but unappreciated Rose Bowl championship team top the nation in scoring and total offense, while giving up only six sacks, three by the first team. He was the short side guard with an aggressive blocking technique. Injured before the '94 Illinois game but came in as a sub and helped with the famous last quarter come-from-behind length-of-field drive that won Big 10 Championship and preserved unbeaten streak. Started at long side tackle in '93 and was in for 156 plays as a "redshirt" frosh. Fine sense of humor and very outspoken. Will always be remembered for his forthright post-game comments, even to the point of criticizing Paterno's play-calling, as he did in controversial four-down failure against Michigan at Beaver Stadium in '93. Continued to play well throughout senior year and helped keep offensive line motivated when team was struggling. Played in '96 Senior Bowl. 6th choice of Green Bay in '96 and a member of the Pack's '97 Super Bowl championship team. Now lives in Brooklyn, NY.

ROBB, HARRY. 1916-17-19. RB & QB, 5'10", 164lbs.; Pittsburgh, PA. One of the stars of his generation but was overshadowed by All-Americans Charlie Way and Glenn Killinger. Holds one of the longest standing team records for most TDs in one game with six scored in 80-0 rout of Gettysburg as junior in '17 and had total of 13 that year. The 13 TDs tied him with "Bull" McCleary, "Light Horse" Harry Wilson and Lenny Moore for the single season record that was not broken until '68 by Charlie Pittman. QB of a excellent '19 team that only lost once in close game with Dartmouth and won unofficial Eastern Championship with 7-1 record. Called one of his biggest plays ever in first four minutes of final game against Pitt: without informing coach Bezdek he sent Harold Hess into punt formation near own goal line, Hess faked and hit E Bob Higgins with short pass of 15 yards and Higgins went rest of way for shocking TD and eventual 20-0 win; the TD pass is still listed as the longest pass play in State history at 92-yards but it should have been recorded as 95 yards. Teamed with QB Way and FB Red Gross in '17 Pitt game to work an unorthodox spread formation featuring a triple pass that brought them national attention; didn't win Pitt game but outplayed Panthers in last three QTs because of the new, radical formation. Was elected co-captain of the '18 team but left for

military and enrolled at Columbia as part of SATC program and became a Second-Team All-American pick by Walter Camp. Returned to be one of team leaders on Bezdek's first great team. Later played pro football. Deceased.

ROBINSON, DAVE. 1960-61-62. G & E, 6'3", 220 lbs.; Moorestown, NJ. The first "honors" graduate of "Linebacker U" and one of the great defensive players in college football history. State's first Black All-American when he was a consensus First-Team selection in senior year, picked by AP, Football Writers, NEA and Time magazine. Also the latest State player to be elected to the National Football Foundation College Football Hall of Fame, inducted in '97. Selected on the All-Time Penn State team in 1967 by *Pittsburgh Press* sports editor Chet Smith, who covered Nittany Lion football for more than a half century. But he says his greatest accomplishment at State was being the first Black to play in the Gator Bowl ('61). Engle called him "the greatest lineman and the greatest natural athlete I've ever coached." He was a ferocious hitter and linebacker. If tackling records had been kept fully in his era, he would probably be among the all-time leaders. Also may hold record in recovered fumbles in a single game when he recovered three in 23-7 win over Maryland in senior year. In junior year he and Bob Mitinger were the best pair of defensive ends in the country, but he was hobbled for much of season with an injury; suffered shoulder dislocation in opening game against Navy but returned to play in seventh game against Maryland and was one of the defensive and offensive standouts in 47-26 win over Pitt, catching three passes for 65 yards in setting up two TDs and being all over Pitt runners on defense. Then followed that with an outstanding all-around performance in the '61 Gator Bowl win over favored Georgia Tech, 30-15: he led all receivers with four receptions for 40 yards (two in crucial first down situations); but it was on defense that he captured the fancy of the fans, and one play in the third QT that sportswriter Larry Merchant called "possibly the play of the century" told it all: with State leading, 14-9, Tech was driving from its 43-yard line when Robinson dived over two blockers to sack QB Stan Gann with one arm around his neck and slammed him to the ground, causing a fumble that Robinson immediately jumped on and recovered at the Tech 35; on the next play Galen Hall threw to a wide open Junior Powell for a TD that broke open the game. That play set up his All-American year. Played what he later called his best game ever at State in defeating Syracuse, 20-19, before a '62 Homecoming crowd, making crucial plays in fourth QT: Syracuse had just scored on an 86-yard drive to take 19-14 lead and, puzzlingly, tried an onside kick which Robinson snatched and ran back five yards to Lion 42, then caught three passes from Pete Liske in TD winning drive, including a clutch fourth down pass at the one-yard line that led to State TD. Also played one of his finest defensive games in the ill-fated '62 Gator Bowl loss to Florida, 17-7, and was State's Outstanding Player-of-the-Game. Played G as soph for seven games and led blocking on a 65-yard punt return by Don Jonas that helped State beat Maryland, 28-9; switched to E on alternate unit in next to last game of season against Holy Cross because of injuries and caught two passes for 55 yards and was a terror on defense in 33-8 win. People forget how good of a pass receiver he was; basically a TE, he caught 17 passes for 178 yards in his senior year and as a junior he was State's leading receiver. Played in '63 Hula Bowl. First choice of NFL Green Bay Packers and third choice of AFL San Diego Chargers in '63 and signed with Packers; went on to an All-Pro career with the Packers from '63-'72 and played two years with Washington ('73-'74) before retiring. Played in the first two Super Bowls with the champion Packers. Now senior vice president of the Superior Beverage Group of Akron and lives in Kent, OH.

ROBINSON, MARK. 1980-81-82-83. S & PR, 5'11", 197 lbs.; Silver Spring, MD. One of the best defensive backs of the Paterno era. All-American in junior year on State's first National Championship team, when selected by Football Writers, Sporting News and NEA. He and Scott Radecic led team in interceptions that year with four (which he returned for 89 yards) and he was second to Radecic in tackles with 70. A punishing tackler who had the instinct to get quickly to the ball carrier. In the 27-23 win over Georgia for the national title in the '83 Sugar Bowl, he and defensive end Walker Lee Ashley were designated to stop Heisman Trophy winner Herschel Walker from getting around the corner, where he could use his speed—and they did; Walker got only 103 yards and one TD on 28 carries and Robinson was credited with nine tackles, several times tackling Walker one-on-one, intercepted two Georgia passes and deflected another. Played another of his outstanding games earlier in season in key 27-24 win over Nebraska, when he led team with 10 tackles and recovered a fumble. Made one of PSU's all-time momentous interceptions as a soph in '81, when he picked off Pitt's Dan Marino and went 91 yards for final TD in come-from-behind 48-14 upset over then number one Panthers. Often ran back punts and his 92-yard return for team's first TD in 49-14 win over Rutgers in '82 is second longest punt runback of all-time; he also set up a TD with an interception that day and was the TV Player-of-the-Game. Fourth choice of Kansas City Chiefs in 1984 and played four years with Chiefs and four years with Tampa Bay before leaving pro ball. Now an investment advisor and lives in Oldsmar, FL.

RODHAM, HUGH. 1934. E, 5'7", 165 lbs.; Scranton, PA. Would be just one of hundreds of virtually unknown but fine players at Penn State if not for the fact that his daughter, Hillary Rodham Clinton, later became the First Lady of the United States. Went out for team during its disastrous period of de-emphasis. He was not a bench warmer but a starter and according to news clippings of the period respected by his teammates. The '34 team was 4-4 but played one of its best games in 3-0 loss to powerful Penn at Franklin Field. Rodham is seen in '34 team photo sitting at end of first row wearing jersey number 69. Deceased.

ROEPKE, JOHNNY. 1925-26-27. HB & PK, 5'11", 170 lbs.; Jersey City, NJ. State's best runner, passer, punter and placekicker of his era. Second and Third-Team All-American and Captain of '27 team that had fine 6-2-1 record. A three-year star on teams where most players didn't measure up to his talent. Injuries kept him out of several games in junior year. Played probably his finest game in 20-0 win over Penn at Franklin Field in '27 that turned around the season: completed 10 passes for 184 yards including a 21-yard TD pass in the fourth quarter when the lead was just 6-0 and two minutes later ran two yards for the final TD, and kicked both extra points. The next week he kicked winning FG of 21-yards late in fourth quarter and made a game saving tackle on the ensuing kickoff return for first win ever over Syracuse, 9-6. Earlier in season, he scored 28 points by catching four TD passes and kicking four PATs in 34-13 victory over Gettysburg and 27 points in 40-6 Homecoming win over Lafayette; the 28 against Gettysburg is still

fourth in all-time one game scoring. After graduation played one year of pro ball with Frankford Yellow Jackets. Deceased.

ROGEL, FRAN. 1947-48-49. FB, 5'10", 195 lbs.; North Braddock, PA. Perhaps the school's best FB of all-time and the prototypical FB of his era of the popular Single-Wing. A bruising runner who punished tacklers with his straight-ahead crunching, "short gainer" smashes into the line and earned the nickname "Punchy" from his teammates. A two-way player who also was a fine LB. Second-Team All-American as a junior and one of State's best known running stars of the '40s. At one time he and Chuck Peters held most of State's rushing records. Tied Peters' record of three games with more than 100-yards rushing which was the school standard until broken by Roger Kochman in '61. (He actually had four games but his 110 yards on 27 carries in 7-0 win over Washington State in last game of '48 was not in record book until 1998.) His best rushing day was the 117 yards and a TD on 16 carries in 21-14 victory over West Virginia in '47; also had 116 yards and two TDs on 25 carries in 34-17 win over West Virginia in '49. Led team in rushing all three years he played and finished career with 1,496 yards and 15 TDs on 372 carries and a 4.02 yards per attempt for 16th place in all time. Best year was as junior when he set a rushing record for fullbacks with 602 yards and five TDs on 152 carries but scored more TDS (seven) and had better average (4.6 yards) as soph standout on State's unbeaten Cotton Bowl team; set up both State TDs and out-gained future Heisman Trophy winner Doak Walker in that game with 95 yards on 25 carries to Walker's 66 yards on 18 attempts. Perhaps his finest game ever was against Penn in '48, when he scored both TDs in a 13-0 victory that snapped Quakers 14-game winning streak: tallied his first TD on a 45-yard run off tackle in the second QT off a fullback half-spinner play where he literally ran right over Penn's All-American Chuck Bednarik; then in fourth QT had his other TD at the end of a 13-yard razzle-dazzle play that started with his handoff to Chuck Drazenovich, who pitched out to Elwood Petchel who threw into the EZ to Rogel who juggled the ball before making a spectacular leaping catch as he fell to the turf. One of the many frosh of '46 who were "farmed out" to California State Teachers College (where they played for "Frosh Coach" Earl Bruce) because of all the World War II vets returning. A star with the Pittsburgh Steelers in the early '50s who ran the ball into the line so often that Steelers fans coined the phrase, "High Diddle, Diddle, Rogel Up the Middle." Retired after the '57 season. Had been a high school teacher and farmer and lives in Bakerstown, PA.

ROMANO, JIM. 1977-78-79-81. G & C, 6'4", 250 lbs.; Glen Head, NY. Perhaps, the epitome of the persevering offensive lineman who lettered four years but had an erratic career. Broke into the starting lineup at G early in his soph season but the next year moved to C, because he couldn't beat out future All-Pros (junior) Irv Pankey (and sophs) Sean Farrell and Mike Munchak. Still couldn't make starting lineup at C because of classmate Bob Jagers and was set to be backup to Co-Captain Jagers in '80 but sat out season because of an injury. His perseverance finally paid off in '81, when he came back to be the starting C on team that finished third in both AP & UPI and beat Southern Cal, 26-10, in '82 Fiesta Bowl. Along with Farrell and Munchak, he was cited by sportswriters for opening the holes that helped Curt Warner make All-American. When Warner broke Shorty Miller's 69-year record for rushing in one game with 256 yards in 26 carries in 41-16 win over

Syracuse in '81, it was Munchak, Farrell and center Jim Romano who were credited with providing the essential blocking. Played in '82 Senior Bowl. Second choice of Oakland Raiders in '82 and played two years with Raiders and three years with Houston before leaving pro ball. Lives in Keller, TX.

ROSDAHL, HARRISON ("HATCH"). 1961-62-63. C & G, 6'3", 225 lbs.; Ridgefield Park, NJ. One of the best interior linemen of his era but overlooked in All-American voting because of presence of such teammates as Bob Mitinger, Dave Robinson and Glenn Ressler. A virtual three-year starter at G who was as good a blocker as he was a tackler. A key member of the front line teams of '61 & '62 that played in the Gator Bowl and finished in the Top 20 both seasons. Seemed to play his best against Syracuse. Played one of his finest games as a soph in 14-0 win over Syracuse at Beaver Stadium, when his blocking and tackling was noted by sportswriters, and then in '62 he blocked a late fourth QT FG attempt by Syracuse to preserve a 20-19 Homecoming victory. Some fans remember him for the inadvertent disturbance he caused as a junior against Army, when he jumped offside in the last seconds of an eventual and controversial 9-6 loss to Army and hundreds of belligerent cadets rushed onto the field before the game was over, causing such a disturbance that West Point's soon-to-be-famous Superintendent, General William Westmoreland, had to apologize nationwide for weeks. His career was cut short when injured in midseason against West Virginia missed last four games. Played in '64 Hula Bowl. Drafted fourth by NFL San Francisco 49ers and 14th by AFL San Diego Chargers in '64 but wound up playing as a DE for a year with Buffalo and three years with Kansas City before retiring. Now works as an independent handyman in Ridgefield Park, NJ.

ROUNDTREE, RAY. 1985-86-87. WR, 6'0", 180 lbs.; Aiken, SC. One of the best wide receivers of the '80s but never quite reached his potential because of an injury midway through senior year that cut short his career. Still, he was a fine receiver on two teams that played for national title. Had a sensational soph debut in '85 as a big-play pass catcher, when he was the leading pass receiver on the team that surprised everyone by going unbeaten in the regular season and playing Oklahoma for the National Championship in the '86 Orange Bowl. He caught just 15 passes for 285 yards (and a 19 yards average) and two TDs. Had an outstanding debut in the '85 season-opening upset of preseason number one Maryland with four catches for 64 yards that kept offense moving in a game that instantly put the Lions into the championship hunt. His best game that year was probably against West Virginia, when he scored two TDs on passes of 51 and 15 yards and caught one other pass in 27-0 win. Was the main WR on '86 championship team and had probably his best game in 24-19 win at Notre Dame that virtually clinched Fiesta Bowl bid when he shared Offensive Player-of-the-Game with QB John Shaffer: his diving reception of a 34-yard pass set up State's first TD, he scored a TD in third QT on a 37-yarder and then set up the game winning TD in fourth QT with a 24-yard catch. In senior year had two games with over 100 yards in receiving with his best being the 114 yards on four catches and TDs of 21 and 61 yards against Alabama, when he was named State's Player-of-the-Game. Followed that up a month later when he was again named PSU's Player-of-the-Game with a spectacular 59-yard reception for a TD against Syracuse, but that was the last reception of his career as an injury sidelined him for rest of year. Third choice of Detroit in '88 but only played one

year before injuries ended his career. Is a sales representative working in Cleveland, OH.

ROWE, DAVE. 1965-66. DG & DT, 6'6", 255 lbs.; Willingboro, NJ. One of the transition players who probably has not received the proper credit for his fine play on defense because both teams finished 5-5 in his two years. Selected on the All-Time Penn State team in 1967 by *Pittsburgh Press* sports editor Chet Smith, who covered Nittany Lion football for more than a half century. Probably the best lineman in the years he played and would have fit in perfectly with the great defensive linemen who followed. Had the size, speed and strength to play any position on the line, in the middle or at the end. Began career as a two-way G in soph year but came down with a virus that sidelined him most of year and he didn't letter. In the first year of NCAA rules allowing separate offensive and defensive teams in '65, he started at defensive middle guard. It was Engle's last team. The next year he started at DT on Paterno's first team. Was noted for his consistent play and sportswriters said he never had a really bad game. If tackle statistics had been kept then he probably would have been among the team leaders. Teammates and coaches called him "Hap" because of his enthusiastic attitude off the field. Played in East-West Shrine game and Hula Bowl in '67. Second choice of New Orleans in '67 and had an outstanding career as a defensive lineman, playing with the Saints ('67-'70), New England ('71-'73), San Diego ('74-'75), Oakland ('75-'77 and a Super Bowl appearance) and Baltimore ('78-'79) before leaving pro ball. Has become a well-known sportscaster and lives in Ashboro, NC.

RUNNELLS, JOHN. 1964-65-66. H & LB, 6'1", 214 lbs., Scotch Plains, NJ. Another of the fine scholar-athletes who helped begin the Paterno era. The first State player ever selected twice to be a First Team Academic All-American (in '65 & '66). A three-year starter at LB. All-East in '66 when he was Co-Captain of Paterno's first squad and probably the most frustrated player on the team. Despite a 5-5 record, Runnells was outstanding as the "Hero" defender. Played one of his finest games in a frustrating loss, 11-0 to Army in '66, with two pass interceptions that set up scoring opportunities and a half dozen tackles in leading a fine defensive effort. Had another outstanding game against then unbeaten and Orange Bowl bound Georgia Tech late in season, leading team in tackles (12) and making an interception in 21-0 loss. Tied with three others for team lead in interceptions that year with three. Won a prestigious NCAA post graduate scholarship for academics and used it to attend Harvard Law School. Drafted number 10 by Boston Patriots but didn't play pro ball. Now involved in capital management in Oldwick, NJ.

RUSLAVAGE, CHUCK. 1956-57-58. C & G, 6'2", 212 lbs.; Coaldale, PA. One of the fine two-way linemen in the mid-50s, who got more out of his desire and aggressive play than his natural talent. Never played HS football but developed into a fine technician. Could play either C or G in era when two platoon football required all-around skills. Played behind Dan Radakovich at C in '56 & and shared starting position in '57 but moved to LG for senior year to get '58s inspirational and tough captain Steve Garban into the lineup. Had one of his finest games on defense as soph in the classic 7-6 upset of OSU in '56. Played one of his best games in 43-0 rout of Pennsylvania in '58 in last game State ever played with Quakers and was selected as Lineman-of-the-Game. Recovered fumble in crucial moment of '58 clobbering of Holy

Cross 32-0 in what was expected to be a tough game. Played in '58 Blue-Gray game and '59 Senior Bowl. Didn't play pro ball but turned to coaching and was long time assistant for teammate Al Jacks at Clarion University and recently retired as a Clarion professor.

RUSSO, MIKE. 1983-84-85-86. DT, NT, 6-1 272. Mahopac, NY. The forgotten man of the outstanding defense on the '85 & '86 teams that played for two national titles and won it all at the 1987 Fiesta Bowl. Three-year starter at DT and when he played NT in '85 and '86 he was usually double teamed, freeing linemates and linebackers such as Shane Conlan, Bob White, Tim Johnson and Trey Bauer to make the tackles. Made one of the biggest plays that helped State go unbeaten in '85: in eighth game of season, Lions were trailing Boston College 12-10 in fourth quarter when he intercepted a pass tipped by Tim Johnson and ran 21 yards for TD that won game, 16-12; it was first TD scored by a PSU lineman since Mike Reid in '69. A week later, his fumble recovery on Cincinnati 30-yard line late in the third quarter led to a D. J. Dozier TD that gave State a 24-10 lead and clinched eventual 31-10 victory. In pivotal opening game victory that year against favored Maryland, he led all tacklers with 13 then was out with injury for two games before returning and making 8 tackles in win over Rutgers. Had one of his finest games in '86 in the 14-10 victory over Miami that won the National Championship in the '87 Fiesta Bowl and recovered one of two Miami fumbles as the defense shut down the potent Hurricane offense. In '86, opposing offenses concentrated on neutralizing him to disrupt Lion defense an often he had three foes hit him during the course of a play. Still, he averaged four tackles per game. Received one of the most unusual accolades when named to the '86 preseason All-Italian teams. Now a sales representative in Lower Burrell, PA.

SABOL, JOE. 1955-56-57. G & FB, 5'11", 187 lbs.; Shamokin, PA. May have been the toughest player pound-for-pound to play for Engle's mid-'50s teams. An exceptional two-way player who, for his size, was one of the best blockers and hardest tacklers on the team. He was quick and mobile and that made him ideal for the type of offense and defense Engle utilized in the era of two-platoon football. Began as a seventh string FB in preseason of soph year, moved to LHB in fall but by opening game against Boston U he was the starter at FB on the second unit because of injuries, and became an immediate star: as one newspaper headline proclaimed, "Moore Overshadowed by Unknown Sophomore" in 35-0 victory: scored one TD on a 34-yard gallop up the middle, plunged one-yard for another and set up a third on an eight-yard pass from Milt Plum and wound up as second leading rusher behind Lenny Moore (who was used a decoy much of the day). He never had a better running day because by the next year he was switched to G and started on second unit behind All-American Sam Valentine, and then was Captain of '57 team that won six and lost three and also upset Syracuse at Archbold Stadium. Teamed with Les Walters in that game to make one of the outstanding goal-line tackles on a muffed fourth-down punt by Syracuse in first quarter that led immediately to a State TD and an eventual 20-12 win. In another game against Syracuse in '55, he made one of his biggest plays ever when, as a soph LB, he intercepted a pass late in the first half: State was trailing

13-0 when Sabol's interception and 28-yard return to the Syracuse 10-yard line set up a TD with 15 seconds left in half; State went on to a thrilling 21-20 win despite one of the outstanding one-man performances ever by an opposing back, the great Jim Brown. Joe's brother Bernie was a fine defensive lineman on the '62 and '63 teams. Played in North-South Shrine All-Star game in Miami in '57. After graduation, Sabol went into football coaching and athletic administration and was long-time Athletic Director at Norwich University until his retirement. Living in Northfield, VT.

SACCA, TONY. 1988-89-90-91. QB, 6'5", 225 lbs.; Delran, NJ. Perhaps the most enigmatic of State's QBs. Forced to play as a true frosh in '88 because of injuries to upperclassmen, he never had the proper practice time to develop his skills until his later years; also hindered in first three years by a "communications problem" with Paterno. Almost left school at one point because of these problems but stayed on, and finally proved himself in senior year, when he led team to 11-2 season, a number three ranking by AP and UPI and a momentous come-from-behind 42-17 victory over Tennessee in '92 Fiesta Bowl. Winner of Hall Award as Outstanding Senior player that year, when he completed 169-of-292 passes for 2,488 yards and 21 TDs with just three interceptions, which places him in the top 10 of most season passing records. Career leader in yardage (5,869) and completions (401) and attempts (824) and tied with Todd Blackledge on career TD passes with 41; second to Blackledge in TD passes in one season with the 21 in '91. Also leads in most TD passes in one game with the five he threw in the 34-22 victory over Georgia Tech in the '91 Kickoff Classic. He was MVP in the game with 13-of-24 passes for 206 yards and TD passes of 52, 39, eight, five & four yards. Career total offense leader (6,000 yards) but only gained 131 yards rushing, 113 in one game (against Pitt in '90) and was not adept as a runner. Tied for second with Chuck Fusina for most games (11) passing over 200 yards; his best was 291 yards and one TD against Boston College in '91. Third best one season passing efficiency with 149.76% and S econd in lowest interception percentage in a season (1.71%) and most one season yardage (2,488 yards in '91) behind Kerry Collins. Perhaps played one of his best games in a losing cause, when he battled South Florida heat and exhaustion and a tough Miami Hurricane team down to the last moments before his final pass was intercepted in EZ and State lost, 26-20, in '91. Had toughest break in frosh year, when potential game-winning TD pass late in fourth QT was slightly overthrown and dropped in the EZ against Rutgers; State lost, 21-16, and the miffed play set the tone for the rest of the season, which was the first losing one for State in 49 years. Talked about transferring prior to soph season but got break when starting QB Tom Bill had personal problems. Started third game of season against Boston College and pulled out a thrilling come-from-behind 7-3 win by leading a 36-yard drive in last two minutes, making the big play on a fourth-and-eight at the BC 21 by scrambling for 13 yards when a screen pass play wouldn't work, then bootlegging one yard for the TD with 43 seconds left in game. Started every game from then until end of career. Played one of his best games in his last, the win over Tennessee in '72 Fiesta Bowl: he passed for four TDs, with 11 completions and 150 yards on 28 attempts; and his late third QT "across-the-field" pass to Kyle Brady wide open in EZ for a 13-yard TD gave State its first lead of the game in what turned into a 42-17 rout. His brother John also started at QB for State in '92 but quit team and left school after third game of '93 season. Played in '92

Senior Bowl. Number two choice of Phoenix Cardinals in '92 and played three years before leaving NFL, then played in the World Football League. Now coaching quarterbacks for LaSalle College in Philadelphia.

SANDUSKY, JERRY. 1963-64-65. E & DE, 6'1", 205 lbs.; Washington, PA. Better known nowadays for his outstanding work as linebackers coach and defensive coordinator in the Paterno regime, but he was a fine E in last three years of Engle era. Was considered an outstanding defensive player. In soph year he was a two-way player and spot starter and scored TD that almost beat Pitt. Cited by sportswriters for his blocking and tackling in first varsity game against Oregon in the famous "Z" Back win. Started at LE in '64 season opener against Navy but was injured and missed four games, then settled in as a defensive specialist and starter under the new "limited" substitution rules. Had one of his best games that year in Columbus, when he, and All-American middle guard Glenn Ressler were cited by sportswriters for holding then number two Ohio State to a total of 103 yards as a 3-4 State team clobbered the Buckeyes, 27-0, in one of outstanding upsets in PSU history. In '65, when college rules changed to permit unlimited substitution, he became a specialist on defense and was one of the team's leading tacklers. After graduation he was an assistant coach at Juniata College and Boston University before joining Paterno's staff full time in '69, first as assistant line coach, then moved to linebacker coach when Radakovich departed. Known as the architect behind the outstanding defensive teams of the late '70s and '80s and was especially singled out for the defensive plan that frustrated Heisman Trophy winner Vinnie Testaverde and the Miami Hurricanes in the '87 Fiesta Bowl victory for State's second National Championship. Some may call him the Senior Tenured Professor of "Linebacker U" and now in his 31st year as a PSU assistant. His son, E. J., was a lineman in '91 & '92. Founder of The Second Mile, a national charity that helps disadvantaged youths. Lives in State College.

SAUL, BILL. 1960-61. C, G & LB, 6'4", 220 lbs.; Butler, PA. Another of the early graduates of "Linebacker U" who reached his full potential in the NFL. Despite his size he was known for his aggressive style and hard hitting. In his first varsity game, as a backup C and LB against Illinois in '59, he was cited by sportswriters for his outstanding play in 20-9 victory; also played E that year but didn't letter because knee injury kept him on sidelines. Couldn't break into starting lineup at C because of three-year starter Jay Huffman so Engle moved him to E & G in '60, then made him C of alternate unit in '61 but played LB with first unit defense. Had an outstanding senior season and continued to get better as year progressed. Cited for his linebacking in several games, including 34-14 win over Holy Cross when teammates presented him with game ball. Played probably his finest game in 14-0 upset over Syracuse in '61 which was turning point game of season; led first quarter goal line stand with four tackles, including three on eventual Heisman Trophy winner Ernie Davis, then forced fumble at Syracuse 15-yard line in third quarter that led to State's clinching TD. Along with Mitinger and Robinson, made another outstanding goal line stand against West Virginia in game that could have prevented team from ultimately getting "breakthrough" Gator Bowl game against Georgia Tech. Drafted number two by NFL Baltimore Colts and number nine by AFL Buffalo Bills in '62 and played with Colts ('62-'63), Pittsburgh ('64, '66-'68), New Orleans ('69) and Detroit ('70) before retiring. Now lives in Baltimore, MD.

SCHAUKOWITCH, CARL. 1970-71-72. OG, 6'2", 220 lbs.; McKees Rocks, PA. One of the forgotten fine offensive linemen of the early '70's. Co-Captain of '72 team that was first to play in Sugar Bowl and part of the offensive line that helped junior John Cappelletti become one of the country's premier running backs. Had good speed and was an "excellent" blocker. Lettered as a soph while a backup at guard then started for two years. Made one of the biggest blocks of his career as senior during a desperate last minute 80-yard drive against Iowa, when his downfield hit helped spring Cappelletti on a fourth down 32-yard run that gave the Lions a come-from-behind 14-10 victory. His recovery of a fumbled Syracuse punt at the Orange 45-yard line in the second quarter of the '72 Homecoming game led to State's first TD that broke open a scoreless tie, giving the Lions the impetus to take a 17-0 win. An honor student in mechanical engineering. Drafted number 15 by New York Giants and played for Denver Broncos in '75 & '77. Now in insurance business in Mitchellville, MD.

SCHLEICHER, MAURICE ("MAURY"). 1956-57-58. FB & E, 6'2", 221 lbs.; Walnut Park, PA. One of the best defensive linemen of Engle's late '50s teams and a good FB but never reached his full potential at FB, because he was switched to E in senior year and became team's best receiver with nine catches for 127 yards. As soph and junior he was the starting FB on second unit behind Babe Caprara and was used in same way, as a blocker or spot runner who helped disrupt defensive schemes concentrating on the running and passing of State's HBs and QB. Played one of his finest games in soph year in 7-6 upset over heavily favored Ohio State, when he made several key tackles at LB, and his 24 yards on seven carries helped keep State's attack on the move. One of best games in junior year was in close 14-13 loss to Pitt, when he helped set up first TD with a 27-yard pass reception and two short runs. In senior year, it took a few games for him to adjust but he had the size, speed and hands to be a TE, though the position he played was actually RE. Had one of his best games in 36-0 win over Furman, when he was named Player-of-the-Week with four receptions for 58 yards and another one for a two-point conversion. But it was his blocking and defensive prowess that made him a key member of the hard-luck '58 team that just missed a bowl game even though it knocked rival Pitt from a major bowl. Played in '58 Blue-Gray Game and '59 Senior Bowl. Drafted by NFL Chicago Cardinals and AFL Los Angeles/San Diego Chargers in '59 and played with Cardinals ('59) and Chargers ('60-'62) before an injury ended his pro career. Works in athletic communications in San Jose, CA.

SCHOLL, LEROY ("HENNY"). 1896-97-98-99-1900-01. LT, 6'0", 193 lbs.; Williamsport, PA. Was one of the toughest players ever and the only player to win six letters for football. Played in an era when few pads were worn and career ending injuries were frequent and some times deaths occurred. Though known for his hard hitting, he was a good runner who scored many TDs in his career. Showed up at his first day of practice in 1896 with a blackjack and a scowl and some teammates immediately feared him. Credited with introducing helmets to Penn State in 1897, when he appeared at fall practice with an old derby hat with the brim cut off and padding stuffed inside. Part of State's so-called "famous trio" front line (so nicknamed by the press and fans) on the 1897 & '98 teams that included guard "Brute" Randolph and Center W.A. (Bill) Murray. Captain of 1900 team but had his finest year in '01, when he scored at least a dozen TDs and several field goals, and scored all the points in State's surprising 11-6 upset of Navy. In final two games of his career, he scored four TDs in 39-0 win over Lehigh and both TDs in 12-0 victory over Dickinson. After graduation played pro football on Connie Mack's Philadelphia Athletics football team in '02 along with such former State teammates as Randolph , Earl Hewitt and Lynn Sweet. Returned to help coach State teams for several years. Deceased.

SCOTT, FREDDIE. 1993-94-95. WR, 6'0", 185 lbs.. Southfield, MI. One of the finest receivers in the Paterno era but never reached his full potential after brilliant soph season. Played in shadow of Bobby Engram for all of his career and then left with one year of eligibility to play pro football. Still, he is seventh in career receptions and yardage with 93 catches for 1,520 yards and 11 TDs. Also fifth in total receptions for one season, when he caught 47 for 973 yards (fourth career best and a 20.7 yards per reception) and nine TDs in '94, when he and Engram were the 1-2 receiving punch on an offense that was one of college football's all-time best; team went unbeaten and won '95 Rose Bowl. Three times in '94 he and Engram both had more than 100 yards in a game, and he had three other 100 yard plus games, with the 145 yards (on six catches and one TD) against Michigan State being his best ever in yardage and 12th in single game records. Broke into the starting lineup in opening game of '94 against Minnesota with a sensation, catching seven passes for 133 yards and a 26-yard TD and followed that up the next week against USC with another 133 yards and a 44-yard TD on six catches. Teamed up with Kerry Collins for an 82-yard pass play in third QT against Rutgers in '94 that is tied for third as the longest in history. Had perhaps his finest day in the "big" game of '94, when State beat Michigan, 31-24, at Ann Arbor to vault into number one: Scott had three receptions for 56 yards before his "hometown" crowd and made the cover of *Sports Illustrated*. In '95 he set record for most receptions in one game with 13 (for 110 yards and one TD) against Wisconsin at Beaver Stadium but he never did "click" with QB Wally Richardson the way he did with Collins. Played in '96 Hula Bowl. Signed as free agent with Atlanta Falcons in '96 and now playing with Indianapolis.

SCOTT, JIMMY. 1971-72-73. WR, 5'11", 160 lbs.; Carlisle, PA. One of the fine corp of receivers when Paterno accelerated his passing game in the early '70s. But injuries impeded his career. Was so fast and quick he could get past opposing defenders before they realized it, and he became one of the school's most exciting receivers. Caught only 23 passes in career but five were "bombs" for TDs. Still holds the records for best receiving yardage average in a career (30.7 yards) and best yardage in a season (36.1 yards in '72). The catches included a 76-yard pass from John Hufnagel that helped "ice" the 45-26 win over Boston College in '72 and a 66-yard pass from Tom Shuman in first QT of '73 Army game that ignited a 54-3 rout. Made another exceptional catch for the go-ahead TD in 42-22 win over Maryland in '73, leaping high in the air to snag the ball high as he was falling backward into the EZ. Had a sensational varsity debut as backup in 56-3 opening season win over Navy with an exciting 86-yard TD catch from QB Steve Joachim that is second only to the 1919 Hess-to-Higgins aerial as the longest pass play in State history. Began soph year as HB, when he also was IC4-A dash champ, but was switched to flanker, where he found his position and was a reserve in '71 and sometimes starter in '72 & '73. Now working in Martinsburg, PA.

SHAFFER, JOHN. 1984-85-86. QB 6'3", 209 lbs.: Cincinnati, OH. Perhaps the most maligned QB (by fans) despite leading the team to back-to-back national title games and the '86 National Championship. He was Co-Captain and one of the inspirational leaders of that championship squad and is more revered today by Lions than he was while he was playing. He wasn't an outstanding passer (neither his career passing efficiency or TD efficiency ranks in the top 10 of all-time) and was not good enough to make an All-American team, but he was intelligent and smart and cool under pressure. He also was the quintessential leader, as exemplified when he was named an Academic All-American in '86. He was the perfect QB for the running of D. J. Dozier, Tim Manoa and Steve Smith and the "bend-but-don't break" defense led by Shane Conlan, Tim Johnson and Bob White that was the heart of the '85 & '86 teams. Still, he seemed to come through in the "clutch," as he did in the "big" '85 game at Syracuse, when team trailed 20-17 late in fourth QT; he had missed receivers all day and had been throwing into tight coverage, but after State recovered a fumble with less than four minutes remaining in the game at the Syracuse 42-yard line, Shaffer tossed three passes including an eight-yarder to Smith for the game winner. Long-time PSU fans often compared him to Chuck Burkhart, QB of the '68 & '69 teams, because "all he could do was win." But he actually was a better passer than Burkhart. He lost only one game in his high school and college career but it was in the championship game against Oklahoma in '86 Orange Bowl, when he played one of his worst games, throwing three interceptions and completing just 10-of-22 pass attempts for 74 yards, but he accepted the blame and vowed to improve passing in '86. He did because he had only four interceptions in '86 while completing 114 passes in 204 attempts for 1,510 yards and nine TDs and a 1.96% interception percentage that is fifth best in history. Played one of his best games in 23-3 midseason "upset" at Alabama that propelled State into national title hunt, when he hit on 13-of-17 passes for 168 yards and was named Offensive Player-of-the-Game. Had perhaps his finest passing day in 24-19 win at Notre Dame, when he was named Player-of-the-Game, hitting on 9-of-13 passes for 162 yards including three bombs to Ray Roundtree, one for a 37-yard TD in third QT that took State from a 13-10 deficit into a lead it never relinquished. Although his passing statistics in the '87 Fiesta Bowl were not good (5-for-16 for 53 yards and one interception), he led a 13-play, 74-yard drive late in the second QT and scored PSU's first TD on a four-yard run. But he kept his poise throughout and the offense stymied Miami's outstanding defense, giving the Lion offense the chance to win the game, 14-10, and Shaffer has the game ball. Seventh in career passing with 3,469 yards and 18 TDs on 262 of 547 pass attempts; completions is sixth best on record. Had only one game over 200 yards passing, with 220 yards and one TD in a 15-for-36 day against Temple as a junior. Not very mobile and never ran unless it was the very last resort and because of that he has a minus 128 yards in career rushing. Still, he is eighth in all-time total offense. Signed as a free agent by Dallas in '87 but quit pro football to return to State to go to graduate school. Now a high yield bond salesman on Wall Street, lives in Summit, NJ.

SHERMAN, TOM. 1965-66-67. QB & PK, 6'0", 190 lbs.; Rimersburg, PA. One of the most versatile players of the '60s, but a QB who may be overlooked because he was the main man between Pete Liske and Chuck Burkhart. Because of his name, he is often confused with another of the "forgotten" QBs, Tom Shuman (see below). An all-around player who was a throwback to the triple-threat players of another generation because he could run, pass, catch, kick and tackle well. Did almost all the FG and PAT kicking in soph and junior years and finished career with 12-for-21 FGs and 29-for-36 extra points and at one time held the school record for most points kicking in one game (14 against West Virginia in '66). Blossomed as a senior and led team to 8-2-1 record and the 17-17 tie with Florida State in the '67 Gator Bowl that established State's image as a team willing to take risks. Was Outstanding Player-of-the-Game in that Gator Bowl, and was involved in all State scoring, passing for two TDs and kicking a 27-yard field goal and two extra points; he hit on 6-of-19 passes for 69 yards (with two interceptions) and also carried the ball six times for 24 yards. Involved in perhaps the most momentous and controversial play of the Paterno era in that Gator Bowl game: with State leading by a surprising 17-0 score early in second half and a fourth-and-inches deep in own territory at about the PSU 15-yard line, Paterno called for a daring QB sneak by Sherman over C Bill Lenkaitis; to this day both Sherman and Lenkaitis swear Sherman was a foot past the scrimmage line, when Sherman was pulled back by FSU players and the official misplaced the ball; FSU was given ball and scored two plays later and eventually held on for 17-17 tie; but Paterno's gamble captured the imagination of the sportswriters and made him an overnight coaching sensation. Sherman was the second team QB behind Jack White in soph year (and last season in Engle era) but also started at SE when Jack Curry was hurt, and played some at RB. In Paterno's first year as head coach, Sherman started at defensive back where he intercepted two passes, but after back-to-back losses Paterno shook up the backfield and disposed of the I-Formation in fourth game of year against Boston College, moving Sherman back to starting QB, where had outstanding debut, leading a second half come back as he completed 13-of-26 passes for 220 yards and two TDs, passing for one two-point conversion and kicking for two more points and playing some defense in a 30-21 victory. He set six records by the time he was done and is still 11th in career and 12th in one-season passing with a career mark of 2,588 yards and 19 TDs on 163-of-347 attempts and 14 interceptions with a '67 season mark of 1,616 yards and 13 TDs on 104-of-205 attempts and nine interceptions. Led team in scoring as junior with 57 points on five TDs while connecting on 6-of-8 field goals and 7-of-10 extra point kicks. His 25 points (on four TDs and one extra point) in 33-15 Homecoming win over California in '66 is sixth best in the game scoring record books. He also was total offense leader during his junior and senior years because of his ability to scramble when needed. For 21 years, he held the record for most TD passes in a game with four he threw in 42-6 win over Pitt in '67 and then shared record with Chuck Fusina and Todd Blackledge until it was broken by Tony Sacca in '91. Also set record in '67 for TD passes in one season that he held for 10 years. Had three games passing over 200 yards with the 221 and two TDs in 30-21 win over Boston College at Beaver Stadium in '66 being his best. His 80-yard TD to Paul Johnson against Maryland in '67 is tied for fourth longest pass completion of all time. Signed as free agent by Boston Patriots in '68 and played for Patriots in '68 & '69 and for Buffalo in part of '69 before leaving pro ball. Had been a long time assistant (football coach) to George Welsh at the University of Virginia, and now working in UVA's athletic administration.

SHERRY, JACK. 1952-53-54. E, 6'2", 185 lbs.; Drexel Hill, PA. One of the best defensive halfbacks of the early Engle era who also was a fine offensive end in the era of two-platoon football. Part of an

exceptional recruiting class that included Jesse Arnelle, Jim Garrity and Rosey Grier that had three shutout victories over arch rival Pitt, and Sherry's playing was instrumental in all three wins. Had a fine soph season on one of Engle's best teams (7-2-1), when he had eight interceptions (for 101 yards) to share team lead with Don Eyer, setting a new team record that wasn't broken until 16 years later by Neal Smith. One of his biggest interceptions that year came in first QT against Penn and turned around a 7-0 deficit as State won 14-7. Then in final game of year at Pittsburgh, his two interceptions set up both TDs in 17-0 win, picking off his first on last play of first QT and running back 21 yards to Pitt 29, then getting his second midway through the fourth QT and returning it 25 yards to Pitt 10. Continued to be steady on defense but also became a fine pass receiver in senior year and tied with Garrity for most receptions with 11 for 165 yards and one TD. The TD came on a 19-yard pass from Bobby Hoffman in the second QT to help beat Pitt, 13-0. Had one of his best defensive games that year in opening game upset of Illinois 14-12 at Champaign as sportswriters noted his "devastating hits" on the highly regarded Illinois runners, Abe Woodson, J.C. Caroline and Mickey Bates. Also a fine basketball player who started on the '54-'55 team that is only State team ever to go to Final Four. Played in '54 Blue-Gray game. Now a manufacturer's representative and frequent visitor to State College for business and athletic events. Currently living in West Chester, PA.

SHULER, MICKEY. 1975-76-77. TE, 6'3 ½", 224 lbs.; Enola, PA. One of State's all-time outstanding TEs and many believe he is second only to Ted Kwalick as the best in history. Second-Team All-American in senior year, when team was 11-1, rated among top five in country, and beat Arizona State in Fiesta Bowl on Christmas Day, 42-30. Began soph season as a backup TE and was the starter before season was over. Won Red Worrell Award in '76 as most improved player in spring practice and showed why in next two years as he became one of the best receivers and blockers. Some sportswriters believed he was a better blocker than receiver even though he is among the all-time Top 20 pass catchers in PSU history. Led all receivers in '76 and '77 and best year was '77, when he caught 33 for 600 yards (13th in all-time one season yardage) and one TD and 18.2 yards per catch. He had two 100 yards games that year, against Rutgers and Houston with four receptions in each game, and was only the second State receiver up to that time to have two such back-to-back 100 yard games. Perhaps his finest game was in the 31-14 win over Houston when a 41-yard reception helped set up a big TD. A 52-yard catch setting up a TD against Utah State helped spark a 16-7 victory and a 41-yard TD catch in the opening minutes of the West Virginia game provided the spark for an 49-28 win. Played one of his best games against Miami in '76 21-7 win, when he caught four passes for 36 yards including a three-yard aerial for final TD. In '77, one of his best was in tight 21-17 win over North Carolina State, when he caught seven passes for 93 yards to help set up two TDs. Tied for 14th in career receptions and 12th in yardage with 66 catches and 1,016 yards and four TDs and a 15.4 yards per reception. Played in '78 Hula and Japan Bowls. Number three choice of New York Jets in '78 and had great career with Jets from '78-'89, then played two years with Philadelphia before retiring after the '91 season. Owns a car wash in Marysville, PA.

SHUMAN, TOM. 1973-74. QB 6'1½", 194 lbs.; Pottstown, PA. Perhaps the most underrated QB in history but a star in his era. Certainly one of the most durable of PSU's QBs. He won 22 of 24 games he started and the two defeats were by a total of six points. His back-ups in '73 & '74 near saw enough playing time to earn a letter. Another of the sometimes "forgotten" QBs, and because of his name, he is often confused with Tom Sherman (see above), but he was the QB on the '73 team Paterno once called "the best I ever had" in first decade of his career. Led that team to an unbeaten 12-0 season and a 16-9 win over Louisiana State in the '74 Orange Bowl, but the team was neglected by the pollsters and could finish only fifth in both AP & UPI. He was the Most Valuable Back in that game, hitting on 6-of-17 passes for 157 yards and a dazzling 72-yard TD to Chuck Herd, who made a spectacular one-handed catch for the first State touchdown . The next year, he quarterbacked the team to a 10-2 record, a 41-20 win over Baylor in the '75 Cotton Bowl and seventh ranking in AP & UPI polls. The Cotton Bowl was one of the best games in his three-year career, and the only time he got over 200 yards, with 226 yards on 10-for-20 passes and a 49-yard TD pass to frosh Jimmy Cefalo; for that performance sportswriters in the press box selected him as the Outstanding Player of the Game. A fine passer who still holds the record for best TD pass percentage in a season with 8.08% in '73, when he hit on 83 of 161 attempts for 1,375 yards and 13 TDs with just five interceptions. Ranks ninth in career passing with 2,886 yards and 28 TDs on 188 of 365 pass attempts and just 12 interceptions for a fourth place in career passing efficiency at 136.48 behind Mike McQueary, John Hufnagel and Kerry Collins; also fifth in career TDs, second in career TD pass percentage with 7.67% and fifth in lowest career interception percentage with 3.29% of his passes being picked off. He is the only QB to have two of the longest TD passes in the record books: he hooked up with Chuck Herd for a 76-yard TD against West Virginia in '73 and again with Herd in the ensuing Orange Bowl for that breath-taking 72-yard score. As soph he backed up John Hufnagel and completed only 8-of-21 passes but three were for TDs with first TD pass of his career a 29-yarder in fourth QT against Maryland. First career start in nationally-televised opening game at Stanford in '73 indicated what would follow: he out-performed preseason All-American QB Mike Boryla in completing 11-of-18 passes for 117 yards, including a 14-yard TD pass to Gary Hayman in the waning moments of the half that broke open a tight game and led to the eventual 20-6 win, and was named offensive Player of the Game by ABC. Played probably his best regular-season game that year in 42-22 win over Maryland: completed 7-of-14 passes for 114 yards and three TDs, including a 17-yarder to Dan Natale on an audible in the second QT and a 21-yarder to Jimmy Scott that broke open the game in the third QT. Played steadily throughout '74 and wound up with great Cotton Bowl win. Sixth choice of Cincinnati in '75 and played with Hamilton in the CFL for a few years. Now vice president in Plano, TX.

SHUMAKER, EARL. 1953-54-55. G, 5'9", 207 lbs.; Beaver Falls, PA. An outstanding offensive and defensive guard and three-year starter for Rip Engle in the mid-50s. Helped open the holes that made Lenny Moore one of the leading rushers in the country in '54 & '55. A hard tackler who smashed into opponents with a "no holds barred" fury. Pitt assistant coach Ernie Hefferle said Shumaker "was the best middle guard" the Panthers faced in '55 when Pitt went to the Sugar Bowl; "He makes at least 50 percent of the tackles for them," Hefferle said. Played one of his best games as senior in the come-from-behind 21-20 win over Syracuse at Beaver Field. Also cited for his defensive work in the classic 14-12 upset over Illinois at Champaign in 1954 when he helped stifle the high-powered offense led by All-American J.C. Caroline. Now a realtor in Reading, PA.

SIDLER, RANDY. 1974-75-76-77. MG, DE & SE, 6'3 ½", 229 lbs.; Danville, PA. One of the most versatile players of the Paterno era, and a First-Team AP All American in his senior year, when he was Co-Captain of a team that may be one of the most "forgotten" great squads of the Paterno era; it won 11 and lost only once in a mid-season upset to Kentucky (24-20) and beat Arizona State in Fiesta Bowl to finish fourth in UPI and fifth in AP polls. Sidler made 65 tackles and four sacks from his MG position, but his '77 performance is often overlooked because of the outstanding performance of his soph defensive line teammates, Bruce Clark and Matt Millen. Played one of his best games in Eastern regional TV win over Maryland, 27-9, in senior year and was recognized as the Defensive Player-of-the-Game; he terrorized Maryland backs all day, blocking a FG attempt, sacking the QB once, nailing another runner for a big loss and making nine tackles. Blocked a punt in opening minutes of midseason game against West Virginia that Millen scooped up and ran in for three-yard TD in 49-28 rout. Also was the center that year for FGs, PATs and punts. Paterno said the former high school QB had the "size, speed, strength and intelligence to play a number of positions" and he did. After playing SE, TE, LB, DT and DE in three previous years he finally found a home at MG in senior year. Became first frosh in 23 years to start a game in '74 when he replaced the injured Dan Natale at TE against Wake Forest. When Natale returned, he continued to start as Paterno used two-TE formation, which helped win '75 Cotton Bowl against Baylor. Caught 10 passes for 200 yards before moving over to defense in soph season. His first reception was for a TD of 18-yards on pass thrown by Tom Shuman that helped Lions come-from-behind to beat Army, 21-14. Also a star on State's baseball team. Played in Hula and Japan Bowls in 78. Number five choice of New York Jets in '78 but didn't play in NFL. Now sells insurance and lives in his hometown of Danville, PA.

SIEMINSKI, CHUCK. 1960-61-62. LT, 6'5", 240 lbs.; Swoyerville, PA. Another of the fine two-way tackles of the Engle era and a Second-Team All-American in senior year. May be one of the most underrated of PSU's outstanding defensive tackles of the last 50 years. Selected on the All-Time Penn State team in 1967 by *Pittsburgh Press* sports editor Chet Smith, who covered Nittany Lion football for more than a half century. Lettered as second unit LT as soph then on first unit in '61 & '62. As steady and consistent as a lineman could be; he was quick and worked hard. Excellent at pass protection and a fine all-around blocker and defensive player. He was the biggest player on the team in junior and senior years. Cited by sportswriters and coaches for his outstanding all-around play in the 30-15 Gator Bowl win over Georgia Tech in '61. Played another of his best games in 34-6 win over West Virginia in '62, when one writer covering the game called him "a tower of strength." Several times in that game he bailed out QB Pete Liske with aggressive pass blocking. Also one of the best pure tacklers on the team. Played in '63 Senior Bowl. Drafted number four by NFL San Francisco & number 14 by AFL Boston Patriots in junior year of '62 and played defensive tackle for 49ers ('63-'65), Atlanta ('66-'67) and Detroit ('68) before leaving pro ball. Now a high school teacher in Mountain Top, PA.

SKORUPAN, JOHN. 1970-71-72. LB, 6'2", 210 lbs.; Beaver, PA. Part of the great linebacking legacy from the '60s and '70s that helped give State the nickname of "Linebacker U." Selected First-Team All-American in senior year by AP, Football Writers and NEA, when he had his best year with 63 solo tackles and 43 assists for a total of 106. Also credited with partially blocking three punts. Played one of his finest games in 28-19 victory over West Virginia in '72: his blocked punt late in the first half resulted in a safety; then late in third QT, with State leading, 25-19, he and teammates Bruce Bannon and Ed O'Neil led a four-down goal line stand that kept WVU out of EZ and was turning point of the game, with Skorupan stopping a WVU runner at the line of scrimmage on a fourth-and-goal at the two-yard line. Had perhaps his best game ever in 21-10 win over Navy in '72, when he had a season high of 17 tackles, 15 unassisted, and actually won game with a 32-yard TD on an interception with less than two minutes left in the game and the Lions winning by just four points. Paterno compared him to two contemporaries, Jack Ham and Dennis Onkotz. Tied with Shane Conlan for fourth in career tackles with 274 total on 144 solos and 130 assists. Also intercepted nine passes in his three years, returning three for TDs. Had another fine year as starter on the '71 team that was loaded with outstanding linebackers, including All-American Charlie Zapiec and Gary Gray and finished season 11-1, beating Texas, 30-6, in "breakthrough" '72 Cotton Bowl. His partially blocked punt helped set up TD in Army game and his interception against Air Force was one of six that helped preserve unbeaten season in 16-14 win. As backup in soph year, he intercepted two passes in fourth game of season against Boston College to help in 28-3 win that ended two-game losing streak following record 31-game unbeaten skein. Originally thought about going to Ohio State but changed is mind after meeting Woody Hayes. Played in '73 Hula Bowl. Number six choice of Buffalo in '73 and played with Bills until '77, then with New York Giants from '78-'80 before closing pro career. Now in commercial sales and living in Zelienople, PA.

SMALTZ, BILL. 1939-40-41. FB & PK, 6'0", 195 lbs.; Aliquippa. A triple threat and the best passer of the Higgins era until Elwood Petchel came along after World War II. The FB position in the Single-Wing formation popular at the time was more like the QB of today. Teamed with E Lenny Krouse to form one of the best passing combinations in school history, especially considering the period of time that they played. Established record in '40 that stood for 53 years for most completed passes in succession, when he had 12 in row against Syracuse (record broken by Kerry Collins' 14 passes against Minnesota in '94). Also set record in '41 for completions with 38 (in 71 attempts for 611 yards) that was not broken until Petchel did it in '48. Led team to first victory over Pitt in 20 years, when he scored the only TD in first QT in 10-0 win at Pitt Stadium in '39. Not much of a runner but could get the tough yardage when needed. Could easily heave a pass 60 yards. Made one of his outstanding passes in late season 13-13 tie with Syracuse in '40: with four minutes left and State trailing, 13-6, he threw the ball 57 yards to Krouse who made a leaping finger-tip catch at the three-yard line surrounded by Orange defenders and bulled into the EZ for an official 53-yard TD; it had been one of Smaltz' finest games as he hit on 14-of-21 passes (including the 12 passes in succession) for 193 yards and both TDs; it was the best passing day ever for a State player up to that time. Had several fine passing days in '41, but his best was probably last game of career against South Carolina, when he hit on 10-of-15 attempts in 19-12 win. Shared punting with Krouse as

senior and also kicked extra points for first time (hitting on 20-of-24 for season) and made only FG of career (for 16 yards) in 31-7 win over Pitt. Played in '42 East-West Shrine Game. For years he was an assistant coach at North Carolina State, serving under another ex-State player, Earle Edwards, and coached against his alma mater in several games. Now retired and living in Raleigh, NC.

SMEAR, STEVE. 1967-68-69. DT, 6'1", 227 lbs.; Johnstown, PA. Had one of the greatest names for the way he played. Teamed with Mike Reid for one of the outstanding defensive tackle combinations in State history but often overlooked because of the super ability of Reid, who started a year earlier. Paterno said was Smear was "one of those unspectacular type players who does a great job, play in and play out." Co-Captain with Reid for both years on the great back-to-back unbeaten teams of '68 & '69 that never got the respect they deserved and finished number two in the country: along with Reid, Jack Ham (his high school teammate), Dennis Onkotz and Neal Smith, this was one of the outstanding defensive teams in the history of college football, nicknamed "The Rover Boys." A Second-Team All-American in '69 and Honorable Mention in '68. Won Red Worrell Award in '68 as most improved offensive and defensive player in spring practice and went on to prove why during season when he led team in total tackles with 56 solos and 36 assists. Fulfilled a lineman's dream in '68 game against Maryland, when he intercepted a pass in first QT and rambled 40 yards for team's first TD in 57-13 rout. Began frosh career as TE but moved to DT in '67 and became starter when Paterno shook up team in second game of season against Miami and inserted a bevy of sophs, including Smear and Smith, into lineup in a move that became the turning point of his career. During that season Smear made 32 solo and 28 unassisted tackles; played one of his best games that year in 50-28 romp over Boston College with nine unassisted tackles and fumble recovery that led to second TD. Had two of his finest games in the back-to-back Orange Bowl victories over Kansas and Missouri. Won the national Swede Nelson Award for sportsmanship as senior. Number four choice of Baltimore Colts in '70 but decided to play in Canadian Football League and spent several years with Montreal Alouettes and Toronto Argonauts. Now an insurance agent in Annapolis, MD.

SMITH, MIKE. 1968-69-70. DB & PR, 5'11", 185 lbs.; Annville, PA. A consistent and well disciplined DB who was a three-year starter and standout DB on the back-to-back unbeaten teams of '68 and '69 which were known for their outstanding defense. Set record in '70 that still stands for most interceptions in one game, when he picked off four against Ohio University, including one for a 28-yard TD in the first QT that led to 32-22 victory. Began career as RB and was leading rusher of frosh team, but by fall practice of soph year he had been moved to DHB. Had one of his finest games in the highest scoring win ever over rival Pitt, 65-9, in '68, when he intercepted one pass in the EZ early in the game to stop a Pitt threat then picked off another to set up a TD in a 35-point second QT. Played a fine game in '68 Orange Bowl win over Kansas, with several key tackles and the return of a Bobby Douglass interception for 24 yards. Also an excellent punt returner. His a 75-yard runback against West Virginia in '70 set up first TD in 42-8 rout. Because he played at same time as Neal Smith, some mistakenly believe they were related but they weren't. Now in insurance and investments in Lebanon, PA.

SMITH, NEAL. 1967-68-69. S & PR, 5'11", 180 lbs.; Port Trevorton, PA. A genuine walk-on in '66 who became a three-year starter on Paterno's first great teams and one of the outstanding "clutch" DBs. A First-Team All-American in senior year, when he led team with 10 interceptions (for 78 yards), including one for 70 yards in 42-3 win over Ohio University. Also one of Paterno's true "scholar athletes" with a 3.5-plus average in civil engineering. The all-time interception leader in a career (19) and one season (the 10 in '69). In three years he had 19 interceptions for 152 yards and the one TD and that is four more interceptions than the all-time runners-up, Pete Harris and Darren Perry, but tied with Harris for most interceptions in one season. Always seemed to play his best in the big games, as he did in the post-season bowls. Had two interceptions in '70 Orange Bowl win over Missouri. His diving interception in '67 Gator Bowl set up State's first TD in an eventual 17-17 tie with Florida State. Perhaps, his finest "clutch" play was his partial block of a Kansas punt with 1:16 left in '69 Orange Bowl and State trailing, 14-7, that led to a quick 51-yard drive and an eventual 15-14 win in the historic "12th man" game that was the true start of the Paterno coaching legacy. Also ran back punts. Now a construction engineer in Selinsgrove, PA.

SMITH, STEVE. 1984-85-86. FB, 6'1", 232 lbs.; DeMatha, MD. Teamed with Tim Minoa in senior year for an outstanding one-two fullback combination that helped unbeaten State win its second National Championship with the historic 14-10 win over Miami at the '87 Fiesta Bowl. They started about equally and played the same amount of time. An excellent blocker and good pass receiver on short sprints out of the backfield. Had good speed which traced to his background as a high school HB. Made one of his biggest TDs in come-from-behind '85 Syracuse game, when he caught an eight-yard pass from John Shaffer with less than two minutes left in game to give team winning points in 24-20 win. In '86 he scored as many TDs on pass receptions as he did on runs. Recorded PSU's first TD of the '86 season on a 10-yard pass from John Shaffer in 45-15 opening season win over Temple and finished game with two more receptions, one for 21 yards setting up a TD, and also was second leading rusher with 54 yards on 12 carries. The next week, he scored first TD of game against Boston College on an eight-yard run that started the Lions off to a 26-14 win. Scored first TD in 24-19 win over Notre Dame that clinched Fiesta Bowl invitation but injured ankle on play and missed Pitt game but came back to start against Miami. Had one of his longest runs ever against Rutgers in '85, when he rambled for 63 yards in 17-10 win at NJ Meadowlands. Twenty-second in all-time rushing with 1,246 yards on 265 carries for 11 TDs. Used more as a blocker to clear way for TBs like D.J. Dozier than a runner in State's offense; his best rushing day was in 37-30 win over Boston College in '84, when he got 126 yards and two TDs on 23 carries, but was second to Dozier in yardage that day. Won Red Worrell award in '84 as the most improved offensive player in spring practice. Played in '87 East-West Shrine game. Drafted third by Los Angeles Raiders in '87 and made immediate impact as FB; played with Raiders ('87-'93) and Seattle ('93-'95) before retiring. Now owns a car wash in the Atlanta area.

SMITH, TERRY. 1988-89-90-91. WR, 5'8", 155 lbs.; Monroeville, PA. Along with O.J. McDuffie and David Daniels, he was part of one of the best group of receivers in State history. Known as a "big play" receiver. Scored State's first TD in thrilling '89 Holiday Bowl

on a 24-yard pass from Tony Sacca, and caught another pass for five yards as State beat BYU in a pass-happy scoring contest, 50-39. Caught a 37-yard TD pass in '90 Blockbuster Bowl loss to Florida State, 24-17, when he had five receptions for 100 yards. Second behind McDuffie and Bobby Engram in receptions for one season with 55 for 846 yards and eight TDS (and a 15.4 per catch average) in his senior year, when he was co-captain. Played one of his finest games that year in opening season Kickoff Classic at Meadowlands, when he scored first two TDs on passes of four and eight yards from Tony Sacca and caught three more to lead all receivers with five receptions (and 51 yards) in 34-22 victory over Georgia Tech. Fifth in career receptions and sixth in career yardage with 108 for 1,825 yards and 15 TDs (and a 16.9 per catch average). Had one of his finest games against Southern Cal in '91, when he was named State's Outstanding Player-of-the-Game with 10 receptions for 165 yards and a 13-yard TD; that was his all-time best statistical game and ties him with Jack Curry for fourth in most receptions in one game and with Engram for sixth most yardage in one game. Tied with Kenny Jackson and Kyle Brady with most receptions in one game by a frosh with four (including a 40-yard TD) at West Virginia in '88. Had a total of five games with 100 or more yards and his 144 yards and one TD on eight receptions against Temple in '91 is 15th best in all-time single game yardage. Was considered an outstanding downfield blocker, who often helped spring big gains with his blocks on DBs. Eleventh choice of Washington in '92 but didn't play pro football. Now an assistant football coach at Duquesne and living in Monroeville, PA.

SNELL, GEORGE. 1919-20-21. FB & QB, 5'10", 170 lbs.; Reading, PA. One of the least known star backs of Bezdek's best teams—the once beaten squad of '19 and undefeated teams of '20 & '21—because he was surrounded by such All-Americans as Glenn Killinger, Charlie Way and Joe Lightner. Captained the '21 team that was 8-0-2. He was the starting FB in junior and senior years. Played one of his best games in what was the biggest game of the '20 season against Dartmouth and scored first TD as State won, 14-7, before a Homecoming crowd at Beaver Field. Considered one of the best defensive players on the team. Sportswriters quoted one teammate as saying "When Snell tackles you he can hit you three times before you hit the ground." He was cited for his defensive work in the secondary during the second half of the 28-7 win over Georgia Tech at New York's Polo Grounds, which is one of the outstanding games in school history. Had one of his best games that season in 24-0 win over Gettysburg, scoring a TD and playing "an exceptional game in running with the ball and defense," as one sportswriter noted. The next week against North Carolina he scored on a 50-yard broken field run to lead a 35-0 win. He never played again after the mid-season Georgia Tech game because of a throat infection. Deceased.

SOBCZAK, SAM. 1958-59-60. FB & H, 5'10", 198 lbs.; Dubois, PA. The first man designated "Hero" in the State defense. Occurred in senior year and unveiled in third game of season against Army, which State won in upset 27-16. But name did not change what role he and other fullback's played in team defense at the time. Because of substitution rules in effect, players played offense and defense and, if an individual left a game at any time during a quarter, he could not return until next quarter. In PSU defensive scheme, FBs normally played left CB on defense. Thus, left CB became "Hero" in '60. Even in his era

FBs were not major ball carriers and he was primarily a blocker. Some sportswriters said if he was two inches taller and 10 pounds heavier he may have been the best FB in the nation. Despite his size, he was a good one, though his first game as soph on the second unit in Nebraska opener was so bad he was instantly demoted to sixth team halfback; but because of injuries he got first start of season at FB against Marquette three games later, and the next week he was leading rusher (74 yards on 15 carries and the first TD) in only televised game of the year, a 34-0 win over Boston University. Made one of the biggest plays of his career in '59's great historic "match of the unbeatens" at Beaver Field with a vicious block on Syracuse's DE Fred Mautino that helped State recover a blocked kick at the Syracuse one-yard line, then scored the ensuing TD that almost beat favored Syracuse; but the Orange won, 20-18, and went on to win the national title that year. In junior year, he usually played on second platoon behind Pat Botula who was Captain in '59, but played fine game in 7-0 win over Alabama in Liberty Bowl with 42 yards on nine carries. As senior, he usually started, and got 36 yards on eight carries in '60 Liberty Bowl win over Oregon. But he was more valuable to those teams as the "Hero" back. Played in Tucson's Copper Bowl All-Star game in '60. Taught high school for more than 20 years and is now with the Pennsylvania Higher Education Association Agency. Lives in Harrisburg and is frequent attendee of PSU football and basketball games.

SPAZIANI, FRANK ("SPAZ"). 1966-67-68. QB & DE, 6'2", 210 lbs.; Clark, NJ. He's mentioned here not because he's Italian or because Paterno is Italian but because the author is Italian. (See below.) Actually, he was a good, versatile player and a fine DE who was aggressive and loved to hit, but he may be best known as the object of many Paterno jokes early in the Paterno era: when accused by some sportswriters of playing favorites to Spaziani, Paterno replied with a jibe that has become part of the Paterno legend: "I don't like 'Spaz' because he's Italian; I like him because I'm Italian." Played six different positions including QB before finally making his mark at DE in '67 & '68, and he was a standout on the unbeaten '68 team that defeated Kansas, 15-14, in the '69 Orange Bowl. Began varsity career as second team QB on Paterno's first team in '66 and started second game of season against Michigan State, when Jack White was injured. But after 42-7 pasting by MSU he was benched, and, eventually, both he and White were replaced by Tom Sherman. Also played some QB early in junior year and TB, WB and FB both years before DL coach Jim O'Hora turned him into a DE in '67 season, and he became so good he was an AP All-East Honorable Mention that year. In third game of season, he hounded UCLA's future Heisman Trophy winner, Gary Beban, all afternoon after replacing an injured starter, and he had three sacks on Beban, even though PSU lost, 17-15. Played one of his finest defensive games that year in 35-14 win over Ohio University; in first half he was getting into OU's backfield so fast that he intercepted a bobbled pitchout; in fourth QT he blocked a punt, picked it up and raced nine-yards for a TD. Went into coaching after graduation and for years was an assistant to George Welsh at Virginia. Now an assistant coach for Calgary in the Canadian Football League.

SPEROS, PETE. 1980-81-82. OT & OG, 6'2", 253 lbs.; Potomac, MD. A bulwark on the offensive line that helped take State to its first National Championship with the '83 Sugar Bowl win over Georgia, 27-23. Being a co-captain of that team was the climax of a solid three-year season that earned him great respect for his efficient blocking. Paterno said Speros was "one of our hardest-working players...He's an ideal kind of player for the offensive line..." Began as a defensive lineman and was a MG before being switched to OT in the fall of soph year and became the prime backup and sometimes starter that year at the short T position. Started in '81 on the great offensive line that also featured All-American guards Sean Farrell and Mike Munchak. Began '82 at LT but was moved to starting LG on the rebuilt offensive line and the tactic helped win the '82 championship. Sportswriters cited the middle of the line featuring Speros and Mike Magginis at guards with Mark Battaglia at center as the keys to QB Todd Blackledge's passing attack. Played one of best games that season in 39-31 win over Maryland, perhaps with extra incentive because his father was once a starter with the Terps. A friendly and outgoing individual off the field with a great sense of humor. Played in '83 Hula Bowl. Number eight choice of Seattle in '83 but went into United States Football League and played with Birmingham ('84-'85) before leaving for career in business. Now a financial planner in Bethesda, MD.

STRAVINSKI, CARL. 1938-39-40. Long Tackle & PK, 6'2", 218 lbs.; Plymouth, PA. Probably one of the most underrated lineman who ever played for State because he played in the shadow of All-American Center Leon Gejecki during the schools' misguided era of football de-emphasis and on the last losing team (in '38) for 49 years. A three-year starter in the long T position that was the key to defending against the popular Single-Wing. The long T was usually double teamed by the opponents' Wing Back and long T; on offense, the long T also had to pull and lead interference on most power running plays. Thus, the long T had to be fast, tough and mobile to fight off the best of the defense and offense. "Stravo"—as his teammates called him—was all of that and more. Entered PSU in '36 but broke leg in the spring of '37 and missed entire year. As a soph he was a major force in the tough '38 defensive team that set three NCAA pass-defense records despite a losing season; the record for fewest yards passing allowed per game (13.1 average) still stands after 60 years. Also one of the stars of the highly regarded '40 front line known as "the Seven Mountains" the helped lead team to the best Penn State record in 19 years, 6-1-1. Had a great leg for kickoffs and frequently kicked into the EZ in the days when kickers did not use tees (for lifts) as they do nowadays. His two kicks against the wind and snow into the Syracuse EZ in '39 is credited with helping State to a 6-6 tie in a 5-1-2 season. Made one of the biggest plays of his career in '39 in beating Pitt for first time in 20 years, 10-0, when he was credited with making the tackle that caused Pitt's great back Dick Cassiano to fumble at own 22-yard line; Leon Gajecki recovered and four plays later State scored only TD of game. After graduation, he played football in the military for the '42 Army All Stars in a five-game, 20-day period against five NFL teams for the Army Emergency Relief Fund, then played and coached for other military and semi-pro teams. Played with Scranton of the American Professional Football League. Now retired after a long career in the parks area of city government in Baltimore, Dayton and Pittsburgh and living in Boalsburg, PA. A regular at Penn State home and away games who is one of the best-known "old-timers" within State's unofficial family.

STUCKRATH, ED. 1962-63-64. FB & H, 5'10", 190 lbs.; Baltimore, MD. One of the most underrated two-way FBs in history. A three-year vet who played the "Hero" position on defense. A fine defensive player who also had the speed to return punts. Overshadowed by some of his now more famous teammates, such as Glenn Ressler and Ralph Baker. A defensive specialist as soph in '62 who got almost as much playing time as many on the first unit. Was one of the standouts of '63 season as starter at FB and Hero. Best known for his blitzing which usually meant losses for opposing QBs and runners. Played one of best all-around games in 28-7 win over Rice when he roamed field tackling on defense and had 64 yards rushing on 12 carries. Also had great game against Maryland and scored a TD in close 16-15 win. Part of the outstanding defense that whipped Ohio State in '63, 10-7. Had probably his best game in 22-21 loss to fourth-ranked Pitt that season; blocked a kick to set up State's first TD, thwarted crucial two-point conversion play with tackle that made Pitt adjust tactics and stopped another Pitt TD opportunity by throwing ball carrier for 11-yard loss. Played in '64 Blue-Gray game. Now a supply manager in Millerville, MD.

STYNCHULA, ANDY. 1957-58-59. T, 6'1", 221 lbs.; Old Crabree, PA. One of the best two-way linemen of the Engle era who got better each year that he played. Made one of the "big plays" ever for an Engle team with a blocked punt in the fourth QT of the historic '59 battle of unbeatens between State and Syracuse; he smashed through four blockers, including two All-Americans, Roger Davis and Maury Youmans, and hit the ball with his left arm; Bob Mitinger recovered at the one-yard line and Sam Sobczak scored the TD but State missed the potential tying two-point conversion and lost, 20-18, as Syracuse went on to win National Championship. Started out as an E in preseason of soph year but was moved to T before first game and became the LT on second Unit. Then won first Red Worrell Award as most improved player in spring practice of '58, and became starter for next two years, although he shared position as senior with Charlie Janerette. Had what may have been the best game of career in 20-9 mid-season win at Illinois, when he had what sportswriters described as "a field day" on defense against the bigger Illini line, "knocking nearly everyone down and throwing guys around like toys." Also praised for his performance in his final game, the 7-0 win over Alabama in the '59 Liberty Bowl. Played in '59 Blue-Gray Game and '60 Senior Bowl. Drafted number three by NFL Washington Redskins and by AFL Los Angeles Chargers in '60 and played defensive line for the Redskins from '60-'63, then was with the New York Giants ('64-'65), Baltimore ('66-'67) and Dallas ('68). Killed in a traffic accident while vacationing in the Caribbean.

SUHEY, LARRY. 1975-76. FB, 6' ½", 202 lbs.; State College, PA. The oldest of the Suhey brothers, who may have had the most talent but who had the worst luck. Tore the ligaments in his right knee during preseason practice of his frosh year ('72) and never fully recovered. But if he had not committed to play at State, it is likely his younger brothers Matt and Paul (see below) would also have played elsewhere. Larry was highly recruited by other schools after an All-State season at SCHS, but chose State. After being redshirted in '73, he was a backup for two years; didn't letter in '74 but was on second team in '75 and had best game against Maryland when he led rushers with 56 yards on 11 carries. His father, Steve (see below) was unhappy at how Larry was being used by Paterno, and, at the time, this had an impact on the recruiting of Matt who was still in HS. Larry convinced Matt to play at State, and in '76 he was slated to be the starting FB in same backfield with Matt at TB. But he injured knee again in preseason and, despite

told by doctors his career was over, he came back in sixth game of season. Couldn't oust Mike Guman from starting FB position but was a solid backup for rest of year. Now a regional sales manager in State College.

SUHEY, MATT. 1976-77-78-79. FB & PR, 5'11½", 212 lbs.; State College, PA. Had an outstanding four year career but will always be remembered most for his frustrating attempt on third-and-two to cross the Alabama goal line late in the fourth QT of the '79 Sugar Bowl game for the National Championship. Neither Suhey nor his backfield mate Mike Guman could penetrate the Alabama line in that classic Alabama goal-line stand and Alabama went on to beat then number one State, 14-7, and win the national title, in what is probably the most disappointing loss in the history of PSU football; what's forgotten is he was the leading rusher in that bruising defensive game with 48 yards on 10 carries. Made a terrific debut starting in the opening game of his frosh season, when he ran for 119 yards and a TD on 23 carries in 15-12 win over Stanford at Beaver Stadium. Was one of the top HS running backs in country in '75 and was planning to attend Ohio State, partly because his father, Steve (see below), was unhappy with Paterno's handling of older brother, Larry. But Larry convinced Matt to attend Penn State, and he became one of the best FBs in school history. Had speed and quickness and was set in frosh year to be the starting TB with brother Larry at FB but shifted to FB when Larry was hurt. Then missed several games that year with an injury. Was the starting FB for next three years and is seventh on all-time career rushing yardage with 2,818 yards and 26 TDs on 633 carries for 4.5 yards per attempt and led team in rushing in sophomore, junior and senior years. Winner of Hall Award in '79, as Outstanding Senior player, when he had his best season rushing: 973 yards and six TDs on 185 carries for a 5.3 yards average. Had best game ever in 24-3 Homecoming win over Army in '79 when he gained 225 yards and two TDs on runs of 17 and 61 yards in 23 carries. Also had seven other games of 100 plus yards including 112 (on 19 carries) when he was the leading rusher in the 9-6 win over Tulane in the '79 Liberty Bowl. Had one of his best days as a sophomore in '77 Fiesta Bowl when he scored two TDs on 13 carries for 76 yards in 42-30 win over Arizona State on Christmas Day. His 53 yard run that set up TD in 31-14 victory over Houston in '77 was the longest run from scrimmage for the season. Played one of his finest games in '78 against SMU, when he helped lead come-from-behind 26-21 victory, scoring winning TD with about two minutes left in game at the end of a 73-yard drive; was leading rusher that day with 96 yards on 28 carries and also caught a pass for 16 yards. Led team in punt returns in the outstanding '78 season with a 15.2 yards average return and 197 yards and one TD on 13 returns. He still holds the punt return record for one game yardage average (29.0 yards) and total yards (145 yards) with the five punt returns against North Carolina State in the 1978 victory that made State number one for the first time ever; his 43-yard return for a TD late in the fourth QT broke open a close game and gave State the 19-10 win; he also had 97 yards rushing that day. Played in '80 Hula Bowl. Number two choice of Chicago in '80 and had an outstanding career with Bears, including a Super Bowl championship ring in '86, until retiring at end of '89 season. Now an investment banker in Chicago and living in Highland Park, IL.

SUHEY, PAUL. 1975-76-77-78. LB, 6'1", 227 lbs.; State College, PA. The lesser known but middle Suhey brother (see above). He was the defensive captain of the '78 team that was the first State team ever to become number one, but had the disappointing and frustrating loss to Alabama in the National Championship game at the '79 Sugar Bowl. Started at outside linebacker on that '78 squad and was a good, aggressive defensive player, but sometimes overshadowed by the super skills and ability of his All-American teammates such as Lance Mehl, Matt Millen and Bruce Clark. Was second to Mehl in tackles that year with 63 on 31 solos and 32 assists. Paterno said he was "one of the finest captains I ever had." Played one of his best games in the close 19-10 win over North Carolina State in the '78 game that made Lions number one for first time in history, when he had nine tackles including a QB sack and was given the game ball for his performance. Almost didn't attend PSU but older brother Larry convinced him to do so. Lettered as frosh as backup FB & TE and played on special teams. Moved to LB in '76 where he found his natural position. Winner of Ridge Riley Award in '78 given to a senior player for "sportsmanship, scholarship, leadership and friendship." Went to medical school after graduation and was an orthopedic surgeon in Jacksonville, FL, until fall of '97 when he returned to State College and joined University Orthopedics and Sports Medicine Center operated by another former player turned physician Dave Joyner.

SUHEY, STEVE. 1942, 1946-47. G, 5'11", 205 lbs.; Cazenovia, NY. One of the "legends" of PSU football with a unique historical significance to State's football tradition, linking the early days of success to the Paterno era: He married the daughter of his college coach, Bob Higgins ('30-'48), who was State's second All-American, as an E in '15 & '19, and three of his seven children—Matt, Paul & Larry—played football for Paterno (and were on '76 team together); and, when Paterno moved here from Brown with Rip Engle, Paterno lived with the Suhey family for one year. A First-Team All-American in senior year when selected by AP, INS and Colliers. One of 14 State players and three coaches named to the National Football Foundation College Football Hall of Fame, inducted in '85. Picked on the All-Time Penn State team in 1950s and again in 1967 by *Pittsburgh Press* sports editor Chet Smith, who covered Nittany Lion football for more than a half century. A frosh on the '42 team but left to serve with Army Air Corps and saw plenty of combat as a gunner on an attack plane in the Pacific during World War II. Returned in time to become part of the great unbeaten team of '47 that tied with SMU, 13-13, in the '48 Cotton Bowl and finished fourth in the country. Started at RG in '46 opening game against Bucknell but was injured in third game against Michigan State, missed several games and didn't start again as his replacement Bob Rutkowski became second-Team All-East. Didn't miss a start in '47, even after a knee injury and two deep facial cuts sidelined him in the first QT of the tough, late season 7-0 win over Temple. Played the next week in the key victory of the year, a 20-7 win over Navy at Annapolis that put the team in line for the Cotton Bowl; cited by sportswriters for his excellent blocking during the game, including two blocks which helped FB Jeff Durkota make two long TD runs. Had great speed for pulling and could get to the linebacker quickly. Used as middle guard on defense where his strength and quickness made him a great tackler. He was considered the spearhead of the outstanding '47 defense on undefeated Cotton Bowl team, which still holds three NCAA defensive records, including fewest yards allowed rushing per game (17.0 yards on a total of 150 yards in nine games) and fewest yards per rush (0.64 yards on 240 carries). Played with Pittsburgh Steelers for two

years, as he completed his degree than quit pro ball to coach high school football in Waynesboro. Returned to State College, where he worked as a salesman for the L.G. Balfour Co. until his unexpected death on his 55th birthday, January 8, 1977.

SZOTT, DAVE. 1987-88-89. DT & OG, 6'4", 234 lbs.; Clifton, NJ. A versatile lineman who played defense most of career but switched to OG as a senior and became a good one, earning Honorable Mention All-American. Began career as a backup DT in soph year and moved to NT in '88 where he was the starter, and made 41 tackles, including seven for losses. Played one of best games in his next-to-last as a NT, when he had six tackles and recovered a fumble in disheartening 14-7 loss at Pitt. In senior year he was moved to OG to replace the graduated Steve Wisniewski but missed opening season game because of injury. Started next game against Temple and by end of season he was a standout. Made a key block to spring Blair Thomas on 38-yard TD run to ignite 34-12 win over Syracuse in 89. Finest game was probably the '89 Holiday Bowl win over BYU, 50-39, when he and his linemates dominated the Cougar defensive line led by Outland Trophy winner Mohammed Elewonibi as the offense racked up 249 yards rushing and 215 yards passing. Played in '90 Senior Bowl. Number seven choice of Kansas City in '90 and a starter at LG for Chiefs since then. Lives in Greenwood, MO.

TAMBURO, SAM. 1945-46-47-48. E, 6'2", 185 lbs.; New Kensington, PA. A four-year starting end in the day of the two-way player. All-American in senior year and leading receiver on the '48 7-1-1 team rated 18th by AP, when he had 17 catches for 301 yards and three TDs. Also leading receiver in '46 with seven receptions for 126 yards and one TD. As frosh he played in '45 Blue-Gray game, when it was one of only two post-season All-Star games, and at a time when frosh were eligible because of World War II. Started at LE as frosh in second game of season against Colgate and was the regular there (or at RE) for the three years ('45, '47, '48) and spot starter in '46. He was an immediate sensation with his blocking and aggressive defensive play. In second game as starter, he blocked two extra point attempts by the Navy kicker, had a QB sack and did a quick-kick punt from the goal line that went for 64 yards. He gained an excellent reputation in four years as a blocker for Elwood Petchel, Wally Triplett, Larry Joe and Fran Rogel. Typical were the two blocks he threw on Navy's highly-touted tackle, Dick Shimschack that sprung FB Jeff Durkota for TD runs of 48 and 42 yards that helped beat Navy 20-7, in the key game of the unbeaten '47 season. His block of a Doak Walker punt in '48 Cotton Bowl helped set up last minute drive for victory which fell short. Also was an outstanding defensive end, who often was cited in game for his defensive play. Part of the '47 defense which still holds three NCAA defensive team records, including fewest yards allowed rushing per game (17.0 yards on a total of 150 yards in nine games) and fewest yards per rush (0.64 yards on 240 carries). Caught two of his few TD passes in back-to-back '48 wins over Syracuse (for seven yards) and West Virginia (for two yards). Involved in one of the most unusual TDs in history before record-setting Homecoming crowd (24,579) against Michigan State in '48: trailing, 14-7, with a first-and-10 at the MSU 20, Petchel completed a pass down the middle to Tamburo, who faked a quick handoff to the nearby Rogel, then gave the ball to guard John Simon who ran in for the TD; and the game ended in a 14-14 tie. Played in first Hula Bowl in '49 along with teammate Elwood Petchel. Played one season with New York Bulldogs of All-American Conference in '49. Worked as an auditor until retiring in New Kensington.

TEPSIC, JOE. 1945. LHB, 5'9", 170 lbs.; Slovan, PA. The war hero. The first genuine star when State opened the '45 season two months after the end of World War II. He had been wounded in hand-to-hand combat at Guadalcanal in one of the heroic early battles of the War in '42. Returned to play only one season (at tailback) but he boosted the spirits of the fans right from opening game against Muhlenberg at Beaver Field: on fourth play from scrimmage he ran off tackle for a 52-yard TD and scored again six minutes later as State won, 47-7. The next week he did it again in 27-7 win over Colgate, scoring two TDs and gaining 76 yards on 18 carries. Played perhaps his finest game when he was temporary Captain for the day against Syracuse: he gained 135 yards on 15 carries and scored one TDs on a 26-yard run and another on a combined 41-yard lateral play from FB Al Bellas in a 26-0 rout of the Orange. Missed next to last game against Michigan State because of injury but came back in final game of career at Pitt and was outstanding on offense and defense, playing all but one play in 60 minute game, gaining 73 yards on 18 carries in tough 7-0 loss. Was one of leading scorers in East that year with 48 points and called the signals from his LHB position as 5-3 team set tone for the three outstanding seasons that followed. Played briefly with Brooklyn Dodgers baseball team in late 1940s. Retired and living in Tyrone, PA.

THOMAS, BLAIR. 1985-86-87-89. TB & KR, 5'11", 190 lbs.; Philadelphia, PA. Another of State's outstanding running backs whom Paterno said was as good as any of them. A First-Team All-American in senior year and Third-Team as a junior. Only back in school history to gain 1,300 or more yards in two seasons ('87 & '89). 10th in Heisman Trophy race in '89. Still holds record for best rushing average in a season (8.4 yards in '86) and in a game (44 yards against Syracuse in '86). Second only to Curt Warner in yards gained for a career (3,301 yards on 606 carries for 21 TDs and 5.4 average), most games over 100 yards (17) and career all-purpose yards (4,512 on 3,301 rushing, 477 receiving and 734 kick returns) and second to O.J. McDuffie for one-season all-purpose yards (1,772 on 1,414 rushing, 300 receiving and 58 kick returns). Held record for most consecutive games rushing over 100 yards (seven) until broken in '97 by Curtis Enis. Had best rushing day in 21-20 victory over Notre Dame at Beaver Field in '87, when he ran for 214 yards and one TD on 35 carries. His 92-yard run against Syracuse as a soph in championship '86 season is the longest run ever from scrimmage by one individual, even though he didn't score a TD. Made impact as soph with his kickoff returns and his 91-yard KO return for a TD against Pitt in '86 helped clinch a 34-14 victory for the unbeaten Lions and a berth in the '87 Fiesta Bowl against then number one Miami. Earlier in year he helped preserve State's unbeaten season with a "clutch" fourth QT performance against upstart Cincinnati that earned him Offensive Player-of-the-Game; it started with a 34-yard return with State trailing, 17-14, and ended in a 75-yard drive for winning TD where he caught a 32-yard pass and ran for 27 yards, as State pulled out a 23-17 win. Led '87 team in scoring (80 points on 13 TDs and one two-point conversion and rushing (1,341 yards and five

TDs on 264 carries for a 5.1 average). Also leading pass receiver in junior year with 300 yards and two TDs on 23 catches. Total offense leader in '87 (1,414 yards) and '89 (1,341 yards) and seventh in career total offense. Sat out '88 season after injuring knee while practicing for Citrus Bowl after '87 season and had reconstructive surgery. Came back in '89 with eight 100-yard rushing games, including six straight at end of season, to lead '89 team in rushing with 1,341 yards on 264 carries for five TDs. Named outstanding senior player in '89. Holds State record for most rushing yards gained in any post-season bowl game with 186 yards on 35 carries and one TD in '89 Holiday Bowl win over Brigham Young, 50-39; shared Player-of-the-Game with BYU QB Ty Detmer. Fourth in all-time average KO return for one season (31.9 yards on nine returns for 293 yards and one TD in '86) and fifth for career (26.3 yards on 18 returns for 658 yards and one TD), led team in returns in '86 (9-for-217 yards) and '87 (12-for-383 yards); also led team in all-purpose yardage in '87 and '89 and second in career all-purpose yards. Played in '90 Senior and Japan Bowls. First choice (and second overall pick) of New York Jets in '90 and played with Jets ('90-'93), New England ('94), Dallas ('94) and Carolina Panthers ('95). Now offensive backfield coach for Temple and living in Rosemont, PA.

TIMPSON, MICHAEL. 1985-87-88. WR & KR, 5'7", 172 lbs.; Miami, FL. Another fine receiver following the tradition of Kenny Jackson but never reached full potential because he gave up his final year of eligibility to turn pro. One of the receivers on the young '85 team that played Oklahoma in the '86 Orange Bowl for the national title. Had a sensational frosh debut in '85 opening season win over Maryland with an over-the-shoulder 50-yard catch that started an eight-play 80-yard drive for State's first offensive TD of the game. He missed the '86 National Championship season when he decided to pass up football in '86 to try out for the Olympics, but never made Olympic team despite his world-class speed as a hurdler. Played one of best games in losing cause in '88 Citrus Bowl against Clemson with six receptions for 55 yards, two punt returns for 40 yards and six KO runbacks for 127 yards. Led team in receiving in '88 with 22 catches for 342 yards and two TDs and a 15.6 yards per reception average. Led team in punt returns every year he played with '88 being his best when he returned 16 for 162 yards and one TD. Had 44 punt returns in career for 488 yards and two TDs and an 11.1 yards per return. A track star who never participated in spring practice, and after the team's first losing season in 49 years in '88, he decided to turn pro. Fourth round choice of New England in '89 and was one of Patriots' star receivers until '95 season, when he signed with the Chicago Bears, Eagles in '96 and Dolphins in '98.

TORETTI, SEVER ("TOR"). 1936-37-38. C & G, 6'1", 202 lbs.; Monongahela, PA. Better known to fans of the Engle and Paterno eras as a line coach and recruiter, but he was a fine lineman for Higgins during the "down" period when football was de-emphasized. Considered one of the best blockers on the team but also a fine tackler. Started at LG as soph, then moved to C for opening game in '37 years but was soon switched to T and G because of the super ability of soph C Leon Gajecki. Started at LG as senior and called defensive signals when team set three NCAA pass-defense records: fewest yards passing allowed per game (13.1 average), lowest average allowed per game (1.78 and lowest completion percentage (16.9 percent); only 10 passes completed against team that year; the 13.1 yards per game average is still an NCAA record. Potential winning season of '38 spoiled by eighth-ranked Pitt, losing, 26-0, but that would be the last losing season for 49 years. Upon graduation, coached high school football and was very successful in Steelton and Williamsport before joining Joe Bedenk's staff in '49. Retained by Engle in '50, he went on to develop some of the best offensive linemen of the '50s and early '60s such as Otto Kneidinger, Joe Sabol and Bill Wehmer. He also was one of the best scouts and his scouting is credited with one of the biggest upsets in history, the 7-6 win over Ohio State in '56. Became assistant athletic director in '63 and, as a full-time recruiter during Paterno era, he was responsible for spotting many of the future stars who launched State into its greatest football seasons; one of his first class of recruits was the 1966 freshmen who included future Hall of Famers and All-Americans Dennis Onkotz and Mike Reid. Retired in 1979. Still lives in State College and frequently attends PSU sporting events.

TRIPLETT, WALLY. 1946-47-48. HB & KR, 5'10", 165 lbs.; Philadelphia, PA. A true racial pioneer who has never been given his proper due as a trailblazer or as a star running and defensive back. The first Black player in PSU history to make the varsity and start ('45), the first to earn a letter ('46) and one of the running and defensive stars of the post-World War II era when State produced its best teams in 25 years. Along with Dennie Hoggard, he integrated the Cotton Bowl in '47. Scored the tying TD in the Cotton Bowl on a six-yard pass from Elwood Petchel in the third QT, made at least three tackles that saved probable SMU TDs and just missed catching the winning TD on a 37-yard pass deflection on the last play of the game; game ended in 13-13 tie and State finished fourth in AP ratings, the best ever national rating up to that time. Started as LHB (or tailback) in Single-Wing as frosh but played at RHB (or wingback) for rest of career. Twice rushed for over 100 yards in era when few players did, getting 154 yards and one TD on eight carries in 34-14 win over Syracuse and 105 yards and one TD on nine carries in 37-7 victory over West Virginia, both in '48; this was Higgins' last team and only loss was to Pitt, 7-0, in next to last game of season. Led '48 team in all-purpose yards with 424 on the ground, 90 on pass receptions and 220 on punt returns and scoring with 36 points on six TDs. Although he wasn't the regular punt returner in any year, he is second in career average yardage (16.5) behind Ron Younker with 17 returns for 280 yards and one TD; that's because the TD came on the end of an 85-yard return against West Virginia in '48, which remains the third longest return ever. Played less than a quarter early in frosh '45 season but made a great impression late in 26-0 win over Syracuse, when he scored the first TD of his career, going in from the six-yard line after three straight carries, and started at LHB two weeks later against powerful Michigan State; played courageously but took such a severe physical beating from MSU he missed last two games and didn't earn a letter. In '46 began to come into his own, catching 29-yard pass for only TD in 9-6 win over Colgate in fourth game of year and scoring TDs on runs of 42 and 53 yards a week later in 68-0 rout of Fordham. By next year he was a star, known as "Mr. Outside," who combined speed, strength and intelligence in his running style. Was the prime kickoff man in '47 & '48. Also an outstanding defensive HB and was particularly effective against the pass; praised for helping thwart the high-powered SMU passing attack in '48 Cotton Bowl, and for interceptions and last-ditch tackles that enabled State to tie Michigan State 14-14 in '48 season. May have played his finest defensive game ever in one of the biggest contests of Higgins era, a 13-0 win over

unbeaten Penn, when he starred in a great goal line stand, breaking up passes and making fourth down tackle short of goal line. Played in NFL with Detroit ('50) and Chicago Cardinals ('52-'53) but his pro career was hampered by the year he spent not playing because of service in the Korean War in '51, when he was one of first two NFL players drafted into Army. After retirement from the NFL in mid-50s, he became first Black mutual clerk in Michigan racing history. Was a businessman in Detroit for many years. Now retired and lives primarily in Detroit.

URBANIK, TOM. 1963-64. FB, 5'11", 220 lbs.; Donora, PA. A real workhorse FB on teams late in the Engle era. Came into his own in the latter part his senior year, when his running helped turn a disastrous 1-4 start in '64 into a 6-4 season and Lambert Trophy winners as best team in the East and 14th ranking nationally. Selected on the All-Time Penn State team in 1967 by *Pittsburgh Press* sports editor Chet Smith, who covered Nittany Lion football for more than a half century. First FB to lead an Engle team in rushing with 625 yards and eight TDs on 134 carries in senior year. Also led in scoring with 48 points. Because he gained much of his yardage running behind the blocks of All-American Glenn Ressler, newspapers started calling the duo "Paul Bunyon and his Ox." Starting with West Virginia, team swept last five games including the historic 27-0 clobbering of then number two and unbeaten Ohio State at Columbus with Urbanik leading all rushers with 74 yards on 16 carries and setting up three TDs with sparkling smashes through the highly-praised OSU defense. Had more than 100 yards in rushing three-of-last-four games, all victories over Maryland, Houston and Pitt: his best running display was in 24-7 win over Houston when he carried the ball for all but 21yards in opening 73-yard drive to score a TD and finished with 122 yards on 19 carries. Then, in final game of career at Pitt, he won Coogan Award as Outstanding Player-of-the-Game, when he ran for 107 yards and two TDs on 20 carries, sometimes lugging ball on five or six successive plays in methodical drives as State won, 28-20. Winner of Red Worrell Award in '63 as most improved player in spring practice and started on first Unit in opening game win over Oregon, 17-7, where he had 45 yards on 12 carries; sometimes shifted to second unit because of FB Ed Stuckrath's defensive ability at LB. Missed latter part of season because of injuries and started '64 pre-season as third team FB but picked it up a notch and became starter and leading rusher in all but two games for rest of season. May not have had the natural talent of other PSU FBs but certainly one of the most determined. A three-year letterman in track while throwing the shotput. Drafted by Washington Redskins but didn't play pro ball. Now teaching and living in Bethel Park, PA.

VALENTINE, SAM. 1954-55-56. G & K, 6'0", 210 lbs.; Sykesville, PA. Engle's first All-American and State's first First-Team All-American in eight years after Sam Tamburo. Was a consensus guard in '56, chosen by Look and Colliers Magazines, Associated Press, International News Service and Newspaper Enterprise Association. Captain of '56 team that stunned the college football world with 7-6 upset over three-TD favorite Ohio State at Columbus; that game meant more to him than most any other he played in because he had been told he was "too small" to play at OSU and in the Big 10. Played one of his finest games on defense, as he and teammates limited OSU's high-powered attack to 253 yards with 80 yards coming on a last minute drive when the Buckeyes scored their only TD. Also was outstanding in the last game of his career, when State knocked Pitt out of Cotton Bowl with surprising 7-7 tie at Pitt Stadium. His '56 team was 6-2-1 with two losses (at Army and at Syracuse) by total of 11 points. Began varsity career as a backup at LG and moved up to second unit in soph season where he also handled some placekicking. Didn't make first start until third game of '55 but never missed another start for rest of career. Played two of his finest games against rivals Syracuse and Pitt in '55 and was cited for his tackling and fumble recovery in 21-20 win over Syracuse. Started off the '56 season where he left off at Pitt in '55, when he was named the Outstanding Lineman in 34-0 opening season win over Penn. Made the weekly All-East team four times and only Pitt's Joe Walton and Syracuse's Jim Brown were similarly honored that year. Engle said Valentine had "the uncanny facility of getting to the right place at the right time...and an exceptionally good sense in diagnosing plays." He also was an inspiring leader with a good sense of humor. The youngest of 10 children who got noticed for his football playing at Dubois High School. Near unanimous All-East and Co-Captain of East team in '57 East-West Shrine game. After graduation, played center for Quantico Marines and was All-Navy and All-Service in '58. Became a division manager for BMI, Inc. in Chicago and lived in Michigan City, IN, until his premature death on January 17, 1985.

VARGO, TOM. 1938-39-40. E, 6'2", 202 lbs.; Johnstown, PA. One of the best ends of his era when blocking and defense was more significant than catching passes. Picked on the All-Time Penn State team in 1950s and again in 1967 by *Pittsburgh Press* sports editor Chet Smith, who covered Nittany Lion football for more than a half century. Was a good blocker who had the speed to take out defensive backs. Also was used to run the ball on an "end around" and rarely lost yardage. Was even better on defense and was known for his hard tackling. A three-year starter and as a soph he was part of the outstanding defensive team that set three NCAA pass-defense records despite a losing season; the record for fewest yards passing allowed per game (13.1 average) still stands after 68 years. Cited for his play that year against Cornell. He also was the starting RE of the so-called "Seven Mountains" of '40, the excellent seven-man line anchored by All-American C Leon Gejecki on a team that only lost the end-of-season finale with Pitt in posting a 6-1-1 record and finishing among top 20 teams in country. Sportswriters who covered the Lions that year say he and Gejecki were the leaders on defense but Vargo never received the credit Gejecki did. Played one of his best games in 17-13 win over West Virginia in '40; he caught two passes that helped set up one TD and was cited by sportswriters along with Gejecki for holding Mountaineers to minus six yards in running and passing. In junior year, had one of his best games in 13-3 opening season win over Bucknell, including pass receptions of 20 and 23 yards that set up TD that broke up 3-3 tie in second half. Played another strong game in 10-0 upset of Penn in '39 and recovered a fumble that kept Lion drive alive and resulted in game's only TD. Retired and living in Montoursville, PA.

VERY, DEX. 1909-10-11-12. E, RB & KR, 5'8", 160 lbs.; Fairdale, PA. State's first great pass receiver who was inducted into the National Football Foundation College Football Hall of Fame in '76. Picked on the All-Time Penn State team in 1950s and again in 1967 by *Pittsburgh Press* sports editor Chet Smith, who covered Nittany Lion football for more than a half century. One of the most durable players in history. Never missed starting a game in four years, mostly at RE, usually played 60 minutes and never known to be removed for injury or fatigue in an era when State won 32 games and lost only two. Even more remarkable, he never wore any head gear, which made him one of the most conspicuous players on the field at that time. Second Team All-American in both '11 and '12 when picked by Walter Camp but at least a half dozen newspapers named him to the First-Team in '12, including three Pittsburgh papers and the Boston Journal. Captain in junior year of '11 team that was 8-0-1 and outscored opponents 199-to-12. Part of the school's first great recruiting class, entering in '09 with such teammates as Pete Mauthe, who, like Very, also was a future member of the collegiate Hall of Fame. First attended State on a State senatorial scholarship after playing at Mercersburg Academy and immediately made first team with his outstanding blocking, pass catching and vicious downfield tackling. Had exceptional speed and mobility and was a fierce competitor despite his small size. Played two of his best games against Penn in junior and senior years. His 70-yard punt return for a TD against Penn in '11 was the school record for 32 years and still remains one of the top 15 longest punt returns in history; he also threw the block that allowed Shorty Miller to score a then record 85-yard TD on the opening kickoff in what eventually was a 22-6 victory. The next year he caught a fourth down TD pass from Miller and set up another TD with his running and receiving in 14-0 win and was praised by sportswriters for defense, offense and kicking as he forced fumbles, recovered them and "pushed Penn's ends and halfbacks out of the play as though they were so many stuffed dolls." That '12 team was the best PSU squad ever up to that time and was unbeaten and untied with Mauthe, Miller and Very forming a great passing-receiving combination in an era when passing was restricted. This also was before Notre Dame's Gus Dorias and Knute Rockne made the forward pass famous. Very finished season with nine TDs, which included 17 end-around carries for 234 yards and 240 yards in kick returns. In second game of season against W & J he caught two TD passes from Miller, including one for 40 yards, in 30-0 win. Had one of his most outstanding games ever in the controversial 37-0 whipping of Ohio State at Columbus when OSU walked off field with seven minutes left in game and Very was accused of being "too rough" in his performance. In final game of his career, a 38-0 win over Pitt, he caught one TD pass from Mauthe for 38 yards and set up another with a spectacular 60-yard catch. Although he had never wrestled before coming to State, he wrestled four years and lost only two matches in 158-lb class, then in '17 won the National AAU titles in both the 175-lb. & heavyweight classes. Was one of the top intercollegiate football officials for 28 years, including refereeing at the Rose Bowl and Army-Navy games, but quit to concentrate on sales in Pittsburgh area. Died on Sept. 20, 1980 at age 91.

VITIELLO, ALBERT ("AL"). 1971-72. K, 5'8", 165 lbs.; East Meadow, NY & Naples, Italy. The first placekicking specialist recruited in Paterno era and PSU's first ever junior college transfer. Also team's first soccer-style PK who kicked left-footed. Broke most school placekicking records in first year of kicking when he booted 59 of 62

PATs and five of 13 FGs for 74 points in '71; his nine PATs in nine attempts in 63-21 win over Maryland also set single game record and had record in most consecutive PATs with 43. In '72 he kicked 39 of 40 PATs and eight of 16 FGs for 63 points. His longest FG was for 48-yards (two short of then record) against Boston College in '72. Set Cotton Bowl record with FGs of 21, 37 & 22 yards in "breakthrough" 30-6 win over Texas on Jan. 1, '73. Finished career with school record in PATs with 43 and tied for then season record of eight FGs with Pete Mauthe. Perhaps his most important kick ever and his first under pressure was a 22-yard FG with four minutes left in fourth QT in come-from-behind 16-14 win over Air Force that kept State unbeaten at time. He may be most forgotten of the fine placekickers coached by Paterno because his records have been surpassed over time. Recruited by assistant John Chuckran out of Nassau (NY) Community College where he set nation's junior college FG record with 60-yard boot against Baltimore Community College in '70. After football eligibility was used up he played half-back on PSU's '73 soccer team and his teammates included Chris Bahr, who succeeded him as the Lions' prime placekicker. A native of Naples, Italy, who migrated to U.S. in '65. Now in the custom furniture and upholstery business in Plainview, NY.

VORHIS, LARRY. 1906-07-08-09. QB & PK, 5'9", 175 lbs.; New York City. The first of State's outstanding quarterbacks and placekickers. Picked to All-Time Penn State team on 40th anniversary of State football in '27 by *New York Sun* sportswriter George Trevor who wrote that Vorhis was State's "most dependable drop kicker, as well as a cagey pilot...rarely missed the target; even when the tension was tightest, his dropkicks (were) game clinchers. Vorhis scored three FGs to beat Pittsburgh in '08, two to trim Cornell in '07, one to tie Cornell in '08 and one to deadlock Carlisle (Indians) in '09, and one to tie Pennsylvania the same season. That's delivery under pressure." His 22 career FGs was the record for almost 60 years until broken by Chris Bahr in '75, and he remains ninth on the all-time career list. One of the first QBs in nation to utilize passing when the rules were extremely restrictive. He threw the type of spiral pass that had never really been seen before. Could run quarter-mile in 51 seconds. Captain of unbeaten '09 team that won five and tied the powerful Carlisle Indians and Penn. The team scored 166 points while only giving up 11, and was declared champion of the mythical "Big Five" by Pittsburgh newspapers because of wins over Pitt and West Virginia; named to All-Western Pennsylvania team by several area newspapers. Scored the first ever TD on New Beaver Field in 31-0 win over Grove City to open '09 season. He returned with 10 other players and Coach Hollenbeck to mark the dedication of Beaver Stadium on September 17, 1960. Deceased.

WALTERS, LES. 1955-56-57. E, 6'0", 185 lbs. ; Hershey, PA. One of the best E's of his era who was as good a receiver as any of those who played under Engle. Second Team All-American in senior year, when he led team in receptions with 24 catches for 440 yards and five TDs and an 18.3 yards per reception; these were the best receiving statistics at State from '54-through-'61 and all the more re-markable when one considers that the team's passing offense was more limited than it is today. Still holds one of the best records for average yards per catch with 18.3 yards. His 72-yard reception for a TD on a pass from Milt Plum in the 40-7 win over Boston University in '56 is still tied for eighth longest in school history; he caught another pass for 28 yards and another TD that day for his first 100 yards receiving day, and had another 100-plus game the next year with 103 yards and two TDs on four catches in a controversial 20-12 loss at Syracuse. Made one of his finest receptions in last minute against North Carolina State in '56 thriller, when he took a six-yard pass from Plum on three-yard line and blasted into EZ with three defenders draped over him for a TD with 15 seconds left and a 14-7 win. Also a very good defensive player, mostly used in secondary. Played the best game in his career in 20-12 win over Syracuse at Archbold Stadium in '57: first, he teamed with captain Joe Sabol to make one of the all-time goal-line tackles on a muffed fourth-down punt by Syracuse in first quarter that led immediately to a State TD; next, he caught a spectacular 51-yard TD pass from Al Jacks in second period, then scored game-winning TD on a pass from soph Richie Lucas who found Walters all alone at five-yard line for 27-yard score, and, finally, ended the last minute threat by Syracuse with a fourth down tackle at the State eight-yard line. Played in East-West Shrine game and Senior Bowl in '58. Drafted by Washington in '58 but wound up playing one year with the Baltimore Colts before leaving pro football. Now a vice president of sales for a company in Chamblee, GA.

WARNER, CURT. 1979-80-81-82. TB & KR, 6'0", 208 lbs.; Wyoming, WV. May be State's best all-around offensive back ever. Two-time First-Team All-American in '81 & '82; finished 10th in Heisman Trophy race as senior. One of the all-time running backs who, along with his roommate Todd Blackledge at QB, led State to its first National Championship in '82 with 27-23 victory over then number one Georgia in '83 Sugar Bowl; he outdueled Heisman Trophy winner Hershel Walker in that game by rushing for 117 yards and two TDs on 18 carries and getting another 35 yards on two pass receptions. With Warner's running and Blackledge's passing, the '82 Lions had one of the most balanced offenses in school history. State's career leader in rushing yardage with 3,398 yards and 24 TDs on 649 attempts—also the record—and career leader in all-purpose yards (4,982 with 3,398 rushing, 662 on receiving and 922 on kick returns). Was also one of best pass receivers of all running backs and his 662 yards is the career record for backs. Holds single game record for rushing and all purpose yards in 41-16 win over Syracuse in junior year; he broke Shorty Miller's 69-year record that day, gaining 256 yards (in 26 carries) on the ground, 20 yards on two pass receptions and 65-yards on three kickoff returns for a total of 341 yards and one TD after a 69-yard run. His 238 yards on 28 carries in 30-24 win at Nebraska earlier that year is sixth best of all-time. Along with John Cappelletti, Ki-Jana Carter and Curtis Enis he is one of only four players with two or more games rushing over 200 yards in a career. Also has record for most games rushing over 100 yards with 18, including the final five games of his career in '82 championship year. Probably had the most impressive debut of any back in modern era, when he started at TB in opening-season game against Rutgers in frosh year and proceeded to run for 100 yards, including TDs of seven and 18 yards, catch two passes for 71 yards, one for a 68-yard TD, and pick up another 109 yards returning kicks in a 45-10 win. Not surprisingly, he led the '82 championship team in rushing

(1,041 yards and eight TDs on 198 carries) and scoring (eight TDs rushing and five on pass receptions). Also led team in rushing in soph and junior years and had best average in '81 when he gained 6.1 yards per carry (and eight TDs) on 1,044 yards in 171 attempts. seventh in career scoring with 33 TDs, and his five TDs on pass receptions in '82 is most ever in one season for a running back. Also an excellent kickoff return man who has career record for most TDs on returns (three) and yardage (922 yards), tied for most TDs in one season (two in 1980) and is second in career returns (32), career average (28.8 yards per return) and season average (35.0 yards per return and two TDs in 1980); led team in returns in freshman and sophomore years. His 95-yard return for TD against Pitt in '79 is tied with six others for fourth longest in history. Selected outstanding offensive player in '80 and '82 Fiesta Bowls; in '80 bowl he scored the first TD on a 64-yard run and totaled 155 yards on 18 carries, as State came from behind to clobber Ohio State, 31-19; in '82 bowl win over Southern Cal, 26-10, he also scored first TD on a 17-yard run and scored another TD in the third quarter on a 21-yard run, as he rushed for 145 yards on 26 carries. May have played his finest game in 24-14 win over Notre Dame in '82, when he sparked State's come-from-behind win in fourth QT: he caught 48-yard TD pass from Blackledge at start of period that gave Lions the lead, then had 44-yard run late in game to set up FG that clinched victory and eventual bid to Fiesta Bowl. Winner of Hall Award as outstanding senior player in '82. Played in '83 Hula Bowl. First choice of Seattle in '83 and had sensational, All-Pro career with Seahawks ('83-'89) and Los Angeles Rams ('90) before retiring. Now owns an auto dealership in Redmond, WA.

WAY, CHARLIE ("ONE-WAY" "GANG-WAY" "PIE-WAY" or 'RABBIT-WAY"). 1917, 1919-20. QB & HB, 5'7", 145 lbs.; Downingtown, PA. Another of the all-time running backs with more nicknames than any of the others. Selected First-Team All-American by Walter Camp in senior year and State's sixth ever AA at the time on an outstanding team that was unbeaten. Picked on the All-Time Penn State team in 1950s and again in 1967 by *Pittsburgh Press* sports editor Chet Smith, who covered Nittany Lion football for more than a half century. Also a Second-Team All-American in '19 on team that lost only to Dartmouth in one of the most significant games in history; made two spectacular plays at Dartmouth, when he took opening kickoff and went 90 yards for TD, then scooped up Dartmouth fumble and ran 85 yards for another TD, but State eventually lost, 19-13; team still won unofficial Eastern Title (with Dartmouth fourth) thanks to a 20-0 win over Pitt when Way's 53-yard TD in third QT clinched victory. Scored three TDs in first QT against Lebanon Valley in '20 in 107-7 win that is still the most points and widest margin of victory by a State team. In first game ever against Nebraska near end of '20 season, he scored the TD that broke up a close game on a 53-yard dash up the middle to set up one TD and ran in for another as State won, 20-0. One week later, he saved the unbeaten 7-0-2 season at Lehigh, when he carried 10 times in late 90-yard drive to get a TD and kicked the PAT that got a 7-7 tie. Was scrawny and light but had breakaway speed, a wonderful change of pace and a great stiff-arm. Still considered a fine "line smasher" because his speed got him through the smallest hole so quickly. Also an outstanding defensive HB who was praised for his ability to break up passes. His last name conjured up so many nicknames from sportswriters but his teammates simply called him "Charlie," and he was probably the most likable and unassuming man on the team. Was so unheralded and light (he then weighed 115 pounds) when he arrived on campus that he didn't play enough to earn a frosh numeral but was encouraged by head coach Dick Harlow to come out the next fall when most varsity players were in the military during World War I. Was a backup halfback early in soph season but made impressive debut in opening game against U.S. Army Ambulance Corps, an All-star college team, with his open field running. Started his first game at quarterback in fifth game against West Virginia Wesleyan after regular Frank Wolf had been hurt the previous game and became a star with a dazzling 40-yard punt return down the sidelines of a muddy field for a TD in last 30 seconds that gave State a come-from-behind 8-7 win. Started at QB rest of season. Teamed with HB Harry Robb and FB Red Gross as soph in '17 Pitt game to work an unorthodox spread formation featuring a triple pass that brought them national attention; didn't win Pitt game but outplayed Panthers in second & third QTs because of the new, radical formation. Went into the Army in '18, added weight and came back to be a star in '19 & '20 under new coach, Hugo Bezdek. Seldom started a game because he was not considered durable or rugged, so Bezdek would let him rest most of first half and then sub him in second half when he was fresh and opponents were tired. Teammates said Way would be so "worked up" he would play with a frenzy, crying and shouting as he carried the ball. Played pro football with the Canton Bulldogs ('21), the Frankford Steamrollers ('24) and the Philadelphia Quakers ('26). Coached football in high school and college at Dayton and VPI before going to work for the Internal Revenue Service until his retirement. Lived in Thorndale, PA, until his death on Jan. 31, 1988.

WEAR, WENDELL ("WINDY" "WENDY" or "RABBIT"). 1935-36-37. QB, HB & P, 5'9", 130 lbs.; Huntingdon, PA. One of the fine pint-sized backs who helped State get through the "down years" when de-emphasis took its toll. He was a very good player who had been recruited by other schools, including Southern Cal, but wanted to play close to home. Might have been better known if he had played on a better team. A speedy back who could pass and catch passes as well as anyone on the team. Also did most of the punting during his career. Called the offensive plays in Higgins' Single-Wing. As senior, he helped Higgins achieve his first winning season (5-3) after eight years of coaching at State. Played one of best games of career in '37 when a Higgins-coached team beat Penn for the first time, 7-0, at Philadelphia, catching a 17-yard pass from "High School" Harry Harrison for the only TD just moments after throwing a 21-yard pass to Harrison to set up the scoring play. Helped give Harrison his nickname in '36 Pitt game, when he completed an 11-TD pass to Harrison on a "sleeper" play that newspapers called "a high school play." Also was a star infielder on the varsity baseball team. After graduation stayed on to assist Higgins, then went into coaching and teaching at Altoona High School and then in West Orange, NJ, until his retirement.

WEAVER, HENNY. 1907-08-09-10. T, 5'10", 170 lbs.; Steelton, PA. One of the weirdest players ever. Seemed very strange to his teammates and played that way, too. But he was a four-year starter at T on some good teams that were improving each year. In senior year he made several All-Western PA squads, which was similar to making All-East today. A tough defensive player who was older than most of his teammates. He loved to hit and be hit. Frequently in the middle of the action, he would often be knocked out cold but after being revived by a trainer he would continue in game and refused to come out. No one ever confirmed the rumor that he had a steel plate in his head as the result of a machete wound suffered in the Spanish American War. But to protect himself, he wore a high head gear stuffed with whatever he could find. Teamed at T with Dick Harlow in '09 on first unbeaten team in 15 years (5-0-2) and on '10 that was 5-2-1. After graduation came back to help coach for a few weeks at a time. Deceased.

WEHMER, BILL. 1956-57-58. T & G, 6'4", 207 lbs.; Turtle Creek, PA. One of the most unknown and underrated of linemen who ever played at State. A true "student-athlete" in the days before the term became popular; often missed practice because of classroom commitments. Despite his size he was a quiet, easy-going person who was a dependable, solid blocker on running plays, a good pass protector and a hard-charging tackler. Made one his biggest tackles to save 14-10 victory over Holy Cross in '57, when on fourth-and-goal from the five-yard line with two minutes left to play, he made initial stop on HC's fine option QB Tom Greene inches short of the EZ; the win preserved State's streak of winning seasons, then at 19 consecutive years. A three-year starter in the late '50s but didn't like the limelight. Stayed in the background while his more flashy linemates such as Sam Valentine, Joe Sabol, Andy Stynchula and "Bull" Smith made more headlines. Now an electrical division director in North Myrtle Beach, SC.

WHITE, BOB. 1983-84-85-86. DE, 6'3", 254 lbs.; Freeport, PA. Part of the "Sack Gang" that played in back-to-back bowl games for the National Championship and won it in '86 with the great 14-10 win over then number one Miami in the '87 Fiesta Bowl. Along with Shane Conlan and Don Graham, the trio had more sacks on opposing QBs than any three defensive teammates before or since the years they played, '83-'86. Played one of his best games against Maryland in '86, when had two sacks and eight tackles and stopped two TDs with tipped passes that were intercepted by teammates and was named TV's Player-of-the-Game; his second tipped pass came after the Terps had driven to the PSU seven-yard line midway in the fourth QT and were poised to score the go-ahead TD but his tip was intercepted by Pete Curkendall and run back a record 82 yards, setting up a D. J. Dozier TD that broke open the game and eventually gave State the 17-15 win. The next week against Notre Dame, his sack of QB Steve Beuerlein with ND at the PSU one-yard line with less than a minute to play saved a 24-19 victory and the unbeaten season. In '85 he made another outstanding "clutch" play that helped preserve the undefeated season in midseason clash at Syracuse: his tackle on FB Roland Grimes caused a fumble at midfield late in fourth QT with State trailing, 20-17; teammate Graham recovered the fumble, and State scored the game-winning TD moments later. Tied for seventh with Graham on the career sack list with 18. Was backup DE in early part of frosh year but got first start at midseason against Syracuse and was there for next three and a half years. Won Jim O'Hora Award in '84 as most improved defensive player in spring practice and went on to lead team in sacks as soph. Played in '87 Senior Bowl. Number six choice of San Francisco in '87 but didn't play pro ball. Returned to State in '89 to work in University Admissions Office and then became an assistant athletic director in '95 and oversees student services, admissions and NCAA affairs. Lives in Boalsburg, PA.

WHITE, JACK. 1965-66. QB, 6'1", 195 lbs.; Wilkinsburg, PA. Had the misfortune of being the transition QB between the Engle and Paterno eras who was a lot better QB than it may seem now because he only had one good season, '65, under Engle. Was one of country's leading passers in '65 when he set team records (since broken) for passes completed, attempted and yardage (98-for-206 and 1,275 yards) and total offense (1,342). Had problems throwing too many interceptions that year with 14, the most for any State QB between 1950-and-1981. In Paterno's first game ever as head coach in '66, White led team to 15-7 win over Maryland and was leading rusher with 85 yards and a TD on 19 carries and also hit on 9-of-17 passes for 112 yards. But in next game against heavily favored Michigan State, he was blindsided in a legal but vicious tackle by All-American Bubba Smith that put him out of the game with a severe kidney injury and he never fully recovered. Two weeks later, he was benched for Tom Sherman as Paterno abandoned the I-Formation for a more power-running Wing-T offense and later explained that White wasn't the type of QB for an offense "where you had to throw back across the field, pitch back and do other things" such as find the secondary receivers. Paterno called White "a tough kid and a great competitor" but that virtually ended his career at QB. Transferred to State after beginning '62 season at Florida and was in the middle of a controversy because of unofficial agreement between State, Pitt, Syracuse and West Virginia over "redshirts' but sat out '63 season and became Pete Liske's backup in '64. Didn't have enough playing time to earn letter but took over as starter in Engle's final season. Played the finest game of his career in heartbreaking and controversial 21-17 loss at California in '65: completed 17-of-27 passes for 227 yards and a 13-yard TD throw to Jack Curry with 42 seconds left in the game, climaxing an 81-yard drive that gave State a come-from-behind 17-14 lead and the apparent victory; but Cal came back 63 yards with some questionable clock management by the referees favoring the home team to win game on a desperation 43-yard "hail mary" pass as time ran out. His son, Dan, played briefly with Lions in early '90s but transferred to Arizona and became a top QB. Drafted number eight at end of junior year by Baltimore but went to dental school instead of playing pro ball. Now a dentist in San Diego, CA.

WILLIAMS, JON. 1980-81-82-83. TB & FB, 5'10", 198 lbs.; Somervile, NJ. A fine running back on two of Paterno's best teams who was willing to sacrifice his own desires for the team and that helped give PSU first National Championship in '82. A natural TB, he moved to FB that year and teamed with Curt Warner to give the Lions a potent running attack. Played one of his finest games in team's only loss that season to Alabama, when he led rushing with 69 yards and a TD on 10 carries and caught two passes for 21 yards and was named State's Player-of-the-Game. Also had a good game against Pitt and made key 25-yard run in last two minutes that set up FG that clinched 19-10 victory. Teamed with Warner as frosh in '80 to run back kickoffs and was backup to TB Booker Moore; threw TD pass against Maryland; then in 31-19 Fiesta Bowl win over Ohio State, he set up his own four-yard TD with a 17-yard punt return in the fourth QT that put game out of reach. Was Warner's backup at TB in '81 and when Warner was injured, he made first start against West Virginia and rushed for over 100 yards for first time (140 yards and a TD on 27 carries) and was named Offensive Player-of-the-Game. With Warner still hobbling, Williams had an even better day against Notre Dame, running for 192 yards and a TD and catching two passes for 27 yards in 24-21 win that put Lions into Fiesta Bowl. He was expected to have a big year as the starting TB in '83 but missed spring practice with a knee injury, then strained ligaments in left knee in fourth game of season against Temple; freshman D.J. Dozier took over and Williams couldn't get back starting job until Dozier was hurt and Williams had finest day rushing with 196 yards and two TDs on 27 carries in 41-23 win over West Virginia. When Dozier returned, Williams went back to FB and was the leading rusher against Pitt and Washington in the Aloha Bowl. He is 12th in career rushing with 2,042 yards and 14 TDs on 380 carries. Played in '84 Senior Bowl. Drafted number three by New England and played for Patriots for two years. Now a hotel sales manager in Norton, MA.

WILLIAMS, ROBERT ("BOBBY"). 1942-43, 46-47. HB & KR, 5'8", 165 lbs.; Pittsburgh, PA. One of the stars of the war-time teams who also came back after service in World War II to be an integral part of the unbeaten Cotton Bowl team of '47. Probably the best pure passer of his era and one of the most popular players on the team. Also one of leading kick returners. As LHB in Single-Wing formation he was the play-caller and passer. Began '42 season as a walk-on on frosh team but was so sensational against Cornell frosh (hitting 20-of-30 passes) that he was moved to varsity, when frosh were declared eligible because of the war, and made a fine impression in his first varsity game in '42: came into Homecoming contest against Colgate in fourth QT with State trailing, 10-6, and a first down on its own 36-yard line; he immediately threw a "bomb" to soph tailback Cliff St. Clair, who caught the ball in stride near the sideline behind the safety at the 20-yard line and dashed into the EZ for the winning TD. Joined Marines for officer training following '42 season but returned to campus for fall of '43 as part of the historic V-12 program, which sent college students back to school until they could be integrated into the service. He was one of the stars that year—including 14-0 opening season win against Bucknell when he led all rushers with 51 yards and passed for one TD— until called up by the Marines at midseason. Returned in '46 and was the starting LHB all year on team that lost only close games to Pitt and Michigan State in 6-2 season. Was considered cool under pressure and the type of leader who could settle a team down and call the right plays in tough situations. Played one of best games in '46 in 12-7 win over Navy as President Truman looked on, when he led all rushers with 47 yards on eight carries and set up both TDs with his running and passing. Also tossed winning TD pass to Jeff Durkota in 9-0 win over Syracuse. In '47 shared LHB, mostly with the Larry Joe, but teammates on that Cotton Bowl team considered him the reliable and durable leader. Played one of best games of career in 7-0 win over upset-minded Temple, when he scored only TD in fourth QT, on two-yard run after he and Fran Rogel carried the ball 16 times on a great 49-yard drive, set up by Williams' 12-yard punt return. Scored first two TDs in 29-0 win over Pitt that put State into Cotton Bowl and setup second TD against SMU in '48 Cotton Bowl with 14-yard punt return. Son Bob played on '85 team. Coached high school football at Kane and Greensburg and was long time teacher in Greensburg school system before retiring. Still a frequent attendee at home games.

WILSON, AL. 1909-10-11-12. E, height and weight unknown; Williamsport, PA. The "other" end on the first outstanding back-to-back unbeaten teams of '11 & '12 who was overshadowed by the great-ness of teammate "Dex" Very. Made unbeaten '09 team as backup frosh and then started at LE for three years. Started at RE on the '12 team that was the school's first ever unbeaten, untied squad (8-0) and had only six points scored against it all season. Played one of his best games in the controversial first meeting with Ohio State at Columbus in '12; was all over field making tackles and blocking for Pete Mauthe and Shorty Miller; game was so vicious Wilson apparently lost several front teeth. Later became an executive of a coal company in West Virginia. Deceased.

WILSON, HARRY ("LIGHT HORSE"). 1921-22-23. HB, 5'9", 170 lbs.; Sharon, PA. Certainly one of State's greatest backs who also became a star at West Point. First-Team All-American in '23 (State's sixth), then went on to West Point and made All-American at Army in '26. One of only 14 State players and three coaches in the National Football Foundation College Football Hall of Fame, inducted in '73. Picked on the All-Time Penn State team in 1950s and again in 1967 by *Pittsburgh Press* sports editor Chet Smith, who covered Nittany Lion football for more than a half century. Originally came to State to play basketball and had little previous football experience. By soph year he was a little used backup until fifth game of season at Harvard, in what a Boston sportswriter later called "one of the greatest football games ever played," when he made a spectacular debut in third QT subbing for Pete Redinger: on his first carry he broke the record for the longest run in Harvard's stadium with a 56-yard dash to the Harvard four-yard line to set up State's second TD; game ended in thrilling 21-21 tie, as Wilson became starter for rest of his career. Forced to carry load almost by self in '22, when team started well but lost three of last four games; still went to first ever bowl game, the '23 Rose Bowl, where he was star in losing effort, rushing for 55 yards on 20 carries, completing two-of-two passes for five yards and catching three passes for only one yard in 14-3 loss to USC. The next year was his best as he scored every TD for State in last six games. Played perhaps his greatest game when heavily favored Navy visited State for first time ever for Homecoming clash in fourth game of '23 season. It was that game that earned him the nickname "Light Horse Harry." State was being outplayed in second QT when Wilson intercepted a pass and went 55 yards for TD; moments later he returned the KO 95 yards for a TD and then in third QT he ran 72 yards off a fake reverse for another TD as State won 21-3. He rushed for 123 yards on 16 carries and had a total of 218 yards, including the kickoff, interception and pass receptions. The next week he scored both TDs in historic 13-13 tie with West Virginia at Yankee Stadium, got only TD in 7-0 win over Georgia Tech at home, then again scored all three TDs on runs of 30 and 48 and a 50 yard interception in 21-0 win over Penn at Franklin Field where he carried the ball 32 times, which was the team record for years. Led State in scoring in '22 (12 TDs) and '23 and his 13 TDs in eight-game '23 season tied the season record of "Bull" McCleary and Harry Robb that was not broken until '68 by Charlie Pittman in 10 game season. One of the most quiet individuals on or off the field who let his running do his "talking." As fast as his teammate Glenn Killinger but had the "fancy maneuvers to break away from a defensive halfback" and was adept at following his interference. Always seemed to play his finest games against Navy and continued to do so at West Point as Army never lost to Navy the entire time he was there. Commissioned as a lieutenant in '28 and rose to the rank of Colonel before retiring in '56. A genuine hero who flew 45 combat missions as a pilot commander in World War II and won the

Distinguished Flying Cross and five oak leaf clusters. Retired to New Smyrna Beach, FL., but died in Rochester, NY at 88 years old.

WISNIEWSKI, LEO. 1979-80-81. DT 6'1", 286 lbs.; Houston, TX. One of the fan favorites in his era because he always seemed to play his heart out. Co-Captain in senior year of team that lost only twice and pulled off one of the biggest upsets over then number one Pitt by coming from 14 point deficit to win, 41-14. He was Defensive Player-of-the-Game in '82 Fiesta Bowl as team went on to beat USC, 26-10 , holding Heisman Trophy winner Marcus Allen to 85 yards on 30 carries; credited with six tackles, including nailing Allen for three big losses, and also recovered a fumble that set up a 23-yard FG. Coaches said he was "a great leader" who made the most of his talent. Began to make an impact as a soph backup in the fifth game, a 24-3 Homecoming win over Army, when he had four tackles, three for losses totaling 16 yards. By the final game of the' 79 season against Pitt, he was a starter and had eight tackles, two behind the line of scrimmage. Injuries hampered him in his junior year, but he was outstanding in '81, when he won the '81 Ridge Riley Award given to the senior for "sportsmanship, scholarship, leadership and friendship." Played one of his finest games in '81, the week after team was knocked out of number one ranking in midseason by Miami, when he had nine tackles including two sacks for 11 yards in losses in 22-15 win over North Carolina State. Brother of All-American Steve (see below). Played in the Hula and Japan Bowls in '82. Second choice of Baltimore in '82 and played nose tackle for Colts ('82) and Indianapolis ('84-'85) before leaving pro football to go into business. Now lives in Pittsburgh, PA.

WISNIEWSKI, STEVE. 1985-86-87-88. G, 6'4", 260 lbs.; Houston, TX. Three-year starter and one of the toughest and meanest offensive linemen who ever played at State. Only the third offensive lineman to be a two-time First-Team All-American; selected by *Sporting News* in '87 and '88 and Football Coaches in '88. That was a major feat considering the teams of his junior and senior years did not come close to the quality of the '85 & '86 squads that played for the national title and that the '88 team was the school's first losing one in 49 years. Was a starter as a soph at short guard on the '86 National Championship team, including the title game in '87 Fiesta Bowl; began year in similar backup position he had as frosh (on the '85 team that also played for national title), but was the starter by third game of season against East Carolina and stayed there the rest of career. Followed older brother Leo (see above) to State but became bigger star. Winner of Hall Award as outstanding senior player in '88. Followed in the footsteps of his brother in post-season games by playing in '89 Hula and Japan Bowls. Second pick of Dallas in '89 draft who traded him immediately to the Los Angeles/Oakland Raiders where he has been a starter and virtual All-Pro ever since. Lives in Pleasanton, CA.

WITMAN, JON. 1992-93-94-95. FB & OLB, 6'3", 230 lbs.; Wrightsville, PA. One of the underrated backs of the '90s who teamed with Brian Milne to give State an outstanding one-two punch at FB on the unbeaten '94 team that won the school's first Big 10 Championship and the '95 Rose Bowl. He usually was the lead block for Ki-Jana Carter and Mike Archie in the running attack and also made key block in leading Milne over the goal line for crucial TDs. He was the starting FB on that '94 team, but sidelined most of last three games because of

a knee injury; still gained 241 yards on 49 carries. Recovered in time to score a nine-yard TD in Rose Bowl win over Oregon. Made one of the clutch plays of his career with a nine-yard TD on a pass reception in third QT of '94 win over Michigan that made team number one in country. Started all 12 games in '95 and his 10 TDs were second only to Bobby Engram: rushed for 316 yards (and nine TDs) on 84 attempts and caught 14 passes for 141 yards. He was an excellent blocker whose running style was built on quickness, speed and strength. Began career as a linebacker and earned letter as frosh backing up Reggie Givens. Switched to FB at spring practice in '93 when injuries decimated State's FB candidates and became prime backup. Played in '96 Senior Bowl. Drafted third by Pittsburgh in '96 and now a valued backup for the Steelers and member of special teams; picked by Pittsburgh Pro Football Writers as Rookie-of-the-Year in '96.

WOLOSKY, JOHN ("SHAG"). 1942, 47. C, 5'11", 205 lbs.; Brownsville, PA. Best remembered as the man who caused the great Doak Walker to miss an extra point kick in State's 13-13 tie with SMU in '48 Cotton Bowl; after Walker had scored SMU's second TD in first Half, Wolosky "crashed" through twice on the PAT attempt, the first time he was so offside that SMU had not centered the ball to the holder, then when he did it again he hurried Walker's attempt and the kick failed. He was the starting C on that unbeaten '47 team but he had missed four seasons because of service in World War II. One of the most highly recruited high school linemen in country in '40 who passed up national powers Pitt, Ohio State and Alabama to play for Lions. Played C on the outstanding unbeaten Frosh team of '41, then backed up captain Lou Palazzi at C on '42 team that lost only to West Virginia. Spent next four years in service but returned after '46 season and started the next year in every game. A good blocker and rugged tackler who was very aggressive. Played one year in NFL with New York Giants after graduation. Retired and living in Isabella, PA.

WYDMAN, GARY. 1961-64. HB & QB, 6'1", 180 lbs.; Corning, NY. One of the most forgotten of Engle's QBs but also one of the most respected for his perseverance and devotion to the team. He will always be known as the QB who led the '64 team to the shocking 27-0 upset over number two Ohio State at Columbus: played the game of his career with his play-calling, ball-handling, passing and spiritual leadership against three-TD favorite OSU; completed 12-of-22 passes for 148 yards, setting up all the TDs, and scored second TD himself on a three-yard run around left end off a pass-run option play. Frustrated by injuries and illness throughout career until senior year. One of the country's top high school QBs, he was such a good runner that Engle used him at HB in soph season rather than keep him on bench at QB. In '61 season-opening win over Navy, 20-10, he caught the only three passes completed by State QBs, gaining 59 yards, and picked up another 24 rushing. But injuries forced him out of several games and by fall practice of '62 he was back vying for QB with Pete Liske and Don Caum; actually was projected starter as preseason practice began but an injury sidelined him for season and he never fully recovered until '64. Got off to a disastrous start in '64, as team lost first three games and four-of-five and fans were pushing Engle to replace him. Engle didn't, and he led team to five straight victories and a 14th ranking by UPI and the Lambert Trophy; by end of season Engle believed this was one of the best teams he ever coached. Wound up year by completing

70-for-149 passes for 832 yards and one TD and six interceptions. Son Steve played basketball for State ('92-'94). Now a recruiting counselor in Dallas, TX.

YECKLEY, ED. 1902-03-04-05. T, E, HB & PK, 6'1", 180 lbs.; Dubois, PA. Perhaps one of the toughest all-around players in State history & known as much for his defensive play as his running and goal kicking. Picked on State's 40th Anniversary All-Time team in 1927 by *New York Sun* sportswriter George Trevor who wrote that Yeckley was "very fast and shifty when he carried the ball. And when he didn't he was a vicious tackler." In one of his first games in '02 against Navy, he recovered a fumbled punt with three minutes left in scoreless tie, which led to winning TD and 6-0 upset victory. Combined with Carl Forkum, Andy Smith, Ed Whitworth and Irish McIlveen in '02 for one of the most potent running attacks in the country. Captain of '05 team that went 8-3. May have played finest game against West Virginia in '05, when he scored winning TD on eight-yard run with time running out and then kicked "goal after" to give State an 8-0 victory at Beaver Field. Often played hurt, including '05 in 11-5 loss to Navy, when he was severely injured but refused to come out of game. After graduation, helped coach in the Hollenback years, then was a major recruiter of Ohio prospects during Bezdek era. Had falling out with Bezdek in late '20s and helped lead alumni revolt that eventually ousted Bezdek in '29. Owned a successful manufacturing business in Lorain, OH, until his death.

YOUNKER, RON. 1953-54. HB & PR, 5'8", 165 lbs.; Windber, PA. Played in the shadow of Lenny Moore and Billy Kane but was one of the all-time best punt returners. An outstanding "clutch" player who made things happen. Small but determined running back who teammates said had "a lot of heart." Also a gutsy fighter on defense who wasn't afraid to stick his head into the middle of the pack. Still holds record for career punt return average with 17.6 yards on 16 returns for 281 yards. A reserve as soph who usually played behind Moore in junior year but sometimes was in same backfield; in senior year started at RHB on '54 team that was 7-2; led team with 12 punt returns for 193 yards, fifth best average for one season. His 80-yard TD run against Virginia in '54 is seventh longest on record and he shares this with eight players, including Moore. Made perhaps the two biggest plays of his career as junior in the famous "snow game" against Fordham at Beaver Field; recovered a fumbled punt by Fordham to set up State's third TD then scored on a 37-yard run late in fourth QT to break a 21-21 tie and give State a 28-21 win. Played one of his finest games in 39-7 win over Holy Cross in senior year when he scored TDs on runs of 35 and 46 yards and the 96 yards he gained was the most ever in one game, but did get 91 against VA thanks to 80-yard run. Now living in Windber, PA.

YUKICA, JOE. 1951-52. E, 6'2", 190 lbs.; Midland, PA. A fine offensive end in the early Engle years who was recruited when Higgins was still coach and was in the first group of scholarship players (1949) since 1927 and spent frosh year at California State Teachers College because of crowded conditions on campus. A reserve as soph but in era of two-platoon football he started at offensive RE as junior and caught many passes in key situations, including opening game with Boston University when his catch early in game set up first TD in 40-34 victory. Started at LE in senior year and was leading team in pass receptions until his career was cut short when injured against Nebraska at midseason and missed rest of year. Had one of his finest games in that 10-0 win over Nebraska with six receptions. Finished year with 15 receptions for 163 yards. Also had another fine game in surprising 20-20 tie with Purdue with receptions that set up two TDs and scored himself on a 17-yard toss from Tony Rados. Went into coaching after graduation and coached future State star Don Caum at Harrisburg's Central Dauphin, then became assistant at Dartmouth; moved on to be head coach at University of New Hampshire and Boston College—where he coached against Paterno several times in late '60s and had several close games. As BC coach in '73 he proposed an Eastern football conference to help increase prestige of area and Paterno was supportive; later Paterno picked up on the idea as athletic director but the move never went anywhere. Paterno has always said one of the reasons BC has never kept up with PSU in football was because of the dismissal of Yukica before the BC program had a full chance to develop. Now a real estate broker in the Grantham, NH area.

ZAPIEC, CHARLIE. 1968-69, 71. G & LB, 6'2", 220 lbs.; Philadelphia, PA. Could have easily played in the era of two-way 60-minute men. Played LB only as senior on '71 team and became a star, making NEA All-American after making 62 tackles and intercepting four passes. Part of great linebacking crew of '71 that included John Skourpan and Gary Gray. Started at G as soph and junior on State's great back-to-back undefeated teams of '68 & '69 that won two Orange Bowls and finished second in nation. Will always be remembered for the crucial block he made on Kansas' All-American defensive end John Zook that sprang Bobby Campbell for the two-point conversion with 30 seconds to play that gave PSU the thrilling 15-14 victory in '68 Orange Bowl and State's first unbeaten, untied season in 56 years. Moved to ILB in spring of senior year and started in '70 season opener against Navy, but while in Colorado the next weekend, he had an emergency appendectomy before game and missed rest of year. Came back as LB and co-captain of powerful '71 team that lost only last game of regular season in upset to Tennessee, and went on to hold Texas to two first half FGs in 30-6 Paterno's "breakthrough" victory at '72 Cotton Bowl; recovered a key fumble early in third QT at Texas 41-yard line leading to a Lydell Mitchell TD that gave State a 10-6 lead it never relinquished. Played one of his best games on national TV Sept. 25, '71, in 44-14 win over Iowa and was named Defensive Player-of-the-Game. Spearheaded outstanding first quarter goal line stand against Air Force that helped set tone for game as Lions came from behind to win, 16-14. Drafted fourth by Dallas in '72 but chose to play in Canadian Football League with Montreal Alouettes and was a star there for several years until retirement. Now works in estate planning in New Hope, PA.

ZORDICH, MICHAEL. 1982-83-84-85. LB, FS, CB & Hero, 6'0", 206 lbs.; Youngstown, OH. All-American as senior when he was Co-Captain and the leader of the young '85 defensive team that shocked the college football world by coming from nowhere to take the team to the national title game in the '86 Orange Bowl against Oklahoma. He set the tone for the entire '85 season when he intercepted a pass on the second play from scrimmage in the first game of year at pre-season number one Maryland and ran it back 32 yards for a TD that sparked State to a 20-18 upset win. Also made an interception which set up FG in 36-6 win over ND that year and finished season with 60 tackles. Played outside LB as frosh and saw plenty of action as backup on first National Championship team. Started to play more in '82 after frustrating early season loss to Alabama, which temporarily bounced State from national title race; in following game against Syracuse he led team in tackles with nine, including two QB sacks in 28-7 win, and two weeks later led team again in tackles with seven and one sack in 52-17 victory over Boston College. Became starter as soph playing at CB, then free safety, then to Hero and was regular for rest of career. Was usually among the top tacklers in every game. Led team in interceptions as soph with three for 19 yards and was a tough, hard-tackling, dependable defensive star who broke up many passes. Winner of '85 Hall Award as Outstanding Senior. Played in '87 Japan Bowl. Ninth choice of San Diego in '86 but cut and signed by New York Jets. Played with Jets in '87 and '88 and then traded to Phoenix Cardinals where he became one of the leaders on defense ('89-'93) and since '94 has been a star defensive back for the Philadelphia Eagles. Lives in Canfield, OH, in off season.

ZUR, ROD. 1975. SE 6'2", 175 lbs.; Endicott, NY. Listed here because he symbolically represents all the hundreds of virtually unknown young men who played football for Penn State in the last 111 years. Many never earned a letter but they worked hard during practice and are part of the tradition. He is the last of all the football lettermen named in alphabetical order and should be the answer to a PSU trivia game. Finally lettered as a reserve SE on '75 team that went to Sugar Bowl but he never caught a pass or carried the ball. Spent his career trying to make it as a flanker and defensive back but never got past third string. His brother, Randy, was a starting QB for Syracuse in early 70s. Now lives in West Jacksonville, FL.

"The Players"

CHAPTER 16

THE LETTERMEN

Abbey, Don, 1967-69, real estate managing partner, Bradbury, Cal.

Abran, Wally, 1967, retired, Coraopolis, Pa.

Adams, Askari, 1996-97, Penn State student, Camp Hill, Pa.

Adams, Charlie, 1969, physician, Encinitas, Cal.

Addie, Walt, 1972-74, teacher/coach, Sterling, Va.

Adessa, Joe, 1936-37, deceased.

Adkins, Henry, 1990, fixed income trading, New York, N.Y.

Ahrenhold, Frank, 1969-71, company vice president, Blue Bell, Pa.

Alberigi, Ray, 1955-56, insurance agent & county commissioner, Jessup, Pa.

Alexander, Dave, 1959-60, vice president & business manager, Huntersville, N.C.

Alexander, Mike, 1987, Sescane, Pa.

Alexander, Rogers, 1982-85, security guard, State College, Pa.

Alguero, Anthony, 1978, bank examiner, Cambria Heights, N.Y.

Alleman, Ronald, 1957-59, area sales manager, Emmaus, Pa.

Allen, Bruce, 1944, Omaha, Neb.

Allen, Doug, 1970, 72-73, NFLPA assistant executive director, Alexandria, Va.

Allen, George, 1968, senior lab engineer, Gilbert, Ariz.

Allen, Robert, 1955, retired high school teacher/coach, Moorestown, N.J.

Allerman, Kurt, 1974-76, wholesale lighting distributor, Hudson, Ohio

Alpert, George, 1983-84, Livingston, N.J.

Alston, Chris, 1997, Chapel Hill, N.C.

Alter, Spike, 1937-39, deceased.

Amprim, L.R., 1949

Anders, Paul, 1950-51, retired, Anaheim, Cal.

Anderson, Bill, 1996, Indiana, Pa.

Anderson, Danne, 1985, corporate finance officer, Bethesda, Md.

Anderson, Dick, 1961-63, Penn State assistant football coach, State College, Pa.

Anderson, Jeff, financial aid officer, State College, Pa.

Anderson, Richie, 1991-92, NFL player, Sandy Spring, Md.

Anderson, Wilson, 1931-33

Andress, John, 1975-76, marketing representative, Pipersville, Pa.

Andrews, Fritz, 1935, retired, Ambler, Pa.

Andrews, Kenn, 1971-72, production manager, Glenshaw, Pa.

Andronici, Bob, 1964-65, business & marketing consultant, Centre Hall, Pa.

Angevine, Leon, 1966-68, Peru, N.Y.

Anthony, Joseph, 1937-38, retired industrial engineer, Jamestown, N.Y.

Arbuthnot, James, 1901-03, deceased.

Archie, Mike, 1992-95, NFL player, Sharon, Pa.

Argenta, Ron, 1975-76, Greensburg, Pa.

Arnelle, Jesse, 1951-54, Penn State trustee, retired attorney, San Francisco, Cal.

Arnst, John, 1956, health care specialist, Coatesville, Pa.

Arrington, Lavar, 1997, Penn State student, Pittsburgh, Pa.

Artelt, Art, 1922-24, deceased.

Ashley, Walker Lee, 1979-82, environmental products marketing, St. Paul, Minn.

Astle, Greg, 1991, sales consultant, Ft. Lauderdale, Fla.

Atherton, Charles, 1890-94, deceased.

Atkins, Todd, 1992-95, Ellwood City, Pa.

Atty, Ferris, 1967-68, teacher, Camp Hill, Pa.

Aull, Charles, 1889-91, deceased.

Aumiller, Jack, 1971, cardiologist, Danville, Ky.

Austin, Bruce, 1977, bank assistant vice president, Pittsburgh, Pa.

Baer, Ray, 1920-21, deceased.

Baggett, Matt, 1988-91, sales manager, Marietta, Ga.

Bahr, Chris, 1973-75, financial advisor, Boalsburg, Pa.

Bahr, Matt, 1976-78, design engineer, Pittsburgh, Pa.

Bailey, Don, 1952-54, manufacturer's representative, Berwyn, Pa.

Baiorunos, Jack, 1972-74, dentist, Ellicott City, Md.

Baker, Ralph, 1961-63, account representative, Greenlawn, N.Y.

Ballou, Vic, 1908, deceased.

Balthaser, Don, 1952-54, watch sales, Atlanta, Ga.

Banks, Bill, 1975-77, York, Pa.

Bannon, Bruce, 1970-72, marketing senior vice president, North Hollywood, Cal.

Baran, Stan, 1969

Barninger, Michael, 1995, Mechanicsburg, Pa.

Banbury, J.R., 1941-42

Barantovich, Alex, 1936-38, retired, Brownsville, Pa.

Barber, Stew, 1958-60, division vice president, Mt. Pleasant, S.C.

Barber, W.B., 1950

Barclay, Watson, 1887, deceased.

Barnett, W.D., 1908, deceased.

Barney, Don, 1950-52, retired, State College, Pa.

Barowski, Sean, 1987, Harrisburg, Pa.

Barr, Adam, 1904-05, deceased.

Barr, Jim, 1949-51, scholastic athletics, Lancaster, Pa.

Barr, Tom, 1981-82, high school teacher, Pottstown, Pa.

Barrett, Dick, 1965, school administrator, Tyrone, Pa.

Barrett, Fritz, 1910, deceased.

Barron, A.M., 1910, 13-14, deceased.

Barry, P.A., 1911, deceased.

Bartek, Len, 1950-51, retired pharmaceutical sales, Stroudsburg, Pa.

Bartek, Lou, 1982, Hampton, Va.

Barth, Lou, 1934-36, deceased.

Barvinchak, Dick, 1973, 75, Long Beach, Cal.

Bassett, Bob, 1977-78, company owner, Enola, Pa.

Batdorf, John, 1930, deceased.

Battaglia, Mark, 1980-82, senior account executive, Pittsburgh, Pa.

Bauer, Trey, 1984-87, account manager, Paramus, N.J.

Baugh, Kevin, 1980-83

Beatty, Charles, 1947-49, retired drywall contractor, Wilmington, Del.

Bebout, James, 1911-13, deceased.

Beck, Carl, 1916, 20, deceased.

Beckish, Mike, 1984-86, orthopedic surgeon, Durham, N.C.

Beckwith, Dan, 1971, deceased.

Bedenk, Joe, 1921-23, deceased.

Bedick, Tom, 1962-63

Bedoski, A.J., 1931-33

Bell, Fred, 1945-47, retired teacher, Southampton, N.J.

Bell, Imani, 1997, Penn State student, Philadelphia, Pa.

Bellamy, Herb, 1984, Staten Island, N.Y.

Bellamy, Irv, 1987, Staten Island, N.Y.

Bellas, Albert, 1944-45, retired, Dallas, Pa.

Bellas, Joe, 1964-65, deceased.

Benfatti, Lou, 1990-93, Oak Ridge, N.J.

Benjamin, Chuck, 1974, 76, lawyer, Ridgewood, N.J.

Bennett, Robert, 1900-01, deceased.

Benson, Brad, 1974-76, Flemington, N.J.

Bentz, Newsh, 1920-22, deceased.

Berfield, Wayne, 1958, 60, high school teacher, New Smyrna Beach, Fla.

Bergman, Bud, 1924, 26, deceased.

Bergstrom, Jeff, 1980-81, advisory client representative, Philadelphia, Pa.

Bernier, Kurt, 1984-87, general manager, Coraopolis, Pa.

Berry, Parker, 1931-33, retired, Hartville, Ohio

Berryman, Punk, 1911-15, deceased.

Betts, Arthur, 1950-51, high school teacher, Murraysville, Pa.

Biesecker, Art, 1901, deceased.

Bill, Tom, 1987-90, Ringoes, N.J.

Biondi, Dan, 1979-82, auto dealership secretary/treasurer, Export, Pa.

Black, Jim, 1917, deceased.

Blackledge, Todd, 1980-82, television analyst, North Canton, Ohio

Blair, R.W., 1905, deceased.

Blair, W.A., 1898, deceased.

Bland, Dave, 1971-73, advertising executive, Oakland, Cal.

Blasentine, Joe, 1960-62, teacher, Cinnaminson, N.J.

Bleamer, Jeff, 1973-74, assistant head football coach, East Tennessee State, Johnson City, Tenn.

Blick, John, 1996-97, Penn State student, Saylorsburg, Pa.

Blockson, Charlie, 1953-55, school district advisor/Afro-American historian, Gwynedd, Pa.

Bochna, Derek, 1990-93, Washington & Jefferson assistant football coach, Pittsburgh, Pa.

Bodle, Dave, 1977, deceased.

Bohart, Joe, 1957-58

Bohn, Wellington, 1899-1900, deceased.

Bonham, Jim, 1941, insurance & real estate, Coraopolis, Pa.

Boone, Ed, 1983, 85, probation officer, Columbus, Ohio

Booth, John, 1971, deceased.

Botts, Mike, 1969, 71, machinist, Elizabethville, Pa.

Botula, Pat, 1957-59, investment broker, Pittsburgh, Pa.

Bowden, A.T., 1952, deceased.

Bower, James, 1964, San Antonio, Tex.

Bowes, Bill, 1962-64, New Hampshire head football coach, Durham, N.H.

Bowman, Kirk, 1980-83, national accounts, Colleyville, Texas

Boyd, James, 1997, Penn State student, Chesapeake, Va.

Boyle, Rusty, 1974

Bozick, John, 1958-60, insurance principal, Pittsburgh, Pa.

Braddock, Edward, 1929, deceased.

Bradley, Dave, 1966-68, steel corporate manager, Lewistown, Pa.

Bradley, Jim, 1973-74, orthopedic surgeon, Pittsburgh, Pa.

Bradley, Matt, 1979-81, Johnstown, Pa.

Bradley, Tom, 1977-78, Penn State assistant football coach, State College, Pa.

Brady, Kyle, 1991-94, NFL player, New Cumberland, Pa.

Bratton, Rod, 1974, physical therapist, Montoursville, Pa.

Brennan, Thad, 1993-94, Lansdale, Pa.

Bresecker, A.S., 1901-03, deceased.

Brewster, Jesse, 1931-32, retired high school teacher, Wallingford, Pa.

Brezna, Steve, 1968, high school teacher, Askam, Pa.

Briggs, Bernard, 1937, retired, Milford, Del.

Brosky, Bernard, 1941, grocer, Moosic, Pa.

Brown, Conrad, 1950, retired school administrator, Fayetteville, Pa.

Brown, Courtney, 1996-97, Penn State student, Alvin, S.C.

Brown, Craig, 1977, terminal operations manager, Chicago, Ill.

Brown, Cuncho, 1995-97, Penn State student, Winston-Salem, N.C.

Brown, Ed, 1895, deceased.

Brown, Gary, 1987-90, NFL player, Houston, Tex.

Brown, George, 1918-20, deceased.

Brown, Ivan, 1918, deceased.

Brown, Jim, 1978-81, Rosalyn, Ga.

Brown, Keith, 1981, company president, Phoenix, Ariz.

Brown, Rick, 1971-72, regional vice president, Tucson, Ariz.

Brown, Sparky, 1940, 42-43, retired, Cazenovia, N.Y.

Brown, Sydney, 1891-92, deceased.

Brubaker, Jeff, 1988, teacher, Denver, Pa.

Bruhn, Earl, 1944, St. Bonafacius, Minn.

Brunie, Jeff, 1982, company owner, Wormleysburg, Pa.

Bruno, John C., 1956, product & market development manager, Pittsburgh, Pa.

Bruno, John, Jr., 1984-86, deceased.

Brzenchek, Dave, 1990, product engineer, Canton, Mich.

Buchan, Sandy, 1962-64, dentist, Amherst, N.H.
Buchman, Barry, 1985, Whitehall, Pa.
Buckwalter, Cliff, 1974, West Chester, Pa.
Bullock, Darryl, 1988, Morgan State assistant head football coach, Cockeysville, Md.
Bulvin, Jerry, 1970, high school teacher, South Fork, Pa.
Bunn, Ken, 1949-50, retired professor, Bangor, Pa.
Burger, Todd, 1989-92, NFL player, Martinsville, N.J.
Burkhart, Chuck, 1968-69, company president, Dallas, Tex.
Burns, Billy, 1899, deceased.
Burns, Harry, 1906-07, deceased.
Bush, John, 1974-75, recreational therapist, Selinsgrove, Pa.
Butterfield, Dick, 1960, restaurant owner, Atlanta, Ga.
Buttle, Greg, 1973-75, sports marketing representative, East Meadow, N.Y.
Butya, Jeff, 1981, restaurant owner, Pittsburgh, Pa.
Buzin, Mike, 1996, Penn State student, Westlake, Ohio
Buzin, Rich, 1966-67, executive vice president, Westlake, Ohio
Bycoskie, Drew, 1984-86, district sales manager, Collegeville, Pa.

Calderone, Jack, 1955-56, real estate broker, Glen Mills, Pa.
Caldwell, J.W., 1955
Campbell, Bob, 1966-68, high school teacher/coach, Frederick, Md.
Campbell, Charles, 1905-06, deceased.
Campbell, Chris, 1994-96, Akron, Ohio
Campbell, Kevin, 1984, medical student, McLean, Va.
Capozzolli, Tony, 1976
Cappelletti, John, 1971-73, sales & manufacturing, Laguna Niguel, Cal.
Cappelletti, Mike, 1976, field supervisor, Berwyn, Pa.
Caprara, Babe, 1956-57, Grand Rapids J.C. athletic director, Rockford, Mich.
Capretto, Bob, 1966-67, orthodontist, Oakmont, Pa.
Caravella, Rich, 1975, insurance sales, Hilliard, Ohio
Carlson, Cory, 1994-95, Penn State student, Medina, Ohio
Carraher, Scott, 1983, regional manager, Macungie, Pa.
Carroll, Mike, 1996, Northbrook, Ill.
Carter, Gary, 1968-70, Fulton, N.Y.
Carter, Ki-Jana, 1992-94, NFL player, Westerville, Ohio
Cartwright, C.R., 1887, 1889-91, deceased.
Cartwright, Mike, 1981, sales representative, Baltimore, Md.
Caruso, Jordan, 1997, Penn State student, Medford, N.J.
Case, Frank, 1980, elementary school teacher, Colorado Springs, Col.
Caskey, Howard, 1944-45, deceased.
Castignola, Jack, 1943, Dayton, Ohio
Caum, Don, 1961-63, senior vice president & chief marketing officer, Topeka, Kan.
Caye, Ed, 1957-60, account executive, Fort Thomas, Ky.
Cefalo, Jim, 1974-77, television sportscaster, Miami, Fla.
Ceh, Bob, 1990-92, school teacher, Wexford, Pa.
Cenci, Aldo, 1941-43, deceased.
Chamberlain, Rich, 1985, territory sales manager, Coral Springs, Fla.

Cherewka, Mark, 1980, dental consultant, Mechanicsburg, Pa.
Cherundolo, Chuck, 1934-36, Des Plaines, Ill.
Cherry, Tom, 1968, high school teacher/coach, Wellington, Fla.
Chizmar, Brian, 1986-89, acute care specialist, Pittsburgh, Pa.
Christian, Greg, 1973, 75, management analyst, Palm Harbor, Fla.
Chuckran, John, 1944, 48-49, deceased.
Cimino, Pete, 1959, high school teacher & assistant dean, Baldwin, N.Y.
Cino, John, 1961, Rockville, Md.
Cirafesi, Wally, 1967, 69, teacher, Miami, Fla.
Cisar, Chris, 1988, 90, 92, sales representative, Randolph, N.J.
Clair, Eric, 1992-95, Elizabethtown, Pa.
Clapper, John, 1896-97, deceased.
Clark, Bruce, 1976-79, Orlando, Fla.
Clark, David, 1985-86, police officer, Lorton, Va.
Clark, Harold, 1913-16, deceased.
Clark, John, 1911-13, deceased.
Clark, Richard, 1952, reliability engineer, Lancaster, Pa.
Clauss, Chris, 1987, insurance & real estate, Clarks Summitt, Pa.
Clayton, Stan, 1985-87, Alabama State assistant football coach, Montgomery, Ala.
Cleary, Anthony, 1995-97, Shippensburg (student), Chambersburg, Pa.
Cleaver, G.G., 1888, deceased.
Clouser, Joe, 1983, sales representative, Roseville, Cal.
Coates, Jim, 1985-87, car care business owner, Girard, Ohio
Coates, Ron, 1962-63, coal sales, Greenville, Pa.
Cobbs, Duffy, 1983-86, marketing representative, Alexandria, Va.
Coccoli, Don, 1967, high school teacher, Newport News, Va.
Coder, Craig, 1977-78, medical sales, Redmond, Wash.
Coder, Ron, 1974-75, independent contractor, Roswell, Ga.
Colbus, H.H., 1916, deceased.
Cole, Clyde, 1932-33, deceased.
Cole, Eric, 1996-97, Penn State student, Kennett Square, Pa.
Cole, Glen, 1970-71, Binghamton, N.Y.
Coles, Joel, 1979-80, 82, Pittsburgh, Pa.
Collins, Aaron, 1994-97, Cinnaminson, N.J.
Collins, Ahmad, 1994, 1996-97, Harrisburg, Pa.
Collins, Andre, 1986-89, Arlington, Va.
Collins, Chris, 1983-86, operations manager, Woodbridge, Va.
Collins, George, 1928, 31-32
Collins, Gerry, 1989-91, professional football player, Cinnaminson, N.J.
Collins, Jason, 1994-95, 97, Cinnaminson, N.J.
Collins, Kerry, 1992-94, NFL player, Charlotte, N.C.
Collins, Phillip, 1993-94, Cinnaminson, N.J.
Colone, Joe, 1942, 46-48, retired high school teacher, Berwick, Pa.
Conforto, Mike, 1978, company president, Woodinvale, Wash.
Conlan, Shane, 1983-86, businessman, Sewickley, Pa.
Conlin, Chris, 1984-86, arena league football coach, Davie, Fla.
Conlin, Keith, 1992-95, Glenside, Pa.
Conlin, Kevin, 1996-97, Glenside, Pa.
Conn, Donald, 1931, deceased.
Conover, Larry, 1916-17, 19, deceased.
Contz, Bill, 1980-82, client systems administrator, Cranberry Township, Pa.
Conway, Brett, 1993-96, NFL player, Lilburn, Ga.
Cooney, Larry, 1944-45, 47-48, deceased.

Cooper, Eufard, 1985, investment banker, Teaneck, N.J.

Cooper, Mike, 1968-70, Harrisburg, Pa.

Cooper, William, 1933, 35, retired, Dallas, Pa.

Corbett, Wayne, 1965-66, professor, Pfafftown, N.C.

Corbin, Cliff, 1977

Correal, Chuck, 1977-78, investment broker, Pittsburgh, Pa.

Coulson, Bob, 1906-07, deceased.

Craft, George, 1900, deceased.

Crawford, Rowan, 1943, retired, Loudon, Tenn.

Cromwell, Troy, 1986, senior manager national account marketing, Naperville, Ill.

Crosby, Ron, 1974-76, distributor account manager, Venetia, Pa.

Crowder, Randy, 1971-73, mortgage broker, Tampa, Fla.

Cripps, R.J., 1950-51, deceased.

Crummy, Bill, 1976, 78, high school teacher, Gibsonia, Pa.

Cubbage, Ben, 1916, 19, deceased.

Cummings, Ralph, 1899-02, deceased.

Cunningham, Eric, 1977-78, deceased.

Cure, Dave, 1897-99, deceased.

Curkendall, Pete, 1985-87, psychiatric case worker, Liverpool, N.Y.

Curry, Jack, 1965-67, insurance & real estate broker, Danville, Pa.

Curry, Tom, 1930-31, deceased.

Curtin, Joe, 1895, 97-98, deceased.

Cyphers, Cy, 1906-08, deceased.

Czarnecki, Stan, 1915-17, deceased.

Czekaj, Ed, 1943, 46-47, retired Penn State athletic director, State College, Pa.

D'Amico, Rich, 1979-81, Pittsburgh, Pa.

Daily, Pat, 1983, business development analysis, Clifton, Va.

Daman, Bob, 1991, Camp Hill, Pa.

Daniels, David, 1988-90, Sarasota, Fla.

Daniels, Maurice, 1996-97, Penn State student, Alexandria, Va.

Dangerfield, Harold, 1925-27, deceased.

Danser, Gene, 1952-54, retired teacher/coach, Delmont, Pa.

Darragh, Scudder, 1926-27, deceased.

Daugherty, George, 1968, auditor, Lake Latrobe, Pa.

Davis, Cliff, 1961, New Kensington, Pa.

Davis, Jeff, 1995, Fredonia, N.Y.

Davis, Larry, 1943, Xenia, Ohio

Davis, Robert, 1941-42, retired, Pittsburgh, Pa.

Davis, Stephen, 1985-87, Vineland, N.J.

Davis, Steve, 1972, school administrator, Concord, N.H.

Davis, Troy, 1987-88, high school teacher/coach, Cary, N.C.

Dean, J.M., 1901, deceased.

Debes, Gary, 1971, 73, vice president of sales, Toms River, N.J.

Debler, Bill, 1941, manufacturing representative, Franklin, Mass.

DeCindis, Ed, 1930, lawyer, Merion Station, Pa.

DeCohen, Daryl, 1987, inhalation toxicologist, Edison, N.J.

DeFalco, Dan, 1952-54, district manager, Glen Allen, Va.

Deibert, John, 1963-64, school superintendent, Bernardsville, N.J.

DellaPenna, Frank, 1954-55, retired, Potomac, Md.

Delmonaco, Al, 1966, office supply dealer, Oil City, Pa.

Delp, George, 1926-28, Dania, Fla.

DeLuca, James, 1958, high school teacher & athletic director, Aliquippa, Pa.

DeLuca, Richard, 1954-56, high school teacher, Rochester, Pa.

DeMarino, Danny, 1935, 37, deceased.

Demler, Fred, 1974, metals broker/economist, Washington Crossing, Pa.

DePaso, Tom, 1975-77, NFLPA attorney, Herndon, Va.

DePasqua, John, 1986, Atlanta, Ga.

Deter, Jim, 1988-91, Sykesville, Pa.

Deuel, Gary, 1968-70, Binghamton, N.Y.

Devlin, Chris, 1972-74, dentist, State College, Pa.

Diange, Joe, 1976-77, commercial real estate broker, Tampa, Fla.

Diedrich, Yutz, 1928-30, retired, Sun City, Ariz.

Diehl, Amby, 1897, deceased.

Dill, Richard, 1958, company president, Erie, Pa.

DiMidio, Dean, 1983-85, sales representative, State College, Pa.

Diminick, Joe, 1976-78, courier, Pfafftown, N.C.

Dimmerling, Carl, 1944-45, North Braddock, Pa.

Dingle, Cliff, 1992-94, Bonneau, S.C.

D'Onofrio, Mark, 1988-91, Teaneck, N.J.

Dodge, Fred, 1900-02, deceased.

Donaldson, Rick, 1976-79, Somerset, N.J.

Donato, Joe, 1976, director of residential areas, Winter Park, Fla.

Donato, Sammy, 1936-37, deceased.

Donchez, Tom, 1971, 73-74, business manager, Bethlehem, Pa.

Donovan, Tom, 1975-76, 78-79, financial consultant, Northport, N.Y.

Dooley, Jim, 1951-52, insurance sales, Allentown, Pa.

Dorney, Keith, 1975-78, time management products, Sebastopol, Cal.

Dougherty, Owen, 1949-50, deceased.

Dowler, Henry, 1889-93, deceased.

Downing, Dwayne, 1985-87, Chesapeake, Va.

Dozier, D.J., 1983-86, minister, Altamonte Springs, Fla.

Drayton, Troy, 1991-92, NFL player, Steelton, Pa.

Drazenovich, Andy, 1978, sanitation manager, Woodhaven, Mich.

Drazenovich, Chuck, 1945, 47-49, deceased.

Drazenovich, Joe, 1947-49, retired, Wexford, Pa.

Dreese, Jamie, 1992, medical school student, Mifflinburg, Pa.

Ducatte, Gregg, 1969-71, investment consultant, St. Petersburg, Fla.

Duffy, Gene, 1990, engineer, Scottsdale, Ariz.

Duffy, Pat, 1990, account representative, Canton, Ohio

Duffy, Roger, 1987-89, NFL player, Pittsburgh, Pa.

Dugan, Bill, 1979-80, plumbing & heating repair, Hornell, N.Y.

Duman, Jack, 1967, professor, South Bend, Ind.

Dunn, John, 1977, N.Y. Giants strength coach, Wayne, N.J.

Dunn, Mother, 1903-06, deceased.

Dunsmore, J.A., 1893-96, deceased.

Dunsmore, James, 1894-95, deceased.

Dunsmore, William, 1893, deceased.

Durkota, Jeff, 1942, 46-47, car dealer, Leola, Pa.

Duvall, Red, 1928-30, deceased.

Eachbach, Herb, 1928-29, deceased.

Eaise, Jim, 1973-74, Haddon Heights, N.J.

Eberle, Gary, 1965, winery owner, Paso Robles, Cal.

Eberly, Chris, 1995-97, Penn State student, Beverly, N.J.

Ebersole, John, 1967-69, county commissioner, Altoona, Pa.

Economos, Jack, 1935-37, deceased.

Edgerton, Robert, 1916, deceased.

Edmonds, Greg, 1968-70, dessert manufacturer, Northfield, Ohio

Edwards, Earle, 1928-30, deceased.

Edwards, Grover, 1977-80, Bayonne, N.J.

Ege, Ed, 1916, deceased.

Ehinger, Chuck, 1964-65, project engineer, Mentor, Ohio

Elbert, J.S., 1897, deceased.

Elder, John, 1902-03, deceased.

Ellis, Buddy, 1971-73, certified public accountant, Bridgeville, Pa.

Ellwood, Pop, 1923, deceased.

Ellwood, W.T., 1937-38, retired high school teacher, Harborcreek, Pa.

Emerson, Bill, 1982-83, account representative, Bloomfield Hills, Mich.

Enders, Paul, 1935, 37

Engle, Dad, 1910-12, deceased.

English, Rocco, 1976, insurance sales, Winter Park, Fla.

Engram, Bobby, 1991, 93-95, NFL player, Chicago, Ill.

Enis, Curtis, 1995-97, NFL player, Union City, Ohio

Enyeart, Craig, 1976, marketing representative, Bethel Park, Pa.

Eppensteiner, John, 1967

Ericsson, Bill, 1970, advertising executive, Erie, Pa.

Etze, Eric, 1987-88, sales representative, Winter Springs, Fla.

Evancho, Matt, 1996, high school teacher, Bethlehem, Pa.

Evans, Tommy, 1928-30, retired, Allentown, Pa.

Ewing, Mark, 1975, district sales manager, Charlotte, N.C.

Ewing, Stan, 1915-16, deceased.

Eyer, Don, 1951-53, retired high school teacher, Chambersburg, Pa.

Fagan, Mike, 1993, Flanders, N.J.

Fagan, Ryan, 1997, Penn State student, Pittsburgh, Pa.

Farkas, Gerry, 1960-62, claims supervisor, Palmyra, Pa.

Farkas, Mike, 1979

Farley, Eugene, 1918, deceased.

Farls, Jack, 1955-57, endodontist, Sewickley, Pa.

Farrell, Sean, 1979-81, Tampa, Fla.

Fawkes, Edward, 1904, deceased.

Fay, Charles, 1891-92, deceased.

Fayak, Craig, 1990-93, consulting analyst, Bryn Mawr, Pa.

Feeney, Chris, 1995, Erie, Pa.

Felbaum, F.V., 1948-49, Greensburg, Pa.

Fields, Chafie, 1996-97, Penn State student, Philadelphia, Pa.

Fields, Ron, 1991, Bronx, N.Y.

Filak, John, 1924-26

Filardi, Gerald, 1994-96, Melville, N.Y.

Filkovski, Greg, 1990, Penn, Pa.

Finley, John, 1945-48, retired construction company owner, Navarre, Fla.

Firshing, William, 1917, deceased.

Fisher, Benjamin, 1888, 92-94, deceased.

Fitzkee, Scott, 1976-78, president commercial/ industrial roofing, Bel Air, Md.

Flanagan, Mike, 1987, 90, Chadds Ford, Pa.

Fleischhauer, David, 1996-97, Penn State student, Clemmons, N.C.

Fletcher, Ambrose, 1994-95, Penn State student, New London, Conn.

Flock, Freddy, 1922, deceased.

Flood, Robert, 1933, deceased.

Flythe, Mark, 1990-91, Monmouth Junction, N.J.

Forbes, Marlon, 1992-94, NFL player, Central Islip, N.Y.

Forkum, Carl, 1902-04, deceased.

Fornadel, Matt, 1995-97, Bethel Park, Pa.

Forney, Travis, 1997, Penn State student, Lock Haven, Pa.

Foster, Phillip, 1888-90, deceased.

Fox, Derek, 1996-97, Penn State student, Canton, Ohio

Franco, Brian, 1979-81, Atlantic Beach, Fla.

Frank, Calvin, 1922-23, deceased.

Franzetta, Chuck, 1968, company president, Ooltewah, Tenn.

Freeman, Tim, 1987-89, Summit, N.J.

French, Coop, 1928-30, deceased.

Frerotte, Mitch, 1985, Redmond, Wash.

Frketich, Len, 1939-40

Fruehan, Mark, 1982-83, regional sales director, Allen, Tex.

Fry, Arthur, 1934-35, retired, Shawnee-on-Delaware, Pa.

Frye, Mel, 1967, junior high school teacher, Altoona, Pa.

Fugate, Thomas, 1900, deceased.

Fuhs, Bill, 1906, deceased.

Funk, Jim, 1981, branch manager, Gaithersburg, Md.

Fusetti, Greg, 1990, Beaver Falls, Pa.

Fusina, Chuck, 1976-78, medical sales representative, Pittsburgh, Pa.

Gabel, Paul, 1972-73, company president, Elkins, W.Va.

Gabriel, Ed, 1967, company president, Moorestown, N.J.

Gabriel, Robert, 1949-50, motion picture sales, Pinehurst, N.C.

Gaertner, Brennan, 1987, seminary student, Brentwood, Mo.

Gajecki, Leon, 1938-40, retired, Pitman, N.J.

Galardi, Joe, 1961-62, insurance sales, Clarks Summit, Pa.

Gallagher, Mac, 1991, company sales, Houston, Tex.

Gallman, Eric, 1995, Irmo, S.C.

Gancitano, Nick, 1982-84, Coconut Creek, Fla.

Ganter, Fran, 1968-70, Penn State assistant football coach, State College, Pa.

Garban, Steve, 1956-58, Penn State trustee, retired Penn State senior vice president, State College, Pa.

Garbinski, Mike, 1939-40, 45, retired, Johnstown, Pa.

Garrett, Mike, 1982, 84, company president, Charlotte, N.C.

Garrity, Gregg, 1980-82, self-employed, Bradford Woods, Pa.

Garrity, Jim, 1952-54, semi-retired, Bradford Woods, Pa.

Garthwaite, Bob, 1969, sales, South Hackensack, N.J.

Gash, Sam, 1988, 90-91, NFL player, Hendersonville, N.C.

Gatten, Aaron, 1997, Penn State student, Washington, Pa.

Gattuso, Greg, 1981-83, Duquesne head football coach, Pittsburgh, Pa.

Gearhart, Tim, 1987-88, Montoursville, Pa.

Geise, Steve, 1975-77, physician, Lock Haven, Pa.

Gelzheiser, Brian, 1991-94, Pittsburgh, Pa.

Gentilman, Victor, 1936-38, retired school teacher, Kane, Pa.

Gerak, John, 1989, 91-92, NFL player, Youngstown, Ohio

Gernard, Robert, 1945, Fort Wayne, Ind.

Gersh, Don, 1971, Pembroke State director of university relations, Fayetteville, N.C.

Gethers, Ivory, 1989-92, landscape supervisor, Johns Island, S.C.

Getty, Charlie, 1971-73, teacher/coach, Blue Springs, Mo.

Giacomarro, Ralph, 1979-82, engineer/project manager, Cumming, Ga.

Giannantonria, A.J., 1937-38

Giannetti, Frank, 1988-90, teacher/personal trainer, Toms River, N.J.

Giftopoulos, Pete, 1985-87, sales, Connellsville, Pa.

Gigliotti, Jason, 1992, Monessen, Pa.

Giles, Darrell, 1983, 85-86, certified public accountant, Melrose Park, Pa.

Gillard, Chuck, 1930, deceased.

Gilmore, Bruce, 1956, 58, commercial officer, Delran, N.J.

Gilmore, Deryk, 1988, cultural programs director, Champaign, Ill.

Gilmour, Robert, 1958, 60, company president, Gibbsboro, N.J.

Gilsenan, Mike, 1978, transportation manager, Staten Island, N.Y.

Gingrich, Dick, 1963-65, attorney, Lewistown, Pa.

Ginnetti, Don, 1983-85, investment executive, Medina, Ohio

Giotto, Tom, 1974-75, labor/employment lawyer, Pittsburgh, Pa.

Girton, B.J., 1934

Givens, Reggie, 1989-92, Emporia, Va.

Gladys, Gene, 1977-80, moving company owner, Fairfax Station, Va.

Glassmire, H.M., 1896, deceased.

Glennon, Bill, 1977, manufacturer's representative, Jarrettsville, Md.

Glocker, Rudy, 1991-92, mortgage analyst, Boston, Mass.

Glunz, Steve, 1976, insurance agent, Charlotte, N.C.

Gob, Scott, 1986-89, banker, Pittsburgh, Pa.

Godlasky, Charles, 1949-50, retired professor, Coraopolis, Pa.

Goedecke, Albert, 1911, deceased.

Goganious, Keith, 1988-91, Virginia Beach, Va.

Golden, Al, 1989-91, Virginia graduate assistant, Charlottesville, Va.

Gordon, Tony, 1977, transportation vice president, Millburn, N.J.

Gorinski, Clarence, 1947, retired, Calumet, Pa.

Gotwals, John, 1905-06, deceased.

Graf, Dave, 1972-73, assistant vice president/financial consultant, Pompano Beach, Fla.

Graham, A., 1889, deceased.

Graham, Don, 1983-86, Columbia, S.C.

Graham, James, 1943, insurance analyst, Ellicott City, Md.

Graham, Jim, 1959, social insurance analyst, Ellicott City, Md.

Graham, Mark, 1990-92, Florham Park, N.J.

Gratson, Joe, 1950-52, deceased.

Gray, Alex, 1907-10, deceased.

Gray, Bas, 1923-25, deceased.

Gray, Carl, 1995, Hershey, Pa.

Gray, Gary, 1969-71, investment banking vice president, Lemont, Pa.

Greeley, Bucky, 1991-94, NFL player, Wilkes-Barre, Pa.

Green, G.R., 1925-26, deceased.

Green, Sam, 1952-53, deputy sheriff, Pottstown, Pa.

Green, Jason, 1994, York, Pa.

Greene, John, 1986-88, investment advisor, State College, Pa.

Greenshields, Donn, 1926-28, deceased.

Grier, Roosevelt, 1951-54, minister, humanitarian & entertainer, Los Angeles, Cal.

Griffiths, Red, 1917, 20, deceased.

Griffiths, Steve, 1979-80, Ellicott City, Md.

Grimes, Paul, 1918, deceased.

Grimes, Roger, 1966-67, builder/developer, Lebanon, Pa.

Grimshaw, John, 1930-32, retired, Frederick, Md.

Groben, Dick, 1962, human resources director, Ogden, Utah

Gross, Red, 1917, deceased.

Grube, Ryan, 1990-93, Northampton, Pa.

Gudger, Eric, 1989, Columbus, Ohio

Guman, Mike, 1976-79, regional vice president/investment manager, Allentown, Pa.

Gurski, John, 1983, contract & service manager, Bloomsbury, N.J.

Gursky, Al, 1960-62, car dealer, Shillington, Pa.

Guthrie, Ed, 1977, Marietta, Ga.

Haden, Nick, 1982-83, company president, Coraopolis, Pa.

Hager, Gary, 1971-73, Cooper City, Fla.

Haines, Hinkey, 1919-20, deceased.

Halderman, O.G., 1952

Haley, Ed, 1891-93, deceased.

Hall, Galen, 1959-61, professional football coach, Orlando, Fla.

Hall, Tracy, 1979, Moorestown, N.J.

Halpin, R.D., 1941

Ham, Jack, 1968-70, general manager sales, Sewickley, Pa.

Hamas, Steve, 1926-28, deceased.

Hamilton, Darren, 1985, East Pennsboro athletic director, Chambersburg, Pa.

Hamilton, Eric, 1985-86, marketing representative, Cleveland, Ohio

Hamilton, Harry, 1980-83, Odenton, Md.

Hamilton, Lance, 1983-85, law clerk, Tampa, Fla.

Hamilton, Neil, 1988-89, Wilkes-Barre, Pa.

Hamilton, William, 1922, deceased.

Hammonds, Shelly, 1990-93, professional football player, Barnwell, S.C.

Hand, Brian, 1979, market analyst, Metuchen, N.J.

Hanley, Dean, 1936-38, retired insurance sales, Coraopolis, Pa.

Hansen, Albert, 1911-12, deceased.

Hapanowicz, Ted, 1943

Harding, Jim, 1955, ROTC commandant, Melbourne, Fla.

Harlow, Dick, 1910-11, deceased.

Harper, Thomas, 1932

Harrington, Bernard, 1927, deceased.

Harris, Al, 1981-82, dentist, Ocean View, N.J.

Harris, Aaron, 1997, Penn State student, Exton, Pa.

Harris, Charles, 1899, deceased.

Harris, Franco, 1969-71, business executive, Sewickley, Pa.

Harris, Giuseppe, 1979-81, Mount Holly, N.J.

Harris, J.L., 1892-94, deceased.

Harris, Pete, 1977-78, 80, Mount Holly, N.J.

Harrison, Harry, 1936-38, deceased.

Hart, Bob, 1960-62, assistant principal, New Hope, Pa.

Hart, Kevin, 1976, financial services, Ponte Vedra Beach, Fla.

Hart, Rob, 1991, Philadelphia, Pa.

Hartenstine, Mike, 1972-74, Chicago, Ill.

Hartenstine, Warren, 1967, company president, Bel Air, Md.

Hartings, Jeff, 1992-95, NFL player, Rochester Hills, Mich.

Harvan, George, 1951, deceased.

Harvey, Dale, 1993, Salem, N.J.

Hastings, Hal, 1925-27, retired engineer, Atlantic Beach, Fla.

Hayes, C.E., 1918

Hayes, Dave, 1960-62, insurance agent, Freeport, N.Y.

Hayes, Lalon, 1897-98, deceased.

Hayman, Gary, 1972-73, attorney, New Castle, Del.

Heckel, Fred, 1896-98, deceased.

Hedderick, Ray, 1948-49, retired high school principal, Transfer, Pa.

Heist, M.L., 1932, deceased.

Helbig, Bill, 1925, deceased.

Helkowski, Doug, 1988-91, teacher/coach, Warrenton, Va.

Heller, Jim, 1970-72, highway maintenance foreman, Lewisberry, Pa.

Heller, Mike, 1991-92, Amityville Harbor, N.Y.

Heller, Ron, 1981-83, manufacturer's representative, Absarokee, Mont.

Henderson, Hernon, 1987, 89-90, Chantilly, Va.

Henderson, Jason, 1994, 1996, Satellite Beach, Fla.

Henderson, Marques, 1985-87, Monaca, Pa.

Henry, H., 1905-06, deceased.

Henry, Lee, 1948, cattle rancher, Matthews, Ala.

Henry, Red, 1918-19, deceased.

Heppenstall, Charles, 1892, deceased.

Heppenstall, G., 1889, deceased.

Herd, Chuck, 1971-73, conference coordinator, State College, Pa.

Hermann, Burke, 1911, deceased.

Herring, Kim, 1993-96, NFL player, Solon, Ohio

Herron, Ross, 1945

Hershey, Frank, 1962-64, Dartmouth assistant football coach, Hanover, N.H.

Hesch, Matty, 1932, retired civil engineer, Ambler, Pa.

Hess, Harold, 1916, 19-20, deceased.

Hettinger, Scott, 1977-79, insurance agent, Mountain Top, Pa.

Hewitt, Earl, 1898-1901, deceased.

Hewitt, Jr., Earl, 1927, deceased.

Hicks, Robert, 1944, 47-49, retired, Millersville, Pa.

Higgins, Bob, 1914-17, 19, deceased.

Hildebrand, Charles, 1887-91, deceased.

Hile, Charles, 1888-91, deceased.

Hill, Chappie, 1956, retired Marine Corps officer, Pittsburgh, Pa.

Hills, Lee, 1921, deceased.

Hines, Joe, 1981-83, Cleveland, Ohio

Hirshman, Charles, 1906-09, deceased.

Hite, Jeff, 1973-75, brewing superintendent, Crown Point, Ind.

Hladun, Bob, 1980, DEA special agent, Sparks, Md.

Hoak, Dick, 1958-60, Pittsburgh Steelers assistant coach, Greensburg, Pa.

Hochberg, Jeff, 1983, State College, Pa.

Hochberg, Jim, 1955, retired Penn State athletic trainer, State College, Pa.

Hockersmith, William, 1951, engineer, Overland Park, Kan.

Hodne, Todd, 1978

Hoffman, Robert, 1954-55, sales manager, Lititz, Pa.

Hoggard, Dennie, 1947-48, deceased.

Holes, Clint, 1994-95, Spring Church, Pa.

Holloway, Alfred, 1901, deceased.

Holmberg, Rob, 1993, NFL player, Mt. Pleasant, Pa.

Holmes, Wayne, 1994, Silver Spring, Md.

Holuba, Bob, 1968-70, company president, HoHoKus, N.J.

Hondru, Bryan, 1965-66, company president, Pittsburgh, Pa.

Hoover, Edward, 1950-51, retired high school principal, Pittsburgh, Pa.

Horn, Keith, 1953-54, consulting forester, Kane, Pa.

Hornfeck, Dave, 1973-74, high school teacher, Belle Vernon, Pa.

Hornyak, John, 1986, pricing services manager, Centreville, Va.

Horst, Tim, 1966, 68, Redmond, Wash.

Hoskins, George, 1892-94, deceased.

Hostetler, Doug, 1976-78, financial consulting, Ellicott City, Md.

Hostetler, Jeff, 1980, NFL player, Washington, D.C.

Hostetler, Ron, 1975-77, teacher, Hershey, Pa.

House, William, 1924-25, deceased.

Huber, Bill, 1963-65, semi-retired, Williamsport, Pa.

Huffman, Jay, 1959-61, cleaning service owner, Guilford, Conn.

Hufford, Squeak, 1920-22, deceased.

Hufnagel, John, 1970-72, arena league football head coach/general manager, Randolph, N.J

Hull, Gary, 1968-70, high school teacher/coach, Jamestown, Pa.

Hull, John, 1970-71, claims examiner, Richmond, Va.

Hull, Tom, 1971-73, company vice president, Cannonsburg, Pa.

Hummel, Alkey, 1975, company vice president, Aliquippa, Pa.

Hummel, Clarence, 1947, retired, Harrisburg, Pa.

Humphries, Leonard, 1989-91, Washington, D.C.

Huntington, Greg, 1990-92, NFL player, Jacksonville, Fla.

Hutton, Neil, 1974, 76-77, computer consultant, Mount Holly, N.J.

Iagrossi, Mike, 1989, account executive, Garden City, N.Y.

Ickes, Lloyd, 1937-39, deceased.

Irwin, Mike, 1964-66, financial advisor, Altoona, Pa.

Isom, Ray, 1984-86, claims adjuster, Harrisburg, Pa.

Jacks, Al, 1956-58, Clarion University professor, Clarion, Pa.

Jackson, Joe, 1973-74, Brimfield, Mass.

Jackson, John, 1887, deceased.

Jackson, Kenny, 1980-83, Penn State assistant football coach, State College, Pa.

Jackson, Roger, 1981-82, South River, N.J.

Jackson, Tom, 1967-69, human resources manager, Bradenton, Fla.

Jackson, Tyoka, 1990-93, NFL player, Forestville, Md.

Jacob, George, 1950, deceased.

Jaffurs, Johnny, 1941-43, deceased.

Jagers, Bob, 1979-80, Washington, D.C.

Jakob, David, 1987-89, Clifton Park, N.Y.

James, Don, 1914

Janerrette, Charlie, 1958-59, deceased.

Japchen, Geoff, 1988-89, financial consultant, North Wales, Pa.

Jeram, Jerry, 1974, banking, Stamford, Conn.
Joachim, Steve, 1971
Joe, Larry, 1942, 47-48, deceased.
Johns, Gregg, 1985, 87, financial consultant, Washington, D.C.
Johnson, Andre, 1993-95, NFL player, South Hampton, N.Y.
Johnson, Barry, 1971, log broker, Kane, Pa.
Johnson, Bill, 1973
Johnson, Brad, 1995, 97, Parkersburg, W. Va.
Johnson, Chan, 1949-51, retired, Lompoc, Cal.
Johnson, Eddie, 1985-88, Sparks, Md.
Johnson, Fred, 1909-10, deceased.
Johnson, G.R., 1888, deceased.
Johnson, Howard, 1899, deceased.
Johnson, Matt, 1985-87, managing director, Summit, N.J.
Johnson, Mike, 1973-75, district sales manager, Philadelphia, Pa.
Johnson, Paul, 1967-69, lumber company owner, Cazenovia, N.Y.
Johnson, Pete, 1967-69, commodity firm president, New Vernon, N.J.
Johnson, Tim, 1983-86, NFL player, Ashburn, Va.
Johnston, Ray, deceased.
Jonas, Don, 1958, 60-61, sales director, Winter Springs, Fla.
Jonassen, Eric, 1987-88, Glen Burnie, Md.
Jones, Brad, 1996, Penn State student, Beaver Falls, Pa.
Jones, Casey, 1916, deceased.
Jones, Corey, 1996, Penn State student, Lancaster, Pa.
Jones, Greg, 1979-80, sales representative, Herndon, Va.
Jones, Richard, 1952-53, sportswear company president, Marshfield, Mass.
Joyner, Dave, 1969-71, orthopedic surgeon, Hummelstown, Pa.
Joyner, Matt, 1996-97, Penn State student, Hummelstown, Pa.
Junk, J.L., 1901-02, deceased.
Jurevicius, Joe, 1994-97, NFL player, Chardon, Ohio

Kab, Vyto, 1979-81, Kinnelon, N.J.
Kane, Billy, 1954-56, Munhall, Pa.
Kane, Bob, 1964-65, lawyer, Pittsburgh, Pa.
Kane, Fred, 1931, deceased.
Kania, Darrell, 1994-96, mortgage broker,State College, Pa.
Kaplan, Mike, 1928-30, deceased.
Karpinski, Keith, 1986-88, teacher/coach, Clawson, Mich.
Kasperian, David, 1957-58, Worcester, Mass.
Kates, Jim, 1967-69, corporate security supervisor, Middletown, Conn.
Kelley, Ken, 1979-82, medical sales, Sewell, N.J.
Kelly, Paul, 1947-49, deceased.
Kemmerer, Ted, 1952, retired realtor, Pine Grove Mills, Pa.
Kerns, Mike, 1940-42
Kerr, Jim, 1958-60, computer sales representative, Mount Pleasant, S.C.
Kerwin, Geff, 1991-93, Kearny, N.J.
Kessler, Charles, 1887, deceased.
Kidwell, George, 1987, Wellsburg, W. Va.
Killens, Terry, 1992-95, NFL player, Cincinnati, Ohio
Killinger, Glenn, 1918, 20-21, deceased.

King, Anthony, 1996-97, Penn State student, Norfolk, Va.
King, Brian, 1992-95, West Chester, Ohio
King, Frank, 1911, deceased.
Kissell, Tim, 1976, teacher, Downingtown, Pa.
Kleist, E.R., 1955, West Mifflin, Pa.
Kline, Bob, 1961, data processing, Easton, Pa.
Klingensmith, Gary, 1963-64, high school teacher/coach, Mifflintown, Pa.
Klossner, Gary, 1971, insurance underwriter, Jamesville, N.Y.
Kmit, Ed, 1964, company vice president, Bloomfield Hills, Mich.
Knabb, Al, 1918, retired, Richmond, Va.
Knapp, Ron, 1933-35
Knechtel, Bob, 1970-71, division controller, Russell, Pa.
Knechtel, Rick, 1975, district laboratory manager, Mathews, N.C.
Kneidinger, Otto, 1953-55, retired Delaware assistant football coach, Altoona, Pa.
Knittle, A.P., 1891, deceased.
Knizner, Matt, 1985-87, insurance executive, Greensburg, Pa.
Kochman, Roger, 1959-62, telephone director of security, Upper Darby, Pa.
Koegel, Warren, 1968-70, Connecticut assistant football coach, South Windsor, Conn.
Koerber, John (Dick), 1950, retired, Bethel Park, Pa.
Kohlhaas, Earl, 1957-59, tire store manager, Mechanicsburg, Pa.
Koiwai, Mark, 1970, senior program evaluator, Washington, D.C.
Kollar, Jim, 1965-66
Kominic, W.E., 1934
Koniszewski, Jack, 1972-73, tax partner, Vienna, Va.
Koontz, Al, senior vice president/finance, Vero Beach, Fla.
Kopach, S.J., 1940
Korbini, Frank, 1958-59, Department of Defense analyst, Sterling, Va.
Kosanovich, Bronco, 1944-46, deceased.
Kraft, Rudy, 1917, deceased.
Krall, Joe, 1926-27
Kratt, George, 1914, deceased.
Kratzke, Ted, 1941, 45, high school teacher, Pittston, Pa.
Kraus, Joe, 1980-81
Kreizman, Louis, 1932-34, retired, Bethesda, Md.
Krenicky, Doug, 1968, Norristown, Pa.
Kriston, Rich, 1973-74, athletic director, Pittsburgh, Pa.
Kroell, Josh, 1993-94, Penn State graduate assistant football coach, Clearfield, Pa.
Krouse, Lenny, 1939-41, elevator company president, Springfield, Pa.
Krupa, Joe, 1934, 36, deceased.
Krushank, Al, 1916
Kuba, Dave, 1962
Kubas, Greg, 1975-76, distribution manager, Phoenix, Ariz.
Kubin, Larry, 1977-80, Union, N.J.
Kugler, Pete, 1979-80, San Francisco, Cal.
Kulka, John, 1966-68, civil engineer/company president, State College, Pa.
Kulka, Todd, 1995, Penn State graduate student, State College, Pa.
Kunit, Don, 1964-65, high school teacher, Alpine, Cal.
Kunkle, Bayard, 1905-06, deceased.
Kurlej, Brian, 1992, Cherry Hill, N.J.
Kurpeikis, Justin, 1997, Penn State student, Pittsburgh, Pa.

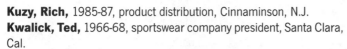

Kuzy, Rich, 1985-87, product distribution, Cinnaminson, N.J.
Kwalick, Ted, 1966-68, sportswear company president, Santa Clara, Cal.
Kwalik, Leo S., 1955, national sales accounts, Overland Park, Kan.
Kyle, Bill, 1946-47, congressional aide,St. Petersburg, Fla.

LaBarca, Chip, 1991-93, high school head football coach, Lakewood, N.J.
Lafferty, E.D., 1923-24, deceased.
LaFleur, Bill, 1943, 47, retired, Coronado, Cal.
Lagler, Regis, 1972, physician, Indianapolis, Ind.
Lally, Joe, 1976-78, financial printing sales, Bryn Mawr, Pa.
Lamb, Levi, 1912-14, deceased.
Landis, George, 1968-70, Schwenksville, Pa.
Lang, Alfred, 1936, deceased.
Lang, Floyd, 1945, retired park superintendent, Odessa, Fla.
Lang, Jon, 1960, management consultant, Sun Lakes, Ariz.
Lankford, Paul, 1980-81, sales manager, Jacksonville, Fla.
LaPointe, Ron, 1977, 79, financial advisor, Bryn Mawr, Pa.
LaPorta, Phil, 1971-73, construction management, Draper, Utah
Lasich, George, 1929-31, deceased.
Laslavic, Jim, 1970-72, television sportscaster, Coronado, Cal.
Latorre, Harry, 1934-35, Berwick, Pa.
Latsko, Mark, 1979, distribution center manager, New Castle, Pa.
Latsko, Mike, 1986, management accounting, Cranberry Township, Pa.
Laube, Dave, 1980-82, wood flooring specialist, River Edge, N.J.
Lavelle, Chris, 1976, Clinton, Mass.
Law, Clint, 1955-56, paper sales, Pottstown, Pa.
Lawn, Mark, 1989, commercial fisherman, Hicksville, N.Y.
Lee, Shawn, 1995-97, Penn State student, Harrisburg, Pa.
Lenda, Ed, 1965-66, account executive, Camp Hill, Pa.
Lenkaitis, Bill, 1965-67, dentist, Canton, Mass.
Leonard, Bill, 1950-52, deceased.
Lesh, Floyd, 1909, deceased.
Lesko, Al, 1926-27
Levinson, James, 1949, company chairman, Ky Largo, Fla.
Lewis, Sid, 1985-86, sales, Farmington Hills, Mich.
Leyden, Harry, 1887-89, deceased.
Libiano, Lance, 1994, Bradbury, Cal.
Light, Hobie, 1923-24, deceased.
Lightner, Joe, 1920-21, deceased.
Linski, Frank, 1967, accountant, Hillsborough, N.J.
Linsz, George, 1887-88, deceased.
Lippincott, Lincoln, 1968, Navy deputy commander, Westcliffe, Colo.
Liske, Pete, 1961-63, Toledo athletic director, Holland, Ohio
Litterelle, Jim, 1966-67, company owner, Wilmington, Del.
Livezey, Jack, 1929-30, retired, Canton, Pa.
Livziey, Jay, 1956, retired, Williamsport, Pa.
Lockerman, James, 1956, branch manager, Washington, Pa.
Logue, Lester, 1918, 22, deceased.
Lohr, William, 1932, retired, Murrysville, Pa.
Lonergan, Dan, 1983, executive vice president, New York, N.Y.
Lonergan, Lance, 1988, institutional sales trader, Westport, Conn.

Lord, N.M., 1890, deceased.
Love, Sean, 1988-89, NFL player, Tamaqua, Pa.
Lucas, Rich, 1957-59, retired Penn State assistant athletic director, State College, Pa.
Lucyk, Dan, 1966-67, dentist, Conyngham, Pa.
Ludwig, Larry, 1971-72, parole supervisor, McKees Rocks, Pa.
Luedeke, Rob, 1990, advertising sales, State College, Pa.
Lundberg, Arthur, 1915, deceased.
Lungreen, Cy, 1925-27, deceased.
Lupold, Ken, 1993, Wallingford, Pa.
Lupo, Bob, 1994, Nesconset, N.Y.
Luther, Bill, 1947-48, deceased.
Luton, John, 1982-83, Coraopolis, Pa.
Lyle, Craig, 1970-71, company president, Poca, W. Va.

Macklin, David, 1996-97, Penn State student, Newport News, Va.
MacKensie, H.T., 1918
Maddigan, Dan, 1959, telecommunications manager, Conneaut Lake, Pa.
Madera, Rags, 1921, deceased.
Maginnis, Dick, 1981-83, deceased.
Mahoney, Rog, 1925-27, deceased.
Malinak, Don, 1951-53, retired, Lock Haven, Pa.
Malinoski, Mike, 1991-93, accountant, Shenandoah, Pa.
Manca, Massimo, 1982, 1985-86, sales representative, Easthampton, N.J.
Manoa, Tim, 1983-86, athlete consultant, Cleveland, Ohio
Marchi, Marino, 1943, 45, Glassmere, Pa.
Mariades, Jim, 1943, Groveton, Pa.
Marino, D.A., 1936, deceased.
Markiewicz, Joe, 1989, West Mifflin, Pa.
Markiewicz, Ron, 1956-57, high school teacher, West Mifflin, Pa.
Markovich, Mark, 1971-73, company president, Peoria, Ill.
Martella, Orient, 1946, deceased.
Martin, Jack, 1928-29, deceased.
Martin, Kirk, 1983, project manager, Ft. Mill, S.C.
Martin, Percival, 1899-1900, deceased.
Martz, William, 1930, Army officer retired, Upland, Cal.
Marczyk, Pete, 1995-96, Penn State student, Absecon, N.J.
Masciantonio, Carmen, 1982-83, district sales manager, Center Valley, Pa.
Masella, Brian, 1972-74, teacher/special assistant, Yardville, N.J.
Matesic, Tony, 1989, 91, specialist assistant, Fairview, N.J.
Mathers, William, 1950, retired, Easton, Pa.
Mattern, Frank, 1891-92, deceased.
Mattern, Louis, 1891, deceased.
Mattern, Roy, 1891-92, deceased.
Matthews, James, 1944-45, retired, Easton, Pa.
Mauthe, Pete, 1909-12, deceased.
Mauti, Rich, 1975-76, marketing manager, Mandeville, La.
Maxwell, Larry, 1906-07, deceased.
Maxwell, William, 1898-99, deceased.
Mazur, Walt, 1955-56, restaurant owner, Tamaqua, Pa.
Mazyck, Chris, 1993-94, Hopkins, S.C.

McAndrews, John, 1932, deceased.
McAndrews, Marty, 1928-29, deceased.
McArthur, Doug, 1968, 70, Fayetteville, N.C.
McBath, Mike, 1965-67, vice president & stockbroker, Orlando, Fla.
McCabe, Joe, 1976, company owner, Wexford, Pa.
McCann, Brian, 1982, company vice president, Holly Springs, N.C.
McCann, Ernie, 1923-25, deceased.
McCartin, Matt, 1988-90, district manager, Albuquerque, N.M.
McCaskey, Walter, 1892-95, deceased.
McClaren, Walter, 1934, deceased.
McCleary, E.H. "Bull", 1906-09, deceased.
McClellan, Ora, 1908, deceased.
McCloskey, Mike, 1979-82, marketing vice president, Lower Gwynedd, Pa.
McCollum, Stan, 1920-21
McCord, Jim, 1969-70, deceased.
McCormick, Jim, 1966-67, regional sales vice president, Mendham, N.J.
McCoy, Karl, 1977-78
McCoy, Robert, 1944-45, retired, Ft. Pierce, Fla.
McDonald, Quintus, 1985-88, Montclair, N.J.
McDowell, Cecil, 1913-15, deceased.
McDuffie, O.J., 1989, 91-92, NFL player, Ft. Lauderdale, Fla.
McGee, George, 1904-05, deceased.
McGrath, Tom, 1967, company president, Marion, Ind.
McIlveen, Irish, 1902-04, deceased.
McKee, W.B., 1933
McKenzie, Kareem, 1997, Penn State student, Willingboro, N.J.
McKenzie, Rich, 1989-92, NFL player, Ft. Lauderdale, Fla.
McKibbin, James, 1894-95, deceased.
McLean, Harvey, 1887-90, deceased.
McLean, Jim, 1964, general sales manager, Nevillewood, Pa.
McMahon, Tiny, 1921-22, deceased.
McMillen, Bill, 1930-31, deceased.
McMillen, Rich, 1956-57, physical therapist, Beaver Falls, Pa.
McMunn, Stuart, 1981-82, deceased.
McNaughton, Dave, 1965, company president, Lancaster, Pa.
McPoland, Patrick, 1950-51, Butler, Pa.
McQueary, Mike, 1996-97, State College, Pa.
Meade, Mike, 1979-81, Dover, Dela.
Mechling, Doug, 1955-56, deceased.
Mehl, Lance, 1977-79, St. Clairsville, Ohio
Menhardt, Herb, 1979-80, Flourtown, Pa.
Mercinko, Dan, 1968, purchasing manager, Derry, Pa.
Mesko, Charlie, 1969-71, company president, Danville, Cal.
Metro, Joe, 1936-38, deceased.
Michalske, August (Mike), 1923-25, deceased.
Mikelonis (Michaels), A.P., 1933-34, deceased.
Mikulski, Rob, 1986, East Stroudsburg strength coach, Easton, Pa.
Miles, Bill, 1901-02, deceased.
Millen, Matt, 1976-79, TV analyst, Whitehall, Pa.
Miller (Bowman), Brian, 1993-96, Donora, Pa.
Miller, Daniel, 1898-1900, deceased.
Miller, Donald, 1964, professor, Shippensburg, Pa.
Miller, Eugene E. (Shorty), 1910-13, deceased.
Miller, Franklin, 1898-1900, deceased.
Miller, Ran, 1913-15

Miller, John, 1928, 30
Miller, Samuel, 1905, deceased.
Miller, Thomas, 1898-1900, deceased.
Miller, William, 1935, buyer, Johnston City, Tenn.
Milne, Brian, 1993-95, NFL player, Southgate, Ky.
Milot, Rich, 1977-78, Haymarket, Va.
Miltenberger, Don, 1944-45, Easton, Pa.
Misiewicz, John, 1943, 47, retired Marine officer, Oceanside, Cal.
Mitchell, Cordell, 1996-97, Penn State student, Syracuse, N.Y.
Mitchell, John, 1887, deceased.
Mitchell, Josh, 1997, Penn State student, Doylestown, Pa.
Mitchell, Lydell, 1969-71, public relations consultant, Baltimore, Md.
Mitchell, Scott, 1973, plant manager, Sandusky, Ohio
Mitinger, Bob, 1959-61, attorney, State College, Pa.
Mock, James, 1887-89, deceased.
Moconyi, Andy, 1956-58, teacher & real estate broker, Bethlehem, Pa.
Moffitt, Sean, 1990, Tunkhannock, Pa.
Monaghan, Brian, 1991-93, Wexford, Pa.
Monaghan, Ed, 1986, 88-89, restaurant manager, Drexel Hill, Pa.
Monaghan, F., 1902, deceased.
Monaghan, Terry, 1961-62, deceased.
Monroe, Pat, 1981, high school head football coach, Pittsburgh, Pa.
Montgomery, Tim, 1966-67, high school teacher/coach, Williamsport, Pa.
Moonves, Philip, 1931, retired builder/developer, Palm Beach, Fla.
Moore, Booker, 1977-80, Flint, Mich.
Moore, Lenny, 1953-55, program specialist, Randallstown, Md.
Moore, Red, 1942-43, retired, Meadville, Pa.
Moorehead, Cal, 1904-05, deceased.
Morgan, Bill, 1956, accountant, Katy, Tex.
Morgan, Dan, 1983-86, brokerage director, Lakeside Park, Ky.
Mori, Wade, 1939-40, deceased.
Morini, Bob, 1934, retired, Pittsburgh, Pa.
Morris, George, 1913-16, deceased.
Morris, John, 1890, deceased.
Morrison, Mac, 1996-97, Penn State student, Port Orchard, Wash.
Morrison, M.B., 1932-34
Morrow, S.E., 1892, deceased.
Moscript, Andrew, 1903-04
Moser, Brian, 1990-92, Langhorne, Pa.
Motz, W.R., 1890, deceased.
Moules, Todd, 1982-85, commercial lending, Cleveland, Ohio
Mrosko, Bob, 1986-88, Wickliffe, Ohio
Muckle, Harry, 1944, Charleroi, Pa.
Mulraney, Tom, 1957-59, retired, Riverview, Mich.
Mumford, Tony, 1982-83, Jersey City, N.J.
Munchak, Mike, 1979, 81, Houston Oilers assistant coach, Brentwood, Tenn.
Mundell, Earle, 1951, school administrator, Dayton, Ohio
Munson, Wayne, 1969, 71, professor, Kent, Ohio
Munz, Paul, 1926, deceased.
Murphy, Greg, 1973-74, construction management, Brooklyn Heights, N.Y.
Murray, Charles, 1949, Uniontown, Pa.
Murray, Don, 1948-49, deceased.
Murray, L.C., 1901, deceased.

Murray, W.A., 1895-97, deceased.
Murrer, Robert, 1952, company president, Sewickley, Pa.
Muscillo, V.J., 1992-93, Long Branch, N.J.

Nagle, Bob, 1972-73, systems engineer, Bergenfield, N.J.
Nardolillo, Matt, 1991-92, Chester, N.J.
Nash, Walter, 1938-40, deceased.
Nastasi, Joe, 1995-97, Penn State student, Woodbury, Pa.
Natale, Dan, 1972-74, sporting goods store owner, North Huntingdon, Pa.
Neff, Norm, 1958-59, salesman, Harrisburg, Pa.
Nelson, Jim, 1995-97, Waldorf, Md.
Nemeth, Ted, 1938-39, deceased.
Nessel, John, 1973-74, technology education instructor, Wilton, Conn.
Nichols, Skeeter, 1982, Cambridge, Md.
Nixon, Jeff, 1996, assistant high school football coach, State College, Pa.
Nobile, Leo, 1942, 46, retired activities director, Coraopolis, Pa.
Noble, Brandon, 1994-96, Virginia Beach, Va.
Nolan, John, 1945-47, deceased.
Nonemaker, Aubrey, 1940
North, Paul, 1955-57, deceased.
Norton, Neg, 1944, 47-49, district manager, Slingerlands, N.Y.
Nye, Dirk, 1964-65, investment consultant, Denver, Col.

O'Bara, Vince, 1949-50, retired school district administrator, Sinking Spring, Pa.
Oberle, Joseph, 1916, deceased.
Ochsner, Pete, 1964, high school teacher, Goshen, N.Y.
Odell, Tom, 1974-75, Madison, N.J.
Oden, Boris, 1995, State College, Pa.
O'Donnell, James, 1916, deceased.
O'Donnell, Mike, 1981, investment broker, Monroeville, Pa.
O'Donnell, Scott, 1981, superintendent grocery distribution, Midlothian, Va.
O'Hora, Frank, 1933, 35-36, deceased.
O'Hora, Jim, 1933-35, retired Penn State associate head football coach, State College, Pa.
Oldziejewski, Tom, 1976, Kings assistant football coach, Wilkes-Barre, Pa.
Olsommer, Keith, 1993-96, Moscow, Pa.
O'Neal, Brian, 1990, 92-93, NFL player, Cincinnati, Ohio
O'Neil, Ed, 1971-73, high school football coach, Amherst, N.Y.
Onkotz, Andy, 1976, branch manager, Catasauqua, Pa.
Onkotz, Dennis, 1967-69, financial advisor, Boalsburg, Pa.
Ontko, Bob, 1983-85, fixed income institutional sales, Naperville, Ill.
Opfar, Dave, 1981-82, Penn State graduate assistant football coach, State College, Pa.
Oppermann, Henry, 1959-60, company vice president, Connellsville, Pa.
Oquendo, Jorge, 1989, Columbus, Ohio

Orbison, T.K., 1889, deceased.
Orsini, Mike, 1971-73, head & neck surgeon, Sewickley, Pa.
Orsini, Tony, 1949-50, retired high school teacher, Hummelstown, Pa.
Osborn, Robert, 1919, deceased.
Ostrosky, Doug, 1997, Pittsburgh, Pa.
Ostrowski, Phil, 1996-97, Wilkes-Barre, Pa.

Pae, Dick, 1959-60, associate professor, Shippensville, Pa.
Paffenroth, Dave, 1980-82, insurance sales, Kansas City, Mo.
Page, George, 1911, deceased.
Painter, Heister, 1915, deceased.
Palazzi, Lou, 1941-42, landscape architect, Santa Fe, N.M.
Palm, Mike, 1922-23, deceased.
Panaccion, Toots, 1927-29
Pannozzo, Romeo, 1956-57, high school teacher, Poughkeepsie, N.Y.
Pankey, Irv, 1977-79, Ithaca, N.Y.
Pantall, Brad, 1993-95, State College, Pa.
Paolone, Bucky, 1957-58
Park, W.B., 1934
Parlavecchio, Chet, 1979-81, high school teacher/head coach, Florham Park, N.J.
Parmer, Brandon, 1996-97, Penn State student, Worthington, Ohio
Parrish, Floyd, 1916, deceased.
Parsons, Bob, 1969-71, Lake Zurich, Ill.
Parsons, Lloyd, 1940, retired, Flourtown, Pa.
Pasqualoni, Paul, 1971, Syracuse head football coach, Fayetteville, N.Y.
Paterno, Jay, 1989, Penn State assistant football coach, State College, Pa.
Paton, Tom, 1963, deceased.
Patrick, John G., 1936, retired high school teacher/coach, Temple City, Cal.
Patrick, John R., 1939-40, Johnstown, Pa.
Patton, Johnny, 1923, deceased.
Patton, Wallace K., 1942, deceased.
Pavlechko, Ron, 1968-69, high school athletic director, Boalsburg, Pa.
Pearl, Tom, 1983, materials manager, Mechanicsburg, Pa.
Peel, Joseph, 1937-38, retired, Charlotte, N.C.
Penrose, F.A., 1898, deceased.
Penzenik, Chuck, 1994-96, Copley, Ohio
Perlman, W.B., 1936, retired executive president, Los Angeles, Cal.
Perri, Ralph, 1974, sales manager, Hagerstown, Md.
Perry, Darren, 1988-91, NFL player, Pittsburgh, Pa.
Perry, Jeff, 1990-91, 93-94, Conway, N.H.
Perry, T.M., 1903, deceased.
Perugini, R.J., 1941-42, deceased.
Petchel, Elwood, Sr., 1944, 46-48, retired, Wind Gap, Pa.
Petchel, Woody, 1974-75, plant manager, Drums, Pa.
Petercuskie, Gary, 1975-77, NFL scout, Centerville, Mass.
Peters, Chuck, 1938-40, deceased.
Petrella, John, 1939-41, deceased.
Petruccio, Tony, 1975-78, sales representative, Yardley, Pa.

Pettigrew, Titcus, 1997, Penn State student, Winston-Salem, N.C.

Pevarnik, Tom, 1951, retired dairy farmer, Carmichaels, Pa.

Pfirman, Carl, 1951-52, rehabilitation director, Williamsport, Pa.

Pickett, Derick, 1991-93, Glenside, Pa.

Pidgeon, Pat, 1997, Penn State student, Mayfield, Pa.

Pinchotti, Chuck, 1968, Monaca, Pa.

Pincura, John, 1925-27, deceased.

Piollet, Tom, 1908-10, deceased.

Pittman, Charlie, 1967-69, publishing vice president, Davenport, Iowa.

Pittman, Tony, 1992-94, systems consultant, Elkins Park, Pa.

Pitts, Stephen, 1992-95, Atlantic Highlands, N.J.

Platt, Frank, 1939-40, retired, Alexandria, Va.

Platt, J.E., 1893, deceased.

Plum, Milt, 1955-56, sporting goods representative, Raleigh, N.C.

Podrasky, J.T., 1949-51, retired, East Orange, N.J.

Polamalu, Aoatoa, 1985, 87, Pottstown, Pa.

Poll, Jack, 1978, recreation director, Cary, N.C.

Pollard, Jim, 1950-51, retired high school administrator, Inwood, N.Y.

Pollard, Robert, 1950-52

Pollock, Ben, 1939-40, deceased.

Pomfret, Paul, 1986-87, investment banker, New York, N.Y.

Pond, Al, 1917, retired, Greensboro, N.C.

Popp, Bill, 1958-60, retired Albright head track coach, Reading, Pa.

Popp, Steve, 1960, 62, Freehold, N.J.

Potsklan, John, 1941, 46-47, deceased.

Potter, Frank, 1964, high school teacher, Swarthmore, Pa.

Pottios, Ray, 1955-57, retired, Milton, Pa.

Powell, Andre, 1987-88, 90-91, York, Pa.

Powell, Harold (Junior), 1961-63, lawyer, Mifflintown, Pa.

Powers, William, 1943, Dayton, Ohio

Prater, Shino, 1994-97, Arlington, Tex.

Pratt, E.J., 1888, deceased.

Prevost, Jules, 1923-24, deceased.

Price, J.C., 1889, deceased.

Price, Jack, 1943, Belle Vernon, Pa.

Pringle, Frank, 1966-67, group vice president, Stamford, Conn.

Pritchard, Bill, 1925-26, deceased.

Prue, Steve, 1968-70, account executive, Longwood, Fla.

Pryts, Ed, 1979-81, company president, Hermitage, Pa.

Putman, S., 1905, deceased.

Puz, Rodger, 1981-82, lawyer, Pittsburgh, Pa.

Pysher, Doug, 1978, senior vice president institutional sales, San Marino, Cal.

Quinn, John, 1973-75, foreman, Columbia, Md.

Quirch, Carlos, 1979, pharmaceutical sales, Miami Lakes, Fla.

Radakovich, Dan, 1955-56, Robert Morris assistant football coach, Strongsville, Ohio

Radakovich, Dave, 1968-69, senior vice president, Frisco, Tex.

Radcliff, Elgin, 1939, retired Army officer, York, Pa.

Radecic, Keith, 1985-86, management, Corpus Christi, Tex.

Radecic, Scott, 1980-83, project engineer, Mission Hills, Kan.

Rados, Tony, 1951-53, deceased.

Rafferty, Tom, 1973-75, Southlake, Tex.

Ragucci, Fred, 1977-78, bank attorney, New York, N.Y.

Raifsnider, Herb, 1952, deceased.

Rainge, Sherrod, 1987-89, Brockton, Mass.

Raisig, Charles, 1962, insurance broker, Middletown, Pa.

Rakiecki, Dave, 1967-69, Grand Junction, Colo.

Rakowsky, Terry, 1979-81, dentist, Doylestown, Pa.

Ramich, Joel, 1968-70, vice president of administration, Mountain Lakes, N.J.

Randolph, Brute, 1895, 97-99, deceased.

Rauch, Dick, 1917, 19-20

Ravotti, Eric, 1989-91, 93, NFL player, Wexford, Pa.

Read, Gus, 1889-92, deceased.

Reber, D.C., 1888, deceased.

Redinger, Pete, 1921

Redman, Sean, 1988-89, substance awareness coordinator, King of Prussia, Pa.

Reich, Frank, 1953-55, high school teacher/coach, Lebanon, Pa.

Reid, Mike, 1966, 68-69, music writer/producer/singer, Nashville, Tenn.

Reihner, George, 1974-76, attorney, Scranton, Pa.

Reihner, John, 1972, 74, dentist, Washington, Pa.

Reitz, Mike, 1969, national accounts manager, Harrisburg, Pa.

Renaud, Paul, 1976-77, contractor, Tallahassee, Fla.

Renkey, Eric, 1988, 91, NFL player, Pittsburgh, Pa.

Ressler, Glenn, 1962-64, restaurant owner, Camp Hill, Pa.

Restauri, Jim, 1978, Margate, Fla.

Rettig, Bill, 1965-67, artist, Cranberry Township, Pa.

Reynolds, George, 1981, 83, Freemont, Cal.

Rhoda, William, 1934, 36, deceased.

Rhule, Matt, 1997, Albright assistant football coach, Reading, Pa.

Rice, Bob, 1957, retired high school teacher/coach, Harrisburg, Pa.

Ricevuto, Charles, 1962, company owner, West Chester, Pa.

Richards, Allen, 1944, Miamisburg, Ohio

Richardson, Wally, 1992, 94-96, NFL player, Sumter, S.C.

Rickenbach, Bob, 1970-72, office furniture dealer, Blackwood, N.J.

Ricker, Ralph, 1927-29, deceased.

Riggle, Bob, 1964-65, Washington, Pa.

Rinkus, Gene, 1962, home construction, Kissimmee, Fla.

Rishell, Bill, 1979-81, fitness center owner, South Glastonbury, Conn.

Ritchey, Jesse, 1907, deceased.

Ritner, Thomas, 1921, deceased.

Rivera, Marco, 1992-95, NFL player, Brooklyn, N.Y.

Robb, Harry, 1916-19, deceased.

Robb, Ray, 1943, deceased.

Robinson, Bernard, 1975-76, Flint, Mich.

Robinson, Dave, 1960-62, district sales manager, Kent, Ohio

Robinson, F.A., 1894, deceased.

Robinson, Mark, 1980-83, investment advisor, Oldsmar, Fla.

Robinson, Tim, 1983, school teacher, Sicklerville, N.J.

Rocco, Dan, 1979-80, Maryland assistant football coach, College Park, Md.

Rocco, Frank, 1980-81, high school athletic director/football coach, Oakmont, Pa.

Rodham, Hugh, 1934, deceased.
Roepke, Johnny, 1925-27, deceased.
Rogel, Fran, 1947-49, high school teacher & farmer, Bakerstown, Pa.
Rohland, Bob, 1954, Savannah, Ga.
Rollins, Steve, 1938-39, deceased.
Romango, Kevin, 1980, consultant, Pittsburgh, Pa.
Romano, Jim, 1977-79, 81, Keller, Tex.
Rosa, Rich, 1991, marketing director, Sparks, Md.
Rosdahl, Harrison, 1961-63, handyman, Ridgefield Park, N.J.
Rose, James, 1887, deceased.
Rosecrans, Jim, 1973-75, company president, Syracuse, N.Y.
Rosenberg, Harold, 1931, 33, retired company president, Cranbury, N.J.
Ross, Dan, 1943, lawyer, Bethesda, Md.
Ross, Robert, 1947-48, engineer, Pittsburgh, Pa.
Rothrock, W.R., 1888, 91, deceased.
Roundtree, Ray, 1985-87, sales representative, Cleveland, Ohio
Rowe, Dave, 1965-66, sportscaster, Ashboro, N.C.
Rowe, Ricky, 1992, Columbia, Md.
Rowell, Lester, 1951-54, insurance executive & Penn State trustee, Berwyn, Pa.
Rubin, Lee, 1990-93, executive recruiter, Manalapan, N.J.
Ruble, C.W., 1901, deceased.
Ruble, Joseph, 1896-97, 99-1900, deceased.
Rucci, Todd, 1990-92, NFL player, Franklin, Mass.
Runnells, John, 1964-66, capital management, Oldwick, N.J.
Ruslavage, Charles, 1956-58, retired professor, Clarion, Pa.
Russell, Samuel, 1901, deceased.
Russo, Mike, 1983-86, sales representative, Lower Burrell, Pa.
Rutkowski, Bob, 1944-46, retired high school teacher, Natrona Heights, Pa.

Saar, Brad, 1982, Chicago, Ill.
Sabatino, Noel, 1964, publishing sales, East Windsor, N.J.
Sabol, Bernie, 1961-62, professor/associate athletic director, Mansfield, Pa.
Sabol, Joe, 1955-57, retired athletic director, Northfield, Vt.
Sabolevski, Joe, 1997, Roxbury, N.H.
Sacca, John, 1992, professional football player, Delran, N.J.
Sacca, Tony, 1988-91, LaSalle assistant football coach, Delran, N.J.
Sain, John, 1966, high school teacher, Brookville, Pa.
Samuels, Bobby, 1989, 91, Farrell, Pa.
Sandusky, E.J., 1991-92, Albright head football coach, Reading, Pa.
Sandusky, Jerry, 1963-66, Penn State assistant football coach, State College, Pa.
San Fillipo, George, 1970, company vice president, Spring, Tex.
Santangelo, Mario, 1950
Sarabok, Joseph, 1946, retired senior medical representative, Palmyra, Pa.
Saul, Bill, 1961, Baltimore, Md.
Saunders, Joseph, 1904, deceased.
Sava, John, 1959, retired school superintendent, Farrell, Pa.
Sayles, Rick, 1990-91, State College, Pa.
Sayre, Ralph, 1913, deceased.

Schaeffer, Dennis, 1960, senior sales representative, Whitefish Bay, Wis.
Schaukowitch, Carl, 1970-72, insurance, Mitchellville, Md.
Scheetz, Stew, 1950-52, retired, Naples, Fla.
Scherer, Rip, 1948, retired school administrator, Coraopolis, Pa.
Schiazza, Guido, 1961, educator, Drexel Hill, Pa.
Schleicher, Maury, 1956-58, athletic communications, San Jose, Cal.
Schoderbek, Pete, 1951-53, professor, Iowa City, Iowa
Scholl, Henny, 1896-1901, deceased.
Schonewolf, Rich, 1986-89, medical sales representative, Williamsport, Pa.
Schoonover, Ken, 1941-42, retired school superintendent, Knoxville, Pa.
Schreckengaust, Steve, 1964-65, executive director, Drexel Hill, Pa.
Schroyer, John, 1942, retired county worker, Connellsville, Pa.
Schuster, Dick, 1920, 23, deceased.
Schuyler, Roy, 1934-36, retired company vice president, Hockessin, Del.
Schwab, Jim, 1961, deceased.
Scioli, Brad, 1994-95, 97, Penn State student, Bridgeport, Pa.
Scott, Charles, 1894-95, deceased.
Scott, Freddie, 1993-95, NFL player, Southfield, Mich.
Scott, Jim, 1971-73, Martinsburg, Pa.
Scovill, Brad, 1978-80, chief financial officer, Hanover, Pa.
Scrabis, Bob, 1958, car dealership owner, Avon-by-the-Sea, N.J.
Seace, Clint, 1996-97, Thorndale, Pa.
Sebastianelli, Ted, 1968, Air National Guard technician, State College, Pa.
Sefter, Steve, 1981-83, sales representative, Windham, N.H.
Seitz, Ellery, 1963-65, Blacksburg, Va.
Shaffer, John, 1984-86, high yield bond sales, Summit, N.J.
Shainer, David, 1941, deceased.
Shalvey, Bernie, 1978, sales manager, Lancaster, Pa.
Shank, Don, 1951-52, deceased.
Shattuck, Ted, 1950-51, deceased.
Shattuck, Paul, 1953, retired, Highland, Ind.
Shawley, Cal, 1928-30, deceased.
Shephard, Len, 1949-51, sales manager, Herndon, Va.
Sherman, Tom, 1965-67, Virginia football administrative assistant, Charlottesville, Va.
Sherry, Jack, 1952-54, manufacturer's representative, West Chester, Pa.
Shields, R.K., 1931
Shoemaker, Tom, 1971-72, company vice president, Hudson, Ohio
Shopa, Peter, 1951-52, retired, Olyphant, Pa.
Short, Brandon, 1996-97, Penn State student, McKeesport, Pa.
Short, Stan, 1982-83, Ft. Belvoir, Va.
Shukri, Dave, 1975-76, Lindenhurst, N.Y.
Shukri, Rob, 1977, Conmack, N.Y.
Shuler, Mickey, 1975-77, car wash owner, Marysville, Pa.
Shumaker, Earl, 1953-55, realtor, Reading, Pa.
Shuman, Tom, 1973-74, regional vice president, Plano, Tex.
Shumock, Joseph, 1950-51, retired high school coach, Willow Grove, Pa.
Sickler, Mark, 1985-87, forester, Tunkhannock, Pa.
Sidler, Randy, 1974-77, insurance sales, Danville, Pa.

Sieminski, Charlie, 1960-62, high school teacher, Mountain Top, Pa.

Sierocinski, Marty, 1977, Bradenton, Fla.

Siever, Paul, 1990-91, Jacksonville, Fla.

Sigel, Harry, 1932-34, high school teacher/coach, Abingdon, Va.

Sills, Frank, 1937, retired university president, St. Petersburg, Fla.

Silock, Andrew, 1950-51, retired high school principal, Stroudsburg, Pa.

Silvano, Thomas, 1934-35, retired, Dunmore, Pa.

Simko, John, 1962-64, industrial engineer, Louisville, Ohio

Simon, David, 1951-52, high school teacher, New Eagle, Pa.

Simon, John, 1944-45, 47-48, retired high school guidance counselor, Emporium, Pa.

Sincek, Frank, 1962, high school principal, Mercer, Pa.

Sink, Robert, 1964

Sisler, Cass, 1943, Barberton, Ohio

Siverling, Brian, 1985-86, structural engineer, Charlotte, N.C.

Skarzynski, Scott, 1970-72, state trooper, South River, N.J.

Skemp, Leo, 1932, retired field construction engineer, Bridgeville, Pa.

Skorupan, John, 1970-72, commercial sales, Zelienople, Pa.

Skrip, Dan, 1991, Mocanaqua, Pa.

Sladki, John, 1965-66, high school teacher, Johnstown, Pa.

Slafkowsky, Joe, 1967, freight supervisor, Cupertino, Cal.

Slamp, Ken, 1925, deceased.

Sload, Jason, 1995-96, Penn State student, Marysville, Pa.

Slobodnjak, Mike, 1943, Harrisburg, Pa.

Slowik, Joe, 1974

Slusser, Tom, 1931-33, deceased.

Smalls, Irv, 1994, Hershey, Pa.

Smaltz, Bill, 1939-41, retired N.C. State assistant football coach, Raleigh, N.C.

Smear, Steve, 1967-69, insurance agent, Annapolis, Md.

Smidansky, John, 1948-50, retired, Chagrin Falls, Ohio

Smith, Andy, 1901, deceased.

Smith, Charles, 1904, deceased.

Smith, Franklin, 1934-36, retired, Newfield, N.J.

Smith, James, 1960-61, company president, San Leandro, Cal.

Smith, Mike, 1968-70, insurance & investments, Lebanon, Pa.

Smith, Neal, 1967-69, construction engineer, Selinsgrove, Pa.

Smith, R.M., 1907-09, deceased.

Smith, Rob, 1984-85, district manager, Carlisle, Pa.

Smith, Robert, 1951-52, deceased.

Smith, Steve, 1984-86, Jonesboro, Ga.

Smith, Terry, 1988-91, Duquesne assistant football coach, Pittsburgh, Pa.

Smith, Thomas, 1948, retired, Norwalk, Conn.

Smith, Willie, 1992-94, professional football player, Ft. Pierce, Fla.

Smith, Wilson, 1955, 57-58, Lititz, Pa.

Smozinsky, E., 1921

Smyth, Bill, 1943, deceased.

Snell, George, 1919-21

Snyder, Chris, 1994-97, Chesapeake, Va.

Snyder, Robert, 1930-31, deceased.

Sobczak, Sam, 1958-60, teacher education director, Harrisburg, Pa.

Sowers, Charles, 1954, company president, Lake Harmony, Pa.

Spaziani, Frank, 1966-68, CFL assistant coach, Calgary, Alberta

Speers, Fred, 1971, Ardmore, Pa.

Spencer, Larry, 1944

Speros, Pete, 1980-82, certified financial planner, Bethesda, Md.

Spires, Mike, 1972, Deerfield Beach, Fla.

Spoor, Bill, 1991, institutional investments, Chicago, Ill.

St. Clair, Cliff, 1942, deceased.

Stahley, Skip, 1928-29, deceased.

Steinbacher, Don, 1965, company controller & vice president, Kennett Square, Pa.

Stellatella, Sam, 1957-59, insurance field representative, Toms River, N.J.

Stellfox, Skip, 1957, management consultant, New Canaan, Conn.

Stempeck, Stan, 1930-31, retired, Ellwood City, Pa.

Stephenson, Bob, 1995-97, Waynesburg, Pa.

Stewart, Ed, 1963-65, general auditor, Coraopolis, Pa.

Stewart, Tony, 1997, Penn State student, Allentown, Pa.

Stewart, Vin, 1992-94, professional football player, Shirley, N.Y.

Stilley, Steve, 1971-72, district sales manager, Medford, N.J.

Stillman, Mike, 1982-84, executive vice president, Lancaster, Pa.

Stofko, Ed, 1967-68, Johnstown, Pa.

Stoken, John, 1944, Aliquippa, Pa.

Storer, Jack, 1950, retired management consultant, Madison, Wis.

Strang, Doug, 1982-83, accountant, West Chester, Pa.

Straub, Bill, 1953-55, tire test manager, Akron, Ohio

Stravinski, Carl, 1938-40, retired, Boalsburg, Pa.

Struchor, J.J., 1950, retired, Merritt Island, Fla.

Strycharz, Joe, 1988, senior financial consultant, Great Falls, Va.

Stuart, Tom, 1966, high school teacher/coach, East Windsor, N.J.

Stuart, W.A., 1893, deceased.

Stuckrath, Ed, 1962-64, supply manager, Millerville, Md.

Stump, Terry, 1968-70, deceased.

Stupar, Steve, 1979, cleaning company owner, Pennsylvania Furnace, Pa.

Sturdifen, Eric, 1997, Penn State student, Richmond, Va.

Sturges, Carl, 1948, resort owner, Bethesda, Md.

Stutts, Dave, 1975, millwright, Mifflintown, Pa.

Stynchula, Andy, 1957-59, deceased.

Suhey, Larry, 1975-76, regional sales representative, State College, Pa.

Suhey, Matt, 1976-79, investment banking, Highland Park, Ill.

Suhey, Paul, 1975-78, orthopedic surgeon, State College, Pa.

Suhey, Steve, 1942, 46-47, deceased.

Sunday, LeRoy, 1936, deceased.

Surma, Vic, 1968-70, dentist, Pittsburgh, Pa.

Susko, John, 1972, high school teacher/coach, Fort Walton Beach, Fla.

Suter, H.M., 1894, deceased.

Suter, Mike, 1982-83, regional sales manager, Lilburn, Ga.

Swain, Ward, 1916, Sterling, Va.

Sweeney, Tim, 1987-88, sales vice president, Troy, Mich.

Sweet, Lynn, 1901, deceased.

Sydnor, Chris, 1982-83, purchasing agent, Ardmore, Pa.

Szajna, Robert, 1951-52

Szott, Dave, 1987-89, NFL player, Greenwood, Mo.

Taccalozzi, Dino, 1944-45

Tamburo, Sam, 1945-48, retired auditor, New Kensington, Pa.

Tarasi, Ray, 1987-89, account executive, Pittsburgh, Pa.

Tate, Dayle, 1979, sales, Richwood, N.J.

Tate, Mark, 1993-96, Erie, Pa.

Tavener, Otho, 1917, deceased.

Taylor, C.F., 1899, deceased.

Taylor, Duane, 1974-75, 77, Braddock, Pa.

Taylor, H.S., 1891-92, deceased.

Tepsic, Joseph, 1945, retired, Tyrone, Pa.

Tesner, Buddy, 1972-74, orthopedic surgeon, Columbus, Ohio

Thomas, Blair, 1985-87, 89, Temple assistant football coach, Philadelphia, Pa.

Thomas, Charlie, 1895, deceased.

Thomas, David, 1993-94, Silver Spring, Md.

Thomas, Kenneth, 1930, deceased.

Thomas, Mark, 1973-75, Tulsa assistant football coach, Tulsa, Okla.

Thomas, Tisen, 1990, 92-93, York, Pa.

Thomas, Willie, 1987-90, Hightstown, N.J.

Thompson, Irving, 1902, deceased.

Thompson, Leroy, 1987-90, Knoxville, Tenn.

Thorpe, Chris, 1988, area sales manager, Allison Park, Pa.

Tielsch, Barry, 1993-96, Pittsburgh, Pa.

Tietjens, Ron, 1961-62, deceased.

Timpson, Michael, 1985, 87-88, NFL player, Attleboro, Mass.

Tincher, Gabe, 1996-97, Penn State student, Cincinnati, Ohio

Tobin, Yeggs, 1912-14, deceased.

Tomlinson, Ken, 1951, retired, Lebanon, Pa.

Toretti, Sever, 1936-38, retired Penn State athletic administrator & assistant football coach, State College, Pa.

Torrey, Bob, 1976-78, Ceres, N.J.

Torris, Buddy, 1960-62, internal audit director, Oak Park, Ill.

Travis, Dean, 1944-45, retired teacher, West Chester, Pa.

Trent, Jim, 1971, Pittsburgh, Pa.

Triplett, Wally, 1946-48, retired company owner, Detroit, Mich.

Troxell, Greg, 1991, Phillipsburg, N.J.

Truitt, Dave, 1960, personal investments, Sarasota, Fla.

Truitt, Greg, 1985-86, 88, NFL player, Sarasota, Fla.

Trumbull, Richard, 1943, sales vice manager, Punta Gorda, Fla.

Tupa, Brian, 1994, Ashburn, Va.

Turinski, Bill, 1962, South Williamsport, Pa.

Twaddle, J.P., 1951

Tyler, Gary, 1974, company vice president, Arlington, Va.

Uhlar, Mike, 1985, Youngstown, Ohio

Ulinski, Ray, 1947, retired Penn State athletic trainer, State College, Pa.

Unger, Frank, 1918, deceased.

Urban, Jack, 1959, university professor, Edinboro, Pa.

Urbanik, Tom, 1963-64, university instructor, Bethel Park, Pa.

Urion, Robert, 1948, retired insurance agent, Swedesboro, N.J.

Urquhart, Micky, 1977-80, vice president sales, West Redding, Conn.

Valentine, Sam, 1954-56, deceased.

Vance, Jerrod, 1991, Massillon, Ohio

Van Allen, John, 1992, State College, Pa.

Van Lenten, Wilbur, 1941-42

Van Sickle, D.P., 1952, retired, Panama City, Fla.

Vargo, Joe, 1963-64, high school teacher/coach, Milton, Pa.

Vargo, Thomas, 1938-40, retired, Montoursville, Pa.

Vendor, Joseph, 1943, Cleveland, Ohio

Ventresco, Ralph, 1941, 45, Allport, Pa.

Vernaglia, Bob, 1988, Brockton, Mass.

Vernaglia, Kip, 1979, regional sales director, Anaheim, Cal.

Very, Dexter, 1909-12, deceased.

Vesling, Keith, 1951-53, retired consultant, Grafton, Ohio

Vierzbicki, Joe, 1965, physical therapist, Hellertown, Pa.

Vitiello, Alberto, 1971-72, custom furniture & upholstery, Plainview, N.Y.

Vogel, Ollie, 1913, deceased.

Voll, Edwin, 1944, retired school administrator, Toms River, N.J.

Vorhis, Larry, 1906-09, deceased.

Vukmer, Bob, 1966, Richmond, Va.

Wagner, Gary, 1979, service supervisor, Whitehall, Pa.

Wagner, Marshall, 1970, high school principal, Philipsburg, Pa.

Wahl, John, 1931, deceased.

Walchack, Ron, 1979, stockbroker, Pittsburgh, Pa.

Walker, Samuel, 1895, deceased.

Wallace, Dan, 1974, development director, State College, Pa.

Walsh, John, 1979-80, physician, Ann Arbor, Mich.

Walter, John, 1981-83, institutional equity sales, Haddonfield, N.J.

Walters, Les, 1955-57, sales vice president, Chamblee, Ga.

Walters, R.L., 1942, 46, deceased.

Wanamaker, Steve, 1975-76, property loss supervisor, Valley Cottage, N.Y.

Wantshouse, Harry, 1932, deceased.

Waresak, Frank, 1962, real estate manager, Chapel Hill, N.C.

Warner, Curt, 1979-82, auto dealership, Redmond, Wash.

Washabaugh, Grover, 1937-39, deceased.

Washington, Darryl, 1986-87, bank branch manager, Smyrna, Ga.

Washington, Rocky, 1982-83, pharmaceutical sales, Beaver Falls, Pa.

Wasilov, Alex, 1974, emerging markets president, Pittsford, N.Y.

Wateska, Mark, 1987-88, Boston College head strength & conditioning coach, Chestnut Hill, Mass.

Watson, Burley, 1909-10, deceased.

Watson, James, 1915, deceased.

Watson, Kenny, 1996, Penn State student, Harrisburg, Pa.

Watson, R.S., 1924, deceased.

Waugaman, Carl, 1936-37, retired high school teacher/coach, Somerset, Pa.

Way, Charley, 1917, 19-20, deceased.

Wayne, Tony, 1961, investment management, Los Angeles, Cal.

Wear, Bob, 1941, deceased.

Wear, Wendell, 1935-37, retired high school teacher/coach, West Orange, N.J.

Weatherspoon, Ray, 1980

Weaver, Henny, 1907-10, deceased.

Weaver, Jim, 1966, Mattawan, Mich.

Weaver, Manny, 1941, 46, deceased.

Weber, Chris, 1963, architect/developer, Boulder, Col.

Weber, Robert, 1933-35, senior engineer, Greensburg, Pa.

Wedderburn, Floyd, 1997, Penn State student, Upper Darby, Pa.

Wehmer, Bill, 1956-58, electrical division director, North Myrtle Beach, S.C.

Weitzel, Robert, 1942, 46-47, retired, DuBois, Pa.

Weller, John, 1887, deceased.

Welsh, Frederick, 1907, deceased.

Welty, Daniel, 1912-14, deceased.

Wentz, Barney, 1922, deceased.

Weston, Harry, 1913, deceased.

Weston, Ken, 1924-26, deceased.

White, Beaver, 1892-93, deceased.

White, Bob, 1983-86, Penn State assistant to the athletic director, Boalsburg, Pa.

White, Craig, 1938-40, deceased.

White, Ed, 1959

White, Jack, 1965-66, dentist, San Diego, Cal.

White, L.R., 1903-04, deceased.

Whitney, Robert, 1912, deceased.

Whitworth, Edward, 1901-03, deceased.

Wible, T.E., 1937, deceased.

Wilk, Tom, 1985, treasury analyst, Bear, Del.

Wilkerson, Gary, 1985-87, Sutherland, Va.

Wille, Carl, 1932, retired, Lewiston, N.Y.

Williams, Benjamin, 1956-57, company president, Ellisville, Mo.

Williams, Bob, 1985, Easton, Pa.

Williams, Frank, 1972, steam fitter, Allentown, Pa.

Williams, Jim, 1962, Penn State administrative assistant, State College, Pa.

Williams, Jon, 1980-83, hotel sales manager, Norton, Mass.

Williams, Justin, 1992-93, 95, Penn State graduate student, State College, Pa.

Williams, Robert, 1942-43, 46-47, retired high school teacher, Greensburg, Pa.

Williams, Ronald, 1918, 20, deceased.

Williams, Tom, 1973-74, restaurant owner, Bethlehem, Pa.

Williott, Tony, 1976-77, attorney, Pittsburgh, Pa.

Wilson, Al, 1911-12, retired, Pompano Beach, Fla.

Wilson, Charles, 1950-51, owner & sales, Fort Lauderdale, Fla.

Wilson, Charlie, 1968-70, vice president sales &-marketing, Indianapolis, Ind.

Wilson, Dick, 1959-61

Wilson, Harry (Light Horse), 1921-23, deceased.

Wilson, Jerome, 1982, Harrisburg, Pa.

Wilson, Odell, 1988, Brockton, Mass.

Wilson, Thomas, 1925, deceased.

Wise, Tom, 1978-80, vice president sales & marketing, Harrisburg, Pa.

Wismer, Frank, 1933-35, retired, Deltona, Fla.

Wisniewski, Leo, 1979-81, Pittsburgh, Pa.

Wisniewski, Steve, 1985-88, NFL player, Pleasanton, Cal.

Witman, Jon, 1992-95, NFL player, Wrightsville, Pa.

Wojtowicz, John, 1978, 80, company vice president, New Castle, Pa.

Wolf, Mike, 1986-87, Philadelphia Eagles strength coach, Medford, N.J.

Wolfe, John, 1988-89, department store buyer, Pittsburgh, Pa.

Wolff, Allie, 1927-28, retired, North Miami Beach, Fla.

Wolfkeil, Wayne, 1953, MIA (Vietnam).

Wolosky, John, 1947, retired, Isabella, Pa.

Wood, Bill, 1913-15, deceased.

Wood, Edwin, 1899, deceased.

Woods, Kevin, 1987, Birmingham, Ala.

Woodward, Charles, 1903-04, deceased.

Woodward, James, 1940, deceased.

Woofter, Jeff, 1983, Cumberland, W. Va.

Woolbert, Richard, 1932-33, deceased.

Woolridge, Rembrandt, 1933, coal company president, Clearfield, Pa.

Wray, Bill, 1904-06, deceased.

Wright, Brett, 1990-92, wholesale sales, Ft. Lauderdale, Fla.

Wydman, Gary, 1961, 64, recruiting consultant, Dallas, Tex.

Yahn, Tom, 1987, teacher, Bronx, N.Y.

Yanosich, Matt, 1951-52, retired laboratory supervisor, Monca, Pa.

Yarabinetz, Tom, 1965, education/personnel director, Greensburg, Pa.

Yeafer, F., 1915

Yeboah-Kodie, Frank, 1993, Montreal, Quebec

Yeboah-Kodie, Phil, 1991-94, Montreal, Quebec

Yeckley, Ed, 1902-05, deceased.

Yerger, Chuck, 1915

Yett, Arthur, 1934, 36, retired, Wadsworth, Ohio

Yoho, Don, 1939-41, retired, Plant City, Fla.

Yost, Bud, 1962-64, hotel/restaurant owner,Lock Haven, Pa.

Young, Todd, 1987-89, Tempe, Ariz.

Younker, Ron, 1953-54, Windber, Pa.

Yowell, Bob, 1967, planner/public administrator, Williamsport, Pa.

Yukica, Joe, 1951-52, real estate broker, Grantham, N.H.

Zapiec, Charlie, 1968-69, 71, vice president estate planning, New Hope, Pa.

Zawacki, Stanley, 1931-32, deceased.

Zelinsky, Joe, 1967, management accountant, Lancaster, Pa.

Zink, Howard, 1907, deceased.

Zmudzin, Dennis, 1974-75, revenue officer, York Springs, Pa.

Zordich, Mike, 1982-85, NFL player, Canfield, Ohio

Zorella, John, 1928-30, retired school administrator, Manville, N.J.

Zubaty, Ed, 1967, deceased.

Zufall, Don, 1965, Punxsutawney, Pa.

Zur, Rod, 1975, West Jacksonville, Fla.

CHAPTER 17

THE ALL-AMERICANS & THE HALL OF FAME INDUCTEES

ALL-AMERICANS

First Team:

1906: W.T. (Mother) Dunn, C

1915: Bob Higgins, E

1919: Bob Higgins, E

1920: Percy W. (Red) Griffiths, G

1920: Charley Way, HB

1921: Glenn Killinger, HB

1923: Harry (Light Horse) Wilson, HB

1923: Joe Bedenk, G

1940: Leon Gajecki, C

1947: Steve Suhey, G

1948: Sam Tamburo, E

1956: Sam Valentine, G

1959: Rich Lucas, QB

1961: Bob Mitinger, E

1962: Dave Robinson, E

1962: Roger Kochman, HB

1964: Glenn Ressler, C & MG

1967: Ted Kwalick, TE

1968: Ted Kwalick, TE

1968: Dennis Onkotz, LB

1969: Dennis Onkotz, LB

1969: Mike Reid, DT

1969: Charlie Pittman, HB

1969: Neal Smith, Saf

1970: Jack Ham, LB

1971: Dave Joyner, T

1971: Lydell Mitchell, HB

1971: Charlie Zapiec, LB

1972: Bruce Bannon, DE

1972: John Hufnagel, QB

1972: John Skorupan, LB

1973: John Cappelletti, HB

1973: Randy Crowder, DT

1973: Ed O'Neil, LB

1974: John Nessel, T

1974: Mike Hartenstine, DE

1975: Chris Bahr, K

1975: Greg Buttle, LB

1975: Tom Rafferty, G

1976: Kurt Allerman, LB

1977: Keith Dorney, T

1977: Randy Sidler, MG

1978: Keith Dorney, T

1978: Matt Bahr, K

1978: Bruce Clark, DT

1978: Chuck Fusina, QB

1978: Pete Harris, Saf

1978: Matt Millen, DT

1979: Bruce Clark, DT

1980: Bill Dugan, T

1980: Sean Farrell, G

1981: Sean Farrell, G

1981: Curt Warner, TB

1982: Curt Warner, TB

1982: Walker Lee Ashley, DE

1982: Kenny Jackson, F

1982: Mark Robinson, Saf

1983: Kenny Jackson, F

1985: Michael Zordich, SS

1985: Shane Conlan, OLB

1986: Shane Conlan, OLB

1986: Chris Conlin, T

1986: D.J. Dozier, HB

1986: Tim Johnson, DT

1987: Steve Wisniewski, G

1988: Steve Wisniewski, G

1989: Andre Collins, ILB

1989: Blair Thomas, TB

1991: Darren Perry, DB

1992: O.J. McDuffie, WR

1993: Lou Benfatti, DT

1994: Kyle Brady, TE

1994: Ki-Jana Carter, RB

1994: Kerry Collins, QB

1994: Bobby Engram, WR

1994: Jeff Hartings, G

1995: Jeff Hartings, G

1996: Kim Herring, FS

1997: Curtis Enis, TB

Second -Team All-Americans:

1911: Dexter Very, E

1912: Dexter Very, E

1915: Bob Higgins, E

1917: Stan Czarnecki, G

1920: George Brown, E

1920: Henry "Hinkey" Haines, HB

1921: Ray Baer, G

1921: Joe Bedenk, G

1921: Joe Lightner, B

1921: Stan McCollum, E

1924: Jules Prevost, T

1943: John Jaffurs, G

1948: Fran Rogel, RB

1952: Jim Dooley, C

1954: Lenny Moore, RB

1955: Lenny Moore, RB

1957: Les Walters, E

1959: Charlie Janerette, T

1962: Chuck Sieminski, T

1967: Rich Buzin, T

1967: Tim Montgomery, Saf

1967: Dennis Onkotz, LB

1968: Mike Reid, DT

1969: Steve Smear, DT

1973: Charlie Getty, T

1973: Mark Markovich, G

1973: Dan Natale, TE

1974: Greg Murphy, DE

1977: Mickey Schuler, TE

1979: Lance Mehl, LB

1979: Irv Pankey, G

1981: Mike Munchak, G

1981: Chet Parlavecchio, LB

1982: Scott Radecic, LB

1992: Ray Isom, DT; Lou Benfatti, DT

1995: Bobby Engram, WR

Third-Team All-Americans:

1898: C.A. "Brute" Randolph, G

1913: Eugene "Shorty" Miller, QB

1915: Bob "Punk" Berryman, B

1919: Charley Way, B

1922: Joe Bedenk, G

1927: John Roepke, B

1948: Paul Kelly, L

1948: Elwood Petchel, B

1974: Jack Baiorunos, C

1983: Harry Hamilton, LB

1985: Todd Moules, G

1985: Tim Johnson, DT

1987: Trey Bauer, LB

1987: Pete Curkendall, DT

1987: Blair Thomas, TB

1988: Eddie Johnson, DB

1990: Frank Giannetti, DT

1992: Troy Drayton, TE

1993: Bobby Engram, WR

HALL OF FAME INDUCTEES

Hugo Bezdek , Fullback

Inducted:

College Hall of Fame – 1954

Helms Foundation Hall of Fame – 1960

John Cappelletti, Running back

Inducted:

College Football Hall of Fame – Dec. 7, 1993

Rib Engle, Coach

Inducted:

College Football Hall of Fame – 1974.

Jack Ham, Linebacker

Inducted:

 College Football Hall of Fame – 1990

Dick Harlow, Coach

Inducted:

College Football Hall of Fame – 1954.

Bob Higgins, End

Inducted:

College Football Hall of Fame – 1954.

Glenn Killinger, Quarterback

Inducted:

College Football Hall of Fame - 1971

Ted Kwalick, Tight end

Inducted:

College Football Hall of Fame – 1989

Rich Lucas, Quarterback

Inducted:

College Football Hall of Fame – 1986

Pete Mauthe, Fullback

Inducted:

College Football Hall of Fame – 1957

Shorty Miller, Quarterback

Inducted:

College Football Hall of Fame – 1974

Dennis Onkotz, Linebacker

Inducted:

College Football Hall of Fame – 1995

Mike Reid, Lineman

Inducted

College Football Hall of Fame – 1987

Dave Robinson, End

Inducted:

College Football Hall of Fame – 1997

Steve Suhey, Guard

Inducted:

College Football Hall of Fame - 1985

Dexter Very, End

Inducted:

College Football Hall of Fame - 1976

Harry Wilson, Halfback

Inducted:

College Football Hall of Fame - 1973

Jersey numbers of players are part of the charisma of sports. The number identifies and immortalizes the individual for all-time, and is as almost as important to many fans as the person's name. No sports trivia game is played without some questions related to jersey numbers. Thousands of fans walk around wearing an athletic shirt in the color of their favorite teams but, of greater importance to some fans, is the number of their favorite player. These days, the actual jerseys of superstars are sold for hundreds, often thousands of dollars. The retirement of a jersey number is a major event and many sports teams display that now unused numbered jersey in a prominent place so everyone can be reminded of the superlative accomplishments of the individual and how the player led that team to the apex of success. Penn State has never retired a jersey. Perhaps that is not too surprising, considering the Nittany Lions' penchant for emphasizing the team over the individual.

Penn State began placing felt numerals on the game shirts of players in 1906. It is probable that leaflets listing the numbers were distributed to spectators at time but little evidence remains in State's historical files. The earliest documentation of numbers in the sports archives at the Patee Library is a 1910 program of the game at Penn. So, until further research uncovers the player numbers from earlier years, this book's list of numbers dates to that year.

Below are selected jersey numbers for the 401 players profiled in Section 3 of the *Penn State Football Encyclopedia*. Certainly, there are other jersey numbers that should be on this list. In fact, it would be in keeping with Penn State's kinship with its former players and the school's bond with its past, to compile a list of every player's number. That remains a future project. It should be noted that some players changed jersey numbers during their time at State. In the early years, it was traditional for the senior captain to wear number 1 when he served as captain in his junior and senior years. In the modern era, the number a player wore depended on his position. For example, Bob Parsons started out with number 13 as a sophomore quarterback in 1969, but wore number 86 as a tight end and kicker in 1970 and 1971. So, for this listing, only the senior number is recorded.

BY NUMBER

1 - Joe Bedenk, Bas Gray, Harold (Bill) Hess, Bob Higgins.

2 - Mike Archie, Levi Lamb.

3 - Kim Herring, Bob (Duke) Osborn.

4 - Paul Johnson, Lou Palazzi.

5 - James (Red) Bebout, Craig Fayak, Calvin (Hap) Frank, Chuck Peters, Michael Timpson, Wendell (Windy) Wear.

6 - Aaron Collins, Larry Conover, Ray Roundtree, George Snell.

7 - Frank (Yutz) Diedrich, Harry (High School Harry) Harrison, Mall Knizner, John (Pepper) Petrella, Jules Prevost, Charlie Way.

8 - Henry (Hinkey) Haines, Roger Mahoney, Eugene (Shorty) Miller, John R. Patrick, Terry Smith.

9 - John Economos, Mike McQueary, Mike Palm, Darren Perry, Bill Pritchard.

10 - Matt Bahr, Robert (Punk) Berryman, Bobby Engram, Glenn Killinger, Rags Madera, Massimo Manca, Tom Odell, Mike Smith.

11 - Kevin Baugh, John Bruno, Earle Edwards, Don Eyer, Sam Gash, Stan McCollum.

12 - Kerry Collins, Paul Lankford, Bill Leonard, Joe Lightner, August (Gus) Michalske, Tim Montgomery, Frank Platt, Tom Shuman, Wally Triplett, Ron Younker.

13 - Dave Alston, Ray Baer, Earl (Sparky) Brown, Nick Gancitano.

14 - Todd Blackledge, Owen Dougherty, Jeff Durkota, Chuck Fusina, Dick Harlow, Bob Pollard, Wally Richardson, Harry Robb, John Shaffer, Frank Spaziani.

15 - Lloyd B. Ickes, Harry (Light Horse Harry) Wilson.

16 - Duffy Cobbs, Brian Gelzheiser, John Hufnagel, Lenny Krouse.

17 - Spike Alter, Jim Bradley, Larry Cooney, A. G. (Red) Duvall, Harry Hamilton, Don Jonas, Billy Kane.

18 - Alex Barantovich, Troy Drayton, Lloyd (Dad) Engle.

19 - Gregg Garrity, Tony Sacca, Jim Scott.

20 - Richie Anderson, Joel Coles, Brett Conway, Johnny Roepke, Dex Very.

21 - Ralph Giacomarro, Jim O'Hora.

22 - Chuck Burkhart, John Cappelletti, Stan Czarnecki, Dick Gingrich, Ray Isom, Brian Milne, Milt Plum, Tony Rados, Sever (Tor) Toretti.

23 - Bobby Campbell, Don Caum, Aldo Cenci, Joe Drazenovich, Dick Hoak, R. A. (Squeak) Hufford, Lydell Mitchell.

24 - Mike Guman, Al Jacks, Pete Liske, O.J. McDuffie, Charlie Pittman.

25 - Don Bailey, Tom Bradley, Mike Cooper, Galen Hall, Chuck Herd, Jay (Tiny) McMahon, Tom Sherman, Curt Warner, Gary Wydman.

26 - Chuck Cherundolo, David Daniels, Leon Gajecki, Neal Smith, Jack White, Al Wilson.

27 - Gary Brown, Pete Harris, Tom Vargo.

28 - Gary Hayman, Rich Milot, Carl Stravinski.

29 - Steve Geise.

30 - Gary Gray, George Reynolds.

31 - Pat Botula, Shane Conlan, Coop French, George Landis, Herb Menhardt, Freddie Scott.

32 - Charlie Blockson, Ki-Jana Carter, Tom Donchez, Mark Robinson, Matt Suhey, Blair Thomas.

33 - Jack Ham, Richie Lucas, Fran Rogel, Steve Smith.

34 - Babe Caprara, Percy (Red) Griffiths, Franco Harris, Brian Miller, Bob White.

35 - Trey Bauer, Derek Bochna, Joe Colone, Anthony Giannantonio, Dennis Onkotz,Ed Stuckrath, Larry Suhey.

36 - Don Abbey, James Lester (Pete) Mauthe, Tom Urbanik & Joe Paterno (at Brown).

37 - Walker Lee Ashley, Ben Pollock, Al Vitiello.

38 - Mark D'Onofrio, Greg Ducatte, Ron Hostetler, Jon Witman.

39 - Curtis Enis, Eddie Johnson.

40 - John Chuckran, Bruce Gilmore, Jeff Hite, Pete Johnson, Stephen Pitts, Harold (Junior) Powell.

41 - Newsh Bentz, Jim Kerr, Gary Klingensmith, Elwood Petchel.

42 - D.J. Dozier, Fran Ganter, Keith Goganious, Lenny Moore, Bill Smaltz, Robert (Bobby) Williams.

43 - Andre Collins, Michael Zordich.

44 - Jim Cefalo, Mike Garbinski, Larry Joe, Tim Manoa, Jon Williams.

45 - Lance Hamilton, Vince O'Bara, Sam Sobczak, Joe Tespic.

46 - Scott Fitzkee, Dave Kasperian, Ted Kemmerer, Roger Kochman, Joel Ramich.

47 - Brian Chizmar, Jim Laslavic.

48 - Rich Mauti, Booker Moore.

49 - Roger Jackson

50 - Jeff Hartings

51 - Jim Dooley, Jay Huffman, Dan Radakovich.

52 - Bill Saul

53 - Kurt Allerman, Keith Conlin, Randy Crowder, Steve Garban, Don Graham, Joe Gratson, Bill Lenkaitis, Glenn Ressler, Jim Romano.

54 - Bruce Clark, Dick Maginnis, Mark Markovich, Marco Rivera.

55 - Jack Baiorunos, Lou Benfatti, Chuck Correal, Tim Johnson, Jim Kates, Frank Reich, John Wolosky.
56 - Warren Koegel, Lance Mehl, Pete Speros.

57 - Kirk Bowman, Chris Conlin, John Gerak.

58 - Reggie Givens

60 - Don Barney, Bucky Greeley, Earl (Bud) Kohlhaas, Matt Millen, Sam Valentine, Charlie Zapiec.

61 - John Nessel, Leo Nobile.

62 - Joe Blasentine, Sean Farrell, Mike Reitz, Steve Suhey.

63 - Tom Jackson, John Jaffurs, Todd Moules, John Runnells.

64 - Ron Crosby, Phil Ostrowski, Billy Popp, Earl Shumaker.

65 - Ron Coder, Paul Suhey.

66 - Chuck Drazenovich, Bill Wehmer, Steve Wisniewski.

67 - Greg Buttle, Bob Holuba, Al Michaels (Mikelonis), Dave Robinson, Harrison (Hatch) Rosdhal, Chuck Ruslavage, Mike Russo, Joe Sabol.

68 - Doug Allen, Ralph Baker, Pete Kugler, Mike Reid, George Reihner.

69 - Dick DeLuca, Hugh Rodham, Carl Schaukowitch, Leo Wisniewski.

70 - Greg Gattuso, Dave Joyner, John Nolan, Irv Pankey.

71 - Brad Benson, Keith Dorney, Negley Norton.

72 - Jim Heller, Harold (Red) Moore, Tom Rafferty.

73 - Dave Bradley, Pete Curkendall.

74 - Jeff Bleamer, Stan Clayton, Roosevelt Grier.

75 - Jack Calderone, Charlie Janerette, Randy Sidler.

76 - Dave Rowe, Steve Smear.

77 - Rich Buzin, Bill Dugan, Charlie Getty, Chuck Sieminski.

78 - Roger Duffy, Ron Heller, John Kulka, Mike Munchak, Andy Stynchula.

79 - Joe Bellas, Bill Contz, Mike Hartenstine, Mike McBath, Dave Szott.

80 - Gary Hull, Don Malinak, Maury Schleicher.

81 - Kyle Brady, Jack Curry, Ed Czekaj, Otto Kneidinger, Brian Masella, Mike McCloskey, John Skorupan, Joe Yukica.

82 - Ted Kwalick, Greg Murphy, Jerry Sandusky, Mickey Shuler.

83 - Bruce Bannon, Kenny Jackson, Joe Jurevicius, John Potsklan.

84 - Joe Lally, Carmen Masciantonio, Jack Sherry.

85 - Dick Anderson, Jim Garrity, Dave Graf, Sam Tamburo.

86 - Stew Barber, Bob Mitinger, Bob Parsons, Les Walters.

87 - Ed O'Neil.

88 - Greg Edmunds, Larry Kubin.

89 - Jesse Arnelle, John Ebersole, Dennie Hoggard, Dan Natale, Henry Opperman.

90 - Pete Giftopoulos.

91 - Andre Johnson, Rod Zur, Terry Killens.

93 - Brandon Noble.

94 - Chet Parlavecchio, Eric Ravotti.

95 - Rogers Alexander.

97 - Tyoka Jackson, Scott Radecic.

99 - Chris Bahr.

Numbers Unavailable - Charles Atherton, Charlie Aull, Dave Cure, Ellis (Cy) Cyphers, Henry Dowler, William (Mother) Dunn, Carl Forkum, Burke (Dutch) Herman, Charles (Heff) Hershman, Earl Hewitt, Sr., Charles (Charlie) Hildebrand, Casey Jones, George (Lucy) Linsz, Walter (Bull) McCaskey, E.H. (Bull) McCleary, Henry (Irish) McILveen, Andy Moscrip, Carlton (Brute) Randolph, Leroy (Henny) Scholl, Larry Vorhis, Henry Weaver, Ed Yeckley.

BY NAME

Don Abbey 36
Rogers Alexander 95
Doug Allen 68
Kurt Allerman 53
Dave Alston 13
Spike Alter 17
Dick Anderson 85
Richie Anderson 20
Mike Archie 2
Jesse Arnelle 89
Walker Lee Ashley 37
Charles Atherton *
Charlie Aull *
Ray Baer 13
Chris Bahr 99
Matt Bahr 10
Don Bailey 25
Jack Baiorunos 55
Ralph Baker 68
Bruce Bannon 83
Alex Barantovich 18
Stew Barber 86
Don Barney 60

Trey Bauer 35
Kevin Baugh 11
James (Red) Bebout 5
Joe Bedenk 1
Joe Bellas 79
Lou Benfatti 55
Brad Benson 71
Newsh Bentz 41
Robert (Punk) Berryman 10
Todd Blackledge 14
Joe Blasentine 62
Jeff Bleamer 74
Charlie Blockson 32
Derek Bochna 35
Pat Botula 31
Kirk Bowman 57
Dave Bradley 73
Jim Bradley 17
Tom Bradley 25
Kyle Brady 81
Alex Barantovich 18
Earl (Sparky) Brown 13
Gary Brown 27
John Bruno 11
Chuck Burkhart 22
Greg Buttle 67
Rich Buzin 77
Jack Calderone 75
Bobby Campbell 23
John Cappelletti 22
Babe Caprara 34
Ki-Jana Carter 32
Don Caum 23
Jim Cefalo 44
Aldo Cenci 23
Chuck Cherundolo 26
Brian Chizmar 47
John Chuckran 40
Bruce Clark 54
Stan Clayton 74
Duffy Cobbs 16
Ron Coder 65
Joel Coles 20
Aaron Collins 6
Andre Collins 43
Kerry Collins 12
Joe Colone 35
Shane Conlan 31
Chris Conlin 57
Keith Conlin 53
Larry Conover 6
Bill Contz 79
Brett Conway 20
Larry Cooney 17
Mike Cooper 25
Chuck Correal 55
Ron Crosby 64

Randy Crowder 53
Dave Cure *
Pete Curkendall 73
Jack Curry 81
Ellis (Cy) Cyphers *
Stan Czarnecki 22
Ed Czekaj 81
Mark D'Onofrio 38
David Daniels 26
Dick DeLuca 69
Frank (Yutz) Diedrich 7
Tom Donchez 32
Jim Dooley 51
Keith Dorney 71
Owen Dougherty 14
Henry Dowler *
D.J. Dozier 42
Troy Drayton 18
Chuck Drazenovich 66
Joe Drazenovich 23
Greg Ducatte 38
Roger Duffy 78
Bill Dugan 77
William. T. (Mother) Dunn *
Jeff Durkota 14
Red Duvall 17
John Ebersole 89
John Economos 9
Greg Edmunds 88
Earle Edwards 11
Lloyd (Dad) Engle 18
Bobby Engram 10
Curtis Enis 39
Don Eyer 11
Sean Farrell 62
Craig Fayak 5
Scott Fitzkee 46
Carl Forkum *
Calvin (Hap) Frank 5
Coop French 31
Chuck Fusina 14
Leon Gajecki 26
Nick Gancitano 13
Fran Ganter 42
Steve Garban 53
Mike Garbinski 44
Gregg Garrity 19
Jim Garrity 85
Sam Gash 11
Greg Gattuso 70
Steve Geise 29
Brian Gelzheiser 16
John Gerak 57
Charlie Getty 77
Ralph Giacomarro 21
Anthony Giannantonio 35
Pete Giftopoulos 90

Bruce Gilmore 40
Dick Gingrich 22
Reggie Givens 58
Keith Goganious 42
Dave Graf 85
Don Graham 53
Joe Gratson 53
Bas Gray 1
Gary Gray 30
Bucky Greeley 60
Roosevelt Grier 74
Percy (Red) Griffiths 34
Mike Guman 24
Henry (Hinkey) Haines 8
Galen Hall 25
Jack Ham 33
Harry Hamilton 17
Lance Hamilton 45
Dick Harlow 14
Franco Harris 34
Pete Harris 27
Harry (High School Harry) Harrison 7
Mike Hartenstine 79
Jeff Hartings 50
Gary Hayman 28
Jim Heller 72
Ron Heller 78
Chuck Herd 25
Burke (Dutch) Herman *
Kim Herring 3
Charles (Heff) Hershman *
Harold (Bill) Hess 1
Earl Hewitt, Sr. *
Bob Higgins 1
Charles (Charlie) Hildebrand *
Jeff Hite 40
Dick Hoak 23
Dennie Hoggard 89
Bob Holuba 67
Ron Hostetler 38
Jay Huffman 51
R. A. (Squeak) Hufford 23
John Hufnagel 16
Gary Hull 80
Lloyd B. Ickes 15
Ray Isom 22
Al Jacks 24
Kenny Jackson 83
Roger Jackson 49
Tom Jackson 63
Tyoka Jackson 97
John Jaffurs 63
Charlie Janerrette 75
Larry Joe 44
Andre Johnson 91
Eddie Johnson 39
Paul Johnson 4

Pete Johnson 40
Tim Johnson 55
Don Jonas 17
Casey Jones *
Dave Joyner 70
Joe Jurevicius 83
Billy Kane 17
Dave Kasperian 46
Jim Kates 55
Ted Kemmerer 46
Jim Kerr 41
Terry Killens 92
Glenn Killinger 10
Gary Klingensmith 41
Otto Kneidinger 81
Matt Knizner 7
Roger Kochman 46
Warren Koegel 56
Earl (Bud) Kohlhaas 60
Lenny Krouse 16
Larry Kubin 88
Pete Kugler 68
John Kulka 78
Ted Kwalick 82
Joe Lally 84
Levi Lamb 2
George Landis 31
Paul Lankford 12
Jim Laslavic 47
Bill Lenkaitis 53
Bill Leonard 12
Joe Lightner 12
George (Lucy) Linsz *
Pete Liske 24
Richie Lucas 33
Rags Madera 10
Dick Maginnis   54
Roger Mahoney 8
Don Malinak 80
Massimo Manca 10
Tim Manoa 44
Mark Markovich 54
Carmen Masciantonio 84
Brian Masella 81
James Lester (Pete) Mauthe 36
Rich Mauti 48
Mike McBath 79
E.H. (Bull) McCaskey *
Walter (Bull) McCleary *
Mike McCloskey 81
Stan McCollum 11
Mike McQueary 9
O.J. McDuffie 24
Henry (Irish) McIlveen *
Jay (Tiny) McMahon 25
Lance Mehl 56
Herb Menhardt 31

Al Michaels (Mikelonis) 67
August (Gus) Michalske 12
Matt Millen 60
Brian Miller 34
Eugene (Shorty) Miller 8
Brian Milne 22
Rich Milot 28
Lydell Mitchell 23
Bob Mitinger 86
Tim Montgomery 12
Booker Moore 48
Harold (Red) Moore 72
Lenny Moore 42
Andy Moscrip *
Todd Moules 63
Mike Munchak 78
Greg Murphy 82
Dan Natale 89
John Nessel 61
Leo Nobile 61
Brandon Noble 93
John Nolan 70
Negley Norton 71
Vince O'Bara 45
Jim O'Hora 21
Ed O'Neil 87
Tom Odell 10
Dennis Onkotz 35
Henry Opperman 89
Bob (Duke) Osborn 3
Phil Ostrowski 64
Lou Palazzi 4
Mike Palm 9
Irv Pankey 70
Chet Parlavecchio 94
Bob Parsons 86
Joe Paterno 36 (Brown)
John R. Patrick 8
Darren Perry 9
Elwood Petchel 41
Chuck Peters 5
John (Pepper) Petrella 7
Charlie Pittman 24
Stephen Pitts 40
Frank Platt 12
Milt Plum 22
Bob Pollard 14
Ben Pollock 37
Billy Popp 64
John Potsklan 83
Harold (Junior) Powell 40
Jules Prevost 7
Bill Pritchard 9
Dan Radakovich 51
Scott Radecic 97
Tony Rados 22
Tom Rafferty 72

Joel Ramich 46
Carlton (Brute) Randolph *
Eric Ravotti 94
Frank Reich 55
Mike Reid 68
George Reihner 68
Mike Reitz 62
Glenn Ressler 53
George Reynolds 30
Wally Richardson 14
Marco Rivera 54
Harry Robb 14
Dave Robinson 67
Mark Robinson 32
Hugh Rodham 69
Johnny Roepke 20
Fran Rogel 33
Jim Romano 53
Harrison (Hatch) Rosdahl 67
Ray Roundtree 6
Dave Rowe 76
John Runnells 63
Chuck Ruslavage 67
Mike Russo 67
Joe Sabol 67
Tony Sacca 19
Jerry Sandusky 82
Bill Saul 52
Carl Schaukowitch 69
Maury Schleicher 80
Leroy (Henny) Scholl *
Freddie Scott 31
Jim Scott 19
John Shaffer 14
Tom Sherman 25
Jack Sherry 84
Mickey Shuler 82
Earl Shumaker 64
Tom Shuman 12
Randy Sidler 75
Chuck Sieminski 77
John Skorupan 81
Bill Smaltz 42
Steve Smear 76
Mike Smith 10
Neal Smith 26
Steve Smith 33
Terry Smith 8
George Snell 6
Sam Sobczak 45
Frank Spaziani 14
Pete Speros 56
Carl Stravinski 28
Ed Stuckrath 35
Andy Stynchula 78
Larry Suhey 35
Matt Suhey 32

Paul Suhey 65
Steve Suhey 62
Dave Szott 79
Sam Tamburo 85
Joe Tespic 45
Blair Thomas 32
Michael Timpson 5
Sever (Tor) Toretti 22
Wally Triplett 12
Tom Urbanik 36
Sam Valentine 60
Tom Vargo 27
Dex Very 20
Al Vitiello 37

Larry Vorhis *
Les Walters 86
Curt Warner 25
Charlie Way 7
Wendell Wear 5
Henry Weaver *
Bill Wehmer 66
Bob White 34
Jack White 26
Jon Williams 44
Robert (Bobby) Williams 42
Al Wilson 26
Harry (Light Horse Harry) Wilson 15
Leo Wisniewski 69

Steve Wisniewski 66
Jon Witman 38
John Wolosky 55
Gary Wydman 25
Ed Yeckley *
Ron Younker 12
Joe Yukica 81
Charlie Zapiec 60
Michael Zordich 43
Rod Zur 91

*No number or number unavailable

HALL OF FAME SCHOLAR-ATHLETES

The National Football Foundation and College Football Hall of Fame honors the nation's outstanding scholar-athletes annually with graduate school fellowships.

A recipient must be a senior and in his final year of eligibility, have shown outstanding football ability and performance, exhibited academic application and performance, demonstrated outstanding leadership and citizenship, and be a candidate for graduate study and must not have received his diploma.

Recipients of the prestigious honor receive an $18,000 fellowship.

Dave Joyner – T, 1971
Bruce Bannon – DE, 1972
Mark Markovich – G, 1973
Jack Baiorunos – C, 1974
Chuck Correal – C, 1978
John Walsh – DHB, 1980
Carmen Masciantonio – ILB, 1984
Lance Hamilton – DHB, 1985
Brian Siverling – TE, 1986
Matt Johnson – DT, 1987
Tony Pittman – CB, 1994

GTE ACADEMIC ALL-AMERICANS

Twenty-two Penn State players have received first-team GTE Academic All-American recognition by the College Sports Information Directors of America (CoSIDA).

A nominee must be a starter or an important reserve, carry at least a 3.2 cumulative average (on a 4.0 scale) for an entire academic career, and have completed at least one full year at their current institution.

In 1995, All-America guard Jeff Hartings became the fourth Nittany Lion to earn first-team Academic All-America honors twice.

Joe Bellas – T, 1965
John Runnells – LB, 1965, 1966
Rich Buzin – T, 1967
Dennis Onkotz – LB, 1969
Charlie Pittman- RB, 1969
Dave Joyner – T, 1971
Bruce Bannon – DE, 1972
Mark Markovich – G, 1973
Chuck Benjamin – DT, 1976
Keith Dorney – T, 1978
Todd Blackledge – QB, 1982
Harry Hamilton – DHB, 1982, 1983
Scott Radecic – LB, 1982
Lance Hamilton – DHB, 1984, 1985
Carmen Masciantonio – ILB, 1984

NCAA POSTGRADUATE SCHOLARSHIPS

Twenty-nine Penn State athletes, including 16 football players, have received National Collegiate Athletic Association Postgraduate Scholarships. The award carries a $5,000 scholarship for postgraduate study at the university or professional school of the student's choice.

To qualify for consideration, each recipient must have earned at least a "B" cumulative average (3.0 on

Penn State's 4.0 grade-point scale) and also much have performed with distinction in his or her sport, thus epitomizing the term "student-athlete."

Penn State's recipients in football, with their year of graduation:

Joe Bellas – 1966
Jonhn Runnells – 1967
Bob Holuba – 1971
Dave Joyner – 1972
Bruce Bannon – 1973
Mark Markovich – 1974
Jack Baiorunos – 1975
Chuck Correal – 1979
Mike Guman – 1979
John Walsh – 1980
Harry Hamilton – 1983
Doug Strang – 1984
Brian Siverling – 1987
Roger Duffy – 1990
Craig Fayak – 1994
Tony Pittman – 1995

NCAA SILVER ANNIVERSARY AWARD

Mike Reid – 1995
Dave Joyner – 1997

HEISMAN TROPHY AWARD

John Cappelletti, tailback on the unbeaten and untied 1973 Penn State team, was the recipient of the 1973 Heisman Trophy, which is given to the "outstanding intercollegiate football player in the United States."

Twelve other Penn State players have finished in the Top 10 in Heisman Trophy balloting. Tailback Ki-Jana Carter and quarterback Kerry Collins placed second and fourth, respectively, in the 1994 balloting for only the eigth top four finish by teammates in the 63-year history of the Heisman Trophy.

Year	Penn Stater (Top 10)	Winner
1959	Rich Lucas, QB (2)	Billy Cannon, LSU, B
1968	Ted Kwalick, TE (4)	O.J. Simpson, Southern Cal., RB
1969	Mike Reid, DT (5)	Steve Owens, Oklahoma, RB
1971	Lydell Mithchell, RB (5)	Pat Sullivan, Auburn, QB
1972	John Hufnagel, QB (6)	Johnny Rodgers, Nebraska, FLK
1973		John Cappelletti, Penn State, RB
1978	Chuck Fusina, QB (2)	Billy Sims, Oklahoma, RB
1982	Todd Blackledge, QB (6)	Herschel Walker, Georgia, RB
1982	Curt Warner, RB (10)	
1986	D.J. Dozier, RB (8)	Vinny Testaverde, Miami (Fla.), QB
1989	Blair Thomas, TB (10)	Andre Ware, Houston, QB
1994	Ki-Jana Carter, TB (2)	Rashaan Salaam, Colorado, RB
	Kerry Collins, QB (4)	
1997	Curtis Enis, TB (6)	Charles Woodson, Michigan, CB

MAXWELL AWARD

Six Penn State players have been honored with the Maxwell Award, given annually to "the outstanding player in collegiate football."

The award is named in honor of Robert W. "Tiny" Maxwell, an Al-America guard at Chicago and Swarthmore. He later worked as a newspaper city editor and sportswriter before his death in an automobile accident at the age of 37.

Rich Lucas – QB, 1959   **John Cappelletti** – RB, 1973

Glenn Ressler – C/G, 1964   **Chuck Fusina** – QB, 1978

Mike Reid – DT, 1969   **Kerry Collins** – QB, 1994

BILETNIKOFF AWARD

Penn State wide receiver Bobby Engram was the inaugural winner of the Biletnikoff Award, presented in February of 1995. This award is given to the nation's top receiver.

The owner of 12 school records, Engram was one of three finalists for the 1995 Biletnikoff Award.

In 1997, Joe Jurevicius was a semifinalist for the Biletnikoff Award.

LOMBARDI AWARD

Penn State defensive tackle Bruce Clark became the first junior to win the Lombardi Award when he was named the recipient in 1979. It is presented annually "to the offensive or defensive lineman or linebacker who, in addition to outstanding performance, best exemplifies the discipline of Lombardi."

Clark and junior defensive tackle teammate Matt Millen both were finalists in 1979. Senior offensive tackle Keith Dorney also finished in the Top 10 in balloting for the award that year.

Clark and Millen were the first finalists from Penn State and only the second and third juniors to be finalists. Guard Sean Farrell was a finalist in 1982.

All-America guard Jeff Hartings was a semifinalist for the 1995 Rotary Lombardi Award.

DAVEY O'BRIEN AWARD

Penn State quarterback Kerry Collins was presented the 1994 Davey O'Brien National Quarterback Award, which includes a scholarship grant to the recipient's school. Todd Blackledge was the Nittany Lions' first recipient of the award in 1982.

The award was established in memory of the late Davey O'Brien, who quarterbacked Texas Christian to the 1938 National Championship and was the winner of the Heisman, Walter Camp and Maxwell trophies. Sponsored by the Davey O'Brien Educational and Charitable Trust and the Fort Worth Club, the award is presented for competitive sportsmanship, academic standing and scholarship, leadership qualities and ability to inspire others, dedication to team success, and quarterback skills and achievements.

Todd Blackledge – 1982   **Kerry Collins** – 1994

OUTLAND TROPHY AWARD

Mike Reid was awarded the Outland Trophy in 1969. Presented annually since 1946, the award is given to "the outstanding interior lineman" by the Football Writers Association of America.

Reid, who was inducted into the National Football Foundation College Football Hall of Fame in 1987, went on to earn All-Pro honors with the Cincinnati Bengals in the National Football League.

JOHN BRUNO, JR. MEMORIAL AWARD

The John Bruno, Jr. Memorial Award is presented to the outstanding member of the special teams.

The award honors former Nittany Lion John Bruno, Jr., who died of cancer in 1992. Bruno was the squad's punter from 1984-86 and his career 41.7-yard average is third-highest in school history. His 42.9 average in 1985 is third-highest in a season and included a career-best 71-yard effort against Boston College.

Chris Cisar– Hero, 1992   **Shelly Hammonds** – CB, 1993

V.J. Muscillo – P, 1993   **Marlon Forbes** – CB, 1994

Brian King – Saf, 1995   **Brett Conway** – K, 1996

Ahmad Collins – OLB, 1997

HALL AWARD

The Hall Award Foundation Athletic Award was established by the Hall Foundation of Mechanicsburg, Pa., to honor Penn State's "outstanding senior player."

Selection is made by a commitee composed of head coach Joe Paterno, National Collegiate Athletic Association faculty athletic representative Dr. John Coyle, a representative of the Hall Foundation and a media member.

Chuch Fusina – 1978	Steve Wisniewski – 1988
Matt Suhey – 1979	Blair Thomas – 1989
Booker Moore – 1980	Leroy Thompson – 1990
Sean Farrell – 1981	Tony Sacca – 1991
Curt Warner – 1982	O.J. McDuffie – 1992
Kenny Jackson – 1983	Lou Benfatti – 1993
Nick Haden – 1984	Kerry Collins – 1994
Michael Zordich – 1985	Bobby Engram – 1995
Shane Conlan – 1986	Brandon Noble – 1996
Matt Knizner – 1987	Mike McQueary – 1997

MAGINNIS AWARD

The Richard Maginnis Memorial Award is presented to the outstanding Penn State offensive lineman who exemplifies the spirit, dedication and commitment which Maginnis displayed as a member of the 1980-83 Nittany Lion teams.

The award was established by the members of the 1982 National Championship team in memory of Maginnis.

Tim Freeman – 1989	Mike Malinoski & Derick Pickett – 1993
Pat Duffy – 1990	Bucky Greeley – 1994
Paul Siever – 1991	Jeff Hartings – 1995
Greg Huntington – 1992	Barry Tielsch – 1996
	Kevin Conlin & Phil Ostrowski – 1997

FRANK PATRICK MEMORIAL AWARD

The Frank Patrick "Total Commitment" Award is presented to the junior squad members who consistently follow through with their responsibilities in all facets of the football program and do so in an exemplary manner. This total commitment is applied to academic pursuits, off-season preparation, in-season commitment and community service.

The award honors Frank Patrick , a member of the Nittany Lion coaching staff from 1949-73. Patrick was instrumental in the academic advising of squad members and remained in an advisory capacity with the program after his retirement in 1973.

Jeff Davis, Carl Gray, Jeff Hartings, Andre Johnson – 1995
Jason Henderson & Wally Richardson – 1996
Mike McQueary & Bob Stephenson – 1997
Maurice Daniels, Chad Kroell & Jon Sandusky – 1998

JIM O'HORA AWARD

The Jim O'Hora Award is presented to a defensive player for "exemplary conduct, loyalty, interest, attitude and improvement" during Penn State's spring practice each year.

The award honors Penn State assistant head coach Jim O'Hora, who retired in 1977 after serving 31 years on the coaching staff.

Joe Lally – 1977	Andre Collins – 1988
Karl McCoy – 1978	Jorge Oquendo – 1989
Gene Gladys – 1979	Keith Goganious – 1990
Grover Edwards – 1980	Mark Flythe – 1991
Walker Lee Ashley – 1981	Vin Stewart – 1992
John Luton – 1982	Tony Pittman – 1993
Brad Saar – 1983	Chris Mazyck – 1994
Bob White – 1984	Shino Prater – 1995
Chris Collins & Tim Johnson – 1985	Matt Fornadel & Chris Snyder – 1996
Mike Beckish – 1986	Mike Buzin – 1997
Quintus McDonald – 1987	Jason Wallace – 1998

RIDGE RILEY AWARD

The Ridge Riley Award honors a senior member of the Penn State team for "sportsmanship, scholarship, leadership and friendship" and includes a $2,500 postgraduate scholarship.

Named in honor of the late executive director of the Penn State alumni Association and author of the Penn State Football Letter for 38 years, the award is sponsored by Richard and Arlene Small, owners of Alumni Holidays, Inc., of Chicago.

Chuck Benjamin – 1976	Darryl Washington – 1987
Tom DePaso – 1977	John Green & Eddie Johnson – 1988
Paul Suhey – 1978	Scott Gob – 1989
Mike Guman – 1979	Dave Brzenchek – 1990
John Walsh – 1980	Al Golden – 1991
Leo Wisniewski – 1981	E.J. Sandusky – 1992
Stuart McMunn – 1982	Lee Rubin – 1993
Scott Radecic – 1983	Willie Smith – 1994
Carmen Masciantonio – 1984	Carl Gray – 1995
Lance Hamilton – 1985	Wally Richardson – 1996
Brian Siverling – 1986	Matt Fornadel – 1997

RED WORRELL AWARD

The Red Worrel Award is presented annually to an offensive player "for exemplary conduct, loyalty, interest, attitude and improvement" during Penn State's spring practice.

The award honors freshman fullback Robert T. "Red" Worrell, who was electrocuted at his home in Denbo, Pa., in December, 1957.

The Worrell Award was restricted to offensive players with the inception of the Jim O'Hora Award for defensive players in 1977, both offensive and defensive players were eligible for the Worrell award from 1958 to 1976.

Andy Stynchula – 1958

Frank Korbini – 1959

Bill Popp – 1960

Joe Galardi – 1961

Ralph Baker – 1962

Tom Urbanik – 1963

Chuck Ehinger – 1964

Ed Lenda – 1965

Jim McCormick – 1966

Tom McGrath – 1967

Steve Smear – 1968

Greg Edmonds – 1969

Fran Ganter – 1970

Mike Botts & Lydell Mitchell – 1971

Larry Ludwig – 1972

Greg Murphy – 1973

Jeff Bleamer – 1974

Dave Strutts – 1975

Mickey Shuler – 1976

Bob Bassett – 1977

Kip Vernaglia – 1978

Bill Dugan – 1979

John Wojtowicz – 1980

Vyto Kab – 1981

George Herina – 1982

Stan Short – 1983

Steve Smith – 1984

Rob Smith – 1985

Mike Wolf – 1986

Tim Freeman & John Greene – 1987

Ed Monaghan & Odell Wilson – 1988

Rob Luedeke – 1989

Sam Gash – 1990

Todd Rucci – 1991

E.J. Sandusky – 1992

Kyle Brady – 1993

Keith Olsommer – 1994

Jason Henderson – 1995

Jason Sload – 1996

Ryan Fagan & Floyd Wedderburn – 1997

John Blick – 1998

COOGAN AWARD

The outstanding player in the Penn State-Pittsburgh game receives the James H. Coogan Memorial Award. It is named in honor of Penn State's long-time Sports Information Director, who later became the school's Public Information Director until his death in April, 1962.

Pete Liske – Penn State, 1962

Fred Mazurek – Pittsburgh, 1963

Tom Urbanik – Penn State, 1964

Kenny Lucas – Pittsburgh, 1965

Bob Campbell – Penn State, 1966

Tom Sherman – Penn State, 1967

Skip Orszulak – Pittsburgh, 1968

Dennis Onkotz – Penn State, 1969

Lydell Mitchell – Penn State, 1970

Lydell Mitchell – Penn State, 1971

John Hufnagel – Penn State, 1972

Chris Bahr – Penn State, 1974

Tony Dorsett – Pittsburgh, 1975

Tony Dorsett – Pittsburgh, 1976

Ron Hostetler – Penn State, 1977

Mike Guman – Penn State, 1978

Randy McMillan - Pittsburgh, 1979

Rick Trocano & Hugh Green – Pittsburgh, 1980

Todd Blackledge – Penn State, 1981

Curt Warner – Penn State, 1982

Bill Wallace – Pittsburgh, 1983

John Congemi – Pittsburgh, 1984

Tim Manoa – Penn State, 1985

Blair Thomas – Penn State, 1986

No Selection – 1987

Curvin Richards – Pittsburgh, 1988

Curvin Richards – Pittsburgh, 1989

Tony Sacca – Penn State, 1990

Richie Anderson – Penn State, 1991

Brian O'Neal – Penn State, 1992

Mike McQueary – Penn State, 1997

SECTION FOUR

THE APPENDICES

CHAPTER 20

THE ASSISTANT COACHES

The listing of Assistant Coaches includes only full-time staff members. Graduate Assitants are not included.

Anderson, Dick, 1973-83, 90-present
Bear, Ray, 1924-25
Bedenk, Joe, 1929-51
Bentz, Newsh, 1926
Bove, John, 1981-84
Bradley, Tom, 1980-present
Brooks, Booker, 1972-83
Bruce, Earl, 1946-69
Caldwell, Jim, 1986-92
Cartmell, N.J., 1923-24
Chuckran, John, 1970-76
Cirbus, Craig, 1987-89, 92-94
Conover, Larry, 1926-30
Crowder, Randy, 1983-84
Davis, E.C., 1932-35
Dickerson, Ron, 1985-90
Ducatte, Gregg, 1974-77
Dunn, W.T., 1907

Hermann, B.M., 1922-23, 25-31
Higgins, Bob, 1928-29
Houck, Leo, 1923-31
Hulme, J.W., 1937
Jackson, Kenny, 1993-present
Johnson, Larry, 1996-present
Kenney, Bill, 1989-91, 93-present
Killinger, Glenn, 1923-25
Leslie, Spike, 1932-35
Martin, C.W., 1922
McAndrews, Marty, 1936, 41-45
McCleary, E.H., 1911
McIlveen, H.C., 1906-09
McMahon, Tiny, 1923
McMullen, Joe, 1963-68
Michaels, Al, 1935-53
Moscrip, A.L., 1905
O'Hora, Jim, 1946-76
Paterno, Jay, 1995-present
Paterno, Joe, 1950-65
Patrick, Frank, 1949-73
Phillips, Bob, 1966-86

Prevost, Jules, 1925
Radakovich, Dan, 1960-69
Rauch, R.H., 1921
Rocco, Frank, 1985
Rosenberg, John, 1975-82
Sandusky, Jerry, 1969-present
Sarra, Joe, 1985-present
Schiano, Greg, 1991-95
Scholl, L.R., 1910
Scott, Zen, 1917
Slusser, T.A., 1936
Snell, George, 1922
Speidel, Charles, 1929-35
Toretti, Sever, 1949-62
Walke, Nels, 1932-35
Weaver, Jim, 1969-72
Welsh, George, 1964-72
White, J.T., 1954-79
Whitney, L.W., 1915-16
Williams, Jim, 1978-92
Wood, E.K., 1910
Yeckley, E.G., 1906-08
Yerger, H.C., 1918

CHAPTER 21

THE MEN AT THE MIKE

The emergence of Penn State as one of the premier football programs in the country under Joe Paterno has paralleled the influence of radio and television on the nation's consciousness. Today, almost every game is televised live either by an over the air or cable network on a national or regional basis or by a syndicator to a series of stations. Occasionally, an away game of limited appeal is beamed back to a single station designated as the primary "home" station for State College, WTAJ in Altoona.

But even in this age of TV omnipresence, thousands of State fans listen to the game via radio over the Penn State Radio Network. At home games, transistor radios are as ubiquitous as Pepsi and hotdogs. State's radio broadcasting team, Fran Fisher and George Paterno, are as well known to the Nittany Lion football fan as Coach Joe Paterno. Fisher, in fact, has been part of the PSU broadcasting football family in one way or another since Paterno's first year as head coach in 1966. He was the general manager and sportscaster of a station in Lewistown when he became a second color commentator for play-by-play broadcaster Tom Bender, then associated with KDKA in Pittsburgh. The other color man at the time was State College broadcaster Mickey Bergstein, who had been involved with State's radio games since the early 1950s. Even after Fisher left the radio booth following the 1982 season, he continued to work with Joe Paterno on the coach's weekly telephone call-in show and made other broadcasting appearances before returning to the play-by-play microphone in 1994.

Joe's brother George, first became involved with broadcasting State football in 1976 when he joined the Telecommunications Systems network of TV stations and cable systems that televised the games on a delayed basis or carried a condensed one hour highlights show. George's first partner was the nationally known Ray Scott, who once did play-by-play on radio as part of a roving group of sportscasters who covered State games in the late 1940s and early 1950s. In 1988, George moved over to the radio side of the PSU network. The college football television environment changed in 1984 because of a federal court order that lifted NCAA restrictions on the televising of college games. Subsequently, Penn State's delayed TV network was dissolved because all games were now available for telecasting live. Additionally, the advent of all-sports networks such as ESPN and Fox, with their repetitive video tape replays of game highlights and special shows featuring college football, has given additional exposure to Penn State and other high profile teams.

The creation and evolution of a weekly television program specializing in Penn State football also has been influential in enhancing the image of the Nittany Lions. The first weekly show was created in 1965 by Marlowe Froke, then general manager of the university-own educational station, WPSX. Froke and PSU president Eric Walker had discussed such a program as a way to get State's football team more visibility. A one hour show known as "Wednesday Night Quarterbacks" premiered in the fall of 1965 with coach Rip Engle. The hosts were Harris Lipez, general manager of WBPZ radio in Lock Haven, and Ken Holderman, vice president of State's Commonwealth campuses. Joe Paterno, in his first year as head coach in 1966, agreed to be involved in the program because of his personal interest in helping educational television. The name was changed to "TV Quarterbacks" and was produced and directed by David Phillips. Paterno was on hand each week to discuss the games and assistant coaches narrated the black and white game films shot by the athletic department primarily for internal use. Occasionally, players also would appear during the hour. In 1967, Fisher joined the program to narrate the game films and in 1968 he became a co-host replacing Lipez. State's sports information director Jim Tarman became the other co-host in 1969. The basic format continued for the life of the program but the black and white coach's film was eventually replaced by original footage shot by WPSX.

After airing solely on WPSX in its first two years, the show expanded to WITF in Hershey in 1967 and by 1974, the show was being carried on seven state educational stations which were part of the new Pennsylvania Public Television Network, spearheaded by Froke, Phillips and WPSX. In 1975, the program was moved to commercial television as part of the new Penn State Television Network and syndicated on television stations and cable systems around the country. "TV Quarterbacks" ended in 1985 and was replaced by "The Joe Paterno Show." In 1988 the "Penn State Football Story" succeeded that Paterno program and that show continues to this day.

Live television coverage of college football games on a regular basis began in the early 1950s. Under the NCAA's television rules, teams were limited in the number of games that could be televised each season. It wasn't until the 1980s that more than three games a season were televised on a regular basis. And that was more than four decades after the first known telecast of a Lion football game and some 60 years after the first radio broadcast. Until the 1950s, radio was the only outlet for live coverage of Penn State games. What follows is a summary of the history of Penn State football on radio and a listing of some of the men who were at "mike" for the local originations. The television portion of this chapter is a brief chronology of significant historical dates in the broadcasting of games on television.

RADIO

1927

- October 1, 1927 - College radio station WPSC broadcasts first Penn State game with assistant coach Larry Conover describing action in 34-13 win over Gettysburg at Beaver Field; Conover goes on to broadcast four more games that season at Beaver Field.

- November 24, 1927- First away game is broadcasted over radio by KDKA in Pittsburgh as undefeated Pitt scores most points against State in 11 years to win 30-0 at Pitt Stadium.

1928

- September 29, 1928- Sophomore Ken Holderman becomes first student to broadcast Penn State game over college station, WPSC. Holderman (later a university vice president and trustee) does Play-by-Play (PBP) in 25-0 victory over Lebanon Valley.

1928 -1937 - Various games were broadcast during this period but at sporadic times and usually over only one or two stations.

1938

-October 1, 1938- First Penn State radio network is established and broadcasts opening game against Maryland at Beaver Field; KDKA Pittsburgh originates broadcast with Bill Sutherland on Play-by-Play and Jack Barry doing "Color;" Penn State wins 38-0.

1939 -1941 - KDKA radio network continues with Bill Sutherland and Jack Barry broadcasting some games but not all each season.

1942 - First radio network organized by KDKA dissolves because of World War II; major gasoline sponsor can't get enough gas to sell.

1943 - 1952 - Various games were broadcast. After World War II, Atlantic Refining Co. purchased broadcast rights and used different announcers from its talent pool to broadcast games. From 1946 through the 1952 season, Bob Wilson of WMAJ radio (and a 1940 PSU graduate) was the color man for the home and away radio broadcasts. But Atlantic Refining Co. and its advertising agency, N.W. Ayer of Philadelphia, assigned the play-by-play announcers and they varied from game to game. Among the play-by-play commentators were several nationally known sportscasters, including Ray Scott, Bob Prince, Claude Haring, Tom McMahon, Chuck Thompson, Woody Wolf and Byron Saam. In 1953 Prince was assigned to be the principal play-by-play announcer but missed one game and the fourth quarter of another due to prior commitments to broadcast games of the Pittsburgh Pirates and Pittsburgh Steelers.

1953 - Bob Prince PBP & Mickey Bergstein Color (Bergstein does first PBP in 4th QT of Syracuse game when Prince leaves be

cause of pro football commitment.
Also, Joe Tucker does PBP in Wisconsin season opener at Madison because of Prince commitment)

1954 - Prince PBP & Bergstein Color
1955 - University Sets up its own Penn State Football Radio Net work with Prince PBP & Bergstein Color

September 29, 1956- First all-Penn State alumni broadcasting team works first game for the Lions football radio network as Mickey Bergstein ('43) moves from color commentary to Play-By-Play and Bob Wilson ('40) takes over Color; State beats Pennsylvania, 34-0, at Franklin Field in Philadelphia

1956 - 1957- Bergstein PBP & Wilson handling Color for home games
1958 - Bergstein PBP & Ridge Riley Color
1959 - Tom Bender PBP & Bergstein Color
1960 - C. D. Chesley Gains Rights
1960 - Gene Kelly PBP & Bender Color
1961 - Bill Campbell PBP & Bender Color
1962 - 1963 - Bender PBP & Randy Hall Color
1964 - 1965 - Bender PBP & Bergstein Color
1966 - Bender PBP & Bergstein & Fran Fisher Color
1967 - 1969 - Bender PBP & Bergstein & Fisher Color
1970 - Fisher PBP & Bergstein Color
1971 - 1979 - Fisher & Jim Tarman Color
1980 - 1982 - Fisher & John Grant Color
1983 - TCS Produces Radio Network
1983 - Gil Santos PBP, Grant Color & Steve Jones at Halftime & Post Game
1984 - 1986 - Santos, Grant & Jones

1987 - Bill Campbell & Lanny Frattare PBP, Grant & Jones with Scott Fitzkee also on Color & interviews

1988 - State sets up own radio network as TCS dissolves; Frank Giardina hired as new marketing and promotions coordinator for Penn State football Radio & TV networks.
- New weekly Joe Paterno Call-In Show established and syndicated by network and airing live on Thursday evenings between 6:06 and 7:00 p.m., with Paterno answering questions from listeners via telephone; Fran Fisher named to host show.

1988 - John Sanders PBP, George Paterno Color & Jones
1989 - Sanders, Paterno & Jones
1990 - Bill Zimpfer PBP, Paterno & Jones
1991 - 1993 - Zimpfer, Paterno & Frank Giardina on Interviews
1994 - 1998 - Fisher, Paterno & Giardina

TELEVISION

October 1, 1949 - This is the first known televising of a State football game as game is carried by WNBT-TV in New York City; State plays 500th game since 1887 and loses to 42-7 to an Army.

October 30, 1954 - State plays first ever game on national television and beats Penn, 35-13, at Franklin Field, scoring most points in long time series against Quakers as Lenny Moore rushes for 140 yards and scores three touchdowns.

September 29, 1955 - First ever game televised from Beaver Field as CBS transmits season opener against Boston University to limited region in East; Lions win 35-0 as unknown, fifth string, sophomore fullback Joe Sabol scores two touchdowns to lead vic tory.

October 26, 1957 - The third game of Engle era is televised by CBS on a regional basis from Syracuse as State beats Orangemen, 21-12.

October 13, 1958 - In the fourth game televised during Engle's tenure, State defeats Boston University, 34 - 0, on regionally tele vised game from Boston University's field.

September 29, 1961 - Athletic Department experiments with closed circuit television by televising first game ever against Mi ami from Orange Bowl Stadium to Rec Hall and Schwab Audito rium on Penn State campus but paid attendance is disappointing when less than 40 percent of the seating capacity is filled.

September, 1965 - WPSX-TV general manager Marlowe Froke creates first weekly Penn State football television show known as "Wednesday Quarterbacks" with Coach Rip Engle, hosted by Harris Lipez and Ken Holderman.

September, 1966 - Name of weekly football show changed from "Wednesday Quarterbacks" to "TV Quarterbacks" with Joe Paterno.

November 5, 1966- Eight games Into Paterno's first season, ABC-TV broadcasts the first ever game under his tenure to a re gional audience and State loses to Syracuse, 12-10, at Beaver Stadium.

October 12, 1968 - Paterno wins his first game on television after two defeats and a tie as Lions beat UCLA 21-6 in regionally-televised game from Los Angeles.

December 7, 1968 - The first nationally televised game of the Paterno era during the regular season is broadcast by ABC from Beaver Stadium as Lions beat Syracuse, 30-12, to finish unbeaten and become first State team to win 10 games.

1970- A six-station Pennsylvania station television network set up by Television Production Company (TPC) of Pittsburgh broadcasts five home games on a delayed basis at 11 p.m.; games are car ried in Philadelphia, Altoona, Harrisburg, Scranton, Lancaster and York as Governor Ray Shafer helps do color commentary of games as does athletic department official Steve Garban with Dick Scherr of WTAF (Philadelphia) and Dick Richards of WFBG (Altoona) han dling play-by-play and other commentary.

1975 - Start of Penn State TV Network by TCS with all games televised in 1975 on 2 1/2 hour game delay with some games also broadcast live plus a one-hour highlights show. Two away games against Ohio State and Iowa also were televised live via closed circuit pay-TV back to Recreation Hall with 2300 turning out for OSU but about 500 for Iowa.

1975 - 1984 - The TCS 2 1/2 Hour delayed game and the one-hour Highlights show ran from 1975 to 1984 but the number of stations and cable systems that aired the programs varied from game to game and year to year. Ray Scott, a Western Pennsylva nia native who became famous as a CBS sportscaster broadcast ing games for the Green Bay Packers, handled the play-by-play with former Packers star Max McGee doing color. Ex-PSU All-Ameri can and former Packers All-Pro Dave Robinson served as analyst for several games in the 1975 season. George Paterno replaced McGee as the color commentator in 1976 and in 1982, Pitts burgh sportscaster Stan Savaran succeeded Scott.

1984 - U.S. Supreme Court ruling against NCAA allows individual colleges to make their own television arrangements; State con tracts with TCS to televise several games live.

September 29, 1984 - ESPN televises its first live regular sea son game of Penn State football after 10 delayed broadcasts be tween 1980-to-1983 and Lions lose to Texas, 28-3, at Giants Sta dium in New Jersey Meadowlands.

1985 - TV Quarterbacks ends and is replaced by new program entitled, The Paterno Show produced by TCS with Jimmy Cefalo as host along with Joe Paterno.

1988 - State sets up own TV network after TCS dissolves.
- Frank Giardina hired as new coordinator for Penn State football on TV & radio
- *Penn State Football Story* highlights show created to replace The Paterno Show
- Eric Clemons of ESPN hired as host.

1989 - *Penn State Football Story* continues with Eric Clemons as host.

1990 - Present - Guy Junker narrates *Penn State Football Story*.

1966 - 1997 - During the Paterno era, Penn State games have been televised 123 times on a national basis and 42 times re gionally. The Paterno record for televised games is: National - 82-40-1; Regional - 30-12; Bowl Games -18-9-1.

CHAPTER 22

THE HEALERS

TEAM PHYSICIANS	YEAR	TEAM TRAINERS	YEAR
Dr. W.S. Forsythe	1915-1916	George Hoskins	1892-1895
Dr. Joseph Ritenour	1917-1938	Dr. B.Sam Newton	1896-1898
Dr. Alfred H. Griess	1939-1965	W.N. Pop Golden	1900-1910
Dr. William Grasley	1965-1971	Dr. Dan Luby	1912-1913
Dr. Samuel Fleagle	1966-1977	C.W. Martin	1913-1923
Dr. Alxander Kalenak	1974-1994	Nate Cartmell	1924-1925
Dr. James Whiteside	1974-1985	Leo Houck	1926-1933
Dr. Harry Weller	1985-1994	W.D. Edwards	1929-1932
Dr. Deborah Waters	1987-1989	Charlie Spiedel	1934-1935
Dr. Michael Lynch	1989-1997	T.A. Slusser	1936
Dr. Margot Putukian	1994-1997	Jack Hulme	1937-1946
Dr. Michael Cordas	1995-1996	Charles E. (Chuck) Medlar	1946-1977
Dr. Thomas Martin	1997	Gerald Slagle	1978-1990
Dr. Wayne Sebastianelli*	1992-199	Jim Hochberg	1981-1982
		George Salvaterra	1990-1997
		Charles Thompson	1991-1997

CHAPTER 23

THE BOSSES & THE HOSSES

ATHLETIC DIRECTORS	YEAR
Hugo Bezdek	1918-1936
Dr. Carl P. Schott	1937-1953
Ernie McCoy	1953-1968
Ed Czekaj	1968-1980
Joe Paterno	1980-1982
Jim Tarman	1982-1993
Tim Curley	1994- Present

SPORTS INFORMATION DIRECTORS	YEAR
George (Pat) Sullivan	1922-1926
Wes Dunlap	1926-1935
Ridge Riley	1935-1943
Jim Coogan	1943-1958
Jim Tarman	1958-1970
John Morris	1970-1979
Dave Baker	1979-1986
L. Budd Thalman	1986-1993
Jeff Nelson	1994-Present

STUDENT MANAGERS	YEAR
J.G. White	1881
John Morris	1887
J. Frank Shields	1891
J.E. Quigley	1893
R.M. McKinley	1896
J.S. Albert	1897
J. Diller	1899
N.R. Wright	1907
P.B. Postlethwaite	1908
J.M. McKee	1909
L.A. Cuthbert	1910
F.W. Orr	1911
William G. Kerr	1912
Neil M. Fleming	1913
C.A. Lord	1914
R.S. Davis	1915
P. Hoffman	1916
R.K. Cochrane	1917
K.B. Kirk	1918
C.W. Brown	1919
K.R. Stark	1920
L.W. Forncrook	1921
W.H. Parsons	1922
R.E. Longacre	1923
B.F. Gotwals	1924
W.W. Allen	1925
J.E. Smart	1926
Harry F. Smith	1927
Bernard Newman	1928
John K. McClements	1929
Ralph Hutchinson	1930
John D.Page	1931
Charles E. Malley, Jr.	1932
William A. Hansen &	1933
Harold J. Muncaster	1933
Alan R. Warehime	1934
Walter J. Kinsey	1935
J.F. Griffith	1936
W.E. Lindenmuth	1937
George W. Yeckley	1938
W.J. Howarth	1939
C.A. Reid	1940
W.F. Finn	1941
Allan I. Moses	1942
Claire Eisenhart	1943
Paul M. Burns	1944-1945
James McMaster	1946
David Barron	1947
Harold Saunders	1948
David F. Owen, Jr.	1949
George Avery, Jr.	1950
Jack Brown	1951
Benjamin Thompson	1952
Richard Crafton	1953
John Greiner	1954
Calvin Orrin Barr	1955
John A. Chaffetz	1956
Paul M. Schonbachler	1957

Edward R. Hintz, Jr.	1958
David F. Williams	1959
John Irvine	1960
Ray Bradford	1961
Dorn Johnstone	1962
Steven Wolfe	1963-64
John A. Tomco	1965-1968
Clarence Thompson	1969
Wayne Cunningham	1970
Gary Crocus	1971
Rick Nichols &Glen Allen	1972
Carl Hartley	1973
Mark Dowd &	1974
John Kuttesch	1974
Greg Nicotera	1975
Mike Gross & Lou Groff	1976
Unknown	1977
Charles Chiampi & Bob Kush	1978
Ron Hileman	1979
Bob Bartolomeo	1980
Bob Celt &	1981
Rob Seitz	1981-1982
Tim Keech & Phil Marguriet	1983
Scott Bouslough & Don Carlino	1984
Tim Keech	1985
Brad Caldwell	1986

Tim Reedy, Ken Brzozowski	1987
& Joe Soprano	
Mark Bonson, Don Hoover	1988
& Doug Badali	
Sam Shuss, Nick Downs	1989
Eric Wayne, Scott McAndrews	1990
Johnny DeCooman, Brad Koontz	1991
Chris Rush, Mark Reedy	1992
Adam Fahrer, Jeremy Smith	1993
Chris Molnar, Mark Ritter	1994
Steve Babinchak	1995
Kirk Diehl, Jeff Koontz	1996
Todd Young, Tom Molnar	1997

EQUIPMENT MANAGERS

Ollie Victor	1920-Mid 1920s
A.P. (Dean) Burell	Mid 1920s-1941
Oscar Buchenhorst	1941-1956
Mel Franks	1956-1963
Bud Thompson	1963-1964
John Tomco	1965-1969
Ed O'Hara	1969-1970
John Nolan	1971-1978
Tim Shope	1979-Present

CHAPTER 24

THE LION

LION MASCOTS

Richard Hoffman	1921-1923
Leon Skinner	1927
Eugene Wettstone	1939
Donald Newberry	1939
George Terwilliger	1939-1941
Tom Kelley	1941-1942
Robert Ritzmann	1942-1946
Peter Bates	1945-1946
Clark Sharon	1946-1947
Wendell Lomady	1947-1949
Michael Kurowki	1949-1950
John Waters	1950-1951
Alex Gregal	1951-1954
Alfred Klimcke	1954-1957
William Hillgartner	1957-1958
John Behler	1957-1960
Jack Lesyk	1960-1961
Paul Seltzer	1962-1963
Unknown	1963-1964
Martin Serota	1965-1967
Danny Kohlhepp	1967-1969
David Lacey	1969-1971
David Brazet	1971-1972
James Schaude	1972-1973
Robert Welsh	1973-1975
Andrew Bailey	1975-1977
Cliff Fiscus	1977-1978
Norman Constantinc	1978-1980
Roy Scott	1980-1982
David Daily	1982-1984
Robert Sterling	1984-1986
Doug Skinner	1986-1988
Peter Garland	1988-1990
Todd Shilkret	1990-1991
Tim Durant	1991-1993
Richard Williams	1993-1995
Brad Cornali	1995-1996
Nick Indeglio	1996-1998

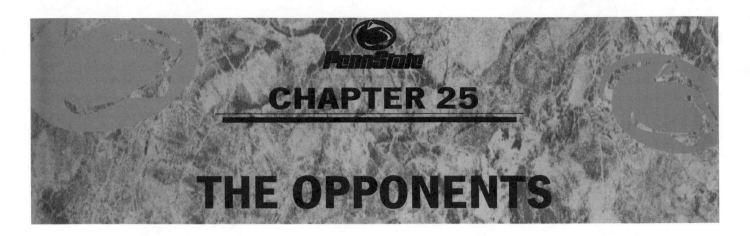

CHAPTER 25

THE OPPONENTS

BIG TEN

ILLINOIS
(5-1)

1954	September 25	W 14-12	Away	54,094
1959	October 24	W 20-9	Cleveland*	15,045
1960	October 22	L 8-10	Away	51,459
1972	October 7	W 35-17	Away	60,349
1993	November 13	W 28-14	Home	90,000
1994	November 12	W 35-31	Away	72,364
1997	October 4	W 41-6	Away	51,523

*Municipal Stadium

INDIANA
(4-0)

1993	November 6	W 38-31	Home	91,000
1994	November 5	W 35-29	Away	47,754
1995	October 28	W 45-21	Home	96,391
1996	October 26	W 48-26	Away	37,354

IOWA
(9-4)

1930	November 15	L 0-19	Away	20,000
1971	September 25	W 44-14	Away	44,303
1972	September 30	W 14-10	Home	58,065
1973	September 29	W 27-8	Home	59,980
1974	September 28	W 27-0	Away	46,500
1975	September 27	W 30-10	Away	52,780
1976	September 25	L 6-7	Home	61,268
1983	September 17	L 34-42	Home	84,628
1984	September 15	W 20-17	Away	66,145
1993	September 18	W 31-0	Away	70,397
1994	September 17	W 61-21	Home	95,834
1995	October 21	W 41-27	Away	70,397
1996	October 19	L 20-21	Home	96,653

MICHIGAN
(3-2)

1993	October 16	L 13-21	Home	96,719
1994	October 15	W 31-24	Away	106,832
1995	November 18	W 27-17	Home	80,000
1996	November 16	W 29-17	Away	105,898
1997	November 9	L 8-34	Home	97,498

MICHIGAN STATE
(5-9-1)

1914	November 13	L 3-6	Home	10,000
1925	October 24	W 13-6	Home	4,000
1945	November 17	L 0-33	Away	NA
1946	October 19	L 16-19	Home	17,149
1948	October 23	T 14-14	Home	24,579
1949	October 22	L 0-24	Away	NA
1951	October 20	L 21-32	Home	30,321
1952	October 25	L 7-34	Away	51,162
1965	September 25	L 0-23	Home	46,121
1966	September 24	L 8-42	Away	64,860
1993	November 27	W 38-37	Away	53,482
1994	November 26	W 59-31	Home	96,493
1995	November 25	W 24-20	Away	66,189
1996	November 23	W 32-29	Home	96,263
1997	November 29	L 14-49	Away	73,623

MINNESOTA
(3-0)

1993	September 4	W 38-20	Home	95,387
1994	September 3	W 56-3	Away	51,134
1997	October 18	W 16-15	Home	96,953

NORTHWESTERN
(4-1)

1993	November 20	W 43-21	Away	30,355
1994	November 19	W 45-17	Home	96,383
1995	November 4	L 10-21	Away	49,256
1996	November 2	W 34-9	Home	96,596
1997	November 1	W 30-27	Away	47,129

OHIO STATE
(8-5)

1912	November 16	W 37-0	Away	3,500
1956	October 20	W 7-6	Away	82,584
1963	November 9	W 10-7	Away	83,519
1964	November 7	W 27-0	Away	84,279
1975	September 20	L 9-17	Away	88,093
1976	September 18	L 7-12	Home	62,503
1978	September 16	W 19-0	Away	88,202
1980	December 26	W 31-19	Fiesta Bowl	66,738
1993	October 30	L 6-24	Away	95,060
1994	October 29	W 63-14	Home	97,079
1995	October 7	L 25-28	Home	96,655

| 1996 | October 5 | L 7-38 | Away | 94,241 |
| 1997 | October 11 | W 31-37 | Home | 97,282 |

PURDUE
(3-1-1)

1951	November 3	L 0-28	Away	21,000
1952	September 27	T 20-20	Home	20,506
1995	October 14	W 26-23	Away	60,445
1996	October 12	W 31-14	Home	96,653
1997	November 15	W 42-17	Away	52,156

WISCONSIN
(3-3)

1953	September 26	L 0-20	Away	49,000
1970	October 3	L 16-29	Away	55,204
1995	September 30	L 9-17	Home	96,540
1996	September 28	W 23-20	Away	79,607
1997	November 22	W 35-10	Home	96,934

OTHER

AIR FORCE
(3-0)

1962	September 29	W 20-6	Home	45,200
1971	October 2	W 16-14	Home	50,459
1973	October 6	W 19-9	Away	37,077

ALLEGHENY
(3-0)

1903	October 3	W 24-5	Home	NA
1904	October 1	W 50-0	Home	NA
1906	September 29	W 26-0	Home	NA

ALTOONA ATHLETIC ASSOCIATION
(2-0)

| 1890 | November 15 | W 68-0 | Home | NA |
| 1907 | September 21 | W 27-0 | Home | NA |

ARIZONA STATE
(1-0)

| 1977 | December 25 | W 42-30 | Fiesta Bowl | 57,766 |

ALABAMA
(5-8)

1959	December 19	W 7-0	Liberty Bowl*	36,211
1975	December 31	L 6-13	Sugar Bowl	75,212
1979	January 1	L 7-14	Sugar Bowl	76,824
1981	November 14	L 16-31	Home	85,133
1982	October 9	L 21-42	Birmingham, AL	76,821
1983	October 8	W 34-28	Home	85,614
1984	October 13	L 0-6	Away	60,210
1985	October 12	W 19-17	Home	85,444

1986	October 25	W 23-3	Away	60,210
1987	September 12	L 13-24	Home	85,619
1988	October 22	L 3-8	Birmingham, AL	75,808
1989	October 28	L 16-17	Home	85,975
1990	October 27	W 9-0	Away	70,123

*Philadelphia Municipal Stadium

ARMY
(13-10-2)

1899	October 7	W 6-0	Away	NA
1900	October 6	T 0-0	Away	NA
1939	November 18	T 14-14	Away	7,412
1949	October 1	L 7-42	Away	27,000
1950	October 7	L 7-41	Away	26,252
1955	October 1	L 6-35	Away	24,200
1956	October 8	L 7-14	Away	24,195
1957	October 5	L 13-27	Home	31,979
1958	October 4	L 0-26	Away	27,250
1959	October 10	W 17-11	Away	27,500
1960	October 8	W 27-16	Away	27,150
1961	October 14	L 6-10	Home	45,306
1962	October 13	L 6-9	Away	31,000
1963	October 12	L 7-10	Home	49,389
1964	October 10	W 6-2	Away	32,268
1966	October 1	L 0-11	Away	31,112
1968	November 2	W 28-24	Home	49,653
1970	October 24	W 38-14	Away	41,062
1971	October 9	W 42-0	Home	49,887
1972	October 14	W 45-0	Away	42,352
1973	October 13	W 54-3	Home	58,194
1974	October 5	W 21-14	Away	41,221
1975	October 25	W 31-0	Home	59,381
1976	October 9	W 38-16	Home	60,436
1979	October 13	W 24-3	Home	77,157

ARMY AMBULANCE CORPS
(1-0)

| 1917 | September 29 | W 10-0 | Allentown, PA | NA |

AUBURN
(1-0)

| 1996 | January 1 | W 43-14 | Outback Bowl | 65,313 |

BAYLOR
(1-0)

| 1975 | January 1 | W 41-20 | Cotton Bowl | 67,500 |

BELLEFONTE ACADEMY
(1-0)

| 1890 | NA | W 23-0 | Away | NA |

BLOOMSBURG
(1-0)

| 1897 | November 20 | W 10-0 | Home | NA |

BOSTON COLLEGE
(19-2)

1949	October 8	W 32-14	Home	18,041
1950	November 4	W 20-13	Away	8,000
1965	October 9	W 17-0	Away	24,300
1966	October 8	W 30-21	Home	30,924
1967	October 14	W 50-28	Away	15,500
1968	October 26	W 29-0	Away	25,272
1969	November 1	W 38-16	Home	46,652
1970	October 10	W 28-3	Away	25,252
1972	November 18	W 45-26	Away	23,119
1981	October 10	W 38-7	Home	84,473
1982	October 30	W 52-17	Away	33,205
1983	October 29	L 17-27	Away*	56,188
1984	November 3	W 37-30	Home	85,690
1985	November 2	W 16-12	Home	82,000
1986	September 20	W 26-14	Away*	42,329
1987	September 26	W 27-17	Away*	50,267
1988	September 17	W 23-20	Home	84,000
1989	September 23	W 7-3	Home	85,651
1990	October 20	W 40-21	Away	32,000
1991	September 28	W 28-21	Home	95,927
1992	October 17	L 32-35	Home	96,130

* Sullivan Stadium, Foxboro

BOSTON UNIVERSITY
(8 -0)

1951	September 29	W 40-34	Home	15,536
1953	October 10	W 35-13	Away	12,000
1955	September 24	W 35-0	Home	20,150
1956	November 10	W 40-7	Home	29,094
1958	October 18	W 34-0	Away	11,000
1959	October 16	W 21-12	Home	NA
1960	September 17	W 20-0	Home	22,559
1961	October 6	W 32-0	Away	10,150

BOWLING GREEN
(1-0)

1987	September 5	W 45-19	Home	85,574

BRIGHAM YOUNG
(2-1)

1989	December 29	W 50-39	Holiday Bowl	61,113
1991	September 21	W 33-7	Home	96,304
1992	October 31	L 17-30	Away	66,016

BUCKNELL
(28-10)

1887	November 5	W 54-0	Away	NA
1887	November 19	W 24-0	Home	NA
1889	November 25	W 12-0	Home	NA
1891	November 7	L 10-12	Away	NA
1892	November 12	W 18-0	Home	NA
1893	November 11	W 36-18	Away	2,000
1894	November 17	W 12-6	Williamsport	NA

1895	October 26	W 16-0	Williamsport	4,000
1896	October 31	L 0-10	Williamsport	NA
1897	November 13	W 27-4	Williamsport	NA
1898	November 5	W 16-0	Williamsport	NA
1899	November 4	L 0-5	Williamsport	3,000
1900	November 3	W 6-0	Williamsport	NA
1908	November 7	W 33-6	Home	NA
1909	November 6	W 33-0	Away	NA
1910	November 12	W 45-3	Home	NA
1916	October 7	W 50-7	Home	NA
1919	October 11	W 9-0	Home	NA
1926	November 13	W 9-0	Home	15,000
1927	October 8	L 7-13	Home	5,000
1928	October 13	L 0-6	Home	16,000
1929	November 16	L 6-27	Home	17,000
1930	November 1	L 7-19	Away	NA
1934	November 24	L 7-13	Home	10,000
1935	November 23	L 0-2	Away	8,500
1936	November 21	W 14-0	Home	9,227
1937	October 9	W 20-14	Home	11,376
1938	October 8	L 0-14	Home	12,071
1939	October 7	W 13-3	Home	11,143
1940	October 5	W 9-0	Home	12,091
1941	October 11	W 27-13	Home	16,000
1942	October 3	W 14-7	Home	10,303
1943	September 25	W 14-0	Home	6,639
1944	October 14	W 20-6	Home	9,000
1945	October 20	W 46-7	Away	5,319
1946	October 5	W 48-6	Home	12,401
1947	October 4	W 54-0	Home	12,294
1948	October 2	W 35-0	Home	14,423

BUFFALO
(0-1)

1900	November 29	L 0-10	Away	NA

CALIFORNIA
(3-1)

1961	October 28	W 33-16	Home	32,497
1962	October 27	W 23-21	Away	31,500
1965	October 30	L 17-21	Away	36,418
1966	October 29	W 35-15	Home	33,332

CALIFORNIA STATE
(1-0)

1905	September 30	W 29-0	Home	NA

CARLISLE INDIANS
(1-4-1)

1896	November 28	L 5-48	Harrisburg	NA
1905	October 7	L 0-11	Harrisburg	8,000
1906	October 6	W 4-0	Williamsport	NA
1907	October 5	L 5-18	Williamsport	NA
1908	October 3	L 5-12	Wilkes-Barre	10,000
1909	October 9	T 8-8	Wilkes-Barre	10,000

CARNEGIE TECH
(6-0)

1910	October 8	W 61-0	Home	NA
1912	October 5	W 41-0	Home	NA
1913	October 4	W 49-0	Home	NA
1921	November 5	W 28-7	Home	6,000
1922	November 11	W 10-0	Home	17,000
1924	November 8	W 22-7	Home	15,000

CINCINNATI
(7-1)

1981	September 12	W 52-0	Home	84,342
1983	September 10	L 3-14	Home	83,683
1985	November 9	W 31-10	Away*	33,528
1986	October 11	W 23-17	Home	84,812
1987	September 19	W 41-0	Home	82,000
1988	October 8	W 35-9	Home	85,693
1991	September 7	W 81-0	Home	94,000
1992	September 5	W 24-20	Away	29,099

*Riverfront Stadium

CLEMSON
(0-1)

1988	January 1	L 10-35	Citrus Bowl	53,152

COLGATE
(9-4-1)

1911	November 11	W 17-9	Home	NA
1930	October 25	L 0-40	Home	8,000
1931	November 8	L 7-32	Home	5,000
1932	October 29	L 0-31	Away	4,000
1941	October 4	L 0-7	Away*	23,467
1942	October 24	W 13-10	Home	11,510
1943	October 9	T 0-0	Home	6,933
1944	October 21	W 6-0	Home	3,000
1945	October 6	W 27-7	Home	9,619
1946	October 26	W 6-2	Away	13,500
1947	November 1	W 46-0	Home	14,014
1948	October 30	W 32-13	Away	10,000
1959	October 3	W 58-20	Home	NA
1980	September 6	W 54-10	Home	78,926

* Buffalo Civic Stadium

COLORADO
(1-1)

1969	September 27	W 27-3	Home	51,402
1970	September 26	L 13-41	Away	42,850

COLUMBIA
(0-2)

1933	October 28	L 0-33	Away	NA
1934	October 27	L 7-14	Away	23,000

CORNELL
(4-7-2)

1895	October 5	T 0-0	Away	1,000
1897	October 30	L 0-45	Away	NA
1907	October 19	W 8-6	Away	NA
1908	October 31	L 4-10	Away	NA
1911	October 14	W 5-0	Away	NA
1912	October 19	W 29-6	Away	NA
1919	November 15	W 20-0	Away	NA
1936	October 24	L 7-13	Away	6,000
1937	September 25	L 19-26	Away	6,000
1938	October 22	L 6-21	Away	7,000
1939	October 21	L 0-47	Away	5,099
1942	October 17	T 0-0	Away	5,000
1943	November 6	L 0-13	Away	6,617

DARTMOUTH
(1-2)

1917	November 3	L 7-10	Away	NA
1919	October 18	L 13-19	Away	4,500
1920	October 9	W 14-7	Home	12,000

DICKINSON
(11-5-1)

1888	October 31	T 6-6	Home	NA
1888	November 7	L 0-16	Away	NA
1891	November 26	W 2-0	Home	NA
1892	November 25	W 16-0	Harrisburg	NA
1896	October 10	W 8-0	Home	NA
1897	November 25	L 0-6	Sunbury	NA
1898	November 26	W 34-0	Williamsport	NA
1899	October 28	W 15-0	Home	NA
1900	October 20	L 0-18	Away	NA
1901	November 23	W 12-0	Home	1,500
1902	November 22	W 23-0	Away	NA
1903	November 14	L 0-6	Williamsport	NA
1904	November 12	W 11-0	Williamsport	NA
1905	November 18	W 6-0	Williamsport	8,000
1906	November 17	W 6-0	Williamsport	8,000
1907	November 2	W 52-0	Williamsport	NA
1931	October 17	L 6-10	Home	5,000

DICKINSON SEMINARY
(2-0)

1902	September 20	W 27-0	Home	NA
1903	September 19	W 60-0	Home	NA

DUQUESNE ATHLETIC CLUB
(0-3)

1898	October 29	L 5-18	Away	NA
1899	November 25	L 5-64	Away	NA
1900	October 27	L 0-29	Away	NA

EAST CAROLINA
(2-0)

1985	September 21	W 17-10	Home	84,266
1986	September 27	W 42-17	Home	84,744

EASTERN MICHIGAN
(1-0)

1992	September 19	W 52-7	Home	94,578

FLORIDA
(0-2)

1962	December 29	L 7-17	Gator Bowl	45,248
1998	January 1	L 6-21	Citrus Bowl	72,940

FLORIDA STATE
(0-2-1)

1967	December 30	T 17-17	Gator Bowl	68,019
1990	December 28	L 17-24	Blockbuster Bowl	74,021

FORDHAM
(3-0)

1946	November 2	W 68-0	Home	10,305
1947	October 11	W 75-0	Away	NA
1953	November 7	W 28-21	Home	13,897

FRANKLIN & MARSHALL
(2-1)

1890	October 12	L 0-10	Away	NA
1891	October 24	W 26-6	Away	NA
1925	October 3	W 13-0	Home	3,500

FURMAN
(1-0)

1958	November 1	W 36-0	Home	28,000

GENEVA
(7-0)

1904	November 19	W 44-0	Home	NA
1905	November 11	W 73-0	Home	NA
1907	September 28	W 34-0	Home	NA
1908	October 17	W 51-0	Home	NA
1909	October 16	W 46-0	Home	NA
1911	September 30	W 57-0	Home	NA
1916	November 4	W 79-0	Home	NA

GEORGETOWN
(1-0)

1950	September 30	W 34-14	Home	16,617

GEORGE WASHINGTON
(3-0)

1926	October 30	W 20-12	Home	3,500
1927	November 5	W 13-0	Home	3,500
1928	November 10	W 50-0	Home	5,000

GEORGIA
(1-0)

1982	January 1	W 27-23	Sugar Bowl	78,124

GEORGIA TECH
(3-3)

1921	October 29	W 28-7	New York***	30,000
1923	November 10	W 7-0	Home	10,000
1924	October 18	L 13-15	Away	30,000
1925	October 10	L 7-16	New York**	8,000
1961	December 30	W 30-15	Gator Bowl	50,000
1966	November 12	L 0-21	Away	50,172
1991	August 28	W 34-22	Kickoff Classic*	77,409

*Giants Stadium
**Yankee Stadium
***Polo Grounds

GETTYSBURG
(27-0-1)

1891	October 27	W 18-0	Away	NA
1894	October 13	W 60-0	Home	NA
1895	September 25	W 8-0	Home	NA
1896	September 26	W 40-0	Home	NA
1897	September 25	W 32-0	Home	NA
1926	October 30	W 20 12	Home	3,500
1927	November 5	W 13-0	Home	3,500
1928	November 10	W 50-0	Home	5,000

GROVE CITY
(3-0)

1907	October 12	W 46-0	Home	NA
1908	September 26	W 31-0	Home	NA
1909	October 2	W 31-0	Home	NA

HARRISBURG ATHLETIC CLUB
(1-0)

1910	October 1	W 58-0	Home	NA

HARVARD
(0-3-2)

1913	October 25	L 0-29	Away	NA
1914	October 24	T 13-13	Away	22,000
1915	October 30	L 0-13	Away	22,000
1921	October 22	T 21-21	Away	38,000
1932	October 15	L 13-46	Away	15,000

HAVERFORD
(1-0)

1891	December 5	W 58-0	Away	NA

HOLY CROSS
(9-0)

1954	November 6	W 39-7	Home	25,383
1956	October 13	W 43-0	Home	25,828
1957	November 16	W 14-10	Away	18,000
1958	November 15	W 32-0	Home	20,000
1959	November 14	W 46-0	Home	NA
1960	November 12	W 33-8	Away	14,856
1961	November 18	W 34-14	Home	32,796
1962	November 17	W 48-20	Away	11,825
1963	November 16	W 28-14	Home	24,644

HOMESTEAD ATHLETIC CLUB
(0-1)

| 1901 | November 2 | L 0-39 | Away | NA |

HOUSTON
(2-0)

| 1964 | November 14 | W 24-7 | Away | 25,000 |
| 1977 | September 17 | W 31-14 | Home | 62,554 |

JERSEY SHORE
(1-0)

| 1904 | October 29 | W 30-0 | Home | NA |

JOHN HOPKINS
(1-0)

| 1933 | November 11 | W 40-6 | Home | 5,000 |

KANSAS
(1-0)

| 1969 | January 1 | W 15-14 | Orange Bowl | 77,719 |

KANSAS STATE
(2-0)

| 1968 | September 28 | W 25-9 | Home | 45,024 |
| 1969 | October 4 | W 17-14 | Away | 37,000 |

KENT STATE
(1-0)

| 1965 | November 6 | W 21-6 | Home | 30,323 |

KENTUCKY
(2-2)

1975	October 4	W 10-3	Home	60,225
1976	October 2	L 6-22	Away	57,723
1977	October 1	L 20-24	Home	62,196
1978	October 7	W 30-0	Away	58,068

LAFAYETTE
(10-5-1)

1889	November 9	L 0-26	Away	NA
1891	October 2	W 14-4	Away	NA
1892	November 23	W 18-0	Wilkes-Barre	NA
1894	October 20	W 72-0	Home	NA
1897	October 2	L 0-24	Away	NA
1898	October 8	W 5-0	Away	NA
1914	October 31	W 17-0	Away	NA
1915	November 13	W 33-3	Away	NA
1916	November 17	W 40-0	Home	NA
1927	October 29	W 40-6	Home	11,000
1928	November 17	L 0-7	Away	NA
1929	October 26	W 6-3	Home	10,000
1930	October 18	T 0-0	Away	NA
1931	November 14	L 0-33	Away	NA
1934	November 17	W 25-6	Home	5,775
1938	November 5	L 0-7	Home	8,274

LEBANON VALLEY
(20-0)

1905	September 16	W 23-0	Home	NA
1906	September 22	W 24-0	Home	NA
1907	October 26	W 75-0	Home	NA
1915	October 2	W 13-0	Home	NA
1920	October 23	W 109-7	Home	2,500
1921	September 24	W 53-0	Home	2,500
1922	October 14	W 32-6	Home	3,000
1923	September 29	W 58-0	Home	3,000
1924	September 27	W 47-3	Home	3,500
1925	September 26	W 14-0	Home	3,500
1926	October 2	W 35-0	Home	3,500
1927	September 24	W 27-0	Home	3,500
1928	September 29	W 25-0	Home	4,000
1929	October 5	W 15-0	Home	4,000
1930	October 4	W 27-0	Home	4,000
1931	October 3	W 19-6	Home	4,000
1932	October 1	W 27-0	Home	2,500
1933	October 7	W 32-6	Home	3,000
1934	October 6	W 13-0	Home	5,422
1935	October 5	W 12-6	Home	5,848

LEHIGH
(16-6-1)

1888	November	L 0-30	Home	NA
1889	November 11	L 0-106	Away	NA
1891	October 3	L 2-24	Away	NA
1901	November 16	W 38-0	Williamsport	1,500
1914	November 7	L 7-20	Away	NA
1915	November 5	W 7-0	Home	NA
1916	November 11	W 10-7	Away	NA
1917	November 10	L 0-9	Home	NA
1918	November 16	W 7-6	Away	NA
1919	November 8	W 20-7	Home	6,000
1920	November 13	T 7-7	Away	5,000
1921	October 15	W 28-7	Home	4,000
1931	November 28	W 31-0	Philadelphia*	2,500
1933	October 21	W 33-0	Home	5,000
1934	October 20	W 31-0	Away	NA
1935	October 19	W 26-0	Home	7,113
1936	October 17	L 6-7	Away	NA
1937	October 16	W 14-7	Home	7,660
1938	October 15	W 59-6	Away	NA
1939	October 14	W 49-7	Home	9,419

1940	October 19	W 34-0	Away	NA
1941	October 25	W 40-6	Home	NA
1942	October 10	W 19-3	Away	NA

*Franklin Field

LOUISIANA STATE
(1-0)

1974	January 1	W 16-9	Orange Bowl	60,477

LOUISVILLE
(2-0)

1996	September 7	W 24-7	Home	95,670
1997	September 28	W 57-21	Away	39,826

MANSFIELD
(1-0)

1899	September 23	W 38-0	Home	NA

MARIETTA
(3-0)

1924	November 22	W 28-0	Home	3,500
1925	October 17	W 13-0	Home	3,500
1926	October 9	W 48-6	Home	4,000

MARQUETTE
(2-0)

1957	November 9	W 20-7	Away	4,719
1958	October 11	W 40-8	Home	22,000

MARSHALL
(2-0)

1929	October 12	W 26-7	Home	5,000
1930	October 11	W 65-0	Home	5,000

MARYLAND
(35-1-1)

1917	November 17	W 57-0	Home	NA
1937	November 13	W 21-14	Home	7,535
1938	October 1	W 33-0	Home	9,846
1939	November 4	W 12-0	Home	7,690
1943	October 23	W 45-0	Away	5,000
1944	November 18	W 34-19	Home	NA
1960	November 5	W 28-9	Home	30,126
1961	November 4	L 17-21	Away	34,000
1962	November 3	W 23-7	Home	41,834
1963	November 2	W 17-15	Away	35,500
1964	October 31	W 17-9	Home	33,500
1965	December 4	W 19-7	Away	24,000
1966	September 17	W 15-7	Home	40,911
1967	November 4	W 38-3	Away	34,700
1968	November 16	W 57-13	Away	30,000
1969	November 15	W 48-0	Home	46,106
1970	November 7	W 34-0	Away	23,400
1971	November 6	W 63-27	Home	50,144
1972	November 4	W 46-16	Home	58,171
1973	November 3	W 42-22	Away	44,135

1974	November 2	W 24-17	Home	60,125
1975	November 1	W 15-13	Away	59,973
1977	September 24	W 27-9	Home	62,079
1978	November 4	W 27-3	Home	78,019
1979	October 6	W 27-7	Away	52,348
1980	October 11	W 24-10	Away	48,123
1982	September 11	W 39-31	Home	84,597
1984	October 6	W 25-24	Home	85,486
1985	September 7	W 20-18	Away	50,750
1986	November 8	W 17-15	Home	85,561
1987	November 7	W 21-16	Baltimore*	62,500
1988	November 5	W 17-10	Home	78,000
1989	November 11	T 13-13	Baltimore*	61,215
1990	November 10	W 24-10	Home	83,000
1991	November 9	W 47-7	Baltimore*	57,416
1992	September 26	W 49-13	Home	95,891
1993	October 2	W 70-7	Away	42,008

*Memorial Stadium

MIAMI
(6-5)

1961	September 29	L 8-25	Away	45,687
1967	September 29	W 17-8	Away	39,516
1968	November 9	W 22-7	Home	50,132
1976	November 13	W 21-7	Away	19,627
1977	October 29	W 49-7	Home	61,853
1979	November 3	L 10-26	Home	75,332
1980	November 1	W 27-12	Home	83,661
1981	October 31	L 14-17	Away	32,117
1987	January 2	W 14-10	Fiesta Bowl	73,098
1991	October 12	L 20-26	Away	75,723
1992	October 10	L 14-17	Home	96,704

MIDDLEBURY
(1-0)

1922	October 21	W 33-0	Home	4,000

MISSOURI
(3-1)

1959	September 19	W 19-8	Away	28,000
1960	October 1	L 8-21	Home	33,613
1969	January 1	W 10-3	Orange Bowl	77,282
1980	October 4	W 29-21	Away	75,298

MUHLENBURG
(5-1)

1914	October 3	W 22-0	Home	NA
1920	September 25	W 27-7	Home	2,500
1933	October 14	L 0-3	Home	4,000
1936	October 3	W 45-0	Home	7,535
1944	September 30	W 58-13	Home	2,799
1945	September 29	W 47-7	Home	5, 048

NAVY
(18-17-2)

1894	November 10	T 6-6	Away	NA
1897	October 20	L 0-4	Away	NA
1898	October 22	L 11-16	Away	NA
1899	October 21	L 0-6	Away	NA

1900	November 10	L 0-44	Away	NA
1901	October 26	W 11-6	Away	NA
1902	November 1	W 6-0	Away	NA
1903	October 31	W 17-0	Away	NA
1904	November 5	L 9-20	Away	NA
1905	November 4	L 5-11	Away	NA
1906	November 3	W 5-0	Away	5,000
1907	November 16	L 4-6	Away	NA
1908	November 14	L 0-5	Away	NA
1911	November 18	T 0-0	Away	NA
1913	November 15	L 0-10	Away	NA
1921	November 12	W 13-7	Philadelphia*	25,000
1922	November 3	L 0-14	Washington**	30,000
1923	October 20	W 21-3	Home	15,000
1924	November 1	W 6-0	Away	NA
1943	October 16	L 6-14	Away	NA
1944	October 7	L 14-55	Away	NA
1945	October 13	L 0-28	Away	16,148
1946	November 16	W 12-7	Away	22,000
1947	November 15	W 20-7	Baltimore***	25,000
1955	October 15	L 14-34	Home	32,209
1961	September 23	W 20-10	Home	38,437
1962	September 22	W 41-7	Home	42,653
1964	September 19	L 8-21	Home	44,800
1965	November 13	W 14-6	Home	47,163
1967	September 23	L 22-23	Away	20,101
1968	September 21	W 31-6	Home	49,273
1969	September 20	W 45-22	Away	28,796
1970	September 19	W 55-7	Home	48,566
1971	September 18	W 56-3	Away	26,855
1972	September 23	W 21-10	Home	50,547
1973	September 22	W 39-0	Away	28,383
1974	September 21	L 6-7	Home	42,000

*Franklin Field
**American League Park
***Memorial Stadium

NEBRASKA
(6-5)

1920	November 6	W 20-0	Home	9,000
1949	October 15	W 22-7	Home	23,956
1950	October 21	L 0-19	Away	38,000
1951	October 13	W 15-7	Away	39,000
1952	October 18	W 10-0	Home	28,551
1958	September 20	L 7-14	Away	30,000
1979	September 29	L 17-42	Away	76,151
1980	September 27	L 7-21	Home	84,585
1981	September 26	W 30-24	Away	76,308
1982	September 25	W 27-24	Home	85,304
1983	August 29	L 6-44	Kickoff Classic*	71,123

*Giants Stadium

NEW YORK UNIVERSITY
(2-1-1)

1927	November 12	T 13-13	Home	9,000
1929	October 19	L 0-7	Away	35,000
1940	November 16	W 25-0	Home	9,449
1941	October 31	W 42-0	Away*	10,690

*NY Polo Grounds

NIAGARA
(2-0)

1929	September 28	W 16-0	Home	4,000
1930	September 27	W 31-14	Home	4,000

NORTH CAROLINA
(0-1)

1943	October 2	L 0-19	Away	9,983

NORTH CAROLINA STATE
(17-2)

1920	October 16	W 41-0	Home	3,500
1921	October 8	W 35-0	Home	3,000
1923	October 6	W 16-0	Home	3,000
1924	October 4	W 51-6	Home	3,500
1956	November 17	W 14-7	Home	22,864
1967	November 11	W 13-8	Home	46,497
1969	November 29	W 33-8	Away	24,150
1971	November 13	W 35-3	Home	50,477
1972	November 11	W 37-22	Home	54,274
1973	November 10	W 35-29	Home	59,424
1974	November 9	L 7-12	Away	47,700
1975	November 8	L 14-15	Home	59,536
1976	November 6	W 41-20	Home	60,426
1977	November 5	W 21-17	Away	44,800
1978	November 11	W 19-10	Home	77,043
1979	November 10	W 9-7	Away	51,200
1980	November 8	W 21-13	Home	83,847
1981	November 7	W 22-15	Away	48,800
1982	November 6	W 54-0	Home	84,837

NORTHERN ILLINOIS
(1-0)

1996	September 14	W 49-0	Home	95,589

NOTRE DAME
(8-8-1)

1913	November 8	L 7-14	Home	NA
1925	November 7	T 0-0	Home	25,000
1926	October 6	L 0-28	Away	28,000
1928	November 3	L 0-9	Philadelphia*	35,000
1976	December 27	L 9-20	Gator Bowl	67,827
1981	November 21	W 24-21	Home	84,175
1982	November 13	W 24-14	Away	59,075
1983	November 12	W 34-30	Home	85,899
1984	November 17	L 7-44	Away	59,075
1985	November 16	W 36-6	Home	84,000
1986	November 15	W 24-19	Away	59,075
1987	November 21	W 21-20	Home	84,000
1988	November 19	L 3-21	Away	59,075
1989	November 18	L 23-34	Home	86,016
1990	November 17	W 24-21	Away	59,075
1991	November 16	W 35-13	Home	96,672
1992	November 14	L 16-17	Away	59,075

*Franklin Field

OBERLIN
(1-0)

1894	November 24	W 9-6	Away	NA

OHIO UNIVERSITY
(5-0)

1967	November 18	W 35-14	Home	29,556
1969	October 25	W 42-3	Home	49,069
1970	November 14	W 32-22	Home	43,000
1973	November 17	W 49-10	Home	51,804
1974	November 16	W 35-16	Home	58,700

OKLAHOMA
(0-2)

1972	December 31	L 0-14	Sugar Bowl	80,123
1985	January 1	L 10-25	Orange Bowl	74,148

OREGON
(3-1)

1960	December 17	W 41-12	Liberty Bowl*	16,697
1963	September 12	W 17-7	Away	33,220
1964	October 3	L 14-22	Home	44,803
1995	January 2	W 38-20	Rose Bowl	102,247

*Philadelphia

PENNSYLVANIA
(18-25-4)

1890	October 10	L 0-20	Away	NA
1892	October 1	L 0-20	Away	NA
1893	October 25	L 6-18	Away	NA
1895	November 9	L 4-35	Away	5,000
1896	November 14	L 0-27	Away	NA
1897	October 16	L 0-24	Away	NA
1898	October 1	L 0-40	Away	NA
1899	November 17	L 0-47	Away	NA
1900	October 17	L 5-17	Away	NA
1901	October 5	L 6-23	Away	NA
1902	October 4	L 0-17	Away	NA
1903	October 10	L 0-39	Away	NA
1904	September 24	L 0-6	Away	NA
1907	November 9	L 0-28	Away	NA
1908	October 10	L 0-6	Away	7,000
1909	October 23	T 3-3	Away	12,000
1910	October 22	L 0-10	Away	NA
1911	October 28	W 22-6	Away	15,000
1912	November 2	W 14-0	Away	15,000
1913	November 1	L 0-17	Away	NA
1915	October 9	W 13-3	Away	NA
1916	October 21	L 0-15	Away	NA
1919	November 1	W 10-0	Away	20,000
1920	October 30	W 28-7	Away	30,000
1922	November 18	L 6-7	Away	50,000
1923	November 17	W 21-0	Away	56,000
1924	November 15	T 0-0	Away	52,000
1926	November 6	L 0-3	Away	55,000
1927	October 15	W 20-0	Away	65,000
1928	October 20	L 0-14	Away	65,000
1929	November 9	W 19-7	Away	60,000

1933	November 18	T 6-6	Away	20,000
1934	November 10	L 0-3	Away	35,000
1935	November 16	L 6-33	Away	40,000
1936	November 14	L 12-19	Away	40,000
1937	November 6	W 7-0	Away	50,000
1938	November 12	T 7-7	Away	50,000
1939	November 11	W 10-0	Away	40,000
1942	November 14	W 13-7	Away	50,000
1948	November 6	W 13-0	Away	71,180
1952	November 1	W 14-7	Away	67,000
1953	October 3	L 7-13	Away	51,000
1954	October 30	W 35-13	Away	33,125
1955	October 29	W 20-0	Away	28,000
1956	September 29	W 34-0	Away	23,390
1957	September 28	W 19-14	Away	21,150
1958	September 27	W 43-0	Away	19,549

PITTSBURGH
(48-41-4)

1893	November 6	W 32-0	Home	NA
1896	October 3	W 10-4	Home	NA
1900	September 30	W 12-0	Bellefonte	1,000
1901	September 29	W 37-0	Bellefonte	NA
1902	September 27	W 27-0	Home	NA
1903	October 24	W 59-0	Away*	NA
1904	November 24	L 5-22	Away*	8,500
1905	November 30	W 6-0	Away*	2,400
1906	November 29	W 6-0	Away*	NA
1907	November 28	L 0-6	Away*	11,000
1908	November 26	W 12-6	Away*	NA
1909	November 25	W 5-0	Away**	NA
1910	November 24	L 0-11	Away**	18,000
1911	November 30	W 3-0	Away**	15,000
1912	November 28	W 38-0	Away**	NA
1913	November 27	L 6-7	Away**	NA
1914	November 26	L 3-13	Away**	17,000
1915	November 25	L 0-20	Away**	30,000
1916	November 30	L 0-31	Away**	NA
1917	November 29	L 6-28	Away**	20,000
1918	November 28	L 6-28	Away**	NA
1919	November 27	W 20-0	Away**	40,000
1920	November 25	T 0-0	Away**	NA
1921	November 24	T 0-0	Away**	34,000
1922	November 30	L 0-14	Away**	35,000
1923	November 29	L 3-20	Away**	33,000
1924	November 27	L 3-24	Away**	33,000
1925	November 26	L 7-23	Away	34,715
1926	November 25	L 6-24	Away	42,915
1927	November 24	L 0-30	Away	57,051
1928	November 29	L 0-26	Away	32,209
1929	November 28	L 7-20	Away	25,755
1930	November 26	L 12-19	Away	15,816
1931	October 31	L 6-41	Home	7,000
1935	October 26	L 0-9	Away	17,310
1936	November 7	L 7-34	Away	15,692
1937	November 20	L 7-28	Away	19,936
1938	November 19	L 0-26	Away	16,881
1939	November 25	W 10-0	Home	20,000
1940	November 23	L 7-20	Away	30,083
1941	November 22	W 31-7	Away	30,696
1942	November 21	W14-6	Home	11,710
1943	November 20	W 14-0	Away	12,242
1944	November 25	L 0-14	Away	8,840
1945	November 24	L 0-7	Away	11,354
1946	November 23	L 7-14	Away	42,124
1947	November 22	W 29-0	Away	47,822
1948	November 20	L 0-7	Away	49,444
1949	November 19	L 0-19	Away	43,308
1950	November 25	W 21-20	Away**	12,250

1951	November 24	L 7-13	Away	22,771
1952	November 22	W 17-0	Away	53,766
1953	November 21	W 17-0	Away	39,642
1954	November 20	W 13-0	Away	NA
1955	November 19	L 0-20	Home	29,361
1956	November 24	T 7-7	Away	51,308
1957	November 23	L 13-14	Away	44,710
1958	November 27	W 25-21	Away	39,479
1959	November 21	L 7-22	Away	46,104
1960	November 19	W 14-3	Away	45,023
1961	November 25	W 47-26	Away	37,261
1962	November 24	W 16-0	Away	45,149
1963	December 7	L 21-22	Away	51,477
1964	November 21	W 28-0	Home	50,144
1965	November 20	L 27-30	Away	35,576
1966	November 19	W 48-24	Away	30,467
1967	November 25	W 42-6	Home	36,008
1968	November 23	W 65-9	Away	31,224
1969	November 22	W 27-7	Away	39,517
1970	November 21	W 35-15	Home	50,017
1971	November 20	W 55-18	Away	39,539
1972	November 25	W 49-27	Home	38,600
1973	November 24	W 35-13	Home	56,600
1974	November 28	W 31-10	Away***	48,895
1975	November 22	W 7-6	Away***	46,846
1976	November 26	L 7-24	Away***	50,360
1977	November 26	W 15-13	Away	56,500
1978	November 24	W 17-10	Home	77,465
1979	December 1	L 14-29	Home	76,958
1980	November 28	L 9-14	Home	82,459
1981	November 28	W 48-14	Away	60,260
1982	November 26	W 19-10	Home	85,522
1983	November 19	T 24-24	Away	60,283
1984	November 24	L 11-31	Home	85,499
1985	November 23	W 31-0	Away	60,134
1986	November 22	W 34-14	Home	85,722
1987	November 14	L 0-10	Away	56,500
1988	November 12	L 7-14	Home	85,701
1989	November 25	W 16-13	Away	57,158
1990	November 24	W 22-17	Home	85,180
1991	November 28	W 32-20	Away	52,519
1992	November 21	W 57-13	Home	91,000
1997	September 6	W 34-17	Home	97,115

*Exposition Park
**Forbes Field
***Three Rivers Stadium

PITTSBURGH ATHLETIC CLUB
(3-1)

1892	November 5	W 16-0	Away	NA
1893	November 30	W 12-0	Away	NA
1894	November 29	W 14-0	Away	NA
1895	November 16	L 10-11	Away	2,000

PRINCETON
(0-5)

1896	October 24	L 0-39	Away	NA
1897	October 13	L 0-34	Away	NA
1898	October 26	L 0-5	Away	NA
1899	October 18	L 0-12	Away	NA
1900	October 10	L 0-26	Away	NA

RICE
(2-0)

1962	October 6	W 18-7	Away	35,982
1963	October 5	W 28-7	Home	38,275

RUTGERS
(22-2)

1918	November 9	L 3-26	Home	NA
1950	November 18	W 18-14	Home	15,299
1951	November 17	W 13-7	Away	15,000
1952	November 15	W 7-6	Home	15,957
1953	November 14	W 54-26	Away	9,500
1954	November 13	W 37-14	Home	16,623
1955	November 12	W 34-13	Away	12,000
1977	September 2	W 45-7	E.Rutherford*	64,790
1978	September 9	W 26-10	Home	77,154
1979	September 15	W 45-10	Home	77,309
1982	September 18	W 49-14	Home	83,268
1983	October 1	W 36-25	E.Rutherford*	32,804
1984	September 8	W 15-12	Home	84,409
1985	September 28	W 17-10	E.Rutherford*	54,560
1986	October 4	W 31-6	Home	84,000
1987	October 10	W 35-21	Home	85,376
1988	September 24	L 16-21	Home	85,531
1989	October 7	W 17-10	E.Rutherford*	57,688
1990	September 22	W 28-0	Home	85,194
1991	October 19	W 37-17	Home	95,729
1992	October 3	W 38-24	E.Rutherford*	61,562
1993	September 25	W 31-7	Home	95,092
1994	September 24	W 55-27	Home	95,379
1995	September 23	W 59-34	E.Rutherford*	58,870

*Giants Stadium

ST. BONAVENTURE
(4-0)

1910	November 5	W 34-0	Home	NA
1911	November 4	W 46-0	Home	NA
1917	October 13	W 99-0	Home	NA
1922	September 23	W 54-0	Home	3,000

SEWANEE
(1-0)

1932	November 5	W 18-6	Home	5,500

SOUTH CAROLINA
(2-0)

1940	November 2	W 12-0	Home	9,346
1941	November 29	W 19-12	Away	NA

SOUTHERN CALIFORNIA
(3-3)

1923	January 1	L 3-14	Rose Bowl	43,000
1981	January 1	W 26-10	Fiesta Bowl	71,053
1990	September 15	L 14-19	Away	70,594
1991	September 14	L 10-21	Away	64,758

1993	September 11	W 21-20	Home	95,992
1994	September 10	W 38-14	Home	96,463
1996	August 25	W 24-7	Kickoff Classic*	77,716

*Giants Stadium

SOUTHERN METHODIST
(1-0-1)

1948	January 1	T 13-13	Cotton Bowl	43,000
1978	September 23	W 26-21	Home	77,704

STANFORD
(4-2)

1973	September 15	W 20-6	Away	57,000
1974	September 14	W 24-20	Home	58,200
1975	September 13	W 34-14	Home	61,325
1976	September 11	W 15-12	Home	61,645
1993	January 1	L 3-24	Blockbuster Bowl	45,554

STEELTON YMCA
(0-1)

1902	November 27	L 5-6	Away	NA

STERLING ATHLETIC CLUB
(1-0)

1910	October 15	W 45-0	Home	NA

SUSQUEHANNA
(6-0)

1898	October 15	W 45-6	Home	NA
1900	September 23	W 17-0	Home	NA
1901	September 22	W 17-0	Home	NA
1902	October 25	W 55-0	Home	NA
1916	September 23	W 27-0	Home	NA
1926	September 25	W 82-0	Home	3,500

SWARTHMORE
(2-0)

1889	NA	W 20-6	Home	NA
1891	October 17	W 44-0	Away	NA

SYRACUSE
(40-23-5)

1922	October 28	T 0-0	New York**	25,000
1923	November 3	L 0-10	Away	25,000
1924	October 25	L 6-10	Away	NA
1925	October 31	L 0-7	Away	NA
1926	October 23	L 0-10	Home	8,000
1927	October 22	W 9-6	Away	25,000
1928	October 27	T 6-6	Home	15,000
1929	November 2	W 6-4	Away	NA
1930	November 8	T 0-0	Home	7,000
1931	October 24	L 0-7	Away	NA
1932	October 22	L 6-12	Home	6,000
1933	November 4	L 6-12	Away	NA

1934	November 3	L 0-16	Home	8,013
1935	November 2	L 3-7	Away	12,000
1936	October 31	W 18-0	Home	7,137
1937	October 30	L 13-19	Away	NA
1938	October 29	W 33-6	Home	10,659
1939	October 28	T 6-6	Away	NA
1940	November 9	T 13-13	Away	NA
1941	November 8	W 34-19	Home	16,000
1942	November 7	W 18-13	Home	8,856
1944	November 4	W 41-0	Away	NA
1945	November 3	W 26-0	Home	8,505
1946	October 12	W 9-0	Away	12,000
1947	October 18	W 40-0	Home	16,632
1948	October 8	W 34-14	Away	14,000
1949	October 29	W 33-21	Home	18,758
1950	October 14	L 7-27	Away	17,500
1951	November 10	W 32-13	Home	16,612
1952	November 8	L 7-25	Away	16,000
1953	October 17	W 20-14	Home	20,712
1954	October 2	W 13-0	Away	18,000
1955	November 5	W 21-20	Home	30,321
1956	November 3	L 9-13	Away	35,475
1957	October 26	W 20-12	Away	35,000
1958	October 25	L 6-14	Home	27,000
1959	November 7	L 18-20	Home	34,000
1960	October 15	L 15-21	Away	40,617
1961	October 21	W 14-0	Home	44,674
1962	October 20	W 20-19	Home	48,356
1963	October 19	L 0-9	Away	39,209
1964	October 17	L 14-21	Home	47,998
1965	October 16	L 21-28	Away	39,000
1966	November 5	L 10-12	Home	45,126
1967	October 28	W 29-20	Away	41,750
1968	December 7	W 30-12	Home	41,393
1969	October 18	W 15-14	Away	42,291
1970	October 17	L 7-24	Home	50,540
1971	October 16	W 31-0	Away	41,382
1972	October 21	W 17-0	Home	60,465
1973	October 20	W 49-6	Away	27,595
1974	October 19	W 30-14	Home	59,100
1975	October 18	W 19-7	Away	28,153
1976	October 16	W 27-3	Home	61,474
1977	October 15	W 31-24	Away	27,029
1978	October 21	W 45-15	Home	77,827
1979	October 20	W 35-7	E.Rutherford*	53,789
1980	October 18	W 24-7	Home	84,000
1981	October 17	W 41-16	Away	50,037
1982	October 16	W 28-7	Home	84,762
1983	October 15	W 17-6	Away	50,010
1984	October 20	W 21-3	Home	85,850
1985	October 19	W 24-20	Away	50,021
1986	October 18	W 42-3	Home	85,512
1987	October 17	L 21-48	Away	50,011
1988	October 15	L 10-24	Home	85,916
1989	October 14	W 34-12	Away	49,876
1990	October 13	W 27-21	Home	86,002

*Giants Stadium
*NY Polo Grounds

TEMPLE
(29-3-1)

1931	October 10	L 0-12	Away	20,000
1932	November 12	L 12-13	Away	15,000
1940	October 26	W 18-0	Away	13,078
1941	October 18	L 0-14	Away	25,000
1943	November 13	W 13-0	Home	4,142
1944	November 11	W 7-6	Away	12,000

1945	November 10	W 27-0	Home	13,135
1946	November 9	W 26-0	Home	13,536
1947	November 8	W 7-0	Away	20,000
1948	November 13	W 47-0	Home	16,555
1949	November 12	W 28-7	Away	18,000
1950	October 28	T 7-7	Home	20,782
1952	September 20	W 20-13	Home	15,889
1975	September 6	W 26-25	Away*	57,112
1976	October 30	W 31-30	Away**	42,005
1977	November 12	W 44-7	Home	61,327
1978	September 1	W 10-7	Away**	53,103
1979	November 17	W 22-7	Home	76,000
1980	November 15	W 50-7	Away**	49,313
1981	October 3	W 30-0	Home	84,562
1982	September 4	W 31-14	Home	80,000
1983	September 24	W 23-18	Away**	35,760
1985	September 14	W 27-25	Home	84,651
1986	September 6	W 45-15	Home	85,732
1987	October 3	W 27-13	Home	84,000
1988	October 1	W 45-9	Away**	66,592
1989	September 16	W 42-3	Home	84,790
1990	October 6	W 48-10	Home	85,874
1991	October 5	W 24-7	Away**	43,808
1992	September 12	W 49-8	Home	94,892
1994	October 1	W 48-21	Away*	38,410
1995	September 16	W 66-14	Home	95,926
1996	September 21	W 41-0	E.Rutherford***	24,847

*Franklin Field
**Veterans Stadium
*** Giants Stadium

TENNESSEE
(2-2)

1971	December 4	L 11-31	Away	59,542
1972	September 16	L 21-28	Away	71,647
1991	January 1	W 42-17	Fiesta Bowl	71,133
1994	January 1	W 31-13	Citrus Bowl	72,456

TEXAS
(3-2)

1972	January 1	W 30-6	Cotton Bowl	72,000
1984	September 29	L 3-28	E.Rutherford*	76,883
1989	September 30	W 16-12	Away	75,232
1990	September 8	L 13-17	Home	85,973
1997	January 1	W 38-15	Fiesta Bowl	65,106

*Giants Stadium

TEXAS A&M
(1-1)

1979	September 22	L 14-27	Home	77,575
1980	September 20	W 25-9	Away	66,234

TEXAS CHRISTIAN
(3-1)

1953	October 24	W 27-21	Home	27,966
1954	October 23	L 7-20	Away	15,000
1971	October 23	W 66-14	Home	51,896
1978	September 30	W 58-0	Home	76,832

TEXAS TECH
(1-0)

1995	September 9	W 24-23	Home	96,035

TULANE
(1-0)

1979	December 22	W 9-6	Liberty Bowl*	50,021

*Memphis

UCLA
(2-4)

1963	September 28	W 17-14	Home	36,327
1964	September 26	L 14-21	Away	34,636
1965	October 2	L 22-24	Home	46,429
1966	October 15	L 11-49	Away	37,271
1967	October 7	L 15-17	Home	46,007
1968	October 12	W 21-6	Away	35,772

URSINUS
(2-0)

1914	October 17	W 30-0	Home	NA
1919	October 25	W 48-7	Home	NA

UTAH STATE
(1-0)

1977	October 8	W 16-7	Home	62,015

VANDERBILT
(0-1)

1957	October 19	L 20-32	Home	26,781

VILLANOVA
(5-3-1)

1902	October 11	W 32-0	Home	NA
1905	October 28	W 29-0	Home	NA
1910	October 29	T 0-0	Home	NA
1911	October 21	W 18-0	Away	NA
1912	November 9	W 71-0	Home	NA
1935	November 9	W 27-13	Home	8,150
1936	October 10	L 0-13	Home	9,593
1949	September 24	L 6-27	Home	22,080
1951	October 6	L 14-20	Away*	NA

*Allentown

VIRGINIA
(4-1)

1893	October 14	W 6-0	Away	NA
1954	October 9	W 34-7	Home	21,820

1955	October 8	W 26-7	Away*	NA
1988	September 10	W 42-14	Away	45,000
1989	September 9	L 6-14	Home	85,956

*Richmond-City Stadium

VMI
(1-0)

| 1959 | September 26 | W 21-0 | Home | NA |

WAKE FOREST
(1-0)

| 1974 | October 12 | W 55-0 | Home | 56,500 |

WASHINGTON
(2-0)

| 1921 | December 3 | W 21-7 | Away | 35,000 |
| 1983 | December 26 | W 13-10 | Aloha Bowl | 37,212 |

WASHINGTON & JEFFERSON
(5-2-2)

1894	November 23	W 6-0	Away	NA
1895	November 18	T 6-6	Away	NA
1898	November 19	W 11-6	Away	NA
1899	October 13	T 0-0	Home	NA
1903	November 26	W 22-0	Away*	7,000
1904	October 22	W 12-0	Away*	NA
1912	October 12	W 30-0	Home	4,000
1913	October 18	L 0-17	Away	7,000
1917	October 20	L 0-7	Away	NA

*Pittsburgh Exposition Park

WASHINGTON STATE
(2-0)

| 1947 | September 20 | W 27-4 | Away* | 15,000 |
| 1948 | November 27 | W 7-0 | Away** | NA |

*Hershey
**Tacoma, Washington

WAYNESBURG
(0-2)

| 1931 | September 26 | L 0-7 | Home | 3,000 |
| 1932 | October 8 | L 6-7 | Home | 4,000 |

WESTERN MARYLAND
(1-0)

| 1935 | October 12 | W 2-0 | Home | 7,140 |

WESTERN RESERVE
(0-0-1)

| 1895 | November 28 | T 8-8 | Away | NA |

WESTMINSTER
(3-0)

1914	September 26	W 13-0	Home	NA
1915	September 25	W 26-0	Home	NA
1916	September 30	W 55-0	Home	NA

WEST VIRGINIA
(48-9-2)

1904	October 15	W 34-0	Home	NA
1905	November 24	W 6-0	Home	NA
1906	November 24	W 10-0	Home	NA
1908	October 24	W 12-0	Home	NA
1909	November 13	W 40-0	Home	NA
1923	October 27	T 13-13	New York*	50,000
1925	November 14	L 0-14	Away	20,000
1931	November 21	L 0-19	Away	6,500
1940	October 12	W 17-13	Home	10,574
1941	November 15	W 7-0	Home	NA
1942	October 31	L 0-24	Away	12,000
1943	October 30	W 32-7	Home	4,494
1944	October 28	L 27-28	Home	5,534
1947	October 25	W 21-14	Home	20,313
1948	October 16	W 37-7	Home	17,814
1949	November 5	W 34-14	Away	21,000
1950	November 11	W 27-0	Home	16,338
1951	October 27	W 13-7	Home	17,206
1952	October 11	W 35-21	Away	18,500
1953	October 31	L 19-20	Home	24,670
1954	October 16	L 14-19	Home	32,384
1955	October 22	L 7-21	Away	34,400
1956	October 27	W 16-6	Home	29,244
1957	November 2	W 27-6	Home	28,712
1958	November 8	T 14-14	Away	26,000
1959	October 31	W 28-10	Away	NA
1960	October 29	W 34-13	Home	37,715
1961	November 11	W 20-6	Away	30,000
1962	November 10	W 34-6	Home	33,212
1963	October 26	W 20-9	Home	45,159
1964	October 24	W 37-8	Away	26,000
1965	October 23	W 44-6	Home	44,230
1966	October 22	W 38-6	Away	15,835
1967	October 21	W 21-14	Home	44,460
1968	October 5	W 31-20	Away	34,500
1969	October 11	W 20-0	Home	52,713
1970	October 31	W 42-8	Home	49,932
1971	October 30	W 35-7	Away	37,000
1972	October 28	W 28-19	Away	37,000
1973	October 27	W 62-14	Home	59,138
1974	October 26	W 21-12	Away	34,500
1975	October 11	W 39-0	Home	59,658
1976	October 23	W 33-0	Away	37,762
1977	October 22	W 49-28	Home	62,108
1978	October 28	W 49-21	Away	34,010
1979	October 27	W 31-6	Home	77,923
1980	October 25	W 20-15	Away	49,000
1981	October 24	W 30-7	Home	85,012
1982	October 23	W 24-0	Away	60,958
1983	October 22	W 41-23	Home	86,309
1984	October 27	L 14-17	Away	64,879
1985	October 26	W 27-0	Home	85,534
1986	November 1	W 19-0	Away	59,184
1987	October 31	W 25-21	Home	85,108
1988	October 29	L 30-51	Away	66,811
1989	November 4	W 19-9	Home	85,911
1990	November 3	W 31-19	Away	66,461
1991	October 26	W 51-6	Home	96,445
1992	October 24	W 40-26	Away	66,663

*Yankee Stadium

WEST VIRGINIA WESLEYAN
(3-0)

1915	October 23	W 28-0	Home	NA
1916	October 14	W 39-0	Home	NA
1917	October 20	W 8-7	Home	NA

WILLIAM & MARY
(4-0)

1922	September 30	W 27-7	Home	3,000
1952	October 4	W 35-23	Home	22,848
1957	October 12	W 21-13	Home	30,462
1984	September 22	W 56-18	Home	84,704

WISSAHICKON ARMY BARRACKS
(0-0-1)

1918	November 2	T 6-6	Home	NA

WYOMING SEMINARY
(1-0)

1892	October 27	W 40-0	Away	NA

YALE
(0-7)

1899	November 11	L 0-42	Away	3,000
1901	October 19	L 0-22	Away	NA
1902	October 18	L 0-11	Away	NA
1903	October 17	L 0-27	Away	NA
1904	October 8	L 0-24	Away	NA
1905	October 21	L 0-12	Away	NA
1906	October 20	L 0-10	Away	NA

Season By Season

1887   Won 2, Lost 0
Coach: None
Captain: George Linsz

N	5	W	at Bucknell	54-0
N	19	W	Bucknell	24-0

1888   Won 0, Lost 2, Tied 1
Coach: None
Captain: George Linsz

O	31	T	Dickinson	6-6
N	7	L	at Dickinson	0-16
N		L	Lehigh	0-30

1889   Won 2, Lost 2
Coach: None
Captain: James Mock

		W	Swarthmore	20-6
N	9	L	at Lafayette	0-26
N	11	L	at Lehigh	0-106
N	25	W	Bucknell	12-0

1890   Won 2, Lost 2
Coach: None
Captain: Harvey McLean

O	10	L	at Pennsylvania	0-20

1890 Continued:

O	12	L	at Franklin & Marshall	0-10
N	15	W	Altoona Athletic Association	68-0
N		W	at Bellefonte Academy	23-0

1891   Won 6, Lost 2
Coach: None
Captain: Charles Aull

O	2	W	at Lafayette	14-4
O	3	L	at Lehigh	2-24
O	17	W	at Swarthmore	44-0
O	24	W	at Franklin & Marshall	26-6
O	27	W	at Gettysburg	18-0
N	7	L	at Bucknell	10-12
N	26	W	Dickinson (forfeit)	2-0
D	5	W	at Haverford	58-0

1892   Won 5, Lost 1
Coach: George Hoskins
Captain: Gus Reed

O	1	L	at Pennsylvania	0-20
O	27	W	at Wyoming Seminary	40-0
N	5	W	at Pittsburgh Athletic Club	16-0
N	12	W	Bucknell	18-0
N	23	W	Lafayette (at Wilkes-Barre)	18-0
N	25	W	Dickinson (at Harrisburg)	16-0

1893   Won 4, Lost 1
Coach: George Hoskins
Captain: Ed Haley

O	14	W	at Virginia	6-0
O	25	L	at Pennsylvania	6-18
N	6	W	Pittsburgh	32-0
N	11	W	at Bucknell	36-18	2,000
N	30	W	at Pittsburgh Athletic Club	12-0

1894   Won 6, Lost 0, Tied 1
Coach: George Hoskins
Captain: Benjamin Fisher

O	13	W	Gettysburg	60-0
O	20	W	Lafayette	72-0
N	10	T	at Navy	6-6
N	17	W	Bucknell (at Williamsport)	12-6
N	23	W	at Washington & Jefferson	6-0
N	24	W	at Oberlin	9-6
N	29	W	at Pittsburgh Athletic Club	14-0

1895   Won 2, Lost 2, Tied 3
Coach: George Hoskins
Captain: Walter McCaskey

S	25	W	Gettysburg	48-0
O	5	T	at Cornell	0-0	1,000
O	26	W	Bucknell (at Williamsport)	16-0	4,000
N	9	L	at Pennsylvania	4-35	5,000
N	16	L	at Pittsburgh Athletic Club	10-11	2,000
N	18	T	at Washington & Jefferson	6-6
N	28	T	at Western Reserve	8-8

1896   Won 3, Lost 4
Coach: Dr. Samuel Newton
Captain: James Dunsmore

S	26	W	Gettysburg	40-0
O	3	W	Pittsburgh	10-4
O	10	W	Dickinson	8-0
O	24	L	at Princeton	0-39
O	31	L	Bucknell (at Williamsport)	0-10
N	14	L	at Pennsylvania	0-27
N	28	L	Carlisle Indians (at Harrisburg)	5-48

1897 Won 3, Lost 6

Coach: Dr. Samuel Newton
Captain: Joe Curtin

S	25	W	Gettysburg	32-0
O	2	L	at Lafayette	0-24
O	13	L	at Princeton	0-34
O	16	L	at Pennsylvania	0-24
O	20	L	at Navy	0-4
O	30	L	at Cornell	0-45
N	13	W	Bucknell (at Williamsport)	27-4
N	20	W	Bloomsburg Normal	10-0
N	25	L	Dickinson (at Sunbury)	0-6

1898 Won 6, Lost 4

Coach: Dr. Samuel Newton
Captain: Lalon Hayes

S	24	W	Gettysburg	47-0
O	1	L	at Pennsylvania	0-40
O	8	W	at Lafayette	5-0
O	15	W	Susquehanna	45-6
O	22	L	at Navy	11-16
O	26	L	at Princeton	0-5
O	29	L	at Duquesne Athletic Club	5-18
N	5	W	Bucknell (at Williamsport)	16-0
N	19	W	at Washington & Jefferson	11-6
N	26	W	Dickinson (at Williamsport)	34-0

1899 Won 4, Lost 6, Tied 1

Coach: Sam Boyle
Captain: Brute Randolph

S	23	W	Mansfield	38-0	
S	30	W	Gettysburg	40-0	
O	7	W	at Army	6-0	
O	13	T	Washington & Jefferson	0-0	
O	18	L	at Princeton	0-12	
O	21	L	at Navy	0-6	
O	28	W	Dickinson	15-0	
N	4	L	Bucknell (at Williamsport)	0-5	3,000
N	11	L	at Yale	0-42	3,000
N	17	L	at Pennsylvania	0-47	
N	25	L	at Duquesne Athletic Club	5-64	

1900 Won 4, Lost 6, Tied 1

Coach: Pop Golden
Captain: Henny Scholl

S	23	W	Susquehanna	17-0	
S	30	W	Pittsburgh (at Bellefonte)	12-0	1,000
O	6	T	at Army	0-0	
O	10	L	at Princeton	0-26	
O	17	L	at Pennsylvania	5-17	
O	20	L	at Dickinson	0-18	
O	27	L	at Duquesne Athletic Club	0-29	
N	3	W	Bucknell (at Williamsport)	6-0	
N	10	L	at Navy	0-44	
N	17	W	Gettysburg	44-0	
N	29	L	at Buffalo	0-10	

1901 Won 5, Lost 3

Coach: Pop Golden
Captain: Earl Hewitt

S	22	W	Susquehanna	17-0	
S	29	W	Pittsburgh (at Bellefonte)	37-0	
O	5	L	at Pennsylvania	6-23	
O	19	L	at Yale	0-22	
O	26	W	at Navy	11-6	
N	2	L	at Homestead Athletic Club	0-39	
N	16	W	Lehigh (at Williamsport)	38-0	1,500
N	23	W	Dickinson	12-0	1,500

1902 Won 7, Lost 3

Coach: Pop Golden
Captain: Ralph Cummings

S	20	W	Dickinson Seminary	27-0
S	27	W	Pittsburgh	27-0
O	4	L	at Pennsylvania	0-17
O	11	W	Villanova	32-0
O	18	L	at Yale	0-11
O	25	W	Susquehanna	55-0
N	1	W	at Navy	6-0
N	8	W	Gettysburg	37-0
N	22	W	at Dickinson	23-0
N	27	L	at Steelton YMCA	5-6

1903 Won 5, Lost 3

Coach: Dan Reed
Captain: Ed Whitworth

S	19	W	Dickinson Seminary	60-0	
O	3	W	Allegheny	24-5	
O	10	L	at Pennsylvania	0-39	
O	17	L	at Yale	0-27	
O	24	W	at Pittsburgh	59-0	
O	31	W	at Navy	17-0	
N	14	L	Dickinson (at Williamsport)	0-6	
N	26	W	Washington & Jefferson (at Pittsburgh)		
22-0		7,000			

1904 Won 6, Lost 4

Coach: Tom Fennell
Captain: Carl Forkum

S	24	L	at Pennsylvania	0-6	
O	1	W	Allegheny	50-0	
O	8	L	at Yale	0-24	
O	15	W	West Virginia	34-0	
O	22	W	Washington & Jefferson (at Pittsburgh)	12-0	
O	29	W	Jersey Shore	30-0	
N	5	L	at Navy	9-20	
N	12	W	Dickinson (at Williamsport)	11-0	
N	19	W	Geneva	44-0	
N	24	L	at Pittsburgh	5-22	8,500

1905 Won 8, Lost 3

Coach: Tom Fennell
Captain: Ed Yeckley

S	16	W	Lebanon Valley	23-0	
S	30	W	California State	29-0	
O	7	L	Carlisle Indians (at Harrisburg)	0-11	8,000
O	14	W	Gettysburg	18-0	
O	21	L	at Yale	0-12	
O	28	W	Villanova	29-0	
N	4	L	at Navy	5-11	
N	11	W	Geneva	73-0	
N	18	W	Dickinson (at Williamsport)	6-0	8,000
N	24	W	West Virginia	6-0	
N	30	W	at Pittsburgh	6-0	2,400

1906 Won 8, Lost 1, Tied 1

Coach: Tom Fennell
Captain: Mother Dunn

S	22	W	Lebanon Valley	24-0	
S	29	W	Allegheny	26-0	
O	6	W	Carlisle Indians (at Williamsport)	4-0	
O	13	T	Gettysburg	0-0	
O	20	L	at Yale	0-10	
N	3	W	at Navy	5-0	5,000
N	12	W	Bellefonte Academy	12-0	
N	17	W	Dickinson (at Williamsport)	6-0	8,000
N	24	W	West Virginia	10-0	
N	29	W	at Pittsburgh	6-0	

1907 Won 6, Lost 4

Coach: Tom Fennell
Captain: Harry Burns

S	21	W	at Altoona Athletic Association	27-0	
S	28	W	Geneva	34-0	
O	5	L	Carlisle Indians (at Williamsport)	5-18	
O	12	W	Grove City	46-0	
O	19	W	at Cornell	8-6	
O	26	W	Lebanon Valley	75-0	
N	2	W	Dickinson (at Williamsport)	52-0	
N	9	L	at Pennsylvania	0-28	
N	16	L	at Navy	4-6	
N	28	L	at Pittsburgh	0-6	11,000

1908 Won 5, Lost 5

Coach: Tom Fennell
Captain: Bull McCleary

S	19	L	Bellefonte Academy	5-6	
S	26	W	Grove City	31-0	
O	3	L	Carlisle Indians (at Wilkes-Barre)	5-12	10,000
O	10	L	at Pennsylvania	0-6	7,000
O	17	W	Geneva	51-0	
O	24	W	West Virginia	12-0	
O	31	L	at Cornell	4-10	
N	7	W	Bucknell	33-6	
N	14	L	at Navy	0-5	
N	26	W	at Pittsburgh	12-6	

1909 Won 5, Lost 0, Tied 2

Coach: Bill Hollenback
Captain: Larry Vorthis

O	2	W	Grove City	31-0	
O	9	T	Carlisle Indians (at Wilkes-Barre)	8-8	10,000
O	16	W	Geneva	46-0	
O	23	T	at Pennsylvania	3-3	12,000
N	6	W	at Bucknell	33-0	
N	13	W	West Virginia	40-0	
N	25	W	at Pittsburgh	5-0	

1910 Won 5, Lost 2, Tied 1

Coach: Jack Hollenback
Captain: Alex Gray

O	1	W	Harrisburg Athletic Club	58-0	
O	8	W	Carnegie Tech	61-0	
O	15	W	Sterling Athletic Club	45-0	
O	22	L	at Pennsylvania	0-10	
O	29	T	Villanova	0-0	
N	5	W	St. Bonaventure	34-0	
N	12	W	Bucknell	45-3	
N	24	L	at Pittsburgh	0-11	18,000

1911 Won 8, Lost 0, Tied 1

Coach: Bill Hollenback
Captain: Dexter Very

S	30	W	Geneva	57-0	
O	7	W	Gettysburg	31-0	
O	14	W	at Cornell	5-0	
O	21	W	Villanova	18-0	
O	28	W	at Pennsylvania	22-6	15,000
N	4	W	St. Bonaventure	46-0	
N	11	W	Colgate	17-9	
N	18	T	at Navy	0-0	
N	30	W	at Pittsburgh	3-0	15,000

1912 Won 8, Lost 0

Coach: Bill Hollenback
Captain: Pete Mauthe

O	5	W	Carnegie Tech	41-0	
O	12	W	Washington & Jefferson	30-0	4,000
O	19	W	at Cornell	29-6	
O	26	W	Gettysburg	25-0	

1912 continued:

N	2	W	at Pennsylvania	14-0	15,000
N	9	W	Villanova	71-0	
N	16	W	at Ohio State	37-0	3,500
N	28	W	at Pittsburgh	38-0	

1913 Won 2, Lost 6

Coach: Bill Hollenback
Captain: Shorty Miller

O	4	W	Carnegie Tech	49-0	
O	11	W	Gettysburg	16-0	
O	18	L	at Washington & Jefferson	0-17	7,000
O	25	L	at Harvard	0-29	
N	1	L	at Pennsylvania	0-17	
N	7	L	Notre Dame	7-14	
N	15	L	at Navy	0-10	
N	27	L	at Pittsburgh	6-7	

1914 Won 5, Lost 3, Tied 1

Coach: Bill Hollenback
Captain: Yegg Tobin

S	26	W	Westminster	13-0	
O	3	W	Muhlenberg	22-0	
O	10	W	Gettysburg	13-0	
O	17	W	Ursinus	30-0	
O	24	T	at Harvard	13-13	22,000
O	31	W	at Lafayette	17-0	
N	7	L	at Lehigh	7-20	
N	13	L	Michigan State	3-6	10,000
N	26	L	at Pittsburgh	3-13	17,000

1915 Won 7, Lost 2

Coach: Dick Harlow
Captain: Bill Wood

S	25	W	Westminster	26-0	
O	2	W	Lebanon Valley	13-0	
O	9	W	at Pennsylvania	13-3	
O	16	W	Gettysburg	27-12	
O	23	W	West Virginia Wesleyan	28-0	
O	30	L	at Harvard	0-13	22,000
N	5	W	Lehigh	7-0	
N	13	W	at Lafayette	33-3	
N	25	L	at Pittsburgh	0-20	30,000

1916 Won 8, Lost 2

Coach: Dick Harlow
Captain: Harold Clark

S	23	W	Susquehanna	27-0	
S	30	W	Westminster	55-0	
O	7	W	Bucknell	50-7	
O	14	W	West Virginia Wesleyan	39-0	
O	21	L	at Pennsylvania	0-15	
O	28	W	Gettysburg	48-2	
N	4	W	Geneva	79-0	
N	11	W	at Lehigh	10-7	
N	17	W	Lafayette	40-0	
N	30	L	at Pittsburgh	0-31	

1917 Won 5, Lost 4

Coach: Dick Harlow
Captains: Larry Conover, Bob Higgins

S	29	W	Army Ambulance Corps (at Allentown)	10-0	
O	6	W	Gettysburg	80-0	
O	13	W	St. Bonaventure	99-0	
O	20	L	at Washington & Jefferson	0-7	
O	27	W	West Virginia Wesleyan	8-7	
N	3	L	at Dartmouth	7-10	
N	10	L	Lehigh	0-9	
N	17	W	Maryland	57-0	
N	29	L	at Pittsburgh	6-28	20,000

1918 Won 1, Lost 2, Tied 1

Coach: Hugo Bezdek
Captains: Harry Robb, Frank Unger

N	2	T	Wissahickon Barracks	6-6	
N	9	L	Rutgers	3-26	
N	16	W	at Lehigh	7-6	
N	28	L	at Pittsburgh	6-28	

1919 Won 7, Lost 1

Coach: Hugo Bezdek
Captain: Bob Higgins

O	4	W	Gettysburg	33-0	
O	11	W	Bucknell	9-0	
O	18	L	at Dartmouth	13-19	4,500
O	25	W	Ursinus	48-7	
N	1	W	at Pennsylvania	10-0	20,000
N	8	W	Lehigh	20-7	6,000
N	15	W	at Cornell	20-0	
N	27	W	at Pittsburgh	20-0	40,000

1920 Won 7, Lost 0, Tied 2

Coach: Hugo Bezdek
Captain: Bill Hess

S	25	W	Muhlenberg	27-7	2,500
O	2	W	Gettysburg	13-0	2,500
O	9	W	Dartmouth (Homecoming)	14-7	6,000
O	16	W	North Carolina State	41-0	3,500
O	23	W	Lebanon Valley	109-7	2,500
O	30	W	at Pennsylvania	28-7	30,000
N	6	W	Nebraska	20-0	9,000
N	13	T	at Lehigh	7-7	5,000
N	25	T	at Pittsburgh	0-0	

1921 Won 8, Lost 0, Tied 2

Coach: Hugo Bezdek
Captain: George Snell

S	24	W	Lebanon Valley	53-0	2,500
O	1	W	Gettysburg	24-0	2,500
O	8	W	North Carolina State	35-0	3,000
O	15	W	Lehigh (Homecoming)	28-7	4,000
O	22	T	at Harvard	21-21	30,000
O	29	W	Georgia Tech (New York, Polo Grounds)	28-7	30,000
N	5	W	Carnegie Tech	28-7	6,000
N	12	W	Navy (Philadelphia, Franklin Field)	13-7	25,000
N	24	T	at Pittsburgh	0-0	34,000
D	3	W	at Washington	21-7	35,000

1922 Won 6, Lost 4, Tied 1

Coach: Hugo Bezdek
Captain: Newsh Bentz

S	23	W	St. Bonaventure	54-0	3,000
S	30	W	William & Mary	27-7	3,000
O	7	W	Gettysburg	20-0	3,000
O	14	W	Lebanon Valley	32-6	3,000
O	21	W	Middlebury (Homecoming)	33-0	4,000
O	28	T	Syracuse (New York, Polo Grounds)	0-0	25,000
N	3	L	Navy (Washington, D.C., American League Park)	0-14	30,000
N	11	W	Carnegie Tech	10-0	17,000
N	18	L	at Pennsylvania	6-7	50,000
N	30	L	at Pittsburgh	0-14	35,000
J	1	L	Southern Cal (Rose Bowl)	3-14	43,000

1923 Won 6, Lost 2, Tied 1

Coach: Hugo Bezdek
Captain: Joe Bedenk

S	29	W	Lebanon Valley	58-0	3,000
O	6	W	North Carolina State	16-0	3,000
O	13	W	Gettysburg	20-0	3,000
O	20	W	Navy (Homecoming)	21-3	20,000

1923 continued:

O	27	T	West Virginia (New York, Yankee Stadium)	13-13	50,000
N	3	L	at Syracuse	0-10	25,000
N	10	W	Georgia Tech	7-0	10,000
N	17	W	at Pennsylvania	21-0	56,000
N	29	L	at Pittsburgh	3-20	33,000

1924 Won 6, Lost 3, Tied 1

Coach: Hugo Bezdek
Captain: Bas Gray

S	27	W	Lebanon Valley	47-3	3,500
O	4	W	North Carolina State	51-6	3,500
O	11	W	Gettysburg	26-0	6,000
O	18	L	at Georgia Tech	13-15	6,000
O	25	L	Syracuse (Homecoming)	6-10	
N	1	W	at Navy	6-0	
N	8	W	Carnegie Tech	22-7	7,000
N	15	T	at Pennsylvania	0-0	52,000
N	22	W	Marietta	28-0	3,500
N	27	L	at Pittsburgh	3-24	33,000

1925 Won 4, Lost 4, Tied 1

Coach: Hugo Bezdek
Captain: Baz Gray

S	26	W	Lebanon Valley	14-0	3,500
O	3	W	Franklin & Marshall	13-0	3,500
O	10	L	Georgia Tech (New York Yankee Stadium)	7-16	8,000
O	17	W	Marietta	13-0	3,500
O	24	W	Michigan State	13-6	4,000
O	31	L	at Syracuse	0-7	
N	7	T	Notre Dame (Homecoming)	0-0	20,000
N	14	L	at West Virginia	0-14	20,000
N	26	L	at Pittsburgh	7-23	34,715

1926 Won 5, Lost 4

Coach: Hugo Bezdek
Captain: Ken Weston

S	25	W	Susquehanna	82-0	3,500
O	2	W	Lebanon Valley	35-0	3,500
O	9	W	Marietta	48-6	4,000
O	16	L	at Notre Dame	0-28	28,000
O	23	L	Syracuse (Homecoming)	0-10	8,000
O	30	W	George Washington	20-12	3,500
N	6	L	at Pennsylvania	0-3	55,000
N	13	W	Bucknell	9-0	6,000
N	25	L	at Pittsburgh	6-24	42,915

1927 Won 6, Lost 2, Tied 1

Coach: Hugo Bezdek
Captain: Johnny Roepke

S	24	W	Lebanon Valley	27-0	3,500
O	1	W	Gettysburg	34-13	4,000
O	8	L	Bucknell	7-13	5,000
O	15	W	at Pennsylvania	20-0	60,000
O	22	W	at Syracuse	9-6	25,000
O	29	W	Lafayette (Homecoming)	40-6	11,000
N	5	W	George Washington	13-0	3,500
N	12	T	New York U.	13-13	9,000
N	24	L	at Pittsburgh	0-30	57,051

1928 Won 3, Lost 5, Tied 1

Coach: Hugo Bezdek
Captains: Don Greenshields, Steve Hamas

S	29	W	Lebanon Valley	25-0	4,000
O	6	W	Gettysburg	12-0	5,000
O	13	L	Bucknell	0-6	12,000
O	20	L	at Pennsylvania	0-14	65,000
O	27	T	Syracuse (Homecoming)	6-6	15,000

1928 continued:

N	3	L	Notre Dame	0-9	35,000
			(Philadelphia, Franklin Field)		
N	10	W	George Washington	50-0	5,000
N	17	L	at Lafayette	0-7	
N	29	L	at Pittsburgh	0-26	32,209

1929   Won 6, Lost 3

Coach: Hugo Bezdek
Captain: Jack Martin

S	28	W	Niagara	16-0	4,000
O	5	W	Lebanon Valley	15-0	4,000
O	12	W	Marshall	26-7	5,000
O	19	L	at New York U.	0-7	35,000
O	26	W	Lafayette (Homecoming)	6-3	10,000
N	2	W	at Syracuse	6-4	
N	9	W	at Pennsylvania	19-7	60,000
N	16	L	Bucknell	6-27	12,000
N	28	L	at Pittsburgh	7-20	25,755

1930   Won 3, Lost 4, Tied 2

Coach: Bob Higgins
Captain: Frank Diedrich

S	27	W	Niagara	31-14	4,000
O	4	W	Lebanon Valley	27-0	4,000
O	11	W	Marshall	65-0	5,000
O	18	T	at Lafayette	0-0	
O	25	L	Colgate (Homecoming)	0-40	8,000
N	1	L	at Bucknell	7-19	
N	8	T	Syracuse	0-0	7,000
N	15	L	at Iowa	0-19	20,000
N	26	L	at Pittsburgh	12-19	15,816

1931   Won 2, Lost 8

Coach: Bob Higgins
Captain: George Lasich

S	26	L	Waynesburg	0-7	3,000
O	3	W	Lebanon Valley	19-6	4,000
O	10	L	at Temple	0-12	20,000
O	17	L	Dickinson	6-10	5,000
O	24	L	at Syracuse	0-7	
O	31	L	Pittsburgh (Homecoming)	6-41	7,000
N	8	L	Colgate	7-32	5,000
N	14	L	at Lafayette	0-33	
N	21	L	at West Virginia	0-19	6,500
N	28	W	Lehigh (Philadelphia, Franklin Field)	31-0	2,500

1932   Won 2, Lost 5

Coach: Bob Higgins
Captain: George Collins

O	1	W	Lebanon Valley	27-0	2,500
O	8	L	Waynesburg	6-7	4,000
O	15	L	at Harvard	13-46	15,000
O	22	L	Syracuse (Homecoming)	6-12	6,000
O	29	L	at Colgate	0-31	4,000
N	5	W	Sewanee (U. of the South)	18-6	5,500
N	12	L	at Temple	12-13	15,000

1933   Won 3, Lost 3, Tied 1

Coach: Bob Higgins
Captain: Tom Slusser

O	7	W	Lebanon Valley	32-6	3,000
O	14	L	Muhlenberg	0-3	4,000
O	21	W	Lehigh (Homecoming)	33-0	5,000
O	28	L	at Columbia	0-33	
N	4	L	at Syracuse	6-12	
N	11	W	Johns Hopkins	40-6	5,000
N	18	T	at Pennsylvania	6-6	20,000

1934   Won 4, Lost 4

Coach: Bob Higgins
Captain: M.B. Morrison

O	6	W	Lebanon Valley	13-0	5,422
O	13	W	Gettysburg	32-6	6,797
O	20	W	at Lehigh	31-0	
O	27	L	at Columbia	7-14	
N	3	L	Syracuse (Homecoming)	0-16	8,013
N	10	L	at Pennsylvania	0-3	35,000
N	17	W	Lafayette	25-6	5,775
N	24	L	at Bucknell	7-13	10,000

1935   Won 4, Lost 4

Coach: Bob Higgins
Captain: Robert Weber

O	5	W	Lebanon Valley	12-6	5,848
O	12	W	Western Maryland	2-0	7,140
O	19	W	Lehigh (Homecoming)	26-0	7,113
O	26	L	at Pittsburgh	0-9	17,310
N	2	L	at Syracuse	3-7	12,000
N	9	W	Villanova	27-13	8,150
N	16	L	at Pennsylvania	6-33	40,000
N	23	L	at Bucknell	0-2	8,500

1936   Won 3, Lost 5

Coach: Bob Higgins
Captain: Chuck Cherundolo

O	3	W	Muhlenberg	45-0	7,535
O	10	L	Villanova (Homecoming)	0-13	9,593
O	17	L	at Lehigh	6-7	
O	24	L	at Cornell	7-13	6,000
O	31	W	Syracuse	18-0	7,137
N	7	L	at Pittsburgh	7-34	15,692
N	14	L	at Pennsylvania	12-19	40,000
N	21	W	Bucknell	14-0	9,227

1937   Won 5, Lost 3

Coach: Bob Higgins
Captain: Sam Donato, John Economos

S	25	L	at Cornell	19-26	6,000
O	2	W	Gettysburg	32-6	8,919
O	9	W	Bucknell (Homecoming)	20-14	11,376
O	16	W	Lehigh	14-7	7,660
O	30	L	at Syracuse	13-19	
N	6	W	at Pennsylvania	7-0	50,000
N	13	W	Maryland	21-14	7,535
N	20	L	at Pittsburgh [1]	7-28	19,936

1938   Won 3, Lost 4, Tied 1

Coach: Bob Higgins
Captain: Dean Hanley

O	1	W	Maryland	33-0	9,846
O	8	L	Bucknell (Homecoming)	0-14	12,071
O	15	W	at Lehigh	59-6	
O	22	L	at Cornell	6-21	7,000
O	29	W	Syracuse	33-6	10,659
N	5	L	Lafayette	0-7	8,274
N	12	T	at Pennsylvania	7-7	50,000
N	19	L	at Pittsburgh	0-26	16,881

1939   Won 5, Lost 1, Tied 2

Coach: Bob Higgins
Captain: Spike Alter

O	7	W	Bucknell	13-3	11,143
O	14	W	Lehigh (Homecoming)	49-7	9,419
O	21	L	at Cornell	0-47	5,099
O	28	T	at Syracuse	6-6	
N	4	W	Maryland	12-0	7,690
N	11	W	at Pennsylvania	10-0	40,000
N	18	T	at Army	14-14	7,412
N	25	W	Pittsburgh	10-0	20,000

1940   Won 6, Lost 1, Tied 1

Coach: Bob Higgins
Captain: Leon Gajecki

O	5	W	Bucknell	9-0	12,091
O	12	W	West Virginia (Homecoming)	17-13	10,574
O	19	W	at Lehigh	34-0	
O	26	W	at Temple	18-0	13,078
N	2	W	South Carolina	12-0	9,346
N	9	T	at Syracuse	13-13	
N	16	W	New York U.	25-0	9,449
N	23	L	at Pittsburgh	7-20	30,083

1941   Won 7, Lost 2

Coach: Bob Higgins
Captain: Lenny Krouse

O	4	L	at Colgate (Buffalo, Civic Stadium)	0-7	23,467
O	11	W	Bucknell (Homecoming)	27-13	16,000
O	18	L	at Temple	0-14	25,000
O	25	W	Lehigh	40-6	
O	31	W	at New York U. (Polo Grounds)	42-0	10,690
N	8	W	Syracuse	34-19	16,000
N	15	W	West Virginia	7-0	
N	22	W	at Pittsburgh	31-7	30,696
N	29	W	at South Carolina	19-12	

1942   Won 6, Lost 1, Tied 1

Coach: Bob Higgins
Captain: Lou Palazzi

O	3	W	Bucknell	14-7	10,303
O	10	W	at Lehigh	19-3	
O	17	T	at Cornell	0-0	5,000
O	24	W	Colgate (Homecoming)	13-10	11,510
O	31	L	at West Virginia	0-24	12,000
N	7	W	Syracuse	18-13	8,856
N	14	W	at Pennsylvania	13-7	50,000
N	21	W	Pittsburgh	14-6	11,710

1943   Won 5, Lost 3, Tied 1

Coach: Bob Higgins
Captain: John Jaffurs

S	25	W	Bucknell	14-0	6,639
O	2	L	at North Carolina	0-19	9,983
O	9	T	Colgate (Homecoming)	0-0	6,933
O	16	L	at Navy	6-14	
O	23	W	at Maryland	45-0	5,000
O	30	W	West Virginia	32-7	4,494
N	6	L	at Cornell	0-13	6,617
N	13	W	Temple	13-0	4,142
N	20	W	at Pittsburgh	14-0	12,242

1944   Won 6, Lost 3

Coach: Bob Higgins
Captain: John Chuckran

S	30	W	Muhlenberg	58-13	2,799
O	7	L	at Navy	14-55	
O	14	W	Bucknell (Homecoming)	20-6	4,753
O	21	W	at Colgate	6-0	3,000
O	28	L	West Virginia	27-28	5,534
N	4	W	at Syracuse	41-0	
N	11	W	at Temple	7-6	12,000
N	18	W	Maryland	34-19	
N	25	L	at Pittsburgh	0-14	8,840

1945   Won 5, Lost 3

Coach: Bob Higgins
Captain: None

S	29	W	Muhlenberg	47-7	5,048
O	6	W	Colgate (Homecoming)	27-7	9,619
O	13	L	at Navy	0-28	16,148
O	20	W	at Bucknell	46-7	5,319

1945 continued:

N	3	W	Syracuse	26-0	8,505
N	10	W	Temple	27-0	13,135
N	17	L	at Michigan State	0-33	
N	24	L	at Pittsburgh	0-7	11,354

1946   Won 6, Lost 2

Coach: Bob Higgins
Captains: Red Moore, Bucky Walters

O	5	W	Bucknell	48-6	12,401
O	12	W	at Syracuse	9-0	12,000
O	19	L	Michigan State (Homecoming)	16-19	17,149
O	26	W	at Colgate	6-2	13,500
N	2	W	Fordham	68-0	10,305
N	9	W	Temple	26-0	13,536
N	16	W	at Navy	12-7	22,000
N	23	L	at Pittsburgh	7-14	42,124

1947   Won 9, Lost 0, Tied 1

Coach: Bob Higgins
Captains: John Nolan, John Potsklan

S	20	W	Washington State (Hershey, HersheyPark Stadium)	27-4	15,000
O	4	W	Bucknell	54-0	12,294
O	11	W	at Fordham	75-0	
O	18	W	Syracuse (Homecoming)	40-0	16,632
O	25	W	West Virginia	21-14	20,313
N	1	W	Colgate	46-0	14,014
N	8	W	at Temple	7-0	20,000
N	15	W	Navy (Baltimore, Memorial Stadium)	20-7	25,000
N	22	W	at Pittsburgh	29-0	47,822
J	1	T	[4] Southern Methodist [3] (Cotton Bowl)	13-13	43,000

Wire Service Rankings: AP 4th

1948   Won 7, Lost 1, Tied 1

Coach: Bob Higgins
Captain: Joe Colone

O	2	W	Bucknell	35-0	14,423
O	8	W	at Syracuse	34-14	14,000
O	16	W	West Virginia	37-7	17,814
O	23	T	Michigan State (Homecoming)	14-14	24,579
O	30	W	at Colgate	32-13	10,000
N	6	W	at Pennsylvania	13-0	71,180
N	13	W	Temple	47-0	16,555
N	20	L	at Pittsburgh	0-7	49,444
N	27	W	at Washington State (Tacoma)	7-0	

Wire Service Rankings: AP 18th

1949   Won 5, Lost 4

Coach: Joe Bedenk
Captains: Bob Hicks, Neg Norton

S	24	L	Villanova	6-27	22,080
O	1	L	at Army	7-42	27,000
O	8	W	Boston College	32-14	18,041
O	15	W	Nebraska (Homecoming)	22-7	23,956
O	22	L	at Michigan State	0-24	
O	29	W	Syracuse	33-21	18,758
N	5	W	at West Virginia	34-14	21,000
N	12	W	at Temple	28-7	18,000
N	19	L	at Pittsburgh	0-19	43,308

1950   Won 5, Lost 3, Tied 1

Coach: Rip Engle
Captain: Owen Dougherty

S	30	W	Georgetown	34-14	16,617
O	7	L	at Army	7-41	26,252
O	14	L	at Syracuse	7-27	17,500
O	21	L	at Nebraska	0-19	38,000
O	28	T	Temple (Homecoming)	7-7	20,782

1950 continued:

N	4	W	at Boston College	20-13	8,000
N	11	W	West Virginia	27-0	16,338
N	18	W	Rutgers	18-14	15,299
D	2	W	at Pittsburgh (Forbes Field)	21-20	12,250

1951   Won 5, Lost 4
Coach: Rip Engle
Captains: Art Betts, Len Shephard

S	29	W	Boston U.	40-34	15,536
O	6	L	Villanova (Allentown)	14-20	
O	13	W	at Nebraska	15-7	39,000
O	20	L	Michigan State (Homecoming)	21-32	30,321
O	27	W	West Virginia	13-7	17,206
N	3	L	at Purdue	0-28	21,000
N	10	W	Syracuse	32-13	16,612
N	17	W	at Rutgers	13-7	15,000
N	24	L	at Pittsburgh	7-13	22,771

1952   Won 7, Lost 2, Tied 1
Coach: Rip Engle
Captains: Joe Gratson, Stewart Scheetz

S	20	W	Temple	20-13	15,889
S	27	T	Purdue	20-20	20,506
O	4	W	William & Mary	35-23	22,848
O	11	W	at West Virginia	35-21	18,500
O	18	W	Nebraska (Homecoming)	10-0	28,551
O	25	L	at Michigan State [1]	7-34	51,162
N	1	W	at Pennsylvania	14-7	67,000
N	8	L	at Syracuse	7-25	16,000
N	15	W	Rutgers	7-6	15,957
N	22	W	at Pittsburgh	17-0	53,766

1953   Won 6, Lost 3
Coach: Rip Engle
Captains: Don Malinak, Tony Rados

S	26	L	at Wisconsin	0-20	49,000
O	3	L	at Pennsylvania	7-13	51,000
O	10	W	at Boston U.	35-13	12,000
O	17	W	Syracuse	20-14	20,712
O	24	W	Texas Christian U. (Homecoming)	27-21	27,966
O	31	L	West Virginia	19-20	24,670
N	7	W	Fordham	28-21	13,897
N	14	W	at Rutgers	54-26	9,500
N	21	W	at Pittsburgh	17-0	39,642

1954   Won 7, Lost 2
Coach: Rip Engle
Captains: Don Balthaser, Jim Garrity

S	25	W	at Illinois	14-12	54,094
O	2	W	at Syracuse	13-0	18,000
O	9	W	Virginia	34-7	21,820
O	16	L	West Virginia (Homecoming)	14-19	32,384
O	23	L	at Texas Christian U.	7-20	15,000
O	30	W	at Pennsylvania	35-13	33,125
N	6	W	Holy Cross	39-7	25,383
N	13	W	Rutgers	37-14	16,623
N	20	W	at Pittsburgh	13-0	
Wire Service Rankings: AP 20th, UPI 16th

1955   Won 5, Lost 4
Coach: Rip Engle
Captains: Otto Kneidinger, Frank Reich

S	24	W	Boston U.	35-0	20,150
O	1	L	at Army	6-35	24,200
O	8	W	at Virginia (Richmond, City Stadium)	26-7	
O	15	L	Navy (Homecoming)	14-34	32,209
O	22	L	at West Virginia	7-21	34,400
O	29	W	at Pennsylvania	20-0	28,000
N	5	W	Syracuse	21-20	30,321

1955 Continued:

N	12	W	at Rutgers	34-13	12,000
N	19	L	Pittsburgh	0-20	29,361

1956   Won 6, Lost 2, Tied 1
Coach: Rip Engle
Captain: Sam Valentine

S	29	W	at Pennsylvania	34-0	23,390
O	8	L	at Army	7-14	24,195
O	13	W	Holy Cross (Homecoming)	43-0	25,828
O	20	W	at Ohio State	7-6	82,584
O	27	W	West Virginia	16-6	29,244
N	3	L	at Syracuse	9-13	35,475
N	10	W	Boston U.	40-7	29,094
N	17	W	North Carolina State	14-7	22,864
N	24	T	at Pittsburgh	7-7	51,308

1957   Won 6, Lost 3
Coach: Rip Engle
Captain: Joe Sabol

S	28	W	at Pennsylvania	19-14	21,150
O	5	L	Army	13-27	31,979
O	12	W	William & Mary	21-13	30,462
O	19	L	Vanderbilt (Homecoming)	20-32	26,781
O	26	W	at Syracuse	20-12	35,000
N	2	W	West Virginia	27-6	28,712
N	9	W	at Marquette	20-7	4,719
N	16	W	at Holy Cross	14-10	18,000
N	23	L	at Pittsburgh	13-14	44,710

1958   Won 6, Lost 3, Tied 1
Coach: Rip Engle
Captain: Steve Garban

S	20	L	at Nebraska	7-14	30,000
S	27	W	at Pennsylvania	43-0	19,549
O	4	L	at Army [3]	0-26	27,250
O	11	W	Marquette (Homecoming)	40-8	22,000
O	18	W	at Boston U.	34-0	11,000
O	25	L	Syracuse	6-14	27,000
N	1	W	Furman	36-0	28,000
N	8	T	at West Virginia	14-14	26,000
N	15	W	Holy Cross	32-0	20,000
N	27	W	at Pittsburgh	25-21	39,479

1959   Won 9, Lost 2
Coach: Rip Engle
Captain: Pat Botula

S	19	W	at Missouri	19-8	28,000
S	26	W	VMI	21-0	
O	3	W	Colgate	58-20	
O	10	W	at Army	17-11	27,500
O	17	W	Boston U. (Homecoming)	21-12	
O	24	W	Illinois (Cleveland, Municipal Stadium)	20-9	15,045
O	31	W	at West Virginia	28-10	
N	7	L	[7] Syracuse [4]	18-20	34,000
N	14	W	Holy Cross	46-0	
N	21	L	[5] at Pittsburgh	7-22	46,104
D	19	W	Alabama [10]	7-0	36,211
			(Liberty Bowl, Philadelphia)		
Wire Service Rankings: AP 11th, UPI 14th

1960   Won 7, Lost 3
Coach: Rip Engle
Captain: Hank Oppermann

S	17	W	Boston U.	20-0	22,559
O	1	L	Missouri (Homecoming)	8-21	33,613
O	8	W	at Army	27-16	27,150
O	15	L	at Syracuse	15-21	40,617
O	22	L	at Illinois	8-10	51,459

1960 Continued:

O	29	W	West Virginia	34-13	37,715
N	5	W	Maryland	28-9	30,126
N	12	W	at Holy Cross	33-8	14,856
N	19	W	at Pittsburgh	14-3	45,023
D	17	W	Oregon (Liberty Bowl, Philadelphia)	41-12	16,697

Wire Service Rankings: AP 16th

1961   Won 8, Lost 3

Coach: Rip Engle
Captain: Jim Smith

S	23	W	Navy	20-10	38,437
S	29	L	at Miami (Fla.)	8-25	45,687
O	6	W	at Boston U.	32-0	10,150
O	14	L	Army	6-10	45,306
O	21	W	Syracuse	14-0	44,674
O	28	W	California (Homecoming)	33-16	32,497
N	4	L	at Maryland	17-21	34.000
N	11	W	at West Virginia	20-6	30,000
N	18	W	Holy Cross	34-14	32,746
N	25	W	at Pittsburgh	47-26	37,261
D	30	W	Georgia Tech (Gator Bowl)	30-15	50,000

Wire Service Rankings: AP 18th, UPI 19th

1962   Won 9, Lost 2

Coach: Rip Engle
Captain: Joe Galardi

S	22	W	Navy	41-7	42,653
S	29	W	Air Force	20-6	45,200
O	6	W	[4] at Rice	18-7	35,982
O	13	L	[3] at Army	6-9	31,000
O	20	W	Syracuse (Homecoming)	20-19	48,356
O	27	W	at California	23-21	31,500
N	3	W	Maryland	23-7	41,834
N	10	W	West Virginia	34-6	33,212
N	17	W	at Holy Cross	48-20	11,825
N	24	W	at Pittsburgh	16-0	45,149
D	29	L	[9] Florida (Gator Bowl)	7-17	45,248

Wire Service Rankings: AP 9th, UPI 9th

1963   Won 7, Lost 3

Coach: Rip Engle
Captain: Ralph Baker

S	21	W	at Oregon	17-7	33,220
S	28	W	UCLA	17-14	36,327
O	5	W	Rice (Homecoming)	28-7	38,275
O	12	L	Army	7-10	49,389
O	19	L	at Syracuse	0-9	39,209
O	26	W	West Virginia	20-9	45,159
N	2	W	at Maryland	17-15	35,500
N	9	W	at Ohio State	10-7	83,519
N	16	W	Holy Cross	28-14	24,644
D	7	L	at Pittsburgh	21-22	51,477

Wire Service Rankings: AP 10th, UPI 16th

1964   Won 6, Lost 4

Coach: Rip Engle
Captain: Bill Bowes

S	19	L	Navy	8-21	44,800
S	26	L	at UCLA	14-21	34,636
O	3	L	Oregon	14-22	44,803
O	10	W	at Army	6-2	32,268
O	17	L	Syracuse (Homecoming)	14-21	47,998
O	24	W	at West Virginia	37-8	26,000
O	31	W	Maryland	17-9	33,500
N	7	W	at Ohio State [2]	27-0	84,279
N	14	W	at Houston	24-7	25,000
N	21	W	Pittsburgh	28-0	50,144

Wire Service Rankings: UPI 14th

1965   Won 5, Lost 5

Coach: Rip Engle
Captain: Bob Andronici

S	25	L	Michigan State	0-23	46,121
O	2	L	UCLA	22-24	46,429
O	9	W	at Boston College	17-0	24,300
O	16	L	at Syracuse	21-28	39,000
O	23	W	West Virginia (Homecoming)	44-6	44,230
O	30	L	at California	17-21	36,418
N	6	W	Kent State	21-6	30,323
N	13	W	Navy	14-6	47,163
N	20	L	at Pittsburgh	27-30	35,576
D	4	W	at Maryland	19-7	24,000

1966   Won 5, Lost 5

Coach: Joe Paterno
Captains: Mike Irwin, John Runnells

S	17	W	Maryland	15-7	40,911
S	24	L	at Michigan State [1]	8-42	64,860
O	1	L	at Army	0-11	31,112
O	8	W	Boston College	30-21	30,924
O	15	L	at UCLA [4]	11-49	37,271
O	22	W	at West Virginia	38-6	15,835
O	29	W	California (Homecoming)	33-15	33,332
N	5	L	Syracuse	10-12	45,126
N	12	L	at Georgia Tech [5]	0-21	50,172
N	19	W	at Pittsburgh	48-24	30,467

1967   Won 8, Lost 2, Tied 1

Coach: Joe Paterno
Captains: Bill Lenkaitis, Jim Litterelle

S	23	L	at Navy	22-23	20,101
S	29	W	at Miami (Fla.)	17-8	39,516
O	7	L	UCLA [3]	15-17	46,007
O	14	W	at Boston College	50-28	15,500
O	21	W	West Virginia (Homecoming)	21-14	44,460
O	28	W	at Syracuse	29-20	41,750
N	4	W	at Maryland	38-3	34,700
N	11	W	North Carolina State	13-8	46,497
N	18	W	Ohio U.	35-14	29,556
N	25	W	Pittsburgh	42-6	36,008
D	30	T	Florida State (Gator Bowl)	17-17	68,019

Wire Service Rankings: AP 10th

1968   Won 11, Lost 0

Coach: Joe Paterno
Captains: John Kulka, Mike Reid, Steve Smear

S	21	W	[10] Navy	31-6	49,273
S	28	W	[4] Kansas State	25-9	45,024
O	5	W	[3] at West Virginia	31-20	34,500
O	12	W	[3] at UCLA	21-6	35,772
O	26	W	[4] at Boston College	29-0	25,272
N	2	W	[4] Army (Homecoming)	28-24	49,653
N	9	W	[4] Miami (Fla.)	22-7	50,132
N	16	W	[3] at Maryland	57-13	30,000
N	23	W	[3] at Pittsburgh	65-9	31,224
D	7	W	[3] Syracuse	30-12	41,393
J	1	W	[3] Kansas [6] (Orange Bowl)	15-14	77,719

Wire Service Rankings: AP 2nd, UPI 3rd

1969   Won 11, Lost 0

Coach: Joe Paterno
Captains: Tom Jackson, Mike Reid, Steve Smear

S	20	W	[2] at Navy	45-22	28,796
S	27	W	[2] Colorado	27-3	51,402
O	4	W	[2] at Kansas State [20]	17-14	37,000
O	11	W	[5] West Virginia [17] (Homecoming)	20-0	52,713
O	18	W	[5] at Syracuse	15-14	42,291
O	25	W	[8] Ohio U.	42-3	49,069
N	1	W	[5] Boston College	38-16	46,652

1969 Continued:

N	15	W	[5] Maryland	48-0	46,106
N	22	W	[5] at Pittsburgh	27-7	39,517
N	29	W	[3] at North Carolina State	33-8	24,150
J	1	W	[2] Missouri [6] (Orange Bowl)	10-3	77,282

Wire Service Rankings: AP 2nd, UPI 2nd

1970   Won 7, Lost 3

Coach: Joe Paterno
Captains: Jack Ham, Warren Koegel

S	19	W	Navy	55-7	48,566
S	26	L	[4] at Colorado [18]	13-41	42,850
O	3	L	at Wisconsin	16-29	55,204
O	10	W	at Boston College	28-3	25,252
O	17	L	Syracuse (Homecoming)	7-24	50,540
O	24	W	at Army	38-14	41,062
O	31	W	West Virginia	42-8	49,932
N	7	W	at Maryland	34-0	23,400
N	14	W	[20] Ohio U.	32-22	43,000
N	21	W	Pittsburgh	35-15	50,017

Wire Service Rankings: AP 18th, UPI 19th

1971   Won 11, Lost 1

Coach: Joe Paterno
Captains: Dave Joyner, Charlie Zapiec

S	18	W	[14] at Navy	56-3	26,855
S	25	W	[12] at Iowa	44-14	44,303
O	2	W	[9] Air Force	16-14	50,459
O	9	W	[9] Army	42-0	49,887
O	16	W	[9] at Syracuse	31-0	41,382
O	23	W	[7] Texas Christian U. (Homecoming)	66-14	51,896
O	30	W	[6] at West Virginia	35-7	37,000
N	6	W	[6] Maryland	63-27	50,144
N	13	W	[5] North Carolina State	35-3	50,477
N	20	W	[6] at Pittsburgh	55-18	39,539
D	4	L	[5] at Tennessee [11]	11-31	59,542
J	1	W	[10] Texas [12] (Cotton Bowl)	30-6	72,000

Wire Service Rankings: AP 5th, UPI 11th

1972   Won 10, Lost 2

Coach: Joe Paterno
Captains: Gregg Ducatte, Jim Heller, John Hufnagel, Carl Schaukowitch

S	16	L	[6] at Tennessee [7]	21-28	71,647
S	23	W	Navy	21-10	50,547
S	30	W	[13] Iowa	14-10	58,065
O	7	W	at Illinois	35-17	60,349
O	14	W	at Army	45-0	42,352
O	21	W	Syracuse (Homecoming)	17-0	60,465
O	28	W	at West Virginia	28-19	37,000
N	4	W	[10] Maryland	46-16	58,171
N	11	W	[8] North Carolina State	37-22	54,274
N	18	W	[7] at Boston College	45-26	23,119
N	25	W	[6] Pittsburgh	49-27	38,600
D	31	L	[5] Oklahoma [2] (Sugar Bowl)		

1973   WON 12, LOST 0

Coach: Joe Paterno
Captains: John Cappelletti, Randy Crowder, Mark Markovich, Ed O'Neil

S	15	W	at Stanford	20-6	57,000
S	22	W	at Navy	39-0	28,383
S	29	W	Iowa (Homecoming)	27-8	59,980
O	6	W	at Air Force	19-9	37,077
O	13	W	Army	54-3	58,194
O	20	W	at Syracuse	49-6	27,595
O	27	W	West Virginia	62-14	59,138
N	3	W	at Maryland	42-22	44,135
N	10	W	North Carolina State	35-29	59,424
N	17	W	Ohio U.	49-10	51,804
N	24	W	Pittsburgh	35-13	56,600
J	1	W	[5] Louisiana State (Orange Bowl)	16-9	60,477

Wire Service Rankings: AP 5th, UPI 5th

1974   WON 10, LOST 2

Coach: Joe Paterno
Captains: Jack Baiorunos, Jim Bradley

S	14	W	Stanford	24-20	58,200
S	21	L	Navy	6-7	42,000
S	28	W	at Iowa	27-0	46,500
O	5	W	at Army	21-14	41,221
O	12	W	Wake Forest (Homecoming)	55-0	56,500
O	19	W	Syracuse	30-14	59,100
O	26	W	at West Virginia	21-12	34,500
N	2	W	Maryland [15]	24-17	60,125
N	9	L	[6] at North Carolina State	7-12	47,700
N	16	W	[10] Ohio U.	35-16	58,700
N	28	W	[10] at Pittsburgh (Three Rivers Stadium)	31-10	48,895
J	1	W	[10] Baylor [16] (Cotton Bowl)	41-20	67,500

Wire Service Rankings: AP 7th, UPI 7th

1975   WON 9, LOST 3

Coach: Joe Paterno
Captains: Greg Buttle, John Quinn, Tom Rafferty

S	6	W	at Temple (Franklin Field)	26-25	57,112
S	13	W	Stanford	34-14	61,325
S	20	L	[7] at Ohio State [3]	9-17	88,093
S	27	W	at Iowa	30-10	52,780
O	4	W	[10] Kentucky (Homecoming)	10-3	60,225
O	11	W	[9] West Virginia [10]	39-0	59,658
O	18	W	at Syracuse	19-7	28,153
O	25	W	Army	31-0	59,381
N	1	W	at Maryland [14]	15-13	59,973
N	8	L	North Carolina State	14-15	59,536
N	22	W	at Pittsburgh (Three Rivers Stadium)	7-6	46,846
D	31	L	[8] Alabama [4] (Sugar Bowl)	6-13	75,212

Wire Service Rankings: AP 10th, UPI 10th

1976   WON 7, LOST 5

Coach: Joe Paterno
Captains: Kurt Allerman, John Andress, Chuck Benjamin, Brad Benson, Ron Crosby, George Reihner, Bernard Robinson

S	11	W	Stanford	15-12	61,645
S	18	L	[7] Ohio State [2]	7-12	62,503
S	25	L	Iowa	6-7	61,268
O	2	L	at Kentucky	6-22	57,723
O	9	W	Army	38-16	60,436
O	16	W	Syracuse (Homecoming)	27-3	61,474
O	23	W	at West Virginia	33-0	37,762
O	30	W	at Temple (Veterans Stadium)	31-30	42,005
N	6	W	North Carolina State	41-20	60,426
N	13	W	at Miami (Fla.)	21-7	19,627
N	26	L	at Pittsburgh [1] (Three Rivers Stadium)	7-24	50,360
D	27	L	Notre Dame [15] (Gator Bowl)	9-20	67,827

1977   WON 11, LOST 1

Coach: Joe Paterno
Captains: John Dunn, Steve Geise, Ron Hostetler, Randy Sidler

S	2	W	at Rutgers (E. Rutherford, Giants Stadium)	45-7	64,790
S	17	W	[10] Houston [9]	31-14	62,554
S	24	W	Maryland	27-9	62,079
O	1	L	Kentucky	20-24	62,196
O	8	W	Utah State (Homecoming)	16-7	62,015
O	15	W	at Syracuse	31-24	27,029
O	22	W	West Virginia	49-28	62,108
O	29	W	Miami (Fla.)	49-7	61,853
N	5	W	at North Carolina State	21-17	44,800
N	12	W	Temple	44-7	61,327
N	26	W	[9] at Pittsburgh [10]	15-13	56,500
D	25	W	[6] Arizona State [15] (Fiesta Bowl)	42-30	57,766

Wire Service Rankings: AP 5th, UPI 4th

1978 WON 11, LOST 1

Coach: Joe Paterno
Captains: Chuck Fusina, Paul Suhey

S	1	W	at Temple (Veterans Stadium)	10-7	53,103
S	9	W	Rutgers	26-10	77,154
S	16	W	[5] at Ohio State [6]	19-0	88,202
S	23	W	Southern Methodist	26-21	77,704
S	30	W	Texas Christian U.	58-0	76,832
O	7	W	at Kentucky	30-0	58,068
O	21	W	Syracuse (Homecoming)	45-15	77,827
O	28	W	at West Virginia	49-21	34,010
N	4	W	[2] Maryland [5]	27-3	78,019
N	11	W	[2] North Carolina State	19-10	77,043
N	24	W	[1] Pittsburgh	17-10	77,465
J	1	L	[1] Alabama [2] (Sugar Bowl)	7-14	76,824

Wire Service Rankings: AP 4th, UPI 4th

1979 WON 8, LOST 4

Coach: Joe Paterno
Captains: Lance Mehl, Matt Millen, Irv Pankey

S	15	W	Rutgers	45-10	77,309
S	22	L	Texas A & M	14-27	77,575
S	29	L	at Nebraska [6]	17-42	76,151
O	6	W	at Maryland	27-7	52,348
O	13	W	Army (Homecoming)	24-3	77,157
O	20	W	Syracuse	35-7	53,789
			(E. Rutherford, Giants Stadium)		
O	27	W	West Virginia	31-6	77,923
N	3	L	Miami (Fla.)	10-26	75,332
N	10	W	at North Carolina State	9-7	51,200
N	17	W	Temple	22-7	76,000
D	1	L	Pittsburgh	14-29	76,958
D	22	W	Tulane (Liberty Bowl, Memphis)	9-6	50,021

Wire Service Rankings: AP 20th, UPI 18th

1980 WON 10, LOST 2

Coach: Joe Paterno
Captains: Bob Jagers, Greg Jones

S	6	W	Colgate	54-10	78,926
S	20	W	[12] at Texas A & M	25-9	66,234
S	27	L	[11] Nebraska [3]	7-21	84,585
O	4	W	[17] at Missouri [9]	29-21	75,298
O	11	W	[12] at Maryland	24-10	48,123
O	18	W	[12] Syracuse (Homecoming)	24-7	84,000
O	25	W	[13] at West Virginia	20-15	49,000
N	1	W	[12] Miami (Fla.)	27-12	83,661
N	8	W	[10] North Carolina State	21-13	83,847
N	15	W	at Temple (Veterans Stadium)	50-7	49,313
N	28	L	[5] Pittsburgh [4]	9-14	82,459
D	26	W	[10] Ohio State [14] (Fiesta Bowl)	31-19	66,738

Wire Service Rankings: AP 8th, UPI 8th

1981 WON 10, LOST 2

Coach: Joe Paterno
Captains: Sean Farrell, Chet Parlavecchio, Leo Wisniewski

S	12	W	[5] Cincinnati	52-0	84,342
S	26	W	[3] at Nebraska [15]	30-24	76,308
O	3	W	Temple	30-0	84,562
O	10	W	Boston College (Homecoming)	38-7	84,473
O	17	W	[2] at Syracuse	41-16	50,037
O	24	W	[1] West Virginia	30-7	85,012
O	31	L	[1] at Miami (Fla.)	14-17	32,117
N	7	W	[6] at North Carolina State	22-15	48,800
N	14	L	[5] Alabama [6]	16-31	85,133
N	21	W	[13] Notre Dame	24-21	84,175
N	28	W	[11] at Pittsburgh [1]	48-14	60,260
J	1	W	[7] Southern Cal [8] (Fiesta Bowl)	26-10	71,053

Wire Service Rankings: AP 3rd, UPI 3rd

1982 WON 11, LOST 1

Coach: Joe Paterno
Captains: Walker Lee Ashley, Ken Kelley, Stuart McMunn, Pete Speros

S	4	W	Temple	31-14	80,000
S	11	W	Maryland	39-31	84,597
S	18	W	Rutgers	49-14	83,268
S	25	W	[8] Nebraska [2]	27-24	85,304
O	9	L	[3] at Alabama [4]	21-42	76,821
			(Birmingham, Legion Field)		
O	16	W	[8] Syracuse (Homecoming)	28-7	84,762
O	23	W	[8] at West Virginia	24-0	60,958
O	30	W	[7] at Boston College	52-17	33,205
N	6	W	[7] North Carolina State	54-0	84,837
N	13	W	[5] at Notre Dame [13]	24-14	59,075
N	26	W	[2] Pittsburgh [5]	19-10	85,522
J	1	W	[2] Georgia [1] (Sugar Bowl)	27-23	78,124

Wire Service Rankings: AP 1st, UPI 1st

1983 WON 8, LOST 4, TIED 1

Coach: Joe Paterno
Captains: Ron Heller, Kenny Jackson, Scott Radecic, Mark Robinson

A	29	L	Nebraska [1]	6-44	71,123
			(E. Rutherford, Giants Stadium)		
S	10	L	Cincinnati	3-14	83,683
S	17	L	Iowa	34-42	84,628
S	24	W	at Temple (Veterans Stadium)	23-18	35,760
O	1	W	at Rutgers	36-25	32,804
			(E. Rutherford, Giants Stadium)		
O	8	W	Alabama [3]	34-28	85,614
O	15	W	at Syracuse	17-6	50,010
O	22	W	West Virginia [5] (Homecoming)	41-23	86,309
O	29	L	at Boston College	17-27	56,188
			(Foxboro, Sullivan Stadium)		
N	5	W	Brown	38-21	84,670
N	12	W	Notre Dame	34-30	85,899
N	19	T	at Pittsburgh	24-24	60,283
D	26	W	[22] Washington (Aloha Bowl)	13-10	37,212

Wire Service Rankings: UPI 17th

1984 WON 6, LOST 5

Coach: Joe Paterno
Captains: Bill Emerson, Nick Haden, Carmen Masciantonio, Stan Short, Doug Strang

S	8	W	Rutgers	15-12	84,409
S	15	W	at Iowa	20-17	66,145
S	22	W	William & Mary	56-18	84,704
S	29	L	[4] Texas [2]	3-28	76,883
			(E. Rutherford, Giants Stadium)		
O	6	W	Maryland	25-24	85,486
O	13	L	at Alabama	0-6	60,210
O	20	W	Syracuse (Homecoming)	21-3	85,850
O	27	L	at West Virginia	14-17	64,879
N	3	W	Boston College	37-30	85,690
N	17	L	at Notre Dame	7-44	59,075
N	24	L	Pittsburgh	11-31	85,499

1985 WON 11, LOST 1

Coach: Joe Paterno
Captains: Rogers Alexander, Todd Moules, Michael Zordich

S	7	W	at Maryland [7]	20-18	50,750
S	14	W	Temple	27-25	84,651
S	21	W	East Carolina	17-10	84,266
S	28	W	at Rutgers	17-10	54,560
			(E. Rutherford, Giants Stadium)		
O	12	W	[8] Alabama [10]	19-17	85,444
O	19	W	at Syracuse	24-20	50,021
O	26	W	West Virginia (Homecoming)	27-0	85,534
N	2	W	Boston College	16-12	82,000
N	9	W	[2] at Cincinnati (Riverfront Stadium)	31-10	33,528

1985 CONTINUED:

N	16	W	[1] Notre Dame	36-6	84,000
N	23	W	[1] at Pittsburgh	31-0	60,134
J	1	L	[1] Oklahoma [2] (Orange Bowl)	10-25	74,148

Wire Service Rankings: AP 3rd, UPI 3rd

1986 WON 12, LOST 0

Coach: Joe Paterno
Captains: Shane Conlan, John Shaffer, Steve Smith, Bob White

S	6	W	[6] Temple	45-15	85,732
S	20	W	a[6] t Boston College (Foxboro, Sullivan Stadium)	26-14	42,329
S	27	W	[7] East Carolina	42-17	84,774
O	4	W	[5] Rutgers	31-6	84,000
O	11	W	[5] Cincinnati	23-17	84,812
O	18	W	[6] Syracuse (Homecoming)	42-3	85,512
O	25	W	[6] at Alabama [2]	23-3	60,210
N	1	W	[2] at West Virginia	19-0	59,184
N	8	W	[2] Maryland	17-15	85,561
N	15	W	[2] at Notre Dame	24-19	59,075
N	22	W	[2] Pittsburgh	34-14	85,722
J	2	W	[2] Miami (Fla.) [1] (Fiesta Bowl)	14-10	73,098

Wire Service Rankings: AP 1st, UPI 1st

1987 WON 8, LOST 4

Coach: Joe Paterno
Captains: Trey Bauer, Marques Henderson, Matt Knizner

S	5	W	Bowling Green	45-19	84,574
S	12	L	[11] Alabama [19]	13-24	85,619
S	19	W	[20] Cincinnati	41-0	82,000
S	26	W	[15] at Boston College (Foxboro, Sullivan Stadium)	27-17	50,267
O	3	W	[14] Temple	27-13	84,000
O	10	W	[14] Rutgers (Homecoming)	35-21	85,376
O	17	L	[10] at Syracuse [13]	21-48	50,011
O	31	W	[18] West Virginia	25-21	85,108
N	7	W	[16] at Maryland (Baltimore, Memorial Stadium)	21-16	62,500
N	14	L	[15] at Pittsburgh	0-10	56,500
N	21	W	Notre Dame [7]	21-20	84,000
J	1	L	[20] Clemson [14] (Citrus Bowl)	10-35	53,152

1988 WON 5, LOST 6

Coach: Joe Paterno
Captains: John Greene, Eddie Johnson, Keith Karpinski, Steve Wisniewski

S	10	W	[20] at Virginia	42-14	45,000
S	17	W	[15] Boston College	23-20	84,000
S	24	L	[15] Rutgers	16-21	85,531
O	1	W	at Temple (Veterans Stadium)	45-9	66,592
O	8	W	Cincinnati (Homecoming)	35-9	85,693
O	15	L	Syracuse	10-24	85,916
O	22	L	at Alabama (Birmingham, Legion Field)	3-8	75,808
O	29	L	at West Virginia [7]	30-51	66,811
N	5	W	Maryland	17-10	78,000
N	12	L	Pittsburgh	7-14	85,701
N	19	L	at Notre Dame [1]	3-21	59,075

1989 WON 8, LOST 3, TIED 1

Coach: Joe Paterno
Captains: Brian Chizmar, Andre Collins, Blair Thomas

S	9	L	[12] Virginia	6-14	85,956
S	16	W	Temple	42-3	84,790
S	23	W	Boston College	7-3	85,651
S	30	W	at Texas	16-12	75,232
O	7	W	at Rutgers (E. Rutherford, Giants Stadium)	17-0	57,688
O	14	W	[23] at Syracuse	34-12	49,876
O	28	L	[14] Alabama [6]	16-17	85,975
N	4	W	[16] West Virginia [13] (Homecoming)	19-9	85,911
N	11	T	[13] at Maryland (Baltimore, Memorial Stadium)	13-13	61,215

1989 CONTINUED:

N	18	L	[17] Notre Dame [1]	23-34	86,016
N	25	W	[22] at Pittsburgh	16-13	57,158
D	29	W	Brigham Young [19] (Holiday Bowl)	50-39	61,113

Wire Service Rankings: AP 15th, UPI 14th

1990 WON 9, LOST 3

Coach: Joe Paterno
Captains: Matt McCartin, Willie Thomas, Leroy Thompson

S	8	L	[21] Texas	13-17	85,973
S	15	L	at Southern Cal [6]	14-19	70,594
S	22	W	Rutgers	28-0	85,194
O	6	W	Temple (Homecoming)	48-10	85,874
O	13	W	Syracuse	27-21	86,002
O	20	W	at Boston College	40-21	32,000
O	27	W	at Alabama	9-0	70,123
N	3	W	[24] at West Virginia	31-19	66,461
N	10	W	[21] Maryland	24-10	83,000
N	17	W	[18] at Notre Dame [1]	24-21	59,075
N	24	W	[11] Pittsburgh	22-17	85,180
D	28	L	[7] Florida State [6] (Blockbuster Bowl)	17-24	74,021

Wire Service Rankings: AP 11th, UPI 10th

1991 WON 11, LOST 2

Coach: Joe Paterno
Captains: Mark D'Onofrio, Sam Gash, Keith Goganious, Al Golden, Darren Perry, Terry Smith

A	28	W	[7] Georgia Tech [8] (E. Rutherford, Giants Stadium)	34-22	77,409
S	7	W	[5] Cincinnati	81-0	94,000
S	14	L	[5] at Southern Cal	10-21	64,758
S	21	W	Brigham Young	33-7	96,304
S	28	W	[10] Boston College	28-21	95,927
O	5	W	[12] at Temple (Veterans Stadium)	24-7	43,808
O	12	L	[9] at Miami (Fla.) [2]	20-26	75,723
O	19	W	[10] Rutgers (Homecoming)	37-17	95,729
O	26	W	[8] West Virginia	51-6	96,445
N	9	W	[8] at Maryland (Baltimore, Memorial Stadium)	47-7	57,416
N	16	W	[8] Notre Dame [12]	35-13	96,672
N	28	W	[6] at Pittsburgh	32-20	52,519
J	1	W	[6] Tennessee [10] (Fiesta Bowl)	42-17	71,133

Wire Service Rankings: AP 3rd, UPI 3rd, USA Today/CNN 3rd

1992 WON 7, LOST 5

Coach: Joe Paterno
Captains: John Gerak, Reggie Givens, O.J. McDuffie, Brett Wright

S	5	W	[8] at Cincinnati	24-20	29,099
S	12	W	[10] Temple	49-8	94,892
S	19	W	[10] Eastern Michigan	52-7	94,578
S	26	W	[9] Maryland	49-13	95,891
O	3	W	[8] at Rutgers (E. Rutherford, Giants Stadium)	38-24	61,562
O	10	L	[7] Miami (Fla.) [2]	14-17	96,704
O	17	L	[9] Boston College (Homecoming)	32-35	96,130
O	24	W	[14] at West Virginia	40-26	66,663
O	31	L	[14] at Brigham Young	17-30	66,016
N	14	L	[22] at Notre Dame [8]	16-17	59,075
N	21	W	[23] Pittsburgh	57-13	91,000
J	1	L	[21] Stanford [13] (Blockbuster Bowl)	3-24	45,554

Wire Service Rankings: UPI 24th, USA Today/CNN 24th

PENN STATE BEGINS PLAY IN THE BIG TEN CONFERENCE.

1993 WON 10, LOST 2; 6-2, 3RD

Coach: Joe Paterno
Captains: Lou Benfatti, Mike Malinoski, Brian O'Neal, Lee Rubin

S	4	W	[17] Minnesota	38-20	95,387
S	11	W	[15] Southern Cal	21-20	95,992

1993 CONTINUED:

S	18	W	[14] at Iowa	31-0	70,397
S	25	W	[9] Rutgers	31-7	95,092
O	2	W	[9] at Maryland	70-7	42,008
O	16	L	[7] Michigan [18]	13-21	96,719
O	30	L	[12] at Ohio State [3]	6-24	95,060
N	6	W	[19] Indiana [13] (Homecoming)	38-31	91,000
N	13	W	[16] Illinois	28-14	90,000
N	20	W	[14] at Northwestern	43-21	30,355
N	27	W	[14] at Michigan State [24]	38-37	53,482
J	1	W	[13] Tennessee [6] (Citrus Bowl)	31-13	72,456

Wire Service Rankings: AP 8th, UPI 7th, USA Today/CNN 7th

1994   WON 12, LOST 0; 8-0, 1ST

Coach: Joe Paterno
Captains: Kerry Collins, Brian Gelzheiser, Bucky Greeley,
Willie Smith, Vin Stewart

S	3	W	[9] at Minnesota	56-3	51,134
S	10	W	[9] Southern California [14]	38-14	96,463
S	17	W	[8] Iowa	61-21	95,834
S	24	W	[6] Rutgers	55-27	95,379
O	1	W	[5] at Temple (Franklin Field)	48-21	38,410
O	15	W	[3] at Michigan [5]	31-24	106,832
O	29	W	[1] Ohio State [21] (Homecoming)	63-14	97,079
N	5	W	[1] at Indiana	35-29	47,754
N	12	W	[2] at Illinois	35-31	72,364
N	19	W	[2] Northwestern	45-17	96,383
N	26	W	[2] Michigan State	59-31	96,493
J	2	W	[2] Oregon [12] (Rose Bowl)	38-20	102,247

Wire Service Rankings: AP 2nd, UPI 2nd, USA Today/CNN 2nd

1995   WON 9, LOST 3; 5-3, 3RD

Coach: Joe Paterno
Captains: Todd Atkins, Bobby Engram, Jeff Hartings, Terry Killens

S	9	W	[4] Texas Tech	24-23	96,035
S	16	W	[7] Temple	66-14	95,926
S	23	W	[6] at Rutgers	59-34	58,870
			(E. Rutherford, Giants Stadium)		
S	30	L	[6] Wisconsin	9-17	96,540
O	7	L	[12] Ohio State [5]	25-28	96,655
O	14	W	[20] at Purdue	26-23	60.445
O	21	W	[19] at Iowa [18]	41-27	70,397
O	28	W	[16] Indiana (Homecoming)	45-21	96,391
N	4	L	[12] at Northwestern [6]	10-21	49,256

1995 CONTINUED:

N	18	W	[19] Michigan [13]	27-17	80,000
N	25	W	[14] at Michigan State	24-20	66,189
J	1	W	[15] Auburn [12] (Outback Bowl)	43-14	65,313

Wire Service Rankings: AP 13th, UPI 12th, USA Today/CNN 12th

1996   WON 11, LOST 2; BIG TEN: 6-2, 3RD

Coach: Joe Paterno
Captains: Kim Herring, Brandon Noble, Wally Richardson, Barry Tielsch

A	25	W	[11] Southern Cal [7]	24-7	77,716
			(at E. Rutherford, Giants Stadium)		
S	7	W	[7] Louisville	24-7	95,670
S	14	W	[6] Northern Illinois	49-0	95,589
S	21	W	[5] Temple	41-0	24,847
			(E. Rutherford, Giants Stadium)		
S	28	W	[3] at Wisconsin	23-20	79,607
O	5	L	[4] at Ohio State [3]	7-38	94,241
O	12	W	[10] Purdue (Homecoming)	31-14	96,653
O	19	W	[10] Iowa	20-21	96,230
O	26	W	[17] at Indiana	48-26	37,354
N	2	W	[15] Northwestern [11]	34-9	96,596
N	16	W	[11] at Michigan [16]	29-17	105,898
N	23	W	[7] Michigan State	32-29	96,263
J	1	W	[7] Texas [20] (Fiesta Bowl)	38-15	65,106

Wire Service Rankings: AP 7th, USA Today/CNN 7th

1997   WON 9, LOST 3; BIG TEN: WON 6, LOST 2

Coach: Joe Paterno
Captains: Aaron Collins, Matt Fornadel, Mike McQueary, Phil Ostrowski

S	6	W	[1] Pittsburgh	38-17	97,115
S	13	W	[1] Temple	52-10	96,735
S	20	W	[1] at Louisville	57-21	39,826
O	4	W	[2] at Illinois*	41-6	51,523
O	11	W	[2] Ohio State* [7]	31-27	97,282
O	18	W	[1] Minnesota*	16-15	96,953
N	1	W	[2] at Northwestern*	30-27	47,129
N	9	L	[2] Michigan* [4]	8-34	97,498
N	15	W	[6] at Purdue* [19]	42-17	52,156
N	22	W	[6] Wisconsin*	35-10	96,934
N	29	L	[4] at Michigan State*	14-49	73,623
J	1	L	[11] Florida [6]	6-21	72,940
			(CompUSA Florida Citrus Bowl)		

*Big Ten Conference games. Season statistics do not include CompUSA Florida Citrus Bowl.

National ranking on day of game in brackets.

Year By Year

Season	W	L	T	Pts.	Opp.	Coach	Captain (s)
1887	2	0	0	78	0	None	George Linsz
1888	0	2	1	6	52	None	George Linsz
1889	2	2	0	32	138	None	James Mock
1890	2	2	0	91	30	None	Harvey McLean
1891	6	2	0	174	46	None	Charles Aull
1892	5	1	0	108	20	George Hoskins	Gus Reed
1893	4	1	0	92	36	George Hoskins	Ed Haley
1894	6	0	1	179	18	George Hoskins	Benjamin Fisher
1895	2	2	3	92	60	George Hoskins	Walter McCaskey
1896	3	4	0	63	128	Dr. Samuel Newton	James Dunsmore
1897	3	6	0	69	141	Dr. Samuel Newton	Joe Curtin
1898	6	4	0	174	91	Dr. Samuel Newton	Lalon Hayes
1899	4	6	1	104	176	Sam Boyle	Brute Randolph
1900	4	6	1	84	144	Pop Golden	Henny Scholl
1901	5	3	0	112	90	Pop Golden	Earl Hewitt
1902	7	3	0	219	34	Pop Golden	Ralph Cummings

1903	5	3	0	182	77	Dan Reed	Ed Whitworth
1904	6	4	0	195	72	Tom Fennell	Carl Forkum
1905	8	3	0	195	34	Tom Fennell	Ed Yeckley
1906	8	1	1	93	10	Tom Fennell	Mother Dunn
1907	6	4	0	251	64	Tom Fennell	Harry Burns
1908	5	5	0	153	51	Tom Fennell	Bull McCleary
1909	5	0	2	166	11	Bill Hollenback	Larry Vorhis
1910	5	2	1	243	24	Jack Hollenback	Alex Gray
1911	8	0	1	199	15	Bill Hollenback	Dexter Very
1912	8	0	0	285	6	Bill Hollenback	Pete Mauthe
1913	2	6	0	78	94	Bill Hollenback	Shorty Miller
1914	5	3	1	121	52	Bill Hollenback	Yeggs Tobin
1915	7	2	0	147	51	Dick Harlow	Bill Wood
1916	8	2	0	348	62	Dick Harlow	Harold Clark
1917	5	4	0	267	61	Dick Harlow	Larry Conover, Bob Higgins
1918	1	2	1	22	66	Hugo Bezdek	Harry Robb, Frank Unger
1919	7	1	0	173	33	Hugo Bezdek	Bob Higgins
1920	7	0	2	259	35	Hugo Bezdek	Bill Hess
1921	8	0	2	251	56	Hugo Bezdek	George Snell
1922	6	4	1	185	62	Hugo Bezdek	Newsh Bentz
1923	6	2	1	159	46	Hugo Bezdek	Joe Bedenk
1924	6	3	1	202	65	Hugo Bezdek	Bas Gray
1925	4	4	1	67	66	Hugo Bezdek	Bas Gray
1926	5	4	0	200	83	Hugo Bezdek	Ken Weston
1927	6	2	1	163	81	Hugo Bezdek	Johnny Roepke
1928	3	5	1	93	68	Hugo Bezdek	Don Greenshields, Steve Hamas
1929	6	3	0	101	75	Hugo Bezdek	Jack Martin
1930	3	4	2	142	111	Bob Higgins	Frank Diedrich
1931	2	8	0	69	167	Bob Higgins	George Lasich
1932	2	5	0	82	115	Bob Higgins	George Collins
1933	3	3	1	117	66	Bob Higgins	Tom Slusser
1934	4	4	0	115	58	Bob Higgins	M.B. Morrison
1935	4	4	0	76	70	Bob Higgins	Robert Weber
1936	3	5	0	109	86	Bob Higgins	Chuck Cherundolo
1937	5	3	0	133	114	Bob Higgins	Sam Donato, John Economos
1938	3	4	1	138	87	Bob Higgins	Dean Hanley
1939	5	1	2	114	77	Bob Higgins	Spike Alter
1940	6	1	1	135	46	Bob Higgins	Leon Gajecki
1941	7	2	0	200	78	Bob Higgins	Lenny Krouse
1942	6	1	1	91	70	Bob Higgins	Lou Palazzi
1943	5	3	1	124	53	Bob Higgins	John Jaffurs
1944	6	3	0	207	141	Bob Higgins	John Chuckran
1945	5	3	0	173	89	Bob Higgins	None
1946	6	2	0	192	48	Bob Higgins	Red Moore, Bucky Walters
1947	9	0	1	332	25	Bob Higgins	John Nolan, John Potsklan
1948	7	1	1	219	55	Bob Higgins	Joe Colone
1949	5	4	0	162	175	Joe Bedenk	Bob Hicks, Neg Norton
1950	5	3	1	141	155	Rip Engle	Owen Dougherty
1951	5	4	0	155	161	Rip Engle	Art Betts, Len Shephard
1952	7	2	1	172	149	Rip Engle	Joe Gratson, Stewart Scheetz
1953	6	3	0	207	148	Rip Engle	Don Malinak, Tony Rados
1954	7	2	0	206	92	Rip Engle	Don Balthaser, Jim Garrity
1955	5	4	0	163	150	Rip Engle	Otto Kneidinger, Frank Reich
1956	6	2	1	177	60	Rip Engle	Sam Valentine
1957	6	3	0	167	135	Rip Engle	Joe Sabol
1958	6	3	1	237	97	Rip Engle	Steve Garban
1959	9	2	0	262	112	Rip Engle	Pat Botula
1960	7	3	0	228	113	Rip Engle	Hank Oppermann
1961	8	3	0	261	143	Rip Engle	Jim Smith
1962	9	2	0	256	119	Rip Engle	Joe Galardi
1963	7	3	0	165	114	Rip Engle	Ralph Baker
1964	6	4	0	189	111	Rip Engle	Bill Bowes
1965	5	5	0	202	151	Rip Engle	Bob Andronici
1966	5	5	0	193	208	Joe Paterno	Mike Irwin, John Runnells
1967	8	2	1	299	158	Joe Paterno	Bill Lenkaitis, Jim Litterelle
1968	11	0	0	354	120	Joe Paterno	John Kulka, Mike Reid, Steve Smear
1969	11	0	0	322	90	Joe Paterno	Tom Jackson, Mike Reid, Steve Smear
1970	7	3	0	300	163	Joe Paterno	Jack Ham, Warren Koegel
1971	11	1	0	484	137	Joe Paterno	Dave Joyner, Charlie Zapiec
1972	10	2	0	358	189	Joe Paterno	Gregg Ducatte, Jim Heller, John Hufnagel, Carl Schaukowitch
1973	12	0	0	447	129	Joe Paterno	John Cappelletti, Randy Crowder, Mark Markovich, Ed O'Neil

1974	10	2	0	322	142	Joe Paterno	Jack Baiorunos, Jim Bradley
1975	9	3	0	240	123	Joe Paterno	Greg Buttle, John Quinn, Tom Rafferty
1976	7	5	0	241	173	Joe Paterno	Kurt Allerman, John Andress, Chuck Benjamin, Brad Benson, Ron Crosby, George Reihner, Bernard Robinson
1977	11	1	0	390	187	Joe Paterno	John Dunn, Steve Geise, Ron Hostetler, Randy Sidler
1978	11	1	0	333	111	Joe Paterno	Chuck Fusina, Paul Suhey
1979	8	4	0	257	178	Joe Paterno	Lance Mehl, Matt Millen, Irv Pankey
1980	10	2	0	321	158	Joe Paterno	Bob Jagers, Greg Jones
1981	10	2	0	371	162	Joe Paterno	Sean Farrell, Chet Parlavecchio, Leo Wisniewski
1982	11	1	0	395	196	Joe Paterno	Walker Lee Ashley, Ken Kelley, Stuart McMunn, Pete Speros
1983	8	4	1	320	312	Joe Paterno	Ron Heller, Kenny Jackson, Scott Radecic, Mark Robinson
1984	6	5	0	209	230	Joe Paterno	Bill Emerson, Nick Haden, Carmen Masciantonio, Stan Short, Doug Strang
1985	11	1	0	275	153	Joe Paterno	Rogers Alexander, Todd Moules, Michael Zordich
1986	12	0	0	340	133	Joe Paterno	Shane Conlan, John Shaffer, Steve Smith, Bob White
1987	8	4	0	286	244	Joe Paterno	Trey Bauer, Marques Henderson, Matt Knizner
1988	5	6	0	231	201	Joe Paterno	John Greene, Eddie Johnson, Keith Karpinski, Steve Wisniewski
1989	8	3	1	209	130	Joe Paterno	Brian Chizmar, Andre Collins, Blair Thomas
1990	9	3	0	280	155	Joe Paterno	Matt McCartin, Willie Thomas, Leroy Thompson
1991	11	2	0	432	167	Joe Paterno	Mark D'Onofrio, Sam Gash, Keith Goganious, Al Golden, Darren Perry, Terry Smith
1992	7	5	0	388	210	Joe Paterno	John Gerak, Reggie Givens, O.J. McDuffie, Brett Wright
1993	10	2	0	357	202	Joe Paterno	Lou Benfatti, Mike Malinoski, Brian O'Neal
1994	12	0	0	526	232	Joe Paterno	Kerry Collins, Brian Gelzheiser, Bucky Greeley, Willie Smith, Vin Stewart
1995	9	3	0	356	245	Joe Paterno	Todd Atkins, Bobby Engram, Jeff Hartings, Terry Killens
1996	11	2	0	362	188	Joe Paterno	Kim Herring, Brandon Noble, Wally Richardson, Barry Tielsch
1997	9	3	0	366	254	Joe Paterno	Aaron Collins, Matt Fornadel, Mike McQueary, Phil Ostrowski
Totals	**715**	**299**	**42**				

Penn State vs. Opponents

Opponent	First Game	Last Game	W	L	T
Air Force	1962	1973	3	0	0
Alabama	1959	1990	5	8	0
Allegheny	1903	1906	3	0	0
Altoona Athletic Association	1890	1907	2	0	0
Arizona State	1977	1977	1	0	0
Army	1899	1979	13	10	2
Army Ambulance Corps	1917	1917	1	0	0
Auburn	1995	1995	1	0	0
Baylor	1975	1975	1	0	0
Bellefonte Academy	1890	1908	2	1	0
Bloomsburg	1897	1897	1	0	0
Boston College	1949	1992	19	2	0
Boston U.	1951	1961	8	0	0
Bowling Green	1987	1987	1	0	0
Brigham Young	1989	1992	2	1	0
Brown	1983	1983	1	0	0
Bucknell	1887	1948	28	10	0
Buffalo	1900	1900	0	1	0
California	1961	1966	3	1	0
California State (Pa.)	1905	1905	1	0	0
Carlisle Indians	1896	1909	1	4	1
Carnegie Tech	1910	1924	6	0	0
Cincinnati	1981	1992	7	1	0
Clemson	1988	1988	0	1	0
Colgate	1911	1980	9	4	1
Colorado	1969	1970	1	1	0
Columbia	1933	1934	0	2	0
Cornell	1895	1943	4	7	2
Dartmouth	1917	1920	1	2	0
Dickinson	1888	1931	11	5	1
Dickinson Seminary	1902	1903	2	0	0
Duquesne Athletic Club	1898	1900	0	3	0
East Carolina	1985	1986	2	0	0
Eastern Michigan	1992	1992	1	0	0

Florida	1962	1997	0	2	0
Florida State	1967	1990	0	1	1
Fordham	1946	1953	3	0	0
Franklin & Marshall	1890	1925	2	1	0
Furman	1958	1958	1	0	0
Geneva	1904	1916	7	0	0
Georgetown	1950	1950	1	0	0
George Washington	1926	1928	3	0	0
Georgia	1982	1982	1	0	0
Georgia Tech	1921	1991	4	3	0
Gettysburg	1891	1937	27	0	1
Grove City	1907	1909	3	0	0
Harrisburg Athletic Club	1910	1910	1	0	0
Harvard	1913	1932	0	3	2
Haverford	1891	1891	1	0	0
Holy Cross	1954	1963	9	0	0
Homestead Athletic Club	1901	1901	0	1	0
Houston	1964	1977	2	0	0
Illinois	1954	1997	6	1	0
Indiana	1993	1996	4	0	0
Iowa	1930	1996	9	4	0
Jersey Shore	1904	1904	1	0	0
Johns Hopkins	1933	1933	1	0	0
Kansas	1968	1968	1	0	0
Kansas State	1968	1969	2	0	0
Kent State	1965	1965	1	0	0
Kentucky	1975	1978	2	2	0
Lafayette	1889	1938	10	5	1
Lebanon Valley	1905	1935	20	0	0
Lehigh	1888	1942	16	6	1
Louisiana State	1974	1974	1	0	0
Louisville	1996	1997	2	0	0
Mansfield	1899	1899	1	0	0
Marietta	1924	1926	3	0	0
Marquette	1957	1958	2	0	0
Marshall	1929	1930	2	0	0
Maryland	1917	1993	35	1	1
Miami (Fla.)	1961	1992	6	5	0
Michigan	1993	1997	3	2	0
Michigan State	1914	1997	5	9	1
Middlebury	1922	1922	1	0	0
Minnesota	1993	1997	3	0	0
Missouri	1959	1980	3	1	0
Muhlenberg	1914	1945	5	1	0
Navy	1894	1974	18	17	2
Nebraska	1920	1983	6	5	0
New York U.	1927	1941	2	1	1
Niagara	1929	1930	2	0	0
North Carolina	1943	1943	0	1	0
North Carolina State	1920	1982	17	2	0
Northern Illinois	1996	1996	1	0	0
Northwestern	1993	1997	4	1	0
Notre Dame	1913	1992	8	8	1
Oberlin	1894	1894	1	0	0
Ohio State	1912	1997	8	5	0
Ohio U.	1967	1974	5	0	0
Oklahoma	1972	1985	0	2	0
Oregon	1960	1994	3	1	0
Pennsylvania	1890	1958	18	25	4
Pittsburgh	1893	1997	48	41	4
Pittsburgh Athletic Club	1892	1895	3	1	0
Princeton	1896	1900	0	5	0
Purdue	1951	1997	3	1	1
Rice	1962	1963	2	0	0
Rutgers	1918	1995	22	2	0
St. Bonaventure	1910	1922	4	0	0
Sewanee	1932	1932	1	0	0
South Carolina	1940	1941	2	0	0
Southern California	1923	1996	4	3	0
Southern Methodist U.	1948	1978	1	0	1
Stanford	1973	1992	4	1	0

Steelton YMCA	1902	1902	0	1	0
Sterling Athletic Club	1910	1910	1	0	0
Susquehanna	1898	1926	6	0	0
Swarthmore	1889	1891	2	0	0
Syracuse	1922	1990	40	23	5
Temple	1931	1997	30	3	1
Tennessee	1971	1993	2	2	0
Texas	1972	1996	3	2	0
Texas A & M	1979	1980	1	1	0
Texas Christian U.	1953	1978	3	1	0
Texas Tech	1995	1995	1	0	0
Tulane	1979	1979	1	0	0
UCLA	1963	1968	2	4	0
Ursinus	1914	1919	2	0	0
Utah State	1977	1977	1	0	0
Vanderbilt	1957	1957	0	1	0
Villanova	1902	1951	5	3	1
Virginia	1893	1989	4	1	0
VMI	1959	1959	1	0	0
Wake Forest	1974	1974	1	0	0
Washington	1921	1983	2	0	0
Washington & Jefferson	1894	1917	5	2	2
Washington State	1947	1948	2	0	0
Waynesburg	1931	1932	0	2	0
Western Maryland	1935	1935	1	0	0
Western Reserve	1895	1895	0	0	1
Westminster	1914	1916	3	0	0
West Virginia	1904	1992	48	9	2
West Virginia Wesleyan	1915	1917	3	0	0
William & Mary	1922	1984	4	0	0
Wisconsin	1953	1997	2	3	0
Wissahickon Barracks	1918	1918	0	0	1
Wyoming Seminary	1892	1892	1	0	0
Yale	1899	1906	0	7	0

Includes bowl games.

Joe Paterno vs. Opponents

Opponent	First Game	Overall Record	Home	Away	Neutral
Air Force	1971	2-0-0	1-0	1-0	0-0
Alabama	1975	4-8-0	2-3	2-3	0-2
Arizona State	1977	1-0-0	0-0	0-0	1-0
Army	1966	9-1-0	6-0	3-1	0-0
Auburn	1995	1-0-0	0-0	0-0	1-0
Baylor	1975	1-0-0	0-0	0-0	1-0
Boston College	1966	16-2-0	8-1	8-1	0-0
Bowling Green	1987	1-0-0	1-0	0-0	0-0
Brigham Young	1989	2-1-0	1-0	0-1	1-0
Brown	1984	1-0-0	1-0	0-0	0-0
California	1966	1-0-0	1-0	0-0	0-0
Cincinnati	1981	7-1-0	5-1	1-0	1-0
Clemson	1988	0-1-0	0-0	0-0	0-1
Colgate	1980	1-0-0	1-0	0-0	0-0
Colorado	1969	1-1-0	1-0	0-1	0-0
East Carolina	1985	2-0-0	2-0	0-0	0-0
Eastern Michigan	1992	1-0-0	1-0	0-0	0-0
Florida	1998	0-1-0	0-0	0-0	0-1
Florida State	1967	0-1-1	0-0	0-0	0-1-1
Georgia	1982	1-0-0	0-0	0-0	1-0
Georgia Tech	1966	1-1-0	0-0	0-1	1-0
Houston	1977	1-0-0	1-0	0-0	0-0
Indiana	1993	4-0-0	2-0	2-0	0-0
Illinois	1972	4-0-0	1-0	3-0	0-0
Iowa	1971	9-3-0	3-3	6-0	0-0
Kansas	1969	1-0-0	0-0	0-0	1-0
Kansas State	1968	2-0-0	1-0	1-0	0-0

Kentucky	1975	2-2-0	1-1	1-1	0-0
Louisiana State	1974	1-0-0	0-0	0-0	1-0
Louisville	1996	2-0-0	1-0	1-0	0-0
Maryland	1966	24-0-1	13-0	9-0	2-0-1
Miami (Fla.)	1967	6-4-0	3-2	2-2	1-0
Michigan	1993	3-2-0	1-2	2-0	0-0
Michigan State	1966	4-2-0	2-0	2-2	0-0
Minnesota	1993	3-0-0	2-0	1-0	0-0
Missouri	1970	2-0-0	0-0	1-0	1-0
Navy	1967	6-2-0	3-1	3-1	0-0
Nebraska	1979	2-3-0	1-1	1-1	0-1
North Carolina State	1967	12-2-0	8-1	4-1	0-0
Northern Illinois	1996	1-0-0	1-0	0-0	0-0
Northwestern	1993	4-1-0	2-0	2-1	0-0
Notre Dame	1976	8-5-0	5-1	3-3	0-1
Ohio State	1975	4-5-0	2-2	1-3	1-0
Ohio U.	1967	5-0-0	5-0	0-0	0-0
Oklahoma	1972	0-2-0	0-0	0-0	0-2
Oregon	1995	1-0-0	0-0	0-0	1-0
Pittsburgh	1966	21-6-1	10-4	9-1-1	2-1
Purdue	1995	3-0-0	1-0	2-0	0-0
Rutgers	1977	16-1-0	10-1	0-0	6-0
Southern California	1982	4-2-0	2-0	0-2	2-0
Southern Methodist U.	1978	1-0-0	1-0	0-0	0-0
Stanford	1973	4-1-0	3-0	1-0	0-1
Syracuse	1966	21-4-0	10-3	10-1	1-0
Temple	1975	21-0-0	12-0	6-0	3-0
Tennessee	1971	2-2-0	0-0	0-2	2-0
Texas	1972	3-2-0	0-1	1-0	2-1
Texas A & M	1979	1-1-0	0-1	1-0	0-0
Texas Christian	1971	2-0-0	2-0	0-0	0-0
Texas Tech	1995	1-0-0	1-0	0-0	0-0
Tulane	1979	1-0-0	0-0	0-0	1-0
UCLA	1966	1-2-0	0-1	1-1	0-0
Utah State	1977	1-0-0	1-0	0-0	0-0
Virginia	1988	1-1-0	0-1	1-0	0-0
Wake Forest	1974	1-0-0	1-0	0-0	0-0
Washington	1984	1-0-0	0-0	0-0	1-0
West Virginia	1966	25-2-0	13-0	12-2	0-0
William & Mary	1984	1-0-0	1-0	0-0	0-0
Wisconsin	1970	2-2-0	1-1	1-1	0-0
Totals		**298-77-3**	**158-32**	**105-33-1**	**35-12-2**

Includes bowl games.

Penn State Coaches Records

Season (s)	Coach	Won	Lost	Tied	Pct.
1892-95	George Hoskins	17	4	4	82.6
1896-98	Samuel Newton	12	14	0	46.2
1899	Sam Boyle	4	6	1	40.9
1900-02	Pop Golden	16	12	1	56.9
1903	Dan Reed	5	3	0	62.5
1904-08	Tom Fennell	33	17	1	65.7
1909, 11-14	Bill Hollenback	28	9	4	73.2
1910	Jack Hollenback	5	2	1	68.8
1915-17	Dick Harlow	20	8	0	71.4
1918-29	Hugo Bezdek	65	30	11	66.5
1930-48	Bob Higgins	91	57	11	60.7
1949	Joe Bedenk	5	4	0	55.6
1950-65	Rip Engle	104	48	4	67.9
1966-	Joe Paterno	298	77	3	79.3

Penn State Individual Records

Rushing Records

RUSHING YARDAGE
Game: 256
Curt Warner at Syracuse, 1981.
By a senior: 239, Bob Campbell vs.Syracuse, 1968.
By a junior: 256, Curt Warner at Syracuse, 1981.
By a sophomore: 241, Curtis Enis vs. Southern Cal, 1996.
By a freshman: 208, Shelly Hammonds at Boston College, 1990.
Half: 207
Bob Campbell (14 carries, 1st half) vs. Syracuse, 1968.
Season: 1567
Lydell Mitchell, 1971.
By a senior: 1567, Lydell Mitchell, 1971.
By a junior: 1539, Ki-Jana Carter, 1994.
By a sophomore: 1210, Curtis Enis, 1996.
By a freshman: 1002, D.J. Dozier, 1983.
Career: 3398
Curt Warner, 1979-82.

RUSHING ATTEMPTS
Game: 41
John Cappelletti vs. N.C. State, 1973
Season: 286
John Cappelletti, 1973.
Career: 649
Curt Warner, 1979-82.

RUSHING AVERAGE
Game: 44.0
Blair Thomas vs. Syracuse, 1986.
Season: 8.4
Blair Thomas, 1986.
Career: 7.2
Ki-Jana Carter, 1992-94.

100-YARD RUSHING GAMES
Season: 9
Ki-Jana Carter, 1994.
Career: 18
Curt Warner, 1979-82.
Consecutive Games: 8
Curtis Enis, 1997.

200-YARD RUSHING GAMES
Season: 3
John Cappelletti, 1973.
Career: 3
John Cappelletti, 1972-73.
Consecutive Games: 3
John Cappelletti, 1973.

RUSHING TOUCHDOWNS
Game: 6
Harry Robb vs. Gettysburg, 1917.
Half: 4
Leroy Thompson vs. Rutgers, 1990;
Ki-Jana Carter vs. Michigan State, 1994.
Season: 26
Lydell Mitchell, 1971.
By a senior: 26, Lydell Mitchell, 1971.
By a junior: 23, Ki-Jana Carter, 1994.
By a sophomore: 13, Bull McCleary, 1907; Harry Robb, 1917, Curtis Enis, 1996.
By a freshman: 7, D.J. Dozier, 1983.
Career: 38
Lydell Mitchell, 1969-71.

GAME RUSHING YARDAGE

Yards	Att.	TD	
256	26	1	Curt Warner at Syracuse, 1981
250	—	—	Shorty Miller vs. Carnegie Tech, 1913
243	14	2	Bob Pollard at Rutgers, 1951
241	27	3	Curtis Enis vs. Southern Cal, 1996.
239	24	2	Bob Campbell vs. Syracuse, 1968
238	28	0	Curt Warner at Nebraska, 1981
227	27	5	Ki-Jana Carter vs. Michigan State, 1994
225	23	2	Matt Suhey vs. Army, 1979
220	41	3	John Cappelletti vs. N.C. State, 1973
214	35	1	Blair Thomas vs. Notre Dame, 1987
211	29	2	Lydell Mitchell at Iowa, 1971
211	23	1	Curtis Enis vs. Ohio State, 1997
210	20	3	Ki-Jana Carter at Minnesota, 1994
209	24	5	Lydell Mitchell vs. Maryland, 1971
208	24	2	Shelly Hammonds at Boston College, 1990
204	25	4	John Cappelletti vs. Ohio U., 1973
202	37	0	John Cappelletti at Maryland, 1973

SEASON LEADERS

Season	Name	Yards	Att.	Avg.	TD
1946	Elwood Petchel	373	71	5.0	7
1947	Fran Rogel	499	110	4.6	7
1948	Fran Rogel	602	152	4.0	5
1949	Fran Rogel	395	110	3.6	3
1950	Tony Orsini	563	146	3.9	5
1951	Ted Shattuck	579	135	4.3	4
1952	Bob Pollard	341	110	3.1	2
1953	Lenny Moore	601	108	5.6	7
1954	Lenny Moore	1082	136	8.0	11
1955	Lenny Moore	697	138	5.1	5
1956	Billy Kane	544	105	5.0	7
1957	Dave Kasperian	469	122	3.8	7
1958	Dave Kasperian	381	98	3.9	5
1959	Rich Lucas	325	99	3.3	6
1960	Jim Kerr	389	93	4.2	6
1961	Roger Kochman	666	129	5.2	6
1962	Roger Kochman	652	120	5.4	4
1963	Gary Klingensmith	450	102	4.4	3
1964	Tom Urbanik	625	134	4.7	8
1965	Dave McNaughton	884	193	4.6	7
1966	Bob Campbell	482	79	6.1	5
1967	Charlie Pittman	580	119	4.9	6
1968	Charlie Pittman	950	186	5.1	14
1969	Charlie Pittman	706	149	4.7	10
1970	Lydell Mitchell	751	134	5.6	6
1971	Lydell Mitchell	1567	254	6.2	26
1972	John Cappelletti	1117	233	4.8	12
1973	John Cappelletti	1522	286	5.3	17
1974	Tom Donchez	880	195	4.5	7
1975	Woody Petchel	621	148	4.2	5
1976	Steve Geise	560	116	4.8	3
1977	Matt Suhey	638	139	4.6	8
1978	Matt Suhey	720	184	3.9	7
1979	Matt Suhey	973	185	5.3	6
1980	Curt Warner	922	196	4.7	6
1981	Curt Warner	1044	171	6.1	8
1982	Curt Warner	1041	198	5.3	8
1983	D.J. Dozier	1002	174	5.8	7
1984	D.J. Dozier	691	125	5.5	4
1985	D.J. Dozier	723	154	4.7	4
1986	D.J. Dozier	811	171	4.7	10
1987	Blair Thomas	1414	268	5.3	11
1988	Gary Brown	689	136	5.1	6
1989	Blair Thomas	1341	264	5.1	5
1990	Leroy Thompson	573	152	3.8	8
1991	Richie Anderson	779	152	5.1	10
1992	Richie Anderson	900	195	4.6	18
1993	Ki-Jana Carter	1026	155	6.6	7
1994	Ki-Jana Carter	1539	198	7.8	23
1995	Curtis Enis	683	113	6.0	4
1996	Curtis Enis	1210	224	5.4	13
1997	Curtis Enis	1363	228	6.0	19

SEASON RUSHING YARDAGE

Yards	Att.	TD	
1567	254	26	Lydell Mitchell, 1971
1539	198	23	Ki-Jana Carter, 1994
1522	286	17	John Cappelletti, 1973
1414	268	11	Blair Thomas, 1987
1363	228	19	Curtis Enis, 1997
1341	264	5	Blair Thomas, 1989
1210	224	13	Curtis Enis, 1996
1117	233	12	John Cappelletti, 1972
1082	136	11	Lenny Moore, 1954
1044	171	8	Curt Warner, 1981
1041	198	8	Curt Warner, 1982
1026	155	7	Ki-Jana Carter, 1993
1002	174	7	D.J. Dozier, 1983

CAREER 1,000 yard RUSHING YARDAGE

		Yards	Att.	TD
1.	Curt Warner, 1979-82	3398	649	24
2.	Blair Thomas, 1985-87, 89	3301	606	21
3.	Curtis Enis, 1995-1997	3256	565	36
4.	D.J. Dozier, 1983-86	3227	624	25
5.	Lydell Mitchell, 1969-71	2934	501	38
6.	Ki-Jana Carter, 1992-94	2829	395	34
7.	Matt Suhey, 1976-79	2818	633	26
8.	John Cappelletti, 1972-73	2639	519	29
9.	Lenny Moore, 1953-55	2380	382	23
10.	Charlie Pittman, 1967-69	2236	454	30
11.	Booker Moore, 1977-80	2072	448	20
12.	Jon Williams, 1980-83	2042	399	14
13.	Franco Harris, 1969-71	2002	380	24
14.	Richie Anderson, 1989-92	1756	363	29
15.	Mike Archie, 1992-95	1694	305	14
16.	Fran Rogel, 1947-49	1496	372	15
17.	Roger Kochman, 1959-62	1485	264	12
18.	Bob Campbell, 1966-68	1480	242	14
19.	Tom Donchez, 1971-74	1422	296	11
20.	Steve Geise, 1975-77	1362	313	11
21.	Gary Brown, 1987-90	1321	260	11
22.	Steve Smith, 1983-86	1246	265	11
23.	Leroy Thompson, 1987-90	1215	334	12
24.	Stephen Pitts, 1992-95	1156	215	5
25.	Mike Guman, 1976-79	1130	276	12
26.	Tony Mumford, 1981-84	1103	245	8
27.	Tim Manoa, 1983-86	1098	223	5
28.	Bob Torrey, 1976-78	1095	222	3
29.	Duane Taylor, 1973-77	1060	228	10
30.	Woody Petchel, 1973-75	1058	257	14

LONGEST RUNS

92*	Duane Taylor (14) & Dan Natale (78) at Syracuse,1973
92**	Blair Thomas vs. Syracuse, 1986
90	Bill Suter at Navy, 1894
87	Bob Campbell vs. Syracuse, 1968
86	Bob Riggle at West Virginia, 1964
84	Chafie Fields vs. Texas, 1997 Fiesta
83	Ki-Jana Carter vs. Oregon, 1995 Rose
80	Chuck Peters vs. Syracuse, 1938
80	Ron Younker vs. Virginia, 1954
80	Lenny Moore at Rutgers, 1955
80	Kevin Baugh vs. Colgate, 1980
80	David Clark vs. William & Mary, 1984
80	Gary Brown at Syracuse, 1987
80	Ki-Jana Carter at Minnesota, 1994
80	Ki-Jana Carter at Indiana, 1994
79	Sparky Brown vs. Bucknell, 1942
79	Lenny Moore at Pittsburgh, 1953
78	Shorty Miller vs. Carnegie Tech, 1912
78	Elwood Petchel at Fordham, 1947
78	Curtis Enis vs. Wisconsin, 1997
77**	Dick Jones at Boston U., 1953
76**	David Clark at Rutgers, 1985
75	Bob Higgins at Pittsburgh, 1919
75	Bob Pollard at Rutgers, 1951
75	John Sacca vs. Cincinnati, 1991
73**	Walt Addie vs. Maryland, 1972
72	Harry Wilson vs. Navy, 1923
71	Bob Pollard at Rutgers, 1951
71	Lydell Mitchell vs. Maryland, 1969

* Fumble recovery
**Non-scoring play

Passing Records

PASSING YARDAGE
Game: 366
Mike McQueary vs. Pittsburgh, 1997.
By a senior: Mike McQueary vs. Pittsburgh, 1997.
By a junior: 352, Kerry Collins at Michigan State, 1993.
By a sophomore: 358, Todd Blackledge at Miami (Fla.), 1981.
By a freshman: 215, Tony Sacca vs. Syracuse, 1988.
First Half: 219
Mike McQueary vs. Wisconsin, 1997.
Second Half: 225
Todd Blackledge at Miami (Fla.), 1981.
Season: 2679
Kerry Collins, 1994.
By a senior: 2679, Kerry Collins, 1994.
By a junior: 2221, Chuck Fusina, 1977.
By a sophomore: 1557, Todd Blackledge, 1981.
By a freshman: 1037, Todd Blackledge, 1980.
Career: 5869
Tony Sacca, 1988-91.

COMPLETIONS
Game: 33
Wally Richardson vs. Wisconsin, 1995.
Season: 193
Wally Richardson, 1995.
Career: 401
Tony Sacca, 1988-91.
Consecutive: 14
Kerry Collins at Minnesota, 1994.

COMPLETION PERCENTAGE
Game: 91.7
Pete Liske at Oregon, 1963.
Season: 66.7
Kerry Collins, 1994.
Career: 56.3
Kerry Collins, 1991-94.

PASS ATTEMPTS
Game: 54
Kerry Collins at Brigham Young, 1992.
Season: 335
Wally Richardson, 1995.
Career: 824
Tony Sacca, 1988-91.

YARDS PER ATTEMPT
Season: 10.15
Kerry Collins, 1994.
Career: 8.69
John Hufnagel, 1970-72.

TOUCHDOWNS
Game: 5
Tony Sacca vs. Georgia Tech, 1991.
Season: 22
Todd Blackledge, 1982.
Career: 41
Todd Blackledge, 1980-82;
Tony Sacca, 1988-91.

TOUCHDOWN PASS IN CONSECUTIVE GAMES
In One Season: 11
Kerry Collins, 1994.
Over Two Seasons: 14
Kerry Collins, 1993-94.

Passing Records continued:

INTERCEPTIONS
Game: 4
Rich Lucas at Illinois, 1959; Bob Parsons vs. Syracuse, 1970;
Todd Blackledge at Alabama, 1982.
Season: 15
Vince O'Bara, 1950.
Career: 41
Todd Blackledge, 1980-82.

PASSING EFFICIENCY RATING
Season: 172.86
Kerry Collins, 1994.
Career: 145.57
Mike McQueary, 1994-97.

200 Yard Game
Season: 10
Kerry Collins, 1994
Career: 16
Kerry Collins, 1992-94.

SEASON LEADERS

Season	Name	Yards	Att.	Cmp.	Int.	TD
1946	Elwood Petchel	287	37	16	4	2
1947	Elwood Petchel	353	38	18	3	5
1948	Elwood Petchel	628	100	48	11	9
1949	Owen Dougherty	281	28	12	5	3
1950	Vince O'Bara	640	103	38	15	3
1951	Bob Szajna	528	86	41	7	3
1952	Tony Rados	937	186	93	10	8
1953	Tony Rados	1025	171	81	12	8
1954	Don Bailey	393	80	33	2	5
1955	Bobby Hoffman	355	53	25	7	1
1956	Milt Plum	675	75	40	7	6
1957	Al Jacks	673	103	53	3	5
1958	Rich Lucas	483	80	36	4	3
1959	Rich Lucas	913	117	58	8	5
1960	Galen Hall	448	89	39	5	5
1961	Galen Hall	951	97	50	5	8
1962	Pete Liske	1037	162	91	4	12
1963	Pete Liske	1117	161	87	5	10
1964	Gary Wydman	832	149	70	6	1
1965	Jack White	1275	205	98	14	6
1966	Tom Sherman	943	135	58	4	6
1967	Tom Sherman	1616	205	104	9	13
1968	Chuck Burkhart	1170	177	87	7	6
1969	Chuck Burkhart	805	114	59	9	1
1970	Mike Cooper	429	64	32	6	4
1971	John Hufnagel	1185	136	86	6	10
1972	John Hufnagel	2039	216	115	8	15
1973	Tom Shuman	1375	161	83	5	13
1974	Tom Shuman	1355	183	97	6	12
1975	John Andress	991	149	71	4	2
1976	Chuck Fusina	1260	168	88	10	11
1977	Chuck Fusina	2221	246	142	9	15
1978	Chuck Fusina	1859	242	137	12	11
1979	Dayle Tate	1179	176	92	11	8
1980	Todd Blackledge	1037	159	76	13	7
1981	Todd Blackledge	1557	207	104	14	12
1982	Todd Blackledge	2218	292	161	14	22
1983	Doug Strang	1944	259	134	7	19
1984	Doug Strang	840	148	57	10	5
1985	John Shaffer	1366	228	103	10	8
1986	John Shaffer	1510	204	114	4	9
1987	Matt Knizner	1478	223	113	12	7
1988	Tony Sacca	821	146	54	5	4
1989	Tony Sacca	694	137	56	5	6
1990	Tony Sacca	1866	249	122	9	10
1991	Tony Sacca	2488	292	169	5	21

Season Leaders continued:

Year	Player					
1992	John Sacca	1118	155	81	3	9
1993	Kerry Collins	1605	250	127	11	13
1994	Kerry Collins	2679	264	176	7	21
1995	Wally Richardson	2198	335	193	6	18
1996	Wally Richardson	1732	279	145	8	7
1997	Mike McQueary	2211	255	146	9	17

GAME PASSING YARDAGE

Yards	Att.	Cmp.	TD	Int	
366	36	21	2	0	Mike McQueary vs. Pittsburgh, 1997.
358	41	26	2	2	Todd Blackledge at Miami (Fla.), 1981
352	42	23	3	1	Kerry Collins at Michigan State, 1993
328	16	14	2	0	Kerry Collins vs. Rutgers, 1994
317	54	28	1	0	Kerry Collins at Brigham Young, 1992
315	36	22	2	2	Chuck Fusina at N.C. State, 1977
303	37	21	3	0	John Sacca at Rutgers, 1992
300	38	24	1	1	Kerry Collins at Illinois, 1994
295	39	23	3	1	Todd Blackledge vs. Nebraska, 1982
293	27	15	4	1	Chuck Fusina vs. Syracuse, 1978
292	22	16	1	0	Tony Sacca vs. Boston College, 1991
290	30	14	1	1	John Hufnagel vs. Maryland, 1972
289	24	16	1	1	Kerry Collins vs. Michigan State, 1994
288	41	20	1	1	John Sacca vs. Boston College, 1992
286	29	19	2	0	Chuck Fusina vs. Maryland, 1977
286	19	12	3	1	Kerry Collins at Temple, 1994
281	29	18	2	1	Wally Richardson at Purdue, 1995
281	31	21	1	0	Wally Richardson vs. Michigan State, 1996
278	30	19	1	0	Kerry Collins at Northwestern, 1993
277	34	20	3	0	Tony Sacca at Notre Dame, 1990
274	24	16	3	0	Doug Strang vs. Notre Dame, 1983
274	32	18	4	0	John Sacca vs. Minnesota, 1993

SEASON PASSING YARDAGE

Yards	Att.	Cmp.	TD	Int	
2679	264	176	21	7	Kerry Collins, 1994
2488	292	169	21	5	Tony Sacca, 1991
2221	246	142	15	9	Chuck Fusina, 1977
2218	292	161	22	14	Todd Blackledge, 1982
2211	255	146	17	9	Mike McQueary, 1997
2198	335	193	18	6	Wally Richardson, 1995
2039	216	115	15	8	John Hufnagel, 1972
1944	259	134	19	7	Doug Strang, 1983
1866	249	122	10	9	Tony Sacca, 1990
1859	242	137	11	12	Chuck Fusina, 1978
1732	279	145	7	8	Wally Richardson, 1996
1616	205	104	13	9	Tom Sherman, 1967
1605	250	127	13	11	Kerry Collins, 1993

CAREER PASSING YARDAGE

Yards	Att.	Cmp.	TD	Int	
5869	824	401	41	24	Tony Sacca, 1988-91
5382	665	371	37	32	Chuck Fusina, 1975-78
5304	657	370	39	21	Kerry Collins, 1991-94
4812	658	341	41	41	Todd Blackledge, 1980-82
4419	692	378	27	14	Wally Richardson, 1992, 1994-96
3545	408	225	26	17	John Hufnagel, 1970-72
3469	547	262	18	24	John Shaffer, 1983-86
2966	438	202	24	20	Doug Strang, 1981-84
2886	365	188	28	12	Tom Shuman, 1972-74
2730	307	167	22	11	Mike McQueary, 1994-97

LONGEST PASS PLAYS

92	Bob Higgins from Harold Hess at Pittsburgh, 1919
86	Jim Scott from Steve Joachim at Navy, 1971
82	Eric Hamilton from Matt Knizner vs. Pittsburgh, 1986
82	Freddie Scott from Kerry Collins vs. Rutgers, 1994
80	Paul Johnson from Tom Sherman at Maryland, 1967
80	Dean DiMidio from Doug Strang vs. Alabama, 1983
79	John Greene from Lance Lonergan vs. Maryland, 1988

Longest Pass Plays continued:

76	Tom Cherry from Chuck Burkhart at UCLA, 1968
76	Jimmy Scott from John Hufnagel at Boston College, 1972
76	Chuck Herd from Tom Shuman vs. West Virginia, 1973
*75	Dick Barvinchak from John Andress at Iowa, 1975
75	David Daniels from Tom Bill vs. Temple, 1989
72	Les Walters from Milt Plum vs. Boston U., 1956
72	Chuck Herd from Tom Shuman vs. LSU, 1974 Orange
72	Scott Fitzkee from Chuck Fusina vs. Miami (Fla.), 1977
70	Rich Mauti from John Andress at Iowa, 1975

*Non-scoring play.

GAME COMPLETIONS

33	Wally Richardson vs. Wisconsin, 1995
28	Kerry Collins at Brigham Young, 1992
26	Todd Blackledge at Miami (Fla.), 1981
24	Tony Sacca at Miami (Fla.), 1991
24	Kerry Collins at Illinois, 1994
24	Wally Richardson at Michigan State, 1995
23	Todd Blackledge vs. Nebraska, 1982
23	Kerry Collins at Michigan State, 1993
22	Chuck Fusina at N.C. State, 1977
21	John Sacca at Rutgers, 1992
21	Wally Richardson vs. Michigan State, 1996
21	Mike McQueary vs. Pittsburgh, 1997
20	Todd Blackledge at Alabama, 1982
20	Tony Sacca at Notre Dame, 1990
20	John Sacca vs. Boston College, 1992
20	Kerry Collins at Michigan, 1994
20	Kerry Collins at Indiana, 1994

SEASON COMPLETIONS

193	Wally Richardson, 1995
176	Kerry Collins, 1994
169	Tony Sacca, 1991
161	Todd Blackledge, 1982
146	Mike McQueary, 1997
145	Wally Richardson, 1996
142	Chuck Fusina, 1977
137	Chuck Fusina, 1978
127	Kerry Collins, 1993

CAREER COMPLETIONS

401	Tony Sacca, 1988-91
378	Wally Richardson, 1992, 94-96
371	Chuck Fusina, 1975-78
370	Kerry Collins, 1991-94
341	Todd Blackledge, 1980-82
262	John Shaffer, 1983-86
225	John Hufnagel, 1970-72

GAME TD PASSES

5	Tony Sacca vs. Georgia Tech, 1991
4	Tom Sherman vs. Pittsburgh, 1967
4	Chuck Fusina vs. Syracuse, 1978
4	Todd Blackledge vs. Temple, 1982
4	Todd Blackledge vs. Maryland, 1982
4	Todd Blackledge vs. Rutgers, 1982
4	John Sacca vs. Minnesota, 1993
4	Kerry Collins vs. Rutgers, 1993
4	Wally Richardson vs. Auburn, 1996 Outback

SEASON TD PASSES

22	Todd Blackledge, 1982
21	Tony Sacca, 1991
21	Kerry Collins, 1994
19	Doug Strang, 1983
18	Wally Richardson, 1995
17	Mike McQueary, 1997
15	John Hufnagel, 1972

Season TD Passes continued:

15	Chuck Fusina, 1977
13	Tom Sherman, 1967
13	Tom Shuman, 1973
13	Kerry Collins, 1993
12	Pete Liske, 1962
12	Tom Shuman, 1974
12	Todd Blackledge, 1981

CAREER TD PASSES

41	Todd Blackledge, 1980-82
41	Tony Sacca, 1988-91
39	Kerry Collins, 1991-94
37	Chuck Fusina, 1975-78
28	Tom Shuman, 1972-74
27	Wally Richardson, 1992, 94-96
26	John Hufnagel, 1970-72
24	Pete Liske, 1961-63
24	Doug Strang, 1981-84
22	Mike McQueary, 1994-97

SEASON TD PASS PCT.

8.08	Tom Shuman, 1973
7.95	Kerry Collins, 1994
7.53	Todd Blackledge, 1982
7.41	Pete Liske, 1962
7.35	John Hufnagel, 1971
7.34	Doug Strang, 1983
7.19	Tony Sacca, 1991
6.94	John Hufnagel, 1972
6.67	Mike McQueary, 1997
6.56	Tom Shuman, 1974
6.55	Chuck Fusina, 1976
6.21	Pete Liske, 1963

CAREER TD PASS PCT.

9.14	Elwood Petchel, 1946-48
7.67	Tom Shuman, 1972-74
7.17	Mike McQueary, 1994-97
6.76	Galen Hall, 1959-61
6.76	Pete Liske, 1961-63
6.48	John Sacca, 1992-93
6.37	John Hufnagel, 1970-72
6.23	Todd Blackledge, 1980-82
5.94	Kerry Collins, 1991-94
5.56	Chuck Fusina, 1975-78

SEASON YARDS/ATTEMPT

10.15	Kerry Collins, 1994
9.44	John Hufnagel, 1972
9.03	Chuck Fusina, 1977
9.00	Milt Plum, 1956
8.71	John Hugnagel, 1971
8.67	Mike McQueary, 1997
8.54	Tom Shuman, 1967
8.52	Tony Sacca, 1991
7.88	Tom Sherman, 1967
7.80	Rich Lucas, 1959
7.68	Chuck Fusina, 1978
7.60	Todd Blackledge, 1981

Career Yards/Attempt

8.89	Mike McQueary, 1994-97
8.69	John Hufnagel, 1970-72
8.09	Chuck Fusina, 1975-78
8.07	Kerry Collins, 1991-94
7.91	Tom Shuman, 1972-74
7.46	Tom Sherman, 1965-67
7.31	Todd Blackledge, 1980-82
7.29	Galen Hall, 1959-61
7.25	Elwood Petchel, 1946-48

Career Yards/Attempt continued:

7.17	Tom Bill, 1987-90
7.12	Rich Lucas, 1957-59
7.12	Tony Sacca, 1988-91

Season Efficiency

172.86	Kerry Collins, 1994
151.84	John Hufnagel, 1971
149.76	Tony Sacca, 1991
148.04	John Hufnagel, 1972
146.38	Chuck Fusina, 1977
145.03	Mike McQueary, 1997
143.73	Tom Shuman, 1973
136.47	Milt Plum, 1956
134.23	Todd Blackledge, 1982
133.64	Doug Strang, 1983

Career Passing Efficiency

140.83	John Hufnagel, 1970-72
137.33	Kerry Collins, 1991-94
136.68	Tom Shuman, 1972-74
132.48	Chuck Fusina, 1975-78
127.71	Pete Liske, 1961-63
127.00	Tom Bill, 1987-90
121.83	Galen Hall, 1959-61
121.32	Todd Blackledge, 1980-82
119.63	Tom Sherman, 1965-67
119.09	Tony Sacca, 1988-91
117.32	Elwood Petchel, 1946-48
117.09	Wally Richardson, 1992, 94-96

Season Interception Pct.

1.46	Kerry Collins, 1992
1.71	Tony Sacca, 1991
1.79	Wally Richardson, 1995
1.94	John Sacca, 1992
1.96	John Shaffer, 1986
2.47	Pete Liske, 1962
2.65	Kerry Collins, 1994
2.69	John Andress, 1975
2.70	Doug Strang, 1983
2.87	Wally Richardson, 1996
2.96	Tom Sherman, 1966
3.11	Pete Liske, 1963
3.11	Tom Shuman, 1973

Career Interception Pct.

2.02	Wally Richardson, 1992, 94-96
2.31	John Sacca, 1992-93
2.82	Pete Liske, 1961-63
3.20	Kerry Collins, 1991-94
3.29	Tom Shuman, 1972-74
3.59	Mike McQueary, 1994-97
3.67	John Andress, 1975-76
3.67	Tom Bill, 1987-90
4.04	Tom Sherman, 1965-67
4.17	John Hufnagel, 1970-72
4.57	Doug Strang, 1981-84

Receiving Records

RECEPTIONS
Game: 13
Freddie Scott vs. Wisconsin, 1995.
By a senior: 11, O.J. McDuffie vs. Boston College, 1992.
By a junior: 13, Freddie Scott vs. Wisconsin, 1995.
By a sophomore: 10, Jack Curry at Syracuse and at California, 1965.
By a freshman: 4, Kenny Jackson, three games, 1980; Terry Smith at West Virginia, 1988; Kyle Brady vs. Notre Dame, 1991.

Receiving Records continued:

Season: 63
O.J. McDuffie, 1992; Bobby Engram, 1995.
By a senior: 63, O.J. McDuffie, 1992; Bobby Engram, 1995.
By a junior: 52, Bobby Engram, 1994.
By a sophomore: 48, Bobby Engram, 1993.
By a freshman: 21, Kenny Jackson, 1980.
By a wide receiver: 63, O.J. McDuffie, 1992.
By a tight end: 36, Troy Drayton, 1992.
By a running back: 32, Curtis Enis, 1996.
Career: 167
Bobby Engram, 1991, 93-95.
By a wide receiver: 167, Bobby Engram, 1991, 93-95.
By a tight end: 86, Ted Kwalick, 1966-68.
By a running back: 70, Mike Archie, 1992-95.

RECEIVING YARDAGE
Game: 212
O.J. McDuffie vs. Boston College, 1992.
By a senior: 212, O.J. McDuffie vs. Boston College, 1992.
By a junior: 155, Len Krouse at Syracuse, 1940.
By a sophomore: 165, Bobby Engram vs. Minnesota, 1993.
By a freshman: 93, Kenny Jackson vs. Nebraska, 1980.
Season: 1084
Bobby Engram, 1995.
By a senior: 1084, Bobby Engram, 1995.
By a junior: 1029, Bobby Engram, 1994.
By a sophomore: 973, Freddie Scott, 1994.
By a freshman: 386, Kenny Jackson, 1980.
By a wide receiver: 1084, Bobby Engram, 1994.
By a tight end: 600, Mickey Shuler, 1977.
By a running back: 335, Curt Warner, 1982.
Career: 3026
Bobby Engram, 1991, 93-95.
By a wide receiver: 3026, Bobby Engram, 1991, 93-95.
By a tight end: 1343, Ted Kwalick, 1966-68.
By a running back: 662, Curt Warner, 1979-82.

100 Yards Receiving
Most Games: 16
Bobby Engram, 1993-95
One Season: 6
Bobby Engram, 1995

RECEIVING YARDAGE AVERAGE
Season: 36.1
Jimmy Scott (12-433-3 TD), 1972.
Career: 30.7
Jimmy Scott (23-705-6 TD), 1971-73.

TOUCHDOWNS
Game: 4
Bobby Engram vs. Minnesota, 1993.
By a senior: 3, Bobby Engram at Rutgers, 1995; Joe Jurevicius at Lousville, 1997.
By a junior: 2, eight times (Last: Joe Jurevicius vs. Northern Illinois, 1996).
By a sophomore: 4, Bobby Engram vs. Minnesota, 1993.
By a freshman: 2, Kyle Brady vs. Cincinnati, 1991.
By a wide receiver: 13, Bobby Engram, 1993.
By a tight end: 5, Bob Parsons, 1971; Dan Natale, 1972.
By a running back: 5, Curt Warner, 1982.
Season: 13
Bobby Engram, 1993.
By a senior: 11, Bobby Engram, 1995.
By a junior: 7, Kenny Jackson, 1982; Bobby Engram, 1994.
By a sophomore: 13, Bobby Engram, 1993.
By a freshman: 5, Kenny Jackson, 1980.
By a wide receiver: 13, Bobby Engram, 1993.
By a tight end: 5, Bob Parsons, 1971; Dan Natale, 1972.
By a running back: 5, Curt Warner, 1982.
Career: 31
Bobby Engram, 1991, 93-95.
By a wide receiver: 31, Bobby Engram,1991, 93-95.
By a tight end: 10, Ted Kwalick, 1966-68.
By a running back: 7, Mike Archie,1992-95.

SEASON LEADERS

Season	Name	Rec.	Yards	Avg.	TD
1946	Sam Tamburo	7	126	18.0	1
1947	Jeff Durkota	6	110	18.5	3
1948	Sam Tamburo	17	301	17.7	3
1949	Robert Hicks	10	196	19.6	2
1950	John Smidansky	23	383	16.7	3
1951	Don Malinak	14	138	9.9	2
1952	Jesse Arnelle	33	291	8.8	2
1953	Jim Garrity	30	349	11.6	1
1954	Jack Sherry	11	160	14.5	1
	Jim Garrity	11	131	11.9	0
1955	Billy Kane	9	184	20.4	2
1956	Billy Kane	16	232	14.4	0
1957	Les Walters	24	440	18.3	5
1958	Maurice Schleicher	9	127	14.1	0
	Dave Kasperian	9	107	11.9	2
	Norm Neff	9	106	11.8	2
1959	Dick Hoak	14	167	11.9	0
1960	Jim Kerr	13	163	12.5	2
	Henry Oppermann	13	131	10.1	1
1961	Jim Schwab	16	257	16.1	0
1962	Junior Powell	32	303	9.5	3
1963	Dick Anderson	21	229	10.9	2
1964	Bill Huber	25	347	13.9	1
1965	Jack Curry	42	572	13.6	2
1966	Jack Curry	34	584	17.2	1
1967	Jack Curry	41	681	16.6	2
1968	Ted Kwalick	31	403	13.0	2
1969	Greg Edmonds	20	246	12.3	0
1970	Greg Edmonds	38	506	13.3	6
1971	Bob Parsons	30	489	15.6	5
1972	Dan Natale	30	460	15.3	5
1973	Gary Hayman	30	525	17.5	3
1974	Jerry Jeram	17	259	15.2	2
	Tom Donchez	17	176	10.4	1
1975	Dick Barvinchak	17	327	19.2	0
1976	Mickey Shuler	21	281	12.9	3
1977	Mickey Shuler	33	600	18.2	1
1978	Scott Fitzkee	37	630	17.0	6
1979	Brad Scovill	26	331	12.7	3
1980	Kenny Jackson	21	386	18.4	5
1981	Gregg Garrity	23	415	18.0	1
1982	Kenny Jackson	41	697	17.0	7
1983	Kevin Baugh	36	547	15.2	5
1984	Herb Bellamy	16	306	19.1	2
1985	Ray Roundtree	15	285	19.0	2
1986	D.J. Dozier	26	287	11.0	2
1987	Blair Thomas	23	300	13.0	2
1988	Michael Timpson	22	342	15.6	2
1989	David Daniels	22	362	16.5	4
1990	David Daniels	31	538	17.4	4
1991	Terry Smith	55	846	15.4	8
1992	O.J. McDuffie	63	977	15.5	9
1993	Bobby Engram	48	873	18.2	13
1994	Bobby Engram	52	1029	19.8	7
1995	Bobby Engram	63	1084	17.2	11
1996	Joe Jurevicius	41	869	21.2	4
1997	Joe Jurevicius	39	817	20.9	10

GAME RECEPTIONS

Rec.	Yards	TD	
13	110	1	Freddie Scott vs. Wisconsin, 1995
12	—	0	Stan McCollum at Washington, 1921
11	212	1	O.J. McDuffie vs. Boston College, 1992
10	155	2	Len Krouse at Syracuse, 1940
10	94	0	Jack Curry at Syracuse, 1965
10	148	1	Jack Curry at California, 1965
10	165	1	Terry Smith at Southern Cal, 1991
9	89	1	Ted Kwalick at Miami (Fla.), 1967
9	140	0	Jack Curry vs. Ohio U., 1967

Game Receptions continued:

9	119	1	David Daniels vs. Pittsburgh, 1990
9	203	1	Bobby Engram at Purdue, 1995

SEASON RECEPTIONS

Rec.	Yards	Avg.	TD	
63	977	15.5	9	O.J. McDuffie, 1992
63	1084	17.2	11	Bobby Engram, 1995
55	846	15.4	8	Terry Smith, 1991
52	1029	19.8	7	Bobby Engram, 1994
48	873	18.2	13	Bobby Engram, 1993
47	973	20.7	9	Freddie Scott, 1994
46	790	17.2	7	O.J. McDuffie, 1991
42	572	13.6	2	Jack Curry, 1965
41	681	16.6	2	Jack Curry, 1967
41	697	17.0	7	Kenny Jackson, 1982
41	869	21.2	4	Joe Jurevicius, 1996
39	817	20.9	10	Joe Jurevicius, 1997
38	506	13.3	6	Greg Edmonds, 1970

CAREER RECEPTIONS

Rec.	Yards	Avg.	TD	
167	3026	18.1	31	Bobby Engram, 1991, 93-95
125	1988	15.9	16	O.J. McDuffie, 1988-92
117	1837	15.7	5	Jack Curry, 1965-67
109	2006	18.4	25	Kenny Jackson, 1980-83
108	1825	16.9	15	Terry Smith, 1988-91
94	1894	20.1	15	Joe Jurevicius, 1994-97
93	1520	16.3	11	Freddie Scott, 1993-95
86	1343	15.6	10	Ted Kwalick, 1966-68
76	940	12.4	9	Kyle Brady, 1991-94
70	534	7.6	7	Mike Archie, 1992-95
69	1222	17.7	9	David Daniels, 1988-90
67	1038	15.5	8	Dan Natale, 1972-74
66	860	13.0	6	Greg Edmonds, 1968-70
66	1016	15.4	4	Mickey Shuler, 1975-77
66	613	9.3	5	D.J. Dozier, 1983-86

GAME RECEPTION YARDAGE

Yards	Rec.	TD	
212	11	1	O.J. McDuffie vs. Boston College, 1992
203	9	1	Bobby Engram at Purdue, 1995
200	8	1	Bobby Engram vs. Rutgers, 1994
175	8	3	Bobby Engram at Rutgers, 1995
169	8	1	Bobby Engram vs. Michigan State, 1994
165	10	1	Terry Smith at Southern Cal, 1991
165	8	4	Bobby Engram vs. Minnesota, 1993
158	5	2	Kenny Jackson at Pittsburgh, 1981
156	4	1	Joe Jurevicius at Indiana, 1996
155	9	2	Len Krouse at Syracuse, 1940
150	7	2	Bobby Engram at Iowa, 1995
150	4	3	Joe Jurevicius at Louisville, 1997
148	10	1	Jack Curry at California, 1965
145	6	1	Freddie Scott vs. Michigan State, 1994
144	8	1	Terry Smith at Temple, 1991
140	9	1	Jack Curry vs. Ohio U., 1967

SEASON RECEPTION YARDAGE

Yards	Rec.	TD	
1084	63	11	Bobby Engram, 1995
1029	52	7	Bobby Engram, 1994
977	63	9	O.J. McDuffie, 1992
973	47	9	Freddie Scott, 1994
873	48	13	Bobby Engram, 1993
869	41	4	Joe Jurevicius. 1996
846	55	8	Terry Smith, 1991
817	39	10	Joe Jurevicius, 1997
790	46	6	O.J. McDuffie, 1991
697	41	7	Kenny Jackson, 1982
681	41	2	Jack Curry, 1967

Season Reception Yardage continued:

630	37	6	Scott Fitzkee, 1978
600	33	1	Mickey Shuler, 1977
584	34	1	Jack Curry, 1966
572	42	2	Jack Curry, 1965
563	33	4	Ted Kwalick, 1967
547	36	5	Kevin Baugh, 1983
538	31	4	David Daniels, 1990
530	29	4	Terry Smith, 1990
525	30	3	Gary Hayman, 1973

CAREER RECEPTION YARDAGE

Yards	Rec.	TD	
3026	167	31	Bobby Engram, 1991, 93-95
2006	109	25	Kenny Jackson, 1980-83
1988	125	16	O.J. McDuffie, 1988-92
1894	94	15	Joe Jurevicius, 1994-97
1837	117	5	Jack Curry, 1965-67
1825	108	15	Terry Smith, 1988-91
1520	93	11	Freddie Scott, 1993-95
1343	86	10	Ted Kwalick, 1966-68
1263	65	11	Scott Fitzkee, 1975-78
1222	69	9	David Daniels, 1988-90
1058	56	7	Jimmy Cefalo, 1974-77
1038	67	8	Dan Natale, 1972-74
1016	66	4	Mickey Shuler, 1975-77
952	58	4	Gregg Garrity, 1980-82

Total Offensive Records

TOTAL OFFENSE YARDAGE
Game: 370
Mike McQueary vs. Pittsburgh, 1997.
By a senior: 370, Mike McQueary vs.Pittsburgh, 1997.
By a junior: 350, Kerry Collins at Michigan State, 1993.
By a sophomore: 360, Todd Blackledge at Miami (Fla.), 1981.
By a freshman: 208, Tony Sacca vs. Syracuse, 1988.
Season: 2660
Kerry Collins, 1994.
By a senior: 2660, Kerry Collins, 1994.
By a junior: 2168, Chuck Fusina, 1977.
By a sophomore: 1576, Todd Blackledge, 1981.
By a freshman: 1144, Todd Blackledge, 1980.
Career: 6000
Tony Sacca, 1988-91.

TOUCHDOWNS
Game: 6
Harry Robb vs. Gettysburg, 1917.
Season: 26
Lydell Mitchell, 1971.
Career: 51
Todd Blackledge, 1980-82.

OFFENSIVE PLAYS
Game: 59
Kerry Collins at Brigham Young, 1992.
Season: 376
Tony Sacca, 1991.
Career: 1051
Tony Sacca, 1988-91.

GAME TOTAL OFFENSE

Yards	Rush	Pass	
370	4	366	Mike McQueary vs. Pittsburgh, 1997
363	92	271	John Hufnagel at Boston College, 1972
360	2	358	Todd Blackledge at Miami (Fla.), 1981
350	-2	352	Kerry Collins at Michigan State, 1993
328	0	328	Kerry Collins vs. Rutgers, 1994
320	3	317	Kerry Collins at Brigham Young, 1992

Game Total Offense continued:

315	12	303	John Sacca at Rutgers, 1992
303	13	290	John Hufnagel vs. Maryland, 1972
303	8	295	Todd Blackledge vs. Nebraska, 1982
300	-15	315	Chuck Fusina at N.C. State, 1977
300	113	187	Tony Sacca vs. Pittsburgh, 1990
300	0	300	Kerry Collins at Illinois, 1994

SEASON TOTAL OFFENSE

Yards	Rush	Pass	
2660	-19	2679	Kerry Collins, 1994
2427	-61	2488	Tony Sacca, 1991
2201	162	2039	John Hufnagel, 1972
2191	-27	2218	Todd Blackledge, 1982
2184	-57	2211	Mike McQueary, 1997
2168	-53	2221	Chuck Fusina, 1977
2077	-121	2198	Wally Richardson, 1995
2003	137	1866	Tony Sacca, 1990
1912	-32	1944	Doug Strang, 1983
1761	145	1616	Tom Sherman, 1967
1743	-116	1859	Chuck Fusina, 1978
1634	-98	1732	Wally Richardson, 1996
1613	8	1605	Kerry Collins, 1993
1576	19	1557	Todd Blackledge, 1981
1567	1567	0	Lydell Mitchell, 1971
1539	1522	17	John Cappelletti, 1973
1539	1539	0	Ki Jana Carter, 1994

CAREER TOTAL OFFENSE

Yards	Rush	Pass	
6000	131	5869	Tony Sacca, 1988-91
5300	-4	5304	Kerry Collins, 1991-94
5162	-220	5382	Chuck Fusina, 1975-78
4911	99	4812	Todd Blackledge, 1980-82
4212	667	3545	John Hufnagel, 1970-72
4182	-237	4419	Wally Richardson, 1992, 1994-96
3398	3398	0	Curt Warner, 1979-82
3341	-128	3469	John Shaffer, 1983-86
3301	3301	0	Blair Thomas, 1985-87, 89
3256	3256	0	Curtis Enis, 1995-97
3227	3227	0	D.J. Dozier, 1983-86
3095	129	2966	Doug Strang, 1981-84

SEASON LEADERS

Season	Name	Yards	Plays	TDR
1946	Elwood Petchel	660	106	8
1947	Elwood Petchel	581	80	8
1948	Elwood Petchel	737	158	12
1949	Owen Dougherty	521	81	5
1950	Vince O'Bara	692	140	5
1951	Ted Shattuck	579	137	4
1952	Tony Rados	876	205	11
1953	Tony Rados	1021	190	11
1954	Lenny Moore	1082	136	10
1955	Lenny Moore	697	138	5
1956	Milt Plum	745	111	6
1957	Al Jacks	675	125	5
1958	Rich Lucas	701	145	9
1959	Rich Lucas	1238	216	10
1960	Dick Hoak	680	112	6
1961	Galen Hall	1034	137	11
1962	Pete Liske	1292	231	16
1963	Pete Liske	1131	217	10
1964	Gary Wydman	956	248	2
1965	Jack White	1342	283	9
1966	Tom Sherman	1058	207	11
1967	Tom Sherman	1058	207	11
1968	Chuck Burkhart	1182	218	6
1969	Chuck Burkhart	773	171	2
1970	Lydell Mitchell	751	134	6
1971	Lydell Mitchell	1567	254	26

Season Leaders continued:

1972	John Hugnagel	2201	138	21
1973	John Cappelletti	1539	288	17
1974	tom Shuman	1397	224	14
1975	John Andress	978	203	4
1976	Chuck Fusina	1172	198	14
1977	Chuck Fusina	2168	275	16
1978	Chuck Fusina	1743	293	13
1979	Dayle Tate	1187	234	8
1980	Todd Blackledge	1144	236	9
1981	Todd Blackledge	1576	252	17
1982	Todd Blackledge	2191	334	25
1983	Doug Strang	1912	319	24
1984	Doug Strang	1019	209	8
1985	John Shaffer	1323	279	12
1986	John Shaffer	1443	257	12
1987	Blair Thomas	1414	269	11
1988	Tony Sacca	809	188	4
1989	Blair Thomas	1341	266	5
1990	Tony Sacca	2003	300	11
1991	Tony Sacca	2427	376	25
1992	John Sacca	1179	180	9
1993	Kerry Collins	1613	276	13
1994	Kerry Collins	2660	276	21
1995	Wally Richardson	2077	375	18
1996	Wally Richardson	1634	308	7
1997	Mike McQueary	2211	308	18

Punt Return Records

PUNT RETURNS
Game: 7
Elwood Petchel vs. West Virginia, 1947; Joe Vargo at Ohio State, 1964; Kevin Baugh vs. Rutgers, 1982; Jim Coates vs. East Carolina, 1986.
Season: 36
Jim Coates, 1986.
Career: 84
O.J. McDuffie, 1988-92.

PUNT RETURN YARDAGE
Game: 145
Matt Suhey vs. North Carolina State, 1978.
Season: 442
Gary Hayman, 1973.
Career: 1059
O.J. McDuffie, 1988-92.

PUNT RETURN AVERAGE YARDAGE
Game: 29.0
Matt Suhey (5 returns) vs. North Carolina State, 1978.
Season: 21.4
Don Jonas, 1960.
Career: 17.6
Ron Younker, 1953-54.

TOUCHDOWNS
Game: 1, by many players
(Last: Chris Campbell vs. Purdue, 1996; Ahmad Collins at Michigan, 1996, blocked punt).
Season: 2
Jimmy Cefalo, 1977; O.J. McDuffie, 1991.
Career: 3
O.J. McDuffie, 1988-92.

SEASON PUNT RETURN AVG. (Min. 6 Returns)

Avg.	Ret.	Yards	TD	
21.4	7	150	1	Don Jonas, 1960
19.2	23	442	1	Gary Hayman, 1973
17.5	13	228	1	Lenny Moore, 1953
17.0	35	396	-	Shorty Miller, 1912

Season Punt Return Avg. (Min. 6 returns) continued:

16.1	12	193	0	Ron Younker, 1954
16.0	14	224	0	Bob Pollard, 1951
15.7	6	94	0	Dick Hoak, 1959
15.2	13	197	1	Matt Suhey, 1978
14.6	19	278	1	O.J. McDuffie, 1989
14.2	11	156	1	Mike Irwin, 1965
13.7	18	247	2	Jimmy Cefalo, 1977

CAREER PUNT RETURN AVG. (Min. 15 Returns)

Avg.	Ret.	Yards	TD	
17.6	16	281	0	Ron Younker, 1953-54
16.5	17	280	1	Wally Triplett, 1946-48
15.9	17	271	2	Don Jonas, 1958-61
15.8	24	378	1	Lenny Moore, 1953-55
15.3	15	229	0	Dick Hoak, 1958-60
14.0	24	337	1	Mike Archie, 1992-95
13.7	18	247	2	Jimmy Cefalo, 1974-77
13.2	47	619	2	Dennis Onkotz, 1967-69
13.0	23	300	1	Joe Vargo, 1963-64
12.8	56	717	2	Gary Hayman, 1972-73
12.6	84	1059	3	O.J. McDuffie, 1988-92

SEASON LEADERS

Season	Name	Ret.	Yards	Avg.	TD
1946	Robert Williams	16	164	10.3	0
1947	Robert Williams	20	214	10.7	0
1948	Elwood Petchel	14	144	10.3	0
1949	Bill Luther	18	241	13.4	0
1950	George Jacob	8	51	6.4	0
1951	Bob Pollard	14	224	16.0	1
1952	Don Bailey	16	213	13.3	0
1953	Lenny Moore	13	228	17.5	1
1954	Ron Younker	12	193	16.1	0
1955	Lenny Moore	4	45	11.3	0
1956	Billy Kane	15	135	9.0	0
1957	Dave Kasperian	6	62	10.3	0
1958	Dick Hoak	9	135	15.0	0
1959	Dick Hoak	6	94	15.7	0
1960	Don Jonas	7	150	21.4	1
1961	Al Gursky	5	49	9.8	0
1962	Junior Powell	5	33	6.6	0
1963	Junior Powell	18	222	12.3	0
1964	Joe Vargo	19	233	12.3	1
1965	Mike Irwin	11	156	14.2	1
1966	Mike Irwin	11	112	10.2	0
1967	Dennis Onkotz	5	86	17.2	1
1968	Dennis Onkotz	18	208	11.6	0
1969	Dennis Onkotz	24	325	13.5	1
1970	Mike Smith	21	200	9.5	1
1971	John Cappelletti	28	274	9.8	0
1972	Gary Hayman	33	275	8.3	1
1973	Gary Hayman	23	442	19.2	1
1974	Jim Eaise	27	187	6.9	0
1975	Gary Petercuskie	11	81	7.4	0
1976	Rich Mauti	17	208	12.2	0
1977	Jimmy Cefalo	18	247	13.7	2
1978	Matt Suhey	13	197	15.2	1
1979	Mike Guman	14	102	7.3	0
1980	Kevin Baugh	5	88	17.6	1
1981	Kevin Baugh	10	101	10.1	0
1982	Kevin Baugh	29	315	10.8	0
1983	Kevin Baugh	18	167	9.3	0
1984	Kevin Woods	13	77	6.8	0
1985	Michael Timpson	13	164	12.6	0
1986	Jim Coates	36	309	8.6	0
1987	Michael Timpson	15	162	10.8	1
1988	Michael Timpson	16	162	10.1	1
1989	O.J. McDuffie	19	278	14.6	1
1990	Tisen Thomas	29	380	13.1	0
1991	O.J. McDuffie	33	358	10.8	2

Season Leaders continued:

1992	O.J. McDuffie	30	398	13.3	0
1993	Bobby Engram	33	402	12.2	0
1994	Mike Archie	11	126	11.5	0
1995	Bobby Engram	19	187	9.8	0
1996	Chris Campbell	24	242	10.1	1
1997	Chris Eberly	25	176	7.0	0

LONGEST PUNT RETURNS

100	Jim Boring vs. Johns Hopkins, 1933
92	Mark Robinson vs. Rutgers, 1982
85	Wally Triplett vs. West Virginia, 1948
85	Mike Guman at West Virginia, 1978
84	O.J. McDuffie at Syracuse, 1989
83	Gary Hayman vs. N.C. State, 1973
80	Fritz Andrews vs. Lehigh, 1935
80	Bill Luther vs. Syracuse, 1949
78	Joe Vargo at Houston, 1964
77	Don Bailey at Syracuse, 1952
75*	Mike Smith vs. West Virginia, 1970
75	Jimmy Cefalo vs. Kentucky, 1977
74	Mike Irwin vs. West Virginia, 1965
71*	Dennis Onkotz at Pittsburgh, 1969
70	Dexter Very at Pennsylvania, 1911

*Non-scoring play.

Kickoff Return Records

KICKOFF RETURNS
Game: 7
Gary Brown at West Virginia, 1988.
Season: 26
Kevin Baugh, 1983.
Career: 62
Kevin Baugh, 1980-83.

KICKOFF RETURN YARDAGE
Game: 201
Gary Brown vs. Texas, 1990.
Season: 503
Kevin Baugh, 1983.
Career: 1216
Kevin Baugh, 1980-83.

KICKOFF RETURN YARDAGE AVERAGE
Game: 40.2
Gary Brown (5 returns) vs. Texas, 1990.
Season: 43.0
Gary Brown, 1990.
Career: 29.6
Larry Joe, 1946-48.

TOUCHDOWNS
Game: 1, by many players
(Last: Blair Thomas vs. Pittsburgh, 1986).
Season: 2
Chuck Peters, 1940; Curt Warner, 1980.
Career: 3
Curt Warner, 1979-82.

SEASON KICKOFF RETURN AVG. (Min. 8 Returns)

Avg.	Ret.	Yards	TD	
43.0	8	344	0	Gary Brown, 1990
35.0	10	350	2	Curt Warner, 1980
32.6	9	293	1	Larry Joe, 1947
31.9	12	383	1	Blair Thomas, 1986
29.6	8	237	1	Gary Hayman, 1973
29.0	17	493	1	Curt Warner, 1979
28.7	10	287	1	Charlie Pittman, 1967
28.0	8	224	1	Rich Mauti, 1975

Season Kickoff Return Avg. (Min. 8 Returns) continued:

27.4	9	247	0	Bob Riggle, 1965
26.5	16	424	0	Shelly Hammonds, 1993
26.3	12	316	1	Paul Johnson, 1969

CAREER KICKOFF RETURN AVG. (Min. 16 Returns)

Avg.	Ret.	Yards	TD	
29.6	16	473	1	Larry Joe, 1946-48
28.8	32	922	3	Curt Warner, 1979-82
28.4	17	483	1	Charlie Pittman, 1967-69
26.9	18	484	1	Gary Hayman, 1972-73
26.3	25	658	1	Blair Thomas, 1985-87, 89
25.7	23	591	1	Roger Kochman, 1959-62
24.6	19	468	0	Lydell Mitchell, 1969-71
24.4	25	609	0	Shelly Hammonds, 1990-93
24.3	23	560	0	Lenny Moore, 1953-55
24.2	38	920	0	Gary Brown, 1987-90
23.9	22	526	0	Leroy Thompson, 1987-90

SEASON LEADERS

Season	Name	Ret.	Yards	Avg.	TD
1940	Chuck Peters	5	261	52.2	2
1946	Robert Williams	3	77	25.7	0
1947	Larry Joe	9	293	32.6	1
1948	Larry Joe	6	147	24.5	0
1949	Owen Dougherty	8	132	16.5	0
1950	Earle Mundell	9	227	25.2	0
1951	Ted Shattuck	9	168	18.7	0
1952	Richard Jones	13	303	23.3	0
1953	Lenny Moore	5	136	27.2	0
1954	Lenny Moore	4	142	35.5	0
1955	Billy Kane	13	273	21.0	0
1956	Billy Kane	7	197	28.1	0
1957	Dave Kasperian	6	191	31.9	0
1958	Dave Kasperian	2	90	45.0	0
1959	Dick Hoak	6	215	35.8	0
1960	Jim Kerr	8	158	19.8	0
1961	Roger Kochman	10	229	22.9	0
1962	Roger Kochman	10	218	21.8	0
1963	Gary Klingensmith	10	245	24.5	0
1964	Don Kunit	9	223	24.8	0
1965	Bob Riggle	9	247	27.4	0
1966	Mike Irwin	16	285	17.9	0
1967	Bob Campbell	5	179	35.8	0
1968	Charlie Pittman	4	110	27.5	0
1969	Paul Johnson	12	316	26.3	1
1970	Lydell Mitchell	16	410	25.6	0
1971	John Cappelletti	15	355	23.7	0
1972	Gary Hayman	10	247	24.7	0
1973	Gary Hayman	8	237	29.6	1
1974	Jimmy Cefalo	9	159	17.7	0
1975	Rich Mauti	8	224	28.0	1
1976	Rich Mauti	13	217	16.7	0
1977	Booker Moore	6	155	25.8	0
1978	Matt Suhey	5	103	20.6	0
1979	Curt Warner	17	493	29.0	1
1980	Curt Warner	10	350	35.0	2
1981	Jon Williams	8	133	16.6	0
1982	Kevin Baugh	18	404	22.4	0
1983	Kevin Baugh	26	503	19.3	0
1984	Jim Coates	12	277	23.1	0
1985	Blair Thomas	9	217	24.1	0
1986	Blair Thomas	12	383	31.9	1
1987	Leroy Thompson	10	245	24.5	0
1988	Gary Brown	22	427	19.4	0
1989	Bobby Samuels	10	197	19.7	0
1990	Gary Brown	8	344	43.0	0
1991	Richie Anderson	9	222	24.7	0
1992	O.J. McDuffie	14	323	23.1	0
1993	Shelly Hammonds	16	424	26.5	0
1994	Mike Archie	11	240	21.8	0

Season Leaders continued:

1995	Stephen Pitts	17	364	21.4	0
1996	Kenny Watson	16	376	23.5	0
1997	Chris Eberly	22	530	24.1	0

LONGEST KICKOFF RETURNS

101	Chuck Peters vs. New York, 1940
100	Fritz Barrett vs. Carnegie Tech, 1910
100	Roger Kochman vs. Syracuse, 1959
100	Rich Mauti at Temple, 1975
98	Thomas Evans vs. Marshall, 1930
98	Gary Hayman at Maryland, 1973
96	Chuck Peters at Lehigh, 1940
95	Shorty Miller at Pennsylvania, 1911
95	Charlie Way vs. Ursinus, 1919
95	Harry Wilson vs. Navy, 1923
95	Cy Lungren vs. Marietta, 1926
95	Larry Joe vs. Bucknell, 1947
95	Curt Warner vs. Pittsburgh, 1979
95*	Gary Brown vs. Texas, 1990
94	Harry Harrison at Pennsylvania, 1936
94	John Patrick vs. Bucknell, 1936
91	Paul Johnson vs. Colorado, 1969
91	Blair Thomas vs. Pittsburgh, 1986

*Non-scoring play.

All Purpose Running Records

YARDAGE

Game: 341
Curt Warner at Syracuse, 1981.
By a senior: 302, Harry Wilson vs. Navy, 1923.
By a junior: 341, Curt Warner at Syracuse, 1981.
By a sophomore: 265, Charlie Pittman vs. West Virginia, 1967.
By a freshman: 280, Curt Warner vs. Rutgers, 1979.

Season: 1831
O.J. McDuffie, 1992.
By a senior: 1831, O.J. McDuffie, 1992.
By a junior: 1772, Blair Thomas, 1987.
By a sophomore: 1364, Curt Warner, 1980.
By a freshman: 1191, D.J. Dozier, 1983.

Career: 4982
Curt Warner, 1979-82.

GAME ALL-PURPOSE RUNNING YARDAGE

Yards	Rush	Rec.	Ret.	
341	256	20	65	Curt Warner at Syracuse, 1981
302	115	0	187	Harry Wilson vs. Navy, 1923
295	88	49	158	Bob Campbell at Navy, 1967
282	132	0	150	Stephen Pitts vs. Iowa, 1995
281	9	112	170	Gary Hayman vs. N.C. State, 1973
280	100	71	109	Curt Warner vs. Rutgers, 1979
280	43	212	25	O.J. McDuffie vs. Boston College, 1992
278	162	42	74	Harry Wilson at Pennsylvania, 1923
278	243	0	35	Bob Pollard at Rutgers, 1951
278	238	26	14	Curt Warner at Nebraska, 1981
269	186	83	0	Curtis Enis at Purdue, 1997
265	137	45	83	Charlie Pittman vs. West Virginia, 1967
259	239	20	0	Bob Campbell vs. Syracuse, 1968
259	167	51	41	Blair Thomas vs. Temple, 1987
258	241	17	0	Curtis Enis vs. Southern Cal, 1996

SEASON ALL-PURPOSE RUNNING YARDAGE

Yards	Rush	Rec.	Ret.	
1831	133	977	721	O.J. McDuffie, 1992
1772	1414	300	58	Blair Thomas, 1987
1754	1567	154	33	Lydell Mitchell, 1971
1743	1539	123	81	Ki-Jana Carter, 1994
1607	1522	69	16	John Cappelletti, 1973
1578	1363	215	0	Curtis Enis, 1997

Season All-Purpose Running Avg.:

1535	1341	118	76	Blair Thomas, 1989
1501	1210	291	0	Curtis Enis, 1996
1486	1082	44	360	Lenny Moore, 1954
1474	1117	138	219	John Cappelletti, 1972
1407	94	1084	229	Bobby Engram, 1995
1397	801	0	596	Shorty Miller, 1912
1376	1041	335	0	Curt Warner, 1982

CAREER ALL-PURPOSE RUNNING YARDAGE

Yards	Rush	Rec.	Ret.	
4982	3398	662	922	Curt Warner, 1979-82
4512	3301	477	734	Blair Thomas, 1985-87, 89
4043	155	3026	862	Bobby Engram, 1991, 93-95
4034	3256	506	272	Curtis Enis, 1995-97
3904	2934	470	500	Lydell Mitchell, 1969-71
3895	3227	613	55	D.J. Dozier, 1983-86
3817	330	1988	1499	O.J. McDuffie, 1988-92
3735	2639	207	889	John Cappelletti, 1971-73
3549	2818	328	403	Matt Suhey, 1976-79
3543	2380	89	1074	Lenny Moore, 1953-55
3229	2829	172	228	Ki-Jana Carter, 1992-94

SEASON LEADERS

Season	Name	Yards	Rush	Rec.	Ret.
1946	Elwood Petchel	495	373	0	122
1947	Larry Joe	656	350	0	306
1948	Wally Triplett	734	424	90	220
1949	Bill Luther	605	200	0	405
1950	Tony Orsini	745	563	29	153
1951	Ted Shattuck	833	579	80	174
1952	Bob Pollard	589	341	84	164
1953	Lenny Moore	1013	601	8	404
1954	Lenny Moore	1486	1082	44	360
1955	Lenny Moore	1044	697	37	310
1956	Billy Kane	1085	530	232	333
1957	Dave Kasperian	830	469	108	253
1958	Dave Kasperian	624	381	107	141
1959	Jim Kerr	710	320	122	268
1960	Jim Kerr	799	389	163	247
1961	Roger Kochman	1154	666	226	262
1962	Roger Kochman	1176	652	254	270
1963	Gary Klingensmith	871	450	173	248
1964	Don Kunit	734	418	94	223
1965	Mike Irwin	974	398	217	359
1966	Bob Campbell	842	482	139	221
1967	Charlie Pittman	927	580	60	287
1968	Charlie Pittman	1262	950	196	116
1969	Charlie Pittman	919	706	127	86
1970	Lydell Mitchell	1271	751	110	410
1971	Lydell Mitchell	1754	1567	154	33
1972	John Cappelletti	1474	1117	138	219
1973	John Cappelletti	1607	1522	69	16
1974	Tom Donchez	1056	880	176	0
1975	Woody Petchel	697	621	14	72
1976	Mike Guman	601	470	127	44
1977	Jimmy Cefalo	872	72	507	293
1978	Matt Suhey	1131	720	111	300
1979	Matt Suhey	1127	973	99	55
1980	Curt Warner	1364	922	92	350
1981	Curt Warner	1227	1044	106	79
1982	Curt Warner	1376	1041	335	0
1983	Kevin Baugh	1224	7	547	670
1984	D.J. Dozier	796	691	50	55
1985	D.J. Dozier	810	723	87	0
1986	D.J. Dozier	1098	811	287	0
1987	Blair Thomas	1772	1414	300	58
1988	Gary Brown	1268	689	152	427
1989	Blair Thomas	1535	1341	118	76
1990	Leroy Thompson	835	573	245	17
1991	O.J. McDuffie	1367	102	790	475

Season Leaders continued:

1992	O.J. McDuffie	1831	133	977	721
1993	Bobby Engram	1324	15	873	436
1994	Ki-Jana Carter	1743	1539	123	81
1995	Bobby Engram	1407	94	1084	229
1996	Curtis Enis	1501	1210	291	0
1997	Curtis Enis	1578	1363	215	0

Punting Records

PUNTS
Game: 14
Joe Colone at Cornell, 1942.
By a senior: 12, by four players (Last: Scott Fitzkee at Temple, 1978).
By a junior: 10, Doug Helkowski at Alabama, 1990; Pat Pidgeon vs. Michigan, 1997.
By a sophomore: 12, Bob Parsons vs. Missouri, 1970 Orange.
By a freshman: 14, Joe Colone at Cornell, 1942.
Season: 79
John Bruno, Jr., 1984.
By a senior: 68, George Reynolds, 1983.
By a junior: 60, John Bruno, Jr., 1985.
By a sophomore: 79, John Bruno, Jr., 1984.
By a freshman: 71, Ralph Giacomarro, 1979.
Career: 241
Doug Helkowski, 1988-91.

PUNTING YARDAGE
Game: 453
Doug Helkowski at Alabama, 1988.
Season: 3273
John Bruno, Jr., 1984.
By a senior: 2899, George Reynolds, 1983.
By a junior: 2575, John Bruno, Jr., 1985.
By a sophomore: 3273, John Bruno, Jr., 1984.
By a freshman: 2822, Ralph Giacomarro, 1979.
Career: 9402
Ralph Giacomarro, 1979-82.

PUNTING YARDAGE AVERAGE
Game: 54.8
Ralph Giacomarro (4 punts) at Syracuse, 1981.
By a senior: 52.4 (5 punts), Bob Campbell vs. Miami (Fla.), 1968.
By a junior: 54.8 (4 punts), Ralph Giacomarro at Syracuse, 1981.
By a sophomore: 48.4 (5 punts), Ralph Giacomarro vs. Miami (Fla.), 1980.
By a freshman: 43.2 (4 punts), Ralph Giacomarro vs. Syracuse, 1979.
Season: 43.6
Ralph Giacomarro, 1981.
By a senior: 42.6, George Reynolds, 1983.
By a junior: 43.6, Ralph Giacomarro, 1981.
By a sophomore: 43.3, Ralph Giacomarro, 1980.
By a freshman: 39.8, Ralph Giacomarro, 1979.
Career: 43.0
George Reynolds, 1980-83.

GAME PUNTING AVERAGE (Min. 4 Punts)

Avg.	Punts	Yards	
54.8	4	219	Ralph Giacomarro at Syracuse, 1981
52.4	5	262	Bob Campbell vs. Miami (Fla.), 1968
51.0	4	204	Doug Helkowski vs. Texas, 1990
48.5	4	194	Chris Bahr vs. Alabama, 1975
48.4	5	242	Ralph Giacomarro vs. Miami (Fla.), 1980
48.3	4	193	Ralph Giacomarro vs. Alabama, 1981
48.3	4	193	Ralph Giacomarro vs. Pittsburgh, 1982
48.1	7	337	Bob Parsons vs. Maryland, 1969

SEASON PUNTing Average (min. 30 punts)

Avg.	Punts	Yards	
43.6	55	2395	Ralph Giacomarro, 1981
43.3	52	2252	Ralph Giacomarro, 1980
42.9	60	2575	John Bruno, Jr., 1985

Season Punting Avg. (Min. 30 Punts) continued:

42.6	68	2899	George Reynolds, 1983	
42.6	55	2341	Pat Pidgeon, 1997	
41.4	34	1408	Chuck Raisig, 1962	
41.4	79	3273	John Bruno, Jr., 1984	
41.1	47	1933	Ralph Giacomarro, 1982	
41.0	39	1599	Jamie Dreese, 1992	
40.9	65	2660	John Bruno, Jr., 1986	
40.6	58	2353	Bob Parsons, 1969	
40.5	62	2511	Chris Clauss, 1987	

Career Punting Average (min. 45 punts)

Avg.	Punts	Yards	
43.0	72	3096	George Reynolds, 1980-83
41.8	225	9402	Ralph Giacomarro, 1979-82
41.7	204	8508	John Bruno, Jr., 1984-86
41.6	72	2994	Pat Pidgeon, 1996-present
40.5	62	2511	Chris Clauss, 1987
39.0	241	9391	Doug Helkowski, 1988-91
38.9	153	5948	Bob Parsons, 1969-71
38.6	56	2163	Chris Bahr, 1973-75
38.4	79	3035	Joe Colone, 1946-48
38.4	119	4568	Darrell Kania, 1994-96
38.0	47	1787	Milt Plum, 1955-56

Season Leaders

Season	Name	Punts	Yards	Avg.	Blk.
1946	Joe Colone	30	1120	37.3	0
1947	Joe Colone	28	1120	40.0	0
1948	Joe Colone	21	795	37.9	0
1949	Bill Luther	34	1180	34.8	1
1950	Vince O'Bara	51	1638	32.1	1
1951	Art Betts	53	1855	35.2	1
1952	Ted Kemmerer	52	1904	36.7	2
1953	Don Eyer	10	330	33.0	2
1954	Don Bailey	26	898	34.5	0
1955	Jim Hochberg	10	436	43.6	0
1956	Milt Plum	33	1297	39.3	0
1957	Rich Lucas	21	750	35.7	0
1958	Rich Lucas	29	1083	37.3	0
1959	Dick Pae	14	492	35.1	0
1960	Chuck Raisig	40	1389	34.7	0
1961	Pete Liske	24	880	36.7	0
1962	Chuck Raisig	34	1408	41.4	0
1963	Frank Hershey	46	1632	35.5	0
1964	Frank Hershey	57	2128	37.3	0
1965	Wayne Corbett	44	1658	37.7	0
1966	Wayne Corbett	63	2365	37.5	2
1967	Bob Campbell	12	541	45.1	0
1968	Steve Brezna	46	1739	37.8	1
1969	Bob Parsons	58	2353	40.6	1
1970	Bob Parsons	54	2009	37.2	0
1971	Bob Parsons	41	1586	38.	0
1972	Brian Masella	55	2085	37.9	0
1973	Brian Masella	48	1757	36.6	0
1974	Brian Masella	56	2201	39.3	0
1975	Chris Bahr	56	2163	38.6	0
1976	Scott Fitzkee	59	2087	35.4	0
1977	Scott Fitzkee	44	1699	38.6	0
1978	Scott Fitzkee	65	2335	35.9	0
1979	Ralph Giacomarro	71	2822	39.8	1
1980	Ralph Giacomarro	52	2252	43.3	2
1981	Ralph Giacomarro	55	2395	43.6	0
1982	Ralph Giacomarro	47	1933	41.1	2
1983	George Reynolds	68	2899	42.6	1
1984	John Bruno, Jr.	79	3273	41.4	0
1985	John Bruno, Jr.	60	2575	42.9	1
1986	John Bruno, Jr.	65	2660	40.9	0
1987	Chris Clauss	62	2511	40.5	0
1988	Doug Helkowski	68	2668	39.2	3

Season Leaders continued:

1989	Doug Helkowski	57	2175	38.2	4
1990	Doug Helkowski	59	2327	39.4	2
1991	Doug Helkowski	57	2221	39.0	0
1992	Jamie Dreese	39	1599	41.0	1
1993	V.J. Muscillo	55	2014	36.6	0
1994	Darrell Kania	23	849	36.9	0
1995	Darrell Kania	45	1682	37.4	0
1996	Darrell Kania	51	2037	39.9	0
1997	Pat Pidgeon	55	2341	42.6	0

Longest Punts

89	Coop French at Iowa, 1930	
76	Chris Clauss vs. Rutgers, 1987	
73	Milt Plum at Ohio State, 1956	
71	Joe Colone at Syracuse, 1946	
71	John Bruno vs. Boston College, 1985	
70	Coop French at Iowa, 1930	
70	Joe Colone at Syracuse, 1946	
69	Bob Parsons at Colorado, 1970	
67	Joe Colone vs. Navy, 1947	
67	Art Betts vs. Michigan State, 1951	
67	Wayne Corbett at Pittsburgh, 1965	
66	Frank Hershey vs. Maryland, 1964	
65	W.G. Cooper vs. Villanova, 1935	
65	Tom Cherry vs. UCLA, 1967	
65	Bob Parsons vs. Colorado, 1969	
64	Brian Masella vs. Maryland, 1972	
64	Scott Fitzkee vs. Maryland, 1977	
64	Ralph Giacomarro at Syracuse, 1981	
64	Ralph Giacomarro at N.C. State, 1981	

Scoring Records

POINTS
Game: 36
Harry Robb vs. Gettysburg, 1917.
By a senior: 32, Charles Atherton vs. Gettysburg, 1894.
By a junior: 30, Ki-Jana Carter vs.Michigan State, 1994.
By a sophomore: 36, Harry Robb vs. Gettysburg, 1917.
By a freshman: 24, Mike Guman vs. Army, 1976.
Season: 174
Lydell Mitchell, 1971.
By a senior: 174, Lydell Mitchell, 1971.
By a junior: 138, Ki-Jana Carter, 1994.
By a sophomore: 93, Craig Fayak, 1991.
By a freshman: 74, Craig Fayak, 1990.
Career: 282
Craig Fayak, 1990-93.

TOUCHDOWNS
Game: 6
Harry Robb vs. Gettysburg, 1917.
Season: 29
Lydell Mitchell, 1971.
Career: 41
Lydell Mitchell, 1969-71.
In Consecutive Games: 14
Curtis Enis, 1996 (3) through 1997 (11).

KICKING POINTS
Game: 18
Massimo Manca vs. Notre Dame, 1985.
Season: 97
Matt Bahr, 1978.
Career: 282
Craig Fayak, 1990-93.

Scoring Records continued:

EXTRA POINTS
Game: 10
Charles Atherton vs. Gettysburg, 1894.
Season: 62
Brett Conway, 1994.
Career: 141
Brett Conway, 1993-96.

EXTRA POINT ATTEMPTS
Game: 10
Charles Atherton vs. Gettysburg, 1894.
Season: 63
Brett Conway, 1994.
Career: 142
Brett Conway, 1993-96.

EXTRA POINT ACCURACY
Game: 100.0
Charles Atherton (10-10) vs. Gettysburg, 1894.
Season: 100.0
Matt Bahr (31-31), 1978; Massimo Manca
(37-37), 1986; Brett Conway (37-37), 1995; (39-39), 1996.
Career: 100.0
Herb Menhardt (54-54), 1978-80.
Consecutive Made: 119
Brett Conway, 1994-96.

FIELD GOALS
Game: 5
Brian Franco at Nebraska, 1981;
Massimo Manca vs. Notre Dame, 1985.
Half: 4
Matt Bahr vs. SMU, 1978.
Season: 22
Matt Bahr, 1978.
Career: 50
Craig Fayak, 1990-93.

FIELD GOAL ATTEMPTS
Game: 6
Massimo Manca at West Virginia, 1986.
Season: 33
Chris Bahr, 1975.
Career: 80
Craig Fayak, 1990-93.
In Consecutive Games: 13
Massimo Manca, 1985-86.

FIELD GOAL ACCURACY
Game: 100.0
Brian Franco (5-5) vs. Nebraska, 1981; Massimo Manca (5-5) vs. Notre Dame, 1985.
Season: 83.3
Brett Conway (10-12), 1994.
Career: 77.6
Nick Gancitano (38-49), 1981-83.
50-Yard Percentage: 40.0
Chris Bahr (6-15), 1973-75.

SEASON LEADERS

Season	Name	Points	TD	PAT	FG
1946	Elwood Petchel	42	7	0	0
1947	Fran Rogel	36	6	0	0
1948	Wally Triplett	36	6	0	0
1949	Vince O'Bara	31	5	1-2	0
1950	Tony Orsini	30	5	0	0
1951	Ted Shattuck	30	5	0	0
1952	Bill Leonard	27	0	21-23	2
1953	Jim Garrity	48	4	17-19	1
1954	Lenny Moore	78	13	0	0
1955	Lenny Moore	30	5	0	0

Season Leaders continued:

		Points	TD	PAT	FG
	Milt Plum	30	3	*12-14	0
1956	Billy Kane	42	7	0	0
1957	Dave Kasperian	48	8	0	0
1958	Dave Kasperian	46	7	*0	0
1959	Rich Lucas	36	6	0	0
	Jim Kerr	36	6	0	0
1960	Jim Kerr	52	8	*0	0
1961	Roger Kochman	56	9	*0	0
1962	Roger Kochman	48	8	0	0
1963	Ron Coates	33	0	18-19	5-13
1964	Tom Urbanik	48	8	0	0
1965	Mike Irwin	42	7	0	0
	Dave McNaughton	42	7	0	0
1966	Tom Sherman	57	5	*7-10	6-8
1967	Don Abbey	88	9	*23-26	3-14
1968	Charlie Pittman	84	14	0	0
1969	Charlie Pittman	66	11	0	0
1970	Franco Harris	48	8	0	0
1971	Lydell Mitchell	174	29	0	0
1972	John Cappelletti	78	13	0	0
1973	John Cappelletti	102	17	0	0
1974	Tom Donchez	48	8	0	0
1975	Chris Bahr	73	0	19-20	18-33
1976	Mike Guman	48	8	0	0
1977	Matt Bahr	81	0	39-41	14-24
1978	Matt Bahr	97	0	31-31	22-27
1979	Herb Menhardt	70	0	28-28	14-20
1980	Herb Menhardt	71	0	26-26	15-21
1981	Brian Franco	81	0	36-37	15-21
1982	Curt Warner	78	13	0	0
1983	Nick Gancitano	85	0	34-36	17-21
1984	Nick Gancitano	49	0	19-19	10-14
1985	Massimo Manca	91	0	28-28	21-26
1986	Massimo Manca	79	0	37-37	14-23
1987	Blair Thomas	80	13	*0	0
1988	Gary Brown	44	7	*0	0
1989	Ray Tarasi	77	0	20-21	19-23
1990	Craig Fayak	74	0	29-30	15-21
1991	Craig Fayak	93	0	42-46	17-26
1992	Richie Anderson	116	19	*0	0
1993	Craig Fayak	79	0	40-42	13-23
1994	Ki-Jana Carter	138	23	0	0
1995	Brett Conway	85	0	37-37	16-24
1996	Brett Conway	93	0	39-39	18-24
1997	Curtis Enis	122	20	*0	0-0

*Does not include one two-point conversion.

GAME SCORING

Points	TD	PAT	FG	
36	6	0	0	Harry Robb vs. Gettysburg, 1917
33	4	9	0	Carl Forkum at Pittsburgh, 1903
32	3	10	0	Charles Atherton vs. Gettysburg, 1894*
30	5	0	0	Shorty Miller vs. Carnegie Tech, 1913
30	5	0	0	Lydell Mitchell at Navy, 1971
30	5	0	0	Lydell Mitchell vs. Maryland, 1971
30	5	0	0	Ki-Jana Carter vs. Michigan State, 1994
28	4	4	0	Johnny Roepke vs. Gettysburg, 1927
25	4	1	0	Tom Sherman vs. California, 1966
24	4	0	0	John Cappelletti vs. West Virginia, 1973
24	4	0	0	John Cappelletti vs. Ohio U., 1973
24	4	0	0	Mike Guman vs. Army, 1976
24	4	0	0	Leroy Thompson vs. Rutgers, 1990
24	4	0	0	Richie Anderson vs. Maryland, 1992
24	4	0	0	Brian O'Neal vs. Pittsburgh, 1992
24	4	0	0	Bobby Engram vs. Minnesota, 1993
24	4	0	0	Ki-Jana Carter vs. Ohio State, 1994
24	4	0	0	Bobby Engram at Rutgers, 1995
24	4	0	0	Curtis Enis at Purdue, 1997

*Prior to 1897, four points were awarded for touchdowns and two points for extra points.

SEASON SCORING

Points	TD	PAT	FG	
174	29	0	0	Lydell Mitchell, 1971
138	23	0	0	Ki-Jana Carter, 1994
122	20	**1	0	Curtis Enis, 1997
119	11	–	–	Pete Mauthe, 1909
116	19	*1	0	Richie Anderson, 1992
102	17	0	0	John Cappelletti, 1973
97	0	31	22	Matt Bahr, 1978
93	0	42	17	Craig Fayak, 1991
93	0	39	18	Brett Conway, 1996
92	0	62	10	Brett Conway, 1994
91	0	28	21	Massimo Manca, 1985
88	9	25	3	Don Abbey, 1967
85	0	34	17	Nick Gancitano, 1983
85	0	37	16	Brett Conway, 1995
84	14	0	0	Charlie Pittman, 1968

CAREER SCORING

Points	TD	PAT	FG	
282	0	132	50	Craig Fayak, 1990-93
276	0	141	45	Brett Conway, 1993-96
246	41	0	0	Lydell Mitchell, 1969-71
230	38	**1	0	Curtis Enis, 1995-97
206	0	86	40	Massimo Manca, 1982, 84-86
204	34	0	0	Ki-Jana Carter, 1992-94
198	33	0	0	Curt Warner, 1979-82
192	32	0	0	Charlie Pittman, 1967-69
192	32	0	0	Bobby Engram, 1991, 93-95
191	0	74	39	Matt Bahr, 1976-78
190	0	76	38	Nick Gancitano, 1981-84
188	31	*1	0	Richie Anderson, 1989-92
180	30	0	0	John Cappelletti, 1971-73
176	29	*1	0	Matt Suhey, 1976-79

*Two-point conversion run; **Two-point conversion reception.

50-yard Field Goals

55	Chris Bahr at Temple, 1975
55	Chris Bahr at Ohio State, 1975
55	Chris Bahr at Syracuse, 1975
54	Herb Menhardt at N.C. State, 1979
53	Massimo Manca vs. Notre Dame, 1985
52	Chris Bahr vs. West Virginia, 1975
52	Eric Etze at Notre Dame, 1988
52	Brett Conway vs. Temple, 1996
51	Pete Mauthe at Pittsburgh, 1912
51	Brett Conway vs. Michigan, 1995
50	Chris Bahr at Syracuse, 1973
50	Chris Bahr at Pittsburgh, 1974
50	Matt Bahr vs. Syracuse, 1978
50	Massimo Manca vs. Alabama, 1985
50	Massimo Manca vs. Notre Dame, 1985
50	Craig Fayak at Alabama, 1990

Game Field Goals

FG	FGA	LG	
5	5	48	Brian Franco at Nebraska, 1981
5	5	50	Massimo Manca vs. Notre Dame, 1985
4	4	50	Chris Bahr at Pittsburgh, 1974
4	5	37	Matt Bahr vs. Rutgers, 1978
4	5	41	Matt Bahr at Ohio State, 1978
4	4	41	Matt Bahr vs. SMU, 1978
4	4	37	Matt Bahr vs. N.C. State, 1978
4	4	35	Massimo Manca vs. Maryland, 1982
4	4	31	Nick Gancitano vs. Pittsburgh, 1982
4	5	50	Massimo Manca vs. Alabama, 1985
4	4	49	Ray Tarasi vs. West Virginia, 1989
4	4	48	Craig Fayak at Pittsburgh, 1991
4	4	42	Brett Conway at Purdue, 1995

Season Field Goals

fg	fga	pct.	lg	
22	27	81.5	50	Matt Bahr, 1978
21	26	80.8	53	Massimo Manca, 1985
19	23	82.6	49	Ray Tarasi, 1989
18	24	75.0	52	Brett Conway, 1996
18	33	54.6	55	Chris Bahr, 1975
17	21	81.0	48	Nick Ganitano, 1983
17	26	65.4	50	Craig Fayak, 1991
16	24	66.7	51	Brett Conway, 1995
15	21	71.4	44	Herb Menhardt, 1980
15	21	71.4	48	Brian Franco, 1981
15	22	68.2	50	Craig Fayak, 1990
14	24	58.3	38	Matt Bahr, 1977
14	20	70.0	54	Herb Menhardt, 1979
14	23	60.9	49	Massimo Manca, 1986

Career Field Goals

fg	fga	pct.	lg	
50	80	62.5	50	Craig Fayak, 1990-93
45	61	73.7	52	Brett Conway, 1993-96
40	59	67.6	53	Massimo Manca, 1982, 84-86
39	61	63.9	50	Matt Bahr, 1976-78
38	49	77.6	48	Nick Gancitano, 1981-84
35	63	55.6	55	Chris Bahr, 1973-75
29	41	70.7	54	Herb Menhardt, 1978-80
27	42	64.3	49	Ray Tarasi, 1986-89
20	–	–	–	Larry Vorhis, 1906-09
17	23	73.9	48	Brian Franco, 1980-81

Interception Records

INTERCEPTIONS
Game: 4
Mike Smith vs. Ohio U., 1970.
Season: 10
Neal Smith, 1969; Pete Harris, 1978.
Career: 19
Neal Smith, 1967-69.

INTERCEPTION RETURN YARDAGE
Game: 108
Mark Robinson at Pittsburgh, 1981.
Season: 179
Dennis Onkotz, 1967.
Career: 299
Darren Perry, 1988-91.

TOUCHDOWNS
Game: 2
Jeff Hite vs. Maryland, 1974.
Season: 2
Dennis Onkotz, 1967; Jeff Hite, 1974;
Scott Radecic, 1982; Darren Perry, 1991.
Career: 3
Dennis Onkotz, 1967-69; Darren Perry, 1988-91.

SEASON INTERCEPTIONS

No.	Yards	TD	
10	78	1	Neal Smith, 1969
10	155	0	Pete Harris, 1978
8	67	0	Don Eyer, 1952
8	101	0	Jack Sherry, 1952
8	74	0	Neal Smith, 1968
7	72	0	Milt Plum, 1956
7	66	0	Dick Gingrich, 1965
7	125	1	Darren Perry, 1990
7	64	0	Kim Herring, 1996
6	43	0	Bob Pollard, 1951
6	96	1	Lenny Moore, 1954

Season Interceptions continued:

6	56	0	Tim Montgomery, 1967
6	179	2	Dennis Onkotz, 1967
6	97	0	Sherrod Rainge, 1989
6	139	1	Leonard Humphries, 1990
6	122	2	Darren Perry, 1991

CAREER INTERCEPTIONS

Int.	Yards	TD	
19	152	1	Neal Smith, 1967-69
15	183	0	Pete Harris, 1976-78, 80
15	299	3	Darren Perry, 1988-91
13	106	1	Kim Herring, 1993-96
12	211	1	Junior Powell, 1961-63
12	30	0	Derek Bochna, 1990-93
12	135	0	Brian Miller, 1993-96
11	143	0	Don Eyer, 1951-53
11	275	3	Dennis Onkotz, 1967-69
10	136	1	Lenny Moore, 1953-55
10	91	0	Milt Plum, 1954-56
10	66	0	Dick Gingrich, 1964-65
10	172	0	Buddy Ellis, 1971-73
10	121	0	Ray Isom, 1983-86

LONGEST INTERCEPTION RETURNS

98	Wayne Berfield at Boston U., 1958
91	Mark Robinson at Pittsburgh, 1981
85	Tom Silvano vs. Gettysburg, 1934
85	Scott Radecic at West Virginia, 1982
82	Coop French at Pennsylvania, 1929
82*	Pete Curkendall vs. Maryland, 1986
80*	Buddy Torris at Holy Cross, 1960
80	Aaron Collins vs. Indiana, 1995

*Non-scoring play.

Season Leaders

Season	Name	Int.	Yards	Avg.	TD
1946	Elwood Petchel	4	40	10.0	0
1947	Bill Luther	5	65	13.0	0
1948	Elwood Petchel	4	15	3.8	0
1949	Bill Luther	4	80	20.0	0
1950	Bill Leonard	3	94	31.3	1
	Chan Johnson	3	55	18.3	0
1951	Bob Pollard	6	43	7.2	0
1952	Jack Sherry	8	101	14.3	0
	Don Eyer	8	67	8.4	0
1953	Lenny Moore	3	40	13.3	0
1954	Lenny Moore	6	96	16.0	1
1955	Sam Valentine	2	40	20.0	0
	Milt Plum	2	9	4.5	0
1956	Milt Plum	7	72	10.3	0
1957	Paul North	2	10	5.0	0
	Dave Kasperian	2	0	0.0	0
1958	Jim Kerr	5	122	24.4	1
1959	Rich Lucas	5	114	22.8	0
1960	Don Jonas	3	45	15.0	0
1961	Junior Powell	3	2	0.7	0
1962	Junior Powell	5	140	28.0	1
1963	Don Caum	4	81	20.3	0
	Junior Powell	4	69	17.3	0
1964	Frank Hershey	3	41	13.7	0
1965	Dick Gingrich	7	66	9.4	0
1966	Bob Capretto	3	6	2.0	0
	Tim Montgomery	3	4	1.3	0
	John Runnells	3	3	1.0	0
	John Sladki	3	0	0.0	0
1967	Dennis Onkotz	6	179	29.8	2
	Tim Montgomery	6	56	9.3	0
1968	Neal Smith	8	74	9.3	0
1969	Neal Smith	10	78	7.8	1
1970	Mike Smith	5	89	19.8	1

Season Leaders continued:

1971	Gary Gray	5	11	2.2	0
1972	Buddy Ellis	3	61	20.3	0
1973	Jim Bradley	4	59	14.8	0
1974	Jeff Hite	3	104	34.7	2
	Greg Buttle	3	7	2.3	0
1975	Tom Odell	4	30	7.5	0
1976	Bill Crummy	3	52	17.3	0
	Matt Millen	3	27	9.0	0
1977	Gary Petercuskie	2	11	5.5	0
	Tom DePaso	2	7	3.5	0
	Pete Harris	2	0	0.0	0
	Ron Hostetler	2	0	0.0	0
1978	Pete Harris	10	155	15.5	0
1979	Giuseppe Harris	3	40	13.3	0
1980	Paul Lankford	4	33	8.3	0
1981	Roger Jackson	5	19	3.8	0
1982	Scott Radecic	4	142	35.5	2
	Mark Robinson	4	89	22.3	0
1983	Michael Zordich	3	19	6.3	0
1984	Chris Sydnor	5	14	2.8	0
1985	Ray Isom	4	39	9.8	0
1986	Duffy Cobbs	4	-6	-1.5	0
1987	Brian Chizmar	3	18	6.0	0
1988	Sherrod Rainge	3	39	13.0	0
1989	Sherrod Rainge	6	97	16.2	0
1990	Darren Perry	7	125	17.9	1
1991	Darren Perry	6	122	20.3	2
1992	Derek Bochna	3	10	3.3	0
1993	Tony Pittman	5	40	8.0	0
1994	Brian Miller	4	25	6.3	0
1995	Brian Miller	5	28	5.6	0
1996	Kim Herring	7	64	9.1	0
1997	Aaron Collins	3	61	20.3	1

Defensive Records

TACKLES
Season: 165
Greg Buttle, 1974.
Solo Tackles: 86
Greg Buttle, 1974.
Assisted Tackles: 79
Greg Buttle, 1974.

QUARTERBACK SACKS
Season: 15
Larry Kubin, 1979.
Career: 30
Larry Kubin, 1977-80.

TACKLES FOR LOSSES
Season: 23
Larry Kubin, 1979.

FUMBLES RECOVERED
Game: 3
Dave Robinson vs. Maryland, 1962.
Season: 5
Tom Odell, 1975.

FUMBLES CAUSED
Season: 5
Mark D'Onofrio, 1990.

BLOCKED PUNTS
Season: 3
Jack Ham, 1968; Andre Collins, 1989.
Career: 4
Jack Ham, 1968-70; Andre Collins, 1986-89.

Defensive Records continued:

SAFETIES
Game: 3
Mike Reid vs. Maryland, 1966.
Season: 3
Mike Reid, 1966.
Career: 3
Mike Reid, 1966, 68-69.

SEASON TACKLES

Total	Solo	Assists	
165	86	79	Greg Buttle, 1974
140	76	64	Greg Buttle, 1975
130	68	62	Andre Collins, 1989
126	72	54	Ed O'Neil, 1972
126	51	75	Brian Gelzheiser, 1994
118	74	44	Dennis Onkotz, 1967
115	60	55	Gary Gray, 1971
113	57	56	Brian Gelzheiser, 1993
112	55	57	Gerald Filardi, 1995
110	63	47	Andre Collins, 1988
110	56	54	Brian Chizmar, 1989
104	57	47	Mike Hartenstine, 1973
102	54	48	Rogers Alexander, 1985
100	53	47	Harry Hamilton, 1983

CAREER TACKLES

Total	Solo	Assists	
343	185	158	Greg Buttle, 1973-75
315	157	158	Brian Gelzheiser, 1991-94
287	165	122	Dennis Onkotz, 1967-69
274	144	130	John Skorupan, 1970-72
274	186	88	Shane Conlan, 1983-86
257	147	110	Andre Collins, 1986-89
256	176	80	Trey Bauer, 1984-87
255	158	97	Jim Nelson, 1994-97
251	143	108	Jack Ham, 1968-70
241	161	80	Brian Chizmar, 1986-89
237	133	104	Jim Heller, 1970-72
235	145	90	Kurt Allerman, 1974-76
230	107	123	Gerald Filardi, 1993-96
227	136	91	Aaron Collins, 1994-97
226	137	89	Rogers Alexander, 1982-85
223	126	97	Bruce Bannon, 1970-72

SEASON TACKLE LEADERS

Season	Name	Total	Solo	Assists
1969	Dennis Onkotz	97	50	47
1970	Gary Gray	96	50	46
1971	Gary Gray	115	60	55
1972	Ed O'Neil	126	72	54
1973	Mike Hartenstine	104	57	47
1974	Greg Buttle	165	86	79
1975	Greg Buttle	140	76	64
1976	Kurt Allerman	87	57	30
1977	Rick Donaldson	86	42	44
1978	Lance Mehl	96	46	50
1979	Lance Mehl	99	68	31
1980	Chet Parlavecchio	72	42	30
1981	Chet Parlavecchio	70	42	28
1982	Scott Radecic	71	48	23
1983	Harry Hamilton	100	53	47
1984	Ray Isom	82	55	27
1985	Rogers Alexander	102	54	48
1986	Shane Conlan	79	63	16
1987	Brian Chizmar	69	57	12
1988	Andre Collins	110	63	47
1989	Andre Collins	130	68	62
1990	Mark D'Onofrio	71	45	26
1991	Lee Rubin	60	45	15

Season Tackle Leaders continued:

1992	Phil Yeboah-Kodie	63	40	23
1993	Brian Gelzheiser	113	57	56
1994	Brian Gelzheiser	126	51	75
1995	Gerald Filardi	112	55	57
1996	Gerald Filardi	96	37	59
1997	Jim Nelson	91	70	21

SEASON QUARTERBACK SACKS

Season	Name	Total
1975	Ron Coder	5
1976	Tony Petruccio	7
1977	Bruce Clark	6
	Matt Millen	6
1978	Larry Kubin	12
1979	Larry Kubin	15
1980	Gene Gladys	6
1981	Walker Lee Ashley	6
1982	Walker Lee Ashley	5
1983	Rogers Alexander	6
1984	Bob White	7
1985	Don Graham	7
1986	Don Graham	9
1987	Pete Curkendall	7
1988	Quintus McDonald	7
1989	Mark D'Onofrio	11
1990	Rich McKenzie	6
1991	Tyoka Jackson	9.5
1992	Rich McKenzie	6
1993	Tyoka Jackson	8
1994	Willie Smith	7
1995	Terry Killens	11
1996	Brandon Noble	8
1997	Chris Snyder	7

Career Quarterback Sacks (since 1975)

Sacks	
30	Larry Kubin, 1977-80
24.5	Tyoka Jackson, 1990-93
22	Matt Millen, 1976-79
21	Todd Atkins, 1992-95
20	Rich McKenzie, 1989-92
19	Bruce Clark, 1976-79
18	Don Graham, 1983-86
18	Bob White, 1983-86
16	Shane Conlan, 1983-86
15	Mark D'Onofrio, 1988-91
15	Terry Killens, 1992-95
14.5	Eric Ravotti, 1989-93
14	Walker Lee Ashley, 1979-82
14	Brandon Noble, 1994-96

The Last Time by Penn state

200 Yards Rushing: 211, Curtis Enis at Purdue, 1997.
30 Rushing Attempts: 37, Curtis Enis at Purdue, 1997.
35 Rushing Attempts: 37, Curtis Enis at Purdue, 1997.
Three Touchdowns Rushing: Curtis Enis at Purdue, 1997.
Four Touchdowns Rushing: Brian O'Neal vs. Pittsburgh, 1992.
Five Touchdowns Rushing: Ki-Jana Carter vs. Michigan State, 1994.
70-Yard Run: 78, Curtis Enis vs. Wisconsin, 1997.
80-Yard Run: 80, Ki-Jana Carter at Indiana, 1994.
90-Yard Run: 92, Blair Thomas vs. Syracuse, 1986.
Two Players Rushing For 100 Yards: Ki-Jana Carter (159) & Mike Archie (120) at Maryland, 1993.
300 Yards Passing: 366, Mike McQueary vs. Pittsburgh, 1997.
350 Yards Passing: 366, Mike McQueary vs. Pittsburgh, 1997.
20 Pass Completions: 21, Mike McQueary vs. Pittsburgh, 1997.
25 Pass Completions: 28, Kerry Collins at Brigham Young, 1992.

The Last Time By Penn State continued:

30 Pass Attempts: 30, Mike McQueary vs. Ohio State, 1997.
40 Pass Attempts: 48, Wally Richardson vs. Wisconsin, 1995.
50 Pass Attempts: 54, Kerry Collins at Brigham Young, 1992.
Four Touchdown Passes: 4, Kerry Collins vs. Rutgers, 1993.
Five Touchdown Passes: 5, Tony Sacca vs. Georgia Tech, 1991.
Four Interceptions Thrown: 4, Todd Blackledge at Alabama, 1982.
300 Yards Total Offense: 370, Mike McQueary (366 pass, 4 rush) vs.Pittsburgh, 1997.
350 Yards Total Offense: 370, Mike McQueary (366 pass, 4 rush) vs.Pittsburgh, 1997.
100 Yards Receiving: 123, Joe Jurevicius at Michigan State, 1997.
150 Yards Receiving: 150, Joe Jurevicius at Louisville, 1997.
200 Yards Receiving: 203, Bobby Engram at Purdue, 1995.
Two Players With 100 Yards Receiving: Bobby Engram (169) & Freddie Scott (145) vs. Michigan State, 1994.
10 Receptions: 13, Freddie Scott vs. Wisconsin, 1995.
80-Yard Reception: 82, Freddie Scott from Kerry Collins vs. Rutgers, 1994.
Three Touchdowns Receiving: 3, Joe Jurevicius at Louisville, 1997.
Four Touchdowns Receiving: 4, Bobby Engram vs. Minnesota, 1993.
Kickoff Return For Touchdown: 91, Blair Thomas vs. Pittsburgh, 1986.
100-Yard Kickoff Return: 100, Rich Mauti at Temple, 1975.
Punt Return For Touchdown: 59, Chris Campbell vs. Purdue, 1996.
80-Yard Punt Return: 84, O.J. McDuffie at Syracuse, 1989.
Interception Return For Touchdown: 27, Maurice Daniels at Purdue, 1997.
Blocked Punt For Touchdown: 2, Ahmad Collins (blocked by David Macklin) at Michigan, 1996.
Safety: Kickoff return brought back into end zone at Louisville, 1997.
50-Yard Field Goal: 52, Brett Conway vs. Temple, 1996.

Penn State Team Records

FIRST DOWNS
Game: 38
vs. West Virginia, 1962
Season: 273
1994 (11 games)
Rushing: 173, 1971 (Low: 109, 1988)
Passing: 131, 1994 (Low: 49, 1969)
Penalty: 17, 1986 (Low: 5, 1967; 1974)

RUSHING ATTEMPTS
Game: 83
vs. West Virginia, 1975
Season: 643
1973 (11 games)

PASSING YARDAGE
Game: 377
vs. Pittsburgh, 1997
Season: 2962
1994 (11 games); (Low: 914, 1960)

PASS ATTEMPTS
Game: 54
at Brigham Young, 1992
Season: 343
1995 (11 games)

MOST INTERCEPTIONS THROWN
Season: 16
1981; 1982; 1987.

PLAYS
Game: 99
at West Virginia, 1966.
Season: 886
1978 (Low: 637, 1960).

Rushing Yardage
Game: 622
vs. Lebanon Valley, 1924
Season: 3347
1971 (Low: 1689, 1973)

Rushing Average
Season: 6.1
1994 (Low: 3.45, 1963)

Completions
Game: 33
vs. Wisconsin, 1995
Season: 197
1995 (11 games); (Low: 68, 1970)

Completion Percentage
Game: 91.7
vs. Oregon, 1963
Season: 64.9
1994 (Low: 41.8, 1966)

Total Offense Yardage
Game: 711
vs. Susquehanna, 1926;
706 vs.Cincinnati, 1991
Season: 5722
1994 (11 games); (Low: 2914, 1960)

Punts
Season: 79
1984 (Low: 36, 1963)

Penn State Team Records continued:

PUNT RETURNS
Punt Return Yardage
vs. Rutgers, 1982.

PENALTIES
Season: 84
1978 (11 games); 88, 1991 (12 games); (Low: 36, 1963, 1996).

FUMBLES
Season: 40
1965 (Low: 13, 1987).

TURNOVERS
Season: 36
1972 (Low: 11, 1994).

Touchdowns
Season: 71
1994 (Low: 21, 1963)
Rushing, Season: 45
1994 (Low: 11, 1989)
Passing, Season: 23
1994 (11 games); 1991 (12 games); (Low: 1, 1969)

TOUCHDOWN RETURNS
Season: 7
1967 (Low: 0, 1966; 1976; 1993)

SCORING DEFENSE
Shutouts, Season: 6
1947
Consecutive Shutouts: 3
1940; 1947
Fewest Points Allowed, Season: 27
1947 (9 games)

WINNING STREAKS
Consecutive Games: 23
1968-70
Season: 12
1973, 1986, 1994
Home Games: 50
1889-1908
Home Games Since 1920: 29
1919-24

Game: 12 Game: 256
vs. Rutgers, 1982

Penalty Yardage
Game: 142.5
at Pittsburgh, 1966
Season: 776
1978 (Low: 287, 1996)

Fumbles Lost
Season: 25
1972 (Low: 4, 1994)

Points
Game: 109
vs. Lebanon Valley (7), 1920
Game Since 1920; 82
vs. Susquehanna (0), 1926; 81 vs. Cincinnati (0), 1991.
Season: 526
1994 (11 games); (Low: 67, 1925, 9 games)
Scoring In Consecutive Games, All Games: 138
1973-84
Regular-Season: 190
1966-84

Field Goals
Season: 22
1978 (Low: 2, 1970)

Interceptions Made
Game: 7
at Boston College, 1970
Season: 28
1971; 1978

Losing Streak
Consecutive Games: 7
1931

Opponent Points
Game: 106
at Lehigh (Penn State 0), 1889
Game Since 1920: 55
at Navy (Penn State 14), 1944

Unbeaten Streaks

Games	Won	Tied	Seasons	Ended By
31	30	1	1967-70	Colorado, 41-13
30	25	5	1919-22	Navy, 14-0
20	20	0	1993-95	Wisconsin, 17-9
19	19	0	1977-78	Alabama, 14-7
19	18	1	1911-13	Washington & Jefferson, 17-0
17	15	2	1947-48	Pittsburgh, 7-0

Milestone Victories

100 vs. Grove City, Oct. 2, 1909 (31-0)
200 vs. Marietta, Oct. 9, 1926 (48-6)
300 vs. Navy, Nov. 15, 1947 (20-7)
400 at Oregon, Sept. 21, 1963 (17-7)
500 vs. Ohio U., Nov.16, 1974 (35-16)
600 vs. West Virginia, Oct. 26, 1985 (27-0)
700 vs. Wisconsin, Sept. 28, 1996 (23-20)

Winning Point Differential
102   vs. Lebanon Valley (109-7), 1920
99   vs. St. Bonaventure (99-0), 1917

Winning Point Differential (Since 1920)
82   vs. Susquehanna (82-0), 1926
81   vs. Cincinnati (81-0), 1991

Winning Point Differential Under Joe Paterno
81   vs. Cincinnati (81-0), 1991
63   vs. Maryland (70-7), 1993

Losing Point Differential
106   at Lehigh (106-0), 1889
47   at Pennsylvania (47-0), 1899

Losing Point Differential (since 1920)
47   at Cornell (47-0), 1939
41   at Navy (55-14), 1944

Losing Point Differential Under Joe Paterno
38   at UCLA (49-11), 1966
38   vs. Nebraska (44-6), 1983

NCAA Leaders/Records

Individual Leaders

Rushing Touchdowns
Season: 26, Lydell Mitchell, 1971.
Passing Efficiency
Season: 148.0, John Hufnagel, 1972; 172.8, Kerry Collins, 1994.
Punt Return Average
Season: 19.2, Gary Hayman, 1973.
Kickoff Return Average
Season: 52.2, Chuck Peters, 1940 (5 returns).
Field Goals Per Game
Season: 2.0, Matt Bahr (22-27), 1978.
Field Goal Percentage (Min. 25 FGA)
Season: 81.5 (22-27), Matt Bahr, 1978.
Interceptions
Season: 10, Pete Harris, 1978.

NCAA Individual Record Holders

Most Four-Field Goal Games
Season: 4, Matt Bahr, 1978.

NCAA Team Records by Penn State

Fewest Yards Allowed
Game: (-47) vs. Syracuse, Oct. 18, 1947 (-107 rushing, 60 passing, 49 plays).
Fewest Yards Allowed Rushing
Per Game: 17.0, 1947 (153 yards, 9 games).
Per Rush: 0.64, 1947 (153 yards, 240 rushes).
Fewest Yards Allowed Passing
Per Game: 13.1, 1938 (105, 8 games).
Consecutive Non-Losing Seasons
49, 1939-87.

Team Leaders

Scoring Offense
Season: 1994, 47.8 points per game.
Total Offense
Season: 1994, 520.2 yards per game.

NCAA Leaders/Records continued:

Rushing Defense
Season: 1947, 17.0 yards per game; 1978, 54.5.
Passing Defense
Season: 1938, 13.1 yards per game.
Total Defense
Season: 1947, 76.8 yards per game; 1978, 203.9.
Scoring Defense
Season: 1947, 2.8 points per game.

Penn State Opponent Records

RUSHING
Yardage: 251
Ted Brown, N.C. State, 1977.
Attempts: 38
Tony Dorsett, Pittsburgh, 1976.
Touchdowns: 4
Allen Pinkett, Notre Dame, 1983; 1984.
Longest Run: 94
Frank Funair, Bucknell, 1938.

Receiving
Receptions: 16
Skip Orszulak, Pittsburgh, 1968.
Receiving Yardage: 285
Thomas Lewis, Indiana, 1993.
Touchdowns: 3
Bill Wallace, Pittsburgh, 1984;
Marco Battaglia, Rutgers, 1995.

TOTAL OFFENSE
Yardage: 507
Doug Flutie, Boston College, 1982.

KICKOFF RETURNS
Returns: 7
Bob Elflein, Navy, 1970.
Yardage: 186
Derrick Mason, Michigan State, 1994.
Longest: 100
Tony Uansa, Pittsburgh, 1928;
Kerry Marbury, West Virginia, 1972;
Derrick Mason, Michigan State, 1994.

SCORING
Touchdowns: 4
Johnny Castan, Boston U., 1951;
Allen Pinkett, Notre Dame, 1983, 1984.
Extra Points: 7
Kurt Zimmerman, UCLA, 1966.
Kicking Points: 15
Charlie Baumann, West Virginia, 1988.

Penn State Opponent Records continued:

INTERCEPTIONS
Interceptions: 3
Tom Myers, Syracuse, 1970;
Jamel Coleman, Purdue, 1996.
Yardage: 100
Tom Pridemore, West Virginia, 1977.
Longest: 100
Tom Pridemore, West Virginia, 1977.

Passing
Yardage: 520
Doug Flutie, Boston College, 1982.
Completions: 34
Tim Schade, Minnesota, 1993.
Completion Percentage: 84.6
Todd Norley (11-13), Syracuse, 1984.
Attempts: 66
Tim Schade, Minnesota, 1993.
Touchdowns: 4
Boyce Smith, Vanderbilt, 1957; John
Hogan, Pittsburgh, 1972; Terry Gregory,
Temple, 1976.
Interceptions: 6
Frank Harris, Boston College, 1970.
Steve Skiver, Ohio U., 1970.
Longest Completion: 99
John Paci to Thomas Lewis, Indiana,
1993.

Punt Returns
Returns: 7
Chris Anderson, Alabama, 1990.
Yardage: 172
Greg Allen, Syracuse, 1969.
Longest: 91
Floyd Little, Syracuse, 1965.

Punting
Punts: 24
Charles Robinson, Cornell, 1942.
Yardage: 936
Charles Robinson, Cornell, 1942.
Average: 49.1
Johnny Evans, N.C. State, 1974.
Longest: 81
Johnny Evans, N.C. State, 1974.

Field Goals
Field Goals: 5
Adam Bailey, Minnesota, 1997.
Longest Field Goal: 57
Gary Homer, Ohio U., 1973.

Fumble Return
Longest: 100
Steve Smoke, Lehigh, 1938

Individual Opponent Rushing Yardage

251	Ted Brown, N.C. State, 1977
238	Sedrick Irvin, Michigan State, 1997
224	Tony Dorsett, Pittsburgh, 1976
220	Bobby Humphrey, Alabama, 1987
217	Allen Pinkett, Notre Dame, 1983
206	Paul Palmer, Temple, 1985
203	Marc Renaud, Michigan State, 1997
200	Warren Heller, Pittsburgh, 1930
192	Tyrone Wheatley, Michigan, 1993
189	Jarvis Redwine, Nebraska, 1980
189	Allen Pinkett, Notre Dame, 1984
184	Curtis Dickey, Texas A & M, 1979

Individual Opponent Passing Yardage

520	Doug Flutie, Boston College, 1982
478	Tim Schade, Minnesota, 1993
447	Doug Flutie, Boston College, 1984
380	Doug Flutie, Boston College, 1983
379	John Paci, Indiana, 1993
378	Joe Germaine, Ohio State, 1997
374	Matt Sherman, Iowa, 1995
367	Rusty Hochberg, Rutgers, 1983
354	Bobby Hoying, Ohio State, 1995
347	Billy Dicken, Purdue, 1997
345	Chuck Long, Iowa, 1983
344	Glenn Foley, Boston College, 1992

Individual Opponent Receiving Yardage

285	Thomas Lewis, Indiana, 1993
229	Scott Nizolek, Boston College, 1982
210	Andrew Baker, Rutgers, 1983
193	Omar Douglas, Minnesota, 1993
190	Oscar Patrick, West Virginia, 1968

Opponent Team Records

First Downs: 34
Alabama, 1983
Rushing Attemps: 75
Kentucky, 1976
Completions: 34
Minnesota, 1993
Interceptions Thrown: 7
Boston Collge, 1970.
Total Offense Plays: 94
Rutgers, 1994.
Penalty Yardage: 141
Nebaraska, 1980.

Rushing Yardage: 452
Michigan State, 1997
Passing Yardage: 595
Boston College, 1982
Pass Attempts: 66
Minnesota, 1993
Total Offense Yardage: 656
Boston College, 1982
Punts: 24
Cornell, 1942
Fumbles Lost: 5
Syracuse, 1970

The Last Time By Opponents

100 Yards Rushing: 238, Sedrick Irvin; 203, Marc Renaud, Michigan State, 1997.
200 Yards Rushing: 238, Sedrick Irvin; 203, Marc Renaud, Michigan State, 1997.
35 Rushing Attempts: 36, Darnell Autry, Northwestern, 1995.
Three Touchdowns Rushing: 3, Sedrick Irvin, Michigan State, 1997.
Four Touchdowns Rushing: 4, Allen Pinkett, Notre Dame, 1984.
70-Yard Run: 71, Todd Bell, Boston College, 1984.
Two Players Rushing For 100 Yards: 238, Sedrick Irvin; 203, Marc Renaud, Michigan State, 1997.
300 Yards Passing: 347, Billy Dicken, Purdue, 1997.
400 Yards Passing: 478, Tim Schade, Minnesota, 1993.

The Last Time by Opponent continued:

25 Pass Completions: 33, Billy Dicken, Purdue, 1997.
30 Pass Completions: 33, Billy Dicken, Purdue, 1997.
40 Pass Attempts: 60, Billy Dicken, Purdue, 1997.
50 Pass Attempts: 60, Billy Dicken, Purdue, 1997.
Four Touchdown Passes: 4, Glenn Foley, Boston College, 1992.
Four Interceptions Thrown: 5, Alex Van Pelt, Pittsburgh, 1991.
400 Yards Total Offense: 536, Tim Schade (478 pass, 59 rush), Minnesota, 1993.
200 Yards Receiving: 285, Thomas Lewis, Indiana, 1993.
10 Receptions: 10, Isaac Jones, Purdue, 1997.
80-Yard Reception: 80, Tyler Anderson from Ryan Hancock, Brigham Young, 1992.
Kickoff Return For Touchdown: 100, Derrick Mason, Michigan State, 1994.
100-Yard Kickoff Return: 100, Derrick Mason, Michigan State, 1994.
Punt Return For Touchdown: 83, Tim Dwight, Iowa, 1996.
80-Yard Punt Return: 83, Tim Dwight, Iowa, 1996.
Interception Return For Touchdown: 68, Quincy Harrison, Southern Cal, 1994.
200 Yards Receiving: 153, David Boston, Ohio State, 1997.
Blocked Punt For Touchdown: 2, Kevin Cary (blocked by James Harris), Temple, 1990.
Safety: Courtney Ledyard (blocked punt out of end zone), Michigan State, 1996.
50-Yard Field Goal: 50, Adam Bailey, Minnesota, 1997.

All-Star Games

Blue-Gray

1942: Kenneth Schoonover	1944: John Chuckran
1944: Donald Miltenberger	1945: Al Bellas
1945: Bob Davis	1945: Sam Tamburo
1946: Larry Joe	1946: Bucky Waters
1949: Joe Drazenovich	1950: Bill Mathers
1950: Vince O'Bara	1951: Len Bartek
1951: Ed Hoover	1952: Don Barney
1952: Jim Dooley	1952: Bill Leonard
1952: Bob Smith	1953: Fred Prender
1953: Tony Rados	1953: Pete Schoderbek
1954: Gene Danser	1954: Jack Sherry
1955: Walt Mazur	1956: Dan Radakovich
1957: Paul North	1958: Dave Kasperian
1958: Charles Ruslavage	1958: Maurice Schleicher
1959: Earl Kohlass	1959: Andy Stynchula
1960: Stew Barber	1963: Dick Anderson
1963: Dan Caum	1964: Billy Bowes
1964: Ed Stuckrath	1964: Gary Wydman
1965: Robert Riggle	1970: Greg Edmonds
1970: Robert Holuba	1984: Tony Munford
	1988: Bob Mrosko
	1988: Keith Karpinski

Coach: Rip Engle
1951, 52, 53, 54, 62

East-West Shrine

1927: Gary Green, B	1927: Bill Pritchard, B
1927: Ken Weston, E	1928: George Delp, E
1930: Skip Stahley, E	1941: Leon Gajecki, C
1942: Len Krouse, B	1942: Bill Smaltz, B
1944: Aldo Cenci, QB	1944: John Jaffurs, G
1946: Chuck Drazenovich, QB	1946: Bronco Kosanovich, C
1947: William Moore, T	1947: Paul Weaver, B
1949: Larry Cooney, B	1949: John Finlay, T
1949: John Simon, G	1955: Don Bailey, QB
1955: Jim Garrity, E	1955: Otto Kneidinger, T
1955: Lenny Moore, B	1955: Frank Reich, C
1957: Ray Alberigi, FB	1957: Milt Plum, QB
1957: Sam Valentine, G	1958: Babe Caprara, B
1958: Les Walters, E	1960: Jim Kerr, B
1963: Ralph Baker, C	1963: Pete Liske, B
1965: Dick Gingrich, B	1965: Glenn Ressler, G
1966: Dave Rowe, G	1971: Jack Ham, LB
1971: Warren Koegel, C	1978: Chuck Correal, C

East-West Shrine continued:

1978: Eric Cunningham, G
1979: Mike Guman, RB
1981: Bill Dugan, T
1982: Sean Farrell, G
1983: Bill Contz, T
1986: Lance Hamilton, DHB
1987: Don Graham, LB
1988: Pete Curkendall, DT
1992: Leonard Humphries, CB
1997: Pete Marczyk, T

1978: Keith Dorney, T
1979: Irv Pankey, T
1981: Booker Moore, RB
1982: Chet Parlavecchio, LB
1984: Greg Gattuso, DT
1987: D.J. Dozier, RB
1987: Steve Smith, RB
1989: Eddie Johnson, DHB
1994: Lou Benfatti, DT
1998: Jim Nelson, LB

Hula Bowl

1949: Elwood Petchel, B
1960: Rich Lucas, B
1962: Bob Mitinger, E
1963: Dave Robinson, B
1964: Pete Liske, B
1965: Glenn Ressler, G
1967: Dave Rowe, T
1968: Bill Lenkaitis, C
1970: Dennis Onkotz, LB
1972: Dave Joyner, T
1973: Bruce Bannon, DE
1974: Randy Crowder, DT
1976: Tom Rafferty, G
1977: Ron Crosby, LB
1978: Mickey Shuler, TE
1979: Matt Bahr, K
1979: Chuck Fusina, QB
1981: Pete Kugler, DT
1983: Pete Speros, T
1984: Harry Hamilton, DHB
1985: Nick Haden, G
1987: Chris Conlin, T
1987: Keith Radecic, C
1988: Mark Sickler, T
1990: Rich Schonewolf, DT
1991: Willie Thomas, Saf
1994: Shelly Hammonds, CB
1996: Brian Milne, FB
1997: Kim Herrin, Saf

1949: Sam Tamburo, E
1961: Jim Kerr, B
1963: Roger Kochman, B
1964: Ralph Baker, C
1964: Harrison Rosdahl, C
1966: Joe Bellas, T
1968: Rich Buzin, T
1970: Jim Kates, MG
1971: Jack Ham, LB
1972: Lydell Mitchell, RB
1974: John Cappelletti, RB
1976: Greg Buttle, LB
1977: Brad Benson, T
1978: Jimmy Cefalo, WR
1978: Randy Sidler, DT
1979: Scott Fitzkee, WR
1980: Lance Mehl, LB
1982: Matt Bradley, DHB
1983: Curt Warner, RB
1984: Kenny Jackson, WR
1986: Rogers Alexander, ILB
1987: Tim Manoa, FB
1988: Pete Giftopoulos, LB
1989: Steve Wisniewski, G
1991: Frank Giannetti, DT
1992: Keith Goganious, LB
1996: Terry Killens, DE
1996: Freddie Scott, WR
1998: Joe Jurevicius, WR

Japan Bowl

1976: Greg Buttle, LB
1977: Brad Benson, T
1978: Jimmy Cefalo, FLK
1978: Mickey Shuler, TE
1979: Matt Bahr, K
1979: Scott Fitzkee, FLK
1980: Irv Pankey, TE
1981: Pete Kugler, DT
1982: Sean Farrell, G
1982: Leo Wisniewski, T
1983: Ken Kelley, LB
1984: Kenny Jackson, WR
1986: Todd Moules, G
1987: Shane Conlan, LB
1987: Tim Johnson, DE
1988: Marques Henderson, DHB
1989: Steve Wisniewski, G
1990: Andre Collins, LB
1990: Blair Thomas, RB
1991: Leroy Thompson, RB
1992: Paul Siever, G
1993: O.J. McDuffie, WR

1976: Tom Rafferty, G
1977: Ron Crosby, DE
1978: Neil Hutton, DHB
1978: Randy Sidler, DT
1979: Scott Fitzkee, FLK
1979: Chuck Fusina, QB
1981: Pete Harris, DGB
1981: Booker Moore, RB
1982: Chet Parlavecchio, LB
1983: Mike McCloskey, TE
1983: Dave Paffenroth, DT
1984: Scott Radecic, LB
1986: Michael Zordich, CB
1987: Ray Isom, Saf
1987: Brian Siverling, TE
1989: Keith Karpinski, LB
1990: Brian Chizmar, LB
1990: Roger Duffy, C
1991: Frank Giannetti, DT
1992: Darren Perry, DHB
1993: Reggie Givens, OLB

Senior Bowl

1953: Don Barney, G
1953: Jim Dooley, C
1953: Stew Scheetz, T
1954: Don Malinak, E
1955: Jim Garrity, E
1957: Walt Mazur, T
1957: Milt Plum, B
1958: Les Walters, E
1959: Charles Ruslavage, C
1959: Maury Scleicher, E
1960: Andy Stynchula, T
1962: Jim Smith, T
1963: Charlie Sieminski, G
1966: Don Kunit, B
1968: Mike McBath, T
1968: Tim Montgomery, DHB
1969: Dave Bradley, T
1969: Bob Campbell, RB
1969: Ted Kwalick, TE
1970: Chuck Burkhart, QB
1970: Charlie Pittman, RB
1970: Mike Reid, DT
1972: Franco Harris, RB
1973: Gregg Ducatte, DHB
1974: John Cappelletti, RB
1974: Gary Hayman, WR
1974: Phil LaPorta, T
1974: Ed O'Neil, LB
1976: Chris Bahr, K
1977: Kurt Allerman, LB
1977: George Reihner, T
1979: Chuck Correal, C
1979: Eric Cunningham, G
1979: Keith Dorney, T
1979: Bob Torrey
1981: Herb Menhardt, K
1982: Vyto Kab, TE
1982: Paul Lankford, DHB
1982: Jim Romano, C
1982: Ralph Giacomarro, P

1984: Kevin Baugh, WR
1984: Ron Heller, T
1984: Jon Williams, RB
1985: Tony Mumford, RB
1985: Stan Short, T
1987: Tim Manoa, FB
1987: Bob White, DT
1988: Trey Bauer, LB
1988: Stan Clayton, T
1989: Eddie Johnson, DHB
1989: Quintus McDonald, LB
1990: Andre Collins, LB
1990: Sherrod Rainge, DHB
1990: Dave Szott, G
1990: Blair Thomas, TB
1991: Gary Brown, TB
1991: Matt McCartin, T
1992: Keith Goganious, LB
1992: Tony Sacca, QB
1993: John Gerak, G
1993: Reggie Givens, OLB
1993: Greg Huntington, T
1994: Lou Benfatti, DT
1994: Tyoka Jackson, DT
1995: Kerry Collins, QB
1995: Brian Gelzheiser, LB
1996: Mike Archie, TB
1996: Keith Conlin, T
1996: Bobby Engram, WR
1996: Andre Johnson, T
1996: Marco Revera, G
1996: Jon Witman, FB
1997: Brett Conway, K
1997: Brandon Noble, DT
1998: Aaron Collins, OLB
1998: Mike McQueary, QB
1998: Phil Ostrowski, G

Penn State Pro Players

Penn Staters in the NFL

The following were on National Football League rosters as of June 1, 1998:

Anderson, Richie; New York Jets, RB
Archie, Mike; Tennessee Oilers, RB
Brady, Kyle; New York Jets, TE
Brown, Gary; New York Giants, RB
Burger, Todd; Chicago Bears, G
Carter, Ki-Jana; Cincinnati Bengals, RB
Collins, Kerry; Carolina Panthers, QB
Conway, Brett; Green Bay Packers, PK
Drayton, Troy; Miami Dolphins, TE
Duffy, Roger; Pittsburgh Steelers, C
Engram, Bobby; Chicago Bears, WR
Forbes, Marlon; Chicago Bears, DB
Gash, Sam; Buffalo Bills, RB
Gerak, John; St. Louis Rams, G
Greeley, Bucky; Carolina Panthers, C
Hartings, Jeff; Detroit Lions, G
Herring, Kim; Baltimore Ravens, DB
Holmberg, Rob; Oakland Raiders, LB
Huntington, Greg; Jacksonville Jaguars, C
Jackson, Tyoka; Tampa Bay Buccaneers, DE
Johnson, Andre; Miami Dolphins, T

Killens, Terry; Tennessee Oilers, LB
Love, Sean; Philadelphia Eagles, G
McDuffie, O.J.; Miami Dolphins, WR
Milne, Brian; Cincinnati Bengals, FB
Noble, Brandon; San Francisco 49ers, DT
Perry, Darren; Pittsburgh Steelers, DB
Ravotti, Eric; Pittsburgh Steelers, LB
Rivera, Marco; Green Bay Packers, G
Rucci, Todd; New England Patriots, G
Scott, Freddie; Indianapolis Colts, WR
Szott, Dave; Kansas City Chiefs, G
Tate, Mark; New England Patriots, G
Timpson, Michael; Miami Dolphins, WR
Truitt, Greg; Cincinnati Bengals, KS
Wisniewski, Steve; Oakland Raiders, G
Witman, Jon; Pittsburgh Steelers, FB
Zordich, Michael; Philadelphia Eagles, DB

Note: List does not include Penn State players selected in the 1998 NFL draft or those signed as free agents. These players are listed under "Pro Football Draft, 1998."

Penn State's All-Time National Football League Roster

(Through the 1997 season)
Ahrenhold, Frank; Pittsburgh, DT, 1973-74
Alexander, Mike; Los Angeles Raiders, WR, 1988-90; Buffalo, 1991
Alexander, Rogers; N.Y. Jets, LB, 1986; New England, 1987
Allen, Doug; Buffalo, LB, 1974-75
Allerman, Kurt; St. Louis, LB, 1977-79, 83-85; Green Bay, 1980-82; Detroit, 1985
Anderson, Richie; N.Y. Jets, RB, 1993-97
Archie, Mike; Houston/Tennessee, RB, 1996-97
Ashley, Walker Lee; Minnesota, LB, 1983-88, 90; Kansas City, 1988-89

Bahr, Chris; Cincinnati, K, 1976-79; Oakland/ Los Angeles Raiders, 1980-88; San Diego, 1989
Bahr, Matt; Pittsburgh, K, 1979-80; San Francisco, 1981; Cleveland, 1981-89; N.Y. Giants, 1990-92; New England, 1993-95
Baker, Ralph; N.Y. Jets, LB, 1964-74
Bannon, Bruce; Miami, LB, 1973-74
Barber, Stew; Buffalo, T, 1961-69
Beck, Clarence; Pottsville, T, 1925
Benfatti, Lou; N.Y. Jets, DT, 1994-96
Benson, Brad; N.Y. Giants, C/G, 1978-86
Berryman, Robert; Frankford, B, 1924
Blackledge, Todd; Kansas City, QB, 1983-87; Pittsburgh, 1988-89
Bleamer, Jeff; Philadelphia, T, 1975-76; N.Y. Jets, 1977; N.Y. Giants, C, 1978
Bradley, Dave; Green Bay, G, 1969-71; St. Louis, 1972
Brady, Kyle; N.Y. Jets, TE, 1995-97
Brown, Gary; Houston, RB, 1991-95; San Diego, 1996-97
Bruno, John; Pittsburgh, P, 1987
Burger, Todd; Chicago, G, 1994-97
Buttle, Greg; N.Y. Jets, LB, 1976-84
Buzin, Rich; N.Y. Giants, T, 1968-70; Los Angeles Rams, 1971; Chicago, 1972

Campbell, Bob; Pittsburgh, RB, 1969
Cappelletti, John; Los Angeles Rams, RB, 1974-78; San Diego, 1980-83
Carter, Ki-Jana; Cincinnati, RB, 1995-97
Case, Frank; Kansas City, DE, 1981
Cefalo, Jimmy; Miami, WR, 1978-84
Cherundolo, Chuck; Cleveland, C, 1937-39; Philadelphia, 1940; Pittsburgh, 1941-42, 45-48
Clark, Bruce; New Orleans, DE, 1983-88; Kansas City, 1989
Clayton, Stan; Atlanta, T, 1988-89; New England, 1990-91
Coder, Ron; Seattle, G, 1976-77, 79; St. Louis, 1980-81
Collins, Andre; Washington, LB, 1990-94; Cincinnati, 1995-97
Collins, Kerry; Carolina, QB, 1995-97
Conlan, Shane; Buffalo, LB, 1987-92; Los Angeles Rams/St. Louis, 1993-95
Conlin, Chris; Miami, T, 1987-88; Indianapolis, 1990-91
Contz, Bill; Cleveland, T, 1983-86; New Orleans, 1986-88
Conover, Larry; Canton, C, 1921-23; Cleveland, 1925; Frankford, 1926

Conway, Brett; Green Bay, K, 1997
Cooper, William; Cleveland, QB, 1936-37; Cincinnati, 1937
Correal, Chuck; Atlanta, C, 1979-80; Cleveland, 1981
Crist, Chuck; N.Y. Giants, DHB, 1972-74; New Orleans, Saf, 1975-77; San Francisco, 1978
Crosby, Ron; Detroit, LB, 1977; New Orleans, 1978; N.Y. Jets, 1979-83
Crowder, Randy; Miami, DT, 1974-76; Tampa Bay, 1978-80
Cubbage, Ben; Massillon, G, 1919
Cunningham, Eric; N.Y. Jets, G, 1979-80; St. Louis, 1980

Daniels, David; Seattle, WR, 1991-92
Davis, Robert; Pittsburgh, E, 1946-50
DePaso, Tom; Cincinnati, LB, 1978
Devlin, Chris; Cincinnati, LB, 1975-76, 78; Chicago, 1978
Donchez, Tom; Chicago, FB, 1975
D'Onofrio, Mark; Green Bay, LB, 1992
Donovan, Tom; New Orleans, WR, 1980
Dorney, Keith; Detroit, G/T, 1979-87
Dozier, D.J.; Minnesota, RB, 1987-90; Detroit, 1991
Drayton, Troy; Los Angeles/St. Louis Rams, TE, 1993-95; Miami, 1996-97
Drazenovich, Chuck; Washington, LB, 1950-59
Duffy, Roger; N.Y. Jets, C, 1990-97
Dugan, Bill; Seattle, G, 1981-83; Minnesota, 1984
Durkota, Jeff; Los Angeles Dons, FB, 1948

Ebersole, John; N.Y. Jets, LB, 1970-77
Engram, Bobby; Chicago, WR, 1996-97
Eschbach, Herb; Providence, C, 1930-31

Farrell, Sean; Tampa Bay, G, 1982-86; New England, 1987-89; Denver, 1990-91
Filak, John; Frankford, T, 1927-29
Fitzkee, Scott; Philadelphia, WR, 1979-80; San Diego, 1981-82
Flythe, Mark; N.Y. Giants, DT, 1993
Forbes, Marlon; Chicago, DB, 1996-97
Franco, Brian; Cleveland, K, 1987
Frerotte, Mitch; Buffalo, G, 1987-92; Seattle, 1993-94
Frketich, Len; Pittsburgh, T, 1945
Fusina, Chuck; Tampa Bay, QB, 1979-82; Green Bay, 1986

Garrity, Gregg; Pittsburgh, WR, 1983; Philadelphia, 1985-89
Gash, Sam; New England, RB, 1992-97
Gerak, John; Minnesota, G, 1993-96;
St. Louis, 1997
Getty, Charlie; Kansas City, T, 1974-82; Green Bay, 1983
Giacomarro, Ralph; Atlanta, P, 1983-85
Giannetti, Frank; Indianapolis, DE, 1991
Gladys, Gene; New Orleans, LB, 1981
Goganious, Keith; Buffalo, LB, 1992-94; Jacksonville, 1995; Baltimore, 1996
Graf, Dave; Cleveland, LB, 1975-79; Washington, 1981
Graham, Don; Tampa Bay, LB, 1987; Buffalo, 1988
Greeley, Bucky; Carolina, C, 1996-97
Gremenshields, Donn; Brooklyn, T, 1932-33
Grier, Roosevelt; N.Y. Giants, DT, 1955-56, 58-62; Los Angeles Rams, 1963-66
Griffiths, Paul; Canton, G, 1921
Guman, Mike; Los Angeles Rams, RB, 1980-88
Gursky, Al; N.Y. Giants, LB, 1963

Haden, Nick; Philadelphia, G/T, 1986
Haines, Hinkey; N.Y. Giants, QB, 1925-28; Staten Island, 1929-31
Hall, Galen; Washington, QB, 1962; N.Y. Jets, 1963
Ham, Jack; Pittsburgh, LB, 1971-82
Hamilton, Harry; N.Y. Jets, Saf, 1984-87; Tampa Bay, 1988-91
Hammonds, Shelly; Minnesota, DB, 1995
Hamas, Steve; Orange, B, 1929
Harris, Franco; Pittsburgh, RB, 1972-83; Seattle, 1984
Hartenstine, Mike; Chicago, DE, 1975-86; Minnesota, 1987
Hartings, Jeff; Detroit, G, 1996-97
Hayman, Gary; Buffalo, RB, 1974-75
Heller, Ron; Tampa Bay, T, 1984-87; Philadelphia, 1988-92; Miami, 1993-95
Herring, Kim; Baltimore, DB, 1997
Higgins, Bob; Canton, E, 1920-21

Hoak, Dick; Pittsburgh, RB, 1961-70
Holmberg, Rob; Los Angeles/Oakland Raiders, LB, 1994-97
Hufnagel, John; Denver, QB, 1974-75
Hull, Tom; San Francisco, LB, 1974; Green Bay, 1975
Humphries, Leonard; Indianapolis, DB, 1994
Huntington, Greg; Washington, G, 1993; Jacksonville, 1996-97

Jacksom, Ray; Tampa Bay, Saf, 1987-88
Jackson, Kenny; Philadelphia, WR, 1984-88, 90-91; Houston, 1989
Jackson, Tyoka; Miami, DT, 1994; Tampa Bay, 1996-97
Jaffurs, John; Washington, G, 1946
Janerette, Charlie; Los Angeles Rams, G, 1960; N.Y. Giants, 1961-62; N.Y. Jets, 1963; Denver, 1964-65
Joe, Larry; Buffalo, RB, 1949
Johnson, Andre; Washington, T, 1996; Miami, 1997
Johnson, Tim; Pittsburgh, DE/DT, 1987-89; Washington, 1990-95; Cincinnati, 1996
Jonas, Don; Philadelphia, B, 1962

Kab, Vyto; Philadelphia, TE, 1982-84; N.Y. Giants, 1985; Detroit, 1987-88
Karpinski, Keith; Detroit, LB, 1989
Kerr, Jim; Washington, DHB, 1961-62
Killens, Terry; Houston/Tennessee, LB, 1996-97
Killinger, Glenn; N.Y. Giants, B, 1926
Klotz, John; N.Y. Titans, T, 1962; San Diego, 1962; N.Y. Jets, 1963; Houston, 1964
Kochman, Roger; Buffalo, HB, 1963
Koegel, Warren; Oakland, C, 1971; St. Louis, 1973; N.Y. Jets, 1974
Kubin, Larry; Washington, LB, 1982-84
Kugler, Pete; San Francisco, NT/DE, 1981-82, 1986-90
Kwalick, Ted; San Francisco, TE, 1969-74; Oakland, 1975-77

Lankford, Paul; Miami, DHB, 1982-91
LaPointe, Ron; Baltimore, TE, 1980
LaPorta, Phil; New Orleans, DT, 1974-75
Laslavic, Jim; Detroit, LB, 1973-77; San Diego, 1978-81; Green Bay, 1982
Lenkaitis, Bill; San Diego, G, 1968-70; New England, G/C, 1971-81
Lewis, Sid; N.Y. Jets, CB, 1987
Liske, Pete; N.Y. Jets, QB/DHB, 1964; Denver, 1969-70; Philadelphia, 1971-72
Love, Sean; Tampa Bay, G, 1994, 1996; Carolina, 1995
Lucas, Rich; Buffalo, QB/DHB, 1960-61
Luce, Len; Washington, B, 1961

Mahoney, Roger; Frankford, C, 1928-30; Minneapolis, 1930
Manca, Massimo; Cincinnati, K, 1987
Manoa, Tim; Cleveland, RB, 1987-90; Indianapolis, 1991
Markovich, Mark; San Diego, G, 1975; Detroit, 1976-77
Mauti, Rich; New Orleans, WR, 1977-83; Washington, 1984
McBath, Mike; Buffalo, DE, 1968-72
McCann, Ernest; Hartford, T, 1926
McCloskey, Mike; Houston, TE, 1983-85; Philadelphia, 1987
McDonald, Quintus; Indianapolis, LB, 1989-91
McDuffie, O.J.; Miami, WR, 1993-97
McKenzie, Rich; Cleveland, LB, 1995; Tampa Bay, 1996
Meade, Mike; Green Bay, RB, 1982-83; Detroit, 1984-85
Mehl, Lance; N.Y. Jets, LB, 1980-87
Michalske, Mike; N.Y. Yankees, G, 1927-28; Green Bay, 1929-35, 37
Millen, Matt; Oakland/Los Angeles Raiders, LB, 1980-88; San Francisco, 1989-90; Washington, 1991
Miller, Shorty; Massillon, QB, 1919
Mills, Tom; Green Bay, B, 1922-23
Milne, Brian; Cincinnati, FB, 1996-97
Milot, Rich; Washington, LB, 1979-87
Mitchell, Lydell; Baltimore, RB, 1972-77; San Diego, 1978-79; Los Angeles Rams, 1980
Mitinger, Bob; San Diego, LB, 1962-64, 66, 68
Moore, Booker; Buffalo, RB, 1983-85
Moore, Cliff; Cincinnati, B, 1934
Moore, Lenny; Baltimore, TB, 1956-67
Moore, Red; Pittsburgh, G, 1947-49
Morgan, Dan; N.Y. Giants, G, 1987
Mrosko, Bob; Houston, TE, 1989; N.Y. Giants, 1990; Indianapolis, 1991
Munchak, Mike; Houston, G, 1982-93

Nobile, Leo; Washington, G, 1947; Pittsburgh, 1948-49
Nolan, John; Boston Yanks, T, 1948; N.Y. Bulldogs, 1949; N.Y. Yankees, 1950

Olszewski, Al; Pittsburgh, E, 1945
O'Neal, Brian; Philadelphia, RB, 1994
O'Neil, Ed; Detroit, LB, 1974-79; Green Bay, 1980
Onkotz, Dennis; N.Y. Jets, LB, 1970
Ontko, Bob; Indianapolis, LB, 1987
Opfar, Dave; Pittsburgh, NT, 1987
Osborn, Robert; Canton, G, 1921-23; Cleveland, 1924; Pottsville, 1925-28

Palazzi, Lou; N.Y. Giants, C, 1946-47
Palm, Mike; N.Y. Giants, QB, 1925-26; Cincinnati, 1933
Panaccion, Vic; Frankford, T, 1930
Pankey, Irv; Los Angeles Rams, T, 1980-90; Indianapolis, 1991-92
Parlavecchio, Chet; Green Bay, LB, 1982; St. Louis, 1983
Parsons, Bob; Chicago, TE/P, 1972-83
Patrick, John; Pittsburgh, G, 1941, 45-46
Perry, Darren; Pittsburgh, Saf, 1992-97
Petrella, John; Pittsburgh, B, 1945
Pittman, Charlie; St. Louis, RB, 1970; Baltimore, 1971
Plum, Milt; Cleveland, QB, 1957-61; Detroit, 1962-67; Los Angeles Rams, 1968; N.Y. Giants, 1969
Powell, Andre; N.Y. Giants, LB, 1993-94
Pritchard, William; Providence, B, 1927; N.Y. Yankees, 1928

Radecic, Keith; St. Louis, C, 1987
Radecic, Scott; Kansas City, LB, 1984-86; Buffalo, 1987-89, Indianapolis, 1990-95
Rafferty, Tom; Dallas, G/C, 1976-89
Rauch, Richard; Columbus, G, 1921; Toledo, 1922; Pottsville, 1925; N.Y. Yankees, 1928; Boston Braves, 1929
Ravotti, Eric; Pittsburgh, LB, 1994-96
Redinger, Otis; Canton, B, 1925
Reid, Mike; Cincinnati, DT, 1970-74
Reihner, George; Houston, G, 1977-80, 82
Ressler, Glenn; Baltimore, G, 1965-74
Richardson, Wally; Baltimore, QB, 1997
Riggle, Bob; Atlanta, Saf, 1966-67
Rivera, Marco; Green Bay, 1996-97
Robb, Harry; Washington, QB, 1921; Canton, 1921-23, 25-26
Robinson, Dave; Green Bay, LB, 1963-72; Washington, 1973-74
Robinson, Mark; Kansas City, DHB, 1984-87; Tampa Bay, 1988-91
Roepke, John; Frankford, B, 1928
Rogel, Fran; Pittsburgh, B, 1950-57
Romano, Jim; Oakland, C, 1982-83; Houston, 1984-86
Rosdahl, Hatch; Buffalo, DF, 1964; Kansas City, 1964-65
Roundtree, Ray; Detroit, WR, 1988
Rowe, Dave; New Orleans, DT, 1967-70; New England, 1971-73; San Diego, 1974-75; Oakland, 1975-78; Baltimore, NT, 1978
Rucci, Todd; New England, T, 1993-97

Sacca, Tony; Phoenix, QB, 1992-93
Saul, Bill; Baltimore, LB, 1962-63; Pittsburgh, 1964, 66-68; New Orleans, 1969; Detroit, 1970
Schaukowitch, Carl; Denver, G, 1975
Schleicher, Maury; Chicago Cardinals, LB, 1959; L.A. Chargers, 1960; San Diego, 1961-62
Schuster, Richard; Canton, E, 1925
Scott, Freddie; Atlanta, WR, 1996-97
Scrabis, Bob; N.Y. Jets, QB, 1960-62
Sherman, Tom; New England, QB, 1968-69; Buffalo, 1969
Shuler, Mickey; N.Y. Jets, TE, 1978-89; Philadelphia, 1990-91
Sieminski, Chuck; San Francisco, DT, 1963-65; Atlanta, 1966-67; Detroit, 1968
Skorupan, John; Buffalo, LB, 1973-77; N.Y. Giants, 1978-80
Smith, Steve; Los Angeles Raiders, RB, 1987-93; Seattle, 1993-95
Smyth, Bill; Los Angeles Rams, DE/DT, 1947-50
Snell, George; Brooklyn, B, 1926; Buffalo, 1927
Stynchula, Andy; Washington, DL, 1960-63; N.Y. Giants, 1964-65; Baltimore, 1966-67; Dallas, 1968
Suhey, Matt; Chicago, RB, 1980-89

Suhey, Steve; Pittsburgh, G, 1948-49
Szott, Dave; Kansas City, G, 1990-97

Tamburo, Sam; N.Y. Bulldogs, E, 1949
Tays, Jim; Kansas City, HB, 1924; Chicago Cardinals, 1925; Dayton, 1927; Newark, 1930; Staten Island, 1930
Thomas, Blair; N.Y. Jets, RB, 1990-93; New England, 1994; Dallas, 1994; Carolina, 1995
Thomas, William; Frankford, B, 1924; Philadelphia Quakers, 1926
Thompson, Leroy; Pittsburgh, RB, 1991-93; New England, 1994; Kansas City, 1995
Timpson, Michael; New England, WR, 1989-94; Chicago, 1995-96; Philadelphia, 1997
Tobin, Elgie; Akron, E, 1919-21
Torrey, Bob; N.Y. Giants, RB, 1979; Miami, 1979; Philadelphia, 1980
Triplett, Wally; Detroit, B, 1949-50; Chicago Cardinals, 1952-53
Truitt, Greg; Cincinnati, KS, 1994-97

Ullery, William; Dayton, B, 1922

Walters, Les; Washington, E, 1958
Warner, Curt; Seattle, RB, 1983-89; Los Angeles Rams, 1990
Way, Charlie; Canton, B, 1921; Frankford, 1924
Wear, Bob; Philadelphia, C, 1942
Williams, Jon; New England, RB, 1984-85
Wisniewski, Leo; Baltimore, NT, 1983; Indianapolis, 1984-85
Wisniewski, Steve; Los Angeles/Oakland Raiders, G, 1989-97
Witman, Jon; Pittsburgh, FB, 1996-97
Wontz, Bryon; Pottsville, B, 1925-28
Wender, Gerald; Buffalo All-Americans, B, 1920

Yeboah-Kodie, Phil; Pittsburgh, LB, 1996
Yerger, Howard; Dayton, B, 1919; Louisville, 1921

Zordich, Michael; N.Y. Jets, Saf, 1987-88; Phoenix, 1989-93; Philadelphia, 1994-97

Special thanks to Michael Signora of the National Football League for his assistance in compiling this list.

Penn State Players in the Pro Draft

Round	Player	Team
1960		
1	Rich Lucas	Washington (NFL)
—	Rich Lucas	Buffalo (AFL)
3	Andy Stynchula	Washington (NFL)
—	Andy Stynchula	Los Angeles (AFL)
5	Charlie Janerette	Los Angeles (AFL)
20	Earl Kohlhass	Washington (NFL)
—	Earl Kohlhass	Oakland (AFL)
—	James Hickman	Boston (AFL)
1961		
3	Stew Barber	Dallas (NFL)
5	Stew Barber	Buffalo (AFL)
7	Dick Hoak	Pittsburgh (NFL)
7	James Kerr	Washington (NFL)
19	James Kerr	New York (AFL)
13	Don Jonas	Philadelphia (NFL)
19	Dick Wilson	Philadelphia (NFL)
1962		
2	Bill Saul	Baltimore (NFL)
9	Bill Saul	Buffalo (AFL)
3	Bob Mitinger	Washington (NFL)
5	Bob Mitinger	San Diego (AFL)
4	Roger Kochman	St. Louis (NFL)
15	Roger Kochman	Buffalo (AFL)
4	Charlie Sieminski	San Francisco (NFL)
14	Charlie Sieminski	Boston (AFL)
5	Jim Smith	Los Angeles (NFL)
16	Jim Smith	New York (AFL)
12	Al Gursky	New York (NFL)
14	Jim Schwab	Philadelphia (NFL)
1963		
1	Dave Robinson	Green Bay (NFL)
3	Dave Robinson	San Diego (AFL)
4	Hatch Rosdahl	San Francisco (NFL)
14	Hatch Rosdahl	San Diego (AFL)
6	Terry Monaghan	Los Angeles (NFL)
8	Dave Hayes	Baltimore (NFL)
11	Dave Hayes	Boston (AFL)
10	Pete Liske	Philadelphia (NFL)
15	Pete Liske	New York (AFL)
17	Dick Anderson	Cleveland (NFL)
1964		
3	Ralph Baker	Pittsburgh (NFL)
6	Ralph Baker	New York (AFL)
13	John Deibert	New York (NFL)
14	Tom Urbanik	Washington (NFL)
1965		
3	Glenn Ressler	Baltimore (NFL)
3	Glenn Ressler	Denver (AFL)
1966		
8	Don Kunit	Dallas (NFL)
8	Jack White	Baltimore (NFL)
20	Bob Riggle	Atlanta (NFL)
1967		
2	Dave Rowe	New Orleans
10	John Runnells	Boston
16	Mike Irwin	Buffalo
1968		
2	Rich Buzin	New York Giants
2	Bill Lenkaitis	San Diego
5	Mike McBath	Buffalo
1969		
1	Ted Kwalick	San Francisco
2	Dave Bradley	Green Bay
4	Bob Campbell	Pittsburgh
7	John Kulka	Miami
15	Leon Angevine	Philadelphia
1970		
1	Mike Reid	Cincinnati
3	Charlie Pittman	St. Louis
3	Dennis Onkotz	New York Jets
4	Steve Smear	Baltimore
4	John Ebersole	New York Jets
7	Don Abbey	Dallas
8	Paul Johnson	Washington
12	Jim Kates	Washington
1971		
2	Jack Ham	Pittsburgh
3	Warren Koegel	Oakland
11	Vic Surma	Miami
16	Greg Edmonds	Minnesota
1972		
1	Franco Harris	Pittsburgh
2	Lydell Mitchell	Baltimore
4	Charlie Zapiec	Dallas
5	Bob Parsons	Chicago
1973		
3	Jim Laslavic	Detroit
5	Bruce Bannon	New York Jets
6	John Skorupan	Buffalo
14	John Hufnagel	Denver
15	Carl Schaukowitch	New York Giants
1974		
1	Ed O'Neil	Detroit
1	John Cappelletti	Los Angeles Rams
2	Doug Allen	Buffalo
2	Charlie Getty	Kansas City
2	Mark Markovich	San Diego
5	Gary Hayman	Buffalo
6	Randy Crowder	Miami
9	Phil LaPorta	New Orleans

10	Chuck Herd	Cincinnati
12	Tom Hull	San Francisco

1975

2	Mike Hartenstine	Chicago
4	John Nessel	Atlanta
4	Tom Donchez	Buffalo
6	Tom Shuman	Cincinnati
7	Chris Devlin	Cincinnati
8	Jeff Bleamer	Philadelphia
9	Dan Natale	San Francisco
10	Joe Jackson	Miami
12	Greg Murphy	Pittsburgh
17	Dave Graf	Cleveland

1976

2	Chris Bahr	Cincinnati
3	Greg Buttle	New York Jets
3	Ron Coder	Seattle
4	Tom Rafferty	Dallas

1977

2	George Reihner	Houston
3	Kurt Allerman	St. Louis
5	Ron Crosby	Detroit
8	Brad Benson	New England

1978

3	Mickey Shuler	New York Jets
3	Jimmy Cefalo	Miami
5	Randy Sidler	New York Jets
6	Steve Geise	Cincinnati
9	Neil Hutton	New York Jets
10	Tom DePaso	Cincinnati
11	Ron Hostetler	Los Angeles Rams

1979

1	Keith Dorney	Detroit
4	Eric Cunningham	New York Jets
5	Scott Fitzkee	Philadelphia
5	Chuck Fusina	Tampa Bay
6	Bob Torrey	New York Giants
6	Matt Bahr	Pittsburgh
7	Rich Milot	Washington
8	Chuck Correal	Philadelphia
10	Tony Petruccio	San Diego

1980

1	Bruce Clark	Green Bay
2	Matt Millen	Oakland
2	Matt Suhey	Chicago
2	Irv Pankey	Los Angeles Rams
3	Lance Mehl	New York Jets
6	Mike Guman	Los Angeles Rams
9	Tom Donovan	Kansas City

1981

1	Booker Moore	Buffalo
3	Bill Dugan	Seattle
6	Pete Kugler	San Francisco
6	Larry Kubin	Washington
7	Brad Scovill	Seattle
8	Gene Gladys	New Orleans
11	Frank Case	Kansas City

1982

1	Mike Munchak	Houston
1	Sean Farrell	Tampa Bay
2	Leo Wisniewski	Baltimore
2	Jim Romano	Oakland
3	Paul Lankford	Miami
4	Vyto Kab	Philadelphia
5	Mike Meade	Green Bay
6	Chet Parlavecchio	Green Bay
9	Matt Bradley	Houston
10	Rich D'Amico	Oakland

1983

1	Curt Warner	Seattle
1	Todd Blackledge	Kansas City

3	Walker Lee Ashley	Minnesota
4	Mike McCloskey	Houston
5	Bill Contz	Cleveland
5	Gregg Garrity	Pittsburgh
8	Pete Speros	Seattle
10	Dave Laube	Detroit
10	Ralph Giacomarro	Atlanta

1984

1	Kenny Jackson	Philadelphia
2	Scott Radecic	Kansas City
3	Jon Williams	New England
4	Mark Robinson	Kansas City
4	Ron Heller	Tampa Bay
7	Harry Hamilton	New York Jets
8	Kevin Baugh	Houston
9	George Reynolds	Los Angeles Rams

1985

6	Stan Short	Detroit
7	Nick Haden	Los Angeles Raiders
9	Chris Sydnor	Los Angeles Raiders
11	Tony Mumford	New England

1986

4	Rogers Alexander	New York Jets
7	Bob Williams	Buffalo
9	Michael Zordich	San Diego

1987

1	Shane Conlan	Buffalo
1	D.J. Dozier	Minnesota
3	Tim Manoa	Cleveland
3	Steve Smith	Los Angeles Raiders
4	Don Graham	Tampa Bay
5	John Bruno	St. Louis
5	Chris Conlin	Miami
6	Tim Johnson	Pittsburgh
6	Bob White	San Francisco
8	Dan Morgan	Denver
9	Bob Ontko	Indianapolis
10	Sid Lewis	New York Jets
11	Brian Siverling	Detroit

1988

3	Ray Roundtree	Detroit
8	Michael Alexander	Los Angeles Raiders
10	Stan Clayton	Atlanta
11	Pete Curkendall	Buffalo

1989

2	Steve Wisniewski	Dallas
4	Michael Timpson	New England
6	Quintus McDonald	Indianapolis
6	Gary Wilkerson	Cleveland
9	Bob Mrosko	Houston
11	Keith Karpinski	Detroit

1990

1	Blair Thomas	New York Jets
2	Andre Collins	Washington
7	Dave Szott	Kansas City
8	Roger Duffy	New York Jets

1991

3	David Daniels	Seattle
6	Leroy Thompson	Pittsburgh
8	Gary Brown	Houston
10	Frank Giannetti	Indianapolis
10	Sean Love	Dallas
12	Rob Luedeke	Indianapolis

1992

2	Mark D'Onofrio	Green Bay
2	Tony Sacca	Phoenix
3	Paul Siever	Washington
3	Keith Goganious	Buffalo
8	Darren Perry	Pittsburgh
8	Sam Gash	New England
8	Andre Powell	Miami

8	Leonard Humphries	Buffalo
11	Terry Smith	Washington

1993

1	O.J. McDuffie	Miami
2	Troy Drayton	Los Angeles Rams
2	Todd Rucci	New England
3	John Gerak	Minnesota
5	Greg Huntington	Washington
6	Richie Anderson	New York Jets
6	Rich McKenzie	Cleveland
8	Reggie Givens	Dallas

1994

3	Lou Benfatti	New York Jets
5	Shelly Hammonds	Minnesota
6	Eric Ravotti	Pittsburgh
7	Rob Holmberg	Los Angeles Raiders

1995

1	Ki-Jana Carter	Cincinnati
1	Kerry Collins	Carolina
1	Kyle Brady	New York Jets
5	Phil Yeboah-Kodie	Denver
6	Brian Gelzheiser	Indianapolis

1996

1	Jeff Hartings	Detroit
1	Andre Johnson	Washington
2	Bobby Engram	Chicago
3	Terry Killens	Houston
3	Jon Witman	Pittsburgh
4	Brian Milne	Indianapolis
6	Keith Conlin	Indianapolis
6	Stephen Pitts	San Francisco
6	Marco Rivera	Green Bay
7	Mike Archie	Houston

1997

2	Kim Herring	Baltimore
3	Brett Conway	Green Bay
7	Wally Richardson	Baltimore

1998

1	Curtis Enis	Cincinnati
2	Joe Jurevicius	New York Giants
5	Phil Ostrowski	San Francisco

Free Agents:
Aaron Collins, Arizona
Mike McQueary, Oakland
Jim Nelson, San Francisco
Shino Prater, Tennessee
Chris Snyder, New York Giants

Penn State Players in the Pro Football Hall of Fame

Four former Penn State players are enshrined in the Professional Football Hall of Fame in Canton, Ohio. Franco Harris, who achieved professional fame primarily with the Pittsburgh Steelers, joined the legends of the pro game in July, 1990. Offensive lineman Mike Michalske was the first Nittany Lion to reach Canton, winning election in 1964.

Jack Ham

LINEBACKER
Inducted 1988
(Penn State 1968-70;
Pittsburgh Steelers, 1971-82)

August Michalske

GUARD
Inducted 1964
(Penn State 1923-25;
New York Yankees (AFL) 1926;
New York Yankees (NFL) 1927-28;
Green Bay Packers 1929-35, 1937)

Franco Harris

FULLBACK
Inducted 1990
(Penn State 1969-71;
Pittsburgh Steelers 1972-83;
Seattle Seahawks 1984)

Lenny Moore

RUNNING BACK
Inducted 1975
(Penn State 1953-55;
Baltimore Colts 1956-67)

Penn State players in the Super Bowl

From the Super Bowl's inception in 1967, there has been at least one Penn State alum on the roster of a participating team in the National Football League's title game for all but three contests: 1970, 1972 and 1975.

1967, Super Bowl I: Dave Robinson, Green Bay.
1968, II: Dave Robinson, Green Bay.
1969, III: Glenn Ressler, Baltimore; Ralph Baker, N.Y. Jets.
1970, IV: None
1971, V: Glenn Ressler, Baltimore.
1972, VI: None
1973, VII: Bruce Bannon (IRL), Miami.
1974., VIII: Bruce Bannon, Miami.
1975, IX: Jack Ham and Franco Harris, Pittsburgh.
1976, X: Jack Ham and Franco Harris, Pittsburgh.
1977, XI: Dave Rowe and Ted Kwalick (IRL).
1978, XII: Tom Rafferty, Dallas
1979, XIII: Tom Rafferty, Dallas; Jack Ham and Franco Harris, Pittsburgh.
1980, XIV: Matt Bahr, Jack Ham and Franco Harris, Pittsburgh.
1981, XV: Chris Bahr and Matt Millen, Oakland; Bob Torrey (IRL), Philadelphia.
1982, XVI: Pete Kugler (IRL), San Francisco.
1983, XVII: Jimmy Cefalo and Paul Lankford, Miami; Larry Kubin and Rich Milot, Washington
1984, XVIII: Chris Bahr, Matt Millen and Jim Romano (IRL), Los Angeles Raiders; Larry Kubin and Rich Milot, Washington.
1985, XIX: Jimmy Cefalo and Paul Lankford, Miami.
1986, XX: Mike Hartenstine and Matt Suhey, Chicago; Jon Williams (IRL), New England.
1987, XXI: Stan Short (IRL), Denver; Brad Benson, N.Y. Giants.
1988, XXII: Rich Milot, Washington.
1989, XXIII: Pete Kugler, San Francisco.
1990, XXIV: Pete Kugler and Matt Millen, San Francisco.
1991, XXV: Shane Conlan and Mitch Frerotte, Buffalo; Matt Bahr and Bob Mrosko, N.Y. Giants.
1992, XXVI: Shane Conlan and Mitch Frerotte, Buffalo; Andre Collins, Tim Johnson and Matt Millen, Washington.
1993, XXVII: Shane Conlan, Mitch Frerotte and Keith Goganious, Buffalo.
1994, XXVIII: Keith Goganious, Buffalo.
1995, XXIX: None
1996, XXX: Darren Perry and Eric Ravotti, Pittsburgh.
1997, XXXI: Marco Rivera, Green Bay: Sam Gash and Todd Rucci, New England.
1998, XXXII: Marco Rivera & Brett Conway (IRL), Green Bay
IRL = Injured Reserve List.

Penn State Season Finishes

(Penn State's seasonal position in the Associated Press National Polls; voting by sportswriters. Only includes the years Penn State was listed within the Top 20)

1942: 19th	1947: 4th	1948: 18th
1954: 20th	1959: 11th	1960: 16th
1961: 18th	1962: 9th	1967: 10th
1968: 2nd	1969: 2nd	1970: 18th
1971: 5th	1972: 10th	1973: 5th
1974: 7th	1975: 10th	1977: 5th

Penn State Season Finishes continued:

1978: 4th		1979: 20th		1980: 8th	
1981: 3rd		1982: 1st		1985: 3rd	
1986: 1st		1989: 15th		1990: 11th	
1991: 3rd		1993: 8th		1994: 2nd	
1995: 13th		1996: 7th		1997: 16th	

Lambert-Meadowlands Trophy

Penn State won an unprecedented 24th Lambert-Meadowlands Trophy in 1997 as Eastern collegiate football's top team.

In 1936, the Lambert brothers, Victor and Henry, of the distinguished New York City jewelry house that bears their name, established a memorial to their father, August. They instituted a trophy to be awarded to the outstanding Division I college football team in the East.

In 1957, the Lambert Cup was instituted for Division II teams and, in 1966, the Lambert Bowl was added for Division III schools.

Fourteen schools have been awarded the Lambert-Meadowlands Trophy. Army has won seven Lambert-Meadowlands trophies; Pittsburgh and Syracuse, six; Boston College and Navy, four; Dartmouth and Princeton, two; and Carnegie Tech, Cornell, Fordham, Virginia Tech and West Virginia, one each. Navy and Yale also shared the title in 1960.

1936: Pittsburgh	1966: Syracuse
1937: Pittsburgh	1967: Penn State
1938: Carnegie Tech	1968: Penn State
1939: Cornell	1969: Penn State
1940: Boston College	1970: Dartmouth
1941: Fordham	1971: Penn State
1942: Boston College	1972: Penn State
1943: Navy	1973: Penn State
1944: Army	1974: Penn State
1945: Army	1975: Penn State
1946: Army	1976: Pittsburgh
1947: Penn State	1977: Penn State
1948: Army	1978: Penn State
1949: Army	1979: Pittsburgh
1950: Princeton	1980: Pittsburgh
1951: Princeton	1981: Penn State
1952: Syracuse	1982: Penn State
1953: Army	1983: Boston College
1954: Navy	1984: Boston College
1955: Pittsburgh	1985: Penn State
1956: Syracuse	1986: Penn State
1957: Navy	1987: Syracuse
1958: Army	1988: West Virginia
1959: Syracuse	1989: Penn State
1960: Navy & Yale	1990: Penn State
1961: Penn State	1991: Penn State
1962: Penn State	1992: Syracuse
1963: Navy	1993: West Virginia
1964: Penn State	1994: Penn State
1965: Dartmouth	1996: Penn State
	1997: Penn State

Beaver Stadium Attendance & Records

Top Ten Crowds

1.	97,498	Nov. 9, 1997	Michigan 34, Penn State 8
2.	97,282	Oct. 11, 1997	Penn State 31, Ohio State 27
3.	97,115	Sept. 6, 1997	Penn State 34, Pittsburgh 17
4.	97,079	Oct. 29, 1994	Penn State 63, Ohio State 14
5.	96,953	Oct. 18, 1997	Penn State 16, Minnesota 15
6.	96,934	Nov. 22, 1997	Penn State 35, Wisconsin 10
7.	96,735	Sept. 13, 1997	Penn State 52, Temple 10
8.	96,719	Oct. 16, 1993	Michigan 21, Penn State 13

Top Ten Crowds continued:

9.	96,704	Oct. 10, 1992	Miami (Fla.) 17, Penn State 14
10.	96,672	Nov. 16, 1991	Penn State 35, Notre Dame 13

*Beaver Stadium attendance figures include the media box, visiting band, ushers and other stadium personnel.

Largest Crowd to See Penn State

1.	106,832	Oct. 15, 1994	Michigan, Michigan Stadium
2.	105,898	Nov. 16, 1996	Michigan, Michigan Stadium
3.	102,247	Jan. 2, 1995	Oregon, Rose Bowl
4.	97,498	Nov. 9, 1997	Michigan, Beaver Stadium
5.	97,282	Oct. 11, 1997	Ohio State, Beaver Stadium
6.	97,115	Sept. 6, 1997	Pittsburgh, Beaver Stadium
7.	97,079	Oct. 29, 1994	Ohio State, Beaver Stadium
8.	96,953	Oct. 18, 1997	Minnesota, Beaver Stadium
9.	96,934	Nov. 22, 1997	Wisconsin, Beaver Stadium
10.	96,735	Sept. 13, 1997	Temple, Beaver Stadium
11.	96,719	Oct. 16, 1993	Michigan, Beaver Stadium
12.	96,704	Oct. 10, 1992	Miami (Fla.), Beaver Stadium
13.	96,672	Nov. 16, 1991	Notre Dame, Beaver Stadium
14.	96,655	Oct. 7, 1995	Ohio State, Beaver Stadium
15.	96,653	Oct. 12, 1996	Purdue, Beaver Stadium

Beaver Stadium Attendance Records

(Previous Capacities)

Capacity	Record	Date	Opponent & Score
46,284	50,144	Nov.	Penn State 28, Pittsburgh 0
48,284	52,713	Oct.	Penn State 20, West Virginia 0
57,723	61,325	Sept.	Penn State 34, Stanford 14
60,203	62,554	Sept.	Penn State 31, Houston 14
76,639	78,019	Nov.	Penn State 27, Maryland 3
83,370	86,309	Oct.	Penn State 41, West Virginia 23

Top Beaver Stadium Season Records

Year	W	L	T
1978	7	0	0
1982	7	0	0
1986	7	0	0
1972	6	0	0
1973	6	0	0
1985	6	0	0
1991	6	0	0
1994	6	0	0
1962	5	0	0
1968	5	0	0
1969	5	0	0
1971	5	0	0

Total Season Attendance

Season	Games	Home	Away	Total
1968	11	234,923	234,493	469,416
1969	11	245,942	250,036	495,978
1970	10	241,055	187,738	428,793
1971	12	252,863	320,621	573,484
1972	12	320,122	314,590	634,712
1973	12	323,725	254,667	578,392
1974	12	345,140	283,316	628,456
1975	12	300,125	407,169	707,294
1976	12	367,788	224,944	592,732
1977	12	434,132	250,465	684,597
1978	12	542,444	310,207	852,651
1979	12	538,264	283,509	821,773

Total Season Attendance continued:

1980	12	498,268	355,900	854,168
1981	12	507,697	338,575	846,272
1982	12	588,290	308,183	896,473
1983	13	510,803	343,380	854,183
1984	11	511,638	327,192	838,830
1985	13	505,895	322,971	828,866
1986	12	595,613	293,896	889,509
1987	12	590,677	272,430	863,107
1988	11	504,841	313,286	818,127
1989	12	514,329	357,282	871,611
1990	12	511,223	372,274	883,497
1991	13	575,077	442,766	1,017,843
1992	12	569,195	327,969	897,164
1993	12	564,190	363,758	927,948
1994	12	577,631	418,741	996,372
1995	12	561,547	370,470	932,017
1996	13	577,001	412,769	989,770
1997	12	582,517	337,197	919,714

Bowl game attendance included in away total.

Beaver Stadium Milestone Victories

1st	Sept.17, 1960 vs. Boston University (20-0)
50th	Oct.21, 1972 vs. Syracuse (17-0)
100th	Sept.11, 1982 vs. Maryland (39-31)
150th	Nov.16, 1991 vs. Notre Dame (35-13)

Beaver Stadium Season Attendance

Season	Games	Attendance	Average
1960	4	124,013	31,003
1961	5	193,660	38,732
1962	5	211,378	42,276
1963	5	193,794	38,759
1964	5	218,401	43,680
1965	5	214,236	42,847
1966	4	148,503	37,125
1967	5	202,528	40,506
1968	5	234,923	46,985
1969	5	245,942	49,188
1970	5	241,055	48,211
1971	5	252,863	50,573
1972	6	320,122	53,354
1973	6	323,725	53,954
1974	6	345,140	57,523
1975	5	300,125	60,025
1976	6	367,788	61,298
1977	7	434,132	62,019
1978	7	542,444	77,492
1979	7	538,264	76,894
1980	6	498,268	83,045
1981	6	507,697	84,616
1982	7	588,290	84,041
1983	6	510,803	85,134
1984	6	511,638	85,273
1985	6	505,895	84,316
1986	7	595,613	85,088
1987	7	590,677	84,382
1988	6	504,841	84,140
1989	6	514,329	85,722
1990	6	511,223	85,204
1991	6	575,077	95,846
1992	6	569,195	94,866
1993	6	564,190	94,032
1994	6	577,631	96,272
1995	6	561,547	93,591

Beaver Stadium Season Attendance continued:

1996	6	577,001	96,167
1997	6	582,517	97,086
Totals	**219**	**15,499,468**	**70,774**

Team Stadium Records

FIRST DOWNS
Most First Downs: 38
vs. West Virginia, 1962.
Combined First Downs: 60
vs. Maryland, 1992.
Fewest First Downs: 3
Pittsburgh, 1970.
Fewest Combined First Downs: 18
vs. Rice, 1963; vs. Army, 1963.

RUSHING
Yardage: 484
vs. TCU, 1971; vs. Cincinnati, 1991.
Low Yardage: -32
Maryland, 1978.
Combined Yardage: 662
vs. Notre Dame, 1989.
Low Combined Yardage: 131
vs. Iowa, 1973.
Attempts: 83
vs. West Virginia, 1975.
Fewest Attempts: 11
West Virginia, 1975.
Combined Attempts: 119
vs. West Virginia, 1975.
Fewest Combined Attempts: 41
vs. Rice, 1963.

PASSING
Yardage: 478
Minnesota, 1993.
Low Yardage: 10
Ohio State, 1976.
Combined Yardage: 752
vs. Minnesota, 1993.
Low Combined Yardage: 70
vs. Boston College, 1969.
Completions: 34
Minnesota, 1993.
Fewest Completions: 1
Ohio State, 1976.
Team Stadium Records continued:

Combined Completions: 52
vs. Minnesota, 1993.
Fewest Combined Completions: 4
vs. Pittsburgh, 1970.
Interceptions Thrown: 6
Ohio U., 1970; Air Force, 1971.
Combined Interceptions: 7
vs. Ohio U., 1970.

TOTAL OFFENSE
Total Yardage: 706
vs. Cincinnati, 1991.
Low Total Yardage: 100
Pittsburgh, 1964.
Combined Total Yardage: 1,095
vs. Minnesota, 1993.
Low Combined Total Yardage: 300
vs. Pittsburgh, 1965.

Team Stadium Records continued:

Offensive Plays: 96
vs. Syracuse, 1974; vs. West Virginia, 1975.
Fewest Offensive Plays: 27
West Virginia, 1965; Pittsburgh, 1970.
Combined Total Offensive Plays: 178
vs. Minnesota, 1993.

TURNOVERS
Total Turnovers: 7,
Three times (Last: N.C State, 1982).
Combined Turnovers: 11
vs. West Virginia, 1960.

PENALTY YARDAGE
Total Yardage: 163
Rutgers, 1991.
Combined Yardage: 314
vs. Rutgers, 1991.

PUNTING
Punts: 13
West Virginia, 1973; Iowa, 1973; Army, 1979; Cincinnati, 1988.
Combined Punts: 24
vs. Cincinnati, 1988.

SCORING
Points: 81
vs. Cincinnati, 1991.
Combined Points: 90
vs. Maryland, 1971; Michigan State, 1994.
Fewest Combined Points: 10
vs. Pittsburgh, 1987; Boston College, 1989.

Individual Stadium Records

Rushing
Yardage: 239
Bob Campbell vs. Syracuse, 1968.
Attempts: 41
John Cappelletti vs. N.C. State, 1973.
Touchdowns: 5
Lydell Mitchell vs. Maryland, 1971;
Ki-Jana Carter vs. Michigan State, 1994
Longest Run: 92
Blair Thomas vs. Syracuse, 1986

Passing
Yardage: 478
Tim Schade, Minnesota, 1993
Completions: 34
Tim Schade, Minnesota, 1993.
Attempts: 66
Tim Schade, Minnesota, 1993.
Touchdowns: 4
10 times (Last: Kerry Collins vs. Rutgers, 1993)
Interceptions Thrown: 6
Steve Skiver, Ohio U., 1970.

Receiving
Yardage: 285
Thomas Lewis, Indiana, 1993
Receptions: 13
Freddie Scott, Wisconsin, 1995
Touchdowns: 4
Bobby Engram vs. Minnesota, 1993
Longest Reception: 99
Thomas Lewis from John Paci, Indiana, 1993.

Individual Stadium Records continued:

Total Offense
Total Yardage: 536
Tim Schade, Minnesota, 1993.
Offensive Plays: 74
Tim Schade, Minnesota, 1993

Punt Returns
Returns: 7
Jim Coates vs. East Carolina, 1986.
Yardage: 145
Matt Suhey vs. N.C. State, 1978.
Longest Return: 92
Mark Robinson vs. Rutgers, 1982.

Kickoff Returns
Returns: 7
Bob Elflein, Navy, 1970.
Yardage: 201
Gary Brown vs. Texas, 1990
Longest Return: 100
Derrick Mason, Michigan State, 1994.

Punting
Punts: 13
Gary Liska, Rutgers, 1982.
Punting Average (Min. 5 Punts) : **52.4**
Bob Campbell (5 punts) vs. Miami (Fla.), 1968.

Scoring
Points: 30
Lydell Mitchell vs. Maryland, 1971;
Ki-Jana Carter vs. Michigan State, 1994.
Touchdowns: 5
Lydell Mitchell vs. Maryland, 1971;
Ki-Jana Carter vs. Michigan State, 1994.
Kicking Points: 18
Massimo Manca vs. Notre Dame, 1985
Extra Points: 9
Al Vitiello vs. TCU & Maryland, 1971.
Extra Point Attempts: 9
Al Vitiello vs. TCU & Maryland, 1971.
Field Goals: 5
Massimo Manca vs. Notre Dame, 1985.
Longest Field Goal: 57
Gary Homer, Ohio U., 1973.
Longest Field Goal Attempt: 61
Chris Bahr vs. Kentucky, 1975;
Massimo Manca vs. Syracuse, 1984.

Interceptions
Interceptions: 4
Mike Smith vs. Ohio U., 1970.
Return Yardage: 100
Jeff Hite vs. Maryland, 1974; Tom Pridemore, West Virginia, 1977
Longest Return: 100
Tom Pridemore, West Virginia, 1977

Largest Campus Stadiums

	School	Stadium	Opened	Capacity
1.	Michigan	Michigan	1927	107,000
2.	Tennessee	Neyland	1921	102,854
3.	PENN STATE	Beaver	1960	93,967
4.	Ohio State	Ohio	1921	89,841
5.	Georgia	Sanford	1929	86,117

Largest Stadiums

Stadium	Location	Capacity
1.	Michigan	Ann Arbor, Mich.	107,000
2.	Neyland	Knoxville, Tenn.	102,854
3.	Rose Bowl	Pasadena, Calif.	100,089
4.	BEAVER	University Park, Pa.	93,967
5.	L.A. Memorial Coliseum	Los Angeles, Calif.	92,000
6.	Ohio	Columbus, Ohio	89,841
7.	Sanford	Athens, Ga.	86,117
8.	Stanford	Palo Alto, Calif.	85,500
9.	Jordan-Hare	Auburn, Ala.	85,214
10.	Legion Field	Birmingham, Ala.	83,091

Sources: 1997 NCAA Football Guide; 1997 NFL Record & Fact Book; and school WWW sites.

Penn State Bowl History

Penn State's Bowl Record

Won 21, Lost 11, Tied 2

1923	L	**Rose:** Jan. 1, 1923

Southern Cal 14, Penn State 3

| 1948 | T | **Cotton:** Jan. 1, 1948 |

Penn State 13, Southern Methodist U. 13

| 1959 | W | **Liberty:** Dec. 19, 1959 |

Penn State 7, Alabama 0
Leftwich Memorial Trophy: Jay Huffman

| 1960 | W | **Liberty:** Dec. 17, 1960 |

Penn State 41, Oregon 12
Leftwich Memorial Trophy: Dick Hoak

| 1961 | W | **Gator:** Dec. 30, 1961 |

Penn State 30, Georgia Tech 15
Burkhalter Award: Galen Hall

| 1962 | L | **Gator:** Dec. 29, 1962 |

Florida 17, Penn State 7
Miller Award: Dave Robinson

| 1967 | T | **Gator:** Dec. 30, 1967 |

Penn State 17, Florida State 17
Burkhalter Award: Tom Sherman

| 1969 | W | **Orange:** Jan. 1, 1969 |

Penn State 15, Kansas 14

| 1970 | W | **Orange:** Jan. 1, 1970 |

Penn State 10, Missouri 3
Most Valuable Back: Chuck Burkhart
Most Valuable Lineman: Mike Reid

| 1972 | W | **Cotton:** Jan. 1, 1972 |

Penn State 30, Texas 6
Outstanding Offensive Player: Lydell Mitchell
Outstanding Defensive Player: Bruce Bannon

| 1972 | L | **Sugar:** Dec. 31, 1972 |

Oklahoma 14, Penn State 0

| 1974 | W | **Orange:** Jan. 1, 1974 |

Penn State 16, Louisiana State U. 9
Most Valuable Back: Tom Shuman
Most Valuable Lineman: Randy Crowder

| 1975 | W | **Cotton:** Jan. 1, 1975 |

Penn State 41, Baylor 20
Outstanding Offensive Player: Tom Shuman

| 1975 | L | **Sugar:** Dec. 31, 1975 |

Alabama 13, Penn State 6

| 1976 | L | **Gator:** Dec. 27, 1976 |

Notre Dame 20, Penn State 9
Outstanding Penn State Player: Jimmy Cefalo

| 1977 | W | **Fiesta:** Dec. 25, 1977 |

Penn State 42, Arizona State 30
Outstanding Defensive Player: Matt Millen

Penn State's Bowl Record continued:

1979	L	**Sugar:** Jan. 1, 1979

Alabama 14, Penn State 7

| 1979 | W | **Liberty:** Dec. 22, 1979 |

Penn State 9, Tulane 6

| 1980 | W | **Fiesta:** Dec. 26, 1980 |

Penn State 31, Ohio State 19
Outstanding Offensive Player: Curt Warner
Outstanding Defensive Player: Frank Case
Sportsmanship Award: Frank Case

| 1982 | W | **Fiesta:** Jan. 1, 1982 |

Penn State 26, Southern Cal 10
Outstanding Offensive Player: Curt Warner
Outstanding Defensive Player: Leo Wisniewski

| 1983 | W | **Sugar:** Jan. 1, 1983 |

Penn State 27, Georgia 23
Outstanding Player: Todd Blackledge

| 1983 | W | **Aloha:** Dec. 26, 1983 |

Penn State 13, Washington 10
Outstanding Defensive Player: George Reynolds

| 1986 | L | **Orange:** Jan. 1, 1986 |

Oklahoma 25, Penn State 10

| 1987 | W | **Fiesta:** Jan. 2, 1987 |

Penn State 14, Miami (Fla.) 10
Most Valuable Offensive Player: D.J. Dozier
Most Valuable Defensive Player: Shane Conlan

| 1988 | L | **Citrus:** Jan. 1, 1988 |

Clemson 35, Penn State 10

| 1989 | W | **Holiday:** Dec. 29, 1989 |

Penn State 50, Brigham Young 39
Player-of-the-Game: Blair Thomas & Ty Detmer
(Brigham Young)

| 1990 | L | **Blockbuster:** Dec. 28, 1990 |

Florida State 24, Penn State 17

| 1992 | W | **Fiesta:** Jan. 1, 1992 |

Penn State 42, Tennessee 17
Most Valuable Offensive Player: O.J. McDuffie
Most Valuable Defensive Player: Reggie Givens

| 1993 | L | **Blockbuster:** Jan. 1, 1993 |

Stanford 24, Penn State 3

| 1994 | W | **Citrus:** Jan. 1, 1994 |

Penn State 31, Tennessee 13
Most Valuable Offensive Player: Bobby Engram
Most Valuable Defensive Player: Lee Rubin

| 1995 | W | **Rose:** Jan. 2, 1995 |

Penn State 38, Oregon 20
Co-Most Valuable Players: Ki-Jana Carter & Danny O'Neil (Oregon)

| 1996 | W | **Outback:** Jan. 1, 1996 |

Penn State 43, Auburn 14
Most Valuable Player: Bobby Engram

| 1997 | W | **Fiesta:** Jan. 1, 1997 |

Penn State 38, Texas 15
Offensive Player-of-the-Game: Curtis Enis
Defensive Player-of-the-Game: Brandon Noble

| 1998 | W | **Citrus:** Jan. 1, 1998 |

Florida 21, Penn State 6
Team Offensive MVP: Chris Eberly
Team Defensive MVP: Brandon Short

Bowl Summaries

1923 ROSE

Penn State	3	0	0	0–3
Southern Cal	0	7	7	0–14

PS-Palm, 20, field goal; USC-Campbell, 1, run (Hawkins kick); USC-Baker, 1, run (Hawkins kick).

1923 rose Continued:

Team Statistics	PS	USC
First Downs	5	13
Total Net Yards	104	293
Net Yards Rushing	98	254
Net Yards Passing	6	39
Passes (Att-Comp-Int)	11-5-3	12-6-1
Punts	12	8
Fumbles-Fumbles Lost	2-1	6-1
Penalties-Yards	2-10	3-35

Individual Statistics
Rushing
PENN STATE-Wilson 20 for 55; Palm 16 for 25; Wentz 4 for 7; Hafford 2 for 6; Flock 1 for 5.
SOUTHERN CAL-Baker 29 for 123, 1 TD; Campbell 17 for 52, 1 TD; Kincaid 6 for 43; Galloway 9 for 22; Leahy 2 for 6; Nelson 1 for 3; Wyhan 2 for 2.
Passing
PENN STATE-Wilson 2 for 2, 5 yds.; Palm 3 for 9, 1 yd., 3 Int.
SOUTHERN CAL-Galloway 1 for 3, 23 yds., 1 Int.; Baker 3 for 4, 12 yds.; Campbell 2 for 5, 4 yds.
Receiving
PENN STATE-Wilson 3 for 1; Palm 2 for 5.
SOUTHERN CAL-Campbell 2 for 8; Pythian 1 for 23; Galloway 1 for 4; Baker 1 for 3; Kincaid 1 for 1.
Attendance: 55,000

1948 COTTON

Penn State	0	7	6	0	—	13
So. Methodist	7	6	0	0	—	13

SMU-Page, 53, pass from Walker (Walker kick); PS-Cooney, 38, pass from Petchel (Czekaj kick); SMU-Walker, 2, run (Kick failed); PS-Triplett, 6, pass from Petchel (Kick failed).

Team Statistics	PS	SMU
First Downs	12	12
Total Net Yards	258	206
Net Yards Rushing	165	92
Net Yards Passing	93	114
Passes (Att-Comp-Int)	15-7-1	25-11-1
Punts-Average	4-33.4	7-33.1
Fumbles Lost	2	1
Penalties-Yards	3-15	1-5

Individual Statistics (Unofficial)
Rushing
PENN STATE-Rogel 25 for 95.
SMU-Walker 18 for 66, 1 TD; McKissick 12 for 36; Ketchel 9 for 25.
Passing
PENN STATE-Petchel 7 for 15, 1 TD.
SMU-Johnson 6 of 16; Walker 5 for 9, 1 TD.
Attendance: 43,000

1959 LIBERTY

Penn State	0	7	0	0	—	7
Alabama	0	0	0	0	—	0

PS-Kochman, 18, pass from Hall (Stellatella kick).

Team Statistics	PS	A
First Downs	18	8
Total Net Yards	319	131
Net Yards Rushing	278	104
Net Yards Passing	41	27
Passes (Att-Comp-Int)	10-2-0	8-2-0
Punts-Average	6-29.0	8-34.4
Fumbles-Fumbles Lost	4-4	7-4
Penalties-Yards	4-45	3-45

1959 Liberty continued:

Individual Statistics
Rushing
PENN STATE-Lucas 9 for 54; Botula 13 for 50; Sobczek 9 for 42; Pae 10 for 40; Hoak 7 for 30; Hall 9 for 24; Kochman 6 for 22; Kerr 5 for 16.
ALABAMA-Trammell 13 for 37; Dyess 7 for 35; Richardson 7 for 21; O'Steen 3 for 13; Skelton 3 for 1; Fuller 1 for 0; Rich 1 for (-1); Wesley 4 for (-2).
Passing
PENN STATE-Lucas 1 for 4, 23 yds.; Hall 1 for 6, 18 yds., 1 TD.
ALABAMA-Trammell 1 for 4, 20 yds.; Skelton 1 for 4, 7 yds.
Receiving
PENN STATE-Bozich 1 for 23; Kochman 1 for 18, 1 TD.
ALABAMA-Brooker 1 for 20; Ronnanet 1 for 7.
Attendance: 36,211

1960 LIBERTY

Penn State	0	21	0	20	—	41
Oregon	6	0	6	0	—	12

O-Grosz, 1, run (Kick failed); PS-Jonas, 1, run (Oppermann kick); PS-Gursky, 2, run (Oppermann kick); PS-Hoak, 6, run (Oppermann kick); O-Grayson, 10, run (Pass failed); PS-Caye, 1, run (Oppermann kick); PS-Hoak, 11, run (Kick failed); PS-Pae, 33, pass from Hoak (Jonas kick).

Team Statistics	PS	O
First Downs	25	17
Total Net Yards	420	360
Net Yards Rushing	301	187
Net Yards Passing	119	173
Passes (Att-Comp-Int)	14-8-0	16-10-2
Punts-Average	4-25	4-34
Fumbles-Fumbles Lost	2-1	4-2
Penalties-Yards	6-40	2-12

Individual Statistics
Rushing
PENN STATE-Hoak 9 for 61, 2 TD; Kerr 12 for 47; Jonas 13 for 40, 1 TD; Sobczak 8 for 36; Gursky 9 for 32, 1 TD; Hall 2 for 29; Hayes 9 for 25; Pae 5 for 12; Torris 1 for 9; Caye 3 for 6, 1 TD; Kline 1 for 2; Wayne 1 for 2.
OREGON-Grayson 10 for 93, 1 TD; Cargill 4 for 32; Josephson 3 for 32; Grosz 6 for 25, 1 TD; Snyder 5 for 7; Bruce 7 for 5; Gaecher 1 for (-7).
Passing
PENN STATE-Hall 4 for 7, 47 yds.; Hoak 3 for 5, 67 yds., 1 TD; Lang 1 for 1, 5 yds.; Jonas 0 for 1.
OREGON-Grosz 9 for 15, 178 yds., 2 Int.; Grayson 1 for 1, (-5) yds.
Receiving
PENN STATE-Oppermann 4 for 49; Pae 1 for 33, 1 TD; Robinson 1 for 18; Kerr 1 for 14; Davis 1 for 5.
OREGON-Bruce 4 for 90; Peterson 2 for 18; Grayson 1 for 43; Bauge 1 for 15; Jones 1 for 12; Grosz 1 for (-5).
Attendance: 16,624

1961 GATOR

Penn State	0	14	6	10	—	30
Georgia Tech	2	7	0	6	—	15

GT-Safety, Penn State quarterback Galen Hall intentional grounding in end zone; GT-Auer, 68, run (Lothridge kick); PS-Gursky, 13, pass from Hall (Jonas kick); PS-Kochman, 27, pass from Hall (Jonas kick); PS-Powell, 35, pass from Hall (Kick failed); GT-Auer, 14, run (Run failed); PS-Jonas, 23, field goal; PS-Torris, 1, run (Jonas kick).

Team Statistics	PS	GT
First Downs	13	19
Total Net Yards	313	412
Net Yards Rushing	138	211
Net Yards Passing	175	201
Passes (Att-Comp-Int)	22-10-0	24-12-2
Punts-Average	8-41.0	5-27.6
Fumbles-Fumbles Lost	1-1	6-3
Penalties-Yards	6-63	2-14

1961 Gator Continued:

Individual Statistics
Rushing
PENN STATE-Kochman 13 for 76; Torris 12 for 27, 1 TD; Gursky 5 for 18; Powell 3 for 17; Sabol 1 for 1; Hall 1 for (-1).
GEORGIA TECH-Auer 10 for 98, 2 TD; Williamson 11 for 44; Gann 6 for 37; McNames 8 for 22; Mendheim 4 for 8; Lothridge 4 for 1; Winingder 1 for 1; Sircy 1 for 0.
Passing
PENN STATE-Hall 12 for 22, 175 yds., 3 TD.
GEORGIA TECH-Lothridge 8 for 16, 154 yds.; Gann 4 for 8, 47 yds., 2 Int.
Receiving
PENN STATE-Robinson 4 for 40; Anderson 3 for 40; Kochman 2 for 36, 1 TD; Powell 1 for 35, 1 TD; Gursky 1 for 13, 1 TD; Schwab 1 for 11.
GEORGIA TECH-Williamson 4 for 102; Martin 3 for 36; Sexton 2 for 34; Davis 2 for 32; Auer 1 for (-3).
Attendance: 50,202

1962 GATOR

Penn State	0	7	0	0	—	7
Florida	3	7	0	7	—	17

F-Lyle, 43, field goal; F-Dupree, 7, pass from Shannon (Hall kick); PS-Liske, 1, run (Coates kick); F-Clarke, 19, pass from Shannon (Hall kick).

Team Statistics	PS	F
First Downs	8	14
Total Net Yards	147	248
Net Yards Rushing	89	162
Net Yards Passing	58	86
Passes (Att-Comp-Int)	21-5-2	13-8-1
Punts-Average	6-40.8	6-23.8
Fumbles-Fumbles Lost	4-3	4-1
Penalties-Yards	2-10	5-42

Individual Statistics
Rushing
PENN STATE-Kochman 6 for 51; Hayes 10 for 25; Gursky 5 for 10; Caum 1 for 6; Stuckrath 1 for 4; Torris 1 for 2; Hershey 1 for (-1); Powell 1 for (-1); Liske 4 for (-7), 1 TD.
FLORIDA-Dupree 25 for 66; Mack 10 for 33; Shannon 12 for 26; Libertore 4 for 20; Newcomer 3 for 13; O'Donnell 4 for 6; Stoner 2 for 5; Kelley 1 for 0; Batten 2 for (-7).
Passing
PENN STATE-Liske 5 for 18, 58 yds., 1 Int.; Coates 0 for 2; Caum 0 for 1, 1 Int.
FLORIDA-Shannon 7 for 9, 79 yds., 2 TD, 1 Int.; Batten 1 for 4, 7 yds.
Receiving
PENN STATE-Powell 4 for 40; Yost 1 for 18.
FLORIDA-Brown 3 for 25; Clarke 2 for 27, 1 TD; Newcomer 1 for 20; Dean 1 for 7; Dupree 1 for 7, 1 TD.
Attendance: 50,026

1967 GATOR

Penn State	3	14	0	0	—	17
Florida State	0	0	14	3	—	17

1967 continued:

PS-Sherman, 27, field goal; PS-Curry, 9, pass from Sherman (Sherman kick); PS-Kwalick, 12, pass from Sherman (Sherman kick); FS-Sellers, 20, pass from Hammond (Guthrie kick); FS-Hammond, 1, run (Guthrie kick); FS-Guthrie, 26, field goal.

Team Statistics	PS	FS
First Downs	12	23
Total Net Yards	244	418
Net Yards Rushing	175	55
Net Yards Passing	69	363
Passes (Att-Comp-Int)	19-6-2	55-38-4
Punts-Average	7-39.9	4-29.8
Fumbles-Fumbles Lost	3-2	1-0
Penalties-Yards	1-5	4-40

Individual Statistics
Rushing
PENN STATE-Pittman 19 for 124; Sherman 6 for 24; Lucyk 7 for 12; Grimes 3 for 8;

1967 Gator Continued:

Kwalick 1 for 7.
FLORIDA STATE-Green 12 for 27; Moreman 3 for 22; Gunter 2 for 15; Hammond 9 for (-9), 1 TD.
Passing
PENN STATE-Sherman 6 for 19, 69 yds., 2 TD, 2 Int.
FLORIDA STATE-Hammond 37 for 53, 362 yds., 1 TD, 4 Int.; Cheshire 1 for 1, 1 yd.; Moreman 0 for 1.
Receiving
PENN STATE-Kwalick 2 for 25, 1 TD; Curry 2 for 22, 1 TD; Lucyk 2 for 22.
FLORIDA STATE-Sellers 14 for 145, 1 TD; Moreman 12 for 106; Fenner 8 for 87; Green 2 for 3; Glass 1 for 11; Taylor 1 for 11.
Attendance: 68,019

1969 ORANGE

Penn State	0	7	0	8	—	15
Kansas	7	0	0	7	—	14

K-Reeves, 2, run (Bell kick); PS-Pittman, 13, run (Garthwaite kick); K-Riggins, 1, run (Bell kick); PS-Burkhart, 3, run (Campbell run).

Team Statistics	PS	K
First Downs	17	16
Total Net Yards	361	241
Net Yards Rushing	207	76
Net Yards Passing	154	165
Passes (Att-Comp-Int)	23-12-2	18-9-1
Punts-Average	9-27.0	10-38.3
Fumbles-Fumbles Lost	2-2	2-0
Penalties-Yards	1-15	2-11

Individual Statistics
Rushing
PENN STATE-Campbell 18 for 101, 1 TD; Pittman 14 for 58; Cherry 13 for 28; Abbey 4 for 15; Burkhart 5 for 5, 1 TD; Ramich 1 for 0.
KANSAS-John Riggins 18 for 47, 1 TD; Shanklin 15 for 20; Reeves 3 for 7, 1 TD; Junior Riggins 2 for 5; Jackson 1 for 5; Douglass 20 for (-8).
Passing
PENN STATE-Burkhart 12 for 23, 154 yds., 2 Int.
KANSAS-Douglas 9 for 17, 165 yds., 1 Int.; Shanklin 0 for 1.
Receiving
PENN STATE-Kwalick 6 for 74; Campbell 2 for 55; Pittman 2 for 12; Edmonds 1 for 12; Cherry 1 for 1.
KANSAS-Mosier 5 for 77; Shanklin 1 for 42; Jackson 1 for 19; McGowan 1 for 16; Junior Riggins 1 for 11.
Attendance: 77,719

1970 ORANGE

Penn State	10	0	0	0	—	10
Missouri	0	3	0	0	—	3

PS-Reitz, 29, field goal; PS-Mitchell, 28, pass from Burkhart (Reitz kick); M-H. Brown, 33, field goal.

1970 Orange continued:

Team Statistics	PS	M
First Downs	12	13
Total Net Yards	244	306
Net Yards Rushing	57	189
Net Yards Passing	187	117
Passes (Att-Comp-Int)	26-11-1	28-6-7
Punts-Average	12-42.6	6-44.7
Fumbles-Fumbles Lost	0-0	4-2
Penalties-Yards	5-40	3-25

Individual Statistics
Rushing
PENN STATE-Pittman 21 for 83; Harris 17 for 46; Abbey 1 for 3; Mitchell 5 for 1; Burkhart 10 for (-76).

1970 Orange continued:

MISSOURI-Staggers 9 for 69; Moore 19 for 62; McMillian 5 for 33; McBride 7 for 24; Harrison 2 for 16; Gray 1 for (-15).
Passing
PENN STATE-Burkhart 11 for 26, 187 yds., 1 TD, 1 Int.
MISSOURI-McMillian 4 for 17, 73 yds., 5 Int.; Roper 2 for 9, 44 yds., 2 Int.; Staggers 0 for 2.
Receiving
PENN STATE-Mitchell 5 for 81, 1 TD; Edmonds 2 for 34; Pittman 2 for 10; Paul Johnson 1 for 56; Harris 1 for 6.
MISSOURI-Shryock 3 for 33; Henley 2 for 44; Moore 1 for 40.
Attendance: 78,282

1972 COTTON

Penn State	0	3	17	10 —	30
Texas	3	3	0	0 —	6

T-Valek, 29, field goal; PS-Vitiello, 21, field goal; T-Valek, 40, field goal; PS-Mitchell, 1, run (Vitiello kick); PS-Skarzynski, 65, pass from Hufnagel (Vitiello kick); PS-Vitiello, 37, field goal; PS-Vitiello, 22, field goal; PS- Hufnagel, 4, run (Vitiello kick).

Team Statistics	PS	T
First Downs	18	15
Total Net Yards	376	242
Net Yards Rushing	239	159
Net Yards Passing	137	83
Passes (Att-Comp-Int)	13-7-1	14-5-0
Punts-Average	5-36	5-33
Fumbles-Fumbles Lost	1-0	5-3
Penalties-Yards	2-30	1-5

Individual Statistics
Rushing
PENN STATE-Mitchell 27 for 146, 1 TD; Harris 11 for 47; Donchez 8 for 29; Hufnagel 8 for 14, 1 TD; Herd 1 for 2; Stilley 1 for 1.
TEXAS-Bertelsen 14 for 58; Ladd 8 for 45; Burrisk 7 for 43; Fleming 6 for 11; Steakley 2 for 9; Lowry 1 for 4; Wigginton 2 for (-1); Phillips 12 for (-10).
Passing
PENN STATE-Hufnagel 7 for 12, 137 yds., 1 TD, 1 Int.; Joachim 0 for 1.
TEXAS-Phillips 3 for 8, 59 yds.; Wigginton 2 for 6, 24 yds.
Receiving
PENN STATE-Parsons 3 for 48; Skarzynski 2 for 81, 1 TD; Debes 1 for 7; Donchez 1 for 1.
TEXAS-Burrisk 3 for 45; Kelly 2 for 38.
Attendance: 72,000

1972 SUGAR

Penn State	0	0	0	0 —	0
Oklahoma	0	7	0	7 —	14

O-Owens, 27, pass from Robertson (Fulcher kick); O-Crosswhite, 1, run (Fulcher kick).

Team Statistics	PS	O
First Downs	11	20
Total Net Yards	196	453
Net Yards Rushing	49	278
Net Yards Passing	147	175
Passes (Att-Comp-Int)	31-12-1	12-7-0
Punts-Average	10-42.9	8-32.8
Fumbles-Fumbles Lost	6-4	8-5
Penalties-Yards	3-15	3-55

Individual Statistics
Rushing
PENN STATE-Nagle 10 for 22; Addie 7 for 18; Hayman 4 for 11; Andrews 1 for 9; Hufnagel 6 for (-11).
OKLAHOMA-Pruitt 21 for 86; Crosswhite 22 for 82, 1 TD; Wylie 10 for 58; Robertson 14 for 32; Welsh 3 for 8; Jackson 3 for 6; Washington 2 for 3; Burget 1 for 3.
Passing
PENN STATE-Hufnagel 12 for 31, 147 yds., 1 Int.

1972 Sugar continued:

OKLAHOMA-Robertson 3 for 6, 88 yds., 1 TD; Wylie 3 for 3, 67 yds.; Jackson 1 for 1, 20 yds.; Owens 0 for 1; Pruitt 0 for 1.
Receiving
PENN STATE-Scott 3 for 59; Bland 3 for 39; Andrews 2 for 25; Addie 2 for 3; Herd 1 for 11; Hayman 1 for 5.
OKLAHOMA-Owens 5 for 132, 1 TD; Pruitt 2 for 43.
Attendance: 80,123

1974 ORANGE

Penn State	3	13	0	0 —	16
LSU	7	0	2	0 —	9

LSU-Rogers, 3, run (Jackson kick); PS-Bahr, 44, field goal; PS-Herd, 72, pass from Shuman (Bahr kick); PS-Cappelletti, 1, run (Kick failed); LSU-Safety, Penn State punter falls on bad snap in end zone.

Team Statistics	PS	LSU
First Downs	9	18
Total Net Yards	185	274
Net Yards Rushing	28	205
Net Yards Passing	157	69
Passes (Att-Comp-Int)	17-6-1	20-9-1
Punts-Average	7-34.7	8-46.9
Fumbles-Fumbles Lost	1-0	3-1
Penalties-Yards	3-37	3-30

Individual Statistics
Rushing
PENN STATE-Cappelletti 26 for 50, 1 TD; Nagle 7 for 29; Donchez 4 for 7; Shuman 5 for (-32).
LSU-Davis 19 for 70; Robiskie 10 for 58; Miley 13 for 41; Broussard 4 for 16; Zeringue 4 for 11; Roger 5 for 10, 1 TD; Addy 1 for 1; Fakler 1 for (-2).
Passing
PENN STATE-Shuman 6 for 17, 157 yds., 1 TD, 1 Int.
LSU-Miley 8 for 18, 73 yds., 1 Int.; Broussard 1 for 2, (-4) yds.
Receiving
PENN STATE-Hayman 3 for 35; Herd 1 for 72, 1 TD; Cappelletti 1 for 40; Scott 1 for 10.
LSU-Davis 6 for 20; Boyd 1 for 21; Romain 1 for 15; Jones 1 for 13.
Attendance: 60,477 (74,154 sold)

1975 COTTON

Penn State	0	3	14	24 —	41
Baylor	7	0	7	6 —	20

B-Beaird, 4, run (Hicks kick); PS-Bahr, 25, field goal; PS-Donchez, 1, run (Reihner kick); B-Thompson, 35, pass from Jeffrey (Hicks kick); PS-Cefalo, 49, pass from Shuman (Reihner kick); PS-Cefalo, 3, run (Reihner kick); PS-Bahr, 33, field goal; PS-Shuman, 2, run (Reihner kick); B-Thompson, 11, pass from M. Jackson (Pass failed); PS-Jackson, 50, kickoff return (Reihner kick).

Team Statistics	PS	B
First Downs	21	16
Total Net Yards	491	313
Net Yards Rushing	265	138
Net Yards Passing	226	175
Passes (Att-Comp-Int)	20-10-0	23-10-2
Punts-Average	2-36.5	7-29.1
Fumbles-Fumbles Lost	3-2	4-0
Penalties-Yards	8-70	7-45

Individual Statistics
Rushing
PENN STATE-Donchez 25 for 116, 1 TD; Hutton 12 for 79; Cefalo 11 for 55, 1 TD; Shuman 5 for 14, 1 TD; Taylor 1 for 3; Petchel 2 for (-2).
BAYLOR-Beaird 21 for 84, 1 TD; McNeil 8 for 36; M. Jackson 3 for 18; Kent 3 for 8; Kilgore 1 for 6; Ebow 1 for 4; Franklin 1 for 2; Jeffrey 4 for (-20).
Passing
PENN STATE-Shuman 10 for 20, 226 yds., 1 TD.
BAYLOR-Jeffrey 7 for 19, 135 yds., 1 TD, 2 Int.; M. Jackson 3 for 4, 40 yds., 1 TD.

1975 Cotton continued:

Receiving
PENN STATE-Donchez 4 for 50; Cefalo 3 for 102, 1 TD; Natale 3 for 74.
BAYLOR-Thompson 3 for 62, 2 TD; Harper 3 for 45; A. Jackson 2 for 38; Kent 1 for 23; Beaird 1 for 7.
Attendance: 67,500

1975 SUGAR

Penn State	0	0	3	3	—	6
Alabama	3	0	7	3	—	13

A-Ridgeway, 25, field goal; PS-Bahr, 42, field goal; A-Stock, 14, run (Ridgeway kick); PS-Bahr, 37, field goal; A-Ridgeway, 28, field goal.

Team Statistics	PS	A
First Downs	12	14
Total Net Yards	214	316
Net Yards Rushing	157	106
Net Yards Passing	57	210
Passes (Att-Comp-Int)	8-14-1	10-12-0
Punts-Average	4-48.5	5-40.8
Fumbles-Fumbles Lost	1-0	1-0
Penalties-Yards	0-0	3-22

Individual Statistics
Rushing
PENN STATE-Geise 8 for 46; Taylor 12 for 36; Andress 5 for 22; Fitzkee 1 for 18; Petchel 5 for 13; Barvinchak 1 for 10; Cefalo 6 for 5; Suhey 1 for 4; Mauti 2 for 3.
ALABAMA-Shelby 8 for 45; Davis 12 for 32; Stock 9 for 21, 1 TD; Culliver 3 for 14; Taylor 1 for 2; Todd 16 for (-8).
Passing
PENN STATE-Andress 8 for 14, 57 yds., 1 Int.
ALABAMA-Todd 10 for 12, 210 yds.
Receiving
PENN STATE-Cefalo 2 for 18; Petchel 2 for 13; Shuler 2 for 11; Barvinchak 1 for 10; Suhey 1 for 5.
ALABAMA-Newsome 4 for 97; Harris 2 for 69; Stock 2 for 24; Brown 1 for 15; Davis 1 for 5.
Attendance: 75,212

1976 GATOR

Penn State	3	0	0	6	—	9
Notre Dame	7	13	0	0	—	20

PS-Capozzolli, 26, field goal; ND-Hunter, 1, run (Reeve kick); ND-Reeve, 23, field goal; ND-Hunter, 1, run (Reeve kick); ND-Reeve, 23, field goal; PS-Matt Suhey, 8, pass from Fusina (Run failed).

Team Statistics	PS	ND
First Downs	16	17
Total Net Yards	274	273
Net Yards Rushing	156	132
Net Yards Passing	118	141
Passes (Att-Comp-Int)	33-14-2	20-10-0
Punts-Average	5-29.2	5-33.2
Fumbles-Fumbles Lost	4-1	2-0
Penalties-Yards	6-55	5-62

Individual Statistics
Rushing
PENN STATE-Torrey 12 for 63; Matt Suhey 9 for 40; Geise 12 for 36; Cefalo 3 for 18; Fusina 2 for 1; Guman 2 for (-2).
NOTRE DAME-Hunter 26 for 102, 2 TD; Ferguson 10 for 22; Browner 3 for 10; Orsini 3 for 7; Slager 6 for (-9).
Passing
PENN STATE-Fusina 14 for 33, 118 yds., 1 TD, 2 Int.
NOTRE DAME-Slager 10 for 19, 141 yds.; Browner 0 for 1.
Receiving
PENN STATE-Cefalo 5 for 60; Torrey 3 for (-3); Matt Suhey 2 for 17, 1 TD; Mauti 1 for 21; Donovan 1 for 11; Shuler 1 for 10; Guman 1 for 2.

1976 Gator continued:

NOTRE DAME-MacAfee 5 for 78; Kelleher 3 for 46; Hunter 1 for 13; Orsini 1 for 4.
Attendance: 67,827

1977 FIESTA

Penn State	14	3	7	18	—	42
Arizona State	0	14	0	16	—	30

PS-Lally, 21, blocked punt return (Bahr kick); PS-Torrey, 3, pass from Fusina (Bahr kick); ASU-Lane, 11, pass from Sproul (Hicks kick); PS-Bahr, 23, field goal; ASU-Washington, 13, pass from Sproul (Hicks kick); PS-Geise, 18, run (Bahr kick); PS-Suhey, 3, run (Bahr kick); ASU-Washington, 30, pass from Sproul (Hicks kick); PS-Bahr, 32, field goal; ASU-Perry, 1, run (Hicks kick); PS-Suhey, 2, run (Geise run); ASU-Safety, Penn State punter Scott Fitzkee tackled in end zone.

Team Statistics	PS	AS
First Downs	18	29
Total Net Yards	351	426
Net Yards Rushing	268	90
Net Yards Passing	83	336
Passes (Att-Comp-Int)	23-9-0	47-23-2
Punts-Average	7-40	6-29
Fumbles-Fumbles Lost	1-0	1-1
Penalties-Yards	12-126	5-33

Individual Statistics
Rushing
PENN STATE-Geise 26 for 111, 1 TD; Torrey 9 for 107; Suhey 13 for 76, 2 TD; Fusina 2 for (-26).
ARIZONA STATE-Harris 20 for 56; Sproul 15 for 16; Lane 4 for 9; N. Williams 3 for 6; Perry 3 for 3, 1 TD.
Passing
PENN STATE-Fusina 9 for 23, 83 yds., 1 TD.
ARIZONA STATE-Sproul 23 for 47, 336 yds., 3 TD, 2 Int.
Receiving
PENN STATE-Cefalo 3 for 39; Geise 2 for 10; Fitzkee 1 for 24; Shuler 1 for 7; Torrey 1 for 3, 1 TD; Moore 1 for 0.
ARIZONA STATE-DeFrance 7 for 123; Jefferson 5 for 56; Washington 4 for 76, 2 TD; Edwards 4 for 60; Lane 2 for 17, 1 TD; Williams 1 for 4.
Attendance: 57,727

1979 SUGAR

Penn State	0	0	7	0	—	7
Alabama	0	7	7	0	—	14

A-Bolton, 30, pass from Rutledge (McElroy kick); PS-Fitzkee, 17, pass from Fusina (Bahr kick); A-Ogilvie, 8, run (McElroy kick).

Team Statistics	PS	A
First Downs	12	12
Total Net Yards	182	299
Net Yards Rushing	19	208
Net Yards Passing	163	91
Passes (Att-Comp-Int)	30-15-4	15-8-2
Punts-Average	10-38.7	10-38.8
Fumbles-Fumbles Lost	2-0	2-1
Penalties-Yards	8-51	11-75

Individual Statistics
Rushing
PENN STATE-Suhey 10 for 48; Guman 9 for 22; Torrey 2 for 7; Moore 9 for 6; Donovan 1 for 0; Fusina 7 for (-64).
ALABAMA-Nathan 21 for 127; Whitman 11 for 51; Ogilvie 14 for 40, 1 TD; Ikner 1 for 9; Jackson 4 for 4; Shealy 1 for (-6); Rutledge 8 for (-17).
Passing
PENN STATE-Fusina 15 for 30, 163 yds., 1 TD, 4 Int.
ALABAMA-Rutledge 8 for 15, 91 yds., 1 TD, 2 Int.
Receiving
PENN STATE-Guman 5 for 59; Fitzkee 3 for 38, 1 TD; Bassett 2 for 28; Scovill 2 for 21; Torrey 1 for 10; Pankey 1 for 5; Suhey 1 for 2.

1979 Sugar continued:

ALABAMA-Bolton 2 for 46, 1 TD; Whitman 2 for 27; Ikner 2 for 5; Neal 1 for 8; Nathan 1 for 5.
Attendance: 76,824

1979 LIBERTY

Penn State	0	6	0	3	—	9
Tulane	0	0	0	6	—	6

PS-Menhardt, 33, field goal; PS-Menhardt, 27, field goal; T-Murray, 26, field goal; T-Murray, 26, field goal; PS-Menhardt, 20, field goal.

Team Statistics	PS	T
First Downs	17	10
Total Net Yards	337	202
Net Yards Rushing	242	(-8)
Net Yards Passing	95	210
Passes (Att-Comp-Int)	11-6-2	39-21-0
Punts-Average	4-45.0	10-36.6
Fumbles-Fumbles Lost	2-2	1-0
Penalties-Yards	1-5	5-40

Individual Statistics
Rushing
PENN STATE-Suhey 19 for 112; Warner 14 for 57; Moore 13 for 49; Rocco 8 for 11; Guman 3 for 11; Coles 1 for 2.
TULANE-Christian 6 for 12; Reginelli 4 for 6; Harris 1 for 4; Jones 1 for 1; Hontas 8 for (-31).
Passing
PENN STATE-Rocco 5 for 10, 56 yds., 2 Int.; Coles 1 for 1, 39 yds.
TULANE-Hontas 21 for 39, 210 yds.
Receiving
PENN STATE- Scovill 3 for 34; Donovan 2 for 53; Guman 1 for 8.
TULANE-Alexis 7 for 77; Holman 4 for 47; Griffin 3 for 50; Anderson 2 for 29; Jones 2 for 9; Christian 2 for (-7); Reginelli 1 for 5.
Attendance: 41,036 (50,021 sold)

1980 FIESTA

Penn State	7	3	7	14	—	31
Ohio State	6	13	0	0	—	19

PS-Warner, 64, run (Menhardt kick); OS-Donley, 23, pass from Schlichter (Kick failed); OS-Williams, 33, pass from Schlichter (Run failed); OS-Donley, 19, pass from Schlichter (Atha kick); PS-Menhardt, 38, field goal; PS-Blackledge, 3, run (Menhardt kick); PS-Williams, 4, run (Menhardt kick); PS-Moore, 37, run (Menhardt kick).

Team Statistics	PS	OS
First Downs	22	23
Total Net Yards	468	412
Net Yards Rushing	351	110
Net Yards Passing	117	302
Passes (Att-Comp-Int)	22-8-0	35-20-1
Punts-Average	5-40.8	7-38.7
Fumbles-Fumbles Lost	1-1	1-0
Penalties-Yards	2-10	2-30

Individual Statistics
Rushing
PENN STATE-Warner 18 for 155, 1 TD; Moore 10 for 76, 1 TD; Coles 6 for 57; Meade 7 for 30; Blackledge 10 for 12, 1 TD; Hostetler 1 for 12; Williams 4 for 9, 1 TD.
OHIO STATE-Murray 10 for 75; Gayle 11 for 39; Spencer 4 for 29; Langley 1 for (-9); Schlichter 13 for (-24).
Passing
PENN STATE-Blackledge 8 for 22, 117 yds.
OHIO STATE-Schlichter 20 for 35, 302 yds., 3 TD, 1 Int.
Receiving
PENN STATE-Baugh 3 for 53; Scovill 3 for 42; McCloskey 1 for 22; Warner 1 for 0.
OHIO STATE-Williams 7 for 112, 1 TD; Donley 5 for 122, 2 TD; Gayle 4 for 29; Langley 2 for 32; Murray 2 for 7.
Attendance: 66,738

1982 FIESTA

Penn State	7	10	9	0	—	26
Southern Cal	7	0	3	0	—	10

PS-Warner, 17, run (Franco kick); USC-Banks, 20, interception return (Jordan kick); PS-Garrity, 52, pass from Blackledge (Franco kick); PS-Franco, 21, field goal; PS-Warner, 21, run (Franco kick); USC-Jordan, 37, field goal; PS-Safety, Paffenroth blocked punt out of end zone.

Team Statistics	PS	USC
First Downs	20	19
Total Net Yards	393	262
Net Yards Rushing	218	60
Net Yards Passing	175	202
Passes (Att-Comp-Int)	24-11-2	32-16-3
Punts-Average	4-50.8	5-40.2
Fumbles-Fumbles Lost	3-2	3-2
Penalties-Yards	7-70	7-49

Individual Statistics
Rushing
PENN STATE-Warner 26 for 145, 2 TD; Meade 9 for 60; Williams 10 for 24; Barr 2 for 7; Jackson 2 for (-6); Blackledge 2 for (-12).
SOUTHERN CAL-Allen 30 for 85; Spencer 3 for 16; MacKenzie 1 for 3; Mazur 4 for (-19); Salisbury 3 for (-25).
Passing
PENN STATE-Blackledge 11 for 24, 175 yds., 1 TD, 2 Int.
SOUTHERN CAL-Mazur 11 for 23, 123 yds., 2 Int.; Salisbury 5 for 8, 79 yds., 1 Int.; Allen 0 for 1.
Receiving
PENN STATE-Jackson 3 for 55; Warner 3 for 10; Kab 2 for 43; Garrity 1 for 52, 1 TD; Williams 1 for 8; McCloskey 1 for 7.
SOUTHERN CAL-Allen 5 for 39; Ware 4 for 75; Simmons 3 for 51; Spencer 3 for 30; Cornwell 1 for 7.
Attendance: 71,053

1983 SUGAR

Penn State	7	13	0	7	—	27
Georgia	3	7	7	6	—	23

PS-Warner, 2, run (Gancitano kick); G-Butler, 27, field goal; PS-Gancitano, 38, field goal; PS-Warner, 9, run (Gancitano kick); PS-Gancitano, 45, field goal; G-Archie, 10, pass from Lastinger (Butler kick); G-Walker, 1, run (Butler kick); PS-Garrity, 47, pass from Blackledge (Gancitano kick); G-Kay, 9, pass from Lastinger (Run failed).

Team Statistics	PS	G
First Downs	19	19
Total Net Yards	367	326
Net Yards Rushing	139	160
Net Yards Passing	228	166
Passes (Att-Comp-Int)	23-13-0	28-12-2
Punts-Average	7-42.6	8-41.8
Fumbles-Fumbles Lost	2-1	3-0
Penalties-Yards	7-42	7-39

Individual Statistics
Rushing
PENN STATE-Warner 18 for 117, 2 TD; Williams 13 for 55; Nichols 5 for 12; Coles 2 for 0; Blackledge 6 for (-45).
GEORGIA-Walker 28 for 103, 1 TD; McCarthy 9 for 36; Lastinger 9 for 21.
Passing
PENN STATE-Blackledge 13 for 23, 228 yds., 1 TD.
GEORGIA-Lastinger 12 for 27, 166 yds., 2 TD, 2 Int.; C. Jones 0 for 1.
Receiving
PENN STATE-Garrity 4 for 116, 1 TD; McCloskey 3 for 53; Jackson 2 for 35; Warner 2 for 23; Williams 2 for 1.
GEORGIA-Kay 5 for 61, 1 TD; Harris 4 for 67; Archie 2 for 23, 1 TD; Walker 1 for 15.
Attendance: 78,124

1983 ALOHA

Penn State	3	0	0	10	—	13
Washington	0	10	0	0	—	10

PS-Gancitano, 23, field goal; W-Greene, 57, punt return (Jaeger kick); W-Jaeger, 39, field goal; PS-Gancitano, 49, field goal; PS-Dozier, 2, run (Gancitano kick).

Team Statistics	PS	W
First Downs	15	18
Total Net Yards	213	279
Net Yards Rushing	95	126
Net Yards Passing	118	153
Passes (Att-Comp-Int)	34-14-1	40-19-0
Punts-Average	8-46.8	9-39.6
Fumbles-Fumbles Lost	0-0	0-0
Penalties-Yards	7-60	6-50

Individual Statistics
Rushing
PENN STATE-Williams 12 for 48; Dozier 15 for 37, 1 TD; Jackson 1 for 15; Emerson 1 for 2; Nichols 1 for 1; Strang 10 for (-8).
WASHINGTON-Jackson 7 for 34; Hinds 9 for 33; Pelluer 4 for 25; Penney 5 for 19; Robinson 6 for 9; Fuimaono 2 for 6.
Passing
PENN STATE-Strang 14 for 34, 118 yds., 1 Int.
WASHINGTON-Pelluer 19 for 40, 153 yds.
Receiving
PENN STATE-DiMidio 4 for 35; Williams 3 for 24; Dozier 3 for 22; Baugh 2 for 25; Bowman 1 for 7; Smith 1 for 5.
WASHINGTON-Pattison 6 for 55; Wroten 4 for 25; Greene 4 for 21; Hinds 2 for 18; Jackson 1 for 17; Stransky 1 for 13; Lutu 1 for 4.
Attendance: 37,212

1986 ORANGE

Penn State	7	3	0	0	—	10
Oklahoma	0	16	3	6	—	25

PS-Manoa, 1, run (Manca kick); O-Lashar, 26, field goal; O-Jackson, 71, pass from Holieway (Lashar kick); O-Lashar, 31, field goal; O-Lashar, 21, field goal; PS-Manca, 27, field goal; O-Lashar, 22, field goal; O-Carr, 61, run (Kick failed).

Team Statistics	PS	O
First Downs	14	12
Total Net Yards	267	319
Net Yards Rushing	103	228
Net Yards Passing	164	91
Passes (Att-Comp-Int)	34-18-4	6-3-0
Punts-Average	6-46.3	5-42.6
Fumbles-Fumbles Lost	2-1	5-1
Penalties-Yards	6-49	7-45

Individual Statistics
Rushing
PENN STATE-Dozier 12 for 39; Smith 9 for 23; Timpson 1 for 21; Manoa 5 for 14, 1 TD; Clark 2 for 5;
OKLAHOMA-Carr 19 for 148, 1 TD; Tillman 7 for 43; Perry 8 for 24; Collins 1 for 18; Holieway 12 for 1; Stafford 4 for (-2); Mitchell 1 for (-4).
Passing
PENN STATE-Shaffer 10 for 22, 74 yds., 3 Int.; Knizner 8 for 11, 90 yds., 1 Int.; Dozier 0 for 1.
OKLAHOMA-Holieway 3 for 6, 91 yds., 1 TD.
Receiving
PENN STATE-DiMidio 6 for 50; E. Hamilton 3 for 39; Siverling 3 for 37; Dozier 3 for 0; Smith 1 for 15; Giles 1 for 14; Manoa 1 for 9.
OKLAHOMA-Jackson 2 for 83, 1 TD; Shepard 1 for 8.
Attendance: 74,178

1987 FIESTA BOWL

Penn State	0	7	0	7	—	14
Miami (Fla.)	0	7	0	3	—	10

M-Bratton, 1, run (Cox kick); PS-Shaffer, 4, run (Manca kick); M-Seelig, 38, field goal; PS-Dozier, 6, run (Manca kick).

Team Statistics	PS	M
First Downs 8	22	
Total Net Yards	162	445
Net Yards Rushing	109	160
Net Yards Passing	53	285
Passes (Att-Comp-Int)	16-5-1	50-26-5
Punts-Average	9-43.4	4-46.0
Fumbles-Fumbles Lost	5-2	4-2
Penalties-Yards	4-39	9-62

Individual Statistics
Rushing
PENN STATE-Dozier 20 for 99, 1 TD; Manoa 8 for 36; Smith 4 for 13; Roundtree 1 for 3; Thomas 1 for (-3); Shaffer 9 for (-39), 1 TD.
MIAMI-Highsmith 18 for 119; Bratton 11 for 31, 1 TD; Williams 5 for 20; Testaverde 9 for (-10).
Passing
PENN STATE-Shaffer 5 for 16, 53 yds., 1 Int.
MIAMI-Testaverde 26 for 50, 285 yds., 5 Int.
Receiving
PENN STATE-Dozier 2 for 12; Hamilton 1 for 23; Manoa 1 for 12; Siverling 1 for 6.
MIAMI-Blades 5 for 81; Irvin 5 for 55; Perriman 4 for 37; Highsmith 3 for 33; Bratton 3 for 32; Henry 3 for 24; Williams 2 for 20; Roberts 1 for 3.
Attendance: 73,098

1988 CITRUS

Penn State	0	7	3	0	—	10
Clemson	7	7	7	14	—	35

C-Johnson, 7, run (Treadwell kick); PS-Alexander, 39, pass from Knizner (Etze kick); C-Johnson, 6, run (Treadwell kick); PS-Etze, 27, field goal; C-Johnson, 1, run (Treadwell kick); C-Allen, 25, run (Treadwell kick); C-Henderson, 4, run (Treadwell kick).

Team Statistics	PS	C
First Downs 12	25	
Total Net Yards	305	499
Net Yards Rushing	111	285
Net Yards Passing	194	214
Passes (Att-Comp-Int)	23-14-2	24-15-0
Punts-Average	5-51.0	5-39.0
Fumbles-Fumbles Lost	2-1	0-0
Penalties-Yards	4-26	8-44

Individual Statistics
Rushing
PENN STATE-Thompson 6 for 55; Brown 13 for 51; Greene 4 for 6; Alexander 1 for 3; Bill 1 for 3; Knizner 3 for (-7).
CLEMSON-Allen 11 for 105, 1 TD; Johnson 18 for 88, 3 TD; Henderson 6 for 54, 1 TD; McFadden 12 for 38; Lancaster 1 for 4; Ohan 1 for 3; Cooper 1 for (-2); Williams 4 for (-5).
Passing
PENN STATE-Knizner 13 for 22, 148 yds., 1 TD, 2 Int.; Roberts 1 for 1, 46 yds.
CLEMSON-Williams 15 for 24, 214 yds.
Receiving
PENN STATE-Timpson 4 for 81; Thompson 3 for 19; Alexander 2 for 43, 1 TD; Brown 2 for 14; Mrosko 1 for 25; Pomfret 1 for 7; Barowski 1 for 5.
CLEMSON-Jennings 7 for 110; Cooper 4 for 56; Coley 1 for 19; Hooper 1 for 17; Pearman 1 for 8; Henderson 1 for 4.
Attendance: 53,152

1989 HOLIDAY

Penn State	3	9	17	21	—	50
Brigham Young	3	10	13	13	—	39

1989 Holiday continued:

PS-Tarasi, 30, field goal; BYU-Chaffetz, 20, field goal; PS-T. Smith, 24, pass from Sacca (Kick failed); BYU-Detmer, 1, run (Chaffetz kick); PS-Tarasi, 36, field goal; BYU-Chaffetz, 22, field goal; PS-Tarasi, 51, field goal; PS-Thompson, 16, run (Tarasi kick); BYU-Detmer, 1, run (Kick failed); PS-Thompson, 14, run (Tarasi kick); BYU-Boyce, 12, pass from Detmer (Chaffetz kick); PS-Thomas, 7, run (Run failed); PS-Daniels, 52, pass from Sacca (Pass failed); BYU-Whittingham, 10, run (Chaffetz kick); BYU-Nyberg, 3, pass from Detmer (Pass failed); PS-Collins, 102, interception return of two-point conversion attempt; PS-Brown, 53, fumble return (Tarasi kick).

Team Statistics	PS	BYU
First Downs	26	35
Total Net Yards	464	651
Net Yards Rushing	249	75
Net Yards Passing	215	576
Passes (Att-Comp-Int)	21-11-1	59-42-2
Punts-Average	2-38.0	1-39.0
Fumbles-Fumbles Lost	0-0	3-1
Penalties-Yards	10-93	10-88

Individual Statistics
Rushing
PENN STATE-B. Thomas 35 for 186, 1 TD; Thompson 14 for 68, 2 TD; Sacca 3 for (-2); McDuffie 2 for (-3).
BRIGHAM YOUNG-Whittingham 9 for 39, 1 TD; Corley 6 for 18; Detmer 8 for 18.
Passing
PENN STATE-Sacca 10 for 20, 206 yds., 2 TD, 1 Int.; T. Smith 1 for 1, 9 yds.
BRIGHAM YOUNG-Detmer 42 for 59, 576 yds., 2 TD, 2 Int.
Receiving
PENN STATE-Daniels 2 for 64, 1 TD; B. Thomas 2 for 46; McDuffie 2 for 36; T. Smith 2 for 29, 1 TD; Thompson 1 for 19, Jakob 1 for 12; T. Thomas 1 for 9.
BRIGHAM YOUNG-Bellini 10 for 124; Boyce 8 for 127, 1 TD; Nyberg 8 for 117, 1 TD; Smith 6 for 74; Frandsen 5 for 85; Whittingham 4 for 39; Odle 1 for 10.
Attendance: 61,113

1990 BLOCKBUSTER

Penn State	7	0	3	7	—	17
Florida State	10	7	7	0	—	24

FS-Andrews, 41, field goal; FS-Lee, 1, run (Andrews kick); PS-Daniels, 56, pass from T. Sacca (Fayak kick); FS-Lee, 7, run (Andrews kick); PS-Fayak, 32, field goal; FS-Weldon, 5, run (Andrews kick); PS-T. Smith, 37, pass from Bill (Fayak kick).

Team Statistic	PS	FS
First Downs	17	19
Total Net Yards	400	400
Net Yards Rushing	122	152
Net Yards Passing	278	248
Passes (Att-Comp-Int)	32-15-3	36-22-2
Punts-Average	6-36.3	7-37.6
Fumbles-Fumbles Lost	2-0	0-0
Penalties-Yards	6-46	4-35

Individual Statistics
Rushing
PENN STATE-Brown 14 for 46; Thompson 8 for 33; T. Sacca 6 for 28; T. Smith 1 for 13; Bill 1 for 2; Fayak 1 for 0.
FLORIDA STATE-Lee 21 for 86, 2 TD; Bennet 9 for 30; Weldon 6 for 22, 1 TD; Moore 1 for 12; Jackson 1 for 2; Dawsey 1 for 0.
Passing
PENN STATE-T. Sacca 12 for 25, 194 yds., 1 TD, 2 Int.; Bill 3 for 7, 84 yds., 1 TD, 1 Int.
FLORIDA STATE-Weldon 22 for 36, 248 yds., 2 Int.
Receiving
PENN STATE-Daniels 7 for 154, 1 TD; T. Smith 5 for 100, 1 TD; T. Thomas 1 for 14; Thompson 2 for 10.
FLORIDA STATE-Dawsey 8 for 107; Lee 5 for 32; Bennet 4 for 49; R. Johnson 2 for 34; Baker 1 for 17; Roberts 1 for 6; Moore 1 for 3.
Attendance: 74,021

1992 FIESTA

Penn State	7	0	14	21	—	42
Tennessee	10	0	7	0	—	17

PS-Gash, 10, pass from T. Sacca (Fayak kick); T-Stewart, 1, run (Becksvoort kick); T-Becksvoort, 24, field goal; T-Fleming, 44, pass from Kelly (Becksvoort kick); PS-LaBarca, 3, pass from T. Sacca (Fayak kick); PS-Brady, 13, pass from T. Sacca (Fayak kick); PS-Anderson, 2, run (Fayak kick); PS-Givens, 23, fumble return (Fayak kick); PS-McDuffie, 37, pass from T. Sacca (Fayak kick).

Team Statistics	PS	T
First Downs	12	25
Total Net Yards	226	441
Net Yards Rushing	76	171
Net Yards Passing	150	270
Passes (Att-Comp-Int)	28-11-0	43-21-1
Punts-Average	9-47.9	6-36.3
Fumbles-Fumbles Lost	0-0	5-3
Penalties-Yards	3-36	3-34

Individual Statistics
Rushing
PENN STATE-Anderson 17 for 57, 1 TD; Gash 7 for 15; Morris 3 for 15; Hammonds 1 for 10; G. Collins 4 for 7; T. Sacca 5 for (-28).
TENNESSEE-Stewart 15 for 84, 1 TD; Hayden 13 for 56; Campbell 3 for 23; Faulkner 2 for 21; Phillips 3 for 6; Brunson 2 for 5; Shuler 1 for (-1); Hutton 1 for (-5); Kelly 5 for (-18).
Passing
PENN STATE-T. Sacca 11 for 28, 150 yds., 4 TD.
TENNESSEE-Kelly 20 for 40, 273 yds., 1 TD, 1 Int.; Shuler 1 for 3, (-3) yds.
Receiving
PENN STATE-McDuffie 4 for 78, 1 TD; Drayton 3 for 35; Brady 1 for 13, 1 TD; Anderson 1 for 11; Gash 1 for 10, 1 TD; LaBarca 1 for 3, 1 TD.
TENNESSEE-Pickens 8 for 100; McCleskey 4 for 36; Fleming 2 for 68, 1 TD; Faulkner 2 for 17; Phillips 2 for 8; Kerr 1 for 27; Stewart 1 for 10; Adams 1 for 4.
Attendance: 71,133

1993 BLOCKBUSTER

Stanford	7	7	10	0	—	24
Penn State	3	0	0	0	—	3

S-Wetnight, 3, pass from Senstrom (Abrams kick); PS-Muscillo, 33, field goal; S-Lasley, 5, run (Abrams kick); S-Abrams, 28, field goal; S-Milburn, 40, pass from Stenstrom (Abrams kick).

Team Statistics	PS	S
First Downs	12	16
Total Net Yards	263	365
Net Yards Rushing	107	155
Net Yards Passing	156	210
Passes (Att-Comp-Int)	40-13-2	29-17-2
Punts-Average	11-38.4	7-42.4
Fumbles-Fumbles Lost	0-0	2-1
Penalties-Yards	3-25	5-41

Individual Statistics
Rushing
PENN STATE-R. Anderson 13 for 40; O'Neal 11 for 38; Archie 2 for 10; Carter 3 for 7; McDuffie 4 for 5; Moser 1 for 4; K. Collins 1 for 3.
STANFORD-Roberts 17 for 98; Lasley 4 for 19; Milburn 9 for 19; Buckley 3 for 16; Butterfield 1 for 10; Brockberg 2 for 6; Allen 1 for 1; Stenstrom 5 for (-14).
Passing
PENN STATE-K. Collins 12 for 30, 145 yds., 1 Int.; Richardson 1 for 8, 11 yds., 1 Int.; Sacca 0 for 2.
STANFORD-Stenstrom 17 for 29, 210 yds., 2 TD, 1 Int.; Armour 0 for 1, 1 Int.
Receiving
PENN STATE-McDuffie 6 for 111; Drayton 3 for 21; Moser 1 for 11; R. Anderson 1 for 6; Grube 1 for 6; T. Thomas 1 for 1.
STANFORD-Wetnight 5 for 71, 1 TD; Cook 4 for 55; Milburn 4 for 54, 1 TD; Armour 2 for 9; Cline 1 for 11; Calomese 1 for 10.
Attendance: 45,554

1994 CITRUS

Penn State	7	10	7	7	—	31
Tennessee	10	3	0	0	—	13

T-Becksvoort, 46, field goal; T-Fleming, 19, pass from Shuler (Becksvoort kick); PS-Carter, 3, rush (Fayak kick); PS-Fayak, 19, field goal; T-Becksvoort, 50, field goal; PS-Carter, 14, rush (Fayak kick); PS-Brady, 7, pass from K. Collins (Fayak kick); PS-Engram, 15, pass from K. Collins (Fayak kick).

Team Statistics	PS	T
First Downs 20	16	
Total Net Yards	371	348
Net Yards Rushing	209	135
Net Yards Passing	162	213
Passes (Att-Comp-Int)	24-15-1	44-23-1
Punts-Average	6-32.0	6-44.2
Fumbles-Fumbles Lost	0-0	0-0
Penalties-Yards	4-30	10-79

Individual Statistics
Rushing
PENN STATE-Carter 19 for 93, 2 TD; Archie 13 for 69; Engram 1 for 35; Milne 3 for 13; O'Neal 5 for 6; K. Collins 1 for (-7).
TENNESSEE-Garner 16 for 89; B. Williams 1 for 38; Stewart 4 for 11; Silvan 1 for 9; Hayden 1 for (-3); H. Shuler 5 for (-4); Colquitt 1 for (-5).
Passing
PENN STATE-K. Collins 15 for 24, 162 yds., 2 TD, 1 Int.
TENNESSEE-H. Shuler 22 for 42, 205 yds., 1 TD, 1 Int; Colquitt 1 for 2, 8 yds.
Receiving
PENN STATE-Engram 7 for 107, 1 TD; O'Neal 2 for 19; Scott 2 for 19; Archie 2 for 5; Brady 1 for 7, 1 TD; LaBarca 1 for 5.
TENNESSEE-Fleming 7 for 101, 1 TD; Phillips 3 for 23; Kent 3 for 19; Faulkner 3 for 18; Silvan 2 for 15; B. Williams 2 for 13; B. Shuler 1 for 13; Stewart 1 for 8; Garner 1 for 3.
Attendance: 72,456

1995 ROSE

Oregon	7	0	7	6	—	20
Penn State	7	7	14	10	—	38

PS-Carter, 83, run (Conway kick); O-Wilcox, 1, pass from O'Neil (Belden kick); PS-Milne, 1, run (Conway kick); O-McLemore, 17, pass from O'Neil (Belden kick); PS-Carter, 17, run (Conway kick); PS-Carter, 3, run (Conway kick); PS-Conway, 43, FG; PS-Witman, 9, run (Barn-inger kick); O-Whittle, 3, run (pass failed).

Team Statistics	PS	O
First Downs 22	27	
Total Net Yards	430	501
Net Yards Rushing	228	45
Net Yards Passing	202	456
Passes (Att-Comp-Int)	31-20-1	61-41-2
Punts-Average	6-41.7	6-42.8
Fumbles-Fumbles Lost	1-1	1-0
Penalties-Yards	5-37	6-52

Individual Statistics
Rushing
PENN STATE-Carter 21 for 156, 3 TD; Milne 9 for 36, 1 TD; Archie 3 for 16; Witman 4 for 11, 1 TD; Engram 1 for 5; Pitts 1 for 4.
OREGON-Whittle 12 for 45, 1 TD; Philyaw 4 for 14; Jones 2 for 6; O'Neil 13 for (-20).
Passing
PENN STATE-K. Collins 19 for 30, 200 yds., 1 Int.; Archie 1 for 1, 2 yds.
OREGON-O'Neil 41 for 61, 456 yds., 2 TD, 2 Int.
Receiving
PENN STATE-Engram 5 for 52; Scott 4 for 41; Archie 3 for 29; Jurevicius 2 for 53; Brady 2 for 15; Milne 2 for 8; Carter 1 for 2; K. Collins 1 for 2.
OREGON-Wilcox 11 for 135, 1 TD; McLemore 10 for 90, 1 TD; Philyaw 6 for 80; Ricketts 6 for 70; Whittle 5 for 46; P. Johnson 2 for 28; Jones 1 for 7.
Attendance: 102,247

1996 OUTBACK

Auburn	0	7	0	7	—	14
Penn State	3	13	27	0	—	43

PS-Conway, 19, FG; A-Baker, 25, pass from Nix (Hawkins kick); PS-Conway, 22, FG; PS-Conway, 38, FG; PS-Archie, 8, pass from Richardson (Conway kick); PS-Engram, 9, pass from Richardson (Conway kick); PS-Pitts, 4, pass from Richardson (pass failed); PS-Enis, 1, run (Conway kick); PS-Engram, 20, pass from Richardson (Conway kick); A-McLeod, 12, run (Hawkins kick).

Team Statistics	PS	A
First Downs 22	19	
Total Net Yards	487	314
Net Yards Rushing	266	220
Net Yards Passing	221	94
Passes (Att-Comp-Int)	29-14-2	33-8-2
Punts-Average	4-35.7	8-39.1
Fumbles-Fumbles Lost	2-1	5-2
Penalties-Yards	6-35	5-59

Individual Statistics
Rushing
PENN STATE-Pitts 15 for 118; Milne 12 for 82; Archie 5 for 41; Enis 12 for 24, 1 TD; Sload 2 for 4; Eberly 1 for (-1); McQueary 1 for (-1); Ostrosky 1 for (-1).
AUBURN-Davis 12 for 119; Morrow 10 for 39; Craig 11 for 34; McLeod 2 for 20, 1 TD; Beasley 2 for 9; Goodson 0 for 4; Nix 3 for (-5).
Passing
PENN STATE-Richardson 13 for 24, 217 yds., 4 TD, 1 Int.; McQueary 1 for 4, 4 yds., 1 Int.; Archie 0 for 1.
AUBURN-Nix 5 for 25, 48 yds., 1 TD, 2 Int.; Craig 3 for 8, 46 yds.
Receiving
PENN STATE-Engram 4 for 113, 2 TD; Olsommer 2 for 21; Scott 2 for 17; Archie 2 for 14, 1 TD; Jurevicius 1 for 43; Milne 1 for 5; Pitts 1 for 4, 1 TD; Stephenson 1 for 4.
AUBURN-Bailey 1 for 32; Baker 1 for 25, 1 TD; Dillard 1 for 12; Hand 1 for 8; Goodson 1 for 6; Gosha 1 for 5; Fuller 1 for 4; McLeod 1 for 2.
Attendance: 65,313

1997 Fiesta

Texas	3	9	3	0	—	15
Penn State	7	0	21	10	—	38

PS-Enis, 4, pass from Richardson (Conway kick); T-Dawson, 28, FG; T-Dawson, 28, FG; T-R. Williams, 7, run (pass failed); PS-Harris, 5, run (Enis pass from Richardson); T-Dawson, 48, FG; PS-Enis, 2, run (Conway kick); PS-Cleary, 1, run (kick failed); PS-Conway, 23, FG; PS-Enis, 12, run (Conway kick).

Team Statistics	T	PS
First Downs 19	19	
Total Net Yards	360	425
Net Yards Rushing	73	330
Net Yards Passing	287	95
Passes (Att-Comp-Int)	43-27-1	20-12-0
Punts-Average	6-37.7	5-35.6
Fumbles-Lost	2-1	0-0
Penalties-Yards	8-57	4-49

Individual Statistics
Rushing
PENN STATE-Enis 16 for 95, 2 TD; Fields 1 for 84; Eberly 7 for 54; Mitchell 6 for 45; Cleary 5 for 31, 1 TD; Harris 4 for 13, 1 TD; Sload 2 for 7; Nixon 1 for 3; Richardson 2 for (-2).
TEXAS-Williams 11 for 48, 1 TD; Mitchell 7 for 24; Holmes 6 for 11; Brown 6 for (-10).
Passing
PENN STATE-Richardson 12 for 20, 95 yds., 1 TD.
TEXAS-Brown 26 for 42, 254 yds., 1 Int.; Danaher 1 for 1, 33 yds.
Receiving
PENN STATE-Cuncho Brown 3 for 32; Jurevicius 2 for 22; Eberly 2 for 19; Enis 2 for 15, 1 TD; Harris 2 for 5; Campbell 1 for 2.
TEXAS-Williams 9 for 24; Davis 5 for 72; Adams 4 for 73; McGarity 3 for 27; Fitzgerald 2 for 31; Holmes 2 for 15; Westbrook 1 for 33; White 1 for 12.
Attendance: 65,106

1998 Citrus Bowl

Florida	14	0	0	7	— 21
Penn State	0	3	3	0	— 6

F-Brindise, 1, run (Cooper kick)
F-Green, 35, pass from Johnson (Cooper kick)
PS-Forney, 42, FG
PS-Forney, 30, FG
F-Green, 37, pass from Palmer (Cooper kick)

Team Statistics	F	PS
First Downs 23	9	
Total Net Yards	397	139
Net Yards Rushing	254	47
Net Yards Passing	143	92
Passes (Att-Comp-Int)	32-10-3	19-9-2
Punts-Average	5-36.4	7 42.1
Fumbles-Lost	2-1	0-0
Penalties-Yards	5-46	1-5

Individual Records
Rushing
PENN STATE-Eberly 14 for 53; Watson 4 for 5; Mitchell 5 for 2; McQueary 6 for (-13).
FLORIDA-Taylor 43 for 234; Carroll 9 for 28; Ross 1 for 9; Brindise 3 for (-1), 1 TD;
Johnson 3 for (-16).

Passing
PENN STATE-McQueary 10 for 32, 92 yds., 3 Int.
FLORIDA-Johnson 5 for 12, 77 yds., 1 TD, 1 Int.; Brindise 3 for 6, 29 yds., 1 Int.; Palmer
1 for 1; 37 yds., 1 TD.

Receiving
PENN STATE-Cuncho Brown 3 for 25; Nastasi 2 for 26; Watson 2 for 15; Mitchell 1 for 9;
Pettigrew 1 for 9; Eberly 1 for 8.
FLORIDA-Green 2 for 72, 2 TD; T. Taylor 1 for 19; McGriff 1 for 19; Kinney 1 for 13;
Richardson 1 for 9; McCaslin 1 for 7; Taylor 1 for 3; Carroll 1 for 1.
Attendance: 72,940 (Florida Citrus Bowl record)

Bowl Appearances

School	Bowls
Alabama	48
Southern California	38
Tennessee	38
Texas	37
Nebraska	36
PENN STATE	34
Georgia	33
Oklahoma	32
Louisiana State	31
Ohio State	30
Michigan	29
Arkansas	28
Auburn	26
Florida State	26
Georgia Tech	26
Mississippi	26

Bowl Victories

Alabama	28
Southern California	25
PENN STATE	21
Tennessee	21
Oklahoma	20
Oklahoma State	20
Georgia Tech	18
Nebraska	18
Texas	17
Florida State	16
Georgia	16

Team Bowl Records

First Downs: 26 1989 Holiday.	**Rushing yardage:** 1980 Fiesta.
Rushing Attempts: 73 1960 Liberty.	**Rushing average per play: 7.5** 1996 Fiesta.
Passing Yardage: 278 1990 Blockbuster.	**Pass Completions: 20** 1995 Rose.
Pass Attempts: 40 1993 Blockbuster.	**Pass completion percentage: 64.5** 1995 Rose.
Touchdown Passes: 4 1992 Fiesta; 1996 Outback.	**interceptions thrown: 4** 1979 Sugar; 1986 Orange.
Total Offense: 491 1975 Cotton.	**total plays: 87** 1960 Liberty.
Fumbles Lost: 4 1959 Liberty; 1972 Sugar.	**turnovers: 5** 1962 Gator, 1972 Sugar, 1986 Orange.
Touchdowns: 3 Ki-Jana Carter, 1995 Rose.	**longest run: 84** Chafie Fields, 1997 Fiesta.

Individual Bowl Records

Rushing
Yardage: 186
Blair Thomas, 1989 Holiday.
Attempts: 35
Blair Thomas, 1989 Holiday.
Average: 8.6
(Min. 10 Attempts)
Curt Warner, 1980 Fiesta.
Touchdowns: 3
Ki-Jana Carter, 1995 Rose.
Longest Run: 84
Chafie Fields, 1997 Fiesta.

PASSING
Yardage: 228
Todd Blackledge, 1983 Sugar.
Completions: 19
Kerry Collins, 1995 Rose.
Attempts: 34
Doug Strang, 1983 Aloha.
Completion Percentage (Min. 10 Attempts): 63.3
Kerry Collins, 1995 Rose.
Touchdown Passes: 4
Tony Sacca, 1992 Fiesta;
Wally Richardson, 1996 Outback.
Interceptions Thrown: 4
Chuck Fusina, 1979 Sugar.

RECEIVING
Yardage: 154
David Daniels, 1990 Blockbuster.
Receptions: 7
David Daniels, 1990 Blockbuster;
Bobby Engram, 1994 Citrus.
Average Reception Yardage (Min. 3 Receptions): 34
Jimmy Cefalo, 1975 Cotton.
Touchdowns: 2
Bobby Engram, 1996 Outback.
Longest Reception: 72
Chuck Herd from Tom Shuman, 1974 Orange.

Individual Bowl Records continued:

TOTAL OFFENSE
Total Yardage: 240
Tom Shuman, 1975 Cotton.
Touchdowns Responsible: 4
Tony Sacca, 1992 Fiesta;
Wally Richardson, 1996 Outback.
Offensive Plays: 37
John Hufnagel, 1972 Sugar;
Chuck Fusina, 1979 Sugar.

PUNT RETURNS
Returns: 5
Kevin Baugh, 1983 Sugar.
Yardage: 106
Kevin Baugh, 1983 Sugar.
Longest Return: 67
Jimmy Cefalo, 1977 Fiesta.

Kickoff Returns
Returns: 6
Leroy Thompson, 1988 Citrus.
Yardage: 128
O.J. McDuffie, 1989 Holiday.
Longest Return: 81
Kenny Watson, 1997 Fiesta.

PUNTING
Punts: 12
Mike Palm, 1923 Rose; Bob Parsons, 1970 Orange.
Punting Average (Min. 3 Punts): 51.0
Chris Clauss, 1988 Citrus (5 punts).
Longest Punt: 68
Bob Campbell, 1967 Gator.

SCORING
Points: 20
Curtis Enis, 1997 Fiesta.
Touchdowns: 3
Ki-Jana Carter, 1995 Rose, Curtis Enis, 1997 Fiesta.
Kicking Points: 12
Al Vitiello, 1972 Cotton; Ray Tarasi, 1989 Holiday.
Extra Points: 6
Craig Fayak, 1992 Fiesta.
Defensive Score: 100 Yards
Andre Collins, 1989 Holiday.
Field Goals: 3
Al Vitiello, 1972 Cotton; Herb Menhardt, 1979 Liberty; Ray Tarasi, 1989 Holiday; Brett Conway, 1996 Outback.

INTERCEPTIONS
Interceptions: 2
Shane Conlan, 1987 Fiesta; Pete Giftopoulos, 1987 Fiesta, Chuck Penzenik, 1995 Rose; Kim Herring, 1996 Outback.

Career Bowl Leaders

RUSHING YARDAGE	Bowls	Att.	Yards	Avg.	TD
Curt Warner	4	76	474	6.2	5
Matt Suhey	4	51	276	5.4	2
Charlie Pittman	3	54	250	4.6	1
Ki-Jana Carter	2	40	249	6.2	5
Steve Geise	3	46	193	4.2	1
Blair Thomas	2	36	183	5.1	1
D.J. Dozier	3	47	178	3.7	2
Bob Torrey	3	23	177	7.7	0
Leroy Thompson	3	34	169	5.0	2
Tom Donchez	3	37	152	4.1	1

Career Bowl Leaders continued:

PASSING YARDAGE	Bowls	Att.	Cmp.	Yards	TD
Tony Sacca	3	73	33	550	7
Todd Blackledge	3	69	32	520	2
Kerry Collins	3	84	46	507	2
Tom Shuman	2	37	16	383	2
Chuck Fusina	3	86	38	363	3
Chuck Burkhart	2	49	23	341	1
Wally Richardson	3	44	25	312	5
John Hufnagel	2	43	19	284	1
Galen Hall	3	35	17	240	4

RECEPTIONS	Bowls	No.	Yards	Avg.	TD
Bobby Engram	4	16	272	17.0	3
Jimmy Cefalo	4	13	219	16.8	1
O.J. McDuffie	3	12	225	18.8	1
Dean DiMidio	3	10	85	8.5	0
David Daniels	2	9	218	24.2	2
Kevin Baugh	4	8	124	15.5	0
Ted Kwalick	2	8	99	12.4	1
Brad Scovill	3	8	97	12.1	0
Freddie Scott	3	8	77	9.6	1
Terry Smith	2	7	129	18.4	2
Troy Drayton	2	6	56	9.3	0
Mike Guman	4	6	61	10.2	0
Leroy Thompson	3	6	49	8.2	0
Jon Williams	4	6	33	5.5	0

TOUCHDOWN RECEPTIONS
3	Bobby Engram; 1994 Citrus (1), 1996 Outback (2)
2	Roger Kochman; 1959 Liberty, 1961 Gator
	Gregg Garrity; 1982 Fiesta, 1983 Sugar
	David Daniels; 1989 Holiday, 1990 Blockbuster
	Terry Smith; 1989 Holiday, 1990 Blockbuster

Top Bowl Performances

RUSHING YARDAGE
186	Blair Thomas, 1989 Holiday
156	Ki-Jana Carter, 1995 Rose
155	Curt Warner, 1980 Fiesta
146	Lydell Mitchell, 1972 Cotton
145	Curt Warner, 1982 Fiesta
124	Charlie Pittman, 1967 Gator
118	Stephen Pitts, 1996 Outback
117	Curt Warner, 1983 Sugar
116	Tom Donchez, 1975 Cotton
112	Matt Suhey, 1979 Liberty
111	Steve Geise, 1977 Fiesta
107	Bob Torrey, 1977 Fiesta
102	D.J. Dozier, 1987 Fiesta
101	Bob Campbell, 1969 Orange

PASSING YARDAGE
228	Todd Blackledge, 1983 Sugar
226	Tom Shuman, 1975 Cotton
217	Wally Richardson, 1996 Outback
206	Tony Sacca, 1989 Holiday
200	Kerry Collins, 1995 Rose
194	Tony Sacca, 1990 Blockbuster
187	Chuck Burkhart, 1970 Orange
175	Galen Hall, 1961 Gator
175	Todd Blackledge, 1982 Fiesta
163	Chuck Fusina, 1979 Sugar
162	Kerry Collins, 1994 Citrus
157	Tom Shuman, 1974 Orange
154	Chuck Burkhart, 1969 Orange

Top Bowl Performances continued:

RECEIVING YARDAGE

154	David Daniels, 1990 Blockbuster	
116	Gregg Garrity, 1983 Sugar	
113	Bobby Engram, 1996 Outback	
111	O.J. McDuffie, 1993 Blockbuster	
107	Bobby Engram, 1994 Citrus	
102	Jimmy Cefalo, 1975 Cotton	
100	Terry Smith, 1990 Blockbuster	
81	Lydell Mitchell, 1970 Orange	
81	Scott Skarzynski, 1972 Cotton	
78	O.J. McDuffie, 1992 Fiesta	
74	Ted Kwalick, 1969 Orange	
74	Bob Nagle, 1975 Cotton	

Team Highs and Lows

RUSHING YARDAGE
High	Low
351, 1980 Fiesta	19, 1979 Sugar

PASSING YARDAGE
High	Low
278, 1990 Blockbuster	6, 1923 Rose

TOTAL OFFENSE
High	Low
491, 1975 Cotton	104, 1923 Rose

FIRST DOWNS
High	Low
26, 1989 Holiday	5, 1923 Rose

RUSHING YARDAGE DEFENSE
Best	Worst
-8, 1979 Liberty	285, 1988 Citrus

PASSING YARDAGE DEFENSE
Best	Worst
27, 1959 Liberty	576, 1989 Holiday

TOTAL OFFENSE DEFENSE
Best	Worst
141, 1959 Liberty	651, 1989 Holiday

Team Highs and Lows continued:

FIRST DOWN DEFENSE
Best	Worst
7, 1959 Liberty	35, 1989 Holiday

Top Bowl Winnng Percentages (min. 10 wins)

School	Record	Pct.
Georgia Tech	18-8-0	69.2
Southern California	25-13-0	65.8
Florida State	16-8-2	65.4
PENN STATE	21-11-2	64.7
Oklahoma	20-11-1	64.1
Alabama	28-17-3	61.4
Notre Dame	13-9-0	59.1
Mississippi	15-11-0	57.7
Auburn	14-10-2	57.7
Washington	13-10-1	56.2

Opponent Individual Bowl Records

RUSHING
Yardage: 234
Fred Taylor, Florida, 1998 Citrus.
Attempts: 43
Fred Taylor, Florida, 1998 Citrus.
Average: 9.9 (Min. 10 Attempts)
Stephen Davis, Auburn, 1996 Outback.

Opponent Individual Bowl Records continued:

Touchdowns: 3
Tracy Johnson, Clemson, 1988 Citrus.
Longest Run: 68
Joe Auer, Georgia Tech, 1961 Gator.

PASSING
Yardage: 576
Ty Detmer, Brigham Young, 1989 Holiday.
Completions: 42
Ty Detmer, Brigham Young, 1989 Holiday.
Attempts: 61
Danny O'Neil, Oregon, 1995 Rose.
Completion Percentage: 83.3 (Min. 10 Attempts)
Richard Todd, Alabama, 1975 Sugar.
Touchdown Passes: 3
Dennis Sproul, Arizona State, 1977 Fiesta; Art Schlichter, Ohio
State, 1980 Fiesta.
Interceptions Thrown: 5
Terry McMillan, Missouri, 1970 Orange; Vinny Testaverde, Miami (Fla.), 1987 Fiesta.

RECEIVING
Yardage: 145
Ron Sellers, Florida State, 1967 Gator.
Receptions: 14
Ron Sellers, Florida State, 1967 Gator.
Average Reception Yardage (Min. 5 Receptions): 26.4
Tinker Owens, Oklahoma, 1972 Sugar.
Touchdowns: 2
Ricky Thompson, Baylor, 1975 Cotton; Ron Washington, Arizona State, 1977 Fiesta Bowl;
Doug Donley, Ohio State, 1980 Fiesta.
Longest Reception: 71
Keith Jackson, Oklahoma, 1986 Orange.

TOTAL OFFENSE
Total Yardage: 594
Ty Detmer, Brigham Young, 1989 Holiday.
Touchdowns Responsible: 4
Ty Detmer, Brigham Young, 1989 Holiday.
Offensive Plays: 74
Danny O'Neil, Oregon, 1995 Rose.

PUNT RETURNS
Returns: 6
David Kintigh, Miami (Fla.), 1987 Fiesta; Dale Carter, Tennessee, 1992 Fiesta.
Yardage: 103
Jon Staggers, Missouri, 1970 Orange.
Longest Return: 62
Lou Ikner, Alabama, 1979 Sugar.

KICKOFF RETURNS
Returns: 7
Dale Carter, Tennessee, 1992 Fiesta.
Yardage: 132
Dale Carter, Tennessee, 1992 Fiesta.
Longest Return: 65
Terry Eurick, Notre Dame, 1976 Gator.

PUNTING
Punts: 10
Woody Umphrey, Alabama, 1979 Sugar.
Punting Average (Min. 3 Punts): 46.8
Steve Jackson, LSU, 1974 Orange (8 punts).
Longest Punt: 60
Dave Pryor, Southern Cal, 1982 Fiesta.

SCORING
Points: 18
Tracy Johnson, Clemson, 1988 Citrus.
Touchdowns: 3
Tracy Johnson, Clemson, 1988 Citrus.

Opponent Individual Bowl Records continued:

Kicking Points: 13
Tim Lashar, Oklahoma, 1986 Orange.
Extra Points: 5
David Treadwell, Clemson, 1988 Citrus.
Field Goals: 4
Tim Lashar, Oklahoma, 1986 Orange.
Longest Field Goal: 43
Bob Lyle, Florida, 1962 Gator.

INTERCEPTIONS
Interceptions: 2
Sonny Brown, Oklahoma, 1986 Orange.
Return Yardage: 46
Dorian Mariable, Clemson, 1988 Citrus.
Longest Return: 46
Dorian Mariable, Clemson, 1988 Citrus.

Opponent Team Bowl Records

First Downs: 35
Brigham Young, 1989 Holiday.
Rushing Yardage: 285
Clemson, 1988 Citrus.
Rushing Attempts: 76
Oklahoma, 1972 Sugar.
Rushing Average Per Play: 5.3
Clemson, 1988 Citrus.
Passing Yardage: 576
Brigham Young, 1989 Holiday.
Pass Completions: 42
Brigham Young, 1989 Holiday.
Pass Attempts: 61
Oregon, 1995 Rose.
Pass Completion Percentage: 83.3
Alabama, 1975 Sugar.
Interceptions Thrown: 7
Missouri, 1970 Orange.
Total Offense: 651
Brigham Young, 1989 Holiday.
Total Plays: 93
Miami (Fla.), 1987 Fiesta.
Fumbles Lost: 5
5, Oklahoma, 1972 Sugar.
Turnovers: 9
Missouri, 1970 Orange.
Total Offense: 651
Brigham Young, 1989 Holiday.
Total Plays: 93
Miami (Fla.), 1987 Fiesta.
Fumbles Lost: 5
5, Oklahoma, 1972 Sugar.
Turnovers: 9
Missouri, 1970 Orange.

Penn State vs. Heisman Trophy Winners

Penn State has played against 16 Heisman Trophy winners —

Pete Dawkins (Army), Ernie Davis (Syracuse), Roger Staubach (Navy), Gary Beban (UCLA), Archie Griffin (Ohio State), Tony Dorsett (Pittsburgh), Marcus Allen (Southern Cal), Herschel Walker (Georgia), Mike Rozier (Nebraska), Doug Flutie (Boston College), Vinny Testaverde (Miami, Fla.), Tim Brown (Notre Dame), Ty Detmer (Brigham Young), Gino Torretta (Miami, Fla.), Eddie George (Ohio State) and Charles Woodson (Michigan)

Six — Staubach, Griffin and Detmer (each won as juniors the year before), Allen, Walker and Testaverde — already had received the award from the Downtown Athletic Club. The other 10 played the Nittany Lions earlier in the season in which they won the award.

Here follows a summary of how the Heisman Trophy winners have fared against Penn State.

1958: Army 26, Penn State 0
Pete Dawkins rushed 12 times for 73 yards and a touchdown, threw two incomplete passes, caught two passes for 91 yards and returned three punts for 14 yards.

1961: Penn State 14, Syracuse 0
Ernie Davis rushed 13 times for 35 yards.

1964: Navy 21, Penn State 8
Roger Staubach was held to 30 yards total offense. The 1963 winner was limited to 44 yards on 5-for-13 passing and minus-14 yards rushing. He was sacked for 30 yards in losses.

1967: UCLA 17, Penn State 15
Gary Beban completed 10-of-16 passes for 108 yards and one touchdown, while rushing 19 times for one yard.

1975: Ohio State 17, Penn State 9
Archie Griffin carried 24 times for 128 yards.

1976: Pittsburgh 24, Penn State 7
Tony Dorsett gained 224 yards and scored twice on 38 carries.

1981: Penn State 26, Southern Cal 10 (1982 Fiesta Bowl)
Marcus Allen rushed 30 times for 85 yards and caught five passes for 39 yards (Penn State's Curt Warner out-played Allen, rushing 26 times for 145 yards and two scores and catching three passes for 10 yards).

1982: Penn State 27, Georgia 23 (1983 Sugar Bowl)
Herschel Walker rushed 28 times for 103 yards and scored one TD (again Warner out-performed the Heisman Trophy winner, carrying 18 times for 117 yards and two TD's and catching a pair of passes for 23 yards).

1983: Nebraska 44, Penn State 6
Mike Rozier carried 16 times for 71 yards and threw a pass interception.

1984: Penn State 37, Boston College 30
Doug Flutie completed 29-of-53 passes for 447 yards, was intercepted twice and threw for one TD. He also carried 10 times for 26 yards.

1986: Penn State 14, Miami (Fla.) 10 (1987 Fiesta Bowl)
Vinny Testaverde was intercepted a season-high five times, with pass thefts setting up the winning touchdown and sealing the Lions' victory. For the only time that season, the Miami quarterback did not throw a touchdown pass. He did complete 26-of-50 passes for 285 yards. The Lions sacked Testaverde four times for 26 yards in losses.

1987: Penn State 21, Notre Dame 20
Penn State limited Tim Brown to four receptions for 80 yards, one carry for nine yards and one incomplete pass attempt.

1991: Penn State 33, Brigham Young 7
Ty Detmer, the first incumbent Heisman Trophy winner to appear in Beaver Stadium since Roger Staubach in 1964, was limited to eight completions and 158 passing yards, career lows as the Cougar starter. The Nittany Lions intercepted him once and sacked him six times for 45 yards in losses.

1992: Miami (FL) 17, Penn State 14
Under heavy pressure from the Penn State defense, Gino Torretta threw for just 80 yards, more than 200 under his per game average. The Miami quarterback was held without a touchdown and completed a miserly 35.5 percent (11-of-31) of his passes. His longest completion was for 15 yards. He was sacked once and had minus-10 yards on three rushing attempts.

1995: Ohio State 28, Penn State 25
The Nittany Lions held Eddie George to 105 yards on 24 carries, 43 yards below his average. He scored once.

1997: Michigan 34, Penn State 8
Charles Woodson scored on a 37-yard pass reception from Brian Griese, lost nine yards on one rushing attempt, returned four punts for two yards, and made two tackles and two pass breakups on defense.